SCOTTINI

dicionário escolar inglês

Inglês - Português
Português - Inglês

60 MIL verbetes

Todolivro

©TODOLIVRO LTDA.

Rodovia Jorge Lacerda, 5086 - Poço Grande
Gaspar - SC | CEP 89115-100

Compilação:
Alfredo Scottini

IMPRESSO NA ÍNDIA
www.todolivro.com.br

Dados Internacionais de Catalogação na Publicação (CIP)
(Câmara Brasileira do Livro, SP, Brasil)

Scottini, Alfredo
Scottini – Dicionário Escolar de Inglês / Gaspar, SC: Todolivro Editora, 2023.

ISBN 978-85-376-3657-2

1. Inglês – Dicionários – Português
2. Português – Dicionários – Inglês I. Título.

17-01480   CDD-423.69

Índices para catálogo sistemático:

1. Inglês: Dicionários: Português   423.69
2. Português: Dicionários: Inglês   469.32

INTRODUÇÃO

Ninguém pode negar a importância do conhecimento e domínio de línguas estrangeiras, principalmente o inglês, que desempenha papel de destaque como instrumento de comunicação entre povos de diversas nacionalidades.

Este minidicionário inglês-português - português-inglês tem o objetivo de servir como fonte de consulta prática e simples, não somente a estudantes, mas a todos os interessados em ter boa noção ou mesmo aprofundar seus conhecimentos da língua inglesa contemporânea. De seus verbetes consta a informação básica necessária para facilitar a tradução e o emprego adequado das palavras.

De fácil transporte e manuseio, é ideal para todos os que procuram incluir, em sua lista de prioridades, a busca incessante de conhecimento e cultura.

Editor

Atualizado, incorporando as normas do
Acordo Ortográfico da Língua Portuguesa
(1990), em vigor desde 1° de janeiro de 2009.

ABREVIAÇÕES USADAS NESTA OBRA

Abreviações	Significados em português	Significados em inglês	Abreviações	Significados em português	Significados em inglês
abrev.	abreviatura	abbreviation	Ecol.	Ecologia	Ecology
adj.	adjetivo	adjective	Econ.	Economia	Economy
adv.	advérbio	adverb	Educ.	Educação	Education
Aeron.	Aeronáutica	Aeronautics	elem.	elemento	Element
Agric.	Agricultura	Agriculture	Eletr.	Eletricidade	Electricity
Al.	alemão	germany	Eletron.	Eletrônica	Electronics
Am.S.	América do Sul	South América	Es.	espanhol	espanish
Anat.	Anatomia	Anatomy	Esp.	Esporte	Sport
Ant.	Antigo	Ancient	excl.	exclamação	exclamation / interjection
Antr.	Antropologia	Antropology	fam.	familiar	informal
Ár.	Árabe	Arabian	Farm.	Farmácia	Pharmacology
Arc.	arcaico	archaic	fem.	feminino	feminine (noun)
Arquit.	Arquitetura	Architecture	fig.	Figurado	Figurative
art. def.	artigo definido	definite article	Filos.	Filosofia	Philosophy
Art.	Artes	Art / Fine Arts	Fís.	Física	Physics
Astron.	Astronomia	Astronomy	Fonol.	Fonologia	Phonology
Astrol.	Astrologia	Astrology	Fot.	Fotografia	Photography
aux.	auxiliar	auxiliary	Fr.	francês	French
Biol.	Biologia	Biology	Geogr.	Geografia	Geography
Bioq.	Bioquímica	Biochemistry	Geom.	Geometria	Geometry
Br. , Bras.	Brasil, Brasileiro	Brazil, Brazilian	ger.	geralmente	gerally
Brit.	Britânico	British	gír.	gíria	dialect / jargon
Cin.	Cinema	Cinema	Gr.	Grego	Greek
col.	coloquial	colloquial	Heb.	Hebreu	Hebrew
Com.	Comércio	Commerce	Her.	Heráldica	Heraldry
Comp.	Computação	Information Technology	Hist.	História	History
conj.	conjunção	conjunction	Ind.	Indústria	Industry
contr.	contração	contraction	indic.	indicativo	indicative
Cul.	Culinária	Culinary	Infor.	Informática	Informatics
des.	desuso	disuse	Ingl.	Inglês	English
			interj.	inerjeição	exclamation

ABREVIAÇÕES USADAS NESTA OBRA

Abreviações	Significados em português	Significados em inglês	Abreviações	Significados em português	Significados em inglês
Ir.	Irlandês	Irish	poss.	possessivo	possessive
It.	Italiano	Italian	Pp	particípio passado	past participle
Jap.	Japonês	Japonese	pref.	prefixo	prefix
Jur.	Jurídico	Juridical / Legal	prep.	preposição	preposition
Ling.	Linguística	Linguistics	pres.	presente	present
Lit.	Literatura	Literature	pron.	pronome	pronoun
Lóg.	Lógica	Logic	pron. dem.	pronome demonstrativo	demonstrative pronoun
Mar.	Marinha	Marine			
m.	masculino	masculine (noun)	Ps	Passado Simples	past simple / tense
Mat.	Matemática	Mathematics	Psic.	Psicologia	Psychology
Med.	Medicina	Medicine	Quím.	Química	Chemistry
Met.	Meteorologia	Meteorology	Rel.	Religião	Religion
Mil.	Militar	Military	Ret.	Retórica	Rhetoric
Min.	Mineralogia	Mineralogy	s.	substantivo	noun
Mit.	Mitologia	Mythology	s. 2 gen.	substantivo de 2 gêneros	noun of 2 genres
Náut.	Náutica	Nautical			
neol.	neologismo	neologism	sing.	Singular	singular
num.	numeral	numeral	Sociol.	Sociologia	Sociology
Odont.	Odontologia	Dentistry	superl.	superlativo	superlative
Oftal.	Oftalmologia	Ophthalmology	Teat.	Teatro	Theatre
Opt.	Óptica	Optics	Tec.	Tecnologia	Technical / technology
Paleont.	Paleontologia	paleontology	Tecel.	Tecelagem	Textile Industry
pas.	passado	past tense	Telef.	Telefonia	Telephony
pej.	pejorativo	pejorative	Tipog.	Tipografia	Typography
pess.	pessoal	personal	v.	verbo	verb
Pint.	Pintura	Painting	Vet.	Veterinária	Veterinary Science
pl.	plural	plural			
Pol.	Política	Politics	Zool.	Zoologia	Zoology
Port.	Portugal, Português	Portugal, Portuguese			

ABREVIATURAS E SIGLAS MAIS COMUNS

AAA . . . . . . American Automobile Association
ABC . . . . . . American Broadcasting Company
AC . . . . alternating current
AD . . . . anno domini - in the year of the Lord
AI . . . . Artificial Intelligence
AIDS . . . . . Acquired Immunity Deficiency Syndrome
am . . . . ante meridian - before noon
ASCAP . . . American Society of Composers, Authors and Publishers
ASPCA . . . American Society for the Prevention of Cruelty to Animals
ATM . . . . . . Automatic Teller Machine
Ave . . . . . . Avenue
AVI . . . . audio and video interface
aw . . . . atomic weight
b & b . . . . . bed and breakfast
BA . . . . Bachelor of Arts
BBC . . . . . . British Broadcast Corporation
BBS . . . . . . Bulletin Board System
BC . . . . before Christ
bps . . . . . . bits per second
BSc . . . . . . Bachelor of Science
C . . . . Centigrade or Celsius
c . . . . circa - about
c/o . . . . care of
CAD . . . . . . Computer Aided Design
CBS . . . . . . Columbia Broadcasting System
CD . . . . Compact Disc
CD-R . . . . . Compact Disc-Recordable
CD-ROM . . Compact Disc-Read-Only-Memory
CD-RW . . . Compact Disc-Rewritable
CEO . . . . . . Chief Executive Officer
CFO . . . . . . Chief Financial Officer
CIA . . . . Central Intelligence Agency
CIO . . . . . . Chief Information Officer
COO . . . . . Chief Operating Officer
CPU . . . . . . Central Processing Unit
DA . . . . District Attorney
DAT . . . . . . Digital Audio Tape
DC . . . . direct current
Dec . . . . . . December
DJ . . . . Disc-Jockey
DNA . . . . . . deoxyribonucleic acid
DOS . . . . . . Disc Operating System
doz . . . . . . dozen or dozens
Dr . . . . Doctor or Drive
DST . . . . . . Daylight Saving Time
DVD . . . . . . Digital Video Disc
DVD-ROM Digital Video Disc- Read-Only-Memory
E . . . . East
eg . . . . exempli gratia - for example

e-mail . . . . electronic mail
et al . . . . . . et alii - and others
ETA . . . . . . estimated time of arrival
etc . . . . et cetera - and so forth
e-zine . . . . electronic magazine
F . . . . Fahrenheit
FAO . . . . . . Food and Agricultural Organization
FAQ . . . . . . Frequently Asked Questions
FBI . . . . Federal Bureau of Investigation
FDA . . . . . . Food and Drug Administration
FF . . . . Fast Forward
FIFA . . . . . . Federation of International Football Associations
FIFO . . . . . first in, first out
ft . . . . foot or feet
GB . . . . Great Britain
Gen . . . . . . General
GI . . . . Governmental Issue
GIF . . . . Graphic Interchange Format
GMT . . . . . . Greenwich Mean Time
GNP . . . . . . Gross National Product
HD . . . . Hard Disk
HIV . . . . Human Immunodeficiency Virus
HMS . . . . . . Her / His Majesty's Service; Her / His Majesty's Ship
Hon . . . . . . Honorable
HTML . . . . Hypertext Markup Language
HTTP . . . . . Hypertext Transfer Protocol
I/O . . . . Input / Output
ICBM . . . . . Intercontinental Ballistic Missile
ICJ . . . . International Court of Justice
ICR . . . . . . Intelligent Character Recognition
ID . . . . Identification Document
ie . . . . id est - that is
in . . . . inches
IP . . . . Internet Protocol
IQ . . . . Intelligence Quotient
IRA . . . . Irish Republic Army
IRS . . . . Internal Revenue service
ISP . . . . Internet Service Provider
IT . . . . Information Technology
Jr . . . . Junior
K . . . . Kilo
KG . . . . Kilograms
KO . . . . Knock out
LA . . . . Los Angeles
LAN . . . . . . Local Area Network
LASER . . . Light Amplification by Stimulated Emission of Radiation
lb . . . . pound (weight)
LIFO . . . . . last in, first out

LSD	......	lysergic acid diethylamide
Ltd	......	Limited
m	....	meter
MA	....	Master of Arts
MD	....	Doctor of Medicine
MIDI	......	Musical Instrument Digital Interface
MIT	....	Massachusetts Institute of Technology
mpg	......	miles per gallon
mph	......	miles per hour
MSc	......	Master of Science
N	....	North
NASA	....	National Aeronautics and Space Administration
NATO	.....	North Atlantic Treaty Organization
NBC	......	National Broadcasting Company
Net	......	Internet
NYC	......	New York City
OS	....	Operating System
oz	....	ounces
PC	......	Personal Computer; Police Constable; Politically Correct
PD	....	Police Department
PDF	......	Portable Document Format
PE	....	Physical Education
PhD	......	Doctor of Philosophy
PIN	....	Personal Identification Number
pm	....	post meridian - after noon
POW	.....	Prisoner of War
Prof	......	Professor
PTA	......	Parent Teacher Association
RAM	.....	Random Access Memory
Rd	....	Road

REM	.....	Rapid Eye Movement
Rep	......	Representative
rev	....	revolution
Rev	......	Reverend
RNA	.....	ribonucleic acid
ROM	.....	Read-Only Memory
rpm	......	revolutions per minute
RSVP	.....	Répondez, s'il vous plaît - please answer
S	....	South
sci-fi	.....	Science Fiction
scuba	....	Self-contained Underwater Breathing Apparatus
Sen	......	Senator
Sgt	......	Sergeant
SOS	......	save our souls
Sr	....	Senior
St	....	Saint; Street
TV	....	television
UCLA	.....	University of California at Los Angeles
UFO	.....	Unidentified Flying Object
UK	....	United Kingdom
URL	......	Uniform Resource Locator
US	....	United States
USA	......	United States of America
VAT	......	Value-Added Tax
VCR	......	video cassette recorder
vs	....	versus
W	....	West
www	.....	World Wide Web
Xmas	.....	Christmas

LISTA DE PRONOMES

		Subject Pronouns / Reto	**Objective Pronouns / Oblíquo**	**Possessive Adjectives / Adjetivos Possessivos**	**Possessive Pronouns / Pronomes Possessivos**	**Reflexive Pronouns / Pronomes Reflexivos**
Singular	1ª pesssoa	I	me	my	mine	myself
	2ª pessoa	you	you	your	yours	yourself
	3ª pessoa	he	him	his	his	himself
		she	her	her	hers	herself
		it	it	its	its	itself
Plural	1ª pessoa	we	us	our	ours	ourselves
	2ª pessoa	you	you	your	yours	yourselves
	3ª pessoa	they	them	their	theirs	themselves

PRONOMES DE TRATAMENTO

Mr. Senhor
*Sir Senhor
Mrs. Senhora (mulheres casadas)

Miss Senhorita (mulheres solteiras)
Ms. Senhora (quando não se sabe o estado civil)
*Ma'am Senhora

*Utilizados para conversar ou chamar alguém que não se sabe o nome.

EXPRESSÕES E TERMOS DA LÍNGUA INGLESA, DE USO FREQUENTE

all right - tudo certo, tudo bem
charter - voo charter - voo fretado com saída e chegada predeterminadas
compact disc - CD - cedê
design - projeto, modelo
disquete - pequeno disco
feeling - sentimento, modo de agir
fifty-fifty - metade do negócio
fine - ótimo, muito bom
game - jogo, partida
go home - vá para casa, afaste-se
handicap - desvantagem, obstáculo
home - casa, lar
hot-dog - cachorro-quente
insight - olhada no interior do indivíduo, ideia que surge rapidamente
jeans - tipo de tecido
know-how - conhecimento, domínio de uma técnica
layout - plano, esquema
light - leve, brilhante
lobby - pressão para obter favor
nice - agradável, bom
ok - tudo bem, certo
on-line - na mesma linha, automático
outlet center - conjunto de lojas para vendas no varejo e atacado
paper - papel, resumo, minuta
partner - sócio, companheiro
point - local de encontro badalado
rafting - canoagem em corredeiras, rio de montanha
shopping center - centro comercial, centro de vendas
short - bermuda, calça curta

show - espetáculo, apresentação
show-room - mostruário, sala para expor produtos
skate - brinquedo para deslizar
soft - leve, suave
software - conteúdo de carga do micro, todos os recursos técnicos e humanos de um indivíduo ou empresa
stand by - espera, aguardo de
stand go - ir para frente, posição de avanço
surf - esporte aquático praticado no mar com uma prancha
tape - fita, filme
top - cûme, ápice
top model - modelo de alto valor
traveler's check - cheque de viagem
upgrade - posição superior, degrau acima
v-chip - consulta para pronta resposta por intermédio da própria TV
very much - muito, grande
videocassette - aparelho para reproduzir fitas
video on demand - filme por pedido
videotape - gravação de um programa de televisão em fita
V.I.P. - (very important person) pessoa muito importante
walkie-talkie - aparelho para transmitir e receber mensagens
water-closet - banheiro
windows - programa de linguagem para computador
windsurf - tipo de disputa por barco
yankee - ianque, americano, designação depreciativa para americano

PONTUAÇÃO NA LÍNGUA INGLESA

Uses	Examples
Capital letter • Primeira letra de uma sentença • Nomes de países, nacionalidades, idiomas, religiões, lugares, eventos, organizações, marcas, dias, meses, títulos, feriados, nomes de pessoas. • Títulos de livros, filmes etc. • Abreviações	Carnival is popular in Brazil. Brazil, Brazilian, Portuguese, Christian, World Trade Center, Ferrari, Sunday, January, Mr., Mrs., Easter, George, Ann. Star Wars, The Fault in Our Stars. AIDS, ONU, FBI, CIA
(.) **Full stop (UK)** **Period (US)** • Final de uma sentença • Em alguns casos, depois de uma abreviação	I am going to the zoo. Mrs. Smith. Dr. William
(?) **Question mark** • Final de uma oração interrogativa direta	How old are you?
(…) **Dots / Ellipsis** • Para indicar que palavras foram omitidas, especialmente de uma citação, ou ao final de uma conversa	…challenging the view of that brilliant scientist… had not changed all that fundamentally.
(!) **Exclamation mark (UK)** **Exclamation point (US)** • No final de uma sentença, para expressar surpresa, choque etc. • Para indicar um som alto	I can't believe it! Wow! Yes! No!
(,) Comma • Adicionar informação extra em uma sentença • Mostrar pausa em uma sentença longa • Entre itens em uma lista	The child, who is crying, is my little sister. She didn't want to eat before I arrived, but I was two hours late. Mom needs some eggs, sugar, butter and flour to make a cake.
(') Apostrophe • Em casos possessivos • Para indicar que uma letra foi omitida (contrações)	Nina's doll, Mike's brother, The Smith's house Don't (do not), she'll (she will), it's (it is)
(:) Colon • Para introduzir listagens ou citação em uma sentença	He just needs the following: money, a new car, a girlfriend and peace.
(;) Semi-colon • Para separar partes de uma sentença	I talked to Ann last week; she won't come to the meeting today.

PONTUAÇÃO NA LÍNGUA INGLESA

Uses	Examples
(-) Hyphen • para mostrar que a palavra foi dividida e continua na linha seguinte • Unir duas ou mais palavras que formam uma unidade	Everybody in the neighborhood was horrified by the news about the crime. Twenty-four
(–) Dash • Para separar partes de uma oração ou explicação dentro de uma frase mais longa	The house – the one with blue walls – is the most expensive in the street.
(' ' " ") Quotation marks (UK) **Also inverted commas** • Para fazer referência a títulos de filmes, livros etc • Para introduzir palavras ou pensamentos de outra pessoa	Have you ever read 'Da Vinci Code'? 'Let's go fishing', Daniel suggested to his friends.
(/) Slash / Oblique • Para separar palavras ou frases alternativas. • Separar diferentes componentes em um endereço da internet. Também chamada de forward slash para se diferenciar da barra invertida (backslash).	Have an ice-cream and / or pudding http://www. todolivro.com.br/tema/apoio-escolar

PAÍSES DO MUNDO, ADJETIVOS PÁTRIOS, MOEDAS E IDIOMAS

TO BE + FROM + COUNTRY = I am from **Brazil**.
TO BE + NATIONALITY = I am **Brazilian**.

Country / País	Nationality / Nacionalidade	Capital / Capital	Currency / Moeda	Language / Idioma
Afghanistan	Afghan	Kabul	Afghani	Afghan
Albania	Albanian	Tirana	Lek	Albanese
Algeria	Algerian	Argel	Dinar	Arabic
Andorra	Andorran	Andorra La Vella	Euro	Catalan
Angola	Angolan	Luanda	Kwanza	Portuguese / English / French
Antigua and Barbuda	Antiguan	St. Johns	Dollar	English
Argentina	Argentinian	Buenos Aires	Nuevo peso	Spanish
Armenia	Armenian	Erevan	Dram	Armenian
Australia	Australian	Canberra	Dollar	English
Austria	Austrian	Vienna	Euro	German

PAÍSES DO MUNDO, ADJETIVOS PÁTRIOS, MOEDAS E IDIOMAS

Country / País	Nationality / Nacionalidade	Capital / Capital	Currency / Moeda	Language / Idioma
Azerbaijan	Azerbaijani	Baku	Manat azeri	Azeri
Bahamas, The	Bahamian	Nassau	Bahamian dollar	English
Bahrain	Bahraini	Manama	Bahraini dinar	Arabic
Bangladesh	Bangladeshi	Dhaka	Taka	Bangla
Barbados	Barbadian	Bridgetown	Bajan dollar	English
Belarus	Belarusian	Minsk	Belarusian ruble	Belarusian
Belgium	Belgian	Brussels	Euro	French / Flemish
Belize	Belizean	Belnopan	Belizean dollar	English
Benin	Beninese	Porto Novo	West African CFA franc	French
Bhutan	Bhutanese	Thimbu	Bhutanese ngul-trum	Bhutanese
Bolivia	Bolivian	La Paz	Boliviano	Spanish
Bosnia-Herze-govina	Bosnian	Sarajevo	Convertible marka	Serbian, Croatian, Bosnian
Botswana	Motswana	Gaborone	Pula	English
Brazil	Brazilian	Brasília	Real	Portuguese
Brunei	Bruneian	Bandar Seri Begawan	Bruneian dollar	Malay
Bulgaria	Bulgarian	Sofiya	Lev	Bulgarian
Burkina Faso	Burkinabe	Uagadugu	West African CFA franc	French
Burundi	Burundian	Bujumbura	Burudian franc	French
Cambodia	Cambodian	Phnom Penh	Riel	Khmer
Cameroon	Cameroonian	Yaoundé	Central African CFA franc	French, English
Canada	Canadian	Ottawa	Dollar	English / French
Cape Verde	Cape Verdean	Praia	Cape Verdean escudo	Portuguese
Central African Republic, The	Central African	Bangui	Central CFA franc	French, Sango
Chad	Chadian	N'Djamena	Central African CFA franc	French, Arabic

PAÍSES DO MUNDO, ADJETIVOS PÁTRIOS, MOEDAS E IDIOMAS

Country / País	Nationality / Nacionalidade	Capital / Capital	Currency / Moeda	Language / Idioma
Chile	Chilean	Santiago	Peso	Spanish
China	Chinese	Peking	Yuan	Chinese
Colombia	Colombian	Bogota	Peso	Spanish
Comoros	Comoran	Moronic	Comorian franc	Comorian, French, Arabic
Côte d'Ivoire	Ivorian	Yamoussoukro	West African CFA franc	French
Croatia	Croat	Zagreb	Croatian kuna	Croatian
Cuba	Cuban	Havana	Peso	Spanish
Cyprus	Cyrpiot	Nicosia	Euro	Greek, Turkish
Czech Republic, The	Czech	Prague	Koruna	Czech
Democratic Republic of Congo, The	Congolese	Brazzaville	Congolese Franc	French
Denmark	Dane	Kopenhagen	Krone	Danish
Djibouti	Djiboutian	Djibouti	Djiboutian franc	French
Dominica	Dominican	Roseau	East Caribean dollar	Spanish
Dominican Republic, The	Dominican	Santo Domingo	Peso	Spanish
Ecuador	Ecuadorian	Quito	US dollar	Spanish
Egypt	Egyptian	Cairo	Pound	Arabic
El Salvador	Salvadoran	San Salvador	US dollar	Spanish
England	English (British)	London	Pound	English
Equatorial Guinea	Equatorial Guinean or Equatoguinean	Malabob	Central CFA franc	French, Spanish, Portuguse
Ethiopia	Ethiopian	Addis Abeba	Birr	Amharic
Finland	Finnish	Helsinki	Euro	Finn
France	French	Paris	Euro	Frenchman
Gabon	Gabanese	Libreville	Central CFA franc	French
Gambia	Gambian	Banjul	Dalasi	English

PAÍSES DO MUNDO, ADJETIVOS PÁTRIOS, MOEDAS E IDIOMAS

Country / País	Nationality / Nacionalidade	Capital / Capital	Currency / Moeda	Language / Idioma
Georgia	Georgian	Atlanta	Lari	Georgian
Germany	German	Berlin	Euro	German
Ghana	Ghanaian	Acra	Cedi	English
Greece	Greek	Athens	Euro	Greek
Grenada	Grenadian	Saint George's	Eastern Caribean dollar	English
Guatemala	Guatemalan	Guatemala City	Quetzal	Spanish
Guinea	Guinean	Conakry	Guinean franc	French
Guinea-Bissau	Guinea-Bissauan	Bissau	West African CFA franc	Portuguese
Guyana	Guyanese	Georgetown	Guyanese dollar	English
Haiti	Haitian	Port-au-Prince	Haitian gourde	French, Haitian Creole
Honduras	Honduran	Tegucigalpa	Lempira	Spanish
Hungary	Hungarian	Budapest	Forint	Hungarian
Iceland	Icelander	Reykjavík	Icelandic Króna	Icelandic
India	Indian	Delhi	Rupee	Hindi / English
India	Indian	New delhi	Indian Rupee	Hindi, English
Indonesia	Indonesian	Jakarta	Rupiah	Indonesian
Iran	Iranian	Tehran	Rial	Irarian
Iraq	Iraqi	Bagdad	Dinar	Arabic
Ireland	Irishman	Dublin	Euro	English
Israel	Israeli	Jerusalem	Shekel	Hebrew
Italy	Italian	Rome	Euro	Italian
Jamaica	Jamaican	Kingston	Dollar	English
Japan	Japanese	Tokyo	Yen	Japanese
Jordan	Jordanian	Amman	Jordanian dinar	Arabic
Kazakhstan	Kazakhstani	Astana	Tenge	kazakh
Kenya	Kenyan	Nairobi	Kenyan shilling	English, Kiswahili
Kiribati	Kiribati	Tarawa	Kiribati dollar, Australian dollar	English, Gilbertese

PAÍSES DO MUNDO, ADJETIVOS PÁTRIOS, MOEDAS E IDIOMAS

Country / País	Nationality / Nacionalidade	Capital / Capital	Currency / Moeda	Language / Idioma
Kuwait	Kuwaiti	Kuwait	Kuwaiti dinar	Arabic
Kyrgyzstan	Kyrgyz	Bishkek	Som	Kyrgyz (national), Russian (official)
Laos	Laotian	Vientiane	Kip	Lao
Latvia	Latvian	Riga	Euro	Latvian
Lebanon	Lebanese	Beyrouth	Pound	Arabic / French
Lesotho	Mosotho	Maseru	Lesotho loti	Sesotho, English
Liberia	Liberian	Monrovia	Liberian dollar	English
Libya	Libyan	Tripoli	Dinar	Arabic
Liechtenstein	Liechtensteiner	Vaduz	Swiss franc	German
Lithuania	Lithuanian	Vilnius	Euro	Lithuanian
Luxembourg	Luxembourger	Luxembourg City	Euro	French, German, Luxembourgish
Macedonia	Macedonian	Skopje	Macedonian denar	Macedonian
Madagascar	Malagasy	Antananarivo	Malagasy ariary	French, Malagasy
Malawi	Malawian	Lilongwe	Kwacha	English
Malaysia	Malaysian	Kuala Lumpur	Ringgit	Bahasa Malaysia
Maldives, The	Maldivian	Malé	Maldivian rufiya	Maldivian (Dhivehi)
Mali	Malian	Bamako	West African CFA franc	French
Malta	Maltese	Valletta	Euro	Maltese, English
Marshall Islands, The	Marshallese	Majuro	US dollar	Marshallese, English
Mauritania	Mauritanian	Nouakchott	Ouguiya	Arabic
Mauritius	Mauritian	Port Louis	Mauritian rupee	English, French, Mauritian Creole
Mexico	Mexican	Mexico City	New peso	Spanish
Micronesia	Micronesean	Palikir	US dollar	English
Moldova	Moldovan	Chișinău	Leu	Romanian
Monaco	Monégasque	Monaco	Euro	French
Mongolia	Mongolian	Ulaanbaatar	Tögrög	Mongolian

PAÍSES DO MUNDO, ADJETIVOS PÁTRIOS, MOEDAS E IDIOMAS

Country / País	Nationality / Nacionalidade	Capital / Capital	Currency / Moeda	Language / Idioma
Morocco	Moroccan	Rabat	Dirham	Arabic
Mozambique	Mozambican	Maputo	Mozambican metical	Portuguese
Myanmar	Burmese	Naypyidaw	Kyat	Burmese
Namibia	Namibian	Windhoek	Nabiam dollar	English
Nauru	Nauruan	Yaren	Australian dollar	Nauruan, English
Nepal	Nepalese	Katmandu	Nepalese rupee	Nepali
Netherlands, The	Dutch	Amsterdam	Euro	Dutch
New Zealand	New Zealander	Wellington	Dollar	English
Nicaragua	Nicaraguan	Managua	Cordoba	Spanish
Niger	Nigerien	Niamey	West African CFA franc	French
Nigeria	Nigerian	Abuja	Naira	English
North Korea	North Korean	Pyongyang	North korean won	korean
Norway	Norwegian	Oslo	Krone	Norwegian
Pakistan	Pakistani	Slamabad	Rupee	English / Urdu
Panama	Panamanian	Panama	Balboa	Spanish
Papua New Guinea	Papua New Guinean	Port Moresby	Papua New Guinean kina	Papua New Guinean
Paraguay	Paraguayan	Asuncion	Guarani	Spanish
Peru	Peruvian	Lima	New sol / Inti	Spanish
Philippines, The	Philippine	Manila	Peso	English
Poland	Pole	Warsaw	New zloty	Polish
Portugal	Portuguese	Lisbon	Euro	Portuguese
Qatar	Qatari	Doha	Riyal	Arabic
Republic of Zaire	Zaïrean	kinshasa	Zaire	French
Romania	Romanian	Bucharest	Leu Romeno	Romanian
Russia	Russian	Moscow	Ruble	Russian
Rwanda	Rwandan	Kigali	Rwandan franc	Kinyarwanda, English, French
Saint kitts and Nevis	Kittitian or Nevisian	Basseterre	East Caribbean dollar	English

PAÍSES DO MUNDO, ADJETIVOS PÁTRIOS, MOEDAS E IDIOMAS

Country / País	Nationality / Nacionalidade	Capital / Capital	Currency / Moeda	Language / Idioma
Saint Lucia	Saint Lucian	Castries	East Caribbean dollar	English
Saint Vincent and the Grenadines	Vincentian, Vincy	Kingstown	East Caribbean dollar	English
Samoa	Samoan	Apia	Tala	Samoan, English
San Marino	Sanmarinese	City of San Marino	Euro	Italian
São Tomé and Príncipe	Sao Tomean	São Tomé	Dobra	Portuguese
Saudi Arabia	Saudi	Riyad	Riyal	Arabic
Senegal	Senegalese	Dakar	Franc	French
Seychelles, The	Seychellois	Victoria	Seychellois rupee	English, French, Seychellois Creole
Sierra Leone	Sierra Leonian	Freetown	Leone	English
Singapore	Singaporean	Singapore	Dollar	English / Tamil / Malay / Mandarin
Slovakia	Slovak	Bratislava	Euro	Slovak
Slovenia	Slovene	Ljubljana	Euro	Slovene
Solomon Islands, The	Solomon Islander	Honiara	Solomon Islands dollar	English
Somalia	Somali	Mogadishu	Dollar / shilling	Somali / Arabic
South Africa	South African	Johannesburg	Rand	Afrikaans / English
South Korea	Korean	Seoul	Dollar	Korean
Spain	Spaniard	Madrid	Euro	Spanish
Sri Lanka	Sri Lankan	Colombo	Sri Lankan rupee	Sinhalese, Tamil
Sudan	Sudanese	Khartoum	Sudanese Pound	Arabic / English
Suriname	Surinamese	Paramaribo	Surinamese dollar	Dutch
Swaziland	swazi	Mbabane	South African rand Swazi lilangeni	Swazi, English
Sweden	Swede	Stockholm	Krona	Swedish
Switzerland	Swiss	Berna	Franc	French / Italian / German
Syria	Syrian	Damascus	Syrian pound	Arabic
Tajikistan	Tajik	Dushanbe	Somoni	Tajik

PAÍSES DO MUNDO, ADJETIVOS PÁTRIOS, MOEDAS E IDIOMAS

Country / País	Nationality / Nacionalidade	Capital / Capital	Currency / Moeda	Language / Idioma
Tanzania	Tanzanian	Dodoma	Tanzanian Shilling	Swahili
Thailand	Thai	Bangkok	Baht	Thai
Togo	Togolese	Lomé	CFA Franc	French
Tonga	Tongan	Nuku'alofa	Pa'anga	Tongan, English
Trinidad and Tobago	Tobagonian	Port of Spain	Trinidadian Dollar	English
Tunisia	Tunisian	Tunes	Dinar	Arabic
Turkey	Turkish	Ankara	Lira	Turkish
Turkmenistan	Turkmen	Ashgabat	Turkmen new manat	Turkmen
Tuvalu	Tuvaluan	Funafuti	Tuvaluan dollar Australian dollar	Tuvaluan, English
Uganda	Ugandan	Kampala	Ugandan Shilling	English / Swahili
Ukraine	Ukrainian	Kiev	Hryvnia	Ukrainian
United Arab Emirates, The	Emirian	Abu Dhabi	Dirham	Arabic
United Kingdom, The	British	London	Pound	English
United States, The	American	Washington	Dollar	English
Uruguay	Uruguayan	Montevideo	New peso	Spanish
Uzbekistan	Uzbek	Tashkent	Uzbekistani Som	Uzbek
Vanuatu	Vanuatuan	Port Vila	Vanuatu Vatu	Bislama, French, English
Vatican City	Vatican	Vatican City	Euro	Italian
Venezuela	Venezuelan	Caracas	Bolivar	Spanish
Vietnam	Vietnamese	Hanoi	Dong	Vietnamese
Yemen	Yemeni	San'a	Yemeni rial	Arabic
Yogoslavia	Yogoslav	Belgrado	Dinar	Serbo-Croato-Slovenian
Zambia	Zambian	Lusaka	Zambian kwacha	English
Zimbabwe	Zimbabwean	Harare	US dollar	Zimbabwean

NUMERAIS

Cardinal	Ordinal	Cardinal	Ordinal
1 One	1st First	23 Twenty-three	23rd Twenty-third
2 Two	2nd Second	24 Twenty-four	24th Twenty-fourth
3 Three	3rd Third	25 Twenty-five	25th Twenty-fifth
4 Four	4th Fourth	26 Twenty-six	26th Twenty-sixth
5 Five	5th Fifth	27 Twenty-seven	27th Twenty-seventh
6 Six	6th Sixth	28 Twenty-eigbt	28th Twenty-eighth
7 Seven	7th Seventh	29 Twenty-nine	29th Twenty-ninth
8 Eight	8th Eighth	30 Thirty	30th Thirtieth
9 Nine	9th Ninth	31 Thirty-one	31st Thirty-first
10 Ten	10th Tenth	40 Forty	40th Fortieth
11 Eleven	11th Eleventh	50 Fifty	50th Fiftieth
12 Twelve	12th Twelfth	60 Sixty	60th Sixtieth
13 Thirteen	13th Thirteenth	70 Seventy	70th Seventieth
14 Fourteen	14th Fourteenth	80 Eighty	80th Eightieth
15 Fifteen	15th Fifteenth	90 Ninety	90th Ninetieth
16 Sixteen	16th Sixteenth	100 One hundred	100th hundredth
17 Seventeen	17th Seventeenth	500 Five hundred	500th Five hundredth
18 Eighteen	18th Eighteenth	1,000 One thousand	1,000th Thousandth
19 Nineteen	19th Nineteenth	100,000 One hundred thousand	100,000th Hundred thousandth
20 Twenty	20th Twentieth	1,000,000 One million	1,000,000 Millionth
21 Twenty-one	21st Twenty-first		
22 Twenty-two	22nd Twenty-second		

COMO DIZER OS NÚMEROS

Over 100 / Acima de 100

121	a / one hundred twenty-one (US), a / one hundred and twenty-one (UK)
999	nine hundred ninety-nine (US), nine hundred and ninety-nine (UK)

Numbers over 1,000 / Acima de 1.000

1001	a / one thousand one (US), a / one thousand and one (UK)
1121	a / one thousand one hundred twenty-one (US), a / one thousand one hundred and twenty-one (UK)
9999	nine thousand nine hundred ninety-nine (US), nine thousand nine hundred and ninety-nine (UK)

NUMERAIS

DATAS

1539	fifteen thirty-nine	1986	nineteen eighty-six
1908	nineteen-oh-eight	2017	two thousand (and) seventeen

O NÚMERO "0"

A figura do número "0" tem diferentes nomes no idioma Inglês, se bem que, no Inglês Americano, o zero é frequentemente utilizado em todos os casos. Aqui estão algumas formas de dizer o "0":

Telephone numbers / Números de telefone: todos os números são ditos separadamente.
32320893 three two three two **oh** eight nine three (também no Inglês Americano: three two three two **zero** eight nine three).
Nil: utilizado para falar sobre a pontuação / placar em um jogo entre equipes, por exemplo, no futebol.
6-0 six nil (**UK**), six to zero (**US**).
Nought: utilizado no Inglês Britânico para falar sobre um número, idade etc;
0.68 nought point six eight (**UK**), zero point six eight (**US**).

Parts of numbers: decimals and fractions
Partes dos números: decimais e fracionários

Para os números decimais, dizemos cada número separadamente depois do ponto (.):
4.5 four point five   24.55 twenty-four point fifty-five   6.92 six point ninety-two

Para frações, dizemos:
3 ¼ three and a quarter   5 ¾ five and three quarters   1/5 one fifth

Contudo, utilizamos os números ordinais para a maioria das frações, mas não para ½, ¼, ¾:
3/8 three eighths   1/12 a twelfth or one twelfth   1/3 a third or one third

SÍMBOLOS MATEMÁTICOS

Symbol / Símbolo	How it is read / Como é lido	Symbol / Símbolo	How it is read / Como é lido
+	plus	[ ]	brackets
-	minus	( )	parentheses
x	times	=	equals
±	plus or minus	≠	is not equal to
÷ or /	divided by	<	is less than
∫	the integral of	≤	is less than or equal to
Σ	the summation of	>	is greater than
!	factorial	≥	is greater than or equal to
√	the square root of	°	degree(s)
%	percent	Π	pi

MEDIDAS INGLESAS E AMERICANAS

LINEAR MEASURE / MEDIDAS DE COMPRIMENTO

		Equivalente Métrico
1 inch		2,54 cm
1 foot	12 inches	30,48 cm
1 yard	3 feet	91,44 cm
1 pole, rod, perch	5 ½ yards	5,03 m
1 chain (ingl.)	4 poles, etc.	20,12 m
1 furlong (200 yards)	10 chains (40 rods)	201,17 m
1 statute mile (1760 yards)	8 furlongs (5280 feet)	1.609 km
1 nautical mile	6080.2 feet	1.853 km
1 league	3 statute miles	4.828 km

SQUARE MEASURE / MEDIDAS DE SUPERFÍCIE

1 square inch		6,45 cm²
1 square foot		9,29 dm²
1 square yard		0,84 m²
1 square pole (Am.: rod)		25,29 m²
1 perch (Brit.)	10 square poles	252,93 m²
1 rood (Brit.)	40 square rodes	1011,71 m²
1 acre (U.S.A.)	160 square rods	0,4047 ha
1 acre (Brit.)	4 roods	0,4047 ha
1 square mile	640 acres	259,00 ha ou 2.590 km²

CUBIC MEASURE / MEDIDAS DE VOLUME

1 cubic inch		16,39 cm³
1 cubic foot	1728 cubic inches	28,32 dm³
1 cubic yard	27 cubic feet	764,53 dm³
1 barrel bulck shipping	5 cubic feet	
1 ton shipping	40 cubic feet	

DRY MEASURE / MEDIDAS DE CAPACIDADE PARA SECOS

1 pint (Brit.; abbr. pt.)	4 gills	568,3 ml
1 pint (U.S.A.)	4 gills	473,2 ml
1 quart (U.S.A.; abbr. qt.)	2 pints	0,9464 l
1 gallon (Brit.; abbr. gal.)	4 quarts	4,546 l
1 gallon (U.S.A.)	4 quarts	4,41 l
1 peck (Brit.; abbr. pk.)	2 gallons	9,092 l
1 peck (U.S.A.)	2 gallons	8,810 l
1 bushel (Brit.; abbr. bu.)	4 pecks	36,37 l
1 bushel (U.S.A.)	4 pecks	35,24 l
1 barrel (Brit.)	36 gallons	1,637 hl
1 barrel (U.S.A.)	36 gallons	1,192 hl
1 quarter (Brit.)	8 bushels	2,909 hl
1 quarter (U.S.A.)	8 bushels	2,421 hl

MEDIDAS INGLESAS E AMERICANAS

LIQUID MEASURE / MEDIDAS DE CAPACIDADE PARA LÍQUIDOS

		Equivalente Métrico
1 minim (Brit.)	0,0592 milliliter	0,0000592 l
1 minim (U.S.A.)		0,0000616 l
1 fluid dram (Brit.)	60 minims	3,552 ml
1 fluid dram (U.S.A.)	60 minims	3,697 ml
1 fluid ounce (Brit.)	8 fluid drams	28,47 ml
1 fluid ounce (U.S.A.)	8 fluid drams	29,57 ml
1 pint (Brit.)	20 fluid ounces	569,4 ml
1 pint (U.S.A.)	16 fluid ounces	473,12 ml
1 pint (Brit.)	4 gills	0,5682 l
1 quart (Brit.)	2 pints	1,1364 l
1 gallon (Brit.)	4 quarts	4,5459 l
1 gallon (U.S.A.)	4 quarts	3,785 l
1 peck (Brit.)	2 gallons	9,092 l
1 bushel (Brit.)	4 pecks	36,368 l
1 quarter (Brit.)	8 bushels	2,909 hl
1 barrel (U.S.A.)	31 ½ gallons	1,43198 hl
1 hogshead (U.S.A.)	2 barrels	2,86396 hl

AVOIRDUPOIS WEIGHT / PESOS AVOIRDUPOIS *

1 ounce (Brit.; abbr. oz.)	16 drams 437 ½ grains troy	28,35 g
1 ounce (U.S.A.); abbr. oz.)		31,10 g
1 pound (Brit.; abbr. lb. av.)	16 ounces	453,6 g
1 stone (Brit.)	14 pounds	6,350 kg
1 quarter (Brit.)	28 pounds	12,70 kg
1 quarter ((U.S.A.)	25 pounds	11,34 kg
1 hundredweight cental (Brit. & U.S.A.; abbr. cwt. sh.)	100 pounds	45,36 kg
1 hundredweight long (Brit.)	4 quarters 112 pounds	50,80 kg
1 long ton	2000 pounds	907,2 kg
1 long ton	2240 pounds	1016,064 kg

* Sistema de pesos usado em todos os países da língua inglesa para qualquer material, com exceção de pedras, metais preciosos e drogas.

MARINERS' MEASURE / MEDIDAS NÁUTICAS (OU MARÍTIMAS)

1 fathom	6 feet	1,83 m
1 nautical mile	1000 fathoms (approx.)	1,853 km
1 league	3 nautical miles	5,559 km

SURVEYORS' MEASURE / MEDIDAS DE AGRIMENSOR

1 link	7.92 inches	20,12 cm
1 chain	100 links	20,12 m
1 mile	80 chains	1609,34 m
1 acre	10 square chains	0,4047 ha

LISTA DE VERBOS IRREGULARES

Simple Present	Simple Past	Past participle	Portuguese
abide	abode *	abode *	continuar, permanecer
arise	arose	arisen	levantar-se
awake	awoke	awoke, awaked	acordar
be	was	been	ser
bear	bore	borne, born	suportar
beat	beat	beaten, beat	bater, vencer
become	became	become	tornar-se
beget	begot	begotten	procriar, produzir
begin	began	begun	começar
behold	beheld	beheld	ver, observar
bend	bent	bent	dobrar, curvar
bereave	bereft *	bereft	privar de, roubar
beseech	besought	besought	pedir, implorar
bespeak	bespoke	bespoken	reservar, tratar
bet	bet	bet	apostar
bid	bade *	bidden	mandar, ordenar
bind	bound	bound	atar, amarrar
bite	bit	bitten,	morder
bleed	bled	bled	sangrar
blow	blew	blown	soprar, ventar
break	broke	broken	quebrar
breed	bred	bred	produzir, dar cria
bring	brought	brought	trazer
build	built	built	construir
burn	burnt *	burnt *	queimar
burst	burst	burst	explodir
buy	bought	bought	comprar
cast	cast	cast	atirar, arremessar
catch	caught	caught	pegar
chide	chid *	chidden *	ralhar, repreender
choose	chose	chosen	escolher
cleave	cleft *	cleft *	rachar(se), fender(se)

LISTA DE VERBOS IRREGULARES

Simple Present	Simple Past	Past participle	Portuguese
cling	clung	clung	agarrar-se
clothe	clad *	clad *	vestir, cobrir
come	came	come	vir, chegar
cost	cost	cost	custar
creep	crept	crept	arrastar-se, mover-se
crow	crew *	crowed	gritar de alegria (bebê), cantar (galo)
cut	cut	cut	cortar
deal	dealt	dealt	negociar, lidar
dig	dug	dug	cavar
do	did	done	fazer
draw	drew	drawn	desenhar
dream	dreamt *	dreamt *	sonhar
drink	drank	drunk, drunken	beber
drive	drove	driven	dirigir, guiar
dwell	dwelt *	dwelt *	habitar, residir
eat	ate	eaten	comer
fall	fell	fallen	cair
feed	fed	fed	alimentar
feel	felt	felt	sentir
fight	fougth	fougth	lutar
find	found	found	encontrar, achar
flee	fled	fled	fugir, escapar
fling	flung	flung	arremessar, lançar
fly	flew	flown	voar
forbear	forbore	forborne	conter, abster-se
forbid	forbade	forbidden	proibir, vetar
forget	forgot	forgotten	esquecer
forsake	forsook	forsaken	renunciar, abandonar
freeze	froze	frozen	congelar
get	got	got	pegar, realizar
gild	gilt *	gilt *	dourar, disfarçar

LISTA DE VERBOS IRREGULARES

Simple Present	Simple Past	Past participle	Portuguese
girt	girt *	girt *	cingir, envolver
give	gave	given	dar, doar
go	went	gone	ir, andar
grind	ground	ground	triturar
grow	grew	grown	crescer
hang	hung *	hung *	pendurar
have	had	had	ter, deter, possuir
hear	heard	heard	ouvir
hide	hid	hid, hidden	esconder
hit	hit	hit	bater
hold	held	held	segurar
hurt	hurt	hurt	ferir, machucar
keep	kept	kept	guardar, segurar
kneel	knelt *	knelt *	ajoelhar(-se)
knit	knit *	knit *	tricotar
know	knew	known	saber, conhecer
lade	laded	laden	carregar
lay	laid	laid	pôr, colocar
lead	led	led	levar, liderar
lean	leant *	leant *	inclinar-se, tender
leap	leapt *	leapt *	pular, saltar
learn	learnt *	learnt *	aprender
leave	left	left	partir, ir embora
lend	lent	lent	emprestar
let	let	let	deixar
lie	lay	lain	jazer, estar deitado(a)
light	lit *	lit *	acender
lose	lost	lost	perder
make	made	made	fazer
mean	meant	meant	significar
meet	met	met	encontrar, reunir
melt	melted	molten *	fundir, derreter

LISTA DE VERBOS IRREGULARES

Simple Present	Simple Past	Past participle	Portuguese
mow	mowed	mown *	ceifar, sugar
pay	paid	paid	pagar
pen	pent *	pent *	escrever, redigir
put	put	put	pôr, colocar
read	read	read	ler
rend	rent	rent	lacerar, despedaçar
rid	rid *	rid *	libertar, livrar-se
ride	rode	ridden	cavalgar
ring	rang	rung	soar, ressonar
rise	rose	risen	erguer-se
rive	rived	riven *	rachar, rasgar
rot	rotted	rotten *	apodrecer, deteriorar
run	run	run	correr
saw	sawed	sawn *	serrar
say	said	said	dizer
see	saw	seen	ver
seek	sought	sought	procurar
seethe	seethed	sodden *	ferver
sell	sold	sold	vender
send	sent	sent	enviar, remeter
set	set	set	colocar, pôr
sew	sewed	sewn *	costurar
shake	shook	shaken	sacudir
shear	shore *	shorn *	tosquiar, tosar
shed	shed	shed	derramar
shine	shone	shone	brilhar
shoe	shod	shod	ferrar, calçar
shoot	shot	shot	atirar com arma de fogo
show	showed	shown	mostrar, exibir
shred	shred *	shred *	rasgar, cortar em tiras
shrink	shrank	shrunk	encolher
shrive	shrove*	shriven *	confessar

LISTA DE VERBOS IRREGULARES

Simple Present	Simple Past	Past participle	Portuguese
shut	shut	shut	fechar
sing	sang	sung	cantar
sink	sank, sunk	sunk, sunken	afundar, ir a pique
sit	sat	sat	sentar-se
sleep	slept	slept	dormir
slide	slid	slid	escorregar
sling	slung	slung	atirar, lançar
slink	slunk	slunk	dar à luz prematuramente
slit	slit	slit	cortar, quebrar
smell	smelt *	smelt *	cheirar
smite	smote	smitten	bater, golpear
sow	sowed	sown *	semear
speak	spoke	spoken	falar
speed	sped	sped	correr
spell	spelt *	spelt	soletrar
spend	spent	spent	gastar
spill	spilt *	spilt *	derramar, entornar
spin	spun, span	spun	girar
spit	spat, spit	spat, spit	cuspir
split	split	split	partir, rachar
spoil	spoilt *	spoilt *	estragar, arruinar
spread	spread	spread	espalhar
spring	sprang	sprung	saltar, pular
stand	stood	stood	aguentar, manter-se
steal	stole	stolen	furtar, roubar
stick	stuck	stuck	grudar, colar
sting	stung	stung	picar, furar
stink	stank	stunk	exalar mau cheiro
strew	strewed	strewn *	espalhar, espargir
stride	strode	stridden	andar com passos largos
strike	struck	struck	surrar, golpear
string	strung	strung	amarrar, segurar

LISTA DE VERBOS IRREGULARES

Simple Present	Simple Past	Past participle	Portuguese
strive	strove	striven	esforçar-se, trabalhar
swear	swore	sworn	jurar
sweat	sweat *	sweat *	suar
sweep	swept	swept	varrer
swell	swelled	swelled, swollen	crescer, inchar
swim	swam	swum	nadar
swing	swang	swung	balançar
take	took	taken	tomar, pegar
teach	taught	taught	ensinar
tear	tore	torn	rasgar
tell	told	told	contar, narrar
think	thought	thought	pensar, raciocinar
throw	threw	thrown	lançar, atirar
thrust	thrust	thrust	empurrar, impelir
tread	trod	trodden	andar, marchar
understand	understood	understood	entender, compreender
wake	woke	waked	acordar, despertar
wear	wore	worn	vestir, pôr roupas
weave	wove	woven	tecer
wed	wed	wed	casar, casar-se
weep	wept	wept	chorar
wet	wet *	wet *	molhar
win	won	won	vencer
wind	wound	wound	girar, fazer girar
wring	wrung	wrung	retorcer, espremer
write	wrote	written	escrever

* Verbs for which there is also a regular form ending in "ed".
* Verbos que admitem, também, a forma regular terminada em "ed".

VERBOS REGULARES

Os verbos Regulares em Inglês são muito fáceis de conjugar e muito fáceis de aprender. Eles são diferentes dos Verbos Irregulares. Enquanto o Passado Simples e o Passado Particípio dos Verbos Regulares terminam em - ed, os Verbos Irregulares têm suas próprias formas e é necessário estudar cada um individualmente.

TOP 100 REGULAR VERBS

Infinitive	Simple past / Past participle	Portuguese translation
accept	accepted	aceitar
achieve	achieved	alcançar, realizar
act	acted	agir, representar, atuar
admit	admitted	admitir, reconhecer
affect	affected	afetar
agree	agreed	concordar
announce	announced	anunciar
answer	answered	responder
appear	appeared	aparecer
apply	applied	aplicar, pôr em prática
argue	argued	discutir, argumentar
arrive	arrived	chegar
ask	asked	pedir, perguntar
attend	attended	frequentar, atender
avoid	avoided	evitar
believe	believed	acreditar, crer
call	called	chamar, telefonar para
carry	carried	carregar
cause	caused	causar
change	changed	mudar
close	closed	fechar
compare	compared	comparar
consider	considered	considerar
contain	contained	conter
continue	continued	continuar
count	counted	contar

VERBOS REGULARES

Infinitive	Simple past / Past participle	Portuguese translation
cover	covered	cobrir
create	created	criar
decide	decided	decidir
define	defined	definir
determine	determined	determinar
develop	developed	desenvolver
die	died	morrer
discover	discovered	descobrir
enter	entered	entrar
establish	established	estabelecer
exist	existed	existir
explain	explained	explicar
finish	finished	terminar
follow	followed	seguir
form	formed	formar, criar
happen	happened	acontecer
help	helped	ajudar
hope	hoped	ter esperanças de
imagine	imagined	imaginar
improve	improved	melhorar
include	included	incluir
increase	increased	aumentar
indicate	indicated	indicar
introduce	introduced	introduzir, apresentar
kill	killed	matar
live	lived	morar, viver
maintain	maintained	manter
mention	mentioned	mencionar
move	moved	mover, mexer, mudar
need	needed	precisar

VERBOS REGULARES

Infinitive	Simple past / Past participle	Portuguese translation
note	noted	observar, reparar em
notice	noticed	reparar em, notar
occur	occurred	ocorrer
offer	offered	oferecer
open	opened	abrir
pass	passed	passar
play	played	jogar, brincar
prepare	prepared	preparar
prevent	prevented	prevenir, evitar, impedir
produce	produced	produzir
protect	protected	proteger
publish	published	publicar
raise	raised	levantar, erguer, edificar
reach	reached	alcançar
receive	received	receber
recognize	recognized	reconhecer
reduce	reduced	reduzir
remember	remembered	lembrar
remove	removed	remover
represent	represented	representar
respond	responded	responder
return	returned	retornar
save	saved	salvar, economizar
seem	seemed	parecer
serve	served	servir
share	shared	dividir, compartilhar
sign	signed	assinar
sound	sounded	soar, parecer
stay	stayed	ficar, permanecer
stop	stopped	parar

VERBOS REGULARES

Infinitive	Simple past / Past participle	Portuguese translation
study	studied	estudar
suffer	suffered	sofrer
support	supported	apoiar
touch	touched	tocar
travel	travelled	viajar
treat	treated	tratar
try	tried	tentar, experimentar
use	used	usar
visit	visited	visitar
walk	walked	caminhar, andar
want	wanted	querer
watch	watched	assistir
work	worked	trabalhar
worry	worried	preocupar

PREPOSIÇÕES DE LUGAR

ABOVE / OVER - indica posição acima, sobre (sem contato de superfície).
The lamp is **above / over** the table.
The temperature is **above** 40 degree Celsius.

ON - indicação de superfícies horizontais ou verticais (sobre, com contato), lugares como farm, island, coast, além de ser usada diante de ruas.

The cake is **on** the table.
He lives **on** the farm.
The museum is **on** Main Street.

UNDER / BELOW - indica posição abaixo / embaixo (de).
The slippers are **under** the bed.
It is very cold. The temperature is **below** zero.

IN FRONT OF / OPPOSITE - em frente a, oposto a.
I parked my car **in front of the** church.
They live **opposite** the shopping center.

IN - expressa a ideia de dentro, diante dos nomes de cidades, países e pontos geográficos.

The documents are **in** the drawer.
She lives **in** New Jersey.
Amazonas is in the **North** of Brazil.

INSIDE / OUTSIDE - enfatizam a ideia da preposição dentro e fora. Podem funcionar também como advérbios.
I met my friend **inside** the theater.
There is an angry crowd **outside**.

BETWEEN - entre dois elementos.
The museum is **between** the church and the bookstore.

AMONG - entre vários elementos.
The castle is **among** the trees.
NEXT TO / BY / BESIDE - ao lado de.
Mary is sitting **next to** July.
Who is the girl **by** the window?
The park is **beside** a school.

AGAINST - contra.
The boys are leaning **against** the wall.

PREPOSIÇÕES DE MOVIMENTO OU DIRECIONAMENTO

UP - ideia de movimento para cima.
Please, go **up** the ladder and change the bulb.

DOWN - ideia de movimento para baixo.
The boy fell **down** the stairs.

ALONG - ao longo de.
The runners were training along the road.

ACROSS - através de (um plano, uma reta).
The plane flyes **across** the Atlantic.
There are several bridges **across** the river.

IN / INTO - movimento para dentro.
We went **into** the supermarket together.
She jumped **into** the pool.
My mother always looks at herself **in** the mirror.

TOWARDS - em direção a.
He is running towards the finish line.

OUT OF - implica em movimento de saída.
He got **out of** the pool because the water was cool.

THROUGH - através de (passando por).
Look **through** the window.
I like driving my car **through** downtown.

OVER - acima.
I had a glance at the clock **over** the door.

AROUND / ROUND / ALL OVER - ao redor, por todo / a.
The earth goes **round** the sun.
The athletes are running **around** the track.
People **all over** the world pray for peace.

ONTO - indica movimento de chegada a uma superfície horizontal ou vertical.
The cat jumped **onto** the table and scratched it all.

FROM - desde de (indica origem).
He flew **from** Brazil to Japan in twenty-five hours.
Where are you from? I'm **from** Brazil.

TO - para.
I went **to** the supermarket.
Nota: não é utilizado diante da palavra home.
I'm going home, because I'm very tired.

TEMPOS VERBAIS

- As formas dos verbos para **I**, **you**, **we** e **they** são as mesmas.
- As formas dos verbos para **he**, **she** e **it** são as mesmas.

REGRAS DE ORTOGRAFIA PARA OS TEMPOS VERBAIS DOS VERBOS REGULARES

Simple Present / Presente Simples

Affirmative	Negative	Interrogative
I walk every morning. He walks every morning. • Verbos terminados em -**y**, remover o -**y** e adicionar -**ies**, para **he**, **she** e **it**. I study English. He studies English. • Verbos terminados em -**y**, precedidos de vogal, adicionar -**s**, para **he**, **she** e **it**. I play soccer with my friends. He plays soccer with his friends. • Verbos terminados em -**ch, sh, -s, -x, -z** ou -**o**, adicionar -**es**, para **he**, **she** e **it**. I wash the dishes for my mother. He washes the dishes for his mother.	• Na forma negativa, ao utilizar **DO+NOT** ou **DOES+NOT**, o verbo retorna para o infinitivo. Forma contraída: • **DO+NOT = DON'T** • **DOES+NOT = DOESN'T** I do not (don't) <u>walk</u> every morning. He does not (doesn't) <u>walk</u> every morning.	• Na forma interrogativa, ao utilizar **DO** ou **DOES**, o verbo retorna para o infinitivo. Do I <u>walk</u> every morning? Does he <u>walk</u> every morning?

Simple Past / Passado Simples

Affirmative	Negative	Interrogative
• Verbos terminados em -**e**, apenas adiciona-se -**d**. I shared my sandwich with the girl. He shared his sandwich with the girl. • Verbos com apenas uma sílaba, terminados em consoante precedida por vogal, duplicar a consoante final e acrescentar -**ed**. I stopped He stopped • Verbos com duas sílabas ou mais, terminados em consoante precedida por vogal, duplicar a consoante final apenas se esta última for tônica, e então, acrescentar-**ed**. I admitted He admitted • Verbos terminados em -**y**, remover o -**y** e adicionar -**ied**, se precedido por consoante. I studied He studied • Verbos terminados em -**y**, precedidos por vogal, apenas adicionar -**ed**. I prayed He prayed	• Na forma negativa, ao utilizar **DID+NOT** o verbo retorna para o infinitivo. Forma contraída: • **DID+NOT = DON'T** I did not (din't) <u>walk</u> yesterday. He did not (din't) <u>walk</u> yesterday.	• Na forma interrogativa, ao utilizar **DID**, o verbo retorna para o infinitivo. Did I <u>walk</u> yesterday? Did he <u>walk</u> yesterday?

TEMPOS VERBAIS

Present Perfect / Presente Perfeito

Affirmative	Negative	Interrogative
I, you, we, they + HAVE + PAST PARTICIPLE He, she, it + HAS + PAST PARTICIPLE I **have studied** for the test. ou I'**ve studied** for the test. He **has studied** for the test. ou He'**s studied** for the test.	I, you, we, they + HAVE NOT + PAST PARTICIPLE He, she, it + HAS NOT + PAST PARTICIPLE Forma contraída: • **HAVE+NOT = HAVEN'T** • **HAS+NOT = HASN'T** I **have not** (haven't) **studied** for the test. He **has not** (hasn't) **studied** for the test.	HAVE + I, you, we, they + PAST PARTICIPLE? HAS + He, she, it + PAST PARTICIPLE? **Have** I **studied** for the test? **Has** he **studied** for the test?

Past Perfect / Passado Perfeito

Affirmative	Negative	Interrogative
I, you, he, she, it, we, they + HAD + PAST PARTICIPLE I **had studied** for the test. ou I'**d studied** for the test. He **had studied** for the test. ou He'**d studied** for the test.	I, you, he, she, it, we, they + HAD NOT + PAST PARTICIPLE Forma contraída: • **HAD+NOT = HADN'T** I **had not** (hadn't) **studied** for the test. He **had not** (hadn't) **studied** for the test.	HAD + I, you, he, she, it, we, they + PAST PARTICIPLE? **Had** I **studied** for the test? **Had** he **studied** for the test?

Simple Future / Futuro Simples

Affirmative	Negative	Interrogative
I, you, he, she, it, we, they + WILL + INFINITIVE I **will study** for the test. ou I'**ll will study** for the test. He **will study** for the test. ou He'**ll will study** for the test.	I, you, he, she, it, we, they + WILL NOT + INFINITIVE Forma contraída: • **WILL+NOT = WON'T** I **will not** (won't) **study** for the test. He **will not** (won't) **study** for the test.	WILL + I, you, he, she, it, we, they + INFINITIVE? **Will** I **study** for the test? **Will** he **study** for the test?

Future Perfect / Futuro Perfeito

Affirmative	Negative	Interrogative
I, you, he, she, it, we, they + WILL HAVE + PAST PARTICIPLE I **will have studied** for the test. ou I'**ll will study** for the test. He **will have studied** for the test. ou He'**ll will have studied** for the test.	I, you, he, she, it, we, they + WILL HAVE + PAST PARTICIPLE Forma contraída: • **WILL+NOT = WON'T** I **will not** (won't) **have studied** for the test. He **will** (won't) **have not study** for the test.	WILL + I, you, he, she, it, we, they + HAVE + PAST PARTICIPLE? **Will** I **have studied** for the test? **Will** he **have studied** for the test?

TEMPOS VERBAIS

Conditional / Condicional

Affirmative	Negative	Interrogative
I, you, he, she, it, we, they + WOULD + INFINITIVE I **would study** for the test, if I had time. ou I**'d study** for the test, if I had time. He **would study** for the test, if he had time. ou He**'d study** for the test, if he had time.	**I, you, he, she, it, we, they + WOULD + INFINITIVE** Forma contraída: • **WOULD+NOT = WOULDN'T** I **would not** (wouldn't) **study** for the test, if I had time. He **would not** (wouldn't) **study** for the test, if he had time.	**WOULD + I, you, he, she, it, we, they + INFINITIVE?** **Would** I **study** for the test, if I had time? **Would** he **study** for the test, if he had time?

Conditional Perfect / Condicional Perfeito

Affirmative	Negative	Interrogative
I, you, he, she, it, we, they + WOULD + HAVE + PAST PARTICIPLE I **would have studied** for the test, if I had time. ou I**'d have studied** for the test, if I had time. He **would have studied** for the test, if he had time. ou He**'d have studied** for the test, if he had time.	**I, you, he, she, it, we, they + WOULD NOT+ HAVE + PAST PARTICIPLE** Forma contraída: • **WOULD+NOT = WOULDN'T** I **would not** (wouldn't) **have studied** for the test, if I had time. He **would not** (wouldn't) **have studied** for the test, if he had time.	**WOULD + I, you, he, she, it, we, they + HAVE + PAST PARTICIPLE?** **Would** I **have studied** for the test, if I had time? **Would** he **have studied** for the test, if he had time?

TEMPOS PROGRESSIVOS

Present Continuous / Presente Contínuo

Affirmative	Negative	Interrogative
• **I + am + -ing form** • **he, she, it + is + -ing form** • **you, we, they + are + -ing form** • verbos terminados em *-e*, remover o *-e* e adicionar *-ing*. I **am** preparing the meal. ou I**'m** preparing the meal. He **is** preparing the meal. ou He**'s** preparing the meal. They **are** preparing the meal. ou They**'re** preparing the meal. • Verbos terminados em **uma vogal tônica** e **uma consoante** (exceto ***W*** e ***Y***), dobrar a última consoante e adicionar *-ing*. I **am** running in the park. ou I**'m** running in the park. He **is** running in the park. ou He**'s** running in the park. They **are** running in the park. ou They**'re** running in the park.	• **I + am not + -ing form** • **he, she, it + is not + -ing form** • **you, we, they + are are + -ing form** Forma contraída: • **AM NOT = 'M NOT** • **IS NOT = ISN'T** • **ARE NOT = AREN'T** I **am not** ('m not) running in the park. He **is not** (isn't) running in the park. They **are not** (aren't) running in the park.	• **Am I + -ing form?** • **Is he, she, it + -ing form?** • **Are + you, we, they + -ing form?** **Am** I running in the park? **Is** he running in the park? **Are** they running in the park?

TEMPOS VERBAIS

Past Continuous / Passado Contínuo

Affirmative	Negative	Interrogative
• I, he, she, it + + was + -ing form • you, we, they + were + -ing form • verbos terminados em -e, remover o -e e adicionar -ing. He was running in the park when she arrived. They were running in the park when she arrived.	• I, he, she, it + + was + -ing form • you, we, they + were + -ing form Forma contraída: • WAS NOT = WASN'T • WERE NOT = WEREN'T He was not (wasn't) running in the park when she arrived. They were not (weren't) running in the park when she arrived.	• Was + I, he, she, it + -ing form? • Were + you, we, they + -ing form? Was he running in the park when she arrived? Were they running in the park when she arrived?

Present Perfect Continuous / Presente Perfeito Contínuo

Affirmative	Negative	Interrogative
• I, you, we, they + HAVE + BEEN + -ing form • he, she, it + HAS + BEEN + -ing form I'm late because I have been preparing the meal. ou I'm late because I've been preparing the meal. He is late because He has been preparing the meal. ou He is late because He's been preparing the meal.	• I, you, we, they + HAVE NOT + BEEN + -ing form • he, she, it + HAS NOT + BEEN + -ing form Forma contraída: • HAVE+NOT = HAVEN'T • HAS+NOT = HASN'T I have not (haven't) been preparing the meal. He has not (hasn't) been preparing the meal.	• HAVE + I, you, we, they + BEEN + -ing form? • HAS + he, she, it + BEEN + -ing form? Have I been preparing the meal? Has he been preparing the meal?

Past Perfect Continuous / Passado Perfeito Contínuo

Affirmative	Negative	Interrogative
• I, you, he, she, it, we, they + HAD + BEEN + -ing form He had been preparing the meal. ou He'd been preparing the meal. They have been preparing the meal. ou They've been preparing the meal.	• I, you, he, she, it, we, they + HAD NOT + BEEN + -ing form Forma contraída: • HAD +NOT = HADN'T He had not (hadn't) been preparing the meal. They had not (hadn't) been preparing the meal.	• HAD + I, you, he, she, it, we, they + BEEN + -ing form? Had he been preparing the meal? Had they been preparing the meal?

Future Continuous / Futuro Contínuo

Affirmative	Negative	Interrogative
• I, you, he, she, it, we, they + WILL + BE + -ing form He will be preparing the meal. He'll be preparing the meal. They will be preparing the meal. They'll be preparing the meal.	• I, you, he, she, it, we, they + WILL NOT + BE + -ing form Forma contraída: • WILL +NOT = WON'T He will not (won't) be preparing the meal. They will not (won't) be preparing the meal.	• WILL + I, you, he, she, it, we, they + BE + -ing form? Will he be preparing the meal? Will they be preparing the meal?

TEMPOS VERBAIS

Future Perfect Continuous / Futuro Perfeito Contínuo

Affirmative	Negative	Interrogative
• I, you, he, she, it, we, they + WILL + HAVE + BEEN + -ing form He **will have been** preparing the meal. He**'ll have been** preparing the meal. They **will have been** preparing the meal. They**'ll have been** preparing the meal.	• I, you, he, she, it, we, they + WILL NOT + HAVE + BEEN + -ing form Forma contraída: • **WILL +NOT = WON'T** He **will not** (won't) **have been** preparing the meal. They **will not** (won't) **have been** preparing the meal.	• WILL + I, you, he, she, it, we, they + HAVE + BEEN + -ing form? Will he **have been** preparing the meal? Will they **have been** preparing the meal?

Conditional Continuous / Condicional Contínuo

Affirmative	Negative	Interrogative
I, you, he, she, it, we, they + WOULD + BE + -ing form I **would be studying** for the test, if I had time. I**'d be studying** for the test, if I had time. He **would be studying** for the test, if he had time. He**'d be studying** for the test, if he had time.	I, you, he, she, it, we, they + WOULD NOT+ BE + -ing form Forma contraída: • **WOULD+NOT = WOULDN'T** I **would not** (wouldn't) **be studying** for the test, if I had time. He **would not** (wouldn't) **be studying** for the test, if he had time.	WOULD + I, you, he, she, it, we, they + BE + -ing form? Would I **be studying** for the test, if I had time? Would he **be studying** for the test, if he had time?

Conditional Perfect Continuous / Condicional Perfeito Contínuo

Affirmative	Negative	Interrogative
I, you, he, she, it, we, they + WOULD + HAVE + BEEN + -ing form I **would have been studying** for the test, if I had time. I**'d have been studying** for the test, if I had time. He **would have been studying** for the test, if he had time. He**'d have been studying** for the test, if he had time.	I, you, he, she, it, we, they + WOULD NOT+ HAVE + BEEN + -ing form Forma contraída: • **WOULD+NOT = WOULDN'T** I **would not** (wouldn't) **have been studying** for the test, if I had time. He **would not** (wouldn't) **have been studying** for the test, if he had time.	WOULD + I, you, he, she, it, we, they + HAVE + BEEN + -ing form? Would I **have been studying** for the test, if I had time? Would he **have been studying** for the test, if he had time?

O VERBO 'TO BE'

Simple Present / Presente Simples

Affirmative	Interrogative	Negative
I am, I'm	Am I?	I am not, I'm not
You are, you're	Are you?	You are not, you're not, you aren't
She is, he's	Is he / she / it?	It is not, he's not, she isn't
We are, they're	Are we / they?	We are not, they're not, we aren't

Simple Past Passado Simples

Affirmative	Interrogative	Negative
I was	Was I?	I was not, I wasn't
You were	Were you?	You were not, you weren't
He, she, it was	Was he / she / it?	She was not, it wasn't
We, they were	Were we / they?	We were not, they weren't

Past Participle: been

AQUISIÇÃO DE VOCABULÁRIO

MEIOS DE TRANSPORTE

automóvel, carro	car	**metrô**	subway (US) underground (UK)
avião	airplane (US) aeroplane (UK)	**microônibus**	minivan
balsa	ferry	**moto**	motorcycle
barco à vela	sailboat (US) sailing boat (UK)	**motor-home**	RV (US) camper (UK)
bicicleta	bicycle	**navio**	ship
caminhão	truck (US) lorry (UK)	**ônibus**	bus (US) coach (UK)
camionete	van	**petroleiro**	oil tanker
helicóptero	helicopter	**táxi**	taxi (US) cab (UK)
jipe	SUV	**trailer**	caravan
lambreta	scooter	**trem**	train
lancha	speedboat		

AQUISIÇÃO DE VOCABULÁRIO

LOJAS

açougue	butcher shop (US) butcher's (UK)	**livraria**	bookstore
balcão	counter	**loja de conveniência**	convenience store
banca de jornais	newsstand	**loja de departamentos**	department store
boutique	boutique		
caixa	checkout	**loja de ferragens**	hardware store (US) hardware shop (UK)
caixa registradora	till		
carrinho	cart (US) trolley (UK)	**loja de roupas**	clothes store (US) clothes shop (UK)
centro comercial	mall shopping center (US) shopping centre (UK)	**mercado, feira**	market
		mercearia, armazém	grocery store (US) grocer's (UK)
cliente, consumidor	customer		
conta	bill	**óptica**	optician
farmácia	drugstore (US) chemist's (UK)	**para levar**	takeout
floricultura	flower shop (US) florist's (UK)	**recibo**	receipt
jornaleiro	news dealer	**sacola, saco**	carrier bag
lavanderia automática	laundromat	**tinturaria**	dry-cleaners

LAZER E PASSATEMPO

acampar	camping	**dança, dançar**	dancing
andar de patins	roller skating	**dardos**	darts
bilhar	billiards	**desenho, desenhar**	drawing
bilhar americano	pool	**discoteca, danceteria**	clubbing
blogar, escrever	blogging	**dominó**	dominoes
boliche	bowling	**encontrar-se com os amigos**	meeting friends
bricolage	DIY		
cartas	cards	**excursionismo**	hiking
culinária	cookery	**fazer exercício**	working out

AQUISIÇÃO DE VOCABULÁRIO

LAZER E PASSATEMPO

fotografia	photography	sinuca	snooker
leitura	reading	skate	skateboarding
mochileiro	backpacking	tocar violão	playing the guitar
passatempo	hobby	tricotar	knitting
patinação sobre rodas	in-line skating or rollerblading	xadrez	chess
pintura	painting		

MÚSICA

violoncelo	cello	banda de música	brass band
clarinete	clarinet	coro	choir
contrabaixo	double bass	compositor	composer
tambor	drum	concerto	concert
bateria	drums	regente	conductor
flauta	flute	clave, tecla do piano	key
piano de cauda	grand piano	músico	musician
violão	guitar	nota	note
teclado	keyboard	percussão	percussion
oboé	oboe	tocar	play
piano	piano	quarteto	quartet
flauta doce	recorder	partitura	score
saxofone	saxophone	instrumentos de corda	strings
trombone	trombone	sintetizador	synthesizer
trumpete	trumpet		
viola	viola	melodia, afinar	tune
violino	violin	instrumentos de sopro de madeira	woodwind
reverência	bow		

AQUISIÇÃO DE VOCABULÁRIO

CORPO HUMANO

amígdala	tonsil	costela	rib
antebraço	forearm	cotovelo	elbow
apêndice	appendix	coxa	thigh
artéria	artery	crânio	skull
axila	armpit	dedo anelar	ring finger
baço	spleen	dedo da mão	finger
barba	beard	dedo do pé	toe
barriga	belly	dedo indicador	forefinger
barriga da perna	calf	dedo médio	middle finger
bexiga	bladder	dedo mínimo	little finger
boca	mouth	dedo polegar	thumb
bochecha	cheek	dente	tooth
braço	arm	dorso	back
cabeça	head	esôfago	esophagus
cabelo	hair	esqueleto	skeleton
calcanhar	heel	estômago	stomach
canela	shin	falange	phalanx
carne	flesh	faringe	pharynx
célula	cell	fêmur	thigh bone
cérebro	brain	fígado	liver
cílios	eyeslash	garganta	throat
cintura	waist	gengiva	gum
clavícula	collar bone	intestinos	bowels
coluna vertebral	spine	íris	iris
coração	heart	joelho	knee
cordas vocais	vocal cords	lábio	lip
coronária	corónary	laringe	larynx
costas	back	língua	tongue

AQUISIÇÃO DE VOCABULÁRIO

CORPO HUMANO

lóbulo	earlobe	punho	fist
mamilo	nipple	pupila	pupil
mandíbula	jaw	quadril	hip
mão	hand	queixo	chin
medula espinhal	spinal cord	região lombar	lumbar region
medula óssea	marrow	rim	kidney
músculo	muscle	rosto	face
nádegas	buttocks	rótula	knee cap, patella
narina	nostril	sangue	blood
nariz	nose	seio	bosom
nuca	nape	sobrancelha	eyebrow
olho	eye	tecido	tissue
ombro	shoulder	têmporas	temples
omoplata	shoulder blade	testa	forehead
osso	bone	tórax	chest
ouvido	ear	tornozelo	ankle
pálpebra	eyelid	traqueia	windpipe
pâncreas	pancreas	tronco	trunk
pé	foot	umbigo	navel
peito (colo)	breast	unha	nail
peito do pé	instep	uretra	urethra
pele	skin	útero	womb
pênis	penis	vagina	vagina
perna	leg	vaso sanguíneo	blood vessel
pescoço	neck	veia	vein
pomo-de-adão	Adam's apple	vértebra	vertebra
pulmão	lung	vesícula	gall bladder
pulso	wrist	virilha	groin

AQUISIÇÃO DE VOCABULÁRIO

VESTUÁRIO

(blusão de) moletom	sweatshirt	cueca	underwear
blusa	blouse	gorro de lã	wooly hat
bolsa tiracolo	shoulder bag	gravata	tie
bone de beisebol	baseball cap	jaqueta de brim	denim jacket
bota	boot	jaqueta de couro	leather jacket
cachecol	scarf	luva	glove
calça	pants (US) trousers (UK)	meia	sock
calça cargo	cargo pants	meia-calça	pantyhose (US) tights (UK)
calça jeans	jeans	óculos de sol	sunglasses
calção	shorts	pasta executiva	briefcase
camisa	shirt	roupa de jogging	tracksuit
camiseta	t-shirt	saia	skirt
camisola curta	crop top	sandália	sandal
capa de chuva	raincoat	sapato	shoe
capuz	hood	sobretudo	overcoat
casaco	coat	suéter	sweater
casaco curto, jaqueta	jacket	tanga, fio-dental	thong
chapéu	hat	terno	suit
cinto	belt	vestido	dress
colete	vest		

AQUISIÇÃO DE VOCABULÁRIO

MATÉRIAS ESCOLARES E SALA DE AULA

apontador	pencil sharpener	intervalo, recreio	break
Arte	Art	lápis	pencil
Biologia	Biology	lição	lesson
borracha	eraser (US) rubber (UK)	lição de casa	homework
caderno	notebook	livro texto	textbook
calculadora	calculator	lixeira	wastebasket
caneta	pen	lousa	board
caneta esferográfica	ballpoint (pen)	mapa	map
caneta hidrográfica	felt-tip (pen)	Matemática	Math (US) Maths (UK)
caneta marcatexto	highlighter	mochila	school bag
chamada	register	Música	Music
compasso	compasses	professor	teacher
dicionário	dictionary	quadro branco	whiteboard
Economia doméstica	Home economics	quadro de avisos	bulletin board (US) noticeboard (UK)
Educação física	Physical Education	Química	Chemistry
estojo	pencil case	recesso, férias	recess
estudante	student	régua	ruler
fichário	file	revisão	review
Física	Physics	série, nota	grade
Geografia	Geography	tabuada	timetable
ginásio	gym	Tecnologia da informação, Computação	IT or Computer Science
grampeador	stapler	teste, prova	test
História	History		
Inglês	English		

AQUISIÇÃO DE VOCABULÁRIO

PROFISSÕES

aprendiz	apprentice	médico(a)	doctor
balconista	salesclerk	padeiro	baker
barbeiro	baber	pescador(a)	fisherman
bombeiro(a), encanador(a)	plumber	piloto	pilot
cabeleireiro(a)	hairdresser	pintor(a)	painter
carpinteiro(a)	carpenter	professor(a)	teacher
carteiro	letter carrier	programador(a)	programmer
cozinheiro(a)	cook	projetista	designer
enfermeiro(a)	nurse	secretário(a)	secretary
fazendeiro(a)	farmer	técnico(a)	technician
gerente	manager		

ATIVIDADES ESPORTIVAS

alpinismo	mountaineering, climbing	críquete	cricket
andar de caiaque	kayaking	croqué	croquet
andar de jet ski	jet-skiing	equitação	horseback riding (US) riding (UK)
atletismo	track and field (US) athletics (UK)	esgrima	fencing
badminton	badminton	espécie de basquetebol	netball
basquete	basketball	esqui	skiing
beisebol	baseball	esqui aquático	waterskiing
boxe, pugilismo	boxing	fazer mountain bike	mountain biking
ciclismo	cycling	futebol	soccer (US) football (UK)
cooper, jogging	jogging	futebol americano	football (US) American football (UK)
corrida pelo campo	cross-country		

AQUISIÇÃO DE VOCABULÁRIO

ATIVIDADES ESPORTIVAS

ginástica (olímpica)	gymnastics	rafting	white-water rafting
golfe	golf	rapel	rappel (US) abseiling (UK)
handebol	handball	remo	rowing
hóquei	hockey	rúgbi	rugby
judô	judo	snowboard, surf na neve	snowboarding
levantamento de pesos	weightlifting	squash	squash
líder de torcida	cheerleader	surfe	surfing
luta livre	wrestling	taekwondo	tae kwon do
megulho com snorkel	snorkeling	tênis	tennis
mergulho (com tubo de oxigênio)	scuba-diving	tênis de mesa	table tennis
muay thai	kickboxing	voleibol	volleyball
natação	swimming	voo livre	hang-gliding
navegação	sailing	windsurfe	windsurfing
parapente	paragliding		

Relacionados:

taco	bat	raia	lane
clube	club	rede	net
curso	course	arremesso, lance	pitch
quadra	court	corrida	race
mergulho	diving	raquete	racket
descida	downhill	marcar ponto, ponto	score
campo	field, ground	pista	slope, track
capacete	helmet		

AQUISIÇÃO DE VOCABULÁRIO

ALIMENTOS E REFEIÇÕES

açúcar	sugar	mostarda	mustard
água mineral	mineral water	óleo	oil
bagel	bagel	ovo frito	fried egg
batata assada	jacket potato	ovos	eggs
batatas fritas	french fries (US) chips (UK)	pão	bread
bolinhos	muffins	pãozinho	roll
cachorro-quente	hot dog	patê	pâté
caril	curry	picles	pickle
cereal	cereal	pimenta	pepper
cerveja	beer	pizza	pizza
creme	cream	presunto	ham
espaguete com molho de tomate	spaghetti with tomato sauce	queijo	cheese
fatia, posta, rodela	slice	rosbife	roast beef
frango assado	roast chicken	sal	salt
guisado, ensopado	stew	salmão	salmon
leite	milk	sanduíche	sandwich
leite batido	milkshake	sopa	soup
macarão, massa(s)	pasta	sorvete	ice cream
maionese	mayonnaise	suco de fruta	fruit juice
manteiga	butter	torta de abóbora	pumpkin pie
margarina	margarine	torta de maçã	apple pie
mingau (de aveia)	porridge	truta	trout
molho	sauce	vinagre	vinegar
molho para servir com salgadinhos	dip	vinho	wine
		waffles	waffles

AQUISIÇÃO DE VOCABULÁRIO

VERDURAS, RAÍZES E SEMENTES

abóbora	pumpkin, squash	couve-flor	caili-flower
abobrinha	zucchini	couve	kale
agrião	water-cress	ervilha	pea
aipo (salsão)	celery	espinafre	spinash
alcachofra	artichoke	feijão	bean
alface	lettuce	gengibre	ginger
alho	garlic	grão-de-bico	chickpea
aspargo	asparagus	mandioca	cassava
azeitona	olive	nabo	turnip
batata	potato	palmito	heart of palm
batata-doce	sweet-potato	pepino	cucumber
berinjela	aubergine, eggplant	pimentão	sweet pepper, pimento
beterraba	beet	quiabo	okra
cebola	onion	rabanete	radish
cenoura	carrot	repolho	cabbage
chicória	chicory	salsão (aipo)	celery
chuchu	chayote	salsinha	parsley
cogumelo	mushroom	vagem	husk

FRUTAS

abacate	avocado	amora	blackberry, mulberry
abacaxi	pineapple	avelã	hazelnut
abóbora	pumpkin	banana	banana
ameixa fresca	plum	cacau	cocoa
ameixa seca	prune	caju	cashew
amêndoa	almond	caqui	persimmon
amendoim	peanut	castanha	chestnut

AQUISIÇÃO DE VOCABULÁRIO

FRUTAS

castanha-do-pará	brazil nut	marmelo	quince
cereja	cherry	melancia	watermelon
coco	coconut	melão	melon
figo	fig	morango	strawberry
framboesa	raspberry	noz	nut, walnut
fruta-do-conde	sweetsop	pera	pear
goiaba	guava	pêssego	peach
groselha	currant, gooseberry	romã	pomegranate
laranja	orange	tâmara	date
limão	lemon	tamarindo	tamarind
maçã	apple	tangerina	tangerine
mamão	papaya	tomate	tomato
manga	mango	uva	grape
maracujá	passion fruit	uva-passa	raisin

REINO ANIMAL

abelha	bee	beija-flor	hummingbird
abutre	vulture	besouro	beetle
águia	eagle	bezerro, terneiro	calf
andorinha	swallow	bicho-da-seda	silkworm
antílope	antelope	bode, cabra	goat
aranha	spider	boi	ox
asno	donkey, ass	borboleta	butterfly
avestruz	ostrich	búfalo	buffalo
bacalhau	code	burro	donkey
baleia	whale	cabrito	kid
barata	cockroach	cachorrinho	puppy

AQUISIÇÃO DE VOCABULÁRIO

REINO ANIMAL

cachorro	dog	ema	rhea
camarão	shrimp	enguia	eel
camelo	camel	escorpião	scorpion
camundongo	mouse	esquilo	squirrel
canguru	kangaroo	faisão	pheasant
caracol	snail	foca	seal
caranguejo	crab	gafanhoto	grasshopper
carneiro	lamb, sheep	gaivota	seagull
carrapato	tick	galinha	chicken
castor	beaver	galo	cock
cavalo	horse	gambá	skunk
cegonha	stork	ganso	goose
cervo	fawn	gato	cat
chipanzé	chimpanzee	gavião	hawk
chita	cheetah	gerbo	gerbil
cisne	swan	girafa	giraffe
coala	koala	golfinho	dolphin
cobra	snake	gorila	gorilla
coelho	rabbit	grilo	cricket
cordeiro	lamb	hamster	hamster
coruja	owl	hipopótamo	hippopotamus hippo (coloq.)
corvo	crow, raven		
coiote	coyote	jacaré	alligator
crocodilo	crocodile	javali	wild boar
cupim	termite	joaninha	lady-bug
cutia	agouti	lagartixa	small lizard
égua	mare	lagarto	lizard
elefante	elephant	lagosta	lobster

AQUISIÇÃO DE VOCABULÁRIO

REINO ANIMAL

leão	lion	porco	pig
lebre	hare	porco-espinho	porcupine
leopardo	leopard	porquinho-da-índia	guinea pig
lhama	illama	potro	foal
libélula	dragonfly	preguiça	sloth
lince	lynx	pulga	flea
lobo	wolf	puma	puma
lontra	otter	rã	frog
macaco	monkey	raposa	fox
macaco (sem rabo)	ape	rena	reindeer
mexilhão	mussel	rinoceronte	rhinoceros rhino (coloq.)
minhoca	earthworm		
morcego	bat	rouxinol	nightingale
ornitorrinco	platypus	sapo	toad
ostra	oyster	tamanduá	anteater
ovelha	ewe, sheep	tartaruga	turtle
pantera	panther	tatu	armadillo
papagaio	parrot	tigre	tiger
pardal	sparrow	toupeira	mole
pato	duck	touro	bull
pavão	peacock	traça	moth
percevejo	bug	tubarão	shark
peru	turkey	urso	bear
pica-pau	woodpecker	urso polar	polar bear
piolho	louse	vaca	cow
polvo	octopus	veado	deer
pombo	pigeon, dove	zangão	drone
pônei	pony	zebra	zebra

AQUISIÇÃO DE VOCABULÁRIO

ESTAÇÕES DO ANO E O CLIMA

arco-íris	raibow	neve	snow
chuva com neve ou granizo	sleet	nevoeiro	fog
		nuvens	clouds
ensolarado	sunny	outono	Fall (US) Autumm (UK)
está chovendo	it's raining		
está ventando	it's windy	pelando (de calor)	boiling
frio, friorento	chilly	pôr-do-sol	sunset
glacial	freezing	primavera	Spring
granizo	hail	relâmpago, raio	lightning
inverno	Winter	tempestade	storm
neblina (leve) névoa (pesada)	mist	trovão, trovoada	thunder
		verão	Summer

MENSAGENS DE TEXTO

Muitas pessoas costumam utilizar formas abreviadas e / ou *emoticons* ao enviarem mensagens de texto pelo celular ou internet, como as que se seguem: **EMOTION (EMOÇÃO) + ICON (ÍCONE) = EMOTICON**

Icon / Ícones, Abbreviation/ Abreviações	Meaning / Significado	Icon / Ícones, Abbreviation/ Abreviações	Meaning / Significado
:-) :-] :-} :o) :^) :c)	happy, happy face, smiley feliz, cara feliz, sorriso	:-o	very surprised, shouting loudly, shocked, yawn muito surpreso, berrando, chocado, bocejo
:-D X-D B^D	laughing, big grin rindo, sorriso enorme	:-@	Screaming gritando
:-))	very happy or double chin muito feliz ou queixo duplo	:-*	sending you a kiss mandando um beijo
:-(:-c :-< :-{ :-[:-@	sad, unhappy, angry, pouting triste, infeliz, zangado, amuado	:-()	I have a mustache Eu tenho bigode
>:-(	very sad, unhappy muito triste, infeliz	8-)	I wear glasses Eu uso óculos
:'-(	Crying chorando	;-) *-) ;^) ;-D	wink, smirk piscada, sorriso falso
:'-)	tears of happiness lágrimas de felicidade	:-p	tongue sticking out mostrando a língua

MENSAGENS DE TEXTO

Icon / Ícones, Abbreviation/ Abreviações	Meaning / Significado
:-/ :/	skeptical, annoyed, undecided cético, aborrecido, indeciso
:-|	straight face, no expression, indecision cara séria, sem expressão, indecisa
:$	embarrassed, blushing envergonhado, ruborizado
:-x :-# :-&	sealed slips or wearing braces, tongue-tied lábios selados ou usando aparelgo, nó na língua
0:-) 0;^)	angel, saint, innocent anjo, santo, inocente
%-)	drunk, confused bêbado, confuso
@	at
2	to, too, two
2day	today
2moro	tomorrow
2nite	tonight
4	for, four
4eva	forever
asap	as soon as possible
b	be
b4	before
brb	be right back
btw	by the way
cn	can
cu	see you
cud	could

Icon / Ícones, Abbreviation/ Abreviações	Meaning / Significado
evry1	everyone
ez	easy
fone	phone
gd	good
gr8	great
l8	late
l8r	later
lol	laugh out loud
luvu	love you
msg	message
ne1	anyone
neway	anyway
no1	no one
pls	please
ppl	people
ruok?	Are you ok?
sn	soon
spksn	speak soon
thanx ou thx	thanks
txt	text
u	you
ur	you are
v	very
w	with
xoxoxo	hugs and kisses
yr	your, you're

VERBOS MODAIS

Os verbos modais servem para expressar ideias como capacidade, possibilidade, obrigação, permissão, ou proibição. Estes verbos posuem somente as formas de presente e passado, com exceção de *must* e *ought to*, que possuem somente formas de presente. Também não possuem infinitivo, nem particípio, nem gerúndio. Os verbos modais são os seguintes:

Possibility and Probability
Possibilidade e Probabilidade

- **MUST / CAN'T** - referir-se a algo que considera-mos certo, algo do qual temos mais certeza. Usa-se *must* em sentenças afirmativas e *can't* em senten-ças negativas.
  You **must** be thirsty – you haven't drunk water all day.
  You **can't** be thirsty – we just drank iced tea!

- **MAY / MIGHT / COULD** - referir-se a algo que é possível, mas não certo de acontecer.
  Mommy **may** be right.
  Daddy **must** be in the bathroom.
  He **may / might** not come to the meeting if he's busy.
  Laura **could** be a famous singer one day.
  It **could** be exciting.
  Obs.: should (US) e **ought to** (UK), podem ser utilizados para prever o futuro.
  Two hundred dollars **should** be enough to pay the expenses.
  John **ought to** pass – he has studied hard.

Obligation and Duty
Obrigação e Dever

- **MUST** - para enfatizar um conselho ou expressar uma obrigação.
  They **must** be back by five.
  You **must** stop drinking.
  You **must** read that novel – it's amazing!
- **HAVE TO / HAVE GOT TO (UK)** - ambos podem ser utilizados para expressar obrigação e dever. De forma geral, utiliza-se **have got to** somente no presente.
  I **have to** finish my Biology work before Thursday.
  She **had to** stop drinking.

Prohibition
Proibição

- **MUSTN'T / CAN'T** - utilizados para expressar algo que é proibido.
  You **mustn't** smoke inside the restaurant.
  She **can't** come in here without an authorization.

Advices
Conselhos

- **SHOULD / OUGHT TO** - utilizados para pedir e dar conselhos.
  The children **should** go to bed – it's late!
  The government **should** do something about it.
  Barbara **ought to** visit her parents more often.
  You **shouldn't** buy this car.
  Should I take my documents with me?

Offers, Suggestions and Requests
Ofertas, Sugestões e Pedidos

- **CAN / COULD / WILL / SHALL / SHOULD (US)** - utilizados para oferecer, sugerir ou pedir algo.
  Can I help you Sir?
  Could you open the window, please?
  Will you go out, please?
  Will she stay for lunch?
  Should I invite them for some tea?

Permission
Permissão

- **CAN / COULD** – utilizados para expressar permis-são para fazer algo, no presente e no passado.
  Can we go now?
  Could I possibly borrow your car this weekend?
  They **can** come if they want.
  É possível utilizar **may** e **might** no presente, porém, expressam mais formalidade.
  May I use you toilet, please?
  DVDs **may** only be borrowed for three days.
  Might a make a suggestion for you?
  I'll go to the party, if I **may**.

PHRASAL VERBS

São verbos acompanhados de preposições ou de partículas adverbiais. Podem ser formados por duas ou três palavras. A primeira palavra sempre será um verbo, seguido de um advérbio (**go up**), uma preposição (**run after**) ou ambos (**carry on with**). A lista abaixo apresenta alguns exemplos de verbos seguidos de preposição ou de partículas adverbiais.

Verbo	Tradução	Exemplo
to break up	separar-se	I've got no ideia why they have broken up.
to break down	quebrar	My car broke down on the highway.
to call off	cancelar	The picnic was called off because of the rain.
to carry on with	continuar	Let's carry on with our work.
to come across	encontrar por acaso	She came across an old friend in Paris.
to come off	sair, desaparecer	I need to wash this now; otherwise, this stain won't come off.
to come out	publicar	William's book is coming out next month.
to cut down	reduzir	She has to cut down on expenses.
to do away with	eliminar	His company has done away with all their competitors.
to find out	averiguar	Jenny, find out how much he has to pay.
to get at	querer dizer	What is she getting at?
to get on with	relacionar-se com	He doesn't really get on with his colleagues at school.
to get on	progredir	How are you getting on at school?
to get over	superar (problemas)	Mary cannot easily get over a bad mark in exams.
to get up	levantar-se	My dad always gets up at 6.
to give up	deixar de (fazer algo)	He has tried to give up smoking more than four times.
to go off	explodir	The building went off some minutes before we left it.
to go on	acontecer, suceder	What's going on there?
to go through	atravessar, passar por	Our country has gone through a financial crisis.
to go with	combinar, coordenar	This blouse does not go with this skirt.
to grow up	crescer	When July grows up, she wants to be a top model.
to hold on	aguardar	Please, hold on. I'm going to call my mother.
to keep on	continuar	I can't keep on eating fast food every week.
to pass away	morrer, falecer	My father passed away in 2008.
to look for	procurar	I'm looking for my red shoes. Have you seen them?
to look forward to	esperar com ansiedade	She's looking forward to see him again.
to look like	parecer	She looks quite like her mother.
to look into	investigar	The detective has been looking into the crime.
to look after	tomar conta de, cuidar	Betty will look after her little cousin tonight.

PHRASAL VERBS

Verbo	Tradução	Exemplo
to look through	examinar	The police has been looking through the crime evidences.
to pick up	pegar, apanhar	He'll pick me up at the bus station at 8.
to put out	apagar	The firefighters finally managed to put out the fire.
to put off	adiar	Never put off until tomorrow what you can do today.
to put up with	tolerar, aguentar	I sick of prejudice. I cannot put up with it anymore.
to run away	escapar	I often hear of prisoners who run away from prison.
to run out of	terminar, acabar (estoque)	We've run out of ice-cream. Let's go to the market and buy some.
to set off	partir	At what time does she set off tomorrow?
to think over	considerar	If I were you, I'd think it over.
to take back	devolver	I took back the T-shirt because it had shrunk.
to take after	parecer-se com (atitudes)	Nora takes after her father.
to take over	assumir o controle	A Japanese firm took over the company last month.
to take off	decolar	The plane took off three hours later.
to throw away	jogar fora	Why did you throw these old magazines away?

DIFERENÇAS ENTRE O INGLÊS AMERICANO E BRITÂNICO

As diferenças entre os dois idiomas não se limitam somente à pronúncia, mas também ao vocabulário, ortografia e estruturas gramaticais, como veremos a seguir.

VOCABULARY / VOCABULÁRIO
Apesar de serem muito parecidos, existem diferenças lexicais importantes entre os dois idiomas. Veja alguns exemplos:

US	UK	Tradução	US	UK	Tradução
candy	sweets	doces	movie theater	cinema	cinema
cell phone	mobile (phone)	telefone celular	pants	trousers	calças
chips	crisps	batata frita	sidewalk	pavement	calçada
closet	wardrobe	guarda-roupas	store	shop	loja
elevator	lift	elevador	trash	rubbish	lixo
fall	autumn	outono	truck	lorry	caminhão
gas	petrol	gasolina	zucchini	courgette	abobrinha
line	queue	fila			

DIFERENÇAS ENTRE O INGLÊS AMERICANO E BRITÂNICO

ORTOGRAPHY / ORTOGRAFIA

No inglês Britânico, o final -l de alguns verbos é duplicado:

US	UK	Tradução
Canceling	Cancelling	Cancelar
Traveled	Travelled	Viajar

A terminação -ter, muda para -tre:

US	UK	Tradução
center	centre	centro
liter	litre	litro
meter	metre	metro
theater	theatre	teatro

A terminação -ense muda para -ence:

US	UK	Tradução
defense	defence	defesa
license	licence	licença
offense	offence	ofensa

Palavras terminadas em -or, são escritas com -our:

US	UK	Tradução
color	colour	cor
colorful	colourful	colorido
favor	favour	favor
honor	honour	honra
labor	labour	trabalho
neighbor	neighbour	vizinho

Palavras que são escritas com -og ou -ogue, são escritas somente com -ogue:

US	UK	Tradução
Catalog	Catalogue	Catálogo
Dialogue / dialog	Dialogue	diálogo

Verbos terminados em -ize, podem terminar em -ize ou -ise, ocorrendo o mesmo com seus derivados:

US	UK	Tradução
realize	realize, realize realization, realisation	realizar realização

Obs.: Há exceções, como por exemplo: **advise**, **surprise**, **exercise**, que tem a mesma escrita em ambos os idiomas.

Outros casos em que a ortografia é diferente:

US	UK	Tradução
analyze	analyse	analisar
anemia	anaemia	anemia
check	cheque	cheque
cozy	cosy	aconchegante
gray	grey	cinza
jewelry	jewellery	jóias
mold	mould	bolor, mofo
pajamas	pyjamas	pijama
plow	plough	arado, arar
practice	practise	praticar
tire	tyre	pneu

DIFERENÇAS ENTRE O INGLÊS AMERICANO E BRITÂNICO

GRAMMAR / GRAMÁTICA
Present Perfect e Simple Past

US	UK
Utiliza-se os advérbios just, yet e already no Simple Past.	Utiliza-se **just, yet** e **already** apenas no **Present Perfect**.
I just had lunch. Did you hear the news yet? He already gave her his present.	I've just had lunch. Have you heard the news yet? He has already given her his present

HAVE em frases interrogativas e negativas

US	UK
Para indicar ideia de posse, utiliza-se somente have quando a frase é negativa ou interrogativa.	Pode-se utilizar **have** ou **have got**.
She doesn't have enough time. Do you have a cell phone?	She hasn't (got) time. / She doesn't have enough time. Have you got a cell phone? / Do you have a cell phone?

GOTTEN / GOT

US	UK
O Passado Particípio de get é gotten.	O Passado Particípio de get é **got**.
Her cooking has gotten much better.	Her cooking has got much better.

WILL / SHALL

US	UK
Utiliza-se somente will para formar a primeira pessoa do futuro.	Pode-se utilizar **shall** e **will**.
I will be here next week.	I shall / will be here next week.
Utiliza-se should para oferecer algo ou fazer uma sugestão.	Utiliza-se **shall** para oferecer algo ou fazer uma sugestão.
Should I open the door?	Shall I open the door?

Prepositions and Adverbs

US	UK
a quarter after ten	a quarter **past** ten
different from / than	different **from / to**
Monday through Friday	Monday **to** Friday
on the weekend	**at** the weekend
to stay home	to stay **at** home

DIFERENÇAS ENTRE O INGLÊS AMERICANO E BRITÂNICO

Irregular Verbs
Os verbos: **burn, dream, lean, leap, learn, smell, spill** e **spoil** apresentam duas formas no Passado Simples e no Passado Particípio, uma regular: **burned, dreamed, leaned, leaped, learned, smelled, spilled** e **spoiled**.

US	UK
Utiliza-se somente a forma regular para o Passado Simples e Passado Particípio.	Utiliza ambas as formas, indistintamente.
They burned the old chair.	They **burned / burnt** the old chair.

FALSOS COGNATOS

Cognatos são palavras que têm a mesma origem, semelhança, ortografia e mesmo significado em diversas línguas. Entretanto, algumas palavras em Inglês são semelhantes ao Português, mas o significado delas é diferente. Vejamos alguns exemplos abaixo:

English	Portuguese
actually (adv) - realmente, na verdade	**atualmente** - nowadays, today
amass (v) - acumular, juntar	**amassar** - crush
application (n) - registro, uso	**aplicação** - investment
appointment (n) - hora marcada, compromisso	**apontamento** - note
appreciation (n) - gratidão, reconhecimento	**apreciação** - judgment
argument (n) - discussão	**argumento** - reasoning, point
assist (n) - ajudar, dar apoio	**assistir** - to attend, to watch
assume (v) - presumir, aceitar como verdadeiro	**assumir** - to take over
attend (v) - assistir, participar	**atender** - to help; to answer; to see; to examine
balcony (n) - sacada	**balcão** - counter
carton (n) - caixa de papelão	**cartão** - card
casualty (n) - baixas (mortes)	**casualidade** - chance
cigar (n) - charuto	**cigarro** - cigarrete
collar (n) - gola, colarinho, coleira	**colar** - necklace
college (n) - faculdade	**colégio** - high school
commodity (n) - artigo, mercadoria	**comodidade** - comfort
comprehensive (adj) - abrangente, amplo, extenso	**compreensivo** - understandable
compromise (v) - entrar em acordo, conceder	**compromisso** - appointment
contest (n) - competição, concurso	**contexto** - context
convenient (adj) - útil, acessível	**conveniente** - appropriate
costume (n) - fantasia, (roupa)	**costume** - custom, habit

FALSOS COGNATOS

English	Portuguese
data (n) - dados (números, informações)	**data** - date
deception (n) - fraude, logro	**decepção** - disappointment
design (v, n) - criar, projetar; projeto	**designar** - to appoint
editor (n) - redator	**editor** - publisher
educated (adj) - instruído, estudado	**educado** - well-mannered, polite
enroll (v) - inscrever-se, alistar-se, registrar-se	**enrolar** - to roll; to wind; to curl
eventually (adv) - finalmente, no final	**eventualmente** - occasionally
exciting (adj) - empolgante	**excitante** - thrilling
exit (n, v) - sair, saída	**êxito** - success
expert (n) - especialista, perito	**esperto** - smart, clever
exquisite (adj) - belo, refinado	**esquisito** - strange, odd
fabric (n) - tecido	**fábrica** - plant, factory
gratuity (n) - gratificação, gorgeta	**grátis** - free, free of change
grip (v) - agarrar firme	**gripe** - flu, cold, influenza
hazard (n, v) - risco, arriscar	**azar** - bad luck
idiom (n) - expressão idiomática	**idioma** - language
ingenuity (n) - engenhosidade	**ingenuidade** - naiveté / naivety
injury (n) - ferimento	**injúria** - insult, offense
inscription (n) - gravação (sobre pedra ou metal)	**inscrição** - application
intend (v) - pretender, ter a intenção de	**entender** - understand
journal (n) - periódico, revista especializada	**jornal** - newspaper
large (adj) - grande, espaçoso	**largo** - wide
lecture (n) - palestra	**leitura** - reading
legend (n) - lenda	**legenda** - subtitle
library (n) - biblioteca	**livraria** - bookshop, bookstore
lunch (n) - almoço	**lanche** - snack
magazine (n) - revista	**magazine** - department store
mayor (n) - prefeito	**maior** - bigger
moisture (n) - umidade	**mistura** - mix, mixture, blend
notice (n, v) - aviso, notar	**notícias** - news
novel (n) - romance	**novela** - soap opera
office (n) - escritório	**ofício** - profession

FALSOS COGNATOS

English	Portuguese
parents (n) - pais	**parentes** - relatives
pasta (n) - massa (macarrão)	**pasta** - briefcase, folder
policy (n) - política	**polícia** - police
porter (n) - carregador	**porteiro** - door keeper
prejudice (n) - preconceito	**prejuízo** - damage, loss
preservative (n) - conservante	**preservativo** - condom
pretend (v) - fingir	**pretender** - to intend, to plan
procure (v) - conseguir, adquirir	**procurar** - to look for, to search
pull (v) - puxar	**pular** - to jump
push (v) - empurrar	**puxar** - to pull
range (n, v) - cadeia (montanhas), variar, descobrir	**ranger** - to creak, to grind
realize (v) - perceber (entender)	**realizar** - to accomplish, to do
recipient (n) - recebedor, beneficiário, destinatário	**recipiente** - container
record (n, v) - gravar, gravação, registro	**recordar** - to remember, to recall
requirement (n) - requisito	**requerimento** - request, petition
resume (v) - retomar, recomeçar	**resumir** - to summarize
retired (adj) - aposentado	**retirado** - removed, secluded
senior (adj) - idoso	**senhor** - gentleman, sir
stranger (adj) - desconhecido	**estrangeiro** - foreigner

SINÔNIMOS E ANTÔNIMOS

above	below	cold	hot	happy	sad
add	subtract	dark	light	hard	soft
after	before	day	night	heavy	light
awake	asleep	east	west	high	low
bad	good	end	begin	hungry	full
better	worse	even	odd	in	out
big	little	fail	pass	last	first
birth	death	false	true	laugh	cry
boy	girl	fat	skinny	learn	teach
clean	dirty	float	sink	less	more
close	open	gentle	rough	lie	truth

SINÔNIMOS E ANTÔNIMOS

long	short	raise	lower	teacher	student
loose	tight	right	wrong	tidy	messy
lost	found	rise	sink	top	bottom
love	hate	rough	smooth	true	false
north	south	same	different	ugly	beautiful
on	off	sell	buy	up	down
over	under	short	long	well	sick
play	work	sour	sweet	wet	dry
polite	rude	start	stop	white	black
poor	rich	stay	leave	wild	tame
present	absent	stop	go	win	lose
quick	slow	strong	weak	young	old

FRASES ÚTEIS

Basic vocabulary / Vocabulário básico

Bom dia / boa tarde / boa noite!	Good morning / afternoon / evening!
Sou brasileiro(a).	I am Brazilian.
Meu passaporte é o (número).	My passport number is…
Eu gostaria de…	I would like to…
Eu preciso (de)…	I need (to)…
Desculpe-me, não falo Inglês muito bem.	Sorry, I don't speak English very well.
Um minutinho, por favor!	Just a moment, please!
Você / O Sr. / A Sra. Fala Português ou Espanhol?	Can you speak Portuguese or Spanish?
Até logo / Tchau / Adeus!	Goodbye!
Muito obrigado!	Thank you!
De nada!	You're welcome!

Arriving at a foreign country / Chegando em um país estrangeiro

Estou viajando sozinho(a).	I'm traveling alone.
Estamos viajando juntos(as).	We are traveling together.
Estou viajando com um(a) amigo(a).	I'm traveling with a friend.
Aqui está o meu passporte.	Here you have my passport.
Somos seis pessoas.	We are six people.

FRASES ÚTEIS

A alfândega é logo ali.	The Customs is right there.
Estou aqui a negócios / por lazer.	I'm here on business / for pleasure.
Só tenho objetos pessoais em minha mala.	I only have personal belongings in my suitcase.
Eu mesmo(a) fiz e fechei minha mala.	I packed and locked my suitcase myself.
Não tenho artigos a declarar.	I have nothing to declare.
Tenho alguns artigos a declarar.	I have some goods to declare.
Esta é toda a bagagem que tenho.	This is all my luggage.
Com licença, por favor!	Excuse me, please!
Minha bagagem não chegou!	My luggage is lost!
Demora para eu recuperar a bagagem?	How long does it take to have my luggage back?
Meu voo era o WT676.	My flight was the WT676.
Onde fica o balcão de informações para turistas?	Where is the tourist information bureau?
Onde fica o banheiro, por favor?	Where is the toilet, please?
Onde posso pegar um táxi?	Where can I get a taxi?
Onde posso reservar um hotel?	Where can I book a hotel room?
Este é o transporte do aeroporto para o hotel?	Is this the hotel shuttle?
Qual o preço de cada volume de bagagem?	What's the price for each piece of luggage?
Isso não pertence a mim.	This is not mine.
A quanto está o dólar / euro?	What are the rates for the dollar / euro?
Eu gostaria de alugar um carro.	I would like to rent a car.
Quanto lhe devo?	How much do I owe you?
Desculpe me, não entendi!	Sorry, I don't understand!
Vou ficar no Hotel Hilton.	I'm staying at the Hilton Hotel.
Por favor, deixe-me no Hotel Hilton.	Please, drop me off at the Hilton Hotel.
Você pode levar minhas bagagens?	Can you carry my luggage?
Por favor, leve-me até Central Park.	Please, take me to Central Park.
Qual é a gorgeta normal por aqui?	What's the usual tip around here?

At the hotel / No hotel

Olá, eu tenho uma reserva.	Hi, I have a reservation.
Está em nome de Smith.	It's under the name of Smith.
O café da manhã está incluído?	Is breakfast included in the daily rate?

FRASES ÚTEIS

Gostaria de um quarto com vista para o mar.	I'd like a room facing the sea.
A que horas tenho que deixar o quarto?	What time is the check-out?
Vocês têm TV a cabo no quarto?	Does the room have cable TV?
Como faço para telefonar do quarto?	How do I get an outside line?
Quero deixar meus objetos de valor no cofre.	I want to leave my valuables in the safe, please.
Quais são as melhores atrações locais?	Can you give me some information on the best local attractions?
É seguro andar a pé por aqui?	Is it safe to take a walk around this neighborhood?
Onde fica a estação de metrô mais próxima?	Where is the nearest subway station?
Onde fica o ponto de ônibus mais próximo?	Where is the nearest bus stop?
Onde posso comprar ingressos para o teatro?	Where can I buy tickets for the theater?
Existe algum ônibus de turismo que circule pela cidade?	Is there any tourist hop-on-hop off bus in this town?
Aqui é do quarto 45. Tenho um problema.	This is room 45. I have a problem.
Não tem água quente.	There's no hot water.
O ralo da pia / do chuveiro está entupido.	The sink / shower drain is clogged.
A Tv / o ar condicionado / o aquecedor não está funcionando.	The TV / air-conditioning / heating is not working.
Tem algum recado para mim?	Is there any messages for me?
Eu quero fechar a conta, por favor.	Check-out, please!
Vocês aceitam cartões de crédito / cheques de viagem?	Do you accept credit cards / traveler's checks?
Vocês poderiam, por favor, mandar alguém buscar minha bagagem?	Could you please send someone for my luggage, please?
Poderia chamar-me um táxi, por favor?	Could you get us a taxi, please?

At a restaurant / No restaurante

Mesa para dois, não fumantes, por favor.	Table for two, non-smokers, please.
Vamos ter de esperar?	Is there a wait?
Gostaria de uma mesa perto da janela.	I would like a table close to the window.
Posso ver o menu, por favor?	Can I see the menu, please?
Vou pedir massa / carne / frango.	I'll have pasta / steak / chicken.
Poderia me trazer mais um guardanapo / um garfo / uma colher / uma faca?	Could you please bring me another napkin / fork / spoon / knife?

FRASES ÚTEIS

Duas cervejas, por favor!	Two beers, please.
Posso ver a carta de vinhos?	Can I see your wine list?
De sobremesa, vou querer frutas / sorvete.	I'll have fruit / ice-cream for dessert.
Estava tudo delicioso, obrigado(a)!	That was great, thank you!
Poderia trazer-me a conta?	Can I have the check, please?
Aqui está, fique com o troco.	Here you are, keep the change.

Health / Saúde

Você não parece estar bem.	You don't look very well.
O que você tem?	What's the matter?
Como você está se sentindo?	How are you feeling?
Estou com uma dor de cabeça terrível.	I have a terrible headache.
Estou com dor de estômago.	I have a stomachache.
Não estou me sentindo muito bem.	I'm not feeling very well.
Minha garganta está inflamada.	My throat is sore.
Meus olhos estão inchados / irritados.	My eyes are swollen / irritated.
Acho que peguei um resfriado.	I think I caught a cold.
Meus pés estão doendo.	My feet hurt.
Preciso descansar.	I need to rest.
Estou gripado.	I got the flu.
Onde fica a farmácia mais próxima?	Where is the nearest drugstore?
Onde posso comprar remédios?	Where can I buy some medicine?
Vocês têm aspirinas?	Do you have some aspirins?
Vocês têm seringas / agulha descartável?	Do you have disposable syringes / needle?
Qual é o número da emergência?	What's the emergency number here?
Como faço para chamar uma ambulância?	How can I call an ambulance?
O hospital mais próximo é muito longe?	How far is the nearest hospital?
Há algum médico de plantão?	Is there any doctor on duty?
Você tem o telefone de algum médico?	Do you know a doctor I could call?
Ajude-me, por favor! Ele teve um ataque cardíaco.	Help me, please! He's had a heart attack.
Vocês têm um kit de primeiros socorros?	Do you have a first-aid kit?
Vocês podem aviar-me esta receita?	Can you prepare this prescription for me?

FRASES ÚTEIS

Vocês têm alguma coisa para picadas de insetos?	Do you have anything for insect bites?
Vocês têm protetor solar?	Do you have any solar-protection cream?

Shopping / Indo às compras.

Estou só olhando, obrigado(a)!	I'm just browsing, thank you!
Isto está em promoção?	Is this on sale?
Isto não é o que está na vitrine.	This is not what you're showing in the window.
Por favor, poderia mostrar-me aquela peça?	Could you please show me that item?
Vocês têm esta peça em cores diversas?	Do you have this item in different collors?
Vocês têm esta peça em tamanhos diversos?	Do you have this item in different sizes?
Onde fica o setor de CD's e DVD's?	Where is the CD and DVD department?
Posso enviar isto para o Brasil?	Can I have this sent to Brazil?
Isto tem isenção de impostos?	Is this tax-free?
É para presente. Vocês embrulham?	It's a gift. Can I have this gift-wrapped?
Este é o preço justo para esta mercadoria?	Is this the fair price for this item?
Você vai me dar um desconto?	Will you offer me a discount?
Qual é o horário desta loja?	What are the hours of this store?
Vocês abrem no fim de semana / domingo?	Are you open on weekends / Sundays?
Vou ficar com esta camiseta / saia.	I'll take this T-shirt / skirt.
As gravatas / meias são muito baratas.	The ties / socks are a bargain here.
Vocês trocam mercadorias?	What is the exchange policy?
Por favor, onde eu pago?	Where do I pay, please?
Preciso de uma nota / recibo, por favor.	I need a receipt, please.
Onde é a seção de achados e perdidos?	Where is the los-and-found section?
Acho que esqueci minha bolsa aqui, hoje cedo.	I think I forgot my purse here this morning.
Você sabe se alguém a encontrou?	Do you happen to know if anybody's found it?
Por favor, onde é a saída?	Could you please show me the exit?

FORMAÇÃO DAS PALAVRAS

Na Língua Inglesa, muitas palavras podem ter seus significados e suas classes gramaticais alteradas, simplesmente adicionando um grupo de letras ao início delas (**prefixos**) ou ao final delas (**sufixos**). Os quadros abaixo apresentam exemplos mais comuns, de como acontece o processo de formação das palavras.

Verb formation / Formação de Palavras

Os finais -**ize** e -**ify** podem ser utilizados para transformar muitos substantivos e adjetivos em verbos.

American		Americanize
legal	-ize	legalize
modern		modernize
popular		popularize

The university wants to make the education system more **modern**.
It wants to **modernize** the education system.

beauty		beautify
liquid	-fy	liquefy
pure		purify
simple		simplify

The filters make the water **pure**.
They **purify** the water.

Adverb formation / Formação de Advérbio

O final -**ly** pode ser utilizado para transformar muitos adjetivos em advérbios.

easy		easily
main	-ly	mainly
quick		quickly
stupid		stupidly

The little girl behavior was **stupid**.
She behaved **stupidly**.

Noun formation / Formação de Substantivo

Os finais -**er**, -**ment**, e -**ation** podem ser utilizados para transformar muitos verbos em substantivos.

drive		driver
fasten	-er	fastener
open		opener
teach		teacher

Peter **drives** a truck. He is a **driver**.
A can **opener** is a tool for **opening** cans.

amaze		amazement
develop	-ment	development
play		payment
retire		retirement

Technology **develops** very quickly.
Its **development** is very quick.

admire		admiration
associate	-ation	association
examine		examination
organize		organization

The nurse **examined** the child carefully.
She gave it a careful **examination**.

Os finais -**ity** e -**ness** podem ser utilizados para transformar muitos adjetivos em substantivos.

cruel		cruelty
odd	-ity	oddity
pure		purity
stupid		stupidity

Don't be so **stupid**.
I hate **stupidity**.

FORMAÇÃO DAS PALAVRAS

dark		darkness
deaf		deafness
happy	-ness	happiness
kind		kindness

She is so **kind**.
Her **kindness** makes people feel good.

Adjective formation / Formação de Adjetivo

Os finais **-y**, **-ic**, **-ical**, **-ful** e **-less** podem ser utilizados para transformar muitos substantivos em adjetivos.

bush		bushy
dirt		dirty
hair	-y	hairy
smell		smelly

She should clean the **dirt** in the kitchen.
The kitchen is very **dirty**.

atom		atomic
biology	-ic	biological
grammar	-ical	grammatical
poetry		poetic

This magazine contains topics on **biology**.
It contains **biological** topics.

pain		painful
hope		hopeful
care	-ful	careful
beauty		beautiful

Her **beauty** is unbelievable.
She is so **beautiful**.

pain		painless
hope		hopeless
care	-less	careless
home		homeless

The storm took her **hope** away.
She is **hopeless**.

O final **-able** pode ser utilizado para transformar muitos verbos em adjetivos.

wash		washable
love		lovable
debate	-able	debatable
break		breakable

Don't be afraid to **wash** this dress.
It is **washable**.

Opposites / Opostos

Os prefixos abaixo podem ser utilizados na frente de muitas palavras para expressar um significado de oposição. Porém, as palavras formadas desta maneira nem sempre são opostos exatos e podem ter um significado um pouco diferente.

un-	block	unblock
	fortunate	unfortunate
	happy	unhappy
	wind	unwind

He's not a **fortunate** person.
In fact, he's an **unfortunate** person.

in-	efficient	inefficient
im-	possible	impossible
il-	literate	illiterate
ir-	regular	irregular

This method is not **efficient**.
It's totally **inefficient**.

FORMAÇÃO DAS PALAVRAS

dis-	honest agree approve	dishonest disagree disapprove

His family does not **approve** his behavior.
They **disapprove** his behavior.

de-	ascend inflate centralize increase	descend deflate decentralize decrease

The government took actions to **increase** the rate of employment last year.
The government has declared that unemployment will **decrease** next year.

non-	conformist payment sense resident	nonconformist nonpayment nonsense nonresident

His attitudes makes **sense** if you know his life history.
His sadness makes **nonsense** because he has everything he wants.

dicionário escolar inglês

Português - Inglês

A, *s.*, the first letter of the Portuguese alphabet; *art. def.*, the; *prep.*, to, on, according, by; *pron.*, that, the one; *contraction of the prep. a* with the *art.* or *pron. a*; **À DIREITA**: on the right.
A.BA, *s.f.*, border, edge, extremity, flap.
A.BA.CA.TE, *s.m., Bot.*, avocado, alligator-pear.
A.BA.CA.TEI.RO, *s.m., Bot.*, avocado tree.
A.BA.CA.XI, *s.m., Bot.*, ananas, pineaple.
A.BA.CHA.RE.LAR, *v.*, to graduate as a bachelor.
Á.BA.CO, *s.m.*, abacus.
A.BA.DA, *s.f.*, quantity (of something).
A.BA.DAR, *v.*, to provide with an abbot (in monastery).
A.BA.DE, *s.m.*, abbot.
A.BA.DES.SA, *s.f.*, abbess.
A.BA.DI.A, *s.f.*, monastery.
A.BA.DO, *adj.*, brimmed, large-brimmed.
A.BA.FA.DI.ÇO, *adj.*, not ventiled, stifling, sultry, chockyng.
A.BA.FA.DO, *adj.*, airless, stuffy, sultry; oppressed, restricted.
A.BA.FA.ÇÃO, *s.f.*, the same that *abafamento*.
A.BA.FA.DO, *adj.*, sultry, chocking, stifling, stuffy.
A.BA.FA.DOR, *s.m.*, something to muffle, maffler; *Mús.*, damper.
A.BA.FA.MEN.TO, *s.m.*, choking, checking, oppression.
A.BA.FAR, *v.*, to choke, to smother, to suffocate, to stifle.
A.BA.FO, *s.m.*, muffler.
A.BA.GUN.ÇA.DO, *adj.*, the same that *bagunçado*: messed-up.
A.BA.GUN.ÇAR, *v.*, the same that *bagunçar*: to provoke disorder.
A.BAI.XA.DO, *adj.*, lowered, downcast; stooped.
A.BAI.XAR, *v.*, to lower, to pull down, to decrease, to fall.
A.BAI.XO, *adv.*, down, under, inferior, below.
A.BAI.XO-AS.SI.NA.DO, *s.m.*, petition, application with the signature of several petitioners.
A.BA.JUR, *s.m.*, lampshade.
A.BA.LA.DO, *adj.*, shaky, loose, touched, upset.
A.BA.LAN.ÇAR, *v.*, to balance.
A.BA.LAR, *v.*, to shake, to move, to jog, to affect.
A.BA.LA.US.TRA.DO, *adj.*, provide with balusters, stanchions.
A.BA.LA.US.TRAR, *v.*, to provide with balusters, stanchions; to shape like a baluster.
A.BA.LÁ.VEL, *adj.*, shakeable.
A.BA.LI.ZA.DO, *adj.*, authoritative, distinguished, renowned.
A.BA.LI.ZA.DOR, *s.m.*, surveyor, stake (for surveying).
A.BA.LI.ZAR, *v.*, to mark out by bounds or buoys; to delimit, to demarcate.
A.BA.LO, *s.m.*, commotion, disturbance, shock, grief, earthquake.
A.BA.LO SÍS.MI.CO, *s.m.*, earthquake.
A.BAL.RO.A.MEN.TO, *s.m.*, collision (vehicles); onset, assault; *Náut.*, grappling.
A.BAL.RO.AR, *v.*, collide, to run into, to attack.
A.BA.NA.DOR, *s.m.*, fan, fanner.

A.BA.NAR, *v.*, to fan, to shake, to agitate.
A.BAN.DA.LHA.DO, *adj.*, degraded, vilified, debased.
A.BAN.DA.LHAR, *v.*, to degrade, to vilify, to debase.
A.BAN.DO.NA.DO, *adj.*, abandoned, forlorn, deserted, helpless, alone.
A.BAN.DO.NAR, *v.*, to abandon, to leave off, to neglect, to forsake, to renounce.
A.BAN.DO.NÁ.VEL, *s.m., adj.*, that may or should be abandoned.
A.BAN.DO.NO, *s.m.*, abandonment, abandoning, forsaking, helplessness, desertion.
A.BA.NI.CO, *s.m.*, small fan.
A.BA.NO, *s.m.*, fire-fan, ventilator, shake, fan.
A.BAR.CA.MEN.TO, *s.m.*, encompassment, containment, inclusion, monopoly.
A.BAR.CAR, *v.*, to contain, to embrace, to monopolize, to obtain, to include, to comprehend.
A.BAR.RO.TA.DO, *adj.*, overfull, overloaded, overfilled.
A.BAR.RO.TAR, *v.*, to overfill, to overload, to overstock, to satiate.
A.BAS.TA.DO, *adj.*, rich, wealthy.
A.BAS.TAN.ÇA, *s.f.*, abundance, sufficiency, plenty.
A.BAS.TAR, *v.*, to supply; to suffice.
A.BAS.TAR.DAR, *v.*, to bastardize.
A.BAS.TE.CE.DOR, *s.m.*, supplier, provider; *adj.*, supplying.
A.BAS.TE.CER, *v.*, to supply, to provide, to refuel.
A.BAS.TE.CI.DO, *adj.*, well supplied, abundant.
A.BAS.TE.CI.MEN.TO, *s.m.*, supply, provision, provisioning, supplying.
A.BA.TE, *s.m.*, discount, abatement, reduction, felling (trees).
A.BA.TE.DOI.RO, *s.m., Port.*, the same that *abatedouro*.
A.BA.TE.DOR, *s.m.*, abater, reducer.
A.BA.TE.DOU.RO, *s.m.*, slaughterhouse, abattoir.
A.BA.TER, *v.*, to abate, to lower, to discount, to lessen, to diminish, to reduce.
A.BA.TI.DO, *adj.*, abated, prostrated, exhausted, low, depressed.
A.BA.TI.MEN.TO, *s.m.*, abatement, lessening, discount, felling, depression, decay.
A.BA.TO.CAR, *v.*, to bung, close with a bung.
A.BAU.LA.DO, *adj.*, incurved, convex.
A.BAU.LA.MEN.TO, *s.m.*, incurvation, bulging; convexity.
A.BAU.LAR, *v.*, to arch, bulge, incurve.
AB.DI.CA.ÇÃO, *s.f.*, abdication, renunciation.
AB.DI.CA.DOR, *s.m., adj.*, abdicator.
AB.DI.CAR, *v.*, to abdicate, to renounce, to leave, to abandon.
AB.DI.CA.TÓ.RI.O, *s.m., adj.*, the same that *abdicador*.
AB.DI.CÁ.VEL, *adj.*, abdicable.
AB.DO.ME, AB.DÔ.MEN, *s.m., Anat.*, abdomen.
AB.DO.MI.NAL, *adj., Anat.*, abdominal; *s.m.*, localized exercise for abdminal muscles.
AB.DU.ÇÃO, *s.f.*, abduction.

ABDUZIR · 73 · ABRIR

AB.DU.ZIR, *v.*, to abduct.
ABECÊ, *s.m.*, ABC; *fig.*, fundamentals; *a-bê-cê*: the alphabet.
A.BE.CE.DÁ.RIO, *s.m.*, abecedary, alphabet.
A.BEI.RAR, *v.*, to bring near, to border.
A.BE.LHA, *s.f.*, *Zool.*, bee, honey bee.
A.BE.LHA-RA.I.NHA, *s.f.*, *Zool.*, queen bee.
A.BE.LHA-MES.TRA, *s.f.*, *Zool.*, queen bee.
A.BE.LHEI.RO, *s.f.*, beekeeper; *Zool.*, beehive, bee-eater.
A.BE.LHU.DO, *adj.*, curious, indiscreet, impudent, nosy.
A.BEN.ÇO.A.DO, *adj.*, blessed.
A.BEN.ÇO.A.DOR, *s.m.*, one who blesses; *adj.*, blessing.
A.BEN.ÇO.AR, *v.*, to bless, to protect, to give blessings, to consecrate.
A.BER.RA.ÇÃO, *s.f.*, aberration, deviation.
A.BER.RAN.TE, *adj.*, incongruous, aberrant.
A.BER.RAR, *v.*, to deviate.
A.BER.TA.MEN.TE, *adv.*, openly.
A.BER.TO, *adj.*, open, opened, exposed, frank.
A.BER.TU.RA, *s.f.*, opening, crevice, gap, overture, inauguration.
A.BES.PI.NHA.DO, *adj.*, irritable, excitable.
A.BES.PI.NHAR, *v.*, to make irritated; to get irritated.
A.BES.TA.LHA.DO, *adj.*, moronic, idiot, stupid.
A.BE.TO, *s.m.*, abies.
A.BE.TU.MAR, *v.*, to bituminise.
A.BI.LO.LA.DO, *adj.*, *fam.*, potty, loony, silly; infatuated.
A.BIS.MA.DO, *adj.*, stupefied, shocked, astonished.
A.BIS.MAL, *adj.*, abysmal; abyssal.
A.BIS.MAR, *v.*, to throw into an abyss, to stupefy, to stun.
A.BIS.MO, *s.m.*, abyss, vortex, precipice.
A.BIS.SAL, *adj.*, deep; the same that *abismal*.
AB.JE.ÇÃO, *s.f.*, abjetion, debasement.
AB.JE.TO, *adj.*, abject, base, contemptible.
AB.JU.GAR, *v.*, to liberate, free.
AB.JU.RA.ÇÃO, *s.f.*, abjuration.
AB.JU.RAR, *v.*, to abjure, to renounce, to repudiate.
A.BLA.TI.VO, *s.m.*, the ablative case; *adj.*, ablative.
AB.LU.ÇÃO, *s.f.*, ablution, washing.
AB.LU.TOR, *s.m.*, purifier, washer.
AB.NE.GA.ÇÃO, *s.f.*, abnegation, self-denial.
AB.NE.GA.DO, *adj.*, unselfish, self-forgetful.
AB.NE.GAR, *v.*, to abnegate, to renounce.
ABNT, *abrev.* of *Associação Brasileira de Normas Técnicas*: Brazilian Technical Standards Association.
A.BÓ.BA.DA, *s.f.*, arch, vault, arched roof.
A.BO.BA.DA.DO, *adj.*, arched, vaulted.
A.BO.BA.DO, *adj.*, foolish, silly, senseless.
A.BO.BA.LHA.DO, *adj.*, the same that *abobado*.
A.BÓ.BO.RA, *s.f.*, *Bot.*, pumpkin.
A.BO.BO.RAL, *s.m.*, *Bot.*, pumpkin-field.
A.BÓ.BO.RA-MO.RAN.GA, *s.f.*, *Bot.*, common pumpkin.
A.BO.BRI.NHA, *s.f.*, *Bot.*, summer-squash.
A.BO.CA.NHAR, *v.*, to bite, to bite off, to snap.
A.BO.CAR, *v.*, to snap, to catch with the mouth.
A.BO.LA.CHA.DO, *adj.*, like a biscuit or cracker.
A.BO.LE.TA.MEN.TO, *s.m.*, *Mil.*, billeting, lodgement.
A.BO.LE.TAR, *v.*, to lodge, to billet.
A.BO.LI.ÇÃO, *s.f.*, abolition, abolishment, revocation, abrogation.
A.BO.LI.DO, *adj.*, abolished, cancelled.
A.BO.LIR, *v.*, to abolish, to suppress, to abrogate, to revoke.

A.BO.MI.NA.ÇÃO, *s.f.*, abomination.
A.BO.MI.NAR, *v.*, to abominate, to abhor, to detest, to loathe.
A.BO.MI.NÁ.VEL, *adj.*, abominable, detestable.
A.BO.NA.DO, *adj.*, well-off (rich); wealthy, rich.
A.BO.NA.DOR, *s.m.*, warrantor, guarantor.
A.BO.NAR, *v.*, to declare good or true, to bail, to guarantee.
A.BO.NO, *s.m.*, advance-money, loan, remuneration, warranty.
A.BOR.DA.GEM, *s.f.*, approach, coming, boarding approaching.
A.BOR.DAR, *v.*, to board, to attack, to approach, to accost.
A.BOR.DÁ.VEL, *adj.*, accessible, approachble.
A.BO.RÍ.GI.NE, *s.m.*, aborigine; *adj.*, aboriginal.
A.BOR.RE.CER, *v.*, to bore, to displease, to disgust, to hassle, to abhor.
A.BOR.RE.CI.DO, *adj.*, disgusted, displeased, weary, bored, annoyed, odious.
A.BOR.RE.CI.MEN.TO, *s.m.*, disgust, annoyance, nuisance, tediousness.
A.BOR.TA.DO, *adj.*, aborted; frustrated.
A.BOR.TAR, *v.*, to abort, to miscarry, to fail.
A.BOR.TI.VO, *s.m.*, abortive; *adj.*, abortive.
A.BOR.TO, *s.m.*, abortion, miscarriage.
A.BO.TO.A.DEI.RA, *s.f.*, buttonhook.
A.BO.TO.A.DU.RA, *s.f.*, set of buttons.
A.BO.TO.AR, *v.*, to button; to pinch.
A.BRA.CA.DA.BRA, *s.m.*, abracadabra.
A.BRA.ÇAR, *v.*, to embrace, to hug, to encircle, to adopt, to follow.
A.BRA.ÇO, *s.m.*, embrace, embracing, hug, embracement.
A.BRAN.DA.MEN.TO, *s.m.*, softening, mitigation.
A.BRAN.DAR, *v.*, to mitigate, to milden, to assuage, to mollify.
A.BRAN.GÊN.CI.A, *s.f.*, range, reach, scope.
A.BRAN.GEN.TE, *adj.*, all-embracing, extensive, comprehensive.
A.BRAN.GER, *v.*, to embrace, to enclose, to comprise, to include, to contain.
A.BRAN.GÍ.VEL, *adj.*, that can be reached or included.
A.BRA.SA.DOR, *adj.*, burning, scorching, blazing, glowing.
A.BRA.SÃO, *s.f.*, abrasion.
A.BRA.SAR, *v.*, to fire, to burn, to consume by fire, devastate, to glow, to inflame.
A.BRA.SI.LEI.RA.DO, *adj.*, Brazilianized.
A.BRA.SI.LEI.RAR, *v.*, to adopt Brazilian ways and manners.
A.BRA.SI.VO, *adj.*, abrasive.
A.BREU.GRA.FI.A, *s.f.*, roentgenfotography.
A.BRE.VI.A.ÇÃO, *s.f.*, abbreviation, shortening, reduction.
A.BRE.VI.A.DO, *adj.*, abbreviated, shortened, reduced, condensed.
A.BRE.VI.AR, *v.*, to abbreviate, to shorten, to reduce, to summarize.
A.BRE.VI.A.TU.RA, *s.f.*, abbreviation, shortening.
A.BRI.CÓ, *s.m.*, *Bot.*, apricot.
A.BRI.DOR, *s.m.*, opener, tool for opening.
A.BRI.GA.DO, *adj.*, sheltered, well-covered.
A.BRI.GAR, *v.*, to shelter, to protect, to exempt, to cover, to hide.
A.BRI.GO, *s.m.*, shelter, guard, protection, covering, asylum.
A.BRIL, *s.m.*, April.
A.BRI.LHAN.TAR, *v.*, to brighten, to enliven, to embellish; *fig.*, to enhance.
A.BRIR, *v.*, to open, to break up, to unlock, to unfold, to

ABROCHAR ··74·· ACAREAR

unfasten.
A.BRO.CHAR, *v.*, to clasp, fasten with a clasp.
AB-RO.GA.ÇÃO, *s.m.*, abrogation, repeal.
AB-RO.GAR, *v.*, to abrogate, to repeal, to abolish, to cancel.
A.BRO.LHO, *s.m.*, thorn; caltrop; reefs.
A.BRUP.TA.MEN.TE, *adv.*, abruptly.
AB-RUP.TO, *adj.*, abrupt, sudden, disconnected.
A.BRU.MAR, *v.*, to fog; to darken.
A.BRU.TA.LHA.DO, *adj.*, brutal, brutish, rude.
A.BRU.TA.LHAR, *v.*, to brutify.
ABS.CES.SO, *s.m.*, abscess.
ABS.CIS.SA, *s.f., Geom.*, abscisse, absciss.
AB.SEN.TE.ÍS.MO, *sm.*, absenteeism (best: *absentismo*); *Bras.*, abstention from voting.
AB.SEN.TIS.MO, *s.m.*, absenteeism; absentee administration of an estate, factory; repeated absence from work.
AB.SIN.TO, *s.m., Bot.*, absinthe, absinth; liquor of wormwood.
AB.SO.LU.TA.MEN.TE, *adv.*, absolutely, completely, entirely.
AB.SO.LU.TIS.MO, *s.m., Hist.*, absolutism.
AB.SO.LU.TIS.TA, *s. 2 gen., Hist.*, absolutist; *adj.*, absolutist, absolutistic.
AB.SO.LU.TO, *adj.*, absolute, unrestricted, unlimited, unconditional, total.
AB.SOL.VER, *v.*, to absolve, to forgive, to clear, to isent, to excuse.
AB.SOL.VI.ÇÃO, *s.f.*, absolution, pardoning.
AB.SOL.VI.DO, *adj.*, absolved, pardoned.
AB.SOR.ÇÃO, *s.f.*, absorption.
AB.SOR.TO, *adj.*, absorbed, distracted.
AB.SOR.VE.DOU.RO, *s.m.*, the same that *sorvedouro*.
AB.SOR.VÊN.CI.A, *s.f.*, absorvency, absorbance
AB.SOR.VEN.TE, *s.m.*, absorbent, tampon; *adj.*, absorbing.
AB.SOR.VEN.TE HI.GI.Ê.NI.CO, *s.m., UK* sanitary towel; *US* sanitary napkin.
AB.SOR.VER, *v.*, to absorb, to consume, to assimilate, to captivate.
ABS.TÊ.MIO, *adj.*, abstemious.
ABS.TEN.ÇÃO, *s.f.*, abstention.
ABS.TER, *v.*, to abstain, to forbear, to refrain, to restrain.
ABS.TI.NÊN.CIA, *s.f.*, abstinence, temperance, abstemiousness.
ABS.TI.NEN.TE, *s. 2 gen.*, abstainer; *adj.*, abstinent.
ABS.TRA.ção, *s.f.*, abstraction.
ABS.TRA.IR, *v.*, to abstract, to take from, to separate.
ABS.TRA.TO, *adj.*, abstract, abstracted, separated; *s.m.*, abstract.
ABS.TRU.SO, *adj.*, abstruse; intricate, confused.
AB.SUR.DO, *s.m.*, absurdity, folly, nonsense; *adj.*, absurd, nonsensical.
A.BU.GA.LHA.DO, *adj.*, wide-open eyes.
A.BU.LI.A, *s.f., Med.*, abulia; apathy.
A.BÚ.LI.CO, *adj., Med.*, abulic.
A.BUN.DÂN.CIA, *s.f.*, abundance, plenty, copiousness.
A.BUN.DAN.TE, *adj.*, abundant, plentiful, copious.
A.BUN.DAR, *v.*, abound, to be rich in.
A.BU.SA.DO, *adj.*, abused, impertinent, presumptuous.
A.BU.SA.DOR, *s.m.*, abuser; *adj.*, abusive.
A.BU.SAR, *v.*, to abuse, to misuse, to delude, to violate, to annoy.
A.BU.SI.VA.MEN.TE, *adv.*, abusively.
A.BU.SI.VO, *adj.*, abusive.

A.BU.SO, *s.m.*, abuse, misuse, overuse, nuisance, annoyance, abhorrence.
A.BUR.GUE.SA.DO, *adj.*, bourgeois.
A.BUR.GUE.SAR, *v.*, to gentrify.
A.BU.TRE, *s.m., Zool.*, vulture.
A.C., *abrev.* of *Antes de Cristo*: Before Christ, B.C.
A/C, *abrev.* of *aos cuidados de*: care of, c/o.
A.CA.BA.DO, *adj.*, finished, accomplished, ready, complete, worn, used, consumed.
A.CA.BA.MEN.TO, *s.m.*, finishing, completion.
A.CA.BAR, *v.*, to finish, to end, to terminate, to conclude, to achieve.
A.CA.BRU.NHA.DO, *adj.*, disheartened, embarrassed.
A.CA.BRU.NHAR, *v.*, to oppress, to lessen, to humiliate.
A.CA.ÇA.PA.DO, *adj.*, shrunk, crouched; thickset, low; flat.
A.CÁ.CI.A, *s.f., Bot.*, acacia.
A.CA.DEI.RAR, *v.*, to have a seat; sit down.
A.CA.DE.MI.A, *s.f.*, accademy, university, college.
A.CA.DE.MI.CIS.MO, *s.m.*, academicism.
A.CA.DE.MI.CIS.TA, *s. 2 gen.*, academicista.
A.CA.DÊ.MI.CO, *s.m., adj.*, academician; *adj.*, academic.
A.ÇA.FLOR, *s.m.*, the same that *açafrão*.
A.ÇA.FRÃO, *s.m.*, saffron.
A.ÇA.Í, *s.m., Bot.*, Açaí palm, cabbage palm.
A.ÇA.I.ZEI.RO, *s.m., Bot.*, cabbage-palm
A.CA.JU, *s.m., Bot.*, acajou, mahogany.
A.CA.LAN.TAR, *v.*, the same that *acalentar*.
A.CA.LAN.TO, *s.m.*, the same that *acalento*.
A.CA.LEN.TAR, *v.*, to lull or rock to sleep.
A.CA.LEN.TO, *s.m.*, lullaby.
A.CAL.MAR, *v.*, to calm, to pacify, to appease, to quiet, to silence, to still, to tranquilize.
A.CA.LO.RA.DO, *adj.*, sweaty; agitated, inflamed; heated.
A.CA.LO.RAR, *v.*, to heat, to warm, to agitate, to excite.
A.CA.MA.DO, *adj.*, abed, lying in bed.
A.CA.MAR, *v.*, stay in bed, to arrange in layers, to lie in bed.
A.CA.MA.RA.DAR, *v.*, to join in fellowship, befriend.
A.ÇAM.BAR.CAR, *v.*, to monopolize, to forestall.
A.CAM.BU.LHAR, *v.*, to put in a helter-skelter way.
A.CAM.PA.MEN.TO, *s.m.*, camp, camping.
A.CAM.PAR, *v.*, to camp, to encamp, live in a camp.
A.CA.MUR.ça.do, *adj.*, chamoislike.
A.CA.NA.LAR, *v.*, to channel, to groove, to flute.
A.CA.NE.LAR, *v.*, to give cinnamon colour to; to flavour of cinnamon.
A.CA.NHA.DO, *adj.*, timid, bashful, shy, awkward, close.
A.CA.NHA.MEN.TO, *s.m.*, shyness, timidity.
A.CA.NHAR, *v.*, to restrict, to lessen, to ashame, to intimidate.
A.CA.NO.AR, *v.*, to shape like a canoe.
A.CAN.TO.A.DO, *adj.*, put or thrown in a corner, occult.
A.CAN.TO.AR, *v.*, to put in a corner; to hide; to put aside.
A.CAN.TO.NA.DO, *adj.*, divided into cantons.
A.CAN.TO.NA.MEN.TO, *s.m.*, cantonment, billeting, military camp.
A.CAN.TO.NAR, *v.*, to canton, to camp.
A.ÇÃO, *s.f.*, action, movement, activity, act, deed, feat, event, operation, engagement, battle.
A.CA.RA.JÉ, *s.m., Cul.*, little cake fried in palm oil and served with pepper sauce and vatapá.
A.CA.RE.A.ÇÃO, *s.f.*, confrontation (of witnesses).
A.CA.RE.AR, *v.*, to contrast one thing with another, to

ACARICIAR   ·· 75 ··   ACINTOSO

confront.

A.CA.RI.CI.AR, *v.*, to caress, to fondle, to pet, to cherish.

A.CA.RI.NHAR, *v.*, to caress, to fondle, to pet.

Á.CA.RO, *s.m., Zool.*, acarus, mite.

A.CAR.RAN.CAR, *v.*, to frown, to scowl.

A.CAR.RE.AR, *v.*, the same that *acarretar*.

A.CAR.RE.TAR, *v.*, to occasion, to cause; to cart (transport in a cart).

A.CA.SA.LA.MEN.TO, *s.m.*, mating, coupling, joining.

A.CA.SA.LAR, *v.*, to mate, to couple, to join.

A.CA.SO, *s.m.*, chance, hazard, fortune, luck; *adv.*, perhaps.

A.CAS.TA.NHA.DO, *adj.*, brownish.

A.CAS.TA.NHAR, *v.*, to give a brownish.

A.CA.TA.DO, *adj.*, respected.

A.CA.TA.MEN.TO, *s.m.*, deference, reverence, regard, respect.

A.CA.TAR, *v.*, to respect, to venerate, to regard, to revere, to follow, to obey.

A.CAU.TE.LA.DO, *adj.*, cautions, prudent, careful.

A.CAU.TE.LAR, *v.*, to warn, to forewarn, to caution, to avoid, to shun; to be careful.

A.CE.BO.LA.DO, *adj.*, seasoned with onions; onion-flavoured.

A.CE.BO.LAR, *v.*, to season with onions.

A.CE.DER, *v.*, to accede, to conform, to comply with, to consent.

A.CE.FÁ.LI.CO, *adj., Med.*, acephalous, headless.

A.CÉ.FA.LO, *adj.*, the same that *acefálico*.

A.CEI.TA.ÇÃO, *s.f.*, acceptance, acceptation, reception, approbation.

A.CEI.TAR, *v.*, to accept, to receive, to take, to admit, to acknowledge.

A.CEI.TÁ.VEL, *adj.*, acceptable, admissible, agreeable.

A.CEI.TO, *adj., v. (part. irreg. de aceitar)*, accepted, received, admitted.

A.CE.LE.RA.ÇÃO, *s.f.*, acceleration, speed.

A.CE.LE.RA.DO, *adj.*, accelerated, quick.

A.CE.LE.RA.DOR, *s.m.*, accelerator; gas pedal (vehicle); *adj.*, accelerating.

A.CE.LE.RAR, *v.*, to accelerate, to press, to speed up, to quicken, to push on.

A.CEL.GA, *s.f., Bot.*, chard.

A.CÉM, *s.m.*, brisket.

A.CE.NAR, *v.*, to beckon, to provoke, to wave.

A.CEN.DE.DOR, *s.m.*, lighter, igniter.

A.CEN.DER, *v.*, to light, to ignite, to kindle, to set on fire.

A.CEN.DI.MEN.TO, *s.m.*, act of lighting; kindling (fire).

A.CE.NO, *s.m.*, nodding, calling, invitation, wink.

A.CEN.TO, *s.m.*, accent, emphasis given to a syllable.

A.CEN.SÃO, *s.m.*, the same that *acendimento*.

A.CEN.TU.A.ÇÃO, *s.f.*, accent, accentuation.

A.CEN.TU.A.ÇÃO GRÁ.FI.CA, *s.f.*, marking with accents.

A.CEN.TU.A.DO, *adj.*, accented, accentuated, stressed, marked, pronounced; *fig.*, evident.

A.CEN.TU.AR, *v.*, to accentuate, to accent, to pronounce.

A.CEP.ÇÃO, *s.f.*, acceptation, meaning, sense, signification.

A.CE.PI.PE, *s.m.*, dainty, tidbit, delicacy.

A.CE.RA.DO, *adj.*, steeled; sharpened; stinging.

A.CER.BA.DA.MEN.TE, *adv.*, bitterly; rigorously; fiercely.

A.CER.BO, *adj.*, acerb, bitter, tart.

A.CER.CA, *adv.*, near, about, almost; *prep.*, concerning, regarding.

A.CER.CAR, *v.*, to surround, to enclose.

A.CE.RO.LA, *s.f., Bot.*, acerola.

A.CER.TA.DO, *adj.*, right, correct; accorded, agreed.

A.CER.TAR, *v.*, to make right, to set right, to adjust, to regulate, to get right.

A.CER.TO, *s.m.*, hit, lucky hit, skill, prudence.

A.CER.VO, *s.m.*, heap, pile, lot, collection.

A.CE.SO, *adj.;* lighted, burning, inflamed.

A.CES.SÃO, *s.f.*, accession, acquisition.

A.CES.SAR, *v., Comp.*, to access.

A.CES.SI.BI.LI.DA.DE, *s.f.*, accessibility, availability.

A.CES.SÍ.VEL, *adj.*, accessible, available.

A.CES.SO, *s.m.*, access, admittance, admission, entrance.

A.CES.SÓ.RIO, *s.m.*, accessory, complement, addition; *adj.*, accessory, additional.

A.CE.TA.TO, *s.m., Quím.*, acetate.

A.CÉ.TI.CO, *adj.*, acetic, acetous.

A.CE.TI.NA.DO, *adj.*, satiny, silky.

A.CE.TO.NA, *s.f., Quím.*, acetone.

A.CE.TO.NÚ.RI.A, *s.f., Med.*, acetonuria (presence of acetone in the urine).

A.CHA.CA.DO, *adj.*, sickly; *gir.*, subjected to extortion, wrested.

A.CHA.CAR, *v., col.*, to steal by threatening, to extort money from; to fall ill, become sick.

A.CHA.DO, *s.m.*, find, discovery; invention; bargain.

A.CHA.QUE, *s.m.*, ailment, illness, indisposition, pretext.

A.CHAR, *v.*, to find, to meet with, to meet, to hit on, to discover, to invent.

A.CHA.TA.DO, *adj.*, flattened, crushed.

A.CHA.TA.MEN.TO, *s.m.*, flattening.

A.CHA.TAR, *v.*, to flatten, to squash, to crush, to humble; to humiliate.

A.CHA.VAS.CAR, *v.*, to give bad finish (work on wood).

A.CHÁ.VEL, *adj.*, that can be found.

A.CHE.GA.DO, *adj.*, near, close.

A.CHE.GA.MEN.TO, *s.m.*, approach, proximity.

A.CHE.GAR, *v.*, to arrange, to adjust, to aproximate.

A.CHIN.CA.LHAR, *v.*, to ridicule, to jest ,to mock.

A.CHIS.MO, *s.m., Bras., pop.*, argumentation based on suppsition.

A.CHO.CO.LA.TA.DO, *adj.*, like chocolate.

A.CI.DAR, *v.*, acidify.

A.CI.DEN.TA.DO, *adj.*, uneven, rough, broken, irregular, bumpy.

A.CI.DEN.TAL, *adj.*, accidental, unexpected, casual, fortuitous, occasional.

A.CI.DEN.TAL.MEN.TE, *adv.*, accidentally.

A.CI.DEN.TAR, *v.*, to cause an accident, to change.

A.CI.DEN.TE, *s.m.*, accident, misfortune, disaster, mishap, casualty.

A.CI.DEZ, *s.f.*, acidity, sourness.

A.CI.DI.FI.CA.ÇÃO, *s.f.*, acidification.

A.CI.DI.FI.CAR, *v.*, to acidify.

Á.CI.DO, *adj.*, acid, sour, tart.

A.CI.DU.LA.ÇÃO, *s.f.*, acidulation.

A.CI.DU.LAN.TE, *adj.*, acidulalent.

A.CI.MA, *adv.*, above, up.

A.CIN.TE, *s.m.*, provocation; *adv.*, intentionally, purposefully.

A.CIN.TO.SA.MEN.TE, *adv.*, purposefully, intentionally, deliberately.

A.CIN.TO.SO, *adj.*, provocative.

ACINZENTADO · · 76 · · ACRIMÔNIA

A.CIN.ZEN.TA.DO, *adv.*, greyish.
A.CIN.ZEN.TAR, *v.*, to make or become gray or grayish.
A.CIO.NAR, *v.*, to put in action, to incorporate, to gesticulate.
A.CIO.NIS.TA, *s. 2 gen.*, shareholder.
A.CIR.RA.DO, *adj.*, intransigent, stubborn; tough; bitter.
A.CIR.RAR, *v.*, to irritate, to incite, to instigate.
A.CLA.MA.ÇÃO, *s.f.*, acclamation, applause.
A.CLA.MA.DO, *adj.*, the same that *proclamado*.
A.CLA.MAR, *v.*, to acclaim, to applaud, to cheer.
A.CLA.MA.TI.VO, *adj.*, acclaimatory.
A.CLA.RA.DO, *adj.*, cleared; explained.
A.CLA.RAR, *v.*, to clear, to make clear, to brighten, to clarify.
A.CLI.MA.ÇÃO, *s.f.*, acclimation.
A.CLI.MA.DO, *adj.*, acclimated, acclimatized.
A.CLI.MA.TA.ÇÃO, *s.f.*, acclimatation.
A.CLI.MA.TAR, *v.*, to acclimatize, to acclimate.
A.CLI.MA.TI.ZA.ÇÃO, *s.f.*, acclimatization.
A.CLI.MA.TI.ZAR, *v.*, acclimatize, acclimantise.
A.CLI.VE, *s.m.*, acclivity, slope, ascent.
AC.ME, *s.m.*, acme, culmination; apex; *Med.*, crisis (desease).
AC.NE, *s.f.*, *Med.*, acne.
A.ÇO, *s.m.*, steel.
A.CO.BAR.DAR, *v.*, *Port.*, the same that *acovardar*.
A.CO.BER.TAR, *v.*, to cover, to cloak, to hide, to conceal, to dissimulate.
A.CO.CO.RA.DO, *adj.*, saquated, squatting.
A.CO.CO.RAR-SE, *v.*, to squat, to crouch.
A.ÇO.DA.DO, *adj.*, hasty, hurried, diligent.
A.ÇO.DA.MEN.TO, *s.m.*, haste, hury, urging.
A.ÇO.DAR, *v.*, to haste, to urge, to speed, to incite, to instigate.
A.ÇOI.TAR, *v.*, to whip, to lash.
A.ÇOI.TE, *s.m.*, whip, lash, scourge.
A.CO.LÁ, *adv.*, there, yonder, over there.
A.COL.CHO.A.DO, *s.m.*, wadding, padding, stuffing.
A.COL.CHO.A.MEN.TO, *s.m.*, wadding, padding.
A.COL.CHO.AR, *v.*, to wad, to pad, to quilt.
A.CO.LHE.DOR, *s.m.*, *adj.*, welcomer; *adj.*, welcoming.
A.CO.LHER, *v.*, to welcome, to receive, to shelter, to lodge.
A.CO.LHI.DA, *s.f.*, reception, welcome.
A.CO.LHI.MEN.TO, *s.m.*, the same that *acolhida*.
A.CÓ.LI.TO, *s.m.*, acolyte, assistant.
A.CO.ME.TER, *v.*, to attack, to assail, to assault, to provoke.
A.CO.ME.TI.DA, *s.f.*, attack, onset, assault, enterprise.
A.CO.MO.DA.ÇÃO, *s.f.*, accomodation, arrangement, room, agreement, adaptation.
A.CO.MO.DA.DO, *adj.*, accomodated, settled, adjusted.
A.CO.MO.DA.MEN.TO, *s.m.*, the same that *acomodação*.
A.CO.MO.DAR, *v.*, to accomodate, to arrange, to put in order.
A.COM.PA.NHA.DO, *adj.*, accompanied.
A.COM.PA.NHA.MEN.TO, *s.m.*, retinue, attendance, train, suite, accompaniment.
A.COM.PA.NHAN.TE, *s. 2 gen.*, companion, escort, follower; *adj.*, accompanying, attendant.
A.COM.PA.NHAR, *v.*, to accompany, come or go along with, escort, follow, wait on, attend.
A.CON.CHE.GA.DO, *adj.*, snug, cosy.
A.CON.CHE.GAN.TE, *adj.*, cosy.
A.CON.CHE.GAR, *v.*, to aproximate, to bring near, to unite.
A.CON.CHE.GO, *s.m.*, shelter, comfort.
A.CON.DI.CI.O.NA.DO, *adj.*, packed, wraped.

A.CON.DI.CI.O.NA.DOR, *s.m.*, packer, conditioning apparatus.
A.CON.DI.CIO.NA.MEN.TO, *s.m.*, conditioning, packing.
A.CON.DI.CIO.NAR, *v.*, to condition, to pack, to box, to adapt, to arrange.
A.CON.SE.LHA.DOR, *s.m.*, advisor, counsellor.
A.CON.SE.LHA.MEN.TO, *s.m.*, advising, counseling.
A.CON.SE.LHAR, *v.*, to advise, to counsel, to persuade.
A.CON.SE.LHÁ.VEL, *adj.*, advisable.
A.CON.TE.CER, *v.*, to happen, to take place, to occur, to come about.
A.CON.TE.CI.DO, *adj.*, past, done.
A.CON.TE.CI.MEN.TO, *s.m.*, occurrence, happening, incident, event.
A.CO.PLA.DO, *adj.*, connected, docked, coupled.
A.CO.PLA.MEN.TO, *s.m.*, coupling, connection, linkage.
A.CO.PLAR, *v.*, to couple.
A.COR.DA.DO, *adj.*, awake, alert, watchful, agreed, determined.
A.CÓR.DÃO, *s.m.*, sentence, judgement.
A.COR.DAR, *v.*, to wake up, awake, awaken, to agree upon, to harmonize, to resolve, to grant.
A.COR.DE, *s.m.*, *Mús.*, chord.
A.COR.DE.ÃO, *s.m.*, accordion.
A.COR.DE.O.NIS.TA, *s.m.*, accordionist.
A.COR.DO, *s.m.*, agreement, harmony, accord, accordance, pact.
A.ço.RES, *s.m.*, *pl.*, the Azores (islands).
A.ço.RI.A.NO, *s.m.*, *adj.*, Azorian.
A.CO.RO.ço.AR, *v.*, to encourage, to animate.
A.COR.REN.TA.DO, *adj.*, chained, fettered.
A.COR.REN.TAR, *v.*, to chain, to fetter, to enslave.
A.COR.RER, *v.*, to run to help, to assist, to succour.
A.COS.SA.DO, *adj.*, harassed, persecuted, hounded.
A.COS.SAR, *v.*, to pursue, to chase.
A.COS.TA.MEN.TO, *s.m.*, hard shoulder (highway), margin.
A.COS.TU.MA.DO, *adj.*, accustomed, used, customary, habituated.
A.COS.TU.MAR, *v.*, to accustom, to habituate, to inure, to familiarize.
A.CO.TO.VE.LAR, *v.*, to elbow, to thrust with the elbow, to push.
A.CO.TUR.NAR, *v.*, to shape like a cothurnus.
A.ÇOU.GUE, *s.m.*, butchery, butcher shop.
A.ÇOU.GUEI.RO, *s.m.*, butcher.
A.ÇOU.TE, *s.m.*, the same that *açoite*.
A.CO.VAR.DA.DO, *adj.*, intimidated, threatened.
A.CO.VAR.DAR, *v.*, to intimidate, discourage.
A.CRE, *adj.*, acre, acrid, sharp, biting, tart; sarcastic, rude.
A.CRE, *s.*, Acre (Brazilian state).
A.CRE.DI.TA.DO, *adj.*, credited, accredited.
A.CRE.DI.TAR, *v.*, believe, trust, to credit, to give credit, to obtain credit.
A.CRE-DO.CE, *adj.*, the same that *agridoce*.
A.CRES.CEN.TAR, *v.*, to add, to increase, to raise, to enlarge.
A.CRES.CEN.TÁ.VEL, *adj.*, addable, addible.
A.CRES.CER, *v.*, to add, to increase, to grow.
A.CRES.CI.DO, *adj.*, added, increased.
A.CRÉS.CI.MO, *s.m.*, addition, increase.
A.CRI.AN.ÇAR, *v.*, to behave or become childish.
A.CRÍ.LI.CO, *s.m.*, acrylic.
A.CRI.MÔ.NI.A, *s.f.*, acrimony.

ACRÍTICO · · 77 · · ADJUDICAÇÃO

A.CRÍ.TI.CO, *adj.*, uncritical.
A.CRO.BA.CI.A, *s.f.*, acrobatics, acrobacy.
A.CRO.BA.TA, *s. 2 gen.*, acrobat.
A.CRO.BÁ.TI.CO, *adj.*, acrobatic.
A.CRÓ.PO.LE, *s.f., Hist.*, acropolis.
A.CRÓS.TI.CO, *s.m.*, acrostic.
A.ÇU, *adj., Bras.*, big., large, grat.
A.CU.A.DO, *adj.*, reared, cornered, trapped.
A.CU.AR, *v.*, to encircle, to corner, to recoil; to contract, to retrogress.
A.ÇÚ.CAR, *s.m.*, sugar.
A.ÇU.CA.RA.DO, *adj.*, sugary, sugared, sweet.
A.ÇU.CA.RAR, *v.*, to sugar, to sweeten with sugar.
A.ÇU.CA.REI.RO, *s.m.*, sugar basin, sugar bowl.
A.ÇU.DE, *s.m.*, dam, weir, sluice.
A.CU.DIR, *v.*, to run to help, to succour, to assist.
A.CUI.DA.DE, *s.f.*, acuity, sharpness, perspicacity.
A.ÇU.LAR, *v.*, to instigate, to incite, to provoke.
A.CUL.TU.RA.DO, *adj.*, acultured.
A.CUL.TU.RAR, *v.*, to acculturate.
A.CU.MU.LA.ÇÃO, *s.f.*, accumulation, storage, pile, concentration.
A.CU.MU.LA.DO, *adj.*, accumulated, increased.
A.CU.MU.LA.DOR, *s.m.*, accumulator, battery.
A.CU.MU.LAR, *v.*, to accumulate, to amass, to pile up, to collect.
A.CÚ.MU.LO, *s.m.*, accumulation.
A.CU.PUN.TOR, *s.m.*, acupuncturist.
A.CU.PUN.TU.RA, *s.f., Med.*, acupuncture.
A.CU.PUN.TU.RIS.TA, *s. 2 gen., Med.*, acupuncturist.
A.CU.RA.DO, *adj.*, accurate, exact.
A.CU.RAR, *v.*, to treat with care, to have acuity.
A.CU.SA.ÇÃO, *s.f.*, accusation, charge, impeachment, indictment.
A.CU.SA.DO, *s.m.*, accused, offender, defendant; *adj.*, accused.
A.CU.SAR, *v.*, to accuse, to charge with, to indict, to impeach.
A.CU.SA.TI.VO, *s.m.*, accusative; *adj.*, accusative, accusatory, accusing.
A.CÚS.TI.CA, *s.f.*, acoustics.
A.CÚS.TI.CO, *adj.*, acoustic.
AD, *abrev.* of *Anno Domini* (*Lat.*), AD.
A.DA.GA, *s.f.*, dagger.
A.DÁ.GIO, *s.m.*, adage, proverb.
A.DA.MAS.CA.DO, *adj.*, mad of or resembling damask; of the color damask.
A.DA.MAS.CAR, *v.*, to damask.
A.DAP.TA.BI.LI.DA.DE, *s.f.*, adaptability, adaptableess.
A.DAP.TA.ÇÃO, *s.f.*, adaptation.
A.DAP.TA.DO, *adj.*, adapted, adjusted.
A.DAP.TA.DOR, *s.m.*, adpter; *adj.*, adapting.
A.DAP.TAR, *v.*, to adapt, to adjust, to suit, to apply, to conform.
A.DAP.TÁ.VEL, *adj.*, adaptable.
A.DE.GA, *s.f.*, cellar, wine cellar.
A.DE.JA.MEN.TO, *s.m.*, flapping.
A.DE.JAR, *v.*, to flutter, to flicker, to flit; to hover.
A.DE.JO, *s.m.*, fluter, fluttering, flickering.
A.DEL.GA.ÇA.DO, *adj.*, thin, slender, thinned.
A.DEL.GA.ÇAR, *v.*, to thin, to make thin, to diminish.
A.DE.MAIS, *adv.*, moreover.
A.DEN.SA.MEN.TO, *s.m.*, densification.

A.DEN.SAR, *v.*, to densify, to condense, to compact.
A.DEN.TRAR, *v.*, to enter, to penetrate.
A.DEN.TRO, *adv.*, inwards, inwardly.
A.DEP.TO, *s.m.*, adept, follower.
A.DE.QUA.DA.MEN.TE, *adv.*, properly, suitably, appropriately.
A.DE.QUA.DO, *adj.*, adequate, fit, suitable, proper.
A.DE.QUAR, *v.*, to adjust, to adapt, to accommodate, to appropriate.
A.DE.RE.ÇAR, *v.*, to address.
A.DE.RE.ÇO, *s.m.*, decoration, adornment.
A.DE.RÊN.CIA, *s.f.*, adherence, adhesion.
A.DE.REN.TE, *s.m.*, adherent, follower; *adj.*, adherent, sticking.
A.DE.RIR, *v.*, to adhere, to approve, to agree, to join.
A.DER.NAR, *v., Náut.*, to, heel (ship); to tilt, incline (for pouring out).
A.DE.SÃO, *s.f.*, adhesion, adherence, agreement.
A.DE.SI.VO, *adj.*, adhesive, sticker, sticking plaster.
A.DES.TRA.DO, *adj.*, skilled, trained, dextrous.
A.DES.TRA.DOR, *s.m.*, instructor, trainer, coach; *adj.*, training, instructive.
A.DES.TRA.MEN.TO, *s.m.*, training, teaching.
A.DES.TRAR, *v.*, to train, to teach, to instruct, to coach.
A.DEUS, *s.m.*, good-bye, farewell, adieu; *interj.*, good-bye, bye-bye, so-long.
A.DI.A.MAN.TAR, *v.*, to make brilliant like a diamond.
A.DI.A.MEN.TO, *s.m.*, postponement, delay, adjournment.
A.DI.AN.TA.DO, *adj.*, advanced, forwarded, interfering, fast.
A.DI.AN.TA.MEN.TO, *s.m.*, advancement, advancing, progress.
A.DI.AN.TAR, *v.*, to advance, to move forward, to pay in advance, to accelerate, to hasten.
A.DI.AN.TE, *adv.*, before, in front of, past, forward, further.
A.DI.AR, *v.*, to adjourn, to postpone, to delay.
A.DI.ÇÃO, *s.f.*, addition, sum, increase.
A.DI.CIO.NA.DO, *adj.*, added, increased.
A.DI.CIO.NAL, *s.m.*, extra, supplement; *adj.*, additional, supplementary.
A.DI.CIO.NAR, *v.*, to add.
A.DIC.TO, *adj.*, addicted.
A.DI.DO, *s.m.*, attaché.
A.DI.NHEI.RA.DO, *adj.*, well-off, wealthy.
A.DI.PO.SE, *s.f.*, adiposis, obesity.
A.DI.PO.SO, *adj.*, adipose.
A.DIR, *v.*, to add, to aggregate, to join.
A.DI.TA.MEN.TO, *s.m.*, additament.
A.DI.TAR, *v.*, to add, to increase; to make happy.
A.DI.TI.VO, *s.m.*, minuend; *adj.*, additive.
A.DI.VI.NHA, *s.f.*, prophecy, prediction, vaticination; premonition; puzzle.
A.DI.VI.NHA.ÇÃO, *s.f.*, puzzle, enigma.
A.DI.VI.NHA.DOR, *s.m.*, soothsayer.
A.DI.VI.NHAR, *v.*, to prophecy, to predict, to vaticinate.
A.DI.VI.NHO, *s.m.*, soothsayer, fortune-teller.
AD.JA.CÊN.CIA, *s.f.*, adjacency, neighbourhood.
AD.JA.CÊN.CIAS, *s.f., pl.*, neighbourhoods.
AD.JA.CEN.TE, *adj.*, adjacent, adjoining.
AD.JA.ZER, *v.*, to be adjacent, to be neighbouring.
AD.JE.TI.VA.ÇÃO, *s.f.*, use of adjectives.
AD.JE.TI.VAR, *v.*, to qualify, to accompany as an adjective.
AD.JE.TI.VO, *s.m., Gram.*, adjective; *adj.*, adjective.
AD.JU.DI.CA.ÇÃO, *s.f., Jur.*, adjucation.

ADJUDICAR •• 78 •• AEROFOTO

AD.JU.DI.CAR, *v., Jur.*, to adjudicate.

AD.JUN.TO, *s.m.*, adjunct, assistant; *adj.*, annexed, joined, contiguous.

AD.JU.RAR, *v.*, to adjure.

AD.JU.TOR, *s.m.*, assistant, helper.

AD.JU.TÓ.RI.O, *s.m.*, assistance, aid, help.

AD.MI.NIS.TRA.ÇÃO, *s.f.*, administration, management, government, direction.

AD.MI.NIS.TRA.DOR, *s.m.*, administrator, manager, executive.

AD.MI.NIS.TRAR, *v.*, manage, direct, govern, conduct.

AD.MI.NIS.TRA.TI.VO, *adj.*, administrative.

AD.MI.RA.BI.LI.DA.DE, *s.f.*, admirableness.

AD.MI.RA.ÇÃO, *s.f.*, admiration, wonder, astonishment, surprise.

AD.MI.RA.DO, *adj.*, admired, astonished.

AD.MI.RA.DOR, *s.m.*, admirer, fan, lover.

AD.MI.RAR, *v.*, to admire, to appreciate, to esteem.

ADMIRÁVEL, *adj.*, admirable, amazing.

AD.MIS.SÃO, *s.f.*, admission, admittance, inlet.

AD.MIS.SÍ.VEL, *adj.*, admissible.

AD.MI.TI.DO, *adj.*, admitted, esteemed.

AD.MI.TIR, *v.*, to admit, to adopt, to acknowledge.

AD.MO.ES.TA.ÇÃO, *s.f.*, admonition, reproof, warning, monition.

AD.MO.ES.TAR, *v.*, to admonish, to reprove, to reprehend.

ADN, *abrev.* of **ÁCIDO DESOXIRRIBONUCLEICO**: deoxyribonucleic acid, DNA.

A.DO.ÇA.DO, *adj.*, sweetened, sugared.

A.DO.ÇA.MEN.TO, *s.m.*, sweetening, softening.

A.DO.ÇAN.TE, *s.m.*, sweetener.

A.DO.ÇÃO, *s.f.*, adoption.

A.DO.ÇAR, *v.*, to sweeten, to soften, to facilitate.

A.DO.CI.CA.DO, *adj.*, slightly sweet, sweetish.

A.DO.CI.CAR, *v.*, to sweeten; to attenuate, to soften.

A.DO.E.CER, *v.*, to become sick or ill, be taken ill.

A.DO.E.CI.DO, *adj.*, sick, ill.

A.DO.E.CI.MEN.TO, *s.m.*, falling sick or ill.

A.DO.EN.TA.DO, *adj.*, ill, sick, indisposed.

A.DO.EN.TAR, *v.*, to sicken, make sickish.

A.DOI.DA.DO, *adj.*, mad, foolish, crazy; *adv.*, madly.

A.DOI.DAR, *v.*, to madden.

A.DO.LES.CÊN.CIA, *s.f.*, adolescence, adolescency.

A.DO.LES.CEN.TE, *s. 2 gen.*, adolescent; *adj.*, adolescent, youthful.

A.DON.DE, *adv., pop., Bras.*, where, from where, wherefrom; *aonde*: wherever; *donde*: from where.

A.DO.RA.ÇÃO, *s.f.*, adoration, veneration, devotion.

A.DO.RA.DO, *adj.*, adored, venerated.

A.DO.RA.DOR, *s.m.*, admirer, worshipper, lover.

A.DO.RAR, *v.*, to adore, to venerate, to worship, to love.

A.DO.RÁ.VEL, *adj.*, adorable, lovely.

A.DO.RA.VEL.MEN.TE, *adv.*, adorably, charmingly.

A.DOR.ME.CER, *v.*, to put to sleep, to fall asleep.

A.DOR.ME.CI.DO, *adj.*, asleep, numb; *a bela adormecida*: the sleeping beauty.

A.DOR.ME.CI.MEN.TO, *s.m.*, falling asleep; lethargy, drowsiness.

A.DOR.NA.DO, *adj.*, adorned, ornate.

A.DOR.NAR, *v.*, to adorn, to embellish, to dress.

A.DOR.NO, *s.m.*, adornment, ornament, decoration.

A.DO.TAR, *v.*, to adopt, to accept, to use, to resolve.

A.DO.TÁ.VEL, *adj.*, adoptable.

A.DO.TI.VO, *adj.*, adoptive.

AD.QUI.REN.TE, *s. 2 gen.*, acquirer; *adj.*, acquiring.

AD.QUI.RI.DO, *adj.*, acquired, purchased.

AD.QUI.RIR, *v.*, to acquire, to obtain, to get.

A.DRE.DE, *adv.*, purpose.

A.DRE.NA.LI.NA, *s.f.*, adrenalin.

A.DRI.Á.TI.CO, *s.m.*, the Adriatic (Sea).

A.DRO, *s.m.*, churchyard.

AD-RO.GAR, *v.*, to adopt.

ADS.CRE.VER, *v.*, to add in writing.

ADS.TRIN.GEN.TE, *adj.*, astringent.

ADS.TRIN.GIR, *v.*, to astringe, to compel.

ADS.TRI.TO, *adj., Med.*, astricted.

A.DU.A.NA, *s.f.*, customs, custom house.

A.DU.A.NEI.RO, *s.m.*, custom house officer.

A.DU.BA.ÇÃO, *s.f.*, fertilization, manuring.

A.DU.BAR, *v.*, to season, to fertilize, to manure.

A.DU.BO, *s.m.*, fertilizer, manure, seasoning, flavouring.

A.DU.LA.ÇÃO, *s.f.*, adulation, flattery.

A.DU.LA.DOR, *adj.*, flattering, adulator.

A.DU.LAR, *v.*, to flatter, to adulate, to coax.

A.DÚL.TE.RA, *s.f.*, adulteress.

A.DUL.TE.RA.ÇÃO, *s.f.*, adulteration, falsification.

A.DUL.TE.RA.DO, *adj.*, adulterated, corrupt.

A.DUL.TE.RA.DOR, *s.m.*, adulterator, falsifier, corrupter.

A.DUL.TE.RAR, *v.*, to adulterate, to falsify, to corrupt.

A.DUL.TÉ.RIO, *s.m.*, adultery.

A.DÚL.TE.RO, *s.m.*, adulterer; *adj.*, adulterous, adulterated.

A.DUL.TO, *s.m., adj.*, adult.

A.DUN.CO, *adj.*, crooked, hooked, curved, unciform.

A.DU.TOR, *s.m.*, adducer, adductor.

A.DU.TO.RA, *s.f.*, water supply network.

A.DU.ZIR, *v.*, to adduce, to expose, to show.

AD.VEN.TÍ.CI.O, *adj.*, foreigner, stranger.

AD.VEN.TIS.TA, *s. 2 gen.*, Adventist (member of Adventism).

AD.VEN.TO, *s.m.*, coming, arrival, approach, Advent.

AD.VER.BI.AL, *adj., Gram.*, adverbial.

AD.VÉR.BIO, *s.m.*, adverb.

AD.VER.SÁ.RIO, *s.m.*, adversary, opponent, enemy; *adj.*, adverse, opposing.

AD.VER.SI.DA.DE, *s.f.*, adversity, misfortune, mishap.

AD.VER.SO, *adj.*, adverse, contrary, opposed.

AD.VER.TÊN.CIA, *s.f.*, admonition, warning, censure.

AD.VER.TI.DA.MEN.TE, *adv.*, attentively, cautiously.

AD.VER.TIR, *v.*, to warn, to admonish, to censure, to advise.

AD.VIN.DO, *adj.*, that has occurred; *~de*: resulting from.

AD.VIR, *v.*, to happen, to occur; to succeed.

AD.VO.CA.CI.A, *s.f.*, advocacy, advocateship.

AD.VO.GA.DO, *s.m.*, lawyer, advocate, attorney.

AD.VO.GAR, *v.*, to act as a lawyer.

A.E.RA.ÇÃO, *s.f.*, aeration, ventilation, airing.

A.É.REO, *adj.*, aerial, living in the air, airlike.

A.E.RO.BAR.CO, *s.m.*, hovercraft.

A.E.RÓ.BI.CA, *s.f.*, aerobics (gymnastics).

A.E.RÓ.BI.CO, *adj.*, aerobic.

A.E.RO.CLU.BE, *s.m.*, flying club.

A.E.RO.DI.NÂ.MI.CA, *adj.*, aerodynamic; *s.f.*, aerodynamics.

A.E.RÓ.DRO.MO, *s.m.*, aerodrome, airdrome.

A.E.RO.ES.PA.CI.AL, *adj.*, aerospace.

A.E.RO.FO.TO, *s.f.*, aerial photograph.

AEROMOÇA   •• 79 •••   AGACHADO

A.E.RO.MO.ÇA, *s.f.*, flight stewardess.

A.E.RO.MO.DE.LIS.MO, *s.m.*, model aeroplane making; *Esp.*, model aeronautics.

A.E.RO.NAU.TA, *s. 2 gen.*, aeronaut.

A.E.RO.NÁU.TI.CA, *s.f.*, aviation, aeronautics.

A.E.RO.NA.VE, *s.f.*, aircraft, airship.

A.E.RO.PLA.NO, *s.m.*, airplan.

A.E.RO.POR.TO, *s.m.*, airport.

A.E.ROS.SOL, *s.m.*, *Quím.*, aerosol.

A.E.RÓS.TA.TO, *s.m.*, airship, balloom.

A.E.RO.VI.Á.RIO, *s.m.*, person employed in the air service.

AFÃ, *s.m.*, diligence, anxiety, eagerness; grat care.

A.FA.BI.LI.DA.DE, *s.f.*, affability, politeness, kindness, suavity.

A.FA.GAR, *v.*, to caress, to fondle, to pet, to comfort.

A.FA.GO, *s.m.*, caress, allurement.

A.FA.MA.DO, *adj.*, famous, notable.

A.FA.SI.A, *s.f.*, *Med.*, aphasia.

A.FA.NAR, *v.*, to strive, to obtain laboriously, to steal.

A.FAS.TA.DO, *adj.*, remote, distant, far off, apart.

A.FAS.TA.MEN.TO, *s.m.*, removal, dismissal, separation, retirement, distance.

A.FAS.TAR, *v.*, to remove, to separate, to repel.

A.FÁ.VEL, *adj.*, polite, courteous, affable, pleasant.

A.FA.ZE.RES, *s.m., pl.*, business, affairs.

A.FE.GA.NIS.TÃO, *s.m.*, Afghanistan.

A.FE.GÃ, A.FE.GA.NE, *s. 2 gen., adj.*, afghan.

A.FE.GÃO, *s.m.*, the same that *afegã/afegane*.

A.FEI.ÇÃO, *s.f.*, affection, love.

A.FEI.ÇO.A.DO, *adj.*, affectionate; attached.

A.FEI.ÇO.A.MEN.TO, *s.m.*, affection, inclination.

A.FEI.ÇO.AR, *v.*, to captivate, to shape, to form, to charm.

A.FEI.TO, *adj.*, accostumed to.

A.FE.MI.NA.DO, *adj.*, effeminate.

A.FE.MI.NAR, *v.*, to become effeminate, to make effeminate.

A.FE.RI.ÇÃO, *s.f.*, gauging, calibrating, checking, collation.

A.FE.RI.DO, *adj.*, gauged, calibrated, checked.

A.FE.RI.DOR, *s.m.*, gauger, standard.

A.FE.RIR, *v.*, to gauge, to calibrate, to check.

A.FER.RA.DO, *adj.*, stubborn, abstinate; attached.

A.FER.RAR, *v.*, to grapple, to grasp; *aferrar-se*: to cling to.

A.FER.RO.LHAR, *v.*, to bolt, to imprision.

A.FER.VEN.TAR, *v.*, to boil; to parboil.

A.FE.TA.ÇÃO, *s.f.*, affectation, affection, pedantism, vanity.

A.FE.TA.DO, *adj.*, affected.

A.FE.TAR, *v.*, to affect, to feign, to simulate.

A.FE.TI.VI.DA.DE, *s.f.*, affectivity.

A.FE.TI.VO, *adj.*, affective, dedicated, devoted.

A.FE.TO, *s.m.*, friendship, sympathy, passion; *adj.*, affectionate, friendly.

A.FE.TU.O.SO, *adj.*, affectionate, affable, kind.

A.FI.A.DO, *adj.*, sharpened, sharp, whetted.

A.FI.AN.ÇAR, *v.*, to warrant, to bail, to guarantee, to assure.

A.FI.AR, *v.*, to sharpen, to improve, to irritate.

A.FI.CI.O.NA.DO, *s.m.*, enthusiast.

A.FI.GU.RAR, *v.*, to figure, to represent; *afigurar-se*: to appear to; to look alike.

A.FI.LA.DO, *adj.*, fine, delicate.

A.FI.LAR, *v.*, to gauge, to standardize.

A.FI.LHA.DA, *s.f.*, goddaughter.

A.FI.LHA.DO, *s.m.*, godson.

A.FI.LHAR, *v.*, to produce offspring.

A.FI.LI.A.ÇÃO, *s.f.*, affiliation, connection.

A.FI.LI.A.DO, *s.m.*, affiliate, member.

A.FI.LI.AR, *v.*, to affiliate, to join:

A.FIM, *s.m.*, kinsman, kinswoman; affinity; similar.

A.FI.NA.ÇÃO, *s.f.*, *Mús.*, tuning, refinement, refining (metals).

A.FI.NA.DO, *adj.*, tuned up, refined.

A.FI.NAL, *adv.*, finally, at last, after all.

A.FI.NAR, *v.*, to fine, to make fine, to refine, to taper.

A.FIN.CO, *s.m.*, attachment, assiduity.

A.FI.NI.DA.DE, *s.f.*, affinity, relation, relationship.

A.FIR.MA.ÇÃO, *s.f.*, affirmation, assertion.

A.FIR.MAR, *v.*, to affirm, to asseverate, to maintain, to assert, to say, to confirm.

A.FIR.MA.TI.VA.MEN.TE, *adv.*, affirmatively.

A.FIR.MA.TI.VO, *adj.*, affirmative.

A.FI.VE.LAR, *v.*, to buckle, to fasten.

A.FI.XAR, *v.*, to fix, to fasten, to make firm, to post.

A.FLI.ÇÃO, *s.f.*, affliction, trouble, grief, anguish.

A.FLI.GIR, *v.*, to afflict, to trouble, to distress, to torment.

A.FLI.TI.VO, *adj.*, afflicting, afflictive.

A.FLI.TO, *adj.*, afflicted, afflictive.

A.FLO.RAR, *v.*, to level, to emerge, to come to the surface.

A.FLU.ÊN.CIA, *s.f.*, affluence, abundance; flush, flood.

A.FLU.EN.TE, *s.m.*, tributary; *adj.*, affluent, confluent.

A.FLU.IR, *v.*, to flow to, flow in, to stream towards.

A.FO.BA.ÇÃO, *s.f.*, hurry, bustle, fatigue.

A.FO.BA.DO, *adj.*, in a haste; flustered.

A.FO.BA.MEN.TO, *s.m.*, the same that *afobação*.

A.FO.BAR, *v.*, to hurry, to bustle, to embarrass.

A.FO.FAR, *v.*, fluff up, to soften.

A.FO.GA.DO, *adj.*, drowned, asphixiated, watered, soaked.

A.FO.GA.DOR, *s.m.*, choke, throttle; *adj.*, stifling.

A.FO.GAR, *v.*, suffocate, asphixiate, stifle, to check, to submerge.

A.FOI.TE.ZA, *s.f.*, courage, fearlessness.

A.FOI.TO, *adj.*, fearless, bold, audacious.

A.FO.NI.A, *s.f.*, aphonia, loss of voice.

A.FÔ.NI.CO, *adj.*, aphonic, voiceless.

A.FO.RA, *adv.*, except, save, excepting, besides.

A.FO.RIS.MO, *s.m.*, aphorism, maxim.

A.FOR.TU.NA.DO, *adj.*, lucky, happy, fortunate.

A.FRES.CA.LHA.DO, *adj.*, *col.*, affeminate, *gír.*, camp.

A.FRES.CO, *s.m.*, afresco (painting).

A.FRE.TAR, *v.*, to freight.

Á.FRI.CA, *s.f.*, **ÁFRICA**.

A.FRI.CA.NO, *s.m., adj.*, African.

A.FRO-A.ME.RI.CA.NO, *s.m., adj.*, Afro-American.

A.FRO-BRA.SI.LEI.RO, *s.m., adj.*, Afro-Brasilian.

A.FRO.DI.SÍ.A.CO, *s.m., adj.*, aphrodisiac.

A.FRON.TA, *s.f.*, insult, offence, affront.

A.FRON.TA.DO, *adj.*, affronted, insulted; importuned.

A.FRON.TAR, *v.*, to affront, to insult, to importune, to tire, exhaust.

A.FROU.XAR, *v.*, to slacken, to relax, to loosen, to release.

AF.TA, *s.f.*, aphtha.

A.FU.GEN.TAR, *v.*, to chase away, to put to flight, to scare away.

A.FUN.DAR, *v.*, to sink, to founder, to submerge, to deepen.

A.FU.NI.LAR, *v.*, to shape like a funnel; to narrow.

A.GÁ, *s.m.*, aitch (the name of the letter H).

A.GA.CHA.DO, *adj.*, squatted, crouched.

AGACHAMENTO · · 80 · · AGULHADA

A.GA.CHA.MEN.TO, *s.m.*, crouching, squatting, cowering.
A.GA.CHAR-SE, *v.*, to crouch, to squat, to cower.
A.GAR.RA.DO, *adj.*, stingy, avaricious, miserly, caught.
A.GAR.RA.MEN.TO, *s.m.*, seizing, holding, catching, stinginess.
A.GAR.RAR, *v.*, to catch, to seize, to clasp, to grip, to snap up.
A.GA.SA.LHA.DO, *adj.*, sheltered, covered, lodged.
A.GA.SA.LHAR, *v.*, to shelter, to lodge, to warm, to protect.
A.GA.SA.LHO, *s.m.*, shelter, warm clothing, wrap.
A.GÊN.CIA, *s.f.*, agency, activity, action, bureau.
A.GEN.CI.A.MEN.TO, *s.m.*, intermediation, representation, negotiation.
A.GEN.CI.AR, *v.*, to negotiate, to work as an agent.
A.GEN.DA, *s.f.*, agenda, notebook.
A.GEN.DAR, *v.*, to schedule.
A.GEN.TE, *s. 2 gen.*, agent.
A.GI.GAN.TAR, *v.*, to make gigantic.
Á.GIL, *adj.*, agile, fast.
A.GI.LI.DA.DE, *s.f.*, agility, quickness, vivacity, nimbleness.
A.GI.LI.ZAR, *v.*, to make agile, to activate.
Á.GIO, *s.m.*, agio.
A.GI.O.TA, *s. 2 gen.*, jobber, usurer, moneylender.
A.GI.O.TA.GEM, *s.f.*, agiotage, usury.
A.GIR, *v.*, to act, to proceed, to do.
A.GI.TA.ÇÃO, *s.f.*, agitation, perturbation, trouble, conflict.
A.GI.TA.DO, *adj.*, agitated, excited.
A.GI.TA.DOR, *s.m.*, agitator, *adj.*, agitating.
A.GI.TAR, *v.*, to agitate, to shake, to shock, to excite, to disturb, to move.
A.GI.TO, *s.m.*, *gír.*, excitement.
A.GLO.ME.RA.ÇÃO, *s.f.*, agglomeration, mass, heap.
A.GLO.ME.RA.DO, *s.m.*, *Geol.*, agglomerate; *adj.*, agglomerated, heaped, massed up.
A.GLO.ME.RAR, *v.*, to agglomerate, to accumulate, to join.
A.GLU.TI.NA.ÇÃO, *s.f.*, agglutination.
A.GLU.TI.NAR, *v.*, to agglutinate, to unite, to join.
A.GO., *abrev.* of *agosto*: August, Ago.
A.GO.NI.A, *s.f.*, agony, pangs of death.
A.GO.NI.A.DO, *adj.*, agonizing, uneasy, anxious.
A.GO.NI.AR, *v.*, to agonize.
A.GO.NI.ZAN.TE, *adj.*, agonizing, dying.
A.GO.NI.ZAR, *v.*, to agonize, to afflict, to distress, to worry.
A.GO.RA, *adv.*, now, at the present time, however; *conj.*, but.
A.GO.RA.FO.BI.A, *s.f.*, *Med.*, agoraphobia.
A.GO.RI.NHA, *adv.*, just now.
A.GOS.TO, *s.m.*, August.
A.GOU.RAR, *v.*, to omen, to forebode, to presage, to augur.
A.GOU.REN.TO, *adj.*, foreboding, superstitious.
A.GOU.RO, *s.m.*, omen, foreboding, prediction.
A.GRA.CI.A.DO, *adj.*, honoured, graced.
A.GRA.CI.AR, *v.*, to grace, to reward, to recompense.
A.GRA.DA.BI.LÍS.SI.MO, *adj.*, (superlative) very pleasant.
A.GRA.DAR, *v.*, to please, to be agreeable.
A.GRA.DÁ.VEL, *adj.*, agreeable, pleasant, enjoyable, nice, good.
A.GRA.DE.CER, *v.*, to thank, to show gratitude.
A.GRA.DE.CI.DO, *adj.*, grateful, thankful, obliged.
A.GRA.DE.CI.MEN.TO, *s.m.*, thanks, thankfulness.
A.GRA.DO, *s.m.*, pleasure, contentment, delight, satisfaction, kindness.
A.GRÁ.RI.O, *adj.*, agrarian.

A.GRA.VA.MEN.TO, *s.m.*, aggravation, worsening.
A.GRA.VAN.TE, *s.m.*, culpability.
A.GRA.VAR, *v.*, to aggravate, to worsen, to oppress, to molest, to offend.
A.GRA.VO, *s.m.*, offence, loss, damage, injury.
A.GRE.DIR, *v.*, to attack, to assault, to aggress, to strike.
A.GRE.GA.ÇÃO, *s.f.*, aggregation, association, agglomeration.
A.GRE.GA.DO, *s.m.*, aggregation, assemblage; *adj.*, aggregate, reunited.
A.GRE.GAR, *v.*, to aggregate, to join, to annex, to associate, to add.
A.GRE.MI.A.ÇÃO, *s.f.*, association, fellowship, reunion.
A.GRE.MI.AR, *v.*, to associate, to reunite.
A.GRES.SÃO, *s.f.*, aggression, wound, injury, blow, assault.
A.GRES.SI.VI.DA.DE, *adv.*, aggressiveness
A.GRES.SI.VO, *adj.*, aggressive, offensive.
A.GRES.SOR, *s.m.*, aggressor.
A.GRES.TE, *s.m.*, agricultural land not in use; dry area in the north-east; *adj.*, rural; rustic.
A.GRI.ÃO, *s.m.*, water-cress.
A.GRÍ.CO.LA, *adj.*, *s. 2 gen.*, agricultural.
A.GRI.CUL.TOR, *s.m.*, agriculturist, farmer; *adj.*, agricultural.
A.GRI.CUL.TU.RA, *s.f.*, agriculture, farming, cultivation.
A.GRI.CUL.TU.RÁ.VEL, *adj.*, farmable, arable.
A.GRI.DO.CE, *adj.*, sour-sweet, sweet and sour.
A.GRI.MEN.SOR, *s.m.*, surveyor.
A.GRO.IN.DÚS.TRI.A, *s.f.*, agroindustry.
A.GRO.IN.DUS.TRI.AL, *adj.*, agroindustrial.
A.GRO.NO.MI.A, *s.f.*, agronomy, agronomics.
A.GRO.NÔ.MI.CO, *adj.*, agronomic.
A.GRÔ.NO.MO, *s.m.*, agronomist.
A.GRO.PE.CU.Á.RI.A, *s.f.*, farming and cattle raising.
A.GRO.PE.CU.Á.RI.O, *s.m.*, mixed farming; *adj.*, mixed-farming.
A.GRO.TÓ.XI.CO, *s.m.*, pesticide.
A.GRU.PA.MEN.TO, *s.m.*, grouping, assembly, group.
A.GRU.PAR, *v.*, to group, to cluster, to gather.
A.GRU.RA, *s.f.*, acrity, roughness.
Á.GUA, *s.f.*, water.
A.GUA.CEI.RO, *s.m.*, a shower of rain; squall.
Á.GUA DE CO.CO, *s.m.*, coconut milk.
Á.GUA-DE-CO.LÔ.NI.A, *s.f.*, Cologne water.
A.GUA.DO, *adj.*, watered down, watery; dilute in water.
Á.GUA-FUR.TA.DA, *s.f.*, garret.
Á.GUA-MA.RI.NHA, *s.f.*, aquamarine.
A.GUAR, *v.*, to water, to dilute.
A.GUAR.DAR, *v.*, to expect, to await, to wait for, to observe.
A.GUAR.DEN.TE, *s.m.*, brandy, fire-water.
A.GUAR.RÁS, *s.f.*, *Quim.*, turpentine.
Á.GUA-VI.VA, *s.f.*, medusa, jelly-fish.
A.GU.ÇA.DO, *adj.*, sharp, sharpened; keen; *fig.*, lively.
A.GU.ÇAR, *v.*, to grind, to sharpen, to whet, to taper, to point, to excite.
A.GU.DE.ZA, *s.f.*, sharpness, keenness.
A.GU.DO, *adj.*, sharp, pointed.
A.GUEN.TA.DOR, *s.m.*, supporter; *adj.*, supporting, sustaining.
A.GUEN.TAR, *v.*, to support, to bear, to sustain, to endure.
A.GUER.RI.DO, *adj.*, warlike, courageous, bellicose.
Á.GUIA, *s.f.*, eagle.
A.GU.LHA, *s.f.*, needle.
A.GU.LHA.DA, *s.f.*, needle prick.

AH   ·· 81 ··   ALEIJAR

AH, *interj.*, ah!

AI, *s.m.*, groan, moan; *interj.*, ah!

AÍ, *adv.*, there, in that place, in this respect.

AI.A.TO.LÁ, *s.m.*, *Rel.*, ayatollah.

AI.DÉ.TI.CO, *adj.*, *Med.*, suffering from AIDS; *s.m.*, person with AIDS; AIDS sufferer.

AIDS (sida), *s.f.*, AIDS (acquired immune deficiency sindrome).

A.IN.DA, *adv.*, still, yet, again.

AI.PIM, *s.m.*, sweet cassava.

AI.PO, *s.m.*, celery.

AI.RO.SO, *adj.*, slender, graceful, elegant.

A.JA.E.ZAR, *v.*, to harness, to adorn.

A.JAR.DI.NA.DO, *adj.*, gardenlike.

A.JAR.DI.NAR, *v.*, to garden, to form into a garden.

A.JEI.TAR, *v.*, to arrange, to dispose, to accomodate, to adapt.

A.JO.E.LHA.DO, *adj.*, kneeling.

A.JO.E.LHAR, *v.*, to kneel, to kneel down.

A.JU.DA, *s.f.*, help, assistance, support, aid, succour.

A.JU.DAN.TE, *s. 2 gen.*, assistant, helper, acolyte.

A.JU.DAR, *v.*, to help, to aid, to assist, to succour, to support.

A.JU.I.ZA.DA.MEN.TE, *adv.*, reasonably, wisely.

A.JU.I.ZA.DO, *adj.*, reasonable, discret, judicious.

A.JU.I.ZAR, *v.*, to judge, to form an opinion, to estimate, to suppose.

A.JU.I.ZÁ.VEL, *adj.*, judgeable, estimable.

A.JUN.TA.MEN.TO, *s.m.*, reunion, meeting, assembly.

A.JUN.TAR, *v.*, to gather, to accumulate, to compile, to add, to collect.

A.JUS.TA.DO, *s.m.*, adjusted; *adj.*, adjusted, proportional; settled.

A.JUS.TA.MEN.TO, *s.m.*, adjustment, adjusting; adaptation.

A.JUS.TAR, *v.*, to adjust, to regulate, to order, to accord, to adapt.

A.JUS.TÁ.VEL, *adj.*, adjustable.

A.JUS.TE, *s.m.*, agreement, understanding, pact, settlement.

A.LA, *s.f.*, line, row, file, guard.

ALÁ, *s.m.*, *Rel.*, Allah.

A.LA.DO, *adj.*, winged.

A.LA.GA.DI.ÇO, *adj.*, subject to flooding, swampish; drenched.

A.LA.GA.DO, *adj.*, full of water, waterlogged.

A.LA.GA.MEN.TO, *s.m.*, widening (road); inundation, overflow.

A.LA.GAR, *v.*, to inundate, to overflow, to flood.

A.LA.GO.AS, *s.*, Alagoas (Brazilian state).

ALALC, *abrev.* of *Associação Latino-Americana de Livre Comércio*: Latin-American Free Trade Association.

A.LAM.BI.CAR, *v.*, to distil, to refine.

A.LAM.BI.QUE, *s.m.*, alembic, still.

A.LA.ME.DA, *s.f.*, lane, alley, grove, avenue, park.

A.LA.RAN.JA.DO, *adj.*, orange, like an orange.

A.LAR.DE, *s.m.*, ostentation, vainglory, pomp, vanity.

A.LAR.DE.AR, *v.*, to parade; to show off.

A.LAR.GA.MEN.TO, *s.m.*, widening, enlargement, dilatation.

A.LAR.GAR, *v.*, to widen, to dilate, to broaden, to enlarge, to amplify.

A.LA.RI.DO, *s.m.*, clamour, row.

A.LAR.MAN.TE, *adj.*, alarming.

A.LAR.MAR, *v.*, to alarm, to frighten, to trouble.

A.LAR.ME, *s.m.*, alarm, signal.

A.LAR.MIS.TA, *s. 2 gen.*, alarmist; *adj.*, alarmist, alarming.

A.LAS.TRA.MEN.TO, *s.m.*, spreading, expansion, diffusion.

A.LAS.TRAR, *v.*, to spread out, to diffuse, to stow.

A.LA.VAN.CA, *s.f.*, lever, handspike, crowbar.

A.LA.VAN.CA.GEM, *s.f.*, *Econ.*, leverage.

A.LA.VAN.CAR, *v.*, to launch; *Econ.*, to leverage.

AL.BA.NÊS, *s.m.*, *adj.*, albanian.

AL.BÂ.NI.A, *s.*, Albânia.

AL.BA.TROZ, *s.m.*, albatross.

AL.BER.GUE, *s.m.*, inn, lodging, hostelry, shelter.

AL.BI.NO, *s.m.*, albino; *adj.*, albinic.

ÁL.BUM, *s.m.*, album.

AL.BU.MI.NA, *s.f.*, *Quím.*, albumin.

ALCA, *abrev.* of Área de Livre Comércio das Américas: Free Trade Area of the Americas, FTAA.

AL.ÇA, *s.f.*, ring, eye, handle, holder, strap.

AL.CA.CHO.FRA, *s.f.*, artichoke.

AL.CA.ÇUZ, *s.m.*, *Bot.*, liquorice plant.

AL.ÇA.DA, *s.f.*, competence, jurisdiction.

AL.CA.GUE.TAR, *v.*, *gír.*, to stool.

ÁL.CA.LI, *s.m.*, *Quím.*, alkali.

AL.CA.LI.NO, *adj.*, *Quím.*, alkaline.

AL.CAN.ÇAR, *v.*, to reach, to fetch, to attain, to obtain, to get, to catch up.

AL.CAN.ÇÁ.VEL, *adj.*, attainable, reachable, achievable.

AL.CAN.CE, *s.m.*, reach, range, grasp, scope, attainment.

AL.ÇA.PÃO, *s.m.*, trapdoor.

AL.ÇAR, *v.*, to raise, to lift, to elevate, to edify, to heave, to exalt.

AL.CA.TEI.A, *s.f.*, pack of wolves; herd.

AL.CA.TRA, *s.f.*, rump steak.

AL.CA.TRÃO, *s.m.*, tar, pitch.

AL.CE, *s.m.*, moose, elk.

ÁL.CO.OL, *s.m.*, alcohol, spirit.

AL.CO.Ó.LA.TRA, *s. 2 gen.*, alcoholic, drunkard; *adj.*, alcoholic.

AL.CO.Ó.LI.CO, *adj.*, alcoholic.

AL.CO.O.LIS.MO, *s.m.*, alcoholism.

AL.CO.O.LI.ZA.DO, *adj.*, drunk; *gír.*, woozy, tipsy.

AL.CO.O.LI.ZAR, *v.*, to alcoholize, to intoxicate.

AL.CO.RÃO, *s.m.*, Alcoran, Koran.

AL.CO.VA, *s.f.*, alcove.

AL.CO.VI.TEI.RO, *s.m.*, panderer, gossiper.

AL.CU.NHA, *s.f.*, nickname.

AL.DE.ÃO, *s.m.*, countryman, peasant, villager.

AL.DEI.A, *s.f.*, village.

AL.DRA.VA, AL.DRA.BA, *s.f.*, door-knocker, rapper.

A.LE.A.TÓ.RIO, *adj.*, aleatoric.

A.LE.CRIM, *s.m.*, rosemary.

A.LE.GA.ÇÃO, *s.f.*, allegation, assertion, exposition.

A.LE.GA.DA.MEN.TE, *adv.*, allegedly.

A.LE.GA.DO, *adj.*, alleged.

A.LE.GAN.TE, *s. 2 gen.*, alleger; *adj.*, alleging.

A.LE.GAR, *v.*, to allege, to cite, to proof, to present, to plead.

A.LE.GÁ.VEL, *adj.*, claimable, allegeable, pleadable.

A.LE.GO.RI.A, *s.f.*, allegory.

A.LE.GÓ.RI.CO, *adj.*, allegoric.

A.LE.GRAR, *v.*, to make happy, rejoice, to gladden.

A.LE.GRE, *adj.*, happy, gay, cheerful, glad, joyful.

A.LE.GRI.A, *s.f.*, cheerfulness, happiness, joy, gladness, pleasure, gaiety.

A.LEI.A, *s.f.*, alley.

A.LEI.JA.DO, *s.m.*, cripple; *adj.*, crippled, disabled.

A.LEI.JAR, *v.*, to deform, to mutilate.

ALEITAMENTO · 82 · ALISTAR

A.LEI.TA.MEN.TO, *s.m.*, breastfeeding, suckling, nursing.
A.LEI.TAR, *v.*, to nurse, to shuckle, to feed on milk.
A.LÉM, *adv.*, there, in that place, over there, farther on, beyond.
A.LE.MA.NHA, *s.*, Germany.
A.LE.MÃO, *s.m., adj.*, German.
A.LÉM-MAR, *s.m.*, oversea country.
A.LEN.TA.DO, *adj.*, courageous, brave, highspirited; bulky, stout.
A.LEN.TAR, *v.*, to encourage, to animate, to enliven, to comfort.
A.LEN.TO, *s.m.*, courage, effort, respiration, diligence.
A.LER.GI.A, *s.f.*, allergy.
A.LÉR.GI.CO, *adj.*, allergic.
A.LER.TA, *s.m.*, alert; *adv.*, alert; *interj.*, attention.
A.LER.TAR, *v.*, to alert, to give alarm.
A.LE.TRI.A, *s.f.*, vermicelli.
AL.FA.BÉ.TI.CO, *adj.*, aphabetic(al).
AL.FA.BE.TI.ZA.ÇÃO, *s.f.*, alphabetization.
AL.FA.BE.TI.ZA.DO, *s.m.*, person literate; *adj.*, literate.
AL.FA.BE.TI.ZAR, *v.*, alphabetize.
AL.FA.BE.TO, *s.m.*, alphabet.
AL.FA.CE, *s.f.*, lettuce.
AL.FA.FA, *s.f., Bot.*, alfalfa, lucern(e).
AL.FAI.A.TA.RI.A, *s.f.*, tailor's workshop.
AL.FAI.A.TE, *s.m.*, tailor.
AL.FÂN.DE.GA, *s.f.*, customs, custom house.
AL.FAN.DE.GÁ.RIO, *adj.*, of or referring to customs.
AL.FA.ZE.MA, *s.f.*, lavender.
AL.FI.NE.TA.DA, *s.f.*, pin-prick.
AL.FI.NE.TAR, *v.*, to pin; prick with a pin; to criticize harshly; to satirize.
AL.FI.NE.TE, *s.m.*, pin, tiepin.
AL.FI.NE.TEI.RA, *s.f.*, pin box, pincushion.
AL.FOR.JE, *s.m.*, bag or sack with two pouches.
AL.FOR.RI.A, *s.f.*, enfranchisement, libertation, release from slavery.
AL.GA, *s.f.*, alga, seaweed.
AL.GA.RIS.MO, *s.m.*, cipher, figure, numeral, number.
AL.GA.ZAR.RA, *s.f.*, clamour, uproar, bawling, mutiny, tumult.
ÁL.GE.BRA, *s.f.*, algebra.
AL.GÉ.BRI.CO, *adj.*, algebric.
AL.GE.MAS, *s.f.*, manacles, shackles, handcuffs.
AL.GE.MAR, *v.*, to shackle, to fetter, to handcuff, to dominate.
AL.GI.BEI.RA, *s.f.*, pocket.
AL.GO, *adv.*, somewhat, a bit, a little; *pron.*, something, anything.
AL.GO.DÃO, *s.m.*, cotton.
AL.GO.DÃO-DO.CE, *s.m.*, cotton candy.
AL.GO.DO.AL, *s.m.*, cotton plantation.
AL.GO.DO.EI.RO, *s.m.*, cotton plant; cotton spiner (manufacturer)
AL.GO.RIT.MO, *s.m., Mat.*, algorithm.
AL.GOZ, *s.m.*, executioner, hangman, torturer, monster.
AL.GUÉM, *pron.*, somebody, someone, anybody, anyone.
AL.GUM, *pron., adj.*, some, any.
AL.GU.RES, *adv.*, somewhere, in some place.
A.LHA.NAR, *v.*, to soften; to make even, to level.
A.LHE.A.MEN.TO, *s.m.*, alienation.
A.LHE.AR, *v.*, to alienate, to deprive, to transfer property.
A.LHEI.O, *adj.*, strange, foreign, alien, distant, contrary.

A.LHO, *s.m.*, garlic.
A.LHO-PO.RÓ, A.LHO-POR.RO, *s.m.*, leek.
A.LHU.RES, *adv.*, elsewhere.
A.LI, *adv.*, there, in that place; then.
A.LI.Á, *s.f., Zool.*, the female elephant.
A.LI.A.DO, *s.m.*, ally; *adj.*, allied, associated.
A.LI.AN.ÇA, *s.f.*, alliance, confederation, association, connection.
A.LI.AN.ÇAR, *v.*, to ally, to unite.
A.LI.AR, *v.*, to ally, to join, to unite, to combine, to harmonize.
A.LI.ÁS, *adv.*, besides, otherwise, moreover, on the other hand.
A.LI.Á.VEL, *adj.*, alliable.
Á.LI.BI, *s.m.*, alibi.
A.LI.CA.TE, *s.m.*, pincers, a pair of pliers.
A.LI.CER.ÇA.DO, *adj.*, based; having a founding.
A.LI.CER.ÇAR, *v.*, to lay the foundation, to found, to base.
A.LI.CER.CE, *s.m.*, foundation, base.
A.LI.CI.A.ÇÃO, *s.f.*, seduction, enticement, allurement; bribery; provocation.
A.LI.CI.A.DOR, *s.m.*, baiter, enticer; bait; *adj.*, alluring, enticing.
A.LI.CI.A.MEN.TO, *s.f.*, seduction, allurement.
A.LI.CI.AR, *v.*, to allure, to bait, to seduce, to attract.
A.LI.E.NA.ÇÃO, *s.f.*, alienation, madness, transfer of ownership.
A.LI.E.NA.ÇÃO, *s.f.*, alienation.
A.LI.E.NA.DO, *adj.*, alienate, abstracted; lunatic, insane; ceded, ransfered; assigned (chattel).
A.LI.E.NAR, *v.*, to alienate, to cede, to transfer, to madden.
A.LI.E.NÍ.GE.NA, *s. 2 gen.*, alien.
A.LI.E.NIS.TA, *s. 2 gen., Med.*, alienist (specialist in mental diseases).
A.LI.GÁ.TOR, *s.m., Zool.*, alligator.
A.LI.GEI.RAR, *v.*, to make haste, to hasten, speed up.
A.LI.JA.MEN.TO, *s.m.*, jettison; lighten, riddance, discard.
A.LI.JAR, *v.*, to jettison, to lighten.
A.LI.MEN.TA.ÇÃO, *s.f.*, alimentation, nourishment, food.
A.LI.MEN.TA.DOR, *s.m.*, feeder; *adj.*, feeding, nourishing.
A.LI.MEN.TAR, *v.*, to nourish, to feed; *adj.*, alimentary, nutritious.
A.LI.MEN.TÍ.CI.O, *adj.*, alimentary, nourishing, nutritious, esculent; *gêneros ~s*: foodstuffs.
A.LI.MEN.TO, *s.m.*, food, provisions, supply.
A.LIM.PAR, *v., pop.*, the same that *limpar*: to clean.
A.LIN.DA.MEN.TO, *s.m.*, embellishment, adornment.
A.LIN.DAR, *v.*, to embellish, to adorn, to ornament.
A.LÍ.NE.A, *s.f.*, paragraph.
A.LI.NHA.DO, *adj.*, alined, lined up; elegant.
A.LI.NHA.MEN.TO, *s.m.*, alignment, arrangement.
A.LI.NHAR, *v.*, to ali(g)n, to range; to dress up.
A.LI.NHA.VA.DO, *adj.*, basted, tacked.
A.LI.NHA.VAR, *v.*, to baste; *UK* to tack.
A.LI.NHA.VO, *s.m.*, bastings, tacking.
A.LÍ.QUO.TA, *s.f.*, aliquot.
A.LI.SA.MEN.TO, *s.f.*, flatting, smoothing.
A.LI.SAR, *v.*, to make plane, to smooth, to level, to equal.
A.LIS.TA.DO, *s.m., Mil., US* draftee, conscript; *adj.*, recruted, conscripted, listed.
A.LIS.TA.MEN.TO, *s.m.*, enrolment; *Mil.*, enlistment, recruitment.
A.LIS.TAR, *v.*, to enlist, to recruit, to list.

ALISTÁVEL · 83 · ALTRUÍSTICO

A.LIS.TÁ.VEL, *adj.*, liable to enrolling.
A.LI.TE.RA.ÇÃO, *s.f.*, alliteration.
A.LI.TE.RAR, *v.*, to alliterate.
A.LI.VI.A.DO, *adj.*, eased, relieved.
A.LI.VI.AR, *v.*, to lighten, to ease, to lessen, to soften, to mitigate, to diminish, to comfort.
A.LÍ.VIO, *s.m.*, relief, softening, ease, comfort, lightening.
AL.JÔ.FAR, *s.m.*, seed-pearl; dew, tears (of pretty woman).
AL.MA, *s.f.*, soul, spirit.
AL.MA.ÇO, *s.m.*, foolscap.
AL.MA.NA.QUE, *s.m.*, almanac.
AL.MEI.A, *s.f.*, oriental balsam; dancer and singer (East woman).
AL.MEI.RÃO, *s.m.*, *Bot.*, wild chicory.
AL.ME.JAR, *v.*, to desire, to long for, to intend.
AL.ME.JÁ.VEL, *adj.*, desirable.
AL.MI.RAN.TA.DO, *s.m.*, admiralty, admiralship.
AL.MI.RAN.TE, *s.m.*, admiral, admiral-ship.
AL.MÍS.CAR, *s.m.*, musk.
AL.MIS.CA.RA.DO, *adj.*, musky.
AL.MIS.CA.RAR, *v.*, to perfume with musk.
AL.MO.ÇAR, *v.*, to lunch, to breakfast.
AL.MO.ÇO, *s.m.*, lunch, breakfast.
AL.MO.CRE.VE, *s.m.*, mule-driver, muleteer.
AL.MO.E.DA, *s.f.*, public sale, auction.
AL.MO.E.DAR, *v.*, to auction.
AL.MO.FA.DA, *s.f.*, cushion, pillow.
AL.MO.FA.DA.DO, *adj.*, cushioned; upholstered.
AL.MO.FA.DI.NHA, *s.f.*, pinchshion; little cushion; *col.*, dandy, coxcomb.
AL.MÔN.DE.GA, *s.f.*, minced meat ball.
AL.MO.XA.RI.FA.DO, *s.m.*, warehouse.
AL.MO.XA.RI.FE, *s.m.*, warehouse person; storekeeper.
A.LÔ!, *interj.*, hallo!, hullo!, hello!
A.LO.CA.ÇÃO, *s.f.*, allocation.
A.LO.CAR, *v.*, to allocate.
A.LO.CU.ÇÃO, *s.f.*, allocution, speech.
A.LOI.RA.DO, *adj.*, the same that *alourado*.
A.LO.JA.DO, *adj.*, *Mil.*, quartered; sheltered, accomodated.
A.LO.JA.MEN.TO, *s.m.*, accommodation; lodging, lodgement; *Mil.*, billet.
A.LO.JAR, *v.*, to receive, to shelter, to lodge.
A.LOM.BA.DO, *adj.*, bowed, arched; lazy, indolent.
A.LOM.BA.MEN.TO, *s.m.*, rounding, arching, bending.
A.LON.GA.DO, *adj.*, elongated, away, lengthened.
A.LON.GA.DOR, *s.m.*, lengthener, prolonger; *adj.*, lengthening, prolonging.
A.LON.GA.MEN.TO, *s.m.*, lengthening, prolongation, elongation.
A.LON.GAR, *v.*, to prolongate, to extend, to lengthen.
A.LO.PA.TA, *s. 2 gen.*, *Med.*, allopath, allopathist.
A.LO.PA.TI.A, *s.f.*, allopathy.
A.LO.PRA.DO, *adj.*, *gír.*, restless, foolish, crazy.
A.LOU.CA.DO, *adj.*, foolish, crazy dangerous.
A.LOU.RA.DO, A.LOI.RA.DO, *adj.*, blondish, fair-haired
A.LOU.SAR, *v.*, to slate.
AL.PA.CA, *s.f.*, *Zool.*, alpaca (variety of lhama).
AL.PAR.CA.TA, AL.PER.CA.TA, *s.f.*, the same that *alpargata*.
AL.PAR.GA.TA, *s.f.*, espadrille.
AL.PEN.DRE, *s.m.*, shed, porch.
AL.PER.CA.TA, *s.f.*, the same that *alpargata*.

AL.PI.NIS.MO, *s.m.*, Alpinism.
AL.PI.NIS.TA, *s. 2 gen.*, Alpinist, mountaineer.
AL.PI.NO, *adj.*, alpine.
AL.PIS.TE, AL.PIS.TA, *s.m.*, canary grass.
AL.PON.DRAS, *s.f.*, *pl.*, stepping-sotnes in a brook.
AL.QUEI.RE, *s.m.*, land measure in Brazil (4,84 hectares in MG, RJ and GO, and 2,42 hectares in SP).
AL.QUE.BRA.DO, *adj.*, weak, feeble, broken down.
AL.QUI.MI.A, *s.f.*, alchemy.
AL.QUÍ.MI.CO, *adj.*, alchemistic, alchemic(al).
AL.QUI.MIS.TA, *s. 2 gen.*, alchemist.
AL.TA, *s.f.*, raising, rise, boom, increase; delay, nobility.
AL.TA-FI.DE.LI.DA.DE, *s.f.*, high-fidelity, hi-fi.
AL.TA.NA.RI.A, *s.f.*, haughtiness, arrogance; hawking.
AL.TA.NEI.RO, *adj.*, soaring, in high spirits; haughty, proud; arrogant, towering.
AL.TAR, *s.m.*, altar.
AL.TAR-MOR, *s.m.*, high altar.
AL.TA-RO.DA, *s.f.*, high society.
AL.TA-TEM.SÃO, *s.m.*, *Eletr.*, high voltage.
AL.TE.AR, *v.*, to raise, make higher.
AL.TE.RA.BI.LI.DA.DE, *s.f.*, alterability, changeability.
AL.TE.RA.ÇÃO, *s.f.*, alteration, change, modification, decay, degeneration, perturbation.
AL.TE.RA.DO, *adj.*, altered, changed; worried.
AL.TER.NÂN.CI.A, *s.f.*, alternation; *Eletr.*, reversal.
AL.TE.RAR, *v.*, to change, to modify, to alter, to disturb, to perturbate, to falsify.
AL.TE.RÁ.VEL, *adj.*, changeable, alterable.
AL.TER.CA.ÇÃO, *s.f.*, altercation, dispute, wrangle, debate.
AL.TER.CAR, *v.*, to altercate, to dispute, to debate.
AL.TER.NA.DA.MEN.TE, *adv.*, alternately.
AL.TER.NA.DOR, *s.m.*, alternator.
AL.TER.NAR, *v.*, to alternate, to interchange, to reverse.
AL.TER.NA.TI.VA, *s.f.*, alternative.
AL.TER.NA.TI.VO, *adj.*, alternative, optional.
AL.TER.NÁ.VEL, *adj.*, variable.
AL.TE.RO.SO, *adj.*, very high, magnificent, tall, grand.
AL.TE.ZA, *s.f.*, highness, elevation.
AL.TI.BAI.XOS, *s.m.*, *pl.*, unevenness; ups and downs.
AL.TI.LO.QUEN.TE, *adj.*, grandiloquent, pompous.
AL.TÍ.ME.TRO, *s.m.*, altimeter.
AL.TI.PLA.NO, *s.m.*, elevated plain, plateau.
AL.TÍS.SI.MO, *adj.*, highest (superlative); *Altíssimo*: The Almighty, God.
AL.TIS.SO.NAN.TE, *adj.*, altissonant, high-sounding.
AL.TI.TU.DE, *s.f.*, altitude.
AL.TI.VEZ, *s.f.*, haughtiness, arrogance, pride.
AL.TI.VO, *adj.*, high, elevated, courageous, dignified, presumptuous.
AL.TO, *adj.*, high, elevated, tall, lofty, excellent, magnificent, loud.
AL.TO-AS.TRAL, *s.m.*, high spirits, good vibes; *adj.*, cool.
AL.TO-CÚ.MU.LO, *s.m.*, *Met.*, high cumulus.
AL.TO-FA.LAN.TE, *s.m.*, loudspeaker.
AL.TO-FOR.NO, *s.m.*, blast furnace.
AL.TO-MAR, *s.m.*, high sea.
AL.TO-RE.LE.VO, *s.m.*, high-relief.
AL.TRU.ÍS.MO, *s.m.*, altruism, unselfishness.
AL.TRU.ÍS.TA, *s. 2 gen.*, altruist.
AL.TRU.ÍS.TI.CO, *adj.*, altruistic.

ALTURA · 84 · AMÁSIO

AL.TU.RA, *s.f.*, height, highness, tallness, top, summit, size; altitude.

A.LU.A.DO, *adj.*, lunatic, moonstruck, crazy.

A.LU.CI.NA.ÇÃO, *s.f.*, hallucination, delusion.

A.LU.CI.NA.DO, *adj.*, hallucinated, possessed, raving.

A.LU.CI.NAN.TE, *adj., col.*, maddening, hallucinating; amazing.

A.LU.CI.NAR, *v.*, to hallucinate, to delude.

A.LU.CI.NÓ.GE.NO, *s.m.*, hallucinogen; *adj.*, hallucinogenic.

A.LU.DE, *s.m., Geol.*, the same that *avalancha*: avalanche.

A.LU.DIR, *v.*, to allude, to mention.

A.LU.GA.DO, *adj.*, hired, let, rented.

A.LU.GAR, *v.*, to rent, to hire, to let, to lease.

A.LU.GUEL, *s.m.*, letting, rent.

A.LU.GUER, *s.m.*, the same that *aluguel*.

A.LU.IR, *v.*, to shake, to tremble, to ruin, to collapse.

A.LUM.BRAR, *v.*, to enlighten, to illuminate.

A.LU.MI.A.ÇÃO, *s.f.*, illumination, lighting.

A.LU.MI.AR, *v.*, to illuminate, to light.

A.LU.MÍ.NIO, *s.m., Quím.*, aluminium.

A.LU.MI.NI.ZAR, *v.*, to aluminize.

A.LU.NA, *s.f.*, pupil, schoolgirl.

A.LU.NAR, *v.*, the same that *alunissagem*.

A.LU.NIS.SA.GEM, *s.f., Astron.*, moonlanding, lunar landing.

A.LU.NIS.SAR, *v., Astron.*, to land on the moon.

A.LU.NO, *s.m.*, pupil, schoolboy, scholar, student, disciple.

A.LU.SÃO, *s.f.*, allusion, reference.

A.LU.SI.VO, *adj.*, allusive, referring; figurative.

A.LU.VI.AL, *adj.*, alluvial.

A.LU.VI.ÃO, *s.f.*, alluvium, inundation, torrent.

AL.VA, *s.f.*, aurora, dawn; white of the eye, sclerotica.

AL.VA.CEN.TO, *adj.*, whitish, whity.

AL.VAR, *adj.*, whitish; foolish, silly.

AL.VA.RÁ, *s.m.*, permit, charter, warrant.

AL.VA.REN.GA, *s.f., Náut., Bras.*, lighter, barge.

AL.VE.JA.MEN.TO, *s.m.*, whitening, bleaching.

AL.VE.JAN.TE, *s.m.*, bleaching, bleach; whitener.

AL.VE.JAR, *v.*, to aim at; to bleach, to whiten.

AL.VE.NA.RI.A, *s.f.*, masonry, the work of a mason.

AL.VÉO.LO, *s.m.*, alveolus, cell of a honeycomb.

AL.VÍS.SA.RAS, *interj.*, announcing good news.

AL.VIS.SA.REI.RO, *s.m.*, bearer of good news; *adj.*, auspicious, promising.

AL.VI.TRE, *s.m.*, reminder, hint, proposal, suggestion, opinion.

AL.VO, *s.m.*, white, target, aim, purpose, object; *adj.*, white, pure, limpid.

AL.VOR, *s.m.*, whiteness, shine, brightness; aurora.

AL.VO.RA.DA, *s.f.*, dawn (of day).

AL.VO.RE.CER, *v.*, to dawn (of day), daybreak.

AL.VO.RO.ÇA.DO, *adj.*, restless, flustered, agitated.

AL.VO.RO.ÇAR, *v.*, to stir up; to agitate, to excite.

AL.VO.RO.ÇO, *s.m.*, agitation, alarm, fluster, haste.

AL.VU.RA, *s.f.*, whiteness, purity.

AM, *abrev.* of *Amplitude Modulada*: Amplitude Modulation, AM.

A.MA, *s.f.*, mistress, governess, nursemaid.

A.MA.BI.LI.DA.DE, *s.f.*, amiability, kindness, friendliness, affection.

A.MA.BI.LÍS.SI.MO, *adj.*, most loving (superlative).

A.MA.CI.A.DO, *adj.*, soft, supple.

A.MA.CI.AN.TE, *s.m.*, softener; ~ *de roupas*: laundry softener.

A.MA.CI.AR, *v.*, to smooth, to soften, to soothe, to ease, to tranquilize.

A.MA.DA, *s.f.*, sweetheart, mistress, girl friend; *adj.*, loved.

A.MA DE LEI.TE, *s.f.*, wet nurse.

A.MA.DO, *adj.*, loved, beloved.

A.MA.DOR, *s.m.*, lover, fan, amateur.

A.MA.DO.RIS.MO, *s.m.*, amateurism, fondeness, diletantism.

A.MA.DO.RÍS.TI.CO, *adj.*, amateurish.

A.MA.DU.RAR, *v.*, the same that *amadurecer*.

A.MA.DU.RE.CER, *v.*, to mature, to ripen, to grow ripe.

A.MA.DU.RE.CI.MEN.TO, *s.m.*, ripening, maturation, ripeness.

Â.MA.GO, *s.m.*, essence, heart.

A.MAI.NAR, *v.*, to calm down, to appease, to soothe, to quell.

A.MAL.DI.ÇO.A.DO, *s.m.*, cursed person; *adj.*, cursed, damned.

A.MAL.DI.ÇO.AR, *v.*, to curse, to execrate, to damn, to abhor, to detest.

A.MÁL.GA.MA, *s.m.*, amalgam.

A.MAL.GA.MAR, *v.*, to amalgamate, to mix, to blend.

A.MA.LU.CA.DO, *adj., col.*, crazy, silly, foolish, maniac.

A.MA.MEN.TA.ÇÃO, *s.f.*, nursing, breast-feeding.

A.MA.MEN.TAR, *v.*, to suckle, to nurse, to nourish.

A.MAN.CE.BAR, *v.*, to live in concubinage.

A.MA.NHÃ, *adv.*, tomorrow.

A.MA.NHAR, *v.*, to cultivate, to till, to prepare, to arrange, to dispose.

A.MA.NHE.CER, *s.m.*, break of the day; *v.*, to dawn, to grow day.

A.MA.NHE.CI.DO, *adj.*, dawned, old; *pão* ~: stale bread.

A.MAN.SAR, *v.*, to tame, to domesticate, to break in, to mitigate, to pacify.

A.MAN.TE, *s. 2 gen.*, lover, boyfriend, girlfriend.

A.MAN.TEI.GA.DO, *s.m., Bras.*, cookie of butter; *adj.*, (bread) buttered, (biscuit) buttery.

A.MAN.TEI.GAR, *v.*, spread butter on, to make buttery.

A.MAR, *v.*, to love, to be in love, to like, to adore.

A.MA.RAN.TO, *s.m., Bot.*, amaranth.

A.MA.RE.LA.DO, *adj.*, yellowish, flavescent.

A.MA.RE.LÃO, *s.m., Med.*, ancylostomiasis; *Bras.*, a kind of rice.

A.MA.RE.LAR, *v.*, to yellow, to fade.

A.MA.RE.LI.DÃO, *s.m.*, yellowness, paleness.

A.MA.RE.LI.NHA, *s.f.*, hop-scotch.

A.MA.RE.LO, *adj.*, yellow, pale, faded.

A.MAR.GAR, *v.*, to embitter, to make bitter.

A.MAR.GO, *adj.*, bitter, acrid, acrimonious, sad.

A.MAR.GOR, *s.m.*, bitterness.

A.MAR.GU.RA, *s.f.*, bitterness, acridity; sorrow, affliction.

A.MAR.GU.RA.DO, *adj.*, bitter, distressed, acrimonious.

A.MAR.GU.RAR, *v.*, to cause sorrow, to afflict, to embitter.

A.MA.RI.CAR, *v.*, to become effeminate.

A.MAR.RA, *s.f., Náut.*, cable, moorings; shakle, chain; *fig.*, support, aid.

A.MAR.RA.ÇÃO, *s.f.*, fastening, tying; *fig.*, amorous entanglement.

A.MAR.RA.DO, *adj.*, tied up; *col.*, committed.

A.MAR.RAR, *v.*, to moor, to bind, to fasten, to close, to chain.

A.MAR.RON.ZA.DO, *adj., col.*, brownish.

A.MAR.RO.TA.DO, *adj.*, wrinkled, crumpled.

A.MAR.RO.TAR, *v.*, to crample, to ruffle, to wrinkle.

A.MA-SE.CA, *s.f.*, dry nurse, baby sitter.

A.MÁ.SIA, *s.f.*, mistress, concubine.

A.MA.SI.AR-SE, *v.*, to live in concubinage.

A.MÁ.SI.O, *s.m.*, lover.

AMASSADO ·· 85 ·· AMOLDAR

A.MAS.SA.DO, adj., squashed, crushed, flattened.

A.MAS.SAR, v., to knead, to mix, to squash, to crush, to crumple.

A.MÁ.VEL, adj., amiable, kind, lovable.

A.MA.VEL.MEN.TE, adv., kindly, courteously.

A.MA.VI.O.SO, adj., alluring, seductive; gentle.

A.MA.ZO.NA, s.f., Amazon, horsewoman.

A.MA.ZO.NAS, s., Amazonas (Brazilian state).

A.MA.ZO.NEN.SE, s.m., Amazonian (native or inhabitant of Amazonas, Brazilian state); adj., Amazonian.

A.MA.ZÔ.NI.A, s.f., Amazon rainforest.

A.MA.ZÔ.NI.CO, adj., Amazonian (for the inhabitants of Amazonia).

A.MÃ, s., Amman (country).

ÂM.BAR, s.m., amber.

AM.BI.ÇÃO, s.f., ambition.

AM.BI.CI.O.NAR, v., to pursue ambitiously, strive after.

AM.BI.CI.O.SO, s.m., ambitious person; adj., ambitious.

AM.BI.DES.TRO, adj., ambidextrous.

AM.BI.EN.TAL, adj., environmental.

AM.BI.EN.TA.LIS.TA, s. 2 gen., environmentalist.

AM.BI.EN.TAR, v., to acclimatize, to adapt, fig., to form an atmosphere.

AM.BI.EN.TE, s.m., environment, ambiance, surrounding, sphere, atmosphere.

AM.BI.GUI.DA.DE, s.f., ambiguity, ambiguousness.

AM.BÍ.GUO, adj., ambiguous, doubtful, dubious, equivocal.

ÂM.BI.TO, s.m., ambit, circuit, circumference.

AM.BI.VA.LÊN.CI.A, s.f., ambivalence.

AM.BI.VA.LEN.TE, adj., ambivalent.

AM.BOS, num., adj., both.

AM.BRO.SI.A, s.f., ambrosia (food and drink of gods); Bras., sweet of milk, sugar and eggs.

ÂM.BU.LA, s.f., Rel., ampulla.

AM.BU.LÂN.CIA, s.f., ambulance.

AM.BU.LAN.TE, s. 2 gen., ambulant, moving.

AM.BU.LA.TÓ.RIO, s.m., ambulatory.

A.ME.A.ÇA, s.f., threat, menace.

A.ME.A.ÇA.DO, s.m., threatened person, adj., threatened.

A.ME.A.ÇA.DOR, adj., threatening, menacing.

A.ME.A.ÇAR, v., to threaten, to menace.

A.ME.A.LHAR, v., to amass, to bargain, to haggle, to economize, to save.

A.ME.BA, s.f., Zool., ameba, amoeba.

A.ME.BÍ.A.SE, s.f., Med., amebiasis, amoebiasis.

A.ME.DRON.TA.DO, adj., frightened, afraid, scared.

A.ME.DRON.TA.DOR, s.m., frightener, intimidator; adj., frightening.

A.ME.DRON.TAR, v., to frighten, to scare, to alarm, to intimidate.

A.MEI.A, s.f., battlement.

A.MEI.GAR, v., to fondle, caress, cherish.

A.MEI.XA, s.f., Bot., plum.

A.MEI.XAL, s.m., plum tree orchard.

A.MEI.XA SE.CA, s.f., prune.

A.MÉM, s.m., amen; interj., amen!.

A.MÊN.DOA, s.f., Bot., almond.

A.MEN.DO.A.DO, adj., almond-shaped (eyes).

A.MEN.DO.AL, s.m., almond plantation.

A.MEN.DO.EI.RA, s.f., Bot., almond tree.

A.MEN.DO.IM, s.m., peanut, groundnut.

A.ME.NI.DA.DE, s.f., amenity, pleasentness, serenity.

A.ME.NI.ZAR, v., to soften, to ease, to soothe.

A.ME.NO, adj., bland, suave, mild, agreeable, delicate.

A.MÉ.RI.CA, s.f., Geogr., America (North America, Central American, South America).

A.MÉ.RI.CA HIS.PÂ.NI.CA, s.f., Geogr., Spanish America.

A.MÉ.RI.CA LA.TI.NA, s.f., Geogr., Latin America.

A.ME.RI.CA.NIS.MO, s.m., Americanism.

A.ME.RI.CA.NI.ZA.DO, adj., Americanized.

A.ME.RI.CA.NI.ZAR, v., to Americanize.

A.ME.RI.CA.NO, s.m., adj., American.

A.ME.RÍN.DI.O, s.m., Amerindian; adj., Amerindian.

A.MES.QUI.NHA.DO, adj., depreciated, disparaged; wretched; humilated.

A.MES.QUI.NHAR, v., to depreciate, to disparage, to humble, to humiliate.

A.MES.TRA.DO, adj., trained, domesticated, instructed.

A.MES.TRA.DOR, s.m., trainer; adj., instructing, training.

A.MES.TRA.MEN.TO, s.m., training, instruction, domestication.

A.MES.TRAR, v., to instruct, to teach, to train.

A.ME.TIS.TA, s.f., Min., amethyst.

A.MI.AN.TO, s.m., Min., amianthus; asbestos.

A.MI.CÍS.SI.MO, adj., (superlative) very friendly.

A.MI.DO, s.m., Quím., starch, amylum.

A.MI.GA, s.f., female friend; mistress, concubine.

A.MI.GAR-SE, v., to live together.

A.MI.GÁ.VEL, adj., amicable, friendly.

A.MÍG.DA.LA, A.MÍ.DA.LA, s.f., amygdala, tonsil.

A.MIG.DA.LI.TE, s.f., amygdalitis.

A.MI.GO, s.m., friend, lover, protector; adj., friendly, favourable, kind.

A.MI.GO DA ON.ÇA, s.m., false-friend.

A.MI.MA.DO, adj., fondled; spoiled.

A.MI.MAR, v., to fondle, to caress, to spoil.

A.MIN.GUAR, v., to diminish, to run short of.

A.MI.NO.Á.CI.DO, s.m., Quím., amino acid.

A.MI.SE.RAR, v., to feel sorry for, to wail, to sympathize with.

A.MIS.TO.SO, adj., friendly, amicable.

A.MI.U.DA.DO, adj., frequent, repeated.

A.MI.U.DAR, v., to do, to happen frequently.

A.MI.Ú.DE, adv., frequent, often, repeated.

A.MI.ZA.DE, s.f., friendship, amity, affection, benevolence.

AM.NÉ.SI.A, s.f., Med., amnesia.

AM.NI.Ó.TI.CO, adj., Anat., amniotic.

A.MO, s.m., master, master of house.

A.MO.DER.NAR, v., to modernize.

A.MO.E.DAR, v., to coin, to monetize.

A.MO.FI.NA.ÇÃO, s.f., annoyance, vexation; worrying.

A.MO.FI.NADO, adj., annoyed, vexed; worried.

A.MO.FI.NAR, v., to annoy, to vex, to worry.

A.MO.LA.ÇÃO, s.f., grinding, whetting, sharpening, affliction.

A.MO.LA.DO, adj., sharpened, whetted; vexed, bothered, annoyed.

A.MO.LA.DOR, s.m., sharpener, whetter; vexer, annoying, bothersome.

A.MO.LAR, v., to whet, to grind, to sharpen, to vex, to annoy, to importune.

A.MOL.DA.DO, adj., moulded, shaped, accustomed.

A.MOL.DAR, v., to mould, to frame; to adjust, to adapt something (to).

AMOLECER • 86 • ANARQUIZAR

A.MO.LE.CER, *v.*, mollify, to soften, to soak, to weaken, to move, to affect.

A.MO.LE.CI.MEN.TO, *s.m.*, mollification, softening.

A.MÔ.NIA, *s.f., Quím.*, ammonia.

A.MO.NÍ.A.CO, *s.m., Quím.*, ammonia, ammoniac.

A.MON.TO.A.DO, *s.m.*, pile, heap.

A.MON.TO.A.MEN.TO, *s.m.*, accumulation, amassment, pile.

A.MON.TO.AR, *v.*, to pile up, to heap up, to accumulate, to amass, to gather.

A.MOR, *s.m.*, love, affection, attachment, devotion, passion, enthusiasm.

A.MO.RA, *s.f., Bot.*, mulberry.

A.MO.RAL, *adj.*, amoral.

A.MO.RA.LIS.MO, *s.m.*, amoralism.

A.MO.RA.LI.ZAR, *v.*, to deprive of morals.

A.MOR.DA.ÇA.MEN.TO, *s.m.*, gagging, muzzling.

A.MOR.DA.ÇAR, *v.*, to gag, to muzzle.

A.MO.RE.CO, *s.m., col.*, honey, darling.

A.MO.RE.NA.DO, *adj.*, swarthy, tanned.

A.MO.RE.NAR, *v.*, to become tawny, tan.

A.MOR.FIS.MO, *s.m.*, amorphism.

A.MOR.FO, *adj.*, amorphous, formless.

A.MO.RI.CO, *s.m.*, flirt.

A.MO.RIS.CAR, *v.*, to fall in love.

A.MOR.NA.DO, *adj.*, lukewarm, tepid.

A.MOR.NAR, *v.*, to warm up.

A.MO.RO.SO, *adj.*, loving, affectionate, fond, kind, affable, soft.

A.MOR-PER.FEI.TO, *s.m., Bot.*, pansy, heartsease.

A.MOR-PRÓ.PRI.O, *s.m.*, self-steem, self-love.

A.MOR.TA.LHA.DO, *adj.*, dressed for the grave, shrouded.

A.MOR.TA.LHAR, *v.*, to shroud.

A.MOR.TE.CE.DOR, *s.m.*, shock absorber, damper; *adj.*, damping.

A.MOR.TE.CER, *v.*, to deaden, to debilitate, to weaken, to lessen.

A.MOR.TE.CI.DO, *adj.*, weakened, debilitated, deadened; dampened (sound).

A.MOR.TE.CI.MEN.TO, *s.m.*, deadening, debilitation, mitigation.

A.MOR.TI.ZA.ÇÃO, *s.f.*, amortization, paying off.

A.MOR.TI.ZAR, *v.*, to amortize, to pay off.

A.MOR.TI.ZÁ.VEL, *adj.*, amortizable, redeemable.

A.MOS.TRA, *s.f.*, sample, specimen, sign, proof, indication.

A.MOS.TRA.GEM, *s.f.*, sampling.

A.MOS.TRAR, *v.*, the same that *mostrar.* to show.

A.MO.TI.NA.ÇÃO, *s.f.*, mutiny, insurrection, revolt; sedition, tumult.

A.MO.TI.NA.DO, *s.m.*, mutineer; *adj.*, mutinous.

A.MO.TI.NAR, *v.*, to mutiny, to rebel, to agitate.

A.MOU.CAR, *v.*, to become partially deaf.

AM.PA.RA.DO, *adj.*, supported; sheltered, protected.

AM.PA.RAR, *v.*, to support, to prop, to sustain, to protect, to favour, to assist.

AM.PA.RO, *s.m.*, support, protection, shelter, assistance, help.

AM.PE.RA.GEM, *s.f.*, amperage.

AM.PÈ.RE, *s.m.*, ampere.

AM.PE.RÍ.ME.TRO, *s.m., Eletr.*, amperimeter.

AM.PLE.XO, *s.m.*, embracement.

AM.PLI.A.ÇÃO, *s.f.*, amplification, enlargement.

AM.PLI.A.DO, *adj.*, amplified, enlarged.

AM.PLI.A.DOR, *s.m.*, amplifier, enlarger; *adj.*, amplifying.

AM.PLI.AR, *v.*, to amplify, to enlarge, to increase.

AM.PLI.DÃO, *s.f.*, amplitude, ampleness, wideness.

AM.PLI.FI.CA.ÇÃO, *s.f.*, amplification, enlargement, widening.

AM.PLI.FI.CA.DOR, *s.m.*, amplifier, amplificator.

AM.PLI.FI.CAR, *v.*, to amplify, to enlarge, to increase, to widen.

AM.PLI.TU.DE, *s.f.*, amplitude, largeness.

AM.PLO, *adj.*, ample, wide, extensive, spacious.

AM.PO.LA, *s.f.*, ampoule, vial.

AM.PU.LHE.TA, *s.f.*, hour-glass, sand-glass.

AM.PU.TA.ÇÃO, *s.f.*, amputation.

AM.PU.TA.DO, *adj.*, amputee, amputated.

AM.PU.TAR, *v.*, to amputate, to cut off, to mutilate, to restrict.

A.MU.A.DO, *adj.*, sulky, surly.

A.MU.AR, *v.*, to make sullen, to disgust, to vex, to annoy.

A.MU.LA.TA.DO, *adj.*, mulatto-like.

A.MU.LE.TO, *s.m.*; amulet, talisman.

A.MU.NI.CI.A.MEN.TO, *s.m., Mil.*, munitioning.

A.MU.NI.CI.AR, *v., Mil.*, to munition.

A.MU.O, *s.m.*, ill humor, sulleness; pout.

A.MU.RA.DA, *s.f.*, wall, high wall; *Náut.*, parapet, side of a ship.

A.MU.RA.LHAR, *v.*, to wall in.

A.MU.RAR, *v.*, the same that *amuralhar.*

A.NÃ, *s.f.*, woman dwarf.

A.NA.CA.RA.DO, *adj.*, nacreous.

A.NA.CRÔ.NI.CO, *adj.*, anachronistic.

A.NA.CO.LU.TO, *s.m., Gram.*, anacoluthon.

A.NA.CON.DA, *s.f., col.*, anaconda (snake species).

A.NA.CO.RE.TA, *s.m.*, anchorite; recluse, unsociable person.

A.NA.CRÔ.NI.CO, *adj.*, anachronistic, anachronic; outdated.

A.NA.CRO.NIS.MO, *s.m.*, anachronism.

A.NA.E.RÓ.BI.O, *s.m., Biol.*, anaerobe; *adj.*, anaerobic.

A.NA.FI.LÁ.TI.CO, *adj., Med.*, anaphylactic.

A.NÁ.FO.RA, *s.f., Gram.*, anaphora.

A.NA.FO.RIS.MO, *s.m.*, excessive use of anaphora.

A.NA.GRA.MA, *s.m.*, anagram.

A.NÁ.GUA, *s.f.*, slip, petticoat.

A.NAIS, *s.m., pl.*, annals.

A.NAL, *adj.*, anal; annual, yearly.

A.NAL.FA.BE.TIS.MO, *s.m.*, analphabetism.

A.NAL.FA.BE.TO, *s.m.*, analphabet; *adj.*, analphabet, letterless.

A.NAL.GE.SI.A, *s.f., Med.*, analgesia.

A.NAL.GÉ.SI.CO, *s.m., Med.*, analgesic; *adj.*, analgesic.

A.NA.LI.SA.DOR, *s.m.*, analyser (analyzer); *adj.*, analyzing.

A.NA.LI.SAR, *v.*, to analyse, to separate, to study the facts.

A.NÁ.LI.SE, *s.f.*, analysis.

A.NA.LIS.TA, *s. 2 gen.*, analyst, writer of annals.

A.NA.LÍ.TI.CO, *adj.*, analytic(al).

A.NA.LO.GI.A, *s.f.*, analogy, conformity, likeness.

A.NA.LÓ.GI.CO, *adj.*, analog, analogic(al).

A.NÁ.LO.GO, *adj.*, analogous, similar, resembling.

A.NAM.NE.SE, *s.f.*, anamnesis.

A.NA.NÁS, *s.m., Bot.*, pine-apple.

A.NÃO, *s.m.*, dwarf; *adj.*, dwarfish, small.

A.NAR.QUI.A, *s.f.*, anarchy, disorder, confusion.

A.NÁR.QUI.CO, *adj.*, anachic, anachical; *fig.*, chaotic.

A.NAR.QUIS.MO, *s.m.*, anarchism.

A.NAR.QUIS.TA, *s. 2 gen.*; anarchist; *adj.*, anarchistic; *fig.*, agitator.

A.NAR.QUI.ZAR, *v.*, to anarchize.

ANÁSTROFE 87 ANIMÁLIA

A.NÁS.TRO.FE, *s.f., Gram.*, anastrophe.
A.NÁ.TE.MA, *s.m., Gram.*, anathema.
A.NA.TO.MI.A, *s.f.*, anatomy, morphology, dissection.
A.NA.TÔ.MI.CO, *adj.*, anatomic, anatomical.
A.NA.TO.MIS.TA, *s. 2 gen.*, anatomist.
A.NA.TO.MI.ZAR, *v.*, to anatomize, to dissect.
A.NA.VA.LHAR, *v.*, to cut with a razor; to shape like a razor.
AN.CA, *s.f.*, buttock, haunch.
AN.CES.TRAL, *adj.*, ancestral; age-old.
AN.CES.TRA.LI.DA.DE, *s.f.*, quality of ancestral.
AN.CHO.VA, *s.f., Zool.*, anchovy.
AN.CI.ÃO, *s.m.*, venerable old man; *adj.*, ancient, old.
AN.CI.NHO, *s.m.*, rake.
AN.CO, *s.m.*, a small bay on the coast.
ÂN.CO.RA, *s.f.*, anchor; refuge, shelter.
AN.CO.RA.DO, *adj.*, anchored.
AN.CO.RA.DOU.RO, *s.m.*, anchorage.
AN.CO.RA.GEM, *s.f.*, anchorage.
AN.CO.RAR, *v.*, to anchor, to cast anchor.
AN.CU.DO, *adj.*, having large buttocks.
AN.DA.DA, *s.f.*, act of taking a walk.
AN.DA.DOR, *s.m.*, someone who walks a lot; walker.
AN.DAI.ME, *s.m.*, scaffold.
AN.DA.MEN.TO, *s.m.*, process, proceeding, course.
AN.DAN.ÇA, *s.f.*, travel, walking, trip.
AN.DAN.TE, *s.m., Mús.*, andante; passer-by; *adj.*, walking, errant, wandering; *cavaleiro* ~: knight-errant.
AN.DAR, *s.m.*, gait, floor, story, speed, velocity; *v.*, to go, to walk, to wander, to drive, to ride.
AN.DA.RI.LHO, *s.m.*, walker.
AN.DI.NO, *adj.*, Andean.
AN.DOR, *s.m.*, a kind of handbarrow to carry statues in a procession; *Hist.*, litter.
AN.DO.RI.NHA, *s.f., Zool.*, swallow.
AN.DOR.RA, *s.*, Andorra.
AN.DRA.JO, *s.m.*, rag, tatter.
AN.DRA.JO.SO, *adj.*, tattered, ragged.
AN.DRO.GE.NI.A, *s.f.*, androgenesis.
AN.DRO.GI.NI.A, *s.f.*, androgyny.
AN.DRÓ.GI.NO, *adj.*, androgynous.
AN.DROI.DE, *s.m.*, android.
AN.DRÔ.ME.DA, *s.f., Astron.*, Andromeda (constellation); *Mit.*, Andromeda (personage in Greek mythology).
A.NE.DO.TA, *s.f.*, anecdote, joke.
A.NE.DÓ.TI.CO, *adj.*, anecdotical.
A.NE.DO.TIS.TA, *s. 2 gen.*, anecdotist.
A.NE.DO.TI.ZAR, *v.*, to tell anecdotes.
A.NE.GRAR, *v.*, to darken, to blacken.
A.NEL, *s.m.*, ring, circle, link.
A.NE.LA.DO, *adj.*, curly.
A.NE.LAR, *v.*, to curl, to shape like a ring, to pant; *adj.*, annular.
A.NE.LEI.RA, *s.f.*, box for keeping rings.
A.NE.LI.FOR.ME, *adj.*, ring-shaped, ringlike.
A.NE.LO, *s.m.*, aspiration, anxiety.
A.NE.MI.AR, *v.*, to cause anemia, to weaken, to enfeeble.
A.NÊ.MI.CO, *adj., Med.*, anemic; bloodless, pale.
A.NE.MI.A, *s.f.*, an(a)emia.
A.NE.MÔ.ME.TRO, *s.m.*, anemometer.
A.NEN.FA.LI.A, *s.f.*, anencephaly.
A.NES.TE.SI.A, *s.f.*, an(a)esthesia.
A.NES.TE.SI.A.DO, *adj.*, an(a)esthetized.

A.NES.TE.SI.AN.TE, *adj.*, an(a)esthetic.
A.NES.TE.SI.AR, *v.*, to an(a)esthetize.
A.NES.TÉ.SI.CO, *s.m.*, anaesthetic; *adj.*, anaesthetic.
A.NES.TE.SI.O.LO.GI.A, *s.f.*, anesthesiology.
A.NES.TE.SIS.TA, *s. 2 gen.*, anesthetist.
A.NEU.RIS.MA, *s.f., Med.*, aneurism, aneurysm.
A.NE.XA.ÇÃO, *s.f.*, annexation.
A.NE.XA.DO, *adj.*, annexed, attached.
A.NE.XAR, *v.*, to annex, to join, to attach.
A.NE.XO, *s.m.*, appurtenance, appendage.
AN.FE.TA.MI.NA, *s.f., Quím.*, amphetamine.
AN.FÍ.BIO, *s.m.*, amphibian.
AN.FI.BI.O.LO.GI.A, *s.f.*, amphibiology.
AN.FI.TE.A.TRO, *s.m.*, amphiteatre.
AN.FI.TRI.ÃO, *s.m.*, amphitryon, host.
ÂN.FO.RA, *s.f.*, amphora.
AN.GA.RI.A.ÇÃO, *s.f.*, enlistment, recruitment; enticement, allurement.
AN.GA.RI.AR, *v.*, to recruit, to engage, to allure.
AN.GE.LI.CAL, *adj.*, pure, beautiful.
AN.GÉ.LI.CO, *adj.*, angelic, angelical.
ÂN.GE.LUS, *s.m., Rel.*, Angelus.
AN.GI.NA, *s.f., Med.*, angina.
AN.GI.O.GRA.FI.A, *s.f., Med.*, angiography.
AN.GI.O.PA.TI.A, *s.f., Med.*, angiopathy.
AN.GLI.CA.NIS.MO, *s.m.*, Anglicanism.
AN.GLI.CA.NO, *s.m., adj.*, Anglican.
AN.GLI.CIS.MO, *s.m.*, Anglicism, Briticism.
AN.GLI.CI.ZAR, *v.*, Anglicize.
AN.GLÓ.FO.NO, *s.m.*, English speaker; *adj.*, English speaking.
AN.GLO-SA.XÃO, *s.m.*, Anglo-Saxon; *adj.*, Anglo-Saxon.
AN.GLO-SA.XÔ.NI.O, *s.m.*, the same that *anglo-saxão.*
AN.GO.LA, *s.*, Angola.
AN.GO.LA.NO, *s., adj.*, Angolan.
AN.GO.RÁ, *s., adj.*, Angora (cat, rabbit or goat).
AN.GRA, *s.f.*, bay, creek.
AN.GU, *s.m., Bras., Cul.*, flour of manioc, porridge; *gír.*, mess, intrigue.
AN.GUÍ.FE.RO, *adj.*, snake-breeding.
AN.GUI.FOR.ME, *adj.*, anguiform (having the form of a snake).
AN.GU.LA.DO, *adj.*, having angles or the form of an angle.
ÂN.GU.LO, *s.m.*, angle, corner, nook.
AN.GU.LO.SO, *adj.*, angled, angulate.
AN.GÚS.TIA, *s.f.*, anguish, affliction, annoyance, agony.
AN.GUS.TI.A.DO, *adj.*, afflicted, annoyed.
AN.GUS.TI.AN.TE, *adj.*, harrowing, afflictive, annoying.
AN.GUS.TI.AR, *v.*, to afflict, to torment, to distress, to annoy.
AN.GUS.TI.O.SO, *adj.*, afflicting, tormenting, annoying.
AN.GUS.TO, *adj.*, narrow, tight.
AN.GU.ZA.DA, *s.f., col., Bras.*, confusion, gossip, intrigue.
A.NHO, *s.m.*, lamb.
A.NI.A.GEM, *s.m.*, burlap.
A.NI.CHAR, *v.*, to niche, place in a niche.
A.NIL, *s.m.*, anil, blue; *adj.*, blue, senile.
A.NI.LAR, *v.*, to dye with a blue colour.
A.NI.LI.NA, *s.f.*, aniline.
A.NI.MA.ÇÃO, *s.f.*, animation, liveliness, enthusiasm, activity.
A.NI.MA.DO, *adj.*, animated.
A.NI.MA.DOR, *s.m.*, animator; *adj.*, encouraging.
A.NI.MAL, *s.m., adj.*, animal.
A.NI.MÁ.LI.A, *s.f.*, irrational animal.

ANIMALESCO ·· 88 ··· ANTIASMÁTICO

A.NI.MA.LES.CO, *adj.*, animal; bestial, brutal.
A.NI.MA.LI.DA.DE, *s.f.*, animality.
A.NI.MA.LI.ZA.ÇÃO, *s.f.*, animalization.
A.NI.MA.LI.ZAR, *v.*, to animalize.
A.NI.MAR, *v.*, to animate, encourage, boost, stimulate.
A.NI.MÁ.VEL, *adj.*, capable of being animated
A.NI.MIS.TA, *s. 2 gen., Filos.*, animist; *adj.*, animistic, animist.
Â.NI.MO, *s.m.*, courage, will, vitality, life, soul, purpose.
A.NI.MO.SI.DA.DE, *s.f.*, animosity.
A.NI.MO.SO, *adj.*, courageous, stout, valiant, brave.
A.NI.NAR, *v.*, to animate, to encourage.
A.NI.NHAR, *v.*, to put in a nest; to shelter, to cudle; to nesttle.
Â.NI.ON, *s.m., Fís., Quím.*, anion.
A.NI.QUI.LA.ÇÃO, *s.f.*, annihilation.
A.NI.QUI.LA.DO, *adj.*, annihilated.
A.NI.QUI.LA.DOR, *s.m.*, annihilator, destroyer; *adj.*, annihilating, destructive.
A.NI.QUI.LA.MEN.TO, *s.m.*, annihilation, extermination.
A.NI.QUI.LAR, *v.*, to annihilate, to extinguish.
A.NIS, *s.m., Bot.*, anise; aniseed.
A.NIS.TI.A, *s.f.*, amnesty.
A.NIS.TI.A.DO, *s.m.*, one who was granted amnesty; *adj.*, amnestied.
A.NIS.TI.AR, *v.*, to amnesty.
A.NI.VER.SA.RI.AN.TE, *s. 2 gen.*, person having a birthday.
A.NI.VER.SA.RI.AR, *v.*, to have (celebrate) one's birthday.
A.NI.VER.SÁ.RIO, *s.m.*, anniversary, birthday.
AN.JO, *s.m.*, angel.
A.NO, *s.m.*, year; ano bissexto, leap year; ano novo, New Year, New Year's Day.
A.NO-BA.SE, *s.m.*, basis-year, fiscal year.
A.NÓ.DI.O, *s.m.*, the same that ânodo.
Â.NO.DO, *s.m., Eletr.*, anode.
A.NOI.TE.CER, *v.*, to darken, to grow dark; *s.m.*, nightfall.
A.NO.JAR, *v.*, to nauseate.
A.NO-LUZ, *s.m., Astron., Fís.*, light-year.
A.NO.MA.LI.A, *s.f.*, anomaly.
A.NÔ.MA.LO, *adj.*, anomalous, anomalistic, abnormal.
A.NO.NI.MA.TO, *s.m.*, anonimity.
A.NO.NÍ.MI.A, *s.f.*, anonymousness, anonymity.
A.NÔ.NI.MO, *s.m.*, anonym; *adj.*, anonymous, nameless, unnamed.
A.NO-NO.VO, *s.m.*, new year; New Year (event).
A.NO.RA.QUE, *s.m.*, anorak (a jacket with hood).
A.NO.RE.XI.A, *s.f., Med.*, anorexia.
A.NO.RÉ.XI.CO, *s.m., adj.*, anorexic.
A.NOR.MAL, *s. 2 gen.*, abnormal person; *adj.*, abnormal, anomalous; mentally defective.
A.NOR.MA.LI.DA.DE, *s.f.*, abnormality, anomaly.
A.NO.SI.DA.DE, *s.f.*, old age.
A.NO.SO, *adj.*, aged, old.
A.NO.TA.ÇÃO, *s.f.*, annotation, notation, note.
A.NO.TA.DOR, *s.m.*, noter, annotator; writer of notes.
A.NO.TAR, *v.*, annotate, take note, mark, note down.
AN.SEI.O, *s.m.*, longing, craving, yearning; anxiety.
ÂN.SIA, *s.f.*, anguish, anxiety, trouble, sorrow.
AN.SI.AR, *v.*, to crave, to hanker, yearn.
AN.SI.E.DA.DE, *s.f.*, anxiety, worry, apprehension, fear, anguish.
AN.SI.O.SO, *adj.*, anxious, uneasy, careworn.
AN.SI.O.SA.MEN.TE, *adv.*, anxiously.

AN.TA, *s.f., Zool.*, tapir.
AN.TA.GÔ.NI.CO, *adj.*, antagonistic, opposit, contrary.
AN.TA.GO.NIS.MO, *s.m.*, antagonism, opposition, incompatibility.
AN.TA.GO.NIS.TA, *s. 2 gen.*, antagonist, oponent; *adj.*, antagonist, opposing, conflicting, incompatible.
AN.TA.GO.NI.ZAR, *v.*, to antagonize.
AN.TA.NHO, *adv.*, last yar, in former times.
AN.TÃO, *adv.*, então (antiquated).
AN.TÁR.TI.CO, *adj.*, antarctic.
AN.TÁR.TI.DA, *s.f.*, the Antarctica (the south polar region).
AN.TE, *prep.*, before, in the face of, in view of.
AN.TE.BRA.ÇO, *s.m.*, forearm, underarm.
AN.TE.BRA.QUI.AL, *adj.*, antebrachial.
AN.TE.CÂ.MA.RA, *s.f.*, vestibule, lobby, antechamber.
AN.TE.CE.DÊN.CIA, *s.f.*, antecedence, priority, precedence.
AN.TE.CE.DEN.TE, *s.m.*, antecedent, predecessor; *adj.*, antecedent, preceding, previous.
AN.TE.CE.DER, *v.*, to antecede, to precede, to anticipate.
AN.TE.CES.SOR, *s.m.*, antecessor, predecessor, foregoer.
AN.TE.CI.PA.ÇÃO, *s.f.*, anticipation, advance, expectation, forestalling.
AN.TE.CI.PA.DA.MEN.TE, *adv.*, beforehand, previousy, ahead.
AN.TE.CI.PA.DO, *adj.*, anticipated, beforehand.
AN.TE.CI.PAR, *v.*, to anticipate, to forestall, to do in advance.
AN.TE.DA.TA, *s.f.*, antedate.
AN.TE.DA.TAR, *v.*, to antedate, to predate.
AN.TE.DI.LU.VI.A.NO, *adj.*, antediluvian.
AN.TE.DI.ZER, *v.*, to predict.
AN.TE.GO.ZAR, *v.*, to foretaste; to have a foretaste of.
AN.TE.MÃO, *adv.*, beforehand, forestall.
AN.TE.MU.RO, *s.m.*, outside wall; barbican.
AN.TE.NA, *s.f.*, antenna.
AN.TE.NA.DO, *adj.*, provided with antenna; *gír.*, attentive.
AN.TE.NUP.CI.AL, *adj.*, antenupcial, prenuptial.
AN.TE.ON.TEM, *adv.*, the day before yesterday.
AN.TE.PA.RA, *s.f., Náut.*, bulkhead; screen.
AN.TE.PA.RO, *s.m.*, any screen (protection), fence, rampart.
AN.TE.PAS.SA.DO, *s.m.*, forefather, ancestor, predecessor.
AN.TE.PAS.TO, *s.m.*, appetizer.
AN.TE.PE.NÚL.TI.MO, *adj.*, antepenult, the last but two.
AN.TE.POR, *v.*, to set, to put before, to place before.
AN.TE.PRO.JE.TO, *s.m.*, project, plan, draft, preliminary sketch.
AN.TE.RI.OR, *adj., s. 2 gen.*, anterior, former, foregoing, front, previous.
AN.TE.RI.O.RI.DA.DE, *s.f.*, anteriority, precedence.
AN.TE.RI.OR.MEN.TE, *adv.*, previously, anteriorly, before.
AN.TES, *adv.*, before, formerly, previously, sooner, ahead.
AN.TES.SA.LA, *s.f.*, antechamber, antecabinet, waiting-room.
AN.TE.VER, *v.*, to foresee.
AN.TE.VÉS.PE.RA, *s.f.*, the day before yesterday.
AN.TE.VI.SÃO, *s.f.*, foresight.
AN.TI-, *pref.*, anti-, non-.
AN.TI.Á.CI.DO, *s.m.*, antacid.
AN.TI.A.DE.REN.TE, *s.m.*, non-stick (surface); *adj.*, non-stick.
AN.TI.A.É.REO, *adj.*, antiaircraft.
AN.TI.A.LÉR.GI.CO, *adj.*, hypo-allergenic; *s.m.*, antihistamine.
AN.TI.A.ME.RI.CA.NO, *adj.*, anti-American.
AN.TI.AS.MÁ.TI.CO, *s.m.*, antiasthmatic; *adj.*, antiasthmatic.

ANTIBACTERIANO ··89·· ANULATÓRIO

AN.TI.BAC.TE.RI.A.NO, s.m., antibacterial substance; adj., antibácterial.
AN.TI.BI.Ó.TI.CO, s.m., antibiotic.
AN.TI.CA.PI.TA.LIS.MO, s.m., anti-capitalism.
AN.TI.CAS.PA, adj., anti-dandruff.
AN.TI.CÉP.TI.CO, adj., antiskeptical.
AN.TI.CLE.RI.CAL, adj., anticlerical.
AN.TI.CLÍ.MAX, s.m., anticlimax.
AN.TI.CO.A.GU.LAN.TE, adj., anticoagulant.
AN.TI.CO.MU.NIS.TA, s. 2 gen., adj., anti-comunist.
AN.TI.CON.CEP.CIO.NAL, s.m., adj., contraceptive.
AN.TI.CON.GE.LAN.TE, s.m., adj., antifreeze.
AN.TI.CONS.TI.TU.CI.O.NAL, adj., anticonstitutional.
AN.TI.COR.PO, s.m., antibody.
AN.TI.COR.RO.SI.VO, adj., anticorrosive, non-corrosive.
AN.TI.CRIS.TO, s.m., Antichrist.
AN.TI.DE.MO.CRA.TA, s. 2 gen., antidemocrat.
AN.TI.DE.MO.CRÁ.TI.CO, adj., antidemocratic.
AN.TI.DE.PRES.SI.VO, s.m., Psic., antidepressant.
AN.TI.DER.RA.PAN.TE, s.m., adj., antiskid, nonskid.
AN.TÍ.DO.TO, s.m., antidote.
AN.TI.ES.TÉ.TI.CO, adj., antiaesthetic.
AN.TI.ES.PAS.MÓ.DI.CO, adj., antispasmodic.
AN.TI.É.TI.CO, adj., contrary to ethics, unethical.
AN.TI.E.VO.LU.CI.O.NIS.TA, s. 2 gen., antievolutionist; adj., antievolutionist.
AN.TI.FE.BRIL, s.m., antipyretic, febrifuge; adj., antipyretic, febrifugal.
AN.TI.GA.MEN.TE, adv., formerly, in the past, anciently, aforetime.
AN.TÍ.GE.NO, s.m., Med., antigen.
AN.TI.GO, adj., ancient, old, olden, antique, archaic, antiquated.
AN.TI.GUI.DA.DE, s.f., antiquity, antique, oldness, ancientry.
AN.TI.GUI.DA.DES, s.f., pl., antiques; loja de ~: antique shop.
AN.TI-HE.RÓI, s.m., anti-hero.
AN.TI-HI.GI.Ê.NI.CO, adj., antihygienic, unsanitary.
AN.TI-HI.PER.TEN.SI.VO,
AN.TI-HIS.TA.MÍ.NI.CO, s.m., adj., antihistamine.
AN.TI-HO.RÁ.RI.O, adj., US counterclockwise, UK anticlockwise.
AN.TI-IN.FLA.MA.TÓ.RI.O, s.m., adj., anti-inflammatory
AN.TI.LHA.NO, s.m., adj., Antilean, West Indian.
AN.TI.LHAS, s.f., pl., Antilles, West Indies.
AN.TÍ.LO.PE, s.m., Zool., antelope; steenbock.
AN.TI.MA.TÉ.RI.A, s.f., Fís., antimatter.
AN.TI.MI.LI.TAR, adj., antimilitary.
AN.TI.MO.NAR.QUIS.TA, s. 2 gen., antimonarchist; adj., antimonarchical, antimonarchic.
AN.TI.MÔ.NIO, s.m., antimony.
AN.TI.NA.CI.O.NAL, adj., antinational.
AN.TI.NA.TU.RAL, adj., unnatural.
AN.TI.NU.CLE.AR, adj., antinuclear.
AN.TI.O.FÍ.DI.CO, adj., antidotal (snake bites).
AN.TI.O.XI.DAN.TE, s.m., antioxidant.
AN.TI.PA.TI.A, s.f., antipathy, aversion, dislike, averseness.
AN.TI.PÁ.TI.CO, adj., antipathetic, averse, unpleasant, unfriendly.
AN.TI.PA.TI.ZAR, v., to dislike, to feel antipathy.
AN.TI.PA.TRI.O.TA, s. 2 gen., person; adj., unpatriotic.
AN.TI.PA.TRI.Ó.TI.CO, adj., unpatriotic.

AN.TI.PERS.PI.RAN.TE, s.m., adj., antiperspirante.
AN.TI.PI.RÉ.TI.CO, s.m., Med., antipyretic, febrifuge; adj., antipyretic.
AN.TÍ.PO.DA, adj., antipodal.
AN.TI.PO.LU.EN.TE, s.m., antipollution agent; adj., antipollution, antipollutant.
AN.TI.QUA.DO, adj., antiquated, antique, old, old-fashioned.
AN.TI.QUÁ.RIO, s.m., antiquary, antiquarian, archaist.
AN.TI.QUÍS.SI.MO, adj., most ancient (superlative), very old, ancient, age-old.
AN.TIR.RÁ.BI.CO, adj., Med., antirabic, antihydrophobic.
AN.TIS.SE.MI.TA, s. 2 gen., anti-Semite.
AN.TIS.SE.MI.TIS.MO, s.m., anti-Semitism.
AN.TIS.SÉP.TI.CO, s.m., Med., antiseptic.
AN.TIS.SO.CI.AL, adj., s. 2 gen., antisocial, unsocial.
AN.TI.TA.BA.GIS.MO, s.m., anti-smoking.
AN.TI.TA.BA.GIS.TA, s. 2 gen., anti-smoker; adj., anti-smoking.
AN.TI.TÉR.MI.CO, s.m., adj., antipyretic.
AN.TI.TER.RO.RIS.MO, s.m., antiterrorism.
AN.TI.TER.RO.RIS.TA, s. 2 gen., adj., antiterrorist.
AN.TÍ.TE.SE, s.f., antithesis, contraposition.
AN.TI.TE.TÂ.NI.CO, adj., antitetanic.
AN.TI.VÍ.RUS, s.m., Biol., antivirus; Comp., antivirus program.
AN.TO.JO, s.m., disgust, nausea; fancy, desire.
AN.TO.LHAR, v., to fancy, to imagine.
AN.TO.LHOS, s.m., pl., blinkers.
AN.TO.LO.GI.A, s.f., anthology, florilegium.
AN.TO.LÓ.GI.CO, adj., anthological, outstanding.
AN.TO.LO.GIS.TA, s. 2 gen., anthologist.
AN.TÔ.NI.MO, s.m., antonym.
AN.TRAZ, s.m., Vet., anthrax.
AN.TRO, s.m., antrum, antre, cave, sty.
AN.TRO.PO.CÊN.TRI.CO, adj., anthropocentric.
AN.TRO.PO.CEN.TRIS.MO, s.m., anthropocentrism.
AN.TRO.PO.FA.GI.A, s.f., cannibalism, anthropophagy.
AN.TRO.PÓ.FA.GO, s.m., cannibal, man-eater; adj., anthropophagous.
AN.TRO.POI.DE, s.m., anthropoid; adj., anthropoid.
AN.TRO.PO.LO.GI.A, s.f., anthropology.
AN.TRO.PO.LÓ.GI.CO, adj., anthropological.
AN.TRO.PO.LO.GIS.TA, s. 2 gen., anthropologist.
AN.TRO.PÓ.LO.GO, s.m., anthropologist.
A.NU, s.m., Zool., the same that anum.
A.NU.AL, adj., annual, yearly.
A.NU.A.LI.DA.DE, s.f., the same that anuidade.
A.NU.AL.MEN.TE, adv., annually, yearly.
A.NU.Á.RIO, s.m., yarbook.
A.NU.ÊN.CIA, s.f., approvement, approval, acquiescence.
A.NU.EN.TE, s. 2 gen., person who consents; adj., consenting, assenting.
A.NU.I.DA.DE, s.f., annuity, yearly payment.
A.NU.IR, v., to assent, to approve, to agree, to consent.
A.NU.LA.ÇÃO, s.f., annulment, nullification, cancellation, rescission.
A.NU.LA.DO, adj., canceled.
A.NU.LA.MEN.TO, s.m., annulment, cancellation.
A.NU.LAN.TE, adj., nullifying, cancelling.
A.NU.LAR, v., to annul, to cancel, to nullify, to make void; to suppress. **DEDO**
A.NU.LA.TI.VO, adj., the same that anulante.
A.NU.LA.TÓ.RI.O, adj., Jur., nullifying.

ANUM · 90 · APEGO

A.NUM, *s.m., Zool., Bras.*, anum, *Crotophaga*.
A.NUN.CI.A.ÇÃO, *s.f.*, annunciation, announcement.
A.NUN.CI.A.DOR, *s.m.*, annunciator, announcer; *adj.*, annunciating.
A.NUN.CI.AN.TE, *s. 2 gen.*, announcer, advertiser.
A.NUN.CI.AR, *v.*, to announce, to annunciate, to advertise, to promulgate, to proclaim.
A.NÚN.CIO, *s.m.*, advertisement, notice, announcement; bill.
A.NU.RO, *s.m., Zool.*, one of the anurans (which has no tail: frogs, toads, tree toads); *adj.*, anurous.
Â.NUS, *s.m.*, anus.
A.NU.VI.A.DO, *adj.*, clouded, overcast.
A.NU.VI.AR, *v.*, to grow cloudy, cloud, becloud, to darken.
AN.VER.SO, *s.m.*, obverse.
AN.ZOL, *s.m.*, fishhood, hook, angle.
AO, *contr.* of the *prep.* **A** and the *art.* **O**: in the, for the, to the, by the.
A.ON.DE, *adv.*, where, wherever, whither.
A.OR.TA, *s.f., Anat.*, aorta.
AOS, *pl., contr.* of the *prep.* **A** and the *def. art. pl.*, masculine **OS**: to the; ~ *amigos*: to the friends.
A.PA.CHE, *s. 2 g.*, Apache (North-American Indian).
A.PA.DRI.NHA.DOR, *s.m.*, protector, supporter; *adj.*, supporting, sponsoring.
A.PA.DRI.NHAR, *v.*, to be a godfather to; to be best man to; to sponsor.
A.PA.GA.DO, *adj.*, extinguished, extinct, dark, unlit, erased.
A.PA.GA.DOR, *s.m.*, extinguisher, quencher, eraser.
A.PA.GÃO, *s.m.*, great black out.
A.PA.GAR, *v.*, to extinguish, to quench, to damp, to smother, to blot.
A.PA.GÁ.VEL, *adj.*, erasable.
A.PAI.XO.NA.DA.MEN.TE, *adj.*, passionately.
A.PAI.XO.NA.DO, *s.m., adj.*, lover, enamoured, passionate, impassioned, flaming.
A.PAI.XO.NAN.TE, *adj.*, exciting, enthralling.
A.PAI.XO.NAR, *v.*, to impassion, to enamour, to enfatuate, to smite.
A.PA.LER.MA.DO, *adj.*, idiot, imbecile, silly.
A.PA.LER.MAR, *v.*, to become silly, to behave stupidly.
A.PAL.PA.ÇÃO, *s.f.*, act or fact of touching; Med percussion.
A.PAL.PA.DE.LA, *s.f.*, the same that *apalpação*.
A.PAL.PA.DOR, *s.m.*, fingerer, groper; *adj.*, catacting, groping.
A.PAL.PAR, *v.*, to touch, to feel, to palp, to palpate, to finger.
A.PAL.PO, *s.m.*, the same that *apalpação*.
A.PA.NI.GUA.DO, *s.m.*, sectarian, follower.
A.PA.NI.GUAR, *v.*, protect, sustain, favour.
A.PA.NHA.DO, *s.m.*, resumé, summary, abstract.
A.PA.NHA.DOR, *s.m.*, harvester, picker; *adj.*, that picks up.
A.PA.NHAR, *v.*, to pick, to pick out, to pluck, to gather, to collect.
A.PA.RA, *s.f.*, shaving, scrap, shred.
A.PA.RA.DO, *adj.*, pared, clipped.
A.PA.RA.DOR, *s.m.*, parer, cropper, parrier, dresser.
A.PA.RA.FU.SAR, *v.*, to bolt, to screw, fasten with a screw.
A.PA.RA.MEN.TAR, *v.*, to adorn, to ornament; dress official vestments.
A.PA.RAR, *v.*, to clip, to trim, to cut, to part, to chip.
A.PA.RA.TAR, *v.*, to adorn, to decorate, to trim.
A.PA.RA.TO, *s.m.*, display, apparatus, grandeur, pomp, device.

A.PA.RA.TO.SO, *adj.*, sumptuous, ostentatious.
A.PA.RE.CER, *v.*, to appear, to show up, to turn up, to arise, to emerge, to begin.
A.PA.RE.CI.DO, *s.m., gir., adj.*, appeared, emerged.
A.PA.RE.CI.MEN.TO, *s.m.*, emersion, appearing, coming, emergence.
A.PA.RE.LHA.DO, *adj.*, prepared, ready, disposed, planed.
A.PA.RE.LHA.GEM, *s.f.*, implements, tools, equipments.
A.PA.RE.LHA.MEN.TO, *s.m.*, apparatus, equipment.
A.PA.RE.LHAR, *v.*, to equip, to outfit, to furnish, to prepare, to prim.
A.PA.RE.LHO, *s.m.*, equipment, arrangement, apparatus, implement, gear.
A.PA.RÊN.CIA, *s.f.*, appearance, aspect, semblance, likelihood, likeness.
A.PA.REN.TA.DO, *adj.*, related, connected, agnate.
A.PA.REN.TAR, *v.*, to pretend, to simulate, have the appearance of, to establish kinship.
A.PA.REN.TE, *adj.*, apparent, semblable, evident.
A.PA.REN.TE.MEN.TE, *adv.*, apparently.
A.PA.RI.ÇÃO, *s.f.*, phantom, ghost, spectre, apparition, vision.
A.PA.RO, *s.m.*, cropping, paring.
A.PAR.TA.MEN.TO, *s.m.*, flat, apartment.
A.PAR.TA.DO, *adj.*, separated, distant, astray, deviated.
A.PAR.TA.DOR, *s.m.*, separator; *adj.*, separating.
A.PAR.TA.MEN.TO, *s.m., US* apartment, *UK* flat; separation.
A.PAR.TAR, *v.*, to separate, to part, to divide, to alienate, to disjoin.
A.PAR.TE, *s.m.*, incidental remark, interruption; an aside.
A.PAR.TE.AR, *v.*, to interrupt an orator.
A.PAR.TI.DÁ.RI.O, *adj.*, non-partisan, contrary to political parties.
A.PAR.VA.LHA.DO, *adj.*, stupid, idiot; confused, perplexed.
A.PAR.VA.LHAR, *v.*, to confuse, to puzzle, to confound.
A.PAS.CEN.TA.DOR, *s.m.*, herdsman; *adj.*, that herds the cattle.
A.PAS.CEN.TAR, *v.*, to take to pasture, feed, herd.
A.PAS.SI.VAR, *v.*, to change to the passive.
A.PA.TE.TA.DO, *adj.*, foolish, stupid.
A.PA.TI.A, *s.f.*, apathy, insensibility, indolence.
A.PÁ.TI.CO, *adj.*, apathetic, indifferent.
A.PÁ.TRI.DA, *adj., s. 2 gen.*, war refugee.
A.PA.VO.RA.DO, *adj.*, panic-stricken, scared.
A.PA.VO.RA.MEN.TO, *s.m.*, panic, terror, act of appalling.
A.PA.VO.RAN.TE, *adj.*, terrifying, appalling.
A.PA.VO.RAR, *v.*, terrify, frighten, horrify.
A.PA.ZI.GUA.DO, *adj.*, pacified, calmed.
A.PA.ZI.GUA.MEN.TO, *s.m.*, peacemaking, pacification.
A.PA.ZI.GUAR, *v.*, to pacify, to appease, to reconcile, to calm, to quiet, to mollify.
A.PA.ZI.GUÁ.VEL, *adj.*, pacifiable, appeasable.
A.PE.A.MEN.TO, *s.m.*, act of dismounting (horse).
A.PE.AR, *v.*, to dismount (horse), to alight from.
A.PE.DEU.TA, *s. 2 gen.*, unlearned person, ignorant.
A.PE.DRE.JA.DO, *adj.*, stoned, hurt by sotones.
A.PE.DRE.JA.DOR, *s.m.*, one who throws stones.
A.PE.DRE.JA.MEN.TO, *s.m.*, stoning, lapidation.
A.PE.DRE.JAR, *v.*, to stone, to lapidate.
A.PE.GA.DO, *adj.*, stuck to, fastened, affectionate.
A.PE.GAR, *v.*, to attach, to infect, to transmit by contagion.
A.PE.GO, *s.m.*, affection, fondness, adherence, adhesion.

APELAÇÃO ••91•• APORTUGUESAR

A.PE.LA.ÇÃO, *s.f.*, appeal, appellation, recourse.
A.PE.LAN.TE, *s. 2 gen.*, appellant.
A.PE.LAR, *v.*, to appeal, to solicit, to plead, to ask.
A.PE.LA.TI.VA.MEN.TE, *adv.*, appellatively.
A.PE.LA.TI.VO, *adj.*, appellative.
A.PE.LÁ.VEL, *adj.*, appealable.
A.PE.LI.DAR, *v.*, to cognominate, to nickname, to denominate.
A.PE.LI.DO, *s.m.*, surname, byname, family name, cognomen.
A.PE.LO, *s.m.*, appellation, appeal, plea.
A.PE.NAR, *v.*, to punish, to make suffer.
A.PE.NAS, *adv.*, scarcely, hardly, only, merely.
A.PÊN.DI.CE, *s.f.*, appendix, supplement, addendum.
A.PEN.DI.CI.TE, *s.f., Med.*, appendicitis.
A.PE.NHO.RAR, *v.*, to pledge, to pawn.
A.PEN.SAR, *v.*, to append, to join, to add.
A.PEN.SO, *s.m.*, enclosure, thing annexed.
A.PE.QUE.NAR, *v.*, to make smaller, to lessen, diminish.
A.PER.CE.BER, *v.*, to prepare, to fit, to adapt, to warn, to inform, to notify.
A.PER.FEI.ÇO.A.DO, *adj.*, improved, polished.
A.PER.FEI.ÇO.A.MEN.TO, *s.m.*, perfection, improvement.
A.PER.FEI.ÇO.AR, *v.*, to improve on, to perfect, to meliorate, to better, to amend.
A.PER.FEI.ÇO.Á.VEL, *adj.*, perfectible, ameliorable, amendable.
A.PE.RI.TI.VO, *s.m.*, aperitif, appetizer.
A.PER.RE.A.ÇÃO, *s.f.*, vexation, act of appression, hardship.
A.PER.RE.A.DO, *adj.*, oppressed, dreary, weak, vexed.
A.PER.RE.AR, *v.*, to vex, to annoy.
A.PER.REI.O, *s.m.*, the same that *aperreação*.
A.PER.TA.DO, *adj.*, pressed, narrow, compressed, scarce, tight, close.
A.PER.TAR, *v.*, to squeeze, to press, to compress, to narrow, to constrict, to limit.
A.PER.TÃO, *s.m.*, strong pressure, crowd; to urge; difficult situation.
A.PER.TO, *s.m.*, squeeze, pressure, stress, tightness, straitness, narrowness.
A.PE.SAR DE, *prep.*, in spite of,despite, although.
A.PES.SO.A.DO, *adj.*, well-shaped, good-looking.
A.PE.TE.CER, *v.*, to have an apetite for, to desire, to hunger for.
A.PE.TE.CÍ.VEL, *adj.*, appetizing, desirable, tempting.
A.PE.TÊN.CI.A, *s.f.*, appetite, appetence, hunger.
A.PE.TEN.TE, *adj.*, appetent, appetitive.
A.PE.TI.TE, *s.m.*, appetite, appetence, hunger.
A.PE.TI.TO.SO, *adj.*, appetizing, savoury, desirable.
A.PE.TRE.CHAR, *v.*, to equip, to provide, to supply.
A.PE.TRE.CHOS, *s.m., pl.*, equipments, supplies; tackle.
A.PE.ZI.NHAR, *v.*, the same that *espezinhar*: to trample on.
A.PI.Á.RIO, *s.m.*, apiary.
Á.PI.CE, *s.m.*, apex, vertex, top, summit.
A.PÍ.CO.LA, *s. 2 gen.*, apiarist; *adj.*, apicultural.
A.PI.CUL.TOR, *s.m.*, apiculturist, beekeeper, apiarist.
A.PI.CUL.TU.RA, *s.f.*, apiculture, beekeeping.
A.PI.E.DAR, *v.*, to pity, to feel sorry for.
A.PI.FOR.ME, *adj.*, having the form of a bee.
A.PI.MEN.TA.DO, *adj.*, peppery, spicy.
A.PI.MEN.TAR, *v.*, to pepper, to spice, to season.
A.PI.NHA.DO, *adj.*, crowded (with people), crammed.
A.PI.NHAR, *v.*, to pile up, to overcrowd.

A.PI.PAR, *v.*, to give the shape of a pipe or barrel to.
A.PI.TA.DOR, *s.m.*, whistler, tooter.
A.PI.TAR, *v.*, to whistle, to blow the whistle.
A.PI.TO, *s.m.*, whistle.
APLACAR, *v.*, to placate, to sooth; to quiet, to tranquilize.
A.PLAI.NA.DO, *adj.*, planed (wood), even, level, smooth.
A.PLAI.NAR, *v.*, to level, to smooth, to plane.
A.PLA.NAR, *v.*, to level out, to equalize; to smooth.
A.PLAU.DIR, *v.*, to applaud, to clap, to acclaim, to cheer, to laud.
A.PLAU.SO, *s.m.*, applause, acclamation, cheering, laudation.
A.PLI.CA.BI.LI.DA.DE, *s.f.*, applicability, relevancy.
A.PLI.CA.ÇÃO, *s.f.*, application, adornment; attention, diligence.
A.PLI.CA.DO, *adj.*, applied, diligent.
A.PLI.CAR, *v.*, to apply, to put into pratice, to adapt, to inflict.
A.PLI.CA.TI.VO, *s.m., Comp.*, application; *adj.*, applicable, *Comp.*, application.
A.PLI.CÁ.VEL, *adj.*, applicable, appropriate.
A.PLI.QUE, *s.m., Fr.*, appliqué.
AP.NEI.A, *s.f., Med.*, apnea, apnoea.
AP.NEI.CO, *adj.*, apneal (refering to apnea).
A.PO.CA.LIP.SE, *s.m.*, apocalypse.
A.PO.CA.LÍP.TI.CO, *adj.*, apocalyptic; terrifying, prophetic.
A.PÓ.CO.PE, *s.f., Gram.*, apocope.
A.PÓ.CRI.FO, *adj.*, apocryphal.
Á.PO.DE, *s.m.*, apode, apod; *adj.*, apodal (without feet).
A.PO.DE.RAR, *v.*, to take possession, to take hold of, to possess, to grab.
A.PO.DRE.CER, *v.*, to putrefy, to rot, to corrupt, to decompose.
A.PO.DRE.CI.DO, *adj.*, putrefied, rotten; corrupt (morally).
A.PO.DRE.CI.MEN.TO, *s.m.*, putrefaction.
A.PO.GEU, *s.m.*, apogee, summit.
A.POI.A.DO, *s.m.*, support, help; *adj.*, supported, approved.
A.POI.AR, *v.*, to support, to stay, to sustain, to prop, to make firm.
A.POI.O, *s.m.*, base, basis, foundation, support, stay, rest, protection.
A.PÓ.LI.CE, *s.f.*, policy, bond, stock, share.
A.PO.LÍ.NE.O, *adj.*, Apollinian, Apollonian (referring to god Apollo).
A.PO.LÍ.TI.CO, *adj.*, apolitical.
A.PO.LO.GÉ.TI.CO, *adj.*, aplogetic, deprecatory.
A.PO.LO.GI.A, *s.f.*, apology, discourse.
A.PO.LO.GIS.TA, *s. 2 gen.*, apologist.
A.PON.TA.DO, *adj.*, pointed, indacated, noted, directed.
A.PON.TA.DOR, *s.m.*, pencil sharpener.
A.PON.TA.MEN.TO, *s.m.*, annotation, note, notice, reference.
A.PON.TAR, *v.*, to indicate, to show, to mark, to label, to mention; to point, to sharpen.
A.PON.TÁ.VEL, *adj.*, that can be pointed.
A.PO.PLÉ.TI.CO, *adj.*, apoplectic.
A.PO.PLE.XI.A, *s.f.*, apoplexy.
A.PO.QUEN.TA.DO, *adj.*, afflicted, troubled.
A.PO.QUEN.TAR, *v.*, to annoy.
A.POR, *v.*, to appose, to put together or above, to attach, to append, to affix.
A.POR.RI.NHA.ÇÃO, *s.f.*, annoyance.
A.POR.RI.NHAR, *v.*, to annoy.
A.POR.TAR, *v.*, to enter a port, to arrive at a port.
A.POR.TU.GUE.SAR, *v.*, to make Portuguese, to give

APÓS ··92·· APROXIMATIVO

Portuguese characteristics to.

A.PÓS, *adv.*, after, thereafter, behind.

A.PO.SEN.TA.DO, *s.m., adj.*, pensioner.

A.PO.SEN.TA.DO.RI.A, *s.f.*, retirement.

A.PO.SEN.TAR-SE, *v.*, to retire, to pension off.

A.PO.SEN.TO, *s.m.*, residence, room, domicile, apartment.

A.PÓS-GUER.RA, *s.m.*, postwar.

A.POS.SAR-SE, *v.*, to take possession of, to put in possession.

A.POS.TA, *s.f.*, bet, betting, wager.

A.POS.TA.DO, *adj.*, wagered, betted.

A.POS.TAR, *v.*, to bet, to make a bet, to risk.

A.PÓS.TA.SE, *s.f., Med.*, apostasis.

A.POS.TA.SI.A, *s.f.*, apostasy.

A.PÓS.TA.TA, *s. 2 gen.*, apostate.

A.POS.TI.LA, *s.f.*, apostil, postil, annotation to a script, comment.

A.POS.TO, *s.m.*, appositive; *adj.*, apposed, appositive.

A.POS.TO.LA.DO, *s.m.*, apostolate.

A.POS.TÓ.LI.CO, *adj.*, apostolic, papal.

A.PÓS.TO.LO, *s.m.*, apostle.

A.POS.TRO.FAR, *v.*, to apostrophize, to apostrophise.

A.PÓS.TRO.FE, *s.f.*, apostrophe, interruption.

A.PÓS.TRO.FO, *s.m., Gram.*, apostrophe.

A.PÓ.TE.MA, *s.m., Mat.*, apothem.

A.PO.TE.O.SE, *s.f.*, apotheosis, glorification.

A.POU.CA.DO, *adj.*, poorly; mean, stingy; faint-hearted.

A.POU.CAR, *v.*, to reduce, to minify.

A.PRA.ZA.MEN.TO, *s.m.*, act of fixing a date for an appointment.

A.PRA.ZAR, *v.*, to convene, to summon, to cite, to mark a day.

A.PRA.ZER, *v.*, to please, to gratify.

A.PRA.ZÍ.VEL, *adj.*, pleasant, delightful, diverting, amusing.

A.PRE.ÇAR, *v.*, to price, to determine the price of, to appraise.

A.PRE.CI.A.ÇÃO, *s.f.*, appreciation, rating, valuation, concept, idea.

A.PRE.CI.A.DOR, *s.m.*, appraiser, appreciator, affectionate.

A.PRE.CI.AR, *v.*, to appreciate, to rate, to compute, to value, to estimate, to judge.

A.PRE.CI.A.TI.VO, *adj.*, appreciating, appreciative.

A.PRE.CI.Á.VEL, *adj.*, appreciable, considerable, notable.

A.PRE.ÇO, *s.m.*, valuation, estimation, deference.

A.PRE.EN.SI.VO, *adj.*, apprehensive.

A.PRE.EN.DER, *v.*, to make apprehension of, to apprehend; to confiscate; to understand.

A.PRE.EN.SÃO, *s.f.*, apprehension, act of apprehending, arrest, capture.

A.PRE.EN.SI.BI.LI.DA.DE, *s.f.*, apprehensiveness.

A.PRE.EN.SI.VO, *s.f.*, apprehensive, fearful.

A.PRE.GO.AR, *v.*, to announce by a crier, proclaim, to divulge, to puff, to boom.

A.PREN.DER, *v.*, to learn, to study, to come to know.

A.PREN.DIZ, *s.m.*, apprentice, beginner, novice.

A.PREN.DI.ZA.DO, *s.m.*, apprenticeship, apprenticement.

A.PREN.DI.ZA.GEM, *s.f.*, apprenticeship, apprenticement.

A.PRE.SA.MEN.TO, *s.m.*, apprehension, capture.

A.PRE.SAR, *v.*, to capture, to apprehend, to seize.

A.PRE.SEN.TA.ÇÃO, *s.f.*, presentation, introduction, personal appearance.

A.PRE.SEN.TA.DOR, *s.m.*, presenter (radio, TV); speaker.

A.PRE.SEN.TAR, *v.*, to present, to introduce, to show, to display, to expose, to exhibit.

A.PRE.SEN.TÁ.VEL, *adj.*, presentable.

A.PRES.SA.DA.MEN.TE, *adv.*, heastily.

A.PRES.SA.DO, *adj.*, hurried, ready, in a hurry; hasty.

A.PRES.SAR, *v.*, to speed up, to accelerate, to hurry, to quicken, to instigate.

A.PRES.TAR, *v.*, to prepare, to equip, to furnish.

A.PRI.MO.RA.DO, *adj.*, refined, excellent, fine.

A.PRI.MO.RA.MEN.TO, *s.m.*, refinement, elegance, improvement.

A.PRI.O.RIS.TA, *s. 2 gen.*, apriorist.

A.PRI.O.RÍS.TI.CO, *adj.*, aprioristic.

A.PRI.MO.RAR, *v.*, to perfect, to improve, to ameliorate, to refine.

A.PRI.SI.O.NA.DO, *adj.*, captive.

A.PRI.SI.O.NA.MEN.TO, *s.m.*, imprisonment, capture.

A.PRI.SI.O.NAR, *v.*, to arrest, to capture, to imprison, to lead captive.

A.PRO.A.MEN.TO, *s.m., Náut.*, act of steering towards, directing to (harbour).

A.PRO.AR, *v., Náut.*, to steer (turn the prow of a ship towards to).

A.PRO.BA.TI.VO, *adj.*, approving, aprobatory.

A.PRO.BA.TÓ.RI.O, *adj.*, the same that *aprobativo*.

A.PRO.FUN.DA.MEN.TO, *s.m.*, deepening, serious study, in-depth examination.

A.PRO.FUN.DAR, *v.*, to deepen, to make deeper, to sink down.

A.PRON.TA.MEN.TO, *s.m.*, preparation, finishing.

A.PRON.TAR, *v.*, to prepare, to get ready, to put in order, to equip.

A.PRO.PRI.A.ÇÃO, *s.f.*, appropriation, assumption, accommodation.

A.PRO.PRI.A.DO, *adj.*, appropriate, proper, adequate, suitable.

A.PRO.PRI.AR, *v.*, to appropriate, to make suitable, to apt, to accommodate.

A.PRO.PRI.Á.VEL, *adj.*, appropriable.

A.PRO.VA.ÇÃO, *s.f.*, approval, approbation, agreement, consent, assent, praise.

A.PRO.VA.DO, *adj.*, approved, sanctioned, accredited.

A.PRO.VAR, *v.*, to approve, to approbe, to approbate, to validate, to ratify.

A.PRO.VEI.TA.DO, *adj.*, utilized, useful, profitable.

A.PRO.VEI.TA.DOR, *s.m.*, profiteer.

A.PRO.VEI.TA.MEN.TO, *s.m.*, utilization, use, profit.

A.PRO.VEI.TAR, *v.*, to use to advantage, make good use of, to utilize, to use.

A.PRO.VEI.TÁ.VEL, *adj.*, profitable, reusable, utilizable, useful.

A.PRO.VI.SI.O.NA.MEN.TO, *s.m.*, supply, catering, provisioning.

A.PRO.VI.SI.O.NAR, *v.*, to provision, to provide with food, supply.

A.PRO.XI.MA.ÇÃO, *s.f.*, approximation, approach.

A.PRO.XI.MA.DA.MEN.TE, *adv.*, approximately, nearly, almost.

A.PRO.XI.MA.DO, *adj.*, approximate, close.

A.PRO.XI.MAR, *v.*, to approach, to approximate, to bring near, colligate.

A.PRO.XI.MA.TI.VO, *adj.*, approximative.

APRUMADO ·· 93 ·· ARDENTE

A.PRU.MA.DO, *adj.*, upright, erect; *Bras.*, well-dressed; *fig.*, correct.
A.PRU.MAR, *v.*, to erect, to put in an upright position.
A.PRU.MO, *s.m.*, straightness, uprightness, rectitude.
AP.TI.DÃO, *s.f.*, aptness, aptitude, ability, capacity, capability.
AP.TO, *adj.*, able, capable, qualified, apt, fit.
A.PU.NHA.LAR, *v.*, to stab, to kill with a dagger.
A.PU.PAR, *v.*, to scoff, to jeer, to boo, to sneer, to hoot.
A.PU.PO, *s.m.*, hoot, jeer, boo.
A.PU.RA.ÇÃO, *s.f.*, examination, verification, purifying, refinement, purification.
A.PU.RA.DO, *adj.*, refined, selected, sharp.
A.PU.RA.MEN.TO, *s.m.*, the same that *apuração*.
A.PU.RAR, *v.*, to perfect, to improve, to clean, to purify, to refine, to select, to choose.
A.PU.RO, *s.m.*, purifying, refinement, purification, precision, accuracy.
A.QUA.PLA.NA.GEM, *s.f.*, landing on water; (vehicle) skidding on a wet surface.
A.QUA.PLA.NAR, *v.*, to slide on a wet surface (vehicle).
A.QUA.RE.LA, *s.f.*, aquarelle, water colour.
A.QUA.RE.LIS.TA, *s. 2 gen.*, watercolourist (painter).
A.QUA.RI.A.NO, *s.m., Astrol.*, Aquarian.
A.QUÁ.RIO, *s.m.,* aquarium; *Astron.*, Aquarius (constellation); *Astrol.*, Aquarius (sign in the Zodiac).
A.QUAR.TE.LA.MEN.TO, *s.m., Mil.*, billeting.
A.QUAR.TE.LAR, *v., Mil.*, to billet, to quarter.
A.QUÁ.TI.CO, *adj.*, aquatic.
A.QUE.CE.DOR, *s.m.*, warmer, heater, radiator.
A.QUE.CER, *v.*, to heat, to warm, to make hot, to make warm.
A.QUE.CI.MEN.TO, *s.m.*, heating, warming, calefaction.
A.QUE.DU.TO, *s.m.*, aqueduct.
A.QUE.LA, A.QUE.LE, *pron.*, that, that one, the one.
A.QUE.LAS, A.QUE.LES, *pron.*, those.
À.QUE.LE(S), À.QUE.LA(S), *pron.*, to that, to those.
A.QUÉ.M, *adv.*, on this side, inferiorly, below, beneath; less.
A.QUI, *adv.*, here, herein, in this, on this place.
A.QUI.ES.CÊN.CI.A, *s.f.*, acquiescence.
A.QUI.ES.CEN.TE, *adj.*, acquiescent.
A.QUI.ES.CER, *v.*, to acquiesce, to consent, to permit, to assent.
A.QUI.E.TA.ÇÃO, *s.f.*, quieting, appeasing, tranquillity, pacification.
A.QUI.E.TAR, *v.*, to quiet, to appease, to pacify, to calm.
A.QUÍ.FE.RO, *adj.*, aquiferous, bearing water.
A.QUI.LA.TAR, *v.*, to appraise, to make an appreciation, to assay.
A.QUI.LI.NO, *adj.*, aquiline.
A.QUI.LO, *pron.*, that.
À.QUI.LO, *pron.*, to that.
A.QUI.NHO.AR, *v.*, to portion, to share out.
A.QUI.SI.ÇÃO, *s.f.*, acquisition, acquirement, acquest; buy.
A.QUI.SI.TI.VO, *adj.*, acquisitive.
A.QUO.SO, *adj.*, aqueous, waterish.
AR, *s.m.*, air, atmosphere, breath, breeze, wind, climate, aspect, look.
Á.RA.BE, *s.m., adj.*, Arab, Arabian, Arabic.
A.RA.BES.CO, *s.m.*, arabesque, flurish.
A.RÁ.BI.A SAU.DI.TA, *s.f.*, Saudi Arabia.
A.RÁ.BI.CO, *s.m.*, Arabic; *adj.*, Arabic, Arabian.
A.RA.DO, *s.m.*, plough, plow.

A.RA.GEM, *s.f.*, whiff, breeze, wind.
A.RA.MA.DO, *s.m.*, wire fence; *adj.*, fenced, enclosed.
A.RA.MA.GEM, *s.f.*, wire grating, wire netting.
A.RA.MAI.CO, *s.m.*, Aramaic; *adj.*, Aramean.
A.RA.MAR, *v.*, fence with wire, to enclose.
A.RA.ME, *s.m.*, wire.
A.RA.NHA, *s.f., Zool.*, spider.
A.RA.NHA-CA.RAN.GUE.JEI.RA, *s.f., Zool.*, bird-catching spider.
A.RA.PON.GA, *s.f., Zool.*, bellbird.
A.RA.PU.CA, *s.f.*, bird-trap; pitfall, snare, trap.
A.RA.QUE, *s.m., Bras.*, chance, hazard; *de ~*: fake, phony, rubbish.
A.RAR, *v.*, to plow, to till.
A.RA.RA, *s.f., Zool.*, macaw (a Brazilian parrot).
A.RA.RI.NHA-A.ZUL, *s.f., Bras., Zool.*, Spix's macaw.
A.RA.RU.TA, *s.f.*, arrowroot.
A.RAU.CÁ.RIA, *s.f.*, araucaria.
A.RAU.TO, *s.m.*, herald, town-crier, public crier.
A.RÁ.VEL, *adj.*, arable, tillable.
AR.BI.TRA.GEM, *s.f.*, arbitration, arbitrament.
AR.BI.TRAR, *v.*, to arbitrate, to decide, to umpire, to mediate.
AR.BI.TRA.RI.E.DA.DE, *s.f.*, arbitrariness.
AR.BI.TRÁ.RIO, *adj.*, arbitrary, despotic, discretionary.
AR.BÍ.TRIO, *s.m.*, will, discretion, judgement, choice, expedient.
ÁR.BI.TRO, *s.m.*, arbiter, umpire, judge, judger.
AR.BÓ.REO, *adj.*, arboreal, arboreous, treelike.
AR.BO.RES.CÊN.CI.A, *s.f.*, arborescence.
AR.BO.RES.CER, *v.*, to grow into a tree.
AR.BO.RÍ.CO.LA, *adj., Zool.*, arboreal.
AR.BO.RI.ZA.ÇÃO, *s.f.*, arborization, forestation.
AR.BO.RI.ZA.DO, *adj.*, arboreous, arbored, forested.
AR.BO.RI.ZAR, *v.*, to forest, to plant with trees.
AR.BUS.TI.VO, *adj.*, undershrub, shrubby.
AR.BUS.TO, *s.m.*, shrub, bush.
AR.CA, *s.f.*, ark, chest, coffer, trunk.
AR.CA.BOU.ÇO, *s.m.*, framework, skeleton, outline.
AR.CA.BUZ, *s.m.*, harquebus.
AR.CA.DA, *s.f.*, arcade, vault, arch; *~ dentária*: dental arch.
AR.CA.DO, *adj.*, arched, bowed, curved.
AR.CAI.CO, *adj.*, archaic, disused, obsolete, antique.
AR.CA.IS.MO, *s.m.*, archaism.
AR.CA.I.ZAN.TE, *adj.*, archaist, archaic, archaizing.
AR.CAN.JO, *s.m.*, archangel.
AR.CA.NO, *s.m.*, arcanum; secret, mistery; *adj.*, arcane, hidden, mysterious.
AR.CAR, *v.*, to bend, to curve, to arch, to bow; to struggle, to grapple.
AR.CE.BIS.PO, *s.m.*, archbishop.
AR.CHO.TE, *s.m.*, torch, torch-light, flambeau.
AR.CO, *s.m.*, arc, arch, squinch, bow, hoop.
AR.CO-DA-VE.LHA, *s.m., coisas do ~*: fantastic things, wondrous things.
AR.CO E FLE.CHA, *s.m., Esp.*, archery, bow and arrow.
AR.CO-Í.RIS, *s.m.*, rainbow.
AR-CON.DI.CI.O.NA.DO, *s.m.*, air conditioning.
AR.CON.TE, *s.m., Gr., Hist.*, archon (magistrate in ancient Athens).
AR.DÊN.CI.A, *s.f.*, burning, ardency, fernvency.
AR.DEN.TE, *adj.*, ardent, burning, torrid, flaming, fervent,

ARDENTEMENTE   •• 94 ••   ARPÃO

violent.

AR.DEN.TE.MEN.TE, *adv.*, ardently.

AR.DER, *v.*, to burn, to flame, to blaze, to smoulder, to shine, to fire.

AR.DI.DO, *adj.*, stinging, burning, burnt, hot (pepper in food).

AR.DIL, *s.m.*, cunning, slyness, craftiness, trickiness, trick; trap, snare.

AR.DI.LO.SO, *adj.*, cunning, artful, crafty, subtle, crooked.

AR.DOR, *s.m.*, heat, burning, hotness, ardour, passion.

AR.DO.RO.SA.MEN.TE, *adv.*, fervently, zealously.

AR.DO.RO.SO, *adj.*, ardent, fervent; amorous, zealous.

AR.DÓ.SI.A, *s.f.*, *Geol.*, slate.

AR.DU.A.MEN.TE, *adv.*, arduously, painfully.

AR.DU.ME, *s.m.*, piquancy, pungency.

ÁR.DU.O, *adj.*, arduous, difficult, laborious, hard.

A.RE, *s.m.*, are, measure of 119,6 square yards.

Á.REA, *s.f.*, area, surface, space, ground, yard.

A.RE.AR, *v.*, to polish, to sand, to scour.

A.RE.AL, *s.m.*, beach, sand dune.

A.RE.EN.TO, *adj.*, sanded, sandy.

A.REI.A, *s.f.*, sand, grit, gravel.

A.RE.JA.DO, *adj.*, aired, ventilated.

A.RE.JA.MEN.TO, *adj.*, airing, ventilation.

A.RE.JAR, *v.*, to air, to expose to the air, to weather, to ventilate.

A.RE.NA, *s.f.*, arena, ring.

A.REN.GA, *s.f.*, harangue, speech; dispute, discussion.

A.REN.GAR, *v.*, to harangue; to dispute, to altercate, to argue.

A.RE.NI.TO, *s.m.*, sandstone, grit.

A.RE.NO.SO, *adj.*, sandy, gravelly, gritty.

A.REN.QUE, *s.m.*, *Zool.*, herring.

A.RÉ.O.LA, *s.f.*, areola, areole.

A.RE.O.LA.DO, *adj.*, areolate, areolar.

A.RE.Ó.PA.GO, *s.m.*, *Gr.*, *Hist.*, Areopagus (Athenian tribunal).

A.RE.O.SO, *adj.*, the same that *arenoso*.

A.RES.TA, *s.f.*, edge, corner, brim, border.

A.RES.TO, *s.m.*, judgement, legal decision, decree, sentence.

A.RÉU, *adj.*, hesitant, puzzled, bewildered.

AR.FAN.TE, *adj.*, gasping, heaving.

AR.FAR, *v.*, to heave, to gasp, to palpitate.

AR.GA.MAS.SA, *s.f.*, mortar, building cement, daub, pug.

AR.GÉ.LI.A, *s.*, Algeria.

AR.GE.LI.NO, *s.m.*, *adj.*, Argelian.

AR.GÊN.TEO, *adj.*, silvery, argentine.

AR.GEN.TI.NA, *s.*, Argentina.

AR.GEN.TI.NO, *s.m.*, *adj.*, Argentinean.

AR.GEN.TO, *s.m.*, *Lit.*, silver.

AR.GI.LA, *s.f.*, argil, clay.

AR.GI.LO.SO, *adj.*, clayey.

AR.GO.LA, *s.f.*, ring, hoop, link, door knocker.

AR.GO.NAU.TA, *s.m.*, *Mit.*, argonaut; *fig.*, a daring navigator.

AR.GÔ.NI.O, *s.m.*, *Quím.*, argon.

AR.GOS, *s.m.*, *Mit.*, Argus (a hundred-eyed monster); *fig.*, a smart person.

AR.GÚ.CIA, *s.f.*, astuteness, smartness, captiousness.

AR.GUI.ÇÃO, *s.f.*, argumentation, arguing, reprimand; oral examination.

AR.GUI.DOR, *s.m.*, arguer; accuser, blamer, reprover.

AR.GUIR, *v.*, to accuse, to reprove, to reprehend, to condemn, to infer.

AR.GUI.TI.VO, *adj.*, conclusive; accusatory.

AR.GUÍ.VEL, *adj.*, censurable; accusable; discussable.

AR.GU.MEN.TA.ÇÃO, *s.f.*, argumentation, reasoning, dispute, debate.

AR.GU.MEN.TAR, *v.*, to argue, to dispute, to debate.

AR.GU.MEN.TA.TI.VO, *adj.*, argumentative.

AR.GU.MEN.TO, *s.m.*, argument, subject, reason, topic.

AR.GU.TO, *adj.*, shrewd, subtle, sagacious.

Á.RIA, *s.f.*, aria, air, song, tune, melody.

A.RI.A.NIS.MO, *s.m.*, Arianism.

A.RI.A.NO, *s.m.*, Arian (person); *Astrol.*, Arian; *adj.*, Aryan (about ethnic group Indo-European).

A.RI.DEZ, *s.f.*, aridity, aridness, dryness.

Á.RI.DO, *adj.*, arid, dry, desert, withered, sterile.

Á.RI.ES, *s.m.*, *Astron.*, Aries (constellation), *Astrol.*, Aries (sign of the zodiac).

A.RI.GÓ, *s.m.*, *Bras.*, rustic, boor.

A.RIS.CO, *adj.*, sandy, shy, skittish, antisocial, untameable.

A.RÍ.E.TE, *s.m.*, *Mil.*, battering ram; hydraulic ram.

A.RIS.TO.CRA.CI.A, *s.f.*, aristocracy, nobility.

A.RIS.TO.CRA.TA, *s. 2 gen.*, aristocrat, noble, patrician.

A.RIS.TO.CRÁ.TI.CO, *adj.*, aristocratic, aristocratical, noble.

A.RIS.TO.CRA.TI.ZAR, *v.*, to render aristocratic.

A.RIS.TO.TÉ.LI.CO, *adj.*, Aristotelian, Aristotelic.

A.RIT.MÉ.TI.CA, *s.f.*, arithmetic.

A.RIT.MÉ.TI.CO, *s.f.*, arithmetic; *adj.*, arithmetic.

AR.LE.QUIM, *s.m.*, harlequin.

AR.MA, *s.f.*, weapon arm, power, might, gun, arm.

AR.MA.ÇÃO, *s.f.*, equipment, tackle, outfit.

AR.MA.DA, *s.f.*, armada, fleet, navy.

AR.MA.DI.LHA, *s.f.*, snare, gin, net, pitfall, trap.

AR.MA.DO, *adj.*, armed, equipped, prepared.

AR.MA.DOR, *s.m.*, shipowner, trapper.

AR.MA.DU.RA, *s.f.*, armour, armament, shell (animal), armature.

AR.MA.MEN.TIS.MO, *s.m.*, arms build-up.

AR.MA.MEN.TIS.TA, *adj.*, concerning the use of military strenght; *corrida ~*: arms race.

AR.MA.MEN.TO, *s.m.*, armament.

AR.MAR, *v.*, to arm, to put in arms, to supply with armament.

AR.MA.RI.A, *s.f.*, arsenal, armoury.

AR.MA.RI.NHO, *s.m.*, *UK* haberdashery; *US* notions store.

AR.MÁ.RIO, *s.m.*, cupboard, buffet, case, locker.

AR.MA.ZÉM, *s.m.*, store, shop, warehouse charges.

AR.MA.ZE.NA.GEM, *s.f.*, storage, warehousing.

AR.MA.ZE.NAR, *v.*, to store, to lay up, to stock-pile.

AR.MEI.RO, *s.m.*, armourer, armoury, gunman.

AR.MÊ.NI.A, *s.*, Armenia.

AR.MÊ.NI.CO, *s.m.*, Armenian; *adj.*, Armenian.

AR.MÊ.NI.O, *s.m.*, *adj.*, Armenian.

AR.MEN.TO, *s.m.*, herd of cattle.

AR.MI.NHO, *s.m.*, ermine.

AR.MIS.TÍ.CIO, *s.m.*, armistice, truce, suspension of hostilities.

AR.NI.CA, *s.f.*, *Bot.*, arnica.

A.RO, *s.m.*, iron or wooden hoop, rim of wheel.

A.RO.EI.RA, *s.f.*, *Bot.*, peppertree.

A.RO.MA, *s.f.*, flavour, smell, scent, bouquet.

A.RO.MÁ.TI.CO, *adj.*, aromatical, balsamic, flavoured.

A.RO.MA.TI.ZA.ÇÃO, *s.f.*, aromatization.

A.RO.MA.TI.ZA.DO, *adj.*, flavoured.

A.RO.MA.TI.ZAR, *v.*, to aromatize, to scent, to flavour.

AR.PÃO, *s.m.*, harpoon, gaff, fish-gig.

ARPAR · · 95 · · ARREMATAR

AR.PAR, *v.*, to harpoon.
AR.PE.JO, *s.m.*, *Mús.*, *arpeggio*.
AR.PO.A.DOR, *s.m.*, harpooner.
AR.PO.AR, *v.*, to harpoon.
AR.QUE.A.ÇÃO, *s.f.*, arching.
AR.QUE.A.DO, *adj.*, arch-shaped, arched, bent.
AR.QUE.AR, *v.*, to arch, to vault, to bow, to curve, to warp.
AR.QUEI.RO, *s.m.*, archer; *Esp.*, goalkeper (soccer).
AR.QUE.JA.MEN.TO, *s.m.*, the same that *arquejo*.
AR.QUE.JAR, *v.*, to puff, to blow, to pant.
AR.QUE.JO, *s.m.*, panting; gasp.
AR.QUE.O.LO.GI.A, *s.f.*, archaeology.
AR.QUE.Ó.LO.GO, *s.m.*, archaeologist.
AR.QUE.TE, *s.m.*, *Mús.*, arch, little bow; burial urn.
AR.QUE.TÍ.PI.CO, *adj.*, archetypal, archetypical.
AR.QUÉ.TI.PO, *s.m.*, archetype.
AR.QUI.BAN.CA.DA, *s.f.*, *Bras.*, rows of seats in a stadium; US bleachers; terrace(s).
AR.QUI.DI.O.CE.SE, *s.f.*, archdiocese.
AR.QUI.DU.QUE, *s.m.*, archduke.
AR.QUI.DU.QUE.SA, *s.f.*, archduchess.
AR.QUI.E.PIS.CO.PAL, *adj.*, archiepiscopal.
AR.QUI-I.NI.MI.GO, *s.m.*, archenemy, archifiend.
AR.QUI.MI.LI.O.NÁ.RI.O, *s.m.*, multimillionaire.
AR.QUI.PÉ.LA.GO, *s.m.*, *Geogr.*, archipelago.
AR.QUI.TE.TAR, *v.*, to build, to construct, to project, to plan.
AR.QUI.TE.TO, *s.m.*, architect, master builder.
AR.QUI.TE.TÔ.NI.CO, *adj.*, architectonic; architectural.
AR.QUI.TE.TU.RA, *s.f.*, architectonics, architecture.
AR.QUI.VA.MEN.TO, *s.m.*, filing (documents); shelving.
AR.QUI.VAR, *v.*, to collect documents, to shelve, to file.
AR.QUI.VIS.TA, *s.* 2 *gen.*, archivist.
AR.QUI.VÍS.TI.CA, *s.f.*, archival science, archival studies.
AR.QUI.VO, *s.m.*, archive, register, index book.
AR.RA.BAL.DE, *s.m.*, adjacency, environs, suburbs.
AR.RAI.A, *s.f.*, *Zool.*, ray, skate; frontier, border.
AR.RAI.AL, *s.m.*, camp, camping ground, country, small village.
AR.RAI.A-MI.Ú.DA, *s.f.*, *col.*, hoi polloi, the populace.
AR.RAI.GA.DO, *adj.*, deep-rooted; inveterate, staunch.
AR.RAI.GAR, *v.*, to root, to take root, to irradicate, to grow.
AR.RA.MAR, *v.*, to spread, to ramify.
AR.RAN.CA.DA, *s.f.*, pull, ready start, jerk, dash.
AR.RAN.CAR, *v.*, to pull or tear away violently, to pluck out, to force.
AR.RAN.CA-RA.BO, *s.m.*, *pop.*, shindy, scuffle, melee.
AR.RAN.CO, *s.m.*, tug, jerk away, sudden pull.
AR.RA.NHA-CÉU, *s.m.*, skyscraper.
AR.RA.NHA.DU.RA, *s.f.*, the same that *arranhão*.
AR.RA.NHÃO, *s.m.*, scratch, light wound.
AR.RA.NHAR, *v.*, to scratch, to graze, to scrabble, to mangle.
AR.RAN.JA.DOR, *s.m.*, *Mús.*, arranger.
AR.RAN.JA.MEN.TO, *s.m.*, arrangement, disposal, composition, agreement.
AR.RAN.JAR, *v.*, to arrange, to provide for, to set in order, to adjust, to dispose.
AR.RAN.JO, *s.m.*, arrangement, settling, fixing.
AR.RAN.QUE, *s.m.*, push, thrust, sudden start.
AR.RA.SA.DO, *adj.*, levelled, laid even, demolished.
AR.RA.SA.DOR, *s.m.*, demolisher, devastating, overwhelming.
AR.RAS, *s.f.*, *pl.*, pledge, token; earnest money; jointure.

AR.RA.SA.DO, *adj.*, levelled, razed, demolished; exhausted.
AR.RA.SAR, *v.*, to demolish, to humiliate, to destroy.
AR.RAS.TA.DI.ÇO, *adj.*, easily dragged.
AR.RAS.TA.DO, *adj.*, sluggish, dragged, miserable.
AR.RAS.TÃO, *s.m.*, wrench, dragging, jerk; draw along; trawl.
AR.RAS.TA-PÉ, *s.m.*, *Bras.*, shindig.
AR.RAS.TAR, *v.*, to drag, to pull, to induce into, to draw.
AR.RAS.TO, *s.m.*, trailing; dragging, drag; trawl.
AR.RA.ZO.A.DO, *s.m.*, defence; *adj.*, reasoned, rational.
AR.RA.ZO.AR, *v.*, to plead, to defend, to reason, to argue.
AR.RE, *interj.*, dammit! geep up! yah!
AR.RE.A.DO, *adj.*, harnessed.
AR.RE.AR, *v.*, to harness, to array, to dress, to adorn.
AR.RE.BA.NHA.DOR, *s.m.*, herder, shepherd; *adj.*, herding.
AR.RE.BA.NHAR, *v.*, to herd; *fig.*, to gather.
AR.RE.BA.TA.DO, *adj.*, impetuous, passionate, tempered.
AR.RE.BA.TA.DOR, *s.m.*, ravishing, charming, ravisher.
AR.RE.BA.TA.MEN.TO, *s.m.*, ravishing, ecstasy.
AR.RE.BA.TAR, *v.*, to snatch, to grab, to take by force, to rash, to rap.
AR.RE.BEN.TA.ÇÃO, *s.f.*, the breaking of the waves.
AR.RE.BEN.TA.DO, *adj.*, broken; *fig.*, battered, worn out.
AR.RE.BEN.TAR, *v.*, to bear, to burst, to crush, to break.
AR.RE.BI.TA.DO, *adj.*, snub, turned up; pert.
AR.RE.BI.TA.MEN.TO, *s.m.*, raising, turning up.
AR.RE.BI.TAR, *v.*, to turn up, to raise, to lift, to rivet.
AR.RE.BI.TE, *s.m.*, rivet.
AR.RE.BOL, *s.m.*, aurora, afterglow; redness of the sunrise.
AR.RE.CA.DA.ÇÃO, *s.f.*, magazine, deposit, depository, collection of taxes.
AR.RE.CA.DA.MEN.TO, *s.m.*, collecting (tax); safekeeping.
AR.RE.CA.DAR, *v.*, to collect duties or taxes, to deposit, to demand.
AR.RE.CI.FE, *s.m.*, reef.
AR.RE.DA.DO, *adj.*, withdrawn, removed.
AR.RE.DAR, *v.*, to remove, to withdraw.
AR.RE.DÁ.VEL, *adj.*, removable.
AR.RE.DI.O, *adj.*, withdrawn, far off, lonesome, apart.
AR.RE.DON.DA.DO, *adj.*, round, roundish.
AR.RE.DON.DA.MEN.TO, *s.m.*, roundness, rounding off.
AR.RE.DON.DAR, *v.*, to make round, to round, to sphere, to circularize.
AR.RE.DOR, *adj.*, adjacent, near; *adv.*, around, about.
AR.RE.DO.RES, *s.m.*, *pl.*, environs, environment, adjacency.
AR.RE.FE.CER, *v.*, to cool, to chill, to allay, to moderate.
AR.RE.FE.CI.MEN.TO, *s.m.*, cooling.
AR.RE.FRI.GE.RA.DO, *s.m.*, air-conditioning.
AR.RE.GA.ÇAR, *v.*, to tuck up, to pin up, to truss.
AR.RE.GA.LA.DO, *adj.*, wide-open (eyes); staring.
AR.RE.GA.LAR, *v.*, to open one's eyes wide, to google.
AR.RE.GA.NHA.DO, *adj.*, gaping, showing the teeth.
AR.RE.GA.NHAR, *v.*, to grin, to laugh, to snarl.
AR.RE.GI.MEN.TAR, *v.*, to regiment, to drum up.
AR.REI.O, *s.m.*, saddlery, harness, gear, array.
AR.RE.LI.A.DO, *adj.*, *pop.*, quarrelsome, insolent.
AR.RE.LI.A, *s.f.*, tease, vexation, bad omen.
AR.RE.LI.AR, *v.*, to tease, to annoy, to bother.
AR.RE.LI.EN.TO, *adj.*, teasing, irritating, disgusting.
AR.RE.MA.TA.ÇÃO, *s.f.*, public sale, auction, finishing.
AR.RE.MA.TAR, *v.*, to finish up, to give the final touch to, to accomplish.

ARREMATE · · 96 · · ARTIFICIOSO

AR.RE.MA.TE, *s.m.*, finish, finishin off, end, conclusion.
AR.RE.ME.DAR, *v.*, to imitate, to mimic, to mock.
AR.RE.ME.DO, *s.m.*, imitation, mimicry; mockery.
AR.RE.MES.SAR, *v.*, to fling, to dart, to throw, to hurl, to cast; to jaculate.
AR.RE.MES.SO, *s.m.*, throw, cast, pitch, act or fact of.
AR.RE.ME.TER, *v.*, to assault, to invade, to attack, to rush violently upon.
AR.RE.ME.TI.DA, *s.f.*, attack, assault, onset, dash.
AR.REN.DA.DO, *adj.*, rented, leased; laced.
AR.REN.DA.MEN.TO, *s.m.*, renting, lease, tenantry.
AR.REN.DAR, *v.*, to rent, to lease, to hire.
AR.REN.DA.TÁ.RIO, *s.m.*, tenant, renter, leaseholder.
AR.RE.NE.GA.DO, *s.m., pop.*, devil; *adj.*, renegate, apostate.
AR.RE.NE.GAR, *v.*, to abjure, to forswear, to execrate.
AR.RE.PEN.DER-SE, *v.*, to repent, to be sorry for, regret, to rue.
AR.RE.PEN.DI.DO, *adj.*, regretful, penitent, rueful.
AR.RE.PEN.DI.MEN.TO, *s.m.*, regret, penitence, repentance, rue, compunction.
AR.RE.PI.A.DO, *adj.*, goose-pimpled (skin); unkempt, hispid, *fig.*, distrustful.
AR.RE.PI.AN.TE, *adj.*, bristly, upstanding, terrifying.
AR.RE.PI.AR, *v.*, to ruffle, to fluff up, to bristle, to roughen.
AR.RE.PI.O, *s.m.*, goose-flesh, shiver, chill.
AR.RES.TA.DO, *s.m., Jur.*, person under an attachment; *adj.*, under an embargo.
AR.RES.TO, *s.m., Jur.*, confiscation, arest; attachment.
AR.RE.TA.DO, *adj., pop.*, lustful; *Bras.*, smart, beautiful, good, assertive.
AR.RE.VE.SA.DO, *adj.*, obscure, intricate, complicated.
AR.RI.A.DO, *adj.*, powerless, prostrated, cheerless, very tired.
AR.RI.AR, *v.*, to break down, to collapse, to flop, to put down.
AR.RI.BA, *adv.*, upward, above; *interj.*, onward!
AR.RI.BAR, *v.*, to land; to migrate; to attain one's aim; to depart.
AR.RI.MAR, *v.*, to support, to lean against, to prop, to rhime.
AR.RI.MO, *s.m.*, support, prop, help, protection.
AR.RIS.CA.DO, *adj.*, dangerous, risky, hazardous, daring.
AR.RIS.CAR, *v.*, to risk, to dare, to gamble.
AR.RIT.MI.A, *s.f., Med.*, arrhythmia.
AR.RÍT.MI.CO, *adj.*, arrhythmical, arrhythmic.
AR.RI.VIS.TA, *s. 2 gen.*, arriviste, opportunist; *adj.*, opportunistic.
AR.RO.BA, *s.f.*, arroba, unit of weight (15 kg).
AR.RO.BUS.TAR, *v.*, to strengthen, invigorate.
AR.RO.CHA.DO, *adj.*, bold, daring, fearless.
AR.RO.CHAR, *v.*, to tighten, to compress, to cram.
AR.RO.CHO, *s.m.*, tightening stick; lessening; garrote.
AR.RO.GÂN.CIA, *s.f.*, arrogance, presumption, pride, haughtiness.
AR.RO.GAN.TE, *adj., s. 2 gen.*, arrogant, superior, disdainful, haughty.
AR.RO.GAR, *v.*, to arrogate, to usurp; *arrogar-se*: to claim.
AR.RO.GO, *s.m.*, the same that *arrogância*.
AR.RO.IO, *s.m.*, arroyo, rivulet, brook.
AR.RO.JA.DO, *adj.*, bold, daring, rash; enterprising, active.
AR.RO.JAR, *v.*, to fling, to throw violently, to drag, to reject, to repel.
AR.RO.JO, *s.m.*, boldness, audacity, fearlessness.
AR.RO.LA.MEN.TO, *s.m.*, enrolment, register, list, roll.
AR.RO.LAR, *v.*, to enroll, to inscribe, to list.

AR.RO.LHAR, *v.*, to corck.
AR.ROM.BA.DO, *adj.*, forced open, broken up.
AR.ROM.BA.MEN.TO, *s.m.*, breaking in, inbreak.
AR.ROM.BAR, *v.*, to break into, to burst, to force.
AR.RO.TAR, *v.*, to belch, to burp, to boast.
AR.RO.TO, *s.m.*, eructation, belch.
AR.ROU.BO, *s.m.*, dellirium, moment of ecstasy; flight.
AR.RO.XA.DO, *adj.*, violet, violaceous, purplish.
AR.RO.XAR, *v.*, to become purplish, make violaceo.
AR.RO.XE.A.DO, *adj.*, the same that *arroxado*.
AR.RO.XE.AR, *v.*, the same that *arroxar*.
AR.ROZ, *s.m.*, rice.
AR.RO.ZAL, *s.m.*, rice field, rice paddy.
AR.ROZ-DO.CE, *s.m., Cul.*, rice pudding.
AR.RO.ZEI.RA, *s.f.*, the same that *arrozal*.
AR.RU.A.ÇA, *s.f.*, uproar, street riot, tumult.
AR.RU.A.CEI.RO, *s.m.*, street rioter; *adj.*, rowdy.
AR.RU.DA, *s.f., Bot.*, rue, herbe-of-grace.
AR.RU.E.LA, *s.f.*, washer, roundel.
AR.RU.I.NA.DO, *adj.*, ruined, spoiled, bankrupt.
AR.RUI.NA.MEN.TO, *s.m.*, ruin.
AR.RU.I.NAR, *v.*, to ruin, to destroy, to devastate, to blight.
AR.RUI.VA.DO, *adj.*, reddish (hair).
AR.RU.LHAR, *v.*, to coo (the birds); to lull asleep.
AR.RU.LHO, *s.m.*, cooing; lullaby; a lully asleep.
AR.RU.MA.ÇÃO, *s.f.*, arrangement, putting in order, placing, disposition, shipment.
AR.RU.MA.DEI.RA, *s.f.*, housemaid, chamber maid.
AR.RU.MAR, *v.*, to arrange, to dispose, to set in order, to settle, to tidy up, to pack.
AR.SE.NAL, *s.m.*, arsenal, repository of provisions.
AR.SÊ.NI.CO, *s.m., Quím.*, arsenic (arsenic trioxide).
AR.SÊ.NI.O, *s.m., Quím.*, arsenic.
AR.TE, *s.f.*, art, skill, craft, workmanship, trade, profession.
AR.TE.FA.TO, *s.m.*, workmanship, artifact; petard.
AR.TE-FI.NAL, *s.f.*, artwork.
AR.TEI.RO, *adj.*, mischievous, naughty; crafty, cunning.
AR.TE.LHO, *s.m., Anat.*, ankle, anklebone.
AR.TÉ.RIA, *s.f.*, artery, blood vessel.
AR.TE.RI.AL, *adj.*, arterial.
AR.TE.RI.OS.CLE.RO.SE, *s.f., Med.*, arteriosclerosis.
AR.TE.SA.NA.TO, *s.m.*, workmanship, handicraft.
AR.TE.SA.NAL, *adj.*, relating to handicraft, craftwork.
AR.TE.SA.NA.TO, *s.m.*, workmanship, handiwork, handicraft.
AR.TE.SÃO, *s.m.*, artisan, craftsman.
AR.TE.SI.A.NO, *adj.*, artesian; *poço ~*: artesian well.
ÁR.TI.CO, *adj., Geogr.*, arctic.
AR.TI.CU.LA.ÇÃO, *s.f.*, articulation, joint, link.
AR.TI.CU.LA.DO, *adj.*, articulated; articulate, hinged, jointed.
AR.TI.CU.LAR, *adj.*, articular; *v.*, to articulate, to join by articulation.
AR.TI.CU.LÁ.VEL, *adj.*, articulable.
AR.TI.CU.LIS.TA, *s. 2 gen.*, newspaper writter.
AR.TÍ.FI.CE, *s. 2 gen.*, craftsman, artificer, artist; *fig.*, author.
AR.TI.FI.CI.AL, *adj., s. 2 gen.*, artificial, artful, unnatural.
AR.TI.FI.CI.A.LI.DA.DE, *s.f.*, artificiality, artificialness.
AR.TI.FI.CI.A.LIS.MO, *s.m.*, the same that *artificialidade*.
AR.TI.FI.CI.A.LI.ZAR, *v.*, to artificialize, make artificial.
AR.TI.FI.CI.AL.MEN.TE, *adv.*, artificially.
AR.TI.FÍ.CIO, *s.m.*, artifice, skilful making, work of art.
AR.TI.FI.CI.O.SO, *adj.*, skillful, cunning, clever, fraudulent.

ARTIGO · 97 · · ASSENTAR

AR.TI.GO, *s.m.*, article, commodity, product, chapter, clause of a contract.
AR.TI.LHA.RI.A, *s.f.*, artillery, gunnery.
AR.TI.LHEI.RO, *s.m.*, gunner, cannoneer; *Bras., Esp.*, striker (soccer).
AR.TIS.TA, *s. 2 gen.*, artist, artisan; *adj.*, artistic, cunning.
AR.TIS.TI.CA.MEN.TE, *adj.*, artistically.
AR.TÍS.TI.CO, *adj.*, artistic, artistical.
AR.TRI.TE, *s.f.*, arthritis.
AR.TRI.TI.CO, *adj.*, arthritic.
AR.TRO.PA.TI.A, *s.f.*, arthropathy.
AR.TRÓ.PO.DE, *s.m.*, *Zool.*, arthropod; *adj.*, arthropodal.
AR.TROS.CO.PI.A, *s.f.*, *Med.*, arthroscopy.
AR.TRO.SE, *s.f.*, *Med.*, arthrosis.
AR.VO.RAR, *v.*, to hoist colours, to raise, to lift the flag, to set up.
ÁR.VO.RE, *s.f.*, arbor, tree, mast.
AR.VO.RE.DO, *s.m.*, grove, stand of tree.
AS, *art. pl.*, the; *pron.*, those, them; the ones.
ÀS, *contr.* of the *art.* **A** with the *prep.* **A**: to the, for the, by the.
ÁS, *s.m.*, ace, star.
A.SA, *s.f.*, wing.
A.SA-DEL.TA, *s.f.*, *Esp.*, hang glider, hang-gliding.
A.SA.DO, *s.m.*, a vase with ears; *adj.*, winged.
A.SAR, *v.*, to furnish with wings.
AS.BES.TO, *s.m.*, asbestos (mining).
AS.CEN.DÊN.CI.A, *s.f.*, ascending line; ascendency, ancestry; influence, superiority.
AS.CEN.DEN.TE, *s.m.*, ancestor; *Astrol.*, ascendent; *adj.*, rising, ascendant.
AS.CEN.DER, *v.*, to ascend, to rise, to climb.
AS.CEN.SÃO, *s.f.*, ascension, ascent, rising.
AS.CEN.SI.O.NAL, *adj.*, *Astron.*, ascensional.
AS.CEN.SO.RIS.TA, *s. 2 gen.*, lift boy, elevator operator.
AS.CE.SE, *s.f.*, ascesis, asceticism.
AS.CE.TA, *s. 2 gen.*, ascetic.
AS.CÉ.TI.CO, *adj.*, ascetic, ascetical.
AS.CE.TIS.MO, *s.m.*, asceticism.
AS.CO, *s.m.*, loathing, aversion, disgust.
AS.CÓR.BI.CO, *adj.*, *Quím.*, ascorbic.
AS.FAL.TA.DO, *adj.*, asphalted.
AS.FAL.TAR, *v.*, to cover with asphalt.
AS.FÁL.TI.CO, *adj.*, asphaltic.
AS.FAL.TO, *s.m.*, asphalt.
AS.FI.XI.A, *s.f.*, asphyxia.
AS.FI.XI.A.DOR, *adj.*, asphyxiating.
AS.FI.XI.AN.TE, *adj.*, asphyxiating, suffocating; *fig.*, oppressive.
AS.FI.XI.AR, *v.*, to asphyxiate, to suffocate.
Á.SIA, *s.*, Asia (the continent).
A.SI.Á.TI.CO, *adj.*, Asiatic.
A.SI.LA.DO, *s.m.*, inmate of an asylum; refugee.
A.SI.LAR, *v.*, to shelter, to give shelter, to refuge.
A.SI.LO, *s.m.*, asylum, refuge, place of refuge.
AS.MA, *s.f.*, asthma.
AS.MÁ.TI.CO, *s.m.*, asthmatic; *adj.*, asthmatic.
AS.NA.DA, *s.f.*, a drove of asses or donkeys.
AS.NEI.RA, *s.f.*, foolishness, stupidity, folly.
AS.NO, *s.m.*, ass, donkey; stupid, ignorant person.
AS.PAR.GO, *s.m.*, asparagus.
AS.PA, *s.f.*, St. Andrew's cross (X); *aspas* (*pl.*): inverted commas.

AS.PAR.GO, *s.m.*, *Bot.*, asparagus.
AS.PAR.TA.ME, *s.m.*, *Quím.*, aspartame.
AS.PAS, *s.f., pl.*, quotation marks (" "), inverted commas; *Bras.*, horns.
AS.PE.AR, *v.*, to place between inverted commas.
AS.PEC.TO, *s.m.*, aspect, look, appearance, form, shape, feature.
AS.PE.RA.MEN.TE, *adv.*, harshly, roughly, austerely.
AS.PE.RE.ZA, *s.f.*, asperity, roughness, rudeness.
AS.PER.GIR, *v.*, to sprinkle, asperse.
ÁS.PE.RO, *adj.*, rough, coarse, rude, crude, rugged.
AS.PER.SÃO, *s.f.*, aspersion, sprinkling.
AS.PER.SO, *adj.*, aspersed, besprinkled.
AS.PI.RA.ÇÃO, *s.f.*, breathing, aspiration, longing.
AS.PI.RA.DOR, *s.m.*, aspirator, exhaustor; ~ *de pó*: vacuum cleaner.
AS.PI.RAN.TE, *s. 2 gen.*, aspirant, candidate; *Mil.*, cadet; *adj.*, aspirant, aspiring.
AS.PI.RAR, *v.*, to aspirate, to breathe in, to inhale.
AS.PI.RI.NA, *s.f.*, aspirin.
AS.QUE.RO.SO, *adj.*, loathsome, nasty, nauseous, detestable.
AS.SA.DEI.RA, *s.f.*, roasting or baking pan.
AS.SA.DO, *s.m.*, roast; *adj.*, roasted, baked.
AS.SA.DOR, *s.m.*, roaster; (roasting) spit.
AS.SA.DU.RA, *s.f.*, napy rash (baby); roasting, baking.
AS.SA.LA.RI.A.DO, *s.m.*, employee; *adj.*, employed.
AS.SA.LA.RI.AR, *v.*, to engage, to employ, to take in pay, to subsidize.
AS.SAL.TAN.TE, *s. 2 gen.*, assailant, burglar, waylayer.
AS.SAL.TAR, *v.*, to assault, to attack, to charge, to storm.
AS.SAL.TO, *s.m.*, assault, attack, onset.
AS.SA.NHA.DO, *adj.*, excited, furious, restless, erotic.
AS.SA.NHA.MEN.TO, *s.m.*, excitement, anger.
AS.SA.NHAR, *v.*, to provoke, to excite, to anger.
AS.SAR, *v.*, to roast, to bake, to grill.
AS.SAS.SI.NA.DO, *adj.*, assassinated, killed, murdered.
AS.SAS.SI.NAR, *v.*, to murder, to assassinate, to kill.
AS.SAS.SI.NA.TO, *s.m.*, assassination, murder, homicide.
AS.SAS.SÍ.NI.O, *s.m.*, the same that *assassinato*.
AS.SAS.SI.NO, *s.m.*, murderer, killer, assassin.
AS.SAZ, *adv.*, quite; sufficiently, enough.
AS.SE.A.DO, *adj.*, clean, neat; spruce, trim.
AS.SE.AR, *v.*, clean up, adorn, trim.
AS.SE.DI.A.DOR, *s.m.*, besieger, *fig.*, bore; *adj.*, besieging; *fig.*, boring.
AS.SE.DI.AR, *v.*, to besiege, to importune, to molest, to annoy.
AS.SÉ.DIO, *s.m.*, siege, insistence, importunement, molestation.
AS.SE.GU.RA.DO, *adj.*, insured, assured.
AS.SE.GU.RAR, *v.*, to assert, to affirm, to guarantee, to assure, to secure.
AS.SEI.O, *s.m.*, cleanliness, neatness, decency.
AS.SEM.BLEI.A, *s.f.*, assembly, meeting, gathering, congregation.
AS.SE.ME.LHAR, *v.*, to assimilate, to liken to.
AS.SE.NHO.RE.AR-SE, *v.*, to take possession (of); to domineer.
AS.SEN.TA.DO, *adj.*, seated, steady, firm.
AS.SEN.TA.MEN.TO, *s.m.*, seating, sitting down, putting into place.
AS.SEN.TAR, *v.*, to seat, to place, to base, to lay, to settle,

ASSENTE ·· 98 ·· ATACANTE

to fix.

AS.SEN.TE, *adj.*, agreed; firm, established; settled.

AS.SEN.TI.MEN.TO, *s.m.*, assent, consent, permission.

AS.SEN.TIR, *v.*, to assent, to agree, to consent.

AS.SEN.TO, *s.m.*, seat, place to sit, chair, base, fundaments.

AS.SEP.SI.A, *s.f., Med.*, asepsis.

AS.SÉP.TI.CO, *adj., Med.*, aseptic.

AS.SER.ÇÃO, *s.f.*, assertion; affirmation, allegation.

AS.SER.TI.VA, *s.f.*, assertion.

AS.SES.SOR, *s.m.*, assessor, adviser, counsellor.

AS.SES.SO.RA.DO, *adj.*, advisee, assisted.

AS.SES.SO.RA.MEN.TO, *s.m.*, assistance, advise.

AS.SES.SO.RAR, *v.*, to advise, to assist.

AS.SES.SO.RI.A, *s.f.*, consultancy, assistance; advisement.

AS.SE.VE.RA.ÇÃO, *s.f.*, assertion; asseveration, affirmation.

AS.SE.VE.RAR, *v.*, to asseverate, to assert, to affirm.

AS.SE.VE.RA.TI.VO, *adj.*, asseverative.

AS.SE.XU.A.DO, *adj.*, assexual, non-sexual.

AS.SI.DU.A.MEN.TE, *adv.*, assiduouly.

AS.SI.DU.I.DA.DE, *s.f.*, assiduity, regular attendance, diligence.

AS.SÍ.DUO, *adj.*, assiduous, sedulous, diligent.

AS.SIM, *adv.*, thus, so, in this manner, like this, such.

ASSIMETRIA, *s.f.*, asymmetry.

ASSIMÉTRICO, *adj.*, asymmetric, asymmetrical. ·

AS.SI.MI.LA.ÇÃO, *s.f.*, assimilation, absorption.

AS.SI.MI.LAR, *v.*, to assimilate, absorb.

AS.SI.MI.LÁ.VEL, *adj.*, assimilable.

AS.SI.NA.DO, *adj.*, signed, subscribed.

ASSINALADO, *adj.*, marked, signalized, distinguished, outstanding.

ASSINALAMENTO, *s.m.*, signalment.

AS.SI.NA.LAR, *v.*, to mark, to provide with a mark, to distinguish.

AS.SI.NA.LÁ.VEL, *adj.*, assignable, remarkable.

AS.SI.NAN.TE, *s. 2 gen.*, subscriber, signatory.

AS.SI.NAR, *v.*, to sign, to underwrite, to subscribe, note.

AS.SI.NA.TU.RA, *s.f.*, signature, subscription.

AS.SI.NÁ.VEL, *adj.*, signable.

AS.SIN.TO.MÁ.TI.CO, *adj., Med.*, asymptomatic.

AS.SIS.TÊN.CIA, *s.f.*, presence, attendance, audience, auditory, assistance, aid.

AS.SIS.TEN.TE, *s. 2 gen.*, assistant, helper, right hand.

AS.SIS.TIR, *v.*, to attend, to be present at, to assist, to aid.

AS.SO.A.LHA.DOR, *s.m.*, floor layer, newsmonger.

AS.SO.A.LHAR, *v.*, to lay a wood floor.

AS.SO.A.LHO, *s.m.*, floor.

AS.SO.AR, *v.*, to wipe or blow one's nose.

AS.SO.BER.BA.DO, *adj.*, snowed under; arrogant, proud.

AS.SO.BER.BA.MEN.TO, *s.m.*, overawing; an arrogant treatment.

AS.SO.BER.BAR, *v.*, to overload (with work); to treat with disdain; to humiliate, to dominate.

AS.SO.BI.A.DOR, *s.m.*, whistler.

AS.SO.BI.AR, *v.*, to whistle, to hiss, to hoot.

AS.SO.BI.O, *s.m.*, whistle, hiss.

AS.SO.CI.A.ÇÃO, *s.f.*, association, community, society, partnership.

AS.SO.CI.A.DO, *s.m.*, associate, partner; *adj.*, associated.

AS.SO.CI.AR-SE, *v.*, to associate with, to join, to unit.

AS.SO.CI.A.TI.VO, *adj.*, associative; sociable.

AS.SO.LAR, *v.*, to desolate, to devastate, to destroy, to ravage.

AS.SO.MA.DO, *adj.*, irascible, rash, overhasty.

AS.SO.MAR, *v.*, to appear (at); to ascend (to the top), to emerge, to loom.

AS.SOM.BRA.ÇÃO, *s.f.*, apparition, ghost, spook, terror.

AS.SOM.BRA.DO, *adj.*, haunted, terrified.

AS.SOM.BRAR, *v.*, to shade, to shadow, to darken, to terrify, to astonish.

AS.SOM.BRO, *s.m.*, surprise, admiration, astonishment, wonder.

AS.SOM.BRO.SO, *adj.*, amazing, terrific, frightening.

AS.SO.MO, *s.m.*, appearance; dawn; sign; irritation.

AS.SO.NÂN.CI.A, *s.f.*, assonance.

AS.SO.PRAR, *v.*, to blow, (sail) to blow out; to whisper, to suggest.

AS.SO.RE.A.MEN.TO, *s.m.*, silting up, accumulation of sand.

AS.SO.RE.AR, *v.*, to silt up.

AS.SO.VI.AR, AS.SO.BI.AR, *v.*, to whistle; to hiss.

AS.SO.VI.O, AS.SO.BI.O, *s.m.*, whistle, hiss.

AS.SU.MI.DO, *adj., col.*, assumed, acknowledge; out of the closet (gay).

AS.SU.MIR, *v.*, to assume, to take over, to shoulder.

AS.SUN.ÇÃO, *s.f.*, assumption; promotion; *Assunção de Nossa Senhora*: the Assumption of our Blessed Lady.

AS.SUN.TO, *s.m.*, subject, topic, theme, affair, matter, proposition.

AS.SUS.TA.DI.ÇO, *adj.*, nervous, easily frightened, skittish.

AS.SUS.TA.DO, *adj.*, frightened, afraid, timid, timorous.

AS.SUS.TA.DOR, *s.m.*, terrifying, alarming, startles.

AS.SUS.TAR, *v.*, to frighten, to startle, to alarm, to terrify.

AS.TE.CA, *s. 2 gen.*, Aztec; *adj.*, Aztect, Aztecan.

AS.TE.RIS.CO, *s.m.*, asterisk, star.

AS.TE.ROI.DE, *s.m.*, asteroid.

AS.TIG.MA.TIS.MO, *s.m., Med.*, astigmatism.

AS.TRAL, *s.m.*, mood, *adj.*, astral, starry; *Astrol.*, astological.

AS.TRO, *s.m., Astron.*, star.

AS.TRO.FÍ.SI.CA, *s.f., Astron.*, astrophysics.

AS.TRO.LÁ.BI.O, *s.m.*, astrolabe.

AS.TRO.LO.GI.A, *s.f.*, astrology.

AS.TRÓ.LO.GO, *s.m.*, astrologer.

AS.TRO.NAU.TA, *s. 2 gen.*, astronaut.

AS.TRO.NÁU.TI.CA, *s.f., Astron.*, astronautics.

AS.TRO.NA.VE, *s.f., Aeron.*, spaceship.

AS.TRO.NO.MI.A, *s.f.*, astronomy.

AS.TRO.NÔ.MI.CO, *adj., Astron.*, astronomic, astronomical, *fig.*, fantastic.

AS.TRÔ.NO.MO, *s.m.*, astronomer.

AS.TÚ.CIA, *s.f.*, astuteness, sagacity, smartness.

AS.TU.CI.O.SA.MEN.TE, *adv.*, astutely, shiftingly, trickishly.

AS.TU.CI.O.SO, *adj.*, astute, cunning, guileful, shifting, foxy.

AS.TU.TO; *adj.*, astute, smart, clever.

A.TA, *s.f.*, record, register, writing.

A.TA.BA.LHO.A.DO, *adj.*, disorderly, confused.

A.TA.BA.LHO.AR, *v.*, to botch, to bungle, to confuse, to flounder.

A.TA.BA.QUE, *s.m., Mús.*, atabaque, small drum.

A.TA.CA.DIS.TA, *s. 2 gen.*, wholesaler.

A.TA.CA.DO, *adj.*, attacked, laced, tied; *s.m.*, wholesale business.

A.TA.CAN.TE, *s. 2 gen.*, agressor, assailant; lineman.

ATACAR · 99 · ATORDOADO

A.TA.CAR, *v.*, to attack, to assault, to seize, to strike.
A.TA.DO, *adj.*, tied, bound, hampered, timid.
A.TA.DU.RA, *s.f.*, tie, band, ligature, string.
A.TA.LAI.A, *s.f.*, sentinel, watchtower.
A.TA.LHAR, *v.*, to block, to intercept, to impede; to short-cut.
A.TA.LHO, *s.m.*, bypath, sideway, bypass, crosscut.
A.TA.PE.TAR, *v.*, to carpet.
A.TA.QUE, *s.m.*, attack, assault, onset, fit, agression.
A.TAR, *v.*, to tie, to fasten, to lace, to bind, to dress.
A.TA.RAN.TA.DO, *adj.*, perplexed, confused, flustered, hectic.
A.TA.RAN.TAR, *v.*, to perplex, to fluster, to bewilder.
A.TA.RE.FA.DO, *adj.*, busy, occupied, engaged.
A.TA.RE.FAR, *v.*, to burden, to overload with work.
A.TAR.RA.CA.DO, *adj.*, thickset, short and stout.
A.TAR.RA.XAR, *v.*, to screw, to bolt (screw), to rivet.
A.TA.Ú.DE, *s.m.*, coffin, bier, tomb, casket.
A.TA.VI.AR, *v.*, to trim, to array, to embellish.
A.TÁ.VI.CO, *adj., Biol.*, atavistic.
A.TA.VIS.MO, *s.m.*, atavism.
A.TA.ZA.NAR, *v.*, to taunt.
A.TÉ, *prep.*, till, untill, by, up to, up till.
A.TE.AR, *v.*, to set fire, to inflame, to kindle.
A.TE.ÍS.MO, *s.m.*, atheism.
A.TE.LI.Ê, *s.m.*, studio (place where artists work).
A.TE.LHA.MEN.TO, *s.m.*, tiling of a roof.
A.TE.MO.RI.ZA.DO, *adj.*, frightened.
A.TE.MO.RI.ZA.DOR, *s.m.*, frightener; *adj.*, alarming, frightening.
A.TE.MO.RI.ZAN.TE, *adj.*, frightening, alarming.
A.TE.MO.RI.ZAR, *v.*, to intimidate, to scare, to daunt, to terrify.
A.TEN.ÇÃO, *s.f.*, attention, concentration, carefulness, vigilance.
A.TEN.CI.O.SA.MEN.TE, *adv.*, respectfully, consideratel.
A.TEN.CI.O.SO, *adj.*, attentive, respectful, considerate, polite, gallant.
A.TEN.DEN.TE, *s.f.*, auxiliary.
A.TEN.DER, *v.*, to attend, to consider, to mind, to pay attention, to listen.
A.TEN.DI.MEN.TO, *s.m.*, attendance, attending; *horário de* ~: opening times.
A.TE.NEU, *s.m.*, athenaeum.
A.TE.NI.EN.SE, *s. 2 gen.*, athenian.
A.TEN.TA.DO, *s.m.*, attack, assault, attempt.
A.TEN.TA.MEN.TE, *adv.*, attentively, closely.
A.TEN.TAR, *v.*, to attempt.
A.TEN.TO, *adj.*, alert, careful, observant.
A.TE.NU.A.ÇÃO, *s.f.*, attenuation, diminishing.
A.TE.NU.A.DOR, *adj.*, attenuating.
A.TE.NU.AN.TE, *s.f.*, attenuating, mitigating.
A.TE.NU.AR, *v.*, to attenuate, to extenuate, to lessen, to diminish.
A.TER, *v.*, to rely on, to lean against; *ater-se*: to stick to.
A.TER.RA.DO, *s.m.*, a filling up with earth, levelling; *adj.*, filled with earth; awe-stricken, frightened.
A.TER.RA.DOR, *adj.*, terrifying, frightful, appaling.
A.TER.RA.GEM, *v.*, the same that *aterrissagem*; a filling up with earth, levelling.
A.TER.RAR, *v.*, to frighten, to terrify; fill or cover with earth; to land.
A.TER.RIS.SA.GEM, *s.f.*, landing.
A.TER.RIS.SAR, *v.*, to land.

A.TER.RO, *s.m.*, embankment, place filled up with earth.
A.TER.RO.RI.ZA.DO, *adj.*, terrorized, terrified, frightened.
A.TER.RO.RI.ZA.DOR, *s.m.*, frightful, terrifying.
A.TER.RO.RI.ZAN.TE, *adj.*, frightful, terrifying.
A.TER.RO.RI.ZAR, *v.*, to terrify, to horrify, to frighten, to dismay.
A.TER-SE, *v.*, to lain against, to rely on, to stick to.
A.TES.TA.DO, *s.m.*, certificate, certification, credential.
A.TES.TAR, *v.*, to attest, to vouch, to witness, to certify.
A.TEU, *s.m.*, atheist; *adj.*, atheistic; godless.
A.TI.ÇA.MEN.TO, *s.m.*, instigation, provocation.
A.TI.ÇAR, *v.*, to poke, to instigate, to incite.
Á.TI.MO, *s.m.*, instant, moment.
A.TI.NA.DO, *adj.*, cautious, wise, heedful, prudent, sensible.
A.TI.NAR, *v.*, to understand using reasoning; to discover, find out; to realize.
A.TI.NEN.TE, *adj.*, referent, relative.
A.TIN.GIR, *v.*, to reach, to attain, to arrive at, to touch.
A.TIN.GÍ.VEL, *adj.*, attainable, achievable, touchable.
A.TÍ.PI.CO, *adj.*, atypical, untypical.
A.TI.RA.DEI.RA, *s.f.*, slingshot.
A.TI.RA.DO, *adj., col.*, bold, daring, forward; given to amorous affairs.
A.TI.RA.DOR, *s.m.*, shooter, rifleman, marksman, soldier.
A.TI.RAR, *v.*, to shoot, to fire, to rifle, to discharge.
A.TI.TU.DE, *s.f.*, attitude, posture, pose; mood, position.
A.TI.VA.ÇÃO, *s.f.*, activation.
A.TI.VA.MEN.TE, *adv.*, actively, busily, efficiently, vivaciously.
A.TI.VAR, *v.*, to activate, to actuate, to push, to bring into action.
A.TI.VI.DA.DE, *s.f.*, activity, energy, stir, bustle, function.
A.TI.VIS.MO, *s.m.*, activism.
A.TI.VIS.TA, *s.m.*, activist.
A.TI.VO, *adj.*, active, busy, brisk, dynamic, alert.
A.TLÂN.TI.CO, *s.m.*, Atlantic Ocean; *adj.*, Atlantic.
A.TLAS, *s.m.*, atlas.
A.TLE.TA, *s. 2 gen.*, athlete.
A.TLÉ.TI.CO, *adj.*, athletic; *fig.*, vigorous.
A.TLE.TIS.MO, *s.m.*, athletics.
AT.MOS.FE.RA, *s.f.*, atmosphere.
AT.MOS.FÉ.RI.CO, *adj.*, atmospheric, atmospherical.
A.TO, *s.m.*, act, performing, function, doing, action, deed.
À TOA, *adj.*, adrift; worthless, insignificant.
A.TO.A.LHA.DO, *adj.*, towelling.
A.TOL, *s.m.*, atoll.
A.TO.LA.DI.ÇO, *adj.*, miry, muddy.
A.TO.LA.DO, *adj.*, mired.
A.TO.LAR, *v.*, to stick in the dirt, to mud, to mir; to bog, to stall.
A.TO.LEI.RO, *s.m.*, quagmire, slough, marshy place, *fig.*, morass.
A.TO.MI.CI.DA.DE, *s.f., Fis., Quím.*, atomicity.
A.TÔ.MI.CO, *adj.*, atomic.
A.TO.MIS.MO, *s.m.*, atomism.
A.TO.MI.ZA.DOR, *s.m.*, atomizer, spray.
A.TO.MI.ZAR, *v.*, to atomize.
Á.TO.MO, *s.m.*, atom, corpuscle.
A.TO.NAL, *adj., Mús.*, atonal.
A.TO.NA.LI.DA.DE, *s.f., Mús.*, atonality.
A.TÔ.NI.TO, *adj.*, astonished, stupefied, aghast, perplexed.
A.TOR, *s.m.*, actor, artist, player; star.
A.TOR.DO.A.DO, *adj.*, stunned, dazed.

ATORDOADOR   •• 100 ••   AUMENTADOR

A.TOR.DO.A.DOR, *adj.*, stunning, stupefying.

A.TOR.DO.A.MEN.TO, *s.m.*, stunning, bewilderment, consciousness.

A.TOR.DO.AN.TE, *adj.*, stunning, stupefying.

A.TOR.DO.AR, *v.*, to stun, to stupefy, to consternate, to puzzle.

A.TOR.MEN.TA.DO, *adj.*, tormented.

A.TOR.MEN.TAR, *v.*, to torment, to torture, to afflict, to trouble.

A.TÓ.XI.CO, *adj.*, non-toxic, non-poisonous.

A.TRA.ÇÃO, *s.f.*, attraction, interest, affinity.

A.TRA.CA.ÇÃO, *s.f.*, docking, mooring; approach; scuffle.

A.TRA.CAR, *v.*, *Náut.*, to come alongside; to moor, to approach; *atracar-se*: to come to blows.

A.TRA.EN.TE, *adj.*, eye-catching, attractive, lovely.

A.TRAI.ÇO.AR, *v.*, to betray, to deceive, to delude, to play foul.

A.TRA.IR, *v.*, to attract, to captivate, to magnetize, to draw.

A.TRA.PA.LHA.ÇÃO, *s.f.*, confusion, disorder, muddle.

A.TRA.PA.LHA.DO, *adj.*, confused, confounded, puzzled.

A.TRA.PA.LHAR, *v.*, to confuse, to disturb, to upset, to perturb, to muddle.

A.TRÁS, *adv.*, behind, back, after, before, ago.

A.TRA.SA.DO, *adj.*, backward, retrograde, tardy, behind, late, slow.

A.TRA.SAR, *v.*, to set back, to delay, to retard, to defer, to postpone, to put off.

A.TRA.SO, *s.m.*, delay, retardation, tardiness, lateness, latecoming.

A.TRA.TI.VI.DA.DE, *s.f.*, attractiveness.

A.TRA.TI.VO, *s.m.*, appeal, charm, incentive; *adj.*, attractive.

A.TRA.VAN.CA.MEN.TO, *s.m.*, obstruction, encumbered.

A.TRA.VAN.CAR, *v.*, to clutter, to encumber, to embarrass, to obstruct.

A.TRA.VÉS, *adv.*, through, over, cross, across, athwart.

A.TRA.VES.SA.DO, *adj.*, crossed, laid across, athwart, oblique.

A.TRA.VES.SA.DOR, *adj.*, person who or thing that crosses; intermediary.

A.TRA.VES.SAR, *v.*, to cross, to pass over, to traverse, to overpass, to transit.

A.TRE.LAR, *v.*, to tie up, to harness, to leash.

A.TRE.VER-SE, *v.*, to dare, to adventure, to venture, to brave.

A.TRE.VI.DO, *adj.*, daring, bold, insolent, cheeky.

A.TRE.VI.MEN.TO, *s.m.*, dare, daring, daringness, boldness, impudence.

A.TRI.BU.I.ÇÃO, *s.f.*, attribution, duty, power, prerogative.

A.TRI.BU.IR, *v.*, to attribute, to impute to, to assign to.

A.TRI.BU.Í.VEL, *adj.*, attributable, ascribable.

A.TRI.BU.LA.ÇÃO, *s.f.*, tribulation, adversity.

A.TRI.BU.LA.DO, *adj.*, wretched, afflicted, troubled.

A.TRI.BU.LAR, *v.*, to afflict, to trouble, to vex.

A.TRI.BU.TI.VO, *adj.*, attributive.

A.TRI.BU.TO, *s.m.*, attribute, predicate, quality.

Á.TRI.O, *s.m.*, atrium; hallway, vestibule; courtyard.

A.TRIS.TAR, *v.*, to sadden, to grieve.

A.TRI.TAR, *v.*, to rub, to cause anguish.

A.TRI.TO, *s.m.*, attrition, friction, rubbing, dissension.

A.TRIZ, *s.f.*, actress, star.

A.TRO, *adj.*, atrous, black, dark; *fig.*, tenebrous.

A.TRO.A.DA, *s.f.*, loud noise; roar.

A.TRO.AR, *v.*, to thunder; to roar; to terrify; to stun.

A.TRO.CI.DA.DE, *s.f.*, atrocity, cruelty, inhumanity.

A.TRO.FI.A, *s.f.*, atrophy.

A.TRO.FI.A.DO, *adj.*, atrophied, atrophic, decayed.

A.TRO.FI.AR, *v.*, to atrophy.

A.TRO.PE.LA.DA.MEN.TE, *adv.*, chaotically.

A.TRO.PE.LA.MEN.TO, *s.m.*, running over; tumult.

A.TRO.PE.LAR, *v.*, to run over, to chash into, to push, *fig.*, to outrage.

A.TRO.PE.LO, *s.m.*, running-over, turmoil, problem.

A.TROZ, *adj.*, atrocious, terrible, cruel.

A.TROZ.MEN.TE, *adv.*, atrociously.

A.TU.A.ÇÃO, *s.f.*, actuation, performance.

A.TU.AL, *adj.*, actual, present, current, real, absolute.

A.TU.A.LI.DA.DE, *s.f.*, the present, the present time, opportunity.

A.TU.A.LI.ZA.ÇÃO, *s.f.*, modernization.

A.TU.A.LI.ZA.DO, *adj.*, up-to-date.

A.TU.A.LI.ZAR, *v.*, to modernize.

A.TU.AL.MEN.TE, *adv.*, nowadays, presently, currently.

A.TU.AN.TE, *adj.*, active, acting.

A.TU.CA.NAR, *v.*, to peck; *gir.*, to razz.

A.TU.AR, *v.*, to actuate, bring into action, put into action, to operate.

A.TU.LHA.MEN.TO, *s.m.*, a filling or heaping up, jam.

A.TU.LHAR, *v.*, to till or heap up; to jam; to overcrowd.

A.TUM, *s.m.*, *Zool.*, tuna, tunny.

A.TU.RAR, *v.*, to support, to suffer, to endure, to tolerate, to bear.

A.TU.RÁ.VEL, *adj.*, tolerable.

A.TUR.DI.DO, *adj.*, dizzy, stunned, perturbed.

A.TUR.DIR, *v.*, to stun, to din, to daze, to bewilder, to surprise.

AU.DÁ.CIA, *s.f.*, audacity, audaciousness, daring, presumption.

AU.DA.CI.O.SA.MEN.TE, *adv.*, boldly, fearlessly.

AU.DA.CI.O.SO, *adj.*, audacious, daring, intrepid; insolent.

AU.DAZ, *adj.*, audacious.

AU.DI.BI.LI.DA.DE, *s.f.*, audibility.

AU.DI.ÇÃO, *s.f.*, audition, reception, hearing.

AU.DI.ÊN.CIA, *s.f.*, audience, audition, assembly.

ÁU.DIO, *s.m.*, audio; sound (electronics); discourse (TV).

AU.DI.O.ME.TRI.A, *s.f.*, *Med.*, audiometry.

AU.DI.O.VI.SU.AL, *s.m.*, projector; *adj.*, audiovisual.

AU.DI.TAR, *v.*, *Jur.*, to audit.

AU.DI.TI.VO, *adj.*, auditive.

AU.DI.TOR, *s.m.*, auditor.

AU.DI.TO.RI.A, *s.f.*, audit; firm of accountants (enterprise).

AU.DI.TÓ.RIO, *s.m.*, audience, listeners, attendance.

AU.DÍ.VEL, *adj.*, audible, hearable.

AU.Ê, *s.m.*, *col.*, uproar, confusion, disorder.

AU.FE.RIR, *v.*, to gain, to profit, to make profit, to obtain.

AU.FE.RIR, *adj.*, that can be gained, obtained, profited.

AU.GE, *s.m.*, summit, height, the highest point, culmination, top, zenith.

AU.GU.RAR, *v.*, to augur, to predict, to forebode, to portend.

AU.GÚ.RIO, *s.m.*, augury, foretoken, presage.

AUGUSTO, *adj.*, august, venerable, majestic.

AU.LA, *s.f.*, class, lesson.

ÁU.LI.CO, *s.m.*, courtier; *adj.*, courtly

AU.LI.DO, *s.m.*, cry or howlling of animals.

AU.MEN.TA.DOR, *s.m.*, augmenter; amplifier; *adj.*, augmentative.

AUMENTAR ·· 101 ·· AVALIADOR

AU.MEN.TAR, *v.*, to augment, to enlarge, to amplify, to increase, to grow, to develop.

AU.MEN.TA.TI.VO, *s.m.*, *Gram.*, augmentative; *adj.*, augmentative.

AU.MEN.TÁ.VEL, *adj.*, augmentable, increasable.

AU.MEN.TO, *s.m.*, augmentation, enlarging, enlargement, amplification, development.

AU.RA, *s.f.*, aura; halo, breath of air; supposed emanation about some people; *fig.*, aura, fame.

ÁU.REO, *adj.*, aureate, golden, brilliant.

AU.RÉ.O.LA, *s.f.*, aureole, nimbus, glory.

AU.RÍ.CU.LA, *s.f.*, *Anat., Bot., Zool.*, auricle.

AU.RI.CU.LAR, *adj.*, auricular.

AU.RÍ.FE.RO, *adj.*, auriferous.

AU.RÍ.FI.CO, *adj.*, auriferous, golden.

AU.RO.RA, *s.f.*, aurora, dawn, daybreak, begin.

AU.RO.RAL, *adj.*, auroral.

AU.RO.RE.AL, *adj.*, auroral.

AUS.CUL.TAR, *v.*, to auscultate; to sound (out).

AU.SÊN.CIA, *s.f.*, absence, nonappearance, privation.

AU.SEN.TAR-SE, *v.*, to go away, to depart.

AU.SEN.TE, *adj.*, absent, away.

AUS.PI.CI.AR, *v.*, to augur, to predict.

AUS.PÍ.CI.O, *s.m.*, auspice, augury, sign.

AUS.PI.CI.O.SA.MEN.TE, *adv.*, auspiciously, fortunately.

AUS.PI.CI.O.SO, *adj.*, auspicious.

AUS.TE.RI.DA.DE, *s.f.*, austerity, severity, rigour.

AUS.TE.RO, *adj.*, austere, severe, rigorous, rigid, strict, grave.

AUS.TRAL, *adj.*, austral, southern.

AUS.TRÁ.LI.A, *s.*, Australia.

AUS.TRA.LI.A.NO, *s.m.*, Autralian; *adj.*, Australian.

ÁUS.TRI.A, *s.*, Austria;

AUS.TRÍ.A.CO, *s.m.*, *adj.*, Austrian.

AUS.TRO, *s.m.*, *Lit.*, southern, Auster.

AU.TAR.QUI.A, *s.f.*, autarchy.

AU.TÁR.QUI.CO, *adj.*, autarchic.

AU.TEN.TI.CA.ÇÃO, *s.f.*, authentication.

AU.TEN.TI.CAR, *v.*, to make authentic, authenticate.

AU.TEN.TI.CI.DA.DE, *s.f.*, authenticity, legality.

AU.TÊN.TI.CO, *adj.*, authentic, legitimate.

AU.TIS.MO, *s.m.*, *Med.*, autism.

AU.TIS.TA, *s. 2 gen.*, autist.

AU.TO, *s.m.*, solemnity, document; *Teat.*, medieval allegorical play; *abrev.* of *automóvel*: motor-car.

AU.TO.A.DE.SI.VO, *s.m.*, self-adhesive.

AU.TO.A.FIR.MA.ÇÃO, *s.f.*, self-affirmation, self-assertion.

AU.TO.A.NÁ.LI.SE, *s.f.*, self-analysis.

AU.TO.A.VA.LI.A.ÇÃO, *s.f.*, self-evaluation.

AU.TO.BI.O.GRA.FI.A, *s.f.*, autobiography.

AU.TO.BI.O.GRÁ.FI.CO, *adj.*, autobiographical.

AU.TO.CAR.RO, *s.m.*, *Port.*, omnibus, bus.

AU.TO.CON.FI.AN.ÇA, *s.f.*, auto-confidence.

AU.TO.CO.NHE.CI.MEN.TO, *s.m.*, self-knowledge.

AU.TO.CON.TRO.LE, *s.m.*, self-control.

AU.TO.CRA.TA, *s. 2 gen.*, autocrat; *adj.*, autocratic.

AU.TO.CRÍ.TI.CA, *s.f.*, self-criticism.

AU.TÓC.TO.NE, *s.m.*, autochthon, native; *adj.*, autochthonal, native.

AU.TO.DE.FE.SA, *s.f.*, self-defense.

AU.TO.DES.TRU.I.ÇÃO, *s.f.*, self-destruction.

AU.TO.DI.DA.TA, *s. 2 gen.*, self-taught person.

AU.TO.DIS.CI.PLI.NA, *s.f.*, self-discipline.

AU.TO.DO.MÍ.NIO, *s.m.*, self-control.

AU.TÓ.DRO.MO, *s.m.*, racetrack, motordrome.

AU.TO.ES.CO.LA, *s.f.*, driving school.

AU.TO.ES.TI.MA, *s.f.*, *Psic.*, self-esteem.

AU.TO.ES.TRA.DA, *s.f.*, arterial road, auto highway, expressway.

AU.TO.GRA.FAR, *v.*, to autograph.

AU.TÓ.GRA.FO, *s.m.*, autograph.

AU.TO.MA.TI.CA.MEN.TE, *adv.*, automatically, mechanically.

AU.TO.MA.ÇÃO, *s.f.*, automation.

AU.TO.MÁ.TI.CO, *adj.*, automatic, self-regulating.

AU.TO.MA.TI.ZA.ÇÃO, *s.f.*, automation, automatization.

AU.TO.MA.TI.ZAR, *v.*, to automatize.

AU.TÔ.MA.TO, *s.m.*, automaton, robot.

AU.TO.ME.DI.CAR-SE, *v.*, to self-medicate.

AU.TO.MO.BI.LIS.MO, *s.m.*, automobilism.

AU.TO.MO.BI.LIS.TA, *s. 2 gen.*, automobilist; *Esp.*, racing driver.

AU.TO.MO.BI.LÍS.TI.CO, *adj.*, automobilistic.

AU.TO.MO.TRIZ, *s.m.*, shuttle car; *adj.*, self-propelling, automotive.

AU.TO.MÓ.VEL, *s.m.*, automobile, motor-car, car.

AU.TO.NO.MI.A, *s.f.*, autonomy, self-government.

AU.TÔ.NO.MO, *adj.*, autonomous, independent.

AU.TO.PE.ÇA, *s.f.*, car part.

AU.TÓP.SIA, *s.f.*, autopsy.

AU.TOR, *s.m.*, author, writer, composer, creator, maker.

AU.TO.RA, *s.f.*, authoress.

AU.TO.RAL, *adj.*, authorial.

AU.TO.RI.A, *s.f.*, authorship, paternity.

AU.TO.RI.DA.DE, *s.f.*, authority, jurisdiction, influence.

AU.TO.RI.TÁ.RIO, *adj.*, despotic, authoritarian.

AU.TO.RI.TA.RIS.MO, *s.m.*, authoritarianism.

AU.TO.RI.ZA.ÇÃO, *s.f.*, authorization, permission, permit.

AU.TO.RI.ZA.DO, *adj.*, authorized, approved; afficial, trustworthy.

AU.TO.RI.ZAR, *v.*, to authorize, to permit, to allow, to sanction, to approve.

AU.TOR.RE.TRA.TO, *s.m.*, self-portrait.

AU.TOS.SU.FI.CI.EN.TE, *adj.*, *s. 2 gen.*, self-sufficient.

AU.TOS.SU.GES.TÃO, *s.f.*, auto-suggestion.

AU.TO.VI.A, *s.f.*, highway, expressway.

AU.TU.A.ÇÃO, *s.f.*, filing, collection of documents for lawsuit.

AU.TU.AR, *v.*, to report (occurrence); to write a statement on a person.

AU.XI.LI.A.DOR, *s.f.*, helper, auxiliary, assistant, supporter.

AU.XI.LI.AR, *s. 2 gen.*, assistant, adjudant; *adj.*, auxiliary, helpful; *v.*, to help, to aid, to assist.

AU.XÍ.LIO, *s.m.*, help, aid, succour, assistance, backing.

AU.XÍ.LI.O-DE.SEM.PRE.GO, *s.m.*, unemployment benefit.

AU.XÍ.LI.O-NA.TA.LI.DA.DE, *s.m.*, maternity grant.

AV., *abrev.* of *avenida*: avenue, Av.

A.VA.CA.LHA.ÇÃO, *s.f.*, negligence, desmoralization.

A.VA.CA.LHA.DO, *adj.*, messy, slipshod, dishevelled.

A.VA.CA.LHAR, *v.*, to demoralize, to depress, to lower.

A.VAL, *s.m.*, guaranty, surety, warranty.

A.VA.LAN.CHA, *s.f.*, the same that *avalanche*.

A.VA.LAN.CHE, *s.f.*, avalanche; *fig.*, deluge.

A.VA.LI.A.ÇÃO, *s.f.*, valuation, estimate, estimation, appraisement.

A.VA.LI.A.DOR, *s.m.*, appraiser, evaluator, estimator, rater.

AVALIAR ·· 102 ·· AZEITAR

A.VA.LI.AR, *v.*, to evaluate, to appraise, to prize, to value, to estimate.

A.VA.LI.Á.VEL, *adj.*, appraisable.

A.VA.LIS.TA, *s. 2 gen.*, bondsman.

A.VA.LI.ZAR, *v.*, to guarantee.

A.VAN.ÇA.DO, *adj.*, advanced, onward, progressive.

A.VAN.ÇAR, *v.*, to attach, to go, to bring forward, to make go on, go, advance.

A.VAN.ÇO, *s.m.*, advance, advancement, progress, progression, improvement.

A.VAN.TA.JA.DO, *adj.*, stout, strong, superior.

A.VAN.TA.JAR, *v.*, to ameliorate, to make better, improve, to be superior.

A.VAN.TE, *adv.*, forward, onward, forth, along; *interj.*, go it!, go ahead!

A.VA.RAN.DA.DO, *s.m.*, building with a veranda; *adj.*, verandahed.

A.VA.REN.TO, *s.m.*, miser, niggard, money-grubber, penny pincher.

A.VA.RE.ZA, *s.f.*, miserliness, avarice, avidity.

A.VA.RI.A, *s.f.*, damage, breakdown (car).

A.VA.RI.A.DO, *adj.*, damaged, averaged, destroyed.

A.VA.RI.AR, *v.*, to cause damage; to fail, to break down.

A.VA.RO, *s.m.*, miser; *adj.*, avaricious.

A.VAS.SA.LA.DOR, *s.m.*, conqueror, dominator; *adj.*, overwhelming, overpowerin.

A.VAS.SA.LAN.TE, *adj.*, vassalizing.

A.VAS.SA.LAR, *v.*, to vassal, to dominate, to subdue; to captivate.

A.VA.TAR, *s.m.*, avatar.

A.VE, *s.f.*, bird, fowl.

A.VE.AL, *s.m.*, field of oats.

A.VEI.A, *s.f.*, oat, oats, oatmeal.

A.VE.LÃ, *s.f.*, hazelnut.

A.VE.LEI.RA, *s.f., Bot.*, hazel.

A.VE.LA.NAL, *s.f.*, plantation of hazels.

A.VE.LU.DA.DO, *adj.*, velvety.

A.VE.LU.DAR, *v.*, to give appearance of velvet.

A.VE-MA.RI.A, *s.f.*, Ave Mary, Hail Mary.

A.VEN.CA, *s.f., Bot.*, maidenhair.

A.VE.NI.DA, *s.f.*, avenue, alley, parkway.

A.VEN.TAL, *s.m.*, apron, pinafore.

A.VEN.TAR, *v.*, to air; to hurl; to suggest (an idea).

A.VEN.TU.RA, *s.f.*, adventure, venture, hazard, risk.

A.VEN.TU.RA.DO, *adj.*, adventurous; fortunate; *bem-~*: blessed.

A.VEN.TU.RAR, *v.*, to risk, to venture.

A.VEN.TU.REI.RO, *s.m.*, adventurer, venturer; *adj.*, venturesome, venturous.

A.VER.BAR, *v.*, to protocol, to annotate, to note, to register, to legalize.

A.VE.RI.GUA.ÇÃO, *s.f.*, inquiry, investigation, finding.

A.VE.RI.GUAR, *v.*, to inquire, to investigate, to verify, to indagate.

A.VE.RI.GUÁ.VEL, *adj.*, examinable, investigable.

A.VER.ME.LHA.DO, *adj.*, reddish, russet.

A.VER.ME.LHA.MEN.TO, *s.m.*, reddening.

A.VER.ME.LHAR, *v.*, to redden, to make red.

A.VER.NAL, *adj.*, infernal, hellish.

A.VER.SÃO, *s.f.*, aversion, averseness, dislike.

A.VES.SO, *s.m.*, contrary, reverse, back, opposite.

A.VES.TRUZ, *s.m., Zool.*, ostrich, emu.

A.VE.XAR, *v.*, the same that *vexar*: to vexate.

A.VI.A.ÇÃO, *s.f.*, aviation, flying.

A.VI.A.DOR, *s.m.*, aviator, flyer, aeronaut.

A.VI.A.MEN.TO, *s.m.*, accessories; dispatching; notions (as for a dress), trimmings.

A.VI.ÃO, *s.f.*, aeroplane, airplane, plane, flying machine.

A.VI.AR, *v.*, to dispatch, to expedit, to ship, to put on the way.

A.VI.á.RIO, *s.m.*, aviary (vivarium of birds); *adj.*, aviam (relating to birds).

A.VI.CUL.TOR, *s.m.*, aviculturist, breeder.

A.VI.CUL.TU.RA, *s.f.*, aviculture, poultry raising.

A.VI.DEZ, *s.f.*, avidity, greediness, impatience, rapacity.

Á.VI.DO, *adj.*, eager, grasping, greedy, covertous.

A.VI.GO.RAR, *v.*, to invigorate, fortify.

A.VI.LA.NAR, *v.*, to become a villain.

A.VIL.TA.MEN.TO, *s.m.*, abasement, abjection, disgrace, dishonour.

A.VIL.TAN.TE, *adj.*, degrading, digraceful.

A.VIL.TAR, *v.*, to abase, to debase, to disgrace, to vilify, to depress.

A.VI.NA.GRA.DO, *adj.*, sourish, sour; *fig.*, ill-natured.

A.VI.NA.GRAR, *v.*, to season or mix with vinegar.

A.VI.SA.DO, *adj.*, discreet, prudent, advised.

A.VI.SAR, *v.*, to advise, to give notice, to inform, to notify.

A.VI.SO, *s.m.*, notice, advice, communication, warning.

A.VIS.TAR, *v.*, to see from a distance, to discover, to espy.

A.VI.VA.MEN.TO, *s.m.*, invigoration, enlivenment, revival.

A.VI.VAR, *v.*, to give life to, to revive, to vivify, to awake.

A.VI.ZI.NHAR, *v.*, to approach, to approximate, to bring near, to put near of.

A.VO, *s.m., Mat.*, fractional part; *um quatorze avos*: one fourteenth (1/14).

A.VÔ, *s.f.*, grandfather.

A.VÓ, *s.f.*, grandmother.

A.VO.A.DO, *adj.*, dizzy, giddy, senseless.

A.VO.CAR, *v., Jur.*, to appeal to a higher court; to arrogate, claim.

A.VO.LU.MAR, *v.*, to augment, to increase the volume of, enlarge.

A.VÓS, *s.m., pl.*, grandparents, forefathers.

A.VUL.SO, *adj.*, detached, pulled out, torn off, single.

A.VUL.TA.DO, *adj.*, large, bulky, voluminous.

A.VUL.TAR, *v.*, to increase, to augment, to enlarge.

A.XI.LA, *s.f.*, axilla, armpit.

A.XI.O.MA, *s.m.*, axiom.

A.XI.O.MÁ.TI.CO, *adj.*, axiomatic, self-evident.

A.ZÁ.FA.MA, *s.f.*, great haste, hurry, flurry.

A.ZA.FA.MA.DO, *adj.*, hasty, bustling, busy.

A.ZA.LEI.A, *s.f.*, azalea (it is also used *azálea*).

A.ZAR, *s.m.*, misfortune, bad luck, mishap.

A.ZA.RA.DO, *adj.*, jinxed, unlucky.

A.ZA.RAR, *v., col.*, to woo; to pull, to cause misfortune to.

A.ZA.RÃO, *s.m.*, a racehorse or team or someone else with little chances to win.

A.ZA.REN.TO, *adj.*, ill-starred.

A.ZE.DA.MEN.TO, *s.m.*, acidification, sourness.

A.ZE.DAR, *v.*, to acidify, to sour, to make sour.

A.ZE.DO, *adj.*, sour, acid., tart, sharp.

A.ZE.DU.ME, *s.m.*, sourness, tartness, acidity.

A.ZEI.TAR, *v.*, to oil, to lubricate, to grease.

AZEITE · 103 · AZURRAR

A.ZEI.TE, *s.m.*, olive-oil.
A.ZEI.TEI.RA, *s.f.*, cruet, oil-can.
A.ZEI.TEI.RO, *s.m.*, oil merchant or manufacturer, oilman.
A.ZEI.TO.NA, *s.f., Bot.*, olive; fruit of the olive tree.
A.ZE.NHA, *s.f.*, water-mil.
A.ZER.BAI.JÃO, *s.*, Azerbaijan.
A.ZER.BAI.JA.NO, *s.m.*, Azerbaijani; *adj.*, Azerbaijani.
A.ZE.VI.CHE, *s.m.*, jet black, bituminous coal.
A.ZI.A, *s.f., Med.*, pyrosis, heartburn.
A.ZI.A.GO, *adj.*, ill-fated, unlucky.
Á.ZI.MO, *adj.*, azymous, without ferment (bread).
A.ZI.MUTE, *s.m., Astron.*, azimuth.
A.ZO, *s.m.*, occasion, opportunity.
A.ZOR.RA.GUE, *s.m.*, scourge, whip.

A.ZO.TO, *s.m., Quím.*, azote.
A.ZU.CRI.NAR, *v.*, to annoy.
A.ZUL, *adj.*, blue; *s.m.*, the firmament, the sky.
A.ZU.LA.DO, *adj.*, bluish.
A.ZU.LAR, *v.*, to blue, to make blue.
A.ZUL-CLA.RO, *adj.*, light-blue.
A.ZU.LE.JA.DO, *adj.*, tiled.
A.ZU.LE.JAR, *v.*, to tile, to set wall tiles.
A.ZU.LE.JO, *s.m.*, wall tile, glazed tile.
A.ZUL-ES.CU.RO, *adj.*, dark-blue.
A.ZUL-MA.RI.NHO, *adj.*, navy blue, blue ultramarine.
A.ZUL-TUR.QUE.SA, *adj.*, turquoise.
A.ZUR.RA.DOR, *s.m.*, brayer; *adj.*, braying.
A.ZUR.RAR, *v.*, to bray.

B

B, *s.m.*, second letter of the Portuguese alphabet.
BA.BA, *s.f.*, saliva, slaver, bib, spit.
BA.BÁ, *s.f.*, wet nurse, nanny.
BA.BA.CA, *adj., gír.*, idiot, stupid.
BA.BA.ÇU, *s.m.*, babassu, palm, oil palm.
BA.BA.ÇU.AL, *s.m.*, forest of babassu palms.
BA.BA.ÇU.ZAL, *s.m.*, the same that *babaçual*.
BA.BA.DOR, *s.m.*, bib, dribble, slobbering.
BA.BÃO, *s.m.*, slobberer; a slavering child; idiot, silly; *adj.*, slobbering, slavering.
BA.BAR, *v.*, to bib.
BA.BAU!, *interj.*, gone it! it's all up!
BA.BEI.RA, *s.f.*, chinpiece of a medieval helmet.
BA.BÉ.LI.CO, *adj.*, concerning Babel; confused.
BA.BO.SA, *s.f., Bot.*, aloe.
BA.BO.SEI.RA, *s.f.*, folly, nonsense, blunder.
BA.BO.SI.CE, *s.f.*, the same that *baboseira*.
BA.BO.SO, *s.m.*, slobberer, passionate lover; *adj.*, slavering, slobbery; in love; silly.
BA.BU.Í.NO, *s.m., Zool.*, baboon.
BA.BY-SIT.TER, *s. 2 gen.*, baby-sitter.
BA.CA.LHAU, *s.m., Zool.*, cod, codfish.
BA.CA.LHO.A.DA, *s.f., Cul.*, dish of salt-cod; large amount of cod; *Bras.*, beating applied with cod, whipping.
BA.CA.MAR.TE, *s.m.*, blunderbuss, harquebus; old, unavailable.
BA.CA.NA, *adj.*, good, splendid, excellent.
BA.CA.NAL, *s.f.*, bacchanal, orgy; *adj.*, bacchanal, bacchanalian, orgiastic.
BA.CAN.TE, *s.f., Gr.*, bacchante (priestess of Bacchus), maenad.
BA.CA.RÁ, *s.m.*, bacarat (a card game).
BA.CHA.REL, *s.m.*, bachelor.
BA.CHA.RE.LA.DO, *s.m.*, bachelor's degree, baccalaureate.
BA.CHA.RE.LAN.DO, *s.m.*, student in the final year of college, senior.
BA.CI.A, *s.f.*, basin, wash-basin, lavabo, tray, pot.
BA.CI.A.DA, *s.f.*, basinful.
BA.CI.LAR, *adj.*, bacillary, bacilliform.
BA.CI.LO, *s.m.*, bacillus, bacterium, bacteria.
BA.ÇO, *s.m., Anat.*, spleen, milt.
BA.CON, *s.m., Ingl.*, bacon.
BÁ.CO.RO, *s.m.*, piglet, pigling, piggy.
BAC.TÉ.RIA, *s.f.*, bacterium, bacillus.
BAC.TE.RI.CI.DA, *s.m.*, bactericide.
BAC.TE.RI.O.LO.GI.A, *s.f.*, bacteriology.
BAC.TE.RI.O.LO.GIS.TA, *s. 2 gen.*, bacteriologist.
BAC.TE.RI.Ó.LO.GO, *s.m.*, bacteriologist.
BÁ.CU.LO, *s.m.*, staff, rod, stick.
BA.DA.LA.DA, *s.f.*, clang of a bell, toll.
BA.DA.LAR, *v.*, to ring, to toll, to tinkle.
BA.DA.LO, *s.m.*, clapper, bell-clapper; *gír.*, flattery.

BA.DE.JO, *s.m., Zool.*, name of several fishes of the family *Serranidae*; *adj.*, showy; extraordinary.
BA.DER.NA, *s.f.*, frolics, riot, conflict, rumpus.
BA.DER.NEI.RO, *s.m.*, rowdy, brawler, rioter.
BA.DU.LA.QUE, *s.m.*, trinket, trash, rubbish.
BA.FA.FÁ, *s.m.*, quarrel, strife, bustle, altercation.
BA.FE.JA.DOR, *s.m.*, whiffer.
BA.FE.JAR, *v.*, to warm (by breathing on), to favour, to protect.
BA.FE.JO, *s.m.*, puff of wind, breath, whiff, air.
BA.FO, *s.m.*, breath, exhalation, respiration.
BA.FO.RA.DA, *s.f.*, expiration, breathing out, puff; puff of smoke (cigar or cigarette).
BA.FO.RAR, *v.*, exhale, blow, to expel.
BA.GA, *s.f.*, berry or berrylike of fruit, drop.
BA.GA.CEI.RA, *s.f.*, remainder, residue; vulgar people; mob; *gír., Teat.*, bad acting.
BA.GA.ÇO, *s.m.*, bagasse.
BA.GA.GEI.RO, *s.m.*, loader, carrying luggage.
BA.GA.GEM, *s.f.*, baggage, lug, luggage, equipage, outfit.
BA.GA.NA, *s.f.*, cigarette or cigar end, dog end.
BA.GA.NHA, *s.f.*, hull of seed, husk.
BA.GA.TE.LA, *s.f.*, bagatelle, trifle, fleabite, straw.
BA.GO, *s.m.*, each fruit of a bunch of grapes or any grapelike fruit, berry, acinus.
BA.GRE, *s.m., Zool.*, sheat-fish, catfish.
BA.GUAL, *s.m.*, untamed colt; horse that turned wild again; *adj.*, untamed; *fig.*, unsociable, unfriendly
BA.GUE.TE, *s.f., It.*, baguette.
BA.GU.LHO, *s.m.*, trinket, grain, trash; *pej.*, an unattractive person.
BA.GUN.ÇA, *s.f.*, tumult, disorder, confusion, mess.
BA.GUN.ÇAR, *v.*, to clutter, feast noisily; *fig.*, to upset.
BA.GUN.CEI.RO, *s.m.*, disorderly person; *adj.*, disorderly, careless, untidy.
BAH!, *interj.*, exclamation expressing surprise.
BAI.A, *s.f.*, stall, box, bail.
BA.Í.A, *s.f.*, bay.
BAI.A.CU, *adj.*, desordenado, desleixado, relaxado.
BAI.A.NO, *s.m.*, Bahian (inhabitant or native of Bahia, state of Brazil); *adj.*, Bahian.
BAI.ÃO, *s.m., Bras.*, baião (folk music and dance).
BAI.LA.DO, *s.m.*, ballet, choreography.
BAI.LAR, *v.*, to dance, to perform a ballet.
BAI.LA.RI.NA, *s.f.*, ballet-dancer, ballerina, dancer.
BAI.LA.RI.NO, *s.m.*, ballet dancer, dance artist.
BAI.LE, *s.m.*, dance, ball function.
BA.I.NHA, *s.f.*, hem, cuff; sheath, scabbard.
BA.I.NHAR, *v.*, to sheathe.
BAI.O.NE.TA, *s.f.*, bayonet.
BAIR.RIS.MO, *s.m.*, regionalism, localism, local patriotism.
BAIR.RIS.TA, *s.m.*, provincialist, regionalist, local patriot; *adj.*, community-based, regionalistic.

BAITA   •• 105 ••   BANDALHEIRA

BAI.TA, *adj., Bras.*, enormous, very great; nice, good.

BAIR.RO, *s.m.*, district, ward, precinct, quarter, region.

BAI.U.CA, *s.f.*, pub, tavern, canteen; *pop.*, dump.

BAI.XA, *s.f.*, reduction, depression, hollow, decrease, decadence, decay.

BAI.XA.DA, *s.f.*, slope, declivity, depression, lowlands.

BAI.XAR, *v.*, to lower, to let down, to shorten, to incline, to stoop.

BAI.XA.RI.A, *s.f., gír.*, gross behaviour; vileness.

BAI.XE.LA, *s.f.*, tableware, tableset.

BAI.XE.ZA, *s.f.*, lowness, inferiority, indignity.

BAI.XI.NHO, *s.m.*, child; person of short stature; *adv.*, in a low voice; secretly, stealthily;

BAI.XO, *s.m.*, lower part, depression, hollow; *Mús.*, bass; *adj.*, low, shallow, shoal, inferior.

BAI.XO-RE.LE.VO, *s.m., Art.*, bas-relief, low-relief.

BAI.XO.TE, *s.m.*, basset; *adj.*, somewhat low or short.

BA.JU.LA.ÇÃO, *s.f.*, flattery, fawning, adulation, cajoling.

BA.JU.LAR, *v.*, to flatter, to adulate, to fawn upon, cringe.

BA.LA, *s.f.*, bullet, missile, shot, ball, projectile; bonbon, sweet, candy.

BA.LA.DA, *s.f.*, ballad, lay (poem and music); *Mús.*, ballade.

BA.LAI.O, *s.m.*, hamper, basket made of straw.

BA.LAN.ÇA, *s.f.*, balance, scales, pair of scales, weighing-machine, ponderation.

BA.LAN.ÇAR, *v.*, to balance, to counter-balance, equilibrate, to swing, to oscillate.

BA.LAN.CE.A.DO, *adj.*, balnced; *Bras.*, foolish.

BA.LAN.CE.A.MEN.TO, *s.m.*, swinging, oscillation, rocking.

BA.LAN.CE.AR, *v.*, to balance (wheels), to sway; *Com.*, to counterbalance.

BA.LAN.CE.TE, *s.m.*, trial, intermediate balance, balance sheet.

BA.LAN.ÇO, *s.m.*, swinging, swing, sway, balance sheet, oscillation.

BA.LAN.GAN.DÃ, *s.m.*, jewelry, trinkets, amulet.

BA.LÃO, *s.m.*, balloon, aerostat.

BA.LÃO DE EN.SAI.O, *s.m.*, trial baloon, pilot baloon.

BA.LAUS.TRA.DA, *s.f.*, balustrade, parapet, railing.

BA.LA.ÚS.TRE, *s.m.*, baluster, rail post.

BAL.BU.CI.A.ÇÃO, *s.f.*, stuttering, stammering, babbling.

BAL.BU.CI.AR, *v.*, to stutter, to stammer, to babble.

BAL.BU.CI.O, *s.m.*, the same that *balbuciação*.

BAL.BÚR.DIA, *s.f.*, confusion, disorder, tumult, messiness.

BAL.CÂ.NI.CO, *adj.*, Balkan, Balkanic.

BAL.CÃO, *s.m.*, balcony, projecting terrace; counter, show counter.

BAL.CO.NIS.TA, *s. 2 gen.*, shop assistant, salesman, shopman.

BAL.DA.DA, *s.f.*, pailful, bucketful, bucket.

BAL.DA.DO, *adj.*, frustrate, useless, unsuccessful.

BAL.DAR, *v.*, to frustrate, to disappoint; to baffle.

BAL.DE, *s.m.*, bucket, pail, scuttle.

BAL.DE.A.ÇÃO, *s.f.*, transfusion, decantation, transshipment, connection.

BAL.DE.AR, *v.*, to transfer, to change, to connect, to transship.

BAL.DI.O, *adj.*, unused, uncultivated, fallow.

BAL.DO, *s.m.*, deficient, wanting, lacking.

BAL.DO.AR, *v.*, to offend, to insult.

BAL.DO.SO, *adj.*, useless, ineffectual; *Bras.*, unruly.

BA.LÉ, *s.m.*, ballet.

BA.LE.A.DO, *adj.*, wounded with a shot (gun).

BA.LE.AR, *v.*, to wound with a shot.

BA.LE.EI.RA, *s.f.*, whaler (ship).

BA.LE.EI.RO, *s.m.*, whaleman, whale-fisher.

BA.LEI.A, *s.f.*, whale.

BA.LEI.RO, *s.m.*, sweet seller (candy).

BA.LE.LA, *s.f.*, false report, lie, rumour.

BA.LE.O.TE, *s.m., Zool.*, baby whale, whale calf.

BA.LES.TI.LHA, *s.f., Náut.*, sextant.

BA.LI, *s.*, Bali.

BA.LI.DO, *s.m.*, bleat (sheep or lamb), baa.

BA.LÍS.TI.CA, *s.f.*, ballistics.

BA.LI.ZA, *s.f.*, mark, landmark, sign, boundary, limit.

BA.LI.ZA.DOR, *s.m.*, marker, mark, sign.

BA.LI.ZA.GEM, *s.f.*, demarcation, marking.

BA.LI.ZA.MEN.TO, *s.m.*, the same that *balizagem*.

BA.LI.ZAR, *v.*, to limit, to set boundaries; to put up signs; to estimate.

BAL.NE.AR, *v.*, to bathe (in the sea).

BAL.NE.Á.RIO, *s.m.*, health-resort, spa, watering-place; *adj.*, balneary.

BA.LO.FO, *adj.*, spongy, flaccid, flabby, fat.

BA.LO.NIS.TA, *s. 2 gen.*, balloonist.

BA.LOU.ÇAR, *v.*, to balance, to swing, to pendulate, to oscillate.

BAL.RÒ.AR, *v.*, the same that *abalroar*: to collide (ship).

BAL.SA, *s.f.*, husks of grapes, raft, ferryboat.

BÁL.SA.MO, *s.m.*, balm, balsam.

BAL.SÂ.MI.CO, *adj.*, balsamic, aromatic.

BAL.SEI.RO, *s.m.*, ferryman, waterman.

BA.LU.AR.TE, *s.m.*, fortress, stronghold, bulwark, fortification.

BAL.ZA.QUI.A.NA, *s.f., Bras.*, woman in her thirties; *adj.*, concerning to such a woman.

BAM.BA, *s.m.*, expert; bigwig; *adj., col.*, expert; braggart.

BAM.BE.AR, *v.*, to falter, to weaken, to slacken.

BAM.BO.LÊ, *s.m.*, hula hoop.

BAM.BO.LE.AN.TE, *adj.*, swinging; dangling.

BAM.BO.LE.AR, *v.*, to wobble; to falter.

BAM.BO.LEI.O, *s.m.*, swinging, oscillation.

BAMBU, *s.m.*, bamboo.

BAM.BU.ZAL, *s.m.*, bamboo ticket, bamboo plantation.

BA.NAL, *adj.*, common, trivial, vulgar.

BA.NA.LI.DA.DE, *s.f.*, banality, triviality.

BA.NA.LI.ZAR, *v.*, to vulgarize, to make common.

BA.NA.NA, *s.f., Bot.*, banana.

BA.NA.NAL, *s.f.*, banana grove.

BA.NA.NEI.RA, *s.f., Bot.*, banana plant.

BAN.CA, *s.f.*, table, stall, writing-table, desk, bureau, business office, lawyer's office.

BAN.CA.DA, *s.f.*, workbench; row of seats, tier; *Pol.*, bench (partido).

BAN.CAR, *v.*, to keep the bank, to finance, to pay, to dissimulate.

BAN.CÁ.RIO, *s.m.*, employee of a bank, bank clerk; *adj.*, of or concerning bank.

BAN.CAR.RO.TA, *s.f.*, bankruptcy, insolvency, suspension of payments.

BAN.CO, *s.m.*, seat, pew, bench, footstool, stool, bank.

BAN.DA, *s.f.*, side, flank, shore, band, strip.

BAN.DA.GEM, *s.f.*, dressing, bandaging, compress.

BAN.DA.LHEI.RA, *s.f.*, mean action, ridiculous, shabby trick.

BANDALHO   •• 106 ••   BARULHENTO

BAN.DA.LHO, *s.m.*, scoundrel, rascal.
BAN.DA.NA, *s.f.*, bandanna, kerchief.
BAN.DE.AR, *v.*, to join, to incline to the side; *bandear-se*: to associate oneself with.
BAN.DEI.RA, *s.f.*, flag, banner, colours, ensign.
BAN.DEI.RA.DA, *s.f.*, basic fare indicated by taximeters.
BAN.DEI.RAN.TE, *s.m., Hist., Bras.*, member of the expeditions called *bandeiras*.
BAN.DEI.RAR, *v., Bras.*, to take part in a campaign.
BAN.DEI.RO.LA, *s.f.*, banderol, streamer, signal-flag.
BAN.DE.JA, *s.f.*, tray, salver, board.
BAN.DE.JÃO, *s.m., gír.*, cafeteria.
BAN.DI.DA.ÇO, *s.m.*, bandit, dangerous outlaw.
BAN.DI.DO, *s.m.*, bandit, outlaw, gangster, brigand.
BAN.DI.TIS.MO, *s.m.*, banditry, brigandism.
BAN.DO, *s.m.*, gang, group, band, faction, multitude.
BAN.DO.LEI.RO, *s.m.*, outlaw, brigand.
BAN.DO.LIM, *s.m., Mús.*, mandolin.
BAN.DÔ.NI.ON, *s.m., Es., Mús.*, bandonion.
BAN.DU.LHO, *s.m.*, potbelly, belly, paunch.
BAN.DUR.RA, *s.f., Mús.*, bandore.
BAN.GA.LÔ, *s.m.*, bungalow.
BAN.GUE-BAN.GUE, *s.m.*, Western (movie).
BAN.GUE.LA, *s.f.*, toothless.
BA.NHA, *s.f.*, fat, grease, lard, drippings.
BA.NHA.DO, *s.m.*, marsh, swamp, bog.
BA.NHAR, *v.*, to bathe, to bath, to wash, to take a bath, to inundate, to flood.
BA.NHEI.RA, *s.f.*, bathtub, bath.
BA.NHEI.RO, *s.m.*, bathroom, closet, toilet.
BA.NHIS.TA, *s. 2 gen.*, bather.
BA.NHO, *s.m.*, bathing, bath, bathroom, wash.
BA.NHO-MA.RI.A, *s.m.*, water-bath.
BA.NI.DO, *s.m.*, outcast, exile; *adj.*, banished, outlawed; deported.
BA.NI.MEN.TO, *s.m.*, banishment, exile, deportation.
BA.NIR, *v.*, to banish, to expatriate, to exile, to outlaw.
BAN.JO, *s.m., Mús.*, banjo.
BAN.NER, *s.m., Comp.*, banner.
BAN.QUEI.RO, *s.m.*, banker, dealer, croupier, capitalist.
BAN.QUE.TA, *s.f.*, stool, footstool.
BAN.QUE.TE, *s.m.*, banquet.
BA.QUE, *s.m.*, collision, thud, collapse, fall.
BA.QUE.AR, *v.*, to fall, to tumble, to plop; to fail.
BA.QUE.LI.TA, *s.f., Quím.*, bakelite.
BAR, *s.m.*, bar, pub, saloon, beershop.
BA.RA.LHO, *s.m.*, cards, pack of playing cards.
BA.RÃO, *s.m.*, baron.
BA.RA.TA, *s.f., Zool.*, cockroach.
BA.RA.TE.AR, *v.*, to sell at a low price, to undervalue.
BA.RA.TEI.RO, *s.m.*, underseller; *adj.*, cut-price.
BA.RA.TI.NA.DO, *adj., gír.*, stressed, upset, disturbed.
BA.RA.TI.NAR, *v.*, to confuse, to overturn; *gír.*, to wig out.
BA.RA.TO, *adj.*, cheap, low-priced; *s.m., gír.*, ecstasy from drugs.
BAR.BA, *s.f.*, beard.
BAR.BA-A.ZUL, *s.m.*, Bluebeard.
BAR.BA.DA, *s.f., gír.*, easy victory.
BAR.BA.DO, *adj.*, bearded, barbed.
BAR.BA.DOS, *s.*, Barbados.
BAR.BAN.TE, *s.m.*, thread, twine, string.

BAR.BA.RA.MEN.TE, *adv.*, brutally, atrociously, barbarously.
BAR.BA.RI.DA.DE, *s.f.*, barbarity, cruelty, inhumanity.
BAR.BÁ.RI.E, *s.f.*, barbarity, inhumanity.
BAR.BA.RIS.MO, *s.m.*, barbarism.
BAR.BA.RI.ZAR, *v.*, to barbarize, to brutalize.
BÁR.BA.RO, *s.m.*, barbarian; *adj.*, barbarous, uncivilized.
BAR.BA.TA.NA, *s.f.*, fin (of a fish), flipper.
BAR.BE.A.DOR, *s.m.*, shaver.
BAR.BE.AR, *v.*, to shave; *barbear-se*: to shave oneself.
BAR.BE.A.RIA, *s.f.*, barbershop.
BAR.BEI.RA.GEM, *s.f., pop.*, bad driving.
BAR.BEI.RO, *s.m.*, shaver, barber; *Zool.*, barbeiro (bug); *pop.*, bad driver; *adj.*, referring to a bad driver.
BAR.BI.CHA, *s.f.*, small beard, goatee.
BAR.BI.TÚ.RI.CO, *adj., Quím.*, barbituric; barbiturate.
BAR.BU.DO, *s.m.*, bearded man; *adj.*, bearded.
BAR.CA, *s.f.*, flatboat, barge.
BAR.CA.ÇA, *s.f., Náut.*, barge, large bark.
BAR.CA.RO.LA, *s.f.*, barcarolle (also musical composition).
BAR.CO, *s.m.*, boat, bark, ship.
BAR.DA.NA, *s.f., Bot.*, burdock, cocklebur.
BAR.DO, *s.m.*, bard, troubadour.
BAR.GA.NHA, *s.f.*, barter, exchange; swindle.
BA.RI.CEN.TRO, *s.m., Fís.*, centre of gravity.
BÁ.RI.O, *s.m., Quím.*, barium.
BÁ.RI.ON, *s.m., Fís.*, baryon.
BA.RÍ.TO.NO, *s.m., Mús.*, barytone, baritone.
BAR.NA.BÉ, *s.m., pop.*, minor civil servant.
BA.RÔ.ME.TRO, *s.m.*, barometer.
BA.RO.NE.SA, *s.f.*, baroness.
BAR.QUEI.RO, *s.m.*, boatman, ferryman.
BAR.RA, *s.f.*, hem, border, fringe, bar; tablet.
BAR.RA.CA, *s.f.*, tent, barrack, hut.
BAR.RA.CO, *s.m.*, cottage, hut; shack; *gír.*, confusion, tumult.
BAR.RA.CU.DA, *s.f., Zool.*, barracuda.
BAR.RA.DO, *adj.*, barred, mudded; covered with clay or mud.
BAR.RA.GEM, *s.f.*, barrage, crawl, barrier, dam.
BARRANCO, *s.f.*, the same that *barranco*.
BAR.RAN.CO, *s.m.*, rut, groove, bank, ravine, gorge, precipice.
BAR.RAN.CO.SO, *adj.*, full of ravines, declivous, rutted, gullied.
BAR.RAN.QUEI.RA, *s.f.*, precipice, slope, steep.
BAR.RA-PE.SA.DA, *s.m.*, awful person; tough situation.
BAR.RAR, *v.*, to clay, to hem, to hinder, to plug, to obstruct.
BAR.REI.RA, *s.f.*, barricade, barrier, palisade, limit, block, obstacle.
BAR.REN.TO, *adj.*, clayey, loamy, muddy.
BAR.RE.TE, *s.m.*, cap, beret, hat.
BAR.RI.CA, *s.f.*, barrel, keg, cask, tub.
BAR.RI.CA.DA, *s.f.*, barricade.
BAR.RI.GA, *s.f.*, belly, tummy, paunch, abdominal cavity.
BAR.RI.GU.DO, *adj.*, pot bellied, paunchy, obese.
BAR.RIL, *s.m.*, cask, barrel, wooden keg, coop.
BAR.RO, *s.m.*, clay, mud, kaolin, loam.
BAR.RO.CO, *adj.*, baroque.
BAR.RO.SO, *adj.*, clayish, loamy.
BAR.RO.TE, *s.m.*, rafter, support, beam.
BA.RU.LHEI.RA, *s.f.*, uproar, racket, clamour, noise.
BA.RU.LHEN.TO, *adj.*, loud, noisy, uproarious, turbulent, tumultuous.

BARULHO · 107 · BELICISTA

BA.RU.LHO, s.m., noise, uproar, clamour, tumult, confusion.

BAS.BA.QUE, adj., foolish, stupid, jacknapes.

BAS.BA.QUI.CE, s.f., foolishness, silliness, stupidity.

BA.SÁL.TI.CO, adj., basaltic.

BA.SAL.TO, s.m., Miner., basalt; Geol., whinstone.

BAS.CO, s., adj., basque.

BAS.CU.LAN.TE, s.m., swivel window.

BA.SE, s.f., base, basis, grounds, support, bottom.

BA.SE.A.DO, adj., based on; weel-founded; s.m., gír., marihuana cigarette.

BA.SE.AR, v., to base, to form, to serve as a base, found, establish.

BÁ.SI.CO, adj., basic, essential, fundamental.

BA.SÍ.LI.CA, s.f., basilica.

BAS.QUE.TE, s.m., the same that basquetebol.

BAS.QUE.TE.BOL, s.m., basketball.

BAS.TA, interj., enough!; s.m., um ~: a stop.

BAS.TAN.TE, adj., enough, sufficient; adv., satisfactory, sufficiently.

BAS.TÃO, s.m., stick, truncheon, baton.

BAS.TAR, v., to be enough, to be sufficient, to suffice, to satisfy.

BAS.TAR.DO, adj., s.m., bastard.

BAS.TI.ÃO, s.m., bastion, bulwark.

BAS.TI.DOR, s.m., embroidery frame, tambour frame.

BAS.TI.LHA, s.f., Hist., defensive tower; Bastilha: the Bastille.

BAS.TO.NE.TE, s.m., rod, stick.

BA.TA.LHA, s.f., battle, combat, action, engagement, conflict, fight.

BA.TA.LHA.DOR, s.m., fighter, warrior, champion; adj., fighting, struggling.

BA.TA.LHÃO, s.m., Mil., battalion; fig., crowd.

BA.TA.LHAR, v., to combat, to contend, to fight.

BA.TA.TA, s.f., Bot., potato.

BA.TA.TA-DO.CE, s.f., sweet potato.

BA.TA.TAL, s.m., potato field.

BA.TA.VO, adj., s.m., Dutchman, Batavian.

BA.TE-BO.CA, s.m., quarrel, discussion, bawling.

BA.TE-BO.LA, s.m., warm up.

BA.TE.DEI.RA, s.f., food-mixer, churn, butter vat.

BA.TE.DOR, s.m., beater, knocker.

BA.TEL, s.m., small bark, canoe.

BA.TEN.TE, s.m., rabbet, hard work, door-post, door-knocker.

BA.TE-PA.PO, s.m., chat; conversation.

BA.TER, v., to hit, to hang, to beat, to mix, to knock about, to fight, to strike, to collide.

BA.TE.RI.A, s.f., Eletr., battery (accumulator, pile); Mús., drum; Mil., battery (basic unit of artillery).

BA.TE.RIS.TA, s.m., Mús., drummer.

BA.TI.DA, s.f., beat, stroke, police raid, tap.

BA.TI.DO, s.m., beaten, hit, worn out.

BA.TI.MEN.TO, s.m., collision, shock, beating, impact; Med., pulsation.

BA.TI.NA, s.f., cassock, soutane.

BA.TIS.CA.FO, s.m., Náut., bathyscaphe.

BA.TIS.MAL, adj., baptismal.

BA.TIS.MO, s.m., baptism.

BA.TI.ZA.DO, s.m., baptism; adj., baptized.

BA.TI.ZAR, v., baptize, christen.

BA.TOM, s.m., lipstick.

BA.TRÁ.QUI.OS, s.m., pl., Zool., Batrachia, Amphibia.

BA.TU.CA.DA, s.f., Afro-Brazilian rhythm with drums and dance.

BA.TU.CAR, v., to drum, to hammer.

BA.TU.QUE, s.m., hammering, drumming.

BA.TU.QUEI.RO, s.m., pop., Bras., drummer; one who plays batucada.

BA.TU.TA, s.f., wand, a conductor's baton; intelligent person; adj., pop., notable, intelligent.

BA.Ú, s.m., trunk, travelling box, chest.

BAU.NI.LHA, s.f., vanilla.

BAU.XI.TA, s.f., Miner., bauxite.

BA.ZAR, s.m., bazaar, oriental market.

BA.ZÓ.FI.A, s.m., vanity, haughtiness, swagger.

BA.ZO.FI.AR, v., to swagger, to boast, to swank.

BA.ZU.CA, s.f., Mil., bazooka.

BE.A.BÁ, s.m., alphabet, the ABC.

BE.A.TA, s.f., pious woman, bigot.

BE.A.TI.CE, s.f., bigotry.

BE.A.TI.FI.CA.ÇÃO, s.f., beatification.

BE.A.TI.TU.DE, s.f., beatitude.

BE.A.TO, s.m., beatified man; bigot; adj., devot, fanatic, hypocritical.

BÊ.BA.DO, s.m., drunk, drunkard; adj., drunk, tipsy.

BE.BÊ, s.m., baby, babe.

BE.BE.DEI.RA, s.f., spree, drunkenness, drinking bout.

BE.BER, v., to drink, to take a drink, to imbibe, to swallow.

BE.BE.RA.GEM, v., decoction, infusion, watered bran; swill; potion.

BE.BE.RI.CAR, v., to sip.

BE.BER.RÃO, s.m., drunkard, boozer, tippler.

BE.BI.DA, s.f., drink, beverage, potion.

BE.BÍ.VEL, adj., drinkable, potable.

BE.CA, s.f., judge's robe, toga; fig., magistracy.

BE.ÇA, s.f., a lot, numerous; à ~: in large numbers.

BE.CO, s.m., alley.

BE.DEL, s.m., school attendant.

BE.DE.LHO, s.m., latch, meter o ~ em: to poke one's nose in.

BE.DU.Í.NO, adj., s.m., Bedouin, Arab.

BE.GE, adj., s. 2 gen., beige.

BE.GÔ.NI.A, s.f., Bot., begonia.

BEI.ÇO, s.m., lip, pout, salience.

BEI.ÇU.DO, adj., s.m., blubber-lipped.

BEI.JA.DO, adj., kissed.

BEI.JA-FLOR, s.m., hummingbird, colibri.

BEI.JAR, v., to kiss, to caress, to osculate.

BEI.JO, s.m., kiss, osculation.

BEI.JO.CA, s.f., col., smack, smackeroo.

BEI.JO.QUEI.RO, s.m., kisser; adj., kissing, caressing.

BEI.RA, s.f., edge, shore, rim, proximity, border.

BEI.RA.DA, s.f., margin, border.

BEI.RAL, s.m., weatherboard.

BEI.RA-MAR, s.m., sea-shore, strand, coast, littoral, waterfront.

BEI.SE.BOL, s.m., Esp., baseball.

BE.LAS-AR.TES, s.f., pl., fine arts.

BEL.DA.DE, s.f., beauty, belle.

BE.LE.ZA, s.f., beauty, prettiness, gracefulness, handsomeness.

BEL.GA, adj., s.m., Belgian.

BE.LI.CHE, s.m., berth, bunk, sleeping berth, cabin.

BE.LI.CIS.TA, s. 2 gen., warrior; adj., warlike.

BÉLICO · 108 · BICAMA

BÉ.LI.CO, *adj.*, warlike, bellicose, litigious.
BE.LI.CO.SI.DA.DE, *s.f.*, bellicosity, hostility.
BE.LI.CO.SO, *adj.*, warlike, bellicose, pugnacious.
BE.LI.GE.RÂN.CIA, *s.f.*, belligerence.
BE.LI.GE.RAN.TE, *adj.*, belligerent, contentious.
BE.LIS.CÃO, *s.m.*, squeeze, nip, pinch.
BE.LIS.CAR, *v.*, to pinch, to squeeze, to peck, to nip.
BE.LO, *adj.*, beautiful, handsome, pretty, fine, harmonious.
BE.LO.NA.VE, *s.f.*, warship, battleship.
BEL-PRA.ZER, *s.m.*, free will, liking, pleasure; *ao seu ~*: to one's heart's content.
BEL.TRA.NO, *s.m.*, Mr. So-and-so; John Doe.
BEL.ZE.BU, *s.m.*, Beelzebub, devil.
BEM, *s.m.*, good, goodness, benefit, virtue; *adv.*, well, very, right.
BEM-A.CA.BA.DO, *adj.*, well finished.
BEM-A.MA.DO, *s.m.*, lover, swetheart; *adj.*, darling, dear.
BEM-A.PES.SO.A.DO, *adj.*, presentable.
BEM-A.VEN.TU.RA.DO, *s.m.*, blessed person; *adj.*, blessed, lucky.
BEM-E.DU.CA.DO, *adj.*, well bred, refined.
BEM-ES.TAR, *s.m.*, comfort, welfare, satisfaction.
BEM-FA.ZER, *v.*, to do good to, to benefit.
BEM FEI.TO, *adj.*, well done.
BEM-HU.MO.RA.DO, *adj.*, good-humoured.
BEM-IN.TEN.CI.O.NA.DO, *adj.*, well-meaning.
BEM-ME-QUER, *s.m.*, *Bot.*, daisy.
BEM PAS.SA.DO, *adj.*, well cooked (meat).
BEM-SU.CE.DI.DO, *adj.*, successful.
BEM-TE-VI, *s.m.*, tyrant flycatcher.
BEM-VIN.DO, *adj.*, welcome.
BEM-VIS.TO, *adj.*, well-beloved.
BÊN.ÇÃO, *s.f.*, blessing.
BEN.DI.TO, *adj.*, blessed, praised.
BE.NE.FI.CA.MEN.TE, *adv.*, beneficially, kindly.
BE.NE.FI.CÊN.CIA, *s.f.*, charity; kindness.
BE.NE.FI.CEN.TE, *adj.*, beneficent, charitable, beneficial.
BE.NE.FI.CI.A.DO, *s.m.*, beneficiary; *adj.*, beneficial, treated.
BE.NE.FI.CI.A.DOR, *s.m.*, benefactor; *adj.*, beneficient, beneficial.
BE.NE.FI.CI.AR, *v.*, to benefit, to be beneficial to, to improve, to better; to process.
BE.NE.FI.CI.Á.RI.O, *s.m.*, beneficiary, payee; *adj.*, beneficiary, favoured.
BE.NE.FI.CI.Á.VEL, *adj.*, susceptible to be beneficed.
BE.NE.FÍ.CIO, *s.m.*, benefit, service.
BE.NÉ.FI.CO, *adj.*, benefic, beneficient, useful, salutary.
BE.NE.MÉ.RI.TO, *s.m.*, worthy person; *adj.*, deserving, worthy, praiseworthy.
BE.NE.PLÁ.CI.TO, *s.m.*, consent, approval, permission.
BE.NÉ.VO.LO, *adj.*, benevolent, kind, charitable, tolerant.
BE.NE.VO.LÊN.CIA, *s.f.*, benevolence, goodwill, amity, friendship.
BE.NE.VO.LEN.TE, *adj.*, benevolent, benign, kind, charitable.
BEN.FA.ZE.JO, *adj.*, beneficent, wholesome.
BEN.FA.ZER, *s.m.*, charity, generosity.
BEN.FEI.TOR, *s.m.*, benefactor, well-doer, amender.
BEN.FEI.TO.RI.A, *s.f.*, improvement, melioration.
BEN.GA.LA, *s.f.*, cane, walking stick.
BE.NIG.NA.MEN.TE, *adv.*, benignly, kindly.
BE.NIG.NI.DA.DE, *s.f.*, benignity.

BEM.JA.MIM, *s.m.*, *Eletr.*, adaptor.
BEM.QUE.REN.ÇA, *s.f.*, affection.
BEN.QUIS.TO, *adj.*, beloved, esteemed.
BEN.TO, *adj.*, sacred, holy, consecrated.
BEN.ZE.DEI.RA, *s.f.*, female healer.
BEN.ZE.DU.RA, *s.f.*, blessing, benediction.
BEN.ZE.NO, *s.m.*, *Quim.*, benzene, benzol.
BEN.ZER, *v.*, to bless, to consecrate, to make happy.
BEN.ZI.NA, *s.f.*, *Quim.*, benzine.
BE.Ó.CIO, *s.m.*, Boeotian; *adj.*, Boeotian, *fig.*, stupid, dull.
BE.QUE, *s.m.*, beak, prow, head of a ship.
BER.ÇÁ.RIO, *s.m.*, nursery.
BER.ÇO, *s.m.*, cradle, cot, crib, bassinet.
BER.GA.MO.TA, *s.f.*, *Bot.*, bergamot, tangerine, mandarin.
BE.RI.BÉ.RI, *s.m.*, *Med.*, beriberi.
BE.RÍ.LI.O, *s.m.*, *Quim.*, berylium.
BE.RIM.BAU, *s.m.*, *Mús.*, berimbau.
BE.RIN.JE.LA, *s.f.*, aubergine, eggplant.
BER.LIN.DA, *s.f.*, *Hist.*, berlin; game of forfeits; *estar na ~*: to be in the hot seat.
BER.LO.QUE, *s.m.*, trinket, pendant.
BER.MU.DA, *s.f.*, Bermuda shorts.
BER.NE, *s.m.*, *Zool.*, *Bot.*, larva of the flee *Dermatobia cyaneventris*.
BER.RAN.TE, *adj.*, crying, vociferous; gaudy (color, adorn).
BER.RAR, *v.*, to cry, to scream, to shout, to roar, to bellow.
BER.REI.RO, *s.m.*, noisy crying, shouting, wailing.
BER.RO, *s.m.*, howl, shout, scream, lowing, clamour.
BE.SOU.RO, *s.m.*, *Zool.*, beetle.
BES.TA, *s.f.*, beast, quadruped, mare, mule; a stupid person, duffer; *adj.*, stupid.
BES.TA.LHÃO, *s.m.*, foolish, fool, silly, stupid.
BES.TEI.RA, *s.f.*, nonsense, absurdity, foolishness, stupidity.
BES.TI.AL, *adj.*, bestial, beastly; irrational, brutal.
BES.TI.A.LI.DA.DE, *s.f.*, bestiality, atrocity.
BES.TI.A.LI.ZAR, *v.*, to bestialize, to brutalize, to stupefy.
BES.TI.FI.CAR, *v.*, to bestialize, to brutalize.
BES.TUN.TO, *s.m.*, dullness, stupidity.
BE.SUN.TAR, *v.*, to anoint, to grease.
BE.TA.CA.RO.TE.NO, *s.m.*, *Bot.*, beta-carotene.
BE.TÃO, *s.m.*, concrete.
BE.TER.RA.BA, *s.f.*, *Bot.*, beet, beetroot.
BE.TO.NEI.RA, *s.f.*, concret mixer.
BE.TU.ME, *s.m.*, bitumen, asphalt, cement.
BE.TU.MI.NO.SO, *adj.*, betuminous.
BE.XI.GA, *s.f.*, *Anat.*, bladder.
BE.ZER.RO, *s.m.*, *Zool.*, bull-calf, male calf, bossy.
BI.BE.LÔ, *s.m.*, bibelot, trinket.
BÍ.BLI.A, *s.f.*, the Bible, the Holy Scriptures.
BÍ.BLI.CO, *adj.*, biblical, scriptural.
BI.BLI.O.GRA.FI.A, *s.f.*, bibliography.
BI.BLI.O.GRÁ.FI.CO, *adj.*, bibliographic.
BI.BLI.Ó.GRA.FO, *s.m.*, bibliographer.
BI.BLI.O.TE.CA, *s.f.*, library, collection of books.
BI.BLI.O.TE.CÁ.RI.O, *s.m.*, librarian; *adj.*, concerning to library.
BI.BLI.O.TE.CO.NO.MI.A, *s.f.*, bibliotheconomy.
BI.BLIS.TA, *s. 2 gen.*, biblicist.
BI.BO.CA, *s.f.*, hut, small shop.
BI.CA, *s.f.*, conduit, pipe, fountain, springlet.
BI.CA.DA, *s.f.*, peck, pecking, beakful.
BI.CA.MA, *s.f.*, couch, sofa bed.

BICAMERAL · 109 · BISNETA

BI.CA.ME.RAL, *adj.*, bicameral.
BI.CÃO, *s.m., col.*, freeloader.
BI.CAR, *v.*, to peck.
BI.CAR.BO.NA.TO, *s.m.*, bicarbonate.
BI.CHA, *s.f.*, worm, leech; gay, homossexual.
BI.CHA.DO, *adj.*, wormy, worm-eaten.
BI.CHA.NO, *s.m., pop.*, kitten, cat.
BI.CHA.RA.DA, *s.f.*, a lot of animals.
BI.CHEI.RO, *s.m.*, bookie (ticket-vendor of a sort of illegal lottery bets); *adj.*, feeding on worms.
BI.CHO, *s.m.*, animal, beast, worm, any animal; ugly, repulsive or unsociable person.
BI.CHO-DA-SEDA, *s.m., Zool.*, silkworm.
BI.CHO-DE-PÉ, *s.m.*, jigger.
BI.CHO DO MA.TO, *s.m.*, shy person, recluse.
BI.CHO-PA.PÃO, *s.m.*, ogre, boogeyman.
BI.CHO-PRE.GUI.ça, *s.m., Zool.*, sloth.
BI.CI.CLE.TA, *s.f.*, bicycle, bike; wheel.
BI.CO, *s.m.*, beak, bill, pecker, peak, spout.
BI.CO-DE-PA.PA.GAI.O, *s.m., Med.*, osteophyte on de the spinal column; hooked noise.
BI.CO.LOR, *adj.*, two-coloured.
BI.CU.DO, *adj.*, beaked, pointed; painful, angry, surly.
BI.DÊ, *s.m.*, bidet.
BI.DI.MEN.SI.O.NAL, *adj.*, two-demensional.
BI.DI.RE.CI.O.NAL, *adj.*, bidirectional.
BI.E.LO-RÚS.SI.A, *s.*, Belarus.
BI.E.LO-RUS.SO, *s.m., adj.*, Belorussian.
BI.E.NAL, *adj.*, biennial.
BI.Ê.NIO, *s.m.*, biennium.
BI.FE, *s.m.*, beefsteak, steak.
BI.FO.CAL, *adj.*, bifocal.
BI.FOR.ME, *adj.*, biform.
BI.FUR.CA.ÇÃO, *s.f.*, bifurcation.
BI.FUR.CAR, *v.*, to bifurcate, to fork, to dichotomize.
BI.GA, *s.f., Hist.*, Roman or Greek chariot.
BI.GA.MI.A, *s.f.*, bigamy.
BÍ.GA.MO, *s.m.*, bigamist.
BIG BANG, *s.m., Astron.*, big bang (the cosmic explosion that marked the beginning of the universe).
BI.GO.DE, *s.m.*, moustache.
BI.GO.DU.DO, *adj.*, moutached.
BI.GOR.NA, *s.f.*, anvil; incus.
BI.GUE-BAN.GUE, *s.m.*, big bang.
BI.JU.TE.RI.A, *s.f.*, bijouterie, trinckets, small jewels.
BI.LA.TE.RAL, *adj.*, bilateral.
BIL.BO.QUÊ, *s.m.*, catchball (children's toy).
BI.LHA, *s.f.*, pitcher, monkey jar.
BI.LHÃO, *num.*, billion.
BI.LHAR, *s.m.*, billiards.
BI.LHE.TE, *s.m.*, note, billet, short letter, notice; ticket.
BI.LHE.TEI.RO, *s.m.*, ticket clerk.
BI.LHE.TE.RI.A, *s.f.*, booking office, box-office, ticket-office.
BI.LI.AR, *adj.*, bilious; *vesícula ~*: gall bladder.
BI.LÍN.GUE, *s.m.*, bilingual.
BI.LI.O.NÁ.RIO, *adj., s.m.*, billionaire.
BI.LI.O.SO, *adj.*, bilious; ill-tempered.
BÍ.LIS, *s.f.*, bile, gall.
BIL.RO, *s.m.*, bobbin.
BIL.TRE, *s.m.*, rascal, scoundrel.
BI.MEN.SAL, *adj.*, bimensal, bimonthly.

BI.MES.TRAL, *adj.*, bimestrial.
BI.MES.TRE, *s.m.*, bimester.
BI.MO.TOR, *s.m.*, twin-engined plane; *adj.*, twin-enguined.
BI.NÁ.RIO, *adj.*, dual, binary.
BIN.GO, *s.m.*, bingo (game).
BI.NÓ.CU.LO, *s.m.*, binocle, binocular, field-glass.
BI.NÔ.MI.O, *s.m.*, binomial.
BI.O.COM.BUS.TÍ.VEL, *s.m.*, biofuel.
BI.O.DE.GRA.DÁ.VEL, *adj.*, biodegradable.
BI.O.FÍ.SI.CA, *s.f.*, biophysics.
BI.O.GRA.FAR, *v.*, to biographize.
BI.O.GRA.FI.A, *s.f.*, biography.
BI.O.GRÁ.FI.CO, *adj.*, biographical.
BI.Ó.GRA.FO, *s.m.*, biographer.
BI.O.LO.GI.A, *s.f.*, biology.
BI.Ó.LO.GO, *s.m.*, biologist.
BI.O.MA, *s.m., Biol.*, biome.
BI.O.MAS.SA, *s.f.*, biomass.
BI.OM.BO, *s.m.*, folding screen, screen; blind.
BI.Ô.NI.CO, *adj.*, bionic.
BI.Ó.PSIA, *s.f.*, biopsy.
BI.O.QUÍ.MI.CA, *s.f.*, biochemistry.
BI.O.QUÍ.MI.CO, *s.m.*, biochemist; *adj.*, biochemical.
BI.OR.RIT.MO, *s.m.*, biorhythm.
BI.OS.FE.RA, *s.f., Biol.*, biosphere.
BI.O.TA, *s.f., Biol.*, biota.
BI.O.TEC.NO.LO.GI.A, *s.f.*, biotechnology.
BIP, *s.m., Bras.*, tone.
BI.PAR.TI.ÇÃO, *s.f.*, bipartition.
BI.PAR.TI.DÁ.RI.O, *adj.*, bipartisan.
BI.PAR.TI.DA.RIS.MO, *s.m.*, bipartisanship.
BI.PAR.TIR, *v.*, to divide into two parts, divide into halves.
BI.PE.DAL, *adj.*, bipedal.
BÍ.PE.DE, *s.m.*, two-footed animal, biped.
BI.PO.LAR, *adj.*, bipolar.
BI.PO.LA.RI.DA.DE, *s.f.*, bipolarity.
BI.QUEI.RA, *s.f.*, tip; gutter.
BI.QUÍ.NI, *s.m.*, bikini.
BIR.MÂ.NI.A, *s.*, Burma.
BIR.MA.NÊS, *s., adj.*, Burmese.
BI.RI.TA, *s.f., Bras.*, booze, any alcoholic drink.
BI.ROS.CA, *s.f.*, small shop, snack bar.
BIR.RA, *s.f.*, obstinacy, stubbornness.
BIR.REN.TO, *adj.*, stubborn, obstinate, mad.
BI.RU.TA, *adj., s. 2 gen.*, crazy, nuts; *s.f.*, wind sleeve (aeronautics).
BIS, *adv.*, bis, again, twice.
BI.SÃO, *s.m.*, bison, buffalo.
BI.SAR, *v.*, to repeat, to do once more.
BI.SA.VÔ, *s.m.*, great-grandfather.
BI.SA.VÓ, *s.f.*, great-grandmother.
BIS.BI.LHO.TAR, *v.*, to snoop, to gossip, to complicate.
BIS.BI.LHO.TEI.RO, *s.m.*, intriguer, telltale; *adj.*, meddling, intruding.
BIS.CA.TE, *s.m.*, odd job, casual earnings, casual work.
BIS.CA.TE.AR, *v.*, to work casually, to live on odd jobs.
BIS.CA.TEI.RO, *s.m., Bras.*, one who does odd jobs.
BIS.COI.TO, *s.m.*, biscuit, sugar bread, scone, cookie.
BIS.MU.TO, *s.m., Quím.*, bismuth.
BIS.NA.GA, *s.f.*, tube, squirt.
BIS.NE.TA, *s.f.*, great-granddaughter.

BISNETO   •• 110 ••   BÓLIDE

BIS.NE.TO, *s.m.*, great-grandson.
BI.SO.NHI.CE, *s.m.*, inability, incapacity.
BI.SO.NHO, *s.m.*, inexperienced recruit, freshman, *adj.*, unable, incapable.
BIS.PA.DO, *s.m.*, bishopric.
BIS.PO, *s.m.*, bishop.
BIS.SEX.TO, *adj.*, bissextile.
BIS.SE.XU.AL, *adj.*, *s. 2 gen.*, bisexed.
BIS.SE.XU.A.LI.DA.DE, *s.f.*, bisexuality.
BIS.SÍ.LA.BO, *adj.*, *Gram.*, disyllabic.
BIS.TU.RI, *s.m.*, scalpel, bistoury.
BI.TO.LA, *s.f.*, gauge, standard measure, tread.
BI.VA.LÊN.CI.A, *s.f.*, bivalence, bivalency.
BI.VA.LEN.TE, *adj.*, bivalent.
BI.VAL.VE, *adj.*, bivalve.
BI.VA.QUE, *s.m.*, bivouac, camp, encampment.
BI.ZAN.TI.NO, *s.m.*, Byzantine.
BI.ZAR.RI.CE, *s.f.*, ostentation, boasting.
BI.ZAR.RO, *adj.*, gentle, generous, bizarre, extravagant.
BLA.BLA.BLÁ, *s.m.*, *gír.*, blab, chatter, excessive talk.
BLACK-TIE, *s.m.*, black-tie.
BLAS.FE.MA.DOR, *s.m.*, blasphemer, *adj.*, blasphemous.
BLAS.FE.MAR, *v.*, to blaspheme, to profane, to damn, to curse.
BLAS.FÊ.MIA, *s.f.*, blasphemy, impiety, profanity.
BLA.SO.NAR, *v.*, to brag, to boast.
BLE.CAU.TE, *s.m.*, black-out.
BLE.FA.DOR, *s.m.*, bluffer.
BLE.FAR, *v.*, to bluff.
BLE.FE, *s.m.*, bluff, thimblerig.
BLÊI.SER, *s.m.*, bazer, coat.
BLE.NOR.RA.GI.A, *s.f.*, blennorhea, gonorrhea.
BLIN.DA.DO, *adj.*, armoured, armored.
BLIN.DA.GEM, *adj.*, armour, armouring.
BLI.NDAR, *v.*, to armour, to plate, to case, to coat, to protect, to cover.
BLITZ, *s.f.*, blitz, blitzkrieg.
BLO.CO, *s.m.*, block; writing pad, date block; bloc: a political group.
BLOG, *s.m.*, *Comp.*, blog.
BLO.QUE.A.DO, *adj.*, blocked, obstructed.
BLO.QUE.A.DOR, *adj.*, blocker, blockader; *adj.*, blocking.
BLO.QUE.AR, *v.*, to block, to obstruct, to blockade, to stop.
BLO.QUEI.O, *s.m.*, block; siege; blockade; obstruction.
BLUES, *s.m.*, *Mús.*, blues.
BLU.SA, *s.f.*, blouse, smock.
BLU.SÃO, *s.m.*, windbraker, sweatshirt.
BO, *abrev.* of *Boletim de Ocorrência*: Brazilian crime report (equivalent to Complaint).
BO.A, *s.f.*, feminine of *bom*: good; *Zool.*, boa, snake; *adj.*, good, fine; *interj.*, *boa!*: excellent! good!
BO.A FÉ, *s.f.*, good faith, plain-dealing.
BO.A NOI.TE, *s.m.*, good night!, good evening! (salutation).
BO.A-PIN.TA, *s. 2 gen.*, good-looking person; *adj.*, good-looking.
BO.AS FES.TAS, *s.f.*, *pl.*, greetings at Christmas and New Year.
BO.A TAR.DE, *s.m.*, good afternoon; *interj.*, good afternoon! (salutation).
BO.A.TO, *s.m.*, rumour, report, hearsay.
BO.BA.GEM, *s.f.*, foolery, buffoonery, nonsense, rot, bullshit, stupidity.

BO.BA.LHÃO, *s.m.*, fool, dunce.
BO.BE.A.DA, *s.f.*, foolishness.
BO.BI.NA, *s.f.*, spool, bobbin, reel.
BO.BI.NAR, *v.*, to wind, to coil.
BO.BO, *s.m.*, fool, imbecile, buffoon, clown; *adj.*, foolish, silly, soft.
BO.BO.CA, *adj.*, stupid, fool.
BO.CA, *s.f.*, mouth, whistle, muzzle.
BO.CA.DA, *s.f.*, mouthful.
BO.CA.DO, *s.m.*, piece, a mouthful, morsel, small portion.
BO.CAL, *s.m.*, mouth, muzzle; mouthpiece.
BO.ÇAL, *s.m.*, stupid, rude.
BO.ÇA.LI.DA.DE, *s.f.*, stupidity, rudeness.
BO.CA-LI.VRE, *s. 2 gen.*, free meal.
BO.CE.JAR, *v.*, to gape, to yawn.
BO.CE.JO, *s.m.*, yawn, gaping.
BO.CE.TA, *s.f.*, little box; *vulg.*, cunt.
BO.CHE.CHA, *s.f.*, cheek.
BO.CHE.CHÁR, *v.*, to rinse the mouth.
BO.CHE.CHO, *s.m.*, cheek.
BO.CHE.CHU.DO, *adj.*, cheeky, fubsy.
BÓ.CI.O, *s.m.*, *Med.*, goitre, goiter, struma.
BO.CÓ, *adj.*, silly, childish.
BO.DA, *s.f.*, wedding party; wedding dinner.
BO.DE, *s.m.*, *Zool.*, he-goat, goat, buck-goat.
BO.DE.GA, *s.f.*, wine-cellar, trash.
BO.DE.GUEI.RO, *s.m.*, tavern-keeper.
BO.Ê.MIA, *s.f.*, folly, dissipation.
BO.ê.MI.O, *s.m.*, *adj.*, bohemian (merrymaker); Bohemian (concerning to or inhabitant in Bohemia).
BO.DO.SO, *adj.*, dirty, filthy, smelly.
BO.DUM, *s.m.*, fetid smell of animal or human sweat.
BO.FE.TA.DA, *s.f.*, box on the ear, slap in the face, flap, cuff; insult, injury.
BO.FE.TÃO, *s.m.*, hard slap on the face.
BOI, *s.m.*, *Zool.*, ox, bull, any bovine, bullock.
BOI.A, *s.f.*, *Náut.*, buoy, seamark, lifebuoy; *pop.*, meal, food.
BOI.A.DA, *s.f.*, herd of oxen, drove.
BOI.A.DEI.RO, *s.m.*, herdsman, cowboy, cattle dealer.
BOI.A-FRI.A, *s.m.*, agricultural dayworker.
BOI.AR, *v.*, to float, to buoy, to be afloat, to driff.
BOI.CO.TAR, *v.*, to boycott, to restrict.
BOI.CO.TE, *s.m.*, boycott.
BOI.NA, *s.f.*, bonnet, berret, cap.
BO.JO, *s.m.*, bulge, paunch; belly (ship).
BO.JU.DO, *adj.*, rounded, paunchy.
BO.LA, *s.f.*, ball, globe, sphere; round, bowl.
BO.LA.CHA, *s.f.*, biscuit, cracker, cookies, snap.
BOL.CHE.VIS.MO, *s.m.*, bolshevism, communism.
BOL.CHE.VIS.TA, *s. 2 gen.*, *adj.*, bolshevist, Bolshevik.
BOL.DO, *s.m.*, *Bot.*, boldo, boldu.
BO.LE.RO, *s.m.*, bolero.
BO.LE.TIM, *s.m.*, bulletin, short notice, report; school report, periodical publication.
BO.LE.TO, *s.m.*, *Com.*, bank payment guide; *Mil.*, requisition; fetlock joint.
BO.LEI.A, *s.f.*, *US* driver's seat (trucks), carriage box; *UK* lorry.
BO.LÉU, *s.m.*, fall, jolt, jerk.
BO.LHA, *s.f.*, blister, bubble, pimple, blain.
BO.LI.CHE, *s.m.*, poolroom, bowling, inn.
BÓ.LI.DE, *s. 2 gen.*, bolide (great meteorite).

BOLINA   •• 111 ••   BOVINO

BO.LI.NA, *s.f., Náut.*, bowline; *pop.*, masher.

BO.LI.NA.DOR, *s.m., pop.*, masher.

BO.LI.NAR, *v.*, to excite, to excite anyone sexually.

BO.LI.NHO, *s.m.*, croquette, tidbit, small fried balls.

BO.LÍ.VI.A, *s.*, Bolivia.

BO.LI.VI.A.NO, *s.m., adj.*, Bolivian.

BO.LO, *s.m.*, cake.

BO.LOR, *s.m.*, mould, mildrew, mustiness.

BO.LO.REN.TO, *adj.*, mouldy, musty, frowzy, rusty.

BO.LO.TA, *s.f.*, acorn, lump.

BOL.SA, *s.f.*, purse, small bag, burse, pocket.

BOL.SEI.RO, *s.m.*, purse maker, purse seller.

BOL.SIS.TA, *s. 2 gen.*, stockbroker, broker.

BOL.SO, *s.m.*, pocket, fob.

BOM, *adj.*, good, fine, right, nice.

BOM.BA, *s.f.*, bomb, bomshell, pump, siphon, suction-pipe.

BOM.BA.CHAS, *s.f., pl.*, gaucho pants (wide breeches).

BOM.BAR.DA, *s.f., Hist.*, bombard.

BOM.BAR.DE.AR, *v.*, to shell, to bombard, to bomb, to cannon.

BOM.BAR.DEI.O, *s.m.*, bombardment, shelling.

BOM.BAR.DEI.RO, *s.m.*, bombardier, bomberder.

BOM.BA-RE.LÓ.GI.O, *s.f.*, time bomb.

BOM.BÁS.TI.CO, *adj.*, bombastic, deafening, magnificent; *adv.*, bombastically.

BOM.BE.A.MEN.TO, *s.m.*, act of pumping fluids.

BOM.BE.AR, *v.*, to pump.

BOM.BEI.RO, *s.m.*, fireman, hoseman.

BOM.BO, *s.m., Mús.*, big drum, bass drum.

BOM.BOM, *s.m.*, bonbon; *UK* sweetie.

BOM.BOR.DO, *s.m., Náut.*, port, portside, larboard.

BOM-DI.A, *s.m.*, good morning! (salutation).

BO.NA.CHÃO, *s.m.*, good-natured, honest fellow.

BO.NAN.ÇA, *s.f.*, calm, peace, tranquility, lull, calmness.

BON.DA.DE, *s.f.*, goodness, kindness, graciousness, affability, benevolence.

BON.DE, *s.m.*, streetcar, trolley.

BON.DO.SA.MEN.TE, *adv.*, kindly, mildly.

BON.DO.SO, *adj.*, good-natured, charitable, kind-hearted, benevolent.

BO.NÉ, *s.m.*, cap, bonnet, kepi.

BO.NE.CA, *s.f.*, doll, toy, baby.

BO.NE.CO, *s.m.*, puppet, marionette, doll.

BO.NI.FI.CA.ÇÃO, *s.f.*, allowance, money grant, bonus, privilege.

BO.NI.FI.CAR, *v.*, to improve, to reward.

BO.NI.TÃO, *s.m.*, handsome man; *adj.*, handsome, good-looking.

BO.NI.TE.ZA, *s.f.*, prettiness, attractiveness, beauty.

BO.NI.TO, *adj.*, pretty, handsome, beautiful, nice, bonny, nifty.

BÔ.NUS, *s.m.*, bonus, bond, paper.

BON.ZO, *s.m.*, bonze (Buddhist priest); *fig.*, person indifferent; charlatan, hypocrite.

BO.QUEI.RA, *s.f., Med., pop.*, chapped lips (the corners).

BO.QUEI.RÃO, *s.m.*, big mouth, estuary; gully.

BO.QUE.JO, *s.m.*, muttering, gape, yawn.

BO.QUI.A.BER.TO, *adj.*, astonished, amazed, agape, gaping.

BO.QUI.LHA, *s.f.*, cigar-holder; *Mús.*, mouthpiece.

BO.QUI.NHA, *s.f.*, little mouth; *col.*, kiss.

BOR.BO.LE.TA, *s.f., Zool.*, butterfly, moth.

BOR.BO.LE.TE.AR, *v.*, to meander, to wander, to flit, to flutter.

BOR.BO.TÃO, *s.m.*, jet, spout, flash, squall.

BOR.BU.LHA, *s.f.*, bubble, burble; *Med.*, pimple, pustule.

BOR.BU.LHAR, *v.*, to bubble.

BOR.BU.LHEN.TO, *adj.*, pimpled; pimplous, gushing.

BOR.DA, *s.f.*, edge, border, brim, lip, rim, skirt, margin.

BOR.DA.DO, *s.m.*, embroidery, needlework; *adj.*, embroidered.

BOR.DA.DU.RA, *s.f.*, embroidery; border; retrenchment, clipping; bordure.

BOR.DÃO, *s.f.*, stick, cudgel, bourdon; pet phrase, slogan.

BOR.DAR, *v.*, to embroider, to hem, to garnish.

BOR.DEL, *s.m.*, whore-house, bawdy-house.

BOR.DO, *s.m., Náut.*, board of a ship, log; border, edge, flange; *Bot.*, maple (tree).

BOR.DÔ, *s.m.*, dark red colour, burgundy (color); wine-red (Bordeaux).

BOR.DO.A.DA, *s.f.*, stroke, knock, punch.

BO.RE.AL, *adj.*, boreal, northern, northerly.

BO.RES.TE, *s.m., Náut.*, starbord.

BÓ.RI.CO, *adj.*, boric, boracic.

BO.RO, *s.m., Quím.*, boron.

BO.RO.CO.XÔ, *s. 2 gen., gír.*, listless, inert; *adj.*, feeble, sluggish, brocken.

BOR.RA, *s.f.*, grounds (coffee); dregs (wine).

BOR.RA-BO.TAS, *s.m.*, good-for-nothing.

BOR.RA.CHA, *s.f.*, rubber, eraser, india-rubber.

BOR.RA.CHEI.RO, *s.m.*, tyre fitter, vulcanizer.

BOR.RA.CHU.DO, *s.m.*, black fly, gnat.

BOR.RA.DO, *adj.*, stained, spotty; *col.*, foul (shit).

BOR.RA.DOR, *s.m.*, blotter, notepad, daybook.

BOR.RÃO, *s.m.*, blot, blemish, dot, stain, spatter.

BOR.RAR, *v.*, to stain, to besmear, to dirty, to smudge.

BOR.RAS.CA, *s.f.*, tempest, storm, hurricane, thunderstorm.

BOR.RI.FA.DOR, *s.m.*, sprinkler, watering can.

BOR.RI.FAR, *v.*, to sprinkle, to spray, to asperse, to perfuse, to damp.

BOR.RI.FO, *s.m.*, sprinkling; drizzle, spray.

BÓS.NIA-HERZEGOVINA, *s.*, Bosnia-Herzegovina.

BOS.NI.A.NO, *s.m.*, Bosnian; *adj.*, Bosnian.

BÓS.NI.O, *s.m., adj.*, Bosnian.

BÓ.SON, *s.m., Fís.*, boson (subatomic particle).

BOS.QUE, *s.m.*, wood, forest, thicket, grove.

BOS.SA, *s.m.*, bruise, bump, boil, aptitude, talent.

BOS.SA-NO.VA, *s.f., Bras.*, Bossa Nova (new style, in especially, popular music from Brazil).

BOS.TA, *s.f.*, cow dropping, cow dung, shit, crap.

BO.TA, *s.f.*, boot, tub, barrel.

BO.TÂ.NI.CA, *s.f.*, botany.

BO.TÂ.NI.CO, *s.m.*, botanist, herbalist; *adj.*, botanic.

BO.TÃO, *s.m.*, bud, button, flower-bud, gemmule.

BO.TAR, *v.*, to throw, to cast, to fling, to put, to lay an egg.

BO.TE, *s.m.*, assault, boat, skiff, cut, stab, blow.

BO.TE.CO, *s.m.*, bar, tavern, stall.

BO.TE.QUIM, *s.m.*, bar, tavern, taphouse.

BO.TI.CA, *s.f.*, apothecary, pharmacy.

BO.TI.CÁ.RI.O, *s.m.*, dispensing chemist.

BO.TI.JA, *s.f.*, flask, stone jug.

BO.TI.JÃO, *s.m.*, cylinder.

BO.TI.NA, *s.f.*, small boot, lady's boot, ankle-boot.

BOU.TI.QUE, *s.f.*, boutique.

BO.VÍ.DE.O, *s.m.*, bovine; *adj.*, bovine.

BO.VI.NO, *adj.*, bovine.

BOXE

•• 112 ••

BRINDE

BO.XE, *s.m.*, boxing, pugilism.
BO.XE.A.DOR, *s.m.*, pugilist, boxer.
BO.XE.AR, *v.*, to box.
BÓ.XER, *s.m.*, boxer (a breed of dogs).
BO.XIS.TA, *s.m.*, *Esp.*, boxer.
BO.ZÓ, *s.m.*, *gír.*, ass, arse, buns, buttocks.
BRA.BE.ZA, *s.f.*, the same that *braveza*.
BRA.BO, *s.m.*, the same that *bravo*.
BRA.ÇA, *s.f.*, fathom.
BRA.ÇA.DA, *s.f.*, armful, stroke.
BRA.ÇA.DEI.RA, *s.f.*, clamp, brace, band.
BRA.ÇAL, *adj.*, relating to the arm, brachial, manual; *s.m.*, bracer, brassard.
BRA.CE.AR, *v.*, brace (sails); struggle.
BRA.CE.JAR, *v.*, to gesticulate, to move the arms.
BRA.CE.LE.TE, *s.m.*, bracelet, armlet.
BRA.ÇO, *s.f.*, arm, branch.
BRA.ÇU.DO, *adj.*, brawny, strong-armed.
BRA.DAR, *v.*, to cry, to hollo, to shout, to scream, to yell, to bawl.
BRA.DE.JAR, *v.*, to cry, to shout, to scream.
BRA.DO, *s.m.*, cry, shout, scream, whoop, acclamation, clamour.
BRA.GUI.LHA, *s.f.*, slit of trousers.
BRAI.LE, *s.m.*, Braille.
BRA.MA.NIS.MO, *s.m.*, *Rel.*, Brahmanism.
BRA.MÂ.NI.CO, *adj.*, *Rel.*, Brahmanic.
BRA.MAR, *v.*, to roar, to shout, to cry.
BRA.MI.DO, *s.m.*, roar, bellow, scream (animals, storm).
BRA.MIR, *v.*, to roar, to bellow, to yell, to howl.
BRA.MO.SO, *adj.*, roaring; *fig.*, tempestuous.
BRAN.CO, *adj.*, white, light, clear; *Branca de Neve*: Snow-White (fairy tale).
BRAN.CU.RA, *s.f.*, white, whiteness, hoar.
BRAN.DE.AR, *v.*, to make mild.
BRAN.DIR, *v.*, to brandish, to shake, to swing.
BRAN.DO, *adj.*, tender, soft, mild, bland, light, temperate.
BRAN.DU.RA, *s.f.*, softness, mildness, mildness, lightness, kindness.
BRAN.QUE.A.DOR, *s.m.*, whitener, bleacher.
BRAN.QUE.A.MEN.TO, *s.m.*, whitening, bleaching.
BRAN.QUE.AR, *v.*, to whiten, to make white.
BRAN.QUE.JAR, *v.*, to whiten, to bleach; to appear.
BRÂN.QUI.A, *s.f.*, *Zool.*, *Anat.*, gill, branchia.
BRAN.QUI.AL, *adj.*, branchial.
BRÂN.QUIAS, *s.f.*, *pl.*, gills.
BRAN.QUI.DÃO, *s.m.*, whiteness, white colour.
BRA.QUI.AL, *adj.*, brachial.
BRA.QUI.CE.FA.LI.A, *s.f.*, *Anat.*, brachycephaly.
BRA.QUI.CÉ.FA.LO *s.m.*, *Anat.*, brachycephal (person); *adj.*, brachycephalic.
BRA.SA, *s.f.*, live or burning coal, incandescence, ember.
BRA.SÃO, *s.m.*, coat of arms, arm; *fig.*, honor, honour, distinction.
BRA.SEI.RO, *s.m.*, brazier, fire remains.
BRA.SIL, *s.m.*, Brazil.
BRA.SI.LEI.RA, *s.f.*, Brazilian woman or girl.
BRA.SI.LEI.RIS.MO, *s.m.*, Brazilianism.
BRA.SI.LEI.RO, *s.m.*, Brazilian: native or inhabitant of Brazil; *adj.*, Brazilian.
BRA.SI.LI.A.NA, *s.f.*, collection of books and studies concerning Brazil.
BRA.VA.MEN.TE, *adv.*, bravely.
BRA.VA.TA, *s.f.*, bravado, boasting; vainglory.
BRA.VA.TEI.RO, *s.m.*, swaggerer, boaster, braggart.
BRA.VE.ZA, *s.f.*, ferocity, savagery, rage.
BRA.VI.O, *s.m.*, wild country; *adj.*, wild, savage, fierce, unruly.
BRA.VO, *adj.*, brave, valiant, bold, furious, courageous, valorous.
BRA.VU.RA, *s.f.*, bravery, courage, prowess, exploit.
BRE.AR, *v.*, to pitch, to tar; to dirty.
BRE.CA, *s.f.*, cramp.
BRE.CA.DA, *s.f.*, putting on the brakes.
BRE.CAR, *v.*, to brake, to put on the brake.
BRE.CHA, *s.f.*, gap, fissure, rupture, chasm, rent.
BRE.CHÓ, *s.m.*, second-hand shop.
BRE.GA, *adj.*, *pop.*, tacky.
BRE.JEI.RO, *s.m.*, tramp, vagrant, loafer; *adj.*, malicious, vagrant, lazy.
BRE.JEN.TO, *adj.*, marshy, swampy, boggy.
BRE.JO, *s.m.*, swamp, bog, fen, slough, slash, morass.
BRE.NHA, *s.f.*, thicket.
BRE.QUE, *s.m.*, brake, break.
BRE.TÃO, *s.m.*, Breton; *adj.*, Breton.
BREU, *s.m.*, pitch, tar, colophony, darkness.
BRE.VE, *adj.*, brief, short, rapid, quick, concise.
BRE.VÊ, *s.m.*, *Aeron.*, certificate who qualifies a pilot, diploma.
BRE.VE.MEN.TE, *adv.*, shortly, briefly, concisely.
BRE.VI.Á.RI.O, *s.m.*, breviary.
BRE.VI.DA.DE, *adj.*, shortness, conciseness, brevity, briefness.
BRI.CA.BRA.QUE, *s.m.*, bric-a-brac, junk shop.
BRI.DA, *s.f.*, bridle, rein.
BRID.GE, *s.m.*, bridge.
BRI.GA, *s.f.*, strife, quarrel, fight, broil.
BRI.GA.DOR, *s.m.*, quarreler, brawler; *adj.*, quarreling, quarrelsome.
BRI.GA.DA, *s.f.*, brigade.
BRI.GA.DEI.RO, *s.m.*, brigadier, brigadier-general.
BRI.GÃO, *s.m.*, brawler; *adj.*, brawling.
BRI.GAR, *v.*, to quarrel, to fight, to combat.
BRI.GUEN.TO, *s.m.*, wrangler, scuffler; *adj.*, quarrelsome, belligerent.
BRI.LHAN.TE, *s.m.*, diamond, brilliant; *adj.*, brilliant, bright, sparkling.
BRI.LHAN.TE.MEN.TE, *adv.*, brilliantly, magnificently.
BRI.LHAN.TI.NA, *s.f.*, brilliantine.
BRI.LHAN.TIS.MO, *s.m.*, brilliancy, brightness, splendour, illustriousness.
BRI.LHAR, *v.*, to shine, to glitter, to scintillate, to star, to flash.
BRI.LHO, *s.m.*, brightness, splendor, brilliancy, luminosity, splendour.
BRI.LHO.SO, *adj.*, brilliant, radiant; bright, lustrous.
BRIM, *s.m.*, sailcloth, canvas, drill.
BRIN.CA.DEI.RA, *s.f.*, entertainment, fun, game, play, sport, merrymaking.
BRIN.CA.LHÃO, *s.m.*, jester, wag, sport.
BRIN.CAR, *v.*, to play, to joke, to toy, to frolic, to amuse, to divert.
BRIN.CO, *s.m.*, earring, drop, pendant, toy.
BRIN.DAR, *v.*, to toast, to drink to a person's health.
BRIN.DE, *s.m.*, toast, wish of health.

BRINQUEDO · 113 · BYTE

BRIN.QUE.DO, *s.m.*, toy, plaything, joke.
BRI.O, *s.m.*, sense of dignity, valour, pride, character.
BRI.O.CHE, *s.f.*, *Cul.*, brioche.
BRI.O.SO, *adj.*, proud, brave, courageous.
BRI.SA, *s.f.*, breeze, light, fresh wind.
BRI.TA, *s.f.*, broken stones, pebble.
BRI.TA.MEN.TO, *s.m.*, breaking, trituratio, crushing.
BRI.TÂ.NI.CO, *adj.*, *s.m.*, British.
BRI.TAR, *v.*, to break, to crush, to spall; to grind.
BRO.A, *s.f.*, bread of maize, pone.
BRO.CA, *s.f.*, drill, bit, auger, gimlet.
BRO.CAR, *v.*, to bore; to drill, to perforate.
BRO.CHA, *s.f.*, tack, peg.
BRO.CHAR, *v.*, to stitch or sew books.
BRO.CHE, *s.m.*, brooch, pin, breast-pin.
BRO.CHU.RA, *s.f.*, brochure, paperback edition, pamphlet, booklet.
BRO.CO.LIS, *s.m.*, *pl.*, *Bot.*, broccoli.
BRO.MA.TO, *s.m.*, *Quím.*, bromate.
BRO.MO, *s.m.*, *Quím.*, bromine.
BRON.CA, *s.f.*, scolding, reprimand.
BRON.CO, *adj.*, rude, dull, stupid, rough.
BRON.CO.PNEU.MO.NI.A, *s.f.*, *Med.*, bronchopneumonia.
BRON.QUE.AR, *v.*, *col.*, to scold, to reprimand.
BRON.QUI.AL, *adj.*, bronchial.
BRÔN.QUI.O, *s.m.*, *Anat.*, bronchial tube, bronchus.
BRON.QUI.TE, *s.f.*, *Med.*, bronchitis.
BRON.TOS.SAU.RO, *s.m.*, *Paleont.*, brontosaurus, brontosaur.
BRON.ZE, *s.m.*, bronze, gun metal.
BRON.ZE.A.DO, *s.m.*, bronzed, bronzy, tanned.
BRON.ZE.A.DOR, *s.m.*, tanning lotion.
BRON.ZE.A.MENT.TO, *s.m.*, tanning; bronzing, brazing.
BRON.ZE.AR, *v.*, to tan.
BRO.QUEL, *s.m.*, buckler, shield.
BRO.TA.MEN.TO, *s.m.*, sprouting, budding.
BRO.TAR, *v.*, to arise, to produce, to grow, to issue, to originate.
BRO.TO, *s.m.*, bud, shoot, eye; young girl.
BRO.TO.E.JA, *s.f.*, sudamen, skin eruption, vesicular eruption.
BRO.XA, *s.f.*, stock brush.
BRU.ços, *s.m.*, *pl.*, face down, prone.
BRU.CU.TU, *s.m.*, *gír.*, armored vehicle used by the police; brute, hulk.
BRU.MA, *s.f.*, thick fog, haze, vapour, cloud, mist.
BRU.MA.DO, *adj.*, foggy.
BRU.MO.SO, *adj.*, foggy, hazy, misty.
BRU.NIR, *v.*, to polish, to burnish, to furbish.
BRUS.CO, *adj.*, sudden, coarse.
BRU.TAL, *adj.*, brutal, cruel, rough, brutish, bestial, savage.
BRU.TA.LI.DA.DE, *s.f.*, brutality, atrocity, brutishness, wildness, bestiality.
BRU.TA.MON.TES, *s. 2 gen.*, hulk.
BRU.TA.LI.ZAR, *v.*, to brutalize, bestialize.
BRU.TO, *s.m.*, animal, beast; *adj.*, rude, rough, dull, raw.
BRU.XA, *s.f.*, witch, sorceress, enchantress.
BRU.XA.RI.A, *s.f.*, witchery, sorcery, witchcraft.
BRU.XO, *s.m.*, wizard, sorcerer, conjurer.
BU.CHA, *s.f.*, bush, sleeve, wad.
BU.CHO, *s.m.*, craw, crop, stomach.
BU.ÇO, *s.m.*, down.
BU.CÓ.LI.CO, *adj.*, pastoral, bucolic.

BU.DIS.MO, *s.m.*, Buddhism.
BU.DIS.TA, *s. 2 gen.*, *adj.*, Buddhist.
BU.EI.RO, *s.m.*, sewer, drainpipe, gutter.
BÚ.FA.LO, *s.m.*, *Zool.*, buffalo.
BU.FAN.TE, *adj.*, puffed out, bouffant.
BU.FAR, *v.*, to puff, to blow, to snuff, to snort.
BU.FÊ, *s.m.*, buffet.
BU.FO.NA.RI.A, *s.f.*, buffoonery, drollery.
BUG, *s.m.*, *Ingl.*, *Comp.*, bug.
BU.GI.GAN.GA, *s.f.*, trifle, gewgaws, gadgets, trinket.
BU.GI.O, *s.m.*, ape, monkey, simian.
BU.GRE, *s.m.*, Indian, savage, aborigine.
BU.JÃO, *s.m.*, plug, sttoper, stopple.
BU.LA, *s.f.*, bull, papal or imperial edict or letter.
BUL.BO, *s.m.*, bulb.
BUL.DÔ.ZER, *s.m.*, bulldozer.
BU.LE, *s.m.*, coffeepot, teapot.
BUL.GÁ.RI.A, *s.*, Bulgaria.
BÚL.GA.RO, *adj.*, *s.m.*, Bulgarian.
BU.LHU.FAS, *pron.*, *gír.*, nothing.
BU.LI.MI.A, *s.f.*, bulimia.
BU.LIR, *v.*, to agitate, to move slightly.
BUM.BUM, *s.m.*, *pop.*, bottom, bum.
BUN.DA, *s.f.*, bum, buttock, posterior.
BU.QUÊ, *s.m.*, bouquet, bunch of flowers.
BU.RA.CO, *s.m.*, hole, gap, hollow, cavity, cave, gully.
BUR.GO, *s.m.*, burgh, borough, village, hamlet, palace.
BUR.GUÊS, *s.m.*, burgher, citizen, bourgeois.
BUR.GUE.SI.A, *s.f.*, bourgeoisie.
BU.RI.LAR, *v.*, to perfect, to chisel, to carve, to adorn.
BUR.LA, *s.f.*, double-dealing; jeering.
BUR.LAR, *v.*, to cheat, to fraud, to trick, to jest, to joke.
BU.RI.LAR, *v.*, to engrave, *fig.*, to perfect.
BUR.LES.CO, *adj.*, burlesque.
BU.RO.CRA.CI.A, *s.f.*, bureaucracy, red-tape, officialism.
BU.RO.CRA.TA, *s. 2 gen.*, bureaucrat, red-tapist.
BU.RO.CRÁ.TI.CO, *adj.*, bureaucratic.
BU.RO.CRA.TI.ZAR, *v.*, to bureaucratize.
BUR.RA.DA, *s.f.*, foolish act, nonsense, drove of asses, mistake.
BUR.RI.CE, *s.f.*, stupidity, foolishness, nonsense.
BUR.RO, *s.m.*, ass, donkey, mule; stupid, dull, foolish.
BUR.SI.TE, *s.f.*, bursitis.
BUS.CA, *s.f.*, search, inquiry, quest, research.
BUS.CA.DOR, *s.m.*, *Comp.*, search engine.
BUS.CA-PÉ, *s.m.*, firecracker.
BUS.CAR, *v.*, to search, to seek, to inquire, to quest, to investigate, to obtain.
BÚS.SO.LA, *s.f.*, magnetic needle, compass.
BUS.TI.Ê, *s.m.*, bustier.
BUS.TO, *s.m.*, bust, bosom, sculture.
BU.TI.QUE, *s.f.*, *Fr.*, boutique.
BU.TU.CA, *s.f.*, gadfly.
BU.ZI.NA, *s.f.*, horn, trumpet, honk, bugle, hooter.
BU.ZI.NAR, *v.*, to sound a horn, to hoot.
BÚ.ZI.O, *s.m.*, conch; helmet shell; *jogar búzios*: to cast shells (in fortune teller).
BY.TE, *s.m.*, *Comp.*, byte.

C

C, *s.m.*, the third letter of the Portuguese alphabet.
C, *num.*, one hundred in Roman numerals.
CÁ, *adv.*, here, in this place, hither, between us.
CÃ, *s.f.*, white hair, *cãs* (*pl.*): white locks.
CA.A.BA, *s.f., Rel.*, Kaaba, Kaabeh.
CA.A.TIN.GA, *s.f.*, a stunted sparse forest, scrub savana.
CA.BA.ÇA, *s.f.*, bottle gourd.
CA.BAL, *adj.*, complete, whole, full, perfect.
CA.BA.LA, *s.f.*, cabbala; *fig.*, cabal.
CA.BA.LAR, *v.*, to cabal, to plot, to intrigue.
CA.BA.LÍS.TI.CO, *adj.*, cabalístic.
CA.BAL.MEN.TE, *adv.*, completely, exactly.
CA.BA.NA, *s.f.*, hut, cottage, shack.
CA.BA.RÉ, *s.m.*, cabaret, honky-tonk.
CA.BE.A.MEN.TO, *s.m.*, cabling.
CA.BE.AR, *v.*, to wire, to install cables.
CA.BE.ÇA, *s.f.*, head, poll, scalp, top, intelligence, chief, leader, sagacity, judgment.
CA.BE.ÇA.DA, *s.f.*, a bump with the head, headstall.
CA.BE.ÇA DE VEM.TO, *s. 2 gen.*, scatterbrain.
CA.BE.ÇA-DU.RA, *s. 2 gen.*, blockhead, stubborn, headstrong person; *adj.*, headstrong.
CA.BE.ÇA-FEI.TA, *adj., pop.*, level-headed.
CA.BE.ÇA.LHO, *s.m.*, letterhead, heading, pillow, head of a bed, title page.
CA.BE.CE.AR, *v.*, to nod, to doze, to head, to deviate.
CA.BE.CEI.RA, *s.f.*, cushion, pillow, head of a bed, headrest.
CA.BE.ÇO.TE, *s.m.*, headstock.
CA.BE.ÇU.DO, *adj.*, big-headed, stubborn; pig-headed, obstinate.
CA.BE.DAL, *s.m.*, stock, funds, capital, means, prosperity.
CA.BE.LEI.RA, *s.f.*, head of hair; tail of a comet.
CA.BE.LEI.REI.RO, *s.m.*, hairdresser, wigmaker.
CA.BE.LO, *s.m.*, hair.
CA.BE.LU.DO, *adj.*, hairy, hirsute, difficult; obscene.
CA.BER, *v.*, to be contained in, to fit in or inside of; to be containable.
CA.BI.DE, *s.m.*, rack, hat-stand, hanger, peg.
CA.BI.MEN.TO, *s.m.*, relevancy, pertinance, acceptance, capacity.
CA.BI.NA, CA.BI.NE, *s.f.*, cabin, box, berth.
CA.BIS.BAI.XO, *adj.*, downcast, depressed.
CA.BÍ.VEL, *adj.*, founded on fact, reasonable, fitting.
CA.BO, *s.m.*, corporal, chief; terminal, end, cape; cable, handle, holder.
CA.BO.CLO, *s.m.*, cabloco, civilized Brazilian Indian, rustic, agricultural labourer.
CA.BO DE GUER.RA, *s.m.*, tug-of-war.
CA.BO.GRA.MA, *s.m.*, cable, cablegram, wire.
CA.BO.TA.GEM, *s.f.*, navigation along the coast, cabotage, coasting.
CA.BO.TI.NO, *s.m.*, itinerant actor; show-off; bad actor; *adj.*, theatrical, charlatanic.
CA.BO VER.DE, *s.*, Cabo Verde (country).
CA.BO-VER.DI.A.NO, *s.m., adj.*, Cabo-Verdean.
CA.BRA, *s.f.*, she-goat.
CA.BRA-CE.GA, *s.f.*, blindman's buff.
CA.BRA-MA.CHO, *s.m.*, tough guy.
CA.BREI.RO, *adj., pop.*, suspicious.
CA.BRES.TAN.TE, *s.m., Náut.*, capstan; winch.
CA.BRES.TO, *s.m.*, halter, tame lead ox.
CA.BRI.O.LÉ, *s.f.*, cabriolet carriage; gig, dogcart.
CA.BRI.TA, *s.f.*, a little goat; a young woman.
CA.BRI.TO, *s.m.*, a little buck, kid.
CA.BU.LAR, *v.*, to play truant, to cut classes.
CA.CA, *s.f.*, feces, dirt, shit, excrement.
CA.ÇA, *s.f.*, hunt, hunting, chasing, game; the animals chased.
CA.ÇA.DA, *s.f.*, hunting party, hunt, safari.
CA.ÇA.DOR, *s.m.*, hunter, huntsman.
CA.ÇAM.BA, *s.f.*, bucket, pail, well-bucket, dump-car.
CA.ÇA-MI.NAS, *s.m.*, mine-sweeper.
CA.ÇA-NÍ.QUEIS, *s.m.*, slot-machine.
CA.ÇÃO, *s.m., Zool.*, shark, dogfish.
CA.ÇA.PA, *s.f.*, pocket (on billiard table).
CA.ÇAR, *v.*, to hunt, to chase, to pursue, to catch.
CA.CA.RE.CO, *s.m.*, piece of junk.
CA.CA.RE.JA.DOR, *adj.*, cackling; chattering.
CA.CA.RE.JAR, *v.*, to cackle, to cluck, to chatter.
CA.CA.RE.JO, *s.m.*, cackling, clucking; chuckle.
CA.CA.RÉUS, *s.m., pl.*, old household utensils; junk, trash.
CA.ÇA.RO.LA, *s.f.*, casserole, saucepan.
CA.CAU, *s.m., Bot.*, cacao, cocoa, cacao-bean.
CA.CAU.EI.RO, *s.m., Bot.*, cacao tree.
CA.CE.TA.DA, *s.f.*, a blow with a club, beating, thrashing.
CA.CE.TE, *s.m.*, club, mace.
CA.CE.TI.NHO, *s.m.*, a small club; *Bras.*, a roll (bread).
CA.CHA.ÇA, *s.f.*, sugar cane brandy, rum.
CA.CHA.CEI.RO, *s.m.*, drunkard; *adj.*, drunken.
CA.CHA.LO.TE, *s.m., Zool.*, cachalot, sperm whale.
CA.CHE, *s.m., Comp.*, cache (fast access device).
CA.CHÊ, *s.m.*, fee (payment made to performances).
CA.CHE.A.DO, *adj., pop.*, curly.
CA.CHE.AR, *v.*, to cluster; *pop.*, to curl (hair).
CA.CHE.COL, *s.m.*, scarf, neck-cloth, muffler.
CA.CHIM.BO, *s.m.*, pipe, tobacco-pipe.
CA.CHO, *s.m.*, curl, cluster, ringlet, raceme.
CA.CHO.EI.RA, *s.f.*, waterfall, river rapids, overfall, cascade, cataract.
CA.CHO.LA, *s.f.*, head, pate, nut.
CA.CHOR.RA.DA, *s.f.*, a pack of dogs, mob, rabble; wickedness.
CA.CHOR.RI.CE, *s.f.*, wickedness, indignity, outrage.
CA.CHOR.RI.NHO, *s.m.*, puppy, whelp.
CA.CHOR.RO, *s.m.*, dog, puppy.

CACHORRO-QUENTE ·· 115 ·· CALÇAMENTO

CA.CHOR.RO-QUEN.TE, *s.m.*, hot dog.
CA.CI.FE, *s.m.*, stake, ante (poker).
CA.CIM.BA, *s.f.*, small pool of stagnant water, dewfall.
CA.CI.QUE, *s.m.*, Indian chief, political boss, big shot.
CA.CO, *s.m.*, bit of broken object; trash; shard.
CA.ÇO.A.DA, *s.f.*, mockery, derision.
CA.ÇO.ÀR, *v.*, to scoff, to sneer, to make fun of, to mock.
CA.CO.E.TE, *s.m.*, nervous tic, a bad.habit, cacoethes.
CA.CO.FO.NI.A, *s.f.*, cacophony.
CAC.TO, *s.m.*, cactus.
CA.ÇU.LA, *s. 2 gen.*, baby, the youngest child of a family.
CA.DA, *pron.*, each, every.
CA.DA.FAL.SO, *s.m.*, scaffold, scaffolding.
CA.DAR.ÇO, *s.m.*, tape, ribbon, floss silk, ferret.
CA.DAS.TRA.MEN.TO, *s.m.*, registration; organizing of a register.
CA.DAS.TRAL, *adj.*, cadastral.
CA.DAS.TRAR, *v.*, to make a cadaster, to register.
CA.DAS.TRO, *s.m.*, cadaster, dossier.
CA.DÁ.VER, *s.m.*, dead body, corpse cadaver, defunct.
CA.DA.VÉ.RI.CO, *adj.*, cadaveric, cadaverous.
CA.DÊ, *adv., pop.*, where is/are?
CA.DE.A.DO, *s.m.*, padlock, snap.
CA.DEI.A, *s.f.*, prison, jail, network, chain.
CA.DEI.RA, *s.f.*, chair, seat, place, stall.
CA.DEI.RA.DA, *s.f.*, a blow with a chair.
CA.DE.LA, *s.f.*, female dog, bitch, she-dog.
CA.DÊN.CI.A, *s.f.*, cadence, rhythm.
CA.DEN.CI.A.DO, *adj.*, cadenced, rhythmic; measured.
CA.DEN.CI.AR, *v.*, to cadence, to harmonize.
CA.DEN.TE, *adj.*, falling (star).
CA.DER.NE.TA, *s.f.*, notebook, school register.
CA.DER.NE.TA DE POU.PAN.ÇA, *s.f.*, savings account.
CA.DER.NO, *s.m.*, copy-book, notebook.
CA.DE.TE, *s.m.*, cadet.
CA.DI.NHO, *s.m.*, crucible; *fig.*, melting pot.
CA.DU.CAR, *v.*, to grow very old, to decay, to become decrepit.
CA.DU.CEU, *s.m.*, caduceus.
CA.DU.CI.DA.DE, *s.f.*, old age, decadence; senility.
CA.DU.CO, *adj.*, falling, senile, decrepit.
CA.FA.JES.TA.DA, *s.f.*, boorishness, churlishness; rabble.
CA.FA.JES.TE, *s. 2 gen.*, boor, churl, common, vulgar, scum.
CA.FÉ, *s.m.*, coffee.
CA.FÉ COM·LEI.TE, *adj.*, coffee-coloured.
CA.FE.EI.RO, *s.m.*, coffee tree, coffee bush; *adj.*, regarding coffee, or their production and trade.
CA.FE.I.CUL.TOR, *s.m.*, coffee planter.
CA.FE.I.CUL.TU.RA, *s.f.*, coffee planting.
CA.FE.Í.NA, *s.f.*, caffeine.
CA.FE.TÃO, *s.m.*, cafetão, cáften.
CA.FE.TEI.RA, *s.f.*, coffee-pot.
CA.FE.ZAL, *s.m.*, coffee plantation.
CA.FE.ZEI.RO, *s.m.*, coffee grower; *Bot.*, coffee tree.
CA.FE.ZI.NHO, *s.m.*, a small cup of coffee.
CA.FO.NA, *s.m.*, person tacky; *adj.*, tacky.
CA.FO.NI.CE, *s.f.*, tackiness.
CA.FU.NÉ, *s.m.*, a soft scratching on the head (to sleep).
CA.FU.ZO, *adj., s.m.*, the offspring of Negro and Indian.
CA.GA.ÇO, *s.m.*, fright, fear.
CÁ.GA.DO, *s.m., Zool.*, terrapin.

CA.GA.NEI.RA, *s.f., vulg.*, diarrhea.
CA.GAR, *v.*, to shit, to defecate.
CA.GUE.TAR, *v., gir.*, the same that *alcaguetar*: to stool.
CA.GUE.TE, *s.m.*, telltale; *gir.*, police informer, stoolpigeon.
CAI.A.QUE, *s.m.*, kayak.
CAI.A.DO, *s.m.*, whitewash; *adj.*, covered with whitewash.
CAI.AR, *v.*, to whitewash, to whiten, to conceal.
CÃI.BRA, *s.f., Med.*, cramp, kink, convulsion.
CAI.BRO, *s.m.*, joist.
CA.Í.DA, *s.f.*, fall, falling, decay, decadence.
CA.Í.DO, *adj.*, fallen, droopy; *fig.*, depressed.
CA.I.MEN.TO, *s.m.*, falling, fall; decadence; hang (clothes).
CAI.PI.RA, *s. 2 gen.*, rustic, backwoodsman, hayseed, redneck, yokel, country dumpkin.
CA.I.PI.RI.NHA, *s.f.*, caipirinha.
CA.IR, *v.*, to fall, to decline, to decay, to collapse, to fall down, to tumble.
CAIS, *s.m.*, quay, wharf, dock, pier, mole.
CAI.XA, *s.f.*, box, case, chest, cashier, kit, set, casing.
CAI.XA-D'Á.GUA, *s.f.*, water tank.
CAI.XA DE FÓS.FO.ROS, *s.f.*, matchbox.
CAI.XA-FOR.TE, *s.f.*, safe; strongbox.
CAI.XA-PRE.TA, *s.f., Aeron.*, black box.
CAI.XÃO, *s.m.*, coffin, great chest, locker.
CAI.XA.RI.A, *s.f.*, a great quantity of boxes.
CAI.XEI.RO, *s.m.*, salesclerk, salesperson, counter clerk, shop-boy.
CAI.XEI.RO-VI.A.JAN.TE, *s.m.*, travelling salesman.
CAI.XI.LHO, *s.m.*, window-sash, casement.
CAI.XI.NHA, *s.f.*, tip, casket.
CAI.XO.LA, *s.f.*, little box, casket.
CAI.XO.TA.RI.A, *s.m.*, box factory.
CAI.XO.TE, *s.m.*, box, crate, packing-box.
CA.JA.DA.DA, *s.f.*, a blow with a stick.
CA.JA.DO, *s.m.*, shepherd's stick, crook.
CA.JU, *s.m., Bot.*, cashew-nut, cashew.
CA.JU.EI.RO, *s.m., Bot.*, cashew-tree.
CAL, *s.f.*, whitewash.
CA.LA.BOU.ÇO, *s.m.*, dungeon, prison, jail, calaboose.
CA.LA.DA, *s.f.*, complete silence; quietness.
CA.LA.DÃO, *s.m.*, a quiet man, taciturn person.
CA.LA.DO, *adj.*, silent, quiet, close, reserved, secret.
CA.LA.FE.TA.DOR, *s.m.*, caulker, caulking iron.
CA.LA.FE.TA.GEM, *s.f.*, caulking, gasket.
CA.LA.FE.TAR, *v.*, to calk.
CA.LA.FRI.O, *s.m.*, chill, shiver, shakes, fit of cold.
CA.LA.MAR, *s.m., pop., Zool.*, calamry, squid.
CA.LA.MI.DA.DE, *s.f.*, calamity, calamitousness, disaster, affliction.
CA.LA.MI.TO.SO, *adj.*, calamitous, disastrous, woeful, tragic.
CA.LAN.GO, *s.m., pop., Zool.*, name popular of several small lizards.
CA.LÃO, *s.m.*, jargon, slang, cant.
CA.LAR, *v.*, not to speak, to shut up, to silence, to stay silent, to conceal, to disguise.
CAL.ÇA, *s.f.*, the same that *calças* (*pl.*).
CAL.ÇA.DA, *s.f.*, pavement, sidewalk, paved street.
CAL.ÇA.DEI.RA, *s.f.*, stamper, rammer; shoe-horn.
CAL.ÇA.DIS.TA, *s. 2 gen.*, shoe manufacturer, shoemaker.
CAL.ÇA.DO, *s.m.*, foot-wear, shoe; *adj.*, paved, shod.
CAL.ÇA.MEN.TO, *s.m.*, paving, pavement.

CALCANHAR · 116 · CAMBALEANTE

CAL.CA.NHAR, *s.m.*, heel.

CAL.ÇÃO, *s.m.*, trunks, shorts, trousers.

CAL.CAR, *v.*, to step on, to smash, to crush, to squeeze, to oppress, to grind, to crunch.

CAL.ÇAR, *v.*, to shoe, to boot, to put on (any footwear); to pave.

CAL.CÁ.RIO, *s.m.*, limestone; *adj.*, calcareous, limy, chalky.

CAL.ÇAS, *s.f., pl.*, trousers, pants, pantaloons; *calcinhas*: panties.

CAL.CE.TAR, *v.*, to pave, to cover with stone.

CAL.CE.TEI.RO, *s.m.*, paver; trouser maker.

CAL.CI.FI.CAÇÃO, *s.f.*, calcification, calcination.

CAL.CI.FI.CAR, *v.*, to calcify, to calcinate.

CAL.CI.NA.ÇÃO, *s.f.*, calcination.

CAL.CI.NAR, *v.*, to calcine, to reduce to lime.

CÁL.CIO, *s.m., Quím.*, calcium.

CAL.ÇO, *s.m.*, wedge, a piece of wood, chock, skid.

CAL.CU.LA.DO, *adj.*, calculated, figured, rated.

CAL.CU.LA.DOR, *s.m.*, calculator, counter; calculating machine; *adj.*, calculating, computing.

CAL.CU.LA.DO.RA, *s.f.*, calculator.

CAL.CU.LAR, *v.*, to calculate, to compute, to reckon, to count, to estimate, to conjecture.

CAL.CU.LÁ.VEL, *adj.*, calculable.

CAL.CU.LIS.TA, *s. 2 gen.*, opportunist, *adj.*, calculating.

CÁL.CU.LO, *s.m.*, calculation, reckoning, computation, counting.

CAL.DA, *s.f.*, syrup, preserves.

CAL.DEI.RA, *s.f.*, kettle, caldron, boiler, seether.

CAL.DEI.RÃO, *s.m.*, caldron, large kettle.

CAL.DO, *s.m.*, soup, broth, sauce.

CA.LE.FA.ÇÃO, *s.f.*, heating, warming, calefaction.

CA.LEI.DOS.CÓ.PIO, *s.m.*, kaleidoscope.

CA.LE.JA.DO, *adj.*, callous, horny, hardy, hardened, experienced.

CA.LE.JAR, *v.*, to make callous, to harden, to indurate.

CA.LEN.DÁ.RIO, *s.m.*, calendar, diary, almanac.

CA.LEN.DA.RIS.TA, *s. 2 gen.*, calendar maker, calendarian.

CA.LÊN.DU.LA, *s.f.*, calendula.

CA.LHA, *s.f.*, drip, gutter, pipe, channel.

CA.LHA.MA.ÇO, *s.m.*, an old book, a big book.

CA.LHAM.BE.QUE, *s.m.*, a small coasting vessel, jaloppy.

CA.LHAR, *v.*, to fit well in, to go into, to be opportune.

CA.LHAU, *s.m.*, pebble, flintstone.

CA.LHE.TA, *s.f.*, narrow bay.

CA.LHOR.DA, *s.m.*, scoundrel, rogue.

CA.LHOR.DI.CE, *s.f.*, dirty trick.

CA.LI.BRA.ÇÃO, *s.f.*, calibration.

CA.LI.BRA.DO, *s.m.*, calibrated.

CA.LI.BRA.DOR, *s.m.*, gauge, calibrator, caliber rule.

CA.LI.BRA.GEM, *s.f.*, calibration.

CA.LI.BRAR, *v.*, to measure the caliber of, to gauge, to calibrate.

CA.LI.BRE, *s.m.*, caliber, gauge, bore, measurement.

CÁ.LI.CE, *s.m.*, cup, chalice, wineglass; calyx of a flower.

CA.LI.DEZ, *s.f.*, warmth, heat.

CÁ.LI.DO, *adj.*, hot, burning, heated, ardent.

CA.LI.FA.DO, *s.m.*, calif, caliph.

CA.LI.FA.DO, *s.m.*, caliphate, califate.

CA.LI.GRA.FI.A, *s.f.*, handwriting, calligraphy.

CA.LÍ.GRA.FO, *s.m.*, calligrapher, teacher of calligraphy.

CAL.MA, *s.f.*, calm, calmness, serenity, silence, piece, tranquility, repose.

CAL.MA.MEN.TE, *adv.*, calmly, evenly.

CAL.MAN.TE, *s.m.*, sedative, calmative; *adj.*, sedative, lenitive, calmative.

CAL.MAR, *v.*, to calm, to quiet, to tranquilize.

CAL.MA.RI.A, *s.f.*, calm, lull, becalmed sea.

CAL.MO, *adj.*, hot, calm, still, quiet, sultry, cool, serene.

CA.LO, *s.m.*, corn, callus, callosity, callousness.

CA.LOM.BEN.TO, *adj.*, pustulate, covered with blisters.

CA.LOM.BO, *s.m.*, swelling, cyst; blister, pustule.

CA.LOR, *s.m.*, heat, warmth, hotness, warmness, torridness.

CA.LO.RÃO, *s.m.*, excessive heat, heat wave.

CA.LO.REN.TO, *adj.*, stifling hot, sensitive to heat.

CA.LO.RI.A, *s.f.*, calorie, calory, heat.

CA.LÓ.RI.CO, *s.m.*, caloric; *adj.*, caloric.

CA.LO.RÍ.FE.RO, *s.m.*, heater; *adj.*, caloriferous, calorific.

CA.LO.RÍ.FI.CO, *adj.*, calorific.

CA.LO.RI.ME.TRI.A, *s.f., Fís.*, calorimetry.

CA.LO.RO.SA.MEN.TE, *adv.*, ardently, effusively, hotly.

CA.LO.RO.SO, *adj.*, warm, hot, sultry, enthusiastic.

CA.LO.SI.DA.DE, *s.f.*, callosity.

CA.LO.SO, *adj.*, callous, horny, having corns.

CA.LO.TA, *s.f.*, cap, skulcap.

CA.LO.TE, *s.m.*, unpaid debt, swindle, cheat.

CA.LO.TE.AR, *v.*, not to pay a debt, to swindle.

CA.LO.TEI.RO, *s.m.*, swindler, cheat.

CA.LOU.RO, *s.m.*, rookie, new student, freshman, beginner, novice.

CA.LÚ.NIA, *s.f.*, calumny, slander, falsehood, scandal.

CA.LU.NI.A.DOR, *s.m.*, calumniator, detractor.

CA.LU.NI.AR, *v.*, to calumniate, to detract, to defame.

CA.LU.NI.O.SA.MEN.TE, *adv.*, calumniously, slanderously.

CA.LU.NI.O.SO, *adj.*, slanderous, libellous.

CAL.VÁ.RIO, *s.m.*, calvary; *Rel.*, *Calvário*: Mount Calvary; *fig.*, labour, suffering.

CAL.VÍ.CIE, *s.f.*, baldness.

CAL.VO, *adj.*, bald, bald-headed, hairless, bare.

CAL.VU.RA, *s.f.*, baldness.

CA.MA, *s.f.*, bed; sofa, couch, resting place.

CA.MA-BE.LI.CHE, *s.f.*, double-decker bed.

CA.MA.DA, *s.f.*, layer, class, stratum.

CA.MA.FEU, *s.m.*, cameo.

CA.MA.LE.ÃO, *s.m., Zool.*, chameleon.

CA.MA.LE.Ô.NI.CO, *adj.*, chameleonic.

CÂ.MA.RA, *s.f.*, chamber, camera, room, bedroom.

CÂ.MA.RA-AR.DEN.TE, *s.f.*, mourning chamber.

CA.MA.RA.DA, *s. 2 gen.*, comrade, roommate, fellow student, mate, fellow, colleague.

CA.MA.RA.DA.GEM, *s.f.*, comradeship, good fellowship.

CÂ.MA.RA DE AR, *s.f.*, inner tube.

CA.MA.RÃO, *s.m., Zool.*, shrimp, prawn.

CA.MA.REI.RA, *s.f.*, chambermaid, housekeeper.

CA.MA.RI.LHA, *s.f.*, clique, cabal.

CA.MA.RIM, *s.m.*, little room, dressing-room.

CA.MA.RÕES, *s.*, Cameroon.

CA.MA.RO.NÊS, *s., adj.*, Cameroonian.

CA.MA.RO.TE, *s.m.*, box, box seat, loge, cabin.

CAM.BA.DA, *s.f.*, gang, mob, rabble.

CAM.BA.LA.CHO, *s.m.*, scam, truck, permutation.

CAM.BA.LE.AN.TE, *adj.*, unsteady.

CAMBALEAR •• 117 •• CANCRO

CAM.BA.LE.AR, *v.*, to sway, to reel, to stagger.
CAM.BA.LEI.O, *s.m.*, staggering, reeling.
CAM.BA.LHO.TA, *s.f.*, caper, skip, somersault, capriole.
CAM.BI.AL, *s.m.*, cambial; *adj.*, cambial, relative to the exchange.
CAM.BI.AR, *v.*, to change, to exchange, to trade, to convert.
CÂM.BIO, *s.m.*, exchange, change, permutation; gear box.
CAM.BIS.TA, *s. 2 gen.*, money-changer, cambist, banker.
CAM.BO.JA, *s.*, Cambodia.
CAM.BO.JA.NO; *s.m.*, *adj.*, Cambodian.
CAM.BRAI.A, *s.f.*, cambric.
CAM.BRI.A.NO, *adj.*, *Geol.*, Cambrian.
CAM.BU.RÃO, *s.m.*, police van.
CA.MÉ.LIA, *s.f.*, camellia.
CA.ME.LO, *s.m.*, *Zool.*, camel.
CA.ME.LÔ, *s.m.*, hawker, street peddler.
CÂ.ME.RA, *s.f.*, camera; *s. 2 gen.*, camera operator.
CA.ME.RA.MAN, *s.m.*, camera operator.
CA.MI.NHA.DA, *s.f.*, walk, walking, ride, stroll, excursion, journey.
CA.MI.NHAN.TE, *s. 2 gen.*, walker, hiker, pedestrian; *adj.*, walking, travelling.
CA.MI.NHÃO, *s.m.*, lorry, truck.
CA.MI.NHAR, *v.*, to walk, to hike, to march, to journey, to go, to travel.
CA.MI.NHO, *s.m.*, way, road, route, path, trail, track, street, course.
CA.MI.NHO.NEI.RO, *s.m.*, *US* truck driver; *UK* lorry driver.
CA.MI.NHO.NE.TE, *s.f.*, pickup, van, truck.
CA.MI.O.NE.TA, *s.f.*, light truck, pickup truck.
CA.MI.SA, *s.f.*, shirt, chemise.
CA.MI.SA DE FOR.ÇA, *s.f.*, straitjacket.
CA.MI.SA DE VÊ.NUS, *s.f.*, preservative.
CA.MI.SÃO, *s.m.*, smock.
CA.MI.SA.RI.A, *s.f.*, shirt factory; shirt shop.
CA.MI.SE.TA, *s.f.*, chemisette, undershirt.
CA.MI.SI.NHA, *s.f.*, condom, preservative.
CA.MI.SO.LA, *s.f.*, nightshirt, nightgown.
CA.MO.MI.LA, *s.f.*, *Bot.*, camomile.
CA.MO.NI.A.NO, *s.m.*, admirer and collector of Camões' works; *adj.*, relative to Camões.
CA.MOR.RA, *s.f.*, *Hist.*, camorra; *Bras.*, quarrel, provocation.
CAM.PA, *s.f.*, gravestone, tomb.
CAM.PA.I.NHA, *s.f.*, bell, small bell, handbell.
CAM.PAL, *s.m.*, *missa ~*: open-air mass; *adj.*, rural.
CAM.PA.NA, *s.f.*, bell, handbell.
CAM.PA.NÁ.RI.O, *s.m.*, bell tower.
CAM.PA.NHA, *s.f.*, campaign, wide plains, lowland, camp.
CAM.PÂ.NU.LA, *s.f.*, *Bot.*, campanula, bellflower; bell jar.
CAM.PA.NU.LÁ.CE.A, *s.f.*, *Bot.*, a plant of the family *Campanulaceae*.
CAM.PAR, *v.*, to camp, to pitch a camp.
CAM.PE.Ã, *s.f.*, championess.
CAM.PE.A.DOR, *s.m.*, cowboy; *adj.*, rural, rustic.
CAM.PE.ÃO, *s.m.*, champion, champ; protagonist.
CAM.PE.AR, *v.*, to camp, to look for, to brag.
CAM.PEI.RO, *s.m.*, cowboy, wrangler, farmhand, rural worker.
CAM.PE.O.NA.TO, *s.m.*, championship, sporting event, bout.
CAM.PE.SI.NHO, *adj.*, the same that *campesino*.
CAM.PE.SI.NO, *adj.*, rural, campestral, rustic.
CAM.PES.TRE, *adj.*, rural, rustic, campestrian, bucolic.

CAM.PI.NA, *s.f.*, prairie, plain, level land.
CAM.PI.NA, *v.*, to live in the country.
CAM.PI.NO *s.m.*, farmer, rural; herdsman; *adj.*, rural, rustic.
CAM.PIS.TA, *s.m.*, cowboy that takes care of cattle; *adj.*, concerning this person.
CAM.PO, *s.m.*, field, corn land, open country, prairie, country-side; space, opportunity.
CAM.PO.NE.SA, *s.f.*, countrywoman, peasant woman.
CAM.PO.NÊS, *s.m.*, peasant, cottager, farmer, yokel, countryman.
CAM.PO.SAN.TO, *s.m.*, cemetery.
CA.MU.FLA.DO, *adj.*, hidden, camouflaged.
CA.MU.FLA.GEM, *s.f.*, camouflage, disguise, disguising.
CA.MU.FLAR, *v.*, to disguise by camouflage, to disguise.
CA.MUN.DON.GO, *s.m.*, *Zool.*, mouse.
CA.MUR.ça, *s.f.*, *Zool.*; mountain goat; *chamois* (animal, color, cloth); *adj.*, chamois-coloured.
CA.MUR.ça.DO, *adj.*, chamois-coloured.
CA.NA, *s.f.*, cane, reed, sugar-cane; prison, jail.
CA.NA.DÁ, *s.*, Canada.
CA.NA-DA-ÍN.DIA, *s.f.*, fine Indian cane.
CA.NA-DE-A.ÇÚ.CAR, *s.f.*, sugar-cane.
CA.NA.DEN.SE, *s. 2 gen.*, *adj.*, Canadian.
CA.NAL, *s.m.*, channel, canal, waterway, stream.
CA.NA.LE.TA, *s.f.*, gutter.
CA.NA.LE.TE, *s.m.*, a small channel.
CA.NA.LHA, *s. 2 gen.*, scum, scoundrel, rabble, mob, crook.
CA.NA.LHI.CE, *s.f.*, knavery, trickery.
CA.NA.LI.ZA.ÇÃO, *s.f.*, drainage, canalization, system of canals, sewerage.
CA.NA.LI.ZA.DOR, *s.m.*, canal or sewer constuctor.
CA.NA.LI.ZAR, *v.*, to channel, to pipe, to canalize, to sluice.
CA.NA.LI.ZÁ.VEL, *adj.*, capable of being canalized.
CA.NA.PÉ, *s.m.*, appetizer; sofa.
CA.NÁ.RI.AS, *s.f.*, *(as Ilhas) Canárias*: the Canary Islands, the Canaries.
CA.NÁ.RIO, *s.m.*, canary.
CA.NAS.TRA, *s.f.*, big basket, dorser, dosser, game of cards.
CA.NAS.TRÃO, *s.m.*, a big hamper; *Teat.*, *gír.*, a bad actor.
CA.NA.VI.AL, *s.m.*, reed plot, sugar-cane plantation.
CA.NA.VI.EI.RA, *s.f.*, *Bot.*, sorghum grass, sorghum.
CAN.ÇÃO, *s.f.*, song, singing, chant, chanson.
CAN.CE.LA, *s.f.*, gate, barrier; railway gate.
CAN.CE.LA.DO, *adj.*, cancelled, abrogated.
CAN.CE.LA.MEN.TO, *s.m.*, cancellation.
CAN.CE.LAR, *v.*, cancel, to cross out, to bloc out, to annul, to put off.
CAN.CE.LÁ.VEL, *adj.*, subject to cancellation; abrogable.
CÂN.CER, *s.m.*, *Med.*, cancer.
CAN.CE.RA.ÇÃO, *s.f.*, *Med.*, canceration.
CAN.CE.RA.DO, *adj.*, affected with cancer, cancered.
CAN.CE.RI.A.NO, *s.m.*, *Astrol.*, Cancerian, *adj.*, Cancerian.
CAN.CE.RI.ZA.ÇÃO, *s.f.*, cancerazation, canceration.
CAN.CE.RÍ.GE.NO, *adj.*, *Med.*, carcinogenic.
CAN.CE.RO.LO.GIS.TA, *s. 2 gen.*, cancer specialist.
CAN.CE.RO.SO, *adj.*, cancered, cankered, affected with cancer, cancerous.
CAN.CHA, *s.f.*, football field, court, ground, playground.
CAN.CI.O.NEI.RO, *s.m.*, collection of songs.
CAN.CRO, *s.m.*, *Med.*, canker, chancre (generic designation of malignant tumours).

CANCROSO   •• 118 •••   CAÓTICO

CAN.CRO.SO, *adj.*, *Med.*, cancerous, chancrous.
CAN.DE.EI.RO, *s.m.*, candle-holder, chandelier, lamp.
CAN.DEI.A, *s.f.*, lamp, candle, light. .
CAN.DE.LA.BRO, *s.m.*, chandelier.
CAN.DÊN.CI.A, *s.f.*, candescence, white heat.
CAN.DEN.TE, *adj.*, *s. 2 gen.*, candescent, glowing.
CAN.DI.DA.MEN.TE, *adv.*, candidly, sincerely, purely.
CAN.DI.DA.TAR-SE, *v.*, to be a candidat for, stand for, run for.
CAN.DI.DA.TO, *s.m.*, candidate, applicant, aspirant.
CAN.DI.DA.TU.RA, *s.f.*, candidateship, candidature, claim, aspiration.
CAN.DI.DEZ, *s.f.*, whiteness, pureness.
CÂN.DI.DO, *adj.*, white, pure, innocent, sincere.
CAN.DOM.BLÉ, *s.m.*, *Rel.*, Candomble (african-Brazilian religion).
CAN.DOR, *s.m.*, *Lit.*, whiteness, pureness.
CAN.DU.RA, *s.f.*, whiteness, pureness, sincerity.
CA.NE.CA, *s.f.*, mug, cup, tankard.
CA.NE.CA.DA, *s.f.*, the quantity a mug holds.
CA.NE.CO, *s.m.*, beer mug.
CA.NE.LA, *s.f.*, cinnamon, cinnamon tree; shin, shinbone.
CA.NE.LA.DA, *s.f.*, a blow on the shinbone.
CA.NE.LA.DO, *adj.*, ribbed, fluted, grooved.
CA.NE.LAR, *v.*, to chanfer; to groove; to channel, to flute.
CA.NE.LEI.RA, *s.f.*, *Bot.*, cinnamon, cinnamon-bark tree; *Esp.*, shin guard (soccer).
CA.NE.TA, *s.f.*, pen, penholder.
CA.NE.TA-TIN.TEI.RO, *s.f.*, fountain-pen.
CÂN.FO.RA, *s.f.*, camphor, gum camphor.
CAN.FO.RA.DO, *adj.*, camphorated.
CAN.FO.RAR, *v.*, to camphorate.
CAN.GA, *s.f.*, a yoke for oxen; oppression.
CAN.GA.CEI.RO, *s.m.*, bandit, brigand.
CAN.GA.ÇO, *s.m.*, the activity or way of life of *cangaceiros*.
CAN.GAR, *v.*, to put the oxen into the yoke, to subdue.
CAN.GO.TE, *s.m.*, back of the neck, occipital region.
CAN.GU.RU, *s.m.*, *Zool.*, kangaroo.
CA.NHA.DA, *s.f.*, deep gorge, ravine, gully.
CÂ.NHA.MO, *s.m.*, hemp; *Bot.*, hemp plant.
CA.NHÃO, *s.m.*, cannon, gun, gorge, defile, ravine, canyon.
CA.NHES.TRO, *adj.*, *s.m.*, clumsy, left-handed, awkward.
CA.NHO.NA.ÇO, *s.m.*, cannon-shot.
CA.NHO.NA.DA, *s.f.*, cannonade.
CA.NHO.TA, *s.f.*, the left hand; feminine of *canhoto*.
CA.NHO.TEI.RO, *s.f.*, the left hand.
CA.NHO.TO, *s.m.*, left-hander, counterfoil; *adj.*, left-handed, left.
CA.NI.BAL, *s. 2 gen.*, cannibal, anthropophagite, brutal, cruel; *adj.*, cruel, barbarous.
CA.NI.BA.LES.CO, *adj.*, cannibalistic; *fig.*, inhuman, cruel.
CA.NI.BA.LIS.MO, *s.m.*, cannibalism, man-eating, anthropophagy.
CA.NI.BA.LI.ZA.ÇÃO, *s.f.*, cannibalization.
CA.NI.BA.LI.ZAR, *v.*, to cannibalize.
CA.NI.ÇO, *s.m.*, fishing-rod, rod.
CA.NÍ.CU.LA, *s.f.*, the hottest period of the year, canicular days; *Astron.*, Canicula, Syrius, dog-star.
CA.NÍ.CU.LAR, *s.f.*, hot, sultry day, canicular; *Astron.*, pertaining to or relative to Syrius or Canicula.
CA.NI.CUL.TU.RA, *s.f.*, breeding of dogs.
CA.NÍ.DEO, *s.m.*, *Zool.*, animal of the family *Canidae* (dogs, wolves, jackals and foxes); *adj.*, canine.

CA.NÍ.DE.OS, *s.m.*, *pl.*, *Zool.*, canids.
CA.NIL, *s.m.*, kennel, dog-house.
CA.NI.NHA, *s.f.*, *pop.*, sugar-cane brandy: *cachaça*.
CA.NI.NO, *s.m.*, canine tooth, eye tooth, fang; *adj.*, canine, doglike.
CA.NI.VE.TE, *s.m.*, pocket-knife, penknife, jack-knife.
CA.NI.VE.TE.AR, *v.*, to wound with pocketknife.
CA.NI.VE.TEI.RO, *s.m.*, pocketknife manufacturer or vendor.
CAN.JA, *s.f.*, chicken soup; easy to do, chicken broth.
CAN.JI.CA, *s.f.*, *Cul.*, grated corn porridge.
CA.NO, *s.m.*, tube, pipe, barrel, barrel of a gun.
CA.NO.A, *s.f.*, canoe, boat, skiff, yawl.
CA.NO.A.GEM, *s.f.*, canoeing.
CA.NO.EI.RO, *s.f.*, canoeist, conoeman.
CA.NO.LA, *s.f.*, *Bot.*, canola; óleo de canola: canola oil.
CA.NON, *s.m.*, canon (rule, decree, critical standar, church law); *Rel.*, Canon (Catholic liturgy).
CÂ.NO.NE, *s.m.*, canon (general rule; general principle).
CA.NO.NIS.TA, *s.m.*, *Rel.*, canonist.
CA.NÔ.NI.CO, *adj.*, canonic.
CA.NO.NI.ZA.ÇÃO, *s.f.*, canonization.
CA.NO.NI.ZA.DO, *adj.*, canonized, sainted.
CA.NO.NI.ZAR, *v.*, to canonize, to declare saint.
CA.NO.RO, *adj.*, canorous, pleasant.
CAN.SA.ÇO, *s.m.*, fatigue, weariness, tiredness, lassitude.
CAN.SA.DA.MEN.TE, *adv.*, tiredly, wearily.
CAN.SA.DO, *adj.*, tired, fatigued, weary, spent, outworn.
CAN.SAR, *v.*, tire, weary, to cause fatigue.
CAN.SA.TI.VO, *adj.*, tiresome, tiring, fatiguing, toilsome.
CAN.SA.TI.VA.MEN.TE, *adv.*, wearisomely, tiresomely.
CAN.SEI.RA, *s.f.*, fatigue, weariness, tiredness.
CAN.TA.DA, *s.f.*, act of singing; chat somebody up; song.
CAN.TA.DOR, *s.m.*, singer; *adj.*, singing, chanting.
CAN.TAN.TE, *s.m.*, *gir.*, vagabond, loafer, swindler; *adj.*, singing, cantative.
CAN.TAR, *v.*, to sing, to chant, to warble.
CÂN.TA.RO, *s.m.*, jar, jug, pitcher, urn.
CAN.TA.RO.LAR, *v.*, to sing with a low voice, to trill.
CAN.TA.TA, *s.f.*, *cantata* (musical or choral composition).
CAN.TEI.RO, *s.m.*, stone-cutter, stone-mason, flower-box.
CÂN.TI.CO, *s.m.*, canticle, chant; symphonic poem.
CAN.TI.GA, *s.f.*, ditty, ballad.
CAN.TIL, *s.m.*, canteen, water-bottle.
CAN.TI.LE.NA, *s.m.*, ballad, ode; ditty, tender love-song; *col.*, a boring tell.
CAN.TI.LÉ.VER, *s.m.*, *Arquit.*, cantilever.
CAN.TI.NA, *s.f.*, canteen, mess, tavern.
CAN.TI.NHO, *s.m.*, diminutive of *canto*; corner, retreat.
CAN.TO, *s.m.*, corner, angle, edge; song, chant, singing.
CAN.TO.CHÃO, *s.m.*, chant; Gregorian chant; church songs hymns.
CAN.TO.NEI.RA, *s.f.*, a corner shelf or stand, corner cupboard.
CAN.TOR, *s.m.*, singer, crooner, songster, chanter.
CAN.TO.RA, *s.f.*, songstress, singer.
CAN.TO.RI.A, *s.f.*, choral singing; troll.
CA.NU.DI.NHO, *s.m.*, diminutive of *canudo*; drinking straw, straw.
CÃO, *s.m.*, dog, hound; hammer of a gun.
CA.O.LHO, *adj.*, *s.m.*, one-eyed, cross-eyed.
CA.OS, *s.m.*, chaos, mess, under confusion.
CA.Ó.TI.CO, *adj.*, chaotic, confused.

CAPA

119

CARA

CA.PA, *s.f.*, coat, cloak, overcoat, cover, mantle.
CA.PA.ÇÃO, *s.f.*, castration.
CA.PA.CE.TE, *s.m.*, helmet, helm, headpiece.
CA.PA.CHO, *s.m.*, door-mat, rug; obeying, servile.
CA.PA.CI.DA.DE, *s.f.*, capacity, ability, volume, capability, competence, talent.
CA.PA.CI.TA.DO, *adj.*, capable, competent, able; qualified.
CA.PA.CI.TÂN.CIA, *s.f., Eletr.*, capacitance.
CA.PA.CI.TAR, *v.*, to capacitate, to qualify, to enable, to persuade.
CA.PA.CI.TOR, *s.m., Eletr.*, capacitor, condenser.
CA.PA.DO, *adj.*, castrated.
CA.PA.DÓ.CI.O, *s.m.*, impostor, charlatan; *Hist.*, Cappadocian; *adj.*, fraudulent; *Hist.*, Cappadocian.
CA.PA.DOR, *s.m.*, castrator.
CA.PAN.GA, *s.m.*, bully, crime associate, mobster; money bag, bag.
CA.PAN.GA.DA, *s.m.*, gang of henchmen.
CA.PÃO, *s.m.*, capon (castrated male chicken); *Bot.*, hurst.
CA.PAR, *v.*, to castrate, to emasculate.
CA.PA.TAZ, *s.m.*, foreman, headman.
CA.PAZ, *adj.*, capable, able, apt, fit, good.
CAP.CI.O.SA.MENTE, *adv.*, captiously, fallaciously.
CAP.CI.O.SO, *adj.*, catchy, captious, fallacious.
CA.PE.A.MEN.TO, *s.m.*, coping of a wall; asphalt coating.
CA.PE.AR, *v.*, to cover with a coat, to hide.
CA.PE.LA, *s.f.*, chapel, sanctuary.
CA.PE.LÃO, *s.m.*, chaplain; priest.
CA.PE.LO, *s.m.*, hood, cowl; cap.
CA.PEN.GA, *s. 2 gen.*, crippled; *adj.*, crippled, lame.
CA.PEN.GAN.TE, *adj.*, crippled, maimed, lame.
CA.PE.TA, *s.m.*, devil; naughty child.
CA.PE.TA.GEM, *s.f., pop.*, prank, lark; devilish trick.
CA.PI.LAR, *adj.*, capillary, capillaceous; hairlike.
CA.PI.LA.RI.DA.DE, *s.f.*, capillarity.
CA.PI.LÉ, *s.m.*, a drink prepared with syrup.
CA.PIM, *s.m.*, grass, hay, sedge.
CA.PIM–CI.DREI.RA, *s.m., Bot.*, lemon grass.
CA.PIM-GOR.DU.RA, *s.m., Bot.*, molasses grass.
CA.PI.NA, *s.f.*, the act of cutting the grass, weeding.
CA.PI.NA.ÇÃO, *s.f.*, act of cutting the grass of a meadow, weeding.
CA.PI.NA.DEI.RA, *s.f.*, weeding machine.
CA.PI.NA.DO, *adj.*, weeded.
CA.PI.NA.DOR, *adj.*, weeder, mower, hoer.
CA.PI.NAR, *v.*, to weed, to hoe.
CA.PI.ZAL, *s.m.*, pasture, hayfield.
CA.PIS.CAR, *v., pop.*, to perceive (intrigue or trap); *Bras.*, to understand something (language or craft).
CA.PI.TAL, *s.f.*, capital, funds, wealth, metropolis; *adj.*, capitalistic, essencial, vital.
CA.PI.TA.LIS.MO, *s.m.*, capitalism, economic system.
CA.PI.TA.LIS.TA, *s. 2 gen.*, capitalist, stockholder; *adj.*, capitalistic.
CA.PI.TA.LI.ZA.ÇÃO, *s.f.*, capitalization.
CA.PI.TA.LI.ZAR, *v.*, to capitalize, to accumulate, to amass money.
CA.PI.TA.LI.ZÁVEL, *adj.*, to capitalizable.
CA.PI.TA.NE.AR, *v.*, to captain, to lead, direct; to command as a captain.
CA.PI.TA.NI.A, *s.f.*, capitainship.

CA.PI.Tâ.NI.A, *s.f., Náut.*, admiralship, flagship; *adj.*, relative to a flagship.
CA.PI.TÃO, *s.m.*, captain, military commander, leader, chief, officer of the army; political boss.
CA.PI.TÃO-MOR, *s.m.*, commander of local police troops; *Hist., Bras.*, governor of a capitania (province).
CA.PI.TEL, *s.m., Arquit.*, capital (heart of a column); chapiter (cushion capital).
CA.PI.TÓ.LI.O, *s.m., Hist.*, the Capitol (Ancient Rome); *fig.*, glory, splendour.
CA.PI.TU.LA.ÇÃO, *s.f.*, capitulation, surrender, rendition.
CA.PI.TU.LA.DOR, *s.m.*, capitulator (one who surrenders).
CA.PI.TU.LAR, *v.*, to capitulate, to surrender, to agree, to enunciate, to compromise.
CA.PÍ.TU.LO, *s.m.*, chapter.
CA.PI.VA.RA, *s.f., Zool.*, capybara, capibara.
CA.PÔ, *s.m.*, hood.
CA.PO.EI.RA, *s.f.*, brushwood, coop; technique of sudden fight.
CA.PO.EI.RA.GEM, *s.f.*, fighting system of capoeiras.
CA.PO.EI.RAR, *v.*, to practice *capoeira*.
CA.PO.EI.RIS.TA, *s. 2 gen.*, practioner; person who uses the *capoeira* technique.
CA.PO.TA, *s.f.*, cap, hood, headdress, capote.
CA.PO.TA.DO, *adj.*, overturned, upset, upturned.
CA.PO.TA.GEM, *s.f.*, capsize, capsizal.
CA.PO.TAR, *v.*, to capsize, to overturn.
CA.PO.TE, *s.m.*, cloak, mantle, overcoat.
CA.PO.TEI.RO, *s.m.*, manufacturer or seller of motorcar or cowlings.
CA.PRI.CHAR, *v.*, to perfect, to excel, to elaborate.
CA.PRI.CHO, *s.m.*, caprice, fancy, whim, freakishness, skittishness.
CA.PRI.CHO.SA.MEN.TE, *adv.*, capriciously, freakishly.
CA.PRI.CHO.SO, *adj.*, fanciful, freakish, capricious, skittish; petulant, obstinate, extravagant.
CA.PRI.CÓR.NIO, *s.m., Astron., Astrol.*, Capricorn.
CA.PRI.NO, *adj.*, caprine, goatlike, hircine.
CÁP.SU.LA, *s.f.*, capsule.
CAP.SU.LA.DO, *adj.*, furnished with a capsule, capsuled.
CAP.SU.LAR, *v.*, to capsulate; *adj.*, capsular.
CAP.TA.ÇÃO, *s.f.*, captation, captivation.
CAP.TA.DOR, *s. 2 gen.*, captivator, inveigler; *adj.*, captivating, inveigling.
CAP.TAN.TE, *s. 2 gen.*, the same that *captador*.
CAP.TAR, *v.*, to captivate, to collect, to catch, to ingratiate.
CAP.TA.TÓ.RI.O, *adj.*, referring to captivation.
CAP.TOR, *s.m.*, capturer, catcher, captor.
CAP.TU.RAR, *v.*, to capture, to seize, to catch, to occupy, to arrest.
CA.PU.CHI.NHO, *s.m.*, small hood or cowl; *Rel.*, Capuchin, monk of the Franciscan order.
CA.PU.CHO, *s.m., Rel.*, a Capuchin friar or monk; *adj.*, relative to the Capuchin order.
CA.PUZ, *s.m.*, cap, hood, bonnet.
CA.QUÉ.TI.CO, *adj., Med.*, cachectic, cachexic.
CA.QUI, *s.m.*, kaki: the fruit of the persimmon tree.
CÁ.QUI, *s.m.*, khaki, khaki-coloured cotton cloth; *adj.*, khaki, khaki-coloured.
CA.QUI.ZEI.RO, *s.m., Bot.*, persimmon tree.
CA.RA, *s.f.*, face, appearance, look, outward appearance,

CARÁ · 120 · CARGO

boldness.

CA.RÁ, *s.m.*, *Bot.*, popular name to the yams.

CA.RA.BI.NA, *s.f.*, rifle.

CA.RA.BI.NA.DA, *s.f.*, rifle-shot, discharge of a carabine.

CA.RA.BI.NEI.RO, *s.m.*, rifleman, carabineer.

CA.RA.ÇA, *s.f.*, a paper mask, mask; *fig.*, a moon-face.

CA.RA.COL, *s.m.*, *Zool.*, snail, caracol; spiral, a spiral line.

CA.RA.CO.LAR, *v.*, to move in caracoles; to spiral.

CA.RA.CO.LE.AR, *v.*, the same that *caracolar*.

CARACTER, *s.m.*, the same that *caráter*.

CA.RAC.TE.RE, *s.m.*, character (letters of the alphabet, numbers, punctuation marks).

CA.RAC.TE.RES, *s.m.*, *pl.*, characters, signs, marks; written letters, printing types.

CA.RAC.TE.RÍS.TI.CA, *s.f.*, characteristic(s), trait, mark.

CA.RAC.TE.RIS.TI.CA.MEN.TE, *adv.*, characteristically, typically, specifically.

CA.RAC.TE.RÍS.TI.CO, *adj.*, characteristic, peculiar, distinctive, typical, discriminative.

CA.RAC.TE.RI.ZA.ÇÃO, *s.f.*, characterization, making-up, artistic representation, personality.

CA.RAC.TE.RI.ZA.DO, *adj.*, characterized.

CA.RAC.TE.RI.ZA.DOR, *s.m.*, characterizer; *Teat.*, character actor; *adj.*, characterizing, impersonating.

CA.RAC.TE.RI.ZAN.TE, *adj.*, characterizing, distinguishing.

CA.RAC.TE.RI.ZAR, *v.*, to characterize, to point out, to describe, to distinguish, to mark.

CA.RA.CU, *s.m.*, bone morrow, medulla.

CA.RA DE PAU, *s. 2 gen.*, brazen, straight-faced person; *adj.*, wooden-faced.

CA.RA.DU.RA, *s. 2 gen.*, the same that *cara de pau*.

CA.RA.MAN.CHÃO, *s.m.*, arbour, bower.

CA.RAM.BO.LA, *s.f.*, *Bot.*, starfruit, carom.

CA.RA.ME.LA.DO, *s.m.*, a caramel candy; *adj.*, caramelized.

CA.RA.ME.LI.ZA.DO, *adj.*, caramelized.

CA.RA.ME.LI.ZAR, *v.*, to caramelize.

CA.RA.ME.LO, *s.m.*, caramel, frozen snow, candy.

CA.RA-ME.TA.DE, *s.f.*, wife.

CA.RA.MIN.GUÁS, *s.m.*, *pl.*, *pop.*, trifles, baubles; small change.

CA.RA.MIN.HO.LA, *s.f.*, forelock; tuft of hair; intrigue; lie; *caraminholas*: invention, imagination; lies.

CA.RA.MU.JO, *s.m.*, *Zool.*, winkle, common periwinkle, snail.

CA.RAN.GUE.JEI.RA, *s.f.*, *Zool.*, bird spider.

CA.RAN.GUE.JO, *s.m.*, *Zool.*, crab; Cancer (zod.)

CA.RÃO, *s.m.*, *pop.*, censure, reprimand.

CA.RA.PA.ÇA, *s.f.*, carapace, cuirass, shell, shard.

CA.RA.PI.NHO, *adj.*, crisp, coarse, curled.

CA.RA.PU.ÇA, *s.f.*, cap, hood, skull cap, hood, cowl.

CA.RA.TÊ, *s.m.*, karate.

CA.RÁ.TER, *s.m.*, character, mark, feature; badge, symbol, type, structure, letter(s).

CA.RA.VA.NA, *s.f.*, caravan.

CA.RA.VA.NEI.RO, *s.m.*, leader of a caravan.

CA.RA.VE.LA, *s.f.*, caravel, small sailing vessel.

CA.RA.VE.LEI.RO, *s.m.*, sailor of a caravelle.

CAR.BO.I.DRA.TO, *s.m.*, carbohydrate.

CAR.BO.NÁ.CE.O, *adj.*, *Quim.*, carbonaceous.

CAR.BO.NA.DO, *s.m.*, *Min.*, a black diamond, carbonado; *adj.*, *Quim.*, carbonized, carbonaceous.

CAR.BO.NAR, *v.*, to carbonate, to carbonize.

CAR.BO.NA.TO, *s.m.*, *Quim.*, carbonate.

CAR.BO.NE.TO, *s.m.*, *Quim.*, carbide.

CAR.BÔ.NI.CO, *adj.*, *Quim.*, carbonic.

CAR.BO.NÍ.FE.RO, *adj.*, carboniferous, carbonaceous.

CAR.BO.NI.ZA.DO, *adj.*, carbonized.

CAR.BO.NI.ZA.ÇÃO, *s.f.*, carbonization.

CAR.BO.NI.ZAR, *v.*, to carbonize, burn out.

CAR.BO.NO, *s.m.*, *Quim.*, carbon (atomic number: 6, symbol: C).

CAR.BU.RA.ÇÃO, *s.f.*, carburetion, carburation.

CAR.BU.RA.DO, *adj.*, carbureted.

CAR.BU.RA.DOR, *s.m.*, carburetor.

CAR.BU.RAN.TE, *s.m.*, *Quim.*, carburetant.

CAR.BU.RAR, *v.*, to carburize, to carburet.

CAR.BU.RE.TO, *s.m.*, *Quim.*, carburet, carbide.

CAR.CA.ÇA, *s.f.*, carcass, carcase, skeleton, framework.

CAR.CE.RA.GEM, *s.f.*, incarceration.

CÁR.CE.RE, *s.m.*, prison, jail.

CAR.CE.REI.RO, *s.m.*, prison guard, director of prison, jailer, warden.

CAR.CO.MA, *s.f.*, woodworm; putridity (tree); worm-dust.

CAR.CO.MI.DO, *adj.*, worm-eaten, wormy; rotten; consumed by use or time; *fig.*, utterly destroyed, old.

CAR.DA, *s.f.*, wool card; separator, teasel; carding.

CAR.DA.ÇÃO, *s.f.*, carding, combing.

CAR.DÁ.PIO, *s.m.*, menu, carte.

CAR.DAR, *v.*, to disentangle; to card, to comb (wool, flax).

CAR.DE.AL, *s.m.*, cardinal, principal chief; prelate; *adj.*, cardinal, principal.

CAR.DÍ.A.CO, *adj.*, cardiac, patient.

CAR.DI.AL, *adj.*, *Med.*, cardiac, cardial.

CAR.DI.GÃ, *s.m.*, cardigan (sweater with front opening).

CAR.DI.NAL, *adj.*, cardinal, basic; *número cardinal*, *s.m.*, cardinal number.

CAR.DI.O.GRA.FI.A, *s.f.*, cardiography, cardiogram.

CAR.DI.O.GRA.MA, *s.m.*, *Med.*, cardiogram.

CAR.DI.O.LO.GI.A, *s.m.*, *Med.*, cardiology.

CAR.DI.O.LO.GIS.TA, *s. 2 gen.*, cardiologist.

CAR.DI.O.PA.TI.A, *s.f.*, *Med.*, cardiopathy.

CAR.DI.O.PÁ.TI.CO, *adj.*, *Med.*, cardiopathic.

CAR.DI.OS.CO.PI.A, *s.f.*, *Med.*, cardioscopy.

CAR.DI.O.VAS.CU.LAR, *adj.*, *Med.*, cardiovascular.

CAR.DU.ME, *s.m.*, shoal of fish, run, flock, cluster.

CA.RE.A.ÇÃO, *s.f.*, confrontation, act of bringing face to face.

CA.RE.AR, *v.*, to bring face to face, to confront.

CA.RE.CA, *s.f.*, baldness; *adj.*, bald, bald-headed.

CA.RE.CEN.TE, *adj.*, carente.

CA.RE.CER, *v.*, to lack, to need, to require, to necessitate.

CA.RE.CI.MEN.TO, *s.m.*, privation, necessity; poverty; scarcity.

CA.REI.RO, *adj.*, costly, expensive.

CA.RE.NA.DO, *adj.*, carinate, carinated.

CA.RE.NAR, *v.*, to careen (plane, ship, motorcar).

CA.RÊN.CIA, *s.f.*, lack, need, necessity, scarcity.

CA.REN.TE, *adj.*, wanting, destitute, shy.

CA.RES.TI.A, *s.f.*, high prices, dearness, costlines, scarcity, need.

CA.RE.TA, *s.f.*, grimace, mask, scowl; person stupid, person obsolete.

CA.RE.TE.AR, *v.*, to make faces, to grimace.

CAR.GA, *s.f.*, load, burden, freight, cargo, loading.

CAR.GO, *s.m.*, load, charge, duty, task, office, employment,

CARGUEIRO ·· 121 ·· CARROCINHA

responsibility.
CAR.GUEI.RO, *s.m.*, cargo boat, cargo vessel, freighter.
CA.RI.A.DO, *adj.*, *Oftal.*, decayed, carious (tooth).
CA.RI.AR, *v.*, *Med., Oftal.*, to decay, to become carious; to rot.
CA.RI.BE, *s.*, *(Mar do) Caribe*: Caribean (Sea).
CA.RI.BE.NHO, *s.m., adj.*, Caribean.
CA.RI.CA.TO, *s.m.*, satirical actor, parodist; *adj.*, burlesque, caricatural; ridiculous, comical.
CA.RI.CA.TU.RA, *s.f.*, caricature, exaggeration; parody, ridiculous person.
CA.RI.CA.TU.RAL, *adj.*, caricatural.
CA.RI.CA.TU.RAR, *v.*, to caricature; to draw a caricature of.
CA.RI.CA.TU.RES.CO, *adj.*, caricatural, grotesque, ridiculous.
CA.RI.CA.TU.RIS.TA, *s. 2 gen.*, cartoonist, caricaturist.
CA.RÍ.CIA, *s.f.*, caress, fondling, affection.
CA.RI.CI.AR, *v.*, to caress, to fondle.
CA.RI.CI.Á.VEL, *adj.*, caressing, fondling; agreeable.
CA.RI.DA.DE, *s.f.*, charity, kindliness; benevolence, mercy, generosity.
CA.RI.DO.SA.MEN.TE, *adv.*, charitably.
CA.RI.DO.SO, *adj.*, charitable, kind, gentle, benevolent.
CÁ.RIE, *s.f.*, caries, tooth decay.
CA.RIL, *s.m.*, curry.
CA.RIM.BA.DO, *adj.*, stamped, sealed.
CA.RIM.BA.DOR, *s.m.*, stamper, rubber-stamper; *adj.*, stamping, marking.
CA.RIM.BA.GEM, *s.f.*, act or process of stamping.
CA.RIM.BAR, *v.*, to stamp, to seal, to imprint.
CA.RIM.BO, *s.m.*, seal, stamp, signet.
CA.RI.NHO, *s.m.*, kindness, gentleness, caress, fondling, love, affection.
CA.RI.NHO.SA.MEN.TE, *adv.*, affectionately; amorously.
CA.RI.NHO.SO, *adj.*, kind, loving, tender, gentle, affectionate.
CA.RI.O.CA, *adj., s. 2 gen.*, carioca, inhabitant of Rio de Janeiro.
CA.RIS.MA, *s.m.*, charism.
CA.RIZ, *s.m.*, face, countenance, aspect, appearance; *Bot.*, caraway; state or looks of the weather.
CA.RIS.MÁ.TI.CO, *adj.*, charismatic.
CAR.MA, *s.m.*, *Filos.*, karma.
CAR.ME.SIM, *s.m.*, crimson; *adj.*, crimson, bluish-red.
CAR.MIM, *s.m.*, carmine; *adj.*, crimson.
CAR.NAL, *adj.*, fleshly, carnal; bodily, libidinous, sensual.
CAR.NA.LI.DA.DE, *s.f.*, carnality, fleshiness, sensuality.
CAR.NAL.MEN.TE, *adv.*, carnally.
CAR.NA.VAL, *s.m.*, carnival.
CAR.NA.VA.LES.CO, *s.m.*, merrymaker, carnivaller; *adj.*, relative to carnaval.
CAR.NE, *s.f.*, flesh, meat, the pulp of fruit; sensuality.
CAR.NE.AR, *v.*, to butcher, to slaughter (cattle).
CAR.NEI.RO, *s.m.*, *Zool.*, sheep, ram, wether, mutton.
CAR.NE-SE.CA, *s.f.*, jerked meat.
CAR.NI.ÇA, *s.f.*, prey, booty.
CAR.NI.ÇAL, *adj.*, carnivorous; voracious; sanguinary.
CAR.NI.CEI.RO, *s.m.*, butcher, slaughterer; *adj.*, carnivorous, sanguinary.
CAR.NI.FI.CI.NA, *s.f.*, bloodshed, massacre, slaughter.
CAR.NÍ.VO.RO, *s.m.*, carnivore; *adj.*, carnivorous.
CAR.NO.SI.DA.DE, *s.f.*, carnosity, fleshiness.
CAR.NO.SO, *adj.*, full of flesh, meaty, carneous.
CAR.NU.DO, *adj.*, meaty, fleshy, carneous.

CA.RO, *adj.*, dear, costly, expensive.
CA.RO.CHA, *s.f.*, *Zool.*, ground beetle, dung beetle.
CA.RO.CHI.NHA, *s.f.*, diminutive of *carocha*; *fig.*, puerility; *conto da ~*: nursery tale.
CA.RO.ÇO, *s.m.*, heart, stone, pit, kernel.
CA.RO.ÇU.DO, *adj.*, kerneled, seedy.
CA.RO.LA, *s. 2 gen.*, piety, devotee, religionist; *adj.*, sanctimonious, pietistic.
CA.RO.LI.CE, *s.f.*, religious fanatism, pietism.
CA.RO.NA, *s.f.*, ride, lift.
CA.RO.NIS.TA, *s. 2 gen.*, hitch-hiker.
CA.RÓ.TI.DA, *s.f.*, *Anat.*, carotid.
CAR.PA, *s.f.*, *Zool.*, carp.
CAR.PIN.TA.RI.A., *s.f.*, carpenter's art, carpentry.
CAR.PIN.TEI.RO, *s.m.*, carpenter, woodworker.
CAR.PIR, *v.*, to gather, to pick, to pluck.
CAR.PO, *s.m.*, *Anat.*, carpus, wrist.
CAR.QUE.JA, *s.f.*, *Bot.*, carqueja (*Baccharis trimera*).
CAR.QUI.LHA, *s.f.*, wrinkle; pleat, fold.
CAR.RA.DA, *s.f.*, regular load of a cart or carriage, cartload, carload.
CAR.RAN.CA, *s.f.*, scowl, frown; an ugly face; severe expression of the face; mask.
CAR.RAN.CU.DO, *adj.*, scowling, frowning, grim.
CAR.RÃO, *s.m.*, a large car, coach, bus.
CAR.RA.PA.TO, *s.m.*, *Zool.*, tick, louse.
CAR.RA.PI.CHO, *s.m.*, *Bot.*, popular designation of the spiny seed kernels of various plants; *pop.*, kinky hair.
CAR.RAS.CO, *s.m.*, hangman, hanger, executioner, torturer.
CAR.RE.AR, *v.*, to cart, to carry, to transport, to haul.
CAR.RE.A.TA, *s.f.*, motorcade.
CAR.RE.GA.DEI.RA, *s.f.*, *Náut.*, brail; a woman who bears loads on her head; *Zool.*, a kind of leaf-cutting ant.
CAR.RE.GA.DO, *adj.*, loaded, charged; full, replete; cloudy; threatening (weather).
CAR.RE.GA.DOR, *s.m.*, loader, packer, porter, trucker, freighter.
CAR.RE.GA.MEN.TO, *s.m.*, lading, loading, cargo, load, oppression.
CAR.RE.GAR, *v.*, to burden, to load, to freight, to bear, to carry, to transport, to charge.
CAR.REI.RA, *s.f.*, profession, career, cartway, route, track.
CAR.REI.RIS.TA, *s. 2 gen.*, careerist.
CAR.RE.TA, *s.f.*, cart, waggon, gig.
CAR.RE.TA.GEM, *s.f.*, cartage.
CAR.RE.TEI.RO, *s.m.*, cart driver, carter, carman, carrier.
CAR.RE.TEL, *s.m.*, spool, bobbin, reel.
CAR.RE.TI.LHA, *s.f.*, small roll or spool; pastry cutter.
CAR.RE.TO, *s.m.*, act of transporting by cart; freight.
CAR.RIL, *s.m.*, rail, steel rail.
CAR.RI.LHÃO, *s.m.*, carillon.
CAR.RI.NHO, *s.m.*, diminutive form of *carro*; a child's play car.
CAR.RI.O.LA, *s.f.*, cariole; cab, gig.
CAR.RO, *s.m.*, car, automobile, cart, carriage, motorcar.
CAR.RO.ÇA, *s.f.*, waggon, cart.
CAR.RO.ÇA.RI.A, *s.f.*, car body.
CAR.RO.ÇÁ.VEL, *adj.*, passible, carriageable.
CAR.RO.CEI.RO, *s.m.*, cart-driver, waggoner.
CAR.RO.CE.RI.A, *s.f.*, the same that *carroçaria*.
CAR.RO-CHE.FE, *s.m.*, leading float; *fig.*, flagship.
CAR.RO.CI.NHA, *s.f.*, a small dump-cart; *~ de cachorro*:

CARRO-FORTE ·· 122 ·· CASSINO

dog vagon.

CARRO-FOR.TE, *s.m.*, armoured car.

CAR.RO-LEI.TO, *s.m.*, wagon lit.

CAR.RO-PI.PA, *s.m.*, tank-waggon, tank-car.

CAR.RO-RES.TAU.RAN.TE, *s.m.*, dining car, dining wagon (train).

CAR.ROS.SEL, *s.m.*, carrousel, roundabout, coach; merry go round; *gír.*, old-fashioned car.

CAR.RO-TAN.QUE, *s.m.*, the same that *carro-pipa*.

CAR.RU.A.GEM, *s.f.*, carriage, coach, car, cart, chariot.

CAR.TA, *s.f.*, letter, missive, map, chart, epistle, playing card; charter, bill; document.

CAR.TA.DA, *s.f.*, act of playing a decisive card on the table (game cards); *fig.*, attempt, effort.

CAR.TÃO, *s.m.*, card.

CAR.TÃO-POS.TAL, *s.m.*, postcard.

CAR.TAZ, *s.f.*, poster, placard.

CAR.TA.ZIS.TA, *s. 2 gen.*, poster maker, poster designer.

CAR.TE.A.DO, *s.m.*, card game.

CAR.TEI.RA, *s.f.*, wallet, purse;

CAR.TEI.RA DE I.DEN.TI.DA.DE, *s.f.*, identity card.

CAR.TEI.RO, *s.m.*, postman, mailman.

CAR.TEL, *s.m.*, letter of challenge; provocation; *Econ.*, coalition between companies, trust, cartel.

CAR.TE.LA, *s.f.*, tablet for inscriptions; portable display of cloth, ribbons etc.

CÁR.TER, *s.m.*, crankcase (car engine).

CAR.TE.SI.A.NIS.MO, *s.m.*, Cartesianism (the philosophy of Descartes).

CAR.TI.LA.GEM, *s.f.*, cartilage, gristle.

CAR.TI.LA.GI.NO.SO, *adj.*, cartilaginous, gristly.

CAR.TI.LHA, *s.f.*, primer, speller, spelling book.

CAR.TO.GRA.FAR, *v.*, make a map, to plat.

CAR.TO.GRA.FI.A, *s.f.*, cartography.

CAR.TO.GRÁ.FI.CO, *adj.*, cartographic, cartographical.

CAR.TÓ.GRA.FO, *s.m.*, cartographer.

CAR.TO.LA, *s.f.*, top-hat, topper; *fig.*, snob; *s.m.*, *pej.*, the manager of a sports club.

CAR.TO.LI.NA, *s.f.*, cardboard, pasteboard.

CAR.TO.MAN.TE, *s. 2 gen.*, fortuneteller, cartomancer.

CAR.TO.NA.DO, *adj.*, in boards, (books) bound in boards.

CAR.TO.NA.GEM, *s.f.*, bookbinding; manufacture of cardboard articles.

CAR.TO.NAR, *v.*, to board, to bind books in pasteboard.

CAR.TÓ.RIO, *s.m.*, register office, registry office, registry, archives.

CAR.TU.CHEI.RA, *s.f.*, cartridge-box, cartouche.

CAR.TU.CHO, *s.m.*, cartridge, shell, cartouche.

CAR.TUM, *s.m.*, cartoon.

CAR.TU.NIS.TA, *s. 2 gen.*, cartoonist.

CA.RUN.CHO, *s.m.*, *Zool.*, woodworm, worm.

CAR.VA.LHO, *s.m.*, *Bot.*, oak; oak tree, oak wood.

CAR.VÃO, *s.f.*, coal, charcoal, cinder.

CAR.VO.A.RI.A, *s.f.*, coal-pit, charcoal works.

CAR.VO.EN.TO, *adj.*, coally, coallike.

CÃS, *s.f.*, white hair.

CA.SA, *s.f.*, house, residence, place, habitation, building; home, family.

CA.SA BAN.CÁ.RIA, *s.f.*, bank.

CA.SA.CA, *s.f.*, dress-coat; *virar a casaca*: to be a turncoat.

CA.SA.CÃO, *s.m.*, top-coat, great-coat.

CA.SA.CO, *s.m.*, coat, jacket, overcoat.

CA.SA.DEI.RO, *adj.*, marriageable.

CA.SA.DO, *adj.*, married, wedded, united.

CA.SA.DOI.RO, *adj.*, the same that *casadouro*.

CA.SA-GRAN.DE, *s.f.*, mansion; *Bras.*, a large house, seat of a farm.

CA.SAL, *s.m.*, couple, pair.

CA.SA.MA.TA, *s.f.*, *Mil.*, casemate, pillbox, bunker.

CA.SA.MEN.TO, *s.m.*, marriage, wedding, matrimony, match, espousal.

CA.SAR, *v.*, to marry, to wed, to match, to mate, to espouse, to unite.

CA.SA.RÃO, *s.m.*, large house, building.

CA.SA.RI.A, *s.f.*, the same that *casario*.

CA.SA.RI.O, *s.m.*, a group of houses.

CAS.CA, *s.f.*, peel, rind, skin, shell, bark; husk.

CAS.CA.LHO, *s.m.*, gravel, pebbles, grit.

CAS.CÃO, *s.m.*, thick bark; hard crust; grime; *Med.*, crust, scab.

CAS.CAR, *v.*, to peel, to remove the skin (peel); to direct harsh words.

CAS.CA.TA, *s.f.*, cascade, waterfall; *gír.*, idle talk, lie.

CAS.CA.TE.AR, *v.*, to cascade; *fig.*, to tell lies, to say boast.

CAS.CA.TEI.RO, *s.m.*, *gír.*, one who is boastful; *adj.*, boastful.

CAS.CA.VEL, *s.f.*, *Zool.*, rattlesnake, rattle.

CAS.CO, *s.m.*, hoof, hull, skul, scalp, keg, skin.

CA.SE.A.DO, *s.m.*, act of making buttonholes.

CA.SE.AR, *v.*, to make buttonholes; to work with buttonhole stitch.

CA.SE.BRE, *s.m.*, little paltry cottage, shack.

CA.SE.I.FI.CAR, *v.*, to transform into cheese.

CA.SE.Í.NA, *s.f.*, *Biol.*, *Quím.*, casein.

CA.SEI.RO, *s.m.*, tenant, farm manager; *adj.*, home-made, domestic.

CA.SER.NA, *s.f.*, barracks, casern.

CA.SER.NEI.RO, *s.m.*, *Mil.*, casern commander; soldier on duty (barracks).

CA.SI.MI.RA, *s.f.*, cashmere.

CA.SI.NHA, *s.f.*, small house, cottage.

CAS.MUR.RI.CE, *s.f.*, obstinacy; sullenness, taciturnity.

CAS.MUR.RO, *s.m.*, a stubborn fellow; *adj.*, obstinate; grumpy, sullen.

CA.SO, *s.m.*, affair, case, event, fact, story, tale, chance, accident, condition.

CA.SO, *conj.*, if, if so, thus.

CA.SÓ.RIO, *s.m.*, marriage.

CAS.PA, *s.f.*, dandruff, scaly skin, scale.

CAS.PEN.TO, *adj.*, dandruffy.

CAS.PO.SO, *adj.*, dandruffy, scurfy.

CAS.QUEI.RO, *s.m.*, place where trees are decorticated for sawing.

CAS.QUEN.TO, *adj.*, having a thick skin or shell.

CAS.QUI.LHA, *s.f.*, small shell; piece of bark.

CAS.QUI.LHO, *s.m.*, dandy; dude; *adj.*, elegant, modish.

CAS.SA.ÇÃO, *s.f.*, abrogation, act of cancelling or annulling, repeal.

CAS.SA.DO, *adj.*, which was abrogated or repealed.

CAS.SAR, *v.*, to annul, to cancel, to repeal, to revoke.

CAS.SE.TE.TE, *s.m.*, truncheon, billy.

CAS.SE.TE, *s.m.*, cassette, tape player.

CAS.SI.NO, *s.m.*, casino, a game at cards; building or club for dancing or gambling.

CASSIOPÉIA ·· 123 ·· CATOLICIDADE

CAS.SI.O.PÉI.A, *s.f., Astron., Mit.,* Cassiopeia.
CAS.SI.TE.RI.TA, *s.f., Min.,* cassiterite.
CAS.TA, *s.f.,* caste, race, lineage, stock.
CAS.TA.MEN.TE, *adv.,* chastely, virginally, continently.
CAS.TA.NHA, *s.f., Bot.,* chestnut.
CAS.TA.NHA-DO-PA.RÁ, *s.f., Bot.,* Brazil nut.
CAS.TA.NHAL, *s.m.,* a grove of chestnut trees.
CAS.TA.NHEI.RA, *s.f.,* woman who sells chestnuts; *Bot.,* wild chestnut tree.
CAS.TA.NHEI.RO, *s.m.,* chestnut tree, chestnut.
CAS.TA.NHO, *adj.,* brown, chestnut.
CAS.TA.NHO.LAS, *s.f., pl.,* castanets.
CAS.TE.LHA.NO, *adj., s.m.,* Castilian; Spanish.
CAS.TE.LÃO, *s.m.,* castellan, lord of castle.
CAS.TE.LO, *s.m.,* castle, fortress, fort.
CAS.TI.ÇAL, *s.m.,* candlestick, candleholder.
CAS.TI.ÇO, *s.m.,* someone who uses the correct and pure language of a region; *adj.,* pure, authentic.
CAS.TI.DA.DE, *s.f.,* chastity, chasteness, purity, continency, virtue.
CAS.TI.GA.DO, *adj.,* punished, chastised.
CAS.TI.GAR, *v.,* to punish, to castigate, to discipline, to chasten.
CAS.TI.GÁ.VEL, *adj.,* punishable.
CAS.TI.GO, *s.m.,* punishment, penalty, chastisement, correction.
CAS.TO, *adj.,* chaste, pure, clean, virginal, virtuous.
CAS.TOR, *s.m., Zool.,* beaver, castor.
CAS.TRA.ÇÃO, *s.f.,* castration.
CAS.TRA.DO, *s.m.,* castrate, eunuch; *adj.,* castrated, gelded; emasculate.
CAS.TRA.DOR, *s.m.,* castrator.
CAS.TRAR, *v.,* to castrate, to geld, to spay.
CA.SU.AL, *adj.,* casual, occasional, incidental.
CA.SU.A.LI.DA.DE, *s.f.,* casualty, fortuity; accident, hazard, contingency, eventuality.
CA.SU.ÍS.MO, *s.m.,* casuistry.
CA.SU.ÍS.TI.CA, *s.f.,* casuistry.
CA.SU.IS.TI.CA.MEN.TE, *adv.,* casuistically.
CA.SU.ÍS.TI.CO, *adj.,* casuistic.
CA.SU.LO, *s.m., Zool.,* cocoon; *Bot.,* boll, seed capsule.
CA.TA, *s.f.,* search; examination, investigation, research.
CA.TA.CLÍS.MI.CO, *adj.,* cataclysmal, cataclysmic.
CA.TA.CLIS.MO, *s.m.,* cataclysm; catastrophe, disaster, ruin.
CA.TA.CRE.SE, *s.f., Gram.,* catachresis.
CA.TA.CUM.BA, *s.f.,* catacomb.
CA.TA.DOR, *s.m.,* one who searches; *adj.,* that searches, scrutinizes.
CA.TA.DU.RA, *s.f.,* outward appearance; aspect, look.
CA.TA.LÃO, *s.m., adj.,* Catalan.
CA.TA.LEP.SI.A, *s.f., Med.,* catalepsy.
CA.TA.LI.SA.ÇÃO, *s.f., Fis., Quim.,* catalysis, activation.
CA.TA.LI.SA.DOR, *s.m., Fis., Quim.,* catalyst, catalyzer, catalyser.
CA.TA.LI.SAR, *v.,* to catalyze.
CA.TÁ.LI.SE, *s.f.,* catalysis.
CA.TA.LÍ.TI.CO, *adj., Fis., Quim.,* catalytic.
CA.TA.LO.GA.ÇÃO, *s.f.,* cataloguing.
CA.TA.LO.GA.DO, *adj.,* catalogued.
CA.TA.LO.GA.DOR, *s.m.,* cataloguer, catalogist, cataloger.
CA.TA.LO.GAR, *v.,* to catologue, to classify, to make a list

of, to register.
CA.TÁ.LO.GO, *s.m.,* catalogue, catalog, roll, register.
CA.TA.MA.RÃ, *s.m.,* catamaran.
CA.TA.NA, *s.f.,* catan (a Japanese sword).
CA.TÃO, *s.m.,* an austere man.
CA.TA-PI.O.LHO, *s.m., Bras., pop.,* the thumb.
CA.TA.PLAS.MA, *s.m.,* cataplasm, plaster.
CA.TA.PLE.XI.A, *s.f., Med., Fisiol.,* cataplexy.
CA.TA.PO.RA, *s.f.,* chicken pox, varicella.
CA.TA.PUL.TA, *s.f.,* catapult.
CA.TAR, *v.,* to collect, to seek, to discover, to scrutinize.
CA.TA.RA.TA, *s.f.,* cataract, waterfall; *Med.,* cataract, amaurosis.
CA.TA.RI.NEN.SE, *s. 2 gen.,* native or inhabitant of Santa Catarina.
CA.TAR.RAL, *s.f., Med., pop.,* catarrhal fever; *adj.,* catarrhal.
CA.TAR.REN.TO, *adj.,* catarrhal.
CA.TAR.RO, *s.m.,* catarrh.
CA.TAR.RO.SO, *adj.,* catarrhal.
CA.TAR.SE, *s.f.,* catharsis, purification, purifying.
CA.TÁR.TI.CO, *s.m.,* cathartic, purgative; *adj.,* cathartic.
CA.TÁS.TRO.FE, *s.f.,* catastrophe, calamity.
CA.TAS.TRÓ.FI.CO, *adj.,* catastrophic.
CA.TAS.TRO.FIS.MO, *s.m., pop.,* catastrophism.
CA.TA.TAU, *s.m.,* physical punishment; blow, rap; *Bras., pop.,* something big or bulky; a short person.
CA.TA-VEN.TO, *s.m.,* weather vane, weathercock, vane.
CA.TE.CIS.MO, *s.m.,* catechism, religious instruction.
CÁ.TE.DRA, *s.f.,* cathedra, chair.
CA.TE.DRAL, *s.m.,* cathedral, dome.
CA.TE.DRÁ.TI.CO, *s.m.,* university professor or lecturer.
CA.TE.GO.RI.A, *s.f.,* category, class, order, grade, series, character, quality.
CA.TE.GO.RI.CA.MEN.TE, *adv.,* categorically, absolutely, definitely.
CA.TE.GÓ.RI.CO, *adj.,* categorical, explicit, absolute, decisive.
CA.TE.GO.RI.ZA.DO, *adj.,* categorized.
CA.TE.GO.RI.ZAR, *v.,* to categorize, to class, to classify.
CA.TE.QUE.SE, *s.f.,* catechesis.
CA.TE.QUÉ.TI.CO, *adj.,* catechetical.
CA.TE.QUIS.TA, *s. 2 gen.,* catechist, catechizer.
CA.TE.QUI.ZA.ÇÃO, *s.f.,* catechization, catechisation.
CA.TE.QUI.ZAR, *v.,* catechize, to teach, to convince.
CA.TI.LI.NÁ.RI.A, *s.f., Hist.,* Cicero's accusatory speeches (criticizing violently Catilina); *fig.,* violent accusation.
CA.TIN.GA, *s.f.,* fetid smell.
CA.TIN.GAL, *s.m.,* a forest of small stunted trees.
CA.TIN.GAN.TE, *adj.,* fetid smelling.
CA.TIN.GAR, *v.,* to bicker; to emit a bad smell, to stink.
CA.TIN.GO.SO, *adj.,* ill-smelling, malodorous.
CA.TIN.GUEN.TO, *adj.,* malodorous.
CÁ.TION, *s.m., Fis., Quim.,* cation, kation.
CA.TI.VA.ÇÃO, *s.f.,* captivation.
CA.TI.VAN.TE, *adj.,* captivating, fascinating, charming.
CA.TI.VAR, *v.,* to captivate, to capture, to hold captive, to charm, to fascinate, to enchant.
CA.TI.VEI.RO, *s.m.,* captivity, slavery, servitude, prison, preoccupation.
CA.TI.VO, *s.m.,* captive, prisoner, slave; *adj.,* captive, confined, charmed, fascinating.
CA.TO.LI.CI.DA.DE, *s.f.,* Catholicity.

CATOLICISMO · 124 · CEDILHA

CA.TO.LI.CIS.MO, *s.m.*, Catholicism, faith.
CA.TÓ.LI.CO, *adj., s.m.*, Roman Catholic, Catholic.
CA.TOR.ZE, *num.*, fourteen.
CA.TRA.CA, *s.f.*, turnstile, ratchet.
CA.TRE, *s.m.*, truckle bed, folding bed, pallet, cot.
CA.TU.CAR, *v.*, to nudge.
CA.TUR.RA, *s. 2 gen.*, cantankerous person; *adj.*, cantankerous, stubborn.
CA.TUR.RA.DA, *s.f.*, obstinacy.
CA.TUR.RI.CE, *s.f.*, obstinacy, unfounded stubbornness.
CA.TUR.RI.TA, *s.f., Zool.*, monk parrot, monk parakeet.
CAU.BÓI, *s.m.*, cowboy.
CAU.ÇÃO, *s.f.*, security, guarantee, guaranty, pledge, bond.
CAU.CA.SI.A.NO, *adj.*, Caucasian.
CAU.CI.O.NAR, *v.*, to bail, to bond, to vouch for, to pledge.
CAU.DA, *s.f.*, tail, rear, rear end; *Astron.*, tail of a comet; *piano de cauda*: grand piano.
CAU.DA.DO, *adj.*, caudate.
CAU.DA.DOS, *s.m., pl., Zool.*, Caudata.
CAU.DAL, *s.m.*, torrent, mighty river; *adj.*, relating to tail.
CAU.DA.LO.SA.MEN.TE, *adv.*, abundantly, copiously.
CAU.DA.LO.SO, *adj.*, torrential, abundant, copious.
CAU.DA.TÁ.RI.O, *s.m.*, trainbearer; *fig.*, servile, submissive; *adj.*, referring to someone submissive.
CAU.DI.LHIS.MO, *s.m.*, caudillismo.
CAU.DI.LHO, *s.m.*, commander, chief, military leader.
CAU.LE, *s.m.*, stalk, stem.
CAU.LES.CÊN.CI.A, *s.f., Bot.*, caulescence.
CAU.SA, *s.f.*, cause, motive, reason, ground, origin.
CAU.SA.ÇÃO, *s.f.*, causation.
CAU.SAL, *adj.*, causal, causative.
CAU.SA.LI.DA.DE, *s.f.*, causality, causation.
CAU.SAR, *v.*, to cause, to motivate, to occasion, to engender, to provoke.
CAU.SÍ.DI.CO, *s.m.*, lawyer, attorney.
CAUS.TI.CA.MEN.TE, *adv.*, caustically.
CAUS.TI.CAN.TE, *adj.*, caustic, cauterant, burning; *fig.*, tedious, wearisome.
CAUS.TI.CAR, *v.*, to cauterize, to sear, to cauterise; to burn; *fig.*, to molest.
CAUS.TI.CI.DA.DE, *s.f.*, causticity, *fig.*, mordacity.
CÁUS.TI.CO, *s.m.*, a caustic agent; *adj.*, caustic; *fig.*, acrid, scathing, bitter; *soda cáustica*: caustic soda.
CAU.TE.LA, *s.f.*, caution, vigilance, watchfulness, prudence.
CAU.TE.LA.MEN.TO, *s.m.*, act of cautioning or warning.
CAU.TE.LAR, *v.*, to caution, to warn, to forearm.
CAU.TE.LO.SA.MEN.TE, *adv.*, cautiously, watchfully, precautiously, prudently.
CAU.TE.LO.SO, *adj.*, cautious, careful, prudent, watchful.
CAU.TE.RI.ZA.ÇÃO, *s.f.*, cautery, cauterization.
CÁU.TE.RI.ZAR, *v.*, cauterize, to sear, to burn.
CAU.TO, *adj.*, cautious, prudent.
CA.VA.CO, *s.m.*, a chip of wood.
CA.VA.DEI.RA, *s.f.*, hoe.
CA.VA.DE.LA, *s.f.*, act of digging; a stroke with a hoe.
CA.VA.DO, *s.m.*, hollow, hole, pit; *adj.*, excavated; low-cut.
CA.VA.DOR, *s.m.*, digger, hoer, ploughman, digging tool.
CA.VA.LA, *s.f., Zool.*, mackerel.
CA.VA.LAR, *adj.*, equine; exaggerated, excessive, huge.
CA.VA.LA.RI.A, *s.f.*, cavalry, chivalry, a group of horsemen.
CA.VA.LA.RI.ÇA, *s.f.*, horse stable.

CA.VA.LA.RI.ÇO, *s.m.*, equerry, hostler; stable-boy, groom.
CA.VA.LEI.RA, *s.f.*, horsewoman.
CA.VA.LEI.RO, *s.m.*, horseman, rider, equestrian, cavalryman.
CA.VA.LE.TE, *s.m.*, trestle, easel; wooden horse, rack, stand.
CA.VAL.GA.DA, *s.f.*, cavalcade, rodeo.
CA.VAL.GA.DU.RA, *s.f.*, beast, saddle animal; stupid, a rude person.
CA.VAL.GAR, *v.*, to ride on horseback, to mount a horse to jockey.
CA.VA.LHA.DA, *s.f.*, horses, donkeys, mules collectively; *Bras.*, cavalhadas (*pl.*): popular amusement or sport.
CA.VA.LHEI.RES.CO, *adj.*, chivalrous, chivalric; knightly, noble.
CA.VA.LHEI.RIS.MO, *s.m.*, chivalrousness, chivalry; knightliness; generous act.
CA.VA.LHEI.RO, *s.m.*, gentleman; *adj.*, noble.
CA.VA.LO, *s.m.*, horse; knight.
CA.VA.LO.AR, *v.*, to cavort, to leap like a horse.
CA.VA.LO-MA.RI.NHO, *s.m.*, sea-horse, hippopotamus.
CA.VA.LO-VA.POR, *s.m.*, horse-power.
CA.VA.NHA.QUE, *s.m.*, goatee, goatee beard.
CA.VA.QUE.AR, *v.*, to chat, to chatter, to tattle.
CA.VA.QUI.NHO, *s.m.*, small guitar.
CA.VAR, *v.*, to dig, to delve, to excavate, to burrow, to cave, to hoe.
CA.VEI.RA, *s.f.*, skull, death's-head.
CA.VEI.RO.SO, *adj.*, resembling a skull; very lean, haggard.
CA.VER.NA, *s.f.*, cave, cavern, grotto, den, crypt.
CA.VER.NAL, *adj.*, cavernous.
CA.VER.NO.SA.MEN.TE, *adv.*, cavernously.
CA.VER.NO.SI.DA.DE, *s.f.*, cavernous character.
CA.VER.NO.SO, *adj.*, cavernous.
CA.VI.AR, *s.m.*, caviar.
CA.VI.DA.DE, *s.f.*, cavity; hole.
CA.VI.LO.SO, *adj.*, captious; fraudulent, deceitful, deceptive.
CA.VOU.CA.DOR, *s.m.*, digger, ditchdigger, delver.
CA.VOU.CAR, *v.*, to dig, to delve; to excavate.
CA.VOU.CO, *s.m.*, ditch, trench; excavation.
CA.VOU.QUEI.RO, *s.m.*, digger, delver.
CA.XI.AS, *s. 2 gen., 2 num.*, a person who is aware of their duties and respect the rules.
CA.XUM.BA, *s.f., Med.*, mumps, parotitis.
CD-ROM, *s.m.*, abrev. of compact disk read only memory.
CE.AR, *v.*, to eat supper, to dine.
CE.A.REN.SE, *s. 2 gen.*, native or inhabitant of the state of Ceará.
CE.BO.LA, *s.f., Bot.*, onion.
CE.BO.LA.DA, *s.f.*, onion stew.
CE.BO.LAL, *s.m.*, onion field, onion plantation.
CE.BO.LÃO, *s.m., pop.*, an old and large watch.
CE.BO.LI.NHA, *s.f., Bot.*, welsh onion.
CE.CE.AR, *v.*, to lisp.
CE.CEI.O, *s.m.*, act of lisping, lisp.
CE.CE.O.SO, *adj.*, lisping.
CÊ-DÊ-EFE, *s. 2 gen., Bras.*, a very hard-working student.
CE.DÊN.CIA, *s.f.*, cession, transfer.
CE.DEN.TE, *s. 2 gen.*, ceder, transferor; *adj.*, transferring, assigning.
CE.DER, *v.*, to cede, to assign, to transfer, to submit.
CE.DI.DO, *adj.*, granted, transferred, relinquished.
CE.DI.LHA, *s.f.*, cedilla mark.

CEDILHAR · 125 · CENTOPEIA

CE.DI.LHAR, *v.*, to mark with a cedilla.
CE.DI.MEN.TO, *s.m.*, cession, transfer, yielding.
CE.DI.NHO, *adv.*, very early.
CE.DÍ.VEL, *adj.*, transferable; alienable, yieldable.
CE.DO, *adv.*, early, soon.
CE.DRO, *s.m.*, *Bot.*, cedar, juniper.
CÉ.DU.LA, *s.f.*, note, short letter, ticket.
CE.FA.LEI.A, *s.f.*, *Med.*, headache, cephalalgia.
CE.FÁ.LI.CO, *adj.*, cephalic.
CE.FA.LI.TE, *s.f.*, cephalitis.
CE.GA.MEN.TE, *adv.*, blindly, rashly, unreasoningly.
CE.GA.MEN.TO, *s.m.*, blindness, deprivation of sight.
CE.GAR, *v.*, to blind, to fascinate, to charm, to deprive of sight, to dazzle, daze.
CE.GAS, *s.f.*, (word used only in the adverbial locution) às cegas: blindly, groping.
CE.GO, *s.m.*, blind man; *adj.*, blind, blunt, sightless, blinded, dazzled.
CE.GO.NHA, *s.f.*, *Zool.*, stork.
CE.GUEI.RA, *s.f.*, blindness, passion, fanatism.
CEI.A, *s.f.*, supper, evening meal.
CEI.FA, *s.f.*, harvesting, reaping, harvest.
CEI.FA.DEI.RO, *s.m.*, the same that *ceifeiro*.
CEI.FA.DOR, *s.m.*, the same that *ceifeiro*.
CEI.FAR, *v.*, to harvest, to shear, to mow.
CEI.FEI.RO, *s.m.*, reaper, harvest-man; cutter, scytheman; *adj.*, pertaining to harvest, harvesting, reaping.
CE.LA, *s.f.*, cell.
CE.LA.GEM, *s.f.*, the colour of the sky at sunrise and sunset; dawn.
CE.LE.BRA.ÇÃO, *s.f.*, celebration, commemoration, solemnity.
CE.LE.BRA.DO, *adj.*, celebrated; famous; glorified.
CE.LE.BRAN.TE, *s. 2 gen.*, celebrant; *adj.*, celebrative, celebrant.
CE.LE.BRAR, *v.*, to celebrate, to commemorate, to officiate.
CE.LE.BRÁ.VEL, *adj.*, praiseworthy.
CÉ.LE.BRE, *adj.*, famous, renowned, celebrated, eminent.
CE.LE.BRE.MEN.TE, *adv.*, celebratedly, famously.
CE.LE.BRI.DA.DE, *s.f.*, celebrity, fame, renown; idol star.
CE.LE.BRI.ZA.ÇÃO, *s.f.*, process of becoming famous.
CE.LE.BRI.ZAR, *v.*, to fame, to render famous.
CE.LEI.RO, *s.m.*, cellar, granary, corn-floor.
CE.LEN.TE.RA.DO, *s.m.*, *Zool.*, coelenterate; adj coelenterate.
CE.LE.RA.DO, *s.m.*, criminal, malefactor, felon.
CÉ.LE.RE, *adj.*, swift, quick.
CE.LE.RI.DA.DE, *s.f.*, celerity; rapidity, quickness.
CE.LES.TE, *adj.*, celestial, heavenly, divine, paradisiac.
CE.LES.TI.AL, *adj.*, celestial.
CE.LES.TI.NO, *adj.*, *Lit.*, celestial blue, sky-blue.
CE.LEU.MA, *s.f.*, noise, clamour; uproar, tumult.
CE.LÍ.A.CO, *adj.*, *Anat.*, coeliac, celiac, abdominal.
CE.LI.BA.TÁ.RI.O, *s.m.*, celibate; *adj.*, unmarried, celibate, celibatarian.
CE.LI.BA.TA.RIS.MO, *s.m.*, celibatarian's situation.
CE.LI.BA.TO, *s.m.*, celibacy, bachelorhood.
CE.LO.FA.NE, *s.m.*, cellophane.
CEL.SO, *adj.*, high, noble; sublime, elevated.
CEL.TA, *s. 2 gen.*, Celt, Kelt; *s.m.*, Celtic, Keltic (language); *adj.*, Celtic, Keltic.
CÉL.TI.CO, *s.m.*, Celt, Kelt; *adj.*, Celtic.

CÉ.LU.LA, *s.f.*, cell, cellule.
CÉ.LU.LA-OVO, *s.f.*, *Biol.*, egg cell, ovum.
CE.LU.LAR, *adj.*, cellular.
CE.LU.LI.TE, *s.f.*, cellulitis.
CE.LU.LOI.DE, *s.f.*, celluloid.
CE.LU.LO.SE, *s.f.*, cellulose.
CE.LU.LO.SI.DA.DE, *s.f.*, adj cellulosity.
CE.LU.LO.SO, *adj.*, cellular.
CEM, *num.*, one hundred, a hundred.
CE.MI.TE.RI.AL, *adj.*, concerning the cemetery.
CE.MI.TÉ.RIO, *s.m.*, cemetery, burial ground, necropolis.
CE.NA, *s.f.*, scene, stage, scenery, picture.
CE.NÁ.CU.LO, *s.m.*, dining-room; where the Last Supper took place; group bound together by common ideals.
CE.NÁ.RIO, *s.m.*, scenery, set, landscape.
CE.NA.RIS.TA, *s. 2 gen.*, scenographer.
CE.NHO, *s.m.*, severe or awe inspiring countenance; scowl, frown.
CE.NHO.SO, *adj.*, cross, surly.
CÊ.NI.CO, *adj.*, scenic, scenical; theatrical.
CE.NO.GRA.FI.A, *s.f.*, scenography.
CE.NO.GRÁ.FI.CO, *adj.*, scenographic, scenographical.
CE.NÓ.GRA.FO, *s.m.*, scenographer.
CE.NO.SI.DA.DE, *s.f.*, filth, dirt; *fig.*, obscenity.
CE.NO.SO, *adj.*, dirty, filthy; obscene.
CE.NOU.RA, *s.f.*, *Bot.*, carrot.
CE.NO.ZOI.CO, *adj.*, *Geol.*, Cenozoic.
CEN.SA.TÁ.RI.O, *s.m.*, renter; a census or taxpayer; *adj.*, liable to pay quit-rent; concerning the census.
CEN.SI.TÁ.RI.O, *s.m.*, the same that *censatário*.
CEN.SO, *s.m.*, census, cense, rank, computation, tribute.
CEN.SOR, *s.m.*, censor, critic, censurer, controller.
CEN.SÓ.RI.O, *adj.*, censorious.
CEN.SU.Á.RI.O, *s.m.*, taxpayer, rent payer; *adj.*, of or related to a census.
CEN.SU.RA, *s.f.*, censorship.
CEN.SU.RA.DO, *adj.*, censured, condemned, reproved.
CEN.SU.RA.DOR, *s.m.*, censor, censurer; *adj.*, censorious, censuring.
CEN.SU.RAR, *v.*, to censure, to control, to subject to censure, to criticize.
CEN.SU.RÁ.VEL, *adj.*, censurable, reprovable, criticizable.
CEN.SU.RA.VEL.MEN.TE, *adv.*, censurably, blameworthily, objectionably.
CEN.TAU.RO, *s.m.*, *Astron.*, Centaurus, Centaur; *Mit.*, centaur.
CEN.TA.VO, *s.m.*, cent, centavo, penny, pence.
CEN.TEI.O, *s.m.*, *Bot.*, rye.
CEN.TE.LHA, *s.f.*, spark, scintilla, flash, sparkle.
CEN.TE.LHA.DOR, *s.m.*, spark discharger.
CEN.TE.LHAR, *v.*, to scintillate, to sparkle.
CEN.TE.NA, *s.f.*, a hundred.
CEN.TE.NÁ.RIO, *s.m.*, centenarian, centennial, centenary; *adj.*, centennial, centenary.
CEN.TE.SI.MAL, *adj.*, centesimal.
CEN.TÉ.SI.MO, *s.m.*, centesimal, hundredth.
CEN.TI.GRA.DO, *adj.*, *s.m.*, centigrade.
CEN.TI.GRA.MA, *s.m.*, centigram, centigramme.
CEN.TI.LI.TRO, *s.m.*, centiliter, centilitre.
CEN.TÍ.ME.TRO, *s.m.*, centimetre, centimeter.
CEN.TO, *num.*, a hundred.
CEN.TO.PEI.A, *s.f.*, *Zool.*, centipede.

CENTRAL ·· 126 ·· CERZIDURA

CEN.TRAL, s.f., central, headquarters; adj., central, centric.

CEN.TRA.LI.DA.DE, s.f., centrality, centricity.

CEN.TRA.LIS.MO, s.m., centralism, centralization.

CEN.TRA.LIS.TA, s. 2 gen., centralist; adj., centralist, centralistic.

CEN.TRA.LI.ZA.ÇÃO, s.f., centralization.

CEN.TRA.LI.ZA.DO, adj., centralized.

CEN.TRA.LI.ZAR, v., to centralize, to concentrate.

CEN.TRAL.MEN.TE, adv., centrically, centrally.

CEN.TRAR, v., to center, to centre, to fix in a center.

CEN.TRÍ.FU.GA, s.f., centrifuge.

CEN.TRI.FU.GA.ÇÃO, s.f., centrifugation.

CEN.TRI.FU.GA.DO.RA, s.f., centrifuge.

CEN.TRI.FU.GA.MEN.TE, adv., centrifugally.

CEN.TRI.FU.GAR, v., to centrifuge.

CEN.TRÍ.FU.GO, adj., centrifugal.

CEN.TRÍ.PE.TO, adj., centripetal; força centrípeta: centripetal force.

CEN.TRO, s.m., center, centre, focal point, middle; nucleus.

CEN.TRO.A.VAN.TE, s.m., Esp., centre-forward (soccer).

CEN.TRO-O.ES.TE, s.m., Geogr., Middle West.

CEN.TU.PLI.CAR, v., to centuple, to multiply by one hundred, to centuplicate.

CÊN.TU.PLO, s.m., centuplicate; adj., centuple, centuplicate.

CEN.TÚ.RI.A, s.f., century; group of a hundred; centenary.

CEN.TU.RI.AL, adj., centurial.

CEN.TU.RI.ÃO, s.m., Hist., centurion (an officer commanding a Roman century).

CE.NU.RO, s.m., Zool., coenurus.

CEP, abrev. of Código de Endereçamento Postal: zip code, post code.

CE.PA, s.f., Bot., cepa, onion; grapevine, stubble; fig., pith; ancestry, stock.

CE.PÁ.CE.O, adj., Bot., cepacious, onionlike.

CEP.TI.CIS.MO, s.m., scepticism, skepticism.

CÉP.TI.CO, s.m., a sceptic, a philosophic doubter; adj., sceptic, agnostic, cynical.

CE.RA, s.f., wax.

CE.RÂ.MI.CA, s.f., ceramics, pottery.

CE.RÂ.MI.CO, adj., ceramic.

CE.RA.MIS.TA, s. 2 gen., ceramist, ceramic artist; adj., ceramic.

CE.RAR, v., to wax; to seal.

CE.RA.TO.SE, s.f., Med., keratosis.

CÉR.BE.RO, s.m., Mit., Cerberus, three-headed dog.

CER.CA, s.f., fence, wire fence, railing, hedge; (loc. prep.) cerca de: approximately, about.

CER.CA.DU.RA, s.f., rim, edge; hem; embroidery.

CER:CA, adv., near, close by, approximate.

CER.CA.DO, s.m., enclosure, yard, park; adj., enclosed, hedged in.

CER.CA.NI.AS, s.f., pl., outskirts.

CER.CAR, v., to surround, to fence in, to enclose, to wall.

CER.CE, adv., close, closely, close to; short.

CER.CE.A.DOR, s.m., one who clips or cuts round.

CER.CE.A.DU.RA, s.f., cutting short, clipping.

CER.CE.A.MEN.TO, s.m., trimming, cutting.

CER.CE.AR, v., to lessen, to restrict, to cut around, to cut short.

CER.CEI.O, s.m., the same that cerceamento.

CER.CO, s.m., circle, siege, encirclement, envelopment.

CER.DA, s.f., bristle.

CER.DO, s.m., the same that porco.

CER.DO.SO, adj., bristly.

CE.RE.AL, s.m., cereal, corn, grain.

CE.RE.A.LIS.TA, s. 2 gen., cereal dealer; adj., which relates to trade in cereals.

CE.RE.BE.LO, s.m., Anat., cerebellum.

CE.RE.BRAL, adj., cerebral.

CE.RE.BRI.NO, adj., cerebral; imaginary, extraordinary, uncommon.

CÉ.RE.BRO, s.m., Anat., brain; intelligence.

CE.RE.JA, s.f., Bot., cherry.

CE.RE.JEI.RA, s.f., Bot., cherry tree.

CE.RES, s.f., Mit., Ceres; Astron., Ceres (dwarf planet); fig., vegetation, field.

CE.RÍ.FE.RO, adj., wax producing, ceriferous.

CE.RI.MÔ.NIA, s.f., ceremony, solemnity, rite, civility.

CE.RI.MO.NI.AL, s.m., rites; adj., ceremonial, ritual.

CE.RI.MO.NI.Á.TI.CO, adj., ceremonious, formal.

CE.RI.MO.NI.O.SO, adj., ceremonious, ceremonial.

CÉ.RI.O, s.m., Quím., cerium (Ce).

CER.NE, s.m., center, core, pith.

CE.ROL, s.m., a mixture of ground glass with glue that goes in line of the kites.

CE.RO.SO, adj., waxy, waxen.

CE.ROU.LAS, s.f., pl., long underwear; long johns.

CER.RA.ÇÃO, s.f., fog, mist, haze, fogginess, darkness.

CER.RA.DÃO, s.m., an extensive tract of barren land.

CER.RA.DO, s.m., fence, hedge, fenced-in land; woodsy pasture; adj., compact, dense, close, thick.

CER.RAR, v., to close, to shut, to join, to clench.

CER.RO, s.m., small hill, hillock, knoll, cliff.

CER.TA.ME, s.m., fight, combat, discussion, argument.

CER.TÂ.MEN, s.m., the same that certame.

CER.TA.MEN.TE, adv., certainly, exactly, surely.

CER.TEI.RO, adj., adequate, right, convenient, correct.

CER.TE.ZA, s.f., certainty, conviction, confidence, security.

CER.TI.DÃO, s.f., certificate, attestation, voucher.

CER.TI.FI.CA.ÇÃO, s.f., certification.

CER.TI.FI.CA.DO, s.m., certification, certificate, attestation, voucher.

CER.TI.FI.CA.DOR, s.m., certifier; adj., certifying.

CER.TI.FI.CAN.TE, s. 2 gen., the same that certificador.

CER.TI.FI.CAR, v., to certify, to attest, to confirm, to authenticate, to affirm.

CER.TI.FI.CA.TI.VO, adj., certificatory, certifiable.

CER.TO, adj., certain, true, exact, evident, sure, correct, assured, positive.

CE.RU.ME, s.m., Med., cerumen.

CE.RU.MI.NO.SO, adj., ceruminous.

CER.VE.JA, s.f., beer, ale.

CER.VE.JA.DA, s.f., glass of beer; a group of beer drinkers, party of beer tipplers.

CER.VE.JA.RI.A, s.f., beershop, ale-house, beerhouse, brewery.

CER.VE.JEI.RO, s.m., brewer.

CER.VI.CAL, adj., Anat., cervical.

CER.VÍ.DE.O, s.m., Zool., Cervidae ; adj., cervine, cervoid.

CER.VO, s.m., Zool., deer.

CER.ZI.DEI.RA, s.f., woman who darns clothes.

CER.ZI.DOR, s.m., darner; adj., darning.

CER.ZI.DU.RA, s.f., darning.

CERZIMENTO

CHAPEADO

CER.ZI.MEN.TO, *s.m.*, darning, fine-drawing.
CER.ZIR, *v.*, to darn, to fine-draw, to knit up.
CE.SA.RI.A.NA, *s.f.*, Caesarian, Caesarian operation.
CÉSIO, *s.m.*, *Quím.*, cesium (Cs, atomic number 55).
CES.SA.ÇÃO, *s.f.*, cessation, ceasing, interruption, break.
CES.SAN.TE, *adj.*, inactive, intermissive.
CES.SÃO, *s.f.*, cession, release.
CES.SAR, *v.*, to cease, to stop, to discontinue, to interrupt.
CES.SI.O.NÁ.RI.O, *s.m.*, assignee.
CES.SÍ.VEL, *adj.*, assignable, transferable.
CES.TA, *s.f.*, basket, coop.
CES.TA.DA, *s.f.*, basketful.
CES.TÃO, *s.m.*, large basket; Fort gabion.
CES.TA.RI.A, *s.f.*, basketmaking, basketry.
CES.TEI.RO, *s.m.*, basketmaker.
CES.TI.NHA, *s.f.*, a small basket; *Esp.*, a player who scores high at a basketball game.
CES.TO, *s.m.*, basket.
CE.SU.RA, *s.f.*, act of cutting, incision; *Mús., Lit.*, caesura, break.
CE.SU.RAR, *v.*, to cut, to make an incision; *Mús., Lit.*, to present a pause or break.
CE.TÁ.CE.O, *s.m.*, *Zool.*, cetacean; *adj.*, cetacean, cetaceous.
CE.TI.CIS.MO, *s.m.*, scepticism.
CÉ.TI.CO, *adj.*, sceptic, cynical.
CE.TIM, *s.m.*, satin.
CE.TO.NA, *s.f.*, *Quím.*, ketone.
CE.TRO, *s.m.*, scepter, sceptre.
CÉU, *s.m.*, sky, heaven, firmament, paradise, sphere.
CE.VA, *s.f.*, act of fattening animals; bait.
CE.VA.DA, *s.f.*, *Bot.*, barley.
CE.VA.DAL, *s.m.*, barley field.
CE.VA.DEI.RA, *s.f.*, nose-bag, feed bag.
CE.VA.DO, *s.m.*, fattened hog; *adj.*, fatted, fat.
CE.VA.DOR, *s.m.*, fattener, one who fattens animals for slaughter.
CE.VAR, *v.*, to make fat, fatten, to bait, to feed, to nourish.
CHÁ, *s.m.*, tea; tea party, tea-plant.
CHÃ, *adj.*, plain, plateau.
CHA.BU, *s.m.*, *Bras.*, the defective explosion of a fire cracker; *dar chabu*: to go wrong.
CHA.CAL, *s.m., Zool.*, jackal.
CHÁ.CA.RA, *s.f.*, country seat, country house, small farm.
CHA.CA.REI.RO, *s.m.*, proprietor of a country house.
CHA.CI.NA, *s.f.*, slaughter, massacre.
CHA.CI.NA.DO, *adj.*, slaughtered; *fig.*, meager.
CHA.CI.NA.DOR, *s.m.*, slaughterer; massacrer, killer.
CHA.CI.NAR, *v.*, to slaughter, to massacre.
CHA.CO.A.LHAR, *v.*, to shake violently; to agitate.
CHA.CO.TA, *s.f.*, mockery, derision, banter, joke.
CHA.CO.TE.A.DOR, *s.m.*, mocker, joker, merry maker.
CHA.CO.TE.AR, *v.*, to joke, to jest; to mock.
CHA.FA.RIZ, *s.m.*, fountain.
CHA.FUR.DAR, *v.*, to roll in the mire; to wallow; *fig.*, to become degraded.
CHA.FUR.DEI.RO, *s.m.*, wallower; pigsty, bog, mire.
CHA.FUR.DI.CE, *s.f.*, wallow, act of wallowing.
CHA.GA, *s.f.*, ulcer, sore, fester.
CHA.GAR, *v.*, to ulcerate; to molest; to torment.
CHA.GUEN.TO, *adj.*, full of sores, ulcerated.
CHA.LA.ÇA, *s.f.*, bon mot, mockery, derision.

CHA.LA.ÇAR, *v.*, to joke, to jest.
CHA.LÉ, *s.m.*, cottage, lodge, chalet.
CHA.LEI.RA, *s.f.*, kettle, tea-kettle.
CHAL.RAR, *v.*, the same that *chalrear*.
CHAL.RE.A.DA, *s.f.*, prattle, gabbling; chirping, twittering.
CHAL.RE.A.DOR, *s.m.*, babbler; chatterbox; *adj.*, babbling, prattling; chirping.
CHAL.RE.AR, *v.*, to prattle, to chatter; to babble.
CHA.LU.PA, *s.f.*, long-boat, shallop, sloop.
CHA.MA, *s.f.*, flame, fire, blaze, light.
CHA.MA.DA, *s.f.*, call, calling, recall, roll-call.
CHA.MA.DO, *s.m.*, call; *adj.*, called.
CHA.MA.DOR, *s.m.*, caller, summoner; oxman.
CHA.MA.MEN.TO, *s.m.*, call, calling; convocation.
CHA.MAR, *v.*, to call, to hail, to summon, to invoke, to evoke, to convoke, to name.
CHA.MA.RIS.CO, *s.m.*, decoy; enticement, attraction.
CHA.MA.RIZ, *s.m.*, lure, bait, advertisement, attraction.
CHÁ-MA.TE, *s.m.*, *Bot., Bras.*, mate: a tea-like beverage drunk especially in South America.
CHA.MA.TI.VO, *adj.*, attracting attention.
CHAM.BRE, *s.m.*, housecoat, dressing gown, robe.
CHA.ME.GO, *s.m.*, state of excitement; flirtation.
CHA.ME.GUEN.TO, *adj.*, infatuated, flirtaceous.
CHA.ME.JA.MEN.TO, *s.m.*, act of flaming.
CHA.ME.JAN.TE, *adj.*, flaming; ablaze, fiery.
CHA.ME.JAR, *v.*, to flame; to blaze, flare.
CHA.MI.NÉ, *s.f.*, chimney, chimney flue.
CHAM.PA.NHA, *s.m.*, champagne.
CHAM.PA.NHE, *s.m.*, champagne.
CHAM.PI.NHOM, CHAM.PIG.NON, *s.m.*, champignon.
CHA.MUS.CA.DO, *adj.*, slightly burned.
CHA.MUS.CA.DU.RA, *s.f.*, act of singeing, slight burn.
CHA.MUS.CAR, *v.*, to singe, to burn slightly, to scorch.
CHA.MUS.CO, *s.m.*, singe, slight burn, skirmish.
CHAN.CE, *s.f.*, chance, opportunity, vantage.
CHAN.CE.LA, *s.f.*, seal, abbreviated signature; *fig.*, assurance, approval.
CHAN.CE.LAR, *v.*, to seal; to sign; *fig.*, to approve.
CHAN.CE.LA.RI.A, *s.f.*, chancellorship, chancellery.
CHAN.CE.LER, *s.m.*, chancellor.
CHAN.CHA.DA, *s.f.*, *Cin., Teat., TV*, a slapstick comedy interspersed with dances and songs.
CHAN.FRA.DO, *adj.*, beveled, chamfered, notched.
CHAN.FRA.DOR, *s.m.*, chamfering plane, chaser.
CHAN.FRA.DU.RA, *s.f.*, bevel, bezel, chamfer.
CHAN.FRAR, *v.*, to chamfer, to groove, to flute.
CHAN.TA.GE.AR, *v.*, to blackmail.
CHAN.TA.GEM, *s.f.*, extortion.
CHAN.TA.GIS.TA, *s. 2 gen.*, blackmailer, extortionist.
CHÃO, *s.m.*, earth, ground, floor, plot, background; *adj.*, plain.
CHA.PA, *s.f.*, metal sheet, plate, lamina, pane, foil, tag, tablet; *gír.*, great friend.
CHA.PA.DA, *s.f.*, plateau; blow, stroke; clearing, mesa (mountain).
CHA.PA.DÃO, *s.m.*, a large area of level land; ridge; plain, prairie.
CHA.PA.DEI.RO, *s.m.*, *Bras.*, yokel, backwoodsman.
CHA.PA.DO, *adj., pop.*, garnished with plate, plated; sprawled, lying on the ground; *gír.*, drug addict.
CHA.PE.A.DO, *s.m.*, veneering; *adj.*, plated.

CHAPELARIA
·· 128 ··
CHICOTAÇO

CHA.PE.LA.RI.A, *s.f.*, hattery, hatmaker's shop.
CHA.PE.LEI.RA, *s.f.*, milliner, hat maker, hatter.
CHA.PE.LEI.RO, *s.m.*, hatter, hatmaker.
CHA.PÉU, *s.m.*, hat, dregs of wine.
CHA.PÉU-CO.CO, *s.m.*, bowler hat.
CHA.PEU.ZI.NHO, *s.m.*, a little hat; *Gram.*, circumflex accent.
CHA.PI.NHA, *s.f.*, a little plate; *gír.*, close friend, comrade.
CHA.PI.NHAR, *v.*, to plash, splash; to beat water with hands or feet.
CHA.PIS.TA, *s. 2 gen.*, *Tipog.*, platemaker.
CHA.RA.DA, *s.f.*, charade, riddle, problem.
CHA.RA.DIS.TA, *s. 2 gen.*, one who composes or likes to solve charades.
CHAR.CO, *s.m.*, bog, dirty, stagnant water, slough.
CHAR.GE, *s.f.*, caricatural drawing satirizing some fact of public knowledge.
char.gis.ta, *s. 2 gen.*, one who draws charges.
CHAR.LA.TA.NA.RI.A, *s.f.*, the same that *charlatanice*.
CHAR.LA.TA.NI.CE, *s.f.*, charlatanism, charlatanry.
CHAR.LA.TA.NIS.MO, *s.m.*, charlatanism, charlatanry.
CHAR.LA.TÃO, *s.m.*, charlatan, quack, impostor, faker.
CHAR.ME, *s.m.*, charm, charms, grace, attraction, pleasant manners.
CHAR.MO.SO, *adj.*, charming, pleasing, graceful.
CHAR.NE.CA, *s.f.*, large area of barren land; heath, moor.
CHAR.QUE, *s.m.*, salted and dried meat, jerked beef.
CHAR.QUE.A.DA, *s.f.*, place where jerked beef is made.
CHAR.QUE.A.DOR, *s.m.*, manufacturer of jerked beef.
CHAR.QUE.AR, *v.*, to salt and dry meat, to jerk.
CHAS.QUE.A.DOR, *s.m.*, mocker, scoffer; *adj.*, scoffing, mocking.
CHAR.RE.TE, *s.f.*, a light two-wheeled cart, drawn by a horse.
CHAR.RU.A, *s.f.*, plough, moldboard plough; *fig.*, agriculture.
CHAR.RU.AR, *v.*, to break up the soil with a plough.
CHA.RU.TA.RI.A, *s.f.*, tobacco shop, cigar shop.
CHA.RU.TEI.RA, *s.f.*, cigar case.
CHA.RU.TEI.RO, *s.m.*, cigar maker, cigar manufacturer.
CHA.RU.TO, *s.m.*, cigar, cheroot, stogy.
CHAS.CO, *s.m.*, mockery, derision; flout, fleer.
CHAS.QUE, *s.m.*, messenger; deliveryman.
CHAS.SI, *s.m.*, chassis, frame, body.
CHA.TA, *s.f.*, *Náut.*, flatboat, barge.
CHA.TE.A.ÇÃO, *s.f.*, bothering, importunity, annoyance, molesting.
CHA.TE.AR, *v.*, to annoy, to importune, to bother, to bore.
CHA.TE.ZA, *s.f.*, flatness; *fig.*, shallowness; annoyance, bother.
CHA.TI.CE, *s.f.*, boredom.
CHA.TO, *s.m.*, crablouse; *adj.*, smooth, plain; importunate, annoying.
CHAU.VI.NIS.MO, *s.m.*, chauvinism.
CHAU.VI.NIS.TA, *s. 2 gen.*, chauvinist; *adj.*, chauvinistic, chauvinistical.
CHA.VÃO, *s.m.*, cliché, household word.
CHA.VA.RI.A, *s.f.*, collection of keys.
CHA.VAS.CA.DA, *s.f.*, stroke, blow.
CHA.VAS.CAR, *v.*, to give bad finish (work on wood).
CHA.VAS.CO, *adj.*, rough, coarse, bungled, imperfect.
CHA.VAS.QUI.CE, *s.f.*, rudeness; coarseness, crudeness.
CHA.VE, *s.f.*, key; keynote (mus.).
CHA.VE.A.MEN.TO, *s.m.*, act of locking with a key.
CHA.VE.AR, *v.*, to lock with a key.

CHA.VEI.RO, *s.m.*, key keeper, doorman, key rack, jailer.
CHÁ.VE.NA, *s.f.*, tea-cup, cup.
CHA.VE.TA, *s.f.*, pin; key, slot key.
CHE.CA.GEM, *s.f.*, checking.
CHE.CAR, *v.*, to check, check out, examine.
CHECK-IN, *s.m.*, check-in.
CHE.FÃO, *s.m.*, political leader, boss, big shot.
CHE.FA.TU.RA, *s.f.*, chieftainship, headquarters.
CHE.FE, *s.m.*, chief, leader, boss, manager, principal.
CHE.FI.A, *s.f.*, leadership, managership.
CHE.FI.AR, *v.*, to direct, to manage, to govern, to chief.
CHE.GA, *s.f.*, *pop.*, censure, reprimand; *interj.*, that's enough!, enough!.
CHE.GA.DA, *s.f.*, arrival, approach, coming.
CHE.GA.DE.LA, *s.f.*, approximation, approach; *pop.*, censure, reprimand.
CHE.GA.DI.ÇO, *s.m.*, *Ant.*, a foreigner; *adj.*, *Ant.*, foreign; *pop.*, intrusive.
CHE.GA.DO, *adj.*, intimate, near; propense; proximate; allied; arrived, landed; fond of.
CHE.GA.DOR, *s.m.*, comer, newcomer, foreigner; fireman; *adj.*, *pop.*, courageous, bold.
CHE.GA.MEN.TO, *s.m.*, coming, landing; approaching.
CHE.GAN.ÇA, *s.f.*, *Ant.*, arrival; *pop.*, popular Christmas festivities and merry-making.
CHE.GAR, *v.*, to come, to arrive, to begin, to start, to border, to be enough.
CHEI.A, *s.f.*, inundation, flood.
CHEI.O, *adj.*, full, filled up, replete, crammed, packed, massive, dense, pregnant.
CHEI.RA.DEI.RA, *s.f.*, snuff-box.
CHEI.RA.DOR, *s.m.*, smeller; professional smeller; *gír.*, person that snorts cocaine.
CHEI.RAR, *v.*, to smell, to sniff, to snuff, to scent, to investigate, to suspect.
CHEI.RO, *s.m.*, smell, scent, odour, perfume, fragrance.
CHEI.RO.SO, *adj.*, fragrant, odoriferous, flavourous, scented; smelly (not usual).
CHE.QUE, *s.m.*, check, cheque.
CHI.A.DA, *s.f.*, hissing, chirping; creak, squeak.
CHI.A.DEI.RA, *s.f.*, squeaking, creaking; clamour, uproar, din; complaint.
CHI.A.DO, *s.m.*, shrill sound, squeaking; *adj.*, squeaky, sly, cunning.
CHI.AR, *v.*, to creak, to squeak, to hiss.
CHI.BAN.TE, *s.m.*, braggart, boaster; *adj.*, bragging, boasting.
CHI.BAN.TE.AR, *v.*, to brag, to boast, to swagger.
CHI.BAR.RO, *s.m.*, *Zool.*, a young he-goat.
CHI.BA.TA, *s.f.*, stick, cane; whip.
CHI.BA.TA.DA, *s.f.*, a blow with a cane; a blow with a whip.
CHI.BA.TAR, *v.*, to cane, to whip.
CHI.BA.TE.AR, *v.*, the same that *chibatar*.
CHI.CA.NA, *s.f.*, chicane, chicanery; subterfuge.
CHI.CA.NAR, *v.*, to chicane, to quibble over, to pettifog.
CHI.CA.NE.AR, *v.*, the same that *chicanar*.
CHI.CHI.AR, *v.*, to creak, to squeak.
CHI.CHIS.BÉU, *s.m.*, a man overly flirtatious.
CHI.CLE, *s.m.*, chicle; chewing gum.
CHI.CLE.TE, *s.m.*, chewing gum.
CHI.CÓ.RIA, *s.f.*, *Bot.*, chicory, endive.
CHI.CO.TA.ÇO, *s.m.*, the same that *chicotada*.

CHICOTADA ·· 129 ·· CHULEIO

CHI.CO.TA.DA, *s.f.*, flogging, whipping, lashing.
CHI.CO.TAR, *v.*, to whip, to flog, to lash.
CHI.CO.TE, *s.m.*, whip, lash.
CHI.CO.TE.A.MEN.TO, *s.m.*, stroking with a whip.
CHI.CO.TE.AR, *v.*, the same that *chicotar*.
CHI.FRA.DA, *s.f.*, a thrust with the horns.
CHI.FRAR, *v.*, to attack with horns, to horn; *gír.*, to be unfaithful.
CHI.FRU.DO, *s.m.*, *pop.*, cuckold; *adj.*, having big horns.
CHI.LE.NAS, *s.f.*, *pl.*, *pop.*, very long spurs.
CHI.FRE, *s.m.*, horn.
CHILE, *s.*, Chile.
CHI.LE.NO, *s.m.*, *adj.*, Chilean.
CHI.LI.QUE, *s.m.*, *pop.*, faint, swoon; fit, seizure.
CHIL.RA.DA, *s.f.*, chirping, twittering; chatter.
CHIL.RAR, *v.*, to chirp, to twitter; to chatter; *fig.*, to sing.
CHIL.RE.A.DA, *s.f.*, the same that *chilrada*.
CHIL.RE.A.DOR, *s.m.*, warbling bird; *fig.*, chatterbox, blabbermouth; *adj.*, chirping, warbling; *fig.*, prattling.
CHIL.RE.AN.TE, *adj.*, chirping, warbling.
CHIL.RE.AR, *v.*, the same that *chilrar*.
CHIL.REI.O, *s.m.*, chirp; twitter; cheep, peep.
CHIL.RO, *s.m.*, the same that *chilreio*.
CHI.MAR.RÃO, *s.m.*, maté, tea or caffee served without sugar; *adj.*, unsweetened (hot beverage).
CHI.MAR.RE.AR, *v.*, *Bras.*, to drink hot (unsweetened maté).
CHI.MAR.RO.NE.AR, *v.*, *Bras.*, the same that *chimarrear*.
CHIM.PAN.ZÉ, *s.m.*, *Zool.*, chimpanzee.
CHI.NA, *s. 2 gen.*, Chinese; *s.f.*, *Bras.*, Indian woman.
CHINA, *s.*, China (country).
CHIN.CHA, *s.f.*, a fishing boat; a small trawling net.
CHIN.CHI.LA, *s.f.*, *Zool.*, chinchilla.
CHIN.CHOR.RO, *s.m.*, a kind of fishing vessel; trawling net.
CHI.NE.LA, *s.f.*, house slipper.
CHI.NE.LA.DA, *s.f.*, a blow with a slipper.
CHI.NE.LO, *s.m.*, slipper, scuff.
CHI.NÊS, *adj.*, *s.m.*, Chinese.
CHI.NE.SI.CE, *s.f.*, Chinese behaviour or mannerisms; bagatelle, trifle, any object made with special patience.
CHIN.FRIM, *s.m.*, disorder, confusion; *adj.*, insignificant, trifling, paltry.
CHIN.FRI.NA.DA, *s.f.*, clamour, uproar; ridiculous thing.
CHIN.FRI.NAR, *v.*, to clamour; to cause a tumult or disorder; *gír.*, to poke fun.
CHIN.FRI.NI.CE, *s.f.*, the same that *chinfrinada*.
CHI.O, *s.m.*, squeak; squeal, shriek.
CHI.QUE, *adj.*, elegant, smart, chic, beautiful, handsome.
CHI.QUEI.RI.NHO, *s.m.*, diminutive form of *chiqueiro*; playpen.
CHI.QUEI.RO, *s.m.*, pigsty, sty.
CHIR.RI.AR, *v.*, to shriek; to hoot (as an owl).
CHI.RU, *s.m.*, *Bras.*, a South American Indian; caboclo, mestizo; *adj.*, of or relative to a caboclo, rural, rustic.
CHIS.PA, *s.f.*, spark; *fig.*, flake; talent, superior intelligence.
CHIS.PA.DA, *s.f.*, a rapid race, stampede, rush.
CHIS.PAR, *v.*, to sparkle, to scintillate; to flare up; to rush along; to whisk; to spank.
CHIS.PE.AR, *v.*, the same that *chispar*.
CHIS.TE, *s.m.*, jocosity, joke, jest, wit, witty remark.
CHIS.TO.SA.MEN.TE, *adv.*, facetiously, wittily.
CHIS.TO.SO, *adj.*, witty, funny, jocular.
CHI.TA, *s.f.*, *Zool.*, cheetah; plain common cotton cloth.
CHO.CA, *s.f.*, a cowbell; bell cow.

CHO.ÇA, *s.f.*, hut, hovel, shack.
CHO.CA.DEI.RA, *s.f.*, a broody hen, brooder.
CHO.CA.LHAR, *v.*, to shake, to stir up, to brattle, to chime.
CHO.CA.LHO, *s.m.*, rattle, clapper, bell; cattle bell.
CHO.CAN.TE, *adj.*, shocking, scandalous, frightful.
CHO.CAR, *v.*, to shock, brood, incubate.
CHO.CHO, *s.m.*, bland, uninteresting; tasteless, insulso; fool, simpleton; *fam.*, child kiss.
CHO.CO, *s.m.*, incubation; *adj.*, being hatched; broody; not fresh; insipid; spoiled, rotten.
CHO.CO.LA.TA.RI.A, *s.f.*, chocolate shop, chocolate factory.
CHO.CO.LA.TE, *s.m.*, chocolate.
CHO.CO.LA.TEI.RA, *s.f.*, chocolate pot, chocolate kettle.
CHO.CO.LA.TEI.RO, *s.m.*, chocolate maker, chocolate manufacturer.
CHO.FER, *s.m.*, driver.
CHO.FE.RAR, *v.*, *Bras.*, to chauffeur.
CHO.FRE, *s.m.*, a sudden blow; *de chofre*: suddenly, unexpectedly.
CHO.PA.DA, *s.f.*, beer party.
CHO.PE, *s.m.*, beer.
CHO.PE.RI.A, *s.f.*, a bar where draft beer is served.
CHO.QUE, *s.m.*, collision, crash, clash, impact, shock.
CHO.RA.DEI.RA, *s.f.*, weeping, crying.
CHO.RA.DO, *adj.*, mournful, sad; bemoaned.
CHO.RÃO, *s.m.*, weeping-willow (Bot.), whimperer; *adj.*, crying, whimpering.
CHO.RAR, *v.*, to weep, to cry, to sob, to mourn, to bemoan.
CHO.RI.NHO, *s.m.*, *Bras.*, *Mús.*, a kind of music; *pop.*, an extra quantity in addition to the usual dose (drink).
CHO.RO, *s.m.*, weeping, crying, sobbing, wail.
CHO.RO.RÓ, *s.m.*, small waterfall; cascade; *Zool.*, a small bird.
CHO.RO.SA.MEN.TE, *adv.*, weepingly, tearfully.
CHO.RO.SO, *adj.*, weeping, weepy, tearful.
CHO.RU.ME, *s.m.*, lard, animal fat; grease; liquid from the waste decomposition; *fig.*, fortune.
CHO.RU.ME.LA, *s.f.*, trifle, bauble.
CHOU.PA.NA, *s.f.*, cottage, hut, hovel, grass shack.
CHOU.PO, *s.m.*, *Bot.*, poplar.
CHOU.RI.ÇA.DA, *s.f.*, a great quantity of sausages.
CHOU.RI.CEI.RO, *s.m.*, sausage maker, sausage dealer.
CHOU.RI.ÇO, *s.m.*, sausage, smoked sausage.
CHOU.TO, *s.m.*, hard trot, jolting gait of a horse.
CHO.VE.DI.ÇO, *adj.*, rainy, showery.
CHO.VE NÃO MO.LHA, *s.m.*, *fam.*, shilly-shallying.
CHO.VER, *v.*, to rain, to pour down.
CHU.ÇA, *s.f.*, spear; harpoon.
CHU.ÇA.DA, *s.f.*, blow with a spear or harpoon.
CHU.ÇAR, *v.*, to throw a spear or harpoon.
CHU.CEI.RO, *s.m.*, lancer.
CHU.CHA, *s.f.*, breast, mother's milk; nutriment.
CHU.CHAR, *v.*, to suck, to suckle.
CHU.CHU, *s.m.*, chayote.
CHU.CRU.TE, *s.m.*, sauerkraut.
CHU.FIS.TA, *s. 2 gen.*, punster, buffoon, joker; *adj.*, witty, funny, scoffing.
CHU.LA, *s.f.*, a popular dance, country dance; street song.
CHU.LÉ, *s.m.*, the rank smell of perspiring feet.
CHU.LE.A.DO, *s.m.*, the same that *chuleio*.
CHU.LE.AR, *v.*, to stitch, whipstitch.
CHU.LEI.O, *s.m.*, stitching; stitch, whipstitch.

CHULETA ·· 130 ·· CIFRÃO

CHU.LE.TA, *s.f., Cul.*, T-bone steak.
CHU.LO, *adj.*, coarse, crude, vulgar, common, jesting.
CHU.MA.ÇAR, *v.*, to pad, to quilt.
CHU.MA.ÇO, *s.m.*, padding, stuffing.
CHUM.BA.DA, *s.f.*, a load of shot, buckshot.
CHUM.BA.DO, *adj.*, soldered with lead; leaded; wounded (by shot); *pop.*, tipsy, drunk.
CHUM.BA.DOR, *s.m.*, anchor bolt; workman who anchors bolts; person who seals with lead.
CHUM.BA.GEM, *s.f.*, anchoring in lead or concrete.
CHUM.BAR, *v.*, to lead, to fasten, to fix, to plug with lead, to solder with lead.
CHUM.BE.A.DO, *adj., Bras., fam.*, drunk.
CHUM.BE.AR, *v.*, to wound with buckshot.
CHUM.BI.NHO, *s.m.*, small bullet (gun); printing type.
CHUM.BO, *s.m.*, lead, shot, lead pellet; *Quím.*, lead (chemical symbol Pb); *levar chumbo*: to fail.
CHU.PA.DA, *s.f.*, sucking; suck, suction.
CHU.PA.DE.LA, *s.f.*, sucking, suck, suction.
CHU.PA.DO, *adj., pop.*, skinny, meager, sucked.
CHU.PA.DOR, *s.m.*, sucker, one who sucks; *Zool.*, proboscis of insects; *adj.*, sucking.
CHU.PA.DOU.RO, *s.m.*, sucking tube.
CHU.PA.MEN.TO, *s.m.*, suck, sucking, suction.
CHU.PÃO, *s.m.*, loud kiss, hickey, slurpy kiss, smack.
CHU.PAR, *v.*, to suck, to absorb, to soak in.
CHU.PE.TA, *s.f.*, pacifier, sucking bag.
CHU.PIM, *s.m., Zool.*, Brazilian bird (*Molothrus bonariensis*); *fig.*, man who lets his wife support him.
CHUR.RAS.CA.RI.A, *s.f.*, grill room.
CHUR.RAS.CA.DA, *s.f.*, barbecue; friends invited to a barbecue.
CHUR.RAS.CA.RI.A, *s.f.*, restaurant specialized in roasted meat.
CHUR.RAS.CO, *s.m.*, barbecue.
CHUR.RAS.QUE.A.DA, *s.f.*, eating and savouring a barbecue.
CHUR.RAS.QUE.AR, *v.*, to prepare meat for barbecuing; eat roasted meat.
CHUR.RAS.QUEI.RA, *s.f.*, portable fireplace.
CHUR.RAS.QUEI.RO, *s.m.*, barbecuer.
CHUR.RAS.QUI.NHO, *s.m.*, chopped barbecue on a small spit.
CHUR.RO, *s.m., Cul.*, a fried-dough-pastry, predominantly choux (light pastry), based snack; *adj.*, coarse, dirty.
CHUS.MA, *s.f.*, great quantity, a lot, a heap of things; crowd, throng.
CHU.TA.DOR, *s.m., gír.*, liar; *Esp.*, kicker, a good football player (soccer).
CHU.TAR, *v.*, to kick the ball, to boot the ball.
CHU.TE, *s.m.*, a kick.
CHU.TEI.RA, *s.f.*, football boat, football shoe.
CHU.VA, *s.f.*, rain, shower.
CHU.VA.RA.DA, *s.f.*, abundant rain, downpour.
CHU.VA.RA.DA, *s.f.*, a quick shower bath.
CHU.VEI.RI.NHO, *s.m., Bras., Esp.*, high ball on the opponent's area (soccer); showerhead.
CHU.VEI.RO, *s.m.*, shower.
CHU.VI.NHA, *s.f.*, drizzle.
CHU.VIS.CAR, *v.*, to drizzle, to mizzle, to dribble.
CHU.VIS.CO, *s.m.*, mizzle, drizzle.
CHU.VO.SO, *adj.*, rainy, showery.

CIA., *abrev.* of *Companhia*: Co. (Company).
CI.A.NE.TO, *s.m., Quím.*, cyanide.
CI.Â.NI.CO, *adj., Quím.*, cyanic.
CI.A.NO, *s.m.*, a greenish-blue color; *adj.*, greenish-blue.
CI.A.NU.RE.TO, *s.m., Quím.*, cyanide.
CI.Á.TI.CA, *s.f.*, sciatica, neuralgia of the sciatic nerve.
CI.Á.TI.CO, *s.m., Anat.*, sciatic nerve; *adj.*, sciatic, ischiatic.
CI.BER.ES.PA.ço, *s.m.*, cyberspace.
CI.BER.NÉ.TI.CA, *s.f.*, cybernetics.
CI.BER.NÉ.TI.CO, *adj.*, cybernetic, cybernetical.
CI.BER.PUNK, *s. 2 gen.*, net hacker, cyberpunk.
CI.CA, *s.f.*, acridity, harshness, astringency.
CI.CA.TRI.CI.AL, *adj., Med.*, cicatricial.
CI.CA.TRIZ, *s.f.*, cicatrix, scar.
CI.CA.TRI.ZA.ÇÃO, *s.f.*, cicatrization.
CI.CA.TRI.ZA.DO, *adj.*, scarred, scarry, cicatrized; *fig.*, cured.
CI.CA.TRI.ZAN.TE, *adj.*, cicatrizant.
CI.CA.TRI.ZAR, *v.*, to cicatrize, to scar, to heal.
CI.CA.TRI.ZÁ.VEL, *adj.*, capable of being healed.
CI.CE.RO.NE, *s.m.*, cicerone, tourist guide.
CI.CI.AR, *v.*, to lisp; to murmur, to whisper.
CI.CI.O, *s.m.*, lisping; murmur, whisper.
CI.CI.O.SO, *adj.*, lisping, murmuring, rustling.
CI.CLA.MA.TO, *s.m., Quím.*, cyclamate.
CÍ.CLI.CO, *adj.*, cyclic, regular.
CI.CLIS.MO, *s.m.*, cyclism.
CI.CLIS.TA, *s. 2 gen.*, cyclist, bicyclist.
CI.CLO, *s.m.*, cycle.
CI.CLOI.DE, *s.f., Geom.*, cycloid, cycloid curve.
CI.CLO.NE, *s.m.*, cyclone, hurricane, tornado, twister.
CI.CLÔ.NI.CO, *adj.*, cyclonic, cyclonical.
CI.CLO.PE, *s.m., Mit.*, Cyclops.
CI.CLÓ.PE.O, *adj., Mit.*, Cyclopean; cyclopean; *fig.*, gigantic.
CI.CLÓ.PI.CO, *adj.*, ciclópeo.
CÍ.CLO.TRON, *s.m., Fís.*, cyclotron (a particles accelerator).
CI.CLO.VI.A, *s.f.*, bike way.
CI.CU.TA, *s.f.*, cicuta, water hemlock.
CI.DA.DÃ, *s.f.*, citizeness.
CI.DA.DA.NI.A, *s.f.*, citizenhood, citizenship.
CI.DA.DÃO, *s.m.*, citizen.
CI.DA.DE, *s.f.*, city, town, capital, burg.
CI.DA.DE-ES.TA.DO, *s.f.*, city-state.
CI.DA.DE.LA, *s.f.*, citadel, fortress; stronghold.
CI.DA.DE-SA.TÉ.LI.TE, *s.f.*, satellite town.
CI.DRA, *s.f., Bot.*, citron (the fruit); citron cider.
CI.DRAL, *s.m.*, citron plantation.
CI.DREI.RA, *s.f., Bot.*, citron (*Citrus medica*).
CI.ÊN.CIA, *s.f.*, science, knowledge, wisdom, learning.
CI.EN.TE, *adj.*, aware, knowing, cognizant.
CI.EN.TE.MEN.TE, *adv.*, knowingly, wittingly.
CI.EN.TI.FI.CA.MEN.TE, *adv.*, scientifically, scientially.
CI.EN.TI.FI.CAR, *v.*, to inform, to notify, to notice.
CI.EN.TI.FI.CIS.MO, *s.m., Filos.*, scientism.
CI.EN.TÍ.FI.CO, *adj.*, scientific, sciential; *ficção científica*: science fiction.
CI.EN.TIS.MO, *s.m.*, the same that *cientificismo*.
CI.EN.TIS.TA, *s. 2 gen.*, scientist, savant.
CI.FO.SE, *s.f., Med.*, kyphosis.
CI.FRA, *s.f.*, cipher, cypher, naught, figure.
CI.FRA.DO, *adj.*, written in code.
CI.FRÃO, *s.m.*, money sign.

CIFRAR ·· 131 ·· CIRCUNAVEGAR

CI.FRAR, *v.*, to cipher, to cypher, to code, to resume, to include.
CI.GA.NA, *s.f.*, gypsy woman; *Zool.*, hoatzin (bird).
CI.GA.NA.DA, *s.f.*, a band of gypsies; gypsy life; *gír.*, underhand tricks.
CI.GA.NE.AR, *v.*, to wander aimlessly around.
CI.GA.NO, *s.m.*, gypsy, horse-dealer.
CI.GAR.RA, *s.f.*, *Zool.*, cicada, grasshopper.
CI.GAR.RA.RI.A, *s.f.*, cigarette and tobacco shop.
CI.GAR.REI.RA, *s.f.*, cigarette case.
CI.GAR.RI.LHA, *s.f.*, cigarillo.
CI.GAR.RI.NHA, *s.f.*, *Zool.*, hopper, frog hopper.
CI.GAR.RIS.TA, *s. 2 gen.*, a cigarette smoker.
CI.GAR.RO, *s.m.*, cigarette.
CI.LA.DA, *s.f.*, ambush, snare, trap, pitfall.
CI.LI.A.DO, *s.m.*, *Zool.*, a ciliate; *adj.*, *Bot.*, *Zool.*, ciliated.
CI.LIN.DRA.DA, *s.f.*, piston displacement.
CI.LÍN.DRI.CO, *adj.*, cylindric, cylindrical.
CI.LIN.DRO, *s.m.*, cylinder, roll, roller.
CI.LIN.DROI.DE, *adj.*, cylindroid, cylindric, cylindrical.
CÍ.LIO, *s.m.*, eyelash, lash; *Bot.*, *Zool.*, cilium.
CI.MA, *s.f.*, top, summit, apex.
CÍM.BA.LO, *s.m.*, *Mús.*, cymbal (percussion).
CI.MEI.RA, *s.f.*, crest of a helmet; summit, top, apex.
CI.MEI.RO, *adj.*, situated on the top; crested; elevated.
CI.MEN.TA.ÇÃO, *s.f.*, cementation, cementing; foundation.
CI.MEN.TA.DO, *adj.*, bound or paved with cement.
CI.MEN.TAR, *v.*, to cement, to unit, to consolidate.
CI.MEN.TO, *s.m.*, cement, concrete.
CI.MO, *s.m.*, top, summit, apex.
CIN.CAR, *v.*, to make a mistake; to lose five points (bowling).
CIN.CEI.RO, *s.m.*, *Bras.*, a thick fog.
CIN.CER.RO, *s.m.*, bell hung about the neck of animal (mule).
CIN.CO, *num.*, five, the number five.
CIN.DIR, *v.*, to cut, to separate.
CIN.DÍ.VEL, *adj.*, dividable.
CI.NE, *s.m.*, short of *cinema*.
CI.NE.AS.TA, *s. 2 gen.*, cineast, cinematographer, moviemaker.
CI.NE.CLU.BE, *s.m.*, film society, cinema club, cineclub.
CI.NÉ.FI.LO, *s.m.*, cinephile, cineast.
CI.NE.GRA.FIS.TA, *s. 2 gen.*, cineast, cinematographer.
CI.NE.MA, *s.m.*, cinema, movies.
CI.NE.MAS.CO.PE, *s.m.*, cinemascope.
CI.NE.MÁ.TI.CA, *s.f.*, *Fís.*, kinematics.
CI.NE.MA.TO.GRA.FI.A, *s.f.*, cinematography.
CI.NE.MA.TO.GRÁ.FI.CO, *adj.*, cinematographic, cinematographical.
CI.NE.MA.TÓ.GRA.FO, *s.m.*, first film projector; picture projector, cinematograph, kinematograph.
CI.NE.RAR, *v.*, to incinerate, to cremate.
CI.NE.RÁ.RI.O, *s.m.*, cinerarium, funeral urn; *adj.*, cinerary.
CI.NES.CÓ.PI.O, *s.m.*, *Eletr.*, kinescope, picture tube.
CI.NES.TE.SI.A, *s.f.*, kinesthesis, kinesthesia.
CI.NES.TÉ.SI.CO, *adj.*, kinesthetic.
CI.NÉ.TI.CA, *s.f.*, *Fís.*, kinematics, kinetics.
CI.NÉ.TI.CO, *adj.*, *Fís.*, kinetic.
CIN.GA.LÊS, *s.m.*, Cingalese (native or inhabitant of Ceylon, India); *adj.*, Cingalese.
CIN.GA.PU.RA, *s.*, Singapore.
CIN.GIR, *v.*, to gird, to surround, to enclasp, to unite, to constrain.

CÍ.NI.CO, *s.m.*, cynic; *adj.*, cynic, impudent.
CI.NIS.MO, *s.m.*, cynicism, impudence.
CI.NO.FI.LI.A, *s.f.*, love for dogs.
CI.NÓ.FI.LO, *adj.*, dog lover.
CI.NO.FO.BI.A, *s.f.*, cynophobia.
CIN.QUEN.TA, *num.*, fifty.
CIN.QUEN.TÃO, *s.m.*, a man in his fifties.
CIN.QUEN.TE.NÁ.RIO, *s.m.*, the fiftieth anniversary.
CIN.TA, *s.f.*, girdle, sash, belt, waistband.
CIN.TA-LI.GA, *s.f.*, garter belt.
CIN.TAR, *v.*, to put on a belt; to belt, to bind, to band.
CIN.TEI.RO, *s.m.*, belt maker or dealer.
CIN.TI.LA.ÇÃO, *s.f.*, scintillation, sparkle, blink.
CIN.TI.LA.DOR, *s.m.*, *Fís.*, *Astron.*, scintillator.
CIN.TI.LAN.TE, *adj.*, scintillant, sparkling.
CIN.TI.LAR, *v.*, to scintillate, to blink.
CIN.TI.LO.GRA.FI.A, *s.f.*, *Med.*, scintigraphy.
CIN.TI.LO.GRÁ.FI.CO, *adj.*, scintigraphic.
CIN.TO, *s.m.*, belt, girdle, buckle, sash.
CIN.TU.RA, *s.f.*, waist, waistline, waisband, belt.
CIN.TU.RA.DO, *adj.*, girt, girded, belted.
CIN.TU.RÃO, *s.m.*, leather belt; broad band; cartridge belt.
CIN.ZA, *s.f.*, ash, gray, ember, cinder.
CIN.ZAR, *v.*, to make gray; *fig.*, to deceive, to fool.
CIN.ZEI.RO, *s.m.*, ash-tray, ash-heap.
CIN.ZEL, *s.m.*, sculptor's chisel, chisel.
CIN.ZE.LA.DOR, *s.m.*, chiseller, engraver; *adj.*, chiseling, engraving.
CIN.ZE.LA.MEN.TO, *s.m.*, chiseling, engraving.
CIN.ZE.LAR, *v.*, to chisel, to engrave.
CIN.ZEN.TO, *s.m.*, gray, gray colour, ash gray; *adj.*, gray, grey, ashen.
CI.O, *s.m.*, rut, heat, oestrus.
CI.O.SA.MEN.TE, *adv.*, jealously.
CI.O.SO, *adj.*, envious, jealous, careful, zealous.
CI.PÓ, *s.m.*, liana, liane, cipo.
CI.PO.AL, *s.m.*, a place where lianas grow; *fig.*, complication, difficulty.
CI.PRES.TAL, *s.m.*, a grove of cypress trees.
CI.PRES.TE, *s.m.*, cypress, cypress tree.
CI.PRI.O.TA, *s. 2 gen.*, Cypriot (native or inhabitant of Cyprus); *adj.*, Cypriot.
CIR.CA.DI.A.NO, *adj.*, circadian.
CIR.CEN.SE, *adj.*, circensian.
CIR.CO, *s.m.*, circus, amphitheater, ring.
CIR.CUI.TO, *s.m.*, circle, circumference, circuit, round.
CIR.CU.LA.ÇÃO, *s.f.*, circulation, rotation, flow, transit, route, orbit.
CIR.CU.LA.DA, *s.f.*, *pop.*, a small tour or walk.
CIR.CU.LA.DOR, *s.m.*, an electric circulator; *adj.*, circulating.
CIR.CU.LAN.TE, *adj.*, circulating, circulatory, circling, current, floating.
CIR.CU.LAR, *v.*, to circulate, to move, to surround; *s.m.*, circular, bill; *adj.*, circular, cyclic.
CIR.CU.LAR.MEN.TE, *adv.*, circular, circlewise, roundly.
CIR.CU.LA.TÓ.RI.O, *adj.*, circulative, circulatory; *sistema ~*, circulatory system.
CÍR.CU.LO, *s.m.*, circle, ring, strip, ring, circumference.
CIR.CUM.PO.LAR, *adj.*, circumpolar.
CIR.CU.NA.VE.GA.ÇÃO, *s.f.*, circumnavigation.
CIR.CU.NA.VE.GAR, *v.*, to circumnavigate, to sail round.

CIRCUNCIDADO   •• 132 ••   CLAMAR

CIR.CUN.CI.DA.DO, *s.m.*, a circumcised man; *adj.*, circumcised.
CIR.CUN.CI.SO, *s.m.*, the same that *circundidado*.
CIR.CUN.CI.SÃO, *s.f.*, circumcision.
CIR.CUN.DA.MEN.TO, *s.m.*, compassing, surrounding.
CIR.CUN.DAN.TE, *adj.*, encircling, surrounding, neighbouring.
CIR.CUN.DAR, *v.*, to circle, to encompass, to surround, to enclose.
CIR.CUN.FE.RÊN.CIA, *s.f.*, circumference, circle, periphery.
CIR.CUN.FE.REN.CI.AL, *adj.*, circumferential.
CIR.CUN.FLE.XO, *adj.*, circumflex, curved; *acento ~*: *Gram.*, circumflex accent.
CIR.CUN.FLU.ÊN.CIA, *s.f.*, circumfluence.
CIR.CUN.FLU.IR, *v.*, to flow around.
CIR.CUN.GI.RAR, *v.*, to circumgyrate, to circle.
CIR.CUN.LO.CU.ÇÃO, *s.f.*, circumlocution.
CIR.CUN.LÓ.QUI.O, *s.m.*, the same that *circunlocução*.
CIR.CUNS.CRE.VER, *v.*, to circumscribe, to encircle, to limit.
CIR.CUNS.CRI.ÇÃO, *s.f.*, circumscription, periphery, district.
CIR.CUNS.CRI.TI.VO, *adj.*, circumscriptive.
CIR.CUNS.CRI.TO, *adj.*, circumscribed.
CIR.CUNS.PEC.TO, *adj.*, circumspect; prudent, cautious.
CIR.CUNS.TÂN.CIA, *s.f.*, circumstance, condition, fact, detail.
CIR.CUNS.TAN.CI.A.DO, *adj.*, circumstanced.
CIR.CUNS.TAN.CI.AL, *adj.*, circumstantial.
CIR.CUNS.TAN.CI.AR, *v.*, to circumstantiate.
CIR.CUNS.TAN.TE, *s. 2 gen.*, onlooker, bystander.
CIR.CUNS.TAR, *v.*, to be present; to be around.
CIR.CUN.VA.GAR, *v.*, to wander about, to move in a circle.
CIR.CUN.VA.GO, *adj.*, wandering about; surrounding.
CIR.CUN.VI.ZI.NHAN.ÇA, *s.f.*, adjacency, environs; neighbourhood.
CIR.CUN.VI.ZI.NHAR, *v.*, to be in the neighbourhood of.
CIR.CUN.VI.ZI.NHO, *adj.*, circumjacent; neighbouring.
CIR.CUN.VO.LU.ÇÃO, *s.f.*, circumvolution.
CIR.CUN.VOL.VER, *v.*, to circumvolve.
CI.RÍ.LI.CO, *s.m.*, Cyrillic alphabet; *adj.*, Cyrillic.
CÍ.RIO, *s.m.*, candle, taper.
CIR.RO, *s.m.*, *Met.*, cirrus cloud, spindrift cloud; *Bot.*, tendril, cirrus.
CIR.RO-CÚ.MU.LO, *s.m.*, *Met.*, cirro-cumulus.
CIR.RO-ES.TRA.TO, *s.m.*, *Met.*, cirro-stratus.
CIR.RO.SE, *s.f.*, cirrhosis.
CIR.RO.SI.DA.DE, *s.f.*, *Med.*, scirrhosity.
CIR.RO.SO, *adj.*, *Med.*, scirrhous; *Met.*, cirrous (clouds).
CIR.RÓ.TI.CO, *adj.*, *Med.*, cirrhotic.
CI.RUR.GI.A, *s.f.*, surgery.
CI.RUR.GI.ÃO, *s.m.*, surgeon.
CI.RUR.GI.ÃO-DEN.TIS.TA, *s.m.*, dental surgeon.
CI.RÚR.GI.CO, *adj.*, surgical.
CI.SAL.PI.NO, *adj.*, cisalpine.
CI.SAN.DI.NO, *adj.*, *s.m.*, cisandine.
CI.SA.TLÂN.TI.CO, *adj.*, cisatlantic.
CI.SÃO, *s.f.*, split, scission, dissension.
CIS.CA.DA, *s.f.*, coal sweepings.
CIS.CAR, *v.*, to weed; to sweep, to rake; to clean up; to scratch the earth (chicken).
CIS.CO, *s.m.*, dust; speck of dust; wood chips, refuse, trash; sweepings.
CIS.MA, *s.m.*, schism, split, division; *s.f.*, daydreaming, doubt, preoccupation.

CIS.MA.DO, *adj.*, suspicious, distrustful.
CIS.MAR, *v.*, to ponder, to meditate, to daydream.
CIS.MA.REN.TO, *adj.*, preoccupied, worried; meditative.
CIS.MÁ.TI.CO, *adj.*, worried, preoccupied, meditative; schismatic, cismático; *s.m.*, schismatic, separatist.
CIS.NE, *s.m.*, *Zool.*, swan, cob.
CIS.SI.PA.RI.DA.DE, *s.f.*, *Biol.*, schizogony.
CIS.SÍ.PA.RO, *adj.*, *Biol.*, schizogonous, schizogonic.
CIS.TER.CI.EN.SE, *adj.*, *Rel.*, Cistercian (order of the Benedictines, in France).
CIS.TER.NA, *s.f.*, cistern, water-tank.
CIS.TI.TE, *s.f.*, *Med.*, cystitis.
CIS.TO, *s.m.*, cyst.
CIS.TOI.DE, *adj.*, *Med.*, cystoid.
CI.TA.ÇÃO, *s.f.*, citation, quotation.
CI.TA.DI.NO, *s.m.*, city-bred, civic, citizen, townsman; *adj.*, civic, urban, citizen.
CI.TA.DO, *adj.*, summoned, arraigned, cited.
CI.TA.DOR, *s.m.*, summoner; one who quotes; *adj.*, summoning.
CI.TAR, *v.*, to cite, to quote, to summon, to mention, to name.
CÍ.TA.RA, *s.f.*, *Mús.*, cithara, cither, zither.
CI.TÁ.VEL, *adj.*, citable, quotable.
CI.TO.GE.NÉ.TI.CA, *s.f.*, *Biol.*, cytogenetics.
CI.TO.LO.GI.A, *s.f.*, cytology.
CI.TO.LÓ.GI.CO, *adj.*, cytological.
CI.TO.LO.GIS.TA, *s. 2 gen.*, cytologist.
CI.TO.PLAS.MA, *s.m.*, *Biol.*, cytoplasm.
CI.TO.PLAS.MÁ.TI.CO, *adj.*, *Biol.*, cytoplasmic.
CI.TRA.TO, *s.m.*, *Quím.*, citrate.
CÍ.TRI.CO, *adj.*, citrus, citrine.
CI.TRI.CUL.TOR, *s.m.*, citriculturist.
CI.TRI.CUL.TU.RA, *s.f.*, citriculture.
CI.U.MA.DA, *s.f.*, sudden outburst of jealousy.
CI.U.MAR, *v.*, to be jealous.
CI.U.MA.RI.A, *s.f.*, a deep-rooted jealousy.
CI.Ú.ME, *s.m.*, jealousy, emulation.
CI.U.MEI.RA, *s.f.*, *pop.*, exaggerated jealousy.
CI.U.MEN.TO, *adj.*, jealous.
CÍ.VEL, *adj.*, civil.
CI.VEL.MEN.TE, *adv.*, civilly.
CI.VI.CA.MEN.TE, *adv.*, civically.
CÍ.VI.CO, *adj.*, civic, civil.
CI.VIL, *s.m.*, civilian, citizen; *adj.*, civil.
CI.VI.LI.DA.DE, *s.f.*, civility, courtesy.
CI.VI.LIS.MO, *s.m.*, civilism.
CI.VI.LIS.TA, *s. 2 gen.*, civilian, civilist; *adj.*, civilist, civilian.
CI.VI.LI.ZA.ÇÃO, *s.f.*, civilization.
CI.VI.LI.ZA.DO, *adj.*, civilized, cultured, cultivated, civil, courteous, polite.
CI.VI.LI.ZA.DOR, *s.m.*, civilizer; *adj.*, civilizing.
CI.VI.LI.ZAR, *v.*, to civilize, to reclaim from, to instruct, to educate.
CI.VI.LI.ZÁ.VEL, *adj.*, civilizable.
CI.VIL.MEN.TE, *adv.*, civilly, sociably, courteously.
CI.VIS.MO, *s.m.*, civism, patriotism.
CI.ZÂ.NI.A, *s.f.*, *Bot.*, darnel; *fig.*, discord, disharmony.
CLÃ, *s.m.*, clan, tribe, family, society.
CLA.MA.DOR, *s.m.*, crier, town-crier, clamourer; *adj.*, crying, clamant, clamouring.
CLA.MAR, *v.*, to cry, to claim, to vociferate, to clamour.

CLAMOR
•• 133 ••
CLORO

CLA.MOR, *s.m.*, clamour, outcry, vociferation, exclamation.
CLA.MO.RO.SA.MEN.TE, *adv.*, clamourously.
CLA.MO.RO.SO, *adj.*, clamourous, vociferous, vociferant.
CLAN.DES.TI.NA.MEN.TE, *adv.*, clandestinely.
CLAN.DES.TI.NI.DA.DE, *s.f.*, clandestineness, clandestinity.
CLAN.DES.TI.NO, *s.m.*, one who acts clandestinely; *adj.*, clandestine; illegal.
CLAN.GOR, *s.m.*, clangour, blare of a trumpe.
CLAN.GO.RAR, *v.*, to blare, clangour.
CLAN.GO.RO.SA.MEN.TE, *adv.*, clangorously.
CLAN.GO.RO.SO, *adj.*, clangorous, plangent.
CLA.QUE, *s.f.*, claque (a group of paid applauders); collapsible opera hat.
CLA.QUE.TE, *s.f.*, *Cin.*, clapboard.
CLA.QUIS.TA, *s. 2 gen.*, claqueur, claquer.
CLA.RA, *s.f.*, egg white.
CLA.RÃO, *s.m.*, glaring radiance.
CLA.RE.A.ÇÃO, *s.f.*, making clear, bleaching.
CLA.RE.AR, *v.*, to clear, to clarify.
CLA.REI.RA, *s.f.*, glade, opening, clearing in the woods.
CLA.RE.JAR, *v.*, the same that *clarear*.
CLA.RE.ZA, *s.f.*, clearness, clarity, explicitness.
CLA.RI.DA.DE, *s.f.*, clarity, brightness, light, shine.
CLA.RI.FI.CA.ÇÃO, *s.f.*, clarification.
CLA.RI.FI.CA.DOR, *s.m.*, clarifier; *adj.*, clarifying.
CLA.RI.FI.CAR, *v.*, to clarify, to make clear, to purify.
CLA.RIM, *s.m.*, *Mús.*, clarion, bugle; clarioner, bugler.
CLA.RI.NA.DA, *s.f.*, clarion call.
CLA.RI.NE.TA, *s.f.*, *Mús.*, the same that *clarinete*.
CLA.RI.NE.TE, *s.m.*, *Mús.*, clarinet; clarinetist.
CLA.RI.NE.TIS.TA, *s. 2 gen.*, clarinetist, clarinet player.
CLA.RI.VI.DÊN.CI.A, *s.f.*, clairvoyance.
CLA.RI.VI.DEN.TE, *adj.*, clairvoyant.
CLA.RO, *adj.*, clear, luminous, bright, shining, lucid, transparent, limpid.
CLAS.SE, *s.f.*, class, category, group, kind, variety, type, degree.
CLAS.SI.CA.MEN.TE, *adv.*, classically.
CLAS.SI.CIS.MO, *s.m.*, classicism.
CLÁS.SI.CO, *s.m.*, *adj.*, classic, classical.
CLAS.SI.FI.CA.ÇÃO, *s.f.*, classification, arrangement, sorting, qualification.
CLAS.SI.FI.CA.DO, *adj.*, classified; selected, approved.
CLAS.SI.FI.CA.DOR, *s.m.*, classifier; *adj.*, classifying.
CLAS.SI.FI.CAR, *v.*, to classify, to class, to assort, to catalogue, to label, to qualify.
CLAS.SI.FI.CA.TÓ.RI.O, *adj.*, classificatory.
CLAS.SI.FI.CÁ.VEL, *adj.*, classifiable.
CLAS.SIS.TA, *s. 2 gen.*, representative or member of a class; *adj.*, divided into social classes.
CLAS.SU.DO, *adj.*, *pop.*, classy, having high class.
CLAU.DI.CA.ÇÃO, *s.f.*, claudication, limping; *fig.*, hesitation.
CLAU.DI.CAN.TE, *adj.*, claudicant, limping; *fig.*, wrong, imperfect.
CLAU.DI.CAR, *v.*, to limp, to hobble, to walk lamely; *fig.*, to err, to go wrong.
CLAUS.TRAL, *s.m.*, the inner patio of a cloiste; *adj.*, claustral, cloistral.
CLAUS.TRO, *s.m.*, monastery, convent.
CLAUS.TRO.FO.BI.A, *s.f.*, *Med.*, claustrophobia.
CLAUS.TRO.FÓ.BI.CO, *adj.*, claustrophobic.

CLÁU.SU.LA, *s.f.*, clause, condition, passage.
CLAU.SU.LAR, *adj.*, clausal; *v.*, to insert clauses in.
CLA.VA, *s.f.*, club, mace, bludgeon.
CLA.VE, *s.f.*, *Mús.*, clef; axle pin.
CLA.VÍ.CU.LA, *s.f.*, *Anat.*, clavicle, collar-bone.
CLA.VI.CU.LA.DO, *adj.*, *Zool.*, claviculate.
CLA.VI.CU.LAR, *adj.*, clavicular.
CLE.MÊN.CIA, *s.f.*, clemency, indulgence, mercy, kindness.
CLE.MEN.CI.AR, *v.*, to treat with clemency.
CLE.MEN.TE, *adj.*, clement, indulgent, merciful.
CLEP.SI.DRA, *s.f.*, clepsydra, water clock.
CLEP.TO.MA.NI.A, *s.f.*, *Med.*, kleptomania.
CLEP.TO.MA.NÍ.A.CO, *s.m.*, *Med.*, kleptomaniac.
CLE.RI.CAL, *adj.*, cleric, clerical; priestly; ecclesiastic(al).
CLE.RI.CA.LIS.MO, *s.m.*, clericalism.
CLE.RI.CA.LIS.TA, *s. 2 gen.*, clericalist.
CLE.RI.CAL.MEN.TE, *adv.*, clerically, priestly.
CLÉ.RI.GO, *s.m.*, cleric, clergyman, churchman.
CLE.RO, *s.m.*, the clergy.
CLI.CAR, *v.*, to click.
CLI.CHÊ, *s.m.*, cliché, stereotype.
CLI.CHE.RI.A, *s.f.*, stereotype manufacture; workshop.
CLI.CHE.RIS.TA, *s. 2 gen.*, a stereotype maker.
CLI.EN.TE, *s. 2 gen.*, client, dependent; customer, patron.
CLI.EN.TE.LA, *s.f.*, clientele, clients, customers.
CLI.EN.TE.LIS.MO, *s.m.*, *Pol.*, political patronage.
CLI.MA, *s.m.*, clime, climate, zone.
CLI.MA.TÉ.RI.O, *s.m.*, *Med.*, menopause, climacterium, climacteric.
CLI.MA.TI.CA.MEN.TE, *adv.*, climatically.
CLI.MÁ.TI.CO, *adj.*, climatic.
CLI.MA.TI.ZA.ÇÃO, *s.f.*, acclimation, air-conditioning.
CLI.MA.TI.ZAR, *v.*, to climatize, to acclimate.
CLI.MA.TO.LO.GI.A, *s.f.*, climatology.
CLI.MA.TO.LÓ.GI.CO, *adj.*, climatologic(al), climatic(al).
CLI.MA.TO.LO.GIS.TA, *s. 2 gen.*, climatologist.
CLÍ.MAX, *s.m.*, climax, culmination, apex.
CLÍ.NI.CA, *s.f.*, clinic, hospital clinic.
CLI.NI.CAR, *v.*, to practise medicine.
CLÍ.NI.CO, *s.m.*, doctor, physician; *adj.*, clinical.
CLI.PE, *s.m.*, clip, paperclip.
CLÍ.PER, *s.m.*, *Náut.*, clipper, clipper ship.
CLI.QUE, *s.m.*, clique, set; *interj.*, click!
CLI.TÓ.RIS, *s.m.*, *2 num.*, *Anat.*, clitoris.
CLI.VA.GEM, *s.f.*, *Min.*, cleavage.
CLI.VAR, *v.*, *Min.*, to cleave.
CLO.A.CA, *s.f.*, sewer, latrine.
CLO.A.CAL, *adj.*, cloacal.
CLO.NA.GEM, *s.f.*, *Biol.*, cloning.
CLO.NAL, *adj.*, *Biol.*, clonal.
CLO.NAR, *v.*, *Biol.*, to clone.
CLO.NE, *s.m.*, *Biol.*, clone.
CLÔ.NI.CO, *Med.*, clonic.
CLO.RA.ÇÃO, *s.f.*, *Quím.*, chlorination.
CLO.RA.DO, *adj.*, *Quím.*, chlorinated.
CLO.RAR, *v.*, to chlorinate.
CLO.RA.TO, *s.m.*, *Quím.*, chlorate.
CLO.RE.TO, *s.m.*, chloride.
CLÓ.RI.CO, *adj.*, *Quím.*, chloric.
CLO.RÍ.TI.CO, *adj.*, *Quím.*, chloritic.
CLO.RO, *s.m.*, *Quim.*, chlorine.

CLOROFILA ·· 134 ·· COCHO

CLO.RO.FI.LA, s.f., Bot., chlorophyll.
CLO.RO.FI.LA.DO, adj., chlorophyllous.
CLO.RO.FÓR.MIO, s.m., chloroform.
CLO.RO.SI.DA.DE, s.m., Quím., chlorinity.
CLO.RO.SO, adj., Quím., chlorous.
CLO.SET, s.m., Ingl., closet.
CLU.BE, s.m., club, club-house, association, society.
CLU.BIS.TA, s. 2 gen., clubber, club member.
CO.A.BI.TA.ÇÃO, s.f., cohabitation.
CO.A.BI.TA.DOR, s.m., cohabitant; adj., cohabiting.
CO.A.BI.TAN.TE, s. 2 gen., cohabitant.
CO.A.BI.TAR, v., to cohabit, to live together.
CO.A.ÇÃO, s.f., coaction, compulsion.
CO.A.CER.VAR, v., to accumulate, to coacervate.
CO.AC.TAR, v., the same that coatar.
CO.A.CU.SA.DO, s.m., Jur., codefendant.
CO.A.DA, s.f., juice strained cooked vegetables.
CO.AD.JU.TOR, s.m., assistant, helper; adj., coadjutor.
CO.AD.JU.VAN.TE, s. 2 gen., coadjuvant.
CO.AD.JU.VAR, v., to help, to aid, to assist.
CO.AD.MI.NIS.TRA.ÇÃO, s.f., coadministration.
CO.A.DO, adj., filtered, strained.
CO.A.DOR, s.m., percolator, filter.
CO.AD.QUI.RIR, v., to acquire jointly.
CO.A.DU.NA.ÇÃO, s.f., coadunation.
CO.A.DU.NA.DO, adj., coadunate.
CO.A.DU.NAR, v., to coadunate, to incorporate.
CO.A.GI.DO, adj., constrained, strained, coerced.
CO.A.GIR, v., to coerce, to constrain, to restrain.
CO.A.GU.LA.ÇÃO, s.f., coagulation.
CO.A.GU.LA.DO, adj., coagulated.
CO.A.GU.LA.DOR, s.m., coagulant; Anat., abomasum; adj., coagulating.
CO.A.GU.LAN.TE, s.m., coagulant (agent); adj., coagulative, coagulating.
CO.A.GU.LAR, v., to coagulate, to curdle, to clot.
CO.A.GU.LÁ.VEL, adj., coagulable.
CO.Á.GU.LO, s.m., coagulum, clot.
CO.A.LA, s.m., Zool., koala.
CO.A.LES.CÊN.CI.A, s.f., coalescence, coalition.
CO.A.LES.CEN.TE, adj., coalescent.
CO.A.LES.CER, v., to coalesce; to combine; to agglutinate.
CO.A.LHA.DA, s.f., curdled milk.
CO.A.LHA.DO, adj., curdled, solidified.
CO.A.LHAR, v., to curdle, to clot, to curd.
CO.A.LHO, s.m., coagulum; Zool., Anat., abomasum; coagulator.
CO.A.LI.ZÃO, s.f., coalition, alliance, union.
CO.A.LI.ZAR, v., to coalize; to unite, to confederate.
CO.AR, v., to filter, to strain, to percolate, to distill, to cast, to found.
CO.AR.REN.DAR, v., co-lease.
CO.A.TAR, v., to coerce.
CO.AU.TO.RI.A, s.f., co-authorship.
CO.A.VA.LIS.TA, s. 2 gen., Com., co-signer.
CO.AU.TOR, s.m., co-author, collaborator.
CO.A.XA.ÇÃO, s.f., croaking (of a frog).
CO.A.XAR, v., to croak.
CO.A.XI.AL, adj., Eletr., coaxial.
CO.BAI.A, s.f., Zool., guinea pig, cavy.
CO.BAL.TO, s.m., Quím., cobalt (symbol: Co); Art., the cobalt blue color.

CO.BAL.TO.SO, adj., Quím., cobaltous.
CO.BER.TA, s.f., cap, cover, covering, coverlet, bedspread, hood.
CO.BAR.DE, s. 2 gen., the same that covarde: coward.
CO.BER.TA, s.f., cover, cap, coverture; blanket, spread; hood; casing, casement.
CO.BER.TO, adj., covered, protected, hooded.
CO.BER.TOR, s.m., blanket, coverlet, quilt.
CO.BER.TU.RA, s.f., cover, coverage, covering, wrapper.
CO.BI.ÇA, s.f., envy, greediness, avarice.
CO.BI.ÇAN.TE, adj., covetous, greedy.
CO.BI.ÇAR, v., to covet, to lust after, to desire, to envy.
CO.BI.ÇÁ.VEL, adj., covetable.
CO.BI.ÇO.SA.MEN.TE, adv., covetously, avariciously.
CO.BI.ÇO.SO, adj., covetous, greedy, avaricious.
CO.BRA, s.f., snake, serpent, adder; picada de ~: snake bite; s. 2 gen., pop., expert.
CO.BRA-CO.RAL, s.f., Zool., coral snake.
CO.BRA-D'Á.GUA, s.f., Zool., water snake.
CO.BRA-DE-VI.DRO, s.f., Zool., glass snake.
CO.BRA.DO, adj., gathered, collected.
CO.BRA.DOR, s.m., bill collector, receiver.
CO.BRAN.ÇA, s.f., collection, encashment, exaction.
CO.BRAR, v., to receive, to charge, to exact.
CO.BRÁ.VEL, adj., chargeable, collectable.
CO.BRE, s.m., copper; money.
CO.BRE,A.MEN.TO, s.m., copper-facing.
CO.BRE.AR, v., to cover or treat with copper; to coat with copper.
CO.BREI.RO, s.m., pop., Med., shingles, herpes zoster.
CO.BRE.JAR, v., to snake, twist, wind, meander.
CO.BRE.LO, s.m., Zool., any small snake; Med., pop., herpes zoster.
CO.BRI.MEN.TO, s.m., coverage, covering; coating.
CO.BRIR, v., to cover, to hide, to conceal, to cloak, to hood, to defend, to protect.
CO.BRO, s.m., end, termination; encashment; fee; any small snake; Med., pop., herpes zoster.
CO.CA, s.f., Bot., coca (Erythroxylon coca), pop., cocaine; Coca-cola®.
CO.CA.DA, s.f., coconut candy; pop., head-butt.
CO.CA.Í.NA, s.f., cocain, cocaine.
CO.CA.I.NÔ.MA.NO, s.m., Med., cocainomaniac, cocaine addict.
CO.CAL, s.m., a grove of coconut palms.
CO.CAR, s.m., cockade, topknot; v., be on the lookout.
COC.ÇÃO, s.f., cooking; digestion of food.
CÓC.CIX, s.m., coccyx.
CÓ.CE.GAS, s.f., pl., tickle, tickling, titillation.
CO.CE.GUEN.TO, adj., ticklish.
CO.CEI.RA, s.f., itch, itching.
CO.CHE, s.m., coach, carriage.
CO.CHEI.RA, s.f., box, coach-house.
CO.CHEI.RO, s.m., coachman.
CO.CHI.CHA.DOR, s.m., whisperer; adj., whispering.
CO.CHI.CHAR, v., to whisper, to murmur, to mutter.
CO.CHI.CHO, s.m., whispering, whisper, buzz.
CO.CHI.LAR, v., to nod off, to nap, to doze.
CO.CHI.LO, s.m., nap, doze, drowse.
CO.CHIN.CHI.NA, s.f., Cochin China (part of Indochina).
CO.CHO, s.m., trug, hod, trough.

COCIENTE   •• 135 ••   COLADOR

CO.CI.EN.TE, *s.m.*, *Mat.*, quotient.
COCKER SPANIEL, *s.m.*, *Zool.*, cocker spaniel (breed of dog).
COCK.PIT, *s.m.*, *Ingl.*, *Autom.*, *Aeron.*, cockpit (airplane, boat or automobile).
CÓ.CLE.A, *s.f.*, *Anat.*, cochlea.
CO.CO, *s.m.*, *Bot.*, coconut, coconut tree.
CO.CO-DA-BA.Í.A, *s.m.*, *Bot.*, common coconut palm; coconut.
CÓ.CO.RAS, *s.f.*, *pl.*, squatting.
CO.CO.RI.CAR, *v.*, to crow.
CO.CO.RI.CÓ, *s.m.*, the same that *cocorocó*.
CO.CO.RO.CÓ, *s.m.*, a cock's crow, crowing.
CO.CO.RO.TE, *s.m.*, a small blow on the head with the knuckles.
CO.CO.TA, *s.f.*, *pop.*, a teenaged girl who wears fashionable clothes.
CO.CU.RU.TO, *s.m.*, top, summit, apex; the crown of the head; knoll; the hump of zebu cattle.
CÔ.DEA, *s.f.*, hull, husk, crust, scab.
CÓ.DI.CE, *s.m.*, codex (ancient manuscript).
CO.DI.FI.CA.ÇÃO, *s.f.*, codification.
CO.DI.FI.CA.DOR, *s.m.*, codifier.
CO.DI.FI.CAR, *v.*, to codify, to systematize, to classify.
CÓ.DI.GO, *s.m.*, code, systematic colletion of laws.
CO.DI.NO.ME, *s.m.*, code name.
CO.DI.RE.TOR, *s.m.*, co-director.
CO.DOR.NA, *s.f.*, *Zool.*, quail; *ovo de ~*: a quail's egg.
CO.DOR.NIZ, *s.f.*, *Zool.*, quail.
CO.E.DI.ÇÃO, *s.f.*, co-edition.
COE.DI.TAR, *v.*, to co-edit.
CO.E.DI.TOR, *s.m.*, co-editor.
CO.E.DU.CAR, *v.*, to coeducate.
CO.E.FI.CI.EN.TE, *s.m.*, coefficient, factor, rate.
CO.E.LHEI.RA, *s.f.*, rabbitry.
CO.E.LHEI.RO, *s.m.*, rabbit-hunter (dog).
CO.E.LHO, *s.m.*, *Zool.*, rabbit.
CO.EN.TRO, *s.m.*, *Bot.*, coriander.
CO.ER.ÇÃO, *s.f.*, coercion, repression.
CO.ER.CI.TI.VO, *adj.*, coercitive, coactive.
CO.ER.CI.BI.LI.DA.DE, *s.f.*, coerciveness.
CO.ER.CI.TI.VI.DA.DE, *s.f.*, compulsiveness.
CO.ER.CI.VA.MEN.TE, *adv.*, coercively.
CO.ER.CÍ.VEL, *adj.*, coercible.
CO.ER.CI.VO, *adj.*, coercive; exerting coercion.
CO.E.RÊN.CIA, *s.f.*, coherence, cohesion, harmony.
CO.E.REN.TE, *adj.*, coherent, consistent.
CO.E.REN.TE.MEN.TE, *adv.*, coherently.
CO.E.SÃO, *s.f.*, cohesion, act of cohering; harmony, coherence.
CO.E.SI.VA.MEN.TE, *adv.*, cohesively.
CO.E.SI.VO, *adj.*, cohesive.
CO.E.SO, *adj.*, cohesive, united.
CO.ES.SÊN.CI.A, *s.f.*, common essence.
CO.E.TÂ.NE.O, *s.m.*, contemporary; *adj.*, coetaneous, contemporary.
CO.E.VO, *s.m.*, coeval, contemporary; *adj.*, coeval, contemporary.
CO.E.XIS.TÊN.CIA, *s.f.*, coexistence.
CO.E.XIS.TEN.TE, *adj.*, coexistent.
CO.E.XIS.TIR, *v.*, to coexist, to exist together.
CO.FA.TOR, *s.m.*, *Mat.*, cofactor, minor.
CO.FI.A.DOR, *s.m.*, co-surety.

CO.FI.AR, *v.*, stroke with the hand (hair, beard or mustache).
CO.FRE, *s.m.*, strongbox, box, chest.
CO.GI.TA.ÇÃO, *s.f.*, cogitation.
CO.GI.TAR, *v.*, to cogitate, to ponder, to recollect; to consider.
COG.NA.TO, *s.m.*, cognate; *adj.*, cognate; *Gram.*, having the same root.
COG.NI.ÇÃO, *s.f.*, cognition.
COG.NI.TI.VO, *adj.*, cognitive.
CÓG.NI.TO, *adj.*, known, cognized.
COG.NO.ME, *s.m.*, cognomen, surname, nickname.
COG.NO.MI.NA.ÇÃO, *s.f.*, cognomination.
COG.NO.MI.NAR, *v.*, to cognominate, to nickname.
COG.NOS.CI.BI.LI.DA.DE, *s.f.*, cognoscibility.
COG.NOS.CI.TI.VA.MEN.TE, *adv.*, cognoscitively.
COG.NOS.CI.TI.VO, *adj.*, cognoscitive.
COG.NOS.CÍ.VEL, *adj.*, cognoscible, cognizable, knowable.
CO.GU.ME.LO, *s.m.*, *Bot.*, mushroom, fungus.
CO.ER.DAR, *v.*, to inherit jointly.
CO.ER.DEI.RO, *s.m.*, coheir, joint heir.
CO.I.BI.ÇÃO, *s.f.*, cohibition, restraint, limitation.
CO.I.BIR, *v.*, to stop, to repress, to cohibit.
CO.I.BI.TI.VO, *adj.*, cohibitive.
COI.CE, *s.m.*, kick, rear, recoil.
COI.CE.AR, *v.*, to kick, to lash out.
COI.FA, *s.f.*, a fine hair-net; coif.
COI.MA, *s.f.*, fine, penalty.
COI.MAR, *v.*, to impose a fine or penalty.
CO.IN.CI.DÊN.CIA, *s.f.*, coincidence, concurrence, concurrency.
CO.IN.CI.DEN.TE, *adj.*, coincident.
CO.IN.CI.DEN.TE.MEN.TE, *adv.*, coincidentally.
CO.IN.CI.DIR, *v.*, to coincide, to contemporize.
CO.IN.CI.DÍ.VEL, *adj.*, capable of coinciding.
COI.Ó, *s.m.*, a ridiculous admirer; *adj.*, silly, ridiculous; *gír.*, coward.
COI.O.TE, *s.m.*, *Zool.*, coyote, prairie wolf.
CO.IR.MÃO, *s.m.*, affiliate, member.
COI.SA, *s.f.*, thing, object, matter, substance, affair, event.
COI.SA À TO.A, *s. 2 gen.*, *pop.*, a person of low morals; unimportant thing.
COI.SA-FEI.TA, *s.f.*, witchcraft, voodoo.
COI.SAR, *v.*, *gír.*, to ponder, meditate.
COI.SA-RU.IM, *s. 2 gen.*, *Bras.*, *pop.*, the devil.
COI.SI.FI.CAR, *v.*, to reduce something or someone on mere thing.
COI.TA.DO, *s.m.*, underdog; *adj.*, poor, pitiful, miserable.
COI.TO, *s.m.*, coitus, copulation, coupling.
COI.VA.RA, *s.f.*, *pop.*, a heap brushwood gathered for final burning.
CO.LA, *s.f.*, glue, gum, adhesive.
CO.LA.BO.RA.ÇÃO, *s.f.*, collaboration, co-operation, common work, help, assistance.
CO.LA.BO.RA.CI.O.NIS.MO, *s.m.*, collaborationism.
CO.LA.BO.RA.CI.O.NIS.TA, *s. 2 gen.*, collaborationist.
CO.LA.BO.RA.DOR, *s.m.*, collaborator, contributor.
CO.LA.BO.RAR, *v.*, to collaborate, to co-operate.
CO.LA.BO.RA.TI.VO, *adj.*, collaborative.
CO.LA.ÇÃO, *s.f.*, comparison, collation; bestowal of a title or degree.
CO.LA.DO, *adj.*, glued, fixed with glue.
CO.LA.DOR, *s.m.*, collator; paster, gluer.

COLAGEM · 136 · COLORÍFICO

CO.LA.GEM, s.f., gluing, pasting.

CO.LÁ.GE.NO, s.m., Biol., Quím., collagen.

CO.LAP.SAR, v., to collapse, to crumble, to break down.

CO.LAP.SO, s.m., collapse, break-down, burst-up.

CO.LAR, v., to glue, to conglutinate, to aglutinate, to gum, to graduate; s.m., necklace, collar.

CO.LA.RI.NHO, s.m., collar, shirt collar, neckband.

CO.LA.TE.RAL, adj., s.m., collateral.

CO.LA.TE.RAL.MEN.TE, adv., collaterally.

CO.LA.TE.RA.LI.DA.DE, s.f., collaterality.

COL.CHA, s.f., blanket, bed-spread, coverlet.

COL.CHÃO, s.m., mattress.

COL.CHEI.A, s.f., Mús., quaver, eighth note.

COL.CHEI.RO, s.m., quilter, bedspread maker.

COL.CHE.TE, s.m., hook, clasp.

COL.CHO.A.RI.A, s.f., mattress factory; mattress shop.

COL.CHO.EI.RO, s.m., mattress maker; mattress vendor.

COL.CHO.NE.TE, s.m., small mattress.

COL.DRE, s.m., holster.

CO.LE.ÇÃO, s.f., collection, compilation, gathering, accumulation.

CO.LE.CI.O.NA.DO, adj., collected, compiled.

CO.LE.CI.O.NA.DOR, s.m., collector, compiler.

CO.LE.CI.O.NAR, v., to collect, to gather, to accumulate.

CO.LE.GA, s. 2 gen., colleague, associate, schoolmate, friend, fellow.

CO.LE.GI.A.DO, adj., collegiate.

CO.LE.GI.AL, s. 2 gen., student; adj., collegiate, collegial.

CO.LÉ.GIO, s.m., college, public school, high school.

CO.LE.GUIS.MO, s.m., collegiality, colleagueship, fellowship.

CO.LEI.RA, s.f., collar (for animals), dog-collar.

CO.LE.ÓP.TE.RO, s.m., Zool., coleopter, coleopteran; adj., coleopterous.

CÓ.LE.RA, s.f., anger, irritation, passion, rage, ira; cholera.

CO.LE.RI.CA.MEN.TE, adv., irately, passionately, wrathfully.

CO.LÉ.RI.CO, adj., choleric, furious, irascible, irate, choleraic (med.)

CO.LES.TE.ROL, s.m., Biol., Quím., cholesterol.

CO.LE.TA, s.f., collection, levy, tax, contribution.

CO.LE.TÂ.NE.A, s.f., collectanea (collection, compilation).

CO.LE.TÂ.NE.O, adj., excerptive, selected, excerpted.

CO.LE.TAR, v., to collect, to gather, to rate.

CO.LE.TÁ.VEL, adj., collectable, collectible.

CO.LE.TE, s.m., waistcoat, jumper.

CO.LE.TEI.RO, s.m., waistcoat maker.

CO.LE.TI.VA.MEN.TE, adv., collectively.

CO.LE.TI.VI.DA.DE, s.f., collectivity, community, society.

CO.LE.TI.VIS.MO, s.m., collectivism.

CO.LE.TI.VIS.TA, s. 2 gen., collectivist; adj., collectivistic.

CO.LE.TI.VI.ZAR, v., to collectivize, to communize.

CO.LE.TI.VO, s.m., tramwaycar, omnibus; collective; adj., collective, social.

CO.LE.TOR, s.m., collector; gatherer; tax collector; adj., collecting.

CO.LE.TO.RI.A, s.f., tax collector's office.

CO.LHÃO, s.m., Bras., vulg., testicle.

CO.LHE.DEI.RA, s.f., harvester, reaper.

CO.LHE.DOR, s.m., gatherer, collector.

CO.LHEI.TA, s.f., harvest, crop, picking.

CO.LHER, s.f., spoon.

CO.LHER, v., to harvest, to pick, to reap, to perceive.

CO.LHE.RA.DA, s.f., spoonful.

CO.LHI.MEN.TO, s.m., gathering, picking (fruit).

CO.LI.BRI, s.m., Zool., colibri, hummingbird.

CÓ.LI.CA, s.f., colic, pain, belly-ache.

CÓ.LI.CO, adj., colic (colon), colicky; cholic (bile).

CO.LI.DIR, v., to collide, to shock, to dash.

CO.LI.GA.ÇÃO, s.f., colligation, coalition, confederation.

CO.LI.GA.DO, adj., confederate, allied.

CO.LI.GAR, v., to colligate, to aproximate, to unite, to join, to connect.

CO.LI.GIR, v., to gather, collect; to compile.

CO.LI.GÍ.VEL, adj., collectable, colligible.

CO.LI.MA.ÇÃO, s.f., Fís., collimation.

CO.LI.MAR, v., Fís., to collimate; to aim at.

CO.LI.NA, s.f., mount, hill, knoll.

CO.LI.NE.AR, adj., collinear.

CO.LI.NE.A.RI.DA.DE, s.f., Geom., collinearity.

CO.LI.NE.AR.MEN.TE, adv., collinearly.

CO.LI.NO.SO, adj., hilly.

CO.LÍ.RIO, s.m., Med., collyrium, eye drops.

CO.LI.SÃO, s.f., collision, crash, shock, clash.

CO.LI.SEU, s.m., coliseum, amphitheater.

CO.LI.TE, s.f., Med., colitis.

COL.LANT, s.m., Fr., leotard; footless tights.

COL.MAR, v., to thatch, to cover with straw.

COL.ME.EI.RO, s.m., apiarist, beekeeper.

COL.MEI.A, s.f., beehive, hive, skep.

COL.MI.LHO, s.m., Zool., Anat., canine, canine tooth.

COL.MI.LHO.SO, adj., having fangs, tusked.

COL.MI.LHU.DO, adj., having long fangs, tusked.

COL.MO, s.m., stem, stalk; straw.

CO.LO, s.m., neck, bosom, lap; colon (anat.)

CO.LO.CA.ÇÃO, s.f., placement, collocation, job, setting, situation.

CO.LO.CA.DO, adj., collocated, situated, placed, appointed, set.

CO.LO.CAR, v., to place, to dispose, to arrange, to employ, to set, to plant.

CO.LOI.DAL, adj., colloidal.

CO.LÔM.BIA, s., Colombia.

CO.LOM.BI.A.NO, s.m., Colombian; adj., Colombian.

CO.LOM.BI.NO, s.m., the same that colombiano.

CO.LÔM.BI.O, s.m., Quím., columbium, niobium (symbol: Cb).

CÓ.LON, s.m., Anat., colon.

CO.LÔ.NIA, s.f., colony, possession, territory.

CO.LO.NI.AL, s. 2 gen., colonial; colonist; adj., colonial.

CO.LO.NI.A.LIS.MO, s.m., colonialism.

CO.LO.NIS.TA, s. 2 gen., colonist (member of a colony).

CO.LO.NI.ZA.ÇÃO, s.f., colonization.

CO.LO.NI.ZA.DO, adj., colonized, settled.

CO.LO.NI.ZAR, v., to colonize.

CO.LO.NI.ZÁ.VEL, adj., colonizable.

CO.LO.NO, s.m., colonist, planter, settler.

CO.LO.QUI.AL, adj., colloquial.

CO.LÓ.QUIO, s.m., colloquy, conversation.

CO.LO.RA.ÇÃO, s.f., colouration, coloration.

CO.LO.RA.DO, adj., reddish, red.

CO.LO.RAN.TE, adj., colorant, dye, pigment.

CO.LO.RAU, s.m., Cul., annatto.

CO.LO.RI.DO, s.m., colour, colouring, coloured.

CO.LO.RÍ.FI.CO, adj., colourific.

COLORIR · 137 · COMETÁRIO

CO.LO.RIR, *v.*, to color, to colour, to paint, to dye, to tinge.
CO.LO.RIS.TA, *s. 2 gen.*, colourist, colorist.
CO.LO.RI.ZA.ÇÃO, *s.f., Cin.*, colorization.
CO.LO.RI.ZAR, *v., Cin.*, to colorize.
CO.LOS.SAL, *adj.*, colossal; enormous; gigantic.
CO.LOS.SAL.MEN.TE, *adv.*, colossally, enormously.
CO.LOS.SO, *s.m.*, colossus.
CO.LOS.TO.MI.A, *s.f., Med.*, colostomy.
CO.LOS.TRO, *s.m., Anat.*, colostrum.
CO.LU.NA, *s.f.*, column, pillar; military column; support; section of a newspaper.
CO.LU.NAR, *v.*, to arrange in columns.
CO.LU.NÁ.RI.O, *adj.*, showing or representing columns.
CO.LU.NA.TA, *s.f.*, a range of columns; colonnade.
CO.LU.NÁ.VEL, *s. 2 gen., pop.*, celebrity; *adj.*, glamorous.
CO.LU.NIS.TA, *s. 2 gen.*, columnist, author of a newspaper column.
CO.LU.NI.ZA.ÇÃO, *s.f., Arquit.*, columniation.
COM, *prep.*, with.
CO.MA, *s.m.*, coma, torpor.
CO.MA.DRE, *s.f.*, godmother.
CO.MAN.CHE, *s. 2 gen.*, Comanche (member of a tribe of North American indian); *adj.*, Comanche.
CO.MAN.DAN.TE, *s. 2 gen.*, commander, commandant, chief.
CO.MAN.DAN.TE EM CHE.FE, *s.m., Mil.*, commander in chief.
CO.MAN.DAR, *v.*, to command, to control, to order, to direct.
CO.MAN.DI.TA, *s.f., Com.*, shareholder in a limited society; limited partnership.
CO.MAN.DI.TÁ.RI.O, *s.m., Com.*, financier of a limited company.
CO.MAN.DO, *s.m.*, command, order, mandate, power, control.
CO.MAR.CA, *s.f.*, judiciary district, district, region.
CO.MA.TO.SO, *adj., Med.*, comatose.
COM.BA.LI.DO, *adj.*, weak, frail, dejected, indisposed.
COM.BA.LIR, *v.*, to weaken, to enfeeble; to despond.
COM.BA.TE, *s.m.*, combat, fight, battle.
COM.BA.TEN.TE, *s. 2 gen.*, fighter, combatant; *adj.*, fighting, combatant.
COM.BA.TER, *v.*, to combat, to strive against, to contend, to contest.
COM.BA.TI.VA.MEN.TE, *adv.*, combatively.
COM.BA.TÍ.VEL, *adj.*, combatable.
COM.BA.TI.VI.DA.DE, *s.f.*, combativeness.
COM.BA.TI.VO, *adj.*, combative.
COM.BI.NA.ÇÃO, *s.f.*, combination, arrangement, aggregation, formation.
COM.BI.NA.DO, *s.m.*, agreement; *adj.*, combined, agreed.
COM.BI.NA.DOR, *s.m.*, combiner; *adj.*, combining.
COM.BI.NAR, *v.*, to combine, to join together, to connect, to assort, to stipulate.
COM.BOI.O, *s.m.*, convoy.
COM.BI.NA.TI.VO, *adj.*, combinative, combinatory.
COM.BI.NA.TÓ.RI.O, *adj.*, combinatory, combinative.
COM.BI.NÁ.VEL, *adj.*, combinable, compoundable.
COM.BOI.AR, *v.*, to guide; to convoy, to escort.
COM.BOI.EI.RO, *s.m.*, escort.
COM.BOI.O, *s.m.*, convoy, transport.
COM.BU.REN.TE, *s. 2 gen.*, fuel; *adj.*, causing combustion, causing inflaming.
COM.BU.RIR, *v.*, to burn.
COM.BUS.TÃO, *s.m.*, combustion, ignition, tumult.

COM.BUS.TI.BI.LI.DA.DE, *s.f.*, combustibility.
COM.BUS.TÍ.VEL, *s.m.*, fuel, combustible, gasoline, gas.
COM.BUS.TI.VO, *adj.*, combustive, combustible.
COM.BUS.TOR, *s.m.*, street lamp.
CO.ME.ÇA.DOR, *s.m.*, beginner, initiator; *adj.*, beginning.
CO.ME.ÇAR, *v.*, to begin, to commence, to start, to enter on.
CO.ME.ÇO, *s.m.*, beginning, commencement, birth, start.
CO.MÉ.DIA, *s.f.*, comedy, sketch, farce.
CO.ME.DI.AN.TE, *s. 2 gen.*, comedian, comedienne.
CO.ME.DI.AR, *v.*, to transform into a comedy, write a farce or comedy.
CO.ME.DI.DO, *adj.*, moderate, unpretentious; cautious; prudent.
CO.ME.DI.MEN.TO, *s.m.*, moderation, unpretentiousness, prudence.
CO.ME.DIR, *v.*, to moderate, to contain, to restrain, to regulate.
CO.ME.DIS.TA, *s. 2 gen.*, author of a comedy.
CO.ME.DOR, *s.m.*, eater, glutton.
CO.ME.DO.RI.A, *s.f.*, food, aliment.
CO.ME.DOU.RO, *s.m.*, feeding place; feedbin, feedbag.
CO.ME.MO.RA.ÇÃO, *s.f.*, commemoration, celebration.
CO.ME.MO.RA.DOR, *s.m.*, commemorator.
CO.ME.MO.RAR, *v.*, to commemorate, to remember, to memorialize, to celebrate.
CO.ME.MO.RA.TI.VA.MEN.TE, *adv.*, commemoratively.
CO.ME.MO.RA.TI.VO, *adj.*, commemorative.
CO.MÉ.MO.RÁ.VEL, *adj.*, commemorable.
CO.MEN.DA, *s.f., Hist.*, commandery, knighthood; distinction.
CO.MEN.DA.DOR, *s.m.*, commander, commendatary.
CO.MEN.DA.TÁ.RI.O, *s.m.*, commendatary.
CO.MEN.SAL, *s. 2 gen.*, commensal.
CO.MEN.SA.LIS.MO, *s.m.*, commensalism.
CO.MEN.SU.RA.BI.LI.DA.DE, *s.f.*, commensurability.
CO.MEN.SU.RAR, *v.*, to measure; to compare.
CO.MEN.SU.RÁ.VEL, *adj.*, commensurable, commensurate.
CO.MEN.SU.RA.VEL.MEN.TE, *adv.*, commensurably.
CO.MEN.TA.DO, *adj.*, commented, discussed.
CO.MEN.TA.DOR, *s.m.*, commentator, expositor.
CO.MEN.TAR, *v.*, to comment, to explain, to annotate.
CO.MEN.TÁ.RIO, *s.m.*, comment, commentary, note, interpretation.
CO.MEN.TA.RIS.TA, *s. 2 gen.*, commentator.
CO.MEN.TÍ.CI.O, *adj.*, invented, fictious.
CO.MER, *v.*, to eat, to consume, to feed.
CO.MER.CI.AL, *s.m.*, commercial; *adj.*, commercial, mercantile.
CO.MER.CI.A.LI.DA.DE, *s.f., Com.*, commerciality.
CO.MER.CI.A.LI.ZA.ÇÃO, *s.f.*, commercialization.
CO.MER.CI.A.LI.ZAR, *v.*, commercialize.
CO.MER.CI.AL.MEN.TE, *adv.*, commercially.
CO.MER.CI.AN.TE, *s. 2 gen.*, merchant, trader, businessman.
CO.MER.CI.AR, *v.*, to trade, to deal.
CO.MER.CI.Á.RI.O, *s.m.*, commercial employee.
CO.MER.CI.Á.VEL, *adj.*, marketable.
CO.MÉR.CIO, *s.m.*, commerce, trade, trading, business.
CO.MES, *s.m., pl., pop.*, comestibles; *comes e bebes*: eating and drinking.
CO.MES.TI.BI.LI.DA.DE, *s.f.*, edibility, edibleness.
CO.MES.TÍ.VEL, *s.m.*, comestible, edible, food; *adj.*, comestible.
CO.ME.TA, *s.f., Astron.*, comet.
CO.ME.TÁ.RI.O, *adj.*, relative to a comet.

COMETER · 138 · COMPLACENTE

CO.ME.TER, *v.*, to commit, to practise, to perform, to perpetrate.

CO.ME.TI.MEN.TO, *s.m.*, committal, commitment; comission, undertaking; crime.

CO.MI.CA.MEN.TE, *adv.*, comically.

CO.MI.CHÃO, *s.f.*, itching; ardent desire.

CO.MI.CHAR, *v.*, to itch.

CO.MI.CI.DA.DE, *s.f.*, comicality, comicalness.

CO.MÍ.CI.O, *s.m.*, meeting, rally, demonstration; assembly.

CÔ.MI.CO, *adj.*, comic, funny.

CO.MI.DA, *s.f.*, food, aliment, eating, fare, meal, feed, feeding.

CO.MI.GO, *pron.*, with me, in my society.

CO.MI.GO-NIN.GUÉM-PO.DE, *s.m.*, *Bras.*, *Bot.*, dieffenbachia (*Dieffenbachia seguine*).

CO.MI.LAN.ÇA, *s.f.*, *pop.*, act of overeating.

CO.MI.LÃO, *s.m.*, a heavy eater, glutton.

CO.MI.NAR, *v.*, to comminate, to threaten, to menace.

CO.MI.NA.TI.VO, *adj.*, comminatory, threatening.

CO.MI.NHO, *s.m.*, cumin, cummin.

CO.MI.SE.RA.ÇÃO, *s.f.*, commiseration.

CO.MI.SE.RAR, *v.*, to commiserate.

CO.MIS.SÃO, *s.f.*, commission, committee, retribution.

CO.MIS.SÁ.RIA, *s.f.*, stewardess.

CO.MIS.SÁ.RIO, *s.m.*, commissary, commissioner, police officer.

CO.MIS.SI.O.NA.DO, *s.m.*, commissioned; *adj.*, commissioned.

CO.MIS.SI.O.NAR, *v.*, to commission.

CO.MI.TÊ, *s.m.*, committee.

CO.MI.TI.VA, *s.f.*, retinue, escort, entourage.

CO.MÍ.VEL, *adj.*, eatable, edible.

COM.MO.DI.TY, *s.f.*, *Ingl.*, *Com.*, commodity (any kind of article of trade or commerce).

CO.MO, *adv.*, how, to what degree, by what means, wherein, for what reason; *conj.*, as, while; *pron.*, why.

CO.MO.ÇÃO, *s.f.*, commotion, agitation, ferment, riot.

CÔ.MO.DA, *s.f.*, commode; chest of drawers.

CO.MO.DA.MEN.TE, *adv.*, commodiously, comfortably.

CO.MO.DI.DA.DE, *s.f.*, comfortableness, cosiness, convenience.

CO.MO.DIS.MO, *s.m.*, selfishness; self-indulgence.

CO.MO.DIS.TA, *s. 2 gen.*, selfish, selfish person; *adj.*, self-indulgent.

CÔ.MO.DO, *s.m.*, room, accomodation, comfort; *adj.*, commodious, useful, suitable.

CO.MO.VEN.TE, *adj.*, moving, touching.

CO.MO.VER, *v.*, to move, to affect, to agitate, to stir up.

CO.MO.VI.DO, *adj.*, upset, shaken, moved, touched.

COM.PAC.TA.ÇÃO, *s.f.*, compactness.

COM.PAC.TA.DOR, *s.m.*, *Comp.*, compressor (file).

COM.PAC.TAR, *v.*, to compact; *Comp.*, ~ *arquivos*: to compress files.

COM.PACT DISC, *s.m.*, *Ingl.*, *Eletr.*, *compact disc*.

COM.PAC.TO, *adj.*, compact, close, massy, massive, dense.

COM.PA.DE.CER, *v.*, to pity, compassionate, sympathize; *compadecer-se*: to feel pity for.

COM.PA.DE.CI.DO, *adj.*, compassionate, sympathetic.

COM.PA.DE.CI.MEN.TO, *s.m.*, compassion, sympathy, commiseration.

COM.PA.DRAR, *v.*, to be or become godfather.

COM.PA.DRE, *s.m.*, godfather.

COM.PA.DRI.O, *s.m.*, relationship between a godfather and the child's parents; sponsorship, favouritism.

COM.PAI.XÃO, *s.f.*, compassion, pity, comiseration.

COM.PA.NHEI.RA, *s.f.*, female companion, wife.

COM.PA.NHEI.RIS.MO, *s.m.*, companionship, comradeship.

COM.PA.NHEI.RO, *s.m.*, companion, friend, fellow, consort, colleague.

COM.PA.NHIA, *s.f.*, company, society, firm, corporation.

COM.PA.RA.ÇÃO, *s.f.*, comparison.

COM.PA.RA.DO, *adj.*, compared, contrasted.

COM.PA.RA.DOR, *s.m.*, confronter.

COM.PA.RAR, *v.*, to compare, to contrast, to liken.

COM.PA.RA.TI.VO, *s.m.*, *Gram.*, comparative degree; adj comparative.

COM.PA.RÁ.VEL, *adj.*, comparable.

COM.PA.RE.CER, *v.*, to attend to, to be present at.

COM.PA.RE.CI.MEN.TO, *s.m.*, attendance, appearance, presence.

COM.PAR.SA, *s. 2 gen.*, *pop.*, accomplice.

COM.PAR.TI.LHAR, *v.*, to share, to participate, to partake.

COM.PA.TI.BI.LI.DA.DE, *s.f.*, compatibility, associability.

COM.PAR.TI.MEN.TO, *s.m.*, compartment, partitioning.

COM.PAR.TIR, *v.*, to distribute; participate; share, partake.

COM.PAS.SA.DA.MEN.TE, *adv.*, measuredly, rhythmically.

COM.PAS.SA.DO, *adj.*, measured; regulated, paced, moderate.

COM.PAS.SAR, *v.*, to cadence, to pace, to calculate.

COM.PAS.SI.VA.MEN.TE, *adv.*, compassionately.

COM.PAS.SÍ.VEL, *adj.*, compassionable.

COM.PAS.SI.VI.DA.DE, *s.f.*, compassionateness.

COM.PAS.SI.VO, *adj.*, compassionate, sympathetic.

COM.PA.TI.BI.LI.DA.DE, *s.f.*, compatibility.

COM.PA.TÍ.VEL, *adj.*, compatible.

COM.PA.TRI.O.TA, *s. 2 gen.*, compatriot, countryman.

COM.PE.LIR, *v.*, to compel, to oblige, to coerce.

COM.PE.LÍ.VEL, *adj.*, compellable.

COM.PEN.DI.AR, *v.*, to summarize, epitomize.

COM.PÊN.DIO, *s.m.*, compendium, text-book, school-book, manual.

COM.PE.NE.TRA.DO, *adj.*, deeply convinced.

COM.PE.NE.TRAR, *v.*, to compenetrate, to convince, to enroot.

COM.PEN.SA.ÇÃO, *s.f.*, compensation, recompense, remuneration, indemnity.

COM.PEN.SA.DO, *s.m.*, compensated; hardboard; cleared (check).

COM.PEN.SAR, *v.*, to compensate, to recompense, to indemnify, to even.

COM.PEN.SA.TÓ.RI.O, *adj.*, compensatory.

COM.PEN.SÁ.VEL, *adj.*, compensable.

COM.PE.TÊN.CIA, *s.f.*, competence, ability, aptitude, efficiency.

COM.PE.TEN.TE, *adj.*, competent.

COM.PE.TI.ÇÃO, *s.f.*, competition, competitiveness.

COM.PE.TI.DOR, *s.m.*, competitor; contender; rival.

COM.PE.TIR, *v.*, to compete, to contest, to contend, to match.

COM.PE.TI.TI.VI.DA.DE, *s.f.*, competitiveness.

COM.PI.LA.DOR, *s.m.*, compiler; *adj.*, compiling.

COM.PI.LA.ÇÃO, *s.f.*, compilation, collection.

COM.PI.LAR, *v.*, to compile, to unite, to collect.

COM.PLA.CÊN.CI.A, *s.f.*, complacence, complacency.

COM.PLA.CEN.TE, *adj.*, complacent.

COMPLACENTEMENTE ·· 139 ·· COMUTAR

COM.PLA.CEN.TE.MEN.TE, *adv.*, complacently.
COM.PLEI.ÇÃO, *s.f.*, complexion, physique, build.
COM.PLE.MEN.TA.ÇÃO, *s.f.*, completion, conclusion; *Mat.*, complemention.
COM.PLE.MEN.TA.DOR, *s.m.*, completer; *adj.*, completing.
COM.PLE.MEN.TAR, *v.*, to complement, to complete; *adj.*, supplementary.
COM.PLE.MEN.TO, *s.m.*, complement.
COM.PLE.TA.DOR, *s.m.*, completer; *adj.*, completing.
COM.PLE.TA.MEN.TE, *adv.*, completely, perfectly, fully.
COM.PLE.TA.MEN.TO, *s.m.*, completion.
COM.PLE.TI.VO, *s.m.*, complement; *adj.*, completive.
COM.PLE.TAR, *v.*, to complete, to complement, to accomplish, to conclude.
COM.PLE.TO, *adj.*, complete, entire, finished, done, concluded.
COM.PLE.XI.DA.DE, *s.f.*, complexity.
COM.PLE.XO, *s.m.*, compound, complex; *adj.*, complex, complicated.
COM.PLI.CA.ÇÃO, *s.f.*, complication, difficulty, complicacy.
COM.PLI.CA.DA.MEN.TE, *adv.*, complicatedly.
COM.PLI.CA.DO, *adj.*, complicated, intricate, complex.
COM.PLI.CA.DOR, *s.m.*, one who complicates; *adj.*, complicating.
COM.PLI.CAR, *v.*, to complicate, to embarass, to confuse.
COM.PLÔ, *s.m.*, conspiracy.
COM.PO.NEN.TE, *s. 2 gen.*, component part; *adj.*, component.
COM.POR, *v.*, to compose, to arrange, to put together, to set up, to write, to produce.
COM.POR.TA, *s.f.*, flood-gate, sluice-gate, sluice.
COM.POR.TA.MEN.TO, *s.m.*, conduct, behaviour, manner, posture.
COM.POR.TAR, *v.*, to hold, to contain, to admit, to suffer.
COM.POR.TÁ.VEL, *adj.*, tolerable, bearable.
COM.PO.SI.ÇÃO, *s.f.*, composition, mixture, compound, disposition.
COM.PO.SI.TOR, *s.m.*, composer, songwriter, typographer.
COM.POS.TO, *adj.*, composed, consisting of, compound, articulate.
COM.POS.TU.RA, *s.f.*, composition, composure, decency.
COM.PO.TA, *s.f.*, compote; *um vidro de ~*: a jar of compote.
COM.PO.TEI.RA, *s.f.*, compote.
COM.PRA, *s.f.*, purchase, acquisition, shopping.
COM.PRA.DOR, *s.m.*, purchaser, buyer, shopper, customer.
COM.PRAR, *v.*, to purchase, to buy, to acquire.
COM.PRÁ.VEL, *adj.*, buyable, purchasable.
COM.PRA.ZER, *v.*, comply with, to gladden.
COM.PRA.ZI.MEN.TO, *s.m.*, pleasing, complaisance.
COM.PRE.EN.DER, *v.*, to comprehend, to comprise, to include, to contain, to consist.
COM.PRE.EN.DI.DO, *adj.*, included, comprised, understood.
COM.PRE.EN.SÃO, *s.f.*, comprehension, apprehension, understanding.
COM.PRE.EN.SI.BI.LI.DA.DE, *s.f.*, comprehensibility.
COM.PRE.EN.SÍ.VEL, *adj.*, comprehensible, understandable.
COM.PRE.EN.SI.VEL.MEN.TE, *adv.*, comprehensibly.
COM.PRE.EN.SI.VO, *adj.*, comprehensive, understanding.
COM.PRES.SA, *s.f.*, compress, dressing.
COM.PRES.SÃO, *s.f.*, compression, compressure.
COM.PRES.SI.VO, *adj.*, compressive.
COM.PRES.SOR, *s.m.*, compressor.

COM.PRI.DO, *s.m.*, length; *adj.*, long, lengthy.
COM.PRI.MEN.TO, *s.m.*, lenght, dimension, extent.
COM.PRI.MI.DO, *s.m.*, pill, tablet; *adj.*, compressed.
COM.PRI.MIR, *v.*, to compress, to squeeze, to condense, to compact.
COM.PRI.MÍ.VEL, *adj.*, compressible.
COM.PRO.BA.ÇÃO, *s.f.*, proof, corroboration.
COM.PRO.BA.TI.VO, *adj.*, corroborative, probative.
COM.PRO.BA.TÓ.RI.O, *adj.*, corroborative, probative.
COM.PRO.ME.TE.DOR, *adj.*, compromising.
COM.PRO.ME.TER, *v.*, to compromise, to promise, to pledge, to engage.
COM.PRO.ME.TI.MEN.TO, *s.m.*, compromising.
COM.PRO.MIS.SO, *s.m.*, liability, obligation, promise, pledge, engagement.
COM.PRO.VA.ÇÃO, *s.f.*, proof, evidence, corroboration, confirmation.
COM.PRO.VA.DOR, *s.m.*, authenticator, verifier; *adj.*, confirming, verifying.
COM.PRO.VAN.TE, *s.m.*, receipt, voucher; evidence; *adj.*, confirming, proving.
COM.PRO.VAR, *v.*, to prove, to confirm, to aver, to verify.
COM.PUL.SÃO, *s.f.*, compulsion, coercion.
COM.PUL.SI.VO, *adj.*, compulsive.
COM.PUL.SO.RI.A.MEN.TE, *adv.*, compulsorily.
COM.PUN.ÇÃO, *s.f.*, compunction.
COM.PUN.GIR, *v.*, to move, to touch; to cause remorse; *compungir-se*: to be sorry for.
COM.PUL.SÓ.RIO, *adj.*, compulsive, compulsory, forced.
COM.PU.TA.ÇÃO, *s.f.*, computation, calculation, representation.
COM.PU.TA.DOR, *s.m.*, computer, calculator.
COM.PU.TAR, *v.*, to compute, to calculate, to count, to estimate.
COM.PU.TÁ.VEL, *adj.*, computable; calculable.
CÔM.PU.TO, *s.m.*, computation, calculation.
CO.MUM, *adj.*, common, usual, regular, habitual, plain, ordinary.
CO.MU.MEN.TE, *adv.*, commonly, usually.
CO.MU.NA, *s.f.*, commune ; community; *pop.*, communist; *adj.*, *pop.*, communist.
CO.MU.NAL, *s. 2 gen.*, inhabitant of a commune ; *adj.*, communal.
CO.MUN.GAR, *v.*, to communicate, to commune; to receive the Lord's Supper.
CO.MU.NHÃO, *s.f.*, Communion, Eucharist, participation.
CO.MU.NI.CA.ÇÃO, *s.f.*, communication, message, connection.
CO.MU.NI.CA.DO, *s.m.*, communication.
CO.MU.NI.CA.DOR, *s.m.*, informant; communicator; *adj.*, communicating.
CO.MU.NI.CAR, *v.*, to communicate, to impart, to tell, to notify.
CO.MU.NI.CA.TI.VO, *adj.*, communicating.
CO.MU.NI.CÁ.VEL, *adj.*, communicable; communicative.
CO.MU.NI.DA.DE, *s.f.*, community, commoness, society.
CO.MU.NIS.MO, *s.m.*, communism.
CO.MU.NIS.TA, *s. 2 gen.*, communist.
CO.MU.NI.TÁ.RI.O, *adj.*, communitarian.
CO.MU.NI.ZAR, *v.*, to communize.
CO.MU.TA.ÇÃO, *s.f.*, commutation; substitution.
CO.MU.TAR, *v.*, to commutate; to commute; to substitute.

COMUTÁVEL ·· 140 ·· CONDENAR

CO.MU.TÁ.VEL, *adj.*, commutable.
CON.CA.TE.NA.ÇÃO, *s.f.*, concatenation; connection.
CON.CA.TE.NA.MEN.TO, *s.m.*, the same that *concatenação*.
CON.CA.VI.DA.DE, *s.f.*, concavity.
CÔN.CA.VO, *s.m.*, concavity; *adj.*, concave.
CON.CE.BER, *v.*, to conceive, to become pregnant, to think out, to ponder.
CON.CE.BI.MEN.TO, *s.m.*, conception, understanding.
CON.CE.BÍ.VEL, *adj.*, conceivable, possible.
CON.CE.DER, *v.*, to concede, to grant, to confer, to impact, to permit, to allow.
CON.CE.DI.DO, *adj.*, permitted, granted, conceded.
CON.CE.DÍ.VEL, *adj.*, permissible, allowable, grantable.
CON.CEI.ÇÃO, *s.f.*, *Rel.*, the dogma of the Immaculate Conception.
CON.CEI.TO, *s.m.*, idea, thought, notion, conception, concept.
CON.CEI.TU.A.DO, *adj.*, conceptualized, highly esteemed; *bem conceituado*: well thought of.
CON.CEI.TU.AL, *adj.*, conceptual.
CON.CEI.TU.AR, *v.*, to judge, to appraise, to evaluate, to repute as.
CON.CEN.TRA.ÇÃO, *s.f.*, concentration.
CON.CEN.TRAR, *v.*, to concentrate, to centralize.
CON.CEP.ÇÃO, *s.f.*, conception, generation, notion, ideation.
CON.CER.NÊN.CI.A, *s.f.*, relation, reference.
CON.CER.NEN.TE, *adj.*, relative to, with regard to, concerning.
CON.CER.NIR, *v.*, to concern, to refer.
CON.CER.TAR, *v.*, to put in order, to adjust, to regulate, to harmonize.
CON.CER.TIS.TA, *s. 2 gen.*, concert performer.
CON.CER.TO, *s.m.*, *Mús.*, concert.
CON.CES.SÃO, *s.f.*, concession, permission, assent.
CON.CES.SI.O.NÁ.RI.O, *s.m.*, concessionaire; *adj.*, concessionary.
CON.CES.SÍ.VEL, *adj.*, concessible, grantable.
CON.CES.SOR, *s.m.*, conceder, grantor.
CON.CHA, *s.f.*, shell, scoop.
CON.CHA.VAR, *v.*, to combine; to join; to collude.
CON.CHA.VO, *s.m.*, collusion, conspiracy, plot.
CON.CHE.A.DO, *adj.*, shell-shaped, shell-like.
CON.CHE.GAR, *v.*, to approach, to make comfortable.
CON.CHE.GO, *s.m.*, comfort, ease.
CON.CI.DA.DÃO, *s.m.*, fellow-citizen.
CON.CI.LI.A.ÇÃO, *s.f.*, conciliation, compromise, agreement.
CON.CI.LI.A.DOR, *s.m.*, conciliator; *adj.*, conciliating.
CON.CI.LI.AR, *v.*, to conciliate, to reconcile; *adj.*, conciliar (related or pertaining to a council).
CON.CI.LI.A.TÓ.RI.O, *adj.*, conciliatory.
CON.CI.LI.Á.VEL, *adj.*, reconcilable.
CON.CÍ.LIO, *s.m.*, council.
CON.CI.SA.MEN.TE, *adv.*, concisely.
CON.CI.SÃO, *s.f.*, briefness, brevity, conciseness.
CON.CI.SO, *adj.*, concise, brief; exact, precise.
CON.CI.TA.DOR, *s.m.*, instigator, inciter.
CON.CI.TA.ÇÃO, *s.f.*, tumult, disorder, incitation.
CON.CI.TAR, *v.*, to incite, to rouse; to instigate.
CON.CLA.MA.ÇÃO, *s.f.*, clamour, acclamation.
CON.CLA.MAR, *v.*, to shout, to yell, to clamour.
CON.CLA.VE, *s.m.*, *Rel.*, conclave (meeting of cardinals to elect a pope).
CON.CLU.DEN.TE, *adj.*, concluding; conclusive.

CON.CLU.Í.DO, *adj.*, concluded, finished.
CON.CLU.I.DOR, *s.m.*, concluder; *adj.*, concluding.
CON.CLU.IR, *v.*, to conclude, to end, to decide, to resolve.
CON.CLU.SÃO, *s.f.*, conclusion, closing, end, inference, decision.
CON.CLU.SI.VA.MEN.TE, *adv.*, conclusively.
CON.CLU.SI.VO, *adj.*, conclusive, illative, final.
CON.CO.MI.TAN.TE, *adj.*, concomitant.
CON.COR.DÂN.CIA, *s.f.*, concordance, agreement, consonance, conformity.
CON.COR.DÂN.CI.A, *s.f.*, concordance, agreement; *Gram.*, concord.
CON.COR.DAN.TE, *adj.*, concordant, agreeing, concurring.
CON.COR.DAR, *v.*, to agree, to concord, to assent, to acquiesce, to harmonize.
CON.COR.DA.TA, *s.f.*, concordat, agreement, contract.
CON.COR.DA.TÁ.RI.O, *s.m.*, *Com.*, businessman who enteres into composition with creditors.
CON.COR.DÁ.VEL, *adj.*, reconcilable.
CON.COR.DE, *adj.*, concordant.
CON.CÓR.DIA, *s.f.*, concordance, harmony, peace.
CON.COR.RÊN.CIA, *s.f.*, affluence, competition, emulation.
CON.COR.REN.TE, *s. 2 gen.*, *Com.*, competitor; contender, contestant, rival; *adj.*, competitive.
CON.COR.RER, *v.*, to compete with, to rival, to contest, to concur.
CON.CRE.ÇÃO, *s.f.*, concretion; *Geol.*, concretions.
CON.CRES.CÊN.CI.A, *s.f.*, *Biol.*, concrescence.
CON.CRES.CEN.TE, *adj.*, *Biol.*, concrescent.
CON.CRE.TA.GEM, *s.f.*, paving, covering with concrete.
CON.CRE.TA.MEN.TE, *adv.*, concretely.
CON.CRE.TAR, *v.*, to concrete.
CON.CRE.TIS.MO, *s.m.*, concretism; *Lit.*, concretism (theory or practice of concrete poetry).
CON.CRE.TIS.TA, *s. 2 gen.*, concretist (adherent of concretism).
CON.CRE.TI.ZA.ÇÃO, *s.f.*, accomplishment, achievement.
CON.CRE.TI.ZAR, *v.*, to materialize.
CON.CRE.TO, *s.m.*, concretion; *Arquit.*, concrete; *adj.*, concrete.
CON.CU.BI.NA, *s.f.*, concubine, mistress.
CON.CU.BI.NA.TO, *s.m.*, concubinage.
CON.CU.PIS.CÊN.CI.A, *s.f.*, concupiscence.
CON.CU.PIS.CEN.TE, *adj.*, concupiscent.
CON.CUR.SA.DO, *adj.*, having passed public service exams.
CON.CUR.SO, *s.m.*, concurrence, confluence, concourse, competition.
CON.CUS.SÃO, *s.f.*, concussion.
CON.CU.TIR, *v.*, to concuss, to shake, tremble.
CON.DA.DO, *s.m.*, county (authority of a count); earldom; shire.
CON.DAL, *adj.*, pertaining or belonging to a count.
CON.DÃO, *s.m.*, magic power, mental power.
CON.DE, *s.m.*, count, earl.
CON.DE.CO.RA.ÇÃO, *s.f.*, decoration, badge of honour.
CON.DE.CO.RA.DO, *s.m.*, decorated man; *adj.*, decorated.
CON.DE.CO.RAR, *v.*, to distinguish, ro honour.
CON.DE.NA.ÇÃO, *s.f.*, condemnation, conviction, censure, penalty.
CON.DE.NA.DO, *s.m.*, convict, felon; *adj.*, condemned, damned, reprobate.
CON.DE.NAR, *v.*, to condemn, to sentence, to declare, to

CONDENATÓRIO · · 141 · · CONFORME

censure.

CON.DE.NA.TÓ.RI.O, *adj.*, condemnatory.

CON.DE.NÁ.VEL, *adj.*, condemnable.

CON.DEN.SA.ÇÃO, *s.f.*, condensation.

CON.DEN.SA.DO, *adj.*, condensed; condensated.

CON.DEN.SAN.TE, *adj.*, condensing.

CON.DEN.SAR, *v.*, to condense, to compact, to concentrate.

CON.DEN.SÁ.VEL, *adj.*, condensable, condensible.

CON.DES.CEN.DÊN.CI.A, *s.f.*, condescendence, condescension.

CON.DES.CEN.DEN.TE, *adj.*, condescending, tolerant.

CON.DES.CEN.DER, *v.*, to condescend.

CON.DES.SA, *s.f.*, countess.

CON.DI.ÇÃO, *s.f.*, condition, circumstance, quality, character.

CON.DI.CI.O.NA.RIO, *adj.*, subject, conditioned.

CON.DI.CI.O.NAL, *adj.*, conditional, conditioned.

CON.DI.CI.O.NA.LI.DA.DE, *s.f.*, conditionality.

CON.DI.CI.O.NAL.MEN.TE, *adv.*, conditionally.

CON.DI.CI.O.NA.MEN.TO, *s.m., Fis.*, conditioning.

CON.DI.CI.O.NAR, *v.*, to stipulate, to condition.

CON.DIG.NI.DA.DE, *s.f.*, merit, value.

CON.DIG.NO, *adj.*, condign.

CON.DI.MEN.TAR, *v.*, to season, to spice.

CON.DI.MEN.TO, *s.m.*, seasoning, condiment, spice.

CON.DI.ZEN.TE, *adj.*, suitable.

CON.DI.ZER, *v.*, to suit, to fit well, to agree, to match.

CON.DO.ER, *v.*, to move to compassion.

CON.DO.Í.DO, *adj.*, pitiful, sympathetic.

CON.DO.LÊN.CIA, *s.f.*, condolence, sympathy, compassion.

CON.DO.LEN.TE, *adj.*, condolatory, condoling.

CON.DO.MÍ.NI.O, *s.m.*, joint ownership; condominium.

CON.DOR, *s.m., Zool.*, condor.

CON.DU.ÇÃO, *s.f.*, conduction, conveyance, transport.

CON.DU.Í.TE, *s.m., Eletr.*, conduit.

CON.DU.TA, *s.f.*, conduct, behaviour, conveyance, procedure, posture.

CON.DU.TI.BI.LI.DA.DE, *s.f., Fis.*, conductibility.

CON.DU.TÍ.VEL, *adj.*, conductible.

CON.DU.TI.VI.DA.DE, *s.f., Eletr.*, conductivity.

CON.DU.TI.VO, *adj., Fis.*, conductive.

CON.DU.TO, *s.m.*, duct, pipe, tube conduit.

CON.DU.TOR, *s.m.*, conductor.

CON.DU.ZIR, *v.*, to conduct, to lead, to direct, to drive.

CO.NE, *s.m., Geom.*, cone.

CO.NEC.TAR, *v.*, to connect, to tie in, to link.

CO.NEC.TI.VO, *s.m.*, the same that *conetivo*.

CÔ.NE.GO, *s.m., Rel.*, canon.

CO.NE.TI.VO, *s.m., Bot.*, connective; *Gram.*, connective; *adj.*, connective, conjunctive.

CO.NE.XÃO, *s.f.*, connection, link, relation.

CO.NE.XO, *adj.*, connected, linked.

CON.FA.BU.LA.ÇÃO, *s.f.*, confabulation.

CON.FA.BU.LAR, *v.*, to confabulate, chat, converse, talk.

CON.FEC.ÇÃO, *s.f.*, making, confection.

CON.FEC.CI.O.NAR, *v.*, to make, to fabricate, to manufacture.

CON.FE.DE.RA.ÇÃO, *s.f.*, confederation, alliance.

CON.FE.DE.RAR, *v.*, to confederate, to unite.

CON.FEI.TA.DO, *adj.*, trimmed, confected.

CON.FEI.TAR, *v.*, to confect, to cover with sugar.

CON.FEI.TA.RI.A, *s.f.*, candy shop.

CON.FEI.TEI.RO, *s.m.*, confectioner.

CON.FEI.TO, *s.m.*, sweet, candy, confection.

CON.FE.RÊN.CIA, *s.f.*, conference, convention, speech, talk.

CON.FE.REN.CI.AR, *v.*, to confer, to lecture; to parley; to have a conversation.

CON.FE.REN.CIS.TA, *s. 2 gen.*, lecturer.

CON.FE.REN.TE, *s. 2 gen.*, conferee; *adj.*, conferential.

CON.FE.RI.ÇÃO, *s.f.*, conferment.

CON.FE.RI.DOR, *s.m.*, conferrer.

CON.FE.RIR, *v.*, to confer, to compare, to check, to control.

CON.FE.RÍ.VEL, *adj.*, conferrable.

CON.FES.SA.DO, *s.m.*, confessant; *adj.*, confessed.

CON.FES.SAR, *v.*, to confess, to declare, to reveal, to admit, to acknowledge.

CON.FES.SÁ.VEL, *adj.*, confessable.

CON.FES.SI.O.NÁ.RI.O, *s.m., Rel.*, confessional.

CON.FE.TE, *s.m.*, confetti; *jogar ~*: to flatter.

CON.FI.A.BI.LI.DA.DE, *s.f.*, trustworthiness, reliability.

CON.FI.A.DO, *adj.*, confident, fiducial.

CON.FI.AN.ÇA, *s.f.*, confidence, trust, assurance, reliability.

CON.FI.AN.TE, *adj.*, confident.

CON.FI.AR, *v.*, to confide, to trust, to believe in, to rely on.

CON.FI.Á.VEL, *adj.*, trustworthy, reliable.

CON.FI.DÊN.CIA, *s.f.*, confidence, trust, secret.

CON.FI.DEN.CI.AL, *adj.*, confidential, classified, private.

CON.FI.DEN.CI.AR, *v.*, to confide, to reveal (secret).

CON.FI.DEN.CI.O.SO, *adj.*, confidential.

CON.FI.DEN.TE, *s. 2 gen.*, confidant, trusted person. *adj.*, confident, trustworthy.

CON.FI.GU.RA.ÇÃO, *s.f.*, configuration, form, aspect, figuration.

CON.FI.GU.RAR, *v.*, to configure.

CON.FIM, *s.m.*, confine; *adj.*, bordering, limiting.

CON.FI.NA.DO, *adj.*, confined.

CON.FI.NA.MEN.TO, *s.m.*, confinement.

CON.FI.NAR, *v.*, to limit; to confine, to bound, to border.

CON.FI.NÁ.VEL, *adj.*, confinable.

CON.FIR.MA.ÇÃO, *s.f.*, confirmation, affirmation, homologation.

CON.FIR.MA.DO, *adj.*, confirmed.

CON.FIR.MA.DOR, *s.m.*, confirmer; *adj.*, confirming.

CON.FIR.MAR, *v.*, to confirm, to affirm, to sustain, to validate.

CON.FIS.CA.ÇÃO, *s.f.*, confiscation, sequestration.

CON.FIS.CA.DO, *adj.*, confiscated.

CON.FIS.CAR, *v.*, to confiscate, to sequestrate.

CON.FIS.CÁ.VEL, *adj.*, confiscable.

CON.FIS.CO, *s.m.*, confiscation, requisition.

CON.FIS.SÃO, *s.f.*, confession; *Rel.*, act of confessing.

CON.FLA.GRA.ÇÃO, *s.f.*, conflagration; *fig.*, revolution, war.

CON.FLA.GRAR, *v.*, to conflagrate, to burn.

CON.FLI.TAN.TE, *adj.*, conflicting, clashing.

CON.FLI.TO, *s.m.*, conflict, disagreement, discord, skirmish.

CON.FLI.TU.O.SO, *adj.*, conflictive, conflicting.

CON.FLU.ÊN.CIA, *s.f.*, confluence.

CON.FLU.EN.TE, *s.m.*, confluent; *adj.*, confluent.

CON.FLU.IR, *v.*, to join, to flow together.

CON.FOR.MA.ÇÃO, *s.f.*, conformation, form, shape.

CON.FOR.MA.DO, *adj.*, resigned, patient.

CON.FOR.MAR, *v.*, to form, to adapt, to conform, to accommodate.

CON.FOR.ME, *adj., s. 2 gen.*, conform, accordant, correspondent; *conj.*, how, according to, as per.

CONFORMIDADE ·· 142 ·· CONSANGUINIDADE

CON.FOR.MI.DA.DE, *s.f.*, conformity, accordance, agreement, convenience.
CON.FOR.MIS.MO, *s.m.*, conformism.
CON.FOR.MIS.TA, *s. 2 gen.*, conformist; *adj.*, conformist, conformistical.
CON.FOR.TA.DO, *adj.*, comforted; strengthened.
CON.FOR.TA.DOR, *s.m.*, comforter, consoler; *adj.*, comforting.
CON.FOR.TAR, *v.*, to comfort, to console, to stimulate.
CON.FOR.TÁ.VEL, *adj.*, comfortable.
CON.FOR.TO, *s.m.*, comfort, well-being, ease.
CON.FRA.DE, *s.m.*, comrade, confrere, fellow.
CON.FRAN.GER, *v.*, to torment, to distress, to oppress, to torture.
CON.FRAN.GI.DO, *adj.*, tormented, distressed, afflicted.
CON.FRA.RI.A, *s.f.*, brotherhood, fraternity.
CON.FRA.TER.NI.ZA.ÇÃO, *s.f.*, confraternization.
CON.FRA.TER.NI.ZAR, *v.*, to fraternize with, to forgather.
CON.FREI, *s.m., Bot.*, comfrey.
CON.FRON.TA.ÇÃO, *s.f.*, confrontation.
CON.FRON.TA.DO, *adj.*, compared, confronted.
CON.FRON.TAR, *v.*, to confront, to compare, to collate.
CON.FRON.TO, *s.m.*, confrontation, comparison.
CON.FUN.DI.DO, *adj.*, confused, concerned.
CON.FUN.DIR, *v.*, to confound, to perplex, to mistake, to humble.
CON.FUN.DÍ.VEL, *adj.*, confusable.
CON.FU.SÃO, *s.f.*, confusion, uproar, tumult, perplexity.
CON.FU.SO, *adj.*, confused, disorderly, woolly.
CON.GA, *s.f.*, conga (dance music).
CON.GE.LA.DO, *s.m.*, frozen; *adj.*, frozen, icy.
CON.GE.LA.DOR, *s.m.*, freezer.
CON.GE.LA.MEN.TO, *s.m.*, frozenness, congelation, congealment, freezing of prices.
CON.GE.LÁ.VEL, *adj.*, freezable, congelable.
CON.GE.LAR, *v.*, to freeze, to ice, to ice up.
CON.GÊ.NE.RE, *s.m.*, congener, congenerousness; *adj.*, congenerous.
CON.GÊ.NI.TO, *adj.*, congenital.
CON.GES.TÃO, *s.f.*, congestion.
CON.GES.TI.O.NA.DO, *adj.*, congested, crowded; apopletic.
CON.GES.TI.O.NA.MEN.TO, *s.m.*, congestion; traffic jam.
CON.GES.TI.O.NAN.TE, *adj.*, congestive.
CON.GES.TI.O.NAR, *v.*, to congest, to crowd.
CON.GLO.ME.RA.ÇÃO, *s.f.*, conglomeration.
CON.GLO.ME.RA.DO, *s.m.*, conglomerate; *adj.*, cnglomerate.
CON.GLO.ME.RAR, *v.*, to conglomerate, to accumulate.
CON.GO, *s.*, Congo.
CON.GO.LÊS, *s., adj.*, congolese.
CON.GRA.ÇA.DOR, *s.m.*, conciliator, pacifier; *adj.*, conciliatory.
CON.GRA.ÇA.MEN.TO, *s.m.*, act of reconciling, harmonizing.
CON.GRA.ÇAR, *v.*, to reconcile, to harmonize.
CON.GRA.TU.LA.ÇÃO, *s.f.*, congratulation.
CON.GRA.TU.LAR, *v.*, to congratulate; *congratular-se*: to congratulate oneself.
CON.GRE.GA.ÇÃO, *s.f.*, congregation, reunion, assembly, fraternity.
CON.GRE.GA.DO, *s.m.*, member of a congregation; *adj.*, congregated.
CON.GRE.GAR, *v.*, to congregate, to assemble, to convene.
CON.GRES.SI.O.NAL, *adj.*, congressional.
CON.GRES.SIS.TA, *s. 2 gen.*, member of Congress,

Congressman; *adj.*, congressional.
CON.GRES.SO, *s.m.*, congress, conference, session.
CON.GRU.ÊN.CI.A, *s.f.*, congruence, congruency.
CON.GRU.EN.TE, *adj.*, congruent.
CO.NHA.QUE, *s.m.*, cognac, brandy.
CO.NHE.CE.DOR, *s.m.*, connoisseur, expert, specialist.
CO.NHE.CER, *v.*, to know, to perceive, to be familiar with, to judge, to be aware of.
CO.NHE.CI.DO, *adj.*, known, public, famous.
CO.NHE.CI.MEN.TO, *s.m.*, knowledge, cognizance, familiarity, information, understanding.
CO.NHE.CÍ.VEL, *adj.*, knowable, cognizable.
CO.NI.CI.DA.DE, *s.f.*, conicity.
CÔ.NI.CO, *adj.*, conical, conic.
CO.NÍ.FE.RA, *s.f., Bot.*, conifer.
CO.NÍ.FE.RO, *adj., Bot.*, coniferous.
CO.NI.FOR.ME, *adj.*, coniform, conic, conoid.
CO.NI.VÊN.CIA, *s.f.*, connivance, connivancy.
CO.NI.VEN.TE, *adj.*, collusive, conniving, connivent.
CON.JE.TU.RA, CON.JEC.TU.RA *s.f.*, conjecture, supposition, guess.
CON.JE.TU.RA.DOR, CON.JEC.TU.RA.DOR, *s.m.*, conjecturer; *adj.*, conjecturing.
CON.JE.TU.RAR, CON.JEC.TU.RAR, *v.*, to conjecture.
CON.JU.GA.ÇÃO, *s.f.*, conjugation, conjunction, union.
CON.JU.GA.DO, *adj.*, conjugate, conjoint, combined.
CON.JU.GAL, *adj., s. 2 gen.*, conjugal, matrimonial, married.
CON.JU.GAR, *v.*, to conjugate, to unite, to coordinate.
CÔN.JU.GE, *s. 2 gen.*, consort, spouse, partner.
CON.JU.MI.NÂN.CI.A, *s.f.*, combination.
CON.JU.MI.NAR, *v., Bras., pop.*, to combine.
CON.JUN.ÇÃO, *s.f.*, conjunction, union.
CON.JUN.TA.MEN.TE, *adv.*, conjunctly.
CON.JUN.TI.VI.TE, *s.f., Med.*, conjunctivitis.
CON.JUN.TI.VO, *s.m.*, conjunctive, subjunctive; *adj.*, conjunctive, connective.
CON.JUN.TO, *s.m.*, whole, set, kit, team, band; *adj.*, conjunct, united, concurrent.
CON.JUN.TU.RA, *s.f.*, conjuncture; happening, opportunity.
CON.JUN.TU.RAL, *adj.*, pertaining to conjuncture.
CON.JU.RA.ÇÃO, *s.f.*, conjuration, conspiracy, conspiration.
CON.JU.RA.DO, *s.m.*, conspirator; *adj.*, conspiring, plotting.
CON.JU.RAR, *v.*, to conjure, to conspire, to plot.
CON.JU.RO, *s.m.*, conjuration, magic, sorcery.
CON.LUI.AR, *v.*, to collude, to plot.
CON.LUI.O, *s.m.*, collusion, collusiveness, plot.
CO.NOS.CO, *pron.*, with us, to us, for us, together with us.
CO.NO.TA.ÇÃO, *s.f.*, connotation.
CO.NO.TA.TI.VO, *adj.*, connotative.
CON.QUAN.TO, *conj.*, although, though.
CON.QUIS.TA, *s.f.*, conquest, acquisition.
CON.QUIS.TA.DOR, *s.m.*, conqueror.
CON.QUIS.TAR, *v.*, to conquer, to defeat, to acquire, to win.
CON.QUIS.TÁ.VEL, *adj.*, conquerable.
CON.SA.GRA.ÇÃO, *s.f.*, consecration, dedication, devotion.
CON.SA.GRA.DO, *adj.*, consecrated, sanctified, celebrated.
CON.SA.GRA.DOR, *s.m.*, consecrator; *adj.*, consecratory.
CON.SA.GRAR, *v.*, to consecrate, to sanctify, to devote.
CON.SAN.GUÍ.NE.O, *s.m.*, kin; *adj.*, consanguine, consanguineous, akin.
CON.SAN.GUI.NI.DA.DE, *s.f.*, consanguinity.

CONSCIÊNCIA · 143 · CONSTRANGER

CONS.CI.ÊN.CIA, *s.f.*, conscience, conscientiousness, scruple.

CONS.CI.EN.CI.O.SO, *adj.*, conscientious, scrupulous.

CONS.CI.EN.TE, *s.m.*, conscious; *adj.*, conscious, conscientious, aware, knowing.

CONS.CI.EN.TE.MEN.TE, *adv.*, consciously.

CONS.CI.EN.TI.ZA.ÇÃO, *s.f.*, act of acquiring knowledge of, awareness.

CONS.CI.EN.TI.ZAR, *v.*, to acquire knowledge of, *conscientizar-se*: to become aware.

CÔNS.CI.O, *adj.*, conscious, cognizant, aware.

CON.SE.CU.ÇÃO, *s.f.*, consecution, success, achievement.

CON.SE.CU.TI.VO, *adj.*, consecutive.

CON.SE.GUIN.TE, *adj.*, consecutive, consequent.

CON.SE.GUIR, *v.*, to obtain, to achieve, to get, to succeed.

CON.SE.LHEI.RO, *s.m.*, counselor, counsel, adviser, council-man; *adj.*, counseling, advising.

CON.SE.LHO, *s.m.*, counsel, council, synod; advice, recommendation.

CON.SEN.SO, *s.m.*, consensus, agreement, consent, accord.

CON.SEN.SU.AL, *adj.*, consensual.

CON.SEN.TÂ.NE.O, *adj.*, consentaneous.

CON.SEN.TI.DOR, *s.m.*, assenter, assentor.

CON.SEN.TI.MEN.TO, *s.m.*, consent, approval, acquiescence, agreement.

CON.SEN.TIR, *v.*, to consent, to approve, to permit.

CON.SE.QUÊN.CIA, *s.f.*, consequence, result, sequel.

CON.SE.QUEN.TE, *adj.*, *Mat.*, consequent; *adj.*, consequent, consequential.

CON.SE.QUEN.TE.MEN.TE, *adv.*, consequently.

CON.SER.TA.DO, *adj.*, repaired, fixed, mended.

CON.SER.TA.DOR, *s.m.*, repairer, repairman, fixer.

CON.SER.TAR, *v.*, to repair, to mend, to adjust.

CON.SER.TÁ.VEL, *adj.*, repairable.

CON.SER.TO, *s.m.*, repair, mending, restoration.

CON.SER.VA, *s.f.*, conserve, comfit, preserve.

CON.SER.VA.ÇÃO, *s.f.*, conservation, maintenance.

CON.SER.VA.DO, *adj.*, preserved, kept.

CON.SER.VA.DOR, *s.m.*, conserver, preserver; curator, conservative.

CON.SER.VAR, *v.*, to maintain, to conserve, to sustain, to keep, to guard.

CON.SER.VA.TI.VO, *adj.*, conservative.

CON.SER.VA.TÓ.RI.O, *s.m.*, conservatory.

CON.SER.VÁ.VEL, *adj.*, conservable, preservable.

CON.SI.DE.RA.ÇÃO, *s.f.*, consideration, appreciation, reflection, respect, regard.

CON.SI.DE.RA.DO, *adj.*, considerate, considered.

CON.SI.DE.RAN.DO, *s.m.*, reason, motive, fundamental consideration; considering.

CON.SI.DE.RAR, *v.*, to consider, to ponder, to esteem, to regard.

CON.SI.DE.RÁ.VEL, *adj.*, considerable.

CON.SI.DE.RA.VEL.MEN.TE, *adv.*, considerably.

CON.SIG.NA.ÇÃO, *s.f.*, consignation, deposit, trust.

CON.SIG.NA.DOR, *s.m.*, consigner; *adj.*, consigning.

CON.SIG.NAN.TE, *s. 2 gen.*, the same that *consignador*.

CON.SIG.NAR, *v.*, to consign, to seal.

CON.SIG.NÁ.VEL, *adj.*, consignable.

CON.SI.GO, *pron.*, with him, with himself.

CON.SIS.TÊN.CIA, *s.f.*, consistence, consistency.

CON.SIS.TEN.TE, *adj.*, consistent, dense, solid.

CON.SIS.TIR, *v.*, to consist in, to rest in, to comprise.

CON.SO.AN.TE, *s.f.*, consonant; *adj.*, consonant, consonantal; *s.m.*, rhyme; *prep.*, conformable, according to.

CON.SO.LAR, *v.*, to comfort, to console, to solace, to relieve.

CON.SO.LA.ÇÃO, *s.f.*, consolation.

CON.SO.LA.DOR, *s.m.*, consoler, comforter.

CON.SO.LAR, *v.*, to console, to comfort, to solace.

CON.SO.LÁ.VEL, *adj.*, consolable.

CON.SO.LE, *s.m.*, *Arquit.*, console; corbel; console table.

CON.SO.LI.DA.ÇÃO, *s.f.*, consolidation, solidification, combination.

CON.SO.LI.DA.DO, *s.m.*, consolidated; *adj.*, consolidated.

CON.SO.LI.DAR, *v.*, to consolidate, to solidify, to become hard.

CON.SO.LO, *s.m.*, consolation, solace, comfort; console.

CON.SO.MÊ, *s.m.*, *Fr.*, *Cul.*, *consommé*.

CON.SO.NÂN.CIA, *s.f.*, consonance, consonancy, harmony.

CON.SO.NAN.TAL, *adj.*, consonant, consonantal.

CON.SO.NAN.TE, *adj.*, consonant.

CON.SOR.CI.AR, *v.*, to associate, to consort.

CON.SÓR.CIO, *s.m.*, consortium, partnership.

CON.SOR.TE, *s. 2 gen.*, spouse, husband, wife, partner.

CONS.PI.CU.I.DA.DE, *s.f.*, conspicuity, conspicuousness.

CONS.PÍ.CUO, *adj.*, conspicuous, prominent, illustrous.

CONS.PI.RA.ÇÃO, *s.f.*, conspiracy, plot, conspiration.

CONS.PI.RA.DOR, *s.m.*, conspirator, complotter.

CONS.PI.RAR, *v.*, to conspire, to complot, to collude, to machinate.

CONS.PI.RA.TÓ.RI.O, *adj.*, conspiratorial.

CONS.PUR.CA.ÇÃO, *s.f.*, conspurcation, defilement.

CONS.PUR.CAR, *v.*, to conspurcate, to defile.

CONS.TÂN.CIA, *s.f.*, constancy, fidelity, firmness, stability.

CONS.TAN.TE, *adj.*, constant, persistent, invariable, stable.

CONS.TAN.TE.MEN.TE, *adv.*, constantly, ever.

CONS.TAR, *v.*, to consist of, to be evident.

CONS.TA.TA.ÇÃO, *s.f.*, verification, confirmation.

CONS.TA.TAR, *v.*, to testify, to find out, to verify.

CONS.TE.LA.ÇÃO, *s.f.*, constellation.

CONS.TER.NA.ÇÃO, *s.f.*, consternation.

CONS.TER.NA.DO, *adj.*, consternated, depressed, aghast.

CONS.TER.NAR, *v.*, to dismay, to confound.

CONS.TI.PA.ÇÃO, *s.f.*, constipation.

CONS.TI.PA.DO, *adj.*, constipated.

CONS.TI.PAR, *v.*, to constipate.

CONS.TI.TU.CI.O.NAL, *adj.*, constitutional.

CONS.TI.TU.CI.O.NA.LI.DA.DE, *s.f.*, constitutionality.

CONS.TI.TU.CI.O.NA.LIS.MO, *s.m.*, constitutionalism.

CONS.TI.TU.CI.O.NA.LIS.TA, *s. 2 gen.*, constitutionalist; *adj.*, constitutional.

CONS.TI.TU.I.ÇÃO, *s.f.*, constitution, formation, organization.

CONS.TI.TU.Í.DO, *adj.*, constituted, formed, composed.

CONS.TI.TU.IN.TE, *s. 2 gen.*, voter, constituent.

CONS.TI.TU.IR, *v.*, to constitute, to form, to put together.

CONS.TI.TU.TI.VO, *adj.*, constitutive.

CONS.TRAN.GE.DOR, *adj.*, constraining, compelling.

CONS.TRAN.GI.DO, *adj.*, constrained, uncomfortable.

CONS.TRAN.GI.MEN.TO, *s.m.*, constraint, compulsion, embarrassment, coercion.

CONS.TRI.ÇÃO, *s.f.*, constriction, contraction.

CONS.TRAN.GER, *v.*, to constrain, to urge, to impel, to oblige.

CONSTRINGIR ·· 144 ·· CONTRA

CONS.TRIN.GIR, *v.*, to constringe, to compress.
CONS.TRI.TO, *adj.*, narrow, constricted, constrained.
CONS.TRU.ÇÃO, *s.f.*, construction, building, edification, structure.
CONS.TRU.Í.DO, *adj.*, constructed, built.
CONS.TRU.IR, *v.*, to construct, to build, to form.
CONS.TRU.TI.VO, *adj.*, constructive.
CONS.TRU.TOR, *s.m.*, constructor, builder.
CONS.TRU.TO.RA, *s.f.*, construction company.
CON.SUBS.TAN.CI.A.ÇÃO, *s.f.*, *Teol.*, consubstantiation.
CON.SUBS.TAN.CI.AR, *v.*, to consubstantiate.
ON.SU.E.TU.DI.NÁ.RI.O, *adj.*, consuetudinary.
CÔN.SUL, *s.m.*, consul.
CON.SU.LA.DO, *s.m.*, consulate, consulship.
CON.SU.LAR, *adj.*, consular.
CON.SUL.TA, *s.f.*, consultation, consult; consulting; appointment; query (search).
CON.SUL.TAR, *v.*, to consult, to refer, to seek information.
CON.SUL.TI.VO, *adj.*, consultive, consultory.
CON.SUL.TOR, *s.m.*, consultant, examiner.
CON.SUL.TO.RI.A, *s.f.*, consultancy.
CON.SUL.TÓ.RIO, *s.m.*, doctor's office.
CON.SU.MA.ÇÃO, *s.f.*, consummation, conclusion, completion.
CON.SU.MA.DO, *adj.*, consummate, accomplished.
CON.SU.MAR, *v.*, to terminate, to finish, to consummate, to complete.
CON.SU.MI.DO, *adj.*, consumed, wasted, worried.
CON.SU.MI.DOR, *s.m.*, consumer; *adj.*, consuming, wasting.
CON.SU.MIR, *v.*, to consume, to eat up, to spend, to use, to destroy, to exhaust.
CON.SU.MIS.MO, *s.m.*, consumerism.
CON.SU.MIS.TA, *s. 2 gen.*, consumerist.
CON.SU.MÍ.VEL, *adj.*, consumable, expendable.
CON.SU.MO, *s.m.*, consumption, use, absorption.
CON.SÚ.TIL, *adj.*, having a seam.
CON.TA, *s.f.*, account, count, calculation, sum, total, bill, note.
CON.TÁ.BIL, *adj.*, accountant, bookkeeping.
CON.TA.BI.LI.DA.DE, *s.f.*, accountancy.
CON.TA.BI.LIS.TA, *s. 2 gen.*, accountant.
CON.TA.BI.LI.ZA.ÇÃO, *s.f.*, *Com.*, bookkeeping, accounting, accountancy.
CON.TA.BI.LI.ZA.DO, *adj.*, booked, registered.
CON.TA.BI.LI.ZAR, *v.*, to do accounting, to do bookkeeping.
CON.TA-COR.REN.TE, *s.m.*, *Com.*, checking account.
CON.TA.DO, *adj.*, counted, calculated, computed.
CON.TA.DOR, *s.m.*, bookkeeper, accountant.
CON.TA.GI.AR, *v.*, to infect, to contaminate, to corrupt.
CON.TA.GEM, *s.f.*, count, reckoning; score.
CON.TA.GI.AN.TE, *adj.*, contagious.
CON.TA.GI.AR, *v.*, to infect, to contaminate, to transmit.
CON.TÁ.GIO, *s.m.*, infection, contagion, pollution.
CON.TA.GI.O.SO, *adj.*, contagious.
CON.TA-GO.TAS, *s.m.*, dropper, filler.
CON.TA.MI.NA.ÇÃO, *s.f.*, contamination, infection, contagion.
CON.TA.MI.NA.DO, *adj.*, contaminated, infected.
CON.TA.MI.NAR, *v.*, to infect, to contaminate, to corrupt.
CON.TA.MI.NÁ.VEL, *adj.*, contaminable.
CON.TAN.TO QUE, *conj.*, as long as, if, as.
CON.TAR, *v.*, to count, to calculate, to recount, to number, to tell, to rely.

CON.TA.TAR, CON.TAC.TAR, *v.*, to contact.
CON.TA.TO, CON.TAC.TO, *s.m.*, contact, proximity, touch.
CON.TÁ.VEL, *adj.*, countable.
CON.TÊI.NER, *s.m.*, container.
CON.TEM.PLA.ÇÃO, *s.f.*, contemplation, meditation.
CON.TEM.PLAR, *v.*, to contemplate, to regard, to ponder, to admire, to observe.
CON.TEM.PLA.TI.VO, *s.m.*, contemplator; *adj.*, contemplative.
CON.TEM.PO.RA.NEI.DA.DE, *s.f.*, contemporaneity.
CON.TEM.PO.RÂ.NEO, *adj.*, contemporaneous.
CON.TEM.PO.RI.ZA.ÇÃO, *s.f.*, temporization.
CON.TEM.PO.RI.ZAR, *v.*, to temporize.
CON.TEN.ÇÃO, *s.f.*, contention, quarrel, dispute.
CON.TEN.CI.O.SO, *adj.*, contentious.
CON.TEN.DA, *s.f.*, contention, quarrel.
CON.TEN.DER, *v.*, to contend, to fight.
CON.TEN.SÃO, *s.f.*, contention, endeavour.
CON.TEN.TA.MEN.TO, *s.m.*, contentment, contentedness, satisfaction.
CON.TEN.TAR, *v.*, to content, to satisfy, to suffice, to please.
CON.TEN.TÁ.VEL, *adj.*, contentable.
CON.TEN.TE, *adj.*, content, contented.
CON.TER, *v.*, to contain, to enclose, to comprise, to refrain.
CON.TER.RÂ.NE.O, *s.m.*, fellow, citizen, countryman.
CON.TES.TA.ÇÃO, *s.f.*, contestation, plea, defense, disputation.
CON.TES.TA.DO, *adj.*, refuted, contradicted.
CON.TES.TA.DOR, *s.m.*, contester, refuter; *adj.*, refuting.
CON.TES.TAR, *v.*, to contest, to refute, to object, to argue.
CON.TES.TÁ.VEL, *adj.*, contestable.
CON.TES.TA.VEL.MEN.TE, *adv.*, contestably.
CON.TE.Ú.DO, *s.m.*, content, matter contained.
CON.TEX.TO, *s.m.*, context, structure, composition.
CON.TI.DO, *adj.*, contained, restrained.
CON.TI.GO, *pron.*, with you, in your company.
CON.TÍ.GUO, *adj.*, contiguous.
CON.TI.NÊN.CI.A, *s.f.*, continence, continency; *Mil.*, honours; salute.
CON.TI.NEN.TE, *s.m.*, continent, mainland, container; *adj.*, including, continental.
CON.TIN.GÊN.CI.A, *s.f.*, contingency, contingence.
CON.TIN.GEN.TE, *s.m.*, contingent; *adj.*, contingent.
CON.TI.NU.A.ÇÃO, *s.f.*, continuation, continuance, continuity, sequel, sequence.
CON.TI.NU.A.DA.MEN.TE, *adv.*, continuedly.
CON.TI.NU.A.DO, *adj.*, continued, prolonged.
CON.TI.NU.A.MEN.TE, *adv.*, continuously.
CON.TI.NU.AR, *v.*, to continue, to pursue, to stay, to extend.
CON.TI.NU.I.DA.DE, *s.f.*, continuity.
CON.TÍ.NUO, *s.m.*, servant, attendant; *adj.*, continued, continuous.
CON.TIS.TA, *s. 2 gen.*, short story writer.
CON.TO, *s.m.*, narrative, short story, tale, fable, invention.
CON.TOR.ÇÃO, *s.f.*, contortion.
CON.TOR.CER, *v.*, to contort, to distort, to twist.
CON.TOR.CI.DO, *adj.*, contorted, twisted.
CON.TOR.CI.O.NIS.TA, *s. 2 gen.*, contortionist.
CON.TOR.NAR, *v.*, to profile, to turn round.
CON.TOR.NÁ.VEL, *adj.*, surmountable.
CON.TOR.NO, *s.m.*, outline, profile.
CON.TRA, *prep.*, against, contrary to, versus; *adv.*, adversely,

CONTRA-ARGUMENTO · 145 · CONVERSADOR

contra.
CON.TRA-AR.GU.MEN.TO, *s.m.*, counter-argument.
CON.TRA-A.TA.CAR, *v.*, to counter-attack.
CON.TRA-A.TA.QUE, *s.m., Esp., Mil.*, counter-attack.
CON.TRA.BAI.XO, *s.m., Mús.*, contrabass, double-bass.
CON.TRA.BA.LAN.ÇAR, *v.*, to counterbalance.
CON.TRA.BAN.DE.AR, *v.*, to contraband, to smuggle.
CON.TRA.BAN.DIS.TA, *s. 2 gen.*, contrabandist, smuggler.
CON.TRA.BAN.DO, *s.m.*, smuggling, smugled goods.
CON.TRA.ÇÃO, *s.f.*, contraction, shrinking, convulsion.
CON.TRA.CA.PA, *s.f.*, inside cover.
CON.TRA.CE.NAR, *v., Teat.*, to perform, to act.
CON.TRA.CEP.ÇÃO, *s.f.*, contraception.
CON.TRA.CEP.TI.VO, *s.m.*, contraceptive.
CON.TRA.CHE.QUE, *s.m.*, payslip.
CON.TRA.COR.REN.TE, *s.f.*, countercurrent.
CON.TRA.CUL.TU.RA, *s.f.*, counterculture.
CON.TRA.DI.ÇÃO, *s.f.*, contradiction, incoherence, variance, opposition.
CON.TRA.DI.TÓ.RIO, *s.m.*, contradictory, contradictive, discordant, incoherent.
CON.TRA.DI.ZER, *v.*, to contradict, to contest, to deny.
CON.TRA.FEI.TO, *adj.*, constrained, counterfeit.
CON.TRA.FI.LÉ, *s.m., Cul.*, sirloin steak, rump steak.
CON.TRA.GOL.PE, *s.m.*, counterblow, counterplot.
CON.TRA.GOS.TO, *s.m.*, dislike, aversion.
CON.TRA.Í.DO, *adj.*, contracted.
CON.TRA.IN.DI.CA.ÇÃO, *s.f., Med.*, contraindication.
CON.TRA.IN.DI.CAR, *v., Med.*, to contraindicate.
CON.TRA.IR, *v.*, to contract, to tighten, to compress, to reduce.
CON.TRAL.TO, *s.m., Mús.*, contralto.
CON.TRA.MÃO, *s.m.*, contraflow lane; *adj.*, out of a one's way; *adv.*, out of the way.
CON.TRA.MES.TRE, *s.m.*, foreman, foremanship; *Náut.*, first mate.
CON.TRA.O.FEN.SI.VA, *s.f., Mil.*, counteroffensive.
CON.TRA.O.FER.TA, *s.f.*, counterproposal, counteroffer.
CON.TRA.PAR.TI.DA, *s.f.*, counterpart.
CON.TRA.PE.SO, *s.m.*, counterbalance.
CON.TRA.PON.TO, *s.m., Mús.*, counterpoint.
CON.TRA.POR, *v.*, to put against, to put in front of.
CON.TRA.PRO.DU.CEN.TE, *adj., s. 2 gen.*, counterproductive.
CON.TRA.PRO.VA, *s.f., Jur.*, counterevidence; counter-proof.
CON.TRA.PRO.VAR, *v.*, to counterprove.
CON.TRA.RI.A.DO, *adj.*, vexed, annoyed, upset.
CON.TRA.RI.A.MEN.TE, *adv.*, oppositely, adversely.
CON.TRA.RI.AR, *v.*, to counter, to oppose, to contest, to refute, to antagonize.
CON.TRA.RI.E.DA.DE, *s.f.*, opposition, resistance, contrariety.
CON.TRÁ.RIO, *adj.*, opposed, opponent, contrary, adverse.
CON.TRAR.RE.FOR.MA, *s.f.*, counter-reformation; *Hist., Rel.*, Counter-Reformation.
CON.TRAR.RE.GRA, *s.m., Teat.*, stage manager.
CON.TRAR.RE.VO.LU.ÇÃO, *s.f.*, counter-revolution.
CON.TRAS.SEN.SO, *s.m.*, nonsense, absurdity.
CON.TRAS.TAN.TE, *adj.*, contrasting.
CON.TRAS.TAR, *v.*, to contrast, to fight against, to defy, to oppose.
CON.TRAS.TE, *s.m.*, contrast, opposition, assay.
CON.TRA.TA.ÇÃO, *s.f.*, contract, recruitment, agreement.

CON.TRA.TA.DO, *s.m.*, a person under contract; *adj.*, contracted.
CON.TRA.TA.DOR, *s.m.*, contractor; *adj.*, contracting.
CON.TRA.TAN.TE, *s. 2 gen.*, contractor, contracting; *adj.*, contracting.
CON.TRA.TAR, *v.*, to contract, to agree upon, to hire, to trade, to ideal.
CON.TRA.TÁ.VEL, *adj.*, contractable.
CON.TRA.TEM.PO, *s.m.*, mischance, mishap, accident.
CON.TRA.TO, *s.m.*, contract, covenant, agreement, bargain.
CON.TRA.VEN.ÇÃO, *s.f.*, contravention, infraction.
CON.TRA.VEN.TOR, *s.m.*, contravener, transgressor; *adj.*, contravening, transgressing.
CON.TRI.BUI.ÇÃO, *s.f.*, contribution, quota, tribute, tax.
CON.TRI.BU.IN.TE, *s. 2 gen.*, contributor, taxpayer; *adj.*, contributory, tributary.
CON.TRI.BU.IR, *v.*, to contribute, to pay taxes, to donate, to concur.
CON.TRI.BU.TI.VO, *adj.*, contributive.
CON.TRI.ÇÃO, *s.f., Rel.*, contrition.
CON.TRO.LA.DO, *adj.*, controlled, dispassionate.
CON.TRO.LA.DOR, *s.m.*, controller.
CON.TRO.LAR, *v.*, to control, to supervise, to dominate.
CON.TRO.LÁ.VEL, *adj.*, controllable.
CON.TRO.LE, *s.m.*, control, controlment, regulation, direction.
CON.TRO.VÉR.SIA, *s.f.*, controversy, contest, contestation, dispute.
CON.TRO.VER.SO, *adj.*, controversial.
CON.TU.DO, *conj.*, however, yet, although.
CON.TU.MÁ.CI.A, *s.f.*, contumacy, obstinacy.
CON.TU.MAZ, *adj.*, contumacious, disobedient.
CON.TUN.DEN.TE, *adj.*, bruising. incisive.
CON.TUN.DIR, *v.*, to contuse, to bruise, to injure.
CON.TUR.BA.ÇÃO, *s.f.*, agitation, commotion, tumult.
CON.TUR.BAR, *v.*, to disturb.
CON.TU.SÃO, *s.f.*, contusion, bruise.
CO.NÚ.BI.O, *s.m.*, marriage, matrimony; *fig.*, union, alliance.
CON.VA.LES.CEN.ÇA, *s.f.*, convalescence.
CON.VA.LES.CEN.TE, *s. 2 gen., adj.*, convalescent.
CON.VA.LES.CER, *v.*, to convalesce, to recover, to fortify.
CON.VEC.ÇÃO, *s.f., Fís.*, convection.
CON.VEN.ÇÃO, *s.f.*, convention, agreement, pact.
CON.VEN.CER, *v.*, to convince, to persuade, to overcome.
CON.VEN.CI.DO, *adj.*, convinced, satisfied, assured.
CON.VEN.CI.MEN.TO, *s.m.*, argument, persuasion; satisfaction.
CON.VEN.CI.O.NAL, *s. 2 gen.*, conventional.
CON.VEN.CI.O.NA.LIS.MO, *s.m.*, conventionalism.
CON.VEN.CI.O.NA.LIS.TA, *s. 2 gen.*, conventionalist.
CON.VEN.CI.O.NAR, *v.*, to stipulate, to contract, to establish, to arbitrate.
CON.VE.NI.ÊN.CIA, *s.f.*, convenience, fittingness.
CON.VE.NI.EN.TE, *adj.*, convenient, suitable, fitting.
CON.VÊ.NIO, *s.m.*, convention, covenant, accord.
CON.VEN.TO, *s.m.*, convent, cloister.
CON.VER.GÊN.CI.A, *s.f.*, convergence, convergency.
CON.VER.GEN.TE, *adj.*, convergent.
CON.VER.GIR, *v.*, to converge, to approach.
CON.VER.SA, *s.f.*, conversation, talk, talking, speech.
CON.VER.SA.ÇÃO, *s.f.*, conversation, colloquy.
CON.VER.SA.DOR, *s.m.*, converser, proser.

CONVERSÃO · 146 · CORISTA

CON.VER.SÃO, *s.f.*, convertion, commutation, change.
CON.VER.SAR, *v.*, to talk, to converse, to discourse.
CON.VER.SI.BI.LI.DA.DE, *s.f.*, convertibility.
CON.VER.SÍ.VEL, *s.m.*, convertible.
CON.VER.SI.VO, *adj.*, conversive.
CON.VER.SOR, *s.m.*, converter.
CON.VER.TER, *v.*, to convert, to transform, to invert, to reduce, to change.
CON.VER.TI.DO, *s.m.*, proselyte; *adj.*, converted.
CON.VER.TI.MEN.TO, *s.m.*, conversion.
CON.VÉS, *s.m.*, deck, shipboard.
CON.VES.CO.TE, *s.m.*, picnic.
CON.VE.XO, *adj.*, convex.
CON.VIC.ÇÃO, *s.f.*, conviction, certitude, belief.
CON.VIC.TO, *s.m.*, convict; *adj.*, convicted.
CON.VI.DA.DO, *s.m.*, guest, visitor; *adj.*, invited.
CON.VI.DAR, *v.*, to invite.
CON.VI.DA.TI.VO, *adj.*, inviting, invitory.
CON.VIN.CEN.TE, *adj.*, convincing, potent, powerful, conclusive.
CON.VIR, *v.*, to suit, to agree to, to befit.
CON.VI.TE, *s.m.*, invitation, call, convocation, engagement.
CON.VI.VA, *s. 2 gen.*, commensal, guest.
CON.VI.VÊN.CIA, *s.f.*, acquaintance, living in society.
CON.VI.VER, *v.*, to live together, to cohabit.
CON.VÍ.VI.O, *s.m.*, closeness, conviviality; banquet.
CON.VO.CA.ÇÃO, *s.f.*, convocation, invitation, convening.
CON.VO.CA.DO, *s.m.*, *Mil.*, draftee; *adj.*, *Mil.*, drafted, summoned.
CON.VO.CAR, *v.*, to convoke, to call together, to call, to convene.
CON.VO.CA.TÓ.RI.A, *s.f.*, notice of convocation.
CON.VOS.CO, *pron.*, with you.
CON.VUL.SÃO, *s.f.*, convulsion, convulsive, fit.
CON.VUL.SI.O.NAR, *v.*, to convulse, to agitate, to disturb.
CON.VUL.SI.VA.MEN.TE, *adv.*, convulsively.
CON.VUL.SI.VO, *adj.*, convulsive, spasmodic.
CO.O.PE.RA.ÇÃO, *s.f.*, co-operation, coaction.
CO.O.PE.RAR, *v.*, to co-operate, to work together.
CO.O.PE.RA.TI.VA, *s.f.*, co-operative, co-operative society.
CO.O.PE.RA.TI.VIS.MO, *s.m.*, co-operativism.
CO.O.PE.RA.TI.VIS.TA, *s. 2 gen.*, cooperativist.
CO.O.PE.RA.TI.VO, *adj.*, co-operative, co-operating.
CO.OR.DE.NA.ÇÃO, *s.f.*, co-ordination.
CO.OR.DE.NA.DOR, *s.m.*, co-ordinator; *adj.*, co-ordinating.
CO.OR.DE.NAR, *v.*, to co-ordenate, to organize, to classify, to arrange.
CO.PA, *s.f.*, cup, chalice; pantry, butler's pantry; pressing vat; top of a tree.
CO.PAR.TI.CI.PA.ÇÃO, *s.f.*, copartnership, communion.
CO.PAR.TI.CI.PAR, *v.*, to share, take part jointly.
CO.PEI.RO, *s.m.*, butler.
CÓ.PIA, *s.f.*, copy, reproduction, transcript, imitation.
CO.PI.A.DOR, *s.m.*, copier, copyist.
CO.PI.AR, *v.*, to copy, to reproduce, to duplicate.
CO.PI.DES.CAR, *v.*, to copy edit, to copy desk.
CO.PI.DES.QUE, *s.m.*, *US* copy-desk; *UK* copy-editing, copy-editor.
CO.PI.LO.TO, *s.m.*, copilot.
CO.PI.O.SA.MEN.TE, *adv.*, copiously, abundantly.
CO.PI.O.SO, *adj.*, copious, plenty, plentiful.

CO.PIS.TA, *s. 2 gen.*, copier, copyist.
CO.PO, *s.m.*, cup, glass, drinking glass.
CO.PRO.DU.ÇÃO, *s.f.*, joint production, co-production.
CO.PRO.DU.TOR, *s.m.*, co-producer.
CO.PRO.DU.ZIR, *v.*, to co-produce.
CO.PRO.FA.GI.A, *s.f.*, *Med.*, *Zool.*, coprophagy.
CO.PRÓ.LI.TO, *s.m.*, *Paleont.*, coprolite.
CO.PRO.PRI.E.DA.DE, *s.f.*, copartnership, joint property.
CO.PRO.PRI.E.TÁ.RI.O, *s.m.*, co-proprietor, co-owner.
CÓ.PU.LA, *s.f.*, coitus, coition, copulation.
CO.PU.LA.ÇÃO, *s.f.*, copulation.
CO.PU.LAR, *v.*, to copulate, to have sexual intercourse.
CO.QUE, *s.m.*, coke.
CO.QUEI.RAL, *s.m.*, a grove of coconut trees.
CO.QUEI.RO, *s.m.*, coconut palm.
CO.QUE.LU.CHE, *s.m.*, whooping-cough.
CO.QUE.TE, *adj.*, coquettish.
CO.QUE.TEL, *s.m.*, cocktail.
CO.QUE.TE.LEI.RA, *s.f.*, cocktail shaker.
CO.QUI.NHO, *s.m.*, a small cocoanut.
COR, *s.f.*, colour, color, hue, tint, paint; wish, heart, desire.
CO.RA.ÇÃO, *s.f.*, heart, courage, feeling.
CO.RA.DO, *adj.*, red-faced, ashamed, ruddy, rosy, florid.
CO.RA.GEM, *s.f.*, courage, daring, fearlessness, valour, gut, grit, bravery.
CO.RA.JO.SA.MEN.TE, *adv.*, courageously.
CO.RA.JO.SO, *adj.*, courageous, daring, valiant, bold, brave.
CO.RAL, *s.m.*, coral, coral plant; chorus, choral, coral snake; *adj.*, choric, choral.
CO.RA.LIS.TA, *s. 2 gen.*, choralist, chorist, chorister.
CO.RAN.TE, *s.m.*, colour, dye, pigment; *adj.*, colouring, dyeing.
CO.RÃO, *s.m.*, *Rel.*, Koran.
CO.RAR, *v.*, to colour, to dye, to paint.
COR.ÇA, *s.f.*, *Zool.*, doe, hind.
COR.CEL, *s.m.*, charger, courser (horse).
COR.ÇO, *s.m.*, *Zool.*, roebuck, roe deer.
COR.CO.VA, *s.f.*, hump, hunch.
COR.CO.VA.DO, *adj.*, humpy, humped.
COR.CO.VAR, *v.*, to curve, to bend
COR.CUN.DA, *s.f.*, humpback, hunchback, crookback.
COR.DA, *s.f.*, cord, rope, line, string.
COR.DÃO, *s.m.*, string, thread, twist, lace.
COR.DA.TO, *adj.*, prudent, sensible, wise.
COR.DEI.RO, *s.m.*, *Zool.*, lamb.
COR.DEL, *s.m.*, twine, string; *Lit.*, *literatura de ~*: popular Brazilian literatura.
COR-DE-RO.SA, *adj.*, pink, damask, rosy, roseate.
COR.DI.AL, *adj.*, cordial, sincere, kind, amicable, genial.
COR.DI.A.LI.DA.DE, *s.f.*, cordiality, sincerity, affection.
COR.DI.AL.MEN.TE, *adv.*, cordially.
COR.DI.LHEI.RA, *s.f.*, mountain range.
COR.DO.A.RI.A, *s.f.*, rope factory.
COR.DO.EI.RO, *s.m.*, rope manufacturer.
CO.RE.A.NO, *s.m.*, *adj.*, Korean.
CO.REI.A, *s.*, Korea: *~ do Norte*: North Korea; *~ do Sul*: South Korea.
CO.RE.O.GRA.FI.A, *s.f.*, choreography, choregraphy.
CO.RE.Ó.GRA.FO, *s.m.*, choreographer.
CO.RE.TO, *s.m.*, bandstand.
CO.RIS.CAR, *v.*, to coruscate, to scintillate.
CO.RIS.TA, *s. 2 gen.*, chorist, chorister; *Teat.*, chorus girl.

CORIZA   •• 147 •••   COSEDURA

CO.RI.ZA, *s.f.*, coryza, nasal catarrh.
COR.JA, *s.f.*, rabble, mob, multitude.
CÓR.NEA, *s.f.*, *Anat.*, cornea.
COR.NE.TA, *s.f.*, *Mús.*, cornet, bugle, horn.
COR.NE.TEI.RO, *s.m.*, trumpeter, bugler.
COR.NE.TIS.TA, *s. 2 gen.*, cornetist.
COR.NO, *s.m.*, horn.
COR.NU.CÓ.PI.A, *s.f.*, cornucopia.
COR.NU.DO, *s.m.*, *vulg.*, cuckold; *adj.*, horned.
CO.RO, *s.m.*, choir, chorus, cornu.
CO.RO.A, *s.f.*, crown.
CO.RO.A.ÇÃO, *s.f.*, crowning, coronation, antlers.
CO.RO.A.MEN.TO, *s.m.*, coronation, crowning.
CO.RO.A.DO, *adj.*, crowned, coroneted.
CO.RO.A.MEN.TO, *s.m.*, coronation.
CO.RO.AR, *v.*, to crown, to enthrone, to acclaim, to top.
CO.RO.I.NHA, *s.f.*, small crown; *s.m.*, altar server.
CO.RO.LÁ.RIO, *s.m.*, corollary, deduction, consequence.
CO.RO.NÁ.RIA, *s.f.*, *Anat.*, coronary artery.
CO.RO.NEL, *s.m.*, *Mil.*, colonel, commander.
CO.RO.NHA, *s.f.*, butt.
CO.RO.NHA.DA, *s.f.*, blow with a rifle butt.
COR.PE.TE, *s.m.*, bodice, camisole.
COR.PO, *s.m.*, body, frame, corpus, society, bulk, regiment, brigade, basis.
COR.PO.RA.ÇÃO, *s.f.*, corporation, association, fraternity.
COR.PO.RAL, *adj.*, corporal.
COR.PO.RA.LI.ZAR, *v.*, to materialize, to give a corporeal form to.
COR.PO.RA.TI.VIS.MO, *s.m.*, corporatism, corporativism.
COR.PO.RA.TI.VIS.TA, *s. 2 gen.*, corporatist, corporativist, collectivist; *adj.*, corporate, collectivistic(al).
COR.PO.RA.TI.VO, *adj.*, corporative, collective.
COR.PÓ.REO, *adj.*, corporal, bodily, material, external.
COR.PU.LÊN.CIA, *s.f.*, corpulence, corpulency.
COR.PU.LEN.TO, *adj.*, corpulent, fat, gross, big.
COR.PUS.CU.LAR, *adj.*, corpuscular.
COR.PÚS.CU.LO, *s.m.*, corpuscule, corpuscle.
COR.RE.ÇÃO, *s.f.*, correction, correctness, rectitude, retification.
COR.RE.CI.O.NAL, *adj.*, correctional; reformatory.
COR.RE-COR.RE, *s.m.*, great haste, mad rush.
COR.RE.DEI.RA, *s.f.*, river rapids.
COR.RE.DI.ÇA, *s.f.*, slide, rail.
COR.RE.DI.ÇO, *adj.*, sliding, gliding.
COR.RE.DOR, *s.m.*, runner, racer, corridor, passage.
COR.RE.GE.DOR, *s.m.*, corregidor.
CÓR.RE.GO, *s.m.*, brook, streamlet, brooklet, runlet.
COR.REI.A, *s.f.*, strap, belt, leash.
COR.REI.O, *s.m.*, mail, mailman, postal service; messenger.
COR.RE.LA.ÇÃO, *s.f.*, correlation.
COR.RE.LA.CI.O.NAR, *v.*, to correlate, to connect.
COR.RE.LA.TAR, *v.*, to correlate, to put in relation with each other.
COR.RE.LA.TI.VO, *adj.*, correlative, correlate.
COR.RE.LA.TO, *adj.*, the same that *correlativo*.
COR.RE.LI.GI.O.NÁ.RI.O, *s.m.*, coreligionist.
COR.REN.TE, *s.f.*, chain, cable, stream, flow, tie; *adj.*, current, common, fluent.
COR.REN.TE.ZA, *s.f.*, current, stream, watercourse, flow.
COR.REN.TIS.TA, *s. 2 gen.*, account holder.

COR.RER, *v.*, to run, to hurry, to pursue, to travel.
COR.RE.RIA, *s.f.*, rush, scurry, running.
COR.RES.PON.DÊN.CIA, *s.f.*, correspondence, letters, conformity, agreement.
COR.RES.PON.DEN.TE, *s. 2 gen.*, correspondent, newspaper correspondent; *adj.*, correspondent.
COR.RES.PON.DER, *v.*, to correspond, to reciprocate, reply, to satisfy.
COR.RES.PON.SÁ.VEL, *adj.*, co-responsible.
COR.RE.TA.GEM, *s.f.*, brokerage.
COR.RE.TAR, *v.*, to work as a broker.
COR.RE.TI.VO, *s.m.*, penalty, punishment; *adj.*, corrective.
COR.RE.TO, *adj.*, correct, right, true, perfect, exact, proper.
COR.RE.TOR, *s.m.*, broker, agent, commission agent, jobber.
COR.RI.DA, *s.f.*, race, scurrying, way, distance.
COR.RI.GIR, *v.*, to correct, to amend, to set right, to reform.
COR.RI.GÍ.VEL, *adj.*, corrigible, amendable.
COR.RI.MÃO, *s.m.*, handrail, stair rail.
COR.RI.MEN.TO, *s.m.*, act of flowing; *Med.*, flowing of humours.
COR.RI.O.LA, *s.f.*, *Bras., gír.*, a band of thieves or rascals.
COR.RI.QUEI.RO, *adj.*, current, everyday.
COR.RO.BO.RA.ÇÃO, *s.f.*, corroboration, confirmation.
COR.RO.BO.RAR, *v.*, to corroborate.
COR.RO.ER, *v.*, to erode, to corrode, to destroy, to deprave.
COR.RO.Í.DO, *adj.*, corroded, eroded.
COR.ROM.PER, *v.*, to corrupt, to spoil, to pervert, to adulterate, to seduce.
COR.ROM.PI.DO, *adj.*, corrupted.
COR.RO.SÃO, *s.f.*, corrosion, erosion.
COR.RO.SI.VO, *adj.*, corrosive.
COR.RUP.ÇÃO, *s.f.*, corruption, spoiling, putrefaction, deterioration.
COR.RUP.TÍ.VEL, *adj.*, corruptible.
COR.RUP.TO, *adj.*, corrupt, depraved, dissolute.
COR.RUP.TOR, *s.m.*, corrupter.
COR.SÁ.RIO, *s.m.*, corsair, privateer, pirate.
COR.TA.DO, *adj.*, cut, interrupted.
COR.TA.DOR, *s.m.*, cutter.
COR.TA.DU.RA, *s.f.*, cut, incision.
COR.TAN.TE, *adj.*, cutting; nipping (cold).
COR.TAR, *v.*, to cut, to chop, to slice, to carve, to shut off.
COR.TE, *s.m.*, cut, incision, section.
CORTE(Ô), *s.f.*, court, sovereign's residence.
COR.TE.JAR, *v.*, to court, to flirt with, to greet, to salute.
COR.TE.JO, *s.m.*, procession, courtship, homage.
COR.TÊS, *adj.*, courteous, polite.
COR.TE.SÃ, *s.f.*, courtesan.
COR.TE.SÃO, *s.m.*, courtier; *adj.*, courtly.
COR.TE.SI.A, *s.f.*, courtesy, politeness, urbanity, civility.
CÓR.TEX, *s.m.*, *Anat., Bot.*, cortex.
COR.TI.ÇA, *s.f.*, cork.
COR.TI.CAL, *adj.*, *Anat., Bot.*, cortical.
COR.TI.COI.DE, *s.m.*, *Med.*, corticoid, corticosteroid.
COR.TI.NA, *s.f.*, curtain, screen.
CO.RU.JA, *s.f.*, *Zool.*, owl, owlet.
CO.RUS.CAR, *v.*, to coruscate.
COR.VE.JAR, *v.*, to caw, to croak.
COR.VI.NA, *s.f.*, *Zool.*, corvina (fish).
COR.VO, *s.m.*, *Zool.*, raven, crow.
CÓS, *s.m.*, waistband of a garment.
CO.SE.DU.RA, *s.f.*, sewing.

COSER ·· 148 ·· CRÉSCIMO

CO.SER, *v.*, to sew, to stitch.
COS.MÉ.TI.CO, *adj.*, *s.m.*, cosmetic.
CÓS.MI.CO, *adj.*, *s.m.*, cosmic.
COS.MO, *s.m.*, cosmos.
COS.MO.LO.GI.A, *s.f.*, cosmology.
COS.MÓ.LO.GO, *s.m.*, cosmologist.
COS.MO.NAU.TA, *s.m.*, astronaut.
COS.MO.NA.VE, *s.f.*, spaceship.
COS.MO.PO.LI.TA, *s. 2 gen.*, cosmopolitan, cosmopolite, citizen of the cosmos.
COS.MO.VI.SÃO, *s.f.*, conception or view of the world.
COS.QUEN.TO, *adj.*, *Bras.*, ticklish (sensible to tickling).
COS.SE.CAN.TE, *s.f.*, *Mat.*, cosecant.
COS.TA, *s.f.*, coast, seashore, declivity; *costas*: back.
COS.TA.DO, *s.m.*, *Anat.*, back; flank, the side of a ship, broadside.
COS.TA-RI.QUE.NHO, *s.m.*, *adj.*, Costa Rican (too *costa-riquense*).
COS.TE.AR, *v.*, to coast, to round, to move alongside of.
COS.TEI.RO, *adj.*, coastal.
COS.TE.LA, *s.f.*, *Anat.*, rib.
COS.TE.LE.TA, *s.f.*, chop, cutlet.
COS.TU.MAR, *v.*, to be accustomed, to be used to.
COS.TU.ME, *s.m.*, custom, habit, practice, usage, use, way, common law.
COS.TU.MEI.RO, *adj.*, usual, customary.
COS.TU.RA, *s.f.*, sewing, needlework, seam, juncture.
COS.TU.RAR, *v.*, to sew, to seam.
COS.TU.REI.RA, *s.f.*, needlewoman, dressmaker.
COS.TU.REI.RO, *s.m.*, seamster.
CO.TA, *s.f.*, share, portion, quota.
CO.TA.ÇÃO, *s.f.*, quotation, assessment.
CO.TA.DO, *adj.*, well-reputed, esteemed, well priced.
CO.TAN.GEN.TE, *s.f.*, *Mat.*, cotangent.
CO.TAR, *v.*, to estimate, to valuate, to tax.
CO.TE.JAR, *v.*, to compare, to confront.
CO.TI.DI.A.NO, *adj.*, daily, everyday, day-to-day, quotidian.
CO.TI.ZAR, *v.*, to tax, to assess, to rate.
CO.TO. *s.m.*, stump.
CO.TO.CO, *s.m.*, *pop.*, the same that *coto*.
CO.TO.NE.TE, *s.m.*, swab.
CO.TO.NI.FÍ.CIO, *s.m.*, cotton mill.
CO.TO.VE.LA.DA, *s.f.*, nudge, dig.
CO.TO.VE.LO, *s.m.*, elbow.
CO.TO.VI.A, *s.f.*, *Zool.*, lark.
CO.TUR.NO, *s.m.*, cothurnus; any shoes with high, thick soles.
COU.RA.ÇA, *s.f.*, cuirass, breastplate.
COU.RA.ÇAR, *v.*, to armour.
COU.REI.RO, *s.m.*, dealer in leather.
COU.RO, *s.m.*, leather, hide.
COU.VE, *s.m.*, *Bot.*, kale, cabbage.
COU.VE-FLOR, *s.m.*, *Bot.*, cauliflower.
CO.VA, *s.f.*, hole, cavity, hollow, pit; grave.
CO.VAR.DE, *s. 2 gen.*, coward; *adj.*, coward.
CO.VAR.DI.A, *s.f.*, cowardice.
CO.VEI.RO, *s.m.*, grave-digger.
CO.VIL, *s.m.*, den.
CO.VI.NHA, *s.f.*, dimple, cleft.
CO.XA, *s.f.*, thigh.
CO.XO, *adj.*, *s.m.*, limping, halting, lame.
CO.ZE.DU.RA, *s.f.*, cookery, cooking.

CO.ZER, *v.*, to cook, to boil, to bake.
CO.ZI.DO, *s.m.*, something that was cooked; *adj.*, cooked.
CO.ZI.MEN.TO, *s.m.*, cooking.
CO.ZI.NHA, *s.f.*, kitchen, cuisine, cookery.
CO.ZI.NHAR, *v.*, to cook, to boil.
CO.ZI.NHEI.RA, *s.f.*, cook (female).
CO.ZI.NHEI.RO, *s.m.*, cook (male).
CPD, *abrev.* of *Centro de Processamento do Dados*: Data-Processing Department.
CPF, *abrev.* of *Cadastro de Pessoa Física*: *UK* National Insurance Number; *US* Social Security Number.
CRÂ.NIO, *s.m.*, cranium, skull, brainpan.
CRÁ.PU.LA, *s.f.*, debauchery, rascal.
CRA.PU.LO.SO, *adj.*, crapulous, licentious.
CRA.QUE, *s.m.*, *Bras.*, excellent race-horse or footballer; *interj.*, crack!, bang!
CRA.SE, *s.f.*, *Gram.*, crasis, contraction of two vowels.
CRA.SE.AR, *v.*, *Gram.*, to put an accent on a vowel to indicate a crasis.
CRAS.SO, *adj.*, crass, gross, coarse, stupid.
CRA.TE.RA, *s.f.*, crater, mouth of a volcano.
CRA.VAR, *v.*, to thrust in, to set, to fix.
CRA.VE.JA.MEN.TO, *s.m.*, gem-setting, nailing.
CRA.VE.JAR, *v.*, to set gems, to stud with nails.
CRA.VO, *s.m.*, horseshoe nail, shoe tack; *Bot.*, carnation, pink; *Mús.*, harpsichord.
CRE.CHE, *s.f.*, nursery.
CRE.DEN.CI.AIS, *s.f.*, *pl.*, credentials.
CRE.DI.Á.RIO, *s.m.*, credit system, instalment system.
CRE.DI.TAR, *v.*, to credit, to guarantee.
CRÉ.DI.TO, *s.m.*, credit, trust; good reputation; power; *carta de* ~: letter of credit.
CRE.DO, *s.m.*, Credo, Creed, symbol of the apostles.
CRE.DOR, *s.m.*, creditor.
CRE.DU.LI.DA.DE, *s.f.*, credulity.
CRÉ.DU.LO, *s.m.*, credulous person; *adj.*, credulous.
CRE.MA.ÇÃO, *s.f.*, cremation, incineration.
CRE.MA.DO, *adj.*, cremated.
CRE.MAR, *v.*, to cremate.
CRE.MA.TÓ.RI.O, *s.m.*, crematorium, crematory.
CRE.ME, *s.m.*, cream, custard.
CREN.ÇA, *s.f.*, belief, creed, faith, opinion.
CREN.DI.CE, *s.f.*, superstition.
CREN.TE, *s. 2 gen.*, believer; *adj.*, believing.
CRE.O.LI.NA, *s.f.*, creolin (disinfectant).
CRE.PE, *s.f.*, crape, gauzy fabric.
CRE.PI.TA.ÇÃO, *s.f.*, crepitation, crackle.
CRE.PI.TAN.TE, *adj.*, crepitant, crackling.
CRE.PI.TAR, *v.*, to crepitate.
CRE.PUS.CU.LAR, *adj.*, crepuscular.
CRE.PÚS.CU.LO, *s.m.*, crepuscle, crepusculum, nightfall, twilight.
CRER, *v.*, to believe, to trust, to think, to judge.
CRES.CEN.TE, *s.m.*, crescent, increasing; the first quarter of the moon.
CRES.CER, *v.*, to grow, to grow up, to increase, to develop, to multiply, to augment.
CRES.CI.DO, *adj.*, grown; adult.
CRES.CI.MEN.TO, *s.m.*, growth, increase, development, augmentation.
CRÉS.CI.MO, *s.m.*, excess, surplus.

CRESOL · · 149 · · CUECAS

CRE.SOL, *s.m.*, *Quím.*, cresol.
CRE.TÁ.CE.O, *s.m.*, *Geol.*, Cretaceous; *adj.*, Cretaceous.
CRE.TI.NIS.MO, *s.m.*, cretinism, stupidity.
CRE.TI.NO, *adj.*, idiot, imbecile, cretin, stupid.
CRI.A, *s.f.*, brood, suckling (animal), breed, litter, calf, foal, kid.
CRI.A.ÇÃO, *s.f.*, creation, invention, universe, institution, nurture, establishment.
CRI.A.CI.O.NIS.MO, *s.m.*, *Rel.*, creationism.
CRI.A.DA.GEM, *s.f.*, the household servants.
CRI.A.DO, *s.m.*, servant, man-servant, domestic; *adj.*, created, bred, raised.
CRI.A.DO-MU.DO, *s.m.*, bedside table.
CRI.A.DOR, *s.m.*, creator; *o Criador:* the Creator.
CRI.AN.ÇA, *s.f.*, child, infant, baby.
CRI.AN.ÇA.DA, *s.f.*, children, fry, bunch of children.
CRI.AN.CI.NHA, *s.f.*, nestling.
CRI.AR, *v.*, to create, to generate, to produce, to originate, to invent.
CRI.A.TI.VO, *adj.*, creative.
CRI.A.TU.RA, *s.f.*, creature, being.
CRI.CRI.LAR, *v.*, to stridulate (chirp as a cricket).
CRI.ME, *s.m.*, crime, felony, delinquency.
CRI.MI.NAL, *adj.*, criminal.
CRI.MI.NA.LI.DA.DE, *s.f.*, criminality, culpability.
CRI.MI.NA.LIS.TA, *s. 2 gen.*, criminalist.
CRI.MI.NA.LÍS.TI.CA, *s.f.*, *Jur.*, criminalistics.
CRI.MI.NA.LI.ZA.ÇÃO, *s.f.*, criminalization.
CRI.MI.NA.LI.ZAR, *v.*, to criminalize.
CRI.MI.NO.SO, *s.m.*, criminal, felon, offender, delinquent, murderer; *adj.*, criminal.
CRI.NA, *s.f.*, mane.
CRI.O.GE.NI.A, *s.f.*, *Fís.*, cryogenics.
CRI.O.GÊ.NI.CO, *adj.*, cryogenic.
CRI.OU.LO, *s.m.*, creole.
CRIP.TA, *s.f.*, crypt, vault, catacomb.
CRÍP.TI.CO, *adj.*, cryptic.
CRIP.TO.GRA.FAR, *v.*, *Comp.*, to encrypt.
CRIP.TO.GRA.FI.A, *s.f.*, cryptography.
CRÍ.QUE.TE, *s.m.*, (game of) cricket.
CRI.SÂN.TE.MO, *s.m.*, *Bot.*, chrysanthemum.
CRI.SE, *s.f.*, crisis.
CRIS.MA, *s.f.*, confirmation, chrism; *s.m.*, consecrated oil.
CRIS.MAR, *v.*, to chrism.
CRI.SOL, *s.m.*, crucible.
CRIS.PAR, *v.*, the same that *encrespar:* to crisp.
CRIS.TA, *s.f.*, crest, cockscomb, comb.
CRIS.TAL, *s.m.*, crystal, crystal glass.
CRIS.TA.LEI.RA, *s.f.*, crystal closet.
CRIS.TA.LI.NO, *adj.*, crystalline, limpid, like crystal.
CRIS.TA.LI.ZA.ÇÃO, *s.f.*, crystallization.
CRIS.TA.LI.ZAR, *v.*, to crystallize.
CRIS.TAN.DA.DE, *s.f.*, Christianity.
CRIS.TÃO, *adj.*, *s.m.*, Christian.
CRI.TÉ.RI.O, *s.m.*, criterion, judgment, discernment.
CRI.TE.RI.O.SO, *adj.*, selective, discerning, judicious.
CRIS.TI.A.NIS.MO, *s.m.*, Christianism.
CRIS.TI.A.NI.ZAR, *v.*, to Christianize.
CRIS.TO, *s.m.*, Christ, Jesus.
CRI.TÉ.RIO, *s.m.*, criterion, rule, discretion.
CRÍ.TI.CA, *s.f.*, criticism, censure, critique.
CRI.TI.CAR, *v.*, to criticize, to judge, to censure.

CRÍ.TI.CO, *s.m.*, critic, reviewer, censurer; *adj.*, critical, crucial, dangerous.
CRI.VAR, *v.*, to riddle, to sift, to sieve, screen; to perforate.
CRÍ.VEL, *adj.*, credible, believable.
CRI.VO, *s.m.*, sieve, screen, colander.
CRO.Á.CI.A, *s.*, Croatia.
CRO.A.TA, *s. 2 gen.*, *adj.*, Croat, Croatian.
CRO.CHÊ, *s.m.*, crochet, crochet work.
CRO.CI.TAR, *v.*, to croak, to caw (raven, crow).
CRO.CO.DI.LO, *s.m.*, *Zool.*, crocodile.
CRO.MAR, *v.*, to chromate.
CRO.MÁ.TI.CO, *adj.*, chromatic.
CRO.MA.TIS.MO, *s.m.*, *Fís.*, chromatism.
CRO.MO, *s.m.*, *Quím.*, chromium.
CRO.MOS.SO.MO, *s.m.*, *Biol.*, chromosome.
CRÔ.NI.CA, *s.f.*, chronicle, narrative, event.
CRÔ.NI.CO, *adj.*, chronic, chronical.
CRO.NIS.TA, *s. 2 gen.*, chronicler, historian.
CRO.NO.GRA.MA, *s.m.*, chronogram.
CRO.NO.LO.GI.A, *s.f.*, chronology.
CRO.NO.ME.TRA.GEM, *s.f.*, timekeeping.
CRO.NO.ME.TRAR, *v.*, to time, to clock.
CRO.NO.ME.TRIS.TA, *s. 2 gen.*, chronometer maker, timekeeper.
CRO.NÔ.ME.TRO, *s.m.*, chronometer, precision watch.
CRO.QUE.TE, *s.m.*, *Cul.*, croquette.
CRO.QUI, *s.m.*, sketch.
CROS.TA, *s.f.*, crust, rind.
CRU, *adj.*, raw, uncooked, crude, unprocessed.
CRU.CI.AL, *adj.*, crucial, decisive.
CRU.CI.AN.TE, *adj.*, mortifying, torturing.
CRU.CI.FI.CA.ÇÃO, *s.f.*, crucifixion.
CRU.CI.FI.CA.DO, *s.m.*, the Crucified; Christ; *adj.*, crucifixed.
CRU.CI.FI.CAR, *v.*, to crucify, to torture, to mortify.
CRU.CI.FI.XO, *s.m.*, crucifix.
CRU.EL, *adj.*, cruel, inhuman, fierce, barbarous.
CRU.EL.DA.DE, *s.f.*, cruelty, inhumanity.
CRU.EL.MEN.TE, *adv.*, cruelly.
CRU.EN.TO, *adj.*, bloody.
CRU.E.ZA, *s.f.*, rawness, crudity.
CRUS.TÁ.CEO, *s.m.*, *Zool.*, crustacean; *adj.*, crustaceous.
CRUZ, *s.f.*, cross; Christian symbol, Cristianism.
CRUZ VER.ME.LHA, *s.f.*, Red Cross (International Committee of the Red Cross).
CRU.ZA.DA, *s.f.*, cruzade.
CRU.ZA.DOR, *s.m.*, crosser; *Náut.*, cruiser.
CRU.ZA.MEN.TO, *s.m.*, crossing, intersection, street crossing.
CRU.ZAR, *v.*, to cross, to traverse, to pass through.
CRU.ZEI.RO, *s.m.*, *Náut.*, cruise; *Astron.*, *Cruzeiro do Sul:* Crux (constellation); *adj.*, crossed.
CU, *s.m.*, *vulg.*, ass, asshole, bum.
CU.BA, *s.f.*, vat.
CU.BA, *s.*, Cuba.
CU.BA.GEM, *s.f.*, cubature.
CU.BA.NO, *adj.*, *s.m.*, Cuban.
CU.BÍ.CU.LO, *s.m.*, cubicle, cubby-hole.
CU.BIS.MO, *s.m.*, *Pint.*, cubism.
CU.CA, *s.f.*, *Bras., pop.*, head.
CU.BO, *s.m.*, cube.
CU.CO, *s.m.*, cuckoo; cuckoo-clock.
CU.E.CAS, *s.f., pl.*, briefs, short drawers.

CUIA · 150 · CUTIA

CUI.A, *s.f., Bras.*, bottle gourd.
CU.Í.CA, *s.f., Bras., Mús.*, a percussion instrument.
CUI.DA.DO.SA.MEN.TE, *adv.*, carefully.
CUI.DA.DO, *s.m.*, care, precaution, caution, attention.
CUI.DA.DOR, *s.m.*, caretaker.
CUI.DA.DO.SO, *adj.*, careful.
CUI.DAR, *v.*, to care, to consider; to take care of, to look after, to suppose.
CU.JO, *pron.*, whose, of whom, of which.
CU.LA.TRA, *s.f.*, breech.
CU.LI.NÁ.RIA, *s.f.*, cookery, culinary art.
CU.LI.NÁ.RIO, *adj.*, culinary.
CUL.MI.NAN.TE, *adj.*, culminant.
CUL.MI.NAR, *v.*, to culminate, to terminate.
CUL.PA, *s.f.*, blame, fault, guilt, offence, delinquency, crime.
CUL.PA.BI.LI.DA.DE, *s.f.*, culpability.
CUL.PA.DO, *s.m.*, culprit, guilty person.
CUL.PAR, *v.*, to accuse, to inculpate, to incriminate.
CUL.PÁ.VEL, *adj.*, culpable, guilty.
CUL.PO.SO, *adj.*, guilty.
CUL.TIS.MO, *s.m.*, cultism, eruditeness.
CUL.TI.VA.DOR, *s.m.*, cultivator.
CUL.TI.VAR, *v.*, to cultivate, to till, to maintain, to develop, to keep up.
CUL.TI.VÁ.VEL, *adj.*, cultivable, cultivatable.
CUL.TI.VO, *s.m.*, cultivation, culture.
CUL.TO, *s.m.*, cult, adoration, veneration; *adj.*, cultured, learned, educated, refined.
CUL.TOR, *s.m.*, the same that *cultivador*.
CUL.TU.AR, *v.*, to worship, to adore.
CUL.TU.RA, *s.f.*, culture, education, civilization, cultivation, breeding.
CUL.TU.RAL, *adj.*, cultural.
CU.ME, *s.m.*, summit, top, peak.
CU.ME.EI.RA, *s.f.*, roof ridge, ridge beam.
CÚM.PLI.CE, *s. 2 gen.*, accomplice, partner.
CUM.PLI.CI.DA.DE, *s.f.*, complicity.
CUM.PRI.DOR, *s.m.*, accomplisher, fulfiller; *adj.*, executant, performing.
CUM.PRI.MEN.TAR, *v.*, to salute, to greet, to bow to, to congratulate.
CUM.PRI.MEN.TO, *s.m.*, accomplishment, compliment, execution, performance.
CUM.PRIR, *v.*, to accomplish, to execute, to fulfil, to carry out, to keep.
CU.MU.LA.TI.VO, *adj.*, cumulative.
CÚ.MU.LO, *s.m.*, cumulus; apex, summit, top; *Met.*, cumulus.
CU.NEI.FOR.ME, *s.m.*, cuneiform.
CU.NHA, *s.f.*, wedge.
CU.NHA.DA, *s.f.*, sister-in-law.
CU.NHA.DO, *s.m.*, brother-in-law.
CU.NHA.GEM, *s.f.*, coinage, mintage.
CU.NHAR, *v.*, to coin, to mint, to stamp, to emboss.
CU.NHO, *s.m.*, stamp; characteristic.
CU.NI.CUL.TU.RA, *s.f.*, rabbit breeding.
CU.PI.DO, *s.m., Mit.*, Cupid.
CU.PIM, *s.m., Zool.*, termite; white ant.
CU.PÃO, *s.m.*, the same that *cupom*.
CÚ.PI.DO, *adj.*, covetous, avid; amorous.
CU.PIN.ZEI.RO, *s.m.*, termitary.
CU.POM, *s.m.*, coupon, voucher.

CÚ.PU.LA, *s.f., Arquit.*, dome; cupule; faculty; *reunião de cúpula*: summit meeting.
CU.RA, *s.f.*, cure, healing, sanation, recovery, medication; *s.m.*, curate, rector.
CU.RA.DO, *adj.*, cured.
CU.RA.DOR, *s.m.*, curator, guardian, tutor.
CU.RAR, *v.*, to cure, to heal, to treat, to remedy, to medicate.
CU.RA.TI.VO, *s.m.*, curative, medication, remedy.
CU.RÁ.VEL, *adj.*, curable, remediable.
CU.RE.TA.GEM, *s.f., Med.*, curettage.
CU.RE.TAR, *v., Med.*, to curette.
CU.RIN.GA, *s.m.*, joker.
CU.RI.Ó, *s.m., Bras., Zool.*, arice finch (bird).
CU.RI.O.SA.MEN.TE, *adv.*, curiously.
CU.RI.O.SI.DA.DE, *s.f.*, curiosity, indiscretion, rarity.
CU.RI.O.SO, *s.m.*, curious, looker on, by-stander; *adj.*, curious, inquisitive, studious.
CUR.RAL, *s.m.*, corral, stable, pound.
CUR.RAR, *v., Bras., pop.*, to rape, to sodomize.
CUR.RÍ.CU.LO, *s.m.*, curriculum.
CUR.RY, *s.m., Cul.*, curry.
CUR.SAR, *v.*, to course, to follow a course of study, to cruise, to navigate.
CUR.SI.NHO, *s.m., Bras.*, a preparatory course for university entry exam.
CUR.SI.VO, *s.m.*, cursine (cursive character or script); *adj.*, cursive; *letra cursiva*: cursive writing.
CUR.SO, *s.m.*, course; run, career, sequence, progress, circulation.
CUR.SOR, *s.m., Comp.*, cursor.
CUR.TA-ME.TRA.GEM, *s.f., Cin.*, a short-feature movie.
CUR.TI.ÇÃO, *s.f.*, tanning (leather); *Bras., fam.*, fun.
CUR.TI.MEN.TO, *s.m.*, tanning, tannage.
CUR.TIR, *v.*, to tan hides, to harden.
CUR.TO, *adj.*, short, brief, scant, scarce.
CUR.TO-CIR.CUI.TO, *s.m.*, short circuit.
CUR.TU.ME, *s.m.*, tanning, tannage; tannery.
CUR.VA, *s.f.*, curve, bend, crook, bow.
CUR.VA.DO, *adj.*, curved, arched.
CUR.VAR, *v.*, to curve, to incurvate, to bend, to arch, to inflect.
CUR.VA.TU.RA, *s.f.*, curvature, bend, flection.
CUR.VO, *adj.*, curved, bent, arched.
CUS.CUZ, *s.m., 2 num., Bras., Cul.*, couscous.
CUS.PA.RA.DA, *s.f., Bras.*, the same that *cuspidura*.
CUS.PE, *s.m.*, spit, saliva, spittle.
CUS.PI.DOR, *s.m.*, spitter.
CUS.PI.DU.RA, *s.f.*, spitting.
CUS.PIR, *v.*, to spit, to expectorate, to eject.
CUS.PO, *s.m.*, the same that *cuspe*.
CUS.TAR, *v.*, to cost, to be worth, to be difficult.
CUS.TE.AR, *v.*, to bear the expense, to finance.
CUS.TEI.O, *s.m.*, defrayal, costs, estimate of costs.
CUS.TO, *s.m.*, cost, expense, difficulty, price, worth.
CUS.TÓ.DI.A, *s.f.*, custody.
CUS.TO.DI.AR, *v.*, to keep in custody.
CUS.TO.SO, *adj.*, expensive, difficult.
CU.TÂ.NEO, *adj.*, cutaneous, of or relating to the skin.
CU.TE.LA.RI.A, *s.f.*, cutlery.
CU.TE.LEI.RO, *s.m.*, cutler.
CU.TE.LO, *s.m.*, chopping knife.
CU.TI.A, *s.f., Bras., Zool.*, agouti.

CUTÍCULA

CU.TÍ.CU.LA, *s.f.*, cuticle, pellicle.
CU.TI.CU.LAR, *adj.*, cuticular, epidermal.
CÚ.TIS, *s.f.*, cutis, derma, skin.
CU.TU.CÃO, *s.m.*, dig, jab.

CU.TU.CAR, *v.*, to jog, to poke, to dig.
CZAR, *s.m.*, *Hist.*, czar, tsar.
CZA.RIS.TA, *s. 2 gen.*, *Hist.*, czarist, tsarist.

D, s.m., the fourth letter of the Portuguese alphabet.
D, num., Roman numeral: 500.
DA, Gram., contr. of the prep. **DE** with the art. fem. **A**.
DA.DA.ÍS.MO, s.m., Dadaism (a short-lived movement in art and literature).
DA.DA.ÍS.TA, s. 2 gen., Dadaist; adj., Dadaist, Dadaistic.
DÁ.DI.VA, s.m., gift, present, donation, godsend.
DA.DI.VO.SO, adj., bountiful, generous.
DA.DO, s.m., die, small cube for playing; datum, figure; licit, permitted, free; conj., in view of.
DA.DOR, s.m., giver, donator.
DA.GUER.RE.Ó.TI.PO, s.m., daguerreotype.
DA.Í, adv., thence, from there, therefore.
DA.LI, adv., thence, therefrom, from there.
DÁ.LIA, s.f., Bot., dahlia.
DÁL.MA.TA, s.m., Dalmatian (breed of dogs); adj., Dalmatian.
DÁL.TON, s.m., Quím., dalton.
DAL.TÔ.NI.CO, s.m., daltonian; adj., colour-blind.
DAL.TO.NIS.MO, s.m., Med., daltonism, colour blindness.
DA.MA, s.f., lady, maid, actress; queen (chess, cards); king (in draughts/checkers).
DA.MAS.CO, s.m., Bot., apricot.
DA.MAS.QUEI.RO, s.m., Bot., apricot (tree).
DA.NA.ÇÃO, s.f., damagement, anger, fury.
DA.NA.DO, adj., damned, condemned, ruined, decayed, furious, angry.
DA.NAR, v., to harm, to hurt, to injure, to damage, to provoke, to annoy.
DAN.ÇA, s.f., dance.
DAN.ÇAN.TE, adj., dancing.
DAN.ÇAR, s.f., to dance, to turn around, to bob.
DAN.ÇA.RI.NA, s.f., dancer, ballerina, dancing-girl.
DAN.ÇA.RI.NO, s.m., dancer.
DÂN.DI, s.m., dandy, fop.
DA.NI.FI.CA.DO, adj., damaged, impaired (machine).
DA.NI.FI.CAR, v., to damage, to harm, to injure, to hurt.
DA.NO, s.m., damage, harm, injury, loss.
DA.NO.SO, adj., prejudicial, damaging.
DAN.TES, adv., formerly, before.
DAN.TES.CO, adj., awful, horrible; Dantesque.
DA.QUE.LE, contr. of the prep. **DE** and the pron. dem. **AQUELE**: from that, of that.
DA.QUÉM, contr. of the prep. **DE** and the adv. **AQUÉM**: from this side.
DA.QUI, contr. of the prep. **DE** and the adv. **AQUI**: from here, within.
DA.QUI.LO, contr. of the prep. **DE** and the pron. dem. **AQUILO**: from that, of that.
DAR, v., to give, to offer, to bestow; to beat, to grant, to concede, to dedicate.
DAR.DE.JAR, v., to throw the javelin or the spear.
DAR.DO, s.m., spear, javelin, dart.

DAR.WI.NIS.MO, s.m., Darwinism.
DAR.WI.NIS.TA, s. 2 gen., adj., Darwinist, Darwinian.
DA.TA, s.f., date.
DA.TA.ÇÃO, s.f., dating.
DA.TAR, v., to date, to start, to reckon from, to persist.
DA.TI.LO.GRA.FAR, v., to typewrite.
DA.TI.LO.GRA.FI.A, s.f., typewriting.
DA.TI.LÓ.GRA.FO, s.m., typist.
DA.TI.VO, s.m., Gram., dative (case); adj., dative.
DE, prep., of, from, by, to, on, in, with.
DE.AM.BU.LA.ÇÃO, s.f., walk, stroll.
DE.AM.BU.LAR, v., to walk around, stroll.
DE.ÃO, s.m., dean.
DE.BAI.XO, adv., under, beneath, below, inferior.
DE.BAL.DE, adv., in vain.
DE.BAN.DA.DA, s.f., flight, escape.
DE.BAN.DAR, v., to flee, to scatter, to put to flight.
DE.BA.TE, s.m., debate, discussion, contest.
DE.BA.TER, v., to discuss, to dispute, to contend, to contest.
DE.BE.LA.ÇÃO, s.f., restraint, subjection, cure.
DE.BE.LAR, v., to subject, to subdue, to conquer, to repress, to restrain, to cure.
DE.BÊN.TU.RE, s.f., debenture.
DÉ.BIL, adj., weak, vacillating, feeble, infirm.
DE.BI.LI.DA.DE, s.f., debility, fragility, weakness.
DE.BI.LI.TAN.TE, adj., weakening, debilitating.
DE.BI.LI.TAR, v., to weaken, to debilitate, to harm.
DE.BIL.MEN.TE, adv., weakly, feebly.
DE.BI.LOI.DE, s. 2 gen., feebleminded person; adj., feebleminded.
DE.BI.TAR, v., to debit, to charge.
DÉ.BI.TO, s.m., debt, obligation, debit.
DE.BO.CHA.DO, adj., licentious, indecent; scoffing, mocking.
DE.BO.CHAR, v., to debauch, to pervert; to jeer, to mock.
DE.BO.CHE, s.m., mockery.
DE.BRU.ÇAR, v., to stoop, to bend forward, to lean over.
DE.BRUM, s.m., hem, edging, border, binding.
DE.BU.LHA, s.f., thrashing, peeling, stripping.
DE.BU.LHAR, v., thrash, to peel.
DE.BU.TAN.TE, s.f., Fr., débutante.
DE.BU.TAR, v., to make a debut.
DÉ.CA.DA, s.f., decade.
DE.CA.DÊN.CIA, s.f., decadence, decline, decay, fall.
DE.CA.DEN.TE, adj., decadent, deteriorating.
DE.CA.DIS.TA, s. 2 gen., adj., decadent.
DE.CA.E.DRO, s.m., Geom., decahedron; adj., decahedral.
DE.CÁ.GO.NO, s.m., Geom., decagon.
DE.CA.Í.DA, s.f., decay, decline.
DE.CA.I.MEN.TO, s.m., decay, decline; Fís., decay, decay heat.
DE.CA.IR, v., to decay, to decline, to fall away, to slip.
DE.CAL.CAR, v., to trace, to copy, to imitate.
DE.CAL.CO, s.m., the same thar decalque.

DECALCOMANIA ·· 153 ·· DEFASAGEM

DE.CAL.CO.MA.NI.A, *s.f.*, decalcomania.
DE.CÁ.LO.GO, *s.m.*, decalogue.
DE.CAL.QUE, *s.m.*, tracing, copying; decalcomania.
DE.CAM.PAR, *v.*, to decamp.
DE.CA.NA.TO, *s.m.*, deanship, deanery.
DE.CA.NO, *s.m.*, dean, elder, senior.
DE.CAN.TA.ÇÃO, *s.f.*, decantation.
DE.CAN.TAR, *v.*, to decant.
DE.CA.PA.GEM, *s.f.*, scouring, pickling.
DE.CA.PAR, *v.*, to scour, to strip, to pickle.
DE.CA.PI.TA.ÇÃO, *s.f.*, decapitation.
DE.CÁ.PO.DE, *s.m.*, *Zool.*, decapod, decapodan; *decápodes*: Decapoda.
DE.CA.PI.TAR, *v.*, to decapitate, to behead.
DE.CAS.SÍ.LA.BO, *s.m.*, *Lit.*, decasyllable; *adj.*, decasyllabic.
DE.CA.TLE.TA, *s.* 2 *gen.*, *Esp.*, decathlete.
DE.CA.TLO, *s.m.*, *Esp.*, decathlon.
DE.CE.NAL, *adj.*, decennial.
DE.CÊN.CIA, *s.f.*, decency, neatness, decorum.
DE.CÊ.NI.O, *s.m.*, decennium (a period of ten years).
DE.CEN.TE, *adj.*, decent, proper, decorous, honest, fair, convenient.
DE.CE.PA.MEN.TO, *s.m.*, cutting off, amputation.
DE.CE.PAR, *v.*, to cut off, to amputate, to sever, to maim, to interrupt, to mutilate.
DE.CEP.ÇÃO, *s.f.*, disappointment, disillusion, fraud.
DE.CEP.CI.O.NAN.TE, *adj.*, disappointing.
DE.CEP.CI.O.NAR, *v.*, to disappoint, to disillusion.
DE.CER.TO, *adv.*, certainly, surely.
DE.CI.BEL, *s.m.*, *Fis.*, decibel.
DE.CI.DI.DA.MEN.TE, *adv.*, resolutely, steadily.
DE.CI.DI.DO, *adj.*, resolute, decided, courageous.
DE.CI.DIR, *v.*, to decide, to resolve, to determine, to settle.
DE.CI.FRA.ÇÃO, *s.f.*, deciphering.
DE.CI.FRA.DOR, *s.m.*, decipherer; *adj.*, deciphering.
DE.CI.FRAR, *v.*, to decipher, to interpret.
DE.CI.FRÁ.VEL, *adj.*, decipherable.
DE.CI.LI.TRO, *s.m.*, decilitre, deciliter.
DE.CI.MAL, *s.m.*, *adj.*, decimal.
DE.CÍ.ME.TRO, *s.m.*, decimeter, decimetre.
DÉ.CI.MO, *num.*, tenth, tenth part.
DE.CI.SÃO, *s.f.*, decision, resolution, determination, judgment, verdict.
DE.CI.SI.VA.MEN.TE, *adv.*, decisively, evidently.
DE.CI.SI.VO, *adj.*, decisive, conclusive, obvious.
DE.CI.SÓ.RI.O, *adj.*, *Jur.*, decisive.
DE.CLA.MA.ÇÃO, *s.f.*, declamation, recitation.
DE.CLA.MA.DOR, *s.m.*, declaimer; *adj.*, declaiming.
DE.CLA.MAR, *v.*, to declaim, to recite, to proclaim.
DE.CLA.MA.TÓ.RI.O, *adj.*, declamatory.
DE.CLA.RA.ÇÃO, *s.f.*, declaration, assertion, statement.
DE.CLA.RA.DO, *adj.*, declared, manifest, proved.
DE.CLA.RA.DOR, *s.m.*, declarer; *adj.*, declaring.
DE.CLA.RAN.TE, *s.* 2 *gen.*, declarant; *adj.*, declaring.
DE.CLA.RAR, *v.*, to declare, to assert, to state, to announce.
DE.CLA.RA.TI.VO, *adj.*, declarativo.
DE.CLA.RA.TÓ.RI.O, *adj.*, declaratory.
DE.CLI.NA.ÇÃO, *s.f.*, declination; decline, decay; *Gram.*, declension.
DE.CLI.NAN.TE, *adj.*, declining; falling, decaying.
DE.CLI.NAR, *v.*, to reject, to refuse, to declare, to reveal.

DE.CLI.NÁ.VEL, *adj.*, declinable.
DE.CLÍ.NI.O, *s.m.*, decline, declination; decadence, decay.
DE.CLI.VE, *s.m.*, descending, declivity; *adj.*, declivous.
DE.CLI.VI.DA.DE, *s.f.*, declivity.
DE.CLÍ.VI.O, *s.m.*, the same that *declive*.
DE.CO.DI.FI.CA.ÇÃO, *s.f.*, decoding.
DE.CO.DI.FI.CA.DOR, *s.m.*, decoder.
DE.CO.DI.FI.CAR, *v.*, to decode, to decipher.
DE.CO.LAR, *v.*, to take off.
DE.COM.POR, *v.*, to decompose, to separate, to analyse, to modify.
DE.COM.PO.SI.ÇÃO, *s.f.*, decomposition, disintegration, separation, analysis.
DE.COM.POS.TO, *adj.*, decomposed.
DE.CO.RA.ÇÃO, *s.f.*, decoration, adornment, ornamentation.
DE.CO.RA.DOR, *s.m.*, decorator.
DE.CO.RAR, *v.*, to know by heart, to remember; to decorate, to adorn, to embellish.
DE.CO.RA.TI.VO, *adj.*, decorative.
DE.CO.RE.BA, *s.f.*, *gír.*, learning by heart, without really understanding.
DE.CO.RO, *s.m.*, decency, honesty, propriety, decorum.
DE.CO.RO.SO, *adj.*, decorous, deserving, decent.
DE.COR.RÊN.CI.A, *s.f.*, consequence, result.
DE.COR.REN.TE, *adj.*, deriving, resulting from; current.
DE.COR.RER, *v.*, to elapse, to pass away, to happen, to occur, to derive.
DE.COR.RI.DO, *adj.*, passed, elapsed.
DE.CO.TAR, *v.*, to cut off, to make low-necked.
DE.CO.TE, *s.m.*, low neck.
DE.CRÉ.PI.TO, *adj.*, decrepit, old, feeble.
DE.CRE.PI.TU.DE, *s.f.*, decrepitude, feebleness.
DE.CRES.CEN.TE, *adj.*, decrescent, decreasing.
DE.CRES.CER, *v.*, to diminish, to decrease, decline.
DE.CRES.CI.MEN.TO, *s.m.*, decrease, lessening, diminution, decrement.
DE.CRÉS.CI.MO, *s.m.*, decrease.
DE.CRIP.TA.ÇÃO, *s.f.*, decryption, decoding.
DE.CRE.TAR, *v.*, to decree, to determine, to proclaim, to order.
DE.CRE.TO, *s.m.*, decree, edict, designation.
DE.CÚ.BI.TO, *s.m.*, decubitus.
DE.CU.PLI.CAR, *v.*, to increase tenfold.
DE.DAL, *s.m.*, thimble.
DE.DÃO, *s.m.*, *pop.*, thumb, big toe.
DE.DAR, *v.*, to accuse, to denounce.
DE.DE.TI.ZA.ÇÃO, *s.f.*, spraying of insecticide.
DE.DE.TI.ZAR, *v.*, to spray insecticide or pesticide.
DE.DI.CA.ÇÃO, *s.f.*, dedication, devotion, affection, fondness.
DE.DI.CA.DO, *adj.*, dedicated, devoted, consecrated.
DE.DI.CAR, *v.*, to dedicate, to devote, to hallow, to consecrate.
DE.DI.CA.TÓ.RIA, *s.f.*, dedication.
DE.DI.LHAR, *v.*, to finger, to play with the fingers.
DE.DO, *s.m.*, finger.
DE.DO-DU.RAR, *v.*, *gír.*, to accuse, to delate.
DE.DO-DU.RO, *s.* 2 *gen.*, *gír.*, stool pigeon, delator, informer.
DE.DU.ÇÃO, *s.f.*, deduction, abatement, allowance.
DE.DU.RAR, *v.*, bras, *gír.*, the same that *dedo-durar*.
DE.DU.TÍ.VEL, *adj.*, deductible.
DE.DU.TI.VO, *adj.*, deductive.
DE.DU.ZIR, *v.*, to deduce, to draw or trace from facts, to infer.
DE.FA.SA.GEM, *s.f.*, *Eletr.*, phase, displacement; *fig.*, difference.

DEFASAR ·· 154 ·· DELICADAMENTE

DE.FA.SAR, v., *Eletr.*, to dephase.
DE.FE.CA.ÇÃO, s.f., defecation.
DE.FE.CAR, v., to defecate, to shit, to poop.
DE.FEC.ÇÃO, s.f., defection, desertion.
DE.FEC.TÍ.VEL, adj., faulty, fallible.
DE.FEC.TI.VO, adj., defective, imperfect.
DE.FEI.TO, s.m., defect, fault, flaw, deformity.
DE.FEI.TU.O.SO, adj., defective, faulty, imperfect.
DE.FEN.DER, v., to defend, to protect, to help, to aid, to support.
DE.FE.NES.TRA.ÇÃO, s.f., defenestration.
DE.FEN.SÁ.VEL, adj., defendable, defensible.
DE.FEN.SI.VO, s.f., defensive; s.m., protection; adj., defensive, protective.
DE.FEN.SOR, s.m., defender, protector.
DE.FE.RÊN.CIA, s.f., deference, respect, regard.
DE.FE.REN.TE, adj., deferent, deferential.
DE.FE.RI.DO, adj., granted, conceded, conferred.
DE.FE.RI.MEN.TO, s.m., grant, concession.
DE.FE.RIR, v., to grant, to approve, to confer.
DE.FE.RÍ.VEL, adj., grantable.
DE.FE.SA, s.f., defence, defense, justification, guard, protection.
DE.FI.CI.ÊN.CIA, s.f., deficiency, lack, want, need, imperfection.
DE.FI.CI.EN.TE, adj., deficient, defective, imperfect.
DÉ.FI.CIT, s.m., deficit, shortage.
DE.FI.CI.TÁ.RIO, adj., deficient.
DE.FI.NHA.MEN.TO, s.m., emaciation, weakening.
DE.FI.NHAR, v., to debilitate, to weaken, to languish.
DE.FI.NI.ÇÃO, s.f., definition, definement, explanation, decision.
DE.FI.NI.DO, adj., defined, determined.
DE.FI.NIR, v., to define, to determine, to fix, to decide.
DE.FI.NI.TI.VA.MEN.TE, adv., definitively, conclusively.
DE.FI.NI.TI.VO, adj., definitive, conclusive.
DE.FI.NÍ.VEL, adj., definable.
DE.FLA.ÇÃO, s.f., *Econ.*, deflation.
DE.FLA.CI.O.NA.DO, adj., *Econ.*, deflated.
DE.FLA.CI.O.NAR, v., *Econ.*, to deflate.
DE.FLA.GRA.ÇÃO, s.f., deflagration.
DE.FLA.GRAR, v., to deflagrate, to burn, to excite.
DE.FLE.XÃO, s.f., deflection.
DE.FLO.RA.ÇÃO, s.f., defloration.
DE.FLO.RA.MEN.TO, s.m., defloration.
DE.FLO.RAR, v., to deflorate, to deflower, to violate.
DE.FLÚ.VI.O, s.m., flowing; emanation (liquid).
DE.FLU.XO, s.m., common cold; coryza.
DE.FOR.MA.ÇÃO, s.f., deformation, disfigurement, deformity.
DE.FOR.MAR, v., to deform, to disfigure, to misshape, to warp.
DE.FOR.MÁ.VEL, adj., deformable.
DE.FOR.MI.DA.DE, s.f., deformity.
DE.FRAU.DA.ÇÃO, s.f., defraudation, cheating.
DE.FRAU.DAR, v., to defraud, to cheat.
DE.FRON.TA.ÇÃO, s.f., confrontation.
DE.FRON.TAR, v., to confront, to face.
DE.FRON.TE, adv., face to face, in front of.
DE.FU.MA.ÇÃO, s.f., smoking, curing.
DE.FU.MA.DO, adj., smoked.
DE.FU.MA.DOR, s.m., smoker.
DE.FU.MAR, v., to smoke-dry, to cure with smoke.

DE.FUN.TO, s.m., corpse, deceased; adj., dead, extinct.
DE.GE.LAR, v., to defrost, to deice.
DE.GE.LO, s.m., defrosting, thawing.
DE.GE.NE.RA.ÇÃO, s.f., degeneration.
DE.GE.NE.RAR, v., to degenerate, to fall off, to deteriorate.
DE.GLU.TI.ÇÃO, s.f., deglutition, swallowing.
DE.GLU.TIR, v., to swallow.
DE.GO.LA, s.f., decollation, decapitation.
DE.GO.LA.ÇÃO, s.f., decollation.
DE.GO.LA.DOR, s.m., cutthroat, fuller, fullering tool.
DE.GO.LAR, v., to decapitate, to behead.
DE.GRA.DA.ÇÃO, s.f., degradation.
DE.GRA.DAN.TE, adj., degrading.
DE.GRA.DAR, v., to degrade, to lower, to decline.
DE.GRAU, s.m., stair, step.
DE.GRE.DA.DO, s.m., deportee; adj., banished, exiled.
DE.GRE.DAR, v., to exile, to banish, to deport.
DE.GRE.DO, s.m., exile, banishment, deportation.
DE.GRIN.GO.LAR, v., to roll down, to fall; to come down.
DE.GUS.TA.ÇÃO, s.f., degustation, tasting.
DE.GUS.TAR, v., to taste, to degust.
DEI.DA.DE, s.f., deity, divinity, god, goddess.
DEI.FI.CA.ÇÃO, s.f., deification.
DE.ÍS.MO, s.m., deism.
DE.ÍS.TA, s. 2 gen., deist.
DEI.TA.DO, adj., lying down; in bed.
DEI.TAR, v., to lie, to lay; to lie down, to incline.
DEI.XA, s.f., *Teat.*, cue; hint.
DEI.XAR, v., to leave, to quit, to abandon, to let go, to forsake, to release.
DÉ.JÀ VU, s.m., *Fr.*, *déjà vu*: old stuff.
DE.JE.TO, s.m., evacuation, defecation.
DE.JU.A.ÇÃO, s.f., the same that *desjejum*.
DE.LA, contr. of the prep. **DE** and the pron. **ELA**: her, hers, of her, from her.
DE.LA.ÇÃO, s.f., delation, accusation.
DE.LA.TAR, v., to delate, to inform against, to denounce.
DE.LA.TOR, s.m., delator, squealer, informer.
DE.LE, contr. of the prep. **DE** and the pron. **ELE**: his, of him, from him.
DE.LE.GA.ÇÃO, s.f., delegation, deputation.
DE.LE.GA.CI.A, s.f., delegateship, police station.
DE.LE.GA.DO, s.m., delegate, police officer.
DE.LE.GAR, v., to delegate, to depute, to authorize, to assign, to appoint.
DE.LEI.TA.ÇÃO, s.f., delight, pleasure, enjoyment.
DE.LEI.TA.MEN.TO, s.m., delight, pleasure.
DE.LEI.TAR, v., to delight, to please, to gratify.
DE.LEI.TE, s.m., delight, pleasure, enjoyment.
DE.LEI.TO.SO, adj., delightful.
DE.LE.TÉ.RI.O, adj., deleterious, noxious, pernicious.
DE.LÉ.VEL, adj., delible, erasable.
DEL.FIM, s.m., *Zool.*, dolphin.
DEL.GA.DO, adj., thin, slender; meagre; fine.
DE.LI.BE.RA.ÇÃO, s.f., deliberation, consideration.
DE.LI.BE.RA.DA.MEN.TE, adv., deliberately.
DE.LI.BE.RA.DO, adj., deliberate, intentional.
DE.LI.BE.RAR, v., to deliberate, to ponder, to reflect upon, to resolve.
DE.LI.BE.RA.TI.VO, adj., deliberative.
DE.LI.CA.DA.MEN.TE, adv., courteously, politely.

DELICADEZA ·· 155 ·· DENÚNCIA

DE.LI.CA.DE.ZA, *s.f.*, politeness, courtesy, fineness.
DE.LI.CA.DO, *adj.*, delicate, polite, courteous.
DE.LÍ.CIA, *s.f.*, delicacy, delight, pleasure.
DE.LI.CI.AR, *v.*, to delight, to please.
DE.LI.CI.O.SO, *adj.*, delicious, delightful.
DE.LI.MI.TA.ÇÃO, *s.f.*, delimitation.
DE.LI.MI.TA.DOR, *s.m.*, delimiter; *adj.*, delimiting.
DE.LI.MI.TAR, *v.*, to delimitate, to delimit, to bound.
DE.LI.NE.A.DOR, *s.m.*, delineator; *adj.*, limiting, sketchin.
DE.LI.NE.A.MEN.TO, *s.m.*, delineation; sketch.
DE.LI.NE.AR, *v.*, to delineate, to sketch out, to draw, to outline.
DE.LIN.QUÊN.CI.A, *s.f.*, delinquency; fault, misdemeanor.
DE.LIN.QUEN.TE, *s. 2 gen.*, delinquent, outlaw, felon, transgressor; *adj.*, delinquent.
DE.LIN.QUIR, *v.*, to commit an offense.
DE.LI.RAN.TE, *adj.*, delirious, insane; excited; extraordinary.
DE.LI.RAR, *v.*, to rave, to talk nonsense.
DE.LÍ.RIO, *s.m.*, delirium, insanity, derangement.
DE.LI.RI.UM TRE.MENS, *s.m., Lat., Med.*, delirium tremens (delirious produced by overabsorption of alcohol).
DE.LI.TO, *s.m.*, delict, fault, crime, transgression.
DE.LI.TU.O.SO, *adj.*, criminal, wrong.
DE.LON.GA, *s.f.*, delay, postponement.
DE.LON.GAR, *v.*, to delay, to postpone.
DEL.TA, *s.m.*, delta.
DE.MA.GO.GI.A, *s.f.*, demagogy, demagogusm.
DE.MA.GÓ.GI.CO, *adj.*, demagogic, demagogical.
DE.MA.GO.GO, *s.m.*, demagogue, demagog.
DE.MAIS, *adv.*, too much, excessive, overmuch; besides, moreover.
DE.MAN.DA, *s.f.*, lawsuit; discussion; *Econ.*, demand.
DE.MAN.DAN.TE, *adj.*, suing, demanding.
DE.MAN.DAR, *v.*, to require, to call for, to demand.
DE.MÃO, *s.f.*, coat, coating (paint, etc.).
DE.MAR.CA.ÇÃO, *s.f.*, demarcation.
DE.MAR.CA.DOR, *s.m.*, demarcator; *adj.*, demarcating.
DE.MAR.CAR, *v.*, to demarcate, to delimit, to define, to mark out.
DE.MAR.CA.TÓ.RI.O, *adj.*, referring to demarcation.
DE.MAR.CÁ.VEL, *adj.*, definable, capable of being demarcated.
DE.MA.SI.A, *s.f.*, surplus, excess, overplus, superabundance.
DE.MA.SI.A.DO, *adj.*, excessive, overmuch, too much, undue.
DE.MÊN.CIA, *s.f.*, dementia, insanity.
DE.MEN.TE, *s., Med.*, demented person; *adj., Med.*, demented; mad, crazy.
DE.MÉ.RI.TO, *s.m.*, demerit; *adj.*, unworthy.
DE.MIS.SÃO, *s.f.*, demission, firing, dismissal, abdication.
DE.MIS.SI.O.NÁ.RI.O, *adj.*, resigning.
DE.MI.TI.DO, *adj.*, dismissed, fired.
DE.MI.TIR, *v.*, to dismiss, to discharge, to fire.
DE.MI.UR.GO, *s.m.*, demiurge.
DE.MO.CRA.CI.A, *s.f.*, democracy.
DE.MO.CRA.TA, *s. 2 gen.*, democrat.
DE.MO.CRA.TI.CA.MEN.TE, *adv.*, democratically.
DE.MO.CRÁ.TI.CO, *adj.*, democratic, democratical.
DE.MO.CRA.TI.ZA.ÇÃO, *s.f.*, democratization.
DE.MO.CRA.TI.ZA.DO, *adj.*, democratized.
DE.MO.CRA.TI.ZAR, *v.*, to democratize.
DE.MO.DÊ, *adj., Fr.*, démodé (out of fashion).
DE.MO.GRA.FI.A, *s.f.*, demography.

DE.MO.GRÁ.FI.CO, *adj.*, demographic, demographical.
DE.MÓ.GRA.FO, *s.m.*, demographer.
DE.MO.LI.ÇÃO, *s.f.*, demolition, demolishment.
DE.MO.LI.DOR, *s.m.*, demolisher, destroyer; *adj.*, demolishing, destroying, destructive.
DE.MO.LIR, *v.*, to demolish, to destroy.
DE.MO.NÍ.A.CO, *adj.*, demoniac, demoniacal, demonic, devilish.
DE.MÔ.NIO, *s.m.*, demon, devil.
DE.MO.NIS.MO, *s.m.*, demonism, demonology.
DE.MO.NIS.TA, *s. 2 gen.*, demonologist.
DE.MONS.TRA.BI.LI.DA.DE, *s.f.*, demonstrability.
DE.MONS.TRA.ÇÃO, *s.f.*, demonstration.
DE.MONS.TRA.DOR, *s.m.*, demonstrator; *adj.*, demonstrative.
DE.MONS.TRAR, *v.*, to demonstrate, to prove by reasoning, to evince.
DE.MONS.TRA.TI.VO, *adj.*, demonstrative.
DE.MONS.TRÁ.VEL, *adj.*, demonstrable.
DE.MO.RA, *s.f.*, delay, retardation, lateness.
DE.MO.RA.DO, *adj.*, delayed, lengthy, protracted.
DE.MO.RAR, *v.*, to delay, to stay, to detain, to retard.
DE.MO.VER, *v.*, to dissuade, to discourage, to divert.
DEN.DÊ, *s.m., Bras., Bot.*, a kind oil palm from Africa; its fruit.
DEN.DE.ZEI.RO, *s.m., Bras., Bot.*, oil palm.
DEN.DRO.LO.GI.A, *s.f.*, dendrology (the study of trees).
DE.NE.GRIR, *v.*, to denigrate, to blacken.
DEN.GO.SO, *adj.*, whining, dainty, coy, finical, affected.
DEN.GUE, *s.m., Med.*, dengue, breakbone fever.
DE.NO.DAR, *v.*, to disentangle, to untie.
DE.NO.DO, *s.m.*, boldness, bravery, courage.
DE.NO.MI.NA.ÇÃO, *s.f.*, denomination, name, naming, designation.
DE.NO.MI.NA.DO, *adj.*, so-called, named.
DE.NO.MI.NA.DOR, *s.m.*, denominator; *adj.*, denominative.
DE.NO.MI.NAR, *v.*, to denominate, to name, to call, to entitle.
DE.NO.TA.ÇÃO, *s.f.*, denotation, sign.
DE.NO.TAR, *v.*, to denote.
DEN.SA.MEN.TE, *adv.*, densely.
DEN.SI.DA.DE, *s.f.*, density, thickness, closeness.
DEN.SO, *adj.*, dense, thick, compact.
DEN.TA.DA, *s.f.*, bite, biting, morsel.
DEN.TA.DU.RA, *s.f.*, denture, set of teeth, false teeth.
DEN.TAL, *s.f., adj.*, dental; *creme dental*: toothpaste; *fio dental*: dental floss.
DEN.TAR, *v.*, to bite, to snap.
DEN.TÁ.RI.O, *adj.*, dental.
DEN.TE, *s.m.*, tooth; *dente de leite*: milk tooth.
DEN.TE.A.ÇÃO, *s.f.*, indentation, denting.
DEN.TE.AR, *v.*, to indent.
DEN.TE-DE-LE.ÃO, *s.m., Bot.*, dandelion.
DEN.TI.ÇÃO, *s.f.*, dentition, teething.
DEN.TI.FRÍ.CIO, *s.m.*, dentifrice, tooth paste.
DEN.TIS.TA, *s. 2 gen.*, dentist.
DEN.TRE, *prep.*, among, in the midst of.
DEN.TRO, *adv.*, inside, within, indoors.
DEN.TU.ÇO, *adj.*, big-toothed.
DEN.TU.DO, *s.m.*, person having big teeth; *adj.*, big-toothed, toothy.
DE.NU.DA.ÇÃO, *s.f.*, denudation, divestment.
DE.NU.DAR, *v.*, to denude, to divest.
DE.NÚN.CIA, *s.f.*, accusation, denunciation, delation.

DENUNCIADO ·· 156 ·· DESACATO

DE.NUN.CI.A.DO, *s.m.*, defendant.

DE.NUN.CI.A.DOR, *s.m.*, denouncer, delator; *adj.*, denouncing.

DE.NUN.CI.AR, *v.*, to denounce, to denunciate, to accuse, to inform.

DE.NUN.CI.AN.TE, *s. 2 gen.*, denouncer; *adj.*, denouncing.

DE.NUN.CI.Á.VEL, *adj.*, denounceable.

DE.PA.RAR, *v.*, to cause to appear suddenly; *deparar-se*: come across.

DE.PAR.TA.MEN.TAL, *adj.*, departmental.

DE.PAR.TA.MEN.TO, *s.m.*, department, bureau.

DE.PAR.TIR, *v.*, to divide, to distribute.

DE.PAU.PE.RA.MEN.TO, *s.m.*, depauperation, impoverishment.

DE.PAU.PE.RA.DO, *adj.*, impoverished, exhausted.

DE.PAU.PE.RAR, *v.*, to depauperate, to impoverish, to enervate.

DE.PE.NAR, *v.*, to pluck, to deplume, to pick; to strip of money.

DE.PEN.DÊN.CIA, *s.f.*, dependence, pendency, subjection, subordination.

DE.PEN.DER, *v.*, to depend on, to be based on, to be pending.

DE.PEN.DU.RA.DO, *adj.*, suspended, hanging.

DE.PEN.DU.RAR, *v.*, the same that *pendurar*: to hang, to suspend.

DE.PI.LA.ÇÃO, *s.f.*, depilation.

DE.PI.LAR, *v.*, to depilate.

DE.PLO.RAR, *v.*, to deplore, to regret, to lament, to bewail.

DE.PLO.RÁ.VEL, *adj.*, deplorable, lamentable.

DE.PO.EN.TE, *s. 2 gen.*, deponent; *adj. Gram.*, deponent.

DE.PO.I.MEN.TO, *s.m.*, deposition, testimony.

DE.POIS, *adv.*, after, afterward, later on, then, besides, moreover.

DE.POR, *v.*, to put down, to lay down, to depose, to put aside, to testify, to witness.

DE.POR.TA.ÇÃO, *s.f.*, deportation, banishment.

DE.POR.TA.DO, *s.m.*, deportee; *adj.*, deported, exiled.

DE.POR.TAR, *v.*, to deport, to banish, to exile.

DE.PO.SI.ÇÃO, *s.f.*, deposition.

DE.PO.SI.TAN.TE, *s. 2 gen.*, depositor; *adj.*, depositing.

DE.PO.SI.TAR, *v.*, to deposit, to lay, to entrust, to commit to for custody.

DE.PO.SI.TÁ.RI.O, *s.m.*, depositary; trustee.

DE.PÓ.SI.TO, *s.m.*, deposit, deposition, act of depositing; storehouse, warehouse.

DE.PRA.VA.ÇÃO, *s.f.*, depravation, perversion, corruption.

DE.PRA.VA.DO, *adj.*, depraved, degenerate, corrupt.

DE.PRA.VAR, *v.*, to deprave, pervert; *depravar-se*: to degenerate.

DE.PRE.CI.A.ÇÃO, *s.f.*, depreciation.

DE.PRE.CI.AR, *v.*, to depreciate, to undervalue, to lessen.

DE.PRE.CI.A.TI.VO, *adj.*, depreciative.

DE.PRE.CI.Á.VEL, *adj.*, depreciable.

DE.PRE.DA.ÇÃO, *s.f.*, depredation, destruction.

DE.PRE.DAR, *v.*, to depredate, to destroy.

DE.PRE.DA.TÓ.RI.O, *adj.*, depredatory.

DE.PRE.EN.DER, *v.*, to infer, to deduce.

DE.PRES.SA, *adv.*, fast, quickly, swiftly, readily.

DE.PRES.SÃO, *s.f.*, depression, stagnation.

DE.PRES.SI.VA.MEN.TE, *adv.*, depressively.

DE.PRES.SI.VO, *adj.*, depressive; depressing.

DE.PRI.MEN.TE, *adj.*, depressing.

DE.PRI.MI.DO, *adj.*, depressed.

DE.PRI.MIR, *v.*, to depress, to lower, to weaken, to depreciate.

DE.PU.RA.ÇÃO, *s.f.*, debugging, purification.

DE.PU.RAR, *v.*, to purify, to clean, to depurate.

DE.PU.TA.ÇÃO, *s.f.*, deputation.

DE.PU.TA.DO, *s.m.*, deputy, delegate, representative, commissioner, congressman.

DE.PU.TAR, *v.*, to depute, to delegate.

DE.RI.VA.ÇÃO, *s.f.*, derivation.

DE.RI.VA.DO, *s.m.*, derivative; *adj.*, derivative.

DE.RI.VAR, *v.*, to derive, to arise from, to deflect, to trace the origin.

DE.RI.VÁ.VEL, *adj.*, derivable.

DER.MA.TI.TE, *s.f., Med.*, dermatitis.

DER.MA.TO.LO.GI.A, *s.f.*, dermatology.

DER.MA.TO.LO.GIS.TA, *s. 2 gen.*, dermatologist.

DER.ME, *s.m., Anat., Zool.*, dermis.

DER.RA.DEI.RO, *adj.*, last, final, conclusive, hindmost.

DER.RA.MA.MEN.TO, *s.m.*, shedding, outflow (liquid); pruning.

DER.RA.MAR, *v.*, to shed, to spill, to lop, to strew, to pour out.

DER.RA.ME, *s.m.*, hemorrhage.

DER.RA.PA.GEM, *s.f., Bras.*, skidding, sideslip.

DER.RA.PAR, *v.*, to skid, to sideslip.

DER.RE.DOR, *adv.*, around, about.

DER.RE.TER, *v.*, to melt, to dissolve, to soften, to liquefy, to fuse.

DER.RE.TI.DO, *adj.*, melted.

DER.RE.TI.MEN.TO, *s.m.*, melting, fusion.

DER.RO.CA.DA, *s.f.*, destruction, demolition.

DER.RO.CA.DO, *adj.*, demolished, ruined.

DER.RO.CAR, *v.*, to demolish, to destroy.

DER.RO.TA, *s.f.*, defeat, overthrow.

DER.RO.TA.DO, *adj.*, defeated.

DER.RO.TAR, *v.*, to defeat, to vanquish, to beat, to foil.

DER.RO.TIS.MO, *s.m.*, defeatism.

DER.RO.TIS.TA, *s. 2 gen., adj.*, defeatist.

DER.RU.BA.DA, *s.f.*, felling (of trees), defeat.

DER.RU.BA.DO, *adj.*, demolished, felled; knocked over.

DER.RU.BA.MEN.TO, *s.m.*, overthrowal, falling dawn.

DER.RU.BAR, *v.*, to throw down, to throw to the ground.

DE.SA.BA.DO, *adj.*, crumble, pulled down, fall down.

DE.SA.BA.FAR, *v.*, to uncover, to expose, to reveal, to open.

DE.SA.BA.FO, *s.m.*, ease, relief, alleviation.

DE.SA.BA.LA.DA.MEN.TE, *adv.*, precipitately.

DE.SA.BA.LA.DO, *adj.*, precipitate, overhasty, hurried.

DE.SA.BA.MEN.TO, *s.m.*, crumbling, falling, tumbling.

DE.SA.BAR, *v.*, to crumble, to fall down, to tumble.

DE.SA.BI.LI.TAR, *v.*, to incapacitate, to disable.

DE.SA.BI.TA.DO, *adj.*, uninhabited, deserted.

DE.SA.BI.TAR, *v.*, to disoccupy, to depopulate.

DE.SA.BO.NAR, *v.*, to discredit, destroy the credit.

DE.SA.BO.TO.A.DU.RA, *s.f.*, unbuttoning.

DE.SA.BO.TO.AR, *v.*, to unbutton, to open, to spread.

DE.SA.BRI.GA.DO, *adj.*, unsheltered, unprotected.

DE.SA.BRI.GAR, *v.*, to uncover.

DE.SA.BRO.CHA.DO, *adj.*, blossomed, blooming; unclasped.

DE.SA.BRO.CHAR, *v.*, to bloom, to sprout, to unclasp, to loosen.

DE.SA.BU.SA.DO, *adj.*, unprejudiced, impartial; impertinent.

DE.SA.CA.TAR, *v.*, to disrespect, to disregard, to affront.

DE.SA.CA.TO, *s.m.*, disrespect, disregard, discourtesy.

DESACELERAÇÃO · · 157 · · DESATENÇÃO

DE.SA.CE.LE.RA.ÇÃO, s.f., deceleration.
DE.SA.CER.TAR, v., to mistake, to miss, to err.
DE.SA.CER.TO, s.m., mistake, error.
DE.SA.COM.PA.NHA.DO, adj., unaccompanied, alone; solitary.
DE.SA.CON.SE.LHAR, v., to dissuade, advise against.
DE.SA.CON.SE.LHÁ.VEL, adj., inadvisable.
DE.SA.COR.DA.DO, adj., unconscious, not aware.
DE.SA.COR.DO, s.m., disagreement.
DE.SA.COS.TU.MA.DO, adj., unaccustomed, not used to.
DE.SA.COS.TU.MAR, v., to disaccustom, to disuse, to dishabituate.
DE.SA.CRE.DI.TA.DO, adj., discredited.
DE.SA.CRE.DI.TAR, v., to discredit, to disparage, to defame.
DE.SA.FE.TO, s.m., disaffection; opponent, enemy; adj., disaffected, disloyal.
DE.SA.FI.A.DO, adj., edgeless, dull.
DE.SA.FI.A.DOR, s.m., challenger, provoker, defier; adj., challenging, defying.
DE.SA.FI.AN.TE, s. 2 gen., challenger, defier.
DE.SA.FI.AR, v., to challenge, to defy, to provoke, to beard.
DE.SA.FI.NA.ÇÃO, s.f., Mús., discord, disharmony.
DE.SA.FI.NA.DO, adj., dissonant, inharmonious.
DE.SA.FI.NAR, v., to sing or play out of tune.
DE.SA.FI.O, s.m., challenge, defiance, provocation, defy.
DE.SA.FO.GAR, v., to relieve, to ease, to disencumber, to disclose.
DE.SA.FO.RA.DO, adj., insolent, impertinent, rude.
DE.SA.FO.RO, s.m., insolence, impudence, insult, injury, affront.
DE.SA.FOR.TU.NA.DO, adj., unfortunate, luckless.
DE.SA.GRA.DAR, v., to displease, dissatisfy, dislike.
DE.SA.GRA.DÁ.VEL, adj., unpleasant, disagreeable.
DE.SA.GRA.DO, s.m., unpleasantness, displeasure, disfavour.
DE.SA.GRA.VO, s.m., revenge, retaliation, redress, requital.
DE.SA.GRE.GA.ÇÃO, s.f., disaggregation, dissolution.
DE.SA.GRE.GAR, v., to disaggregate, to disintegrate, to disperse; desagregar-se: to crumble.
DE.SA.GUAR, v., to drain, to dry.
DE.SA.JEI.TA.DO, adj., unskillful, clumsy, awkward.
DE.SA.JEI.TAR, v., to disarrange, to turn awkward.
DE.SA.JU.I.ZA.DO, adj., witless, unwise, thoughtless.
DE.SA.JUS.TA.DO, adj., disarranged, unadjusted.
DE.SA.JUS.TAR, v., to disagree, disadjust, to disarrange, to disturbe.
DE.SA.JUS.TE, s.m., disagreement, conflict.
DE.SA.LEN.TA.DO, adj., discouraged, depressed.
DE.SA.LEN.TA.DOR, s.m., discourager; adj., discouraging.
DE.SA.LEN.TAR, v., to discourage, to depress.
DE.SA.LEN.TO, s.m., discouragement, faintness, prostration.
DE.SA.LI.NHA.DO, adj., sloppy, disheveled; out of line.
DE.SA.LI.NHO, s.m., dishevelment, disorder, disarray.
DE.SAL.MA.DO, adj., soulless.
DE.SA.LO.JA.MEN.TO, s.m., displacement, dislodgment.
DE.SA.LO.JAR, v., to dislodge, to remove, to unhouse, to drive out.
DE.SA.MAR.RAR, v., to untie, to cast off, to unfasten, to loosen.
DE.SA.MOR, s.m., lovelessness, disaffection.
DE.SAM.PA.RA.DO, adj., abandoned, unhelped, unsupported.
DE.SAM.PA.RAR, v., to abandon, to leave, to quit, to forsake.

DE.SAM.PA.RO, s.m., abandonment, helplessness, lurch.
DE.SAN.DAR, v., to turn or draw back.
DE.SA.NE.XAR, v., disconnect, dissolve, detach.
DE.SA.NI.MA.ção, s.f., discouragement, disheartenment.
DE.SA.NI.MA.DO, adj., discouraged, down, downhearted, depressed.
DE.SA.NI.MAR, v., to discourage, to depress, to dispirit.
DE.SÂ.NI.MO, s.m., discouragement, dispiriteness, dismay, depression.
DE.SA.PAI.XO.NA.DO, adj., dispassionate.
DE.SA.PAI.XO.NAR, v., to free from passion, to stop loving.
DE.SA.PA.RA.FU.SAR, v., to unscrew, to screw off.
DE.SA.PA.RE.CER, v., to disappear, to vanish, to die, to be lost.
DE.SA.PA.RE.CI.DO, adj., disappeared.
DE.SA.PA.RE.CI.MEN.TO, s.m., disappearance.
DE.SA.PA.RI.ção, s.f., disappearance.
DE.SA.PER.CE.BER, v., to deprive of.
DE.SA.PER.CE.BI.DO, adj., unbeknown.
DE.SA.PE.GO, s.m., unattachment, disaffection.
DE.SA.PER.TAR, v., to loosen, to unlace, to unbrace, to unscrew.
DE.SA.PON.TA.DO, adj., disappointed, frustrated.
DE.SA.PON.TA.MEN.TO, s.m., disappointment.
DE.SA.PON.TAR, v., to disappoint.
DE.SA.PRO.PRI.A.ÇÃO, s.f., dispossession, expropriation.
DE.SA.PRO.PRI.AR, v., to dispossess, to deprive, to expropriate.
DE.SA.PRO.VA.ÇÃO, s.f., disapproval.
DE.SA.PRO.VAR, v., disapprove, disfavor.
DE.SAR.MA.DO, adj., unarmed.
DE.SAR.MA.MEN.TIS.MO, s.m., disarmamentism.
DE.SAR.MA.MEN.TO, s.m., disarmament.
DE.SAR.MAR, v., to disarm, to unarm, to unrig, to unship.
DE.SAR.MO.NI.A, s.f., Mús., disharmony; discord.
DE.SAR.MÔ.NI.CO, adj., inharmonious.
DE.SAR.MO.NI.ZAR, v., to disharmonize.
DE.SAR.RAI.GA.MEN.TO, s.m., uprooting.
DE.SAR.RAI.GAR, v., to uproot.
DE.SAR.RAN.JAR, v., to disarrange.
DE.SAR.RAN.JO, s.m., disarrangement, disorder, mishap, distemper.
DE.SAR.RO.LHAR, v., to uncork, unplug.
DE.SAR.RU.MA.DO, adj., untidy.
DE.SAR.RU.MA.ÇÃO, s.f., disorder, untidiness.
DE.SAR.RU.MAR, v., to disarrange, to displace, to disorder, to dislocate.
DE.SAR.TI.CU.LA.ÇÃO, s.f., disarticulation.
DE.SAR.TI.CU.LAR, v., to disjoint, to disconnect, to dislocate, to luxate.
DE.SAS.SIS.TI.DO, adj., unaided.
DE.SAS.SIS.TIR, v., to abandon, to desert.
DE.SAS.SOM.BRO, s.m., frankness, firmness, resolution.
DE.SAS.SOS.SE.GAR, v., to bother, to disturb.
DE.SAS.SOS.SE.GO, s.m., unquietness, uneasiness.
DE.SAS.TRA.DO, adj., disastrous, clumsy, awkward.
DE.SAS.TRE, s.m., disaster, accident, calamity, misfortune, loss.
DE.SAS.TRO.SO, adj., disastrous, hazardous, calamitous.
DE.SA.TAR, v., to unfasten, to untie, to unhind, to release.
DE.SA.TEN.ÇÃO, s.f., absence of mind, carelessness,

DESATENTO · 158 · DESCONTROLADO

inattention.

DE.SA.TEN.TO, *adj.*, careless, negligent, heedless, forgetful.

DE.SA.TI.NA.DO, *adj.*, crazy, mad, insane.

DE.SA.TI.NAR, *v.*, to make crazy, to madden.

DE.SA.TI.NO, *s.m.*, madness, nonsense.

DE.SA.TI.VA.ÇÃO, *s.f.*, deactivation, shutting down.

DE.SA.TI.VA.DO, *adj.*, deactivated.

DE.SA.TI.VAR, *v.*, to switch off, to turn off, to power down.

DE.SAU.TO.RI.ZA.ção, *s.f.*, loss of authority.

DE.SAU.TO.RI.ZA.DO, *adj.*, unauthorized.

DE.SAU.TO.RI.ZAR, *v.*, to disauthorize.

DE.SA.VEN.ÇA, *s.f.*, dissension, disagreement, discord, differ.

DE.SA.VER.GO.NHA.DO, *adj.*, shameless, unblushing.

DE.SA.VI.SA.DO, *adj.*, unwary.

DES.BAN.CAR, *v.*, to surpass, to excel.

DES.BA.RA.TAR, *v.*, to waste, to squander.

DES.BAS.TAR, *v.*, to cut off, to pare, to thin out.

DES.BLO.QUE.AR, *v.*, to unblock, to unplug.

DES.BLO.QUEI.O, *s.m.*, raising of a blockade.

DES.BO.CA.DO, *s.m.*, big-mouth; *adj.*, unrestrained, shocking, indecent.

DES.BO.TA.DO, *adj.*, washed-out, weathered, paled.

DES.BO.TA.MEN.TO, *s.m.*, discoloration.

DES.BO.TAR, *v.*, to discolor, to wash out.

DES.BRA.VA.DOR, *s.m.*, pioneer, explorer.

DES.BRA.VAR, *v.*, to tame, to domesticate, to break, to cultivate.

DES.CA.BE.LA.DO, *adj.*, dishevelled, hairless.

DES.CA.BE.LAR, *v.*, to ruffle the hair of.

DES.CA.FEI.NA.DO, *adj.*, decaffeinated.

DES.CAL.ÇAR, *v.*, to take or slip off (shoes, stockings, etc.), to unboot.

DES.CAL.ÇO, *adj.*, unshod, shoeless, barefoot.

DES.CA.MAR, *v.*, to flake off.

DES.CAM.PA.DO, *s.m.*, open field, clearing, desert.

DES.CAN.SA.DO, *adj.*, quiet, undisturbed, rested, easy, calm, tranquil.

DES.CAN.SAR, *v.*, to rest, to relax, to repose, to pause.

DES.CAN.SO, *s.m.*, break, rest, resting, restfulness, repose, refreshment.

DES.CA.RAC.TE.RI.ZAR, *v.*, to decharacterize, to deprive of the characteristics.

DES.CA.RA.DO, *adj.*, shameless, brazen.

DES.CA.RA.MEN.TO, *s.m.*, shamelessness, impudence.

DES.CAR.GA, *s.f.*, discharge, unloading, unlading.

DES.CAR.RE.GAR, *v.*, to discharge, to unload, to unburden, to disembark.

DES.CAR.RI.LAR, *v.*, to derail.

DES.CAR.TAR, *v.*, to discard, to reject, to dismiss, to throw aside.

DES.CAR.TÁ.VEL, *adj.*, disposable, expendable.

DES.CAS.CA.DO, *adj.*, peeled, shelled out.

DES.CAS.CAR, *v.*, to peel, to skin, to rind, to bark.

DES.CA.SAR, *v.*, to divorce, to dissolve marriage.

DES.CA.SO, *s.m.*, negligence, disregard, indifference.

DES.CEN.DÊN.CIA, *s.f.*, descent, family, lineage, generation.

DES.CEN.DEN.TE, *adj.*, descendant, descendent.

DES.CEN.DER, *v.*, to descend, to proceed, to come from, to be derived.

DES.CEN.TRA.LI.ZA.ÇÃO, *s.f.*, decentralization.

DES.CEN.TRA.LI.ZA.DO, *adj.*, decentralized.

DES.CEN.TRA.LI.ZAR, *v.*, to decentralize.

DES.CER, *v.*, to descend, to go down, to come down, to dismount, to step down.

DES.CI.DA, *s.f.*, descent, descending, going down, fall.

DES.CLAS.SI.FI.CA.ÇÃO, *s.f.*, disqualification.

DES.CLAS.SI.FI.CA.DO, *adj.*, disqualified.

DES.CLAS.SI.FI.CAR, *v.*, to disqualify.

DES.CO.BER.TA, *s.f.*, discovery, invention, finding.

DES.CO.BER.TO, *adj.*, discovered.

DES.CO.BRI.DOR, *s.m.*, discoverer; *adj.*, discovering.

DES.CO.BRI.MEN.TO, *s.m.*, discovery, invention.

DES.CO.BRIR, *v.*, to discover, to uncover, to disclose, to expose, to show.

DES.CO.LAR, *v.*, to unglue, to unpaste.

DES.CO.LO.NI.ZAR, *v.*, to decolonize.

DES.CO.LO.RIR, *v.*, to discolor.

DES.CO.ME.DI.DO, *adj.*, exorbitant; unbridled; rude.

DES.COM.PAS.SA.DO, *adj.*, out of measure, excessive; in disorder.

DES.COM.POR, *v.*, to discompose, to disarrange, to derange.

DES.COM.POS.TO, *adj.*, disordered, confused.

DES.COM.PRES.SÃO, *s.f.*, decompression.

DES.CO.MU.NAL, *adj.*, extraordinary, uncommon, rare.

DES.CON.CER.TAR, *v.*, to disconcert, to disarrange, to disorder.

DES.CON.CER.TO, *s.m.*, disorder, disarrangement, confusion.

DES.CO.NE.XÃO, *s.f.*, disconnection.

DES.CO.NE.XO, *adj.*, disconnected, unconnected, separate; fragmentary.

DES.CON.FI.A.DO, *adj.*, suspicious, distrustful.

DES.CON.FI.AN.ÇA, *s.f.*, suspicion, suspiciousness, distrust.

DES.CON.FI.AR, *v.*, to suspect, to mistrust, to doubt, to distrust.

DES.CON.FOR.MI.DA.DE, *s.f.*, disconformity; disproportion.

DES.CON.FOR.TO, *s.m.*, discomfort, comfortlessness, uncomfortableness.

DES.CON.GE.LA.MEN.TO, *s.m.*, thaw, melting ice.

DES.CON.GE.LAR, *v.*, to thaw, defrost.

DES.CON.GES.TI.O.NAN.TE, *s.m.*, *Med.*, decongestant; *adj.*, decongestant.

DES.CO.NHE.CER, *v.*, to ignore, to disown, to dissemble.

DES.CO.NHE.CI.DO, *s.m.*, stranger; *adj.*, unknown, anonymous.

DES.CO.NHE.CI.MEN.TO, *s.m.*, ignorance; non-acquaintance.

DES.CON.SI.DE.RA.ÇÃO, *s.f.*, disrespect, disregard, slight.

DES.CON.SI.DE.RAR, *v.*, to disrespect, to disregard.

DES.CON.SO.LA.DO, *adj.*, disconsolate, desolate.

DES.CON.SO.LAR, *v.*, to become sad, be afflicted.

DES.CON.SO.LO, *s.m.*, desolation, distress, sorrow.

DES.CON.TAR, *v.*, to discount, diminish.

DES.CON.TEN.TA.MEN.TO, *s.m.*, discontentment, displeasure, disgust.

DES.CON.TEN.TAR, *v.*, to discontent, to displease, to dissatisfy, to disoblige.

DES.CON.TEN.TE, *adj.*, discontent, unsatisfied.

DES.CON.TO, *s.m.*, discount, abatement, deduction, reduction.

DES.CON.TRA.ÇÃO, *s.f.*, spontaneity, relaxation.

DES.CON.TRA.IR, *v.*, to become spontaneous, to become relaxed, to eliminate formality.

DES.CON.TRO.LA.DO, *adj.*, uncontrolled, out of control.

DESCONTROLAR · 159 · DESEQUILIBRADO

DES.CON.TRO.LAR, *v.*, to lose control, to be out of control.
DES.CON.TRO.LE, *s.m.*, lack of control.
DES.CO.RA.DO, *adj.*, discoloured, colourless; pale.
DES.CO.RAR, *v.*, to discolour, discolor; to fade.
DES.COR.TÊS, *adj.*, unkind, impolite, discourteous, rude.
DES.COR.TE.SI.A, *s.f.*, discourteousness, impoliteness, unkindness.
DES.COR.TI.NAR, *v.*, to pull the curtain; to reveal, to bring to light.
DES.CRÉ.DI.TO, *s.m.*, discredit.
DES.CREN.ÇA, *s.f.*, incredulity, disbelief, doubt.
DES.CREN.TE, *s. 2 gen.*, unbeliever, infidel; *adj.*, incredulous, unbelieving.
DES.CRE.VER, *v.*, to describe, to relate, to portray.
DES.CRI.ÇÃO, *s.f.*, description, report, picture.
DES.CRI.MI.NAR, *v.*, to absolve (from crime).
DES.CRI.TI.VO, *adj.*, descriptive.
DES.CRU.ZAR, *v.*, to uncross.
DES.CUI.DA.DO, *s.m.*, negligence, carelessness; *adj.*, careless, incautious.
DES.CUI.DAR, *v.*, to neglect, to disregard, to overlook, to slight.
DES.CUI.DO, *s.m.*, carelessness, lapse, disregard, incautiousness.
DES.CUL.PA, *s.f.*, excuse, pardon, apology, defence.
DES.CUL.PAR, *v.*, to excuse, to pardon, to apologize, to forgive, to exculpate.
DES.CUL.PÁ.VEL, *adj.*, excusable, pardonable.
DES.CUM.PRIR, *v.*, to disobey, disregard.
DES.DE, *prep.*, since, from, after.
DES.DÉM, *s.m.*, disdain, disdainfulness, disregard, depreciation.
DES.DE.NHAR, *v.*, to disdain, to scorn, to despise, to condemn.
DES.DE.NHO.SA.MEN.TE, *adv.*, disdainfully.
DES.DE.NHO.SO, *adj.*, disdainful, scornful.
DES.DEN.TA.DO, *adj.*, *Zool.*, edentate.
DES.DI.TA, *s.f.*, misfortune, unluckiness.
DES.DI.ZER, *v.*, to unsay, to deny, to contradict.
DES.DO.BRA.MEN.TO, *s.m.*, unrolling, unfolding; development.
DES.DO.BRAR, *v.*, to unfold, to unroll; to develop, to extend.
DE.SE.JAR, *v.*, to wish, to want, to will, to desire, to covet.
DE.SE.JÁ.VEL, *adj.*, desirable.
DE.SE.JO, *s.m.*, desire, wish, will, mind.
DE.SE.JO.SO, *adj.*, desirous, wishful, solicitous.
DE.SE.LE.GÂN.CI.A, *s.f.*, inelegance, inelegancy.
DE.SE.LE.GAN.TE, *adj.*, inelegant, ungraceful.
DE.SEM.BA.I.NHAR, *v.*, to unseam, to unsew; unsheathe (as a sword).
DE.SEM.BA.RA.ÇAR, *v.*, disembarrass, extricate, disentangle.
DE.SEM.BA.RA.ÇA.DO, *adj.*, unembarrassed, disengaged; adroit, dexterous, clever.
DE.SEM.BA.RA.ÇO, *s.m.*, disembarrassment; unrestraint; agility.
DE.SEM.BA.RA.LHAR, *v.*, to disintricate.
DE.SEM.BAR.CAR, *v.*, to disembark, to debark, to land.
DE.SEM.BAR.GA.DOR, *s.m.*, chief judge, judge at the Court of Appeals.
DE.SEM.BAR.QUE, *s.m.*, disembarkation, landing.

DE.SEM.BOL.SAR, *v.*, to disburse, to spend, to lay out, to expend.
DE.SEM.BOL.SO, *s.m.*, disbursement.
DE.SEM.BRU.LHAR, *v.*, to unpack, to unroll, to unwrap.
DE.SEM.PA.CO.TAR, *v.*, to unpack, to unwrap.
DE.SEM.PA.TAR, *v.*, to decide, to resolve, to give the casting vote.
DE.SEM.PA.TE, *s.m.*, decision; *Esp.*, playoff game, tiebreak.
DE.SEM.PE.NHAR, *v.*, to perform; to execute, to practice, to attend; to carry out; to pay off (one's debts).
DE.SEM.PE.NHO, *s.m.*, performance, discharge, practice.
DE.SEM.PRE.GA.DO, *s.m.*, unemployed; *adj.*, unemployed, unengaged, unoccupied.
DE.SEM.PRE.GAR, *v.*, to dismiss, to lay off.
DE.SEM.PRE.GO, *s.m.*, unemployment.
DE.SEN.CA.DE.AR, *v.*, to unleash, to unchain.
DE.SEN.CAI.XAR, *v.*, to disjoint, to dislocate, to displace.
DE.SEN.CAI.XE, *s.m.*, dislocation, disarticulation.
DE.SEN.CA.MI.NHAR, *v.*, to misguide, mislead, misdirect.
DE.SEN.CAN.TAR, *v.*, to disenchant, to disillusion.
DE.SEN.CAR.NAR, *v.*, to leave the body (as the soul); to die.
DE.SEN.CON.TRAR, *v.*, to fail to meet one another.
DE.SEN.CON.TRO, *s.m.*, failure in meeting, disagreement.
DE.SEN.CO.RA.JAR, *v.*, to discourage, to depress.
DE.SEN.FER.RU.JAR, *v.*, to remove the rust; *fig.*, to begin to exercise (body).
DE.SEN.FRE.A.DO, *adj.*, unruled, ungoverned, uncontrolled.
DE.SEN.FRE.AR, *v.*, to let loose, to set free, to unbridle.
DE.SEN.GA.NAR, *v.*, to undeceive, to disillusion.
DE.SEN.GA.NO, *s.m.*, disillusion, disappointment, undeceiving.
DE.SEN.GA.VE.TAR, *v.*, to take out of a drawer.
DE.SEN.GON.ÇA.DO, *adj.*, awkward, clumsy; unhinged, discoordinated.
DE.SE.NHAR, *v.*, to design, to draw, to trace, to outline, to create.
DE.SE.NHIS.TA, *s. 2 gen.*, sketcher, designer, tracer, drawer.
DE.SE.NHO, *s.m.*, design, sketch, drawing, draft, outline, draught.
DE.SEN.LA.CE, *s.m.*, unfolding, outcome, conclusion, end; *Lit.*, epilogue.
DE.SEN.RO.LAR, *v.*, to unroll, to uncurl, to unwind.
DE.SEN.ROS.CAR, *v.*, to untwine, to untwist, to unscrew.
DE.SEN.TEN.DER, *v.*, to misunderstand.
DE.SEN.TEN.DI.MEN.TO, *s.m.*, misunderstanding, disagreement, ignorance.
DE.SEN.TER.RA.DO, *adj.*, exhumed; dug up, unearthed; removed from the earth.
DE.SEN.TER.RAR, *v.*, to unbury, to dig up, to unearth.
DE.SEN.TRO.SA.DO, *adj.*, disorganized, lacking.
DE.SEN.TU.PI.DO, *adj.*, free from an obstruction, unstopped.
DE.SEN.TU.PI.MEN.TO, *s.m.*, unstopping, clearing, unblocking.
DE.SEN.TU.PIR, *v.*, to unstop, to clear, to cleanse.
DE.SEN.VOL.TO, *adj.*, agile, nimble, brisk, light, quick.
DE.SEN.VOL.TU.RA, *s.f.*, agility, nimbleness.
DE.SEN.VOL.VER, *v.*, to develop, to explain, to unwrap, to unrol, to unfold.
DE.SEN.VOL.VI.MEN.TO, *s.m.*, development, growth, evolution, improvement.
DE.SE.QUI.LI.BRA.DO, *adj.*, unbalanced, unsteady,

DESEQUILIBRAR ·· 160 ·· DESMANCHAR

unequaled; *fig.*, insane.

DE.SE.QUI.LI.BRAR, *v.*, to unbalance, to throw out of balance.

DE.SE.QUI.LÍ.BRIO, *s.m.*, unbalance, instability, distemper.

DE.SER.ÇÃO, *s.f.*, desertion.

DE.SER.DA.DO, *adj.*, disinherited, ungifted, untalented.

DE.SER.DAR, *v.*, to disinherit, to deprive of heritage.

DE.SER.TAR, *v.*, to desert, to abandon; to unpeople.

DE.SER.TI.FI.CA.ÇÃO, *s.f.*, desertification.

DE.SER.TO, *s.m.*, desert, wilderness; *adj.*, desert, uninhabited, wild.

DE.SER.TOR, *s.m.*, deserter, runaway, fugitive.

DE.SES.PE.RA.DO, *adj.*, hopeless, desperate.

DE.SES.PE.RA.DOR, *adj.*, despairing.

DE.SES.PE.RAN.ÇA, *s.f.*, despair, desperation.

DE.SES.PE.RAR, *v.*, to despair, to dishearten; *desesperar-se*: to give up hope.

DE.SES.PE.RO, *s.m.*, despair, hopelessness, desperation.

DES.FA.ÇA.TEZ, *s.f.*, impudence, shamelessness, insolence.

DES.FA.LE.CER, *v.*, to faint, to swoon, to decay.

DES.FAL.CAR, *v.*, to defalcate, to embezzle; to steal.

DES.FA.LE.CER, *v.*, to faint, to swoon.

DES.FA.LE.CI.MEN.TO, *s.m.*, faintness, weakness.

DES.FAL.QUE, *s.m.*, defalcation, peculation, misappropriation.

DES.FA.VO.RÁ.VEL, *adj.*, unfavourable, bad, unpropitious.

DES.FA.VO.RE.CI.DO, *adj.*, unprotected, not supported.

DES.FA.ZER, *v.*, to undo, to unmake, to unpack, to demolish.

DES.FE.CHO, *s.m.*, outcome, conclusion, solution, issue.

DES.FEI.TA, *s.f.*, affront, insult, outrage.

DES.FEI.TO, *adj.*, undone, dissolved, disfigured.

DES.FE.RIR, *v.*, to fling, to throw, to brandish (as a sword).

DES.FI.AR, *v.*, to unweave.

DES.FI.GU.RA.DO, *adj.*, disfigured.

DES.FI.GU.RAR, *v.*, to disfigure.

DES.FI.LA.DEI.RO, *s.m.*, ravine, canyon, gorge, pass, defile, narrow.

DES.FI.LAR, *v.*, to parade, to march, to file, to defile.

DES.FI.LE, *s.m.*, parade, march, pageant, filling off, review.

DES.FLO.RAR, *v.*, to deflorate (flowers); to deflower, to take away the virginity of a woman, to violate.

DES.FLO.RES.TA.MEN.TO, *s.m.*, deforestation.

DES.FLO.RES.TAR, *v.*, to deforest.

DES.FO.LHAR, *v.*, to defoliate, to exfoliate.

DES.FOR.RA, *s.f.*, revenge, retaliation, retribution.

DES.FRU.TAR, *v.*, to usufruct;to hold in usufruct.

DES.FRU.TÁ.VEL, *adj.*, that may be usufructed or enjoyed.

DES.FRU.TE, *s.m.*, usufruct, enjoyment.

DES.GAR.RAR, *v.*, to lead astray, mislead; *desgarrar-se*: to break out.

DES.GAS.TAR, *v.*, to consume, to wear down.

DES.GAS.TE, *s.m.*, wearing, consuming, wastage.

DES.GOS.TO, *s.m.*, disgust, sorrow, displeasure.

DES.GOS.TO.SO, *adj.*, displeased, dissatisfied.

DES.GO.VER.NA.DO, *adj.*, ungoverned, misgoverned.

DES.GRA.ÇA, *s.f.*, misfortune, misadventure, disaster, catasthrophe.

DES.GRU.DAR, *v.*, to unglue, to unstick.

DE.SI.DRA.TAR, *v.*, to anhydrate, to dehydrate.

DE.SIGN, *s.m., Ingl.*, design.

DE.SIG.NA.ÇÃO, *s.f.*, designation, indication, denomination, denotation.

DE.SIG.NAR, *v.*, to designate, to appoint, to determinate, to mark.

DE.SIG.NER, *s. 2 gen., Ingl.*, designer.

DE.SI.GUAL, *adj.*, unequal, unlike, different, irregular.

DE.SI.GUAL.DA.DE, *s.f.*, inequality, dissimilarity, unlikeness.

DE.SI.LU.DI.DO, *adj.*, disillusioned, disenchanted.

DE.SI.LU.DIR, *v.*, to disillusion, to disenchant, to undeceive.

DE.SI.LU.SÃO, *s.f.*, disillusion.

DE.SIN.CHAR, *v.*, to reduce a swelling.

DE.SIM.PE.DIR, *v.*, disencumber, disengage, disembarrass.

DE.SIN.DE.XAR, *v.*, to deindex.

DE.SIN.FEC.ÇÃO, *s.f.*, disinfection.

DE.SIN.FEC.CI.O.NAR, *v.*, to disinfect, to sterilize.

DE.SIN.FE.TAR, *v.*, to disinfect, to purify, to antisepticize, to deodorize.

DE.SIN.FOR.MA.ÇÃO, *s.f.*, disinformation.

DE.SIN.FOR.MA.DO, *adj.*, not informed, disinformed.

DE.SIN.FOR.MAR, *v.*, to misinform.

DE.SI.NI.BI.DO, *adj.*, disinhibited.

DE.SIN.TE.GRAR, *v.*, to disintegrate.

DE.SIN.TE.RES.SA.DO, *adj.*, disinterested, uninterested.

DE.SIN.TE.RES.SAN.TE, *adj.*, uninteresting.

DE.SIN.TE.RES.SAR, *v.*, to disinterest.

DE.SIN.TE.RES.SE, *s.m.*, indifference, disinterest, nonchalance.

DE.SIN.TO.XI.CAR, *v.*, to disintoxicate, to detoxify.

DE.SIS.TÊN.CIA, *s.f.*, cessation, desistance, nonsuit.

DE.SIS.TIR, *v.*, to give up, to stop, to renounce, to quit.

DES.JE.JUM, *s.m.*, breaking of one's fast, breakfast.

DES.LA.VA.DO, *adj.*, discoloured; *fig.*, shameless.

DES.LE.AL, *adj.*, disloyal, false, dishonest, perfidious.

DES.LE.AL.DA.DE, *s.f.*, disloyalty.

DES.LE.GI.TI.MAR, *v.*, to delegitimize.

DES.LEI.XA.DO, *adj.*, careless, untidy, neglectful, negligent.

DES.LEI.XO, *s.m.*, negligence, carelessness, indifference, disregard.

DES.LI.GA.DO, *adj.*, disconnected, disjoint; switched off, off, out.

DES.LI.GA.MEN.TO, *s.m.*, disconnection.

DES.LI.GAR, *v.*, to untie, to unfasten, to undo, to unlink.

DES.LI.ZA.MEN.TO, *s.m.*, sliding, slipping.

DES.LI.ZAR, *v.*, to slide, to glide, to skid, to slip, to overlook.

DES.LI.ZE, *s.m.*, slip, sliding, gliding, skidding.

DES.LO.CA.DO, *adj.*, dislocated, out of place.

DES.LO.CAR, *v.*, to dislocate, to disjoint, to displace, to transfer; to luxate.

DES.LUM.BRA.MEN.TO, *s.m.*, dazzling; fascination, captivation.

DES.LUM.BRAN.TE, *adj.*, dazzling, flaring, blinding, fulgent.

DES.LUM.BRAR, *v.*, to dazzle, to blind, to overpower with light, to fascinate.

DES.MAG.NE.TI.ZA.ÇÃO, *s.f.*, demagnetization.

DES.MAG.NE.TI.ZAR, *v.*, to demagnetize.

DES.MAI.AR, *v.*, to faint, to swoon, to fainting.

DES.MAI.O, *s.m.*, swoon, faint, collapse.

DES.MA.MA.DO, *adj.*, weanling.

DES.MA.MAR, *v.*, to wean.

DES.MAN.CHA-PRA.ZE.RES, *s. 2 gen., 2 num.*, to spoil-sport, to kill-joy.

DES.MAN.CHAR, *v.*, to undo, to unmake, to break up, to disarrange, to ruffle, to disorder.

DESMANCHE   ·· 161 ··   DESPOVOAR

DES.MAN.CHE, *s.m., Bras.*, chop shop.
DES.MAN.DO, *s.m.*, disobedience, insubordination.
DES.MAR.CAR, *v.*, to cancel.
DES.MAS.CA.RAR, *v.*, to unmask, to expose, to reveal.
DES.MA.TA.MEN.TO, *s.m.*, deforestation.
DES.MA.TAR, *v.*, to deforest, to clear.
DES.MA.ZE.LA.DO, *adj.*, negligent, careless.
DES.MA.ZE.LO, *s.m.*, negligence, carelessness, untidiness.
DES.ME.DI.DO, *adj.*, excessive, immense, immoderate.
DES.MEM.BRA.MEN.TO, *s.m.*, dismemberment, detachment.
DES.MEM.BRAR, *v.*, to separate, to dismember, to dislimb.
DES.MEN.TIR, *v.*, to contradict, to belie, to deny.
DES.ME.RE.CER, *v.*, to demerit, not to deserve, to undeserve.
DES.ME.RE.CI.MEN.TO, *s.m.*, demerit, unworthiness.
DES.MI.O.LA.DO, *s.m.*, rattlebrain; *adj.*, rattle-brained.
DES.MIS.TI.FI.CAR, *v.*, to demystify.
DES.MO.BI.LI.ZA.ÇÃO, *s.f.*, demobilization.
DES.MO.BI.LI.ZAR, *v.*, to demobilize, to disarm.
DES.MON.TAR, *v.*, to disjoint, to disassemble, to pull down; to unhorse.
DES.MO.RA.LI.ZA.ÇÃO, *s.f.*, demoralization.
DES.MO.RA.LI.ZAR, *v.*, to pervert, to deprave, to demoralize, to corrupt, to undermine.
DES.MO.RO.NA.MEN.TO, *s.m.*, collapse, tumbling, falling in.
DES.MO.RO.NAR, *v.*, to demolish, to pull down, to ruin, to undermine.
DES.NA.CI.O.NA.LI.ZAR, *v.*, to denationalize.
DES.NA.TA.DO, *adj.*, skimmed; *leite desnatado*: skim milk.
DES.NA.TAR, *v.*, to skim.
DES.NE.CES.SÁ.RIO, *adj.*, unnecessary, needless.
DES.NÍ.VEL, *s.m.*, unevenness.
DES.NI.VE.LAR, *v.*, to unlevel, to make uneven.
DES.NOR.TE.A.DO, *adj.*, bewildered, confused, lost.
DES.NU.DAR, *v.*, to undress.
DES.NU.TRI.ÇÃO, *s.f.*, malnutrition, underfeeding.
DES.NU.TRIR, *v.*, to unfeed, to emaciate.
DE.SO.BE.DE.CER, *v.*, to disobey, to transgress, to disregard.
DE.SO.BE.DI.ÊN.CIA, *s.f.*, disobedience, insubordination, rebellion, indiscipline.
DE.SO.BE.DI.EN.TE, *adj.*, disobedient, contumacious, insubordinate.
DE.SOBS.TRU.IR, *v.*, to remove obstructions, to free.
DE.SO.CU.PA.ÇÃO, *s.f.*, inoccupation, leisure, vacancy.
DE.SO.CU.PA.DO, *s.m.*, unemployed person; *adj.*, unemployed, disengaged, idle.
DE.SO.CU.PAR, *v.*, to vacate, to empty, to disoccupy.
DE.SO.DO.RAN.TE, *s.m.*, deodorant.
DE.SO.DO.RI.ZAR, *v.*, to deodorize.
DE.SO.LA.ÇÃO, *s.f.*, desolation.
DE.SO.LA.DO, *adj.*, desolate, lonely, sad.
DE.SO.LA.DOR, *s.m.*, desolator; *adj.*, desolating.
DE.SO.LAR, *v.*, to lay waste, to desolate, to depopulate.
DE.SO.NES.TI.DA.DE, *s.f.*, dishonesty, crookedness.
DE.SO.NES.TO, *s.m.*, dishonest person; *adj.*, dishonest, corrupt, foul.
DE.SON.RA, *s.f.*, dishonour, disgrace, defame.
DE.SON.RAR, *v.*, to dishonour, to discredit.
DE.SON.RO.SO, *adj.*, dishonourable, discreditable.
DE.SOR.DEI.RO, *s.m.*, rowdy, ruffian, rioter, hooligan, *adj.*, turbulent, rowdy, rough.
DE.SOR.DEM, *s.f.*, disorder, confusion, disturbance, jumble,
disarray.
DE.SOR.DE.NA.DO, *adj.*, disordered, untidy, messy.
DE.SOR.GA.NI.ZA.ÇÃO, *s.f.*, disorganization, disorder.
DE.SOR.GA.NI.ZA.DO, *adj.*, disorganized, disorderly.
DE.SOR.GA.NI.ZAR, *v.*, to disorganize, to disorder.
DE.SO.RI.EN.TA.ÇÃO, *s.f.*, disorientation.
DE.SO.RI.EN.TA.DO, *adj.*, disorientated, confused.
DE.SO.RI.EN.TAR, *v.*, to lead astray, to bewilder.
DE.SOS.SAR, *v.*, to bone, to debone.
DE.SO.VA, *s.f.*, spawning.
DE.SO.XI.DAN.TE, *adj.*, deoxidizing.
DE.SO.XI.GE.NA.ÇÃO, *s.f.*, deoxygenation.
DES.PA.CHA.NTE, *s. 2 gen.*, dispatcher, forwarder, forwarding agent; *adj.*, forwarding.
DES.PA.CHAR, *v.*, to forward, to dispatch, to send, to discharge, to clear.
DES.PA.CHO, *s.m.*, dispatch, forwarding, shipping, expedition.
DES.PA.RA.FU.SAR, *v.*, to unscrew.
DES.PE.DA.ÇA.DO, *adj.*, broken to pieces, disrupted.
DES.PE.DA.ÇAR, *v.*, to tear into pieces.
DES.PE.DI.DA, *s.f.*, farewell, departure, adieu, valediction, dismissal.
DES.PE.DIR, *v.*, to discharge, to dismiss, to disband, to discard, to fire.
DES.PEI.TAR, *v.*, to despise.
DES.PEI.TO, *s.m.*, spite, despite, resentment.
DES.PE.JAR, *v.*, to spill, to pour, to dump, to effuse.
DES.PE.JO, *s.m.*, pouring out, dump, spilling, eviction.
DES.PE.NHA.DEI.RO, *s.m.*, precipice, cliff, slop, crag.
DES.PEN.SA, *s.f.*, pantry, store-room.
DES.PEN.TE.A.DO, *adj.*, unkempt, disheveled.
DES.PEN.TE.AR, *v.*, to tousle, to dishevel.
DES.PER.DI.ÇAR, *v.*, to waste, to throw away, to squander, to scatter, to dissipate.
DES.PER.DÍ.CIO, *s.m.*, wastefulness, waste, wastage.
DES.PER.TA.DOR, *s.m.*, alarm clock; *adj.*, arousing.
DES.PER.TAR, *s.m.*, awakening; *v.*, to awake, to rouse from sleep, to excite.
DES.PER.TO, *adj.*, awake.
DES.PE.SA, *s.f.*, disbursement, expense, outgo.
DES.PI.DO, *adj.*, undressed, unclothed, naked.
DES.PIR, *v.*, to undress, to strip, to bare, to unclothe, to divest.
DES.PIS.TAR, *v.*, to mislead, to misguide, to foil.
DES.PO.JA.MEN.TO, *s.m.*, robbing, dispossession, divestiture, deposal.
DES.PO.JAR, *v.*, to deprive, to divest, dispossess, to strip.
DES.PO.LA.RI.ZA.ÇÃO, *s.f., Fís., Quím.*, depolarization.
DES.PO.LU.I.ÇÃO, *s.f.*, elimination of pollution, depollution.
DES.PO.LU.IR, *v.*, to depollute, to eliminate pollution.
DES.PON.TAR, *v.*, to blunt, to break, to unfold, to rise.
DES.POR.TIS.TA, *s. 2 gen.*, athlete, sportsman.
DES.POR.TI.VO, *adj.*, athletic, sporting.
DES.POR.TO, *s.m.*, sport, play, game.
DES.PO.SAR, *v.*, to marry, to wed, to affiance, to betroth.
DES.POS.SU.IR, *v.*, to deprive of a possession, to dispossess.
DÉS.PO.TA, *s.m.*, despot, tyrant, oppressor.
DES.PÓ.TI.CO, *adj.*, despotical, tyrannical.
DES.PO.TIS.MO, *s.m.*, despotism, absolutism, tyranny.
DES.PO.VO.A.DO, *s.m.*, desert place; *adj.*, unpeopled, desert, depopulated.
DES.PO.VO.AR, *v.*, to depopulate.

DESPRAZER · 162 · DESVIO

DES.PRA.ZER, *s.m.*, displeasure, disgust, dissatisfaction; *v.*, to displease, to disgust, to dissatisfy.

DES.PRE.GAR, *v.*, to unfasten, to unhook, to unpin.

DES.PRE.GUI.ÇAR, *v.*, to idle, to lounge; *despreguiçar-se*: to stretch.

DES.PREN.DER, *v.*, to loosen, to unfasten, to unhood, to unfix.

DES.PREN.DI.DO, *adj.*, loose, unfastened, untied.

DES.PRE.O.CU.PA.ÇÃO, *s.f.*, carefreeness.

DES.PRE.O.CU.PA.DO, *adj.*, carefree.

DES.PRE.O.CU.PAR, *v.*, to ride, to ease, to free from care.

DES.PRE.PA.RA.DO, *adj.*, unprepared.

DES.PRE.PA.RO, *s.m.*, unpreparedness, lack of preparation.

DES.PRES.TI.GI.AR, *v.*, to depreciate, to discredit.

DES.PRES.TÍ.GIO, *s.m.*, discredit, disreputation.

DES.PRE.TEN.SI.O.SO, *adj.*, unpretentious.

DES.PRE.VE.NI.DO, *adj.*, unprepared, unprovided.

DES.PRE.ZA.DO, *adj.*, despised, abandoned.

DES.PRE.ZAR, *v.*, to despise, to scorn, to disdain, to contemn, to slight.

DES.PRE.ZÍ.VEL, *adj.*, despicable, pitiable, contemptible.

DES.PRE.ZO, *s.m.*, disdain, disdainfulness, disregard, contempt.

DES.PRO.POR.ÇÃO, *s.f.*, disproportion.

DES.PRO.POR.CI.O.NAL, *adj.*, unproportional.

DES.PRO.PO.SI.TA.DO, *adj.*, unreasonable, absurd; purposeless.

DES.PU.DOR, *s.m.*, shamelessness, impudence.

DES.QUA.LI.FI.CA.ÇÃO, *s.f.*, disqualification, elimination.

DES.QUA.LI.FI.CA.DO, *adj.*, disqualified, eliminated.

DES.QUA.LI.FI.CAR, *v.*, to disqualify, to unfit, to incapacitate.

DES.QUI.TAR, *v.*, Bras, *Jur.*, to separate legally.

DES.QUI.TE, *s.m.*, divorce, separation, disunion.

DES.RE.GRA.DO, *adj.*, disorderly, unruly, dissolute.

DES.RE.GRAR, *v.*, to disorder.

DES.RES.PEI.TAR, *v.*, to disrespect, to disregard, to affront.

DES.RES.PEI.TO, *s.m.*, disrespect, contempt, affront.

DES.RES.PEI.TO.SO, *adj.*, disrespectful.

DES.SA, *contr.* of the *prep.* **DE** and the *pron.* **ESSA**: from that, of that.

DES.SE, *contr.* of the *prep.* **DE** and the *pron.* **ESSE**: from that, of that.

DES.SER.VI.ÇO, *s.m.*, desservice.

DES.TA, *contr.* of the *prep.* **DE** and the *pron.* **ESTA**: of this, from this.

DES.TA.CA.DO, *adj.*, detached.

DES.TA.CA.MEN.TO, *s.m.*, detachment.

DES.TA.CAR, *v.*, detach, emphatisize, to exceed, to overtop.

DES.TA.CÁ.VEL, *adj.*, detachable.

DES.TA.QUE, *s.m.*, prominence, eminence, distinction, notability.

DES.TE, *contr.* of the *prep.* **DE** and the *pron.* **ESTE**: of this, from this.

DES.TE.MI.DO, *adj.*, fearless, dreadless, daring, bold.

DES.TEM.PE.RO, *s.m.*, intemperance, distemper, disorder, impertinence.

DES.TER.RA.DO, *s.m.*, exile; *adj.*, exiled, expatriated.

DES.TER.RAR, *v.*, to exile, to expatriate.

DES.TER.RO, *s.m.*, exile, deportation, expatriation.

DES.TI.LAR, *v.*, to distill.

DES.TI.LA.RI.A, *s.f.*, distillery.

DES.TI.NAR, *v.*, to destine, to apply, to appropriate, to appoint, to doom, to consecrate.

DES.TI.NA.TÁ.RIO, *s.m.*, addressee, receiver, recipient, consignee.

DES.TI.NO, *s.m.*, destiny, fate, fortune, predestination, destination, purpose.

DES.TI.TU.I.ÇÃO, *s.f.*, dismissal, deposing, need, want.

DES.TI.TU.IR, *v.*, to depose, to dismiss, to displace, to fire, to demit.

DES.TO.AN.TE, *adj.*, dissonant, discordant.

DES.TO.AR, *v.*, to discord, to sound out of tune, to diverge, to jar.

DES.TRA.TAR, *v.*, to insult, to affront, to abuse.

DES.TRA.VAR, *v.*, to unlock, to unshackle, to unfetter.

DES.TRE.ZA, *s.f.*, ability, skill, craft, dexterity, handiness, knack.

DES.TRIN.CHAR, *v.*, Bras., to resolve, to explain, to disentangle.

DES.TRI.PAR, *v.*, to eviscerate, to disembowel.

DES.TRO, *adj.*, desterous, right-handed, habile, skillful, deft.

DES.TRO.ÇO, *s.m.*, destruction, devastation, havock.

DES.TRO.NAR, *v.*, to dethrone, to decrown, to unthrone.

DES.TRU.Í.DO, *adj.*, destroyed, ruined.

DES.TRU.I.ÇÃO, *s.f.*, destruction, devastation, demolition, ruination, ravage.

DES.TRU.IR, *v.*, to destroy, to demolish, to crush, to devastate, to subvert.

DES.TRU.TI.VO, *adj.*, destructive, ruinous.

DE.SU.MA.NI.DA.DE, *s.f.*, inhumanity, cruelty.

DE.SU.MA.NI.ZA.ÇÃO, *s.f.*, dehumanization.

DE.SU.MA.NI.ZAR, *v.*, to dehumanize.

DE.SU.MA.NO, *adj.*, inhuman, brutal, cruel, barbarous, savage.

DE.SU.ME.DE.CER, *v.*, to dehumidify.

DE.SU.NI.ÃO, *s.f.*, disunion, separation.

DE.SU.NI.FI.CAR, *v.*, to eliminate a unit.

DE.SU.NIR, *v.*, to disunite, to disjoint, to separate, to divide, to disengage.

DE.SU.SO, *s.m.*, disuse.

DES.VAI.RA.DO, *s.m.*, a crazy person; *adj.*, crazy, confused.

DES.VA.LO.RI.ZA.ÇÃO, *s.f.*, depreciation, devaluation, discredit.

DES.VA.LO.RI.ZA.DO, *adj.*, devaluated, depreciated.

DES.VA.LO.RI.ZAR, *v.*, to devaluate, to depreciate.

DES.VAN.TA.GEM, *s.f.*, disadvantage, prejudice, handicap, detriment.

DES.VAN.TA.JO.SO, *adj.*, disadvantageous, prejudicial.

DES.VA.RI.O, *s.m.*, derangement, loss of wits, delirium, absurdity.

DES.VE.LA.DO, *adj.*, watchful, careful.

DES.VE.LAR, *v.*, to watch, care for.

DES.VE.LO, *s.m.*, attention, carefulness, zeal.

DES.VEN.DAR, *v.*, to take the blindfold from the eyes.

DES.VEN.TU.RA, *s.f.*, misadventure, misfortune, unhappiness, unluckiness.

DES.VEN.TU.RO.SO, *adj.*, unhappy, unlucky, unfortunate.

DES.VI.AR, *v.*, to turn aside, to deviate, to divert, to remove, to deflect.

DES.VIN.CU.LA.ÇÃO, *s.f.*, disentail.

DES.VIN.CU.LAR, *v.*, to disentail, to detach.

DES.VI.O, *s.m.*, deviation, detour, deflection, bypass.

DESVIRGINAR ·· 163 ··· DIFERENÇA

DES.VIR.GI.NAR, v., to deflower.
DES.VI.RI.LI.ZAR, v., to unman, to emasculate.
DES.VIR.TU.AR, v., to depreciate, to misinterpret.
DE.TA.LHA.DO, adj., detailed.
DE.TA.LHAR, v., to detail, to specify.
DE.TA.LHE, s.m., detail, circumstance.
DE.TEC.TAR, v., to detect, to discover.
DE.TEN.ÇÃO, s.f., detention, arrest, imprisonment, confinement.
DE.TEN.TO, s.m., Bras., prisoner.
DE.TER, v., to arrest, to hold, to retain, to keep, to stop, to retard.
DE.TER.GEN.TE, s.m., detergent.
DE.TE.RI.O.RAR, v., to deteriorate.
DE.TER.MI.NA.ÇÃO, s.f., determination, resolution, decision, order.
DE.TER.MI.NA.DO, adj., determinate, definitive.
DE.TER.MI.NAN.TE, s.f., determinant; Gram., determiner; adj., determinative.
DE.TER.MI.NAR, v., to determine, to order, to command, to enjoin.
DE.TER.MI.NIS.MO, s.m., Filos., determinism.
DE.TER.MI.NIS.TA, s. 2 gen., determinist.
DE.TES.TAR, v., to detest, to abhor, to abominate, to dislike, to loathe, to execrate.
DE.TES.TÁ.VEL, adj., detestable.
DE.TE.TI.VE, s. 2 gen., detective.
DE.TI.DO, adj., detained.
DE.TO.NAR, v., to detonate.
DE.TRÁS, adv., after, behind, back.
DE.TRI.MEN.TO, s.m., detriment, damage, loss, disadvantage.
DE.TRI.TO, s.m., remains, detritus, debris.
DE.TUR.PA.ÇÃO, s.f., disfigurement, alteration., falsification.
DE.TUR.PAR, v., to disfigure, to falsify, to deform.
DEUS, s.m., God, Lord, divinity, Creator of the Universe, Spirit.
DEU.SA, s.f., goddess.
DEU.TÉ.RI.O, s.m., Quím., deuterium.
DE.VA.GAR, adv., slow, slowly, softly.
DE.VA.NE.AR, v., to daydream.
DE.VA.NEI.O, s.m., day-dream, reverie, chimera.
DE.VAS.SA, s.f., inquiry, inquest.
DE.VAS.SAR, v., to trespass, to invade, to divulgate, to penetrate.
DE.VAS.SI.DÃO, s.f., debauchery, licentiousness.
DE.VAS.SO, s.m., debauchee; adj., debauched.
DE.VAS.TA.ÇÃO, s.f., devastation.
DE.VAS.TAR, v., to devastate, to lay waste, to destruct, to destroy.
DE.VE.DOR, s.m., debtor; adj., in debt, owing.
DE.VER, s.m., obligation, duty, task, business, job; v., to need, to owe, must, shall.
DE.VI.DA.MEN.TE, adv., duly, orderly.
DE.VI.DO, adj., due, just, owing.
DE.VIR, s.m., Filos., series of transformations; v., to become, to turn out.
DE.VO.ÇÃO, s.f., devotion, adoration, cult, dedication, religion.
DE.VO.LU.ÇÃO, s.f., devolution, restoration, return, restitution, reversion.
DE.VO.LU.TO, adj., returned, empty, vacant, uninhabited.
DE.VOL.VER, v., to return, to devolve, to remise, to render.
DE.VOL.VI.DO, adj., returned.

DE.VO.RA.DOR, s.m., devourer; adj., devouring.
DE.VO.RAR, v., to devour, to ingurgitate, to wolf.
DE.VO.TA.MEN.TO, s.m., devotement, dedication.
DE.VO.TAR, v., to devote, to dedicate, to consecrate.
DE.VO.TO, s.m., devotee, cultist; adj., devoted, pious.
DEZ, num., ten.
DE.ZEM.BRO, s.m., December.
DE.ZE.NA, s.f., ten, a set of ten.
DE.ZE.NO.VE, num., nineteen.
DE.ZES.SEIS, num., sixteen.
DE.ZES.SE.TE, num., seventeen.
DE.ZOI.TO, num., eighteen.
DI.A, s.m., day, daylight, daytime; Dia do Trabalho: Labor Day; Dia de Natal: Christmas Day.
DI.A.BE.TES, s. 2 gen., Med., diabetes.
DI.A.BO, s.m., demon, devil, evil spirit, Satan, Beelzebub.
DI.A.BÓ.LI.CO, adj., devilish, hellish.
DI.A.BRU.RA, s.f., diablerie, develish trick.
DI.A.CHO, s.m., Bras., devil, demon; interj., the devil!
DI.Á.CO.NO, s.m., deacon.
DI.Á.FA.NO, adj., diaphanic, diaphanous, transparent, translucent.
DI.A.FRAG.MA, s.m., diaphragm.
DI.AG.NOS.TI.CAR, v., to diagnose.
DI.AG.NÓS.TI.CO, s.m., diagnosis; adj., diagnostic.
DI.A.GO.NAL, adj., diagonal, oblique.
DI.A.GRA.MA, s.m., diagram.
DI.AL, s.m., dial (radio); adj., daily.
DI.A.LÉ.TI.CA, s.f., Filos., dialectic, dialectics.
DI.A.LÉ.TI.CO, adj., dialectic.
DI.A.LE.TO, s.m., dialect.
DI.A.LO.GAR, v., to dialogue.
DI.Á.LO.GO, s.m., dialogue, conversation, talk.
DI.A.MAN.TE, s.m., diamond.
DI.A.MAN.TI.NO, adj., diamantine, adamantine.
DI.Â.ME.TRO, s.m., diameter.
DI.AN.TE, adv., before, in front.
DI.AN.TEI.RA, s.f., forepart, front, lead, foreside.
DI.A.PA.SÃO, s.m., Mús., diapason.
DI.Á.RIA, s.f., daily wages.
DI.Á.RIO, s.m., diary, daybook, journal, daily newspaper; adj., diurnal, daily, quotidian.
DI.A.RIS.TA, s. 2 gen., journalist, diarist; dayworker.
DI.AR.REI.A, s.f., Med., diarrhea.
DI.ÁS.PO.RA, s.f., diaspora.
DI.A.TRI.BE, s.f., diatribe.
DI.CA, s.f., gír., hint, cue.
DIC.ÇÃO, s.f., diction, expression.
DI.CI.O.NÁ.RIO, s.m., dictionary, wordbook, lexicon.
DI.CI.O.NA.RIS.TA, s. 2 gen., lexicographer.
DI.DÁ.TI.CA, s.f., didactics.
DI.DÁ.TI.CO, adj., didactic, instructive, pedagogical.
DI.DA.TIS.MO, s.m., didacticism.
DI.E.TA, s.f., diet, regimen.
DI.E.TÉ.TI.CO, adj., Med., dietary, dietetic, dietetical.
DI.FA.MA.ÇÃO, s.f., defamation, libel, calumny.
DI.FA.MAN.TE, adj., defaming, slanderous, detractory.
DI.FA.MAR, v., to defame, to vilify, to blemish.
DI.FA.MA.TÓ.RI.O, adj., defamatory, calumnious.
DI.FE.REN.ÇA, s.f., difference, unlikeness, disparity, divergence, dissimilarity, deviation.

DIFERENCIAÇÃO ·· 164 ·· DISCORDÂNCIA

DI.FE.REN.CI.A.ÇÃO, s.f., differentiation.
DI.FE.REN.CI.AR, v., to differentiate, to difference, to distinguish.
DI.FE.REN.TE, adj., different, unlike, unequal, dissimilar, distinct.
DI.FE.RIR, v., to differ, to disagree, to postpone, to delay, to retard.
DI.FÍ.CIL, adj., difficult, hard, uneasy, painful, intricate, arduous, laborious.
DI.FI.CUL.DA.DE, s.f., difficulty, hardness, laboriousness, complication.
DI.FI.CUL.TAR, v., to make difficult, to difficultate, to render difficult.
DI.FI.CUL.TO.SO, adj., difficult, laborious.
DI.FRA.ÇÃO, s.f., Fís., diffraction.
DIF.TE.RI.A, s.f., Med., diphtheria, diphtheritis.
DI.FUN.DIR, v., to diffuse, to spread, to disseminate, to pour out, to scatter.
DI.FU.SÃO, s.f., diffusion, scattering, dissemination, infiltration.
DI.FU.SO, adj., diffuse.
DI.FU.SOR, s.m., diffuser.
DI.FU.SO.RA, s.f., broadcasting or television station.
DI.GE.RIR, v., to digest, to assimilate, to tolerate.
DI.GE.RÍ.VEL, adj., digestible.
DI.GES.TÃO, s.f., digestion, concoction.
DI.GES.TOR, s.m., digestor; adj., digestive.
DI.GI.TA.ÇÃO, s.f., digitation.
DI.GI.TA.DO, adj., digitate, digitiform.
DI.GI.TAL, adj., digital.
DI.GI.TA.LI.ZAR, v., Comp., to digitize.
DI.GI.TAR, v., Comp., to key in.
DÍ.GI.TO, s.m., Lit., finger; Mat., any number from 0 to 9; adj., Mat., digital.
DI.GLA.DI.AR, v., to digladiate.
DIG.NAR-SE, v., to condescend, to deign, to be pleased.
DIG.NI.DA.DE, s.f., dignity, nobleness, honourableness.
DIG.NO, adj., worthy, deserving, respectable.
DI.LA.CE.RA.ÇÃO, s.f., dilaceration.
DI.LA.CE.RAR, v., to lacerate, to tear, to dilacerate.
DI.LA.PI.DAR, v., to dilapidate.
DI.LA.TA.ÇÃO, s.f., dilation, expansion.
DI.LA.TA.DO, adj., dilated.
DI.LA.TA.DOR, s.m., dilator; adj., dilating.
DI.LA.TAR, v., to dilate, to enlarge, to widen, to expand, to diffuse.
DI.LE.MA, s.m., dilemma, problem.
DI.LE.TAN.TE, s. 2 gen., dilettante.
DI.LE.TAN.TIS.MO, s.m., dilletantism, dilletanteism.
DI.LI.GEN.TE, adj., diligent, assiduous, industrious, active.
DI.LU.EN.TE, adj., diluent, diluting.
DI.LU.IR, v., to dilute.
DI.LÚ.VIO, s.m., deluge, flood, inundation.
DI.MEN.SÃO, s.f., measurement, dimension, size, extension.
DI.MEN.SI.O.NAL, adj., dimensional.
DI.MI.NU.I.ÇÃO, s.f., diminution, decrease, reduction, subtraction, abatement.
DI.MI.NU.IR, v., to diminish, to reduce, to lessen, to abate.
DI.MI.NU.TI.VO, s.m., adj., diminutive.
DI.MI.NU.TO, adj., minute, diminutive, small, little.
DI.NA.MAR.QUÊS, s.m., adj., Dane, Danish.
DI.NÂ.MI.CA, s.f., dynamics.

DI.NÂ.MI.CO, adj., Fís., dynamic, dynamical.
DI.NA.MIS.MO, s.m., dynamism.
DI.NA.MI.TAR, v., to dynamite.
DI.NA.MI.TE, s.f., Quím., dynamite, blasting powder.
DI.NA.MI.ZAR, v., to dynamize, to expedite.
DÍ.NA.MO, s.m., Eletr., dynamo, generator.
DI.NAS.TI.A, s.f., dynasty.
DI.NÁS.TI.CO, adj., dynastic, dynastical.
DIN.DI.NHA, s.f., pop., godmother, grandmother.
DIN.DI.NHO, s.m., pop., godfather, grandfather.
DI.NHEI.RA.DA, s.f., a lot of money.
DI.NHEI.RÃO, s.m., the same that dinheirada.
DI.NHEI.RO, s.m., money, currency, cash, capital.
DI.NOS.SAU.RO, s.m., dinosaur.
DI.O.CE.SE, s.f., diocese.
DI.O.DO, s.m., Eletr., diode.
DI.PLO.CO.CO, s.m., Biol., diplococcus.
DI.PLO.MA, s.m., diploma, certificate, document.
DI.PLO.MA.ÇÃO, s.f., Bras., the granting of a diploma.
DI.PLO.MA.CI.A, s.f., diplomacy, tact, skill.
DI.PLO.MA.TA, s.m., diplomat, ambassador; tactful person.
DI.QUE, s.m., dike, embankment, flood-gate; obstacle.
DI.RE.ÇÃO, s.f., direction, course, route, run, administration, government.
DI.RE.CI.O.NAL, adj., directional.
DI.RE.CI.O.NAR, v., to direct, to orientate.
DI.REI.TA, s.f., right hand, right side; the conservative party.
DI.REI.TIS.MO, s.m., Pol., rightism, conservatism.
DI.REI.TIS.TA, s. 2 gen., rightist; adj., rightist.
DI.REI.TO, s.m., right, law, jurisprudence, justice; adj., right, straight, even, flat.
DI.RE.TA.MEN.TE, adv., directly.
DI.RE.TO, adj., direct, straight, nonstop, immediate.
DI.RE.TOR, s.m., director, headmaster, manager.
DI.RE.TO.RI.A, s.f., direction, administration, management, directorship.
DI.RE.TÓ.RI.O, s.m., directory.
DI.RE.TRIZ, s.f., Geom., directrix; guideline, route.
DI.RI.GEN.TE, s. 2 gen., director, leader, controller.
DI.RI.GI.BI.LI.DA.DE, s.f., dirigibility.
DI.RI.GIR, v., to direct, to conduct, to govern, to rule, to command, to head.
DI.RI.MIR, v., to nullify, to cancel, to annul.
DIS.CA.GEM, s.f., Bras., dialing (pulse signal).
DIS.CAR, v., to dial.
DIS.CEN.TE, s.m., pupil, student; adj., learning; corpo ~: student body.
DIS.CER.NI.MEN.TO, s.m., discernment, criterion, perception.
DIS.CER.NIR, v., to discern.
DIS.CI.PLI.NA, s.f., discipline, order, correction, education, instruction.
DIS.CI.PLI.NA.DO, adj., disciplined.
DIS.CI.PLI.NA.DOR, s.m., disciplinarian, discipliner.
DIS.CI.PLI.NAR, v., to discipline, to educate, to train, to instruct, to correct.
DIS.CÍ.PU.LO, s.m., disciple, follower, pupil, scholar, student.
DISC-JÓ.QUEI, s.m., disc-jockey (radio).
DIS.CO, s.m., disk, disc, record, dial, discus.
DIS.CO.GRA.FI.A, s.f., Mús., discography.
DIS.COR.DÂN.CIA, s.f., disagreement, divergence, discordancy.

DISCORDAR · 165 · DITADURA

DIS.COR.DAR, *v.*, to disagree, to disaccord.
DIS.CÓR.DIA, *s.f.*, disharmony, variance, discord, strife, dissension.
DIS.COR.RER, *v.*, to talk about something at length; to discourse.
DIS.CO.TE.CA, *s.f.*, discotheque, record collection.
DIS.CRE.PÂN.CI.A, *s.f.*, discrepancy, disagreement, difference.
DIS.CRE.PAN.TE, *adj.*, discrepant, disagreeing.
DIS.CRE.TA.MEN.TE, *adv.*, discreetly.
DIS.CRE.TO, *adj.*, discreet, wise, prudent.
DIS.CRI.ÇÃO, *s.f.*, discretion, reserve.
DIS.CRI.MI.NA.ÇÃO, *s.f.*, discrimination, separation, segregation.
DIS.CRI.MI.NA.DO, *adj.*, discriminate, distinguished, segregated.
DIS.CRI.MI.NAR, *v.*, to discriminate, to distinguish, to select.
DIS.CRI.MI.NA.TÓ.RI.O, *adj.*, discriminatory.
DIS.CUR.SAR, *v.*, to discourse, to declaim, to speech.
DIS.CUR.SI.VO, *adj.*, discursive.
DIS.CUR.SO, *s.m.*, discourse, speech.
DIS.CUS.SÃO, *s.f.*, discussion, debate, argument, disputation.
DIS.CU.TIR, *v.*, to discuss, to argue, to dispute, to agitate.
DIS.CU.TÍ.VEL, *adj.*, discussible.
DI.SEN.TE.RI.A, *s.f.*, *Med.*, dysentery.
DIS.FAR.ÇA.DO, *adj.*, disguised.
DIS.FAR.ÇAR, *v.*, to disguise.
DIS.FAR.CE, *s.m.*, disguise, mask, veil.
DIS.FOR.ME, *adj.*, deformed, defaced.
DIS.FUN.ÇÃO, *s.f.*, *Med.*, dysfunction.
DIS.JUN.TOR, *s.m.*, *Eletr.*, circuit breaker.
DIS.LE.XI.A, *s.f.*, *Med.*, dyslexia.
DIS.LÉ.XI.CO, *s.m.*, *Med.*, one who suffers from dyslexia; *adj.*, dyslexic.
DIS.PA.RA.DO, *adj.*, fearless, discharged, fired; high speed.
DIS.PA.RA.DOR, *s.m.*, trigger; *Fot.*, shutter release.
DIS.PA.RAR, *v.*, to discharge, to shoot, to fire off, to let fly.
DIS.PA.RA.TE, *s.m.*, folly, nonsense, foolishness, absurdity.
DIS.PA.RI.DA.DE, *s.f.*, disparity.
DIS.PA.RO, *s.m.*, discharge, shot.
DIS.PÊN.DIO, *s.m.*, expense.
DIS.PEN.SA, *s.f.*, dispense, dispensation, leave.
DIS.PEN.SAR, *v.*, to dispense, to exempt, to excuse, to release.
DIS.PEN.SÁ.VEL, *adj.*, dispensable, expendable.
DIS.PER.SAR, *v.*, to disperse.
DIS.PER.SI.VO, *adj.*, dispersive.
DIS.PER.SO, *adj.*, dispersed.
DIS.PLI.CÊN.CIA, *s.f.*, negligence, carelessness, displeasure, annoyance.
DIS.PLI.CEN.TE, *s. 2 gen.*, disorderly person; *adj.*, disagreeable, negligent, careless.
DIS.PO.NI.BI.LI.DA.DE, *s.f.*, availability, disposability.
DIS.PO.NÍ.VEL, *adj.*, available.
DIS.POR, *v.*, to dispose, to arrange, to regulate, to adjust, to fit, to place.
DIS.PO.SI.ÇÃO, *s.f.*, disposition, disposal, arrangement, classification, control.
DIS.PO.SI.TI.VO, *s.m.*, gadget, device, appliance.
DIS.POS.TO, *s.m.*, rule, determination; *adj.*, disposed, ordered; willing, ready, eager.

DIS.PU.TA, *s.f.*, dispute, discussion, controversy, debate, altercation.
DIS.PU.TAR, *v.*, to dispute, to debate, to discuss, to argue.
DIS.QUE.TE, *s.m.*, diskette, floppy disk.
DIS.RIT.MI.A, *s.f.*, *Med.*, dysrhythmia.
DIS.RÍT.MI.CO, *adj.*, dysrhythmic.
DIS.SA.BOR, *s.m.*, disgust, contrariety, annoyance, insipidity.
DIS.SE.CA.ÇÃO, *s.f.*, dissection.
DIS.SE.CAR, *v.*, to dissect.
DIS.SER.TA.ÇÃO, *s.f.*, dissertation.
DIS.SER.TAR, *v.*, to dissert, to talk, to speech, to write dissertation.
DIS.SI.DÊN.CI.A, *s.f.*, dissidence, dissent, disagreement.
DIS.SI.DEN.TE, *s. 2 gen.*, dissident; *adj.*, dissident.
DIS.SÍ.DI.O, *s.m.*, dissension, divergence; ~ *coletivo*: collective bargaining.
DIS.SI.MU.LA.ÇÃO, *s.f.*, dissimulation.
DIS.SI.MU.LA.DO, *s.m.*, dissimulator; *adj.*, dissimulative, dissembling, stealthy, veiled.
DIS.SI.MU.LAR, *v.*, to dissimulate, to hide, to feign.
DIS.SI.PA.DOR, *s.m.*, squanderer; *adj.*, squandering, wasting, dissipating.
DIS.SI.PAR, *v.*, to dissipate, to scatter, to disperse, to waste, to consume.
DIS.SO, *contr.* of the *prep.* **DE** and the *pron.* **ISSO**: of that, thereof, about that, therefrom.
DIS.SO.CI.AR, *v.*, to dissociate.
DIS.SO.LU.ÇÃO, *s.f.*, dissolution, breakup, separation.
DIS.SOL.VER, *v.*, to dissolve, to liquefy, to melt.
DIS.SO.NÂN.CI.A, *s.f.*, *Mús.*, dissonance.
DIS.SU.A.DIR, *v.*, to dissuade, to bring off, to turn, to discourage.
DIS.SU.A.SÃO, *s.f.*, dissuasion.
DIS.TÂN.CIA, *s.f.*, distance, extension, farness, space.
DIS.TAN.CI.A.DO, *adj.*, distant.
DIS.TAN.CI.AR, *v.*, to distance, to separate, to situate.
DIS.TAN.TE, *adj.*, distant, far, remote, far-away, cool, reserved.
DIS.TAR, *v.*, to be distant.
DIS.TIN.ÇÃO, *s.f.*, distinction.
DIS.TIN.GUIR, *v.*, to distinguish, differentiate, to discriminate, to discern.
DIS.TIN.TI.VO, *s.m.*, badge, emblem, symbol; *adj.*, distinctive, characteristic.
DIS.TIN.TO, *adj.*, distinct, different, distinguished, diverse, individual, special.
DIS.TO, *contr.* of the *prep.* **DE** and the *pron.* **ISTO**: of this, of it, at it, hereof, herefrom.
DIS.TOR.CER, *v.*, to distort.
DIS.TRA.ÇÃO, *s.f.*, distraction, pastime, diversion.
DIS.TRA.IR, *v.*, to distract, to draw away.
DIS.TRI.BU.I.ÇÃO, *s.f.*, distribution, delivery, division, parcelling.
DIS.TRI.BU.I.DOR, *s.m.*, distributor; *adj.*, distributing.
DIS.TRI.BU.IR, *v.*, to distribute, to divide, to deliver, to allocate.
DIS.TRI.TO, *s.m.*, district, quarter, county, zone, circuit, territory.
DIS.TRO.FI.A, *s.f.*, *Med.*, dystrophy.
DIS.TÚR.BIO, *s.m.*, disturb, disturbance, riot, trouble, noise.
DI.TA.DO, *s.m.*, dictation, proverb, sentence.
DI.TA.DOR, *s.m.*, dictator, despot, tyrant.
DI.TA.DU.RA, *s.f.*, dictatorship, despotism.

DITAME ·· 166 ·· DOMINGO

DI.TA.ME, *s.m.*, rule, precept, principle.
DI.TAR, *v.*, to dictate, to impose, to command.
DI.TA.TO.RI.AL, *adj.*, dictatorial, absolute, authoritative.
DI.TO, *s.m.*, ditto, the same, axiom, sentence; *adj.*, said, stated.
DI.TO-CU.JO, *s.m., pop.*, Mr. So-And-So.
DI.TON.GO, *s.m., Gram.*, diphthong.
DI.UR.NO, *s.m.*, daytime; *adj.*, diurnal, daytime.
DI.U.TUR.NO, *adj.*, lasting, being of a long duration.
DI.VA, *s.f.*, diva.
DI.VÃ, *s.m.*, couch, divan.
DI.VA.GAR, *v.*, to divagate, to wander, to deviate.
DI.VER.GÊN.CIA, *s.f.*, divergence, disagreement, divergency.
DI.VER.SÃO, *s.f.*, diversion, entertainment, amusement.
DI.VER.SI.DA.DE, *s.f.*, diversity, variety, dissimilarity, unlikeness.
DI.VER.SI.FI.CA.ÇÃO, *s.f.*, diversification.
DI.VER.SI.FI.CA.DO, *adj.*, diversified.
DI.VER.SI.FI.CAN.TE, *adj.*, diversifying, varying.
DI.VER.SI.FI.CAR, *v.*, to diversify.
DI.VER.SI.FI.CÁ.VEL, *adj.*, that can be diversified.
DI.VER.SO, *adj.*, different, various, unlike, divers, manifold.
DI.VER.TI.CU.LI.TE, *s.f., Med.*, diverticulitis.
DI.VER.TI.DO, *adj.*, deviated, funny, amusing, diverting.
DI.VER.TI.MEN.TO, *s.m.*, diversion, amusement, pastime, entertainment, play.
DI.VER.TIR, *v.*, to divert, to draw away, to turn aside, to distract, to amuse.
DÍ.VI.DA, *s.f.*, debt, duty, due, liability, obligation, arrears, debit.
DI.VI.DEN.DO, *s.m.*, dividend.
DI.VI.DI.DO, *adj.*, divided (feeling), separated, disunited, split.
DI.VI.DIR, *v.*, to divide, to share, to separate, to disjoin, to break, to split, to parcel out.
DI.VI.NA.ÇÃO, *s.f.*, divination.
DI.VIN.DA.DE, *s.f.*, divinity, sanctity.
DI.VI.NI.ZAR, *v.*, to divinize.
DI.VI.NO, *adj.*, divine, holy, deific, excellent.
DI.VI.SA, *s.f.*, symbol, emblem; device, motto, slogan; frontier, boundary.
DI.VI.SÃO, *s.f.*, division, section, segment, category, partition, split.
DI.VI.SI.BI.LI.DA.DE, *s.f.*, divisibility, partibility.
DI.VI.SÍ.VEL, *adj.*, divisible.
DI.VI.SOR, *s.m.*, divisor, divider.
DI.VI.SÓ.RI.A, *s.f.*, partition, demarcation.
DI.VI.SÓ.RI.O, *adj.*, dividing, parting, separating.
DI.VOR.CI.AR, *v.*, to divorce, to disunite, to separate.
DI.VÓR.CIO, *s.m.*, divorce.
DI.VUL.GA.ÇÃO, *s.f.*, divulgation, conveyance.
DI.VUL.GA.DOR, *s.m.*, the one who makes discloses; *adj.*, divulging, publicizing, making public.
DI.VUL.GAR, *v.*, to divulge, to publish, to make public, to disclose, to betray.
DI.ZER, *v.*, to say, to speak, to tell, to talk, to declare.
DI.ZI.MA.ÇÃO, *s.f.*, decimation.
DI.ZI.MAR, *v.*, to decimate.
DÍ.ZI.MO, *s.m.*, tithe (a tenth part as a voluntary contribution for the support of the church).
DIZ QUE DIZ, *s.m.*, rumour, gossip, report.
DO, *contr.* of the *prep.* DE and the *art.* O: of the, from the.
DÓ, *s.m., Mús.*, C, do; pity, compassion, empathy.

DO.A.ÇÃO, *s.f.*, donation, bounty, gift, present.
DO.A.DO, *adj.*, donated.
DO.A.DOR, *s.m.*, donor, giver, donator.
DO.AR, *v.*, to donate, to give.
DO.BRA, *s.f.*, fold, plait, plication.
DO.BRA.DI.ÇA, *s.f.*, hinge, joint.
DO.BRA.DO, *s.m., Bras., Mil.*, marching music; *adj.*, folded, doubled, double.
DO.BRAR, *v.*, to double, to bend, to fold, to bow, to ply.
DO.BRÁ.VEL, *adj.*, foldable.
DO.BRO, *s.m.*, double, duplication.
DO.CA, *s.f.*, dock, quay.
DO.CE, *s.m.*, sweets, sweetmeat, comfit, bonbon, candy, cooky.
DO.CEN.TE, *s. 2 gen.*, teacher, professor, instructor, lecturer, prelector.
DÓ.CIL, *adj.*, docile, amenable, teachable, sweet tempered, ductile.
DO.CI.LI.DA.DE, *s.f.*, docility, teachableness.
DO.CU.MEN.TA.ÇÃO, *s.f.*, documentation.
DO.CU.MEN.TAR, *v.*, to document, to prove, to bring evidence.
DO.CU.MEN.TO, *s.m.*, document, paper, record, writ, act, voucher, bill.
DO.ÇU.RA, *s.f.*, sweetness, honey.
DO.DÓI, *s.m., pop.*, wound, woe, pain; *adj.*, sick, ill.
DO.EN.ÇA, *s.f.*, disease, illness, sickness, affection, ailment.
DO.EN.TE, *s.m.*, patient; *adj.*, sick, ill, diseased.
DO.EN.TI.O, *adj.*, sickly, unhealthy.
DO.ER, *v.*, to ache, to hurt.
DOG.MA, *s.m.*, dogma, principle, maxim, doctrine.
DOG.MÁ.TI.CO, *adj.*, dogmatic, dogmatical.
DOG.MA.TIS.MO, *s.m.*, dogmatism.
DOI.DI.CE, *s.f.*, madness, foolishness.
DOI.DO, *s.m.*, madman, foolish; *adj.*, mad, crazy, insane.
DO.Í.DO, *adj.*, aching, painful, hurt, troubled.
DOI.RA.DO, *s.m., adj.*, the same that *dourado*.
DOI.RAR, *v.*, the same that *dourar*.
DOIS, *num.*, two; deuce.
DÓ.LAR, *s.m.*, dollar; buck.
DO.LO, *s.f.*, fraud, deceit, duplicity.
DO.LO.RI.DO, *adj.*, dolorific, dolorous, painful.
DO.LO.RO.SO, *adj.*, dolorous, aching, sore, cruel.
DO.LO.SO, *adj.*, deceitful, premeditated, fraudulent.
DOM, *s.m.*, gift, talent, ability, present, donation.
DO.MA.DOR, *s.m.*, tamer, horse-breaker; *adj.*, taming.
DO.MAR, *v.*, to tame, to domesticate, to vanquish, to overcome, to subdue.
DO.MÁ.VEL, *adj.*, tamable.
DO.MES.TI.CA.ÇÃO, *s.f.*, domestication.
DO.MES.TI.CAR, *v.*, to domesticate, to tame, to civilize, to break in.
DO.MÉS.TI.CO, *adj.*, domestic, internal, familiar, private, tame.
DO.MI.CI.LI.AR, *v.*, to domiciliate, to domicile, to establish in a place; *adj.*, home.
DO.MI.CÍ.LIO, *s.m.*, domicile, dwelling, residence, home.
DO.MI.NA.ÇÃO, *s.f.*, domination, dominance, command, rule, control.
DO.MI.NAR, *v.*, to dominate, to rule, to command, to control, to govern.
DO.MIN.GO, *s.m.*, Sunday.

DOMINICAL ·· 167 ·· DÚZIA

DO.MI.NI.CAL, *adj.*, dominical.

DO.MÍ.NIO, *s.m.*, power, control, domain, command, domination.

DO.MI.NÓ, *s.m.*, domino, *pl.* dominos(oes).

DO.NA, *s.f.*, lady, donna, proprietress; woman, wife.

DO.NA.TÁ.RI.O, *s.m.*, donee.

DO.NA.TI.VO, *s.m.*, donation.

DON.DE, *adv.*, where, from where, wherefrom.

DON.DO.CA, *s.f., pop., pej.*, snooty woman, posh.

DO.NO, *s.m.*, master, keeper, owner, proprietor, lord, landlord, holder.

DON.ZE.LA, *s.f.*, maiden, damsel, virgin.

DO.PAR, *v.*, to dope, to drug.

DOP.ING, *s.m., Ingl.*, dope; *Esp.*, doping.

DOR, *s.m.*, ache, pain, ail, grief, sorrow, dolour; *dor de barriga*: bellyache; *dor de cabeça*: headache.

DO.RA.VAN.TE, *adv.*, from now on, hereafter, henceforth.

DOR.MÊN.CI.A, *s.f.*, dormancy.

DOR.MEN.TE, *s.m.*, railway sleeper; *adj.*, dormant, sleeping; numb, torpid.

DOR.MI.NHO.CO, *s.m.*, sleepyhead; *adj.*, sleepy, drowsy, dozy.

DOR.MIR, *v.*, to sleep, to slumber, to fall asleep, to repose, to lie, to rest.

DOR.MI.TÓ.RIO, *s.m.*, bedroom.

DOR.SO, *s.m.*, back, reverse, dorsum.

DO.SA.GEM, *s.f.*, dosage, dose.

DO.SAR, *v.*, to dose, to portion.

DO.SE, *s.f.*, dose, quantity, proportion, measure.

DOS.SEL, *s.m.*, dossal.

DOS.SI.Ê, *s.m.*, dossier.

DO.TA.ÇÃO, *s.f.*, endowment, budget, foundation.

DO.TA.DO, *adj.*, gifted, endowed with.

DO.TAR, *v.*, to endow, to dower.

DO.TE, *s.m.*, dot, dotal gift, fortune.

DOU.RA.DO, *adj.*, golden, gilt, gilded.

DOU.RAR, *v.*, to gild, to gild over, to embellish.

DOU.TO, *adj.*, learned, erudite.

DOU.TOR, *s.m.*, doctor, lawyer.

DOU.TO.RA, *s.f.*, doctoress, lady doctor.

DOU.TO.RA.DO, *s.m.*, doctorate, doctorship.

DOU.TRI.NA, *s.f.*, doctrine, precept, instruction, teaching.

DOU.TRI.NAR, *v.*, to doctrinize, to teach.

DO.ZE, *num.*, twelve.

DRA.GA, *s.f.*, drag, dredger.

DRA.GA.GEM, *s.f.*, dredging.

DRA.GÃO, *s.m.*, dragon.

DRA.GAR, *v.*, to drag.

DRÁ.GE.A, *s.f.*, tablet, medicinal pill, *dragée*.

DRAG QUEEN, *s.f., Ingl.*, drag queen.

DRA.MA, *s.m.*, drama, play, tragedy.

DRA.MA.TI.CI.DA.DE, *s.f., pop.*, the quality of what is dramatic.

DRA.MA.TI.ZA.ÇÃO, *s.f., Teat.*, dramatization.

DRA.MA.TI.ZAR, *v.*, to dramatize; *fig.*, to exaggerate.

DRA.MA.TUR.GI.A, *s.f.*, dramaturgy.

DRA.MA.TUR.GO, *s.m.*, playwright, dramatist.

DRÁS.TI.CO, *adj., Med.*, drastic, powerful.

DRE.NA.GEM, *s.f.*, drainage.

DRE.NAR, *v.*, to drain, to draw off.

DRE.NO, *s.m.*, drain.

DRI.BLAR, *v., Esp.*, to dribble (soccer).

DRIN.QUE, *s.m.*, drink.

DRO.GA, *s.f.*, drug, rubbish.

DRO.GAR, *v.*, to drug, to dope, to store.

DRO.GA.RI.A, *s.f.*, drugstore, pharmacy.

DRO.ME.DÁ.RIO, *s.m., Zool.*, dromedary.

DRUI.DA, *s.m.*, druid.

DU.A.LI.DA.DE, *s.f.*, duality.

DU.A.LIS.MO, *s.m.*, dualism.

DU.A.LÍ.ZAR, *v.*, to dualize, to make dual.

DU.AS, *num.*, two; *adj.*, twain, two.

DU.BI.E.DA.DE, *s.f.*, dubiety.

DÚ.BI.O, *adj.*, dubious.

DU.BLAR, *v.*, to dub.

DU.BLA.GEM, *s.f.*, dubbing.

DU.CAL, *adj.*, ducal (pertaining to a duke).

DU.CHA, *s.f.*, shower, douche.

DÚC.TIL, *adj.*, ductile.

DU.E.LAR, *v.*, to duel, to fight a duel.

DU.E.LO, *s.m.*, duel, duetto, single combat.

DU.EN.DE, *s.m.*, dwarf, elf, boglin.

DU.E.TO, *s.m.*, duet, *duetto*.

DUL.CI.FI.CAR, *v.*, to dulcify.

DU.NA, *s.f.*, dune, sand dune, sand hill.

DUN.GA, *s.m., pop.*, chief, boss; joker (cards).

DU.O, *s.m.*, duo, duet.

DU.O.DE.NAL, *adj.*, duodenal.

DU.PLA, *adj., s.f.*, couple, pair, two-some.

DU.PLI.CAR, *v.*, to double, to duplicate, to copy, to repeat.

DU.PLI.CA.TA, *s.f.*, duplicate, copy, bill.

DU.PLI.CI.DA.DE, *s.f.*, duplicity, doubleness.

DU.PLO, *s.m.*, the double; *adj.*, double, duplex, twofold, dual, duplicate.

DU.QUE, *s.m.*, duke.

DU.QUE.SA, *s.f.*, duchess.

DU.RA.BI.LI.DA.DE, *s.f.*, durability.

DU.RA.ÇÃO, *s.f.*, duration, lasting, run, continuance, endurance.

DU.RA.DOU.RO, *adj.*, lasting, durable.

DU.RAN.TE, *prep.*, during, while, in the time of, in the course of, for, by.

DU.RAR, *v.*, to last, to continue, to remain, to abide, to be resistent.

DU.RÁ.VEL, *adj.*, durable, lasting.

DU.RE.ZA, *s.f.*, hardness, consistency, solidity, stiffness, severity.

DU.RO, *adj.*, hard, firm, solid, consistent, compact, dense, strong, vigorous, difficult.

DÚ.VI.DA, *s.f.*, doubt, dubiety, incertainty, incertitude, discredit.

DU.VI.DAR, *v.*, to doubt, to be uncertain, to descredit, suspect.

DU.VI.DO.SO, *adj.*, dubious, doubtful, uncertain, questionable, problematic.

DU.ZEN.TOS, *num.*, two hundred.

DÚ.ZIA, *s.f.*, dozen; **ÀS DÚZIAS** (*pl.*): by the dozen; *meia dúzia*: half a dozen.

E, *s.m.*, the fifth letter of the Portuguese alphabet; *conj.*, and.
É.BA.NO, *s.m.*, ebony.
E.BRI.E.DA.DE, *s.f.*, inebriation, drunkenness.
É.BRIO, *s.m.*, drunkard, bum; *adj.*, drunk.
E.BU.LI.ÇÃO, *s.f.*, ebullition, boiling, ebullience.
E.BU.LIR, *v.*, to boil.
E.BÚR.NE.O, *adj.*, of or like ivory; ivory-coloured.
E.CHAR.PE, *s.f.*, scarf.
E.CLAMP.SI.A, *s.f.*, *Med.*, eclampsia.
E.CLE.SI.ÁS.TI.CO, *adj.*, ecclesiastic, clerical, canonical.
E.CLÉ.TI.CO, *adj.*, eclectic.
E.CLE.TIS.MO, *s.m.*, eclecticism.
E.CLIP.SAR, *v.*, to eclipse.
E.CLIP.SE, *s.m.*, eclipse.
E.CLÍP.TI.CA, *s.f.*, *Astron.*, ecliptic.
E.CLU.SA, *s.f.*, floodgate, dam, canal lock, sluicegate.
E.CLO.SÃO, *s.f.*, emergence, appearance; development; *Zool.*, eclosion; *Bot.*, blooming (flower).
E.CO, *s.m.*, echo, repetition, ressonance, resound.
E.CO.AR, *v.*, to echo, to reflect the sound, to repeat.
E.CO.LO.GI.A, *s.f.*, ecology.
E.CO.LÓ.GI.CO, *adj.*, *Biol.*, ecologic, ecological.
E.CO.LO.GIS.TA, *s. 2 gen.*, ecologist.
E.CO.NO.MI.A, *s.f.*, economy, regulation, method, economics.
E.CO.NÔ.MI.CO, *adj.*, economic, cheap, thrifty, frugal.
E.CO.NO.MIS.TA, *s. 2 gen.*, economist.
E.CO.NO.MI.ZAR, *v.*, to save, to spare, to cut corners, to economize, to husband, to be frugal.
E.COS.SIS.TE.MA, *s.m.*, ecosystem.
E.CO.TU.RIS.MO, *s.m.*, eco-tourism.
E.CU.MÊ.NI.CO, *adj.*, ecumenical, oecumenical.
E.CU.ME.NIS.MO, *s.m.*, *Rel.*, ecumenismo.
EC.ZE.MA, *s.m.*, *Med.*, eczema.
E.DE.MA, *s.f.*, *Med.*, edema, oedema.
É.DEN, *s.m.*, Eden, paradise.
E.DÊ.NI.CO, *adj.*, Edenic.
E.DI.ÇÃO, *s.f.*, edition, issue, publication, impression.
E.DÍ.CU.LA, *s.f.*, little house, oratory, niche.
E.DI.FI.CA.ÇÃO, *s.f.*, edification, erection, construction, edifying, building.
E.DI.FI.CA.ÇÃO, *s.f.*, building, construction, edifying.
E.DI.FI.CAN.TE, *adj.*, edifying, instructive, constructive.
E.DI.FI.CAR, *v.*, to construct, to build, to elevate, to erect, to found.
E.DI.FÍ.CIO, *s.m.*, building.
E.DIL, *s.m.*, councilman, alderman.
É.DI.PO, *s.m.*, Oedipus; *complexo de* ~: Oedipus complex.
E.DI.TAL, *s.m.*, proclamation, edict.
E.DI.TAR, *v.*, to edit, to publish.
É.DI.TO, *s.m.*, edict, proclamation.
E.DI.TOR, *s.m.*, publisher, editor.
E.DI.TO.RA, *s.f.*, publishinghouse, company.
E.DI.TO.RA.ÇÃO, *s.f.*, editorial business, publishing, publication.
E.DI.TO.RI.A, *s.f.*, section.
E.DRE.DÃO, *s.m.*, comforter.
E.DRE.DOM, *s.m.*, comforter.
E.DU.CA.ÇÃO, *s.f.*, education, instruction, knowledge, teaching, breeding, development.
E.DU.CA.CIO.NAL, *adj.*, educational.
E.DU.CA.DO, *adj.*, educated.
E.DU.CA.DOR, *s.m.*, educator.
E.DU.CAN.DÁ.RIO, *s.m.*, educational establishment, school.
E.DU.CAR, *v.*, to educate, to bring up, to teach, to instruct.
E.DU.CA.TI.VO, *adj.*, educative, educational.
E.FE, *s.m.*, name of the letter *f*.
E.FEI.TO, *s.m.*, effect, result, consequence, realization, efficacy, intention.
E.FE.ME.RI.DA.DE, *s.f.*, ephemerality.
E.FE.MÉ.RI.DES, *s.f., pl.*, ephemeris, ephemerides; *Astron.*, astronomical table.
E.FÊ.ME.RO, *adj.*, ephemeral, short-lived.
E.FE.MI.NA.DO, *adj.*, effeminate, fag, queer, fagot, womanlike.
E.FE.TI.VA.ÇÃO, *s.f.*, effectuation.
E.FE.TI.VA.MEN.TE, *adv.*, effectively, actually.
E.FE.TI.VAR, *v.*, to execute, to effect, to accomplish, to realize.
E.FE.TI.VI.DA.DE, *s.f.*, effectiveness, reality.
E.FE.TI.VO, *adj.*, effective.
E.FE.TU.AR, *v.*, to effectuate.
E.FI.CÁ.CIA, *s.f.*, efficacy, efficiency.
E.FI.CAZ, *adj.*, efficacious.
E.FI.CI.ÊN.CIA, *s.f.*, efficiency.
E.FI.CI.EN.TE, *adj.*, efficient, efficacious.
E.FLU.EN.TE, *adj.*, effluent, emanating.
E.FLÚ.VI.O, *s.m.*, effluvium.
E.FU.SÃO, *s.f.*, effusion.
E.FU.SI.VO, *adj.*, effusive, expressive, gushing, effluent.
É.GI.DE, *s.f.*, aegis, egis.
E.GÍP.CIO, *adj., s.m.*, Egyptian.
E.GIP.TO.LO.GI.A, *s.f.*, Egyptology.
É.GLO.GA, *s.f.*, eclogue.
E.GO.CÊN.TRI.CO, *s.m.*, egocentric; *adj.*, egocentric.
E.GO.ÍS.MO, *s.m.*, egoism, selfishness.
E.GO.ÍS.TA, *adj.*, egoistic, selfish.
E.GRÉ.GI.O, *adj.*, distinguished, prominent, eminent.
E.GRES.SO, *s.m.*, egress, exit, departure; ex-prisoner; *adj.*, egressed.
É.GUA, *s.f.*, *Zool.*, mare.
EI, *interj.*, hey!
EIS, *adv.*, here is, this is, here are, these are.
EI.XO, *s.m.*, axis, axle, axle-tree.
E.JA.CU.LA.ÇÃO, *s.f.*, ejaculation.
E.JA.CU.LAR, *v.*, to ejaculate.
E.JE.ÇÃO, *s.f.*, ejection, expulsion.

EJETAR ·· 169 ·· EMBICAR

E.JE.TAR, *v.*, to eject.

E.LA, *pron.*, she, it, her; elas, they, them.

E.LA.BO.RA.ÇÃO, *s.f.*, elaboration, preparation, working up.

E.LA.BO.RAR, *v.*, to elaborate, to organize, to prepare.

E.LAS.TI.CI.DA.DE, *s.f.*, elasticity, resilience; flexibility.

E.LÁS.TI.CO, *s.m.*, elastic cord, elastic band, rubber band; *adj.*, elastic, flexible, stringy.

E.LE, *pron.*, he, it, him; *eles*: they, them.

E.LE.FAN.TA, *s.f., Zool.*, she-elephant.

E.LE.FAN.TE, *s.m., Zool.*, elephant.

E.LE.FAN.TÍ.A.SE, *s.f.*, elephantiasis.

E.LE.FAN.TI.NO, *adj.*, elephantine.

E.LE.GÂN.CIA, *s.f.*, elegance, grace, smartness.

E.LE.GAN.TE, *s.f.*, elegant.

E.LE.GER, *v.*, to elect, to choose by vote, to select.

E.LE.GI.A, *s.f.*, elegy.

E.LE.GÍ.VEL, *adj.*, elegible.

E.LEI.ÇÃO, *s.f.*, election, poll, choice, selection.

E.LEI.TO, *s.m.*, elect; *adj.*, elect, elected, selected.

E.LEI.TOR, *s.m.*, elector, voter, constituent.

E.LEI.TO.RA.DO, *s.m.*, electorate.

E.LEI.TO.RAL, *adj.*, electoral.

E.LEI.TO.REI.RO, *adj., pej.*, vote-catching.

E.LE.MEN.TAR, *adj., s.m.*, elementary, elemental.

E.LE.MEN.TO, *s.m.*, element, component, ingredient.

E.LEN.CAR, *v.*, to list.

E.LEN.CO, *s.m.*, cast, list, catalogue.

E.LE.TI.VO, *adj.*, elective.

E.LE.TRI.CI.DA.DE, *s.f.*, electricity.

E.LE.TRI.CIS.TA, *s. 2 gen.*, electrician.

E.LÉ.TRI.CO, *adj.*, electric.

E.LE.TRI.FI.CAR, *v., Eletr.*, to electrify.

E.LE.TRI.ZAN.TE, *adj., fig.*, electrifying.

E.LE.TRI.ZAR, *v.*, to electrize.

E.LE.TRO.CAR.DI.O.GRA.MA, *s.m., Med.*, electrocardiogram.

E.LE.TRO.CHO.QUE, *s.m., Med.*, electroconvulsive therapy.

E.LE.TRO.CU.TAR, *v.*, to electrocute.

E.LE.TRO.DI.NÂ.MI.CA, *s.f., Fís.*, electrodynamics.

E.LE.TRO.DO, *s.m., Eletr.*, electrode.

E.LE.TRO.DO.MÉS.TI.CO, *s.m.*, electric appliance.

E.LE.TRO.Í.MÃ, *s.m.*, electromagnet.

E.LE.TRÓ.LI.SE, *s.f., Fís., Quím.*, electrolysis.

E.LE.TRO.MAG.NÉ.TI.CO, *adj.*, electromagnetic, electromagnetical.

E.LE.TRO.MAG.NE.TIS.MO, *s.m.*, electromagnetism.

E.LÉ.TRON, *s.m., Quím.*, electron.

E.LE.TRÔ.NI.CA, *s.f.*, electronics.

E.LE.TRÔ.NI.CO, *adj.*, electronic.

E.LE.TROS.TÁ.TI.CA, *s.f., Eletr.*, electrostatics.

E.LE.VA.ÇÃO, *s.f.*, elevation, rïse, increase.

E.LE.VA.DO, *adj.*, elevated, high, lifted up, raised.

E.LE.VA.DOR, *s.m.*, elevator, lift.

E.LE.VAR, *v.*, to elevate, to raise, to lift, to exalt, to ennoble.

EL.FO, *s.m., Mit.*, elf.

E.LI.MI.NA.ÇÃO, *s.f.*, elimination.

E.LI.MI.NA.TÓ.RI.O, *adj.*, eliminatory, eliminating.

E.LI.MI.NAR, *v.*, to eliminate, to remove, to expel, to delete.

E.LIP.SE, *s.f.*, ellipsis, ellipse.

E.LÍP.TI.CO, *adj.*, elliptic, elliptical.

E.LI.TE, *s.f.*, elite.

E.LI.TIS.MO, *s.m.*, elitism.

E.LI.XIR, *s.m.*, elixir, panacea.

E.LO, *s.m.*, link, chain, connexion.

E.LO.CU.ÇÃO, *s.f.*, elocution.

E.LO.GI.AR, *v.*, to praise, to compliment, to extol, to commend.

E.LO.GI.O, *s.m.*, praise, compliment, eulogy.

E.LO.GI.O.SO, *adj.*, eulogious, laudatory, eulogistic; flattering.

E.LO.QUÊN.CI.A, *s.f.*, eloquence.

E.LU.CI.DA.ÇÃO, *s.f.*, elucidation, explanation, clearing up, exposition.

E.LU.CI.DAR, *v.*, to elucidate, to explain, to make clear, to illuminate.

E.LU.CI.DA.TI.VO, *adj.*, elucidative, elucidating.

EM, *prep.*, in, into, up, at, on, upon, during, within, by, to.

E.MA, *s.f., Zool.*, rhea (Brazilian ostrich).

E.MA.GRE.CER, *v.*, to emaciate, to lose weight, to grow thin, to reduce.

E.MA.GRE.CI.MEN.TO, *s.m.*, thinning, slimming.

E.MA.NA.ÇÃO, *s.f.*, emanation.

E.MAN.CI.PA.ÇÃO, *s.f.*, emancipation.

E.MAN.CI.PAR, *v.*, to emancipate, to liberate.

E.MA.RA.NHA.DO, *adj.*, tangled, matted.

E.MA.RA.NHA.MEN.TO, *s.m.*, entanglement, intricacy; tangle, confusion.

E.MA.RA.NHAR, *v.*, to embarrass, to tangle, to entangle, to complicate.

E.MAS.CU.LA.ÇÃO, *s.f.*, emasculation.

E.MAS.CU.LA.DO, *adj.*, emasculate, effeminate.

E.MAS.CU.LAR, *v.*, to emasculate.

EM.BA.ÇA.DO, *adj.*, dimmed, dull; obfuscated.

EM.BA.ÇAR, *v.*, to dim, to dull; to obfuscate.

EM.BA.CI.A.DO, *adj.*, the same that *embaçado*.

EM.BAI.XA.DA, *s.f.*, embassy.

EM.BAI.XA.DOR, *s.m.*, ambassador.

EM.BAI.XA.TRIZ, *s.f.*, ambassadress.

EM.BAI.XO, *adv.*, below, beneath, downstairs.

EM.BA.LA.GEM, *s.f.*, package, packaging.

EM.BA.LAN.ÇAR, *v.*, to balance, to swing; to oscillate.

EM.BAL.SA.MA.MEN.TO, *s.m.*, embalmment.

EM.BAL.SA.MAR, *v.*, to embalm.

EM.BA.RA.ÇA.DO, *adj.*, embarrassed, perplexed, puzzled.

EM.BA.RA.ÇAR, *v.*, to embarrass, to distress.

EM.BA.RA.ÇO, *s.m.*, embarrassment.

EM.BA.RA.ÇO.SO, *adj.*, embarrassing.

EM.BA.RA.LHAR, *v.*, to shuffle (cards); to mix (up), to confuse.

EM.BAR.CA.ÇÃO, *s.f.*, vessel, ship, craft.

EM.BAR.CAR, *v.*, to embark.

EM.BAR.GA.DO, *adj.*, blocked, seized, stopped.

EM.BAR.GAR, *v.*, to block, to embargo, to seize.

EM.BAR.GO, *s.m.*, seizure, embargo, arrest.

EM.BAR.QUE, *s.m.*, embarkment, shipping.

EM.BA.SAR, *v.*, to base, to found.

EM.BE.BE.DAR, *v.*, to intoxicate, to make drunk.

EM.BE.BER, *v.*, to soak up, to steep.

EM.BE.BI.DO, *adj.*, soaked, drenched; enraptured.

EM.BE.LE.ZA.MEN.TO, *s.m.*, embellishment.

EM.BE.LE.ZAR, *v.*, to embellish, to beautify.

EM.BE.VE.CER, *v.*, to enrapture, to delight.

EM.BE.VE.CI.DO, *adj.*, enraptured, delighted.

EM.BI.CAR, *v.*, to shape like a beak, to sharpen, bras to

EMBLEMA ·· 170 ·· EMPLACAR

drink, sip.

EM.BLE.MA, *s.m.*, emblem, badge, ensign, allegory.

EM.BLE.MÁ.TI.CO, *adj.*, emblematic, emblematical, representative.

EM.BO.LAR, *v.*, to shape into a ball; *Bras.*, to tangle, to entangle.

EM.BO.LI.A, *s.f., Med.*, embolism.

ÊM.BO.LO, *s.m., Mec.*, piston; *Med.*, embolus.

EM.BOL.SAR, *v.*, to pocket, to pouch, to purse.

EM.BO.RA, *adv.*, though, although, even though, albeit, however, in despite of.

EM.BOS.CA.DA, *s.f.*, ambush, ambuscade.

EM.BOR.CAR, *v.*, to upside down; to drain off; to empty.

EM.BOS.CA.DA, *s.f.*, ambuscade, ambush.

EM.BOS.CAR, *v.*, to ambush.

EM.BO.TA.DO, *adj.*, edgeless; benumbed, dull.

EM.BO.TAR, *v.*, to blunt; to benumb; to grow feeble.

EM.BRAN.QUE.CER, *v.*, to whiten, to make white.

EM.BRAN.QUE.CI.MEN.TO, *s.m.*, whitening.

EM.BRE.A.GEM, *s.f.*, clutch.

EM.BRI.A.GA.DO, *adj.*, drunk, drunken, tipsy, intoxicated.

EM.BRI.A.GAR, *v.*, to make drunk, to intoxicate, to alcoholize.

EM.BRI.A.GUEZ, *s.f.*, drunkenness, inebriety; *fig.*, ecstasy, enthusiasm.

EM.BRI.ÃO, *s.f., Biol.*, embryo, germ.

EM.BRI.O.LO.GI.A, *s.f., Biol.*, embriologia.

EM.BRI.O.NÁ.RI.O, *adj., Med.*, embryonic.

EM.BRO.MA.ÇÃO, *s.f., Bras., pop.*, delaying, putting off; deceiving, cheating; false promise.

EM.BRO.MAR, *v., Bras., pop.*, to deceive, to swindle; to delay; to defraud, to make false promises.

EM.BRU.LHA.DA, *s.f.*, confusion, complication, disorder.

EM.BRU.LHAR, *v.*, to wrap up, to pack up.

EM.BRU.LHO, *s.m.*, bundle, packet, package; *fig.*, intrigue.

EM.BRU.TE.CER, *v.*, to brutalize, to make brutal.

EM.BRU.TE.CI.MEN.TO, *s.m.*, brutalization.

EM.BU.CHA.DO, *adj.*, stuffed, glutted.

EM.BU.CHAR, *v.*, to stuff (belly), to glut.

EM.BUR.RA.DO, *adj., pop.*, sulky, moody.

EM.BUS.TE, *s.m.*, deception; imposture, hoax.

EM.BUS.TEI.RO, *s.m.*, liar, impostor; *adj.*, lying, cheating; deceptive.

EM.BU.TI.DO, *s.m.*, inlaid work; *adj., Arquit.*, built-in.

EM.BU.TIR, *v.*, to inlay, to incrust.

E.ME, *s.m.*, name of the letter *m*.

E.MEN.DA, *s.f.*, correction; amendment, rectification.

E.MEN.DAR, *v.*, to correct, to amend, to emend, to ameliorate.

E.MEN.TA, *s.f.*, list; annotation, summary; syllabus.

E.MER.GÊN.CIA, *s.f.*, emergency, incident, crisis.

E.MER.GEN.TE, *adj.*, emergent; emerging.

E.MER.GIR, *v.*, to emerge, to appear.

E.MÉ.RI.TO, *adj.*, emeritus.

E.MER.SÃO, *s.f.*, emersion; gradual appearance.

E.MER.SO, *adj.*, emersed, emerged.

E.MI.GRA.ÇÃO, *s.f.*, emigration.

E.MI.GRAN.TE, *s. 2 gen.*, emigrant.

E.MI.GRAR, *v.*, to emigrate, to migrate.

E.MI.NÊN.CIA, *s.f.*, eminence.

E.MI.NEN.TE, *adj.*, eminent, high, prominent, elevated.

E.MIR, *s.m.*, emir.

E.MI.RA.DO, *s.m.*, emirate.

E.MIS.SÃO, *s.f.*, emission, issuing.

E.MIS.SÁ.RI.O, *s.m.*, emissary, messenger, agent.

E.MIS.SOR, *s.m.*, sender, emitter; *adj.*, issuing, emitting, emissive.

E.MIS.SO.RA, *s.f.*, broadcasting station.

E.MI.TEN.TE, *s. 2 gen.*, issuing, emitter.

E.MI.TIR, *v.*, to emit, to issue, to discharge, to send out.

E.MO.ÇÃO, *s.f.*, emotion, thrill, excitement.

E.MO.CI.O.NAL, *adj.*, emotional.

E.MO.CI.O.NAN.TE, *adj.*, exciting, thrilling.

E.MO.CI.O.NAR, *v.*, to thrill, to touch.

E.MOL.DAR, *v.*, to mold.

E.MOL.DU.RAR, *v.*, to frame.

E.MO.TI.VO, *adj.*, emotional, emotive.

EM.PA.CAR, *v., Bras.*, to balk, stop short (horse or beast); to stand still.

EM.PA.CO.TA.DOR, *s.m.*, packer; *adj.*, packing.

EM.PA.CO.TA.MEN.TO, *s.m.*, wrappage.

EM.PA.CO.TAR, *v.*, to pack, to wrap up, to package.

EM.PA.DA, *s.f.*, patty, pie.

EM.PA.DI.NHA, *s.f.*, patty, a little pie.

EM.PA.LHAR, *v.*, to stuff with straw (animals); to cover with straw.

EM.PA.LI.DE.CER, *v.*, to pale.

EM.PA.NAR, *v.*, to cover (with cloth); *Cul.*, to coat with flour.

EM.PAN.TUR.RAR, *v.*, to stuff, to glut, to cram, to gorge.

EM.PAN.ZI.NAR, *v.*, to surfeit, to stuff, to glut.

EM.PA.PAR, *v.*, to drench, to sop.

EM.PA.RE.DAR, *v.*, to wall in, to cloister, to shut up between walls.

EM.PA.RE.LHAR, *v.*, to pair, to couple, to match, to unite, to join, to link.

EM.PAS.TAR, *v.*, to paste, to plaster.

EM.PAS.TE.LAR, *v.*, to become disarranged; to destroy the installations of a newspaper.

EM.PA.TA.DO, *adj.*, drawn, tied (game); invested (money).

EM.PA.TAR, *v.*, to make equal, to equalize, to tie up.

EM.PA.TE, *s.m.*, equality, draw, tie.

EM.PA.TI.A, *s.f., Psic.*, empathy.

EM.PE.CI.LHO, *s.m.*, impediment, difficulty, obstruction, snag, hitch.

EM.PE.DER.NI.DO, *adj.*, petrified; *fig.*, harsh, insensible.

EM.PE.DER.NIR, *v.*, to petrify; *fig.*, to harden, to make insensible.

EM.PE.DRAR, *v.*, to pave, to convert into stone.

EM.PE.NAR, *v.*, to warp, to feather.

EM.PE.NHA.DO, *adj.*, indebt, pledged, engaged.

EM.PE.NHAR, *v.*, to pawn, to mortgage, hypothecate, to induce.

EM.PE.NHO, *s.m.*, pledge, pawn, promise.

EM.PER.RAR, *v.*, to stick fast, to get jammed.

EM.PI.LHA.DO, *adj.*, piled up, heaped up.

EM.PI.LHAR, *v.*, to heap up, to pille, to stack, to accumulate.

EM.PI.NAR, *v.*, to raise up, to lift up, to put straight, to tope.

EM.PÍ.RI.CO, *s.m.*, empiric; *adj.*, empiric, empirical, experimental.

EM.PI.RIS.MO, *s.m.*, empiricism.

EM.PI.RIS.TA, *s.m.*, empiricist; *adj.*, empiric, empirical.

EM.PLA.CA.MEN.TO, *s.m., Bras.*, method of supplying with a plate (licence and number plate).

EM.PLA.CAR, *v.*, to supply with a plate.

EMPLASTRO ·· 171 ·· ENCARNAÇÃO

EM.PLAS.TRO, *s.m.*, plaster.
EM.PLU.MAR, *v.*, to feather.
EM.PO.BRE.CER, *v.*, to make poor, to impoverish, to pauperize.
EM.PO.BRE.CI.MEN.TO, *s.m.*, impoverishment.
EM.PO.ÇAR, *v.*, to put into a puddle; to form a puddle.
EM.PO.EI.RA.DO, *adj.*, dusty.
EM.PO.EI.RAR, *v.*, to dust.
EM.PO.LA.DO, *adj.*, swollen; blistered; *fig.*, pompous.
EM.PO.LAR, *v.*, to blister; to swell.
EM.POL.GA.ÇÃO, *s.f.*, excitement, enthusiasm.
EM.POL.GAN.TE, *adj.*, exciting, thrilling.
EM.POL.GAR, *v.*, to thrill, to excite arrest, to fill with enthusiasm.
EM.POR.CA.LHAR, *v.*, to dirty.
EM.POS.SA.DO, *adj.*, installed in office, vested.
EM.POS.SAR, *v.*, to give possession to, to put in possession of.
EM.POS.SAR, *v.*, to install in office.
EM.PRE.EN.DE.DOR, *s.m.*, enterpriser, entrepreneur; *adj.*, enterprising; adventurous.
EM.PRE.EN.DER, *v.*, to undertake, to attempt, to enterprise.
EM.PRE.EN.DI.MEN.TO, *s.m.*, undertaking, enterprise.
EM.PRE.GA.DA, *s.f.*, maid, servant-girl, domestic servant.
EM.PRE.GA.DO, *s.m.*, servant, employee; *adj.*, employed.
EM.PRE.GA.DOR, *s.m.*, employer.
EM.PRE.GAR, *v.*, to employ.
PRE.GA.TÍ.CI.O, *adj.*, employment.
EM.PRE.GÁ.VEL, *adj.*, employable.
EM.PRE.GO, *s.m.*, employment, job, work, occupation.
EM.PRE.GUIS.MO, *s.m.*, job handouts, nepotism.
EM.PREI.TA.DA, *s.f.*, contract job, piecework, taskwork.
EM.PREI.TAR, *v.*, to job, to take over on a contract basis.
EM.PREI.TEI.RA, *s.f.*, contracting company, enterprise.
EM.PREI.TEI.RO, *s.m.*, contractor.
EM.PRE.SA, *s.f.*, enterprise, firm, business, company.
EM.PRE.SA.RI.A.DO, *s.m.*, class of undertakers, employers, contractors, entrepreneurs.
EM.PRE.SA.RI.AL, *adj.*, managerial, company.
EM.PRE.SÁ.RIO, *s.m.*, entrepreneur, contractor, manager, undertaker, impresario.
EM.PRES.TA.DO, *adj.*, lent, loaned, borrowed.
EM.PRES.TAR, *v.*, to lend to, to loan to.
EM.PRÉS.TI.MO, *s.m.*, loan, lending, borrowing.
EM.PRO.A.DO, *adj.*, *Náut.*, sailing towards; *fig.*, proud, arrogant.
EM.PRO.AR, *v.*, *Náut.*, to head for; emproar-se: *fig.*, to be proud, to be arrogant.
EM.PU.NHAR, *v.*, to grasp, to lay hold of.
EM.PUR.RÃO, *s.m.*, push, shove, thrust, jostle, poke.
EM.PUR.RAR, *v.*, to push, to thrust, to shove, to hustle.
E.MU.DE.CER, *v.*, to silence, to still.
E.MU.LA.ÇÃO, *s.f.*, emulation.
E.MU.LAR, *v.*, to emulate.
Ê.MU.LO, *s.m.*, emulator; *adj.*, emulous.
E.MUL.SÃO, *s.f.*, emulsion.
E.NAL.TE.CER, *v.*, to exalt, to honour.
E.NAL.TE.CI.MEN.TO, *s.m.*, exaltation, extolment.
E.NA.MO.RA.DO, *adj.*, enamo(u)red, in love.
E.NA.MO.RAR, *v.*, to enchant, to enamo(u)r, to fascinate, to charm.
EN.CA.BE.ÇAR, *v.*, to head, to lead.

EN.CA.BU.LA.DO, *adj.*, embarrassed, ashmed, timid, shy.
EN.CA.BU.LAR, *v.*, to abash, to constrain, to ashame.
EN.CA.ÇA.PAR, *v.*, to pocket (a billiard ball).
EN.CA.DE.A.MEN.TO, *s.m.*, chaining, linkage, series; enchainment, concatenation.
EN.CA.DE.AR, *v.*, to enchain, to fetter, to link, to connect, to joint.
EN.CA.DER.NA.ÇÃO, *s.f.*, bookbinding.
EN.CA.DER.NA.DO, *adj.*, bound.
EN.CA.DER.NAR, *v.*, to bind books.
EN.CAI.XAR, *v.*, to box, to case, to incase, to mortise.
EN.CAI.XE, *s.m.*, fitting, mortise, splice, groove, joint.
EN.CAI.XO.TA.DO, *adj.*, boxed.
EN.CAI.XO.TAR, *v.*, to box, to incase, to pack (goods) in boxes.
EN.CA.LA.CRAR, *v.*, to lead into difficulties, to let someone down; encalacrar-se: to get into difficulties.
EN.CAL.ÇO, *s.m.*, pursuit, chase, footprint, trail, track.
EN.CA.LHA.DO, *adj.*, aground, stranded.
EN.CA.LHAR, *v.*, to run aground (ship); to remain unsold (goods).
EN.CA.LHE, *s.m.*, stranding (ship); unsold merchandise.
EN.CA.MI.NHA.MEN.TO, *s.m.*, direction, guiding, leading.
EN.CA.MI.NHAR, *v.*, to conduct, to lead, to guide, to direct, to orient.
EN.CAM.PAR, *v.*, to rescind (contract); to take over, to take into administration.
EN.CA.NA.DOR, *s.m.*, plumber, drainer.
EN.CA.NA.MEN.TO, *s.m.*, plumbing, piping, canalization.
EN.CA.NAR, *v.*, to channel, to lay pipes, to convey in pipes.
EN.CAN.TA.DO, *adj.*, enchanted, bewitched.
EN.CAN.TA.DOR, *s.m.*, enchanter; *adj.*, enchanting, charming.
EN.CAN.TA.DO.RA.MEN.TE, *adv.*, enchantingly.
EN.CAN.TA.MEN.TO, *s.m.*, enchantment, charming, fascination.
EN.CAN.TAR, *v.*, to enchant, to charm, to delight.
EN.CAN.TO, *s.m.*, enchantment, delight, wonder, marvel.
EN.CA.PA.DO, *adj.*, covered.
EN.CA.PAR, *v.*, to put a cover on (book).
EN.CA.PO.TA.DO, *s.m.*, person wearing an overcoat or cape; *adj.*, cloaked, covered.
EN.CA.PO.TAR, *v.*, to cloak, to muffle.
EN.CAP.SU.LAR, *v.*, to encapsulate.
EN.CA.PU.ZAR, *v.*, to hood.
EN.CA.RA.CO.LA.DO, *adj.*, curly, crisp (hair).
EN.CA.RA.CO.LAR, *v.*, to spiral; to curl, to crisp.
EN.CA.RAR, *v.*, to look at, to stare at, to face.
EN.CAR.CE.RA.MEN.TO, *s.m.*, imprisonment.
EN.CAR.CE.RAR, *v.*, to imprison, to shut up, to confine, to encarcerate.
EN.CAR.DI.DO, *adj.*, dirty, filthy, grimy.
EN.CAR.DIR, *v.*, to soil, to grime.
EN.CA.RE.CER, *v.*, to raise the prices, to endear, to grow dear, to exaggerate.
EN.CA.RE.CI.DA.MEN.TE, *adv.*, entreatingly; pedir ~: to implore insistently.
EN.CA.RE.CI.MEN.TO, *s.m.*, increase in price; raising (of prices); enhancement.
EN.CAR.GO, *s.m.*, responsibility, duty, mission, charge, incumbency.
EN.CAR.NA.ÇÃO, *s.f.*, incarnation.

ENCARNADO ·· 172 ·· ENDOIDECER

EN.CAR.NA.DO, *adj.*, incarnate, personified; red, scarlet.

EN.CAR.NAR, *v.*, to incarnate, to embody, to personify.

EN.CA.RO.ÇAR, *v.*, to come up in bumps (skin), to break out in pustules.

EN.CAR.QUI.LHAR, *v.*, to wrinkle, to crumple.

EN.CAR.RE.GA.DO, *s.m.*, person in charge; *adj.*, charged.

EN.CAR.RE.GAR, *v.*, to charge, to intrust, to put in charge in, to take charge of.

EN.CAR.RI.LHAR, *v.*, to put on the rails; to follow the right way.

EN.CAR.TAR, *v.*, to insert.

EN.CAR.TE, *s.m.*, insertion, insert.

EN.CAS.QUE.TAR, *v.*, to persuade; to put an idea in one's head.

EN.CA.VA.LAR, *v.*, superpose.

EN.CE.FA.LI.TE, *s.f.*, *Med.*, encephalitis.

EN.CÉ.FA.LO, *s.m.*, *Anat.*, brain, encephalon.

EN.CE.FA.LO.GRA.FI.A, *s.f.*, *Med.*, encephalography.

EN.CE.FA.LO.GRA.MA, *s.m.*, *Med.*, encephalogram.

EN.CE.NA.ÇÃO, *s.f.*, staging; simulation.

EN.CE.NAR, *v.*, to stage, to show, to exhibit, to display.

EN.CE.RA.DEI.RA, *s.f.*, floor polisher.

EN.CE.RA.DO, *s.m.*, tarpaulin, waxed cloth; *adj.*, waxed.

EN.CE.RAR, *v.*, to wax, to polish.

EN.CER.RA.MEN.TO, *s.m.*, closing, finishing; enclosure, closure; confinement.

EN.CER.RAR, *v.*, to enclose, to bring to an end, to contain, to hold, to include, to conclude, to keep.

EN.CES.TAR, *v.*, to basket; *Esp.*, to score.

EN.CE.TAR, *v.*, to begin, to start.

EN.CHAR.CA.DO, *adj.*, flooded, soppy; soaking wet; swampy.

EN.CHAR.CAR, *v.*, to flood, to soak, to drench, to form into a puddle, to inundate.

EN.CHEN.TE, *s.f.*, inundation, flood.

EN.CHER, *v.*, to fill, to make full, to satisfy, to saturate, to satiate, to glut, to abound, to stuff.

EN.CHI.MEN.TO, *s.m.*, filling; stuffing.

EN.CHO.VA, *s.f.*, *Zool.*, anchovy; bluefish.

EN.CÍ.CLI.CA, *s.f.*, encyclic.

EN.CI.CLO.PÉ.DIA, *s.f.*, *US* encyclopedia, *UK* encyclopaedia.

EN.CI.CLO.PÉ.DI.CO, *adj.*, *US* encyclopedic, *UK* encyclopaedic.

EN.CI.CLO.PE.DIS.TA, *s. 2 gen.*, *US* encyclopedist, *UK* encyclopaedist.

EN.CI.U.MAR, *v.*, to make or become jealous.

EN.CLAUS.TRAR, *v.*, to cloister; *enclaustrar-se*: to retire as in a convent.

EN.CLAU.SU.RA.MEN.TO, *s.m.*, act of shutting oneself up in.

EN.CLAU.SU.RAR, *v.*, to cloister; to refrain from society.

ÊN.CLI.SE, *s.f.*, *Gram.*, enclisis.

EN.CLÍ.TI.CO, *s.f.*, *Gram.*, enclitic.

EN.CO.BER.TO, *adj.*, covered, hidden.

EN.CO.BRI.MEN.TO, *s.m.*, covering, concealing, hiding.

EN.CO.BRIR, *v.*, to cover, to hide.

EN.CO.LE.RI.ZAR, *v.*, to make angry, to enrage, to infuriate, to irritate.

EN.CO.LHER, *v.*, to shrink, to contract, to draw up, to cramp.

EN.CO.LHI.MEN.TO, *s.m.*, shrinking.

EN.CO.MEN.DA, *s.f.*, order, thing ordered, indent, task.

EN.CO.MEN.DAR, *v.*, to order, to ask for, to charge, to command.

EN.COM.PRI.DAR, *v.*, to lengthen, to prolong.

EN.CON.TRÃO, *s.m.*, collision, shock, jostle.

EN.CON.TRAR, *v.*, to meet, to encounter, to find, to find out, to discover.

EN.CON.TRO, *s.m.*, meeting, appointment, date, impact, shock, collision.

EN.CO.RA.JA.MEN.TO, *s.m.*, encouragement.

EN.CO.RA.JAR, *v.*, to encourage, to foster, to hearten, to give courage to, to stimulate.

EN.COR.PA.DO, *adj.*, full-bodied, dense; close-woven.

EN.COR.PAR, *v.*, to thicken, to grow fat, to make thicker, to increase the body.

EN.CO.RU.JAR, *v.*, to be sad; to seclude oneself from society.

EN.COS.TA, *s.f.*, hillside, slope, ascent, declivity, acclivity.

EN.COS.TA.DO, *s.m.*, *fig.*, hanger-on, parasite, dependent; *adj.*, leaning on, propped, supported.

EN.COS.TAR, *v.*, to lean, to prop, to place against, to ask for money.

EN.COS.TO, *s.m.*, support; back (chair); a spirit that hampers a living being.

EN.COU.RA.ÇA.DO, *s.m.*, battleship; *adj.*, armoured, ironclad.

EN.CRA.VA.DO, *adj.*, nailed; inlaid; *unha encravada*: ingrowing nail.

EN.CRA.VAR, *v.*, to nail; to inlay; to prick, to wound with horseshoe nails.

EN.CREN.CA, *s.f.*, obstacle, difficulty, trouble, complication.

EN.CREN.CAR, *v.*, to break down, seize up, to embarrass, to embroil.

EN.CREN.QUEI.RO, *s.m.*, troublemaker.

EN.CRES.PA.ÇÃO, *s.f.*, curling.

EN.CRES.PA.DO, *adj.*, crisp, curled; choppy (sea); *fig.*, furious, angry.

EN.CRES.PAR, *v.*, to curl, crisp (hair); to ripple (sea); *encrespar-se*: to become choppy; *fig.*, to become angry.

EN.CRU.AR, *v.*, to harden.

EN.CRU.ZI.LHA.DA, *s.f.*, cross, crossroad, crossway.

EN.CU.CA.DO, *adj.*, *gír.*, worried, confused.

EN.CU.CAR, *v.*, *gír.*, to worry, to confound, to disturb.

EN.CUR.RA.LA.DO, *adj.*, cornered.

EN.CUR.RA.LAR, *v.*, to corner; to corral, to herd.

EN.CUR.TAR, *v.*, to shorten, to diminish, to abbreviate, to curtail, to cut short.

EN.CUR.VAR, *v.*, to incurvate, to bend, to curve.

EN.DE.MI.A, *s.f.*, *Med.*, endemic disease.

EN.DÊ.MI.CO, *adj.*, endemic, endemical.

EN.DE.MO.NI.NHA.DO, *adj.*, possessed by an evil spirit, devilish, mischievous.

EN.DE.RE.ÇA.MEN.TO, *s.m.*, address; *Comp.*, addressing.

EN.DE.RE.ÇAR, *v.*, to address.

EN.DE.RE.ÇO, *s.m.*, address.

EN.DEU.SA.MEN.TO, *s.m.*, divinization.

EN.DEU.SAR, *v.*, to deify.

EN.DI.A.BRA.DO, *adj.*, devilish, mad, demoniac, impish.

EN.DI.NHEI.RA.DO, *adj.*, moneyed, rich, opulent.

EN.DI.REI.TAR, *v.*, to straighten, to set to right, to rectify, to make straight, to reform.

EN.DI.VI.DA.DO, *adj.*, in debt.

EN.DI.VI.DA.MEN.TO, *s.m.*, indebtedness.

EN.DI.VI.DAR, *v.*, to indebt, to lay under obligation.

EN.DOI.DE.CER, *v.*, to become insane, to go crazy, to get mad, to madden.

ENDÓCRINO · 173 · ENGAVETAMENTO

EN.DÓ.CRI.NO, *adj., Med.,* endocrine. .
EN.DO.CRI.NO.LO.GI.A, *s.f., Med.,* endocrinology.
EN.DO.CRI.NO.LO.GIS.TA, *s. 2 gen.,* endocrinologist.
EN.DOI.DAR, *v.,* to go mad.
EN.DOI.DE.CER, *v.,* to madden, to go crazy.
EN.DOR.FI.NA, *s.f., Biol., Quím.,* endorphin.
EN.DOS.CO.PI.A, *s.f., Med.,* endoscopy.
EN.DOS.CÓ.PIO, *s.m.,* endoscope.
EN.DOS.PER.MA, *s.m., Bot.,* endosperm.
EN.DOS.SA.DO, *s.m.,* endorsee.
EN.DOS.SAR, *v.,* to endorse, to give sanction, to defend, to protect.
EN.DOS.SO, *s.m.,* endorsement.
EN.DO.VE.NO.SO, *adj.,* intravenous.
EN.DU.RE.CER, *v.,* to harden, to toughen, to stiffen, to become hard.
EN.DU.RE.CI.MEN.TO, *s.m.,* hardening, callosity.
EN.DU.RO, *s.m., Esp.,* enduro.
E.NE.GRE.CER, *v.,* to blacken, darken.
E.NE.GRE.CI.MEN.TO, *s.m.,* blackening, darkening.
E.NER.GÉ.TI.CO, *adj.,* energetic.
E.NER.GI.A, *s.f.,* energy, power, strenght, force, vigour, soul, zip.
E.NER.GI.CA.MEN.TE, *adv.,* energetically, vigorously.
E.NÉR.GI.CO, *adj.,* energetic, powerful, strenuous, vigorous.
E.NER.GI.ZA.DO, *adj.,* energized.
E.NER.GI.ZAR, *v.,* to energize.
E.NER.GÚ.ME.NO, *s.m.,* energumen; a fanatical enthusiast.
E.NER.VAN.TE, *adj.,* enervating, irritant.
E.NER.VAR, *v.,* to enervate, unnerve.
E.NÉ.SI.MO, *adj., Mat.,* it is said of the number that occupies the order nth.
EN.FA.DO, *s.m.,* unpleasantness, annoyance, boredom, displeasure.
EN.FA.DO.NHO, *adj.,* tiresome, irksome, boring, tedious.
EN.FAI.XAR, *v.,* to swathe.
EN.FAR.TA.DO, *adj.,* infarcted (that suffered a heart attack).
EN.FAR.TAR, *v., Med.,* to have a heart attack; to have a clot, obstruct, congest.
EN.FAR.TE, *s.m., Med.,* heart attack, infarct, clot.
ÊN.FA.SE, *s.f.,* emphasis, stress, accent, ostentation.
EN.FAS.TI.A.DO, *adj.,* bored.
EN.FAS.TI.AR, *v.,* to tire, to bore, to annoy; *enfastiar-se:* to get bored.
EN.FA.TI.CA.MEN.TE, *adv.,* emphatically.
EN.FÁ.TI.CO, *adj.,* emphatic.
EN.FA.TI.ZAR, *v.,* to emphasize, to stress.
EN.FEI.TA.DO, *adj.,* adorned, trimmed, decorated.
EN.FEI.TAR, *v.,* to adorn, to decorate, to ornament, to trim, to embellish.
EN.FEI.TE, *s.m.,* ornament, decoration, trimming, embellishment.
EN.FEI.TI.ÇA.DO, *adj.,* enchanted, bewitched, charmed.
EN.FEI.TI.ÇAR, *v.,* to bewitch, to charm, to fascinate.
EN.FER.MA.GEM, *s.f.,* nursing.
EN.FER.MAR, *v.,* to sicken; to weaken.
EN.FER.MA.RI.A, *s.f.,* infirmary, ward, sickroom.
EN.FER.MEI.RA, *s.f.,* nurse.
EN.FER.MEI.RO, *s.m.,* male nurse.
EN.FER.MI.DA.DE, *s.f.,* disease, sickness, infirmity, ailment.
EN.FER.MO, *s.m.,* patient, sick person, sufferer; *adj.,* sick, diseased, infirm.

EN.FER.RU.JA.DO, *adj.,* rusty.
EN.FER.RU.JAR, *v.,* to rust, to become affected with rust.
EN.FE.ZA.DO, *adj.,* annoyed, exasperated.
EN.FE.ZAR, *v.,* to annoy, to irritate.
EN.FI.AR, *v.,* to thread (needle); to slip on (dresses, shoes, etc.); to range into files.
EN.FI.LEI.RAR, *v.,* to range in a file, to align, to set in a row, to form a line.
EN.FIM, *adv.,* at last, finally, after all.
EN.FI.SE.MA, *s.m., Med.,* emphysema.
EN.FO.CAR, *v.,* to focus, to focalize.
EN.FO.QUE, *s.m., Bras.,* focus.
EN.FOR.CA.DO, *s.m.,* hanged person; *adj.,* hanged.
EN.FOR.CA.MEN.TO, *s.m.,* hanging.
EN.FOR.CAR, *v.,* to hang, to squander.
EN.FRA.QUE.CER, *v.,* to weaken, to debilitate, to lose courage.
EN.FRA.QUE.CI.MEN.TO, *s.m.,* weakness, feebleness, debility.
EN.FREN.TA.MEN.TO, *s.m.,* confrontation.
EN.FREN.TAR, *v.,* to face, to meet, to brave, to defy, to confront.
EN.FRO.NHAR, *v.,* to put the pillow into the pillowcase; ~ *alguém em algo:* to instruct someone in something.
EN.FU.MA.ÇA.DO, *adj.,* smoky.
EN.FU.MA.ÇAR, *v.,* to make smoky.
EN.FU.RE.CER, *v.,* to infuriate, to enrage, to make furious, to be furious.
EN.FU.RE.CI.DO, *adj.,* infuriated, furious.
EN.GA.BE.LA.ÇÃO, *s.f., pop.,* deceit.
EN.GA.BE.LAR, *v., pop.,* to deceive, to coax, to decoy.
EN.GAI.O.LAR, *v.,* to cage; *fig.,* to imprison.
EN.GA.JA.DO, *s.m.,* person committed to a cause; *adj.,* engaged.
EN.GA.JA.MEN.TO, *s.m.,* engagement, involvement, employment.
EN.GA.JAR, *v.,* to engage, to employ, to take an employment.
EN.GAL.FI.NHAR, *v.,* to wrestle, to grapple; *engalfinhar-se:* to get entangled.
EN.GAM.BE.LAR, *v.,* the same that *engabelar:* to deceive.
EN.GA.NA.DO, *adj.,* wrong, mistaken.
EN.GA.NAR, *v.,* to deceive, to mislead, to cheat, to trick.
EN.GAN.CHAR, *v.,* to hook.
EN.GA.NO, *s.m.,* mistake, error, fault, swindle, fraud, delusion, deception.
EN.GA.NO.SO, *adj.,* deceiving, deceitful, illusory; fallacious.
EN.GAR.RA.FA.DO, *adj.,* bottled; *trânsito ~:* heavy traffic.
EN.GAR.RA.FA.MEN.TO, *s.m.,* bottling; traffic jam.
EN.GAR.RA.FAR, *v.,* to bottle.
EN.GAS.GA.DO, *adj.,* choked, gagged.
EN.GAS.GAR, *v.,* to choke, to gag.
EN.GAS.GO, *s.m.,* choking.
EN.GAS.TAR, *v.,* to set (gems).
EN.GAS.TE, *s.m.,* setting.
EN.GA.TAR, *v.,* to clamp, to leash.
EN.GA.TE, *s.m.,* clamp, leash, hook, coupling gear.
EN.GA.TI.LHAR, *v.,* to cock, to prepare.
EN.GA.TI.NHAR, *v.,* to creep, to crawl.
EN.GA.VE.TA.MEN.TO, *s.m.,* putting into a drawer; *fig.,* postponement; smash (of cars in a collision).

ENGAVETAR   •• 174 ••   ENSABOADO

EN.GA.VE.TAR, *v.*, to put into a drawer, to postpone.
EN.GEN.DRAR, *v.*, to engender; to create, to produce.
EN.GE.NHAR, *v.*, to engineer.
EN.GE.NHA.RI.A, *s.f.*, engineering.
EN.GE.NHEI.RO, *s.m.*, engineer.
EN.GE.NHO, *s.m.*, inventive power, ingeniousness, wit, ability.
EN.GE.NHO.CA, *s.f.*, gadget.
EN.GE.NHO.SO, *adj.*, ingenious, artful.
EN.GES.SA.DO, *adj.*, plastered.
EN.GES.SAR, *v.*, to plaster.
EN.GLO.BAR, *v.*, to embody, encompass, to conglobate, to unite.
EN.GO.DO, *s.m.*, allure, decoy.
EN.GO.LIR, *v.*, swallow, ingest, devour, to gulp down, to englut, to absorb.
EN.GO.MA.DO, *adj.*, starched.
EN.GO.MAR, *v.*, to starch.
EN.GOR.DAR, *v.*, to fatten, to grow fat.
EN.GOR.DU.RA.DO, *adj.*, greasy, oily, fatty.
EN.GOR.DU.RA.MEN.TO, *s.m.*, greasing.
EN.GOR.DU.RAR, *v.*, to grease.
EN.GRA.ÇA.DO, *adj.*, funny, amusing, comic, merry, jocose, jolly.
EN.GRA.ÇAR, *v.*, to grace, to make gracious; *engraçar-se*: *pop.*, to become cheeky.
EN.GRA.DA.DO, *s.m.*, crate, packing box.
EN.GRAN.DE.CER, *v.*, to increase, to raise, to enlarge, to augment.
EN.GRA.VA.TAR-SE, *v.*, to dress well, to present oneself well-dressed.
EN.GRA.VI.DAR, *v.*, to make pregnant, to become pregnant, to render pregnant.
EN.GRA.XA.MEN.TO, *s.m.*, shining (shoes).
EN.GRA.XAR, *v.*, to shine, to polish, to smear.
EN.GRA.XA.TE, *s.m.*, shoeshiner.
EN.GRE.NA.GEM, *s.f.*, gear, gearing, works, set of gears; *fig.*, organization.
EN.GRE.NAR, *v.*, to gear, to mesh; to put in gear (auto).
EN.GROS.SAR, *v.*, to enlarge, to thicken, to swell, to augment, to increase.
EN.GUI.A, *s.f.*, *Zool.*, eel.
EN.GUI.ÇA.DO, *adj.*, broken down, broken, bewitched.
EN.GUI.ÇAR, *v.*, to break down (car, machine); to stunt; to stop (clock).
EN.GUI.ÇO, *s.m.*, impediment, breakdown.
EN.GU.LHO, *s.m.*, nausea.
E.NIG.MA, *s.m.*, enigma, riddle, puzzle.
E.NIG.MÁ.TI.CO, *adj.*, enigmatic.
EN.JAM.BRAR, *v.*, to warp.
EN.JAU.LAR, *v.*, to jail, to cage, to imprison, to confine.
EN.JEI.TA.DO, *adj.*, abandoned, rejected.
EN.JEI.TAR, *v.*, to despise, to reject, to abandon.
EN.JO.A.DO, *adj.*, nauseated, airsick, seasick.
EN.JO.AR, *v.*, to nauseate, to be sick, to cause nausea, to annoy.
EN.JO.A.TI.VO, *adj.*, nauseating, nauseous; repugnant.
EN.JO.O, *s.m.*, nausea, sickness, repugnance.
EN.LA.ÇAR, *v.*, to interlace, to entwine, to tie up; to entangle.
EN.LA.CE, *s.m.*, interlacing, union, marriage, enlacement, concatenation.
EN.LA.ME.A.DO, *adj.*, muddied, muddy; slandered.

EN.LA.ME.AR, *v.*, to dirty, to soil with mud, to spatter, to stain.
EN.LA.TAR, *v.*, to tin, to can, to trellis.
EN.LE.VA.ÇÃO, *s.f.*, rapture, enchantment, delight, wonder.
EN.LE.VAR, *v.*, to enrupture, to enchant; to delight, to captivate, to entrance.
EN.LE.VO, *s.m.*, rapture, enchantment; delight, overjoy.
EN.LOU.QUE.CER, *v.*, to madden, to craze.
EN.LOU.QUE.CI.MEN.TO, *s.m.*, insanity, madness, mental illness.
EN.LU.A.RA.DO, *adj.*, moonlit.
EN.LU.TA.DO, *adj.*, in mourning, mournful.
EN.LU.TAR, *v.*, to put on mourning.
E.NO.BRE.CE.DOR, *s.m.*, ennobler; *adj.*, ennobling.
E.NO.BRE.CER, *v.*, to ennoble.
E.NO.BRE.CI.MEN.TO, *s.m.*, ennoblement.
E.NO.JA.DO, *adj.*, nauseated, disgusted.
E.NO.JAR, *v.*, to nauseate, to disgust; *enojar-se*: to feel nausea for, to become bored.
E.NO.LO.GI.A, *s.f.*, enology (the study of wines).
E.NO.LO.GIS.TA, *s. 2 gen.*, enologist.
E.NÓ.LO.GO, *s.m.*, enologist.
E.NOR.ME, *adj.*, enormous, vast, colossal.
E.NOR.MI.DA.DE, *s.f.*, enormity, hugeness, enormousness.
EN.QUA.DRA.MEN.TO, *s.m.*, framing.
EN.QUA.DRAR, *v.*, to frame, to fit.
EN.QUAN.TO, *conj.*, while, as long as, whereas.
EN.QUE.TE, *s.f.*, survey, inquiry.
EN.RA.BI.CHA.DO, *adj.*, infatuated, in love.
EN.RAI.VE.CER, *v.*, to enrage, to irritate, to infuriate, to anger.
EN.RAI.VE.CI.DO, *adj.*, enraged, angry, infuriated.
EN.RA.I.ZA.DO, *adj.*, rooted.
EN.RA.I.ZAR, *v.*, to root, to take root, to strike root.
EN.RAS.CA.DA, *s.f.*, *pop.*, difficulty, trouble, embarrassment.
EN.RAS.CAR, *v.*, to snarl, to tangle, to complicate; *enrascar-se*: to become embarrassed, to get in a fix.
EN.RE.DA.DO, *adj.*, netlike, tangled.
EN.RE.DAR, *v.*, to complicate, to net, to catch in a net, to snarl, to embroil.
EN.RE.DO, *s.m.*, plot of a drama, story, intrigue.
EN.RE.GE.LA.DO, *adj.*, frozen, congealed.
EN.RE.GE.LA.MEN.TO, *s.m.*, freezing.
EN.RE.GE.LAR, *v.*, to freeze, to congeal; *enregelar-se*: to be frozen.
EN.RI.JE.CER, *v.*, to rigidify.
EN.RI.QUE.CER, *v.*, to enrich, to make rich, to embellish, to adorn, to increase.
EN.RI.QUE.CI.MEN.TO, *s.m.*, enrichment.
EN.RO.BUS.TE.CER, *v.*, to make robust.
EN.RO.DI.LHAR, *v.*, to wind around; to twist, twine.
EN.RO.LA.DO, *adj.*, rolled up, coiled; wound up.
EN.RO.LAR, *v.*, to roll, to roll up, to coil, to twist.
EN.ROS.CA.DO, *adj.*, threadlike; coiled, entangled.
EN.ROS.CAR, *v.*, to twine, to twist; *enroscar-se*: to entangle.
EN.ROU.QUE.CER, *v.*, to hoarsen.
EN.RU.BES.CER, *v.*, to redden, to blush, to flush.
EN.RU.BES.CI.MEN.TO, *s.m.*, blushing.
EN.RU.GA.DO, *adj.*, wrinkled, furrowed.
EN.RU.GAR, *v.*, to wrinkle, to crinkle, to crease.
EN.RUS.TI.DO, *adj.*, *pop.*, completely introverted; closeted, closet gay.
EN.SA.BO.A.DO, *adj.*, soapy, lathery.

ENSABOAR ··· 175 ··· ENTRISTECIMENTO

EN.SA.BO.AR, *v.*, to soap, to wash with soap, to reprove.
EN.SA.CA.DO, *adj.*, sacked, bagged.
EN.SA.CAR, *v.*, to sack, to bag.
EN.SAI.AR, *v.*, to test, to rehearse, to run in, to assay, to analyze, to try.
EN.SAI.O, *s.m.*, assay, an analysis, trial, test, examination.
EN.SA.ÍS.TA, *s. 2 gen.*, essayist (a writer of essays).
EN.SAN.GUEN.TA.DO, *adj.*, blooded, bloody.
EN.SAN.GUE.NTAR, *v.*, to stain with blood, to bloody.
EN.SE.A.DA, *s.f.*, inlet, small bay, cove, lagoon.
EN.SE.BA.DO, *adj.*, greasy; covered with grease; *fig.*, soiled.
EN.SE.BAR, *v.*, to grease; to cover with grease; *fig.* to soil.
EN.SE.JAR, *v.*, to give a good opportunity.
EN.SE.JO, *s.m.*, opportunity, chance, occasion.
EN.SI.MES.MA.DO, *adj.*, concentrated, introverted.
EN.SI.NA.DO, *adj.*, instructed, trained, learned; educated.
EN.SI.NA.MEN.TO, *s.m.*, teaching, training, instruction, education.
EN.SI.NAR, *v.*, to teach, to instruct, to train, to coach, to drill.
EN.SI.NO, *s.m.*, teaching, instruction, train, education.
EN.SO.LA.RA.DO, *adj.*, sunny.
EN.SOM.BRAR, *v.*, to shadow.
EN.SO.PA.DO, *s.m., Cul.*, stew.
EN.SO.PA.DI.NHO, *s.m., Cul.*, stew.
EN.SO.PAR, *v.*, to soak, to drench, to sop in; to stew; *ensopar-se*: to get sopping wet; to be drenched.
EN.SUR.DE.CE.DOR, *s.m.*, deafening.
EN.SUR.DE.CER, *v.*, to deafen, to make deafen, to stun with noise.
EN.TA.BU.LAR, *v.*, to prepare, to arrange; *fig.*, to open, to start (conversation).
EN.TA.LA.DO, *adj.*, stuck.
EN.TA.LAR, *v.*, to splint, to put between splints, to put in a tight spot.
EN.TA.LHA.DOR, *s.m.*, wood carver.
EN.TA.LHAR, *v.*, to carve, to engrave, to sculpture (in wood).
EN.TA.LHE, *s.m.*, notch, cut, groove.
EN.TAN.TO, *adv.*, in the meantime, meanwhile.
EN.TÃO, *adv.*, then, at that time, on this occasion, in that case.
EN.TAR.DE.CER, *s.m.*, late afternoon, nightfall; *v.* to grow dark, to grow night.
EN.TE, *s.m.*, being, person, living creature, life.
EN.TE.A.DA, *s.f.*, stepdaughter.
EN.TE.A.DO, *s.m.*, stepson.
EN.TE.AR, *v.*, to weave.
EN.TE.DI.AN.TE, *adj.*, boring.
EN.TE.DI.AR, *v.*, to bore, to tire.
EN.TEN.DE.DOR, *s.m.*, comprehensive or quick-witted person; expert.
EN.TEN.DER, *v.*, to understand, to apprehend, to learn, to figure out, to perceive, to know.
EN.TEN.DI.DO, *s.m.*, expert, knower; *adj.*, understood, learned, erudite.
EN.TEN.DI.MEN.TO, *s.m.*, understanding, agreement, comprehension, perception.
EN.TER.NE.CE.DOR, *adj.*, touching, moving.
EN.TER.NE.CER, *v.*, to touch, to affect.
EN.TER.NE.CI.MEN.TO, *s.m.*, compassion, commiseration.
EN.TER.RAR, *v.*, to bury, to inter, to hide.
EN.TER.RO, *s.m.*, burial, interment, entombment.
EN.TE.SOU.RAR, *v.*, to treasure; to hoard.

EN.TI.DA.DE, *s.f.*, entity, being, essence, corporation, existence.
EN.TO.A.ÇÃO, *s.f.*, chanting; intonation.
EN.TO.AR, *v.*, to sing, to chant, to tune, to intone, to vocalize.
EN.TO.NA.ÇÃO, *s.f.*, intonation.
EN.TOR.NAR, *v.*, to spill, to upset, to overturn.
EN.TOR.PE.CEN.TE, *s.m.*, any narcotic; *adj.*, narcotic.
EN.TOR.PE.CER, *v.*, to torpify, to make torpid, to numb, to paralyse, to weaken.
EN.TOR.PE.CI.DO, *adj.*, torpid, benumbed, numb.
EN.TOR.PE.CI.MEN.TO, *s.m.*, torpor, numbness, torpid condition.
EN.TOR.TAR, *v.*, to crook, to curve, to bend, to bow, to twist, to warp, to mislead.
EN.TRA.DA, *s.f.*, entrance, entry, inlet, opening, gate, passage, access, admission, ingress.
EN.TRA.NHA, *s.f.*, viscera, entrails, bowels.
EN.TRA.NHAR, *v.*, to pierce, to penetrate.
EN.TRAR, *v.*, to enter, to come in, to go in, to get into, to go inside of, to become a member.
EN.TRA.VAR, *v.*, to obstruct, to block, to impede, to trammel.
EN.TRA.VE, *s.m.*, fetter; *fig.*, obstacle, hindrance.
EN.TRE, *prep.*, between, among, amongst, during the interval.
EN.TRE.A.BER.TO, *adj.*, half-open (eye), ajar (door, window).
EN.TRE.A.BRIR, *v.*, to open partially, to bloom.
EN.TRE.COR.TA.DO, *adj.*, intermittent; disconnected.
EN.TRE.COR.TAR, *v.*, to cut off; to interrupt.
EN.TRE.CRU.ZAR, *v.*, to cross mutually.
EN.TRE.GA, *s.f.*, delivery, surrender, treachery, cession.
EN.TRE.GA.DOR, *s.m.*, deliverer, delivery man, traitor.
EN.TRE.GAR, *v.*, to deliver, to hand over, to remit, to restore, to return.
EN.TRE.GUIS.MO, *s.m., Pol.*, selling out.
EN.TRE.GUIS.TA, *adj., Pol.*, supportive or typical of seeling out.
EN.TRE.LA.ÇA.MEN.TO, *s.m.*, interlacement, interlinking.
EN.TRE.LA.ÇAR, *v.*, to interlace, to intertwine.
EN.TRE.LI.NHA, *s.f.*, space between two lines, interlineation.
EN.TRE.ME.AR, *v.*, to intermix, to intermingle, to interpose.
EN.TRE.MEN.TES, *adv.*, meantime, meanwhile.
EN.TRE.O.LHAR-SE, *v.*, to look at one another; to exchange glances.
EN.TRE.OU.VIR, *v.*, to hear but indistinctly.
EN.TRE.POR, *v.*, to interpose, to place between.
EN.TRE.POS.TO, *s.m.*, warehouse, emporium.
EN.TRES.SA.FRA, *s.f.*, period between harvests.
EN.TRE.TAN.TO, *adv.*, meantime, meanwhile, in the meantime.
EN.TRE.TE.NI.MEN.TO, *s.m.*, entertainment, diversion.
EN.TRE.TER, *v.*, to entertain, to amuse, to divert, to recreate, to delay.
EN.TRE.VA.DO, *s.m.*, maimed person; *adj.*, maimed, paralytic.
EN.TRE.VAR, *v.*, to maim, to cripple, to paralyse.
EN.TRE.VER, *v.*, to see indistinctily, to have a pressentiment.
EN.TRE.VE.RO, *s.m., pop.*, melee.
EN.TRE.VIS.TA, *s.f.*, interview, meeting, conference.
EN.TRE.VIS.TA.DOR, *s.m.*, interviewer.
EN.TRE.VIS.TAR, *v.*, to interview.
EN.TRIS.TE.CE.DOR, *adj.*, saddening.
EN.TRIS.TE.CER, *v.*, to sadden, to make sad, to afflict, to grieve.
EN.TRIS.TE.CI.MEN.TO, *s.m.*, sadness, sorrow.

ENTRONCAMENTO · 176 · EPISTEMOLOGIA

EN.TRON.CA.MEN.TO, *s.m.*, crossing point, junction.
EN.TRON.CAR, *v.*, to make a junction, to make robust.
EN.TRO.PI.A, *s.f., Fís.*, entropy.
EN.TRÓ.PI.CO, *adj., Fís.*, entropic.
EN.TRO.SA.MEN.TO, *s.m.*, adaptation, integration, adjustment.
EN.TRO.SAR, *v.*, to gear, to mesh.
EN.TU.LHAR, *v.*, to cram (something with); to fill up with rubbish; to heap up.
EN.TU.LHO, *s.m.*, rubbish, debris.
EN.TU.PI.DO, *adj.*, obstructed, blocked up.
EN.TU.PI.MEN.TO, *s.m.*, blockage, clogging; obstruction.
EN.TU.PIR, *v.*, to block, to choke up, to obstruct, to clog.
EN.TUR.MA.DO, *adj.*, in a group.
EN.TUR.MAR, *v., pop.*, to form a group; *enturmar-se*: to get together in a group; to make friends.
EN.TU.SI.AS.MA.DO, *adj.*, excited, ravished, exalted.
EN.TU.SI.AS.MAR, *v.*, to ravish, to enrapture, to excite, to animate.
EN.TU.SI.AS.MO, *s.m.*, enthusiasm, excitement, zeal.
EN.TU.SI.ÁS.TI.CO, *adj.*, enthusiastic.
E.NU.ME.RA.ÇÃO, *s.f.*, enumeration.
E.NU.ME.RAR, *v.*, to enumerate, to count, to number.
E.NU.ME.RÁ.VEL, *adj.*, enumerable.
E.NUN.CI.A.DO, *s.m.*, statement, proposition; *adj.*, stated, declared.
E.NUN.CI.AR, *v.*, to enunciate, to state, to utter, to express.
E.NU.VI.AR, *v.*, to overcast (cloud).
EN.VAI.DE.CER, *v.*, to make vain, to flatter; *envaidecer-se*; to become vain; to feel flattered.
EN.VA.SAR, *v.*, to put into vessels; to bottle, to barrel.
EN.VA.SI.LHAR, *v.*, the same that *envasar*.
EN.VE.LHE.CER, *v.*, to age, to grow old, to make old.
EN.VE.LHE.CI.MEN.TO, *s.m.*, aging (or ageing).
EN.VE.LO.PAR, *v., pop.*, to envelop.
EN.VE.LO.PE, *s.m.*, envelope.
EN.VE.NE.NA.DO, *adj.*, poisoned; *pop.*, souped up (car).
EN.VE.NE.NA.MEN.TO, *s.m.*, poisoning, intoxication.
EN.VE.NE.NAR, *v.*, to poison, to put poison in, to give poison.
EN.VER.GO.NHA.DO, *adj.*, ashamed, bashful.
EN.VE.RE.DAR, *v.*, to make one's way (to or toward); to head for; to guide.
EN.VER.GA.DU.RA, *s.f., Aeron.*, span; wingspan (dimension); *fig.*, capacity.
EN.VER.GA.MEN.TO, *s.m.*, curvature; *Náut.*, fastening of the sails.
EN.VER.GAR, *v.*, to bend, to curve; to wear; to warp; *Náut.*, to fasten the sails; *envergar-se*: to bend over.
EN.VER.GO.NHA.DO, *adj.*, ashamed; shy; embarrassed.
EN.VER.GO.NHAR, *v.*, to shame; to make ashamed; *envergonhar-se*: to be ashamed, to be embarrassed.
EN.VER.NI.ZA.DO, *adj.*, varnished.
EN.VER.NI.ZAR, *v.*, to varnish, to polish.
EN.VI.A.DO, *s.m.*, messenger, envoy; *adj.*, sent, dispatched.
EN.VI.AR, *v.*, to send, to dispatch, to forward, to depute.
EN.VI.DAR, *v.*, to challenge, to endeavour.
EN.VI.DRA.ÇA.DO, *adj.*, glazed.
EN.VI.DRA.ÇAR, *v.*, to glaze, to cover with glass.
EN.VI.E.SA.DO, *adj.*, biased, slanting.
EN.VI.E.SAR, *v.*, to put at an alngle; to slant.

EN.VI.NA.GRAR, *v.*, to add vinegar to.
EN.VI.O, *s.m.*, sending, forwarding, remittance, dispatch; shipment.
EN.VI.U.VAR, *v.*, to widow.
EN.VOL.TO, *adj.*, wrapped, covered, mixed.
EN.VOL.TÓ.RI.O, *s.m.*, wrapper, wrapping.
EN.VOL.VEN.TE, *adj.*, involving, compelling.
EN.VOL.VER, *v.*, to involve, to wrap up, to cover, to envelop, to contain, to hold.
EN.VOL.VI.DO, *adj.*, wrapped up, involved in.
EN.VOL.VI.MEN.TO, *s.m.*, involvement.
EN.XA.DA, *s.f.*, hoe, spade.
EN.XA.DRIS.TA, *s. 2 gen.*, chess player.
EN.XA.GUA.DA, *s.f.*, rinse.
EN.XA.GUAR, *v.*, to rinse, to wash lightly (as clothes, dishes).
EN.XÁ.GUE, *s.m.*, rinsing, rinse.
EN.XAI.MEL, *s.m.*, timber framing: pillar of a mud hut (Southern Brazil).
EN.XA.ME, *s.m.*, a swarm of bees, hive.
EN.XA.QUE.CA, *s.f.*, migraine, megrim.
EN.XER.GAR, *v.*, to see, to discover, to discern, to descry.
EN.XER.TAR, *v.*, to graft.
EN.XER.TO, *s.m.*, graft.
EN.XO.FRE, *s.m., Quím.*, brimstone; *UK* sulphur, *US* sulfur.
EN.XO.TAR, *v.*, to scare, to frighten away, to chase away, to expel, to banish.
EN.XO.VAL, *s.m.*, trousseau (for newlyweds); layette (baby).
EN.XO.VA.LHAR, *v.*, to dirty, to stain, to soil; to crumple; *fig.*, to affront.
EN.XU.GAR, *v.*, to dry, to wipe, to wipe out.
EN.XUR.RA.DA, *s.f.*, downpour, torrent, rushing stream of water.
EN.XUR.RAR, *v.*, to overflow, to inundate; to stream.
EN.XU.TO, *adj.*, dry.
EN.ZI.MA, *s.f., Quím.*, enzyme.
E.O.CÊ.NI.O, *s.m., Geol.*, Eocene.
E.Ó.LI.CO, *adj., Hist.*, Aeolian, Aeolic.
E.PA.NÁS.TRO.FE, *s.f., Gram.*, epanastrophe.
E.PI.CE.NO, *adj., Gram.*, epicene.
E.PI.CEN.TRO, *s.m.*, epicenter (Geofísics).
é.pi.co, *s.m., Lit.*, an epic poet; *adj.*, epic, epical.
E.PI.CU.RIS.MO, *s.m., Filos.*, Epicureanism.
E.PI.DÊ.MI.CO, *adj., Med.*, epidemic, epidemical.
E.PI.DE.MI.A, *s.f.*, epidemic.
E.PI.DE.MI.O.LO.GI.A, *s.f., Med.*, epidemiology.
E.PI.DE.MI.O.LO.GIS.TA, *s. 2 gen., Med.*, epidemiologist.
E.PI.DER.ME, *s.f., Anat.*, epidermis.
E.PI.DÉR.MI.CO, *adj., Anat.*, epidermic, epidermical.
E.PI.FA.NI.A, *s.f.*, epiphany.
E.PI.GLO.TE, *s.f., Anat.*, epiglottis.
E.PI.GRA.FAR, *v.*, to epigraph.
E.PÍ.GRA.FE, *s.f.*, epigraph.
E.PI.GRA.FI.A, *s.f.*, epigraphy.
E.PI.GRA.MA, *s.m.*, epigram.
E.PI.LEP.SI.A, *s.f., Med.*, epilepsy.
E.PI.LÉP.TI.CO, *s.m.*, epileptic.
E.PÍ.LO.GO, *s.m.*, epilog, epilogue, summary, conclusion.
E.PIS.CO.PA.DO, *s.m.*, episcopate.
E.PIS.CO.PAL, *adj.*, episcopal.
E.PI.SÓ.DIO, *s.m.*, episode.
E.PIS.TE.MO.LO.GI.A, *s.f., Filos.*, epistemology.

EPISTEMOLÓGICO ·· 177 ·· ESCABECHE

E.PIS.TE.MO.LÓ.GI.CO, *adj., Filos.*, epistemological.
E.PÍS.TO.LA, *s.f.*, epistle, a letter.
E.PIS.TO.LAR, *adj.*, epistolary.
E.PIS.TO.LÁ.RI.O, *s.m.*, epistolary, collection of letters.
E.PI.TÁ.FIO, *s.m.*, epitaph.
E.PI.TÉ.LI.O, *s.m., Med.*, epithelium.
E.PÍ.TE.TO, *s.m.*, epithet.
É.PO.CA, *s.f.*, epoch, era, period, age, season, time, tide, cycle.
E.PO.PEI.A, *s.f.*, epopee, epopoeia.
E.PO.PEI.CO, *adj.*, epic.
E.PÓ.XI, *s.m., Quím.*, epoxy (a flexible resin).
EP.SÍ.LON, *s.m.*, epsilon (the fifth letter of the Greek alphabet).
E.QUA.ÇÃO, *s.f.*, equation.
E.QUA.DOR, *s.m.*, equator.
E.QUA.DOR, *s.m.*, Ecuador (country).
E.QUA.LI.ZA.ÇÃO, *s.f.*, equalization.
E.QUA.LI.ZA.DOR, *s.m.*, equalizer.
E.QUA.LI.ZAR, *v.*, to equalize.
E.QUÂ.NI.ME, *adj.*, equanimous.
E.QUA.NI.MI.DA.DE, *s.f.*, equanimity.
E.QUA.TO.RI.AL, *adj.*, equatorial.
E.QUA.TO.RI.A.NO, *adj., s.m.*, Ecuadorian.
E.QUES.TRE, *adj.*, equestrian.
E.QUI.DA.DE, *s.f.*, equity, fairness.
E.QUI.DIS.TÂN.CI.A, *s.f.*, equidistance.
E.QUI.DIS.TAN.TE, *adj.*, equidistant.
E.QUI.DIS.TAR, *v.*, to be equidistant.
E.QUI.LÁ.TE.RO, *adj.*, equilateral.
E.QUI.LI.BRAR, *v.*, to equilibrate, to balance.
E.QUI.LI.BRIO, *s.m.*, balance, equilibrium, poise.
E.QUI.LI.BRIS.TA, *s. 2 gen.*, equilibrist.
E.QUI.NO, *adj.*, equine.
E.QUI.NO.CI.AL, *adj.*, equinoctial.
E.QUI.NÓ.CIO, *s.m.*, equinox.
E.QUI.PA.MEN.TO, *s.m.*, equipment, apparatus, outfit, takle.
E.QUI.PAR, *v.*, to equip, to fit, to man.
E.QUI.PA.RA.ÇÃO, *s.f.*, equalization.
E.QUI.PA.RAR, *v.*, to equal, to equalize, to compare, to make equal.
E.QUI.PA.RÁ.VEL, *adj.*, comparable (that can be equalized).
E.QUI.PE, *s.f.*, team, squad, staff, group.
E.QUI.TA.ÇÃO, *s.f.*, equitation, horsemanship.
E.QUI.TA.TI.VA.MEN.TE, *adv.*, equitably.
E.QUI.TA.TI.VO, *adj.*, equitable.
E.QUI.VA.LÊN.CIA, *s.f.*, equivalence.
E.QUI.VA.LEN.TE, *s.m.*, equivalent.
E.QUI.VA.LER, *v.*, to be equivalent to, to amount; to equivale.
E.QUI.VO.CA.DO, *adj.*, mistaken.
E.QUI.VO.CAR, *v.*, to mistake; *equivocar-se*: to make a mistake.
E.QUÍ.VO.CO, *s.m.*, mistake, error, ambiguity, equivocation.
E.RA, *s.f.*, era, epoch, period of time.
E.RÁ.RIO, *s.m.*, exchequer.
E.RE.ÇÃO, *s.f.*, erection.
E.RE.MI.TA, *s. 2 gen.*, hermit, recluse.
E.RE.MI.TÉ.RI.O, *s.m.*, hermitage; monastery.
E.RÉ.TIL, *adj.*, erectile.
E.RE.TO, *adj.*, erected, erect, raised, upright.
ER.GO.ME.TRI.A, *s.f.*, ergometrics.
ER.GO.MÉ.TRI.CO, *adj.*, ergometric.

ER.GO.NO.MI.A, *s.f.*, ergonomics.
ER.GUER, *v.*, to raise, to lift, to elevate, to rear.
ER.GUI.DO, *adj.*, raised, lifted; elevated.
E.RI.ÇA.DO, *adj.*, bristly, brushy; standing on end (bristle).
E.RI.ÇAR, *v.*, to bristle; to ruffle.
E.RI.GIR, *v.*, to erect; to build, to found.
ER.MI.TÃO, *s.m.*, hermit.
ER.MO, *s.m.*, hermitage, wilderness, desert; *adj.*, solitary, retired, desert.
E.RO.SÃO, *s.f.*, erosion, corrosion.
E.RO.SI.VO, *adj.*, erosive, corrosive.
E.RÓ.TI.CO, *adj.*, erotic, sensual.
E.RO.TIS.MO, *s.m.*, eroticism.
E.RO.TI.ZA.ÇÃO, *s.f.*, erotization, eroticization.
ER.RA.BUN.DO, *adj.*, vagrant, errant.
ER.RA.DI.CA.ÇÃO, *s.f.*, eradication.
ER.RA.DI.CAR, *v.*, to eradicate, to extirpate.
ER.RA.DO, *adj.*, mistaken, wrong, false, erroneous.
ER.RAN.TE, *adj.*, wandering, erring, errant.
ER.RAR, *v.*, to miss, to mistake, to misunderstanding, to fail.
ER.RA.TA, *s.f.*, erratum.
ER.RÁ.TI.CO, *adj.*, erratic.
ER.RO, *s.m.*, error, fault, mistake.
ER.RÔ.NEO, *adj.*, erroneous, false.
E.RU.DI.ÇÃO, *s.f.*, erudition, learning.
E.RU.DI.TO, *adj., s.m.*, erudit.
E.RUP.ÇÃO, *s.f.*, eruption, outbreak.
E.RUP.TI.VO, *adj.*, eruptive.
ER.VA, *s.f.*, herb, grass.
ER.VA-CI.DREI.RA, *s.f., Bot.*, lemon balm, balm mint (*Melissa officinalis*).
ER.VA-DO.CE, *s.f., Bot.*, fennel; fennel seed.
ER.VAL, *s.m., Bras.*, maté plantation.
ER.VA-MA.TE, *s.f., Bras., Bot.*, maté.
ER.VI.LHAL, *s.m.*, pea plantation.
ER.VI.LHA, *s.f.*, pea.
ER.VO.SO, *adj.*, grassy, herbous.
ES.BA.FO.RI.DO, *adj.*, hasty; panting, tired.
ES.BA.FO.RIR, *v.*, to pant, to puff; to grow weary.
ES.BAN.JA.DOR, *s.m.*, spendthrift; *adj.*, squandering.
ES.BAN.JA.MEN.TO, *s.m.*, dissipation, squandering.
ES.BAN.JAR, *v.*, to waste, to squander, to lavish, to dissipate, to misspend.
ES.BAR.RÃO, *s.m.*, shock, collision, bump.
ES.BAR.RAR, *v.*, to dash, to collide with.
ES.BEL.TO, *adj.*, svelte, slender, slim; elegant.
ES.BO.ÇAR, *v.*, to sketch, to roughdraw, to draft, to delineate.
ES.BO.ÇO, *s.m.*, sketch, outline.
ES.BO.DE.GA.DO, *adj., col.*, panting, worn out; spoiled.
ES.BO.DE.GAR, *v., col.*, to spoil, to squander.
ES.BO.FE.TE.AR, *v.*, to slap, to strike.
ES.BÓR.NI.A, *s.f., Bras.*, orgy; wild party.
ES.BOR.RA.CHAR(-SE), *v.*, to burst, to crush, to squash.
ES.BRAN.QUI.ÇA.DO, *adj.*, whitish.
ES.BRA.VE.JAR, *v.*, to roar, to shout, to cry out.
ES.BU.GA.LHA.DO, *adj.*, bulging, pop-eyed.
ES.BU.GA.LHAR, *v.*, to bulge, to pop out (eyes).
ES.BU.RA.CA.DO, *adj.*, bored, perfurated, full of holes, broken.
ES.BU.RA.CAR, *v.*, to make holes, to bore, to perforate.
ES.CA.BE.CHE, *s.m.*, marinade.

ESCABROSO ·· 178 ··· ESCORREGÃO

ES.CA.BRO.SO, *adj.*, scabrous, rough; difficult, hard.

ES.CA.DA, *s.f.*, staircase, stairs, ladder.

ES.CA.DA.RI.A, *s.f.*, a flight of stairs, stairway.

ES.CA.FAN.DRIS.TA, *s. 2 gen.*, deep-sea diver.

ES.CA.FAN.DRO, *s.m.*, diving-dress.

ES.CA.FE.DER.SE, *v., pop.*, to run away, to slip off.

ES.CA.LA, *s.f.*, scale, stopover, ladder.

ES.CA.LA.ÇÃO, *s.f.*, selection.

ES.CA.LA.DA, *s.f.*, climbing, scaling.

ES.CA.LÃO, *s.m.*, echelon, step, stair, level.

ES.CA.LAR, *v.*, to scale.

ES.CAL.DA.DO, *adj.*, scalded, burned; *fig.*, wary.

ES.CAL.DAR, *v.*, to scald, to burn, to parch, to inflame, to heat.

ES.CA.LER, *s.m.*, launch, ship, boat.

ES.CA.LO.NA.MEN.TO, *s.m.*, assignment, scheduling.

ES.CA.LO.NAR, *v.*, to schedule.

ES.CA.LO.PE, *s.m., Cul.*, escalope.

ES.CAL.PE.LAR, *v.*, to scalp.

ES.CAL.PE.LO, *s.m.*, scalpel.

ES.CAL.PO, *s.m.*, scalp.

ES.CA.MA, *s.f.*, scale.

ES.CA.MAR, *v.*, to scale.

ES.CAM.BO, *s.m.*, barter, trade, change.

ES.CA.MO.SO, *adj.*, scaly, squamous.

ES.CA.MO.TE.AR, *v.*, to filch, to pilfer.

ES.CAN.CA.RA.DO, *adj.*, wide-open; brazen; manifest.

ES.CAN.CA.RAR, *v.*, to set wide open, to open, to show.

ES.CAN.DA.LI.ZAR, *v.*, to scandalize, to offend, to shock, to defame.

ES.CÂN.DA.LO, *s.m.*, scandal, offense, opprobrium.

ES.CAN.DA.LO.SO, *adj.*, scandalous.

ES.CAN.DI.NÁ.VI.A, *s.*, Scandinavia.

ES.CAN.DI.NA.VO, *adj., s.m.*, Scandinavian.

ES.CA.NE.AR, *v., Comp.*, to scan.

ES.CAN.GA.LHAR, *v., pop.*, to break, to spoil, to destroy.

ES.CA.NI.NHO, *s.m.*, pigeonhole.

ES.CAN.TEI.O, *s.m.*, corner.

ES.CA.PA.DA, *s.f.*, escape; escapade.

ES.CA.PA.MEN.TO, *s.m.*, exhaust pipe, muffler.

ES.CA.PAR, *v.*, to escape, to get out, to run away.

ES.CA.PA.TÓ.RI.A, *s.f.*, excuse, pretext; subterfuge, way out.

ES.CA.PE, *s.m.*, escape, flight, evasion, leakage.

ES.CA.PIS.MO, *s.m.*, escapism.

ES.CA.PIS.TA, *s. 2 gen.*, escapist.

ES.CA.PU.LI.DA, *s.f.*, scape, outing, runaway.

ES.CA.PU.LIR, *v.*, to escape, to run away.

ES.CA.RA.FUN.CHAR, *v.*, to scratch, to scrape; to rummage in.

ES.CA.RA.MU.ÇA, *s.f.*, skirmish.

ES.CAR.LA.TE, *s.m.*, scarlet.

ES.CAR.LA.TI.NA, *s.f., Med.*, scarlatina, scarlet fever.

ES.CAR.NE.CER, *v.*, to mock, to make fun of.

ES.CÁR.NIO, *s.m.*, mockery, derision.

ES.CAR.PA, *s.f.*, scarp, slope, cliff.

ES.CAR.PA.DO, *adj.*, sloped, steep.

ES.CAR.RA.DO, *adj.*, expectorated, spat.

ES.CAR.RAR, *v.*, to spit, to expectorate.

ES.CAR.RO, *s.m.*, phlegm, spittle, mucus.

ES.CAS.SE.AR, *v.*, to make or become scarce.

ES.CAS.SEZ, *s.f.*, scarcity, scarceness, need, privation, dearth, want, lack, parsimony.

ES.CAS.SO, *adj.*, scarce, sparing, insufficient.

ES.CA.TO.LO.GI.A, *s.f.*, scatology.

ES.CA.VA.DEI.RA, *s.f.*, digging machine, digger.

ES.CA.VAR, *v.*, to excavate, to hollow, to scoop.

ES.CLA.RE.CER, *v.*, to clear, to elucidate.

ES.CLA.RE.CI.DO, *adj.*, explained, solved, well informed; illustrious, educated.

ES.CLA.RE.CI.MEN.TO, *s.m.*, clearing up, explanation, elucidation, light, clearness.

ES.CLE.RO.SA.DO, *adj.*, sclerosed, senile.

ES.CLE.RO.SE, *s.f., Med.*, sclerosis.

ES.CO.A.DOU.RO, *s.m.*, drain.

ES.CO.A.MEN.TO, *s.m.*, flowing off, drainage, flowage, outlet, filtration.

ES.CO.AR, *v.*, to drain, to flow off, to decant.

ES.CO.CÊS, *adj., s.m.*, Scottish, Scotch, Scot.

ES.CÓ.CI.A, *s.f.*, Scotland.

ES.CO.LA, *s.f.*, school, schoolhouse.

ES.CO.LA.DO, *adj., pop.*, smart, experienced.

ES.CO.LAR, *s. 2 gen.; adj.*, scholar; scholastic, school.

ES.CO.LA.RI.ZA.ÇÃO, *s.f.*, school education.

ES.CO.LA.RI.ZAR, *v.*, to educate.

ES.CO.LÁS.TI.CA, *s.f., Filos.*, scholasticism.

ES.CO.LÁS.TI.CO, *s.m.*, scholastic; *adj.*, scholastic.

ES.CO.LHA, *s.f.*, choice, election, selection, option.

ES.CO.LHER, *v.*, to choose, to make a choice of, to select.

ES.CO.LHI.DO, *adj.*, chosen, elected.

ES.CO.LI.O.SE, *s.f., Med.*, scoliosis.

ES.COL.TA, *s.f.*, guard, escort.

ES.COL.TAR, *v.*, to escort.

ES.COM.BRO, *s.m.*, rubbish.

ES.CON.DER, *v.*, to hide, to conceal, to put, to occult, to weil.

ES.CON.DE.RI.JO, *s.m.*, hiding-place, hiding corner.

ES.CON.DI.DAS, *s.f., pl.*, hide-and-seek; às ~: secretly, furtively.

ES.CON.DI.DO, *adj.*, hidden, occult, secret.

ES.CON.JU.RAR, *v.*, to exorcize, to curse, to adjure; to conjure; to swear.

ES.CON.JU.RO, *s.m.*, exorcism; conjuration.

ES.CO.PE.TA, *s.f.*, shotgun; carabine.

ES.CO.PO, *s.m.*, scope, purpose.

ES.CO.RA, *s.f.*, prop, stay, support, aid, help, brace.

ES.CO.RAR, *v.*, to support, to prop up, to brace, to uphold, to sustain; *escorar-se*: to seek shelter.

ES.COR.BU.TO, *s.m., Med.*, scurvy.

ES.COR.CHAN.TE, *adj.*, stripping, peeling; *fig.*, fleecing, despoiling; abusive.

ES.COR.CHAR, *v.*, to flay, to skin; to scratch; *fig.*, to despoil, to rob; to scorch.

ES.CÓ.RIA, *s.f.*, dross, slag, dregs, scum, scoria, refuse.

ES.CO.RI.A.ÇÃO, *s.f.*, excoriation.

ES.CO.RI.AR, *v.*, to excoriate, to strip off the skin, to fly.

ES.COR.PI.ÃO, *s.m., Zool.*, scorpion; *Escoprião: Astron.*, Scorpio.

ES.COR.RA.ÇAR, *v.*, to throw out; to banish, to expulse.

ES.COR.RE.DOR, *s.m.*, drainer; ~ *de pratos*: dish drainer.

ES.COR.RE.GA.DI.ÇO, *adj.*, slippery.

ES.COR.RE.GA.DI.O, *adj.*, slippery.

ES.COR.RE.GA.DOR, *s.m.*, child's slide; *adj.*, slipping, sliding.

ES.COR.RE.GÃO, *s.m.*, slip, slipping, sliding.

ESCORREGAR · 179 · ESGOTADO

ES.COR.RE.GAR, *v.*, to slide, to slip, to skid, to glide.
ES.COR.RER, *v.*, to let flow off, to drain, to drop, to trickle, to drip.
ES.COR.RI.DO, *adj.*, drained, emptied; straight (hair).
ES.CO.TEI.RIS.MO, ES.CO.TIS.MO, *s.m.*, scouting.
ES.CO.TEI.RO, *s.m.*, Boy Scout; a scout.
ES.CO.VA.ÇÃO, *s.f.*, brushing.
ES.CO.VA, *s.f.*, brush; *escova de cabelo*: hairbrush.
ES.CO.VAR, *v.*, to brush.
ES.CRA.CHA.DO, *adj., fam.*, scruffy.
ES.CRA.CHAR, *v., fam.*, to unmask, to tick off.
ES.CRA.CHO, *s.m., fam.*, shambles.
ES.CRA.VA.TU.RA, *s.f.*, slave-trade; slavery.
ES.CRA.VI.DÃO, *s.f.*, slavery, servitude.
ES.CRA.VI.ZAR, *v.*, to enslave, to reduce to slavery.
ES.CRA.VIS.MO, *s.m.*, proslavery, proslaver system.
ES.CRA.VIS.TA, *s. 2 gen.*, proslaver.
ES.CRA.VI.ZAR, *v.*, to enslave; *fig.*, to dominate.
ES.CRA.VO, *s.m.*, slave; *adj.*, slave, slavish.
ES.CRA.VO.CRA.TA, *s. 2 gen.*, enslave-owner, proslaver; *adj.*, enslave-owning, proslavery.
ES.CRE.TE, *s.m., Esp.*, scratch team (soccer).
ES.CRE.VEN.TE, *s. 2 gen.*, clerk, copyist.
ES.CRE.VER, *v.*, to write.
ES.CRE.VI.NHAR, *v.*, to scribble.
ES.CRI.TA, *s.f.*, writing, handwriting.
ES.CRI.TO, *s.m.*, writing, *adj.*, written, described.
ES.CRI.TOR, *s.m.*, writer, author.
ES.CRI.TO.RA, *s.f.*, writer, authoress.
ES.CRI.TÓ.RIO, *s.m.*, office, bureau, counting-house.
ES.CRI.TU.RA, *s.f.*, deed, legal document, writ, contract.
ES.CRI.TU.RA.ÇÃO, *s.f.*, book-keeping.
ES.CRI.TU.RAR, *v.*, keep books, keep account.
ES.CRI.TU.RÁ.RIO, *s.m.*, bookkeeper, clerk, scribe.
ES.CRI.VA.NI.NHA, *s.f.*, desk, writing desk.
ES.CRI.VÃO, *s.m.*, notary, notary public, clerk, copyist.
ES.CRO.TAL, *adj.*, scrotal.
ES.CRO.TO, *s.m., Anat.*, scrotum; *adj., gír.*, ordinary, sordid, dirt.
ES.CRÚ.PU.LO, *s.m.*, scruple, susceptibility, remorse.
ES.CRU.PU.LO.SO, *adj.*, scrupulous.
ES.CRU.TI.NA.DOR, *s.m.*, scrutineer.
ES.CRU.TI.NAR, *v.*, to scrutinize.
ES.CRU.TÍ.NIO, *s.m.*, scrutiny, balloting, ballot-box.
ES.CU.DEI.RO, *s.m.*, squire.
ES.CU.DE.RI.A, *s.f.*, car racing team.
ES.CU.DO, *s.m.*, shield, buckler, arms; Portuguese currency.
ES.CU.LA.CHA.DO, *s.m., pop.*, a sloppy person; *adj., pop.*, messed up; careless, demoralized.
ES.CU.LA.CHAR, *v., pop.*, to mess up; to blow.
ES.CU.LA.CHO, *s.m., pop.*, telling off; blow.
ES.CU.LHAM.BA.ÇÃO, *s.f., pop.*, confusion, disarray; demoralization.
ES.CU.LHAM.BAR, *v., pop.*, to trash, to shatter, to destroy; to ridicule.
ES.CUL.PIR, *v.*, to sculpt.
ES.CUL.TOR, *s.m.*, sculptor.
ES.CUL.TU.RA, *s.f.*, sculpture.
ES.CUL.TU.RAL, *adj.*, sculptural.
ES.CU.MA.DEI.RA, *s.f.*, skimmer.
ES.CU.MAR, *v.*, to skim.
ES.CU.NA, *s.f., Náut.*, schooner.

ES.CU.RE.CER, *v.*, to darken, to blacken, to obscure, to make dark.
ES.CU.RE.CI.MEN.TO, *s.m.*, darkening, blackout.
ES.CU.RI.DÃO, *s.f.*, darkness, blackness, obscurity.
ES.CU.RO, *adj.*, dark, shadowy, black, obscure, lightless, tenebrous.
ES.CU.SA, *s.f.*, excuse, pardon, apology.
ES.CU.SA.DO, *adj.*, useless, needless, unnecessary.
ES.CU.SAR, *v.*, to excuse, to forgive.
ES.CU.SÁ.VEL, *adj.*, excusable.
ES.CU.SO, *adj.*, underhand, secret, suspicious; excused, useless.
ES.CU.TAR, *v.*, to hearken, to give ear to, to listen, to hear.
ES.DRÚ.XU.LO, *adj.*, weird, odd; *Gram.*, proparoxytone.
ES.FA.CE.LA.MEN.TO, *s.m.*, destruction, laceration.
ES.FA.CE.LAR, *v.*, to spoil, to destroy; *esfacelar-se*: to ruin oneself.
ES.FAI.MA.DO, *s.m.*, famished.
ES.FA.QUE.A.DO, *adj.*, knifed.
ES.FA.QUE.AR, *v.*, to stab, to knife, to cut with a knife.
ES.FA.RE.LA.DO, *adj.*, crumbled.
ES.FA.RE.LAR(-SE), *v.*, to crumble.
ES.FA.RI.NHAR, *v.*, to crumble, to reduce to flour.
ES.FAR.RA.PA.DO, *adj.*, tattered, ragged, shabby, scruffy.
ES.FAR.RA.PAR, *v.*, to tear, to rend, to reduce to tatters.
ES.FE.RA, *s.f.*, sphere, globe, ball, orb.
ES.FE.RI.CI.DA.DE, *s.f.*, sphericity, sphericalness.
ES.FÉ.RI.CO, *adj.*, spherical.
ES.FE.RO.GRÁ.FI.CA, *s.f.*, ball-point pen.
ES.FI.A.PAR, *v.*, to ravel, to fray.
ES.FÍNC.TER, *s.m., Anat.*, sphincter.
ES.FIN.GE, *s.f.*, sphinx.
ES.FO.LA.MEN.TO, *s.m.*, flaying.
ES.FO.LAR, *v.*, to flay, to skin, to scratch, to chafe, to rap, to abrade, to excoriate.
ES.FO.LI.A.ÇÃO, *s.f.*, exfoliation.
ES.FO.LI.AR, *v.*, to exfoliate.
ES.FO.ME.A.DO, *adj.*, hungry, famished, ravenous.
ES.FOR.ÇA.DO, *s.m.*, diligent person; *adj.*, committed, valiant, courageous.
ES.FOR.ÇAR, *v.*, to make strong, to encourage, to incite, to strengthen, to stimulate.
ES.FOR.ÇO, *s.m.*, effort, endeavour, struggle, attempt, exertion, courage, valour.
ES.FRAL.DAR, *v.*, to unfurl.
ES.FRE.GÃO, *s.m.*, mop, rubbing cloth, rubber, scrubber.
ES.FRE.GAR, *v.*, to rub, to mop, to scour, to scrub, to scrape.
ES.FRI.A.MEN.TO, *s.m.*, refrigeration, cooling.
ES.FRI.AR, *v.*, to cool, to chill, to make cool, to refresh, to refrigerate.
ES.FU.MA.ÇA.DO, *adj.*, smoky.
ES.FU.MA.ÇAR, *v.*, to smoke out.
ES.FU.ZI.AN.TE, *adj.*, effusive; whistling, hissing.
ES.GA.NA.DO, *s.m.*, glutton or famished person; *adj.*, famished, gluttonish, greedy, desirous.
ES.GA.NAR, *v.*, to strangle, to suffocate.
ES.GA.NI.ÇA.DO, *adj.*, shrieking, shrill, howling.
ES.GA.RA.VA.TAR, *v.*, to rake, to pick the teeth or ears; *fig.*, to search, to ask about.
ES.GAR.ÇAR, *v.*, to tear, to slit; to wear thin.
ES.GO.TA.DO, *adj.*, drained, emptied, exhausted, finished.

ESGOTAMENTO · 180 · ESPECTRO

ES.GO.TA.MEN.TO, *s.m.*, prostration, weakness, debility, fatigue.

ES.GO.TAR, *v.*, exhaust, to drain to the last drop, to dry.

ES.GO.TÁ.VEL, *adj.*, drainable, exhaustible.

ES.GO.TO, *s.m.*, drain, drainage, sewer, sewerage.

ES.GRI.MA, *s.f.*, fencing.

ES.GRI.MIR, *v.*, to fence, to brandish, to dispute.

ES.GRI.MIS.TA, *s. 2 gen.*, fencer.

ES.GUE.LHA, *s.f.*, obliquity, slant, bias; *de esguelha*: aslant.

ES.GUEI.RAR, *v.*, to steal artfully; *esgueirar-se*: to steal away.

ES.GUI.CHAR, *v.*, to squirt, to jet; to gush.

ES.GUI.CHO, *s.m.*, squirt, jet, waterspout.

ES.GUI.O, *adj.*, lanky, slender; willowy.

ES.LA.VO, *s.m., adj.*, Slavonian, Slavic, Slavonic, Slav.

ES.LO.VA.CO, *s.m.*, Slovak; *adj.*, Slovakian.

ES.LO.VÁ.QUI.A, *s.*, Slovakia.

ES.LO.VÊ.NI.A, *s.*, Slovenia.

ES.LO.VE.NO, *s.m., adj.*, Slovene.

ES.MA.GA.DOR, *adj.*, overwhelming.

ES.MA.GA.MEN.TO, *s.m.*, smashing, crushing; *fig.*, destruction.

ES.MA.GAR, *v.*, to compress; to squeeze, to press, to crush.

ES.MAL.TA.DO, *adj.*, enamelled.

ES.MAL.TAR, *v.*, to enamel.

ES.MAL.TE, *s.m.*, enamel.

ES.ME.RA.DO, *adj.*, performed with care, meticulous, accurate, accomplished.

ES.ME.RAL.DA, *s.f., Min.*, emerald.

ES.ME.RAR, *v.*, to perform with care, to accomplish; *esmerar-se*: to work with care.

ES.ME.RIL, *s.m.*, emery.

ES.ME.RI.LAR, *v.*, to rub or polish with emery.

ES.ME.RI.LHAR, *v.*, the same that *esmerilar*.

ES.ME.RO, *s.m.*, care, diligence, carefulness, perfection.

ES.MI.GA.LHAR, *v.*, to crumb, to crumble, to break into fragments, to triturate.

ES.MI.U.ÇAR, *v.*, to explain in details, to scrutinize, to examine.

ES.MO, *s.m.*, estimate, estimation; conjecture, guess; *a esmo*: at random.

ES.MO.LA, *s.f.*, alms, charity, almsdeed, benefit.

ES.MO.LAM.BA.DO, *adj. pop.*, tattered, ragged, in tatters.

ES.MO.LAR, *v.*, to give alms, to beg, to live by begging.

ES.MO.RE.CER, *v.*, to dismay, to discourage, to depress, to love heart.

ES.MO.RE.CI.MEN.TO, *s.m.*, discouragement.

ES.MUR.RAR, *v.*, to box, to sock, to beat, to punch, to pummel.

ES.NO.BE, *s. 2 gen.*, snob; snobbish.

ES.NO.BIS.MO, *s.m.*, snobbishness.

E.SO.FA.GI.TE, *s.f., Med.*, esophagitis.

E.SÔ.FA.GO, *s.m., Anat.*, gullet, esophagus.

E.SO.TÉ.RI.CO, *adj.*, esoteric.

E.SO.TE.RIS.MO, *s.m.*, esotericism, esoterism.

ES.PA.ÇA.DO, *adj.*, spaced (set at intervals); sluggish, slow.

ES.PA.ÇA.MEN.TO, *s.m.*, spacing.

ES.PA.CI.AL, *adj., s.m.*, spatial, space.

ES.PA.ÇO, *s.m.*, space, area, place.

ES.PA.ÇO.NA.VE, *s.f.*, spacecraft, spaceship.

ES.PA.ÇO.SO, *adj.*, spacious.

ES.PA.DA, *s.f.*, sword.

ES.PA.DA.CHIM, *s.m.*, swordsman.

ES.PA.DA.Ú.DO, *adj.*, broad-shouldered; corpulent.

ES.PA.DIM, *s.m.*, a small sword.

ES.PÁ.DUA, *s.f.*, shoulder, shoulder blade.

ES.PA.GUE.TE, *s.m., Cul.*, spaghetti.

ES.PAI.RE.CER, *v.*, to amuse, to recreate, to entertain, to divert.

ES.PAI.RE.CI.MEN.TO, *s.m.*, relaxation, recreation.

ES.PAL.DAR, *s.m.*, back (of a chair).

ES.PA.LHA.DO, *adj.*, scattered, dispersed.

ES.PA.LHA.FA.TO, *s.m.*, disorder, confusion, commotion.

ES.PA.LHA.FA.TO.SO, *adj.*, fussy, noisy, ostentatious.

ES.PA.LHAR, *v.*, to spread, to scatter about, to disperse, to dispel, to divulge.

ES.PAL.MA.DO, *adj.*, flattened, palmated, laminated.

ES.PAL.MAR, *v.*, to flatten, to spread, to make flat.

ES.PA.NA.DOR, *s.m.*, duster, feather broom.

ES.PA.NAR, *v.*, to dust.

ES.PAN.CA.MEN.TO, *s.m.*, spanking, beating.

ES.PAN.CAR, *v.*, to spank, to beat, to drub, to thrash.

ES.PA.NHA, *s.*, Spain (country).

ES.PA.NHOL, *adj., s.m.*, Spaniard, Spanish.

ES.PAN.TA.DO, *adj.*, startled, astonished, surprised.

ES.PAN.TA.LHO, *s.m.*, scarecrow.

ES.PAN.TAR, *v.*, to astonish, to frighten, to terrify, to alarm, to scare, to surprise.

ES.PAN.TO, *s.m.*, fright, terror, scare, fear, astonishment.

ES.PAN.TO.SO, *adj.*, startling, frightening, amazing, astounding.

ES.PA.RA.DRA.PO, *s.m.*, adhesive tape.

ES.PAR.GIR, *v.*, to spray, to spill, to shed.

ES.PAR.RA.MA.DO, *adj.*, scattered, to dispersed, to splashed, to sprawled.

ES.PAR.RA.MAR, *v.*, to scatter about, to spread, to strew, to disperse.

ES.PAR.RA.MO, *s.m.*, scattering.

ES.PAR.SO, *adj.*, sparse; diffuse; scarce.

ES.PAR.TA.NO, *adj.*, Spartan; *fig.*, austere, rigorous.

ES.PAR.TI.LHO, *s.m.*, corset.

ES.PAS.MO, *s.m., Med.*, spasm.

ES.PAS.MÓ.DI.CO, *adj.*, spasmodic, convulsive.

ES.PA.TI.FAR, *v.*, to shatter, to smash, to splinter.

ES.PÁ.TU.LA, *s.f.*, spatula, slice, spattle, trowel.

ES.PA.VO.RI.DO, *adj.*, frightened, terrified.

ES.PE.CI.AL, *adj.*, special, particular, excellent, individual.

ES.PE.CI.A.LI.DA.DE, *s.f.*, speciality, particularity, peculiarity.

ES.PE.CI.A.LIS.TA, *s. 2 gen.*, specialist, expert; *adj.*, specialist, specialistic.

ES.PE.CI.A.LI.ZA.ÇÃO, *s.f.*, specialization, speciality.

ES.PE.CI.A.LI.ZA.DO, *adj.*, specialized.

ES.PE.CI.A.LI.ZAR, *v.*, to specialize, to differentiate, to particularize.

ES.PE.CI.AL.MEN.TE, *adv.*, especially.

ES.PE.CI.A.RI.A, *s.f.*, spice; spicery.

ES.PÉ.CIE, *s.f.*, species, sort, kind, variety, class, order, group.

ES.PE.CI.FI.CAR, *v.*, to specify, to indicate, to particularize, to stipulate.

ES.PÉ.CI.ME, ESPÉCIMEN, *s.m.*, specimen.

ES.PEC.TA.DOR, *s.m.*, spectator, looker-on, viewer, observer, onlooker.

ES.PEC.TRAL, *adj.*, spectral.

ES.PEC.TRO, *s.m.*, ghost, spectre, spirit, apparition, phantom.

ESPECTROSCÓPIO •• 181 •• ESPREMER

ES.PEC.TROS.CÓ.PI.O, *s.m., Ópt.*, spectroscope.
ES.PE.CU.LA.ÇÃO, *s.f.*, speculation.
ES.PE.CU.LAR, *v.*, to speculate.
ES.PE.CU.LA.TI.VO, *adj.*, speculative.
ES.PE.LE.O.LO.GI.A, *s.f., Geol.*, speleology.
ES.PE.LHA.DO, *adj.*, mirrored.
ES.PE.LHAR, *v.*, to mirror; to polish, to bright.
ES.PE.LHO, *s.m.*, mirror, looking-glass.
ES.PE.LUN.CA, *s.f.*, honky-tonk, cavern, hole, den.
ES.PE.RA, *s.f.*, expectation, waiting-for, a wait.
ES.PE.RA.DO, *adj.*, expected, wished, awaited.
ES.PE.RAN.ÇA, *s.f.*, hope, expectation.
ES.PE.RAN.ÇO.SO, *adj.*, hopeful.
ES.PE.RAN.TO, *s.m.*, Esperanto.
ES.PE.RAR, *v.*, to hope for, to wait, to expect, to await.
ES.PE.RÁ.VEL, *adj.*, probable.
ES.PER.MA, *s.m., Biol.*, sperm, semen.
ES.PER.MA.TO.ZOI.DE, *s.m.*, spermatozoid, spermatozoon.
ES.PER.MI.CI.DA, *s.m.*, spermcide; *adj.*, spermcidal.
ES.PER.TE.ZA, *s.f.*, briskness, quickness, smartness, liveliness, vivacity.
ES.PER.TO, *adj.*, brisk, lively, smart, clever.
ES.PES.SO, *adj.*, thick, dense.
ES.PES.SU.RA, *s.f.*, thickness.
ES.PE.TA.CU.LAR, *adj.*, spectacular.
ES.PE.TÁ.CU.LO, *s.m.*, spectacle, show, entertainment, view, scene.
ES.PE.TA.CU.LO.SO, *adj.*, spectacular, showy, pompous.
ES.PER.TA.LHÃO, *s.m.*, sly, smart operator, rascal; *adj.*, crafty.
ES.PE.TAR, *v.*, to spit, to impale, to prick.
ES.PE.TO, *s.m.*, spit, skewer, broach.
ES.PE.VI.TA.DO, *adj.*, lively, brisk.
ES.PE.VI.TAR, *v.*, to make pretentious or affected; to incite; *espevitar-se*: to show off (affected).
ES.PE.ZI.NHAR, *v.*, to trample on, to oppress, to vex.
ES.PI.A.DA, *s.f., pop.*, peep, glance, squint, look.
ES.PI.ÃO, *s.m.*, spy, secret agent, intelligencer.
ES.PI.AR, *v.*, to spy, to watch, to observe, to look at, to dog, to pry into.
ES.PI.CA.ÇAR, *v.*, to peck; to strike, to hit; *fig.*, to torture, torment.
ES.PI.CHA.DO, *adj.*, to stretched out.
ES.PI.CHAR, *v.*, to stretch out, to extend; to shoot up.
ES.PI.GA, *s.f.*, ear (corn, maize).
ES.PI.GÃO, *s.m.*, great ear or spike; *Bras., pop.*, building.
ES.PI.GAR, *v.*, to ear, to seed; to grow up.
ES.PI.NA.FRAR, *v., pop.*, to reprimand, to ridicule, to lambaste.
ES.PI.NA.FRE, *s.m., Bot.*, spinach.
ES.PI.NAL, *adj.*, spinal.
ES.PIN.GAR.DA, *s.f.*, rifle, shotgun.
ES.PI.NHA, *s.f.*, spine, backbone, spinal column.
ES.PI.NHA.ÇO, *s.m.*, backbone; mountain chain, ridge.
ES.PI.NHAR, *v.*, to prick; *fig.*, to nettle; to offend.
ES.PI.NHEI.RAL, *s.m.*, plantation of any prickly shrub.
ES.PI.NHEI.RO, *s.m., Bot.*, thornbush.
ES.PI.NHEN.TO, *adj.*, thorny, prickly; bony (fish).
ES.PI.NHO, *s.m.*, thorn, prickle, sting, spine.
ES.PI.NHO.SO, *adj.*, thorny.
ES.PI.O.NA.GEM, *s.f.*, espionage, spying.
ES.PI.O.NAR, *v.*, to spy, to observe.

ES.PI.RAL, *s.f.*, spiral, wreath.
ES.PI.RA.LA.DO, *adj.*, spiralled.
ES.PI.RA.LAR, *v.*, to spiral.
ES.PÍ.RI.TA, *s. 2 gen.*, spiritist; *adj.*, spiritualistic.
ES.PI.RI.TEI.RA, *s.f.*, chafing fuel, spirit lamp.
ES.PI.RI.TIS.MO, *s.m.*, spiritism.
ES.PÍ.RI.TO, *s.m.*, spirit, soul, mind, a ghost, spectre; energy; ~ *esportivo*: competitive spirit.
ES.PI.RI.TU.AL, *adj.*, spiritual, immaterial.
ES.PI.RI.TU.A.LI.DA.DE, *s.f.*, spirituality, immateriality.
ES.PI.RI.TU.A.LIS.MO, *s.m.*, spiritualism.
ES.PI.RI.TU.A.LIS.TA, *s. 2 gen.*, spiritualist.
ES.PI.RI.TU.A.LI.ZAR, *v.*, to spiritualize.
ES.PI.RI.TU.O.SO, *adj.*, spirituous, alcoholic, witty, spirited.
ES.PIR.RAR, *v.*, to sneeze, to splash, to crepitate.
ES.PIR.RO, *s.m.*, sneeze.
ES.PLA.NA.DA, *s.f.*, esplanade.
ES.PLÊN.DI.DO, *adj.*, splendid, brilliant, magnificent, shining, grand, admirable.
ES.PLEN.DOR, *s.m.*, splendor, glory, pomp, refulgence, magnificence.
ES.PLEN.DO.RO.SO, *adj.*, splendorous; magnificent.
ES.PO.CAR, *v.*, to burst (corn); to explode.
ES.PO.LE.TA, *s.f.*, detonator.
ES.PO.LI.A.ÇÃO, *s.f.*, spoliation, spoliating, plunder.
ES.PO.LI.AR, *v.*, to spoliate, to plunder.
ES.PÓ.LI.O, *s.m.*, inheritance; *Jur.*, assets, estate; spoil; remains.
ES.PON.JA, *s.f.*, sponge.
ES.PON.JO.SO, *adj.*, spongeous, spongy.
ES.PON.TA.NEI.DA.DE, *s.f.*, spontaneity, spontaneousness, free will.
ES.PON.TÂ.NEO, *adj.*, spontaneous, voluntary.
ES.PO.RA, *s.f.*, spur.
ES.PO.RA.DI.CA.MEN.TE, *adv.*, sporadically.
ES.PO.RÁ.DI.CO, *adj.*, sporadic, sporadical.
ES.PO.RÃO, *s.m.*, spur.
ES.PO.RAR, *v.*, to spur.
ES.PO.RO, *s.m., Bot., Zool.*, spore.
ES.PO.RO.CIS.TO, *s.m., Biol.*, sporocyst.
ES.POR.RO, *s.m., Bras., gír.*, reprimand, reproof, brawl; *vulg.*, semen.
ES.POR.TE, *s.m.*, sport, sports.
ES.POR.TIS.TA, *s. 2 gen.*, sportsman, sportswoman.
ES.POR.TI.VI.DA.DE, *s.f.*, sportiness, sportsmanship.
ES.POR.TI.VO, *adj.*, sportive, sporting.
ES.PO.SA, *s.f.*, wife, consort, spouse.
ES.PO.SAR, *v.*, to marry, to espouse.
ES.PO.SO, *s.m.*, husband, consort.
ES.PRAI.A.DO, *s.m.*, seashore; *adj.*, cast on the shore; *fig.*, scattered.
ES.PRAI.AR, *v.*, to drive ashore, to spread, to scatter; to sprawl, to wash ashore.
ES.PRE.GUI.ÇA.DEI.RA, *s.f.*, deck chair, reclining chair, chaise longue.
ES.PRE.GUI.ÇAR, *v.*, to stretch.
ES.PREI.TA, *s.f.*, peep, pry, sly close look; on the lookout (for).
ES.PREI.TAR, *v.*, to peep, to watch, to observe, to pry, to spy.
ES.PRE.ME.DOR, *s.m.*, squeezer, smasher.
ES.PRE.MER, *v.*, to press, to squeeze, to compress, to crush, to express, to constrict.

ESPUMA · 182 · ESTARRECER

ES.PU.MA, *s.f.*, foam, froth, scum, spume.
ES.PU.MAN.TE, *adj.*, sparkling, foaming, bubbly; fizzy; *vinho ~*: sparkling wine.
ES.PU.MAR, *v.*, to scum, skim, to foam, to bubble, to froth.
ES.PU.MO.SO, *adj.*, foamy.
ES.PÚ.RI.O, *adj.*, spurious.
ES.QUA.DRA, *s.f.*, squadron, naval fleet.
ES.QUA.DRÃO, *s.m.*, squadron.
ES.QUA.DRI.A, *s.f.*, frame, sash, square.
ES.QUA.DRI.LHA, *s.f.*, squadron, wing, flotilla.
ES.QUA.DRO, *s.m.*, square.
ES.QUA.LI.DEZ, *s.f.*, squalidness, squalour.
ES.QUÁ.LI.DO, *adj.*, squalid.
ES.QUAR.TE.JA.MEN.TO, *s.m.*, quartering.
ES.QUAR.TE.JAR, *v.*, to quarter.
ES.QUE.CER, *v.*, to forget, to disremember, to neglect.
ES.QUE.CI.DO, *adj.*, forgotten, forgetful.
ES.QUE.CI.MEN.TO, *s.m.*, forgetfulness, oblivion.
ES.QUEI.TIS.TA, *s.m.*, skateboarder.
ES.QUE.LÉ.TI.CO, *adj.*, skeleton.
ES.QUE.LE.TO, *s.m.*, skeleton.
ES.QUE.MA, *s.m.*, scheme, project, plan, model, design.
ES.QUE.MÁ.TI.CO, *adj.*, schematic.
ES.QUE.MA.TI.ZA.ÇÃO, *s.f.*, schematization.
ES.QUE.MA.TI.ZAR, *v.*, to schematize.
ES.QUEN.TA.DO, *adj.*, heated; *fig.*, irritated.
ES.QUEN.TAR, *v.*, to heat, to warm, to make warm, to overheat, to animate.
ES.QUER.DA, *s.f.*, the left side or hand, the opposition.
ES.QUER.DIS.MO, *s.m.*, *Pol.*, leftism.
ES.QUER.DIS.TA, *s. 2 gen.*, *Pol.*, leftist; *adj.*, leftist.
ES.QUER.DO, *adj.*, left.
ES.QUE.TE, *s.m.*, sketch.
ES.QUI, *s.m.*, ski.
ES.QUI.A.DOR, *s.m.*, skier.
ES.QUI.AR, *v.*, to ski.
ES.QUI.FE, *s.m.*, coffin, caske.
ES.QUI.LO, *s.m.*, *Zool.*, squirrel.
ES.QUI.MÓ, *adj.*, *s. 2 gen.*, Eskimo.
ES.QUI.NA, *s.f.*, corner, street corner.
ES.QUI.SI.TI.CE, *s.f.*, extravagance, eccentricity.
ES.QUI.SI.TO, *adj.*, exquisite, singular, rare, strange.
ES.QUI.VA, *s.f.*, avoidance; dodge, ducking (of a blow).
ES.QUI.VAR, *v.*, to shun, to dodge, to avoid, to duck.
ES.QUI.VO, *adj.*, aloof; hard to find (person); untractable, rude.
ES.QUI.ZO.FRE.NI.A, *s.f.*, schizophrenia.
S.QUI.ZO.FRÊ.NI.CO, *s.m.*, *Med.*, schizophrenic.
ES.SA, *pron. dem.*: that; *essas pl.*: those.
ES.SE, *pron. dem.*: that, that one; *esses pl.*: those.
ES.SÊN.CIA, *s.f.*, essence, substance.
ES.SEN.CI.AL, *adj.*, essential, main.
ES.SEN.CI.AL.MEN.TE, *adv.*, essentially.
ES.SÊ.NI.O, *s.m.*, *Hist.*, Essene.
ES.TA, *pron. dem.*, this, the latter; *estas (pl.)*: these, these ones.
ES.TA.BA.NA.DO, *adj.*, clumsy, overhasty, headlong, careless.
ES.TA.BE.LE.CER, *v.*, to establish, to settle, to fix, to set up, to found, to determine.
ES.TA.BE.LE.CI.MEN.TO, *s.m.*, establishment, shop, store, institution.
ES.TA.BI.LI.DA.DE, *s.f.*, stability, stableness, firmness.
ES.TA.BI.LI.ZA.ÇÃO, *s.f.*, stabilization.

ES.TA.BI.LI.ZA.DOR, *s.m.*, *Comp.*, surge protector.
ES.TA.BI.LI.ZAR, *v.*, to stabilize, to fix, to fixate.
ES.TÁ.BU.LO, *s.m.*, stall, stable.
ES.TA.CA, *s.f.*, stake, post, picket; support.
ES.TA.CA.DA, *s.f.*, stockade; picket fence.
ES.TA.ÇÃO, *s.f.*, station, season, term, stand.
ES.TA.CAR, *v.*, to stake, to stop short.
ES.TA.CIO.NA.MEN.TO, *s.m.*, parking, parking lot, car park.
ES.TA.CIO.NAR, *v.*, to park, to station.
ES.TA.CI.O.NÁ.RI.O, *adj.*, stationary; *Econ.*, stagnant.
ES.TA.DA, *s.f.*, stay, sojourn, stop.
ES.TA.DI.A, *s.f.*, stay, sojourn; lay days.
ES.TÁ.DIO, *s.m.*, stadium.
ES.TA.DIS.TA, *s. 2 gen.*, statesman, stateswoman.
ES.TA.DO, *s.m.*, state, condition, circumstance.
ES.TA.DO-MAI.OR, *s.m.*, *Mil.*, general staff; army/air staff.
ES.TA.DU.AL, *adj.*, state.
ES.TA.DU.NI.DEN.SE, *s. 2 gen.*, North American; *adj.*, American.
ES.TA.FA, *s.f.*, stress, fatigue, hard work.
ES.TA.FA.DO, *adj.*, exhausted, fatigued, tired.
ES.TA.FAN.TE, *adj.*, exhausting, fatiguing, tiring.
ES.TA.FAR, *v.*, to exhaust, to tire, to weary, to fatigue.
ES.TA.FE.TA, *s.m.*, courier.
ES.TA.GI.AR, *v.*, to train.
ES.TA.GI.Á.RIO, *s.m.*, trainee.
ES.TÁ.GIO, *s.m.*, training, probation.
ES.TAG.NA.ÇÃO, *s.f.*, stagnation.
ES.TAG.NA.DO, *adj.*, stagnant.
ES.TAG.NAR, *v.*, to stagnate.
ES.TA.LAC.TI.TE, *s.f.*, *Min.*, stalactite.
ES.TA.LA.GEM, *s.f.*, inn, lodge, auberge; hostel.
ES.TA.LA.JA.DEI.RO, *s.m.*, innkeeper.
ES.TA.LAR, *v.*, to crack; to crackle, to crepitate; to snap.
ES.TA.LEI.RO, *s.m.*, shipyard, dockyard.
ES.TA.LI.DO, *s.m.*, snapping, clapping, smacking.
ES.TA.LO, *s.m.*, snap, crack; cracking, crackling.
ES.TA.MEN.TO, *s.m.*, assembly as a legislative body, parliament or congress.
ES.TAM.PA, *s.f.*, impression, print, model, picture.
ES.TAM.PA.DO, *s.m.*, *pop.*, printed cloth; *adj.*, printed, impressed; *fig.*, etched.
ES.TAM.PAR, *v.*, to print, to imprint, to impress, to stamp.
ES.TAM.PA.RI.A, *s.f.*, print shop room; printworks, printery.
ES.TAM.PI.DO, *s.m.*, clap, crack; explosion, detonation.
ES.TAN.CAR, *v.*, to stanch, to stop, *UK* to stem; to hinder from running (as blood).
ES.TÂN.CIA, *s.f.*, stay, ranch, state, country, residence, resort, strophe.
ES.TAN.CI.EI.RO, *s.m.*, *Bras.*, rancher, owner of a ranch.
ES.TAN.DAR.TE, *s.m.*, standard, flag, banner, guidon.
ES.TAN.DE, *s.f.*, stand.
ES.TA.NHO, *s.m.*, *Quím.*, tin, pewter.
ES.TAN.QUE, *adj.*, tight, wattertight; stanch.
ES.TAN.TE, *s.f.*, shelf, rack, bookstand, bookcase.
ES.TA.PA.FÚR.DI.O, *adj.*, heedless, outlandish.
ES.TAR, *v.*, to be, to stay, to remain, to lie, to exist, to be present, to attend.
ES.TAR.DA.LHA.ÇO, *s.m.*, bustle; confusion; racket; *fig.*, ostentation, flamboyance.
ES.TAR.RE.CER, *v.*, to frighten, to strike with fear, terrorize.

ESTATAL ··· 183 ··· ESTRAÇALHAR

ES.TA.TAL, s.f., state-owned company; adj., of or referring to the state.

ES.TA.TE.LA.DO, adj., sprawled; motionless; stretched out; astonished.

ES.TA.TE.LAR, v., to throw, to be stretched, to fall flat.

ES.TÁ.TI.CA, s.f., Fís., statics.

ES.TÁ.TI.CO, adj., static.

ES.TA.TIS.MO, s.m., statism.

ES.TA.TÍS.TI.CA, s.f., statistics.

ES.TA.TÍS.TI.CO, s.m., statistician; adj., statistic.

ES.TA.TI.ZA.ÇÃO, s.f., nationalization.

ES.TA.TI.ZAR, v., to nationalize.

ES.TÁ.TUA, s.f., statue.

ES.TA.TU.E.TA, s.f., statuette.

ES.TA.TU.RA, s.f., tallness, size, stature.

ES.TA.TU.TÁ.RI.O, adj., statutory.

ES.TA.TU.TO, s.m., statute, decree, rule, law.

ES.TÁ.VEL, adj., stable, solid, firm, fixed.

ES.TE, pron. dem., this, the latter; estes pl.: these, these ones.

ES.TEI.O, s.m., shore, prop, support; fig., breadwinner.

ES.TEI.RA, s.f., mat; ~ rolante: treadmill; fig., course, direction.

ES.TE.LI.O.NA.TÁ.RI.O, s.m., swindler.

ES.TE.LI.O.NA.TO, s.m., swindle; fraud.

ES.TÊN.CIL, s.m., stencil.

ES.TEN.DER, v., to extend, to stretch out, to enlarge, to expand, to amplify.

ES.TE.NO.DAC.TI.LO.GRA.FI.A, s.f., shorthand typing.

ES.TE.NO.DAC.TI.LÓ.GRA.FO, s.m., shorthand typist.

ES.TE.NO.GRA.FI.A, s.f., stenography.

ES.TE.NÓ.GRA.FO, s.m., stenographer, shorthand typist.

ES.TE.PE, s.f., steppe.

ÉS.TER, s.m., Quím., ester.

ES.TER.CAR, v., to manure, to dung, to fertilize.

ES.TER.CO, s.m., manure, dung, excrement.

ES.TÉ.RE.O, s.m., stereo.

ES.TE.RE.O.FO.NI.A, s.f., stereophony.

ES.TE.RE.O.FÔ.NI.CO, adj., stereophonic.

ES.TE.RE.O.TI.PA.DO, adj., stereotypical, stereotyped.

ES.TE.RE.O.TI.PAR, v., to stereotype.

ES.TE.RE.Ó.TI.PO, s.m., stereotype.

ES.TÉ.RIL, adj., infertile, sterile, unfruitful, barren.

ES.TE.RI.LI.DA.DE, s.f., sterility, infertility.

ES.TE.RI.LI.ZA.ÇÃO, s.f., sterilization.

ES.TE.RI.LI.ZAR, v., to sterilize, to make barren or sterile.

ES.TER.NO, s.m., Anat., sternum, breastbone.

ES.TE.ROI.DE, s.m., Quím., steroid.

ES.TER.TOR, s.m., Med., death-rattle.

ES.TE.TA, s. 2 gen., esthete, aesthete.

ES.TÉ.TI.CA, s.f., esthetics, aesthetics.

ES.TE.TI.CIS.TA, adj., estheticism, aestheticism; s. 2 gen., esthetician, aesthetician.

ES.TE.TOS.CÓ.PIO, s.m., stethoscope.

ES.TI.A.GEM, s.f., drought, dryness.

ES.TI.AR, v., to stop raining; to be dry, to dry up.

ES.TI.BOR.DO, s.m., starboard.

ES.TI.CA.DA, s.f., pop., well-dressed, stretched.

ES.TI.CAR, v., to extend, to stretch out, to dilate.

ES.TIG.MA, s.m., stigma, mark, spot.

ES.TIG.MA.TI.ZAR, v., to stigmatize.

ES.TI.LE.TE, s.m., probe, sound, stiletto.

ES.TI.LHA.ÇAR, v., to shatter, to splinter.

ES.TI.LHA.ÇO, s.m., splinter, shard, fragment, chip.

ES.TI.LÍS.TI.CA, s.f., stylistic, stylistics.

ES.TI.LÍS.TI.CO, adj., stylistic.

ES.TI.LI.ZA.ÇÃO, s.f., stylization.

ES.TI.LI.ZAR, v., to stylize.

ES.TI.LO, s.m., style, method, fashion.

ES.TI.MA, s.f., esteem, respect, regard, affection, fondness.

ES.TI.MA.ÇÃO, s.f., affection, esteem; cachorro de ~: a pet dog.

ES.TI.MAR, v., to esteem, to regard with respect, to prize, to consider.

ES.TI.MA.TI.VA, s.f., estimation, valuation.

ES.TI.MÁ.VEL, adj., estimable; respectable; appraisable.

ES.TI.MU.LA.ÇÃO, s.f., stimulation, incitation, excitement.

ES.TI.MU.LAN.TE, adj., s.m., stimulant, incitant.

ES.TI.MU.LAR, v., to stimulate, to incite, to instigate, to excite.

ES.TÍ.MU.LO, s.m., stimulus, incentive, impulse.

ES.TI.O, s.m., summer; adj., estival, aestival.

ES.TI.PU.LAR, v., to stipulate, to contract, to covenant.

ES.TI.RA.MEN.TO, s.m., Med., strain; stretch.

ES.TI.RAR, v., to stretch, to extend, to distend, to strain.

ES.TIR.PE, s.f., race, origin, stock, lineage.

ES.TI.VA, s.f., stowage.

ES.TI.VA.DOR, s.m., stower, docker.

ES.TI.VAL, adj., estival, aestival.

ES.TO.CA.DA, s.f., thrust, stab.

ES.TO.CA.GEM, s.f., Bras., stock (stocks of goods).

ES.TO.CAR, v., Bras., to stock (goods); to strike with a rapier.

ES.TO.FA.DO, s.m., upholstered.

ES.TO.FA.MEN.TO, s.m., upholstering, upholstery; stuffing.

ES.TO.FAR, v., to stuff, to upholster.

ES.TOI.CIS.MO, s.m., stoicism.

ES.TOI.CO, s.m., stoic; adj., Stoic, Stoical.

ES.TO.JO, s.m., case, box, kit, set, container.

ES.TO.LA, s.f., stole.

ES.TO.MA.CAL, adj., stomachic.

ES.TÔ.MA.GO, s.m., Anat., stomach.

ESTÔNIA, s., Estonia.

ES.TO.NI.A.NO, s.m., adj., Estonian.

ES.TON.TE.AN.TE, adj., stunning.

ES.TO.PA, s.f., tow, hards, hurds, oakum.

ES.TO.PIM, s.m., quickmatch, fuse.

ES.TO.QUE, s.m., stock, reserve.

ES.TOR.NAR, v., Com., to cancel (credit or debit).

ES.TOR.RI.CA.DO, adj., overroasted, toasted, parched; dry, arid.

ES.TOR.RI.CAR, v., to scorch, to dry; to toast, to overroast.

ES.TOR.VAR, v., to hinder, to embarrass, to obstruct, to impede.

ES.TOR.VO, s.m., hindrance, impediment, embarrassment, obstacle.

ES.TOU.RA.DO, adj., turbulent, rattlebrained, boisterous, knackered.

ES.TOU.RAR, v., to explode; to break up; to split, to crack; to blow out.

ES.TOU.RO, s.m., explosion, detonation; crack, clap, peal.

ES.TOU.VA.DO, adj., foolhardy; hotheaded.

ES.TRÁ.BI.CO, s.m., a cross-eyed person; adj., cross-eyed, strabismic, squinting.

ES.TRA.BIS.MO, s.m., Med., squint, strabismus.

ES.TRA.ÇA.LHAR, v., to cut, to slash, to tear, to shred;

ESTRADA ·· 184 ··· ETÉREO

to shatter.

ES.TRA.DA, *s.f.*, road, highway, main road.

ES.TRA.DO, *s.m.*, mattress, frame, bedframe.

ES.TRA.GA.DO, *adj.*, rotten, deteriorated, damaged; damnified.

ES.TRA.GÃO, *s.m., Bot.*, tarragon.

ES.TRA.GAR, *v.*, to destroy, to spoil, to danger, to ruin, to blemish, to damage, to waste.

ES.TRA.GO, *s.m.*, damage, prejudice, harm, injury.

ES.TRA.LAR, *v.*, to crack, to crackle, to burst.

ES.TRAM.BÓ.TI.CO, *adj.*, extravagant, odd, freakish.

ES.TRAN.GEI.RIS.MO, *s.m.*, loan word, the usage of foreign words.

ES.TRAN.GEI.RO, *s.m.*, foreigner, stranger.

ES.TRAN.GU.LA.DOR, *s.m.*, strangler; *adj.*, strangling.

ES.TRAN.GU.LA.MEN.TO, *s.m.*, strangulation, suffocation; blocking.

ES.TRAN.GU.LAR, *v.*, to strangle, suffocate.

ES.TRA.NHA.MEN.TO, *s.m.*, unfamiliarity; surprise (amazement).

ES.TRA.NHAR, *v.*, to find queer, to odd, to strange, to wonder.

ES.TRA.NHE.ZA, *s.f.*, queerness, amazement, surprise, shyness.

ES.TRA.NHO, *s.m.*, stranger, foreigner; *adj.*, foreign, strange, alien, odd, wonderful, exotic.

ES.TRA.TA.GE.MA, *s.m.*, stratagem, cunning, ruse, artifice.

ES.TRA.TÉ.GIA, *s.f.*, strategy.

ES.TRA.TÉ.GI.CO, *s.m.*, strategist; *adj.*, strategic, strategical.

ES.TRA.TE.GIS.TA, *s. 2 gen.*, strategist.

ES.TRA.TI.FI.CAR, *v.*, to stratify.

ES.TRA.TO, *s.m., Geol.*, stratum, layer; *Met.*, stratus.

ES.TRA.TO-CIR.RO, *s.m., Met.*, cirrostratus.

ES.TRA.TO-CÚ.MU.LO, *s.m., Met.*, cumulostratus, stratocumulus.

ES.TRA.TO.GRA.FI.A, *s.f.*, stratography.

ES.TRA.TOS.FE.RA, *s.f.*, stratosphere.

ES.TRE.AN.TE, *s. 2 gen.*, debutant, beginner; *adj.*, beginning.

ES.TRE.AR, *v.*, to premiere (film, show.); to inaugurate, to iniciate, to begin.

ES.TRE.BA.RIA, *s.f.*, horse stable.

ES.TRE.BU.CHAR, *v.*, to writhe; to flounder, to toss.

ES.TREI.A, *s.f.*, handsel, première, beginning, debut.

ES.TREI.TA.MEN.TO, *s.m.*, narrowing, straitening, tightening, shrinking.

ES.TREI.TAR, *v.*, to narrow, to straiten, to crimp.

ES.TREI.TE.ZA, *s.f.*, narrowness, straitness.

ES.TREI.TO, *s.m.*, strait; *adj.*, narrow, strait, close.

ES.TRE.LA, *s.f.*, star, guide, fate, fortune, destiny.

ES.TRE.LA-D'AL.VA, *s.f.*, morning star, evening star (Venus).

ES.TRE.LA.DO, *adj.*, starry, starred; fried (egg).

ES.TRE.LA-DO-MAR, *s.f., Zool.*, starfish.

ES.TRE.LAR, *v.*, to star; to fry (eggs).

ES.TRE.LA.TO, *s.m., Bras.*, stardom.

ES.TRE.LI.NHA, *s.f.*, little star; sparkler (firework); starlet.

ES.TRE.ME.CER, *v.*, to tremble, to shake, to quake, to excite, to affect.

ES.TRE.ME.CI.DO, *adj.*, shocked, startled, shaken.

ES.TRE.ME.CI.MEN.TO, *s.m.*, shudder, trembling.

ES.TRE.PAR-SE, *v., pop.*, to come unstuck.

ES.TRÉ.PI.TO, *s.m.*, great noise; peal, thunder, crack, crash.

ES.TRE.PI.TO.SO, *adj.*, noisy, clamorous, thundering.

ES.TRES.SAN.TE, *adj., Med.*, stressful.

ES.TRES.SAR, *v.*, to wear down.

ES.TRES.SE, *s.m.*, stress, strain.

ES.TRI.A, *s.f.*, groove, channel; stria, stretch mark (skin).

ES.TRI.BEI.RA, *s.f.*, step, foot-board; stirrup.

ES.TRI.BI.LHO, *s.m., Lit.*, refrain; *Mús.*, chorus.

ES.TRI.BO, *s.m.*, stirrup; step, foot-board.

ES.TRI.DEN.TE, *adj.*, strident.

ES.TRI.PU.LI.A, *s.f., pop.*, naughtiness, tumult, racket, mischief.

ES.TRI.TO, *adj.*, strict.

ES.TRO.BOS.CÓ.PI.O, *s.m.*, stroboscope.

ES.TRO.FE, *s.f.*, strophe, stanza.

ES.TRÓ.GE.NO, *s.m., Biol., Quím.*, estrogen.

ES.TRO.GO.NO.FE, *s.m., Cul.*, stroganoff.

ES.TRÔN.CI.O, *s.m., Quím.*, strontium.

ES.TRON.DO, *s.m.*, noise, cracking, boom, blast, thundering, rumble.

ES.TRON.DO.SO, *adj.*, strepitous, clamorous; roaring; fig., famous, pompous, spectacular.

ES.TRO.PI.A.DO, *adj.*, maimed, crippled; hobbling (horse).

ES.TRO.PI.AR, *v.*, to maim, to cripple; to overfatigue.

ES.TRU.ME, *s.m.*, dung, manure, fertilizer.

ES.TRU.PÍ.CI.O, *s.m.*, stupidity, blunder; mutiny, revolt.

ES.TRU.TU.RA, *s.f.*, structure, framework, framing.

ES.TRU.TU.RA.ÇÃO, *s.f.*, structuring.

ES.TRU.TU.RAL, *adj.*, structural.

ES.TRU.TU.RA.LIS.MO, *s.m.*, structuralism.

ES.TRU.TU.RAR, *v.*, to structure.

ES.TU.Á.RIO, *s.m.*, estuary.

ES.TU.DAN.TE, *s. 2 gen.*, student, scholar.

ES.TU.DAN.TIL, *adj.*, pertaining to a student.

ES.TU.DAR, *v.*, to study, to learn, to investigate.

ES.TÚ.DIO, *s.m.*, studio, atelier.

ES.TU.DI.O.SO, *s.m.*, expert; *adj.*, studious.

ES.TU.DO, *s.m.*, study, application.

ES.TU.FA, *s.f.*, stove, hothouse, greenhouse.

ES.TU.FAR, *v.*, to stew; to heat; to stuff.

ES.TUL.TÍ.CI.A, *s.f.*, foolishness, stupidity, silliness.

ES.TU.PE.FA.TO, *adj.*, stupefied.

ES.TU.PEN.DO, *adj.*, stupendous, amazing, admirable, extraordinary.

ES.TU.PI.DEZ, *s.f.*, stupidity, foolishness, silliness, dullness.

ES.TÚ.PI.DO, *adj.*, stupid, dull, silly, idiotic.

ES.TU.PRA.DOR, *s.m.*, raper, violator, deflowerer.

ES.TU.PRAR, *v.*, to rape, to deflower.

ES.TU.PRO, *s.m.*, rape.

ES.TU.QUE, *s.m.*, stucco.

ES.TUR.JÃO, *s.m., Zool.*, sturgeon (fish).

ES.TUR.RI.CA.DO, *adj.*, too roasted, very dry.

ES.TUR.RI.CAR, *v.*, to dry, to become dry.

ES.VA.IR, *v.*, to disperse, to dissipate; *esvair-se*: to disappear, to faint; to become exhausted.

ES.VA.ZI.A.MEN.TO, *s.m.*, emptying, exhaustion.

ES.VA.ZI.AR, *v.*, to empty, evacuate.

ES.VER.DE.A.DO, *adj.*, greeny, greenish.

ES.VIS.CE.RAR, *v.*, to eviscerate.

ES.VO.A.ÇAN.TE, *adj.*, fluttering.

E.TA.PA, *s.f.*, stage, stopping place.

É.TER, *s.m., Quím.*, ether.

E.TÉ.RE.O, *adj.*, ethereal; fig., aerial, celestial, sublime.

ETERNIDADE ·· 185 ··· EXCLUÍDO

E.TER.NI.DA.DE, *s.f.*, eternity.
E.TER.NI.ZAR, *v.*, to eternalize, eternize.
E.TER.NO, *adj.*, eternal, immortal, timeless.
É.TI.CA, *s.f.*, ethics.
É.TI.CO, *adj.*, ethic, moral.
E.TI.LE.NO, *s.m.*, *Quím.*, ethylene.
E.TÍ.LI.CO, *adj.*, *Quím.*, ethylic.
E.TI.MO.LO.GI.A, *s.f.*, etymology.
E.TI.MO.LÓ.GI.CO, *adj.*, etymologic, etymological.
E.TI.MO.LO.GIS.TA, *s. 2 gen.*, etymologist.
E.TÍ.O.PE, *adj.*, *s.m.*, Ethiopian.
E.TI.Ó.PI.A, *s.*, Ethiopia.
E.TI.QUE.TA, *s.f.*, etiquette, formality, ticket, tag.
E.TI.QUE.TAR, *v.*, to label, to ticket.
ET.NI.A, *s.f.*, ethnic group.
ÉT.NI.CO, *adj.*, ethnic, ethnical.
ET.NO.GRA.FI.A, *s.f.*, ethnography.
ET.NO.LO.GI.A, *s.f.*, ethnology.
E.TRUS.CO, *adj.*, *s.m.*, Etruscan, Etrurian.
EU, *pron.*, I, the ego, the self-conscious subject; me.
EU.CA.LIP.TO, *s.m.*, *Bot.*, eucalyptus.
EU.CA.RIS.TI.A, *s.f.*, *Rel.*, Eucharist.
EU.CA.RÍS.TI.CO, *adj.*, Eucharistic.
EU.FE.MIS.MO, *s.m.*, euphemism.
EU.FO.NI.A, *s.f.*, euphony.
EU.FÔ.NI.CO, *adj.*, euphonic, euphonical, agreeable.
EU.FO.RI.A, *s.f.*, euphoria; a sense of well-being.
EU.FÓ.RI.CO, *adj.*, euphoric.
EU.GE.NI.A, *s.f.*, eugenics.
EU.NU.CO, *s.m.*, eunuch.
EU.RO, *s.m.*, euro (currency).
EU.RO.PE.I.ZAR, *v.*, to Europeanize.
EU.RO.PEU, *adj.*, *s.m.*, European.
EU.TA.NÁ.SI.A, *s.f.*, euthanasia.
E.VA.CU.A.ÇÃO, *s.f.*, evacuation.
E.VA.CU.AR, *v.*, to evacuate, to empty, to void, to excrete.
E.VA.DIR, *v.*, to escape, to avoid, to shun, to delude.
E.VA.NES.CEN.TE, *adj.*, evanescent.
E.VAN.GE.LHO, *s.m.*, Evangel, Gospel.
E.VAN.GÉ.LI.CO, *adj.*, evangelic, evangelical.
E.VAN.GE.LIS.TA, *s. 2 gen.*, Evangelist.
E.VAN.GE.LI.ZA.ÇÃO, *s.f.*, evangelization.
E.VAN.GE.LI.ZA.DOR, *s.m.*, evangelist, preacher.
E.VAN.GE.LI.ZAR, *v.*, to evangelize.
E.VA.PO.RA.ÇÃO, *s.f.*, evaporation.
E.VA.PO.RAR, *v.*, to evaporate, to vaporize, to exale, to dissipate.
E.VA.SÃO, *s.f.*, evasion, escape, elopement.
E.VA.SI.VA, *s.f.*, evasion, subterfuge, pretext.
E.VEN.TO, *s.m.*, event, ocurrence, happening.
E.VEN.TU.AL, *adj.*, fortuitous, occasional, casual.
E.VEN.TU.A.LI.DA.DE, *s.f.*, eventuality, event.
E.VI.DÊN.CIA, *s.f.*, evidence, clearness.
E.VI.DEN.CI.AR, *v.*, to evidence, to make evident, to make clear.
E.VI.DEN.TE, *adj.*, evident, clear, plain, obvious.
E.VIS.CE.RAR, *v.*, to eviscerate.
E.VI.TAR, *v.*, to avoid, to shun, to escape.
E.VO.CA.ÇÃO, *s.f.*, evocation.
E.VO.CAR, *v.*, to evocate.
E.VO.LU.ÇÃO, *s.f.*, evolution.

E.VO.LU.CI.O.NÁ.RI.O, *adj.*, evolutionary.
E.VO.LU.CI.O.NIS.MO, *s.m.*, evolutionism.
E.VO.LU.CI.O.NIS.TA, *s. 2 gen.*, evolutionist.
E.VO.LU.IR, *v.*, to develop, to unfold, to progress.
E.VO.LU.TI.VO, *adj.*, evolutive, evolutionary.
E.XA.CER.BAR, *v.*, to exacerbate, to aggravate, to provoke; *exacerbar-se*: to be exacerbated.
E.XA.GE.RA.DO, *adj.*, exaggerating, excessive.
E.XA.GE.RAR, *v.*, to exaggerate, to amplify, to magnify.
E.XA.GE.RO, *s.m.*, exaggeration, amplification.
E.XA.LA.ÇÃO, *s.f.*, exhalation.
E.XA.LAR, *v.*, to exhale, to emit, to emanate.
E.XAL.TA.ÇÃO, *s.f.*, exaltation.
E.XAL.TA.DO, *adj.*, exalted, exaggerated; fanatical.
E.XAL.TAR, *v.*, to exalt, to glorify, to praise, to magnify.
E.XA.ME, *s.m.*, examination, interrogatory.
E.XA.MI.NA.DOR, *s.m.*, examiner, examinator.
E.XA.MI.NAR, *v.*, to examine, to search, to inquire into, to interrogate, to investigate.
E.XA.MI.NÁ.VEL, *adj.*, examinable.
E.XAN.GUE, *adj.*, bloodless, *fig.*, feeble, faint.
E.XAS.PE.RA.ÇÃO, *s.f.*, exasperation.
E.XAS.PE.RA.DO, *adj.*, exasperated.
E.XAS.PE.RAN.TE, *adj.*, exasperating.
E.XAS.PE.RAR, *v.*, to exasperate.
E.XA.TA.MEN.TE, *adv.*, exactly.
E.XA.TI.DÃO, *s.f.*, exactness, preciseness, precision, punctuality.
E.XA.TO, *adj.*, exact, accurate, precise, correct, right, strict.
E.XAU.RIR, *v.*, to exhaust, to drain, to draw out.
E.XAUS.TI.VO, *adj.*, exhaustive, exhausting.
E.XAUS.TO, *adj.*, exhausted, drained, emptied.
E.XAUS.TOR, *s.m.*, exhaust fun, suction fan, extractor fan; ventilator.
EX.CE.ÇÃO, *s.f.*, exception, excepting.
EX.CE.DEN.TE, *s.m.*, excess, surplus, remainder.
EX.CE.DER, *v.*, to exceed, to overstep, to surpass, to excel.
EX.CE.LÊN.CIA, *s.f.*, excellence, excellency.
EX.CE.LEN.TE, *adj.*, excellent, eminent, admirable.
EX.CEL.SO, *adj.*, high, exalted, sublime, excellent.
EX.CEN.TRI.CI.DA.DE, *s.f.*, eccentricity.
EX.CÊN.TRI.CO, *s.m.*, eccentric.
EX.CEP.CI.O.NAL, *adj.*, exceptional, peculiar, irregular, unusual.
EX.CER.TO, *s.m.*, excerpt, extract, choice.
EX.CES.SI.VO, *adj.*, excessive, exceeding, immoderate.
EX.CES.SO, *s.m.*, excess, abuse, outrage, immoderation, exorbitance.
EX.CE.TO, *prep.*, except, excepting, save, unless, but, excluding.
EX.CE.TU.AR, *v.*, to except, to exclude.
EX.CI.TA.ÇÃO, *s.f.*, excitation, excitement, heat, simulation, agitation.
EX.CI.TA.MEN.TO, *s.m.*, excitement.
EX.CI.TAR, *v.*, to excite, to stimulate, to incite, to instigate.
EX.CLA.MA.ÇÃO, *s.f.*, exclamation; *ponto de exclamação*: exclamation mark.
EX.CLA.MAR, *v.*, to exclaim, to cry out.
EX.CLA.MA.TI.VO, *adj.*, exclamative, exclamatory.
EX.CLU.DEN.TE, *adj.*, excluding.
EX.CLU.Í.DO, *adj.*, excluded.

EXCLUIR

EX.CLU.IR, *v.*, to exclude, to preclude, to shut out.

EX.CLU.SÃO, *s.f.*, exclusion, elimination.

EX.CLU.SI.VI.DA.DE, *s.f.*, exclusiveness.

EX.CLU.SI.VO, *adj.*, exclusive, restricted, limited.

EX.CO.MUN.GA.DO, *s.m.*, excommunicate; excommunicated.

EX.CO.MUN.GAR, *v.*, to excommunicate.

EX.CO.MU.NHÃO, *s.f., Rel.*, excommunication.

EX.CRE.ÇÃO, *s.f.*, excretion.

EX.CRE.MEN.TO, *s.m.*, excrement, feces, shit, crap, fecal matter.

EX.CRES.CÊN.CI.A, *s.f.*, excrescence, excrescency.

EX.CRE.TAR, *v.*, to excrete, to expel; to evacuate.

EX.CRE.TOR, *adj.*, excretory.

EX.CUR.SÃO, *s.f.*, excursion, trip, tour, journey, sally, raid.

EX.CUR.SI.O.NIS.TA, *s. 2 gen.*, excursionist.

E.XE.CRAR, *v.*, to execrate.

E.XE.CRÁ.VEL, *adj.*, execrable.

E.XE.CU.ÇÃO, *s.f.*, execution, performance.

E.XE.CU.TAR, *v.*, to execute, to perform, to realize, to effectuate.

E.XE.CU.TÁ.VEL, *adj.*, executable.

E.XE.CU.TI.VO, *s.m.*, executive; *adj.*, executive, resolute, active, brisk.

E.XEM.PLAR, *s.m.*, exemplar, model, specimen, copy, issue; *adj.*, exemplary.

E.XEM.PLI.FI.CA.ÇÃO, *s.f.*, exemplification.

E.XEM.PLI.FI.CAR, *v.*, to exemplify.

E.XEM.PLO, *s.m.*, example, model, instance.

E.XÉ.QUI.AS, *s.f., pl.*, funeral rites.

E.XE.QUÍ.VEL, *adj.*, feasible.

E.XER.CER, *v.*, to exercise, to practise, to exert.

E.XER.CÍ.CIO, *s.m.*, exercise, practice, drill, exercitation, work.

E.XER.CI.TAR, *v.*, to exercise, to practise.

E.XÉR.CI.TO, *s.m.*, army, troops.

E.XI.BI.ÇÃO, *s.f.*, exhibition, display, exposition, ostentation.

E.XI.BI.CI.O.NIS.MO, *s.m.*, exhibitionism.

E.XI.BI.CI.O.NIS.TA, *s. 2 gen.*, exhibitionist.

E.XI.BI.DO, *s.m.*, exhibitionist; *adj.*, flamboyant.

E.XI.BI.DOR, *s.m., Cin.*, cinema owner; *adj.*, exhibiting.

E.XI.BIR, *v.*, to exhibit, to show, to display, to expose, to show off.

E.XI.GÊN.CIA, *s.f.*, exigence, exigency, request, demand, necessity, need.

E.XI.GEN.TE, *adj.*, exigent, demanding.

E.XI.GIR, *v.*, to claim, to exact, to demand, to require, to urge.

E.XÍ.GUO, *adj.*, exiguous, small, tiny, meagre.

E.XI.LA.DO, *s.m.*, exile; *adj.*, exiled, banished.

E.XI.LAR, *v.*, to exile, to banish, to deport, to expatriate.

E.XÍ.LIO, *s.m.*, exile, banishment.

E.XÍ.MIO, *adj.*, conspicuous, excellent, extraordinary.

E.XI.MIR, *v.*, to exempt, to exonerate; to clear; *eximir-se*: to refuse to, to escape from; shun.

E.XIS.TÊN.CIA, *s.f.*, existence, reality, life.

E.XIS.TEN.CI.AL, *adj.*, existential.

E.XIS.TEN.CI.A.LIS.MO, *s.m.*, existentialism.

E.XIS.TEN.CI.A.LIS.TA, *s. 2 gen., adj.*, existentialist.

E.XIS.TEN.TE, *s. 2 gen.*, existent; *adj.*, existent, existing.

E.XIS.TIR, *v.*, to exist, to be, to live, to subsist.

Ê.XI.TO, *s.m.*, effect, result, outcome, sucess, triumph.

Ê.XO.DO, *s.m.*, exodus, migration.

E.XO.NE.RA.ÇÃO, *s.f.*, exoneration, dismissal, discharge.

EXPRESSÃO

E.XO.NE.RAR, *v.*, to exonerate, to dismiss, to free.

E.XOR.BI.TÂN.CIA, *s.f.*, exorbitance, exorbitancy, extravagance.

E.XOR.BI.TAR, *v.*, to exorbitate, exceed.

E.XOR.CIS.MO, *s.m.*, exorcism.

E.XOR.CIS.TA, *s. 2 gen.*, exorcist, exorcizer.

E.XOR.CI.ZAR, *v.*, to exorcise, to conjure.

E.XOR.TAR, *v.*, to exhort.

E.XÓ.TI.CO, *adj.*, exotic, foreign, odd, extravagant.

E.XO.TIS.MO, *s.m.*, exoticism.

EX.PAN.DIR, *v.*, to expand, to enlarge, to unfold, to extend.

EX.PAN.SÃO, *s.f.*, expansion, expansiveness.

EX.PAN.SI.O.NIS.TA, *s. 2 gen.*, expansionist.

EX.PAN.SI.VI.DA.DE, *s.f.*, expansivity.

EX.PAN.SI.VO, *adj.*, expansive.

EX.PA.TRI.A.ÇÃO, *s.f.*, expatriation, banishment, exile.

EX.PA.TRI.AR, *v.*, to expatriate, to exile, to banish, to deport.

EX.PEC.TA.DOR, *s.m.*, expectant, expectator.

EX.PEC.TA.TI.VA, *s.f.*, expectancy, expectation.

EX.PEC.TO.RAN.TE, *s.m., adj., Med.*, expectorant.

EX.PEC.TO.RAR, *v.*, to expectorate.

EX.PE.DI.ÇÃO, *s.f.*, expedition, despatch; trek, excursion.

EX.PE.DI.EN.TE, *s.m.*, expedient, office hours, working day, business.

EX.PE.DIR, *v.*, to expel, to eject, to dispatch, to express.

EX.PE.LIR, *v.*, to expel, to eject.

EX.PE.RI.ÊN.CIA, *s.f.*, experience, practice, knowledge, proof.

EX.PE.RI.MEN.TA.ÇÃO, *s.f.*, experimentation, experiment, test, trial.

EX.PE.RI.MEN.TAR, *v.*, to experiment, to try, to test.

EX.PE.RI.MEN.TO, *s.m.*, experiment, trial, test, proof.

EX.PI.A.ÇÃO, *s.f.*, expiation, atonement.

EX.PI.AR, *v.*, to expiate, to atone for, to pay for a crime.

EX.PI.A.TÓ.RI.O, *adj.*, expiatory; *bode expiatório*: scapegoat.

EX.PI.RAR, *v.*, to expire, to die, to end, to exhale, to conclude.

EX.PLA.NA.ÇÃO, *s.f.*, explanation, explication, elucidation.

EX.PLA.NAR, *v.*, to explain, to elucidate, to explicate.

EX.PLI.CA.ÇÃO, *s.f.*, explication, explanation, elucidation.

EX.PLI.CAR, *v.*, to explain, to elucidate, to explicate, to interpret.

EX.PLI.CÁ.VEL, *adj.*, explainable, explicable.

EX.PLI.CI.TAR, *v.*, to make explicit.

EX.PLÍ.CI.TO, *adj.*, explicit.

EX.PLO.DIR, *v.*, to explode, to blast, to detonate, to blow-up.

EX.PLO.RA.ÇÃO, *s.f.*, exploration, investigation.

EX.PLO.RAR, *v.*, to explore, to search, to inquire into.

EX.PLO.RA.TÓ.RI.O, *adj.*, exploratory, exploring.

EX.PLO.SÃO, *s.f.*, explosion, blast, outburst, detonation.

EX.PLO.SI.VO, *s.m.*, explosive.

EX.PO.EN.TE, *s. 2 gen.*, exponent (important person); *s.m., Mat.*, exponent.

EX.POR, *v.*, to expose, to lay out, to exhibit, to show, to display.

EX.POR.TA.ÇÃO, *s.f.*, exportation, export.

EX.POR.TA.DOR, *s.m.*, exporter; *adj.*, exporting.

EX.POR.TAR, *v.*, to export.

EX.PO.SI.ÇÃO, *s.f.*, exposition, exhibition, explanation, interpretation.

EX.PO.SI.TOR, *s.m.*, exhibitor; exposer.

EX.POS.TO, *s.m.*, something exposed; *adj.*, exposed.

EX.PRES.SÃO, *s.f.*, expression, utterance, countenance,

EXPRESSAR   ••• 187 •••   EXUMAR

term, phrase, sentence.

EX.PRES.SAR, *v.*, to express.

EX.PRES.SI.O.NIS.MO, *s.m., Art.*, expressionism.

EX.PRES.SI.O.NIS.TA, *s. 2 gen.*, expressionist.

EX.PRES.SI.VI.DA.DE, *s.f.*, expressiveness.

EX.PRES.SO, *s.m.*, express, courier; *adj.*, express, plain, explicit.

EX.PRI.MIR, *v.*, to express, to speak, to utter.

EX.PRO.PRI.A.ÇÃO, *s.f.*, expropriation, dispossession.

EX.PRO.PRI.AR, *v.*, to expropriate.

EX.PUG.NAR, *v.*, to expugn, to storm.

EX.PUL.SÃO, *s.f.*, expulsion, exclusion, dismissal.

EX.PUL.SAR, *v.*, to expel, to drive away, to turn out, to dismiss.

EX.PUL.SO, *adj.*, expelled, driven away.

EX.PUR.GAR, *v.*, to expurgate, to purge, to clean.

EX.PUR.GO, *s.m.*, purge.

ÊX.TA.SE, *s.f.*, ecstasy, rapture, trance.

EX.TA.SI.AR, *v.*, enrapture, to ravish; *extasiar-se*: to be entranced.

EX.TEM.PO.RÂ.NE.O, *adj.*, extemporaneous, extempory.

EX.TEN.SÃO, *s.f.*, extension, stretching, length, range, enlargement.

EX.TEN.SO, *adj.*, extensive, ample, vast.

EX.TE.NU.A.DO, *adj.*, exhausted, worn out.

EX.TE.NU.AN.TE, *adj.*, exhausting, debilitating.

EX.TE.NU.AR, *v.*, to extenuate, to exhaust, to weaken, to wear out; *extenuar-se*: to lose strength, to be debilitate.

EX.TE.RI.OR, *s.m.*, exterior, outside; *adj.*, exterior, external, outer.

EX.TE.RI.O.RI.DA.DE, *s.f.*, appearance; externality, exteriority.

EX.TE.RI.O.RI.ZA.ÇÃO, *s.f.*, externalization, manifestation.

EX.TE.RI.O.RI.ZAR, *v.*, to express, to utter.

EX.TER.MI.NA.ÇÃO, *s.f.*, extermination.

EX.TER.MI.NAR, *v.*, to exterminate, to destroy, to annihilate.

EX.TER.MÍ.NIO, *s.m.*, extermination, extirpation.

EX.TER.NA.TO, *s.m.*, day-school.

EX.TER.NO, *adj.*, external, exterior, outside.

EX.TIN.ÇÃO, *s.f.*, extinction, destruction.

EX.TIN.GUIR, *v.*, to extinguish, to put out, to stifle.

EX.TIN.TO, *adj.*, extinct, extinguished, dead, defunct.

EX.TIN.TOR, *s.m.*, extinguisher.

EX.TIR.PAR, *v.*, to extirpate.

EX.TOR.QUIR, *v.*, to extort.

EX.TOR.SÃO, *s.f.*, extortion, exaction, blackmail, usurpation.

EX.TRA, *s. 2 gen.*, extra; *adj.*, extra, additional, supplementary.

EX.TRA.ÇÃO, *s.f.*, extraction, derivation, drawing.

EX.TRA.CON.JU.GAL, *adj.*, extramarital.

EX.TRA.CUR.RI.CU.LAR, *adj.*, extracurricular.

EX.TRA.DI.ÇÃO, *s.f.*, extradition.

EX.TRA.DI.TAR, *v.*, to extradite.

EX.TRA.IR, *v.*, to extract, to draw out, to withdraw.

EX.TRA.JU.DI.CI.AL, *adj.*, extrajudicial.

EX.TRA.O.FI.CI.AL, *adj.*, unofficial.

EX.TRA.OR.DI.NÁ.RIO, *adj.*, extraordinary, unusual, extra.

EX.TRA.PO.LA.ÇÃO, *s.f.*, extrapolation.

EX.TRA.PO.LAR, *v.*, to extrapolate.

EX.TRA.TER.RE.NO, *adj.*, extraterrestrial.

EX.TRA.TER.RES.TRE, *s. 2 gen.*, extraterrestrial being; *adj.*, extraterrestrial.

EX.TRA.TO, *s.m.*, extract, summary.

EX.TRA.VA.GÂN.CIA, *s.f.*, extravagance, garishness, absurdity, folly.

EX.TRA.VA.GAN.TE, *s. 2 gen.*, an extravagant person; *adj.*, extravagant.

EX.TRA.VA.SAR, *v.*, to flow out, to extravasate.

EX.TRA.VI.A.DO, *adj.*, astray, lost, amiss, depraved, corrupt.

EX.TRA.VI.AR, *v.*, to lead astray, to misplace, to put out of the way.

EX.TRA.VI.O, *s.m.*, misleading, deviation, miscarriage, loss.

EX.TRE.MA-UN.ÇÃO, *s.f., Rel.*, extreme unction.

EX.TRE.MI.DA.DE, *s.f.*, extremity, edge, end, border; misery.

EX.TRE.MIS.MO, *s.m.*, extremism.

EX.TRE.MIS.TA, *s. 2 gen.*, extremist.

EX.TRE.MO, *s.m.*, extreme, extremity, end; *adj.*, extreme, last, final, utmost.

EX.TRE.MO O.RI.EN.TE, *s.m.*, Far East.

EX.TRO.VER.SÃO, *s.f.*, extroversion.

EX.TRO.VER.TI.DO, *s.m.*, extrovert.

E.XU, *s.m., Bras.*, Orisha in the Yoruba religion; *pop.*, the devil (erroneously).

E.XU.BE.RÂN.CIA, *s.f.*, exuberance, exuberancy.

E.XU.BE.RAN.TE, *adj.*, exuberant, rich, copious, luxuriant.

E.XUL.TA.ÇÃO, *s.f.*, exultation, jubilation.

E.XUL.TAN.TE, *adj.*, exultant.

E.XUL.TAR, *v.*, to exult, to crow, to rejoice, to jubilate.

E.XU.MA.ÇÃO, *s.f.*, exhumation.

E.XU.MAR, *v.*, to exhume, to disinter.

E

F, *s.m.*, the sixth letter of the Portuguese alphabet.
FÃ, *s. 2 gen.*, fan, admirer, devotee.
FÁ, *s.m., Mús.*, fa, the fourth musical note.
F.A.B., *abrev.* of *Força Aérea Brasileira*: Brazilian Air Force.
FÁ.BRI.CA, *s.f.*, factory, workshop, mill, plant, industry.
FA.BRI.CA.ÇÃO, *s.f.*, fabrication, manufacture, production.
FA.BRI.CAN.TE, *s. 2 gen.*, manufacturer, producer, maker, fabricant.
FA.BRI.CAR, *v.*, to make, to produce, to manufacture, to edify.
FA.BRIL, *adj.*, industrial.
FÁ.BU.LA, *s.f.*, fable, tale, legend.
FA.BU.LO.SO, *adj.*, fabulous.
FA.CA, *s.f.*, knife.
FA.CA.DA, *s.f.*, stab, thrust with a knife.
FA.ÇA.NHA, *s.f.*, achievement, effort, performance, exploit.
FA.CÃO, *s.m.*, large knife.
FAC.ÇÃO, *s.f.*, feat, faction, part, wing, set.
FA.CE, *s.f.*, face, side, look, visage, appearance, surface.
FAC.CI.O.SO, *adj.*, factious, factional, partial.
FA.CEI.RO, *adj.*, cheerful, coquettish, foppish, graceful.
FA.CE.TA.DO, *adj.*, faceted.
FA.CHA.DA, *s.f.*, front, face, façade.
FA.CHO, *s.m.*, torch; lighthouse; lantern, signal light, beam.
FA.CI.AL, *adj.*, facial.
FÁ.CIL, *adj.*, easy, simple, fluent, ready, flowing, fast.
FA.CI.LI.DA.DE, *s.f.*, facility, easiness, simplicity, readiness, agility.
FA.CI.LI.TA.DOR, *s.m.*, facilitator; *adj.*, facilitative.
FA.CI.LI.TAR, *v.*, to facilitate, make easy.
FA.CÍ.NO.RA, *s.m.*, criminal, villain, gangster.
FAC-SÍ.MI.LE, *s.m.*, facsimile.
FAC.TÍ.VEL, *adj.*, feasible.
FAC.TÓ.TUM, *s.m.*, factotum.
FA.CUL.DA.DE, *s.f.*, faculty, capacity, ability, talent, reach, power.
FA.CUL.TAR, *v.*, to grant, to permit, to facilitate.
FA.CUL.TA.TI.VO, *adj.*, facultative, optional.
FA.DA, *s.f.*, fairy.
FA.DA.DO, *adj.*, predestinate, fated, destined.
FA.DAR, *v.*, to predestine, to fate; to presage, augur; to endow with (talent).
FA.DI.GA, *s.f.*, fatigue, tiredness, lassitude.
FA.DIS.TA, *s. 2 gen., Mús.*, player or singer of fados.
FA.DO, *s.m.*, destiny, fate; *Mús.*, Portuguese folk song, dance and music.
FA.GO.TE, *s.m., Mús.*, bassoon.
FA.GO.TIS.TA, *s. 2 gen., Mús.*, bassoonist.
FA.GUEI.RO, *adj.*, tender, affectionate, loving, sweet, pleasant; happy.
FA.GU.LHA, *s.f.*, spark, flash.
FAI.A, *s.f., Bot.*, beech tree.
FAI.NA, *s.f.*, work, labour.
FAI.SÃO, *s.m., Zool.*, pheasant.
FA.ÍS.CA, *s.f.*, spark, flashing, gleam, flake, fire.
FA.IS.CAN.TE, *adj.*, flickering, scintillating, sparkling.
FA.IS.CAR, *v.*, to spark, to flash, to sparkle, to scintillate, to coruscate.
FAI.XA, *s.f.*, band, banner, strip, range, belt, ribbon, bandage; zone, area.
FA.JU.TO, *adj., gír.*, of poor quality, shoddy, fake.
FA.LA, *s.f.*, speech, talk, conversation, discourse, words, allocution.
FA.LA.ÇÃO, *s.f., pop.*, discourse, speech, idle talk.
FA.LÁ.CI.A, *s.f.*, fallacy.
FA.LA.CI.O.SO, *adj.*, fallacious.
FA.LA.DO, *adj.*, talked over, famous.
FA.LA.DOR, *s.m.*, talker, indiscret; *adj.*, talkative, indiscret, communicative.
FA.LAN.GE, *s.f.*, phalanx, phalange, digital bones of the hand or foot.
FA.LAN.TE, *adj.*, speaking, talking.
FA.LAR, *v.*, to speak, to say, to tell, to communicate, to talk, to express.
FA.LA.TÓ.RI.O, *s.m.*, voices, whisper, slander, diatribe.
FAL.CÃO, *s.m., Zool.*, falcon, hawk.
FAL.CA.TRU.A, *s.f.*, fraud, imposture.
FAL.CO.A.RI.A, *s.f.*, falconry.
FAL.CO.EI.RO, *s.m.*, falconer, hawker.
FA.LE.CER, *v.*, to decease, to die, to expire.
FA.LE.CI.DO, *s.m.*, deceased; *adj.*, dead, deceased.
FA.LE.CI.MEN.TO, *s.m.*, death, dying, decease, departure.
FA.LÊN.CIA, *s.f.*, insolvency, bankruptcy, crash, collapse.
FA.LÉ.SI.A, *s.f.*, sea cliff.
FA.LHA, *s.f.*, crack, fissure, rent, error, imperfection, fault.
FA.LHAR, *v.*, to fail, to err, to miss.
FA.LHO, *adj.*, faulty, flawed, bad, lame.
FÁ.LI.CO, *adj.*, phallic.
FA.LI.DO, *adj.*, broken, bankrupt.
FA.LIR, *v.*, to fail, to break, to be unable to pay.
FA.LÍ.VEL, *adj.*, fallible.
FA.LO, *s.m.*, phallus.
FAL.SÁ.RI.O, *s.m.*, falsifier, forger, perjurer.
FAL.SE.AR, *v.*, to falsify, to misrepresent, to deceive, to cheat, to betray.
FAL.SE.TE, *s.m., Mús.*, falsetto.
FAL.SI.DA.DE, *s.f.*, falseness, falsehood, mendacity, hypocrisy.
FAL.SI.FI.CA.ÇÃO, *s.f.*, falsification, forgery.
FAL.SI.FI.CA.DOR, *s.m.*, forger, falsifier; *adj.*, falsifying.
FAL.SI.FI.CAR, *v.*, to falsify, to counterfeit, to fake, to forge.
FAL.SO, *adj.*, untrue, false, fraudulent, spurious, fake, wrong, sham, simulate.
FAL.SO-TES.TE.MU.NHO, *s.m.*, false witness.
FAL.TA, *s.f.*, need, lack, absence, privation, deficiency, failure.

FALTAR · 189 · FAVORÁVEL

FAL.TAR, *v.*, to miss, to be absent, to fail, to neglect, to omit.
FAL.TO, *adj.*, needy, necessitous, lacking.
FAL.TO.SO, *adj.*, faulty, delinquent.
FA.MA, *s.f.*, fame, glory, reputation.
FA.MÉ.LI.CO, *adj.*, hungry, famished, ravenous.
FA.MÍ.LIA, *s.f.*, family, folk, people, tribe, clan, lineage.
FA.MI.LI.AR, *adj.*, familiar, domestic, familial; known.
FA.MI.LIA.RI.DA.DE, *s.f.*, familiarity, intimacy, frankness.
FA.MI.LI.A.RI.ZA.ÇÃO, *s.f.*, domestication, familiarization.
FA.MI.LIA.RI.ZAR, *v.*, familiarize, to become familiar, to habituate, to vulgarize.
FA.MIN.TO, *adj.*, hungry, starving, famishing, voracious.
FA.MO.SO, *adj.*, famous, renowned, famed, noted.
FA.NÁ.TI.CO, *s.m.*, fanatic, fan, bigot; *adj.*, fanatic, fan, bigoted.
FA.NA.TIS.MO, *s.m.*, fanaticism, bigotry, passion.
FA.NA.TI.ZAR, *v.*, to fanaticize.
FAN.DAN.GO, *s.m.*, fandango (a lively Spanish dance).
FAN.FAR.RA, *s.f.*, fanfare; brass band.
FAN.FAR.RÃO, *s.m.*, boaster, braggart; *adj.*, boastful, rowdy.
FAN.FAR.RI.CE, *s.f.*, boasting, blow, fanfaronade, bragging.
FA.NHO, *adj.*, *Bras.*, the same that *fanhoso*.
FA.NHO.SO, *adj.*, snuffling, nasal.
FA.NI.QUI.TO, *s.m.*, *pop.*, nervous fit, fainting fit.
FAN.TA.SI.A, *s.f.*, fantasy, imagination, fancy, illusion, extravagancy.
FAN.TA.SI.AR, *v.*, to fantasy, to fancy, to daydream.
FAN.TA.SI.O.SO, *adj.*, fantastic, fanciful; imaginary.
FAN.TA.SIS.TA, *s. 2 gen.*, dreamer; imaginative person, whimsical; *adj.*, fanciful, fantastic.
FAN.TAS.MA, *s.f.*, phantom, ghost, apparition.
FAN.TAS.MA.GÓ.RI.CO, *adj.*, phantasmagoric.
FAN.TÁS.TI.CO, *adj.*, fantastic, imaginary, unreal.
FAN.TO.CHE, *s.m.*, puppet, marionette.
FAN.ZO.CA, *s. 2 gen.*, *pop.*, enthusiastic fan, junkie.
FA.QUEI.RO, *s.m.*, knife box.
FA.QUIR, *s.m.*, fakir, fakeer.
FA.RA.Ó, *s.m.*, Pharaoh.
FA.RA.Ô.NI.CO, *adj.*, pharaonic.
FAR.DA, *s.f.*, uniform, military dress.
FAR.DAR, *v.*, to uniform, to put in uniform.
FAR.DO, *s.m.*, bundle, pack, package, bale, bunch.
FA.RE.JAR, *v.*, to scent, to smell out, to trace.
FA.RE.LEN.TO, *adj.*, crumbly, mealy.
FA.RE.LO, *s.m.*, bran, crumb, sawdust, pollard.
FAR.FA.LHAN.TE, *adj.*, rustling.
FAR.FA.LHAR, *v.*, to rustle.
FA.RIN.GE, *s.f.*, pharynx.
FA.RI.NÁ.CE.O, *adj.*, farinaceous; *farináceos (pl.)*: starchy foods.
FA.RIN.GE, *s.f.*, *Anat.*, pharynx.
FA.RIN.GI.TE, *s.f.*, *Med.*, pharyngitis.
FA.RI.NHA, *s.f.*, flour, meal, breadstuff, farina; *farinha de aveia*, *s.f.*: oatmeal.
FA.RI.NHEN.TO, *adj.*, floury.
FA.RI.SEU, *s.m.*, Pharisee.
FAR.MA.CÊU.TI.CO, *s.m.*, pharmacist, apothecary, druggist.
FAR.MÁ.CIA, *s.f.*, pharmacy, pharmaceutics, drugstore.
FÁR.MA.CO, *s.m.*, medicine.
FAR.MA.CO.LO.GI.A, *s.f.*, pharmacology.
FAR.MA.CO.LÓ.GI.CO, *adj.*, pharmacologic, pharmacological.
FAR.NEL, *s.m.*, packed meal, lunch box (sack, bag).

FA.RO, *s.m.*, sense of smell; *fig.*, nose.
FA.RO.ES.TE, *s.m.*, *Bras.*, western (movie, motion picture).
FA.RO.FA, *s.f.*, manioc flour.
FA.RO.FEI.RO, *s.m.*, boaster, braggart; *fam.*, beach bum; *adj.*, boastful, bragging.
FA.ROL, *s.m.*, lighthouse, light, warning light, pharos, seamark.
FA.RO.LEI.RO, *s.m.*, lighthouse keeper.
FAR.PA, *s.f.*, splinter, barb.
FAR.PA.DO, *adj.*, barbed, pronged; *arame ~*: barbed wire.
FAR.RA, *s.f.*, binge, fun, revelry, bust, bender.
FAR.RA.PO, *s.m.*, rag, ragamuffin, shred, clout, junk.
FAR.RE.AR, *v.*, to rave, to carouse.
FAR.RIS.TA, *s. 2 gen.*, carouser, raver; *adj.*, fun-loving.
FAR.SA, *s.f.*, farce, burlesque, satirical composition.
FAR.SAN.TE, *s. 2 gen.*, buffoon, trickster, fake.
FAR.SES.CO, *adj.*, *Teat.*, farcical.
FAR.TAR, *v.*, to satiate, saturate, to surfeit, to sate.
FAR.TO, *adj.*, satiated, full, satisfied, tired, weary.
FAR.TU.RA, *s.f.*, abundance, profusion, wealth, plenty.
FAS.CÍ.CU.LO, *s.m.*, fascicle.
FAS.CI.NA.ÇÃO, *s.f.*, fascination, enchantment, captivation, charm.
FAS.CI.NAN.TE, *adj.*, fascinating, charming, amazing.
FAS.CI.NAR, *v.*, to fascinate, to captivate, to attract, to dazzle.
FAS.CÍ.NI.O, *s.m.*, fascination.
FAS.CIS.MO, *s.m.*, Fascism.
FAS.CIS.TA, *s. 2 gen.*, Fascist.
FA.SE, *s.f.*, phase, stage, period, phasis, aspect, side, angle.
FAS.TI.DI.O.SO, *adj.*, fastidious, critical; tedious, troublesome.
FAS.TÍ.GI.O, *s.m.*, apex, summit.
FAS.TI.O, *s.m.*, lack of appetite, disgust, aversion, dislike.
FA.TAL, *adj.*, fatal, fateful, ruinous, deadly.
FA.TA.LI.DA.DE, *s.f.*, fatality, destiny, disaster.
FA.TA.LIS.MO, *s.m.*, fatalism.
FA.TA.LIS.TA, *s. 2 gen.*, fatalist; *adj.*, fatalistic.
FA.TAL.MEN.TE, *adv.*, fatally.
FA.TI.A, *s.f.*, slice, chop, chip, piece, section.
FA.TI.AR, *v.*, to slice.
FA.TÍ.DI.CO, *adj.*, fatidic, fateful.
FA.TI.GAN.TE, *adj.*, tiresome, wearing, tiring; tedious.
FA.TI.GAR, *v.*, to fatigue, to tire, to bore, to wear out, to exhaust, to flog.
FA.TO, *s.m.*, fact, deed, event, occurence.
FA.TOR, *s.m.*, factor.
FÁ.TUO, *adj.*, fugacious, transitory, fatuous; foolish, vain, smug.
FA.TU.RA, *s.f.*, invoice, bill, voucher.
FA.TU.RA.MEN.TO, *s.m.*, invoicing, billing; *Com.*, turnover.
FA.TU.RAR, *v.*, to invoice, to bill.
FAU.NA, *s.f.*, fauna.
FAU.NO, *s.m.*, *Mit.*, faunus, faun.
FAUS.TO, *s.m.*, ostentation, pomp, luxury; *adj.*, fortunate, lucky.
FAUS.TO.SO, *adj.*, sumptuous, pompous, luxurious.
FA.VA, *s.f.*, *Bot.*, broad bean, fava bean.
FA.VE.LA, *s.f.*, slum, shanty-town.
FA.VE.LA.DO, *adj.*, slum dweller.
FA.VO, *s.m.*, honeycomb; sweet.
FA.VOR, *s.m.*, favor, help, benefit, privilege, attention, courtesy, regard, interest.
FA.VO.RÁ.VEL, *adj.*, favourable, suitable, propitious, benefic.

FAVORECER
190
FERIDA

FA.VO.RE.CER, *v.*, to favour, to help, to aid, to support, to patronize.

FA.VO.RE.CI.DO, *s.m.*, beneficiary; *adj.*, favourit, protected, supported.

FA.VO.RI.TIS.MO, *s.m.*, favoritism, preference, nepotism.

FA.VO.RI.TO, *adj.*, favorite, fond, preferred.

FA.XI.NA, *s.f.*, cleaning, fascine.

FA.XI.NEI.RO, *s.m.*, cleaner.

FAZ DE CON.TA, *s.m., 2 num.*, make-believe; imagination, fantasy.

FA.ZEN.DA, *s.f.*, farm, ranch, estate, property; public finances, treasury; cloth, textile material.

FA.ZEN.DEI.RO, *s.m.*, farmer, landholder.

FA.ZER, *v.*, to make, to do, to build, to produce, to perform, to form, to write.

FAZ-TU.DO, *s.m., 2 num.*, handy man, factotum.

FÉ, *s.f.*, faith, creed, belief, conviction, persuasion, trust, credit.

FE.AL.DA.DE, *s.f.*, ugliness.

FE.BO, *s.m.*, phoebus, the sun.

FE.BRE, *s.f.*, fever, temperature, pyrexia.

FE.BRIL, *adj.*, febril, feverous, feverish, agitated.

FE.CAL, *adj.*, fecal, faecal, excremental.

FE.CHA.DO, *adj.*, closed, close, shut, shut in, locked, unopened.

FE.CHA.DU.RA, *s.f.*, lock.

FE.CHA.MEN.TO, *s.m.*, closure, closing, stopping.

FE.CHAR, *v.*, to close, to shut, to shut up, to lock up, to unite, to finish, to stop, to belt.

FE.CHO, *s.m.*, bolt, latch; device to shut or lock; conclusion; *Arquit.*, keystone.

FE.CHO, *s.m.*, bolt, latch, clasp, clip, fastener, conclusion, closure.

FÉ.CU.LA, *s.f.*, fecula, starch.

FE.CUN.DA.ÇÃO, *s.f.*, fecundation, fertilization.

FE.CUN.DAR, *v.*, to fecundate, to fructify, to fertilize, to develop.

FE.CUN.DI.DA.DE, *s.f.*, fecundity, abundance, pregnancy, productivity.

FE.CUN.DO, *adj.*, fecund, fertile; *fig.*, creative, inventive.

FE.DE.LHO, *s.m., pop.*, brat, bantling.

FE.DEN.TI.NA, *s.f.*, stink, stench.

FE.DER, *v.*, to stink, to reek, to smell badly, to bore.

FE.DE.RA.ÇÃO, *s.f.*, federation, union, federacy, confederation, alliance.

FE.DE.RAL, *adj.*, federal, allied.

FE.DE.RA.LIS.MO, *s.m.*, federalism.

FE.DE.RA.LI.ZA.ÇÃO, *s.f.*, federalization.

FE.DE.RA.LI.ZAR, *v.*, to federalize.

FE.DE.RA.TI.VO, *adj.*, federative, federal.

FE.DI.DO, *adj.*, fetid, stinking.

FE.DOR, *s.m.*, stink, stench.

FE.DO.REN.TO, *adj.*, fetid, stinking, rammy.

FEED.BACK, *s.m., Ingl.*, feedback.

FEI.ÇÃO, *s.f.*, feature, aspect, appearance, look, manner, humour.

FEI.JÃO, *s.m.*, bean; ~ *preto*: black bean.

FEI.JO.A.DA, *s.f., Cul., Bras.*, dish of beans and pork.

FEI.JO.AL, *s.m.*, field of beans.

FEI.JO.EI.RO, *s.m., Bot.*, bean plant, kidney bean.

FEI.O, *adj.*, ugly, disagreeable, insightly, haggish.

FEI.O.SO, *adj.*, unsightly, plain.

FEI.RA, *s.f.*, fair, street market.

FEI.RAN.TE, *s. 2 gen.*, stalholder, marketer, merchant.

FEI.TA, *s.f.*, action, occasion, opportunity; *certa* ~: once.

FEI.TI.ÇA.RI.A, *s.f.*, witchcraft, sorcery, magic, charm.

FEI.TI.CEI.RA, *s.f.*, witch, sorceress.

FEI.TI.CEI.RO, *s.m.*, sorcerer, wizard, enchanter.

FEI.TI.ÇO, *s.m.*, witchcraft, sorcery, enchantment, charm, magic power.

FEI.TI.O, *s.m.*, shape, make, fabric, pattern, manner.

FEI.TO, *s.m.*, fact, deed, act, action; *adj.*, made, done, built, finished, fashioned, ready, prepared.

FEI.TOR, *s.m.*, administrator, manager, foreman.

FEI.TO.RI.A, *s.f.*, factorship, management; commercial establishment, factory.

FEI.TU.RA, *s.f.*, make up, work, structure; production.

FEI.U.RA, *s.f.*, ugliness; indignity.

FEI.XE, *s.m.*, sheaf, bundle, faggot, cluster, bunch, handful.

FEL, *s.m.*, bile, gall.

FELDS.PA.TO, *s.m., Min.*, feldspar.

FE.LI.CI.DA.DE, *s.f.*, happiness, bliss, contentment, felicity, luckiness.

FE.LÍ.DE.O, *s.m., Zool.*, feline (cat family); *adj.*, feline.

FE.LI.CI.TA.ÇÃO, *s.f.*, felicitation, congratulation.

FE.LI.CI.TAR, *v.*, to felicitate, to congratulate, to make happy, to compliment.

FE.LI.NO, *adj.*, feline, felid.

FE.LIZ, *adj.*, happy, lucky, fortunate, blessed, felicitous, fain, sunny, blissful.

FE.LI.ZAR.DO, *adj.*, lucky fellow.

FE.LIZ.MEN.TE, *adv.*, happily, fortunately.

FEL.PA, *s.f.*, nap; down; felt, fur, pile.

FEL.PU.DO, *adj.*, fluffy, downy.

FEL.TRO, *s.m.*, felt.

FÊ.MEA, *s.f.*, female.

FE.MI.NI.LI.DA.DE, *s.f.*, femininity, womanishness, feminineness.

FE.MI.NI.NO, *adj.*, female, feminine, womanly, womanlike.

FE.MI.NIS.MO, *s.m.*, feminism.

FE.MI.NIS.TA, *s. 2 gen.*, feminist.

FÊ.MUR, *s.m., Anat.*, femur, thighbone.

FEN.DA, *s.f.*, crack, fissure, chink, chap, gap, cleft.

FEN.DER, *v.*, to split, to cleave, to cut.

FE.NE.CER, *v.*, to end, to finish; to die out, to terminate; to die.

FE.NÍ.CIO, *s.m., adj.*, Phoenician.

FE.NIL, *s.m., Quím.*, phenyl.

FÊ.NIX, *s.f.*, phoenix.

FE.NO, *s.m.*, hay.

FE.NOL, *s.m., Quím.*, phenol, carbolic acid.

FE.NO.ME.NAL, *adj.*, phenomenal, extraordinary, remarkable, wonderful.

FE.NO.ME.NA.LI.DA.DE, *s.f.*, quality of phenomenal, remarkability.

FE.NÔ.ME.NO, *s.m.*, phenomenon.

FE.NO.ME.NO.LO.GI.A, *s.f.*, phenomenology.

FE.NO.ME.NO.LÓ.GI.CO, *adj.*, phenomenological.

FE.RA, *s.f.*, wild animal, wild beast.

FÉ.RE.TRO, *s.m.*, funeral, funeral procession, grave, coffin.

FÉ.RIA, *s.f.*, weekday; salary, rest, recreation, repose.

FE.RI.A.DO, *s.m.*, holiday, feast day, vacation.

FÉRIAS, holidays, vacations.

FE.RI.DA, *s.f.*, wound, sore, trauma, hurt.

FERIDO ··· 191 ··· FILANTROPIA

FE.RI.DO, *s.m.*, injured person; *adj.*, wounded, hurt.
FE.RI.MEN.TO, *s.m.*, wound, trauma, injury.
FÉR.MI.O, *s.m.*, *Quím.*, fermium (radioactive metallic elemen).
FÉR.MION, *s.m.*, *Fis.*, fermion (subatomic particle).
FE.RIR, *v.*, to wound, to hurt, to injure, to bruise, to beat.
FER.MEN.TA.ÇÃO, *s.f.*, fermentation, leavening, working.
FER.MEN.TAR, *v.*, to leaven, to ferment, to yeast.
FER.MEN.TO, *s.m.*, ferment, leaven, yeast.
FE.RO.CI.DA.DE, *s.f.*, ferocity, ferociousness.
FE.ROZ, *adj.*, ferocious, wild, savage, fierce.
FER.RA.DO, *adj.*, shod (horse); *fig.*, *fam.*, falling apart; ~ *no sono*: fast asleep; *gír.*, very difficult situation.
FER.RA.DU.RA, *s.f.*, horseshoe.
FER.RA.GEM, *s.f.*, hardware, iron tools.
FER.RA.MEN.TA, *s.f.*, tool, instrument, utensil, implement.
FER.RA.MEN.TAL, *s.m.*, tool kit.
FER.RÃO, *s.m.*, sting, prickle, ferret.
FER.RA.RI.A, *s.f.*, ironworks, iron mill.
FER.REI.RO, *s.m.*, smith, blacksmith, forger.
FER.RE.NHO, *adj.*, ironlike, inflexible; tenacious, obstinate.
FÉR.REO, *adj.*, ferrous, iron, ferric.
FER.RO, *s.m.*, *Quím.*, iron (symbol: Fe); cutting blade; tool, implement; ~ *de passar*: pressing iron; *pop.*, worry; *ferros* (*pl.*): chains.
FER.RO.A.DA, *s.f.*, sting, prick.
FER.RO.AR, *v.*, to sting, to prickle.
FER.RO.LHO, *s.m.*, bolt, push bolt, door bolt, latch.
FER.RO.SO, *adj.*, ferrous.
FER.RO-VE.LHO, *s.m.*, scrapyard, scrap metal; junk, scrap.
FER.RO.VI.A, *s.f.*, railway, railroad.
FER.RO.VI.Á.RIO, *s.m.*, railway man, railroader.
FER.RU.GEM, *s.m.*, rust, rustiness, ferric oxyde.
FÉR.TIL, *adj.*, fertile, fruitful, fructuous, fecund.
FER.TI.LI.DA.DE, *s.f.*, fertility, fruitfulness, prolificacy.
FER.TI.LI.ZA.ÇÃO, *s.f.*, fertilization.
FER.TI.LI.ZAN.TE, *s.m.*, fertilizer, manure.
FER.TI.LI.ZAR, *v.*, to fertilize, to fecundate, to impregnate, to fructify.
FER.VEN.TE, *adj.*, boiling, ebullient; fervent; ardent.
FER.VER, *v.*, to boil, to cook, to seethe.
FER.VI.LHAR, *v.*, to boil; to simmer; *fig.*, to effervesce, bubble; to be very vivacious.
FER.VOR, *s.m.*, boiling, seething, ebulition, heat, hotness.
FER.VO.RO.SO, *adj.*, fervent; devoted, vehement.
FER.VU.RA, *s.f.*, ebullition, boiling; *fig.*, fervour, agitation.
FES.TA, *s.f.*, party, feast, feasting, entertainment; *Boas Festas!*: a Merry Christmas and happy New Year!
FES.TAN.ÇA, *s.f.*, big party, revelry, celebration.
FES.TEI.RO, *s.m.*, host, entertainer; *adj.*, party-going, merrymaking.
FES.TE.JAR, *v.*, to feast, to celebrate, to entertain, to commemorate.
FES.TE.JO, *s.m.*, feast, festivity, celebration, frolic, entertainment.
FES.TIM, *s.m.*, feast, party, banquet; *bala de* ~: blank cartridge.
FES.TI.VAL, *s.m.*, festival.
FES.TI.VI.DA.DE, *s.f.*, festivity, celebration, feast.
FES.TI.VO, *adj.*, festive, joyful, cheerful.
FE.TAL, *adj.*, *US* fetal, *UK* foetal.
FE.TO, *s.m.*, *US* fetus, *UK* foetus.
FEU.DAL, *s.m.*, *adj.*, feudal, feudalistic.

FEU.DA.LIS.MO, *s.m.*, feudalism.
FEU.DA.TÁ.RI.O, *s.m.*, feudatory, vassal; *adj.*, feudatory, feudal.
FEU.DO, *s.m.*, feud, feudal; vassalage.
FE.VE.REI.RO, *s.m.*, February.
FE.ZES, *s.f.*, *pl.*, feces, excrement.
FI.A.ÇÃO, *s.f.*, spinning, spinnery.
FI.A.DO, *s.m.*, trusting, trustful; varn, filament; *adj.*, on credit, trusting; spun.
FI.A.DOR, *s.m.*, warrantor, truster, guarantor.
FI.AM.BRE, *s.m.*, ham, cold ham; food for a trip.
FI.AN.ÇA, *s.f.*, security, bail, pledge, warrant, deposit, responsibility.
FI.AN.DEI.RA, *s.f.*, spinster, female spinner; *Zool.*, spinneret.
FI.A.PO, *s.m.*, fine thread.
FI.AR, *v.*, to spin, to weave, to guarantee, to give security.
FI.AS.CO, *s.m.*, fiasco, failure, washout, fizzle, frost.
FI.BRA, *s.f.*, fibre, fiber, filament, nerve, energy, strength.
FI.BRI.LA.ÇÃO, *s.f.*, fribrillation.
FI.BRI.LAR, *adj.*, fibrillar.
FI.BRO.SE, *s.f.*, *Med.*, fibrosis.
FI.BRO.SO, *adj.*, fibrose, fibrous.
FI.CAR, *v.*, to remain, to stay, to stand, to tarry, to rest, to sojourn.
FIC.ÇÃO, *s.f.*, fiction, invention, legend, romance.
FIC.CI.O.NAL, *adj.*, *Lit.*, fictional.
FIC.CI.O.NIS.TA, *s. 2 gen.*, *Lit.*, fictionist.
FI.CHA, *s.f.*, card, counter, check, chip.
FI.CHA.DO, *adj.*, on file; *ser* ~ *na polícia*: to have a police record.
FI.CHAR, *v.*, to register, to annotate, to mark, to note down, to record, to card.
FI.CHÁ.RIO, *s.m.*, card index, card registry, file.
FIC.TÍ.CIO, *adj.*, fictitious, imaginary, unreal, fabulous.
FI.DAL.GO, *s.m.*, noble, peer.
FI.DAL.GUI.A, *s.f.*, nobility, the nobles.
FI.DE.DIG.NI.DA.DE, *s.f.*, trustworthiness, reliability.
FI.DE.DIG.NO, *adj.*, trustworthy, reliable; authentical.
FI.DE.LI.DA.DE, *s.f.*, fidelity, fealty, faithfulness, loyalty, integrity.
FI.DU.CI.Á.RI.O, *s.m.*, fiduciary, trustee; *adj.*, fiduciary, fiducial.
FI.EL, *s.m.*, follower, *Rel.*, *fiéis* (*pl.*): churchgoers; *adj.*, faithful, loyal, true, trusty.
FI.EL.MEN.TE, *adv.*, faithfully.
FI.GA, *s.f.*, charm, talisman.
FÍ.GA.DO, *s.m.*, *Anat.*, liver.
FI.GO, *s.m.*, fig (fruit).
FI.GUEI.RA, *s.f.*, *Bot.*, fig tree.
FI.GU.RA, *s.f.*, figure, form.
FI.GU.RA.DO, *adj.*, figurative, figured.
FI.GU.RAN.TE, *s. 2 gen.*, *Teat.*, *Cin.*, extra.
FI.GU.RÃO, *s.m.*, big shot, bigwig.
FI.GU.RAR, *v.*, to figure, to portray, to draw, to shape; *Teat.*, *Cin.*, to act as an extra.
FI.GU.RA.TI.VO, *adj.*, figurative, representative.
FI.GU.RI.NIS.TA, *s.f.*, clothes designer.
FI.GU.RI.NO, *s.m.*, model, fashion plate.
FI.JI, *s.*, Fiji.
FI.LA, *s.f.*, file, line, row, queue, rank, tier.
FI.LA.MEN.TO, *s.m.*, filament, fibre, string.
FI.LAN.TRO.PI.A, *s.f.*, philanthropy, goodwill.

FILANTRÓPICO ··· 192 ··· FLÁCIDO

FI.LAN.TRÓ.PI.CO, *adj.*, philanthropic.
FI.LAN.TRO.PO, *s.m.*, philanthropist.
FI.LÃO, *s.m., Min.*, lode, vein; *fig.*, opportunity.
FI.LAR, *v.*, to fasten, to grusp; *fam.*, to cadge.
FI.LAR.MÔ.NI.CA, *s.f.*, Philharmonic.
FI.LAR.MÔ.NI.CO, *adj., Mús.*, philharmonic.
FI.LA.TE.LI.A, *s.f.*, philately.
FI.LÉ, *s.m.*, filet, steak.
FI.LEI.RA, *s.f.*, row, rank, tier, range, line, string.
FI.LE.TE, *s.m.*, thin thread; *Arquit.*, fillet; filament.
FI.LHA, *s.f.*, daughter.
FI.LHA.RA.DA, *s.f.*, large family, many sons and daughters.
FI.LHO, *s.m.*, son, descendant; offspring; *filhos pl.*: children.
FI.LHO.TE, *s.m.*, nestling, native, descendant.
FI.LI.A.ÇÃO, *s.f.*, affiliation, filiation, descent, adoption.
FI.LI.AL, *s.f.*, branch, branch office or establishment.
FI.LI.AR, *v.*, to adopt, to affiliate, to branch out.
FI.LI.GRA.NA, *s.f.*, filigrane.
FI.LI.PI.NAS, *s.*, Philippines.
FI.LI.PI.NO, *s.m., adj.*, Filipino.
FIL.MA.DO.RA, *s.m.*, movie camera.
FIL.MA.GEM, *s.f.*, filming, motion picture shot.
FIL.MAR, *v.*, to film, to shoot.
FIL.ME, *s.m.*, film, movie, motion picture.
FIL.MO.GRA.FI.A, *s.f.*, filmography.
FIL.MO.TE.CA, *s.f.*, collection of films; film library.
FI.LO, *s.m., Biol.*, phylum.
FI.LÓ.LO.GO, *s.m.*, philologist.
FI.LO.LO.GI.A, *s.f.*, philology.
FI.LO.SO.FAL, *adj.*, philosophic, philosophical.
FI.LO.SO.FAR, *v.*, to philosophize.
FI.LO.SO.FI.A, *s.f.*, philosophy.
FI.LO.SÓ.FI.CO, *adj.*, philosophic, philosophical.
FI.LÓ.SO.FO, *s.m.*, philosopher.
FIL.TRA.DO, *s.m.*, filtrated.
FIL.TRA.DOR, *adj.*, filtering.
FIL.TRA.ÇÃO, *s.f.*, filtration.
FIL.TRA.GEM *s.f.*, filtration.
FIL.TRAR, *v.*, to filter, to filtrate, to percolate.
FIL.TRO, *s.m.*, filter, strainer, percolator.
FIM, *s.m.*, end, conclusion, termination, ending, expiration, closure.
FI.MO.SE, *s.f., Med.*, phimosis.
FI.NA.DO, *s.m.*, deceased, dead, defunct; *adj.*, dead, defunct.
FI.NAL, *s.m.*, conclusion, end, finish, terminal; *adj.*, last, terminal, terminative.
FI.NA.LI.DA.DE, *s.f.*, purpose, end, goal, finality, effect.
FI.NA.LIS.TA, *s. 2 gen.*, finalist; *adj.*, finalist.
FI.NA.LI.ZA.ÇÃO, *s.f.*, conclusion, termination, finalization.
FI.NA.LI.ZA.DO, *adj.*, finished.
FI.NA.LI.ZAR, *v.*, to finish, to terminate, to conclude, to accomplish.
FI.NAL.MEN.TE, *adv.*, finally, at last, lastly.
FI.NAN.ÇAS, *s.f., pl.*, finances, funds capital.
FI.NAN.CEI.RA.MEN.TE, *adv.*, financially.
FI.NAN.CEI.RO, *adj.*, financial.
FI.NAN.CIA.MEN.TO, *s.m.*, financing.
FI.NAN.CI.AR, *v.*, to finance, to provide capital for, to support.
FI.NAN.CIS.TA, *s. 2 gen.*, financier.
FIN.CAR, *v.*, to stick, to plunge, to drive in.
FIN.DAR, *v.*, to finish, to conclude, to complete, to terminate.

FIN.DÁ.VEL, *adj.*, terminable.
FIN.DO, *adj.*, finished, ended, over.
FI.NE.ZA, *s.f.*, slimness, thinness, gracefulness, perfection, delicacy.
FIN.GI.DO, *adj.*, insincere, false, feigned.
FIN.GI.MEN.TO, *s.m.*, simulation, hypocrisy, dissimulation.
FIN.GIR, *v.*, to pretend, to simulate, to dissimulate, to feign.
FI.NI.DA.DE, *s.f., Filos.*, finiteness, finitude, finite.
FI.NI.TO, *s.m.*, finite.
FI.NI.TU.DE, *s.m.*, finitude, finite nature.
FIN.LAN.DÊS, *adj., s.m.*, Finn, Finnish.
FIN.LÂN.DI.A, *s.*, Finland.
FI.NO, *adj.*, thin, slim, slender, thread, string; delicate, gentle, pure.
FI.NU.RA, *s.f.*, slimness, thinness; fineness, refinement.
FI.O, *s.m.*, thread, twine, varn; file, row, line, string.
FI.OR.DE, *s.m.*, fiord, fjord.
FIR.MA, *s.f.*, firm, business; signature, seal.
FIR.MA.ÇÃO, *s.f.*, act of signing.
FIR.MA.MEN.TO, *s.m.*, sky, heaven, firmament.
FIR.MAR, *v.*, to firm, to fix, to set, to secure.
FIR.ME, *adj.*, firm, fixed, strong, rigid, stable.
FIR.ME.ZA, *s.f.*, firmness, steadiness, fortitude, fixedness.
FIS.CAL, *s.m.*, custom officer; inspector, overseer; *adj. 2 gen.*, fiscal.
FIS.CA.LI.ZA.ÇÃO, *s.f.*, fiscalization, control, inspection.
FIS.CA.LI.ZAR, *v.*, to fiscalize, to subject to fiscal control, to inspect, to examine.
FIS.CO, *s.m.*, public revenue, public treasury.
FIS.GA.DA, *s.f.*, stabbing pain, sharp pain.
FIS.GAR, *v.*, to hook, to catch, to gaff.
FÍ.SI.CA, *s.f.*, physics.
FÍ.SI.CO, *s.m.*, constitution, build, physique, physicist; *adj.*, physical, material, personal, corporeal.
FÍ.SI.CO-QUÍ.MI.CA, *s.f.*, physicochemistry.
FI.SIO.LO.GI.A, *s.f.*, physiology.
FI.SI.O.LÓ.GI.CO, *adj.*, physiologic, physiological.
FI.SI.O.LO.GIS.MO, *s.m., Pol.*, self-interest.
FI.SIO.NO.MI.A, *s.f.*, physio(g)nomy, face, semblance, look, brow, aspect.
FI.SI.O.NO.MIS.TA, *s. 2 gen.*, physiognomist.
FI.SI.O.TE.RA.PEU.TA, *s. 2 gen.*, physiotherapist.
FI.SIO.TE.RA.PI.A, *s.f.*, physiotherapy.
FIS.SÃO, *s.f.*, fission.
FIS.SU.RA, *s.f.*, chink, split, crack, rime, fissure.
FIS.SU.RA.DO, *adj.*, fissured; *col.*, anxious, mad about.
FIS.SU.RAR, *v.*, to crack.
FÍS.TU.LA, *s.f., Med.*, fistula.
FI.TA, *s.f.*, ribbon, band, string, snood, ferret; tape.
FI.TAR, *v.*, to stare, to gaze, to eye, to envisage.
FI.TO, *s.m.*, target, aim, mark.
FI.VE.LA, *s.f.*, buckle, clasp, loop.
FI.XA.ÇÃO, *s.f.*, fixation, fixing, fastening.
FI.XA.DO, *adj.*, fixed.
FI.XA.DOR, *s.m.*, hairspray, *Quím.*, fixing agent, fixative; *adj.*, fixative
FI.XA.MEN.TE, *adv.*, fixedly.
FI.XAR, *v.*, to fasten, to attach, to fix, to firm, affix, to steady.
FI.XO, *adj.*, fixed, firm, stable, steady, durable.
FLA.CI.DEZ, *s.f.*, flaccidity.
FLÁ.CI.DO, *adj.*, flaccid, flabby.

FLAGELADO ··· 193 ··· FOLHETIM

FLA.GE.LA.DO, *s.m.*, flagellate; *adj.*, flagellate, tortured.
FLA.GE.LAN.TE, *adj.*, flagellant.
FLA.GE.LAR, *v.*, to flagellate.
FLA.GE.LO, *s.m.*, scourge, whip, punishment, calamity, plague.
FLA.GRAN.TE, *s.m.*, moment, instant, chance; *adj.*, flagrant, ardent, pressing, urgent.
FLA.GRAR, *v.*, to glow, to burn, to inflame.
FLA.MA; *s.f.*, flame, blaze; ardour,
FLAM.BAR, *v.*, to buckle; *Fr., Cul.*, to flambé.
FLA.ME.JAN.TE, *adj.*, flaming, ablaze; flashy, alight.
FLA.ME.JAR, *v.*, to flame, to blaze, to burn, to glow.
FLA.MEN.CO, *s.m., adj.*, flamenco.
FLA.MEN.GO, *s.m., adj.*, Flemish.
FLÂ.MU.LA, *s.f.*, pennant, banner, small flame.
FLAN.CO, *s.m.*, flank, side.
FLA.NE.LA, *s.f.*, flannel.
FLAN.QUE.AR, *v.*, to flank; to attack in the flank.
FLASH-BACK, *s.m., Ingl.*, flash-back.
FLA.TU.LÊN.CI.A, *s.f.*, flatulence.
FLAU.TA, *s.f., Mús.*, pipe, flute.
FLAU.TIM, *s.m., Mús.*, piccolo.
FLAU.TIS.TA, *s. 2 gen.*, flutist, flute player.
FLE.BI.TE, *s.f., Med.*, phlebitis.
FLE.CHA, *s.f.*, arrow, spire, dart, shaft, bolt.
FLE.CHA.DA, *s.f.*, arrow shot.
FLER.TAR, *v.*, to flirt.
FLER.TE, *s.m.*, flirt, flirtation.
FLEU.MA, *s.f.*, phlegm, apathy, indifference.
FLEU.MÁ.TI.CO, *adj.*, phlegmatic, phlegmatical, dull.
FLE.XÃO, *s.f.*, flexion, bending; *Gram.*, inflexion.
FLE.XI.BI.LI.DA.DE, *s.f.*, flexibility, flexibleness, pliancy.
FLE.XI.BI.LI.ZAR, *v.*, to make flexible, to make pliable.
FLE.XIO.NA.DO, *adj.*, inflected.
FLE.XIO.NAR, *v.*, to inflect, to bend, to deflect.
FLE.XÍ.VEL, *adj.*, flexible, versatile, deflective.
FLI.PE.RA.MA, *s.m.*, pinball machine.
FLO.CO, *s.m.*, flake, flock; fuzz; ~ *de milho*: cornflake.
FLOR, *s.f.*, flower, bloom, blossom.
FLO.RA, *s.f.*, Flora, the goddess of flowers; flora, botany.
FLO.RA.ÇÃO, *s.f.*, blooming.
FLO.RA.DO, *adj.*, covered with flowers.
FLO.RAL, *adj.*, floral.
FLO.RAR, *v.*, to flower, to bloom, to flourish.
FLOR-DE-LIS, *s.f., Bot.*, fleur-de-lis, lily flower.
FLO.RE.A.DO, *s.m.*, ornament, adornment; *adj.*, adorned with flowers, floriated, decorated.
FLO.RE.AR, *v.*, to flourish, to embellish, to bear flowers.
FLO.REI.O, *s.m.*, flourish.
FLO.REI.RA, *s.f.*, flowerpot, flower vase.
FLO.REN.TI.NO, *s.m., adj.*, Florentine.
FLO.RES.CÊN.CI.A, *s.f.*, florescence.
FLO.RES.CEN.TE, *adj.*, florescent, flowering, blooming.
FLO.RES.CER, *v.*, to blossom, to bud, to flower, to florish, to grow.
FLO.RES.TA, *s.f.*, forest, wood, wildwood.
FLO.RES.TAL, *adj.*, forestal, forestial.
FLO.RE.TE, *s.m.*, rapier.
FLO.RI.CUL.TOR, *s.m.*, floriculturist, florist; *adj.*, floricultural.
FLO.RI.CUL.TU.RA, *s.f.*, floriculture.
FLO.RI.DO, *adj.*, flowery, flowering; in flower.

FLO.RIR, *v.*, to flower, to blossom; to grow.
FLO.RIS.TA, *s. 2 gen.*, florist, flower seller; flower girl.
FLO.TI.LHA, *s.f., flotilla* (a small fleet).
FLU.ÊN.CIA, *s.f.*, fluency, flux, flow.
FLU.EN.TE, *adj.*, fluent, flowing, fluid, liquid, easy.
FLUI.DEZ, *s.f.*, fluidity, fluidness, fluency.
FLU.I.DI.FI.CAR, *v.*, to fluidify; to dilute.
FLUI.DO, *s.m.*, fluid, liquid, gas; *adj.*, fluid, fluent.
FLU.IR, *v.*, to flow, to run, to stream, to emanate.
FLÚ.OR, *s.m., Quím.*, fluor, fluorite.
FLU.O.RES.CÊN.CI.A, *s.f., Fís.*, fluorescence.
FLU.O.RES.CEN.TE, *adj., Fís.*, fluorescent.
FLU.TU.A.ÇÃO, *s.f.*, flotation, fluctuation, surging.
FLU.TU.AN.TE, *adj.*, fluctuant, floating, fluctuating.
FLU.TU.AR, *v.*, to float, to wave, to drift, to fluctuate, to roll.
FLU.TU.Á.VEL, *adj.*, fluctuable, floatable; navigable.
FLU.VI.AL, *adj.*, fluvial, fluviatic.
FLU.XO, *s.m.*, flow, stream, flood, flux.
FLU.XO.GRA.MA, *s.m.*, flow-chart.
FO.BI.A, *s.f.*, phobia; aversion.
FO.CA, *s.f., Zool.*, seal, phoca.
FO.CAL, *adj.*, focal.
FO.CA.LI.ZA.ÇÃO, *s.f.*, focalization.
FO.CA.LI.ZAR, *v.*, to focalize, to focus.
FO.CAR, *v.*, to focus, to focalize.
FO.CI.NHO, *s.m.*, muzzle, snout, mouth, trunk.
FO.CI.NHEI.RA, *s.f.*, muzzle.
FO.CO, *s.m.*, focus, focal point.
FO.DI.DO, *adj., col.*, screwed-up, ruined, looser; *vulg.*, fucked.
FO.FO, *adj.*, light, soft, smooth, mild, gentle.
FO.FO.CA, *s.f.*, gossip.
FO.FO.CAR, *v.*, to gossip.
FO.FO.QUEI.RO, *s.m.*, gossiper.
FO.FU.RA, *s.f.*, cuteness.
FO.GÃO, *s.m.*, stove, hearth, cooker.
FO.GA.REI.RO, *s.m.*, burner, cooker, little stove.
FO.GA.RÉU, *s.m.*, little flame; bonfire, torch.
FO.GO, *s.m.*, fire, blaze, energy, vigor, flame, conflagration; home.
FO.GO.SO, *adj.*, fiery, hot; flamming; ardent.
FO.GUEI.RA, *s.f.*, bonfire, fire, pyre.
FO.GUE.TE, *s.m.*, rocket; admonition.
FO.GUE.TEI.RO, *s.m.*, pyrotechnist.
FO.GUE.TÓ.RI.O, *s.m.*, noise of fireworks.
FOI.CE, *s.f.*, scythe, sickle, hedgebill.
FOL.CLO.RE, *s.m.*, folklore.
FOL.CLÓ.RI.CO, *adj.*, folkloric.
FO.LE, *s.m.*, bellows.
FÔ.LE.GO, *s.m.*, breath, wind, respiration, rest, relaxation.
FOL.GA, *s.f.*, pause, leisure, rest, repose, slackness.
FOL.GA.DO, *adj.*, loose, idle, lazy, broad, ample, baggy.
FOL.GUE.DO, *s.m.*, recreation; joke, prank; revelry, spree, frolic.
FO.LHA, *s.f.*, leaf, list, sheet, report, journal, paper, newspaper.
FO.LHA.DO, *s.m., Cul.*, puff paste, puff pastry; *adj.*, leaf-shaped, leafy.
FO.LHA.GEM, *s.f.*, foliage.
FO.LHAR, *v.*, to leaf, to cover with leaves.
FO.LHE.A.DO, *adj.*, foliaged, foliate, foliaceous.
FO.LHE.AR, *v.*, to leaf, to turn over the pages of a book.
FO.LHE.TIM, *s.m.*, newspaper serial; rag.

FOLHETO

•• 194 ••

FOSSILIZADO

FO.LHE.TO, *s.m.*, pamphlet, leaflet, prospectus, brochure.
FO.LHI.NHA, *s.f.*, calendar.
FO.LI.A, *s.f.*, merry-making, revelry, spree.
FO.LI.ÃO, *s.m.*, buffoon, reveller, merry-maker.
FO.LÍ.CU.LO, *s.m., Bot., Anat.*, follicle.
FO.ME, *s.f.*, hunger, famine, hungriness, scarcity.
FO.MEN.TA.DOR, *s.m.*, fomenter.
FO.MEN.TAR, *v.*, to foment, to promote, to develop.
FO.MEN.TO, *s.m.*, fomentation, incitement.
FO.MI.NHA, *adj., gír.*, avaricious, greedy, mean.
FO.NA.DOR, *adj.*, phonic; *aparelho ~*: speech apparatus.
FO.NE, *s.m.*, phone, receiver, telephone.
FO.NE.MA, *s.m.*, phoneme.
FO.NÉ.TI.CA, *s.f.*, phonetics.
FO.NÉ.TI.CO, *adj.*, phonetic.
FÔ.NI.CO, *adj.*, phonic.
FO.NO.AU.DI.O.LO.GI.A, *s.f.*, speech therapy.
FO.NO.AU.DI.Ó.LO.GO, *s.m.*, speech therapist.
FO.NO.GRA.FI.A, *s.f.*, phonography.
FO.NÓ.GRA.FO, *s.m.*, phonograph, victrola.
FO.NO.LO.GI.A, *s.f.*, phonology.
FO.NÔ.ME.TRO, *s.m.*, phonometer.
FON.TE, *s.f.*, fountain, font, origin, source, headspring.
FO.RA, *s.m.*, rejection, elimination; *adv.*, out, outside, outdoors, outlying, beyond, abroad, off, away; *prep.*, except.
FO.RA.GI.DO, *s.m.*, fugitive, refugee, absconder, outlaw; *adj.*, fugitive, flighty, erratic.
FO.RA.GIR, *v.*, to emigrate; foragir-se: to take shelter, to flee.
FO.RAS.TEI.RO, *s.m.*, foreigner, stranger, outlander; *adj.*, foreign, strange.
FOR.CA, *s.f.*, gallows, gibbet, scaffold.
FOR.ÇA, *s.f.*, force, strength, power, energy, vigour; fibre.
FOR.CA.DO, *s.m.*, fork, pitchfork.
FOR.ÇA.DO, *adj.*, compelled, obliged, compulsory.
FOR.ÇAR, *v.*, to force, to oblige, to impel, to compel, to constrain.
FOR.ÇA-TA.RE.FA, *s.f.*, task force.
FÓR.CEPS, *s.m., 2 num., Med.*, forceps.
FOR.ÇO.SA.MEN.TE, *adv.*, forcibly, necessarily.
FOR.ÇO.SO, *adj.*, forcible, necessary; vigorous, violent.
FO.REN.SE, *adj.*, forensic, judicial, judiciary.
FOR.JA, *s.f.*, forge, smithy, foundry.
FOR.JA.DO, *adj.*, forged, wrought; counterfeit, fabricated (news).
FOR.MA, *s.f.*, form, shape, configuration, structure, appearance, build; mould, last.
FOR.MA.ÇÃO, *s.f.*, formation, forming, development, origin, forming, arrangement.
FOR.MA.DO, *adj.*, formed, shaped; graduated.
FOR.MA.DOR, *s.m.*, former, moulder, modeller; *adj.*, forming, formative, shaping.
FOR.MAL, *adj.*, formal, conventional; solemn.
FOR.MAL.DE.Í.DO, *s.m., Quím.*, formaldehyde.
FOR.MA.LI.DA.DE, *s.f.*, formality, ceremony, etiquette, conventionalism.
FOR.MA.LIS.MO, *s.m.*, formalism, pedantry.
FOR.MA.LIS.TA, *s. 2 gen.*, formalist; *adj.*, formalistic, conventional.
FOR.MA.LI.ZAR, *v.*, to formalize.
FOR.MAN.DO, *s.m.*, finalist (college, school, course).
FOR.MÃO, *s.m.*, chisel, former.

FOR.MAR, *v.*, to form, to shape, to model, to instruct, to produce, to establish.
FOR.MA.TAR, *v.*, to format.
FOR.MA.TO, *s.m.*, format, shape, size.
FOR.MA.TU.RA, *s.f.*, formation, development, arrangement, graduation.
FOR.MI.DÁ.VEL, *adj.*, formidable.
FOR.MI.CI.DA, *s.m.*, poison for killing ants.
FOR.MI.GA, *s.f., Zool.*, ant, pismire.
FOR.MI.GA.MEN.TO, *s.m., Med.*, formication, pins and needles.
FOR.MI.GAR, *v.*, to formicate; to tingle.
FOR.MI.GUEI.RO, *s.m.*, anthill, ants'nest.
FOR.MOL, *s.m.*, formaldehyde.
FOR.MO.SO, *adj.*, beautiful, handsome, pretty, fair, comely.
FOR.MO.SU.RA, *s.f.*, beauty, handsomeness, prettiness.
FÓR.MU.LA, *s.f.*, formula, form.
FOR.MU.LA.ÇÃO, *s.f.*, formulation.
FOR.MU.LAR, *v.*, to formulate, to prescribe, to formul, to enounce.
FOR.MU.LÁ.RIO, *s.m.*, formulary, collection, form.
FOR.NA.LHA, *s.f.*, furnace, firebox, stove; forge.
FOR.NE.CE.DOR, *s.m.*, furnisher, supplier, contractor, provisioner.
FOR.NE.CER, *v.*, to furnish, to supply, to provide, to purvey, to stock.
FOR.NE.CI.MEN.TO, *s.m.*, furnishing, supply, supplying, delivery.
FOR.NI.CAR, *v.*, to fornicate, to afflict, to vex.
FOR.NO, *s.m.*, oven, hearth, stove, kiln.
FO.RO, *s.m.*, forum.
FOR.QUI.LHA, *s.f.*, pitchfork.
FOR.RA, *s.f., pop.*, revenge, retaliation.
FOR.RA.ÇÃO, *s.f.*, furring.
FOR.RA.GEM, *s.f.*, feed, forage, silage.
FOR.RAR, *v.*, to cover with, to face, to line, to case.
FOR.RO, *s.m.*, covering, doubling, lining, padding, ceiling; *adj.*, freed, emancipated.
FOR.RÓ, *s.m., pop.*, a popular dance in Brazil.
FOR.TA.LE.CER, *v.*, to fortify, to invigorate, to strengthen.
FOR.TA.LE.CI.MEN.TO, *s.m.*, strengthening, fortification; encouragement.
FOR.TA.LE.ZA, *s.f.*, fortress, fort, fortification.
FOR.TE, *s.m.*, fort, fortification, fortress; *adj.*, strong, vigorous, robust, valiant.
FOR.TI.FI.CAR, *v.*, to fortify, to make strong, to encourage.
FOR.TI.FI.CA.ÇÃO, *s.f.*, fortification.
FOR.TI.FI.CAN.TE, *s.m.*, tonic, fortifier; *adj.*, fortifying, invigorant.
FOR.TI.FI.CAR, *v.*, to fortify, to invigorate; fortificar-se: to become strong, to fortify oneself.
FOR.TUI.TO, *adj.*, fortuitous, accidental, casual.
FOR.TU.NA, *s.f.*, fortune, good luck, destiny, prosperity, success.
FOS.CO, *adj.*, tarnished, dim, dull, opaque.
FOS.FA.TO, *s.m., Quím.*, phosphate.
FOS.FO.RES.CÊN.CI.A, *s.f.*, phosphorescence.
FOS.FO.RES.CEN.TE, *adj.*, phosphorescent.
FÓS.FO.RO, *s.m., Quím.*, phosphorus; match.
FOS.SA, *s.f.*, cesspool, cesspit, sinkhole, gully.
FÓS.SIL, *s.m.*, fossil.
FOS.SI.LI.ZA.DO, *adj.*, fossilized, petrified.

FOSSILIZAÇÃO · 195 · FREQUENTADOR

FOS.SI.LI.ZA.ÇÃO, *s.f.*, fossilization, petrification.
FOS.SI.LI.ZAR, *v.*, to fossilize, petrify.
FOS.SO, *s.m.*, ditch, moat, trench.
FO.TO, *s.f.*, photo.
FO.TO.CÉ.LU.LA, *s.f.*, *Fís.*, photoelectric cell, photocell.
FO.TO.COM.PO.SI.ÇÃO, *s.f.*, *Art.*, photocomposition, filmsetting.
FO.TO.CÓ.PIA, *s.f.*, photocopy.
FO.TO.FO.BI.A, *s.f.*, *Med.*, photophobia.
FO.TO.GÊ.NI.CO, *adj.*, photogenic.
FO.TO.GRA.FAR, *v.*, to photograph, to shoot.
FO.TO.GRA.FI.A, *s.f.*, photography, snapshot, photo.
FO.TO.GRÁ.FI.CO, *adj.*, photographic, photographical.
FO.TÓ.GRA.FO, *s.m.*, photographer.
FO.TO.JOR.NA.LIS.MO, *s.m.*, photojournalism.
FO.TO.LI.TO.GRA.FI.A, *s.f.*, *art. Gráf.*, photolithography.
FO.TÔ.ME.TRO, *s.m.*, photometer.
FO.TO.MON.TA.GEM, *s.f.*, *Fot.*, photomontage, composite picture.
FÓ.TON, *s.m.*, *Fís.*, photon.
FO.TO.NO.VE.LA, *s.f.*, photostrip story.
FO.TOS.FE.RA, *s.f.*, photosphere.
FO.TO.TE.RA.PI.A, *s.f.*, *Med.*, phototherapy.
FO.TOS.SÍN.TE.SE, *s.f.*, photosynthesis.
FOX.TRO.TE, *s.m.*, foxtrot.
FOZ, *s.f.*, estuary, mouth of a river, outfall.
FRA.ÇÃO, *s.f.*, fraction, quantum; rupture, part, fragment.
FRA.CAS.SAR, *v.*, to fail, to break, to shatter, to miscarry.
FRA.CAS.SO, *s.m.*, crash, smash, failure, ruin, disaster.
FRA.CI.O.NA.MEN.TO, *s.m.*, fragmentation, fractionation, division.
FRA.CIO.NAR, *v.*, to shatter, to fragment, to divide, to split.
FRA.CI.O.NÁ.RI.O, *adj.*, fractionary, fractional.
FRA.CO, *adj.*, feeble, weak, faint, fragile, debile, slim, slender.
FRA.DE, *s.m.*, friar, monk.
FRA.GA.TA, *s.f.*, *Náut.*, frigate.
FRÁ.GIL, *adj.*, fragile, weak, frail, feeble, transitory.
FRA.GI.LI.DA.DE, *s.f.*, fragility, weakness, delicateness.
FRA.GI.LI.ZAR, *v.*, to make vulnerable.
FRAG.MEN.TA.ÇÃO, *s.f.*, fragmentation.
FRAG.MEN.TA.DO, *adj.*, fragmented.
FRAG.MEN.TAR, *v.*, to fragment, to break up, to shatter, to split.
FRAG.MEN.TO, *s.m.*, fragment, fraction, scrap, piece, part, portion.
FRA.GOR, *s.m.*, crash, loud repport.
FRA.GO.RO.SO, *adj.*, clamorous, noisy, loud.
FRA.GRÂN.CIA, *s.f.*, fragrance, flavor, perfume, pleasant scent.
FRA.GRA.NTE, *adj.*, fragrant, odoriferous, odorous, balmy.
FRA.JO.LA, *adj.*, *gír.*, elegant, dandyish.
FRAL.DA, *s.f.*, diaper, nappy, lap, flap, brim.
FRAM.BO.E.SA, *s.f.*, *Bot.*, raspberry (fruit).
FRAM.BO.E.SEI.RA, *s.f.*, raspberry bush.
· **FRANÇA**, *s.*, France.
FRAN.CA.MEN.TE, *adv.*, frankly, sincerely.
FRAN.CÊS, *s.m.*, *adj.*, French, Frenchman, Gaul.
FRÂN.CI.O, *s.m.*, *Quím.*, francium (symbol: Fr).
FRAN.CIS.CA.NO, *s.m.*, *adj.*, Franciscan; friar of the Franciscan order.
· **FRAN.CO**, *s.m.*, franc; monetary unit in France, Belgium and

Switzerland; *adj.*, frank, candid, outspoken.
FRAN.CO.A.TI.RA.DOR, *s.m.*, sniper.
FRAN.CO-BRA.SI.LEI.RO, *s.m.*, *adj.*, Franco-Brazilian.
FRAN.CO-CA.NA.DEN.SE, *s. 2 gen.*, *adj.*, Franco-Canadian.
FRAN.CÓ.FO.BO, *s.m.*, *adj.*, Francophobe.
FRAN.GA.LHO, *s.m.*, tatter, frazzle, rag.
FRAN.GO, *s.m.*, chicken, young cock.
FRAN.JA, *s.f.*, fringe, edging.
FRAN.JA.DO, *adj.*, fringed, fringy; *fig.*, affected, pretentious.
FRAN.JAR, *v.*, to fringe, to adorn with a lace; to decorate.
FRAN.QUE.A.DO, *s.m.*, franchise; *adj.*, patent; prepaid.
FRAN.QUE.AR, *v.*, to free, to exempt, to facilitate, to clear; to frank (from taxes or duties).
FRAN.QUE.ZA, *s.f.*, frankness, candour, sincerity, liberality.
FRAN.QUI.A, *s.f.*, postage, postage stamp, franchise, exemption, privilege.
FRAN.ZI.DO, *s.m.*, pleat, gathering; *adj.*, pleated, rugged, wrinkly.
FRAN.ZI.NO, *adj.*, slender; weak, frail, fine.
FRAN.ZIR, *v.*, to wrinkle, to plait, to pleat.
FRA.QUE.JAR, *v.*, to weaken, to lose courage, to succumb.
FRA.QUE.ZA, *s.f.*, weakness, debility, powerlessness.
FRA.SAL, *adj.*, phrasal.
FRAS.CO, *s.m.*, flask, bottle, flagon.
FRA.SE, *s.f.*, phrase, sentence, proposition, expression.
FRA.SE.A.DO, *s.m.*, phrasing.
FRA.SE.O.LO.GI.A, *s.f.*, phraseology.
FRA.SIS.TA, *s. 2 gen.*, phraseologist.
FRAS.QUEI.RA, *s.f.*, bottle rack, cellaret.
· **FRA.TER.NAL**, *adj.*, fraternal, brotherlike, brotherly.
FRA.TER.NI.DA.DE, *s.f.*, fraternity, brotherhood.
FRA.TER.NO, *adj.*, fraternal, brotherly.
FRA.TRI.CI.DA, *s. 2 gen.*, fratricide; *adj.*, fratricidal.
FRA.TRI.CÍ.DI.O, *s.m.*, fratricide; *fig.*, civil war.
FRA.TU.RA, *s.f.*, fracture, breaking; *Geol.*, faulting, rock fissure.
FRA.TU.RAR, *v.*, to fracture, to break.
FRAU.DA.DOR, *s.m.*, defrauder.
FRAU.DAR, *v.*, to defraud.
FRAU.DE, *s.f.*, swindle, fraud, hoax.
FRAU.DU.LEN.TO, *adj.*, fraudulent.
FRE.A.DA, *s.f.*, *pop.*, sudden braking.
FRE.AR, *v.*, to brake, to repress, to refrain, to control.
FRE.Á.TI.CO, *adj.*, *Geol.*, phreatic; *lençol ~*: water table.
REE.LAN.CE, *s. 2 gen.*, *Ingl.*, freelancer.
FRE.GUÊS, *s.m.*, customer, client, patron.
FRE.GUE.SI.A, *s.f.*, community, customers, parish, clientele.
FREI, *s.m.*, friar, monk.
FREI.O, *s.m.*, bridle, bit, brake, rein, repression.
FREI.RA, *s.f.*, nun, sister, religious.
FREI.XO, *s.m.*, *Bot.*, ash.
FRE.MEN.TE, *adj.*, roaring, thundering; thrilled.
FRE.MIR, *v.*, to roar, to tremble, to shudder, to vibrate.
FRÊ.MI.TO, *s.m.*, roar, thunder, shudder, clangour, thrill.
FRE.NE.SI, *s.m.*, frenzy, madness.
FRE.NÉ.TI.CO, *adj.*, frenetic, frenetical.
FREN.TE, *s.f.*, front, forefront, façade, face, head, front side, frontage.
FREN.TIS.TA, *s.m.*, *Bras.*, forecourt atendant; gas station attendant.
FRE.QUÊN.CIA, *s.f.*, frequency, periodicity, concourse.
FRE.QUEN.TA.DOR, *s.m.*, frequenter, visitor, regular; *adj.*,

FREQUENTAR · 196 · FUNCIONALISMO

frequenting, visiting.
FRE.QUEN.TAR, *v.*, to frequent, to attend, to visit.
FRE.QUEN.TE, *adj.*, frequent, recurrent, repeated.
FRES.CAL, *adj.*, fresh, new; saltish.
FRES.CO, *adj.*, fresh, new, recent, vigorous, green.
FRES.COR, *s.m.*, freshness, coolness; liveliness.
FRES.CU.RA, *s.f.*, freshness; *pop.*, vulgarity; *pop.*, picky, choosy.
FRES.TA, *s.f.*, slit, opening, gap, aperture.
FRE.TA.DO, *adj.*, chartered; *UK* hired (car).
FRE.TA.MEN.TO, *s.m.*, charter; *US* renting (car, truck, etc.), *UK* hiring.
FRE.TAR, *v.*, to charter, to freight,.*US* to rent, *UK* to hire.
FRE.TE, *s.m.*, freight, freightage, carriage, portage.
FREU.DI.A.NO, *s.m.*, *Psic.*, Freudian; *adj.*, Freudian.
FRI.A.GEM, *s.f.*, cold(ness), chill(ness).
FRIC.ÇÃO, *s.f.*, friction, attrition, rub, fret.
FRIC.CIO.NAR, *v.*, to rub, to grit.
FRI.CO.TE, *s.m.*, cunning, slyness, vanity.
FRI.EI.RA, *s.f.*, *Med.*, chilblain.
FRI.E.ZA, *s.f.*, coldness; *fig.*, indifference.
FRI.GI.DEI.RA, *s.f.*, frying pan.
FRI.GI.DEZ, *s.f.*, coldness; frigidity.
FRÍ.GI.DO, *adj.*, frigid; cold, frozen; indifferent.
FRI.GIR, *v.*, to fry, to cook in hot fat.
FRI.GO.RÍ.FI.CO, *s.m.*, freezer, refrigerator; *adj.*, frigorific, frigorifical.
FRI.LA, *s.* 2 *gen.*, *gir.*, freelance.
FRI.O, *s.m.*, cold, coldness, iciness, frost, low temperature; indifference; *adj.*, cold, icy, frosty, algid; indifferent.
FRI.O.REN.TO, *adj.*, sensitive to cold, chilly.
FRI.SA, *s.f.*, *Teat.*, box, dress box.
FRI.SA.DO, *adj.*, frizzled, curled, curly.
FRI.SAN.TE, *adj.*, fitting, accurate; *vinho* ~: sparkling wine.
FRI.SAR, *v.*, to nap, to curl, to emphasize.
FRI.SO, *s.m.*, frieze.
FRI.TAR, *v.*, to fry, to roast.
FRI.TAS, *s.f., pl., Cul.*, French fries.
FRI.TO, *adj.*, fried.
FRI.TU.RA, *s.f.*, fried food.
FRI.VO.LI.DA.DE, *s.f.*, frivolousness, futility, frivolity, emptiness, lightness.
FRÍ.VO.LO, *adj.*, frivolous, wanton, trivial, futil, light.
FRON.DO.SO, *adj.*, frondose, leafy.
FRO.NHA, *s.f.*, pillowcase, pillow.
FRONT, *s.m., Mil., Ingl.*, battle front.
FRON.TE, *s.f.*, forehead, head, brow.
FRON.TEI.RA, *s.f.*, frontier, border, bound, boundary, limit, mark.
FRON.TEI.RI.ÇO, *s.m.*, borderer; *adj.*, frontier, border line.
FRON.TEI.RO, *adj.*, frontier, bordering, facing, opposite.
FRON.TIS.PÍ.CI.O, *s.m.*, frontispiece.
FRO.TA, *s.f.*, fleet, navy, shipping.
FROU.XO, *adj.*, weak, feeble, slack, sluggish, lax.
FRU.FRU, *s.f.*, froufrou, frill.
FRU.GAL, *adj.*, frugal, sparing, moderate.
FRU.GA.LI.DA.DE, *s.f.*, frugality, frugalness, parsimony, economy.
FRU.GÍ.FE.RO, *adj.*, fructiferous, frugiferous.
FRU.I.ÇÃO, *s.f.*, fruition.
FRU.IR, *v.*, to enjoy, to find pleasure in; to usufruct.
FRUS.TRA.ÇÃO, *s.f.*, frustration, failure, defeat.

FRUS.TRA.DO, *s.m.*, a frustrated person; *adj.*, frustrate, disappointed.
FRUS.TRAN.TE, *adj.*, frustrating.
FRUS.TRAR, *v.*, to frustrate, to foil, to balk, to baffle, to defeat; to disappoint.
FRU.TA, *s.f.*, fruit, fruitage.
FRU.TA-DE-CON.DE, *s.f., Bot.*, sweetsop.
FRU.TEI.RA, *s.f.*, fruit bowl or plate.
FRU.TEI.RO, *s.m.*, fruit dealer, fruiterer; *adj.*, fruit-bearing, fruitful, fruit-loving.
FRU.TI.CUL.TOR, *s.m.*, pomologist, horticulturist, fruiter.
FRU.TI.CUL.TU.RA, *s.f., Bot.*, horticulture.
FRU.TÍ.FE.RO, *adj.*, fruitful, fructiferous, fecund, fertile.
FRU.TI.FI.CAR, *v.*, to fructify.
FRU.TÍ.VO.RO, *adj.*, frugivorous.
FRU.TO, *s.m.*, fruit, fruitage, offspring; produce, result, profit, gain.
FRU.TO.SE, *s.f., Quím.*, fruit sugar, fructose.
FU.BÁ, *s.m.*, flour, maize, corn meal.
FU.ÇA, *s.f., pop.*, nose, snout, face.
FU.ÇAR, *v.*, to root, to nuzzle, to meddle, to dig, to excavate.
FÚC.SI.A, *s.f., Bot.*, fuchsia.
FU.GA, *s.f.*, escape, flight, escapement, run, runaway.
FU.GA.CI.DA.DE, *s.f.*, fugacity.
FU.GAZ, *adj.*, transitory, rapid, fugacious, fugitive.
FU.GI.DA, *s.f.*, escape.
FU.GI.DI.O, *adj.*, fugacious, fugitive, evanescent, fleeting.
FU.GIR, *v.*, to flee, to run away, to escape, to run.
FU.GI.TI.VO, *s.m.*, fugitive, exile, deserter, runaway; *adj.*, fugitive, flying, fleeing.
FU.LA.NO, *s.m.*, (Mr.) So-and-so.
FU.LEI.RO, *adj., gir.*, worthless, corny, tacky.
FÚL.GI.DO, *adj.*, dazzling.
FUL.GIR, *v.*, to shine, to glitter; to dazzle.
FUL.GOR, *s.m.*, fulgency, effulgence, fulgor.
FUL.GU.RAN.TE, *adj.*, fulgurant, fulgurous, shining, sparkling.
FU.LI.GEM, *s.f.*, soot, smoke-black.
FU.LI.GI.NO.SO, *adj.*, fuliginous.
FUL.MI.NAN.TE, *adj.*, fulminant, sudden, detonating, fulminating, lethal.
FUL.MI.NAR, *v.*, to fulminate, to lighten, to strike, to kill instantaneously.
FU.LO, *adj.*, irritated, furious.
FÚL.VI.DO, *adj.*, fulvous, tawny.
FUL.VO, *adj.*, fulvous, tawny.
FU.MA.ÇA, *s.f.*, smoke, fume, vapour, steam, reek.
FU.MA.CEI.RA, *s.f.*, dense smoke.
FU.MA.CEN.TO, *adj.*, smoky.
FU.MAN.TE, *s.* 2 *gen.*, smoker; *adj.*, smoking, smoky.
FU.MAR, *v.*, to smoke.
FU.MA.REN.TO, *adj.*, smoky, vaporous, fumous.
FU.ME.GAN.TE, *adj.*, steaming, smoking, fuming.
FU.MI.CUL.TOR, *s.m.*, tobacco planter.
FU.MI.CUL.TU.RA, *s.f.*, cultivation of tobacco .
FU.MO, *s.m.*, tobacco; smoke, fume, vapour.
FUN.ÇÃO, *s.f.*, function, activity, operation, action, duty, occupation, performance.
FUN.CHO, *s.m., Bot.*, fennel.
FUN.CI.O.NAL, *adj.*, functional, functionary.
FUN.CIO.NA.LIS.MO, *s.m.*, functionalism, public functionaries, officialism.

FUNCIONAMENTO ·· 197 ·· FUZUÊ

FUN.CIO.NA.MEN.TO, *s.m.*, functioning, action, acting.
FUN.CIO.NAR, *v.*, to function, to work, to perform, to officiate.
FUN.CIO.NÁ.RIO, *s.m.*, employee, official, public functionary.
FUN.DA.ÇÃO, *s.f.*, foundation.
FUN.DA.DOR, *s.m.*, founder.
FUN.DA.MEN.TAL, *adj.*, fundamental, basic.
FUN.DA.MEN.TA.LIS.MO, *s.m., Rel.*, fundamentalism.
FUN.DA.MEN.TA.LIS.TA, *s. 2 gen.*, fundamentalist.
FUN.DA.MEN.TAR, *v.*, to found, to ground, to base, to establish, to evidence.
FUN.DA.MEN.TO, *s.m.*, basis, foundation, origin, motive, cause.
FUN.DAR, *v.*, to found, to establish, to build, to originate.
FUN.DE.AR, *v., Náut.*, to drop anchor.
FUN.DI.Á.RIO, *adj.*, agrarian, landed.
FUN.DI.ÇÃO, *s.f.*, foundry, smeltry, forge, melt.
FUN.DI.LHO, *s.m.*, seat of trousers, seat, botton.
FUN.DI.DOR, *s.m.*, founder, moulder.
FUN.DIR, *v.*, to found, to cast, to fuse, to melt, to liquefy, to unite.
FUN.DO, *s.m.*, bottom, remotest, profoundest, floor, depth, depress; *adj.*, deep, fordless, hollowed.
FUN.DU.RA, *s.f.*, profundity, depth, deepness.
FÚ.NE.BRE, *adj.*, funeral, mortuary, macabre.
FU.NE.RAL, *s.m.*, funeral, obsequies; *adj.*, funeral.
FU.NE.RÁ.RIO, *adj.*, funerary, funereal.
FU.NÉ.RE.O, *adj.*, funeral, mortuary.
FU.NES.TO, *adj.*, funest, fatal, sinister, disastrous, unlucky.
FUN.GAR, *v.*, to snuff, to sniff.
FUN.GI.CI.DA, *s.f.*, fungicide.
FUN.GO, *s.m.*, fungus, fungal.
FU.NI.CU.LAR, *s.m.*, funicular; *adj.*, funicular.
FU.NIL, *s.m.*, funnel, filler.
FU.NI.LA.RI.A, *s.f.*, a tinsmith's, panel beating.
FU.NI.LEI.RO, *s.m.*, tinsmith's shop; tinker, beater.
FU.RA.CÃO, *s.m.*, hurricane, ciclone, tornado, whirlwind.
FU.RA.DEI.RA, *s.f.*, drill, drilling machine.
FU.RA.DO, *adj.*, bored, pierced, perforated, punctured (tyre).
FU.RA.DOR, *s.m.*, awl, bradawl, perforator, bodkin.
FU.RA-GRE.VE, *s. 2 gen.*, strikebreaker, blackleg, scab.

FU.RÃO, *s.m., Zool.*, ferret.
FU.RAR, *v.*, to bore, to pierce, to drill, to perforate, to hole, to puncture.
FUR.GÃO, *s.m.*, delivery van.
FÚ.RIA, *s.f.*, fury, furiosity, furiousness, rage, extreme rage, rave.
FU.RI.O.SO, *adj.*, furious, mad, ragefull.
FUR.NA, *s.f.*, cavern, grotto, hole, den.
FU.RO, *s.m.*, hole, bore, boring, perforation, puncture, orifice.
FU.ROR, *s.m.*, furor, fury, rage, passion, tantrum, madness.
FUR.TA-COR, *adj.*, iridescent, changeable, chatoyant.
FUR.TAR, *v.*, to steal, to thieve, to rob, to pick.
FUR.TI.VO, *adj.*, stealthy, secret, clandestine.
FUR.TO, *s.m.*, theft, stealing, thievery, robbery.
FU.RÚN.CU.LO, *s.m., Med.*, furuncle, boil.
FU.SÃO, *s.f.*, fusion, melting, blend, amalgam, union.
FU.SE.LA.GEM, *s.f.*, fuselage.
FU.SÍ.VEL, *s.m.*, fuse; *adj.*, fusile, fusible.
FU.SO, *s.m.*, spindle, spool, screw.
FUS.TI.GAN.TE, *adj.*, vexatious.
FUS.TI.GAR, *v.*, to fustigate, to punish, to castigate.
FU.TE.BOL, *s.m.*, football, soccer.
FU.TE.BO.LIS.TA, *s. 2 gen.*, footballer, *US* soccer player.
FU.TE.BO.LÍS.TI.CO, *adj., Esp.*, of football/soccer.
FU.TE.VÔ.LEI, *s.m., Bras., Esp.*, a kind of volleyball played with the feet.
FÚ.TIL, *adj.*, futile, heedless, careless.
FU.TI.LI.DA.DE, *s.f.*, futility, triviality, frivolousness.
FU.TRI.CAR, *s.f.*, to rag, to intrigue, to gossip.
FU.TU.RIS.TA, *s. 2 gen., Art.*, futurist; *adj.*, futurist, futuristic.
FU.TU.RO, *s.m.*, future, destiny, fate; *adj.*, future, coming.
FU.XI.CAR, *v.*, to intrigue, to wrinkle, to gossip.
FU.XI.CO, *s.m.*, intrigue, plot.
FU.XI.QUEI.RO, *s.m.*, intriguer, intrigant.
FU.ZIL, *s.m.*, rifle.
FU.ZI.LA.MEN.TO, *s.m.*, shooting; execution.
FU.ZI.LAR, *v.*, to shoot, to fusillade.
FU.ZI.LA.RI.A, *s.f.*, shooting, continuous firing.
FU.ZI.LEI.RO, *s.m.*, fusileer, rifleman; ~ *naval*: marine.
FU.ZU.Ê, *s.m.*, noise, clamour, confusion; party.

G

G, s.m., the seventh letter of the Portuguese alphabet.
GA.BAR, v., to praise, to laud, to eulogize, to flatter.
GA.BAR.DI.NA, s.f., .gabardine.
GA.BA.RI.TA.DO, adj., qualified; high-calibre.
GA.BA.RI.TO, s.m., mould, form, model, pattern, gauge.
GA.BI.NE.TE, s.m., cabinet, study, closet, office, chamber, room.
GA.BO.LI.CE, s.f., bragging, boast.
GA.DA.NHA, s.m., scythe; col., hand.
GA.DO, s.m., cattle, stock, livestock, herd, drove.
GA.FA.NHO.TO, s.m., Zool., grasshopper, locust.
GA.FE, s.f., involuntary indiscretion.
GA.FI.EI.RA, s.f., Bras., pop., gaff, honky-tonk.
GA.GÁ, s 2 gen., decrepit, senile, enfeebled.
GA.GO, s.m., stutterer, stammerer; adj., stammering, stuttering.
GA.GUEI.RA, s.f., stuttering, stammering.
GA.GUE.JAR, v., to stammer, to stutter.
GA.GUEZ, s.f., stutter, stammer, impediment of speech.
GAI.A.TO, s.m., guy, rascal; adj., mischievous, joyous, naughty.
GAI.O.LA, s.f., cage, bird-cage, prison, coop.
GAI.TA, s.f., Mús., shepherd's pipe or flute, reed; gaita de folo: bagpipe.
GAI.TEI.RO, s.m., bagpipe, mouth-organ player.
GAI.VO.TA, s.f., Zool., gull, sea-gull, pewit-gull.
GA.LA, s.f., gala, pomp, solemnity, celebration.
GA.LÃ, s.m., leading gentleman; lover.
GA.LÁC.TI.CO, adj., Astron., galactic.
GA.LAN.TE, s 2 gen., gallant.
GA.LAN.TE.AR, v., to gallant.
GA.LAN.TEI.O, s.m., gallantry, courtesy, politeness.
GA.LÃO, s.m., galloon, strap; stripe.
GA.LAR.DÃO, s.m., reward, premium, recompense.
GA.LÁ.XIA, s.f., galaxy.
GA.LE.RI.A, s.f., gallery, art gallery, passage.
GA.LÉ, s.f., galley.
GA.LE.ÃO, s.m., Náut., galleon.
GA.LÊS, adj., s.m., Welsh.
GA.LE.GO, s.m., Galician.
GA.LE.NO, s.m., physician.
GA.LE.TO, s.m., spring chicken; Bras., Cul., roasted spring chicken.
GAL.GAR, v., to speed along, to climb, to pass over, to ascend, to pass beyond.
GA.LHA.DA, s.f., antlers, branches.
GA.LHAR.DI.A, s.f., gallantry, chivalry, bravery.
GA.LHAR.DO, adj., chivalrous, graceful, gallant, elegant, brave.
GA.LHO, s.m., branch of tree, limb, arm, twig, offshoot.
GA.LHO.FA, s.f., jest, mockery, joke.
GA.LI.CIS.MO, s.m., Gallicism.
GA.LI.NHA, s.f., hen, chicken, fowl, biddy.
GA.LI.NHA-D'AN.GO.LA, s.f., Zool., guinea fowl.
GA.LI.NHA.GEM, s.f., vulg., necking; philandering.
GA.LI.NHEI.RO, s.m., poultry yard, poulterer, henhouse.
GA.LO, s.m., cock, rooster, chanticleer.
GA.LO.PAN.TE, adj., galloping.
GA.LO.PAR, v., to gallop, to run by leaps.
GA.LO.PE, s.m., gallop.
GAL.PÃO, s.m., hangar, shed, haven, coach house.
GAL.VÂ.NI.CO, adj., Fís., galvanic, galvanical.
GAL.VA.NI.ZA.ÇÃO, s.f., galvanization, plating.
GAL.VA.NI.ZA.DO, adj., galvanized.
GAL.VA.NI.ZAR, v., to galvanize, to coat with metal, to zinc.
GA.MA, s.f., gamma (third letter of the Greek alphabet), scale, series of theories.
GA.MÃO, s.m., backgammon.
GA.MA.DO, adj., gír., hooked.
GA.MAR, v., gír., to love, to be hooked, to fall for.
GAM.BÁ, s.m., Zool., opossum.
GÂMBIA, s., Gambia (country).
GAM.BI.TO, s.m., gambit (chess).
GA.ME.LA, s.f., wooden trough, tray.
GA.ME.TA, s.m., Biol., gamete.
GA.MO, s.m., Zool., fallow deer, deer, buck, stag.
GA.NA, s.f., hunger, appetite, desire, will, ill will, spite.
GA.NA, s., Ghana (country).
GA.NÂN.CIA, s.f., greed, greediness, rapacity, gain, profit.
GA.NAN.CI.O.SO, adj., greedy, avaricious, profitable.
GAN.CHO, s.m., hook, grapple, crook, cramp.
GAN.DAI.A, s.f., fig., dissipation, vagrancy, idleness.
GÂN.GLI.O, s.m., Anat., ganglion (cell); Med., ganglion.
GAN.GOR.RA, s.f., seesaw, teeter, snare.
GAN.GRE.NA, s.f., Med., gangrene, necrosis.
GAN.GRE.NAR, v., Med., to gangrene, to canker, to pervert, to corrupt.
GAN.GRE.NO.SO, adj., gangrenous.
GAN.GUE, s.f., Bras., pop., gang.
GA.NHA.DOR, s.m., winner; adj., winning.
GA.NHA-PÃO, s.m., livelihood, means of living.
GA.NHAR, v., to acquire, to earn, to get, to obtain, to receive, to procure, to gain.
GA.NHO, s.m., gain, profit, acquisition, advantage, lucre.
GA.NI.DO, s.m., yelping, yelp, whine.
GA.NI.ME.DES, s.m., Mit., Astron., Ganymede.
GA.NIR, v., to bark, to yelp, to yap.
GAN.SO, s.m., Zool., goose, gander.
GA.RA.GEM, s.f., garage.
GA.RA.GIS.TA, s 2 gen., garage man.
GA.RA.NHÃO, s.m., stallion (horse); col., stud (man).
GA.RAN.TI.A, s.f., guarantee, guaranty, warranty, bail, pawn, responsibility.
GA.RAN.TI.DO, adj., warranted, assured, safe, secure.
GA.RAN.TIR, v., to guarantee, to warrant, to pledge, to secure.
GA.RA.PA, s.f., Bras., garapa, juice of sugar cane.

GARATUJA ··· 199 ··· GENIOSO

GA.RA.TU.JA, *s.f.*, scribble, scrawl, doodle.
GAR.BO, *s.m.*, elegance, garb, dress, gracefulness.
GAR.BO.SO, *adj.*, elegant, graceful, doggie; distinguished.
GAR.ÇA, *s.f.*, *Zool.*, heron.
GAR.ÇOM, *s.m.*, waiter, potman.
GAR.ÇO.NE.TE, *s.f.*, waitress, barmaid.
GAR.FA.DA, *s.f.*, forkful.
GAR.FAR, *v.*, to fork, to graft.
GAR.FO, *s.m.*, fork, pitchfork.
GAR.GA.LHA.DA, *s.f.*, laughter.
GAR.GA.LHAR, *v.*, to laugh loudly, to burst into laughter.
GAR.GA.LO, *s.m.*, neck of a bottle.
GAR.GAN.TA, *s.f.*, *Anat.*, throat; larynx, weasand; abyss, gulf.
GAR.GAN.TI.LHA, *s.f.*, neckband, necklace, collarband.
GAR.GA.RE.JAR, *v.*, to gargle.
GAR.GA.RE.JO, *s.m.*, gargling, gargle.
GÁR.GU.LA, *s.f.*, gargoyle.
GA.RI, *s. 2 gen.*, sweeper, street cleaner.
GA.RIM.PAR, *v.*, to prospect (for diamonds or other precious minerals).
GA.RIM.PEI.RO, *s.m.*, diamond or gold seeker, prospector.
GA.RIM.PO, *s.m.*, *Miner.*, prospecting.
GA.RO.A, *s.f.*, drizzle, mizzle.
GA.RO.AR, *v.*, to drizzle, to mizzle.
GA.RO.TA, *s.f.*, girl, baby, lass.
GA.RO.TA.DA, *s.f.*, a lot of boys or kids.
GA.RO.TO, *s.m.*, boy, lad, kid.
GA.ROU.PA, *s.f.*, *Zool.*, grouper.
GAR.RA, *s.f.*, claw, courage, talon, pounce.
GAR.RA.FA, *s.f.*, bottle, flask, carboy.
GAR.RA.FAL, *adj.*, bottle-shaped; large, big.
GAR.RA.FÃO, *s.m.*, large bottle, demijohn.
GAR.RAN.CHO, *s.m.*, brushwood; *col.*, bad handwriting, illegible writing.
GAR.RO.TE, *s.m.*, garrote, garrotte, iron collar, tourniquet.
GA.RU.PA, *s.f.*, haunch, croup, hindquarters (of a horse); rump, pillion.
GÁS, *s.m.*, gas, vapour, fume; animation.
GA.SEI.FI.CAR, *v.*, to gasify.
GA.SES, *s.m., pl.*, flatus.
GA.SO.DU.TO, *s.m.*, gas pipeline.
GA.SO.GÊ.NI.O, *s.m.*, gazogene, gasogene.
GA.SO.LI.NA, *s.f.*, petrol, gas.
GA.SÔ.ME.TRO, *s.m.*, gasmeter, gasometer .
GA.SO.SA, *s.f.*, soda, soda water, fizz.
GA.SO.SO, *adj.*, gaseous, gassy, aeriform.
GAS.TA.DOR, *s.m.*, waster, dissipater; *adj.*, wasteful, thriftless.
GAS.TAR, *v.*, to consume, to use up, to spend, to diminish, to deteriorate, to defray, to disburse.
GAS.TO, *s.m.*, expense, disbursement, expenditure, outlay, cost, waste.
GÁS.TRI.CO, *adj.*, gastric.
GAS.TRI.TE, *s.f.*, *Med.*, gastritis, gastric fever.
GAS.TRO.EN.TE.RI.TE, *s.f.*, *Med.*, gastroenteritis.
GAS.TRO.EN.TE.RO.LO.GI.A, *s.f.*, gastroenterology.
GAS.TRO.LO.GI.A, *s.f.*, gastrology.
GAS.TRO.NO.MI.A, *s.f.*, gastronomy.
GAS.TRO.NÔ.MI.CO, *adj.*, gastronomic, gastronomical.
GAS.TRÔ.NO.MO, *s.m.*, gastronome.
GA.TA, *s.f.*, *Zool.*, cat; beautiful girl.
GA.TI.LHO, *s.m.*, trigger; dog-head.

GA.TI.NHA, *s.f.*, kitten, pussy.
GA.TI.NHAR, *v.*, to go on all fours, to crawl.
GA.TI.NHO, *s.m.*, pussycat, kitty, cattling.
GA.TO, *s.m.*, *Zool.*, cat, tom-cat, miauler.
GA.TU.NO, *s.m.*, thief, stealer, robber, sharper.
GA.TU.RA.MO, *s.m.*, *Zool.*, tanager.
GA.U.CHES.CO, *adj.*, *Bras.*, relative to gauchos.
GA.Ú.CHO, *s.m.*, gaucho.
GA.VE.TA, *s.f.*, drawer, locker.
GA.VE.TEI.RO, *s.m.*, a drawer-runner.
GA.VI.ÃO, *s.m.*, *Zool.*, hawk, sparrow-hawk.
GAY, *s. 2 gen.*, *Ingl.*, homosexual, gay.
GA.ZE, *s.f.*, gauze, tissue.
GA.ZE.LA, *s.f.*, *Zool.*, gazelle.
GA.ZE.TA, *s.f.*, gazette, journal, newspaper.
GA.ZU.A, *s.f.*, picklock, skeleton-key.
GE.A.DA, *s.f.*, frost, hoar, hoar-frost.
GE.AR, *v.*, to frost, to chill, to freeze, to rime.
GÊI.SER, *s.m.*, geyser.
GEL, *s.m.*, gel.
GE.LA.DEI.RA, *s.f.*, refrigerator, freezer, cooler, ice-box.
GE.LA.DO, *s.m.*, sherbet, ice-cream; *adj.*, icy, frozen, frosty.
GE.LAR, *v.*, to freeze, to chill, to ice, to congeal.
GE.LA.TI.NA, *s.f.*, gelatin, jelly.
GE.LA.TI.NO.SO, *adj.*, gelatinous, jellying.
GE.LEI.A, *s.f.*, fruit-jelly, marmalade.
GE.LEI.RA, *s.f.*, ice-cap, glacier, ice-cave.
GE.LEI.RO, *s.m.*, ice manufacturer.
GÉ.LI.DO, *adj.*, gelid, icy; frozen.
GE.LO, *s.m.*, ice, chill.
GE.LO-SE.CO, *s.m.*, dry ice.
GE.MA, *s.f.*, egg yolk, yellow; shoot, germ.
GE.MA.DA, *s.f.*, eggnog (drink of eggs).
GÊ.MEO, *s.m.*, twin(s); *adj.*, twin.
GÊ.ME.OS, *s.m., pl.*, *Astron.*, *Astrol.*, Gemini.
GE.MER, *v.*, to groan, to moan; to lament, to wail, to bewail.
GE.MI.DO, *s.m.*, groan, moan, wailing, lamentation.
GE.MI.NA.DO, *adj.*, geminate, binate.
GEN.DAR.ME, *s.m.*, gendarme.
GE.NE, *s.m.*, *Biol.*, gene.
GE.NE.A.LO.GI.A, *s.f.*, genealogy.
GE.NE.A.LÓ.GI.CO, *adj.*, genealogical.
GE.NE.RAL, *s.m.*, general.
GE.NE.RA.LI.DA.DE, *s.f.*, generality, bulk.
GE.NE.RA.LIS.TA, *s. 2 gen.*, generalist.
GE.NE.RA.LI.ZAR, *v.*, to generalize.
GE.NÉ.RI.CO, *adj.*, generic, general.
GÊ.NE.RO, *s.m.*, class, order, kind, genus, sort, line, style.
GE.NE.RO.SI.DA.DE, *s.f.*, generosity, liberality, freeness.
GE.NE.RO.SO, *adj.*, generous, liberal, noble.
GÊ.NE.SE, *s.f.*, genesis.
GE.NÉ.TI.CA, *s.f.*, *Biol.*, genetics.
GE.NE.TI.CIS.TA, *s. 2 gen.*, geneticist.
GE.NÉ.TI.CO, *adj.*, genetic, genic.
GEN.GI.BRE, *s.f.*, *Bot.*, ginger.
GEN.GI.VA, *s.f.*, *Anat.*, gum.
GEN.GI.VI.TE, *s.f.*, *Med.*, gingivitis.
GE.NI.AL, *adj.*, ingenious, inspired, brilliant.
GE.NI.A.LI.DA.DE, *s.f.*, geniality, genius.
GÊ.NI.O, *s.m.*, genius, temper, talent, character, spirit.
GE.NI.O.SO, *adj.*, ill-tempered, ill-natured.

GENITAL ··· 200 ··· GLORIFICAÇÃO

GE.NI.TAL, *adj.*, genital, reproductive.
GE.NI.TI.VO, *s.m.*, genitive; *adj.*, genitive.
GE.NI.TOR, *s.m.*, genitor, father.
GE.NO.CÍ.DIO, *s.m.*, genocide.
GE.NO.MA, *s.m., Biol.*, genome.
GEN.RO, *s.m.*, son-in-law.
GEN.TA.LHA, *s.f.*, rabble, pleb, populace.
GEN.TE, *s.f.*, people, population, humanity, folk, nation.
GEN.TIL, *adj.*, gentle, noble, pleasant, agreeable, kind.
GEN.TI.LE.ZA, *s.f.*, courtesy, kindness, gentility, niceness.
GEN.TÍ.LI.CO, *s.m., Gram.*, the gentilic adjective (nationality); *adj., Gram.*, that indicates nationality.
GEN.TIL.MEN.TE, *adv.*, genteelly, gracefully.
GEN.TI.O, *s.m.*, pagan, heathen; *adj.*, pagan, savage.
GE.NU.FLE.XÓ.RI.O, *s.m.*, praying-chair, kneeler.
GE.NU.I.NI.DA.DE, *s.f.*, genuineness, authenticity.
GE.NU.Í.NO, *adj.*, genuin, authentic.
GE.O.CÊN.TRI.CO, *adj., Astron.*, geocentric.
GE.O.CI.ÊN.CI.AS, *s.f., pl.*, geoscience.
GE.O.DÉ.SI.CO, *adj.*, geodetic.
GE.O.GRA.FIA, *s.f.*, geography.
GE.O.GRÁ.FI.CO, *adj.*, geographic, geographical.
GE.Ó.GRA.FO, *s.m.*, geographer.
GE.O.LO.GI.A, *s.f.*, geology.
GE.Ó.LO.GO, *s.m.*, geologist.
GE.Ô.ME.TRA, *s. 2 gen.*, geometer.
GE.O.ME.TRI.A, *s.f.*, geometry.
GE.O.MÉ.TRI.CO, *adj.*, geometric, geometrical.
GE.O.PO.LÍ.TI.CA, *s.f.*, geopolitics.
GE.RA.ÇÃO, *s.f.*, creation, offspring, generation, lineage, progeny.
GE.RA.DOR, *s.m.*, generator; *adj.*, generating.
GE.RAL, *adj.*, common, generic, general, usual.
GE.RAL.MEN.TE, *adv.*, generally, usually.
GE.RÂ.NIO, *s.m., Bot.*, geranium.
GE.RAR, *v.*, to beget, to engender, to father, to generate.
GE.RA.TI.VO, *adj.*, generative.
GE.RÊN.CIA, *s.f.*, management, administration, managership.
GE.REN.CI.AL, *adj.*, managerial.
GE.REN.CI.A.MEN.TO, *s.m.*, management.
GE.REN.CI.AR, *v.*, to manage, to direct, to supervise, to administrate.
GE.REN.TE, *s. 2 gen.*, manager, administrator, supervisor, director, conductor.
GER.GE.LIM, *s.m., Bot.*, sesame.
GE.RI.A.TRI.A, *s.f., Med.*, geriatrics.
GE.RI.Á.TRI.CO, *adj.*, geriatric.
GE.RIN.GON.ÇA, *s.f.*, contraption.
GE.RIR, *v.*, to manage, to administrate, to direct, to supervise.
GER.MÂ.NI.CO, *adj., s.m.*, Germanic.
GER.MÂ.NI.O, *s.m., Quím.*, germanium.
GER.MA.NIS.MO, *s.m.*, Germanism, Teutonism.
GER.MA.NIS.TA, *s. 2 gen.*, Germanist.
GER.MA.NI.ZA.ÇÃO, *s.f.*, Germanization.
GER.MA.NI.ZAR, *v.*, to Germanize.
GER.ME, *s.m.*, germ, germen, microbe; cause, origin; rudiments.
GÉR.MEN, *s.m.*, germen; the same that *germe*.
GER.MI.CI.DA, *s.m.*, germicide.
GER.MI.NA.ÇÃO, *s.f.*, germination.
GER.MI.NAR, *v.*, to germinate, to bud, to sprout.

GE.RÚN.DIO, *s.m., Gram.*, gerund.
GES.SO, *s.m.*, plaster, cast, gypsum.
GES.TA.ÇÃO, *s.f.*, gestation, pregnancy.
GES.TAN.TE, *s.f.*, pregnant woman; *adj.*, pregnant, gravid.
GES.TÃO, *s.f.*, management, administration.
GES.TI.CU.LA.ÇÃO, *s.f.*, gesticulation.
GES.TI.CU.LAR, *v.*, to gesticulate, to motion.
GES.TO, *s.m.*, gesture, sign, gesticulation.
GES.TU.AL, *adj.*, gestural.
GI.BI, *s.m.*, comic strip.
GI.GA.BY.TE, *s.m., Comp.*, gigabyte.
GI.GAN.TE, *s.m.*, giant, titan, colossus; *adj.*, giant, gigantic.
GI.GAN.TES.CO, *adj.*, enormous, huge, gigantic, gigantean.
GI.GO.LÔ, *s.m.*, gigolo.
GI.LE.TE, *s.f.*, Gillette; shaving tackle.
GIM, *s.m.*, gin.
GI.NA.SI.AL, *adj.*, gymnasial.
GI.NÁ.SIO, *s.m.*, high school, gymnasium, secondary school.
GI.NAS.TA, *s. 2 gen.*, gymnast.
GIN.CA.NA, *s.f.*, gymkhana, scavenger hunt.
GI.NÁS.TI.CA, *s.f.*, gymnastics.
GI.NE.CO.LO.GI.A, *s.f.*, gynecology.
GI.NE.CO.LÓ.GI.CO, *adj.*, gynecologic, gynecological.
GI.NE.CO.LO.GIS.TA, *s. 2 gen.*, gynecologist.
GI.NE.TE, *s.m.*, thoroughbred, well-bred horse.
GIN.GA, *s.f.*, oar, nimble, shimmy.
GI.RA.FA, *s.f., Zool.*, giraffe.
GI.RAR, *v.*, to go, move, swing or turn (a)round, to circle, to rotate.
GI.RAS.SOL, *s.m.*, sunflower.
GI.RA.TÓ.RI.O, *adj.*, gyratory, rotating, revolving; *cadeira giratória*: swivel chair.
GÍ.RI.A, *s.f.*, slang, dialect, jargon.
GI.RO, *s.m.*, rotation, spin, revolution, circuit, turn, circulation.
GI.ROS.CÓ.PI.O, *s.m.*, gyroscope.
GIZ, *s.m.*, chalk, chalk-pencil.
GLA.CÊ, *s.m.*, glacé silk, icing.
GLA.CI.A.ÇÃO, *s.f.*, glaciation.
GLA.CI.AL, *adj.*, glacial, icy, freezing, frigid.
GLA.CI.AR, *s.m.*, glacier.
GLA.DI.A.DOR, *s.m.*, gladiator.
GLÁ.DI.O, *s.m.*, daggerlike sword.
GLA.MOUR, **GLA.MUR**, *s.m.*, glamour, glamor.
GLA.MOU.RO.SO, **GLA.MU.RO.SO**, *adj.*, glamorous.
GLAN.DE, *s.f., Anat.*, glans.
GLÂN.DU.LA, *s.f., Biol.*, glandula, gland, small gland.
GLAN.DU.LAR, *adj.*, glandular.
GLAU.CO.MA, *s.m., Med.*, glaucoma.
GLE.BA, *s.f.*, soil; glebe, clod of earth.
GLI.CE.RI.NA, *s.f.*, glycerin, glycerol.
GLI.CO.SE, *s.f.*, glucose, dextrose, grap sugar.
GLO.BAL, *adj.*, global, total, spherical, integral, over-all.
GLO.BA.LI.ZA.ÇÃO, *s.f.*, globalization.
GLO.BA.LI.ZA.DO, *adj.*, globalized.
GLO.BA.LI.ZAN.TE, *adj.*, globalizing.
GLO.BA.LI.ZAR, *v.*, to globalize; to integrate.
GLO.BO, *s.m.*, sphere, ball, globe.
GLO.BU.LAR, *adj.*, globular, globe-shaped.
GLÓ.BU.LO, *s.m.*, globule, little globe.
GLÓ.RI.A, *s.f.*, glory, praise, honour, renown, pomp.
GLO.RI.FI.CA.ÇÃO, *s.f.*, glorification, praise, beatification.

GLORIFICAR ••• 201 ••• GRAFOLOGIA

GLO.RI.FI.CAR, *v.*, to glorify, to extol, to apotheosize, to make glorious, to exalt.

GLO.RI.O.SO, *adj.*, glorious, illustrious, splendid, bright.

GLO.SA, *s.f.*, gloss, comment, commentary, *Lit.*, a kind of rondel.

GLO.SAR, *v.*, to gloss, to comment, to annotate.

GLOS.SÁ.RI.O, *s.m.*, glossary, vocabulary, dictionary.

GLO.TE, *s.f.*, *Anat.*, glottis.

GLP, *abrev.* of *Gás Liquefeito de Petróleo*: liquefied petroleum gas.

GLU.CO.SE, *s.f.*, the same that *glicose*.

GLU.TÃO, *s.m.*, glutton, gormandizer; *adj.*, voracious, gluttonous.

GLÚ.TEN, *s.m.*, gluten.

GLÚ.TE.O, *adj.*, *Anat.*, gluteal.

GLU.TO.NA.RI.A, *s.f.*, gluttony, gulosity.

GNO.MO, *s.m.*, gnome, goblin; sprite.

GNOS.TI.CIS.MO, *s.m.*, Gnosticism.

GO.DÊ, *s.m.*, *Fr.*, godet (small pan of water-colour).

GO.E.LA, *s.f.*, throat, gullet, esophagus.

GO.GÓ, *s.m.*, *Bras.*, Adam's apple; throat.

GOI.A.BA, *s.f.*, guava.

GOI.A.BA.DA, *s.f.*, guava jam.

GOI.A.BEI.RA, *s.f.*, *Bot.*, guava tree.

GOI.ÁS, *s.*, Goiás (a state of Brazil).

GOL, *s.m.*, goal.

GO.LA, *s.f.*, collar, shirt-collar.

GO.LA.ÇO, *s.m.*, *Bras.*, *Esp.*, great goal (soccer).

GO.LE, *s.m.*, gulp, sip, draught, swallow.

GO.LE.A.DA, *s.f.*, hammering, heavy.

GO.LE.AR, *v.*, to score many goals (soccer).

GO.LEI.RO, *s.m.*, goalkeeper.

GOL.FA.DA, *s.f.*, gush; vomit, spurt.

GOL.FAR, *v.*, to spew, to vomit, to spurt out.

GOL.FE, *s.m.*, golf.

GOL.FI.NHO, *s.m.*, *Zool.*, dolphin.

GOL.FO, *s.m.*, gulf, large open bay.

GOL.PE, *s.m.*, blow, punch, stroke, wound, injury, hit, knock; *Pol.*, putsch.

GOL.PE.AR, *v.*, to strike, to beat, to knock, to hit.

GOL.PIS.MO, *s.m.*, coup, putschism.

GOL.PIS.TA, *s. 2 gen.*, putschist, trickster, rascal; *adj.*, tricky.

GO.MA, *s.f.*, gum, latex, gumma, glue.

GO.MO, *s.m.*, bud, shoot, gemma, button.

GÔN.DO.LA, *s.f.*, gondola; Venetian boat.

GON.DO.LEI.RO, *s.m.*, gondolier.

GON.GO, *s.m.*, gong.

GO.NOR.REI.A, *s.f.*, *Med.*, gonorrhea, gonorrhoea.

GO.RAR, *v.*, to miscarry, to go wrong.

GOR.DO, *adj.*, obese, adipose, fat, corpulent.

GOR.DU.CHO, *s.m.*, fatty, paunch; *adj.*, plump, fubsy, chubby, chuffy.

GOR.DU.RA, *s.f.*, obesity, adiposity; fatness, fat.

GOR.DU.REN.TO, *adj.*, unctuous, fatty.

GOR.DU.RO.SO, *adj.*, greasy, fatty, lardy, oily.

GO.RI.LA, *s.m.*, gorilla.

GOR.JE.AR, *v.*, to warble, to quaver, to trill.

GOR.JEI.O, *s.m.*, warble, trill, twitter, quaver.

GOR.JE.TA, *s.f.*, tip, gratuity, gratification.

GO.RO.RO.BA, *s.f.*, *fam.*, grub, nosh, slop, muck.

GOR.RO, *s.m.*, cap, bonnet.

GOS.MA, *s.f.*, spittle.

GOS.MEN.TO, *adj.*, phlegmy; *col.*, slimy.

GOS.TAR, *v.*, to like, to enjoy, to relish, to find palatable.

GOS.TO, *s.m.*, taste, gustation, flavour, relish, savour.

GOS.TO.SO, *adj.*, tasty, savoury, sapid, flavorous.

GOS.TO.SU.RA, *s.f.*, *Bras.*, *col.*, great pleasure, delightful thing, delicious food or cookie.

GO.TA, *s.f.*, drop, raindrop, dewdrop; minim.

GO.TEI.RA, *s.f.*, gutter, leak, eaves; drain.

GO.TE.JAN.TE, *adj.*, dropping, trickling, dripping.

GO.TE.JAR, *v.*, to drip.

GÓ.TI.CO, *adj.*, Gothic.

GO.TÍ.CU.LA, *s.f.*, droplet.

GO.TI.NHA, *s.f.*, droplet.

GOUR.MET, *s.m.*, gourmet.

GO.VER.NA.BI.LI.DA.DE, *s.f.*, governability.

GO.VER.NA.DOR, *s.m.*, governor, commander; *adj.*, governing.

GO.VER.NA.MEN.TAL, *adj.*, governmental, civil.

GO.VER.NAN.TA, *s.f.*, governess, tutoress, nurse.

GO.VER.NAN.TE, *s. 2 gen.*, ruler, governor; *adj.*, governing.

GO.VER.NAR, *v.*, to govern, to command, to rule, to dominate.

GO.VER.NIS.TA, *s. 2 gen.*, government supporter; *adj.*, pro-government.

GO.VER.NO, *s.m.*, government, authority, domination, direction.

GO.ZA.ÇÃO, *s.f.*, mocking, mockery, teasing.

GO.ZA.DO, *adj.*, *Bras.*, *gír.*, comical, funny; amusing, strange.

GO.ZA.DOR, *s.m.*, enjoyer.

GO.ZAR, *v.*, to derive pleasure from, to enjoy oneself, to profit.

GO.ZO, *s.m.*, joy, enjoyment, pleasure, delight, contentment, utility.

GPS, *abrev.* of Global Positioning System: *Sistema de Posicionamento Global*.

GRÃ-BRE.TA.NHA, *s.*, Grat Britain.

GRA.ÇA, *s.f.*, grace, favor, joke, goodwill, benevolence, kindness, charm, mercy.

GRA.CE.JA.DOR, *s.m.*, jester, wag, joker; *adj.*, that jokes.

GRA.CE.JAR, *v.*, to joke, to jest, to banter, to droll, to frolic.

GRA.CE.JO, *s.m.*, joke, jest, mirth, merriness, gracefulness.

GRA.CI.O.SI.DADE, *s.f.*, grace, gracefulness, amenity.

GRA.CI.O.SO, *adj.*, gracious, graceful, elegant, charming, lovely, adorable.

GRA.DA.ÇÃO, *s.f.*, gradation, gradual increase or diminution.

GRA.DA.TI.VO, *adj.*, gradual, gradational.

GRA.DE, *s.f.*, grate, grid, grille, barrier.

GRA.DE.A.DO, *s.m.*, grating, fencing; *adj.*, fenced, with a grating.

GRA.DE.AR, *v.*, to fence in, to put bars on.

GRA.DO, *s.m.*, will, wish.

GRA.DU.A.ÇÃO, *s.f.*, gradation, graduation, gradation scale.

GRA.DU.A.DO, *s.m.*, graduate, grad; *adj.*, graduated, graded.

GRA.DU.AL, *adj.*, gradual, successive, slow.

GRA.DU.AR, *v.*, to graduate, to calibrate, to gauge, to classify, to divide into grade.

GRA.DU.Á.VEL, *adj.*, adjustable; that can be graduated.

GRA.FAR, *v.*, to spell, to write, to express by letters.

GRA.FI.A, *s.f.*, style of writing; orthography.

GRÁ.FI.CO, *s.m.*, graph, chart, diagram; *adj.*, graphic.

GRÃ-FI.NO, *s.m.*, aristocrat, snob; *col.*, toff, dude; *adj.*, posh.

GRA.FI.TE, *s.f.*, *Quím.*, graphite; graffiti.

GRA.FO.LO.GI.A, *s.f.*, graphology.

GRAMA
•• 202 ••
GRUDADO

GRA.MA, *s.f.*, grass, grama; *s.m.*, gram, gramme.
GRA.MA.DO, *s.m.*, lawn, turf, grass, green.
GRA.MAR, *v.*, to sow with grass, to plant grass, to sward; to scutch.
GRA.MÁ.TI.CA, *s.f.*, grammar, grammar book.
GRA.MA.TI.CAL, *adj.*, grammatic, grammatical.
GRA.MÁ.TI.CO, *s.m.*, grammarian, grammatist; *adj.*, grammatic, grammatical.
GRA.MO.FO.NE, *s.m.*, gramophone.
GRAM.PE.A.DOR, *s.m.*, stapler.
GRAM.PE.AR, *v.*, to staple, to clip, to cramp.
GRAM.PO, *s.m.*, cramp, clip, clasp, staple, brace.
GRA.NA, *s.f.*, money.
GRA.NA.DA, *s.f.*, grenade, bomb, shell.
GRAN.DA.LHÃO, *adj.*, huge, enormous.
GRAN.DE, *adj.*, great, big, large, bulky, tall, high, vast, ample.
GRAN.DE.ZA, *s.f.*, largeness, greatness, bigness, tallness, height, ampleness.
GRAN.DI.LO.QUÊN.CI.A, *s.f.*, grandiloquence.
GRAN.DI.LO.QUEN.TE, *adj.*, grandiloquent.
GRAN.DI.O.SI.DA.DE, *s.f.*, grandiosity.
GRAN.DI.O.SO, *adj.*, grandioso, grand, elevated, lofty, sublime, strong.
GRA.NEL, *s.m.*, barn, granary; *a ~*: in bulk.
GRA.NÍ.TI.CO, *adj.*, granitic.
GRA.NI.TO, *s.m.*, granite.
GRA.NI.ZO, *s.m.*, hail, hailstorm, hailstone.
GRAN.JA, *s.f.*, farm, grange, ranch.
GRAN.JE.AR, *v.*, to cultivate, to acquire, to obtain.
GRA.NU.LA.ÇÃO, *s.f.*, granulation, graining.
GRA.NU.LA.DO, *adj.*, granulated.
GRA.NU.LAR, *v.*, to granulate, to corn.
GRÂ.NU.LO, *s.m.*, granule, corn.
GRÃO, *s.m.*, grain, cereal, corn.
GRÃO-DE-BI.CO, *s.m.*, UK chick-pea, US garbanzo bean.
GRAS.NAR, *v.*, to caw, to croak, to quack, to clang.
GRAS.SAR, *v.*, to develop gradually; to rage.
GRA.TI.DÃO, *s.f.*, gratitude, gratefulness, thankfulness.
GRA.TI.FI.CA.ÇÃO, *s.f.*, gratification, reward, recompense.
GRA.TI.FI.CAN.TE, *adj.*, gratifying.
GRA.TI.FI.CAR, *v.*, to gratify, to reward, to recompense.
GRA.TI.NA.DO, *s.m.*, gratin; *adj.*, *gratiné* (*Fr.*), au gratin.
GRÁ.TIS, *adv.*, gratis, gratuitously, free, costless.
GRA.TO, *adj.*, grateful, thankful, gratified.
GRA.TUI.DA.DE, *s.f.*, gratuitousness; gratuity.
GRA.TUI.TO, *adj.*, gratis, gratuitous, free, costless.
GRAU, *s.m.*, step, pace, degree, grade, measure, extent, lenght, dimension.
GRA.Ú.DO, *adj.*, great, distinguished, developed.
GRA.VA.ÇÃO, *s.f.*, engraving, recording, record, aggravation.
GRA.VA.DO, *adj.*, engraved, incised.
GRA.VA.DOR, *s.m.*, tape recorder, engraver, chaser, graver.
GRA.VAR, *v.*, to engrave, to sculpture, to record, to save.
GRA.VA.TA, *s.f.*, tie, neckcloth.
GRA.VA.TA-BOR.BO.LE.TA, *s.f.*, bow tie.
GRA.VE, *adj.*, grave, serious, heavy, weighty, ponderous, solemn.
GRA.VE.MEN.TE, *adv.*, gravely, seriously.
GRA.VE.TO, *s.m.*, piece of kindling wood.
GRÁ.VI.DA, *adj.*, pregnant, expectant.
GRA.VI.DA.DE, *s.f.*, gravity, seriousness, graveness, solemnity, ponderation.
GRA.VI.DEZ, *s.f.*, pregnancy.
GRA.VI.O.LA, *s.f.*, sweetsop.
GRA.VI.TA.ÇÃO, *s.f.*, gravitation.
GRA.VI.TAR, *v.*, to gravitate, to be affected by gravitation.
GRA.VU.RA, *s.f.*, engraving; gravure, print, picture.
GRA.XA, *s.f.*, grease.
GRÉ.CIA, *s.f.*, Greece.
GRE.GÁ.RIO, *adj.*, gregarious.
GRE.GO, *adj.*, *s.m.*, Greek.
GRE.GO.RI.A.NO, *adj.*, Gregorian.
GRE.LAR, *v.*, to sprout, to germinate, to grow.
GRE.LHA, *s.f.*, grill, grate, fire grate.
GRE.LHA.DO, *s.m.*, *Cul.*, grill; *adj.*, grilled.
GRE.LHAR, *v.*, to grill, to fry.
GRÊ.MIO, *s.m.*, bosom, lap, community, club, society, circle.
GRE.NÁ, *s.m.*, grenadine red; *adj.*, dar red.
GRE.TA, *s.f.*, cleft, crack, fissure, hiatus.
GRE.VE, *s.f.*, strike, turn-out.
GRE.VIS.TA, *s. 2 gen.*, striker, worker on strike.
GRIFADO,
GRI.FAR, *v.*, to underline, to curl; to emphasize.
GRI.FE, *s.f.*, *Ingl.*, designer label.
GRI.FO, *s.m.*, italic type, italics; *Mit.*, griffin, griffon.
GRI.LA.DO, *adj.*, *Bras.*, *gír.*, worried, suspicious.
GRI.LA.GEM, *s.f.*, *Bras.*, landgrab, falsification of property deeds.
GRI.LAR(-SE), *v.*, to worry; to get annoyed.
GRI.LEI.RO, *s.m.*, *Bras.*, land-grabber, forger of property deeds.
GRI.LHÃO, *s.m.*, chain, fetters, shackles, leg irons.
GRI.LO, *s.m.*, cricket.
GRI.NAL.DA, *s.f.*, garland, wreath.
GRIN.GO, *s.m.*, gringo, foreigner, greenhorn.
GRI.PA.DO, *adj.*, with the flu; seized with influenza.
GRI.PAL, *adj.*, grippal.
GRI.PAR-SE, *v.*, to get the flu.
GRI.PE, *s.f.*, influenza, cold, grip, catarrh.
GRI.SA.LHO, *adj.*, grey, greyish, grizzled.
GRI.TAN.TE, *adj.*, chiding, crying.
GRI.TAR, *v.*, to cry, to shout, to clamour, to bawl, to exclaim.
GRI.TA.RI.A, *s.f.*, crying, shouting, bawling.
GRI.TO, *s.m.*, cry, shout, yell, scream, call, clamour, vociferation.
GRO.EN.LÂN.DIA, *s.*, Greenland.
GRO.GUE, *s.m.*, grog; *adj.*, groggy, toddy.
GRO.SA, *s.f.*, gross, rasp.
GRO.SAR, *v.*, to rasp; to file; *Ant.*, to comment, to gloss.
GRO.SE.LHA, *s.f.*, gooseberry, currant.
GRO.SE.LHEI.RA, *s.f.*, *Bot.*, red currant bush.
GROS.SEI.RO, *adj.*, gross, impolite, crude, rustic, clumsy.
GROS.SE.RI.A, *s.f.*, roughness, rudeness, uncivility, grossness, indelicacy.
GROS.SO, *s.m.*, main part, bulk; *adj.*, bulky, big, great, dense, compact.
GROS.SU.RA, *s.f.*, thickness, stoutness, bulkiness.
GRO.TA, *s.f.*, *Bras.*, deep, dark valley.
GRO.TÃO, *s.f.*, large cavern.
GRO.TES.CO, *adj.*, grotesque, ridiculous.
GROU, *s.m.*, crane.
GRU.A, *s.f.*, crane.
GRU.DA.DO, *adj.*, glued.

GRUDAR

203

GUTURALIZAR

GRU.DAR, *v.*, to glue, to paste, to joint, to unite.
GRU.DE, *s.m.*, glue, size, paste.
GRU.DEN.TO, *adj.*, sticky, tac, gummy.
GRU.ME.TE, *s.m.*, *Náut.*, cabin-boy.
GRU.NHI.DO, *s.m.*, grunting, grunt.
GRU.NHIR, *v.*, to grunt.
GRU.PO, *s.m.*, group, class, party, clan, bunch, ring, cluster, collection, gang.
GRU.TA, *s.f.*, grot, grotto, cavern, cave.
GUA.CHE, *s.m.*, *Art.*, gouache.
GUA.RA.NÁ, *s.m.*, guarana.
GUA.RA.NI, *s.*, *adj.*, Guarani.
GUAR.DA, *s.f.*, guard, vigilance, prudence, caution; *s.m.*, keeper, officer, caretaker.
GUAR.DA-CHU.VA, *s.m.*, umbrella.
GUAR.DA-COS.TAS, *s. 2 gen.*, bodyguard; coast-guard vessel.
GUAR.DA.DOR, *s.m.*, guardian, watchman, guard; *adj.*, watching.
GUAR.DA-FLO.RES.TAL, *s.m.*, ranger, forest ranger.
GUAR.DA-JOI.AS, *s.m.*, jewel-case.
GUAR.DA-LI.VROS, *s.m.*, book-keeper, accountant.
GUAR.DA-LOU.ÇA, *s.m.*, cupboard.
GUAR.DA-NA.PO, *s.m.*, napkin, serviette.
GUAR.DA-NO.TUR.NO, *s.m.*, night watchman.
GUAR.DA-PÓ, *s.m.*, dust-coat, smock-frock.
GUAR.DAR, *v.*, to guard, to protect, to defend, to store, to shield, to check, to retain, to keep.
GUAR.DA-ROU.PA, *s.m.*, wardrobe.
GUAR.DA-SOL, *s.m.*, sunshade, parasol, umbrella.
GUAR.DA-VO.LU.MES, *s.m.*, *2 num.*, baggage room.
GUAR.DI.ÃO, *s.m.*, guardian, custodian.
GUA.RI.DA, *s.f.*, shelter, den, protection.
GUA.RI.TA, *s.f.*, lodge, sentry-box.
GUAR.NE.CER, *v.*, to provide, to supply, to furnish, to equip.
GUAR.NI.ÇÃO, *s.f.*, crew, garrison, personnel, post.
GUA.TE.MA.LA, *s.*, Guatemala.
GUA.TE.MAL.TE.CO, *s.m.*, *adj.*, Guatemalan.
GU.DE, *s.m.*, game played with marbles.
GUEI.XA, *s.f.*, geisha.
GUEL.RA, *s.f.*, gills.
GUER.RA, *s.f.*, war,warfare,conflict, battle, strife.
GUER.RE.AR, *v.*, to war, to make war, to fight, to combat, to struggle.

GUER.REI.RO, *s.m.*, warrior, fighter, soldier, combatant.
GUER.RI.LHA, *s.f.*, guerilla.
GUER.RI.LHAR, *v.*, to engage in guerrilla warfare.
GUER.RI.LHEI.RO, *s.m.*, guerrilla; *adj.*, guerrilla.
GUE.TO, *s.m.*, ghetto.
GUI.A, *s.f.*, guidance, guidebook, manual, guide, courier, pass bill, permit.
GUI.A.NA, *s.*, Guyana.
GUI.A.NEN.SE, *s.m.*, *adj.*, Guyanese.
GUI.AR, *v.*, to guide, to lead, to conduct, to direct, to drive, to advise, to teach.
GUI.CHÊ, *s.m.*, sliding window, ticket-office window, information counter.
GUI.DÃO, GUI.DOM, *s.m.*, handle bar.
GUI.LHO.TI.NA, *s.f.*, guillotine.
GUIM.BA, *s.f.*, stub.
GUI.NA.DA, *s.f.*, veer (auto); *Náut.*, yaw, leeway; change of course.
GUIN.CHAR, *v.*, to scream, to shriek, to screech, to ululate.
GUIN.CHO, *s.m.*, tow-car, squeal, crab.
GUI.NE.A.NO, *s.m.*, *adj.*, Guinean.
GUI.NÉ-BIS.SAU, *s.*, Guinea-Bissau.
GUI.NÉ E.QUA.TO.RI.AL, *s.*, Equatorial Guinea.
GUIN.DAS.TE, *s.m.*, crane, hoist, crab.
GUIR.LAN.DA, *s.f.*, garland, festoon.
GUI.SA, *s.f.*, mode, fashion, manner.
GUI.SA.DO, *s.m.*, stew, ragout, hash.
GUI.SAR, *v.*, to stew.
GUI.TAR.RA, *s.f.*, guitar.
GUI.TAR.RIS.TA, *s. 2 gen.*, guitar player.
GUI.ZO, *s.m.*, cascabel; gingle bell.
GU.LA, *s.f.*, gluttony, voracity, greed, gorge.
GU.LO.DI.CE, *s.f.*, delicacy, dainty, sweetmeat.
GU.LO.SEI.MA, *s.f.*, titbit, dainties, sweets, delicacy.
GU.LO.SO, *adj.*, gluttonous, greedy, lickerish.
GU.ME, *s.m.*, edge, knife-edge, cutting or sharp edge.
GU.RI, *s.m.*, boy, kid, child.
GU.RI.A, *s.f.*, *Bras., pop.*, little girl, girl.
GU.RI.ZA.DA, *s.f.*, *Bras.*, *s. 2 gen.*, a lot of little girls and boys.
GU.RU, *s.m.*, guru.
GU.SA, *s.f.*, cast-iron, pig-iron.
GU.TU.RAL, *adj.*, guttural, throaty.
GU.TU.RA.LI.ZAR, *v.*, to gutturalize.

G

H

H, *s.m.*, the eighth letter of the Portuguese alphabet.
HÃ, *interj.*, huh (reflection); *hã?*: sorry.
HÁ.BIL, *adj.*, skilful, skilled, able, dexterous, capable, fit.
HA.BI.LI.DA.DE, *s.f.*, ability, aptitude, capacity, talent, intelligence, skill.
HA.BI.LI.DO.SO, *adj.*, skilful, skilled, handy, dexterous, clever, witty, able.
HA.BI.LI.TA.ÇÃO, *s.f.*, qualification, habilitation, fitness, capacity, competence.
HA.BI.LI.TA.DO, *adj.*, qualified, competent, capable.
HA.BI.LI.TAR, *v.*, to habilitate, to qualify, to entitle, to enable, to prepare, to make ready.
HA.BI.TA.ÇÃO, *s.f.*, habitation, house, residence.
HA.BI.TA.CI.O.NAL, *adj.*, housing, dwelling.
HA.BI.TA.DO, *adj.*, inhabited.
HA.BI.TAN.TE, *s. 2 gen.*, inhabitant, resident, habitant, dweller, lodger, colonist.
HA.BI.TAR, *v.*, to inhabit, to reside, to lodge, to live in.
HA.BI.TAT, *s.m.*, habitat.
HÁ.BI.TO, *s.m.*, custom, habit, usage; dress, garment.
HA.BI.TU.AL, *adj.*, habitual, customary, usual, regular, common.
HA.BI.TU.AR, *v.*, to habituate, to familiarize, to accustom, to inure.
HACK.ER, *s.m., Comp.*, hacker.
HA.CHU.RA, *s.f.*, hachure.
HA.DO.QUE, *s.m., Zool.*, haddock (fish).
HAITI, *s.*, Haiti.
HAI.TI.A.NO, *adj., s.m.*, Haitian.
HÁ.LI.TO, *s.m.*, breath, respiration, exhalation.
HAL.TE.RE, *s.m.*, barbell, dumbbell.
HAL.TE.RO.FI.LIS.MO, *s.m., Bras.*, weight-lifting.
HAL.TE.RO.FI.LIS.TA, *s. 2 gen., Bras.*, weight-lifter.
HAM.BÚR.GUER, *s.m.*, hamburger.
HAN.GAR, *s.m.*, hangar, shed, dock.
HAN.SE.NI.A.NO, *s.m.*, lazar, leper; *adj.*, leprous.
HA.RAS, *s.m.*, stud, horse breeding farm.
HA.RÉM, *s.m.*, harem, seraglio.
HAR.MO.NI.A, *s.f.*, harmony, accord, consonance, concord.
HAR.MÔ.NI.CO, *adj.*, harmonious, harmonic, consonant, regular.
HAR.MO.NI.O.SO, *adj.*, harmonious, melodious, musical.
HAR.MO.NI.ZA.ÇÃO, *s.f.*, harmonization.
HAR.MO.NI.ZAR, *v.*, to harmonize, to make harmonious, to conciliate.
HAR.PA, *s.f.*, harp.
HAR.PI.A, *s.f., Mit.*, harpy; *Zool.*, harpy eagle.
HAR.PIS.TA, *s. 2 gen.*, harpist, harper.
HAS.TE, *s.f.*, staff, stick, stem, stalk, long stick.
HAS.TE.A.MEN.TO, *s.m.*, hoist, hoisting.
HAS.TE.AR, *v.*, to hoist, to run up, to heave.
HA.VA.Í, *s.*, Hawaii.
HA.VAI.A.NO, *adj., s.m.*, Hawaiian.
HA.VER, *s.m.*, credit, fortune; *v.*, to have, to possess, to own, to occur.
HA.XI.XE, *s.m.*, hashish.
HE.BRAI.CO, *adj., s.m.*, Hebrew, Hebraist.
HE.BREU, *adj., s.m.*, Hebrew.
HEC.TA.RE, *s.m.*, hectare.
HEC.TO.GRA.MA, *s.m.*, hectogram.
HEC.TO.LI.TRO, *s.m.*, hectoliter.
HE.DI.ON.DO, *adj.*, hideous, dreadful.
HE.DO.NIS.MO, *s.m., Gr., Filos.*, hedonism.
HE.DO.NIS.TA, *s. 2 gen., Gr., Filos.*, hedonist.
HE.GE.MO.NI.A, *s.f.*, hegemony, predominance.
HE.GE.MÔ.NI.CO, *adj.*, hegemoniac, hegemoniacal.
HÉ.LI.CE, *s.f.*, helix, propeller.
HE.LI.COI.DAL, *adj.*, helicoid, helical.
HE.LI.COI.DE, *s. 2 gen.*, helicoid; *adj.*, helicoid, helicoidal.
HE.LI.CÓP.TE.RO, *s.m.*, helicopter, chopper.
HE.LI.POR.TO, *s.m.*, heliport.
HEL.VÉ.CIO, *adj., s.m.*, Helvetian, Swiss.
HE.MA.TO.LO.GI.A, *s.f.*, hematology.
HE.MA.TO.MA, *s.m.*, bruise, hematoma.
HE.MIS.FÉ.RI.CO, *adj.*, hemispherical.
HE.MIS.FÉ.RIO, *s.m.*, hemisphere.
HE.MO.DI.Á.LI.SE, *s.f., Med.*, hemodialysis.
HE.MO.FI.LI.A, *s.f.*, hemophilia.
HE.MO.FÍ.LI.CO, *adj.*, hemophiliac.
HE.MOR.RÁ.GI.CO, *adj.*, hemorrhagic.
HE.MOR.RA.GI.A, *s.f.*, hemorrhage.
HE.MOR.ROI.DAS, *s.f.*, hemorrhoids.
HE.NA, *s.f., Bot.*, henna.
HE.PÁ.TI.CO, *adj.*, hepatic, hepatical.
HE.PA.TI.TE, *s.f.*, hepatitis.
HEP.TÁ.GO.NO, *s.m., Geom.*, heptagon.
HE.RA, *s.f., Bot.*, ivy.
HE.RÁL.DI.CA, *s.f.*, heraldry, heraldic art.
HE.RAN.ÇA, *s.f.*, inheritance, heritage, legacy, heredity, birthright.
HER.BA.NÁ.RIO, *s.m.*, herb shop, herbarium.
HER.BÁ.RIO, *s.m.*, herbarium.
HER.BI.CI.DA, *s.m.*, herbicide; *adj.*, herbicidal.
HER.BÍ.VO.RO, *s.m.*, herbivore; *adj.*, herbivorous.
HER.CÚ.LE.O, *adj.*, Herculean; *fig.*, strong, vigorous.
HER.DAR, *v.*, to inherit, to bequeath, to legate.
HER.DEI.RA, *s.f.*, heiress, inheritress.
HER.DEI.RO, *s.m.*, heir, inheritor.
HE.RE.DI.TA.RI.E.DA.DE, *s.f.*, heredity.
HE.RE.DI.TÁ.RIO, *adj.*, hereditary; hereditable.
HE.RE.GE, *s. 2 gen.*, heretic, dissenter, misbeliever, sectary.
HE.RE.SI.A, *s.f.*, heresy.
HE.RÉ.TI.CO, *s.m.*, heretic; *adj.*, heretic, heretical.
HER.MA.FRO.DI.TA, *s. 2 gen.*, hermaphrodite.

HERMENÊUTICA ·· 205 ··· HISTRIÔNICO

HER.ME.NÊU.TI.CA, *s.f.*, hermeneutics.
HÉR.NIA, *s.f.*, hernia, rupture.
HE.RÓI, *s.m.*, hero.
HE.ROI.CO, *adj.*, heroic, noble, bold, courageous.
HE.RO.Í.NA, *s.f.*, heroess, heroine; heroin.
HE.RO.ÍS.MO, *s.m.*, heroism, courage, intrepidity, valour.
HER.PES, *s.f., pl.*, herpes.
HE.SI.TA.ÇÃO, *s.f.*, hesitation, hesitance, vacillation.
HE.SI.TAN.TE, *s. 2 gen.*, hesitant, wavering, irresolute, indecisive.
HE.SI.TAR, *v.*, to hesitate, to vacillate, to waver, to halt, to doubt.
HE.TE.RO.GÊ.NEO, *adj.*, heterogeneous, unlike, dissimilar, motley.
HE.TE.ROS.SE.XU.AL, *s. 2 gen.*, heterosexual; *adj.*, heterosexual.
HE.TE.ROS.SE.XU.A.LI.DA.DE, *s.f.*, heterosexuality.
HE.XA.GO.NAL, *adj.*, hexagonal.
HE.XÁ.GO.NO, *s.m.*, hexagon.
HE.XÂ.ME.TRO, *s.m.*, hexameter.
HI.A.TO, *s.m.*, hiatus, gap, opening.
HI.BER.NA.ÇÃO, *s.f., Zool.*, hibernation, winter-sleep.
HI.BER.NAL, *adj.*, hibernal, winterly.
HI.BER.NAR, *v.*, to hibernate.
HI.BIS.CO, *s.m., Bot.*, hibiscus.
HI.BRI.DIS.MO, *s.m.*, hybridism, hybridity.
HÍ.BRI.DO, *adj.*, hybrid.
HI.DRA.MÁ.TI.CO, *adj.*, Hydra-Matic.
HI.DRAN.TE, *s.m.*, hydrant.
HI.DRA.TA.ÇÃO, *s.f.*, hydration.
HI.DRA.TA.DO, *adj.*, hydrated.
HI.DRA.TAN.TE, *s.m.*, moisturizer; *adj.*, moisturizing, hydrating.
HI.DRA.TAR, *v.*, to hydrate.
HI.DRA.TO, *s.m., Quím.*, hydrate.
HI.DRÁU.LI.CO, *adj.*, hydraulic.
HI.DRE.LÉ.TRI.CA, *s.f.*, hydroelectric power station; hydro-electric company.
HI.DRE.LÉ.TRI.CO, *adj.*, hydroelectric.
HÍ.DRI.CO, *adj.*, hydric.
HI.DRO.A.VI.ÃO, *s.m.*, hydro-airplane.
HI.DRO.CAR.BO.NE.TO, *s.m., Quím.*, hydrocarbon.
HI.DRO.DI.NÂ.MI.CA, *s.f.*, hydrodynamics.
HI.DRÓ.FI.LO, *adj.*, hydrophilic; *Bot.*, hydrophilous.
HI.DRO.FO.BI.A, *s.f.*, hydrophobia, rabies.
HI.DRO.GÊ.NIO, *s.m., Quím.*, hydrogen.
HI.DRO.MAS.SA.GEM, *s.f.*, hydromassage.
HI.DRÔ.ME.TRO, *s.m.*, hydrometer.
HI.DRO.PLA.NO, *s.m.*, sea-plane.
HI.DRO.TE.RA.PI.A, *s.f.*, hydrotherapeutics, hydrotherapy.
HI.E.NA, *s.f., Zool.*, hyena.
HI.E.RAR.QUI.A, *s.f.*, hierarchy.
HI.E.RÁR.QUI.CO, *adj.*, hierarchic, hierarchical.
HI.E.RAR.QUI.ZA.ÇÃO, *s.f.*, act of hierarchizing.
HI.E.RAR.QUI.ZAR, *v.*, to hierarchize.
HI.E.RÓ.GLI.FO, *s.m.*, hieroglyph.
HÍ.FEN, *s.m.*, hyphen.
HI.FE.NI.ZAR, *v.*, to hyphenate.
HI-FI, *s.m., abrev.* of High Fidlity: *Alta Fidelidade*, hi-fi.
HI.GI.E.NE, *s.f.*, hygienics, hygiene, cleanliness.
HI.GI.Ê.NI.CO, *adj.*, hygienic, hygienical, sanitary, clean.
HI.GI.E.NI.ZAR, *v.*, to hygienize.

HI.LA.RI.AN.TE, *adj.*, hilarious.
HI.LÁ.RIO, *adj.*, hilarious.
HÍ.MEN, *s.m., Anat.*, hymen.
HIN.DI, *s.m.*, Hindi.
HIN.DU, *s. 2 gen.*, Hindu, Hindo; *adj.*, Hindu, Hindoo.
HIN.DU.ÍS.MO, *s.m.*, Hinduism.
HI.NO, *s.m.*, hymn, anthem.
HI.PÉR.BO.LE, *s.f.*, hyperbole.
HI.PE.RIN.FLA.ÇÃO, *s.f.*, hyperinflation.
HI.PER.MER.CA.DO, *s.m.*, hypermarket.
HI.PER.ME.TRO.PI.A, *s.f., Med.*, hypermetropia.
HI.PER.SEN.SÍ.VEL, *adj.*, hypersensitive.
HI.PER.TEN.SÃO, *s.f.*, hypertension.
HI.PER.TEN.SO, *s.m.*, hypertensive; *adj.*, hypertensive.
HI.PER.TEX.TO, *s.m.*, hypertext.
HI.PER.TRO.FI.A, *s.f.*, hypertrophy.
HI.PER.TRO.FI.AR, *v.*, to hypertrophy.
HÍ.PI.CO, *adj.*, hippic, equine.
HI.PIS.MO, *s.m.*, horsemanship, equestrianism.
HIP.NO.SE, *s.f.*, hypnosis, hypnotism.
HIP.NÓ.TI.CO, *s.m., Med.*, hypnotic; *adj.*, hypnotic.
HIP.NO.TIS.MO, *s.m.*, hypnotism.
HIP.NO.TI.ZA.ÇÃO, *s.f.*, hypnotization.
HIP.NO.TI.ZA.DO, *adj.*, hypnotized.
HIP.NO.TI.ZA.DOR, *s.m.*, hypnotist, hypnotizer.
HIP.NO.TI.ZAR, *v.*, to hypnotize.
HI.PO.CON.DRI.A, *s.f., Med.*, hypochondria, hypochondriasis.
HI.PO.CON.DRÍ.A.CO, *s.m.*, hypochondriac; *adj.*, hypochondriac.
HI.PO.CRI.SI.A, *s.f.*, hypocrisy.
HI.PÓ.CRI.TA, *s. 2 gen.*, hypocrite, pretender, dissimulator.
HI.PO.DÉR.MI.CO, *adj.*, hypodermic.
HI.PÓ.DRO.MO, *s.m.*, hippodrome, race-course.
HI.PÓ.FI.SE, *s.f., Anat.*, hypophysis, pituitary.
HI.PO.GLI.CE.MI.A, *s.f., Med.*, hypoglycemia.
HI.PO.PÓ.TA.MO, *s.m., Zool.*, hippopotamus.
HI.PO.TE.CA, *s.f.*, hypothec, mortgage.
HI.PO.TE.CAR, *v.*, to mortgage, to hypothecate, to bond.
HI.PO.TE.CÁ.RI.O, *adj.*, hypothecary.
HI.PO.TE.NU.SA, *s.f.*, hypotenuse.
HI.PÓ.TE.SE, *s.f.*, hypothesis, supposition, theory.
HI.PO.TÉ.TI.CO, *adj.*, hypothetic, hypothetical.
HIR.SU.TO, *adj.*, hirsute, hairy.
HIS.PÂ.NI.CO, *adj.*, Hispanic.
HIS.PA.NO, *s. 2 gen., adj.*, Hispanic.
HIS.PA.NO-A.ME.RI.CA.NO, *s.m.*, Hispano-American; *adj.*, Hispano-American.
HIS.TE.REC.TO.MI.A, *s.f.*, hysterectomy.
HIS.TE.RI.A, *s.f.*, hysteria.
HIS.TÉ.RI.CO, *adj.*, hysteric, excited.
HIS.TE.RIS.MO, *s.m., Med.*, hysterics, hysterism.
HIS.TO.LO.GI.A, *s.f., Anat.*, histology.
HIS.TÓ.RIA, *s.f.*, history, tale, narration, story, legend, fable.
HIS.TO.RI.A.DOR, *s.m.*, historian, historiographer.
HIS.TO.RI.AR, *v.*, to historize.
HIS.TO.RI.CI.DA.DE, *s.f.*, historicity, historicalness.
HIS.TÓ.RI.CO, *s.m.*, description, narration, review; *adj.*, historical, true, veracious.
HIS.TO.RI.E.TA, *s.f.*, historiette, tale, short story.
HIS.TRI.ÃO, *s.m.*, histrion, comedian, buffoon.
HIS.TRI.Ô.NI.CO, *adj.*, histrionic.

HIV · 206 · HUMILHAR

HIV, *s.m., abrev.* of Immunodeficiency Virus, HIV.
HOB.BY, *s.m.,* hobby.
HO.JE, *adv.,* today, this day, actually.
HO.LAN.DA, *s.f.,* Holland, Netherlands.
HO.LAN.DÊS, *adj., s.m.,* Hollander, Netherlander, Dutchman.
HOL.DING, *s.f., Ingl., Com.,* holding company.
HO.LO.CAUS.TO, *s.m.,* holocaust.
HO.LO.FO.TE, *s.m.,* holophote, projector, spotlight.
HO.LO.GRA.MA, *s.m.,* hologram.
HOM.BRI.DA.DE, *s.f.,* decency, magnanimity.
HO.MEM, *s.m.,* man, human being, mankind, humanity, male, husband.
HO.MEM-RÃ, *s.m.,* frogman.
HO.ME.NA.GE.A.DO, *adj.,* celebrated, venerated, honoured.
HO.ME.NA.GE.AR, *v.,* to homage, to honor, to pay tribute to.
HO.ME.NA.GEM, *s.f.,* homage, tribute, allegiance, reverence, respect.
HO.MEN.ZAR.RÃO, *s.m.,* tall, stout man.
HO.ME.O.PA.TA, *s. 2 gen.,* homeopathist.
HO.ME.O.PA.TI.A, *s.f.,* homeopathy.
HO.ME.O.PÁ.TI.CO, *adj., Med.,* homeopathic.
HO.MÉ.RI.CO, *adj., Hist.,* Homeric; *fig.,* epic, extraordinary.
HO.MI.CI.DA, *s. 2 gen.,* murderer, slayer, homicide; *adj.,* murderous, homicidal.
HO.MI.CÍ.DIO, *s.m.,* homicide, murder, assassination.
HO.MI.LI.A, *s.f.,* homily.
HO.MO.GE.NEI.DA.DE, *s.f.,* homogeneity.
HO.MO.GE.NEI.ZA.DO, *adj.,* homogenized.
HO.MO.GE.NEI.ZAR, *v.,* to homogenize.
HO.MO.GÊ.NEO, *adj.,* homogeneous, uniform, smooth.
HO.MO.LO.GA.ÇÃO, *s.f.,* homologation, ratification, confirmation.
HO.MO.LO.GAR, *v.,* to homologate, to ratify, to confirm.
HO.MÓ.LO.GO, *adj.,* homologous.
HO.MÔ.NI.MO, *s.m.,* homonym, namesake.
HO.MOS.SE.XU.AL, *adj., s. 2 gen.,* homosexual, gay, fag.
HO.MOS.SE.XU.A.LI.DA.DE, *s.f.,* homosexuality.
HO.MOS.SE.XU.A.LIS.MO, *s.m.,* homosexualism.
HON.DU.RAS, *s.,* Honduras.
HON.DU.RE.NHO, *adj., s.m.* Honduran.
HO.NES.TA.MEN.TE, *adv.,* honestly.
HO.NES.TI.DA.DE, *s.f.,* honesty, honour, integrity, uprightness, truth.
HO.NES.TO, *adj.,* honest, honourable, frank, sincere.
HO.NO.RA.BI.LI.DA.DE, *s.f.,* honourableness, reputability.
HO.NO.RÁ.RIO, *adj.,* honorary, honorific.
HO.NO.RÁ.RI.OS, *s.m., pl.,* honorarium, remuneration, pay.
HO.NO.RÍ.FI.CO, *adj.,* honorific, honorary.
HON.RA, *s.f.,* honor, reputation, honour, repute, respect, reverence.
HON.RA.DEZ, *s.f.,* honour, probity, honesty, righteousness.
HON.RA.DO, *adj.,* honourable, reputable, honest, sincere, worthy.
HON.RAR, *v.,* to honor, to esteem, to respect, to revere.
HON.RO.SO, *adj.,* honourable, honest, praiseworthy.
HÓ.QUEI, *s.m., Esp.,* hockey.
HO.RA, *s.f.,* hour, time, opportunity.
HO.RÁ.RIO, *s.m.,* timetable, schedule; *adj.,* hourly; ~ *de expediente*: working hours.
HOR.DA, *s.f.,* horde, gang, troop.
HO.RIS.TA, *s. 2 gen.,* employee paid by the hour; *adj.,* paid

by the hour.
HO.RI.ZON.TAL, *adj.,* horizontal.
HO.RI.ZON.TE, *s.m.,* horizon, skyline, sealine.
HOR.MÔ.NIO, *s.m.,* hormone.
HO.RÓS.CO.PO, *s.m.,* horoscope.
HOR.REN.DO, *adj.,* horrendous, fearful, frightful.
HOR.RI.PI.LAN.TE, *adj.,* horrifying.
HOR.RI.PI.LAR, *v.,* to horripilate, horrify; *horripilar-se*: to become horripilated.
HOR.RÍ.VEL, *adj.,* horrible, terrible, horrid, dreadful.
HOR.ROR, *s.m.,* horror, terror, hate, repulsion, aversion.
HOR.RO.RI.ZAR, *v.,* to horrify, to terrify, to frighten.
HOR.RO.RO.SO, *adj.,* horrible, terrible, horrific, fearful.
HOR.TA, *s.f.,* vegetable garden, kitchen garden.
HOR.TA.LI.ÇA, *s.f.,* green-stuff, vegetable.
HOR.TE.LÃ, *s.f., Bot.,* mint, spearmint.
HOR.TE.LÃ-PI.MEN.TA, *s.f., Bot.,* peppermint.
HOR.TÊN.SIA, *s.f., Bot.,* hydrangea.
HOR.TI.CUL.TU.RA, *s.f.,* horticulture.
HOR.TI.CUL.TOR, *s.m.,* horticulturist.
HOR.TO, *s.m.,* little garden, allotment.
HOS.PE.DA.GEM, *s.f.,* hospitality, lodging, accomodation.
HOS.PE.DAR, *v.,* to house, to lodge, to accomodate.
HOS.PE.DA.RI.A, *s.f.,* inn, lodging house, hotel, guest house.
HÓS.PE.DE, *s. 2 gen.,* guest, visitor, lodger.
HOS.PE.DEI.RO, *s.m.,* host, innkeeper.
HOS.PÍ.CIO, *s.m.,* hospice, hospitium, mental hospital, asylum, mad house.
HOS.PI.TAL, *s.m.,* hospital, clinic, sanatorium.
HOS.PI.TA.LAR, *adj.,* pertaining to a hospital, nosocomial.
HOS.PI.TA.LEI.RO, *adj.,* hospitable.
HOS.PI.TA.LI.DA.DE, *s.f.,* hospitality, hospitableness.
HOS.PI.TA.LI.ZA.ÇÃO, *s.f.,* hospitalization.
HOS.PI.TA.LI.ZAR, *v.,* to hospitalize, to intern in a hospital.
HOS.TE, *s.f.,* troop, army; *fig.,* gang; enemy.
HÓS.TIA, *s.f.,* Host, holy bread, Eucharist.
HOS.TIL, *adj.,* hostile, inimical, adverse, antagonistic, belligerent.
HOS.TI.LI.DA.DE, *s.f.,* hostility, enmity.
HOS.TI.LI.ZAR, *v.,* to hostilize, to antagonize, to persecute, to oppose.
HO.TEL, *s.m.,* hotel, inn, lodging house.
HO.TE.LA.RI.A, *s.f.,* hotel management; hotels.
HO.TE.LEI.RO, *s.m.,* hotelkeeper.
HUM, *interj.,* hum!
HU.MA.NI.DA.DE, *s.f.,* humanity, mankind, human nature.
HU.MA.NIS.MO, *s.m.,* humanism.
HU.MA.NIS.TA, *s. 2 gen.,* humanist.
HU.MA.NI.TÁ.RIO, *s.m.,* humanitarian, philantropist; *adj.,* humanitarian, humane.
HU.MA.NI.TA.RIS.MO, *s.m.,* humanitarianism.
HU.MA.NI.ZA.ÇÃO, *s.f.,* humanization.
HU.MA.NI.ZAR, *v.,* to humanize.
HU.MA.NO, *adj., s.m.* human; *humanos (pl.)*: humans.
HU.MA.NOI.DE, *s.m.,* humanoid; *adj.,* humanoid.
HU.MIL.DA.DE, *s.f.,* humbleness, humility, modesty, submission.
HU.MIL.DE, *adj.,* humble, modest, submissive, poor.
HU.MI.LHA.ÇÃO, *s.f.,* humiliation, abasement.
HU.MI.LHAN.TE, *adj.,* humiliating, humiliative.
HU.MI.LHAR, *v.,* to humiliate, to humble, to mortify.

HOMINÍDEO · 207 · HURRA

HO.MI.NÍ.DE.O, *s.m.*, hominid; *hominídeos* (*pl.*): Hominidae.

HU.MOR, *s.m.*, humor, mood, moisture, mental state, disposition, temper.

HU.MO.RA.DO, *adj.*, humoured, tempered.

HU.MO.RIS.MO, *s.m.*, humorism.

HU.MO.RIS.TA, *s. 2 gen.*, humorist.

HÚ.MUS, *s.m.*, humus, earth.

HÚN.GA.RO, *adj., s.m.*, Hungarian.

HUN.GRI.A, *s.*, Hungary.

HUR.RA, *interj.*, hurrah, hooray.

I, *s.m.*, ninth letter of the Portuguese alphabet.
I, *num.*, number one in the Roman notation.
IAN.QUE, *adj., s.m.*, Yankee.
IA.TE, *s.m.*, yacht.
IA.TIS.MO, *s.m.*, yachting.
I.BI.DEM, *adv.*, ibid., ibidem.
I.ÇAR, *v.*, to hoist, to hoist up, to lift, to jack.
ICE.BERG, *s.m.*, iceberg.
Í.CO.NE, *s.m.*, icon.
I.CO.NO.CLAS.TA, *s. 2 gen.*, iconoclast; *adj.*, iconoclastic.
I.CO.NO.CLAS.TI.A, *s.f.*, iconoclasm.
I.CO.NO.GRA.FI.A, *s.f.*, iconography.
I.CO.NO.GRÁ.FI.CO, *adj.*, iconographic, iconographical.
IC.TE.RÍ.CI.A, *s.f.*, jaundice, icterus.
I.DA, *s.f.*, departure, setting out, starting, going, leaving.
I.DA.DE, *s.f.*, age, time, lifetime, epoch, maturity.
I.DE.A.ÇÃO, *s.f.*, ideation; notion, idea.
I.DE.AL, *s.m.*, ideal, model, example; *adj.*, ideal, imaginary.
I.DE.A.LIS.MO, *s.m.*, idealism.
I.DE.A.LIS.TA, *s. 2 gen.*, idealist; *adj.*, idealistic.
I.DE.A.LI.ZA.ÇÃO, *s.f.*, idealization, idealisation.
I.DE.A.LI.ZA.DOR, *s.m.*, idealizer, idealist; planner.
I.DE.A.LI.ZAR, *v.*, to idealize, to imagine, to organize.
I.DE.AR, *v.*, to ideate, idealize.
IDEÁRIO, *s.m.*, ideas; *Pol.*, ideology.
I.DEI.A, *s.f.*, idea, thought, notion, concept, image, imagination.
I.DEM, *pron.*, ditto, the same; idem.
I.DÊN.TI.CO, *adj.*, identical, equal, similar, analogous.
I.DEN.TI.DA.DE, *s.f.*, identity, identicalness, sameness, exactness, individuality.
I.DEN.TI.FI.CA.ÇÃO, *s.f.*, identification.
I.DEN.TI.FI.CA.DOR, *s.m.*, identifier; *adj.*, identifying.
I.DEN.TI.FI.CAR, *v.*, to identify, to recognize, to make identical.
I.DEN.TI.FI.CÁ.VEL, *adj.*, identifiable.
I.DE.O.LO.GI.A, *s.f.*, ideology.
I.DE.O.LÓ.GI.CO, *adj.*, ideologic, ideological.
I.DE.Ó.LO.GO, *s.m.*, ideologist.
Í.DI.CHE, *s.m.*, the same that *iídiche*.
I.DÍ.LI.CO, *adj.*, idyllic.
I.DÍ.LIO, *s.m.*, idyl, rural poem.
I.DI.O.MA, *s.m.*, idiom, language, tongue.
I.DI.O.MÁ.TI.CO, *adj.*, idiomatic.
I.DI.OS.SIN.CRA.SI.A, *s.f.*, idiosyncrasy.
I.DI.O.TA, *s. 2 gen.*, idiot, fool, cretin; *adj.*, idiotic, idiotical, stupid, foolish.
I.DI.O.TI.A, *s.f.*, idiocy.
I.DI.O.TI.CE, *s.f.*, foolishness, madness.
I.DO, *adj.*, departed, past, gone.
I.DÓ.LA.TRA, *s. 2 gen.*, idolater, idol worshipper; *fig.*, adorer; *adj.*, idolatrous.
I.DO.LA.TRAR, *v.*, to idolize, to adore, to admire, to worship.
I.DO.LA.TRI.A, *s.f.*, idolatry, idolism.

Í.DO.LO, *s.m.*, idol, image, icon, effigy.
I.DO.NEI.DA.DE, *s.f.*, decency, honesty, aptitude, competence.
I.DÔ.NEO, *adj.*, idoneous, apt, competent, fit.
I.DOS, *s.m., pl.*, bygone times.
I.DO.SO, *adj., s.m.*, old-aged, elder, advanced in years.
IG.NA.RO, *adj.*, unlearned; ignorant.
IG.NI.ÇÃO, *s.f.*, ignition, combustion.
IG.NO.MÍ.NIA, *s.f.*, ignominy, dishonour, disgrace.
IG.NO.MI.NI.AR, *v.*, to treat ignominiously.
IG.NO.MI.NI.O.SO, *adj.*, ignominious.
IG.NO.RA.DO, *adj.*, unknown, obscure.
IG.NO.RÂN.CI.A, *s.f.*, ignorance.
IG.NO.RAN.TE, *s. 2 gen.*, ignorant, illiterate, idiot, know-nothing, unlearned, stupid.
IG.NO.RAR, *v.*, to ignore, not to know, to be ignorant of.
IG.NO.TO, *adj.*, unknown, obscure.
I.GRE.JA, *s.f.*, church.
I.GUAL, *adj.*, equal, even, identic, equable, uniform, like, alike.
I.GUA.LAR, *v.*, to equalize, to make equal, to equal, to match, to cap.
I.GUA.LÁ.VEL, *adj.*, that can be equalized.
I.GUAL.DA.DE, *s.f.*, equality, equity, equalness, equation, uniformity.
I.GUA.LI.TÁ.RI.O, *adj.*, equalitarian.
I.GUAL.MEN.TE, *adv.*, equally, identically.
I.GUA.NA, *s.m.*, *Zool.*, iguana.
I.GUA.RI.A, *s.f.*, delicacy.
IH!, *interj.*, eek!.
I.Í.DI.CHE, Í.DI.CHE, *s.m.*, Yiddish.
I.LE.GAL, *adj.*, illegal, illicit, lawless, injudicial, wrong.
I.LE.GA.LI.DA.DE, *s.f.*, illegality, unlawfulness.
I.LE.GI.BI.LI.DA.DE, *s.f.*, illegibility, illegibleness.
I.LE.GI.TI.MI.DA.DE, *s.f.*, illegitimacy.
I.LE.GÍ.TI.MO, *adj.*, illegitimate, illegal, unlawful, spurious, criminal.
I.LE.GÍ.VEL, *adj.*, illegible.
I.LESO, *adj.*, unhurt, uninjured.
I.LE.TRA.DO, *s.m.*, illiterate; *adj.*, illiterate, unlearned, rude, uncultured.
I.LHA, *s.f.*, island, isle, islet.
I.LHAL, *s.m.*, flank (of an animal: horse, cattle).
I.LHAR, *v.*, to isolate, to insulate; *ilhar-se*: to become incommunicable.
I.LHAR.GA, *s.f., Anat.*, flank.
I.LHÉU, *s.m.*, islander, islet.
I.LHÓS, *s. 2 gen.*, eyelet.
I.LHO.TA, *s.f.*, islet.
I.LÍ.CI.TO, *adj.*, illicit, illegal, unlawful, lawless.
I.LI.MI.TA.DO, *adj.*, unlimited, limitless, free, unrestricted.
I.LÓ.GI.CO, *adj.*, illogical.
I.LU.DIR, *v.*, to deceive, to cheat, to dupe.
I.LU.DÍ.VEL, *adj.*, deceptible; illusory.

ILUMINAÇÃO   209   IMPASSE

I.LU.MI.NA.ÇÃO, *s.f.*, illumination, explication.

I.LU.MI.NA.DO, *adj.*, illuminated, lighted, illustrated.

I.LU.MI.NA.DOR, *s.m.*, illuminator; *Cin., Teat., TV,* lighting technician.

I.LU.MI.NAR, *v.*, to illuminate, to light up, to illumine, elucidate.

I.LU.MI.NIS.MO, *s.m.*, illuminism.

I.LU.MI.NIS.MO, *s.m., Hist.,* Enlightenment.

I.LU.MI.NIS.TA, *s. 2 gen.*, illuminist; member of the Enlightenment.

I.LU.SÃO, *s.f.*, illusion, illusiveness, fantasy, fancy.

I.LU.SI.O.NIS.MO, *s.m.*, illusionism.

I.LU.SI.O.NIS.TA, *s. 2 gen.*, illusionist.

I.LU.SÓ.RIO, *adj.*, illusory, delusive, deceptive, delusory.

I.LUS.TRA.ÇÃO, *s.f.*, illustration, knowledge, culture, erudition, picture.

I.LUS.TRA.DO, *adj.*, illustrated, erudite, learned, cultured.

I.LUS.TRA.DOR, *s.m.*, illustrator.

I.LUS.TRAR, *v.*, to illustrate, to illuminate, to illumine, to elucidate, to explain.

I.LUS.TRA.TI.VO, *adj.*, illustrative, elucidative.

I.LUS.TRE, *adj., s. 2 gen.*, illustrious, eximious, famous, egregious, brilliant.

I.LUS.TRÍS.SI.MO, *superl.*, honorable gentleman; very illustrious.

Í.MÃ, *s.m.*, magnet, loadstone.

I.MA.CU.LA.DO, *adj.*, immaculate, spotless.

I.MA.CU.LÁ.VEL, *adj.*, that cannot be maculated.

I.MA.GEM, *s.f.*, image, drawing, painting, likeness, semblance, picture.

I.MA.GÉ.TI.CO, *s.f.*, fully illustrated.

I.MA.GI.NA.ÇÃO, *s.f.*, imagination.

I.MA.GI.NAR, *v.*, to imagine, to suppose, to conjecture, to invent.

I.MA.GI.NÁ.RIO, *adj.*, imaginary, fantastic, fictive.

I.MA.GI.NA.TI.VO, *adj.*, imaginative, creative, inventive.

I.MA.GI.NÁ.VEL, *adj.*, imaginable.

I.MA.GI.NO.SO, *adj.*, fanciful, imaginary, illusory.

I.MA.NÊN.CI.A, *s.f.*, immanence, immanency.

I.MA.NEN.TE, *adj.*, immanent, inherent.

I.MAN.TAR, *v.*, to magnetize.

I.MA.TE.RI.AL, *adj.*, immaterial.

I.MA.TE.RI.A.LI.DA.DE, *s.f.*, immateriality.

I.MA.TU.RI.DA.DE, *s.f.*, immaturity, precocity, untimeliness.

I.MA.TU.RO, *adj.*, immature, unripe, premature.

IM.BA.TÍ.VEL, *adj.*, unbeatable.

IM.BE.CIL, *s. 2 gen.*, feeble-minded, imbecile, fool; *adj.*, feeble-minded, idiot, imbecile, silly, stupid.

IM.BE.CI.LI.DA.DE, *s.f.*, imbecility.

IM.BE.CI.LI.ZAR, *v.*, to make imbecile.

IM.BER.BE, *adj.*, beardless, unbearded.

IM.BRI.CA.ÇÃO, *s.f.*, imbrication.

IM.BRI.CAR, *v.*, to imbricate.

IM.BU.Í.DO, *adj.*, imbued.

IM.BU.IR, *v.*, to imbue; *imbuir-se*: to become imbued.

I.ME.DI.A.ÇÃO, *s.f.*, immediacy; neighbourhood.

I.ME.DI.A.TA.MEN.TE, *adv.*, immediately.

I.ME.DI.A.TIS.MO, *s.m.*, immediatism.

I.ME.DI.A.TIS.TA, *s.m.*, immediate.

I.ME.DI.A.TO, *s.m.*, chief officer; *adj.*, immediate, direct, proximate, near, close.

I.ME.MO.RÁ.VEL, *adj.*, immemorial.

I.ME.MO.RI.AL, *adj.*, immemorial, long forgotten.

I.ME.MO.RI.Á.VEL, *adj.*, the same that *imemorial*.

I.MEN.SI.DA.DE, *s.f.*, immensity, immenseness.

I.MEN.SI.DÃO, *s.f.*, the same that *imensidade*.

I.MEN.SO, *adj.*, immense, immeasurable, unlimited, great, huge, vast.

I.MEN.SU.RÁ.VEL, *adj.*, immensurable.

I.ME.RE.CI.DO, *adj.*, gratuitous, unworthy, immerited.

I.MER.GIR, *v.*, to immerse, to immerge, to plunge into, to penetrate.

I.MER.SÃO, *s.f.*, immersion, plunge.

I.MER.SÍ.VEL, *adj.*, immersible.

I.MER.SO, *adj.*, immersed.

I.MI.GRA.ÇÃO, *s.f.*, immigration.

I.MI.GRAN.TE, *s. 2 gen.*, immigrant.

I.MI.GRAR, *v.*, to immigrate, migrate.

I.MI.NÊN.CI.A, *s.f.*, imminence.

I.MI.NEN.TE, *adj.*, imminent.

I.MI.TA.ÇÃO, *s.f.*, imitation, copy; sham, mock.

I.MI.TA.DO, *adj.*, imitated, imitative, copied, sham.

I.MI.TAR, *v.*, to imitate, to copy, to reproduce, to assume, to pretend.

I.MI.TA.TI.VO, *adj.*, imitative, imitational.

Í.MO, *adj.*, intimate, inmost.

I.MO.BI.LI.Á.RI.A, *s.f.*, real estate office.

I.MO.BI.LI.Á.RIO, *s.m.*, immovable, real estate, property; *adj.*, of, pertaining to or relative to immovable property.

I.MO.BI.LI.DA.DE, *s.f.*, immobility, immovability.

I.MO.BI.LIS.MO, *s.m., Pol.*, immobilism.

I.MO.BI.LI.ZA.ÇÃO, *s.f.*, immobilization.

I.MO.BI.LI.ZA.DOR, *adj.*, immobilizing.

I.MO.BI.LI.ZAR, *v.*, to immobilize, to fix, to impede.

I.MO.DE.RA.ÇÃO, *s.f.*, immoderation.

I.MO.DE.RA.DO, *adj.*, immoderate, excessive, intemperate.

I.MO.DÉS.TI.A, *s.f.*, immodesty.

I.MO.DES.TO, *adj.*, immodest, arrogant.

I.MO.LA.ÇÃO, *s.f.*, immolation.

I.MO.LAR, *v.*, to immolate, sacrifice.

I.MO.RAL, *adj.*, immoral, vicious, indecent.

I.MO.RA.LI.DA.DE, *s.f.*, immorality, vice, wickedness.

I.MO.RA.LIS.MO, *s.m.*, immoralism.

I.MOR.RE.DOU.RO, *adj.*, immortal, deathless.

I.MOR.TAL, *adj.*, immortal, undying, deathless, eternal.

I.MOR.TA.LI.DA.DE, *s.f.*, immortality, eternity.

I.MOR.TA.LI.ZAR, *v.*, to immortalize, to eternalize, to become famous.

I.MÓ.VEL, *s.m.*, real estate, landed property, property, building; *adj.*, immobile, immovable.

IM.PA.CI.ÊN.CIA, *s.f.*, impatience, restlessness, anxiety, irritability.

IM.PA.CI.EN.TAR, *v.*, to grow impatient.

IM.PA.CI.EN.TE, *adj.*, impatient, eager, restive, hasty, quick.

IM.PAC.TAN.TE, *adj.*, shattering (shocking).

IM.PAC.TO, *s.m.*, impact, discharge, shot, shock, hit.

IM.PAC.TAR, *v.*, to shatter; to crash into.

IM.PA.GÁ.VEL, *adj.*, impayable, not payable.

IM.PAL.PÁ.VEL, *adj.*, impalpable.

ÍM.PAR, *adj.*, odd, uneven, unique.

IM.PAR.CI.AL, *adj.*, impartial, fair.

IM.PAR.CIA.LI.DA.DE, *s.f.*, impartiality.

IM.PAS.SE, *s.m.*, impasse, predicament, dilemma.

IMPASSIBILIDADE ·· 210 ··· IMPRENSA

IM.PAS.SI.BI.LI.DA.DE, *s.f.*, impassibility.
IM.PAS.SÍ.VEL, *adj.*, impassive, impassible.
IM.PÁ.VI.DO, *adj.*, impavid, fearless, brave.
IM.PE.CÁ.VEL, *adj.*, impeccable.
IM.PE.DÂN.CI.A, *s.f.*, *Eletr.*, impedance.
IM.PE.DI.DO, *adj.*, hindered, obstructed, blocked.
IM.PE.DI.MEN.TO, *s.m.*, hindrance, obstruction, impediment, impeachment.
IM.PE.DIR, *v.*, to impede, to hinder, to obstruct, to intercept, to deter, to restrain.
IM.PE.LIR, *v.*, to impel, to push on, to throw, to thrust, to incite.
IM.PE.NE.TRÁ.VEL, *adj.*, impenetrable, not penetrable.
IM.PEN.SA.DO, *adj.*, thoughtless, heedless, wild.
IM.PEN.SÁ.VEL, *adj.*, unthinkable, inconceivable.
IM.PE.RA.DOR, *s.m.*, emperor.
IM.PE.RAR, *v.*, to reign, to rule, to command, to govern, to dominate.
IM.PE.RA.TI.VO, *s.m.*, imperative, *Gram.*, imperative mood; *adj.*, imperative, absolute, obligatory.
IM.PE.RA.TRIZ, *s.f.*, imperatrix, empress.
IM.PER.CEP.TÍ.VEL, *adj.*, imperceptible, insensible.
IM.PER.DÍ.VEL, *adj.*, unmissable.
IM.PER.DO.Á.VEL, *adj.*, unpardonable, inexcusable, unforgivable.
IM.PE.RE.CÍ.VEL, *adj.*, imperishable.
IM.PER.FEI.ÇÃO, *s.f.*, imperfection, fault, defectiveness.
IM.PER.FEI.TO, *s.m.*, *Gram.*, imperfect tense; *adj.*, imperfect, defective, deficient.
IM.PE.RI.AL, *adj.*, imperial.
IM.PE.RIA.LIS.MO, *s.m.*, imperialism.
IM.PE.RI.A.LIS.TA, *s. 2 gen.*, imperialist; *adj.*, imperialistic.
IM.PE.RÍ.CIA, *s.f.*, unskilfulness, incapacity, incompetence.
IM.PÉ.RIO, *s.m.*, empire, imperium, monarchy.
IM.PE.RI.O.SA.MEN.TE, *adv.*, imperiously.
IM.PE.RI.O.SO, *adj.*, imperious, commanding, urgent.
IM.PER.ME.A.BI.LI.DA.DE, *s.f.*, impermeability.
IM.PER.ME.A.BI.LI.ZAN.TE, *s.m.*, waterproofer *adj.*, waterproofing.
IM.PER.ME.A.BI.LI.ZAR, *v.*, to render impermeable.
IM.PER.ME.Á.VEL, *s.m.*, raincoat; *adj.*, impermeable, impenetrable, waterproof.
IM.PER.TI.NÊN.CIA, *s.f.*, impertinence, irrelevance, annoyance.
IM.PER.TI.NEN.TE, *adj.*, impertinent, insolent, petulant, importune.
IM.PER.TUR.BÁ.VEL, *adj.*, imperturbable.
IM.PES.SO.AL, *adj.*, impersonal.
IM.PES.SO.A.LI.DA.DE, *s.f.*, impersonality.
ÍM.PE.TO, *s.m.*, impulse, rashness, emotion.
IM.PE.TRA.ÇÃO, *s.f.*, impetration.
IM.PE.TRAR, *v.*, to impetrate, to supplicate, to petition.
IM.PE.TU.O.SI.DA.DE, *s.f.*, impetuosity, impetuousness.
IM.PE.TU.O.SO, *adj.*, impetuous, hasty, furious, vehement.
IM.PI.E.DA.DE, *s.f.*, impiety.
IM.PI.E.DO.SO, *adj.*, merciless, ruthless.
IM.PIN.GIR, *v.*, to impinge, to strike, to dash, to force.
ÍM.PIO, *s.m.*, impious man; *adj.*, impious, ungodly, profane.
IM.PLA.CÁ.VEL, *adj.*, implacable, inexorable, unappeasable.
IM.PLAN.TA.ÇÃO, *s.f.*, implantation.
IM.PLAN.TAR, *v.*, to introduce, to establish, to implant, to insert, to instil.

IM.PLAN.TE, *s.m.*, implant.
IM.PLE.MEN.TO, *s.m.*, implement, accessory.
IM.PLI.CA.ÇÃO, *s.f.*, implication.
IM.PLI.CAR, *v.*, to implicate, to involve, to entangle, to imply, to embarrass, to hint, to include.
IM.PLÍ.CI.TO, *adj.*, implicit, implicate, implied, inferred.
IM.PLO.DIR, *v.*, to implode.
IM.PLO.RA.ÇÃO, *s.f.*, imploration.
IM.PLO.RAR, *v.*, to implore, to entreat, to supplicate, to beseech.
IM.PLO.SÃO, *s.f.*, implosion.
IM.PO.LU.TO, *adj.*, unpolluted.
IM.PON.DE.RA.DO, *adj.*, inconsiderate, heedless, rash.
IM.PON.DE.RÁ.VEL, *adj.*, imp0nderable.
IM.PO.NÊN.CIA, *s.f.*, portliness, imposingness, majesty.
IM.PO.NEN.TE, *adj.*, imponent, impressive, imposing.
IM.PON.TU.AL, *adj.*, unpunctual.
IM.PON.TU.A.LI.DA.DE, *s.f.*, impunctuality.
IM.PO.PU.LAR, *adj.*, unpopular.
IM.PO.PU.LA.RI.DA.DE, *s.f.*, unpopularity.
IM.POR, *v.*, to impose, to burden, to lay on, to encumber, to direct, to command.
IM.POR.TA.ÇÃO, *s.f.*, importation, import(s), entry.
IM.POR.TA.DOR, *s.m.*, importer.
IM.POR.TÂN.CIA, *s.f.*, importance, sum, consideration, regard, emphasis, preciousness.
IM.POR.TAN.TE, *adj.*, important, essential, significant, pretentious.
IM.POR.TAR, *v.*, to import, to interest, to matter, to aggregate, to concern.
IM.POR.TE, *s.m.*, total amount; sum, cost.
IM.POR.TU.NA.ÇÃO, *s.f.*, importunity, annoyance.
IM.POR.TU.NAR, *v.*, to importune, to annoy, to molest, to embarrass.
IM.POR.TU.NO, *s.m.*, annoyer, molester; *adj.*, importunate, importune, worrysome, obstrusive.
IM.PO.SI.ÇÃO, *s.f.*, imposition, assessment, tax, tribute, order.
IM.POS.SI.BI.LI.DA.DE, *s.f.*, impossibility.
IM.POS.SI.BI.LI.TA.DO, *adj.*, unable.
IM.POS.SI.BI.LI.TAR, *v.*, to make impossible, to weaken, to enfeeble.
IM.POS.SÍ.VEL, *adj.*, impossible, unfeasible, unattainable, impracticable.
IM.POS.TA.ÇÃO, *s.f.*, diction, voice placement.
IM.POS.TO, *s.m.*, tax, tribute, duty; *adj.*, forced, enforced; *imposto de renda*: income tax.
IM.POS.TOR, *s.m.*, impostor.
IM.POS.TU.RA, *s.f.*, imposture.
IM.PO.TÊN.CIA, *s.f.*, impotence, impotency.
IM.PO.TEN.TE, *adj.*, impotent.
IM.PRA.TI.CA.BI.LI.DA.DE, *s.f.*, impracticability, impracticableness.
IM.PRA.TI.CÁ.VEL, *adj.*, impracticable, impossible.
IM.PRE.CAR, *v.*, to imprecate, to invoke.
IM.PRE.CAU.ÇÃO, *s.f.*, imprudence, carelessness.
IM.PRE.CI.SÃO, *s.f.*, imprecision, inexactness.
IM.PRE.CI.SO, *adj.*, imprecise, inaccurate, inexact.
IM.PREG.NA.DO, *adj.*, impregnated, saturated.
IM.PREG.NAR, *v.*, to impregnate, to permeate, to fecundate, to steep.
IM.PREN.SA, *s.f.*, press, printing press, newspaper,

IMPRENSADO
•• 211 ••
INAPETENTE

typography.
IM.PREN.SA.DO, *adj.*, pressed, printed.
IM.PREN.SAR, *v.*, to press, to compress, to print, to imprint.
IM.PRES.CIN.DÍ.VEL, *adj.*, necessary, vital, indispensable.
IM.PRES.CRI.TÍ.VEL, *adj.*, imprescriptible.
IM.PRES.SÃO, *s.f.*, feeling, idea, impression, printing, imprint, edition.
IM.PRES.SIO.NAN.TE, *adj.*, impressive, impressing, striking.
IM.PRES.SIO.NAR, *v.*, to impress, to mark, to stamp in, to affect, to touch.
IM.PRES.SI.O.NÁ.VEL, *adj.*, impressionable, impressible.
IM.PRES.SI.O.NIS.MO, *s.m., Art.*, impressionism.
IM.PRES.SI.O.NIS.TA, *s. 2 gen.*, impressionist; *adj.*, impressionist.
IM.PRES.SO, *s.m.*, printed matter; *adj.*, printed.
IM.PRES.SOR, *s.m.*, pressman, printer.
IM.PRES.SO.RA, *s.f.*, printer, printing press.
IM.PRES.TÁ.VEL, *adj.*, useless, worthless, unhelpful.
IM.PRE.TE.RÍ.VEL, *adj.*, unsurpassable, implicit, unconditional, undeclinable.
IM.PRE.VI.DÊN.CI.A, *s.f.*, improvidence, imprudence.
IM.PRE.VI.DEN.TE, *adj.*, improvident, imprudent.
IM.PRE.VI.SÃO, *s.f.*, improvidence, carelessness.
IM.PRE.VI.SÍ.VEL, *adj.*, unexpected, unforeseeable.
IM.PRE.VIS.TO, *s.m.*, unforeseen, unexpected, surprising.
IM.PRI.MIR, *v.*, to print, to imprint, to impress, to stamp.
IM.PRO.BA.BI.LI.DA.DE, *s.f.*, improbability.
IM.PRO.BI.DA.DE, *s.f.*, improbity.
ÍM.PRO.BO, *adj.*, dishonest.
IM.PRO.CE.DEN.TE, *adj.*, unjustified, unfounded, groundless.
IM.PRO.CE.DÊN.CI.A, *s.f.*, groundlessness, unfoundedness.
IM.PRO.DU.TI.VI.DA.DE, *s.f.*, unproductiveness.
IM.PRO.DU.TI.VO, *adj.*, unproductive, barren, nonproductive.
IM.PRO.FÍ.CU.O, *adj.*, useless.
IM.PRO.PÉ.RIO, *s.m.*, affront, insult, outrage.
IM.PRÓ.PRIO, *adj.*, improper, inappropriate, inadequate, inexact, indecorous.
IM.PROR.RO.GÁ.VEL, *adj.*, undelayable, unpostponable, nonpostponable.
IM.PRO.VÁ.VEL, *adj.*, improbable, unlikely.
IM.PRO.VI.DEN.TE, *adj.*, improvident.
IM.PRO.VI.SA.ÇÃO, *s.f.*, improvisation, extemporization.
IM.PRO.VI.SA.DO, *adj.*, improvised, unprepared, extempore.
IM.PRO.VI.SAR, *v.*, to improvise, to improvisate, to extemporize.
IM.PRO.VI.SO, *s.m.*, improvisation, extemporization.
IM.PRU.DÊN.CIA, *s.f.*, imprudence, rashness, heedlesness, indiscretion.
IM.PRU.DEN.TE, *adj.*, imprudent, rash, precipitate, headless, incautious.
IM.PU.DÊN.CI.A, *s.f.*, impudence.
IM.PU.DEN.TE, *adj.*, impudent, shameless, insolent.
IM.PU.DI.CO, *adj.*, shameless, impudent, insolent.
IM.PUG.NA.ÇÃO, *s.f.*, impugnation, impugnment.
IM.PUG.NAR, *v.*, to refute, to contest, to contradict.
IM.PUL.SÃO, *s.f.*, impulse.
IM.PUL.SAR, *v.*, to give impulse, to impel.
IM.PUL.SIO.NAR, *v.*, to animate, to stimulate, to boast.
IM.PUL.SI.VI.DA.DE, *s.f.*, impulsiveness, impetuosity.
IM.PUL.SI.VO *adj.*, impulsive.
IM.PUL.SO, *s.m.*, impulse, impelling force, drive, thrust, push.

IM.PU.NE, *adj.*, unpunished.
IM.PU.NI.DA.DE, *s.f.*, impunity, exemption from penalty.
IM.PU.NÍ.VEL, *adj.*, unpunishable.
IM.PU.RE.ZA, *s.f.*, impurity, uncleanness, muddiness, lees.
IM.PU.RO, *adj.*, impure, dirty, foul.
IM.PU.TA.BI.LI.DA.DE, *s.f.*, imputability.
IM.PU.TA.ÇÃO, *s.f.*, imputation.
IM.PU.TAR, *v.*, to impute, to attribute, to accuse.
IM.PU.TÁ.VEL, *adj.*, imputable.
I.MUN.DÍ.CI.A, *s.f.*, uncleanness.
I.MUN.DÍ.CIE, *s.f.*, uncleanness, filthiness, foulness.
I.MUN.DO, *adj.*, dirty, filthy, unclean, foul, impure, feculent.
I.MU.NE, *adj.*, immune, exempt.
I.MU.NI.DA.DE, *s.f.*, immunity, exemption, franchise.
I.MU.NI.ZA.ÇÃO, *s.f.*, immunization.
I.MU.NI.ZA.DO, *adj.*, immunized.
I.MU.NI.ZA.DOR, *s.m.*, immunizing agent; *adj.*, immunizing.
I.MU.NI.ZAR, *v.*, to immunize.
I.MU.NO.DE.FI.CI.ÊN.CI.A, *s.f., Med.*, immunodeficiency.
I.MU.NO.LO.GI.A, *s.f., Med.*, immunology.
I.MU.TA.BI.LI.DA.DE, *s.f.*, immutability.
I.MU.TÁ.VEL, *adj.*, immutable.
I.NA.BA.LÁ.VEL, *adj.*, unshakeable, unshakable.
I.NÁ.BIL, *adj.*, unfit, incapable, unapt, unskilled.
I.NA.BI.LI.DA.DE, *s.f.*, inability, incapacity, incompetence, inaptness.
I.NA.BI.LI.DO.SO, *adj.*, inept.
I.NA.BI.LI.TA.ÇÃO, *s.f.*, disablement, incapacitation.
I.NA.BI.LI.TAR, *v.*, to disable, to incapacitate, to disqualify; *inabilitar-se*: to fail.
I.NA.BI.TA.DO, *adj.*, uninhabited, unoccupied, untenanted.
I.NA.BI.TÁ.VEL, *adj.*, uninhabitable.
I.NA.CA.BA.DO, *adj.*, unfinished, uncompleted.
I.NA.CA.BÁ.VEL, *adj.*, unfinishable, interminable, unending.
I.NA.ÇÃO, *s.f.*, inaction.
I.NA.CEI.TÁ.VEL, *adj.*, unacceptable.
I.NA.CES.SI.BI.LI.DA.DE, *s.f.*, inaccessibility.
I.NA.CES.SÍ.VEL, *adj.*, inacessible, impervious, unapproachable, exclusive.
I.NA.CRE.DI.TÁ.VEL, *adj.*, incredible, unbelievable, doubtful.
I.NA.DAP.TA.ÇÃO, *s.f.*, inadaptation, inadaptability.
I.NA.DE.QUA.DO, *adj.*, inadequate, improper, inappropriate, unfit.
I.NA.DI.Á.VEL, *adj.*, undelayable, pressing.
I.NA.DIM.PLÊN.CI.A, *s.f., Jur.*, non-compliance.
I.NAD.MIS.SÍ.VEL, *adj.*, inadmissible, unpermissible.
I.NAD.VER.TÊN.CI.A, *s.f.*, inadvertence.
I.NAD.VER.TI.DA.MEN.TE, *adv.*, inadvertently.
I.NAD.VER.TI.DO, *adj.*, inadvertent, headless, careless.
I.NA.LA.ÇÃO, *s.f.*, inhalation.
I.NA.LA.DOR, *s.m.*, inhaler.
I.NA.LAR, *v.*, to inhale, to breath in.
I.NAL.CAN.ÇÁ.VEL, *adj.*, inaccessible, unachievable.
I.NA.LI.E.NA.BI.LI.DA.DE, *s.f.*, inalienability.
I.NA.LI.E.NA.DO, *adj.*, not alienated.
I.NA.LIE.NÁ.VEL, *adj.*, inalienable.
I.NA.NI.ÇÃO, *s.f.*, inanition, starvation.
I.NA.NI.MA.DO, *adj.*, inanimate, lifeless, dead.
I.NA.PE.LÁ.VEL, *adj.*, inappellable.
I.NA.PE.TÊN.CI.A, *s.f.*, inappetence, inappetency.
I.NA.PE.TEN.TE, *adj.*, inappetent.

INAPLICÁVEL ·· 212 ·· INCOMUNICÁVEL

I.NA.PLI.CÁ.VEL, *adj.*, inapplicable.
I.NA.PRO.PRI.A.DO, *adj.*, impropriate, unsuitable.
I.NAP.TI.DÃO, *s.f.*, inaptness, inability, inaptitude.
I.NAP.TO, *adj.*, inapt, unfit.
I.NA.TA.CÁ.VEL, *adj.*, unassailable, unimpeachable.
I.NA.TEN.ÇÃO, *s.f.*, inattention, negligence.
I.NA.TIN.GÍ.VEL, *adj.*, unachievable, unattainable.
I.NA.TI.VI.DA.DE, *s.f.*, inactivity, inertness.
I.NA.TI.VO, *adj.*, inactive, inert, passive, idle, indolent.
I.NA.TO, *adj.*, innate, native, inborn, connate.
I.NAU.DI.TO, *adj.*, unprecedented, unheard; extraordinary.
I.NAU.DÍ.VEL, *adj.*, inaudible.
I.NAU.GU.RA.ÇÃO, *s.f.*, inauguration, initiation, beginning, opening.
I.NAU.GU.RAL, *adj.*, inaugural.
I.NAU.GU.RAR, *v.*, to inaugurate, to initiate.
IN.CA, *s. 2 gen.*, Inca; *adj.*, Incan.
IN.CA.BÍ.VEL, *adj.*, irrelevant, unreasonable.
IN.CAI.CO, *adj.*, Incan.
IN.CAL.CU.LÁ.VEL, *adj.*, incalculable.
IN.CAN.DES.CÊN.CIA, *s.f.*, incandescence, incandescency.
IN.CAN.DES.CEN.TE, *adj.*, incandescent, red hot, aglow, fervent.
IN.CAN.SÁ.VEL, *adj.*, tireless, unweariable, untiring.
IN.CA.PA.CI.DA.DE, *s.f.*, incapacity.
IN.CA.PA.CI.TAR, *v.*, to incapacitate.
IN.CA.PA.CI.TÁ.VEL, *adj.*, impossible of being capacitated.
IN.CA.PAZ, *adj.*, incapable, inapt, unfit, incompetent, inefficient.
IN.CAU.TO, *adj.*, incautious, unwary, heedless, imprudent.
IN.CEN.DI.AR, *v.*, to ignite, to set on fire, to enkindle, to inflame, to excite.
IN.CEN.DI.Á.RI.O, *s.m.*, incendiary.
IN.CÊN.DIO, *s.m.*, fire, blaze, burning, conflagration.
IN.CEN.SAR, *v.*, to incense, to aromatise.
IN.CEN.SO, *s.m.*, incense, aromatic fumes, perfume; flattery, adulation.
IN.CEN.TI.VA.DOR, *s.m.*, stimulator; *adj.*, stimulating, motivating.
IN.CEN.TI.VAR, *v.*, to stimulate, to animate, to encourage, to incite.
IN.CEN.TI.VO, *s.m.*, incentive, impulse, incitement, encouragement.
IN.CER.TE.ZA, *s.f.*, uncertainty, uncertainness, dubiety, incertitude, hesitance, hesitation.
IN.CER.TO, *adj.*, uncertain, hesitating, doubtful, dubious, insecure.
IN.CES.SAN.TE, *adj.*, incessant, permanent.
IN.CES.TO, *s.m.*, incest.
IN.CES.TU.O.SO, *adj.*, incestuous.
IN.CHA.ÇÃO, *s.f.*, swelling, tumour, tumefaction.
IN.CHA.ÇO, *s.m., pop.*, swelling, bump, lump.
IN.CHA.DO, *adj.*, swollen, turgid, turgescent, inflated, exalted.
IN.CHA.MEN.TO, *s.m.*, the same that *inchação*.
IN.CHAR, *v.*, to swell, to intumesce, to inflate, to bulge, to rise, to belly.
IN.CI.DÊN.CIA, *s.f.*, incidence, incidency.
IN.CI.DEN.TAL, *adj.*, incidental.
IN.CI.DEN.TE, *s.m.*, incident.
IN.CI.DIR, *v.* to happen, to occur, to fall on or fall upon.
IN.CI.NE.RA.ÇÃO, *s.f.*, incineration.

IN.CI.NE.RA.DOR, *s.m.*, incinerator; *adj.*, incinerating.
IN.CI.NE.RAR, *v.*, to incinerate, to cremate.
IN.CI.PI.EN.TE, *adj., s. 2 gen.*, incipient.
IN.CI.SÃO, *s.f.*, cut, incision.
IN.CI.SI.VO, *adj.*, incisive, cutting, sharp, keen.
IN.CI.TA.ÇÃO, *s.f.*, incitation, incitement, encouragement, sedition.
IN.CI.TA.DOR, *s.m.*, inciter, instigator; *adj.*, inciting, stimulating.
IN.CI.TA.MEN.TO, *s.m.*, incitement, incitation.
IN.CI.TAN.TE, *adj.*, incitant, inciting.
IN.CI.TAR, *v.*, to incite, to stimulate, to inspire, to encourage, to excite.
IN.CI.VIL, *adj.*, discorteous, incivil.
IN.CI.VI.LI.DA.DE, *s.f.*, incivility, discourtesy, disrespect.
IN.CI.VI.LI.ZA.DO, *adj.*, uncivilized.
IN.CI.VI.LI.ZÁ.VEL, *adj.*, incapable of being civilized, benighted.
IN.CLAS.SI.FI.CÁ.VEL, *adj.*, unclassifiable, untidy, disorderly.
IN.CLE.MÊN.CIA, *s.f.*, inclemency.
IN.CLE.MEN.TE, *adj.*, inclement, merciless, ruthless.
IN.CLI.NA.ÇÃO, *s.f.*, incline, inclination, bow, nod, bending, vocation, tendency.
IN.CLI.NAR, *v.*, to incline, to recline, to tilt, to slope, to bow, to bend, to be fond.
ÍN.CLI.TO, *adj.*, prominent, distinguished, eminent, famous.
IN.CLU.IR, *v.*, to include, to enclose, to comprise, to comprehend, to contain, to add in, to involve.
IN.CLU.SÃO, *s.f.*, inclusion, inclosure, enclosure.
IN.CLU.SI.VE, *adv.*, inclusively.
IN.CLU.SI.VO, *adj.*, inclusive, included, including.
IN.CLU.SO, *adj.*, included, enclosed.
IN.CO.E.RÊN.CI.A, *s.f.*, incoherence.
IN.CO.E.REN.TE, *adj.*, incoherent, disjointed.
IN.CÓG.NI.TA, *s.f.*, unknown quantity.
IN.CÓG.NI.TO, *s.m.*, incognito; *adj.*, incognito, unknown.
IN.COG.NOS.CÍ.VEL, *adj.*, incognoscible.
IN.CO.LOR, *adj.*, colourless.
IN.CÓ.LU.ME, *adj.*, unhurt, scarless, entire, whole.
IN.CO.MEN.SU.RÁ.VEL, *adj.*, incommensurable, unmeasurable.
IN.CO.MO.DAR, *v.*, to incommode, to trouble, to disturb, to importune.
IN.CÔ.MO.DO, *s.m.*, indisposition, disease, discomfort, trouble, disturbance, nuisance, fatigue.
IN.COM.PA.RÁ.VEL, *adj.*, incomparable, matchless, peerless.
IN.COM.PAS.SÍ.VEL, *adj.*, uncompassionate.
IN.COM.PA.TI.BI.LI.DA.DE, *s.f.*, incompatibility.
IN.COM.PA.TI.BI.LI.ZAR, *v.*, to make incompatible, to make irreconcilable.
IN.COM.PE.TÊN.CIA, *s.f.*, incompetence, incapacity, inability.
IN.COM.PE.TEN.TE, *adj.*, incompetent, unfit.
IN.COM.PLE.TO, *adj.*, incomplete, unfinished, uncompleted, fragmentary.
IN.COM.PRE.EN.DI.DO, *adj.*, misunderstood.
IN.COM.PRE.EN.SÃO, *s.f.*, incomprehension.
IN.COM.PRE.EN.SÍ.VEL, *adj.*, incomprehensible, inconceivable, impenetrable.
IN.COM.PRE.EN.SI.VO, *adj.*, uncomprehending.
IN.CO.MUM, *adj.*, uncommon, unusual, scarce, rare.
IN.CO.MU.NI.CÁ.VEL, *adj.*, cut off ; incommunicable; *fig.*, unsociable.

INCONCEBÍVEL · 213 · INDESCULPÁVEL

IN.CON.CE.BÍ.VEL, *adj.*, inconceivable, incomprehensible, extraordinary.

IN.CON.CI.LI.Á.VEL, *adj.*, irreconcilable.

IN.CON.CLU.SI.VO, *adj.*, inconclusive.

IN.CON.CLU.SO, *adj.*, unfinished.

IN.CON.DI.CIO.NAL, *adj.*, unconditional, absolute, categorical.

IN.CON.FES.SÁ.VEL, *adj.*, unconfessable.

IN.CON.FES.SO, *adj.*, unconfessed.

IN.CON.FI.DÊN.CIA, *s.f.*, unconfidence, infidelity, treachery, distrust.

IN.CON.FI.DEN.TE, *adj.*, disloyal, unfaithful.

IN.CON.FOR.MI.DA.DE, *s.f.*, unconformity.

IN.CON.FUN.DÍ.VEL, *adj.*, unconfoundable, unmistakable, distinct.

IN.CON.GRU.ÊN.CIA, *s.f.*, incongruence, incongruity.

IN.CON.GRU.EN.TE, **IN.CÔN.GRU.O**, *adj.*, incongruent, incongruous.

IN.CONS.CI.ÊN.CIA, *s.f.*, unconsciousness.

IN.CONS.CI.EN.TE.MEN.TE, *adv.*, unconsciously.

IN.CONS.CI.EN.TE, *s. 2 gen.*, unconscious; *adj.*, unconscious, unaware, insensible.

IN.CON.SE.QUÊN.CI.A, *s.f.*, inconsequence, inconsistency, incongruence.

IN.CON.SIS.TÊN.CI.A, *s.f.*, inconsistence, inconsistency, weakness.

IN.CON.SIS.TEN.TE, *adj.*, inconsistent, flimsy, incongruous.

IN.CON.SO.LÁ.VEL, *adj.*, inconsolable, disconsolate.

IN.CONS.TÂN.CIA, *s.f.*, inconstancy, instability.

IN.CONS.TAN.TE, *adj.*, inconstant, changeable.

IN.CONS.TI.TU.CIO.NAL, *adj.*, unconstitutional.

IN.CONS.TI.TU.CI.O.NA.LI.DA.DE, *s.f.*, unconstitutionality.

IN.CON.TÁ.VEL, *adj.*, countless, uncountable.

IN.CON.TES.TÁ.VEL, *adj.*, incontestable, certain.

IN.CON.TI.DO, *adj.*, unrestricted.

IN.CON.TI.NÊN.CIA, *s.f.*, incontinence.

IN.CON.TI.NEN.TE, *s. 2 gen.*, licentious person; *adj., Med.*, incontinent, unrestrained.

IN.CON.TOR.NÁ.VEL, *adj.*, that cannot be bypassed.

IN.CON.TRO.LÁ.VEL, *adj.*, uncontrollable.

IN.CON.TRO.VER.SO, *adj.*, incontrovertible, uncontroverted.

IN.CON.VE.NI.ÊN.CIA, *s.f.*, inconvenience, impoliteness, inconveniency.

IN.CON.VE.NI.EN.TE, *s.m.*, disadvantage, nuisance, obstacle; *adj.*, inconvenient, unsuitable.

IN.COR.PO.RA.ÇÃO, *s.f., Com.*, incorporation, embodiment; annexation.

IN.COR.PO.RA.DO, *adj.*, incorporated, consolidated.

IN.COR.PO.RA.DOR, *s.m.*, incorporator.

IN.COR.PO.RAR, *v.*, to incorporate, to embody, to connect.

IN.COR.RE.ÇÃO, *s.f.*, incorrection, inaccuracy.

IN.COR.RER, *v.*, to incur, to run into.

IN.COR.RE.TO, *adj.*, incorrect, faulty, wrong.

IN.COR.RI.GÍ.VEL, *adj.*, incorrigible, incurable, hopeless.

IN.COR.RUP.TÍ.VEL, *adj.*, incorruptible.

IN.CRE.DU.LI.DA.DE, *s.f.*, incredulity, ungodliness, unbelief.

IN.CRÉ.DU.LO, *s.m.*, sceptic, agnostic, unbeliever; *adj.*, incredulous, ungodly, impious.

IN.CRE.MEN.TA.ÇÃO, *s.f.*, the same that *incremento*.

IN.CRE.MEN.TAR, *v.*, to develop, to augment, to increase, to swell.

IN.CRE.MEN.TO, *s.m.*, increment, incrementation, development, increase.

IN.CRI.MI.NA.ÇÃO, *s.f.*, incrimination.

IN.CRI.MI.NAR, *v.*, to incriminate, to accuse, to blame, to criminate.

IN.CRÍ.VEL, *adj.*, incredible, unbelievable, extraordinary.

IN.CRUS.TA.ÇÃO, *s.f.*, incrustation, inlay.

IN.CRUS.TA.DO, *adj.*, inlaid.

IN.CRUS.TAR, *v.*, to incrust, to inlay.

IN.CU.BA.ÇÃO, *s.f.*, incubation.

IN.CU.BA.DO.RA, *s.f.*, incubator.

IN.CU.BAR, *v.*, to incubate, to hatch.

ÍN.CU.BO, *s.m.*, incubus; *adj.*, lying, recumbent.

IN.CUL.CAR, *v.*, to inculcate.

IN.CUL.TI.VÁ.VEL, *adj.*, uncultivable.

IN.CUL.TO, *adj.*, uncultivated, uncultured, fallow, rough.

IN.CUM.BÊN.CIA, *s.f.*, incumbency, task, duty, responsibility.

IN.CUM.BIR, *v.*, to encharge, to charge with, to entrust, to assign a duty.

IN.CU.RÁ.VEL, *adj.*, incurable, irremediable.

IN.CÚ.RIA, *s.f.*, negligence, carelessness.

IN.CUR.SÃO, *s.f.*, incursion, raid, foray, attack.

IN.CU.TIR, *v.*, to infuse, to instil, to inspire, to inculcate, to suggest.

IN.DA.GA.ÇÃO, *s.f.*, searching, search, indagation, quest, inquiry.

IN.DA.GAR, *v.*, to inquire, to investigate, to query, to quest, to scan, to search.

IN.DE.CÊN.CIA, *s.f.*, indecency, indelicacy, immorality, obscenity.

IN.DE.CEN.TE, *adj., s. 2 gen.*, indecent, indecorous, vulgar, improper.

IN.DE.CI.FRÁ.VEL, *adj.*, undecipherable, indecipherable, illegible; *fig.*, intricate.

IN.DE.CI.SÃO, *s.f.*, indecision, irresolution, vacillation, hesitation, doubt.

IN.DE.CI.SO, *adj.*, undecided, undecisive, hesitant, vacillating, unconfirmed.

IN.DE.CO.RO, *s.m.*, indecorum, impropriety, indecency.

IN.DE.CO.RO.SO, *adj.*, indecorous, unseemly.

IN.DE.FEC.TÍ.VEL, *adj.*, indefectible, unfailable.

IN.DE.FEN.SÁ.VEL, *adj.*, indefensible.

IN.DE.FE.RI.DO, *adj.*, rejected, refused.

IN.DE.FE.RI.MEN.TO, *s.m.*, denial, refusal, rejection.

IN.DE.FE.RIR, *v.*, to refuse, to reject a demand.

IN.DE.FE.SO, *adj.*, defenceless, unprotected, undefended.

IN.DE.FI.NI.DA.MEN.TE, *adv.*, indefinitely.

IN.DE.FI.NI.DO, *s.m.*, vagueness, indefiniteness; *adj.*, indefinite, vague, uncertain.

IN.DE.LÉ.VEL, *adj.*, indelible, indeleble.

IN.DE.LI.CA.DE.ZA, *s.f.*, indelicacy, discourtesy, incivility, unkindness.

IN.DE.LI.CA.DO, *adj.*, indelicate, indecent, impolite, rude.

IN.DE.NI.ZA.ÇÃO, *s.f.*, indemnity, indemnification, reparation, damage.

IN.DE.NI.ZAR, *v.*, to indemnify, to repay, to reimburse, to compensate.

IN.DE.PEN.DÊN.CIA, *s.f.*, independence, autonomy, freedom, liberty, independency.

IN.DE.PEN.DEN.TE, *adj.*, independent, free, autonomous.

IN.DES.CRI.TÍ.VEL, *adj.*, unspeakable, indescribable.

IN.DES.CUL.PÁ.VEL, *adj.*, inexcusable, unforgivable.

INDESEJADO ··214·· INEQUAÇÃO

IN.DE.SE.JA.DO, *adj.*, undesired, unwished.
IN.DE.SE.JÁ.VEL, *s. 2 gen.*, undesired person; *adj.*, undesirable.
IN.DES.TRU.TÍ.VEL, *adj.*, undestroyable.
IN.DE.TER.MI.NA.ÇÃO, *s.f.*, undetermination, hesitation.
IN.DE.TER.MI.NA.DO, *adj.*, indeterminate, imprecise, indefinite.
IN.DE.TER.MI.NAR, *v.*, to make indetermined.
IN.DE.TER.MI.NÁ.VEL, *adj.*, indeterminable, undeterminable.
IN.DE.VAS.SÁ.VEL, *adj.*, inaccessible.
IN.DE.VI.DA.MEN.TE, *adv.*, unduly, wrongly.
IN.DE.VI.DO, *adj.*, undue, improper.
ÍN.DEX, *s.m.*, index.
IN.DE.XA.ÇÃO, *s.f.*, indexing.
IN.DE.XAR, *v.*, to index.
ÍN.DIA, *s.*, India.
IN.DI.A.NO, *adj.*, *s.m.*, Indian.
IN.DI.CA.ÇÃO, *s.f.*, indication, nomination, designation, manifestation, sign, evidence.
IN.DI.CA.DO, *adj.*, designate.
IN.DI.CA.DOR, *s.m.*, indicator; index-finger, dial; *adj.*, indicatory, indicative, indicant.
IN.DI.CAR, *v.*, to indicate, to denote, to appoint, to show, to determine.
IN.DI.CA.TI.VO, *s.m.*, sign, mark, indication, indicative mod; *adj.*, indicative, expressive.
ÍN.DI.CE, *s.m.*, index, catalogue, table.
IN.DI.CI.A.ÇÃO, *s.f.*, circumstantial evidence, indictment.
IN.DI.CI.AR, *v.*, to denounce, to accuse.
IN.DÍ.CIO, *s.f.*, indicium, indication, clue, trace, vestige.
ÍN.DI.CO, *s.*, the Indian (the Oean); *adj.*, Indian (pertaining to or relating to India or the Ocean).
IN.DI.FE.REN.ÇA, *s.f.*, indifference, indifferency, unconcern, negligence, apathy.
IN.DI.FE.REN.TE, *adj.*, indifferent, unconcerned, negligent, careless.
IN.DÍ.GE.NA, *s. 2 gen.*, indigene, native, aborigine.
IN.DI.GÊN.CI.A, *s.f.*, poverty, indigence, poorness.
IN.DI.GEN.TE, *s. 2 gen.*, beggar, pauper, poor; *adj.*, indigent, poor.
IN.DI.GES.TÃO, *s.f.*, indigestion.
IN.DI.GES.TO, *adj.*, indigestible, indigestive; *fig.*, boring.
IN.DIG.NA.ÇÃO, *s.f.*, indignation, vexation.
IN.DIG.NA.DO, *adj.*, indignant.
IN.DIG.NAR, *v.*, to cause indignation, to provoke.
IN.DIG.NI.DA.DE, *s.f.*, indignity, unworthiness.
IN.DIG.NO, *adj.*, unworthy, worthless.
ÍN.DIO, *adj.*, *s.m.*, Indian.
IN.DI.RE.TA, *s.f.*, allusion, hint.
IN.DI.RE.TO, *adj.*, indirect, oblique, disguised, simulated.
IN.DIS.CI.PLI.NA, *s.f.*, indiscipline, insubordination, disorder, unruliness.
IN.DIS.CI.PLI.NA.DO, *adj.*, undisciplined, indisciplined.
IN.DIS.CRE.TO, *adj.*, indiscreet, imprudent, injudicious.
IN.DIS.CRI.ÇÃO, *s.f.*, indiscretion.
IN.DIS.CRI.MI.NA.ÇÃO, *s.f.*, indiscrimination.
IN.DIS.CRI.MI.NA.DO, *adj.*, indiscriminate.
IN.DIS.CU.TÍ.VEL, *adj.*, incontestable, unquestionable.
IN.DIS.FAR.ÇÁ.VEL, *adj.*, undisguisable.
IN.DIS.PEN.SÁ.VEL, *adj.*, indispensable, essential.
IN.DIS.PO.NI.BI.LI.DA.DE, *s.f.*, unavailability, unavailableness.

IN.DIS.PO.NÍ.VEL, *adj.*, unavailable.
IN.DIS.POR, *v.*, to indispose, disincline, to irritate, to upset, to alienate.
IN.DIS.PO.SI.ÇÃO, *s.f.*, indisposition, ailment, dislike, aversion.
IN.DIS.POS.TO, *adj.*, indisposed, unwell, sick, ailing, disliking.
IN.DIS.SO.LU.ÇÃO, *s.f.*, *Quím.*, state of being undissolved.
IN.DIS.SO.LÚ.VEL, *adj.*, indissoluble, not dissolvable.
IN.DI.VI.DU.AL, *adj.*, individual, personal, single, singular.
IN.DI.VI.DUA.LI.DA.DE, *s.f.*, individuality, identity.
IN.DI.VI.DUA.LIS.MO, *s.m.*, individualism.
IN.DI.VI.DU.A.LIS.TA, *s. 2 gen.*, individualist; *adj.*, individualistic.
IN.DI.VI.DU.A.LI.ZA.ÇÃO, *s.f.*, individualization.
IN.DI.VI.DUA.LI.ZAR, *v.*, to individualize.
IN.DI.VÍ.DUO, *s.m.*, being, person, fellow, guy.
IN.DI.VI.SI.BI.LI.DA.DE, *s.f.*, indivisibility.
IN.DI.VI.SÍ.VEL, *adj.*, indivisible.
IN.DI.VI.SO, *adj.*, undivided, indivisive, whole.
IN.DI.ZÍ.VEL, *adj.*, unspeakable, inexpressible, extraordinary.
IN.DÓ.CIL, *adj.*, indocile, unruly, wayward, restive, stubborn.
IN.DO.CI.LI.DA.DE, *s.f.*, indocility.
IN.DO-EU.RO.PEU, *s.m.*, *adj.*, Indo-European.
ÍN.DO.LE, *s.f.*, nature, temper, sort, type, character, propensity.
IN.DO.LÊN.CIA, *s.f.*, indolence.
IN.DO.LEN.TE, *adj.*, indolent, negligent, apathetic.
IN.DO.LOR, *adj.*, painless.
IN.DO.NÉ.SI.A, *s.*, Indonesia.
IN.DO.NÉ.SI.O, *s.m.*, Indonesian; *adj.*, Indonesian.
IN.DU.BI.TÁ.VEL, *adj.*, undoubted, certain, assured.
IN.DU.ÇÃO, *s.f.*, induction, suggestion.
IN.DÚC.TIL, *adj.*, inductile.
IN.DUL.GÊN.CIA, *s.f.*, indulgence, clemency.
IN.DU.MEN.TÁ.RI.A, *s.f.*, attire, clothing, garments, apparel.
IN.DÚS.TRIA, *s.f.*, industry, works, diligence.
IN.DUS.TRI.AL, *s. 2 gen.*, manufacturer, producer; *adj.*, industrial, manufacturing.
IN.DUS.TRIA.LI.ZA.ÇÃO, *s.f.*, industrialization.
IN.DUS.TRI.A.LI.ZA.DO, *adj.*, industrialized.
IN.DUS.TRIA.LI.ZAR, *v.*, to industrialize.
IN.DUS.TRI.Á.RIO, *s.m.*, industrial employer.
IN.DUS.TRI.O.SO, *adj.*, industrious.
IN.DU.ZI.DO, *s.m.*, *Eletr.*, armature; *adj.*, induced.
IN.DU.ZIR, *v.*, to induce, to prompt, to incite, to persuade, to conclude.
I.NE.BRI.AN.TE, *adj.*, inebriant, intoxicant.
I.NE.BRI.AR, *v.*, to inebriate, to make drunk, to intoxicate.
I.NE.DI.TIS.MO, *s.m.*, quality of being unpublished.
I.NÉ.DI.TO, *adj.*, inedited, unpublished.
I.NE.FÁ.VEL, *adj.*, ineffable.
I.NE.FI.CÁ.CIA, *s.f.*, inefficacy.
I.NE.FI.CAZ, *adj.*, inefficacious, inoperative, powerless.
I.NE.FI.CI.ÊN.CIA, *s.f.*, inefficiency.
I.NE.FI.CI.EN.TE, *adj.*, inefficient.
I.NE.LE.GI.BI.LI.DA.DE, *s.f.*, inelegibility.
I.NE.LE.GÍ.VEL, *adj.*, ineligible.
I.NE.LU.TÁ.VEL, *adj.*, ineluctable.
I.NE.NAR.RÁ.VEL, *adj.*, incapable of being narrated, unspeakable, inexpressible.
I.NÉP.CI.A, *s.f.*, ineptitude, ineptness.
I.NEP.TO, *adj.*, inept.
I.NE.QUA.ÇÃO, *s.f.*, *Mat.*, inequation.

INEQUÍVOCO ·· 215 ·· INFORTUNADO

I.NE.QUÍ.VO.CO, *adj.*, inequivocal.
I.NÉR.CIA, *s.f.*, inertness, inactivity, indolence.
I.NER.CI.AL, *adj.*, *Fís.*, inertial.
I.NE.REN.TE, *adj.*, inherent, intrinsic, native.
I.NER.TE, *adj.*, inert, inactive, lazy.
I.NES.CRU.PU.LO.SO, *adj.*, unscrupulous.
I.NES.CRU.TÁ.VEL, *adj.*, inscrutable.
I.NES.GO.TA.DO, *adj.*, unexhausted, unspent.
I.NES.GO.TÁ.VEL, *adj.*, inexhaustible, exhaustless, copious, profuse.
I.NES.PE.RA.DO, *adj.*, unexpected, unforeseen, sudden, abrupt.
I.NES.QUE.CÍ.VEL, *adj.*, unforgettable.
I.NE.VI.TÁ.VEL, *adj.*, unavoidable, fatal, unpreventable.
I.NE.XA.TI.DÃO, *s.f.*, inexactitude, inexactness.
I.NE.XA.TO, *adj.*, inexact, incorrect.
I.NE.XAU.RÍ.VEL, *adj.*, inexhaustible.
I.NEX.CE.DÍ.VEL, *adj.*, unsurpassable.
I.NE.XE.CU.TÁ.VEL, *adj.*, inexecutable.
I.NE.XE.QUI.VEL, *adj.*, unfeasible, inexecutable.
I.NE.XIS.TÊN.CIA, *s.f.*, inexistence.
I.NE.XIS.TEN.TE, *adj.*, inexistent, nonexistent.
I.NE.XIS.TIR, *v.*, not to exist.
I.NE.XO.RA.BI.LI.DA.DE, *s.f.*, inexorability.
I.NE.XO.RÁ.VEL, *adj.*, inexorable, inflexible, merciless.
I.NEX.PE.RI.ÊN.CIA, *s.f.*, inexperience, rawness.
I.NEX.PE.RI.EN.TE, *s. 2 gen.*, rookie; *adj. 2 gen.*, inexperienced, green, raw.
I.NEX.PLI.CÁ.VEL, *adj.*, inexplicable, incomprehensible, obscure.
I.NEX.PLO.RA.DO, *adj.*, unexplored.
I.NEX.PRES.SI.VI.DA.DE, *s.f.*, inexpressiveness.
I.NEX.PRES.SI.VO, *adj.*, inexpressive, expressionless.
I.NEX.PRI.MÍ.VEL, *adj.*, inexpressible, unspeakable, unutterable.
I.NEX.PUG.NÁ.VEL, *adj.*, inexpugnable.
IN.FAC.TÍ.VEL, *adj.*, infeasible, impracticable.
IN.FA.LÍ.VEL, *adj.*, infallible, certain, sure.
IN.FA.MAR, *v.*, to defame.
IN.FA.ME, *adj.*, *s. 2 gen.*, infamous, odious, shameful.
IN.FÂ.MIA, *s.f.*, infamy, dishonour, disgrace.
IN.FÂN.CIA, *s.f.*, infancy, childhood.
IN.FAN.TA.RI.A, *s.f.*, *Mil.*, infantry.
IN.FAN.TE, *s. 2 gen.*, infante, child; infant; *s.m.*, infantryman.
IN.FAN.TI.CÍ.DA, *s. 2 gen.*, infanticide.
IN.FAN.TI.CÍ.DI.O, *s.m.*, infanticide.
IN.FAN.TIL, *adj.*, infantile, childish, innocent.
IN.FAN.TI.LI.DA.DE, *s.f.*, childlike nature, childishness.
IN.FAN.TI.LI.ZAR, *v.*, to infantilize.
IN.FAR.TA.DO, *adj.*, infarcted.
IN.FAR.TO, *s.m.*, *Med.*, the same that *enfarte*.
IN.FEC.ÇÃO, *s.f.*, infection, contamination, contagion.
IN.FEC.CI.O.NA.DO, *adj.*, infected, contaminated.
IN.FEC.CIO.NAR, *v.*, to infect, to contaminate, to corrupt, to taint.
IN.FEC.CI.O.SO, *adj.*, infective, infectious, contagious.
IN.FEC.TA.DO, *adj.*, the same that *infeccionado*.
IN.FEC.TO, *adj.*, contaminated; *fig.*, very bad, sick.
IN.FE.CUN.DO, *adj.*, infecund, sterile.
IN.FE.LI.CI.DA.DE, *s.f.*, infelicity, unhappiness, misfortune, adversity.

IN.FE.LIZ, *adj.*, unhappy, unfortunate, unlucky, disastrous.
IN.FE.LIZ.MEN.TE, *adv.*, unfortunately, unhappily.
IN.FEN.SO, *adj.*, adverse, hostile.
IN.FE.RÊN.CI.A, *s.f.*, inference.
IN.FE.RI.OR, *s. 2 gen.*, inferior, subordinate; *adj.*, inferior, low.
IN.FE.RIO.RI.DA.DE, *s.f.*, inferiority.
IN.FE.RI.O.RI.ZAR, *v.*, to make inferior.
IN.FE.RIR, *v.*, to infer.
IN.FER.NAL, *adj.*, infernal, hellish, atrocious, diabolic, terrible.
IN.FER.NI.ZAR, *v.*, to render to hellish, to afflict, to doom.
IN.FER.NO, *s.m.*, hell, underworld.
IN.FES.TAR, *v.*, to infest, attack, molest.
IN.FÉR.TIL, *adj.*, infertile.
IN.FI.DE.LI.DA.DE, *s.f.*, infidelity, disloyalty, falseness.
IN.FI.EL, *adj.*, infidel, unfaithful, disloyal, dishonest, false.
IN.FIL.TRA.ÇÃO, *s.f.*, infiltration.
IN.FIL.TRAR, *v.*, to infiltrate, to infilter, to seep, to penetrate.
ÍN.FI.MO, *adj.*, lowermost, undermost, inferior.
IN.FIN.DÁ.VEL, *adj.*, interminable, boundless, unending.
IN.FI.NI.DA.DE, *s.f.*, infinity, infiniteness.
IN.FI.NI.TI.VO, *s.m.*, infinitive; *adj.*, *Gram.*, infinitive.
IN.FI.NI.TO, *s.m.*, infinite, infinity; *adj.*, infinite, infinitive, boundless, timeless, eternal.
IN.FLA.ÇÃO, *s.f.*, inflation, swelling, pride.
IN.FLA.CIO.NAR, *v.*, to inflate.
IN.FLA.DO, *adj.*, inflated, swollen; *fig.*, conceited.
IN.FLA.MA.ÇÃO, *s.f.*, inflammation, ignition.
IN.FLA.MA.DO, *adj.*, inflamed.
IN.FLA.MAR, *v.*, to inflame, to ignite, to kindle, to excite, to stimulate.
IN.FLA.MÁ.VEL, *adj.*, inflammable.
IN.FLE.XÃO, *s.f.*, inflection, inflexion, variation.
IN.FLE.XI.BI.LI.DA.DE, *s.f.*, inflexibility.
IN.FLE.XÍ.VEL, *adj.*, inflexible, unpliant, stiff, rigid.
IN.FLE.XI.VO, *adj.*, *Gram.*, uninflexed.
IN.FLI.GIR, *v.*, to inflict, to impose.
IN.FLU.ÊN.CIA, *s.f.*, influence, hold, influx, action, power.
IN.FLU.EN.CI.AR, *v.*, to influence, to sway over, to modify, to affect.
IN.FLU.EN.CI.Á.VEL, *adj.*, influenciable.
IN.FLU.EN.TE, *s. 2 gen.*, influencer, big shot; *adj.*, influential, influent.
IN.FLU.EN.ZA, *s.f.*, *Med.*, influenza, flu, grippe.
IN.FLU.IR, *v.*, to influence, to excite, to implant, to impel, to actuate.
IN.FLU.XO, *s.m.*, influx, inflow; high tide.
IN.FOR.MA.ÇÃO, *s.f.*, information, intelligence, report.
IN.FOR.MA.DO, *adj.*, informed, aware, knowing.
IN.FOR.MA.DOR, *s.m.*, informer.
IN.FOR.MAL, *adj.*, informal.
IN.FOR.MA.LI.DA.DE, *s.f.*, informality.
IN.FOR.MAN.TE, *s. 2 gen.*, informer; *adj.*, informant, informative.
IN.FOR.MAR, *v.*, to inform, to teach, to instruct, to confirm, to tell, to notify.
IN.FOR.MÁ.TI.CA, *s.f.*, informatics, computer science.
IN.FOR.MA.TI.VO, *s.m.*, bulletin; *adj.*, informative.
IN.FOR.MA.TI.ZA.ÇÃO, *s.f.*, *Comp.*, computerization.
IN.FOR.MA.TI.ZAR, *v.*, to computerize.
IN.FOR.ME, *s.m.*, information, advice; *Mil.*, intelligence; *adj.*, shapeless.
IN.FOR.TU.NA.DO, *adj.*, unfortunate, fortuneless, unhappy.

INFORTÚNIO ··· 216 ··· INSANO

IN.FOR.TÚ.NIO, s.m., misfortune, infelicity, adversity, unhappiness, misery.

IN.FRA.ÇÃO, s.f., infraction, infringement, breach, transgression.

IN.FRA.TOR, s.m., infractor, transgressor, violator, offender.

IN.FRIN.GIR, v., to infringe, to infract, to violate, to transgress, to break.

IN.FRIN.GÍ.VEL, adj., that can be infringed, breakable.

IN.FRU.TÍ.FE.RO, adj., fruitless, unfruitful.

IN.FUN.DA.DO, adj., unfounded, groundless.

IN.FUN.DIR, v., to infuse, to instill, to inspire.

IN.FU.SÃO, s.f., infusion, maceration.

IN.GÁ, s.m., Bot., inga tree, fruit of these trees.

IN.GA.ZEI.RO, s.m., Bot., inga (tropical shrubs and trees of the mimosa family, genus Inga).

IN.GE.NU.I.DA.DE, s.f., ingenuity, simplicity, naiveness, frankness.

IN.GÊ.NUO, adj., naïve, simple, ingenuous, frank.

IN.GE.RÊN.CI.A, s.f., intervention, interference, meddling.

IN.GE.RIR, v., to ingest, to swallow, to introduce, to interfere in.

IN.GES.TÃO, s.f., ingestion.

IN.GLA.TER.RA, s., England.

IN.GLÊS, adj., s.m., English, British.

IN.GLÓ.RI.O, adj., inglorious.

IN.GO.VER.NÁ.VEL, adj., ungovernable, unruly.

IN.GRA.TI.DÃO, s.f., ingratitude, ungratefulness.

IN.GRA.TO, adj., ungrateful, thankless, ingrate.

IN.GRE.DI.EN.TE, s.m., ingredient, element.

ÍN.GRE.ME, adj., steep, sheer, abrupt.

IN.GRES.SAR, v., to enter, to go in, to ingress.

IN.GRES.SO, s.m., ingress, entry, entrance, admission, admittance, ticket.

ÍN.GUA, s.f., Med., inguinal bubo, bubo of the groin.

IN.GUI.NAL, adj., inguinal.

I.NHA.ME, s.m., Bot., yam.

I.NI.BI.ÇÃO, s.f., inhibition, prohibition.

I.NI.BI.DO, adj., inhibited.

I.NI.BI.DOR, s.m., inhibitor, inhibiter; adj., inhibiting.

I.NI.BIR, v., to inhibit, to check, to forbid, to prohibit, to interdict.

I.NI.CI.A.ÇÃO, s.f., initiation, start.

I.NI.CI.A.DO, adj., initiate, adept.

I.NI.CI.A.DOR, s.m., initiator, founder.

I.NI.CI.AL, s.f., initial; adj., initial; iniciais (pl.): initials.

I.NI.CI.AR, v., to initiate, to begin, to start, to commence, to introduce, to induct.

I.NI.CI.A.TI.VA, s.f., iniciative, enterprise, activity.

I.NÍ.CIO, s.m., beginning, start, commencement, outset, opening.

I.NI.GUA.LÁ.VEL, adj., unequalled.

I.NI.MA.GI.NÁ.VEL, adj., unimaginable.

I.NI.MI.GO, s.m., enemy, adversary, foe, opponent, antagonist; adj., averse, inimical.

I.NI.MI.TÁ.VEL, adj., inimitable.

I.NI.MI.ZA.DE, s.f., enmity, hostility, animosity.

I.NIN.TE.LI.GÍ.VEL, adj., unintelligible.

I.NIN.TER.RUP.TO, adj., uninterrupted, unbroken.

I.NI.QUI.DA.DE, s.f., iniquity.

I.NÍ.QUO, adj., iniquous, iniquitous.

IN.JE.ÇÃO, s.f., injection, shot.

IN.JE.TAR, v., to inject, to introduce, to insert.

IN.JE.TÁ.VEL, adj., injectable.

IN.JÚ.RIA, s.f., injury, offense, harm, affront, wrong, insult, outrage.

IN.JU.RI.AR, v., to injure, to do harm, to hurt, to affront, to offend.

IN.JU.RI.O.SO, adj., injurious, offending, insulting.

IN.JUS.TI.ÇA, s.f., injustice, wrong, inequity, iniquity.

IN.JUS.TA.MEN.TE, adv., unjustly, unrighteously, wrong.

IN.JUS.TI.FI.CA.DO, adj., unjustified.

IN.JUS.TI.FI.CÁ.VEL, adj., unjustifiable, unjustified.

IN.JUS.TO, adj., unfair, unjust, dishonest.

I.NOB.SER.VA.DO, adj., unobserved, unregarded.

I.NOB.SER.VÂN.CIA, s.f., inobservance.

I.NOB.SER.VAN.TE, adj., inobservant.

I.NO.CÊN.CIA, s.f., innocence, innocency, harmlessness.

I.NO.CEN.TAR, v., to pronounce not guilty, acquit.

I.NO.CEN.TE, adj., innocent, inoffensive, chaste.

I.NO.CU.LA.ÇÃO, s.f., inoculation.

I.NO.CU.LAR, v., to inoculate, to insert, to transmit.

I.NÓ.CUO, adj., innocuous, harmless.

I.NO.DO.RO, adj., inodorous, scentless.

I.NO.FEN.SI.VO, adj., inoffensive, harmless, unoffending.

I.NOL.VI.DÁ.VEL, adj., unforgettable.

I.NO.MI.NÁ.VEL, adj., unnamable, unnameable, nameless; fig., abject, intolerable.

I.NOR.GÂ.NI.CO, adj., inorganic.

I.NO.PE.RAN.TE, adj., inoperative.

I.NO.PI.NA.DO, adj., unopinionated, unforeseen, unexpected; extraordinary.

I.NO.PI.NÁ.VEL, adj., unforeseeable, unexpected.

I.NO.POR.TU.NO, adj., inopportune.

I.NOR.GÂ.NI.CO, adj., Quím., inorganic.

I.NÓS.PI.TO, adj., inhospitable, wild.

I.NO.VA.ÇÃO, s.f., innovation, change, alteration, newness.

I.NO.VAR, v., to innovate, to renew.

I.NO.XI.DAR, v., to inoxidize.

I.NO.XI.DÁ.VEL, adj., inoxidable, rustproof, stainless.

IN.QUA.LI.FI.CÁ.VEL, adj., unqualifiable.

IN.QUE.BRAN.TÁ.VEL, adj., Lit., unbreakable, infrangible.

IN.QUE.BRÁ.VEL, adj., unbreakable, nonbreakable, infrangible.

IN.QUÉ.RI.TO, s.m., inquiry, investigation, question, examination.

IN.QUI.E.TA.ÇÃO, s.f., inquietude, unrest, disquiet, anxiety, disturbance.

IN.QUI.E.TAN.TE, adj., disturbing, troubling, worrying.

IN.QUI.E.TAR, v., to disquiet, to disturb, to alarm, to worry.

IN.QUI.E.TO, adj., unquiet, disturbed, uneasy, anxious.

IN.QUIE.TU.DE, s.f., unquietness.

IN.QUI.LI.NO, s.m., tenant, lodger, occupant.

IN.QUI.RI.ÇÃO, s.f., inquest, inquiry, investigation.

IN.QUI.RI.DOR, s.m., inquirer, inquisitor, investigator; adj., inquiring, inquisitorial.

IN.QUI.RIR, v., to inquire, to query, to interrogate.

IN.QUI.SI.ÇÃO, s.f., inquisition.

IN.QUI.SI.DOR, s.m., inquisitor.

IN.QUI.SI.TI.VO, adj., inquisitive.

IN.SA.CI.Á.VEL, adj., insatiable, insatiate, voracious.

IN.SA.LU.BRE, adj., insalubrious.

IN.SA.LU.BRI.DA.DE, s.f., insalubrity.

IN.SA.NI.DA.DE, s.f., insanity, insaneness.

IN.SA.NO, adj., insane, crazy, mad, demented, foolish.

INSATISFAÇÃO ••• 217 ••• INSUCESSO

IN.SA.TIS.FA.ÇÃO, *s.f.*, dissatisfaction.
IN.SA.TIS.FA.TÓ.RI.O, *adj.*, unsatisfactory.
IN.SA.TIS.FEI.TO, *adj.*, dissatisfied, unhappy, discontented.
IN.SA.TU.RA.DO, *adj.*, unsaturated.
INS.CRE.VER, *v.*, to inscribe, to engrave, to register.
INS.CRI.ÇÃO, *s.f.*, inscription, lettering, legend, matriculation, registry.
INS.CRI.TO, *adj.*, inscribed, registered.
IN.SE.GU.RAN.ÇA, *s.f.*, insecurity, unsafeness.
IN.SE.GU.RO, *adj.*, insecure, unsafe, unsure.
IN.SE.MI.NA.ÇÃO, *s.f.*, insemination.
IN.SEN.SA.TEZ, *s.f.*, folly, nonsense, madness, stupidity.
IN.SEN.SA.TO, *adj.*, senseless, insensate, irrational, foolish.
IN.SEN.SI.BI.LI.DA.DE, *s.f.*, insensitivity, insensibility.
IN.SEN.SI.BI.LI.ZAR, *v.*, to desensitize, to render insensible; *insensibilizar-se*: to harden oneself.
IN.SEN.SÍ.VEL, *adj.*, unfeeling, insensitive, hard, unaffected.
IN.SE.PA.RÁ.VEL, *adj.*, inseparable.
IN.SE.PUL.TO, *adj.*, unburied.
IN.SER.ÇÃO, insertion.
IN.SE.RIR, *v.*, to insert, to introduce, to put in, to implant.
IN.SER.TO, *adj.*, insert, put in.
IN.SE.TI.CI.DA, *s.m.*, insecticide; *adj.*, insecticidal.
IN.SE.TO, *s.m.*, insect.
IN.SÍ.DIA, *s.f.*, ambush, treachery.
IN.SI.DI.O.SO, *adj.*, insidious.
IN.SIGHT, *s.m.*, *Ingl.*, *Psic.*, insight.
IN.SIG.NE, *adj.*, notable, remarkable, celebrated, extraordinary.
IN.SÍG.NIA, *s.f.*, sign, mark, emblem, symbol.
IN.SIG.NI.FI.CÂN.CIA, *s.f.*, insignificance.
IN.SIG.NI.FI.CAN.TE, *adj.*, insignificant, trivial, unimportant.
IN.SIN.CE.RI.DA.DE, *s.f.*, insincerity.
IN.SIN.CE.RO, *adj.*, insincere, hypocritical.
IN.SI.NU.A.ÇÃO, *s.f.*, insinuation, hint, allegation.
IN.SI.NU.AN.TE, *adj.*, insinuating.
IN.SI.NU.AR, *v.*, to insinuate, to suggest, to imply, to allege.
IN.SI.PI.DEZ, *s.f.*, insipidity, flatness; *fig.*, bad taste; monotony.
IN.SÍ.PI.DO, *adj.*, insipid, tasteless, flat.
IN.SI.PI.EN.TE, *adj.*, *s. 2 gen.*, insipient.
IN.SIS.TÊN.CIA, *s.f.*, insistence, perseverance, persistence.
IN.SIS.TEN.TE, *adj.*, insistent, persistent.
IN.SIS.TIR, *v.*, to insist, to persist, to stand upon.
IN.SO.CI.A.BI.LI.DA.DE, *s.f.*, insociability, unsociableness.
IN.SO.CI.AL, *adj.*, unsocial.
IN.SO.CI.Á.VEL, *adj.*, unsociable, not sociable.
IN.SO.LA.ÇÃO, *s.f.*, insolation, sunstroke.
IN.SO.LÊN.CIA, *s.f.*, insolence, impertinence, arrogance.
IN.SO.LEN.TE, *adj.*, *s. 2 gen.*, insolent, arrogant.
IN.SO.LU.BI.LI.DA.DE, *s.f.*, insolubility.
IN.SO.LÚ.VEL, *adj.*, insoluble, unsolvable.
IN.SOL.VÊN.CIA, *s.f.*, insolvency, bankruptcy.
IN.SOL.VEN.TE, *adj.*, *s. 2 gen.*, insolvent.
IN.SON.DÁ.VEL, *adj.*, unfathomable, fathomless.
IN.SO.NE, *s. 2 gen.*, insomniac; *adj.*, insomnious, sleepless.
IN.SÔ.NIA, *s.f.*, insomnia, restlessness, sleeplessness.
IN.SOS.SO, *adj.*, saltless, tasteless, dull.
INS.PE.ÇÃO, *s.f.*, inspection, survey, check, controlment, review.
INS.PE.CIO.NAR, *v.*, to inspect, to examine, to survey, to control.

INS.PE.TOR, *s.m.*, inspector, supervisor, overseer.
INS.PE.TO.RI.A, *s.f.*, inspectorate, inspectorship.
INS.PI.RA.ÇÃO, *s.f.*, inspiration, creative impulse, instinct.
INS.PI.RA.DO, *adj.*, inspired.
INS.PI.RA.DOR, *s.m.*, inspirer; *adj.*, inspiring, inspired.
INS.PI.RAR, *v.*, to inspire, to inhale, to breathe in, to imbue.
INS.TA.BI.LI.DA.DE, *s.f.*, instability, instableness.
INS.TA.BI.LI.ZAR, *v.*, to unsettle.
INS.TA.LA.ÇÃO, *s.f.*, installation, instalment, facilities, construction.
INS.TA.LA.DO, *adj.*, installed.
INS.TA.LA.DOR, *s.m.*, installer, fitter.
INS.TA.LAR, *v.*, to instal, to place in a seat.
INS.TÂN.CIA, *s.f.*, instance, instancy, urgency, law court.
INS.TAN.TÂ.NEO, *adj.*, instantaneous, rapid.
INS.TAN.TE, *s.m.*, instant, moment, minute, second, flash.
INS.TAR, *v.*, to press, to urge.
INS.TAU.RA.ÇÃO, *s.f.*, instauration.
INS.TAU.RA.DOR, *s.m.*, founder; *adj.*, establishing, instituting.
INS.TAU.RAR, *v.*, to begin, to initiate, to establish, to start.
INS.TÁ.VEL, *adj.*, unstable, unsteady, changeable.
INS.TI.GA.ÇÃO, *s.f.*, instigation.
INS.TI.GA.DO, *adj.*, instigated, induced.
INS.TI.GA.DOR, *s.m.*, instigator; *adj.*, instigating, inciting.
INS.TI.LA.ÇÃO, *s.f.*, instillation, instilment, instillment.
INS.TI.LAR, *v.*, to instil, to instill, to infuse; *fig.*, to insinuate.
INS.TI.GAR, *v.*, to instigate, to goad on, to urge, to spur.
INS.TIN.TI.VO, *adj.*, instinctive, conative, natural.
INS.TIN.TO, *s.m.*, instinct, intuition, flair.
INS.TI.TU.CI.O.NAL, *adj.*, institutional.
INS.TI.TU.CI.O.NA.LI.ZA.ÇÃO, *s.f.*, institutionalization.
INS.TI.TU.CI.O.NA.LI.ZAR, *v.*, to institutionalize.
INS.TI.TU.I.ÇÃO, *s.f.*, institution, establishment, constitution.
INS.TI.TU.I.DOR, *s.m.*, institutor, establisher.
INS.TI.TU.IR, *v.*, to institute, to establish, to found, to instruct.
INS.TI.TU.TO, *s.m.*, institute, institution, order.
INS.TRU.ÇÃO, *s.f.*, instruction, education, schooling, coaching, knowledge.
INS.TRU.CI.O.NAL, *adj.*, instructional.
INS.TRU.Í.DO, *adj.*, learned, educated, wise, initiate.
INS.TRU.IR, *v.*, to instruct, to teach, to educate, to train, to inform.
INS.TRU.MEN.TA.ÇÃO, *s.f.*, instrumentation.
INS.TRU.MEN.TA.DOR, *s.m.*, *Mús.*, score writer; *Med.*, theatre nurse (surgery).
INS.TRU.MEN.TAL, *s.m.*, instruments.
INS.TRU.MEN.TAR, *v.*, *Mús.*, to instrument, to write scores.
INS.TRU.MEN.TIS.TA, *s.*, instrumentalist.
INS.TRU.MEN.TO, *s.m.*, instrument, means, agency, tool, implement.
INS.TRU.TI.VO, *adj.*, instructive, informative, instructional.
INS.TRU.TOR, *s.m.*, instructor, teacher, trainer, coach, tutor.
IN.SUB.MIS.SÃO, *s.f.*, unsubmissiveness, disobedience.
IN.SUB.MIS.SO, *s.m.*, draft dodger, deserter; *adj.*, unsubmissive, disobedient.
IN.SU.BOR.DI.NA.ÇÃO, *s.f.*, insubordination, subversion, mutiny, rebellion.
IN.SU.BOR.DI.NA.DO, *adj.*, *s.m.*, insubordinate.
IN.SU.BOR.DI.NAR, *v.*, to revolt, to rebel.
IN.SUBS.TI.TU.Í.VEL, *adj.*, irreplaceable.
IN.SU.CES.SO, *s.m.*, ill success, failure.

INSUFICIÊNCIA ·· 218 ·· INTERLOCUTOR

IN.SU.FI.CI.ÊN.CI.A, *s.f.*, insufficience, insufficiency.
IN.SU.FI.CI.EN.TE, *adj.*, insufficient, meager, deficient, scanty.
IN.SU.FLAR, *v.*, to insufflate.
IN.SU.LAR, *s. 2 gen.*, islander; *adj.*, insular; *v.*, to isolate, to insulate.
IN.SU.LI.NA, *s.f.*, insulin.
IN.SUL.TAN.TE, *s. 2 gen.*, insulter; *adj.*, insultant, insulting.
IN.SUL.TAR, *v.*, to insult, to abuse, to affront, to offend.
IN.SUL.TO, *s.m.*, insult, abuse, affront, offence.
IN.SUL.TU.O.SO, *adj.*, insulting.
IN.SU.MO, *s.m., Econ.*, input.
IN.SU.PE.RÁ.VEL, *adj.*, insuperable, insurmountable.
IN.SU.POR.TÁ.VEL, *adj.*, intolerable, unbearable.
IN.SUR.GÊN.CI.A, *s.f.*, insurgence, insurgency.
IN.SUR.GEN.TE, *s. 2 gen.*, insurgent, rebel; *adj.*, insurgent, rebellious.
IN.SUR.GIR, *v.*, to revolt, to rebel, to insurrection, to protest.
IN.SUR.REI.ÇÃO, *s.f.*, insurrection.
IN.SUR.RE.TO, *s.m.*, insurgent; *adj.*, insurgent.
IN.SUS.PEI.TO, *adj.*, beyond suspicion, unsuspicious, unsuspected.
IN.SUS.TEN.TÁ.VEL, *adj.*, unsustainable, baseless.
IN.TAC.TO, *adj.*, the same that *intato*.
IN.TAN.GI.BI.LI.DA.DE, *s.f.*, intangibility.
IN.TA.TO, to **IN.TAC.TO**, *adj.*, intact, untouched, whole.
ÍN.TE.GRA, *s.f.*, totality, completeness.
IN.TE.GRA.ÇÃO, *s.f.*, integration.
IN.TE.GRA.DO, *adj.*, integrated.
IN.TE.GRA.DOR, *s.m.*, integrator; *adj.*, integrative.
IN.TE.GRAL, *adj.*, integral, complete, entire, total, whole.
IN.TE.GRA.LI.ZAR, *v.*, to integrate.
IN.TE.GRAL.MEN.TE, *adv.*, integrally.
IN.TE.GRAN.TE, *s. 2 gen.*, a member of a group; *adj.*, integrant, component.
IN.TE.GRAR, *v.*, to integrate, to complete, to form.
IN.TE.GRI.DA.DE, *s.f.*, integrity, entireness.
ÍN.TE.GRO, *adj.*, complete, entire, intact, inviolate, honest, righteous.
IN.TEI.RAR, *v.*, to complete, to integrate, to inform, to acquaint.
IN.TEI.RE.ZA, *s.f.*, entirety, integrity.
IN.TEI.RO, *s.m.*, whole number, integer; *adj.*, entire, whole, exact, perfect, complete.
IN.TE.LEC.TO, *s.m.*, intellect, intelligence, mind.
IN.TE.LEC.TU.AL, *adj., s.m.*, intellectual.
IN.TE.LEC.TU.A.LI.DA.DE, *s.f.*, intellect, intellectuality; intelligentsia.
IN.TE.LEC.TUA.LIS.MO, *s.m.*, intellectualism.
IN.TE.LI.GÊN.CIA, *s.f.*, intelligence, knowledge, intellect.
IN.TE.LI.GEN.TE, *adj.*, clever, intelligent, acute, sagacious.
IN.TE.LI.GÍ.VEL, *adj.*, intelligible, comprehensible, clear, plain.
IN.TEM.PE.RAN.ÇA, *s.f.*, intemperance.
IN.TEM.PÉ.RIE, *s.f.*, bad weather, inclemency.
IN.TEM.PES.TI.VO, *adj.*, untimely, inopportune.
IN.TEN.ÇÃO, *s.f.*, intention, intent, purpose, aim.
IN.TEN.CIO.NA.DO, *adj.*, intentioned, affected, disposed.
IN.TEN.CIO.NAL, *adj.*, intentional, intended.
IN.TEN.CI.O.NAR, *v.*, to intend, to plan.
IN.TEN.DÊN.CIA, *s.f.*, intendency, administration.
IN.TEN.DEN.TE, *s. 2 gen.*, administrator, intendant, superintendant.

IN.TEN.DER, *v.*, to administrate, to superintend.
IN.TEN.SÃO, *s.f.*, intensity.
IN.TEN.SI.DA.DE, *s.f.*, intensity.
IN.TEN.SI.FI.CA.ÇÃO, *s.f.*, intensification.
IN.TEN.SI.FI.CAR, *v.*, to intensify, to amplify, to enhance.
IN.TEN.SI.VO, *adj.*, intensive.
IN.TEN.SO, *adj.*, intense, intensive, active, vivid.
IN.TEN.TAR, *v.*, to attempt, to intent, to plan; to aim at, to commit; *Jur.*, to bring an action against.
IN.TEN.TO, *s.m.*, intention, intent, plan, project, aim.
IN.TEN.TO.NA, *s.f.*, complot, conspiracy.
IN.TE.RA.ÇÃO, *s.f.*, interaction.
IN.TE.RA.GIR, *v.*, to interact.
IN.TE.RA.ME.RI.CA.NO, *adj.*, inter-American.
IN.TE.RA.TI.VI.DA.DE, *s.f., Comp.*, interactivity.
IN.TE.RA.TI.VO, *adj.*, interactive.
IN.TER.CA.LAR, *adj.*, intercalary; *v.*, to intercalate, to interpolate; *intercalar-se*: to intermingle.
IN.TER.CAM.BI.AR, *v.*, to interchange, to exchange.
IN.TER.CAM.BI.Á.VEL, *adj.*, interchangeable.
IN.TER.CÂM.BIO, *s.m.*, exchange, interchange, barter, reciprocity.
IN.TER.CE.DER, *v.*, to intercede, to mediate, to plead for, to intervene.
IN.TER.CEP.TA.ÇÃO, *s.f.*, interception, interruption, obstruction.
IN.TER.CEP.TAR, *v.*, to intercept, interrupt, obstruct.
IN.TER.CES.SÃO, *s.f.*, intercession.
IN.TER.CES.SOR, *s.m.*, intercessor, interceder.
IN.TER.CO.NE.XÃO, *s.f.*, interconnection.
IN.TER.CON.TI.NEN.TAL, *adj.*, intercontinental.
IN.TER.DE.PEN.DEN.TE, *adj.*, interdependent.
IN.TER.DI.ÇÃO, *s.f.*, interdiction, ban, prohibition, closure.
IN.TER.DIS.CI.PLI.NAR, *adj.*, interdisciplinary.
IN.TER.DI.TA.DO, *adj.*, banned, closed.
IN.TER.DI.TAR, *v.*, to interdict, to forbid, to prohibit.
IN.TE.RES.SA.DO, *adj.*, interested, concerned, biased.
IN.TE.RES.SAN.TE, *adj.*, interesting.
IN.TE.RES.SAR, *v.*, to interest, to concern, to affect.
IN.TE.RES.SE, *s.m.*, interest, benefit, advantage, profit, gain, regard.
IN.TE.RES.SEI.RO, *s.m.*, a self-seeking person, egotist; *adj.*, self-seeking.
IN.TE.RES.TA.DU.AL, *adj., s. 2 gen.*, interstate.
IN.TER.FA.CE, *s.f., Comp.*, interface.
IN.TE.RES.TE.LAR, *adj., Astron.*, interstellar.
IN.TER.FE.RÊN.CIA, *s.f.*, interference, intervention.
IN.TER.FE.RIR, *v.*, to interfere, to intervene, to interpose, to restrict.
IN.TER.FO.NE, *s.m.*, interphone.
ÍN.TE.RIM, *s.m.*, meantime, interim.
IN.TE.RI.NO, *adj.*, interim, temporary, conditional.
IN.TE.RI.OR, *s.m.*, interior, inland, countryside, inside, province; *adj.*, interior, inner, inward, internal.
IN.TE.RIO.RA.NO, *adj.*, provincial, upcountry.
IN.TE.RI.O.RI.ZAR, *v.*, to interiorize.
IN.TER.JEI.ÇÃO, *s.f.*, interjection.
IN.TER.LI.GA.ÇÃO, *s.f.*, interconnection.
IN.TER.LI.GAR, *v.*, to interconnect.
IN.TER.LO.CU.ÇÃO, *s.f.*, interlocution, dialogue.
IN.TER.LO.CU.TOR, *s.m.*, interlocutor, speaker.

INTERLOCUTORA · 219 · INTRODUTOR

IN.TER.LO.CU.TO.RA, s.f., interlocutress.
IN.TER.LÚ.DI.O, s.m., Mús., interlude.
IN.TER.ME.DI.AR, v., to intermediate, to mediate, to intermix, to mix.
IN.TER.ME.DI.Á.RIO, s.m., intermediate, intermediary,broker; adj., intermediate, interposed.
IN.TER.MÉ.DIO, s.m., intermediary, agent, mediator, way; adj., intervening, intermediate.
IN.TER.MEZ.ZO, s.m., It., Mús., intermezzo.
IN.TER.MI.NÁ.VEL, adj., interminable, endless, limitless.
IN.TER.MI.TEN.TE, adj., intermittent.
IN.TER.MUN.DI.AL, adj., intercontinental, intermundane.
IN.TER.MUS.CU.LAR, adj., intermuscular.
IN.TER.NA.ÇÃO, s.f., internation, internment.
IN.TER.NA.CIO.NAL, adj., international.
IN.TER.NA.CIO.NA.LI.DA.DE, s.f., internationality.
IN.TER.NA.CIO.NA.LIS.MO, s.m., internationalism.
IN.TER.NA.CIO.NA.LI.ZAR, v., to internationalize.
IN.TER.NA.DO, adj., interned.
IN.TER.NA.MEN.TO, s.m., internment, confinement, restraint.
IN.TER.NAR, v., to intern, to confine, to introduce, to insert.
IN.TER.NA.TO, s.m., boarding school, orphanage.
IN.TER.NAU.TA, s. 2 gen., Comp., user, surfer (internet).
IN.TER.NO, s.m., internee; adj., internal, intern, interior, inside, inner.
IN.TER.PE.LA.ÇÃO, s.f., interpellation, questioning.
IN.TER.PE.LAN.TE, s. 2 gen., interpellant.
IN.TER.PE.LAR, v., to interpellate, to question, to interrogate.
IN.TER.PO.LA.ÇÃO, s.f., interpolation, insertion.
IN.TER.PO.LAR, v., to interpolate, to insert.
IN.TER.POR, v., to interpose, to place between, to interrupt, to intervene.
IN.TER.POS.TO, adj., interposing, interposed.
IN.TER.PRE.TA.ÇÃO, s.f., interpretation, explanation, explication, version.
IN.TER.PRE.TAR, v., to interpret, to expound, to elucidate.
IN.TER.PRE.TA.TI.VO, adj., interpretative.
IN.TÉR.PRE.TE, s. 2 gen., interpreter, translator, performer, artist.
IN.TER.REG.NO, s.m., interregnum.
IN.TER.RO.GA.ÇÃO, s.f., interrogation, questioning, interrogatory, inquiry.
IN.TER.RO.GA.DO, adj., questioned, interrogated.
IN.TER.RO.GA.DOR, s.m., interrogator.
IN.TER.RO.GAR, v., to interrogate, to inquire, to examine, to ask.
IN.TER.RO.GA.TI.VO, adj., questioning; Gram., interrogative.
IN.TER.RO.GA.TÓ.RIO, s.m., interrogatory, hearing, interrogation, questioning.
IN.TER.ROM.PER, v., interrupt, discontinue, cease, break off, stop, desist.
IN.TER.ROM.PI.DO, adj., interrupted.
IN.TER.RUP.ÇÃO, s.f., interruption, cessation, intermission, suspension, break.
IN.TER.RUP.TOR, s.m., circuit breaker, switch; adj., interrupting.
IN.TER.SE.ÇÃO, s.f., intersection.
IN.TERS.TÍ.CI.O, s.m., interstice.
IN.TE.RUR.BA.NO, adj., interurban; between cities.
IN.TER.VA.LO, s.m., interval, space, intermission, interact.
IN.TER.VEN.ÇÃO, s.f., intervention, interference.
IN.TER.VEN.CI.O.NIS.MO, s.m., interventionism.

IN.TER.VEN.CI.O.NIS.TA, s. 2 gen., interventionist.
IN.TER.VEN.TOR, s.m., interventor, temporary governor.
IN.TER.VIR, v., to intervene, to interfere, to interpose, to intermediate.
IN.TES.TI.NAL, adj., intestinal.
IN.TES.TI.NO, s.m., intestine, bowel, entrails; adj., intestine, internal, inward.
IN.TI.FA.DA, s.f., intifada.
IN.TI.MA.DOR, s.m., intimater, summoner; adj., that intimates.
IN.TI.MA.ÇÃO, s.f., notification, citation, announcement, summons, writ.
IN.TI.MA.MEN.TE, adv., intimately, confidentially, familiarly.
IN.TI.MAR, v., to summon, to cite, to convoke, to notify, to inform.
IN.TI.MI.DA.ÇÃO, s.f., intimidation.
IN.TI.MI.DA.DE, s.f., intimacy, privacy, familiarity, nearness, friendship.
IN.TI.MI.DA.DOR, s.m., intimidator; adj., intimidating, intimidator.
IN.TI.MI.DAR, v., to intimidate, to frighten, to discourage, to bully.
ÍN.TI.MO, adj., intimate, inner, internal, innermost, inmost, close, near.
IN.TI.TU.LA.ÇÃO, s.f., intitulation.
IN.TI.TU.LA.DO, adj., entitled.
IN.TI.TU.LAR, v., to intitule, to give a right to, to entitle, to name.
IN.TO.CA.DO, adj., untouched.
IN.TO.CÁ.VEL, adj., untouchable.
IN.TO.LE.RÂN.CIA, s.f., intolerance, bigotry, intolerancy, impatience.
IN.TO.LE.RAN.TE, s. 2 gen., intolerant, intransigent.
IN.TO.LE.RÁ.VEL, adj., intolerable, unbearable, insupportable.
IN.TO.XI.CA.ÇÃO, s.f., intoxication, poisoning.
IN.TO.XI.CA.DO, adj., intoxicated.
IN.TO.XI.CAR, v., to poison, to intoxicate.
IN.TRA.CE.LU.LAR, adj., intracellular.
IN.TRA.CRA.NI.A.NO, adj., Anat., intracranial.
IN.TRA.DU.ZÍ.VEL, adj., untranslatable, inexpressible.
IN.TRA.GÁ.VEL, adj., unpalatable, uneatable.
IN.TRA.MUS.CU.LAR, adj., intramuscular.
IN.TRAN.QUI.LI.DA.DE, s.f., intranquility.
IN.TRAN.QUI.LO, adj., uneasy, afflicted, restless.
IN.TRANS.FE.RÍ.VEL, adj., untransferable.
IN.TRAN.SI.GÊN.CIA, s.f., intransigence.
IN.TRAN.SI.TÁ.VEL, adj., impassable, untransitable, pathless.
IN.TRAN.SI.TI.VO, adj., intransitive.
IN.TRANS.PO.NÍ.VEL, adj., unsurmountable.
IN.TRA.TÁ.VEL, adj., intractable, stubborn, dogged, haughty.
IN.TRA.TO.RÁ.CI.CO, adj., Anat., intrathoracic.
IN.TRA.VE.NO.SO, adj., intravenous.
IN.TRÉ.PI.DO, adj., intrepid, bold, fearless, brave.
IN.TRI.CA.DO, adj., intricate, complicated, difficult.
IN.TRI.CAR, v., to intricate, to complicate.
IN.TRI.GA, s.f., intrigue, plot, scheme, conspiracy, snare, trap.
IN.TRI.GAR, v., to intrigue, to involve, to entangle, to plot for, to scheme.
IN.TRIN.CAR, v., the same that intricar.
IN.TRÍN.SE.CO, adj., intrinsic, inherent, inward.
IN.TRO.DU.ÇÃO, s.f., introduction, importation, preface.
IN.TRO.DU.TOR, s.m., introducer.

INTRODUTÓRIO ·· 220 ·· IRLANDA

IN.TRO.DU.TÓ.RI.O, adj., introductory.
IN.TRO.DU.ZIR, v., to introduce, to lead in, to bring in, to import, to insert.
IN.TRO.ME.TER, v., to introduce, to intrude, to insert, to intromit.
IN.TRO.ME.TI.DO, s.m., intruder; adj., intrusive, importunate, meddlesome.
IN.TRO.MIS.SÃO, s.f., intromission, interference, introduction.
IN.TRO.VER.SÃO, s.f., introversion.
IN.TRO.VER.TI.DO, s.m., introvert; adj., introverted.
IN.TRU.SÃO, s.f., intrusion.
IN.TRU.SO, s.m., intruder, trespasser; adj., intruded, intrusive.
IN.TU.BAR, v., Med., to intubate.
IN.TU.I.ÇÃO, s.f., intuition, feeling.
IN.TU.I.TI.VO, adj., intuitive.
IN.TUI.TO, s.m., design, intention, plan, scheme, aim.
I.NU.MA.NO, adj., inhuman, cruel, brutal.
I.NU.ME.RÁ.VEL, adj., innumerable, unnumbered.
I.NUN.DA.ÇÃO, s.f., inundation, flood, overflow, cataclysm.
I.NUN.DA.DO, adj., flooded, awash.
I.NUN.DAR, v., to inundate, to flood, to overflow, to deluge.
I.NUN.DÁ.VEL, adj., subject to inundation.
I.NÚ.TIL, adj., worthless person; adj., inutile, useless, unnecessary, superfluous, hopeless, needless.
I.NU.TI.LI.DA.DE, s.f., inutility, uselessness, worthlessness.
I.NU.TI.LI.ZAR, v., to nullify, to make useless, to frustrate.
IN.VA.DIR, v., to invade, to conquer, to encroach.
IN.VA.LI.DAR, v., to invalidate, to render invalid, to disable.
IN.VA.LI.DEZ, s.f., invalidity, infirmity, disability, invalidism.
IN.VÁ.LI.DO, s.m., invalid; adj., infirm, disabled, invalid.
IN.VA.RI.A.BI.LI.DA.DE, s.f., invariability.
IN.VA.RI.Á.VEL, adj., invariable, unchangeable, unalterable, constant.
IN.VA.SÃO, s.f., invasion, incursion, inroad.
IN.VA.SI.VO, adj., aggressive, invasion; Med., invasive.
IN.VA.SOR, s.m., invader, forayer.
IN.VEC.TI.VA, s.f., invective, diatribe; insult.
IN.VE.JA, s.f., envy, jealousy, enviousness, emulation.
IN.VE.JA.DO, adj., that is envied.
IN.VE.JAR, v., to envy, to feel envious of, to grudge, to desire.
IN.VE.JO.SO, s.m., envier, grudger; adj., envious, jealous.
IN.VEN.ÇÃO, s.f., invention, creation, discovery.
IN.VEN.CI.BI.LI.DA.DE, s.f., invincibility, invincibleness, insuperability.
IN.VEN.CI.O.NI.CE, s.f., lie, artifice, fabrication.
IN.VEN.CÍ.VEL, adj., invincible, insuperable.
IN.VEN.TA.DO, adj., invented.
IN.VEN.TAR, v., to invent, to create.
IN.VEN.TA.RI.AR, v., to inventory.
IN.VEN.TÁ.RIO, s.m., inventory, schedule, register, stock.
IN.VEN.TO, s.m., invention.
IN.VEN.TOR, s.m., inventor, discoverer, author, fabricator.
IN.VER.DA.DE, s.f., untruthfulness, lie.
IN.VER.NAL, adj., hibernal, wintery.
IN.VER.NAR, v., to winter, to hibernate.
IN.VER.NO, s.m., winter, winter season, winter time.
IN.VE.ROS.SÍ.MIL, adj., improbable, unlikely.
IN.VE.ROS.SI.MI.LHAN.ÇA, s.f., unlikeliness, improbability.
IN.VER.SÃO, s.f., inversion, reversion, reversal.
IN.VER.SI.VO, adj., inversive.
IN.VER.SO, s.m., contrary, reverse, inverse; adj., inverse, reciprocal.
IN.VER.TE.BRA.DO, s.m., invertebrate animal; adj., invertebrate.
IN.VER.TER, v., to invert, to reverse, to transpose, to change, to modify.
IN.VER.TI.DO, adj., inverted, inverse, reverse.
IN.VÉS, s.m., reverse side, opposite.
IN.VES.TI.DA, s.f., attack, assault, charge, rush.
IN.VES.TI.DO, adj., vested.
IN.VES.TI.DOR, adj., investor.
IN.VES.TI.DU.RA, s.f., investiture.
IN.VES.TI.GA.ÇÃO, s.f., investigation, inquiry, research.
IN.VES.TI.GA.DO, adj., that is investigated; Jur., that is subject to investigation.
IN.VES.TI.GA.DOR, s.m., investigator, detective, researcher; adj., investigating.
IN.VES.TI.GAR, v., to investigate, examine, to search into.
IN.VES.TI.MEN.TO, s.m., investment, attack, assault.
IN.VES.TIR, v., to invest, to attack, to assault.
IN.VE.TE.RA.DO, adj., deep-rooted, obstinate, inveterate, old.
IN.VI.A.BI.LI.DA.DE, s.f., impracticability.
IN.VI.A.BI.LI.ZAR, v., to make impracticable, not viable.
IN.VI.Á.VEL, adj., unviable.
IN.VIC.TO, adj., unvanquished, unconquered.
IN.VI.O.LA.BI.LI.DA.DE, s.f., inviolability.
IN.VI.O.LÁ.VEL, adj., inviolable.
IN.VI.SI.BI.LI.DA.DE, s.f., invisibility.
IN.VI.SÍ.VEL, adj., invisible, unseen.
IN.VO.CA.ÇÃO, s.f., invocation.
IN.VO.CA.DO, adj., that was invoked; pop., worried, suspicious, preoccupied; inconssitent, bizarre.
IN.VO.CAR, v., to invoke, to implore, to call for protection or aid.
IN.VO.CA.TI.VO, adj., invocatory, invoking.
IN.VO.LU.ÇÃO, s.f., Biol., retrogressive development; Mat., involution.
IN.VÓ.LU.CRO, s.m., involucre, wrapping, cover, wrappage.
IN.VO.LUN.TÁ.RIO, adj., s.m., involuntary.
IN.VUL.GAR, adj., invulgar, rare, unusual, exceptional.
IN.VUL.NE.RA.BI.LI.DA.DE, s.f., invulnerability.
IN.VUL.NE.RÁ.VEL, adj., invulnerable.
I.O.DA.DO, adj., Quím., iodized.
IO.DO, s.m., iodine.
IO.GA, s.f., yoga.
IO.IÔ, s.m., yo-yo.
IO.GUR.TE, s.m., yoghurt.
íp.si.lon, **ÍP.SI.LÃO**, s.m., wye, upsilon.
IR, v., to go, to move, to depart, to go away, to proceed, to row, to sail, to travel.
IR, s.m., abrev. of Imposto de Renda: income tax.
I.RA, s.f., ranger, rage, wrath, ire, passion, exasperation.
I.RÃ, s., Iran.
I.RA.DO, adj., irate, ireful, angry, wrathful, furious.
I.RA.NI.A.NO, adj., s.m., Iranian.
I.RA.QUE, s.m., Iraq.
I.RA.QUI.A.NO, adj., s.m., Iraqi, Iraki.
I.RAR, v., to make angry, to enrage, to irritate, to provoke.
I.RAS.CÍ.VEL, adj., irascible.
I.RI.DES.CEN.TE, adj., iridescent.
Í.RIS, s.f., iris.
IR.LAN.DA, s., Ireland; ~ do Norte: Northern Ireland.

IRLANDÊS ·· 221 ·· IUGOSLAVO

IR.LAN.DÊS, *adj., s.m.*, Irish, Irishman.
IR.MÃ, *s.f.*, sister.
IR.MA.NAR, *v.*, to fraternize, to fellow, to couple.
IR.MAN.DA.DE, *s.f.*, brotherhood, sisterhood, fraternity.
IR.MÃO, *s.m.*, brother, twin.
I.RO.NI.A, *s.f.*, irony, mockery, sarcasm.
I.RÔ.NI.CO, *adj.*, ironic, sarcastic.
IR.RA.CIO.NAL, *adj.*, irrational, illogical.
IR.RA.CIO.NA.LI.DA.DE, *s.f.*, irrationality, unreason.
IR.RA.DI.A.ÇÃO, *s.f.*, irradiation, irradiance.
IR.RA.DI.AR, *v.*, to irradiate, to emit rays, to radiate.
IR.RE.AL, *adj.*, unreal, illusive, visionary.
IR.RE.A.LI.DA.DE, *s.f.*, unreality, unsubstantiality.
IR.RE.A.LI.ZA.DO, *adj.*, unrealized.
IR.RE.A.LI.ZÁ.VEL, *adj.*, unachievable.
IR.RE.CON.CI.LI.Á.VEL, *adj.*, irreconcilable.
IR.RE.CO.NHE.CÍ.VEL, *adj.*, irrecognizable.
IR.RE.COR.RÍ.VEL, *adj.*, unappealable.
IR.RE.CU.PE.RÁ.VEL, *adj.*, irretrievable, irrecoverable.
IR.RE.CU.SÁ.VEL, *adj.*, irrecusable
IR.RE.DU.TÍ.VEL, *adj.*, indominable, irreducible.
IR.RE.FLE.TI.DO, *adj.*, irreflective, thoughtless; rash, precipitate.
IR.RE.FRE.Á.VEL, *adj.*, irrepressible, uncontrollable.
IR.RE.FU.TÁ.VEL, *adj.*, irrefutable, unquestionable.
IR.RE.GU.LAR, *adj.*, irregular, illegal, lawless.
IR.RE.GU.LA.RI.DA.DE, *s.f.*, irregularity.
IR.RE.LE.VÂN.CI.A, *s.f.*, irrelevance.
IR.RE.LE.VAN.TE, *adj.*, irrelevant.
IR.RE.ME.DI.Á.VEL, *adj.*, irremediable, irreparable.
IR.RE.MO.VÍ.VEL, *adj.*, irremovable.
IR.RE.PA.RÁ.VEL, *adj.*, irreparable.
IR.RE.PRE.EN.SÍ.VEL, *adj.*, irreproachable.
IR.RE.PRI.MÍ.VEL, *adj.*, irrepressible.
IR.RE.QUI.E.TA.ÇÃO, *s.f.*, restlessness.
IR.RE.QUIE.TO, *adj.*, unquiet, restless, fussy, turbulent.
IR.RE.SIS.TÍ.VEL, *adj.*, irresistible, resistless, overpowering.
IR.RE.SO.LU.TO, *adj.*, irresolute.
IR.RES.PON.SA.BI.LI.DA.DE, *s.f.*, irresponsibility.
IR.RES.PON.SÁ.VEL, *adj.*, irresponsible.
IR.RES.TRI.TO, *adj.*, unrestricted, unrestrained.
IR.RE.VE.RÊN.CIA, *s.f.*, irreverence, disrespect.
IR.RE.VE.REN.TE, *adj., s. 2 gen.*, irreverent.
IR.RE.VER.SÍ.VEL, *adj.*, irreversible.
IR.RE.VO.GÁ.VEL, *adj.*, irrevocable, unchangeable.
IR.RI.GA.ÇÃO, *s.f.*, irrigation.
IR.RI.GAR, *v.*, to irrigate, to water.

IR.RI.SÃO, *s.f.*, irrision, derision, sneering.
IR.RI.SÓ.RIO, *adj.*, derisive, scornful.
IR.RI.TA.BI.LI.DA.DE, *s.f.*, irritability.
IR.RI.TA.ÇÃO, *s.f.*, irritation, anger, enragement.
IR.RI.TA.DI.ÇO, *adj.*, irritable, querulous.
IR.RI.TAN.TE, *s.m.*, irritant; *adj.*, irritating, annoying.
IR.RI.TAR, *v.*, to irritate, to anger, to annoy, to enrage.
IR.RI.TÁ.VEL, *adj.*, irritable.
IR.ROM.PER, *v.*, to rush in, to urge forward, to break out, to emerge.
IS.CA, *s.f.*, bait, lure, tinder, allurement.
I.SEN.ÇÃO, *s.f.*, exemption, freedom, immunity.
I.SEN.TAR, *v.*, to exempt, to free from, to release, to relieve.
I.SEN.TO, *adj.*, exempt, free, immune.
IS.LÃ, *s.m.*, Islam.
IS.LÂ.MI.CO, *adj., s.m.*, Islamic.
IS.LA.MIS.MO, *s.m., Rel.*, Islam, Islamism.
IS.LA.MI.TA, *s. 2 gen.*, Mohammedan, Islamist; *adj.*, Islamic.
IS.LAN.DÊS, *adj., s.m.*, Icelander, Icelandic.
IS.LÂN.DIA, *s.f.*, Iceland.
I.SÓ.BA.RO, *s.m., Quím., Fís.*, isobar.
I.SO.LA.CI.O.NIS.MO, *s.m.*, isolationism.
I.SO.LA.DO, *adj.*, isolated, separate, alone, segregate.
I.SO.LA.MEN.TO, *s.m.*, isolation, separation, insulation.
I.SO.LAN.TE, *s.m.*, isolating, insulating material; *adj.*, isolating.
I.SO.LAR, *v.*, to isolate, to detach, to separate, to insulate.
I.SO.NO.MI.A, *s.f.*, isonomy, equality.
I.SO.POR, *s.m., Quím.*, polystyrene.
IS.QUEI.RO, *s.m.*, lighter, fire-lighter.
IS.RA.EL, *s.m.*, Israel.
IS.RA.E.LEN.SE, *adj., s. 2 gen.*, Israeli.
IS.RA.E.LI.TA, *adj., s. 2 gen.*, Israelite, Hebrew.
IS.SO, *pron.*, that; *isso mesmo*: exactly.
IST.MO, *s.m.*, isthmus.
IS.TO, *pron.*, this.
I.TÁ.LIA, *s.f.*, Italy.
I.TA.LI.A.NO, *adj., s.m.*, Italian.
Í.TA.LO, *adj., s.m.*, Italian.
I.TEM, *s.m.*, item, article.
I.TE.RA.ÇÃO, *s.f.*, iteration, repetition.
I.TE.RA.DO, *adj.*, iterated, reiterated.
I.TE.RA.TI.VO, *adj.*, iterative.
I.TI.NE.RAN.TE, *s.2 gen.*, itinerant; *adj.*, itinerary.
I.TI.NE.RÁ.RIO, *s.m.*, itinerary, route, schedule.
IU.GOS.LÁ.VI.A, *s.*, Yugoslavia (ex-Yugoslavia).
IU.GOS.LA.VO, *adj., s.m.*, Yugoslav.

J, *s.m.*, tenth letter of the Portuguese alphabet.
JÁ, *adv.*, now, at once, immediately, then, presently; *conj.*, already, since, once.
JA.BU.RU, *s.m., Zool.*, jabiru stork.
JA.BU.TI, *s.m., Zool.*, land turtle.
JA.BU.TI.CA.BA, *s.f., Bras.*, jaboticaba fruit.
JA.BU.TI.CA.BAL, *s.m., Bras.*, grove of jaboticaba.
JA.BU.TI.CA.BEI.RA, *s.f.*, jaboticaba tree.
JA.CA, *s.f.*, jack-fruit; *Bras.*, top hat.
JA.CA.RAN.DÁ, *s.m., Bras., Bot.*, rosewood (tree).
JA.CA.RÉ, *s.m., Zool.*, alligator, jacare, cayman.
JA.CIN.TO, *s.m.*, hyacinth.
JAC.TÂN.CI.A, *s.f.*, boasting, vanity, pride, arrogance.
JAC.TAN.CI.O.SO, *adj.*, vain, boastful, ostentatious.
JAC.TAN.TE, *adj.*, the same that *jactancioso*.
JAC.TAR-SE *v.*, to be boastful, to boast, to swagger to brag.
JA.DE, *s.m., Min.*, jade.
JA.EZ, *s.m.*, harness, quality, sort.
JA.GUAR, *s.m., Zool.*, jaguar.
JA.GUA.TI.RI.CA, *s.f., Zool.*, leopard cat.
JA.GUN.ÇO, *s.m., Bras.*, hired rowdy, body guard, gunman, assassin.
JA.LE.CO, *s.m.*, a short jacket, coat.
JA.MAI.CA, *s.f.*, Jamaica.
JA.MAI.CA.NO, *adj., s.m.*, Jamaican.
JA.MAIS, *adv.*, never, ever, at no time.
JA.MAN.TA, *s.f.*, articulated truck.
JA.NEI.RO, *s.m.*, January.
JA.NE.LA, *s.f.*, window.
JAN.GA.DA, *s.f.*, raft.
JAN.GA.DEI.RO, *s.m.*, raft owner, raftsman.
JÂN.GAL, *s.m.*, jungle.
JAN.TA, *s.f.*, dinner.
JAN.TAR, *s.m.*, dinner; *v.*, to dine.
JAN.TAR DAN.ÇAN.TE, *s.m.*, dinner dance.
JAPÃO, *s.*, Japan.
JA.PO.NA, *s.f.*, short jacket.
JA.PO.NÊS, *adv., s.m.*, Japanese.
JA.QUEI.RA, *s.f., Bot.*, jack-tree.
JA.QUE.TA, *s.f.*, jacket, jumper.
JA.QUE.TÃO, *s.m.*, double-breasted coat.
JA.RA.GUÁ, *s.m., Bot., Bras.*, forage grass; *Bras.*, a fantastic character of the *bumba meu boi*.
JA.RA.RA.CA, *s.f., Zool., Bras.*, jararaca (venomous snake); *fig.*, venomous or spiteful person.
JA.RA.RA.CU.ÇU, *s.m., Zool.*, jararacuçu, a very dangerous Brazilian viper (*Bothrops jararacussu*).
JAR.DA, *s.f.*, yard (36 inches; 0,9144m).
JAR.DIM, *s.m.*, garden, flower-garden.
JAR.DIM BO.TÂ.NI.CO, *s.m.*, botanical garden.
JAR.DIM DE IN.FÂN.CI.A, *s.m.*, kindergarten.
JAR.DIM DE IN.VER.NO, *s.m., Arquit.*, conservatory.
JAR.DIM ZO.O.LÓ.GI.CO, *s.m.*, zoological garden, zoo.
JAR.DI.NA.GEM, *s.f.*, gardening.
JAR.DI.NAR, *v.*, to garden.
JAR.DI.NEI.RA, *s.f., Bras.*, skirt, pants or shorts with front covering the chest and suspenders; jardiniere.
JAR.DI.NEI.RO, *s.m.*, gardener.
JAR.GÃO, *s.m.*, jargon, slang, gibberish.
JAR.RA, *s.f.*, jar, pitcher, jug, vase, flowerpot.
JAR.RO, *s.m.*, pitcher, jar.
JAS.MIM, *s.m.*, jasmin, jessamin.
JAS.MI.NEI.RO, *s.m., Bot.*, jasmine shrub.
JA.TO, *s.m.*, gush, jet, outpour, stream.
JAU, *s.m.*, Javanese, *adj.*, Javanese.
JA.Ú, *s.m., Zool.*, Amazon catfish (*Paulicea luetkeni*).
JAU.LA, *s.f.*, cage.
JA.VA, *s.*, Java.
JA.VA.LI, *s.m.*, wild pig, wild boar.
JA.VA.NÊS, *adj., s.m.*, Javanese.
JA.ZER, *v.*, to lie, to be stretched out, to rest.
JA.ZI.DA, *s.f.*, resting-place, couch, natural deposit of ores.
JA.ZI.GO, *s.m.*, grave, sepulcher, tomb, burial monument.
JAZZ, *s.m., Ingl.*, jazz.
JAZ.ZIS.TA, *s. 2 gen., Mús.*, jazzman.
JEANS, *s.m.*, jeans.
JE.CA, *s.m., gír.*, rube, rustic; *adj.*, awkward, rustic.
JE.GUE, *s.m., Zool., Bras.*, donkey (*Equus asinus*).
JEI.TÃO, *s.m., Bras.*, a very personal way of being or acting.
JEI.TO, *s.m.*, aptitude, aptness, way, knack, skill, dexterity.
JEI.TO.SO, *adj.*, skilful, adroit, dexterous, clever, handy.
JE.JU.A.DOR, *s.m.*, fasting person; *adj.*, fasting.
JE.JU.AR, *v.*, to fast, to be ignorant.
JE.JUM, *s.m.*, fast(ing), abstinence.
JE.O.VÁ, *s.m.*, Jehovah, God.
JE.RI.MUM, *s.m.*, pumpkin.
JÉR.SEI, *s.m.*, jersey (clothing).
JE.SU.Í.TA, *s.m.*, Jesuit; *adj.*, jesuitical.
JE.SU.Í.TI.CO, *adj.*, Jesuitic, Jesuitical.
JE.TOM, *s.m.*, payment, the pay itself; jetton.
JI.BOI.A, *s.f.*, boa constrictor.
JI.LÓ, *s.m.*, jiló, fruit of the *jiloeiro*.
JI.LO.EI.RO, *s.m., Bot., Bras.*, plant of the family *Solanaceae* (*Solanum gilo*).
JIN.GLE, *s.m., Ingl.*, jingle (music for advertisement TV/Radio/Cinema).
JI.PE, *s.m.*, jeep.
JIU-JÍT.SU, *s.m.*, ju-jitsu.
JO.A.LHA.RI.A, *s.f.*, the same that *joalheria*.
JO.A.LHEI.RO, *s.m.*, jeweler.
JO.A.LHE.RI.A, *s.f.*, jewelry store; jeweller's shop.
JO.A.NE.TE, *s.m.*, bunion; *Náut.*, topgallant sail.
JO.A.NI.NHA, *s.f., Zool., Bras.*, lady-bug.
JO.ÃO-DE-BAR.RO, *s.m., Zool.*, oven-bird (family Furnarius).

JOÃO-NINGUÉM ·· 223 ··· JUSTIFICADO

JO.ÃO-NIN.GUÉM, *pron.*, nobody.
JO.ÇA, *s.f., gír.*, mess.
JO.CO.SI.DA.DE, *s.f.*, jocosity.
JO.CO.SO, *adj.*, jocular, jocose, humorous.
JO.EI.RA, *s.f.*, large sieve, winnowing basket.
JO.E.LHA.DA, *s.f.*, hit or stroke with the knee.
JO.E.LHEI.RA, *s.f.*, kneepad, kneepiece (armour).
JO.E.LHO, *s.m.*, knee, joint.
JO.E.LHU.DO, *adj.*, big-kneed.
JO.GA.DA, *s.f.*, play, game, move, stroke, cast.
JO.GA.DO, *adj.*, gambled, played; thrown (in a game); *Bras.*, abandoned.
JO.GA.DOR, *s.m.*, player, gambler.
JO.GAR, *v.*, to play, to take part in a game, to gamble, to stake.
JO.GA.TI.NA, *s.f.*, gambling.
JOG.GING, *s.m., Ingl.*, jogging, tracksuit.
JO.GO, *s.m.*, game, match, play, gamble.
JO.GO DA VE.LHA, *s.m., US* tic-tac-toe, *UK* noughts and crosses.
JO.GOS O.LÍM.PI.COS, *s.m., pl.*, Olympic Games.
JO.GRAL, *s.m.*, jester, scoffer.
JO.GUE.TE, *s.m.*, plaything, toy; laughing-stock, fool.
JOI.A, *s.f.*, jewel, trinket, gem.
JOI.O, *s.m., Bot.*, darnel.
JO.JO.BA, *s.f., Bot.*, jojoba.
JÓ.QUEI, *s.m.*, jockey.
JÓ.QUEI-CLU.BE, *s.m.*, Jockey Club.
JOR.NA.DA, *s.f.*, journey, treck, a day's work, expedition.
JOR.NAL, *s.m.*, newspaper, journal, diary.
JOR.NA.LE.CO, *s.m.*, rag, badly written newspaper.
JOR.NA.LEI.RO, *s.m.*, newsboy, newspaper boy, newsdealer; *adj.*, daily.
JOR.NA.LIS.MO, *s.m.*, journalism, press.
JOR.NA.LIS.TA, *s. 2 gen.*, journalist, reporter, newspaperman.
JOR.NA.LÍS.TI.CO, *adj.*, journalistic.
JOR.RA.MEN.TO, *s.m.*, the same that *jorro*.
JOR.RAR, *v.*, to gush, to spur, to spout out, to pour, to belly out.
JOR.RO, *s.m.*, outpour, gush, jet, spurt, spate, stream.
JO.VEM, *s. 2 gen.*, young person; *adj.*, young, youthful.
JO.VI.AL, *adj.*, jovial, merry, gay, jolly.
JO.VI.A.LI.DA.DE, *s.f.*, joviality, merriment, jollity, gaiety, good humour.
JOY.STICK, *s.m.*, joystick.
JU.Á, *s.m., Bot., Bras.*, fruit of the *juazeiro*.
JU.A.ZEI.RO, *s.m., Bot.*, Brazilian tall tree (*Zizyphus joazeiro*).
JU.BA, *s.f.*, a lion's mane.
JU.BI.LA.ÇÃO, *s.f.*, jubilation, exultation; (university) retirement.
JU.BI.LA.DO, *adj.*, (university) retired; (student) dismissed.
JU.BI.LAR, *v.*, to jubilate; *adj.*, referring to a jubilee.
JU.BI.LEU, *s.m.*, jubilee.
JÚ.BI.LO, *s.m.*, jubilation, exultation, joy, rejoicing, satisfaction.
JU.BI.LO.SO, *adj.*, jubilating, exultant, elated, joyful.
JU.DAI.CO, *adj.*, Jewish, Judaic.
JU.DA.ÍS.MO, *s.m.*, Judaism.
JU.DAS, *s.m., 2 num., fig.*, traitor, false friend.
JU.DEU, *s.m.*, Jew; *adj.*, Jewish.
JU.DI.A, *adj.*, feminine of *judeu*: jewish.
JU.DI.AR, *v.*, to torment, to mistreat, to mock.

JU.DI.CI.AL, *adj.*, judicial, juridical.
JU.DI.CI.Á.RI.O, *s.m.*, the judiciary; *adj.*, judicial, forensic.
JU.DI.CI.O.SO, *adj.*, judicious.
JU.DÔ, *s.m., Esp.*, judo.
JU.DO.CA, *s. 2 gen.*, judoka (judo player).
JU.DO.ÍS.TA, *s. 2 gen.*, the same that *judoca*.
JU.GO, *s.m.*, yoke, submission, servitude.
JU.IZ, *s.m.*, judge, referee, arbiter.
JU.Í.ZA, *s.f.*, female judge.
JU.Í.ZA.DO, *s.m.*, judgeship; location or position of a judge.
JU.Í.ZO, *s.m.*, judgement, trial, brains, reason, opinion.
JU.Í.ZO FI.NAL, *s.m.*, the Judgement Day.
JU.JU.BA, *s.f., Bot.*, jujube; jujube (flavoured boiled sweet).
JU.JUT.SU, *s.m., Jap.*, the same that *jiu-jitsu*.
JUL.GA.DOR, *s.m.*, judge, arbiter; *adj.*, judging.
JUL.GA.MEN.TO, *s.m.*, judgement, verdict, sentence, opinion, court session, trial.
JUL.GAR, *v.*, to judge, to try, to pass sentence on, to think, to deem, to believe.
JU.LHO, *s.m.*, July.
JU.MEN.TO, *s.m.*, ass, donkey.
JUN.CAL, *s.m.*, a growth of rushes.
JUN.ÇÃO, *s.f.*, junction, connection, joint, linking.
JUN.CO, *s.m., Bot.*, rush (Juncaceae), Chinese junk; reed.
JUN.GIR, *v.*, to yoke, to unite, to couple, to join, to link.
JU.NHO, *s.m.*, June.
JU.NI.NO, *adj., Bras.*, pertaining to June; *festas juninas*: traditional celebrations held in June.
JÚ.NIOR, *adj.*, junior, younger.
JUN.TA, *s.f.*, junction, board, juncture, union, pair, yoke, team.
JUN.TA.MEN.TE, *adv.*, the same that *junto*.
JUN.TAR, *v.*, to join, to connect, to associate, to collect, to adjoin.
JUN.TO *adj.*, united, jointed, next to, near, close, together.
JU.RA, *s.f.*, curse, oath, vow, blasphemy; *Bras.*, a kind of rum.
JU.RA.DO, *s.m.*, member of the jury; *adj.*, sworn to.
JU.RA.MEN.TA.DO, *adj.*, under oath.
JU.RA.MEN.TAR, *v.*, to pledge by oath.
JU.RA.MEN.TO, *s.m.*, swearing, oath, vow, imprecation.
JU.RAR, *v.*, to swear, to vow, to pledge.
JÚ.RI, *s.m.*, jury.
JU.RÍ.DI.CO, *adj.*, juridical, forensic, legal.
JU.RIS.CON.SUL.TO, *s.m.*, jurisconsult; *US* jurist, *UK* legal expert.
JU.RIS.DI.ÇÃO, *s.f.*, jurisdiction, power, authority.
JU.RIS.DI.CI.O.NAL, *adj.*, jurisdictional.
JU.RIS.PRU.DÊN.CIA, *s.f.*, jurisprudence, the science of law.
JU.RIS.TA, *s. 2 gen.*, lawyer, jurist.
JU.RO, *s.m.*, interest, right.
JU.RU.RU, *adj., Bras.*, melancholic, moody, gloomy.
JUS, *s.m.*, right.
JU.SAN.TE, *s.f.*, low tide, low water; *a ~ de*: downstream of.
JUS.TA.MEN.TE, *adv.*, just, justly, fairly.
JUS.TA.POR, *v.*, to juxtapose.
JUS.TA.PO.SI.ÇÃO, *s.f.*, juxtaposition.
JUS.TA.POS.TO, *adj.*, juxtaposed.
JUS.TE.ZA, *s.f.*, justness, righteousness, precision.
JUS.TI.ÇA, *s.f.*, justice, rightness, justness, equity.
JUS.TI.CEI.RO, *s.m., Bras.*, revenger; *adj.*, just, righteous.
JUS.TI.FI.CA.ÇÃO, *s.f.*, justification.
JUS.TI.FI.CA.DO, *adj.*, justified.

JUSTIFICADOR   ••• 224 •••   JUVENTUDE

JUS.TI.FI.CA.DOR, *s.m.*, justifier; *adj.*, justifying.
JUS.TI.FI.CAN.TE, *s.m.*, that intends to justify; *adj.*, justifying.
JUS.TI.FI.CAR, *v.*, to justify, to prove, to warrant, to vindicate.
JUS.TI.FI.CA.TI.VA, *s.f.*, justification.
JUS.TI.FI.CÁ.VEL, *adj.*, justifiable.
JUS.TO, *s.m.*, fair, correct; *adj.*, just, fair, equitable, right, righteous, honest.

JU.TA, *s.f.*, jute.
JU.VE.NES.CER, *v.*, to rejuvenate, to become young.
RE.JU.VE.NES.CI.MEN.TO, *s.m.*, rejuvenation.
JU.VE.NIL, *adj.*, juvenile, youthful, young.
JU.VEN.TUDE, *s.f.*, youth, young people.

K

K, *s.m.*, letter not included in the Portuguese alphabet; used only in foreign words (internationally known symbols and abbreviations).

KAF.KI.A.NO, *adj.*, Kafkaesque, relating to the Franz Kafka (1883-1924).

KAN.TIS.MO, *s.m.*, Kantism.

KA.RA.O.KÊ, *s.m., Jap.,* karaoke.

KAR.DE.CIS.MO, *s.m.*, religious doctrine of the Allan Kardec (1804-1869).

KAR.TIS.MO, *s.m.*, karting (a kart racing).

KAR.TÓ.DRO.MO, *s.m.*, a kart racing track.

KETCH.UP, *s.m., Cul.,* ketchup.

KG, *s.m.*, kg, kilogram.

KIT, *s.m.*, kit.

KIT.CHE.NET.TE, *s.f., Ingl.,* studio flat.

KITSCH, *adj.*, kitsch.

KM, *s.m.*, km, kilometer.

KU.WAIT, *s.*, Kuwait.

KU.WAI.TI.A.NO, *adj.*, kuwaiti.

KW, *s.m.*, kw, kilowatt.

L, *s.m.*, the eleventh letter of the Portuguese alphabet.
L, *num.*, Roman numeral for fifty.
LÁ, *s.m.*, la, a (musical note); *adv.*, there, beyond.
LÃ, *s.f.*, wool.
LA.BA.RE.DA, *s.f.*, flame, blaze, flare, fire.
LÁ.BA.RO, *s.m.*, standard, flag; *Hist.*, labarum.
LÁ.BI.A, *s.f.*, smooth talk; cunning.
LA.BI.AL, *adj.*, labial, of the lips.
LÁ.BIO, *s.m.*, lip, labium.
LA.BI.O.DEN.TAL, *s. 2 gen.; adj.*, labiodental.
LA.BI.O.NA.SAL, *s. 2 gen., adj.*, labionasal.
LA.BI.RIN.TO, *s.m.*, labyrinth, embarrassment.
LA.BOR, *s.m.*, labour, work, toil, task, handiwork.
LA.BO.RAR, *v.*, to labour, to toil, to work, to function.
LA.BO.RA.TO.RI.AL, *adj.*, pertaining to a laboratory.
LA.BO.RA.TÓ.RIO, *s.m.*, laboratory.
LA.BO.RA.TO.RIS.TA, *s. 2 gen.*, laboratory technician.
LA.BO.RI.O.SO, *adj.*, laborious, toilsome.
LA.BU.TA, *s.f.*, toil, labour, drudgery, work.
LA.BU.TAR, *v.*, to struggle, to drudge, to labour.
LA.CA, *s.f.*, lac; shellac, lacquer.
LA.ÇA.DA, *s.f.*, bowknot, tie, loop.
LA.ÇA.DOR, *s.m.*, lassoer.
LA.CAI.O, *s.m.*, lackey, valet.
LA.ÇAR, *v.*, to lace, to tie, to bind, to lasso.
LA.ÇA.RO.TE, *s.m.*, large bow.
LA.ÇO, *s.m.*, bowknot, bond, bow, tie, loop.
LA.CÔ.NI.CO, *adj.*, Laconian, laconic, curt, brief, succinct, concise.
LA.CRAI.A, *s.f., Zool., Bras.*, centipede.
LA.CRAR, *v.*, to seal, to plumb.
LA.CRE, *s.m.*, sealing wax.
LA.CRE.A.DA, *s.f.*, ornament made of lacquer.
LA.CRI.MAL, *adj.*, lachrymal, lacrimal.
LA.CRI.ME.JA.MEN.TO, *s.m.*, shedding of tears.
LA.CRI.ME.JAN.TE, *adj.*, tearful.
LA.CRI.ME.JAR, *v.*, to shed tears.
LA.CRI.MO.GÊ.NEO, *adj.*, lachrymatory.
LA.CRI.MO.SO, *adj.*, lachrymose, tearful.
LAC.TA.ÇÃO, *s.f.*, lactation.
LAC.TAN.TE, *s.f.*, nursing woman; *adj.*, lactating, nursing.
LÁC.TEO, *adj.*, milky.
LÁC.TI.CO, *adj., Quím.*, lactic.
LAC.TO.SE, *s.f., Quím.*, lactose, milk sugar.
LA.CU.NA, *s.f.*, gap, blank, omission.
LA.CUS.TRE, *adj.*, lacustrine.
LA.DA.I.NHA, *s.f.*, litany.
LA.DE.AR, *v.*, to flank, to border, to run alongside; to skirt, to sidestep.
LA.DEI.RA, *s.f.*, declivity, hill, steep street, slope, ascent.
LA.DEI.REN.TO, *adj.*, steep, sloped, sloping, inclined.
LA.DO, *s.m.*, side, flank.
LA.DRA.DOR, *adj.*, barking.
LA.DRÃO, *s.m.*, thief, burglar, robber, bandit, gangster.
LA.DRAR, *v.*, to bark, to bay.
LA.DRI.DO, *s.m.*, bark, barking, yelping, baying.
LA.DRI.LHA.DO, *adj.*, tiled, paved with tiles.
LA.DRI.LHAR, *v.*, to tile.
LA.DRI.LHO, *s.m.*, tile, floor tile, brick.
LA.DRO.A.GEM, *s.m.*, thievery, robbery, theft.
LA.DRO.EI.RA, *s.f.*, the same that *ladroagem*.
LA.GAR.TA, *s.f.*, caterpillar; track.
LA.GAR.TE.AR, *v., Bras.*, to bask in the sun (as a lizard).
LA.GAR.TI.XA, *s.f.*, gecko, hiker.
LA.GAR.TO, *s.m.*, lizard.
LA.GO, *s.m.*, lake, pool, pond.
LA.GO.A, *s.f.*, lagoon, pond, pool, marsh.
LA.GOS.TA, *s.f.*, lobster.
LA.GOS.TIM, *s.m., Zool.*, crayfish, small lobster.
LÁ.GRI.MA, *s.f.*, tear, teardrop, drop.
LA.GU.NA, *s.f.*, lagoon.
LAI.A, *s.f.*, quality, kind, sort, nature, race, ilk.
LAI.CI.DA.DE, *s.f.*, laicity.
LAI.CIS.MO, *s.m.*, laicism.
LAI.CI.ZAR, *v.*, to laicize, to secularize.
LAI.CO, *adj.*, lay, secular.
LAI.VO, *s.m.*, spot, blot, speck.
LA.JE, *s.f.*, flag, flagstone, flagging.
LA.JE.A.DO, *s.m.*, flagging, slab covering.
LA.JE.AR, *v.*, to flag, pave with flagstones.
LA.JO.TA, *s.f.*, small flagstone.
LA.MA, *s.f.*, mud, dirt, sludge, mire, slime.
LA.MA.ÇAL, *s.m.*, slough, muddy place, bog, swamp.
LA.MA.CEN.TO, *adj.*, muddy, miry.
LAM.BA.DA, *s.f.*, blow, stroke, lash, rap.
LAM.BE-BO.TAS, *s. 2 gen., 2 num.*, bootlicker, flatterer.
LAM.BE.DOR, *s.m.*, licker; flatterer, wheedler.
LAM.BER, *v.*, to lick, to touch slightly, to polish.
LAM.BI.ÇÃO, *s.f., Bras.*, adulation, flattery.
LAM.BI.DA, *s.f.*, licking, lick; flattery.
LAM.BI.DO, *adj.*, overrefined; ungraceful, ungainly.
LAM.BIS.CA.DA, *s.f.*, nibbling, nibble.
LAM.BIS.CAR, *v.*, to nibble.
LAM.BIS.GOI.A, *s.f.*, haughty woman, busybody.
LAM.BRE.TA, *s.f.*, scooter.
LAM.BRI, *s.m.*, wainscot; panelling.
LAM.BU.JA, *s.f.*, sweetmeat, gain.
LAM.BU.JEM, *s.f.*, sweetmeat, dainty; gain.
LAM.BU.ZA.DO, *adj.*, dirty, smeared.
LAM.BU.ZAR, *v.*, to dirty, to stain.
LAM.BU.ZEI.RA, *s.f.*, mess, dirtiness.
LA.MEI.RA, *s.f.*, the same that *lamaçal*: muddy place.
LA.MEN.TA.ÇÃO, *s.f.*, lamentation, wailing, outcry.
LA.MEN.TAR, *v.*, to lament, to regret, to pity.

LAMENTÁVEL · 227 · LATINIDADE

LA.MEN.TÁ.VEL, *adj.*, lamentable, doleful, mournful, grievous.
LA.MEN.TA.VEL.MEN.TE, *adv.*, lamentably.
LA.MEN.TO, *s.m.*, lament, moan, groan, complaint.
LÂ.MI.NA, *s.f.*, blade, sheet, platter, strip.
LA.MI.NA.ÇÃO, *s.f.*, lamination.
LA.MI.NA.DO, *s.m.*, laminate; *adj.*, laminated.
LA.MI.NAR, *v.*, to laminate, to roll.
LÂM.PA.DA, *s.f.*, lamp, bulb; light.
LAM.PA.RI.NA, *s.f.*, oil lamp, small lamp.
LAM.PE.JAN.TE, *adj.*, flashing, glittering, sparkling, shining.
LAM.PE.JAR, *v.*, to sparkle, to coruscate.
LAM.PE.JO, *s.m.*, flash (of light); glitter, sparkle.
LAM.PI.ÃO, *s.m.*, lantern, large lamp.
LA.MÚ.RIA, *s.f.*, lamentation, complaint.
LA.MU.RI.AN.TE, *adj.*, lamenting; complaining, plaintive, crying.
LA.MU.RI.AR, *v.*, to lament; *lamuriar-se*: to (be) moan, to become woeful.
LAN, *s.m.*, *abrev.* of Local Area Network: *Rede de Área Local*.
LAN.ÇA, *s.f.*, lance, spear, javelin.
LAN.ÇA-CHA.MAS, *s.m.*, *2 num.*, flame-thrower.
LAN.ÇA.DEI.RA, *s.f.*, sewing shuttle; *pop.*, restless person.
LAN.ÇA.MEN.TO, *s.m.*, cast, casting, throw, pitch, release, publication, edition.
LAN.ÇA-PER.FU.ME, *s.m.*, perfume squirter.
LAN.ÇAR, *v.*, to cast, to throw, to release, to pitch, to fling, to launch.
LAN.CE, *s.m.*, throw, cast, casting, hurl, conjuncture, risk.
LAN.CEI.RO, *s.m.*, lancer; lance maker; *lanceiros pl.*: lancers.
LAN.CHA, *s.f.*, motorboat, launch, barge.
LAN.CHAR, *v.*, to take a snack, to eat.
LAN.CHE, *s.m.*, snack.
LAN.CHEI.RA, *s.f.*, lunch box.
LAN.CHO.NE.TE, *s.f.*, snack bar.
LAN.CI.NAN.TE, *adj.*, lancinating, painful, piercing.
LAN.GOR, *s.m.*, languor.
LAN.GUI.DEZ, *s.f.*, languidness, languor.
LÂN.GUI.DO, *adj.*, languid, languishing.
LA.NHAR, *v.*, to wound, to hurt, to injure, to bruise.
LA.NHO, *s.m.*, scratch, slash, cut.
LA.NÍ.FE.RO, *adj.*, lanigerous.
LA.NÍ.GE.RO, *adj.*, lanigerous.
LA.NO.LI.NA, *s.f.*, lanolin.
LAN.TE.JOU.LA, *s.f.*, sequin.
LAN.TER.NA, *s.f.*, lantern.
LAN.TER.NEI.RO, *s.m.*, lantern maker, lantern bearer, lighthouseman.
LAN.TER.NI.NHA, *s.f.*, a small lantern; tail-light; *s. 2 gen., Bras., Cin.*, usher.
LA.PA, *s.f.*, formetion by an over-hanging stone, grotto; *Zool.*, limpet; *Bras.*, bit, fraction.
LA.PA.ROS.CO.PI.A, *s.f.*, *Med.*, laparoscopy.
LA.PA.RO.TO.MI.A, *s.f.*, *Med.*, laparotomy.
LA.PE.LA, *s.f.*, lapel.
LA.PI.DA.ÇÃO, *s.f.*, stone-cutting, refining, lapidation.
LA.PI.DAR, *v.*, to lapidate, to polish gems, to polish.
LA.PI.DÁ.RI.O, *s.m.*, lapidary, stone-cutter; *adj.*, lapidary.
LÁ.PI.DE, *s.f.*, gravestone, tombstone, ledger.
LÁ.PIS, *s.m.*, pencil.
LA.PI.SEI.RA, *s.f.*, pencil-case, port-crayon.
LÁ.PIS-LA.ZÚ.LI, *s.m.*, lapis-lazuli.

LAP.SO, *s.m.*, lapse, slip, error.
LA.QUÊ, *s.m.*, hairspray, hair spray.
LA.QUE.A.DU.RA, *s.f.*, *Med.*, tubal ligation.
LA.QUE.AR, *s.m.*, to gloss; *Med.*, to ligate.
LAR, *s.m.*, home, residence.
LA.RAN.JA, *s.f.*, orange.
LA.RAN.JA.DA, *s.f.*, orangeade.
LA.RAN.JAL, *s.m.*, orangery.
LA.RAN.JEI.RA, *s.f.*, orange (tree).
LA.RÁ.PIO, *s.m.*, pilferer, filcher, thief.
LA.REI.RA, *s.f.*, fireplace.
LAR.GA.DA, *s.f.*, start, departure, prowess.
LAR.GA.DO, *adj.*, abandoned, despised.
LAR.GAR, *v.*, to release, to let go, to free, to relax, to leave, to ease, to abandon.
LAR.GO, *s.m.*, breadth, width, plaza, public square, high sea; *adj.*, broad, large, wide, ample.
LAR.GUE.ZA, *s.f.*, breadth, width; *fig.*, largesse, liberality.
LAR.GU.RA, *s.f.*, breadth, width, wideness, broadness.
LA.RI.CA, *s.f.*, *gír.*, hunger.
LA.RIN.GE, *s.f.*, *Anat.*, larynx.
LA.RÍN.GE.O, *adj.*, laryngeal, laryngal.
LA.RIN.GI.TE, *s.f.*, *Med.*, laryngitis.
LAR.VA, *s.f.*, larva, worm.
LAR.VAL, *adj.*, larval.
LAS.CA, *s.f.*, sliver, splint, splinter.
LA.SA.NHA, *s.f.*, lasagna, lasagne.
LAS.CA.DO, *adj.*, split, splintered, cracked, chip; *fig., Bras.*, wretched.
LAS.CAR, *v.*, to splinter, to chip, to crack, to cleave.
LAS.CÍ.VI.A, *s.f.*, lasciviousness, wantonness.
LAS.CI.VO, *adj.*, lascivious, wanton, lewd.
LA.SER, *s.m.*, laser.
LAS.SI.DÃO, *s.f.*, lassitude, tiredness.
LÁS.TI.MA, *s.f.*, pity, pain, grief, sorrow, lamentation, compassion.
LAS.TI.MAR, *v.*, to lament, to regret, to grieve, to deplore, to commiserate.
LAS.TI.MÁ.VEL, *adj.*, disgraceful, pitiable, regrettable.
LAS.TI.MO.SO, *adj.*, pitiful, doleful.
LAS.TRE.AR, *v.*, to ballast.
LAS.TRO, *s.m.*, *Náut.*, ballast; *Econ.*, guaranty; standard; *fig.*, grounding.
LA.TA, *s.f.*, tin, can, tin plate, canister.
LA.TA.DA, *s.f.*, a blow on with a tin can; lattice, trellis.
LA.TÃO, *s.m.*, brass.
LA.TA.RI.A, *s.f.*, bodywork (auto); large quantity of tins.
LÁ.TE.GO, *s.m.*, whip, scourge.
LA.TE.JAN.TE, *adj.*, throbbing, pulsating.
LA.TE.JAR, *v.*, to pulsate, to throb, to palpitate, to pulse.
LA.TE.JO, *s.m.*, throbbing, pulsation, beat.
LA.TÊN.CI.A, *s.f.*, latency.
LA.TEN.TE, *adj.*, latent, hidden, concealed.
LA.TE.RAL, *adj.*, lateral, transversal.
LA.TI.CÍ.NI.O, LAC.TI.CÍ.NI.O, *s.m.*, dairy, creamery.
LÁ.TI.CO, *adj.*, *Quím.*, the same that *láctico*: lactic.
LA.TI.DO, *s.m.*, bark, barking, yelp, baying.
LA.TI.FUN.DI.Á.RIO, *s.m.*, the owner of a latifundium.
LA.TI.FÚN.DIO, *s.m.*, latifundium, a large farm.
LA.TIM, *s.m.*, Latin.
LA.TI.NI.DA.DE, *s.f.*, Latinity.

LATINIZAR ·· 228 ··· LENTE

LA.TI.NI.ZAR, *v.*, to Latinize.
LA.TI.NO, *adj., s.m.*, Latin.
LA.TI.NO-A.ME.RI.CA.NO, *adj., s.m.*, Latin-American.
LA.TIR, *v.*, to bark, to yap, to yelp, howl.
LA.TI.TU.DE, *s.f.*, latitude, breadth, scope.
LA.TI.TU.DI.NAL, *adj.*, latitudinal.
LA.TO, *adj.*, wide, broad.
LA.TO.A.RI.A, *s.f.*, a tinsmith's shop.
LA.TO.EI.RO, *s.m.*, tinsmith, tinker.
LA.TRI.NA, *s.f.*, latrine, privy.
LA.TRO.CÍ.NIO, *s.m.*, armed robbery, hold-up.
LAU.DA, *s.f.*, page, page of a book; standard writing page.
LÁU.DA.NO, *s.m.*, laudanum.
LAU.DA.TÓ.RI.O, *adj.*, laudative, laudatory.
LAU.DO, *s.m.*, report, award, report of experts.
LÁU.REA, *s.f.*, laurel.
LAU.RE.A.DO, *s.m.*, laureate; *adj.*, laureate.
LAU.RE.AR, *v.*, to laureate, to praise, to applaud.
LAU.REL, *s.m.*, laurel; *fig.*, honour, award, prize.
LAU.RÊN.CI.O, *s.m., Quím.*, lawrencium (radioactive element).
LAU.TO, *adj.*, sumptuous, splendid, abundant.
LA.VA, *s.f.*, lava, torrent, fire.
LA.VA.BO, *s.m.*, any wash-basin.
LA.VA.DEI.RA, *s.f.*, laundress, washing-machine.
LA.VA.DO, *adj.*, washed.
LA.VA.DO.RA, *s.f., Bras.*, washing machine.
LA.VA.GEM, *s.f.*, wash, cleansing, ablution.
LA.VAN.DA, *s.f.*, lavender.
LA.VAN.DE.RI.A, *s.f.*, laundry.
LA.VAR, *v.*, to wash, to bathe, to cleanse, to purify, to purge.
LA.VA.TÓ.RIO, *s.m.*, lavatory, wash-basin.
LA.VOU.RA, *s.f.*, farming, agriculture, tillage.
LA.VRA, *s.f.*, cultivation, fabrication, production.
LA.VRA.DOR, *s.m.*, farmer, tiller, peasant.
LA.VRAR, *v.*, to cultivate, to till, to plough, to plow.
LA.XAN.TE, *s.m.*, purgative, laxative; *adj.*, laxative, purgative.
LA.XA.TI.VO, *adj.*, laxative, purgative.
LÁ.ZA.RO, *s.m.*, lazar.
LA.ZER, *s.m.*, leisure, spare time, recreation.
LE.AL, *adj.*, loyal, true, devoted, sincere.
LE.AL.DA.DE, *s.f.*, loyalty, faithfulness, fidelity.
LE.ÃO, *s.m.*, lion.
LE.ÃO DE CHÁ.CA.RA, *s.m.*, bouncer.
LE.ÃO-MA.RI.NHO, *s.m.*, sea-lion.
LEAS.ING, *s.m., Econ.*, leasing.
LE.BRE, *s.f.*, hare.
LE.CI.O.NAR, *v.*, to teach, to lecture, to doctrinate, to instruct, to study.
LE.GA.ÇÃO, *s.f.*, legation, diplomacy, legacy.
LE.GA.DO, *s.m.*, legate, envoy, legacy, bequest.
LE.GAL, *adj.*, legal, lawful, right.
LE.GA.LI.DA.DE, *s.f.*, legality, lawfulness.
LE.GA.LI.ZA.ÇÃO, *s.f.*, legalization.
LE.GA.LI.ZAR, *v.*, to legalize, to authenticate, to validate, to legitimate.
LE.GAR, *v.*, to delegate, to pass on; *Jur.*, to bequeath.
LE.GEN.DA, *s.f.*, story, inscription, legend, caption.
LE.GEN.DAR, *v., Cin.*, to subtitle; to captions (typography, photo).
LE.GI.ÃO, *s.f.*, legion, multitude, host.
LE.GI.BI.LI.DA.DE, *s.f.*, legibility.

LE.GI.O.NÁ.RI.O, *s.m.*, legionary; *adj.*, legionary.
LE.GIS.LA.ÇÃO, *s.f.*, legislation.
LE.GIS.LA.DOR, *s.m.*, legislator, lawgiver.
LE.GIS.LAR, *v.*, to legislate, to make laws.
LE.GIS.LA.TI.VO, *s.m.*, legislative, the legislative power; *adj.*, legislative.
LE.GIS.LA.TU.RA, *s.f.*, legislature.
LE.GIS.TA, *s. 2 gen.*, legist, jurist, lawyer; doctor-legist.
LE.GÍ.TI.MA, *s.f., Júr.*, legitim.
LE.GI.TI.MA.ÇÃO, *s.f.*, legitimation.
LE.GI.TI.MA.DO, *adj.*, legitimated.
LE.GI.TI.MAR, *v.*, to legitimate, to make legitimate, to legalize.
LE.GI.TI.MI.DA.DE, *s.f.*, legitimacy, legality.
LE.GÍ.TI.MO, *adj.*, legitimate, lawful, legal, rightful, true, genuine, authentic.
LE.GÍ.VEL, *adj.*, readable, legible.
LÉ.GUA, *s.f.*, league, measure of 6,000 meters.
LE.GU.ME, *s.m.*, legume, vegetables.
LE.GU.MI.NO.SA(S), *s.f., (pl.)* leguminous plant.
LEI, *s.f.*, law, rule, commandment.
LEI.AU.TE, *s.m., Bras.*, layout.
LEI.GO, *s.m.*, layman, outsider, laic; *adj.*, laic, lay, secular, unprofessional.
LEI.LÃO, *s.m.*, auction, outcry.
LEI.LO.AR, *v.*, to auction, to sell by auction.
LEI.LO.EI.RO, *s.m.*, auctioneer.
LEI.TÃO, *s.m., Zool.*, piglet, shoat.
LEI.TE, *s.m.*, milk; *leite condensado*: condensed milk; *dente de leite*: milk tooth.
LEI.TEI.RA, *s.f.*, milk jug, milkpot; dairy woman.
LEI.TEI.RO, *s.m.*, milkman.
LEI.TE.RI.A, *s.f.*, dairy, creamery, milkshop.
LEI.TO, *s.m.*, bed, berth; couch, bunk.
LEI.TO.A, *s.f., Zool.*, female sucking pig.
LEI.TOR, *s.m.*, reader, lecturer.
LEI.TO.SO, *adj.*, milky.
LEI.TU.RA, *s.f.*, read, read out, reading, lecture.
LE.LÉ, *s.m., Bras., gír.*, crazy person; *adj.*, nuts, crazy.
LE.MA, *s.m.*, lemma, motto, slogan, premise.
LEM.BRA.DO, *adj.*, mindful.
LEM.BRAN.ÇA, *s.f.*, remembrance, recollection, souvenir, keepsake, recall, memory, mind.
LEM.BRAR, *v.*, to recall, to remember, to remind, to suggest.
LEM.BRE.TE, *s.m.*, reminder, note, memorandum.
LE.ME, *s.m.*, rudder, government, direction, helm.
LEN.ÇO, *s.m.*, handkerchief.
LEN.ÇOL, *s.m.*, sheet.
LEN.DA, *s.f.*, legend, folk tale, myth, fable, fiction.
LEN.DÁ.RIO, *adj.*, legendary, mythical.
LÊN.DE.A, *s.f.*, nit (the egg of a louse); fragment, piece, insignificance.
LEN.GA-LEN.GA, *s.f.*, tedious narrative, rigmarole.
LE.NHA, *s.f.*, firewood, fuel.
LE.NHA.DOR, *s.m.*, woodcutter, lumberman.
LE.NHO, *s.m.*, xylem, wood, log.
LE.NHO.SO, *adj.*, ligneous, woody.
LE.NI.NIS.MO, *s.m., Pol.*, Leninism.
LE.NI.NIS.TA, *s. 2 gen., adj.*, Leninist.
LE.NI.TI.VO, *s.m.*, lenitive, palliative.
LE.NO.CÍ.NIO, *s.m.*, panderage.
LEN.TE, *s.f.*, lens; *s.m.*, university professor, teacher.

LENTIDÃO ·· 229 ·· LICENCIAR

LEN.TI.DÃO, *s.f.*, slowness, lentitude, sluggishness, delay, indolence.
LEN.TO, *adj.*, slow, sluggish, tardy.
LE.O.A, *s.f.*, lioness.
LE.O.NI.NO, *adj.*, leonine.
LE.O.PAR.DO, *s.m.*, leopard.
LÉ.PI.DO, *adj.*, gay, happy, jovial; nimble, swift.
LE.PO.RI.NO, *adj.*, leporine.
LE.PRA, *s.f.*, leprosy.
LE.PRO.SÁ.RIO, *s.m.*, leprosery.
LE.PRO.SO, *s.m.*, leper, lazar; *adj.*, leprous.
LE.QUE, *s.m.*, fan.
LER, *v.*, to read, to peruse, to interpret, to recite.
LER.DE.ZA, *s.f.*, slowness, sluggishness.
LER.DI.CE, *s.f.*, *Bras.*, the same that *lerdeza*.
LER.DO, *adj.*, slow, sluggish, laggard, dull, stupid.
LE.RO-LE.RO, *s.m.*, *Bras.*, *gír.*, idle talk, chit-chat.
LE.SA.DO, *adj.*, injured, wounded, hurt, damaged.
LE.SA-HU.MA.NI.DA.DE, *s.f.*, lese-humanity.
LE.SÃO, *s.f.*, lesion, hurt, wound, injury.
LE.SAR, *v.*, to injure, to hurt, to wound, to damage, to bruise, to wrong.
LES.BI.A.NIS.MO, *s.m.*, lesbianism.
LÉS.BI.CA, *s.f.*, Lesbian.
LÉS.BI.CO, *adj.*, Lesbian.
LE.SEI.RA, *s.f.*, laziness, indolence; *Bras.*, foolishness, stupidity.
LE.SI.O.NAR, *v.*, to injure, to wound.
LE.SI.VO, *adj.*, injurious, offensive, harmful.
LES.MA, *s.f.*, snail, slug.
LE.SO, *adj.*, injured, offended, wronged; *Bras.*, foolish, crazy.
LES.TE, *s.m.*, east, the Orient.
LE.TAL, *adj.*, lethal, deadly, mortal, fatal.
LE.TÃO, *s.m.*, Latvian; *adj.*, Lettish, Latvian.
LE.TAR.GI.A, *s.f.*, *Med.*, lethargy.
LE.TÁR.GI.CO, *adj.*, lethargic, lethargical; *fig.*, indolent.
LE.TI.VO, *adj.*, concerning school or a period of learning.
LE.TÔ.NI.A, *s.*, Latvia.
LE.TRA, *s.f.*, letter, character, type, inscription.
LE.TRA.DO, *s.m.*, man of letters, literate; *adj.*, lettered, erudite, literate, well read.
LE.TREI.RO, *s.m.*, lettering, label, ticket, inscription.
LÉU, *s.m.*, time, leisure, opportunity, occasion, chance.
LEU.CE.MI.A, *s.f.*, leukemia.
LEU.CÊ.MI.CO, *adj.*, leukemic.
LEU.CÓ.CI.TO, *s.m.*, leucocyte.
LE.VA, *s.f.*, *Náut.*, weighing of anchor; batch; *pop.*, group.
LE.VA.DI.ÇO, *adj.*, mobile, movable.
LE.VAN.TA.DO, *adj.*, upright, erect, up.
LE.VAN.TA.DOR, *s.m.*, levator; *adj.*, lifting, raising.
LE.VAN.TA.MEN.TO, *s.m.*, survey, elevation, lifting, raising, rise, erection.
LE.VAN.TAR, *v.*, to lift, to raise, to elevate, to rise up, to upload.
LE.VAR, *v.*, to carry, to lead, to remove, to convey, to run, to transport, to lead.
LE.VE, *adj.*, light, slight, nimble, quick, agile.
LE.VE.DAR, *v.*, to leaven, to yeast.
LÊ.VE.DO, *s.m.*, yeast; *adj.*, leavened, fermented.
LE.VE.DU.RA, *s.f.*, yeast, leaven.
LE.VE.MEN.TE, *adv.*, lightly.

LE.VE.ZA, *s.f.*, lightness.
LE.VI.AN.DA.DE, *s.f.*, levity, imprudence, rashness, frivolity.
LE.VI.A.NO, *adj.*, rash, frivolous, flighty.
LE.VI.A.TÃ, *s.m.*, *Rel.*, leviathan.
LE.VI.TA.ÇÃO, *s.f.*, levitation.
LE.VI.TAR, *v.*, to levitate.
LE.XI.CAL, *adj.*, lexical.
LÉ.XI.CO, *s.m.*, lexicon, dictionary.
LE.XI.CO.GRA.FI.A, *s.f.*, lexicography.
LE.XI.CO.GRÁ.FI.CO, *adj.*, lexicographic.
LE.XI.CO.LO.GI.A, *s.f.*, lexicology.
LE.XI.CÓ.LO.GO, *s.m.*, lexicologist.
LHA.MA, *s.m.*, *Zool.*, llama.
LHA.NE.ZA, *s.f.*, sincerity, honesty, kindness.
LHA.NO, *adj.*, sincere, honest, gracious, kind, affable.
LHE, *pron.*, him, her, it, to him, to it, her, to her.
LHU.FAS, *pron.*, *Bras.*, nothing.
LI.A, *s.f.*, lees, sediment, mother of wine.
LI.A.ME, *s.m.*, bond, tie; *Náut.*, strengthening pieces, cordage.
LI.BA.ÇÃO, *s.f.*, libation.
LI.BA.NÊS, *adj.*, *s.m.*, Lebanese.
LÍBANO, *s.*, Lebanon.
LI.BE.LO, *s.m.*, lampoon; *Jur.*, indictment, libel.
LI.BÉ.LU.LA, *s.f.*, dragonfly.
LI.BE.RA.ÇÃO, *s.f.*, liberation, release, liquidation, discharge.
LI.BE.RAL, *s.* 2 *gen.*, liberalist; *adj.*, liberal, munificent, befitting.
LI.BE.RA.LI.DA.DE, *s.f.*, liberality, generosity. ·
LI.BE.RA.LIS.MO, *s.m.*, liberalism.
LI.BE.RA.LI.ZA.ÇÃO, *s.f.*, liberalization, freedom from controls.
LI.BE.RA.LI.ZAN.TE, *adj.*, liberalizing.
LI.BE.RA.LI.ZAR, *v.*, to liberalize, to lavish.
LI.BE.RAR, *v.*, to discharge, to liquidate, to settle.
LI.BER.DA.DE, *s.f.*, liberty, freedom, permission, frankness, exemption.
LI.BER.TA.ÇÃO, *s.f.*, liberation, relief, release, delivery.
LI.BER.TAR, *v.*, to liberate, to set free, to free, to deliver, to release.
LIBÉRIA, *s.*, Liberia.
LÍ.BE.RO, *s.m.*, *Bras.*, libero (soccer).
LI.BER.TÁ.RI.O, *s.m.*, libertarian; *adj.*, libertarian.
LI.BER.TI.NA.GEM, *s.f.*, libertinism, licentiousness; loose living.
LI.BER.TI.NO, *adj.*, libertine, licentious, dissolute.
LI.BER.TO, *s.m.*, freedman; *adj.*, free, at liberty; independent; liberated.
LÍBIA, *s.*, Libya.
LI.BI.DI.NA.GEM, *s.f.*, libidinousness.
LI.BI.DI.NO.SO, *adj.*, libidinous.
LI.BI.DO, *s.f.*, libido.
LÍ.BI.O, *s.m.*, Libyan; *adj.*, Libyan.
LI.BRA, *s.f.*, pound, the weight and the monetary unit.
LI.BRE.TO, *s.m.*, libretto.
LI.BRI.A.NO, *s.m.*, *adj.*, Libran.
LI.ÇÃO, *s.f.*, lesson, example, task, school-work, explanation.
LI.CEN.ÇA, *s.f.*, license, permission, consent, liberty.
LI.CEN.CI.A.MEN.TO, *s.m.*, licensing, permission, discharge.
LI.CEN.CI.A.DO, *s.m.*, licentiate; graduate; *adj.*, licensed; graduated; *Mil.*, discharged.
LI.CEN.CI.A.MEN.TO, *s.m.*, licensing; discharge.
LI.CEN.CI.AR, *v.*, to license, to authorize, to discharge.

LICENCIATURA ·· 230 ·· LISURA

LI.CEN.CI.A.TU.RA, *s.f.*, degree course; bachelor's degree.
LI.CEN.CI.O.SO, *adj.*, licentious.
LI.CEU, *s.m.*, lyceum, a secondary school.
LI.CI.TA.ÇÃO, *s.f.*, *Econ.*, bid, bidding, tender.
LI.CI.TA.DOR, LI.CI.TAN.TE, *s.m.*, *Econ.*, bidder, estimating company.
LÍ.CI.TO, *adj.*, licit, lawful.
LI.CI.TU.DE, *s.f.*, quality of being licit.
LI.COR, *s.m.*, liqueur, liquor.
LI.CO.RO.SO, *adj.*, sweet and strong (wine).
LI.DA, *s.f.*, work, toil, chore.
LI.DE, *s.f.*, work, toil; fight, dispute; *Júr.*, case.
LÍ.DER, *s.m.*, leader, chief, commander, guide.
LI.DE.RAN.ÇA, *s.f.*, leadership, lead.
LI.DE.RAR, *v.*, to lead, to guide, to conduct.
LI.DO, *adj.*, *Lit.*, well read, studied, erudite.
LI.GA, *s.f.*, league, union, alliance; garter (stocking); alloy (metals).
LI.GA.ÇÃO, *s.f.*, ligation, joining, junction, connection, bond, binding.
LI.GA.DO, *adj.*, joint, connected, intimate, close.
LI.GA.DU.RA, *s.f.*, bandage; *Mús.*, ligature.
LI.GA.MEN.TO, *s.m.*, ligament, bandage, bond.
LI.GAR, *v.*, to tie, to bind, to link, to fasten, to attach, to connect, to pay attention to.
LI.GEI.RE.ZA, *s.f.*, quickness, lightness, swiftness.
LI.GEI.RO, *adj.*, quick, swift, fast, speedy, rapid, light, alert.
LI.LÁS, *s.m.*, lilac; *adj.*, lilac (colour).
LI.MA, *s.f.*, file (steel instrument); *Bot.*, sweet lime (fruit).
LI.MÃO, *s.m.*, *Bot.*, lemon.
LI.MAR, *v.*, to sand, to file, to polish.
LIM.BO, *s.m.*, limb, edge, border; Limbo.
LI.MI.AR, *s.m.*, threshold; *fig.*, doorway.
LI.MI.NAR, *s.f.*, preliminary, introductory.
LI.MI.TA.ÇÃO, *s.f.*, limitation, restriction, check.
LI.MI.TA.DO, *adj.*, limited.
LI.MI.TAR, *v.*, to limit, to delimit, to circumscribe, to border.
LI.MI.TE, *s.m.*, limit, bound, border, frontier, end.
LI.MÍ.TRO.FE, *adj.*, adjacent, limitrophe.
LI.MO, *s.m.*, *Bot.*, slime; mud, ooze.
LI.MO.AL, *s.m.*, lemon orchard.
LI.MO.EI.RO, *s.m.*, lemon tree.
LI.MO.NA.DA, *s.f.*, lemonade.
LIM.PA.DOR, *s.m.*, cleaner, wiper; *limpador de para-brisa*: windshield wiper.
LIM.PAR, *v.*, to clarify, to clean, to purify, to wash.
LIM.PE.ZA, *s.f.*, cleanness, neatness, cleaning.
LIM.PI.DEZ, *s.f.*, limpidity, limpidness.
LÍM.PI.DO, *adj.*, limpid, clear, transparent, lucid, bright.
LIM.PO, *adj.*, clean, neat, trim, tidy, clear, pure, clearly, immaculate.
LI.MU.SI.NE, *s.f.*, limousine, limo.
LIN.CE, *s.m.*, lynx.
LIN.CHA.MEN.TO, *s.m.*, lynching.
LIN.CHAR, *v.*, to lynch.
LIN.DE.ZA, *s.f.*, beauty, prettiness.
LIN.DO, *adj.*, pretty, beautiful, handsome, nice, fine, elegant, graceful, good.
LI.NE.AR, *adj.*, linear, lineal.
LI.NE.A.RI.DA.DE, *s.f.*, linearity.
LI.NE.AR.MEN.TE, *adv.*, lineally.

LIN.FÁ.TI.CO, *adj.*, lymphatic.
LIN.GO.TE, *s.m.*, ingot.
LÍN.GUA, *s.f.*, *Anat.*, tongue, speech, language, idiom; interpreter.
LIN.GUA.DO, *s.m.*, *Zool.*, sole; a long blade.
LIN.GUA.GEM, *s.f.*, language, idiom, dialect.
LIN.GUA.JAR, *s.m.*, talk, speech, dialect.
LIN.GUA.RU.DO, *s.m.*, gossipy, chatterbox, gabbler.
LIN.GUE.TA, *s.f.*, a little tongue; languet; catch; tongue (of a shoe).
LIN.GUI.ÇA, *s.f.*, sausage.
LIN.GUIS.TA, *s. 2 gen.*, linguist.
LIN.GUÍS.TI.CA, *s.f.*, linguistics.
LIN.GUÍS.TI.CO, *adj.*, linguistic.
LI.NHA, *s.f.*, line, thread, string, lineage, cord, rail; *linha férrea*: railway.
LI.NHA.ÇA, *s.f.*, linseed, flaxseed.
LI.NHA-DU.RA, *s. 2 gen.*, *Bras., col.*, hardliner; *adj.*, hard-line.
LI.NHA.GEM, *s.f.*, lineage, genealogy, race, pedigree.
LI.NHO, *s.m.*, linen (cloth made of flax); *Bot.*, flax.
LI.NHO.SO, *adj.*, flaxen.
LINK, *s.m.*, *Comp.*, link.
LI.NÓ.LE.O, *s.m.*, linoleum.
LI.NO.TI.PO, *s.m.*, linotype.
LI.PÍ.DIO, *s.m.*, lipid.
LI.PO.AS.PI.RA.ÇÃO, *s.f.*, *Med.*, liposuction.
LI.PO.SO, *adj.*, bleary, blear-eyed.
LI.QUE.FA.ÇÃO, *s.f.*, liquefaction.
LI.QUE.FA.ZER, *v.*, to liquefy, to reduce to a liquid.
LI.QUE.FEI.TO, *adj.*, liquefied; molten.
LÍ.QUEN, *s.m.*, *Bot.*, lichen.
LI.QUES.CER, *v.*, to liquesce.
LI.QUI.DA.ÇÃO, *s.f.*, liquidation, sale, clearing.
LI.QUI.DA.DO, *adj.*, liquidated, finished.
LI.QUI.DAR, *v.*, to liquidate, to settle, to adjust, to shut down.
LI.QUI.DEZ, *s.f.*, liquidness.
LI.QUI.DI.FI.CA.ÇÃO, *s.f.*, liquidification.
LI.QUI.DI.FI.CA.DOR, *s.m.*, mixer, blender, liquidizer, liquifier.
LI.QUI.DI.FI.CAN.TE, *adj.*, liquidifier.
LI.QUI.DI.FI.CAR, *v.*, to liquefy.
LÍ.QUI.DO, *s.m.*, liquid; *adj.*, liquid, fluid, net, clear, evident.
LI.RA, *s.f.*, *Mús.*, lyre.
LÍ.RI.CA, *s.f.*, lyric poem.
LÍ.RI.CO, *adj.*, lyric; romantic, sentimental.
LÍ.RIO, *s.m.*, *Bot.*, lily.
LI.RIS.MO, *s.m.*, lyrism, lyricism; *Lit.*, romance.
LIS, *s.m.*, lily.
LIS.BO.A.NO, *s. 2 gen.*, *adj.*, Lisbon.
LIS.BO.E.TA, *s. 2 gen.*, *adj.*, Lisbon.
LI.SO, *adj.*, smooth, even, sleeky, lank, soft, flat, sincere.
LI.SON.JA, *s.f.*, flattery, adulation, coaxing, cajolery.
LI.SON.JA.RI.A, *s.f.*, flattery, adulation.
LI.SON.JE.AR, *v.*, to flatter, to court, to fawn, to adulate, to cajole, to please.
LI.SON.JEI.RO, *adj.*, flattering, pleasing, adulatory, satisfactory.
LIS.TA, *s.f.*, list, roll, roster, catalogue; ribbon, band, slip.
LIS.TA.DO, *adj.*, the same that *listrado*.
LIS.TRA, *s.f.*, stripe.
LIS.TRA.DO, *adj.*, striped, ribboned.
LI.SU.RA, *s.f.*, smoothness, softness, sincerity, frankness.

LITANIA ·· 231 ·· LONGÍNQUO

LI.TA.NI.A, *s.f.*, litany.
LI.TEI.RA, *s.f.*, litter.
LI.TE.RAL, *adj.*, literal, exact, true.
LI.TE.RÁ.RIO, *adj.*, literary.
LI.TE.RA.TIS.MO, *s.m.*, mania of writing.
LI.TE.RA.TO, *s.m.*, literate.
LI.TE.RA.TU.RA, *s.f.*, literature, letters, learning, literary profession.
LI.TI.GAN.TE, *adj., s. 2 gen.*, litigant, litigator.
LI.TI.GAR, *v.*, to litigate, to contend.
LI.TÍ.GIO, *s.m.*, litigation, lawsuit, dispute.
LI.TI.GI.OS.O, *adj.*, litigious; *Jur.*, contentious.
LI.TO.GRA.FAR, *v.*, to lithograph.
LI.TO.GRA.FI.A, *s.f.*, lithography.
LI.TO.GRÁ.FI.CO, *adj.*, lithographical.
LI.TO.GRA.VU.RA, *s.f.*, lithograph.
LI.TO.RAL, *s.m.*, coast, littoral, seaside, seabord; *adj.*, littoral, coastal.
LI.TO.RÂ.NEO, *adj.*, littoral, coastal.
LI.TRA.GEM, *s.f.*, quantity expressed in liters.
LI.TRO, *s.m.*, liter, litre.
LITUÂNIA, *s.*, Lithuania.
LI.TU.A.NO, *adj., s.m.*, Lithuanian.
LI.TUR.GI.A, *s.f.*, liturgy, ritual.
LI.TÚR.GI.CO, *adj.*, liturgical.
LI.VI.DEZ, *s.f.*, lividity, lividness.
LÍ.VI.DO, *adj.*, livid, ashy.
LI.VRA.MEN.TO, *s.m.*, liberation, release.
LI.VRAR, *v.*, to liberate, to free, to release, to save, to deliver.
LI.VRA.RI.A, *s.f.*, bookshop, bookstore.
LI.VRE, *adj.*, free, independent, at liberty, exempt, absolved, released.
LI.VRE-AR.BÍ.TRI.O, *s.m., Filos.*, free will.
LI.VRE-DO.CÊN.CI.A, *s.f., Bras., Educ.*, the degree; title university.
LI.VRE-DO.CEN.TE, *s. 2 gen., Bras., Educ.*, research professor (title); *adj.*, research professor.
LI.VREI.RO, *s.m.*, bookseller.
LI.VRES.CO, *adj.*, bookish.
LI.VRO, *s.m.*, book.
LI.VRO-TEX.TO, *s.m.*, textbook.
LI.ÇA, *s.f.*, sandpaper, glasspaper.
LI.XA.ÇÃO, *s.f.*, act of sandpapering.
LI.XA.DEI.RA, *s.f.*, sander.
LI.XA.DOR, *s.m.*, sander; *adj.*, sanding.
LI.XÃO, *s.m.*, landfill.
LI.XAR, *v.*, to sandpaper, to paper, to sand, to polish.
LI.XEI.RA, *s.f.*, garbage can.
LI.XEI.RO, *s.m.*, garbage man, dustman.
LI.XÍ.VIA, *s.f.*, lixivium.
LI.XO, *s.m.*, trash, garbage, waste, rubbish, sweepings, dirtiness.
LO.A, *s.f., Teat.*, prologue of a play, laudatory speech.
LO.BA, *s.f.*, she-wolf.
LOB.BY, *s.m.*, lobby.
LÓ.BI, *s.m.*, lobby.
LO.BI.NHO, *s.m.*, a little wolf, boy scout.
LO.BI.SO.MEM, *s.m.*, werewolf.
LO.BIS.TA, *s. 2 gen.*, lobbyist.
LO.BO, *s.m.*, wolf.
LO.BO-MA.RI.NHO, *s.m., Zool.*, sea-lion.

LO.BO.TO.MI.A, *s.f., Med.*, lobotomy.
LO.BO.TO.MI.ZAR, *v., Med.*, to lobotomize.
LO.BU.LAR, *adj.*, lobular.
LÓ.BU.LO, *s.m.*, lobule.
LO.CA.ÇÃO, *s.f.*, location, situation, place, hiring, lease.
LO.CA.DOR, *s.m.*, lessor, landlord, hirer.
LO.CAL, *s.m.*, place, spot, site, locality.
LO.CA.LI.DA.DE, *s.f.*, locality, place, settlement, situation.
LO.CA.LI.ZA.ÇÃO, *s.f.*, localization, location, position.
LO.CA.LI.ZA.DO, *adj.*, localized, situated.
LO.CA.LI.ZAR, *v.*, to localize, to locate, to place.
LO.CA.LI.ZÁ.VEL, *adj.*, localizable.
LO.ÇÃO, *s.f.*, lotion.
LO.CA.TÁ.RIO, *s.m.*, lodger, tenant, lessee.
LO.CO.MO.ÇÃO, *s.f.*, locomotion.
LO.CO.MO.TI.VA, *s.f.*, locomotive, train engine.
LO.CO.MO.TI.VI.DA.DE, *s.f.*, locomotivity.
LO.CO.MO.TI.VO, *adj.*, locomotive.
LO.CO.MO.TOR, *adj.*, locomotor.
LO.CO.MO.VER-SE, *v.*, to move about.
LO.CU.ÇÃO, *s.f.*, locution, expression, phrase, phraseology.
LO.CU.PLE.TA.ÇÃO, *s.f.*, enrichment.
LO.CU.PLE.TAR, *v.*, to enrich, to satiate.
LO.CU.TOR, *s.m.*, speaker, radio announcer.
LO.DA.ÇAL, *s.m.*, mud, bog, swamp.
LO.DA.CEN.TO, *adj.*, muddy, boggy, swampy.
LO.DO, *s.m.*, mud, mire, clay, slime, dirt, slop, slush.
LO.DO.SO, *adj.*, muddy, miry, slimy, sloppy.
LO.GA.RIT.MO, *s.m.*, logarithm.
LÓ.GI.CA, *s.f.*, logic.
LÓ.GI.CO, *adj.*, logical, rational, coherent.
LO.GÍS.TI.CA, *s.f.*, logistics.
LO.GÍS.TI.CO, *adj.*, logistic.
LO.GO, *adv.*, immediately, at once, right away, soon, before long.
LO.GO.TI.PO, *s.m.*, logotype.
LO.GRA.DOU.RO, *s.m.*, public area (avenue, street, square, etc.).
LO.GRAR, *v.*, to cheat, to trick, to deceive, to defraud, to swindle.
LO.GRO, *s.m.*, cheat, swindle, fraud, trick.
LOI.ÇA, *s.f.*, the same that *louça*.
LOI.RO, LOU.RO, *adj., s.m.*, blond.
LO.JA, *s.f.*, shop, store, baz(a)ar, workshop.
LO.JIS.TA, *s. 2 gen.*, shopkeeper, storekeeper.
LOM.BA, *s.f.*, ridge, elevated plain.
LOM.BA.DA, *s.f.*, range of hills, mountain-ridge.
LOM.BAR, *adj.*, lumbar; *Anat.*, *vértebras lombares* (*pl.*): lumbar vertebrae.
LOM.BI.NHO, *s.m.*, tenderloin.
LOM.BO, *s.m.*, loin, reins, back, pork loin.
LOM.BRI.GA, *s.f.*, roundworm, worm.
LO.NA, *s.f.*, canvas, sailcloth, tarpaulin.
LON.DRES, *s.*, London.
LON.DRI.NO, *s.m.*, Londoner; *adj.*, London.
LON.GA.MEN.TE, *adv.*, for a long way; for a long time.
LON.GA-ME.TRA.GEM, *s.m., Cin.*, feature film.
LON.GE, *adj.*, remote, distant; *adv.*, far, far-off.
LON.GE.VI.DA.DE, *s.f.*, longevity, long life.
LON.GE.VO, *adj.*, longevous; long-lived; elderly.
LON.GÍN.QUO, *adj.*, distant, far-away, far-off.

LONGITUDE · 232 · LYCRA

LON.GI.TU.DE, s.f., longitude.
LON.GI.TU.DI.NAL, adj., longitudinal.
LON.GO, adj., long, lenghty, prolix.
LON.JU.RA, s.f., distance, great distance.
LON.TRA, s.f., otter.
LO.QUA.CI.DA.DE, s.f., loquacity.
LO.QUAZ, adj., talkative, eloquent.
LOR.DE, s.m., lord.
LO.RO.TA, s.f., lie, idle, fib, nonsense.
LO.RO.TEI.RO, s.m., lier, fibber; adj., lying, false.
LO.SAN.GO, s.m., Geom., lozenge.
LOS.NA, s.f., wormwood.
LO.TA.ÇÃO, s.f., allotment, capacity, a little bus.
LO.TA.DO, adj., replete, full.
LO.TAR, v., to fill; to allot (distribute by lots).
LO.TE, s.m., lot, allotment, portion, parcel, share.
LO.TE.A.MEN.TO, s.m., division of land into lots.
LO.TE.AR, v., to divide land into lots.
LO.TE.RI.A, s.f., lottery.
LO.TÉ.RI.CO, adj., concerning lotteries.
LO.TO, s.m., lotto, lottery.
LOU.ÇA, s.f., chinaware, dishware, dishes, ceramics.
LOU.CO, s.m., madman, lunatic; adj., mad, lunatic, crazy, insane, bold.
LOU.CU.RA, s.f., madness, craziness, insanity, folly, extravagance.
LOU.RO, s.m., laurel, parrot; a blond man; Bot., laurel tree; louros: fig., triumph, glory; adj., blond (man).
LOU.SA, s.f., blackboard, gravestone.
LOU.VA-A-DEUS, s.m., Zool., mantis, praying mantis.
LOU.VA.ÇÃO, s.f., laudation, praise.
LOU.VA.DO, adj., praised.
LOU.VAR, v., to praise, to laud, to extol, to exalt, to glorify.
LOU.VÁ.VEL, adj., praiseworthy, laudable.
LOU.VOR, s.m., praise, laud, laudation, glorification.
LU.A, s.f., moon; lua de mel: honeymoon.
LU.AR, s.m., moonlight, moonshine.
LU.AU, s.m., luau (a Hawaiian party).
LÚ.BRI.CO, adj., lubricous, slippery.
LU.BRI.FI.CA.ÇÃO, s.f., lubrication.
LU.BRI.FI.CAN.TE, adj., s.m., lubricant.
LU.BRI.FI.CAR, v., to lubricate, to grease, to oil.
LU.CI.DEZ, s.f., lucidity, brightness, perspicacity.
LÚ.CI.DO, adj., lucid, shining, bright, clear.
LU.CRAR, v., to profit, to benefit, to gain.
LU.CRA.TI.VO, adj., lucrative, profitable, gainful.
LU.CRO, s.m., profit, gain, returns, earning, utility.
LU.CU.BRAR, v., to lucubrate.
LU.DI.BRI.AR, v., to deceive, to cheat, to swindle.
LÚ.DI.CO, adj., ludic, playful.
LU.FA.DA, s.f., gust of wind, flurry.
LU.FA-LU.FA, s.f., bustle, fuss, ado.
LU.GAR, s.m., place, space, room, site, locality, seat, spot.
LU.GAR CO.MUM, s.m., commonplace.

LU.GA.RE.JO, s.m., hamlet, small village.
LU.GAR-TE.NEN.TE, s.m., locum tenens, deputy.
LÚ.GU.BRE, adj., lugubrious, doleful, sad.
LU.LA, s.f., Zool., squid, calamary.
LUM.BA.GO, s.m., Med., lumbago.
LU.ME, s.m., fire, flame, light, candle.
LÚ.MEN, s.m., lumen (unit of light).
LU.MI.NÁ.RIA, s.f., luminary.
LU.MI.NES.CÊN.CI.A, s.f., luminescence.
LU.MI.NES.CEN.TE, adj., luminescent.
LU.MI.NO.SI.DA.DE, s.f., luminosity.
LU.MI.NO.SO, adj., luminous, shining, bright, brilliant, radiant.
LU.NAR, adj., lunar.
LU.NÁ.TI.CO, s.m., madman, lunatic; adj., lunatic, mad.
LU.NE.TA, s.f., field-glass, spyglass, lunette, eye-glass.
LU.PA, s.f., lens, magnifying glass.
LÚ.PU.LO, s.m., Bot., hop (Humulus lupulus).
LÚ.PUS, s.m., Med., lupus.
LUS.CO-FUS.CO, s.m., dusk, nightfall, twilight.
LU.SI.TA.NO, adj., s.m., Lusitanian, Portuguese.
LU.SO, s.m., Lusitanian, Portuguese; adj., Lusitanian, Portuguese.
LU.SO-BRA.SI.LEI.RO, s.m., adj., Portuguese-Brazilian.
LU.SÓ.FO.NO, s.m., Portuguese speaker; adj., Portuguese-speaking.
LUS.TRA.DOR, s.m., polisher, glosser; adj., polishing, glossing.
LUS.TRA-MÓ.VEIS, s.m., 2 num., furniture polish.
LUS.TRAR, v., to polish, to shine, to burnish.
LUS.TRE, s.m., chandelier, gloss, shine; luster.
LUS.TRO, s.m., gloss, sheen, shine; lustrum, quinquennium.
LUS.TRO.SO, adj., lustrous, polished.
LU.TA, s.f., fight, contest, combat, conflict, war, battle.
LU.TA.DOR, s.m., fighter, wrestler, boxer, contender.
LU.TAR, v., to fight, to combat, to wrestle, to contend.
LU.TÉ.CI.O, s.m., Quím., lutecium (symbol: Lu, atomic number: 71).
LU.TE.RA.NO, adj., s.m., Lutheran.
LU.TO, s.m., mourning, sorrow, grief, affliction.
LU.VA, s.f., glove, socket.
LU.XA.ÇÃO, s.f., luxation, dislocation.
LU.XAR, v., to luxate, to dislocate, to disjoint.
LU.XEN.TO, adj., Bras., fussy, picky.
LU.XO, s.m., luxury, splendour, magnificence, ostentation, pomp.
LU.XU.O.SO, adj., luxurious, sumptuous.
LU.XÚ.RIA, s.f., luxury, luxuriance, lust, libertinism.
LU.XU.RI.AN.TE, adj., luxuriant, copious, plenty, sensual.
LU.XU.RI.O.SO, adj., luxuriant, exuberant; sensual.
LUZ, s.f., light, luminosity, illumination, radiance, clearness.
LU.ZER.NA, s.f., light, flash, skylight.
LU.ZI.DI.O, adj., bright, shining.
LU.ZIR, v., to shine, to light, to glitter, to glisten, to radiate.
LY.CRA, s.f., Ing., Lycra ®.

M, *s.m.*, twelfth letter of the Portuguese alphabet.
M, *num.*, 1000 in Roman numerals.
MÁ, *adj.*, feminine of *mau*: bad, evil; *de má vontade*: unwillingly.
MA.CA, *s.f.*, stretcher, litter.
MA.ÇA, *s.f.*, bat, mace, club.
MA.ÇÃ, *s.f.*, apple; *maçãs do rosto*: cheek.
MA.CA.BRO, *adj.*, macabre, gruesome.
MA.CA.CÃO, *s.m.*, big monkey; *Bras.*, overalls, dungaree; rompers (child).
MA.CA.CO, *s.m.*, monkey, ape, hoist, jack.
MA.CA.DA.ME, *s.m.*, macadam.
MA.CAM.BÚ.ZI.O, *adj.*, sullen, morose.
MA.ÇA.NE.TA, *s.f.*, knob, pommel, door handle, doorknob.
MA.CA.QUE.AR, *v.*, to monkey around, to mimic.
MA.CA.QUI.CE, *s.f.*, foolishness, foolery, apishness.
MA.ÇA.RI.CO, *s.m.*, torch, blowtorch, blowpipe.
MA.ÇA.RO.CA, *s.f.*, tangle, mess; bundle, sheaf.
MA.CAR.RÃO, *s.m.*, macaroni, pasta.
MA.CAR.RO.NA.DA, *s.f.*, *Cul.*, pasta served with tomato sauce.
MA.CAR.RÔ.NI.CO, *adj.*, macaronic, burlesque.
MA.CE.RA.ÇÃO, *s.f.*, maceration.
MA.CE.RA.DO, *adj.*, macerated.
MA.CE.RAR, *v.*, to macerate; to mortify.
MA.CE.TE, *s.m.*, little mallet.
MA.CHA.DA.DA, *s.f.*, blow with an axe.
MA.CHA.DI.NHA, *s.f.*, hatcher.
MA.CHA.DI.A.NO, *s.m.*, *Bras., Lit.*, connoisseur of Machado de Assis; *adj.*, referring to this writer.
MA.CHA.DI.NHA, *s.f.*, small axe, hatchet, cleaver.
MA.CHA.DO, *s.m.*, ax, axe, hatchet.
MA.CHÃO, *s.m.*, fearless, bossy.
MA.CHE.TE, *s.m.*, machete (large knife).
MA.CHIS.MO, *s.m.*, machismo.
MA.CHIS.TA, *s.m.*, male chauvinist; *adj.*, macho.
MA.CHO, *s.m.*, male, tough guy.
MA.CHO.NA, *s.f., gír.*, virago, termagant; lesbian.
MA.CHU.CA.DO, *s.m.*, wound, bruise, hurt, injured.
MA.CHU.CA.DU.RA, *s.f.*, wound, injury, bruise, contusion.
MA.CHU.CAR, *v.*, to wound, to hurt, to injure, to crush.
MA.CI.ÇO, *s.m.*, dense forest; *Geol.*, massif; *adj.*, massive, compact, solid.
MA.CI.EI.RA, *s.f.*, apple tree.
MA.CI.EZ, *s.f.*, softness, smoothness, sleekness.
MA.CI.LEN.TO, *adj.*, emaciated, pale, lean.
MA.CI.O, *adj.*, soft, smooth, sleek, supple, flexible.
MA.ÇO, *s.m.*, mallet, bundle, bunch, wad, pile, pack.
MA.ÇOM, *s.m.*, mason, Freemason.
MA.ÇO.NA.RI.A, *s.f.*, Freemasonry.
MA.CO.NHA, *s.f.*, marijuana, marihuana.
MA.CO.NHA.DO, *adj.*, *Bras.*, stoned.
MA.CO.NHEI.RO, *s.m.*, *Bras.*, marijuana smoker, addict; *adj.*, addicted.
MA.ÇÔ.NI.CO, *adj.*, masonic.
MÁ-CRI.A.ÇÃO, *s.f.*, ill breeding, bad manners, discourtesy.
MA.CRO.BI.Ó.TI.CA, *s.f.*, macrobiotics.
MA.CRO.CÉ.FA.LO, *s.m.*, an abnormally large head; *adj.*, macrocephalic.
MA.CRO.COS.MO, *s.m.*, macrocosm.
MA.CRO.E.CO.NO.MI.A, *s.f.*, *Econ.*, macroeconomics.
MÁ.CU.LA, *s.f.*, macula, spot, stain, blemish.
MA.CU.LA.DO, *adj.*, maculate, spotted, stained, impure.
MA.CU.LAR, *v.*, to maculate, to stain, to spot, to blemish.
MA.CUM.BA, *s.f.*, *Bras., Rel.*, macumba (Afro-Brazilian religion).
MA.CUM.BEI.RO, *s.m.*, macumba initiate; *adj.*, macumba.
MA.DA.GAS.CAR, *s.*, Madagascar.
MA.DA.GAS.CA.REN.SE, *s. 2 gen., adj.*, Madagascan.
MA.DA.ME, *s.f.*, madam, lady, mistress.
MA.DEI.RA, *s.f.*, wood, timber, lumber.
MA.DEI.RA.MEN.TO, *s.m.*, framework, framing, timberwork.
MA.DEI.RAR, *v.*, to set up a frame, to work with wood.
MA.DEI.REI.RO, *s.m.*, wood merchant, woodworker, logger.
MA.DEI.XA, *s.f.*, tress, lock of hair.
MA.DO.NA, *s.f.*, Madonna; the Virgin Mary.
MA.DRAS.TA, *s.f.*, stepmother.
MA.DRE, *s.f.*, mother, professed nun.
MA.DRE.PÉ.RO.LA, *s.f.*, nacre, mother-of-pearl.
MA.DRES.SIL.VA, *s.f.*, *Bot.*, honeysuckle.
MA.DRI.GAL, *s.m.*, madrigal (lyric poem; pastoral poems).
MA.DRI.NHA, *s.f.*, godmother.
MA.DRU.GA.DA, *s.f.*, dawn, day-break, early morning.
MA.DRU.GA.DOR, *s.m.*, early riser.
MA.DRU.GAR, *v.*, to get up early in the morning.
MA.DU.RAR, *v.*, to mature, to ripen.
MA.DU.RE.ZA, *s.f.*, ripeness, maturity.
MA.DU.RO, *adj.*, ripe, mature, seasoned, mallow.
MÃE, *s.f.*, mother, Mummy.
MA.ES.TRI.A, *s.f.*, mastery; *com ~*: masterfully.
MA.ES.TRI.NA, *s.f.*, *Mús.*, female conductor.
MA.ES.TRO, *s.m.*, maestro, composer.
MÁ-FÉ, *s.f.*, bad faith.
MÁ.FI.A, *s.f.*, Mafia, Cosa Nostra.
MA.FI.O.SO, *s.m.*, Mafioso; *adj.*, Mafioso (of the Mafia).
MÁ-FOR.MA.ÇÃO, *s.f.*, malformation.
MA.FU.Á, *s.m.*, *Bras.*, amusement park; *col.*, shambles.
MA.GA.ZI.NE, *s.m.*, magazine.
MA.GEN.TA, *s. 2 gen., adj.*, reddish purple.
MA.GÉR.RI.MO, *adj.*, extremely thin, thinnest.
MA.GI.A, *s.f.*, magic, sorcery, witchcraft, fascination.
MA.GI.AR, *s. 2 gen.*, Magyar, Hungarian; *adj.*, Hungarian.
MÁ.GI.CA, *s.f.*, magic, sorcery.
MÁ.GI.CO, *s.m.*, magician, juggler; *adj.*, magic.
MA.GIS.TÉ.RIO, *s.m.*, professorship, mastership, teaching

MAGISTRADO ·· 234 ··· MALHAR

profession.

MA.GIS.TRA.DO, *s.m.*, magistrate, judge.

MA.GIS.TRAL, *adj.*, magisterial, masterly; *fig.*, excellent.

MA.GIS.TRA.LI.DA.DE, *s.f.*, magistracy; *fig.*, pedantry.

MA.GIS.TRA.TU.RA, *s.f.*, magistrature, magistracy, function of a magistrate.

MAG.MA, *s.m.*, magma.

MAG.MÁ.TI.CO, *adj.*, magmatic.

MAG.NA-CAR.TA, *s.f., Lat.*, Magna Carta.

MAG.NA.NI.MI.DA.DE, *s.f.*, magnanimity.

MAG.NÂ.NI.MO, *adj.*, magnanimous.

MAG.NA.TA, *s.m.*, magnate.

MAG.NÉ.SIA, *s.f.*, magnesia.

MAG.NÉ.TI.CO, *adj.*, magnetic, magnetical.

MAG.NE.TIS.MO, *s.m.*, magnetism.

MAG.NE.TI.TA, *s.f., Min.*, magnetite.

MAG.NE.TI.ZA.ÇÃO, *s.f.*, magnetization.

MAG.NE.TI.ZAR, *v.*, to magnetize, to influence, to attract, to enchant.

MAG.NE.TI.ZÁ.VEL, *adj.*, magnetizable.

MAG.NI.FI.CÊN.CI.A, *s.f.*, magnificence, grandeur, splendour.

MAG.NI.FI.CEN.TE, *adj.*, magnificent, extraordinary.

MAG.NÍ.FI.CO, *adj.*, magnificent, magnific, superb.

MAG.NI.TU.DE, *s.f.*, magnitude, size, extent.

MAG.NÓ.LIA, *s.f.*, magnolia.

MA.GO, *s.m.*, magus, sorcerer, magician.

MÁ.GOA, *s.f.*, bruise, sore, hurt, sorrow, grief.

MA.GO.A.DO, *adj.*, hurt, sore, sad, woeful; offended.

MA.GO.AR, *v.*, to hurt, to injure, to bruise, to wound, to afflict, to upset.

MA.GO.TE, *s.m.*, crowd of people; lot of things.

MA.GRE.LO, *s.m., adj., Bras.*, the same that *magricela*.

MA.GRE.ZA, *s.f.*, slenderness, thinness, slimness.

MA.GRI.CE.LA, *s. 2 gen.*, skinny person; *adj.*, skinny, lean.

MA.GRO, *adj.*, thin, skinny, lean, meager, slim, bony.

MAI.ÊU.TI.CA, *s.f., Filos.*, maieutics.

MAI.O, *s.m.*, May.

MAI.Ô, *s.m.*, bathing suit.

MAI.O.NE.SE, *s.f.*, mayonnaise.

MAI.OR, *s.m.*, adult, major; *adj.*, comparative of *grande*, larger, higher, bigger.

MAI.O.RAL, *s.m.*, head, chief, boss.

MAI.O.RI.A, *s.f.*, majority, the greater number.

MAI.O.RI.DA.DE, *s.f.*, majority, full legal age.

MAIS, *adv.*, more, also, besides, over, preferentially, further.

MAI.SE.NA, *s.f.*, industrialized corn starch.

MAIS-QUE-PER.FEI.TO, *s.m.*, pluperfect.

MAIS-VA.LI.A, *s.f., Econ.*, surplus value, added vallue, rise.

MAI.ÚS.CU.LO, *adj.*, capital.

MA.JES.TA.DE, *s.f.*, majesty, magnificence.

MA.JES.TO.SO, *adj.*, majestic, august, regal.

MA.JOR, *s.m., Mil.*, major.

MA.JO.RA.ÇÃO, *s.f., Bras.*, increase, rise, augment.

MA.JO.RAR, *v.*, to rise, to raise, to increase.

MA.JO.RI.TÁ.RI.O, *adj., Bras.*, majoritarian.

MAL, *s.m.*, evil, illness, disease, pain, maleficence, wrong, harm; *adj.*, bad, ill; *adv.*, scarcely, hardly, badly.

MA.LA, *s.f.*, bag, handbag, suitcase, valise, box.

MA.LA.BA.RIS.MO, *s.m.*, juggling.

MA.LA.BA.RIS.TA, *s. 2 gen.*, juggler, conjurer.

MAL-A.CA.BA.DO, *adj., Bras.*, badly finished; (body) in poor shape.

MA.LA-DI.RE.TA, *s.m.*, direct mail.

MAL-A.FA.MA.DO, *adj.*, ill-famed, infamous.

MAL-A.GRA.DE.CI.DO, *adj., s.m.*, ungrateful.

MA.LA.GUE.TA, *s.f.*, malagueta pepper.

MA.LAI.O, *s.m.; adj.*, Malay; Malay, Malayan.

MAL-A.JAM.BRA.DO, *adj., Bras.*, scruffy.

MA.LAN.DRA.GEM, *s.f.*, roguery, trickery.

MA.LAN.DRO, *s.m.*, scoundrel, rascal, swindler.

MA.LÁ.RIA, *s.f.*, malaria.

MA.LÁ.SI.A, *s.*, Malaysia.

MAL.BA.RA.TAR, *v.*, to sell at a loss, to dissipate.

MAL.CHEI.RO.SO, *adj.*, stinking, stinky.

MAL.COM.POR.TA.DO, *adj.*, ill-mannered, badly behaved.

MAL.CON.CEI.TU.A.DO, *adj.*, badly thought of, poorly conceived, having a bad reputation.

MAL.CON.SER.VA.DO, *adj.*, poorly preserved.

MAL.CRI.A.DO, *adj.*, ill-bred, impolite, rude.

MAL.DA.DE, *s.f.*, badness, wickedness, malice, iniquity, cruelty.

MAL.DI.ÇÃO, *s.f.*, imprecation, spell, curse.

MAL.DIS.POS.TO, *adj.*, ill-humoured, ill-disposed.

MAL.DI.TO, *adj.*, devil, damned, cursed.

MAL.DI.ZER, *v.*, to curse, to slander, to defame, backbite, to execrate.

MAL.DO.SO, *adj.*, wicked, bad, spiteful, malign, nasty, pernicious.

MA.LE.A.BI.LI.DA.DE, *s.f.*, malleability, ductility.

MA.LE.Á.VEL, *adj.*, malleable.

MA.LE.DI.CÊN.CIA, *s.f.*, slander, calumny.

MA.LE.DI.CEN.TE, *s. 2 gen.*, slanderer; *adj.*, slanderous.

MAL-E.DU.CA.DO, *adj.*, ill-bred, impolite.

MA.LE.FÍ.CIO, *s.m.*, harm, misdeed, malefaction.

MA.LÉ.FI.CO, *adj.*, evil, malign, malefic, harmful.

MA.LEI.TA, *s.f.*, malaria.

MA.LE.MO.LÊN.CI.A, *s.f., Bras., pop.*, sluggishness, lazyness; bad luck.

MA.LE.MO.LEN.TE, *adj., Bras., pop.*, sluggish, lazy; unlucky.

MAL-EM.PRE.GA.DO, *adj.*, ill-used, misused.

MAL-EN.CA.RA.DO, *adj.*, ill-favoured, evil-looking, shady.

MAL-ES.TAR, *s.m.*, indisposition, unrest.

MA.LE.TA, *s.f.*, handbag, small suitcase.

MA.LE.VO.LÊN.CI.A, *s.f.*, malevolence.

MA.LE.VO.LEN.TE, *adj.*, malevolent.

MA.LÉ.VO.LO, *adj.*, malevolent.

MAL.FA.DA.DO, *adj.*, unlucky, ill-fated, ill-starred.

MAL.FA.ZE.JO, *adj.*, maleficent, malignant.

MAL.FA.ZER, *v.*, to evil, to harm, to hurt, to wrong.

MAL.FEI.TO, *adj.*, ill-done, badly-finished, deformed; bad.

MAL.FEI.TOR, *s.m.*, malefactor, evil-doer, criminal, villain.

MAL.FEI.TO.RI.A, *s.f.*, malefaction, misdeed, offense.

MAL.FOR.MA.ÇÃO, *s.f., Med.*, malformation.

MAL.FOR.MA.DO, *adj.*, malformed.

MAL.GA.XE, *s. 2 gen., adj.*, Madagascan.

MAL.GRA.DO, *prep.*, in spite of.

MA.LHA, *s.f.*, mesh, stich in knitting, spot, speckle.

MAL-HA.BI.TU.A.DO, *adj.*, badly accustomed.

MA.LHA.ÇÃO, *s.f.*, act of beating; *col.*, bashing; working out; weight training.

MA.LHA.DO, *adj.*, mottled (animal), in good shape (body).

MA.LHAR, *v.*, to thresh; to hammer, beat with a mallet; to

MALHARIA   •• 235 ••   MANEMOLENTE

knock (critcism); to work out; to weight train.

MA.LHA.RI.A, *s.f.*, textile mill, knitwear products.

MA.LHO, *s.m.*, sledgehammer, flail, maul.

MAL-HU.MO.RA.DO, *adj.*, ill-humoured, tempered.

MA.LÍ.CIA, *s.f.*, malice, evil intention, spite.

MA.LI.CI.AR, *v.*, to impute malice to somebody.

MA.LI.CI.O.SO, *adj.*, malicious, malevolent; artful, crafty, catty, foxy.

MA.LIG.NI.DA.DE, *s.f.*, malignity.

MA.LIG.NO, *s.m.*, the devil; *adj.*, malign, pernicious, baleful, bad, harmful.

MÁ-LÍN.GUA, *s.f.*, scandalmonger, slanderousness.

MAL-IN.TEN.CI.O.NA.DO, *adj.*, malicious, evil-minded, perfidious.

MAL.ME.QUER, *s.m.*, *Bot.*, marigold, English daisy.

MAL.NAS.CI.DO, *adj.*, lowborn, ill-starred, ill-natured.

MAL.NU.TRI.DO, *adj.*, malnourished.

MA.LO.CA, *s.f.*, *Bras.*, Indian village, encampment.

MA.LO.GRA.DO, *adj.*, frustrated, failed, unsuccessfull.

MA.LO.GRAR, *v.*, to frustrate, to fail, to spoil, to wreck, to overthrow, to waste.

MA.LO.GRO, *s.m.*, frustration, failure.

MA.LO.TE, *s.m.*, bag, pouch; mail; courier.

MAL.PAS.SA.DO, *adj.*, *Bras.*, rare (meat).

MAL.QUE.RER, *s.m.*, animosity, aversion, enmity.

MAL.QUIS.TO, *adj.*, disliked, detested, unpopular.

MAL.SU.CE.DI.DO, *adj.*, unsuccessful, unlucky.

MAL.TA, *s.*, Malta.

MAL.TA, *s.f.*, rabble, mob, gang, pack.

MAL.TE, *s.m.*, malt.

MAL.TÊS, *s.m.*, Maltese; *adj.*, Maltese.

MAL.TRA.PI.LHO, *s.m.*, ragamuffin, beggar; *adj.*, ragged, tattered.

MAL.TRA.TA.DO, *adj.*, maltreated, abused, hurt.

MAL.TRA.TAR, *v.*, to mishandle, to receive badly, to insult, to vex.

MAL.TRA.TO, *s.m.*, mistreatment, maltreatment; insult.

MA.LU.CO, *s.m.*, nut, crackpot, fool; *adj.*, wacky, nutty, mad, crazy, insane.

MA.LU.QUI.CE, *s.f.*, craziness, madness, wackiness.

MAL.VA, *s.f.*, mallow.

MAL.VA.DE.ZA, **MAL.VA.DEZ**, *s.f.*, wickedness, perversity.

MAL.VA.DO, *adj.*, mean, wicked, perverse.

MAL.VER.SA.ÇÃO, *s.f.*, malversation.

MAL.VIS.TO, *adj.*, disliked, suspected, distrusted.

MA.MA, *s.f.*, breast, teat, udder.

MA.MA.DEI.RA, *s.f.*, nursing bottle.

MA.MÃE, *s.f.*, mamma, mammy, mother.

MA.MÃO, *s.m.*, papaya.

MA.MAR, *v.*, to suck.

MA.MÁ.RI.O, *adj.*, mammary.

MA.MA.TA, *s.f.*, shady business, theft.

MAM.BEM.BE, *s.m.*, *Bras.*, travelling theatre; *adj.*, second-rate (circus); *pop.*, mediocre, inferior.

MA.ME.LU.CO, *s.m.*, *Bras.*, mestizo, son of an Indian and of a white person.

MA.MÍ.FE.RO, *s.m.*, mammifer, mammal; *adj.*, mammalian, mammiferous.

MA.MI.LO, *s.m.*, nipple.

MA.MI.NHA, *s.f.*, *Cul.*, thick flank, rump steak.

MA.MO.EI.RO, *s.m.*, *Bot.*, papaya tree, papaw tree.

MA.MO.GRA.FI.A, *s.f.*, *Med.*, mammography.

MA.MO.GRA.MA, *s.f.*, *Med.*, mammogram.

MA.NA, *s.f.*, sister.

MA.NÁ, *s.m.*, manna.

MA.NA.DA, *s.f.*, herd (of cattle).

MA.NAN.CI.AL, *s.m.*, fountainhead, spring, source.

MAN.CA.DA, *s.f.*, *Bras.*, *fam.*, gaffe, mistake, error.

MAN.CAL, *s.m.*, bearing, pillow.

MAN.CAR, *v.*, to fail, to limp, to hobble, to go lame, to cripple.

MAN.CHA, *s.f.*, stain, spot, speck, fleck, blotch; disgrace, reproach.

MAN.CHA.DO, *adj.*, stained, spotted, mottled, soiled.

MAN.CHAR, *v.*, to spot, to blot, to stain, to soil, to blemish.

MAN.CHE, *s.m.*, *Bras.*, *Aeron.*, control lever.

MAN.CHE.TE, *s.f.*, headline.

MAN.CO, *s.m.*, lame person, cripple; *adj.*, lame, hobbling, mutilated, unable.

MAN.CO.MU.NA.DO, *adj.*, combined, conspired, plotted, colluded.

MAN.CO.MU.NAR, *v.*, to combine, to plot, to conspire, to collude; *mancomunar-se*: to collude with.

MAN.DA.CHU.VA, *s.m.*, boss; chief; influential person; *Bras.*, tycoon.

MAN.DA.DO, *s.m.*, order, command, court order, commission, message; *adj.*, ordered, sent.

MAN.DA.MEN.TO, *s.m.*, command, order, commandment, jurisdiction.

MAN.DAN.TE, *s. 2 gen.*, commander, boss; *adj.*, commanding.

MAN.DÃO, *s.m.*, boss, bully; *adj.*, *fam.*, bossy, tyrannical.

MAN.DAR, *v.*, to order, to command, to rule, to govern, to dominate, to send.

MAN.DA.RIM, *s.m.*, (title) mandarin; (dialect) Mandarin.

MAN.DA.TÁ.RIO, *s.m.*, mandatory, executive, attorney, person holding a mandate.

MAN.DA.TO, *s.m.*, mandate, commission, power of attorney.

MAN.DÍ.BU.LA, *s.f.*, mandible, jaw, jawbone.

MAN.DI.BU.LAR, *adj.*, mandibular.

MAN.DI.O.CA, *s.f.*, cassava, manioc.

MAN.DI.O.CAL, *s.m.*, *Bras.*, manioc plantation, manioc field.

MAN.DO, *s.m.*, power, authority, command, right.

MA.NÉ, *s.m.*, *Bras.*, nincompoop, fool; untidy individual.

MA.NE.A.BI.LI.DA.DE, *s.f.*, manageability; *US* maneuverability.

MA.NE.AR, *v.*, the same that *manejar*.

MA.NEI.RA, *s.f.*, way, manner, form, fashion, kind, opportunity.

MA.NEI.RAR, *v.*, *Bras.*, *gír.*, to sort out and control the situation; to accomodate shrewdly.

MA.NEI.RO, *adj.*, easy, simple, manageable; portable; *gír.*, great, cool.

MA.NEI.RO.SO, *adj.*, mannered, mannerly.

MA.NE.JA.DOR, *s.m.*, handler, tugger, plier.

MA.NE.JAR, *v.*, to handle, to carry out, to direct, to move, to manage, to govern.

MA.NE.JÁ.VEL, *adj.*, easily handled; manageable, controllable.

MA.NE.JO, *s.m.*, management, administration, handling, attendance.

MA.NE.MO.LÊN.CI.A, *s.f.*, *Bras.*, *pop.*, the same that *malemolência*.

MA.NE.MO.LEN.TE, *adj.*, *Bras.*, *pop.*, the same that *malemolente*.

MANENTE · 236 · MARAVILHADOR

MA.NEN.TE, *adj.*, the same that *permanente*.
MA.NE.QUIM, *s.m.*, model, dummy, mannequin.
MAN.GA, *s.f.*, mango(fruit), sleeve(clothes).
MAN.GA.NÊS, *s.m.*, manganese.
MAN.GUE, *s.m.*, swamp, bayou, mangrove, marsh.
MAN.GUEI.RA, *s.f.*, rubber or canvas hose, mango tree.
MA.NHA, *s.f.*, slyness, cunningness, malice, dexterity, trick.
MA.NHÃ, *s.f.*, morning, forenoon, dawn.
MA.NHÃ.ZI.NHA, *s.f.*, diminutive of *manhã*; day break, dawn.
MA.NHO.SO, *adj.*, foxy, cunning, crafty, smart, whimsical, vicious.
MA.NI.A, *s.f.*, mania, excentricity, obsession, whim, kink.
MA.NÍ.A.CO, *adj.*, *s.m.*, maniac.
MA.NÍ.A.CO-DE.PRES.SI.VO, *s.m.*, manic-depressive person; *adj.*, manic-depressive.
MA.NI.CÔ.MIO, *s.m.*, asylum, bedlam, mad-house.
MA.NI.CU.RE, *s. 2 gen.*, manicurist.
MA.NI.FES.TA.ÇÃO, *s.f.*, manifestation, gathering, meeting.
MA.NI.FES.TAN.TE, *s. 2 gen.*, manifestant, manifester; *adj.*, manifesting.
MA.NI.FES.TAR, *v.*, to manifest, to make public, to reveal, to disclose, to show.
MA.NI.FES.TO, *s.m.*, manifest, public declaration; *adj.*, manifest, evident, obvious, clear.
MA.NI.LHA, *s.f.*, armlet, shackle, fetter.
MA.NI.PU.LA.ÇÃO, *s.f.*, manipulation, handling.
MA.NI.PU.LA.DO, *adj.*, manipulated, processed.
MA.NI.PU.LA.DOR, *s.m.*, manipulator, handler, operator; *adj.*, manipulating, handling.
MA.NI.PU.LAR, *v.*, to manipulate, to handle, to process, to work.
MA.NI.PU.LÁ.VEL, *adj.*, manipulable.
MA.NI.QUE.ÍS.MO, *s.m.*, Manichaeism.
MA.NI.QUE.ÍS.TA, *s. 2 gen.*, Manichaean.
MA.NI.VE.LA, *s.f.*, handle, crank.
MAN.JA.DO, *adj.*, *Bras.*, *pop.*, broadly known, observed, spied.
MAN.JAR, *s.m.*, any foodstuff, tidbit, dainty.
MAN.JE.DOU.RA, *s.f.*, manger, crib, feeding place.
MAN.JE.RI.CÃO, *s.m.*, basil.
MAN.JE.RO.NA, *s.f.*, *Bot.*, marjoram.
MA.NO, *s.m.*, brother, friend.
MA.NO.BRA, *s.f.*, maneuver, a skillful move, scheme.
MA.NO.BRAR, *v.*, to maneuver, to manipulate, to handle, to conduct.
MA.NO.BRÁ.VEL, *adj.*, manoeuvrable.
MA.NO.BRIS.TA, *s. 2 gen.*, maneuverer, parking valet.
MA.NÔ.ME.TRO, *s.m.*, manometer.
MAN.SÃO, *s.f.*, mansion.
MAN.SAR.DA, *s.f.*, *Arquit.*, mansard.
MAN.SI.DÃO, *s.f.*, tameness, meekness, gentleness, docility.
MAN.SI.NHO, *adj.*, diminutive of *manso*; tame, docile; softly, slowly, step by step.
MAN.SO, *adj.*, tame, domesticated, meek, gentle, docile.
MAN.TA, *s.f.*, blanket, travelling rug, shawl.
MAN.TEI.GA, *s.f.*, butter.
MAN.TEI.GUEI.RA, *s.f.*, butter dish.
MAN.TE.NE.DOR, *s.m.*, maintainer.
MAN.TER, *v.*, to maintain, to sustain, to keep, to support, to pay for, to conserve.
MAN.TI.LHA, *s.f.*, mantilla, veil; mantelet.
MAN.TI.MEN.TO, *s.m.*, maintainance, provisions, supply, food.

MAN.TO, *s.m.*, mantle, cloak, robe, veil.
MAN.TÔ, *s.m.*, ladies' coat.
MA.NU.AL, *s.m.*, manual, handbook; *adj.*, manual.
MA.NU.AL.MEN.TE, *adv.*, manually.
MA.NU.FA.TU.RA, *s.f.*, manufacture, factory.
MA.NU.FA.TU.RA.ÇÃO, *s.f.*, manufacturing.
MA.NU.FA.TU.RA.DO, *adj.*, handmade; manufactured.
MA.NU.FA.TU.RAR, *v.*, to manufacture, to make by hand, to produce.
MA.NU.FA.TU.RÁ.VEL, *adj.*, manufacturable (that can be manufactured).
MA.NUS.CRI.TO, *s.m.*, manuscript, document, letter; *adj.*, handwritten.
MA.NU.SE.AR, *v.*, to handle, to manage, to touch, to feel, to soil.
MA.NU.TEN.ÇÃO, *s.f.*, maintenance, keeping, support, administration, management.
MÃO, *s.f.*, hand, side, each of the directions of the traffic, help.
MÃO-A.BER.TA, *s. 2 gen.*, *Bras.*, generous person, prodigal; *adj.*, generous.
MÃO-CHEI.A, *s.f.*, fiirst rate, handful.
MÃO DE FER.RO, *s.f.*, iron hand.
MÃO DE O.BRA, *s.f.*, manual work on a job.
MÃO DE VA.CA, *s. 2 gen.*, stingy person, scrooge.
MÃO-LE.VE, *s. 2 gen.*, *Bras.*, *gír.*, stealer, robber, thief.
MAO.IS.TA, *s. 2 gen.*, *adj.*, Maoist.
MA.O.ME.TA.NO, *s.m.*, *adj.*, Mohammedan, Mahometan.
MA.PA, *s.f.*, map, chart, graph.
MA.PA-MÚN.DI, *s.m.*, map of the world.
MA.QUE.TE, *s.f.*, maquette.
MA.QUI.A.DO, *adj.*, made-up, painted (face).
MA.QUI.A.DOR, *s.m.*, make-up artist.
MA.QUI.A.GEM, *s.f.*, make-up, maquillage.
MA.QUI.AR, *v.*, to make up.
MA.QUI.A.VÉ.LI.CO, *adj.*, astute, sly, Machiavellian.
MA.QUI.LA.DO, *adj.*, the same that *maquiado*.
MA.QUI.LA.DOR, *s.m.*, the same that *maquilador*.
MA.QUI.LA.GEM, *s.f.*, the same that *maquiagem*.
MA.QUI.LAR, *v.*, to make up; to diguise; *maquilar-se*: to make oneself up.
MÁ.QUI.NA, *s.f.*, machine, engine, car, automobile.
MA.QUI.NA.ÇÃO, *s.f.*, machination.
MA.QUI.NA.DOR, *s.m.*, machinator, schemer, plotter; *adj.*, machinating.
MA.QUI.NAR, *v.*, to machinate, plot, scheme.
MA.QUI.NA.RI.A, *s.f.*, machinery.
MA.QUI.NÁ.RI.O, *s.m.*, machinery.
MA.QUI.NIS.TA, *s. 2 gen.*, engine driver, machinist, locomotive driver.
MAR, *s.m.*, sea, ocean; *Mar Morto*: the Dead Sea.
MA.RA.CU.JÁ, *s.m.*, passion fruit; maracock.
MA.RA.CU.JA.ZEI.RO, *s.m.*, *Bras.*, *Bot.*, passion fruit tree.
MA.RA.CU.TAI.A, *s.f.*, *Bras.*, *gír.*, monkey business.
MA.RA.JÁ, *s.m.*, maharaja(h).
MA.RA.TO.NA, *s.f.*, *Esp.*, marathon, marathon race.
MA.RA.TO.NIS.TA, *s. 2 gen.*, marathoner.
MA.RAS.MO, *s.m.*, marasmus, moral apathy, indifference.
MA.RA.VI.LHA, *s.f.*, wonder, marvel, prodigy.
MA.RA.VI.LHA.DO, *adj.*, amazed, astounded.
MA.RA.VI.LHA.DOR, *s.m.*, one who causes wonder; *adj.*, amazing, wondrous.

MARAVILHAMENTO · 237 · MAS

MA.RA.VI.LHA.MEN.TO, *s.m.*, amazement, wonder.

MA.RA.VI.LHAR, *v.*, to marvel, to amaze, to cause admiration.

MA.RA.VI.LHO.SO, *adj.*, wonderful, marvellous, amazing, admirable.

MAR.CA, *s.f.*, mark, brand, type, seal, stamp, token, signature, impression, limit.

MAR.CA.ÇÃO, *s.f.*, act of marking.

MAR.CA.DO, *adj.*, marked; flagged.

MAR.CA.DOR, *s.m.*, marker, scoreboard, scorer; *adj.*, marking, scoring.

MAR.CAN.TE, *adj.*, marked, marking.

MAR.CA-PAS.SO, *s.m., Med.*, pacemaker.

MAR.CAR, *v.*, to mark, to brand, to seal, to label, to book, to stamp.

MAR.CE.NA.RI.A, *s.f.*, cabinetry, joinery.

MAR.CE.NEI.RO, *s.m.*, joiner.

MAR.CHA, *s.f.*, march, progress, walk, route, gear, journey.

MAR.CHA.DOR, *s.m., Bras.*, pacer (horse); *adj.*, pacing, marching.

MAR.CHAND, *s.m., Fr.*, art dealer.

MAR.CHAR, *v.*, to march, to run, to turn, to work.

MAR.CHE.TAR, *v.*, to inlay, to incrust.

MAR.CHI.NHA, *s.f.*, diminutive of *marcha*: little march; *Mús., Bras.*, carnival march.

MAR.CI.AL, *adj.*, martial; *arte marcial*: martial art; *corte ~*: court martial.

MAR.CI.A.NO, *s.m.*, Martian; *adj.*, Martian.

MAR.CO, *s.m.*, mark, limit, boundary, land-mark, demarcation, sign, mark.

MAR.ÇO, *s.m.*, March.

MA.RÉ, *s.f.*, tide; flood-tide.

MA.RE.A.DO, *adj.*, seasick; *fam.*, tipsy.

MA.RÉ AL.TA, MA.RÉ CHEI.A, *s.f.*, high tide.

MA.RE.AR, *v.*, to steer (a ship), to navigate, to become seasick.

MA.RE.CHAL, *s.m.*, marshal.

MA.RE.JAR, *v.*, to shed (tears), to flow; *marejar-se*: to fill (with tears).

MA.RE.MO.TO, *s.m.*, seaquake.

MA.RE.SI.A, *s.f.*, rollers, whitecaps.

MAR.FIM, *adj.*, *s.m.*, ivory.

MAR.GA.RI.DA, *s.f.*, daisy.

MAR.GA.RI.NA, *s.f.*, margarine.

MAR.GE.AR, *v.*, to marginate, to border.

MAR.GEM, *s.f.*, margin, border, limit, edge, shore, bank, rim.

MAR.GI.NA.DO, *adj.*, marginate, marginated.

MAR.GI.NAL, *s.m.*, delinquent; *adj.*, marginal.

MAR.GI.NA.LI.DA.DE, *s.f., Sociol.*, marginality.

MAR.GI.NA.LI.ZA.DO, *adj.*, marginalized.

MAR.GI.NA.LI.ZA.ÇÃO, *s.f.*, marginalization.

MAR.GI.NA.LI.ZAR, *v.*, to marginalize.

MA.RI.A-FU.MA.ÇA, *s. 2 gen., Bras., pop.*, steam-engine, steam-locomotive.

MA.RI.A-SEM-VER.GO.NHA, *s.f., Bot.*, busy Lizzie (Impatiens walleriana).

MA.RI.CAS, *s.m.*, sissy, coward.

MA.RI.DO, *s.m.*, husband, spouse.

MA.RIM.BON.DO, *s.m.*, wasp.

MA.RI.NA, *s.f.*, marina, a berthing area for yacht.

MA.RI.NAR, *v.*, *Cul.*, to marinate.

MA.RI.NHA, *s.f.*, navy, marine, naval force, naval service.

MA.RI.NHEI.RO, *s.m.*, sailor, seaman, mariner, seafarer.

MA.RI.NHO, *s.m.*, navy; *adj.*, *Náut.*, marine.

MA.RI.O.NE.TE, *s.f.*, marionette, puppet.

MA.RI.PO.SA, *s.f., Zool.*, moth.

MA.RIS.CO, *s.m.*, shellfish.

MA.RI.TAL, *adj.*, marital.

MA.RÍ.TI.MO, *adj.*, maritime, marine.

MAR.KET.ING, *s.m., Ingl.*, marketing.

MAR.MAN.JO, *s.m.*, adult male, grown man.

MAR.ME.LA.DA, *s.f.*, quince jam.

MAR.ME.LO, *s.m.*, quince.

MAR.MI.TA, *s.f.*, metal pan with a lid.

MAR.MO.RA.RI.A, *s.f.*, marble industry, marble work.

MAR.MO.RÁ.RI.O, *s.m.*, marble cutter; *adj.*, marble, marmoreal.

MÁR.MO.RE, *s.m.*, marble.

MAR.MÓ.RE.O, *adj.*, marble.

MA.RO.LA, *s.f., Bras.*, small wave.

MA.RO.TO, *s.m.*, scoundrel, rascal, rogue; *adj.*, malicious, artful, lascivious.

MAR.QUÊS, *s.m.*, marquis.

MAR.QUE.SA, *s.f.*, marchioness, marquise.

MAR.QUE.SA.DO, *s.m.*, marquisate.

MAR.QUI.SE, *s.f., Arquit.*, marquise, marquee.

MAR.RA, *s.f.*, sledge hammer; *na marra*: *Bras.*, forcedly.

MAR.RE.CO, *s.m., Zool.*, wild duck, teal.

MAR.RE.TA, *s.f.*, hammer, mallet.

MAR.RE.TA.DA, *s.f.*, blow.

MAR.RE.TEI.RO, *s.m.*, worker who handles a stone-mason's hammer; *Bras.*, street vendor, hawker.

MAR.RO.COS, *s.*, Morocco.

MAR.ROM, *s.m.*, brown colour; *adj.*, brown, hazel.

MAR.ROM-GLA.CÊ, *s.m.*, marron glacé.

MAR.RO.QUI.NO, *s.*, *adj.*, Moroccan.

MAR.SE.LHE.SA, *s.f.*, Marseillaise (national anthem of France).

MAR.SU.PI.AL, *adj.*, *s.m.*, marsupial.

MAR.TA, *s.f., Zool.*, marten.

MAR.TE, *s.m., Mit.*, Mars (ancient Roman god of war); *Astron.*, planet fourth in order from the sun.

MAR.TE.LA.DA, *s.f.*, blow with a hammer.

MAR.TE.LAR, *v.*, to hammer, to pound, to beat, to bother, to annoy.

MAR.TE.LO, *s.m.*, hammer.

MAR.TIM-PES.CA.DOR, *s.m., Zool.*, kingfisher (bird).

MÁR.TIR, *s.m.*, martyr, sufferer.

MAR.TÍ.RIO, *s.m.*, martyrdom, suffering, torment.

MAR.TI.RI.ZA.ÇÃO, *s.f.*, martyrization.

MAR.TI.RI.ZA.DOR, *s.m.*, martyrizor; *adj.*, torturing, tormenting.

MAR.TI.RI.ZAN.TE, *adj.*, martyrizing, tormenting, torturing.

MAR.TI.RI.ZAR, *v.*, to martyrize, to torment.

MA.RU.IM, *s.m., Bras., Zool.*, Amazonian mosquito.

MA.RU.JA.DA, *s.f.*, crowd of sailors.

MA.RU.JO, *s.m.*, sailor, seaman, marine.

MA.RU.LHAR, *v.*, to surge, to rage (the sea), to roar.

MA.RU.LHO, *s.m.*, agitation, roaring (of sea); *fig.*, tumult, noise.

MA.RU.LHO.SO, *adj.*, surgy, murmurous, roaring.

MAR.XIS.MO, *s.m.*, Marxism.

MAR.XIS.TA, *s. 2 gen.*, Marxist.

MAR.ZI.PÃ, *s.m., Cul.*, marzipan.

MAS, *conj.*, but, however, still, yet, even, only.

MASCADOR ··238·· MAURÍCIO

MAS.CA.DOR, *s.m.*, chewer; *adj.*, chewing.
MAS.CAR, *v.*, to chew, to mumble, to mutter, to grumble.
MÁS.CA.RA, *s.f.*, mask.
MAS.CA.RA.DO, *s.m.*, masqued, mask; *adj.*, masked, disguised.
MAS.CA.RAR, *v.*, to mask, to disguise, to hide.
MAS.CA.TE, *s.m.*, peddler, hawker.
MAS.CA.TE.AR, *v.*, *Bras.*, to peddle, to hawk.
MAS.CA.VO, *s.m.*, the Brown sugar.
MAS.CO.TE, *s.m.*, mascot.
MAS.CU.LI.NI.DA.DE, *s.f.*, masculinity.
MAS.CU.LI.NI.ZA.DO, *adj.*, masculinized, masculine.
MAS.CU.LI.NI.ZAR, *v.*, to make masculine.
MAS.CU.LI.NO, *adj.*, masculine, male, manly, virile.
MÁS.CU.LO, *adj.*, pertaining to the male sex, virile, manly, masculine, gender.
MAS.MOR.RA, *s.f.*, dungeon, subterraneous prison.
MA.SO.QUIS.MO, *s.m.*, masochism.
MA.SO.QUIS.TA, *s. 2 gen.*, masochist; *adj.*, masochistic.
MAS.SA, *s.f.*, mass, pasta; totality.
MASSA-CORRIDA, *s.f.*, plaster skim applied before painting.
MAS.SA.CRAN.TE, *adj.*, dull, very boring, annoying.
MAS.SA.CRAR, *v.*, to massacre, to kill.
MAS.SA.CRE, *s.m.*, massacre, slaughter, butchery.
MAS.SA.GE.AR, *v.*, to (do) massage.
MAS.SA.GEM, *s.f.*, massage.
MAS.SA.GIS.TA, *s. 2 gen.*, masseur, masseuse.
MAS.SI.FI.CA.ÇÃO, *s.m.*, massification; popularization; effect of influencing through the mass media.
MAS.SI.FI.CA.DO, *adj.*, popular; influenced or guided through mass media.
MAS.SI.FI.CAR, *v.*, to popularize, to influence or guide through mass media; to sell to the masses.
MAS.SU.DO, *adj.*, massive, heavy, bulky, compact.
MAS.TEC.TO.MI.A, *s.f.*, *Med.*, mastectomy.
MAS.TI.GA.ÇÃO, *s.f.*, mastication, chewing.
MAS.TI.GA.DO, *adj.*, masticated, chewed.
MAS.TI.GAR, *v.*, to chew, to masticate, to crunch, to munch, to ponder.
MAS.TI.GÁ.VEL, *adj.*, masticable, chewable.
MAS.TIM, *s.m.*, mastiff, cur, tyke.
MAS.TI.TE, *s.f.*, *Med.*, mastitis.
MAS.TO.DON.TE, *s.m.*, *Paleont.*, mastodon.
MAS.TO.LO.GI.A, *s.f.*, the study of the breast.
MAS.TRO, *s.m.*, flagstaff, flagpole.
MAS.TUR.BA.ÇÃO, *s.f.*, masturbation, onanism.
MAS.TUR.BAR, *v.*, to masturbate.
MA.TA, *s.f.*, wood, forest, jungle, thicket.
MA.TA-BA.RA.TAS, *s.m.*, *pl.*, cockroach killer.
MA.TA-BOR.RÃO, *s.m.*, blotting paper; blotter.
MA.TA.CÃO, *s.m.*, *Geol.*, a large and round stone; *fig.*, piece or large slice.
MA.TA.DOR, *s.m.*, killer, assassin, murderer.
MA.TA.DOU.RO, *s.m.*, slaughterhouse, shambles, butchery.
MA.TA.GAL, *s.m.*, jungle, bush, thicket.
MA.TA-MOS.CAS, *s.m.*, *2 num.*, fly-swat.
MA.TA-MOS.QUI.TO, *s.m.*, *Bras.*, mosquito spray.
MA.TAN.ÇA, *s.f.*, killing, massacre, slaughter, butchery.
MA.TAR, *v.*, to kill, to assassin, to murder, to slaughter, to extinguish, to eliminate.
MA.TA-RA.TO, *s.m.*, rat poison; *Bras.*, cancer slick (cigarretes).

MA.TE, *s.m.*, checkmate, Paraguay tea, *maté*.
MA.TE.MÁ.TI.CA, *s.f.*, mathematics.
MA.TE.MÁ.TI.CO, *s.m.*, mathematician; *adj.*, mathematical.
MA.TÉ.RIA, *s.f.*, matter, substance, stuff, material, subject, topic.
MA.TE.RI.AL, *s.m.*, material, stuff, matter, substance; *adj.*, material, solid, crude, raw.
MA.TE.RI.A.LI.DA.DE, *s.f.*, materiality.
MA.TE.RI.A.LIS.MO, *s.m.*, materialism.
MA.TE.RI.A.LIS.TA, *s. 2 gen.*, materialist; *adj.*, materialistic.
MA.TE.RI.A.LI.ZA.ÇÃO, *s.f.*, materialization.
MA.TE.RI.A.LI.ZA.DOR, *adj.*, materializing (that makes material, that materializes).
MA.TE.RI.A.LI.ZAR(-SE), *v.*, to materialize, to become corporeal, to produce crude.
MA.TÉ.RIA-PRI.MA, *s.f.*, raw material.
MA.TER.NAL, *adj.*, maternal, motherlike.
MA.TER.NI.DA.DE, *s.f.*, maternity, motherhood, maternity hospital.
MA.TER.NO, *adj.*, maternal, motherly, kind.
MA.TI.LHA, *s.f.*, pack of hounds or wolves.
MA.TI.NA, *s.f.*, dawn, daybreak.
MA.TI.NAL, *adj.*, matutinal, matutine, morning.
MA.TI.NÊ, *s.f.*, matinée.
MA.TIZ, *s.m.*, nuance, tone, tint, tincture.
MA.TI.ZAR, *v.*, to variegate, to adorn.
MA.TO, *s.m.*, wood, forest, brushwood.
MA.TO-GROS.SEN.SE, *s. 2 gen.*, *Bras.*, inhabitant of the Mato Grosso; *adj.*, pertaining to Mato Grosso.
MA.TRA.CA, *s.f.*, *Mús.*, rattle; (person) chatterbox.
MA.TRA.QUE.AR, *v.*, *Mús.*, to rattle; (person) to chatter.
MA.TREI.RI.CE, *s.f.*, slyness, shrewdness, smartness.
MA.TREI.RO, *adj.*, sly, smart, shrewd, crafty.
MA.TRI.AR.CA, *s.f.*, matriarch.
MA.TRI.AR.CAL, *adj.*, matriarchal.
MA.TRI.CI.DA, *s. 2 gen.*, matricide.
MA.TRI.CÍ.DI.O, *s.m.*, matricide.
MA.TRÍ.CU.LA, *s.f.*, registration, enrollment, matriculation fee.
MA.TRI.CU.LA.DO, *adj.*, matriculated, registered.
MA.TRI.CU.LAR, *v.*, to matriculate, to register, to enroll.
MA.TRI.MO.NI.AL, *adj.*, matrimonial, nuptial, conjugal, spousal.
MA.TRI.MÔ.NIO, *s.m.*, matrimony, marriage.
MÁ.TRI.O, *adj.*, pertaining to the mother.
MA.TRIZ, *s.f.*, matrix, source, mold; *adj.*, original, primitive, primordial.
MA.TRO.NA, *s.f.*, matron, woman.
MA.TRO.NAL, *adj.*, matronly.
MA.TU.RA.ÇÃO, *s.f.*, maturation.
MA.TU.RA.DO, *adj.*, ripe, seasoned, mature; maturated.
MA.TU.RAR, *v.*, to mature, to ripen, to season.
MA.TU.RI.DA.DE, *s.f.*, maturity, maturedness, ripeness.
MA.TU.TAR, *v.*, *pop.*, to think, to muse, to ponder, to meditate.
MA.TU.TI.NO, *adj.*, matutinal, early.
MA.TU.TO, *s.m.*, *Bras.*, fieldworker, hillbilly; rustic.
MAU, *s.m.*, evil, bad; *adj.*, bad, evil, harmful, noxious, pernicious, perverse.
MAU-CA.RÁ.TER, *s.m.*, a knave person, a villainous person.
MAU-O.LHA.DO, *s.m.*, evil eye.
MAU.RI.CI.NHO, *s.m.*, *fam.*, posh kid, dandy.
MAU.RÍ.CI.O, *s.*, Mauritius.

MAUSOLÉU ·· 239 ·· # MELÃO

MAU.SO.LÉU, *s.m.*, mausoleum.
MAUS-TRATOS, *s.m., pl.*, abuse, mistreatment.
MA.VI.O.SO, *adj.*, affectionate, suave, compassionate.
MA.XI.LA, *s.f., Anat.*, maxilla, jaw, jawbone.
MA.XI.LAR, *s.m., Anat.*, jaw, jawbone; *adj.*, maxillary.
MÁ.XI.MA, *s.f.*, maxim, precept, aphorism.
MA.XI.MA.LIS.MO, *s.m.*, maximalism.
MA.XI.MA.LIS.TA, *s. 2 gen.*, maximalist; *adj.*, pertaining to maximalism.
MÁ.XI.ME, *adv.*, principally.
MA.XI.MI.ZA.ÇÃO, *s.f.*, maximization.
MA.XI.MI.ZAR, *v.*, to maximize.
MÁ.XI.MO, *adj.*, maximum, greatest, utmost.
MA.XI.XE, *s.m.*, Maxixe (Brazilian dance); *Bot.*, fruit of the anguria (*Cucumis anguria*).
MA.XI.XEI.RO, *s.m., Bot.*, cucurbitaceous plant; dancer of the maxixe; *adj.*, that enjoys dancing the maxixe.
MA.ZE.LA, *s.f.*, wound, sore, bruise.
ME, *pron.*, me, to me, myself, to myself.
ME.A.DA, *s.f.*, skein.
ME.A.DO, *s.m.*, middle, mean; *adj.*, halved.
ME.AN.DRO, *s.m.*, meander; *fig.*, intrigue.
ME.CA, *s.*, Mecca.
ME.CÂ.NI.CA, *s.f.*, mechanics.
ME.CÂ.NI.CO, *s.m.*, mechanic; *adj.*, mechanical.
ME.CA.NIS.MO, *s.m.*, mechanism, device, gear, machinery.
ME.CA.NI.ZA.ÇÃO, *s.f.*, mechanization.
ME.CA.NI.ZAR, *v.*, US to mechanize; UK to mechanise.
ME.CE.NA.TO, *s.m.*, patronage.
ME.CE.NAS, *s.m., 2 num.*, Maecenas; patron.
ME.CHA, *s.f.*, fuse, lunt, match, strand of hair.
ME.DA.LHA, *s.f.*, medal.
ME.DA.LHÃO, *s.m.*, medallion, locket.
ME.DA.LHIS.TA, *s. 2 gen.*, medalist.
MÉ.DIA, *s.f.*, mean, medium, average.
ME.DI.A.ÇÃO, *s.f.*, mediation, intervention, interposition.
ME.DI.A.DOR, *s.m.*, mediator, intermediary, interposer, arbiter.
ME.DI.A.NO, *adj.*, average, median, mean, ordinary.
ME.DI.AN.TE, *prep.*, by means of, by, through, against.
ME.DI.AR, *v.*, to halve, to mediate, to intervene, to interpose, to interfere.
ME.DI.CA.ÇÃO, *s.f.*, medical treatment, medication.
ME.DI.CAL, *adj.*, medical.
ME.DI.CA.MEN.TAR, *v.*, to medicate.
ME.DI.CA.MEN.TO, *s.m.*, medicine, remedy, medicament.
ME.DI.CA.MEN.TO.SO, *adj.*, medicamentous, medicamental.
ME.DI.ÇÃO, *s.f.*, measurement.
ME.DI.CAR, *v.*, to medicate.
ME.DI.CI.NA, *s.f.*, medicine, medicament.
ME.DI.CI.NAL, *adj.*, medicinal.
MÉ.DI.CO, *s.m.*, physician, doctor, medico, practitioner, surgeon.
MÉ.DI.CO-CI.RUR.GI.ÃO, *s.m.*, surgeon.
MÉ.DI.CO-HOS.PI.TA.LAR, *adj.*, hospital and medical.
MÉ.DI.CO-LE.GAL, *adj.*, forensic.
MÉ.DI.CO-LE.GIS.TA, *s. 2 gen.*, coroner, forensic expert.
ME.DI.DA, *s.f.*, measure, dimension, size.
ME.DI.DOR, *s.m.*, measurer, meter.
ME.DI.E.VAL, *adj.*, medieval.
MÉ.DIO, *adj.*, mean, medium, middle, median.
ME.DÍ.O.CRE, *adj.*, mediocre, ordinary, commonplace.

ME.DI.O.CRI.DA.DE, *s.f.*, mediocrity, commonness.
ME.DIR, *v.*, to measure, to gauge, to mete, to survey, to consider.
ME.DI.TA.ÇÃO, *s.f.*, meditation, thought, cogitation, ponderation, reflection.
ME.DI.TAR, *v.*, to meditate, to cogitate, to think, to ponder.
ME.DI.TA.TI.VO, *adj.*, meditative, pondering, meditating.
ME.DI.TER.RÂ.NEO, *s.m.*, Mediterranean; *adj.*, mediterranean.
ME.DI.Ú.NI.CO, *adj.*, mediumistic, referring to a spiritualistic medium.
ME.DI.U.NI.DA.DE, *s.f.*, mediumship.
ME.DO, *s.m.*, fear, fright, awe, terror.
ME.DO.NHO, *adj.*, awful, frightful, horrible, dreadful, terrible.
ME.DRAR, *v.*, to prosper, to grow, to develop, to flourish.
ME.DRO.SO, *adj.*, fearful, frightful, timid, timorous.
ME.DU.LA, *s.f.*, medula, marrow.
ME.DU.SA, *s.f., Mit.*, Medusa; *Zool.*, medusa, jellyfish.
MEGA.BYTE, *s.m., Comp.*, megabyte.
ME.GA.E.VEN.TO, *s.m.*, huge event.
ME.GA.FO.NE, *s.m.*, megaphone.
ME.GA-HERTZ, *s.m., 2 num., Fís.*, megahertz.
ME.GA.LO.CE.FA.LI.A, *s.f., Anat.*, megacephaly.
ME.GA.LO.MA.NI.A, *s.f.*, megalomania.
ME.GA.LO.MA.NÍ.A.CO, *s.m., Psic.*, megalomaniac.
ME.GA.TÉ.RI.O, *s.m., Paleont.*, megatherium.
ME.GA.TON, *s.m., Fís.*, megaton (Nuclear physics).
ME.GE.RA, *s.f.*, Megaera, cruel woman, shrew.
MEI.A, *s.f.*, sock, stocking, hose.
MEI.A-Á.GUA, *s.f.*, one plane roof.
MEI.A-CAL.ÇA, *s.f.*, tights, pantyhose.
MEI.A-EN.TRA.DA, *s.f.*, half-price ticket.
MEI.A-ES.TA.ÇÃO, *s.f.*, mid-season.
MEI.A-I.DA.DE, *s.f.*, middle age.
MEI.A-IR.MÃ, *s.f.*, half sister.
MEI.A-LU.A, *s.f.*, half-moon, crescent.
MEI.A-LUZ, *s.f.*, half light, twilight.
MEI.A-NOI.TE, *s.f.*, midnight.
MEI.A-VI.DA, *s.f., Fís.*, half-life (Nuclear physics).
MEI.A-VOL.TA, *s.f., Mil.*, about-face.
MEI.GO, *adj.*, sweet, tender, gentle, loving, kind, mild, amiable.
MEI.GUI.CE, *s.f.*, tenderness, gentleness, sweetness, affability.
MEI.O, *s.m.*, middle, centre, medium, expedient, means; *adj.*, half, mean, middle, undecided.
MEI.O AM.BI.EN.TE, *s.m.*, environment, milieu.
MEI.O-CAM.PIS.TA, *s. 2 gen., Esp.*, midfielder (soccer).
MEI.O-DI.A, *s.m.*, midday.
MEI.O-FI.O, *s.m.*, US curb; UK kerb.
MEI.O-IR.MÃO, *s.m.*, half brother.
MEI.O-TEM.PO, *s.m.*, half-time; nesse ~: meanwhile.
MEI.O-TOM, *s.m.*, half-tone (color); *Mús.*, semitone.
MEL, *s.m.*, honey.
ME.LA.ÇO, *s.m.*, molasses.
ME.LA.DO, *s.m., Bras.*, (cookie) molasses; *adj.*, sweetened with honey; sticky.
ME.LAN.CI.A, *s.f.*, watermelon.
ME.LAN.CI.EI.RA, *s.f.*, watermelon plant.
ME.LAN.CO.LI.A, *s.f.*, melancholy, melancholia, gloom, dismalness.
ME.LAN.CÓ.LI.CO, *adj.*, melancholic, gloomy, dreary.
ME.LÃO, *s.m.*, melon.

M

MELAR ·· 240 ·· MERENDAR

ME.LAR, v., to sweeten, to cover or sweeten with honey; *gír.*, to frustrate.

ME.LE.CA, *s.f., Bras., pop.*, nasal secretion, bogey; *gír.*, something bad or frustrating.

ME.LE.NA, *s.f.*, long hair.

ME.LHOR, *s.m.*, the best; *adj.*, better, superior, preferable, best; *adv.*, better, preferably.

ME.LHO.RA, *s.f.*, improvement, amelioration.

ME.LHO.RA.DA, *s.f., Bras., fam.*, change for the better.

ME.LHO.RA.DO, *adj.*, better, bettered, ameliorated.

ME.LHO.RA.MEN.TO, *s.m.*, advance, progress, enrichment, profit, improvement.

ME.LHO.RAR, v., to improve, to get better, to ameliorate, to reform, to amend.

ME.LHO.RI.A, *s.f.*, advance, improvement, amelioration, superiority.

ME.LI.AN.TE, s. 2 gen., gír., scoundrel, thief, vagabond.

ME.LÍ.FLUO, *adj.*, mellifluous, mellifluent.

ME.LIN.DRAR, v., to hurt the feelings of, to wound, to pique, to scandalize.

ME.LIN.DRE, *s.m.*, politeness, sensitivity, susceptibility, coyness, prudery.

ME.LIN.DRO.SO, *adj.*, susceptible, squeamish; affected; tricky, risky.

ME.LO.DI.A, *s.f.*, melody, tune, air, sweetness.

ME.LÓ.DI.CO, *adj.*, melodious, melodic.

ME.LO.DI.O.SO, *adj.*, melodious, harmonious.

ME.LO.DRA.MA, *s.m.*, melodrama.

ME.LO.DRA.MÁ.TI.CO, *adj.*, melodramatic.

ME.LO.SO, *adj.*, sticky, syrupy, sweet.

MEL.RO, *s.m.*, blackbird, ouzel.

MEM.BRA.NA, *s.f.*, membrane.

MEM.BRA.NO.SO, *adj.*, membranous.

MEM.BRO, *s.m.*, member, limb; fellow, associate.

ME.MO.RAN.DO, *s.m.*, memorandum, memorial, notification, note.

ME.MO.RAR, v., to memorize, to remind.

ME.MO.RÁ.VEL, *adj.*, memorable, notable, remarkable.

ME.MÓ.RIA, *s.f.*, memory, storage, remembrance, reminescence.

ME.MO.RI.AL, *s.m.*, memorial; *adj.*, memorialmemorable.

ME.MO.RI.ZA.ÇÃO, *s.f.*, memorization.

ME.MO.RI.ZAR, v., to memorize.

MEN.ÇÃO, *s.f.*, mention, reference, citation, notice.

MEN.CIO.NAR, v., to mention, to refer to, to cite, to name, to narrate.

MEN.DI.CÂN.CI.A, *s.f.*, mendicity, beggary, begging.

MEN.DI.CAN.TE, s. 2 gen., mendicant, beggar.

MEN.DI.GAR, v., to beg, to go begging, to cadge.

MEN.DI.GO, *s.m.*, beggar, mendicant, cadger, pauper.

ME.NE.AR, v., to waggle, to wriggle, to shake.

ME.NEI.O, *s.m.*, wagging, waggling, shaking.

ME.NI.NA, *s.f.*, girl, maiden, young woman.

ME.NI.NA.DA, *s.f.*, a group of boys and girls.

ME.NIN.GI.TE, *s.f., Med.*, meningitis.

ME.NI.NI.CE, *s.f.*, childhood, infancy.

ME.NI.NO, *s.m.*, boy, infant, lad.

ME.NIS.CO, *s.m., Anat.*, meniscus.

ME.NO.PAU.SA, *s.f., Med.*, menopause.

ME.NOR, s. 2 gen., minor, person under legal age; *adj.*, smaller, lesser, younger, minor.

ME.NO.RI.DA.DE, *s.f.*, minority.

ME.NOS, *s.m.*, the least; *adv.*, less, least; *conj.*, but, save, except, less.

ME.NOS.PRE.ZA.DO, *adj.*, underestimated.

ME.NOS.PRE.ZAR, v., to despise, to scorn, to contemn, to disdain, to disparage.

ME.NOS.PRE.ZO, *s.m.*, contempt, despite, disdain.

MEN.SA.GEI.RO, *s.m.*, messenger, courier, bell-boy, emissary, announcer, herald.

MEN.SA.GEM, *s.f.*, message, communication, dispatch, summons.

MEN.SAL, *adj.*, monthly.

MEN.SA.LI.DA.DE, *s.f.*, monthly fee, allowance.

MEN.SA.LIS.TA, s. 2 gen., temporary worker, monthly paid employee.

MEN.SAL.MEN.TE, *adv.*, monthly.

MENS.TRU.A.ÇÃO, *s.f.*, menstruation, menses.

MENS.TRU.A.DA, *adj.*, (to be) menstruating; in the menstrual period.

MENS.TRU.AL, *adj.*, menstrual.

MENS.TRU.AR, v., to menstruate.

MEN.SU.RA.ÇÃO, *s.f.*, mensuration.

MEN.SU.RAR, v., to measure.

MEN.SU.RÁ.VEL, *adj.*, measurable, mensurable.

MEN.TA, *s.f.*, mint.

MEN.TAL, *adj.*, mental.

MEN.TA.LI.DA.DE, *s.f.*, mentality.

MEN.TA.LI.ZAR, v., to think; to conceptualize, to imagine.

MEN.TE, *s.f.*, mind, intellect, spirit, intention, intent.

MEN.TE.CAP.TO, *s.m.*, insane, fool, madcap, madman.

MEN.TIR, v., to lie, to tell a lie, to illude, to deceive.

MEN.TI.RA, *s.f.*, lie, untruth, falsehood, deceit, falseness, illusion.

MEN.TI.RO.SO, *s.m.*, liar, false; *adj.*, lying, untruthful, false.

MEN.TOL, *s.m., Med.*, menthol.

MEN.TO.LA.DO, *adj.*, mentholated.

MEN.TOR, *s.m.*, mentor, guide.

MENU, *s.m., carte*, menu; *Comp.*, menu.

ME.RA.MEN.TE, *adv.*, merely.

MER.CA.DO, *s.m.*, market, market place, fair, emporium.

MER.CA.DO.LO.GI.A, *s.f.*, marketing.

MER.CA.DO.LÓ.GI.CO, *adj.*, referring to marketing.

MER.CA.DOR, *s.m.*, merchant, trader, dealer.

MER.CA.DO.RI.A, *s.f.*, merchandise, goods, commodity.

MER.CAN.TE, s. 2 gen., merchant; *adj.*, trade, mercantile.

MER.CAN.TIL, *adj.*, mercantile.

MER.CAN.TI.LIS.MO, *s.m.*, mercantilism.

MER.CAN.TI.LIS.TA, *s.m.*, merchantilist; *adj.*, mercantilistic.

MER.CÊ, *s.f.*, indult, grace, mercy, favour.

MER.CE.A.RI.A, *s.f.*, grocery, grocery store.

MER.CE.NÁ.RIO, *s.m.*, mercenary, hireling.

MER.CO.SUL, *abrev. de Mercado Comum do Sul*: Southern Common Market.

MER.CÚ.RIO, *s.m.*, mercury, quicksilver.

MER.DA, *s.f.*, shit, crap.

ME.RE.CE.DOR, *adj.*, meritorious, worthy.

ME.RE.CER, v., to earn, to deserve, to merit.

ME.RE.CI.DO, *adj.*, merited, deserved, just, due.

ME.RE.CI.MEN.TO, *s.m.*, merit, desert, worthiness.

ME.REN.DA, *s.f.*, snack; ~ *escolar*: free school meal.

ME.REN.DAR, v., to have a snack.

MERENDEIRA ·· 241 ·· MEXIDO

ME.REN.DEI.RA, *s.f.*, snackbox, lunchbox; *Bras.*, a woman that serves the snack at school.

ME.REN.GUE, *s.m.*, meringue (dance and music from Haiti).

ME.RE.TRÍ.CI.O, *s.m.*, prostitution; *adj.*, pertaining to prostitutes.

ME.RE.TRIZ, *s.f.*, prostitute, harlot, whore, hooker.

MER.GU.LHA.DOR, *s.m.*, diver, plunger.

MER.GU.LHAR, *v.*, to dive, to plunge, to sink, to duck, to immerse.

MER.GU.LHO, *s.m.*, dive, plunge, dip.

ME.RI.DI.A.NO, *s.m.*, meridian.

ME.RI.DIO.NAL, *adj.*, meridional, austral, southern.

ME.RI.TÍS.SI.MO, *adj.*, most worthy, Your Honor.

MÉ.RI.TO, *s.m.*, aptitude, superiority.

ME.RI.TÓ.RIO, *adj.*, meritorious, worthy.

MER.LU.ZA, *s.f.*, *Zool.*, hake (fish).

ME.RO, *adj.*, mere, sheer, simple, pure.

MER.RE.CA, *s.f.*, trifle.

MER.TI.O.LA.TE, *s.m.*, Merthiolate (trademark used for thimerosal).

MÊS, *s.m.*, month.

ME.SA, *s.f.*, table, board.

ME.SA.DA, *s.f.*, monthly allowance.

ME.SA DE CA.BE.CEI.RA, *s.f.*, bedside table.

ME.SA-RE.DON.DA, *s.f.*, round table.

ME.SÁ.RI.O, *s.m.*, board member; polling officer; committee member.

MES.CA.LI.NA, *s.f.*, *Quím.*, mescaline.

MES.CLA, *s.f.*, mixture, miscellany; blend (mixed cloth); *adj.*, *Bras.*, blend.

MES.CLAR, *v.*, to mix, to add, to intercalate, to variegate.

MES.MI.CE, *s.f.*, sameness.

MES.MO, *s.m.*, the same, *adj.*, same, like, equal, identical; *adv.*, exactly, precisely, even.

ME.SÓ.CLI.SE, *s.f.*, *Gram.*, tmesis.

ME.SO.PO.TÂ.MI.A, *s.f.*, region between rivers.

MES.QUI.NHA.RI.A, *s.f.*, avarice, stinginess.

MES.QUI.NHEZ, *s.f.*, the same that *mesquinharia*.

MES.QUI.NHO, *adj.*, stingy, paltry, skimpy, mean, little.

MES.QUI.TA, *s.f.*, mosque.

MES.SI.Â.NI.CO, *adj.*, messianic.

MES.SI.A.NIS.MO, *s.m.*, *Rel.*, messianism.

MES.SI.AS, *s.m.*, 2 *num.*, *Rel.*, Messiah.

MES.TI.ÇA.GEM, *s.f.*, miscegenation.

MES.TI.ÇO, *s.m.*, half-breed, mongrel; *adj.*, mestizo, crossbred.

MES.TRA, *s.f.*, mistress, teacher.

MES.TRA.DO, *adj.*, masters (degree ou course).

MES.TRAN.DO, *s.m.*, student about to complete a master's degree.

MES.TRE, *s.m.*, master, expert, principal, instructor.

MES.TRE-CU.CA, *s.m.*, chef, cook.

MES.TRE DE CE.RI.MÔ.NI.AS, *s.m.*, master of ceremonies.

MES.TRE DE O.BRAS, *s.m.*, foreman.

MES.TRE-SA.LA, *s.m.*, *Bras.*, leader of a Brazilian escola de samba during carnival; master of ceremonies.

MES.TRI.A, *s.f.*, mastership, mastery.

ME.SU.RA, *s.f.*, reverence, bow, curtsy.

ME.TA, *s.f.*, aim, goal, purpose, mark.

ME.TA.BÓ.LI.CO, *adj.*, metabolic.

ME.TA.BO.LIS.MO, *s.m.*, metabolism.

ME.TA.BO.LI.ZAR, *v.*, to metabolize.

ME.TA.CAR.PO, *s.m.*, *Anat.*, metacarpus.

ME.TA.DE, *s.f.*, half, moiety.

ME.TA.FÍ.SI.CA, *s.f.*, metaphysics.

ME.TA.FÍ.SI.CO, *s.m.*, metaphysician; *adj.*, metaphysical, supernatural.

ME.TÁ.FO.RA, *s.f.*, metaphor, trope.

ME.TA.FÓ.RI.CO, *adj.*, metaphoric (figure of speech).

ME.TA.FO.RI.ZAR, *v.*, to express metaphorically.

ME.TAL, *s.m.*, metal, brass.

ME.TA.LEP.SE, *s.f.*, metalepsis.

ME.TÁ.LI.CO, *adj.*, metallic.

ME.TA.LIN.GUA.GEM, *s.f.*, metalanguage (language used to talk about language).

ME.TA.LUR.GI.A, *s.f.*, metallurgy.

ME.TA.LÚR.GI.CA, *s.f.*, foundry (workshop of metallurgy).

ME.TA.LÚR.GI.CO, *s.m.*, metallurgist, metalworker; *adj.*, metallurgic.

ME.TA.MOR.FO.SE, *s.f.*, metamorphosis.

ME.TA.MOR.FO.SE.AR, *v.*, to metamorphose.

ME.TA.NO, *s.m.*, *Quím.*, methane, marsh-gas.

ME.TÁS.TA.SE, *s.f.*, *Med.*, metastasis.

ME.TE.Ó.RI.CO, *adj.*, meteoric.

ME.TE.O.RI.TO, *s.m.*, meteorite, fallen meteor.

ME.TE.O.RO, *s.m.*, meteor, bolide, fireball.

ME.TE.O.RO.LO.GI.A, *s.f.*, meteorology.

ME.TE.O.RO.LÓ.GI.CO, *adj.*, meteorologic.

ME.TE.O.RO.LO.GIS.TA, *s.* 2 *gen.*, meteorologist.

ME.TER, *v.*, to put, to put into, to introduce, to place, to lay, to set, to deposit.

ME.TI.CU.LO.SI.DA.DE, *s.f.*, meticulosity.

ME.TI.CU.LO.SO, *adj.*, meticulous, overcareful.

ME.TI.DO, *adj.*, meddling, busy.

ME.TÓ.DI.CO, *adj.*, methodic, sistematical, orderly.

ME.TO.DIS.MO, *s.m.*, Methodism.

ME.TO.DIS.TA, *s.* 2 *gen.*, methodist.

MÉ.TO.DO, *s.m.*, method, mode, system, form.

ME.TO.DO.LO.GI.A, *s.f.*, methodology.

ME.TO.DO.LÓ.GI.CO, *adj.*, methodological.

ME.TO.NÍ.MI.A, *s.f.*, metonymy (figure of speech).

ME.TRA.GEM, *s.f.*, lenght, lenght in meters.

ME.TRA.LHA.DO.RA, *s.f.*, machine gun.

ME.TRA.LHAR, *v.*, to machine-gun.

MÉ.TRI.CO, *adj.*, metric, relating to the meter.

ME.TRO, *s.m.*, meter, meter stick.

ME.TRÔ, *s.m.*, subway, underground, tube.

ME.TRO.LO.GI.A, *s.f.*, metrology.

ME.TRÓ.PO.LE, *s.f.*, metropolis, capital, town.

ME.TRO.PO.LI.TA.NO, *s.m.*, metropolitan, subway, underground railway.

ME.TRO.VI.Á.RI.O, *s.m.*, *UK* underground worker; *US* subway worker.

MEU, *pron.*, my, mine.

ME.XER, *v.*, to move, to stir, to shuffle, to shake, to fidget, to touch.

ME.XE.RI.CA, *s.f.*, *Bot.*, tangerine.

ME.XE.RI.CAR, *v.*, to gossip.

ME.XE.RI.CO, *s.m.*, gossip, intrigue.

ME.XE.RI.QUEI.RO, *s.m.*, gossip, busybody.

ME.XI.CA.NO, *adj.*, *s.m.*, Mexican.

MÉ.XI.CO, *s.*, Mexico.

ME.XI.DO, *s.m.*, *Cul.*, scrambled (eggs); muddled (papers).

MEXILHÃO ·· 242 ·· MINISTRANTE

ME.XI.LHÃO, *s.m.*, *Zool.*, mussel, muscle.
ME.ZA.NI.NO, *s.m.*, mezzanine, entresol.
MI, *s.m.*, *Mús.*, mi or E (third note of the diatonic scale).
MI.A.DO, *s.m.*, mew, mewing of a cat.
MI.AR, *v.*, to mew, to miaul.
MI.AS.MA, *s.m.*, miasma (exhalation).
MI.AU, *s.m.*, mew, miaow.
MI.ÇAN.GA, *s.f.*, glass bead, beads.
MIC.ÇÃO, *s.f.*, urination.
MI.CO, *s.m.*, name for several species of monkeys.
MI.CO-LE.ÃO-DOU.RA.DO, *s.m.*, *Zool.*, golden lion tamarin.
MI.CO.LO.GI.A, *s.f.*, mycology, mycetology.
MI.CRO, *s.m.*, micron.
MI.CRO.BI.A.NO, *adj.*, microbial, microbic, microbian.
MI.CRÓ.BIO, *s.m.*, microbe, germ, microorganism.
MI.CRO.BI.O.LO.GI.A, *s.f.*, microbiology.
MI.CRO.BI.O.LÓ.GI.CO, *adj.*, microbiological.
MI.CRO.CI.RUR.GI.A, *s.f.*, *Med.*, microsurgery.
MI.CRO.COM.PU.TA.DOR, *s.m.*, micro, microcomputer, personal computer.
MI.CRO.COS.MO, *s.m.*, microcosm.
MI.CRO.E.CO.NO.MI.A, *s.f.*, *Econ.*, microeconomics.
MI.CRO.EM.PRE.SA, *s.f.*, small business.
MI.CRO.EM.PRE.SÁ.RI.O, *s.m.*, *Econ.*, small-business owner.
MI.CRO.FIL.ME, *s.m.*, microfilm.
MI.CRO.FO.NE, *s.m.*, microphone.
MI.CRO.FO.NI.A, *s.f.*, *Med.*, microphony.
MI.CRO.FO.TO.GRA.FI.A, *s.f.*, microphotography; microphotograph (microscopic photograph).
MI.CRO.LO.GI.A, *s.f.*, micrology.
MI.CRO.ME.TRI.A, *s.f.*, micrometry.
MI.CRÔ.ME.TRO, *s.m.*, micrometer.
MI.CRO-ON.DAS, *s.m.*, microwaves.
MI.CRO-Ô.NI.BUS, *s.m.*, *2 num.*, microbus.
MI.CRO-OR.GA.NIS.MO, *s.m.*, microorganism, microbe.
MI.CRO.PRO.CES.SA.DOR, *s.m.*, *Comp.*, microprocessor.
MI.CROS.CÓ.PIO, *s.m.*, microscope.
MIC.TÓ.RIO, *s.m.*, urinal, public convenience.
MÍ.DIA, *s.f.*, media, mass communication.
MI.GA.LHA, *s.f.*, crumb, bit, small portion.
MI.GRA.ÇÃO, *s.f.*, migration, wandering.
MI.GRA.DOR, *adj.*, migrant.
MI.GRAN.TE, *s. 2 gen.*, migrant.
MI.GRAR, *v.*, to migrate.
MI.GRA.TÓ.RIO, *adj.*, migratory.
MI.JA.DA, *s.f.*, *pop.*, *vulg.*, act of urination; *col.*, reprehension.
MI.JA.DO, *adj.*, wet from urine; that urinated.
MI.JAR, *v.*, to piss, to piddle, to urinate.
MI.JO, *s.m.*, *col.*, urine, piss.
MIL, *num.*, thousand; great number.
MI.LA.GRE, *s.m.*, miracle, wonder, marvel.
MI.LA.GREI.RO, *s.m.*, wonder-worker; *adj.*, credulous.
MI.LA.GRO.SO, *adj.*, miraculous, wonderful, marvelous.
MI.LE.NAR, *adj.*, millenary; *fig.*, age old.
MI.LE.NÁ.RIO, *s.m.*, millenary; *adj.*, millenial, millenarian.
MI.LÊ.NIO, *s.m.*, millenium.
MI.LÉ.SI.MO, *s.m.*, millesimal.
MIL-FO.LHAS, *s.f.*, *2 num.*, *Cul.*, millefeuille; *Bot.*, milfoil.
MI.LHA, *s.f.*, mile.
MI.LHAL, *s.m.*, maize field.
MI.LHÃO, *s.m.*, million.

MI.LHAR, *num.*, thousand.
MI.LHA.RAL, *s.m.*, maize field, cornfield.
MI.LHO, *s.m.*, maize, corn.
MI.LI.AR.DÁ.RI.O, *s.m.*, *adj.*, multimillionaire.
MI.LI.GRA.MA, *s.f.*, milligramme.
MI.LI.LI.TRO, *s.m.*, milliliter.
MI.LÍ.ME.TRO, *s.m.*, millimeter.
MI.LI.O.NÁ.RIO, *s.m.*, *adj.*, millionnaire.
MI.LI.O.NÉ.SI.MO, *num.*, millionth.
MI.LI.TÂN.CI.A, *s.f.*, militancy.
MI.LI.TAN.TE, *adj.*, *s. 2 gen.*, militant.
MI.LI.TAR, *s.m.*, soldier; *v.*, to fight, to serve as a soldier, to militate.
MI.LI.TA.RIS.MO, *s.m.*, militarism.
MI.LI.TA.RIS.TA, *s. 2 gen.*, militarist.
MI.LI.TA.RI.ZA.ÇÃO, *s.f.*, militarization.
MI.LI.TA.RI.ZAR, *v.*, to militarize.
MIM, *pron.*, me.
MI.MA.DO, *adj.*, spoiled.
MI.MAR, *v.*, to pet, to fondle, to spoil, to pamper, to cocker.
MI.ME.O.GRA.FAR, *v.*, *Bras.*, to mimeograph.
MI.ME.Ó.GRA.FO, *s.m.*, mimeograph.
MÍ.MI.CA, *s.f.*, mime, mimic.
MÍ.MI.CO, *adj.*, mimic, mimical.
MI.MO, *s.m.*, gift, offering, present, tenderness.
MI.MO.SO, *adj.*, tender, sweet, exquisite.
MI.NA, *s.f.*, mine, quarry, pit.
MI.NAR, *v.*, to mine, to excavate, to undermine, to sap, to corrode.
MI.NA.RE.TE, *s.m.*, minaret.
MIN.DI.NHO, *s.m.*, the little finger; *fam.*, pinky.
MI.NEI.RO, *s.m.*, miner, collier, native of the State of Minas Gerais; *adj.*, mining.
MI.NE.RA.ÇÃO, *s.f.*, mining.
MI.NE.RA.DOR, *s.m.*, miner; *adj.*, mining.
MI.NE.RAL, *s.m.*, mineral; *adj.*, mineral, inorganic.
MI.NE.RA.LO.GI.A, *s.f.*, mineralogy.
MI.NÉ.RIO, *s.m.*, ore.
MIN.GAU, *s.m.*, porridge; *fig.*, sloppy, mush.
MÍN.GUA, *s.f.*, lack, need, scarcity, shortage.
MIN.GUA.DO, *adj.*, scarce, lacking, wanting.
MIN.GUAN.TE, *s.m.*, *Astron.*, (moon) last quarter, waning quarter.
MIN.GUAR, *v.*, to wane, to decrease, to diminish.
MI.NHA, *pron.*, mine, my.
MI.NHO.CA, *s.f.*, *Zool.*, earthworm.
MI.NI, *s. 2 gen.*, mini, miniskirt, minidress; *adj.*, mini.
MI.NI.A.TU.RA, *s.f.*, miniature, summary.
MI.NI.A.TU.RI.ZAR, *v.*, to miniaturize.
MI.NI.MA.LIS.MO, *s.m.*, *Art.*, minimalism.
MI.NI.MA.LIS.TA, *s. 2 gen.*, minimalist.
MI.NI.MI.ZAR, *v.*, to minimize.
MÍ.NI.MO, *s.m.*, minimum, the least; *adj.*, minimal, least, remote.
MI.NIS.SAI.A, *s.f.*, miniskirt.
MI.NIS.SÉ.RI.E, *s.f.*, miniseries.
MI.NIS.TE.RI.AL, *adj.*, ministerial.
MI.NIS.TE.RI.A.LIS.TA *s. 2 gen.*, *adj.*, ministerialist.
MI.NIS.TE.RI.Á.VEL, *adj.*, ministerial candidate.
MI.NIS.TÉ.RIO, *s.m.*, ministry, cabinet, state department, charge, office.
MI.NIS.TRA.NTE, *s.m.*, ministrant, acolyte; *adj.*, ministering.

MINISTRAR · 243 · MOÇO

MI.NIS.TRAR, *v.*, to minister, to furnish, to give, to administer, to supply.

MI.NIS.TRO, *s.m.*, minister, minister of state; clergyman.

MI.NOI.CO, *s.m., adj., Hist.,* Minoan (inhabitant or relating to a Bronze Age culture of Crete).

MI.NO.RAR, *v.*, to diminish, to decrease.

MI.NO.RI.A, *s.f.,* minority.

MI.NO.RI.TÁ.RI.O, *adj.,* minority.

MI.NU.A.NO, *s.m., Bras.,* cold and dry southwestern winter wind.

MI.NÚ.CIA, *s.f.,* minute, detail, nicety, insignificance.

MI.NU.CI.O.SI.DA.DE, *s.f.,* minuteness, particularity, accuracy, exactness.

MI.NU.CI.O.SA.MEN.TE, *adv.,* minutely.

MI.NU.CI.O.SO, *adj.,* minute, circumstantial, particular.

MI.NÚS.CU.LO, *adj.,* minuscule, tiny.

MI.NU.TA, *s.f.,* minute, draft of a document.

MI.NU.TE.RI.A, *s.f.,* timer.

MI.NU.TO, *s.m.,* minute, moment, instant.

MI.O.CÁR.DI.O, *s.m., Anat.,* myocardium.

MI.O.CE.NO, *s.m., adj., Geol.,* Miocene.

mi.o.lo, *s.m.,* brain, medulla, soft part of bread.

MI.O.MA, *s.m., Med.,* myoma.

MÍ.O.PE, *s.m.,* myopic person; *adj.,* myopic.

MI.O.PI.A, *s.f.,* myopia, nearsightedness.

MI.O.SÓ.TIS, *s. 2 gen.,* myosotis, forget-me-not.

MI.RA, *s.f.,* sight, aim, mark, purpose, scope, end.

MI.RA.BO.LAN.TE, *adj.,* incredible, showy, gaudy, ridiculously.

MI.RA.CU.LO.SO, *adj.,* miraculous.

MI.RA.DA, *s.f.,* look.

MI.RA.GEM, *s.f.,* optical illusion, deception, mirage.

MI.RA.MAR, *s.m.,* sea-view belvedere.

MI.RAN.TE, *s.m.,* belvedere, mirador.

MI.RAR, *v.*, to eye, to examine, to look at, to see.

MI.RÍ.A.DE, *s.f.,* myriad.

MI.RIM, *adj.,* small.

MIR.RA, *s.f.,* myrrh.

MI.SAN.TRO.PI.A, *s.f.,* misanthropy.

MI.SAN.TRO.PO, *s.m.,* misanthrope; *adj.,* misanthropic.

MIS.CE.LÂ.NEA, *s.f.,* miscellanea, miscellany, confusion.

MIS.CI.GE.NA.ÇÃO, *s.f.,* miscegenation.

MIS.CI.GE.NAR, *v.*, to miscegenate.

MI.SE.RÁ.VEL, *s. 2 gen.,* miserable, miser, skinflint; *adj.,* unhappy, miserable, woeful, pitiful.

MI.SE.RA.VEL.MEN.TE, *adv.,* miserably.

MI.SÉ.RIA, *s.f.,* misery, distress, poverty, calamity, unhappiness.

MI.SE.RI.CÓR.DIA, *s.f.,* mercy, compassion, commiseration, pity.

MI.SE.RI.COR.DI.O.SO, *adj.,* merciful, clement.

MI.SE.RO, *adj.,* disgraced, miserable, unhappy.

MI.SO.GI.NI.A, *s.f., Med.,* misogyny.

MI.SÓ.GI.NO, *s.m.,* misogynist; *adj.,* misogynic, misogynical, misogynous.

MISS, *s.f., Ingl.,* the same that *misse*.

MIS.SA, *s.f.,* mass.

MIS.SAL, *s.m.,* missal.

MIS.SÃO, *s.f.,* mission, delegation, commission, vocation, missionary station.

MIS.SE, *s.f.,* beauty queen.

MÍS.SIL, *s.m.,* missile.

MIS.SI.O.NÁ.RIO, *s.m.,* missionary.

MIS.SI.VA, *s.f.,* missive.

MIS.SI.VIS.TA, *s. 2 gen., Bras.,* the person who writes a letter.

MIS.TER, *s.m.,* occupation, employment, office.

MIS.TÉ.RIO, *s.m.,* mystery, enigma, secret.

MIS.TE.RI.O.SO, *adj.,* mysterious, enigmatic.

MÍS.TI.CA, *s.f.,* study of divine or spiritual things.

MIS.TI.CIS.MO, *s.m.,* mysticism.

MÍS.TI.CO, *s.m.,* mystic; *adj.,* mystic, spiritually, allegorical.

MIS.TI.FI.CA.ÇÃO, *s.f.,* mystification.

MIS.TI.FI.CA.DOR, *adj.,* mystifying.

MIS.TI.FI.CAR, *v.*, to mystify, to puzzle, to bewilder.

MIS.TO, *adj.,* mixed, variegated, confused.

MIS.TO-QUEN.TE, *s.m., Bras., Cul.,* a hot ham and cheese sandwich.

MIS.TU.RA, *s.f.,* mixture, blend.

MIS.TU.RA.DOR, *s.m.,* mixer.

MIS.TU.RAR, *v.*, to mix, to blend, to mingle, to shuffle, to confuse.

MIS.TU.RÁ.VEL, *adj.,* mixable.

MIS.TU.RE.BA, *s.f., fam.,* hotchpotch.

MÍ.TI.CO, *adj.,* mythical.

MI.TI.FI.CAR, *v.*, to mythicize.

MI.TI.GAR, *v.*, to mitigate, to alleviate, to moderate.

MI.TO, *s.m.,* myth.

MI.TO.CÔN.DRI.A, *s.f., Biol.,* mitochondrion.

MI.TO.LO.GI.A, *s.f.,* mythology.

MI.TO.LÓ.GI.CO, *adj.,* mythologic, mythological.

MI.TRA, *s.f.,* miter, mitre.

MI.U.DA.GEM, *s.f., Bras.,* lots of little things, trifles.

MI.U.DE.ZA, *s.f.,* minuteness, smallness.

MI.U.DI.NHO, *s.m., Bras.,* popular dance; *adj.,* tiny.

MI.Ú.DO, *adj.,* small, little, minute; *s.m., pl.* giblets.

MI.XA.GEM, *s.f., Mús.,* mixing.

MI.XAR, *v., gír.,* to finish, to end.

MI.XAR, *v., Mús.,* to mix.

MI.XA.RI.A, *s.f., fam.,* peanuts; rubbish.

MI.XÓR.DIA, *s.f.,* confusion, mix-up, medley.

MI.XU.RU.CA, *adj., Bras.,* worthless, lifeless (party).

MNE.MÔ.NI.CA, *s.f.,* mnemonics.

MNE.MÔ.NI.CO, *adj.,* mnemonic.

MÓ, *s.f.,* millstone.

MO.A.GEM, *s.f.,* grinding, milling; grist.

MÓ.BI.LE, *s.m.,* mobile.

MO.BÍ.LIA, *s.f.,* furniture.

MO.BI.LI.AR, *v.*, to furnish.

MO.BI.LI.Á.RI.O, *s.m.,* furniture; *adj.,* pertaining to furniture.

MO.BI.LI.DA.DE, *s.f.,* mobility.

MO.BI.LI.ZA.ÇÃO, *s.f.,* mobilization.

MO.BI.LI.ZAR, *v.*, to mobilize, to render mobile, to put in motion.

MO.BI.LI.ZÁ.VEL, *adj.,* mobilizable.

MO.ÇA, *s.f.,* girl, young woman, miss.

MO.ÇA.DA, *s.f.,* youngsters.

MO.ÇÃO, *s.f.,* motion, movement, commotion.

MO.CAS.SIM, *s.m.,* moccasin.

MO.CHI.LA, *s.f.,* backpack, rucksack, haversack.

MO.CI.DA.DE, *s.f.,* youth, youthfulness.

MO.CI.NHO, *s.m.,* diminutive of *moço*: young man; *Bras.,* hero in adventure films.

MO.ÇO, *s.m.,* boy, young man; *adj.,* young, youthful.

M

MOCORONGO · 244 · MONÓGAMO

MO.CO.RON.GO, *s.m., Bras.*, backwoodsman, boor.

MO.DA, *s.f.*, fashion, manner, vogue, custom, way, method, song.

MO.DAL, *adj.*, modal.

MO.DA.LI.DA.DE, *s.f.*, modality, manner, way.

MO.DE.LA.ÇÃO, *s.f.*, modelling, moulding.

MO.DE.LA.DOR, *s.m.*, modeller, girdle ; *adj.*, modelling.

MO.DE.LA.GEM, *s.f.*, modelling, moulding.

MO.DE.LAR, *v.*, to model, to shape, to mould, to form; *adj.*, model.

MO.DE.LIS.TA, *s. 2 gen.*, designer, a maker of models.

MO.DE.LO, *s.m.*, model, mould, standard, example, ideal.

MO.DEM, *s.m., Ingl., Comp.*, modem.

MO.DE.RA.ÇÃO, *s.f.*, moderation.

MO.DE.RA.DO, *adj.*, moderate.

MO.DE.RA.DOR, *s.m.*, moderator; *adj.*, moderating.

MO.DE.RAR, *v.*, to moderate, to temper, to diminish, to mitigate, to restrain.

MO.DER.NI.DA.DE, *s.f.*, modernity.

MO.DER.NIS.MO, *s.m.*, modernism.

MO.DER.NIS.TA, *s. 2 gen.*, modernist.

MO.DER.NI.ZA.ÇÃO, *s.f.*, modernization.

MO.DER.NI.ZAR, *v.*, to modernize, to render modern.

MO.DER.NO, *adj.*, new, modern, actual.

MO.DER.NO.SO, *adj., Bras., pej.*, pretentiously or doubtfully modern.

MO.DES.TA.MEN.TE, *adv.*, modestly.

MO.DÉS.TIA, *s.f.*, modesty, humbleness, simplicity.

MO.DES.TO, *adj.*, modest, unpretentious, moderate.

MÓ.DI.CO, *adj.*, small, slight, low.

MO.DI.FI.CA.ÇÃO, *s.f.*, modification, alteration.

MO.DI.FI.CAR, *v.*, to modify, to change, to alter.

MO.DI.FI.CÁ.VEL, *adj.*, modifiable.

MO.DI.NHA, *s.f.*, popular Brazilian song, tune.

MO.DIS.MO, *s.m.*, trend, fashion.

MO.DIS.TA, *s.f.*, dressmaker, fashion designer.

MO.DO, *s.m.*, mode, manner, fashion, style, form, custom, method, humour.

MO.DOR.RA, *s.f.*, sleepiness, somnolence, sturdy.

MO.DU.LA.ÇÃO, *s.f.*, modulation.

MO.DU.LA.DO, *adj.*, mudular, modulated.

MO.DU.LAR, *v.*, to modulate, to inflect; *adj.*, modular.

MÓ.DU.LO, *s.m.*, module, modulus, coefficient.

MO.E.DA, *s.f.*, coin, currency.

MO.E.DOR, *s.m.*, grinder, pounder; *adj.*, grinding.

MO.E.LA, *s.f.*, gizzard.

MO.EN.DA, *s.f.*, sugar mill, millwork.

MO.ER, *v.*, to grind, to crush, to triturate, to bray, to press.

MO.FA, *s.f.*, mockery.

MO.FA.DO, *adj.*, musty, mouldy.

MO.FA.DOR, *s.m.*, scoffer, mocker.

MO.FAR, *v.*, to mock, to scorn, to deride, to jeer.

MO.FO, *s.m.*, mould, mildew, must.

MOG.NO, *s.m., Bot.*, mahogany.

MO.Í.DO, *adj.*, ground, crushed.

MO.I.NHO, *s.m.*, mill, flour-mill.

MOI.SÉS, *s.m., 2 num.*, Moses basket, carrycot.

MOI.TA, *s.f.*, bush, thicket, scrub, tuft.

MO.LA, *s.f.*, spring, coil, motive, incentive.

MO.LAM.BEN.TO, *s.m., Bras.*, rundown, ragged.

MO.LAM.BO, *s.m., Bras.*, rag, rags, tatter.

MO.LAR, *s.m.*, molar, grinding.

MOL.DA.DO, *adj.*, moulded, mould, moulding.

MOL.DA.DOR, *s.m.*, moulder; *adj.*, moulding.

MOL.DA.GEM, *s.f.*, moulding.

MOL.DAR, *v.*, to mould, to cast, to make moulds, to shape, to model.

MOL.DÁ.VI.A, *s.*, Moldova, Moldavia.

MOL.DÁ.VI.O, *s., adj.*, Moldovan, Moldavian.

MOL.DE, *s.m.*, mould, pattern, norm.

MOL.DU.RA, *s.f.*, frame, borders.

MO,LE, *adj.*, soft, tender, lazy, sluggish.

MO.LE.CA.DA, *s.f.*, bunch of kids.

MO.LE.CA.GEM, *s.f., Bras.*, trick, prank.

MO.LÉ.CU.LA, *s.f.*, molecule.

MO.LE.CU.LAR, *adj.*, molecular.

MO.LE.CU.LA.RI.DA.DE, *s.f., Fís., Quím.*, molecularity.

MO.LE.QUE, *s.m.*, young boy; dude; *adj.*, funny, mocking.

MO.LES.TA.DOR, *s.m.*, molester; *adj.*, molesting.

MO.LES.TAR, *v.*, to molest, to disturb, to annoy, to offend.

MO.LÉS.TIA, *s.f.*, disease, sickness, malady, illness.

MO.LE.TOM, *s.m.*, brushed cotton, flannel.

MO.LE.ZA, *s.f.*, softness, tenderness, laziness, indolence.

MO.LHA.DO, *adj.*, moist, wet.

MO.LHAR, *v.*, to wet, to dampen, to moisten, to soak.

MO.LHE, *s.m.*, breakwater, pier, jetty.

MO.LHEI.RA, *s.f.*, sauce boat.

MO.LHO(ó), *s.m.*, bunch, bundle, faggot, sheaf.

MO.LHO(ô), *s.m.*, sauce, gravy.

MO.LIB.DÊ.NI.O, *s.m., Quím.*, molybdenum (a metallic element).

MO.LI.NE.TE, *s.m.*, moulinet; fishing reel.

MO.LUS.CO, *s.m., Zool.*, mollusc, shellfish.

MO.MEN.TÂ.NEO, *adj.*, momentary, instantaneous, transitory.

MO.MEN.TO, *s.m.*, moment, instant, circumstance.

MO.MO, *s.m.*, Momus, pantomine.

MO.NA.CAL, *adj.*, monachal, monastic.

MO.NAR.CA, *s.f.*, monarch, sovereign.

MO.NAR.QUI.A, *s.f.*, monarchy, sovereignty.

MO.NAR.QUIS.MO, *s.m.*, monarchism.

MO.NAS.TÉ.RIO, *s.m.*, monastery.

MO.NÁS.TI.CO, *adj.*, monachal, monastic.

MON.ÇÃO, *s.f.*, monsoon.

MO.NE.TÁ.RIO, *adj.*, monetary.

MO.NE.TA.RIS.MO, *s.m., Econ.*, monetarism.

MO.NE.TA.RIS.TA, *s. 2 gen., adj.*, monetarist.

MON.GE, *s.m.*, monk, friar.

MON.GOL, *s. 2 gen.*, Mongol; *adj.*, Mongol, Mongolian.

MON.GÓ.LI.A, *s.*, Mongolia.

MON.GO.LIS.MO, *s.m., Med.*, Down's syndrome.

MON.GO.LOI.DE, *s. 2 gen.*, mongoloid (person with Down's syndrome); *adj., Med.*, Mongoloid (Down's syndrome).

MO.NI.TOR, *s.m.*, monitor.

MO.NI.TO.RAR, *v.*, to monitor.

MO.NI.TÓ.RIA, *s.f.*, monitory, advice, reproof.

MON.JA, *s.f.*, nun.

MO.NO, *s.m.*, monkey, ape.

MO.NO.CRO.MÁ.TI.CO, *adj.*, monochrome, monochromic, monochromical.

MO.NÓ.CU.LO, *s.m.*, monocle, single eyeglass.

MO.NO.GA.MI.A, *s.f.*, monogamy.

MO.NÓ.GA.MO, *s.m.*, monogamist; *adj.*, monogamous.

MONOGRAFIA ·· 245 ·· MOTEJAR

MO.NO.GRA.FI.A, *s.f.*, monograph.
MO.NO.GRA.MA, *s.m.*, monogram.
MO.NO.LÍ.TI.CO, *adj.*, monolithic.
MO.NO.LO.GAR, *v.*, to monologize; to speak to oneself; *Teat.*, to recite monologues.
MO.NÓ.LO.GO, *s.m.*, monologue, soliloquy.
MO.NO.NU.CLE.O.SE, *s.f.*, *Med.*, mononucleosis.
MO.NO.PÓ.LIO, *s.m.*, monopoly.
MO.NO.PO.LIS.TA, *s. 2 gen.*, monopolist.
MO.NO.PO.LI.ZA.ÇÃO, *s.f.*, monopolization.
MO.NO.PO.LI.ZAR, *v.*, to monopolize.
MO.NOS.SÍ.LA.BO, *s.m.*, monosyllable; *adj.*, monosyllabic.
MO.NO.TE.ÍS.MO, *s.m.*, monotheism.
MO.NO.TO.NI.A, *s.f.*, monotony, sameness.
MO.NÓ.TO.NO, *adj.*, monotone, tedious, tiresome, irksome.
MO.NÓ.XI.DO, *s.m.*, *Quím.*, monoxide.
MON.SE.NHOR, *s.m.*, Monsignor.
MONS.TREN.GO, *s.m.*, monster, monstrosity, awkward, scarecrow.
MONS.TRO, *s.m.*, monster; prodigy.
MONS.TRU.O.SI.DA.DE, *s.f.*, monstrosity, monstrousness.
MONS.TRU.O.SO, *adj.*, monstrous, abnormal, huge.
MON.TA, *s.f.*, amount, importance, sum.
MON.TA.DO, *adj.*, mounted; assembled.
MON.TA.DOR, *s.m.*, fitter, assembler; *Cin.*, (film) editor.
MON.TA.GEM, *s.f.*, mounting, erecting, erection, assembly.
MON.TA.NHA, *s.f.*, mountain, pile.
MON.TA.NHA-RUS.SA, *s.f.*, roller coaster.
MON.TA.NHÊS, *s.m.*, mountaineer, highlander; *adj.*, mountain.
MON.TA.NHIS.MO, *s.m.*, mountaineering.
MON.TA.NHIS.TA, *s. 2 gen.*, mountaineer; *adj.*, mountaineering.
MON.TA.NHO.SO, *adj.*, mountainous.
MON.TAN.TE, *s.m.*, amount, sum.
MON.TÃO, *s.m.*, heap, disorderly pile.
MON.TAR, *v.*, to mount, to ride, to assemble, to erect, to furnish.
MON.TA.RI.A, *s.f.*, riding horse.
MON.TE, *s.m.*, mount, hill, heap, pile, accumulation.
MON.TE.PI.O, *s.m.*, trust fund.
MON.TÊS, *adj.*, montane, rustic, wild.
MON.TO.EI.RA, *s.f.*, *Bras.*, a heap of; large quantity.
MO.NU.MEN.TAL, *adj.*, monumental, magnificent, extraordinary.
MO.NU.MEN.TO, *s.m.*, monument, memorial, memory.
MO.QUE.CA, *s.f.*, *Bras., Cul.*, fish, mussels or chicken simmered in oil, coconut milk, onions and pepper.
MO.RA, *s.f.*, delay, respite.
MO.RA.DA, *s.f.*, residence, habitation, dwelling.
MO.RA.DIA, *s.f.*, residence.
MO.RA.DOR, *s.m.*, resident, lodger, inhabitant, tenant.
MO.RAL, *s.f.*, morals, ethics, morality, morale; *adj.*, moral, ethical.
MO.RA.LI.DA.DE, *s.f.*, morality.
MO.RA.LIS.MO, *s.m.*, moralism.
MO.RA.LIS.TA, *s. 2 gen.*, moralist.
MO.RA.LI.ZA.ÇÃO, *s.f.*, moralization.
MO.RA.LI.ZAR, *v.*, to moralize, to censure.
MO.RAN.GO, *s.m.*, *Bot.*, strawberry.
MO.RAR, *v.*, to live, to inhabit, to reside, to abide.
MO.RA.TÓ.RI.A, *s.f.*, moratorium.
MOR.BI.DEZ, *s.f.*, morbidness, morbidity.

MÓR.BI.DO, *adj.*, morbid, diseased, sickly.
MOR.CE.GO, *s.m.*, *Zool.*, bat, flickermouse.
MOR.DA.ÇA, *s.f.*, muzzle, gag.
MOR.DA.ÇAR, *v.*, to mordant.
MOR.DA.CI.DA.DE, *s.f.*, mordacity, mordancy.
MOR.DAZ, *adj.*, biting, snappish.
MOR.DE.DE.LA, *s.f.*, *col.*, the same that *mordedura*.
MOR.DE.DOR, *s.m.*, biter; *adj.*, biting, caustic.
MOR.DE.DU.RA, *s.f.*, bite, teethmark.
MOR.DER, *v.*, to bite, to nip, to snap, to sink the teeth into.
MOR.DI.DA, *s.f.*, bite, teethmark.
MOR.DI.DE.LA, *s.f.*, *col.*, the same that *mordedura*.
MOR.DI.DO, *adj.*, bitten; *Bras.*, angry, furious.
MOR.DO.MI.A, *s.f.*, stewardship, perks, comfort.
MOR.DO.MO, *s.m.*, butler, majordomo.
MO.RE.NO, *s.m.*, brunet; *adj.*, brunet, brown, dark.
MOR.FE.MA, *s.m.*, *Ling.*, morpheme.
MOR.FI.NA, *s.f.*, *Farm.*, morphine.
MOR.FO.LO.GI.A, *s.f.*, morphology.
MO.RI.BUN.DO, *s.m.*, moribund; *adj.*, moribund, dying, expiriting.
MO.RIN.GA, *s.f.*, *Bras.*, water cooler.
MOR.MA.CEN.TO, *adj.*, sultry.
MOR.MA.ÇO, *s.m.*, sweltry.
MOR.MEN.TE, *adv.*, mainly, especially.
MÓR.MON, *s.m.*, Mormon.
MOR.NO, *adj.*, lukewarm, tepid.
MO.RO.SI.DA.DE, *s.f.*, slowness, tardiness, moroseness.
MO.RO.SO, *adj.*, morose, glum, gloomy.
MOR.RER, *v.*, to die, to perish, to decease, to pass away, to decay.
MOR.RO, *s.m.*, mount, mound, hill.
MOR.TA.DE.LA, *s.f.*, large Italian sausage.
MOR.TAL, *adj.*, mortal, lethal, deadly, fatal.
MOR.TA.LHA, *s.f.*, hearse cloth.
MOR.TA.LI.DA.DE, *s.f.*, mortality.
MOR.TAL.MEN.TE, *adv.*, mortally, deadly.
MOR.TAN.DA.DE, *s.f.*, slaughter.
MOR.TE, *s.f.*, death, decease, dying, destruction.
MOR.TEI.RO, *s.m.*, mortar.
MOR.TÍ.FE.RO, *adj.*, mortal, lethal, murderous.
MOR.TI.FI.CA.DO, *adj.*, mortified.
MOR.TI.FI.CAR, *v.*, to mortify, to afflict, to torment, to torture.
MOR.TO, *s.m.*, dead, deceased, defunct; *adj.*, dead, deceased, killed, wilted, withered.
MOR.TU.Á.RIO, *adj.*, mortuary, funerary.
MO.SAI.CO, *s.m.*, mosaic.
MOS.CA, *s.f.*, fly.
MOS.CO.VI.TA, *s. 2 gen.*, *adj.*, Muscovite.
MOS.QUI.TEI.RO, *s.m.*, mosquito-net.
MOS.QUI.TO, *s.m.*, mosquito.
MOS.TAR.DA, *s.f.*, mustard.
MOS.TEI.RO, *s.m.*, monastery, convent.
MOS.TRA, *s.f.*, show, exhibition, display.
MOS.TRA.DOR, *s.m.*, dial; *adj.*, showing.
MOS.TRAR, *v.*, to show, to display, to present, to signify, to denote.
MOS.TRU.Á.RIO, *s.m.*, showcase, collection.
MO.TE, *s.m.*, theme.
MO.TE.JAR, *v.*, to scoff; to censure, to criticize; to make mottoes, to epigraphs.

M

MOTEJO ··246·· MURMURANTE

MO.TE.JO, *s.m.*, scorn, jest, joke.
MO.TEL, *s.m.*, motel.
MO.TIM, *s.m.*, mutiny, revolt, uproar.
MO.TI.VA.ÇÃO, *s.f.*, motivation, argumentation.
MO.TI.VA.DO, *adj.*, motivated.
MO.TI.VA.DOR, *s.m.*, person (or thing) that is motivator; *adj.*, giving a motive or reason.
MO.TI.VAR, *v.*, to motivate, to incite, to reason.
MO.TI.VO, *s.m.*, motive, ground, cause, reason, intent.
MO.TO, *s.m.*, motto, device; *s.f.*, motorcycle.
MO.TO.CA, *s.f.*, *Bras., pop.*, motorcycle.
MO.TO.CI.CLE.TA, *s.f.*, motorcycle, bike, motorbike.
MO.TO.CI.CLIS.MO, *s.m.*, motorcycling.
MO.TO.CI.CLIS.TA, *s. 2 gen.*, motorcyclist.
MO.TO-CON.TÍ.NUO, *s.m., Fís.*, moto perpétuo.
MO.TO.CROSS, *s.m., Esp.*, motocross.
MO.TO.NE.TA, *s.f.*, scooter.
MO.TO.QUEI.RO, *s.m., Bras., pop.*, motorcyclist.
MO.TOR, *s.m.*, motor, engine; *adj.*, motor, moving.
MO.TO.RIS.TA, *s. 2 gen.*, driver, motorist, engineer.
MO.TO.RI.ZA.DO, *adj.*, motorized.
MO.TO.RI.ZAR, *v.*, to motorize.
MO.TOR.NEI.RO, *s.m., Bras.*, motorman (professional who drives tram car).
MO.TOS.SER.RA, *s.f.*, chainsaw.
MO.TRIZ, *adj.*, motor, motive.
MOU.CO, *s.m.*, deaf person; *adj.*, deaf.
MOUN.TAIN-BIKE, *s.f.*, mountain bike.
MOU.RÃO, *s.m.*, pole, stake, post.
MOU.RE.JAR, *v.*, to work hard, to toil.
MOU.RIS.CO, *adj.*, Moorish.
MOU.RO, *s.m.*, Moor, Saracen; *adj.*, Moorish.
MOUSE, *s.m., Comp.*, mouse (pointing device).
MO.VE.DI.ÇO, *adj.*, movable, unstable.
MÓ.VEL, *s.m.*, piece of furniture; *adj.*, movable, moveable, changeable.
MO.VE.LEI.RO, *s.m., Bras.*, furniture dealer; furniture maker.
MO.VER, *v.*, to move, to put in motion, to advance, to progress.
MO.VI.DO, *adj.*, moved, impelled.
MO.VI.MEN.TA.ÇÃO, *s.f.*, movement, moving.
MO.VI.MEN.TA.DO, *adj.*, lively, busy, active.
MO.VI.MEN.TAR, *v.*, to move, to stir, to animate.
MO.VI.MEN.TO, *s.m.*, movement, motion, move, moving.
MO.VÍ.VEL, *adj.*, movable, moveable.
MP, *abrev.* of *Ministério Público*: Brazilian state government.
MPB, *abrev.* of *Música Popular Brasileira*: Popular Brazilian Music.
MU.AM.BA, *s.f.*, smuggling, theft, fraud.
MU.AM.BEI.RO, *s.m., Bras.*, smuggler.
MU.CO, *s.m.*, mucus, slime, phlegm.
MU.CO.SA, *s.f., Anat.*, mucous membrane.
MU.CO.SI.DA.DE, *s.f.*, mucosity; mucus.
MU.ÇUL.MA.NO, *adj., s.m.*, Mussulman, Moslem.
MU.DA, *s.f.*, change, shift, move, moving.
MU.DAN.ÇA, *s.f.*, change, alteration, move, substitution.
MU.DAR, *v.*, to change, to shift, to move, to exchange, to alter.
MU.DEZ, *s.f.*, muteness, dumbness.
MU.DO, *s.m.*, speechless, mute; *adj.*, speechless, voiceless, dumb, mute.
MU.GI.DO, *s.m.*, moo.

MU.GIR, *v.*, to moo.
MUI.TO, *adj.*, much, plenty, very, a good deal; *muitos*: many, a great many; *adv.*, very, most, much, too much.
MU.LA, *s.f.*, mule, she-hinny.
MU.LA.TA, *s.f.*, mulatto woman.
MU.LA.TO, *s.m.*, mulatto.
MU.LE.TA, *s.f.*, crutch, support.
MU.LHER, *s.f.*, woman, wife.
MU.LHE.RA.ÇA, **MU.LHE.RÃO**, *s.f.*, aumentative of *mulher*; *Bras., col.*, a very attractive woman.
MU.LHE.REN.GO, *s.m.*, skirt chaser, milksop; *adj.*, unmanly.
MU.LHE.RI.O, *s.m.*, women; group of women.
MUL.TA, *s.f.*, fine, penalty, forfeiture.
MUL.TAR, *v.*, to fine, to mulct.
MUL.TI.BI.LI.O.NÁ.RI.O, *s.m.*, person who has several billions; *adj.*, very wealthy.
MUL.TI.CO.LOR, *adj.*, multicoloured.
MUL.TI.CUL.TU.RAL, *adj.*, multicultural.
MUL.TI.DÃO, *s.f.*, multitude, crowd, throng.
MUL.TI.FA.CE.TA.DO, *adj.*, multifaceted.
MUL.TI.FO.CAL, *adj.*, having many focal points.
MUL.TI.FOR.ME, *adj.*, multiform.
MUL.TI.LA.TE.RAL, *adj.*, multilateral.
MUL.TI.MI.LI.O.NÁ.RIO, *s.m., adj.*, multimillionaire.
MUL.TI.NA.CI.O.NAL, *s.f.*, multinational (company); *adj.*, multinational.
MUL.TI.PAR.TI.DA.RIS.MO, *s.m.*, multipartyism.
MUL.TI.PLI.CA.ÇÃO, *s.f.*, multiplication, increase in number.
MUL.TI.PLI.CA.DOR, *s.m.*, multiplier, coefficient.
MUL.TI.PLI.CAR, *v.*, to multiply, to increase in number.
MUL.TI.PLI.CÁ.VEL, *adj.*, multipliable.
MUL.TI.PLI.CI.DA.DE, *s.f.*, multiplicity.
MÚL.TI.PLO, *adj.*, multiple.
MUL.TIR.RA.CI.AL, *adj.*, multiracial.
MUL.TI.U.SO, *adj.*, multipurpose.
MUL.TI.U.SU.Á.RI.O, *adj., Comp.*, multiuser.
MÚ.MIA, *s.f.*, mummy.
MUN.DA.NA, *s.f.*, dissolute, prostitute, whore.
MUN.DA.NO, *adj.*, mundane, worldly, earthly.
MUN.DI.AL, *adj.*, worldwide, general.
MUN.DO, *s.m.*, world, universe, earth, humanity.
MUN.GUN.ZÁ, **MUN.GU.ZÁ**, *s.m., Bras.*, a dish made out of corn grains cooked in sugar syrup and in milk.
MU.NHE.CA, *s.f.*, wrist; *Bras.*, hand.
MU.NI.ÇÃO, *s.f.*, munition, supplies.
MU.NI.CI.PAL, *adj.*, municipal.
MU.NI.CI.PA.LI.DA.DE, *s.f.*, municipality, town hall; local authority.
MU.NI.CI.PA.LI.ZAR, *v.*, to municipalize.
MU.NI.CÍ.PIO, *s.m.*, municipal district.
MU.NIR, *v.*, to munition, to provide, to supply.
MU.QUE, *s.m., Bras., gír.*, muscles, muscular force, brute force.
MU.QUI.RA.NA, *s. 2 gen., Bras., col.*, niggard, miser.
MU.RA.DA, *s.f., Náut.*, board, side of a ship; wall.
MU.RA.DO, *adj.*, walled (enclosed with a wall).
MU.RAL, *adj.*, mural.
MU.RA.LHA, *s.f.*, wall, rampart, battlement.
MU.RAR, *v.*, to wall, to immure, to enclose, to fence in.
MUR.CHAR, *v.*, to wilt, to dry up, to wither, to wizen.
MUR.CHO, *adj.*, wilted, faded, drooping, wizened.
MUR.MU.RAN.TE, *adj.*, murmuring, murmurous.

MURMURAR · 247 · MUXOXO

MUR.MU.RAR, *v.*, to murmur, to whisper, to mumble.
MUR.MU.RI.NHO, *s.m.*, murmuring (of voices); rustling (of leaves).
MUR.MU.RO.SO, *adj.*, murmurous.
MUR.MÚ.RIO, *s.m.*, murmur, murmur of many voices.
MU.RO, *s.m.*, wall, enclosure.
MUR.RO, *s.m.*, punch, blow, slug.
MU.SA, *s.f.*, muse.
MUS.CU.LA.ÇÃO, *s.f.*, musculation; bodybuilding.
MUS.CU.LAR, *adj.*, muscular.
MUS.CU.LA.TU.RA, *s.f.*, musculature, muscularity.
MÚS.CU.LO, *s.m.*, muscle, brawn.
MUS.CU.LO.SO, *adj.*, muscular, sinewy.
MU.SE.O.LO.GI.A, *s.f.*, museology.
MU.SE.O.LO.GIS.TA, *s. 2 gen.*, museologist.
MU.SE.Ó.LO.GO, *s.m.*, museologist.
MU.SEU, *s.m.*, museum.
MUS.GO, *s.m.*, moss.
MUS.GO.SO, *adj.*, mossy.
MÚ.SI.CA, *s.f.*, music, melody, harmony.
MU.SI.CA.DO, *adj.*, musical, set to music.
MU.SI.CAL, *adj.*, musical.
MU.SI.CA.LI.DA.DE, *s.f.*, musicality.

MU.SI.CAR, *v.*, to set to music; to sing, to chant.
MU.SI.CIS.TA, *s. 2 gen.*, musician; musicologist.
MÚ.SI.CO, *s.m.*, musician, artist, performer; *adj.*, musical, harmonious.
MU.SI.CO.LO.GI.A, *s.f., Mús.*, musicology.
MU.SI.CÓ.LO.GO, *s.m., Mús.*, musicologist.
MUS.SE, *s.f., Cul.*, mousse.
MUS.SE.LI.NA, *s.f.*, muslin.
MU.TA.BI.LI.DA.DE, *s.f.*, mutability.
MU.TA.ÇÃO, *s.f.*, mutation, change, alteration, variation.
MU.TÁ.VEL, *adj.*, mutable, changeable.
MU.TI.LA.ÇÃO, *s.f.*, mutilation.
MU.TI.LA.DO, *s.m.*, mutilated person, cripple; *adj.*, mutilated.
MU.TI.LAR, *v.*, to mutilate, to maim, to cripple, to disable.
MU.TI.RÃO, *s.m.*, joint effort.
MU.TIS.MO, *s.m.*, mutism, muteness.
MU.TRE.TA, *s.f., Bras., col.*, fraud, cheat.
MU.TU.A.MEN.TE, *adv.*, mutually.
MU.TU.Á.RIO, *s.m.*, borrower.
MÚ.TUO, *s.m.*, loan, insurance; *adj.*, mutual, reciprocal, interchangeable.
MU.XO.XO, *s.m.*, smack, kiss, caress.
MU.XO.XO, *s.m., Bras.*, tutting; smack.

N, *s.m.*, thirteenth letter of the Portuguese alphabet.
NA, *contr.* of the *art.* **A** with the *prep.* **IN**: in the.
NA.BA.BES.CO, *adj.*, rich, pompous, opulent.
NA.BO, *s.m.*, turnip.
NA.ÇÃO, *s.f.*, nation, country, land, state, people, folk.
NÁ.CAR, *s.m.*, nacre, mother-of-pearl.
NA.CA.RA.DO, *adj.*, nacreous, pearly.
NA.CA.RAR, *v.*, to make pearly; to redden, to make pink.
NA.CE.LA, *s.f.*, Aeron., the same that *nacele*.
NA.CE.LE, *s.f.*, Aeron., nacelle.
NA.CI.O.NAL, *adj.*, national, inlandish.
NA.CI.O.NA.LI.DA.DE, *s.f.*, nationality.
NA.CI.O.NA.LIS.MO, *s.m.*, nationalism.
NA.CI.O.NA.LIS.TA, *s. 2 gen.*, nationalist; *adj.*, nationalistic.
NA.CI.O.NA.LI.ZA.ÇÃO, *s.f.*, nationalization.
NA.CI.O.NA.LI.ZAR, *v.*, to nationalize, naturalize.
NA.CO, *s.m.*, large piece, lump, chop, portion.
NA.DA, *s.m.*, nothing, nil, nought, insignificance; *adv.*, nothing, not at all.
NA.DA-CONS.TA, *s.m.*, deed of indemnity.
NA.DA.DEI.RA, *s.f.*, fin, flipper.
NA.DA.DOR, *s.m.*, swimmer; *adj.*, swimming.
NA.DAN.TE, *adj.*, natant, swimming.
NA.DAR, *v.*, to swim, to float, to wallow.
NÁ.DE.GA, *s.f.*, buttock, rump, backside, crupper.
NA.DE.GU.DO, *adj.*, having large buttocks.
NA.DI.NHA, *s.m.*, little, insignificance, trifle; *adv.*, absolutely nothing.
NAF.TA, *s.f.*, Quím., naphtha.
NAF.TA.LI.NA, *s.f.*, Quím., naphtalin, naphtalene.
NAF.TOL, *s.m.*, Quím., naphthol.
NÁI.LON, *s.m.*, nylon.
NAI.PE, *s.m.*, suit.
NA.MO.RA.DA, *s.f.*, sweetheart, ladylove, flame.
NA.MO.RA.DEI.RA, *adj.*, flirtatious, coquettish.
NA.MO.RA.DO, *s.m.*, sweetheart, boyfriend, lover.
NA.MO.RA.DOR, *s.m.*, flirter, gallant; *adj.*, flirtatious.
NA.MO.RAR, *v.*, to court, to go out with, to make love, to woo.
NA.MO.RI.CAR, *v.*, to flirt.
NA.MO.RI.CO, *s.m.*, flirt, flirtation.
NA.MO.RO, *s.m.*, courtship, going out, love-making, wooing.
NA.NA, *s.f.*, fam., lullaby.
NA.NAR, *v.*, fam., to sleep (children).
NA.NI.CO, *s.m.*, dwarfish, stunted.
NA.NO.CE.FA.LI.A, *s.f.*, Med., microcephaly, microcephalia.
NA.NO.CE.FÁ.LI.CO, *adj.*, Med., microcephalous.
NA.NÔ.ME.TRO, *s.m.*, nanometer.
NA.NO.TEC.NO.LO.GI.A, *s.f.*, nanotechnology.
NAN.QUIM, *s.m.*, US India ink, UK Indian ink (or Chinese ink).
NÃO, *s.m.*, no, refusal, denial; *adv.*, no, not.
NÃO A.GRES.SÃO, *adj.*, non-aggression.
NÃO A.LI.NHA.DO, *adj.*, non-aligned.
NÃO GO.VER.NA.MEN.TAL, *adj.*, non-governmental.
NÃO IN.TER.VEN.ÇÃO, *adj.*, non-intervention.
NÃO-ME-TO.QUES, *s.m., 2 num., Bot.*, touch-me-not.
NA.PA, *s.f.*, napa leather.
NA.QUE.LA, *contr.* of the *prep.* **EM** and the *pron.* **AQUELA**: at that.
NA.QUE.LE, *contr.* of the *prep.* **EM** and the *pron.* **AQUELE**: in that, thereat, at that, therein, on that.
NA.QUI.LO, *contr.* of the *prep.* **EM** and the *pron.* **AQUILO**: on that.
NAR.CI.SIS.MO, *s.m.*, narcissism.
NAR.CI.SIS.TA, *s. 2 gen.*, narcissist; *adj.*, narcissistic.
NAR.CI.SO, *s.m.*, narcissus.
NAR.CO.LEP.SI.A, *s.f., Med.*, narcolepsy.
NAR.CO.SE, *s.f., Med.*, narcosis.
NAR.CÓ.TI.CO, *s.m.*, narcotic, drug, stuff; *adj.*, narcotic.
NAR.CO.TI.ZA.ÇÃO, *s.f.*, narcotization.
NAR.CO.TI.ZAR, *v.*, to narcotize, to dope, to drug.
NAR.CO.TRÁ.FI.CO, *s.m.*, drug traffic.
NAR.GUI.LÉ, *s.m.*, narghile, hookah.
NA.RI.GÃO, *s.m.*, a big nose.
NA.RI.GU.DO, *adj.*, with a large nose.
NA.RI.NA, *s.f.*, nostril; Zool., blowhole.
NA.RIZ, *s.f.*, nose; smeller, pecker.
NAR.RA.ÇÃO, *s.f.*, narration, narrative, narrating.
NAR.RA.DO, *s.m.*, report; *adj.*, reported, told.
NAR.RA.DOR, *s.m.*, narrator, story-teller; *adj.*, narrative.
NAR.RAR, *v.*, to narrate, to relate, to report, to tell.
NAR.RA.TI.VA, *s.f.*, narrative, narration.
NAR.RA.TI.VO, *adj.*, narrative, descriptive.
NAS, *contr.* of the *prep.* **EM** and the definite article (in plural) **AS**: at the.
NASA, *s.f., abrev.* of National Aeronautics and Space Administration: NASA.
NA.SAL, *adj.*, nasal.
NA.SA.LA.ÇÃO, *s.f.*, nasalization.
NA.SA.LA.DO, *adj.*, nasal.
NA.SA.LAR, *v.*, to nasalize.
NA.SA.LI.DA.DE, *s.f.*, nasality.
NAS.CE.DOU.RO, *s.m.*, birthplace.
NAS.CEN.ÇA, *s.f.*, birth, origin, source, nascency.
NAS.CEN.TE, *s.f.*, fountain, source, origin, beggining, rise, spring; *adj.*, nascent, being born.
NAS.CER, *s.m.*, rising; *v.*, to be born, to see the light, to come to light.
NAS.CI.DO, *adj.*, born.
NAS.CI.MEN.TO, *s.m.*, birth, origin, source, nativity.
NAS.CI.TU.RO, *s.m.*, unborn child; *adj.*, unborn.
NA.TA, *s.f.*, cream, skim.
NA.TA.ÇÃO, *s.f.*, swimming, natation.
NA.TAL, *s.m.*, Christmas, birthday; *adj.*, native, natal.
NA.TA.LÍ.CIO, *s.m.*, natal; *aniversário* ~: birthday.

NATALIDADE ·· 249 ·· NELA

NA.TA.LI.DA.DE, *s.f.*, natality, birth.
NA.TA.LI.NO, *adj.*, Christmas; *festas natalinas*: Christmas celebrations.
NA.TI.MOR.TO, *adj.*, *s.m.*, stillborn.
NA.TI.VI.DA.DE, *s.f.*, nativity, birth.
NA.TI.VIS.TA, *s. 2 gen.*, nativist; *adj.*, nativistic.
NA.TI.VO, *s.m.*, native, homeborn; *adj.*, native, indigenous, national.
NA.TO, *adj.*, born, native, alive, innate.
NA.TU.RAL, *adj.*, natural, nature, genuine, spontaneous.
NA.TU.RA.LI.DA.DE, *s.f.*, naturalness, simplicity.
NA.TU.RA.LIS.MO, *s.m.*, naturalism.
NA.TU.RA.LIS.TA, *s. 2 gen.*, naturalist; *adj.*, naturalistic.
NA.TU.RA.LI.ZA.ÇÃO, *s.f.*, naturalization.
NA.TU.RA.LI.ZA.DO, *s.m.*, naturalized citizen; *adj.*, naturalized.
NA.TU.RA.LI.ZAR, *v.*, to naturalize, to nationalize, to familiarize.
NA.TU.RA.LI.ZÁ.VE, *adj.*, that may be naturalized.
NA.TU.RAL.MEN.TE, *adv.*, naturally.
NA.TU.RE.BA, *s. 2 gen., col.*, health freak.
NA.TU.RE.ZA, *s.f.*, nature, forces of nature, character.
NA.TU.RE.ZA-MOR.TA, *s.f.*, still life.
NAU, *s.f., Lit.*, ship.
NAU.FRA.GA.DO, *adj.*, (ship) wrecked.
NAU.FRA.GAN.TE, *s. 2 gen.*, shipwrecked person; *adj.*, shipwrecked.
NAU.FRA.GAR, *v.*, to wreck, to shipwreck, to fail.
NÁU.FRÁ.GIO, *s.m.*, wreck, failure, shipwreck, failure.
NÁU.FRA.GO, *s.m.*, shipwrecked person.
NÁU.SEA, *s.f.*, nausea, sickness, repugnance, qualm.
NAU.SE.A.BUN.DO, *adj.*, nauseous, nauseating; *fig.*, sickening.
NAU.SE.A.DO, *adj.*, nauseated, sick.
NAU.SE.AN.TE, *adj.*, the same that *nauseabundo*: nauseous.
NAU.SE.AR, *v.*, to nauseate, to sicken, to repugnate, to disgust.
NÁU.TI.CA, *s.f.*, nautics, navigation.
NÁU.TI.CO, *adj.*, nautical, marine, navigational, naval.
NA.VAL, *adj.*, naval, marine, maritime.
NA.VA.LHA, *s.f.*, razor.
NA.VA.LHA.DA, *s.f.*, stroke with a razor, stab.
NA.VA.LHAR, *v.*, to wound or slash with a razor.
NA.VE, *s.f., Arquit.*, nave; *Náut.*, ship; ~ *espacial*: spaceship.
NA.VE.GA.ÇÃO, *s.f.*, navigation, shipping, sailing.
NA.VE.GA.DOR, *s.m.*, navigator.
NA.VE.GAN.TE, *s. 2 gen.*, navigator.
NA.VE.GAR, *v.*, to navigate, to sail, to travel by sea.
NA.VE.GÁ.VEL, *adj.*, navigable.
NA.VI.O, *s.m.*, ship, vessel, craft, boat.
NA.VI.O-ES.CO.LA, *s.m.*, training ship.
NA.VI.O-PE.TRO.LEI.RO, *s.m., Náut.*, oil tanker.
NA.VI.O-TAN.QUE, *s.m.*, tank steamer; tanker.
NA.ZA.RE.NO, *s.m.*, Nazarene (inhabitant of Nazareth); *o Nazareno*: the Christ; *adj.*, Nazarene.
NA.ZI.FAS.CIS.MO, *s.m.*, Nazi-Fascism.
NA.ZI.FAS.CIS.TA, *adj.*, Nazi-Fascist.
NA.ZIS.MO, *s.m.*, Nazism.
NA.ZIS.TA, *s. 2 gen.*, Nazi; *adj.*, Nazi.
NE.BLI.NA, *s.f.*, mist, fog, haze, gauze.
NE.BU.LI.ZAR, *v.*, to nebulize.
NE.BU.LO.SA, *s.f., Astron.*, nebula.

NE.BU.LO.SI.DA.DE, *s.f.*, nebulosity, mistiness.
NE.BU.LO.SO, *adj.*, misty, foggy, hazy, vaporous.
NÉ.CES.SAIRE, *s.f., Fr.*, sponge bag.
NE.CES.SA.RI.A.MEN.TE, *adv.*, necessarily.
NE.CES.SÁ.RIO, *adj.*, necessary, indispensable, exigent.
NE.CES.SI.DA.DE, *s.f.*, necessity, necessariness, must, need, poverty.
NE.CES.SI.TA.DO, *s.m.*, needer, indigent person; *adj.*, necessitous; very poor; ~ *de*: in need (of).
NE.CES.SI.TAR, *v.*, to need, to necessitate, to demand.
NE.CRO.FO.BI.A, *s.f., Psic.*, necrophobia.
NE.CRO.FÓ.BI.CO, *adj., Psic.*, necrophobic.
NE.CRO.LO.GI.A, *s.f.*, necrology.
NE.CRO.LÓ.GI.CO, *adj.*, necrological, necrologic.
NE.CRO.LÓ.GI.O, *s.m.*, obituary.
NE.CRÓ.PO.LE, *s.f.*, necropolis, cemetery.
NE.CROP.SI.A, *s.f.*, necropsy, autopsy.
NE.CRO.TÉ.RIO, *s.m.*, mortuary, morgue.
NÉC.TAR, *s.m.*, nectar.
NEC.TA.RI.NA, *s.f., Bot.*, nectarine.
NE.FAN.DO, *adj.*, nefarious, abominable.
NE.FAS.TO, *adj.*, disastrous, disgraceful, tragic.
NE.FE.LO.ME.TRI.A, *s.f., Quím.*, nephelometry.
NE.FRAL.GI.A, *s.f., Med.*, nephralgia.
NE.FRÁL.GI.CO, *adj., Med.*, nephralgic.
NE.FRI.TE, *s.f., Med.*, nephritis.
NE.FRO.LO.GI.A, *s.f., Med.*, nephrology.
NE.FRO.LO.GIS.TA, *s. 2 gen., Med.*, nephrologist.
NE.GA.ÇÃO, *s.f.*, negation, negative, denial.
NE.GA.CE.AR, *v.*, to entice, to shake; to refuse; to decoy; to deceive; to provoke.
NE.GAR, *v.*, to deny, to say no, to negate, to contradict.
NE.GA.TI.VA, *s.f.*, negative, refusal.
NE.GA.TI.VI.DA.DE, *s.f.*, negativity, negativeness.
NE.GA.TI.VIS.MO, *s.m.*, negativism.
NE.GA.TI.VIS.TA, *s. 2 gen.*, negativist; *adj.*, negativistic.
NE.GA.TI.VO, *s.m., Fot.*, negative; *adj.*, negative (not positive).
NÉ.GLI.GÉ, *s.m., Fr.*, negligé, negligee.
NE.GLI.GÊN.CIA, *s.f.*, negligence, neglect, omit.
NE.GLI.GEN.CI.A.DO, *adj.*, neglected.
NE.GLI.GEN.CI.AR, *v.*, to neglect, to disregard, to omit.
NE.GLI.GEN.TE, *adj., s. 2 gen.*, negligent, neglectful, lazy; lax.
NEGO, *s.m., fam.*, mate, black.
NE.GO.CI.A.BI.LI.DA.DE, *s.f.*, negotiability.
NE.GO.CI.A.ÇÃO, *s.f.*, negotiation, transaction, deal.
NE.GO.CI.A.DOR, *s.m.*, negotiator; *adj.*, negotiating.
NE.GO.CI.AN.TE, *s. 2 gen.*, merchant, merchandiser, trader, businessman.
NE.GO.CI.AR, *v.*, to negotiate, to trade in, to do business.
NE.GO.CI.A.TA, *s.f.*, suspicious business; swindle.
NE.GO.CI.Á.VEL, *adj.*, negotiable.
NE.GÓ.CIO, *s.m.*, business, trade, commerce, transaction.
NE.GRI.DÃO, *s.f.*, blackness, obscurity.
NE.GRA, *s.f.*, feminine of *negro*: negress.
NE.GRI.TO, *s.m., Tip.*, boldface, bold type; *adj.*, bold-faced.
NE.GRI.TU.DE, *s.f.*, black awareness.
NE.GRO, *s.m.*, Negro, black; *adj.*, black, dark, negro, African.
NE.GRU.ME, *s.m.*, darkness, obscurity.
NE.GRU.RA, *s.f.*, blackness.
NE.LA, *contr.* of the *prep.* **EM** with the *pron.* **ELA**: in her, on

NELE — 250 — NÍVEL

her, in it, on it.

NE.LE, *contr.* of the *prep.* **EM** with the *pron.* **ELE**: in him, on him, in it, on it.

NEM, *conj.*, neither, nor, not even.

NE.NÊ, *s.m.*, baby, newborn.

NE.NHUM, *adj.*, null, void, any, neither; *adv.*, none, nobody, not any.

NE.NÚ.FAR, *s.m., Bot.*, nenuphar, nuphar, water-lily.

NE.O.CLÁS.SI.CO, *adj.*, neoclassic.

NE.O.DAR.WI.NIS.MO, *s.m., Biol.*, Neo-Darwinism.

NE.O.FAS.CIS.MO, *s.m.*, Neofascism.

NE.O.FAS.CIS.TA, *s. 2 gen.*, Neofascist; *adj.*, Neofascist.

NE.Ó.FI.TO, *s.m.*, neophite, proselite, novice.

NE.O.LA.TI.NO, *adj., s.m.*, Neolatin.

NE.O.LI.BE.RAL, *s. 2 gen.*, neoliberal; *adj.*, neoliberal.

NE.O.LI.BE.RA.LIS.MO, *s.m.*, neoliberalismo.

NE.O.LÍ.TI.CO, *adj.*, the Neolithic period; *adj.*, Neolithic.

NE.O.LO.GIS.MO, *s.m.*, neologism.

NÉ.ON, NE.Ô.NI.O, *s.m.*, neon.

NE.O.NA.ZIS.MO, *s.m.*, neo-Nazism.

NE.O.NA.ZIS.TA, *s. 2 gen., Pol.*, neo-Nazi; *adj.*, neo-Nazi.

NE.OR.RE.A.LIS.MO, *s.m., Art.*, neorealism.

NE.O.ZE.LAN.DÊS, *s.m.*, New Zealander; *adj.*, New Zealand.

NE.PAL, *s.*, Nepal.

NE.PA.LÊS, *s.m., adj.*, Nepalese, Nepali.

NE.PO.TIS.MO, *s.m.*, nepotism.

NER.VO, *s.m.*, nerve.

NER.VO.SI.DA.DE, *s.f.*, nervousness.

NER.VO.SIS.MO, *s.m.*, nerves, nervousness, excitability.

NER.VO.SO, *adj.*, nervous, energetic, vigorous, irritable, nervy.

NER.VU.RA, *s.f.*, nervure, rib; *Bot.*, vein.

NÉS.CI.O, *s.m.*, stupid person; *adj.*, foolish, stupid.

NES.GA, *s.f.*, gore, piece; small.

NES.SA, *contr.* of the *prep.* **EM** with the *pron.* **ESSA**: in that, on that; **NESSAS** (*pl.*): in those, on those.

NES.SE, *contr.* of the *prep.* **EM** with the *pron.* **ESSE**: in that, on that; **NESSES** (*pl.*): in those, on those.

NES.TA, *contr.* of the *prep.* **EM** with the *pron.* **ESTA**: in this, on this; **NESTAS** (*pl.*): in these, on these.

NES.TE, *contr.* of the *prep.* **EM** with the *pron.* **ESTE**: in this, on this; **NESTES** (*pl.*): in these, on these.

NET, *s.f., Comp.*, net.

NE.TA, *s.f.*, granddaughter.

NE.TO, *s.m.*, grandson.

NE.TU.NI.A.NO, *adj.*, Neptunian.

NE.TÚ.NI.O, *s.m., Quím.*, neptunium.

NE.TU.NO, *s.m., Mit., Astron.*, Neptune.

NEU.RAL.GI.A, *s.f., Med.*, neuralgia.

NEU.RAS.TE.NI.A, *s.f.*, neurasthenia.

NEU.RAS.TÊ.NI.CO, *adj., Med.*, neurasthenic.

NEU.RO.CI.RUR.GI.A, *s.f., Med.*, neurosurgery.

NEU.RO.CI.RUR.GI.ÃO, *s.m., Med.*, neurosurgeon.

NEU.RO.LIN.GUIS.TA, *s. 2 gen., Ling.*, neurolinguist.

NEU.RO.LO.GI.A, *s.f.*, neurology.

NEU.RO.LÓ.GI.CO, *adj., Med.*, neurologic.

NEU.RO.LO.GIS.TA, *s. 2 gen., Med.*, neurologist.

NEU.RO.SE, *s.f.*, neurosis.

NEU.RÓ.TI.CO, *adj.*, neurotic.

NEU.RO.TRANS.MIS.SOR, *s.m., Med.*, neurotransmitter.

NEU.RO.VE.GE.TA.TI.VO, *adj.*, neurovegetative.

NEU.TRA.LI.DA.DE, *s.f.*, neutrality, impartiality.

NEU.TRA.LI.ZA.DOR, *s.m.*, neutralizer.

NEU.TRA.LI.ZAR, *v.*, to neutralize; to kill, to destroy.

NEU.TRO, *s.m.*, neuter; *adj.*, neuter, neutral, impartial.

NÊU.TRON, *s.m., Fis.*, neutron (Nuclear physics).

NE.VA.DA, *s.f.*, snow-fall.

NE.VA.DO, *adj.*, snow-covered; snow-white.

NE.VAR, *v.*, to snow, to cover with snow.

NE.VAS.CA, *s.f.*, snow-storm, blizzard.

NE.VE, *s.f.*, snow.

NE.VIS.CAR, *v.*, to snow slightly.

NÉ.VOA, *s.f.*, fog, mist.

NE.VO.EI.RO, *s.m.*, fog, mist.

NE.VRAL.GI.A, *s.f.*, neuralgia.

NE.VRÁL.GI.CO, *adj., Med.*, neuralgic.

NE.XO, *s.m.*, connection, nexus, link, tie.

NHEM-NHEM-NHEM, *s.m., Bras., col.*, grumbling; chattering, gossip.

NHO.QUE, *s.m., It., Cul.*, gnocchi.

NI.CA.RÁ.GUA, *s.*, Nicaragua.

NI.CA.RA.GUEN.SE, *s. 2 gen., adj.*, Nicaraguan.

NI.CHO, *s.m.*, niche.

NICK, *s.m., Comp.*, nickname.

NI.CO.TI.NA, *s.f.*, nicotine.

NI.DI.FI.CAR, *v.*, to nidificate, to nidify.

NI.GÉ.RI.A, *s.*, Nigeria.

NI.GE.RI.A.NO, *s.m., adj.*, Nigerian.

NI.I.LIS.MO, *s.m.*, nihilism.

NI.I.LIS.TA, *s. 2 gen.*, nihilist.

NI.LO, *s.m.*, Nilo (river).

NI.LO, *adj., Bras.*, white-headed (cattle).

NIM.BO, *s.m., Met.*, nimbus (rain-cloud).

NI.NAR, *v.*, to lull to sleep.

NIN.FA, *s.f.*, nymph.

NIN.FE.TA, *s.f.*, nymphet.

NIN.FO.MA.NI.A, *s.f.*, nymphomania.

NIN.FO.MA.NÍ.A.CA, *adj., Med.*, nymphomaniac.

NIN.GUÉM, *pron.*, nobody, no one, no man, no person.

NI.NHA.DA, *s.f.*, nide, clutch, covery.

NI.NHA.RI.A, *s.f.*, trifle, insignificance.

NI.NHO, *s.m.*, nest, hole, den.

NI.PO-BRA.SI.LEI.RO, *s.m.*, a person of Japanese and Brazilian origin; *adj.*, relating to Japan and Brazil.

NI.PÔ.NI.CO, *adj., s.m.*, Japanese.

NÍ.QUEL, *s.m.*, nickel.

NI.QUE.LAR, *v.*, to nickel.

NIR.VA.NA, *s.m., Rel.*, nirvana.

NIS.SEI, NI.SEI, *s. 2 gen., Jap.*, nisei.

NIS.SO, *contr.* of the *prep.* **EM** with the *pron.* **ISSO**: at that, in that, on that, thereat, herein, thereon, thereby.

NIS.TO, *contr.* of the *prep.* **EM** with the *pron.* **ISTO**: at this, in this, on this, hereat, herein, hereon, hereby.

NI.TI.DEZ, *s.f.*, clearness, distinctness, brightness, brilliance.

NI.TI.DA.MEN.TE, *adv.*, clearly. ele escreve muito nitidamente/ he writes a very clear hand.

NÍ.TI.DO, *adj.*, clear, sharp, explicit, neat, fair.

NI.TRA.TO, *s.m., Quím.*, nitrate.

NÍ.TRI.CO, *adj., Quím.*, nitric.

NI.TRI.FI.CA.ÇÃO, *s.f., Quím.*, nitrification.

NI.TRO.GÊ.NIO, *s.m., Quím.*, azote, nitrogen.

NI.TRO.GLI.CE.RI.NA, *s.f., Quím.*, nitroglycerin(e).

NÍ.VEL, *s.m.*, level; situation; *nível social*: social level.

NIVELAMENTO ·· 251 ·· NOTORIEDADE

NI.VE.LA.MEN.TO, *s.m.*, levelling, grading.
NI.VE.LAR, *v.*, to level, to grade, to equalize.
NO, *contr.* of the *prep.* **EM** and the article **O**: in the, on the.
NO, *pron.*, him (enclitic form of the *pron.* **O** after a nasal sound); *respeitam-no*: they respect him.
NO, *abrev.* of *Noroeste*: NW (northwest).
NÓ, *s.m.*, node, knot; problem, difficulty.
NO.BI.LI.Á.RI.O, *s.m.*, peerage book; *adj.*, nobiliary.
NO.BI.LI.AR.QUI.A, *s.f.*, rule by bobles.
NO.BI.LÍS.SI.MO, *adj.*, superlative of *nobre*: most noble.
NO.BI.LI.TAR, *v.*, to ennoble.
NO.BRE, *s.m.*, noble, nobleman, aristocrat; *adj.*, noble, generous, gallant.
NO.BRE.ZA, *s.f.*, nobility, aristocracy, nobleness.
NO.ÇÃO, *s.f.*, notion, conception, impression, idea.
NO.CAU.TE, *s.m.*, knockout.
NO.CAU.TE.AR, *v.*, *Esp.*, to knock-out.
NO.CEN.TE, *adj.*, harmful, noxious.
NO.CI.O.NAL, *adj.*, notional.
NO.CI.VI.DA.DE, *s.f.*, noxiousness, harmfulness.
NO.CI.VO, *adj.*, harmful, bad, noxious, ruinous.
NOC.TÂM.BU.LO, *s.m.*, *Med.*, noctambulist; *adj.*, noctambulous.
NOC.TÍ.VA.GO, *s.m.*, night-walker; *adj.*, noctivagant, noctivagous.
NO.DAL, *adj.*, nodal.
NÓ.DOA, *s.f.*, blot, spot, stain, mark, blur, fleck.
NO.DO.AR, *v.*, to spot, to stain.
NO.DO.SI.DA.DE, *s.f.*, nodosity, knottiness.
NO.DO.SO, *adj.*, nodose, knotty.
NÓ.DU.LO, *s.m.*, nodule, node, knot.
NO.GUEI.RA, *s.f.*, walnut tree.
NO.GUEI.RAL, *s.m.*, walnut plantation.
NOI.TA.DA, *s.f.*, vigil, watch, night's period.
NOI.TE, *s.f.*, night, darkness, obscurity.
NOI.TE.ZI.NHA, *s.f.*, the same that *noitinha*.
NOI.TI.NHA, *s.f.*, late afternoon, nightfall, dusk.
NOI.VA, *s.f.*, bride, fiancée.
NOI.VA.DO, *s.m.*, engagement, betrothal.
NOI.VAR, *v.*, to become engaged, to court, to woo.
NOI.VO, *s.m.*, fiancé, bridegroom.
NO.JA.DO, *adj.*, disgustful, disgusted, sad.
NO.JEI.RA, *s.f.*, filth, disgusting.
NO.JEN.TO, *adj.*, nauseating, sickening, repulsive.
NO.JO, *s.m.*, nausea, disgust, loathing, qualm, repugnance.
NO.JO.SO, *adj.*, disgustful, loathsome, sickening.
NÔ.MA.DE, *s. 2 gen.*, nomad; *adj.*, nomad, nomadic, errant.
NO.MA.DIS.MO, *s.m.*, nomadism.
NO.ME, *s.m.*, name, designation, denomination, noun, nick-name, reputation, renown.
NO.ME.A.ÇÃO, *s.f.*, nomination, appointment.
NO.ME.A.DA, *s.f.*, reputation, renown, fame.
NO.ME.A.DA.MEN.TE, *adv.*, namely.
NO.ME.A.DO, *adj.*, nominated.
NO.ME.AR, *v.*, to name, to denominate, to call, to designate.
NO.MEN.CLA.TU.RA, *s.f.*, nomenclature.
NO.ME PRÓ.PRI.O, *s.m.*, *Gram.*, proper noun.
NO.MI.NA.ÇÃO, *s.f.*, coining or giving a name to, denomination.
NO.MI.NAL, *adj.*, nominal.
NO.MI.NAL.MEN.TE, *adv.*, nominally.
NO.MI.NA.TI.VO, *s.m.*, nominative.

NO.NA.DA, *s.f.*, trifle, bagatelle.
NO.NA.GE.NÁ.RIO, *adj.*, *s.m.*, nonagenarian.
NO.NA.GÉ.SI.MO, *num.*, ninetieth.
NO.NO, *num.*, ninth.
NO.RA, *s.f.*, daughter-in-law.
NOR.DES.TE, *s.m.*, northeast; *adj.*, northeastern.
NOR.DES.TI.NO, *s.m.*, Northeasterner (inhabitant of north-eastern Brazil); *adj.*, Northeastern.
NÓR.DI.CO, *adj.*, *s.m.*, Nordic.
NOR.MA, *s.f.*, norm, principle, rule, direction, precept.
NOR.MAL, *adj.*, normal, regular, natural.
NOR.MA.LI.DA.DE, *s.f.*, normality, normalness.
NOR.MA.LIS.TA, *s. 2 gen.*, student of a normal school; *adj.*, said of student of a normal school.
NOR.MA.LI.ZA.ÇÃO, *s.f.*, normalization.
NOR.MA.LI.ZAR, *v.*, to normalize, to adjust.
NOR.MAL.MEN.TE, *adv.*, normally, usually, as expected.
NOR.MA.TI.VO, *adj.*, normative, prescriptive.
NO.RO.ES.TE, *s.m.*, northwest; *adj.*, north-west.
NOR.TE, *s.m.*, north, northward; *adj.*, north, northern.
NOR.TE.A.DOR, *adj.*, guiding, directing.
NOR.TE.A.MEN.TO, *s.m.*, guidance, direction.
NOR.TE-A.ME.RI.CA.NO, *s.m.*, *adj.*, North American.
NOR.TE.AR, *v.*, to guide, to direct, to lead, to indicate the north.
NOR.TIS.TA, *s. 2 gen.*, northerner; *adj.*, northern.
NO.RU.E.GA, *s.*, Norway.
NO.RU.E.GUÊS, *adj.*, *s.m.*, Norwegian.
NOS, *contr. prep.* **EM** with *art. m. pl.* **OS**: at the, in the, on the.
NÓS, *pron.*, we; us.
NO.SO.CÔ.MIO, *s.m.*, hospital.
NO.SO.FO.BI.A, *s.f.*, *Med.*, nosophobia.
NO.SÓ.FO.BO, *s.m.*, *Med.*, nosophobe.
NOS.SO, *pron.*, our, ours.
NOS.TAL.GI.A, *s.f.*, homesickness, nostalgia.
NOS.TÁL.GI.CO, *adj.*, nostalgic, homesick.
NO.TA, *s.f.*, note, reminder, bill, account, annotation, chit.
NO.TA.BI.LI.DA.DE, *s.f.*, notability.
NO.TA.BI.LI.ZAR, *v.*, to distinguish; *notabilizar-se*: to become notable.
NO.TA.ÇÃO, *s.f.*, notation.
NO.TA.DA.MEN.TE, *adv.*, notedly.
NO.TAR, *v.*, to notice, to observe, to note, to remark.
NO.TÁ.RIO, *s.m.*, notary.
NO.TÁ.VEL, *adj.*, notable.
NOTE.BOOK, *s.m.*, *Comp.*, notebook.
NO.TÍ.CIA, *s.f.*, news, information, report, tidings.
NO.TI.CI.A.DOR, *s.m.*, informer; *adj.*, informative.
NO.TI.CI.AR, *v.*, to inform, to announce, to publish, to advertise.
NO.TI.CI.Á.RIO, *s.m.*, news, news service.
NO.TI.CI.A.RIS.TA, *s. 2 gen.*, reporter, news writer.
NO.TI.CI.O.SO, *adj.*, news, informative.
NO.TI.FI.CA.ÇÃO, *s.f.*, notification.
NO.TI.FI.CA.DOR, *s.m.*, notifier; *adj.*, notifying.
NO.TI.FI.CAR, *v.*, to notify, to inform, to announce, to intimate, to warn.
NO.TI.FI.CA.TI.VO, *adj.*, informative, that notifies.
NO.TI.FI.CÁ.VEL, *adj.*, notifiable.
NO.TÍ.VA.GO, *s.m.*, *adj.*, the same that *noctívago*.
NO.TO.RI.E.DA.DE, *s.f.*, notoriety, notoriousness, publicity.

NOTÓRIO ··252·· NUVEM

NO.TÓ.RIO, *adj.*, notorious, public.
NO.TUR.NO, *adj.*, nocturnal, nightly.
NOU.TRO, *contr. prep.* EM with indefinite pronoun **OUTRO**; ~ *dia*: another day.
NO.VAS, *s.f., pl.*, news, novelty; *boas novas*: good news.
NO.VA-I.OR.QUI.NO, *s.m.*, New Yorker; *adj.*, New York.
NO.VA.MEN.TE, *adv.*, again, newly, over and again.
NO.VA.TO, *s.m.*, beginner, apprentice, newcomer, rookie, freshman; *adj.*, inexperienced, raw.
NO.VA YORK, *s.*, New York.
NO.VA ZE.LÂN.DI.A, *s.*, New Zealand.
NO.VE, *num.*, nine.
NO.VE.CEN.TOS, *num.*, nine hundred.
NO.VE-HO.RAS, *s.f., pl., col., fam.*, airs, ceremonies; fussy, fancy.
NO.VEL, *adj.*, new, beginning; inexperienced.
NO.VE.LA, *s.f.*, novel, soap opera, tale, story.
NO.VE.LES.CO, *adj.*, novelistic; *pej.*, soppy.
NO.VE.LIS.TA, *s. 2 gen.*, novelist, a soap-opera writer.
NO.VE.LO, *s.m.*, ball of yarn.
NO.VEM.BRO, *s.m.*, November.
NO.VE.NA, *s.f.*, novena, space of nine days.
NO.VE.NAL, *adj.*, referring to a novena.
NO.VEN.TA, *num.*, ninety.
NO.VI.CI.A.DO, *s.m., Rel.*, novitiate.
NO.VI.CI.AR, *v., Rel.*, to be a novice.
NO.VI.ÇO, *s.m.*, begginer, novice, neophyte.
NO.VI.DA.DE, *s.f.*, newness, recentness, novelty, news.
NO.VI.DA.DEI.RO, *s.m.*, who likes news; newsmonger, gossiper.
NO.VI.LHA, *s.f.*, heifer.
NO.VI.LHO, *s.m.*, bullock, steer.
NO.VO, *adj.*, young, new, recent, fresh, novel, green.
NO.VO-RI.CO, *s.m.*, nouveau riche.
NOZ, *s.f.*, nut, walnut.
NOZ-MOS.CA.DA, *s.f.*, nutmeg.
NU, *s.m.*, nude, *adj.*, nude, bare, naked, undressed, uncovered.
NU.AN.ÇA, *s.f.*, nuance, shade.
NU.BEN.TE, *s. 2 gen.*, betrothed; *adj.*, betrothed.
NÚ.BIL, *adj.*, marriageable, nubile.
NU.BI.LAR, *s.m.*, wheat barn.
NU.BI.LI.DA.DE, *s.f.*, marriageability, nubility.
NU.BI.LO.SO, *adj.*, cloudy, foggy.
NU.BLA.DO, *adj.*, cloudy, dark, obscure, somber, skyless.
NU.BLAR, *v.*, to cloud, to darken, to overcloud, to obscure, to shadow.
NU.BLO.SO, *adj.*, cloudy; *fig.*, gloomy.
NU.CA, *s.f.*, nape, scruff, neck.
NU.CÍ.FRA.GO, *adj.*, nut-cracking.
NU.CÍ.VO.RO, *adj.*, nucivorous (nut-eating).
NU.CLE.A.DO, *adj.*, nucleated.

NU.CLE.AL, *adj.*, nuclear.
NU.CLE.AR, *adj.*, nuclear, *v.*, to nucleate.
NÚ.CLEO, *s.m.*, nucleous, center.
NU.CLÉ.O.LO, *s.m.*, nucleolus.
NU.DEZ, *s.f.*, nakedness, nudity, bareness.
NU.DIS.MO, *s.m.*, nudism.
NU.DIS.TA, *s. 2 gen.*, nudist.
NU.LI.DA.DE, *s.f.*, nullity, invalidity, voidness.
NU.LO, *adj.*, null, void, zero, none, inept.
NUM, *contr.* of the *prep.* EM and UM (masculine): at a (one), in a (one).
NU.MA, *contr.* of the *prep.* EM and UMA (feminine): at a (one), in a (one).
NU.ME.RA.ÇÃO, *s.m.*, numbering, numeration.
NU.ME.RA.DO, *adj.*, numbered; in numerical order.
NU.ME.RA.DOR, *s.m.*, numerator; *adj.*, numerative.
NU.ME.RAL, *s.m.*, numeral, *adj.*, numeric, numeral.
NU.ME.RAR, *v.*, to number, to enumerate, to expose.
NU.ME.RÁ.RI.O, *s.m.*, money, cash; *adj.*, nummary.
NU.ME.RÁ.VEL, *adj.*, numerable.
NU.ME.RI.CA.MEN.TE, *adv.*, numerically.
NU.MÉ.RI.CO, *adj.*, numeric, numerical.
NÚ.ME.RO, *s.m.*, number, cypher, mark, quantity.
NU.ME.RO.LO.GI.A, *s.f.*, numerology.
NU.ME.RO.LO.GIS.TA, *s. 2 gen.*, numerologist.
NU.ME.RO.SO, *adj.*, numerous, plentiful.
NUN.CA, *adv.*, never, at no time, ever.
NUN.CI.A.TU.RA, *s.f.*, nunciature.
NÚN.CIO, *s.m.*, nuncio, legate.
NUN.CU.PA.ÇÃO, *s.m., Jur.*, nuncupation.
NUNS, *contr.* of the *prep.* EM and *art. ind. pl.*, **UNS**: ~ *restaurantes*: in some restaurants.
NUP.CI.AL, *adj.*, nuptial, bridal.
NÚP.CIAS, *s.f., pl.*, nuptials, marriage, wedding.
NU.TA.ÇÃO, *s.f., Astron.*, nutation; oscillation.
NU.TAR, *v.*, to nutate; to oscillate.
NU.TO, *s.m.*, nutation; *fig.*, wish, desire.
NU.TRI.ÇÃO, *s.f.*, nutrition, feed, nourishment, alimentation.
NU.TRI.CI.O.NAL, *adj.*, nutritional.
NU.TRI.CI.O.NIS.TA, *s. 2 gen.*, nutritionist.
NU.TRI.DO, *adj.*, fed, nourished, robust.
NU.TRI.DOR, *s.m.*, nourisher, feeder; *adj.*, nutritious, nutrient, nourishing.
NU.TRI.EN.TE, *s.m.*, nutrient; *adj.*, nutritional.
NU.TRI.MEN.TAL, *adj.*, nutrimental, nutritious.
NU.TRIR, *v.*, to nourish, to feed, to maintain, to sustain, to foster.
NU.TRI.TI.VA.MEN.TE, *adv.*, nutritiously.
NU.TRI.TI.VO, *adj.*, nutritious, nutrient.
NU.VEM, *s.f.*, cloud, haze, mist.

O, *s.m.*, the fourteenth letter of the Portuguese alphabet; article (m.) the; zero, cypher; *pron.*, it, him, to him; you, to you.
Ó!, Ô, OH!, *interj.*, oh! wo!
OAB, abrev. of *Ordem dos Advogados do Brasil*: Brazilian Law Society.
O.Á.SIS, *s.m.*, oasis.
O.BA!, *interj.*, whoopee! great! hi!
OB.CE.CA.ÇÃO, *s.f.*, blindness, obduracy.
OB.CE.CA.DO, *adj.*, obsessive.
OB.CE.CAR, *v.*, to blind, to obscure, to obfuscate, to obsess.
O.BE.DE.CER, *v.*, to obey, to comply, to execute, to submit.
O.BE.DI.ÊN.CIA, *s.f.*, obedience, submission, compliance, dependence.
O.BE.DI.EN.TE, *adj.*, obedient, submissive.
O.BE.DI.EN.TE.MEN.TE, *adv.*, obediently.
O.BÉ.LI.O, *s.m.*, Anat., obelion.
O.BE.LIS.CAL, *adj.*, obeliscal.
O.BE.LIS.CO, *s.m.*, obelisk.
ó.be.lo, *s.m.*, obelus.
O.BE.RA.DO, *adj.*, indebted; pawned, mortgaged.
O.BE.SI.DA.DE, *s.f.*, obesity, fatness.
O.BE.SO, *adj.*, fat, obese.
Ó.BI.CE, *s.m.*, hindrance, impediment, obstacle.
Ó.BI.TO, *s.m.*, death, decease, obit.
O.BI.TU.Á.RIO, *s.m.*, obituary.
O.BI.TU.A.RIS.TA, *s. 2 gen.*, obituarist.
OB.JE.ÇÃO, *s.f.*, objection, opposition, contestation.
OB.JE.TAR, *v.*, to object, to oppose, to refute.
OB.JE.TÁ.VEL, *adj.*, objectionable.
OB.JE.TI.VA, *s.f.*, Ópt., objective.
OB.JE.TI.VA.ÇÃO, *s.f.*, objectification.
OB.JE.TI.VA.MEN.TE, *adv.*, objectively.
OB.JE.TI.VAR, *v.*, to objectify, to materialize.
OB.JE.TI.VI.DA.DE, *s.f.*, objectivity.
OB.JE.TI.VIS.MO, *s.m.*, objectivism.
OB.JE.TI.VO, *s.m.*, objective, end, aim, object.
OB.JE.TO, *s.m.*, object, matter, topic, purpose, motive, reason.
O.BLA.ÇÃO, *s.f.*, oblation.
O.BLA.TA, *s.f.*, oblation (offering to God).
O.BLI.QUI.DA.DE, *s.f.*, obliquity.
O.BLÍ.QUO, *adj.*, oblique, slanting, skew.
O.BLI.TE.RA.ÇÃO, *s.f.*, obliteration; obstruction.
O.BLI.TE.RA.DO, *adj.*, obliterated.
O.BLI.TE.RA.DOR, *s.m.*, obliterator.
O.BLI.TE.RAR, *v.*, to obliterate, to erase, to efface; Med., to block.
O.BLI.TE.RÁ.VEL, *adj.*, capable of being obliterated.
O.BLON.GO, *adj.*, oblong, elongated, oval.
OB.NU.BI.LA.ÇÃO, *s.f.*, Med., obnubilation.
OB.NU.BI.LAR, *v.*, to obnubilate, to obscure.
O.BO.É, *s.m.*, Mús., oboe.
O.BO.ÍS.TA, *s. 2 gen.*, Mús., oboist.
Ó.BO.LO, *s.m.*, obolus; *fig.*, alms, donation.
O.BRA, *s.f.*, work, job, handwork.
O.BRA.DOR, *s.m.*, worker, laborer; *adj.*, working.
OBRA-PRI.MA, *s.f.*, masterpiece.
O.BRAR, *v.*, to work, to operate; to do, to produce.
O.BREI.RO, *s.m.*, wrighter, wright, workman.
O.BRI.GA.ÇÃO, *s.f.*, obligation, duty.
O.BRI.GA.CI.O.NAL, *adj.*, obligational.
O.BRI.GA.DO, *adj.*, obliged, compelled, thankful.
O.BRI.GAR, *v.*, to oblige, to force, to compel, to subject.
O.BRI.GA.TO.RI.A.MEN.TE, *adv.*, obligatorily, compulsorily.
O.BRI.GA.TO.RI.E.DA.DE, *s.f.*, obligatoriness.
O.BRI.GA.TÓ.RIO, *adj.*, obligatory, forceable, mandatory.
OBS.CE.NI.DA.DE, *s.f.*, obscenity, indecency.
OBS.CE.NO, *adj.*, obscene, indecent, filthy, impure, sensual.
OBS., abrev. of *observação*: observation.
OBS.CE.NA.MEN.TE, *adv.*, obscenely, bawdily.
OBS.CE.NI.DA.DE, *s.f.*, obscenity, obsceneness.
OBS.CE.NO, *adj.*, obscene.
OBS.CU.RAN.TE, *s. 2 gen.*, obscurant, obscurantist.
OBS.CU.RAN.TIS.MO, *s.m.*, obscurantism.
OBS.CU.RAN.TIS.TA, *s. 2 gen.*, obscurantist; *adj.*, obscurantist.
OBS.CU.RE.CER, *v.*, to darken, to obscure, *fig.*, to confuse, to trouble; *obscurecer-se*: to become obscure.
OBS.CU.RE.CI.DO, *adj.*, obscured; *fig.*, vague; *fig.*, forgotten.
OBS.CU.RI.DA.DE, *s.f.*, obscurity, obscureness, darkness.
OBS.CU.RO, *adj.*, obscure, dark, dim, cloudy, enigmatic, misty, unknown.
OB.SE.CRA.ÇÃO, *s.f.*, obsecration, supplication.
OB.SE.CRAR, *v.*, to obsecrate, to supplicate.
OB.SE.CRÁ.VEL, *adj.*, obsecratory, supplicatory.
OB.SE.DAN.TE, *adj.*, Bras., obsessive, obsessing.
OB.SE.DAR, *v.*, to obsess, to annoy.
OB.SE.DI.AR, *v.*, the same that *obsedar*.
OB.SE.QUI.A.DOR, *s.m.*, obliger; *adj.*, obliging.
OB.SE.QUI.AR, *v.*, to oblige, to captivate, to do a favour.
OB.SÉ.QUI.AS, *s.f., pl.*, obsequies.
OB.SÉ.QUIO, *s.m.*, favour, courtesy.
OB.SE.QUI.O.SI.DA.DE, *s.f.*, benevolence, complaisance.
OB.SE.QUI.O.SO, *adj.*, obliging, respectful, complaisantly.
OB.SER.VA.ÇÃO, *s.f.*, observation, remark, note.
OB.SER.VA.DOR, *s.m.*, observer, watcher, spectator, onlooker.
OB.SER.VÂN.CIA, *s.f.*, observance.
OB.SER.VAN.TE, *s. 2 gen.*, observer, spectator; *adj.*, observant, watchful.
OB.SER.VAR, *v.*, to observe, to watch, to look at, to notice, to perceive.
OB.SER.VA.TÓ.RIO, *s.m.*, observatory.
OB.SER.VÁ.VEL, *adj.*, observable, perceptible.
OB.SES.SÃO, *s.f.*, obsession, mania.
OB.SES.SI.VO, *s.m.*, obsessor; *adj.*, obsessive.

OBSIDENTE   •• 254 •••   OFEGOSO

OB.SÌ.DEN.TE, *s. 2 gen.*, besieger; *adj.*, besieging, obsessive.
OB.SI.DI.A.NA, *s.f., Geol.*, obsidian.
OB.SI.DI.AR, *v.*, to besiege, *fig.*, to spy, annoy, to importune.
OB.SO.LE.TO, *adj.*, obsolete, archaic, antiquated.
OBS.TA.CU.LI.ZAR, *v.*, to raise obstacles or difficulties.
OBS.TÁ.CU.LO, *s.m.*, obstacle, hindrance, obstruction, difficulty.
OBS.TAN.TE, *adj., s. 2 gen.*, hindering, obstructive; *não obstante*: in spite of, despite of, however.
OBS.TAR, *v.*, to oppose, to thwart, to resist.
OBS.TE.TRA, *s. 2 gen.*, obstetrician.
OBS.TE.TRÍ.CIA, *s.f.*, obstetrics.
OBS.TÉ.TRI.CO, *adj.*, obstetric, obstetrical.
OBS.TI.NA.ÇÃO, *s.f.*, obstinacy, stubbornness, pertinacity.
OBS.TI.NA.DO, *adj.*, obstinate, obdurate, persistent.
OBS.TI.NAR, *v.*, to become obstinate, to persevere.
OBS.TI.PAR, *v.*, to cause obstipation.
OBS.TRIN.GIR, *v.*, to press, to bind, to constrain.
OBS.TRU.ÇÃO, *s.f.*, obstruction, blockage.
OBS.TRU.IR, *v.*, to obstruct, to block up, to engorge, to shut, to close.
OBS.TRU.TI.VO, *adj.*, obstructive.
OB.TEM.PE.RAR, *v.*, to obtemper, to obtemperate.
OB.TEN.ÇÃO, *s.f.*, obtainment, acquirement, obtention, acquisition.
OB.TE.NÍ.VEL, *adj.*, obtainable.
OB.TER, *v.*, to obtain, to gain, to achieve, to get, to attain, to secure, to bay.
OB.TI.DO, *adj.*, obtained, attained.
OB.TU.RA.ÇÃO, *s.f.*, obturation, filling, stopping.
OB.TU.RA.DOR, *s.m.*, obturator; *Fot.*, shutter; *Odont.*, filler.
OB.TU.RAR, *v.*, to obturate, to fill, to close, to stop, to plug.
OB.TU.SÂN.GU.LO, *adj.*, obtuse-angled, obtuse-angular.
OB.TU.SI.DA.DE, *s.f.*, obtusity, obtuseness.
OB.TU.SO, *adj.*, obtuse, rounded, blunt.
OB.VI.A.MEN.TE, *adv.*, obviously.
OBVIEDADE, *s.f.*, obviousness.
ÓB.VIO, *adj.*, obvious, plain, evident, clear.
OB.VIR, *v.*, to accrue, to escheat.
O.CA, *s.f., Bras.*, hut of Indians (Tupi).
O.CA.SI.ÃO, *s.f.*, occasion, time, opportunity, motive, reason, place.
O.CA.SI.O.NA.DO, *adj.*, occasioned, caused.
O.CA.SI.O.NA.DOR, *s.m.*, causer; *adj.*, causing.
O.CA.SI.O.NAL, *adj.*, occasional, eventual, casual.
O.CA.SI.O.NAL.MEN.TE, *adv.*, occasionally.
O.CA.SI.O.NAR, *v.*, to occasion, to cause, to originate, to provoke.
O.CA.SO, *s.m.*, sunset, west, decline, occident.
OC.CI.PI.TAL, *s.m.*, occipital.
O.CE.Â.NE.O, *adj.*, oceanic.
O.CE.A.NI.A, *s.*, Oceania.
O.CE.Â.NI.CO, *adj.*, oceanic; Oceanian (pertaining to Oceania).
O.CE.A.NO, *s.m.*, ocean, sea.
O.CE.A.NO.GRA.FI.A, *s.f.*, oceanography.
O.CE.A.NO.GRÁ.FI.CO, *adj.*, oceanographic, oceanographical.
O.CE.A.NÓ.GRA.FO, *s.m.*, oceanographer.
O.CE.A.NO.LO.GI.A, *s.f.*, oceanology.
O.CI.DEN.TAL, *adj.*, occidental, western.

O.CI.DEN.TA.LI.DA.DE, *s.f.*, occidentality.
O.CI.DEN.TA.LIS.MO, *s.m.*, occidentalism.
O.CI.DEN.TA.LI.ZA.ÇÃO, *s.f.*, occidentalization.
O.CI.DEN.TA.LI.ZAR, *v.*, to occidentalize, to westernize.
O.CI.DEN.TE, *s.m.*, occident, west.
Ó.CIO, *s.m.*, leisure, rest, inactivity, laziness, indolence.
O.CI.O.SI.DA.DE, *s.f.*, laziness, idleness, indolence.
O.CI.O.SO, *s.m.*, laybones, truant, idler; *adj.*, idle, lazy, indolent.
O.CO, *adj.*, hollow, empty, deep, addle.
O.COR.RÊN.CIA, *s.f.*, occurrence, incident, event, fact, chance.
O.COR.REN.TE, *adj.*, occurring, occurrent.
O.COR.RER, *v.*, to occur, happen, befall, to appear, to come out.
O.CRE, *adj.*, UK ochre, US ocher.
O.CRE.O.SO, *adj.*, ocherous.
OC.TA.E.DRO, *s.m., Geom.*, octahedron.
OC.TAN.GU.LAR, *adj., Geom.*, the same that *octogonal*.
OC.TA.NO, *s.f., Quím.*, octane.
OC.TO.GE.NÁ.RIO, *adj., s.m.*, octogenarian.
OC.TO.GÉ.SI.MO, *num.*, eightieth.
OC.TO.GO.NAL, *adj., Geom.*, octagonal.
OC.TÓ.GO.NO, *s.m.*, octagon; *adj.*, octagonal.
O.CU.LAR, *adj., s. 2 gen.*, ocular.
O.CU.LIS.TA, *s. 2 gen.*, oculist, optician, eye-doctor.
Ó.CU.LOS, *s.m., pl.*, spectacles, glasses.
O.CUL.TA.ÇÃO, *s.f.*, occultation.
O.CUL.TA.DOR, *s.m.*, concealer; *adj.*, concealing.
O.CUL.TAR, *v.*, to occult, to hide, to conceal, to cover, to eclipse.
O.CUL.TAS, *loc. adv.*, ÀS OCULTAS: secretly.
O.CUL.TÁ.VEL, *adj.*, that can be occulted.
O.CUL.TIS.MO, *s.m.*, occultism.
O.CUL.TO, *adj.*, occult, hidden, secret, covered, secret.
O.CU.PA.ÇÃO, *s.f.*, occupation, job, business, employment.
O.CU.PA.CI.O.NAL, *adj.*, occupational.
O.CU.PA.DO, *adj.*, occupied, busy, engaged, taken.
O.CU.PAN.TE, *s.m.*, occupant, occupier.
O.CU.PAR, *v.*, to occupy, to possess, to live in, to reside, to tenant.
O.DA.LIS.CA, *s.f.*, odalisque, odalisk.
O.DE, *s.f.*, ode, the poem.
O.DE.ÃO, *s.m., Hist.*, odeum.
O.DI.A.DO, *adj.*, hated, detested.
O.DI.AR, *v.*, to hate, to detest, to dislike, to abhor, to abominate.
O.DI.EN.TO, *adj.*, hateful, odious.
Ó.DIO, *s.m.*, hate, hatred, odium, enmity, aversion.
O.DI.O.SO, *adj.*, hateful, loathsome, abominable, spiteful.
O.DIS.SEI.A, *s.f., fig.*, series of adventures; *Hist.*, Odyssey.
O.DÔ.ME.TRO, *s.m.*, odometer.
O.DON.TI.TE, *s.f., Odont.*, odontitis.
O.DON.TO.LO.GI.A, *s.f.*, odontology, dentistry.
O.DON.TO.LO.GIS.TA, *s. 2 gen.*, dentist, odontologist.
O.DOR, *s.m.*, smell, scent, odor, aroma, fragrance.
O.DO.RAR, *v.*, to emit odour.
O.DO.RÍ.FE.RO, *adj.*, odoriferous, odôrous, fragrant.
O.ES.TE, *s.m.*, west, occident; *adj.*, west, western.
O.FE.GAN.TE, *adj.*, panting, breathless.
O.FE.GAR, *v.*, to pant, to puff, to gasp.
O.FE.GO.SO, *adj.*, the same that *ofegante*.

OFENDEDOR ••• 255 ••• OMS

O.FEN.DE.DOR, *s.m.*, offender.

O.FEN.DER, *v.*, to offend, to insult, to hurt, to pique, to displease.

O.FEN.DI.DO, *adj.*, offended, insulted.

O.FEN.SA, *s.f.*, offense, insult, affront, wound, hurt.

O.FEN.SI.VA, *s.f.*, offensive, aggression, assault.

O.FEN.SI.VO, *adj.*, offensive, aggressive, attacking.

O.FEN.SO, *adj.*, the same that *ofendido*.

O.FEN.SOR, *s.m.*, offender, wounder.

O.FE.RE.CE.DOR, *s.m.*, offerer, offeror. adj offering.

O.FE.RE.CER, *v.*, to offer, to give, to tender, to proffer, to expose.

O.FE.RE.CI.DO, *adj.*, offered; *pej.*, easy.

O.FE.RE.CI.MEN.TO, *s.m.*, offer, proffer, proposal.

O.FE.REN.DA, *s.f.*, offer, proffer; *Rel.*, offering.

O.FE.REN.DAR, *v.*, to offer, present; to make an offering.

O.FER.TA, *s.f.*, offer, donation, present.

O.FER.TAR, *v.*, to present, to offer, to proffer.

O.FER.TÓ.RIO, *s.m.*, offertory.

OF.FICEBOY, *s.m.*, *Ingl.*, office boy, errand boy.

OFF-LINE, *adv.*, *Comp.*, off-line.

OFF.SET, *s.m.*, *Ingl.*, offset.

O.FI.CI.AL, *s. 2 gen.*, officer; *adj.*, official.

O.FI.CI.A.LA.TO, *s.m.*, officialdom.

O.FI.CI.A.LI.DA.DE, *s.f.*, officiality, officialdom.

O.FI.CI.A.LI.ZA.ÇÃO, *s.f.*, officialization.

O.FI.CI.A.LI.ZA.DO, *adj.*, officially recognized.

O.FI.CI.A.LI.ZAR, *v.*, to officialize.

O.FI.CI.AR, *v.*, to officiate; to serve Mass.

O.FI.CI.NA, *s.f.*, workshop, shop, pantry.

O.FÍ.CIO, *s.m.*, profession, service, art, work, job.

O.FI.CI.O.SO, *adj.*, obliging, accommodating.

O.FÍ.DIO, *s.m.*, ophidian, snake.

O.FÍ.DI.CO, *adj.*, ophidian.

OF.TAL.GI.A, *s.f.*, *Med.*, ophthalmalgia.

OF.TAL.MO.LO.GI.A, *s.f.*, ophthalmology.

OF.TAL.MO.LÓ.GI.CO, *adj.*, ophtalmologic, ophtalmological.

OF.TAL.MO.LO.GIS.TA, *s. 2 gen.*, ophthalmologist.

O.FUS.CA.ÇÃO, *s.f.*, obfuscation, darkness, hiding.

O.FUS.CA.DO, *adj.*, obfuscated; *fig.*, overshadowe.

O.FUS.CAN.TE, *adj.*, dazzling, blinding, flaring.

O.FUS.CAR, *v.*, to obfuscate to obscure, to dazzle, to darken, to dim.

O.GI.VA, *s.f.*, ogive.

O.GRO, *s.m.*, ogre.

O.GUM, *s.m.*, god of war in Afro-Brazilian cults.

OH!, *interj.*, ó!, oh!

OII, *interj.*, hallo!, hello!

OI.TAN.TE, *s.m.*, *Geom.*, octant.

OI.TA.VA, *s.f.*, octave.

OI.TA.VO, *num.*, eighth.

OI.TEN.TA, *num.*, eighty.

OI.TO.CEN.TIS.TA, *s.m.*, artist of the nineteenth century; *adj.*, pertaining to the nineteenth century.

OI.TO, *num.*, eight.

OI.TO.CEN.TOS, *num.*, eight hundred.

O.JE.RI.ZA, *s.f.*, grudge, ill will, antipathy.

OLA, *s.f.*, Mexican wave.

O.LÁ, *interj.*, hallo!, hi!, hey!, hello!

O.LA.RI.A, *s.f.*, pottery, brickyard.

O.LE.A.DO, *s.m.*, oilcloth, tarpaulin; *adj.*, oily, greasy.

O.LE.A.GI.NO.SO, *adj.*, oleaginous.

O.LE.AR, *v.*, to oil.

O.LE.Í.FE.RO, *adj.*, oleiferous.

O.LEI.RO, *s.m.*, brickmaker, potter.

Ó.LEO, *s.m.*, oil.

O.LE.O.DU.TO, *s.m.*, pipeline, oleoduct.

O.LE.O.SI.DA.DE, *s.f.*, oiliness, oleaginousness.

O.LE.O.SO, *adj.*, greasy, fatty, oleaginous.

OL.FA.ÇÃO, *s.f.*, olfaction.

OL.FA.TI.VO, *adj.*, olfactive, olfactory.

OL.FA.TO, *s.m.*, smell, scent.

O.LHA.DA, *s.f.*, glimpse, glance, look, peep.

O.LHA.DE.LA, *s.f.*, the same that *olhada*.

O.LHA.DO, *s.m.*, evil eye, bewitching; *adj.*, looked at, eyed.

O.LHAR, *s.m.*, look, glance; *v.*, to look, to eye, to stare at, to gaze, to view.

O.LHEI.RAS, *s.f.*, *pl.*, shades, shadows around the eyes.

O.LHEI.RO, *s.m.*, foreman, overseer; informer.

O.LHO, *s.m.*, eye; eyesight, view, look.

O.LHO-D'Á.GUA, *s.m.*, water spring.

O.LHO-DE-BOI, *s.m.*, *Zool.*, yellowtail, amber jack.

OLHO DE GATO, *s.m.*, reflector.

O.LI.GAR.CA, *s.m.*, oligarch.

O.LI.GAR.QUI.A, *s.f.*, oligarchy.

O.LI.GÁR.QUI.CO, *adj.*, oligarchic, oligarchical.

O.LI.GO.CE.NO, *s.m.*, *Geol.*, Oligocene.

O.LI.GO.PÓ.LI.O, *s.m.*, *Econ.*, oligopoly.

O.LIM.PÍ.A.DA, *s.f.*, Olympiad, Olympic games.

O.LÍM.PI.CO, *adj.*, Olympic.

O.LIM.PO, *s.m.*, *Mit.*, Olympus (the abode of gods); the gods of Olympus; *fig.*, heaven.

O.LI.VA, *s.f.*, olive, olive tree.

O.LI.VAL, *s.m.*, olive grove.

O.LI.VEI.RA, *s.f.*, olive tree.

OL.MO, *s.m.*, *Bot.*, elm (tree of the genus Ulmus).

OLP, *abrev.* of *Organização para a Libertação da Palestina*: Palestine Liberation Organization, PLO.

OL.VI.DAR, *v.*, to forget, to omit, to neglect.

OL.VI.DÁ.VEL, *adj.*, forgettable.

OL.VI.DO, *s.m.*, forgetfulness, oblivion.

OMÃ, *s.*, Oman.

OM.BRE.AR, *v.*, to shoulder, to compare, to equal.

OM.BREI.RA, *s.f.*, shoulder piece (clothes).

OM.BRO, *s.m.*, *Anat.*, shoulder, dilligence.

OMC, *abrev.* of *Organização Mundial do Comercio*: World Trade Organization, WTO.

Ó.ME.GA, *s.m.*, omega (the last letter of the Greek alphabet); *fig.*, the end.

O.ME.LE.TE, *s.f.*, omelet.

Ô.MI.CRON, *s.m.*, omicron (the fifteenth letter of the Greek alphabet).

O.MI.NAR, *v.*, to omen.

O.MI.NO.SO, *adj.*, ominous, inauspicious, bodeful.

O.MIS.SÃO, *s.f.*, omission, neglect, oversight, default, negligence.

O.MIS.SO, *adj.*, omissive, negligent.

O.MI.TI.DO, *adj.*, suppressed, omitted.

O.MI.TIR, *v.*, to omit, to overlook, to neglect, to overslip, to fail.

O.MO.PLA.TA, *s.f.*, omoplate, shoulder blade.

OMS, *abrev. Organização Mundial da Saúde*: World Health Organization, WHO.

ONANISMO · 256 · ORALMENTE

O.NA.NIS.MO, *s.m.*, onanism, masturbation.
O.NA.NIS.TA, *s. 2 gen.*; *adj.*, onanistic.
ON.ÇA, *s.f.*, *Zool.*, jaguar(animal), ounce(unit of weight).
ON.CO.LO.GI.A, *s.f.*, *Med.*, oncology.
ON.CO.LO.GIS.TA, *s. 2 gen.*, *Med.*, oncologist.
ON.DA, *s.f.*, wave, billow, comber, surge, undulation, vibration, oscillation, fashion.
ON.DE, *adv.*, where; *pron.*, wherein, in which.
ON.DE.A.DO, *s.m.*, undulation; *adj.*, wavy, undulate; rippled.
ON.DE.A.MEN.TO, *s.m.*, the act of waving.
ON.DE.AR, *v.*, to wave, to ripple, to undulate.
ON.DU.LA.ÇÃO, *s.f.*, undulation, fluctuation, waving, vibration.
ON.DU.LA.DO, *adj.*, wavy.
ON.DU.LAN.TE, *adj.*, undulant, wavy.
ON.DU.LAR, *v.*, to wave, to undulate.
ON.DU.LA.TÓ.RI.O, *adj.*, undulatory.
ON.DU.LO.SO, *adj.*, undulous, undulating, wavy.
O.NE.RA.ÇÃO, *s.f.*, burdening financially, taxation.
O.NE.RA.DO, *adj.*, taxed, overburdened, oppressed.
O.NE.RAR, *v.*, to burden, to tax, to load, to oppress.
O.NE.RO.SO, *adj.*, onerous, oppressive, weighty, heavy.
ONG, *abrev.* of *Organização Não Governamental*: Non-Governmental Organization, NGO.
Ô.NI.BUS, *s.m.*, bus, coach, omnibus.
O.NI.PO.TÊN.CIA, *s.f.*, omnipotence.
O.NI.PO.TEN.TE, *adj.*, omnipotent, almighty.
O.NI.PRE.SEN.ÇA, *s.f.*, omnipresence.
O.NI.PRE.SEN.TE, *adj.*, omnipresent.
O.NÍ.RI.CO, *adj.*, oniric, oneiric.
O.NIS.CI.ÊN.CI.A, *s.f.*, omniscience.
O.NIS.CI.EN.TE, *adj.*, omniscient.
O.NÍ.VO.RO, *adj.*, omnivorous.
Ô.NIX, *s.m.*, *2 num.*, onyx.
ON-LI.NE, *adj.*, *Ingl.*, on-line.
O.NO.MÁS.TI.CA, *s.f.*, onomasticon.
O.NO.MÁS.TI.CO, *s.m.*, onomasticon; *adj.*, onomastic.
O.NO.MA.TO.PAI.CO, *adj.*, *Gram.*, onomatopoeical.
O.NO.MA.TO.PEI.A, *s.f.*, onomatopoeia.
ON.TEM, *adv.*, yesterday.
ON.TO.LO.GI.A, *s.f.*, ontology.
ON.TO.LÓ.GI.CO, *adj.*, ontological.
ONU, *abrev.* of *Organização das Nações Unidas*: United Nations, UN.
Ô.NUS, *s.m.*, onus, burden, charge.
ON.ZE, *num.*, eleven!
O.PA, *interj.*, oh!, wow!
O.PA.CI.DA.DE, *s.f.*, opacity.
O.PA.CO, *adj.*, opaque, dull, obscure, dark.
O.PA.LA, *s.f.*, *Min.*, opal.
O.PA.LES.CÊN.CI.A, *s.f.*, opalescence
OP.ÇÃO, *s.f.*, option, choice, selection.
OP.CI.O.NAL, *adj.*, optional.
O.PEN MAR.KET, *s.m.*, open market.
OPEP, *abrev.* *Organização dos Países Exportadores de Petróleo*: Organization of the Petroleum Exporting Countries, OPEC.
Ó.PE.RA, *s.f.*, opera.
O.PE.RA.ÇÃO, *s.f.*, operation, action.
O.PE.RA.CI.O.NAL, *adj.*, operational.
O.PE.RA.CI.O.NA.LI.DA.DE, *s.f.*, operating efficiency.
O.PE.RA.DO, *s.m.*, surgery patient; *adj.*, operated.

O.PE.RA.DOR, *s.m.*, operator, surgeon; *adj.*, operative, operating.
O.PE.RAN.TE, *adj.*, operative, operating.
O.PE.RAR, *v.*, to produce, to work, to function, to perform.
O.PE.RA.RI.A.DO, *s.m.*, working class, proletariat.
O.PE.RÁ.RIO, *s.m.*, worker, workman, labourer.
O.PE.RA.TÓ.RIO, *adj.*, operative, operating.
O.PE.RE.TA, *s.f.*, *Teat.*, *Mús.*, operetta.
O.PE.RÍS.TI.CO, *adj.*, *Bras.*, operatic.
O.PE.RO.SI.DA.DE, *s.f.*, operoseness.
O.PE.RO.SO, *adj.*, operose, laborious, diligent.
O.PI.LA.ÇÃO, *s.f.*, oppilation, obstruction.
O.PI.LAR, *v.*, to oppilate; *opilar-se*: to become oppilated.
O.PI.NAR, *v.*, to judge, to opine, to consider, to think, to vote.
O.PI.NA.TI.VO, *adj.*, opinionative, opinionated.
O.PI.NI.ÃO, *s.f.*, opinion, point of view, idea, judgment.
O.PI.NI.O.SO, *adj.*, opinionative, opinionated.
Ó.PIO, *s.m.*, *Farm.*, opium.
O.PO.NEN.TE, *s. 2 gen.*, opponent, antagonist, adversary; *adj.*, opponent.
O.POR, *v.*, to oppose, to refuse, to resist, to hinder, to prevent.
O.POR.TU.NA.MEN.TE, *adv.*, opportunely.
O.POR.TU.NI.DA.DE, *s.f.*, opportunity, chance, occasion.
O.POR.TU.NIS.MO, *s.m.*, opportunism.
O.POR.TU.NIS.TA, *s. 2 gen.*, opportunist; *adj.*, opportunistic.
O.POR.TU.NO, *adj.*, opportune, suitable, timely, handy, propitious, convenient.
O.PO.SI.ÇÃO, *s.f.*, opposition, resistance, antagonism.
O.PO.SI.CI.O.NIS.MO, *s.m.*, oppositionism.
O.PO.SI.CI.O.NIS.TA, *s. 2 gen.*, oppositionist.
O.PO.SI.TOR, *s.m.*, opposer, opponent, antagonist; *adj.*, opposing, opponent.
O.POS.TO, *adj.*, opposite, contrary.
O.PRES.SÃO, *s.f.*, oppression, hardship, pressure, tyranny.
O.PRES.SI.VO, *adj.*, opressive, tyrannical.
O.PRES.SOR, *s.m.*, oppressor, despot, tyrant; *adj.*, oppressive.
O.PRI.MI.DO, *s.m.*, oppressed person; *adj.*, oppressed, persecuted.
O.PRI.MIR, *v.*, to oppress, tyrannize over, torment, suppress, persecute.
OP.TAN.TE, *s. 2 gen.*, optant; *adj.*, optative.
OP.TAR, *v.*, to opt, to choose, to prefer, to select, to make a choice.
OP.TA.TI.VO, *s.m.*, optative; *adj.*, optative, optional; elective.
ÓP.TI.CA, *s.f.*, optics.
ÓP.TI.CO, *adj.*, optic, optical.
O.PU.LÊN.CIA, *s.f.*, opulence, opulency, riches, wealthiness.
O.PU.LEN.TO, *adj.*, opulent, rich, wealthy, plentiful.
O.PUS, *s.m.*, *Mús.*, opus (work or composition).
O.PUS.CU.LAR, *adj.*, opuscular.
O.PÚS.CU.LO, *s.m.*, opuscule.
O.RA, *adv.*, now, at present; *conj.*, but, however, nevertheless.
O.RA.ÇÃO, *s.f.*, prayer, supplication, rogation, clause, sentence.
O.RA.CI.O.NAL, *adj.*, *Gram.*, pertaining to sentence.
O.RA.CU.LAR, *v.*, to oracle; *adj.*, oracular, oraculous.
O.RÁ.CU.LO, *s.m.*, oracle.
O.RA.DOR, *s.m.*, orator, public speaker.
O.RAL, *adj.*, oral, verbal, vocal, spoken.
O.RA.LI.DA.DE, *s.f.*, orality.
O.RAL.MEN.TE, *adv.*, orally, verbally.

ORANGOTANGO ·· 257 ·· ORVALHO

O.RAN:GO.TAN.GO, *s.m., Zool.*, orangutan, orangoutang.
O.RAR, *v.*, to pray, to supplicate, to beseech, to preach, to orate.
O.RA.TÓ.RIA, *s.f.*, oratory.
O.RA.TÓ.RI.O, *s.m.*, oratory.
OR.BE, *s.m.*, orb; globe, sphere.
OR.BI.CU.LAR, *s.m., Anat.*, orbicularis; *adj.*, orbicular.
ÓR.BI.TA, *s.f.*, orbit, eye socket.
OR.BI.TAL, *adj.*, orbital.
OR.BI.TAR, *v.*, to orbit.
OR.CA, *s.f., Zool.*, orca, killer whale, grampus.
OR.ÇA.MEN.TÁ.RI.O, *adj.*, budgetary, budget.
OR.ÇA.MEN.TO, *s.m.*, budget, calculation.
OR.ÇAR, *v.*, to calculate, to compute, to estimate, to rate, to apprize, to budget for.
OR.DEI.RO, *adj.*, orderly.
OR.DEM, *s.f.*, order, disposition, method, regularity, tidiness, neatness, rule, regulation.
OR.DE.NA.ÇÃO, *s.f.*, ordering; *Rel.*, ordination.
OR.DE.NA.DO, *s.m.*, salary, wage; *adj.*, in order, orderly, arranged.
OR.DE.NA.DOR, *s.m.*, orderer, ordainer; *adj.*, ordering, ordaining.
OR.DE.NA.MEN.TO, *s.m.*, ordainment.
OR.DE.NAN.ÇA, *s.f.*, ordinance; orderly.
OR.DE.NAR, *v.*, to order, to arrange, to organize, to dispose.
OR.DI.NA.RI.A.MEN.TE, *adv.*, ordinarily, usualy.
OR.DI.NÁ.RI.O, *adj.*, ordinary, usual; of poor quality.
OR.DE.NHAR, *v.*, to milk.
OR.DI.NAL, *adj.*, ordinal.
OR.DI.NÁ.RIO, *adj.*, ordinary, habitual, common, usual, customary.
O.RÉ.GA.NO, *s.m., Bot.*, oregano.
O.RE.LHA, *s.f., Anat.*, ear, the organ of earing.
O.RE.LHA.DA, *s.f., de ~:* by ear.
O.RE.LHÃO, *s.m.*, big ear; *Bras.*, opentelephone booth.
O.RE.LHU.DO, *adj.*, long-eared, stupid, ignorant.
OR.FA.NA.TO, *s.m.*, orphanage, orphan asylum.
OR.FAN.DA.DE, *s.f.*, orphanhood, orphanage.
ÓR.FÃO, *s.m.*, orphan; *adj.*, orphan, fatherless.
OR.GA.NE.LA, *s.f., Biol.*, organelle.
OR.GÂ.NI.CO, *adj.*, organic.
OR.GA.NIS.MO, *s.m.*, organism, body, formation.
OR.GA.NIS.TA, *s. 2 gen.*, organist.
OR.GA.NI.ZA.ÇÃO, *s.f.*, organization, arrangement, order, institution.
OR.GA.NI.ZA.CI.O.NAL, *adj.*, organizational.
OR.GA.NI.ZA.DO, *adj.*, organized.
OR.GA.NI.ZA.DOR, *s.m.*, organizer.
OR.GA.NI.ZAR, *v.*, to organize, to arrange, to systematize, to establish.
OR.GA.NI.ZÁ.VEL, *adj.*, organizable, arrangeable.
OR.GA.NO.GE.NI.A, *s.f., Biol.*, organogenesis.
OR.GA.NO.GÊ.NI.CO, *adj., Biol.*, organogenic.
OR.GA.NO.GRA.MA, *s.m.*, organization chart.
ÓR.GÃO, *s.m.*, organ, pipe organ, instrument, agency.
OR.GAS.MO, *s.m.*, orgasm.
OR.GI.A, *s.f.*, orgy, revelry, debauch.
OR.GÍ.A.CO, *adj.*, orgiastic.
OR.GU.LHAR, *v.*, to make proud of.
OR.GU.LHO, *s.m.*, pride, vanity.

OR.GU.LHO.SO, *s.m.*, a proud person; *adj.*, proud; arrogant, self-satisfied.
O.RI.EN.TA.ÇÃO, *s.f.*, orientation, direction.
O.RI.EN.TA.DOR, *s.m.*, advisor; *fig.*, guide, leader; *adj.*, orienting, guiding, directing.
O.RI.EN.TAL, *adj.*, oriental, eastern.
O.RI.EN.TA.LI.DA.DE, *s.f.*, Orientality.
O.RI.EN.TAR, *v.*, to orient, to guide, to direct, to orientate.
O.RI.EN.TE, *s.m.*, east, orient.
O.RI.FÍ.CIO, *s.m.*, orifice, hole, opening.
O.RI.GA.MI, *s.m.*, origami.
O.RI.GEM, *s.f.*, origin, source, ancestry, cause, ascendance.
O.RI.GI.NA.DOR, *s.m.*, originator; *adj.*, originating, originative.
O.RI.GI.NAL, *s.m.*, original, archetype, pattern; *adj.*, original, inventive, primitive, primary.
O.RI.GI.NA.LI.DA.DE, *s.f.*, originality.
O.RI.GI.NAL.MEN.TE, *adv.*, originally.
O.RI.GI.NAR, *v.*, to originate, to cause, to rise, to start, to produce, to create.
O.RI.GI.NÁ.RIO, *adj.*, originary, primitive, derived, descended.
Ó.RI.ON, *s.m., Astron.*, Orion (constellation); *Mit.*, Orion (a giant hunter in Greek mythology).
O.RI.UN.DO, *adj.*, derived, native.
O.RI.XÁ, *s.m., Bras.*, orixá (a pagan African divinity).
OR.LA, *s.f.*, border, edge, margin, rim; coastline.
OR.LAR, *v.*, to border, to edge.
OR.NA.DO, *adj.*, ornate, ornated, decorated.
OR.NA.MEN.TA.ÇÃO, *s.f.*, ornamentation.
OR.NA.MEN.TA.DO, *adj.*, ornamented.
OR.NA.MEN.TAL, *adj.*, ornamental.
OR.NA.MEN.TAR, *v.*, to ornament, to adorn, to decorate.
OR.NA.MEN.TIS.TA, *s. 2 gen.*, ornamentist, ornamenter.
OR.NA.MEN.TO, *s.m.*, ornament, decoration, adornment.
OR.NAR, *v.*, to adorn, to ornament, to decorate, to embellish.
OR.NA.TO, *s.m.*, ornament.
OR.NI.TO.LO.GI.A, *s.f.*, ornithology.
OR.NI.TO.LO.GIS.TA, *s. 2 gen.*, ornithologist.
OR.NI.TÓ.LO.GO, *s.m.*, ornithologist.
OR.QUES.TRA, *s.f.*, orchestra.
OR.QUES.TRA.ÇÃO, *s.f., Mús.*, orchestration
OR.QUES.TRA.DOR, *s.m.*, orchestrator; *adj.*, orchestrating.
OR.QUES.TRAL, *adj.*, orchestral.
OR.QUES.TRAR, *v.*, to orchestrate.
OR.QUI.DÁ.RI.O, *s.m.*, orchid-house.
OR.QUÍ.DEA, *s.f., Bot.*, orchid.
OR.QUI.DÓ.FI.LO, *s.m.*, orchidist.
OR.TO.DON.TI.A, *s.f., Odont.*, orthodontics.
OR.TO.DÔN.TI.CO, *adj., Odont.*, orthodontic.
OR.TO.DON.TIS.TA, *s. 2 gen., Odont.*, orthodontist.
OR.TO.DO.XI.A, *s.f.*, orthodoxy.
OR.TO.DO.XO, *adj., s.m.*, orthodox, Orthodox.
OR.TO.GO.NAL, *adj.*, orthogonal.
OR.TO.GRA.FI.A, *s.f.*, orthography.
OR.TO.GRÁ.FI.CO, *adj.*, orthographic.
OR.TO.PE.DI.A, *s.f., UK*orthopaedics, *US* orthopedics.
OR.TO.PÉ.DI.CO, *adj.*, orthopaedic(al), *US* orthopedic(al).
OR.TO.PE.DIS.TA, *s. 2 gen., Med., UK* orthopaedist, *US*orthopedist.
OR.VA.LHA.DO, *adj.*, dewy; *fig.*, wet.
OR.VA.LHAR, *v.*, to bedew, to dew, to drop moisture.
OR.VA.LHO, *s.m.*, dew, morning dew, mist.

ORVALHOSO · 258 · OZONIZAR

OR.VA.LHO.SO, *adj.*, dewy; drizzly.
OS.CI.LA.ÇÃO, *s.f.*, oscillation, vibration, fluctuation, variation.
OS.CI.LAN.TE, *adj., s. 2 gen.*, oscillating, oscillatory.
OS.CI.LAR, *v.*, to oscillate, to swing, to sway, to vibrate.
OS.CI.LA.TÓ.RI.O, *adj.*, oscillatory, oscillating.
OS.CU.LAR, *v.*, to osculate, to kiss.
ÓS.CU.LO, *s.m.*, osculum, kiss.
OS.MO.SE, *s.f., Biol., Quím.*, osmosis, osmose.
OS.MÓ.TI.CO, *adj., Biol., Fís., Quím.*, osmotic.
OS.SA.DA, *s.f.*, skeleton, ruins, heap of bones.
OS.SA.RI.A, *s.f.*, the same that *ossaria*.
OS.SÁ.RI.O, *s.m.*, ossuary, bone house, ossarium.
OS.SA.TU.RA, *s.f.*, skeleton, skeletal structure; framework.
ÓS.SEO, *adj.*, osseous, bony.
OS.SI.FI.CA.ÇÃO, *s.f.*, ossification.
OS.SI.FI.CAR, *v.*, to ossify.
OS.SO, *s.m., Anat.*, bone; *fig.*, difficulty.
OS.SU.DO, *adj.*, big-boned, bony.
OS.TEN.SI.VO, *adj.*, ostensive, demonstrative.
OS.TEN.TA.ÇÃO, *s.f.*, ostentation, show, vanity, display, pomp.
OS.TEN.TA.DOR, *s.m.*, ostentatious person; *adj.*, ostentious.
OS.TEN.TAR, *v.*, to exhibit, make a show of.
OS.TEN.TO.SO, *adj.*, ostentatious.
OS.TE.O.PA.TA, *s. 2 gen.*, osteopath.
OS.TE.O.PA.TI.A, *s.f., Med.*, osteopathy.
OS.TE.O.PO.RO.SE, *s.f., Med.*, osteoporosis.
OS.TRA, *s.f.*, oyster.
OS.TRA.CIS.MO, *s.m.*, ostracism, relegation.
OTAN, *abrev.* of *Organização do Tratado do Atlântico Norte*: North Atlantic Treaty Organization, NATO.
O.TÁ.RIO, *s.m.*, sucker, dull, gull, dupe.
Ó.TI.CA, *s.f.*, otics.
Ó.TI.CO, *adj.*, otic.
O.TI.MA.MEN.TE, *adv.*, excellently.
O.TI.MIS.MO, *s.m.*, optimism.
O.TI.MIS.TA, *s. 2 gen.*, optimist, hopeful.
O.TI.MI.ZA.ÇÃO, *s.f.*, optimization.
O.TI.MI.ZAR, *v.*, to optimize.
Ó.TI.MO, *adj.*, excellent, very good, best, fine.
O.TI.TE, *s.f., Med.*, otitis.
O.TOR.RI.NO.LA.RIN.GO.LO.GI.A, *s.f., Med.*, otorhinolaryngology.
O.TOR.RI.NO.LA.RIN.GO.LO.GIS.TA, *s. 2 gen., Med.*, otorhinolaryngologist.
O.TO.MA.NO, *adj., s.m.*, Ottoman, Turk.
OU, *conj.*, or, either.
OU.RE.LA, *s.f.*, border; margin.
OU.RI.ÇA.DO, *adj., fam.*, prickly.
OU.RI.ÇAR, *v.*, to bristle.
OU.RI.ÇO, *s.m.*, hedgehog.
OURIÇO-DO-MAR, *s.m., Zool.*, sea urchin.
OU.RI.VES, *s.m.*, goldsmith, jeweler.
OU.RI.VE.SA.RI.A, *s.f.*, jewelry, goldsmithery.
OU.RO, *s.m.*, gold.
OU.SA.DI.A, *s.f.*, daring, boldness, courage, audacity, bravery.
OU.SA.DO, *adj.*, bold, audacious, brave, insolent.
OU.SAR, *v.*, to dare, to risk, to attempt.
OUT.DOOR, *s.m., Ingl.*, billboard, hoarding.
OU.TEI.RO, *s.m.*, hillock, small hill.
OU.TO.NAL, *adj.*, autumnal.

OU.TO.NO, *s.m.*, autumn, fall.
OU.TOR.GA, *s.f.*, grant, bestowal.
OU.TOR.GA.DO, *s.m., Jur.*, grantee; *adj.*, granted.
OU.TOR.GAN.TE, *s. 2 gen., Jur.*, grantor; *adj.*, granting.
OU.TOR.GAR, *v.*, to approve, to sanction, to grant, to warrant, to confer.
OU.TREM, *pron.*, somebody else, other people.
OU.TRO, *pron.*, other, another; *outros*: others; *outra vez*: again, another time.
OU.TRO.RA, *adv.*, formerly, of old, long ago.
OU.TROS.SIM, *adv.*, also, likewise.
OU.TU.BRO, *s.m.*, October.
OU.VI.DO, *s.m.*, ear, audition.
OU.VI.DOR, *s.m.*, listener; special magistrate; *Hist., Bras.*, judge appointed by the king of Portugal.
OU.VI.DO.RI.A, *s.f.*, magistracy.
OU.VIN.TE, *s. 2 gen.*, listener, hearer.
OU.VIR, *v.*, to hear, to listen, to attend to, to pay attention to.
O.VA, *s.f.*, fish ovary, spawn.
O.VA.ÇÃO, *s.f.*, ovation, applause.
O.VA.CI.O.NAR, *v.*, to acclaim, to applaud, to homage.
O.VAL, *adj.*, oval, ovate, oviform.
O.VA.LA.DO, *adj.*, ovate, elliptical.
O.VA.LAR, *v.*, to ovalize, to make oval.
O.VA.RI.A.NO, *adj., Anat.*, ovarian.
O.VÁ.RIO, *s.m., Anat.*, ovary, ovarium.
O.VE.LHA, *s.f., Zool.*, ewe, sheep; member of a spiritual flock.
O.VE.LHI.NHA, *s.f.*, lamb.
O.VER.DO.SE, *s.f.*, overdose.
O.VÍ.FE.RO, *adj.*, oviferous.
O.VI.FOR.ME, *adj.*, oviform, egg-shaped.
O.VIL, *s.m.*, sheep-cote.
O.VI.NO, *adj.*, ovine, sheeplike.
O.VI.NO.CUL.TOR, *s.m.*, sheepman, sheep breeder.
O.VI.NO.CUL.TU.RA, *s.f.*, sheep raising.
ÓV.NI, *s.m., abrev.* of *objeto voador não identificado*: unidentified flying object, UFO.
O.VO, *s.m.*, egg; *clara do ovo*: egg white; *gema do ovo*: egg yolk.
O.VOI.DE, *adj.*, ovoid.
O.VU.LA.ÇÃO, *s.f.*, ovulation.
O.VU.LA.DO, *adj.*, ovulate.
O.VU.LAR, *v.*, to ovulate (to release ova from the ovary; to form ova); *adj.*, ovular (resembling an egg or ova).
Ó.VU.LO, *s.m.*, ovule, small ovum.
O.XA.LÁ, *interj.*, would to God!
O.XI.DA.ÇÃO, *s.f.*, rust, oxidation, corrosion.
O.XI.DAN.TE, *adj.*, oxidant, oxidizer.
O.XI.DAR, *v.*, to oxidate, to oxidize, to rust.
O.XI.DÁ.VEL, *adj.*, oxidable.
Ó.XI.DO, *s.m.*, oxid.
O.XI.GE.NA.ÇÃO, *s.f.*, oxygenation.
O.XI.GE.NA.DO, *adj.*, oxygenated.
O.XI.GE.NAR, *v.*, to oxygenate, to treat.
O.XI.GÊ.NIO, *s.m.*, oxygen.
O.XÍ.TO.NO, *adj., s.m.*, oxytone.
O.XUM, *s.m., Bras., Folc., Rel.*, Oxum (god of the rivers and streams).
O.ZÔ.NIO, *s.m.*, ozone.
O.ZO.NI.ZAR, *v.*, to ozonize.

P

P, *s.m.*, fifteenth letter of the Portuguese alphabet.
PÁ, *s.f.*, spade, shovel, scoop, peel.
PA.CA, *s.f., Zool.*, paca (*Cuniculus paca*); *adv., Bras., gir.*, great quantity, very good.
PA.CA.TEZ, *s.f.*, tranquility, placidity.
PA.CA.TO, *adj.*, quiet, peaceful.
PA.CHOR.RA, *s.f.*, phlegm, sluggishness, apathy.
PA.CHOR.REN.TO, *adj.*, phlegmatic, sluggish.
PA.CI.ÊN.CIA, *s.f.*, patience, solitaire (card game).
PA.CI.EN.TE, *adj. s 2 gen.*, patient.
PA.CI.FI.CA.ÇÃO, *s.f.*, pacification, reconciliation.
PA.CI.FI.CA.DOR, *s.m.*, pacifier, pacificator, pacifist.
PA.CI.FI.CA.MEN.TE, *adv.*, pacifically.
PA.CI.FI.CAR, *v.*, to pacify, to pacificate, to tranquilize, to calm, to conciliate.
PA.CI.FI.CÁ.VEL, *adj.*, pacifiable.
PA.CÍ.FI.CO, *s.m.*, pacific; (the Ocean) Pacific; *adj.*, pacific, calm, peaceful, tranquil.
PA.CI.FIS.MO, *s.m.*, pacifism.
PA.CI.FIS.TA, *s 2 gen.*, pacifist; *adj.*, pacifistic.
PA.ÇO, *s.m.*, palace; *fig.*, the court; courtiers.
PA.CO.BA, *s.f., Bras.*, banana.
PA.ÇO.CA, *s.f., Bras., Cul.*, sweet crushed peanut with brown sugar; *Cul.*, a kind of dried meat cooked mixed with cassava flour.
PA.CO.TE, *s.m.*, package, packet, pack, parcel, bundle.
PAC.TO, *s.m.*, pact, agreement, compact.
PAC.TU.AL, *adj.*, referring to a pact.
PAC.TU.AR, *v.*, to make a pact with.
PA.DA.RIA, *s.f.*, bakery, baker's shop.
PA.DE.CE.DOR, *s.m.*, sufferer.
PA.DE.CER, *v.*, to suffer, to endure pain, tolerate.
PA.DE.CI.MEN.TO, *s.m.*, suffering, affliction.
PA.DEI.RO, *s.m.*, baker.
PA.DI.O.LA, *s.f.*, handbarrow, litter.
PA.DRÃO, *s.m.*, standard, gauge, model, pattern.
PA.DRAS.TO, *s.m.*, stepfather.
PA.DRE, *s.m.*, priest, father, clergyman.
PA.DRE-NOS.SO, *s.m.*, Pater Noster.
PA.DRI.NHO, *s.m.*, godfather, protector, sponsor.
PA.DRO.EI.RO, *s.m.*, patron, protector, patron saint.
PA.DRO.NI.ZA.ÇÃO, *s.f.*, standardization.
PA.DRO.NI.ZA.DO, *adj.*, standardized.
PA.DRO.NI.ZAR, *v.*, to standardize, to gauge.
PA.DRO.NI.ZÁ.VEL, *adj.*, that can be standardized.
PA.E.LHA, *s.f., Cul.*, paella (Spanish typical dish).
PA.E.TÊ, *s.m.*, spangle, sequin.
PA.GA.DOR, *s.m.*, payer, paymaster.
PA.GA.MEN.TO, *s.m.*, payment, salary.
PA.GÃO, *adj., s.m.*, pagan.
PA.GAR, *v.*, to pay, to remunerate, to reimburse, to compensate, to repay.

PA.GÁ.VEL, *adj.*, payable.
PÁ.GI.NA, *s.f.*, page.
PA.GI.NA.ÇÃO, *s.f.*, pagination, paging.
PA.GI.NA.DOR, *s.m.*, pager.
PA.GI.NAR, *v.*, to paginate, to page.
PA.GO, *s.m.*, pay, retribution; *adj.*, paid.
PA.GO.DE, *s.m.*, pagoda (a towerlike templo in Asia); *Bras.*, an informal singing and dancing popular party.
PA.GO.DEI.RO, *s.m., Bras., col.*, frequenter of a popular party (pagode).
PAI, *s.m.*, father; pais, parents.
PAI DE SAN.TO, *s.m.*, spiritual candomblé leader.
PAI.NEL, *s.m.*, panel, picture.
PAI-NOS.SO, *s.m.*, the Lord's Prayer; *Pai Nosso*: Our Father.
PAI.O, *s.m., Bras.*, salamelle; salami of pork sausage.
PAI.OL, *s.m.*, storehouse, barn.
PAI.RAR, *v.*, to hover, to scud, to hang (over).
PA.ÍS, *s.m.*, country, nation, land, region.
PAI.SA.GEM, *s.m.*, landscape, scenery.
PAI.SA.GIS.MO, *s.m.*, landscape gardening, landscaping.
PAI.SA.GIS.TA, *s 2 gen.*, landscapist; landscape architect, landscape painter, landscape gardener.
PAI.SA.GÍS.TI.CO, *adj.*, referring to a landscape.
PAI.SA.NO, *s.m.*, compatriot, fellow countryman; *adj.*, compatriot; *loc. adv.*, à paisana: in mufti.
PA.ÍS BAS.CO, *s.*, Basque Country.
PA.Í.SES BAI.XOS, *s.*, Netherlands
PAI.XÃO, *s.f.*, passion, love, infatuation.
PAI.XO.NI.TE, *s.f., Bras., col.*, infatuation, a crush, madly in love.
PA.JÉ, *s.m.*, peai, shaman.
PA.JE.LAN.ÇA, *s.f., Bras.*, witchcraft, healing, conjuration.
PA.JEM, *s.m.*, page, attendant, baby sitter.
PA.LA, *s.f.*, peak, yoke, tongue; sun visor, visor.
PA.LA.CE.TE, *s.m.*, a small palace.
PA.LA.CI.A.NO, *s.m.*, courtier; *adj.*, palatial.
PA.LÁ.CIO, *s.m.*, palace.
PA.LA.DAR, *s.m.*, taste, liking, palate.
PA.LA.DI.NO, *s.m.*, paladin; knight-errant.
PA.LA.FI.TA, *s.f., Arquit.*, palafitte, stilts, house built on stilts.
PA.LAN.QUE, *s.m.*, stand, scaffold.
PA.LA.TAL, *adj.*, palatal (pertaining to the palate).
PA.LA.TÁ.VEL, *adj.*, palatable; *fig.*, acceptable.
PA.LA.TO, *s.m., Anat.*, palate, taste, savour.
PA.LA.VRA, *s.f.*, word, term, expression, vocable, promise.
PA.LA.VRA-CHA.VE, *s.f.*, keyword.
PA.LA.VRÃO, *s.m.*, swear word, curse word.
PA.LA.VRE.A.DO, *s.m.*, chatter, gabble, idle talk.
PAL.CO, *s.m.*, stage.
PA.LE.AN.TRO.PO.LO.GI.A, *s.f.*, paleoanthropology.
PA.LE.AN.TRO.PO.LO.GIS.TA, *s 2 gen.*, paleoanthropologist.
PA.LE.AN.TRO.PÓ.LO.GO, *s.m.*, the same that paleoantropologista.

PALEOCENO ·· 260 ·· PANTANEIRO

PA.LE.O.CE.NO, *s.m., adj., Geol., UK* Palaeocene, *US* Paleocen.

PA.LE.O.LÍ.TI.CO, *adj.*, palaeolithic.

PA.LE.O.LO.GIA, *s.f.*, palaeology.

PA.LE.Ó.LO.GO, *s.m., UK* palaeologist, *US* paleologist.

PA.LE.ON.TO.LO.GI.A, *s.f., UK* palaeontology, *US* paleontology.

PA.LE.ON.TÓ.LO.GO, *s.m., UK* palaeontologist, *US* paleontologist.

PA.LER.MA, *s.m.*, idiot, fool, imbecile; *adj.*, foolish, idiotic, dull, silly.

PA.LER.MI.CE, *s.f.*, foolishness, idiotism.

PA.LES.TI.NA, *s.*, Palestina.

PA.LES.TI.NO, *s.m., adj.*, Palestinian.

PA.LES.TRA, *s.f.*, lecture, talk, conversation.

PA.LES.TRAN.TE, *s. 2 gen.*, speaker (at conference).

PA.LES.TRAR, *v.*, to give a talk; to converse, to chat.

PA.LE.TA, *s.f.*, shoulder-blade.

PA.LE.TÓ, *s.m.*, coat, jacket.

PA.LHA, *s.f.*, straw, dry grass.

PA.LHA.ÇA.DA, *s.f.*, clowning; *pej.*, ridiculous sight.

PA.LHA.ÇO, *s.m.*, clown, buffoon, jester.

PA.LHEI.RO, *s.m.*, hayloft, haystack.

PA.LHE.TA, *s.f.*, plectrum, reed (of musical instruments); slat (of a Venetian blind); blade (ventilador).

PA.LHO.ÇA, *s.f.*, thatched hut; straw hut.

PA.LI.A.TI.VO, *s.m.*, a palliative medicine.

PA.LI.ÇA.DA, *s.f.*, palisade.

PA.LI.DEZ, *s.f.*, paleness, wanness, whiteness.

PÁ.LI.DO, *adj.*, pale, shallow, wan, pallid, whitish.

PA.LI.TAR, *v.*, to pick (the teeth).

PA.LI.TEI.RO, *s.m.*, one who makes toothpicks; toothpick holder.

PA.LI.TO, *s.m.*, stick, toothpick.

PAL.MA, *s.f.*, palm (of the hand); *Bot.*, palm leaf, palm tree; *palmas* (*pl.*): applause.

PAL.MÁ.CE.AS, *s.f., pl., Bot.*, palm family (*Arecaceae*).

PAL.MA.DA, *s.f.*, slap, rap, cuff.

PAL.MA.TÓ.RIA, *s.f.*, ferule, a pandy.

PAL.MEI.RA, *s.f.*, palm tree.

PAL.MEI.RAL, *s.m., Bot.*, palmery, a grove of palm trees.

PAL.MI.LHA, *s.f.*, insole.

PAL.MI.LHAR, *v.*, to provide an insole; to mend stockings; to go on foot.

PAL.MÍ.PE.DE, *s.m.*, palmiped.

PAL.MI.TAL, *s.m.*, palmetto plantation.

PAL.MI.TO, *s.m., Bot.*, palmetto; *Cul.*, heart of palm.

PAL.MO, *s.m.*, span (of the hand), palm.

PAL.PA.BI.LI.DA.DE, *s.f.*, palpability.

PAL.PAR, *v.*, to palpate.

PAL.PÁ.VEL, *adj.*, palpable, touchable; evident.

PÁL.PE.BRA, *s.f., Anat.*, eyelid.

PÁL.PE.BRA, *s.f.*, eyelid.

PAL.PI.TA.ÇÃO, *s.f.*, palpitation, throb.

PAL.PI.TAN.TE, *adj., s. 2 gen.*, palpitant.

PAL.PI.TAR, *v.*, to palpitate, to throb, to pulsate, to pulse.

PAL.PI.TE, *s.m.*, suggestion, tip.

PAL.PI.TEI.RO, *s.m.*, tipster, tout.

PAL.RA, *s.f.*, talk, chatter, babble.

PAL.RA.DOR, *s.m.*, prattler, chatterer, twitter, *adj.*, garrulous, chattering.

PAL.RAR, *v.*, to jabber, to chatter, to converse.

PAL.RA.RI.A, *s.f.*, talk, chatter, babble.

PA.LU.DA.MEN.TO, *s.m.*, paludamentum (the cloak worn by an ancient Roman general).

PA.LU.DE, *s.m.*, lagoon, swamp.

PA.LU.DIS.MO, *s.m., Med., col.*, paludism, malaria.

PA.LU.DO.SO, *adj.*, paludous, marshy, swampy.

PA.LUS.TRE, *adj.*, swampy, marshy.

PA.MO.NHA, *s.f., Bras.*, a kind of sweet corn paste, baked in fresh corn husk; *s. 2 gen.*, sluggard, dull; *adj.*, sluggard, dullard.

PAM.PAS, *s.m., pl.*, vast treeless plains in South America.

PAM.PEI.RO, *s.m., Bras.*, pampero (wind from the pampas).

PA.NA.CA, *s. 2 gen.*, fool, simpleton; *adj.*, silly, simple, foolish.

PA.NA.CEI.A, *s.f.*, panacea.

PA.NA.DO, *adj.*, breaded.

PANAMÁ, *s.*, Panama (country).

PA.NA.ME.NHO, *adj., s.m.*, Panamanian.

PAN-A.ME.RI.CA.NO, *adj., s.m.*, Pan-American.

PAN.CA, *s.f.*, a wooden lever; *fig.*, style, mode of expression.

PAN.ÇA, *s.f.*, rumen; paunch.

PAN.CA.DA, *s.f.*, blow, knock, bang, hit.

PAN.CA.DA.RI.A, *s.f.*, scuffle, fray, brawl, beating, spanking.

PÂN.CREAS, *s.m., Anat.*, pancreas.

PAN.CRE.Á.TI.CO, *adj., Med.*, pancreatic.

PAN.ÇU.DO, *adj.*, big-bellied, paunchy, parasitic.

PAN.DA, *s.m., Zool.*, giant panda.

PAN.DA.RE.COS, *s.m., pl.*, chips, splinters, shattered.

PÂN.DE.GO, *s.m.*, reveler, funny person; *adj.*, reveling, funny.

PAN.DEI.RO, *s.m.*, tambourine.

PAN.DE.MI.A, *s.f., Med.*, pandemia, pandemic.

PAN.DE.MÔ.NIO, *s.m.*, pandemonium.

PA.NE, *s.f.*, failure or breakdown of a motor of an automobile, airplane, etc.

PA.NE.GÍ.RI.CO, *s.m.*, panegyric; *adj.*, panegyrical.

PA.NE.GI.RIS.TA, *s. 2 gen.*, panegyrist.

PA.NE.LA, *s.f.*, pot, pan, saucepan.

PA.NE.LA.ÇO, *s.m.*, banging of pots and pans as a sign of protest.

PA.NE.LA.DA, *s.f.*, potful, panful.

PA.NE.LI.NHA, *s.f.*, a small pot; *fig.*, any closed group of people; plot, intrigue.

PAN.FLE.TA.GEM, *s.f., Bras.*, act of writing or distributing pamphlets.

PAN.FLE.TAR, *v., Bras.*, to hand out pamphlets, to pamphleteer.

PAN.FLE.TO, *s.m.*, pamphlet, brochure.

PAN.GA.RÉ, *s.m., Bras.*, nag; unruly horse, worthless horse.

PÂ.NI.CO, *s.m.*, panic, terror, alarm; *adj.*, panic.

PA.NI.FI.CA.ÇÃO, *s.f.*, panification, breadmaking.

PA.NI.FI.CA.DOR, *s.m.*, baker, breadmaker, breadman.

PA.NI.FI.CA.DO.RA, *s.f.*, bakery.

PA.NI.FI.CAR, *v.*, to produce breads to sell in bakery.

PA.NO, *s.m.*, cloth.

PA.NO.RA.MA, *s.f.*, panorama, landscape, view, scene.

PA.NO.RÂ.MI.CA, *s.f., Fot., Cin.*, camera movement that rotates on its own horizontal or vertical axis.

PA.NO.RÂ.MI.CO, *adj.*, panoramic, panoramical.

PAN.QUE.CA, *s.f.*, pancake.

PAN.TA.LO.NAS, *s.f., pl.*, pantaloons, trousers.

PAN.TA.NAL, *s.m.*, swampland.

PAN.TA.NEI.RO, *s.m.*, a cattle breeder, a farmer; *adj., Bras.*,

PÂNTANO · 261 · PARAQUEDAS

referring to a kind of cattle in the state of Mato Grosso.

PÂN.TA.NO, *s.m.*, swamp, marsh, bog, morass.

PAN.TA.NO.SO, *adj.*, swampy, marshy, boggy.

PAN.TE.ÃO, *s.m.*, pantheon.

PAN.TE.ÍS.MO, *s.m.*, pantheism.

PAN.TE.ÍS.TA, *s. 2 gen.*, pantheist.

PAN.TE.RA, *s.f., Zool.*, panther.

PAN.TÓ.GRA.FO, *s.m.*, pantograph.

PAN.TO.MI.MA, *s.f., Teat.*, pantomime; *fig.*, farce.

PAN.TO.MÍ.MI.CO, *adj.*, pantomimic, pantomimical.

PAN.TU.FA, *s.f.*, slipper.

PAN.TUR.RI.LHA, *s.f.*, calf of the leg.

PÃO, *s.m.*, bread, loaf, roll; *pão caseiro*: home-baked bread.

PÃODE LÓ, *s.m.*, sponge-cake.

PÃO-DU.RIS.MO, *s.m., Bras., col.*, avariciousness, niggardliness, stinginess.

PÃO-DU.RO, *s.m.*, miser, niggard.

PÃO.ZI.NHO, *s.m.*, little bread.

PA.PA, *s.m.*, pope; *s.f.*, pap.

PA.PA.DA, *s.f.*, double chin, gills, dewlap.

PA.PA.GAI.A.DA, *s.f., Bras., fam.*, farce, ostentatious.

PA.PA.GAI.AR, *v.*, to parrot, to talk idly.

PA.PA.GAI.O, *s.m., Zool.*, parrot, kite.

PA.PAI, *s.m.*, dad, daddy, father, pappy.

PA.PAI.A, *s.f., Bot.*, papaya, papaw tree (*Carica papaya*).

PA.PAI-NO.EL, *s.m., Bras.*, Christmas gift; *Papai Noel*: Father Christmas.

PA.PAL, *adj.*, papal, pontifical.

PA.PÃO, *s.m.*, bugbear, hobgoblin.

PA.PAR, *v., fam.*, to gabble, to eat; *col.*, to win.

PA.PA.RI.CAR, *v.*, to mollycoddle.

PA.PA.RI.COS, *s.m., pl.*, smotherings; excessive care.

PA.PE.AR, *v.*, to chat (with), to jabber, to talk.

PA.PEI.RA, *s.f.*, parotitis.

PA.PEL, *s.m.*, paper, role; *papéis*: documents; *papel almaço*: foolscap paper.

PA.PE.LA.DA, *s.f.*, a lot of papers; a stack of papers.

PA.PEL-A.LU.MÍ.NI.O, *s.m.*, aluminum foil.

PA.PE.LÃO, *s.m.*, cardboard.

PA.PE.LA.RI.A, *s.f.*, stationery, stationer's shop.

PA.PEL-BÍ.BLI.A, *s.m.*, Bible paper.

PA.PEL-CAR.BO.NO, *s.m.*, carbon paper.

PA.PEL-MAN.TEI.GA, *s.m.*, tracing paper.

PA.PEL-MO.E.DA, *s.f.*, paper currency.

PA.PE.LO.TE, *s.m., Bras., gír.*, a small package of powder drug, twist.

PA.PI.LA, *s.f., Anat.*, papilla.

PA.PI.RO, *s.m.*, papyrus.

PA.PO, *s.m.*, crop, pouch, craw.

PA.POU.LA, *s.f., Bot.*, poppy.

PÁ.PRI.CA, *s.f.*, paprika.

PA.PU.A-NO.VA GUI.NÉ, *s.*, Papua New Gunea.

PA.PU.A, *s. 2 gen., adj.*, Papuan.

PA.PU.DO, *s.m., Bras.*, boaster, swaggerer; *adj.*, boastful, swaggering.

PA.QUE.RA, *s. 2 gen., Bras., gír.*, flirt, flirtation, casual affair; pick up.

PA.QUE.RAR, *v., Bras., gír.*, to flirt; to pull.

PA.QUE.TE, *s.m.*, packet.

PA.QUI.DER.ME, *s.m.*, pachyderm.

PA.QUI.DÉR.MI.CO, *adj.*, pachydermatous, pachydermous.

PA.QUIS.TÃO, *s.*, Pakistan.

PA.QUIS.TA.NÊS, *s. 2 gen., adj.*, Pakistani.

PAR, *s.m.*, pair, couple, peer, brace, partner; *adj.*, equal, like, similar, equivalent.

PA.RA, *prep.*, for, to, toward, in, in(to), in order to, about to.

PA.RA.BÉNS, *s.m., pl.*, congratulations, felicitations.

PA.RÁ.BO.LA, *s.f.*, parable, parabola.

PA.RA.BÓ.LI.CO, *adj.*, parabolic.

PA.RA-BRI.SA, *s.f.*, windshield.

PA.RA-CHO.QUE, *s.m.*, bumper.

PA.RA.DA, *s.f.*, parade, stop, pause, rest, halt.

PA.RA.DEI.RO, *s.m.*, whereabouts.

PA.RA.DI.DÁ.TI.CO, *adj.*, paradidactic.

PA.RA.DIG.MA, *s.m.*, paradigm.

PA.RA.DIG.MÁ.TI.CO, *adj.*, paradigmatic, paradigmatical.

PA.RA.DI.SÍ.A.CO, *adj.*, paradisiac, idilic, celestial.

PA.RA.DO, *adj.*, motionless, immovable, quiet.

PA.RA.DO.XAL, *adj.*, paradoxical.

PA.RA.DO.XO, *s.m.*, paradox.

PA.RA.ES.TA.TAL, *adj., Bras.*, public (partially controlled by the state).

PA.RA.FER.NÁ.LI.A, *s.f.*, paraphernalia.

PA.RA.FI.NA, *s.f.*, paraffin.

PA.RÁ.FRA.SE, *s.f.*, paraphrase.

PA.RA.FRA.SE.AR, *v.*, to paraphrase.

PA.RA.FU.SAR, *v.*, to screw, to fasten with a screw.

PA.RA.FU.SO, *s.m.*, screw, bolt.

PA.RA.GEM, *s.f.*, stopping, stoppage, elsewhere.

PA.RÁ.GRA.FO, *s.m.*, paragraph.

PA.RA.GUAI, *s.*, Paraguay.

PA.RA.GUAI.O, *adj., s.m.*, Paraguayan.

PA.RA.Í.SO, *s.m.*, paradise, heaven, the garden of Eden.

PA.RA-LA.MA, *s.m.*, mudguard, fender, dashboard.

PA.RA.LA.XE, *s.f., Astron.*, parallax.

PA.RA.LE.LA, *s.f.*, parallel.

PA.RA.LE.LA.MEN.TE, *adv.*, parallelly.

PA.RA.LE.LE.PÍ.PE.DO, *s.m.*, parallelepiped.

PA.RA.LE.LO, *s.m.*, parallel, confrontation, comparison.

PA.RA.LI.SA.ÇÃO, *s.f.*, paralyzation, stoppage, weakness, interruption.

PA.RA.LI.SAR, *v.*, to paralize, to weaken, to neutralize.

PA.RA.LI.SIA, *s.f.*, paralysis, palsy.

PA.RA.LÍ.TI.CO, *adj., s.m.*, paralytic.

PA.RA.MÉ.DI.CO, *s.m.*, paramedic, rescuer; *adj.*, paramedic, paramedical.

PA.RA.MEN.TA.DO, *adj.*, dressed up, vested; adorned.

PA.RA.MEN.TAR, *v.*, to decorate, to ornament, to vest; *paramentar-se*: to dress oneself up.

PA.RA.MEN.TO, *s.m.*, ornament, adornment.

PA.RÂ.ME.TRO, *s.m., Mat.*, parameter.

PA.RA.MI.LI.TAR, *adj.*, semimilitary.

PA.RA.NIN.FO, *s.m.*, sponsor, patron, paranymph.

PA.RA.NOI.A, *s.f.*, paranoia.

PA.RA.NOI.CO, *adj.*, paranoiac.

PA.RA.NOR.MAL, *s. 2 gen.*, psychic; *adj.*, paranormal.

PA.RA.PEI.TO, *s.m.*, parapet, window sill.

PA.RA.PEN.TE, *s.m.*, paragliding.

PA.RA.PLE.GI.A, *s.f., Med.*, paraplegia.

PA.RA.PLÉ.GI.CO, *adj., s.m.*, paraplegic.

PA.RA.PSI.CO.LO.GIA, *s.f.*, parapsychology.

PA.RA.QUE.DAS, *s.m.*, parachute.

PARAQUEDISMO ·· 262 ·· PARTIDÁRIO

PA.RA.QUE.DIS.MO, *s.m.*, parachuting.
PA.RA.QUE.DIS.TA, *s. 2 gen.*, parachutist.
PA.RAR, *v.*, to stop, to quit, to pause, to halt, to discontinue, to stay.
PA.RA-RAI.OS, *s.m., pl.*, lightning-rod, lightning-conductor.
PA.RA.SI.TA, *s. 2 gen.*, parasite.
PA.RA.SI.TAR, *v.*, to parasitize, to sponge.
PA.RA.SI.TÁ.RI.O, *adj.*, parasitic.
PA.RA.SÍ.TI.CO, *adj.*, parasitic.
PA.RA.SI.TIS.MO, *s.m.*, parasitism.
PA.RA.SI.TO, *s.m.*, parasite; *adj.*, parasitic.
PA.RA.SI.TO.LO.GI.A, *s.f.*, parasitology.
PA.RA.SI.TO.LÓ.GI.CO, *adj.*, parasitological.
PA.RA.SI.TO.LO.GIS.TA, *s. 2 gen.*, parasitologist.
PA.RA.SI.TÓ.LO.GO, *s.m.*, the same that *parasitologista*.
PA.RÁ.VEL, *adj.*, that can be stoped.
PAR.CEI.RO, *s.m.*, partner, associate, companion; *adj.*, similar, like, equal.
PAR.CEL, *s.m.*, reef, shelf.
PAR.CE.LA, *s.f.*, parcel, portion, fragment, quota.
PAR.CE.LA.DO, *adj.*, made in parcels.
PAR.CE.LA.MEN.TO, *s.m.*, payment by instalments.
PAR.CE.LAR, *v.*, to parcel, to divide into parcels.
PAR.CE.RIA, *s.f.*, partnership, association.
PAR.CI.AL, *adj.*, partial, biased, unfair, prejudiced.
PAR.CI.A.LI.DA.DE, *s.f.*, partiality, unfairness, bias, faction.
PAR.CI.A.LIS.MO, *s.m.*, partiality.
PAR.CI.AL.MEN.TE, *adv.*, partially.
PAR.CI.MÔ.NIA, *s.f.*, parsimony, economy.
PAR.CI.MO.NI.O.SO, *adj.*, parsimonious.
PAR.CO, *adj.*, economic, frugal, poor.
PAR.DA.CEN.TO, *adj.*, brownish, dark grey, greyish.
PAR.DAL, *s.m., Zool.*, sparrow (bird).
PAR.DI.EI.RO, *s.m.*, ruin (house).
PAR.DO, *s.m.*, mulatto, pard; *adj.*, brown, dusky.
PA.RE.CEN.ÇA, *s.f.*, similarity; affinity, analogy.
PA.RE.CER, *s.m.*, aspect, opinion, concept, point of view; *v.*, to appear, to seem, to look, to resemble.
PA.RE.CI.DO, *adj.*, similar, like, resembling.
PA.RE.DÃO, *s.m.*, high wall; steep slope.
PA.RE.DE, *s.f.*, wall, barrier, partition.
PA.RE.LHA, *s.f.*, team, yoke, pair, couple.
PA.RE.LHO, *adj.*, similar, equal, like.
PA.REN.CÉ.FA.LO, *s.m., Anat.*, parencephalon.
PA.RÊ.NE.SE, *s.f.*, parenesis, exhortation.
PA.RÊN.QUI.MA, *s.m., Anat.*, parenchyma.
PA.REN.QUI.MA.TO.SO, *adj., Anat.*, parenchymatous.
PA.REN.TAL, *adj.*, parental (pertaining to family ties).
PA.REN.TA.LHA, *s.f., pej.*, kinsfolk.
PA.REN.TE, *s. 2 gen.*, relative, kindfolk, kinsman.
PA.REN.TE.LA, *s.f.*, kindred, relations, relatives, kinsfolk.
PA.REN.TE.RAL, *adj., Med.*, parenteral.
PA.REN.TES.CO, *s.m.*, kinship, relationship, kinsfolk.
PA.RÊN.TE.SE, *s.m.*, parenthesis, bracket.
PA.RÊN.TE.SIS, *s.m., 2 num.*, the same that *parêntese*.
PÁ.REO, *s.m.*, horse race, running match.
PÁ.RI.A, *s.m.*, pariah; *fig.*, a social outcast.
PA.RI.ÇÃO, *s.f.*, parturiation (of animals).
PA.RI.DA.DE, *s.f.*, parity, equality.
PA.RI.DEI.RA, *adj., Bras.*, that gives birth annually.
PA.RI.DO, *adj.*, that has just given birth.

PA.RI.E.TAL, *s.m., Anat.*, a parietal bone; *adj.*, pertaining to wall.
PA.RIR, *v.*, to bring forth, to give birth to, to have a baby; to cause.
PA.RI.SI.EN.SE, *adj., s. 2 gen.*, Parisian.
PA.RIS.SÍ.LA.BO, *adj., Gram.*, parisyllabic.
PAR.LA.MEN.TA.ÇÃO, *s.f.*, parleying.
PAR.LA.MEN.TAR, *s. 2 gen.*, parliamentary; *v.*, to parley, to treat, to negotiate.
PAR.LA.MEN.TA.RIS.MO, *s.m.*, parliamentarism.
PAR.LA.MEN.TA.RIS.TA, *s. 2 gen., adj.*, parliamentarian.
PAR.LA.MEN.TO, *s.m.*, parliament, legislative body.
PAR.ME.SÃO, *s.m.*, Parmesan, Parmesan cheese.
PAR.NA.SI.A.NIS.MO, *s.m.*, Parnassianism.
PAR.NA.SI.A.NO, *adj., s.m.*, Parnassian.
PÁ.RO.CO, *s.m.*, parish priest, vicar, curate.
PA.RÓ.DIA, *s.f.*, parody.
PA.RO.DI.AR, *v.*, to parody, to imitate, to mimic.
PA.RO.DIS.TA, *s. 2 gen.*, parodist (person who writes a parody).
PA.RÓ.QUIA, *s.f.*, parish.
PA.RO.QUI.AL, *adj.*, parochial.
PA.RO.QUI.A.NO, *s.m.*, parishioner; *adj.*, parochial.
PA.RO.XIS.MO, *s.m.*, paroxysm.
PA.RO.XÍ.TO.NO, *s.m.*, paroxytone word; *adj.*, paroxytone.
PAR.QUE, *s.m.*, park, public square, garden.
PAR.QUÍ.ME.TRO, *s.m.*, parking meter.
PAR.QUI.NHO, *s.m.*, a small park; playground for chidren.
PAR.REI.RA, *s.f.*, vine, grapevine, trellis.
PAR.REI.RAL, *s.m.*, trellised vines.
PAR.RI.CI.DA, *s. 2 gen.*, parricide.
PAR.RI.CÍ.DI.O, *s.m.*, parricide.
PAR.RU.DO, *adj.*, squat, dumpy; *fig.*, bulky, strong.
PAR.TE, *s.f.*, part, portion, piece, fraction, spot, particle, side, region, place.
PAR.TEI.RA, *s.f.*, midwife, accoucheuse.
PAR.TE.JAR, *v.*, to give birth to; assist in childbirth; to help a woman to give birth.
PAR.TE.NO.GÊ.NE.SE, *s.f., Biol.*, parthenogenesis.
PAR.TI.ÇÃO, *s.f.*, partition, division.
PAR.TI.CI.PA.ÇÃO, *s.f.*, participation, notice, communication, notification, advice.
PAR.TI.CI.PAN.TE, *s. 2 gen.*, participant; *adj.*, participating.
PAR.TI.CI.PAR, *v.*, to communicate, to announce, to report, to take part in, to inform, to share in.
PAR.TI.CI.PÁ.VEL, *adj.*, able to participate.
PAR.TÍ.CI.PE, *s. 2 gen.*, informer, participant; *adj.*, informing, participant.
PAR.TI.CÍ.PIO, *s.m.*, participle.
PAR.TÍ.CU.LA, *s.f.*, particle.
PAR.TI.CU.LA.DO, *adj., Quím.*, particulate.
PAR.TI.CU.LAR, *s.m.*, private person, particulars; *adj.*, particular, private, individual, special, specific.
PAR.TI.CU.LA.RI.DA.DE, *s.f.*, characteristic, detail.
PAR.TI.CU.LA.RIS.MO, *s.m.*, particularism.
PAR.TI.CU.LA.RI.ZA.ÇÃO, *s.f.*, particularization.
PAR.TI.CU.LA.RI.ZAR, *v.*, to particularize.
PAR.TI.CU.LAR.MEN.TE, *adv.*, privately.
PAR.TI.DA, *s.f.*, departure, leaving, start, party; game, shipment.
PAR.TI.DÁ.RIO, *s.m.*, adherent, sectarian, partisan.

PARTIDARISMO · 263 · PATRIARCALISTA

PAR.TI.DA.RIS.MO, *s.m.*, partisanship.
PAR.TI.DA.RIS.TA, *s. 2 gen.*, party follower; *adj.*, that follows a party.
PAR.TI.DO, *s.m.*, party, faction, side, part; *adj.*, broken, fractured.
PAR.TI.LHA, *s.f.*, partition, division, repartition, allotment, share.
PAR.TI.LHAR, *v.*, to partition, to share with, to divide.
PAR.TI.LHÁ.VEL, *adj.*, that can be shared.
PAR.TIR, *v.*, to break, to shatter, to split, to depart, to leave, to go away.
PAR.TI.TI.VO, *s.m.*, partitive; *adj.*, partitive.
PAR.TI.TU.RA, *s.f.*, *Mús.*, sheet music; partitur, score.
PAR.TO, *s.m.*, parturition, delivery, childbirth.
PAR.TU.RI.EN.TE, *s.f.*, a parturient woman.
PAR.VA.LHI.CE, *s.f.*, silliness, foolishness.
PAR.VO, *s.m.*, fool, stupid person; *adj.*, foolish, silly.
PAS.CAL, *adj.*, paschal.
PÁS.COA, *s.f.*, Easter.
PAS.MA.CEI.RA, *s.f.*, apathy; amazement, stupefaction.
PAS.MA.DO, *adj.*, amazed, stupefied.
PAS.MAR, *v.*, to amaze, to astonish, to surprise, to stupefy.
PAS.MO, *adj.*, amazed.
PAS.MO.SO, *adj.*, admirable, wonderful, amazing.
PAS.PA.LHÃO, *s.m.*, stupid person, fool; *adj.*, stupid, foolish.
PAS.PA.LHO, *s.m.*, stupid person, fool.
PAS.SA, *s.f.*, raisin.
PAS.SA.DA, *s.f.*, footstep, step.
PAS.SA.DEI.RA, *s.f.*, stepping-stones, stair carpet; ironing woman.
PAS.SA.DI.ÇO, *s.m.*, passageway, sidewalk; *Náut.*, bridge; *adj.*, passing.
PAS.SA.DO, *s.m.*, the past; *adj.*, past, gone, bygone, ended, old-fashioned; last.
PAS.SA.GEI.RO, *s.m.*, passenger, traveller; *adj.*, transitory, temporary, ephemeral.
PAS.SA.GEM, *s.f.*, passage, crossing, ticket.
PAS.SA.POR.TE, *s.m.*, passport.
PAS.SAR, *v.*, to pass, to cross, to traverse, to go, to around, to employ.
PAS.SA.RA.DA, *s.f.*, birds collectively.
PAS.SA.RE.DO, *s.m.*, the same that *passarada*.
PAS.SA.RE.LA, *s.f.*, platform, bridge, runway, ramp.
PAS.SA.RI.NHAR, *v.*, to bird; *Bras.*, to be startled (horse).
PAS.SA.RI.NHO, *s.m.*, small bird, birdie, bird.
PÁS.SA.RO, *s.m.*, bird.
PAS.SA.TEM.PO, *s.m.*, pastime, amusement, diversion, hobby.
PAS.SÁ.VEL, *adj.*, passable, tolerable.
PAS.SE, *s.m.*, pass, permission, pass bill.
PAS.SE.A.DOR, *s.m.*, person fond of walking; *adj.*, walking for amusement.
PAS.SE.AR, *v.*, to promenade, to walk, to stroll, to journey.
PAS.SE.A.TA, *s.f.*, parade, demonstration, stroll.
PAS.SEI.O, *s.m.*, walk, promenade, stroll, jaunt.
PAS.SI.BI.LI.DA.DE, *s.f.*, passibility.
PAS.SÍ.VEL, *adj.*, passible, susceptible.
PAS.SI.VI.DA.DE, *s.f.*, passivity, passiviness.
PAS.SI.VO, *adj.*, passive, inactive, inert, indifferent.
PAS.SO, *s.m.*, pace, step, footstep, walk, march, passage.
PAS.TA, *s.f.*, paste, dough, pulp, portfolio, folder, briefcase.

PAS.TA.GEM, *s.f.*, pasture, pasturage.
PAS.TAR, *v.*, to pasture, to graze.
PAS.TEL, *s.m.*, pastry, pie.
PAS.TE.LÃO, *s.m.*, a big pie; *Bras.*, *Cin.*, slapstick.
PAS.TE.LA.RI.A, *s.f.*, pastry shop.
PAS.TE.LEI.RO, *s.m.*, pastryman, pastry-cook, pastry-maker.
PAS.TEU.RI.ZA.ÇÃO, *s.f.*, pasteurization.
PAS.TEU.RI.ZA.DO, *adj.*, pasteurized.
PAS.TEU.RI.ZAR, *v.*, to pasteurize.
PAS.TI.CHE, *s.m.*, pastiche, pasticcio.
PAS.TI.LHA, *s.f.*, pastille, tablet, lozenge.
PAS.TO, *s.m.*, pasture, pasturage.
PAS.TOR, *s.m.*, herdsman, shepherd, priest, clergyman, vicar.
PAS.TO.RAR, *v.*, the same that *pastorear*.
PAS.TO.RAL, *s.f.*, pastoral.
PAS.TO.RE.AR, *v.*, to pasture, to guide (animals), *fig.*, to tend.
PAS.TO.REI.O, *s.m.*, pasturing (business); *Bras.*, grazing (cattle).
PAS.TO.RIL, *adj.*, pastoral.
PAS.TO.SO, *adj.*, pasty, viscous, gummy, sticky.
PA.TA, *s.f.*, paw, foot; female duck.
PA.TA.DA, *s.f.*, a kick, stamping with the paws or foot.
PA.TA.MAR, *s.m.*, platform, stairhead, landing.
PA.TA.VI.NA, *s.f.*, nothing.
PA.TÊ, *s.m.*, pâté.
PA.TE.LA, *s.f.*, *Anat.*, patella, kneecap.
PA.TEN.TE, *s.f.*, patent; *adj.*, patent, evident, manifest, obvious.
PA.TEN.TE.AR, *v.*, to patent (an invention); to make patent.
PA.TER.NAL, *adj.*, paternal, fatherly.
PA.TER.NA.LIS.MO, *s.m.*, paternalism.
PA.TER.NA.LIS.TA, *adj.*, paternalistic.
PA.TER.NI.DA.DE, *s.f.*, paternity, fatherhood, fathership.
PA.TER.NO, *adj.*, paternal, fatherly.
PA.TE.TA, *s. 2 gen.*, dotard, simpleton, fool.
PA.TE.TI.CE, *s.f.*, dotage, stupidity, nonsense.
PA.TÉ.TI.CO, *adj.*, pathetic.
PA.TÍ.BU.LO, *s.m.*, gallows, gibbet.
PA.TI.FA.RI.A, *s.f.*, knavery, rascality, villainy.
PA.TI.FE, *s. 2 gen.*, rascal, villain, rogue, rotter; *adj.*, scoundrel.
PA.TIM, *s.m.*, roller-skate, ice-skate.
PÁ.TI.NA, *s.f.*, patina.
PA.TI.NA.ÇÃO, *s.f.*, *Bras.*, skating.
PA.TI.NA.DOR, *s.m.*, skater; *adj.*, skating.
PA.TI.NAR, *v.*, to skate, to skid.
PA.TI.NE.TE, *s.m.*, toy scooter.
PA.TI.NHAR, *v.*, to splash, to play in the water; to slosh about.
PA.TI.NHO, *s.m.*, *Zool.*, duckling; leg of beef; *fig.*, fool, idiot.
PÁ.TIO, *s.m.*, courtyard, yard, court.
PA.TO, *s.m.*, duck, drake.
PA.TO.LO.GI.A, *s.f.*, pathology.
PA.TO.LÓ.GI.CO, *adj.*, pathologic, pathological.
PA.TO.LO.GIS.TA, *s. 2 gen.*, pathologist.
PA.TO.TA, *s.f.*, *fam.*, group, gang (of friends).
PA.TRA.NHA, *s.f.*, a great lie; untruthful story.
PA.TRÃO, *s.m.*, master, boss, employer, chief, foreman.
PÁ.TRIA, *s.f.*, native country, home, homeland.
PA.TRI.AR.CA, *s.m.*, patriarch.
PA.TRI.AR.CA.DO, *s.m.*, patriarchate.
PA.TRI.AR.CAL, *adj.*, patriarchal.
PA.TRI.AR.CA.LIS.MO, *s.m.*, patriarchalism.
PA.TRI.AR.CA.LIS.TA, *s. 2 gen.*, a follower of patriarchalism;

PATRICIADO ·· 264 ·· PEDERASTA

adj., that follows patriarchalism; relating to patriarchalism.
PA.TRI.CI.A.DO, *s.m.,* patriciate.
PA.TRI.CI.NHA, *s.f., Bras., pej.,* posh girl.
PA.TRÍ.CIO, *s.m.,* patrician, aristocrat; *adj.,* distinct, elegant.
PA.TRI.MO.NI.AL, *adj.,* patrimonial.
PA.TRI.MÔ.NIO, *s.m.,* patrimony, property, inheritance.
PÁ.TRI.O, *adj.,* native, paternal.
PA.TRI.O.TA, *s. 2 gen.,* patriot; *adj.,* patriot, patriotic.
PA.TRI.O.TA.DA, *s.f., pej.,* a show of patriotism.
PA.TRI.O.TI.CE, *s.f., pej.,* chauvinism; false patriotism.
PA.TRI.Ó.TI.CO, *adj.,* patriotic.
PA.TRI.O.TIS.MO, *s.m.,* patriotism.
PA.TRO.A, *s.f.,* mistress, housekeeper.
PA.TRO.CI.NA.DOR, *s.m.,* sponsor, patron; *adj.,* patronizing; protecting.
PA.TRO.CI.NAR, *v.,* to sponsor, to patronize, to support, to defend.
PA.TRO.CÍ.NIO, *s.m.,* patronage, protection, support, aid, sponsorship.
PA.TRU.LHA, *s.f.,* patrol, a patrolling.
PA.TRU.LHA.MEN.TO, *s.m.,* patrolling.
PA.TRU.LHAR, *v.,* to patrol.
PA.TRU.LHEI.RO, *s.m.,* patrolman.
PAU, *s.m.,* stick, wood, timber, lath.
PAU-BRA.SIL, *s.m., Bot.,* brazilwood, redwood (*Caesalpinia echinata*).
PAU-D'Á.GUA, *s.m., Bras., pop.,* drunkard.
PAU.LA.DA, *s.f.,* a blow with a cudgel.
PAU.LA.TI.NA.MEN.TE, *adv.,* gradually.
PAU.LA.TI.NO, *adj.,* gradual, slow.
PAU.LI.CEI.A, *s.f.,* the city of São Paulo.
PAU.LIS.TA, *s. 2 gen.,* Paulista (inhabitant of the State of São Paulo).
PAU.PE.RIS.MO, *s.m.,* pauperism; poverty.
PAU.PÉR.RI.MO, *adj., superl.,* very poor.
PAUS, *s.m., pl.,* club (cards); *rei de paus:* king of clubs.
PAU.SA, *s.f.,* pause, stop, interruption, interval.
PAU.SA.DA.MEN.TE, *adv.,* pausingly.
PAU.SAR, *v.,* to pause, to make a pause.
PAU.TA, *s.f.,* stave, staff; list, roll, agenda.
PAU.TA.DO, *adj.,* ruled (paper); correct, regular, methodic, measured.
PAU.TA.DOR, *s.m.,* who determines the agenda or ruled lines.
PAU.TAR, *v.,* to rule, to mark.
PAU.ZI.NHOS, *s.m., pl., col., mexer os pauzinhos:* to pull strings.
PA.VÃO, *s.m., Zool.,* peacock.
PA.VÊ, *s.m., Cul.,* cream cake made of biscuits imbibed in liquor with a chocolate paste or cream as a filling.
PÁ.VI.DO, *adj.,* pavid, frightful, timid, fearful.
PA.VI.LHÃO, *s.m.,* pavillion, the external ear, canopy.
PA.VI.MEN.TA.ÇÃO, *s.f.,* paving.
PA.VI.MEN.TA.DO, *adj.,* paved.
PA.VI.MEN.TAR, *v.,* to pave, to floor, to cover with asphalt.
PA.VI.MEN.TO, *s.m.,* pavement, paving, floor.
PA.VIO, *s.m.,* wick, fuse.
PA.VÓ, *s.m., Bras.,* certain Brazilian bird (*Pyroderus scutatus*).
PA.VO.NA.DA, *s.f., fig.,* boasting, vainglory.
PA.VO.NE.AR, *v.,* to peacock.
PA.VOR, *s.m.,* fright, dread, terror.

PA.VO.RO.SO, *adj.,* dreadful, terrible, horrific, frightful.
PAZ, *s.f.,* peace, tranquillity, calm, repose, rest.
PA.ZI.GUAR, *v.,* to conciliate, to pacify.
PC, *abrev., Comp.,* Personal Computer.
PÇA., *(abrev. de Praça)* Sq. (Square).
PÉ, *s.m.,* foot, linear measure (12 in.), foundation, bottom, stalk; *a pé:* on foot; *dar no pé:* run away.
PE.ÃO, *s.m.,* walker, farm hand, footman.
PE.ÇA, *s.f.,* piece, fragment, portion, division, section, play, musical composition.
PE.CA.DI.LHO, *s.m.,* peccadillo.
PE.CA.DO, *s.m.,* sin, offense, misdeed, error, fault, transgression.
PE.CA.DOR, *s.m.,* sinner, offender, wrongdoer.
PE.CA.DO.RA, *s.f.,* sinner, sinful woman.
PE.CA.MI.NO.SO, *adj.,* sinful.
PE.CAR, *v.,* to sin, to commit sin, to err, to offend.
PE.CHA, *s.f.,* defect, failing.
PE.CHAR, *v., Bras.,* to collide with, to crash; to ask for money.
PECH.BLEN.DA, *s.f., Min.,* pitchblende.
PE.CHIN.CHA, *s.f.,* bargain.
PE.CHIN.CHAR, *v.,* to bargain, to barter.
PE.CHIN.CHEI.RO, *s.m.,* bargainer; *adj.,* bartering.
PE.ÇO.NHA, *s.f.,* poison; *fig.,* wickedness.
PE.ÇO.NHEN.TO, *adj.,* poisonous, venomous.
PE.CU.Á.RIA, *s.f.,* cattle breeding, cattle raising.
PE.CU.Á.RI.O, *adj.,* cattle.
PE.CU.A.RIS.TA, *s. 2 gen.,* person skilled in cattle raising. 2 cattleman.
PE.CU.LA.DOR, *s.m.,* peculator.
PE.CU.LA.TO, *s.m.,* peculation.
PE.CU.LI.AR, *adj.,* peculiar, special, singular, uncommon, individual.
PE.CU.LI.A.RI.DA.DE, *s.f.,* peculiarity, peculiarness.
PE.CU.LI.A.RI.ZAR, *v.,* to be peculiar; to make peculiar.
PE.CÚ.LI.O, *s.m.,* peculium.
PE.CÚ.NIA, *s.f.,* money.
PE.CU.NI.Á.RIO, *adj.,* pecuniary, monetary.
PE.CU.NI.O.SO, *adj.,* rich, moneyed, opulent.
PE.DA.ÇO, *s.m.,* piece, bit, fragment, fraction, bite, slice, portion, parcel.
PE.DÁ.GIO, *s.m.,* toll.
PE.DA.GO.GI.A, *s.f.,* pedagogy.
PE.DA.GÓ.GI.CO, *adj.,* pedagogic, pedagogical.
PE.DA.GO.GO, *s.m.,* pedagog, pedagogue.
PÉ-D'Á.GUA, *s.m.,* shower, deluge.
PE.DAL, *s.m.,* pedal.
PE.DA.LA.DA, *s.f.,* pedalling.
PE.DA.LAR, *v.,* to pedal.
PE.DA.LI.NHO, *s.m., Bras.,* pedalo.
PE.DAN.TE, *s. 2 gen.,* pedant; *adj.,* pedantic.
PE.DAN.TIS.MO, *s.m.,* pedantism, pedantry.
PÉ DE A.TLE.TA, *s.m.,* athlete's foot.
PÉ DE CA.BRA, *s.m.,* crowbar.
PÉ-DE-GA.LI.NHA, *s.m., Bot.,* cocksfoot, *pés-de-ga.li.nha* (*pl.*): cow's foot.
PÉ-DE-MEI.A, *s.m.,* nest egg.
PÉ DE MO.LE.QUE, *s.m.,* (sweetmeat) peanut brittle.
PÉ DE OU.VI.DO, *s.m.,* (slap) clip round the ear.
PÉ-DE-PA.TO, *s.m.,* flipper.
PE.DE.RAS.TA, *s.m.,* a pederast.

PEDERASTIA •• 265 •• PENDOR

PE.DE.RAS.TI.A, *s.f.*, pederasty.

PE.DER.NEI.RA, *s.f.*, flint.

PE.DES.TAL, *s.m.*, basis, pedestal, socle.

PE.DES.TRE, *s. 2 gen.*, pedestrian, a walker; *adj.*, pedestrian, walking.

PÉ DE VAL.SA, *s.m., pop.*, expert dancer.

PÉ DE VEN.TO, *s.m.*, squall.

PE.DI.A.TRA, *s. 2 gen.*, pediatrist, pediatrician.

PE.DI.A.TRI.A, *s.f.*, pediatrics.

PE.DI.CU.RO, *s.m.*, pedicure.

PE.DI.DO, *s.m.*, petition, demand, request, solicitation, prayer.

PED.I.GREE, *s.m.*, pedigree.

PE.DIN.TE, *s. 2 gen.*, beggar, mendicant; *adj.*, mendicant.

PE.DIR, *v.*, to ask, to beg, to demand, to claim, to appeal, to pray, to implore.

PE.DRA, *s.f.*, stone, gravel, rock, flint; calculus.

PE.DRA.DA, *s.f.*, throw of a stone.

PE.DRA.DO, *adj.*, rock-paved.

PE.DRA-PO.MES, *s.f.*, pumicestone.

PE.DRAL, *adj.*, stony.

PE.DRA-SA.BÃO, *s.f.*, soap-stone.

PE.DRE.GO.SO, *adj.*, stony, full of stones.

PE.DRE.GU.LHO, *s.m.*, gravel stone, boulder.

PE.DREI.RA, *s.f.*, quarry, stone-pit.

PE.DREI.RO, *s.m.*, mason, bricklayer, stonemason.

PÉ-FRI.O, *s.m., Bras.*, person who also brings bad luck.

PE.GA, *s.f.*, discussion, quarrel.

PE.GA.DA, *s.f.*, footstep, footprint.

PE.GA.DI.NHA, *s.f., Bras., gír.*, catch.

PE.GA.DO, *adj.*, near to, close to, next to.

PE.GA.DOR, *s.m.*, catcher.

PE.GA.JO.SO, *adj.*, clammy, sticky, viscous, adhesive.

PE.GA-LA.DRÃO, *s.m., pop.*, safety catch.

PE.GAR, *v.*, to catch, to hold, to take, to connect, to adhere, to begin.

PE.GA-RA.PAZ, *s.m., Bras., pop.*, kiss-curl, spit curl.

PEI.A, *s.f.*, fetters for animals, tether; *fig.*, hindrance, obstacle.

PEI.DAR, *v., vulg.*, to fart.

PEI.DO, *s.m., vulg.*, a fart.

PEI.TAR, *v.*, to bribe.

PEI.TI.LHO, *s.m.*, bosom (part of a dress, shirt, etc.).

PEI.TO, *s.m.*, chest, breast, bosom, guts; heart, courage.

PEI.TO.RAL, *s.m.*, pectoral; *Anat.*, pectoral muscle; *adj.*, pectoral (pertaining to thorax).

PEI.TO.RIL, *s.m.*, parapet; windowsill.

PEI.TU.DO, *adj.*, a big chest, valiant.

PEI.XA.DA, *s.f., Cul.*, a stew of fish.

PEI.XA.RI.A, *s.f.*, fish market, fish store.

PEI.XE, *s.m.*, fish.

PEI.XE-BOI, *s.m.*, manatee, cowfish.

PEI.XEI.RA, *s.f.*, woman who sells fish; *Bras.*, heavy knife; small and sharp knife.

PEI.XEI.RO, *s.m.*, fishmonger.

PEI.XES, *s.m., pl., Astron.*, Pisces (constellation); *Astrol.*, Pisces (sign of the zodiac).

PE.JO, *s.m.*, encumbrance, embarrassment.

PE.JO.RA.TI.VO, *adj.*, pejorative, depreciative.

PE.LA, *contr. of the prep.* **POR** *with art.* **A**: by, through, at, for the, in the.

PE.LA.DA, *s.f.*, naked (girl); *Bras.*, a football game played between friends.

PE.LA.DO, *adj.*, without hair, shorn; skinless; *fig.*, naked; poor.

PE.LA.GEM, *s.f.*, pelage.

PE.LAN.CA, *s.f.*, wrinkled skin, flabby skin; poor quality meat.

PE.LAN.CU.DO, *adj.*, flaccid (skin), flabby (arm).

PE.LAR, *v.*, to peel, to bark, to make bald, to skin.

PE.LE, *s.f.*, skin, epidermis, hide, fur, leather; hull.

PE.LE.A.DOR, *s.m.*, the same that pelejador.

PE.LE.AR, *v., Bras.*, to fight, to contend.

PE.LE.GO, *s.m.*, sheepskin (used over the saddle); *Bras.*, syndicalist who serves the bosses; lickspittle.

PE.LEI.A, *s.f., Bras.*, the same that peleja.

PE.LEI.RO, *s.m.*, furrier (dealer in furs or fur goods); skinner.

PE.LE.JA, *s.f.*, fight, struggle, battle, combat, conflict, contention, discussion.

PE.LE.JA.DOR, *s.m.*, combatant, fighter; *adj.*, fighting, battling.

PE.LE.JAR, *v.*, to fight, to combat, to struggle with, to contend.

PE.LE.RI.NE, *s.f.*, pelerine.

PE.LE-VER.ME.LHA, *s. 2 gen.*, Red Indian.

PE.LI.CA, *s.f.*, kid (leather), used to make gloves, shoes, etc.

PE.LI.CA.NO, *s.m., Zool.*, pelican.

PE.LÍ.CU.LA, *s.f.*, pellicle, cuticle; film, motion picture.

PE.LO, *contr.* of the *prep.* **POR** with *art.* **O**: by, for the, at, through, in the.

PE.LO, *s.m.*, hair, down, flue.

PE.LO.TA, *s.f.*, bullet; *US* a soccer ball.

PE.LO.TA.DA, *s.f., Bras., Esp.*, a kick at the ball (football).

PE.LO.TÃO, *s.m.*, platoon, troop.

PE.LO.TE, *s.m.*, a small ball.

PE.LOU.RI.NHO, *s.m.*, pillory.

PE.LÚ.CIA, *s.f.*, plush.

PE.LU.DO, *adj.*, hairy, shaggy, shy.

PEL.VE, *s.f., Anat.*, pelvis.

PÉL.VI.CO, *adj., Anat.*, pelvic.

PÉL.VIS, *s.f., Anat.*, the same that *pelve*.

PE.NA, *s.f.*, feather, plume, quill; punishment, penalty, pity; style, writer.

PE.NA.CHO, *s.m.*, plume; crest.

PE.NA.DA, *s.f.*, penful (trace of pen; writing pen); *fig.*, opinion.

PE.NA.DO, *adj.*, feathered; afflicted.

PE.NAL, *adj.*, penal, punitive.

PE.NA.LI.DA.DE, *s.f.*, penalty, punishment, castigation.

PE.NA.LI.ZAR, *v.*, to pain, to afflict, to distress, to grieve, to torment.

PE.NA.LO.GI.A, *s.f.*, penology.

PE.NA.LÓ.GI.CO, *adj.*, penological.

PE.NA.LO.GIS.TA, *s. 2 gen.*, penologist.

PÊ.NAL.TI, *s.m., Bras., Esp.*, penalty (the foul inside the area in soccer-*US*, football-*UK*).

PE.NAR, *v.*, to pain, to suffer, to endure, to grieve.

PE.NA.RO.SO, *adj., Bras.*, painful, sorrowful, pungent.

PEN.CA, *s.f.*, stalk, bunch.

PEN.DÃO, *s.m.*, banner, pennant, flag, labarum.

PEN.DÊN.CIA, *s.f.*, quarrel, dispute, scuffle, fight.

PEN.DEN.CI.AR, *v.*, to dispute, to disagree, to quarrel.

PEN.DEN.GA, *s.f.*, dispute, squabble, quarrel.

PEN.DEN.TE, *adj.*, hanging, pending, pendent, imminent, sloping.

PEN.DER, *v.*, to hang, to lean, to slope, to bend, to tend, to incline.

PEN.DO.AR, *v.*, to adorn with tassels.

PEN.DOR, *s.m.*, declivity, slope, incline, bent, inclination.

PÊNDULA · 266 · PÉ-RAPADO

PÊN.DU.LA, *s.f., Ant.,* pendulum clock.
PEN.DU.LAR, *adj.,* pendular.
PÊN.DU.LO, *s.m.,* pendulum.
PEN.DU.RA.DO, *adj.,* hanging (on); suspended, pending; *fig.,* on tick (indebted).
PEN.DU.RAR, *v.,* to hang, to suspend.
PEN.DU.RI.CA.LHO, *s.m.,* pendant, trinket; *penduricalhos*: fripperies.
PE.NE.DAL, *s.m.,* the same that *penedia.*
PE.NE.DI.A, *s.f.,* a rocky place.
PE.NE.DO, *s.m.,* a great stone, stone.
PE.NE.GO, *s.m.,* a pillow or cushion filled with feathers.
PE.NEI.RA, *s.f.,* bolter, sieve, screen, strainer.
PE.NEI.RA.ÇÃO, *s.f.,* sifting, screening.
PE.NEI.RA.DA, *s.f.,* quantity sifted at a time.
PE.NEI.RA.MEN.TO, *s.m.,* sifting, screening.
PE.NEI.RAR, *v.,* to sift, to screen, to strain, to sieve.
PE.NEI.RÁ.VEL, *adj.,* that can be sifted.
PE.NE.TRA, *s. 2 gen.,* gatecrasher.
PE.NE.TRA.BI.LI.DA.DE, *s.f.,* penetrability.
PE.NE.TRA.ÇÃO, *s.f.,* penetration.
PE.NE.TRA.DOR, *adj.,* the same that *penetrante.*
PE.NE.TRAN.TE, *adj.,* penetrant, penetrative, piercing.
PE.NE.TRAR, *v.,* to penetrate, to invade, to enter, to go in.
PE.NE.TRÁ.VEL, *adj.,* penetrable.
PE.NHA, *s.f.,* rock, cliff.
PE.NHAS.CAL, *s.m.,* a series of crags.
PE.NHAS.CO, *s.m.,* cliff, crag, rock.
PE.NHAS.CO.SO, *adj.,* cragged, cliffy, rocky, full of rocks.
PE.NHO.AR, *s.m.,* peignoir, robe.
PE.NHOR, *s.m.,* pawn, pledge, mortgage; proof.
PE.NHO.RA, *s.f.,* distress, seizure, attachment.
PE.NHO.RA.DO, *adj.,* pawned, pledged.
PE.NHO.RAN.TE, *adj.,* pledging, engaging, obliging.
PE.NHO.RAR, *v.,* to pledge, to pawn, to warrant, to oblige, to engage.
PE.NI.A.NO, *adj., Anat.,* penile, penial.
PE.NI.CI.LI.NA, *s.f., Med.,* penicillin.
PE.NI.CO, *s.m., pop.,* chamber pot, potty.
PE.NÍ.FE.RO, *adj.,* the same that *penígero.*
PE.NÍ.GE.RO, *adj.,* feathered, having feathers.
PE.NÍN.SU.LA, *s.f.,* peninsula, spit.
PE.NIN.SU.LAR, *adj.,* peninsular.
PÊ.NIS, *s.m.,* penis, cock.
PE.NI.TÊN.CIA, *s.f.,* penitence, contrition.
PE.NI.TEN.CI.AL, *s.m., Rel.,* penitential; *adj.,* penitential.
PE.NI.TEN.CI.AR, *v.,* to penance; to do penance.
PE.NI.TEN.CI.Á.RIA, *s.f.,* penitentiary, prison.
PE.NI.TEN.CI.Á.RI.O, *s.m.,* prisoner; *adj.,* penitentiary.
PE.NI.TEN.TE, *adj., s. 2 gen.,* penitent.
PE.NO.SA, *s.f., gír.,* a chicken.
PE.NO.SA.MEN.TE, *adv.,* painfully.
PE.NO.SO, *adj.,* painful, hard, difficult.
PEN.SA.BUN.DO, *adj.,* the same that *pensativo.*
PEN.SA.DO, *adj.,* thought of, considered, deliberate.
PEN.SA.DOR, *s.m.,* thinker, philosopher.
PEN.SA.MEN.TO, *s.m.,* thought, thinking, imagination, mind, idea, spirit.
PEN.SAN.TE, *adj.,* thinking, thoughtful.
PEN.SÃO, *s.f.,* pension, allowance, boarding house.
PEN.SAR, *v.,* to think, to ponder, to meditate, to imagine, to consider, to reflect, to judge.
PEN.SA.TI.VA.MEN.TE, *adv.,* pensively.
PEN.SA.TI.VO, *adj.,* thoughtful, meditative; melancholic.
PÊN.SIL, *adj.,* suspended, hanging.
PEN.SI.O.NAR, *v.,* to pension, to pay a pension.
PEN.SI.O.NÁ.RI.O, *s.m.,* the same that *pensionista; adj.,* referring to pension.
PEN.SI.O.NA.TO, *s.m.,* boarding school, boarding house.
PEN.SI.O.NIS.TA, *s. 2 gen.,* pensioner; boarder.
PEN.SO, *s.m.,* food treatment; nursing (of children); food ration (cattle); *adj.,* inclined.
PEN.TA.CAM.PE.ÃO, *s.m.,* five times champion.
PEN.TÁ.CU.LO, *s.m.,* pentacle.
PEN.TA.DÁC.TI.LO, *adj.,* pentadactyle.
PEN.TÁ.GO.NO, *s.m.,* pentagon.
PEN.TA.GRA.MA, *s.m.,* pentagram.
PEN.TA.TLO, *s.m., Hist.,* pentathlon.
PEN.TE, *s.m.,* comb, card.
PEN.TE.A.DEI.RA, *s.f.,* dressingtable.
PEN.TE.A.DO, *s.m.,* hairdressing, coiffure; *adj.,* well groomed.
PEN.TE.A.DOR, *s.m.,* comber, hairdresser.
PEN.TE.AR, *v.,* to comb, to dress the hair.
PEN.TE.COS.TES, *s.m.,* Pentecost.
PEN.TE-FI.NO, *s.m., pop.,* fine-toothcomb; *fig.,* screening, close scrutiny; close examination.
PEN.TE.LHAR, *v., Bras., gír.,* to annoy, to bore, to aggravate.
PEN.TE.LHO, *s.m., pop.,* pubic hair; *pop.,* an annoying person; *adj.; gír.,* annoying, aggravating.
PE.NU.DO, *adj.,* feathered.
PE.NU.GEM, *s.f.,* fluff, down, fuzz.
PE.NU.GEN.TO, *adj.,* covered with feathers; downy.
PE.NÚL.TI.MO, *adj.,* last but one, penultimate.
PE.NUM.BRA, *s.f.,* shade, half-light, partial shadow.
PE.NUM.BRO.SO, *adj.,* penumbrous, shadowy.
PE.NÚ.RIA, *s.f.,* penury, indigence, extreme poverty, misery, need.
PE.PI.NAL, *s.m.,* plantation of cucumbers.
PE.PI.NAR, *v.,* to eat slowly; to cut into small pieces.
PE.PI.NEI.RA, *s.f.,* field of cucumbers; plant nursery; spree; *fig.,* easy business; bargain.
PE.PI.NO, *s.m., Bot.,* cucumber.
PE.PI.TA, *s.f.,* nugget, lump.
PE.QUE.NA, *s.f., pop.,* young woman, girl, sweetheart.
PE.QUE.NEZ, *s.f.,* smallness, littleness; infancy.
PE.QUE.NI.NI.NHO, *adj.,* tiny, little tiny.
PE.QUE.NI.NO, *s.m.,* young boy; *adj.,* very little.
PE.QUE.NO, *adj.,* small, little, short.
PE.QUE.NO-BUR.GUÊS, *adj.,* petit bourgeois (*Fr.*).
PE.QUI.NÊS, *s.m., adj.,* Pekingese, Pekinese (inhabitant or pertaining to Beijing); *Zool.,* race of dogs.
PE.RA, *s.f., Bot.,* pear.
PE.RAL, *s.m.,* orchard of pear-trees.
PE.RAL.TA, *s. 2 gen.,* mischievous child; *adj.,* mischievous (child).
PE.RAL.TI.CE, *s.f.,* mischievousness.
PE.RAL.TIS.MO, *s.m.,* the same that *peraltice.*
PE.RAL.VI.LHO, *s.m.,* fop, coxcomb, dude.
PE.RAM.BU.LA.ÇÃO, *s.f., Bras.,* perambulation.
PE.RAM.BU.LAR, *v.,* to perambulate, to walk about.
PE.RAN.TE, *prep.,* in the presence of, before, in front of.
PÉ-RA.PA.DO, *s.m., Bras.,* very poor person, loser.

PERCALÇAR   •• 267 ••   **PERGUNTADOR**

PER.CAL.ÇAR, *v., Ant.*, to win, to obtain, to profit.
PER.CAL.ÇO, *s.m.,* disturbance, trouble.
PER.CA.LI.NA, *s.f.,* percaline.
PER CAPITA, *loc. adj.,* per capita.
PER.CE.BER, *v.,* to perceive, to know, to discern, to note, to discry, to hear.
PER.CE.BI.MEN.TO, *s.m.,* perception.
PER.CE.BÍ.VEL, *adj.,* the same that *perceptível*.
PER.CEN.TA.GEM, *s.f.,* percentage.
PER.CEN.TU.AL, *s.m.,* percentage, percent; *adj.,* percent.
PER.CEP.ÇÃO, *s.f.,* perception, feeling, comprehension, perceptivity.
PER.CEP.TI.BI.LI.DA.DE, *s.f.,* perceptibility.
PER.CEP.TÍ.VEL, *adj.,* perceptible, sensible, noticeable.
PER.CEP.TI.VEL.MEN.TE, *adv.,* perceptibly.
PER.CEP.TI.VI.DA.DE, *s.f.,* perceptivity, perceptiveness.
PER.CEP.TI.VO, *adj.,* perceptive.
PER.CE.VE, *s.m., Zool.,* a kind of shellfish (*Lepas anatifera*).
PER.CE.VE.JO, *s.m., Zool.,* bedbug (Cimex lectularius); thumbtack.
PER.CO.LA.ÇÃO, *s.f.,* percolation.
PER.CO.LA.DOR, *s.m.,* percolator.
PER.CO.LAR, *v.,* to percolate.
PER.COR.RER, *v.,* to go through, to visit, to travel, to traverse.
PER.CUR.SO, *s.m.,* course, route, way, trajectory, journey, circuit.
PER.CUS.SÃO, *s.f.,* percussion.
PER.CUS.SI.O.NIS.TA, *s. 2 gen., Bras., Mús.,* percussionist.
PER.CUS.SOR, *s.m., Ant.,* percussioncap; *adj.,* striking, percussive.
PER.CU.TIR, *v.,* to percuss, to reverberate.
PER.DA, *s.f.,* loss, damage, casualty, prejudice, detriment, calamity.
PER.DÃO, *s.m.,* pardon, forgiveness, indulgence.
PER.DE.DOR, *s.m., loser; adj.,* losing.
PER.DER, *v.,* to lose, to miss, to fail, to ruin, to deprave, to waste, to squander.
PER.DI.ÇÃO, *s.f.,* perdition, damnation, ruin, destruction, disgrace, eternal death.
PER.DI.DA.MEN.TE, *adv.,* desperately.
PER.DI.DO, *adj.,* lost, dispersed, ruined, gone.
PER.DI.DO.SO, *adj.,* prejudicial.
PER.DI.GÃO, *s.m., Zool.,* male partridge.
PER.DI.GO.TO, *s.m., Zool.,* young partridge; *pop.,* sputter (saliva emitted in speaking).
PER.DI.GUEI.RO, *s.m.,* pointer (race of dogs); *adj.,* hunting partridges.
PER.DÍ.VEL, *adj.,* losable.
PER.DIZ, *s.f., Zool.,* female partridge.
PER.DO.A.DOR, *s.m., forgiver; adj.,* forgiving.
PER.DO.AR, *v.,* to pardon, to forgive, to excuse, to absolve, to remit.
PER.DO.Á.VEL, *adj.,* excusable.
PER.DO.E, *s.f., Bras.,* straw purse used by mendicants.
PER.DU.LÁ.RIO, *s.m., prodigal, lavisher; adj.,* prodigal, lavish, wasteful.
PER.DU.RA.ÇÃO, *s.f.,* perdurability, duration.
PER.DU.RAR, *v.,* to last, to persist, to remain, to forever, to persist.
PER.DU.RÁ.VEL, *adj.,* perdurable, very durable.
PE.RE.BA, *s.f., Bras.,* sore, abscess.

PE.RE.BEN.TO, *adj., Bras.,* covered with sores, mangy.
PE.RE.CE.DOR, *adj.,* decaying, endable, dying.
PE.RE.CER, *v.,* to perish, to die, to decay, to end, to finish.
PE.RE.CI.MEN.TO, *s.m.,* perishing, extinction.
PE.RE.CÍ.VEL, *adj.,* perishable.
PE.RE.GRI.NA.ÇÃO, *s.f.,* pilgrimage, peregrination, journey.
PE.RE.GRI.NA.DOR, *s.m.,* pilgrim; peregrinator, traveller; *adj.,* peregrinating, wandering, travelling.
PE.RE.GRI.NAR, *v.,* to travel, to go on a pilgrimage.
PE.RE.GRI.NO, *s.m.,* pilgrim, traveller, peregrinator; *adj.,* pilgrim.
PE.REI.RA, *s.f.,* pear-tree.
PE.REI.RAL, *s.m.,* the same that *peral*.
PE.REMP.TO, *adj., Jur.,* extinct, null.
PE.REMP.TO.RI.A.MEN.TE, *adv.,* peremptorily.
PE.REMP.TÓ.RI.O, *adj.,* peremptory.
PE.RE.NE, *adj.,* perennial, unceasing, continual, incessant, permanent, eternal.
PE.RE.NI.DA.DE, *s.f.,* perenniality, perpetuity.
PE.RE.RE.CA, *s.f., Zool.,* tree-frog.
PER.FA.ZER, *v.,* to complete, to finish, to perform.
PER.FEC.CI.O.NIS.MO, *s.m.,* perfectionism.
PER.FEC.CI.O.NIS.TA, *s. 2 gen.,* perfectionist; *adj.,* perfectionist.
PER.FEC.TI.BI.LI.DA.DE, *s.f.,* perfectibility.
PER.FEC.TÍ.VEL, *adj.,* perfectible.
PER.FEC.TI.VO, *adj.,* perfecting.
PER.FEI.ÇÃO, *s.f.,* perfection, excellence, completeness, finishing.
PER.FEI.TA.MEN.TE, *adv.,* perfectly; *interj.,* of course!
PER.FEI.TO, *adj.,* perfect, completed, finished, correct, entire.
PER.FI.CI.EN.TE, *adj.,* perfect, complete.
PER.FI.DA.MEN.TE, *adv.,* perfidiously.
PER.FÍ.DIA, *s.f.,* perfidy, perfidiousness.
PÉR.FI.DO, *adj.,* treacherous, perfidious, disloyal.
PER.FIL, *s.m.,* profile, outline; aspect.
PER.FI.LAR, *v.,* to profile, to stand.
PER.FI.LHA.MEN.TO, *s.m.,* adoption.
PER.FI.LHAR, *v.,* to adopt; *fig.,* to protect; *fig.,* to espousea cause or principle; *Bot.,* to sprout.
PER.FOR.MAN.CE, *s.f., Ingl.,* performance.
PER.FUL.GÊN.CI.A, *s.f.,* refulgence, splendour.
PER.FUL.GEN.TE, *adj.,* refulgent, brilliant, splendid.
PER.FU.MA.DO, *adj.,* perfumed, odorous, fragrant.
PER.FU.MA.DOR, *s.m.,* censer, perfuming pan; *adj.,* perfuming.
PER.FU.MAR, *v.,* to perfume, to aromatize, to scent.
PER.FU.MA.RI.A, *s.f.,* perfume shop; perfumery; *fig., pej.,* nonsense.
PER.FU.ME, *s.m.,* perfume, fragrance, scent.
PER.FU.MIS.TA, *s. 2 gen.,* perfumer.
PER.FU.RA.ÇÃO, *s.f.,* perforation, drill.
PER.FU.RA.DO, *adj.,* perforated, punched, pierced.
PER.FU.RAN.TE, *adj.,* perforating, piercing, perforative.
PER.FU.RAR, *v.,* to perforate, to bore, to drill, to penetrate, to enter.
PER.FU.RA.TRIZ, *s.f.,* drill, drilling machine.
PER.GA.MI.NHA.RI.A, *s.f.,* the making of parchment.
PER.GA.MI.NHO, *s.m.,* parchment.
PÉR.GU.LA, *s.f.,* pergola.
PER.GUN.TA, *s.f.,* question, inquiry, enquiry, interrogation.
PER.GUN.TA.DOR, *s.m.,* questioner, interrogator; *adj.,*

PERGUNTANTE ·· 268 ·· PERPETUAR

questioning, inquiring.

PER.GUN.TAN.TE, *s. 2 gen.*, questioner.

PER.GUN.TAR, *v.*, to ask, to interrogate, to question, to query, to ask for.

PE.RI.CI.A, *s.f.*, investigation, know-how; expertise, invetigators.

PE.RI.CI.AL, *adj.*, expert, skillful.

PE.RI.CLI.TAN.TE, *adj.*, perilous; exposed to danger.

PE.RI.CLI.TAR, *v.*, to run a risk, to endanger.

PE.RI.CU.LO.SI.DA.DE, *s.f., Jur.*, highly perilous.

PE.RI.DEN.TAL, *adj., Odont.*, periodontal.

PE.RI.DU.RAL, *s.f., adj., Anat., Med.*, epidural.

PE.RI.FE.RI.A, *s.f.*, outskirts, suburbs, circumference.

PE.RI.FÉ.RI.CO, *s.m.*, peripheral.

PE.RÍ.FRA.SE, *s.f.*, periphrasis.

PE.RI.FRA.SE.AR, *v.*, to periphrase.

PE.RI.GA.DOR, *adj.*, dangerous.

PE.RI.GAR, *v.*, to be in danger.

PE.RI.GEU, *s.m., Astron.*, perigee.

PE.RI.GI.NI.A, *s.f., Bot.*, perigyny.

PE.RI.GI.NO, *adj., Bot.*, perigynous.

PE.RI.GO, *s.m.*, danger, hazard, peril, risk.

PE.RI.GO.SA.MEN.TE, *adv.*, dangerously.

PE.RI.GO.SO, *adj.*, dangerous, hazardous, perilous.

PE.RI.ME.TRAL, *adj.*, perimetral.

PE.RI.ME.TRI.A, *s.f., Geom.*, perimetry.

PE.RÍ.ME.TRO, *s.m.*, perimeter.

PE.RI.O.DI.CI.DA.DE, *s.f.*, periodicity.

PE.RI.Ó.DI.CO, *s.m.*, periodical, publication; *adj.*, periodic, periodical.

PE.RÍO.DO, *s.m.*, period, cycle, circuit, age, era, lapse of time, term.

PE.RI.PA.TÉ.TI.CO, *s.m., adj.*, Peripatetic.

PE.RI.PÉ.CIA, *s.f.*, peripetia.

PÉ.RI.PLO, *s.m.*, periplus, circumnavigation.

PE.RI.QUI.TO, *s.m., Zool.*, paraquito, parrakeet.

PE.RIS.CÓ.PI.CO, *adj.*, periscopic.

PE.RIS.CÓ.PIO, *s.m.*, periscope.

PE.RIS.PER.MA, *s.f., Bot.*, perisperm.

PE.RIS.SO.LO.GI.A, *s.f.*, perissology.

PE.RI.TO, *s.m.*, expert, specialist, tecnician; *adj.*, skilful, expert, proficient, dexterous.

PE.RI.TO.NE.AL, *adj.*, peritoneal.

PE.RI.TÔ.NI.O, *s.m., Anat.*, peritoneum.

PE.RI.TO.NI.TE, *s.f., Med.*, peritonitis.

PE.RI.TU.RO, *adj.*, perishable.

PER.JU.RAR, *v.*, to perjure, to forswear.

PER.JÚ.RIO, *s.m.*, perjury, false oath.

PER.JU.RO, *s.m.*, perjurer; *adj.*, perjuring, perjured.

PER.MA.NE.CER, *v.*, to stay, to continue, to stand, to remain, to last, maintain.

PER.MA.NÊN.CIA, *s.f.*, permanence, stableness, durability, stability.

PER.MA.NEN.TE, *s. 2 gen.*, perm (abbrev. of permanent wave); *adj.*, permanent, lasting, durable, enduring, constant, fixed.

PER.MA.NEN.TE.MEN.TE, *adv.*, permanently.

PER.ME.A.BI.LI.DA.DE, *s.f.*, permeability.

PER.ME.A.BI.LI.ZA.ÇÃO, *s.f.*, act of making or becoming permeable.

PER.ME.A.BI.LI.ZAR, *v.*, to make or become permeable.

PER.ME.A.ÇÃO, *s.f.*, permeation.

PER.ME.AR, *v.*, to permeate.

PER.ME.Á.VEL, *adj.*, permeable.

PER.MEI.O, *adv., de permeio*: in between, in the middle of.

PER.MI.A.NO, *s.m., Geol.*, Permian; *adj.*, Permian.

PER.MIS.SÃO, *s.f.*, permission, allowance, permit, consent, licence.

PER.MIS.SÍ.VEL, *adj.*, permissible.

PER.MIS.SI.VI.DA.DE, *s.f.*, permissiveness; *Eletr.*, permittivity.

PER.MIS.SI.VO, *adj.*, permissive.

PER.MIS.TÃO, *s.f.*, mixture, confusion.

PER.MI.TIR, *v.*, to permit, to allow, to consent, to authorize, to admit, to tolerate.

PER.MU.TA, *s.f.*, exchange, interchange, barter.

PER.MU.TA.BI.LI.DA.DE, *s.f.*, permutability.

PER.MU.TA.ÇÃO, *s.f.*, permutation.

PER.MU.TA.DOR, *s.m.*, one who permutes; *adj.*, permuting.

PER.MU.TAR, *v.*, to exchange, to interchange, to truck, to barter.

PER.MU.TÁ.VEL, *adj.*, permutable.

PER.NA, *s.f.*, leg; *barriga da perna*: calf.

PER.NA.DA, *s.f.*, kick, spurn; large or big stride.

PER.NA DE PAU, *s.m., Bras., Zool.*, Hudsonian curlew, jack curlew.

PER.NA-LON.GA, *s.f., Zool.*, the same that *mosquito*.

PER.NAL.TAS, *s.f., Zool.*, wading birds.

PER.NAM.BU.CO, *s.*, Pernambuco.

PER.NAM.BU.CA.NO, *s.m., adj.*, pernambucano.

PER.NA.ME, *s.m., Bras., pop.*, legs; fat legs.

PER.NE.AR, *v.*, to kick or shake one's legs.

PER.NE.TA, *s. 2 gen.*, one-legged person.

PER.NI.CI.O.SI.DA.DE, *s.f.*, perniciousness.

PER.NI.CI.O.SO, *adj.*, pernicious, destructive, malign, bad, noxious.

PER.NIL, *s.m.*, thighbone, a thin leg.

PER.NI.LON.GO, *s.m.*, mosquito.

PER.NOI.TAR, *v.*, to stay overnight; to sleep.

PER.NOI.TE, *s.m.*, an overnight stay.

PER.NOS.TI.CIS.MO, *s.m.*, presumptuousness.

PER.NÓS.TI.CO, *adj.*, presumptuous.

PE.RO.BA, *s.f., Bot.*, Peroba (*Aspidosperma polyneuron*).

PE.RO.BAL, *s.m.*, place where peroba trees grow.

PÉ.RO.LA, *s.f.*, pearl, bead.

PE.RO.LA.DO, *adj.*, pearly.

PE.RO.LAR, *v.*, to pearl.

PE.RO.LÍ.FE.RO, *adj.*, producing pearls.

PE.RO.LI.NO, *adj.*, of pearl.

PE.RO.NE.AL, *adj., Anat.*, peroneal.

PE.RÔ.NIO, *s.m., Anat.*, fibula.

PE.RO.NIS.MO, *s.m.*, Peronism.

PE.RO.NIS.TA, *s. 2 gen.*, Peronist; *adj.*, referring to Peronism.

PER.PAS.SAR, *v.*, to pass-by, to graze, to move.

PER.PAS.SÁ.VEL, *adj.*, passable; tolerable.

PER.PEN.DI.CU.LAR, *s.f., Geom.*, perpendicular; *adj.*, perpendicular.

PER.PEN.DI.CU.LA.RI.DA.DE, *s.f.*, perpendicularity.

PER.PEN.DI.CU.LAR.MEN.TE, *adv.*, perpendicularly.

PER.PE.TRA.ÇÃO, *s.f.*, perpetration.

PER.PE.TRA.DOR, *s.m.*, perpetrator; *adj.*, perpetrating.

PER.PE.TRAR, *v.*, to perpetrate.

PER.PE.TU.A.ÇÃO, *s.f.*, perpetuation.

PER.PE.TU.AR, *v.*, to perpetuate, to immortalize, to

PERPETUAÇÃO   ·· 269 ··   **PESCARIA**

propagate.

PER.PE.TU.A.ÇÃO, *s.f.*, perpetuation.

PER.PE.TU.A.DOR, *s.m.*, perpetuator; *adj.*, perpetuating.

PER.PE.TU.A.MEN.TE, *adv.*, perpetually.

PER.PE.TU.A.MEN.TO, *s.m.*, the same that *perpetuação*.

PER.PÉ.TUO, *adj.*, perpetual, constant, ceaseless, eternal, immortal.

PER.PLE.XÃO, *s.f.*, the same that *perplexidade*.

PER.PLE.XI.DA.DE, *s.f.*, perplexity, amazement, bewilderment, hesitation.

PER.PLE.XI.DEZ, *s.f.*, the same that *perplexidade*.

PER.PLE.XO, *adj.*, perplexed, uncertain, astonished.

PER.QUI.RI.ÇÃO, *s.f.*, thorough investigation; scrutiny.

PER.QUI.RIR, *v.*, to investigate minutely, scrutinize.

PER.SA, *adj.*, *s. 2 gen.*, Persian.

PERS.CRU.TA.ÇÃO, *s.f.*, minute search or inquiry.

PERS.CRU.TA.DOR, *s.m.*, investigator; one who scrutinizes; *adj.*, searching, scrutinizing.

PERS.CRU.TAR, *v.*, to search, to scrutinize, to scan, to examine.

PERS.CRU.TÁ.VEL, *adj.*, that can be investigated.

PER.SE.CU.ÇÃO, *s.f.*, the same that *perseguição*.

PER.SE.CU.TÓ.RI.O, *adj.*, involving persecution.

PER.SE.GUI.ÇÃO, *s.f.*, persecution, oppression, pursuit, chase.

PER.SE.GUI.DOR, *s.m.*, pursuer, persecutor; *adj.*, pursuing, persecuting.

PER.SE.GUIR, *v.*, to persecute, pursue, to trace, to chase, to hunt, to oppress, to annoy.

PER.SE.VE.RAN.ÇA, *s.f.*, perseverance, persistence, constancy.

PER.SE.VE.RAN.TE, *adj.*, persevering.

PER.SE.VE.RAR, *v.*, to persevere, to persist, to continue, to remain, to stay, to last.

PÉR.SI.A, *s.*, Persia.

PER.SI.A.NA, *s.f.*, Persian blinds, persiennes, Venetian blinds.

PÉR.SI.CO, *adj.*, the same thar *persa*.

PER.SIG.NAR(-SE), *v.*, to cross (oneself).

PER.SIS.TÊN.CIA, *s.f.*, persistence, perseverance, constancy, stability.

PER.SIS.TEN.TE, *adj.*, persistent, persisting, persevering.

PER.SIS.TIR, *v.*, to persist, to continue, to persevere, to insist.

PER.SO.NA.GEM, *s. 2 gen.*, personage, character.

PER.SO.NA.LI.DA.DE, *s.f.*, personality, individuality.

PER.SO.NA.LIS.MO, *s.m.*, personalism.

PER.SO.NA.LIS.TA, *s. 2 gen.*, personalist; *adj.*, personalist, personalistic.

PER.SO.NA.LI.ZA.ÇÃO, *s.f.*, personalization.

PER.SO.NA.LI.ZA.DO, *adj.*, personalized.

PER.SO.NA.LI.ZAR, *v.*, to personalize.

PER.SO.NI.FI.CA.ÇÃO, *s.f.*, personification.

PER.SO.NI.FI.CAR, *v.*, to personify, to represent, to typify.

PERS.PEC.TI.VA, *s.f.*, perspective, view, outlook, prospect.

PERS.PEC.TI.VA.ÇÃO, *s.f.*, act of putting in perspective.

PERS.PEC.TI.VAR, *v.*, to put in perspective.

PERS.PI.CÁ.CI.A, *s.f.*, perspicacity, perspicaciousness.

PERS.PI.CAZ, *adj.*, *Zool.*, perspicacious, astute, keen, sharp-sighted.

PERS.PI.CU.I.DA.DE, *s.f.*, perspicuity.

PERS.PÍ.CUO, *adj.*, perspicuous.

PERS.PI.RA.ÇÃO, *s.f.*, perspiration.

PERS.PI.RAR, *v.*, to perspire, sweat.

PERS.PI.RA.TÓ.RI.O, *adj.*, *Med.*, perspiratory.

PER.SU.A.DI.MEN.TO, *s.m.*, the same that *persuasão*.

PER.SU.A.DIR, *v.*, to persuade, to influence, to convince, to advise, to counsel.

PER.SU.A.DÍ.VEL, *adj.*, persuadable, persuasible.

PER.SU.A.SÃO, *s.f.*, persuasion, conviction.

PER.SU.A.SÍ.VEL, *adj.*, the same that *persuasivo*.

PER.SU.A.SI.VO, *adj.*, persuasive, persuading.

PER.SU.A.SOR, *s.m.*, persuader; *adj.*, persuading.

PER.SU.A.SÓ.RI.O, *adj.*, the same that *persuasivo*.

PER.TEN.CE, *s.m.*, appurtenance, appendage.

PER.TEN.CEN.TE, *adj.*, pertaining, belonging, proper.

PER.TEN.CER, *v.*, to pertain, to be part of, to belong to, to be owned by, to concern.

PER.TI.NÁ.CI.A, *s.f.*, obstinacy, pertinaciousness.

PER.TI.NAZ, *adj.*, pertinacious.

PER.TI.NÊN.CI.A, *s.f.*, pertinence, pertinency.

PER.TI.NEN.TE, *adj.*, pertinent.

PER.TO, *adj.*, near, close, proximate; *adv.*, near, nearby, nearly, close, towardly.

PER.TUR.BA.ÇÃO, *s.f.*, perturbation, commotion, trouble, disturbance, disorder.

PER.TUR.BA.DO, *adj.*, perturbed, upset, uneasy.

PER.TUR.BA.DOR, *s.m.*, perturbator, disturber; *adj.*, disturbing, perturbing.

PER.TUR.BAR, *v.*, to perturb, to molest, to disturb, to agitate, to disorder, to confuse.

PER.TUR.BA.TI.VO, *adj.*, perturbative.

PER.TUR.BÁ.VEL, *adj.*, perturbable.

PE.RU, *s.m.*, *Zool.*, turkey.

PE.RU, *s.*, Peru.

PE.RUA, *s.f.*, van, station wagon; turkey hen; drunkenness.

PE.RU.A.NO, *adj.*, *s.m.*, Peruvian.

PE.RU.AR, *v.*, to kibitz in a game; to size up, to speculate.

PE.RU.CA, *s.f.*, wig, periwig.

PE.RU.EI.RO, *s.m.*, minibus driver.

PER.VA.GAN.TE, *adj.*, travelling; crossing; roving.

PER.VA.GAR, *v.*, to traverse; to cross; to roam.

PER.VER.SÃO, *s.f.*, perversion, depravation; alteration.

PER.VER.SI.DA.DE, *s.f.*, perversity, perverseness.

PER.VER.SO, *adj.*, perverse, wicked, evil, devilish.

PER.VER.SOR, *s.m.*, perverter; *adj.*, perverting, perversive.

PER.VER.TER, *v.*, to pervert, to make perverse, to corrupt, to distort.

PER.VER.TI.DO, *adj.*, perverted, corrupt.

PE.SA.DA.MEN.TE, *adv.*, heavily.

PE.SA.DÃO, *adj.*, very heavy.

PE.SA.DO, *adj.*, weighty, heavy, hard, onerous, difficult.

PE.SA.GEM, *s.f.*, weighing, weighage.

PÊ.SA.MES, *s.m.*, *pl.*, condolences.

PE.SAR, *s.m.*, sorrow, regret, grief, sadness; *v.*, to weigh, to ponder, to consider, to balance, to examine.

PE.SA.RO.SA.MEN.TE, *adv.*, sorrowfully, condolingly.

PE.SA.RO.SO, *adj.*, sorrowful, sorry.

PES.CA, *s.f.*, fishing, fishery.

PES.CA.DA, *s.f.*, *Zool.*, a weakfish (Cynoscion).

PES.CA.DO, *s.m.*, quantity of fish caught; catch of fish.

PES.CA.DOR, *s.m.*, fisherman, fisher.

PES.CAR, *v.*, to fish, to catch fish, to net, to entrap.

PES.CA.RI.A, *s.f.*, fishery, fishing.

PESCOÇADA ·· 270 ·· PIEDOSAMENTE

PES.CO.ÇA.DA, *s.f.*, a blow on the neck.
PES.CO.ÇÃO, *s.m.*, the same that *pescoçada*.
PES.CO.ÇO, *s.m., Anat.*, neck, throat.
PES.CO.ÇU.DO, *adj.*, thick-necked.
PE.SE.TA, *s.f., Ant.*, peseta (Spanish silver coin).
PE.SO, *s.m.*, weight, heaviness, power, burden, load, oppression, onus; *peso bruto*: gross weight.
PE.SO-GA.LO, *s.m., Esp.*, bantamweight(Boxe).
PE.SO-LE.VE, *s.m., Esp.*, lightweight(Boxe).
PE.SO-MÉ.DI.O, *s.m., Esp.*, middle-weight(Boxe).
PE.SO-MOS.CA, *s.m., Esp.*, flyweight.
PE.SO-PE.NA, *s.m., Esp.*, featherweight(Boxe).
PE.SO-PE.SA.DO, *s.m., Esp.*, heavyweight (Boxe).
PES.PE.GAR, *v.*, to apply blow, to hit; to impose (something); to fool (someone).
PES.PON.TAR, *v.*, to backstitch, to quilt, stitch.
PES.PON.TO, *s.m.*, quilting stitch, backstitch.
PES.QUEI.RO, *s.m.*, fishing ground.
PES.QUI.SA, *s.f.*, search, inquiry, investigation, examination.
PES.QUI.SA.DOR, *s.m.*, researcher; *adj.*, search, searching.
PES.QUI.SAR, *v.*, to search, to inquire, to research, to examine, to investigate.
PES.SE.GA.DA, *s.f.*, peach jam.
PES.SE.GAL, *s.m.*, peachery, peach grove.
PÊS.SE.GO, *s.m., Bot.*, peach.
PES.SE.GUEI.RO, *s.m., Bot.*, peach tree.
PES.SI.MA.MEN.TE, *adv.*, very badly.
PES.SI.MIS.MO, *s.m.*, pessimism.
PES.SI.MIS.TA, *s. 2 gen.*, pessimist.
PÉS.SI.MO, *adj.*, very bad.
PES.SO.A, *s.f.*, person, human being, individual.
PES.SO.AL, *adj.*, personnel, folks; *adj.*, personal, individual.
PES.SO.A.LI.DA.DE, *s.f.*, individuality, personality.
PES.SO.A.LI.ZAR, *v.*, to personalize.
PES.SO.AL.MEN.TE, *adv.*, personally, individually, in person.
PES.TA.NA, *s.f.*, eyelash.
PES.TA.NE.JAN.TE, *adj.*, twinkling.
PES.TA.NE.JAR, *v.*, to twinkle, to blink.
PES.TE, *s.f.*, plague, pest.
PES.TI.CI.DA, *s.f.*, pesticide.
PES.TI.LÊN.CI.A, *s.f.*, pestilence.
PES.TI.LEN.CI.O.SO, *adj.*, pestilent, pernicious, pestilential.
PES.TI.LEN.TO, *adj.*, pestilent, pestilential.
PE.TA, *s.f.*, lie, story, humbug.
PÉ.TA.LA, *s.f.*, petal.
PE.TAR.DO, *s.m.*, petard, bomb.
PE.TE.CA, *s.f., Bras.*, shuttlecock.
PE.TE.LE.CO, *s.m., Bras.*, fillip, slap, rap.
PE.TI.ÇÃO, *s.f.*, petition, request, suit, appeal, solicitation.
PE.TI.CI.O.NAR, *v.*, to petition.
PE.TI.CI.O.NÁ.RI.O, *s.m.*, petitioner, applicant.
PE.TIS.CAR, *v.*, to nibble, to snack; to pick at food.
PE.TIS.CO, *s.m.*, tidbit, dainty, morsel.
PE.TRE.CHOS, *s.m., pl.*, equipment, utensils; *Mil.*, munition.
PÉ.TRE.O, *adj.*, petrous, rocky, stony.
PE.TRI.FI.CA.ÇÃO, *s.f.*, petrification.
PE.TRI.FI.CA.DO, *adj.*, petrified.
PE.TRI.FI.CA.DOR, *adj.*, petrifying.
PE.TRI.FI.CAR, *v.*, to petrify, to change to stone, to paralyze.
PE.TRO.DÓ.LAR, *s.m.*, petrodollar.
PE.TRO.GRA.FI.A, *s.f.*, petrography.

PE.TRO.GRÁ.FI.CO, *adj.*, petrographic, petrographical.
PE.TRO.LEI.RO, *s.m.*, oil tanker, pétroleur.
PE.TRÓ.LEO, *s.m.*, petroleum, oil.
PE.TRO.LÍ.FE.RO, *adj.*, petroliferous, bearing petroleum.
PE.TRO.LO.GI.A, *s.f., Geol.*, petrology.
PE.TRO.QUÍ.MI.CA, *s.f.*, petrochemistry, petrochemicals.
PE.TRO.QUÍ.MI.CO, *s.m.*, petrochemist; *adj.*, petrochemical.
PE.TU.LÂN.CIA, *s.f.*, petulance, sauciness, insolence.
PE.TU.LAN.TE, *adj.*, petulant.
PE.TÚ.NIA, *s.f., Bot.*, petunia.
PEZ, *s.m.*, pitch, resin.
PE.ZU.DO, *adj.*, big-footed.
PI.A, *s.f.*, sink, wash-basin.
PI.Á, *s.m., Bras.*, a young Indian; *col.*, kid, boy, lad.
PI.A.ÇA.BA, *s.f., Bot.*, piassaba palm.
PI.A.ÇA.BAL, *s.m., Bras.*, place where piassava palms grow.
PI.A.DA, *s.f.*, joke, peep, chirp, bird.
PI.A.DI.NHA, *s.f., pop.*, a little joke; *pej.*, ironic comment.
PI.A.DIS.TA, *s. 2 gen.*, joker.
PI.A.DO, *s.m.*, peep, bird call.
PI.A.MEN.TE, *adv.*, earnestly.
PI.AN.ÇAR, *v., Bras.*, to hanker, to tong for.
PI.A.NIS.TA, *s. 2 gen.*, pianist; piano player.
PI.A.NO, *s.m.*, piano.
PI.A.NO.LA, *s.f.*, pianola.
PI.ÃO, *s.m.*, spinningtop.
PI.AR, *v.*, to chirp, to tweet (bird); to cheep, to peep (chick); to hoot (owl); *gir.*, to talk.
PI.CA.DA, *s.f.*, prick, sting, bite; peck; trail.
PI.CA.DEI.RO, *s.m.*, circus ring.
PI.CA.DE.LA, *s.f.*, bite (insect, snake), sting (bee); prick (needle).
PI.CA.DI.NHO, *s.m.*, minced meat, hash.
PI.CA.DO, *s.m.*, minced (meat); *adj.*, pricked; stung; bitten.
PI.CA.NHA, *s.f.*, rump cover, rump cap.
PI.CAN.TE, *s. 2 gen.*, whet, appetizer; *adj.*, appetizing, piquant.
PI.CA-PAU, *s.m., Zool.*, woodpecker.
PI.CAR, *v.*, to sting, to bite, to prick, to peck.
PI.CAR.DI.A, *s.f.*, knavery, crookedness; spite, spitefulness.
PI.CA.RES.CO, *adj.*, picaresque, burlesque, funny, jocose.
PI.CA.RE.TA, *s.f.*, pickax.
PI.CA.RE.TA.GEM, *s.f.*, cheating, swindling.
PI.CA.RE.TAR, *v.*, to cheat, to swindle.
PI.CHA.ÇÃO, *s.f.*, act of covering with pitch; *col.*, written on a street wall, graffitti.
PI.CHA.MEN.TO, *s.m.*, the same that *pichação*.
PI.CHA.DOR, *s.m.*, workman who covers the streets with asphalt; *col.*, graffitist.
PI.CHAR, *v.*, to pitch, to tar, to cover, to paint into graffito.
PI.CHE, *s.m.*, pitch, tar, betumen, asphalt.
PI.CHEL, *s.m.*, a sort of vessel.
PI.CLES, *s.m., pl.*, pickles.
PI.CO, *s.m.*, peak, top, summit, apex, sharp point.
PI.CO.LÉ, *s.m., Bras.*, icelolly.
PI.CO.TA.DO.RA, *s.f.*, a paper-perforating machine.
PI.CO.TA.GEM, *s.f.*, perforation, punching.
PI.CO.TAR, *v.*, to perforate, to punch.
PI.CO.TE, *s.m.*, picot, purl, perforation.
PI.CU.I.NHA, *s.f.*, cheep, chirp, peep, jest.
PI.E.DA.DE, *s.f.*, pity, compassion, mercy, devotion.
PI.E.DO.SA.MEN.TE, *adv.*, piously.

PIEDOSO · 271 · PIPOQUEIRO

PI.E.DO.SO, *adj.*, pious, religious, godly, devout.
PI.E.GAS, *adj.*, soppy.
PI.E.GUI.CE, *s.f.*, sopiness.
PÍ.ER, *s.m.*, pier.
PIERC.ING, *s.m., Ingl.,* body piercing.
PI.ER.RÔ, *s.m.*, pierrot.
PI.FA.DO, *adj., Bras., col.,* broken down.
PI.FÃO, *s.m.*, drunkenness, a drinking spree.
PI.FAR, *v., col.,* to breack down.
PÍ.FA.RO, *s.m., Ant.,* fife (a small flute).
PI.GAR.RE.AR, *v.*, to hawk, to hem.
PI.GAR.REN.TO, *adj.*, phlegmy.
PI.GAR.RO, *s.m.*, phlegm.
PIG.MEN.TA.ÇÃO, *s.f.*, pigmentation, coloration.
PIG.MEN.TA.DO, *adj.*, pigmented.
PIG.MEN.TAR, *v.*, to pigment.
PIG.MEN.TO, *s.m.*, pigment, colouring matter.
PIG.MEU, *s.m.*, Pigmy; *adj.*, pigmy.
PI.JA.MA, *s.m.*, pyjamas, pajama.
PI.LA.DO, *adj.*, pounded; peeled, hulled.
PI.LA.DOR, *s.m.*, pounder, crusher; *adj.*, pounding, crushing.
PI.LAN.TRA, *s. 2 gen.,* rascal, scamp, scoundrel.
PI.LAN.TRA.GEM, *s.f.*, rascality, dishonesty.
PI.LÃO, *s.m.*, pestle, crusher.
PI.LAR, *s.m.*, pillar, column, post.
PI.LAS.TRA, *s.f., Arquit.,* pilaster.
PI.LA.TES, *s.m.*, Pilates (a physical fitness).
PI.LE.QUE, *s.m.*, drunkenness.
PI.LHA, *s.f.*, pile, heap; *Eletr.,* battery, electric battery; plunder, pillage.
PI.LHA.GEM, *s.f.*, plunder, sacking, pillage.
PI.LHAR, *v.*, to plunder, to pillage, to sacking, to sack.
PI.LHÉ.RIA, *s.f.*, quip, jest, joke.
PI.LHÉ.RI.CO, *adj.*, jesting, playful, mocking.
PI.LHE.RI.AR, *v.*, to quip, to jest, to joke.
PI.LO.TA.GEM, *s.f.*, pilotage, flying.
PI.LO.TAR, *v.*, to pilot, to direct, to fly.
PI.LO.TI, *s.m.*, stilt.
PI.LO.TO, *s.m.*, pilot, steersman, flyer, aviator.
PÍ.LU.LA, *s.f.*, pill.
PIM.BA, *interj.*, gee! wow!
PI.MEN.TA, *s.f., Cul.,* pepper.
PI.MEN.TA-DO-REI.NO, *s.f.*, black pepper.
PI.MEN.TA-MA.LA.GUE.TA, *s.f., Bot., Cul.,* malaguetta pepper, chilli pepper.
PI.MEN.TÃO, *s.m., Bot.,* pimento, green pepper, red pepper.
PI.MEN.TEI.RA, *s.f., Bot.,* pepper tree.
PIM.PO.LHO, *s.m.*, kid, child.
PI.NA.CO.TE.CA, *s.f.*, pinacotheca.
PI.NÁ.CU.LO, *s.m.*, pinnacle.
PIN.ÇA, *s.f.*, tweezers, nippers.
PÍN.CA.RO, *s.m.*, apex, pinnacle, summit.
PIN.CEL, *s.m.*, brush.
PIN.CE.LA.DA, *s.f.*, a stroke with a brush.
PIN.CE.LA.GEM, *s.f.*, the same that *pincelada.*
PIN.CE.LAR, *v.*, to paint with a brush.
PIN.CE.NÊ, *s.m., Fr.,* pince-nez.
PIN.DA.Í.BA, *s.f., Bot.,* a kind ofpalm-fiber rope; *Bras., gír.,* lack of money.
PIN.DO.RA.MA, *s.m., Tupi,* region of the palms (referes to Brazil or South America).

PI.NE.AL, *adj., Anat.,* pineal.
PI.NEL, *s. 2 gen., Bras., gír.,* a crazy person; *adj.*, crazy.
PIN.GA, *s.f.*, a drop, rum.
PIN.GA.DO, *s.m., Bras., col.,* coffee with a drop of milk; *adj.*, splashed with something.
PIN.GAR, *v.*, to drip, to fall in drops, to sprinkle, to drizzle.
PIN.GEN.TE, *s.m.*, pendant, earring, drop.
PIN.GO, *s.m.*, drop, dripping.
PIN.GU.ÇO, *s.m., Bras., pop.,* heavy drinker; *adj.*, drunk.
PIN.GUE-PON.GUE, *s.m., Esp.,* ping-pong.
PIN.GUE.LA, *s.f.*, a wood bridge used as a footbridge.
PIN.GUIM, *s.m., Zool.,* penguim.
PIN.GUI.NHO, *s.m.*, droplet; *Bras., col.,* a tiny bit.
PI.NHA, *s.f., Bot.,* pine cone.
PI.NHAL, *s.m.*, a grove of pine trees.
PI.NHÃO, *s.m., Bras., Bot.,* pine nut.
PI.NHEI.RAL, *s.m., Bras.,* the same that *pinhal.*
PI.NHEI.RO, *s.m.*, pine tree.
PI.NHO, *s.m.*, pinewood.
PI.NI.CA.DA, *s.f.*, pinch; peck (needle); stab (thorn).
PI.NI.CAR, *v., Bras.,* to be itchy; to peck, to pinch; to jab.
PI.NI.CO, *s.m., Bras.,* a sharp point; beak.
PI.NIM.BA, *s.f., col.,* annoyance; stubbornness.
PI.NO, *s.m.*, pin, peg, bolt, pivot, top, apex.
PI.NOI.A, *s.f.*, bore, junk; *uma ~:* my foot!
PI.NO.TE, *s.m.*, jump, bound, leap.
PI.NO.TE.AR, *v.*, to leap, to jump.
PIN.TA, *s.f.*, spot, mark; *o cara é boa ~:* the guy is looking good.
PIN.TA BRA.VA, *adj.*, shady character.
PIN.TA.DO, *adj.*, painted; coloured; *col.,* freckled.
PIN.TA.I.NHO, *s.m.*, young chicken.
PIN.TAR, *v.*, to paint, to draw; to set in colours, to tinge.
PIN.TAS.SIL.GO, *s.m., Bras., Zool.,* goldfinch (*Spinus ictericus*).
PIN.TI.NHO, *s.m.*, a small chick.
PIN.TO, *s.m.*, young chicken, kid; *vulg.,* penis.
PIN.TO-CAL.ÇU.DO, *s.m., Bras., fam.,* boy who begins to use long trousers.
PIN.TOR, *s.m.*, painter.
PIN.TO.RA, *s.f.*, paintress.
PIN.TU.RA, *s.f.*, picture, painting, image.
PIN.TU.RES.CO, *adj.*, picturesque.
PI.O, *s.m.*, peep, cheep; *adj.*, pious, godly, devout.
PI.O.DER.MI.TE, *s.f., Med.,* pyoderma.
PI.O.GÊ.NE.SE, *s.f.*, pyogenesis (formation or secretion of pus).
PI.O.LHA.DA, *s.f.*, a great quantity of lice.
PI.O.LHEN.TO, *adj.*, lousy.
PI.O.LHO, *s.m.*, louse.
PI.O.NEI.RIS.MO, *s.m.*, pioneering nature.
PI.O.NEI.RO, *s.m.*, pioneer, precursor, explorer.
PI.OR, *s.m.*, the worst; *adj.*, worse, worst.
PI.O.RA, *s.f.*, deterioration, aggravation.
PI.O.RAR, *v.*, to worsen, to aggravate, to complicate.
PI.PA, *s.f.*, kite; cask, barrel.
PI.PA.RO.TE, *s.m.*, flick, fillip.
PI.PE.TA, *s.f.*, pipette (measuring tube in lab).
PI.PI, *s.m., fam.,* piss (children's language).
PI.PO.CA, *s.f.*, popcorn.
PI.PO.CAR, *v.*, to pop, to burst, to crackle.
PI.PO.QUEI.RO, *s.m.*, popcorn seller.

PIQUE

PI.QUE, *s.m., col.,* enthusiasm; catch; notch; *Náut.,* ir à ~: to sink.
PI.QUE.NI.QUE, *s.m.,* picnic.
PI.QUE.TA.GEM, *s.f.,* act of picketing.
PI.QUE.TAR, *v.,* to picket.
PI.QUE.TE, *s.m.,* picket.
PI.RA, *s.f.,* pyre; *pop.,* fire, bonfire; ~ olímpica: Olympic torch.
PI.RA.ÇÃO, *s.f., gír.,* madness.
PI.RA.DO, *adj., Bras., col.,* crazy, insane.
PI.RAM.BEI.RA, *s.f., Bras.,* precipice, cliff; steep bluff.
PI.RA.MI.DAL, *adj.,* pyramidal; *fig.,* colossal.
PI.RÂ.MI.DE, *s.f.,* pyramid.
PI.RA.NHA, *s.f., Zool.,* piranha, caribe; *vulg.,* whore, prostitute.
PI.RÃO, *s.m., Bras., Cul.,* cassava porridge.
PI.RAR, *v., Bras., gír.,* to go insane.
PI.RA.RU.CU, *s.m., Bras., Zool.,* great fresh-water fish (*Arapaima gigas*).
PI.RA.TA, *s.m.,* pirate, corsair, buccaneer, sea-robber.
PI.RA.TA.RIA, *s.f.,* piracy, fraud, robbery.
PI.RA.TE.AR, *v.,* to pirate, to fraud, to rob.
PI.RES, *s.m.,* saucer.
PI.RÉ.TI.CO, *adj., Med.,* febrile.
PI.RI.FOR.ME, *adj.,* pyriform (pear-shaped).
PI.RI.LAM.PE.AR, *v., Bras.,* to glow (as a firefly).
PI.RI.LÂM.PI.CO, *adj.,* phosphorescent.
PI.RI.LAM.PO, *s.m., Zool.,* firefly.
PI.RI.TA, *s.f.,* pyrites.
PI.RO.GA, *s.f.,* piragua, pirogue.
PI.RO.MA.NI.A, *s.f.,* pyromania.
PI.RO.TEC.NIA, *s.f.,* pyrotechnics.
PI.RO.TÉC.NI.CO, *s.m.,* pyrotechnist; *adj.,* pyrotechnic.
PIR.RA.ÇA, *s.f.,* spite, roguish trick.
PIR.RA.ÇAR, *v.,* to play roguish tricks.
PIR.RA.CEN.TO, *adj.,* stubborn, obstinate, spiteful.
PIR.RA.LHO, *s.m., Bras., pop.,* kid, boy; small person.
PI.RU.E.TA, *s.f.,* pirouette.
PI.RU.E.TAR, *v.,* to pirouette.
PI.RU.LI.TO, *s.m.,* lollypop, lollipop.
PI.SA.DA, *s.f.,* footstep.
PI.SA.DE.LA, *s.f.,* treading, stamping.
PI.SA.DO, *adj.,* trodden, stepped on.
PI.SÃO, *s.m.,* fulling-mill, footstep.
PI.SAR, *v.,* to tread on, to trample, to step on, to offend.
PIS.CA.DE.LA, *s.f.,* blink, wink.
PIS.CA-PIS.CA, *s.m.,* flasher, blinker, indicator.
PIS.CAR, *v.,* to wink, to blink, to twinkle.
PIS.CI.A.NO, *s.m., Astrol.,* Pisces (born under the sign of Pisces); *adj.,* related to the sign of Pisces.
PIS.CI.CUL.TU.RA, *s.f.,* pisciculture.
PIS.CI.NA, *s.f.,* swimming pool, basin.
PI.SO, *s.m.,* floor, pavement, gait.
PI.SO.TE.AR, *v.,* to trample (on); *fig.,* to trample over, to treat harshly, to humiliate.
PIS.TA, *s.f.,* track, racecourse, race track, clue.
PIS.TA.CHE, *s.f.,* pistachio; *Bot.,* pistachio tree.
PIS.TÃO, PIS.TOM, *s.m.,* piston (auto mechanic); *Mús.,* cornet.
PIS.TO.LA, *s.f.,* pistol.
PIS.TO.LÃO, *s.m.,* recomendation, big shot.
PIS.TO.LEI.RO, *s.m.,* gunfighter, bandit, gunman.
PI.TA.DA, *s.f.,* pinch, small quantity.
PI.TA.GÓ.RI.CO, *s.m.,* Pythagorist, Pythagorean; *adj.,* Pythagoric, Pythagorical, Pythagorean.

PLANÍCIE

PI.TAN.GA, *s.f., Bot.,* Brazilian cherry, Suriname cherry (a kind of fleshy red berry).
PI.TAR, *v.,* to smoke.
PI.TE.CAN.TRO.PO, *s.m.,* Pithecanthropus (ancient name for *Homo erectus*).
PI.TEI.RA, *s.f.,* cigarette-holder; *Bot.,* maguey (*Agave americana, Furcraea foetida*).
PI.TI.RÍ.A.SE, *s.f., Med.,* pityriasis.
PI.TO.CO, *adj., Bras.,* bobtailed.
PÍ.TON, *s.m., Zool.,* python, serpent.
PI.TO.NI.SA, *s.f.,* pythoness, fortune-teller(female).
PI.TO.RES.CA.MEN.TE, *adv.,* picturesquely.
PI.TO.RES.CO, *adj.,* picturesque, pictorial.
PI.TOS.GA, *s. 2 gen., pop.,* a myopic person; person who blinks; *adj.,* short-sighted; blinking.
PI.TU.Á, *s.m.,* a sort of fine-haired brush.
PI.TUI.TÁ.RI.A, *s.f., Anat.,* pituitary.
PI.TUI.TÁ.RI.O, *adj.,* pituitary.
PI.TUI.TO.SO, *adj.,* pituitous (full of mucus).
PI.VE.TE, *s.m., pop., pej.,* childthief.
PI.VÔ, *s.m.,* pivot, pin tooth, central factor.
PI.XA.IM, *s.m., Bras.,* frizzy hair; *adj.,* frizzy.
PIXEL, *s.m.,* pixel.
PIXOTE, *s.m.,* smal child.
PI.ZI.CA.TO, *s.m., It., Mús.,* pizzicato.
PIZ.ZA, *s.f., It.,* pizza.
PIZ.ZA.RI.A, *s.f., It.,* pizzeria.
PLA.CA, *s.f.,* plate, board, card, plaque.
PLA.CA.BI.LI.DA.DE, *s.f.,* placability.
PLA.CAR, *s.m.,* placard, scoreboard, poster bill.
PLA.CÁ.VEL, *adj.,* placable.
PLACEBO, *s.m.,* placebo.
PLA.CEN.TA, *s.f., Anat.,* placenta.
PLA.CEN.TA.ÇÃO, *s.f., Anat.,* placentation.
PLA.CEN.TÁ.RI.O, *s.m.,* placentary; *adj.,* placental.
PLA.CI.DEZ, *s.f.,* placidity, placidness.
PLÁ.CI.DO, *adj.,* placid, quiet, tranquil, calm.
PLÁ.CI.TO, *s.m.,* approval, consent; a vow of chastity of the bishops, agreement.
PLA.GA, *s.f.,* region, country, land.
PLA.GI.A.DOR, *s.m.,* plagiarist; *adj.,* plagiaristic.
PLA.GI.AR, *v.,* to plagiarize, crib.
PLA.GI.Á.RI.O, *s.m.,* plagiarist; *adj.,* plagiaristic.
PLÁ.GI.O, *s.m.,* plagiarism.
PLAI.NA, *s.f.,* plane.
PLAI.NO, *s.m.,* prairie, plain; *adj.,* plain, flat.
PLA.NA.DOR, *s.m.,* glider.
PLÂNC.TON, PLANC.TO, *s.m., Bot.,* plankton.
PLA.NAL.TO, *s.m.,* plateau, upland.
PLA.NAR, *v.,* to plane, to glide.
PLA.NE.AR, *v.,* the same that *planejar.*
PLA.NE.JA.DOR, *s.m.,* planner.
PLA.NE.JA.MENTO, *s.m.,* projection, planning.
PLA.NE.JAR, *v.,* to plan, to project.
PLA.NE.TA, *s.m., Astron.,* planet.
PLA.NE.TÁ.RIO, *s.m.,* planetarium.
PLAN.GER, *v.,* to lament, to mourn, to beat.
PLAN.GÊN.CI.A, *s.f.,* plangency; sadness.
PLAN.GEN.TE, *adj.,* plangent, plaintive, sad.
PLAN.GER, *v.,* to lament; ro mourn.
PLA.NÍ.CIE, *s.f.,* plain, lowland.

PLANIFICAÇÃO ·· 273 ·· PODOLOGISTA

PLA.NI.FI.CA.ÇÃO, *s.f.*, planning.
PLA.NI.FI.CAR, *v.*, to design, to plan out, to delineate.
PLA.NI.LHA, *s.f.*, table; *Comp.*, spreadsheet, worksheet.
PLA.NI.ME.TRI.A, *s.f.*, planimetry.
PLA.NO, *s.m.*, plan, scheme, project, plane.
PLA.NO.GRA.FI.A, *s.f.*, planography
PLAN.TA, *s.f.*, plant, plan, blueprint.
PLAN.TA.ÇÃO, *s.f.*, plantation, planting.
PLAN.TA.DO, *adj.*, planted.
PLAN.TA.DOR, *s.m.*, planter, grower; *adj.*, planting.
PLAN.TÃO, *s.m.*, duty, service.
PLAN.TAR, *v.*, to plant, to cultivate, to sow.
PLAN.TEL, *s.m.*, *Bras.*, breeding stock (animals as a cattle); group of athletes.
PLAN.TI.O, *s.m.*, plantation.
PLAN.TO.NIS.TA, *s. 2 gen.*, person on duty.
PLA.QUE.TA, *s.f.*, small plaque, plaquette; *Comp.*, chip.
PLAS.MA, *s.m.*, plasma, protoplasm.
PLAS.MAR, *v.*, to model.
PLÁS.TI.CA, *s.f.*, plastic surgery.
PLAS.TI.CI.DA.DE, *s.f.*, plasticity.
PLAS.TI.CI.ZAR, *v.*, to plasticize.
PLÁS.TI.CO, *adj.*, plastic.
PLAS.TI.FI.CA.ÇÃO, *s.f.*, act of covering something with plastic materials.
PLAS.TI.FI.CAR, *v.*, to laminate.
PLA.TA.FOR.MA, *s.f.*, platform, programme, political programme.
PLÁ.TA.NO, *s.m.*, *Bot.*, platan, platane, plane-tree.
PLA.TEI.A, *s.f.*, pit, auditorium, audience.
PLA.TI.NA, *s.f.*, platinum.
PLA.TI.NA.DO, *s.m.*, contact-point (in old car engines); *adj.*, platinated, platinized.
PLA.TÔ, *s.m.*, plateau.
PLA.TÔ.NI.CO, *adj.*, Platonic, ideal, mental.
PLAU.SI.BI.LI.DA.DE, *s.f.*, plausibility, plausibleness.
PLAU.SÍ.VEL, *adj.*, plausible; reasonable, sensible.
PLAY.BACK, *s.m.*, *Ingl.*, *Mús.*, playback.
PLAY.BOY, *s.m.*, *Ingl.*, playboy.
PLAY.GROUND, *s.m.*, *Ingl.*, playground.
PLE.BE, *s.f.*, the common people, mob, rabble.
PLE.BEU, *s.m.*, plebeian.
PLE.BIS.CI.TÁ.RI.O, *adj.*, plebiscitary.
PLE.BIS.CI.TO, *s.m.*, plebiscite, referendum.
PLÊI.A.DE, *s.f.*, Pleiad; *Plêiades:* *Astron.*, the Pleiades.
PLEI.TE.A.DOR, *s.m.*, pleader, demandant; *adj.*, pleading, demanding.
PLEI.TE.AR, *v.*, to plead, to go to law, to demand, to dispute.
PLEI.TO, *s.m.*, lawsuit, process, plea.
PLE.NA.MEN.TE, *adv.*, fully, quite, completely, entirely, wholly, absolutely.
PLE.NÁ.RIO, *s.m.*, court, plenary assembly, jury.
PLE.NI.PO.TÊN.CI.A, *s.f.*, plenipotence.
PLE.NI.PO.TEN.CI.Á.RI.O, *s.m.*, *adj.*, plenipotentiary.
PLE.NI.TU.DE, *s.f.*, plenitude, fullness.
PLE.NO, *adj.*, full, absolute, plenary, complete.
PLE.O.NAS.MO, *s.m.*, pleonasm.
PLE.O.NÁS.TI.CO, *adj.*, pleonastic, pleonastical.
PLE.TO.RA, *s.f.*, *Med.*, plethora; *fig.*, plenty of vitality.
PLEU.RA, *s.f.*, pleura.
PLIS.SA.DO, *adj.*, pleated.

PLIS.SA.GEM, *s.f.*, pleating.
PLIS.SAR, *v.*, to pleat.
PLU.GA.DO, *adj.*, plugged.
PLU.GAR, *v.*, to plug.
PLU.GUE, *s.m.*, *Eletr.*, plug.
PLU.MA, *s.f.*, plume, feather.
PLU.MA.GEM, *s.f.*, plumage, feathers, plume, crest.
PLU.MAR, *v.*, to plume.
PLU.RAL, *adj.*, *s.m.*, plural.
PLU.RA.LI.DA.DE, *s.f.*, plurality.
PLU.RA.LIS.MO, *s.m.*, diversity; *Filos.*, *Pol.*, pluralism.
PLU.TÃO, *s.m.*, *Astron.*, Pluto; *Mit.*, Pluto (the Greek god of the underworld).
PLU.RA.LIS.TA, *s. 2 gen.*, pluralist; *adj.*, pluralist.
PLU.TO.CRA.CIA, *s.f.*, plutocracy.
PLU.TO.CRA.TA, *s. 2 gen.*, plutocrat.
PLU.TÔ.NIO, *s.m.*, *Quím.*, *Fís.*, plutonium; *adj.*, *Mit.*, Plutonian (pertaining to Pluto).
PLU.VI.AL, *adj.*, pluvial, rainy.
PLU.VI.O.MÉ.TRI.CO, *adj.*, pluviometric, pluviometrical.
PLU.VI.Ô.ME.TRO, *s.m.*, pluviometer.
PNEU, *s.m.*, tire; *pneu furado:* a flat tire.
PNEU.MÁ.TI.CA, *s.f.*, *Fís.*, pneumatics.
PNEU.MÁ.TI.CO, *adj.*, pneumatic.
PNEU.MA.TO.LO.GI.A, *s.f.*, pneumatology.
PNEU.MA.TO.LÓ.GI.CO, *adj.*, pneumatological.
PNEU.MA.TO.LO.GIS.TA, *s. 2 gen.*, pneumatologist.
PNEU.MA.TÓ.LO.GO, *s.m.*, pneumatologist.
PNEU.MO.CO.CO, *s.m.*, pneumococcus (bacterium).
PNEU.MO.GÁS.TRI.CO, *adj.*, *Med.*, pneumogastric.
PNEU.MO.LO.GI.A, *s.f.*, *Med.*, pneumology.
PNEU.MO.LÓ.GI.CO, *adj.*, *Med.*, pneumological.
PNEU.MO.NIA, *s.f.*, *Med.*, pneumonia.
PNEU.MOR.RA.GI.A, *s.f.*, *Med.*, pneumorrhagia.
PNEU.MO.TÓ.RAX, *s.m.*, *2 num.*, *Med.*, pneumothorax.
PÓ, *s.m.*, powder, dust.
PO.BRE, *s.m.*, pauper, beggar; *adj.*, poor, needy, indigent.
PO.BRE.MEN.TE, *adv.*, poorly.
PO.BRE.TÃO, *s.m.*, a poor person.
PO.BRE.ZA, *s.f.*, poverty, indigence, need.
PO.ÇA, *s.f.*, plash, pool.
PO.ÇÃO, *s.f.*, potion.
PO.CEI.RO, *s.m.*, workman that diggs wells; basket used for washing wool.
PO.CIL.GA, *s.f.*, sty, pigsty.
PO.ÇO, *s.m.*, well, pit.
PO.DA, *s.f.*, pruning.
PO.DA.DOR, *s.m.*, pruner; *adj.*, pruning.
PO.DÃO, *s.m.*, pruning shears, pruning knife.
PO.DAR, *v.*, to prune, to cut.
PÓ DE ARROZ, *s.m.*, face powder.
PO.DER, *s.m.*, power, might, strenght, authority; *v.*, to be able to, to can, to may, to have power to.
PO.DE.RI.O, *s.m.*, power, might, force.
PO.DE.RO.SA.MEN.TE, *adv.*, powerfully.
PO.DE.RO.SO, *adj.*, powerful, mighty, efficacious, potent, intense.
PÓ.DI.O, *s.m.*, podium.
PO.DO.DÁC.TI.LO, *s.m.*, *Anat.*, toe.
PO.DO.LO.GI.A, *s.f.*, podology.
PO.DO.LO.GIS.TA, *s. 2 gen.*, podologist.

PODRE   •• 274 •••   POMBO

PO.DRE, *adj.*, rotten, putrid, carious.
PO.DRE.DOU.RO, *s.m.*, place where things rot, dunghill.
PO.DRI.DÃO, *s.f.*, rottenness, putridity, putrefaction.
PO.DRI.GUEI.RA, *s.f., Bras.*, the same that *podridão*.
PO.E.DEI.RA, *s.f.*, laying hen.
PO.E.DOU.RO, *s.m.*, place where hens lay eggs.
PO.EI.RA, *s.f.*, dust, powder.
PO.EI.RA.DA, *s.f.*, dust cloud.
PO.EI.REN.TO, *adj.*, dusty.
PO.E.MA, *s.m.*, poem.
PO.E.MA.TI.ZAR, *v.*, poeticize.
PO.EN.TE, *s.m.*, the west, occident; *adj.*, setting.
PO.EN.TO, *adj.*, dusty.
PO.E.SI.A, *s.f.*, poetry, poesy.
PO.E.TA, *s.m.*, poet, bard.
PO.E.TAR, *v.*, to poetize, to poeticize.
PO.É.TI.CO, *adj.*, poetic, poetical.
PO.E.TI.SA, *s.f.*, poetess, poetress.
PO.E.TI.ZA.ÇÃO, *s.f.*, poeticizing.
PO.E.TI.ZAR, *v.*, to poeticize, to write poetry.
PO.GO.NÍ.A.SE, *s.f., Med.*, pogoniasis.
POIS, *conj.*, since, because, whereas, therefore, as, for.
PO.LA.CO, *s.m.*, Pole; *adj.*, Polish.
PO.LAI.NAS, *s.f., pl.*, gaiters.
PO.LAR, *adj.*, polar.
PO.LA.RI.DA.DE, *s.f.*, polarity.
PO.LA.RI.ZA.ÇÃO, *s.f., Fís.*, polarization.
PO.LA.RI.ZA.DOR, *s.m.*, polarizer; *adj.*, polarizing.
PO.LA.RI.ZAR, *v.*, to polarize.
PO.LA.RI.ZÁ.VEL, *adj.*, polarizable.
POL.CA, *s.f.*, polka.
PO.LE.GA.DA, *s.f.*, inch (2, 54 cm).
PO.LE.GAR, *s.m.*, thumb, the big toe.
PO.LEI.RO, *s.m.*, roost, perch, hen-roost.
PO.LÊ.MI.CA, *s.f.*, polemic(s), controversy.
PO.LÊ.MI.CO, *adj.*, polemic, polemical.
PO.LE.MIS.TA, *s. 2 gen.*, polemist; *adj.*, argumentative.
PO.LE.MI.ZAR, *v.*, to polemize.
PÓ.LEN, *s.m., Bot.*, pollen.
PO.LEN.TA, *s.f., Cul.*, polenta.
PO.LIA, *s.f.*, pulley, sheave.
PO.LI.A.MI.DA, *s.f., Quím.*, polyamide.
PO.LI.AN.DRI.A, *s.f.*, polyandry.
PO.LI.CHI.NE.LO, *s.m., Teat., UK* Mr Punch, Punchinello; buffon.
PO.LÍ.CIA, *s.f.*, police.
PO.LI.CI.A.DO, *adj.*, policed; civilized.
PO.LI.CI.AL, *s. 2 gen.*, officer, policeman, cop.
PO.LI.CI.A.MEN.TO, *s.m.*, patrolling.
PO.LI.CI.AR, *v.*, to police, to patrol, to guard.
PO.LI.CLÍ.NI.CA, *s.f.*, polyclinic.
PO.LI.CLÍ.NI.CO, *s.m.*, physician for general medicine; *adj.*, polyclinic.
PO.LI.CRO.MÁ.TI.CO, *adj.*, polychromatic.
PO.LI.CRO.MIA, *s.f.*, polychromy.
PO.LI.CUL.TU.RA, *s.f., Agric.*, mixed farming.
PO.LI.DÁ.TI.LO, **PO.LI.DÁC.TI.LO**, *adj.*, polydactyl.
PO.LI.DA.MEN.TE, *adv.*, brightly, smoothly; politely.
PO.LI.DEZ, *s.f.*, politeness, courtesy, civility.
PO.LI.DO, *adj.*, polished, smoothed, varnished, bright.
PO.LI.DOR, *s.m.*, polisher; *adj.*, polishing.

PO.LI.E.DRO, *s.m., Geom.*, polyhedron.
PO.LI.ÉS.TER, *s.m., Quím.*, polyester.
PO.LI.E.TI.LE.NO, *s.m., Quím.*, polyethylene.
PO.LI.GA.MI.A, *s.f.*, polygamy.
PO.LÍ.GA.MO, *s.m.*, polygamist; *adj.*, polygamous.
PO.LI.GLO.TA, *s. 2 gen.*, polyglot; *adj.*, polyglot.
PO.LI.GO.NAL, *adj.*, polygonal.
PO.LÍ.GO.NO, *s.m.*, polygon.
PO.LI.MEN.TO, *s.m.*, polish, shine, burnish.
PO.LI.MOR.FO, *adj.*, polymorphic.
PO.LI.ME.RI.ZA.ÇÃO, *s.f., Quím.*, polymerization.
PO.LI.ME.RI.ZAR, *v., Quím.*, to polymerize.
PO.LÍ.ME.RO, *s.m., Quím.*, polymer.
PO.LI.NI.ZA.ÇÃO, *s.f.*, pollination.
PO.LI.NI.ZAR, *v.*, to pollinate.
PO.LI.NÔ.MI.O, *s.m., Mat.*, polynomial, polynomial expression.
PÓ.LIO, *s.f., Med.*, the same that *poliomielite*.
PO.LIO.MI.E.LI.TE, *s.f., Med.*, poliomyelitis.
PÓ.LI.PO, *s.m., Med.*, polyp.
PO.LIR, *v.*, to polish, varnish, civilize.
PO.LIS.SÍ.LA.BO, *s.m.*, polysyllable.
PO.LIS.SÍN.DE.TO, *s.m., Ret.*, polysyndeton.
PO.LI.TÉC.NI.CA, *s.f.*, polytechnic, polytechnical school.
PO.LI.TÉC.NI.CO, *adj.*, polytechnic, polytechnical.
PO.LI.TE.ÍS.MO, *s.m.*, polytheism.
PO.LI.TE.ÍS.TA, *s. 2 gen.*, polytheist.
PO.LÍ.TI.CA, *s.f.*, politics, policy, agility.
PO.LI.TI.CA.GEM, *s.f.*, petty politics.
PO.LI.TI.CA.MEN.TE, *adv.*, politically.
PO.LÍ.TI.CO, *s.m.*, politician, statesman; *adj.*, politic, diplomatic.
PO.LI.TI.QUEI.RO, *s.m.*, petty politician.
PO.LI.TI.ZA.ÇÃO, *s.f.*, politicization.
PO.LI.TI.ZA.DO, *adj.*, politicized, politicalized.
PO.LI.TI.ZAR, *v.*, to politicize, to politicalize.
PO.LI.VA.LEN.TE, *adj., Quím.*, polyvalent.
PO.LO, *s.m.*, pole, terminal, polar region; polo (sport).
PO.LO.NÊS, *s.m.*, Pole; *adj.*, Polish.
PO.LÔ.NI.A, *s.*, Poland.
PO.LÔ.NIO, *s.m., Quím.*, polonium (symbol: Po).
POL.PA, *s.f.*, pulp; the meat of fruits.
POL.PU.DO, *adj.*, pulpy, fleshy.
POL.TRÃO, *s.m.*, coward.
POL.TRO.NA, *s.f.*, easy chair, armchair; seat.
PO.LU.ÇÃO, *s.f., Med.*, pollution.
PO.LU.I.ÇÃO, *s.f.*, pollution, desecration.
PO.LU.Í.DO, *adj.*, polluted, contaminated.
PO.LU.I.DOR, *s.m.*, polluter.
PO.LU.IR, *v.*, to pollute, to defile, to soil.
PO.LU.Í.VEL, *adj.*, subject to pollution; corruptible.
POL.VI.LHAR, *v.*, to powder, to dust.
POL.VI.LHO, *s.m.*, manioc flour.
POL.VO, *s.m., Zool.*, octopus.
PÓL.VO.RA, *s.f.*, gunpowder, powder.
POL.VO.RO.SA, *s.f.*, disorder, confusion, in a flap, in a mess.
PO.MA.DA, *s.f.*, salve, ointment, cream, pomade, unction.
PO.MAR, *s.m.*, orchard.
PO.MA.REI.RO, *s.m.*, orchardist, orchardman; *adj.*, relative to an orchard.
POM.BA, *s.f.*, pigeon, female dove.
POM.BAL, *s.m.*, pigeon house, dove-cot.
POM.BO, *s.m.*, dove, pigeon.

POMBO-CORREIO •• 275 •• PORTA-BAGAGEM

POM.BO-COR.REI.O, *s.m., Zool.*, carrier pigeon (bird).
PO.MI.CUL.TOR, *s.m.,* pomiculturist, orchardist.
PO.MI.CUL.TU.RA, *s.f.,* pomiculture.
PO.MO, *s.m.,* fruit, pome.
PO.MO DE A.DÃO, *s.m.,* the Adam's apple.
PON.CHE, *s.m.,* punch; *Bras.,* fruit juice.
PO.MO.LO.GI.A, *s.f.,* pomology.
PO.MÓ.LO.GO, *s.m.,* pomologist.
POM.PA, *s.f.,* pomp, pagentry, splendour, ostentation.
POM.POM, *s.m.,* pompon (tuft or ball of silk).
POM.PO.SO, *adj.,* pompous, ostentatious, grandiose.
PON.DE.RA.ÇÃO, *s.f.,* ponderation, consideration, deliberation.
PON.DE.RA.DO, *adj.,* weighed, cautions.
PON.DE.RA.DOR, *s.m.,* ponderer; *adj.,* pondering.
PON.DE.RAR, *v.,* to ponder, to weigh, to reflect, to think over, to deliberate, to consider.
PÔ.NEI, *s.m.,* pony.
PO.NEN.TE, *s.m., adj.,* the same that *poente.*
PON.TA, *s.f.,* point, peak, top, extremity, corner, nib, jag.
PON.TA-CA.BE.ÇA, *s.f.,* head over heels; headlong, *de ponta-cabeça:* upside down.
PON.TA.DA, *s.f.,* jab, stab, pang, twinge.
PON.TA-DI.REI.TA, *s.m., Esp.,* outside-right (soccer, futball).
PON.TA-ES.QUER.DA, *s.m., Esp.,* outside-left (soccer, futball).
PON.TAL, *s.m.,* promontory.
PON.TÃO, *s.m.,* pontoon; flatboat, float bridge.
PON.TA.PÉ, *s.m.,* kick, blow with the foot.
PON.TA.RI.A, *s.f.,* aim, sight, target, sighting.
PON.TE, *s.f.,* bridge, deck, dental bridge; bridgework.
PON.TE.AR, *v.,* to dot; to sew; *Mús.,* to finger a string instrument.
PON.TEI.O, *s.m.,* marking with points; *Mús.,* playing and to finger a string instrument.
PON.TEI.RO, *s.m.,* pointer, fescue, indicator, point.
PON.TI.A.GU.DO, *adj.,* pointed, sharp, peaky, acerose.
PON.TI.FI.CA.DO, *s.m.,* pontificate, popedom.
PON.TI.FI.CAL, *adj.,* pontifical; *fig.,* pompous.
PON.TI.FI.CAN.TE, *s.m.,* pontifical priest; *adj.,* pontifical, pontifying.
PON.TI.FI.CAR, *v.,* to pontify, to pontificate.
PON.TÍ.FI.CE, *s.m.,* pontiff, pontifex, bishop.
PON.TI.LHA.DO, *s.m.,* dotted line; *adj.,* dotted.
PON.TI.LHAR, *v.,* to stipple, to dot, to baste.
PON.TO, *s.m.,* point, dot, tittle, mark, period, full stop, spot, speck, stitch.
PON.TO DE VEN.DA, *s.m., Com.,* outlet.
PON.TO-LI.MI.TE, *s.m., Mat.,* limit point.
PON.TU.A.ÇÃO, *s.f.,* punctuation, pointing.
PON.TU.A.DO, *adj.,* punctated, dotted.
PON.TU.AL, *adj.,* punctual, precise, exact, strict.
PON.TU.A.LI.DA.DE, *s.f.,* punctuality, punctualness, accuracy.
PON.TU.AL.MEN.TE, *adv.,* punctually, accurately.
PON.TU.AR, *v.,* to punctuate, to point, to dot.
PON.TU.DO, *adj.,* pointed, peaked, pricked, spiky.
POO.DLE, *s.m., Ingl.,* poodle (race of dogs).
POOL, *s.m., Ingl., Econ.,* pool.
PO.PA, *s.f.,* poop, stern.
PO.PU.LA.ÇÃO, *s.f.,* population, inhabitants, people, class.
PO.PU.LA.CHO, *s.m.,* populace; *pej.,* plebs, herd.
PO.PU.LA.CI.O.NAL, *adj.,* population.

PO.PU.LAR, *adj.,* popular, public, common, communal.
PO.PU.LA.RES.CO, *adj.,* completely popular; that mimics what is popular.
PO.PU.LA.RI.DA.DE, *s.f.,* popularity.
PO.PU.LA.RIS.MO, *s.m.,* popularism.
PO.PU.LA.RI.ZA.ÇÃO, *s.f.,* popularization.
PO.PU.LA.RI.ZAR, *v.,* to popularize, to divulge.
PO.PU.LIS.MO, *s.m., Pol.,* populism.
PO.PU.LIS.TA, *s. 2 gen., Pol.,* Populist; *adj.,* Populist, Populistic.
PO.PU.LO.SO, *adj.,* populous, crowded.
PÔ.QUER, *s.m.,* poker.
POR, *prep.,* at, by, for, from, per, to, through, by means of, in behalf of, by order of, in order to, out of.
PÔR, *v.,* to put, to place, to lay, to set, to put on, to include, to deposit, to add, to inculcate.
PO.RÃO, *s.m.,* cellar, basement, stowage.
POR.CA, *s.f.,* sow; nut, screw-nut.
POR.CA.DA, *s.f.,* a herd of swine, dirt.
POR.CA.LHÃO, *s.m.,* a very dirty person; *adj.,* dirty, nasty, filthy.
POR.ÇÃO, *s.f.,* portion, part, piece, snack, bit, slice, share, dose.
POR.CA.RIA, *s.f.,* dirtiness, filthiness, nastiness, rubbish.
POR.CA.RI.A.DA, *s.f.,* a lot of trash.
POR.CE.LA.NA, *s.f.,* porcelain, chinaware, dishware, earthenware.
POR.CEN.TA.GEM, *s.f.,* percentage.
POR.CI.NO, *adj.,* porcine, swinish.
POR.CO, *s.m.,* swine, pig, hog, porker, grunter; *adj.,* swinish, hoggish, dirty, filthy, obscene.
POR.CO-ES.PI.NHO, *s.m., Zool.,* porcupine.
PÔR DO SOL, *s.m.,* sunset.
PO.RÉM, *conj.,* but, yet, however, still, notwithstanding, nevertheless.
POR.FI.A, *s.f.,* discussion, argument.
POR.ME.NOR, *s.m.,* particularity, particular, detail.
POR.ME.NO.RI.ZA.DO, *adj.,* detailed, particularized, circumstantial.
POR.ME.NO.RI.ZAR, *v.,* to particularize.
POR.NÔ, *s.f., col.,* pornfilm or movie; *adj.,* porn.
POR.NO.CHAN.CHA.DA, *s.f., Bras.,* soft porn film or movie.
POR.NO.GRA.FIA, *s.f.,* pornography.
POR.NO.CRÁ.TI.CO, *adj.,* pornocratic, pornocratical.
PO.RO, *s.m.,* pore.
PO.RO.RO.CA, *s.f., Bras.,* tidal wave which enters a river.
PO.RO.SI.DA.DE, *s.f.,* porosity.
PO.RO.SO, *adj.,* porous.
POR.QUAN.TO, *conj.,* as, when, while, whereby, because.
POR.QUE, *conj.,* because, since, as, in as much as.
POR.QUÊ, *s.m.,* the cause or reason.
PORQUÊ?, *pron.,* why?, for what reason.
POR.QUI.CE, *s.f.,* dirt, filth.
POR.QUI.NHO, *s.m.,* piglet.
POR.QUI.NHO-DA-ÍN.DIA, *s.m.,* guinea pig.
POR.RE, *s.m.,* binge, swallow.
POR.RA.DA, *s.f., gír.,* a blow with a cudgel, punch, knock, hit; *Bras.,* loads of.
POR.RE.TA.DA, *s.f., gír.,* a blow with a club, beating.
POR.RE.TE, *s.m.,* club, cudgel.
POR.TA, *s.f.,* door, entrance, gateway, entry, gate, access.
POR.TA-A.VI.ÕES, *s.m.,* aircraft carrier.
POR.TA-BA.GA.GEM, *s.m.,* parcel rack, rack.

PORTA-BANDEIRA ··276·· POSTERIOR

POR.TA-BAN.DEI.RA, *s.m.*, standard-bearer, flag-bearer.
POR.TA-CHA.VES, *s.m.*, key-ring.
POR.TA.DOR, *s.m.*, porter, carrier, messenger.
POR.TA-ES.TAN.DAR.TE, *s. 2 gen.*, standard-bearer.
POR.TA-FER.RA.MEN.TA, *s.m.*, tool-holder.
POR.TA-GUAR.DA.NA.PO, *s.m.*, napkin ring.
POR.TA-JOI.AS, *s.m.*, jewel case, jewel box.
POR.TA-JOR.NAIS, *s.m., 2 num.*, newspaper holder.
POR.TAL, *s.m.*, portal, the main door of a building.
POR.TA-LÁ.PIS, *s.m., 2 num.*, pencil case, port-crayon.
POR.TA-LEN.TES, *s.m., 2 num., Fot.*, lens carrier.
POR.TA-LU.VAS, *s.m.*, glove compartment.
POR.TA-MA.LAS, *s.m.*, boot, trunk.
POR.TA-MO.E.DAS, *s.m.*, coin holder, purse.
POR.TA-NÍ.QUEIS, *s.m., 2 num.*, coin purse.
POR.TAN.TO, *adv.*, therefore, hence, thus; *conj.*, as, in so far as, in as much as.
POR.TÃO, *s.m.*, gate, gateway, portal, entrance.
POR.TA-PA.PEL, *s.m.*, paper stand, toilet-roll holder.
POR.TA-SA.BÃO, *s.m.*, soap dispenser.
POR.TAR, *v.*, to carry, to land, to enter a port, to go on.
POR.TA-RE.TRA.TOS, *s.m.*, picture frame.
POR.TA-RE.VIS.TAS, *s.m.*, magazine rack.
POR.TA.RI.A, *s.f.*, entrance, reception desk, order, regulation.
POR.TA-TEM.PE.RO, *s.m.*, spice rack.
POR.TÁ.TIL, *adj.*, portable, handy, small, light.
POR.TA-TO.A.LHAS, *s.m.*, towel rack.
POR.TA-VOZ, *s.m.*, spokesman, megaphone.
POR.TE, *s.m.*, transport fee, importance, carriage, load, burden.
POR.TEI.RO, *s.m.*, doorman, doorkeeper, gatekeeper.
POR.TE.LA, *s.f.*, a small door or gate.
POR.TE.NHO, *s.m.*, inhabitant of Buenos Aires; *adj.*, pertaining to Buenos Aires.
POR.TEN.TO, *s.m.*, marvel, prodigy, miracle.
POR.TEN.TO.SO, *adj.*, marvellous, portentous.
PORT.FÓ.LI.O, *s.m.*, portfolio.
PÓR.TI.CO, *s.m., Arquit.*, portico, colonnade.
POR.TI.NHO.LA, *s.f.*, small door; *col.*, trapdoor.
POR.TO, *s.m.*, port, harbor, haven, refuge.
POR.TO RI.CO, *s.*, Puerto Rico.
POR.TO-RI.QUE.NHO, *adj., s.m.*, Puerto Rican.
POR.TU.Á.RIO, *s.m.*, dock worker.
POR.TU.GAL, *s.*, Portugal.
POR.TU.GUÊS, *s.m.*, Portuguese; *adj.*, Portuguese.
POR.TU.NHOL, *s.m., Bras., col.*, a mixed language using Portuguese and Spanish.
POR.VEN.TU.RA, *adv.*, by chance, possibly, perhaps.
POR.VIR, *s.m.*, future, time to come, destiny.
PÓS, *prep.*, post, after, behind; *pref.*, post.
PO.SAR, *v.*, to pose, to posture, to sit for.
PÓS-DA.TA, *s.f.*, postdate.
PÓS-DA.TA.DO, *adj.*, post-dated.
PÓS-DA.TAR, *v.*, to postdate.
PO.SE, *s.f.*, pose, position, posture, posing.
PÓS-ES.CRI.TO, *s.m.*, postscript.
PÓS-GLA.CI.AL, *adj., Geol.*, post-glacial.
PÓS-GRA.DU.A.ÇÃO, *s.f.*, *US* graduation, graduate; *UK* postgraduation, postgraduate.
PÓS-GRA.DU.A.DO, *s.m.*, postgraduate.
PÓS-GUER.RA, *s.m.*, postwar.

PO.SI.ÇÃO, *s.f.*, position, attitude, posture, rank, disposition.
PO.SI.CI.O.NA.MEN.TO, *s.m.*, positioning, position (opinion).
PO.SI.CI.O.NAR, *v.*, to position, to locate; *posicionar-se*: to place oneself.
PÓS-IN.DUS.TRI.AL, *adj.*, postindustrial.
PO.SI.TI.VI.DA.DE, *s.f.*, positivity.
PO.SI.TI.VIS.MO, *s.m.*, positivism, Comtist.
PO.SI.TI.VIS.TA, *s. 2 gen.*, positivist, Comtist; *adj.*, positivistic, positivistical.
PO.SI.TI.VO, *adj.*, positive, real, actual, evident, clear, obvious, sure, certain.
PÓS-ME.DI.E.VAL, *adj.*, postmedieval.
PÓS-MENS.TRU.AL, *adj.*, postmenstrual.
PÓS-MO.DER.NIS.MO, *s.m.*, postmodernism.
PÓS-MO.DER.NIS.TA, *s. 2 gen.*, postmodernist.
PÓS-MO.DER.NO, *adj.*, postmodern.
PÓS-MOR.TE, *s.f.*, postmortem; *adj.*, postmortem.
PÓS-NA.TAL, *adj.*, postnatal.
PÓS-NUP.CI.AL, *adj.*, postnuptial.
PO.SO.LO.GI.A, *s.f., Med.*, posology, dosology.
PÓS-O.PE.RA.TÓ.RI.O, *s.m., adj., Med.*, post-operative.
PÓS-PAR.TO, *adj., Med.*, postpartum.
POS.POR, *v.*, to postpone, to omit, to neglect.
POS.PO.SI.ÇÃO, *s.f.*, postposition.
POS.POS.TO, *adj.*, postponed, postpositive, put after.
PÓS-RO.MA.NO, *adj., Hist.*, post-Roman (after Roman empire).
POS.SAN.TE, *adj.*, powerful, mighty.
POS.SE, *s.f.*, ownership; posses, possessions, riches, property.
POS.SEI.RO, *s.m.*, leaseholder.
POS.SES.SÃO, *s.f.*, possession, estate, dominion, landed property.
POS.SES.SI.VA.MEN.TE, *adv.*, possessively.
POS.SES.SÍ.VEL, *adj.*, possessable.
POS.SES.SI.VO, *adj.*, possessive, proprietary.
POS.SES.SO, *s.m.*, demoniac; *adj.*, possessed, mad.
POS.SI.BI.LI.DA.DE, *s.f.*, possibility, contingency, chance, odds.
POS.SI.BI.LI.TAR, *v.*, to enable, to make possible, allow.
POS.SÍ.VEL, *adj.*, possible, feasible.
POS.SI.VEL.MEN.TE, *adv.*, possibly.
POS.SU.Í.DO, *adj.*, possessed.
POS.SU.I.DOR, *s.m.*, owner, possessor; *adj.*, possessing; *ser ~ de*: to be the owner of.
POS.SUIR, *v.*, to possess, to have, to hold, to own, to occupy, to inhabit.
POS.TA, *s.f., Cul.*, slice of fish; *~ de peixe*: fish steak.
POS.TA.GEM, *s.f., Bras.*, postage.
POS.TAL, *s.m.*, postcard; *adj.*, postal; *caixa postal*: P.O. Box.
POS.TAR, *v.*, to post, to mail, to dispose.
POS.TE, *s.m.*, stake, stud, post, pillar, mast.
POS.TEI.RO, *s.m., Bras.*, herdsman, watchman, guard.
POS.TE.MA, *s.f., Med.*, aposteme.
PÓS-TEM.PO.RA.DA, *s.f.*, after-season.
PÓS.TER, *s.m.*, poster.
POS.TER.GA.ÇÃO, *s.f.*, postponement.
POS.TER.GAR, *v.*, to postpone, to put off, to pass over, to omit.
POS.TER.GÁ.VEL, *adj.*, delayable.
POS.TE.RI.DA.DE, *s.f.*, posterity, descendants, issue.
POS.TE.RI.OR, *s.m.*, posterior; *adj.*, posterior, later, behind,

POSTIÇO ·· 277 ·· PRÉ-ADOLESCENTE

ulterior.

POS.TI.ÇO, *adj.*, false, artificial, counterfeit.

POS.TI.GO, *s.m.*, peephole, scuttle (a small opening in a door or window); small door.

POS.TI.LA, *s.f.*, copybook, class notes, commentary (about the lesson).

POS.TI.TE, *s.f.*, *Med.*, inflammation of the prepuce.

POS.TO, *s.m.*, post, place, position, station, stand, office; *adj.*, put, disposed, arranged.

POS.TU.LA.ÇÃO, *s.f.*, postulation.

POS.TU.LA.DO, *s.m.*, *Filos.*, postulate, assumption.

POS.TU.LAN.TE, *s. 2 gen.*, postulant, candidate, petitioner; *adj.*, postulating.

POS.TU.LAR, *v.*, to postulate.

POS.TU.MA.MEN.TE, *adv.*, posthumously.

PÓS.TU.MO, *adj.*, posthumous.

POS.TU.RA, *s.f.*, posture, position, situation, state attitude, pose.

PO.SU.DO, *adj.*, *Bras., col.*, affected, posey.

PO.TA.BI.LI.DA.DE, *s.f.*, potability.

PO.TA.GEM, *s.f.*, potage.

PO.TA.MO.LO.GI.A, *s.f.*, potamology.

PO.TÁS.SI.O, *s.m.*, *Quím.*, potassium, kalium (atomic number: 19, symbol: K).

PO.TÁ.VEL, *adj.*, drinkable, potable.

PO.TE, *s.m.*, pot, vessel, water jug.

PO.TÊN.CIA, *s.f.*, potency, power, might, strength, potence, authority.

PO.TEN.CI.A.ÇÃO, *s.f.*, *Mat.*, exponentiation; potentiation.

PO.TEN.CI.AL, *s.m.*, potential, *adj.*, powerful, potential, mighty.

PO.TEN.CI.A.LI.DA.DE, *s.f.*, potentiality; potencial.

PO.TEN.CI.A.LI.ZAR, *v.*, to potentize, to make potent.

PO.TEN.CI.AL.MEN.TE, *adv.*, potentially.

PO.TEN.CI.AR, *v.*, *Mat.*, to potentiate.

PO.TEN.TA.DO, *s.m.*, potentate, monarch.

PO.TEN.TE, *adj.*, potent, powerful, mighty, potential, strong.

POT-POURRI, *s.m.*, *Mús.*, potpourry; medley.

PO.TRA, *s.f.*, filly, colt.

PO.TRI.LHO, *s.m.*, *Bras.*, colt.

PO.TRO, *s.m.*, colt, foal, young horse.

POU.CA-VER.GO.NHA, *s.f.*, shamelessness, rascality.

POU.CO, *s.m.*, a little, small quantity; *adj.*, little; *adv.*, little, insufficiently, nearly, rather.

POU.PA.DOR, *s.m.*, thrifty.

POU.PAN.ÇA, *s.f.*, economy, savings, parsimony.

POU.PAR, *v.*, to spare, to save, to preserve, to economize, to lay up.

POU.QUÍS.SI.MO, *adj.*, superlativeof*pouco*: precious little.

POU.SA.DA, *s.f.*, stopping, resting, inn, lodging.

POU.SA.DO, *adj.*, perched, resting; lodged.

POU.SAR, *v.*, to rest, to lodge, to stop, to lay down, to perch, to repose.

POU.SI.O, *s.m.*, fallow ground; *adj.*, uncultivated, fallow.

POU.SO, *s.m.*, resting place, landing, slip.

PO.VA.RÉU, *s.m.*, rabble.

PO.VÃO, *s.m.*, augmentativeof*povo*; *Bras., pej.*, rabble, populace, mob.

PO.VA.RÉU, *s.m.*, a big crowd; *pej.*, rabble, mob.

PO.VI.NHO, *s.m.*, diminutive of *povo*: *Bras., pej.*, rabble, populace, mob.

PO.VO, *s.m.*, people, folk, nation, race, crowd, mob.

PO.VO.A.ÇÃO, *s.f.*, village, settlement, population.

PO.VO.A.DO, *s.m.*, settlement, village; *adj.*, populated.

PO.VO.A.MEN.TO, *s.m.*, population, populating.

PO.VO.AR, *v.*, to populate, to settle, to fill, to colonize.

PO.XA, *interj.*, gosh! my goodness!

PRA, *contr. prep.* **PARA** (*p'ra*): for, to, toward; *contr. prep.* **PRA** with *art.* or *pron. f.* **A**: to the.

PRA.ÇA, *s.f.*, square, market-place.

PRA.CI.NHA, *s.m.*, *Bras.*, diminutive of *praça*; a soldier who fought in the II World War.

PRA.DA.RIA, *s.f.*, prairie, meadow.

PRA.DO, *s.m.*, meadow, plain, grassy land.

PRA-FREN.TE, *adj.*, *2 num., gír.*, very modern, fashionable.

PRA.GA, *s.f.*, curse, malediction, damnation, imprecation, plague, blasphemy.

PRAG.MÁ.TI.CO, *adj.*, pragmatic.

PRAG.MA.TIS.MO, *s.m.*, pragmatism.

PRA.GUE.JA.DOR, *s.m.*, curser, blasphemer; *adj.*, cursing.

PRA.GUE.JAR, *v.*, to curse, to imprecate, to blaspheme, to swear.

PRA.GUEN.TO, *adj.*, cursing, imprecatory.

PRAI.A, *s.f.*, beach, seashore, coast, strand.

PRAI.A.NO, *s.m.*, inhabitant of the seaside; *adj.*, relating to the beach or seaside.

PRAI.EI.RO, *s.m.*, the same that *praiano*.

PRAN.CHA, *s.f.*, plank, board.

PRAN.CHE.TA, *s.f.*, drawing board, small board.

PRAN.TE.A.DOR, *s.m.*, mourner, weeper; *adj.*, mourning, weeping.

PRAN.TE.AR, *v.*, to cry (for someone), to mourn, to lament, to weep; *prantear-se*: to complain (oneself).

PRAN.TO, *s.m.*, weeping, lamentation, wailing.

PRA.TA, *s.f.*, *Quím.*, silver (atomic number 47, symbol: Ag); silverware; *fig.*, money

PRA.TA.RIA, *s.f.*, silverware.

PRA.TE.A.DO, *adj.*, silvered.

PRA.TE.A.MEN.TO, *s.m.*, process of silvering; silver-plating.

PRA.TE.AR, *v.*, to silver, to cover with silver.

PRA.TE.LEI.RA, *s.f.*, shelf, rack.

PRÁ.TI.CA, *s.f.*, *US* practice, *UK* practise, usage, custom, perfomance, habit, function, experience.

PRA.TI.CA.BI.LI.DA.DE, *s.f.*, practicability.

PRA.TI.CA.MEN.TE, *adv.*, practically.

PRA.TI.CAN.TE, *s. 2 gen.*, practitioner; *adj.*, *UK* practising, *US* practicing.

PRA.TI.CAR, *v.*, *US* to practice, *UK* to practise, to execute, to perform, to profess.

PRA.TI.CÁ.VEL, *adj.*, practicable.

PRÁ.TI.CO, *s.m.*, pilot, practician; *adj.*, practical, skilled.

PRA.TO, *s.m.*, plate, dish, food, meal.

PRA.VI.DA.DE, *s.f.*, pravity, perverseness.

PRA.XE, *s.f.*, practice, praxis, use, habit, custom.

PRÁ.XIS, *s.f.*, *2 num., Fil.*, praxis.

PRA.ZEN.TEI.RO, *adj.*, festive, pleasant, merry, gay.

PRA.ZER, *s.m.*, pleasure, joy, delight, satisfaction.

PRA.ZE.RO.SA.MEN.TE, *adv.*, pleasantly.

PRA.ZE.RO.SO, *adj.*, joyful, merry.

PRA.ZO, *s.m.*, time, term, stated period, delay.

PRÉ.Á, *s.f.*, *Bras., Zool.*, cavy.

PRÉ-A.DO.LES.CÊN.CI.A, *s.f.*, preadolescence.

PRÉ-A.DO.LES.CEN.TE, *adj.*, preadolescent.

PRÉ-AJUSTAR ·· 278 ·· PREFERENTE

PRÉ-A.JUS.TAR, *v.*, to prearrange.
PRE.A.MAR, *s.f.*, flood, high water, high tide.
PRE.ÂM.BU.LO, *s.m.*, preamble, foreword.
PRÉ-A.NES.TÉ.SI.CO, *s.m., Med.*, preanesthetic.
PRE.A.NUN.CI.AR, *v.*, to preannounce.
PRE.A.QUE.CER, *v.*, to preheat, prewarm.
PRÉ-A.VI.SO, *s.m.*, advance notice.
PRE.CA.ÇÃO, *s.f.*, supplication.
PRÉ-CAM.BRI.A.NO, *adj., Geol.*, pre-Cambrian, Precambrian.
PRE.CA.RI.A.MEN.TE, *adv.*, precariously.
PRE.CA.RI.E.DA.DE, *s.f.*, precariousness.
PRE.CÁ.RIO, *adj.*, precarious, uncertain, insecure.
PRE.CA.TAR, *v.*, to precaution, to forewarn.
PRE.CA.TÓ.RI.A, *s.f., Jur.*, writ.
PRE.CA.TÓ.RI.O, *s.m.*, petition; *adj.*, precatory.
PRE.CAU.ÇÃO, *s.f.*, precaution, caution, foresight, care.
PRE.CA.VER, *v.*, to prevent, to obviate, to provide.
PRE.CA.VI.DO, *adj.*, precautious, wary.
PRE.CE, *s.f.*, prayer, petition, invocation.
PRE.CE.DÊN.CIA, *s.f.*, precedence, priority, anteriority.
PRE.CE.DEN.TE, *adj., s. 2 gen.*, precedent.
PRE.CE.DER, *v.*, to precede, to go before in time, to anticipate.
PRE.CEI.TO, *s.m.*, precept, principle, maxim, rule.
PRE.CEI.TU.AR, *v.*, to prescribe, to order.
PRE.CI.O.SI.DA.DE, *s.f.*, preciousness.
PRE.CI.O.SIS.MO, *s.m.*, preciosity, over-refinement.
PRE.CI.O.SO, *adj.*, precious, valuable, splendid, excellent.
PRE.CI.PÍ.CIO, *s.m.*, precipice, abyss, ruin.
PRE.CI.PI.TA.ÇÃO, *s.f.*, precipitation, haste, rush, abruptness, rainfall.
PRE.CI.PI.TA.DA.MEN.TE, *adv.*, precipitately.
PRE.CI.PI.TA.DO, *adj.*, precipitate, heedless.
PRE.CI.PI.TA.DOR, *s.m.*, precipitator; *adj.*, precipitative.
PRE.CI.PI.TAR, *v.*, to precipitate, to deposit, to extract.
PRE.CI.PI.TÁ.VEL, *adj.*, precipitable.
PRE.CI.SA.DO, *adj.*, needy; ~ *de*: in need of.
PRE.CI.SÃO, *s.f.*, precision, exactness, accuracy, need.
PRE.CI.SAR, *v.*, to need, to require, to exact, to fix.
PRE.CI.SO, *adj.*, precise, exact, just, definite, distinct.
PRE.ÇO, *s.m.*, price, cost, value, charge.
PRE.CO.CE, *adj.*, precocious, premature.
PRE.CO.CI.DA.DE, *s.f.*, precocity, prematurity.
PRE.CO.GI.TAR, *v.*, to consider beforehand, to premeditate.
PRÉ-CO.LOM.BI.A.NO, *adj., Hist.*, pre-Columbian.
PRE.CON.CE.BER, *v.*, to preconceive.
PRE.CON.CE.BI.DO, *adj.*, preconceived.
PRE.CON.CEI.TO, *s.m.*, preconceit, preconception, conclusion, prejudice.
PRE.CON.CEP.ÇÃO, *s.f.*, preconception.
PRE.CON.DI.ÇÃO, *s.f.*, precondition.
PRE.CO.NI.ZA.ÇÃO, *s.f.*, preconization.
PRE.CO.NI.ZA.DO, *adj.*, preconized.
PRE.CO.NI.ZAR, *v.*, to preconize, to profess, to proclaim.
PRÉ-CO.ZER, *v.*, to precook.
PRÉ-CO.ZI.DO, *adj.*, precooked.
PRE.CUR.SOR, *s.m.*, forerunner, pioneer; *adj.*, precursory, preceding.
PRE.DA.DOR, *s.m.*, predator.
PRE.DA.TÓ.RI.O, *adj.*, predatory.
PRÉ-DA.TA.DO, *adj.*, predated.

PRÉ-DA.TAR, *v.*, to predate.
PRE.DE.CES.SOR, *s.m.*, predecessor, precursor.
PRE.DE.FI.NI.ÇÃO, *s.f.*, predefinition.
PRE.DE.FI.NIR, *v.*, to predefine.
PRE.DES.TI.NA.ÇÃO, *s.f.*, predestination, fate, destiny, election.
PRE.DES.TI.NA.DO, *s.m., Teol.*, elect saint; *adj.*, predestinated, predetermined.
PRE.DE.TER.MI.NA.ÇÃO, *s.f.*, predetermination.
PRE.DE.TER.MI.NA.DO, *adj.*, predetermined.
PRE.DES.TI.NAR, *v.*, to predestinate, predestine.
PRE.DE.TER.MI.NAN.TE, *adj.*, predetermining.
PRE.DE.TER.MI.NAR, *v.*, to predetermine, preordain, preorder.
PRE.DI.AL, *adj.*, predial; *imposto predial*: house tax.
PRÉ.DI.CA, *s.f.*, preaching, sermon.
PRE.DI.CA.ÇÃO, *s.f.*, preaching, sermon.
PRE.DI.CA.DO, *s.m.*, quality, attribute, talent, faculty; *Gram.*, predicate.
PRE.DI.ÇÃO, *s.f.*, prediction, presage.
PRE.DI.LE.ÇÃO, *s.f.*, predilection, favour.
PRE.DI.LE.TO, *adj.*, favourite, beloved, dear.
PRÉ.DIO, *s.m.*, estate, landed property, building, edifice.
PRE.DIS.POR, *v.*, to predispose, to prearrange, to prepare.
PRE.DIS.PO.SI.ÇÃO, *s.f.*, predisposition.
PRE.DIS.POS.TO, *adj.*, predisposed, prone.
PRE.DI.ZER, *v.*, to predict, to foretell, to prophesy.
PRE.DO.MI.NA.ÇÃO, *s.f.*, predomination.
PRE.DO.MI.NÂN.CIA, *s.f.*, predominance, domination, prevalence.
PRE.DO.MI.NAN.TE, *adj.*, predominant, prevailing, superior.
PRE.DO.MI.NAR, *v.*, to predominate, to preponderate, to rule.
PRE.DO.MÍ.NIO, *s.m.*, power, predominancy, supremacy.
PRÉ-E.LEI.ÇÃO, *s.f.*, pre-election.
PRÉ-E.LEI.TO.RAL, *adj., Bras.*, pre-election.
PRE.E.MI.NÊN.CI.A, *s.f.*, pre-eminence.
PRE.E.MI.NEN.TE, *adj.*, pre-eminent.
PRE.EMP.ÇÃO, *s.f.*, pre-emption, forestallment.
PRE.EN.CHER, *v.*, to fulfill, to fill in, to perform, to supply.
PRE.EN.CHI.MEN.TO, *s.m.*, filling out, fulfilling.
PRE.EN.SÃO, *s.f.*, prehension, seizing.
PRE.ÊN.SIL, *adj.*, prehensile, seizing.
PRÉ-ES.CO.LAR, *adj.*, preschool.
PRE.ES.TA.BE.LE.CER, *v.*, to pre-establish.
PRÉ-ES.TREI.A, *s.f.*, preview.
PRE.EX.CEL.SO, *adj.*, sublime, eminent.
PRE.E.XIS.TÊN.CI.A, *s.f.*, pre-existence.
PRE.E.XIS.TEN.TE, *adj.*, pre-existent.
PRE.E.XIS.TIR, *v.*, to pre-exist.
PRÉ-FA.BRI.CA.DO, *adj.*, prefabricated.
PRE.FA.CI.A.DOR, *s.m.*, prologizer, prefacer.
PRÉ-FA.BRI.CAR, *v.*, to prefabricate.
PRE.FA.CI.AL, *adj.*, prefatorial, prefatory.
PRE.FA.CI.AR, *v.*, to preface.
PRE.FÁ.CIO, *s.m.*, preface, preamble, introduction.
PRE.FEI.TO, *s.m.*, mayor, prefect.
PRE.FEI.TU.RA, *s.f.*, town hall, city hall, prefecture.
PRE.FE.RÊN.CIA, *s.f.*, preference, choise, selection, favouritism, liking.
PRE.FE.REN.CI.AL, *adj.*, preferential.
PRE.FE.REN.TE, *s.*, preferrer; *adj.*, preferential, preferring.

PREFERIDO ·· 279 ·· PRESCREVER

PRE.FE.RI.DO, *adj.*, favoured, preferred, elected.
PRE.FE.RIR, *v.*, to prefer, to give preference to, to select, to opt.
PRE.FE.RÍ.VEL, *adj.*, preferable, better.
PRE.FI.GU.RA.ÇÃO, *s.f.*, prefiguration.
PRE.FI.GU.RAR, *v.*, to prefigure.
PRE.FI.GU.RA.TI.VO, *adj.*, prefigurative.
PRE.FI.XA.ÇÃO, *s.f.*, prefixation; *Gram.*, use of prefixes.
PRE.FI.XAR, *v.*, to prefix; *Gram.*, add as a prefix.
PRE.FI.XO, *s.m.*, *Gram.*, prefix; affix; *adj.*, prefixed.
PRÉ-FRON.TAL, *adj.*, prefrontal.
PRE.GA, *s.f.*, pleat, crease.
PRE.GA.ÇÃO, *s.f.*, preachment.
PRE.GA.DO, *adj.*, nailed, fixed, fastened; *Bras.*, exhausted.
PRE.GA.DOR, *s.m.*, preacher, nailer; *adj.*, preaching.
PRE.GÃO, *s.m.*, proclamation, cry; trading (stock exchange); bidding (auction).
PRE.GAR, *v.*, to nail, to fix, to fasten, to attach, to stick; to predicate, to preach.
PRE.GO, *s.m.*, nail, sprig.
PRÉ-GRA.VA.DO, *adj.*, prerecorded (TV, Radio).
PRE.GRES.SO, *adj.*, previous, antecedent, earlier.
PRE.GUE.AR, *v.*, to tuck; to put a crease in (trousers); *Bras.*, to be exhausted.
PRE.GUI.ÇA, *s.f.*, sluggishness, laziness, indolence; *Zool.*, sloth.
PRE.GUI.ÇO.SO, *s.m.*, lazy-bones, idler; *adj.*, lazy, idle, indolent, laggard.
PRÉ-HIS.TÓ.RI.A, *s.f.*, prehistory.
PRÉ-HIS.TÓ.RI.CO, *adj.*, prehistoric.
PREI.A, *s.f.*, the same that *presa*.
PRE.JU.DI.CA.DO, *adj.*, prejudiced, damaged.
PRE.JU.DI.CAR, *v.*, to prejudice, to damage, to hurt, to wrong, to injure.
PRE.JU.DI.CI.AL, *adj.*, prejudicial, hurtful, harmful, evil.
PRE.JU.DI.CI.AL.MEN.TE, *adv.*, prejudicially.
PRE.JU.Í.ZO, *s.m.*, prejudice, prejudgement, bias, leaning.
PRE.JUL.GAR, *v.*, to prejudge, judge beforehand, decide in anticipation.
PRE.JUL.GA.DO, *adj.*, prejudged.
PRE.LA.ÇÃO, *s.f.*, prelation, preference.
PRE.LA.DO, *s.m.*, *Rel.*, prelate.
PRE.LE.ÇÃO, *s.f.*, prelection, reading, sermon.
PRE.LI.MI.NAR.MEN.TE, *adv.*, preliminarily.
PRE.LI.MI.NAR, *adj.*, *s.f.*, preliminary.
PRÉ.LI.O, *s.m.*, *Lit.*, combat, battle, fight.
PRE.LO, *s.m.*, printing press.
PRE.MA.TU.RA.MEN.TE, *adv.*, prematurely.
PRE.MA.TU.RI.DA.DE, *s.f.*, prematureness, precocity.
PRE.MA.TU.RO, *adj.*, premature, immature.
PRE.ME.DI.TA.ÇÃO, *s.f.*, premeditation.
PRE.ME.DI.TA.DA.MEN.TE, *adv.*, deliberately.
PRE.ME.DI.TA.DO, *adj.*, premeditated, deliberate, studied.
PRE.ME.DI.TAR, *v.*, to premeditate, to plan.
PRE.MÊN.CI.A, *s.f.*, *Bras.*, pressure, urgency.
PRE.MEN.TE, *adj.*, pressing, urgent.
PRE.MI.A.ÇÃO, *s.f.*, act of rewarding; awarding of prizes.
PRE.MI.A.DO, *s.m.*, prizewinner; *adj.*, prizewinner, awarded.
PRE.MI.AR, *v.*, to reward, award a prize to.
PRE.MI.Á.VEL, *adj.*, awardable.
PRE.MI.ER, **PRE.MI.Ê**, *s.m.*, *Fr.*, premier, prime minister.

PRÊ.MIO, *s.m.*, reward, prize, award, remuneration, gain.
PRE.MIS.SA, *s.f.*, premise, reason, supposition.
PRÉ-MOL.DA.DO, *s.m.*, breeze block, cinder block; *adj.*, premolded, precast.
PRE.MO.NI.ÇÃO, *s.f.*, premonition.
PRE.MO.NI.TÓ.RI.O, *adj.*, premonitory.
PRÉ-NA.TAL, *adj.*, prenatal.
PREN.DA, *s.f.*, present, gift; forfeit (game); *Bras.*, young woman.
PREN.DA.DO, *adj.*, gifted, talented.
PREN.DAR, *v.*, to give a present to, to gift.
PREN.DE.DOR, *s.m.*, fastener, clip, arrester, seizer.
PREN.DER, *v.*, to fasten, to tie, to fix, to bind, to grip, to gasp.
PRE.NHE, *adj.*, gravid, pregnant.
PRE.NHEZ, *s.f.*, pregnancy.
PRE.NO.ME, *s.m.*, first name, Christian name.
PRE.NO.MI.NAR, *v.*, to give a first name.
PREN.SA, *s.f.*, press, printing press.
PREN.SAR, *v.*, to press, to compress, to crush.
PRE.NUN.CI.AR, *v.*, to foretell, foreshadow, prophesy, predict, adumbrate.
PRE.NÚN.CI.O, *s.m.*, adumbration, presage, foretoken, sign, prognostic, prediction.
PRÉ-NUP.CI.AL, *adj.*, antenuptial, premarital.
PRE.O.CU.PA.ÇÃO, *s.f.*, worry, preoccupation, apprehension, anxiety.
PRE.O.CU.PAN.TE, *s. 2 gen.*, preoccupant; *adj.*, worrying.
PRE.O.CU.PAR, *v.*, to worry, to preoccupy.
PRE.PA.RA.ÇÃO, *s.f.*, preparation, preparing, training.
PRE.PA.RA.DO, *adj.*, prepared, ready.
PRE.PA.RA.DOR, *s.m.*, preparer; preparator; *adj.*, preparatory, preparing.
PRE.PA.RAR, *v.*, to prepare, to make ready, to arrange, to provide.
PRE.PA.RA.TI.VOS, *s.m.*, *pl.*, preparatives, preparatories.
PRE.PA.RO, *s.m.*, preparation, education, competence, ability.
PRE.PON.DE.RÂN.CI.A, *s.f.*, preponderance, predominance.
PRE.PON.DE.RAN.TE, *adj.*, preponderant, predominant.
PRE.PON.DE.RAR, *v.*, to preponderate, to overbear, to predominate.
PRE.POR, *v.*, to preplace.
PRE.PO.SI.ÇÃO, *s.f.*, preposition.
PRE.PO.SI.CI.O.NAL, *adj.*, *Gram.*, prepositional.
PRE.PO.SI.TI.VO, *adj.*, prepositive.
PRE.PO.SI.TU.RA, *s.f.*, prepositure.
PRE.POS.TE.RAR, *v.*, to preposterate.
PRE.POS.TO, *adj.*, preferred.
PRE.PO.TÊN.CIA, *s.f.*, prepotence, prepotency, superiority, despotism.
PRE.PO.TEN.TE, *adj.*, prepotent, all-powerful.
PRE.PÚ.CI.O, *s.m.*, *Anat.*, prepuce, foreskin.
PRER.RO.GA.TI.VA, *s.f.*, prerogative.
PRE.SA, *s.f.*, prey, fang, capture, catch, tusk.
PRES.BI.TE.RI.A.NO, *s.m.*, Presbyterian; *adj.*, Presbyterian.
PRES.BÍ.TE.RO, *s.m.*, presbyter, elder.
PRES.CI.ÊN.CI.A, *s.f.*, prescience, foresight.
PRES.CI.EN.TE, *adj.*, prescient, foreknowing.
PRES.CIN.DIR, *v.*, to prescind, to dispense, to leave out, to renounce.
PRES.CIN.DÍ.VEL, *adj.*, prescindent, dispensable.
PRES.CRE.VER, *v.*, to prescribe, to order the use of, to ordain,

PRESCRIÇÃO ·· 280 ·· PREVER

to assign, to fall into desuse.

PRES.CRI.ÇÃO, *s.f.*, prescription, precept, lapse, order, instruction.

PRES.CRI.TÍ.VEL, *adj.*, prescriptible, prescribable.

PRE.SEN.ÇA, *s.f.*, presence, aspect, appearance.

PRE.SEN.CI.AL, *adj.*, present.

PRE.SEN.CI.A.LI.DA.DE, *s.f.*, presentiveness.

PRE.SEN.CI.AR, *v.*, to be present, to witness, to observe.

PRE.SEN.TE, *s.m.*, present, actuality, gift, donative; *adj.*, present, actual, current.

PRE.SEN.TE.A.DOR, *s.m.*, presenter; *adj.*, presenting.

PRE.SEN.TE.AR, *v.*, to present, to offer as a gift.

PRE.SE.PA.DA, *s.f.*, *Bras.*, boasting, ostentation; *Bras.*, nonsense.

PRE.SÉ.PIO, *s.m.*, stable, stall, crèche.

PRE.SE.PIS.TA, *s. 2 gen.*, one who mounts a Nativity scene.

PRE.SER.VA.ÇÃO, *s.f.*, preservation, conservation.

PRE.SER.VAR, *v.*, to preserve, to protect, to guard, to defend, to save, to retain.

PRE.SER.VA.TI.VO, *s.m.*, preservative, condom; *adj.*, preservative.

PRE.SI.DÊN.CIA, *s.f.*, presidency, chairmanship.

PRE.SI.DEN.CI.AL, *adj.*, presidential.

PRE.SI.DEN.CI.A.LIS.MO, *s.m.*, *Pol.*, presidentialism.

PRE.SI.DEN.CI.Á.VEL, *s. 2 gen.*, presidential candidate; *adj.*, elegible to be president.

PRE.SI.DEN.TE, *s.m.*, president, chairman, manager; *adj.*, presiding.

PRE.SI.DI.Á.RI.O, *s.m.*, convict, prisoner; *adj.*, presidiary, presidial.

PRE.SÍ.DIO, *s.m.*, prison, fortress, garrison, penitentiary.

PRE.SI.DIR, *v.*, to preside, to manage, to direct, to administer, to coordinate.

PRE.SI.LHA, *s.f.*, fastening belt, strap; hairslide.

PRE.SO, *s.m.*, prisoner, captive; *adj.*, captive, imprisoned, arrested.

PRES.SA, *s.f.*, haste, hurry, rush, velocity, urgency.

PRES.SA.GI.A.DOR, *s.m.*, foreboder; *adj.*, foreboding.

PRES.SA.GI.AR, *v.*, to foretell, to presage, to forebode.

PRES.SÁ.GIO, *s.m.*, presage, sign, omen, augury.

PRES.SÃO, *s.f.*, pressure, compulsion, stress, strain, pressing, oppression.

PRES.SÃOSANGUÍNEA, *s.f.*, blood pressure.

PRES.SEN.TI.MEN.TO, *s.m.*, presentiment, foreboding, apprehension.

PRES.SEN.TIR, *v.*, to foresee, anticipate, suspect.

PRES.SI.O.NAR, *v.*, to press, to compress.

PRES.SU.POR, *v.*, to presuppose, to assume.

PRES.SU.PO.SI.ÇÃO, *s.f.*, presupposition.

PRES.SU.POS.TO, *s.m.*, pretext, purpose; *adj.*, presupposed, assumed.

PRES.SU.RI.ZA.ÇÃO, *s.f.*, pressurization.

PRES.SU.RI.ZA.DO, *adj.*, pressurized.

PRES.SU.RI.ZAR, *v.*, to pressurize.

PRES.SU.RO.SO, *adj.*, speedy, swift, quick, prompt.

PRES.TA.ÇÃO, *s.f.*, installment, contribution.

PRES.TA.DOR, *adj.*, serviceable, obliging.

PRES.TA.MIS.TA, *s. 2 gen.*, moneylender.

PRES.TAR, *v.*, to lend, to load, to render, to give, to perform, to be useful.

PRES.TA.TI.VO, *adj.*, serviceable, useful, helpful.

PRES.TES, *adj.*, ready, prepared; about to; *estar ~ a fazer algo*: to be about to do something.

PRES.TE.ZA, *s.f.*, quickness, readiness, promptness, rapidity, celerity.

PRES.TI.DI.GI.TA.ÇÃO, *s.f.*, prestidigitation, jugglery, magic.

PRES.TI.DI.GI.TA.DOR, *s.m.*, prestidigitator, magician, wizar, juggler.

PRES.TI.GI.A.DOR, *s.m.*, the same that *prestidigitador*.

PRES.TI.GI.AR, *v.*, to esteem, to give prestige to.

PRES.TÍ.GIO, *s.m.*, fascination, prestige, reputation, influence, charm.

PRES.TI.GI.O.SO, *adj.*, prestigious.

PRÉS.TI.MO, *s.m.*, utility, usefulness, service, fitness.

PRES.TI.MO.SO, *adj.*, helpful, useful, serviceable.

PRÉS.TI.TO, *s.m.*, *cortège*, train.

PRE.SU.MI.DO, *adj.*, arrogant, presumptuous.

PRE.SU.MIR, *v.*, to presume, to suppose, to surmise, to suspect.

PRE.SU.MÍ.VEL, *adj.*, presumable, probable, presumptive.

PRE.SUN.ÇÃO, *s.f.*, presumption, supposition, arrogance, guess, pride.

PRE.SUN.ÇO.SO, *adj.*, presumptuous, vainglorious, arrogant.

PRE.SUN.TO, *s.m.*, ham.

PRE.TEN.DE.DOR, *s.m.*, claimer, claimant, aspirant; *adj.*, claiming.

PRE.TEN.DEN.TE, *s. 2 gen.*, pretender, candidate; *adj.*, pretending, expecting.

PRE.TEN.DER, *v.*, to claim, to demand, to aspire, to wish, to intend, to contemplate, to expect.

PRE.TEN.DI.DO, *adj.*, claimed, intended.

PRE.TEN.SA.MEN.TE, *adv.*, supposedly.

PRE.TEN.SÃO, *s.f.*, pretension, claim, demand, intention, design.

PRE.TEN.SI.O.SO, *adj.*, pretentious, arrogant, ambitious, snobbish.

PRE.TEN.SO, *adj.*, assumed, supposed, presumed, alleged.

PRE.TE.RIR, *v.*, to pretermit, to neglect, to defer, to slight.

PRE.TÉ.RI.TO, *s.m.*, past, The Past Time; *adj.*, past, preterit, bygone.

PRE.TE.RÍ.VEL, *adj.*, that may be pretermitted.

PRE.TEX.TO, *s.m.*, pretext, excuse, pretension, cloak.

PRE.TI.DÃO, *s.f.*, blackness, black colour, darkness.

PRE.TO, *s.m.*, Negro, black; *adj.*, black, dark, jet, sombre.

PRE.TO.RI.A, *s.f.*, pretorship.

PRE.TO.RI.A.NO, *s.m.*, *Hist.*, praetorian (soldier of the praetorian guard (Roam Empire)); *adj.*, praetorian.

PRE.TU.ME, *s.m.*, darkness.

PRE.VA.LE.CEN.TE, *adj.*, prevalent.

PRE.VA.LE.CER, *v.*, to prevail, to predominate, to preponderate.

PRE.VA.LE.CI.DO, *adj.*, impertinent, arrogant, snobbish.

PRE.VA.LÊN.CI.A, *s.f.*, prevalence.

PRE.VA.RI.CA.ÇÃO, *s.f.*, prevarication.

PRE.VA.RI.CAR, *v.*, to prevaricate, to transgress.

PRE.VEN.ÇÃO, *s.f.*, prevention, precaution, warning, prejudice.

PRE.VE.NI.DO, *adj.*, advised, forewarmed, cautious, informed.

PRE.VE.NIR, *v.*, to prevent, to avert, to forestall, to alarm, to alert.

PRE.VEN.TI.VO, *s.m.*, preventive; *adj.*, preventive.

PRE.VER, *v.*, to foresee, to calculate.

PRÉ-VESTIBULAR ·· 281 ·· PROCURAR

PRÉ-VES.TI.BU.LAR, *s.m.*, course to the entrance examinations for university.

PRE.VI.A.MEN.TE, *adv.*, previously.

PRE.VI.DÊN.CIA, *s.f.*, providence, precaution, provision.

PRE.VI.DEN.CI.Á.RI.O, *s.m., Bras.*, employee or the institutional system of social welfare.

PRE.VI.DEN.TE, *adj.*, provident, cautious, prudent.

PRÉ.VIO, *adj.*, previous, precedent, prior, former, foregoing, precedent.

PRE.VI.SÃO, *s.f.*, prevision, foresight, forecast.

PRE.VI.SI.BI.LI.DA.DE, *s.f.*, foreseeability.

PRE.VI.SÍ.VEL, *adj.*, foreseeable.

PRE.VIS.TO, *adj.*, foreseen, anticipated.

PRE.ZA.DO, *adj.*, dear, esteemed.

PRE.ZAR, *v.*, to esteem, to value, to respect, to honour.

PRE.ZÁ.VEL, *adj.*, estimable, respectable.

PRI.MA, *s.f.*, cousin.

PRI.MA.DO, *s.m.*, primacy, primateship; *Rel.*, primate.

PRI.MA-DO.NA, *s.f.*, prima donna.

PRI.MAR, *v.*, to excell; to be superior.

PRI.MÁ.RIO, *adj.*, basic, primary, primitive, original.

PRI.MA.TA, *s.m., Zool.*, primate; *primatas*: primates (the order of primatic mammals).

PRI.MA.VE.RA, *s.f.*, spring, springtime; primrose (flower).

PRI.MA.VE.RIL, *adj.*, vernal.

PRI.MAZ, *s.m., Rel.*, primate, archbishop; *adj.*, prime.

PRI.MA.ZI.A, *s.f.*, primacy, superiority.

PRI.MEI.RA-DA.MA, *s.f.*, first lady.

PRI.MEI.RA.MEN.TE, *adv.*, first, firstly, primely.

PRI.MEI.RA.NIS.TA, *s. 2 gen.*, first-year student.

PRI.MEI.RO, *s.m.*, the first; *adj.*, first, prime, foremost, main, chief, original, principal.

PRI.MEI.RO-MI.NIS.TRO, *s.m.*, prime minister.

PRI.MI.TI.VO, *adj.*, primitive, original, early, simple, rude.

PRI.MO, *s.m.*, cousin; *adj.*, prime, excellent, perfect.

PRI.MO.GÊ.NI.TO, *s.m.*, first-born, eldest born; *adj.*, firstborn.

PRI.MO.GE.NI.TOR, *s.m.*, primogenitor, forefather, ancestor.

PRI.MO-IR.MÃO, *s.m.*, first cousin.

PRI.MOR, *s.m.*, beauty, delicacy.

PRI.MOR.DI.AL, *adj.*, primordial, original, prime.

PRI.MÓR.DI.O, *s.m.*, primordium.

PRI.MO.RO.SO, *adj.*, grateful, magnificent, excellent, perfect.

PRIN.CE.SA, *s.f.*, princess.

PRIN.CI.PA.DO, *s.m.*, principality, princedom.

PRIN.CI.PAL, *adj.*, principal, main, essential, chief, superior.

PRIN.CI.PAL.MEN.TE, *adv.*, principally, mainly.

PRÍN.CI.PE, *s.m.*, prince.

PRIN.CI.PES.CO, *adj.*, princely, magnificent.

PRIN.CI.PI.AN.TE, *s. 2 gen.*, principiant, beginner, novice, tyro; *adj.*, beginning.

PRIN.CI.PI.AR, *v.*, to begin, to initiate, to start.

PRIN.CÍ.PIO, *s.m.*, start, beginning, source, origin, maxim, axiom.

PRI.OR, *s.m.*, prior, rector.

PRI.O.RA.DO, *s.m.*, priorate, priorship.

PRI.O.RI.DA.DE, *s.f.*, priority, preference, precedence.

PRI.O.RI.ZAR, *v.*, to priorize.

PRI.SÃO, *s.f.*, prison, jail, ward, capture, apprehension, imprisonment.

PRI.SI.O.NAL, *adj.*, relating to a prison.

PRI.SI.O.NEI.RO, *s.m.*, prisoner, captive.

PRIS.MA, *s.f.*, prisma.

PRIS.MÁ.TI.CO, *adj.*, prismatic, prismatical.

PRI.VA.ÇÃO, *s.f.*, privation, want, destitution.

PRI.VA.CI.DA.DE, *s.f.*, privacy.

PRI.VA.DA, *s.f.*, privy, water-closet, toilet.

PRI.VA.DO, *s.m., adj.*, private.

PRI.VAR, *v.*, to prive, to deprive, to prohibit, to forbid.

PRI.VA.TI.VO, *adj.*, privative, peculiar, particular, private.

PRI.VA.TI.ZA.ÇÃO, *s.f., Bras.*, privatization.

PRI.VA.TI.ZAR, *v., Bras.*, to privatize.

PRI.VI.LE.GI.A.DO, *adj.*, privileged, favoured.

PRI.VI.LE.GI.AR, *v.*, to privilege, to favour, to exempt, to invest.

PRI.VI.LÉ.GIO, *s.m.*, privilege, advantage, prerogative, immunity.

PRÓ, *adv.*, pro, in favor of.

PRO.A, *s.f.*, stem, prow, bow, nose.

PRO.AR, *v., Náut.*, to steer for.

PRO.BA.BI.LI.DA.DE, *s.f.*, probability, likelihood, chance.

PRO.BA.BI.LIS.MO, *s.m., Fil.*, probabilism.

PRO.BA.TÓ.RI.O, *adj.*, probationary, probational.

PRO.BI.DA.DE, *s.f.*, probity, honesty, integrity.

PRO.BLE.MA, *s.m.*, problem, proposition, trouble, doubt.

PRO.BLE.MÁ.TI.CA, *s.f.*, problematic.

PRO.BLE.MÁ.TI.CO, *adj.*, problematic.

PRO.BO, *adj.*, honest.

PRO.CE.DÊN.CIA, *s.f.*, origin, derivation, provenance, source, genealogy.

PRO.CE.DEN.TE, *adj.*, proceeding, derived, descended.

PRO.CE.DER, *v.*, to procede, to go on, to come, to arise from, to result, to originate.

PRO.CE.DI.MEN.TO, *s.m.*, proceeding, procedure, dealing, transaction.

PRO.CES.SA.DOR, *s.m., Comp.*, processor.

PRO.CES.SA.MEN.TO, *s.m.*, processing; ~ *de dados*: data processing.

PRO.CES.SAR, *v.*, to process, to carry on a lawsuit, to law, to prosecute.

PRO.CES.SO, *s.m.*, process, legal proceedings, method, procedure.

PRO.CIS.SÃO, *s.f.*, procession, cortège.

PRO.CLA.MA.ÇÃO, *s.f.*, proclamation, publication, ban, declaration.

PRO.CLA.MA.DOR, *s.m.*, proclaimer; *adj.*, proclaiming.

PRO.CLA.MAR, *v.*, to proclaim, to promulgate, to announce.

PRO.CRAS.TI.NA.ÇÃO, *s.f.*, procrastination, putting off.

PRO.CRAS.TI.NAR, *v.*, to procrastinate, to put off.

PRO.CRI.A.ÇÃO, *s.f.*, procreation, generation.

PRO.CRI.A.DOR, *s.m.*, procreator; *adj.*, procreative.

PRO.CRI.AR, *v.*, to procreate, to beget, to engender, to generate.

PROC.TO.LO.GI.A, *s.f., Med.*, proctology.

PRO.CU.RA, *s.f.*, search, pursuit, demand.

PRO.CU.RA.ÇÃO, *s.f.*, procuration, mandate.

PRO.CU.RA.DO, *adj.*, demanded, sought after; ~ *pela polícia*: wanted by the police.

PRO.CU.RA.DOR, *s.m.*, procurator, attorney, proxy, proctor, mandatary.

PRO.CU.RA.DO.RA, *s.f.*, female procurator.

PRO.CU.RA.DO.RI.A, *s.f.*, procuracy, procuratorship.

PRO.CU.RAR, *v.*, to look for, to seek, to search, to try to

PRODIGALIDADE ···282··· PROLONGAMENTO

attempt, to visit, to call.

PRO.DI.GA.LI.DA.DE, s.f., prodigality, lavishness, profusion.

PRO.DÍ.GIO, s.m., prodigy, marvel, sign.

PRO.DI.GI.O.SA.MEN.TE, adv., prodigiously.

PRO.DI.GI.O.SO, adj., prodigious.

PRÓ.DI.GO, s.m., prodigal, waster, squanderer.

PRO.DU.ÇÃO, s.f., production, producing, manufacturing, output.

PRO.DU.CEN.TE, adj., producing, causing.

PRO.DU.TI.BI.LI.DA.DE, s.f., productiveness.

PRO.DU.TI.VA.MEN.TE, adv., productively.

PRO.DU.TÍ.VEL, adj., producible.

PRO.DU.TI.VI.DA.DE, s.f., productivity.

PRO.DU.TI.VO, adj., productive.

PRO.DU.TO, s.m., product, production, produce, proceeds, output.

PRO.DU.TOR, s.m., producer, creator, manufacturer.

PRO.DU.ZI.DO, adj., produced; trendy.

PRO.DU.ZIR, v., to produce, to bear, to yield, to cause, to effect, to afford.

PRO.E.MI.NÊN.CI.A, s.f., prominence.

PRO.E.MI.NEN.TE, adj., prominent.

PRO.E.ZA, s.f., prowess, bravery, courage, valor.

PRO.FA.NA.ÇÃO, s.f., profanation; sacrilege, violation; profanity.

PRO.FA.NA.DOR, s.m., profaner, sacrilegist; adj., profanatory, sacrilegious.

PRO.FA.NAR, v., to profane, to pollute, to abuse.

PRO.FA.NÁ.VEL, adj., capable of being profaned.

PRO.FA.NO, s.m., profane, layman; adj., profane, secular, irreligious.

PRO.FE.CIA, s.f., prophecy, prediction, forecast.

PRO.FE.RIR, v., to pronounce, utter, speak, say.

PRO.FE.RÍ.VEL, adj., that can be pronounced.

PRO.FES.SAR, v., to profess, to avow, to acknowledge, affirm, to teach, to educate.

PRO.FES.SO, s.m., professed person; adj., professed, avowed, seasoned.

PRO.FES.SOR, s.m., teacher, professor, master, educator, instructor.

PRO.FES.SO.RA, s.f., school mistress, instructress, woman teacher.

PRO.FES.SO.RA.DO, s.m., professorship, faculty.

PRO.FES.SO.RAL, adj., professorial.

PRO.FE.TA, s. 2 gen., prophet, predictor, foreteller.

PRO.FÉ.TI.CO, adj., prophetic, prophetical, predictive, presageful, pythonic.

PRO.FE.TI.SA, s.f., prophetess, pythoness.

PRO.FE.TI.ZAR, v., to prophetize, to prophesy, to predict.

PRO.FI.CI.ÊN.CIA, s.f., proficiency, skill, adeptness.

PRO.FI.CI.EN.TE, adj., proficient.

PRO.FI.CUI.DA.DE, s.f., utility, profitableness, usefulness.

PRO.FÍ.CUO, adj., useful, advantageous.

PRO.FI.LA.XIA, s.f., prophylaxis.

PRO.FIS.SÃO, s.f., profession, occupation, career, employment.

PRO.FIS.SI.O.NAL, adj., professional, occupational.

PRO.FIS.SI.O.NA.LIS.MO, s.m., professionalism.

PRO.FIS.SI.O.NA.LI.ZA.ÇÃO, s.f., profissionalization.

PRO.FIS.SI.O.NA.LI.ZAN.TE, adj., vocational.

PRO.FIS.SI.O.NA.LI.ZAR, v., to profissionalize;

profissionalizar-se: to become professional.

PRO.FUN.DA.MEN.TE, adv., deeply, profoundly.

PRO.FUN.DE.ZA, s.f., profundity, depth, abyss, deepness.

PRO.FUN.DE.ZAS, s.f., pl., depths.

PRO.FUN.DI.DA.DE, s.f., depth, profundity.

PRO.FUN.DO, s.m., profundity, depth; adj., deep, profound, impenetrable.

PRO.FU.SÃO, s.f., profusion, prodigality.

PRO.FU.SO, adj., profuse.

PRO.GE.NI.TOR, s.m., progenitor, forefather.

PRO.GES.TE.RO.NA, s.m., Bioq., progesterone.

PROG.NOS.TI.CAR, v., to prognosticate, to foretell, to predict.

PROG.NÓS.TI.CO, s.m., omen, presage, prognostic, prediction, prognosis.

PRO.GRA.MA, s.m., program, programme, plan.

PRO.GRA.MA.ÇÃO, s.f., programming, program; planing.

PRO.GRA.MA.DO, adj., programmed.

PRO.GRA.MA.DOR, s.m., programmer.

PRO.GRA.MAR, v., to program, to plan.

PRO.GRA.MÁ.VEL, adj., programmable.

PRO.GRE.DIR, v., to progress, to proceed, to advance.

PRO.GRES.SÃO, s.f., progression.

PRO.GRES.SIS.TA, s. 2 gen., progressist; adj., progressive.

PRO.GRES.SI.VO, adj., progressive, advancing, gradual.

PRO.GRES.SO, s.m., progress, advancement, improvement, growth, development.

PRO.I.BI.ÇÃO, s.f., prohibition, ban, interdiction, forbidding.

PRO.I.BI.DO, adj., prohibited, forbidden.

PRO.I.BIR, v., to prohibit, forbid, deny.

PRO.I.BI.TI.VA.MEN.TE, adv., prohibitively.

PRO.I.BI.TI.VO, adj., prohibitive.

PRO.JE.ÇÃO, s.f., projection, plan, delineation, scheme.

PRO.JE.TAR, v., to project, to throw out, to design, to cast forth, to shoot.

PRO.JE.TÁ.VEL, adj., projectable.

PRO.JÉ.TIL, s.m., projectile, missile, bullet, shot, bomb.

PRO.JE.TIS.TA, s. 2 gen., planner, designer; adj., planning, design.

PRO.JE.TO, s.m., project, plan, scheme, design, sketch.

PRO.JE.TOR, s.m., projector.

PROL, s. 2 gen., advantage, benefit.

PRÓ-LA.BO.RE, s.m., remuneration.

PRO.LAP.SO, s.m., Med., prolapse, prolapsus.

PRO.LE, s.f., offspring, progeny, descendants.

PRO.LE.GÔ.ME.NOS, s.m., pl., prolegomenon.

PRO.LEP.SE, s.f., Ret., prolepsis.

PRO.LE.TA.RI.A.DO, s.m., proletariat.

PRO.LE.TÁ.RIO, s.m., proletarian.

PRO.LI.FE.RA.ÇÃO, s.f., proliferation.

PRO.LI.FE.RAR, v., to proliferate, reproduce, grow rapidly.

PRO.LÍ.FE.RO, adj., prolific, proliferous.

PRO.LÍ.FI.CO, adj., prolific, productive, fertile.

PRO.LI.XI.DA.DE, s.f., prolixity, diffuseness.

PRO.LI.XO, adj., prolix, diffuse, tedious.

PRÓ.LO.GO, s.m., prologue, preamble, introduction.

PRO.LON.GA.ÇÃO, s.f., prolongation, elongation.

PRO.LON.GA.DA.MEN.TE, adv., extendedly, lengthily.

PRO.LON.GA.DO, adj., prolonged, delayed, protracted.

PRO.LON.GA.DOR, s.m., prolonger; adj., prolonging, extending.

PRO.LON.GA.MEN.TO, s.m., prolongation, delay.

PROLONGAR ·· 283 ·· PROTAGONISTA

PRO.LON.GAR, v., to prolong, to lenghten, to extend, to delay.
PRO.MES.SA, s.f., promise, assurance, word.
PRO.ME.TER, v., to promise, to pledge.
PRO.ME.TI.DO, adj., promised.
PRO.MIS.CUI.DA.DE, s.f., promiscuity.
PRO.MIS.CU.IR-SE, v., to mingle with; to mix (with).
PRO.MÍS.CUO, adj., promiscuous, mixed.
PRO.MIS.SOR, s.m., promiser; adj., promising.
PRO.MIS.SÓ.RIA, s.f., promissory note.
PRO.MO.ÇÃO, s.f., promotion, preference, preferment.
PRO.MO.CI.O.NAL, adj., promotional.
PRO.MON.TÓ.RI.O, s.m., Geol., promontory.
PRO.MO.TOR, s.m., promoter, sponsor, inciter, instigator;
 PROMOTOR DE JUSTIÇA, attorney, prosecutor.
PRO.MO.TO.RI.A, s.f., state prosecutor'soffice.
PRO.MO.VER, v., to promote, to foster, to raise.
PRO.MUL.GA.ÇÃO, s.f., promulgation.
PRO.MUL.GAR, v., to promulgate, to publish.
PRO.NO.ME, s.m., pronoun.
PRO.NO.MI.NAL, adj., Gram., pronominal.
PRON.TI.DÃO, s.f., promptitude, promptness, readiness.
PRON.TI.FI.CAR, v., to make ready, prepare; prontificar-se:
 to volunteerfor/to do (something).
PRON.TO, adj., ready, prompt, prepared, disposed.
PRON.TO-SO.COR.RO, s.m., first-aid clinic.
PRON.TU.Á.RIO, s.m., dossier, promptuary, record.
PRO.NÚN.CIA, s.f., pronunciation, enunciation.
PRO.NUN.CI.A.DO, adj., pronounced, articulate; well-marked.
PRO.NUN.CI.A.MEN.TO, s.m., pronouncement; Jur., judgment.
PRO.NUN.CI.AR, v., to pronounce, to enunciate, to utter.
PRO.NUN.CI.Á.VEL, adj., pronounceable.
PRO.PA.GA.ÇÃO, s.f., propagation, diffusion, dissemination.
PRO.PA.GA.DOR, s.m., propagator, spreader; adj., propagative.
PRO.PA.GAN.DA, s.f., advertising, publicity, advertisement, propaganda.
PRO.PA.GAN.DIS.TA, s. 2 gen., propagandist.
PRO.PA.GAR, v., to propagate, to multiply, to reproduce, to diffuse, to spread, to scatter.
PRO.PA.LAR, v., to blab, to divulge.
PRO.PE.DÊU.TI.CA, s.f., propaedeutics.
PRO.PE.LEN.TE, s.m., propellant, propellent.
PRO.PE.LIR, v., to propel, to impel.
PRO.PEN.DER, v., to be inclined; ~ para: to lean towards.
PRO.PE.NO, s.m., Quím., propene, propylene.
PRO.PEN.SÃO, s.f., propensity, propension, tendency, disposition.
PRO.PEN.SO, adj., propense, inclined, prone, ready.
PRO.PI.CI.A.DOR, s.m., propitiator; adj., propitiating.
PRO.PI.CI.AR, v., to propitiate, to conciliate.
PRO.PÍ.CIO, adj., propitious, promising, benevolent, kind.
PRO.PI.NA, s.f., propine, gratuity, tip.
PRO.PI.NAR, v., to propine.
PRÓ.PO.LIS, s.f., propolis.
PRO.POR, v., to propose, to suggest, to recommend, to offer.
PRO.POR.ÇÃO, s.f., proportion, rate, ratio, symmetry.
PRO.POR.CI.O.NA.DO, adj., proportionate, proportioned.
PRO.POR.CI.O.NAL, adj., proportional.
PRO.POR.CI.O.NA.LI.DA.DE, s.f., proportionateness.
PRO.POR.CI.O.NAR, v., to proportion, to proportionate, to adjust, to provide.

PRO.PO.SI.ÇÃO, s.f., proposition, proposal.
PRO.PO.SI.TA.DA.MEN.TE, adv., on purpose, purposively.
PRO.PO.SI.TA.DO, adj., intentional, purposed, deliberate.
PRO.PO.SI.TAL, s. 2 gen., intentional.
PRO.PÓ.SI.TO, s.m., purpose, aim, intention, matter.
PRO.POS.TA, s.f., proposal, bid, offer, proposition.
PRO.POS.TO, adj., offered, proposed.
PRO.PRI.A.MEN.TE, adv., properly; suitably.
PRO.PRI.E.DA.DE, s.f., propriety, accuracy, quality, real estate.
PRO.PRI.E.TÁ.RIO, s.m., proprietor, owner.
PRÓ.PRIO, adj., proper, peculiar, private, own, fit, suitable, correct, appropriate, right.
PRO.PUG.NAR, v., to defend, to vindicate.
PRO.PUL.SÃO, s.f., propulsion.
PRO.PUL.SOR, s.m., propellor; adj., propelling.
PROR.RO.GA.ÇÃO, s.f., prorogation, deferment.
PROR.RO.GA.DO, adj., deferred, prolonged.
PROR.RO.GAR, v., to prorogate, to prorogue, to put off.
PROR.RO.GÁ.VEL, adj., prolongable.
PROR.ROM.PER, v., to break out, to burst.
PRO.SA, s.f., prose, talk, chatter, courtship.
PRO.SA.DOR, s.m., prose writer.
PRO.SAI.CO, adj., prosaic, dull, commonplace.
PROS.CÊ.NI.O, s.m., proscenium.
PROS.CRE.VER, v., to proscribe; to banish, to exile; to prohibit, to do away with.
PROS.CRI.TO, s.m., outlaw; adj., proscribed, outlawed.
PRO.SE.A.DOR, s.m., Bras., chatter, talker; adj., talkative.
PRO.SE.AR, v., Bras., to chat, to talk; to show off, to vaunt.
PRO.SE.LI.TIS.MO, s.m., proselytism.
PRO.SÉ.LI.TO, s.m., proselyte, convert.
PRO.SÓ.DIA, s.f., prosody.
PRO.SO.PO.PEI.A, s.f., Ret., prosopopoeia.
PROS.PEC.ÇÃO, s.f., Geol., prospecting.
PROS.PEC.TAR, v., to prospect.
PROS.PEC.TI.VO, adj., prospective.
PROS.PEC.TO, s.m., prospectus, prospect; leaflet.
PROS.PEC.TOR, s.m., Geol., prospector.
PROS.PE.RA.MEN.TE, adv., prosperously.
PROS.PE.RAR, v., to prosper, to thrive, to flourish.
PROS.PE.RI.DA.DE, s.f., prosperity, success, welfare.
PRÓS.PE.RO, adj., prosperous, successful, propitious.
PROS.SE.GUI.MEN.TO, s.m., pursuit, continuation, following.
PROS.SE.GUIR, v., to follow, to continue, to proceed, to go on, to pursue.
PRÓS.TA.TA, s.f., Anat., prostate, the prostate gland.
PROS.TA.TEC.TO.MI.A, s.f., Med., prostatectomy.
PROS.TA.TO.TO.MI.A, s.f., Med., prostatotomy.
PROS.TER.NAR, v., to prostrate.
PROS.TÍ.BU.LO, s.m., brothel, whore-house.
PROS.TI.TU.I.ÇÃO, s.f., prostitution.
PROS.TI.TU.Í.DO, adj., prostituted.
PROS.TI.TU.IR, v., to prostitute, to corrupt.
PROS.TI.TU.TA, s.f., prostitute, courtesan, whore.
PROS.TRA.ÇÃO, s.f., prostration.
PROS.TRA.DO, adj., prostrate, prostrated.
PROS.TRA.ÇÃO, s.f., prostration, debility.
PROS.TRAR, v., to prostrate, to humiliate, to weaken, to humble.
PRO.TA.GO.NIS.TA, s. 2 gen., protagonist.

PROTAGONIZAR ·· 284 ·· PUDIM

PRO.TA.GO.NI.ZAR, *v., Cin., Teat.*, to feature in, to star in; to be at the center of (event).

PRO.TE.ÇÃO, *s.f.*, protection, patronage, support, security, help, favour.

PRO.TE.CI.O.NIS.MO, *s.m., Econ.*, protectionism.

PRO.TE.CI.O.NIS.TA, *s. 2 gen., Econ.*, protectionist; *adj.*, protectionist.

PRO.TE.GER, *v.*, to protect, to defend, to support, shield.

PRO.TE.GI.DO, *adj.*, protected, favoured.

PRO.TEI.CO, *adj.*, proteinaceous, próteinic.

PRO.TE.Í.NA, *s.f.*, protein.

PRO.TE.LA.ÇÃO, *s.f.*, delay, postponement.

PRO.TE.LA.DOR, *s.m.*, delayer, procrastinator; *adj.*, delaying, putting off.

PRO.TE.LAR, *v.*, to delay, to postpone, to prolong.

PRO.TE.LÁ.VEL, *adj.*, delayable, postponable.

PRÓ.TE.SE, *s.f.*, prosthesis.

PRO.TES.TAN.TE, *s. 2 gen.*, Protestant; *adj.*, Protestant, protesting.

PRO.TES.TAN.TIS.MO, *s.m.*, Protestantism.

PRO.TES.TAR, *v.*, to protest, to make a protest against, to object.

PRO.TES.TO, *s.m.*, protest, disapproval, objection, asseveration.

PRO.TE.TOR, *s.m.*, protector, supporter, guardian; *adj.*, protecting, protective, shielding.

PRO.TE.TO.RA.DO, *s.m.*, protectorate.

PRO.TE.TO.RAL, *adj.*, protectoral.

PRO.TO.CO.LO, *s.m.*, protocol, ceremony, register, record.

PRO.TÓ.TI.PO, *s.m.*, prototype, model, pattern.

PRO.TU.BE.RÂN.CIA, *s.f.*, protuberance, projection, bulge.

PRO.TU.BE.RAN.TE, *adj.*, protuberant, prominent.

PRO.VA, *s.f.*, proof, experiment, essay, trial, examen, test, demonstration, testimony.

PRO.VA.ÇÃO, *s.f.*, probation, proving, trial.

PRO.VA.DO, *adj.*, proved, proven, confirmed, examined, tried.

PRO.VA.DOR, *s.m.*, prover; *adj.*, proving.

PRO.VAR, *v.*, to prove, to try, to experiment, to test, to check, to verify, to testify.

PRO.VÁ.VEL, *adj.*, probable, likely, provable.

PRO.VA.VEL.MEN.TE, *adv.*, probably.

PRO.VE.DOR, *s.m.*, purveyor.

PRO.VEI.TO, *s.m.*, profit, advantage, gain, benefit, progress.

PRO.VEI.TO.SO, *adj.*, profitable, advantageous, lucrative.

PRO.VEN.ÇAL, *s. 2 gen.*, Provençal; *adj.*, Provençal.

PRO.VE.NI.EN.TE, *adj.*, deriving from, coming, proceeding.

PRO.VEN.TO, *s.m.*, produce, profit.

PROVENTOS, *s.m., pl.*, proceeds, remuneration, pay.

PRO.VER, *v.*, to provide, to furnish, to supply, to give, to grant, to confer.

PRO.VER.BI.AL, *adj.*, proverbial.

PRO.VÉR.BIO, *s.m.*, proverb, saying.

PRO.VE.TA, *s.f.*, cylinder.

PRO.VI.DÊN.CIA, *s.f.*, Providence, God, providence, foresight, precaution.

PRO.VI.DEN.CI.AL, *adj.*, providential.

PRO.VI.DEN.CI.AR, *v.*, to provide, to make arrangement for, to arrange, to prepare.

PRO.VI.MEN.TO, *s.m.*, stocking up, provision; *Jur.*, granting.

PRO.VÍN.CIA, *s.f.*, province, region, territory, district.

PRO.VIN.CI.AL, *adj.*, provincial.

PRO.VIN.CI.A.NIS.MO, *s.m.*, provincialism.

PRO.VIN.CI.A.NO, *s.m.*, provincial; *adj., pej.*, provincial.

PRO.VIN.DO, *adj.*, proceeding, coming from.

PRO.VIR, *v.*, to proceed, to come, to issue.

PRO.VI.SÃO, *s.f.*, provision, supply, store, storage.

PRO.VI.SI.O.NAR, *v.*, to provision.

PRO.VI.SÓ.RIO, *adj.*, temporary, transitory.

PRO.VO.CA.ÇÃO, *s.f.*, provocation, provoking, affront, challenge.

PRO.VO.CA.DOR, *s.m.*, provoker; *adj.*, provocative.

PRO.VO.CAN.TE, *adj.*, provocative.

PRO.VO.CAR, *v.*, to provoke, to affront, to incite, to insult.

PRO.VO.CA.TI.VO, *adj.*, provocative, irritating.

PRO.XE.NE.TA, *s. 2 gen.*, procurer, pimp.

PRO.XI.MI.DA.DE, *s.f.*, proximity, nearness, kinship.

PRÓ.XI.MO, *s.m.*, fellow man, neighbor; *adj.*, next, coming, near, close, adjacent.

PRU.DÊN.CIA, *s.f.*, prudence, caution, circumspection.

PRU.DEN.TE, *adj.*, careful, prudent, discreet, provident.

PRU.MO, *s.m.*, plumb bob, plummet.

PRU.RI.DO, *s.m., Med.*, prurigo, pruritus; itch, itching.

PSEU.DÔ.NI.MO, *s.m.*, pseudonym.

PSI.CA.NÁ.LI.SE, *s.f.*, psychoanalysis.

PSI.CA.NA.LIS.TA, *s. 2 gen.*, psychoanalyst.

PSI.CO.DÉ.LI.CO, *adj.*, psychodelic, psychedelic.

PSI.CO.DRA.MA, *s.m., Psic.*, psychodrama.

PSI.CO.GRA.FAR, *v.*, to write through spiritual agency.

PSI.CO.GRA.FI.A, *s.f.*, psychography.

PSI.CO.LIN.GUÍS.TI.CA, *s.f., Ling.*, psycholinguistics.

PSI.CO.LO.GIA, *s.f.*, psychology.

PSI.CO.LÓ.GI.CO, *adj.*, psychological.

PSI.CÓ.LO.GO, *s.m.*, psychologist.

PSI.CO.PA.TA, *s. 2 gen.*, psychopath.

PSI.CO.SE, *s.f.*, psychosis.

PSI.COS.SO.MÁ.TI.CO, *adj.*, psychosomatic.

PSI.CO.TÉC.NI.CO, *adj.*, referring to psychotechnics.

PSI.CO.TE.RA.PEU.TA, *s. 2 gen.*, psychotherapist.

PSI.CO.TE.RA.PI.A, *s.f.*, psychotherapy.

PSI.CÓ.TI.CO, *adj.*, psychotic.

PSI.QUE, *s.f.*, psyche, soul, spirit, mind.

PSI.QUI.A.TRA, *s. 2 gen.*, psychiatrist.

PSI.QUI.A.TRI.A, *s.f.*, psychiatry.

PSI.QUI.Á.TRI.CO, *adj.*, psychiatric, psychiatrical.

PSÍ.QUI.CO, *adj.*, psychic.

PSIU!, *interj.*, pst! hush!

PSO.RÍ.A.SE, *s.f., Med.*, psoriasis.

PU.A, *s.f.*, prick, point, bit.

PU.BER.DA.DE, *s.f.*, puberty.

PÚ.BE.RE, *adj.*, pubescent.

PU.BI.A.NO, *adj.*, pubic; *Anat.*, pubis.

PU.BLI.CA.ÇÃO, *s.f.*, publication.

PU.BLI.CAR, *v.*, to publish, to announce, to edit, to spread.

PU.BLI.CÁ.VEL, *adj.*, publishable.

PU.BLI.CI.DA.DE, *s.f.*, publicity, advertisement, advertising.

PU.BLI.CI.TÁ.RI.O, *s.m.*, adman; *adj., Bras.*, referring to publicity.

PÚ.BLI.CO, *s.m.*, public, audience, spectators; *adj.*, public.

PÚ.BLI.CO-AL.VO, *s.m.*, target audience.

PU.DE.RA!, *interj.*, small wonder! why!

PU.DI.CO, *adj.*, chaste, modest, bashful, shy.

PU.DIM, *s.m.*, pudding.

PUDOR

PU.DOR, *s.m.*, chastity, shyness, modesty.
PU.E.RI.CUL.TU.RA, *s.f.*, childcare, child welfare.
PU.E.RIL, *adj.*, puerile, childish.
PU.E.RI.LI.DA.DE, *s.f.*, puerility, childishness, foolishness.
PU.FE, *s.m.*, pouffe, ottoman.
PU.GI.LA.TO, *s.m.*, boxing.
PU.GI.LIS.MO, *s.m.*, pugilism, boxing.
PU.GI.LIS.TA, *s. 2 gen.*, pugilist, boxer.
PUG.NAZ, *adj.*, pugnacious, combative.
PU.Í.DO, *adj.*, threadbare, frayed.
PU.IR, *v.*, to polish, to abrade.
PU.JAN.TE, *adj.*, puissant, strong, powerful.
PU.LA-PU.LA, *s.m.*, bouncy castle, pogo (toy); *Zool.*, a warbler (bird).
PU.LAR, *v.*, to leap, to bounce, to hop, to spring.
PUL.GA, *s.f., Zool.*, flea.
PUL.GÃO, *s.m., Zool.*, aphid.
PUL.GUEI.RO, *s.m., pop.*, fleapit.
PUL.GUEN.TO, *adj.*, infested with fleas.
PUL.MÃO, *s.m.*, lung.
PUL.MO.NAR, *adj.*, pulmonary.
PU.LO, *s.m.*, jump, leap, skip, vault.
PU.LÔ.VER, *s.m.*, pullover.
PÚL.PI.TO, *s.m.*, pulpit.
PUL.SA.ÇÃO, *s.f.*, pulsation, pulse.
PUL.SAR, *v.*, to pulsate, to pulse, to impel, to vibrate.
PUL.SEI.RA, *s.f.*, bracelet, wristband.
PUL.SO, *s.m.*, pulse, wrist, strength, vigor.
PU.LU.LAR, *v.*, to pullulate, to proliferate, to grow rankly.
PUL.VE.RI.ZA.ÇÃO, *s.f.*, pulverization.
PUL.VE.RI.ZA.DOR, *s.m.*, pulverizer, spray; *adj.*, pulverizing, spraying.
PUL.VE.RI.ZAR, *v.*, to pulverize, to spray, to destroy.
PUM!, *interj.*, boom, pang.
PU.MA, *s.f.*, puma, cougar.
PUN.ÇÃO, *s.f.*, puncture, perforation.
PUN.GÊN.CI.A, *s.f.*, pungency.
PUN.GEN.TE, *adj.*, pungent, poignant.
PUN.GIR, *v.*, to prick, to pierce, to hurt.
PUN.GUIS.TA, *s.m.*, pickpocket.
PU.NHA.DO, *s.m.*, handful, a few, bunch.
PU.NHAL, *s.m.*, dagger, poniard.
PU.NHA.LA.DA, *s.f.*, stab.
PU.NHO, *s.m.*, fist, wrist, handle.
PU.NI.ÇÃO, *s.f.*, punishment, penalty.

PUXA-SACO

PU.NIR, *v.*, to punish, to reprimand.
PU.NI.TI.VO, *adj.*, punitive.
PU.PI.LA, *s.f.*, pupil; the opening of the iris.
PU.PI.LO, *s.m.*, pupil, ward.
PU.RÊ, *s.m.*, purée, pap.
PU.RE.ZA, *s.f.*, pureness, purity, innocence, perfection.
PUR.GA.ÇÃO, *s.f.*, purgation, purge; purification; cleansing.
PUR.GAN.TE, *s.m.*, purgative; *adj.*, purgative, laxative.
PUR.GAR, *v.*, to purge.
PUR.GA.TÓ.RIO, *s.m.*, purgatory.
PUR.GA.TI.VO, *s.m.*, purgative medicine; *adj.*, purgative.
PU.RI.FI.CA.ÇÃO, *s.f.*, purification.
PU.RI.FI.CA.DOR, *s.m.*, purifier, refiner.
PU.RI.FI.CAR, *v.*, to purify, to clean, to clear, to refine.
PU.RIS.MO, *s.m.*, purism.
PU.RIS.TA, *s. 2 gen.*, purist.
PU.RI.TA.NIS.MO, *s.m.*, Puritanism.
PU.RI.TA.NO, *s.m.*, Puritan; *adj.*, puritan, prudish.
PU.RO, *adj.*, pure, clear, clean, unmingled, unspoiled, blameless, innocent.
PU.RO-SAN.GUE, *s. 2 gen.*, thoroughbred; *adj.*, referring to a high-bred animal.
PÚR.PU.RA, *s.f.*, purple; purple cloth.
PUR.PÚ.RE.O, *adj.*, purple, crimson.
PUR.PU.RI.NA, *s.f., Quím.*, purpurin.
PU.RU.LEN.TO, *adj.*, purulent, suppurative.
PUS, *s.m.*, pus, matter.
PU.SI.LÂ.NI.ME, *s. 2 gen.*, fainthearted person, coward; *adj.*, pusillanimous, coward.
PU.SI.LA.NI.MI.DA.DE, *s.f.*, pusillanimity.
PÚS.TU.LA, *s.f.*, pustule, pimple.
PUS.TU.LEN.TO, *adj.*, pustuled.
PU.TA, *s.f.*, whore, hooker, prostitute, bitch.
PU.TRE.FA.ÇÃO, *s.f.*, putrefaction, decomposition.
PU.TRE.FA.TO, *adj.*, putrefied, putrid.
PU.TRE.FA.ZER, *v.*, to putrefy, to rot, to corrupt.
PÚ.TRI.DO, *adj.*, putrid, putrefied, decayed; corrupt.
PU.XA!, *interj.*, why!, now!, gee.
PU.XA.DA, *s.f.*, draft, pull.
PU.XA.DOR, *s.m.*, handle, knob.
PU.XÃO, *s.m.*, pull, tug, jerk.
PU.XA-PU.XA, *s.m.*, toffee; *adj.*, toffee.
PU.XAR, *v.*, to pull, to draw, to haul, to drag, to tug, to pluck.
PU.XA-SA.CO, *s.m.*, cajoler, flatterer, bootlicker, toady.

Q

Q, *s.m.*, sixteenth letter of the Portuguese alphabet.
QATAR, *s.*, Qatar.
QG, *s.m., abrev.* of *Quartel-General*: general headquarters, HQ.
QUA.DRA, *s.f.*, square place, court, block, yard.
QUA.DRA.DO, *s.m.*, square; *adj.*, square, quadrate.
QUA.DRA.GE.NÁ.RIO, *adj., s.m.*, quadragenarian.
QUA.DRA.GÉ.SI.MO, *num.*, fortieth.
QUA.DRAN.GU.LAR, *adj.*, quadrangular: having four sides and four angles.
QUA.DRÂN.GU.LO, *s.m.*, quadrangle.
QUA.DRAN.TE, *s.m.*, quadrant, circle, dial.
QUA.DRA.TU.RA, *s.f.*, quadrature.
QUA.DRI.CI.CLO, *s.m.*, quad bike.
QUA.DRI.CU.LA.DO, *adj.*, checkered.
QUA.DRI.CU.LAR, *adj.*, checker; *v.*, to checker, to divide, to crossline.
QUA.DRI.E.NAL, *adj.*, quadrennial.
QUA.DRI.Ê.NIO, *s.m.*, quadrennium.
QUA.DRIL, *s.m.*, hip, haunch.
QUA.DRI.LÁ.TE.RO, *s.m.*, quadrilateral.
QUA.DRI.LHA, *s.f.*, gang, band.
QUA.DRI.MES.TRAL, *adj.*, happening every fourth month; occurring once in four months.
QUA.DRI.MES.TRE, *s.m.*, a period of four months.
QUA.DRI.MO.TOR, *s.m.*, four-engined plane; *adj.*, four-engined.
QUA.DRI.NHO, *s.m.*, small frame; *quadrinhos* (*pl.*): comic strip, cartoon.
QUA.DRO, *s.m.*, picture, painting, portrait, board, panel, list, staff, image, figure.
QUA.DRO-NE.GRO, *s.m.*, blackboard.
QUA.DRÚ.PE.DE, *s.m.*, quadruped, four-footed, animal.
QUA.DRU.PLI.CA.ÇÃO, *s.f.*, quadruplication.
QUA.DRU.PLI.CAR, *v.*, to quadruplicate.
QUÁ.DRU.PLO, *s.m.*, quadruple.
QUAL, *pron.*, which, that which, that one, such as, who, whom.
QUA.LI.DA.DE, *s.f.*, quality, kind, characteristic, class.
QUA.LI.FI.CA.ÇÃO, *s.f.*, qualification.
QUA.LI.FI.CA.DO, *adj.*, qualified, competent, able.
QUA.LI.FI.CA.ÇÃO, *s.f.*, qualification.
QUA.LI.FI.CA.DOR, *s.m.*, qualifier; *adj.*, qualifying.
QUA.LI.FI.CAR, *v.*, to qualify, designate, consider, to classify, to denominate.
QUA.LI.FI.CA.TI.VO, *adj.*, qualificative, qualifying.
QUA.LI.FI.CÁ.VEL, *adj.*, qualifiable.
QUA.LI.TA.TI.VO, *adj.*, qualitative.
QUAL.QUER, *pron.*, any, some, a, an, every, either, whatever, certain; *a qualquer hora*: any time.
QUAN.DO, *adv.*, when, how soon, at what time; *conj.*, when, at which, as soon as, at the time that.
QUAN.TI.A, *s.f.*, sum, amount, quantity.
QUÂN.TI.CO, *adj., Fís.*, quantum.
QUAN.TI.DA.DE, *s.f.*, quantity, quantum, amount, sum.
QUAN.TI.FI.CA.ÇÃO, *s.f.*, quantification; *Fís.*, quantization.
QUAN.TI.FI.CAR, *v.*, to quantify.
QUAN.TI.TA.TI.VA.MEN.TE, *adv.*, quantitatively.
QUAN.TI.TA.TI.VO, *s. 2 gen.*, quantitative.
QUAN.TO, *adj.*, how much, whatever, as much as; *adv.*, how, as to; *pron.*, how much?, how many?, whatever.
QUÃO, *adv.*, how, as.
QUA.RA.DOR, *s.m.*, bleachground, bleachyard.
QUA.RAR, *v., Bras.*, to bleach; to exposewhite clothesto sunlight.
QUA.REN.TA, *num.*, forty.
QUA.REN.TÃO, *s.m.*, quadragenarian.
QUA.REN.TE.NA, *s.f.*, quarantine.
QUA.RES.MA, *s.f.*, Lent.
QUAR.TA, *s.f.*, quarter, forth part.
QUAR.TA-FEI.RA, *s.f.*, Wednesday.
QUAR.TA.NIS.TA, *s. 2 gen.*, a fourth-year student.
QUAR.TEI.RÃO, *s.m.*, block.
QUAR.TE.JAR, *v.*, to quarter (divide into quarters).
QUAR.TEL, *s.m.*, quarter, barrack, caserne.
QUAR.TE.LA.DA, *s.f., Bras., pej.*, military mutiny.
QUAR.TEL-GE.NE.RAL, *s.m.*, general headquarters.
QUAR.TE.TO, *s.m.*, quartet.
QUAR.TO, *s.m.*, the fourth part, a quarter, room, bedroom.
QUART.ZO, *s.m., Min.*, quartz.
QUA.SAR, *s., Astron.*, quasar.
QUA.SE, *adv.*, almost, near, nearly, closely, about.
QUA.TER.NÁ.RI.O, *s.m., Geol.*, Quaternary; *adj.*, quaternary.
QUA.TI, *s.m., Zool.*, coati (*genus Nasua*).
QUA.TOR.ZE, *num.*, fourteen.
QUA.TRI.Ê.NIO, *s.m.*, quadrennium.
QUA.TRI.LHÃO, *s.m.*, quadrillion.
QUA.TRO, *num.*, four.
QUA.TRO.CEN.TÃO, *adj., Bras.*, with four hundred year of tradition (São Paulo); *col.*, traditionary.
QUA.TRO.CEN.TIS.MO, *s.m., Hist.*, quattrocentism.
QUA.TRO.CEN.TIS.TA, *s. 2 gen., Hist.*, quattrocentist; *adj.*, referring to the quattrocento.
QUA.TRO.CEN.TOS, *num.*, four hundred.
QUE, *pron.*, that, which, who, whom, what; *adv.*, what, how; *conj.*, as, for, than, however.
QUÊ, *s.m.*, anything, something, difficulty, obstacle.
QUE.BRA, *s.f.*, break, breakage, breaking, fracture, interruption, hillside.
QUE.BRA-CA.BE.ÇA, *s.f.*, puzzle.
QUE.BRA.DA, *s.f.*, slope, hillside; *Bras.*, bend of a road.
QUE.BRA.DEI.RA, *s.f., Bras.*, lack of money; bankruptcies (due to economic crisis); *Bras.*, exhaustion, weakness.
QUE.BRA.DI.ÇO, *adj.*, fragile, delicate.
QUE.BRA.DO, *adj.*, broken, fragmented.

QUEBRADOR · 287 · QUINTA-COLUNA

QUE.BRA.DOR, *s.m.*, breaker; *adj.*, breaking.

QUE.BRA-GA.LHO, *s.m.*, Mr Fixit, troubleshooter; contrivance.

QUE.BRA-GE.LO, *s.m.*, *Náut.*, icebreaker.

QUE.BRA-MAR, *s.m.*, breakwater; mole.

QUE.BRA-MO.LAS, *s.m.*, *2 num.*, speed bump.

QUE.BRA-NO.ZES, *s.m.*, *2 num.*, nutcracker.

QUE.BRAN.TAR, *v.*, to break; to let down; to debilitate; to damage; to conquer; to soften; *fig.*, to transgress.

QUE.BRAN.TO, *s.m.*, evil eye; prostration, exhaustion; run-down state.

QUE.BRAR, *v.*, to break, to shatter, to violate, to transgress, to go bankrupt, to interrupt.

QUE.BRA-VEN.TO, *s.m.*, windbreak; fanlight (auto).

QUE.DA, *s.f.*, fall, decadence, destruction, drop, tendency, bent.

QUE.DA-D'Á.GUA, *s.f.*, waterfall.

QUE.DO, *adj.*, quiet, still, stationary.

QUEI.JA.DA, *s.f.*, *Cul.*, a small pie made with flour, milk, eggs, cheese and sugar; cheesecake.

QUEI.JEI.RO, *s.m.*, cheese maker.

QUEI.JO, *s.m.*, *Cul.*, cheese.

QUEI.MA.ÇÃO, *s.f.*, the same that *queima*; *Med.*, pyrosis, heartburn; *fig.*, annoyance.

QUEI.MA.DA, *s.f.*, burn.

QUEI.MA.DO, *adj.*, burned, burnt, scorched, carbonized.

QUEI.MA.DU.RA, *s.f.*, burn.

QUEI.MAR, *v.*, to burn, to destroy by fire, to cremate.

QUEI.MA-ROU.PA, *s.f.*, at point-blank range, point-blank; *fig.*, face to face.

QUEI.XA, *s.f.*, complaint, formal accusation, charge, offence, protest.

QUEI.XA-CRI.ME, *s.f.*, *Jur.*, citation.

QUEI.XA.DA, *s.f.*, proeminet jaw; jawbone, mandible.

QUEI.XAR, *v.*, to complain; to lament; to clamour; to protest; *queixar-se*: to complain about something.

QUEI.XO, *s.m.*, chin, mandible, lower jaw.

QUEI.XO.SA.MEN.TE, *adv.*, complainingly.

QUEI.XO.SO, *s.m.*, complainant; *adj.*, complaining, querulous, plaintiff.

QUEI.XU.ME, *s.m.*, lamentation, complaint, whine.

QUE.LÍ.CE.RA, *s.f.*, *Zool.*, *Anat.*, chelicera (anterior pair of appendages of the Arachnida).

QUEM, *pron.*, who, whom, one or anybody who.

QUÊ.NI.A, *s.*, Kenya.

QUE.NI.A.NO, *s.m.*, Kenyan; *adj.*, Kenyan.

QUEN.TÃO, *s.m.*, mulledwine.

QUEN.TE, *adj.*, hot, burning.

QUEN.TI.NHA, *s.f.*, *Bras.*, hot snackpacked (for delivery).

QUEN.TU.RA, *s.f.*, warmth, heat.

QUE.PE, *s.m.*, kepi.

QUER, *conj.*, or, whether or though, notwithstanding.

QUE.RE.LA, *s.f.*, quarrel; *Jur.*, charge, complaint, action, lawsuit.

QUE.RE.LAN.TE, *s.m.*, *Jur.*, complainant, accuser; *adj.*, complaining, accusing.

QUE.RE.LAR, *v.*, to quarrel, to complain; *Jur.*, to sue.

QUE.RER, *v.*, to wish, to will, to desire, to want, to intend, to aspire.

QUE.RI.DO, *adj.*, dear, darling, beloved, favourite.

QUE.RI.DI.NHO(A), *s. 2 gen.*, deary.

QUER.MES.SE, *s.f.*, kermis, kermess.

QUE.RO-QUE.RO, *s.m.*, *Bras.*, *Zool.*, Southern lapwing (*Vanellus chilensis*).

QUE.RO.SE.NE, *s.m.*, kerosene, oil.

QUE.RU.BIM, *s.m.*, cherub.

QUÉ.RU.LO, *adj.*, *Lit.*, querulous, mournful.

QUE.SI.TO, *s.m.*, inquiry, query, question.

QUES.TÃO, *s.f.*, question, inquiry, query, interrogation.

QUES.TI.O.NA.DOR, *s.m.*, questioner.

QUES.TI.O.NA.MEN.TO, *s.m.*, questioning.

QUES.TI.O.NAR, *v.*, to question, to debate, to discuss, to argue.

QUES.TI.O.NÁ.RIO, *s.m.*, questionnaire.

QUES.TI.O.NÁ.VEL, *adj.*, questionable.

QUI.A.BO, *s.m.*, okra.

QUI.BE, *s.m.*, *Cul.*, kibbe (kind of croquette of Arab origin).

QUI.ÇÁ, *adv.*, perhaps, maybe, possibly.

QUI.CAR, *v.*, to bounce; *Bras.*, *Esp.*, to make the ball jump (football).

QUICHE, *s. 2 gen.*, *Fr.*, *Cul.*, quiche.

QUÍ.CHUA, *s. 2 gen.*, *adj.*, Quechuan.

QUI.E.TA.ÇÃO, *s.f.*, stillness, harmony, calmness.

QUI.E.TAR, *v.*, to quiet.

QUI.E.TO, *adj.*, quiet, still, placid, serene, tranquil.

QUI.E.TU.DE, *s.f.*, quietude, peacefulness, calmness, serenity.

QUI.LA.TA.ÇÃO, *s.f.*, assaying.

QUI.LA.TAR, *v.*, to assay.

QUI.LA.TE, *s.m.*, carat, karat; *fig.*, superiority, excellence.

QUI.LHA, *s.f.*, keel, bottom, hull.

QUI.LO, *s.m.*, kilo; chyle, kilogram.

QUI.LO.GRA.MA, *s.m.*, kilogram, kilogramme.

QUI.LOM.BO, *s.m.*, *Bras.*, *Hist.*, Quilombo (fortified village where runaway slaves lived).

QUI.LO.ME.TRA.GEM, *s.f.*, a distance or a measuring in kilometers.

QUI.LO.MÉ.TRI.CO, *adj.*, kilometric, kilometrical; *fig.*, mile, very extensive.

QUI.LÔ.ME.TRO, *s.m.*, kilometer, kilometre.

QUI.LO.WATT, *s.m.*, kilowatt.

QUI.LO.WATT-HO.RA, *s.m.*, *Eletr.*, kilowatt-hour.

QUIM.BAN.DA, *s.m.*, *Bras.*, Umbanda branch allegedly practicing black magic.

QUI.ME.RA, *s.f.*, chimera.

QUI.MÉ.RI.CO, *adj.*, chimeric, chimerical.

QUÍ.MI.CA, *s.f.*, chemistry.

QUÍ.MI.CO, *s.m.*, chemist; *adj.*, chemic, chemical.

QUI.MI.O.TE.RA.PI.A, *s.f.*, *Med.*, chemotherapy.

QUI.MO.NO, *s.m.*, kimono.

QUI.NA, *s.f.*, edge, corner, five spots (cards).

QUIN.DIM, *s.m.*, *Bras.*, *Cul.*, a cake made with egg, sugar and coconut.

QUIN.GEN.TÉ.SI.MO, *num.*, five hundredth.

QUI.NHÃO, *s.m.*, portion, parcel, partition.

QUI.NHEN.TIS.TA, *s. 2 gen.*, cinquecentist; *adj.*, pertaining to the 16th century.

QUI.NHEN.TOS, *num.*, five hundred.

QUI.NI.NO, *s.m.*, quinine.

QUIN.QUA.GÉ.SI.MO, *num.*, fiftieth.

QUIN.QUÊ.NIO, *s.m.*, quinquennium.

QUIN.QUI.LHA.RI.AS, *s.f.*, *pl.*, trinkets, fripperies, junk.

QUIN.TA, *s.f.*, estate, farm; Thursday.

QUIN.TA-CO.LU.NA, *s.f.*, *s. 2 gen.*, fifth column; fifth columnist.

QUINTA-ESSÊNCIA · · 288 · · QUOTIZAR

QUIN.TA-ES.SÊN.CI.A, *s.f.*, quintessence.
QUIN.TA-FEI.RA, *s.f.*, Thursday.
QUIN.TAL, *s.m.*, yard, backyard.
QUIN.TES.SÊN.CI.A, *s.f.*, the same that *quinta-essência*.
QUIN.TE.TO, *s.m.*, quintet.
QUIN.TO, *num.*, fifth, quint; *adj.*, fifth.
QUIN.TU.PLI.CA.ÇÃO, *s.f.*, quintuplication.
QUIN.TU.PLI.CA.DO, *adj.*, quintuplicate, fivefold.
QUIN.TU.PLI.CAR, *v.*, to quintuple, to quintuplicate.
QUÍN.TU.PLO, *s.m.*, quintuple; *adj.*, quintuple, fivefold.
QUIN.ZE, *num.*, fifteen.
QUIN.ZE.NA, *s.f.*, fortnight.
QUIN.ZE.NAL, *adj.*, fortnightly, biweekly.
QUI.OS.QUE, *s.m.*, kiosk, news stand.
QUI.PRO.QUÓ, *s.m., Lat.*, confusion, mix-up.
QUI.RO.LO.GI.A, *s.f.*, dactylology.
QUI.RO.MAN.CI.A, *s.f.*, chiromancy.
QUI.RO.MAN.TE, *s.2 gen.*, fortuneteller, chiromancer.

QUIS.TO, *s.m., Med.*, cyst, wen.
QUI.TA.ÇÃO, *s.f.*, quittance, repayment.
QUI.TA.DO, *adj.*, quit, quits.
QUI.TAN.DA, *s.f.*, greengrocery.
QUI.TAN.DEI.RO, *s.m.*, greengrocer.
QUI.TAR, *v.*, to quit, to exempt, to desist from, to free, to liberate.
QUI.TE, *adj.*, quit, free, settled.
QUI.TU.TE, *s.m., Bras., UK* titbit, *US* tidbit.
QUI.XO.TES.CO, *adj.*, quixotic.
QUI.XO.TIS.MO, *s.m.*, quixotism.
QUI.ZUM.BA, *s.f., Bras., gír.*, brawl, confusion.
QUO.CI.EN.TE, *s.m.*, quotient.
QUO.RUM, *s.m.*, quorum.
QUO.TA, *s.f.*, quota, share.
QUO.TI.DI.A.NO, *adj.*, daily.
QUO.TI.ZAR, *v.*, to parcel out.

R, *s.m.*, the seventeenth letter of the Portuguese alphabet.
RÃ, *s.f.*, frog.
RA.BA.DA, *s.f.*, tail, caudal fin, rump.
RA.BA.NA.DA, *s.f.*, French toast; *Cul.*, oxtail stew.
RA.BA.NE.TE, *s.m.*, *Bot.*, radish.
RA.BA.VEN.TO, *adj.*, flying or sailing before the wind.
RA.BE.CA, *s.f.*, *Mús.*, violin, fiddle.
RA.BE.CÃO, *s.m.*, *Mús.*, bass fiddle; *Bras., pop.,* hearse.
RA.BEI.RA, *s.f.*, track, trace. 2 chaff. 3 tail of a gown; *col.*, back part of anything.
RA.BI, *s.m.*, rabbi.
RA.BI.CHO, *s.m.*, pigtail, crupper, tail.
RÁ.BI.CO, *adj.*, *Med.*, rabic (veterinary).
RA.BI.CÓ, *adj.*, bobtailed, tailless.
RA.BI.NO, *s.m.*, rabbi.
RA.BIS.CA.DO, *adj.*, scrawly.
RA.BIS.CAR, *v.*, to scribble, scrawl, to scrabble.
RA.BIS.CO, *s.m.*, scribble, scrawl, doodle.
RA.BO, *s.m.*, tail, brush, handle.
RA.BO DE CA.VA.LO, *s.m.*, ponytail.
RA.BO DE FO.GUE.TE, *s.m.*, problem difficult to solve.
RA.BO DE SAI.A, *s.m.*, piece of skirt.
RA.BU.DO, *s.m.*, *gír.*, devil; *adj.*, long-tailed; *gír.* lucky.
RA.BU.GEN.TO, *adj.*, morose, cross, sullen, ill-humoured, peevish.
RA.BU.GI.CE, *s.f.*, grumpiness.
RÁ.BU.LA, *s.f.*, pettifogger, shyster.
RA.ÇA, *s.f.*, race, generation, origin, descent, species, pedigree, family.
RA.ÇÃO, *s.f.*, ration, portion.
RA.CHA, *s.f.*, crack, fissure; split; splinter.
RA.CHA.DO, *adj.*, split, cracked, cleft,.
RA.CHA.DU.RA, *s.f.*, crack; splitting.
RA.CHAR, *v.*, to split, to cleave, to splinter, to shiver, to chap.
RA.CIAL, *adj.*, racial.
RA.CI.O.CI.NAR, *v.*, to reason, to ratiocinate, to think, to consider.
RA.CI.O.CÍ.NIO, *s.m.*, ratiocination, reasoning, thought.
RA.CI.O.NA.DO, *adj.*, rationed, stinted.
RA.CI.O.NAL, *adj.*, rational, reasonable.
RA.CI.O.NA.LI.DA.DE, *s.f.*, rationality.
RA.CI.O.NA.LIS.MO, *s.m.*, rationalism.
RA.CI.O.NA.LIS.TA, *s. 2 gen.*, rationalist.
RA.CI.O.NA.LI.ZA.ÇÃO, *s.f.*, rationalization.
RA.CI.O.NA.LI.ZAR, *v.*, to rationalize.
RA.CI.O.NAL.MEN.TE, *adv.*, rationally.
RA.CI.O.NA.MEN.TO, *s.m.*, rationing, ration.
RA.CI.O.NAR, *v.*, to ration.
RA.CI.O.NÁ.VEL, *adj.*, reasonable.
RA.CIS.MO, *s.m.*, racism.
RA.CIS.TA, *s. 2 gen.*, racist.
RACK, *s.m.*, *Ing.*, rack.

RA.DAR, *s.m.*, radar.
RA.DI.A.ÇÃO, *s.f.*, radiation.
RA.DI.A.DO, *s.m.*, radiate; *adj.*, radiate; radial.
RA.DI.A.DOR, *s.m.*, radiator.
RA.DI.AL, *adj.*, radial.
RA.DI.A.LIS.TA, *s. 2 gen.*, broadcaster.
RA.DI.ÂN.CI.A, *s.f.*, radiance, radiancy.
RA.DI.A.NO, *s.m.*, *Mat.*, radian.
RA.DI.AN.TE, *adj.*, radiant, beautiful, splendid, gleeful.
RA.DI.CA.DO, *adj.*, radicated, rooted; *fig.*, inveterate.
RA.DI.CAL, *adj.*, radical, basic, fundamental.
RA.DI.CA.LIS.MO, *s.m.*, radicalism.
RA.DI.CA.LI.ZA.ÇÃO, *s.f.*, radicalization.
RA.DI.CA.LI.ZAR, *v.*, to radicalize.
RA.DI.CAR, *v.*, to radicate, to take root, to root, to settle down.
RÁ.DIO, *s.m.*, radius, radium, radio.
RA.DI.O.A.MA.DOR, *s.m.*, a radio ham.
RA.DI.O.AS.TRO.NO.MI.A, *s.f.*, *Astron.*, radio astronomy.
RA.DI.O.A.TI.VI.DA.DE, *s.f.*, radioactivity.
RA.DI.O.A.TI.VO, *adj.*, radioactive.
RA.DI.O.DI.AG.NÓS.TI.CO, *s.m.*, *Med.*, radiodiagnosis.
RA.DI.O.DI.FUN.DIR, *v.*, to radiobroadcast.
RA.DI.O.DI.FU.SÃO, *s.f.*, broadcasting.
RA.DI.O.DI.FU.SOR, *s.m.*, radio broadcaster; *adj.*, radio broadcasting.
RA.DI.O.GRA.FAR, *v.*, to radiograph.
RA.DI.O.GRA.FIA, *s.f.*, radiography, roentgenogram.
RA.DI.O.GRÁ.FI.CO, *adj.*, radiographic, radiographical.
RA.DI.O.GRA.MA, *s.m.*, radiogram.
RA.DI.O.JOR.NAL, *s.m.*, radio news.
RA.DI.O.LA, *s.f.*, radiophonograph.
RA.DI.O.LO.GIA, *s.f.*, radiology.
RA.DI.O.LÓ.GI.CO, *adj.*, radiologic, radiological.
RA.DI.O.LO.GIS.TA, *s. 2 gen.*, radiologist.
RA.DI.O.NO.VE.LA, *s.f.*, *Bras.*, radio soap opera.
RA.DI.O.O.PE.RA.DOR, *s.m.*, radio operador.
RA.DI.O.PA.TRU.LHA, *s.f.*, flying squad, radio patrol.
RA.DI.O.SO, *adj.*, radiant, brilliant, ecstatic.
RA.DI.O.TÁ.XI, *s.m.*, radio cab.
RA.DI.O.TE.RA.PI.A, *s.f.*, *Med.*, radiotherapy.
RA.DI.OU.VIN.TE, *s. 2 gen.*, radio listener.
RÁ.FI.A, *s.f.*, raffia.
RA.GU, *s.m.*, *Cul.*, ragout.
RAI.A, *s.f.*, line, stroke, streak, race-course, limit.
RAI.A.DO, *adj.*, striped; radiated; marked (lane); rifled.
RAI.AR, *v.*, to break, to dawn, to emit rays, to radiate.
RA.I.NHA, *s.f.*, queen; queen bee.
RA.I.NHA-MÃE, *s.f.*, queen mother.
RAI.O, *s.m.*, ray, beam, thunderbolt, radius, sign, indication.
RAI.VA, *s.f.*, rage, fury, hydrophobia, rabies, hate.
RAI.VEN.TO, *adj.*, furious, choleric.
RAI.VO.SA.MEN.TE, *adv.*, ragefully.

RAIVOSO ••• 290 ••• RASPADO

RAI.VO.SO, *adj.*, angry, furious.
RA.IZ, *s.f.*, root, base, bottom, origin.
RA.I.ZA.DA, *s.f.*, rootage, quantity of roots.
RA.JÁ, *s.m.*, raja, rajah.
RA.JA.DA, *s.f.*, gust of wind, squall.
RA.JA.DO, *s.m.*, rajaship; *adj.*, striped, streaked.
RA.LA.ÇÃO, *s.f.*, act of grating; *fig.*, work hard; weariness.
RA.LA.DOR, *s.m.*, rasper, grater.
RA.LA.DU.RA, *s.f.*, act of grating; scrapings.
RA.LAR, *v.*, to rasp, to grate, to annoy.
RA.LÉ, *s.f.*, common people, rabble.
RA.LE.A.MEN.TO, *s.m.*, act of thinning out.
RA.LE.AR, *v.*, make sparse, to thin out.
RA.LHA.ÇÃO, *s.f.*, scolding, rebuke.
RA.LHAR, *v.*, to rail, to scold, to chide.
RA.LHO, *s.m.*, scolding, rebuke, reprimand.
RA.LI, *s.m.*, rally, rallye.
RA.LO, *s.m.*, grater, rasper, strainer.
RA.MA, *s.f.*, branches, boughs (of a tree).
RA.MA.DÃ, *s.m.*, Ramadan, Ramadhan.
RA.MA.DO, *adj.*, branchy, branched, ramate.
RA.MA.LHAR, *v.*, to rustle, to sough.
RA.MA.GEM, *s.f.*, branches, boughs, foliage.
RA.MAL, *s.m.*, extension line, railroad branch line.
RA.MA.LHE.TE, *s.m.*, bunch of flowers, bouquet, nosegay.
RA.MEI.RA, *s.f.*, prostitute, whore.
RA.ME.LA, *s.f.*, the same that *remela*.
RA.ME.LO.SO, *adj.*, blear-eyed.
RA.MI.FI.CA.ÇÃO, *s.f.*, ramification, branching.
RA.MI.FI.CA.DO, *adj.*, branched, ramified, forked, furcate.
RA.MI.FI.CAR, *v.*, to divide into branches, ramify, to furcate.
RA.MI.NHO, *s.m.*, twig.
RA.MO, *s.m.*, branch, bough, twig, sprig.
RA.MO.SI.DA.DE, *s.f.*, branchiness.
RA.MO.SO, *adj.*, ramous, branchy, twiggy.
RAM.PA, *s.f.*, ramp, stage.
RA.NÁ.RI.O, *s.m.*, froggery, frog farm.
RAN.CHE.RI.A, *s.f.*, the same that *ranchería*.
RAN.CHA.RI.A, *s.f.*, *Bras.*, group of huts, hut camp.
RAN.CHEI.RO, *s.m.*, regimental cook; farmer; homely.
RAN.CHO, *s.m.*, fare, ranch, farm; food.
RAN.ÇO, *s.m.*, rancidity, rancid taste, rancidness; rank smell; *adj.*, rancid.
RAN.COR, *s.m.*, rancour, resentment.
RAN.ÇO.RO.SO, *adj.*, rancorous, resentful.
RAN.ÇO.SO, *adj.*, rancid, rank; *fig.*, antiquated.
RAN.DÔ.MI.CO, *adj.*, random, haphazard.
RAN.DO.MI.ZA.ÇÃO, *s.f.*, randomization.
RAN.GE.DOR, *adj.*, creaking, grating.
RAN.GEN.TE, *adj.*, creaking, grating.
RAN.GER, *v.*, to screak, to creak, to grit.
RAN.GI.DO, *s.m.*, creaking, screak.
RAN.GO, *s.m.*, *Bras.*, *gír.*, food, meal.
RA.NHE.TA, *s. 2 gen.*, curmudgeon; *adj.*, impertinent, ill-tempered.
RA.NHO, *s.m.*, snivel, snot.
RA.NHO.SO, *adj.*, snotty, snot-nosed.
RA.NHU.RA, *s.f.*, groove, slot, slit, notch.
RAN.ZIN.ZA, *s.f.*, sullen, sulky, ill-humoured, unruly.
RA.PA.CE, *adj.*, rapacious, ravening.
RA.PA.CI.DA.DE, *s.f.*, rapacity, rapaciousness.

RA.PA.DO, *adj.*, scraped, rasped.
RA.PA.DU.RA, *s.f.*, scraping; *Cul.*, raw brown sugar.
RA.PA.GÃO, *s.m.*, healthy lad, burly person.
RA.PA.PÉ, *s.m.*, curtsy; servile greeting, adulation.
RA.PAR, *v.*, to scrape, to scratch, to wear out.
RA.PA.RI.GA, *s.f.*, girl, maiden.
RA.PAZ, *s.m.*, boy, guy, lad, youngster, young man, fellow.
RA.PA.ZI.A.DA, *s.f.*, a lot of boys, lads, group of youths.
RA.PA.ZI.NHO, *s.m.*, kid, little boy.
RA.PA.ZO.TE, *s.m.*, kid, little boy.
RA.PI.DA.MEN.TE, *adv.*, rapidly.
RA.PI.DEZ, *s.f.*, rapidity, quickness, swiftness, speed.
RÁ.PI.DO, *adj.*, rapid, quick, swift, speedy.
RA.PI.NA, *s.f.*, rapine, robbery.
RA.PI.NA.GEM, *s.f.*, robbery, plunder.
RA.PO.SA, *s.f.*, *Zool.*, fox, vixen.
RAP.SÓ.DIA, *s.f.*, rhapsody.
RAP.SO.DIS.TA, *s. 2 gen.*, rhapsodist.
RAP.TA.DO, *adj.*, kidnapped.
RAP.TAR, *v.*, to ravish, to abduct, to kidnap, to rob.
RAP.TO, *s.m.*, abduction, ravishment, kidnapping.
RAP.TOR, *s.m.*, abductor, kidnapper.
RA.QUE, *s.f.*, *Anat.*, rachis, spinal, spinal column.
RA.QUE.TA.DA, *s.f.*, a stroke with a racket.
RA.QUE.TE, RA.QUE.TA, *s.f.*, racket, racquet.
RA.QUE.TIS.TA, *s. 2 gen.*, *Bras.*, tennis player.
RA.QUI.A.NO, *adj.*, the same that *raquidiano*.
RA.QUI.DI.A.NA, *s.f.*, *Med.*, epidural (rachidian anesthesia).
RA.QUI.DI.A.NO, *adj.*, *Med.*, rachidian.
RA.QUÍ.TI.CO, *adj.*, rachitic, richety, scrubby.
RA.QUI.TIS.MO, *s.m.*, *Med.*, rickets, rachitis.
RA.RA.MEN.TE, *adv.*, rarely, seldom.
RA.RE.AR, *v.*, to rarefy, to diminish.
RA.RE.FA.ÇÃO, *s.f.*, rarefaction, rarefication.
RA.RE.FA.CI.EN.TE, *adj.*, rarefactive, rarefying.
RA.RE.FA.TO, *adj.*, rarefied.
RA.RE.FA.TOR, *s.m.*, rarefactor; *adj.*, rarefactive, rarefying.
RA.RE.FA.ZER, *v.*, to rarefy, to make thin.
RA.RE.FEI.TO, *adj.*, rarefied, less dense, thin.
RA.RI.DA.DE, *s.f.*, rareness, rarity, scarcity.
RA.RO, *adj.*, rare, thin, seldom, unusual.
RÁS, *s.m.*, ras (Abyssinian prince).
RA.SAN.TE, *adj.*, *s. 2 gen.*, levelling, smoothing, skimming.
RA.SAR, *v.*, to become shallow, to become full; to raze, to equalize.
RAS.CU.NHAR, *v.*, to sketch, to outline..
RAS.CU.NHO, *s.m.*, draft, sketch, rough copy.
RAS.GA.DO, *adj.*, torn, rent, frank, open.
RAS.GÃO, *s.m.*, gash, rip, tear, rent.
RAS.GA.MEN.TO, *s.m.*, act of rending or tearing; breach; laceration.
RAS.GAR, *v.*, to tear, to rend, to split, to cleave.
RAS.GO, *s.m.*, rip, tear, split, cleft, scratch.
RA.SO, *s.m.*, plain; *adj.*, level, flat, low, vulgar.
RAS.PA, *s.f.*, scrapings, chip, shaving.
RAS.PA.DEI.RA, *s.f.*, scraper, rasp, eraser.
RAS.PA.DE.LA, *s.f.*, act of rasping; abrasion.
RAS.PA.DI.NHA, *s.f.*, *Bras.*, Italian ice; scratchcard (lottery).
RAS.PÃO, *s.m.*, scratch, sore caused by friction; *de ~*: obliquely, slightly.
RAS.PA.DO, *adj.*, shaven.

RASPADOR ··291·· REAPRESENTAÇÃO

RAS.PA.DOR, *s.m.*, scraper; rasper, rubber, raker; *adj.*, scraping, rasping.

RAS.PAR, *v.*, to scrape, to scratch, to erase.

RAS.TÃO, *s.m.*, vine's branch while pruning.

RAS.TA.QUE.RA, *s. 2 gen.*, parvenu, upstart, show-off.

RAS.TE.AR, *v.*, to track down, to look for something.

RAS.TEI.RA, *s.f.*, trip.

RAS.TE.JA.DOR, *s.m.*, searcher, tracer, tracker; *adj.*, searching, tracing, tracking.

RAS.TE.JA.MEN.TO, *s.m.*, act ofcrawl or trailing; *fig.*, inquiry, investigation.

RAS.TE.JAN.TE, *adj.*, creeping, crawling.

RAS.TE.JAR, *v.*, to trace, to track, to follow the track, to crawl.

RAS.TI.LHO, *s.m.*, fuse.

RAS.TO, *s.m.*, trace, track.

RAS.TRE.A.DOR, *adj.*, tracker, tracer.

RAS.TRE.A.MEN.TO, *s.m.*, tracking.

RAS.TRE.AR, *v.*, to trace, to track, to pursue, to trace down.

RAS.TRI.LHO, *s.m.*, portcullis, harrow.

RAS.TRO, *s.m.*, trace, track, vestige.

RA.SU.RA, *s.f.*, erasure.

RA.SU.RAR, *v.*, to cross out, to erase, blot out.

RA.TA.ZA.NA, *s.f.*, Zool., Norway rat; *Bras., gír.*, thief.

RA.TE.AR, *v.*, to prorate, to distribute, to share out, to stall.

RA.TEI.O, *s.m.*, share, apportionment.

RA.TI.CI.DA, *s.m.*, raticide, rat poison.

RA.TI.FI.CA.ÇÃO, *s.f.*, ratification.

RA.TI.FI.CA.DO, *adj.*, ratified, confirmed.

RA.TI.FI.CAR, *v.*, to ratify, to confirm, to validate.

RA.TI.FI.CÁ.VEL, *adj.*, ratifiable, confirmable.

RA.TO, *s.m.*, Zool., mouse, rat.

RA.TO-DE-ES.GO.TO, *s.m.*, Zool., brown rat.

RA.TO-DO.MÉS.TI.CO, *s.m.*, Zool., black rat.

RA.TO.EI.RA, *s.f.*, mousetrap, rat-trap.

RA.VI.NA, *s.f.*, Bot., ravine, mountain steam.

RA.VI.NO.SO, *adj.*, ravined.

RA.VI.Ó.LI, *s.m.*, It., Cul., ravioli.

RA.ZÃO, *s.f.*, reason, reasoning, ground, justice, right, rate, proportion, moral law.

RA.ZI.A, *s.f.*, Fr., *razzia*, incursion; *fig.*, atack, destruction.

RA.ZO.A.DO, *s.m.*, defense, discourse; *adj.*, reasonable, rational.

RA.ZO.AR, *v.*, to reason, to conclude, to argue; to defend, to discourse.

RA.ZO.Á.VEL, *adj.*, reasonable, sensible, rational, sane.

RA.ZO.A.VEL.MEN.TE, *adv.*, reasonably, justly, rightly.

RÉ, *s.f.*, female criminal; *s.m.*, re, the second musical note; *s.f.*, *marcha à ré*: reverse speed.

RE.A.BAS.TE.CER, *v.*, to supply, to replenish, to supply with fresh provisions.

RE.A.BAS.TE.CI.MEN.TO, *s.m.*, replenishment, restocking.

RE.A.BER.TU.RA, *s.f.*, reopening.

RE.A.BI.LI.TA.ÇÃO, *s.f.*, rehabilitation.

RE.A.BI.LI.TA.DO, *adj.*, rehabilitated, reinstated.

RE.A.BI.LI.TAR, *v.*, to rehabilitate, to reinstate.

RE.A.BRIR, *v.*, to reopen, open again.

RE.AB.SOR.ÇÃO, *s.f.*, reabsorption.

RE.AB.SOR.VER, *v.*, to reabsorb.

RE.A.ÇA, *s. 2 gen., Bras., gír.*, the same that *reacionário*.

RE.A.ÇÃO, *s.f.*, reaction, resistance.

RE.A.CEN.DER, *v.*, to relight, to light again, to rekindle.

RE.A.CI.O.NÁ.RIO, *adj.*, reactionary.

RE.A.CI.O.NA.RIS.MO, *s.m.*, reactionarism.

RE.A.CO.MO.DAR, *v.*, to readapt to, to accomodate again.

RE.A.DAP.TA.ÇÃO, *s.f.*, readaptation.

RE.A.DAP.TAR, *v.*, to readapt, adapt again.

RE.AD.MIS.SÃO, *s.f.*, readmission, readmittance.

RE.AD.MI.TIR, *v.*, to readmit, to admit again.

RE.A.DO.ÇÃO, *s.f.*, readoption.

RE.A.DO.TAR, *v.*, to readopt.

RE.AD.QUI.RIR, *v.*, to reacquire. 2 to recover, get back, retrieve.

RE.A.FIR.MA.ÇÃO, *s.f.*, reaffirmation, reassertment.

RE.A.FIR.MAR, *v.*, to reaffirm, to reassert.

RE.A.GEN.TE, *s.m.*, reagent; *adj.*, reactive.

RE.A.GIR, *v.*, to react, to answer, to resist.

RE.A.GRA.DE.CER, *v.*, to thank again.

RE.A.GRA.VAR, *v.*, to renew an offense.

RE.A.GRU.PA.MEN.TO, *s.m.*, reassemblage, rally.

RE.A.GRU.PAR, *v.*, to regroup.

RE.A.JUS.TA.MEN.TO, *s.m.*, readjustment.

RE.A.JUS.TAR, *v.*, to readjust, rearrange.

RE.A.JUS.TÁ.VEL, *adj.*, readjustable.

RE.A.JUS.TE, *s.m.*, readjustment.

RE.AL, *adj.*, real, actual, factual, genuine, royal, kingly.

RE.AL.ÇAR, *v.*, to enhance, to emphasize, to intensify.

RE.AL.CE, *s.m.*, distinction, enhancement.

RE.A.LE.GRAR, *v.*, to make happy again.

RE.A.LE.JO, *s.m.*, barrel organ.

RE.A.LEN.GO, *adj.*, royal, kingly; *Bras.*, unclaimed, public.

RE.A.LE.ZA, *s.f.*, royalty, regality, kingship.

RE.A.LI.DA.DE, *s.f.*, reality, actuality, fact, truth, verity.

RE.A.LI.MEN.TA.ÇÃO, *s.f.*, action or result of feeding again; regeneration; *Eletr.*, self-excitation.

RE.A.LIS.MO, *s.m.*, realism; royalism.

RE.A.LIS.TA, *s. 2 gen., Art., Lit.*, realist; *adj.*, realistic, realistical.

RE.A.LÍS.TI.CO, *adj.*, realistic.

RE.A.LI.ZA.ÇÃO, *s.f.*, accomplishment, fulfillment, achievement, attainment.

RE.A.LI.ZA.DO, *adj.*, accomplished, fulfilled.

RE.A.LI.ZA.DOR, *s.m.*, realizer, producer; *adj.*, realizing, performing, enterprising.

RE.A.LI.ZAR, *v.*, to accomplish, to consummate, to realize, to achieve.

RE.A.LI.ZÁ.VEL, *adj.*, realizable, achievable.

RE.AL.MEN.TE, *adv.*, really, actually.

RE.A.NE.XAR, *v.*, to reannex, to reoccupy, to reincorporate.

RE.A.NI.MA.ÇÃO, *s.f.*, reanimation, revivification.

RE.A.NI.MA.DO, *adj.*, reanimated, revived.

RE.A.NI.MA.DOR, *s.m.*, encourager, reviver; *adj.*, reanimating, reviving, encouraging.

RE.A.NI.MAR, *v.*, to reanimate, to restore to life, to revive, to revivify.

RE.A.PA.RE.CER, *v.*, to reappear, to appear again.

RE.A.PA.RE.CI.MEN.TO, *s.m.*, reappearance.

RE.A.PA.RE.LHA.MEN.TO, *s.m.*, re-equipment.

RE.A.PA.RE.LHAR, *v.*, to re-equip, to refit.

RE.A.PLI.CA.ÇÃO, *s.f.*, reapplication.

RE.A.PLI.CAR, *v.*, reapply.

RE.A.PREN.DER, *v.*, to learn again.

RE.A.PRE.SEN.TA.ÇÃO, *s.f.*, representation, new performance.

REAPRESENTAR ·· 292 ·· RECEBER

RE.A.PRE.SEN.TAR, *v.*, to represent; *reapresentar-se*: to reappear.

RE.A.PRO.VEI.TAR, *v.*, to reuse.

RE.A.PRO.XI.MAR, *v.*, to get close again; *reaproximar-se*: to grow closer again.

RE.A.QUE.CER, *v.*, to reheat.

RE.A.QUE.CI.MEN.TO, *s.m.*, reheating; *Econ.*, revival.

RE.AR.MA.MEN.TO, *s.m.*, rearmament.

RE.AR.MAR, *v.*, to rearm.

RE.AR.RAN.JAR, *v.*, to rearrange.

RE.AR.RAN.JO, *s.m.*, rearrangement.

RE.AR.TI.CU.LAR, *v.*, to rearticulate.

RE.AS.CEN.DER, *v.*, to reascend.

RE.AS.SEN.TAR, *v.*, resettle.

RE.AS.SU.MIR, *v.*, to reacquire, to retake, to recover.

RE.AS.SU.MÍ.VEL, *adj.*, resumable.

RE.AS.SUN.ÇÃO, *s.f.*, reassumption.

RE.A.TA.DO, *adj.*, bound or tied again.

RE.A.TA.MEN.TO, *s.m.*, reattachment; re-establishment, continuation.

RE.A.TAR, *v.*, to rebind, to reattach, to renew.

RE.A.TI.VAR, *v.*, to reactivate, to revive, to reanimate, reobtain.

RE.A.TI.VI.DA.DE, *s.f.*, reactivity.

RE.A.TI.VO, *s.m.*, *Quím.*, reactive agent; *adj.*, reactive.

RE.A.TOR, *s.m.*, reactor, reagent.

RE.A.VA.LI.A.ÇÃO, *v.*, re-evaluation; revaluation.

RE.A.VER, *v.*, to get back, to reobtain, to recover, to recuperate.

RE.A.VI.SAR, *v.*, to advise or warn again.

RE.A.VI.VAR, *v.*, to revive, to recall, to renew.

RE.BAI.XA.DO, *adj.*, lowered, let down; cut; *fig.*, discredited, relegated.

RE.BAI.XA.MEN.TO, *s.m.*, lowering, reduction, degradation.

RE.BAI.XAR, *v.*, to lower, to let down, to depreciate.

RE.BA.NHAR, *v.*, to form a flock, to reunite, to gather; to agglomerate.

RE.BA.NHO, *s.m.*, flock of sheep, herd of cattle, drove, cattle.

RE.BA.TE, *s.m.*, repelling, act or effect of striking again.

RE.BA.TE.DOR, *s.m.*, *Com.*, discounter; *adj.*, striking or beating again; discounting.

RE.BA.TER, *v.*, to strike again, to repel, to refute.

RE.BA.TI.DO, *adj.*, repelled, disproved, discounted.

RE.BA.TI.DA, *s.f.*, repellence; *Esp.*, return, hit.

RE.BA.TI.MEN.TO, *s.m.*, striking, beating again; repulsion; *Com.*, discount, deduction.

RE.BE.LA.DO, *s.m.*, rebel, mutineer.

RE.BE.LAR, *v.*, to cause to revolt, to rebel, to revolt.

RE.BEL.DE, *s. 2 gen.*, rebel, insurgent; *adj.*, rebel, revolutionary.

RE.BEL.DIA, *s.f.*, rebellion, revolt, insurrection, opposition.

RE.BE.LI.ÃO, *s.f.*, rebellion, revolt, mutiny.

RE.BEN.QUE, *s.m.*, *Bras.*, quirt.

RE.BEN.QUE.AR, *v.*, *Bras.*, to whip, to flog.

RE.BEN.TA.ÇÃO, *s.f.*, act of bursting, pounding of waves.

RE.BEN.TAR, *v.*, to burst, to split open, to blow up, to explode, to roar.

RE.BEN.TO, *s.m.*, shoot, sprout; *fig.*, offspring.

RE.BI.TAR, *v.*, to rivet, to clinch.

RE.BI.TE, *s.m.*, rivet, clinch.

RE.BO.AN.TE, *adj.*, resounding, reverberating.

RE.BO.AR, *v.*, to resound, reverberate.

RE.BO.BI.NAR, *v.*, to rewind, reel again.

RE.BO.CA.DO, *adj.*, plastered, coated, over made up.

RE.BO.CA.DOR, *s.m.*, tug, *Náut.*, towboat.

RE.BO.CAR, *v.*, to plaster, to coat with stucco, to tow.

RE.BO.CO, *s.m.*, plaster, roughcast.

RE.BO.LA.DO, *s.m.*, swinging movement of the hips.

RE.BO.LAR, *v.*, to roll, to shake the hips, hipswing.

RE.BO.QUE, *s.m.*, towing, plaster, rough-cast.

RE.BOR.DO.SA, *s.f.*, censure, reprimand; difficult situation; recurrence of an illness.

RE.BRO.TAR, *v.*, to sprout again.

RE.BU, *s.m.*, *gir.*, rumpus, confusion, disorder.

RE.BU.LI.ÇO, *s.m.*, clamour, commotion, tumult.

RE.BUS.CA.DO, *adj.*, highly cultured, accomplished; searched for, looked after; affected.

RE.BUS.CAR, *v.*, to search thoroughly, to refine, to perfect, to search again.

RE.CA.DAS.TRA.MEN.TO, *s.m.*, reregistration.

RE.CA.DAS.TRAR, *v.*, to record again in a cadastre.

RE.CA.DO, *s.m.*, message, word, information.

RE.CAÍ.DA, *s.f.*, act or effect of falling back; *Med.*, relapse, setback.

RE.CA.I.MEN.TO, *s.m.*, the same that *recaída*.

RE.CA.IR, *v.*, to fall again, to fall back, to befall.

RE.CAL.CA.DO, *adj.*, depressed, beaten down.

RE.CAL.CA.MEN.TO, *s.m.*, repression, suppression.

RE.CAL.CAR, *v.*, to step on, to press down.

RE.CAL.CI.TRÂN.CI.A, *s.f.*, recalcitrance, recalcitration.

RE.CAL.CI.TRAN.TE, *s. 2 gen.*, recalcitrant; *adj.*, recalcitrant, reluctant, renitent.

RE.CAL.CI.TRAR, *v.*, to recalcitrate; to refuse obedience; to insist on, to persist in.

RE.CAL.CU.LAR, *v.*, to recalculate, to recount.

RE.CÁL.CU.LO, *s.m.*, recalculation.

RE.CAL.QUE, *s.m.*, pressing down, repression, suppression.

RE.CAM.BI.AR, *v.*, to rechange, change again.

RE.CAN.TO, *s.m.*, place, corner, hiding place, retreat, recess, nook.

RE.CA.PA.CI.TAR, *v.*, to enable or render capable again.

RE.CA.PA.GEM, *s.f.*, retreading.

RE.CA.PE.A.MEN.TO, *s.m.*, covering with a new layer of asphalt.

RE.CA.PI.TA.LI.ZAR, *v.*, *Econ.*, to recapitalize.

RE.CA.PI.TU.LA.ÇÃO, *s.f.*, recapitulation.

RE.CA.PI.TU.LAR, *v.*, to recapitulate, to repeat.

RE.CAP.TU.RAR, *v.*, to recapture, to capture again.

RE.CAR.GA, *s.f.*, fresh load, reload.

RE.CAR.RE.GA.MEN.TO, *s.m.*, reloading.

RE.CAR.RE.GAR, *v.*, to reload, to recharge.

RE.CAR.RE.GÁ.VEL, *adj.*, that can be reloaded.

RE.CA.TA.DO, *adj.*, modest, moderate, prudent, proper.

RE.CA.TO, *s.m.*, modesty, honesty, bashfulness.

RE.CAU.CHU.TA.DO, *adj.*, retreaded (tires), *UK* remoulded, *US* remolded.

RE.CAU.CHU.TAR, *v.*, to recap, to retread.

RE.CE.A.DO, *adj.*, causing apprehension, feared.

RE.CE.AR, *v.*, to fear, to dread, to be apprehensive, to doubt.

RE.CE.Á.VEL, *adj.*, capable of causing fear, dreadful.

RE.CE.BE.DOR, *s.m.*, receiver, gatherer; *adj.*, receiving, gathering.

RE.CE.BER, *v.*, to accept, to take, to get, to receive, to cash in.

RECEBIMENTO ···293··· RECOMPENSÁVEL

RE.CE.BI.MEN.TO, *s.m.*, receiving, reception, receipt.
RE.CE.BÍ.VEL, *adj.*, receivable, acceptable.
RE.CEI.O, *s.m.*, fear, dread, terror, apprehension.
RE.CEI.TA, *s.f.*, income, revenue, recipe, prescription, budget.
RE.CEI.TAN.TE, *adj.*, prescribing.
RE.CEI.TAR, *v.*, to prescribe, to advise, to counsel.
RE.CEI.TU.Á.RI.O, *s.m.*, prescription; prescription pad.
RE.CÉM-CA.SA.DO, *adj.*, married or wed, newly married, just married.
RE.CÉM-CHE.GA.DO, *s.m.*, newcomer; *adj.*, recently arrived.
RE.CÉM-FA.LE.CI.DO, *s.m.*, recently deceased person; *adj.*, recently deceased.
RE.CÉ-FOR.MA.DO, *s.m.*, newly qulified person; *adj.*, newly qulified.
RE.CÉM-NAS.CI.DO, *s.m.*, a newborn baby; *adj.*, newborn.
RE.CÉM-PU.BLI.CA.DO, *adj.*, recently published.
RE.CEN.DER, *v.*, to smell (of something), to exhale a strong aroma.
RE.CEN.SE.A.DO, *s.m.*, person included in a census; *adj.*, registered, included in a census.
RE.CEN.SE.A.DOR, *s.m.*, census taker; *adj.*, registering, polling.
RE.CEN.SE.A.MEN.TO, *s.m.*, census, survey.
RE.CEN.SE.AR, *v.*, to take a census, to poll, to survey, to verify.
RE.CEN.TE, *adj.*, recent, modern, new, fresh.
RE.CEN.TE.MEN.TE, *adv.*, recently.
RE.CE.O.SO, *adj.*, afraid, fearful, anxious, apprehensive, timid.
RE.CEP.ÇÃO, *s.f.*, reception, receipt, admittance.
RE.CEP.CI.O.NAR, *v.*, to receive guests, to entertain.
RE.CEP.CI.O.NIS.TA, *s. 2 gen., Bras.*, receptionist.
RE.CEP.TA.DOR, *s.m.*, fence; *adj.*, receiving, fencing.
RE.CEP.TA.ÇÃO, *s.f.*, receiving of stolen goods.
RE.CEP.TÁ.CU.ŁO, *s.m.*, receptacle, container.
RE.CEP.TA.DOR, *s.m.*, receiver of stolen goods, *gír.*, fence; *adj.*, receiving.
RE.CEP.TAR, *v.*, to receive, to conceal.
RE.CEP.TI.BI.LI.DA.DE, *s.f.*, receptibility.
RE.CEP.TI.VA.MEN.TE, *adv.*, receptively.
RE.CEP.TÍ.VEL, *adj.*, receptible.
RE.CEP.TI.VI.DA.DE, *s.f.*, receptivity, receptiveness.
RE.CEP.TI.VO, *adj.*, receptive.
RE.CEP.TOR, *s.m.*, receiver, receptor.
RE.CES.SÃO, *s.f.*, recession.
RE.CES.SI.VI.DA.DE, *s.f., Biol.*, recessiveness.
RE.CES.SIVO, *adj.*, recessive.
RE.CES.SO, *s.m.*, recess, corner, niche, retreat.
RE.CHA.ÇAR, *v.*, to repel, to reject, to repulse, to decline, *fig.*, to refute.
RE.CHE.A.DO, *adj.*, stuffed, filled.
RE.CHE.AR, *v.*, to stuff, to fill.
RE.CHEI.O, *s.m.*, stuffing, farcing, dressing.
RE.CHON.CHU.DO, *adj.*, chubby, fat.
RE.CI.BO, *s.m.*, receipt, voucher, acquittance.
RE.CI.CLA.GEM, *s.f.*, recycling.
RE.CI.CLAR, *v.*, to recycle, to retrain.
RE.CI.FE, *s.m.*, reef, skerry.
RE.CIN.GIR, *v.*, to gird again.
RE.CIN.TO, *s.m.*, area, enclosure, enclosed space.
RE.CI.PI.EN.TE, *s.m.*, recipient, receiver, vessel.
RE.CI.PRO.CA.MEN.TE, *adv.*, reciprocally.

RE.CI.PRO.CAR, *v.*, to reciprocate.
RE.CI.PRO.CI.DA.DE, *s.f.*, reciprocity.
RE.CÍ.PRO.CO, *adj.*, reciprocal, reciprocative, mutual.
RÉ.CI.TA, *s.f., Teat.*, performance; recital.
RE.CI.TAL, *s.m.*, recital, concert.
RE.CI.TA.LIS.TA, *s. 2 gen.*, recitalist.
RE.CI.TAN.TE, *s. 2 gen.*, reciter; *adj.*, reciting.
RE.CI.TAR, *v.*, to recite, to declaim.
RE.CLA.MA.ÇÃO, *s.f.*, complaint, reclamation, demand.
RE.CLA.MA.DO, *adj.*, claimed.
RE.CLA.MA.DOR, *s.m.*, the same that *reclamante*.
RE.CLA.MAN.TE, *s. 2 gen.*, claimer, claimant; *adj.*, claiming, demanding.
RE.CLA.MAR, *v.*, to object, to protest, to complain, to oppose, to require.
RE.CLA.MÁ.VEL, *adj.*, claimable.
RE.CLA.ME, *s.m.*, advertisement.
RE.CLI.NA.ÇÃO, *s.f.*, reclination, reclining.
RE.CLI.NA.DO, *adj.*, reclinate, turned, reclining.
RE.CLI.NAR, *v.*, to lean back, to recline.
RE.CLI.NA.TÓ.RI.O, *s.m.*, headrest (for reclining), pillow, cushion.
RE.CLI.NÁ.VEL, *adj.*, reclining.
RE.CLU.SÃO, *s.f.*, reclusion, recluseness.
RE.CLU.SO, *s.m.*, recluse, prisoner; *adj.*, recluse, reclusive, shut up.
RE.CO.BRA.MEN.TO, *s.m.*, recovery.
RE.CO.BRAR, *v.*, to recover, to recuperate, to regain, to retrieve.
RE.CO.BRÁ.VEL, *adj.*, recoverable, retrievable.
RE.CO.BRI.MEN.TO, *s.m.*, act of covering again; *Geol.*, deposition of older rock formations on younger layers.
RE.CO.BRIR, *v.*, to cover again, to recover.
RE.CO.LHE.DOR, *s.m.*, collector, gatherer.
RE.CO.LHER, *v.*, to pick up, to collect, to guard, to preserve.
RE.CO.LHI.DO, *adj.*, retired, reserved, solitary.
RE.CO.LHI.MEN.TO, *s.m.*, retiring, retirement, shelter, refuge, home.
RE.CO.LO.CAR, *v.*, to put back, to restore.
RE.CO.LO.NI.ZA.ÇÃO, *s.f.*, recolonization.
RE.CO.LO.NI.ZAR, *v.*, to recolonize.
RE.CO.LO.RIR, *v.*, to paint again.
RE.COM.BI.NA.ÇÃO, *s.f.*, recombination.
RE.COM.BI.NAR, *v.*, to recombine, to rearrange.
RE.CO.ME.ÇA.DO, *adj.*, recommenced, renewed.
RE.CO.ME.ÇAR, *v.*, to begin again, to resume, to continue, to start over, to renew.
RE.CO.ME.ÇO, *s.m.*, recommencement.
RE.CO.MEN.DA.ÇÃO, *s.f.*, recommendation, advice, suggestion.
RE.CO.MEN.DA.DO, *s.m.*, one who is recommended; *adj.*, recommended.
RE.CO.MEN.DAR, *v.*, to recommend, to commend, to praise.
RE.CO.MEN.DÁ.VEL, *adj.*, recommendable, advisable.
RE.COM.PEN.SA, *s.f.*, reward, prize, recompense.
RE.COM.PEN.SA.DO, *adj.*, recompensed, rewarded.
RE.COM.PEN.SA.DOR, *s.m.*, rewarder, recompenser; *adj.*, rewarding, requiting.
RE.COM.PEN.SAR, *v.*, to retribute, to reward, to premiate, to compensate.
RE.COM.PEN.SÁ.VEL, *adj.*, recompensable, rewardable.

RECOMPILAR ·· 294 ·· REDATOR

RE.COM.PI.LAR, *v.*, to recompile.
RE.COM.POR, *v.*, to recompose, to renew, to reorganize.
RE.COM.PO.SI.ÇÃO, *s.f.*, recomposition.
RE.COM.POS.TO, *adj.*, recomposed, rearranged.
RE.COM.PRAR, *v.*, to repurchase, to buy again.
RE.CÔN.CA.VO, *s.m.*, deep cave, grotto, hollow.
RE.CON.CEI.TU.A.ÇÃO, *s.f.*, reconceptualization.
RE.CON.CEI.TU.AR, *v.*, to reconceptualize.
RE.CON.CI.LI.A.ÇÃO, *s.f.*, reconciliation, reconcilement.
RE.CON.CI.LI.A.DO, *adj.*, reconciled.
RE.CON.CI.LI.A.DOR, *s.m.*, reconciler, conciliator.
RE.CON.CI.LI.AR, *v.*, to reconcile, to conciliate, to establish peace.
RE:CON.DI.CI.O.NAR, *v.*, to recondition.
RE.CON.DI.TO, *s.m.*, secluded, hidden corner; *adj.*, hidden, occult; unknown; intimate, innermost.
RE.CON.DU.ÇÃO, *s.f.*, act of reconducting; devolution, renewing.
RE.CON.DU.ZIR, *v.*, to lead back, to return, to reconduct.
RE.CON.FIR.MAR, *v.*, to reconfirm.
RE.CON.FOR.TAN.TE, *adj.*, comforting, relaxing.
RE.CON.FOR.TAR, *v.*, to recomfort, to refresh, to stimulate, to console.
RE.CO.NHE.CE.DOR, *s.m.*, recognizer, acknowledger; *adj.*, recognizing, acknowledging.
RE.CO.NHE.CER, *v.*, to recognize, to acknowledge, to admit, to know again, to verify.
RE.CO.NHE.CI.DA.MEN.TE, *adv.*, gratefully, thankfully.
RE.CO.NHE.CI.DO, *adj.*, grateful, thankful; recognized, acknowledged.
RE.CO.NHE.CI.MEN.TO, *s.m.*, recognition, acknowledgement, cognizance.
RE.CO.NHE.CÍ.VEL, *adj.*, recognizable, acknowledgeable.
RE.CON.QUIS.TA, *s.f.*, reconquest, reconquering.
RE.CON.QUIS.TAR, *v.*, to reconquer, to retake, to conquer again.
RE.CON.SI.DE.RA.ÇÃO, *s.f.*, reconsideration.
RE.CON.SI.DE.RAR, *v.*, to reconsider, to ponder.
RE.CONS.TI.TU.I.ÇÃO, *s.f.*, reconstitution, recomposition, reform.
RE.CON.SO.LI.DAR, *v.*, to reconsolidate.
RE.CONS.TI.TU.I.ÇÃO, *s.f.*, reconstitution.
RE.CONS.TI.TU.IN.TE, *s.m.*, *Med.*, tonic; *adj.*, reconstituent, restoring; *Med.*, restorative.
RE.CONS.TI.TU.IR, *v.*, to reconstitute, constitute again. 2 to recompose, restore. 3 to rebuild, re-establish. 4 to strengthen, invigorate.
RE.CONS.TRU.ÇÃO, *s.f.*, reconstruction, rebuilding.
RE.CONS.TRU.Í.DO, *adj.*, reconstructed, rebuilt.
RE.CONS.TRU.IR, *v.*, to reconstruct, to rebuild, to reorganize.
RE.CONS.TRU.TOR, *s.m.*, reconstructor, rebuilder; *adj.*, reconstructive.
RE.CON.TA.DO, *adj.*, recounted.
RE.CON.TA.GEM, *s.f.*, recount.
RE.CON.TAR, *v.*, to recount, to count again.
RE.CON.VA.LES.CER, *v.*, to recover from illness, to get better.
RE.COR.DA.ÇÃO, *s.f.*, remembrance, recollection, reminiscence.
RE.COR.DAR, *v.*, to remember, to recall, to recollect.
RE.COR.DE, *s.m.*, record, feat, special prowess.
RE.COR.DIS.TA, *s. 2 gen.*, record holder, record breaker; *adj.*,

record-holding, record breaking.
RE.COR.RÊN.CI.A, *s.f.*, recurrence.
RE.COR.REN.TE, *s. 2 gen.*, *Jur.*, appellant; *adj.*, recurring.
RE.COR.RER, *v.*, to run over, to go through again, to search, to scrutinize.
RE.COR.RI.DO, *s.m.*, *Jur.*, appellee.
RE.COR.RÍ.VEL, *adj.*, appealable.
RE.COR.TA.DO, *adj.*, indented, denticulate, crenate.
RE.COR.TAR, *v.*, to cut out, to trim, to clip, to slash, to slice.
RE.COR.TE, *s.m.*, newspaper clipping, press cutting.
RE.COS.TO, *s.m.*, back of a chair or sofa; pillow or cushion for reclining.
RE.COS.TAR, *v.*, to recline, to lean back, to bend, to rest on.
RE.CO.ZER, *v.*, to cook again; cook too much.
RE.CO.ZI.MEN.TO, *s.m.*, cooking, boiling, overcooking.
RE.CRE.A.ÇÃO, *s.f.*, recreation, entertainment, amusement, enjoyment.
RE.CRE.AR, *v.*, to recreate, to entertain, to divert, to play.
RE.CRE.A.TI.VA.MEN.TE, *adv.*, recreationally.
RE.CRE.A.TI.VO, *adj.*, recreative, refreshing, amusing.
RE.CREI.O, *s.m.*, recreation, relaxation, diversion, interval.
RE.CRI.A.ÇÃO, *s.f.*, recreation.
RE.CRI.AR, *v.*, to recreate.
RE.CRI.MI.NA.ÇÃO, *s.f.*, recrimination, exprobation.
RE.CRI.MI.NA.DOR, *s.m.*, recriminator; *adj.*, recriminating, recriminatory.
RE.CRI.MI.NAR, *v.*, to recriminate, reproach, to censure.
RE.CRI.MI.NA.TÓ.RI.O, *adj.*, recriminatory.
RE.CRU.DES.CÊN.CI.A, *s.f.*, recrudescence.
RE.CRU.DES.CEN.TE, *adj.*, recrudescent; aggravating.
RE.CRU.DES.CER, *v.*, to recrudesce, to intensify.
RE.CRU.DES.CI.MEN.TO, *s.m.*, recrudescence, intensification.
RE.CRU.TA, *s.m.*, recruit, rookie, novice.
RE.CRU.TA.DO, *adj.*, recruited, conscript.
RE.CRU.TA.DOR, *s.m.*, recruiter.
RE.CRU.TA.MEN.TO, *s.m.*, recruitment, recruiting, enlistment.
RE.CRU.TAR, *v.*, to recruit, to enlist, to draft.
RE.CU.A.DO, *adj.*, backward, distant, remote.
RE.CU.AR, *v.*, to draw back, to step back, to pull back, to back out of, to move back; to retreat.
RE.CUO, *s.m.*, retrocession, recoiling, recoil, recession, retreat.
RE.CU.PE.RA.ÇÃO, *s.f.*, recuperation, recovery.
RE.CU.PE.RA.DO, *adj.*, recuperated, recovered.
RE.CU.PE.RAR, *v.*, to recuperate, to recover.
RE.CU.PE.RÁ.VEL, *adj.*, recuperable, recoverable.
RE.CUR.SO, *s.m.*, appeal, petition, recourse, claim, reclamation, complaint.
RE.CUR.VA.DO, *adj.*, recurved, curved, arched.
RE.CUR.VAR, *v.*, to recurve, to curve again, to curve back.
RE.CU.SA, *s.f.*, denial, refusal, rejection.
RE.CU.SA.DO, *adj.*, rejected, refused.
RE.CU.SA.SAR, *v.*, to refuse, to deny, to resist, to rebel, to reject, to oppose.
RE.DA.ÇÃO, *s.f.*, redaction, composition, editorship, editorial staff, editorial room.
RE.DAR.GUI.ÇÃO, *s.f.*, retort, retortion; rejoinder; refutation.
RE.DAR.GUIR, *v.*, to retort; to rejoin; to refute.
RE.DA.TOR, *s.m.*, editor, newspaper editor, redactor, writer, journalist.

REDATORA ··295·· REFERIR

RE.DA.TO.RA, *s.f.*, editress.
RE.DA.TOR-CHE.FE, *s.m.*, editor in chief.
RE.DE, *s.f.*, net, network.
RÉ.DEA, *s.f.*, reins, bridle, control.
RE.DE.CO.RA.ÇÃO, *s.f.*, redecoration.
RE.DE.CO.RAR, *v.*, to redecorate.
RE.DE.FI.NI.ÇÃO, *s.f.*, redefinition.
RE.DE.FI.NIR, *v.*, to redefine.
RE.DE.MO.CRA.TI.ZA.ÇÃO, *s.f.*, redemocratization.
RE.DE.MO.CRA.TI.ZAR, *v.*, to redemocratize.
RE.DE.MO.I.NHO, *s.m.*, swirpool, whirlwind; swirl (hair).
RE.DEN.ÇÃO, *s.f.*, redemption, redeeming, ransom.
RE.DEN.TOR, *s.m.*, redeemer, saviour.
RE.DES.CO.BRI.DOR, *s.m.*, rediscoverer.
RE.DES.CO.BRI.MEN.TO, *s.m.*, rediscovery.
RE.DES.CO.BRIR, *v.*, to rediscover, to reveal again.
RE.DES.CON.TAR, *v.*, to rediscount.
RE.DES.CON.TO, *s.m.*, rediscount.
RE.DE.SE.NHA.DO, *adj.*, redrawn.
RE.DE.SE.NHAR, *v.*, to design (or draw) again.
RE.DI.GIR, *v.*, to write, to write down, to compose.
RE.DI.MEN.SI.O.NA.MEN.TO, *s.m.*, act of dimensioning again.
RE.DI.MEN.SI.O.NAR, *v.*, to dimension again.
RE.DI.MIR, *v.*, to redeem, to regain.
RE.DI.MÍ.VEL, *adj.*, redeemable.
RE.DI.TO, *adj.*, said again.
RE.DI.ZER, *v.*, to say again.
RE.DO.BRA.DO, *adj.*, reduplicate; intensified.
RE.DO.BRA.MEN.TO, *s.m.*, redoubling, reduplicating.
RE.DO.BRAR, *v.*, to redouble, to reduplicate, to increase; to intensify.
RE.DO.MA, *s.f.*, glass shade, vial.
RE.DON.DA.MEN.TE, *adv.*, roundly, utterly, absolutely.
RE.DON.DE.ZA, *s.f.*, round, roundness, rotundness, environs.
RE.DON.DO, *adj.*, round, circular, globular, spherical, cylindrical.
RE.DOR, *s.m.*, circle, circuit, contour, outline.
RE.DU.ÇÃO, *s.f.*, reduction, decrease, shortening, reducing.
RE.DU.CEN.TE, *adj.*, reducing, reductive.
RE.DU.CI.O.NIS.MO, *s.m.*, reductionism.
RE.DU.CI.O.NIS.TA, *adj.*, reductionist.
RE.DUN.DÂN.CIA, *s.f.*, redundance, pleonasm, redundancy.
RE.DUN.DAN.TE, *adj.*, redundant; pleonastic.
RE.DUN.DAR, *v.*, to overflow, to spill over, to be redundant; to happen.
RE.DU.TI.BI.LI.DA.DE, *s.f.*, reductibility.
RE.DU.TÍ.VEL, *adj.*, reducible.
RE.DU.TO, *s.m.*, redoubt, outwork.
RE.DU.TOR, *s.m.*, reducer, reducing device; reducing agent; *adj.*, reducing, reductive.
RE.DU.ZI.DO, *adj.*, reduced, diminished, cut, bated.
RE.DU.ZIR, *v.*, to reduce, to decrease, to restrict, to compress.
RE.DU.ZÍ.VEL, *adj.*, reducible.
RE.E.DI.ÇÃO, *s.f.*, re-ediction, new edition.
RE.E.DI.FI.CA.ÇÃO, *s.f.*, re-edification, rebuilding.
RE.E.DI.FI.CA.DO, *adj.*, re-edified, rebuilt.
RE.E.DI.FI.CAR, *v.*, to rebuild, to re-edify.
RE.E.DI.TAR, *v.*, to re-edit, to republish, to reprint.
RE.E.DU.CA.ÇÃO, *s.f.*, re-education.
RE.E.DU.CAR, *v.*, to re-educate.
RE.E.LE.GER, *v.*, to re-elect, to elect again.

RE.E.LE.GÍ.VEL, *adj.*, re-eligible.
RE.E.LEI.ÇÃO, *s.f.*, re-election.
RE.E.LEI.TO, *s.m.*, re-elected person; *adj.*, re-elected.
RE.EM.BAR.CAR, *v.*, to re-embark.
RE.EM.BAR.QUE, *s.m.*, re-embarkation.
RE.EM.BOL.SA.DO, *adj.*, reimbursed.
RE.EM.BOL.SAR, *v.*, to reimburse, to pay back, to repay.
RE.EM.BOL.SÁ.VEL, *adj.*, reimbursable.
RE.EM.BOL.SO, *s.m.*, reimbursement, refund.
RE.EM.POS.SAR, *v.*, to re-empower.
RE.EM.PRE.GAR, *v.*, to re-employ.
RE.EN.CA.MI.NHAR, *v.*, to lead again, to send again.
RE.EN.CA.PAR, *v.*, to put a new cover; as to protect.
RE.EN.CAR.NA.ÇÃO, *s.f.*, reincarnation.
RE.EN.CAR.NAR, *v.*, to reincarnate.
RE.EN.CE.NAR, *v.*, to restage (to play or perform again).
RE.EN.CHI.MEN.TO, *s.m.*, refilling, refill.
RE.EN.CON.TRAR, *v.*, to meet or find again.
RE.EN.CON.TRO, *s.m.*, a new or second meeting.
RE.EN.TRA.DA, *s.f.*, re-entrance, return.
RE.EN.TRÂN.CI.A, *s.f.*, re-entrance, recess.
RE.EN.TRAN.TE, *adj.*, re-entrant, forming a recess.
RE.EN.TRAR, *v.*, to re-enter, to enter again.
RE.ER.GUER, *v.*, to re-erect, to reconstruct, to raise again.
RE.ER.GUI.MEN.TO, *s.m.*, re-erection, reanimation.
RE.ES.CA.LO.NA.MEN.TO, *s.m.*, rescheduling (of a debt).
RE.ES.CA.LO.NAR, *v.*, to reschedule (debt).
RE.ES.CRE.VER, *v.*, to rewrite.
RE.ES.TA.BE.LE.CER, *v.*, to re-establish, restore.
RE.ES.TRU.TU.RA.ÇÃO, *s.f.*, re-structuration.
RE.ES.TRU.TU.RAR, *v.*, to re-structure.
RE.ES.TU.DAR, *v.*, to re-study.
RE.ES.TU.DO, *s.m.*, re-study.
RE.E.XA.ME, *s.m.*, re-examination.
RE.E.XA.MI.NAR, *v.*, to re-examine, examine again.
RE.E.XI.BI.ÇÃO, *s.f.*, re-exhibition.
RE.E.XI.BIR, *v.*, to re-exhibit.
RE.EX.PE.DIR, *v.*, to reship, to dispatch again.
RE.EX.POR.TA.ÇÃO, *s.f.*, re-exportation, re-export.
RE.EX.POR.TA.DOR, *s.m.*, re-exporter.
RE.EX.POR.TAR, *v.*, to re-export, to reship.
RE.FAL.SE.AR, *v.*, to betray, to be disloyal to, to delude.
RE.FA.ZE.DOR, *s.m.*, remaker; *adj.*, remaking, repairing.
RE.FA.ZER, *v.*, to remake, to make over again.
RE.FEI.ÇÃO, *s.f.*, meal, repast.
RE.FEI.TO, *adj.*, restored, recovered. 2 mended, repaired. 3 fat, thickset, plump.
RE.FEI.TÓ.RIO, *s.m.*, refectory, dining-hall.
RE.FÉM, *s.m.*, hostage.
RE.FE.RÊN.CIA, *s.f.*, reference, indication, allusion, mention, remark.
RE.FE.REN.CI.AL, *adj.*, referential.
RE.FE.REN.DA.DO, *adj.*, countersigned, authorized.
RE.FE.REN.DAR, *v.*, to countersign, to attest, to endorse.
RE.FE.REN.DÁ.RI.O, *s.m.*, referendary.
RE.FE.REN.DO, *s.m.*, referendum.
RE.FE.REN.TE, *adj.*, referring, relating to, relative, concerning, regarding.
RE.FE.RI.DO, *adj.*, mentioned, aforesaid, cited.
RE.FE.RI.MEN.TO, *s.m.*, reference, remark.
RE.FE.RIR, *v.*, to refer, to narrate, to tell, to relate, to report.

REFERÍVEL   ••• 296 •••   REGENERAR

RE.FE.RÍ.VEL, *adj.*, referrable, referrible.
RE.FES.TE.LA.DO, *adj.*, sprawling.
RE.FES.TE.LAR, *v.*, to loll, to recline; *refestalar-se*: to sprawl.
RE.FIL, *s.m.*, refill.
RE.FI.LA.DOR, *adj.*, obstinate, stubborn.
RE.FIL.MA.GEM, *s.f.*, re-filming; remake.
RE.FIL.MAR, *v.*, to film again; to shoot a new version of a movie.
RE.FI.NA.DA.MEN.TE, *adv.*, refinedly.
RE.FI.NA.DO, *adj.*, pure, purified, polished.
RE.FI.NA.MEN.TO, *s.m.*, refining, refinement, culture.
RE.FI.NAN.CI.A.MEN.TO, *s.m., Econ.*, refinancing.
RE.FI.NAN.CI.AR, *v., Econ.*, to re-finance.
RE.FI.NAR, *v.*, to refine, to civilize, to cultivate, to perfect.
RE.FI.NA.RI.A, *s.f.*, refinery.
RE.FLE.TI.DA.MEN.TE, *adv.*, reflectively, reflectedly.
RE.FLE.TI.DO, *adj.*, reflected, considered, cautious.
RE.FLE.TIR, *v.*, to reflect, to consider, to ponder.
RE.FLE.TI.VO, *adj.*, reflective, pondering.
RE.FLE.TOR, *s.m.*, reflector.
RE.FLE.XÃO, *s.f.*, reflection, meditation, consideration, contemplation.
RE.FLE.XI.BI.LI.DA.DE, *s.f.*, reflexibility, reflectiveness.
RE.FLE.XI.VO, *adj.*, reflexive, reflective.
RE.FLE.XO, *s.m.*, reflection, reaction.
RE.FLO.RES.CÊN.CI.A, *s.f.*, reflorescence.
RE.FLO.RES.CEN.TE, *adj.*, reflorescent, reflowering.
RE.FLO.RES.CER, *v.*, to blossom again, to reflourish, to reflower.
RE.FLO.RES.CI.MEN.TO, *s.m.*, act of reflowering, reflorescence.
RE.FLO.RES.TA.DOR, *s.m.*, planter of forests; *adj.*, reforesting.
RE.FLO.RES.TA.MEN.TO, *s.m.*, reforestation, reforestment.
RE.FLO.RES.TAR, *v.*, reforest.
RE.FLU.ÊN.CI.A, *s.f.*, refluence.
RE.FLU.EN.TE, *adj.*, refluent.
RE.FLU.IR, *v.*, to flow back, to reflow, to recede.
RE.FLU.XO, *s.m.*, reflow, refluence.
RE.FO.GA.DO, *s.m.*, butter sauce, meat gravy, stew; *adj.*, sautéed.
RE.FO.GAR, *v.*, to stew, to sauté.
RE.FOL.GAR, *v.*, to repose, to rest.
RE.FO.LHAR, *v.*, to wrap in leaves.
RE.FO.LHO, *s.m.*, fold, ruffle; *fig.*, dissimulation.
RE.FOR.ÇA.DO, *adj.*, reinforced, strong, vigorous.
RE.FOR.ÇAR, *v.*, to reinforce, to amplify, to intensify.
RE.FOR.ÇO, *s.m.*, reinforcement, reinforcing, succour, help.
RE.FOR.MA, *s.f.*, reform, reformation; Reforma, the Reformation.
RE.FOR.MA.DO, *adj.*, reformed, retired, converted.
RE.FOR.MA.DOR, *s.m.*, reformer, redresser, remodeller.
RE.FOR.MAR, *v.*, to reform, to remodel, to reconstruct, to rebuild, to renovate.
RE.FOR.MA.TÓ.RIO, *s.m.*, reformatory; *adj.*, reformatory, reformative.
RE.FOR.MÁ.VEL, *adj.*, reformable, renewable.
RE.FOR.MU.LAR, *v.*, to reformulate, to formulate again.
RE.FRA.ÇÃO, *s.f.*, refraction, deflection.
RE.FRAN.GER, *v.*, to refract.
RE.FRÃO, *s.m.*, refrain, adage, proverb.
RE.FRA.TAR, *v.*, to refract; *refratar-se*: to be reflected.

RE.FRA.TÁ.RIO, *s.m.*, refractory; *adj.*, refractory, intractable, unruly.
RE.FRA.TOR, *adj.*, refractive.
RE.FRE.A.DO, *adj.*, curbed, restrained. 2 moderate.
RE.FRE.A.MEN.TO, *s.m.*, restraining, refraining.
RE.FRE.AR, *v.*, to refrain, to restrain, to repress.
RE.FRE.Á.VEL, *adj.*, restrainable.
RE.FRE.GA, *s.f.*, fight, combat, fray.
RE.FRES.CAN.TE, *adj.*, refreshing, cooling.
RE.FRES.CAR, *v.*, to refresh, to refrigerate, to cool, to cool down.
RE.FRES.CO, *s.m.*, refreshment, drink.
RE.FRI.GE.RA.ÇÃO, *s.f.*, refrigeration, cooling, chilling.
RE.FRI.GE.RA.DOR, *s.m.*, refrigerator, fridge, freezer, cooler, ice-box.
RE.FRI.GE.RAN.TE, *s.m.*, refreshment, cooling; *adj.*, refrigerant, refreshing.
RE.FRI.GE.RAR, *v.*, to refresh, to cool, to make fresh.
RE.FRI.GE.RA.TI.VO, *s.m.*, refrigerant, refreshment; *adj.*, refreshing, refrigerative.
RE.FRI.GÉ.RI.O, *s.m.*, refrigeration, freezing, refreshment.
RE.FU.GAR, *v.*, to reject, to refuse.
RE.FU.GI.A.DO, *s.m.*, refugee, fugitive; *adj.*, fugitive.
RE.FU.GI.AR(-SE), *v.*, to take refuge, to seek shelter.
RE.FÚ.GIO, *s.m.*, refuge, rejection.
RE.FU.GO, *s.m.*, refuse, garbage, rejection.
RE.FUL.GÊN.CI.A, *s.f.*, refulgence, refulgency.
RE.FUL.GEN.TE, *adj.*, refulgent, radiant, shining.
RE.FUL.GIR, *v.*, to shine, to glitter, to sparkle, to stand out.
RE.FU.TA.ÇÃO, *s.f.*, refutation, refute.
RE.FU.TA.DOR, *s.m.*, refuter; *adj.*, refuting.
RE.FU.TAR, *v.*, to refute, to contradict, to disprove.
RE.FU.TÁ.VEL, *adj.*, refutable.
RE.GA, *s.f.*, irrigation, watering.
RE.GA-BO.FE, *s.m.*, a party with a lot of food and drink.
RE.GA.ÇAR, *v.*, to tuck up.
RE.GA.ÇO, *s.m.*, lap, bosom, breast, shelter.
RE.GA.DOR, *s.m.*, waterer, sprinkler.
RE.GA.LA.DO, *adj.*, dainty; rich; delicious, agreeable; pampered.
RE.GA.LAR, *v.*, to regale, to entertain, to please, to delight.
RE.GA.LI.A, *s.f.*, regal rights, prerogative.
RE.GA.LO, *s.m.*, regalement, pleasure, gift.
RE.GAR, *v.*, to water, to irrigate, to sprinkle, to wash.
RE.GA.TA, *s.f., Esp.*, regatta.
RE.GA.TE.A.DOR, *s.m.*, bargainer, haggler; *adj.*, bargaining, haggling.
RE.GA.TE.AR, *v.*, to haggle over, to bargain.
RE.GA.TEI.O, *s.m.*, haggling, bargaining.
RE.GA.TO, *s.m.*, rivulet, rill, creek.
RE.GE.LAN.TE, *adj.*, freezing.
RE.GE.LAR, *v.*, to freeze.
RE.GE.LO, *s.m.*, refreezing, glazed frost, *fig.*, indifference.
RE.GÊN.CIA, *s.f.*, regency, government, administration.
RE.GEN.CI.AL, *adj.*, relative to regency.
RE.GE.NE.RA.ÇÃO, *s.f.*, regeneration.
RE.GE.NE.RA.DO, *adj.*, regenerated, reformed.
RE.GE.NE.RA.DOR, *s.m.*, regenerator; *adj.*, regenerative.
RE.GE.NE.RAN.TE, *adj.*, regenerating.
RE.GE.NE.RAR, *v.*, to regenerate, to reproduce, to restore, to reorganize.

REGENERATIVO ••• 297 ••• REJUNTAR

RE.GE.NE.RA.TI.VO, *adj.*, regenerative.

RE.GEN.TE, s. 2 gen., regent; *Mús.*, maestro, conductor; *Pol.*, leader; *adj.*, regent, governing.

RE.GER, *v.*, to reign, to rule, to govern, to manage, to administer, to direct, to guide.

RE.GE.RAR, *v.*, to generate again.

RÉ.GI.A, *s.f.*, palace or royal residence, castle.

RE.GIÃO, *s.f.*, area, country, province, region, section.

RE.GI.CI.DA, s. 2 gen., regicide.

RE.GI.CÍ.DI.O, *s.m.*, regicide.

RE.GI.ME, *s.m.*, regime, regimen, political system; diet.

RE.GI.MEN.TA.DO, *adj.*, having rules; administered, governed.

RE.GI.MEN.TAL, *adj.*, regimental.

RE.GI.MEN.TAR, *adj.*, regimental, regulatory.

RE.GI.MEN.TO, *s.m.*, regiment, administration, guide, rule.

RÉ.GI.O, *adj.*, royal, regal, kingly.

RE.GIO.NAL, *adj.*, regional, sectional.

RE.GI.O.NA.LIS.MO, *s.m.*, regionalism.

RE.GI.O.NA.LIS.TA, s. 2 gen., regionalist, provincialist; *adj.*, regionalistic.

RE.GI.O.NA.LI.ZAR, *v.*, to regionalize.

RE.GIS.TRA.DO, *s.m.*, registered letter; registrant; *adj.*, registered, recorded; *marca registrada*: trademark.

RE.GIS.TRA.DOR, *s.m.*, registrant, registrar, recorder; *adj.*, recording.

RE.GIS.TRA.DO.RA, *s.f.*, cash register.

RE.GIS.TRAR, *v.*, to register, to book, to list.

RE.GIS.TRÁ.VEL, *adj.*, registrable, recordable.

RE.GIS.TRO, *s.m.*, register, record, registry; *registro civil*: registry office.

RE.GO, *s.m.*, channel, duct, ditch, drain, furrow; *vulg.*, bum crack.

RE.GO.ZI.JA.DO, *adj.*, cheerful, rejoicing.

RE.GO.ZI.JA.DOR, *s.m.*, merrymaker; *adj.*, joyful, cheerful.

RE.GO.ZI.JAR, *v.*, to rejoice, to delight, to please.

RE.GO.ZI.JO, *s.m.*, pleasure, joy, glee, gladness.

RE.GRA, *s.f.*, ruler, norm, standard, rule, principle, law.

RE.GRA.DO, *adj.*, sensible, reasonable.

RE.GRAR, *v.*, to rule, to control, to regulate.

RE.GRAS, *s.f.pl.*, period, menstruation.

RE.GRE.DIR, *v.*, to retrograde, to recede.

RE.GRES.SÃO, *s.f.*, regression, retrocession.

RE.GRES.SAR, *v.*, to return, to go back, to come back.

RE.GRES.SI.VO, *adj.*, regressive, retrogressive.

RE.GRES.SO, *s.m.*, return, returning.

RÉ.GUA, *s.f.*, ruler, rule.

RÉ.GUA-TÊ, *s.f.*, T-square.

RE.GU.LA.ÇÃO, *s.f.*, regulation.

RE.GU.LA.DO, *adj.*, regulated, regular.

RE.GU.LA.DOR, *s.m.*, regulator, governor, corrector.

RE.GU.LA.GEM, *s.f.*, tuning.

RE.GU.LA.MEN.TA.ÇÃO, *s.f.*, regulation.

RE.GU.LA.MEN.TAR, *v.*, to regulate, to arrange, to control, to order.

RE.GU.LA.MEN.TO, *s.m.*, regulation, rule, ordinance, resolution, precept.

RE.GU.LAR, *v.*, to regulate, to direct, to guide; *adj.*, regular, constant, legal, lawful.

RE.GU.LA.RI.DA.DE, *s.f.*, regularity.

RE.GU.LA.RI.ZA.ÇÃO, *s.f.*, regularization.

RE.GU.LA.RI.ZA.DOR, *s.m.*, regulator; *adj.*, regulating.

RE.GU.LA.RI.ZAR, *v.*, to regularize, to regulate, to make uniform.

RE.GU.LAR.MEN.TE, *adv.*, regularly.

RE.GUR.GI.TA.ÇÃO, *s.f.*, regurgitation.

RE.GUR.GI.TAR, *v.*, to regurgitate.

REI, *s.m.*, king, monarch, sovereign.

RE.I.DRA.TA.ÇÃO, *s.f.*, rehydration.

RE.I.DRA.TAR, *v.*, to rehydrate.

RE.IM.PRI.MIR, *v.*, to reprint, to republish.

REI.NA.ÇÃO, *s.f.*, merrymaking, high jinks, revelry.

REI.NA.DO, *s.m.*, reign, govern, rule, supremacy.

REI.NAN.TE, s. 2 gen., king, queen; *adj.*, prevailing, predominant; ruling, governing.

REI.NAR, *v.*, to reign, to govern, to rule, to dominate.

RE.IN.CI.DÊN.CIA, *s.f.*, recidivation, reincidence.

RE.IN.CI.DEN.TE, *adj.*, reincident, obstinate; recidivistic, relapsing.

RE.IN.CI.DIR, *v.*, to relapse, to repeat once again; to fall back.

RE.IN.CI.TA.MEN.TO, *s.m.*, reincitation.

RE.IN.CI.TAR, *v.*, to reincite.

RE.IN.COR.PO.RA.ÇÃO, *s.f.*, reincorporation.

RE.IN.COR.PO.RAR, *v.*, to reincorporate.

RE.I.NI.CI.AR, *v.*, to start over, to begin again.

RE.I.NÍ.CI.O, *s.m.*, new start, new beginning.

REI.NO, *s.m.*, kingdom, realm, monarchy, domain.

RE.IN.TE.GRA.ÇÃO, *s.f.*, reintegration, restoration.

RE.IN.TE.GRA.DOR, *s.m.*, reintegrator, restorer; *adj.*, reintegrating.

RE.IN.TE.GRAR, *v.*, to reintegrate, to restore, to renew, to reinstall.

RE.IN.TE.GRO, *s.m.*, reintegration, restoration.

RE.IN.TRO.DU.ÇÃO, *s.f.*, reintroduction.

RE.IN.TRO.DU.ZIR, *v.*, to reintroduce.

REI.TE.RA.ÇÃO, *s.f.*, reiteration, repetition.

REI.TE.RA.DA.MEN.TE, *adv.*, reiteratedly.

REI.TE.RA.DO, *adj.*, reiterated, repeated.

REI.TE.RAR, *v.*, to reiterate, to repeat, to reaffirm, to renew.

REI.TE.RÁ.VEL, *adj.*, reiterable.

REI.TOR, *s.m.*, rector, head of a university or college, principal, dean.

REI.VIN.DI.CA.ÇÃO, *s.f.*, vindication, claim, demand, reclamation.

REI.VIN.DI.CA.DOR, *s.m.*, claimer; *adj.*, claiming.

REI.VIN.DI.CAN.TE, *adj.*, claiming, demanding.

REI.VIN.DI.CAR, *v.*, to revindicate, to vindicate, to demand.

REI.VIN.DI.CA.TI.VO, *adj.*, revendicative.

REI.VIN.DI.CÁ.VEL, *adj.*, claimable.

RE.JEI.ÇÃO, *s.f.*, rejection, refusal, exclusion.

RE.JEI.TA.DO, *adj.*, rejected, castoff, castaway.

RE.JEI.TAR, *v.*, to reject, to cast or throw away, to refuse, to repudiate.

RE.JEI.TÁ.VEL, *adj.*, rejectable.

RE.JEI.TO, *s.m.*, act of rejection; *Ant.*, javelin; *rejeitos*: refuse, waste.

RE.JU.BI.LA.ÇÃO, *s.f.*, jubilation, exultation.

RE.JU.BI.LAN.TE, *adj.*, rejubilant.

RE.JU.BI.LAR, *v.*, to jubilate, to cause great joy.

RE.JÚ.BI.LO, *s.m.*, rejoicing, exultation, joyfulness.

RE.JU.BI.LO.SO, *adj.*, rejoicing, jubilant, glad.

RE.JUN.TA.DO, *adj.*, articulate, jointed, segmented.

RE.JUN.TAR, *v.*, *Arquit.*, to seal the joints.

REJURAR ··298·· REMENDADO

RE.JU.RAR, *v.*, to swear again,

RE.JU.VE.NES.CER, *v.*, to rejuvenate, to make young again, to renew.

RE.JU.VE.NES.CI.MEN.TO, *s.m.*, rejuvenescence, rejuvenation.

RE.LA.ÇÃO, *s.f.*, report, roll, list, relationship, connection; analogy.

RE.LA.CI.O.NA.DO, *adj.*, related, connected.

RE.LA.CI.O.NA.MEN.TO, *s.m.*, relationship.

RE.LA.CI.O.NAR, *v.*, to relate, to tell, to include in a list, to register, to inscribe, to catalogue, to confront.

RE.LA.ÇÕES-PÚ.BLI.CAS, *s. 2 gen., 2 num.*, public relations.

RE.LÂM.PA.GO, *s.m.*, lightning, thunderbolt, flash of lightning.

RE.LAM.PE.JAN.TE, *adj.*, flashing (like a thunderbolt), glittering, sparkling.

RE.LAM.PE.JAR, *v.*, to lighten; to glitter, sparkle. 3 to appear like a flash of lightning.

RE.LAM.PE.JO, *s.m.*, lightning, flash of light.

RE.LAN.ÇA.MEN.TO, *s.m.*, relaunching.

RE.LAN.ÇAR, *v.*, to relaunch, launch again.

RE.LAN.CE, *s.m.*, glance, glimpse.

RE.LAP.SO, *s.m.*, relapser, recidivist, backslider; *adj.*, relapsing, backsliding, obstinate.

RE.LA.TAR, *v.*, to mention, to tell, to narrate, to refer to, to explain, to report.

RE.LA.TI.VA.MEN.TE, *adv.*, relatively.

RE.LA.TI.VI.DA.DE, *s.f.*, relativity, relativeness, conditionality.

RE.LA.TI.VIS.MO, *s.m.*, relativism.

RE.LA.TI.VO, *adj.*, relative, relating to.

RE.LA.TO, *s.m.*, report, account, narration, description.

RE.LA.TOR, *s.m.*, relator, reporter.

RE.LA.TÓ.RIO, *s.m.*, report, account, relation.

RE.LAX, *s.m.*, **INGL RELAXATION: ACT OF RELAXING.**

RE.LA.XA.DO, *adj.*, loose, slack, relaxed, careless, remiss.

RE.LA.XA.MEN.TO, *s.m.*, slackness, negligence, relax, relaxing, demoralization.

RE.LA.XAN.TE, *s.m.*, relaxing, relaxant.

RE.LA.XAR, *v.*, to relax, to slacken, to loosen, to make less severe, to corrupt.

RE.LÉ, *s.m.*, *Eletr.*, relay.

RE.LE.GAR, *v.*, to relegate, to exile, to banish, to expatriate.

RE.LEI.TU.RA, *s.f.*, rereading.

RE.LEM.BRAN.ÇA, *s.f.*, remembrance, reminiscence.

RE.LEM.BRAR, *v.*, to remember again, to put in mind, to recollect.

RE.LEM.BRÁ.VEL, *adj.*, rememorable.

RE.LEN.TO, *s.m.*, dew, moisture.

RE.LER, *v.*, to reread, to read again.

RE.LES, *adj.*, *s. 2 gen.*, despicable, shabby, poor, worthless, feeble.

RE.LE.VA.DO, *adj.*, salient, raised.

RE.LE.VA.MEN.TO, *s.m.*, pardon, indulgence; release, relief; apology.

RE.LE.VÂN.CIA, *s.f.*, prominence, importance, significance, consequence.

RE.LE.VAN.TE, *adj.*, important, considerable, weighty.

RE.LE.VAR, *v.*, to permit, to allow, to exempt, to excuse, to forgive.

RE.LE.VÁ.VEL, *adj.*, pardonable, excusable.

RE.LE.VO, *s.m.*, relief, salience, relievo, salience; *alto-relevo*: high relief; *baixo-relevo*: low relief.

RE.LI.CÁ.RIO, *s.m.*, reliquary, tabernacle.

RE.LI.CI.TA.ÇÃO, *s.f.*, new public sale, new public auction.

RE.LI.CI.TAR, *v.*, to expose for sale at an auction once more.

RE.LI.GAR, *v.*, to retie, to bind again.

RE.LI.GIÃO, *s.f.*, religion, religiousness, piety.

RE.LI.GI.O.SA.MEN.TE, *adv.*, religiously, devoutly.

RE.LI.GI.O.SI.DA.DE, *s.f.*, religiosity.

RE.LI.GI.O.SO, *s.m.*, member of a monastic order, monk; *adj.*, religious, pious, devout, spiritual, godly.

RE.LI.MAR, *v.*, to polish again, to file again.

RE.LIN.CHAR, *v.*, to neigh, to whinny.

RE.LIN.CHO, *s.m.*, neigh, whinny.

RE.LÍ.QUIA, *s.f.*, relic, venerated object.

RE.LÓ.GIO, *s.m.*, watch, clock.

RE.LO.JO.A.RIA, *s.f.*, a watchmaker's shop.

RE.LO.JO.EI.RO, *s.m.*, watchmaker, clockmaker.

RE.LUS.TRAR, *v.*, to give new lustre, to repolish.

RE.LU.TÂN.CIA, *s.f.*, resistance, aversion, reluctance.

RE.LU.TAN.TE, *adj.*, reluctant, averse, unwilling.

RE.LU.TAR, *v.*, to fight again, to struggle against, to resist, to reluct.

RE.LU.ZEN.TE, *adj.*, brilliant, refulgent, shining.

RE.LU.ZIR, *v.*, to shine brightly, to sparkle, to glitter, to glow.

REL.VA, *s.f.*, grass, to turf, to lawn, sward.

REL.VA.DO, *s.m.*, grassplot, turf, lawn.

RE.MA.DA, *s.f.*, act of rowing.

RE.MA.DOR, *s.m.*, rower, boatmann, oarsman.

RE.MA.NE.JA.MEN.TO, *s.m.*, rehandling.

RE.MA.NE.JAR, *v.*, to rehandle.

RE.MA.NES.CEN.TE, *s. 2 gen.*, remainder; *adj.*, remaining.

RE.MA.NES.CER, *v.*, to be leftover, to rest, to remain, to survive.

RE.MAN.SAR, *v.*, to stand still.

RE.MAN.SO, *s.m.*, immobility, calmness, stillness.

RE.MAN.SO.SO, *adj.*, peaceful, calm, still, slow.

RE.MAR, *v.*, to row, to paddle, to oar, to swim.

RE.MAR.CA.ÇÃO, *s.f.*, relabelling; adjustement; *Com.*, price alteration.

RE.MAR.CAR, *v.*, to re-mark, to give a new designation to, to relabel.

RE.MA.TA.DO, *adj.*, complete, perfect.

RE.MA.TAR, *v.*, finish, to conclude, to achieve, to accomplish, to complete.

RE.MA.TE, *s.m.*, end, conclusion, finish, finishing.

RE.ME.DAR, *v.*, to imitate, to mimic; to mock.

RE.ME.DI.A.DO, *adj.*, comfortably off.

RE.ME.DI.A.DOR, *s.m.*, improver, repairer; *adj.*, improving, attenuating.

RE.ME.DI.AR, *v.*, to remedy, to relieve, to attenuate, to repair, to amend, to hinder.

RE.ME.DI.Á.VEL, *adj.*, remediable, rectifiable.

RE.MÉ.DIO, *s.m.*, remedy, medicine, medicament, help.

RE.ME.LA, *s.f.*, gummy secretion from the eyes.

RE.ME.LAR, *v.*, to become blear-eyed.

RE.ME.LEN.TO, *adj.*, blear-eyed.

RE.ME.LE.XO, *s.m.*, *Bras.*, swaying.

RE.ME.MO.RA.ÇÃO, *s.f.*, remembrance, recollection.

RE.ME.MO.RAR, *v.*, to remember, to recollect, to recall.

RE.ME.MO.RA.TI.VO, *adj.*, rememorative.

RE.ME.MO.RÁ.VEL, *adj.*, rememberable, memorable.

RE.MEN.DA.DO, *adj.*, patched, mended.

REMENDAGEM ··299·· RENÚNCIA

RE.MEN.DA.GEM, *s.f.*, act of patching, darning, mending.
RE.MEN.DAR, *v.*, to patch, to mend, to repair.
RE.MEN.DO, *s.m.*, patch, botch, mending.
RE.ME.RE.CE.DOR, *adj.*, meritorious, well-deserving.
RE.MES.SA, *s.f.*, remittance, remitting, transmittal, delivery, letter.
RE.ME.TEN.TE, *s. 2 gen.*, remitter, forwarder; *adj.*, shipmail, post, remitting, sending.
RE.ME.TER, *v.*, to remit, to send, to forward, to ship, to mail, to post, to expedite, to postpone.
RE.ME.TI.DA, *s.f.*, attack, charge, thrust.
RE.ME.TI.MEN.TO, *s.m.*, attack, charge, thrust.
RE.ME.XER, *v.*, to stir or mix again, to move, to shake, to rummage, to jumble, to agitate.
RE.ME.XI.DO, *adj., col.*, restless, unquiet; turbulent, boisterous.
RE.MI.ÇÃO, *s.f.*, redemption, redeeming, ransom.
RE.MI.DO, *adj.*, redeemed, liberated, freed.
RE.MI.DOR, *s.m.*, redeemer, liberator; *adj.*, redeeming, liberating.
RE.MI.NIS.CÊN.CI.A, *s.f.*, reminiscence, memory, recollection.
RE.MIR, *v.*, to redeem, to repurchase, to free, to save, to pay off.
RE.MI.RAR, *v.*, to look again, to observe with great attention.
RE.MIS.SÃO, *s.f.*, remission, forgiveness, absolution, mitigation.
RE.MIS.SÍ.VEL, *adj.*, remissible.
RE.MIS.SI.VO, *adj.*, remissive, forgiving, abating.
RE.MIS.SO, *adj.*, remiss, lax, negligent, indolent, lazy.
RE.MI.TIR, *v.*, to remit, to forgive, to pardon, to absolve, to excuse.
RE.MO, *s.m.*, oar, paddle.
RE.MO.BI.LIAR, *v.*, to refurnish.
RE.MO.BI.LI.ZA.ÇÃO, *s.f.*, remobilization.
RE.MO.BI.LI.ZAR, *v.*, to remobilize.
RE.MO.ÇA.DO, *adj.*, rejuvenated, reinvigorated.
RE.MO.ÇA.DOR, *s.m.*, rejuvenator; *adj.*, rejuvenating.
RE.MO.ÇÃO, *s.f.*, removal, remotion, transfer.
RE.MO.ÇAR, *v.*, to rejuvenate, to renew, to renovate.
RE.MO.DE.LA.ÇÃO, *s.f.*, remodelment, recast, transformation.
RE.MO.DE.LA.DOR, *s.m.*, remodeler, reformer; *adj.*, remodeling, reforming.
RE.MO.DE.LA.GEM, *s.f.*, remodelment.
RE.MO.DE.LAR, *v.*, to remodel, to recast, to reform.
RE.MO.ER, *v.*, to grind again, to grind slowly and thoroughly, to ruminate.
RE.MON.TA.DO, *adj.*, very high, lofty; *fig.*, sublime.
RE.MON.TA.GEM, *s.f.*, reconstitution, reassemblage.
RE.MON.TAR, *v.*, to ascend, to go up, to lift up, to raise.
RE.MON.TE, *s.m.*, act of remounting, ascension.
RÊ.MO.RA, *s.f., Zool.*, remora.
RE.MOR.DER, *v.*, to bite again, to slander, to backbite.
RE.MOR.DI.MEN.TO, *s.m.*, act of biting again, remorse.
RE.MOR.SO, *s.m.*, remorse.
RE.MO.TA.MEN.TE, *adv.*, remotely.
RE.MO.TO, *adj.*, remote, distant, out of the way.
RE.MO.VE.DOR, *s.m.*, solvent, cleaning fluid.
RE.MO.VER, *v.*, to move again, to remove, to transfer, to drive away, to displace.
RE.MO.VI.BI.LI.DA.DE, *s.f.*, removability.
RE.MO.VI.MEN.TO, *s.m.*, act of removing, removal.
RE.MO.VÍ.VEL, *adj.*, removable.

RE.MU.NE.RA.ÇÃO, *s.f.*, remuneration, salary, wages, gratification.
RE.MU.NE.RA.DO, *adj.*, remunerated, salaried, paid.
RE.MU.NE.RA.DOR, *s.m.*, remunerator; *adj.*, remunerating.
RE.MU.NE.RAR, *v.*, to remunerate, to recompense, to reward, to satisfy.
RE.MU.NE.RA.TI.VO, *adj.*, remunerative.
RE.MU.NE.RA.TÓ.RI.O, *adj.*, remunerative, remunetory; profitable.
RE.MU.NE.RÁ.VEL, *adj.*, remunerable, rewardable.
RE.NA, *s.f., Zool.*, reindeer, caribou.
RE.NAL, *adj.*, renal.
RE.NAS.CEN.ÇA, *s.f.*, renascence, renascency; Renaissance.
RE.NAS.CEN.TE, *adj.*, renascent.
RE.NAS.CEN.TIS.TA, *s. 2 gen.*, Renaissancist; *adj.*, Renaissant.
RE.NAS.CER, *v.*, to be born again, to grow again, to reborn.
RE.NAS.CI.DO, *adj.*, newborn, reborn.
RE.NAS.CI.MEN.TO, *s.m.*, renascence, revival, renewal, rebirth.
REN.DA, *s.f.*, lace, lacework, gains, revenue.
REN.DA.DO, *s.m.*, lacework; *adj.*, lace, lacy.
REN.DAR, *v.*, to decorate with lacework.
REN.DEI.RO, *s.m.*, lacemaker; tenant farmer.
REN.DER, *v.*, to subject, to subjugate, to conquer, to produce, to yield.
REN.DI.ÇÃO, *s.f.*, surrender, capitulation.
REN.DI.DO, *adj.*, rent, split, submissive, obedient.
REN.DI.LHA.DO, *adj.*, ornamented with fine lace, lacy.
REN.DI.LHAR, *v.*, to adorn with lacework.
REN.DI.MEN.TO, *s.m.*, revenue, income, profit, yield.
REN.DO.SA.MEN.TE, *adv.*, profitably, lucratively.
REN.DO.SO, *adj.*, profitable, lucrative, fruitful, productive, yielding.
RE.NE.GA.DO, *s.m.*, ; *Mil.*, deserter; *adj.*, renegade, apostate.
RE.NE.GA.DOR, *s.m.*, renegade, apostate, blasphemer; *adj.*, faithless, treacherous, renegading.
RE.NE.GAR, *v.*, to deny, to abjure, to renounce, to betray, to detest, to refute.
RE.NE.GO.CI.A.ÇÃO, *s.f.*, renegotiation.
RE.NE.GO.CI.AR, *v.*, to renegotiate.
RE.NE.GO.CI.Á.VEL, *adj.*, renegotiable.
RE.NI.TÊN.CI.A, *s.f.*, stubbornness, obstinacy, resistance, opposition.
RE.NI.TEN.TE, *adj.*, renitent, stubborn, obstinate.
RE.NI.TIR, *v.*, to resist, to withstand, to oppose.
RE.NO.MA.DO, *adj.*, renowned, reputed, famous.
RE.NO.ME, *s.m.*, reputation, fame, glory, prestige, renown.
RE.NO.VA.ÇÃO, *s.f.*, renovation, revival.
RE.NO.VA.DOR, *s.m.*, renovator, renewer, reformer.
RE.NO.VAR, *v.*, to renew, to renovate, to furbish.
REN.QUE, *s.m.*, row, rank.
REN.TA.BI.LI.DA.DE, *s.f.*, profitability, lucrativeness.
REN.TAR, *v.*, to affront, to insult, to flirt.
REN.TÁ.VEL, *adj.*, profitable, lucrative.
REN.TE, *adj.*, close by, near; *adv.*, closely, even with.
RE.NU.EN.TE, *adj.*, renouncing.
RE.NU.Í.DO, *s.m.*, rejecting with the head (movement); *adj.*, rejecting, negative.
RE.NU.IR, *v.*, to renounce, to reject.
RE.NÚN.CIA, *s.f.*, renunciation, renouncement, rejection, desistance.

RENUNCIAÇÃO ·· 300 ·· REPREENSÍVEL

RE.NUN.CI.A.ÇÃO, *s.f.*, renunciation.
RE.NUN.CI.A.DOR, *s.m.*, renouncer; *adj.*, renouncing.
RE.NUN.CI.AR, *v.*, to renounce, to resign, to reject, to refuse, to desist.
RE.NUN.CI.A.TI.VO, *adj.*, renunciative, renunciatory.
RE.NUN.CI.A.TÓ.RI.O, *s.m.*, *Jur.*, transferee.
RE.O.CU.PA.ÇÃO, *s.f.*, reoccupation.
RE.O.CU.PAR, *v.*, to reoccupy.
RE.OR.DE.NA.ÇÃO, *s.f.*, reorganizing, reordering; *Rel.*, reordination.
RE.OR.DE.NAR, *v.*, *Rel.*, to reordain; to rearrange, to put again in order.
RE.OR.GA.NI.ZA.ÇÃO, *s.f.*, reorganization, rearrangement, reform.
RE.OR.GA.NI.ZA.DOR, *s.m.*, reorganizer; *adj.*, reorganizing.
RE.OR.GA.NI.ZAR, *v.*, to reorganize, to organize anew, to improve, to better.
RE.O.RI.EN.TA.ÇÃO, *s.f.*, reorientation.
RE.PA.GI.NA.ÇÃO, *s.f.*, *Tipog.*, repagination.
RE.PA.GI.NAR, *v.*, *Tipog.*, to repaginate.
RE.PA.RA.BI.LI.DA.DE, *s.f.*, reparability.
RE.PA.RA.ÇÃO, *s.f.*, reparation, repair, repairing, reform, indemnity, satisfaction.
RE.PA.RA.DEI.RA, *s.f.*, inquisitive woman.
RE.PA.RA.DO, *adj.*, repaired, mended, fixed up.
RE.PA.RA.DOR, *s.m.*, repairer, restorer, mender; *adj.*, repairing.
RE.PA.RAR, *v.*, to repair, to mend, to observe, to restore, to retouch, to remedy.
RE.PA.RA.TÓ.RI.O, *adj.*, reparative, reparatory.
RE.PA.RÁ.VEL, *adj.*, reparable.
RE.PA.RO, *s.m.*, repair, repairing, restoration, notice, remark.
RE.PAR.TI.ÇÃO, *s.f.*, partition, department, division, section.
RE.PAR.TI.DO, *adj.*, parted, divided.
RE.PAR.TI.DOR, *s.m.*, divider, distributor; *adj.*, dividing, distributing.
RE.PAR.TI.MEN.TO, *s.m.*, partition, distribution, division, sharing.
RE.PAR.TIR, *v.*, to separate, to slice, to share, to split, to distribute.
RE.PAR.TI.TI.VO, *adj.*, distributive.
RE.PAR.TÍ.VEL, *adj.*, distributable, dividable.
RE.PAS.SA.DO, *adj.*, repassed, that was again read (text passed again); transferred; impregnated.
RE.PAS.SAR, *v.*, to repass, to read over again, to drench, to soak.
RE.PAS.SE, *s.m.*, act of reading over again; *Econ.*, tansfer.
RE.PAS.TAR, *v.*, to repast, to nourish.
RE.PAS.TO, *s.m.*, repast, banquet.
RE.PA.TRI.A.ÇÃO, *s.f.*, repatriation, remigration.
RE.PA.TRI.A.DO, *s.m.*, repatriate; *adj.*, repatriated.
RE.PA.TRI.A.DOR, *s.m.*, repatriator; *adj.*, repatriating.
RE.PA.TRI.A.MEN.TO, *s.m.*, repatriation.
RE.PA.TRI.AR, *v.*, to repatriate, to remigrate.
RE.PE.LÃO, *s.m.*, hard push, shock, clash.
RE.PE.LÊN.CI.A, *s.f.*, repellence, repellency.
RE.PE.LEN.TE, *s.m.*, repellent, repugnant, repulsive.
RE.PE.LI.DO, *s.m.*, violent push, shock; *adj.*, repelled, repulsed.
RE.PE.LIR, *v.*, to repel, to repulse, to drive, to expulse, to reject.
RE.PEN.SAR, *v.*, to rethink, ponder, reconsider.
RE.PEN.TE, *s.m.*, suddenness, impulsive act; *de repente*: suddenly.

RE.PEN.TI.NA.MEN.TE, *adv.*, suddenly.
RE.PEN.TI.NI.DA.DE, *s.f.*, suddenness.
RE.PEN.TI.NO, *adj.*, sudden, abrupt, instantaneous, rapid, acute.
RE.PEN.TIS.TA, *s. 2 gen.*, improvisator; *adj.*, improvising, extemporary.
RE.PER.CUS.SÃO, *s.f.*, repercussion, reverberation, echo.
RE.PER.CUS.SI.VO, *adj.*, repercussive.
RE.PER.CU.TIR, *v.*, to reverberate, to rebound, to reflect, to deflect.
RE.PER.TÓ.RIO, *s.m.*, repertory, index, list, catalogue.
RE.PE.TE.CO, *s.m.*, *Bras., gír.*, repetition, act of repeating.
RE.PE.TÊN.CI.A, *s.f.*, repetition, repeating.
RE.PE.TEN.TE, *s. 2 gen., Educ.*, repeater; *adj.*, repeating.
RE.PE.TI.ÇÃO, *s.f.*, repetition, reiteration, recurrence.
RE.PE.TI.DA.MEN.TE, *adv.*, repeatedly, frequently,
RE.PE.TI.DO, *adj.*, repeated, reiterant.
RE.PE.TI.DOR, *s.m.*, repeater; *adj.*, repeating.
RE.PE.TIR, *v.*, to repeat, to recur, to spread, to do over again.
RE.PE.TI.TÍ.VEL, *adj.*, that can be repeated.
RE.PE.TI.TI.VO, *adj.*, repetitive, repetitious.
RE.PI.CAR, *v.*, to prick again; to ring, to chime.
RE.PI.CA.GEM, *s.f.*, ringing of bells; *Agric.*, transplantation.
RE.PI.QUE, *s.m.*, tolling of bells, alarm.
RE.PI.SA.DO, *adj.*, well-trodden; *fig.*, rehashed, repeated.
RE.PI.SAR, *v.*, to retread, to trample, to tread over again, to insist on.
RE.PI.SA.TI.VO, *adj.*, repetitious.
RE.PLA.NE.JA.MEN.TO, *s.m.*, replanning.
RE.PLA.NE.JAR, *v.*, to plan again, replan.
RE.PLAN.TAR, *v.*, to replant, to plant again.
RE.PLAN.TI.O, *s.m.*, replantation, replanting.
RE.PLAY, *s.m.*, *Ingl.*, replay (TV); *col.*, repetition.
RE.PLE.TO, *adj.*, replete, very full, stuffed, congested.
RÉ.PLI.CA, *s.f.*, response, reply, replication.
RE.PLI.CA.ÇÃO, *s.f.*, the same that *réplica*.
RE.PLI.CA.DOR, *s.m.*, replicator, replier; *adj.*, replying.
RE.PLI.CAR, *v.*, to answer, to reply, to rejoin, to rebut, to object.
RE.PO.LHAL, *s.m.*, cabbage plantation.
RE.PO.LHO, *s.m.*, *Bot.*, cabbage.
RE.PO.LHU.DO, *adj.*, cabbage-shaped, *fig.*, plump, fat.
RE.POR, *v.*, to replace, to put back, to restitute, to refund.
RE.POR.TA.GEM, *s.f.*, newspaper report, interview.
RE.POR.TAR, *v.*, to transport, to resolve, to turn back.
RE.PÓR.TER, *s.m.*, reporter, journalist, news writer.
RE.PO.SI.ÇÃO, *s.f.*, replacement, restitution.
RE.PO.SI.TÓ.RI.O, *s.m.*, repository; *adj.*, referring to a repository.
RE.POS.SU.IR, *v.*, to repossess
RE.POS.TAR, *v.*, to give a sharp answer; to give a coarse answer.
RE.POU.SAN.TE, *adj.*, restful.
RE.POU.SAR, *v.*, to rest, to repose, to calm, to quiet, to sleep.
RE.POU.SO, *s.m.*, rest, repose, tranquility, calmness, ease.
RE.PRE.EN.DE.DOR, *s.m.*, reprehender, reproacher; *adj.*, reprehending.
RE.PRE.EN.DER, *v.*, to reprehend, to reprimand, to censure.
RE.PRE.EN.SÃO, *s.f.*, reprehension, reprimand, reproach.
RE.PRE.EN.SÍ.VEL, *adj.*, reprehensible, censurable.

REPREENSIVELMENTE ·· 301 ·· RESENHAR

RE.PRE.EN.SI.VEL.MEN.TE, *adv.*, reprehensibly.
RE.PRE.EN.SI.VO, *adj.*, reprehensive.
RE.PRE.SA, *s.f.*, dam, dike, sluice, weir, reservoir.
RE.PRE.SÁ.LIA, *s.f.*, retaliation, revenge, reprisal.
RE.PRE.SA.MEN.TO, *s.m.*, act of damming, repression.
RE.PRE.SAR, *v.*, to dam up, to dike, to restrain.
RE.PRE.SEN.TA.ÇÃO, *s.f.*, representation, exhibition, presentation.
RE.PRE.SEN.TA.DO, *adj.*, represented.
RE.PRE.SEN.TAN.TE, *s. 2 gen.*, representative, minister, ambassador, delegate; *adj.*, representing, representative.
RE.PRE.SEN.TAR, *v.*, to personate, to impersonate, to represent, to play.
RE.PRE.SEN.TA.TI.VI.DA.DE, *s.f.*, representativity, representation.
RE.PRE.SEN.TA.TI.VO, *adj.*, representative, figurative.
RE.PRES.SÃO, *s.f.*, repression, suppression, check.
RE.PRES.SI.VO, *adj.*, repressive.
RE.PRES.SOR, *s.m.*, represser, coercer.
RE.PRI.MEN.DA, *s.f.*, reprimand, reprehension, correction.
RE.PRI.MI.DO, *adj.*, repressed, pent-up; dammed up, oppressed.
RE.PRI.MIR, *v.*, to curb, to check, to stop, to repress, to restrain.
RE.PRI.MÍ.VEL, *adj.*, repressible.
RE.PRI.SAR, *v.*, to replay, to repeat.
RE.PRI.SE, *s.f.*, rerum, replay.
RÉ.PRO.BO, *s.m.*, reprobate; *adj.*, reprobate, castaway.
RE.PRO.CES.SA.MEN.TO, *s.m.*, reprocessing.
RE.PRO.CES.SAR, *v.*, to reprocess.
RE.PRO.CHAR, *v.*, to reproach, to censure.
RE.PRO.CHE, *s.m.*, reproach, censure.
RE.PRO.DU.ÇÃO, *s.f.*, reproduction, copy, replication, propagation, duplicate.
RE.PRO.DU.TI.BI.LI.DA.DE, *s.f.*, reproductibility.
RE.PRO.DU.TÍ.VEL, *adj.*, reproducible.
RE.PRO.DU.TI.VO, *adj.*, reproductive.
RE.PRO.DU.TOR, *s.m.*, reproducer, procreator, studhorse.
RE.PRO.DU.ZIR, *v.*, to reproduce, to transcribe, to copy, to multiply, to propagate.
RE.PRO.DU.ZÍ.VEL, *adj.*, reproducible.
RE.PRO.VA.ÇÃO, *s.f.*, reproving, rejection, reproof, reproach.
RE.PRO.VA.DO, *adj.*, reproved, damned, condemned.
RE.PRO.VA.DOR, *s.m.*, reprover; *adj.*, reprobative, reprobatory.
RE.PRO.VAR, *v.*, to disapprove, to reprove, to censure, to reject, to admonish.
RE.PRO.VA.TI.VO, *adj.*, reprobative.
RE.PRO.VÁ.VEL, *adj.*, reprovable.
REP.TAR, *v.*, to defy, to provoke, to oppose.
RÉP.TIL, *s.m.*, reptile; *adj.*, crawling, creeping.
REP.TI.LI.A.NO, *adj.*, reptilian.
RE.PÚ.BLI.CA, *s.f.*, republic, commonwealth.
RE.PÚ.BLI.CA CEN.TRO-A.FRI.CA.NA, *s.*, Central African Republic.
RE.PÚ.BLI.CA DA Á.FRI.CA DO SUL, *s.*, Republic of South Africa.
RE.PÚ.BLI.CA DO.MI.NI.CA.NA, *s.* Dominican Republic.
RE.PU.BLI.CA.NIS.MO, *s.m.*, republicanism.
RE.PU.BLI.CA.NI.ZAR, *v.*, to republicanize.
RE.PU.BLI.CA.NO, *adj., s.m.*, republican.
RE.PU.BLI.CAR, *v.*, to republish.

RE.PÚ.BLI.CA TCHE.CA, *s.*, Czech Republic.
RE.PU.BLI.CI.DA, *s. 2 gen.*, destroyer of a republic; antirepublican.
RE.PU.DI.A.DO, *adj.*, repudiated.
RE.PU.DI.AN.TE, *s. 2 gen.*, repudiator; *adj.*, repudiating.
RE.PU.DI.AR, *v.*, to repudiate, to divorce, to disclaim, to reject.
RE.PU.DI.Á.VEL, *adj.*, repudiable.
RE.PÚ.DI.O, *s.m.*, repudiation, abjuration.
RE.PUG.NÂN.CIA, *s.f.*, repugnance, aversion, disgust, antipathy, repulsion, averseness.
RE.PUG.NAN.TE, *adj.*, repugnant, repellent.
RE.PUG.NAR, *v.*, to repugn, to react, to reject, to repel.
RE.PUL.SA, *s.f.*, repulse, repellence, aversion.
RE.PUL.SÃO, *s.f.*, repulsion; *Fís.*, rejection.
RE.PUL.SI.VO, *adj.*, repulsive, repugnant, repellent.
RE.PUL.SOR, *adj.*, repulsive, repellent.
RE.PU.TA.ÇÃO, *s.f.*, reputation, renown, fame, credit.
RE.PU.TAR, *v.*, to repute, to consider, to regard.
RE.PU.XA.DO *adj.*, stretched, puckered, snagged.
RE.PU.XAR, *v.*, to pull, to pull violently.
RE.PU.XO, *s.m.*, fountain.
RE.QUE.BRA.DO, *s.m.*, swaying.
RE.QUE.BRAR, *v.*, to waddle, to wiggle, to walk in a languishing manner.
RE.QUE.BRO, *s.m.*, languishing or voluptuous movement, swaying.
RE.QUEI.JÃO, *s.m.*, cheesecurds, cottage cheese.
RE.QUEN.TA.DO, *adj.*, reheated.
RE.QUEN.TAR, *v.*, to heat or warm up again.
RE.QUE.RE.DOR, *s.m.*, petitioner, procurator; *adj.*, petitioning, claiming.
RE.QUE.REN.TE, *s. 2 gen.*, petitioner, solicitant, applicant, procurator.
RE.QUE.RER, *v.*, to request, to ask or apply for, to petition, to appeal to.
RE.QUE.RI.DO, *adj.*, required, petitioned, requested.
RE.QUE.RI.MEN.TO, *s.m.*, request, requirement, solicitation, demand.
RE.QUE.RÍ.VEL, *adj.*, requirable, demandable.
RÉ.QUI.EM, *s.m.*, Requiem; *Mús.*, requiem.
RE.QUIN.TA.DO, *adj.*, refined.
RE.QUIN.TAR, *v.*, to refine, to purify, to perfect.
RE.QUIN.TE, *s.m.*, refinement.
RE.QUI.SI.ÇÃO, *s.f.*, requisition, solicitation, demand.
RE.QUI.SI.TAN.TE, *s. 2 gen.*, requirer, requester.
RE.QUI.SI.TAR, *v.*, to requisition, to require, to order, to request.
RE.QUI.SI.TO, *s.m.*, qualification, requisite, requirement.
RE.QUI.SI.TÓ.RI.O, *s.m., Jur.*, requisitor; *adj.*, requisitory.
RÊS, *s.f.*, cattle, livestock, any quadruped bred.
RÉS, *s.m.*, level, close.
RES.CAL.DA.DO, *adj.*, scalded, overheated, experienced.
RES.CAL.DAR, *v.*, to scald again, to overheat.
RES.CAL.DO, *s.m.*, reflected heat.
RES.CIN.DI.MEN.TO, *s.m., Jur.*, abrogation, annulment.
RES.CIN.DIR, *v.*, to break, to dissolve, to sever.
RES.CI.SÃO, *s.f.*, rescission, repeal, annulment, cancellation, revocation.
RES.CI.SÓ.RI.O, *adj.*, rescissory.
RE.SE.NHA, *s.f.*, review, summary, abridgement, digest.
RE.SE.NHAR, *v.*, to recount, to write a detailed report.

RESERVA ·· 302 ·· RESSURGIMENTO

RE.SER.VA, *s.f.*, reservation, restriction, store, stock.

RE.SER.VA.ÇÃO, *s.f.*, act of reserving, reservation.

RE.SER.VA.DA.MEN.TE, *adv.*, reservedly.

RE.SER.VA.DO, *s.m.*, private room; men's room, ladies' room; *adj.*, reserved; private, particular, secretive.

RE.SER.VAR, *v.*, to reserve, to set apart.

RE.SER.VA.TI.VO, *adj.*, reserving, saving.

RE.SER.VA.TÓ.RIO, *s.m.*, reservoir, tank, deposit, store.

RE.SER.VIS.TA, *s. 2 gen.*, reservist.

RES.FO.LE.GAN.TE, *adj.*, puffy, puffing, panting.

RES.FO.LE.GAR, *v.*, to breathe; to pant, to puff.

RES.FRI.A.DO, *s.m.*, cold, catarrh; *adj.*, cold, chilly, iced, frozen.

RES.FRI.A.DOR, *s.m.*, cooler, refrigerator; *adj.*, cooling.

RES.FRI.A.DOU.RO, *s.m.*, cooling place, refrigerator.

RES.FRI.A.MEN.TO, *s.m.*, cooling, cold, chilly.

RES.FRI.AR, *v.*, to cool again, to cool, to freeze, to become chilly.

RES.GA.TA.DOR, *s.m.*, rescuer; *adj.*, redeeming, rescuing.

RES.GA.TAR, *v.*, to ransom, to redeem, to pay off.

RES.GA.TÁ.VEL, *adj.*, ransomable, rescuable.

RES.GA.TE, *s.m.*, ransom, redemption, deliverance.

RES.GUAR.DA.DO, *adj.*, protected, cautious, covered.

RES.GUAR.DAR, *v.*, to guard, to defend, to shelter.

RES.GUAR.DO, *s.m.*, guard, protection, watch.

RE.SI.DÊN.CIA, *s.f.*, residence, residency, dwelling, home.

RE.SI.DEN.CI.AL, *adj.*, residential, residentiary.

RE.SI.DEN.TE, *s. 2 gen.*, resident, diplomatic, agent; *adj.*, resident, residential.

RE.SI.DIR, *v.*, to reside, to live, to dwell, to inhabit.

RE.SI.DU.AL, *adj.*, residual.

RE.SI.DU.Á.RI.O, *adj.*, residuary.

RE.SÍ.DUO, *s.m.*, rest, remainder, residue, refuse.

RE.SIG.NA.ÇÃO, *s.f.*, resignation, abnegation.

RE.SIG.NA.DO, *adj.*, resigned.

RE.SIG.NAR, *v.*, to resign, to give up, to surrender, to abdicate.

RE.SI.LI.ÊN.CI.A, *s.f.*, *Fís.*, resiliency, resilience.

RE.SI.LI.EN.TE, *adj.*, resilient.

RE.SI.NA, *s.f.*, resin, rosin.

RE.SIS.TÊN.CIA, *s.f.*, resistance, opposition, obstacle, reaction.

RE.SIS.TEN.TE, *adj.*, strong, durable, resistant; ~ *a*: resistant to; *Med.*, tolerant.

RE.SIS.TI.BI.LI.DA.DE, *s.f.*, resistibility.

RE.SIS.TIR, *v.*, to resist, to oppose, to withstand, to endure, to hold out.

RE.SIS.TÍ.VEL, *adj.*, resistible.

RES.MA, *s.f.*, ream, 500 sheets of paper.

RES.MUN.GAR, *v.*, to mumble, to grumble.

RES.MUN.GO, *s.m.*, mutter, mumble.

RE.SO.LU.ÇÃO, *s.f.*, resolution, deliberation, decision, purpose.

RE.SO.LU.TO, *adj.*, resolute, courageous.

RE.SOL.VER, *v.*, to resolve, to decide, to solve, to conclude, to determine, to liquidate.

RE.SOL.VI.DO, *adj.*, resolved, settled, decided.

RES.PAL.DAR, *s.m.*, back of a chair; *v.*, to smooth down, to polish; to back.

RES.PEC.TI.VA.MEN.TE, *adv.*, respectively.

RES.PEC.TI.VO, *adj.*, respective, concerning.

RES.PEI.TA.BI.LI.DA.DE, *s.f.*, respectability.

RES.PEI.TA.DO, *adj.*, respected, considered.

RES.PEI.TA.DOR, *s.m.*, respecter; *adj.*, respecting, respectful.

RES.PEI.TAR, *v.*, to respect, to esteem, to honour, to venerate.

RES.PEI.TÁ.VEL, *adj.*, respectable.

RES.PEI.TO, *s.m.*, respect, regard, esteem, consideration, reverence, veneration.

RES.PEI.TO.SO, *adj.*, respectful, dutiful.

RES.PIN.GAR, *v.*, to sprinkle, to spray.

RES.PIN.GO, *s.m.*, splash, aspersion, spatter.

RES.PI.RA.ÇÃO, *s.f.*, respiration, breath.

RES.PI.RA.DOR, *s.m.*, respirator; *adj.*, breathing.

RES.PI.RAR, *v.*, to breathe, to respire, to be, to live.

RES.PI.RA.TÓ.RIO, *adj.*, respiratory.

RES.PI.RO, *s.m.*, respiration, breath; *fig.*, rest, vent.

RES.PLAN.DE.CEN.TE, *adj.*, resplendent, shining, refulgent, splendid (day).

RES.PLAN.DE.CER, *v.*, to shine, to glitter, to sparkle.

RES.PLEN.DOR, *s.m.*, resplendence, resplendency.

RES.PON.DÃO, *s.m.*, cheeky person, backbiter; *adj.*, backbiting, snappish, churlish.

RES.PON.DER, *v.*, to respond, to reply, to answer, to communicate, to answer back.

RES.PON.SA.BI.LI.DA.DE, *s.f.*, responsibility.

RES.PON.SA.BI.LI.ZAR, *v.*, to make or consider responsible.

RES.PON.SÁ.VEL, *adj.*, responsible.

RES.PON.SO, *s.m.*, antiphon, response.

RES.POS.TA, *s.f.*, response, answer, reply.

RES.QUÍ.CIO, *s.m.*, residue, rest, remainder, trace, mark.

RES.SA.BI.A.DO, *adj.*, suspicious, distrustful, resentful.

RES.SA.BI.AR, *v.*, to distrust, to take offense; *ressabiar-se*: to be offended.

RES.SAI.BO, *s.m.*, unpleasant taste, bad taste; *fig.*, resentment, sign (indicium).

RES.SA.CA, *s.f.*, surf, flux and reflux, hangover.

RES.SAL.TA.DO, *adj.*, jutting out, salient.

RES.SAL.TAR, *v.*, to stick out, to stand out, to project.

RES.SAL.TO, *s.m.*, jutting out, projection, rebound.

RES.SAL.VA, *s.f.*, reservation, exception, safety clause.

RES.SAR.CI.DO, *adj.*, compensated, repaired, indemnified.

RES.SAR.CI.MEN.TO, *s.m.*, compensating, compensation, reparation.

RES.SAR.CIR, *v.*, to compensate, to make amends for, to indemnify.

RES.SEN.TI.DO, *s.m.*, a resented person; *adj.*, resentful.

RES.SEN.TI.MEN.TO, *s.m.*, resentment, offense.

RES.SEN.TIR, *v.*, to resent, to feel again, to feel anew, to take offense.

RES.SE.QUI.DO, *adj.*, dried up, parched.

RES.SO.A.DOR, *s.m.*, resonator; *adj.*, resounding.

RES.SO.AN.TE, *adj.*, resonant, resounding; vibrant.

RES.SO.AR, *v.*, to tune, to intone, to resound.

RES.SO.NA.DOR, *s.m.*, resonator; snorter; *adj.*, resounding.

RES.SO.NÂN.CIA, *s.f.*, resonance, echo.

RES.SO.NAN.TE, *adj.*, resonant, resounding; vibrant; snoring.

RES.SO.NAR, *v.*, to resound, to reverberate.

RES.SUR.GÊN.CI.A, *s.f.*, resurgence.

RES.SUR.GEN.TE, *adj.*, resurgent.

RES.SUR.GI.DO, *adj.*, resuscitated, revived, resurrected.

RES.SUR.GI.MEN.TO, *s.m.*, resuscitation, resurgence.

RESSURGIR ··· 303 ··· RETRAÇÃO

RES.SUR.GIR, *v.*, to resurge, to rise again, to revive.
RES.SUR.REC.TO, *adj.*, resurrected, revived.
RES.SUR.REI.ÇÃO, *s.f.*, resurrection, resuscitation.
RES.SUS.CI.TA.ÇÃO, *s.f.*, resuscitation, resurrection.
RES.SUS.CI.TA.DO, *adj.*, resuscitated, revivified.
RES.SUS.CI.TA.DOR, *s.m.*, resuscitator; *adj.*, resuscitating, reviving.
RES.SUS.CI.TA.MEN.TO, *s.m.*, the same that *ressuscitação*.
RES.SUS.CI.TAR, *v.*, to revive, to resuscitate, to resurrect.
RES.SUS.CI.TÁ.VEL, *adj.*, resuscitable.
RES.TA.BE.LE.CER, *v.*, to restore, to re-establish.
RES.TA.BE.LE.CI.DO, *adj.*, re-established.
RES.TA.BE.LE.CI.MEN.TO, *s.m.*, re-establishing, restoration.
RES.TAN.TE, *s.m.*, remainder, rest; *adj.*, remaining, residual.
RES.TAR, *v.*, to rest, to remain.
RES.TAU.RA.ÇÃO, *s.f.*, restoration, restoring, repair.
RES.TAU.RA.DO, *adj.*, restored, repaired.
RES.TAU.RA.DOR, *s.m.*, restorer, liberator.
RES.TAU.RAN.TE, *s.m.*, restaurant.
RES.TAU.RAR, *v.*, to restore, to recuperate, to recapture, to repair, to renovate.
RÉS.TIA, *s.f.*, rope, rope braided from reeds or sedge grass.
RES.TIN.GA, *s.f.*, sandbank, shoal.
RES.TI.TU.I.ÇÃO, *s.f.*, restitution, restoration, returning.
RES.TI.TU.Í.DO, *adj.*, returned, restored.
RES.TI.TU.IR, *v.*, to restitute, to restore, to return, to replace.
RES.TI.TU.Í.VEL, *adj.*, repayable, refundable, returnable.
RES.TO, *s.m.*, rest, remain, residue, end.
RES.TO.LHO, *s.m.*, stubbles.
RES.TRI.ÇÃO, *s.f.*, restriction, limitation, restraint.
RES.TRIN.GIR, *v.*, to restrict, to restringe, to straiten, to narrow, to restrain.
RES.TRIN.GÍ.VEL, *adj.*, restrainable, limitable.
RES.TRI.TI.VO, *adj.*, restrictive.
RES.TRI.TO, *adj.*, restricted, limited.
RE.SUL.TA.DO, *s.m.*, result, consequence, effect, deliberation.
RE.SUL.TAN.TE, *s.f.*, *Fís.*, resultant force; *adj.*, resultant, resulting, consequent.
RE.SUL.TAR, *v.*, to result, to proceed, to spring or arise from, to derive from.
RE.SU.MI.DA.MEN.TE, *adv.*, concisely, succinctly.
RE.SU.MI.DO, *adj.*, resumed, condensed, abridged, concise.
RE.SU.MIR, *v.*, to abbreviate, to abridge, to reduce, to synthetize.
RE.SU.MO, *s.m.*, abridgement, abbreviation, summary.
RES.VA.LAR, *v.*, to let slip or fall, to slide, to slip, to slither.
RE.TA, *s.f.*, straight line, trace or stroke.
RE.TA.GUAR.DA, *s.f.*, rearguard, back.
RE.TAL, *adj.*, *Anat.*, rectal.
RE.TA.LHA.ÇÃO, *s.f.*, act of cutting.
RE.TA.LHA.DO, *adj.*, cut up, chopped, shredded.
RE.TA.LHA.MEN.TO, *s.m.*, act of cutting.
RE.TA.LHAR, *v.*, to cut into small pieces, to stab, to slash, to rend.
RE.TA.LI.A.ÇÃO, *s.f.*, retaliation.
RE.TA.LI.A.DO, *adj.*, retaliated.
RE.TA.LI.A.DOR, *s.m.*, retaliator; *adj.*, retaliatory.
RE.TA.LI.AR, *v.*, to retaliate.
RE.TAN.GU.LAR, *adj.*, rectangular, right-angled.
RE.TAN.GU.LA.RI.DA.DE, *s.f.*, rectangularity.
RE.TÂN.GU.LO, *s.m.*, rectangle, square.

RE.TAR.DA.DO, *s.m.*, *pej.*, *Psic.*, retarded person; *adj.*, delayed, *Psic.*, retarded.
RE.TAR.DA.MEN.TO, *s.m.*, retardation, retarding, delay.
RE.TAR.DAR, *v.*, to retard, to delay, to impede.
RE.TAR.DA.TÁ.RIO, *s.m.*, latecomer, laggard, straggler; *adj.*, tardy, slow.
RE.TAR.DA.TI.VO, *adj.*, retardative, retardatory.
RE.TAR.DO, *s.m.*, delay, lag; *Psic.*, retardedness.
RE.TEM.PE.RAR, *v.*, to retemper.
RE.TEN.ÇÃO, *s.f.*, retention, retaining, restraint, suppression.
RE.TEN.TOR, *s.m.*, retainer, keeper, retentor.
RE.TER, *v.*, to keep, to hold back, to guard, to detain, to remember.
RE.TI.CÊN.CIA, *s.f.*, reticence, omission points.
RE.TI.CEN.TE, *adj.*, reticent, reserved, silent.
RE.TÍ.CU.LA, *s.f.*, reticle, a small net.
RE.TI.DÃO, *s.f.*, rightness, honesty, integrity.
RE.TI.DO, *adj.*, restrained, curbed.
RE.TI.FI.CA, *s.f.*, *Bras.*, shop which reconditions (autos).
RE.TI.FI.CA.ÇÃO, *s.f.*, rectification, rectifying, emendation.
RE.TI.FI.CA.DO, *adj.*, rectified, corrected.
RE.TI.FI.CA.DOR, *s.m.*, rectifier.
RE.TI.FI.CAR, *v.*, to rectify, to straighten, to correct, to amend.
RE.TI.FI.CA.TI.VO, *adj.*, rectificative.
RE.TI.FI.CÁ.VEL, *adj.*, rectifiable, emendable.
RE.TI.LÍ.NEO, *adj.*, rectilineal, rectilinear.
RE.TI.NA, *s.f.*, *Anat.*, retina.
RE.TI.NIR, *v.*, to jingle, to tinkle.
RE.TI.NI.TE, *s.f.*, *Med.*, retinitis.
RE.TIN.TO, *adj.*, redyed, coloured again.
RE.TI.RA.DA, *s.f.*, retreat, evacuation, withdrawal.
RE.TI.RA.DO, *adj.*, retired; retiring, solitary, isolated.
RE.TI.RAN.TE, *s. 2 gen.*, migrant; *adj.*, retiring, retreating.
RE.TI.RAR, *v.*, to draw back, to withdraw, to remove, to take away, to retract.
RE.TI.RÁ.VEL, *adj.*, that can be withdrawn, removable.
RE.TI.RO, *s.m.*, solitary place, seclusion, retreat, privacy, exile, nest.
RE.TO, *s.m.*, rectum; *adj.*, straight, right, direct, plain, just.
RE.TO.CA.DO, *adj.*, retouched.
RE.TO.CA.DOR, *s.m.*, retoucher; *adj.*, retouching.
RE.TO.CAR, *v.*, to retouch, to finish, to complete, to correct, to ameliorate.
RE.TO.CÁ.VEL, *adj.*, that can be retouched.
RE.TO.MA.DA, *s.f.*, retaking, recovery.
RE.TO.MAR, *v.*, to retake, to take again, to recover.
RE.TO.QUE, *s.m.*, retouching.
RE.TOR.CER, *v.*, to twist again, to retwuist, to wrench, to rewind.
RE.TOR.CI.DO, *adj.*, twisted, winding.
RE.TÓ.RI.CA, *s.f.*, rhetoric, eloquence, oratory.
RE.TO.RI.CA.MEN.TE, *adv.*, rhetorically.
RE.TÓ.RI.CO, *adj.*, rhetorical, rhetorician, declamatory.
RE.TOR.NAR, *v.*, to return, to turn, to get back.
RE.TOR.NÁ.VEL, *adj m+f.*, returnable.
RE.TOR.NO, *s.m.*, return, regress, coming back.
RE.TOR.QUIR, *v.*, to answer back, to reply, to retort, to talk back.
RE.TOR.QUÍ.VEL, *adj.*, refutable, answerable.
RE.TOR.TA, *s.f.*, retort.
RE.TRA.ÇÃO, *s.f.*, retractation, retracting.

RETRÁCTIL ·· 304 ·· REVESTIMENTO

RE.TRÁC.TIL, *adj.*, the same that *retrátil*.

RE.TRA.Í.DO, *adj.*, retracted, retired, reserved.

RE.TRA.Í.MEN.TO, *s.m.*, retraction; retreat, withdrawal.

RE.TRA.IR, *v.*, to draw back, to withdraw, to retract, to shrink.

RE.TRAN.CA, *s.f., Esp.*, when all the players remain in the defense (soccer); *fig.*, defensive, reserved attitude.

RE.TRANS.CRE.VER, *v.*, to retranscribe.

RE.TRANS.CRI.ÇÃO, *s.f.*, retranscription.

RE.TRANS.MIS.SÃO, *s.f.*, retransmission, reconveyance.

RE.TRANS.MIS.SOR, *s.m.*, retransmitter; *adj.*, retransmitter.

RE.TRANS.MIS.SO.RA, *s.f.*, rebroadcast station (rádio, TV).

RE.TRANS.MI.TIR, *v.*, to retransmit, to transmit again.

RE.TRA.TA.ÇÃO, *s.f.*, retractation.

RE.TRA.SA.DO, *adj.*, before last; delayed, late.

RE.TRA.SAR, *v.*, to delay, to retard, to set back.

RE.TRA.TA.ÇÃO, *s.f.*, retractation, recantation; portrayal.

RE.TRA.TA.DO, *adj.*, portrayed, painted; drawn.

RE.TRA.TAR, *v.*, to portray, to paint, to draw, to photograph.

RE.TRA.TÁ.VEL, *adj.*, portrayable, retractable.

RE.TRÁ.TIL, *adj.*, retractable, retractile.

RE.TRA.TIS.TA, *s. 2 gen.*, portraitist, portrait photographer.

RE.TRA.TO, *s.m.*, picture, portrait, photograph.

RE.TRI.BU.I.ÇÃO, *s.f.*, retribution, recompense, payment, remuneration.

RE.TRI.BU.Í.DO, *adj.*, retributed, rewarded.

RE.TRI.BU.I.DOR, *s.m.*, retributor; *adj.*, retributing.

RE.TRI.BU.IR, *v.*, to retribute, to reward, to repay, to recompense.

RE.TRI.BU.Í.VEL, *adj.*, rewardable, returnable, requitable.

RE.TRO.A.ÇÃO, *s.f.*, retroaction.

RE.TRO.A.GIR, *v.*, to retroact, to react, to act backward.

RE.TRO.A.LI.MEN.TA.ÇÃO, *s.f., Eletr.*, feedback.

RE.TRO.A.TI.VI.DA.DE, *s.f.*, retroactivity.

RE.TRO.A.TI.VO, *adj.*, retroactive.

RE.TRO.CE.DEN.TE, *adj.*, retrocedent.

RE.TRO.CE.DER, *v.*, to retrocede, to go back, to decline.

RE.TRO.CE.DI.MEN.TO, *s.m.*, retrocession.

RE.TRO.CES.SO, *s.m.*, retrocession, backspacer, retrogression.

RE.TRO.GRA.DAR, *v.*, to retrograde, to retrogress, to degenerate, to turn back, reverse.

RE.TRO.GRE.DIR, *v.*, to retrogress.

RE.TRÓ.GRA.DO, *s.m.*, retrograde, reactionary; *adj.*, retrograde, backward.

RE.TROS.PEC.ÇÃO, *s.f.*, retrospection.

RE.TRO.PRO.JE.TOR, *s.m.*, overhead projector.

RE.TROS.PEC.ÇÃO, *s.f.*, retrospection, retrospect.

RE.TROS.PEC.TI.VA, *s.f.*, retrospective.

RE.TROS.PEC.TI.VA.MEN.TE, *adv.*, retrospectively.

RE.TROS.PEC.TI.VO, *adj.*, retrospective.

RE.TROS.PEC.TO, *s.m.*, retrospection, retrospect.

RE.TRO.VER.TER, *v.*, to retrovert.

RE.TRO.VER.TI.DO, *adj.*, retroverse, reverted.

RE.TRO.VÍ.RUS, *s.m., Biol.*, retrovirus.

RE.TRO.VI.SOR, *s.m.*, rear view mirror.

RE.TRU.CAR, *v.*, to reply, to answer, to retort.

RE.TUM.BAN.TE, *adj.*, reverberating, resounding, resonant, sounding.

RE.TUM.BAR, *v.*, to resound, to reverberate.

RE.TUR.NO, *s.m., Bras., Esp.*, return march, return play, revanche.

RÉU, *s.m.*, defendant, the accused, respondent.

RE.U.MA.NI.ZAR, *v.*, to become human again.

REU.MÁ.TI.CO, *adj., Med.*, rheumatic.

REU.MA.TIS.MO, *s.m., Med.*, rheumatism, arthritis.

REU.MA.TOI.DE, *adj., Med.*, rheumatoid, rheumatoidal.

REU.MA.TO.LO.GI.A, *s.f., Med.*, rheumatology.

REU.MA.TO.LO.GIS.TA, *s. 2 gen.*, rheumatologist.

RE.U.NI.ÃO, *s.f.*, reunion, meeting, gathering, meet, party.

RE.U.NI.DO, *adj.*, reunited, assembled.

RE.U.NI.FI.CA.ÇÃO, *s.f.*, reunification

RE.U.NI.FI.CAR, *v.*, to reunify, reconsolidate.

RE.U.NIR, *v.*, to reunite, to assemble, to congregate, to meet, to rejoin.

RE.U.TI.LI.ZA.ÇÃO, *s.f.*, reutilization, reuse.

RE.U.TI.LI.ZAR, *v.*, to reutilize, to reuse.

RE.U.TI.LI.ZÁ.VEL, *adj.*, reutilizable, reusable.

RE.VA.LI.DA.ÇÃO, *s.f.*, revalidation.

RE.VA.LI.DAR, *v.*, to revalidate, to renew.

RE.VA.LO.RI.ZA.ÇÃO, *s.f.*, revalorization.

RE.VA.LO.RI.ZAR, *v.*, to revalorize.

RÉ.VEIL.LON, *s.m., Fr.*, New Year's Eve.

RE.VE.LA.ÇÃO, *s.f.*, revelation, revealment, disclosure, eye-opener, discovery.

RE.VE.LA.DO, *adj.*, revealed; *Fot.*, developed.

RE.VE.LA.DOR, *s.m.*, revealer; *Fot.*, developer.

RE.VE.LAR, *v.*, to unveil, to unmask, to reveal, to disclose, to divulge, to expose.

RE.VE.LÁ.VEL, *adj.*, revealable; *Fot.*, developable.

RE.VE.LI.A, *s.f.*, default, nonsuit, non-appearance.

RE.VEN.DA, *s.f.*, resale, second sale.

RE.VEN.DE.DOR, *s.m.*, reseller; dealer; *adj.*, resale, reselling.

RE.VEN.DER, *v.*, to resale, to resell, to sell again.

RE.VER, *v.*, to see again, to review, to revise.

RE.VER.BE.RA.ÇÃO, *s.f.*, reverberation, repercussion.

RE.VER.BE.RAN.TE, *adj.*, reverberating, reverberant.

RE.VER.BE.RAR, *v.*, to reverberate, to reflect.

RE.VER.BE.RA.TÓ.RI.O, *adj.*, reverberatory.

RE.VER.DE.CI.MEN.TO, *s.m.*, verdancy.

RE.VER.DE.CER, *v.*, to make green again.

RE.VE.RÊN.CIA, *s.f.*, reverence, deference, veneration.

RE.VE.REN.CI.A.DOR, *s.m.*, reverencer, venerator; *adj.*, reverencing.

RE.VE.REN.CI.AR, *v.*, to treat with reverence, to respect.

RE.VE.REN.CI.O.SO, *adj.*, reverential, ceremonious, respectful.

RE.VE.REN.DÍS.SI.MO, *s.m.*, Right Reverend.

RE.VE.REN.DO, *s.m.*, Reverend.

RE.VE.REN.TE, *adj.*, reverent, reverential.

RE.VER.SÃO, *s.f.*, reversion, reversal.

RE.VER.SI.BI.LI.DA.DE, *s.f.*, reversibility.

RE.VER.SI.VA.MEN.TE, *adv.*, reversively, reversibly.

RE.VER.SÍ.VEL, *adj.*, reversible.

RE.VER.SI.VO, *adj.*, reversive.

RE.VER.SO, *s.m.*, backside, opposite; *adj.*, reverse, contrary, opposite.

RE.VER.TER, *v.*, to return, to go back, to revert.

RE.VER.TÉ.RI.O, *s.m., pop.*, a turn for the worse.

RE.VER.TÍ.VEL, *adj.*, revertible.

RE.VÉS, *s.m.*, reverse, backside, contrary.

RE.VES.TI.DO, *adj.*, covered, coated.

RE.VES.TI.MEN.TO, *s.m.*, revetment, revetting, coating,

REVESTIR ··· 305 ··· RISPIDEZ

facing.
RE.VES.TIR, *v.*, to revest, to dress up, to coat, to cover, to line, to overlay.
RE.VE.ZA.DO, *adj.*, alternate.
RE.VE.ZA.MEN.TO, *s.m.*, alternation, rotation, relay.
RE.VE.ZAR, *v.*, to alternate, to rotate, to relieve, to relay.
RE.VI.DAR, *v.*, to retort, to correspond, to requite, to retribute.
RE.VI.DE, *s.m.*, retaliation, reprisal.
RE.VI.GO.RA.MEN.TO, *s.m.*, reinvigoration.
RE.VI.GO.RAN.TE, *adj.*, reinvigorating.
RE.VI.GO.RAR, *v.*, to reanimate, to revive, to revigorate.
RE.VI.RA.DO, *s.m.*, *Bras.*, untidy (home), turned over.
RE.VI.RA.MEN.TO, *s.m.*, reversal.
RE.VI.RAR, *v.*, to turn, to turn over again, to twist.
RE.VI.RA.VOL.TA, *s.f.*, reversal of position, turn; turnabout.
RE.VI.SÃO, *s.f.*, revision, revisal, revise, review.
RE.VI.SAR, *v.*, to revise, to review, to check, to recense.
RE.VI.SI.O.NIS.MO, *s.m.*, revisionism.
RE.VI.SI.O.NIS.TA, *s. 2 gen.*, revisionist; *adj.*, revisionist.
RE.VI.SI.TAR, *v.*, to revisit.
RE.VI.SOR, *s.m.*, reviewer, reviser, proofreader, reader, revisor, correcter.
RE.VIS.TA, *s.f.*, magazine, review, inspection, revisal.
RE.VI.SI.TA.ÇÃO, *s.f.*, revisitation.
RE.VIS.TA.DO, *adj.*, revised, reviewed, examined.
RE.VIS.TAR, *v.*, to examine, to review, to revise, to search.
RE.VI.TA.LI.ZA.ÇÃO, *s.f.*, revitalization.
RE.VI.TA.LI.ZAR, *v.*, to revitalize, to animate again.
RE.VI.VER, *v.*, to revive, to revivify, to resuscitate.
RE.VI.VES.CER, *v.*, to revive, revivify.
RE.VI.VI.FI.CA.ÇÃO, *s.f.*, revivification.
RE.VO.A.DA, *s.f.*, flying back; flock of birds.
RE.VO.AR, *v.*, to fly again, to fly back, to soar.
RE.VO.CAR, *v.*, to revoke; to recall, to evocate, to annul.
RE.VO.GA.ÇÃO, *s.f.*, revocation, revokement.
RE.VO.GA.DO, *adj.*, revoked.
RE.VO.GAR, *v.*, to revoke, to revocate, to annul, to cancel, to recall.
RE.VOL.TA, *s.f.*, revolt, rebellion, uprising.
RE.VOL.TA.DO, *adj.*, revolted.
RE.VOL.TAN.TE, *adj.*, revolting, revolting, disgusting, repulsive.
RE.VOL.TAR, *v.*, to revolt, to rebel, to raise up against, to disgust, to resent.
RE.VOL.TO.SO, *s.m.*, rebel; *adj.*, revolted.
RE.VO.LU.ÇÃO, *s.f.*, revolution, rebellion, circular motion, rotation, insurrection.
RE.VO.LU.CI.O.NA.DOR, *s.m.*, revolutionizer; *adj.*, revolutionizing.
RE.VO.LU.CI.O.NAR, *v.*, to revolutionize.
RE.VO.LU.CI.O.NÁ.RIO, *s.m.*, revolutionary, revolutionist.
RE.VO.LU.TO, *adj.*, revolved.
RE.VÓL.VER, *s.m.*, revolver, gun, pistol.
RE.VOL.VER, *v.*, to revolve, to turn round, to turn over again.
RE.VOL.VI.DO, *adj.*, revolved, stirred.
RE.ZA, *s.f.*, prayer, praying, oration.
RE.ZA.DOR, *s.m.*, devotee; *Bras.*, faith-healer; *adj.*, praying.
RE.ZAR, *v.*, to pray, to supplicate, to mention, to say, to tell.
RI.A.CHO, *s.m.*, brook, creek, rivulet, streamlet.
RI.BAL.TA, *s.f.*, limelight, row of footlights.
RI.BAN.CEI.RA, *s.f.*, ravine, cliff, bank.

RI.BEI.RA, *s.f.*, river bank, shore; stream, streamlet, brook.
RI.BEI.RÃO, *s.m.*, stream, large brook.
RI.BEI.RI.NHO, *s.m.*, riverain dweller; *adj.*, riverside, riverine.
RI.BEI.RO, *s.m.*, rivulet, streamlet, brook, creek.
RI.BOM.BAR, *v.*, to rumble, to boom, to resound, to thunder.
RI.CA.ÇO, *s.m.*, moneygrubber.
RI.CA.MEN.TE, *adv.*, richly, prosperously, splendidly.
RÍ.CI.NO, *s.m.*, ricinus, castor-oil plant.
RI.CO, *adj.*, rich, wealthy, abundant, fertile.
RI.CO.CHE.TE.AR, *v.*, to ricochet.
RI.CO.TA, *s.f.*, *Cul.*, ricotta.
RI.DI.CU.LA.MEN.TE, *adv.*, ridiculously.
RI.DI.CU.LA.RI.ZA.ÇÃO, *s.f.*, satire, act of exciting laughter.
RI.DI.CU.LA.RI.ZAR, *v.*, to ridicule, to make fan of, to mock.
RI.DI.CU.LA.RI.ZÁ.VEL, *adj.*, that can be ridiculed.
RI.DÍ.CU.LO, *adj.*, ridiculous, comic, foolish.
RI.FA, *s.f.*, raffle.
RI.FAR, *v.*, to raffle.
RI.FLE, *s.m.*, rifle, carbine, gun.
RE.GI.CI.DA, *s. 2 gen.*, regicide (assassin of a monarch).
RE.GI.CÍ.DI.O, *s.m.*, regicide (act of killing a monarch).
RI.GI.DA.MEN.TE, *adv.*, rigidly, severely.
RI.GI.DEZ, *s.f.*, rigidity, severity, stiffness.
RÍ.GI.DO, *adj.*, rigid, stiff, severe, austere.
RI.GOR, *s.m.*, rigidity, severity, strictness, hardness.
RI.GO.RIS.MO, *s.m.*, rigorism, rigourism.
RI.GO.RO.SA.MEN.TE, *adv.*, rigorously.
RI.GO.RO.SO, *adj.*, rigorous, inflexible, rigid, severe, strict.
RI.JE.ZA, *s.f.*, hardness, rigidness.
RI.JO, *adj.*, rigid, hard, inflexible, solid, firm.
RI.LHAR, *v.*, to grind (the teeth), to gnaw, to chew.
RIM, *s.m.*, kidney.
RI.MA, *s.f.*, rhyme.
RI.MA.DO, *adj.*, rhymed, versified.
RI.MA.DOR, *s.m.*, rhymer; *adj.*, rhyming.
RI.MAR, *v.*, to rhyme, to versify.
RIN.CÃO, *s.m.*, hidden corner, sylvan retreat, nook.
RIN.ÇAR, *v.*, to rinse.
RIN.GUE, *s.m.*, ring.
RI.NHA, *s.f.*, *Bras.*, cockfights.
RI.NO.CE.RON.TE, *s.m.*, *Zool.*, rhinoceros.
RI.NO.FA.RIN.GE, *s.f.*, *Anat.*, rhinopharynx.
RI.NO.FA.RIN.GI.TE, *s.f.*, *Med.*, rhinopharyngitis.
RI.NO.LO.GI.A, *s.f.*, rhinology.
RIN.QUE, *s.m.*, *Esp.*, a roller-skating rink.
RIO, *s.m.*, river, stream, water, watercourse.
RI.O-PLA.TEN.SE, *s.*, 2 g., inhabitant of the River Plate, Argentina; *adj.*, pertaining to this region.
RI.PA, *s.f.*, lath, batten.
RI.QUE.ZA, *s.f.*, wealth, riches, abundance, money.
RIR, *v.*, to laugh, to smile.
RI.SA.DA, *s.f.*, loud laughter, laughter, laughing.
RIS.CA, *s.f.*, stripe, streak; line, ray; stroke dash; parting (of the hair).
RIS.CAR, *v.*, to scratch out, to rub out, to delete, to cross.
RIS.CO, *s.m.*, scratch, stroke, stripe, danger, hazard, risk.
RI.SÍ.VEL, *adj.*, laughable, risible.
RI.SO, *s.m.*, laughter, laughing, smile.
RI.SO.NHO, *adj.*, smiling, cheerful.
RI.SO.TO, *s.m.*, *Cul.*, risotto.
RIS.PI.DEZ, *s.f.*, roughness, severity, sternness.

RÍSPIDO · 306 · RONCADOR

RÍS.PI.DO, *adj.*, harsh, rough, severe, stern.
RIS.SO.LE, *s.m.*, rissole.
RIS.TE, *s.m., dedo em ~* : pointing finger.
RIT.MA.DO, *adj.*, rhythmic, cadenced.
RIT.MAR, *v.*, to give rhythm to, to cadence.
RÍT.MI.CA, *s.f.*, rhythmics.
RÍT.MI.CO, *adj.*, rhythmic, rhythmical.
RIT.MIS.TA, *s. 2 gen., Bras.*, percussionist.
RIT.MO, *s.m.*, rhythm, cadence.
RI.TO, *s.m.*, ceremony, rite, cult, sect.
RI.TU.AL, *s.m.*, ritual, cerimonial; *adj.*, ritual.
RI.TU.A.LIS.MO, *s.m.*, ritualism.
RI.TU.A.LIS.TA, *s. 2 gen.*, ritualist.
RI.VAL, *s. 2 gen.*, rival, antagonist, opponent.
RI.VA.LI.DA.DE, *s.f.*, rivalry, rivalship, antagonism.
RI.VA.LI.ZAR, *v.*, to rival, to compete, to dispute, to oppose.
RI.VA.LI.ZÁ.VEL, *adj.*, that can be rivalled.
RI.XA, *s.f.*, quarrel, dispute, wrangle, brawl.
RI.XAR, *v.*, to quarrel, to wrangle.
RI.XEN.TO, *adj.*, quarrelsome.
RI.ZI.CUL.TOR, *s.m.*, rice grower, rice planter.
RI.ZI.CUL.TU.RA, *s.f.*, rice-growing, rice-planting.
RO.BA.LO, *s.m., Zool.*, robalo (fish), snook (*Centropomus*).
RO.BE, *s.m., Fr.*, robe, bathrobe.
RO.BÔ, *s.m.*, robot.
RO.BO.RA.ÇÃO, *s.f.*, roboration, confirmation.
RO.BO.RAR, *v.*, to corroborate, to confirm.
RO.BÓ.TI.CA, *s.f.*, robotics.
RO.BUS.TE.CE.DOR, *adj.*, fortifying, strengthening.
RO.BUS.TE.CER, *v.*, to make strong, to strengthen, to consolidate.
RO.BUS.TEZ, *s.f.*, robustness, burliness.
RO.BUS.TO, *adj.*, robust, strong, vigorous.
RO.CA, *s.f., Tecel.*, distaff; rocks, broken stones.
RO.ÇA, *s.f.*, plantation, country, clearing, clearance.
RO.ÇA.DO, *s.m.*, cleared land, field, clearing, plantation.
RO.CAM.BO.LE, *s.m., Cul.*, roll (a kind of sweet or salty cake).
RO.CAM.BO.LES.CO, *adj.*, complicate; full of adventure and incidents.
RO.ÇAR, *v.*, to clear the land of underwood, to graze.
RO.CHA, *s.f.*, rock, stone.
RO.CHE.DO, *s.m.*, steep, rugged rock, rock, crag.
RO.CHO.SO, *adj.*, rocky, stony.
ROCK, *s.m., Ingl., Mús.*, rock-and-roll.
ROCK-AND-ROLL, *s.m., Ingl., Mús.*, rock-and-roll.
RO.DA, *s.f.*, wheel, circle, circumference, social group, clique.
RO.DA-D'Á.GUA, *s.f.*, waterwheel.
RO.DA.DA, *s.f.*, round (of drinks, cards).
RO.DA.DO, *s.m.*, wheels of a cart or carriage, track; *adj.*, equipped with wheels.
RO.DA-GI.GAN.TE, *s.f.*, Ferris wheel, big wheel.
RO.DA.MO.I.NHO, *s.m., Bras.*, the same that *redemoinho*.
RO.DA.PÉ, *s.m.*, footer, skirting board, baseboard.
RO.DAR, *v.*, to roll, to twirl, to gyrate.
RO.DA-VI.VA, *s.f.*, commotion, confusion; incessant movement.
RO.DE.A.DO, *adj.*, surrounded, encircled.
RO.DE.AR, *v.*, to surround, to encircle, to circle.
RO.DEI.O, *s.m.*, surrounding, circumlocution, evasion.
RO.DE.LA, *s.f.*, a small wheel; slice.
RO.DÍ.ZIO, *s.m.*, shift, turn, relay work.

RO.DO, *s.m.*, squeegee, rake, wooden scraper.
RO.DO.A.NEL, *s.m., UK* ring road, *US* beltway.
RO.DO.DEN.DRO, *s.m., Bot.*, rhododendron.
RO.DO.FER.RO.VI.Á.RI.O, *adj.*, rail-motor.
RO.DO.PI.AR, *v.*, to whirl about, to twirl, to spin, to circle.
RO.DO.PI.O, *s.m.*, rotation, whirl, spin, spinning, gyration.
RO.DO.VIA, *s.f., US* highway, *UK* motorway.
RO.DO.VI.Á.RI.A, *s.f.*, bus station.
RO.DO.VI.Á.RIO, *adj.*, of, pertaining to or relative to a highway.
RO.E.DOR, *s.m.*, rodent, rodents; *adj.*, rodent.
RO.ER, *v.*, to gnaw, to nibble, to bite, to chew, to corrode.
RO.GA.ÇÃO, *s.f.*, rogation.
RO.GA.DO, *adj.*, supplicated; fazer-se de ~ : to play hard to get.
RO.GA.DOR, *s.m.*, supplicant, intercessor, mediator.
RO.GAR, *v.*, to implore, to supplicate, to beg, to pray for.
RO.GA.TI.VA, *s.f.*, prayer, supplication.
RO.GO, *s.m.*, supplication, prayer, request.
RO.Í.DO, *adj.*, corroded, gnawed.
RO.JÃO, *s.m.*, rocket.
ROL, *s.m.*, roll, list, register, file, scroll.
RO.LA, *s.f., Zool.*, turtle dove.
RO.LA.GEM, *s.f., Econ.*, postponement (of debt).
RO.LA.MEN.TO, *s.m.*, rolling, welter, bearing.
RO.LAN.TE, *adj.*, rolling, rotating, revolving.
RO.LAR, *v.*, to roll, to move in circle, to tumble.
RO.LDA.NA, *s.f.*, pulley.
ROL.DÃO, *s.m.*, disorder, confusion, precipitation.
RO.LE.TA, *s.f.*, roulette.
RO.LHA, *s.f.*, cork, stopper.
RO.LI.ÇO, *adj.*, round; chubby.
RO.LO, *s.m.*, cylinder, roll, road roller.
ROM, *abrev.*, Read Only Memory: ROM.
RO.MA, *s.*, Rome.
RO.MÃ, *s.f., Bot.*, pomegranate.
RO.MAN.CE, *s.m.*, novel, fiction, love affair, tale, fable.
RO.MAN.CE.A.DO, *adj., Lit.*, novelized; romanticized, fanciful.
RO.MAN.CE.AR, *v.*, to novelize, to romanticize.
RO.MAN.CIS.TA, *s. 2 gen.*, romancist, novelist.
RO.MÂ.NI.CO, *adj.*, Romanic.
RO.MA.NO, *s.m., adj.*, Roman.
RO.MÂN.TI.CO, *adj.*, Romantic, dreamy.
RO.MAN.TIS.MO, *s.m.*, romanticism, romantism.
RO.MAN.TI.ZAR, *v.*, to romanticize.
RO.MA.RI.A, *s.f.*, pilgrimage, peregrination, procession.
RÔM.BI.CO, *adj.*, rhombic, rhombical.
ROM.BI.FOR.ME, *adj.*, rhombiform, rhomboid.
ROM.BO, *s.m.*, hole, gap, rift, split.
ROM.BU.DO, *adj.*, blunt, not sharp; *fig.*, stupid, dull.
RO.MEI.RO, *s.m.*, pilgrim, peregrinator.
RO.MÊNIA, *s.*, Rumania.
RO.ME.NO, *s.m., adj.*, Rumanian, Romanian.
ROM.PAN.TE, *s.m.*, fury, impetuosity, vehemence; *adj.*, arrogant, proud.
ROM.PE.DOR, *s.m.*, destroyer, breaker; *adj.*, breaking, destroying.
ROM.PE.DU.RA, *s.f.*, rupture, disruption, fracture.
ROM.PER, *v.*, to break, to break up, to destroy, to tear.
ROM.PI.MEN.TO, *s.m.*, breaking, disruption, split, rupture.
RON.CA.DOR, *s.m.*, snorer; *Bras., pop.*, waterfall; *adj.*, snoring; roaring.

RONCAR · 307 · RUM

RON.CAR, *v.*, to snore.
RON.CO, *s.m.*, snore, snoring.
RON.DA, *s.f.*, patrol, rounds, prowl.
RON.DA.DOR, *s.m.*, *adj.*, rondante.
RON.DAN.TE, *s. 2 gen.*, patrolman, watchman; *adj.*, patrolling, inspecting.
RON.DAR, *v.*, to round, to watch, to walk around.
RO.SA, *s.f.*, *Bot.*, rose; *adj.*, rosy, rose-coloured, pink.
RO.SÁ.CEA, *s.f.*, rosette, plant of the rose family.
RO.SA-CHO.QUE, *s.m.*, shocking pink colour; *adj.*, shocking pink.
RO.SA.DO, *adj.*, rose-coloured, rosy, rosate.
RODA DOS VENTOS, *s.f.*, wind rose.
RO.SÁ.RIO, *s.m.*, rosary.
RO.SA-SHOCKING, *s.m.*, *adj.*, the same that *rosa-choque*.
ROS.BI.FE, *s.m.*, roast-beef.
ROS.CA, *s.f.*, thread, screw thread, spiral.
RO.SEI.RA, *s.f.*, *Bot.*, rosebush.
RO.SEI.RAL, *s.m.*, *Bot.*, rosary, rosetum.
RÓ.SEO, *adj.*, rose, rose-coloured.
RO.SE.TA, *s.f.*, a little rose; rosette; rowel.
ROS.MA.NI.NHO, *s.m.*, *Bot.*, rosemary.
ROS.NA.DOR, *s.m.*, grumbler; *adj.*, snarling, growling.
ROS.NAR, *v.*, to snarl, to growl.
ROS.NEN.TO, *adj.*, snarling.
ROS.QUE.A.DO, *adj.*, provided with screw threads.
ROS.QUE.AR, *v.*, to provide with screw threads.
ROS.QUI.LHA, *s.f.*, ring-shaped small loaf, doughnut.
ROS.QUI.NHA, *s.f.*, ring-shaped cooky, doughnut.
ROS.TO, *s.m.*, face, visage, physiognomy.
RO.TA, *s.f.*, direction, route, course, path.
RO.TA.ÇÃO, *s.f.*, rotation, gyration, rolling.
RO.TÁ.CE.O, *adj.*, wheel-shaped.
RO.TA.TI.VA, *s.f.*, rotary press.
RO.TA.TI.VI.DA.DE, *s.f.*, turning; turnover.
RO.TA.TI.VO, *adj.*, rotative, rotational, rotary.
RO.TA.TÓ.RI.O, *adj.*, rotatory, rotating, rotative, rotational.
RO.TEI.RIS.TA, *s. 2 gen.*, scriptwriter.
RO.TEI.RI.ZAR, *v.*, *Bras.*, *Cin.*, to write anscreenplay.
RO.TEI.RO, *s.m.*, itinerary, route, schedule, road-book, norm; *Cin.*, screenplay, script.
RO.TI.NA, *s.f.*, routine, custom, practice, rut.
RO.TI.NEI.RO, *adj.*, routine, routinish, habitual, customary.
RO.TIS.SE.RI.A, *s.f.*, a shop where broiled meats, cold cuts and cheese are sold.
RO.TO, *adj.*, ragged, ratty, shabby.
RÓ.TU.LA, *s.f.*, *Anat.*, knee-cap, rotula, patella; grating.
RO.TU.LA.ÇÃO, *s.f.*, labelling.
RO.TU.LA.DO, *adj.*, labelled, *fig.*, designated.
RO.TU.LAR, *v.*, to label, to mark, to designate.
RÓ.TU.LO, *s.m.*, label, mark, ticket.
RO.TUN.DO, *adj.*, rotund, round, roundish.
ROU.BA.DO, *adj.*, robbed, stolen, despoiled.
ROU.BA.LHEI.RA, *s.f.*, robbery.
ROU.BAR, *v.*, to rob, to steal, to plunder, to hold up.
ROU.BO, *s.m.*, robbery, theft, loot.
ROU.CA.MEN.TE, *adv.*, hoarsely.
ROU.CO, *adj.*, hoarse, raucous, harsh, husky.
ROU.FE.NHO, *adj.*, raucous, hoarse, husky.
ROUND, *s.m.*, *Ingl.*, *Esp.*, round (boxing).
ROU.PA, *s.f.*, clothes, clothing, vesture, wear, dress, garment; *roupa-branca*: body linen.
ROU.PA.GEM, *s.f.*, clothing, garments.
ROU.PÃO, *s.m.*, dressing gown, bathing gown.
ROU.PA.RI.A, *s.f.*, heap of clothes, clothes shop.
ROU.PEI.RO, *s.m.*, wardrobe, clothes closet.
ROU.QUEI.RA, *s.f.*, the same that *rouquidão*.
ROU.QUE.JAR, *v.*, to caw, to croak, to suffer from hoarseness.
ROU.QUI.DÃO, *s.f.*, hoarseness, huskiness.
ROU.XI.NOL, *s.m.*, *Zool.*, nightingale.
RO.XE.AR, *v.*, to purple.
RO.XO, *s.m.*, purple hue; *adj.*, violet, purple.
ROYALTY, *s.m.*, *Ingl.*, royalty.
RU.A, *s.f.*, street, way; *interj.*, rua!: get out!, out you go!
RU.BÉO.LA, *s.f.*, *Med.*, rubeola.
RU.BI, *s.m.*, *Min.*, ruby.
RU.BI.Á.CE.A, *s.f.*, *Bot.*, Rubiaceae, a family of the coffee plant, coffee (*Coffea arabica*).
RU.BI.FI.CAR, *v.*, to rubify.
RU.BOR, *s.m.*, redness, shame, modesty.
RU.BO.RES.CER, *v.*, to make red, redden; *fig.*, to feel shame; *ruborescer-se*: to become red.
RU.BO.RI.ZA.ÇÃO, *s.f.*, blushing.
RU.BO.RI.ZAR, *v.*, to redden, to rubify, to become red.
RU.BRI.CA, *s.f.*, rubric, initials, sign.
RU.BRI.CA.DO, *adj.*, rubricated, countersigned.
RU.BRI.CA.DOR, *s.m.*, rubricator; *adj.*, rubricating.
RU.BRI.CAR, *v.*, to rubricate, to countersign.
RU.BRI.CIS.TA, *s. 2 gen.*, an expert in rubrics.
RU.BRO, *adj.*, rouge, ruby-red, rubious.
RU.DE, *adj.*, rude, uncultivated, indelicate, rough, harsh.
RU.DE.MEN.TE, *adv.*, rudely.
RU.DEZ, **RU.DE.ZA**, *s.f.*, rudeness, crudity, roughness.
RU.DI.MEN.TAR, *adj.*, rudimental.
RU.DI.MEN.TO, *s.m.*, rudiment, element, beginning.
RU.EI.RO, *s.m.*, person who likes to live on the streets; street dweller; *adj.*, gadabout.
RU.E.LA, *s.f.*, bystreet, alley.
RU.FA.DOR, *s.m.*, drummer; *adj.*, drumming.
RU.FAR, *v.*, to drum; to beat (the drum).
RU.FI.ÃO, *s.m.*, ruffian, hooligan.
RU.GA, *s.f.*, wrinkle, corrugation.
RÚG.BI, *s.m.*, *Esp.*, rugby.
RU.GE, *s.m.*, rouge.
RU.GI.DO, *s.m.*, roar, bellow, growl.
RU.GI.DOR, *s.m.*, roarer; *adj.*, roaring.
RU.GIR, *v.*, to bellow, to roar.
RU.GO.SI.DA.DE, *s.f.*, rugosity.
RU.GO.SO, *adj.*, rugose, rugous.
RU.Í.DO, *s.m.*, noise, sound, din, hubbub, uproar, clamour, tumult, row.
RU.I.DO.SA.MEN.TE, *adv.*, noisily, boisterously.
RU.I.DO.SO, *adj.*, noisy, loud, boisterous.
RU.IM, *adj.*, bad, ill, miserable, wicked.
RU.Í.NA, *s.f.*, ruin, wreck, collapse, downfall, deterioration.
RU.IN.DA.DE, *s.f.*, wickedness.
RU.I.NO.SA.MEN.TE, *adv.*, ruinously.
RU.I.NO.SO, *adj.*, ruinous, pernicious, destructive.
RU.IR, *v.*, to collapse, to fall into ruins, to crash.
RUI.VO, *s.m.*, redhead; *adj.*, red-haired, rufous.
RU.LÊ, *adj.*, *gola rulê*: turtleneck collar.
RUM, *s.m.*, rum.

RUMAR

RUVINHOSO

RU.MAR, *v.*, to steer to, to head for, to set a course.
RUM.BA, *s.f.*, rumba (Afro-Cuban dance and music).
RUM.BEI.RO, *s.m.*, a rumba singer or dancer.
RU.MI.NA.ÇÃO, *s.f.*, rumination; *fig.*, reflection, consideration.
RU.MI.NA.DOR, *s.m.*, ruminant; *adj.*, ruminating.
RU.MI.NAN.TE, *s. 2 gen.*, ruminant, ruminator.
RU.MI.NAR, *v.*, to ruminate, to chew the cud.
RU.MO, *s.m.*, route, course, direction, setting, set.
RU.MOR, *s.m.*, rumour, gossip, din, murmur.
RU.MO.RAR, *v.*, the same that *rumorejar*.
RU.MO.RE.JAN.TE, *adj.*, murmuring, rustling, soughing.
RU.MO.RE.JAR, *v.*, to rustle, to buzz, to murmur.
RU.MO.RE.JO, *s.m.*, rustle, buzz, murmur (of voices).
RU.MO.RO.SO, *adj.*, loud, noisy, clamorous.
RU.NA, *s.f., Hist.*, character of the runic alphabet.
RU.PES.TRE, *adj.*, growing on rocks, rupestrian.
RÚP.TIL, *adj.*, breakable.

RUP.TU.RA, *s.f.*, breakage, rupture, breach, disruption.
RU.RAL, *adj.*, rural, rustic.
RU.RA.LIS.MO, *s.m.*, ruralism.
RU.RA.LIS.TA, *s. 2 gen.*, ruralist.
RU.RA.LI.ZAR, *v.*, to ruralize, *ruralizar-se*: to become rural.
RUS.GA, *s.f.*, noise, confusion, brawl, row.
RUS.GUEN.TO, *adj.*, quarrelsome, noisy.
RUSH, *s.m., Ingl.*, rush; *hora do ~*: rush hour.
RÚS.SIA, *s.f.*, Russia.
RUS.SI.FI.CAR, *v.*, to Russify, Russianize.
RUS.SO, *adj., s.m.*, Russian.
RUS.TI.CA.MEN.TE, *adv.*, rustically.
RUS.TI.CI.DA.DE, *s.f.*, rusticity, rusticalness.
RÚS.TI.CO, *adj.*, rustic, rural, bucolic, rough.
RU.TI.LAN.TE, *adj.*, rutilant, bright, shining.
RU.TI.LAR, *v.*, to rutilate, to shine, to glitter, to gleam.
RU.VI.NHO.SO, *adj.*, rusty.

S, s.m., eighteenth letter of the Portuguese alphabet.
SÃ, adj. fem., healthy.
S.A., s.f., abrev. of *Sociedade Anônima*: limited company, Ltd.
SAARIANO, s.m., adj., Saharian.
SA.BÁ, s.m., supposed midnight reunion of witches.
SÁ.BA.DO, s.m., Saturday.
SA.BÃO, s.m., soap; *sabão de coco*: coconut soap.
SA.BÁ.TI.CO, adj., sabbatical, referring to Saturday.
SA.BA.TI.NA, s.f., schoolar examination (usually on Saturdays); fig., discussion (in Saturday).
SA.BA.TI.NAR, v., to recapitulate, to review; to summarize.
SA.BE.DOR, s.m., learned person; adj., learned, knowing.
SA.BE.DO.RI.A, s.f., wisdom, knowledge.
SA.BER, s.m., knowledge; learning, erudition, wisdom.
SA.BER, v., to know, to be aware or cognizant of, to recognize, to identify.
SA.BI.Á, s.m., Zool., song-thrush.
SA.BI.Á-LA.RAN.JEI.RA, s.m., Bras, Zool., rufous bellied thrush (*Turdus rufiventris*).
SA.BI.A.MEN.TE, adv., wisely.
SA.BI.CHÃO, s.m., smarty, wise-guy, egghead; adj., clever, learned, erudite.
SA.BI.DA.MEN.TE, adv., clearly, evidently.
SA.BI.DO, adj., known, wise, intelligent, learned.
SA.BI.NO, s.m., Sabine (member of an ancient people of the Apennines); adj., Sabine.
SÁ.BIO, s.m., scientist, wise, adj., learned, erudite, scholarly.
SA.BÍ.VEL, adj., knowable.
SA.BO.NE.TE, s.m., toilet soap.
SA.BO.NE.TEI.RA, s.f., soap dish, soap bowl.
SA.BOR, s.m., flavor, taste, savour.
SA.BO.RE.AR, v., to taste, to relish, to savour.
SA.BO.RE.Á.VEL, adj., that can be tasted or savoured.
SA.BO.RO.SA.MEN.TE, adv., pleasantly.
SA.BO.RO.SO, adj., savoury, tasty, palatable.
SA.BO.TA.DOR, s.m., saboteur (Fr.).
SA.BO.TA.GEM, s.f., sabotage, intentional damage.
SA.BO.TAR, v., to sabotage, to sabotage, to wreck, to sap.
SA.BU.GAL, s.m., field of the elderberry trees.
SA.BU.GAR, v., Bras., to spank, to flog.
SA.BU.GO, s.m., slough, pith.
SA.BU.GUEI.RO, s.m., Bras., Bot., elder tree.
SA.BU.JAR, v., to flatter, to cajole.
SA.BU.JI.CE, s.f., fawning, wheedling.
SA.BU.JO, s.m., hunting dog; fig., fawner, toady; adj., referring to a fawner.
SA.CA, s.f., bag, surf.
SA.CA.DA, s.f., balcony, terrace.
SA.CA.DE.LA, s.f., pull, yank.
SA.CA.DO, s.m., Com., Jur., drawee.
SA.CA.DOR, s.m., Com., Jur., drawer; adj., Com., drawing.
SA.CAL, adj., gír., boring, annoying.

SA.CA.NA, s.m., gír., rascal fellow; adj., gír., filthy, rascal.
SA.CA.NA.GEM, s.f., Bras., gír., filthy behaviour, derision, raillery, mockery.
SA.CA.NE.AR, v., Bras., gír., to rascal; to infamous behaviour.
SA.CAR, v., to draw out, to tear out, to pull out, to extract, to drag.
SA.CA.RI.A, s.f., a quantity of sacks.
SA.ÇA.RI.CAR, v., to wriggle, to squirm (in dancing).
SA.ÇA.RI.CO, s.m., Bras., pop., act of wriggling in dancing.
SA.CA.RÍ.FE.RO, adj., saccharic, sacchariferous.
SA.CA.RI.FI.CA.ÇÃO, s.f., saccharification.
SA.CA.RI.FI.CA.DOR, adj., that saccharifies.
SA.CA.RI.FI.CAR, v., to saccharify (convert into sugar).
SA.CA.RI.NA, s.f., saccharin.
SA.CA-RO.LHAS, s.m., corkscrew.
SA.CER.DÓ.CIO, s.m., priesthood.
SA.CER.DO.TAL, adj., sacerdotal, priestly.
SA.CER.DO.TA.LIS.MO, s.m., sacerdotalism.
SA.CER.DO.TE, s.m., priest, clergyman.
SA.CER.DO.TI.SA, s.f., priestess.
SA.CHÊ, s.m., Fr., sachet.
SA.CHO, s.m., spud.
SA.CI, s.m., Bras., pop., Saci Pererê (fantastic entity: black boy with one leg).
SA.CI.A.ÇÃO, s.f., action of satiating oneself.
SA.CI.A.DO, adj., satiated, satisfied.
SA.CI.AR, v., to satiate, to appease, to satisfy, to gratify, to satisfy.
SA.CI.Á.VEL, adj., satiable.
SA.CIE.DA.DE, s.f., satiety.
SA.CO, s.m., sack, bag, ball, sac, sackcloth.
SA.CO.LA, s.f., wallet, knapsack.
SA.CO.LÃO, s.m., greengrocer's.
SA.CO.LEI.RO, s.m., UK pedlar, US peddler.
SA.CO.LE.JAR, v., to shake, agitate.
SA.CO.LE.JO, s.m., shaking.
SA.CRA, s.f., Rel., canon of the mass.
SA.CRA.LI.ZA.ÇÃO, s.f., act of making sacred.
SA.CRA.LI.ZAR, v., to make sacred.
SA.CRA.MEN.TA.DO, s.m., person who has received a sacrament; adj., said of such a person.
SA.CRA.MEN.TAL, adj., sacramental; fig., consuetudinary, customary.
SA.CRA.MEN.TAR, v., to administer or receive the sacrament.
SA.CRA.MEN.TO, s.m., sacrament.
SA.CRI.FI.CA.DOR, s.m., sacrificer; adj., sacrificing.
SA.CRI.FI.CAL, adj., sacrificial.
SA.CRI.FI.CAN.TE, s. 2 gen., sacrificer; adj., sacrificing.
SA.CRI.FI.CAR, v., to sacrifice, to offer.
SA.CRI.FI.CA.TÓ.RI.O, adj., sacrificial.
SA.CRI.FI.CÁ.VEL, adj., that which can be sacrificed.
SA.CRI.FÍ.CIO, s.m., sacrifice, self-denial, immolation.

SACRILÉGIO — 310 — SALOBRO

SA.CRI.LÉ.GIO, *s.m.*, sacrilege, profanation, irreverence.
SA.CRÍ.LE.GO, *adj.*, sacrilegious, irreverent.
SA.CRIS.TÃO, *s.m.*, sacristan, sexton.
SA.CRIS.TI.A, *s.f.*, sacristy.
SA.CRO, *s.m.*, sacrum; *adj.*, holy, sacred, venerable.
SA.CROS.SAN.TO, *adj.*, sacrosanct.
SA.CU.DI.DA, *s.f.*, shake, toss, tossing, shaking.
SA.CU.DI.DE.LA, *s.f.*, shaking, jolt.
SA.CU.DI.DO, *adj.*, shaken, jerked, quick, agile.
SA.CU.DI.DOR, *s.m.*, shaker; *adj.*, shaking.
SA.CU.DIR, *v.*, to shake, to shake off, to move, to rock, to vibrate.
SÁ.DI.CO, *s.m.*, sadist; *adj.*, sadistic.
SA.DI.O, *adj.*, healthy, healthful, sound.
SA.DIS.MO, *s.m.*, sadism.
SA.DO.MA.SO.QUIS.MO, *s.m.*, sadomasochism.
SA.DO.MA.SO.QUIS.TA, *s. 2 gen.*, sadomasochist individual; *adj.*, sadomasochist.
SA.FA.DA.GEM, *s.f.*, *Bras.*, rascality, trickishness, shamelessness.
SA.FA.DE.ZA, *s.f.*, knavishness, rascality, baseness.
SA.FA.DIS.MO, *s.m.*, *Bras.*, knavishness, trickishness.
SA.FA.DO, *s.m.*, trickster, rogue; *adj.*, shameless, immoral, roguish.
SA.FA.NÃO, *s.m.*, flounce, fling, push, jerk.
SA.FAR, *v.*, to take away, to wear out, to steal.
SA.FAR.DA.NA, *s.m.*, rascal, scoundrel, contemptible.
SA.FÁ.RI, *s.m.*, safari.
SA.FA.RI.A, *adj.*, designative of a sort of pomegranate.
SA.FE.NA, *s.f.*, *Anat.*, saphena.
SA.FI.RA, *s.f.*, sapphire(color and precious stone).
SA.FRA, *s.f.*, crop, harvest.
SA.FREI.RO, *s.m.*, *Bras.*, auxiliary farm hand during harvest.
SA.FRE.JAR, *v.*, to run a sugar mill.
SA.GA, *s.f.*, saga, tale, story.
SA.GA.CI.DA.DE, *s.f.*, sagacity, perspicacity.
SA.GAZ, *adj.*, sagacious, astute, intelligent, apprehensive.
SA.GI.TA.RI.A.NO, *s.m.*, *adj.*, Sagittarian.
SA.GI.TÁ.RI.O, *s.m.*, *Astron.*, Sagittarius (constellation); *Astrol.*, sign of the Zodiac.
SA.GRA.ÇÃO, *s.f.*, consecration.
SA.GRA.DO, *adj.*, sacred, holy, hallowed.
SA.GRAR, *v.*, to consecrate, to sanctify.
SA.GUÃO, *s.m.*, entrance-hall, lobby, vestibule.
SA.GUI, *s.m.*, *Bras.*, *Zool.*, tamarin, marmoset.
SAI.A, *s.f.*, skirt.
SAI.A-CAL.ÇA, *s.f.*, culottes.
SAI.BRO, *s.m.*, gross sand.
SAI.BRO.SO, *adj.*, gravelly, sandy.
SA.Í.DA, *s.f.*, departure, output, exit, check up.
SA.Í.DA DE PRAI.A, *s.f.*, beach wrap.
SA.I.DEI.RA, *s.f.*, *Bras.*, *gír.*, one for the road.
SAI.O.TE, *s.m.*, petticoat.
SA.IR, *v.*, to go, to come or step out, to quit, to leave.
SAL, *s.m.*, salt.
SA.LA, *s.f.*, room, saloon, hall.
SA.LA.CI.DA.DE, *s.f.*, lewdness, lechery.
SA.LA.DA, *s.f.*, salad, mess, confusion; *salada de frutas*: fruit salad.
SA.LA.DEI.RA, *s.f.*, salad dish.
SA.LA.DEI.RIS.TA, *s.m.*, *Bras.*, owner of a dried meat industry.

SA.LA.FRÁ.RI.O, *s.m.*, *pop.*, bounder, scoundrel.
SA.LA.MA.LE.QUE, *s.m.*, salaam (Turkish salutation).
SA.LA.MAN.DRA, *s.f.*, *Zool.*, salamander.
SA.LA.ME, *s.m.*, salami, sausage.
SA.LA.MI.NHO, *s.m.*, a small salami, a variety of salami.
SA.LÃO, *s.m.*, saloon, salon, ball-room.
SA.LA.RI.A.DO, *s.m.*, wage earner.
SA.LA.RI.AL, *adj.*, *Bras.*, of or referring to salaries or wages.
SA.LÁ.RIO, *s.m.*, salary, wages.
SA.LÁ.RIO-BA.SE, *s.m.*, basic wage, base pay.
SA.LÁ.RIO-FA.MÍ.LI.A, *s.m.*, *Bras.*, extra pay for employees with dependants.
SA.LÁ.RIO-HO.RA, *s.m.*, a wage paid for one hour of work.
SAL.DA.DO, *adj.*, settled (account), paid-up, free from obligations.
SAL.DA.DOR, *s.m.*, person who settles accounts; *adj.*, that settles accounts.
SAL.DAR, *v.*, to liquidate, to pay.
SAL.DO, *s.m.*, balance, remainder.
SA.LEI.RO, *s.m.*, salt-cellar, salt-shaker.
SA.LE.SI.A.NO, *s.m.*, *adj.*, *Rel.*, Salesian.
SA.LE.TA, *s.f.*, small hall, sitting-room.
SAL.GA.ÇÃO, *s.f.*, salting.
SAL.GA.DI.NHOS, *s.m.*, *pl.*, appetizers.
SAL.GA.DO, *adj.*, salted, salty.
SAL.GA.DOR, *s.m.*, salter; *adj.*, referring to a salter.
SAL.GAR, *v.*, to salt, to cure.
SAL.GUEI.RAL, *s.m.*, where they grow the willows.
SAL.GUEI.RO, *s.m.*, willow.
SA.LI.CÍ.LI.CO, *adj.*, *Quím.*, salicylic.
SA.LI.ÊN.CIA, *s.f.*, salience, prominence.
SA.LI.EN.TAR, *v.*, to point out, to accentuate, to emphasize, to jut out.
SA.LI.EN.TE, *adj.*, salient, prominent.
SA.LÍ.FE.RO, *adj.*, saliferous.
SA.LI.FI.CA.ÇÃO, *s.f.*, *Quím.*, salification.
SA.LI.FI.CAR, *v.*, *Quím.*, to salify.
SA.LI.FI.CÁ.VEL, *adj.*, salifiable.
SA.LI.NA, *s.f.*, saline, salt-works, salt-pit, salt-mine.
SA.LI.NA.ÇÃO, *s.f.*, *Quím.*, salt manufacturing process.
SA.LI.NAR, *v.*, to make salt formthrough the evaporation of water.
SA.LI.NÁ.VEL, *adj.*, salifiable.
SA.LI.NI.DA.DE, *s.f.*, saltishness, saltiness, salinity.
SA.LI.NI.ZA.ÇÃO, *s.f.*, salinization.
SA.LI.NI.ZA.DO, *adj.*, salinized.
SA.LI.NO, *adj.*, saline, salt.
SA.LI.TRE, *s.m.*, salpettre, nitre.
SA.LI.TREI.RO, *s.m.*, saltpetre-man, saltpetre-maker; *adj.*, producing saltpetre.
SA.LI.VA, *s.f.*, spittle, saliva.
SA.LI.VA.ÇÃO, *s.f.*, salivation.
SA.LI.VAL, *adj.*, salivary.
SA.LI.VAN.TE, *adj.*, salivating.
SA.LI.VAR, *v.*, to salivate, to drivel.
SA.LI.VO.SO, *adj.*, salivary.
SAL.MÃO, *s.m.*, salmon.
SAL.MO, *s.m.*, psalm.
SAL.MO.NE.LA, *Biol.*, salmonella.
SAL.MOU.RA, *s.f.*, brine, pickle, reproof.
SA.LO.BRO, *adj.*, briny, brackish.

SALPICADO   ·· 311 ··   SÃO

SAL.PI.CA.DO, *adj.*, sprinkled with salt; *fig.*, speckled.
SAL.PI.CÃO, *s.m.*, smoked hamor sausage; *Bras., Cul.*, a dish prepared with chopped chicken, bacon or pork.
SAL.PI.CAR, *v.*, to besprinkle, splash.
SAL.PI.CO, *s.m.*, sprinkle, splash, speck.
SAL.SA, *s.f.*, garden parsley, sharp sauce.
SAL.SÃO, *s.m., Bot.*, celery (*Apium graveolens*).
SAL.SEI.RO, *s.m.*, downpour; *Bras.*, disorder, discord, brawl.
SAL.SI.CHA, *s.f.*, sausage.
SAL.SI.CHÃO, *s.m.*, largesausage.
SAL.SI.CHA.RI.A, *s.f.*, factory or shop of sausage.
SAL.SI.NHA, *s.f.*, diminutive of *salsa*; parsley.
SAL.TA.DO, *adj.*, projecting, protruding.
SAL.TA.DOR, *s.m.*, leaper, jumper; *adj.*, leaping, jumping.
SAL.TAR, *v.*, to leap, to jump, to skip, to spring, to bound.
SAL.TE.A.DA, *s.f.*, big leap; assault.
SAL.TE.A.DO, *adj.*, attacked, assaulted.
SAL.TE.A.DOR, *s.m.*, bandit, brigant, footpad.
SAL.TE.AR, *v.*, to assault, to rob.
SAL.TEI.RO, *s.m.*, person who makes heels for shoes.
SAL.TIM.BAN.CO, *s.m.*, juggler, acrobat.
SAL.TI.TAN.TE, *adj.*, saltatory; skipping, tripping.
SAL.TI.TAR, *v.*, to hop, to jump, to digress.
SAL.TO, *s.m.*, leap, bound, hop, jump, vault; shoe heel.
SAL.TO MOR.TAL, *s.m.*, somersault.
SA.LU.BRE, *adj.*, salutary, salubrious.
SA.LU.BRI.DA.DE, *s.f.*, salubrity, salubriousness, wholesomeness, healthfulness.
SA.LU.BRI.FI.CA.ÇÃO, *s.f.*, act of making salubrious.
SA.LU.BRI.FI.CAR, *v.*, to make healthy; to cleanse.
SA.LU.TAR, *adj.*, salutary, profitable, healthful.
SA.LU.TÍ.FE.RO, *adj., Lit.*, salutary, wholesome.
SAL.VA, *s.f.*, salvia, sage.
SAL.VA.ÇÃO, *s.f.*, salvation, salvage.
SAL.VA.DOR, *s.m.*, savior, rescuer, deliverer, redeemer.
SAL.VA.GEM, *s.f.*, ancient piece of artillery; savage, barbarian; *adj., Ant.*, savage.
SAL.VA.GUAR.DA, *s.f.*, safeguard, protection.
SAL.VA.GUAR.DAR, *v.*, to safeguard, to defend, to protect.
SAL.VA.MEN.TO, *s.m.*, salvation, rescue.
SAL.VAR, *v.*, to save, to rescue, to free, to deliver.
SAL.VA-VI.DAS, *s.m.*, life-saver, life-belt.
SAL.VE!, *interj.*, hail!
SAL.VE-RA.I.NHA, *s.f., Rel.*, Hail Mary (a Catholic prayer).
SÁL.VI.A, *s.f., Bot.*, sage.
SAL.VÍ.NI.A, *s.f., Bot.*, salvinia.
SAL.VO, *adj.*, safe, unhurt, secure, unmolested; *prep.*, save, except, unless.
SAL.VO-CON.DU.TO, *s.m.*, safe-conduct.
SA.MAM.BAI.A, *s.f., Bot.*, fern.
SA.MAM.BAI.AL, *s.m., Bot.*, place rich offerns.
SAM.BA, *s.m.*, samba.
SAM.BA-CAN.ÇÃO, *s.m., Mús.*, modality of samba song.
SAM.BA-EN.RE.DO, *s.m., Mús.*, a samba song that tells a story or has a plot.
SAM.BAR, *v., Bras.*, to dance the samba; *fig.*, to dance.
SAM.BIS.TA, *s. 2 gen., Bras.*, a samba composer.
SAM.BO.CAR, *v., Bras., pop.*, to extract, to draw out.
SAM.BÓ.DRO.MO, *s.m.*, track along which samba schools parade.

SA.MO.VAR, *s.m.*, samovar.
SA.NAR, *v.*, to cure, to heal.
SA.NA.TI.VO, *adj.*, sanative, curative.
SA.NA.TÓ.RIO, *s.m.*, sanatorium, health resort.
SA.NÁ.VEL, *adj.*, curable, healable.
SAN.ÇÃO, *s.f.*, sanction, ratification, decree.
SAN.CIO.NA.DO, *adj.*, sanctioned.
SAN.CI.O.NA.DOR, *s.m.*, ratifier; *adj.*, sanctioning, ratifying.
SAN.CIO.NAR, *v.*, to sanction, to confirm, to approbate.
SAN.DÁ.LIA, *s.f.*, sandal.
SÂN.DA.LO, *s.m.*, sandalwood (tree and perfume).
SAN.DI.CE, *s.f.*, folly, stupidity, nonsense.
SAN.DU.Í.CHE, *s.m.*, sandwich.
SAN.DU.I.CHEI.RA, *s.f.*, hot sandwich-making machine.
SA.NE.A.DOR, *s.m.*, sanitary, improving, curing.
SA.NEA.MEN.TO, *s.m.*, sanitation, cleaning.
SA.NE.AR, *v.*, to sanitate, to clean.
SA.NE.Á.VEL, *adj.*, that can be improved.
SAN.FO.NA, *s.f.*, accordion, hurdy-gurdy.
SAN.FO.NA.DO, *adj.*, pleated or folded; folding (door).
SAN.FO.NEI.RO, *s.m.*, an accordionist, a hurdy-gurdy playe.
SAN.GRA.DEI.RA, *s.f.*, tool used for rubber latex extraction.
SAN.GRA.DO, *adj.*, bloody, wounded; *fig.*, exhausted.
SAN.GRA.DOR, *s.m.*, bleeder, blood-letter. adj that bleeds.
SAN.GRA.DOU.RO, *s.m., Bras.*, water furrow, drainage ditch; *Bras.*, throat or canyon.
SAN.GRAR, *v.*, to bleed, to open a vein.
SAN.GREN.TA.MEN.TE, *adv.*, bloodily.
SAN.GREN.TO, *adj.*, bloody, sanguinary.
SAN.GRI.A, *s.f.*, bleeding, sangria.
SAN.GUE, *s.m.*, blood; race, lineage.
SAN.GUE-DE-BOI, *s.m., Bras., Zool.*, vermilion flycatcher (bird).
SAN.GUES.SU.GA, *s.f.*, leech, bloodsucking worm.
SAN.GUI.FI.CA.ÇÃO, *s.f., Med.*, sanguification.
SAN.GUI.FI.CAR, *v.*, to sanguify.
SAN.GUI.NÁ.RIO, *adj.*, sanguinary.
SAN.GUÍ.NEO, *adj.*, sanguine, sanguineous.
SA.NHA, *s.f.*, wrath, fury, rage.
SA.NHA.ÇO, *s.m., Bras., Zool.*, common name for birds especially of the genus Thraupis.
SA.NI.DA.DE, *s.f.*, sanity, sanitation, hygiene.
SA.NI.FI.CA.ÇÃO, *s.f.*, sanitization.
SA.NI.FI.CAR, *v.*, to sanitate.
SA.NI.O.SO, *adj., Med.*, sanious.
SA.NI.TA.RI.A.MEN.TE, *adv.*, sanitarily.
SA.NI.TÁ.RIO, *s.m.*, toilet, adj., sanitary.
SA.NI.TA.RIS.TA, *s. 2 gen.*, sanitarian, sanitarist, hygienist.
SÂNS.CRI.TO, *s.m.*, Sanskrit.
SAN.TA CA.TA.RI.NA, *s.*, Santa Catarina (state of Brazil).
SAN.TI.DA.DE, *s.f.*, holiness, sanctity.
SAN.TI.FI.CA.ÇÃO, *s.f.*, sanctification, sanctifying.
SAN.TI.FI.CA.DO, *adj.*, sanctified, blessed, sacred.
SAN.TI.FI.CAN.TE, *adj.*, sanctifying.
SAN.TI.FI.CAR, *v.*, to sanctify, to hallow, to glorify.
SAN.TI.FI.CÁ.VEL, *adj.*, sanctifiable.
SAN.TI.NHO, *s.m.*, diminutive of *santo*; little image of a saint; *col.*, well-behaved person.
SAN.TO, *s.m.*, saint; *adj.*, saint, saintly, holy, pure; *Dia de Todos os Santos*: All Saints'Day.
SAN.TU.Á.RIO, *s.m.*, sanctuary, a holy place, temple, refuge.
SÃO, *s.m.*, saint; *adj.*, sound, healthy, sane, robust.

SAPA · 312 · SAUDOSO

SA.PA, *s.f.*, spade, shovel.
SA.PA.RI.A, *s.f.*, a lot of frogs.
SA.PA.TA, *s.f., Arquit.*, console bracket on the foundation; low shoe, slipper.
SA.PA.TA.DA, *s.f.*, blow with a shoe.
SA.PA.TÃO, *s.m.*, augmentative of *sapato*: a large shoe; clodhopper; *Bras., pop.*, lesbian.
SA.PA.TA.RI.A, *s.f.*, shoe store, shoemaking.
SA.PA.TE.A.DO, *s.m.*, tap-dance, tap-dancing.
SA.PA.TE.A.DOR, *s.m.*, tap-dancer.
SA.PA.TE.AR, *v.*, to tap-dance.
SA.PA.TEI.O, *s.m.*, tap-dancing.
SA.PA.TEI.RA, *s.f.*, shoe closet.
SA.PA.TEI.RO, *s.m.*, shoemaker.
SA.PA.TI.LHA, *s.f.*, ballet shoe, ballet slipper; pump.
SA.PA.TI.NHO, *s.m.*, diminutive of *sapato*: small shoe; child's shoe.
SA.PA.TO, *s.m.*, shoe.
SA.PÉ, SA.PÊ, *s.m., Bras.*, satintail (much used for thatching, covering); *Bras.*, basket.
SA.PE.AR, *v., Bras.*, to look on.
SA.PE.CA, *s.f.*, flirt, coquette.
SA.PE.CAR, *v., Bras.*, to dry, to singe, to scorch; *Bras., fig.*, to flirt, to loaf.
SA.PI.ÊN.CI.A, *s.f.*, wisdom, scholarship.
SA.PI.EN.TE, *adj.*, sapient, wise.
SA.PI.NHO, *s.m.*, diminutive of *sapo*: little toad; *Med.*, the same that *sapinhos*.
SA.PI.NHOS, *s.m., pl., Med.*, little white patches in the mouth.
SA.PO, *s.m.*, toad.
SA.PO-BOI, *s.m., Bras., Zool.*, cururu toad (*Rhinella schneideri*).
SA.PO.NÁ.CEO, *adj.*, saponaceous.
SA.PO.NÁ.RI.O, *adj.*, said of a medicine containing soap.
SA.PO.NI.FI.CAR, *v.*, to saponify.
SA.QUE, *s.m.*, draw, drawing, service, bill; sack, robbery.
SA.QUÊ, *s.m.*, sake, saki (a Japanese alcoholic beverage).
SA.QUEA.DOR, *s.m.*, plunderer, pillager.
SA.QUE.AR, *v.*, to sack, to plunder, to pillage, to devastate.
SA.RA.CO.TE.AR, *v.*, to ramble, to sway, to walk about; to flirt.
SA.RA.DO, *adj.*, healed, cured.
SA.RAI.VA, *s.f.*, hail, hailstone.
SA.RAI.VA.DA, *s.f.*, hail, hailstorm; *fig.*, hail of things.
SA.RAI.VAR, *v.*, to hail; *fig.*, to fall as hail.
SA.RAM.PO, *s.m.*, measles.
SA.RA.PA.TEL, *s.m., Cul.*, a dish made with blood and viscera of hogs; *fig.*, medley.
SA.RA.PIN.TA.DO, *adj., pop.*, freckled, spotted.
SA.RAR, *v.*, to heal, to cure, to recover.
SA.RA.RÁ, *s. 2 gen., Bras.*, a albinicperson, albino; *adj.*, albinic.
SA.RAU, *s.m.*, soirée.
SAR.CAS.MO, *s.m.*, sarcasm, bitter irony.
SAR.CAS.TI.CA.MEN.TE, *adv.*, sarcastically.
SAR.CÁS.TI.CO, *adj.*, sarcastic, ironical.
SAR.CÓ.FA.GO, *s.m.*, sarcophagus.
SAR.DA, *s.f.*, freckle.
SAR.DEN.TO, *adj.*, freckled, freckly.
SAR.DI.NHA, *s.f., Zool.*, sardine.
SAR.DÔ.NI.CO, *adj.*, sardonic, sardonian.
SAR.GA.ÇO, *s.m., Bot.*, sargasso, sargassum, gulfweed, seaweed.
SAR.GEN.TO, *s.m.*, sergeant.

SA.RI, SÁ.RI, *s.m.*, sari (sareea Hindu woman's chief garment).
SAR.JA, *s.f.*, serge.
SAR.JA.ÇÃO, *s.f.*, scarifying, slight incision, cupping.
SAR.JA.DOR, *s.m., Med.*, scarifier; scarificator; *adj.*, scarifying.
SAR.JE.TA, *s.f.*, gutter, drain.
SAR.NA, *s.f.*, scabies, itch.
SAR.NEN.TO, *adj.*, scabious, itchy, rancid.
SAR.NO.SO, *s.m., adj.*, the same that *sarnento*.
SAR.RA.CE.NO, *adj., s.m.*, Saracen, Moor, Arab.
SAR.RA.BU.LHO, *s.m., Cul.*, a dish with curdled blood of a hog; a dish made of pork; *fig.*, tumult, noise.
SAR.RA.FA.DA, *s.f.*, a blow with a lath; *Bras., gír.*, kick on the opponent player (futebol).
SAR.RA.FE.AR, *v.*, to cut into laths; *Bras.*, to play violently (futebol).
SAR.RA.FO, *s.m.*, lath, slat.
SAR.REN.TO, *adj.*, tartarous; *Med.*, coated with lees wine.
SAR.RO, *s.m.*, tartar; fur, crust; *Bras., gír.*, kisses, hugs and caresses.
SAS.SA.FRÁS, *s.m., Bras., Bot.*, sassafras.
SA.TÃ, *s.m.*, Satan, devil, Lucifer.
SA.TA.NÁS, *s.m.*, Satan, the devil.
SA.TA.NI.CA.MEN.TE, *adv.*, satanically.
SA.TÂ.NI.CO, *adj.*, satanic.
SA.TA.NIS.MO, *s.m.*, Satanism.
SA.TA.NIS.TA, *s. 2 gen., adj.*, Satanist.
SA.TÉ.LI.TE, *s.m.*, satellite.
SÁ.TI.RA, *s.f.*, satire, sarcasm, lampoon.
SA.TI.RI.CA.MEN.TE, *adv.*, satirically.
SA.TÍ.RI.CO, *adj.*, satiric.
SA.TI.RIS.TA, *s. 2 gen.*, satirista.
SA.TI.RI.ZAR, *v.*, to satirize, to lampoon.
SÁ.TI.RO, *s.m.*, satyr; lecherous man.
SA.TIS.FA.ÇÃO, *s.f.*, satisfaction, pleasure, pride, explanation, compensation.
SA.TIS.FA.TO.RI.A.MEN.TE, *adv.*, satisfactorily.
SA.TIS.FA.TÓ.RIO, *adj.*, satisfactory, satisfying, sufficient.
SA.TIS.FA.ZER, *v.*, to satisfy, to please, to satiate.
SA.TIS.FEI.TO, *adj.*, satisfied, content, contented, happy.
SA.TU.RA.BI.LI.DA.DE, *s.f., Quím.*, saturability.
SA.TU.RA.ÇÃO, *s.f.*, saturation.
SA.TU.RA.DO, *adj.*, saturated, intense, deep.
SA.TU.RA.DOR, *s.m., Quím.*, saturator; *adj.*, saturating.
SA.TU.RAN.TE, *adj., Quím.*, saturant, saturating; *fig.*, tedious.
SA.TU.RAR, *v.*, to saturate, to soak, to impregnate, to satiate.
SA.TU.RÁ.VEL, *adj., Quím.*, saturable.
SA.TUR.NAL, *s.f.*, saturnalia; *adj.*, Saturnian, Saturnalian.
SA.TUR.NO, *s.m., Astron.*, Saturn (planet); *Mit.*, Saturn (god of time in ancient Rome).
SAU.DA.ÇÃO, *s.f.*, salutation, greeting, welcome, salute.
SAU.DA.DE, *s.f.*, longing, yearning, nostalgia.
SAU.DA.DOR, *s.m.*, person who salutes, saluter; *adj.*, saluting.
SAU.DAR, *v.*, to salute, to greet, to hail.
SAU.DÁ.VEL, *adj.*, sound, healthy, wholesome, salutary.
SA.Ú.DE, *s.f.*, health, soundness.
SAU.DI.TA, *s. 2 gen.*, Saudi, Saudi-Arabian; *adj.*, Saudi.
SAU.DO.SIS.MO, *s.m.*, a yearning for bygone days.
SAU.DO.SIS.TA, *s. 2 gen.*, eulogizer of the past, nostalgist; *adj.*, that is nostalgist of the past.
SAU.DO.SO, *adj.*, longing, yearning, ardent.

SAUNA · 313 · SEGURÁVEL

SAU.NA, *s.f.*, sauna; *fig.*, a very hot place.
SÁU.RIO, *s.m.*, saurian.
SA.VA.NA, *s.f.*, savannah.
SA.VEI.RO, *s.m.*, boat with mast and sails used for transport, fishing and tourism.
SA.XÃO, *adj., s.m.*, Saxon.
SA.XO.FO.NE, *s.m.*, saxophone.
SA.XO.FO.NIS.TA, *s. 2 gen.*, saxophonist.
SA.ZÃO, *s.f.*, season.
SA.ZO.NA.DO, *adj.*, seasoned; *fig.*, experienced, competent.
SA.ZO.NAL, *adj.*, seasonal.
SA.ZO.NA.LI.DA.DE, *s.f.*, seasonal variation.
SA.ZO.NAR, *v.*, to season, to ripen, to mellow.
SCAN.NER, *s.m., Comp.*, scanner.
SE, *refl. pers. pron.*, himself, herself, itsefl, oneself, yourself, yourselves, themselves; *conj.*, if, whether, provided, in case that.
SÉ, *s.f.*, see, cathedral.
SE.A.RA, *s.f.*, cornfield, harvest.
SE.BÁ.CE.O, *adj.*, sebaceous, fatty.
SE.BE, *s.f.*, quickset, fence, hedge.
SE.BEN.TO, *s.m.*, dirtyfellow; *adj.*, tallowy, dirty, greasy.
SE.BO, *s.m.*, fat, tallow, suet.
SE.BOR.REI.A, *s.f., Med.*, seborrhoea.
SE.BOR.REI.CO, *adj., Med.*, seborrhoeic.
SE.BO.SO, *adj.*, tallowish, tallowy.
SE.CA, *s.f.*, drought, dryness, aridity.
SE.CA.DOR, *s.m.*, dryer, desiccator.
SE.CA.DO.RA, *s.f.*, tumble-dryer.
SE.CA.GEM, *s.f.*, the act of drying.
SE.ÇÃO, *s.f.*, section, division, department, partition, (var. secção).
SE.CAR, *v.*, to dry, to drain, to wipe, to desiccate, to evaporate.
SEC.ÇÃO, *s.f.*, the same that *seção*.
SE.CI.O.NAL, *adj.*, sectional.
SEC.CI.O.NAR, *v.*, the same that *secionar*.
SE.CES.SÃO, *s.f.*, separation, secession.
SE.CIO.NAR, *v.*, to section, to divide.
SE.CO, *adj.*, dry, arid, droughty.
SE.CRE.ÇÃO, *s.f.*, secretion.
SE.CRE.TA.MEN.TE, *adv.*, secretly.
SE.CRE.TAR, *v., Med.*, to secrete.
SE.CRE.TA.RI.A, *s.f.*, secretaryship, bureau, office, secretariat, ministry.
SE.CRE.TÁ.RIA, *s.f.*, woman secretary.
SE.CRE.TA.RI.A.DO, *s.m.*, secretariate.
SE.CRE.TA.RI.AR, *v.*, to be a secretary.
SE.CRE.TÁ.RIO, *s.m.*, secretary, minister of state; confidant.
SE.CRE.TÁ.RIO-GE.RAL, *s.m.*, secretary general.
SE.CRE.TO, *adj.*, secret, private, hidden, occult.
SEC.TÁ.RI.O, *s.m.*, sectarian, sectary; *adj.*, sectarian.
SEC.TA.RIS.MO, *s.m.*, sectarianism.
SEC.TOR, *s.m.*, the same that *setor*.
SE.CU.LAR, *adj.*, lay, secular, archaic, profane.
SE.CU.LA.RI.DA.DE, *s.f.*, secularity.
SE.CU.LA.RI.ZA.ÇÃO, *s.f.*, secularization.
SE.CU.LA.RI.ZAR, *v.*, to secularize.
SÉ.CU.LO, *s.m.*, century, secular life.
SE.CUN.DAR, *v.*, to second, to assist, to sustain, to aid.
SE.CUN.DÁ.RIO, *adj.*, secondary, subordinate, minor.
SE.CUN.DA.RIS.TA, *s. 2 gen., Bras.*, high school student.

SE.CU.RA, *s.f.*, dryness, lack of moisture, thirst.
SE.CU.RI.TÁ.RI.O, *s.m., Bras.*, employee in an insurance company; *adj.*, referring to insurance.
SE.DA, *s.f.*, silk; *bicho-da-seda*: silkworm.
SE.DÃ, *s.m.*, sedan.
SE.DA.ÇÃO, *s.f.*, sedation.
SE.DAR, *v.*, to sedate, to assuage, to calm.
SE.DA.TI.VO, *s.m.*, sedative, depressant; *adj.*, sedative.
SE.DE, *s.f.*, seat, headquarters, ground, place; dryness, thirst, thirstiness.
SE.DEN.TÁ.RIO, *adj.*, sedentary, stationary.
SE.DEN.TA.RIS.MO, *s.m.*, sedentariness.
SE.DEN.TO, *adj.*, thirsty.
SE.DI.A.DO, *adj.*, headquartered.
SE.DI.ÇÃO, *s.f.*, sedition, rebellion.
SE.DI.CI.O.SO, *s.m.*, rioter; *adj.*, seditious, insurgent.
SE.DI.MEN.TA.ÇÃO, *s.f.*, sedimentation; subsidence.
SE.DI.MEN.TA.DO, *adj.*, sedimented, solid.
SE.DI.MEN.TAR, *adj.*, sedimentary, mothery.
SE.DI.MEN.TO, *s.m.*, sediment, settlings, lees.
SE.DI.MEN.TO.SO, *adj.*, sedimentary.
SE.DO.SI.DA.DE, *s.f.*, silkiness.
SE.DO.SO, *adj.*, silken, silky; hairy.
SE.DU.ÇÃO, *s.f.*, seduction, seducement, temptation.
SE.DU.TOR, *s.m.*, seducer; *adj.*, seducing.
SE.DU.ZIR, *v.*, to seduce, to tempt, to mislead.
SE.DU.ZÍ.VEL, *adj.*, seducible.
SEG.MEN.TA.ÇÃO, *s.f.*, segmentation
SEG.MEN.TA.DO, *adj.*, segmented, segmentate.
SEG.MEN.TAR, *v.*, to segment, to divide; *adj.*, segmental, segmentary.
SEG.MEN.TÁ.RI.O, *adj.*, segmentary.
SEG.MEN.TO, *s.m.*, segment, section, division.
SE.GRE.DAR, *v.*, to confide, to tell in secret.
SE.GRE.DIS.TA, *s. 2 gen.*, whisperer, person who keeps secrets.
SE.GRE.DO, *s.m.*, secret, mistery, secrecy.
SE.GRE.GA.ÇÃO, *s.f.*, segregation, apartheid, separation.
SE.GRE.GAR, *v.*, to segregate, to secrete, to isolate.
SE.GUI.DA, *s.f.*, following, pursuing.
SE.GUI.DA.MEN.TE, *adv.*, continually, continuously.
SE.GUI.DO, *adj.*, followed, continued, continuous.
SE.GUI.DOR, *s.m.*, follower, sectarian, adherent.
SE.GUI.MEN.TO, *s.m.*, following, pursuance.
SE.GUIN.TE, *s.m.*, the next, the following; *adj.*, next, following, subsequent.
SE.GUIR, *v.*, to follow, to pursue, to chase, to watch, to spy.
SE.GUN.DA, *s.f.*, short for *segunda-feira*.
SE.GUN.DA-FEI.RA, *s.f.*, Monday.
SE.GUN.DA.NIS.TA, *s. 2 gen.*, second-year student.
SE.GUN.DO, *s.m.*, second; *adj.*, second, next, secondary; *adv.*, secondly.
SE.GU.RA.DO, *s.m.*, policyholder, insured person; *adj.*, insured.
SE.GU.RA.DOR, *s.m.*, insurer, underwriter; *adj.*, insured, insuring.
SE.GU.RA.MEN.TE, *adv.*, safely.
SE.GU.RAN.ÇA, *s.f.*, security, certainty, assurance, safety, safeguard, insurance, sureness.
SE.GU.RAR, *v.*, to secure, to guard, to shield, to support, to hold, to catch, to guarantee.
SE.GU.RÁ.VEL, *adj.*, assurable, insurable.

SEGURO ··· 314 ··· SENIL

SE.GU.RO, *s.m.*, insurance, security, guarantee; *adj.*, secure, safe, firm, steady, reliable.

SE.GU.RO-DE.SEM.PRE.GO, *s.m.*, *US* unemployment compensation, *UK* unemployment benefit.

SE.GU.RO-SA.Ú.DE, *s.m.*, health insurance.

SEI.O, *s.m.*, breast, bosom, tit, core.

SEIS, *num.*, six.

SEIS.CEN.TIS.MO, *s.m.*, style and school of the 17th century.

SEIS.CEN.TIS.TA, *s. 2 gen.*, artist of the 17th century; *adj.*, referring to the 17th century.

SEIS.CEN.TOS, *num.*, six hundred.

SEI.TA, *s.f.*, sect, faction.

SEI.VA, *s.f.*, sap, juice of a plant.

SEI.VO.SO, *adj.*, *Bot.*, sappy, succulent.

SEI.XO, *s.m.*, pebble, flint.

SE.JA, *conj.*, *interj.*, be it; *ou ~*: that is; *~ como for*: come what may.

SE.LA, *s.f.*, saddle.

SE.LA.DO, *adj.*, stamped, sealed.

SE.LA.DOR, *s.m.*, saddler; sealer; *adj.*, saddling; sealing.

SE.LA.DOU.RO, *s.m.*, part of a horse's back where the saddle is placed.

SE.LA.GEM, *s.f.*, act of sealing with a stamp.

SE.LAR, *v.*, to stamp, to saddle, to seal.

SE.LE.ÇÃO, *s.f.*, selection.

SE.LE.CIO.NA.DO, *adj.*, eclectic.

SE.LE.CIO.NA.DOR, *s.m.*, selector; *adj.*, selecting.

SE.LE.CIO.NAR, *v.*, to select, to sort, to pick, to choose.

SE.LEI.RO, *s.m.*, saddler.

SE.LE.TA, *s.f.*, select; *Lit.*, anthology.

SE.LE.TI.VA.MEN.TE, *adv.*, selectively.

SE.LE.TI.VI.DA.DE, *s.f.*, selectivity; *adj.*, selective.

SE.LE.TI.VO, *adj.*, selective.

SE.LIM, *s.m.*, saddle of a bicycle.

SE.LO, *s.m.*, seal, cachet, postage stamp, stamp.

SEL.VA, *s.f.*, jungle, forest.

SEL.VA.GEM, *s.m.*, a savage, rough fellow; *adj.*, savage, wild, rude, brutal.

SEL.VA.GE.RI.A, *s.f.*, savagery, wildness, brutality.

SEL.VA.JA.RI.A, *s.f.*, the same that *selvageria*.

SEM, *prep.*, without, lacking, wanting, less.

SE.MÁ.FO.RO, *s.m.*, semaphore, traffic light, ligths.

SE.MA.NA, *s.f.*, week; *fim de semana*: week end.

SE.MA.NAL, *adj.*, weekly.

SE.MA.NAL.MEN.TE, *adv.*, weekly.

SE.MA.NÁ.RI.O, *s.m.*, weekly; *adj.*, weekly, hebdomadary.

SE.MAN.TE.MA, *s.m.*, *Ling.*, semanteme.

SE.MÂN.TI.CA, *s.f.*, *Ling.*, semantics.

SE.MÂN.TI.CO, *adj.*, semantic, semantical.

SEM.BLAN.TE, *s.f.*, face, look, visage, physiognomy.

SE.ME.A.ÇÃO, *s.f.*, sowing.

SE.ME.A.DOR, *s.m.*, sower; *adj.*, sowing.

SE.ME.A.DU.RA, *s.f.*, sowing, seeding.

SE.ME.AR, *v.*, to sow, to plant, to spread, to disseminate.

SE.ME.Á.VEL, *adj.*, that is fit for sowing or planting.

SE.ME.LHAN.ÇA, *s.f.*, likeness, resemblance, similarity.

SE.ME.LHAN.TE, *s.2 gen.*, fellow creature; *adj.*, analogous, like, similar.

SE.ME.LHAR, *v.*, to resemble, to be similar.

SE.ME.LHÁ.VEL, *adj.*, that can be resembled to.

SÊ.MEN, *s.m.*, semen, sperm.

SE.MEN.TE, *s.f.*, seed, semen, sperm.

SE.MEN.TEI.RA, *s.f.*, sowing; seed plot, seed field.

SE.MES.TRAL, *adj.*, half-yearly.

SE.MES.TRA.LI.DA.DE, *s.f.*, semestral allowance, semestral payment.

SE.MES.TRAL.MEN.TE, *adv* bi-annually.

SE.MES.TRE, *s.m.*, semester, half-year; *adj.*, semestral.

SEM-FIM, *s.m.*, endless amount of, unlimited space.

SE.MI.A.NAL.FA.BE.TO, *adj.*, semiliterate.

SE.MI.Á.RI.DO, *adj.*, semiarid.

SE.MI.BRE.VE, *s.f.*, *Mús.*, semibreve.

SE.MI.CER.RAR, *v.*, to half-close.

SE.MI.CIR.CU.LAR, *adj.*, semicircular.

SE.MI.CÍR.CU.LO, *s.m.*, semicircle.

SE.MI.CON.DU.TOR, *s.m.*, *Fís.*, semiconductor.

SE.MI.CONS.CI.EN.TE, *adj.*, semiconscious.

SE.MI.DEUS, *s.m.*, demigod.

SE.MI.FI.NAL, *s.f.*, semifinal; *adj.*, semifinal.

SE.MI.FI.NA.LIS.TA, *s. 2 gen.*, semifinalist; *adj.*, participating in a semifinal.

SE.MI.MOR.TO, *adj.*, half dead, torpid.

SE.MI.NAL, *adj.*, seminal.

SE.MI.NÁ.RIO, *s.m.*, seminar, seminary.

SE.MI.NA.RIS.TA, *s.m.*, seminarist.

SE.MI.NU, *adj.*, half-naked.

SE.MI.Ó.TI.CA, *s.f.*, semiotics, semeiotics.

SE.MI.PRE.CI.O.SO, *adj.*, semiprecious.

SE.MI.TA, *adj.*, *s.m.*, Semire, *adj.*, Semitic.

SE.MÍ.TI.CO, *adj.*, Semitic.

SE.MI.TIS.MO, *s.m.*, Semitism.

SEM-NÚ.ME.RO, *s.m.*, numberless; *um ~ de*: a countless number of.

SE.MI.TOM, *s.m.*, semitone.

SÊ.MO.LA, *s.f.*, semolina.

SE.MO.LI.NA, *s.f.*, the same that *sêmola*.

SEM-PAR, *adj.*, peerless.

SEM.PRE, *adv.*, always, ever, constantly.

SEM.PRE-VI.VA, *s.f.*, *Bot.*, strawflower.

SEM-VER.GO.NHA, *adj.*, shameless.

SE.NÁ.CU.LO, *s.m.*, seat of the Senatus (ancient Roman Senate).

SE.NA.DO, *s.m.*, senate.

SE.NA.DOR, *s.m.*, senator.

SE.NÃO, *s.m.*, fault, defect; *adv.*, except, save, else, otherwise; *conj.*, but, saving.

SEN.CI.EN.TE, *adj.*, sentient.

SEN.DA, *s.f.*, narrow road, footpath.

SE.NE.GAL, *s.*, Senegal.

SE.NHA, *s.f.*, password, signal.

SE.NHOR, *s.m.*, owner, proprietor, possessor, master, sir, mister, lord.

SE.NHO.RA, *s.f.*, lady, wife, housewife; *Nossa Senhora*: Our Lady.

SE.NHO.RE.AR, *v.*, to rule, to conquer, to master, to govern.

SE.NHO.RI.A, *s.f.*, lordship, ladyship; landlady.

SE.NHO.RI.AL, *adj.*, seignorial.

SE.NHO.RIL, *adj.*, lordly, lordlike.

SE.NHO.RI.O, *s.m.*, landlord, lordship.

SE.NHO.RI.TA, *s.f.*, miss.

SE.NIL, *adj.*, old, senile.

SENILIDADE ··315·· SERPENTANTE

SE.NI.LI.DA.DE, *s.f.*, senility, old age.
SÉ.NIOR, *s.m.*, senior, older; *adj.*, senior, older, elder.
SEN.SA.BOR, *s. 2 gen.*, tastelessness, insipity; *adj.*, insipid, having no taste.
SEN.SA.ÇÃO, *s.f.*, sensation.
SEN.SA.CIO.NAL, *adj.*, sensational, remarkable.
SEN.SA.CI.O.NA.LIS.MO, *s.m.*, *Filos.*, sensationalism.
SEN.SA.CI.O.NA.LIS.TA, *adj.*, sensationalistic, sensationalist.
SEN.SA.TEZ, *s.f.*, sensibleness, judiciousness, understanding.
SEN.SA.TO, *adj.*, judicious, sensible, rational.
SEN.SI.BI.LI.DA.DE, *s.f.*, sensibility, sensitiveness.
SEN.SI.BI.LI.ZA.ÇÃO, *s.f.*, sensitization.
SEN.SI.BI.LI.ZA.DO, *adj.*, sensitized.
SEN.SI.BI.LI.ZA.DOR, *adj.*, sensitizing.
SEN.SI.BI.LI.ZAN.TE, *adj.*, the same that *sensibilizador*.
SEN.SI.BI.LI.ZAR, *v.*, to sensitize, to penetrate, to touch.
SEN.SI.TI.VA.MEN.TE, *adv.*, sensitively, sentiently.
SEN.SI.TI.VO, *adj.*, sensitive, sensory.
SEN.SÍ.VEL, *adj.*, sensitive.
SEN.SI.VEL.MEN.TE, *adv.*, sensibly.
SEN.SO, *s.m.*, sense, sagacity, keenness, wisdom, reasoning, meaning, understanding, signification.
SEN.SOR, *s.m.*, sensor.
SEN.SO.RI.AL, *adj.*, sensorial.
SEN.SÓ.RI.O, *s.m.*, *Anat.*, sensorium; *adj.*, sensorial.
SEN.SÓ.RIO-MO.TOR, *adj.*, sensorimotor.
SEN.SU.AL, *adj.*, sensual, luxurious, voluptuous, libidinous.
SEN.SUA.LI.DA.DE, *s.f.*, sensuality, fleshlines.
SEN.SUA.LIS.MO, *s.m.*, sensualism.
SEN.SU.A.LIS.TA, *s. 2 gen.*, sensualist; *adj.*, sensualistic.
SEN.SU.A.LI.ZAR, *v.*, to sensualize.
SEN.TA.DO, *adj.*, sitting; sit-down (dinner).
SEN.TAR, *v.*, to seat; *sentar-se*:to seat down, to take a seat.
SEN.TEN.ÇA, *s.f.*, sentence, proverb, maxim, verdict, decision, a judicial decision.
SEN.TEN.CI.A.DO, *s.m.*, convict; *adj.*, sentenced, condemned.
SEN.TEN.CI.A.DOR, *s.m.*, sentencer, judge.
SEN.TEN.CI.AR, *v.*, to judge, to convict.
SEN.TEN.CI.O.SO, *adj.*, sententious.
SEN.TI.DO, *s.m.*, each of the five senses, feeling, meaning, sense; *adj.*, sensible, sorry, sad, grieved.
SEN.TI.MEN.TA.LI.DA.DE, *s.f.*, sentimentality.
SEN.TI.MEN.TAL, *adj.*, sentimental, emotional, romantic.
SEN.TI.MEN.TA.LIS.MO, *s.m.*, sentimentalism; sentimentality.
SEN.TI.MEN.TA.LIS.TA, *s.*, 2 g., sentimentalist; *adj.*, sentimental.
SEN.TI.MEN.TA.LI.ZAR, *v.*, to sentimentalize.
SEN.TI.MEN.TA.LOI.DE, *adj.*, oversentimental.
SEN.TI.MEN.TO, *s.m.*, sentiment, feeling, emotion, perception, passion.
SEN.TI.NE.LA, *s.f.*, sentinel, watchman, guard.
SEN.TIR, *v.*, to feel, to experience, to suffer, to think, to be moved.
SEN.ZA.LA, *s.f.*, slave house.
SE.PA.RA.ÇÃO, *s.f.*, separation, dissociation, division.
SE.PA.RA.DA.MEN.TE, *adv.*, separately.
SE.PA.RA.DO, *adj.*, separate, severed, disunited.
SE.PA.RA.DOR, *s.m.*, separator; *adj.*, separating.
SE.PA.RAR, *v.*, to separate, to disconnect, to disunite, to sever.
SE.PA.RA.TA, *s.f.*, offprint, separatum.

SE.PA.RA.TIS.MO, *s.m.*, separatism.
SE.PA.RA.TIS.TA, *s. 2 gen.*, separatist; *adj.*, separatist.
SE.PA.RÁ.VEL, *adj.*, separable, partible.
SÉ.PI.A, *s.f.*, sepia; *adj.*, sepia.
SEP.TI.CE.MI.A, *s.f.*, septicemia.
SEP.TUA.GÉ.SI.MO, *num.*, seventieth.
SE.PUL.CRAL, *adj.*, sepulchral.
SE.PUL.CRO, *s.m.*, sepulchre, grave, tomb.
SE.PUL.TA.DOR, *s.m.*, grave-digger; *adj.*, that buries.
SE.PUL.TA.MEN.TO, *s.m.*, burial, funeral, sepulture.
SE.PUL.TAR, *v.*, to bury, to inhumate, to sepulchre.
SE.PUL.TU.RA, *s.f.*, sepulture, grave, tomb, sepulchre.
SE.QUAZ, *adj.*, sequacious, following, adherent.
SE.QUE.LA, *s.f.*, sequel, consequence, result; *Med.*, sequela.
SE.QUÊN.CIA, *s.f.*, sequence, continuation, continuity.
SE.QUEN.CI.AL, *adj.*, sequential.
SE.QUEN.CI.A.DOR, *s.m.*, sequencer.
SE.QUEN.TE, *adj.*, sequent, successive.
SE.QUER, *adv.*, at least, even, not even, so much as.
SE.QUES.TRA.ÇÃO, *s.f.*, sequestration.
SE.QUES.TRA.DOR, *s.m.*, sequestrator, kidnapper; *adj.*, sequestering.
SE.QUES.TRAN.TE, *s. 2 gen.*, sequestrant; *adj.*, sequestrating.
SE.QUES.TRAR, *v.*, to sequestrate, to confiscate, to kidnap.
SE.QUES.TRÁ.VEL, *adj.*, sequestrable, attachable.
SE.QUES.TRO, *s.m.*, sequestration, kidnapping.
SE.QUI.AR, *v.*, *Bras.*, to talk, to discuss.
SE.QUI.DÃO, *s.f.*, dryness, roughness, indifference.
SE.QUI.O.SA.MEN.TE, *adv.*, thirstily.
SE.QUI.O.SO, *adj.*, arid, dry, desirous, avid.
SÉ.QUI.TO, *s.m.*, suite, train, attendance.
SER, *s.m.*, being, creature, existence, life, substance; *v.*, to be, to exist, to become, to happen, to belong.
SE.RA.FIM, *s.m.*, seraph.
SE.RÃO, *s.m.*, overtime, soirée.
SE.REI.A, *s.f.*, siren, mermaid.
SE.RE.LE.PE, *s.m.*, *Bras.*, ground squirrel; *adj.*, lively.
SE.RE.NA.GEM, *s.f.*, act of exposing to dew.
SE.RE.NAR, *v.*, to serene, to calm, to pacify.
SE.RE.NA.TA, *s.f.*, serenade.
SE.RE.NA.TIS.TA, *s. 2 gen.*, *Bras.*, serenader.
SE.RE.NI.DA.DE, *s.f.*, serenity, tranquility, calmness.
SE.RE.NO, *s.m.*, serene, dew, mist; *adj.*, serene, cheerful, placid, tranquil.
SE.RES.TA, *s.f.*, serenade.
SE.RES.TEI.RO, *s.m.*, serenader.
SE.RI.A.ÇÃO, *s.f.*, seriation.
SE.RI.A.DO, *s.m.*, seriate, series of TV programs.
SE.RI.AL, *adj.*, serial.
SÉ.RIE, *s.f.*, series, row, set, continuation, succession.
SE.RIE.DA.DE, *s.f.*, seriousness, integrity, sobriety.
SE.RIN.GA, *s.f.*, syringe, squirt.
SE.RIN.GAL, *s.m.*, *Bras.*, place where abound the rubber trees; *Bras.*, property usually at riversides.
SE.RIN.GA.LIS.TA, *s.m.*, *Bras.*, proprietor of a rubber plantation.
SE.RIN.GUEI.RA, *s.f.*, rubber tree.
SE.RIN.GUEI.RO, *s.m.*, *Bras.*, rubber tapper.
SÉ.RIO, *adj.*, serious, grave, reliable, earnest.
SER.MÃO, *s.m.*, discourse, sermon, preach, telling-off.
SER.PEN.TAN.TE, *adj.*, the same that *serpeante*.

SERPEANTE ·· 316 ··· SIDA

SER.PE.AN.TE, *adj.*, winding, meandering.
SER.PE.AR, *v.*, to meander, to twine, to wind.
SER.PEN.TÁ.RI.O, *s.m.*, *Zool.*, serpent eater, secretary-bird; *Bras.*, serpentarium.
SER.PEN.TE, *s.f.*, serpent, snake.
SER.PEN.TE.AN.TE, *adj.*, the same that *serpeante*.
SER.PEN.TE.AR, *v.*, to coil.
SER.PEN.TI.FOR.ME, *adj.*, serpentiform.
SER.PEN.TI.NA, *s.f.*, coil, worm, serpentin.
SER.RA, *s.f.*, saw, mountain ridge, mountain range, elevation.
SER.RA.ÇÃO, *s.f.*, sawing, act ofsawing.
SER.RA.DOR, *s.m.*, sawyer; *adj.*, sawing.
SER.RA.GEM, *s.f.*, sawdust, scobs.
SER.RA LE.O.A, *s.*, Sierra Leone.
SER.RA.LHA.RI.A, *s.f.*, workshop locksmith's.
SER.RA.LHEI.RO, *s.m.*, locksmith.
SER.RA.NO, *s.m.*, mountaineer; *adj.*, mountainous.
SER.RAR, *v.*, to saw.
SER.RA.RIA, *s.f.*, sawframe, sawmill.
SER.RI.LHA, *s.f.*, serration; a serrated ornament.
SER.RI.LHA.DO, *adj.*, serrulate(d), serrate, milled.
SER.RI.LHAR, *v.*, to serrate, to rim.
SER.RO.TE, *s.m.*, hand-saw.
SER.TA.NE.JO, *s.m.*, inlander, backwoodsman; *adj.*, rude, rough.
SER.TA.NI.A, *s.f.*, *Bras.*, the backwoods.
SER.TA.NIS.TA, *s.m.*, *Bras.*, member of an group of early explorers in Brazil.
SER.TÃO, *s.m.*, interior, midland part, hinterland, heart of the country.
SER.VEN.TE, *s.2 gen.*, servant, attendant, helper, jobber; *adj.*, serving, attendant.
SER.VEN.TIA, *s.f.*, usefulness, utility, service.
SER.VI.ÇAL, *s. 2 gen.*, servant; *adj.*, relating to servants or slaves.
SER.VI.ÇO, *s.m.*, service, work, employment, job, performance.
SER.VI.DÃO, *s.f.*, servitude, slavery, vassalage, service.
SER.VI.DI.ÇO, *adj.*, worn out.
SER.VI.DO, *adj.*, served, used.
SER.VI.DOR, *s.m.*, servant, server, public functionary; *adj.*, attendant, serving.
SER.VIL, *adj.*, servile, sequacious, slavish.
SER.VI.LIS.MO, *s.m.*, servility, servileness.
SER.VI.LI.ZAR, *v.*, to render, to become servile.
SER.VIL.MEN.TE, *adv.*, servilely.
SER.VIR, *v.*, to serve, to wait, to supply, to attend on, to help, to benefit.
SER.VÍ.VEL, *adj.*, serviceable.
SER.VO, *s.m.*, servant, slave, drudge.
SER.VO-CRO.A.TA, *s. 2 gen.*, *adj.*, Serbo-Croatian, Serbo-Croat.
SES.SÃO, *s.f.*, session, assembly.
SES.SAR, *v.*, *Bras.*, to sift; to winnow.
SES.SEN.TA, *num.*, sixty.
SES.SEN.TÃO, *s.m.*, *adj.*, sexagenarian.
SÉS.SIL, *adj.*, *Bot.*, sessile.
SES.TA, *s.f.*, siesta.
SE.TA, *s.f.*, arrow, dart, pointer.
SE.TE, *num.*, the number seven, seven.
SE.TE.CEN.TIS.MO, *s.m.*, styleand school of the artists of the 18th century.
SE.TE.CEN.TIS.TA, *s. 2 gen.*, artist of the 18th century; *adj.*, referring to the 18 th century or to its artists.
SE.TE.CEN.TOS, *num.*, seven hundred.
SE.TE E MEI.O, *s.m.*, a kind of card game.
SE.TEM.BRO, *s.m.*, September.
SE.TEN.TA, *num.*, seventy.
SE.TEN.TÃO, *s.m.*, septuagenerian; *adj.*, septuagenary.
SE.TEN.TRIO.NAL, *adj.*, northern, septentrional.
SÉ.TI.MO, *s.m.*, seventh part; *adj.*, seventh.
SE.TOR, *s.m.*, sector, section.
SE.TO.RI.AL, *adj.*, sector.
SE.TUA.GE.NÁ.RIO, *s.m.*, septuagenarian; *adj.*, septuagenary.
SE.TU.A.GÉ.SI.MO, *num.*, seventieth.
SEU, *pron.*, his, her, its, your, their, theirs, yours, hers.
SE.VE.RA.MEN.TE, *adv.*, severely.
SE.VE.RI.DA.DE, *s.f.*, severity, rigidity, harshness, rigorousness.
SE.VE.RO, *adj.*, severe, austere, rigorous, harsh, bitter, grave, accurate, exact.
SE.VI.CIA.DOR, *s.m.*, person who ill-treats; *adj.*, who ill-treats.
SE.VI.CI.AR, *v.*, to ill-treat, maltreat.
SE.VÍ.CIAS, *s.f.*, ill-treatment, inhumanity.
SE.VO, *adj.*, cruel, inhuman, ferocious.
SE.XA.GE.NÁ.RIO, *s.m.*, sexagenarian.
SE.XA.GÉ.SI.MO, *num.*, sixtieth.
SE.XIS.MO, *s.m.*, sexism.
SE.XO, *s.m.*, sex; *ambos os sexos*: man and woman; *fazer sexo*: have sex.
SE.XO.LO.GI.A, *s.f.*, sexology.
SE.XO.LÓ.GI.CO, *adj.*, sexological.
SE.XÓ.LO.GO, *s.m.*, sexologist.
SEX.TA, *s.f.*, short for *sexta-feira*; sext (one of the Canonical hours).
SEX.TA.NIS.TA, *s. 2 gen.*, a sixth-year student.
SEX.TA-FEI.RA, *s.f.*, Friday; *Sexta-Feira Santa*: Good Friday.
SEX.TAN.TE, *s.m.*, *Mat.*, sextant; *Astron.*, Sextant(an equatorial constallation), sextant (instrument).
SEX.TA.VA.DO, *adj.*, hexagonal, six-sided.
SEX.TO, *s.m.*, sixth part; *adj.*, sixth.
SÊX.TU.PLO, *sm* sextuple. adj sextuple, sixfold, six times.
SE.XU.AL, *adj.*, sexual.
SE.XU.A.LI.DA.DE, *s.f.*, sexuality.
SE.XY, *adj.*, *Ingl.*, sexy.
SHOP.PING CEN.TER, *s.m.*, *Ingl.*, *Com.*, mall.
SHORT, *s.m.*, *Ingl.*, shorts.
SHOW, *s.m.*, *Ingl.*, show; *fig.*, scene, scandal.
SI, *s.m.*, *Mús.*, si, B; *pron.*, himself, herself, itself, oneself, yourself, yourselves, themselves.
SIA.MÊS, *s.m.*, Siamese.
SI.BE.RI.A.NO, *adj.*, *s.m.*, Siberian.
SI.BI.LA, *s.f.*, sibyl.
SI.BI.LA.ÇÃO, *s.f.*, sibilation, hissing.
SI.BI.LAN.TE, *adj.*, sibilant, hissing.
SI.BI.LAR, *v.*, to sibilate, to hiss, to whistle.
SI.BI.LO, *s.m.*, sibilation, whistle, zip.
SIC, *adv.*, *Lat.*, sic (intentionally so written).
SI.CÁ.RIO, *s.m.*, sicarian, criminal.
SI.CA.TI.VI.DA.DE, *s.f.*, siccative quality.
SI.CI.LI.A.NO, *adj.*, *s.m.*, Sicilian.
SIDA, *s.f.*, AIDS (Acquired Immune Deficiency Syndrome).

SIDERAL · 317 · SINCRONIZADO

SI.DE.RAL, *adj.*, sideral, astral.
SI.DE.RAR, *v.*, to fulminate; to amaze, to stupefy.
SI.DE.RO.GRA.FI.A, *s.f.*, siderography.
SI.DE.RO.TÉC.NI.CO, *adj.*, the same that *siderúrgico*.
SI.DE.RUR.GI.A, *s.f.*, siderurgy, metallurgy, ironworks.
SI.DE.RÚR.GI.CO, *adj.*, metallurgic, metallurgical, siderurgic.
SI.DRA, *s.f.*, cider, apple-wine.
SI.FÃO, *s.m.*, siphon, syphon.
SÍ.FI.LIS, *s.f.*, *Med.*, syphilis, lues.
SI.FI.LÍ.TI.CO, *s.m., adj., Med.*, syphilitic.
SI.GI.LA.ÇÃO, *s.f.*, the act of sealing.
SI.GI.LO, *s.m.*, seal, sigil, secret, signet.
SI.GLA, *s.f.*, abbreviature.
SIG.NA.TÁ.RIO, *s.m.*, signatory, signer.
SIG.NI.FI.CA.ÇÃO, *s.f.*, signification, significance.
SIG.NI.FI.CA.DO, *s.m.*, meaning, sense.
SIG.NI.FI.CA.DOR, *s.m.*, signifier; *adj.*, signifying.
SIG.NI.FI.CAN.TE, *adj.*, significant.
SIG.NI.FI.CAR, *v.*, to signify, to mean, to denote, to imply.
SIG.NI.FI.CA.TI.VA.MEN.TE, *adv.*, significantly.
SIG.NI.FI.CA.TI.VO, *adj.*, significative, significant.
SIG.NO, *s.m.*, sign.
SÍ.LA.BA, *s.f.*, syllable.
SI.LA.BA.ÇÃO, *s.f.*, syllabication.
SI.LA.BAR, *v.*, to syllable, to syllabize.
SI.LEN.CI.A.DOR, *s.m.*, silencer; *adj.*, silencing.
SI.LEN.CI.AR, *v.*, to silence, to keep silent, to hush.
SI.LÊN.CIO, *s.m.*, silence, stillness, calm, quiet.
SI.LEN.CI.O.SA.MEN.TE, *adv.*, silently.
SI.LEN.CI.O.SO, *adj.*, silent, speechless, still, quiet, noiseless, voiceless, mute.
SI.LEN.TE, *adj., Lit.*, silent.
SI.LHU.E.TA, *s.f.*, silhouette, profile.
SÍ.LI.CA, *s.f.*, silica, silex.
SI.LI.CA.TA.DO, *adj., Quím.*, silicated.
SI.LI.CO.NE, *s.m., Quím.*, silicone.
SI.LO, *s.m.*, silo, garner.
SI.LO.GIS.MO, *s.m.*, syllogism.
SI.LO.GÍS.TI.CO, *adj., Lóg.*, syllogistic, syllogistical.
SIL.VA, *s.f., Bot.*, bramble.
SIL.VAR, *v.*, to whistle, to sibilate.
SIL.VEI.RA, *s.f.*, blackberry; *Bot.*, bramble.
SIL.VES.TRE, *adj.*, silvan, savage, woodsy.
SIL.VÍ.CO.LA, *s.2 gen.*, savage, barbarian, aborigine.
SIL.VO, *s.m.*, whistle, hiss.
SIM, *adv.*, yes, yea, all right, absolutely, exactly.
SIM.BI.ON.TE, *s.m., Biol.*, symbiont.
SIM.BI.O.SE, *s.f.*, symbiosis.
SIM.BI.Ó.TI.CO, *adj., Biol.*, symbiotic.
SIM.BO.LI.CA.MEN.TE, *adv.*, symbolically, figuratively.
SIM.BÓ.LI.CO, *adj.*, symbolic, symbolical.
SIM.BO.LIS.MO, *s.m.*, symbolism.
SIM.BO.LIS.TA, *s. 2 gen.*, symbolist.
SIM.BO.LI.ZA.ÇÃO, *s.f.*, symbolization.
SIM.BO.LI.ZA.DO, *adj.*, symbolized, figured.
SIM.BO.LI.ZA.DOR, *s.m.*, symbolizer; *adj.*, symbolizing.
SIM.BO.LI.ZAR, *v.*, to symbolize, to symbol, to typify.
SÍM.BO.LO, *s.m.*, symbol, figure, image, token, sign.
SIM.BO.LO.GI.A, *s.f.*, symbology.
SI.ME.TRI.A, *s.f.*, symmetry, harmony, proportion.
SI.MÉ.TRI.CO, *adj.*, symmetric, harmonious.

SI.ME.TRI.ZAR, *v.*, to symmetrize.
SI.MI.LAR, *adj.*, similar, alike, uniform.
SI.MI.LA.RI.DA.DE, *s.f.*, similarity, likeness, resemblance.
SÍ.MI.LE, *s.m., Ret.*, simile; analogy.
SI.MI.LI.TU.DE, *s.f.*, similitude.
SÍ.MIO, *s.m.*, simian, monkey, ape.
SIM.PA.TI.A, *s.f.*, sympathy, affinity, compatibility, appeal.
SIM.PÁ.TI.CO, *adj.*, friendly, helpful, nice, sympathetic.
SIM.PA.TI.ZAN.TE, *s. 2 gen.*, sympathizer, supporter, follower, adherent.
SIM.PA.TI.ZAR, *v.*, to like, to sympathize, to feel an affection.
SIM.PLES, *adj.*, simple, plain, clear, ingenuous, unadorned, evident, clear.
SIM.PLES.MEN.TE, *adv.*, simply.
SIM.PLI.CI.DA.DE, *s.f.*, simplicity, naturalness.
SIM.PLI.FI.CA.ÇÃO, *s.f.*, simplification, facilitation.
SIM.PLI.FI.CA.DO, *adj.*, simplified.
SIM.PLI.FI.CA.DOR, *s.m.*, simplifier; *adj.*, simplifying.
SIM.PLI.FI.CAR, *v.*, to simplify, to facilitate, to clarify.
SIM.PLIS.MO, *s.m.*, simplism; oversimplification.
SIM.PLIS.TA, *s. 2 gen.*, simplicist, simplist; *adj.*, simplicistic, simplicistical.
SIM.PLÓ.RIO, *adj.*, simpleton, simple-minded.
SIM.PÓ.SIO, *s.m.*, symposium, feast.
SI.MU.LA.ÇÃO, *s.f.*, simulation, pretense.
SI.MU.LA.CRO, *s.m.*, simulacrum, effigy, imitation.
SI.MU.LA.DO, *adj.*, simulate, mock, sham, false.
SI.MU.LA.DOR, *s.m.*, simulator, faker, pretender; *adj.*, simulating.
SI.MU.LAR, *v.*, to simulate, to feign, to camouflage, to imitate.
SI.MU.LA.TÓ.RI.O, *adj.*, simulatory.
SI.MUL.TA.NE.A.MEN.TE, *adv.*, simultaneously.
SI.MUL.TA.NEI.DA.DE, *s.f.*, simultaneity, synchronism.
SI.MUL.TÂ.NEO, *adj.*, simultaneous, synchronous.
SI.NA, *s.f.*, fate, destiny, flag.
SI.NA.GO.GA, *s.f.*, synagogue, Jewish temple.
SI.NAL, *s.m.*, signal, sign, mark, indication, signature, gesture.
SI.NA.LAR, *v.*, to signalize, to designate, to mark.
SI.NAL DA CRUZ, *s.m.*, act of crossing.
SI.NA.LEI.RA, *s.f., Bras.*, traffic light.
SI.NA.LEI.RO, *s.m.*, flagman, signalman.
SI.NA.LI.ZA.ÇÃO, *s.f.*, signalizing, traffic signs or signals.
SI.NA.LI.ZAR, *v.*, to signal, to telegraph, to mark.
SIN.CE.RA.MEN.TE, *adv.*, sincerely.
SIN.CE.RI.DA.DE, *s.f.*, sincerity, frankness, openness.
SIN.CE.RO, *adj.*, sincere, frank, open, honest, truthful, simpled.
SIN.CO.PA.DO, *adj., Mús.*, syncopated.
SIN.CO.PAR, *v., Mús.*, to syncopate.
SÍN.CO.PE, *s.f.*, syncope, temporary loss of consciousness.
SIN.CRÉ.TI.CO, *adj.*, syncretic.
SIN.CRE.TIS.MO, *s.m.*, syncretism.
SIN.CRE.TIS.TA, *s. 2 gen.*, syncretist; *adj.*, syncretistic.
SIN.CRE.TI.ZAR, *v.*, to syncretize.
SIN.CRO.NI.A, *s.f.*, synchronization, synchronicity.
SIN.CRÔ.NI.CA.MEN.TE, *adv.*, synchronously.
SIN.CRÔ.NI.CO, *adj.*, synchronous, simultaneous.
SIN.CRO.NIS.MO, *s.m.*, synchronism, synchronicity.
SIN.CRO.NIS.TA, *s. 2 gen.*, synchronizer; *adj.*, synchronizing.
SIN.CRO.NI.ZA.ÇÃO, *s.f.*, synchronization.
SIN.CRO.NI.ZA.DO, *adj.*, synchronized.

SINCRONIZADOR ··· 318 ··· SOALHADO

SIN.CRO.NI.ZA.DOR, *s.m.*, synchronizer.
SIN.CRO.NI.ZAR, *v.*, to synchronize, to adjust.
SIN.DI.CA.ÇÃO, *s.f.*, syndication, investigation.
SIN.DI.CAL, *adj.*, syndical.
SIN.DI.CA.LIS.MO, *s.m.*, syndicalism.
SIN.DI.CA.LIS.TA, *s. 2 gen.*, syndicalist; *adj.*, syndicalistic.
SIN.DI.CA.LI.ZA.ÇÃO, *s.f.*, syndicalization.
SIN.DI.CA.LI.ZA.DO, *adj.*, relating to a member of a trade union.
SIN.DI.CA.LI.ZAR, *v.*, to syndicalize, to syndicate.
SIN.DI.CÂN.CIA, *s.f.*, syndication, inquiry, inquest.
SIN.DI.CAN.TE, *s. 2 gen.*, syndic; public investigator; *adj.*, investigating.
SIN.DI.CAR, *v.*, to investigate, to inquire into.
SIN.DI.CA.TO, *s.m.*, syndicate.
SÍN.DI.CO, *s.m.*, syndic, janitor, lawyer.
SÍN.DRO.ME, *s.m., Med.*, syndrome.
SI.NE.CU.RA, *s.f.*, sinecure.
SI.NE.CU.RIS.MO, *s.m.*, sinecurism.
SI.NE.CU.RIS.TA, *s. 2 gen.*, sinecurist.
SI.NE.TA, *s.f.*, a small bell.
SIN.FO.NI.A, *s.f.*, symphony.
SIN.FÔ.NI.CA, *s.f.*, symphony orchestra.
SIN.FÔ.NI.CO, *adj.*, symphonic.
SIN.GE.LE.ZA, **SIN.GE.LEZ**, *s.f.*, singleness, simplicity.
SIN.GE.LO, *adj.*, simple, plain, sincere, single.
SIN.GU.LAR, *s.m.*, singular, the singular number; *adj.*, single, individual, singular.
SIN.GU.LA.RI.DA.DE, *s.f.*, singularity, uniqueness, oddity, remark.
SIN.GU.LA.RI.ZAR, *v.*, to singularize, to single out, to particularize.
SI.NIS.TRA.DO, *s.m.*, victim of an accident; *adj.*, injured by an accident, damaged.
SI.NIS.TRA.MEN.TE, *adv.*, sinisterly, sinistrously.
SI.NIS.TRAR, *v.*, to suffer an accident, to loss or damage.
SI.NIS.TRO, *s.m.*, accident, casualty, disaster, damage, ruin, loss; *adj.*, left, sinister, ominous, fatal, evil.
SI.NIS.TRO.GI.RO, *adj.*, sinistrogyrate.
SI.NO, *s.m.*, bell.
SI.NO.DAL, *adj.*, synodal.
SÍ.NO.DO, *s.m.*, synod.
SI.NO.NÍ.MI.CO, *adj.*, synonymic, synonymical.
SI.NO.NI.MI.ZAR, *v.*, to synonymize.
SI.NÔ.NI.MO, *s.m.*, synonym.
SI.NOP.SE, *s.f.*, synopsis, analysis, summary.
SIN.TAG.MA, *s.m.*, syntagma.
SIN.TAG.MÁ.TI.CO, *adj.*, syntagmatic.
SIN.TA.TI.CA.MEN.TE, *adv.*, syntactically.
SIN.TÁ.TI.CO, *adj.*, syntactic.
SIN.TA.XE, *s.f.*, syntax.
SIN.TÁ.XI.CO, *adj., Gram.*, the same that *sintático*.
SÍN.TE.SE, *s.f.*, synthesis, composition.
SIN.TE.TI.CA.MEN.TE, *adv.*, synthetically.
SIN.TÉ.TI.CO, *adj.*, synthetic, synthetical, resumed, abbreviated.
SIN.TE.TI.ZA.DOR, *s.m., Mùs.*, synthesizer.
SIN.TE.TI.ZAR, *v.*, to synthesize, to synthetize.
SIN.TO.MA, *s.m.*, sympton, sign, indication.
SIN.TO.MÁ.TI.CO, *adj.*, symptomatic, symptomatical.
SIN.TO.MA.TIS.MO, *s.m., Med.*, symptomatics; symptomatic

medicine.
SIN.TO.MA.TO.LO.GI.A, *s.f., Med.*, symptomatology.
SIN.TO.MA.TIS.TA, *s. 2 gen.*, supporter of sintomatic medicine.
SIN.TO.NI.A, *s.f.*, syntony.
SIN.TO.NI.ZA.ÇÃO, *s.f.*, syntonization.
SIN.TO.NI.ZA.DO, *adj.*, syntonized, tuned in (radio, TV).
SIN.TO.NI.ZA.DOR, *s.m.*, tuner; sytonizer.
SIN.TO.NI.ZAR, *v.*, to syntonize, to tune in.
SI.NU.CA, *s.f.*, snooker.
SI.NU.O.SA.MEN.TE, *adv.*, windingly, sinuously.
SI.NUO.SI.DA.DE, *s.f.*, sinuosity, flexuosity, tortuosity.
SI.NU.O.SO, *adj.*, sinuous, winding, bending.
SI.NU.SI.TE, *s.f., Med.*, sinusitis.
SI.O.NIS.MO, *s.m.*, Zionism.
SI.O.NIS.TA, *s. 2 gen.*, Zionist; *adj.*, Zionistic.
SI.RE.NA, *s.f., Mit.*, siren, mermaid; the same that *sirene*.
SI.RE.NE, *s.f.*, sirenalarm.
SI.RI, *s.m., Zool.*, a type of crab.
SÍRIA, *s.*, Syria.
SI.RI.GAI.TA, *s.f., gír.*, livelyhigh-spirited woman; flirt.
SÍ.RIO, *adj., s.m.*, Syrian.
SI.SAL, *s.m.*, sisal, sisal-hemp.
SIS.MAL, *adj.*, seismic.
SÍS.MI.CO, *adj.*, seismic, seismal, cataclysmic.
SIS.MO, *s.m.*, seismism, move, earthquake.
SIS.MO.GRA.FI.A, *s.f.*, seismography.
SIS.MÓ.GRA.FO, *s.m., Fís.*, seismograph.
SIS.MO.LO.GI.A, *s.f.*, seismology.
SIS.MO.LÓ.GI.CO, *adj.*, seismologic, seismological.
SI.SO, *s.m.*, judgment, criterion, prudence.
SIS.TE.MA, *s.m.*, system, scheme, organization, structure.
SIS.TE.MÁ.TI.CA, *s.f.*, systematics, taxonomy.
SIS.TE.MA.TI.CA.MEN.TE, *adv.*, systematically.
SIS.TE.MÁ.TI.CO, *adj.*, systematic.
SIS.TE.MA.TI.ZA.ÇÃO, *s.f.*, systematization.
SIS.TE.MA.TI.ZA.DOR, *s.m.*, systematizer; *adj.*, systematizing.
SIS.TE.MA.TI.ZAR, *v.*, to systemize, systematize.
SI.SU.DEZ, **SI.SU.DE.ZA**, *s.f.*, circumspection, prudence, wisdom.
SI.SU.DO, *adj.*, serious, judicious, wise, sensible, serious.
SI.TE, *s.m., Ingl.*, site.
SI.TI.A.DO, *s.m.*, besieged person or place; *adj.*, be sieged.
SI.TI.AN.TE, *s. 2 gen.*, besieger; *adj.*, besieging.
SI.TI.AR, *v.*, to besiege, to beset; to harrass.
SÍ.TIO, *s.m.*, place, locality, soil, farm, ranch, country.
SI.TO, *adj.*, situated, located.
SI.TUA.ÇÃO, *s.f.*, situation, position, location, place, circumstances.
SI.TU.A.CI.O.NIS.MO, *s.m., Bras.*, situationism (the predominant political party).
SI.TU.A.CI.O.NIS.TA, *s. 2 gen.*, a member of the governing political party.
SI.TU.A.DO, *adj.*, situated.
SI.TU.AR, *v.*, to place, to situate, to position.
SKATE, *s.m., Ingl., Esp.*, skateboarding, skateboard.
SLIDE, *s.m., Ingl.*, slide.
SLOGAN, *sm Ingl.*, slogan.
SÓ, *adj.*, alone, unique, single, sole, lone, solitary.
SO.A.BER.TO, *adj.*, half-open.
SO.A.BRIR, *v.*, to open partly.
SO.A.LHA.DO, *s.m.*, flooring, floor.

SOADO ··319·· SOCIALITE

SO.A.DO, *adj.*, sounded, sounding.
SO.A.LHO, *s.m.*, floor, flooring, ground.
SO.AR, *v.*, to sound, to clang, to jingle.
SOB, *prep.*, sub, under, below, beneath.
SO.BE.JA.DO, *adj.*, more than enough.
SO.BE.JA.MEN.TE, *adv.*, excessively.
SO.BE.JAR, *v.*, to overabound, to superabound.
SO.BE.JI.DÃO, *s.f.*, superabundance, redundancy.
SO.BE.JO, *s.m.*, refuse, candle-end, excess.
SO.BE.RA.NA.MEN.TE, *adv.*, sovereignly, supremely.
SO.BE.RA.NI.A, *s.f.*, sovereignty, domain, rule, reign.
SO.BE.RA.NI.ZAR, *v.*, to raise to position of a sovereign; to exalt.
SO.BE.RA.NO, *s.m.*, sovereign, imperator, monarch.
SO.BER.BA, *s.f.*, arrogance, presumption, pride.
SO.BER.BA.MEN.TE, *adv.*, superbly.
SO.BER.BO, *adj.*, superb, proud, splendid, sumptuous, prideful.
SO.BER.BO.SO, *adj.*, superb, magnificent.
SO.BRA, *s.f.*, surplus, excess, overplus, overmuch.
SO.BRA.ÇAR, *v.*, to put under the arm; to embrace.
SO.BRA.DAR, *v.*, to construct a house with floors.
SO.BRA.DO, *s.m.*, two-store house.
SO.BRAL, *s.m.*, a cork oak plantation.
SO.BRAN.ÇA.RI.A, *s.f.*, pride, haughtiness.
SO.BRAN.CE.AR, *v.*, to be arrogant, to exceed, to surpass.
SO.BRAN.CEI.RO, *adj.*, superior, predominant, distinguished.
SO.BRAN.CE.LHA, *s.f.*, brow, eyebrow.
SO.BRAR, *v.*, to overabound, to be in excess of, to be superfluous.
SO.BRAS, *s.f., pl.*, scrap, garbage.
SO.BRE, *prep.*, about, above, concerning, over, across, besides, over and above.
SO.BRE.A.BUN.DÂN.CI.A, *s.f.*, the same that *superabundância*.
SO.BRE.A.VI.SO, *s.m.*, precaution, forethought, prevention.
SO.BRE.CA.PA, *s.f.*, overcoat, raglan.
SO.BRE.CAR.GA, *s.f.*, overburden, overload, surcharge, overcharge.
SO.BRE.CAR.RE.GA.DO, *adj.*, overloaded, surcharged, supercharged.
SO.BRE.CAR.RE.GAR, *v.*, to overload, to overburden, to overfreight.
SO.BRE.CAR.TA, *s.f.*, envelope, cover; confirmatory letter.
SO.BRE-E.XAL.TAR, *v.*, to superexalt.
SO.BRE-EX.CI.TAR, *v.*, to superexcite; to incite.
SO.BRE-HU.MA.NO, *adj.*, superhuman.
SO.BRE.LE.VAN.TE, *adj.*, elevating to excess, overtopping.
SO.BRE.LE.VAR, *v.*, to elevate to excess; to be higher than, to elevate.
SO.BRE.LO.JA, *s.f.*, mezzanine.
SO.BRE.MA.NEI.RA, *s.f.*, greatly, extremely, excessively.
SO.BRE.ME.SA, *s.f.*, dessert.
SO.BRE.MO.DO, *adv.*, the same that *sobremaneira*.
SO.BRE.NA.TU.RAL, *adj.*, supernatural.
SO.BRE.NA.TU.RA.LI.DA.DE, *s.f.*, supernaturalness.
SO.BRE.NO.ME, *s.m.*, surname, family name.
SO.BRE.NO.ME.AR, *v.*, to surname, to nickname.
SO.BRE.PAI.RAR, *v.*, to hover over.
SO.BRE.PE.SAR, *v.*, to weigh heavily, to be cumbersome.
SO.BRE.PE.SO, *s.m.*, surcharge, overweight.

SO.BRE.POR, *v.*, to put on or upon, to lean against, to superpose, to juxtapose, to connect.
SO.BRE.PO.SI.ÇÃO, *s.f.*, overlapping, superposing.
SO.BRE.POS.TO, *s.m., adj.*, superimposed; ~ a: placed on top of.
SO.BRE.PO.VO.AR, *v.*, to further the population of.
SO.BRE.PU.JA.MEN.TO, *s.m.*, surpassing, outstripping.
SO.BRE.PU.JAR, *v.*, to surmount, to raise above, to surpass.
SO.BRES.CRE.VER, *v.*, to superscribe, to address a letter.
SO.BRES.CRI.TAR, *v.*, to write the address (of a letter or document), to prepare the envelope.
SO.BRES.CRI.TO, *s.m.*, name and address writen on envelope; destination (of a letter or parcel).
SO.BRES.SA.IR, *v.*, to salient, to be projecting, to jut out.
SO.BRES.SA.LEN.TE, *s.m.*, spare; *adj.*, spare.
SO.BRES.SAL.TA.DO, *adj.*, jumpy, apprehensive, fearful.
SO.BRES.SAL.TAR, *v.*, to assail, to attack, to surprise, to take by surprise, to jump over.
SO.BRES.SAL.TA.DO, *adj.*, startled; worried.
SO.BRES.SAL.TO, *s.m.*, dread, fear, alarm, start.
SO.BRES.SA.LEN.TE, *s.m.*, surplus, overplus, rest, remainder, spare part.
SO.BRE.TA.XA, *s.f.*, surtax, supercharge, surcharge.
SO.BRE.TA.XAR, *v.*, to surtax.
SO.BRE.TEN.SÃO, *s.f., Eletr.*, power surge.
SO.BRE.TO.A.LHA, *s.f.*, a towel laid over another one (for protection ou adornment).
SO.BRE.TU.DO, *adv.*, over all, above all, chiefly, mainly, essencially.
SO.BRE.VI.DA, *s.f.*, life span after diagnosis of a lethal disease.
SO.BRE.VIR, *v.*, to befall, to happen, to come to pass.
SO.BRE.VI.VÊN.CIA, *s.f.*, survival.
SO.BRE.VI.VEN.TE, *s.2 gen.*, survivor, outliver; *adj.*, surviving.
SO.BRE.VI.VER, *v.*, to survive, to outlive, to outlast, to continue, to exist.
SO.BRE.VO.AR, *v.*, to fly over.
SO.BRE.VÔ.O, *s.m.*, overflying.
SO.BRI.A.MEN.TE, *adv.*, soberly, moderately.
SO.BRIE.DA.DE, *s.f.*, sobriety, temperance, seriousness, frugality.
SO.BRI.NHA, *s.f.*, niece.
SO.BRI.NHO, *s.m.*, nephew.
SÓ.BRIO, *adj.*, sober, abstinent, temperate, austere.
SO.BRO.LHO, *s.m.*, eyebrow.
SO.CA, *s.f.*, rhizome or stemof a plant; the second harvest of sugar cane.
SO.CA.DO, *adj.*, pounded, crushed, trodden down or upon; stuck; squat.
SO.CA.DOR, *s.m.*, pestle; stamper.
SO.ÇAI.TE, *s.m., col., Ingl.*, society.
SO.CAR, *v.*, to strike with the fist, to beat, to bruise, to hurt.
SO.CIA.BI.LI.DA.DE, *s.f.*, sociability, sociality, communicativeness.
SO.CIA.BI.LI.ZAR, *v.*, to make sociable, to form a society.
SO.CI.AL, *adj.*, social, social-minded, sociable.
SO.CI.AL-DE.MO.CRA.CI.A, *s.f.*, social democracy.
SO.CI.AL-DE.MO.CRA.TA, *s. 2 gen.*, social democrat.
SO.CIA.LIS.MO, *s.m.*, socialism.
SO.CIA.LIS.TA, *s.2 gen.*, socialist.
SO.CI.A.LI.TE, *s. 2 gen., Ingl.*, socialite.

SOCIALIZAÇÃO ·· 320 ·· SOLO

SO.CIA.LI.ZA.ÇÃO, *s.f.*, socialization.
SO.CIA.LI.ZAR, *v.*, to socialize.
SO.CI.Á.VEL, *adj.*, social, sociable, urban, associable.
SO.CI.A.VEL.MEN.TE, *adv.*, sociably, companionably.
SO.CIE.DA.DE, *s.f.*, society, friendly intercourse, association, corporation.
SO.CI.E.TÁ.RI.O, *s.m.*, member of a group or society; associate, companion.
SÓ.CIO, *s.m.*, member, associate, partner, shareholder.
SO.CI.O.CRA.CI.A, *s.f.*, sociocracy.
SO.CI.O.CRA.TA, *s. 2 gen.*, sociocrat; *adj.*, sociocratic, sociocratical.
SO.CI.O.CUL.TU.RAL, *adj.*, sociocultural.
SO.CI.O.E.CO.NÔ.MI.CO, *adj.*, socioeconomic.
SO.CI.O.LIN.GUIS.TA, *s. 2 gen., Ling.*, sociolinguist.
SO.CI.O.LIN.GUÍS.TI.CA, *s.f., Ling.*, sociolinguistics.
SO.CIO.LO.GIA, *s.f.*, sociology.
SO.CI.O.LÓ.GI.CO, *adj.*, sociologic, sociological.
SO.CI.Ó.LO.GO, *s.m.*, sociologist.
SO.CI.O.PO.LÍ.TI.CO, *adj.*, sociopolitical.
SO.CO, *s.m.*, blow, punch.
SO.ÇO.BRA.DO, *adj.*, foundered, capsized, stranded.
SO.ÇO.BRAR, *v.*, to subvert, to turn upside down, to founder.
SO.CO-IN.GLÊS, *s.m.*, knuckleduster.
SO.COR.RER, *v.*, to protect, to aid, to help, to assist, to relieve.
SO.COR.RI.DO, *adj.*, helped, relieved.
SO.COR.RO, *s.m.*, relief, aid, assistance, succour.
SO.DA, *s.f.*, soda, fizzy water.
SÓ.DI.CO, *adj., Quím.*, sodic.
SÓ.DIO, *s.m., Quím.*, sodium (symbol: Na).
SO.DO.MI.A, *s.f.*, sodomy, pederasty.
SO.DO.MI.TA, *s. 2 gen.*, sodomite.
SO.DO.MI.ZAR, *v.*, to sodomize.
SO.FÁ, *s.m.*, sofa, couch.
SO.FÁ-CA.MA, *s.m.*, sofa-bed.
SO.FIS.MA, *s.m.*, sophism, fallacy.
SO.FIS.MAR, *v.*, to act or talk in a sophisticated manner.
SO.FIS.TA, *s. 2 gen.*, sophist.
SO.FIS.TI.CA.ÇÃO, *s.f.*, sophistication, sophistry.
SO.FIS.TI.CA.DO, *adj.*, sophistecated, falsified.
SO.FIS.TI.CA.DOR, *s.m.*, sophisticator.
SO.FIS.TI.CAR, *v.*, to sophisticate, to falsify.
SO.FRE.AR, *v.*, to bridle, to curb, to check, to refrain.
SO.FRE.DOR, *s.m.*, sufferer, endurer.
SO.FRE.GA.MEN.TE, *adv.*, greedily, avidly.
SÔ.FRE.GO, *adj.*, voracious, avid, greedy.
SO.FRE.GUI.DÃO, *s.f.*, greediness, voraciousness, avidity.
SO.FRER, *v.*, to suffer, to bear, to endure, to sustain, to support, to undergo.
SO.FRI.DO, *adj.*, long-suffering, suffering.
SO.FRI.MEN.TO, *s.m.*, suffering, sufferance, pain, agony, torment.
SO.FRÍ.VEL, *adj.*, sufferable, bearable.
SOFT.WARE, *s.m., Comp.*, software.
SO.GRA, *s.f.*, mother-in-law.
SO.GRO, *s.m.*, father-in-law.
SOI.RÉE, *s.f., Fr.*, soirée.
SO.JA, *s.f., Bot.*, soybean, soja, soy.
SOL, *s.m.*, sun, *Astron.*, Sun; *Mús.*, *sol*: the fifth musical note.
SO.LA, *s.f.*, sole-leather, sole of a shoe.

SO.LA.DO, *s.m.*, sole (of a shoe); *adj.*, flat; new-soled (shoes).
SO.LÃO, *s.m.*, very hot sun.
SO.LA.PA.DO, *adj.*, excavated, undermined, hidden.
SO.LA.PA.MEN.TO, *s.m.*, act of excavating, undermining.
SO.LA.PAR, *v.*, to hollow out, to undermine, to sap.
SO.LAR, *s.m.*, manor-house, manor, mansion; *adj.*, solar; *v.*, to sole a shoe, to play solo.
SO.LÁ.RI.O, *s.m.*, solarium, sun porch.
SO.LA.VAN.CAR, *v.*, to jolt, to bump.
SO.LA.VAN.CO, *s.m.*, jolt; bump.
SOL.DA, *s.f.*, solder, weld, soldering.
SOL.DA.DES.CA, *s.f., pej.*, troops; military classes; mercenary soldiers.
SOL.DA.DES.CO, *adj.*, soldierly.
SOL.DA.DO, *s.m.*, soldier, private; *soldados* (*pl.*): troops; *adj.*, soldered, welded, joined.
SOL.DA.DOR, *s.m.*, welder; *adj.*, soldering.
SOL.DA.DU.RA, *s.f.*, act of soldering; soldering.
SOL.DA.GEM, *s.f.*, soldering, welding.
SOL.DAR, *v.*, to solder, to weld, to join, to fasten.
SOL.DO, *s.m.*, soldier's pay.
SO.LE.CIS.MO, *s.m.*, solecism, error, guilt.
SO.LE.DA.DE, *s.f.*, solitude, isolation, solitariness, retirement.
SO.LEI.RA, *s.f.*, sill, door-sill.
SO.LE.NE, *adj.*, solemn, pompous, ominous, serious.
SO.LE.NE.MEN.TE, *adv.*, solemnly.
SO.LE.NI.DA.DE, *s.f.*, solemnity, celebration, festivity.
SO.LE.NI.ZA.ÇÃO, *s.f.*, solemnization, commemoration.
SO.LE.NI.ZAR, *v.*, to solemnize, to celebrate.
SO.LE.TRA.DOR, *s.m.*, speller.
SO.LE.TRAR, *v.*, to spell, to read badly.
SO.LI.CI.TA.ÇÃO, *s.f.*, solicitation, request, appeal.
SO.LI.CI.TA.DO, *adj.*, solicited.
SO.LI.CI.TA.DOR, *s.m., Jur.*, solicitor; *adj.*, soliciting, requesting.
SO.LI.CI.TAN.TE, *adj., s.2 gen.*, solicitant.
SO.LI.CI.TAR, *v.*, to solicit, to seek, to search for, to look for, to obtain.
SO.LI.CI.TÁ.VEL, *adj.*, that may be solicited.
SO.LÍ.CI.TO, *adj.*, solicitous, diligent, careful, thoughtful.
SO.LI.CI.TU.DE, *s.f.*, solicitude, carefulness, diligence.
SO.LI.DA.MEN.TE, *adv.*, solidly.
SO.LI.DÃO, *s.f.*, solitude, seclusion, loneliness.
SO.LI.DAR, *v.*, to solidify; to confirm.
SO.LI.DA.RI.A.MEN.TE, *adv.*, solidarily.
SO.LI.DA.RIE.DA.DE, *s.f.*, solidarity, sympathy.
SO.LI.DÁ.RIO, *adj.*, sympathetyc, solidary, mutual.
SO.LI.DA.RIS.MO, *s.m.*, solidarism.
SO.LI.DA.RI.ZAR, *v.*, to solidarize, to make solidary.
SO.LI.DEZ, *s.f.*, solidity, solidness, firmness.
SO.LI.DI.FI.CA.ÇÃO, *s.f.*, solidification.
SO.LI.DI.FI.CA.DO, *adj.*, solidified, solid.
SO.LI.DI.FI.CAR, *v.*, to solidify, to coagulate, to congeal, to set, to settle.
SÓ.LI.DO, *adj.*, solid, consistent, compact, durable.
SO.LI.LÓ.QUI.O, *s.m.*, soliloquy.
SO.LIS.TA, *s.2 gen.*, solist.
SO.LI.TÁ.RIA, *s.f., Zool.*, tapeworm; solitary cell (prison).
SO.LI.TA.RI.A.MEN.TE, *adv.*, solitarily.
SO.LI.TÁ.RIO, *adj.*, solitary, lonely, secluded.
SO.LI.TU.DE, *s.f., Lit.*, solitude ; solitariness.
SO.LO, *s.m.*, soil, solo, earth.

SOLSTICIAL • 321 • SORTE

SOLS.TI.CI.AL, *adj.*, solstitial.
SOLS.TÍ.CIO, *s.m.*, solstice.
SOL.TA.DOR, *s.m.*, liberator; *adj.*, releasing, liberating.
SOL.TAR, *v.*, to unfasten, to untie, to unbind, to loosen, to free, to release.
SOL.TEI.RA, *s.f.*, single woman, spinster; *adj.*, single, unmarried.
SOL.TEI.RÃO, *s.m.*, bachelor.
SOL.TEI.RO, *s.m.*, single man, single.
SOL.TEI.RO.NA, *s.f.*, spinster.
SOL.TO, *adj.*, free, slack, loose, released.
SOL.TU.RA, *s.f.*, freeing, liberation.
SO.LU.BI.LI.DA.DE, *s.f., Fís., Quím.*, solubility.
SO.LU.BI.LI.ZAR, *v.*, to solubilize.
SO.LU.ÇAN.TE, *adj.*, sobbing, weeping.
SO.LU.ÇÃO, *s.f.*, solution, conclusion, answer.
SO.LU.ÇAR, *v.*, to sob, to hiccup, to whimper, to whine.
SO.LU.CIO.NAR, *v.*, to give a solution, to resolve.
SO.LU.ÇO, *s.m.*, hiccup, sob, sobbing, din.
SO.LU.ÇO.SO, *adj.*, sobbing.
SO.LÚ.VEL, *adj.*, dissoluble, soluble.
SOL.VÊN.CIA, *s.f.*, solvency.
SOL.VEN.TE, *s.m., Quím.*, solvent; *adj.*, solvent, soluble.
SOL.VER, *v.*, to solve, to explain, to resolve, to pay, to settle a debt.
SOL.VI.BI.LI.DA.DE, *s.f., Quím.*, solvability; *Com.*, solvency.
SOL.VÍ.VEL, *adj., Com.*, solvent, solvable.
SOM, *s.m.*, sound, tone.
SO.MA, *s.f.*, sum, addition, total, totality.
SO.MA.LI, *s. 2 gen.*, Somali; *adj.*, pertaining to or relative to Somalia.
SO.MÁ.LIA, *s.*, Somalia.
SO.MA.LI.A.NO, *s.m., adj.*, somali.
SO.MAR, *v.*, to add, to sum up, to total.
SO.MÁ.TI.CO, *adj., Med.*, somatic.
SO.MA.TÓ.RI.O, *s.m.*, sum, sum total, total; *adj.*, referring to a sum.
SOM.BRA, *s.f.*, shadow, shade, darkness.
SOM.BRE.A.DO, *adj.*, shaded.
SOM.BRE.AR, *v.*, to shade, to shadow, to darken.
SOM.BREI.RO, *s.m.*, sombrero.
SOM.BRE.JAR, *v.*, to shadow, to shade.
SOM.BRI.NHA, *s.f.*, umbrella (for ladies), parasol.
SOM.BRIO, *adj.*, shady, shadowy, obscure, dark, sad, dismal, cloudy, moody.
SO.ME.LI.Ê, *s.m.*, sommelier.
SO.ME.NOS, *adj.*, inferior, paltry, vulgar, ordinary, common.
SO.MEN.TE, *adv.*, only.
SO.NAM.BÚ.LI.CO, *adj.*, somnambulic, somnambulistic.
SO.NAM.BU.LIS.MO, *s.m., Med.*, somnambulism.
SO.NÂM.BU.LO, *s.m.*, sleepwalker, somnambulist; *adj.*, somnambulistic.
SO.NÂN.CI.A, *s.f.*, sonance, sonancy.
SO.NAN.TE, *adj.*, sonant, sounding; ringing, toned.
SO.NAR, *s.m.*, sonar.
SO.NA.TA, *s.f.*, sonata.
SON.DA, *s.f.*, sounding lead, style, catheter.
SON.DA.DOR, *s.m.*, sounder, delver; *adj.*, sounding, delving.
SON.DA.GEM, *s.f.*, sounding investigation, perforation, drilling, exploration.
SON.DAR, *v.*, to sound, to search, to evaluate, to probe.

SON.DÁ.VEL, *adj.*, soundable.
SO.NE.CA, *s.f.*, somnolence, nap, doze, sleepiness.
SO.NE.GA.ÇÃO, *s.f.*, defraudation, misappropriation.
SO.NE.GA.DOR, *s.m.*, withholder, defrauder; *adj.*, defrauding.
SO.NE.GAR, *v.*, to withhold, to defraud, to misapply, to steal.
SO.NE.TIS.TA, *s.*, sonnetist.
SO.NE.TO, *s.m.*, sonnet.
SO.NHA.DOR, *s.m.*, visionary, dreamer, dozer.
SO.NHAR, *v.*, to dream, to imagine, to fancy.
SO.NHO, *s.m.*, dream, reverie; *sonho (rosquinha de massa)*: dough-nut.
SO.NO, *s.m.*, sleep, slumber, rest, repose, sleepiness.
SO.NO.LÊN.CIA, *s.f.*, somnolence, sleepiness.
SO.NO.LEN.TO, *adj.*, somnolent, sleepy, drowsy, inert.
SO.NO.RI.DA.DE, *s.f.*, sonority, loudness.
SO.NO.RI.ZAR, *v.*, to render sonorous, to sound.
SO.NO.RI.ZA.ÇÃO, *s.f.*, sound recording (act, process or result of making sonorous).
SO.NO.RI.ZAR, *v.*, to render sonorous; to sound; to make the soundtrack for.
SO.NO.RO.SI.DA.DE, *s.f.*, sonorousness, sonority.
SO.NO.RO, *adj.*, sonorous, loud.
SO.NO.TE.RA.PI.A, *s.f., Med.*, sleep therapy.
SON.SO, *adj.*, sly, artful, cunning, clever, crafty.
SO.PA, *s.f.*, soup, sop, broth.
SO.PA.PO, *s.m.*, slap, wipe.
SO.PÉ, *s.m.*, foothill, foot (of the mountain).
SO.PEI.RA, *s.f.*, tureen, soup dish.
SO.PEI.RO, *s.m.*, person fond of soup; *adj.*, pertaining to soup; fond of soup.
SO.PE.SAR, *v.*, to weight by liftingwith hand; to counterweigh.
SO.PIS.TA, *s. 2 gen.*, person fond of soup.
SO.PI.TA.DO, *adj.*, sleepy, asleep; lazy.
SO.PI.TAR, *v.*, to lull to sleep, to sopite; to tranquillize.
SO.PO.RA.DO, *adj.*, sleepy, drowsy, soporiferous.
SO.PO.RÍ.FE.RO, *adj., s.m.*, soporific.
SO.PO.RÍ.FI.CO, *s.m., Farm.*, soporific; *adj.*, soporiferous.
SO.PRA.NO, *s. 2 gen., Mús.*, soprano.
SO.PRAR, *v.*, to blow, to puff.
SO.PRO, *s.m.*, puff of air, whiff, exhalation, blowing, blast.
SO.QUE.A.DO, *adj.*, pounded, battered.
SO.QUE.AR, *v.*, to strike with the fist, to punch.
SO.QUE.TE, *s.m., Mil.*, ramrod (for gun); rammer; socket, lamp socket.
SOR.DI.DEZ, **SOR.DI.DEZ**, *s.f.*, sordidness, paltriness, dirtiness.
SÓR.DI.DO, *adj.*, dirty, filthy, sordid, vile, base, nasty, repulsive.
SO.RO, *s.m.*, serum.
SO.RO.LO.GI.A, *s.f.*, serology.
SO.RO.LO.GIS.TA, *s. 2 gen.*, serologist.
SO.RO.NE.GA.TI.VO, *adj.*, seronegative.
SO.RO.PO.SI.TI.VO, *adj.*, seropositive.
SO.ROR, *s.f.*, sister, nun.
SO.RO.TE.RA.PI.A, *s.f.*, serum therapy.
SOR.RA.TEI.RA.MEN.TE, *adv.*, furtively, stealthily.
SOR.RA.TEI.RO, *adj.*, sneaky, stealthy; cunning, shrewd.
SOR.RI.DEN.TE, *adj.*, smiling, radiant, beaming, genial.
SOR.RIR, *v.*, to smile, to laugh gently.
SOR.RI.SO, *s.m.*, smile, act of smiling, grin.
SOR.TE, *s.f.*, fate, destiny, fortune, chance, luck, doom, lot,

SORTEADO ··· 322 ··· SUBITÂNEO

hazard, risk.

SOR.TE.A.DO, *s.m.*, person raffled; *adj.*, selected, chosen, reffled.

SOR.TE.AR, *v.*, to choose or pick out by lot, to draw lots.

SOR.TEI.O, *s.m.*, sortition, allotment, raffle, lottery.

SOR.TI.DO, *adj.*, assorted, sorted.

SOR.TI.LÉ.GI.O, *s.m.*, sortilege, sorcery, enchantment.

SOR.TI.MEN.TO, *s.m.*, classification, assortment, supply.

SOR.TIR, *v.*, to supply, to furnish, to provide, to variegate.

SOR.TU.DO, *s.m.*, lucky person; *adj.*, lucky, fortunate.

SO.RUM.BÁ.TI.CO, *adj.*, glum, gloomy, moody.

SOR.VE.DOU.RO, *s.m.*, whirlpool, drain, vortex, chasm.

SOR.VER, *v.*, to sip, to suck, to absorb, to engulf.

SOR.VE.TE, *s.m.*, ice-cream.

SOR.VE.TEI.RO, *s.m.*, ice-cream man.

SOR.VE.TE.RI.A, *s.f.*, ice-cream shop.

SÓS, *adj.*, lonely; *adv.*, just, only; *loc. adv.*, a sós: all by oneself.

SÓ.SIA, *s.f.*, double, counterpart, second self.

SOS.LAI.O, *s.m.*, obliquity.

SOS.SE.GA.DA.MEN.TE, *adv.*, calmly, tranquilly.

SOS.SE.GA.DO, *adj.*, quiet, calm, tranquil, restful, sleepy, drowsy.

SOS.SE.GA-LE.ÃO, *s.m.*, *Bras.*, *pop.*, a pen for children; *pop.*, sedative.

SOS.SE.GAR, *v.*, to calm, to quiet, to tranquilize, to soothe, to pacify.

SOS.SE.GO, *s.m.*, tranquility, calmness, calm, peace.

SO.TAI.NA, *s.f.*, soutane; *pop.*, clergyman.

SÓ.TÃO, *s.m.*, attic, garret.

SO.TA.QUE, *s.m.*, accent, brogue.

SO.TA.VEN.TO, *s.m.*, *Náut.*, lee, leeward; leeside.

SO.TER.RA.DO, *adj.*, covered with earth.

SO.TER.RAR, *v.*, to bury, to cover with earth.

SO.TUR.NO, *s.m.*, darkness, obscurity; *adj.*, saturnine.

SOU.TI.EN, **SU.TI.Ã**, *s.m.*, *Fr.*, brassière, *col.*, bra.

SO.VA, *s.f.*, beating, thrashing, caning.

SO.VA.DO, *adj.*, crumpled, crushed, wrinkled, trodden.

SO.VA.CO, *s.m.*, axilla, armpit.

SO.VA.QUEI.RA, *s.f.*, *Bras.*, armhole, underarm; perspiration from the armpit.

SO.VAR, *v.*, to knead, to batter, to drub.

SO.VE.LA, *s.f.*, bradawl, awl, pricker, broach.

SO.VI.É.TI.CO, *adj.*, *s.m.*, Russian, soviet, sovietic.

SO.VI.NA, *s.f.*, miser, skinflint; *adj.*, miserly, avaricious, parsimonious.

SO.VI.NAR, *v.*, to perforate with an awl; *fig.*, to offend, to pester, to annoy.

SO.VI.NI.CE, *s.f.*, avariciousness, greediness, parsimony.

SO.ZI.NHO, *adj.*, alone, lonely, solo; *adv.*, all alone, solely, all by oneself.

STRIP-TEASE, *s.m.*, *Ingl.*, striptease.

SU.A, *pron.*, his, her, its, your, their, his, hers, its, yours, theirs.

SU.A.DO, *adj.*, sweaty, perspiring.

SU.A.DOR, *s.m.*, sweater; sudorific; hard job; *adj.*, sweating, sudorific.

SU.A.DOU.RO, *s.m.*, act of sweating; *Med.*, sudorific, sweater.

SU.AR, *v.*, to sweat, to perspire, to transpire, to exhale, to exude.

SU.A.SI.VO, *adj.*, suasive, persuasive.

SU.ÁS.TI.CA, *s.f.*, swastica, fylfot.

SU.A.VE, *adj.*, agreeable, pleasant, mild, gentle, kind, affable, delicate, sweet, lenient.

SUA.VI.DA.DE, *s.f.*, amenity, mildness, suaveness, gentleness.

SU.A.VI.ZA.ÇÃO, *s.f.*, act of making suave or sweet, mitigation.

SU.A.VI.ZA.DO, *adj.*, mitigated, softened.

SU.A.VI.ZA.DOR, *adj.*, mitigating, sweetening, softening.

SUA.VI.ZAR, *v.*, to soothe, to soften, to milden.

SU.BA.GÊN.CI.A, *s.f.*, subagency.

SU.BA.LI.MEN.TA.ÇÃO, *s.f.*, undernourishment.

SU.BA.LI.MEN.TA.DO, *adj.*, undernourished.

SU.BA.LI.MEN.TAR, *v.*, to undernourish, to underfeed.

SU.BAL.TER.NI.DA.DE, *s.f.*, subalternity, subordination.

SU.BAL.TER.NI.ZAR, *v.*, to make subaltern, to subordinate.

SU.BAL.TER.NO, *s.m.*, subaltern, subordinate; *adj.*, subaltern, subordinate, inferior, secondary.

SU.BA.LU.GAR, *v.*, to sublet, to underlet.

SU.BA.LU.GUEL, *s.m.*, subletting, subrenting.

SUB.CA.PI.LAR, *adj.*, subcapillary.

SUB.CAR.BO.NÍ.FE.RO, *adj.*, *Geol.*, subcarboniferous.

SUB.CHE.FE, *s.m.*, subchief.

SUB.CO.MIS.SÁ.RI.O, *s.m.*, subcommissioner.

SUB.CONS.CI.ÊN.CI.A, *s.f.*, semiconsciousness; *Psic.*, subconsciousness.

SUB.CONS.CI.EN.TE, *s.m.*, *Psic.*, the subconscious, subconsciousness; *adj.*, subconscious.

SUB.CON.TI.NEN.TE, *s.m.*, subcontinent.

SUB.CUL.TU.RA, *s.f.*, subculture.

SUB.CU.TÂ.NEO, *adj.*, *Anat.*, subcutaneous.

SUB.DE.LE.GA.ÇÃO, *s.f.*, subdelegation.

SUB.DE.LE.GA.DO, *s.m.*, subdelegate, inspector, controller.

SUB.DE.SEN.VOL.VER, *v.*, to underdevelop.

SUB.DE.SEN.VOL.VI.DO, *adj.*, underdeveloped.

SUB.DE.SEN.VOL.VI.MEN.TO, *s.m.*, underdevelopment.

SUB.DI.RE.ÇÃO, *s.f.*, act of being subdirector; dignity and authority of a subdirector.

SUB.DI.RE.TOR, *s.m.*, subdirector.

SUB.DIS.TRI.TO, *s.m.*, subdistrict.

SUB.DI.VI.DIR, *v.*, to subdivide.

SUB.DI.VI.SÃO, *s.f.*, subdivision, suballocation.

SUB.DI.VI.SÍ.VEL, *adj.*, subdivisable.

SU.BE.MEN.DA, *s.f.*, subamendment.

SU.BEM.PRE.GO, *s.m.*, underemployment.

SU.BEM.PREI.TA.DA, *s.f.*, subcontract.

SU.BEM.PREI.TAR, *v.*, to subcontract.

SU.BEN.TEN.DER, *v.*, to perceive or interpret correctly an implication, to suppose.

SU.BEN.TEN.DI.DO, *s.m.*, innuendo, implicitness; *adj.*, inferred, implicit, supposed, presumed.

SU.BES.PÉ.CIE, *s.f.*, subspecies.

SU.BES.TA.ÇÃO, *s.f.*, substation.

SU.BES.TI.MA.DO, *adj.*, underestimated.

SU.BES.TI.MAR, *v.*, to underestimate.

SU.BI.DA, *s.f.*, ascension, ascent, raise, rise, rising, acclivity.

SU.BIN.TEN.DÊN.CI.A, *s.f.*, subintendancy, position of subintendant.

SU.BIN.TEN.DEN.TE, *s.m.*, subintendant.

SU.BIR, *v.*, to ascend, to rise, to go up, to mount up, to scale, to increase, to lift.

SU.BI.TA.MEN.TE, *adv.*, suddenly.

SU.BI.TÂ.NE.O, *adj.*, subitaneous, sudden.

SÚBITO

SUBTROPICAL

SÚ.BI.TO, *adj.*, sudden, abrupt, unexpected, swift; *adv.*, suddenly.

SUB.JA.CEN.TE, *adj.*, subjacent, *fig.*, implied.

SUB.JA.ZER, *v.*, to be subjacent, to implied.

SUB.JE.ÇÃO, *s.f., Ret.*, subjection.

SUB.JE.TI.VA.ÇÃO, *s.f.*, subjectiveness, subjectivity.

SUB.JE.TI.VA.MEN.TE, *adv.*, subjectively.

SUB.JE.TI.VAR, *v.*, to render subjective.

SUB.JE.TI.VI.DA.DE, *s.f.*, subjectivity.

SUB.JE.TI.VIS.MO, *s.m.*, subjectivism.

SUB.JE.TI.VO, *adj.*, subjective.

SUB JU.DI.CE, *adj., Lat., Jur.*, under judicial consideration.

SUB.JU.GA.ÇÃO, *s.f.*, subjugation.

SUB.JU.GA.DO, *adj.*, subjugated, dominated.

SUB.JU.GAN.TE, *adj.*, subjugating, subjugator.

SUB.JU.GAR, *v.*, to subjugate, to submit, to subdue.

SUB.JU.GÁ.VEL, *adj.*, that can be subjugated.

SUB.JUN.ÇÃO, *s.f.*, subjunction.

SUB.JUN.TI.VO, *s.m.*, subjunctive mood, subjunctive; *adj.*, subjunctive.

SUB.LE.VA.ÇÃO, *s.f.*, uprising, sublevation.

SUB.LE.VAR, *v.*, to rebel, to revolt, to mutiny; to lift, to raise.

SU.BLI.MA.ÇÃO, *s.f.*, sublimation.

SU.BLI.MA.DO, *s.m., Quím.*, sublimate; *adj.*, sublimated; elevated; exalted.

SU.BLI.MAR, *v.*, to sublime; to make sublime; to exalt.

SU.BLI.MÁ.VEL, *adj.*, sublimable.

SU.BLI.ME, *adj.*, sublime, splendid, glorious, divine.

SU.BLI.NE.AR, *adj.*, sublinear.

SU.BLI.NHA.DOR, *s.m.*, underliner; *adj.*, underlining.

SU.BLI.NHAR, *v.*, to underline.

SUB.LO.CA.ÇÃO, *s.f.*, act of subletting; subtenancy.

SUB.LO.CA.DOR, *s.m.*, sublessor; *adj.*, subletting.

SUB.LO.CAR, *v.*, to underlet, to sublet.

SUB.LO.CA.TÁ.RI.O, *s.m.*, sublessee.

SUB.MA.RI.NO, *s.m.*, submarine; *adj.* submarine.

SUB.MER.GIR, *v.*, to submerge, to inundate, to overflow, to deluge.

SUB.MER.SÃO, *s.f.*, submergence, submersion.

SUB.MER.SÍ.VEL, *adj.*, submergible.

SUB.MER.SO, *adj.*, submerged.

SUB.ME.TER, *v.*, to submit, to subdue, to subject.

SUB.ME.TI.DO, *adj.*, submitted, subordinated.

SUB.ME.TI.MEN.TO, *s.m.*, submission, subjection.

SUB.ME.TRA.LHA.DO.RA, *s.f.*, submachine-gun.

SUB.MI.NIS.TRAR, *v.*, to subministrate, to subminister.

SUB.MIS.SÃO, *s.f.*, submission, submissiveness, subjection.

SUB.MIS.SO, *adj.*, submissive, obedient, dutiful, subordinate.

SUB.MUN.DO, *s.m.*, underworld.

SUB.NU.TRI.ÇÃO, *s.f.*, underfeeding, undernourishment.

SUB.NU.TRI.DO, *adj.*, underfed, undernourished.

SUB.NU.TRIR, *v.*, to undernourish.

SU.BOR.DEM, *s.f.*, suborder.

SU.BOR.DI.NA.ÇÃO, *s.f.*, subordination, obedience.

SU.BOR.DI.NA.DA, *s.f., Gram.*, subordinate clause.

SU.BOR.DI.NA.DO, *adj.*, subordinate.

SU.BOR.DI.NA.DOR, *s.m.*, subordinator; *adj.*, subordinating.

SU.BOR.DI.NAN.TE, *adj.*, subordinating, subordinative.

SU.BOR.DI.NAR, *v.*, to subordinate, to subject, to subdue.

SU.BOR.NAR, *v.*, to suborn, to bribe.

SU.BOR.NO, *s.m.*, subornation, embracery, bribery.

SU.BOR.NÁ.VEL, *adj.*, bribable.

SUB.PO.LAR, *adj.*, subpolar.

SUB.PRE.FEI.TO, *s.m.*, assistant mayor.

SUB.PRE.FEI.TU.RA, *s.f.*, administrative subdistrict of a municipality.

SUB.PRO.DU.ÇÃO, *s.f., Econ.*, underproduction.

SUB.PRO.DU.TO, *s.m.*, subproduct, byproduct.

SUB-RA.ÇA, *s.f.*, subrace.

SUB-RE.GI.ÃO, *s.f.*, subregion.

SUB-RE.GI.O.NAL, *adj.*, subregional.

SUB-REP.TI.CI.A.MEN.TE, *adv.*, subreptitiously.

SUB-REP.TÍ.CI.O, *adj.*, subreptitious, furtive.

SUBS.CRE.VER, *v.*, to subscribe, to underwrite, to sign, to endorse.

SUBS.CRI.ÇÃO, *s.f.*, subscription, subscribing, agreement.

SUBS.CRI.TO, *s.m.*, subscript; *adj.*, subscript; subscribed, signed.

SUB.SE.CRE.TÁ.RI.O, *s.m.*, undersecretary.

SUB.SE.QUEN.TE, *adj.*, subsequent, sequent, ensuing.

SUB.SER.VI.EN.TE, *adj.*, subservient.

SUB.SI.DI.A.DO, *s.m.*, one who received a subsidy; *adj.*, subsidized.

SUB.SI.DI.AR, *v.*, to subsidize.

SUB.SI.DI.Á.RI.A, *s.f.*, subsidiary (enterprise).

SUB.SI.DI.Á.RIO, *adj.*, subsidiary.

SUB.SÍ.DIO, *s.m.*, subsidy, aid, assistance, help, grant, subvention.

SUB.SIS.TE.MA, *s.m.*, subsystem.

SUB.SIS.TÊN.CIA, *s.f.*, subsistence, sustenance.

SUB.SIS.TEN.TE, *adj.*, subsistent.

SUB.SIS.TIR, *v.*, to subsist, to exist, to survive, to persist.

SUB.SO.LO, *s.m.*, subsoil, substrate, underground.

SUB.SÔ.NI.CO, *adj., Fís.*, subsonic.

SUBS.TA.BE.LE.CER, *v.*, to substitute, to appoint as substitute; to subrogate.

SUBS.TÂN.CIA, *s.f.*, substance, matter, stuff, essence, amount.

SUBS.TAN.CI.AL, *adj.*, essential, nutritive, nourishing.

SUBS.TAN.CI.A.LI.DA.DE, *s.f.*, substantiality.

SUBS.TAN.CI.O.SO, *adj.*, substantial.

SUBS.TAN.TI.VA.ÇÃO, *s.f., Gram.*, act of changing aword into a noun.

SUBS.TAN.TI.VAR, *v.*, to substantivize.

SUBS.TAN.TI.VO, *s.m.*, substantive, noun; *adj.*, substantive.

SUBS.TI.TUI.DO, *adj.*, substituted.

SUBS.TI.TUI.ÇÃO, *s.f.*, substitution, substituting.

SUBS.TI.TU.IR, *v.*, to substitute, to put, to replace.

SUBS.TI.TU.Í.VEL, *adj.*, replaceable, substitutable.

SUBS.TI.TU.TI.VO, *s.m.*, substitution, replacement.

SUBS.TI.TU.TO, *s.m.*, substitute, successor, proxy.

SUB.TE.NEN.TE, *s.m., Mil.*, sublieutenant, second lieutenant.

SUB.TER.FÚ.GIO, *s.m.*, subterfuge, excuse, shift, text.

SUB.TER.FU.GIR, *v.*, to make use of subterfuges, to escape.

SUB.TER.RÁ.NEO, *s.m.*, a subterranean place, cave, basement, cavern; *adj.*, subterranean.

SUB.TÍ.TU.LO, *s.m.*, sub-title, sub-heading.

SUB.TÔ.NI.CA, *s.f., Mús.*, subtonic.

SUB.TO.TAL, *s.m.*, subtotal.

SUB.TRA.ÇÃO, *s.f.*, subtraction, diminution, deduction.

SUB.TRA.IR, *v.*, to subtract, to withdraw, to defalcate.

SUB.TRO.PI.CAL, *adj.*, subtropical.

SUBUMANO · 324 · SUMO

SU.BU.MA.NO, *adj.*, subhuman, inhuman.
SU.BUR.BA.NI.ZAR, *v.*, to suburbanize.
SU.BUR.BA.NO, *adj.*, suburban, suburbial, uptown.
SU.BÚR.BIO, *s.m.*, suburb, environs.
SUB.VEN.ÇÃO, *s.f.*, subvention, subsidy.
SUB.VEN.CI.O.NA.DO, *adj.*, subventioned.
SUB.VEN.CI.O.NAL, *adj.*, subventionary.
SUB.VEN.CI.O.NAR, *v.*, to subsidize.
SUB.VER.SÃO, *s.f.*, subversion, overthrow, revolt.
SUB.VER.SI.VO, *s.m.*, a subversive person; *adj.*, subversive.
SUB.VER.TER, *v.*, to subvert, to overturn, to destroy, to ruin, to disturb.
SU.CA.TA, *s.f.*, scrap(s), scrap iron, junk iron.
SU.CA.TEI.RO, *s.m.*, person who deals with scrap metal.
SUC.ÇÃO, *s.f.*, suction, suck, aspiration.
SU.CE.DÂ.NE.O, *s.m.*, succedaneum; substitute; *adj.*, succedaneous, substitute.
SU.CE.DER, *v.*, to succeed, to happen, to occur, to follow after.
SU.CE.DI.DO, *adj.*, occurred, successful.
SU.CES.SÃO, *s.f.*, succession, sequence, progression.
SU.CES.SI.VA.MEN.TE, *adv.*, successively.
SU.CES.SÍ.VEL, *adj.*, capable of succession.
SU.CES.SI.VO, *adj.*, successive, succeeding.
SU.CES.SO, *s.m.*, outcome, success.
SU.CES.SOR, *s.m.*, successor, aftercomer.
SU.CES.SÓ.RI.O, *adj.*, successional, successive.
SÚ.CIA, *s.f.*, gang, mob, rabble.
SU.CIN.TO, *adj.*, succinct, brief, short.
SU.CO, *s.m.*, juice, sap, essence.
SÚ.CU.BO, *s.m.*, succubus; *adj.*, pertaining to or relative to a succubus.
SU.CU.LÊN.CI.A, *s.f.*, succulence, juiciness.
SU.CU.LEN.TO, *adj.*, succulent, sappy, pulpy, rich.
SU.CUM.BIR, *v.*, to succumb, to yield, to submit, to perish, to despair.
SU.CU.RI, *s.f.*, anaconda.
SU.CUR.SAL, *s.f.*, *Com.*, succursal; *adj.*, succursal.
SU.DA.NÊS, *s.m.*, *adj.*, Sudanese.
SU.DÃO, *s.*, Sudan.
SU.DÁ.RIO, *s.m.*, sudarium, sweat cloth.
SU.DES.TE, *s.m.*, south-east; *adj.*, south-east, south-eastern.
SÚ.DI.TO, *s.m.*, subject, vassal, liege.
SU.DO.ES.TE, *s.m.*, southwest.
SU.DO.RE.SE, *s.f.*, diaphoresis.
SU.É.CIA, *s.*, Sweden.
SU.E.CO, *s.m.*, Swede; *adj.*, Swedish.
SU.É.TER, *s.m.*, sweater.
SU.FI.CI.ÊN.CIA, *s.f.*, sufficiency, adequacy, ability, capacity.
SU.FI.CI.EN.TE, *adj.*, sufficient, adequate, enough.
SU.FI.XA.ÇÃO, *s.f.*, *Gram.*, suffixation, suffixion.
SU.FI.XAR, *v.*, to suffix.
SU.FI.XO, *s.m.*, suffix, postfix, affix.
SU.FO.CA.ÇÃO, *s.f.*, suffocation, choke, strangulation.
SU.FO.CA.MEN.TO, *s.m.*, asphyxiation.
SU.FO.CAN.TE, *adj.*, suffocating, suffocative; sultry, oppressive.
SU.FO.CAR, *v.*, to suffocate, to choke, to smother, to strangle.
SU.FRA.GAR, *v.*, to suffragate, to suffrage.
SU.FRÁ.GIO, *s.m.*, suffrage, vote, voting.
SU.GA.DOR, *s.m.*, sucker; *adj.*, sucking; suction
SU.GAR, *v.*, to suck, to absorb, to extort.

SU.GE.RIR, *v.*, to suggest, to insinuate, to inspire, to prompt.
SU.GE.RÍ.VEL, *adj.*, suggestible.
SU.GES.TÃO, *s.f.*, suggestion, proposal, hint, intimation.
SU.GES.TI.O.NA.BI.LI.DA.DE, *s.f.*, suggestibility.
SU.GES.TI.O.NA.DO, *adj.*, suggestible (influenced by suggestion).
SU.GES.TI.O.NA.MEN.TO, *s.m.*, suggesting, suggestibility (influencing by suggestion).
SU.GES.TIO.NAR, *v.*, to suggestion, to influence, to inspire.
SU.GES.TI.O.NÁ.VEL, *adj.*, suggestible.
SU.GES.TI.VO, *adj.*, suggestive, significant.
SU.Í.ÇA, *s.*, Switzerland.
SUÍ.ÇAS, *s.f.*, *pl.*, sideburns.
SU.I.CI.DA, *s.2 gen.*, suicide(suicidal person); *adj.*, suicidal.
SUI.CI.DAR-SE, *v.*, to suicide, to commit suicide.
SUI.CÍ.DIO, *s.m.*, suicide, self-murder.
SU.Í.ÇO, *adj.*, *s.m.*, Swiss.
SU.IN.GUE, *s.m.*, *Mús.*, swing.
SU.Í.NO, *s.m.*, swine, pig; *adj.*, swinish.
SU.I.NO.CUL.TOR, *s.m.*, pig farmer, pig breeder.
SU.I.NO.CUL.TU.RA, *s.f.*, pig farming, pig breeding.
SU.Í.TE, *s.f.*, *Mús.*, suite; series; a group of connected rooms.
SU.JAR, *v.*, to dirty, to stain, to spot, to maculate, to blot.
SU.JEI.ÇÃO, *s.f.*, subjection, subordination; bondage.
SU.JEI.RA, *s.f.*, dirt, filth, slosh.
SU.JEI.TAR, *v.*, to subject, to submit, to obligate, to dominate.
SU.JEI.TO, *s.m.*, subject, citizen, individual, fellow, chap.
SU.JO, *adj.*, dirty, filthy, sordid, indecorous, greasy, soiled.
SUL, *s.m.*, south, south wind.
SUL-A.FRI.CA.NO, *s.m.*, *adj.*, South African.
SUL-A.ME.RI.CA.NO, *adj.*, *s.m.*, South American.
SUL-A.SI.Á.TI.CO, *s.m.*, native or inhabitant of South Asia; *adj.*, referring to South Asia.
SUL.CA.DO, *adj.*, sulcate.
SUL.CAR, *v.*, to sulcate, to furrow, to ridge.
SUL.CO, *s.m.*, furrow.
SUL.FA.TI.ZAR, *v.*, *Quím.*, to sulphatize, to sulphate.
SUL.FA.TO, *s.m.*, *Quím.*, sulphate.
SUL.FE.TO, *s.m.*, *Quím.*, sulphide, sulfide.
SUL.FÍ.DRI.CO, *adj.*, *Quím.*, hydrosulphuric.
SUL.FI.TE, *adj.*, sulphitic.
SÚL.FUR, *s.m.*, *Quím.*, sulphur.
SUL.FU.RA.DO, *adj.*, *Quím.*, sulphurated, sulphurized.
SUL.FÚ.RI.CO, *adj.*, *Quím.*, sulphuric.
SU.LIS.TA, *s.2 gen.*, southerner; *adj.*, southern.
SUL.TA.NA, *s.f.*, sultana, sultaness.
SUL.TA.NA.TO, *s.m.*, sultanship, sultanate.
SUL.TA.NE.AR, *v.*, to live like a sultan.
SUL.TÃO, *s.m.*, sultan, ruler, sovereign.
SU.MA, *s.f.*, summary, sum, total.
SU.MA.MEN.TE, *adv.*, extremely.
SU.MA.REN.TO, *adj.*, juicy, succulent.
SU.MÁ.RIO, *s.m.*, summary, digest, abbreviation, synopsis; *adj.*, summary, concise, succint.
SU.MI.DA.DE, *s.f.*, prominence; summit.
SU.MI.ÇO, *s.m.*, disappearance, escape, vanishing.
SU.MI.DI.ÇO, *adj.*, evanescent.
SU.MI.DO, *adj.*, evanished, hidden, disappeared; low (voice); faint.
SU.MIR, *v.*, to disappear, to vanish, to lose, to submerge.
SU.MO, *s.m.*, juice, sap, lushness; *adj.*, lofty, superior, supreme.

SUMÔ ·· 325 ·· SURGIR

SU.MÔ, s.m., Esp., sumo (a traditional Japanese sport).
SÚ.MU.LA, s.f., summula, epitome, summary, compendium.
SUN.DAE, s.m., Ingl., sundae.
SUN.GA, s.f., Bras., swim trunks.
SUN.TUO.SI.DA.DE, s.f., sumptuosity.
SUN.TU.O.SO, adj., sumptuous, magnificent, luxurious, splendid.
SU.OR, s.m., sweat, perspiration.
SU.PER-, pref., over, above, superior, beyond, excess, higher.
SU.PE.RA.BUN.DÂN.CI.A, s.f., superabundance.
SU.PE.RA.BUN.DAN.TE, adj., superabundant.
SU.PE.RA.BUN.DAR, v., to superabound, overabound.
SU.PE.RA.ÇÃO, s.f., overcoming.
SU.PE.RA.DO, adj., overcome, outmoded.
SU.PE.RA.QUE.CER, v., to superheat, to overheat.
SU.PE.RA.QUE.CI.MEN.TO, s.m., overheating, superheating.
SU.PE.RAR, v., to overcome, to dominate, to subjugate, to subdue.
SU.PE.RÁ.VEL, adj., superable.
SU.PE.RÁ.VIT, s.m., superavit; surplus.
SU.PE.RA.VI.TÁ.RI.O, adj., Econ., that presents superavit.
SU.PER.CÍ.LIO, s.m., eyebrow.
SU.PER.DI.MEN.SI.O.NA.DO, adj., oversized.
SU.PER.DO.TA.DO, s.m., Bras., genius; gifted person; adj., gifted, talented, endowed; vulg., well endowed.
SU.PE.RE.GO, s.m., Psic., superego; fig., model, example.
SU.PE.RES.TI.MA, s.f., overestimate, overestimation.
SU.PE.RES.TI.MAR, v., Bras., to overestimate.
SU.PE.RES.TRU.TU.RA, s.f., superstructure.
SU.PER.FI.CI.AL, adj., superficial, external, outside.
SU.PER.FI.CIA.LI.DA.DE, s.f., superficiality.
SU.PER.FI.CI.A.LIS.MO, s.m., superficialness.
SU.PER.FI.CI.AL.MEN.TE, adv., superficially.
SU.PER.FÍ.CIE, s.f., surface, superficies, outside.
SU.PÉR.FLUO, adj., superfluous, unnecessary.
SU.PER-HO.MEM, s.m., superman.
SU.PE.RIN.TEN.DÊN.CI.A, s.f., superintendency.
SU.PE.RIN.TEN.DEN.TE, s.2 gen., superintendent.
SU.PE.RI.OR, s.m., superior, head of a monastery; adj., higher, upper, loftier, greater.
SU.PE.RIO.RI.DA.DE, s.f., superiority.
SU.PER.LA.TI.VO, s.m., superlative; adj., superlative.
SU.PER.LO.TA.ÇÃO, s.f., overcrowding.
SU.PER.LO.TA.DO, adj., overcrowded.
SU.PER.LO.TAR, v., to overcrowd, to overload.
SU.PER.MER.CA.DO, s.m., supermarket.
SU.PER.PO.PU.LA.ÇÃO, s.f., overpopulation.
SU.PER.POR, v., to superpose.
SU.PER.PO.SI.ÇÃO, s.f., superposition.
SU.PER.PO.TÊN.CI.A, s.f., superpower.
SU.PER.PO.VO.A.DO, adj., overpopulated.
SU.PER.PO.VO.A.MEN.TO, s.m., overpopulation.
SU.PER.PRO.DU.ÇÃO, s.f., overproduction.
SU.PER.PRO.TE.GER, v., overprotect.
SU.PER.SEN.SI.BI.LI.DA.DE, s.f., supersensitiveness, oversensitivity.
SU.PER.SEN.SÍ.VEL, adj., supersensible.
SU.PER.SÔ.NI.CO, adj., supersonic.
SU.PERS.TI.ÇÃO, s.f., superstition.
SU.PERS.TI.CI.O.SO, adj., superstitious.
SU.PER.VA.LO.RI.ZA.ÇÃO, s.f., overvaluation.

SU.PER.VE.NI.ÊN.CI.A, s.f., supervenience.
SU.PER.VE.NI.EN.TE, adj., supervenient.
SU.PER.VI.SÃO, s.f., supervision.
SU.PER.VI.SIO.NAR, v., to supervise, to oversee.
SU.PER.VI.SOR, s.m., supervisor.
SU.PE.TÃO, adv., suddenly, unexpectedly; de ~: all of a sudden.
SU.PIM.PA, adj., Bras., col., fine, spanking, terrific.
SU.PLAN.TA.ÇÃO, s.f., supplantation.
SU.PLAN.TAR, v., to supplant, to supersede.
SU.PLE.MEN.TAR, v., to supplement; adj., supplemental, additional.
SU.PLE.MEN.TO, s.m., supplement, appendix.
SU.PLÊN.CI.A, s.f., supplying, substituting.
SU.PLEN.TE, s. 2 gen., substitute, proxy.
SU.PLEN.TE, s.2 gen., substitute; adj., substitutional.
SU.PLI.CAN.TE, s. 2 gen., supplicant, implorer; adj., supplicant, supplicating, suppliant.
SU.PLI.CAR, v., to supplicate, to implore; to pray.
SU.PLI.CI.AR, v., to torture, to hurt; to execute.
SU.PLÍ.CI.O, s.m., torture; death; fig., pain, torment.
SU.POR, v., to suppose, to assume, to think, to imagine.
SU.POR.TA.BI.LI.DA.DE, s.f., supportableness.
SU.POR.TAR, v., to support, to suffer, to endure, to stand.
SU.POR.TÁ.VEL, adj., supportable, tolerable.
SU.POR.TE, s.m., support, stay, prop.
SU.PO.SI.ÇÃO, s.f., supposition, conjecture, presumption.
SU.PO.SI.TI.VO, adj., supositious, suppositional.
SU.PO.SI.TÓ.RIO, s.m., suppository.
SU.POS.TA.MEN.TE, adv., supposedly.
SU.POS.TO, adj., supposed, presumed, assumed.
SU.PRA.CI.TA.DO, adj., aforementioned, foresaid, mentioned before.
SU.PRA.NA.CI.O.NAL, adj., supranational.
SU.PRAS.SU.MO, s.m., top, utmost, highest, ideal.
SU.PRE.MA.CI.A, s.f., supremacy, sovereignty.
SU.PRE.MO, s.m., Supreme Court; adj., supreme, highest, utmost.
SU.PRES.SÃO, s.f., suppression.
SU.PRES.SI.VO, adj., suppressive.
SU.PRES.SOR, adj., the same that supressivo.
SU.PRI.MEN.TO, s.m., supply, subsidy, aid, loan.
SU.PRI.MI.DO, adj., suppressed, abolished.
SU.PRI.MIR, v., to suppress, to abolish, to omit.
SU.PRI.MÍ.VEL, adj., suppressible.
SU.PRIR, v., to supply, to furnish, to help, to aid, to compensate.
SU.PRÍ.VEL, adj., suppliable.
SU.PU.RA.ÇÃO, s.f., suppuration.
SU.PU.RA.DO, adj., suppurating, purulent.
SU.PU.RAR, v., to suppurate.
SU.PU.RA.TI.VO, s.m., Farm., suppurative; adj., suppurative.
SUR.DEZ, s.f., deafness.
SUR.DI.NA, s.f., mute, sourdine.
SUR.DO, adj., deaf, unable to hear.
SUR.DO-MU.DO, adj., s.m., deaf-mute.
SUR.FAR, v., to surf, to ride the surf (as on a surfboard).
SUR.FE, s.m., Esp., surfing.
SUR.FIS.TA, s. 2 gen., Bras., surfboarder, surfer.
SUR.GI.MEN.TO, s.m., appearance, emergence.
SUR.GIR, v., to arise, to appear, to emerge, to arouse, to well.

SURINAME ·· 326 ·· SUVENIR

SU.RI.NA.ME, *s.*, Surinam.
SUR.PRE.EN.DEN.TE, *adj.*, surprising, astonishing, amazing.
SUR.PRE.EN.DEN.TE.MEN.TE, *adv.*, surprisingly.
SUR.PRE.EN.DER, *v.*, to surprise, to astonish, to amaze, to startle.
SUR.PRE.SA, *s.f.*, surprise, surprisal, astonishment.
SUR.PRE.SO, *adj.*, surprised, amazed, startled.
SUR.RA, *s.f.*, thrashing, spanking.
SUR.RA.DO, *adj.*, worn, worn out, curried.
SUR.RAR, *v.*, to beat, to spank, to curry, to tan, to beat, to flog.
SUR.RE.A.LIS.MO, *s.m.*, surrealism.
SUR.RE.A.LIS.TA, *s. 2 gen.*, surrealist; *adj.*, surrealistic.
SUR.RU.PI.AR, *v.*, to steal.
SUR.SIS, *s.m.*, *Jur.*, suspended sentence.
SUR.TAR, *v.*, *fam.*, to go berserk.
SUR.TIR, *v.*, to occasion, to result in.
SUR.TO, *s.m.*, outbreak, boom.
SUS.CE.TI.BI.LI.DA.DE, *s.f.*, susceptibility, touchiness.
SUS.CE.TI.BI.LI.ZAR, *v.*, to hurt, to offend, to grieve.
SUS.CE.TÍ.VEL, *s.m.*, sensitive person; *adj.*, susceptible.
SUS.CI.TA.ÇÃO, *s.f.*, suscitation, arousal, stimulation.
SUS.CI.TAR, *v.*, to suscitate, to excite, to rouse, to cause, to provoke.
SUS.CI.TÁ.VEL, *adj.*, that may give rise to.
SUS.PEI.ÇÃO, *s.f.*, suspicion, distrust, mistrust.
SUS.PEI.TA, *s.f.*, suspicion, diffidence, doubt.
SUS.PEI.TAR, *v.*, to suspect, to distrust, to suppose.
SUS.PEI.TO, *adj.*, suspect, suspected, suspicious.
SUS.PEN.DER, *v.*, to hang, to suspend, to hang up, to hoist, to postpone.
SUS.PEN.SÃO, *s.f.*, suspension, interruption, postponement, suspending.
SUS.PEN.SE, *s.m.*, suspense.

SUS.PEN.SI.VO, *adj.*, suspensive.
SUS.PEN.SO, *adj.*, suspended, hanging, interrupted.
SUS.PEN.SÓ.RIO, *s.f.*, suspensory, shoulder straps.
SUS.SUR.RAN.TE, *adj.*, rustling, whispering, murmuring.
SUS.PI.RAR, *v.*, to sigh, to lament.
SUS.PI.RO, *s.m.*, sigh, suspiration; meringue (candy).
SUS.PI.RO.SO, *adj.*, sighing, lamenting.
SUS.SUR.RAR, *v.*, to whisper, to murmur, to rustle.
SUS.SUR.RO, *s.m.*, rustle, whisper, whispering.
SUS.TA.ÇÃO, *s.f.*, act of suspending, stopping.
SUS.TÂN.CI.A, *s.f.*, *pop.*, vigour, strength.
SUS.TAR, *v.*, to stop, to halt, to suspend.
SUS.TÁ.VEL, *adj.*, capable of being stopped.
SUS.TE.NI.DO, *s.m.*, sharp.
SUS.TEN.TA.ÇÃO, *s.f.*, sustentation, subsistence, holding.
SUS.TEN.TÁ.CU.LO, *s.m.*, support, *fig.*, mainstay, supporter.
SUS.TEN.TA.DO, *adj.*, supported.
SUS.TEN.TA.DOR, *s.m.*, supporter, sustainer; *adj.*, supporting, sustaining.
SUS.TEN.TAR, *v.*, to sustain, to support, to maintain, to uphold, to defend.
SUS.TEN.TO, *s.m.*, maintenance, support.
SUS.TER, *v.*, to support, to prop, to sustain.
SUS.TO, *s.m.*, fright, shock, alarm.
SU.TI.Ã, *s.m.*, brassière, bust bodice.
SU.TIL, *adj.*, subtile, subtle, tenous, rarefied, wily, crafty.
SU.TI.LE.ZA, *s.f.*, subtileness, subtility, subtlety.
SU.TI.LI.DA.DE, *s.f.*, subtleness, subtlety.
SU.TIL.MEN.TE, *adv.*, subtly.
SU.TU.RA, *s.f.*, suture, sewing, seam.
SU.TU.RAR, *v.*, to suture, to join by suture or sewing.
SU.VE.NIR, *s.m.*, souvenir.

T, *s.m.*, the nineteenth letter of the Portuguese alphabet.
TÁ, *fam.*, short of *está; interj.*, stop!, hold!; ok!.
TA.BA, *s.f.*, Indian village.
TA.BA.CA.RI.A, *s.f.*, tobacco shop, cigar store.
TA.BA.CO, *s.m.*, tobacco.
TA.BA.GIS.MO, *s.m., Med.*, tobaccoism.
TA.BA.GIS.TA, *s. 2 gen.*, smoker.
TA.BE.FE, *s.m.*, whey, slap.
TA.BE.LA, *s.f.*, table, chart, list, catalogue, schedule, index, roster.
TA.BE.LA.DO, *adj.*, controlled price, fixed.
TA.BE.LA.MEN.TO, *s.m.*, control of prices.
TA.BE.LAR, *v.*, to control, to put on the official price list, to regulate.
TA.BE.LI.ÃO, *s.m.*, notary public.
TA.BE.LI.AR, *v.*, to exercise the functions of a notary.
TA.BE.LI.NHA, *s.f., Bras., Esp.*, repeated exchange of the ballbetween players (soccer).
TA.BE.LIO.NA.TO, *s.m.*, office of a notary.
TA.BER.NA, *s.f.*, tavern, pot-house, inn.
TA.BER.NÁ.CU.LO, *s.m.*, tabernacle.
TA.BI.CAR, *v.*, to separate with a wedge, to cleave.
TÁ.BI.DO, *adj.*, rotten, foul, corrupt.
TA.BI.QUE, *s.m.*, thin wooden partition.
TA.BLA.DO, *s.m.*, stage, raised platform.
TA.BLA.TU.RA, *s.f., Mús.*, tablature.
TA.BLE.TE, *s.m.*, tablet, bar, pastille.
TA.BLOI.DE, *s.m.*, tabloid.
TA.BU, *s.m.*, taboo.
TÁ.BUA, *s.f.*, board; *tábua de passar roupa*:ironing board.
TA.BU.A.DA, *s.f.*, multiplication table.
TA.BU.LA.ÇÃO, *s.f.*, tabulation.
TA.BU.LA.DOR, *s.m.*, tabulator.
TA.BU.LAR, *v.*, to tabularize; *adj.*, arranged in columns, tabular.
TA.BU.LE, *s.m., Cul.*, tabbouleh, tabouli (Arab delicacy).
TA.BU.LEI.RO, *s.m.*, checkerboard, flower bed.
TA.BU.LE.TA, *s.f.*, signboard.
TA.ÇA, *s.f.*, cup.
TA.CA.DA, *s.f.*, blow, stroke with a stick; *Esp.*, strike.
TA.CA.NHI.CE, *s.f.*, stupidity, niggardliness, narrow-mindedness.
TA.CA.NHO, *adj.*, short, not tall, avaricious, niggard.
TA.CHA, *s.f.*, tack, sharp.
TA.CHAR, *v.*, to tax, to censure, to brand, to stigmatize.
TA.CHE.A.DO, *adj.*, tacked, studded.
TA.CHI.NHA, *s.f.*, US thumbtack, UK drawing pin.
TA.CHO, *s.m.*, bowl, pot, pan, boiler.
TA.CHO.NAR, *v.*, to fasten with tacks; to cover with stains and spots, to speckle.
TA.CI.TA.MEN.TE, *adv.*, tacitly.
TÁ.CI.TO, *adj.*, tacit, silent, reserved, implicit.
TA.CI.TUR.NI.DA.DE, *s.f.*, taciturnity.

TA.CI.TUR.NO, *adj.*, taciturn, reserved.
TA.CO, *s.m.*, billiard cue, golf club, hockey stick.
TA.CÓ.GRA.FO, *s.m.*, tachograph.
TA.CO.ME.TRI.A, *s.f.*, tachometry.
TA.CÔ.ME.TRO, *s.m.*, tachometer.
TA.DI.NHO, *interj.*, the same that *coitado*.
TA.FE.TÁ, *s.m.*, taffeta.
TA.GAN.TAR, *v., Ant.*, to whip, to lash, to scourge.
TA.GAN.TE, *s.m., Ant.*, whip, scourge.
TA.GA.RE.LA, *s. 2 gen.*, chatterer, talkative, babbler.
TA.GA.RE.LAR, *v.*, to chatter, to babble, to jabber.
TA.GA.RE.LI.CE, *s.f.*, talkativeness, indiscretion, loquacity, blab.
TA.I.LAN.DÊS, *s.m., adj.*, Thai.
TA.I.LÂN.DIA, *s.*, Thailand.
TAIL.LEUR, *s.m., Fr.*, (women's) suit.
TAI.NE, *s.m., Cul.*, tahina, tahini (Arab delicacy).
TA.I.NHA, *s.f.*, mullet.
TAI.PA, *s.f.*, stucco, lath-and-plaster wall.
TAI.PA.DO, *adj.*, walled of lath-and-plaster.
TAI.PAR, *v.*, to make a wall of lath-and-plaster; to partition; to pug.
TA.I.TI, *s.*, Tahiti.
TAI.WAN, *s.*, Taiwan.
TAI.WA.NÊS, *s. 2 gen., adj.*, taiwanese.
TAL, *adj.*, such, like, similar; *adv.*, so, thus, accordingly; *pron.*, this, that.
TA.LA, *s.f.*, champ, splice, splint.
TA.LA.BAR.TE, *s.m.*, baldric.
TA.LÃO, *s.m.*, coupon stub; *talão de cheque*:checkbook.
TAL.CO, *s.m.*, talc, talcum powder.
TAL.CO.SO, *adj.*, talcose, talcous.
TA.LEN.TO, *s.m.*, talent, ability, ingenuity, aptitude.
TA.LEN.TO.SO, *adj.*, talented, able, smart.
TA.LHA.DA, *s.f.*, slice, cutting; *col.*, reprimand, reproof.
TA.LHA.DEI.RA, *s.f.*, chisel, splitter; cleaver.
TA.LHA.DO, *s.m., Bras.*, cliff, precipice; *adj.*, cut, engraved, sliced.
TA.LHA.DOR, *s.m.*, cutter, chopper, cleaver, butcher; *adj.*, slicing, cutting, carving, chopping.
TA.LHAR, *v.*, to cut, to cut off, to cut out, to slice.
TA.LHA.RIM, *s.m.*, noodles.
TA.LHE, *s.m.*, cut, fashion, style, form.
TA.LHER, *s.m.*, set of knife, fork and spoon.
TA.LHO, *s.m.*, cutting, chopping.
TA.LI.ÃO, *s.m.*, talion, retaliation
TA.LIM, *s.m.*, baldric, sword-belt.
TA.LIS.MÃ, *s.m.*, talisman, amulet, charm, fetish.
TA.LO, *s.m.*, stalk, petiole, bind.
TA.LO.SO, *adj.*, stalky, with long stalks.
TA.LU.DE, *s.m.*, talus, inclination, acclivity.
TA.LU.DO, *adj.*, stalky, caulescent; vigorous, corpulent, tall,

TALVEZ ···328··· TATARAVÔ

strong.

TAL.VEZ, *adv.*, perhaps, maybe, possibly.

TA.MAN.CA, *s.f.*, wooden shoe, sabot, clog.

TA.MAN.CO, *s.m.*, clog, sabot.

TA.MAN.DU.Á, *s.m., Zool.*, tamandua, anteater.

TA.MA.NHO, *s.m.*, size, bulk, proportion, volume.

TA.MA.NHO-FA.MÍ.LI.A, *adj.*, family-size, big size.

TÂ.MA.RA, *s.f., Bot.*, date (fruit of the date palm).

TAM.BÉM, *adv.*, also, so, besides, too, likewise, either.

TAM.BOR, *s.m.*, drum, tambour, drummer.

TAM.BO.RE.TE, *s.m.*, tabouret, footstool, short person.

TAM.BO.RI.LAR, *v.*, to drum, to pelt.

TAM.PA, *s.f.*, cover, covering, lid, cap, stopple.

TAM.PA.DO, *adj.*, covered, stopped, thick.

TAM.PÃO, *s.m.*, large lid; big cork, tampion, dowel, plug; *Med.*, compress.

TAM.PAR, *v.*, to cover, to cap, to shut, to top, to stopper.

TAM.PI.NHA, *s.f.*, bottle cap.

TAM.PO, *s.m.*, barrel top; toilet seat cover.

TAM.PO.NA.MEN.TO, *s.m.*, plugging.

TAM.PO.NAR, *v.*, to plug, to bung.

TAM.POU.CO, *adv.*, either, neither, no more.

TA.NA.GEM, *s.f.*, tannage, tanning.

TA.NA.JU.RA, *s.f., Bras., Zool.*, common name of female species of ants.

TA.NA.TO.LO.GI.A, *s.f.*, thanatology.

TAN.GA, *s.f.*, loincloth, thong.

TAN.GÊN.CI.A, *s.f.*, tangency.

TAN.GEN.CI.AR, *v.*, to tangency, be tangent to.

TAN.GEN.TE, *s.f.*, tangent; *adj.*, tangent, touching.

TAN.GER, *v.*, to play, to sound, to ring.

TAN.GE.RI.NA, *s.f., Bot.*, tangerine, mandarin.

TAN.GE.RI.NEI.RA, *s.f., Bot.*, tangerine tree (*Citrus reticulata*).

TAN.GI.BI.LI.DA.DE, *s.f.*, tangibleness, tangibility.

TAN.GÍ.VEL, *adj.*, tangible, palpable, impressionable.

TAN.GI.VEL.MEN.TE, *adv.*, tangibly.

TAN.GO, *s.m., Mús.*, tango.

TAN.GUIS.TA, *s. 2 gen.*, tango dancer.

TA.NI.NO, *s.m., Quím.*, tannin.

TA.NO.A.RI.A, *s.f.*, cooperage.

TA.NO.EI.RO, *s.m.*, cooper, barrelmaker, tubber.

TAN.QUE, *s.m.*, tank, reservoir, cistern, basin.

TAN.TÃ, *adj., col.*, crazy.

TÂN.TA.LO, *s.m., Quím.*, tantalum.

TAN.TO, *s.m.*, an indeterminate quantity, sum; *adj.*, as much, so much, as many; *adv.*, thus,

to such a degree.

TAN.ZÂ.NIA, *s.*, Tanzania.

TÃO, *adv.*, so, such, that, as, so much.

TAO.IS.MO, *s.m.*, Taoism.

TAO.IS.TA, *s. 2 gen.*, Taoist.

TÃO SÓ, *adv.*, only, simply.

TÃO SO.MEN.TE, *adv.*, only, simply.

TA.PA, *s.m.*, slap, rap, flap.

TA.PA-BU.RA.CO, *s. 2 gen., col.*, one who replaces another in an emergency.

TA.PA.DO, *adj.*, covered, thick.

TA.PAR, *v.*, to close, to plug, to fill up, to block, to cover.

TA.PEA.ÇÃO, *s.f.*, swindle, cheat, trickery, fake.

TA.PE.A.DOR, *s.m., Bras., pop.*, cheat, swindler, faker; *adj.*, cheating, deceitful, faking, tricking.

TA.PE.AR, *v.*, to deceive, to fake, to trick, to humbug.

TA.PE.ÇA.RI.A, *s.f.*, tapestry, hangings, carpet shop.

TA.PE.CEI.RO, *s.m.*, maker or seller of carpets or curtains.

TA.PE.RA, *s.f., Bras.*, ruined house, bad and ugly place, abandoned place.

TA.PE.TAR, *v.*, to carpet.

TA.PE.TE, *s.m.*, carpet, rug, matting.

TA.PI.NHA, *s.f.*, slap, pat.

TA.PI.O.CA, *s.f., Bras.*, tapioca.

TA.PU.ME, *s.m.*, hedge, boarding, screen, fence.

TA.QUA.RA, *s.f., Bras., Bot.*, a variety of bamboo.

TA.QUA.RAL, *s.m., Bras.*, bamboo growth.

TA.QUI.CAR.DI.A, *s.f., Med.*, tachycardia.

TA.QUI.CÁR.DI.CO, *adj.*, tachycardic.

TA.QUI.GRA.FAR, *v.*, to stenograph.

TA.QUI.GRA.FI.A, *s.f.*, tachygraphy, shorthand.

TA.QUI.GRÁ.FI.CO, *adj.*, tachygraphic, stenographic.

TA.QUÍ.GRA.FO, *s.m.*, tachygrapher, stenographer.

TA.RA, *s.f.*, defect, flaw, degeneration.

TA.RA.DO, *adj.*, perverted, sex maniac.

TA.RAR, *v.*, to tare, to determine tare of, to behave in sexually perverted way.

TA.RA.RÁ, *s.m., Bras.*, onomatopoeic word of the sound of a trumpet.

TAR.DA.MEN.TO, *s.m.*, slowness, delay, retardation.

TAR.DAN.ÇA, *s.f.*, act of tarrying.

TAR.DAR, *v.*, to delay, to lag, to procrastinate, to postpone.

TAR.DE, *s.f.*, afternoon, evening; *adj.*, late; *adv.*, tardly.

TAR.DE.ZI.NHA, *s.f.*, late in the afternoon.

TAR.DI.A.MEN.TE, *adv.*, slowly, lately.

TAR.DI.NHA, *s.f.*, late afternoon.

TAR.DIO, *adj.*, slow, late.

TA.RE.CO, *s.m.*, old thing without usefulness; stuff; *Bras.*, a sort of biscuit.

TA.RE.FA, *s.f.*, task, duty, assignment, function, job.

TA.RI.FA, *s.f.*, tariff, rate, fare, charge, tax, fee.

TA.RI.FA.ÇÃO, *s.f.*, fixing of tariff; clearance.

TA.RI.FAR, *v.*, to fix a tariff upon, to tariff.

TA.RI.FÁ.RI.O, *adj.*, referring to a tariff.

TA.RIM.BA, *s.f.*, experience; long practice; military life.

TA.RIM.BA.DO, *adj., Bras.*, experienced, well-practiced.

TA.RIM.BAR, *v.*, to serve in the army.

TA.RÔ, *s.m.*, tarot.

TAR.RA.FA, *s.f.*, fishing net, casting net.

TAR.RA.FAR, *v.*, to fish with a casting net.

TAR.RA.FE.AR, *v.*, to fish with a casting net.

TAR.RA.XA, *s.f.*, screw or twist of a screw, wedge, peg, plug.

TAR.RA.XAR, *v.*, to screw, to rivet.

TAR.TA.MU.DO, *s.m.*, stammerer; *adj.*, stammering, faltering.

TAR.TA.MU.DE.AR, *v.*, to stammerer.

TÁR.TA.RO, *s.m., Lit.*, Tartarus (hell, Hades); tartar of wine; *Odont.*, tartar of teeth.

TAR.TA.RU.GA, *s.f., Zool.*, turtle, tortoise.

TAR.TU.FI.CE, *s.f.*, Tartuffism, hypocrisy.

TAR.TU.FO, *s.m.*, tartuffe, hypocrite.

TA.RU.GO, *s.m.*, wooden pin, slug.

TAS.CA, *s.f.*, beating, scutching; *Bras., pop.*, beating, whipping.

TAS.CAR, *v.*, to beat, to chew, to bite, to crunch, to nibble.

TA.TA.ME, *s.m., Jap.*, a type of mat.

TA.TA.RA.NE.TO, *s.m.*, great-great-grandson.

TA.TA.RA.VÔ, *s.m.*, great-great-grandfather.

TATARAVÓ ·· 329 ··· TELENOVELA

TA.TA.RA.VÓ, *s.f.*, great-great-grandmother.
TA.TE.AN.TE, *adj.*, fumbling, touching, groping.
TA.TE.AR, *v.*, to grope, to touch, to feel, to probe.
TA.TE.Á.VEL, *adj.*, touchable.
TÁ.TI.CA, *s.f.*, tactics, method, policy.
TÁ.TI.CO, *adj.*, tactical.
TÁ.TIL, *adj.*, tactile, touchable.
TA.TO, *s.m.*, touch, feeling, tact, sensibility, discretion, prudence, sense.
TA.TU, *s.m.*, armadillo.
TA.TU.A.DOR, *s.m.*, tattoer, tattoist.
TA.TU.A.GEM, *s.f.*, tattooage, tattooing.
TA.TU.AR, *v.*, to tattoo.
TA.TU-BO.LA, *s.m.*, *Bras.*, *Zool.*, the three-banded armadillo.
TAU.MA.TUR.GI.A, *s.f.*, thaumaturgy, conjuring, magic.
TAU.MA.TUR.GO, *s.m.*, thaumaturge, magician.
TAU.TO.LO.GI.A, *s.f.*, tautology.
TA.VER.NA, *s.f.*, tavern, pub, inn, pothouse.
TA.VER.NEI.RO, *s.m.*, taverner, innkeeper, publican.
TÁ.VO.LA, *s.f.*, board for games (like draughts).
TA.XA, *s.f.*, tribute, tax, tariff, fee, duty, toll.
TA.XA.ÇÃO, *s.f.*, taxation, appraisement, rating.
TA.XA.DO, *adj.*, taxed.
TA.XA.DOR, *s.m.*, taxer, appraiser, valuer; *adj.*, that rates, that taxes.
TA.XAR, *v.*, to rate, to regulate, to fix a value or a price, to tax.
TA.XA.TI.VA.MEN.TE, *adv.*, valuationally.
TA.XA.TI.VO, *adj.*, rating, taxing.
TÁ.XI, *s.m.*, taxi, cab, taxicab.
TA.XI.DER.MI.A, *s.f.*, taxidermy.
TA.XI.DER.MIS.TA, *s. 2 gen.*, taxidermist.
TA.XÍ.ME.TRO, *s.m.*, taximeter.
TA.XO.NO.MI.A, *s.f.*, taxonomy.
TCHAU, *interj.*, *It.*, see you later, bye-bye.
TCHE.CO, *s.m.*, Czech (inhabitant of Czech Republic); *adj.*, Czechish, Czech.
TCHE.CO-ES.LO.VA.CO, *s.m.*, *Hist.*, Czechoslovakian; *adj.*, Czechoslovakian.
TCHE.COS.LO.VÁ.QUI.A, *s.*, *Hist.*, Czechoslovakia.
TE, *pron.*, you, to you.
TEAR, *s.m.*, weaver's loom, clockwork.
TEA.TRAL, *adj.*, theatrical.
TE.A.TRA.LI.DA.DE, *s.f.*, theatricalism, theatricality.
TE.A.TRA.LIS.MO, *s.m.*, *Bras.*, theatricalism.
TE.A.TRA.LI.ZA.ÇÃO, *s.f.*, theatricalization, dramatization.
TE.A.TRA.LI.ZAR, *v.*, to dramatize, to theatricalize.
TE.A.TRO, *s.m.*, theater, playhouse, stage.
TE.A.TRÓ.LO.GO, *s.m.*, playwright, dramatist.
TE.A.TRO-RE.VIS.TA, *s.m.*, *Bras.*, variety show, vaudeville show.
TE.CE.DEI.RA, *s.f.*, female weaver.
TE.CE.DOR, *s.m.*, weaver, knitter; *adj.*, weaving, knitting.
TE.CE.LA.GEM, *s.f.*, textile industry.
TE.CE.LÃO, *s.m.*, weaver, knitter, cloth-weaver.
TE.CER, *v.*, to weave, to web, to spin.
TE.CI.DO, *s.m.*, tissue, texture, cloth, textile; *adj.*, woven, designed.
TE.CLA, *s.f.*, key.
TE.CLA.DIS.TA, *s. 2 gen.*, *Mús.*, keyboardist.
TE.CLA.DO, *s.m.*, keyboard.
TE.CLAR, *v.*, *Bras.*, to tap (typewriter), to strike (keys).

TÉC.NI.CA, *s.f.*, technic, technique, know-how.
TEC.NI.CA.MEN.TE, *adv.*, technically.
TEC.NI.CI.DA.DE, *s.*, technicality.
TEC.NI.CIS.MO, *s.m.*, excessive use of technicality.
TEC.NI.CIS.TA, *adj.*, referring to an excess of technicality.
TÉC.NI.CO, *s.m.*, technicist, technician, expert; *adj.*, technical.
TEC.NI.CO.LOR, *s.m.*, Technicolor; *adj.*, Technicolored.
TEC.NO.CRA.CI.A, *s.f.*, technocracy.
TEC.NO.CRA.TA, *s. 2 gen.*, technocrat.
TEC.NO.CRÁ.TI.CO, *adj.*, technocratic.
TEC.NO.LO.GI.A, *s.f.*, technology.
TEC.NO.LÓ.GI.CO, *adj.*, technologic.
TEC.NÓ.LO.GO, *s.m.*, technologist.
TÉ.DIO, *s.m.*, tedium, boredom.
TE.DI.O.SA.MEN.TE, *adv.*, tediously.
TE.DI.O.SO, *adj.*, tedious, wearisome, dull.
TEI.A, *s.f.*, texture, tissue, cloth, textile, plot, intrigue, scheme.
TEI.MA, *s.f.*, obstinacy, obstinateness, wilfulness.
TEI.MAR, *v.*, to insist, to persist, to persevere.
TEI.MO.SI.A, *s.f.*, obstinacy, stubbornness, pertinacity.
TEI.MO.SI.CE, *s.f.*, the same that *teimosia*.
TEI.MO.SO, *adj.*, stubborn, obstinate, insistent.
TE.ÍS.MO, *s.m.*, theism.
TE.ÍS.TA, *s. 2 gen.*, theist.
TE.LA, *s.f.*, canvas, screen.
TE.LÃO, *s.m.*, a big screen (placed in public places to watch major events).
TE.LE.CI.NE, *s.m.*, film on TV.
TE.LE.CI.NÉ.SI.A, *s.f.*, telekinesis.
TE.LE.CO.MAN.DO, *s.m.*, remote control.
TE.LE.CO.MU.NI.CA.ÇÃO, *s.f.*, telecommunication.
TE.LE.CON.FE.RÊN.CI.A, *s.f.*, teleconference.
TE.LE.CUR.SO, *s.m.*, telecourse (TV, Computer).
TE.LE.DI.FU.SÃO, *s.f.*, telediffusion.
TE.LE.DRA.MA, *s.m.*, teledrama.
TE.LE.FÉ.RI.CO, *s.m.*, cable car, gondola.
TE.LE.FO.NAR, *v.*, to telephone, to phone, to call.
TE.LE.FO.NE, *s.m.*, telephone, phone.
TE.LE.FO.NE.MA, *s.m.*, telephone call.
TE.LE.FO.NI.A, *s.f.*, telephony.
TE.LE.FÔ.NI.CO, *adj.*, telephonic.
TE.LE.FO.NIS.TA, *s. 2 gen.*, telephone operator, operator.
TE.LE.FO.TO, *s.f.*, telephoto.
TE.LE.FO.TO.GRA.FI.A, *s.f.*, telephotography.
TE.LE.FO.TO.GRÁ.FI.CO, *adj.*, telephotographic.
TE.LE.GRA.FAR, *v.*, to telegraph, to cable, to wire.
TE.LE.GRA.FI.A, *s.f.*, telegraphy.
TE.LE.GRA.FI.CA.MEN.TE, *adv.*, telegraphically.
TE.LE.GRÁ.FI.CO, *adj.*, telegraphic, cabled.
TE.LE.GRA.FIS.TA, *s. 2 gen.*, telegrapher, telegraphist.
TE.LÉ.GRA.FO, *s.m.*, telegraph.
TE.LE.GRA.MA, *s.m.*, telegram, cable, wire.
TE.LE.GUI.A.DO, *s.m.*, a guided missile; *adj.*, referring to guided missile.
TE.LE.GUI.AR, *v.*, control from a distance.
TE.LE.JOR.NAL, *s.m.*, TV news, TV news broadcast.
TE.LE.JOR.NA.LIS.MO, *s.m.*, *Bras.*, telejournalism.
TE.LE.MAR.KE.TING, *s.m.*, *Ingl.*, *Com.*, telemarketing.
TE.LE.ME.TRI.A, *s.f.*, telemetry.
TE.LÊ.ME.TRO, *s.m.*, telemeter.
TE.LE.NO.VE.LA, *s.f.*, soap opera.

TELEOBJETIVA ••330•• TENTO

TE.LE.OB.JE.TI.VA, *s.f.*, telephoto lens.
TE.LE.O.LO.GI.A, *s.f.*, teleology.
TE.LE.O.LÓ.GI.CO, *adj.*, teleologic, teleological.
TE.LE.PA.TI.A, *s.f.*, telepathy.
TE.LE.PÁ.TI.CO, *adj.*, telepathic.
TE.LE.PRO.CES.SA.MEN.TO, *s.m.*, teleprocessing.
TE.LE.PROMP.TER, *s.m., Ingl.*, teleprompter (TV).
TE.LES.CÓ.PI.CO, *adj.*, telescopic.
TE.LES.CÓ.PIO, *s.m.*, telescope.
TE.LES.PEC.TA.DOR, *s.m., Bras.*, TV viewer; *adj.*, that watches TV.
TE.LE.TE.A.TRO, *s.m., Bras.*, teleplay (theater play broadcasted on TV).
TE.LE.TI.PIS.TA, *s. 2 gen.*, teletypist.
TE.LE.TI.PO, *s.m.*, teletype.
TE.LE.TRANS.MIS.SÃO, *s.f.*, transmission of television.
TE.LE.VI.SÃO, *s.f.*, television, telly, video, TV, TV set.
TE.LE.VI.SAR, *v.*, the same that *televisionar*.
TE.LE.VI.SI.O.NA.MEN.TO, *s.m.*, act of broadcasting on TV.
TE.LE.VI.SI.O.NAR, *v.*, to televise.
TE.LE.VI.SOR, *s.m.*, television receiver.
TE.LEX, *s.m.*, telex.
TE.LHA, *s.f.*, tile, whim, fancy.
TE.LHA.DO, *s.m.*, roof.
TE.LHA-VÃ, *s.f.*, unlined roof.
TE.LÚ.RI.CO, *adj.*, teluric.
TE.LÚ.RI.O, *s.m., Quím.*, tellurium.
TE.LU.RIS.MO, *s.m.*, tellurism.
TE.MA, *s.m.*, theme, topic, subject, thesis.
TE.MÁ.TI.CA, *s.f.*, set of themes for an artistic or literary work.
TE.MÁ.TI.CO, *adj.*, thematic.
TE.MER, *v.*, to fear, to doubt, to reverence, to respect, to venerate, apprehend.
TE.ME.RA.RI.A.MEN.TE, *adv.*, temerariously.
TE.ME.RÁ.RIO, *adj.*, temerarious, rash, foolhardy.
TE.ME.RI.DA.DE, *s.f.*, temerity.
TE.ME.RO.SO, *adj.*, fearful, dreadful, affraid, terrible.
TE.MI.DO, *adj.*, feared, dreaded.
TE.MÍ.VEL, *adj.*, appalling, dreadful, terrible.
TE.MI.VEL.MEN.TE, *adv.*, dreadfully.
TE.MOR, *s.m.*, dread, fear, fright, anxiety, awe.
TEM.PÃO, *s.m., Bras., pop.*, a long time.
TÊM.PE.RA, *s.f.*, temper, seasoning, flavour, spice.
TEM.PE.RA.DA.MEN.TE, *adv.*, temperately.
TEM.PE.RA.DO, *adj.*, temperate, seasoned, spiced.
TEM.PE.RA.MEN.TAL, *adj.*, temperamental.
TEM.PE.RA.MEN.TO, *s.m.*, temperament, mentality, mood, character.
TEM.PE.RAN.ÇA, *s.f.*, temperance.
TEM.PE.RAR, *v.*, to season, to flavour, to spice, to moderate, to calm, to soften.
TEM.PE.RA.TU.RA, *s.f.*, temperature.
TEM.PE.RO, *s.m.*, seasoning, spice, condiment.
TEM.PES.TA.DE, *s.f.*, tempest, storm, rainstorm, thunderstorm, tumult.
TEM.PES.TI.VI.DA.DE, *s.f.*, timely character, opportunity, season.
TEM.PES.TI.VO, *adj.*, in time, well-timed, opportune, seasonable.
TEM.PES.TU.O.SI.DA.DE, *s.f.*, storminess, tempestuousness.
TEM.PES.TU.O.SO, *adj.*, stormy.

TEM.PLÁ.RI.O, *s.m.*, Templar.
TEM.PLO, *s.m.*, temple.
TEM.PO, *s.m.*, time, period, era, season, weather, tense, duration, opportunity.
TEM.PO-QUEN.TE, *s.m., Bras.*, heated words, tumult, disorder.
TÊM.PO.RA, *s.f., Anat.*, temple.
TEM.PO.RA.DA, *s.f.*, period, season, era, stay.
TEM.PO.RAL, *s.m.*, tempest, rainstorm, hailstorm; *adj.*, temporary, secular, mundane.
TEM.PO.RA.LI.DA.DE, *s.f.*, temporality, temporariness.
TEM.PO.RA.LI.ZAR, *v.*, to make temporal.
TEM.PO.RA.RI.A.MEN.TE, *adv.*, temporarily.
TEM.PO.RA.RI.E.DA.DE, *s.f.*, temporary, transient.
TEM.PO.RÁ.RIO, *adj.*, temporary, provisory.
TEM.PO.RI.ZA.ÇÃO, *s.f.*, temporization, temporizing, procrastination.
TEM.PO.RI.ZA.DOR, *s.m.*, temporizer, procrastinator; *adj.*, temporizing, procrastinating; *Eletr.*, timer.
TEM.PO.RI.ZAR, *v.*, to temporize, to procrastinate.
TE.NA.CI.DA.DE, *s.f.*, tenacity, obstinacy.
TE.NAZ, *s.f.*, tongs, forceps, pliers; *adj.*, tenacious, stubborn, persistent.
TEN.ÇÃO, *s.f.*, intention, purpose, plan, aim.
TEN.CI.O.NAR, *v.*, to intend, to purpose, to contemplate.
TEN.CI.O.NÁ.RI.O, *s.m.*, pensioner; person that receives a pension.
TEN.DA, *s.f.*, tent, canvas.
TEN.DÃO, *s.m.*, tendon, sinew.
TEN.DÊN.CIA, *s.f.*, tendency, inclination, trend, fall.
TEN.DEN.CI.O.SA.MEN.TE, *adv.*, tendentiously.
TEN.DEN.CI.O.SI.DA.DE, *s.f.*, tendenciousness.
TEN.DEN.CI.O.SO, *adj.*, tendentious, partial.
TEN.DEN.TE, *adj.*, tending, prone, inclined.
TEN.DER, *v.*, to tend, to incline, to verge, to trend.
TÊN.DER, *s.m.*, tender.
TEN.DI.NI.TE, *s.f., Med.*, tendinitis.
TEN.DI.NO.SO, *adj.*, tendinous, tendonous.
TE.NE.BRO.SI.DA.DE, *s.f.*, tenebrosity, darkness, obscurity.
TE.NE.BRO.SO, *adj.*, tenebrous, dark, obscure, gloomy.
TE.NÊN.CI.A, *s.f., Ant.*, lieutenancy.
TE.NEN.TE, *s.m.*, lieutenant.
TE.NEN.TE-CO.RO.NEL, *s.m., Mil.*, lieutenant-colonel.
TÊ.NI.A, *s.f., Zool.*, taenia, tapeworm.
TE.NÍ.A.SE, *s.f., Med.*, taeniasis.
TÊ.NIS, *s.m.*, tennis, sneakers.
TE.NIS.TA, *s. 2 gen.*, tennis player.
TE.NOR, *s.m., Mús.*, tenor.
TEN.RO, *adj.*, tender, mild, soft, immature, sensible.
TEN.SÃO, *s.f.*, tension, stress, strain, tensity.
TEN.SO, *adj.*, tense, tight.
TEN.TA.ÇÃO, *s.f.*, temptation, allurement.
TEN.TA.CU.LA.DO, *adj.*, tentaculated, tentacled.
TEN.TA.CU.LAR, *adj.*, tentacular.
TEN.TÁ.CU.LO, *s.m.*, tentacle.
TEN.TA.DO, *adj.*, tempted; incited.
TEN.TA.DOR, *s.m.*, tempter, seducer; *adj.*, tempting, seductive.
TEN.TA.DO.RA.MEN.TE, *adv.*, seductively.
TEN.TAR, *v.*, to try, to test, to experiment, to attempt, to tempt.
TEN.TA.TI.VA, *s.f.*, experiment, trial, attempt, effort.
TEN.TA.TI.VO, *adj.*, experimental, trial.
TEN.TO, *s.m.*, caution, attention, maulstick; score, point.

TÊNUE ·· 331 ·· TESAR

TÊ.NUE, *adj.*, fragile, weak, feeble, insignificant.
TE.NU.E.MEN.TE, *adv.*, tenuously.
TE.NU.I.DA.DE, *s.f.*, tenuousness, weakness.
TE.O.LO.GI.A, *s.f.*, theology.
TE.O.LÓ.GI.CO, *adj.*, theological.
TE.O.LO.GIS.MO, *s.m.*, theologism.
TE.O.LO.GI.ZAR, *v.*, to theologize.
TE.Ó.LO.GO, *s.m.*, theologian, theologician.
TE.OR, *s.m.*, tenor, text, meaning, style.
TE.O.RE.MA, *s.m.*, *Mat.*, theorem.
TE.O.RI.A, *s.f.*, theory.
TE.O.RE.TI.CA.MEN.TE, *adv.*, theoretically.
TE.Ó.RI.CO, *adj.*, theoretical, abstract.
TE.O.RIS.TA, *s. 2 gen.*, theorist.
TE.O.RI.ZA.ÇÃO, *s.f.*, theorization.
TE.O.RI.ZA.DOR, *s.m.*, theorizer; *adj.*, theorizing.
TE.O.RI.ZAR, *v.*, to theorize.
TE.PI.DEZ, *s.f.*, tepidity, tepidness.
TÉ.PI.DO, *adj.*, tepid.
TER, *v.*, to have, to possess, to own, to hold, to keep, to occupy, to retain.
TE.RA.PEU.TA, *s. 2 gen.*, therapist, counselor.
TE.RA.PÊU.TI.CA, *s.f.*, therapeutics.
TE.RA.PEU.TI.CA.MEN.TE, *adv.*, therapeutically.
TE.RA.PÊU.TI.CO, *adj.*, therapeutic, therapeutical.
TE.RA.PI.A, *s.f.*, therapy.
TÉR.BI.O, *s.m.*, *Quím.*, terbium.
TER.ÇA, *s.f.*, the third part; tierce; short of *terça-feira*: Tuesday.
TER.ÇÃ, *s.f.*, *Med.*, tertian fever.
TER.ÇA.DO, *s.m.*, short, broad sword; large knife.
TER.ÇA-FEI.RA, *s.f.*, Tuesday.
TER.CEI.RA.NIS.TA, *s. 2 gen.*, third year student.
TER.CEI.RI.ZA.ÇÃO, *s.f.*, outsourcing.
TER.CEI.RI.ZAR, *v.*, to outsource.
TER.CEI.RO, *num.*, third, third part; *adj.*, third.
TER.CEI.ROS, *s.m., pl.*, the others, other parties.
TER.CE.TO, *s.m.*, tercet, triplet, trio.
TER.CI.Á.RI.O, *adj.*, tertiary; *Geol.*, pertaining to the Tertiary.
TER.ÇO, *s.m.*, third part; chaplet, string of beads.
TER.ÇOL, *s.m.*, *Med.*, stye, eyesore.
TE.RE.BIN.TI.NA, *s.f.*, turpentine.
TER.GAL, *s.m.*, a kind of cloth of synthetic fiber; *adj.*, *Anat.*, dorsal, tergal.
TER.GI.VER.SA.ÇÃO, *s.f.*, tergiversation.
TER.GI.VER.SAR, *v.*, to tergiversate.
TER.MAL, *adj.*, thermal.
TER.MA.LI.DA.DE, *s.f.*, nature of thermal water.
TER.MAS, *s.f., pl.*, thermae.
TER.ME.LÉ.TRI.CA, *s.f.*, a thermal power plant.
TER.ME.LE.TRI.CI.DA.DE, *s.f.*, thermoelectricity.
TER.ME.LÉ.TRI.CO, *adj.*, thermoelectric.
TÉR.MI.CO, *adj.*, thermic.
TER.MI.DOR, *s.m.*, *Hist.*, Thermidor.
TER.MI.NA.ÇÃO, *s.f.*, termination, end.
TER.MI.NAL, *s.m.*, terminal; *adj.*, terminal, terminating.
TER.MI.NAN.TE, *adj.*, terminative, conclusive, deciding.
TER.MI.NAN.TE.MEN.TE, *adv.*, terminatively, utterly.
TER.MI.NAR, *v.*, to terminate, to end, to finish, to close, to complete, to expire.
TER.MI.NA.TI.VA.MEN.TE, *adv.*, terminatively.
TÉR.MI.NO, *s.m.*, conclusion, ending, expiration.

TER.MI.NO.LO.GI.A, *s.f.*, terminology.
TER.MI.NO.LÓ.GI.CO, *adj.*, terminological.
TER.MO, *s.m.*, term, limit, limitation, boundary, landmark, expression, word, vocable.
TER.MO.DI.NÂ.MI.CA, *s.f.*, *Fís.*, thermodynamics.
TER.MO.DI.NÂ.MI.CO, *adj.*, thermodynamic.
TER.MO.FO.BI.A, *s.f.*, excessive fear of heat.
TER.MÓ.GRA.FO, *s.m.*, *Met.*, thermograph.
TER.MO.LO.GI.A, *s.f.*, *Fís.*, thermology.
TER.MO.MAG.NE.TIS.MO, *s.m.*, *Fís.*, thermomagnetism.
TER.MO.ME.TRI.A, *s.f.*, *Fís.*, thermometry.
TER.MO.MÉ.TRI.CO, *adj.*, thermometric.
TER.MÔ.ME.TRO, *s.m.*, thermometer.
TER.MO.NU.CLE.AR, *adj.*, thermonuclear.
TER.MO.QUÍ.MI.CA, *s.f.*, thermochemistry.
TER.MOS.FE.RA, *s.f.*, thermosphere.
TER.MOS.TÁ.TI.CO, *adj.*, *Fís.*, thermostatic.
TER.MOS.TA.TO, *s.m.*, thermostate.
TER.NA.MEN.TE, *adv.*, tenderly.
TER.NÁ.RI.O, *adj.*, ternary, ternal.
TER.NEI.RA.GEM, *s.f.*, *Bras.*, herd of calves.
TER.NEI.RO, *s.m.*, *Bras.*, calf.
TER.NO, *s.m.*, man's suit, ternary; *adj.*, tender, delicate, mild.
TER.NU.RA, *s.f.*, tenderness, kindness, love, affection.
TER.RA, *s.f.*, earth, world, globe, land, grand, soil, country, nation, birthplace.
TER.RA.ÇO, *s.m.*, terrace, platform.
TER.RA.CO.TA, *s.f.*, terracotta.
TER.RA.MI.CI.NA, *s.f.*, *Farm.*, Terramycin.
TER.RA.PLA.NA.GEM, **TER.RA.PLE.NA.GEM**, *s.f.*, earth-work, embankment, levelling of the ground.
TER.RA.PLA.NAR, **TER.RA.PLE.NAR**, *v.*, to embank, to fill with earth, to level.
TER.RE.AL, *adj.*, the same that *terrenal*.
TER.REI.RO, *s.m.*, yard, square.
TER.RE.MO.TO, *s.m.*, earthquake.
TER.RE.NAL, *adj.*, the same that *terrestrial*.
TER.RE.NHO, *adj.*, terrestrial.
TER.RE.NO, *s.m.*, land, terrain, ground, soil, glebe, site; *adj.*, terrestrial, earthy.
TÉR.REO, *adj.*, ground, earthy; *andar térreo*: ground floor; *casa térrea*: one-story house.
TER.RES.TRE, *adj.*, terrestrial, wordly.
TER.RI.BI.LI.DA.DE, *s.f.*, terribleness, fearfulness.
TER.RI.ER, *s.m.*, terrier.
TER.RI.FI.CAN.TE, *adj.*, terrifying, horrifying, frightful.
TER.RI.FI.CAR, *v.*, to terrify, to horrify, to frighten.
TER.RI.NA, *s.f.*, tureen.
TER.RI.TO.RI.AL, *adj.*, territorial.
TER.RI.TO.RI.A.LI.DA.DE, *s.f.*, territoriality.
TER.RI.TÓ.RIO, *s.m.*, territory, land, country, region.
TER.RÍ.VEL, *adj.*, terrible, awful, dreadful.
TER.ROR, *s.m.*, terror, horror, awe, fright, fear, dread.
TER.RO.RIS.MO, *s.m.*, terrorism, reign of terror.
TER.RO.RIS.TA, *s. 2 gen.*, terrorist.
TER.RO.RI.ZAR, *v.*, to terrorize, to frighten.
TER.RO.SO, *adj.*, earthen dim, lusterless; *Quím.*, *alcalino terroso*: alkaline earth.
TE.SÃO, *s.f.*, tension, rigidity, rigour; *gír.*, cool, nice; *vulg.*, sexual desire.
TE.SAR, *v.*, to toughen, stiffen, stretch, make taut.

TESE ··· 332 ··· TÍMIDO

TE.SE, *s.f.*, thesis, proposition, theory, hypothesis.
TE.SO, *s.m.*, hilltop; *adj., fam.*, skint; tense, taut, tight.
TE.SOU.RA, *s.f.*, scissors, a pair of scissors.
TE.SOU.RA.DA, *s.f.*, cut or stroke with the scissors, cutting remark.
TE.SOU.RAR, *v.*, to scissor, to cut with scissors.
TE.SOU.RA.RI.A, *s.f.*, treasury, treasurership.
TE.SOU.REI.RO, *s.m.*, treasurer.
TE.SOU.RI.NHA, *s.f.*, small scissors; *Bras., Zool.*, a bird from Brazil (*Phibalura flavirostris*).
TE.SOU.RO, *s.m.*, treasure, riches, treasury.
TES.TA, *s.f.*, forehead, brow, front.
TES.TA.DA, *s.f.*, sudden blow with the head; *Bras.*, foolishness, blunder.
TES.TA DE FER.RO, *s. 2 gen.*, dummy, man of straw.
TES.TA.DO, *adj.*, tested (that which was was considered good or safe).
TES.TA.DOR, *s.m.*, testator, person who makes a will; *adj.*, testate.
TES.TA.MEN.TAL, *adj.*, testamental, testamentary.
TES.TA.MEN.TÁ.RIO, *adj.*, testamentarious, testamentary.
TES.TA.MEN.TEI.RO, *s.m.*, executor of a will; *adj.*, referring to someone who is always making wills.
TES.TA.MEN.TO, *s.m.*, will, last will, testament.
TES.TAR, *v.*, to test, to try, to legate, to testify.
TES.TE, *s.m.*, test, examination, research, trial.
TES.TEI.RA, *s.f.*, front, frontage; frontpiece; headband.
TES.TE.MU.NHA, *s.f.*, witness, evidence, testimony, proof.
TES.TE.MU.NHA.DOR, *s.m.*, witness; *adj.*, giving evidence, testifying.
TES.TE.MU.NHAL, *adj.*, testimonial.
TES.TE.MU.NHAR, *v.*, to bear witness, to testify, to attest.
TES.TE.MU.NHÁ.VEL, *adj.*, testimonial, confirmatory, credible.
TES.TE.MU.NHO, *s.m.*, testimony, evidence, proof.
TES.TI.CU.LAR, *adj., Anat.*, testicular, testiculate.
TES.TÍ.CU.LO, *s.m., Anat.*, testicle, ball.
TES.TI.FI.CA.ÇÃO, *s.f.*, testification, evidence, attestation, testifying.
TES.TI.FI.CAR, *v.*, to testify, to bear witness, to certify.
TES.TU.DO, *s.m.*, one who is large-headed; *adj.*, stubborn, pig-headed, headstrong.
TE.TA, *s.f.*, teat, tit, nipple.
TE.TA, *s.m.*, theta (the eighth letter of the Greek alphabet).
TE.TÂ.NI.CO, *adj., Med.*, tetanic.
TÉ.TA.NO, *s.m.*, lockjaw.
TÊ.TE-À-TÊ.TE, *s.m., 2 num., Fr.*, a private conversation between two persons.
TE.TEI.A, *s.f.*, charm, trinket.
TÉ.TIS, *s.f., Mit.*, Thetis.
TE.TO, *s.m.*, ceiling, roof, cover, refuge.
TE.TRA.CAM.PE.ÃO, *s.m.*, four times champion; *adj.*, referring to four-time championship.
TE.TRA.CÍ.CLI.CO, *adj., Bot.*, tetracyclic.
TE.TRA.CLO.RE.TO, *s.m., Quím.*, tetrachloride.
TE.TRA.LO.GI.A, *s.f.*, tetralogy.
TE.TRA.PLE.GI.A, *s.f.*, tetraplegia.
TE.TRA.PLÉ.GI.CO, *adj.*, tetraplegic.
TE.TRAR.CA, *s.m.*, tetrarch.
TE.TRAR.QUI.A, *s.f.*, tetrarchy.
TE.TRI.CA.MEN.TE, *adv.*, sadly, awfully.
TE.TRI.CI.DA.DE, *s.f.*, sadness, gloominess.

TÉ.TRI.CO, *adj.*, sad, gloomy, mournful, sorrowful.
TE.TRO, *adj.*, dark, black, dusky, horrible.
TEU, TUA, *pron.*, your, yours.
TEU.TO, *adj.*, Teutonic.
TE.VÊ, *s.f.*, the same that *televisão*.
TÊX.TIL, *adj.*, textile.
TEX.TO, *s.m.*, text.
TEX.TU.AL, *adj.*, literal, textual.
TEX.TU.A.LI.DA.DE, *s.f.*, the quality of what is textual.
TEX.TU.A.LIS.TA, *s. 2 gen.*, textuality.
TEX.TU.AL.MEN.TE, *adv.*, textually.
TEX.TU.RA, *s.f.*, texture, structure.
TEZ, *s.f.*, complexion, epidermis, cutis.
TI, *pron.*, you, yourself,
TI.A, *s.f.*, aunt.
TI.A-A.VÓ, *s.f.*, great aunt.
TI.A.RA, *s.f.*, tiara.
TI.BE.TA.NO, *s.m., adj.*, Tibetan.
TI.BE.TE, *s.*, Tibet.
TÍ.BIA, *s.f., Anat.*, shinbone, tibia.
TI.BI.AL, *adj., Anat.*, tibial.
TI.BI.E.ZA, TI.BI.EZ, *s.f.*, lukewarmness, indolence.
TÍ.BIO, *adj.*, tepid, lukewarm.
TI.ÇÃO, *s.m.*, firebrand, ember; dark person; *fig.*, devil.
TI.CAR, *v.*, to tick, to check.
TI.CO, *s.m.*, a bit, bite, a little; tic, twitch.
TI.CO-TI.CO, *s.m., Bras., Zool.*, crown sparrow, rufous-collared sparrow (*Zonotrichia capensis*).
TI.É, *s.m., Bras., Zool.*, bird of the tanager family.
TI.E.TA.GEM, *s.f., Bras., gír.*, fan behavior.
TI.E.TAR, *v., Bras., gír.*, to act as a groupie.
TI.E.TE, *s. 2 gen.*, fan.
TI.FLO.LO.GI.A, *s.f.*, typhlology.
TI.FO, *s.m., Med.*, typhoid fever.
TI.FOI.DE, *adj., Med.*, typhoid.
TI.FO.SO, *adj.*, typhous.
TI.GE.LA, *s.f.*, bowl, cup, dish, drinking vessel.
TI.GRA.DO, *adj.*, striped like a tiger.
TI.GRE, *s.m.*, tiger.
TI.GRE.SA, *s.f., Bras., Zool.*, tigress.
TI.JO.LEI.RO, *s.m.*, brickmaker.
TI.JO.LO, *s.m.*, brick.
TI.JU.CO, *s.m.*, swamp, slough, marsh, mud.
TIL, *s.m., Gram.*, tilde(diacritical mark indicating nasalization: vão, cão, pão).
TIL.BU.RI, *s.m.*, tilbury.
TI.LIN.TAR, *v.*, to tinkle, to clink.
TI.MA.ÇO, *s.m., pop., Esp.*, a great team, a winner team.
TI.MÃO, *s.m.*, tiller, pole, rudder, helm; *fig.*, direction, leadership; *gír., Esp.*, a great team.
TIM.BA.LE, *s.m., Ant.*, tymbal, kettledrum.
TIM.BRA.DO, *adj.*, (having a) letterhead.
TIM.BRA.GEM, *s.f.*, marking with a crest, stamping.
TIM.BRAR, *v.*, to stamp, to class, to mark with an emblem.
TIM.BRE, *s.m.*, letterhead, emblem, stamp, seal; *Mús.*, expression, tone.
TIM.BRO.SO, *adj.*, having timbre; careful, meticulous.
TI.ME, *s.m.*, team.
TI.MI.DA.MEN.TE, *adv.*, timidly.
TI.MI.DEZ, *s.f.*, shyness, timidity, timidness.
TÍ.MI.DO, *adj.*, shy, timid, coy, bashful.

TIMO · 333 · TOCANTE

TI.MO, *s.m., Anat.,* thymus.

TI.MO.CRA.CI.A, *s.f.,* timocracy (government of the wealthy class).

TI.MO.CRÁ.TI.CO, *adj.,* timocratic, timocratical.

TI.MO.NE.AR, *v., Bras.,* to helm, to steer (a ship).

TI.MO.NEI.RO, *s.m., Náut.,* helmsman.

TIM.PA.NAL, *adj.,* tympanic (relating to the tympanum).

TIM.PA.NI.TE, *s.m., Med.,* tympanitis.

TÍM.PA.NO, *s.m.,* timpanum; *Mús.,* timbal, bell, Kettledrum; *Anat.,* eardrum.

TI.NA, *s.f.,* tub, wooden vessel.

TIN.ÇÃO, *s.f.,* tincture, dye, tint.

TÍ.NER, *s.m.,* thinner.

TIN.GI.DO, *adj.,* dyed.

TIN.GI.DOR, *s.m.,* dyer; *adj.,* dyeing, tinging.

TIN.GI.MEN.TO, *s.m.,* dye, tincture, tinge of colour.

TIN.GIR, *v.,* to dye, to stain, to tint, to colour.

TIN.GÍ.VEL, *adj.,* tingible, colourable.

TI.NHA, *s.f., Med.,* tinea; *fig.,* imperfection, defect.

TI.NI.DO, *s.m.,* clinking, tinkling, ringing sound.

TI.NIR, *v.,* to clink, to clank, to ding, to tinkle.

TI.NHO.SO, *s.m.,* person suffering from tinea; *pop.,* the devil; *adj.,* nauseation; stubborn.

TI.NI.DO, *s.m.,* tinkling, clinking, ringing sound.

TI.NI.DOR, *s.m.,* object that tinkles; *adj.,* tinkling, ringing.

TI.NIR, *v.,* to clink, to ring; ~ *de fome:* to be extremely hungry; ~ *de raiva:* tobe extremely furious.

TI.NO, *s.m.,* discernment, good sense, intelligence.

TIN.TA, *s.f.,* paint, ink, tincture.

TIN.TEI.RO, *s.m.,* inkpot, inkwell, inkholder.

TIN.TIM, *s.m.,* sound of glasses during a toast; *interj., tintim!:* cheers!

TIN.TI.NAR, *v.,* the same that *tilintar:* to tinkle.

TIN.TO, *adj.,* dyed, coloured, red (wine).

TIN.TO.RI.AL, *adj.,* tinctorial; pertaining to colour or dyes.

TIN.TU.RA, *s.f.,* dyeing, dye, colour, tint, hue.

TIN.TU.RA.RI.A, *s.f.,* dyeing, dye works; dry-cleaner's.

TIN.TU.REI.RO, *s.m.,* dyer, dry-cleaner.

TIO, *s.m.,* uncle.

TI.O-A.VÔ, *s.m.,* great-uncle.

TI.PI.CA.MEN.TE, *adv.,* typically.

TÍ.PI.CO, *adj.,* typic, typical, characteristic, symbolic.

TI.PI.FI.CA.ÇÃO, *s.f.,* typification.

TI.PI.FI.CAR, *v.,* to typify.

TI.PO, *s.m.,* type, kind, sort, variety, fashion, norm.

TI.PO.GRA.FI.A, *s.f.,* typography.

TI.PO.GRÁ.FI.CO, *adj.,* typographical.

TI.PÓ.GRA.FO, *s.m.,* typographer.

TI.POI.A, *s.f.,* sling (arm sling etc.).

TI.QUE, *s.m.,* tic, twitch, bad habit.

TI.QUE-TA.QUE, *s.m.,* tick-tock, tick-tack, tick.

TI.QUE.TA.QUE.AR, *v.,* to ticktock.

TÍ.QUE.TE, *s.m.,* ticket.

TI.QUI.NHO, *s.m., Bras.,* a little bit; a shred (of something).

TI.RA, *s.f.,* band, ribbon, strip; *s.m., gír.,* policeman.

TI.RA.ÇÃO, *s.f.,* act of taking or remove something; *Bras.,* felling of wood.

TI.RA.CO.LO, *s.m.,* shoulder belt, baldric; a ~: across the shoulder.

TI.RA.DA, *s.f.,* tirade, rant.

TI.RA.GEM, *s.f.,* drawing, circulation, issue, printing, edition, hauling, draft.

TI.RA.NI.A, *s.f.,* tyranny, despotism, oppression.

TI.RÂ.NI.CO, *adj.,* tyrannical, tyrannous, despotic.

TI.RA.NI.ZA.DOR, *s.m.,* tyrannizer; *adj.,* tyrannical, oppressive.

TI.RA.NI.ZAR, *v.,* to tyrannize, to oppress.

TI.RA.NO, *s.m.,* tyrant, despot, oppressor, autocrat; *adj.,* tyrannical, despotic.

TI.RAN.TE, *s.m.,* harness (belt motor), connecting rod; *adj.,* excepting, saving; *prep.,* except, save.

TI.RAR, *v.,* to draw, to pull, to remove, to extract, to exclude, to suppress.

TI.RE.OI.DE, *s.f., Anat.,* thyroid gland.

TI.RI.RI.CA, *adj., Bras., pop.,* mad, irate, angry; *ficar ~:* to be hopping mad.

TI.RI.TAN.TE, *adj.,* shivering, trembling (with cold).

TI.RI.TAR, *v.,* to shiver, to quiver, to shake.

TI.RO, *s.m.,* shot, pop, shooting, firing.

TI.RO.CÍ.NIO, *s.m.,* tyrocinium, apprenticeship.

TI.RO.LÊS, *s.m.,* Tyrolese (inhabitant of Tyrol); *adj.,* Tyrolese (pertaining to Tyrol).

TI.RO.LE.SA, *s.f.,* Tyrolienne (a Tyrolese peasant dance and song).

TI.RO.TEI.O, *s.m.,* shooting, firing.

TÍ.SI.CA, *s.f.,* phthisis.

TÍ.SI.CO, *s.m.,* phthisic; *adj.,* phthisical.

TI.TÃ, *s.m.,* Titan.

TI.TÂ.NI.CO, *adj.,* titanic; *Quím.,* that contain titanium.

TI.TÂ.NI.O, *s.m., Quím.,* titanium (symbol: Ti, atomic number: 22).

TÍ.TE.RE, *s.m.,* puppet, marionette.

TI.TI.A, *s.f.,* auntie; *fam.,* aunty.

TI.TI.CA, *s.f., Bras.,* birds' excrement; *fig.,* worthless person.

TI.TI.LAN.TE, *adj.,* tickling, thrilling.

TI.TI.LAR, *v.,* to titillate, to tickle; *fig.,* to cuddle; to flatter.

TI.TI.TI, *s.m., Bras., col.,* tittle-tattle, gossip; hubbub, confusion, brawl.

TI.TU.BE.A.ÇÃO, *s.f.,* titubation, staggering, hesitation.

TI.TU.BE.AN.TE, *adj.,* staggering, unsteady; hesitating, vacillating.

TI.TU.BE.AR, *v.,* to stagger, to totter.

TI.TU.LA.ÇÃO, *s.f.,* act of giving a title.

TI.TU.LA.DO, *adj.,* having a title, titled.

TI.TU.LAR, *s.m.,* titleholder, office holder; *adj.,* titular, honorary; *v.,* to title, to entitle, to call.

TÍ.TU.LO, *s.m.,* title, heading, caption, denomination, label, top line, inscription, voucher, bond.

TO.A.DA, *s.f., Mús.,* tune, melody; sound, noise, report.

TO.A.LE.TE, *s.m.,* toilet.

TO.A.LHA, *s.f.,* towel.

TO.A.LHEI.RO, *s.m.,* towel rack.

TO.AN.TE, *adj.,* sounding; rhyming.

TO.AR, *v.,* to sound, to resound, to thunder.

TO.BO.GÃ, *s.m.,* toboggan.

TO.CA, *s.f.,* den, burrow.

TO.CA-DIS.COS, *s.m.,* record player.

TO.CA.DO, *adj.,* groped, touched; *fam.,* tipsy, jolly; *pop.,* turned out, expelled.

TO.CA-FI.TAS, *s.m.,* tape recorder.

TO.CAI.A, *s.f.,* trap, ambush, blind.

TO.CAI.AR, *v.,* to ambush, to lurk.

TO.CAN.TE, *adj.,* touching, feeling, affecting.

TOCAR ·· 334 ··· TORNEADO

TO.CAR, *v.,* to touch, to feel, to contact, to brush, to play, to perform, to ring.

TO.CA.TA, *s.f.,* musical performance; *Mús.,* toccata.

TO.CÁ.VEL, *adj.,* playable.

TO.CHA, *s.f.,* torch, flambeau, firebrand.

TO.CO, *s.m.,* stub, stump.

TO.DA.VI.A, *conj.,* but, yet, still, however, nevertheless, though.

TO.DO, *s.m.,* the whole, totality, mass; *todos (pl.):* each and every, one and all, every one; *adj.,* all, whole, complete, every, entire; *todo mundo:* everybody.

TO.DO-PO.DE.RO.SO, *s.m.,* The Almighty; *adj.,* almighty, omnipotent.

TO.GA, *s.m.,* toga; *fig.,* magistracy.

TO.GA.DO, *s.m.,* judge, magistrate; *adj.,* wearing a toga.

TOI.CI.NHO, *s.m.,* the same that *toucinho:* lard, bacon.

TOL.DAR, *v.,* to cover with an awning; to blur, to darken, to obscure.

TOL.DO, *s.m.,* sun blind, awning.

TO.LEI.RÃO, *s.m.,* simpleton, fool, imbecile; *adj.,* foolish, silly, stupid.

TO.LE.RA.BI.LI.DA.DE, *s.f.,* tolerability.

TO.LE.RÁN.CIA, *s.f.,* tolerance, endurance, toleration, allowance.

TO.LE.RAN.TE, *adj., s. 2 gen.,* tolerant, enduring, indulgent.

TO.LE.RAR, *v.,* to tolerate, to endure, to bear, to stand, to abide, to allow.

TO.LE.RÁ.VEL, *adj.,* tolerable.

TO.LE.RA.VEL.MEN.TE, *adv.,* tolerably.

TO.LHER, *v.,* to hinder, to hamper, to prevent, to restrain, to stop.

TO.LHI.DO, *adj.,* paralysed, disabled, lame, crippled.

TO.LHI.MEN.TO, *s.m.,* obstacle, hindrance, impediment, obstruction, disability.

TO.LI.CE, *s.f.,* foolishness, silliness, folly, vanity, stupidity.

TO.LO, *s.m.,* fool, simpleton, idiot; *adj.,* foolish, crazy, daft, ignorant.

TOM, *s.m.,* tone, sound, inflection, key, intonation.

TO.MA.DA, *s.f.,* taking, seizure, conquest; plug, plug socket.

TO.MA.DO, *s.m.,* which was conquered, subjugated; *adj.,* taken, seized, caught; *fig.,* tipsy.

TO.MAR, *v.,* to take, to seize, to catch, to capture, to grasp, to conquer, to gather, to take possession.

TO.MA.RA, *interj., Bras.,* let's hope so!; God grant!

TO.MA.TE, *s.m., Bot.,* tomato.

TO.MA.TEI.RO, *s.m., Bot.,* tomato plant.

TOM.BA.DI.LHO, *s.m., Náut.,* deck (poop).

TOM.BA.DO, *adj.,* fallen, tumbled, inclined, bent.

TOM.BA.DOR, *s.m.,* stumbler, tumbler; *adj.,* stumbling, tumbling.

TOM.BA.MEN.TO, *s.m.,* act of falling, stumbling.

TOM.BAR, *v.,* to throw or fall down; to register lands.

TOM.BO, *s.m.,* fall, tumble, cropper.

TÔM.BO.LA, *s.f.,* lotto, bingo, tombola.

TO.MO, *s.m.,* tome, volume.

TO.MO.GRA.FI.A, *s.f., Med.,* tomography.

TO.MO.GRÁ.FI.CO, *adj.,* tomographic.

TO.MÓ.GRA.FO, *s.m., Med.,* tomograph.

TO.NA, *s.f.,* surface, skin.

TO.NAL, *adj.,* tonal.

TO.NA.LI.DA.DE, *s.f.,* tonality, character of tone.

TO.NA.LI.ZA.ÇÃO, *s.f., Mús., Art.,* art of giving a tone to.

TO.NA.LI.ZAR, *v., Mús., Art.,* to give a tone to.

TO.NEL, *s.m.,* barrel, cask.

TO.NE.LA.DA, *s.f.,* ton (weight of 1, 000 kg).

TO.NE.LA.GEM, *s.f.,* tonnage.

TO.NER, *s.m.,* toner (ink to printer).

TÔ.NI.CA, *s.f.,* tonic water; *Mús.,* tonic; *fig.,* keynote.

TO.NI.CI.DA.DE, *s.f.,* tonicity.

TÔ.NI.CO, *s.m.,* tonic, corroborative; *adj.,* tonic, restorative, fundamental, stressed, predominant.

TO.NI.FI.CAN.TE, *adj.,* invigorating.

TO.NI.FI.CAR, *v.,* to tone; to invigorate.

TON.TE.AR, *v.,* to fool, to stupefy.

TON.TEI.RA, *s.f.,* foolishness, foolery; dizziness.

TON.TU.RA, *s.f.,* giddiness, dizziness, vertigo.

TÔ.NUS, *s.m., 2 num.,* tonus; ~ *muscular:* muscle tone.

TOP, *s.m.,* bodice (vestment); ~ *de linha:* top of the range.

TO.PA.DA, *s.f.,* trip, tripping, stumbling, tumbling.

TO.PAR, *v.,* to meet, to encounter, to find.

TO.PÁ.ZIO, *s.m.,* topaz.

TO.PE, *s.m.,* top, summit.

TO.PE.TE, *s.m.,* topknot, forelock, crest, tuft.

TO.PE.TU.DO, *adj.,* quiff; *fig.,* daring.

TÓ.PI.CO, *s.m.,* topic, subject, theme, heading, matter, text, argument; *adj.,* topical.

TOP.LESS, *s.m., Ingl.,* topless bikini; *adj.,* topless.

TO.PO, *s.m.,* summit, top, peak, acme.

TO.PO.GRA.FI.A, *s.f.,* topography.

TO.PO.GRÁ.FI.CO, *adj.,* topographic, topographical.

TO.PÓ.GRA.FO, *s.m.,* topographer.

TO.PO.NÍ.MI.A, *s.f.,* toponymy.

TO.PÔ.NI.MO, *s.m.,* toponym.

TO.QUE, *s.m.,* touch, contact, feeling, keystroke, call.

TO.RA, *s.f.,* trunk of a tree; *gír.,* portion, share; portion of meat; *Rel.,* Torah (Law of Moses).

TO.RÁ.CI.CO, *adj.,* thoracic.

TO.RAN.JA, *s.f., Bot.,* grapefruit.

TO.RAN.JEI.RA, *s.f., Bot.,* grapefruit tree.

TO.RAR, *v.,* to cut wood trunks; to cut into stumps or legs.

TÓ.RAX, *s.m., Anat.,* thorax, chest.

TOR.ÇÃO, *s.f.,* torsion, twisting, intorsion.

TOR.CE.DE.LA, *s.f.,* twisting, twist, wrench.

TOR.CE.DOR, *s.m.,* supporter, twister, throwster; *adj.,* inciting, cheering.

TOR.CE.DU.RA, *s.f.,* twist, act of twisting, wrench.

TOR.CER, *v.,* to twist, to turn, to wrench, to distort, to support, to crick.

TOR.CI.CO.LO, *s.m., Med.,* stiff neck.

TOR.CI.DA, *s.f.,* wick, group of cheerers.

TOR.CI.DO, *adj.,* tortuous, sinuous, twisted, wrested.

TOR.CÍ.VEL, *adj.,* twistable.

TOR.DO, *s.m., Zool.,* thrush (bird).

TÓ.RI.O, *s.m., Quím.,* thorium (radioactive element, symbol: Th, atomic number 90).

TOR.MEN.TA, *s.f.,* tempest, violent storm.

TOR.MEN.TO, *s.m.,* torment, affliction, distress, agony.

TOR.MEN.TO.SO, *adj.,* stormy, tempestuous, *fig.,* tormenting.

TOR.NA.DO, *s.m.,* tornado.

TOR.NAR, *v.,* to return, to go, to turn, to come back, to send back.

TOR.NE.A.DO, *adj.,* turned, roundish, well-turned, shapely.

TORNEAMENTO ·· 335 ·· TRACOMA

TOR.NE.A.MEN.TO, *s.m.*, turning on a lathe.
TOR.NE.AR, *v.*, to turn, to turn round, to shape, to mold.
TOR.NE.Á.VEL, *adj.*, turnable, shapeable.
TOR.NEI.O, *s.m.*, tournament, tourney, cup.
TOR.NEI.RA, *s.f.*, tap, faucet, cock.
TOR.NEI.RO, *s.m.*, turner.
TOR.NI.QUE.TE, *s.m., Med.*, tourniquet.
TOR.NO, *s.m.*, lathe, vice, spigot.
TOR.NO.ZE.LEI.RA, *s.m., Bras.*, an ankle support.
TO.RÓ, *s.m., Met.*, downpour.
TOR.NO.ZE.LO, *s.m.*, ankle, ancle.
TOR.PE, *adj.*, torpid, dirty, vile.
TOR.PE.DE.AR, *v.*, to torpedo, to destroy.
TOR.PE.DEI.RO, *s.m., Náut.*, torpedo-boat.
TOR.PE.DO, *s.m.*, torpedo.
TOR.PEN.TE, *adj.*, torpid, numb, benumbed.
TOR.PE.ZA, *s.f.*, foulness, turpitude, vileness, , dirtiness, indecency.
TOR.POR, *s.m.*, torpor, torpidity, lethargy.
TOR.QUE, *s.m., Mec.*, torque.
TOR.QUÊS, *s.f.*, pincers.
TOR.RA.ÇÃO, *s.f.*, act of toasting; *col.*, fire sale.
TOR.RA.DA, *s.f.*, toast.
TOR.RA.DEI.RA, *s.f.*, toaster.
TOR.RA.DO, *adj.*, toasted, roasted.
TOR.RA.DOR, *s.m.*, toaster, roaster.
TOR.RAR, *v.*, to toast, to roast, to grill, to brown.
TOR.RE, *s.f.*, tower, pylon, castle, rook.
TOR.RE.A.DO, *adj.*, towered.
TOR.RE.ÃO, *s.m.*, turret, small turret, pavilion (a larger building).
TOR.RE.AR, *v.*, to surround with towers; to tower.
TOR.RE.FA.ÇÃO, *s.f.*, torrefaction.
TOR.RE.FA.ZER, *v.*, to torrefy, to toast.
TOR.RE.FEI.TO, *adj.*, torrefied, toasted, roasted.
TOR.REN.CI.AL, *adj.*, torrential.
TOR.REN.TE, *s.f.*, torrent, stream, flood, flow, cataract.
TOR.REN.TO.SO, *adj.*, rushing, rapid.
TOR.RES.MO, *s.m.*, crackling, scrap.
TÓR.RI.DO, *adj.*, torrid, very hot, burning.
TOR.RI.FI.CAR, *v.*, the same that *torrefazer*.
TOR.TA, *s.f.*, tart, pie.
TOR.TI.LHA, *s.f., Cul.*, tortilha.
TOR.TI.NHA, *s.f.*, tartlet, small pie.
TOR.TO, *adj.*, twisted, crooked, bent, curved, oblique, deformed.
TOR.TU.O.SI.DA.DE, *s.f.*, tortuosity, tortuousness.
TOR.TU.O.SO, *adj.*, tortuous, curved, crooked, sinuous.
TOR.TU.RA, *s.f.*, torture, pain, anguish.
TOR.TU.RA.DO, *s.m.*, the victim of torture; *adj.*, tortured.
TOR.TU.RA.DOR, *s.m.*, torturer; *adj.*, torturing.
TOR.TU.RAN.TE, *adj.*, tormenting, torturing, afflictive.
TOR.TU.RAR, *v.*, to torture, to torment, to afflict, to grieve.
TOR.VA.ÇÃO, *s.f.*, perturbation, confusion, disturbance.
TOR.VAR, *v.*, to perturb, to disturb, to agitate, to disturb.
TOR.VE.LI.NHAR, *v.*, to whirl, to twirl.
TOR.VE.LI.NHO, *s.m.*, whirl, eddy, vortex.
TO.SA, *s.f.*, shearing (sheep); trimming (pelage, hair).
TO.SA.DOR, *s.m.*, shearer, groomer (dogs).
TO.SÃO, *s.m.*, fleece (of a sheep).
TO.SAR, *v.*, to shear, to fleece, to clip.

TOS.CO, *adj.*, rough, rude, uncouth, coarse.
TOS.QUI.A, *s.f.*, shearing, scolding, shearing time.
TOS.QUI.A.DO, *adj.*, sheared, clipped.
TOS.QUI.A.DOR, *s.m.*, shearer; *adj.*, shearing.
TOS.QUI.AR, *v.*, to shear, to clip, to fleece, to poll.
TOS.SE, *s.f.*, cough, coughing.
TOS.SI.DE.LA, *s.f., pop.*, coughing.
TOS.SIR, *v.*, to cough.
TOS.TA.DEI.RA, *s.f.*, toaster.
TOS.TA.DO, *adj.*, toasted, sunburnt.
TOS.TÃO, *s.m., Ant.*, Brazilian coin; *fig.*, cash.
TOS.TAR, *v.*, to toast, to roast.
TO.TAL, *s.m.*, total, totality, whole, sum; *adj.*, total, whole, entire, integral, complete.
TO.TA.LI.DA.DE, *s.f.*, totality, entirety, universality.
TO.TA.LI.TÁ.RIO, *adj.*, totalitarian.
TO.TA.LI.TA.RIS.MO, *s.m.*, totalitarianism.
TO.TA.LI.TA.RIS.TA, *s. 2 gen.*, totalitarian.
TO.TA.LI.ZA.ÇÃO, *s.f.*, totalization.
TO.TA.LI.ZAR, *v.*, to totalize.
TO.TAL.MEN.TE, *adv.*, totally.
TOU.CA, *s.f.*, toque.
TOU.CA.DOR, *s.m.*, hairdresser, vanity table, toilet table; toilet set.
TOU.CEI.RA, *s.f.*, a big shrub; stump of a tree.
TOU.CI.NHO, *s.m.*, lard, bacon.
TOU.PEI.RA, *s.f., Zool.*, mole, talpa; *adj., col.*, idiot.
TOU.RA.DA, *s.f.*, bullfighting; drove of bulls.
TOU.RE.AR, *v.*, to fight bulls, to be a bullfighter.
TOU.REI.RO, *s.m.*, bullfighter, torero.
TOU.RO, *s.m., Zool.*, bull; *Astron.*, Taurus.
TO.XE.MI.A, *s.f., Med.*, toxemia, toxaemia.
TO.XI.CI.DA.DE, *s.f.*, toxicity.
TÓ.XI.CO, *s.m.*, toxin, poison; *adj.*, toxicant.
TO.XI.CO.MA.NI.A, *s.f.*, drug addiction, toxicomania.
TO.XI.DEZ, *s.f.*, toxicity.
TO.XI.NA, *s.f.*, toxin.
TRA.BA.LHA.DEI.RA, *s.f.*, hard-working woman; *adj.*, laborious, hard-working (woman).
TRA.BA.LHA.DO, *adj.*, worked, laboured, elaborate.
TRA.BA.LHA.DOR, *s.m.*, worker, laborer, toiler; *adj.*, laborious, busy, diligent.
TRA.BA.LHÃO, *s.m.*, tiring work, drudgery job; hard work.
TRA.BA.LHAR, *v.*, to work, to labor.
TRA.BA.LHÁ.VEL, *adj.*, workable.
TRA.BA.LHEI.RA, *s.f.*, hard work, drudgery; effort.
TRA.BA.LHIS.MO, *s.m.*, labourism.
TRA.BA.LHIS.TA, *s.m.*, labourist, labourite; *adj.*, pertaining to the working classes or labour parties.
TRA.BA.LHO, *s.m.*, work, job, service.
TRA.BA.LHO.SO, *adj.*, hard, arduous, difficult.
TRA.ÇA, *s.f., Zool.*, moth, clothes moth.
TRA.ÇA.DO, *s.m.*, trace, tracing, drawing, design; *adj.*, drawn, traced, sketchy.
TRA.ÇA.DOR, *s.m.*, designer, tracer, draftsman, liner, sketcher.
TRA.ÇÃO, *s.f.*, traction, pull, tension, pulling.
TRA.ÇAR, *v.*, to trace, to draw, to delineate, to outline, to sketch.
TRA.ÇO, *s.m.*, trace, line, stroke of a pen, feature, aspect.
TRA.CO.MA, *s.m., Med.*, trachoma.

TRADIÇÃO · 336 · TRANSCREVER

TRA.DI.ÇÃO, *s.f.*, tradition; memory.
TRA.DI.CI.O.NAL, *adj.*, traditional, habitual.
TRA.DI.CI.O.NA.LIS.MO, *s.m.*, traditionalism.
TRA.DI.CI.O.NA.LIS.TA, *s. 2 gen.*, traditionalist.
TRA.DI.CI.O.NAL.MEN.TE, *adv.*, traditionally.
TRA.DU.ÇÃO, *s.f.*, translation, version.
TRA.DU.TOR, *s.m.*, translator, interpreter; *adj.*, translating.
TRA.DU.ZIR, *v.*, to translate, to express.
TRA.DU.ZÍ.VEL, *adj.*, translatable.
TRA.FE.GA.BI.LI.DA.DE, *s.f.*, trafficability.
TRA.FE.GAR, *v.*, to transit, to pass through, to traffic.
TRA.FE.GÁ.VEL, *adj.*, trafficable, capable of bein passed through.
TRÁ.FE.GO, *s.m.*, traffic, transit, transport, business, commerce.
TRA.FI.CÂN.CI.A, *s.f.*, trade, business, commerce.
TRA.FI.CAN.TE, *s. 2 gen.*, trafficker, dealer, trader; swindler, rascal.
TRA.FI.CAR, *v.*, to traffic, to trade, to swindle, to trick.
TRÁ.FI.CO, *s.m.*, traffic, trade.
TRA.GA.DA, *s.f.*, draught, pull, swig.
TRA.GA.DOR, *s.m.*, devourer, swallower, glutton. adj devouring, swallowing, engulfing.
TRA.GA.MEN.TO, *s.m.*, engulfing, swallowing, devouring.
TRA.GAR, *v.*, to devour, to swallow, to absorb, to gulp down.
TRA.GÁ.VEL, *adj.*, that which can be swigged or devoured.
TRA.GÉ.DIA, *s.f.*, tragedy, calamity, disaster, drama, story.
TRA.GI.CA.MEN.TE, *adv.*, tragically.
TRA.GI.CI.DA.DE, *s.f.*, the quality of what is tragic.
TRÁ.GI.CO, *adj.*, sad, tragic, terrible, mournful.
TRA.GI.CO.MÉ.DI.A, *s.f.*, tragicomedy.
TRA.GI.CÔ.MI.CO, *adj.*, tragicomic(al).
TRA.GO, *s.m.*, draft, gulp, swallow, drink.
TRAI.ÇÃO, *s.f.*, treason, treachery, perfidy.
TRAI.ÇO.EI.RA.MEN.TE, *adv.*, treasonably, treacherously.
TRAI.ÇO.EI.RO, *adj.*, treacherous, perfidious.
TRA.Í.DO, *adj.*, having been betrayed.
TRAI.DOR, *s.m.*, traitor, betrayer; *adj.*, perfidious, treacherous.
TRAI.LER, *s.m.*, *Ingl.*, trailer.
TRAI.NEI.RA, *s.f.*, trawlboat; *Bras.*, net for catching sardines.
TRAIN.ING, *s.m.*, *Ingl.*, training suit, track suit.
TRA.IR, *v.*, to betray, to be false.
TRA.Í.RA, *s.f.*, *Bras.*, a species of voracious freshwater fish; *fig.*, traitor.
TRA.JAR, *v.*, to wear, to dress, to vesture.
TRA.JE, *s.m.*, dress, cloth(es), costume, garb.
TRA.JE.TO, *s.m.*, stretch, distance, course.
TRA.JE.TÓ.RIA, *s.f.*, trajectory.
TRA.JO, *s.m.*, the same that *traje*.
TRA.LHA, *s.f.*, small fishing net; *Bras.*, baggage; *col.*, old household articles, rubbish.
TRA.MA, *s.f.*, plot, scheme, woof, weft.
TRA.MA.DOR, *s.m.*, weaver, plotter; *adj.*, weaving.
TRA.MAR, *v.*, to weave, to plot, to scheme.
TRAM.BI.QUE, *s.m.*, *Bras.*, *gír.*, hoax, trickery.
TRAM.BI.QUEI.RO, *s.m.*, *Bras.*, *gír.*, a hoaxer, trickster, cheater; *adj.*, tricky, cheating.
TRAM.BO.LHO, *s.m.*, clog.
TRAM.BO.LHÃO, *s.m.*, *pop.*, fussy fall, tumble; *fig.*, misadventure, mishap; piece of bad luck.
TRAM.BO.LHO, *s.m.*, *pop.*, anything big and heavy that bothers

and disturbs; obstacle, hindrance.
TRA.MI.TA.ÇÃO, *s.f.*, *Bras.*, normal course through legal channels (documents, process, etc.).
TRA.MI.TAR, *v.*, *Bras.*, to follow legal channels (documents, process, etc.).
TRÂ.MI.TE, *s.m.*, path, course, way.
TRA.MOI.A, *s.f.*, chicane, trick, intrigue.
TRAM.PAR, *v.*, *Bras.*, *gír.*, to work.
TRAM.PO, *s.m.*, *Bras.*, *gír.*, work.
TRAM.PO.LIM, *s.m.*, springboard, diving board.
TRAM.PO.LI.NAR, *v.*, to swindle, to cheat, to take in.
TRAN.CA, *s.f.*, bar, crossbar, hindrance, obstacle.
TRAN.CA.DO, *adj.*, locked up, fast, shut; barred, locked, fastened with bars.
TRAN.ÇA.DO, *s.m.*, tress, braid, plait; plaitwork; *adj.*, braided, plaited.
TRAN.CA.FI.AR, *v.*, *Bras.*, *pop.*, lock up, incarcerate, imprison, arrest.
TRAN.CAR, *v.*, to fasten, to latch, to lock, to bolt.
TRAN.ÇAR, *v.*, to tress, to interlace, to weave, to braid, to twist.
TRAN.CO, *s.m.*, collision, push, jolt, jog, hump.
TRAN.QUEI.RA, *s.f.*, set of discarded objects; stockade, fence.
TRAN.QUI.LA.MEN.TE, *adv.*, quietly.
TRAN.QUI.LI.DA.DE, *s.f.*, tranquility, peace, serenity, rest, silence.
TRAN.QUI.LI.ZA.DOR, *s.m.*, tranquilizer; *adj.*, reassuring, soothing.
TRAN.QUI.LI.ZAN.TE, *s.m.*, *Med.*, tranquilizer; *adj.*, tranquilizing, soothing.
TRAN.QUI.LI.ZAR, *v.*, to tranquilize, to quiet, to still, to appease, to pacify.
TRAN.QUI.LO, *adj.*, calm, tranquil, peaceful, easy, quiet.
TRAN.SA, *s.f.*, *Bras.*, *gír.*, business, affair; *vulg.*, sexual intercourse.
TRAN.SA.ÇÃO, *s.f.*, transaction, dealing, business.
TRAN.SA.CI.O.NAL, *adj.*, transactional.
TRAN.SA.CI.O.NAR, *v.*, to transact, to negotiate, to deal.
TRAN.SA.DO, *adj.*, *Bras.*, *gír.*, well-arranged, well-prepared.
TRAN.SAL.PI.NO, *adj.*, transalpine.
TRAN.SA.MA.ZÔ.NI.CO, *adj.*, crossing the Amazon region.
TRAN.SAR, *v.*, *Bras.*, *gír.*, to deal in; to machinate, to plan; *vulg.*, to get laid, to have sexual intercourse.
TRAN.SA.TLÂN.TI.CO, *s.m.*, transatlantic.
TRANS.BOR.DA.MEN.TO, *s.m.*, overflow, overflowing.
TRANS.BOR.DAN.TE, *adj.*, overflowing, inundating.
TRANS.BOR.DAR, *v.*, to overflow.
TRANS.BOR.DO, *s.m.*, overflowing, overflow; trans-shipment.
TRANS.CEN.DÊN.CI.A, *s.f.*, transcendence, transcendency.
TRANS.CEN.DEN.TAL, *adj.*, transcendental.
TRANS.CEN.DEN.TA.LI.DA.DE, *s.f.*, state of being transcendental.
TRANS.CEN.DEN.TA.LIS.MO, *s.m.*, transcendentalism.
TRANS.CEN.DEN.TA.LI.ZAR, *v.*, to give transcendental features to.
TRANS.CEN.DEN.TE, *adj.*, transcendent.
TRANS.CEN.DER, *v.*, to transcend, overpass, overtop, excel.
TRANS.CON.TI.NEN.TAL, *adj.*, transcontinental.
TRANS.COR.RER, *v.*, to elapse, to go by, to pass.
TRANS.CRE.VER, *v.*, to transcribe, to copy, to transfer.

TRANSCRIÇÃO · 337 · TRAPACEAR

TRANS.CRI.ÇÃO, *s.f.*, transcription, transcribing.
TRANS.CRI.TO, *s.m.*, transcript, copy, translation; *adj.*, transcript.
TRANS.CUL.TU.RA.ÇÃO, *s.f.*, transculturation.
TRANS.CUR.SAR, *v.*, to pass, to elapse.
TRANS.CUR.SO, *s.m.*, course, passage of time.
TRAN.SE, *s.m.*, trance, anguish, trouble, distress, difficulty.
TRAN.SE.CU.LAR, *adj.*, occurring through the centuries.
TRAN.SE.UN.TE, *s. 2 gen.*, transient, pedestrian; *adj.*, transient, transitory.
TRAN.SE.XU.AL, *s. 2 gen.*, transexual.
TRAN.SE.XU.A.LIS.MO, *s.m.*, transsexualism.
TRANS.FE.RÊN.CIA, *s.f.*, transference, transfer.
TRANS.FE.RI.DOR, *s.m.*, transferrer; *Mat.*, protractor.
TRANS.FE.RIR, *v.*, to transfer, to remove, to convey, to transport.
TRANS.FE.RÍ.VEL, *adj.*, transferable.
TRANS.FI.GU.RA.ÇÃO, *s.f.*, transfiguration.
TRANS.FI.GU.RA.DO, *adj.*, transfigured.
TRANS.FI.GU.RAR, *v.*, to transfigure.
TRANS.FOR.MA.ÇÃO, *s.f.*, transformation.
TRANS.FOR.MA.CI.O.NAL, *adj.*, transformational.
TRANS.FOR.MA.DOR, *s.m.*, transformer; *adj.*, transforming, changing.
TRANS.FOR.MAN.TE, *adj.*, transforming.
TRANS.FOR.MAR, *v.*, to transform, to alter, to change, to modify, to transfigure.
TRANS.FOR.MA.TI.VO, *adj.*, transformative.
TRANS.FOR.MÁ.VEL, *adj.*, transformable.
TRANS.FOR.MIS.MO, *s.m.*, transformism.
TRANS.FOR.MIS.TA, *s. 2 gen.*, *Biol.*, transformist.
TRANS.FU.SÃO, *s.f.*, transfusion.
TRANS.GÊ.NI.CO, *adj.*, *Biol.*, transgenic.
TRANS.GRE.DIR, *v.*, to transgress, to infringe, to violate, to infract.
TRANS.GRES.SÃO, *s.f.*, transgression, lawbreaking.
TRANS.GRES.SI.VO, *adj.*, transgressive.
TRANS.GRES.SOR, *s.m.*, transgressor, violator, offender; *adj.*, offending, transgressive.
TRAN.SI.BE.RI.A.NO, *s.m.*, trans-Siberian way; *adj.*, trans-Siberian.
TRAN.SI.ÇÃO, *s.f.*, transition, passage.
TRAN.SI.CI.O.NAL, *adj.*, transitional.
TRAN.SI.DO, *adj.*, numb, benumbed.
TRAN.SI.EN.TE, *adj.*, transient.
TRAN.SI.GÊN.CIA, *s.f.*, compromise, agreement, acquiescence.
TRAN.SI.GEN.TE, *s. 2 gen.*, acquiescent person; *adj.*, condescending, acquiescent, complying.
TRAN.SI.GIR, *v.*, to compromise, to condescend, to agree.
TRAN.SI.TAR, *v.*, to transit, to pass.
TRAN.SI.TÁ.VEL, *adj.*, passable, usable.
TRAN.SI.TI.VI.DA.DE, *s.f.*, transitivity.
TRAN.SI.TI.VO, *adj.*, transitive, transitional.
TRÂN.SI.TO, *s.m.*, transit, passage, conveyance, traffic.
TRAN.SI.TO.RI.E.DA.DE, *s.f.*, transitoriness.
TRAN.SI.TÓ.RIO, *adj.*, transitory, passing, brief.
TRANS.LA.DA.ÇÃO, *s.f.*, the same that *trasladação*.
TRANS.LA.ÇÃO, *s.f.*, transfer, remove, metaphor.
TRANS.LA.TO, *adj.*, transferred; *Gram.*, metaphorical, figurative.

TRANS.LI.TE.RA.ÇÃO, *s.f.*, transliteration.
TRANS.LI.TE.RAR, *v.*, to transliterate.
TRANS.LU.CI.DEZ, *s.f.*, translucency, translucence.
TRANS.LÚ.CI.DO, *adj.*, translucent, limpid, clear.
TRANS.LU.ZEN.TE, *adj.*, translucent, transparent.
TRANS.MI.GRA.ÇÃO, *s.f.*, transmigration.
TRANS.MI.GRAR, *v.*, to transmigrate.
TRANS.MIS.SÃO, *s.f.*, transmission.
TRANS.MIS.SI.BI.LI.DA.DE, *s.f.*, transmissibility.
TRANS.MIS.SÍ.VEL, *adj.*, transmissible.
TRANS.MIS.SOR, *s.m.*, transmitter.
TRANS.MI.TÂN.CI.A, *s.f.*, *Fís.*, transmittance.
TRANS.MI.TIR, *v.*, to transmit, to transfer, to send, to deliver, to pass on, to hand over, to convey.
TRANS.PA.RE.CER, *v.*, to become visible, to be evident.
TRANS.PA.REN.TAR, *v.*, to make transparent.
TRANS.PA.RÊN.CIA, *s.f.*, transparency, pellucidity, diaphaneity.
TRANS.PA.REN.TE, *s.m.*, transparence; *adj.*, transparent, translucent, limpid, clear.
TRANS.PA.REN.TE.MEN.TE, *adv.*, transparently.
TRANS.PAS.SA.DO, *adj.*, passed over, crossed over, transferred.
TRANS.PAS.SAR, *v.*, to pass over, to go beyond; to trespass, to exceed.
TRANS.PI.RA.ÇÃO, *s.f.*, transpiration.
TRANS.PI.RAR, *v.*, to transpire, to sweat, to perspire, to become known.
TRANS.PI.RÁ.VEL, *adj.*, transpirable.
TRANS.PLAN.TA.ÇÃO, *s.f.*, transplantation.
TRANS.PLAN.TAR, *v.*, to transplant, to translocate.
TRANS.PLAN.TÁ.VEL, *adj.*, transplantable.
TRANS.PLAN.TE, *s.m.*, transplant, transplantation.
TRANS.PO.NÍ.VEL, *adj.*, capable of being transposed.
TRANS.POR, *v.*, to transpose, to cross over, to overrun.
TRANS.POR.TA.BI.LI.DA.DE, *s.f.*, transportability.
TRANS.POR.TA.DOR, *s.m.*, transporter, conveyer.
TRANS.POR.TAR, *v.*, to transport, to carry, to convey, to entrance.
TRANS.POR.TÁ.VEL, *adj.*, transportable.
TRANS.POR.TE, *s.m.*, transport, transportation, conduction, vehicle.
TRANS.PO.SI.ÇÃO, *s.f.*, transposition.
TRANS.POS.TO, *adj.*, transposed, transferred.
TRANS.TOR.NA.DO, *adj.*, disturbed, perturbed, perplexed.
TRANS.TOR.NA.DOR, *adj.*, disturbing, confusing.
TRANS.TOR.NAR, *v.*, to overturn, to disturb, to perturb, to alter.
TRANS.TOR.NO, *s.m.*, disappointment, perturbation, disturbance, inconvenience.
TRANS.VER.BE.RAR, *v.*, reflect, shine through.
TRANS.VER.SAL, *adj.*, transverse, transversal.
TRANS.VER.SA.LI.DA.DE, *s.f.*, transversality.
TRANS.VER.SAL.MEN.TE, *adv.*, transversally, obliquely.
TRANS.VER.SO, *s.m.*, *Anat.*, transversum (transverse muscle); *adj.*, transverse.
TRANS.VI.A.DO, *adj.*, led astray; perverted.
TRANS.VI.AR, *v.*, to wander, to err, to deviate.
TRANS.VI.O, *s.m.*, deviation.
TRA.PA.ÇA, *s.f.*, fraud, knavery, deceit, trick, swindle.
TRA.PA.CE.AR, *v.*, to swindle, to trick, to cheat.

TRAPACEIRO · 338 · TREPIDANTE

TRA.PA.CEI.RO, *s.m.*, trickster, swindler, crook.
TRA.PA.LHA.DA, *s.f.*, confusion, misunderstanding, topsy-turvy.
TRA.PA.LHÃO, *s.m.*, fumbler, bungler; *adj.*, clumsy, tricky.
TRA.PEI.RO, *s.m.*, ragman, ragpicker, scavenger.
TRA.PÉ.ZIO, *s.m.*, trapezium, trapeze, trapezoid.
TRA.PE.ZIS.TA, *s. 2 gen.*, trapezist.
TRA.PI.CHE, *s.m., Bras.*, old sugar mill; *Bras.*, pier, wharf.
TRA.PO, *s.m.*, rag, tatter, shred, frazzle.
TRA.QUE.AL, *adj.*, tracheal.
TRA.QUEI.A, *s.f., Anat.*, trachea, windpipe.
TRA.QUE.JO, *s.m.*, practice, experience.
TRA.QUE.OS.TO.MI.A, *s.f., Med.*, tracheostomy.
TRA.QUE.O.TO.MI.A, *s.f., Med.*, tracheotomy.
TRA.QUI.NA, *s.m.*, the same that *traquinas*.
TRA.QUI.NA.GEM, *s.f., Bras.*, the same that *traquinice*.
TRA.QUI.NAR, *v.*, to frolic, to frisk, to be restless, to naughty.
TRA.QUI.NAS, *s. 2 gen., 2 num.*, frisker, mischief-maker; *adj.*, mischievous.
TRA.QUI.NI.CE, *s.f.*, mischie, frisk, prank, frolic.
TRÁS, *prep.*, behind, after, back.
TRA.SEI.RA, *s.f.*, rear, hinder part, back.
TRA.SEI.RO, *s.m.*, bum, butt, buttocks; *adj.*, back, posterior, rear.
TRAS.LA.DA.ÇÃO, *s.f.*, translation, copy, transcription.
TRAS.LA.DA.DO, *adj.*, translated.
TRAS.LA.DAR, *v.*, to transfer, to remove, to transport.
TRAS.LA.DÁ.VEL, *adj.*, capable of being translated.
TRAS.LA.DO, *s.m.*, transfer, removal, copy, transcript, translation.
TRAS.PAS.SA.DO, *adj.*, the same that *transpassado*.
TRAS.PAS.SAR, *v.*, the same that *transpassar*.
TRA.TA.BI.LI.DA.DE, *s.f.*, tractability.
TRA.TA.DO, *s.m.*, treaty, agreement, pact, accord.
TRA.TA.DOR, *s.m.*, negotiator; caretaker; cattle feeder, groom; *adj.*, taking care of.
TRA.TA.MEN.TO, *s.m.*, treatment, treating, handling, usage, daily ration.
TRA.TAN.TE *s. 2 gen.*, rascal, crook, scoundrel.
TRA.TAR, *v.*, to treat, to deal with, to handle, to transact, to attend.
TRA.TÁ.VEL, *adj.*, tractable, treatable.
TRA.TIS.TA, *s. 2 gen.*, the same that *tratante*.
TRA.TO, *s.m.*, deal, agreement, contract, dealing.
TRA.TOR, *s.m.*, tractor.
TRA.TO.RIA, *s.f.*, restaurant specialized in Italian cuisine.
TRA.TO.RIS.TA, *s. 2 gen.*, tractor driver.
TRAU.MA, *s.m.*, trauma.
TRAU.MÁ.TI.CO, *adj.*, traumatic.
TRAU.MA.TIS.MO, *s.m., Med., Psic.*, traumatism, trauma.
TRAU.MA.TI.ZA.DO, *adj.*, traumatized.
TRAU.MA.TI.ZAN.TE, *adj.*, traumatizing.
TRAU.MA.TI.ZAR, *v., Med., Psic.*, to traumatize.
TRA.VA, *s.f.*, block, lock, key bolt.
TRA.VA.DA, *s.f., Bras.*, the act of braking (a vehicle).
TRA.VA.DO, *adj.*, connected, joined, linked.
TRA.VA-LÍN.GUA, *s.m.*, tongue twister.
TRA.VAR, *v.*, to join, to connect, to brace, to unite.
TRA.VE, *s.f.*, bar, crossbar; *Esp.*, each of the vertical bars of the goal (soccer).
TRA.VÉS, *s.m.*, bias, slant, traverse, diagonal.

TRA.VES.SA, *s.f.*, beam, crossbar, crossroad, transom, batten.
TRA.VES.SÃO, *s.m.*, dash, division; cross-wind; *Esp.*, horizontal bar over beams of the goal (soccer).
TRA.VES.SAR, *v.*, the same that *atravessar*: to cross over.
TRA.VES.SEI.RO, *s.m.*, pillow.
TRA.VES.SIA, *s.f.*, crossing.
TRA.VES.SU.RA, *s.f.*, prank, gambol, frisk.
TRA.VES.TI, *s.m.*, transvestite, drag-queen; travesty.
TRA.VES.TI.DO, *s.m.*, transvestite; *adj.*, relating to a transvestite.
TRA.VES.TIR, *v.*, to transvest; to disguise oneself.
TRA.VES.TIS.MO, *s.m.*, transvestism.
TRA.ZER, *v.*, to bring, to fetch, to carry, to convey, to introduce.
TRE.CEN.TIS.TA, *s.*, trecentist (artist of the 14th century).
TRE.CHO, *s.m.*, period, space, section, distance, interval.
TRÉ.GUA, *s.f.*, armistice, truce, rest.
TRÊI.LER, *s.m.*, the same that *trailer*.
TREI.NA.DO, *adj.*, trained, drilled.
TREI.NA.DOR, *s.m.*, trainer, coach.
TREI.NA.MEN.TO, *s.m.*, training, coaching.
TREI.NAR, *v.*, to train, to drill, to coach, to exercise, to practise.
TREI.NO, *s.m.*, training, coaching.
TRE.JEI.TO, *s.m.*, grimace, wry face.
TRE.LA, *s.f.*, leash, dog lead; *pop.*, talk, chat, gossip.
TRE.LI.ÇA, *s.f.*, trellis, latticework.
TREM, *s.m.*, train; *Bras.*, a worthless fellow; *trens* (*pl.*): goods and chattels.
TRE.MA, *s.m.*, diaresis.
TRE.MA.DO, *adj.*, marked with a dieresis; unravelled.
TRE.MAR, *v.*, to mark with a dieresis; to unravel.
TRE.ME.DEI.RA, *s.f.*, trembling, quaking, fit, shivering.
TRE.ME.LI.CAN.TE, *adj.*, tremulous, tremulant.
TRE.ME.LI.CAR, *v.*, to tremble, to quake, to quiver.
TRE.ME.LI.QUE, *s.m.*, shake, shiver, tremble.
TRE.MEN.DO, *adj.*, tremendous, terrifying, awful, frightful, terrible.
TRE.MER, *v.*, to tremble, to quake, to shake, to quiver, to vibrate.
TRE.MO.ÇAL, *s.m.*, lupine plantation.
TRE.MO.ÇO, *s.m.*, lupine, lupine bean.
TRE.MOR, *s.m.*, tremor, shake, thrill, quiver.
TRE.MU.LA.ÇÃO, *s.f.*, tremble, trembling, flicker.
TRE.MU.LAN.TE, *adj.*, waving, shaking, fluttering.
TRE.MU.LAR, *v.*, to tremble, to quaver, to wave, to flicker, to twinkle, vascillate.
TRÊ.MU.LO, *adj.*, trembling, fearful, hesitant.
TRE.MU.RA, *s.f.*, tremor, trembling, tremble.
TRE.NA, *s.f.*, measuring tape.
TRE.NÓ, *s.m.*, sled, sleigh, sledge, toboggan.
TRE.PA.ÇÃO, *s.f.*, calumny, defamation; censure, jeering; *Bras., vulg.*, a series of copulas.
TRE.PA.DA, *s.f.*, ascent, climb; reprimand; slope; *Bras., vulg.*, copula.
TRE.PA.DEI.RA, *s.f.*, creeper, creeping.
TRE.PA.DOR, *s.m.*, calumniator; *Bras., vulg.*, one who practices sex; *adj.*, creeping, climbing; slanderous.
TRE.PAR, *v.*, to climb, to ascend, to rise, to scale.
TRE.PI.DA.ÇÃO, *s.f.*, trepidation, vibration, agitation.
TRE.PI.DAN.TE, *adj.*, tremulous, trepidant, trepidatory.

TREPIDANTEMENTE ·· 339 ·· TRITURAR

TRE.PI.DAN.TE.MEN.TE, *adv.*, tremulously.

TRE.PI.DAR, *v.*, to tremble, to shake, to oscillate, to vibrate, to vacillate.

TRÊS, *num.*, three.

TRES.LOU.CA.DO, *adj.*, crazy, mad, deranged.

TRÊS MA.RI.AS, *s.f., pl., Astron.*, Orion's belt.

TRE.VA, *s.f.*, darkness.

TRE.VAS, *s.f., pl.*, darkness, obscurity, ignorance, gloom, mirkiness.

TRE.VO, *s.m.*, clover, intersection, shamrock.

TRE.ZE, *num.*, thirteen.

TRE.ZEN.TOS, *num.*, three hundred.

TRÍ.A.DE, *s.f.*, triad.

TRI.A.GEM, *s.f.*, selection, classification; sorting machine.

TRI.AN.GU.LA.ÇÃO, *s.f.*, triangulation.

TRI.AN.GU.LA.RI.DA.DE, *s.f.*, triangularity.

TRI.ÂN.GU.LO, *s.m.*, triangle, trigon.

TRI.ÁS.SI.CO, TRI.Á.SI.CO, *adj., Geol.*, Triassic.

TRI.A.TLE.TA, *s. 2 gen., Esp.*, triathlete.

TRI.A.TLO, *s.m., Esp.*, triathlon.

TRI.BAL, *adj.*, tribal.

TRI.BO, *s.m.*, tribe, clan, race, folk, family.

TRI.BU.LA.ÇÃO, *s.f.*, tribulation, grief, trouble.

TRI.BU.NA, *s.f.*, tribune, rostrum, pulpit, gallery.

TRI.BU.NAL, *s.m.*, court of justice, tribunal, council.

TRI.BU.LAR, *v.*, the same that *atribular*.

TRI.BU.NO, *s.m.*, tribune.

TRI.BU.TA.ÇÃO, *s.f.*, taxation, assessment.

TRI.BU.TA.DO, *adj.*, taxed, assessed.

TRI.BU.TAR, *v.*, to lay a tribute on, to tax.

TRI.BU.TA.RI.A.MEN.TE, *adv.*, tributarily.

TRI.BU.TÁ.RIO, *s.m.*, tributary; *adj.*, tributary, contributary.

TRI.BU.TÁ.VEL, *adj.*, taxable, , tributary.

TRI.BU.TO, *s.m.*, tribute, duty, tax, toll, due.

TRI.CAM.PE.ÃO, *s.m.*, trichampion.

TRI.CAM.PE.O.NA.TO, *s.m.*, trichampionship.

TRI.CEN.TE.NÁ.RIO, *adj.*, tricentenary.

TRI.CEN.TÉ.SI.MO, TRE.CEN.TÉ.SI.MO, *s.m.*, the three hundredth part; *adj.*, three-hundredth.

TRÍ.CEPS, *s.m., 2 num., Anat.*, triceps; *adj.*, triceps.

TRI.CI.CLO, *s.m.*, tricycle, velocipede, tricar.

TRI.CÔ, *s.m.*, knitting, tricot.

TRI.CO.LOR, *adj.*, tricolour, tricoloured.

TRI.CÓR.NI.O, *s.m.*, tricorn, tricorne, three-cornered hat.

TRI.CO.TAR, *v.*, to knit.

TRI.DÁC.TI.LO, TRI.DÁ.TI.LO, *adj., Zool.*, tridactilous.

TRI.DEN.TE, *s.m.*, trident; *adj.*, tridental, tridentate.

TRI.DI.MEN.SI.O.NAL, *adj.*, tridimensional.

TRI.E.NA.DO, *s.m.*, triennial.

TRI.Ê.NIO, *s.m.*, triennial, a period of three years.

TRI.FO.CAL, *s.m.*, trifocal; *adj.*, trifocal.

TRI.GAL, *s.m.*, wheat field, cornfield.

TRI.GÊ.MEO, *s.m.*, triplet, trilling.

TRI.GÉ.SI.MO, *adj.*, thirtieth.

TRI.GO, *s.m.*, wheat.

TRI.GO.NO.ME.TRI.A, *s.f.*, trigonometry.

TRI.GO.NO.MÉ.TRI.CO, *adj.*, trigonometric, trigonometrical.

TRI.LAR, *v.*, to quaver, to trill.

TRI.LA.TE.RAL, *adj., Geom.*, trilateral.

TRI.LÁ.TE.RO, *s.m.*, triangle; *adj.*, trilateral.

TRI.LHA, *s.f.*, trail, track.

TRI.LHA.DO, *adj.*, thrashed, beaten; common.

TRI.LHÃO, *s.m.*, trillion (corresponds to an English billion).

TRI.LHAR, *v.*, to thrash, to thresh, to flail, to beat.

TRI.LHO, *s.m.*, trail, track, rail.

TRI.LÍN.GUE, *s. 2 gen.*, person who speaks three languages; *adj.*, trilingual.

TRI.LO.BI.TE, *s.m., Paleont.*, trilobite.

TRI.LO.GI.A, *s.f.*, trilogy.

TRI.MEN.SAL, *adj.*, trimestrial.

TRI.MES.TRAL, *adj.*, trimestrial.

TRI.MES.TRA.LI.DA.DE, *s.f., Bras.*, trimestrial payment.

TRI.MES.TRAL.MEN.TE, *adv.*, trimestrially.

TRI.MES.TRE, *s.m.*, quarter, period of three months.

TRI.NA.DO, *s.m.*, trill, twitter, chirp.

TRI.NA.DOR, *s.m.*, triller; *adj.*, trilling, warbling.

TRI.NAR, *v.*, to trill, to shake, to quaver.

TRIN.CA, *s.f.*, trine, gang, scratch, crack.

TRIN.CA.DO, *adj.*, cracked, scratched, split.

TRIN.CAR, *v.*, to crush, to bite, to crunch.

TRIN.CO, *s.m.*, door latch, latch bolt.

TRIN.DA.DE, *s.f.*, Trinity, triad, trine.

TRI.NI.DAD E TO.BA.GO, *s.*, Trinidad and Tobago.

TRI.NÔ.MI.O, *s.m., Biol., Mat.*, trinomial.

TRIN.TA, *num.*, thirty.

TRIN.TÃO, *s.m.*, person of thirty years old (and less than forty); *adj.*, thirtyish.

TRI.O, *s.m.*, trio, a set of three.

TRI.PA, *s.f.*, intestine, gut, tripe.

TRI.PA.NOS.SO.MO, *s.m.*, trypanosome.

TRI.PÉ, *s.m.*, tripod, trivet, spider.

TRÍ.PLEX, *s.m., 2 num., Bras.*, a triplex apartment; *adj.*, triplex.

TRI.PLI.CA.ÇÃO, *s.f.*, triplication.

TRI.PLI.CA.DO, *adj.*, tripled, triplicate, triple.

TRI.PLI.CAR, *v.*, to triplicate, to triple.

TRÍ.PLI.CE, *adj.*, triplo.

TRI.PLI.CI.DA.DE, *s.f.*, triplicity.

TRI.PLO, *s.m.*, triple, triplex; *adj.*, triple, threefold.

TRI.PU.DI.AR, *v.*, to tripudiate, to exult, to rejoice.

TRI.PU.LA.ÇÃO, *s.f.*, crew, personnel.

TRI.PU.LA.DO, *adj.*, manned (spaceship); crewed (ship, boat).

TRI.PU.LAN.TE, *s. 2 gen.*, member of the crew, seaman, sailor.

TRI.PU.LAR, *v.*, to man (a ship, an airplane), to crew (to command, to govern).

TRI.SA.NU.AL, *adj.*, triennal.

TRI.SA.VÓ, *s.f.*, great-great-grandmother.

TRI.SA.VÔ, *s.m.*, great-great-grandfather.

TRIS.TE, *adj.*, dreary, melancholic, sorrowful, unhappy, depressed.

TRIS.TE.MEN.TE, *adv.*, sadly.

TRIS.TE.ZA, *s.f.*, sorrow, grief, unhappiness, melancholy, depression.

TRIS.TO.NHO, *adj.*, unhappy, depressed, dejected.

TRI.TÃO, *s.m., Mit.*, Triton (semigod of the sea); *Astron.*, moon of the planet Neptune.

TRI.TI.CUL.TU.RA, *s.f.*, wheat growing.

TRÍ.TI.O, *s.m., Quím.*, tritium (isotope of hydrogen).

TRI.TON.GO, *s.m., Gram.*, triphtong.

TRI.TU.RA.ÇÃO, *s.f.*, trituration.

TRI.TU.RA.DOR, *s.m.*, pulverizer, triturator.

TRI.TU.RAN.TE, *adj.*, pulverizing, triturating.

TRI.TU.RAR, *v.*, to grind, to mill, to triturate.

TRIUNFAL ·· 340 ·· TUNDRA

TRI.UN.FAL, *adj.*, triumphal.
TRI.UN.FA.LIS.MO, *s.m.*, triumphalism.
TRI.UN.FA.LIS.TA, *s. 2 gen.*, triumphalist.
TRI.UN.FAN.TE, *adj.*, triumphant, victorious.
TRI.UN.FAR, *v.*, to triumph, to win, to conquer, to be successful.
TRI.UN.FO, *s.m.*, triumph, victory, conquest, success.
TRI.VA.LÊN.CI.A, *s.f.*, *Quím.*, trivalence.
TRI.VA.LEN.TE, *adj.*, *Quím.*, trivalent.
TRI.VAL.VAR, *adj.*, trivalvular, trivalved.
TRI.VI.AL, *adj.*, trivial, common, trifling, banal, petty.
TRI.VI.A.LI.DA.DE, *s.f.*, trivialism, triviality, trivialness.
TRI.VI.A.LI.ZAR, *v.*, to trivialize, become trivial, become common.
TRI.VI.AL.MEN.TE, *adv.*, trivially.
TRIZ, *s.m.*, moment, trice.
TRO.AN.TE, *adj.*, roaring, thundering, rumbling.
TRO.AR, *s.m.*, thunder; *v.*, to thunder; to rumble, to roar, to boom.
TRO.CA, *s.f.*, change, mutation, conversion, small cash.
TRO.CA.DI.LHO, *s.m.*, pun, quibble, play on words.
TRO.CA.DO, *s.m.*, change (money); *adj.*, changed, exchanged, in coins (money); wrong.
TRO.CA.DOR, *s. 2 gen.*, conductor (bus), exchanger; *adj.*, exchanging.
TRO.ÇA.DOR, *s.m.*, mocker, joker; *adj.*, joking, mocking.
TRO.CAR, *v.*, to change, to turn, to alter, to replace, to commute, to substitute.
TROM.BA, *s.f.*, trunk (of an elephant or tapir).
TROM.BA.DA, *s.f.*, impact, crash, collision.
TROM.BA.DI.NHA, *s.m.*, *Bras.*, *gír.*, very young thief.
TROM.BAR, *v.*, *Bras.*, to collide, to crash.
TROM.BE.TA, *s.f.*, *Mús.*, trumpet, tuba, horn.
TROM.BE.TE.AR, *v.*, to trumpet; to announce.
TROM.BO.NE, *s.m.*, trombone.
TROM.BO.NIS.TA, *s. 2 gen.*, trombonist.
TROM.BO.SE, *s.f.*, *Med.*, thrombosis.
TROM.BU.DO, *adj.*, having a great snout; *fig.*, sulky, grouchy.
TROM.PA, *s.f.*, *Mús.*, trumpet, trump, bugle.
TROM.PA DE FA.LÓ.PI.O, *s.f.*, *Anat.*, uterine tube (*Anat.*, Fallopian tube).
TROM.PE.TE, *s.m.*, *Mús.*, trumpet.
TROM.PE.TIS.TA, *s. 2 gen.*, trumpeter (trumpet player).
TRON.CHO, *s.m.*, stump, stub (of a tree); *adj.*, curtailed, crooked, bent.
TRON.CO, *s.m.*, trunk, stem of a tree, body, main body.
TRON.CU.DO, *adj.*, *Bras.*, sturdy, strong.
TRO.NO, *s.m.*, throne.
TRO.PA, *s.f.*, troop, band, host.
TRO.PE.ÇÃO, *s.f.*, stumbling, stumble, trip, slip.
TRO.PE.ÇAR, *v.*, to stumble, to trip, to slip.
TRO.PE.ÇO, *s.m.*, stumble, false step, obstacle.
TRÔ.PE.GO, *adj.*, unsteady, shaky, tottery.
TRO.PI.CAL, *adj.*, tropical.
TRO.PI.CA.LIS.MO, *s.m.*, *Mús.*, tropicalism (Brazilian musical movement, Tropicalia).
TRO.PI.CA.LIS.TA, *s. 2 gen.*, specialist in tropical subjects; *Mús.*, Tropicalia movement's participant.
TRO.PI.CÃO, *s.m.*, *Bras.*, *col.*, stumble, false step, slip.
TRO.PI.CAR, *v.*, *Bras.*, *col.*, to stumble.
TRÓ.PI.CO, *s.m.*, tropic.

TRO.TAR, *v.*, to trot, to lope.
TRO.TE, *s.m.*, trot, jog, lope; hoax, hazing, mockery.
TROU.XA, *s.f.*, bundle of clothes, fardel, truss; sucker, booby, fool; *adj.*, foolish, simple, stupid
TRO.VA, *s.f.*, ballad.
TRO.VA.DOR, *s.m.*, troubadour.
TRO.VA.DO.RES.CO, *adj.*, like a troubadour, of or pertaining to a troubadour.
TRO.VÃO, *s.m.*, thunder.
TRO.VAR, *v.*, to compose or sing ballads.
TRO.VE.JAN.TE, *adj.*, thundering.
TRO.VE.JAR, *v.*, to thunder, to rumble, to roar, to lighten, to flash.
TRO.VO.A.DA, *s.f.*, thunderstorm.
TRO.VO.AR, *v.*, to thunder, to roar.
TRU.CA.GEM, *s.f.*, trucage, truquage.
TRU.CI.DA.DO, *adj.*, slaughtered, murdered.
TRU.CI.DAR, *v.*, to murder, to kill, to slaughter, to savage.
TRU.CU.LÊN.CIA, *s.f.*, truculence, truculentness, truculency.
TRU.CU.LEN.TO, *adj.*, truculent, savage, cruel.
TRU.FA, *s.f.*, truffle.
TRU.ÍS.MO, *s.m.*, truism.
TRU.ÍS.TA, *adj.*, of or referring to truism.
TRUM.BI.CAR-SE, *v.*, *Bras.*, *gír.*, to turn out badly, go down the tubes.
TRUN.CA.DO, *adj.*, fragmented, truncated, incomplete.
TRUN.CAR, *v.*, to truncate, to cut off, to ruff.
TRUN.FO, *s.m.*, rump card.
TRU.PE, *s.m.*, troupe; *fig.*, *pej.*, group of followers.
TRU.QUE, *s.m.*, trick, artifice, dodge.
TRUS.TE, *s.m.*, trust.
TRU.TA, *s.f.*, trout.
TU, *pron.*, you.
TU.A, *pron.*, your, yours.
TU.BA.RÃO, *s.m.*, *Zool.*, shark.
TU.BÉR.CU.LO, *s.m.*, tubercle.
TU.BER.CU.LO.SE, *s.f.*, tubercolosis.
TU.BER.CU.LO.SO, *s.m.*, person suffering from tuberculosis; *adj.*, tuberculosis.
TU.BO, *s.m.*, tube, pipe, duct, chute.
TU.BU.LA.ÇÃO, *s.f.*, pipeline, tubulation, piping.
TU.BU.LA.DO, *adj.*, tubulate, tubulated.
TU.BU.LAR, *adj.*, tubular, tubulate.
TU.CA.NO, *s.m.*, *Zool.*, toucan.
TU.DO, *s.m.*, all, everything, the whole; *pron.*, all, everything.
TU.FÃO, *s.m.*, hurricane, typhoon, tornado, windstorm.
TU.FO, *s.m.*, tuft (of feathers, hairs, grass), bunch, cluster.
TU.LI.PA, *s.f.*, *Bot.*, tulip.
TUM.BA, *s.f.*, tomb, grave, tombstone.
TÚ.MI.DO, *adj.*, tumid, turgid, swollen.
TU.MOR, *s.m.*, tumor, tumour.
TU.MO.RO.SO, *adj.*, tumorous, swollen, tumid.
TU.MU.LAR, *adj.*, tumulary; *v.*, to bury, to entomb.
TÚ.MU.LO, *s.m.*, tomb, grave, sepulcher, vault.
TU.MUL.TU.A.DO, *adj.*, agitated, disturbed, tumultuous.
TU.MUL.TO, *s.m.*, tumult, uproar, turbulence, commotion, clamour, ruckus.
TU.MUL.TU.AN.TE, *adj.*, tumultuous, causing a tumult.
TU.MUL.TU.AR, *v.*, to tumultuate, to riot, to mob, to excite.
TU.NAR, *v.*, to idle, drift, loaf, ramble, tramp.
TUN.DRA, *s.f.*, tundra.

TÚNEL ··341·· TV

TÚ.NEL, *s.m.*, tunnel.
TÚ.NI.CA, *s.f.*, tunic.
TU.PI, *s. 2 gen., Bras.*, Tupi (Indian and language of the Tupi tribe); *adj.*, Tupian.
TU.PI-GUA.RA.NI, *s. 2 gen., Bras.*, Tupi-Guarani; *adj.*, Tupi-Guaranian.
TU.PI.NI.QUIM, *s.m.*, Brazilian Indian; *adj.*, Brazilian Indian; *pej.*, Brazilian.
TUR.BA, *s.f.*, crowd, mob, rout, rabble.
TUR.BA.ÇÃO, *s.f.*, disorder, perturbation, trouble, confusion.
TUR.BA.MEN.TO, *s.m.*, the same that *turbação*.
TUR.BAN.TE, *s.m.*, turban.
TUR.BI.DEZ, *s.f.*, turbidness, turbidity.
TÚR.BI.DO, *adj.*, turbid, cloudy; confused, disturbed.
TUR.BI.LHÃO, *s.m.*, vortex, whirlpool, tornado, whirlwind, tumult, eddy, abyss.
TUR.BI.LHO.NAR, *v.*, to swirl, to twirl, to whirl, to spin.
TUR.BI.NA, *s.f.*, turbine.
TUR.BI.NA.DO, *adj.*, turbinate; turbocharged (motor).
TUR.BI.NA.GEM, *s.f.*, industrial processing of a substance by centrifugal force.
TUR.BI.NAR, *v.*, to whirl, to spin, to swirl.
TUR.BU.LÊN.CIA, *s.f.*, turbulence, disturbance, turmoil, agitation.
TUR.BU.LEN.TO, *adj.*, turbulent, troublesome, inquiet, factious.
TUR.CO, *s.m.*, Turk; *adj.*, Turkish.
TUR.FA, *s.f.*, turf, peat.
TUR.FE, *s.m.*, the turf, race-course.
TUR.FIS.TA, *s. 2 gen., Bras.*, turfman, turfite.
TUR.GÊN.CI.A, *s.f.*, turgidity.
TUR.GES.CÊN.CI.A, *s.f.*, turgescence, turgidity.
TUR.GES.CER, *v.*, swell, tumefy.

TUR.GI.DEZ, *s.f.*, turgidity, swelling.
TÚR.GI.DO, *adj.*, turgid, swollen.
TUR.RÍ.BU.LO, *s.m.*, thurible, incense-burner.
TU.RI.FI.CA.ÇÃO, *s.f.*, thurification.
TU.RI.FI.CAR, *v.*, to incense, to burn incense.
TU.RIS.MO, *s.m.*, tourism, touring.
TU.RIS.TA, *s. 2 gen.*, tourist.
TU.RÍS.TI.CO, *adj.*, touristic.
TUR.MA, *s.f.*, group, gang, people, division.
TUR.MA.LI.NA, *s.f.*, tourmaline.
TUR.NÊ, *s.f.*, a trip with programmed route, stops and visits.
TUR.NO, *s.m.*, turn, shift.
TUR.QUE.SA, *s.f.*, turquoise.
TUR.QUIA, *s.*, Turkey.
TUR.RA, *s.f.*, stubborn dispute, bickering, altercation; *viver à ~*: to argue all the time; *adj.*, stubborn.
TUR.RÃO, *s.m., pop.*, stubborn person, blockhead; *adj.*, stubborn.
TUR.VA.ÇÃO, *s.f.*, perturbation, disturbance, overcasting.
TUR.VA.DO, *adj.*, turbid, muddy.
TUR.VAR, *v.*, to darken, to dim, to dazzle, to trouble.
TUR.VO, *adj.*, muddy, cloudy, darkish.
TU.TA.NO, *s.m.*, marrow, medulla.
TU.TE.LA, *s.f.*, tutelage, guardianship, tutorship, custody.
TU.TE.LA.ÇÃO, *s.f.*, the incumbency of tutoring.
TU.TE.LA.DO, *s.m.*, tutored person; *adj.*, tutored, protected.
TU.TE.LAR, *adj.*, tutelar, protective; *v.*, to tutor, to protect, to guard.
TU.TOR, *s.m.*, tutor, preceptor, guardian.
TU.TU, *s.m., Bras., Cul.*, a dish prepared of beans, bacon and cassava flour; *Bras., gír.*, buck, money.
TV, *s.f.*, TV, television.

U

U, *s.m.*, the twentieth letter of the Portuguese alphabet.
U.BER.DA.DE, *s.f.*, uberty.
Ú.BE.RE, *s.m.*, udder, dug; *adj.*, abundant, fertile.
U.BE.RO.SO, *adj.*, uberous.
U.BI.QUI.DA.DE, *s.f.*, ubiquity, omnipresence.
U.BÍ.QUO, *adj.*, ubiquitous, omnipresent.
U.CRÂ.NI.A, *s.*, Ukraine.
U.CRA.NI.A.NO, *adj., s.m.*, Ukrainian.
U.FA, *interj.*, whew! wow!; expressing admiration, irony or fatigue.
U.FA.NAR, *v.*, to render proud, to flatter, to boast.
U.FA.NIS.MO, *s.m., Bras.*, an overoptimistic patriotic attitude towards one's country.
U.FA.NO, *adj.*, vainglorious, boasting, proud.
U.FA.NO.SO, *adj.*, conceited, arrogant.
U.FO, *s.m., abrev.* of unidentified flying object:the same that *OVNI*.
U.FO.LO.GI.A, *s.f.*, ufology.
U.FO.LO.GIS.TA, *s. 2 gen.*, ufologist (specialist in UFO's).
U.FÓ.LO.GO, *s.m.*, the same that *ufologista*.
U.GAN.DA, *s.*, Uganda.
UÍS.QUE, *s.m.*, whisky.
U.IS.QUE.RI.A, *s.f., Bras.*, bar where whiskey is served.
UI.VA.DA, *s.f., Bras.*, an acute and long howl.
UI.VA.DOR, *s.m.*, howler; *adj.*, howling.
UI.VAN.TE, *adj.*, the same that *uivador*.
UI.VAR, *v.*, to howl.
UI.VO, *s.m.*, howl.
ÚL.CE.RA, *s.f.*, ulceration.
UL.CE.RA.ÇÃO, *s.f., Med.*, ulceration, fester.
UL.CE.RA.DO, *adj.*, ulcerous, ulcerated.
UL.CE.RAR, *v.*, to ulcerate, to suppurate, to rankle.
UL.CE.RA.TI.VO, *adj.*, ulcerative, ulcerous.
UL.CE.RÁ.VEL, *adj.*, capable of causing an ulcer.
UL.TE.RI.OR, *adj.*, ulterior.
UL.TE.RI.O.RI.DA.DE, *s.f.*, quality of ulterior, remoteness.
UL.TE.RI.OR.MEN.TE, *adv.*, ulteriorly.
ÚL.TI.MA, *s.f.*, the latest news; *sabe da ~?*: have you heard the latest news?
UL.TI.MA.ÇÃO, *s.f.*, finishing, termination; finishing touch; closing.
UL.TI.MA.DO, *adj.*, concluded, finished, completed.
UL.TI.MA.MEN.TE, *adv.*, lately.
UL.TI.MAR, *v.*, to terminate, to finish, to end, to close.
ÚL.TI.MAS, *s.f., pl.*, last moments, utter misery; latest news.
UL.TI.MA.TO, *s.m.*, ultimatum.
ÚL.TI.MO, *adj.*, last, latter, late, latest.
UL.TRA.CON.SER.VA.DOR, *adj.*, ultra-conservative.
UL.TRA-HU.MA.NO, *adj.*, ultrahuman.
UL.TRA.JA.DO, *adj.*, outraged, insulted.
UL.TRA.JA.DOR, *s.m.*, slanderer; insulter, affronter; *adj.*, outrageous, slanderous.
UL.TRA.JAN.TE, *adj.*, outrageous, slanderous.
UL.TRA.JAR, *v.*, to revile, to slander, to insult, to affront, to offend.
UL.TRA.JE, *s.m.*, affront, offence, insult, defamation.
UL.TRA.JO.SO, *adj.*, the same that *ultrajante*.
UL.TRA.LE.VE, *s.m.*, hang-glider; *adj.*, ultra-light.
UL.TRA.MAR, *s.m.*, overseas (territory, possession or colony); ultramarine.
UL.TRA.MA.RI.NO, *adj.*, ultramarine, overseas.
UL.TRA.MI.CROS.CO.PI.A, *s.f., Ópt.*, ultramicroscopy.
UL.TRA.MI.CROS.CÓ.PI.CO, *adj., Ópt.*, ultramicroscopic.
UL.TRA.MO.DER.NO, *adj.*, ultramodern.
UL.TRA.PAS.SA.DO, *adj.*, overshot, surpassed.
UL.TRA.PAS.SA.GEM, *s.f.*, *UK* overtaking, *US* passing.
UL.TRA.PAS.SAR, *v.*, to surpass, to exceed, to pass over or beyond, to outdate, to leave behind.
UL.TRA.PAS.SÁ.VEL, *adj.*, surpassable.
UL.TRAR.RE.A.LIS.MO, *s.m.*, ultrarealism.
UL.TRAR.RE.A.LIS.TA, *s. 2 gen.*, ultrarealist; *adj.*, ultrarealistic.
UL.TRAR.RE.FI.NA.DO, *adj.*, overrefined.
UL.TRAR.RO.MÂN.TI.CO, *s.m.*, ultraromanticist; *adj.*, ultraromantic.
UL.TRAR.RO.MAN.TIS.MO, *s.m.*, ultraromanticism.
UL.TRAS.SEN.SÍ.VEL, *adj.*, supersensitive.
UL.TRAS.SOM, *s.m.*, supersonic, ultrasonic.
UL.TRAS.SÔ.NI.CO, *adj.*, ultrasonic.
UL.TRAS.SO.NO.GRA.FI.A, *s.f.*, ultrasonography.
UL.TRA.VER.ME.LHO, *adj.*, ultrared, infrared.
UL.TRA.VI.O.LE.TA, *adj., s.m.*, ultraviolet.
UL.TRA.VÍ.RUS, *s.m., 2 num.*, ultravirus.
U.LU.LA.ÇÃO, *s.f.*, ululation, howling, wailing.
U.LU.LA.DOR, *s.m.*, howler, bawler; *adj.*, ululant, ululatinghowling.
U.LU.LAN.TE, *adj.*, ululant, ululating.
U.LU.LAR, *v.*, to ululate, to howl (dog).
U.LU.LO, *s.m.*, the same that *ululação*.
UM, *num.*, one, cardinal number; *Art.*, the, a, an; some; *era uma vez*: once upon a time.
UM.BAN.DA, *s.m., Bras.*, afro-Brazilian cult.
UM.BAN.DIS.TA, *s. 2 gen.*, a follower of theumbanda.
UM.BI.GO, *s.m., Anat.*, navel, umbilicus.
UM.BI.LI.CAL, *adj.*, umbilical; *cordão ~*: navel-string, umbilical cord.
UM.BRAL, *s.m.*, doorjamb, doorpost, threshold.
UM.BRI.A, *s.f., Lit.*, umbrageous place; shadowy of a mountain.
U.MEC.TAN.TE, *adj.*, humectant, moisturizing.
U.MEC.TAR, *v., Med.*, to humect, moisten.
U.ME.DE.CE.DOR, *s.m.*, moistener, moisturizer; *adj.*, moisturizing.
U.ME.DE.CER, *v.*, to moisten, dampen, to wet, to humidify.
U.ME.DE.CI.DO, *adj.*, wettish, wet, damp.
U.ME.DE.CI.MEN.TO, *s.m.*, moistening, wetting, wetness.

UMIDADE   ••• 343 •••   URSA

U.MI.DA.DE, s.f., humidity, moistness, dampness.
U.MI.DI.FI.CA.ÇÃO, s.f., humidification.
U.MI.DI.FI.CA.DOR, s.m., humidifier.
U.MI.DI.FI.CAR, v., to humidify, to moisturize.
Ú.MI.DO, adj., humid, dank, damp, moist.
U.NA.NI.MAR, v., to agree, to make unanimous.
U.NÂ.NI.ME, adj., unanimous.
U.NA.NI.ME.MEN.TE, adv., unanimously.
U.NA.NI.MI.DA.DE, s.f., unanimity, consensus.
U.NA.NI.MIS.MO, s.m., unanimism.
U.NA.NI.MIS.TA, s. 2 gen., Fil., unanimist; adj., unanimistic.
UN.ÇÃO, s.f., unction, anointment.
UN.GI.DO, s.m., anointed person; adj., anointed; consecrated.
UN.GI.MEN.TO, s.m., anointment.
UN.GIR, v., to anoint, to oil; to purify; to invest.
UN.GUEN.TO, s.m., unguent, balm.
UN.GU.LA.DO, s.m., Zool., ungulate; adj., ungulate.
U.NHA, s.f., nail; unha encravada: ingrowing nail.
U.NHA.DA, s.f., a nail scratch.
U.NHAR, v., to scratch.
U.NI.ÃO, s.f., union, alliance, association, junction.
U.NI.CA.MEN.TE, adv., only, exclusively.
U.NI.CA.ME.RAL, adj., Pol., unicameral.
U.NI.CE.LU.LAR, adj., Bot., unicellular.
U.NI.CI.DA.DE, s.f., unicity, oneness.
Ú.NI.CO, s.m., unique; adj., unique, single, alone, sole, only, one, one and only.
U.NI.CO.LOR, adj., unicoloured.
U.NI.CÓR.NI.O, s.m., Mit., unicorn.
U.NI.DA.DE, s.f., unity, oneness, unit, union, drive.
U.NI.DI.MEN.SI.O.NAL, adj., unidimensional.
U.NI.DI.RE.CI.O.NAL, adj., unidirectional.
U.NI.DO, adj., united, joined, allied.
U.NI.FI.CA.ÇÃO, s.f., unification.
U.NI.FI.CA.DO, adj., unified.
U.NI.FI.CA.DOR, s.m., unifier; adj., unifying.
U.NI.FI.CAR, v., to unify, to gather, to standardize, to unite.
U.NI.FI.CÁ.VEL, adj., unifiable.
U.NI.FOR.MAR, v., the same that uniformizar.
U.NI.FOR.ME, s.m., uniform; adj., uniform, identic, same, regular.
U.NI.FOR.ME.MEN.TE, adv., uniformly.
U.NI.FOR.MI.DA.DE, s.f., uniformity.
U.NI.FOR.MI.ZA.ÇÃO, s.f., uniformization.
U.NI.FOR.MI.ZA.DO, adj., uniformed, uniform.
U.NI.FOR.MI.ZA.DOR, s.m., person who uniformizes; adj., that uniformizes.
U.NI.FOR.MI.ZAR, v., to uniformize, to make uniform, to unify.
U.NI.LA.TE.RAL, adj., unilateral.
U.NI.LA.TE.RA.LI.DA.DE, s.f., unilaterality.
U.NI.LA.TE.RA.LIS.MO, s.m., unilateralism.
U.NI.LA.TE.RA.LIS.TA, s. 2 gen., unilateralist.
U.NI.LA.TE.RAL.MEN.TE, adv., unilaterally.
U.NIR, v., to unite, to join, to connect, to adjoin, to unify, to fasten, to attach.
U.NIS.SEX, adj., unisex.
U.NÍS.SO.NO, s.m., unison; adj., unisonant, unisonous.
U.NI.TÁ.RI.O, s.m., Rel., Unitarian; unitarist; adj., unitarian.
U.NI.VA.LÊN.CI.A, s.f., univalence.
U.NI.VA.LEN.TE, adj., s.2 gen., univalent, monovalent.
U.NI.VAL.VE, adj., Bot., Zool., univalve.

U.NI.VER.SAL, adj., universal.
U.NI.VER.SA.LI.DA.DE, s.f., universality, totality.
U.NI.VER.SA.LIS.MO, s.m., universalism.
U.NI.VER.SA.LI.ZA.ÇÃO, s.f., universalization.
U.NI.VER.SA.LI.ZAR, v., to universalize.
U.NI.VER.SAL.MEN.TE, adv., universally.
U.NI.VER.SI.DA.DE, s.f., university.
U.NI.VER.SI.TÁ.RIO, adj., universitarian, academic.
U.NI.VER.SO, s.m., universe, the solar system, a whole; adj., universal.
U.NO, adj., one, sole, only one, single.
U.NÓ.CU.LO, s.m., one-eyed person; adj., having only one eye.
UN.TAR, v., to anoint, to daub, to grease.
UN.TU.O.SI.DA.DE, s.f., unctuosity, greasiness.
UN.TU.O.SO, adj., unctuous, greasy; lubricated, slippery.
U.PA, interj., jump!, hop!, quick!, go!, oops!, gee up! (horse).
U.RÂ.NI.A, s.f., Mit., Urania (the Muse of astronomy).
U.RÂ.NI.CO, adj., uranic.
U.RÂ.NIO, s.m., Quím., uranium (atomic number: 92, symbol: U).
U.RA.NO, s.m., Mit., Uranus (father of the Titans); Astron., Uranus (seventh planet).
U.RA.NO.GRA.FI.A, s.f., uranography.
U.RA.NO.LO.GI.A, s.f., uranology, astronomy.
UR.BA.NI.DA.DE, s.f., urbanity, urbaneness, politeness.
UR.BA.NIS.MO, s.m., city planning.
UR.BA.NIS.TA, s.2 gen., urbanist.
UR.BA.NÍS.TI.CO, adj., urbanistic.
UR.BA.NI.ZA.ÇÃO, s.f., urbanization.
UR.BA.NI.ZA.DO, adj., built up, urbanized.
UR.BA.NI.ZAR, v., to urbanize, to civilize.
UR.BA.NO, adj., urban, civic, townish.
UR.DI.DOR, s.m., warper, weaver.
UR.DI.DU.RA, s.f., warping; fig., intrigue, plot.
UR.DIR, v., to warp, to weave, to plot, to intrigue.
UR.DU, s.m., Urdu (language spoken in Pakistan).
U.REI.A, s.f., urea.
U.REI.CO, adj., ureal.
U.RE.TER, s.m., ureter.
U.RE.TÉ.RI.CO, adj., ureteric, ureteral.
U.RE.TRA, s.f., Anat., urethra.
U.RE.TRAL, adj., urethral.
UR.GÊN.CIA, s.f., urgency, haste, need, exigence.
UR.GEN.TE, adj., urgent, urging, pressing.
UR.GEN.TE.MEN.TE, adv., urgently.
UR.GEN.TÍS.SI.MO, adj., sup abs sint de urgente: with dispatch.
UR.GIR, v., to urge, to instigate; to demand, to claim.
Ú.RI.CO, adj., Quím., uric; ÁCIDO ~: uric acid.
U.RI.NA, s.f., urine.
U.RI.NA.ÇÃO, s.f., urination.
U.RI.NAR, v., to urinate, to piss.
U.RI.NÁ.RI.O, adj., urinary.
U.RI.NOL, s.m., urinal, chamber pot.
UR.NA, s.f., urn, coffin.
U.RÓ.LI.TO, s.m., Med., urolith.
U.RO.LO.GI.A, s.f., urology.
U.RO.LO.GIS.TA, s. 2 gen., Med., urologist.
UR.RAR, v., to roar, to howl, to bawl.
UR.RO, s.m., roar, howl, bawl.
UR.SA, s.f., Zool., she-bear; Astron., Ursa Maior: Great Bear;

URSINHO ··344·· UVULITE

Astron., Ursa Menor: Little Bear.

UR.SI.NHO, *s.m.,* small bear; cub; teddy-bear (kid's toy).

UR.SO, *s.m., Zool.,* bear.

UR.TI.CAN.TE, *adj.,* urticant, stinging.

UR.TI.CÁ.RI.A, *s.f., Med.,* urticaria, nettle-rash.

UR.TI.GA, *s.f., Bot.,* nettle, Urtica.

U.RU, *s.m., Zool.,* capueira partridge (bird).

U.RU.BU, *s.m., Zool.,* vulture.

U.RU.BU.ZAR, *v.,* to watch like a hawk.

U.RU.CU.BA.CA, *s.f., Bras.,* bad luck, unlucky.

U.RU.GUAI, *s.,* Uruguay.

U.RU.GUAI.O, *adj., s.m.,* Uruguayan.

U.RU.TU, *s.f., Zool.,* urutu (Brazilian venomous viper).

U.SA.DO, *adj.,* usual, used, spent, old.

U.SAN.ÇA, *s.f.,* usance, use, employment.

U.SAR, *v.,* to use, to employ, to accustom, to habituate, to utilize, to spend.

U.SÁ.VEL, *adj.,* usable, wearable.

U.SEI.RO, *adj.,* usual, used, customary, wonted.

US.ER.NAME, *s.m., Comp.,* username.

U.SI.NA, *s.f.,* work, workshop, works, mill, plant, factory.

U.SI.NEI.RO, *s.m., Bras.,* sugar mill owner.

U.SO, *s.m.,* use, employ, utilization.

U.SU.AL, *adj.,* usual, normal, habitual, customary, commonplace.

U.SU.AL.MEN.TE, *adv.,* usually.

U.SU.Á.RIO, *s.m.,* user, usuary.

U.SU.CA.PI.ÃO, *s.m.,* usucapion, udal.

U.SU.FRU.IR, *v.,* to usufruct.

U.SU.FRU.TAR, *v.,* the same that *usufruir.*

U.SU.FRU.TO, *s.m.,* usufruct, fruition, enjoyment.

U.SU.FRU.TU.Á.RI.O, *s.m., Jur.,* usufructuary; *adj.,* usufructuary.

U.SU.RA, *s.f.,* usury, interest, avarice, shabbiness.

U.SU.RÁ.RIO, *s.m.,* usurer.

U.SUR.PA.ÇÃO, *s.f.,* usurpation, encroachment, arrogation.

U.SUR.PA.DOR, *s.m.,* usurper, encroacher; *adj.,* usurping.

U.SUR.PAR, *v.,* to usurp, encroach, assume, to arrogate.

U.TEN.SÍ.LIO, *s.m.,* utensil, tool, implement, ware.

U.TE.RI.NO, *adj.,* uterine.

U.TE.RI.TE, *s.f., Med.,* uteritis.

Ú.TE.RO, *s.m., Anat.,* uterus, womb.

Ú.TIL, *adj.,* useful, practical, handy, helpful.

U.TI.LI.DA.DE, *s.f.,* utility, use, convenience.

U.TI.LI.TÁ.RIO, *s.m.,* jeep, station wagon.

U.TI.LI.TA.RIS.MO, *s.m.,* utilitarism.

U.TI.LI.TA.RIS.TA, *s. 2 gen.,* utilitarian; *adj.,* utilitarian.

U.TI.LI.ZA.ÇÃO, *s.f.,* utilization.

U.TI.LI.ZAR, *v.,* to utilize, to make useful, to profit, to apply.

U.TI.LI.ZÁ.VEL, *adj.,* utilizable, applicable.

U.TO.PI.A, *s.f.,* Utopia, dream, chimera, fancy.

U.TÓ.PI.CO, *adj.,* Utopian, fanciful, visionary, fantastic.

U.TO.PIS.MO, *s.m.,* utopianism.

U.TO.PIS.TA, *s. 2 gen.,* utopist, visionary.

U.VA, *s.f., Bot.,* grape.

Ú.VU.LA, *s.f., Anat.,* uvula.

U.VU.LAR, *adj., Anat.,* uvular: of or pertaining to the uvula.

U.VU.LI.TE, *s.f., Med.,* uvulitis.

V

V, *s.m.*, the twenty-first letter of the Portuguese alphabet.

VA.CA, *s.f.*, cow, beef.

VA.CÂN.CI.A, *s.f.*, vacancy.

VA.CAN.TE, *adj.*, vacant, free, empty.

VA.CA-PRE.TA, *s.f.*, *Bras.*, a mixture of soft drink and ice-cream.

VA.CI.LA.ÇÃO, *s.f.*, vacillation, hesitation, oscillation.

VA.CI.LAN.TE, *adj.*, vacillating, hesitating, oscillating.

VA.CI.LAN.TE.MEN.TE, *adv.*, vacillatingly.

VA.CI.LAR, *v.*, to vacillate, to hesitate, to waver, to falter.

VA.CI.NA, *s.f.*, vaccine.

VA.CI.NA.ÇÃO, *s.f.*, vaccination, inoculation.

VA.CI.NAR, *v.*, to vaccinate.

VA.CU.I.DA.DE, *s.f.*, vacuity, vacuousness, emptiness.

VA.CUM, *s.m.*, cattle, oxen; *adj.*, bovine.

VÁ.CUO, *s.m.*, vacuum, hollow, gap, void, vacuity.

VA.CÚ.O.LO, *s.m.*, *Biol.*, vacuole.

VA.DE.A.ÇÃO, *s.f.*, wading, fording.

VA.DE.AR, *v.*, to ford, to wade through.

VA.DI.A.ÇÃO, *s.f.*, vagrancy, idleness, vagabondage.

VA.DI.A.GEM, *s.f.*, idleness, indolence.

VA.DI.AR, *v.*, to idle, to laze, to loaf, to lounge.

VA.DI.O, *s.m.*, idler, lounger, loafer; *adj.*, vagrant, idle, vagabond.

VA.GA, *s.f.*, vacancy, leisure, wave, billow.

VA.GA.BUN.DA.GEM, *s.f.*, vagabondage, vagrancy.

VA.GA.BUN.DE.AR, *v.*, to vagabond; to laze, to idle.

VA.GA.BUN.DO, *s.m.*, vagabond, vagrant, idler, tramp, bum; *adj.*, idle, lazy, vagrant, roving.

VA.GA.ÇÃO, *s.f.*, the same that *vacância*.

VA.GA.LHÃO, *s.m.*, billow.

VA.GA-LU.ME, *s.m.*, firefly, glowworm.

VA.GA.MEN.TE, *adv.*, vaguely, blankly.

VA.GA.MUN.DO, *s.m.*, vagabond, tramp.

VA.GÃO, *s.m.*, railway car, waggon.

VA.GÃO-RES.TAU.RAN.TE, *s.m.*, dining car (train).

VA.GAR, *v.*, to vacate, to become vacant, to rove, to run, to ramble.

VA.GA.REN.TO, *adj.*, the same that *vagaroso*.

VA.GA.RE.ZA, *s.f.*, slowness, sluggishness, tardiness.

VA.GA.RO.SA.MEN.TE, *adv.*, slowly.

VA.GA.RO.SO, *adj.*, slow, sluggish, dull, languid.

VA.GEM, *s.f.*, kidney beams, French beams.

VA.GI.DO, *s.m.*, crying (a newborn child's); wailing, moan.

VA.GI.NA, *s.f.*, *Anat.*, vagina.

VA.GI.NAL, *adj.*, *Anat.*, vaginal.

VA.GIR, *s.m.*, *v.*, to cry (babies); to groan, to lament.

VA.GO, *adj.*, vacant, vacuous, vague, empty, indistinct.

VA.GO.NE.TE, *s.m.*, wagonette, tilting cart, trolley.

VA.GUE.A.ÇÃO, *s.f.*, wandering, roving, rambling; vagabondage.

VA.GUE.AR, *v.*, to wander about; to rove, to ramble, to drift.

VA.GUE.JAR, *s.m.*, *v.*, the same that *vaguear*.

VAI.A, *s.f.*, hiss, catcall, hoot, mockery.

VAI.A.DOR, *s.m.*, hooter, hisser.

VAI.AR, *v.*, to hoot, to hiss at, to boo.

VAI.DA.DE, *s.f.*, vanity, vainness, pride.

VAI.I.DO.SA.MEN.TE, *adv.*, vainly, presumptuously.

VAI.DO.SO, *adj.*, vain, proud, flatulent, conceited.

VAI.VÉM, *s.m.*, teeter, seasaw, ups and downs, rocking motion.

VA.LA, *s.f.*, trench, ditch.

VA.LA.DI.O, *adj.*, said of a roof with loose tiles; said of a piece of land cut by trenches.

VA.LA.DO, *s.m.*, ditch-and-hedge surrounding a rural property.

VA.LAR, *v.*, to surround with ditches; to open gutters or drains.

VA.LE, *s.m.*, valley, dale, plain; credit note, bill.

VA.LE.DI.O, *adj.*, valid.

VA.LÊN.CI.A, *s.f.*, *Quím.*, valence, valency.

VA.LEN.TÃO, *s.m.*, bully, rowdy, braggart, burly. *adj.*, burly.

VA.LEN.TE, *adj.*, valiant, intrepid, brave, bold.

VA.LEN.TI.A, *s.f.*, valiantness, bravery, valour.

VA.LER, *v.*, to value, to be worth, to be valuable, to cost, to protect, to help.

VA.LE-RE.FEI.ÇÃO, *s.m.*, meal ticket.

VA.LE.TA, *s.f.*, ditch, channel, drain.

VA.LE.TE, *s.m.*, knave, jack (card); valet.

VA.LE-TRANS.POR.TE, *s.m.*, travel voucher.

VA.LE-TU.DO, *s. 2 gen.*, *Bras.*, free-for-all.

VA.LI.A, *s.f.*, worth, value, price, merit, favour.

VA.LI.DA.ÇÃO, *s.f.*, validation.

VA.LI.DA.DE, *s.f.*, validity, legality, force.

VA.LI.DA.MEN.TE, *adv.*, validly.

VA.LI.DAR, *v.*, to validate, to legalize, to authenticate, to acknowledge.

VA.LI.DEZ, *s.f.*, the same that *validade*.

VÁ.LI.DO, *adj.*, valid, sound, legal, binding.

VA.LI.O.SO, *adj.*, valuable, worthy, precious, rich.

VA.LI.SA, *s.f.*, the same that *valise*.

VA.LI.SE, *s.f.*, valise, gripsack, small suitcase.

VA.LOR, *s.m.*, value, worth, courage, effort, merit, price, force, feck.

VA.LO.RI.ZA.ÇÃO, *s.f.*, valorization.

VA.LO.RI.ZA.DOR, *s.m.*, estimator; *adj.*, valorizing.

VA.LO.RI.ZAR, *v.*, to valorize, to value, to prize, to appraise.

VA.LO.RO.SI.DA.DE, *s.f.*, valorousness.

VA.LO.RO.SO, *adj.*, valorous, worthy, valiant, manly.

VAL.QUÍ.RI.A, *s.f.*, *Mit.*, Valkyrie (goddesses who conducts the slain from the battlefield to Valhalla).

VAL.SA, *s.f.*, waltz.

VAL.SAR, *v.*, to waltz (dance the waltz).

VAL.VA, *s.f.*, *Bot.*, *Zool.*, valve.

VAL.VAR, *adj.*, valvelike, valvar.

VÁL.VU.LA, *s.f.*, valve.

VAL.VU.LAR, *adj.*, valvular, valval.

VAMPÍRICO   •• 346 ••   VEADO

VAM.PÍ.RI.CO, *adj.*, vampiric.
VAM.PI.RIS.MO, *s.m.*, vampirism.
VAM.PI.RO, *s.m.*, vampire.
VA.NÁ.DI.O, *s.m.*, *Quím.*, vanadium (atomic number: 23, symbol: V).
VAN.DA.LIS.MO, *s.m.*, vandalism.
VÂN.DA.LO, *s.m.*, Vandal; *adj.*, vandalic.
VAN.GLÓ.RI.A, *s.f.*, vainglory, boasting, vaunting.
VAN.GLO.RI.AR, *v.*, to puff up, to praise, to flatter.
VAN.GLO.RI.O.SO, *adj.*, vainglorious, boastful.
VAN.GUAR.DA, *s.f.*, vanguard, advance guard, van.
VAN.TA.GEM, *s.f.*, advantage, benefit, profit, boot.
VAN.TA.JO.SA.MEN.TE, *adv.*, advantageously.
VAN.TA.JO.SO, *adv.*, profitable, advantageous, favourable.
VÃO, *s.m.*, void, vacuum, interspace; *adj.*, vain, void, futile, empty, useless.
VA.POR, *s.m.*, vapour, steam, fume, steamship, ship.
VA.PO.RA.ÇÃO, *s.f.*, evaporation.
VA.PO.RAR, *v.*, to evaporate, to turn into vapor, to steam.
VA.PO.RÁ.VEL, *adj.*, evaporable, vaporable.
VA.PO.RÍ.FE.RO, *adj.*, vaporiferous, vaporific.
VA.PO.RI.ZA.ÇÃO, *s.f.*, vaporization.
VA.PO.RI.ZA.DOR, *s.m.*, *Med.*, vaporizer; pulverizer, spray; *adj.*, vaporizing.
VA.PO.RI.ZAR, *v.*, to vaporize, to evaporate.
VA.PO.RO.SI.DA.DE, *s.f.*, vaporousness.
VA.PO.RO.SO, *adj.*, vaporous, vapourish, steamy; see-through (cloth), diapnanous.
VA.QUEI.RAR, *v.*, to work as a cowboy.
VA.QUEI.RO, *s.m.*, cowboy, herdsman.
VA.QUE.JA.DA, *s.f.*, rodeo (roundup of cattle).
VA.QUI.NHA, *s.f.*, young cow, heifer; pool of money.
VA.RA, *s.f.*, stick, rod, cane, switch, staff.
VA.RA.ÇÃO, *s.f.*, *Náut.*, beaching; *Bras.*, land transport of watercraft to avoid waterfalls.
VA.RA.DA, *s.f.*, blow with a whip.
VA.RAL, *s.m.*, clothes-line.
VA.RAN.DA, *s.f.*, veranda, balcony, terrace.
VA.RAN.DA.DO, *s.m.*, *Bras.*, a sort of building with a veranda.
VA.RÃO, *s.m.*, man, male; *adj.*, male.
VA.RA.PAU, *s. 2 gen.*, beanpole.
VARAR, *v.*, to pierce, to stick; to go beyond, to cross; to go through.
VA.RE.AR, *v.*, to measure by varas; to punt (boat).
VA.REI.O, *s.m.*, *Bras.*, *col.*, restlessness that leads the individual to make foolishness; shock, fright.
VA.RE.JÃO, *s.m.*, large staff, pole or rod; barge-pole.
VA.RE.JEI.RA, *s.f.*, *Zool.*, blowfly.
VA.RE.JIS.TA, *s. 2 gen.*, retail dealer, retailer.
VA.RE.JO, *s.m.*, retail.
VA.RI.A.BI.LI.DA.DE, *s.f.*, variability, alterability.
VA.RI.A.ÇÃO, *s.f.*, change, modification, diversification.
VA.RI.A.DO, *adj.*, varied, diverse, assorted, inconstant.
VA.RI.AN.TE, *s.f.*, variant, deviation; *adj.*, variant.
VA.RI.AR, *v.*, to vary, to change, to alter, to diversify, to alternate, to shade.
VA.RI.Á.VEL, *adj.*, variable, changeable, inconstant.
VA.RI.CE.LA, *s.f.*, chickenpox, varicella.
VA.RI.E.DA.DE, *s.f.*, variety, diversity, variousness, inconstancy.
VA.RI.E.GA.DO, *adj.*, variegated, varying.

VA.RI.E.GAR, *v.*, to variegate.
VA.RI.NHA, *s.f.*, a little stick or rod, wand; switch; ~ *de condão*: magic wand.
VÁ.RIO, *adj.*, different, various, variegated.
VA.RÍ.O.LA, *s.f.*, *Med.*, variola, smallpox.
VA.RIZ, *s.f.*, *Med.*, varix; *varizes* (*pl.*): varicose veins.
VA.RO.NIL, *adj.*, manly, manlike, manful.
VAR.RE.DOR, *s.m.*, sweeper; *adj.*, sweeping.
VAR.RE.DU.RA, *s.f.*, sweep, sweeping; *Comp.*, scan.
VAR.RER, *v.*, to sweep, to broom, to clean, to clear up.
VAR.RI.ÇÃO, *s.f.*, sweep, sweeping.
VAR.RI.DO, *s.m.*, sweep, sweeping; *adj.*, swept, cleaned; *doido* ~: raving lunatic.
VÁR.ZEA, *s.f.*, lea, plain.
VAS.CA, *s.f.*, convulsion; nausea; pangs of death.
VAS.CO.SO, *adj.*, convulsive (having nausea).
VAS.CU.LAR, *adj.*, vascular.
VAS.CU.LA.RI.DA.DE, *s.f.*, vascularity.
VAS.CU.LHAR, *v.*, to sweep, to clean; to research, ferret, to rummage through.
VA.SEC.TO.MI.A, *s.f.*, *Med.*, vasectomy.
VA.SEC.TO.MI.ZAR, *v.*, *Med.*, to vasectomize.
VA.SE.LI.NA, *s.f.*, vaseline.
VA.SEC.TO.MI.A, *s.f.*, vasectomy.
VA.SI.LHA, *s.f.*, vessel, pail, basin.
VA.SI.LHA.ME, *s.m.*, vessels, casks, bottles.
VA.SO, *s.m.*, vase, flowerpot.
VAS.SA.LA.GEM, *s.f.*, vassalage.
VAS.SA.LAR, *v.*, to render tribute as a vassal.
VAS.SA.LO, *s.m.*, vassal, liege; *adj.*, of or like a vassal subservient.
VAS.SOI.RA, *s.f.*, the same that *vassoura*.
VAS.SOU.RA, *s.f.*, broom, besom.
VAS.SOU.RA.DA, *s.f.*, blow with a broom; sweeping.
VAS.SOU.REI.RO, *s.m.*, broommaker, broom seller.
VAS.TI.DÃO, *s.f.*, vastness, wideness, ampleness, amplitude.
VAS.TO, *adj.*, vast, great, colossal, huge, ample.
VA.TA.PÁ, *s.m.*, *Cul.*, Brazilian dish made of manioc flour, oil, pepper, fish and shrimp.
VA.TI.CA.NO, *s.m.*, Vatican.
VA.TI.CI.NA.ÇÃO, *s.f.*, the same that *vaticínio*.
VA.TI.CI.NA.DOR, *s.m.*, diviner, vaticinator; *adj.*, vaticinal.
VA.TI.CI.NAN.TE, *adj.*, vaticinal.
VA.TI.CI.NAR, *v.*, to vaticinate, predict.
VA.TI.CÍ.NIO, *s.m.*, vaticination, foretelling, prediction.
VAU, *s.m.*, ford (river), crossing, passage; *Náut.*, beam.
VAU.DE.VIL.LE, *s.m.*, *Fr.*, vaudeville, variety show.
VA.ZA, *s.f.*, cards played in one round; ebb.
VA.ZA-BAR.RIS, *s.m.*, *2 num.*, reefy coast causing many ship-wrecks; *fig.*, place of hidden treasures; *col.*, ruin.
VA.ZA.DO, *adj.*, empty, hollow.
VA.ZA.DOR, *s.m.*, goldsmith; boring tool, melter, founder. *adj.*, boring, melting.
VA.ZA.MEN.TO, *s.m.*, leak, leakage, leakiness, seepage.
VA.ZAN.TE, *s.f.*, ebb tide, low water.
VA.ZÃO, *s.f.*, flowing out, outflow, emptying.
VA.ZAR, *v.*, to empty, to pour out, to drain, to discharge, to spill.
VA.ZI.O, *s.m.*, emptiness, vaccuum, vacuity; *adj.*, empty, vacant, vold, vain.
VE.A.DO, *s.m.*, *Zool.*, deer, hart, stag; *Bras.*, *vulg.*, queer, a

VEDAÇÃO ·· 347 ·· VERBALIZAÇÃO

male homosexual.

VE.DA.ÇÃO, *s.f.*, prohibition, impediment, hindrance, stoppage, closing, barrier, blocking, enclosure.

VE.DA.DO, *adj.*, forbidden, prohibited.

VE.DAR, *v.*, to hinder, to prohibit, to forbid, to interdict, to stop, to bar.

VE.DÁ.VEL, *adj.*, that can be impeded, prohibited.

VE.DE.TE, *s.f.*, star.

VE.E.MÊN.CIA, *s.f.*, vehemence, vehemency, passion.

VE.E.MEN.TE, *adj.*, vehement, impetuous, enthusiastic, violent.

VE.GE.TA.BI.LI.DA.DE, *s.f.*, vegetability.

VE.GE.TA.ÇÃO, *s.f.*, vegetation.

VE.GE.TAL, *adj.*, vegetable.

VE.GE.TAN.TE, *adj.*, vegetating.

VE.GE.TAR, *v.*, to vegetate.

VE.GE.TA.RI.A.NIS.MO, *s.m.*, vegetarianism.

VE.GE.TA.RI.A.NO, *adj.*, *s.m.*, vegetarian.

VE.GE.TA.TI.VO, *adj.*, vegetative.

VEI.A, *s.f.*, vein, tendency, vocation.

VEI.CU.LA.DOR, *s.m.*, propagator; *adj.*, propagating; transmitting.

VEI.CU.LAR, *adj.*, vehicular; *v.*, to transport in a vehicle, to transmit, to propagate.

VE.Í.CU.LO, *s.m.*, vehicle.

VEI.O, *s.m.*, *Geol.*, vein, lode, thread, streak; *Mec.*, shaft, spindle, axle; *fig.*, main point.

VE.LA, *s.f.*, sail, canvas, sheet; candle.

VE.LA.DO, *adj.*, veiled, hidden, covered, concealed.

VE.LA.ME, *s.m.*, *Náut.*, sails.

VE.LAR, *v.*, to veil, to hide, to keep secret; to wake, to watch, to guard; *s.f.*, *Gram.*, velar sound; *adj.*, velar.

VE.LEI.DA.DE, *s.f.*, velleity, whim inclination.

VE.LEI.RO, *s.m.*, sailing ship, sailing boat; candlemaker; *adj.*, fast-sailing.

VE.LE.JAR, *v.*, to sail.

VE.LHA, *s.f.*, old woman, crone.

VE.LHA.CA.RI.A, *s.f.*, knavery, roguery, deceit, roguish trick.

VE.LHA.CO, *s.m.*, knave, rogue, villain; *adj.*, knavish, roguish, crafty, foxlike.

VE.LHI.CE, *s.f.*, old age, oldness.

VE.LHO, *s.m.*, old man; *adj.*, old, aged, ancient, obsolete, archaic, worn out, shabby.

VE.LHO.TE, *s.m.*, elderly man, old man; *adj.*, old.

VE.LO.CI.DA.DE, *s.f.*, velocity, speed, fastness, swiftness.

VE.LO.CÍ.ME.TRO, *s.m.*, speedometer.

VE.LO.CI.NO, *s.m.*, sheepskin, fell; *Mit.*, o ~ de ouro: the Golden Fleece.

VE.LO.CÍ.PE.DE, *s.m.*, velocipede, bicycle.

VE.LO.CI.PE.DIS.TA, *s. 2 gen.*, cyclist.

VE.LO.CÍS.SI.MO, *adj.*, (superlative) very swift.

VE.LO.CIS.TA, *s. 2 gen.*, sprinter.

VE.LÓ.DRO.MO, *s.m.*, velodrome.

VE.LÓ.RIO, *s.m.*, deathwatch.

VE.LOZ, *adj.*, swift, quick, speedy, fast.

VE.LOZ.MEN.TE, *adv.*, quickly, fast.

VE.LU.DO, *s.m.*, velvet, velveting, velure.

VE.LU.DO.SO, *adj.*, velvetlike, soft like velvet.

VE.NAL, *adj.*, venal; *adj.*, veined.

VEN.CE.DOR, *s.m.*, winner, victor; *adj.*, winning.

VEN.CER, *v.*, to win, to succeed, to triumph, to vanquish, to overcome, to get, to surpass.

VEN.CI.BI.LI.DA.DE, *s.f.*, vincibility.

VEN.CI.DO, *adj.*, vanquished, overcome, conquered.

VEN.CI.MEN.TO, *s.m.*, overcoming, deadline, expiring date, expiration, salary.

VEN.DA, *s.f.*, sale, selling, bandage, blindfold.

VEN.DA.DO, *adj.*, veiled, blindfold.

VEN.DA.GEM, *s.f.*, sales commission. blindfolding.

VEN.DAR, *v.*, to blindfold, hood, veil.

VEN.DA.VAL, *s.m.*, windstorm, whirlwind.

VEN.DÁ.VEL, *adj.*, saleable, negotiable, vendible.

VEN.DE.DOR, *s.m.*, salesman, seller, vendor, agent.

VEN.DEI.RO, *s.m.*, innkeeper, grocer.

VEN.DER, *v.*, to sell, to vend, to make sales, to deal in.

VEN.DE.TA, *s.f.*, vendetta.

VE.NE.NO, *s.m.*, poison, venom, toxine.

VE.NE.NO.SO, *adj.*, poisonous, venomous.

VE.NE.RA.BI.LI.DA.DE, *s.f.*, venerability.

VE.NE.RA.ÇÃO, *s.f.*, veneration, worship.

VE.NE.RA.DO, *adj.*, venerated, worshipped, adored.

VE.NE.RA.DOR, *s.m.*, adorer, worshipper, venerator; *adj.*, worshipful.

VE.NE.RAN.DO, *adj.*, the same that *venerável*.

VE.NE.RAR, *v.*, to venerate, to adore, to worship.

VE.NE.RÁ.VEL, *adj.*, venerable, worshipful, worthy of veneration, reverend, revered.

VE.NÉ.REO, *adj.*, venereal.

VE.NE.ZU.E.LA, *s.*, Venezuela.

VE.NE.ZU.E.LA.NO, *adj.*, *s.m.*, Venezuelan.

VÊ.NIA, *s.f.*, leave, permission, bow.

VE.NI.AL, *adj.*, venial, pardonable, forgiveable.

VEN.TA, *s.f.*, nostril;

VEN.TAS, *s.m.*, *pl.*, nose; *fig.*, face.

VEN.TA.NE.JAR, *v.*, to blow, to wind.

VEN.TA.NI.A, *s.f.*, windstorm, blow.

VEN.TAR, *v.*, to wind, to blow.

VEN.TA.RO.LA, *s.f.*, a little fan.

VEN.TI.LA.ÇÃO, *s.f.*, ventilation, airing.

VEN.TI.LA.DOR, *s.m.*, ventilator, aerator, fan.

VEN.TO, *s.m.*, wind, air, drift.

VEN.TO.I.NHA, *s.f.*, weathercock, vane; blower, fan.

VEN.TO.SA, *s.f.*, *Med.*, cupping glass, cup.

VEN.TO.SI.DA.DE, *s.f.*, windiness, flatulence.

VEN.TO.SO, *adj.*, windy, blowy, airy.

VEN.TRE, *s.m.*, womb, belly, abdomen.

VEN.TU.RO.SO, *adj.*, lucky, fortunate, happy, felicitous.

VÊ.NUS, *s.f.*, Venus (the Roman goddess of love and beauty); *Astron.*, Venus (planetof the solar system).

VER, *v.*, to see, to behold, to look, to watch at, to observe.

VE.RA.CI.DA.DE, *s.f.*, veracity, truthfulness.

VE.RA.NE.AR, *v.*, to summer, to spend the summer.

VE.RA.NEI.O, *s.m.*, summer resort.

VE.RA.NI.CO, *s.m.*, Indian summer, St.Martin's summer.

VE.RA.NIS.TA, *s. 2 gen.*, *US* summer vacationer; *UK* summer holydaymaker.

VE.RÃO, *s.m.*, summer.

VE.RAZ, *adj.*, veracious, truthful.

VER.BA, *s.f.*, available sum or amount, budget, clause.

VER.BAL, *adj.*, verbal, oral.

VER.BA.LIS.MO, *s.m.*, verbalism.

VER.BA.LI.ZA.ÇÃO, *s.f.*, verbalization.

VERBALIZAR · 348 · VESTUÁRIO

VER.BA.LI.ZAR, *v.*, to verbalize.
VER.BAL.MEN.TE, *adv.*, verbally.
VER.BE.RA.ÇÃO, *s.f.*, verberation; lashing, whipping, censure, reproof.
VER.BE.RAR, *v.*, to verberate; to beat, to punish, to censure.
VER.BE.TE, *s.m.*, note, a brief message; entry of a dictionary.
VER.BO, *s.m.*, verb, word, expression.
VER.BOR.RA.GI.A, *s.f.*, verbiage, verbosity.
VER.BOR.RÁ.GI.CO, *adj.*, verbose, wordy, prolix.
VER.BOR.REI.A, *s.f.*, verbiage, verbosity.
VER.BOR.REI.CO, *adj.*, verbose, wordy, prolix.
VER.BO.SI.DA.DE, *s.f.*, verbosity, verbiage, loquaciousness.
VER.DA.DE, *s.f.*, truth, reality, fact, true.
VER.DA.DEI.RA.MEN.TE, *adv.*, trully.
VER.DA.DEI.RO, *adj.*, true, veracious, real, actual, exact, certain.
VER.DE, *s.m.*, green colour; *adj.*, green.
VER.DE-A.BA.CA.TE, *s.m.*, avocado-green colour; *adj.*, avocado-green.
VER.DE-A.MA.RE.LO, *s.m.*, yellowish-green colour; *adj.*, yellowish-green.
VER.DE.AR, *v.*, *Bras.*, to green (especially of pastures).
VER.DE-CLA.RO, *s.m.*, color light green; *adj.*, light green.
VER.DE-ES.CU.RO, *s.m.*, a color dark green; *adj.*, dark green.
VER.DE.JAR, *v.*, to green.
VER.DE-O.LI.VA, *s.m.*, olive green colour; *adj.*, olive green.
VER.DOR, *s.m.*, verdure, viridity, verdancy.
VER.DU.GO, *s.m.*, hangman, executioner.
VER.DU.RA, *s.f.*, greens, vegetable.
VER.DU.REI.RO, *s.m.*, greengrocer.
VE.RE.A.ÇÃO, *s.f.*, office or dignity of a member of a town council; period of such an office.
VE.RE.A.DOR, *s.m.*, town councillor.
VE.RE.AN.ÇA, *s.f.*, city council, councilorship.
VE.RE.AR, *v.*, to act as an alderman.
VE.RE.DA, *s.f.*, path.
VE.RE.DIC.TO, *s.m.*, the same that *veredicto*.
VE.RE.DI.TO, *s.m.*, verdict, judgement, opinion.
VER.GA, *s.f.*, stick, switch; metal rod or bar.
VER.GA.LHÃO, *s.m.*, square iron bar.
VER.GÃO, *s.m.*, weal, welt.
VER.GAR, *v.*, to bend, to curve, to sag; to submit.
VER.GAS.TA, *s.f.*, switch, twig, rod.
VER.GAS.TAR, *v.*, to whip, to flog.
VER.GO.NHA, *s.f.*, shame, ashamedness, bashfulness.
VER.GO.NHO.SO, *adj.*, shameful, disreputable.
VE.RÍ.DI.CO, *adj.*, veracious, veridical, true.
VE.RI.FI.CA.ÇÃO, *s.f.*, verification, checking.
VE.RI.FI.CA.DOR, *s.m.*, verifier, controller; *adj.*, controlling, checking.
VE.RI.FI.CAR, *v.*, to verify, to examine, to check, to control, to find out, to test.
VE.RI.FI.CÁ.VEL, *adj.*, verifiable, checkable.
VER.ME, *s.m.*, worm.
VER.ME.LHI.DÃO, *s.f.*, redness, reddishness.
VER.ME.LHO, *adj.*, red, scarlet.
VER.MI.CI.DA, *s.m.*, vermicide, vermifuge.
VER.MI.CU.LAR, *adj.*, vermicular, wormlike.
VER.MÍ.FU.GO, *s.m.*, vermicide.
VER.MU.TE, *s.m.*, vermouth.
VER.NA.CU.LIS.TA, *s. 2 gen.*, vernacularist.

VER.NÁ.CU.LO, *s.m.*, vernacular, mother tongue; *adj.*, vernacular, native.
VER.NAL, *adj.*, vernal.
VER.NIS.SA.GE, *s.m.*, *Fr.*, opening.
VER.NIZ, *s.m.*, varnish, shellac, lake.
VE.ROS.SÍ.MIL, *adj.*, probable, likely.
VE.ROS.SI.MI.LHAN.ÇA, *s.f.*, verisimilitude.
VE.ROS.SI.MI.LI.TU.DE, *s.f.*, verisimilitude.
VER.RU.GA, *s.f.*, wart.
VER.SA.DO, *adj.*, versed, experienced, expert, skilled, well-informed.
VER.SAL, *s.m.*, capital letter; *adj.*, capital, initial letter.
VER.SA.LE.TE, *s.m.*, small capital.
VER.SÃO, *s.f.*, version, translation.
VER.SAR, *v.*, to versify.
VER.SÁ.TIL, *adj.*, versatile.
VER.SA.TI.LI.DA.DE, *s.f.*, versatility, versatiliness.
VER.SE.JA.DOR, *s.m.*, versifier, poetaster.
VER.SE.JAR, *v.*, to versify, verse.
VER.SÍ.CU.LO, *s.m.*, versicle.
VER.SI.FI.CA.ÇÃO, *s.f.*, versification, metrical version.
VER.SI.FI.CAR, *v.*, to versify, verse.
VER.SO, *s.m.*, verse, rime, rhyme, poetry; back, reverse.
VÉR.TE.BRA, *s.f.*, vertebra, spondyl.
VER.TE.BRA.DO, *adj.*, *s.m.*, vertebrate.
VER.TE.BRAL, *adj.*, vertebral.
VER.TE.DOU.RO, *s.m.*, *Náut.*, scoop; spillway.
VER.TEN.TE, *s.f.*, hillside, downhill; watershed; *Geol.*, hogback; *adj.*, overflowing.
VER.TER, *v.*, to flow, to gush, to pour, to spout, to spill, to shed, to translate, to overflow.
VER.TI.CAL, *adj.*, vertical, upright.
VER.TI.CA.LI.DA.DE, *s.f.*, verticality, verticalness.
VÉR.TI.CE, *s.m.*, vertex.
VER.TI.GEM, *s.f.*, vertigo, giddiness.
VER.TI.GI.NO.SI.DA.DE, *s.f.*, vertiginousness.
VER.TI.GI.NO.SO, *adj.*, vertiginous.
VER.VE, *s.f.*, verve, energy.
VES.GO, *s.m.*, squint-eyed person; *adj.*, cross-eyed, strabismal, squinting.
VE.SÍ.CU.LA, *s.f.*, *Anat.*, vesicle, bladder, blister.
VE.SI.CU.LAR, *adj.*, vesicular, bladdery.
VES.PA, *s.f.*, *Zool.*, wasp.
VES.PEI.RO, *s.m.*, wasps' nest, vespiary.
VÉS.PE.RA, *s.f.*, eve, evening, afternoon.
VES.PE.RAL, *s.m.*, *Rel.*, vesperal book (prayer book); *Bras.*, any afternoon entertainment; *adj.*, vesperal.
VES.PER.TI.NO, *adj.*, vesper, vespertine.
VES.TAL, *s.f.*, vestal (pure or virginal woman); *adj.*, vestal, virginal, pure.
VES.TE, *s.f.*, vest, vestment, clothes, garment, vesture.
VES.TI.Á.RI.O, *s.m.*, dressing-room, cloakroom, changing room.
VES.TI.BU.LAN.DO, *s.m.*, *Bras.*, university candidate.
VES.TI.BU.LAR, *s.m.*, vestibular (university entrance exam).
VES.TÍ.BU.LO, *s.m.*, hall, entrance hall, lobby; *Teat.*, foyer.
VES.TI.DO, *s.m.*, dress, garment.
VES.TÍ.GIO, *s.m.*, vestige, footprint, trail, clue, mark, trace.
VES.TI.MEN.TA, *s.f.*, garment; *Rel.*, vestment.
VES.TIR, *v.*, to dress, to wear, to clothe, to equip, to array.
VES.TU.Á.RIO, *s.m.*, clothes, clothing, garment.

VETAR   •• 349 •••   VINCULAR

VE.TAR, *v.*, to veto, to refuse, to interpose.

VE.TE.RA.NO, *s.m.*, veteran, vet; *adj.*, veteran, senior.

VE.TE.RI.NÁ.RI.A, *s.f.*, veterinary medicin.

VE.TE.RI.NÁ.RIO, *s.m.*, veterinarian, veterinary.

VE.TO, *s.m.*, veto, interdiction.

VÉU, *s.m.*, veil, veling, covering.

VE.XA.ÇÃO, *s.f.*, vexation, molestation.

VE.XA.DO, *adj.*, vexed, annoyed.

VE.XA.ME, *s.m.*, vexation, shame, blunder.

VE.XAR, *v.*, to vexate; to humiliate.

VE.XA.TÓ.RI.O, *adj.*, vexatious, vexatory.

VEZ, *s.f.*, time, turn, occasion, opportunity.

VI.A, *s.f.*, way, path, street, road, route, means, manner, direction, channel; *Via Láctea*: The Milky Way.

VI.A.BI.LI.DA.DE, *s.f.*, practicability.

VI.A.BI.LI.ZA.ÇÃO, *s.f.*, act of making practical or feasible.

VI.A.BI.LI.ZAR, *v.*, to make practical.

VI.A.ÇÃO, *s.f.*, traffic, highways, road system; bus company.

VI.A.DU.TO, *s.m.*, viaduct, overpass.

VI.A.GEM, *s.f.*, travel, voyage, journey, trip, tour, excursion.

VI.A.JA.DO, *adj.*, *UK* well-travelled, *US* well-traveled.

VI.A.JAN.TE, *s. 2 gen.*, *UK* traveller, *US*traveler, voyager; *adj.*, travelling, itinerant, wandering.

VI.A.JAR, *v.*, to travel, to journey, to tour, to voyage, to wander.

VI.Á.RI.O, *adj.*, relating to means and ways of transport.

VI.A.TU.RA, *s.f.*, vehicle.

VI.Á.VEL, *adj.*, practicable (way); feasible.

VÍ.BO.RA, *s.f.*, viper, adder.

VI.BRA.ÇÃO, *s.f.*, vibration, vibrancy, oscillation.

VI.BRA.DOR, *s.m.*, vibrator; *Eletr.*, trembler; *adj.*, vibrating.

VI.BRA.FO.NE, *s.m.*, vibraphone.

VI.BRAN.TE, *adj.*, vibrant.

VI.BRAR, *v.*, to vibrate, to oscillate, to pulse, to pulsate.

VI.BRÁ.TIL, *adj.*, vibratile, vibratory.

VI.BRA.TÓ.RI.O, *adj.*, vibratile, vibratory.

VI.BRI.ÃO, *s.m.*, vibrio (bacterium).

VI.CÁ.RI.O, *adj.*, vicarious.

VI.CE-CAM.PE.ÃO, *s.m.*, runner-up.

VI.CE-CHAN.CE.LER, *s.m.*, vice-chancellor.

VI.CE-GO.VER.NA.DOR, *s.m.*, vice-governor.

VI.CE.JAN.TE, *adj.*, thriving, luxuriant, exuberant.

VI.CE.JAR, *v.*, to flourish, to exuberantly; to exuberate.

VI.CE-PRE.SI.DEN.TE, *s.*, vice-president.

VI.CE-REI, *s.m.*, viceroy.

VI.CE-REI.NA.DO, *s.m.*, viceroyalty.

VI.CE-REI.TOR, *s.m.*, prorector.

VI.CE-VER.SA, *adv.*, vice versa.

VI.CI.A.DO, *adj.*, addicted, addict, vicious.

VI.CI.AR, *v.*, to vitiate, to corrupt, to pervert, to infect, to contaminate.

VI.CI.NAL, *adj.*, vicinal, neighbouring.

VÍ.CIO, *s.m.*, vice, addiction, immorality.

VI.CI.O.SO, *adj.*, vicious.

VI.CIS.SI.TU.DE, *s.f.*, vicissitude (the ups and downs of life).

VI.ÇO, *s.m.*, rankness, freshness, lushness, exuberance, vigour, energy.

VI.ÇO.SO, *adj.*, rank, luxuriant, exuberant, flourishing, glowind.

VI.DA, *s.f.*, life.

VI.DÃO, *s.m.*, *Bras.*, opulent, easygoing life.

VI.DEI.RA, *s.f.*, *Bot.*, grapevine.

VI.DEN.TE, *s. 2 gen.*, visionary, prophet; *adj.*, clairvoyant.

VÍ.DEO, *s.m.*, video, video cassette.

VI.DE.O.CÂ.MA.RA, *s.f.*, video camera.

VI.DE.O.CAS.SE.TE, *s.m.*, videocassette.

VI.DE.O.CLI.PE, *s.m.*, music video.

VI.DE.O.CON.FE.RÊN.CIA, *s.f.*, video-conference.

VI.DE.O.GA.ME, *s.m.*, videogame.

VI.DE.O.LO.CA.DORA, *s.f.*, video rental.

VI.DE.O.TE.CA, *s.f.*, video library.

VI.DE.O.TEI.PE, *s.m.*, videotape.

VI.DRA.ÇA, *s.f.*, windowpane, window glass.

VI.DRA.ÇA.RI.A, *s.f.*, glass factory; glazier's shop; glazing.

VI.DRA.CEI.RO, *s.m.*, glazier.

VI.DRA.DO, *adj.*, glazed, vitreous; *Bras.*, *gír.*, charmed, in love.

VI.DRO, *s.m.*, glass, bottle, flask, phial.

VI.E.LA, *s.f.*, lane, alley, narrow, pass.

VI.ÉS, *s.m.*, obliquity, sloping.

VI.ET.CON.GUE, *s. 2 gen.*, Vietcong; *adj.*, referring to the Vietcongs.

VI.ET.NA.MI.TA, *s. 2 gen.*, Vietnamese; *adj.*, Vietnamese.

VI.GA, *s.f.*, beam, girder.

VI.GA.MEN.TO, *s.m.*, framework, framing, rafters.

VI.GA.RI.CE, *s.f.*, swindle.

VI.GÁ.RI.O, *s.m.*, vicar.

VI.GA.RIS.TA, *s. 2 gen.*, swindler, bilker, trickster.

VI.GÊN.CIA, *s.f.*, legality, force, validity.

VI.GEN.TE, *adj.*, valid, effective, in force, current.

VI.GER, *v.*, to be in force, to be valid.

VI.GÉ.SI.MO, *num.*, twentieth; *adj.*, twentieth.

VI.GI.A, *s.f.*, watch, watchman, guard, sentinel.

VI.GI.AR, *v.*, to watch, to guard, to be vigilate.

VI.GI.LÂN.CIA, *s.f.*, vigilance, guard, alertness.

VI.GI.LAN.TE, *s. 2 gen.*, guard, watcher; *adj.*, vigilant, attentive, alert.

VI.GI.LAR, *v.*, the same that *vigiar*.

VI.GÍ.LIA, *s.f.*, night-watch, vigil.

VI.GOR, *s.m.*, vigor, force, strenght.

VI.GO.RAN.TE, *adj.*, alive, in force, invigorating.

VI.GO.RAR, *v.*, to invigorate, to be in force, to rule.

VI.GO.RO.SA.MEN.TE, *adv.*, vigorously.

VI.GO.RO.SO, *adj.*, vigorous, robust, active, strong, energetic.

VIL, *adj.*, vile, cheap, worthless.

VI.LA, *s.f.*, villa, small town.

VI.LA.NES.CO, *adj.*, referring to a villain.

VI.LA.NI.A, *s.f.*, villainy, depravity.

VI.LÃO, *s.m.*, villain, rascal, scoundrel, dirty.

VI.LA.RE.JO, *s.m.*, hamlet, , village; *adj.*, referring to a village.

VI.LE.ZA, *s.f.*, vileness, villainy, meanness.

VI.LI.PEN.DI.AR, *v.*, to vilipend, to velify, to belittle.

VI.LI.PÊN.DI.O, *s.m.*, slander, contempt, vilification.

VI.ME, *s.m.*, osier, willow, withe.

VI.MEI.RO, *s.m.*, *Bot.*, osier, willow.

VI.NA.GRE, *s.m.*, vinegar.

VI.NA.GREI.RA, *s.f.*, vinegar cruet.

VI.NA.GRE.TE, *adj.*, *Fr.*, *Cul.*, vinaigrette.

VIN.CA.DO, *adj.*, wrinkled, wrinkly, creased, pressed.

VIN.CAR, *v.*, to crease, to wrinkle; *fig.*, to furrow.

VIN.CO, *s.m.*, crease, wrinkle, groove, furrow.

VIN.CU.LA.ÇÃO, *s.f.*, link, linking.

VIN.CU.LA.DO, *adj.*, entailed, bound, linked.

VIN.CU.LAR, *v.*, to entail, to bond, to link, to annex.

VINCULATÓRIO · 350 · VITAL

VIN.CU.LA.TÓ.RI.O, *adj.*, binding, linking.
VÍN.CU.LO, *s.m.*, entail, entailment, bond, link.
VIN.DA, *s.f.*, coming, arrival, forthcoming.
VIN.DI.CA.ÇÃO, *s.f.*, vindication.
VIN.DI.CAR, *v.*, to vindicate; to claim; to avenge.
VIN.DI.CA.TI.VO, *adj.*, vindicative, vindicating.
VIN.DI.MA, *s.f.*, vintage, harvest.
VIN.DI.MA.DO, *adj.*, harvested, gathered.
VIN.DI.MO, *adj.*, pertaining to vintage; autumnal.
VIN.DO, *adj.*, arrived, come.
VIN.DOU.RO, *adj.*, coming, future, towardly.
VIN.GA.DOR, *s.m.*, avenger, revenger.
VIN.GAN.ÇA, *s.f.*, vengeance, revenge, retaliation.
VIN.GAR, *v.*, to avenge, to revenge, to retaliate, to punish.
VIN.GA.TI.VA.MEN.TE, *adv.*, vindictively.
VIN.GA.TI.VO, *adj.*, vindictive, retaliatory, revengeful, vindicatory.
VI.NHA, *s.f.*, vine, vineyard.
VI.NHAL, *s.m.*, vineyard, variety of grapes.
VI.NHE.DO, *s.m.*, extensive vineyard.
VI.NHE.TA, *s.f.*, vignette.
VI.NHE.TIS.TA, *s. 2 gen.*, vignettist.
VI.NHO, *s.m.*, vine.
VI.NÍ.CO.LA, *s.f.; adj.*, wine-growing.
VI.NI.CUL.TOR, *s.m.*, viniculturist, winegrower.
VI.NI.CUL.TU.RA, *s.f.*, viniculture, viticulture.
VI.NIL, *s.m.*, *Quím.*, vinyl.
VIN.TE, *num.*, twenty.
VIN.TÉM, *s.m.*, Brazilian and Portuguese coin; *fig.*, money.
VIN.TE.NA, *s.f.*, group of twenty, score (of).
VI.O.LA, *s.f.*, viola.
VI.O.LA.BI.LI.DA.DE, *s.f.*, violability.
VI.O.LA.ÇÃO, *s.f.*, violation, rape, infraction, trespass.
VI.O.LÁ.CE.O, *adj.*, violaceous.
VI.O.LA.DOR, *s.m.*, violator, transgressor; *adj.*, violative, profanatory.
VI.O.LÃO, *s.m.*, guitar.
VI.O.LAR, *v.*, to violate, to transgress, to rape.
VI.O.LEI.RO, *s.m.*, guitarist, *Bras.*, violist.
VI.O.LÊN.CIA, *s.f.*, violence, impetuosity, ferocity.
VI.O.LEN.TA.DO, *adj.*, violated, forced.
VI.O.LEN.TA.DOR, *s.m.*, violator; *adj.*, that violates.
VI.O.LEN.TA.MEN.TE, *adv.*, violently.
VI.O.LEN.TAR, *v.*, to violate, to force, to coerce, to rape.
VI.O.LEN.TO, *adj.*, violent, powerful.
VI.O.LE.TA, *s.f.*, violet.
VI.O.LE.TEI.RA, *s.f.*, *Bras.*, *Bot.*, golden dewdrop; a woman who sells violets.
VI.O.LI.NIS.TA, *s. 2 gen.*, violinist, fiddler.
VI.O.LI.NO, *s.m.*, violin, fiddle.
VI.O.LON.CE.LIS.TA, *s. 2 gen.*, cellist.
VI.O.LON.CE.LO, *s.m.*, violoncello, cello.
VI.O.LO.NIS.TA, *s. 2 gen.*, guitarist.
VIP, *s. 2 gen.*, *abrev.* of very important person.
VIR, *v.*, to come, to arrive, to come from, to result, to happen, to proceed from.
VI.RA.BRE.QUIM, *s.m.*, crankshaft (automobilemechanics).
VI.RA.ÇÃO, *s.f.*, breeze, gale, fresh wind.
VI.RA-CA.SA.CA, *s.*, 2 g., turncoat.
VI.RA.DA, *s.f.*, turning, swerve; *Esp.*, sudden turnaround.
VI.RA.DO, *adj.*, overturned, upside down.

VI.RA-LA.TA, *s.m.*, street-dog.
VI.RAR, *v.*, to turn, to reverse, to invert, to change.
VI.RA.VOL.TA, *s.f.*, turning, spin, somersault, turnabout.
VIR.GEM, *s.f.*, virgin; *adj.*, virginal, innocent, pure, untouched, spotless.
VIR.GI.NAL, *s.m.*, *Mús.*, virginal; *adj.*, virginal.
VIR.GIN.DA.DE, *s.f.*, virginity.
VIR.GI.NI.A.NO, *s.m.*, Virgo, Virgoan; *adj.*, Virgoan.
VÍR.GU.LA, *s.f.*, comma.
VIR.GU.LA.ÇÃO, *s.f.*, *Gram.*, setting of commas.
VIR.GU.LAR, *v.*, to punctuate, to insert commas.
VI.RIL, *adj.*, virile, vigorous, energetic, masculine, manlike.
VI.RI.LHA, *s.f.*, *Anat.*, groin.
VI.RI.LI.DA.DE, *s.f.*, virility.
VI.RO.LO.GI.A, *s.f.*, virology.
VI.RO.SE, *s.f.*, *Med.*, virosis.
VI.RÓ.TI.CO, *adj.*, referring to a virus or characterized by a virus.
VIR.TU.AL, *adj.*, virtual, practical, actual.
VIR.TU.DE, *s.f.*, virtue, morality, moral action, purity.
VIR.TU.O.SE, *s. 2 gen.*, virtuoso.
VIR.TU.O.SI.DA.DE, *s.f.*, virtuosity.
VIR.TU.O.SIS.MO, *s.m.*, the same that *virtuosidade*.
VIR.TU.O.SO, *s.m.*, virtuoso; *adj.*, virtuous.
VI.RU.LÊN.CI.A, *s.f.*, virulence, virulency.
VI.RU.LEN.TO, *adj.*, virulent.
VÍ.RUS, *s.m.*, virus.
VI.SA.DO, *adj.*, visaed, watched, valid (check).
VI.SÃO, *s.f.*, vision, sight, eyesight, view.
VI.SAR, *v.*, to aim at, to drive at, to seek, to look at.
VIS-À-VIS, *adv.*, Fr., vis-à-vis, face-to-face.
VÍS.CE.RA, *s.f.*, viscera, entrails.
VIS.CE.RAL, *adj.*, visceral; *fig.*, deep-rooted.
VIS.CON.DE, *s.m.*, viscount.
VIS.CO.SI.DA.DE, *s.f.*, viscosity.
VIS.CO.SO, *adj.*, viscous.
VI.SEI.RA, *s.f.*, visor; *fig.*, disguise.
VI.SI.BI.LI.DA.DE, *s.f.*, visibility.
VI.SI.O.NÁ.RI.O, *s.m.*, visionary; *adj.*, visionary.
VI.SI.TA, *s.f.*, visit, visiting, visitation, inspection.
VI.SI.TA.ÇÃO, *s.f.*, visitation, visit; *aberto à ~ pública*: open to the public.
VI.SI.TA.DOR, *s.m.*, visitor, visitant; *adj.*, visiting.
VI.SI.TAN.TE, *s. 2 gen.*, visitant, visitor, caller.
VI.SI.TAR, *v.*, to visit, to call on, to see, to pay a visit.
VI.SÍ.VEL, *adj.*, visible, perceptible, manifest.
VI.SI.VEL.MEN.TE, *adv.*, visibly.
VIS.LUM.BRAR, *v.*, to glimpse.
VIS.LUM.BRE, *s.m.*, glimpse.
VI.SOM, *s.m.*, vison; mink; *casaco de ~*: mink coat.
VI.SOR, *s.m.*, view finder, spy-hole.
VÍS.PO.RA, *s.f.*, *Bras.*, lotto.
VIS.TA, *s.f.*, sight, eyesight, vision, glimpse, view.
VIS.TO, *s.m.*, visa; *adj.*, accepted, seen, known.
VIS.TO.RI.A, *s.f.*, inspection, survey.
VIS.TO.RI.AR, *v.*, to inspect, to examine, to search.
VIS.TO.SO, *adj.*, eye-catching, good-looking, sightly, beautiful.
VI.SU.AL, *adj.*, visual.
VI.SU.A.LI.ZA.ÇÃO, *s.f.*, visualization.
VI.SU.A.LI.ZAR, *v.*, to visualize.
VI.TAL, *adj.*, vital.

VITALÍCIO · · 351 · · · VOLUPTUOSO

VI.TA.LÍ.CIO, *adj.*, lifelong, for life.
VI.TA.LI.DA.DE, *s.f.*, vitality.
VI.TA.LIS.MO, *s.m.*, *Biol.*, vitalism.
VI.TA.LI.ZA.ÇÃO, *s.f.*, vitalization.
VI.TA.LI.ZA.DOR, *s.m.*, vitalizer.
VI.TA.LI.ZAN.TE, *adj.*, vitalizing, invigorating.
VI.TA.LI.ZAR, *v.*, to vitalize.
VI.TA.MI.NA, *s.f.*, vitamin.
VI.TA.MI.NA.DO, *adj.*, vitaminized.
VI.TA.MÍ.NI.CO, *adj.*, vitaminic.
VI.TE.LA, *s.f.*, heifer, calf, a young of a cow.
VI.TI.CUL.TOR, *s.m.*, viticulturist; *adj.*, viticultural.
VI.TI.CUL.TU.RA, *s.f.*, viticulture, viniculture.
VI.TI.LI.GO, *s.m.*, *Med.*, vitiligo.
VÍ.TI.MA, *s.f.*, victim, prey.
VI.TI.MAR, *v.*, to victimize.
VI.TÓ.RIA, *s.f.*, victory, triumph, conquest.
VI.TÓ.RIA-RÉ.GI.A, *s.f.*, *Bot.*, victoria regia.
VI.TO.RI.O.SA.MEN.TE, *adv.*, victoriously.
VI.TO.RI.O.SO, *adj.*, victorious, triumphant.
VI.TRAL, *s.m.*, stained glass window.
VÍ.TREO, *adj.*, vitreous, vitric, glassy.
VI.TRI.FI.CA.ÇÃO, *s.f.*, vitrification.
VI.TRI.FI.CA.DO, *adj.*, vitrified.
VI.TRI.FI.CAR, *v.*, to vitrify.
VI.TRI.FI.CÁ.VEL, *adj.*, vitrifiable.
VI.TRI.NA, *s.f.*, window, display window, shopwindow.
VI.TRI.NIS.TA, *s.* 2 *gen.*, *Bras.*, window dresser.
VI.TRÔ, *s.m.*, glass window, glass.
VI.TRO.LA, *s.f.*, gramophone, phonograph, pickup; *fig.*, *fam.*, gossip.
VI.Ú.VA, *s.f.*, widow.
VI.U.VAR, *v.*, to become a widow or widower.
VI.U.VEZ, *s.f.*, widowhood.
VI.Ú.VO, *s.m.*, widower.
VI.VA, *s.m.*, viva; *interj.*, hooray; ~ *a rainha!*: long live the Queen! *viva a liberdade!*: liberty for ever!
VI.VA.CI.DA.DE, *s.f.*, vivacity.
VI.VAL.DI.NO, *s.m.*, *Bras.*, *gír.*, a great rascal, rogue.
VI.VA.MEN.TE, *adv.*, vividly, vivaciously.
VI.VAZ, *adj.*, lively, vivacious.
VI.VEI.RO, *s.m.*, nursery, aquarium, fishpond.
VI.VÊN.CI.A, *s.f.*, life, existence, being, experienced.
VI.VEN.CI.AR, *v.*, to live through.
VI.VEN.DA, *s.f.*, dwelling, home, abode, house.
VI.VEN.TE, *s.* 2 *gen.*, living being, human being; *adj.*, alive, living.
VI.VER, *v.*, to live, to be alive, to exist, to be, to endure, to last.
VÍ.VE.RES, *s.m.*, *pl.*, provisions.
VI.VI.DEZ, *s.f.*, vividness.
VI.VI.DO, *adj.*, experienced in life.
VÍ.VI.DO, *adj.*, vivid, lively.
VI.VI.FI.CA.ÇÃO, *s.f.*, vivification.
VI.VI.FI.CA.DOR, *s.m.*, vivifier; *adj.*, vivifying.
VI.VI.FI.CAN.TE, *adj.*, vivifying, life-giving.
VI.VI.FI.CAR, *v.*, to vivify, to animate, to vitalize.
VI.VO, *adj.*, alive, living, lively, smart, quick, alert.
VI.ZI.NHAN.ÇA, *s.f.*, neighbourhood, vicinity.
VI.ZI.NHO, *s.m.*, neighbour.
VI.ZIR, *s.m.*, vizier.
VO.A.DOR, *s.m.*, flyer; *adj.*, flying, volant; *fig.*, quick; *disco* ~:

flying saucer.
VO.AN.TE, *adj.*, flying, volant; *fig.*, transient, quick.
VO.AR, *v.*, to fly, to soar.
VO.CA.BU.LAR, *adj.*, pertaining to a vocable.
VO.CA.BU.LÁ.RIO, *s.m.*, vocabulary.
VO.CA.BU.LA.RIS.TA, *s.* 2 *gen.*, author of a vocabulary.
VO.CA.BU.LIS.TA, *s.* 2 *gen.*, the same that *vocabularista*.
VO.CÁ.BU.LO, *s.m.*, vocable, word, term, name.
VO.CA.ÇÃO, *s.f.*, vocation.
VO.CA.CI.O.NA.DO, *adj.*, gifted, endowed, talented.
VO.CA.CI.O.NAL, *adj.*, vocational.
VO.CAL, *adj.*, vocal, oral.
VO.CÁ.LI.CO, *adj.*, vocalic, vowel.
VO.CA.LIS.TA, *s.* 2 *gen.*, vocalist, singer.
VO.CA.LI.ZA.ÇÃO, *s.f.*, vocalization.
VO.CA.LI.ZA.DOR, *s.m.*, vocalizer; *adj.*, vocalizing.
VO.CA.LI.ZAR, *v.*, to vocalize, to vowelize.
VO.CÊ, *pron.*, you.
VO.CI.FE.RA.ÇÃO, *s.f.*, vociferation.
VO.CI.FE.RAN.TE, *s.m.*, vociferant; *adj.*, vociferant, vociferous.
VO.CI.FE.RAR, *v.*, to vociferate, to clamour.
VOD.CA, *s.f.*, vodka.
VO.DU, *s.m.*, voodoo.
VO.GA, *s.f.*, vogue; *s.m.*, stroke-oar, row, pulling.
VO.GAL, *s.f.*, vowel, vocal, voter.
VO.GAR, *v.*, to sail, to row, to navigate; to circulate; to be in vogue.
VOI.LE, *s.m.*, voile.
VO.LAN.TE, *s.m.*, gauze, wheel; *adj.*, movable.
VO.LÁ.TIL, *adj.*, volatile.
VO.LA.TI.LI.DA.DE, *s.f.*, volatility.
VO.LA.TI.ZA.ÇÃO, *s.f.*, volatization.
VÔ.LEI, *s.m.*, short of *voleibol*: volleyball.
VO.LEI.BOL, *s.m.*, volleyball.
VO.LEI.O, *s.m.*, volley.
VOLT, *s.m.*, *Eletr.*, volt (symbol: V).
VOL.TA, *s.f.*, return, regress, curve, change; recurrency, alteration, replacement, gyre.
VOL.TA.DO, *adj.*, facing; *estar* ~ *para*: to be focussed on.
VOL.TA.GEM, *s.f.*, voltage, tension.
VOL.TAI.CO, *adj.*, voltaic.
VOL.TAR, *v.*, to return, to come or go back, to regress, to recur, to devolve.
VOL.TE.AR, *v.*, to turn, to go round, to circle about, to rotate, to revolve; to flutter.
VOL.TEI.O, *s.m.*, spin, bend, movement; turning, rotating.
VOL.TÍ.ME.TRO, *s.m.*, *Eletr.*, voltmeter.
VO.LU.BI.LI.DA.DE, *s.f.*, fickleness.
VO.LU.MAR, *adj.*, *Geom.*, volumetric.
VO.LU.ME, *s.m.*, volume, capacity, content, book, pack, packet, bundle, extent, size.
VO.LU.MÉ.TRI.CO, *adj.*, volumetric, volumetrical.
VO.LUN.TA.RI.A.DO, *s.m.*, volunteers collectively.
VO.LUN.TA.RI.E.DA.DE, *s.f.*, voluntariness.
VO.LUN.TÁ.RIO, *s.m.*, volunteer; *adj.*, voluntary, spontaneous, gratuitous.
VO.LUN.TA.RI.O.SO, *adj.*, willful, whimsical, capricious.
VO.LUN.TA.RIS.MO, *s.m.*, *Filos.*, voluntarism.
VO.LÚ.PIA, *s.f.*, sensuality, voluptuousness.
VO.LUP.TU.O.SI.DA.DE, *s.f.*, voluptuousness.
VO.LUP.TU.O.SO, *adj.*, voluptuous.

VOLÚVEL ··· 352 ··· VURMOSO

VO.LÚ.VEL, *adj.*, voluble, inconstant, fickle, fluky.
VOL.VER, *v.*, to turn, to revolve, to rotate, to spin.
VO.MI.TAR, *v.*, to vomit, to throw up, to puke, to regurgitate, to spew, to cat.
VÔ.MI.TO, *s.m.*, vomit, spew, puke.
VON.TA.DE, *s.f.*, will, volition, wish, desire, mind, intention, purpose, determination, fancy.
VO.O, *s.m.*, flight; *levantar ~*: to take off.
VO.RA.CI.DA.DE, *s.f.*, voracity, voraciousness.
VO.RA.GEM, *s.f.*, whirlpool, chasm, vortex, maelstrom (water).
VO.RAZ, *adj.*, voracious, avid.
VÓR.TI.CE, *s.m.*, vortex, whirlpool, eddy, hurricane, tempest, chasm, maelstrom.
VOS, *pron. pess.*, you, to you.
VÓS, *pron.*, you.
VOS.SO, *pron.*, your, yours.
VO.TA.ÇÃO, *s.f.*, voting, poll, election.
VO.TA.DO, *adj.*, voted, approved.
VO.TAN.TE, *s. 2 gen.*, voter, elector; *adj.*, voting.
VO.TAR, *v.*, to vote, to elect, to poll.
VO.TO, *s.m.*, vote, promise, vow, ballot, election.
VO.VÔ, *s.m.*, grandpa.
VO.VÓ, *s.f.*, grandma, granny.
VOY.EUR, *s. 2 gen., Fr.*, voyeur.
VOY.EU.RIS.MO, *s.m.*, voyeurism.
VOZ, *s.f.*, voice, right to speak.
VO.ZEI.RÃO, *s.m.*, a strong voice, thundering voice.
VO.ZE.RI.O, *s.m.*, uproar, shouting, yelling, crying.

VUL.CÂ.NI.CO, *adj.*, volcanic, vulcanian.
VUL.CA.NIS.MO, *s.m.*, volcanism.
VUL.CA.NIS.TA, *s.m.*, volcanist, volcanologist.
VUL.CA.NI.ZA.ÇÃO, *s.f.*, vulcanization.
VUL.CA.NI.ZA.DOR, *s.m.*, vulcanizer.
VUL.CA.NI.ZAR, *v.*, to vulcanize, to volcanize.
VUL.CA.NO.LO.GI.A, *s.f., Geol.*, vulcanology, volcanology.
VUL.CÃO, *s.m.*, volcano.
VUL.GAR, *adj.*, vulgar, common, popular, banal.
VUL.GA.RI.DA.DE, *s.f.*, vulgarity, coarseness, vulgarism, banality.
VUL.GA.RI.ZA.ÇÃO, *s.f.*, vulgarization.
VUL.GA.RI.ZA.DOR, *s.m.*, vulgarizer; *adj.*, vulgarizing.
VUL.GA.RI.ZAR, *v.*, to vulgarize, to make vulgar, to divulge, to propagate.
VUL.GAR.MEN.TE, *adv.*, vulgarly.
VUL.NE.RA.BI.LI.DA.DE, *s.f.*, vulnerability.
VUL.NE.RAR, *v.*, to hurt, to wound, to offend.
VUL.NE.RÁ.VEL, *adj.*, vulnerable.
VUL.TO, *s.m.*, shadow, shape, face, body, figure.
VUL.TO.SO, *adj.*, voluminous, bulky, important.
VUL.TU.O.SI.DA.DE, *s.f., Med.*, congestion of the face.
VUL.TU.O.SO, *adj., Med.*, attacked by congestion of the face.
VUL.VA, *s.f., Anat.*, vulva.
VUL.VAR, *adj., Anat.*, vulvar (pertaining to the vulva).
VUR.MO, *s.m.*, the pus of ulcers.
VUR.MO.SO, *adj.*, purulent (containing pus).

W, *s.m.*, the twenty-third letter of the Portuguese alphabet.
WAG.NE.RI.A.NO, *s.m.*, Wagnerian (an admirer of the musical of Wagner); *adj.*, Wagnerian.
WAG.NE.RIS.MO, *s.m., Mús.*, Wagnerism, Wagnerianism.
WAL.KIE-TAL.KIE, *s.m., Ingl.*, walkie-talkie.
WALK.MAN, *s.m., Ingl.*, Walkman.
WATT, *s.m.*, watt.
WATT-HO.RA, *s.m., Fís.*, watt-hour.
WAT.TÍ.ME.TRO, *s.m., Fís.*, wattmeter.
WC, *abrev. s.m., Ingl.*, de water closet.
WEB, *s.f., Ingl., Comp.*, short of World Wide Web: Web.
WEB.MAIL, *s.f., Ingl.*, webmail.
WEB.CAM, *s.f., Ingl.*, webcam.
WEB.MAS.TER, *s.m., Ingl., Comp.*, webmaster.
WEST.ERN, *s.m., Ingl.*, western, faroeste (film).
WIL.DI.A.NO, *s.m.*, admirer of Oscar Wilde's literature.
WIND.SUR.FE, *s.m., Ingl., Esp.*, windsurf.
WIND.SUR.FIS.TA, *s.m., Esp.*, windsurfer.
WORK.SHOP, *s.m., Ingl.*, workshop.
WURT.ZI.TA, *s.f., Min.*, wurtzite.
WWW, *s.f., abrev.* of World Wide Web: WWW.

X, *s.m.*, the twenty-fourth letter of the Portuguese alphabet; Roman numeral for ten (X).
XÁ, *s.m.*, Shah, soberano, na língua persa.
XA.BO.QUE, *s.m.*, *Bras., col.*, piece of torn anything with the tooth.
XA.DREZ, *s.m.*, chess, chessboard, check, mosaic, prison.
XA.DRE.ZA.DO, *adj.*, checked.
XA.DRE.ZAR, *v.*, to checker, to chequer.
XA.DRE.ZIS.TA, *s. 2 gen.*, chess player.
XA.LE, *s.m.*, shawl, plaid.
XA.MÃ, *s.m.*, shaman.
XA.MA.NIS.MO, *s.m.*, *Rel.*, shamanism.
XA.MA.NIS.TA, *s. 2 gen.*, shamanist; *adj.*, shamanist, shamanistic.
XAM.PU, *s.m.*, shampoo.
XA.RÁ, *s. 2 gen.*, namesake, homonym.
XA.RO.PA.DA, *s.f.*, cough medicine, sirup, syrup; *Bras., fam.*, drag.
XA.RO.PE, *s.m.*, syrup.
XA.VAN.TE, *s. 2 gen.*, Chavante (Indian of the tribe of Chavantes); *adj.*, referring to the Chavantes.
XA.VE.CO, *s.f.*, *Bras.*, piece of junk; old worthless thing.
XA.XA.DO, *s.m.*, *Bras.*, xaxado (a kind of folkloric dance performed by men).
XA.XIM, *s.m.*, *Bras., Bot.*, fibrous-stemmed plant (family Cyatheaceae).
XEI.QUE, *s.m.*, *Ár.*, Sheikh.
XE.LIM, *s.m.*, shilling.
XE.NO.FI.LI.A, *s.f.*, xenophilism, attraction to foreign things (as styles or people).
XE.NÓ.FI.LO, *s.m.*, xenophile; *adj.*, xenophile.
XE.NO.FO.BI.A, *s.f.*, xenophobia.
XE.NÓ.FO.BO, *s.m.*, xenophobe.
XE.PA, *s.f.*, meal, food.
XE.PEI.RO, *s.m.*, *Bras.*, soldier who lives in quarters; person who does odd jobs.
XE.QUE, *s.m.*, check (chess); sheik.
XE.QUE-MA.TE, *s.m.*, checkmate, mate.
XE.RE.TA, *s. 2 gen.*, snoopy, nosy, prying.
XE.RE.TAR, *v.*, *Bras.*, to snoop into; to interfere.
XE.REZ, *s.m.*, sherry.
XE.RI.FE, *s.m.*, sheriff.
XE.RO.CAR, *v.*, to photocopy.
XE.RO.CÓ.PI.A, *s.f.*, a Xerox copy, photocopy.
XE.RO.CO.PI.AR, *v.*, the same that *xerocar*.
XÉ.ROX, *s.m.*, photocopy.
XE.XE.LEN.TO, *s.m.*, *Bras., fam.*, gross; disagreeable.
XE.XÉU, *s.m.*, *Bras.*, rank smell, pong.
XI, *interj.*, oh, no!, pish!
XÍ.CA.RA, *s.f.*, cup.
XI.I.TA, *s. 2 gen.*, Shiite (a Muslim); *adj.*, Shiite.
XI.FO.PA.GI.A, *s.f.*, characteristic of the xiphopagus.
XI.FÓ.PA.GO, *s.m.*, xiphopagus; *adj.*, xiphopagic, xiphopagous.
XI.LIN.DRÓ, *s.m.*, jail, gaol, prison.
XI.LO.FO.NE, *s.m.*, *Mús.*, xylophone.
XIN.GA.ÇÃO, *s.f.*, chiding, abuse, scolding.
XI.LO.GRA.FI.A, *s.f.*, *Art.*, xylography.
XI.LO.GRA.VU.RA, *s.f.*, *Art.*, xylograph.
XIN.GA.ÇÃO, *s.f.*, *Bras.*, swearing, insulting.
XIN.GA.MEN.TO, *s.m.*, calling names, swear-word.
XIN.GAR, *v.*, to chide, to scold, to rail, to offend.
XIN.XIM, *s.m.*, *Bras., Cul.*, ragout of chicken (with onion, garlic, oil, shrimps and pumpkin).
XIS.TO, *s.m.*, schist; xisto argiloso, shale.
XI.XI, *s.m.*, urine.
XO.DÓ, *s.m.*, flirtation, sweetheart.
XU.CRO, *adj.*, *Bras.*, unbroken (horse), untamed (animal); foolish, rude, ignorant.

Y, *s.m.*, the twenty-fifth letter of the Portuguese alphabet.
YANG, *s.m.*, *Fil.*, yang (the masculine active principle in nature that combines with yin to produce all that comes to be).
YEAT.SI.A.NO, *adj.*, concerning the work or the Irish poet William B. Yeats (1865-1939).
YEN, *s.m.*, *Econ.*, Japan's currency.

YIN AND YANG, *s.*, In Chinese philosophy represents the passive principle (female) and active (male).
Y.O.GA, *s.f.*, the same that *ioga*.
YUAN, *s.m.*, China's currency.
YUP.PIE, *s. 2 gen.*, yuppie (young professional urban, ambitious and prosperous).

Z, *s.m.*, the twenty-sixth and last letter of the Portuguese alphabet.
ZA.BUM.BA, *s.m.*, a big bass drum.
ZA.BUM.BAR, *v.*, to beat a bass drum.
ZA.GA, *s.f., Esp.*, backfield, fullback position (soccer).
ZAI.NO, *s.m.*, a zain horse; *adj.*, zain, a dark-brown horse.
ZAI.RE, *s.*, Zaire.
ZÂM.BIA, *s.m.*, Zambia.
ZA.GUEI.RO, *s.m.*, back, fullback.
ZAN.GA, *s.f.*, annoyance, aversion, indignation, anger.
ZAN.GA.DO, *adj.*, angry, vexed, annoyed.
ZÂN.GA.NO, *s.m.*, a person that runs a business for any others; *fig.*, parasite; pettifogger; fool, jester.
ZAN.GÃO, *s.m.*, drone, humble-bee, male honeybee.
ZAN.GAR, *v.*, to annoy, to make angry, to molest.
ZAN.GA.RE.LHA, *s.f., Port.*, sweep net, dragnet.
ZAN.ZAR, *v.*, to rove, to ramble, to wander.
ZA.RA.BA.TA.NA, *s.f.*, blowtube, blow-pipe, blowgun, puttyblower.
ZA.RA.GA.TA, *s.f.*, tumult, confusion, disorder, muddle; turmoil.
ZA.RAN.ZA, *s. 2 gen.*, person stunned, dazed; what does not make sense; *adj.*, stunned; reckless.
ZAR.CÃO, *s.m.*, minium, red lead.
ZAR.CO, *adj.*, light blue-eyed; said of horses with a white speck or circle around the eyes.
ZA.RO.LHO, *adj.*, squint-eyed, cross-eyed.
ZAR.PAR, *v.*, to weigh anchor, to sail.
ZE.BRA, *s.f., Zool.*, zebra.
ZE.BRA.DO, *adj.*, zebrine (having stripes like zebras).
ZE.BROI.DE, *s.m., Zool.*, zebrula, zebrule; *adj.*, zebroid; *col.*, fool, stupid.
ZE.BU, *s.m., Zool.*, zebu.
ZE.FIR, *s.m.*, zephyr cloth (kind of cotton fabric).
ZÉ.FI.RO, *s.m.*, zephyr, the West wind.
ZE.LA.ÇÃO, *s.f., Bras.*, bolide, shooting star.
ZE.LA.DOR, *s.m.*, janitor, watcher, keeper, overseer, inspector.
ZE.LA.DO.RA, *s.f.*, janitress.
ZE.LA.DO.RI.A, *s.f.*, the office of a janitor; a janitor's job.
ZE.LAN.DÊS, *s.m.*, Zeelander (native or inhabitant of Zeeland); *adj.*, of or relative to Zeeland.
ZE.LAN.TE, *s. 2 gen.*, the same that *zelador*.
ZE.LAR, *v.*, to watch over, to administer, to manage.
ZE.LO, *s.m.*, zeal, devotion, dedication, diligence.
ZE.LO.SA.MEN.TE, *adv.*, zealously, carefully.
ZE.LO.SO, *adj.*, zealous, careful, watchful, diligent, dedicated.
ZE.LO.TE, *s.m., Hist., Rel.*, zealot; one who feigns to be zealous; *adj.*, feigning to be zealous.
ZÉ-MA.NÉ, *s.m., fam.*, fool, idiot, air-head.
ZEN, *s.m., Rel.*, Zen; Zenic.
ZEN-BU.DIS.MO, *s.m.*, Zen-Buddhism.
ZEN-BU.DIS.TA, *s. 2 gen.*, Zenist; *adj.*, of or referring to the followers of Zen.
ZÉ-NIN.GUÉM, *s.m., col.*, *um ~*: a nobody (person).
ZE.NI.TAL, *adj.*, zenithal.
ZÊ.NI.TE, *s.m.*, zenith, vertex.
ZE.Ó.FA.GO, *adj.*, feeding on maize (animal).
ZE.PE.LIM, *s.m.*, zeppelin.
ZÉ-PO.VI.NHO, *s.m., Bras.*, the people, populace, pleb, rabble.
ZE.RAR, *v.*, to zero, to reduce to zero; to wipe out.
ZE.RO, *s.m.*, zero, a cipher, nobody, ought.
ZE.RO-QUI.LÔ.ME.TRO, *s.m., 2 num., Bras.*, brand new car; *adj.*, brand new.
ZEUG.MA, *s.m.*, zeugma.
ZEUG.MÁ.TI.CO, *adj.*, zeugmatic.
ZI.GO.DÁC.TI.LO, *adj.*, zygodactylic, zygodactyle, zygodactylous.
ZI.GO.MA, *s.m., Anat.*, zygoma.
ZI.GUE-ZA.GUE, *s.m.*, zigzag.
ZI.GUE.ZA.GUE.AN.TE, *adj.*, zigzagging.
ZI.GUE.ZA.GUE.AR, *v.*, to zigzag.
ZI.GU.RA.TE, *s.m.*, ziggurat.
ZIM.BÁ.BU.E, *s.*, Zimbabwe.
ZI.MO.LO.GI.A, *s.f.*, zymology.
ZI.MO.SE, *s.f., Quím.*, zymosis (fermentation).
ZIN.CA.DO, *adj.*, zincified (coated with zinc).
ZIN.CA.GEM, *s.f., Quím.*, zincification, galvanization.
ZIN.CAR, *v., Quím.*, to zinc, to zincify, to galvanize.
ZIN.CO, *s.m.*, zinc (metalic element, atomic number: 30, symbol: Zn).
ZIN.CO.GRA.FI.A, *s.f.*, zincography.
ZIN.CO.GRA.VU.RA, *s.f.*, zincograph, zincography, zincography.
ZI.PAR, *v., Comp.*, to zip.
ZÍ.PER, *s.m.*, zipper, slide fastener.
ZO.A.DA, *s.f.*, whiz, whizzing, hum, confusion.
ZO.AN.TE, *adj.*, whizzing, humming.
ZO.AR, *v.*, to whiz, to hum, to buzz.
ZO.DI.A.CAL, *adj.*, zodiacal.
ZO.DÍ.A.CO, *s.m.*, zodiac.
ZO.EI.RA, *s.f., Bras.*, hum, whiz, whizzing; *Bras., gír.*, tumult, disorder, noise.
ZOM.BA.DOR, *s.m.*, scoffer, jester, jeerer, mocker.
ZOM.BAR, *v.*, to mock, to make jokes, to make fun of, to flout.
ZOM.BA.RI.A, *s.f.*, mockery, sarcasm, ridicule, derision.
ZOM.BE.TE.AR, *v.*, to mock.
ZOM.BE.TEI.RO, *s.m.*, mocker, joker; *adj.*, mocking, joking.
ZO.NA, *s.f.*, zone, area, region, country; *gír.*, mess; *vulg.*, the red-light district.
ZO.NA E.LEI.TO.RAL, *s.f.*, electoral district.
ZO.NA FRAN.CA, *s.f.*, freetrade area.
ZO.NAL, *adj.*, zonal.
ZO.NE.A.MEN.TO, *s.m.*, zoning.
ZO.NE.AR, *v.*, to zone; *Bras., gír.*, to mess.

ZONZEAR   ·· 357 ··   ZURRO

ZON.ZE.AR, *v., Bras.,* to stun, be stunned.

ZON.ZEI.RA, *s.f., Bras.,* dizziness, giddiness.

ZON.ZO, *adj., Bras.,* stunned, dizzy, giddy.

ZO.O, *s.m., abrev.* of *zoológico*: zoo.

ZO.O.BI.O.LO.GI.A, *s.f.,* the science of animal life.

ZO.O.E.CO.LO.GI.A, *s.f.,* animal ecology.

ZO.O.LA.TRI.A, *s.f.,* zootheism, zoolatry.

ZO.O.LO.GIA, *s.f.,* zoology.

ZO.O.LÓ.GI.CO, *adj.,* zoologic, zoological; *jardim* ~ : zoological garden, zoo.

ZO.O.LO.GIS.TA, *s. 2 gen.,* zoologist.

ZO.Ó.LO.GO, *s.m.,* the same that *zoologista*.

ZO.O.TEC.NI.A, *s.f.,* zootechny.

ZO.O.TE.RA.PI.A, *s.f.,* zootherapy (veterinary therapeutics).

ZOOM, *s.m., Ingl.,* zoom.

ZO.RO.AS.TRIS.MO, *s.m.,* Zoroastrianism.

ZOR.RA, *s.f., Bras., gír.,* mess, confusion, disorder.

ZU.IR, *v.,* the same that *zumbir*.

ZUM, *s.m.,* zoom lens; zoom.

ZUM.BI, *s.m., Bras.,* the Negro leader of the Palmares quilombo; *Bras.,* a ghost in the Afro-Brazilian.

ZUM.BI.DO, *s.m.,* hum, buzz.

ZUM.BIR, *v.,* to hum, to buzz, to whir, to whiz.

ZU.NI.DO, *s.m.,* whiz, whir, buzz.

ZU.NIR, *v.,* to buzz, to hum, to whistle.

ZUN.ZU.NIR, *v.,* to produce a humming or buzzing sound.

ZU.RE.TA, *s. 2 gen., Bras.,* halfwit, insane, lunatic person; *adj.,* insane, crazy.

ZUR.RAR, *v.,* to bray, to heehaw.

ZUR.RO, *s.m.,* bray, braying, heehaw, rattle.

Z

dicionário escolar inglês

Inglês - Português

A, s., a primeira letra do alfabeto; *mús.* lá.
A, *art. indef.*, um, uma.
A.BACK, *adv.*, para trás. atrás.
AB.A.CUS, s., ábaco;
A.BAFT, *adv.*, à popa; *prep.*, atrás.
A.BAN.DON, v., abandonar, largar, ceder; desamparar, conceder.
A.BAN.DONED, *adj., part.*, abandonado, largado, cedido.
A.BAN.DON.MENT, s., abandono, desamparo.
A.BASE, v., humilhar, rebaixar.
A.BASE.MENT, s., humilhação, rebaixamento, degradação.
A.BASH, v., rebaixar, envergonhar, humilhar.
A.BASHED, *adj.*, envergonhado.
A.BASH.MENT, s., humilhação, rebaixamento.
A.BAS.ING, *adj.*, vergonhoso.
A.BATE, v., abater, enfraquecer, diminuir, reduzir.
A.BATE.MENT, s., abatimento, enfraquecimento.
A.BATER, s., aquele que abate, reduz ou diminui.
A.BAT.TOIR, s., matadouro.
AB.BESS, s., abadessa.
AB.BEY, s., abadia, mosteiro.
AB.BOT, v., abade.
AB.BREV, ABBR, *abrev.*, abreviação de *abbreviation*.
AB.BRE.VI.ATE, v., abreviar, resumir, condensar.
AB.BRE.VI.ATION, s., abreviação, resumo, condensação.
ABC, s., abecedário; *fig.*, princípios, rudimentos.
AB.DI.CA.BLE, *adj.*, abdicável.
AB.DI.CATE, v., abdicar, renunciar, deixar de.
AB.DI.CA.TION, s., abdicação.
AB.DO.MEN, s., abdome, ventre.
AB.DOM.INAL, *adj.*, abdominal.
AB.DU.CENT, *adj.*, abdutor, abducente.
AB.DUCT, v., sequestrar, raptar.
AB.DUCTION, s., rapto, sequestro.
A.BE.CE.DAR.I.AN, s., estudante do alfabeto; *fig.*, principiante.
ABEAR, v., aguentar, suportar, ajeitar.
ABED, *adj.*, deitado, acamado.
AB.ER.RANCE, s., aberração, anomalia.
AB.ER.RANT, *adj.*, aberrante, anômalo.
AB.ER.RA.TION, s., aberração, aleijão, desvio.
ABET, v., instigar, estimular, incitar, provocar.
A.BET.TER, s., instigador, estimulador.
ABEY.ANCE, s., suspensão, inatividade, ócio, pausa.
A.BEY.ANT, *adj.*, pendente, em suspenso.
AB.HOR, v., abominar, odiar, detestar, ter aversão.
AB.HOR.RENCE, s., repugnância, aversão, ódio.
A.BID.ANCE, s., continuidade; fidelidade, conformidade.
ABIDE, v., continuar, permanecer, suportar.
A.BID.ER, s.o., o que continua; o que suporta, espera.
A.BID.ING, *adj.*, duradouro.
ABID.ING.LY, *adv.*, fixamente, permanentemente.
ABIL.I.TY, s., habilidade, capacidade, perícia, competência.

A.BI.OT.IC, *adj.*, abiótico.
AB.JECT, *adj.*, abjeto, desprezível, vil.
AB.JEC.TION, s., abjeção, desprezo, vileza.
AB.JU.RA.TION, s., abjuração, renúncia.
AB.JURE, v., abjurar, renunciar, renegar, deixar de.
ABJURER, s., abjurador, abjurante.
AB.LA.TIVE, s., *adj.*, ablativo.
A.BLAZE, *adj.*, inflamado, queimante, em chamas, brilhante.
A.BLE, *adj.*, hábil, perito, capaz, esperto.
A.BLE-BOD.IED, *adj.*, robusto, apto fisicamente.
A.BLOOM, *adj.*, florido, florescente, em flor.
AB.LU.TION, s., ablução, lavagem, limpeza, purificação.
A.BLY, *adv.*, habilmente, com perícia.
AB.NE.GATE, v., abnegar, negar, renunciar, desistir.
AB.NOR.MAL, *adj.*, anormal, anômalo.
AB.NOR.MAL.LY, *adv.*, de modo anormal, irregularmente.
AB.NOR.MAL.I.TY s., anormalidade, defeito.
ABNORMITY, s., monstruosidade, deformidade; anormalidade.
A.BOARD *adv.*, a bordo.
A.BODE, s., domicílio, s., residência; v., *part.*, de abide.
AB.OL.ISH, v., abolir, anular, desfazer.
AB.O.LI.TION, s., abolição, anulamento.
AB.O.LI.TION.ISM, s., abolicionismo.
AB.O.LI.TION.IST, s., abolicionista.
A-BOMB, s., bomba A (de atômica).
ABOM.I.NA.BLE, *adj.*, abominável, detestável, nojento.
A.BOM.I.NA.BLY, *adv.*, abominavelmente.
ABOM.I.NATE, v., abominar, detestar.
A.BOM.I.NA.TION, s., abominação, repulsão; coisa horrenda.
AB.ORIG.I.NE, s., aborígene, indígena.
A.BORT, v., abortar, cancelar, anular.
A.BOR.TION, s., aborto, abortamento.
A.BOR.TIVE, *adj.*, abortivo.
A.BOUND, v., abundar, ser abundante.
A.BOUT, *adv.*, quase, em torno, ao redor, na vizinhança, a respeito.
A.BOUT-TURN, *(UK)* s., meia-volta.
A.BOUT-FACE, s., meia-volta; *fig.*, guinada.
ABOVE, *adv.*, acima, por sobre, em cima.
A.BOVE.BOARD, *adj.*, legítimo, limpo.
AB.RA.CA.DAB.RA, *interj.*, abracadabra!
A.BRA.SION, s., esfolamento.
ABRA.SIVE, *adj., s.*, abrasivo.
A.BREAST, *adv.*, lado a lado
ABRIDGE, v., abreviar, resumir, condensar.
A.BRIDGED, *adj.*, compacto, resumido.
A.BREAST, *adv.*, lado a lado; diante de; na mesma altura.
A.BRIDGE.ABLE, *adj.*, que pode ser resumido; abreviável.
A.BRIDGE, v., abreviar, resumir; encurtar.
A.BROACH, *adj.*, perfurado; pronto para ser tirado do barril.
A.BROAD, *adv.*, no exterior, fora; *to live ~:* viver/morar no

ABROGATION ···361··· ACCOMMODATIVE

exterior.

AB.RO.GA.TION, s., ab-rogação, anulação.

ABRUPT, adj., abrupto, íngreme, ríspido.

A.BRUPT.LY, adv., abruptamente, repentinamente.

ABRUPT.NESS s., rispidez, brusquidão.

ABS, s., (abrev. de anti-lock breaking system) ABS (freio).

AB.SCESS , s., abcesso.

AB.SCIS.SA, s., Mat., abscissa.

AB.SCOND, v., esconder-se; sumir-se.

AB.SCOND.ENCE, s., evasão, fuga.

AB.SCOND.ER, s., fugitivo, foragido.

A.BSEIL, v., fazer/praticar rapel (prática desportiva).

AB.SENCE, s., ausência, falta, lacuna.

AB.SENT, adj., ausente, faltante, abstrato.

AB.SEN.TEE, s., ausente.

AB.SEN.TEE.ISM, s., absenteísmo.

AB.SENT-MIND.ED, adj., distraído(a)

AB.SENT-MIND.ED.NESS, s., distração.

AB.SENT-MIND.E.DLY, adv., distraidamente.

AB.SINTH(E), s., absinto.

AB.SO.LUTE, adj., absoluto, infinito, total.

AB.SO.LUTE.LY, adv., certamente, absolutamente.

AB.SO.LUTE.NESS, s., integridade, condicionalidade; independência absoluta.

AB.SO.LU.TION, s., absolvição, perdão.

AB.SO.LUT.ISM, s., absolutismo.

AB.SO.LU.TIST, s. e adj., absolutista.

AB.SOLVE, v., absolver, perdoar.

ABSOLVER, s., aquele que absolve, absolvedor.

AB.SORB, v., absorver, assimilar, apreender.

AB.SOR.BENT, adj., absorvente.

AB.SOR.BING, adj., cativante.

AB.SORP.TION, s., absorção, apreensão.

AB.SORP.TIVE, adj., absortivo, absorcível.

AB.STAIN, v., abster-se, deixar de, privar-se.

AB.STE.MI.OUS, adj., abstêmio.

AB.STEN.TION, s., abstenção, abstinência.

AB.STI.NENCE, s., abstinência, renúncia.

AB.STI.NENT, adj., abstinente, abstêmio.

AB.STRACT, adj., abstrato, ideal, extrato, resumo.

AB.STRACT.ED, adj., abstraído, absorto.

AB.STRACT.ED.NESS, s., abstração, distração.

AB.STRAC.TION, s., abstração, divagação, furto.

AB.STRAC.TION.ISM, s., Art., abstracionismo.

AB.STRAC.TION.IST, s., Art., abstracionista.

AB.STRUSE, adj., confuso(a).

AB.STRUSE.LY, adv., abstrusamente, incompreensivelmente.

AB.SURD, adj., absurdo, estúpido, anormal.

AB.SUR.DI.TY, s., absurdidade, disparate, estupidez.

AB.SURD.LY, adv., incrivelmente.

AB.SURD.NESS, s., absurdo, disparate, incongruência.

ABTA, (abrev. de Association of British Travel Agents) s., Associação Britânica de Agentes de Viagem.

A.BUN.DANCE, s., abundância, copiosidade.

A.BUN.DANT, adj., abundante, copioso, farto.

A.BUND.ANT.LY, adv., abundantemente, em abundância.

A.BUSE, s., abuso, desaforo, engano, maus tratos; v., abusar, desaforar, enganar, maltratar.

A.BUSER, s., o que abusa, abusador, insultador.

A.BU.SIVE, adj., abusivo, desaforado.

A.BUT, v., limitar, confinar, restringir.

A.BUT.MENT, s., ponto de contato ou apoio, contiguidade; pilar.

A.BUT.TING, adj., adjacente, contíguo.

A.BYS.MAL, adj., abismal, fundo; ruim, péssimo.

A.BYS.MAL.LY, adv., terrivelmente.

A.BYSS, s., abismo.

A.BYS.SAL, adj., relativo a abismo; abismal.

A.BYS.SIN.I.AN, adj., abissínio(nia).

A/C, abrev., (de account current) conta corrente: c.c.

ACACIA, s., Bot., acacia.

AC.A.DEM.IC, adj., acadêmico; universitário.

AC.A.DE.MI.CIAN, s., acadêmico; lente, docente.

AC.A.DEM.I.CISM, s., academicismo; academismo.

A.CAD.E.MY, s., academia.

AC.A.RUS, s., ácaro.

AC.CEDE, v., aceder, alcançar, permitir; **ACCEDE** to – conceder.

AC.CED.ER, s., o que consente ou adere.

AC.CEL.ER.ATE, v., acelerar, impulsionar.

AC.CEL.ER.AT.ED, adj., acelerado; antecipado.

AC.CEL.ER.A.TION, s., aceleração, aceleramento.

AC.CEL.ER.A.TOR, s., acelerador.

AC.CENT, s., acento, sotaque, pronúncia; acento gráfico.

AC.CEN.TU.AL, adj., acentuado, destacado, rítmico.

AC.CEN.TU.ATE, v., acentuar, destacar, enfatizar.

ACCENTUATION, s., acentuação, ênfase.

AC.CEPT, v., aceitar, receber, suportar, adotar.

AC.CEPT.ABIL.I.TY, s., aceitabilidade, aceitação, recepção.

AC.CEPT.A.BLE, adj., aceitável, admissível.

AC.CEPT.A.BLY, adv., apropriadamente.

AC.CEP.TANCE, s., aceitação.

AC.CEP.TA.TION, s., aceitação, aceitamento, acepção.

AC.CEPT.ED, adj., aceito, reconhecido.

AC.CESS, s., acesso, aproximação, entrada; v., acessar, entrar.

AC.CES.SI.BIL.I.TY, s., acessibilidade.

AC.CES.SI.BLE, adj., acessível, disponível.

AC.CES.SION, s., ascensão.

AC.CES.SO.RI.AL, adj., de ou relativo a acessório, suplementar.

ACCESSORY, s., adj., acessório, suplementar.

AC.CI.DENT, s., acidente, incidente; acaso.

AC.CI.DENT.AL, adj., acidental, fortuito.

AC.CI.DENT.AL.LY, adv., acidentalmente.

AC.CI.DENT.AL.NESS, s., acidência, casualidade, acidentalidade.

AC.CLAIM, s., aplauso, aclamação, ovação.

AC.CLAIM.ER, s., aclamador.

AC.CLA.MA.TION, s., aclamação, ovação.

AC.CLAM.A.TO.RY, adj., aclamatório.

AC.CLI.MATE, v., aclimar, aclimatar, adaptar.

AC.CLI.MAT.ED, adj., aclimatado, adaptado.

AC.CLI.MA.TI.ZA.TION, s., aclimatação.

AC.CLI.MA.TIZE, v., aclimatar, aclimar.

AC.CLIV.I.TY, s., aclive, ladeira, encosta.

AC.CO.LADE, s., honra, elogio; acolada, ascensão à dignidade de cavalheiro.

AC.COM.MO.DATE, v., acomodar, abrigar, alojar.

AC.COM.MO.DAT.ING, adj., complacente.

AC.COM.MO.DA.TION, s., acomodação, alojamento.

AC.COM.MO.DA.TIVE, adj., acomodável, acomodativo.

ACCOMPANIMENT •• 362 •• ACROPOLIS

AC.COM.PANI.MENT, *s.*, acompanhamento.
AC.COM.PA.NIST, *s.*, *Mús.*, aquele(a) que canta ou toca junto com alguém.
AC.COM.PA.NY, *v.*, acompanhar, seguir junto.
AC.COM.PLICE, *s.*, cúmplice, comparsa.
AC.COM.PLISH, *v.*, concluir, terminar, finalizar.
AC.COM.PLISHED, *adj.*, competente, excelente.
AC.COM.PLISH.MENT, *s.*, conclusão, finalização.
AC.CORD; *s.*, tratado, acordo, pacto; *v.*, acordar, concordar.
AC.COR.DANCE, *s.*, acordo, concordância.
AC.COR.DANT, *adj.*, conforme, concorde.
AC.COR.DER, *s.*, o que está de acordo, partidário.
AC.CORD.ING, *adj.*, concorde, acordado, de acordo.
AC.CORD.ING.LY, *adv.*, apropriadamente, consequentemente.
AC.COR.DI.ON, *s.*, acordeão, gaita, sanfona.
AC.COR.DI.ON.IST, *s.*, acordeonista, sanfoneiro(a).
AC.COST, *v.*, abordar.
AC.COUNT, *s.*, conta, soma, cálculo, cômputo; *v.*, contar, somar, calcular.
AC.COUNT.A.BIL.I.TY, *s.*, responsabilidade.
AC.COUNT.A.BLE, *adj.*, responsável; justificável, explicável.
AC.COUNT.AN.CY, *s.*, contabilidade.
AC.COUN.TANT, *s.*, contabilista, contador.
AC.COUNT.ANT.SHIP, *s.*, cargo e responsabilidade de contador.
AC.COUNT-CUR.RENT, *s.*, conta-corrente.
AC.COUNT.ING, *s.*, contabilidade.
AC.COUNT.RE.MENTS, *s. pl.*, parafernália.
ACCOUNT SALES, *s.*, prestação de contas.
AC.CRED.IT, *v.*, acreditar, aceitar, abonar.
AC.CREDIT.ED, *adj.*, acreditado, aceito.
AC.CRE.TION, *s.*, acréscimo, aumento, crescimento.
AC.CRUE, *v.*, advir, provir, resultar.
ACCT, *abrev.*, abreviatura de *account* (conta); *accountant* (contador).
AC.CUL.TUR.ATE, *v.*, aculturar.
AC.CUL.TUR.A.TION, *s.*, aculturação.
AC.CU.MU.LATE, *v.*, acumular, amontoar.
AC.CU.MU.LAT.ED, *adj.*, acumulado.
AC.CU.MU.LA.TION, *s.*, acumulação, amontoamento.
AC.CU.MU.LA.TIVE, *adj.*, acumulativo.
AC.CU.MU.LA.TOR, *s.*, acumulador.
AC.CU.RA.CY, *s.*, exatidão, precisão.
AC.CU.RATE, *adj.*, acurado, preciso, exato.
AC.CU.RATE.LY, *adv.*, com exatidão, precisamente.
AC.CURSE, *v.*, amaldiçoar, maldizer.
AC.CURSED, *adj.*, amaldiçoado, desgraçado, maldito.
AC.CUS.ABLE, *adj.*, acusável, condenável.
AC.CUS.AL, *s.*, acusação (formal).
AC.CU.SA.TION, *s.*, acusação.
AC.CU.SA.TIVE, *s.*, acusativo.
AC.CUSE, *v.*, acusar, delatar, denunciar.
AC.CUSED, *s.*, *adj.*, acusado, réu.
AC.CUS.ER, *s.*, acusador, procurador público.
AC.CUS.ING, *adj.*, acusador(a).
AC.CUS.ING.LY, *adv.*, acusatoriamente.
AC.CUS.TOM, *v.*, acostumar, ter por hábito.
AC.CUS.TOMED, *adj.*, acostumado, habituado.
ACE, *s.*, ás; ponto; bagatela.
A.CEPH.A.LOUS, *adj.*, acéfalo; *fig.*, sem líder ou chefe.
ACERB, *adj.*, acerbo, duro, rigoroso, amargo.

A.CER.BIC, *adj.*, acerbo(a), ferino, duro, ácido.
A.CER.BI.TY, *s.*, amargura, acerbidez, acidez.
AC.E.TATE, *s.*, acetato.
A.CE.TIC, *adj.*, acético; *acetic acid*: ácido acético.
AC.E.TONE, *s.*, acetona.
ACE.TOUS, *adj.*, acetoso, azedo.
A.CET.Y.LENE, *s.*, acetileno.
A.CE.TYL.SA.LIC.Y.LIC A.CID, *s.*, *Quím.*, *Farm.*, ácido acetilsalicílico, aspirina.
ACHE, *v.*, doer, sofrer; *s.*, dor, sofrimento.
A.CHIEV.A.BLE, *adj.*, realizável.
A.CHIEVE, *v.*, concluir, acabar, terminar, alcançar.
A.CHIEVE.MENT, *s.*, acabamento, conclusão, término.
ACH.ING, *s.*, dor, sofrimento: *adj.*, dolorido.
ACH.RO.MAT.IC, *adj.*, acromático.
A.CHRO.MA.TISM, *s.*, acromatismo.
A.CHRO.MA.TIZE, *v.*, acromatizar.
AC.ID, *s.*, *adj.*, ácido.
A.CID.I.FI.CA.TION, *s.*, acidificação.
ACID.I.FY, *v.*, acidificar, azedar.
ACID.I.TY, *s.*, acidez.
A.CID.U.LATE, *v.*, acidular, tornar ácido.
A.CID.U.LATION, *s.*, acidulação.
AC.KNOWL.EDGE, *v.*, reconhecer, conhecer, vir a saber.
AC.KNOWL.EDGE.MENT, *s.*, reconhecimento, conhecimento.
AC.ME, *s.*, cume, pico, culminância.
AC.NE, *s.*, acne.
AC.O.LYTE, *s.*, acólito; ajudante, assistente; coroinha.
A.CORN, *s.*, bolota, glande (fruto do carvalho).
A.COUS.TIC, *adj.*, acústico.
A.COUS.TICS, *s.*, acústica.
AC.QUAINT, *v.*, comunicar, informar, conhecer.
AC.QUAIN.TANCE, *s.*, conhecimento, habilidade, capacidade.
AC.QUAINT.ANCE.SHIP, *s.*, relações pessoais.
AC.QUI.ESCE, *v.*, aquiescer, concordar, acordar, aceitar.
AC.QUI.ES.CENCE, *s.*, aquiescência, concordância.
AC.QUI.ES.CENT, *adj.*, aquiescente, complacente, condescendente.
AC.QUIR.A.BLE, *adj.*, adquirível.
AC.QUIRE, *v.*, adquirir, obter, conquistar.
AC.QUIRED, *adj.*, adquirido, obtido, ganho.
AC.QUIRE.MENT, *s.*, aquisição; conhecimento.
AC.QUI.SI.TION, *s.*, aquisição, compra.
AC.QUI.SI.TIVE, *adj.*, ambicioso, consumista.
AC.QUIT, *v.*, absolver, desobrigar-se, inocentar.
AC.QUIT.TAL, *s.*, *Jur.*, absolvição.
AC.QUIT.TANCE, *s.*, recibo, quitação.
AC.QUIT.TER, *s.*, pagador, pagante.
ACRE, *s.*, acre, med. agrária de 4.046,84 m2.
AC.RID, *adj.*, acre, azedo.
A.CRID.I.TY, *s.*, asperaza.
AC.RI.MO.NIOUS, *adj.*, acrimonioso.
AC.RI.MO.NY, *s.*, acrimônia, amargor; rudeza.
AC.RO.BAT, *s.*, acrobata.
AC.RO.BAT.IC, *adj.*, acrobático; *fig.*, astuto.
AC.RO.BAT.ICS, *s.*, acrobacias.
AC.RO.BAT.ISM, *s.*, acrobatismo.
AC.RO.NYM, *s.*, acrônimo.
AC.RO.PHO.BI.A, *s.*, acrofobia.
A.CROP.O.LIS, *s.*, acrópole.

ACROSS · 363 · ADMINISTRABLE

ACROSS, *prep., adv.,* através de, do outro lado, obliquamente.
A.CROS.TIC, *s. e adj.,* acróstico.
A.CRYL.IC, *s., adj.,* acrílico.
ACT, *s.,* ação, ato, procedimento; *v.,* agir, proceder, comportar-se.
ACT.A.BLE, *adj.,* representável, apresentável (peça de teatro).
ACT.ING, *s.,* ação, realização; *adj.,* ativo, efetivo, interino.
AC.TION, *s.,* ação, ato, efeito, atitude.
AC.TION.ABLE, *adj.,* acionável, litigável.
AC.TI.VATE, *v.,* ativar, colocar em movimento.
AC.TI.VA.TION, *s.,* ativação; radiação.
AC.TIVE, *adj.,* ativo, aplicado, diligente.
AC.TIVE.LY, *adv.,* ativamente, incessantemente.
AC.TIV.IST, *s.,* ativista (político).
AC.TIV.I.TY, *s.,* atividade, ação, presteza.
AC.TIV.I.TIES, *s. pl.,* ações, atividades.
AC.TOR, *s.,* ator, figurante.
AC.TRESS, *s.,* atriz.
AC.TU.AL, *adj.,* atual, real, verdadeiro.
AC.TU.AL.I.TY, *s.,* atualidade, realidade.
AC.TU.AL.I.ZA.TION, *s.,* realização, efetuação.
AC.TU.AL.LY, *adv.,* realmente, na verdade.
AC.TU.A.RY, *s.,* estatístico(a).
AC.TU.ATE, *v.,* acionar, atuar, movimentar.
AC.TU.A.TION, *s.,* ação, efetivação, acionamento.
AC.TU.A.TOR, *s.,* acionador, efetivador.
ACU.MEN, *s.,* perspicácia, sagacidade.
A.CU.I.TY, *s.,* acuidade.
ACU.MI.NATE, *v.,* afiar, aguçar.
A.CU.MI.NA.TION, *s.,* aguçamento; ação de tornar afiado, pontiagudo.
AC.U.PUNC.TURE, *s.,* acupuntura.
AC.U.PUNC.TU.RIST, *s.,* acupuntor, acupunturista.
ACUTE, *adj.,* agudo, pontudo, apontado.
A.CUTE AN.GLE, *s.,* ângulo agudo.
A.CUTE.LY, *adv.,* acentuadamente.
A.CUTE.NESS, *s.,* agudez,perspicácia, sagacidade.
A.CYC.LIC, *adj.,* acíclico.
AD, *s.,* (abrev. de *advertisement*) anúncio de jornal, propaganda de tv.
AD, *abrev.,* (de *Anno Domini*) d.C.
AD.AGE, *s.,* adágio, provérbio.
AD.A.MANT, *s.,* pedra ou algo de extrema dureza; magnetita; *adj.,* adamantino, inflexível.
AD.A.MAN.TINE, *adj.,* adamantino; inflexível, impenetrável.
A.DAPT, *v.,* adaptar, ajustar, acomodar.
A.DAPT.A.BIL.I.TY, *s.,* adaptabilidade, acomodação.
A.DAPT.A.BLE, *adj.,* adaptável, acomodável.
AD.AP.TA.TION, *s.,* adaptação, acomodação.
A.DAPT.ER, ADAPTOR, *s.,* adaptador.
A.DAPT.IVE, *adj.,* adaptável, adaptativo.
A.DAPT.IVE.LY, *adv.,* adaptativamente.
ADD, *v.,* adir, acrescentar, somar.
ADD.A.BLE, *adj.,* adicionável, acrescentável.
AD.DEN.DUM, *s.,* adendo, aditamento.
AD.DER1, *s.,* adicionador, máquina de somar.
AD.DER2, *s.,* víbora, serpente.
AD.DICT, *s.,* dependente (químico), viciado, fanático; *v.,* dedicar-se, devotar-se.
AD.DICT.ED, *adj.,* viciado (em algo), fanático (por algo).
AD.DIC.TION, *s.,* devoção, inclinação, apego.

AD.DI.TION, *s.,* adição, soma, acréscimo.
AD.DI.TION.AL, *adj.,* adicional.
AD.DI.TIVE, *adj.,* aditivo.
AD.DLE, *v.,* confundir, aturdir.
AD.DLE-BRAINED, *adj.,* confuso, excêntrico.
AD.DLED, *adj.,* podre; *fig.,* confuso.
AD.DRESS, *s.,* endereço, discurso; *v.,* remeter, endereçar.
AD.DRESS.EE, *s.,* destinatário.
AD.DUCE, *v.,* aduzir, alegar.
AD.DUCE.A.BLE, *adj.,* aduzível.
AD.DUC.TION, *s.,* adução, alegação, referência.
A.DEEM, *v., Jur.,* revogar uma doação, cancelar um legado.
A.DEMP.TION, *s., Jur.,* adenção (revogação de doação ou legado).
AD.E.NOIDS, *s. pl.,* adenoides.
AD.EPT, *s.,* especialista, perito; *adj.,* hábil, perito.
AD.E.QUA.CY, *s.,* suficiência.
AD.E.QUATE, *adj.,* adequado.
AD.E.QUATE.LY, *adv.,* adequadamente, suficientemente.
AD.HERE, *v.,* aderir, optar.
AD.HER.ENCE, *s.,* aderência, colagem, união.
AD.HER.ENT, *adj.,* aderente, unido, ligado.
AD.HE.SION, *s.,* adesão.
AD.HE.SIVE, *adj., s.,* adesivo.
AD.HIB.IT, *v.,* aderir, adicionar, juntar.
AD.HI.BI.TION, *s.,* aplicação, uso, emprego.
AD.I.POSE, *adj.,* adiposo, gordo.
ADJ, *abrev.,* abreviatura de *adjective* (adjetivo).
AD.JA.CEN.CY, *s.,* adjacência.
AD.JA.CENT, *adj.,* adjacente, próximo.
AD.JA.CENT ANGLES, *s., Geom.,* ângulos adjacentes.
AD.JEC.TIVE, *s.,* adjetivo.
AD.JOIN, *v.,* achegar, aproximar, ajuntar, acrescer.
AD.JOIN.ING, *adj.,* contíguo, próximo, adjacente.
AD.JOURN, *v.,* adiar, protelar, transferir.
AD.JUDGE, *v.,* decretar, *Júr.,* sentenciar.
AD.JU.DI.CATE, *v.,* julgar, sentenciar; examinar.
AD.JU.DI.CA.TION, *s.,* julgamento.
AD.JU.DI.CA.TIVE, *adj.,* adjucativo, judicatório.
ADJU.DICATOR, *s.,* juiz, árbitro.
AD.JUNCT, *s., adj.,* adjunto, adido, assessor.
AD.JUNC.TION, *s.,* junção, ligação, união.
AD.JURE, *v.,* adjurar, imprecar, esconjurar.
AD.JUST, *v.,* ajustar, conectar, regular, acertar.
AD.JUST.A.BLE, *adj.,* ajustável, regulável; conciliável.
AD.JUST.A.BLY, *adv.,* ajustavelmente.
AD.JUST.ED, *adj.,* ajustado, equilibrado (emocionalmente).
AD.JUST.ABLE, *adj.,* ajustável, regulável.
AD.JUS.TER, *s.,* ajustador.
AD.JUST.MENT, *s.,* ajuste, ajustamento, acerto, reajuste.
AD.JU.TAGE, *s.,* bocal (cano, rosca etc.), gárgula, bica (de fonte).
AD.JU.TANT, *s.,* ajudante, assistente.
AD.JU.VANT, *s.,* assistente, adido, ajudante, assessor.
AD.MAN, *s.,* publicitário, anunciante.
AD.MASS, *s.,* público influenciável pela comunicação de massa; *adj.,* relativo à sociedade de consumo.
AD.MEAS.URE, *v.,* repartir, partilhar.
ADMIN *(UK)*, *abrev.,* administração (Informática).
AD.MIN.IS.TER, *v.,* administrar, governar, ministrar.
AD.MIN.IS.TRA.BLE, *adj.,* administrável.

ADMINISTRANT ···364··· AERIE

AD.MIN.IS.TRANT, s. e adj., administrante.
AD.MIN.IS.TRA.TION, s., administração, direção, orientação.
AD.MIN.IS.TRA.TIVE, adj., administrativo.
AD.MIN.IS.TRA.TOR, s., administrador.
AD.MIN.IS.TRA.TOR.SHIP, s., administração.
AD.MI.RA.BLE, adj., admirável.
AD.MI.RA.BLY, adv., admiravelmente.
AD.MI.RAL, s., almirante.
AD.MI.RAL.TY (UK), s., Ministério da Marinha.
AD.MI.RA.TION, s., admiração, veneração.
AD.MIRE, v., admirar, venerar, respeitar.
AD.MIR.ER, s., admirador, fã.
AD.MIR.ING, adj., admiração.
AD.MIR.ING.LY, adv., com admiração (pasmo).
AD.MIS.SI.BLE, adj., aceitável.
AD.MIS.SION, s., entrada, admissão, ingresso.
AD.MIT, v., admitir, aceitar, concordar.
AD.MIT.TA.BLE, adj., admissível, permissível.
AD.MIT.TANCE, s., admissão, permissão; direito de ingresso, entrada.
AD.MIT.TE.DLY, adv., reconhecidamente.
AD.MIX, v., misturar.
AD.MIX.TURE, s., mistura.
AD.MON.ISH, v., admoestar, advertir.
AD.MON.ISH.MENT, s., admoestação, advertência.
AD.NATE, adj., Bot., adnato: que nasce junto de.
AD.NOM.I.NAL, adj., adnominal, adjunto.
A.DO.BE, s., adobe, tijolo cru; lodo seco pelo sol; adj., construído com adobes.
AD.O.LES.CENCE, s., adolescência, juventude.
AD.O.LES.CENT, s., adolescente.
A.DO.NIS, s., Mit., Adônis; homem bonito.
A.DOPT, v., adotar, aceitar.
A.DOPT.A.BLE, adj., adotável.
A.DOPT.ED, adj., adotado, aceito.
A.DOP.TER, s., adotante.
A.DOP.TION, s., adoção.
A.DOP.TIVE, adj., s., adotivo.
A.DOR.ABIL.I.TY, s., adorabilidade.
A.DOR.A.BLE, adj., adorável, divino.
AD.O.RA.TION, s., adoração, respeito, veneração.
A.DORE, v., adorar.
A.DOR.ING, adj., admiração (olhar); encantador(a) (sorriso).
A.DORN, v., adornar, enfeitar, embelezar.
A.DORN.ER, s., adornador, decorador.
A.DORN.ING, adj., adornador, enfeitador.
A.DORN.MENT, s., adorno.
A.DOWN, prep., adv., para baixo, de cima para baixo; prep., ao longo de ou sobre.
A.DREN.A.LIN, s., adrenalina.
A.DRIFT, s., à deriva, sem rumo, desorientado.
A.DROIT, adj., hábil.
A.DRY, adj., ant., seco, sedento.
AD.SORB, v., Quím., adsorver.
AD.SORB.ENT, s., Quím., adsorvente.
AD.SORP.TION, s., Quím., adsorção.
AD.U.LATE, v., adular, bajular, lisonjear.
AD.U.LA.TION, s., adulação, bajulação.
AD.U.LA.TO.RY, adj., adulatório.
A.DULT, adj., s., adulto.
A.DUL.TER.ATE, v., adulterar; adj., adulterado.

A.DUL.TER.ATE.LY, adv., falsificadamente.
A.DUL.TER.A.TION, s., adulteração.
A.DUL.TER.ER, s., adúltero.
A.DUL.TER.ESS, s., adúltera.
A.DUL.TERY, s., adultério.
A.DULT.HOOD, s., maioridade.
A.DUM.BRATE, v., prenunciar,sombrear, eclipsar.
A.DUST, adj., queimado, seco, ressecado.
AD.VANCE, s., avanço, antecipação; v., avançar.
AD.VANCED, adj., avançado(a).
AD.VANCE.MENT, s., avanço, progresso.
AD.VAN.TAGE, s., vantagem, superioridade.
AD.VAN.TA.GEOUS, adj., vantajoso(a).
AD.VENT, s., advento.
AD.VENT.IST, s., adventista.
AD.VEN.TURE, s., aventura, ação.
AD.VEN.TUR.ER, s., aventureiro.
AD.VEN.TUR.OUS, adj., aventureiro(a), intrépido(a).
AD.VERB, s., advérbio.
AD.VER.BI.AL, adj., adverbial.
AD.VER.SARY, s., adversário.
AD.VER.SA.TIVE, adj., adversativo.
AD.VERSE, adj., adverso, contrário.
AD.VERSE.LY, adv., negativamente.
AD.VER.SI.TY, s., adversidade; desgraça.
AD.VERT, v., advertir, admoestar.
AD.VER.TENCE, s., advertência.
AD.VER.TENT, adj., atencioso, cuidadoso, atento.
AD.VER.TISE, v., anunciar.
AD.VER.TISE.MENT, s., anúncio.
AD.VER.TIS.ER, s., anunciante.
AD.VER.TIS.ING, s., propaganda, publicidade.
AD.VICE, s., aviso, conselho, recomendação.
AD.VIS.A.BIL.I.TY, s., conveniência.
AD.VIS.A.BLE, adj., avisável.
AD.VISE, v., avisar, aconselhar, recomendar.
AD.VISED, adj., avisado, advertido.
AD.VIS.ED.LY, adv., deliberadamente.
AD.VIS.ED.NESS, s., prudência, juízo.
AD.VIS.ER (UK), **ADVISOR** (US), s., assessor(a).
AD.VI.SO.RI.LY, adv., consultivamente.
AD.VI.SO.RY, adj., consultivo, aconselhador.
AD.VO.CA.CY, s., advocacia.
AD.VO.CATE, v., advogar, defender, litigar.
AD.VO.CATION, s., defesa, proteção.
AD.VO.CATE.SHIP, s., advocacia.
AD.VO.CAT.ESS, s., advogada.
AD.VOC.A.TO.RY, adj., advocatório, pertencente à advocacia.
AD.Y.TUM, s., ádito, santuário; antiga câmara secreta de templos.
AE.DILE, s., edil.
AE.GIS, s., égide.
AE.ON (UK), **EON** (US), s., Geol., éon; fig., século.
AE.RA, s., era, época, tempo.
A.ER.ATE, v., arejar, ventilar; oxidar, oxigenar.
A.ER.AT.ED, adj., exposto ao ar.
A.ER.A.TION, s., ventilação, arejamento.
A.ER.A.TOR, s., ventilador, aerador.
A.ER.I.AL, s., antena; adj., aéreo.
AERIE, s., ninho de ave de rapina; fig., habitação ou castelo construído a grande altura.

AERIFICATION   ··· 365 ···   AGGLOMERATION

A.ER.I.FI.CA.TION, s., aerificação; vaporização.
AER.O.BAT.IC, adj., aeróbica.
AER.A.O.BICS, s., aeróbica.
A.ER.O.DROME, s., aeródromo.
A.ER.O.DY.NAM.IC, adj., aerodinâmica.
A.ER.O.DY.NAM.ICS, s., aerodinâmica.
A.ER.O.ME.CHAN.IC, adj., aeromecânico(a).
A.ER.O.NAUT, s., aeronauta.
A.ER.O.NAU.TIC, adj., aeronáutico(a).
A.ER.O.NAU.TICS, s., aeronáutica.
A.ER.O.PLANE, s., aeroplano.
A.ER.O.SOL, s., aerossol.
AEROSPACE, s., aeroespacial (refere-se à indústria).
AES.THETE, ES.THETE, s., esteta.
AES.THET.I.CAL.LY, ES.THET.I.CAL.LY, adv., esteticamente.
AES.THET.ICS, s., estética.
AES.TI.VAL, adj., estival, relativo ao verão.
AES.TI.VATE, v., veranear.
AE.THER, s., éter.
AE.TI.OL.O.GY, s., etiologia.
A.FEAR, v., ant., assustar, amedrontar.
A.FAR, adv., à distância.
A.FE.BRILE, adj., sem febre.
AF.FA.BIL.I.TY, s., afabilidade.
AF.FA.BLE, adj., afável.
AF.FA.BLE.NESS, s., afabilidade.
AF.FA.BLY, adv., afavelmente, bondosamente.
AF.FAIR, s., negócio, assunto, objetivo.
AF.FECT, v., afetar, influir.
AF.FEC.TA.TION, s., afetação, influência.
AF.FECT.ED, adj., afetado, influenciado.
AF.FEC.TION, s., afeto, afeição, apego, carinho.
AF.FEC.TION.AL, adj., afetivo.
AF.FEC.TION.ATE, adj., afetuoso(a).
AF.FEC.TION.ATE.LY, adv., afetuosamente
AF.FEC.TION.ATE.NESS, s., afetividade, carinho.
AF.FEC.TIVE, adj., afetivo, afeiçoado, emocional.
AF.FIL.I.ATE, s., filiado; v., filiar, afiliar; ligar, fundir, agregar.
AF.FIL.I.A.TION, s., afiliação.
AF.FINE, s., parente não consanguíneo (através do casamento).
AF.FINED, adj., afim, ligado.
AF.FIN.I.TY, s., afinidade, parentesco.
AF.FIRM, v., afirmar, assegurar, confirmar.
AF.FIRM.A.BLE, adj., afirmável.
AF.FIR.MANCE, s., afirmação, confirmação.
AF.FIR.MA.TION, s., afirmação solene, confirmação.
AF.FIR.MA.TIVE, adj., afirmativo.
AF.FIX, v., afixar, pregar, fixar.
AF.FLA.TION, s., sopro.
AF.FLICT, v., afligir, angustiar.
AF.FLICT.ED, adj., aflito.
AF.FLIC.TING, adj., aflitivo, penoso, desolador.
AF.FLIC.TION, s., aflição, dor, sofrimento.
AF.FLIC.TIVE, adj., aflitivo.
AF.FLU.ENCE, s., riqueza, abundância, fartura; afluência.
AF.FLU.ENT, adj., rico, opulento; afluente.
AF.FLUX, s., afluxo.
AF.FORD, v., ter recursos, ter dinheiro para pagar, ter tempo disponível.
AF.FORD.A.BLE, adj., acessível, disponível.

AF.FOR.EST.A.TION, s., florestamento.
AF.FRAN.CHISE, v., liberar, libertar.
AF.FRAN.CHISE.MENT, s., libertação, liberação, emancipação.
AF.FRAY, s., briga, confusão.
AF.FRIGHT, s., pavor, terror.
AF.FRONT, v., ofender, injuriar, insultar; s., ofensa, injúria.
AF.FRONTED, adj., insultado, ofendido.
AF.GHAN, AFGHANI, adj., afegão(ã); s., afegão(ã), afegane.
A.FIELD, adv., longe de casa, no exterior.
AFIRE, adv., em chamas, que está queimando.
A.FLOAT, adj., flutuante; desgovernado; desimpedido, livre; fig., em dia (com pagamentos).
AFOOT, adv., a pé.
A.FORE.MEN.TIONED, adj., supramencionado.
A.FORE.SAID, adj., supracitado.
A.FORE.THOUGHT, adj., planejado, premeditado.
A.FRAID, adj., assustado, amedrontado, receoso.
AFRESH, adv., novamente, outra vez, de novo.
AF.RI.CAN, adj., e s., africano.
AF.RI.CAN.ISM, s., africanismo.
AF.RI.CAN.IST, s., especialista em culturas e línguas africanas, africanista.
AF.RI.CAN.I.ZA.TION, s., africanização.
AF.RI.KAANS, s., africâner.
AF.RI.KA.NER, s. 2 gen., africâner.
AF.RO-A.MER.I.CAN, s. e adj., afro-americano.
AF.RO-BRA.ZIL.IAN, s. e adj., afro-brasileiro.
AF.TER, adv., depois, após, em seguida.
AF.TER-BIRTH, s., placenta.
AF.TER.CARE, s., cuidados que se tem após um período de tratamento (hospitalar).
AF.TER.DAYS, s. pl., futuro.
AF.TER.EF.FECT, s., efeitos posteriores, consequências.
AF.TER.GROWTH, s., renovo, vergôntea, rama de árvore.
AF.TER.LIFE, s., pós-morte.
AF.TER.MATH, s., consequências, resultado.
AF.TER.NOON, s., tarde, período vespertino.
AF.TER-SEA.SON, s., pós-temporada.
AF.TER.SHAVE, s., loção pós-barba.
AF.TER.SHOCK, s., pequenos tremores (após terremoto).
AF.TER.TASTE, s., ressaibo, ranço, sabor ruim.
AF.TER.THOUGHT, s., reflexão tardia; malícia.
AF.TER-TIMES, s. pl., os tempos vindouros.
AF.TER.WARDS, adv., posteriormente, mais tarde, depois.
AF.TER.WORD, s., epílogo.
A.GAIN, adv., novamente, outra vez, de novo.
A.GAINST, prep., contra, em oposição, ao contrário.
AGE, s., idade, época, momento, velhice.
AGED, adj., velho, idoso, sazonado, maturado.
AG.ED.NESS, s., idade, velhice.
AGE.ING, adj., idoso; velho, ultrapassado; s., ver aging.
AGE.LESS, adj., imutável, eterno.
A.GEN.CY, s., agência, repartição, seção, setor.
A.GEN.CY BUSINESS,
A.GEN.DA, s., agenda, programa, roteiro.
A.GENT, s., agente, encarregado, delegado.
AGE-OLD, adj., antigo(a).
AGE-WORN, adj., senil, decrépito.
AG.GLOM.ER.ATE, adj., aglomerado; v., aglomerar, juntar.
AG.GLOM.ER.A.TION, s., aglomeração, ajuntamento.

AGGLOMERATIVE ··· 366 ··· AIRING

AG.GLOM.ER.A.TIVE, *adj.*, aglomerativo, aglomerante.
AG.GLU.TI.NATE, *v.*, aglutinar, reunir, juntar.
AG.GLU.TI.NA.TION, *s.*, aglutinação, ligação.
AG.GRAN.DIZE, *v.*, engrandecer, tornar grande, aumentar.
AG.GRA.VATE, *v.*, agravar, irritar, provocar.
AG.GRA.VAT.ING, *adj.*, agravante, irritante.
AG.GRA.VA.TION, *s.*, agravamento, aborrecimento, irritação.
AG.GRA.VA.TOR, *s.*, o que ou quem agrava, agravador.
AG.GRE.GATE, *v.*, agregar; *adj.*, *s.*, agregado; *s.*, massa, conjunto aposto.
AG.GRE.GA.TION, *s.*, agregação, ajuntamento, acúmulo.
AG.GRE.GA.TIVE, *adj.*, agregativo, coletivo, acumulativo.
AG.GRESS, *v.*, agredir, atacar, insultar, ofender.
AG.GRES.SION, *s.*, agressão, ataque, ofensa, insulto.
AG.GRES.SIVE, *adj.*, agressivo, ofensivo.
AG.GRES.SIVE.LY, *adv.*, agressivamente.
AG.GRES.SOR, *s.*, agressor, atacante.
AG.GRIEVE, *v.*, agredir, affligir, incomodar, magoar.
AG.GRIEVED, *adj.*, *part.*, agredido, aflito, ofendido.
AG.GRO *(UK)*, *s.*, arruaça (ling. internet).
A.GHAST, *adj.*, espantado.
AG.ILE, *adj.*, ágil, rápido, leve.
AGIL.I.TY, *s.*, agilidade, rapidez.
AG.ING, *s.*, envelhecimento.
A.GIN.NER, *s.*, *gir.*, pessoa que se opõe a mudanças, reaça.
AGIO, *s.*, ágio.
AG.IO.TAGE, *s.*, agiotagem.
AG.I.TATE, *v.*, agitar, sacudir, mover, provocar.
AG.I.TATED, *adj.*, agitado(a).
AG.I.TA.TION, *s.*, agitação, incômodo, movimento.
AG.I.TA.TOR, *s.*, agitador, provocador.
AG.LET, *s.*, agulheta; adorno metálico usado em roupas.
A.GLOW, *adj.*, incandescente; *adv.*, de modo incandescente.
AG.NA.TION, *s.*, parentesco paterno, agnação.
AG.NO.MEN, *s.*, sobrenome.
AG.NOM.I.NATE, *v.*, denominar.
AG.NO.SI.A, *s.*, *Med.*, agnosia.
AG.NOS.TIC, *adj.*, agnóstico, incrédulo.
AG.NOS.TI.CISM, *s.*, agnosticismo.
A.GO, *prep.*, desde, atrás.
A.GOG, *adj.*, impaciente, ansioso; *adv.*, impacientemente.
A.GO.ING, *adv.*, em movimento; *v.*, andando.
A.GO.NIC, *adj.*, agônico, ágono, que não forma ângulo.
A.GO.NIST.IC, *adj.*, agonístico, combativo (atleta).
AG.O.NIZE, *v.*, agonizar, morrer; massacrar, affligir.
AG.O.NIZED, *adj.*, agoniado(a).
AG.O.NIZ.ING, *adj.*, agonizante, moribundo.
AG.O.NIZ.INGLY, *adv.*, angustiosamente, dolorosamente.
AG.O.NY, *s.*, agonia, dor, sofrimento.
A.GRAPH.I.A, *s.*, *Med.*, agrafia, perda da capacidade de escrever por falta de coordenação motora.
A.GRAR.I.AN, *adj.*, agrário; *s.*, agrariano.
A.GREE, *v.*, ceder, corresponder, ser do agrado de.
A.GREE.ABLE, *adj.*, agradável, prazeroso.
A.GREE.ABLY, *adv.*, agradavelmente.
A.GREE.MENT, *s.*, consentimento, acordo, aceitação.
A.GRES.TIC, *adj.*, agreste, rústico, bruto.
A.GRI.BUSI.NESS, *s.*, agronegócio.
AG.RI.CUL.TUR.AL, *adj.*, agrícola, relativo à agricultura.
AG.RI.CUL.TUR.ALIST, *s.*, agricultor, fazendeiro.
AG.RI.CUL.TURE, *s.*, agricultura.

AG.RI.CUL.TUR.IST, *s.*, agricultor.
AG.RO.BI.OL.O.GY, *s.*, agrobiologia.
AG.RO.CHEM.I.CAL, *s.*, agente agroquímico.
AG.RO.IN.DUS.TRI.AL, *adj.*, agroindustrial.
AG.RO.IN.DUS.TRY, *s.*, agroindústria.
AG.RO.NOM.IC, *adj.*, agronômico(a).
AG.RO.NOM.ICS, *s.*, agronomia.
AG.RON.O.MIST, *s.*, agrônomo.
AG.RON.O.MY, *s.*, agronomia.
AG.ROUND, *adj.*, *adv.*, parado, encalhado.
AH, *interj.*, ah!
A.HA!, *interj.*, ah! ah!
A.HEAD, *adv.*, a frente, para diante; primeiro.
A.HOY, *interj.*, *Náut.*, à vista!
AID, *s.*, auxílio, ajuda, socorro, apoio.
AID-DE-CAMP, *s.*, *Mil.*, ajudante de campo.
AIDE, *s.*, *Mil.*, assistente, ajudante.
AID.ER, *s.*, o que socorre, dá ajuda.
AIDS, *Abrev.* (de *acquired immune deficency syndrome*) síndrome de imunodeficiência adquirida.
AI.GUILLE, *s.*, agulha (pico de montanha pontuda); aguilhão.
AIL, *v.*, perturbar, incomodar, affligir.
AIL.ING, *adj.*, doente; *fig.*, debilitado.
AIL.MENT, *s.*, doença.
AIM, *v.*, apontar, mirar; *s.*, mira, pontaria.
AIM.LESS, *adj.*, sem objetivo, sem propósito, incerto.
AIM.LESS.LY, *adv.*, a esmo, sem rumo.
AIN'T, contração das expressões: *am not, are not, is not, have not, has not.*
AIR, *s.*, ar, atmosfera, céu, espaço, firmamento; jeito, atitude.
AIR-A.LARM, *s.*, alarme aéreo.
AIR-A.LERT, *s.*, mesmo que *air-alarm.*
AIR.BAG, *s.*, *Aut.*, airbag (bolsa inflável de segurança em veículos).
AIR.BASE, *s.*, base aérea.
AIR.BED *(UK)*, *s.*, colchão inflável.
AIR.BLAST, *s.*, *Tecnol.*, ar soprado.
AIR.BORNE, *adj.*, transportado por via aérea; em voo.
AIR.BRAKE, *s.*, freio a ar.
AIR.BRUSH, *s.*, aerógrafo; *v.*, pintar com aerógrafo.
AIR.BUS, *s.*, ônibus aéreo.
AIR-COM.PRES.SOR, *s.*, compressor de ar.
AIR-CON.DI.TION.ED, *adj.*, climatizado.
AIR CON.DI.TION.ER, *s.*, aparelho de ar condicionado.
AIR-CON.DI.TION.ING, *s.*, ar condicionado.
AIR.CRAFT, *s.*, aeronave; avião.
AIR.DROP, *s.*, lançamento de medicamentos, víveres etc. de avião para pessoas isoladas.
AIR-DRY, *v.*, secar ao ar por exposição.
AIR.DUCT, *s.*, canal de ar.
AIR-EN.GINE, *s.*, máquina de ar comprimido ou quente.
AIR.ER, *s.*, secador de roupa.
AIR.FIELD, *s.*, aeródromo.
AIR FIGHT.ING, *s.*, combate aéreo.
AIR FORCE, *s.*, força aérea de um país.
AIR FREIGHT, *s.*, frete aéreo.
AIR FRESH.EN.ER, *s.*, purificador de ar.
AIR.GUN, *s.*, arma de ar comprimido.
AIR.HOLE, *s.*, *Tecnol.*, respiradouro; *Aeron.*, poço de ar.
AIR.I.LY, *adv.*, alegremente, despreocupadamente.
AIR.ING, *s.*, ventilação, arejamento.

AIRLESS ••• 367 ••• ALIENATION

AIR.LESS, *adj.*, abafado.
AIR LET.TER, *s.*, carta aérea.
AIR.LIFT, *s.*, transporte aéreo; *v.*, transportar por via aérea.
AIR.LINE, *s.*, companhia aérea.
AIR.LINER, *s.*, avião de passageiros.
AIR.LOCK, *s.*, retentor de ar, câmara de vácuo.
AIR.MAIL, *s.*, correio aéreo.
AIR.MAN, *s.*, aviador, piloto de avião.
AIR-NAV.I.GA.TION, *s.*, navegação aéra, aeronáutica.
AIR-PHO.TO.GRAPH, *s.*, fotografia aérea.
AIR-PICT.URE, *s.*, imagem aérea (da atmosfera).
AIR PI.RA.CY, *s.*, priataria aérea.
AIR.PLANE, *s.*, aeroplano, avião.
AIR PLANT, *s.*, *Bot.*, epífita, planta que cresce sobre outra.
AIR.PLAY, *s.*, divulgação (por ondas de rádio).
AIR.PORT, *s.*, aeroporto.
AIR.SHIP, *s.*, dirigível, aeróstato.
AIR.SICK, *adj.*, enjoado, nauseado (devido à viagem aérea).
AIR.SPACE, *s.*, espaço aéreo.
AIR.SPEED, *s.*, velocidade no ar.
AIR.STRIP, *s.*, pista de pouso.
AIR TAX.I, *s.*, taxi aéreo.
AIR TER.MI.NAL, *s.*, terminal aéreo (terminal de ônibus em aeroportos).
AIR.TIGHT, *adj.*, hermético.
AIR-TO-AIR, *adj.*, *Mil.*, de avião a avião.
AIR TRAF.FIC, *s.*, tráfego aéreo.
AIR.WAVES, *s. pl.*, ondas de rádio.
AIR.WAY, *s.*, linha aérea; canal de ventilação.
AIR.Y, *adj.*, aéreo, etéreo, leve, arejado.
AISLE, *s.*, nave lateral (de igreja); corredor em plateia de teatro, igreja, escola etc.
AITCH, *s.*, h, letra h.
A.JAR, *adj.*, entreaberta (porta).
A.KIN, *adj.*, *s.*, parente, parecido, consanguíneo.
AL.A.BAS.TER, *s.*, alabastro.
A.LAC.RI.TY, *s.*, vivacidade, prontidão, diligência; boa vontade.
A.LA.ME.DA, *s.*, alameda.
A.LAND, *adv.*, em terra.
A.LARM, *s.*, alarme, aviso, sinal de perigo.
A.LARM BELL, *s.*, campainha de alarme.
A.LARM CLOCK, *s.*, despertador.
A.LARM.ING, *adj.*, alarmante.
A.LARM.ING.LY, *adv.*, assustadoramente.
A.LARM.ISM, *s.*, alarmismo.
A.LARM.IST, *s.*, alarmista.
A.LARM POST, *s.*, posto de alarme.
A.LARM-RA.DI.O, *s.*, radiorrelógio.
A.LATE, *adj.*, alado.
A.LAT.ED, *adj.*, alado (o mesmo que *alate*).
AL.BA.NI.AN, *s. e adj.*, albanês.
AL.BA.TROSS, *s.*, albatroz.
AL.BE.IT, *conj.*, embora, não obstante, todavia.
AL.BIN.IC, *adj.*, albínico, albino.
AL.BI.NISM, *s.*, albinismo.
AL.BI.NO, *adj.*, *s.*, albino.
AL.BU.GO, *s.*, *Med.*, albugem, leucoma.
AL.BUM *s.*, álbum.
AL.BUMEN, *s.*, albume, clara de ovo; albumina.
AL.BU.ME.NI.ZA.TION, *s.*, tratamento com albumina.

AL.BU.MIN, *s.*, albumina.
AL.CAI.DE, *s.*, *Es.*, alcaide (governador de um castelo).
AL.CAY.DE, *s.*, o mesmo que *alcaide*.
AL.CA.ZAR, *s.*, alcácer, castelo, fortaleza.
AL.CHEM.IC, *adj.*, alquímico(a).
AL.CHEM.I.CAL, *s.*, alquímico.
AL.CHE.MIST, *s.*, alquimista.
AL.CHE.MY, *s.*, alquimia.
AL.CO.GEL, *s.*, alcogel (gel com porcentagem de álcool).
AL.CO.HOL, *s.*, álcool.
AL.CO.HOL.IC, *adj.*, alcoólico.
AL.CO.HOL.ISM, *s.*, alcoolismo.
AL.CO.HOL.I.ZA.TION, *s.*, alcoolização.
AL.CO.HOL.IZE, *v.*, alcoolizar, encher com álcool.
AL.CO.HOL.OM.E.TER, *s.*, *Quím.*, alcoômetro, pesa-álcool.
AL.CO.HOL.OM.E.TRY, *s.*, *Quím.*, alcoometria.
ALCORAN, *s.*, Alcorão (livro sagrado dos maometanos).
AL.COVE, *s.*, alcova.
AL.DER, *s.*, *Bot.*, âmieiro, alno (árvore ornamental).
AL.DER.MAN *(UK)*, *s.*, vereador.
AL.DER.MAN.IC, *adj.*, relativo à vereador ou funcionário municipal, edilício.
ALE, *s.*, cerveja.
ALE.A.TO.RY, *adj.*, aleatório.
A.LEE, *adj.*, *Náut.*, sotavento; *adv.*, a sotavento.
ALE.HOUSE, *s.*, cervejaria, taberna, bar.
ALEM.BIC, *s.*, alambique.
A.LE.RION, *s.*, alerião (na heráldica, águia de asas abertas, sem bico nem pés).
A.LERT, *adj.*, alerta, pronto, preparado; alerta; *v.*, alertar.
AL.ERT.NESS, *s.*, precaução, vigilância, agilidade.
AL.E.UT, *s.*, esquimó das ilhas aleútas.
A.LE.VIN, *s.*, alevino (cria de peixe após a fase larval).
ALE-WIFE, *s.*, propietária de cervejaria, bar ou botequim.
AL.EX.AN.DRI.AN, *s. e adj.*, natural ou habitante de Alexandria.
AL.EX.AN.DRINE, *s. e adj.*, alexandrino (poesia com versos de doze sílabas).
AL.FAL.FA, *s.*, alfafa.
AL.FIL.A.RIA, *s.*, *Bot.*, bico-de-cegonha.
AL.FRES.CO, *adj.*, ao fresco, ao ar livre; *adv.*, ao ar livre.
AL.GA, *s.*, alga.
AL.GE.BRA, *s.*, álgebra.
AL.GE.BRA.IC, *adj.*, algébrico.
AL.GE.BRA.I.CAL, *adj.*, o mesmo que *algebraic*.
AL.GE.BRA.IC NUM.BER, *s.*, *Mat.*, número algébrico.
AL.GE.BRA.IST, *s.*, algebrista.
AL.GE.RI.AN, *adj. e s.*, argelino(a).
AL.GE.SI.A, *s.*, *Med.*, algesia (muita sensibilidade à dor).
AL.GI.CIDE, *s.*, *Quím.*, algicida (produto que mata algas).
AL.GID, *adj.*, álgido, frio, gelado.
AL.GID.I.TY, *s.*, frio intenso, algidez.
AL.GO.RITHM, *s.*, algoritmo.
A.LI.AS, *s.*, pseudônimo, nome falso; *adv.*, outrora, aliás; vulgo.
AL.I.BI, *s.*, álibi.
AL.IEN, *s.*, alienígena, estrangeiro, estranho.
AL.IEN.ABIL.I.TY, *s.*, alienabilidade.
AL.IEN.ABLE, *adj.*, alienável.
AL.IEN.AGE, *s.*, situação legal e social de um estrangeiro.
AL.IEN.ATE, *v.*, alienar, transferir, mandar adiante, vender.
AL.IEN.ATION, *s.*, alienação, venda, transferência.

ALIENEE — 368 — ALMOND

AL.IEN.EE, *s., Jur.,* alienatário, cessionário.

AL.IEN.ISM, *s.,* alienismo; *Psic.,* tratamento de doenças mentais.

AL.IEN.IST, *s.,* alienista.

AL.IEN.OR, *s.,* alienador, alienante.

AL.IEN RES.ID.ENT CARD, *s.,* carteira de identidade de estrangeiro.

AL.I.FORM, *adj.,* aliforme (que tem forma de asa).

ALIGHT, *adv.,* iluminado, brilhante, aceso, inflamado.

ALIGN, *v.,* alinhar, colocar em ordem.

A.LIGN.MENT, *s.,* alinhamento, enfileiramento; aliança (com alguém ou partido).

A.LIGN.ER, *s.,* alinhador.

A.LIKE, *adj.,* semelhante, parecido.

AL.I.MENT, *s.,* alimento; *v.,* alimentar.

AL.I.MENT.AL, *adj.,* nutritivo.

AL.I.MEN.TA.RY, *adj.,* alimentar, nutritivo, alimentício.

AL.I.MEN.TA.TION, *s.,* alimentação.

AL.I.MEN.TA.TIVE, *adj.,* alimentício, nutritivo.

AL.I.MO.NY, *s., Jur.,* pensão (alimentícia).

A.LINE, *v.,* o mesmo que *align.*

ALINE.MENT, *s.,* alinhamento.

AL.I.PED, *adj., Zool.,* alípede.

AL.I.PHAT.IC, *adj., Quím.,* alifático.

ALIVE, *adj.,* vivo, alegre, satisfeito, ágil, esperto.

AL.KA.LI, *s.,* álcali.

AL.KA.LIM.E.TER, *s., Quím.,* alcalímetro.

AL.KA.LIM.E.TRY, *s., Quím.,* alcalimetria.

AL.KA.LINE, *adj.,* alcalino(a).

AL.KA.LIN.I.TY, *s., Quím.,* alcalinidade.

AL.KAL.I.FY, *v.,* alcalinizar.

AL.KA.LI.ZATION, *s., Quím.,* alcalização.

AL.KA.LIZE, *v.,* tornar alcalino, alcalinizar.

AL.KOR.AN, *s.,* alcorão, corão.

ALL, *adj.,* todo, tudo; *pl.,* todos, todas; *adv.,* de todo, completamente.

ALLAH, *s.,* Alá.

ALL-A.ROUND, *adj.,* versátil, bom para todos (os propósitos).

AL.LAY, *v.,* acalmar, aliviar, pacificar.

AL.LAY.ING, *s.,* alívio, consolo, consolação, paz.

AL.LAY.MENT, *s.,* apaziguamento, alívio, moderação.

AL.LE.GA.TION, *s.,* alegação, desculpa.

AL.LEGE, *v.,* alegar, aduzir, dizer, declarar.

AL.LEG.ED, *adj.,* suposto.

AL.LEG.ED.LY, *adv.,* supostamente.

AL.LE.GIANCE, *s.,* lealdade, amizade, fidelidade.

AL.LE.GIANT, *adj.,* fiel, obediente, leal.

AL.LE.GOR.IC, *adj.,* alegórico.

AL.LE.GOR.I.CAL, *adj.,* alegórico.

AL.LE.GO.RIST, *s.,* alegorista.

AL.LE.GO.RIS.TIC, *adj.,* alegórico.

AL.LE.GO.RIZE, *v.,* alegorizar, figurar, metaforizar.

AL.LE.GO.RY, *s.,* alegoria, parábola.

AL.LE.LU.IA, *s.,* aleluia.

AL.LER.GEN, *s., Med.,* alergênico (substância que provoa alergia).

AL.LER.GIC, *adj.,* alérgico (a algo).

AL.LER.GIST, *s., Med.,* alergista.

AL.LER.GY, *s.,* alergia.

AL.LE.VI.ATE, *v.,* aliviar, diminuir, decrescer.

AL.LE.VI.A.TION, *s.,* alívio, consolo.

AL.LEY, *s.,* aleia, alameda, viela, beco.

AL.LI.ANCE, *s.,* aliança.

AL.LIED, *adj., s.,* aliado.

AL.LIES, *s. pl.,* aliados das duas guerras mundiais.

AL.LI.GA.TOR, *s.,* aligátor, jacaré, crocodilo.

ALL-IM.POR.TANT, *adj.,* importantíssimo, crucial.

ALL-IN *(UK), adj.,* tudo incluído.

ALL-IN.CLUS.IVE, *adj.,* que inclui ou abrange tudo.

ALL-IN-ONE, *s.,* macaquinho (roupa de baixo para ciclistas); macacão (com calças compridas).

AL.LIT.ER.ATE, *v.,* aliterar; empregar aliteração (figura de linguagem).

AL.LIT.ER.A.TION, *s.,* aliteração (figuira de linguagem).

ALL-NIGHT, *adv.,* toda a noite.

AL.LO.CA.BLE, *adj.,* aquinhoável, designável.

AL.LO.CATE, *v.,* alocar.

AL.LO.CA.TION, *s.,* alocação, localização, situação.

AL.LO.CA.TOR, *s.,* distribuidor, o que partilha.

AL.LO.CU.TION, *s.,* alocução, fala, discurso.

AL.LO.MORPH, *s., Ling.,* alomorfe (variante de um morfema).

AL.LO.PATH, AL.LO.PATH.IST, *s.,* alopata.

AL.LO.PA.THY, *s.,* alopatia.

AL.LOT, *v.,* aquinhoar, ratear, destinar.

AL.LOT.A.BLE, *adj.,* distribuível.

AL.LOT.ER, *s.,* distribuidor.

AL.LOT.MENT, *s.,* partilha, distribuição.

AL.LO.TROPE, *s., Quím.,* alótropo.

AL.LO.TROP.IC, *adj., Quím.,* alotrópico.

AL.LOT.RO.PY, *s., Quím.,* alotropia, alotropismo.

ALL-OUT, *adj.,* máximo, o maior; *adv.,* com tudo.

AL.LOW, *v.,* permitir, ceder, aceitar, admitir.

AL.LOW.A.BLE, *adj.,* aceitável, permitido.

AL.LOW.ANCE, *s.,* mesada, ajuda, pensão, diária.

AL.LOY, *v.,* ligar,juntar metais; *s.,* fusão de metais.

AL.LOY.ING, *s.,* fusão de metais.

ALL-POW.ER.FUL, *adj.,* todo-poderoso.

ALL-PUR.POSE, *adj.,* para muitas finalidades, multi-utilidades.

ALL RIGHT, *adj.,* certo, correto.

ALL-ROUND, *adj., (linguagem coloquial),* em redor, por todos os lados, global.

ALL-ROUND.ER *(UK), s., Fut.,* jogador que se destaca em várias posições.

ALL.SPICE, *s., Bot.,* pimenta-da-jamaica.

AL.LUDE, *v.,* aludir, referir, dizer de.

AL.LURE, *s.,* fascinação, encantamento; *v.,* fascinar, encantar; persuadir, seduzir.

AL.LURE.MENT, *s.,* encantamento, fascinação; sedução; engodo.

AL.LUR.ER, *s.,* tentador, sedutor.

AL.LUR.ING, *adj.,* fascinante, encantador(ora).

AL.LU.SION, *s.,* alusão, referência.

AL.LU.SIVE, *adj.,* referente, alusivo.

AL.LU.VI.ON, *s.,* aluvião.

ALL-WEATH.ER, *adj.,* para qualquer tempo (clima).

AL.LY, *s.,* aliado; *v.,* aliar-se, juntar-se.

AL.MA.NAC, *s.,* almanaque, calendário, folhinha.

AL.MIGHT.I.LY, *adv.,* poderosamente; extraordinariamente.

AL.MIGHT.I.NESS, *s.,* onipotência.

AL.MIGHT.Y, *adj.,* onipotente, todo-poderoso; poderoso, grande.

AL.MOND, *s.,* amêndoa; amendoeira.

ALMONER · ·· 369 ··· AMBIGUOUSLY

AL.MO.NER, *s.*, esmoleiro.
AL.MOST, *adv.*, quase.
ALMS, *s.*, esmola, dádiva, donativo.
AL.OE, *s., Bot.*, aloés, babosa.
AL.O.ETIC, *adj.*, que contém aloés, aloético.
A.LOFT, *adv.*, no ar, nas alturas; *Náut.*, no topo do mastro.
A.LONE, *adj.*, sozinho, solitário, só.
A.LONG, *prep.*, ao longo de, ao lado de.
A.LONG.SHORE, *adv.*, na costa, ao longo da praia.
A.LONG.SIDE, *prep.*, ao lado de, junto a.
A.LOOF, *adj.*, indiferente, desinteressado; *adv.*, de longe, à distância.
A.LOUD, *adv.*, em voz alta.
A.LOW, *adv.*, baixo.
ALP, *s.*, montanha, cume, pico.
AL.PAC.A, *s.*, alpaca.
AL.PEN.GLOW, *s.*, arrebol das montanhas.
AL.PEN.STOCK, *s.*, bastão de alpinista.
AL.PHA, *s.* alfa; início.
AL.PHA.BET, *s.*, alfabeto, abecê.
AL.PHA.BET.IC, *adj.*, alfabético.
AL.PHA.BET.I.CAL, *adj.*, alfabético.
AL.PHA.BET.I.CAL.LY, *adv.*, em ordem alfabética.
AL.PHA.BET.I.ZA.TION, *s.*, alfabetização.
AL.PHA.BET.IZE (-ISE), *v.*, alfabetizar.
AL.PHA.NU.MER.IC, *adj.*, alfanumérico.
AL.PINE, *adj.*, alpino.
AL.PIN.ISM, *s.*, alpinismo.
ALPINIST, *s.*, alpinista.
AL.READ.Y, *adv.*, já, agora, neste momento.
AL.SO, *adv.*, também, igualmente, além disso.
AL.SO-RAN, *s., Esp.*, bom cavalo competidor, mas que não tem colocação.
ALT, *abrev.* de *alternate* (substituto); *abrev.* de *altitude* (altitude).
AL.TAR, *s.*, altar.
AL.TER, *v.*, alterar, mudar, modificar.
AL.TER.A.BIL.I.TY, *s.*, variabilidade.
AL.TER.A.BLE, *adj.*, alterável, mutável.
AL.TER.A.BLY, *adv.*, de modo alterável.
AL.TER.A.TION, *s.*, alteração.
AL.TER.A.TIVE, *s., adj.*, alterativo; *Med.*, alterante.
AL.TER.CATE, *v.*, altercar, litigar, lutar, disputar.
AL.TER.CA.TION, *s.*, altercação, discussão, briga.
AL.TER E.GO, *s.*, o segundo "eu"; amigo íntimo.
AL.TER.NANT, *adj.*, alternante.
AL.TER.NATE, *v.*, alternar, alterar; *adj.*, alternado.
AL.TER.NATE.LY, *adv.*, alternadamente.
AL.TER.NA.TION, *s.*, alternação, alternância.
AL.TER.NA.TIVE, *s.*, alternativa, opção; *adj.*, alternativo(a).
AL.TER.NA.TIVE.LY, *adv.*, por outro lado, de outro modo.
AL.TER.NATOR, *s.*, alternador (eletricidade).
AL.THORN, *s., Mús.*, saxotrompa.
AL.THOUGH, *conj.*, apesar de, embora, ainda que.
AL.TIM.E.TER, *s.*, altímetro.
ALTIM.E.TRI.CAL, *adj.*, altimétrico.
AL.TIM.E.TRY, *s.*, altimetria.
AL.TI.TUDE, *s.*, altitude, altura.
AL.TI.TU.DI.NAL, *adj.*, altitudinal.
AL.TO, *s., Mús.*, contralto; *adj.*, relativo à contralto.
AL.TO.CU.MU.LUS, *s., Lat., Meteor.*, altocúmulo.
AL.TO.GETH.ER, *adv.*, completamente, de todo.

AL.TO-RI.LIE.VO, *s., It., Art.*, alto-relevo.
AL.TO.STRA.TUS, *s., Lat., Meteor.*, alto-estrato.
AL.TRU.ISM, *s.*, altruísmo.
AL.TRU.IST, *s.*, altruísta.
AL.TRU.IS.TIC, AL.TRU.IS.TI.CAL, *adj.*, altruístico(a).
ALU.MI.NATE, *s., Quim.*, aluminato.
AL.U.MIN.I.UM, *s.*, alumínio.
A.LU.MI.NOUS, *adj.*, aluminoso (que contém alumínio).
A.LUM.NUS, *s., (Lat. pl. alumni)* ex-aluno (já graduado).
AL.VE.O.LAR, *adj.*, alveolar.
AL.VE.O.LATE, *adj.*, alveolado.
AL.VE.O.LUS, *s.*, alvéolo.
AL.VINE, *adj., Med.*, alvino, intestinal.
AL.WAYS, *adv.*, sempre.
AM, *v.*, 1ª pessoa do sing., pres. do indic., verbo aux. *to be*.
A.MAIN, *adv.*, com rapidez, com energia.
A.MAL.GAM, *s.*, amálgama.
A.MAL.GAM.A.BLE, *adj.*, amalgamável.
A.MAL.GAM.ATE, *v.*, amalgamar, misturar, ligar, unir-se.
A.MAL.GAM.A.TION, *s.*, amalgamação.
AM.A.NI.TA, *s., Bot.*, amanita (fungo venenoso).
A.MAN.U.EN.SIS, *s.*, amanuense, secretário, escrevente.
AM.A.RANTH, *s., Bot.*, amaranto; *Poet.*, planta que murcha; a cor púrpura.
AM.A.RYL.LIS, *s., Bot.*, amarílis, açucena.
AMASS, *v.*, juntar, amontoar, acumular.
A.MASS.A.BLE, *adj.*, acumulável, amontoável.
A.MASS.MENT, *s.*, aglomeração, amontoado, montão.
AM.A.TEUR, *adj., s.*, amador, diletante.
AM.A.TEUR.ISH, *adj.*, amador.
AM.A.TEUR.ISH.NESS, *s.*, amadorismo, diletantismo.
AM.A.TO.RY, *adj.*, amador, erótico, sensual.
AM.A.TIVE, *adj.*, amativo, amoroso, sensual.
AM.A.TIVE.LY, *adv.*, amorosamente, sensualmente.
AM.A.TO.RI.AL, *adj.*, o mesmo que *amatory*.
AM.A.TORY, *adj.*, amatório, amoroso, erótico.
A.MAZE, *v.*, espantar, assustar.
A.MAZED, *adj.*, surpreso(a), assombrado(a).
A.MAZE.MENT, *s.*, surpresa, assombro.
A.MAZ.ING, *adj.*, incrível, surpreendente.
A.MAZ.ING.LY, *adv.*, surpreendentemente, assombrosamente.
AM.A.ZON, *s.*, amazona.
AM.A.ZO.NI.AN, *adj.*, amazônico(a).
AM.BAS.SA.DOR, *s.*, embaixador.
AM.BAS.SA.DO.RI.AL, *adj.*, diplomático, representativo.
AM.BAS.SA.DOR.SHIP, *s.*, embaixada, incluindo cargo e missão de embaixador.
AM.BAS.SA.DRESS, *s.*, embaixadora ou embaixatriz.
AM.BER, *s.*, âmbar, cor de âmbar, amarelo ambarino; *adj.*, ambárico, ambarino.
AM.BER.GRIS, *s.*, âmbar cinzento ou pardo.
AM.BI.ANCE, *s.*, ver *ambience*.
AM.BIENT, *adj.*, ambiente, circunvizinho.
AM.BI.DEX.TER *s.*, ambidestro.
AM.BI.DEX.TROUS, *adj.*, ambidestro; *fig.*, muito ágil, ardiloso.
AM.BI.ENCE, *s.*, ambiência; ambiente (atmosfera)
AM.BI.ENT, *s.*, ambiente.
AM.BI.GU.I.TY, *s.*, ambiguidade.
AM.BIG.U.OUS, *adj.*, ambíguo(a).
AM.BIG.U.OUS.LY, *adv.*, de modo ambíguo.

AMBIT — 370 — AN

AM.BIT,s., âmbito.
AM.BI.TION, s., ambição.
AM.BI.TIOUS, adj., ambicioso, ganancioso.
AM.BI.TIOUS.NESS, s., ambição, ganância.
AM.BIV.A.LENCE, s., incerteza, ambivalência.
AM.BIV.A.LENT, adj., ambivalente.
AM.BI.VER.SION, s., Psic., ambiversão.
AM.BI.VERT, s., Psic., ambiverso.
AM.BLE, v., passear.
AM.BLER, s., cavalo que anda a passo ligeiro, esquipador.
AM.BRO.SI.A, s., ambrosia ; Mit., alimento dos deuses.
AM.BRY, s., armário, guarda-louça; Bib., armário para adornos.
AM.BU.LANCE, s., ambulância.
AM.BU.LANT, adj., ambulante, ambulatório.
AM.BU.LATE, v., andar, perambular.
AM.BU.LA.TO.RY, s., galeria coberta, corredor; adj., ambulatório, ambulativo; variável, modificável.
AM.BUS.CADE, s., emboscada; v., emboscar, fazer uma cilada.
AM.BUS.CAD.ER, s., o que fica de emboscada.
AM.BUSH, s., emboscada; v., emboscar.
A.ME.LIO.RATE, v., melhorar, arrumar, aperfeiçoar.
A.ME.LIO.RA.TION, s., melhoria, melhoramento, aperfeiçoamento.
A.MEN, interj., amém.
A.ME.NA.BLE, adj., receptivo (a algo), acessível, afável; obediente.
A.ME.NA.BLY, adv., responsavelmente; de maneira submissa.
A.MEND, v., emendar, corrigir.
A.MEND.A.BLE, adj., emendável, melhorável.
A.MEND.A.TORY, adj., corretivo, modificativo.
A.MEND.MENT, s., emenda, correção.
A.MENDS, s., indenização, reparação.
A.MEN.IT.IES, s. pl., comodidades, conforto.
A.MEN.I.TY, s., amenidade, afabilidade, suavidade.
A.MENT, s., Bot., amentilho, amento.
A.MER.ASI.AN, s., filho de pai americano e mãe asiática.
A.MERCE, v., multar, punir, castigar.
A.MERCE.A.BLE, adj., sujeito a multa ou punição.
A.MER.I.CAN, adj., s., americano.
A.MER.I.CAN.ISM, s., americanismo.
A.MER.I.CAN.IZE, v., americanizar.
A.MER.I.CAN.IZED, adj., americanizado.
AM.ER.I.CI.UM, s., Quím., amerício.
AM.ER.IND, s., forma abreviada de American Indian.
AM.ER.IN.DI.AN, adj., ameríndio.
AM.ER.IN.DIC, adj., o mesmo que Amerindian.
AM.E.THYST, s., ametista.
AMI.A.BLE, adj., amável, afável, bondoso.
A.MI.A.BLY, adv., amavelmente.
AM.I.AN.THUS, s., Min., amianto.
AM.I.CA.BIL.I.TY, s., amizade, afeto.
AM.I.CA.BLE, adj., amigável.
AM.I.CA.BLE.NESS, s., amabilidade, gentileza, cordialidade.
AM.I.CA.BLY, adv., amigavelmente.
A.MID, prep., no meio, entre, de per meio de.
AM.IDE, s., amido.
AM.I.DOL, s., Quím., amidol.
A.MINE, s., Quím., amina.
A.MI.NO A.CIDS, s. pl., aminoácidos, ácidos aminados.

A.MISS, adj., defeituoso, impróprio, errado.
A.MISS.I.BLE, adj., que pode ser perdido.
AM.I.TY, s., amizade.
AM.ME.TER, s., Elet., amperômetro.
AM.MO, s., Mil., munição.
AM.MO.NIA, s., amônia.
AM.MO.NI.AC, s., amoníaco.
AM.MO.NI.A.CAL, adj., amoniacal, amôniaco.
AM.MO.NI.ATE, v., Quím., combinar com amônia.
AM.MON.I.FI.CA.TION, s., Quím., amonificação.
AM.MO.NITE, s., amonite.
AM.MO.NI.UM, s., Quím., amônio.
AM.MU.NI.TION, s., munições.
AM.NE.SIA, s., amnésia.
AM.NES.TY, s., anistia; v., anistiar.
AM.NI.O.CEN.TE.SIS, s., Med., amniocêntese.
A.MOE.BA, AMEBA, s., Zool., ameba.
A.MOE.BI.FORM, A.ME.BI.FORM, adj., amebiforme.
A.MONG, prep., entre, no meio de.
A.MOR.AL, adj., amoral.
AM.OR.IST, s., namorador, amante, amador.
A.O.ROUS, adj., amoroso, afetuoso, carinhoso.
A.MOR.PHISM, s., amorfismo, amorfia.
A.MOR.PHOUS, adj., amorfo.
AM.OR.TIS.A.BLE, AM.OR.TIZ.A.BLE, adj., amortizável.
AM.OR.TI.ZA.TION, s., amortização.
AM.OR.TIZE, v., amortizar.
A.MOUNT, s., soma, quantia, monte, valor; v., importar, elevar.
A.MOUR, s., galanteio, amor, namoro.
AM.PER.AGE, s., Eletric., amperagem.
AM.PERE, s., Eletric., ampère.
AM.PER.SAND, s., sinal gráfico "&", sinal tironiano ou eitza.
AM.PHET.A.MINE, s., anfetamina.
AM.PHIB.IA, s. pl., anfíbios, batráquios.
AM.PHIB.I.AN, adj., s., anfíbio, batráquio.
AM.PHIB.I.OUS, adj., anfíbio.
AM.PHI.BOL.O.GY, s., anfibologia, ambiguidade.
AM.PHI.THE.ATRE, s., anfiteatro.
AM.PHO.RA, s., ânfora.
AM.PLE, adj., amplo, vasto, extenso.
AM.PLE.NESS, s., amplidão,imensidão, vastidão.
AM.PLI.ATE, v., ampliar, aumentar.
AM.PLI.A.TION, s., ampliação, aumento.
AM.PLI.FI.CA.TION, s., amplificação.
AM.PLI.FI.ER, s., amplificador.
AM.PLI.FY, v., ampliar, aumentar.
AM.PLI.TUDE, s., amplitude, grandeza.
AM.PLI.TUDE MOD.U.LA.TION, s., Eletron., modulação de amplitude.
AM.PLY, adv., amplamente, consideravelmente.
AM.PU.TATE, v., amputar, cortar algo.
AM.PU.TA.TION, s., amputação.
AM.PU.TA.TOR, s., o que amputa, amputador.
AM.PU.TEE, s., amputado, mutilado.
AM.U.LET, s., amuleto.
A.MUSE, v., divertir, agradar, distrair.
A.MUSED, adj., divertido, entretido, distraído.
A.MUSE.MENT, s., diversão, divertimento, agrado, folga.
A.MUS.ING, adj., agradável, divertido, folgado.
A.MYG.DA.LA, s., amêndoa; Anat., amígdala.
AN, art. ind. um, uma – usado antes de vogal ou "h" mudo.

ANABAPTIST ••• 371 ••• ANGLOMANIAC

AN.A.BAP.TIST, *s., Rel.*, anabatista.
AN.A.CHRON.IC, *adj.*, anacrônico.
AN.A.CHRON.I.CAL, *adj.*, o mesmo que *anachronic*.
AN.A.CHRO.NISM, *s.*, anacronismo.
AN.A.CHRO.NIS.TIC, *adj.*, anacrônico.
AN.A.CHRO.NIS.TI.CAL, *adj.*, o mesmo que *anachronistic*.
AN.A.CO.LU.THON, *s., Gram.*, anacoluto (figura de linguagem).
AN.A.CON.DA, *s., Zool.*, anaconda, sucuri; pitão, jiboia.
A.NAC.RE.ON.TIC, *s.*, anacreôntico (poema); *adj.*, anacreôntico(a), festivo.
A.NAE.MIA, *s.*, anemia.
A.NAE.MIC, *adj.*, anêmico.
AN.AE.RO.BI.UM, *s., Biol.*, anaeróbio.
AN.AES.THE.SIA, *s.*, anestesia.
AN.AES.THE.TIZE, *v.*, anestesiar.
AN.A.GRAM, *s.*, anagrama.
A.NAL, *adj.*, anal.
AN.AL.GE.SIC, *adj.*, analgésico.
AN.A.LECTS, *s.*, anacleto, antologia.
AN.A.LEP.TIC, *s., Med.*, analéptico; *adj.*, analéptico, que restaura.
AN.AL.GE.SI.A, *s., Med.*, analgesia.
AN.AL.GE.SIC, *s. e adj.*, analgésico.
AN.A.LOG, *adj.*, analógico.
AN.A.LOG.IC, *adj.*, analógico.
ANAL.O.GIZE, *v.*, analogizar, representar por analogia.
ANAL.O.GOUS, *adj.*, análogo, semelhante, parecido.
AN.A.LOGUE *(UK)*, **ANALOG** *(US)*, *s.*, análogo; *adj.*, analógico,
A.NAL.O.GY, *s.*, analogia.
AN.AL.PHA.BET, *s. e adj.*, analfabeto.
AN.AL.PHA.BET.IC, *adj.*, analfabeto, iletrado, ignorante.
AN.A.LYS.A.BLE, AN.A.LYZ.A.BLE, *adj.*, analisável.
AN.A.LYSE, *v.*, analisar, examinar.
A.NAL.Y.SIS, *s.*, análise.
AN.A.LYST, *s.*, analista.
AN.A.LYT.IC, AN.A.LYT.I.CAL, *adj.*, analítico.
AN.A.LYT.ICS, *s.*, analítica (ciência).
AN.A.LYZE, ANALYSE, *v.*, analizar, decompor; examinar.
AN.AM.NE.SIS, *s.*, anamnese; *Med.*, dados de uma doença.
AN.APH.O.RA, *s.*, anáfora.
AN.APH.RO.DIS.I.AC, *s.* anafrodisíaco; *adj., Med.*, anafrodisíaco(a).
AN.A.PHY.LAC.TIC, *adj., Med.*, anafilático.
AN.A.PHY.LAX.IS, *s., Med.*, anafilaxia.
AN.AR.CHIC, *adj.*, anárquico.
AN.AR.CHISM, *s.*, anarquismo.
AN.AR.CHIST, *s.*, anarquista.
AN.AR.CHY, *s.*, anarquia.
A.NATH.E.MA, *s.*, anátema.
AN.A.TOM.IC, *adj.*, anatômico.
AN.A.TOM.ICAL, *adj.*, anatômico.
A.NAT.O.MIST, *s.*, anatomista; analista.
A.NAT.O.MIZE, *v.*, anatomizar.
A.NAT.O.MY, *s.*, anatomia.
AN.CES.TOR, *s.*, antepassado, antenato.
AN.CES.TRAL, *adj.*, ancestral.
AN.CES.TRY, *s.*, ascendência.
AN.CHOR, *s.*, âncora; *v.*, fundear, ancorar, atracar.
AN.CHOR.AGE, *s.*, ancoragem, porto.

AN.CHOR.MAN, *s.*, âncora (apresentador de tv).
AN.CHOR.WOM.AN, *s.*, âncora (apresentadora de tv).
AN.CHO.VY, *s.*, anchova.
AN.CIENT, *adj.*, velho, antigo, vetusto.
AN.CIENT.RY, *s.*, antiguidade.
AN.CIL.LA.RY, *adj.*, auxiliar; subordinado, ancilar.
AND, *conj.*, bem como, assim como, também, além disso.
AN.DAN.TE, *s., It., Mus.*, andante; *adj., Mus.*, vagaroso; *adv.*, lentamente, andante.
AN.DRO.GEN, *s.*, andrógeno.
AN.DROG.Y.NOUS, *adj.*, andrógino(a).
AN.DROG.Y.NY, *s.*, androginia.
AN.DROID, *s.*, androide, robô.
AN.DROL.O.GY, *s., Med.*, andrologia.
AN.DROM.E.DA, *s., Mit. e Astron.*, Andrômeda.
AN.EC.DO.TAL, *adj.*, anecdotal.
AN.EC.DOTE, *s.*, anedota, pilhéria.
AN.EC.DOTIC, *adj.*, anedótico.
AN.EC.DOTIST, *s.*, anedotista.
ANE.MIA, *s.*, anemia, debilidade.
ANE.MIC, *adj.*, anêmico, fraco, debilitado.
AN.E.MOM.E.TER, *s.*, anemômetro.
A.NEM.O.NE, *s.*, anêmona.
AN.EN.CEPH.A.LY, *s., Med.*, anencefalia.
AN.GE.LE.NO, AN.GE.LI.NO, *s.*, habitante ou nativo de Los Angeles.
AN.ES.THE.TIC, *s. e adj., Med.*, anestético, anestesiante.
ANESTHETIST, *s., Med.*, anestesista.
AN.ES.THE.TI.ZA.TION, *s., Med.*, ato ou processo de anestesiar; estado de anesthesia.
ANES.THE.TIZE, *v.*, anestesiar.
AN.EU.RISM, *s.*, aneurisma.
ANEW, *adv.*, de novo, outra vez, novamente.
AN.GEL, *s.*, anjo.
AN.GEL.IC, *adj.*, angélico, angelical, divino.
AN.GEL.I.CAL, *adj.*, o mesmo que *angelic*.
AN.GEL.I.CAL.LY, *adv.*, angelicamente.
AN.GE.LUS, *s., Rel.*, ângelus (oração que reza em horários específicos); hora da ave-maria (18 horas).
AN.GER, *s.*, raiva, ira, fúria, cólera.
AN.GI.CO, *s., Bot.*, angico.
AN.GI.NA, *s.*, angina.
AN.GI.OL.O.GY, *s., Anat.*, angiologia.
AN.GI.O.MA, *s., Med.*, angioma.
AN.GI.O.SPERM, *s., Bot.*, angiosperma.
AN.GI.O.SPER.MOUS, *adj.*, angiospermo.
AN.GLE, *s.*, ângulo, esquina, curva.
AN.GLED, *adj.*, angular, anguloso.
AN.GLER, *s.*, pescador.
AN.GLI.CAN, *adj., s.*, anglicano.
AN.GLI.CISM, *s.*, anglicismo.
AN.GLI.CIST, *s.*, estudante da língua inglesa.
AN.GLI.CI.ZA.TION, *s.*, anglicização, processo de anglizar(-se).
AN.GLI.CIZE, *v.*, inglesar.
AN.GLING, *s.*, pesca (de caniço).
AN.GLIST, *s.*, o mesmo que *anglicist*.
AN.GLO-, *prefix.*, elemento que denota "inglês" ou "Inglaterra".
AN.GLO-AM.ER.I.CAN, *s. e adj.*, anglo-americano.
AN.GLO.MA.NI.A, *s.*, anglomania.
AN.GLO.MA.NI.AC, *s.*, anglomaníaco.

ANGLOPHILE ···372··· ANTARCTIC CIRCLE

AN.GLO.PHILE, *s.*, anglófilo.
AN.GLO.PHIL.I.A, *s.*, anglofilia.
AN.GLO-SA.XON, *adj.*, *s.*, anglo-saxão.
AN.GO.LAN, *adj.*, angolano(a); *s.*, angolano(a), nativo ou habitante de Angola.
AN.GO.RA, *s.*, angorá.
AN.GOS.TU.RA, *s.*, *Farm.*, agostura (casca).
AN.GRI.LY, *adj.*, raivoso, furioso.
AN.GRI.NESS, *s.*, raiva, ira, fúria.
AN.GRY, *adj.*, irado, zangado, furioso.
ANGST, *s.*, ânsia.
ANG.STROM, *s.*, *Fís.*, angström.
AN.GUISH, *s.*, dor, sofrimento, desconforto.
AN.GUISHED, *adj.*, angustiado(a).
AN.GU.LAR, *adj.*, angular.
AN.GU.LAR.I.TY, *s.*, angularidade; magreza; *fig.*, rudeza.
AN.GU.LATE, *adj.*, angulado, anguloso.
AN.GU.LA.TION, *s.*, formação angular.
AN.HY.DRIDE, *s.*, *Quím.*, anidrido.
AN.HY.DROUS, *adj.*, anidro.
ANIL, *s.*, anil.
AN.I.LINE, *s.*, anilina.
AN.I.MAL, *adj.*, *s.*, animal.
AN.I.MAL.CULE, *s.*, animálculo.
AN.I.MAL.ISM, *s.*, animalismo; carnalidade.
AN.I.MAL.IST, *s.*, *Art.*, animalista.
AN.I.MAL.IS.TIC, *adj.*, relativo a animalismo; animalesco.
AN.I.MAL.I.TY, *s.*, animalidade, sensualidade.
AN.I.MAL.I.ZA.TION, *s.*, animalização.
AN.I.MAL.IZE, *v.*, animalizar, bestializar.
AN.I.MATE, *v.*, animar, avivar, entusiasmar; *adj.*, animado, vivo.
AN.I.MAT.ED, *adj.*, animado(a).
AN.I.MAT.ING, *adj.*, animador, estimulante; tonificante.
AN.I.MA.TION, *s.*, animação.
AN.I.MA.TIVE, *adj.*, animador, animante.
AN.I.MA.TOR, *s.*, aquele que faz desenhos animados.
AN.I.MISM, *s.*, *Fil.*, animismo.
AN.I.MIST, *s.*, animista.
AN.I.MIS.TIC, *adj.*, animista.
AN.I.MOS.I.TY, *s.*, animosidade.
AN.I.MUS, *s.*, ódio, contrariedade, aversão, repulsa.
AN.ISE, *s.*, anis, erva-doce.
AN.I.SEED, *s.*, semente de anis.
AN.I.SETTE, *s.*, aniseta, anisete (licor de anis).
AN.KLE, *s.*, tornozelo.
AN.NAL.IST, *s.*, cronista, historiador.
AN.NALS, *s.*, anais, crônicas, histórias.
AN.NEAL, *v.*, recozer (vidro, metal etc.); temperar; *fig.*, fortalecer.
AN.NEX, *v.*, anexo, adendo, aditamento; *v.*, anexar, conectar, ligar.
AN.NEX.ABLE, *adj.*, anexável.
AN.NEX.ATION, *s.*, anexação, aditamento.
AN.NEXE, *s.*, anexo.
AN.NI.HI.LA.BLE, *adj.*, aniquilável, destrutível.
AN.NI.HI.LATE, *v.*, aniquilar.
AN.NI.HI.LA.TION, *s.*, aniquilação.
AN.NI.HI.LA.TIVE, *adj.*, aniquilador, destrutivo.
AN.NI.HI.LA.TOR, *s.*, aniquilador, destruidor.
AN.NI.VER.SA.RY, *s.*, aniversário.
AN.NO DO.MI.NI, *Lat.*, no ano do Senhor, qualquer ano da era Cristã (*abrev.*: A.D.).

AN.NO.TATE, *v.*, anotar, escrever, referir.
AN.NO.TA.TED, *adj.*, comentado(a).
AN.NO.TA.TION, *s.*, anotação, referência.
AN.NOUNCE, *v.*, anunciar, dizer, proclamar.
AN.NOUNCE.MENT, *s.*, anúncio, declaração.
AN.NOUNCER, *s.*, locutor de tv/rádio.
AN.NOY, *v.*, aborrecer, incomodar, enjoar.
AN.NOY.ANCE, *s.*, enjoo, aborrecimento, incômodo.
AN.NOY.ING, *adj.*, irritante.
AN.NU.AL, *adj.*, anual; *s.*, anuário.
AN.NUAL.LY, *adv.*, anualmente.
AN.NUAL RATE, *s.*, *Com.*, taxa annual.
AN.NUAL RE.PORT, *s.*, *Com.*, *(UK)* balanço annual.
AN.NU.I.TANT, *s.*, anuitário, beneficiário de uma anuidade.
AN.NU.I.TY, *s.*, anuidade.
AN.NUL, *v.*, anular, invalidar.
AN.NU.LAR, *v.*, anelado.
AN.NU.LAR ECLIPSE, *s.*, *Astron.*, eclipse anular.
AN.NU.LA.RI.TY, *s.*, a forma anular.
AN.NU.LA.TION, *s.*, formação de anéis.
AN.NU.LET, *s.*, anelzinho, pequeno anel.
AN.NUL.MENT, *s.*, anulação, cancelamento.
ANNUM, *s.*, *Lat.*, *per annum*: por ano.
AN.NUN.CI.ATE, *v.*, anunciar, proclamar, declarar.
AN.NUN.CI.A.TION, *s.*, anunciação.
AN.NUN.CI.A.TOR, *s.*, anunciador, sinal luminoso ou auditivo.
AN.ODE, *s.*, *Tecnol.*, ânodo.
A.NOD.IC, *adj.*, *Eletr.*, anódico.
A.NOINT, *v.*, ungir, untar, azeitar.
A.NOINT.MENT, *s.*, unção.
A.NOM.A.LISM, *s.*, anomalia, anomalismo.
A.NOM.A.LIS.TIC, *adj.*, anomalístico.
A.NOM.A.LOUS, *adj.*, anômalo, diferente.
A.NOM.A.LOUS.NESS, *s.*, anormalidade, disformidade.
A.NOM.A.LY, *s.*, anomalia, anormalidade.
AN.O.NYM, *s.*, anônimo.
AN.O.NYM.I.TY, *s.*, anonimato.
ANON.Y.MOUS, *adj.*, anônimo.
ANON.Y.MOUS.LY, *adv.*, anonimamente.
A.NOPH.E.LES, *s.*, *Zool.*, anófele (mosquito comum, do gên. *Anopheles*).
AN.O.RAK *(UK)*, *s.*, anoraque.
AN.O.RECT.IC, *adj.*, anorético.
AN.O.REX.IA, *s.*, *Med.*, anorexia.
AN.O.REX.IC, *adj.*, anoréxico.
AN.O.RE.XY, *s.*, *Med.*, o mesmo que *anorexia*.
AN.OTH.ER, *pron.*, *adj.*, outro, outra.
AN.SER.INE, *adj.*, de ou relativo a gansos; *fig.*, estúpido.
AN.SWER, *v.*, responder, retrucar; *s.*, resposta, solução.
AN.SWER.ABLE, *adj.*, responsável, respondível.
AN.SWER.ABLY, *adv.*, responsavelmente; refutavelmente.
ANT, *s.*, *Zool.*, formiga.
AN.TA, *s.*, *Zool.*, anta.
ANT.AC.ID, *s.*, antiácido.
AN.TAG.O.NISM, *s.*, antagonismo, adversidade.
AN.TAG.O.NIST, *s.*, antagonista, opositor.
AN.TAG.O.NIS.TIC, *adj.*, antagônico.
AN.TAG.O.NIZE, *v.*, contrariar, antagonizar, opor.
ANT.ARC.TIC, *s.*, Antártica; *adj.*, antártico(a).
ANT.ARC.TIC CIR.CLE, *s.*, Círculo Polar Antártico.

ANTARCTIC OCEAN ··· 373 ··· ANTONYM

ANT.ARC.TIC O.CEAN, *s.*, Oceano Antártico.
ANT-BEAR, *s., Zool.*, tamanduá-bandeira; porco-da-terra.
ANT.EAT.ER, *s.*, tamanduá.
AN.TE.CEDE, *v.*, anteceder, preceder.
AN.TE.CED.ENCE, *s.*, antecedência, preferência.
AN.TE.CED.ENT, *adj.*, antecedente, precedente.
AN.TE.CES.SOR, *s.*, antecessor.
AN.TE.CHAM.BER, *s.*, antecâmara.
AN.TE.CHOIR, *s.*, antecoro.
AN.TE CHRIS.TUM, *Lat.*, antes de Cristo (*abrev.:* a.C.).
AN.TE.DATE, *s.*, antedata; *v.*, antedatar; preceder.
AN.TE.DI.LU.VI.AN, *adj.*, antediluviano.
AN.TE.LOPE, *s.*, antílope.
AN.TE.ME.RID.I.AN, *adj.*, antemeridiano.
AN.TE.NA.TAL, *adj.*, pré-natal.
AN.TEN.NA, *s.*, antena.
AN.TE.NUP.TIAL, *adj.*, antenupcial.
AN.TE.RI.OR, *adj.*, anterior, precedente.
AN.TE.RI.OR.I.TY, *s.*, anterioridade, precedência; prioridade.
AN.TE.RI.OR.LY, *adv.*, anteriormente, previamente.
AN.TE.RI.OR.NESS, *s.*, anterioridade.
AN.TE.ROOM, *s.*, antessala.
AN.THEM, *s.*, hino.
AN.THER, *s., Bot.*, antera.
AN.THER.ID.I.UM, *s., Bot.*, anterídio.
AN.THE.SIS, *s., Bot.*, antese, florescência.
ANT.HILL, *s.*, formigueiro.
AN.THO.LOG.IC.AL, *adj.*, antológico.
AN.THOL.O.GIST, *s.*, antologista.
AN.THOL.O.GY, *s.*, antologia.
AN.THRAX, *s.*, antraz.
AN.THRO.POID, *s.*, antropoide.
AN.THRO.POCENTRIC, *adj.*, antropocêntrico.
AN.THRO.POID, *s.* e *adj.*, antropoide.
AN.THRO.PO.LOG.IC, *adj.*, antropológico.
AN.THRO.POL.O.GIST, *s.*, antropólogo.
AN.THRO.POL.O.GY, *s.*, antropologia.
AN.THRO.PO.MOR.PHIC, *adj.*, antropomorfo, semelhante à forma humana.
AN.THRO.PO.MOR.PHI.CAL, *adj.*, o mesmo que *anthropomorphic*.
AN.THRO.PO.MOR.PHOUS, *adj.*, antropomorfo.
AN.THRO.POPH.A.GOUS, *adj.*, antropófago.
AN.THRO.POPH.A.GY, *s.*, antropofagia.
AN.THRO.POS.O.PHY, *s.*, antroposofia.
AN.THU.RI.UM, *s., Bot.*, antúrio.
AN.TI-, *pref.*, anti, contra, contrário a.
AN.TI, *s.*, oponente; aquele que é do contra.
AN.TI-AIR.CRAFT, *adj.*, antiaéreo(a).
AN.TI.BI.OT.IC, *adj.*, *s.*, antibiótico.
AN.TI.BODY, *s.*, anticorpo.
AN.TI.CHLOR, *s., Quím.*, anticloro.
AN.TIC.I.PANT, *s.*, o que antecipa, prevê; *adj.*, antecipador, expectante.
AN.TIC.I.PATE, *v.*, prever, prognosticar, vaticinar, prevenir.
AN.TIC.I.PA.TION, *s.*, antecipação, vaticínio, expectativa.
AN.TIC.I.PA.TIVE, *adj.*, antecipado.
AN.TIC.I.PA.TIVELY, *adv.*, previdentemente; preventivamente.
AN.TI.CLER.I.CAL, *s.*, anticlerical; *adj.*, anticlerical.
AN.TI.CLER.I.CAL.ISM, *s.*, anticlericalismo.
AN.TI.CLI.MAX, *s.*, anticlímax.

AN.TI.CLOCK.WISE, *adj.*, em sentido anti-horário.
AN.TI.CO.AG.U.LANT, *s.* e *adj., Med.*, anticoagulante.
AN.TICS, *s. pl.*, palhaçadas; *pej.*, trapaças.
AN.TI.CY.CLONE, *s., Meteor.*, anticiclone.
AN.TI.DE.PRES.SANT, *adj.*, antidepressivo(a); *s.*, antidepressivo (o remédio).
AN.TI.DOTE, *s.*, antídoto.
AN.TI.FE.BRILE, *s.*, antipirético, antifebril; *adj.*, antipirético.
AN.TI.FREEZE, *s.* e *adj.*, anticongelante.
AN.TI.FRIC.TION, *s.*, antifricção; *adj.*, que reduz o atrito ou fricção.
AN.TI.FLU, *adj.*, antigripal.
AN.TI.GOV.ERN.MENT, *adj.*, antigovernamental.
AN.TI.HE.RO, *s.*, anti-herói.
AN.TI.HIS.TA.MINE, *adj.*, anti-histamínico(a); *s.*, anti-histamínico (o remédio).
AN.TI-IM.PE.RI.AL.ISM, *s.*, anti-imperialismo.
AN.TI-IN.FLA.TION.A.RY, *s.*, anti-inflacionário.
AN.TIL.O.GY, *s.*, antilogia, contradição.
AN.TI.MAT.TER, *s., Fís.*, antimatéria.
AN.TI.MIS.SILE, *s.*, antimíssil.
AN.TI.MO.NY, *s.*, antimônio.
AN.TI.NATION.AL, *adj.*, antinacional.
AN.TI.NO.MI.AN, *s.* e *adj., Rel.*, antinomiano.
AN.TIN.O.MY, *s.*, antinomia, oposição, contrariedade.
AN.TI.PA.THET.IC, *adj.*, antipático.
AN.TIP.A.THY, *s.*, antipatia.
AN.TI.PER.SON.NEL, *adj., Mil.*, que combate pessoas (diz-se de arma de fogo).
AN.TI.PER.SPI.RANT, *s., ant.*, desodorante.
AN.TI.PHON, *s.*, antífona.
AN.TIPH.O.NAL, *s.*, antifonário; *adj.*, antifônico.
AN.TI.PODE, *s.*, antípoda.
AN.TI.PY.RET.IC, *s.* e *adj., Med.*, antipirético.
AN.TI.QUAR.I.AN, *adj.*, *s.*, antiquário.
AN.TI.QUARY, *s.*, antiquário.
AN.TI.QUATE, *adj.*, antiquado, velho, antigo.
AN.TI.QUAT.ED, *adj.*, antiquado(a).
AN.TIQUE, *adj.*, antigo; *s.*, antiguidade.
AN.TIQ.UI.TY, *s.*, antiguidade.
AN.TI-SE.MIT.IC, *adj.*, antissemita.
AN.TI-SEM.I.TISM, *s.*, antissemitismo.
AN.TI.SEP.TIC, *adj.*, *s.*, antisséptico.
AN.TI.SO.CIAL, *adj.*, antissocial.
AN.TI.SO.CIAL.IST, *adj.*, antissocialista.
AN.TI.SPAS.MOD.IC, *adj.*, antiespasmódico.
AN.TIS.TAT.IC, *adj.*, antiestético(a).
AN.TI-TANK, *adj., Mil.*, antitanque.
AN.TI.TER.ROR.IST, *s.*, antiterrorista.
AN.TITH.E.SIS, *s.*, antítese.
AN.TI.THET.I.CAL, *adj.*, antiético.
AN.TI.TOX.IC, *adj.*, atitóxico; relativo às antitoxinas.
AN.TI.TOX.IN, *s.*, antídoto, antitóxico, contraveneno.
AN.TI.TOX.INE, *s.*, o mesmo que *antitoxin*.
AN.TI.TRUST, *adj.*, antitruste.
AN.TI.TYPE, *s., Teol.*, antítipo (figura que representa outra).
AN.TI.VI.RUS, *s., Med.*, antivírus.
AN.TI.WORLD, *s., Fís.*, mundo hipotético.
AN.TLER.ED, *adj.*, que tem armação ou cornos, galhada.
AN.TLERS, *s. pl.*, tipo de cornos em cervídeos, esgalhos.
AN.TO.NYM, *s.*, antônimo.

ANTONYMY ·· 374 ·· APPELLANT

AN.TON.Y.MY, s., antonímia.
ANTS *(US)*, s., desconforto, irritação, impaciência.
AN.U.RI.A, s., *Med.*, anúria, anurese, supressão da urina.
A.NUS, s., ânus.
AN.VIL, s., bigorna.
ANX.I.ETY, s., inquietação, ansiedade.
ANX.IOUS, *adj.*, ansioso, preocupante, angustiante.
ANX.IOUS.LY, *adv.*, ansiosamente, nervosamente.
ANX.IOUS.NESS, s., ansiosidade, ansiedade.
AN.Y, *adj., pron.*, algum, alguma, alguns, algumas, certo, certos.
AN.Y.BODY, *pron.*, alguém, qualquer um, fulano.
AN.Y.HOW, *adv.*, de qualquer maneira, de qualquer modo.
AN.Y.ONE, *pron.*, alguém, um tipo indeterminado.
AN.Y.PLACE, *adv.*, ver *anywhere*.
AN.Y.THING, *pron.*, alguma coisa, algo.
AN.Y.WAY, *adv.*, de qualquer maneira.
AN.Y.WHEN, *adv.*, de qualquer jeito.
AN.Y.WHERE, *adv.*, em qualquer lugar, em todo lugar.
A.OR.TA, s., aorta.
A.PACE, *adv.*, depressa, com rapidez.
A.PACH.E, s., apache (membro de tribo guerreira).
A.PA.RE.JO *(US)*, s., albarda de couro estofada de origem mexicana.
A.PART, *adv.*, à parte, separadamente, isoladamente; ao lado, independentemente; em pedaços.
A.PART.HEID, s., segregação na África; apartaide.
A.PART.MENT, s., apartamento.
A.PART.NESS, s., separação, isolamento.
AP.A.THET.IC, *adj.*, apático, abúlico, indiferente.
AP.A.THY, s., apatia, indiferença.
APE, s., macaco, símio, bugio, mono.
A.PEAK, *adv.*, a pique, vertical, perpendicular.
A.PEN.NINES, *s. pl.*, Apeninos (montes).
A.PEPSY, s., apepsia.
A.PE.RI.ENT, s., *Med.*, laxante, purgante; *adj.*, laxativo.
A.PE.RI.OD.IC, *adj.*, aperiódico.
A.PE.RI.O.DIC.I.TY, s., aperiodicidade.
APE.RI.TIF, s., aperitivo.
AP.ER.TURE, s., orifício, buraco, abertura.
A.PEX, s., ápice, cume, pico.
A.PHA.SIA, s., afasia, rouquidão.
A.PHAS.I.AC, APHASIC, *adj.*, afásico.
A.PHE.LI.ON, s., *Astron.*, afélio.
A.PHID, s., pulgão.
A.PHO.NIA, s., afonia.
A.PHO.NIC, *adj.*, afônico.
APH.O.RISM, s., aforismo.
APH.O.RIST, s., aforista.
APH.RO.DIS.I.AC, *adj., s.*, afrodisíaco.
APH.THA, s., afta.
A.PI.AN, *adj.*, de ou relativo a abelhas.
A.PI.A.RIST, s., apicultor.
A.PI.AR.Y, s., apiário, colmeia.
AP.IC.AL, *adj.*, apical, relativo ao ápice.
A.PIC.U.LATE, *adj., Bot.*, apiculado (que é provido de pequena ponta ou apículo).
A.PI.CUL.TUR.AL, *adj.*, apicultural, apícola (relativo à apicultura).
API.CUL.TURE, s., apicultura.
A.PI.CUL.TUR.IST, s., apicultor.

A.PIECE, *adv.*, cada, cada um, um por vez.
AP.ISH, *adj.*, macaqueiro; que arremeda; ridículo.
A.PLOMB, s., desenvoltura, postura.
A.POC.A.LYPSE, s., apocalipse.
A.POC.A.LYP.TIC, *adj.*, apocalíptico.
A.POC.RY.PHA, s., escritos falsos, apócrifos.
A.POD, *adj.*, ápode, sem pés.
AP.O.GEE, s., apogeu, clímax, ápice.
A.PO.LIT.I.CAL, *adj.*, apolítico, neutro.
A.POL.O.GET.IC, *adj.*, apologético.
APOL.O.GET.I.CAL, *adj.*, apologético.
A.POL.O.GET.I.CAL.LY, *adv.*, apologeticamente, em tom de desculpas.
APOL.O.GET.ICS, s., apologia.
A.POL.O.GISE(ZE), v., apologizar, apresentar desculpas.
AP.O.LOGUE, s., apólogo, fábula.
A.POL.O.GY, s., apologia, defesa.
AP.O.PLEC.TIC, *adj.*, apoplético(a); *fig.*, furioso(a).
AP.O.PLEXY, s., apoplexia.
A.POS.TATE, s., apóstata, renegado.
A.POS.TA.TISE(ZE), v., apostatar, cometer apostasia, abjurar.
A.POS.TA.SY, s., apostasia.
A.POS.TA.TIZE, v., apostatar.
A.POS.TIL, s., apostila.
A.POS.TLE, s., apóstolo.
A.POS.TLE.SHIP, s., apostolado.
A.POS.TO.LATE, s., *Rel.*, apostolado; *p. ext.*, difusão de uma doutrina.
AP.OS.TO.LIC, *adj., Rel.*, apostólico (relativo aos doze Apóstolos); relativo ao papa.
AP.OS.TO.LI.CAL, *adj.*, o mesmo que *apostolic*.
AP.OS.TO.LI.CISM, s., apostolicismo.
A.POS.TRO.PHE, s., apóstrofo, apóstrofe.
A.POS.TRO.PHIZE, v., apostrofar, admoestar.
AP.O.THEM, s., *Mat.*, apótema.
A.POTH.E.O.SIS, s., apoteose, deificação; glorificação, exaltação.
AP.PAL, v., horrorizar, apavorar, amedrontar.
AP.PA.LA.CHIANS, *s. pl.*, Apalaches (montes).
AP.PALL, v., intimidar, assustar, amedrontar.
AP.PALL.ED, *adj.*, horrorizado.
AP.PALL.ING, *adj.*, terrível, horrorizante, apavorante.
AP.PALL.ING.LY, *adv.*, espantosamente; *fig.*, terrivelmente.
AP.PA.NAGE, s., apanágio (bem de família, propriedade legítima; dotação).
AP.PA.RAT.US, s., *Lat.*, aparelho, aparelhamento; instrumento; sistema, organização.
AP.PAR.EL, s., traje, vestuário, roupa; v., vestir, trajar, adornar.
AP.PAR.ENT, *adj.*, aparente, claro, evidente.
AP.PAR.ENT.LY, *adv.*, aparentemente.
AP.PA.RI.TION, s., aparição, fantasmas.
AP.PEAL, v., apelar, chamar a atenção; s., apelo, pedido.
AP.PEAL.ER, *adj., s.*, apelante.
AP.PEAL.ING, *adj.*, atraente, sedutor, fascinante.
AP.PEAR, v., aparecer, parecer.
AP.PEAR.ANCE, s., aparecimento, aparência.
AP.PEASE, v., pacificar, apaziguar, acalmar.
AP.PEASE.MENT, s., apaziguamento, pacificação.
AP.PEAS.ING, *adj.*, apaziguante, mitigante, conciliante.
AP.PEL.LANT, s., *Jur.*, apelante, recorrente ; *adj.*, apelante, suplicante.

APPELLATE ••375•• ARABIC NUMERALS

AP.PEL.LATE, *adj., Jur.,* apelatório; relativo à Corte de Apelação.

AP.PEL.LA.TION, *s.,* nome, título; ato ou modo de denominar ou designar.

AP.PEL.LA.TIVE, *s.,* apelativo (substantivo comum: nome, designação); *adj.,* apelativo, designativo.

APPELLEE, *s., Jur.,* apelado, recorrido.

AP.PEND, *v.,* juntar, anexar, conectar, colocar junto.

AP.PEND.AGE, *s.,* apêndice.

AP.PEN.DANT, *adj.,* ligado, unido, junto, conexo.

AP.PEN.DI.CES, *s. pl.,* ver *appendix.*

AP.PEN.DI.CI.TIS, *s.,* apendicite.

AP.PEND.I.CLE, *s.,* apendículo (pequeno apêndice).

AP.PEN.DI.CU.LAR, *adj., Anat., Zool.,* apendicular.

AP.PEN.DIX, *s.,* apêndice.

AP.PER.CEP.TION, *s.,* percepção.

AP.PER.TAIN, *v.,* pertencer, ser de.

AP.PER.TI.NENT, *adj.,* pertencente.

AP.PE.TENCE, *s.,* apetite, vontade, desejo.

AP.PE.TITE, *s.,* apetite.

AP.PE.TI.TIVE, *adj.,* apetitivo, apetitoso.

AP.PE.TIZ.ER, *s.,* entrada (comida); aperitivo (bebida).

AP.PE.TIZ.ING, *s.,* apetitoso (comida).

AP.PLAUD, *v.,* aplaudir, ovacionar, aclamar.

AP.PLAUSE, *s.,* aplauso, ovação.

AP.PLE, *s.,* maçã.

AP.PLI.ABLE, *adj.,* aplicável.

AP.PLI.ANCE, *s.,* aparelho.

AP.PLI.CA.BIL.I.TY, *s.,* aplicabilidade.

AP.PLI.CA.BLE, *adj.,* aplicável.

AP.PLI.CANT, *s.,* pretendente, candidato (a emprego).

AP.PLI.CA.TION, *s.,* aplicação, requerimento.

AP.PLI.CA.TIVE, *adj.,* aplicativo, aplicável, prático.

AP.PLI.CA.TOR, *s.,* aplicador, quem ou o que aplica; *Med., Tec.,* aparelho aplicador.

AP.PLIED, *adj.,* aplicado, usado, colocado.

AP.PLI.ER, *s.,* aplicador, quem aplica; o que está sendo aplicado.

AP.PLY, *v.,* aplicar, colocar, usar, praticar.

AP.POINT, *v.,* apontar, indicar, nomear.

AP.POINT.A.BLE, *adj.,* que pode ser designado.

AP.POINT.EE, *s.,* indivíduo designado para cargo ou dignidade.

AP.POINT.ER, *s.,* nomeador, designador.

AP.POINT.IVE, *adj.,* designativo, que está sujeito à nomeação.

AP.POINT.MENT, *s.,* agenda, encontro marcado, nomeação.

AP.POR.TION, *v.,* dividir (dinheiro, responsabilidade).

AP.POR.TION.MENT, *s.,* partilha, aquinhoamento, rateio.

AP.POSE, *v.,* observar, analisar, examinar.

AP.PO.SITE, *adj.,* próprio, apropriado, exato, certo.

AP.PO.SI.TION, *s.,* justaposição, aposição, colocação.

AP.PRAIS.ABLE, *adv.,* apreciável, aprazível.

AP.PRAIS.AL, *s.,* apreciação, análise.

AP.PRAISE, *v.,* apreciar, examinar, observar.

AP.PRE.CIA.BLE, *adj.,* apreciável, apreciativo(a).

AP.PRE.CIA.BLY, *adj.,* visivelmente.

AP.PRE.CI.ATE, *v.,* apreciar, avaliar, estimar, agradecer.

AP.PRE.CI.A.TION, *s.,* apreciação.

AP.PRE.CI.A.TIVE, *adj.,* apreciativo(a).

AP.PRE.HEND, *v.,* apreender, prender, temer.

AP.PRE.HEN.SION, *s.,* apreensão, temor.

AP.PRE.HEN.SIVE, *adj.,* apreensivo, temeroso.

AP.PRE.HEN.SIVE.LY, *adv.,* apreensivamente.

AP.PREN.TICE, *s.,* aprendiz, estagiário.

AP.PREN.TICE.SHIP, *s.,* aprendizagem.

AP.PRISE, AP.PRIZE, *v.,* informar, referir, avisar.

AP.PROACH, *v.,* aproximar, ir para, dirigir-se, achegar-se.

AP.PROACH.ABIL.I.TY, *s.,* ser acessível, acessibilidade.

AP.PROACH.A.BLE, *adj.,* acessível.

AP.PROACH.ING, *adj.,* achegado, próximo.

AP.PRO.BATE, *v.,* aprovar, sancionar, deferir.

AP.PRO.BA.TION, *s.,* aprovação, sanção.

AP.PRO.PRI.ATE, *adj.,* apropriado(a); *v.,* apropriar-se de; destinar; atribuir.

AP.PRO.PRI.A.TION, *s.,* apropriação.

AP.PRO.PRI.ATE.LY, *adv.,* adequadamente.

AP.PRO.PRI.A.TIVE, *adj.,* relativo à apropriação, apropriador; ávido.

AP.PROV.ABLE, *adj.,* aprovável.

AP.PROV.AL, *s.,* aprovação, deferimento, consentimento.

AP.PROVE, *v.,* aprovar, liberar, autorizar, conceder.

AP.PROV.ED, *adj.,* aprovado.

AP.PROV.ER, *s.,* aprovador; *Jur.,* réu que depõe contra os cúmplices de um crime.

AP.PROV.ING, *adj.,* favorável.

AP.PROX.I.MAL, *adj., Anat.,* proximal.

AP.PROX.I.MATE, *v.,* aproximar, aproximar-se, avizinhar-se.

AP.PROX.I.MATE.LY, *adv.,* aproximadamente.

AP.PROX.I.MA.TION, *s.,* aproximação.

APRI.COT, *s.,* damasco.

APRIL, *s.,* abril.

APRI.ORIST, *s.,* apriorista.

APRI.OR.I.TY, *s.,* apriorismo, prioridade.

APRON, *s.,* avental.

AP.RO.POS, *adj.,* concernente, pertinente; *adv.,* oportunamente; *prep.,* a propósito (de).

APT, *adj.,* apto, capaz, hábil, capacitado.

AP.TI.TUDE, *s.,* aptidão, capacidade, pendor.

AP.TI.TUDE TEST, *s.,* teste de aptidão.

APT.LY, *adv.,* apropriadamente.

APT.NESS, *s.,* aptidão.

AQ.UA.LUNG, *s.,* aparelho para respiração debaixo d'água.

AQ.UA.MA.RINE, *s.,* água-marinha.

AQ.UA.NAUT, *s.,* aquele que é treinado para permanecer debaixo da água para pesquisas.

AQ.UA.PLANE *(UK)*, *v.,* aquaplanar.

AQ.UA.RELLE, *s.,* aquarela.

AQ.UA.RIST, *s.,* aquarista, auqriófilo.

AQUA.R.IUM, *s.,* aquário.

A.QUAR.I.US, *s., Astron.,* constelação aquário; *Astrol.,* signo aquário.

AQUAT.IC, *adj.,* aquático.

A.QUAT.ING, *s., Art.,* aquatinta (processo de gravação); *v.,* gravar pelo processo de aquatinta.

AQ.UE.DUCT, *s.,* aqueduto.

AR.AB, *adj., s.,* árabe.

A.RA.BES.QUE, *s.,* arabesco; *adj.,* arabesco, cinzelado ou pintado em estilo arabesco; fantástico, excêntrico.

ARA.BI.AN, *adj.,* árabe.

AR.A.BIC, *adj.,* arábico(a), árabe; *s.,* arábico (língua escrita e cultura).

AR.A.BIC NU.ME.RALS, *s. pl.,* números arábicos.

ARABIST · 376 · ARMATURE

AR.A.BIST, *s.*, arabista.
AR.A.BLE, *adj.*, arável.
A.RACH.NID, *s.*, aracnídeo.
A.RACH.NOID, *s.*, *Anat.*, aracnoide; *adj.*, aracnóideo.
A.RACH.NO.PHO.BI.A, *s.*, aracnofobia (medo mórbido de aranhas).
AR.A.MA.IC, *s.* e *adj.*, aramaico.
AR.A.PON.GA, *s.*, *Zool.*, araponga.
AR.AU.CAR.IA, *s.*, araucária, pinheiro.
AR.BI.TER, *s.*, árbitro, juiz.
AR.BIT.RAGE, *s.*, arbitragem.
AR.BIT.RA.MENT, *s.*, arbitramento.
AR.BI.TRARY, *adj.*, arbitrário.
AR.BI.TRATE, *v.*, arbitrar, julgar, avaliar.
AR.BI.TRA.TION, *s.*, arbitragem.
AR.BO.RE.OUS, *adj.*, arbóreo; arborizado; arborescente.
AR.BO.RES.CENCE, *s.*, arborescência.
AR.BO.RES.CENT, *adj.*, arborescente.
AR.BOR.I.CUL.TURE, *s.*, arboricultura.
AR.BOR.I.CUL.TUR.IST, *s.*, arboricultor.
AR.BOR.I.ZA.TION, *s.*, arborização.
ARC, *s.*, arco.
AR.CADE, *s.*, arcada.
AR.CAD.ED, *adj.*, arcado, com arcos.
AR.CA.DI.AN, *s.*, árcade; *adj.*, árcade, bucólico, idílico.
AR.CAD.I.AN.ISM, *s.*, arcadismo.
AR.CANE, *adj.*, arcano, enigmático.
AR.CA.NUM, *s.*, arcano, grande segredo ou mistério.
ARCH, *s.*, arco; *v.*, arquear, fazer com arcos.
AR.CHAE.O.LOG.IC.AL, *adj.*, arqueológico(a).
AR.CHAE.OLO.GIST, *s.*, arqueólogo.
AR.CHAE.OL.O.GY, *s.*, arqueologia.
AR.CHA.IC, *adj.*, arcaico.
AR.CHA.ISM, *s.*, arcaísmo.
AR.CHA.IZE, *v.*, arcaizar.
ARCH.AN.GEL, *s.*, arcanjo, anjo.
ARCH.BISH.OP, *s.*, arcebispo.
ARCH.DEA.CON, *s.*, arcediago, arquidiácono.
ARCH.DEA.CON.RY, *s.*, dignidade ou residência do arcediago.
ARCH.DI.O.CESE, *s.*, arquidiocese.
ARCH.DU.CAL, *adj.*, arquiducal.
ARCH.DUCH.ESS, *s.*, arquiduquesa.
ARCH.DUKE, *s.*, arquiduque.
AR.CHED, *adj.*, arqueado(a), em arco; curvado.
ARCH.EN.E.MY, *s.*, arqui-inimigo.
AR.CHE.OL.O.GIST, *s.*, o mesmo que *archaeologist*.
AR.CHE.OL.O.GY, *s.*, o mesmo que *archaeology*.
ARCH.E.O.ZO.IC, *s.* e *adj.*, *Geol.*, arqueozoico.
ARCH.ER, *s.*, arqueiro.
ARCH.ER.Y, *s.*, arco e flecha (arte e equipamento).
AR.CHE.TYP.AL, *s.*, arquétipo.
AR.CHE.TYPE, *s.*, arquétipo.
AR.CHE.TYP.I.CAL, *adj.*, o mesmo que *archetypal*.
AR.CHI.PEL.A.GO, *s.*, arquipélago.
AR.CHI.TECT, *s.*, arquiteto.
AR.CHI.TEC.TON.IC, *adj.*, arquitetônico.
AR.CHI.TEC.TURE, *s.*, arquitetura.
AR.CHIVE, *s.*, arquivo.
AR.CH.IVIST, *s.*, arquivista.
ARCH.LY, *adv.*, maliciosamente; engenhosamente.

AR.CHON, *s.*, *Hist.*, arconte (magistrado da Grécia Antiga).
ARCH.WAY, *s.*, viaduto.
ARC.TIC, *s.*, Ártico; *adj.*, ártico.
ARC.TIC CIR.CLE, *s.*, Círculo Polar Ártico.
ARC.TIC O.CEAN, *s.*, Oceano Glacial Ártco.
ARC.U.ATE, *adj.*, arqueado (curvado como um arco).
AR.CU.A.TION, *s.*, arqueamento, arqueação.
AR.DEN.CY, *s.*, ardência, calor.
AR.DENT, *adj.*, ardente, quente, caloroso, apaixonado.
AR.DOUR *(UK)*, **AR.DOR** *(US)*, *s.*, ardor, fervor, zelo.
AR.DOUS, *adj.*, árduo(a).
ARE, *v.*, ver conjugação do verbo *to be*.
A.RE.A, *s.*, área, zona, região, superfície.
A.RE.A.WAY, *s.*, rebaixo (rebaixamento ou passagem entre edifícios).
AR.E.FY, *v.*, secar, ressecar.
ARENA, *s.*, arena, estádio.
AR.E.O.MET.RY, *s.*, areometria.
AREN'T, *v.*, contração de *are not*.
A.RE.O.LA, *s.*, aréola.
AR.E.OP.A.GUS, *s.*, *do Gr.*, areópago.
AR.GENT, *s.*, *Poet.*, prata; *adj.*, argênteo, prateado.
AR.GEN.TIN.E.AN, **AR.GEN.TINE**, *adj.*, *s.*, argentino.
AR.GIL, *s.*, argila, barro.
AR.GILACEOUS, *adj.*, agiláceo (que contém argila).
AR.GO.NAUT, *s.*, *do Gr.*, *Mit.*, argonauta.
AR.GO.SY, *s.*, grande navio mercante ou frota desses navios; grande suprimento.
AR.GOT, *s.*, calão, linguagem chula.
AR.GU.ABLE, *adj.*, discutível.
AR.GU.ABLY, *adv.*, possivelmente, talvez.
AR.GUE, *v.*, discutir, argumentar, convencer.
AR.GU.MENT, *s.*, argumento, contenda, discussão.
AR.GU.MEN.TA.TION, *s.*, argumentação, discussão.
AR.GU.MEN.TA.TIVE, *adj.*, argumentativo, questionador(a).
AR.GUS, *s.*, argos; *Mit.*, personagem de cem olhos; *fig.*, guardião atento.
AR.GUTE, *adj.*, arguto, aguçado, agudo.
ARIA, *s.*, *Mús.*, ária, melodia.
AR.I.AN.ISM, *s.*, arianismo.
AR.ID, *adj.*, árido, seco, ressecado.
A.RID.I.TY, *s.*, aridez, secura.
A.RI.ES, *s.*, *Astron.*, constelação; *Astrol.*, signo Carneiro.
A.RIGHT, *adv.*, corretamente, com acerto.
A.RISE, *v.*, levantar-se, subir, alçar-se, erguer-se.
A.RIS.TOC.RA.CY, *s.*, aristocracia.
A.RIS.TO.CRA.TIC, *adj.*, aristocrático.
A.RIS.TO.CRAT, *s.*, aristocrata.
A.RIS.TO.TE.LI.AN, *s.* e *adj.*, aristotélico.
A.RIS.TO.TYPE, *s.*, *Fot.*, aristótipo (espécie de papel fotográfico muito sensível).
A.RITH.ME.TIC, *s.*, aritmética.
A.RITH.ME.TI.CIAN, *s.*, aritmético.
ARK, *s.*, arca, refúgio, esconderijo.
ARM, *s.*, braço, manga; seção, setor.
AR.MA.DA, *s.*, *Mar.*, armada (frota de barcos ou navios).
AR.MA.DIL.LO, *s.*, tatu.
AR.MA.GED.DON, *s.*, *Bíb.*, Armagedom; *fig.*, grande conflito final.
AR.MA.MENT, *s.*, armamento.
AR.MA.TURE, *s.*, armadura; couraça, blindagem.

ARMBAND •• 377 •• ASEXUALREPRODUCTION

ARM.BAND, s., braçadeira.
ARM.CHAIR, s., poltrona.
ARMED, adj., armado.
ARMED FORC.ES, s. pl., forças armadas (terra, mar e ar).
ARMED SER.VI.CES, s. pl., forças armadas (em tempos de paz).
AR.ME.NI.AN, adj., armênio(a); s., habitante ou nativo da Armênia.
ARM.FUL, s., braçada.
ARM.HOLE, s., cava.
AR.MI.STICE, s., armistício.
ARM.LET, s., pulseira, bracelete.
AR.MOR (US), **AR.MOUR** (UK), s., armadura; blindagem; couraça; fig., proteção; v., blindar, courar.
AR.MOURED, adj., blindado, encouraçado.
ARM.PIT, s., axila, sovaco.
ARM.REST, s., braço (de poltrona etc.).
ARMS, s. pl., armas (peças ou instrumentos de defesa e ataque); brasões e desenhos heráldicos.
AR.MY, s., exército.
AR.NI.CA, s., Bot., arnica.
ARO.MA, s., aroma, perfume. ·
AR.O.MAT.IC, adj., aromático.
ARO.MA.TIZE, v., aromatizar, perfumar.
AROUND, adv., prep., ao redor, em volta, perto.
AROUS.AL, s., excitação, o despertar de desejos, sentimentos, interesses.
A.ROUSE, v., acordar, despertar.
AR.RAIGN, v., processar, levar a juízo, denunciar.
AR.RAIGN.MENT, s., acusação, denúncia, processo.
AR.RANGE, v., arranjar, organizar, ordenar.
AR.RANGE.MENT, s., arranjo, acerto, acordo.
AR.RANT, adj., completo, reconhecido, notório.
AR.RAY, s., formação militar, ordem; série (objetos etc.); ostentação, pompa; v., enfeitar.
AR.REARS, s., dívida em atraso, dívidas.
AR.REST, v., arrestar, prender, deter; s., arresto, prisão.
AR.REST.A.TION, s., prisão, encarceramento, arresto.
AR.REST.ING, adj., interessante, impressionante.
AR.REST.MENT, s., arresto, prisão.
AR.RHYTH.MI.A, s., Med., arritmia.
AR.RIS, s., Arq., aresta, canto.
AR.RIV.AL, s., chegada, vinda.
AR.RIVE, v., chegar, vir.
AR.RO.GANCE, s., arrogância, presunção.
AR.RO.GANT, adj., arrogante, presunçoso.
AR.RO.GANT.LY, adv., arrogantemente.
AR.ROW, s., flecha, seta.
AR.ROW.ROOT, s., araruta, maranta.
AR.ROY.O, s., do Es., arroio; riacho; barranco, ravina.
ARSE, s., ânus, traseiro.
AR.SE.NAL, s., arsenal.
AR.SE.NATE, s., Quím., arseniato.
AR.SE.NIC, s., arsênico.
AR.SON, s., Jur., incêndio premeditado.
AR.SO.NIST, s., incendiário.
ART, s., arte, jeito, habilidade, engenho.
AR.TE.FACT, s., artefato.
AR.TE.RI.AL, adj., arterial.
AR.TE.RI.O.SCLE.RO.SIS, s., arteriosclerose.
AR.TER.Y, s., artéria.

AR.TE.SIAN, adj., artesanato.
ART.FUL, adj., astuto.
ART.FUL.NESS, s., astúcia, sagacidade.
AR.THRIT.IC, adj., artrítico.
AR.THRI.TIS, s., artrite.
AR.THRO.SIS, s., Med., artrose (doença de uma articulação).
AR.TI.CHOKE, s., alcachofra.
AR.TI.CLE, s., artigo, cláusula, objeto, peça.
AR.TIC.U.LAR, adj., articular.
AR.TIC.U.LATE, adj., articulado(a), bem pronunciado, nítido(a); v., articular, pronunciar.
AR.TIC.U.LAT.ED, adj., o mesmo que articulative.
AR.TIC.U.LA.TION, s., articulação.
AR.TIC.U.LA.TIVE, adj., que tem articulações, articulado.
AR.TIC.U.LA.TOR, s., articulador.
AR.TI.FACT, s., artefato.
AR.TI.FICE, s., artifício, artimanha, engano.
AR.TI.FI.CIAL, adj., artificial.
AR.TI.FI.CI.AL.I.TY, s., artificialidade, artificialismo.
AR.TI.FI.CIAL.LY, adv., artificialmente.
AR.TIL.LER.IST, s., artilheiro.
AR.TIL.LERY, s., artilharia.
AR.TIL.LERYMAN, s., o mesmo que artillerist.
AR.TI.SAN, s., artesão, artista. ·
ART.IST, s., artista.
AR.TISTE, s., artista.
AR.TIS.TIC, adj., artístico.
AR.TIS.TIC.AL.LY, adv., artisticamente.
AR.TIST.RY, s., obra artística; talento artístico.
ART.LESS, adj., ingênuo(a), simples.
AS, conj., quanto, como, tão; prep., como.
AS.BES.TOS, s., Min., asbesto, amianto.
AS.CA.RI.A.SIS, s., Med., ascaríase.
AS.CEND, v., ascender, subir, alçar-se.
AS.CEND.A.BLE, adj., acessível, atingível.
AS.CEND.AN.CY, s., domínio.
AS.CEND.ANT, s., ascendência, superioridade.
AS.CEND.ENCE, s., ascendência.
AS.CEND.ENT, s., o mesmo que ascendant.
AS.CEND.ING, adj., ascendente.
AS.CEN.SION, s., ascensão, subida.
AS.CENT, s., subida, aclive, rampa, ladeira.
AS.CER.TAIN, v., verificar, examinar.
AS.CER.TAIN.MENT, s., investigação, busca, demanda.
AS.CE.SIS, s., ascese (prática do asceticismo).
AS.CET.IC, s., asceta; adj., ascético.
AS.CET.I.CISM, s., ascetismo.
AS.CID.I.AN, s., Zool., ascídio (animais acéfalos que se fixam rochas).
ASCII, abrev., American Standard Code for Information Interchange: Padrão Internacional para Representação de Caracteres.
A.SCOR.BIC, s. e adj., Quím., ascórbico.
AS.CRIBE, v., atribuir.
AS.CRIP.TION, s., atribuição, imputação; declaração.
A.SEP.TIC, adj., asséptico.
A.SEP.T.I.CISE, **A.SEP.T.I.CIZE**, v., assepsiar, asseptizar.
ASEX.U.AL, adj., assexuado.
ASEX.U.AL.I.TY, s., assexualidade.
ASEX.U.AL.LY, adv., assexualmente.
ASEX.U.AL RE.PRO.DUC.TION, s., Biol., reprodução asexual.

ASH   ···378···   ASTOUND

ASH, s., cinza.
A.SHAMED, adj., envergonhado.
A.SHAM.ED.NESS, s., vergonha.
ASH-CAN, ASH.CAN, s., lixeira.
A.SHORE, adv., em terra.
ASH-TRAY, ASH.TRAY, s., cinzeiro.
ASHY, adj., cinzento, pálido, cor cinza.
ASIA, s., Ásia.
ASIAN, adj., asiático.
ASI.AT.IC (US), adj., asiático.
ASIDE, adj., à parte, apartado; s., aparte.
AS.I.NINE, adj., asinino, tolo.
AS.I.NIN.I.TY, s., burrice, tolice, estupidez.
ASK, v., perguntar, indagar.
A.SKANCE, adv., desconfiadamente; de viés, de soslaio.
A.SKANT, adv., o mesmo que askance.
A.SKEW, adv., torto.
ASK.ING, s., pedido, petição, súplica.
A.SLEEP, adj., dormente, adormecido; v., dormir.
A.SLOPE, adj., inclinado, oblíquo; adv., inclinadamente.
AS.PAR.A.GINE, s., Quím., asparagina, alteína.
AS.PAR.A.GUS, s., aspargo.
AS.PECT, s., aspecto, aparência, expressão.
AS.PECT.ABLE, adj., visível, admirável.
AS.PEN, s., álamo.
AS.PER.GE, v., aspergir, benzer.
AS.PER.I.TY, s., aspereza, rispidez.
AS.PERSE, v., difamar, falar mal, caluniar.
AS.PERS.ER, s., caluniador, difamador.
AS.PER.SIONS, s. pl., calúnias, suspeitas, maledicências.
AS.PHALT, s., asfalto; v., asfaltar.
AS.PHAL.TIC, adj., asfáltico.
AS.PHYX.IA, s., asfixia.
AS.PHYX.I.ATE, v., asfixiar, sufocar.
AS.PHYX.I.A.TION, s., ato de asfixiar, sufocamento.
AS.PHYX.Y, s., o mesmo que asphyxia.
AS.PIC, s., geleia (de carne ou peixe); Bot., alfazema.
AS.PIR.ANT, s. e adj., aspirante.
AS.PIR.ATE, v., aspirar, sorver; s., som aspirado; adj., aspirado(a).
AS.PI.RA.TION, s., aspiração, ruído; desejo.
AS.PIRE, v., aspirar, desejar, querer.
AS.PI.RIN, s., aspirina.
AS.PIR.ING, adj., desejoso, ganancioso.
AS.PIR.ING.NESS, s., ambição, ganância.
ASS, s., burro, jumento, jegue; idiota, imbecil.
AS.SAIL, v., assaltar, roubar, atacar.
AS.SAIL.ANT, s., assaltante, agressor.
AS.SAIL.ER, s., o mesmo que assailant.
AS.SAS.SIN, s., assassino.
AS.SAS.SI.NATE, v., assassinar.
AS.SAS.SI.NA.TION, s., assassínio.
AS.SAS.SI.NA.TOR, s., assassino.
AS.SAULT, s., assalto, ataque; v., assaltar, atacar.
AS.SAULT.ER, s., assaltante.
AS.SAY, v., analisar, examinar, verificar; s., análise de metais.
AS.SAY.ER, s., constrasteador (no processo de mineração).
AS.SEM.BLAGE, s., assembleia, coleção.
AS.SEM.BLE, v., reunir, congregar; colecionar.
AS.SEM.BLER, s., montador, mecânico; Comp., programa de computador de uso geral.

AS.SEM.BLY, s., assembleia, reunião, sessão.
AS.SENT, s., aprovação; v., aprovar, consentir.
AS.SENT.ER, s., consentidor.
AS.SERT, v., afirmar, manter, confirmar.
AS.SER.TION, s., afirmação, assertiva.
AS.SER.TIVE, adj., assertivo, afirmativo, positivo.
AS.SESS, v., avaliar, sopesar, taxar, tributar.
AS.SESS.A.BLE, adj., tributável.
AS.SESS.MENT, s., avaliação.
AS.SES.SOR, s., assessor; tributarista.
AS.SET, s., bens, haveres, ativos.
AS.SETS, s., espólio; massa falida.
AS.SEV.ER.ATE, v., asseverar, assegurar.
AS.SEV.ER.A.TION, s., asseveração, confirmação, afirmação.
AS.SI.DU.I.TY, s., assiduidade, diligência, aplicação.
AS.SID.U.OUS, adj., assíduo, aplicado, atento.
AS.SID.U.OUS.LY, adv., assiduamente, zelosamente.
AS.SIGN, v., designar, nomear; determinar; s., Jur., cessionário.
AS.SIG.NA.TION, s., partilha, divisão.
AS.SIGN.MENT, s., designação, indicação.
AS.SIM.I.LATE, v., assimilar, absorver.
AS.SIM.I.LA.TION, s., assimilação.
AS.SIM.I.LA.TOR, s., assimilador.
AS.SIST, v., assistir, auxiliar, socorrer.
AS.SIS.TANCE, s., assistência, socorro, ajuda.
AS.SIST.ANT, s. e adj., que ou quem assiste, assistente; que ou quem auxilia, auxiliar.
AS.SOCI.A.BIL.I.TY, s., sociabilidade.
AS.SO.CI.ATE, s., companheiro, camarada, sócio; v., associar-se.
AS.SO.CI.A.TION, s., associação, sociedade.
AS.SO.CI.A.TIVE, adj., associativo.
AS.SON.ANCE, s., assonância.
AS.SON.ANT, s., palavra ou sílaba assonante; adj., assonante.
AS.SORT, v., agrupar, classificar.
AS.SORT.MENT, s., sortimento, agrupamento.
AS.SUAGE, v., suavizar, diminuir, mitigar, aliviar.
AS.SUAGE.MENT, s., alívio, suavização.
AS.SUME, v., supor, imaginar, presumir.
AS.SUM.ING, adj., pretensioso, presunçoso.
AS.SUMP.TION, s., suposição, presunção; arrogância; Rel., Assunção.
AS.SUR.ANCE, s., garantia, certeza, segurança, seguro.
AS.SURE, v., assegurar, garantir, afirmar.
AS.SURED, adj., autoconfiante.
AS.SURED.LY, adv., certamente, com certeza.
AS.SURED.NESS, s., certeza, garantia.
AS.SUR.GENT, adj., ascendente; Bot., assurgente.
AS.SYR.I.AN, s., assírio.
AS.TER.ISK, s., asterisco.
A.STERN, adv., Náut., à popa, à ré; atrás.
AS.TER.OID, s., asteroide.
ASTH.MA, s., asma.
ASTH.MAT.IC, adj., asmático(a); s., asmático.
ASTH.MA.TIC.AL, adj., asmático.
ASTIG.MA.TISM, s., astigmatismo.
AS.TON.ISH, v., espantar, estontear, maravilhar.
AS.TON.ISH.ED, adj., espantado, maravilhado, pasmado.
AS.TON.ISH.ING, adj., espantoso.
AS.TON.ISH.MENT, s., espanto, admiração.
AS.TOUND, v., espantar, pasmar, surpreender.

ASTOUNDED ··· 379 ··· ATTORNEY

AS.TOUND.ED, *adj.*, pasmado.
AS.TOUND.ING, *adj.*, espantoso(a).
AS.TRA.KHAN, *s.*, astracã.
AS.TOUND.MENT, *s.*, assombro, terror.
AS.TRAL, *adj.*, astral.
A.STRAY, *adv.*, extraviado, sem rumo.
A.STRICT, *v.*, comprimir, apertar, restringir.
A.STRIC.TION, *s.*, compressão, pressão.
AS.TRIN.GE, *v.*, restringir, oprimir, apertar.
AS.TRIN.GENT, *adj.*, adstringente; severo; *s.*, adstringente.
AS.TROLABE, *s.*, *Astron.*, astrolábio.
AS.TROL.O.GER, *s.*, astrólogo.
AS.TRO.LOG.IC, *adj.*, astrológico.
AS.TRO.LOG.I.CAL, *adj.*, astrológico.
AS.TROL.O.GIST, *s.*, astrólogo.
AS.TROL.O.GY, *s.*, astrologia.
AS.TRO.NAUT, *s.*, astronauta.
AS.TRON.O.MER, *s.*, astrônomo.
AS.TRO.NOM.IC, *adj.*, astronômico.
AS.TRO.NOM.I.CAL, *adj.*, astronômico.
AS.TRON.O.MY, *s.*, astronomia.
AS.TRO.PHO.TOG.RA.PHY, *s.*, astrofotografia.
AS.TRO.PHYS.ICS, *s.*, astrofísica.
AS.TUTE, *adj.*, astuto, esperto, sagaz, vivo.
AS.TUTE.NESS, *s.*, esperteza, sagacidade, astúcia.
A.SUNDER, *adj.*, separado, distante; *fig.*, remoto; *adv.*, à parte, separadamente.
ASY.LUM, *s.*, asilo, abrigo, albergue.
A.SYM.MET.RI.CAL, *adj.*, assimétrico(a).
ASYM.ME.TRY, *s.*, assimetria.
A.SYMP.TO.MAT.IC, *adj.*, *Med.*, assintomático.
A.SYN.CHRO.NISM, *s.*, assincronismo.
A.SYN.DET.IC, *adj.*, *Gram.*, assindético.
A.SYN.DE.TON, *s.*, assíndeto.
A.SYN.TAC.TIC, *adj.*, *Gram.*, assindético.
AT, *prep.*, em, a, de, no, na.
AT.A.VIC, *adj.*, atávico.
AT.A.VISM, *s.*, atavismo.
A.TE.LIER, *s.*, *do Fr.*, oficina, estúdio.
A.THE.ISM, *s.*, ateísmo.
A.THE.IST, *adj.*, *s.*, ateu, ateísta.
A.THE.IS.TIC, *adj.*, ateísta, ateístico, ateu.
A.THE.NI.AN, *adj. e s.*, ateniense.
ATH.ER.O.SCLE.RO.SIS, *s.*, *Med.*, aterosclerose.
ATH.LETE, *s.*, atleta.
ATH.LETE'S FOOD, *s.*, *Med.*, pé de atleta, tricofitose.
ATH.LE.TIC, *adj.*, atlético.
ATH.LET.I.CISM, *s.*, atletismo.
ATH.LET.ICS, *s. pl.*, jogos desportivos.
ATH.RONG, *adv.*, em tropel, com pressa.
AT.LAN.TES, *s. pl.*, *Ant.*, atlante, télamon.
AT.LAN.TIC, *adj.*, atlântico.
AT.LAN.TIS, *s.*, Atlântida
AT.LAS, *s.*, atlas.
AT.LAS, *s.*, Atlas (montes).
AT.MO.SPHERE, *s.*, atmosfera.
ATMO.SPHER.IC, *adj.*, atmosférico.
ATOLL, *s.*, atol, abrolho.
AT.OM, *s.*, átomo.
AT.OM BOMB, *s.*, bomba atômica.
A.TOM.IC, *adj.*, atômico.

A.TOM.IC BOMB, *s.*, bomba atômica.
A.TOM.IC EN.ER.GY, *s.*, energia atômica.
A.TOM.IC NUM.BER, *s.*, *Fis.*, número atômico.
AT.OM.ISM, *s.*, atomismo.
AT.OM.IZA.TION, *s.*, atomização.
AT.OM.ISE, AT.OM.IZE, *v.*, atomizar.
AT.OM.IS.ER, AT.OMI.Z.ER, *s.*, atomizador, vaporizador.
AT.OM.Y, *s.*, átomo, corpúsculo, particular.
A.TON.AL, *adj.*, *Mus.*, relative à atonalidade.
A.TONE, *v.*, reconciliar, congraçar; reparar, resgatar.
A.TON.IC, *adj.*, atônico, debilitado, fraco.
AT.O.NY, *s.*, atonia, fraqueza, debilidade.
A.TOP, *adv.*, *prep.*, no cimo, no tope, na crista.
A.TRI.UM, *s.*, *do Lat.*, átrio; *Anat.*, aurícula do coração.
ATRO.CIOUS, *adj.*, atroz, cruel, perverso, ruim, mau, malvado.
ATROC.I.TY, *s.*, atrocidade, maldade, crueldade.
ATRO.PHIC, *adj.*, atrófico, enfraquecido.
AT.RO.PHY, *v.*, atrofiar, enfraquecer, debilitar; *s.*, atrofia.
AT.TACH, *v.*, prender, afixar, conectar, anexar.
AT.TACH.A.BLE, *adj.*, afixável, anexável, embargável.
AT.TACH.ED, *adj.*, anexado(a).
AT.TA.CHÉ, *s.*, adido; *adj.*, ligado.
AT.TACH.MENT, *s.*, ligação, união, anexo.
AT.TACK, *v.*, atacar, agredir; *s.*, ataque, agressão, assalto.
AT.TACK.ABLE, *adj.*, atacável.
AT.TACK.ER, *s.*, agressor, atacante, assaltante.
AT.TAIN, *v.*, alcançar, obter, conseguir, lograr.
AT.TAIN.ABIL.I.TY, *s.*, possibilidade de obter.
AT.TAIN.DER, *s.*, perda dos cireitos civis; *fig.*, mancha, desonra.
AT.TAIN.MENT, *s.*, realização, feito, qualificação; obtenção.
AT.TAINT, *s.*, mancha, nódoa, mácula; *v.*, macular, desonrar, manchar.
AT.TAIN.TURE, *s.*, o mesmo que *attainder*.
AT.TEMP.ER, *v.*, condimentar, temperar, moderar.
AT.TEMP.ER.ANCE, *s.*, temperança, comedimento.
AT.TEMPT, *s.*, tentativa; *v.*, tentar, provar.
AT.TEMPT.A.BLE, *adj.*, que se pode tentar empreender ou atacar.
AT.TEMPT.ER, *s.*, empreendedor; agressor.
AT.TEND, *v.*, assistir, participar, estar presente, tratar.
AT.TEN.DANCE, *s.*, comparecimento, frequência, assistência.
AT.TEN.DANT, *s.*, assistente, servidor; *adj.*, assistente.
AT.TENT, *adj.*, atencioso, atento.
AT.TEN.TION, *s.*, atenção, cuidado, respeito.
AT.TEN.TIVE, *adj.*, atento(a), atencioso(a).
AT.TEN.TIVE.LY, *adv.*, atentamente, cuidadosamente.
AT.TEN.U.ANT, *s.*, diluente; *adj.*, diluente; *Med.*, atenuante.
AT.TENUATE, *v.*, atenuar, minorar, suavizar.
AT.TEN.U.A.TION, *s.*, atenuação, suavizamento.
AT.TEST, *v.*, atestar, afirmar, testemunhar.
AT.TES.TA.TION, *s.*, atestado, testemunho.
AT.TEST.OR, *s.*, testemunha.
AT.TIC, *s.*, sótão.
AT.TIRE, *v.*, ornar, enfeitar, ataviar;*s.*, ornato, ornamento, enfeite.
AT.TIRE.MENT, *s.*, ornato, adorno, atavio, enfeite.
AT.TIR.ING, *s.*, enfeite.
AT.TI.TUDE, *s.*, atitude, postura, faceta, comportamento.
AT.TI.TU.DI.NAL, *adj.*, relativo a atitudes pessoais.
AT.TOR.NEY, *s.*, advogado.

ATTORNMENT ·· 380 ·· AUTOINTOXICATION

AT.TORN.MENT, s., Jur., reconhecimento do senhorio pelo arrendatário.
AT.TRACT, v., atrair, puxar, seduzir, persuadir.
AT.TRACT.A.BLE, adj., que atrai.
AT.TRAC.TION, s., atração, sedução.
AT.TRAC.TIVE, adj., atraente, sedutor, interessante.
AT.TRAC.TIVE.LY, adv., atrativamente.
AT.TRACT.OR, s., quem ou o que atrai.
AT.TRAHENT, adj., atraente.
AT.TRIB.U.TA.BLE, adj., atribuível (a alguém), imputável.
AT.TRIB.UTE, s., atributo; v., atribuir, dar, oferecer.
AT.TRI.BU.TION, s., atribuição, dom.
AT.TRI.BU.TIVE, s., palavra ou frase atributiva; adj., atributivo; Gram., que atribui.
AT.TRIST, v., entristecer, contristar, tornar triste.
AT.TRITE, adj., atritado, gasto, puído.
AT.TRITE.NESS, s., atrito, fricção.
AT.TRI.TION, s., desgaste, atrito, fricção.
AT.TUNE, v., harmonizar, acertar, concertar.
AT.TUNED, adj., acostumado(a).
A.TYP.IC.AL, adj., atípico(a).
A.TYP.I.CAL.LY, adv., atipicamente.
AU.BER.GINE, s., berinjela.
AU.BURN, adj., castanho-avermelhado(a).
AUC.TION, s., leilão; v., leiloar.
AUC.TION.EER, s., leiloeiro.
AUC.TO.RI.AL, adj., próprio de um autor.
AU.DA.CIOUS, adj., audacioso, ousado, valente.
AU.DA.CIOUS.NESS, s., audácia, valentia, ousadia.
AU.DAC.I.TY, s., audácia, ousadia, valentia.
AU.DI.BLE, adj., audível, ouvível.
AU.DI.ENCE, s., audiência, plateia.
AU.DI.ENT, adj., s., ouvinte.
AU.DI.O, adj., auditivo; pref., audio-.
AU.DI.O-FRE.QUEN.CY, s., audiofrequência.
AU.DI.OL.O.GY, s., Med., audiologia (ciência que estuda audição).
AU.DI.O.TY.PIST, s., transcritor.
AU.DIO.VI.SU.AL, s., audiovisual.
AU.DIT, s., auditoria.
AU.DI.TION, s., audição.
AU.DI.TIVE, adj., auditivo.
AU.DI.TOR, s., auditor.
AU.DI.TO.RI.UM, s., auditório.
AU.DI.TO.RY, s., Ant., espectadores; auditório; adj., auditivo.
AU.GER, s., broca, verruma.
AUG.MENT, v., aumentar, ampliar, expandir.
AUG.MEN.TA.TION, s., aumento, acréscimo.
AU.GUR, s., áugure, adivinho; v., vaticinar.
AU.GU.RY, s., augúrio.
AU.GUST, adj., augusto(a).
AU.GUST, s., agosto.
AU.GUS.TIN.I.AN, s. e adj., agostiniano.
AU.GUS.TIN.I.AN.ISM, s., agostinianismo (doutrinas inspiradas na teologia de Santo Agostinho).
AU.LIC, adj., áulico.
AU.MAIL, v., esmaltar.
AUNT, s., tia.
AUNT.IE, AUNTY, s., tia, tiazinha, titia.
AU.RA, s., ar, fisionomia, aparência.
AU.RAL, adj., auditivo(a), auricular.

AU.RAL.LY, adv., auditivamente.
AU.RE.OLA, s., auréola.
AU.RIC, adj., áureo.
AU.RI.CLE, s., aurícula.
AU.RO.RA, s., aurora, madrugada.
AUS.CUL.TA.TION, s., auscultação, busca.
ÁUS.PICE, s., auspício, augúrio; presságio, agouro.
AUS.PIC.ES, s. pl., auspícios, sob o patrocínio de.
AUS.PI.CIOUS, adj., auspicioso, propício.
AUS.PI.CIOUS.LY, adv., auspiciosamente; venturosamente.
AUS.SIE, adj. e s., australiano.
AUS.TER, s., vento do sul, austro, suão.
AUS.TERE, adj., austero, severo, rigoroso.
AUS.TERE.NESS, s., austeridade.
AUS.TER.I.TY, s., austeridade, rigor, simplicidade.
AUS.TRAL, adj., austral, meridional.
AUS.TRA.LA.SIAN, s., australasiano; adj., australásico, australásio.
AUS.TRA.LIAN, adj., s., australiano.
AUS.TRA.LIC, adj., Etnog., relativo aos abrígenes australianos.
AUS.TRI.AN, adj., s., austríaco.
AU.TAR.CHY, s., autarquia, autocracia.
AU.THEN.TIC, adj., autêntico, real, genuíno.
AU.THEN.TI.CATE, v., autenticar.
AU.THEN.TI.CA.TION, s., autenticação.
AU.THEN.TIC.I.TY, s., autenticidade, realidade.
AU.THOR, s., autor.
AU.THOR.ESS, s., autora.
AU.THO.RI.SA.TION, AU.THO.RI.ZA.TION, s., autorização.
AU.THO.RISE, AU.THO.RIZE, v., autorizar, deferir.
AU.THOR.ISED, adj., autorizado, legitimado.
AU.THOR.I.TAR.I.AN, adj., autoritário.
AU.THO.RI.TA.TIVE, adj., autoritário, ditatorial; official, autorizado, compentente.
AU.THOR.I.TA.TIVE.NESS, s., autoritarismo.
AU.THOR.I.TY, s., autoridade, comando, jurisdição.
AU.THOR.IZ.ABLE, adj., autorizável.
AU.THOR.I.ZA.TION, s., autorização.
AU.THOR.SHIP, s., autoria.
AU.TISM, s., Psic., autismo.
AU.TIST, s., autista.
AU.TIS.TIC, adj., autista.
AU.TO, s., carro, veículo.
AU.TO.BI.OG.RA.PHER, s., autobiógrafo.
AU.TO.BI.OG.RA.PHIC, adj., autobiográfico.
AU.TO.BI.OG.RA.PHICAL, adj., autobiográfico.
AU.TO.BI.OG.RA.PHY, s., autobiografia.
AU.TO.BUS, s., ônibus.
AU.TOCH.THON, s., autóctone, indígena, silvícola.
AU.TOC.RA.CY, s., autocracia.
AU.TO.CRAT, s., autocrata.
AU.TO.CRAT.IC, adj., autocrático.
AU.TO.CROSS (UK), s., autocross.
AU.TO.DI.DACT, s., autodidata.
AU.TO.GRAPH, s., autógrafo; v., autografar.
AU.TO.GRAPHY, s., autografia.
AU.TO.GY.RO, s., helicóptero, autogiro.
AU.TO-IM.MUN.I.ZA.TION, s., Med., autoimunização.
AU.TO.IN.FEC.TION, s., Med., autoinfecção.
AU.TO.IN.OC.U.LA.TION, s., Med., autoinoculação.
AU.TO.IN.TOX.I.CA.TION, s., autointoxicação.

AUTOLOADING ·· 381 ·· AZURE

AU.TO.LOAD.ING, *adj.*, relativo a carregamento semiautomático (armas de fogo).
AU.TO.MATE, *v.*, automatizar.
AU.TO.MAT.IC, *adj.*, automático; arma automática.
AU.TO.MAT.I.CAL.LY, *adv.*, automaticamente.
AU.TO.MA.TION, *s.*, automação.
AU.TOM.A.TISM, *s.*, automatismo.
AU.TOM.A.TIZE, *v.*, automatizar.
AU.TOM.A.TON, *s.*, automata, robô; *pej.*, robô.
AU.TO.MO.BILE, *s.*, carro, automóvel.
AU.TO.MO.BIL.ISM, *s.*, automobilismo.
AU.TO.MO.BIL.IST, *s.*, automobilista.
AU.TO.MO.TIVE, *adj.*, automóvel, automotriz.
AU.TON.O.MIST, *s.*, autonomista.
AU.TON.O.MOUS, *adj.*, autônomo.
AU.TON.O.MY, *s.*, autonomia.
AU.TO.PHA.GI.A, *s.*, *Med.*, *Biol.*, autofagia, autofagismo.
AU.TOP.SY, *s.*, autópsia.
AU.TO.SUG.GES.TION, *s.*, autossugestão.
AU.TO.TROPH.IC, *adj.*, *Biol.*, autotrófico.
AU.TO.TRUCK, *s.*, caminhão.
AU.TO.TYPE, *s.*, fac-símile; *Tipog.*, autotipia, fotogravura; *v.*, reproduzir por autotipia.
AU.TUMN, *s.*, outono.
AU.TUM.NAL, *adj.*, outonal.
AUX.IL.IA.RY, *adj.* e *s.*, auxiliar.
AVAIL, *s.*, vantagem, benefício, lucro; *v.*, aproveitar-se, beneficiar-se.
AVAIL.ABIL.I.TY, *s.*, viabilidade, disponibilidade.
AVAIL.ABLE, *adj.*, viável, disponível.
AV.A.LANCHE, *s.*, avalanche, alude, avalancha.
AVANT-GARDE, *s.*, *Fr.*, vanguarda.
AV.A.RICE, *s.*, avareza, usura.
AV.A.RI.CIOUS, *adj.*, avarento, avaro, unha de fome.
AV.A.RI.CIOUS.NESS, *s.*, avareza, usura.
A.VAST, *interj.*, pare!, basta! (Náutica).
AV.A.TAR, *s.*, *Rel.*, encarnação de um deus hindu em forma humana ou animal; manifestação; exaltação.
AVE., *abrev.*, (*avenue*) Av.
AVENGE, *v.*, vingar.
AVENGE.MENT, *s.*, vingança.
AVENG.ER, *s.*, vingador.
AV.E.NUE, *s.*, avenida, alameda, bulevar.
AVER, *v.*, afirmar, confirmar, asseverar.
AV.ER.AGE, *s.*, média, proporção; avaria, dano; *v.*, calcular, ratear.
AVER.MENT, *s.*, afirmação, asseveramento.
AVERSE, *adj.*, contrário, oposto, ao avesso.
AVERSE.NESS, *s.*, oposição, contrariedade.
AVER.SION, *s.*, aversão.
AVERT, *v.*, advertir, prevenir; desviar.
AVERT.IBLE, *adj.*, advertível, previsível.
AVI.AR.IST, *s.*, avicultor.
AVI.ARY, *s.*, aviário.
AVI.ATE, *v.*, viajar de avião, voar.
AVI.A.TION, *s.*, aviação.
AVI.A.TOR, *s.*, aviador, piloto.
A.VI.CUL.TURE, *s.*, avicultura.
A.VI.CUL.TUR.IST, *s.*, avicultor.
AV.ID, *adj.*, ávido, cobiçoso.
AVID.ITY, *s.*, avidez, cupidez.

AV.O.CA.DO, *s.*, abacate.
AV.O.CA.TION, *s.*, distração, lazer, divertimento, folga.
A.VOC.A.TO.RY, *adj.*, avocatório, que chama a atenção.
A.VOID, *v.*, evitar, escapar; esquivar-se.
AVOID.ABLE, *adj.*, evitável.
A.VOID.ANCE, *s.*, vacância; fuga, escape.
A.VOID.ER, *s.*, aquele que se esquiva (de obrigações).
AVOUCH, *s.*, garantia, segurança.
AVOUCH.ABLE, *adj.*, garantível.
A.VOUCH.MENT, *s.*, declaração, afirmação, testemunho.
A.VOW, *v.*, confessar, declarar, proclamar.
A.VOW.ABLE, *adj.*, confessável.
A.VOW.AL, *s.*, confissão, declaração.
A.VOWED, *adj.*, declarado.
A.VUL.SION, *s.*, avulsão, separação, extração.
A.WAIT, *v.*, esperar.
A.WAIT.ER, *s.*, aquilo ou aquele que espera.
A.WAKE, *adj.*, acordado(a), depsertado(a); *v.*, acordar, despertar; estimular.
A.WAK.EN, *v.*, acordar.
A.WAK.EN.ING, *adj.*, despertante; *s.*, o ato de acordar.
A.WARD, *s.*, prêmio, recompensa; *v.*, premiar, recompensar.
A.WARD.A.BLE, *adj.*, premiável, recompensável; arbitrável.
A.WARE, *adj.*, precavido, avisado.
AWARE.NESS, *s.*, consciência, conhecimento.
A.WASH, *adj.*, inundado, flutuante.
A.WAY, *adv.*, longe, ao longe.
AWE, *s.*, medo, receio, respeito.
AWE-COM.MAND.ING, *adj.*, que impõe respeito.
AWE.SOME, *adj.*, terrível.
AWE.STRUCK, *adj.*, aterrorizado(a).
AW.FUL, *adj.*, terrível, medonho, horrendo, horrível.
AW.FUL.LY, *adv.*, muito.
A.WHILE, *adv.*, por certo tempo.
AWK.WARD, *adj.*, desajeitado, incômodo, deselegante.
AWK.WARD.LY, *adv.*, desajeitadamente, inconvenientemente.
AWK.WARD.ISH, *adj.*, desastrado, incapaz, inepto.
AWK.WARD.NESS, *s.*, inépcia, incapacidade, ignorância.
AWL, *s.*, sovela, pua.
AWN.ER, *s.*, maquina que retira praganas dos cereais.
AW.NING, *s.*, toldo, barraca.
A.WRY, *adj.*, desleixado, deselegante.
AXE, *s.*, machado; *v.*, abandonar, largar.
AX.EL, *s.*, *Esp.*, salto de um patim para outro.
AXE.MAN, *s.*, lenhador.
AX.I.AL, *adj.*, axial.
AX.IL, *s.*, axila.
AX.IL.LARY, *adj.*, axilar.
AX.I.OM, *s.*, axioma.
AX.I.OM.AT.IC, *adj.*, axiomático.
AX.IS, *s.*, eixo.
AX.LE, *s.*, eixo.
AYAH, *s.*, aia, ama, babá.
AYE, *adv.*, sempre, sem fim; sim, voto afirmativo.
AZA.LEA, *s.*, azaleia, azálea.
AZER.BAI.JAN, *adj.* e *s.*, azerbaijano.
AZE.RI, *adj.* e *s.*, azeri.
AZ.I.MUTH, *s.*, *Astron.*, azimute.
AZ.OTE, *s.*, azoto.
AZ.TEC, *adj.* e *s.*, asteca.
AZ.URE, *adj.*, azul-celeste.

B

B, segunda letra do alfabeto inglês.
BA.AL, s., Baal (deus dos cananeus e fenícios); *fig.*, falso deus, ídolo.
BA.BA, s., *Cul.*, babá (pudim feito de farinha, leite, ovos e açúcar, mergulhado em calda de rum).
BA.BAS.SU, s., *Bot.*, babaçu.
BAB.BLE, s., fala incompreensível, murmúrio; v., balbuciar.
BAB.BLER, s., tagarela, palrador.
BAB.BLE.MENT, s., balbucio; tolice.
BAB.BLING, s., balbuciação, palrice.
BABE, s., bebê; garota, boneca (afetuoso).
BA.BEL, s., *Geog.*, Babilônia; *fig.*, confusão de sons, utopia.
BAB.OON, s., *Zoo.*, babuíno.
BA.BOUCHE, s., chinela bordada do Oriente, babucha.
BA.BY, s., bebê, nenê.
BA.BY BEEF, s., comida de bebê.
BA.BY DOLL, s., boneca em forma de bebê; *Vest.*, roupa de dormir feminina.
BA.BY.HOOD, s., infância, meninice.
BA.BY.ISH, *adj.*, infantil, pueril.
BA.BY.ISH.LY, *adv.*, puerilmente.
BA.BY.ISH.NESS, s., infantilidade, puerilidade.
BA.BY.LIKE, *adj.*, pueril.
BA.BY LIN.EN, s., roupa de criança.
BA.BY.NURS.ERY, s., creche.
BA.BY-SIT, v., tomar conta de crianças; trabalhar como babá.
BA.BY-SIT.TER, s., babá.
BA.BY TALK, s., voz ou fala de bebê.
BA.BY TOOTH, s., dente de leite.
BA.BY-WALK.ER, s., andador (de bebê).
BA.BY WIPE, s., toalha de papel umedecida descartável (para bebês).
BAC.CA.RA, s., bacará (jogo de azar que se joga com dois baralhos).
BAC.CHA.NAL, s., bacanal, orgia.
BACH.E.LOR, s., solteiro, bacharel.
BACH.E.LOR.HOOD, s., estado de solteiro, bacharelado.
BA.CIL.LA.RY, *adj.*, bacilar.
BA.CIL.LI.FORM, *adj.*, baciliforme, bacilar.
BA.CIL.LUS, s., bacilo.
BACK, s., costas, dorso, fundos.
BACK.ACHE, s., dor nas costas.
BACK AWAY, v., voltar, recuar.
BACK.BENCH.ER, s., na Inglaterra, membro do parlamento sem cargo oficial.
BACK.BENCH.ES, s. pl., na Inglaterra, cadeiras reservadas a membros sem cargo oficial.
BACK.BI.TING, s., calúnia, maledicência.
BACK.BOARD, s., encosto (de cadeira).
BACK.BONE, s., espinha dorsal.
BACK.BREAK.ING, *adj.*, estafante.
BACK.CHAT, s., *col.*, *UK* contestações.
BACK.DATE, v., antedatar.
BACK DOWN, v., desistir, entregar-se.
BACK.DROP, s., pano de fundo (teatro).
BACKER, s., defensor, zagueiro.
BACK.FIRE, v., dar errado; dar tiro pela culatra; s., tiro pela culatra.
BACK.GAM.MON, s., gamão (jogo).
BACK.GROUND, s., fundo, motivo, fato; prática, conhecimento.
BACK.HAND, s., caligrafia.
BACK.HAND.ED, *adj.*, desajeitado; falso, insincero.
BACK.HAND.ER, s., bofetada, bofetão.
BACK.ING, s., apoio, auxílio, ajuda.
BACK.LASH, s., revolta.
BACK.LESS, *adj.*, *US* sem encosto, sem costas; *UK* frente-única.
BACK.LOG, s., acúmulo.
BACK NUMBER, s., número atrasado.
BACK OFF, v., afastar-se.
BACK OUT, v., desistir, ir atrás.
BACK.PACK, s., mochila.
BACK.PACK.ER, s., mochileiro.
BACK.PACK.ING, s., com a mochila nas costas.
BACK.PED.AL, v., desistir, dar para trás.
BACK SEAT, s., banco de trás; *fig.*, papel secundário.
BACK.SET, s., revés, retrocesso.
BACK.SIDE, s., traseiro, nádegas.
BACK.SLAP.PING, s., saudações.
BACK.SLASH, s., *Comp.*, barra invertida.
BACK.SLIDE, v., ter uma recaída.
BACK.SPACE, s., *Comp.*, tecla de retorno; v., retornar (uma ação).
BACK.STAGE, *adj.* e *adv.*, nos bastidores.
BACK.STROKE, s., braçada em nado de costas; recuo, retrocesso.
BACK.UP, s., cópia de segurança, arquivo reserva.
BACK UP, v., reforçar, copiar para segurança.
BACK.WARD, *adj.*, para trás, reverso.
BACK.WARDS, *adv.*, de trás para frente; ao contrário.
BACK.WASH, s., repercussão (de alguma novidade ou evento).
BACK.WA.TER, s., água represada.
BACK.WOODS, s., sertão, região distante e selvagem.
BACK.WOODS.MAN, s., *US* pessoa rústica, caipira.
BACK.YARD, s., quintal, jardim.
BA.CON, s., bacon, toucinho.
BACON.IZE, v., transformar em toucinho, engordar.
BAC.TE.RIA, s., bactéria.
BAC.TE.RI.CIDE, s., bactericida.
BAC.TE.RI.OL.O.GIST, s., bacteriologista.
BAC.TE.RI.OL.O.GY, s., bacteriologia.
BAD, *adj.*, mau, ruim, maldoso, malvado.

BADDISH   ••• 383 •••   BANISTER

BAD.DISH, *adj.*, menos mau, inferior.
BAD.DY, *s.*, *col.*, vilão(ã).
BADGE, *s.*, crachá; distintivo; selo.
BADG.ER, *s.*, texugo; *v.*, convencer alguém a fazer algo.
BAD.LY, *adv.*, maldosamente.
BAD.MAN, *s.*, fora da lei, bandido.
BADLY-OFF, *adj.*, carente.
BAD-MAN.NER.ED, *adj.*, mal-educado.
BAD.MIN.TON, *s.*, *Esp.*, badminton.
BAD-MOUTH, *v.*, falar mal de (algo ou alguém).
BAD.NESS, *s.*, maldade, ruindade.
BAD-TEM.PERED, *adj.*, mal-humorado.
BAF.FLE, *v.*, desnortear.
BAF.FLER, *s.*, enganador, falsário.
BAF.FLING, *adj.*, desnorteante.
BAF.FLE.MENT, *s.*, engano, desfeita.
BAG, *s.*, saco, sacola, bolsa; mala.
BAGGED, *adj.*, ensacado; *fig.* bêbado.
BA.GEL, *s.*, pão enrolado.
BAG.GAGE, *s.*, bagagem.
BAG.GY, *adj.*, largo, folgado, aberto.
BAG.PIPES, *s.*, gaita de foles.
BAG.SNATCH.ER, *s.*, batedor de carteira.
BA.GUETTE, *s.*, baguete.
BAH!, *excl.*, bah!
BAH.RAINI, BAH.REINI, *adj.* e *s.*, bareinita, baremês.
BAG UP, *v.*, ensacar, pôr em sacos.
BAIL, *s.*, fiança, caução; *v.*, liberar sob fiança.
BAI.LEE, *s.*, depositário.
BAIL.IFF, *s.*, oficial de justiça; administrador de propriedades.
BAIL.A.BLE, *adj.*, afiançável.
BAIL.ER, *s.*, balde; baldeador (quem baldeia a água).
BAIL.OR, *s.*, fiador.
BAIT, *s.*, isca,engodo,engano; *v.*, engodar, enganar.
BAIZE, *s.*, feltro.
BAKE, *v.*, cozer no forno, assar.
BA.KE.LITE, *s.*, baquelita.
BAK.ER, *s.*, padeiro.
BAKER.Y, *s.*, padaria.
BAK.ING, *s.*, cozimento.
BAK.ING POW.DER, *s.*, fermento em pó.
BAK.ING TIN, *s.*, forma (de bolo).
BAK.ING TRAY, *s.*, assadeira.
BAL.A.CLAVA, *s.*, *UK* balaclava, touca ninja.
BAL.A.LAI.KA, *s.*, *Mús.*, balalaica (tipo de bandolim de três cordas russo).
BAL.ANCE, *s.*, balança, equilíbrio; balanço, saldo.
BAL.ANCED, *adj.*, equilibrado.
BAL.ANC.ER, *s.*, acrobata.
BAL.ANCE SHEET, *s.*, balancete; demonstração dos resultados.
BAL.CO.NY, *s.*, balcão, varanda; galeria.
BALD, *s.*, careca, calvo.
BALD EA.GLE, *s.*, águia americana.
BALD.HEAD.ED, *adj.*, calvo, careca.
BALD.ING, *adj.*, careca, calvo.
BALD.LY, *adv.*, secamente, grosseiramente.
BALD.NESS, *s.*, calvície.
BALE, *s.*, fardo.
BAL.E.AR.IC IS.LAND, BAL.E.AR.ICS, *s. pl.*, Ilhas Baleares.
BALE.FUL, *adj.*, maligno, pernicioso, triste, tristonho.

BALK, *s.*, obstáculo, empecilho; *v.*, obstaculizar, impedir.
BAL.KAN, *adj.*, balcânico.
BAL.KANS, *s. pl.*, Bálcãs.
BALK.ING, *adj.*, contrário, obstinado.
BALK.Y, *adj.*, teimoso.
BALL, *s.*, bola, novelo.
BAL.LAD, *s.*, balada.
BAL.LAST, *s.*, lastro em navio.
BALL BOY, *s.*, *Fut.*, gandula.
BALLCOCK, *s.*, boia.
BAL.LE.RI.NA, *s.*, bailarina.
BAL.LET, *s.*, balé, bailado.
BALL GIRL, *s.*, *Fut.*, gandula (mulher).
BAL.LIS.TICS, *s.*, balística.
BAL.LOON, *s.*, balão.
BAL.LOON.ING, *s.*, balonismo.
BAL.LOON.IST, *s.*, balonista, aeronauta.
BAL.LOT, *s.*, voto; *v.*, votar.
BAL.LOT BOX, *s.*, urna eleitoral.
BAL.LOT PA.PER, *s.*, cédula de votação.
BALL.POINT, *s.*, esferográfica.
BALL.ROOM, *s.*, salão de danças.
BALM, *s.*, bálsamo.
BALMY, *adj.*, balsâmico, perfumado, suave.
BAL.SAM, *s.*, bálsamo.
BAL.SAM.IC, *adj.*, balsâmico.
BAL.SA WOOD, *s.*, balsa, jangada.
BAL.TIC, *adj.*, báltico; *s.*, Báltico.
BAL.US.TRADE, *s.*, balaustrada.
BAM.BOO, *s.*, bambu.
BAM.BOO.ZLE, *v.*, lograr, enganar.
BAN, *s.*, proibição, interdição, veto.
BA.NAL, *adj.*, banal, trivial.
BA.NAL.I.TY, *s.*, banalidade.
BA.NANA, *s.*, banana.
BAND, *s.*, banda, orquestra; banda, faixa; *v.*, ligar, unir.
BAN.DAGE, *s.*, ligadura, bandagem; *v.*, enfaixar, ligar.
BAND.AID, *s.*, curativo rápido, bandeide.
BAN.DAN.NA, BAN.DA.NA, *s.*, bandana.
BAN.DIT, *s.*, bandido, delinquente.
BAND.MAS.TER, *s.*, maestro, maestrina.
BAN.DOG, *s.*, mastim, cão.
BAND SHELL, *s.*, concha acústica (para concertos).
BANDS.MAN, *s.*, músico.
BAND.STAND, *s.*, palanque.
BAND.WAG.ON, *s.*, carro para propaganda política; *fig.*, popularidade.
BAN.DY, *adj.*, cambaio, arqueado; *v.*, atirar para lá e para cá; alternar.
BANE, *s.*, veneno, tóxico.
BANE.FUL, *adj.*, venenoso, nocivo, prejudicial.
BANG, *s.*, estalo, estrondo, explosão.
BANG DOWN *v.*, atirar no chão, cair.
BANG.ER, *s.*, *UK* salsicha; rojão; *pej.*, carroça.
BANG.LA.DESH, *s.*, Bangladesh.
BANG.LAD.ESHI, *adj.* e *s.*, bangaldeciano, bengalês, bengalense.
BAN.GLE, *s.*, bracelete, pulseira.
BAN.ISH, *v.*, banir, exilar, desterrar.
BAN.ISH.MENT, *s.*, exílio, desterro, deportação.
BAN.IS.TER, *s.*, corrimão; balaústre.

BANJO · 384 · BASQUE

BAN.JO, s., banjo.
BANK, s., banco, ribanceira; ladeira.
BANK.A.BLE, adj., negociável em banco.
BANK AC.COUNT, s., conta bancária.
BANK.BOOK, s., UK extrato bancário; US caderneta bancária.
BANK DIS.COUNT, s., desconto bancário.
BANK.ER, s., banqueiro.
BANK.ING, s., negócio de banco.
BANK.ING.HOUSE, s., casa bancária.
BANK LOAN, s., empréstimo bancário.
BANK MAN.AG.ER, s., gerente de banco.
BANK NOTE, s., CÉDUAL.
BANK PAPER, s., papel-moeda.
BANK.RUPT, adj., falido, quebrado; v., falir, quebrar.
BANK.RUPT.CY, s., falência, bancarrota.
BANK STATE.MENT, s., extrato bancário.
BAN.NER, s., bandeira, faixa de publicidade.
BAN.QUET, s., banquete; v., banquetear.
BAN.TAM, s., garnizé.
BAN.TAM.WEIGHT, s., Esp., peso-galo (boxe etc.).
BAN.TER, s., gracejo, ironia, sarcasmo.
BAN.TER.ING, s., escárnio, zombaria.
BANT.ING, s., fedelho, moleque.
BAP, s., UK bisnaguinha.
BAP.TISM, s., batismo.
BAP.TIS.MAL, adj., batismal.
BAP.TIST, s., Rel., batista.
BAP.TIS.TERY, s., batistério.
BAP.TIZE, v., batizar.
BAR, s., bar; barra, vara; empecilho, tribunal.
BAR.BAR.IAN, adj., bárbaro.
BAR.BAR.IC, adj., bárbaro, barbárico.
BAR.BA.RISM, s., barbarismo, barbaridade.
BAR.BA.RIZE, v., barbarizar, brutalizar.
BAR.BAR.OUS, adj., bárbaro.
BAR.BATE, adj., barbado.
BAR.BE.CUE, s., churrasco.
BARBED, adj., farpado, espinhento.
BAR.BER, s., barbeiro; v., barbear.
BAR.BI.TU.RIC, s., barbitúrico.
BAR.BI.TU.RATE, s., Quím., barbiturato.
BARE, adj., nu, despido; descoberto; mínimo (necessário); vazio; deserto; v., exibir, mostrar.
BARE.BACK, adj. e adv., em pelo (cavalgar sem sela).
BARE.FACED, adj., descarado, safado, sem vergonha.
BARE.FOOT, adj., descalço.
BARE.HEAD.ED, adj. e adv., sem chapéu.
BARE.LEGGED, adj. e adv., de pernas de fora.
BARE.LY, adv., apenas, mal, somente.
BARE.NESS, s., pobreza, miséria, carência.
BAR.GAIN, s., barganha, negócio, acordo; regatear, pechinchar.
BAR.GAIN.ING, s., barganha.
BARGE, s., barcaça, chata, barca.
BARG.EE, s., barqueiro.
BAR.IT.ONE, s., Mús., barítono (voz).
BARK, s., casca de árvore; v., curtir.
BAR.KEEP.ER, s., dono de botequim.
BARK.ER, s., cão que ladra; gritalhão (camelô); descascadeira.

BARK.ING, s., latido, ladrido; adj., ladrador, latidor.
BAR.LEY, s., cevada.
BARM, s., levedura, fermento.
BAR.MAID, s., garçonete.
BAR.MAN, s., empregado de bar.
BARN, s., celeiro.
BAR.NA.CLE, s., Zool., crustáceos cirrípedes que grudam em navios e rochas; fig., figura importuna, sarna.
BARN.EY, s., discussão, altercação, briga.
BARN.STORM, v., UK sair em turnê (pelo país).
BARN.STORM.ING, adj., UK vigoroso(a).
BA.ROM.E.TER, s., barômetro.
BAR.ON, s., barão, ricaço, magnata.
BAR.ON.ESS, s., baronesa.
BAR.ON.ET, s., baronete.
BA.ROQUE, adj., barroco(a).
BAR.RACK, v., aquartelar tropas; montar barracas.
BAR.RACK.ING, s., UK gritaria.
BAR.RACKS, s., quartel, caserna, exército.
BAR.RA.CU.DA, s., Zool., barracuda.
BAR.RAGE, s., barragem, dique; fogo de artilharia.
BARRED, adj., trancado.
BAR.REL, s., barril; v., embarrilar.
BAR.REL OR.GAN, s., realejo.
BAR.REN, adj., infecundo, estéril, seco.
BAR.REN.NESS, s., infertilidade, esterilidade.
BAR.RETTE, s., tiara ou pente que prende os cabelos.
BAR.RI.CADE, s., barricada; v., bloquear com barricadas.
BAR.RI.ER, s., barreira, empecilho, obstáculo.
BAR.RI.ER CREAM, s., UK loção protetora.
BAR.RING, prep., exceto, salvo, com exceção.
BAR.ROW, s., carrinho de mão.
BAR.TEND.ER, s., garçom, garçonete (esp. US).
BAR.TER, s., troca, permuta; v., trocar, cambiar, permutar.
BA.SALT, s., basalto.
BASE, s., base, fundamento, apoio; v., embasar, apoiar, basear.
BASE.BALL, s., beisebol.
BASE.BORN, adj., popular, plebeu, vulgar, bastardo.
BASE.LESS, adj., infundado, sem base.
BASE.LINE, s., Esp., linha de base (beisebol).
BASE.MENT, s., porão; fundamento, embasamento.
BASE METAL, s., metal não precioso.
BASE.NESS, s., baixeza, vileza.
BASH, v., soquear, esmurrar, dar socos.
BASH.FUL, adj., acanhado, tímido.
BA.SIC, adj., básico, fundamental, essencial.
BASIC, abrev. de Beginner's All-purpose Symbolic Instruction Code: BASIC.
BA.SI.CAL.LY, adv., basicamente.
BA.SIC WAGE, s., salário-base.
BA.SIL, s., manjericão.
BA.SIL.I.CA, s., basílica.
BA.SIN, s., bacia.
BA.SIS, s., base, fundamento.
BASK, v., aquecer.
BAS.KET, s., cesto, cesta.
BAS.KET.BALL, s., basquete, bola ao cesto.
BAS.KET.WORK, s., trabalho em vime; produtos em vime.
BASLE, s., Basileia.
BASQUE, adj. e s., basco.

BASRELIEF · 385 · BEAN SPROUTS

BAS.RE.LIEF, *s., Fr.*, baixo relevo.

BASS1, *s., Mús.*, baixo (voz); contrabaixo (instrumento); som ou tom baixo; *adj.*, baixo, grave, profundo.

BASS2, *s., Zool.*, lobo-do-mar, perca.

BASS CLEF, *s., Mús.*, clave de fá.

BASS DRUM, *s., Mús.*, tambor baixo.

BAS.SET, *s.*, cão basset.

BASS GUITAR, *n., Mús.*, baixo (violão ou guitarra elétrica).

BAS.SOON, *s., Mús.*, fagote.

BAS.SOON.IST, *s.*, fagotista.

BAS.TARD, *adj.*, bastardo, ilegítimo.

BAS.TARD.IZE, *v.*, abastardar.

BAS.TARD.LY, *adv.*, ilegitimamente.

BASTE, *v.*, untar carne com gordura; alinhavar; *fig.*, perverter; surrar; atacar com palavras.

BAST.ER, *s.*, colher para molho de gordura.

BAS.TING, *s.*, o molho que se despeja sobre a carne para untá-la; alinhavo; sova, bordoada.

BAS.TION, *s.*, bastião, baluarte, fortaleza.

BAT, *s.*, morcego; bastão: *v.*, usar um bastão.

B.TCH, *s.*, porção, pilha (de coisas); grupo (de pessoas); fornada.

BATE, *s.*, redução, abatimento.

BATED, *adj.*, diminuído, reduzido; *with ~ breath*: segurando a respiração.

BATH, *s.*, banho, banheira; *v.*, banhar-se, tomar banho.

BATH CHAIR, *s.*, carrinho para nenê ou deficiente físico.

BATH CUBE, *s.*, cubos de sais de banho.

BATHE, *v.*, banhar-se, tomar banho.

BATH.ER, *s.*, banhista, quem toma banho.

BATH.ING, *s.*, banho.

BATH.ING CAP, *s.*, touca de banho.

BATH.ING COS.TUME, *s.*, roupa de banho, maiô.

BATH.ING SUIT, *s.*, maiô.

BATH.ING TRUNKS, *s.*, calção de banho.

BATH MAT, *s.*, tapete de banheiro.

BATH OIL, *s.*, óleo de banho.

BATH.ROBE, *s.*, saída de banho; roupão de banho.

BATH.ROOM, *s., UK* banheiro.

BATH SALTS, *s. pl.*, sais de banho.

BATH TOWEL, *s.*, toalha de banho.

BATH.TUB, *s.*, banheira.

BA.TIK, *s.*, batique.

BA.TON, *s.*, batuta, bastão; *UK* cassetete de polícia.

BA.TRA.CHIA, *s.*, batráquios.

BA.TRA.CHI.AN, *s.*, batráquio.

BATS.MAN, *s., Esp.*, batedor (de cricket).

BAT.TAL.ION, *s.*, batalhão.

BAT.TEN, *s.*, tábua de assoalho, ripa; *v.*, engordar, tornar-se gordo.

BAT.TER, *v.*, espancar, castigar; *s.*, massa de farinha.

BAT.TERED, *adj.*, maltratado (pessoa, criança); arruinado (velho, carro); surrado (chapéu, roupa).

BAT.TER.ER, *s.*, demolidor, destruidor.

BAT.TER.ING, *adj.*, de cerco; *fig.*, de crítica; *to take a ~*: sofrer uma derrota.

BAT.TER.ING RAM, *s.*, aríete.

BAT.TER.ING BAT.TER.Y, *s.*, bateria de sítio.

BAT.TER.Y, *s.*, bateria de carro; trem de cozinha; bateria.

BAT.TE.RY CHAR.GER, *s.*, carregador de baterias.

BAT.TE.RY HEN, *s., UK* frango de granja.

BAT.TLE, *s.*, batalha, combate, guerra, luta.

BAT.TLE.DRESS, *s., UK* uniforme de combate.

BAT.TLE.FIELD, BAT.TLE.GROUND, *s.*, campo de batalha.

BAT.TLE.MENTS, *s. pl.*, ameias (de castelo).

BAT.TLE.SHIP, *s.*, couraçado.

BAT.TUE, *s.*, batida, diligência, captura.

BAT.TY, *s.*, maluco, pateta.

BAU.BLE, *s.*, bugiganga, ninharia.

BAUX.ITE, *s.*, bauxita.

BA.VAR.I.AN, *adj. e s.*, bávaro.

BAWD, *s.*, alcoviteira.

BAWD.RY, *s.*, linguagem chula, calão.

BAWD.Y, *adj.*, obsceno, indecente.

BAWD.Y HOUSE, *s.*, lupanar, bordel, casa de meretrício.

BAWL, *v.*, berrar, gritar.

BAY, *s.*, baía, enseada; latido; *v.*, latir, ladrar.

BAY LEAF, *s.*, folha de louro.

BAY.O.NET, *s.*, baioneta.

BAY TREE, *s.*, loureiro.

BA.ZAAR, *s.*, bazar, loja.

BA.ZOO.KA, *s.*, bazuca (arma).

B & B, *abrev.* de *bed and breakfast*: leito e café da manhã (pousada).

BBC, *abrev.* de *British Broadcasting Corporation*, companhia estatal de rádio e televisão britânica.

BC, *abrev.* de *before Christ*: antes de Cristo, a.C.

BE, *v.*, ser, existir, continuar, acontecer, estar.

BEACH, *s.*, praia; *v.*, encalhar, vir para terra firme.

BEACH BALL, *s.*, bola de praia.

BEACH BUG.GY, *s.*, carro de pneus largos que roda na areia (da praia).

BEACH.COMB.ER, *s., US* vagalhão, onda grande de praia; *UK* vagabundo de praia.

BEACH.HEAD, *s., Mil.*, cabeça de ponte.

BEACH WEAR, *s.*, roupa de praia.

BEACH.Y, *adj.*, praiano, de praia.

BEA.CON, *s.*, farol, faixa; *v.*, brilhar.

BEAD, *s.*, conta (de rosário ou de madeira, metal, etc.); gota, lágrima.

BEAD.ED, *adj.*, enfeitado com contas.

BEAD.ING, *s.*, moldura; ornato de contas; listra, filete.

BEA.DLE, *s.*, bedel, atendente, porteiro.

BEAD.Y, *adj.*, pequeno e brilhante, como contas; coberto com gotas ou bolhas.

BEA.GLE, *s.*, cão de caça.

BEAK, *s.*, bico; *v.*, bicar, atingir com o bico.

BEAKED, *adj.*, possuidor de bico.

BEAK.ER, *s.*, béquer, proveta.

BEAK IRON, *s.*, bigorna.

BEAM, *s.*, trave, viga; raio de luz; *v.*, brilhar, sorrir.

BEAM.FUL, *adj.*, luminoso, brilhante.

BEAM.I.NESS, *s.*, brilho, esplendor, luminosidade.

BEAM.ING, *adj.*, brilhante, luminoso.

BEAM.LESS, *adj.*, opaco, sem brilho.

BEAM.Y, *adj.*, brilhante, luminoso, claro.

BEAN, *s.*, feijão, grão.

BEANBAG, *s.*, saquinho cheio de feijões (brinquedo infantil); *UK* almofada cheia de flocos de espuma.

BEAN.SHOOT, *s., UK* broto de feijão.

BEANS.PROUT, *s., US* broto de feijão.

BEAN SPROUTS, *s. pl.*, vagem.

BEAR ··386·· BEETLE

BEAR, *s.*, urso; indivíduo que espera a queda de preços.
BEAR.A.BLE, *adj.*, suportável, aceitável.
BEAR.ABLE.NESS, *s.*, tolerância, ato de suportar.
BEAR.A.BLY, *adv.*, suportavelmente.
BEARD, *s.*, barba; *v.*, pegar pela barba.
BEARD.ED, *adj.*, barbado, barbudo.
BEAR.ER, *s.*, carregador, transportador, condutor; portador; detentor.
BEAR HUG, *s.*, abraço forte.
BEAR.ING, *s.*, comportamento, postura, porte, contato.
BEAR.ISH, *adj.*, bruto, brutamontes, grosseiro.
BEAR.ISH.NESS, *s.*, brutalidade, grosseria, estupidez.
BEAR OUT, *v.*, apoiar, confirmar, dar forças.
BEAR.SKIN, *s.*, pele de urso.
BEAR UP, *v.*, resistir, manter a calma.
BEAST, *s.*, bicho, animal, besta.
BEAST.I.NESS, *s.*, bestialidade, animalidade.
BEAST.LY, *adv.*, bestialmente, brutalmente.
BEAT, *s.*, batida; compasso, ritmo; *v.*, bater em, derrotar, superar.
BEAT.EN, *adj.*, batido, gasto, cansado.
BEAT.ER, *s.*, batedor, martelo, malho.
BEAT GEN.ER.A.TION, *s.*, geração beat.
BE.AT.I.FI.CA.TION, *s.*, beatificação.
BE.AT.I.FY, *v.*, beatificar.
BEAT.ING, *s.*, surra, sova.
BE.AT.I.TUDE, *s.*, beatitude.
BEAT ON, *v.*, surrar, bater em.
BEAT UP, *v.*, *UK* espancar, surrar.
BEAT-UP, *adj., col., US* velho, malconservado, surrado (carro, mala, etc.).
BEAU, *adj., s.*, janota, almofadinha, mauricinho.
BEAU.TE.OUS, *adj.*, belo, formoso, elegante.
BEAU.TE.OUS.NESS, *s.*, beleza, formosura, elegância.
BEAU.TI.CIAN, *s.*, esteticista (salão de beleza).
BEAU.TI.FUL, *adj.*, belo, formoso, elegante.
BEAU.TI.FUL.LY, *adv.*, formosamente, maravilhosamente.
BEAU.TI.FY, *v.*, embelezar.
BEAU.TY, *s.*, beleza, formosura, elegância, maravilha.
BEAU.TY CON.TEST, *s.*, concurso de beleza.
BEAU.TY PAR.LOR, *s.*, salão de beleza.
BEAU.TY QUEEN, *s.*, miss (que venceu concurso de miss).
BEAU.TY SPOT, *s.*, pinta (na pele); recanto, bela paisagem.
BEA.VER, *s.*, castor.
BE.BOP, *s.*, tipo de jaz cheio de dissonâncias.
BE.CALL, *v.*, injuriar, ofender, desrespeitar.
BE.CALM, *v.*, acalmar, aquietar, pacificar.
BE.CALMED, *adj.*, parado por falta de vento.
BE.CAME, *v.*, passado de *become*.
BE.CAUSE, *conj.*, porque, visto que, porquanto.
BE.CHAM, *v.*, seduzir, persuadir, convencer.
BECK, *s.*, aceno, sinal, gesto.
BE.CKON, *s.*, aceno, sinal; *v.*, acenar, gesticular.
BE.CLOUD, *v.*, obscurecer, ensombrar.
BE.COME, *v.*, tornar-se, vir a ser, chegar a ser, assentar.
BE.COM.ING, *adj.*, adequado, próprio, conveniente, certo.
BED, *s.*, cama, colchão; canteiro de flores; *v.*, acamar, ajeitar.
BED AND BRAK.FAST, *s.*, hospedagem com café da manhã (pousada, hotel etc.).
BE.DASH, *v.*, molhar, regar.
BE.DAUB, *v.*, sujar, emporcalhar.

BED-BATH, *s.*, banho na cama.
BED.BUG, *s.*, percevejo.
BED.CHAMB.ER, *s.*, quarto de dormir, dormitório.
BED.CLOTHES, *s. pl.*, roupas de cama.
BED.COV.ER, *s.*, colcha.
BED.DING, *s.*, roupa de cama; forragem para animais dormirem.
BED DOWN, *v.*, pôr na casa, deitar-se.
BE.DECK, *v.*, ornar, decorar, enfeitar.
BE.DE.VIL, *v.*, atormentar, maltratar; torturar; estragar, atrapalhar.
BE.DEV.IL.MENT, *s.*, feitiçaria; possessão por demônio.
BED HEAD, *s.*, cabeceira de cama.
BE.DIGHT, *adj.*, adornado, enfeitado; *v.*, adornar, enfeitar.
BE.DIM, *v.*, toldar, obscurecer.
BE.DIMMED, *adj.*, toldado, turvado, obscurecido.
BED.LAM, *s.* confusão, balbúrdia.
BED LIN.EN, *s.*, roupa de cama.
BED.MAK.ER, *s.*, arrumadeira.
BED.OU.IN, *adj.* e *s.*, beduíno.
BED.PAN, *s.*, comadre (urinol).
BE.DRAG.GLE, *v.*, sujar (roupa), molhar.
BE.DRAGGLED, *adj.*, enlameado.
BED.RID.DEN, *adj.*, acamado.
BED.ROCK, *s., Geol.*, leito de rocha firme; alicerce.
BED.ROOM, *s.*, quarto de dormir.
BED SE.TEE, *s.*, sofá-cama.
BED.SIDE, *s.*, cabeceira.
BED-SIT(TER), *s., UK* conjugado, quitinete.
BED.SORE, *s.*, assadura.
BED.SPREAD, *s.*, colcha.
BED-SPRING, *s.*, estrado de molas.
BED TA.BLE, *s.*, criado-mudo; mesa para comer na cama.
BED.TIME, *s.*, hora de dormir; hora de ir para a cama.
BED-WET.TING, *s.*, incontinência urinária.
BEE, *s.*, abelha.
BEECH, *s.*, faia.
BEEF, *s.*, bife, carne bovina, bisteca.
BEEF.BUR.GER, *s.*, hambúrguer.
BEEF.EAT.ER, *n.*, guarda da Torre de Londres.
BEEF.STEAK, *s.*, bife, bife pequeno.
BEEF.TEA, *s.*, caldo de carne.
BEEF.Y, *adj.*, carnudo; vigoroso, musculoso.
BEE.HIVE, *s.*, colmeia.
BEE.KEEP.ER, *s.*, apicultor.
BEE.KEEP.ING, *s.*, apicultura.
BEE.LINE, *s.*, linha reta; ir direto a alguém/algo.
BEEL.ZE.BUB, *s.*, belzebu, diabo, demônio.
BEEN, *v.*, particípio passado do verbo *to be*.
BEEP, *s., Inform.*, bipe; *v.*, bipar.
BEEP.ER, *s.*, bipe; dispositivo que bipa.
BEER, *s.*, cerveja.
BEER.GLASS, *s.*, copo de cerveja.
BEER HOUSE, *s.*, cervejaria.
BEER.I.NESS, *v.*, ficar bêbado com cerveja.
BEER JUG, *s.*, jarra para cerveja.
BEER MAT, *s.*, apoio para copo de cerveja, bolacha.
BEER MUG, *s.*, caneca de cerveja.
BEES.WAX, *s.*, cera de abelha.
BEET, *s.*, beterraba.
BEE.TLE, *s.*, besouro; malho, maço, macete; *v.*, malhar, bater.

BEETLESTOCK · 387 · BENZINE

BEE.TLE.STOCK, *s.*, cabo de pá.
BEETROOT,
BE.FALL, *v.*, acontecer, sobrevir.
BE.FIT, *v.*, convir a; ser próprio para.
BE.FIT.TING, *adj.*, próprio, conveniente, adequado.
BE.FOG, *v.*, enevoar, cobrir de nevoeiro, escurecer.
BE.FOOL, *v.*, enganar, iludir, lograr.
BE.FORE, *prep.*, antes de, perante; *conj.*, antes que; *adv.*, anteriormente.
BE.FORE.HAND, *adv.*, de antemão, antecipadamente.
BE.FOUL, *v.*, sujar, emporcalhar, imundar.
BE.FRIEND, *v.*, favorecer, apoiar, auxiliar.
BE.FUD.DLED, *adj.*, atordoado(a).
BEG, *v.*, mendigar, esmolar, pedir esmola.
BE.GAN, *v.*, passado de *begin*.
BE.GET.TER, *s.*, progenitor, gerador, criador, provocador.
BEG.GAR, *s.*, mendicante, mendigo, pedinte.
BEG.GAR.LI.NESS, *s.*, pobreza, miséria.
BEG.GARY, *s.*, pobreza, miséria, carência, necessidade.
BE.GIN.NER, *s.*, principiante, iniciante, neófito.
BE.GIN.NING, *s.*, início, começo, princípio.
BE.GONE, *interj.*, fora!, rua!, saia!
BE.GO.NIA, *s.*, begônia.
BE.GRUDGE, *v.*, cobiçar, desejar, querer.
BE.GUILE, *v.*, seduzir, enganar, iludir.
BE.GUIL.ING, *adj.*, encantador(a).
BE.GUN, *v.*, particípio passado de *begin*.
BE.HALF, *s.*, interesse, favor.
BE.HAVE, *v.*, comportar-se, portar-se.
BE.HAV.IOUR, **BE.HAV.IOR** *US*, *s.*, comportamento, postura.
BE.HAV.IOUR.ISM *UK*, **BE.HAV.IORISM** *US*, *s.*, behaviorismo.
BE.HEAD, *v.*, decapitar, degolar, cortar a cabeça.
BE.HEAD.ER, *s.*, carrasco, verdugo.
BE.HEAD.ING, *s.*, decapitação, degolamento.
BE.HELD, *v.*, passado e particípio passado de *behold*.
BE.HIND, *prep.*, atrás de; *adv.*, para trás, depois; *s.*, traseiro.
BE.HOLD, *v.*, ver; observar, contemplar; *interj.*, olhe!
BE.HOLD.EN, *adj.*, grato, agradecido.
BE.HOLD.ER, *s.*, espectador.
BE.HOOF, *s.*, interesse, uso, benefício.
BEIGE, *adj.*, bege.
BEI.JING, *s.*, capital da China: Pequim ou Beijing.
BE.ING, *s.*, existência, vida.
BEI.RUT, *s.*, capital do Líbano: Beirute.
BE.KNOWN, *adj.*, reconhecido, grato.
BE.LAT.ED, *adj.*, atrasado, demorado.
BE.LAT.EDLY, *adv.*, tardiamente.
BE.LAUD, *v.*, elogiar, louvar.
BE.LAY, *v.*, amarrar, trancar.
BELCH, *s.*, arroto, vômito; *v.*, vomitar, arrotar.
BELCH.ING, *s.*, vômito, arroto.
BE.LEA.GUER, *v.*, sitiar, cercar; assediar, importunar.
BE.LEA.GUERED, *adj.*, *Mil.*, sitiado; cercado; *fig.*, assediado.
BE.LEA.GUER.MENT, *s.*, sítio, cerco.
BEL.FRY, *s.*, campanário, torre.
BEL.GIAN, *adj.*, *s.*, belga.
BE.LIE, *v.*, esconder, ocultar, desmentir.
BE.LIEF, *s.*, fé, credo, ideia, opinião.
BE.LIEV.ABLE, *adj.*, crível, acreditável, verossímil.
BE.LIEVE, *v.*, acreditar, crer, confiar.

BE.LIEV.ER, *s.*, crente, fiel, seguidor, partidário.
BE.LIEV.ING, *adj.*, confiante, seguidor, crente.
BE.LIT.TLE, *v.*, decrescer, diminuir, reduzir.
BELL, *s.*, sino, campainha; *v.*, colocar sinos, dar forma de sino.
BELL-BIRD, *s.*, *Zool.*, araponga (pássaro).
BELL-BOT.TOMS, *s. pl.*, *Vest.*, calça boca de sino.
BELL-BOY, *s.*, mensageiro, carregador (de hortel).
BELL CLAP.PER, *s.*, badalo de sino.
BELLE, *s.*, mulher bonita, beldade; namorada.
BEL.LIG.ER.ENCE, *s.*, beligerância.
BEL.LIG.ER.ENT, *s.*, beligerante, lutador.
BEL.LOW, *s.*, mugido, grito de dor; mugir, bramir, berrar.
BEL.LOWS, *s. pl.*, *Mús.*, fole; pulmões.
BELL PUSH, *s.*, *UK* campainha, *US* botão de campainha.
BELL RINGER, *s.*, sineiro.
BELL SHAPED, *adj.*, no formato de sino, campânula.
BEL.LY, *s.*, ventre, barriga; *pop.*, pança.
BEL.LY.ACHE, *s.*, dor de estômago, cólica; *v.*, reclamar (queixando-se).
BEL.LY BUT.TON, *s.*, *col.*, umbigo.
BEL.LY DAN.CER, *s.*, dançarina do ventre.
BEL.LY DAN.CING, *s.*, dança do ventre.
BE.LONG, *v.*, referir-se, pertencer a.
BE.LONG.INGS, *s. pl.*, pertences.
BE.LOVED, *adj.*, amado, querido, quisto.
BE.LOW, *prep.*, sob, por baixo de, embaixo de.
BELT, *s.*, cinto, cinturão; *v.*, amarrar, segurar.
BEL.VE.DERE, *s.*, mirante, belvedere.
BELT.WAY, *s.*, anel viário, rodoanel.
BE.MOAN, *v.*, chorar, lamentar, deplorar.
BE.MOCK, *v.*, zombar, escarnecer.
BE.MUSE, *v.*, tontear, confundir; preocupar-se.
BE.MUSED, *adj.*, bestificado.
BENCH, *s.*, banco (madeira ou pedra); bancada; assento de juízes; juízes, juizado.
BENCH MARK, *s.*, marca de nível (ou de referência etc.).
BEND, *s.*, curva, dobra; *v.*, encurvar, dobrar.
BEND.A.BLE, *adj.*, flexível.
BEND.ING, *s.*, curva, dobradura.
BEND.Y, *adj.*, flexível.
BE.NEATH, *prep.*, abaixo de, sob, mais baixo, inferior.
BEN.E.DICK, *s.*, recém-casado.
BENE.DIC.TION, *s.*, bênção.
BEN.E.FAC.TOR, *s.*, benfeitor.
BEM.E.FAC.TRESS, *s.*, benfeitora.
BE.NEF.ICE, *s.*, benefício.
BE.NEF.I.CENCE, *s.*, beneficência.
BE.NEF.I.CENT, *adj.*, beneficente, filantrópico.
BEN.E.FI.CIAL.LY, *adv.*, vantajosamente.
BEN.E.FI.CIA.RY, *s.*, beneficiário, beneficiado.
BEN.E.FIT, *s.*, benefício, vantagem, proveito.
BEM.E.LUX, *s.*, Benelux (Bélgica, países baixos e Luxemburgo).
BE.NEV.O.LENCE, *s.*, benevolência.
BE.NEV.O.LENT, *adj.*, benévolo.
BE.NIGN, *adj.*, benigno, bondoso, amável.
BE.NIG.NI.TY, *s.*, benignidade, bondade.
BENT, *s.*, tendência; disposição, propensão; *adj.*, torto, curvado; *v.*, passado e particípio passado de *bend*.
BE.NUMB, *v.*, entorpecer.
BEN.ZI.NE, *s.*, benzina.

BENZOL — 388 — BIG MOUTH

BEN.ZOL, s., benzol.
BE.QUEATH, v., deixar em testamento, legar, testamentar.
BE.QUEST, s., herança.
BE.RATE, v., repreender, censurar, recriminar.
BER.BER, adj. e s., bérbere.
BE.REAVED, adj., enlutado.
BE.REAVE.MENT, s., luto.
BE.REFT, adj., liter., desolado(a); part. pas. de bereave.
BE.RET, s., boina, boné.
BER.GA.MOT, s., bergamota, tangerina.
BERK, s., UK palhaço.
BERM, s., berma, margem de um canal; acostamento.
BER.MU.DA, s., Bermudas (Ilhas).
BER.MU.DA SHORTS, s. pl., bermuda (calção).
BER.RY, v., produzir bagas; s., baga, semente.
BER.SERK, adj., furioso, frenético; s., guerreiro nórdico enfurecido.
BERTH, s., beliche, camarote, cabina.
BER.THAGE, s., ancoradouro.
BE.SEECH, v., suplicar, pedir, implorar.
BE.SEECH.ING, s., súplica, pedido.
BE.SET, v., atacar; cercar, sitiar, envolver; perturbar.
BE.SEEM, v., convir; ser conveniente, ser adequado.
BE.SEEM.ING, adj., conveniente, adequado.
BE.SIDE, prep., ao lado de, junto de.
BE.SIDES, adv., além disso, de qualquer modo; prep., além de.
BE.SIE.GE, v., sitiar, cercar; assediar.
BE.SMEAR, v., lambuzar, sujar.
BE.SMOKE, v., sujar com fumo.
BE.SOT.TED, adj., obcecado; apatetado; embriagado.
BE.SOUGHT, v., passado e particípio passado de beseech.
BE.SPEAK, v., pedir com antecedência.
BE.SPEC.TA.CLED, adj., com óculos.
BE.SPOKE, adj., feito sob medida; v., passado de bespeak.
BEST, adj., melhor; s., o melhor.
BE.STAIN, v., macular, manchar, sujar.
BES.TIAL, adj., bestial, animal, brutal, selvagem.
BES.TI.AL.I.TY, s., bestialidade, selvageria.
BES.TIAL.IZE, v., bestializar, brutalizar.
BES.TI.A.RY, s., bestiário.
BE.STIR, v., pôr em movimento, fazer mover.
BEST MAN, s., padrinho de casamento (do noivo).
BE.STOW, v., conceder, dar, outorgar, deferir.
BE.STOW.AL, s., concessão, graça, favor, mercê.
BEST-SELL.ER, s., bestseler, o livro mais vendido.
BEST-SEL.LING, adj., mais vendido.
BET, s., aposta, quantia; v., apostar, jogar.
BE.TAKE, v., ir para, mudar-se, transladar-se.
BETH.EL, s., santuário, lugar sagrado.
BE.TRAY, v., trair, atraiçoar.
BE.TRAY.AL, s., traição; revelação (de segredo).
BE.TRAY.ER, s., traidor.
BE.TROTHED, s., prometido(a) (para casar), adj., ant., noivo(a).
BET.TER, adj., adv., melhor; v., melhorar.
BET.TER HALF, s., cara-metade.
BET.TER.MENT, s., melhoria, melhoramento.
BET.TER OFF, adj., melhor (para uma situação).
BET.TING, s., aposta, ato de apostar; chance.
BET.TING SHOP, s., casa de apostas.
BET.TOR, s., apostador.
BE.TWEEN, prep., no meio de, entre.

BEV.EL, s., chanfradura; v., chanfrar; adj., chanfrado.
BEV.EL.LED UK, **BEVELED** US, adj., chanfrado(a).
BEV.ER.AGE, s., bebida.
BEVY, s., revoada, bando de pássaros, grupo.
BE.WAIL, v., chorar, lamentar.
BE.WAIL.ING, s., lamentação, choro.
BE.WARE, v., precaver-se, cuidar-se.
BE.WIL.DER, v., desnortear, confundir.
BE.WIL.DERED, adj., confuso(a), desnorteado(a).
BE.WIL.DER.ING, adj., desconcertante, desnorteante.
BE.WIL.DER.MENT, s., confusão; espanto.
BE.WITCH, v., fascinar, seduzir, encantar.
BE.WITCHED, adj., encantado.
BE.WITCH.ING, s., encantador, sedutor.
BE.WITCH.MENT, s., encanto, sedução, encantamento.
BE.YOND, prep., além de, acima de, fora de; adv., além.
BI-, prefix., bi, duas vezes; duplamente; dois, duas.
BI.AN.NU.AL, adj., duas vezes por ano, semestral.
BIAS, s., preconceito, tendência, inclinação.
BI.ASED, adj., preconceituoso, tendencioso, parcial, polarizado.
BI.AX.I.AL, adj., com dois eixos.
BIB, s., babador; parte superior (de avental, etc.); v., sorver, bebericar.
BI.BLE, s., Bíblia.
BIB.LI.CAL, adj., bíblico.
BIB.LI.OG.RA.PHER, s., bibliógrafo.
BIB.LI.OG.RA.PHY, s., bibliografia.
BIB.U.LOUS, adj., alcoólatra, viciado em bebida alcoólica.
BI.CAR.BON.ATE s., bicarbonato.
BI.CEN.TE.NA.RY, s., bicentenário.
BI.CEPS, s., bíceps.
BICK.ER, v., brigar, altercar.
BICK.ER.ING, s., briga.
BICK.ER.ER, s., briguento, brigão.
BI.CY.CLE, s., bicicleta.
BI.CY.CLE PATH, s., UK ciclovia.
BI.CY.CLE PUMP, s., bomba de ar (de bicicleta).
BID, s., oferta, lance; v., oferecer.
BID.DER, s., licitante.
BID.DING, s., licitação.
BIDE, v., esperar, aguardar; ant., viver, morar; tolerar.
BI.DET, s., bidê.
BI.EN.NIAL, adj., que ocorre a cada dois anos, bienal; s., bienal (evento).
BIER, s., caixão, esquife.
BI.FO.CALS, s., óculos bifocais.
BI.FUR.CATE, v., bifurcar.
BI.FUR.CA.TION, s., bifurcação.
BIG, adj., grande, imenso, volumoso.
BIG.A.MIST, s., bígamo.
BIG.A.MOUS, adj., bígamo.
BIG.A.MY, s., bigamia.
BIG DEAL, s., coisa grande; excl., grande coisa! (ironia).
BIG.GIN, s., touca.
BIG HAND, s., ponteiro dos minutos; salva de palmas.
BIG-HEADED, adj., metido, enxerido.
BIG HEART.ED, adj., generoso, bondoso.
BIG HOUSE, s., penitenciária.
BIGHT, s., baía, enseada; curva de rio; curva; esquina.
BIG MOUTH, s., pessoa linguaruda.

BIGNESS ··389·· BITTER LEMON

BIG.NESS, *s.*, grandeza, imensidão, volume.
BIG.OT, *s.*, fanático.
BIG.OT.ED, *adj.*, intolerante, fanático.
BIG.OT.RY, *s.*, fanatismo.
BIG SHOT, *s.*, figurão, costa larga.
BIG TIME, *s.*, o auge; posto mais alto; grande divertimento.
BIG TOE, *s.*, dedão do pé.
BIG TOP, *s.*, circo (lona).
BIG TREE, *s.*, *US* sequoia.
BIG WHEEL, *s.*, *UK* roda-gigante.
BIG.WIG, *s.*, figurão, manda chuva.
BIKE, *s.*, bicicleta.
BIKE.WAY, *s.*, *US* ciclovia.
BI.KI.NI, *s.*, biquíni.
BI.LA.BI.AL, *adj.*, *s.*, bilabial.
BI.LAT.ER.AL, *adj.*, *s.*, bilateral.
BIL.BER.RY, *s.*, baga de mirtilo; *Bot.*, uva do monte, mirtilo.
BILE, *s.*, bílis; mau humor.
BILGE, *s.*, *Náut.*, porão (de navio); *col.*, bobagem.
BIL.I.ARY, *adj.*, biliar, próprio da bílis.
BI.LIN.GUAL, *adj.*, *s.*, bilíngue.
BI.LIN.GUIST, *s.*, bilíngue.
BIL.I.OUS, *adj.*, bilioso; nauseado; de mau humor.
BILK, *v.*, enganar, iludir, falsear.
BILK.ER, *s.*, trapaceiro, vigarista.
BILK.ING, *s.*, fraude, trapaça.
BILL, *s.*, conta, fatura, nota; despesa em restaurante.
BILL.BOARD, *s.*, quadro de anúncio.
BIL.LET, *s.*, alojamento.
BILL.FOLD, *s.*, *US* carteira.
BIL.LIARDS, *s.*, bilhar.
BILL.ING, *s.*, faturamento.
BIL.LINGS.GATE, *s.*, *UK* linguagem vulgar.
BIL.LION, *s.*, bilhão.
BIL.LION.AIRE, *s.*, bilionário.
BILOCULAR, *adj.*, bilocular (dividido em duas células).
BIL.LOW, *s.*, onda, vaga.
BILL.POST.ER, *s.*, aquele que cola ou afixa cartazes.
BIL.LY.CAN, *s.*, panela com alça, caldeirão.
BIL.LY.COCK, *s.*, *col.*, chapéu coco.
BIL.LY GOAT, *s.*, *col.*, bode.
BI.MAN.U.AL, *adj.*, bímano, feito com as duas mãos.
BI.MONTH.LY, *s.*, periódico bimensal; *adj.*, bimestral; *adv.*, bimestralmente.
BIN, *s.*, caixa; *v.*, encaixotar, colocar em caixa.
BI.NA.RY, *adj.*, binário.
BIND, *v.*, atar, amarrar, ligar, unir.
BIND.ING, *s.*, ligadura, cinta; encadernação.
BIND UP, *v.*, ligar.
BINGE, *s.*, farra, bebedeira.
BIN.GO, *s.*, bingo.
BIN-LIN.ER, *s.*, *UK* saco de lixo.
BIN.OC.U.LARS, *s.*, binóculos.
BI.NO.MI.AL, *s.*, binômio.
BI.O.CHEM.IS.TRY, *s.*, bioquímica.
BI.O.DE.GRAD.A.BLE, *adj.*, biodegradável.
BI.O.DI.VER.SI.TY, *s.*, biodiversidade.
BI.O.ETH.ICS, *s.*, bioética.
BIO.GEN.E.SIS, *s.*, biogênese.
BI.OG.RA.PHER, *s.*, biógrafo.
BI.OG.RA.PHIC, **BI.O.GRAPH.IC.AL**, *adj.*, biográfico(a).

BI.OG.RA.PHY, *s.*, biografia.
BI.O.FUEL, *s.*, biocombustível.
BI.O.LOG.IC, **BI.O.LOG.I.CAL**, *adj.*, biológico.
BI.O.LOG.IST, *s.*, biólogo.
BI.OL.O.GY, *s.*, biologia.
BI.O.MASS, *s.*, biomassa.
BI.OME, *s.*, *Ecol.*, bioma.
BI.OM.E.TRY, *s.*, biometria.
BI.ON.IC, *adj.*, biônico.
BI.O.PIC, *s.*, *abrev.* de *biographical picture*: filme biográfico.
BI.OP.SY, *s.*, biopsia.
BI.O.SPHERE, *s.*, biosfera.
BI.O.TECH.NOL.O.GY, *s.*, biotecnologia.
BI.O.TER.ROR.ISM, *s.*, bioterrorismo.
BI.PAR.TITE, *adj.*, bipartido (dividido em duas partes).
BI.PED, *adj.*, *s.*, bípede.
BI.PLANE, *s.*, biplano.
BI.PO.LAR, *adj.*, com dois polos, bipolar.
BI.PO.LAR DIS.OR.DER, *s.*, transtorno bipolar.
BIRCH, *s.*, *Bot.*, bétula.
BIRCH.ING, *s.*, açoite, castigo, pena.
BIRD, *s.*, ave, pássaro.
BIRD CAGE, *s.*, gaiola.
BIRD.IE, *s.*, passarinho; *Esp.*, birdie (no golf).
BIRD OF PREY, *s.*, ave de rapina.
BIRD SEED, *s.*, alpiste (alimento de passarinho).
BIRD'S-EYE VIEW, *s.*, *UK* vista panorâmica.
BIRD-WATCH.ER, *s.*, observador de pássaros.
BI.RO, *s.*, esferográfica.
BIRTH, *s.*, nascimento; linhagem.
BIRTH CER.TIF.I.CATE, *s.*, certidão de nascimento.
BIRTH.DAY, *s.*, aniversário, dia de nascimento.
BIRTH.DOM, *s.*, direito de nascimento.
BIRTH.MARK, *s.*, sinal de nascença.
BIRTH.PLACE, *s.*, local de nascimento; terra natal.
BIRTH RATE, *s.*, taxa de natalidade.
BIRTH.RIGHT, *s.*, direito nato; patrimônio hereditário.
BIS.CUIT, *s.*, biscoito, bolacha.
BI.SECT, *v.*, *Geom.*, cortar ao meio; dividir em duas partes.
BI.SEX.U.AL, *adj.*, bissexual.
BISH.OP, *s.*, bispo.
BISH.OP.RIC, *s.*, bispado, diocese.
BI.SON, *s.*, bisão, bisonte.
BIS.SEX.TILE, *adj.*, bissexto; *s.*, ano bissexto.
BIS.TOU.RY, *s.*, bisturi.
BIT, *s.*, pedaço (pequeno); bocado; *fig.*, criançola; momentinho; pouco freio; refreio; broca, verruma; *Comp.*, bit; *v.*, colocar o freio na boca do cavalo; passado de *bite*.
BITCH, *s.*, cadela, cachorra; prostituta, meretriz, rameira.
BITE, *s.*, bocado cortado com os dentes, dentada; boquinha; picada, ferida; dor aguda; ato de agarrar; *v.*, morder; perfurar; roer; ferroar; abocanhar.
BITER, *s.*, mordedor.
BIT.ING, *s.*, cortante, mordente, picante, sarcástico.
BIT.LESS, *adj.*, sem freio, desenfreado.
BIT.MAP, *s.*, *Comp.*, mapa de bits, bitmap.
BIT PART, *s.*, ponta.
BIT.STOCK, *s.*, arco de pua; verruma.
BIT.TEN, *v.*, particípio passado de *bite*.
BIT.TER, *s.*, tipo de cerveja; *adj.*, amargo.
BIT.TER LEM.ON, *s.*, batida de limão.

BITTERLY   •• 390 •••   BLINDLY

BIT.TER.LY, *adv.*, amargamente.
BIT.TER.NESS, *s.*, amargura, amargo, rancor.
BIT.TERS, *s.*, licor doce-amargo.
BIT.TER.SWEET, *adj.*, agridoce.
BI.TU.MEN, *s.*, betume.
BIV.OUAC, *s.*, bivaque, acampamento; *v.*, acampar, acantonar.
BI.WEEK.LY, *s.*, periódico quinzenal, quinzenário; *adj.*, quinzenal.
BI.ZARRE, *adj.*, bizarro, exótico.
BLAB, *v.*, dar com a língua nos dentes, falar demais.
BLAB.BER, *v.*, falar de modo indiscreto.
BLACK, *adj.*, preto, negro, escuro, sinistro, sujo; *s.*, cor preta.
BLACK.A.MOOR, *s.*, negro.
BLACK.BALL, *v.*, votar contra; *s.*, voto contrário.
BLACK BEER, *s.*, cerveja preta.
BLACK BELT, *s.*, faixa preta.
BLACK.BER.RY, *s.*, amora preta; *Bot.*, silva, sarça.
BLACK.BIRD, *s.*, *Zool.*, melro.
BLACK.BOARD, *s.*, quadro-negro, lousa.
BLACK BOX, *s.*, caixa-preta (de avião).
BLACK.CAT.TLE, *s.*, gado vacum, bovinos.
BLACK COMEDY, *s.*, comédia de humor negro.
BLACK.CUR.RANT, *s.*, groselha preta.
BLACK E.CON.O.MY, *s.*, economia informal.
BLACK.EN, *v.*, empretecer, pintar de preto, tingir de preto; difamar.
BLACK EYE, *s.*, olho machucado, olho roxo.
BLACK.GUARD, *s.*, velhaco, safado, cafajeste.
BLACK.HEAD, *s.*, cravo (escuro).
BLACK.HEARTED, *adj.*, mau, maldoso, perverso.
BLACK HOLE, *s.*, *Astron.*, buraco negro.
BLACK.ING, *s.*, graxa.
BLACK.JACK, *s.*, vinte-e-um (jogo de cartas); cassetete; bandeira de piratas.
BLACK.LEAD, *s.*, grafite.
BLACK.LEG, *s.*, fura-greve.
BLACK.LIST, *s.*, lista negra.
BLACK.MAIL, *s.*, chantagem; *v.*, chantagear.
BLACK MAR.KET, *s.*, mercado negro.
BLACK.NESS, *s.*, escuridão.
BLACK OUT, *v.*, desmaiar, cerrar cortinas, desligar, apagar algo.
BLACK.OUT, *s.*, desmaio, queda geral de luz, escuridão, boicote.
BLACK SHEEP, *s.*, *fig.*, ovelha negra.
BLACK.SMITH, *s.*, ferreiro.
BLACK SPOT, *s.*, ponto cego.
BLAC-KTIE, *adj.*, black-tie (terno de gala).
BLACK.Y, *s.*, negro *m.*, negra *f.*
BLADE, *s.*, lâmina; espada; pá (de remo etc.); *fig.*, rapaz esperto.
BLAD.DER, *s.*, bexiga.
BLAM.A.BLE, *adj.*, censurável.
BLAM.A.BLE.NESS, *s.*, culpabilidade, censurabilidade.
BLAME, *s.*, culpa; *v.*, culpar, advertir.
BLAME.LESS, *adj.*, inocente.
BLAME.LESS.NESS, *s.*, inocência.
BLANCH, *adj.*, embranquecido; *v.*, embranquecer.
BLANCH.ING, *s.*, branqueamento.
BLANC.MANGE, *s.*, manjar branco.
BLAND, *adj.*, suave, brando, meigo.

BLAN.DISH, *v.*, adular, lisonjear.
BLAN.DISH.MENT, *s.*, lisonja, adulação, bajulação.
BLANK, *adj.*, em branco, vazio, com lacuna; *s.*, espaço em branco.
BLAN.KET, *adj.*, na íntegra; *s.*, cobertor; colcha, manta; *v.*, cobrir; aplicar-se (a todos); impedir.
BLANK.LY, *adv.*, inexpressivamente.
BLANK.NESS, *s.*, palidez.
BLARE, *s.*, clangor; *v.*, soar em volume muito alto; proclamar em voz alta.
BLAR.NEY, *s.*, lisonja, bajulação; *v.*, bajular, lisonjear.
BLAS.PHEME, *v.*, blasfemar, praguejar, amaldiçoar.
BLAS.PHEM.ER, *s.*, blasfemo, blasfemador.
BLAS.PHEM.ING, *s.*, blasfêmia.
BLASPHEMOUS, *adj.*, blasfemo(a).
BLAS.PHE.MY, *s.*, blasfêmia.
BLAST, *s.*, rajada de vento, pé de vento, explosão; *v.*, explodir, arrasar.
BLA.TAN.CY, *s.*, barulho, ruído.
BLAST.ED, *adj.*, maldito; detestável; arruinado.
BLAST FUR.NACE, *s.*, alto-forno.
BLAST-OFF, *s.*, decolagem (de foguete).
BLA.TANT, *adj.*, descarado.
BLA.TANT.LY, *adv.*, descaradamente.
BLAZE, *s.*, fogo, incêndio; *v.*, arder, brilhar.
BLAZ.ER, *s.*, casaco, blusa; bleizer.
BLAZ.ING, *adj.*, brilhante, luminoso.
BLEACH, *v.*, branquear; branqueamento.
BLEACH.ED, *adj.*, descolorido, desbotado.
BLEACH.ER, *s.*, alvejador, branqueador.
BLEACH.ERS, *s. pl.*, *US* arquibancadas.
BLEACH.ING, *s.*, alvejamento, descoramento.
BLEAK, *adj.*, desolado, sombrio.
BLEAK.NESS, *s.*, frio, frialdade.
BLEAR, *adj.*, turvo, escuro, opaco.
BLEAR.Y, *adj.*, turvo(a).
BLEAT, *s.*, balido; *v.*, balir.
BLEED, *v.*, sangrar, tirar o sangue.
BLEED.ING, *adj.*, ensanguentado; *s.*, hemorragia.
BLEEP, *n.*, apito, som estridente; *v.*, apitar, emitir som estridente.
BLEEPER, *s.*, bip, aparelho para receber chamadas.
BLEM.ISH, *s.*, marca, cicatriz; *fig.*, mácula (na reputação); *v.*, manchar; difamar.
BLEND, *s.*, mistura; *v.*, misturar.
BLENDER, *s.*, liquidificador.
BLEND.ING, *s.*, mistura, combinação.
BLESS, *v.*, abençoar.
BLESS.ED, *s.*, abençoado, santo.
BLESSING, *s.*, bênção; oração, pedido.
BLIGHT, *v.*, frustrar, impedir.
BLIN, *v.*, suspender, terminar.
BLIND, *adj.*, cego; *v.*, cegar; *s.*, persiana.
BLIND.AGE, *s.*, blindagem.
BLINDAL.LEY, *s.*, beco; *fig.*, beco sem saída.
BLIND.ED, *adj.*, cego.
BLIND.ER, *s.*, o que cega; antolhos de animal.
BLIND.ERS, *s. pl.*, *US* antolhos.
BLIND.FOLD, *s.*, venda; *adv.*, de olhos vendados; *v.*, vendar.
BLIND.ING, *adj.*, ofuscante, cegante.
BLIND.LY, *adv.*, cegamente; às cegas, *fig.*, sem saber.

BLINDNESS   ••391••   BLUSTERY

BLIND.NESS, *s.*, cegueira; *fig.*, falta de visão para algo.
BLIND SPOT, *s.*, ponto cego.
BLINK, *s.*, piscadela, piscada; cintilação, brilho; *v.*, piscar; cintilar, brilhar.
BLINK.ER, *s.*, antolhos; *v.*, pôr antolhos em.
BLINK.ERED, *adj., fig.*, bitolado.
BLINK.ERS, *s. pl., UK* antolhos.
BLIP, *s.*, bipe; ponto luminoso no radar; *fig.*, problema temporário.
BLISS, *s.*, felicidade, alegria, ventura; bem-aventurança.
BLISS.FUL, *adj.*, feliz, abençoado, bem-aventurado.
BLISS.FUL.LY, *adv.*, maravilhosamente; com felicidade.
BLIS.TER, *s.*, bolha, pústula; farol, sinal luminoso.
BLIS.TER.ING, *adj.*, abrasador; intenso; mordaz, cruel.
BLITHE, *adj.*, alegre, feliz, contente.
BLITHE.LY, *adv.*, despreocupadamente, alegremente.
BLITHE.NESS, *s.*, felicidade, alegria.
BLITZ, *s.*, ataque aéreo, ataque repentino; vistoria policial.
BLIZ.ZARD, *s.*, nevasca.
BLOAT, *v.*, inchar, intumescer; envaidecer.
BLOAT.ED, *adj.*, inchado, intumescido, empanturrado.
BLOAT.ER, *s.*, arenque (salgado e defumado).
BLOB, *s.*, gota, pingo; ponto distante indistinguível, borrão.
BLOC, *s.*, bloco, coligação partidária.
BLOCK, *s.*, bloco, laje; obstrução; *v.*, bloquear, obstruir, trancar.
BLOCK.ADE, *s.*, bloqueio.
BLOCK.AGE, *s.*, obstrução.
BLOCK.BUS.TER, *s.*, arrasa-quarteirão (bomba); grande sucesso (livro ou filme).
BLOCK.HEAD, *s.*, cabeça dura; *adj.*, ignorante.
BLOCK.ISH.NESS, *s.*, ignorância.
BLOG, *s., Inf.*, blog (sítio eletrônico atualizável).
BLOG.GER, *s., Inf.*, blogueiro *Bras*; bloguista *Port.*
BLOKE, *s., UK* cara; homem, sujeito.
BLOND, BLONDE *adj.*, e *s.*, louro, loura.
BLOOD, *s.*, sangue, linhagem, descendência; *v.*, sangrar.
BLOOD BANK, *s.*, banco de sangue.
BLOOD BATH, *s.*, banho de sangue.
BLOOD BROTH.ER, *s.*, irmão de sangue, irmão; amigo.
BLOOD-CUR.DLING, *adj.*, de gelar o sangue.
BLOOD.GUILT.Y, *s.*, homicida.
BLOOD.LESS, *adj.*, pálido; inanimado; sem derramamento de sangue; cruel.
BLOOD.LET.TING, *s.*, sangria; *fig.*, carnificina, matança.
BLOOD PRESSURE, *s.*, pressão sanguínea.
BLOOD.SHED, *s.*, derramamento de sangue, matança.
BLOOD.SHOT, *adj.*, injetado (olhos).
BLOOD.STAINED, *adj.*, manchado de sangue.
BLOOD.STREAM, *s.*, circulação sanguínea.
BLOOD TEST, *s.*, exame de sangue.
BLOOD.THIRST.Y, *adj.*, sanguinário.
BLOODY, *adj.*, sangrento, ensanguentado.
BLOOM, *s.*, flor, florescência, vigor; juventude; *v.*, florir, ser jovem.
BLOOM.ING, *adj.*, florido, florescente.
BLOS.SOM, *s.*, flor; florescência; *v.*, florir; florescer, desabrochar.
BLOS.SOM.Y, *adj.*, florido(a).
BLOT, *s.*, borrão de tinta, mancha, mácula; *v.*, borrar, manchar.
BLOTCH, *s.*, mancha na pele, grande mancha.

BLOTCH.Y, *adj.*, manchado.
BLOT.TER, *s.*, mata-borrão.
BLOUSE, *s.*, blusa.
BLOU.SON, *s., UK* blusão.
BLOW, *s.*, soco, golpe, pancada; *v.*, soprar, ventar, ofegar, bufar.
BLOW BACK, *v.*, trazer de volta.
BLOW-BY-BLOW, *adj.*, detalhado
BLOW-DRY, *s.*, secagem; *v.*, secar o cabelo (com secador de mão).
BLOW.FLY, *s.*, mosca varejeira.
BLOW.ER, *s.*, ventilador.
BLOW.GUN, *s.*, zarabatana.
BLOW.ING, *s.*, ventilação, hausto, sopro.
BLOW.LAMP, *s., UK* maçarico.
BLOW.OUT, *s.*, furo (de pneu); escape de ar; *fig.*, arroubo impulsivo; comilança.
BLOW.PIPE, *s., UK* zarabatana.
BLOW.TORCH, *s.*, maçarico elétrico.
BLUB.BER, *v.*, chorar, prantear.
BLUDG.EON, *s.*, clava, maça; *v.*, bater com clava; espancar; *fig.*, ameaçar.
BLUE, *s.*, azul, cor azul, firmamento; *adj.*, azul; *v.*, pintar de azul.
BLUE BLOOD, *s.*, sangue azul.
BLUE.BELL, *s., Bot.*, espécie de jacinto do Reino Unido, conhecida como campainha.
BLUE.BER.RY, *s., Bot.*, mirtilo.
BLUE.BIRD, *s., Zool.*, azulão (pássaro norte-americano)
BLUE-BLOOD.ED, *adj.*, de sangue azul, de descendência aristocrática.
BLUE.BOT.TLE, *s., Bot.*, escovinha (centáurea-azul); *Zool.*, varejeira-azul.
BLUE COL.LAR, *adj.*, operário (de produção).
BLUE JEANS, *s. pl., US* jeans; calça comprida azul de brim.
BLUE.PRINT, *s.*, planta, cópia heliográfica; *fig.*, plano; *v.*, tirar cópia heliográfica.
BLUE.STOCK.ING, *s., pej.*, sabichona, literata.
BLUFF, *s.*, simulação, blefe; *v.*, fingir, simular.
BLU.ISH, *adj.*, azulado.
BLUN.DER, *s.*, erro, asneira, bobagem; *v.*, fazer tolices, errar.
BLUN.DER.ING, *adj.*, desajeitado; precipitado.
BLUNGE, *v.*, amassar barro.
BLUNT, *v.*, embotar, cegar; *adj.*, embotado, cego; *s.*, agulha grossa.
BLUNT.LY, *adv.*, com franqueza; asperamente.
BLUNT.NESS, *s.*, embotamento; falta de visão.
BLUR, *s.*, borrão, mácula, obscuridade; *v.*, obscurecer, toldar, turvar.
BLURB, *s.*, sinopse, resumo.
BLURRED, *adj.*, desfocado; obscuro.
BLURRED.NESS, *s.*, indistinto, sumido, mal contornado.
BLUSH, *v.*, corar, enrubescer; *s.*, enrubescimento, rubor.
BLUSH.ER, *s.*, ruge.
BLUSH.FUL, *adj.*, envergonhado, corado, enrubescido.
BLUSH.ING, *s.*, vermelhidão, rubor; *adj.*, envergonhado.
BLUS.TER, *v.*, bramir, roncar, vociferar; *s.*, berro, violência, ruído.
BLUS.TER.ING, *adj.*, barulhento; estrondoso; violento.
BLUS.TER.ING.LY, *adv.*, estrondosamente.
BLUS.TER.Y, *s.*, gabolice, fanfarronice.

BOA   •• 392 •••   BOOKSACK

BOA, *s.*, boa, jiboia.
BOAR, *s.*, porco macho; javali.
BOARD, *s.*, tábua, prancha; quadro, tabuleiro; palco; mesa de conselho.
BOARD.ER, *s.*, aluno interno, pensionista.
BOARD.ING-CARD, *s.*, o mesmo que *boarding pass*.
BOARD GAME, *s.*, jogo de tabuleiro.
BOARD.ING HOUSE, *s.*, pensão, casa para pensão.
BOARD.ING PASS, *s.*, cartão de embarque.
BOARD.ING SCHOOL, *s.*, colégio interno, internato.
BOARD.ROOM, *s.*, sala da diretoria.
BOAST, *s.*, ostentação; *v.*, gabar-se, vangloriar-se, jactar-se.
BOAST.FUL, *adj.*, vaidoso, fanfarrão.
BOAST.ING, *s.*, presunção, ostentação.
BOAT, *s.*, bote, barco, canoa, navio; *v.*, levar em barco.
BOAT.ER, *s.*, chapéu de palha; barqueiro.
BOAT.ING, *s.*, passeio em barco.
BOAT.MAN, *s.*, barqueiro.
BOAT.SWAIN, *s.*, *Náut.*, contramestre.
BOB, *s.*, truque, logro; *v.*, enganar, lograr; *s.*, rapaz, pessoa, estudante.
BOB.BIN, *s.*, bobina, carretel; bilro.
BOB.BLE, *n.*, pompom; sacolejo, balanço.
BOB.BY, *s.*, *UK* policial, tira.
BOB.BY PIN, *s.*, *US* grampo para cabelo.
BOB.BY SOCKS, BOB.BY SOX, *s. pl., col.*, *US* meias soquete.
BOB.SLEIGH, *s.*, trenó de corrida; *v.*, andar de trenó.
BOCK, *s.*, cerveja.
BODE, *v.*, pressagiar, vaticinar.
BODE.MENT, *s.*, vaticínio, presságio.
BOD.ICE, *s.*, corpete.
BOD.I.LY, *adj.*, físico; *adv.*, em peso.
BOD.Y, *s.*, corpo, cadáver; tronco; grupo de pessoas; corpo sólido.
BOD.Y BAG, *s.*, saco mortuário.
BOD.Y BUILD.ER, *s.*, aquele que pratica musculação.
BOD.Y BUILD.ING, *s.*, fisiculturismo, musculação.
BOD.Y.GUARD, *s.*, guarda-costas.
BOD.Y.WORK, *s.*, carroceria (veículo); funilaria.
BOG, *s.*, pântano, charco, atoleiro; *v.*, atolar, afundar na lama.
BO.GEY, *s.*, fantasma, espectro; *UK* meleca de nariz.
BO.GEY.MAN, *s.*, bicho-papão.
BOG.GED DOWN, *adj.*, atolado(a).
BOG.GLE, *v.*, confundir, enganar.
BOG.GY, *adj.*, pantanoso, lodoso.
BO.GIE, *s.*, *Esp.*, um par (golfe); truque (trilho de trem); *UK gír.*, meleca (de nariz).
BO.GLE, *s.*, fantasma.
BOG-STAN.DARD, *adj., col.*, comum
BO.GUS, *adj.*, farsante,adulterado; *s.*, falsificação.
BO.HE.MI.A, *s.*, boemia, vida livre.
BO.HE.MI.AN, *adj. e s.*, natural ou habitante da Boêmia, boêmio.
BOIL, *s.*, ebulição, fervura; *v.*, ferver, estar inchado, aquecer para ferver.
BOILED, *adj.*, cozido(a).
BOI.LER, *s.*, caldeira.
BOIL.ING, *s.*, fervura, ebulição; fervente.
BOIL.ING POINT, *s.*, ponto de ebulição.
BOIS.TER.OUS, *adj.*, tumultuoso, barulhento, violento, rude.
BOIS.TER.OUS.NESS, *s.*, truculência, violência, rudeza.

BOLD, *adj.*, corajoso, valente, audaz, arrojado.
BOLD.LY, *adv.*, audaciosamente, corajosamente.
BOLD.NESS, *s.*, coragem, valentia, audácia.
BO.LIV.I.AN, *adj. e s.*, boliviano.
BOL.LARD, *s.*, *Náut.*, poste de sinalização ou amarração (para navios).
BOL.SHEVIK, *adj.*, bolchevique.
BOL.STER, *s.*, travesseiro.
BOL.STER.ING, *s.*, apoio, suporte; estofamento, almofada.
BOLT, *s.*, trinco, pino, parafuso; *v.*, trancar, aferrolhar; peneirar.
BOMB, *s.*, bomba, projétil; *v.*, bombardear, atacar.
BOM.BARD, *v.*, bombardear.
BOM.BARD.MENT, *s.*, bombardeio, bombardeamento.
BOM.BAS.TIC, *adj.*, bombástico.
BOMB.ER, *s.*, bombardeiro.
BOMB.ING, *s.*, bombardeio.
BOMB.PROOF, *adj.*, à prova de bombas.
BOMB.SHELL, *s.*, bomba.
BOMB.SITE, *s.*, área bombardada.
BOND, *s.*, vínculo, laço, obrigação; bônus; *v.*, ligar, unir, hipotecar.
BOND.AGE, *s.*, cativeiro, escravidão.
BOND.MAID, *s.*, escrava.
BOND.MAN, *s.*, escravo, servo.
BONE, *s.*, osso, espinha, chifre; *v.*, desossar, tirar as espinhas.
BONED, *adj.*, ossudo.
BONE-DRY, *adj.*, completamente seco(a).
BONE.HEAD, *s., col.*, estúpido.
BONE.LESS, *adj.*, sem osso(s).
BONE MARROW, *s.*, tutano, medula óssea.
BON.FIRE, *s.*, fogueira.
BON.GO, *s., Mús.*, bongô (percussão).
BO.NUS, *s.*, bônus, bonificação, dividendo.
BON.Y, *adj.*, ossudo, ósseo, cheio de ossos.
BOO, *excl.*, vaia; *v.*, vaiar.
BOOB, *s.*, *US* simplório, tolo; *UK* gafe; *boobs pl., col.:* seios, tetas.
BOOB TUBE, *s.*, *US* telinha (tevê); *UK* tomara que caia (roupa).
BOO.BY, *s.*, pessoa tola; *adj.*, bobo, ignorante.
BOO.BY HATCH, *s.*, manicômio, hospício; *Náut.*, escotilha da ré.
BOO.BY.ISH, *adj.*, tolo, imbecil, idiota.
BOO.BY PRIZE, *s., Esp.*, prêmio de consolação.
BOO.DLE, *s.*, luvas, suborno; cambada; *v.*, subornar, induzir a.
BOOGIE, *s., gír.*, balanço (dança); *v.*, sacudir (dança).
BOOK, *s.*, livro, caderno, obra literária; *v.*, registrar, pôr em livro.
BOOK.BIND.ER, *s.*, encadernador.
BOOK.BIND.ING, *s.*, encadernação; gráfica para encadernar.
BOOK.CASE, *s.*, estante, prateleira.
BOOK.COV.ER, *s.*, capa de livro.
BOOK.END, *s.*, suporte para livros; *bookends pl.*, prateleiras.
BOOK IN, *v.*, reservar quarto em hotel, anotar.
BOOK.ING OFFICE, *s.*, bilheteria.
BOOK.ISH, *adj.*, estudioso, aplicado; livresco.
BOOK.KEEP.ER, *s.*, guarda-livros.
BOOK.LET, *s.*, brochura.
BOOK.MAK.ER, *s.*, agenciador de apostas, bukmeiquer.
BOOK.MARK, *s.*, marcador de páginas.
BOOK.SACK, *s.*, *US* mochila.

BOOKSELLER ···393··· BOYFRIEND

BOOK.SELL.ER, s., livreiro, vendedor de livros.
BOOK.SELL.ING, s., venda de livros.
BOOK.SHELF, s., prateleira ou estante para livros.
BOOK.SHOP, s., livraria.
BOOK.STORE, s., US livraria, loja de livros.
BOOK TOKEN, s., UK vale-livro.
BOOK.WORM, s., traça de livro; fig., rato de biblioteca.
BOOM, s., estouro, estrondo; v., soar, ressoar, estourar.
BOO.MER.ANG, s., bumerangue.
BOON, s., bênção; favor, obséquio, ajuda; adj., alegre, feliz; Poet., bondoso.
BOOR, s., tipo rústico; camponês.
BOOR.ISH, adj., rústico, rude, grosseiro.
BOOR.ISH.NESS, s., rusticidade, grosseria.
BOOST, s., auxílio, estímulo; v., estimular, impulsionar, auxiliar.
BOOST.ER, s., incentivador; Med., reforço (de vacina).
BOOST.ER SEAT, s., esp. UK bebê conforto.
BOOT, s., bota, botina, chuteira, pontapé, chute; v., calçar botas, chutar.
BOO.TEE, s., botina.
BOOTH, s., barraca; cabine (telefônica etc.)
BOOT.LEG, s., cano de bota; adj., contrabando, ilícito.
BOOT.LEG.GER, s., col., contrabandista.
BOOT.LESS, adj., inútil, imprestável.
BOOT.LESS.NESS, s., inutilidade.
BOOT.Y, s., saque; butim, pilhagem; prêmio.
BOOZE, s., col., trago; v., tomar umas e outras.
BOOZER, s., col., UK bebum.
BOOZ.Y, s., embriagado.
BOP, s., murro; UK festa dançante; abrev. de bebop: tipo de jazz; v., esmurrar.
BOR.DER, s., margem, borda, orla, limite; v., limitar, orlar, bordejar.
BOR.DER.ING, s., borda, margem; adj., limítrofe, confinante.
BOR.DER.LAND, s., área fronteiriça.
BOR.DER.LINE, adj., fronteiriço; limítrofe; fig., limite.
BORE, v., esburacar, cavar, escavar; aborrecer; s., aborrecedor.
BO.RE.AL, adj., boreal.
BORED, adj., entediado.
BORE.DOM, s., tédio, fastio, aborrecimento.
BOR.ER, s., perfurador; furadeira; broca.
BORE.SOME, adj., enfadonho, cansativo.
BOR.ING, adj., aborrecido, enfadonho, enjoativo.
BORN, adj., part., nascido, nato.
BORNE, v., particípio passado de bear.
BO.ROUGH, s., município, distrito; Hist., burgo.
BOR.ROW, s., empréstimo; v., pedir emprestado.
BOR.ROW.ER, s., pessoa que pede ou toma emprestado.
BOR.ROW.ING, s., empréstimo.
BOR.STAL, s., UK programa correcional para jovens.
BOS.NI.AN, adj. e s., natural ou habitante da Bósnia, bósnio.
BOSS, s., chefe, patrão, dono; v., mandar, impor algo.
BOSS.Y, adj., mandão, metido, autoritário.
BO.TAN.IC, adj., botânico.
BOT.A.NIST, s., botânico.
BOT.A.NY, s., botânica.
BOTCH, s., remendo, remendão, serviço mal feito; v., remendar mal.
BOTH, pron., ambos, os dois, as duas.
BOTH.ER, s., preocupação, incômodo; v., incomodar, perturbar.
BOTH.ER.ATION, s., aborrecimento, incômodo.
BOTH.ERED, adj., preocupado, chateado.
BOT.TLE, s., garrafa, vasilhame, frasco; v., engarrafar.
BOT.TLED, adj., engarrafado.
BOT.TLE-FEED, v., alimentar com mamadeira.
BOT.TLE.NECK, s., engarrafamento.
BOT.TLE.OPEN.ER, s., abridor de garrafas.
BOT.TOM, s., fundo, parte mais baixa, traseiro, rodapé; adj., ínfimo, baixo; v., chegar ao fundo, ir à parte mais baixa.
BOT.TOM.LESS, adj., sem fundo.
BOT.U.LISM, s., Med., butolismo.
BOUGH, s., ramo, galho.
BOUGHT, v., passado e particípio passado de buy.
BOUL.DER, s., seixo, pedregulho.
BOU.LE, s., Quim., cristal sintético puro.
BOU.LE.VARD, s., do Fr., bulevar; alameda.
BOUNCE, s., pulo, vivacidade; v., saltar, pular, quicar; sair repentinamente; refletir.
BOUNC.ER, s., objeto que salta muito; leão de chácara; col., fanfarrão.
BOUNC.Y, adj., vivaz, exuberante; saltitante.
BOUND1, adj., com destino a, prestes a ir; s., pulo, salto; ricochete; v., pular, saltar.
BOUND2, v., passado e particípio passado de bind.
BOUND3, s., limite, fronteira; v., limitar, confinar.
BOUND.A.RY, s., fronteira, limite; fig., fronteiras.
BOUND.LESS, adj., ilimitado(a); infinito.
BOUN.TI.FUL, adj., beneficente, generoso.
BOUN.TI.FUL.NESS, s., bondade, generosidade.
BOUN.TY, adj., generoso, bondoso.
BOU.QUET, s., buquê; maço; aroma, perfume.
BOUR.BON, s., bourbon (uísque).
BOUR.GEOIS, adj., s., burguês.
BOUR.GEOI.SIE, s., burguesia; classe média.
BOUT, s., vez, turno, ataque, golpe.
BOU.TIQUE, s., do Fr., butique.
BO.VINE, adj., bovino.
BOW, s., laço, arco para flechas; desculpa, escusa; v., curvar-se, inclinar.
BOW.EL, s., intestino, tripa.
BOW.ELS, s., intestinos, entranhas, vísceras.
BOWL, s., tigela, bola; v., atirar uma bola.
BOWL.ER, s., lançador de bola.
BOWL.FUL, s., baciada, tigelada.
BOWL.ING, s., jogo de boliche; críquete.
BOWL.ING-AL.LEY, s., pista de boliche.
BOWL.ING-GREEN, s., US gramado para jogo de críquete; UK cancha de bocha.
BOW.MAN, s., arqueiro.
BOW-TIE, s., gravata-borboleta.
BOX, s., caixa, camarote; box; v., encaixotar, colocar em caixa, boxear.
BOXED, adj., encaixotado, empacotado.
BOX.ER, s., boxeador, pugilista; Zool., raça de cachorro.
BOX.ER SHORTS, s. pl., cuecas samba-canção.
BOX.ING, s., boxe, pugilato, luta.
BOX-OF.FICE, s., bilheteria.
BOY, s., rapaz, moço, menino, garoto.
BOY.COTT, s., boicote; v., boicotar.
BOY.FRIEND, s., namorado.

BOYHOOD · 394 · BREW

BOY.HOOD, *s.*, infância, meninice, adolescência.
BOY.ISH, *adj.*, criançola, infantil, pueril.
BOY.ISH.NESS, *s.*, criancice, infantilidade.
BOY SCOUT, *s.*, escoteiro.
BRA, *s.*, sutiã.
BRACE.LET, *s.*, bracelete, pulseira.
BRACK, *s.*, fenda, falha, defeito.
BRACK.ET, *s.*, suporte, classe, faixa, parêntese; *v.*, pôr entre parênteses.
BRACH.I.AL, *adj.*, *Anat.*, *Zool.*, braquial (relativo ao braço).
BRACH.Y.CEPH.A.LY, *s.*, braquicefalia (forma curta e arredondada d crânio).
BRAC.ING, *adj.*, revigorante.
BRACK.EN, *s.*, samambaia.
BRACK.ISH, *adj.*, salobre.
BRAD, *s.*, prego sem cabeça.
BRAG, *s.*, jactância, vaidade; *v.*, gabar-se, jactar-se.
BRAH.MAN, *s.*, brâmane.
BRAID, *s.*, cadarço, galão; trança; *v.*, trançar, entrelaçar.
BRAILLE, *s.*, braile.
BRAIN, *s.*, cérebro, miolos, inteligência, intelecto.
BRAIN.CHILD, *s.*, invenção.
BRAIN DEATH, *s.*, morte cerebral.
BRAIN FE.VER, *s.*, meningite.
BRAIN.LESS, *adj.*, sem miolos; desmiolado, irresponsável.
BRAIN.STORM, *s.*, *UK* bobeira; *US* ideia luminosa.
BRAIN.STORM.ING, *s.*, tempestade de ideias.
BRAIN-TEASER, *s.*, quebra-cabeça.
BRAIN WAVE, *s.*, *col.*, ideia luminosa.
BRAIN.Y, *adj.*, inteligente, perspicaz.
BRAKE, *s.*, trava, travão; *v.*, travar.
BRAKE-LIGHT, *s.*, luz de freio.
BRAMBLE, *s.*, *Bot.*, amoreira silvestre; amora silvestre.
BRAN, *s.*, farelo.
BRANCH, *s.*, ramo, galho; sucursal, filial; *v.*, ramificar.
BRAN.CHI.A, *s.*, brânquias, guelras.
BRANCH.ING, *s.*, ramagem, ramificação, ramo, galho.
BRANCH.Y, *adj.*, ramificado, ramado.
BRAND, *s.*, tição, marca de fogo no gado, sinal; *v.*, marcar, manchar.
BRAND.ISH, *v.*, brandir.
BRAND NAME, *s.*, *UK* marca registrada.
BRAN.DY, *s.*, conhaque, licor, aguardente.
BRAN.GLE, *s.*, latão; *v.*, cobrir com latão.
BRASH, *adj.*, *pej.*, atrevido.
BRASS, *s.*, latão, metal; *Mús.*, metais (instrumentos).
BRASS BAND, *s.*, fanfarra.
BRAS.SARD, *adj.*, braçal.
BRAS.SE.RIE, *s.*, restaurante barato.
BRAS.SIERE, *s.*, sutiã.
BRASS KNUCK.LES, *s. pl.*, *US* soco-inglês.
BRAT, *s.*, criança mal-educada, capeta.
BRA.VA.DO, *s.*, desafio, bravata.
BRAVE, *adj.*, bravo, corajoso, valente, atrevido; *v.*, desafiar.
BRAVE.LY, *adv.*, bravamente, corajosamente.
BRAV.ER.Y, *s.*, coragem, valentia.
BRA.VO, *interj.*, bravo!, muito bem!
BRAWL, *s.*, briga.
BRAWN, *s.*, músculo, força física.
BRAWN.Y, *adj.*, musculoso, forte, vigoroso.
BRAY, *v.*, zurrar; *s.*, zurro.

BRA.ZEN, *adj.*, descarado; *v.*, ser descarado.
BRA.ZEN.NESS, *s.*, descaramento.
BRA.ZI.ER, *s.*, braseiro.
BRA.ZIL, *s.*, Brasil.
BRA.ZIL.IAN, *adj.*, *s.*, brasileiro.
BRA.ZIL NUT, *s.*, castanha-do-pará.
BRA.ZIL.WHOOD, *s.*, pau-brasil.
BREACH, *s.*, brecha, fenda, abertura; *v.*, abrir brecha, fender.
BREAD, *s.*, pão.
BREAD.BOARD, *s.*, tábua de cortar pão.
BREAD.BOX, *s.*, caixa para pão.
BREAD.CRUMB, *s.*, migalha de pão.
BREAD.CRUMBS, *s. pl.*, farinha de rosca.
BREAD.ED, *adj.*, empanado.
BREAD.LESS, *adj.*, sem pão; desempregado.
BREAD.LINE, *s.*, fila para receber pão ou alimento; *fig.*, limite da pobreza.
BREADTH, *s.*, largura.
BREAD.WIN.NER, *s.*, o ganha-pão; arrimo (de família).
BREAK, *v.*, quebrar, partir, transgredir; *s.*, abertura, fratura, quebra.
BREAK.A.BLE, *adj.*, frágil, quebradiço.
BREAK.AGE, *s.*, rotura, fratura, quebradura.
BREAK.A.WAY, *adj.*, dissidente.
BREAK.DOWN, *s.*, quebra, avaria; detalhamento; desarranjo; *Med.*, colapso nervoso.
BREAK.ER, *s.*, rebentação (de onda); britador; violador (quebrador de regras).
BREAK-E.VEN, *s.*, ponto de equilíbrio.
BREAK.FAST, *s.*, desjejum, primeira refeição do dia; *v.*, tomar café.
BREAK-IN, *s.*, arrombamento.
BREAK.ING, *s.*, fratura, arrombamento.
BREAK.ING POINT, *s.*, limite; ponto de ruptura.
BREAK.NECK, *adj.*, arriscado, perigoso.
BREAK.THROUGH, *s.*, *Mil.*, avanço (sobre as linhas inimigas).
BREAK-UP, *s.*, dissolução, rompimento; decaída.
BREAST, *s.*, peito, tórax; mama, teta; sentimentos; *v.*, peitar, enfrentar.
BREAST.STROKE, *s.*, *Esp.*, nado de peito.
BREATH, *s.*, respiração, hálito, alento, bafo, fôlego, brisa.
BREATHE, *v.*, respirar, tomar fôlego, descansar, ventar.
BREATH.ER, *s.*, pausa.
BREATH.ING, *s.*, respiração.
BREATH.LESS, *adj.*, ofegante, esbaforido; ansioso, radiante; abafado (clima).
BREATH.TAK.ING, *adj.*, surpreendente, excitante, incrível.
BREATH TEST, *s.*, teste de bafômetro.
BREECH, *s.*, traseiro, nádegas.
BREED, *s.*, raça (animal); *fig.*, tipo; *v.*, criar; produzir; *fig.*, gerar; passado e particípio passado de *bred*.
BREED.ER, *s.*, reprodutor, produtor.
BREED.ING, *s.*, reprodução, educação.
BREED.ING-GROUND, *s.*, local de procriação; *fig.*, origem.
BREEZE, *s.*, brisa, aragem, vento suave.
BREEZ.I.NESS, *s.*, jovialidade, alegria, contentamento.
BRE.VET, *s.*, patente, licença; *v.*, deferir a patente, licenciar.
BRE.VI.ATE, *v.*, abreviar, resumir; *adj.*, abreviado, resumido; *s.*, resumo.
BREV.I.TY, *s.*, brevidade, resumo, concisão.
BREW, *s.*, bebida fermentada, bebida; *v.*, fazer cerveja.

BREWAGE ···395··· BROWN

BREW.AGE, *s.*, fabricação de cerveja, cerveja.
BREW.ER, *s.*, cervejeiro.
BREW.ERY, *s.*, cervejaria.
BRIBE, *s.*, suborno; *v.*, subornar.
BRIBE.LESS, *adj.*, insubornável.
BRIB.ER, *s.*, subornador.
BRIB.ERY, *s.*, suborno.
BRIC-A-BRAC, *s.*, bricabraque, bugigangas, quinquilharias.
BRICK, *s.*, tijolo, coisa.
BRICK.LAY.ER, *s.*, pedreiro.
BRICK.LED, *adj.*, frágil, quebradiço.
BRICK.MAK.ER, *s.*, fabricante de tijolos.
BRICK.WORK, *s.*, construção com tijolos.
BRID.AL, *adj.*, nupcial.
BRIDE, *s.*, noiva.
BRIDE.BED, *s.*, leito nupcial, tálamo.
BRIDE.CAKE, *s.*, bolo da noiva, bolo de casamento.
BRIDE.GROOM, *s.*, noivo.
BRIDGE, *s.*, ponte; ponte de comando; jogo de cartas.
BRI.DLE, *s.*, rédea, freio, cabeçada; *v.*, reprimir, sufocar, restringir.
BRI.DLE-PATH, *s.*, trilha, pista (para cavaleiros).
BRIEF, *s.*, sumário, síntese; *adj.*, breve; *v.*, resumir, sintetizar.
BRIEF.CASE, *s.*, pasta executiva.
BRIEF.ING, *s.*, instruções.
BRIEF.LY, *adv.*, resumidamente, rapidamente.
BRIEF.NESS, *s.*, brevidade, concisão, síntese.
BRIER, *s.*, *Bot.*, roseira brava; *Bot.*, urze-branca; cachimbo feito dessa planta.
BRIG, *s.*, brigue, navio.
BRI.GADE, *s.*, *Mil.*, brigada.
BRIG.A.DIER, *s.*, brigadeiro.
BRIG.AND, *s.*, bandido, criminoso, salteador.
BRIGHT, *adj.*, brilhante, luminoso; inteligente, feliz, alegre.
BRIGHT.EN, *v.*, animar, alegrar, clarear, iluminar.
BRIGHT.LY, *adv.*, brilhantemente, alegremente, fortemente; inteligentemente.
BRIGHT.NESS, *s.*, brilho, esplendor, luminosidade.
BRIL.LIANCE, *s.*, brilho, esplendor, claridade.
BRIL.LIANT, *adj.*, brilhante; maravilhoso.
BRIL.LIANT.LY, *adv.*, brilhantemente; em cores vivas.
BRIM.STONE, *s.*, enxofre.
BRIM, *s.*, borda, oral; aba; beira; *v.*, estar cheio até a borda.
BRINE, *s.*, salmoura; *fig.*, água do mar.
BRING, *v.*, trazer, transportar, carregar.
BRING ALONG, *v.*, carregar consigo.
BRING BACK, *v.*, devolver, recompor.
BRING.ER, *s.*, portador.
BRING IN, *v.*, introduzir, tirar de dentro, trazer.
BRING.ING, *s.*, transporte.
BRING TO.GETH.ER, *v.*, apresentar pessoas, reconciliar.
BRINK, *s.*, orla, margem.
BRINY, *adj.*, salgado, salobro.
BRISK, *v.*, animar, estimular; *adj.*, vivo, forte, vigoroso.
BRIS.KET, *s.*, carne de peito (de boi, de animal).
BRISK.LY, *adv.*, desembaraçadamente, vivamente.
BRISK.NESS, *s.*, viveza, força, estímulo.
BRIS.TLE, *s.*, pelo, cerda, barba dura; *v.*, irritar-se, enraivar-se.
BRIS.TLY, *adj.*, duro, hirsuto, resistente.
BRIT.AIN, *s.*, Grã-Bretanha.
BRI.TAN.NIC, *adj.*, *s.*, britânico.

BRIT.TAN.Y, *s.*, Bretanha.
BRIT.I.CISM, *s.*, britanicismo.
BRIT.ISH, *adj.*, britânico.
BRIT.ON, *adj.*, bretão, nativo ou habitante da Grã-Bretanha.
BRIT.TLE, *adj.*, frágil, quebradiço.
BRIT.TLE.NESS, *s.*, fragilidade, fraqueza.
BROACH, *v.*, abordar, começar, iniciar; *s.*, sovela, furador, mandril.
BROAD, *adj.*, largo, amplo.
BROAD BAND, *s.*, banda larga.
BROAD BEAN, *s.*, fava.
BROAD.CAST, *s.*, transmissão de rádio ou TV; *v.*, transmitir.
BROAD.CAST.ER, *s.*, locutor (de rádio ou TV).
BROAD.CAST.ING, *s.*, transmissão (de rádio ou TV).
BROAD.EN, *v.*, alargar, aumentar.
BROAD.LY, *adv.*, geralmente; largamente, abertamente.
BROUD.LY-BASED, *adj.*, bases amplas.
BROAD.MIND.ED, *adj.*, tolerante, compreensivo.
BROAD.NESS, *s.*, largura, amplitude.
BROAD.SHEET, *s.*, folha grande de papel; cartaz.
BRO.CADE, *s.*, brocado.
BROC.CO.LI, *s.*, brócolos, brócolis.
BRO.CHURE, *s.*, brochura, livreto, folheto.
BROGUE, *s.*, sotaque; *UK* chanca, sapato grande.
BROI.DERY, *s.*, bordado.
BROIL, *v.*, grelhar, assar na grelha.
BROIL.ER, *s.*, grelha.
BROKE, *adj.*, falido(a); *v.*, passado de *break*.
BRO.KEN, *adj.*, *part.*, quebrado, partido.
BRO.KEN-DOWN, *adj.*, falido, arruinado, destruído.
BRO.KER, *s.*, corretor.
BRO.KER.AGE, *s.*, corretagem, ato de fazer a corretagem.
BROKERY, *s.*, corretagem.
BROL.LY, *s.*, guarda-chuva.
BRO.MINE, *s.*, *Quím.*, bromo.
BRONCHIA, *s. pl.*, brônquios.
BRON.CHIT.IC, *adj.*, próprio da bronquite.
BRON.CHI.TIS, *s.*, bronquite.
BRONZE, *s.*, bronze; *v.*, bronzear, dar cor de bronze.
BRONZED, *adj.*, bronzeado(a).
BRONZY, *adj.*, bronzeado, revestido de bronze.
BROOCH, *s.*, broche, alfinete.
BROOD, *v.*, pensar, cismar, refletir.
BROOD.Y, *s.*, pensativo; choco(a) (ave).
BROOK, *s.*, regato, arroio, ribeiro.
BROOK.LET, *s.*, regato, arroio.
BROOM, *s.*, vassoura.
BROOM.STICK, *s.*, cabo de vassoura.
BROS, **BROS**, *s. pl.*, *abrev.* de *brothers*: irmãos.
BROTH, *s.*, caldo.
BROTH.EL, *s.*, bordel, lupanar.
BROTH.ER, *s.*, irmão.
BROTH.ER.HOOD, *s.*, irmandade, fraternidade, família.
BROTH.ER.IN.LAW, *s.*, cunhado.
BROTH.ER.LY, *adj.*, fraternal; *adv.*, fraternalmente.
BROUGHT, *v.*, passado e particípio passado de *bring*.
BROW, *s.*, testa, fronte, sobrancelha; cume, pico; *v.*, estar na orla.
BROW.BEAT, *v.*, intimidar.
BROW.BEAT.EN, *adj.*, intimidado(a).
BROWN, *adj.*, castanho, pardo, moreno; *s.*, cor castanha.

BROWN RICE ··· 396 ··· BUNG

BROWN RICE, *s.*, arroz integral.
BROWN.ISH, *adj.*, acastanhado, amorenado.
BROWN SUG.AR, *s.*, açúcar mascavo.
BROWSE, *s.*, ato de pastar; *v.*, dar uma olhada (sem compromisso); pastar; *Inform.*, navegar na Web.
BROWS.ER, *s.*, *Inform.*, navegador.
BRUCKLE, *adj.*, frágil, fraco.
BRUISE, *s.*, contusão, hematoma, machucadura; *v.*, machucar, magoar.
BRU.MOUS, *adj.*, brumoso, enevoado.
BRUNCH, *s.*, almoço depois da hora.
BRU.NETTE, *s.*, morena.
BRUNT, *s.*, parte mais difícil; perigo ou crise.
BRUSH, *s.*, escova, pincel, ato de escovar; *v.*, escovar, varrer, limpar.
BRUSHED, *adj.*, fio (de algodão).
BRUSH.ING, *s.*, escovadela, pequena escovada.
BRUSH UP, *v.*, retocar, refazer.
BRUSH.WOOD, *s.*, gravetos, galhos; matagal.
BRUSH.WORK, *s.*, pincelada (de pintor).
BRUSQUE, *adj.*, brusco, áspero, rude.
BRU.TAL, *adj.*, brutal.
BRU.TAL.ISM, *s.*, brutalismo, brutalidade.
BRU.TAL.I.TY, *s.*, brutalidade.
BRU.TAL.IZA.TION, *s.*, brutalização, perversidade, animalismo.
BRU.TAL.IZE, *v.*, brutalizar, bestializar.
BRUTE, *adj.*, *s.*, bruto, animal.
BUB.BLE, *s.*, bolha; *v.*, borbulhar.
BUB.BLE BATH, *s.*, banho de espuma.
BUB.BLE GUM, *s.*, chiclete de bola.
BUB.BLING, *s.*, fervura, ebulição.
BUB.BLY, *s.*, efervescente; champanha; *adj.*, espumante.
BUC.CAL, *adj.*, bucal, próprio da boca.
BUCK, *s.*, macho (humanos ou animais); pinote; pulo; resistir, ir contra; derrubar (cavalo); *US gír.*, dólar.
BUCK.ET, *s.*, balde.
BUCK.LE, *s.*, fivela; *v.*, afivelar.
BUCK.SHEE, *s.*, gorjeta, gratificação.
BUCK.SHOT, *s.*, chumbo (de arma de caça).
BUCK.SKIN, *s.*, pele de cervo.
BUCK.TEETH, *s. pl.*, destes salientes.
BUCK.THORN, *s.* espinheiro.
BU.COL.IC, *adj.*, bucólico.
BUD, *s.*, botão, broto; *v.*, brotar, nascer.
BUD.DHISM, *s.*, budismo.
BUD.DHIST, *adj.* e *s.*, budista.
BUD.DING, *adj.*, que está iniciando, principiante.
BUD.DY, *s.*, *col.*, camarada, amigo, companheiro.
BUDGE, *v.*, mover-se, mexer-se, fazer mover.
BUD.GER.I.GAR, *s.*, *Zool.*, periquito australiano.
BUD.GET, *s.*, orçamento, receita; bolsa de couro; *v.*, fazer orçamento.
BUD.GET.A.RY, *adj.*, orçamentário.
BUD.GIE, *s.*, *col.*, periquito.
BUFF, *adj.*, pardo; da cor do couro; *s.*, couro ou casaco de couro de búfalo; fã; experto.
BUF.FA.LO, *s.*, búfalo.
BUFF.ER, *s.*, para-choque.
BUF.FET, *s.*, bufê; bufete; guarda-louça; restaurante (com refeição disposta para o cliente se servir).

BUF.FOON, *s.*, bobo, tolo, palhaço.
BUF.FOON.ERY, *s.*, tolice, idiotice; palhaçada.
BUG, *s.*, bicho, inseto, besouro.
BUG.BEAR, *s.*, bicho-papão, fantasma.
BUG.GER, *s.*, velhaco; *UK* porre; desgraçado (pessoa).
BU.GLE, *s.*, trombeta; clarim; trompa de caça.
BUG.GY, *s.*, carrinho para nenê.
BUILD, *s.*, construção, estilo, talhe, manequim; *v.*, construir.
BUILD.ER, *s.*, construtor, empreiteiro.
BUILD.ING, *s.*, construção, edifício.
BUILD.ING CON.TRAC.TOR, *s.*, constructor(a), empreiteira.
BUILD.ING-SITE, *s.*, canteiro de obras.
BUILD-UP, *s.*, desenvolvimento, formação, progresso.
BUILT, *adj.*, e *part.*, construído, edificado.
BUILT-UP, *adj.*, área urbanizada, muito construído.
BULB, *s.*, lâmpada elétrica; coisa bulbiforme; *Bot.*, bulbo.
BULB.OUS, *adj.*, bulboso, bulbiforme.
BUL.GAR.I.AN, *adj.* e *s.*, nativo ou habitante da Bulgária, búlgaro.
BULGE, *s.*, protuberância, inchação; *v.*, inchar; estufar.
BULG.ING, *adj.*, protuberante; abarrotado; musculoso.
BU.LIM.IA, *s.*, *Med.*, bulimia.
BULK, *s.*, volume, massa; tamanho; *Náut.*, porão de navio; *adj.*, a ganel; *v.*, ter tamanho, importância.
BULK.HEAD, *s.*, divisória, biombo.
BULK.Y, *adj.*, volumoso, corpulento.
BULL, *s.*, touro, macho; bula, escrito.
BULL.DOG, *s.*, buldogue.
BULL.DOZE, *v.*, aplainar; terraplenar; *fig.*, coagir.
BULL.DOZ.ER, *s.*, escavadeira; *fig.*, intimidador.
BUL.LET, *s.*, bala (de arma de fogo), projétil; marcador (usado em texto).
BUL.LE.TIN, *s.*, boletim, publicação.
BUL.LET-PROOF, *adj.*, à prova de bala.
BULL.FIGHT, *s.*, tourada.
BULL.FIGHT.ER, *s.*, toureiro.
BULL.FIGHT.ING, *s.*, touradas; o mesmo que *bullfight*.
BUL.LION, *s.*, barras de ouro ou prata.
BULL.ISH, *adj.*, em alta (bolsa de valores); relativo a ou semelhante a um touro.
BULL MAR.KET, *s.*, mercado em alta.
BUL.LOCK, *s.*, boi.
BULL.RING, *s.*, arena para touradas.
BULL.SHIT, *s.*, *vulg.*, papo furado.
BUL.LY, *s.*, brigão; *v.*, ameaçar, intimidar.
BUL.LY.ING, *s.*, maus-tratos.
BUL.RUSH, *s.*, *Bot.*, junco, papiro.
BUM, *s.*, vagabundo, farra; *vulg.*, nádegas, traseiro.
BUM BAG, *s.*, *col.*, pochete, capanga (bolsa de cinto).
BUM.BLE-BEE, *s.*, *Zool.*, abelhão.
BUM.BLING, *adj.*, *col.*, inútil.
BUMF, *s.*, *UK* papelada, documentos.
BUMP, *s.*, impacto, batida, choque; *v.*, bater, chocar-se.
BUMP.ER, *s.*, para-choque.
BUMP.ER-TO-BUM.PER, *adj.*, trânsito congestionado.
BUMP.TIOUS, *adj.*, *pej.*, presunçoso, arrogante.
BUMP.Y, *adj.*, esburacado, acidentado; ventoso.
BUN, *s.*, bolo, pãozinho, doce de passas.
BUNCH, *s.*, buquê de flores, maço; molho, feixe, cacho.
BUN.DLE, *s.*, trouxa, pacote, embrulho.
BUNG, *s.*, rolha, tampão, batoque; *v.*, tampar, fechar.

BUNGALOW
··397··
BYROAD

BUN.GA.LOW, s., bangalô, chalé.
BUN.GEE-JUMP.ING, s., Esp., bungee jumping.
BUN.GLE, s., trabalho mal feito; v., estragar, fazer mal um serviço.
BUN.ION, s., Med., joanete.
BUNK, s., beliche, cama; v., dormir em beliche.
BUNK BED, s., beliche.
BUN.KER, s., mina de carvão; casamata, búnquer.
BUNK.HOUSE, s., alojamento, construção rústica.
BUN.NY, s., coelho.
BUNTING, s., bandeirolas.
BUOY, s., boia, salva-vidas; v., boiar, flutuar.
BUOY.ANCE, BUOYANCY, s., capacidade de flutuar; otimismo, ânimo.
BUOY.ANT, adj., flutuante, que boia.
BUR.DEN.OUS, adj., pesado, difícil.
BU.REAU, s., escrivaninha, cômoda, escritório, agência, departamento.
BU.REAU.CRA.CY, s., burocracia.
BU.REAU.CRAT, s., burocrata.
BU.REAU.CRAT.IC, adj., burocrático.
BURG, s., burgo, cidade, vila.
BURG.ER, s., hambúrguer.
BUR.GESS, s., burguês, cidadão.
BUR.GLAR, s., ladrão, assaltante.
BUR.GLARY, s., roubo, assalto.
BUR.GLE, v., assaltar, roubar.
BURI.AL, s., enterro, sepultamento.
BURI.I.AL-GROUND, s., cemitério.
BURI.ER, s., coveiro.
BURK, s., UK idiota.
BUR.LY, adj., robusto, forte; rude, áspero.
BUR.MESE, adj., e s., natural ou habitante da Birmânia, birmanês.
BURN, v., queimar, incendiar, arder.
BURN.A.BLE, adj., combustível, queimável.
BURN.ER, s., queimador, bico de gaz.
BURN.ING, adj., em chamas, escaldante, ardente; s., incêndio, queimadura.
BURN.ISH, s., lustro, brilho; v., lustrar, polir.
BURN.OUT, s., combustão, destruição por fogo; fig., exaustão.
BURP, s., col., arroto; v., arrotar.
BUR.ROW, s., toca, esconderijo; v., entocar-se, esconder-se, refugiar-se.
BUR.SAR, s., tesoureiro (em escolas etc.).
BUR.SA.RY, s., tesouraria; UK bolsa de estudos.
BURSE, s., bolsa de estudos.
BURST, s., estouro, explosão, eclosão, fenda; v., estourar, explodir.
BURST.ING, adj., repleto(a).
BURY, v., sepultar, enterrar, sepultar.
BURY.ING, s., sepultamento, enterro.
BURY.ING PLACE, s., cemitério, campo santo.
BUS, s., ônibus.
BUS CON.DUC.TOR, s., cobrador de ônibus.
BUS DRIV.ER, s., motorista de ônibus.
BUSH, s., arbusto, moita; mato.
BUSH.EL, s., alqueire (medida variável por região).
BUSH.Y, adj., espesso (mato), cerrado (bosque).
BUSI.NESS, s., negócio, comércio, tema, assunto, objeto.
BUSI.NESS CARD, s., cartão de visita comercial.

BUSI.NESS CLASS, s., classe executiva.
BUSI.NESS.LIKE, adj., capaz, eficiente, hábil.
BUSI.NESS.MAN, s., homem de negócios.
BUSI.NESS TRIP, s., viagem de negócios.
BUSI.NESS.WO.MAN, s., mulher de negócios.
BUSK.ER, s., UK artista de rua.
BUS LANE, s., faixa exclusiva de ônibus.
BUS STA.TION, s., estação rodoviária.
BUS.STOP, s., parada de ônibus.
BUST, s., busto; explosão, estouro; v., explodir.
BUS.TLE, s., afã, animação, alvoroço; v., animar-se, apressar-se.
BUS.TLING, adj., movimentado(a).
BUST-UP, s., quebra-pau; separação, dissolução.
BUS.Y, adj., ocupado, atarefado; v., ocupar, manter-se ocupado, agir.
BUS.Y.BOD.Y, s., intrometido.
BUSY LIZ.ZIE, s., Bot., maria-sem-vergonha.
BUS.Y SIG.NAL, s., US sinal de ocupado.
BUT, conj., mas, porém, contudo, todavia.
BU.TANE, s., butano.
BUTCH.ER, s., açougueiro, carniceiro; assassino; v., matar, assassinar.
BUTCH.ERY, s., açougue, matadouro.
BUT.LER, s., mordomo.
BUT.LERY, s., despensa.
BUTT, s., col., bagana (cigarro); coronha (rifle); alvo (de riso); v., dar cabeçada em; US vul., traseiro.
BUT.TER, manteiga; v., passar manteiga.
BUT.TER.ED, adj., com manteiga, amanteigado.
BUT.TER FIN.GERS, s., estabanado.
BUT.TER.FLY, s., borboleta; mariposa.
BUT.TER.MILK, s., soro; leite desnatado, leitelho.
BUT.TER.SCOTCH, s., bala feita de manteiga e caramelo.
BUT.TOCK, s., nádega; butocks, s. pl.: nádegas.
BUT.TON, s., botão, emblema; v., abotoar.
BUT.TON-DOWN, adj., abotoado(a).
BUT.TON.HOLE, s., casa de botão.
BUT.TRESS, s., Arquit., contraforte, pilar; v., reforçar, apoiar (com pilastra).
BUX.OM, adj., gordo, rechonchudo.
BUY, v., comprar; s., compra.
BUY.ABLE, adj., comprável.
BUY.ER, s., comprador.
BUY.OUT, s., compra majoritária das ações de uma empresa.
BUZZ, s., zumbido, zunido; v., zumbir, zunir.
BUZ.ZARD, s., Zool., UK gavião; US abutre; fig., pessoa desprezível.
BUZZ.ER, s., campainha.
BUZZ.ING, s., zumbido.
BUZZ.WORD, s., palavra da moda para impressionar.
BY, prep., por, de, com, perto de, conforme, segundo.
BY.LAW, s., lei municipal.
BYE, interj., adeus.
BY.GONE, adj., antigo, passado.
BY.LAW, s., estatuto; regimento interno.
BY.PASS, s., via secundária.
BY.PRO.DUCT, s., subproduto, derivado.
BY-PUR.POSE, s., fim secundário.
BYRE, s., abrigo para vacas, estrebaria.
BYROAD, s., via secundária, atalho, vereda, senda.

BYSTANDER · 398 · BYWORD

BY.STAND.ER, *s.*, espectador, curioso.
BY-STREET, *s.*, viela, beco, ruela.
BYTE, *s.*, bite.

BY.WAY, *s.*, via secundária, atalho, vereda.
BY.WORD, *s.*, provérbio, máxima, sentença.

C, terceira letra do alfabeto inglês.
C, *s.*, dó (música); 100 C (alg. romano).
CAB, *s.*, táxi, cabina; *v.*, andar de táxi, andar de carro.
CA.BAL, *s.*, cabala, intriga, trama; *v.*, intrigar, tramar.
CAB.A.LA, *s.*, cabala.
CAB.A.LISM, *s.*, cabalismo.
CAB.A.LIST, *s.*, cabalista.
CAB.A.LIS.TIC, *adj.*, cabalístico.
CAB.A.RET, *s.*, cabaré.
CAB.BAGE, *s.*, repolho, couve.
CAB.BY, CAB.BIE, *s., col.*, o mesmo que *cab-driver*.
CAB-DRIV.ER, *s., col.*, taxista, motorista de táxi; cocheiro.
CA.BER.NET, *adj.*, cabernet (vinho cabernet).
CAB.IN, *s.*, cabana, choupana; camarote de navio, cabina.
CAB.IN CREW, *s.*, tripulação.
CAB.IN CRUISER, *s.*, iate.
CAB.I.NET, *s.*, gabinete; ministério do governo; armário; *adj.*, relativo a gabinete; privado; valioso.
CAB.I.NET.MAK.ER, *s.*, marceneiro.
CA.BLE, *s.*, cabo, cabograma, telegrama; *v.*, remeter cabograma.
CA.BLE BOX, *s., Tec.*, caixa de distribuição de cabos.
CA.BLE CAR, *s., Tec.*, teleférico.
CA.BLE CAST.ING, *s.*, transmissão de TV a cabo.
CA.BLE.GRAM, *s.*, cabograma.
CA.BLE TEL.E.VI.SION, *s.*, televisão a cabo, TV a cabo.
CA.BLE TV, *s.*, o mesmo que *cable television*.
CAB.MAN, *s.*, taxista; *Ant.*, cocheiro.
CAB.O.TAGE, *s.*, cabotagem.
CAB.RI.O.LET, *s.*, conversível (carro).
CA.CAO, *s.*, cacau; cacaueiro.
CACHE, *s.*, esconderijo; *Infor.*, cache; *v.*, esconder; *Infor.*, pôr em cache.
CACH.ET, *s.*, prestígio; distintivo; *Med.*, cápsula.
CACK.LE, *s.*, cacarejo; *v.*, cacarejar; tagarelar.
CAK.LER, *s.*, ave que cacareja; tagarela.
CACK.LING, *s.*, tagarelice.
CA.COG.RA.PHY, *s.*, cacografia (grafia errada).
CAC.O.MIS.TLE, *s., Zool.*, carnívoro semelhante ao guaxinim.
CA.COPH.O.NOUS, *adj.*, cacofônico.
CA.COPH.O.NY, *s.*, cacofonia.
CAC.TOID, *adj.*, cactoide, cactiforme.
CAC.TUS, *s.*, cacto.
CAD, *s.*, pessoa grosseira, malcriada.
CA.DAS.TRAL, *adj.*, cadastral.
CA.DAS.TRE, *s.*, cadastro.
CA.DAV.ER.OUS, *adj.*, cadavérico.
CAD.DIE, *s., Esp.*, carregador de tacos (de golfe).
CAD.DIS.FLY, *s., Zool.*, mosca d'água.
CAD.DISH, *adj.*, grosseiro, malcriado; vil.
CAD.DISH.LY, *adv.*, grosseiramente.
CAD.DISH.NESS, *s.*, gosseria; vileza.

CAD.DY, *s.*, pequena ciaxa para lápis; porta-chá.
CADE, *adj.*, criado à mão (animal).
CA.DENCE, *s.*, cadência, compasso.
CA.DENCED, *adj.*, cadenciado, com harmonia.
CA.DEN.CY, *s.*, cadência.
CA.DENT, *adj.*, cadenciado.
CA.DET, *s.*, cadete.
CA.DET.SHIP, *s.*, posição de cadete.
CADGE, *v.*, mendigar.
CAD.MI.UM, *s., Quím.*, cádmio.
CA.DRE, *s., Mil.*, grupo militar; quadro, armação.
CA.DU.CI.TY, *s.*, caducidade.
CAE.SAR.E.AN, *s., Med.*, cesariana (operação); *adj.*, cesáreo; imperial.
CAE.SI.UM, *s., Quím.*, césio.
CA.FÉ, *s.*, café, restaurante.
CAF.E.TE.RIA, *s.*, bar ou restaurante de autosserviço.
CAF.FE.IN, *s.*, cafeína.
CAF.FEINE, *s.*, o mesmo que *caffein*.
CAGE, *s.*, gaiola, viveiro, jaula.
CAGE BIRD, *s.*, pássaro de gaiola.
CAGED, *adj.*, enjaulado, engaiolado.
CAG.EY, *adj.*, cauteloso, cuidadoso.
CAG.I.NESS, *s.*, cautela, precaução.
CA.GOULE, *s., UK* capa de chuva.
CAHOOTS, *s. pl.*, sociedade, parceria, coligação.
CAI.MAN, *s., Zool.*, caimão (jacaré pequeno).
CA.IQUE, *s.*, caíque.
CAIRN, *s.*, monte de pedras (em túmulo) ou como marco.
CA.JOLE, *v.*, persuadir, convencer; bajular, adular.
CA.JOLE.MENT, *s.*, bajulação, adulação, engodo.
CA.JOL.ER, *s.*, bajulador, adulador.
CAKE, *s.*, bolo, doce, torta; *v.*, endurecer.
CAKE PAN, *s., US* forma de bolo.
CAKE TIN, *s., UK* forma de bolo; pote.
CAL, *s., abrev.* de *calorie*.
CAL.A.BASH, *s.*, cabaça.
CAL.A.BOOSE, *s.*, calabouço, enxovia, cadeia.
CA.LAM.I.TOUS, *adj.*, calamitoso, desastroso.
CA.LAM.I.TOUS.LY, *adv.*, calamitosamente; funestamente.
CA.LAM.I.TOUS.NESS, *s.*, calamidade.
CA.LAM.I.TY, *s.*, calamidade.
CAL.CAR, *s., Bot., Zool.*, esporão.
CAL.CAR.E.OUS, *s.*, calcário.
CAL.CIC, *adj.*, cálcico.
CAL.CI.NA.TION, *s.*, calcinação.
CAL.CINE, *v.*, calcinar.
CAL.CI.UM, *s.*, cálcio.
CAL.CU.LA.BLE, *adj.*, calculável.
CAL.CU.LA.BLY, *adv.*, seguramente, previsivelmente.
CAL.CU.LATE, *v.*, calcular, computar.
CAL.CU.LATED, *adj.*, calculado, premeditado.

CALCULATING ••• 400 ••• CANASTA

CAL.CU.LAT.ING, *adj.*, calculista, astuto; ~ *machine*: máquina de calcular.

CAL.CU.LA.TION, *s.*, *Mat.*, cálculo.

CAL.CU.LA.TIVE, *adj.*, relativo a cálculo; calculador; cauteloso.

CAL.CU.LA.TOR, *s.*, calculadora, máquina de calcular; calculista.

CAL.CU.LUS, *s.*, *Mat.*, cálculo; *Med.*, cálculo.

CAL.E.FY, *v.*, aquecer, escaldar.

CAL.EN.DAR, *s.*, calendário, folhinha.

CAL.EN.DAR MONTH, *s.*, mês civil.

CAL.EN.DAR YEAR, *s.*, ano civil.

CA.LEN.DU.LA, *s.*, *Bot.*, calêndula.

CALF, *s.*, bezerro, cria, filhote de bicho.

CALF DOZ.ER, *s.*, trator que remove a terra.

CALF LOVE, *s.*, namorico.

CALF.SKIN, *s.*, couro ou pele de bezerro.

CAL.I.BRATE, *v.*, calibrar.

CAL.I.BRA.TION, *s.*, calibragem.

CAL.I.BRA.TOR, *s.*, calibrador.

CAL.I.BRE, *s.*, calibre, capacidade.

CAL.I.BRED, *adj.*, calibrado.

CAL.I.CO, *s.*, tecido branco e fino de algodão da Índia, morim.

CAL.I.PER, *s.*, **CAL.I.PERS**, *s. pl.*, compasso de calibre.

CALI.PH, *s.*, califa.

CA.LIX, *s.*, cálice.

CALL, *v.*, chamar, denominar, intitular, apelar; *s.*, chamado, apelo, grito.

CALL BOX, *s.*, cabina telefônica.

CALL GIRL, *s.*, garota de programa.

CAL.LER, *s.*, visitante, chamador.

CAL.LIG.RA.PHER, *s.*, calígrafo.

CAL.LIG.RA.PHY, *s.*, caligrafia.

CALL.ING, *s.*, vocação, tendência, pendor.

CALL.ING CARD, *s.*, *US* cartão de visita.

CAL.LI.PERS *UK*, **CAL.I.PERS** *US*, *s.*, *Mat.*, compasso de calibre ou medição; *Med.*, aparelho ortopédico.

CAL.LOS.I.TY, *s.*, calosidade.

CAL.LOUS, *adj.*, insensível; caloso; calejado.

CAL.LOUS.LY, *adv.*, insensivelmente; com calosidade.

CAL.LOUS.NESS, *s.*, calosidade.

CALL OUT, *v.*, berrar, gritar, chamar.

CAL.LOW, *adj.*, imaturo; implume (ave).

CAL.LOW.NESS, *s.*, imaturidade; estado de implume (ave).

CALL UP, *v.*, telefonar, evocar, invocar.

CAL.LUS, *s.*, *Med.*, calo (ósseo).

CALM, *adj.*, calmo, tranquilo, sereno; *s.*, calma; *v.*, acalmar, sossegar.

CALM.ATIVE, *s.*, calmante.

CALM.LY, *adv.*, calmamente, tranquilamente.

CALM.NESS, *s.*, calma, serenidade.

CALMY, *adj.*, calmo, sereno, sossegado.

CA.LOR.IC, *adj.*, calorífico; *s.*, calórico; calor.

CAL.O.RIE, *s.*, caloria.

CAL.O.RIF.IC, *adj.*, calorífico.

CA.LO.RIF.I.CAL.LY, *adv.*, calorificamente.

CAL.O.RIM.ETER, *s.*, *Fís.*, calorímetro.

CA.LOTTE, *s.*, solidéu.

CAL.U.MET, *s.*, *US* cachimbo da paz.

CA.LUM.NI.ATE, *v.*, caluniar, difamar.

CA.LUM.NI.A.TION, *s.*, calúnia.

CA.LUM.NI.A.TOR, *s.*, caluniador.

CA.LUM.NI.A.TO.RY, *adj.*, caluniador.

CA.LUM.NI.OUS, *adj.*, calunioso, difamatório.

CA.LUM.NI.OUS.LY, *adv.*, caluniosamente.

CAL.UM.NY, *s.*, calúnia.

CAL.VA.RY, *s.*, *Rel.*, Calvário.

CALVE, *v.*, parir, dar cria (animal, esp. a vaca).

CALVES, *s. pl.*, plural de *calf*: bezerros.

CALV.ING, *s.*, parto (de animais).

CAL.VIN.ISM, *s.*, *Rel.*, calvinismo.

CAL.VIN.IST, *s.*, *Rel.*, calvinista.

CA.LYP.SO, *s.*, *Mús.*, calipso (tipo de música do caribe).

CAM.A.RA.DE.RIE, *s.*, camaradagem, coleguismo.

CAM.A.RIL.LA, *s.*, camarilha.

CAM.BER, *s.*, curvatura, arqueamento; camba; câmber.

CAM.BIST, *s.*, cambista; tabela de conversão (moedas etc.).

CAM.BO.DI.AN, *adj. e s.*, cambojano (do Camboja).

CAM.BRI.AN, *adj.*, *Geol.*, cambriano (período da era paleozoica).

CAM.BRIC, *s.*, cambraia.

CAM.COR.DER, *s.*, filmadora que filma em videotape.

CAME, *v.*, passado de *come*.

CAM.EL, *s.*, camelo.

CAM.EL.EER, *s.*, cameleiro.

CA.MEL.LIA, *s.*, camélia.

CAM.EL.RY, *s.*, *Mil.*, tropas montadas em camelos.

CAM.EO, *s.*, camafeu; *Lit.*, descrição breve e inteligente.

CAM.ERA, *s.*, câmara fotográfica, de TV ou cinema.

CAM.ER.AL, *adj.*, relativo à câmara legislativa.

CAM.ERAMAN, *s.*, operador de câmera (vídeo ou cinema).

CAM.ER.OO.NIAN, *adj. e s.*, camaronês (de Camarões).

CA.MION, *s.*, caminhão.

CAM.I.SOLE, *s.*, corpete, blusinha.

CAM.O.MILE, *s.*, camomila.

CAM.OU.FLAGE, *s.*, camuflagem; *v.*, camuflar.

CAMP, *s.*, campo, acampamento, setor.

CAM.PAIGN, *s.*, campanha; *v.*, fazer campanha.

CAM.PAIGN.ER, *s.*, soldado, veterano.

CAM.PA.NI.LE, *s.*, campanário.

CAMP BED, *s.*, cama de armar.

CAMP CHAIR, *s.*, cadeira de armar.

CAMP.ER, *s.*, indivíduo acampado, campista.

CAMP.FIRE, *s.*, fogueira de acampamento (escoteiros).

CAMP.GROUND, *s.*, *US* camping.

CAM.PHOR, *s.*, cânfora.

CAMP.ING, *s.*, campismo.

CAMP.ING SITE, **CAMP.SITE**, *s.*, área de acampamento.

CAM.PUS, *s.*, *Lat.*, terreno e prédios de uma universidade.

CAMP STOOL, *s.*, banqueta de armar (dobrável).

CAN, *s.*, lata; *v.*, enlatar; *v. aux.*, poder, saber.

CA.NA.DI.AN, *adj.*, *s.*, canadense.

CA.NA.DI.AN FRENCH, *s.*, francês falado no Canadá.

CA.NAL, *s.*, canal; *v.*, canalizar, fazer um canal.

CA.NA.LI.ZA.TION, *s.*, canalização.

CAN.A.LIZE, *v.*, canalizar.

CA.NA.PÉ, *s.*, *Fr.*, canapé; sofá.

CA.NARD, *s.*, boato; peta (notícia mentirosa); *Fr.*, pato.

CA.NARY, *s.*, canário.

CA.NARY-GRASS, *s.*, *Bot.*, alpiste (planta).

CA.NARY-SEED, *s.*, alpiste (grão).

CA.NAS.TA, *s.*, canastra (jogo de cartas).

CANCAN   •• 401 •••   CAPITAL GOODS

CAN.CAN, *s.*, cancã (dança agitada em cabarés franceses).
CAN.CEL, *v.*, cancelar, anular, desfazer.
CAN.CEL.LA.TION, *s.*, cancelamento.
CAN.CEL OUT, *v.*, anular, cancelar.
CAN.CER, *s.*, câncer, cancro.
CAN.CER.OUS, *adj.*, canceroso.
CAN.CRI.FORM, *adj., Med.*, canceriforme, cancroide.
CAN.DE.LA.BRUM, *s.*, candelabro (*pl., candelabra*).
CAN.DES.CENCE, *s.*, incandescência.
CAN.DES.CENT, *adj.*, incandescente.
CAN.DID, *adj.*, sincero, franco; ingênuo.
CAN.DI.DA.CY, *s.*, o mesmo que *candidature*.
CAN.DI.DATE, *s.*, candidato; *v.*, candidatar-se.
CAN.DI.DATE.SHIP, *s.*, o mesmo que *candidature*.
CAN.DI.DA.TURE, *s.*, candidatura.
CAN.DID.LY, *adv.*, sinceramente, francamente; imparcialmente.
CAN.DID.NESS, *s.*, candidez, sinceridade, boa-fé.
CAN.DIED, *adj.*, cristalizado, confeitado; *fig.*, lisonjeiro.
CAN.DLE, *s.*, vela.
CAN.DLE.LIGHT, *s.*, luz de vela.
CAN.DLE.LIT, *s.*, à luz de velas.
CAN.DLE.POW.ER, *s.*, intensidade medida em luz de velas.
CAN.DLE.STICK, *s.*, castiçal.
CAN.DLE.WICK, *s.*, pavio da vela.
CAN.DOUR *UK*, **CAN.DOR** *US*, *s.*, candura, sinceridade, imparcialidade.
CAN.DY, *s.*, açúcar, bombom, caramelo.
CAN.DY FLOSS *UK*, *s.*, algodão-doce; o mesmo que *cotton candy* (*US*).
CAN.DY SHOP, *s.*, confeitaria.
CAN.DY STORE, *s.*, *US* confeitaria.
CAN.DY-STRIPED, *adj.*, de listras coloridas (doces).
CANE, *s.*, cana, junco, taquara, vara, vareta; *v.*, bater com vara.
CANE.BRAKE, *s.*, bambuzal, taquaral.
CA.NEPH.O.RUS, *s., Arq.*, canéfora.
CANE-SUGAR, *s.*, cana-de-açúcar.
CA.NI.CU.LAR, *adj.*, canicular.
CA.NINE, *s.*, canino, dente canino, próprio de cão.
CA.NINE TEETH, *s. pl., Anat.*, dentes caninos.
CAN.ING, *s.*, tunda, surra, sova.
CAN.IS.TER, *s.*, lata ou vasilha de metal; tubo.
CAN.KERED, *adj.*, canceroso, chagado.
CAN.KER.OUS, *adj.*, canceroso.
CAN.NA, *s., Bot.*, cana, caité.
CAN.NA.BIS, *s., Bot.*, planta da maconha, cânhamo.
CANNED, *adj.*, enlatado, em conserva; *Mús.*, gravado(a).
CANNED GOODS, *s. pl.*, enlatados, conservas.
CANNED MEAT, *s.*, carne em conserva ou enlatada.
CAN.NE.LURE, *s., Arq.*, canelura.
CAN.NE.RY, *s.*, fábrica de enlatados ou conservas.
CAN.NI.BAL, *s.*, canibal, antropófago.
CAN.NI.BAL.ISM, *s.*, canibalismo.
CAN.NI.BALIZE, *v., Tec.*, desmontar ou desmanchar máquina ou veículo para aproveitar as peças.
CAN.NI.LY, *adv.*, astuciosamente; gentilmente; cautelosamente.
CAN.NI.NESS, *s.*, astúcia, esperteza, argúcia.
CAN.NON, *s.*, canhão.
CAN.NON.ADE, *s.*, canhonada; bombardeio; *v.*, atacar com canhões; bombardear.
CAN.NON BALL, *s.*, bala de canhão.
CAN.NON.EER, *s.*, artilheiro, canhoneiro.
CAN.NON.RY, *s.*, artilharia.
CAN.NON-SHOT, *s.*, canhonaço, tiro de canhão.
CAN.NOT, *v.*, contração de *can not*.
CAN.NY, *adj.*, esperto, astuto, arguto.
CA.NOE, *s.*, canoa.
CA.NOE.ING, *s., Esp.*, canoagem.
CA.NOE.IST, *s.*, canoeiro.
CA.NON, *s.*, **CÂNONE, CÂNON; Rel.**, cônego.
CA.NON.IC, *adj.*, canônico.
CA.NON.I.CAL.LY, *adv.*, canonicamente.
CAN.ON.I.ZA.TION, *s.*, canonização, santificação.
CAN.ON.IZE, *v.*, canonizar.
CAN.OO.DLE, *v.*, acariciar; *UK gír.*, amassar-se, agarrar-se.
CAN.O.PY, *s.*, dossel; *fig.*, abrigo, cobertura.
CA.NO.ROUS, *adj.*, canoro.
CA.NO.ROUS.NESS, *s.*, harmonia, sonoridade, musicalidade.
CANT, *s., col.*, jargão; hipocrisia; *pej.*, papo-furado; *adj.*, hipócrita.
CAN'T, *v.*, contração de *can not*; o mesmo que *cannot*.
CAN.TAN.KER.OUS, *adj.*, intratável, rabugento.
CAN.TEEN, *s.*, cantina.
CAN.TEEN, *s.*, cantina (em escola, faculdade, fábrica, quartel etc.); bufê; caixa de faqueiro.
CAN.TER, *s., Esp.*, meio-galope (cavalo); *v.*, cavalgar a meio galope.
CAN.TI.CLE, *s.*, cântico.
CAN.TI.LE.VER, *s., Arq.*, viga em balance, cantilever.
CANT.ING, *s.*, hipocrisia; *adj.*, hipócrita.
CAN.TLE, *s.*, parte, porção (de algo); parte posterior elevada do selim (bicicleta) ou da sela (cavalo).
CAN.TON, *s.*, cantão (pequeno distrito).
CAN.TO.NAL, *adj.*, relativo a cantão, cantonal.
CAN.TON.MENT, *s., Mil.*, acantonamento, aquartelamento.
CAN.VAS, *s.*, lona; tenda, barraca (de lona); tela.
CAN.VASS, *s.*, sondagem, exame; angariação de votos; *v.*, examinar; pedir votos.
CAN.VAS.SER, *s.*, cabo eleitoral.
CAN.VASS.ING, *s.*, angariação de votos.
CAN.YON, *s.*, desfiladeiro, garganta.
CAP, *s.*, gorro, tampa; *v.*, cobrir, tapar.
CA.PA.BIL.I.TY, *s.*, capacidade.
CA.PA.BLE, *adj.*, capaz, habilitado.
CA.PA.BLE.NESS, *s.*, capacidade, competência, habilidade.
CA.PA.BLY, *adv.*, habilmente.
CA.PA.CIOUS, *adj.*, espaçoso.
CA.PA.CIOUS.LY, *adv.*, espaçosamente, amplamente.
CA.PA.CIOUS.NESS, *s.*, amplidão.
CA.PAC.I.TANCE, *s., Elet.*, capacitância.
CA.PAC.I.TATE, *v.*, capacitar, tornar capaz.
CA.PAC.I.TOR, *s., Tecnol.*, condensador; capacitor.
CA.PAC.I.TY, *s.*, capacidade, lotação.
CAPE, *s.*, capa; cabo.
CA.PER, *s.*, alcaparra.
CAP.IL.LAR.I.TY, *s.*, capilaridade.
CAP.IL.LA.RY, *s.*, vaso capilar; *adj.*, capilar.
CAP.I.TAL, *s.*, capital, metrópole; bens, dinheiro.
CAP.I.TAL GAIN, *s.*, lucros com a venda de ações, imóveis.
CAP.I.TAL GOODS, *s.*, bens de capital (máquinas etc.).

CAPITALISM ·· 402 ·· CAREEN

CAP.I.TAL.ISM, s., capitalismo.
CAP.I.TAL.IST, adj. e s., capitalista.
CAP.I.TAL.IS.TI.CAL.LY, adv., ao modo capitalista.
CAP.I.TAL.I.ZA.TION, s., capitalização.
CAP.I.TAL.IZE, v., capitalizar.
CAP.I.TAL LET.TER, s., letra maiúscula.
CAP.I.TAL LEV.Y, s., imposto sobre capital.
CAP.I.TAL PUN.ISH.MENT, s., pena capital; pena de morte.
CAP.I.TOL, s., Capitólio; Ant., templo dedicado a Júpiter.
CAP.I.TOL HILL, s., Congresso dos Estados Unidos ou Colina do Capitólio.
CA.PIT.U.LAR, s., Rel., cônego; adj., capitular.
CA.PIT.U.LARY, s., capitular.
CA.PIT.U.LATE, v., render-se (a algo); capitular.
CA.PIT.U.LA.TION, s., capitulação.
CA.PRICE, s., capricho; excentricidade.
CA.PRI.CIOUS, adj., caprichoso.
CA.PRI.CIOUS.LY, adv., caprichosamente.
CAP.RI.CORN, s., Capricórnio (constelação e signo do zodíaco).
CAPS, s., abrev. de capital letters: letras maiúsculas; ver Caps Lock.
CAP.SI.CUM, s., Bot., pimentão, cápsico.
CAP.SIZE, v., emborcar; soçobrar, virar de cabeça para baixo.
CAPS LOCK, s., Inform., tecla que aciona o modo caixa alta; maiúscula.
CAP.SU.LAR, adj., capsular; conciso.
CAP.SU.LATE, adj., capsulado, encapsulado.
CAP.SULE, s., cápsula.
CAP.SUL.ISE, v., capsular, encapsular, colocar em cápsula.
CAPT., s., abrev. de captain: capitão, Cap.
CAP.TAIN, s., capitão, comandante.
CAP.TAIN.CY, s., capitania.
CAP.TAIN.CY-GENERAL, s., Mil., estado-maior.
CAP.TION, s., captura, prisão, confisco.
CAP.TIOUS, adj., capcioso, malicioso, astuto.
CAP.TIOUS.NESS, s., capciosidade, malícia, fraude.
CAP.TI.VATE, v., cativar, seduzir.
CAP.TI.VAT.ING, adj., cativante, encantador.
CAP.TI.VAT.ING.LY, adv., atraentemente.
CAP.TI.VA.TION, s., sedução, cativamento, fascinação.
CAP.TI.VA.TOR, s., encantador, sedutor.
CAP.TIVE, s., cativo, prisioneiro; adj., cativo(a), preso(a); encatado(a).
CAP.TIV.I.TY, s., cativeiro, servidão; prisão.
CAP.TOR, s., capturador, captor.
CAP.TURE, v., capturar, prender, aprisionar; s., captura, prisão.
CAP.TUR.ER, s., capturador, captor.
CA.PUT, s., Anat., cabeça extremidade; Bot., perídio.
CAR, s., carro, automóvel.
CAR.A.BI.NEER, s., carabineiro.
CA.RAFE, s., garrafa de mesa (para água ou vinho).
CAR.A.MEL, s., caramelo, açúcar.
CAR.A.PACE, s., carapaça.
CAR.AT, s., quilate.
CAR.A.VAN, s., caravana; UK casa sobre rodas (trailer).
CAR.A.VAN.NING, s., viagem em casa sobre rodas.
CAR.A.VEL, s., caravela.
CAR.A.WAY, s., Bot., alcaravia, cominho-armênio (condimento).
CAR.BIDE, s., Quím., carboneto, carbureto.

CAR.BINE, s., carabina.
CAR.BI.NEER, s., carabineiro.
CAR.BO.HY.DRATE, s., Quím., carboidrato.
CAR.BON, s., carbono.
CAR.BON.ATE, s., Quím., carbonato; v., carbonatar.
CAR.BON.AT.ED DRINK, adj., com gás (água, refrigerante).
CAR.BON COP.Y, s., cópia em papel carbono.
CAR.BON DAT.ING, s., datação por carbono 14.
CAR.BON DI.OX.IDE, s., dióxido de carbono.
CAR.BON FI.BRE, s., fibra de carbono.
CAR.BON.IC, adj., Quím., carbônico.
CAR.BON.IC OX.IDE, s., óxido de carbono.
CAR.BON.IF.ER.OUS, adj., carbonífero.
CAR.BON.IF.ER.OUS AGE, s., Geol., Era Carbonífera.
CAR.BON.I.ZA.TION, s., carbonização.
CAR.BON.IZE, v., carbonizar.
CAR.BON MO.NOX.IDE, s., monóxido de carbono.
CAR.BON PA.PER, s., papel carbono.
CAR.BU.RE.TOR, s., carburador.
CAR.CASS, s., carcassa.
CAR.CIN.O.GEN, s., Med., carcinógeno, carcinogênio.
CAR.CIN.O.GEN.IC, adj., cancerígeno.
CAR.CI.NO.MA, s., Med., carcinoma, câncer.
CAR.CI.NO.MA.TOUS, adj., Med., carcinomatoso, canceroso.
CARD, s., carta de baralho, cartão, bilhete, cardápio.
CAR.DA.MOM, s., Bot., cardamomo.
CARD.BOARD, s., papelão; cartolina; adj., de papelão.
CARD.BOARD BOX, s., caixa de papelão.
CARD-CAR.RY.ING, adj., associado (de agremiação); col., ativo; legítimo.
CARD CAT.A.LOGUE, s., US fichário de catálogo.
CAR.DI.AC, adj., cardíaco.
CAR.DI.AC AR.REST, s., Med., parada cardíaca.
CAR.DI.AC PACE.MAK.ER, s., Med., marca-passo (para o coração).
CAR.DI.AL.GY, s., Med., cardialgia.
CAR.DI.GAN, s., casaco aberto na frente, casaco de lã, jaqueta.
CAR.DI.NAL, adj., cardeal, cardinal; s., cardeal.
CAR.DI.NAL.LY, adv., principalmente, fundamentalmente.
CAR.DI.NAL NUM.BER, s., Mat., número ou numeral cardinal.
CAR.DI.NAL POINT, s., ponto principal.
CAR.DI.NAL POINTS, s. pl., pontos cardeais.
CARD IN.DEX, s., UK fichário.
CARD.ING, s., cardação.
CAR.DI.O.GRAM, s., Med., cardiograma.
CAR.DI.O.GRAPH, s., Med., cardiógrafo.
CAR.DI.OG.RA.PHY, s., Med., cardiografia.
CAR.DI.OL.O.GIST, s., cardiologista.
CAR.DI.OL.O.GY, s., cardiologia.
CAR.DI.O.VAS.CU.LAR, adj., cardiovascular.
CARD PLAY.ER, s., jogador de cartas.
CARD READ.ER, s., Inform., leitora de cartão.
CARD.SHARP, s., trapaceiro (no jogo de cartas).
CARD TA.BLE, s., mesa de jogo.
CARD VOTE, s., UK voto de delegado (que representa uma classe ou os membros de uma organização).
CARE, s., cuidado, preocupação, empenho, guarda; v., cuidar, preocupar.
CA.REEN, s., carenagem; v., Náut., carenar; virar de carena, adernar.

CAREER ··403·· CARVEL

CA.REER, s., carreira (profissão); v., sair em disparada; desgovernar-se.
CA.REER.IST, s., pessoa que exacerba nas ambições profissionais; pej., carreirista.
CA.REERS, s. pl., orientação profissional; ocupação profissional.
CARE.FREE, adj., despreocupado.
CARE.FUL, adj., cuidadoso, zeloso, cauteloso.
CARE.FUL.LY, adv., cuidadosamente.
CARE.LESS, adj., descuidado, negligente, relaxado, desleixado.
CARE.LESS.LY, adv., descuidadamente, negligentemente.
CARE.LESS.NESS, s., descuido, negligência, relaxamento.
CAR.ER, s., cuidador de pessoas doentes ou incapacitadas.
CA.RESS, s., carícia, afago, carinho, agrado; v., acariciar, afagar.
CA.RESS.ING, adj., carinhoso, amoroso.
CA.RESS.ING.LY, adv., carinhosamente.
CARE.TAK.ER, s., zelador, vigia, guarda.
CARE.TAK.ER GOV.ERN.MENT, s., governo de transição.
CAR FER.RY, s., balsa.
CAR.GO, s., carga, frete.
CAR.GO BOAT, s., embarcação de carga, cargueiro.
CAR.GO SHIP, s., o mesmo que *cargo boat*.
CAR.HOP, s., atendente de *drive-in*.
CA.RIB.BE.AN, adj., s., caribenho.
CAR.I.BOO, **CAR.I.BOU**, s., Zool., caribu (cervo norte-americano).
CAR.I.CA.TUR.AL, adj., caricatural.
CAR.I.CA.TURE, s., caricatura; v., caricaturar.
CAR.I.CA.TUR.IST, s., caricaturista.
CAR.IES, s., cárie.
CAR.IL.LON, s., carrilhão (conjunto de sinos).
CAR.ING, adj., afetuoso(a), atencioso(a).
CAR.I.OUS, adj., cariado, carioso.
CAR.LING, s., Náut., carlinga.
CAR.MINE, s., carmim, cor vermelha.
CAR.NAGE, s., mortandade, morticínio.
CAR.NAL, adj., carnal, sensual, lascivo.
CAR.NAL.I.TY, s., carnalidade, sensualismo.
CAR.NAL KNOW.LEDGE, s., Jur., relação sexual.
CAR.NAL.LY, adv., carnalmente, sensualmente.
CAR.NA.TION, adj., encarnado (cor); s., cor de carne, rosa- -pálido; Bot., craveiro, cravo.
CAR.NI.VAL, s., carnaval, entrudo.
CAR.NI.VAL.ESQUE, adj., carnavalesco.
CAR.NI.VORE, s., Zool., carnívoro.
CAR.NIV.O.ROUS, adj., carnívoro.
CAR.NIV.O.ROUS.LY, adv., de modo carnívoro.
CA.ROCHE, s., Ant., carruagem de luxo (séc. XVII).
CAR.OL, v.; Christmas ~: cântico de Natal.
CAR.OL.LER, s., cantor(a) de peças natalinas.
CA.ROUS.AL, s., farra; beberronia.
CAR.OUSE, v., farrear.
CAR.OU.SEL, s., carrossel; esteira (de aeroporto).
CA.ROT.ID, s., carótida.
CARP, s., Zool., carpa; v., criticar, censurar.
CAR PARK, s., UK estacionamento.
CAR.PEN.TER, s., carpinteiro.
CAR.PEN.TRY, s., carpintaria.
CAR.PER, s., crítico, maldizente, praguejador.

CAR.PET, s., carpete, tapete; v., acarpetar, atapetar.
CAR.PET-BAG.GER, s., US aventureiro político.
CAR.PET BRUSH, s., escova de carpete.
CAR.PET.ING, s., tecido para tapetes.
CAR.PET SLIP.PER, s., pantufas.
CAR.PET SWEEP.ER, s., limpador de carpete, vassoura mágica, feiticeira.
CAR.PHOL.O.GY, s., Med., carfologia.
CAR.PORT, s., abrigo para carro, cobertura.
CAR.PUS, s., Anat., carpo (osso), punho, pulso.
CAR RENTAL, s., aluguel de carro.
CAR.RIAGE, s., carruagem; vagão.
CAR.RIAGE.WAY, s., UK pista simples de uma rodovia.
CAR.RI.ER, s., transportador; empresa de transportes.
CAR.RIER BAG, s., UK sacola comum para levar compras.
CAR.RIER PI.GEON, s., pombo-correio.
CAR.RI.ON, s., carniça, carne putrefata; fig., repugnante.
CAR.ROU.SEL, s., o mesmo que *carousel*.
CAR.ROT, s., cenoura.
CAR.ROTY, adj., cor de cenoura.
CAR.RY, v., transportar, carregar, levar.
CARRYALL, s., bolsa de viagem.
CARRYCOT, s., UK moisés (cesto para levar bebê).
CAR.RY.ING, s., transporte.
CAR.RY.ING CHARGE, s., juros de prestação.
CAR.RY-ON, s., UK bagunça, alvoroço.
CAR.RY.OUT, s., US comida para viagem, quentinha.
CAR-SICK, adj., enjoado, nauseado (de viagem de carro).
CART, s., carroça; carreta; carrinho de mão; carrinho de compras; v., carregar; carrear, carregar.
CAR.TAGE, s., carretagem, carreto.
CARTE, s., Fr., cardápio, menu.
CARTEL, s., cartel.
CAR.TER, s., carroceiro, carreteiro.
CAR.TE.SIAN, s., cartesiano; adj., relativo ao cartesianismo.
CAR.TE.SIAN.ISM, s., cartesianismo (filosofia de René Descartes).
CAR.TI.LAGE, s., cartilagem.
CAR.TI.LAG.I.NOUS, adj., cartilaginoso.
CART-LOAD, **CAR.LOAD**, s., carrada, carroçada.
CAR.TOG.RA.PHER, s., cartógrafo.
CAR.TO.GRAPH.IC, adj., cartográfico.
CAR.TO.GRAPH.I.CAL.LY, adv., de modo cartográfico.
CAR.TOG.RA.PHY, s., cartografia.
CAR.TOM.AN.CY, s., cartomancia.
CAR.TON, s., caixa (de papelão); embalagem tipo longa-vida.
CAR.TOON, s., cartão, papelão, cartaz.
CAR.TOON.IST, s., cartunista, caricaturista.
CAR TOP.PA.BLE, adj., que pode se carregado sobre o carro.
CAR.TRIDGE, s., cartucho (para arma de fogo); cartucho (para impressora); carga de caneta.
CAR.TRIDGE BELT, s., cinturão de cartucheira.
CAR.TRIDGE CLIP, s., Mil., pente para balas (de armas de fogo).
CART.WHEEL, s., pirueta; roda de carro; v., fazer pirueta.
CART.WRIGHT, s., fabricante de carroças.
CARVE, v., trinchar carne, cortar carne.
CARV.ER, s., escultor, entalhador; trinchante.
CAR.VER.Y, s., restaurante que trincha a carne, cozinha ou assa e serve na hora.
CAR.VEL, s., o mesmo que *caravel*.

CARVING · 404 · CATARRHAL

CARV.ING, *s.*, escultura, entalhe.
CAR WASH, *s.*, lavagem de carro; lava-rápido.
CAS.CADE, *s.*, cascata, queda-d'água; *v.*, cair, cair em cascata.
CASE, *s.*, estojo, caixa, cápsula; caso, desinência, acidente.
CASE.BOOK, *s.*, livro de registro.
CASE-HARD.EN, *v.*, cementar (aço, ferro); *fig.*, calejar.
CASE-HARD.ENED, *adj.*, cementado (aço, ferro); *fig.*, calejado.
CASE HISTORY, *s.*, *Med.*, prontuário.
CA.SEIN, *s.*, *Quím.*, caseína.
CASE.KNIFE, *s.*, faca de bainha.
CASE.MENT, *s.*, caixilho, batente de janela.
CASE.MENT WIN.DOW, *s.*, janela de batente.
CA.SERN, CA.SERNE, *s.*, *Mil.*, caserna.
CASE STUD.Y, *s.*, estudo de caso.
CASE.WORK, *s.*, estudo de assistência social.
CASE.WORK.ER, *s.*, assistente social.
CASE.WORM, *s.*, *Zool.*, larva que ainda não saiu do casulo.
CASH, *s.*, dinheiro vivo, caixa; *v.*, pagar com dinheiro.
CASH AND CARRY, *s.*, sistema "pague e leve" do setor atacadista.
CASH.BOOK, *s.*, livro-caixa.
CASH BOX, *s.*, *UK* cofre.
CASH CARD, *s.*, cartão para movimentação bancária.
CASH DESK, *s.*, caixa (lugar para pagamentos em lojas).
CASH DIS.COUNT, *s.*, desconto em pagamento à vista.
CASH DIS.PENS.ER, *s.*, *UK* caixa automático fora da agência bancária.
CASH.EW, *s.*, *Bot.*, cajueiro; caju; ~ *nut*: castanha de caju.
CASH FLOW, *s.*, *Com.*, fluxo de caixa.
CASH.IER, *s.*, caixeiro; *v.*, despedir, demitir.
CASH.IER.MENT, *s.*, demissão de alguém.
CASH-KEEP.ER, *s.*, caixa, caixeiro.
CASH.LESS, *adj.*, sem dinheiro.
CASH.MERE, *s.*, caxemira.
CASH.POINT, *s.*, caixa automático.
CASH PRICE, *s.*, preço à vista.
CASH REG.IS.TER, *s.*, caixa registradora.
CASH SALE, *s.*, venda à vista.
CAS.ING, *s.*, invólucro, revestimento.
CA.SI.NO, *s.*, o mesmo que *cassino*.
CASK, *s.*, barril, tonel, pipa, invólucro; *v.*, engarrafar, envasilhar.
CAS.KET, *s.*, guarda-joias, cofrezinho; *v.*, colocar no cofre.
CASQUE, *s.*, capacete, elmo.
CAS.SA.TION, *s.*, cassação, anulação, cancelamento.
CAS.SE.ROLE, *s.*, caçarola, panela.
CAS.SETTE, *s.*, cassete.
CAS.SETTE PLAY.ER, *s.*, toca-fitas.
CAS.SETTE RE.CORD.ER, *s.*, gravador cassete.
CAS.SI.NO, *s.*, jogo de cartas para quatro jogadores; clube onde se joga, aposta e se diverte.
CAS.SIT.ER.ITE, *s.*, *Min.*, cassiterita.
CAS.SOCK, *s.*, batina, sotaina; *fig.*, sacerdócio.
CAST, *s.*, elenco; lance, arremesso, distância, trajeto.
CAS.TA.NETS, *s. pl.*, *Mús.*, castanholas.
CAST A.SIDE, *v.*, exilar, expatriar.
CAST.AWAY, *s.*, náufrago; *adj.*, abandonado.
CASTE, *s.*, casta (Índia).
CAS.TEL.LAN, *s.*, intendente ou diretor de um castelo, castelão.
CAS.TEL.LA.TED, *adj.*, fortificado, acastelado; que possui castelos.
CAST.ER, *s.*, rodízio (de mesa); galheta (vidro para temperos); roldana; arremessador.
CAST.ER SUG.AR, CAS.TOR SUG.AR, *s.*, *UK* açúcar de confeiteiro.
CAS.TI.GATE, *v.*, castigar, corrigir, punir.
CAS.TI.GA.TION, *s.*, castigo, punição.
CAS.TIL.LIAN, *s.*, castelhano; língua espanhola.
CAST.ING, *s.*, *Cin.*, *Teat.*, distribuição de papéis; fundição; peça fundida; arremesso.
CAST.ING-VOICE, *s.*, voto de desempate, voto de minerva.
CAST.ING-VOTE, *s.*, o mesmo que *casting-voice*.
CAST-I.RON, *s.*, ferro fundido; *adj.*, inflexível, incostentável.
CAS.TLE, *s.*, castelo, fortaleza, torre.
CAS.TLED, *adj.*, encastelado.
CAST-OFF, *s.*, refugo; *adj.*, de ferro fundido; *fig.*, rejeitado, refugado; *v.*, livrar-se (de algo).
CAS.TOR, *s.*, *Zool.*, castor.
CAS.TRATE, *v.*, castrar, capar.
CAS.TRA.TION, *s.*, castração, castramento.
CAST-STEEL, *s.*, aço fundido.
CA.SU.AL, *adj.*, casual, fortuito, acidental; *s.*, trabalhador avulso; chapa.
CAS.U.AL JACK.ET, *s.*, blusa esportiva.
CAS.U.AL.LY, *adv.*, casualmente, informalmente.
CAS.U.AL.LY DE.PART.MENT, *s.*, *UK* pronto-socorro.
CAS.U.AL.NESS, *s.*, casualidade, acaso; negligência.
CAS.U.AL SHIRT, *s.*, camisa esportiva.
CA.SU.AL.TIES, *s.*, perdas, danos; baixas (de guerra); vítimas.
CA.SU.AL.TY, *s.*, perda, dano; acidente, desastre; desventura, infortúnio; pronto-socorro.
CA.SU.AL.TY DE.PART.MENT, *s.*, *UK* setor de emergência; pronto-socorro.
CA.SU.AL.TY IN.SUR.ANCE, *s.*, *US* seguro contra acidentes.
CA.SU.IST, *s.*, casuísta.
CA.SU.IS.TIC, *adj.*, casuístico.
CA.SU.IS.TI.CAL.LY, *adv.*, casuisticamente.
CAT, *s.*, gato.
CAT.A.CLYSM, *s.*, cataclismo, desgraça, calamidade.
CAT.A.CLYS.MAL, *adj.*, cataclísmico; sísmico.
CAT.A.CLYS.MIC, *adj.*, cataclísmico.
CAT.A.COMB, *s.*, catacumba.
CAT.A.LAN, *s. e adj.*, catalão(ã).
CAT.A.LEP.SY, *s.*, catalepsia.
CAT.A.LEP.TIC, *adj.*, cataléptico.
CAT.A.LOG, *s.*, catálogo.
CAT.A.LOGUE, *s.*, catálogo; *v.*, catalogar.
CAT.A.LOGU.ER, CAT.A.LOG.ER, *s.*, catalogador.
CAT.A.LYS.ER, *s.*, catalisador.
CA.TAL.Y.SIS, *s.*, *Quím.*, catálise.
CAT.A.LYST, *s.*, *Quím.*, catalisador.
CAT.A.MA.RAN, *s.*, *Náut.*, catamarã.
CAT.A.MOUNT, *s.*, *Zool.*, gato selvagem; puma, lince.
CAT.A.PLASM, *s.*, cataplasma.
CAT.A.PULT, *s.*, catapulta.
CAT.A.RACT, *s.*, catarata; queda-d'água, cachoeira.
CA.TARRH, *s.*, catarro.
CA.TARRH.AL, *adj.*, catarral, catarrento.

CATASTROPHE · 405 · CAW

CA.TAS.TRO.PHE, *s.*, catástrofe, cataclismo.
CA.TAS.TRO.PHIC, *adj.*, catastrófico.
CAT.A.TO.NI.A, *s., Med.*, catatonia.
CAT.A.TON.IC, *adj.*, catatônico.
CAT.BOAT, *s.*, veleiro pequeno de um mastro.
CAT.CALL, *s.*, vaia (com gritos imitando miados e assovios depreciativos).
CATCH, *v.*, pagar, apanhar, prender, reter, deter, surpreender, atrair.
CATCH-ALL, *s., US* cesto de bugigangas; *adj., UK* que engloba tudo.
CATCH.ER, *s.*, pegador, apanhador; quem pega a bola no basebol.
CATCH.ING, *adj.*, contagioso; cativante, fascinante.
CATCH PHRASE, *s., slogan*, bordão, frase chamativa.
CATCH.UP, *s.*, molho de tomates, catchup.
CATCH.WORD, *s., US Tipogr.*, chamada; *Teat.*, deixa; lema; *UK slogan*.
CATCH.Y, *adj.*, cativante, fascinante.
CAT.E.CHE.SIS, *s.*, catequese, doutrinação.
CAT.E.CHI.SA.TION, *s.*, catequização.
CAT.E.CHET.IC, *adj.*, catequético.
CAT.E.CHET.ICS, *s. pl.*, catequese.
CAT.E.CHISM, *s.*, catecismo.
CAT.E.CHIST, *s.*, catequista.
CAT.E.CHIZE (-ISE), *v.*, catequizar.
CAT.E.CHIZER (-ISER), *v.*, catequizador.
CAT.E.CHU.MEN, *s.*, catecúmeno; *fig.*, noviço.
CAT.E.GOR.I.CAL, *adj.*, categórico.
CAT.E.GOR.I.CAL.LY, *adv.*, categoricamente.
CAT.E.GO.RIZE, -ISE, *v.*, categorizar.
CAT.E.GO.RY, *s.*, categoria.
CAT.E.NATE, *v.*, concatenar, reunir, ligar.
CAT.E.NA.TION, *s.*, encadeamento, concatenação.
CA.TER, *v.*, aprovisionar, prover, suprir.
CA.TER.ER, *s.*, serviço de bufê.
CA.TER.ING, *s.*, fornecimento de bufê a grande número de pessoas.
CAT.ER.PIL.LAR, *s.*, lagarta.
CAT.FISH, *s.*, peixe-gato, lampreia.
CAT FLAP, *s., UK* portinhola para gatos.
CAT.GUT, *s., Med.*, categute (fio para suturas); *Mús.*, corda para instrumentos.
CA.THAR.SIS, *s.*, catarse.
CA.THAR.TIC (-ICAL), *adj.*, catártico.
CA.THE.DRA, *s.*, **CÁTEDRA.**
CA.THE.DRAL, *s.*, catedral.
CATH.E.TER, *s., Med.*, cateter.
CATH.E.TER.I.ZA.TION, *s., Med.*, cateterização.
CATH.ODE, *s.*, cátodo.
CATH.O.LIC, *adj.*, universal; *adj., s.*, católico.
CA.THOL.I.CISM, *s.*, catolicismo.
CA.THOL.I.CIZE, *v.*, catolicizar, converter ao catolicismo.
CATKIN, *s., Bot.*, amentilho, amento.
CAT.LIKE, *adj.*, semelhante a gato, felíneo.
CAT.HOUSE, *s., col.*, pensão mal frequentada.
CAT.KIN, *s., Bot.*, amentilho, amento.
CAT LITTER, *s., UK* ganulado higiênico para gatos.
CAT.NAP, *s.*, sono leve; *v.*, tirar uma soneca.
CAT SUIT, *s.*, colante feminino de corpo inteiro.
CAT.TISH, *adj.*, felino; *fig.*, traiçoeiro, malicioso.

CAT.TLE, *s.*, gado; rebanho.
CAT.TLE GRID, *s.*, mata-burro.
CAT.TLE-BREED.ING, *s.*, pecuária.
CAT.TLE-DEALER, *s.*, pessoa que compra gado, abate e revende para abatedouros.
CAT.TY, *adj.*, malicioso; o mesmo que *cattish*.
CAT.WALK, *s.*, passarela (para desfile de moda); andaime (de construção).
CAU.CA.SIAN, *adj.*, caucásio, caucasiano, do Cáucaso; *s.*, caucásio; *Antrop.*, caucasoide.
CAU.CUS, *s., US* reunião de líderes para escolher candidatos; eleições primárias.
CAUGHT, *v.*, passado e pretérito perfeito de *catch*.
CAUL.DRON, *s.*, caldeirão.
CAU.LIF.ER.OUS, *adj., Bot.*, caulífero.
CAU.LI.FLOW.ER, *s., Bot.*, couve-flor.
CAULK, *v., Náut.*, calafetar.
CAULK.ING, *s., Náut.*, calafetagem.
CAUS.AL, *adj.*, causal.
CAU.SAL.I.TY, *s.*, causalidade.
CAU.SA.TION, *s.*, ato de causar, causação.
CAUS.A.TIVE, *adj.*, causativo, causal.
CAUSE, *s.*, causa, motivo, porquê; *v.*, provocar, causar.
CAUSE.LESS, *adj.*, sem causa, sem motivo.
CAUSE.LESS.LY, *adv.*, infundadamente, de modo injusto, infundado, sem causa.
CAU.SE.RIE, *s.*, conversa informal; texto informal.
CAUSE.WAY, *s.*, calçada; passadiço elevado sobre água ou pântano.
CAUS.TIC, *adj.*, cáustico; irônico.
CAUS.TIC.AL.LY, *adv.*, causticamente.
CAUS.TIC.I.TY, *s.*, causticidade.
CAUS.TIC SO.DA, *s.*, soda cáustica.
CAU.TER, *s., Med.*, cautério (instrumento para cauterizar).
CAU.TER.IZA.TION, *s.*, cauterização.
CAU.TE.RIZE, *v.*, cauterizar.
CAU.TE.RY, *s.*, cautério; cáustico.
CAU.TION, *s.*, advertência, aviso; prudência, cautela, cuidado; *v.*, advertir; acautelar.
CAU.TION.A.RY, *adj.*, preventivo; que adverte.
CAU.TIOUS, *adj.*, cauteloso, cuidadoso.
CAU.TIOUS.LY, *adv.*, com cautela.
CAU.TIOUS.NESS, *s.*, cautela, cuidado, prudência.
CAV.AL.CADE, *s.*, cavalhada, cavalgada.
CAV.A.LIER, *s.*, cavaleiro.
CAV.AL.RY, *s.*, cavalaria.
CA.VA.TI.NA, *s., Mús.*, cavatina.
CAVE, *s.*, caverna, gruta, subterrâneo.
CAVE-MAN, *s.*, troglodita; rude, inculto.
CAV.ERN, *s.*, caverna.
CAV.ERN.OUS, *adj.*, cavernoso; *UK* imenso(a).
CAV.ERN.OUS.LY, *adv.*, cavernosamente.
CAV.I.AR, *s.*, caviar.
CAV.IL, *s.*, cavilação, chicana; *v.*, cavilar, chicanar.
CAV.ING, *s.*, espeleologismo (estudioso das cavernas); espeleologia (estudo das cavernas).
CAV.I.TY, *s.*, cavidade, buraco, cárie.
CA.VORT, *v.*, cabriolar, saracotear.
CA.VY, *s., Zool.*, capivara.
CAW, *s.*, crocito (voz da gralha, condor etc.); *v.*, crocitar, voz do corvo, grasnar.

CAYENNE ·· 406 ·· CEREBELLUM

CAY.ENNE, *s.*, malagueta, pimenta malagueta.
CAY.MAN, *s.*, *Zool.*, caimão.
CD, *s.*, *abrev.* de *Copact Disc*.
CD PLAYER, *s.*, toca-CDs, tocador de CD.
CD-R, *s.*, *abrev.* de *compact disc recordable*, CD-R.
CD-ROM, *s.*, *abrev.* de *compact disc read-only memory*, CD-ROM.
CD-RW, *s.*, *abrev.* de *compact disc rewritable*, CD-RW.
CEASE, *v.*, cessar, terminar, acabar.
CEASE-FIRE, *s.*, cessar-fogo.
CEASE.LESS, *adj.*, incessante.
CEASE.LESS.LY, *adj.*, incessantemente.
CEASE.LESS.NESS, *s.*, ininterrupção.
CEAS.ING, *s.*, cessação.
CE.DAR, *s.*, *Bot.*, cedro.
CEDE, *v.*, ceder, deixar, renunciar.
CE.DIL.LA, *s.*, cedilha.
CEIL.ING, *s.*, teto (de sala); forro do teto.
CEIL.ING-PRICE, *s.*, preço máximo.
CEL.E.BRANT, *s.*, celebrante; sacerdote.
CEL.E.BRATE, *v.*, celebrar; comemorar.
CEL.E.BRAT.ED, *adj.*, célebre, famoso.
CEL.E.BRA.TION, *s.*, celebração, solenidade, festa.
CEL.E.BRA.TO.RY, *adj.*, comemorativo.
CE.LEB.RI.TY, *s.*, celebridade, fama.
CE.LE.RI.AC, *s.*, *Bot.*, aipo-rábano.
CE.LER.I.TY, *s.*, celeridade, rapidez.
CEL.ERY, *s.*, *Bot.*, aipo.
CE.LES.TIAL, *adj.*, celestial.
CEL.I.BA.CY, *s.*, celibato.
CEL.I.BATE, *adj.*, *s.*, solteiro, celibatário.
CELL, *s.*, cela, cubículo; pilha, célula.
CEL.LAR, *s.*, celeiro, porão, adega.
CEL.LAR.ER, *s.*, adegueiro.
CEL.LIST, *s.*, violoncelista.
CEL.LO, *s.*, violoncelo.
CEL.LO.PHANE, *s.*, celofane.
CEL.LO.PHANE TAPE, *s.*, fita adesiva transparente.
CELL PHONE, *s.*, telefone celular.
CEL.LU.LAR, *adj.*, celular, celuloso.
CEL.LULE, *s.*, célula.
CEL.LU.LI.TIS, *s.*, *Med.*, celulite.
CEL.LU.LOID, *s.*, celuloide, película.
CEL.LU.LOSE, *s.*, celulose.
CEL.SI.US, *adj.*, célsius; centígrado; *s.*, centígrado (unidade em escala Célsius).
CELT, *adj.*, *s.*, celta.
CEL.TIC, *adj.*, celta, céltico; *s.*, celta.
CE.MENT, *s.*, cimento; *v.*, cimentar, ligar com cimento.
CE.MENT.ER, *s.*, cimentador, ligame.
CE.MENT MIXER, *s.*, betoneira, misturador de cimento.
CEM.E.TERY, *s.*, cemitério, campo-santo.
CENSE, *v.*, incensar.
CEN.SOR, *s.*, censor; *v.*, censurar.
CEN.SO.RI.AL, *adj.*, censório (relativo a censor ou censura).
CEN.SOR.SHIP, *s.*, censura.
CEN.SUR.A.BLE, *adj.*, censurável, repreensível.
CEN.SUR.A.BLY, *adv.*, repreensivelmente.
CEN.SURE, *v.*, censurar, criticar.
CEN.SUR.ER, *s.*, censurador.
CEN.SUS, *s.*, censo.

CENT, *s.*, cêntimo.
CENT.AGE, *s.*, percentagem, porcentagem.
CENT.AUR, *s.*, *Mit.*, centauro; **CENT.AUR**, *Astron.*, Centauro (constelação).
CEN.TE.NAR.I.AN, *adj.*, *s.*, centenário.
CEN.TE.NA.RY, *adj.*, *s.*, centenário.
CEN.TEN.NI.AL, *s.*, centenário; *adj.*, secular.
CEN.TEN.NI.AL.LY, *adv.*, de cem em cem anos.
CENTER, *s.*, *US* centro; *v.*, *US* centralizar; ver *centre UK*.
CEN.TER.FOLD, *s.*, *US* mulher glamourosa (cf. *centrefold UK*).
CEN.TER.ING, *s.*, centragem; *Arq.*, cambota.
CEN.TES.I.MAL, *s.*, centésimo; *adj.*, centesimal.
CEN.TI.GRADE, *s.*, centígrado.
CEN.TI.GRAM *US*, **CEN.TI.GRAMME** *UK*, *s.*, centigrama.
CEN.TI.LI.TER *US*, **CEN.TI.LI.TRE**, *s.*, centilitro.
CEN.TI.ME.TER *US*, **CEN.TI.ME.TRE** *UK*, *s.*, centímetro.
CEN.TI.PEDE, *s.*, *Zool.*, centopeia, lacraia.
CEN.TRAL, *adj.*, central.
CEN.TRAL AF.RI.CAN, *adj.* e *s.*, centro-africano.
CEN.TRAL A.MER.I.CAN, *adj.* e *s.*, centro-americano.
CEN.TRAL.I.TY, *s.*, centralidade, centralização.
CEN.TRAL.I.ZA.TION, *s.*, ato de centralizar, centralização.
CEN.TRAL.IZE, *v.*, centralizar.
CEN.TRAL.IZ.ER, *s.*, centralizador.
CEN.TRAL.LY, *adv.*, no centro, centralmente.
CEN.TRAL RES.ER.VA.TION, *s.*, *UK* canteiro central (divisão entre faixas nas estradas).
CEN.TRE, *v.*, *UK* centro; *v.*, centrar, centralizar.
CEN.TRE.FOLD, *s.*, *UK* página central (de revista); (cf. *centerfold US*).
CEN.TRE.PIECE *UK*, **CEN.TER.PIECE** *US*, *s.*, peça decorativa central (no centro de mesa); *fig.*, ponto central.
CEN.TRIC (ICAL), *adj.*, cêntrico.
CEN.TRIC.AL.LY, *adv.*, centralmente.
CEN.TRIC.I.TY, *s.*, centralidade.
CEN.TRIF.U.GAL, *adj.*, centrífugo.
CEN.TRIF.U.GAL FORCE, *s.*, *Fís.*, força centrífuga.
CEN.TRIF.U.GAL MA.CHINE, *s.*, centrífuga (máquina de centrifugar).
CEN.TRI.FUGE, *s.*, centrifugador; *v.*, centrifugar.
CEN.TRI.OLE, *s.*, *Biol.*, centríolo.
CEN.TRIP.E.TAL, *adj.*, *Fís.*, centrípeto.
CEN.TRIST, *s.*, pessoa moderada (em política); *adj.*, moderado.
CEN.TUPLE, *s.*, cêntuplo.
CEN.TU.RI.AL, *adj.*, centurial; secular.
CEN.TU.RI.ON, *s.*, centurião.
CEN.TU.RY, *s.*, século; centúria.
CEO, *s.*, *abrev.* de *Chief Executive Officer:* diretor-chefe executivo, CEO.
CE.PHAL.IC, *adj.*, cefálico.
CEPH.A.LI.TIS, *s.*, *Med.*, cefalite.
CEPH.A.LOID, *adj.*, cefaloide.
CEPH.A.LO.POD, *s.*, *Zool.*, cefalópode.
CE.RAM.IC, *s.*, cerâmica.
CE.RAM.ICS, *s. pl.*, louças.
CER.A.MIST, *s.*, ceramista.
CER.BER.US, *s.*, *Mit.*, Cérbero.
CE.RE.AL, *s.*, cereal.
CER.E.BEL.LUM, *s.*, cerebelo.

CEREBRAL   ··407··   CHANNEL

CE.RE.BRAL, *adj.*, cerebral.
CER.E.BRAL PAL.SY, *s.*, *Med.*, paralisia cerebral.
CER.E.BRATE, *v.*, refletir, pensar.
CE.RE.BRUM, *s.*, cérebro.
CER.E.MO.NI.AL, *s.*, cerimonial.
CER.E.MO.NI.OUS, *adj.*, cerimonioso, formal.
CER.E.MO.NI.OUS.LY, *adv.*, cerimoniosamente.
CER.E.MO.NI.OUS.NESS, *s.*, cerimonialista.
CER.E.MO.NY, *s.*, cerimônia, rito, ritual.
CE.RE.OUS, *adj.*, de cera.
CE.RISE, *s.*, cor de cereja; *adj.*, da cor de cereja.
CE.RI.UM, *s.*, *Quím.*, cério (elemento).
CERT, *s.*, barbada, coisa certa; *abrev.* de *certificate.*
CER.TAIN, *adj.*, certo, seguro.
CER.TAIN.LY, *adv.*, certamente, seguramente.
CER.TAIN.TY, *s.*, certeza, firmeza.
CER.TI.FI.A.BLE, *adj.*, certificativo, certificável; *Med.*, demente, louco.
CER.TIF.I.CATE, *s.*, certidão, certificado; *v.*, certificar, atestar.
CER.TIF.I.CAT.ED, *adj.*, certificado, assegurado, asseverado.
CER.TI.FI.CA.TION, *s.*, certificação.
CER.TI.FIED, *adj.*, habilitado, autenticado.
CER.TI.FI.ER, *s.*, certificador.
CER.TI.O.RA.RI, *s.*, *Jur.*, rogatória.
CER.TI.FY, *v.*, certificar, atestar.
CER.VI.CAL, *adj.*, cervical.
CER.VINE, *adj.*, de cervo ou semelhante a, cervino.
CER.VIX, *s.*, *Anat.*, colo do útero.
CE.SI.UM, *s.*, *Quím.*, o mesmo que *caesium.*
CES.SA.TION, *s.*, cessação, suspensão, pausa.
CES.SION, *s.*, cessão, cedimento, ação de ceder.
CES.SION.A.RY, *s.*, *Jur.*, cessionário.
CESS.PIT, *s.*, fossa, cloaca, esgoto.
CE.TA.CEAN, *s.*, cetáceo.
CE.TA.CEOUS, *adj.*, o mesmo que *cetacean.*
CET.OL.O.GY, *s.*, *Zool.*, cetologia.
CHAFE, *v.*, roçar.
CHA.FER, *s.*, besouro.
CHAFF, *s.*, palhiço, debulha; *fig.*, traste; picuinha; *v.*, troçar.
CHAF.FER, *v.*, pechinchar, regatear.
CHAF.FER.ER, *s.*, regateador.
CHAF.FINCH, *s.*, *Zool.*, tentilhão.
CHAF.ING, *s.*, fricção; irritação, aquecimento.
CHA.GRIN, *s.*, tristeza, desgosto; *v.*, desgostar, entristecer.
CHAIN, *s.*, cadeia, corrente, grupo, cadeia de montanhas; *v.*, acorrentar.
CHAIN.ING, *s.*, encadeamento, ligação.
CHAIN-SAW, *s.*, serra articulada; motosserra.
CHAIN-SMOKE, *v.*, fumar continuamente.
CHAIN-SMOK.ER, *s.*, fumante inveterado.
CHAIN STORE, *s.*, sucursal, filial.
CHAIR, *s.*, cadeira, poltrona.
CHAIR.LIFT, *s.*, teleférico.
CHAIR.MAN, *s.*, presidente.
CHAIR.MAN.SHIP, *s.*, presidência.
CHAIR.PER.SON, *s.*, aquele(a) que preside (reunião ou debate); presidente(a).
CHAIR.WOM.AN, *s.*, presidenta.
CHAISE LONGUE, *s.*, espreguiçadeira.
CHAL.DA.IC, *s. e adj.*, caldeu, caldaico.
CHA.LET, *s.*, chalé.

CHAL.ICE, *s.*, cálice.
CHALK, *s.*, giz.
CHALK.BOARD, *s.*, *UK* quadro-negro.
CHALK-PIT, *s.*, mina calcária.
CHALK.Y, *adj.*, calcário; gredoso.
CHAL.LENGE, *s.*, desafio; *v.*, desafiar, provocar.
CHAL.LENGE.A.BLE, *adj.*, contestável.
CHAL.LENG.ER, *s.*, desafiador, competidor, rival.
CHAL.LENG.ING, *s.*, desafiante, provocador.
CHAL.LENG.ING.LY, *adv.*, provocantemente.
CHAL.LIS, *s.*, tecido fino de lã.
CHAM.BER, *s.*, câmara, sala de audiências.
CHAM.BER-MU.SIC, *s.*, música de câmara.
CHAM.BER OF COM.MERCE, *s.*, câmara de comércio.
CHAM.BER OR.CHES.TRA, *s.*, orquestra de câmara.
CHAM.BER-POT, *s.*, urinol.
CHAM.BER.LAIN, *s.*, camareiro, camarista.
CHAM.BER.MAID, *s.*, criada de quarto, camareira.
CHAM.BRAY, *s.*, cambraia.
CHA.ME.LEON, *s.*, *Zool.*, camaleão.
CHA.ME.LE.ON.IC, *adj.*, camaleônico.
CHAM.FER, *s.*, chanfradura; *v.*, chanfrar.
CHAM.MY, *s.*, pele de camurça.
CHAM.OIS, *s.*, camurça.
CHAM.O.MILE, *s.*, camomila.
CHAMP, *v.*, mastigar, morder.
CHAM.PAGNE, *s.*, *Fr.*, champanhe, champanha.
CHAM.PAIGN, *s.*, campina, planície, várzea.
CHAM.PERS, *s.*, champanha.
CHAM.PI.GNON, *s. Fr.*, *Bot.*, cogumelo, champinhom.
CHAM.PI.ON, *s.*, campeão.
CHAM.PI.ON.SHIP, *s.*, campeonato.
CHANCE, *s.*, chance, oportunidade, momento; *v.*, arriscar, aproveitar.
CHANCE.FUL, *adj.*, cheio de possibilidades.
CHAN.CEL.LERY, *s.*, chancelaria.
CHAN.CEL.LOR, *s.*, chanceler (governo); reitor (universidade).
CHANC.ER, *s.*, *col.*, oportunista.
CHAN.CER.Y, *s.*, corte de justiça; supremo tribunal.
CHAN.CRE, *s.*, úlcera ou cancro venéreo.
CHAN.CROUS, *adj.*, cancroso.
CHAN.CY, *adj.*, duvidoso, incerto, arriscado.
CHAN.DE.LIER, *s.*, lustre.
CHANGE, *v.*, cambiar, trocar, mudar.
CHANGE.A.BIL.I.TY, *s.*, mutabilidade, instabilidade.
CHANGE.A.BLE, *adj.*, inconstante, instável.
CHANGE.A.BLY, *adv.*, inconstantemente.
CHANGED, *adj.*, mudado, modificado; trocado.
CHANGE.FUL, *adj.*, variável, inconstante, mutável.
CHANGE.FUL.LY, *adv.*, variavelmente.
CHANGE.FUL.NESS, *s.*, inconstância, volubilidade.
CHANGE.LESS, *adj.*, invariável, constante.
CHANGE.LESS.LY, *adv.*, invariavelmente, constantemente.
CHANGE.LESS.NESS, *s.*, invariabilidade, constância.
CHANGE.O.VER, *s.*, mudança (de trabalho, atividade).
CHANG.ER, *s.*, mudador, o que muda.
CHANG.ING, *adj.*, variável, instável; *s.*, troca, mudança; baldeação.
CHANG.ING ROOM, *s.*, vestiário; provador.
CHAN.NEL, *s.*, canal, ranhura, leito de rio; *v.*, canalizar.

CHANNELER 408 CHECKMATE

CHAN.NEL.ER, *s.*, canalizador; médium (pessoa que se comunica com espíritos).
CHAN.NEL.ING, *s.*, canalização; mediunidade.
CHAN.NEL.IZE, *v.*, canalizar.
CHANT, *s.*, canto; cântico, salmo; *v.*, cantar, entoar; salmodiar.
CHANT.ER, *s.*, cantor de igreja; chantre.
CHANT.EY, *s., Náut.*, cantiga no ritmo do trabalho dos marujos.
CHAN.TI.CLEER, *s., Ant.*, galo.
CHA.OS, *s.*, caos.
CHA.OT.IC, **CHA.OT.I.CAL**, *adj.*, caótico.
CHA.OT.I.CAL.LY, *adv.*, caoticamente, confusamente.
CHAP, *s.*, rachadura (na pele), greta; *UK* camarada, chapa.
CHA.PAR.RAL, *s., Bot.*, chaparral (mata de chaparros).
CHA.PA.TI, **CHAP.PA.TI**, *s.*, tipo de pão indiano muito famoso.
CHAP.BOOK, *s.*, livro de contos populares.
CHAP.EL, *s.*, capela.
CHAP.ER.ON, **CHAP.ER.ONE**, *s.*, aia, acompanhante; *v.*, acompanhar.
CHAP.FALL.EN, *adj.*, de queixo caído; *fig.*, desanimado, humilhado.
CHAP.I.TER, *s., Arq.*, capitel.
CHAP.LAIN, *s.*, capelão.
CHAP.LET, *s.*, terço, grinalda.
CHAP.MAN, *s.*, vendedor, ambulante.
CHAPPED, *adj.*, rachado (pele, lábios); *fig.*, bravo, irritado.
CHAPPED.LIPS, *s. pl.*, lábios rachados.
CHAP.TER, *s.*, capítulo.
CHAR, *s.*, carvão animal; faxineira; *v.*, tostar, queimar, carbonizar; biscatear.
CHAR.AC.TER, *s.*, caráter, temperamento; personagem, papel de artista; cargo.
CHAR.AC.TER.IS.TIC, *adj.*, característico.
CHAR.AC.TER.IST.I.CAL, *adj.*, o mesmo que *characteristic*.
CHAR.AC.TER.IST.I.CAL.LY, *adv.*, caracteristicamente.
CHAR.AC.TER.IZATION, *s.*, caracterização.
CHAR.AC.TER.IZE, *v.*, caracterizar.
CHAR.AC.TER.LESS, *adj.*, sem interesse; ordinário.
CHA.RADE *s.*, charada.
CHAR.COAL, *s.*, carvão vegetal; lápis de carvão; *v.*, desenhar com carvão.
CHARD, *s., Bot.*, acelga.
CHARGE, *s.*, carga (de pólvora); acusação, encargo; preço; custo; *v.*, carregar, cobrar, atacar.
CHARGE.A.BIL.I.TY, *s.*, direito de taxar; taxação; responsabilidade; generosidade.
CHARGE.A.BLE, *adj.*, debitável, cobrável; custoso; imputável, atribuível.
CHARGE.A.BLY, *adv.*, dispendiosamente.
CHARG.ER, *s.*, cavalo de batalha; *Eletr.*, carregador de baterias (celular etc.).
CHAR.I.NESS, *s.*, cuidado, cautela.
CHAR.I.LY, *adv.*, cuidadosamente; parcimoniosamente.
CHAR.I.OT, *s.*, biga (carro da Roma Antiga).
CHA.RIS.MA, *s.*, carisma.
CHAR.IS.MAT.IC, *adj.*, carismático.
CHAR.I.TA.BLE, *adj.*, caridoso, generoso; (organização) beneficente.
CHAR.I.TA.BLE.NESS, *s.*, caridade.
CHAR.I.TA.BLY, *adv.*, caridosamente.
CHAR.I.TY, *s.*, caridade, donativo, amor puro.
CHAR.LA.TAN, *s.*, charlatão.

CHAR.LA.TAN.ISM, *s.*, charlatanismo.
CHAR.LES'S WAIN, *s., Astron.*, Ursa Maior.
CHARLES.TON, *s.*, dança da década de 1920.
CHARM, *s.*, charme, encanto, fascínio; *v.*, encantar, fascinar; seduzir.
CHARMED, *adj.*, encantado, enfeitiçado.
CHARM.ER, *s.*, encantador.
CHARM.FUL, *adj.*, cheio de charme.
CHARM.ING, *adj.*, encantador, fascinante, agradável.
CHARM.ING.LY, *adv.*, encantadoramente.
CHARM.LESS, *adj.*, sem charme, sem encanto.
CHAR.NEL, *s.*, cemitério; *adv.*, sepulcral.
CHARRED, *adj.*, carbonizado, chamuscado.
CHART, *s.*, gráfico, lista; *v.*, traçar.
CHAR.TER, *v.*, fretar, alugar; *s.*, frete, voo fretado, alvará.
CHAR.TER.ER, *s.*, fretador.
CHAR.WOM.AN, *s.*, faxineira.
CHAR.Y, *adj.*, cuidadoso, cauteloso, prudente, solícito.
CHASE, *v.*, perseguir, afugentar.
CHAS.ER, *s.*, bebida fraca de entrada; perseguidor, caçador; entalhador.
CHAS.ING, *s.*, perseguição.
CHASM, *s.*, abismo; *fig.*, divergência de opiniões.
CHAS.SIS, *s. pl.*, chassis; chassi.
CHASTE, *s.*, casto, puro, cândido.
CHAS.TEN, *v.*, disciplinar, castigar; apurar, refinar.
CHAS.TEN.ER, *s.*, disciplinador, castigador; refinador.
CHASTE.NESS, *s.*, castidade, pureza.
CHAS.TISE, *v.*, castigar, punir, açoitar.
CHAS.TI.TY, *s.*, castidade.
CHAT, *s.*, palestra, tagarelice, colóquio; *v.*, tagarelar, conversar.
CHAT.E.LAINE, *s.*, castelã; corrente usada para prender chaves etc.
CHAT ROOM, *s.*, sala de bate-papo (internet).
CHAT SHOW, *s.*, program de entrevistas de rádio ou TV.
CHAT.TER, *s.*, tagarelice; chilro; *v.*, tagarelar, chilrar.
CHAT.TER.BOX, *s., col.*, tagarela, palrador.
CHAT.TY, *adj.*, tagarela, palrador.
CHAUF.FEUR, *s., Fr.*, chofer, motorista.
CHAU.VIN.ISM, *s.*, chauvinismo.
CHAU.VIN.IST, *s.*, chauvinista.
CHAU.VIN.IS.TIC, *adj.*, chauvinista.
CHEAP, *adj.*, barato, sem valor, ordinário, comum.
CHEAP.EN, *v.*, degradar, depreciar.
CHEAP.LY, *adv.*, barato, preço baixo.
CHEAP.NESS, *s.*, preço baixo, barateza.
CHEAP.SKATE, *s.*, pão-duro, muquirana.
CHEAT, *v.*, trapacear, enganar, lograr.
CHEAT.ER, *s.*, trapaceiro.
CHEAT.ING, *adj.*, blefe, fraudulento.
CHECK, *s.*, controle, inspeção, conta, cheque; *v.*, controlar, verificar.
CHECKED, *adj.*, quadriculado, xadrezado.
CHECK.ER, *s.*, controlador.
CHECK.ERED, *adj.*, quadriculado; diversificado.
CHECK.ERS, *s., US* jogo de damas.
CHECK-IN, *s.*, recepção; *check-in*.
CHECK.ING AC.COUNT, *s., US* conta-corrente.
CHECK LIST, *s.*, lista de verificação.
CHECK.MATE, *s.*, xeque-mate (jogo de xadrez).

CHECKOUT ···409··· CHILI

CHECK.OUT, *s.*, caixa de mercado.
CHECK POINT, *s.*, posto de controle (na fronteira).
CHECK-UP, *s.*, consulta, verificação total da saúde.
CHECK.Y, *adj.*, xadrezado, enxadrezado.
CHED.DAR, *s.*, queijo amarelo inglês.
CHEEK, *s.*, bochecha, face; *col.*, audácia; *vul.*, nádega.
CHEEKED, *adj.*, de face, de rosto.
CHEEK.I.NESS, *s.*, descaramento, insolência.
CHEEK.Y, *adj.*, atrevido, petulante, descarado.
CHEEP, *s.*, pio (de pássaro); *v.*, piar.
CHEER, *s.*, vivas, aclamação; regozijo; *v.*, ovacionar; animar.
CHEER.FUL, *adj.*, alegre, satisfeito.
CHEER.FUL.LY, *adv.*, alegremente, de boa vontade.
CHEER.FUL.NESS, *s.*, alegria; animação.
CHEER.ING, *adj.*, animador; *s.*, animação.
CHEER.I.LY, *adv.*, alegremente, jovialmente.
CHEER.I.NESS, *s.*, alegria.
CHEER.I.O, *interj.*, até logo!; viva!; saúde!
CHEER.LEAD.ER, *s.*, *Esp.*, chefe de torcida, animador.
CHEER.LESS, *adj.*, triste, desconsolado.
CHEER.LESS.LY, *adv.*, tristemente, desconsoladamente.
CHEER.LESS.NESS, *s.*, tristeza, desânimo.
CHEER.Y, *adj.*, alegre, contente; cordial.
CHEESE, *s.*, queijo; *v.*, *col.*, cessar; calar-se.
CHEESE.BOARD, *s.*, tábua de queijos.
CHEESE.BURG.ER, *s.*, sanduíche de hambúrguer com queijo quente.
CHEESE CAKE, *s.*, bolo de queijo.
CHEESED OFF, *adj.*, *UK* chateado, desapontado.
CHEESE-PAR.ING, *s.*, aparas de queijo; *fig.*, sovinice; bugigangas; *adj.*, mesquinho.
CHEES.Y, *adj.*, (com cheiro e gosto) de queijo; (sorriso) forçado; cafona; *US* estragado.
CHEE.TAH, *s.*, *Zool.*, guepardo.
CHEF, *s.*, cozinheiro-chefe.
CHEI.ROP.TER.A, *s.*, *Zool.*, quiróptero (ordem a que pertence o morcego).
CHE.LIF.ER.OUS, *adj.*, quelífero.
CHE.LOID, *adj.*, *Med.*, queloide.
CHEL.O.NI.A, *s.*, *Zool.*, quelônios (ordem a que pertence a tartaruga).
CHEM, *abrev.* de *chemical*, *chemist* ou *chemistry*.
CHEM.IC, *adj.*, químico.
CHEM.I.CAL, *s.*, substância química; *adj.*, químico.
CHEM.I.CAL.LY, *adv.*, quimicamente.
CHE.MISE, *s.*, camisa de mulher.
CHEM.I.SETTE, *s.*, camiseta de mulher que cobre o busto (com ou sem rendas).
CHEM.IST, *s.*, químico, farmacêutico.
CHEM.IS.TRY, *s.*, química.
CHEM.IST'S, *s.*, farmácia, drogaria.
CHEM.O.THE.RA.PY, *s.*, *Med.*, quimioterapia.
CHEQUE, *s.*, cheque.
CHEQUE ACCOUNT, *s.*, *UK* conta corrente.
CHEQUE.BOOK, *s.*, talão de cheques, talonário.
CHE.QUERED *UK*, *adj.*, o mesmo que *checkered*.
CHER.ISH, *v.*, acarinhar, tratar com carinho.
CHER.ISH.ED, *adj.*, querido, estimado, precioso.
CHER.RY, *s.*, *Bot.*, cereja.
CHER.RY TO.MA.TO, *s.*, tomate-cereja.
CHER.RY-WOOD, *s.*, madeira de cerejeira.

CHER.UB, **CHER.U.BIM**, *s.*, querubim, anjo.
CHE.RU.BIC, *adj.*, próprio de querubim.
CHER.VIL, *s.*, *Bot.*, cerefólio (planta semelhante à salsa).
CHESS, *s.*, jogo de xadrez.
CHESS.BOARD, *s.*, tabuleiro de xadrez.
CHEST, *s.*, peito, caixa, cofre.
CHEST.NUT, *s.*, castanha.
CHEST.Y, *adj.*, com tosse seca, com catarro; *vulg.*, seios grandes.
CHEV.A.LIER, *s.*, *Fr.*, *Ant.*, cavaleiro; cavalheiro.
CHE.VE.LURE, *s.*, cabeleira.
CHEV.RON, *s.*, *Mil.*, divisa (uniforme); placa de sinalização; *Her.*, chaveirão.
CHEV.Y, *s.*, *UK* grito (usado na caça); *v.*, caçar, perseguir; importunar, aborrecer.
CHEW, *v.*, mastigar.
CHEW.ING, *s.*, mastigação.
CHEW.ING-GUM, *s.*, goma de mascar, chicle.
CHEWY, *adj.*, duro de mastigar.
CHIC, *adj.*, chique, elegante.
CHI.CANE, *s.*, chicana, tramoia, enredo; *v.*, chicanar.
CHI.CA.NE.RY, *s.*, chicana, tramoia, ardil.
CHICK, *s.*, pintinho; *fig.*, *col.*, criança.
CHICK.EN, *s.*, pinto; *US* galinha, frango.
CHICK.EN BROTH, *s.*, canja, caldo de galinha.
CHICK.EN COOP, *s.*, galinheiro.
CHICK.EN-POX, *s.*, *Med.*, catapora, varicela.
CHICK.EN SOUP, *s.*, canja; *fig.*, *col.*, conforto alívio.
CHICK.EN WIRE, *s.*, tela de arame (para galinheiros).
CHICK.PEA, *s.*, *Bot.*, grão-de-bico.
CHIC.LE, *s.*, goma de mascar.
CHIC.O.RY, *s.*, *Bot.*, chicória.
CHIDE, *s.*, repreensão; *v.*, ralhar, admoestar.
CHID.ING, *s.*, repreensão, gritaria; *adj.*, barulhento; repreensivo.
CHIEF, *adj.*, principal, superior, chefe.; *s.*, chefe, superior, cabeça; cacique.
CHIEF COM.MAND, *s.*, comando supremo.
CHIEF.DOM, *s.*, supremacia.
CHIEF.LY, *adv.*, principalmente, sobretudo.
CHIEF.TAIN, *s.*, chefe (de tribo); comandante.
CHIF.FON, *s.*, gaze.
CHI.HUA.HUA, *s.*, *Zool.*, chihuahua (raça de cão).
CHIL.BLAIN, *s.*, **CHIL.BLAINS**, *s. pl.*, frieira.
CHILD, *s.*, criança, filho.
CHILD.BEAR.ING, *s.*, gravidez; parto.
CHILD.BIRTH, *s.*, parto.
CHILD CARE, *s.*, assistência governamental ou não-governamental à infância.
CHILD.HOOD, *s.*, infância.
CHILD.ISH, *adj.*, infantil.
CHILD.ISH.LY, *adv.*, *pej.*, infantilmente.
CHILD.LESS, *adj.*, sem filhos.
CHILD.LIKE, *adj.*, infantil, pueril, inocente.
CHILD.MIND.ER, *s.*, *UK* babá.
CHILD PROOF, *adj.*, que é seguro para crianças, à prova de crianças.
CHIL.DREN, *s.*, prole, filhos.
CHIL.DREN'S BOOKS, *s.*, livros infantis.
CHILE.AN, *adj.*, *s.*, chileno.
CHIL.I *US*, **CHIL.LI** *UK*, *s.*, pimenta malagueta.

CHILL   •• 410 •••   CHONICLER

CHILL, *s.*, frio, friagem, arrepio.
CHILL.ER, *s.*, resfriador.
CHILL.I.LY, *s.*, com frieza, frialdade.
CHIL.LING, *adj.*, que esfria, gelado; arrepiante, indiferente.
CHILL.NESS, *s.*, frio; frieza.
CHILL.Y, *adj.*, frio, friorento; indiferente.
CHI.ME, *s.*, batida de carrilhão (sino, relógio); *v.*, repicar sinos; tocar carrilhão.
CHI.ME.RA, **CHI.MAE.RA**, *s.*, quimera.
CHI.MER.IC, *adj.*, quimérico.
CHIM.NEY, *s.*, chaminé.
CHIM.NEY.POT, *s.*, chaminé; cano de chaminé.
CHIM.NEY.SWEEP.ER, *s.*, limpador de chaminés.
CHIMP, *s.*, *Zool., col.*, chimpanzé.
CHIM.PAN.ZEE, *s.*, *Zool.*, chimpanzé.
CHIN, *s.*, queixo.
CHI.NA, *s.*, porcelana, louça.
CHI.NA-INK, *s.*, nanquim, tinta nanquim.
CHINE, *s.*, espinha dorsal (de animal); lombo; crista, cume; *v.*, cortar (carne do lombo).
CHI.NESE, *adj.*, *s.*, chinês.
CHINK, *s.*, fresta, fenda; tinido (som); *v.*, tilintar, tinir; rachar-se.
CHINTZ, *s.*, tecido de algodão estampado; chita.
CHINWAG, *s.*, *col.*, conversa informal; *UK* bate-papo.
CHIP, *s.*, lasca, caco de qualquer coisa; *Inform.*, circuito; *v.*, lascar; **CHIPS**, *s. pl.*, batatas fritas; refugo.
CHIP.BOARD, *s.*, compensado (material de construção); papelão barato.
CHIP.MUNK, *s.*, *Zool.*, tâmia (esquilo da América do Norte).
CHIPPED, *adj.*, lascado.
CHIPPED BEEF, *s.*, carne seca em fatias.
CHIP.PING, *s.*, estilhaço, lasca, caco.
CHI.ROG.RA.PHY, *s.*, quirografia.
CHI.ROL.O.GY, *s.*, quirologia.
CHI.ROP.O.DIST, *s.*, quiropodista, calista, pedicuro.
CHI.ROP.O.DY, *s.*, tratamento dos pés, serviço de pedicuro.
CHI.RO.PRAC.TOR, *s.*, *Med.*, quiroprático (terapia para reduzir dores).
CHIRP, *s.*, chilro, pio; *v.*, chilrar, piar.
CHIRP.ING, *s.*, chilro, chilreio; *adj.*, chilrador; *fig.*, que anima.
CHIRP.Y, *adj.*, *col.*, alegre, vivo; animado.
CHIS.EL, *s.*, formão, talhadeira, cinzel; *v.*, esculpir; *fig.*, tapear, enganar.
CHIT, *s.*, penhor, garantia, talão; nota; criança, moça atrevida.
CHIT.CHAT, *s.*, conversa mole, conversa fiada.
CHIV.AL.RIC, *adj.*, cavalheiresco.
CHIV.AL.ROUS, *adj.*, nobre, cavalheiresco.
CHI.VAL.RY, *s.*, cavalheirismo, bravura; *Literat.*, cavalaria.
CHIVE, *s.*, *Bot.*, cebolinha.
CHIV.Y, *s.*, o mesmo que *chevy*.
CHLO.RATE, *s.*, *Quím.*, clorato.
CHLO.RIDE, *s.*, *Quím.*, cloreto.
CHLO.RI.NATE, *v.*, clorar; tratar com cloro.
CHLO.RI.NAT.ED, *adj.*, clorado.
CHLO.RINE, *s.*, *Quím.*, cloro.
CHLO.RO.FLU.OR.CARB.ON, *s.*, *Quím.*, clorofluorcarbono.
CHLO.RO.FORM, *s.*, clorofórmio; *v.*, cloroformizar.
CHLO.RO.PHYL, *s.*, clorofila.
CHLO.ROUS, *adj.*, *Quím.*, cloroso.
CHOCK, *s.*, calço, escora, cunha; *v.*, calçar, cunhar.
CHOCK-FULL, *adj.*, apinhado, abarrotado, repleto.

CHOCO.LATE, *s.*, chocolate.
CHOCO.LATE NUT, *s.*, cacau (fruto do cacaueiro).
CHOICE, *s.*, escolha, seleção; *adj.*, seleto, escolhido, preferido.
CHOIR, *s.*, coro.
CHOIR.MAS.TER, *s.*, *Mús.*, maestro de coro.
CHOKE, *s.*, sufocar, engasgar, obstruir.
CHOK.ER, *s.*, abafador; sufocador; gravata apertada; tipo de gargantilha justa.
CHOK.ING, *s.*, sufocação, asfixia; abafamento; *adj.*, asfixiante.
CHO.KY, *adj.*, sufocado, abafado, engasgado.
CHOL.ER, *s.*, *fig.*, mau humor, ira; *Ant.*, bílis.
CHOL.ERA, *s.*, *Med.*, cólera.
CHO.LER.IC, *adj.*, irado, raivoso, colérico.
CHO.LES.TER.OL, *s.*, colesterol.
CHOOSE, *v.*, escolher; preferir, eleger; selecionar.
CHOOS.ER, *s.*, escolhedor, selecionador.
CHOOS.EY, *adj.*, exigente.
CHOOS.ING, *s.*, escolha, seleção.
CHOP, *s.*, corte, talha; fatia; costeleta (carne); *v.*, cortar, talhar; picar; sacudir.
CHOP-CHOP!, *interj.*, rápido!, sem demora!
CHOP.PER, *s.*, cutelo, talhador; cortador.
CHOP.PING, *s.*, corte, rachadura; *adj.*, cortante.
CHOP.PING BOARD, *s.*, tábua de cozinha (para picar carne e vegetais).
CHOP.PY, *adj.*, agitado.
CHOP.STICKS, *s. pl.*, hashi (pausinhos chineses usados para comer).
CHO.RAL, *s.*, coral.
CHORD, *s.*, *Mús.*, acorde; corda, *vocal* ~: corda vocal.
CHORE, *s.*, afazeres, trabalho doméstico.
CHO.REO.GRAPH, **CHO.RE.OG.RA.PHER**, *s.*, coreógrafo.
CHO.RE.OG.RA.PHY, *s.*, coreografia.
CHO.RIST, *s.*, *Teat.*, corista.
CHO.RIS.TER, *s.*, *Mús.*, corista.
CHO.ROG.RA.PHY, *s.*, *Geo.*, corografia (descrição geográfica).
CHO.RUS, *s.*, *Mús.*, coro; refrão.
CHOSE, *v.*, passado de *choose*.
CHO.SEN, *v.*, pretérito perfeito de *choose*.
CHOW, *s.*, chow-chow (raça de cão chinês).
CHOW.DER, *s.*, *US* sopa de frutos do mar.
CHRISM, *s.*, crisma.
CHRISM.AL, *adj.*, crismal.
CHRIST, *s.*, Cristo.
CHRIST.EN.ING, *s.*, batismo, batizado.
CHRIS.TIAN, *adj.*, *s.*, cristão.
CHRIS.TIAN.ISM, *s.*, cristianismo.
CHRIS.TIAN.I.TY, *s.*, cristandade.
CHRIS.TIAN.IZE, *v.*, cristianizar.
CHRIST.MAS, *s.*, Natal; *Happy* ~!: Feliz Natal!; *adj.*, natal, natalício.
CHRIST.MAS-TREE, *s.*, árvore de Natal.
CHRO.MAT.IC, *adj.*, cromático.
CHROME, *s.*, *Quím.*, cromo; *v.*, cromar.
CHRO.MI.UM, *s.*, *Quím.*, cromo.
CHRO.MO.SOME, *s.*, cromossoma.
CHRON.IC, *adj.*, crônico.
CHRON.I.CAL.LY, *adv.*, cronicamente.
CHRON.I.CLE, *s.*, crônica; *v.*, escrever crônica; narrar.
CHON.I.CLER, *s.*, cronista.

CHRONOGRAM ·· 411 ·· CITROUS

CHRO.NO.GRAM, s., cronograma.
CHRO.NOG.RA.PHY, s., cronografia.
CHRON.O.LOG.IC, adj., cronológico.
CHRON.O.LOG.I.CAL, adj., o mesmo que *chronologic*.
CHRON.O.LOG.I.CAL.LY, adv., cronologicamente.
CHRO.NOL.O.GY, s., cronologia.
CHRO.NOM.E.TER, s., cronômetro.
CHRO.NOM.E.TRY, s., cronometria.
CHRYS.A.LID, s., Zool., crisálida; adj., relativo à crisálida.
CHRYS.A.LIS, s., Zool., crisálida, casulo.
CHRYS.AN.THE.MUM, s., Bot., crisântemo.
CHTHON.I.AN, adj., ctônico, ctoniano.
CHUB.BI.NESS, s., gordura, adiposidade.
CHUB.BY, adj., gordo.
CHUCK, v., atirar, jogar, sair, deixar.
CHUCK IN, v., despedir-se.
CHUCK.LE, v., rir à socapa.
CHUFFED, adj., UK orgulhoso, satisfeito.
CHUG, s., US som de escape de motor; UK v., ratear.
CHUM, s., companheiro, amigo.
CHUM.MY, adj., col., amigo íntimo.
CHUMP, s., col., pessoa estúpida, tolo.
CHUNK, s., col., pedaço grande; naco.
CHUNK.Y, adj., corpulento, parrudo; grosso, maciço.
CHURCH, s., igreja, templo cristão, serviço religioso.
CHURCH.GO.ER, s., devoto, fiel, carola.
CHURCH.MAN, s., membro da igreja, clérigo, pastor.
CHURCH.SERVICE, s., serviço religioso.
CHURCH.YARD, s., terreno em volta de igreja, adro; Hist., cemitério.
CHURL, s., camponês, tipo rude.
CHURL.ISH, adj., rude, rústico, grosseiro.
CHURN, s., batedeira (de manteiga); latão (de leite); agitação; v., fazer manteiga; mexer, agitar.
CHUTE, s., US cachoeira, corredeira; rampa, calha; tobogã.
CI.CA.DA, s., Zool., cigarra.
CI.CA.TRI.CE, s., cicatriz.
CI.CA.TRI.ZA.TION, s., cicatrização.
CIC.A.TRIZE, s., cicatrizar.
CI.DER, s., sidra, vinho de maçã.
CI.GAR, s., charuto.
CIG.A.RETTE, s., cigarro.
CIG.A.RETTE-HOLD.ER, s., piteira (para fumar cigarros).
CIG.A.RETTE PA.PER, s., papel de enrolar cigarros.
CIG.A.RIL.LO, s., cigarrilha.
CINC.TURE, s., cinta, cinto, cinturão.
CIN.DER, s., cinza; braza de carvão; **CIN.DERS** s. pl., cinzas.
CIN.DER BLOCK, s., bloco de cimento, laje de concreto.
CINE-CAM.E.RA, s., filmadora; câmera cinematográfica.
CIN.E.MA, s., cinema.
CIN.E.MAT.IC, adj., cinemático, cinematográfico.
CIN.E.MAT.O.GRAPH, s., cinematógrafo (projetor de filmes).
CIN.E.MA.TOG.RA.PHY, s., cinematografia.
CIN.E.RA.TION, s., incineração, cremação.
CIN.ER.A.TOR, s., incinerador; crematório.
CIN.NA.MON, s., canela; casca de caneleira; adj., do aroma ou da cor de canela.
CI.PHER, s., cifra, algarismo arábico, zero; v., cifrar, calcular.
CIR.CA, prep., adv., cerca, aproximadamente.
CIR.CE, s., Mit., Circe; fig., feiticeira.
CIR.CLE, s., círculo, balcão; v., rodear, dar voltas.

CIR.CUIT, s., circuito, volta.
CIR.CUIT BREAK.ER, s., disjuntor, interruptor.
CIR.CU.I.TOUS, adj., que dá voltas, tortuoso; fig., rodeio (fala evasiva), indireto.
CIR.CU.I.TOUS.NESS, s., rodeio, circuito.
CIR.CU.LAR, adj., s., circular.
CIR.CU.LAR.I.TY, s., circularidade, forma circular.
CIR.CU.LAR LET.TER, s., carta-circular.
CIR.CU.LAR.LY, adv., circularmente.
CIR.CU.LATE, v., circular.
CIR.CU.LAT.ING, adj., circulante, corrente.
CIR.CU.LA.TION, s., circulação, tiragem de jornais e revistas.
CIR.CU.LA.TOR, s., quem ou o que circula; distribuidor.
CIR.CU.LA.TO.RY, adj., circulatório.
CIR.CUM.CISE, v., circuncidar.
CIR.CUM.CI.SION, s., circuncisão.
CIR.CUM.FER.ENCE, s., circunferência, periferia.
CIR.CUM.FLEX, s., acento circunflexo.
CIR.CUM.NAV.I.GATE, v., circunavegar.
CIR.CUM.NAV.I.GA.TION, s., circunavegação.
CIR.CUM.NAV.I.GA.TOR, s., circunavegador.
CIR.CUM.SCRIBE, v., circunscrever.
CIR.CUM.SCRIP.TION, s., circunscrição.
CIR.CUM.SPECT, adj., circunspecto, grave, sério.
CIR.CUM.SPEC.TION, s., circunspeção, prudência.
CIR.CUM.STANCE, s., circunstância, situação; v., circunstanciar.
CIR.CUM.STANCED, adj., circunstanciado, detalhado.
CIR.CUM.STAN.TIAL, adj., circunstancial; promenorizado; acidental.
CIR.CUM.STAN.TI.ATE, v., circunstanciar, detalhar, pormenorizar.
CIR.CUM.STAN.TI.A.TION, s., pormenorização.
CIR.CUM.VAL.LATE, v., circunvalar (cercar de fortificações).
CIR.CUM.VAL.LA.TION, s., circunvalação.
CIR.CUM.VENT, v., driblar, enganar, lograr.
CIR.CUM.VEN.TION, s., engano, logro.
CIR.CUM.VENT.IVE, adj., enganoso.
CIR.CUM.VO.LU.TION, s., circunvolução, rotação; circunlóquio.
CIR.CUM.VOLVE, v., circunvolver, rotar.
CIR.CUS, s., circo, anfiteatro.
CIR.RHO.SIS, s., Med., cirrose.
CIR.ROSE, adj., cirroso.
CIS.AL.PINE, adj., cisalpino.
CIS.MON.TANE, adj., cismontano.
CIS.TERN, s., cisterna, poço, reserva de água.
CIS.TUS, s., Bot., cisto.
CIT.A.BLE, adj., citável.
CIT.A.DEL, s., cidadela, foratleza; fig., refúgio.
CI.TA.TION, s., citação, intimação, apelo, menção.
CITE, v., citar, mencionar, referir, chamar; Jur., intimar.
CITH.A.RA, s., Mús., cítara.
CIT.I.FIED, adj., próprio de citadino ou urbano.
CIT.I.ZEN, s., cidadão; pessoa civil; habitante.
CIT.I.ZEN.RY, s., conjunto de cidadãos, povo.
CIT.I.ZEN.SHIP, s., cidadania.
CIT.RIC, adj., cítrico.
CIT.RI.CUL.TURE, s., citricultura.
CIT.RON, s., cidra, lima.
CIT.ROUS, adj., relativo às plantas do gên. Citrus, cítrico.

CITY — 412 — CLEANUP

CIT.Y, s., cidade, metrópole, centro urbano.
CIT.Y FATHER, s., vereador, edil.
CIT.Y HALL, s., prefeitura.
CIT.Y-STATE, s., cidade-estado.
CIV.IC, *adj.*, cívico, urbano.
CIV.IC.AL.LY, *adv.*, civicamente.
CIV.IL, *adj.*, civil, cívico, próprio do governo; cortês, delicado, polido.
CIV.IL DE.FENSE, s., defesa civil.
CIV.IL DIS.O.BE.DI.ENCE, s., desobediência civil.
CIV.IL EN.GI.NEER, s., engenheiro civil.
CI.VIL.IAN, s., cidadão civil, paisano; não militar.
CI.VIL.I.TY, s., civilidade, polidez, cortesia.
CIV.I.LI.ZA.TION, s., civilização, desenvolvimento, educação.
CIV.I.LIZE, v., civilizar, desenvolver, educar.
CIV.I.LIZED, *adj.*, *part.*, civilizado, educado.
CIV.IL.IZ.ER, s., civilizador.
CIV.IL LAW, s., direito civil.
CIV.IL LIB.ER.TIES, *s. pl.*, liberdades civis.
CIV.IL RIGHTS, *s. pl.*, direitos civis.
CIV.IL-SERV.ICE, s., funcionalismo público, serviço público.
CIV.IL WAR, s., guerra civil.
CIV.ISM, s., civismo.
CLAD, *adj.*, *Lit.*, vestido (de traje ou adereço).
CLAD.DING, s., *US* revestimento de azulejo ou madeira.
CLAIM, s., reivindicação, exigência, pretensão; v., exigir, postular.
CLAIM.ANT, s., pretendente, candidato, reclamante.
CLAIR.VOY.ANCE, s., clarividência, esperteza, argúcia.
CLAIR.VOY.ANT, s., clarividente, vidente.
CLAM, s., *Zool.*, molusco, marisco.
CLAM.BER, s., subida, ladeira, escalada íngreme; v., subir, escalar.
CLAM.BER.ER, s., escalador.
CLAM.MY, *adj.*, viscoso, pegajoso.
CLAM.OR, s. e v., o mesmo que *clamour*.
CLAM.OR.OUS, *adj.*, clamoroso, barulhento, evidente.
CLAM.OR.OUS.NESS, s., clamor, clamorosidade.
CLAM.OUR, s., clamor, grito; queixa; v., clamar, berrar, pedir; queixar-se.
CLAM.OUR.ER, s., clamador, reclamador.
CLAM.OR.OUS, *adj.*, clamoroso, vociferante.
CLAM.OR.OUS.LY, *adv.*, clamorosamente.
CLAM.OR.OUS.NESS, s., clamor, vozerio.
CLAMP, v., grampear, fixar, prender; s., braçadeira, fita.
CLAMP.DOWN, s., restrição (de autoridade sobre algo).
CLAN, s., clã, tribo.
CLAN.DES.TINE, *adj.*, clandestino, secreto, oculto.
CLAN.DES.TINE.LY, *adv.*, clandestinamente.
CLAN.DES.TINE.NESS, s., clandestinidade.
CLANG, s., tinido, clangor; v., tinir, soar, ressoar.
CLANG.ER, s., *UK* mancada, gafe, fora.
CLAN.GOUR, s., clangor, ruído, estrondo, estrépito.
CLANK, s., ruído, barulho; v., provocar ruído.
CLAP, v., aplaudir, ovacionar, bater palmas.
CLAP.BOARD, s., tábua, ripa; *US* tábua para revestimento externo de casa; v., revestir.
CLEPPED-OUT, *adj.*, *UK* caindo aos pedaços.
CLAP.PER, s., quem bate palmas, ovacionador.
CLAP.PERBOARD, s., *Cin.*, claquete.
CLAP.PING, s., palmas, aplausos, ovações.

CLAP.TRAP, s., *col.*, conversa mole; *fig.*, reclame.
CLAR.I.FI.CA.TION, s., clarificação; *fig.*, esclarecimento.
CLAR.I.FIED, *adj.*, clarificado, esclarecido.
CLAR.I.FIER, s., clarificador.
CLAR.I.FY, v., clarificar, esclarecer.
CLAR.I.NET, s., *Mús.*, clarineta.
CLAR.I.TY, s., clareza.
CLASH, s., estrondo, divergência; v., chorar, entrar em confronto.
CLASP, s., zíper; fivela, grampo; v., apertar; enganchar.
CLASS, s., classe, categoria; espécie; aula, classe (estudo); grau, qualidade.
CLASS-CON.SCIOUS, *adj.*, que tem consciência de classe; *pej.*, esnobe.
CLAS.SIC, s., obra clássica, clássico, literatura clássica; *adj.*, clássico.
CLAS.SICAL, *adj.*, clássico.
CLAS.SICAL MU.SIC, s., música clássica.
CLAS.SI.CISM, s., classicismo.
CLAS.SI.CIST, s., classicista.
CLAS.SI.CIZE, v., tornar clássico.
CLAS.SI.FI.A.BLE, *adj.*, classificável.
CLAS.SI.FI.CA.TION, s., classificação, ordenamento.
CLAS.SI.FIED, *adj.*, confidencial, secreto; restrito.
CLAS.SI.FIED AD, s., anúncio classificado.
CLAS.SI.FY, v., classificar.
CLASS.LESS, s., sem classe (social); *adj.*, que não pertence a nenhuma classe social.
CLASS.MATE, s., colega de classe.
CLASS.ROOM, s., sala de aula.
CLASS.Y, *adj.*, bacana, chique, elegante.
CLAT.TER, s., barulho, ruído; v., fazer barulho.
CLAT.TER.ING, s., ruído, barulho; tagarelice; *adj.*, ruidoso.
CLAT.TER.ING.LY, *adv.*, ruidosamente.
CLAU.DI.CA.TION, s., claudicação, coxeadura.
CLAUSE, s., cláusula, regra; frase, oração.
CLAUS.TRAL, s., claustral.
CLAUS.TRA.TION, s., enclausuramento.
CLAUS.TRO.PHO.BIA, s., claustrofobia.
CLAUS.TRO.PHO.BIC, *adj.*, claustrofóbico.
CLAV.I.CLE, s., clavícula.
CLA.VIER, s., *Mús.*, teclado; instrumento com teclado.
CLAW, s., garra, pata; unha afiada.
CLAW.BAR, s., pé-de-cabra.
CLAY, s., barro, argila, terra; v., cobrir com argila.
CLAY.EY, *adj.*, argiloso, de barro, terroso.
CLEAN, *adj.*, limpo, puro, inocente; v., limpar, purificar, assear.
CLEAN.ER, s., limpador, faxineiro; produto de limpeza.
CLEAN.ERS, *s. pl.*, tinturaria, lavanderia; tintureiros.
CLEAN.ING, s., limpeza.
CLEAN.ING WOM.AN, s., diarista, faxineira.
CLEAN.LI.NESS, s., limpeza, asseio.
CLEAN.LY, *adj.*, asseado, limpo; *adv.*, asseadamente; com precisão.
CLEAN.NESS, s., limpeza, asseio.
CLEANSE, v., limpar, purificar, assear.
CLEANS.ER, s., creme de limpeza.
CLEAN-SHAV.EN, *adj.*, imberbe, sem barba.
CLEANS.ING, s., limpeza; purificação; *adj.*, de limpeza; *fig.*, purificante.
CLEAN.UP, s., limpeza (total); faxina; *fig.*, grande lucro.

CLEAR ··413·· CLOSE-CROPPED

CLEAR, *adj.*, claro, nítido, diáfano, limpo, evidente; *v.*, abrir, absolver.
CLEAR.ANCE, *s.*, remoção; liberação; desobstrução.
CLEAR.ANCE SALE, *s.*, *Com.*, liquidação total.
CLEAR-CUT, *adj.*, bem definido; nítido, claro.
CLEAR.ER, *s.*, limpador.
CLEAR-HEAD.ED, *adj.*, esperto, perspicaz.
CLEAR.ING, *s.*, clareira.
CLEAR.ING HOUSE, *s.*, câmara de compensação; central de informações.
CLEAR.ING UP, *s.*, limpeza, arrumação.
CLEAR.LY, *adv.*, claramente, nitidamente.
CLEAR.NESS, *s.*, clareza, evidência.
CLEAR-OUT, *s.*, *UK* faxina geral.
CLEAR-SIGHT.ED, *adj.*, perspicaz.
CLEAR UP, *v.*, limpar, solucionar, esclarecer.
CLEAR.WAY, *s.*, acostamento; *UK* via expressa.
CLEAV.A.BLE, *adj.*, que se pode rachar ou fender.
CLEAV.AGE, *s.*, ato de fender, rachadura.
CLEAVE, *v.*, rachar(-se); partir(-se); perfurar; apegar(-se).
CLEAV.ER, *s.*, cutelo de açougueiro; talhador.
CLEF, *s.*, *Mús.*, clave.
CLEFT, *s.*, fenda, racha, fissura; *adj.*, rachado, fendido.
CLEFT PAL.ATE, *s.*, *Med.*, fenda palatina.
CLEM.A.TIS, *s.*, *Bot.*, clematite.
CLEM.EN.CY, *s.*, clemência.
CLEM.ENT, *adj.*, clemente.
CLER.GY, *s.*, clero.
CLER.GY.MAN, *s.*, clérigo, padre, religioso, sacerdote, pastor.
CLER.IC, *s.*, clérigo.
CLER.I.CAL, *adj.*, relativo a escritório; clerical; *s.*, clérigo, padre.
CLERK, *s.*, balconista, escriturário, escrevente.
CLEV.ER, *adj.*, perspicaz, inteligente, engenhoso, hábil.
CLEV.ER.LY, *adv.*, habilmente, inteligentemente.
CLEV.ER.NESS, *s.*, engenhosidade, esperteza, habilidade.
CLI.CHÉ, *s.*, clichê, nariz de cera, coisa pronta, chavão.
CLICK, *s.*, clique, tique-taque, ruído; lingueta; *v.*, estalar, fazer estalidos.
CLI.ENT, *s.*, cliente, freguês.
CLI.ENT.AGE, *s.*, clientela, freguesia.
CLI.EN.TELE, *s.*, o mesmo que *clientage*.
CLIFF, *s.*, penhasco, despenhadeiro.
CLIFF.HANG.ER, *s.*, *col.*, suspense (situação).
CLI.MAC.TER.IC, *s.*, *Med.*, climatério, menopausa; momento crítico; *adj.*, climatérico; crítico.
CLI.MAC.TIC, *adj.*, relativo a clímax.
CLI.MATE, *s.*, clima.
CLIMATE CHANGE, *s.*, mudança climática.
CLI.MAT.IC, *adj.*, climático.
CLI.MA.TIZE, *v.*, climatizar.
CLI.MA.TOL.O.GIST, *s.*, climatologista.
CLI.MA.TOL.O.GY, *s.*, climatologia.
CLI.MAX, *s.*, clímax, auge, ápice.
CLIMB, *v.*, trepar, subir, ascender; *s.*, subida, escarpa, escalada.
CLIMB-DOWN, *s.*, retratação, admissão de erro.
CLIMB.ER, *s.*, alpinista; trepadeira.
CLIMB.ERS, *s. pl.*, ganchos para subir em postes ou coqueiros.
CLIMB.ING, *s.*, alpinismo, montanhismo.

CLINCH, *v.*, fechar (acordo), decidir; fixar; *fig.*, assentar, encerrar (assunto).
CLINCH.ER, *s.*, grampo (para pregar ou fixar); *fig.*, prova decisiva.
CLING, *s.*, agarração; agarrar, segurar; *fig.*, apegar(-se).
CLINGFILM, *s.*, *UK* filme de PVC para proteger alimentos.
CLING.ING, *adj.*, adesivo; apertado; apegado demais, pegajoso.
CLING.Y, *adj.*, adesivo.
CLIN.IC, *s.*, clínica.
CLIN.I.CAL, *adj.*, clínico.
CLIN.I.CAL.LY, *adv.*, clinicamente.
CLI.NI.CIAN, *s.*, clínico.
CLINK, *v.*, tinir, soar.
CLINK.ING, *adj.*, tinidor; *col.*, perfeito; *adv.*, altamente.
CLIP, *s.*, gancho para cabelos, clipe, grampo; *v.*, grampear cabelos.
CLIP-BOARD, *s.*, prancheta; *Infor.*, área de transferência.
CLIP-ON, *adj.*, clipado.
CLIP.PED, *adj.*, entrecortado (fala); aparado (cabelo).
CLIP.PING, *s.*, recorte, apara.
CLIQUE, *s.*, grupo fechado (de pessoas), roda, panelinha, camarilha; *v.*, formar panelinhas.
CLIQU.ISH, *adj.*, exclusivo; faccioso.
CLIQU.ISH.LY, *adv.*, exclusivamente; facciosamente.
CLIT, *s.*, *vulg.*, abrev. de clitóris.
CLIT.O.RIS, *s.*, *Anat.*, clitóris.
CLO.A.CA, *s.*, cloaca, esgoto.
CLOAK, *s.*, capa, manto; disfarce; *v.*, encobrir, ocultar.
CLOAK-AND-DAG.GER, *adj.*, *Lit.*, *Cin.*, de capa-e-espada (envolve drama, ação, mistério e espionagem).
CLOAK.ROOM, *s.*, vestiário; chapeleira; *UK* lavabo, lavatório.
CLOB.BER, *s.*, *col.*, roupa costumeira; *v.*, espancar (alguém); derrotar.
CLOCK, *s.*, relógio; medidor; taxímetro.
CLOCK-CARD, *s.*, cartão de ponto.
CLOCK.CASE, *s.*, caixa de relógio.
CLOCK.HAND, *s.*, ponteiro de relógio.
CLOCK.MAK.ER, *s.*, relojoeiro.
CLOCK RA.DIO, *s.*, rádio-relógio.
CLOCK.WISE, *adj. e adv.*, em sentido horário (dos ponteiros do relógio).
CLOCK.WORK, *s.*, mecanismo de relógio; *adj.*, automático.
CLOD, *s.*, torrão, terra, solo, barro.
CLOD.DISH, *adj.*, grosseiro, rude, tosco.
CLOD.DISH.LY, *adv.*, grosseiramente.
CLOD.DY, *adj.*, cheio de barro grosso; *fig.*, terrestre; atarracado.
CLOD.HOP.PER, *s.*, lavrador; rústico; *vulg.*, sapatão.
CLOD.LY, *adv.*, estupidamente.
CLOG, *s.*, tamanco; obstáculo, impedimento; trava; *v.*, entupir-se; obstruir; frear; sapatear (com tamancos).
CLOG.GY, *adj.*, embaraçoso; pegajoso.
CLOIS.TER, *s.*, claustro; *v.*, enclausurar, ir para o convento.
CLOIS.TERED, *adj.*, enclausurado, recluso.
CLONE, *s.*, clone.
CLON.ING, *s.*, clonagem.
CLOSE, *s.*, fim; conclusão; luta; *v.*, fechar; encerrar, confinar; *adj.*, próximo.
CLOSE-CROP.PED, *adj.*, bem rente (barba, cabelo); cortado à escovinha.

CLOSED ·· 414 ·· COBRA

CLOSED, *adj., part.,* fechado.
CLOSE.DOWN, *v.,* fechar em definitivo.
CLOSE-FIT.TING, *adj.,* apertado (roupa).
CLOSE-KNIT, *adj.,* que é muito unido, ligado.
CLOSE.LY, *adv.,* intimamente.
CLOSE.NESS, *s.,* intimidade; proximidade; solidez.
CLOSE.OUT, *s., US* liquidação.
CLOSE-PEO.PLED, *adj.,* densamente povoado.
CLOSE QUAR.TERS, *s. pl.,* proximidade; *Mil.,* contato direto (com o inimigo).
CLOS.ER, *adj.,* mais perto; *s.,* fechador de negócios (negociante); concluidor.
CLOS.ET, *s.,* cubículo, quarto, despensa; gabinete; *v.,* fechar em quarto; *adj.,* particular, reservado.
CLOSE-UP, *s., Cin., US* primeiro plano; foto tirada de perto.
CLOS.ING, *s.,* conclusão, fim; *adj.,* de encerramento, final.
CLOS.ING TIME, *s.,* hora de fechamento.
CLO.SURE, *s.,* fechamento (escritório), conclusão; *v.,* encerrar (debate).
CLOT, *s.,* coágulo; *v.,* coagular.
CLOTH, *s.,* pano, tecido, fazenda.
CLOTHE, *v.,* vestir.
CLOTHES, *s. pl.,* roupa, vestuário.
CLOTHES-BRUSH, *s.,* escova de roupa.
CLOTHES.LINE, *s.,* varal.
CLOTH.ING, *s.,* roupa, vestuário; coberta.
CLOUD, *s.,* nuvem; *v.,* escurecer, nublar.
CLOUD.BURST, *s.,* aguaceiro, toró.
CLOUD.ED, *adj.,* nublado; *fig.,* sombrio.
CLOUD.I.LY, *adv.,* nebulosamente; sombriamente.
CLOUD.I.NESS, *s.,* nebulosidade; escuridão.
CLOUD.LESS, *adj.,* sem nuvens, céu limpo.
CLOUD.Y, *adj.,* nublado, escuro, sombrio, triste.
CLOUT, *s.,* bofetão, golpe; *US* influência; *v.,* esbofetear.
CLOVE, *s., Bot.,* cravo-da-índia.
CLO.VER, *s., Bot.,* trevo.
CLOWN, *s.,* palhaço; *v.,* fazer palhaçadas.
CLOWN.ER.Y, *s.,* brincadeira de palhaço; palhaçada.
CLOWN.ISH, *adj.,* como palhaço, igual a palhaço.
CLOWN.ISH.NESS, *s.,* palhaçada; grosseria.
CLOY, *v.,* saciar, fartar, enjoar.
CLOY.ING, *adj.,* enjoativo.
CLUB, *s.,* clube; boate; taco (de golf); clava, porrete; naipe de paus (baralho); *v.,* bater, golpear (com algo); reunir-se, associar-se; *adj.,* relativo a clube.
CLUB.BA.BLE, *adj.,* sociável.
CLUB.BER, *s., col.,* farrista, boêmio.
CLUB.BITE, *s.,* clubista (membro de clube).
CLUB.HOUSE, *s.,* clube; sede.
CLUB TO.GETH.ER, *v.,* unir-se; cotizar-se.
CLUCK, *s.,* cacarejo; *v.,* cacarejar; estalar a língua.
CLUE, *s.,* pista, indício, solução.
CLUED UP, *adj.,* bem informado, antenado.
CLUE.LESS, *adj., UK,* estúpido, tapado.
CLUMP, *s.,* moita, arvoredo, cepo; *v.,* plantar árvores, andar forte.
CLUMP.ISH, *adj.,* pesado, desajeitado.
CLUM.SY, *adj.,* desajeitado, desgracioso, malfeito.
CLUS.TER, *s.,* cacho, grupo, bando, quantidade; *v.,* crescer em cachos.
CLUTCH, *s.,* aperto, garra; embreagem, alavanca; *v.,* embrear, arrebatar.
CLUTCH BAG, *s.,* bolsa feminina sem alça.
CLUTCH PEDAL, *s.,* pedal de embreagem.
CLUT.TER, *s.,* confusão, desordem; *v.,* desarrumar.
COACH, *s.,* carruagem; *US* vagão, ônibus; *Esp.,* treinador, técnico; *v.,* ensinar, treinar, viajar.
COACH DOG, *s.,* cão dálmata.
COACH.ING, *s.,* treino, preparo, ensino.
COACH.MAN, *s.,* cocheiro.
COACH STA.TION, *s., UK* rodoviária.
COACH-WRENCH, *s.,* chave de boca
CO.AC.TION, *s.,* cooperação; coação, coerção.
CO.AC.TIVE.LY, *adv.,* compulsoriamente.
CO.AD.JU.TOR, *s.,* coadjutor, assistente.
CO.AG.U.LATE, *v.,* coagular, coalhar.
CO.AG.U.LA.TION, *s.,* coagulação.
CO.AG.U.LA.TOR, *s.,* coágulo, coalho.
COAL, *s.,* carvão de pedra; brasa, tição; *v.,* abastecer, fornecer carvão.
COAL BED, *s., Min.,* jazida de carvão.
COAL-BOX, *s.,* carvoeira (caixa para o carvão).
COAL.ER, *s.,* navio ou trem carvoeiro; negociante de carvão.
CO.A.LESCE, *v.,* fundir-se, misturar-se, coalescer.
COAL.FIELD, *s., Min.,* jazida carbonífera.
COAL GAS, *s.,* gás de carvão, gás de iluminação.
CO.A.LI.TION, *s.,* coalizão, união; coalescência.
COAL.MAN, *s.,* carvoeiro.
COAL.MINE, *s.,* mina de carvão.
COARSE, *adj.,* áspero, grosseiro, grosso.
COARSE.BREAD, *s.,* pão integral.
COARS.EN, *v.,* embrutecer, tornar grosseiro.
COAST, *s.,* costa, litoral, beira-mar, praia.
COAST.AL, *adj.,* costeiro.
COAST.ER, *s.,* descanso para copos; *UK Náut.,* navio costeiro.
COAST GUARD, *s.,* guarda costeira.
COAST.ING, *s.,* navegação costeira, cabotagem.
COAST.LAND, *s.,* região costeira, litoral.
COAST.LINE, *s.,* linha da costa, litoral.
COAST.WARD, *adj.,* costeiro; *adv.,* em direção à costa.
COAST.WISE, *adj.,* costeiro; *adv.,* ao longo da costa.
COAT, *s.,* paletó, casaco, pintura, demão; cobrir com tinta, revestir.
COAT.ED, *adj.,* vestido; coberto, revestido.
COAT-HANG.ER, *s.,* cabide (de armário).
COAT.ING, *s.,* revestimento, pintura, camada.
COAT OF ARMS, *s., Her.,* brasão, escudo de armas.
COAT OF PAINT, *s.,* demão; camada de tinta.
COAT.ROOM, *s.,* vestiário (em clube etc.).
COAT STAND, *s.,* mancebo (cabide alto para casaco, chapéu etc.).
COAT-TAILS, *s. pl.,* abas (de casaco).
CO.AU.THOR, *s.,* coautor.
COAX, *v.,* persuadir, influenciar, lisonjear, convencer.
COAXER, *s.,* lisonjeador, bajulador; *col.,* puxa-saco.
COAX.ING, *adj.,* bajulador, lisonjeador.
COB, *s.,* espiga de milho, sabugo; *UK* pão redondo.
CO.BALT, *s., Quím.,* cobalto.
COB.BLE, *s.,* pedra redonda; *v.,* pavimentar com pedras; consertar sapatos.
COB.BLER, *s.,* sapateiro, remendão.
COBRA, *s., Zool.,* naja.

COBWEB ··415·· COLESLAW

COB.WEB, s., teia de aranha.
CO.CA, s., *Bot.*, coca (arbusto e folha).
CO.CAINE, s., cocaína.
COC.CYX, s., *Anat.*, cóccix.
COCK, s., *Zool.*, galo, frango; macho (ave); torneira, bica; *vulg.*, pênis; v., engatilhar uma arma.
COCK-A-DOODLE-DOO, s., cocorocó (canto do galo).
COCK-A-HOOP, *adj.*, *UK* exultante, pra cima.
COCK.A.LO.RUM, s., *Zool.*, garnisé; *fig.*, baixinho invocado.
COCK-AND-BULL STORY, s., *exp.*, história para boi dormir.
COCK.A.TOO, s., *Zool.*, cacatua.
COCK.ER.EL, s., frango, galo novo.
COCK.ER, s., cocker (raça de cão).
COCK.FIGHT, s., rinha, briga de galos.
COCK.I.NESS, s., afetação, insolência, petulância.
COCK.LE, s., *Zool.*, berbigão; ruga; v., enrugar.
COCK.NEY, s., habitantes dos bairros de Londres.
COCK.PIT, s., cabina de pilotagem no avião.
COCK.ROACH, s., barata.
COCK.SPUR, s., espora de galo.
COCK.SURE, *adj.*, *col.*, convencido; *adv.*, na certa.
COCK.TAIL, s., coquetel, mistura de bebidas, salada mista.
COCK-UP, s., ponta ou aba virada para cima; *UK* erro estúpido.
COCKY, *adj.*, vaidoso, afetado.
CO.COA, s., *Bot.*, cacau; chocolate (bebida).
CO.CO.NUT, s., *Bot.*, coco.
CO.COON, s., casulo.
COD, s., *Zool.*, bacalhau.
COD.DLE v., afagar, acarinhar, acariciar; cozer em fogo lento.
CODE, s., código, cifra; folheto.
COD.ED, *adj.*, em código, codificado.
CODE NAME, s., pseudônimo, codinome.
CODG.ER, s., *col.*, esquisitão; rabugento; avaro.
COD.I.CIL, s., codicilo.
COD.I.FY, v., codificar.
COD-LIV.ER OIL, s., óleo de fígado de bacalhau.
CODS.WAL.LOP, s., *UK* asneira, tolice.
CO.ED.U.CA.TION, s., coeducação, cocapacitação.
CO.ED.U.CA.TION.AL, *adj.*, coeducacional, coeducativo.
CO.EF.FI.CIENT, s., coeficiente.
COE.LEN.TER.ATE, s., *Zool.*, celenterado; *adj.*, que pertence aos celenterados.
CO.EQUAL.I.TY, s., igualdade.
CO.ERCE, v., coagir, obrigar, reprimir, refrear.
CO.ERC.ER, s., o que coage; repressor.
CO.ERC.IBLE, *adj.*, coercível.
CO.ER.CION, s., coerção.
CO.ER.CIVE, *adj.*, coercivo, coercitivo.
CO.E.VAL, *adj.*, coevo, contemporâneo.
CO.EX.IST, v., coexistir.
CO.EX.IS.TENCE, s., coexistência.
CO.EX.IS.TENT, s., coexistente.
COF.FEE, s., café, bebida, grão, local onde se toma café.
COF.FEE.POT, s., cafeteira.
COF.FEE.CUP, s., xícara para café.
COF.FEE-MAKER, s., cafeteira.
COF.FEE MIL, s., moedor de café.
COF.FEE-POT, s., bule (para café).
COF.FEE SHOP, s., *US* cafeteria; *UK* café (bar que serve café).

COF.FEE TREE, s., cafezeiro, cafeeiro.
COF.FER, s., cofre, arca, baú; v., colocar no cofre.
COF.FIN, s., esquife, caixão.
COG, s., dente de roda dentada, roda dentada; v., enganar, lograr.
CO.GENT, *adj.*, convincente, persuasivo.
COG.I.TATE, v., cogitar, pensar, refletir, meditar.
COG.I.TA.TION, s., cogitação, meditação, pensamento.
CO.GNAC, s., conhaque.
COG.NATE, *adj.*, s., cognato, análogo, idêntico.
COG.NI.TION, s., cognição, conhecimento.
COG.NI.TION.AL, *adj.*, cognitivo.
COG.NI.TIVE, *adj.*, o mesmo que *cognitional*.
COG.NI.ZANCE, s., conhecimento, reconhecimento, percepção.
COG.NI.ZANT, *adj.*, conhecedor, informado.
COG.NO.MEN, s., cognome.
COG.WHEEL, s., roda dentada.
CO.HAB.IT, v., coabitar, viver junto.
CO.HAB.I.TA.TION, s., coabitação.
CO.HEIR, s., coerdeiro.
CO.HER.ENCE, s., coerência.
CO.HER.ENT, *adj.*, s., coerente.
CO.HER.ENT.LY, *adv.*, coerentemente.
CO.HE.SION, s., coesão.
CO.HORT, s., grupo (de soldados), magote; *pej.*, bando.
COIF, s., coifa, touca.
COIF.FEUR, s., cabeleireiro.
COIL, s., rolo, bobina, espiral; v., enrolar, bobinar.
COIL.ED, *adj.*, enrolado.
COIN, s., moeda, esquina; v., cunhar moedas, inventar.
COIN.AGE, s., cunhagem de moedas; moedas, sistema monetário.
CO.IN.CIDE, v., coincidir.
CO.IN.CI.DENCE, s., coincidência.
CO.IN.CI.DEN.TAL, *adj.*, coincidente.
CO.IN.CI.DEN.TAL.LY, *adv.*, coincidentemente.
CO.IN.CI.DENT.LY, *adv.*, coincidentemente.
COIN-OP.ER.AT.ED, *adj.*, que funciona com moedas.
CO.IN.STAN.TA.NE.OUS, *adj.*, simultâneo.
CO.I.TION, s., coito, cópula carnal.
CO.I.TUS, s., coito.
CO.LA, s., *Bot.*, cola; refrigerante de cola.
COL.AN.DER, s., coador ou escorredor de macarrão.
COKE, s., *abrev.*, cocaína.
COLD, *adj.*, s., frio; s., resfriado, constipação.
COLD-BLOOD.ED, *adj.*, desumano, cruel, perverso.
COLD-BLOOD.ED.NESS, s., desumanidade, crueldade, sangue frio.
COLD CREAM, s., creme para a pele.
COLD CUTS, s. pl., *US* frios (sortidos).
COLD-HEART.ED, *adj.*, insensível, frio.
COLD.LY, *adv.*, friamente.
COLD.NESS, s., friagem, frialdade; indiferença, frieza.
COLD SHOUL.DER, s., indiferença, desprezo; v., mostrar indiferença.
COLD-SHOUL.DER, v., mostrar indiferença; ignorar friamente.
COLD WAR, s., guerra fria.
COLE, s., couve (qualquer variedade).
COLE.SLAW, s., salada de repolho cru.

COLIC •••416••• COMFORTABLY

COL.IC, s., cólica.
COL.LAB.O.RATE, v., colaborar.
COL.LAB.O.RA.TION, s., colaboração.
COL.LAB.O.RA.TIVE, adj., colaborativo, colaborador.
COL.LAB.O.RA.TOR, s., colaborador.
COL.LAGE, s., colagem.
COL.LA.GEN, s., colágeno.
COL.LAPSE, s., colapso, tombamento, queda; v., cair, tombar, sucumbir.
COL.LAPS.I.BLE, adj., desmontável, dobradiço.
COL.LAR, s., colarinho, gola; v., pôr o colarinho.
COL.LAR.BONE, s., clavícula.
COL.LATE, v., confrontar, cotejar, conferir; ordenar.
COL.LAT.ER.AL, adj., colateral; paralelo; secundário, indireto.
COL.LAT.ER.AL.LY, adv., colateralmene; secundariamente.
COL.LA.TION, s., colação, desjejum, exame, verificação.
COL.LEAGUE, s., colega; v., tornar-se colega, aliar-se.
COL.LECT, v., colecionar, recolher, cobrar, reunir.
COL.LECT.A.BLE, adj., colecionável; acumulável; cobrável.
COL.LECT.ED, adj., part., reunido, agrupado, calmo, sereno.
COL.LECT.ED.NESS, s., calma, paz, tranquilidade.
COL.LECT.ING, s., reunião, encontro.
COL.LEC.TION, s., coleção.
COL.LEC.TIVE, adj., coletivo; s., cooperativa.
COL.LEC.TIVE.LY, adv., coletivamente.
COL.LEC.TIV.ISM, s., coletivismo.
COL.LEC.TIV.I.TY, s., coletividade.
COL.LEC.TIV.IZE, v., coletivizar.
COL.LEC.TOR, s., colecionador, coleto; cobrador.
COL.LEC.TOR.SHIP, s., ofício de coletor ou cobrador.
COL.LEGE, s., colégio superior, faculdade.
COL.LE.GI.AL, adj., colegial.
COL.LE.GIAN, s., colegial, membro de um colégio.
COL.LIDE, v., colidir.
COL.LIE, s., collie (raça de cão).
COL.LIER.Y, s., UK mina de carvão (com instalações).
COL.LI.MATE, v., colimar, objetivar.
COL.LI.SION, s., colisão, choque, batida.
COL.LO.CATE, v., colocar, pôr, dispor.
COL.LO.CA.TION, s., colocação, disposição.
COL.LO.QUI.AL, adj., coloquial.
COL.LO.QUI.AL.ISM, s., coloquialismo.
COL.LO.QUI.AL.LY, adv., coloquialmente, familiarmente.
COL.LO.QUY, s., colóquio, fala.
COL.LUDE, v., conspirar, tramar, conluiar.
COL.LUD.ER, s., conspirador.
COL.LU.SION, s., conspiração, tramoia, conluio.
COL.LYR.I.UM, s., Med., colírio.
COL.OG.A.RITHM, s., Mat., cologaritmo.
CO.LOM.BI.AN, adj., s., colombiano.
CO.LON, s., Anat., cólon; Gram., dois-pontos; colono (rural).
COLONEL, s., coronel.
CO.LO.NIAL, adj., colonial.
CO.LO.NIAL.ISM, s., colonialismo.
COL.O.NIST, s., colono, agricultor.
COL.O.NI.ZA.TION, s., colonização, desbravamento.
COL.O.NIZE, v., colonizar.
COL.O.NIZ.ER, v., colonizador.
COL.ON.NADE, s., Arq., colunata.
COL.O.NY, s., colônia.
COL.OR.A.TION, s., coloração.

COL.ORED, adj., colorido; corado; de cor; de raça negra.
COL.OR.FAST, adj., de cores firmes (não desbota).
COL.OR.FUL, adj., colorido, animado, vivaz.
COL.OR.FUL.LY, adv., com brilho, vivazmente.
COL.OR.ING, s., coloração, colorido, tez, matiz; pigmento; disfarce.
COL.OR.LESS, adj., sem cor ou brilho, descolorido, apagado; desinteressante.
CO.LOS.SAL, adj., colossal, imenso.
CO.LOS.SUS, adj., colosso.
CO.LOS.TO.MY, s., Med., colostomia.
COL.OUR, s., cor, coloração.
COL.OUR BAR, s., discriminação racial.
COL.OUR-BLIND, adj., s., daltônico.
COL.OUR CODED, adj., codificado por cores.
COL.OURED UK, adj., o mesmo que colored.
COL.OUR.FAST UK, adj., o mesmo que colorfast.
COL.OUR.FUL UK, adj., o mesmo que colorful.
COL.OUR.ING UK, s., o mesmo que coloring.
COL.OUR.LESS UK, adj., o mesmo que colorless.
COLT, s., potro; tipo sem experiência.
COL.UMN, s., fila, fileira, coluna, pilar.
COL.UMN.IST, s., colunista de jornal, colaborador, cronista.
CO.MA, s., Med., coma, inconsciência.
COM.A.TOSE, adj., Med., comatoso, em coma.
COMB, s., pente, rastelo, crista; v., pentear, alisar, rastelar.
COM.BAT, s., combate, luta; v., combater, lutar.
COM.BAT.ANT, s., combatente, lutador.
COM.BA.TIVE, adj., combativo.
COM.BAT.IVE.NESS, adj., combatividade.
COMBE UK, s., vale estreito e profundo.
COMB.ED, adj., part., penteado, alisado.
COM.BIN.ABLE, adj., combinável.
COM.BI.NA.TION, s., combinação.
COM.BINE, v., combinar, acertar, reunir; s., associação.
COM.BU.RENT, adj., Fís., comburente.
COM.BUST, adj., queimado.
COM.BUS.TI.BIL.I.TY, s., combustibilidade.
COM.BUS.TI.BLE, s., combustível; adj., inflamável.
COM.BUS.TION, s., combustão.
COM.BUS.TIVE, adj., combustivo, combustível.
COME, v., vir, chegar, aproximar-se, resultar, suceder, tornar-se.
COME ABOUT, v., acontecer, suceder.
COME AF.TER, v., suceder, vir após.
COME AWAY, v., ir embora, despedir-se.
COME BACK, v., voltar, regressar; recordar, vir à memória.
CO.ME.DI.AN, s., comediante, cômico, humorista.
CO.ME.DI.ENNE, s., comediante.
COME-DOWN, s., col., retrocesso, ruína.
COM.E.DY, s., comédia, humor.
COME IN, v., entrar, adentrar, participar de.
COME.LI.NESS, s., elegância.
COME.LY, adj., elegante, sedutor.
COME ROUND, v., voltar a si.
CO.MES.TI.BLE, s., comestível, alimento.
COM.ET, s., cometa.
COM.FIT, s., confeito, fruta cristalizada.
COM.FORT, s., conforto, bem-estar.
COM.FORT.ABLE, adj., confortável.
COM.FORT.A.BLY, adv., confortavelmente.

COMFORTLESS ··417·· COMPATIBLE

COM.FORT.LESS, *adj.*, sem conforto.
COM.FORT.ING, *adj.*, consolador, confortante.
COM.IC, *adj.*, cômico; *s.*, cômico, humorista.
COM.I.CAL, *adj.*, engraçado, cômico.
COM.I.CAL.NESS, *s.*, comicidade.
COM.I.CAL.LY, *adv.*, comicamente.
COM.ING, *s.*, chegada, vinda.
COM.I.TY, *s.*, cortesia; civilidade.
COM.MA, *s.*, vírgula.
COM.MAND, *s.*, mando, ordem, comando.
COM.MAN.DANT, *s.*, comandante, chefe, dirigente.
COM.MAN.DEER, *v.*, confiscar; requisitar; recrutar.
COM.MAND.ER, *s.*, comandante; capitão de navio, chefe.
COM.MAND.ER.SHIP, *s.*, comando.
COM.MAND.ING, *adj.*, que manda; de comando; autoritário; dominante.
COM.MAND.ING OF.FI.CER, *s.*, *Mil.*, comandante.
COM.MAND.MENT, *s.*, mandamento.
COM.MAND MODULE, *s.*, *Aér.*, módulo de comando.
COM.MAN.DO, *s.*, *Mil.*, unidade de assalto; comando.
COM.MEM.O.RATE, *v.*, comemorar, celebrar, festejar.
COM.MEM.O.RA.TION, *s.*, comemoração.
COM.MEM.O.RA.TIVE, *adj.*, comemorativo.
COM.MENCE, *v.*, começar, iniciar, principiar.
COM.MENCE.MENT, *s.*, começo, princípio, início.
COM.MEND, *v.*, elogiar, louvar, recomendar.
COM.MEND.ABLE, *adj.*, louvável, elogiável.
COM.MEN.DA.TION, *s.*, condecoração; aprovação; encargo.
COMMENSURATE, *adj.*, proporcional (a algo).
COM.MEN.SAL, *s.* e *adj.*, comensal.
COM.MEN.SAL.ISM, *s.*, comensalismo.
COM.MEN.SU.RA.BLE, *adj.*, comensurável; proporcional.
COM.MEN.SU.RATE, *adj.*, comensurado; proporcionado.
COM.MEN.SU.RATE.LY, *adv.*, comensuravelmente.
COM.MENT, *s.*, comentário; *v.*, comentar.
COM.MEN.TATE, *v.*, comentar; explicar; narrar (rádio).
COM.MEN.TARY, *s.*, comentário, referência.
COM.MEN.TA.TOR, *s.*, comentador, comentarista.
COM.MERCE, *s.*, comércio.
COM.MER.CIAL, *adj.*, comercial; *s.*, anúncio, propaganda.
COM.MER.CIAL.ISM, *s.*, comercialismo, mercantilismo.
COM.MER.CIAL.IZA.TION, *s.*, comercialização.
COM.MER.CIAL.IZE, *v.*, comercializar; tornar comercial.
COM.MER.CIAL.LY, *adv.*, comercialmente.
COM.MIE, *s.* *adj.*, *col.*, *US* comunista; *UK* comuna.
COM.MIN.ATE, *v.*, cominar, reunir; anatemizar.
COM.MIS.ER.A.TION, *s.*, comiseração, pena.
COM.MIS.SAR.I.AT, *s.*, comissariado.
COM.MIS.SARY, *s.*, comissário.
COM.MIS.SION, *s.*, comissão, empreitada; *v.*, encomendar.
COM.MIS.SION.AIRE, *s.*, porteiro.
COM.MIS.SION.ER, *s.*, comissário; delegado.
COM.MIT, *v.*, cometer, praticar, depositar, entregar.
COM.MIT.MENT, *s.*, compromisso, engajamento.
COM.MIT.TED, *adj.*, comprometido.
COM.MIT.TEE, *s.*, comitê, delegação.
COM.MODE, *s.*, cômoda, pia, lavatório.
COM.MOD.I.TY, *s.*, mercadoria.
COM.MO.DORE, *s.*, comodoro (oficial da marinha).
COM.MON, *adj.*, comum, ordinário, vulgar; *s.*, área pública.
COM.MON.AL.I.TY, *s.*, povo, população, vulgo, plebe.

COM.MON DE.NOM.I.NA.TOR, *s.*, *Mat.*, denominador comum.
COM.MON.ER, *s.*, homem do povo, plebeu; *UK* membro da Câmara dos Comuns.
COM.MON KNOWL.EDGE, *s.*, conhecimento geral.
COM.MON.LY, *adv.*, comumente; geralmente.
COM.MON.PLACE, *adj.*, trivial; lugar-comum; *s.*, trivialidade, generalidade.
COM.MON ROOM, *s.*, quarto de hóspede; sala de recreação.
COM.MONS, *s.* *pl.*, povo; refeitório popular; alimento.
COM.MON SENSE, *s.*, senso comum; bom senso.
COM.MON.WEALTH, *s.*, população de,um Estado; comunidade de língua inglesa.
COM.MO.TION, *s.*, comoção, agitação; tumulto.
COM.MOVE, *v.*, comover.
COM.MU.NAL, *adj.*, comum, comunal.
COM.MUNE, *s.*, comuna; comunidade; *v.*, comungar; conversar com intimidade.
COM.MU.NI.CA.BIL.I.TY, *s.*, comunicabilidade.
COM.MU.NI.CA.BLE, *adj.*, comunicável.
COM.MU.NI.CATE, *v.*, comunicar.
COM.MU.NI.CA.TION, *s.*, comunicação.
COM.MU.NI.CA.TIVE, *adj.*, relativo à comunicação; comunicativo; falador.
COM.MU.NI.CA.TOR, *s.*, comunicador.
COM.MU.NION, *s.*, comunhão, eucaristia.
COM.MU.NISM, *s.*, comunismo.
COM.MU.NIST, *s.*, comunista.
COM.MU.NI.TY, *s.*, comunidade.
COM.MU.NI.TY CEN.TER, *s.*, *US* centro comunitário.
COM.MU.NI.TY HOME, *s.*, *UK* centro socioeducativo para adolescentes.
COM.MU.NI.TY PO.LIC.ING, *s.*, policiamento comunitário.
COM.MU.NI.TY SER.VICE, *s.*, trabalho comunitário.
COM.MU.TA.BLE, *adj.*, comutável, permutável.
COM.MU.TA.TION, *s.*, comutação, redução de pena, permuta.
COM.MUTE, *v.*, viajar habitualmente.
COM.MUT.ER, *s.*, *US* pessoa que vai e volta de casa para o trabalho somente.
COMMY, *s.*, *col.*, o mesmo que *commie*.
COM.PACT, *s.*, estojo, acordo; *adj.*, compacto.
COM.PACT DISC, *s.*, disco a *laser*; *abrev.*: CD.
COM.PACT DISC PLAYER, *s.*, toca-CD.
COM.PAN.ION, *s.*, companheiro.
COM.PAN.ION.A.BLE, *adj.*, amigável, sociável.
COM.PAN.ION.SHIP, *s.*, companhia, companheirismo.
COM.PA.NY, *s.*, companhia, sociedade; *v.*, associar-se.
COM.PA.RA.BLE, *adj.*, comparável.
COM.PAR.A.TIVE, *adj.*, relativo, comparativo; *s.*, *Gram.*, comparativo (grau).
COM.PAR.A.TIVE.LY, *adv.*, relativamente.
COM.PARE, *v.*, comparar.
COM.PAR.I.SON, *s.*, comparação.
COM.PART.MENT, *s.*, compartimento, divisão, seção.
COM.PART.MEN.TAL.IZE, *v.*, compartimentar.
COM.PASS, *s.*, bússola, compasso, limite; *v.*, circular, compreender.
COM.PAS.SION, *s.*, compaixão.
COM.PAS.SION.ATE, *adj.*, compassível, compassivo; *v.*, compadecer-se.
COM.PAT.I.BIL.I.TY, *s.*, compatibilidade.
COM.PAT.I.BLE, *adj.*, compatível.

COMPATRIOT ··418·· CONCEIVABLE

COM.PA.TRI.OT, s., compatriota.
COM.PEL, v., compelir, obrigar, forçar.
COM.PEL.LA.TION, s., interpelação, saudação.
COM.PEL.LER, s., aquele que constrange ou força.
COM.PEL.LING, adj., que obriga; convincente; envolvente.
COM.PEN.DI.UM, s., compêndio.
COM.PEN.SATE, v., compensar, contrabalançar, estabilizar.
COM.PEN.SA.TION, s., compensação, recompensa.
COM.PERE, s., *UK* apresentador; v., apresentar (como mestre-de-cerimônias).
COM.PETE, v., competir, concorrer, rivalizar, emular.
COM.PE.TENCE, s., competência, habilidade, capacidade.
COM.PE.TENT, adj., competente; qualificado.
COM.PE.TENT.LY, adv., competentemente.
COM.PET.ING, adj., conflitante, em que há competição.
COM.PE.TI.TION, s., concurso, competição.
COM.PET.I.TIVE, adj., competitivo.
COM.PET.I.TIVE.LY, adv., competitivamente.
COM.PET.I.TOR, s., competidor, concorrente.
COM.PI.LA.TION, s., compilação.
COM.PILE, v., compilar, compor.
COM.PLA.CEN.CY, s., complacência, satisfação pessoal.
COM.PLA.CENT, adj., complacente, enfatuado.
COM.PLA.CENT.LY, adv., complacentemente.
COM.PLAIN, v., queixar-se.
COM.PLAIN.ER, s., queixoso.
COM.PLAIN.ING, s., queixa; adj., queixoso.
COM.PLAINT, s., queixa, reclamação; enfermidade.
COM.PLE.MENT, s., complemento; tripulação; v., complementar.
COM.PLE.MEN.TA.RY, adj., complementar.
COM.PLE.MEN.TA.TION, s., complementação.
COM.PLETE, adj., completo, inteiro; v., completar, encher.
COM.PLETE.LY, adv., completamente.
COM.PLETE.NESS, s., perfeição.
COM.PLE.TION, s., conclusão, término.
COM.PLEX, adj., s., complexo; complexo de edifícios.
COM.PLEX.ION, s., aparência; compleição; caráter, natureza.
COM.PLEX.I.TY, s., complexidade.
COM.PLI.ANCE, s., cumprimento, obediência; submissão, complacência.
COM.PLI.ANT, adj., obediente; complacente.
COM.PLI.CATE, v., complicar.
COM.PLI.CATED, adj., complicado, complexo.
COM.PLI.CA.TION, s., complicação, problema.
COM.PLIC.I.TY, s., cumplicidade.
COM.PLI.MENT, s., cumprimento, elogio; saudação; v., cumprimentar, saudar.
COM.PLI.MEN.TA.RY, adj., lisonjeiro, cortês; *US* gratuito.
COM.PLY, v., condescender; consentir; cumprir.
COM.PO, s., estuque, argamassa.
COM.PO.NENT, adj., componente, acessório; s., peça acessória.
COM.PORT, v., comportar-se.
COM.PORT.MENT, s., conduta, comportamento, atitude.
COM.POSE, v., compor.
COM.POSED, adj., tranquilo, calmo.
COM.POS.ER, s., compositor.
COM.POS.ITE, adj., composto; s., composto; *Bot.*, coposta (espécime).
COM.PO.SI.TION, s., composição.

COM.POS.I.TOR, s., compositor.
COM.POST, s., adubo.
COM.PO.SURE, s., compostura, calma.
COM.POTE, s., compota.
COM.POUND, adj., composto; s., composto, mistura; v., compor, misturar; agravar.
COM.POUND FRAC.TURE, s., *Med.*, fratura exposta.
COM.POUND IN.TEREST, s., *Com.*, juros compostos.
COM.PRE.HEND, v., compreender, entender, perceber.
COM.PRE.HEN.SION, s., compreensão.
COM.PRE.HEN.SI.BIL.I.TY, s., compreensibilidade.
COM.PRE.HEN.SI.BLE, adj., compreensível.
COM.PRE.HEN.SIVE, adj., inclusivo, abrangente, amplo.
COM.PRE.HEN.SIVE.LY, adv., completamente; abrangentemente, inclusivamente.
COM.PRESS, v., comprimir, reduzir.
COM.PRESS.I.BIL.I.TY, s., compressibilidade.
COM.PRES.SION, s., compressão.
COM.PRES.SIVE, adj., compressivo.
COM.PRES.SOR, s., compressor.
COM.PRISE, v., compreender, constituir, ser parte, incluir.
COM.PRO.MISE, s., compromisso, ajuste; v., ajustar, acordar.
COM.PRO.MIS.ING, adj., comprometedor; condescendente.
COM.PUL.SION, s., compulsão, coação.
COM.PUL.SIVE, adj., compulsório, obrigatório.
COM.PUL.SIVE.LY, adv., compulsoriamente, obrigatoriamente.
COM.PUL.SO.RY, adj., compulsório, coercivo.
COM.PUNC.TION, s., compunção, arrependimento; escrúpulo.
COM.PUNC.TION.LESS, adj., sem escrúpulos.
COM.PUNC.TIOUS, adj., arrependido, compungido.
COM.PUT.ABLE, adj., computável.
COM.PU.TA.TION, s., computação, cômputo.
COM.PUTE, v., computar, calcular, avaliar.
COM.PUT.ER, s., computador.
COM.PUT.ER GRAPH.ICS, s. pl., *Inform.*, infografia; computação gráfica.
COM.PU.TER.I.ZA.TION, s., informatização.
COM.PU.TER.IZE, v., informatizar.
COM.PU.TER.IZED, adj., informatizado, computadorizado.
COM.PU.TER-LIT.ER.ATE, adj., com conhecimento de informática.
COM.PUT.ING, s., computação, informática.
COM.RADE, s., camarada.
COM.RADE.SHIP, s., camaradagem.
CON, s., trapaça, vigarice; v., enganar, trapacear; estudar, decorar.
CON.CAT.E.NATE, v., concatenar, encadear, unir.
CON.CAT.E.NA.TION, s., concatenação, ligação.
CON.CAVE, s., côncavo, concavidade; adj., côncavo, cavado.
CON.CAVE.NESS, s., concavidade.
CON.CAV.I.TY, s., concavidade.
CON.CEAL, v., ocultar, esconder, guardar segredo.
CON.CEAL.ED, adj., oculto, escondido, secreto.
CON.CEAL.MENT, s., ocultamento, segredo, esconderijo.
CON.CEDE, v., conceder, admitir, reconhecer.
CON.CEIT, s., presunção, vaidade, dito chistoso.
CON.CEIT.ED, adj., vaidoso, presunçoso.
CON.CEIT.ED.NESS, s., vaidade, presunção.
CON.CEIV.A.BLE, adj., concebível.

CONCEIVABLY ··419··· CONFESSEDLY

CON.CEIV.A.BLY, *adv.*, de modo concebível, possivelmente.
CON.CEIVE, *v.*, conceber, imaginar; engravidar, compreender.
CON.CEIV.ING, *s.*, concepção.
CON.CEN.TER, *v.*, concentrar, convergir.
CON.CEN.TRATE, *v.*, concentrar.
CON.CEN.TRA.TED, *adj.*, concentrado.
CON.CEN.TRA.TION, *s.*, concentração.
CON.CEN.TRA.TION CAMP, *s.*, campo de concentração.
CON.CEN.TRIC, *adj.*, concêntrico.
CON.CEPT, *s.*, conceito.
CON.CEP.TION, *s.*, concepção, ideia, pensamento.
CONCEP.TUAL, *adj.*, conceitual, conceptual.
CONCEP.TU.AL.ISM, *s.*, conceitualismo.
CONCEP.TUAL.IZE, *v.*, conceituar.
CON.CERN, *s.*, concernência, negócio, inquietação; *v.*, concernir.
CON.CERNED, *adj.*, preocupado, inquieto; interessado.
CON.CERN.ING, *prep.*, referente, a respeito de, concernente.
CON.CERT, *s.*, concerto; *v.*, concertar, ajustar.
CON.CERT.ED, *adj.*, de comum acordo, em conjunto.
CON.CERT.GO.ER, *s.*, frequentador de concertos.
CON.CER.TI.NA, *s.*, *Mús.*, concertina (tipo de sanfona).
CON.CER.TO, *s.*, *Mús.*, concerto.
CON.CES.SION, *s.*, concessão.
CON.CES.SION.ARY, *s.*, concessionário.
CON.CIL.I.ATE, *v.*, conciliar, reconciliar, harmonizar.
CON.CIL.I.A.TION, *s.*, conciliação, harmonização, acordo.
CON.CIL.I.A.TOR, *s.*, conciliador.
CON.CIL.I.A.TORY, *adj.*, conciliatório.
CON.CISE, *adj.*, conciso.
CON.CISE.LY, *adv.*, concisamente.
CON.CI.SION, *s.*, concisão.
CON.CLAVE, *s.*, conclave.
CON.CLUDE, *v.*, concluir, acabar, acordar.
CON.CLU.SION, *s.*, conclusão.
CON.CLU.SIVE, *adj.*, conclusivo.
CON.COCT, *v.*, fabricar, preparar, planejar.
CON.COC.TION, *s.*, mistura, preparação; *fig.*, trama.
CON.COC.TIVE, *adj.*, preparativo.
CON.COM.I.TANT, *s.*, concomitante.
CON.CORD, *s.*, concórdia, paz.
CON.COR.DANCE, *s.*, concordância.
CON.COR.DAT, *s.*, acordo, pacto; concordata.
CON.COURSE, *s.*, saguão; multidão; afluência, concurso.
CON.CRETE, *s.*, concreto, massa de cimento; *v.*, fazer com concreto.
CON.CRETE.LY, *adv.*, concretamente.
CON.CRETE MIX.ER, *s.*, betoneira.
CON.CRET.IZE, *v.*, concretizar.
CON.CU.BI.NAGE, *s.*, concubinato.
CON.CU.BINE, *s.*, concubina.
CON.CUR, *v.*, estar de acordo, acordar, concordar.
CON.CUR.RENCE, *s.*, concordância, cooperação.
CON.CUR.RENT, *adj.*, coincidente, simultâneo.
CON.CUR.RENTLY, *adv.*, concomitantemente, simultaneamente.
CON.CUSS, *v.*, sacudir, abalar.
CON.CUS.SED, *adj.*, que sofreu concussão.
CON.CUS.SION, *s.*, concussão.
CON.DEMN, *v.*, denunciar, condenar, censurar.
CON.DEM.NA.TION, *s.*, condenação, censura, reprovação.

CON.DENS.ABLE, *adj.*, condensável.
CON.DEN.SATE, *s.*, condensado.
CON.DEN.SA.TION, *s.*, condensação.
CON.DENSE, *v.*, condensar.
CON.DENSED MILK, *s.*, leite condensado.
CON.DE.SCEND, *v.*, condescender; tratar com superioridade.
CON.DE.SCEND.ENCE, *s.*, condescendência.
CON.DE.SCEND.ING, *adj.*, condescendente, transigente.
CON.DIGN, *adj.*, justo, certo, merecido.
CON.DI.MENT, *s.*, condimento, tempero; *v.*, temperar.
CON.DI.TION, *s.*, condição, situação, estado, circunstância.
CON.DI.TION.AL, *adj.*, condicional.
CON.DI.TION.AL.I.TY, *s.*, condicionalidade.
CON.DI.TION.AL.LY, *adv.*, condicionalmente.
CON.DI.TIONED, *adj.*, condicionado.
CON.DI.TION.ER, *s.*, aquele que condiciona; condicionador (de cabelo); amaciante (de roupas).
CON.DI.TION.ING, *s.*, condicionamento.
CON.DOLE, *v.*, condoer-se.
CON.DOLE.MENT, *s.*, o mesmo que *condolence(s)*.
CON.DO.LENCES, *s. pl.*, condolências, pêsames.
CON.DOL.ING, *adj.*, pesaroso, condolente.
CON.DOM, *s.*, preservativo.
CON.DO.MIN.I.UM, *s.*, *US* condomínio.
CON.DONE, *v.*, perdoar, aceitar, reconhecer.
CON.DOR, *s.*, *Zool.*, condor.
CON.DUCE, *v.*, levar a, conduzir.
CON.DUCE.MENT, *s.*, tendência.
CON.DU.CIVE, *adj.*, conducente, tendente; útil.
CON.DU.CIVE.NESS, *s.*, tendência, contribuição.
CON.DUCT, *s.*, conduta, comportamento; *v.*, conduzir, dirigir.
CON.DUCT.ED TOUR, *s.*, excursão com guia.
CON.DUCT.I.BIL.I.TY, *s.*, condutibilidade.
CON.DUCT.I.BLE, *adj.*, condutível.
CON.DUCT.ING, *adj.*, condutor.
CON.DUCT.ING WIRE, *s.*, fio condutor.
CON.DUC.TION, *s.*, condução.
CON.DUCT.IVE, *adj.*, condutivo.
CON.DUC.TIV.I.TY, *s.*, condutividade.
CON.DUC.TOR, *s.*, *Fís.*, condutor (de calor, eletricidade etc.); cobrador (ônibus); chefe, guia.
CON.DUC.TRESS, *s.*, condutora, diretora; cobradora (ônibus).
CON.DUIT, *s.*, canal, conduto, cano, tubo.
CONE, *s.*, cone, peça com forma de cone.
CO.NEY, *s.*, *Zool.*, coelho (europeu); pele de coelho.
CON.FAB.U.LATE, *v.*, confabular, conversar.
CON.FAB.U.LA.TION, *s.*, colóquio, conversa familiar.
CON.FECT, *v.*, preparar doce; pôr em conserva.
CON.FEC.TION, *s.*, confecção, preparação; *v.*, confeccionar, fazer.
CON.FEC.TION.ER, *s.*, confeiteiro.
CON.FEC.TION.ERY, *s.*, doces, confeitos.
CON.FED.ER.A.CY, *s.*, confederação, aliança, união.
CON.FED.ER.ATE, *adj.*, *s.*, confederado, aliado, unido.
CON.FED.ER.A.TION, *s.*, confederação.
CON.FER, *v.*, conferir, avaliar, conceder, dar.
CON.FER.ENCE, *s.*, conferência, congresso, reunião.
CON.FER.ENCE HALL, *s.*, salão de conferência.
CON.FER.ENC.ING, *s.*, sistema de teleconferência.
CON.FESS, *v.*, admitir, confessar, contar, dizer.
CON.FESS.ED.LY, *adv.*, reconhecidamente.

CONFESSION ·· 420 ·· CONNEXION

CON.FES.SION, *s.*, confissão, reconhecimento, admissão.
CON.FES.SION.AL, *s.*, confessionário; *adj.*, confessional.
CON.FES.SION.A.RY, *adj.*, confessório.
CON.FES.SOR, *s.*, confessor.
CON.FET.TI, *s. pl., It.*, confete.
CON.FI.DANT, *s.*, confidente.
CON.FI.DANTE, *s.*, confidente (mulher).
CON.FIDE, *v.*, confiar, fiar-se em.
CON.FI.DENCE, *s.*, confiança, fé.
CON.FI.DENT, *adj.*, confiante, convicto.
CON.FI.DEN.TIAL, *adj.*, confidencial, sigiloso.
CON.FI.DENT.IAL.I.TY, *s.*, sigilo, confidência; confidencialidade.
CON.FI.DEN.TIAL.LY, *adv.*, em particular, confidencialmente.
CON.FI.DENT.LY, *adv.*, com confiança, confiantemente.
CON.FID.ING, *adj.*, que confia, confiante.
CON.FIG.U.RA.TION, *s.*, configuração.
CON.FIG.U.RA.TIVE, *adj.*, configurativo.
CON.FIG.U.RE, *v.*, configurar.
CON.FINE, *v.*, confinar, prender, encarcerar.
CON.FINED, *adj.*, confinado, restringido; preso.
CON.FINE.MENT, *s.*, aprisionamento.
CON.FIRM, *v.*, confirmar.
CON.FIR.MA.TION, *s.*, confirmação; crisma.
CON.FIRM.ED, *adj.*, confirmado; convicto.
CON.FIRM.ED.LY, *adv.*, comprovadamente.
CON.FIRM.ER, *v.*, corroborador.
CON.FIS.CATE, *v.*, confiscar.
CON.FIS.CA.TION, *s.*, confisco, apreensão.
CON.FIS.CA.TOR, *s.*, confiscador.
CON.FLA.GRANT, *adj.*, conflagrado; incendiado.
CON.FLA.GRA.TION, *s.*, conflagração.
CON.FLATE, *v.*, fundir; unir, confundir.
CON.FLA.TION, *s.*, fusão, mistura.
CON.FLICT, *s.*, conflito, divergência, embate; *v.*, divergir, conflitar.
CON.FLICT.ING, *adj.*, conflitante, contraditório.
CON.FLICT.IVE, *adj.*, conflitivo, antagônico.
CON.FLU.ENCE, *s.*, confluência.
CON.FLU.ENT, *adj.*, confluente; *s.*, afluente, caudatário.
CON.FORM, *v.*, conformar; acomodar-se.
CON.FORM.ABIL.I.TY, *s.*, conformabilidade.
CON.FOR.MA.TION, *s.*, conformação.
CON.FOR.MIST, *s.*, conformista; *adj., pej.*, conformista.
CON.FOR.MI.TY, *s.*, conformidade.
CON.FOUND, *v.*, confundir; misturar; desconcertar.
CON.FOUND.ED, *adj.*, confuso; *col.*, maldito.
CON.FRA.TER.NI.TY, *s.*, confraria, fraternidade.
CON.FRONT, *v.*, enfrentar, defrontar.
CON.FRON.TA.TION, *s.*, confrontação, enfrentamento; acareação.
CON.FRON.TATION.AL, *adj.*, confrontante, confrontamento.
CON.FU.CIAN, *s.*, confucionista; *adj.*, relativo a Confúcio.
CON.FUS.A.BLE, *adj.*, confundível; confuso.
CON.FUSE, *v.*, confundir, desordenar, desconcertar.
CON.FUSED, *adj.*, confuso.
CON.FUS.ING, *adj.*, confuso, atrapalhado.
CON.FU.SION, *s.*, confusão, mal-entendido.
CON.GA, *s.*, conga (dança cubana).
CON.GEAL, *v.*, coagular.
CON.GEAL.MENT, *s.*, coagulação.

CON.GE.LA.TION, *s.*, congelamento, solidificação.
CON.GE.NER, *adj.*, congênere.
CON.GE.NIAL, *adj.*, agradável, apropriado, congenial.
CON.GE.NIAL.I.TY, *s.*, simpatia.
CON.GEN.I.TAL, *adj.*, congênito, inato.
CON.GER EEL, *s., Zool.*, enguia marinha.
CON.GEST, *v.*, congestionar, acumular.
CON.GEST.ED, *adj.*, congestionado.
CON.GES.TION, *s.*, congestão, congestionamento.
CON.GLOM.ER.A.TION, *s.*, conglomeração, aglomeração.
CON.GRAT.U.LATE, *v.*, congratular, dar parabéns, cumprimentar.
CON.GRAT.U.LA.TIONS, *s.*, congratulações, cumprimentos.
CON.GRAT.U.LA.TOR, *s.*, congratulador.
CON.GRAT.U.LA.TO.RY, *adj.*, de felicitações, congratulatório.
CON.GRE.GATE, *v.*, congregar, reunir, ajuntar.
CON.GRE.GA.TION, *s.*, congregação, grupo de pessoas.
CON.GRE.GA.TIVE, *adj.*, congregante.
CON.GRESS, *s.*, congresso, assembleia; câmara e senado.
CON.GRES.SION.AL, *adj.*, congressional; *US* parlamentar.
CON.GRESS.MAN, *s.*, congressista, homem do congresso.
CON.GRESS.WOM.AN, *s.*, congressista (mulher).
CON.GRU.ENCE, *s.*, congruência; coerência.
CON.GRU.ENT, *adj.*, congruente.
CON.IC, *adj.*, cônico.
CON.I.CAL, *adj.*, o mesmo que *conic*.
CO.NI.CI.TY, *s.*, conicidade
CO.NI.FER, *s., Bot.*, conífera (espécie das coníferas).
CON.IF.ER.OUS, *adj.*, conífero.
CON.JEC.TU.RAL, *adj.*, conjetural.
CON.JEC.TURE, *s.*, conjetura, ideia; *v.*, conjeturar, imaginar, achar.
CON.JOIN, *v.*, reunir, unir, ligar, conectar.
CON.JOINT, *adj.*, unido, ligado, conectado, reunido.
CON.JOINT.LY, *adv.*, conjuntamente.
CON.JU.GAL, *adj.*, conjugal.
CON.JU.GATE, *v.*, conjugar, unir; *adj.*, conjugado, ligado.
CON.JU.GAT.ED, *adj.*, conjugado.
CON.JU.GA.TION, *s.*, conjugação, ligamento, união.
CON.JUNCT, *adj.*, conjunto, ligado; *s.*, par, parceiro.
CON.JUNC.TION, *s.*, conjunção; coincidência; ligação.
CON.JUNC.TIVE, *s., Gram.*, conjunção; *adj.*, conjuntivo; ligado, unido.
CON.JUNC.TI.VI.TIS, *s.*, conjuntivite.
CON.JUNCT.LY, *adv.*, conjuntamente.
CON.JUNC.TURE, *s.*, conjuntura, momento, situação.
CON.JU.RA.TION, *s.*, conjuração, trama, sedição.
CON.JURE, *v.*, conjurar; praticar magia; fazer truques (de mágica); implorar.
CON.JUR.ER, *s.*, conjurador; mágico, encantador.
CON.JUR.OR, *s.*, o mesmo que *conjurer*.
CON.MAN, *s.*, vigarista, trapaceiro.
CON.NATE, *adj.*, congênito, inato.
CON.NECT, *v.*, conectar, ligar, unir.
CON.NECT.ED, *adj.*, conectado, relacionado; associado.
CON.NECT.ING, *adj.*, de conexão (voo, trem).
CON.NECT.ING ROD, *s., Mec.*, biela.
CON.NEC.TION, *s.*, conexão, ligação, união.
CON.NEC.TIVE, *s.* e *adj., Gram.*, conectivo.
CON.NECT.IVE.LY, *adv.*, em conexão.
CON.NEX.ION, *s., UK* o mesmo que *connection*.

CONNIVANCE ·· 421 ·· CONSTRUCTOR

CON.NIV.ANCE, *s.*, conivência, cumplicidade.
CON.NIVE, *v.*, ser conivente, ser cúmplice.
CON.NIV.ENT, *adj.*, conivente.
CON.NIV.ER, *s.*, cúmplice.
CON.NOIS.SEUR, *s.*, *Fr.*, conhecedor, especialista.
CON.NO.TA.TION, *s.*, conotação, palavra figurada.
CON.NO.TA.TIVE, *adj.*, conotativo.
CON.NOTE, *v.*, conotar, implicar.
CON.NU.BI.AL, *s.*, conjugal.
CON.NU.BI.AL.I.TY, *s.*, conúbio, matrimônio.
CON.QUER, *v.*, conquistar, apoderar-se de.
CON.QUER.ING, *adj.*, conquistador, vitorioso.
CON.QUER.OR, *s.*, conquistador.
CON.QUEST, *s.*, conquista.
CON.SAN.GUINE, *adj.*, consanguíneo.
CON.SAN.GUIN.I.TY, *s.*, consanguinidade.
CON.SCIENCE, *s.*, consciência.
CON.SCIENCE.LESS, *adj.*, sem consciência, inescrupuloso.
CON.SCI.EN.TIOUS, *adj.*, consciencioso.
CON.SCI.EN.TIOUS.LY, *adv.*, conscienciosamente.
CON.SCI.EN.TIOUS.NESS, *s.*, consciência, escrúpulo.
CON.SCIOUS, *adj.*, consciente; ciente, sabedor.
CON.SCIOUS.LY, *adv.*, conscientemente, intencionalmente.
CON.SCIOUS.NESS, *s.*, consciência, escrúpulo.
CON.SCRIPT, *s.*, recruta, alistado no exército; *v.*, recrutar, alistar.
CON.SCRIP.TION, *s.*, serviço militar obrigatório, conscrição.
CON.SE.CRATE, *adv.*, consecutivamente.
CON.SE.CRA.TION, *s.*, consagração, sagração.
CON.SEC.U.TIVE, *adj.*, consecutivo.
CON.SEC.U.TIVE.LY, *adv.*, conecutivamente, sucessivamente.
CON.SEN.SUS, *v.*, consenso.
CON.SENT, *s.*, consentimento; *v.*, consentir.
CON.SENT.ER, *s.*, aquele que consente.
CON.SENT.ING, *adj.*, em que teve consentimento das partes.
CON.SE.QUENCE, *s.*, consequência.
CON.SE.QUENT, *adj.*, consequente.
CON.SE.QUENT.LY, *adv.*, consequentemente.
CON.SERV.A.BLE, *adj.*, conservável.
CON.SER.VA.TION, *s.*, conservação, preservação.
CON.SER.VA.TION.IST, *s.*, conservacionista.
CON.SERV.A.TISM, *s.*, conservadorismo.
CON.SERV.A.TIVE, *s.*, conservador; preservador; *adj.*, que conserva, conservador, moderado.
CON.SER.VA.TOR, *s.*, protetor.
CON.SER.VA.TORY, *s.*, estufa (para plantas); *Mús.*, conservatório.
CON.SERVE, *v.*, conservar, preservar.
CON.SID.ER, *v.*, considerar, respeitar, ter em consideração.
CON.SID.ER.A.BLE, *adj.*, considerável.
CON.SID.ER.A.BLY, *adv.*, consideravelmente.
CON.SID.ER.ATE, *adj.*, atencioso, respeitoso.
CON.SID.ER.ATION, *s.*, consideração, exame, deliberação, estima.
CON.SID.ERED, *adj.*, considerado; estimado; ~ *opinion*: opinião sincera.
CON.SID.ER.ING, *prep.*, referente a, em consideração de.
CON.SIGN, *v.*, consignar; destinar, despachar; confiar.
CON.SIGN.MENT, *s.*, consignação; remessa, despacho.
CON.SIST, *v.*, consistir.

CON.SIS.TEN.CE, *s.*, consistência; solidez, estabilidade.
CON.SIS.TEN.CY, *s.*, consistência, coerência.
CON.SIS.TENT, *adj.*, consistente, firme; constante; coerente.
CON.SIST.ENT.LY, *adv.*, constantemente, coerentemente.
CON.SOL.A.BLE, *adj.*, consolável.
CON.SO.LA.TION, *s.*, consolo, consolação, conforto.
CON.SOLE, *v.*, consolar, confortar, aliviar; *s.*, consolo.
CON.SOL.ER, *s.*, consolador.
CON.SOL.I.DATE, *s.*, consolidar, firmar.
CON.SOL.I.DA.TED, *adj.*, consolidado; fortalecido; combinado.
CON.SOL.I.DA.TION, *s.*, consolidação, afirmação, unificação.
CON.SOL.ING, *adj.*, consolador, confortador.
CON.SO.NANCE, *s.*, consonância.
CON.SO.NANT, *s.*, *Gram.*, consoante; *adj.*, consoante, harmonioso; *Fís.*, ressonante.
CON.SORT, *v.*, acompanhar, associar-se, ligar-se.
CON.SOR.TI.UM, *s.*, consórcio.
CON.SPIC.U.OUS, *adj.*, conspícuo, distinto, evidente.
CON.SPIC.U.OUS.LY, *adv.*, conspicuamente.
CON.SPIR.A.CY, *s.*, conspiração.
CON.SPIR.A.TOR, *s.*, conspirador.
CON.SPIR.A.TO.RI.AL, *adj.*, conspiratório, conspirador.
CON.SPIRE, *v.*, conspirar, tramar.
CON.STA.BLE, *s.*, *UK* guarda, policial.
CON.STAB.U.LA.RY, *s.*, *UK* força policial; *adj.*, relativo à polícia.
CON.STAN.CY, *s.*, constância, persistência, lealdade.
CON.STANT, *adj.*, constante.
CON.STANT.LY, *adv.*, constantemente.
CON.STEL.LA.TION, *s.*, *Astron.*, constelação.
CON.STER.NATE, *v.*, consternar, entristecer.
CON.STER.NA.TION, *s.*, consternação.
CON.STI.PATE, *v.*, constipar (obstrução intestinal); *fig.*, emperrar.
CON.STI.PAT.ED, *adj.*, constipado (prisão de ventre).
CON.STI.PA.TION, *s.*, constipação, prisão de ventre.
CON.STIT.U.EN.CY, *s.*, distrito eleitoral; *fig.*, freguesia.
CON.STIT.U.EN.CY PARTY, *s.*, *UK* partido local.
CON.STIT.U.ENT, *s.*, eleitor.
CON.STI.TUTE, *v.*, constituir, representar.
CON.STI.TU.TION, *s.*, constituição; forma, compleição.
CON.STI.TU.TION.AL, *adj.*, constitucional.
CON.STI.TU.TION.AL.ISM, *s.*, constitucionalismo.
CON.STI.TU.TION.AL.IST, *s.*, constitucionalista.
CON.STI.TU.TION.AL.I.TY, *s.*, constitucionalidade.
CON.STI.TU.TION.AL.IZE, *s.*, constitucionalizar.
CON.STI.TU.TION.AL.LY, *adv.*, constitucionalmente.
CON.STI.TU.TIVE, *adj.*, constitutivo.
CON.STRAIN, *v.*, constranger, reprimir, forçar.
CON.STRAINED, *adj.*, constrangido, contido; coagido.
CON.STRAINT, *s.*, pressão, coação, repressão.
CON.STRICT, *v.*, constringir.
CON.STRIC.TION, *s.*, constrição; aperto.
CON.STRICT.ING, *adj.*, apertado (roupa), limitado (estilo de vida).
CON.STRUCT, *v.*, construir.
CON.STRUC.TION, *s.*, construção, edificação.
CON.STRUC.TIVE, *adj.*, construtivo.
CON.STRUC.TIVE.LY, *adv.*, construtivamente.
CON.STRUCT.OR, *s.*, construtor.

CONSTRUE ··422·· CONTROL PANEL

CON.STRUE, v., interpretar; explicar; taduzir.
CON.SUL, s., cônsul.
CON.SU.LAR, adj., consular.
CON.SUL.ATE, s., consulado.
CON.SULT, v., consultar; s., consultório médico.
CON.SULT.AN.CY, s., consulta; empresa de consultoria.
CON.SULT.ANT, s., consultor; consultante; UK especialista (médico).
CON.SUL.TA.TION, s., consulta; discussão, disputa.
CON.SUL.TING ROOM, s., consultório (médico).
CON.SUME, v., consumir, alimentar-se.
CON.SUM.ER, s., consumidor.
CON.SUM.ER GOODS, s. pl., bens de consumo.
CON.SUM.ER.ISM, s., consumismo, consumo exagerado.
CON.SUM.ING, adj., ardente, profundo.
CON.SUM.MATE, adj., consumado; perfeito; v., consumar; realizar.
CON.SUM.MA.TION, s., consumação.
CON.SUMP.TION, s., consumação; consumo; devastação; tuberculose.
CON.TACT, s. contato; v., contatar.
CON.TACT LENS, s., lente de contato.
CON.TAC.TOR, s., Eletr., interruptor.
CON.TA.GION, s., contágio.
CON.TA.GIOUS, adj., contagioso.
CON.TAIN, v., conter, reter.
CON.TAIN.A.BLE, adj., que pode conter ou ser contido.
CON.TAIN.ED, adj., contido, refreado; calmo.
CON.TAIN.ER, s., recipiente, contêiner.
CON.TAIN.ER.IZE, -ISE, v., transportar em contêiner.
CON.TAIN.MENT, s., contenção; refreamento, restrição.
CON.TAM.I.NATE, v., contaminar, afetar.
CON.TAM.I.NAT.ED, adj., contaminado.
CON.TAM.I.NA.TION, s., contaminação.
CON.TEM.PLATE, v., contemplar, olhar, considerar.
CON.TEM.PLA.TION, s., contemplação; reflexão.
CON.TEM.PLA.TIVE, adj., contemplativo, meditativo.
CON.TEM.PO.RA.NE.I.TY, s., contemporaneidade.
CON.TEM.PO.RA.NE.OUS, adj., contemporâneo.
CON.TEM.PO.RA.RY, s., contemporâneo; adj., contemporâneo; simultâneo.
CON.TEMPT, s., desprezo; desdém; presunção.
CON.TEMPT.I.BLE, adj., contemptível, vil, desprezível.
CON.TEMP.TU.OUS, adj., desdenhoso, que despreza.
CON.TEND, v., contender, enfrentar.
CON.TEND.ER, s., contendor, lutador, rival.
CON.TENT, v., contentar; adj., contente, satisfeito; s., conteúdo, teor.
CON.TENT.ED, adj., satisfeito.
CON.TENT.ED.LY, adv., com satisfação.
CON.TEN.TION, s., disputa,contenda, altercação.
CON.TEN.TIOUS, adj., contencioso, disputado.
CON.TENT.MENT, s., contentamento, satisfação.
CON.TEST, v., contestar, opor; s., contenda, disputa, competição.
CON.TEST.A.BLE, adj., contestável.
CON.TEST.ANT, s., concorrente.
CON.TES.TA.TION, s., contestação, contenda.
CON.TEXT, s., contexto, momento, situação.
CON.TI.NENT, s., continente; adj., continente, controlado.
CON.TI.NEN.TAL, adj., continental.

CON.TIN.GENCE, s., contato; contingência.
CON.TIN.GEN.CY, s., contingência.
CON.TIN.GENT, adj., contingente, incerto; s., Mil., contingente.
CON.TIN.U.AL, adj., contínuo.
CON.TIN.U.AL.LY, adv., continuamente, continuadamente.
CON.TIN.U.ANCE, s., duração, durabilidade, permanência; Jur., adiamento.
CON.TIN.U.A.TION, s., continuação, prolongamento.
CON.TIN.UE, v., continuar, retomar.
CON.TI.NU.I.TY, s., continuidade.
CON.TIN.U.O, s., Mús., baixo contínuo.
CON.TIN.U.OUS, adj., contínuo, constante.
CON.TIN.U.OUS CUR.RENT, s., Eletr., corrente contínua.
CON.TIN.UOUS.LY, adv., continuamente.
CON.TIN.U.OUS.NESS, s., continuidade.
CON.TORT, v., contorcer, torcer, distorcer.
CON.TOR.TION, s., contorção.
CON.TOR.TION.IST, s., contorcionista.
CON.TOUR, s., contorno.
CON.TRA.BAND, s., contrabando.
CON.TRA.BAND.IST, s., contrabandista.
CON.TRA.CEP.TION, s., contracepção; controle da natalidade.
CON.TRA.CEP.TIVE, adj., anticonceptivo, anticoncepcional.
CON.TRACT, s., contrato; v., contrair, encolher.
CON.TRAC.TION, s., contração.
CON.TRAC.TOR, s., contratante.
CON.TRAC.TU.AL, adj., contratual.
CON.TRA.DICT, v., contradizer, desmentir, negar.
CON.TRA.DIC.TION, s., contradição.
CON.TRA.DIC.TO.RY, adj., contraditório.
CON.TRA.FLOW, s., contramão, contrafluxo.
CON.TRAL.TO, s., Mús., contralto.
CON.TRA.PO.SI.TION, s., contraposição.
CON.TRAP.TION, s., col., geringonça.
CON.TRAR.I.NESS, s., oposição.
CON.TRA.RY, adj., contrário.
CON.TRAST, s., contraste; v., comparar.
CON.TRAST.ING, adj., o mesmo que contrastive.
CON.TRAST.IVE, adj., contrastante.
CON.TRA.VENE, v., transgredir, infringir, desrespeitar.
CON.TRA.VEN.TION, s., contravenção, infração.
CON.TRIB.UTE, v., contribuir, participar.
CON.TRI.BU.TION, s., contribuição, doação, participação.
CON.TRIB.U.TIVE, adj., contributivo.
CON.TRIB.U.TOR, s., contribuinte, colaborador de órgão de imprensa.
CON.TRIB.U.TORY, s., contributário; adj., contribuinte, contributivo, contributário.
CON.TRITE, adj., contrito, arrependido.
CON.TRIV.ANCE, s., dispositivo, instrumento; sagacidade; artifício.
CON.TRIVE, v., inventar, idear, imaginar.
CON.TRIVED, adj., elaborado, trabalhado; pej., arranjado.
CON.TRIV.ER, s., inventor.
CON.TROL, s., controle, direção: v., controlar, dirigir, guiar.
CON.TROL.LA.BLE, adj., controlável.
CON.TROLLED, adj., controlado; refreado.
CON.TROL.LER, s., controlador, diretor, executivo, contrôler.
CON.TROL.LING, s., verificação.
CON.TROL PAN.EL, s., painel de controle.

CONTROVERSIAL ··423·· COQUETRY

CON.TRO.VER.SIAL, *adj.*, controverso, polemic.
CON.TRO.VER.SY, *s.*, controvérsia.
CON.TRO.VERT, *v.*, discutir, polemizar.
CON.TU.MA.CY, *s.*, contumácia.
CON.TUSE, *v.*, contundir, machucar, magoar.
CON.TU.SION, *s.*, contusão, machucadura.
CO.NUN.DRUM, *s.*, enigma, charada, problema.
CO.NUR.BA.TION, *s.*, conurbação.
CON.VA.LESCE, *v.*, convalescer.
CON.VA.LES.CENCE, *s.*, convalescença.
CON.VA.LES.CENT, *s.* e *adj.*, convalescente.
CON.VEC.TION, *s.*, *Fís.*, convecção.
CON.VE.NE, *v.*, convocar; conveniar; reunir-se, encontrar-se.
CON.VE.NI.ENCE, *s.*, conveniência, facilidade.
CON.VE.N.I.ENT, *adj.*, conveniente.
CON.VEN.I.ENT.LY, *adv.*, convenientemente.
CON.VEN.ING, *s.*, chamada, convocação.
CON.VENT, *s.*, convento.
CON.VEN.TION.AL, *adj.*, convencional.
CON.VEN.TION.AL.ISM, *s.*, convencionalismo.
CON.VEN.TION.AL.I.TY, *s.*, convencionalidade, formalidade.
CON.VEN.TION.AL.IZE, *v.*, convencionalizar.
CON.VEN.TION.AL.LY, *adv.*, convencionalmente.
CON.VERGE, *v.*, convergir, ir para, dirigir-se para.
CON.VER.GENCE, *s.*, convergência.
CON.VER.SANT, *adj.*, familiarizado, conhecedor.
CON.VER.SA.TION, *s.*, conversação, colóquio.
CON.VER.SA.TION.AL.IST, *s.*, conversador, inivíduo sociável.
CON.VER.SA.TION.AL.LY, *adv.*, sociavelmente.
CON.VERSE, *s.*, conversa; trato; contrário, inverso; *adj.*, oposto, contrário; *v.*, conversar.
CON.VERSE.LY, *adv.*, inversamente; reciprocamente.
CON.VERS.ER, *s.*, conversador; palestrante.
CON.VER.SION, *s.*, conversão, mudança.
CON.VERT, *v.*, converter; *s.*, convertido.
CON.VERT.ED, *adj.*, transformado, adaptado; *Rel.*, convertido.
CON.VERT.ER, *s.*, convertedor.
CON.VERT.I.BLE, *s.*, conversível (carro); *adj.*, conversível, convertível.
CON.VEX, *adj.*, convexo.
CON.VEY, *v.*, transportar, levar, carregar.
CON.VEY.ANCE, *s.*, transporte, transmissão, transferência.
CON.VEY.AN.CING, *s.*, transferência de posse, ato de tabeliar; tabelionato.
CON.VEY.ER, *s.*, transportador, entregador.
CON.VEY.OR, *s.*, transportador, carregador.
CON.VICT, *v.*, condenar; *s.*, condenado, presidiário, preso.
CON.VIC.TED, *adj.*, *Jur.*, condenado.
CON.VIC.TION, *s.*, *Jur.*, condenação; convicção, certeza.
CON.VINCE, *v.*, convencer, garantir, assegurar.
CON.VINC.ED, *adj.*, convencido (de algo).
CON.VINC.ING, *adj.*, convincente.
CON.VIV.IAL, *adj.*, sociável, festivo, alegre.
CON.VIV.I.AL.I.TY, *s.*, sociabilidade, convívio, convivência.
CON.VO.CA.TION, *s.*, convocação, reunião, assembleia.
CON.VO.CA.TOR, *s.*, aquele que convoca ou que participa de uma convocação.
CON.VO.LUT.ED, *adj.*, convoluto, enrolado.
CON.VO.LU.TION, *s.*, convolução, enrolamento.
CON.VOLVE, *v.*, enrolar, envolver.

CON.VOY, *v.*, escoltar; *s.*, escolta.
CON.VULSE, *v.*, convulsionar, agitar, sacudir.
CON.VUL.SION, *s.*, convulsão.
CON.VUL.SIVE, *adj.*, convulsivo.
CO.NY, *s.*, coelho.
COO, *s.*, arrulho, fala suave; *v.*, arrulhar, namorar, falar com doçura.
COOK, *v.*, cozinhar, preparar a comida; *s.*, cozinheiro.
COOK.BOOK, *s.*, livro de receitas culinárias; o mesmo que *cookery book (UK)*.
COOK.ED, *adj.*, cozido (comida, refeição); *gír.*, frito (em situação ruim).
COOK.ER, *s.*, fogão, fogareiro.
COOK.ERY, *s.*, arte culinária; culinária.
COOK.ERY BOOK, *s.*, *UK* livro de receitas.
COOK.IE, *s.*, biscoito, bolacha.
COOK.ING, *s.*, cozinha, arte culinária.
COOK.OUT, *s.*, *US* refeição ao ar livre.
COOK.WARE, *s.*, utensílio de cozinha (pote, panela etc.).
COOL, *v.*, esfriar, refrescar; *adj.*, fresco, frio; *col.*, "legal"; *s.*, frescor, frescura.
COOL.ER, *s.*, geladeira; refrigerante; esfriadouro; *col.*, prisão.
COOL.ISH, *adj.*, ameno, fresco.
COOL.LY, *adv.*, calmamente (sangue-frio); friamente.
COOL.NESS, *s.*, frieza; friagem; frialdade.
COOP, *s.*, gaiola; viveiro (para galinhas e coelhos); *col.*, cadeia; *v.*, engaiolar; prender, confinar.
CO-OP, *s.*, *abrev.* de *co-operative*: cooperativa (sociedade).
CO.OP.E.RATE, *v.*, cooperar, colaborar, ajudar.
CO.OP.E.RA.TION, *s.*, cooperação, colaboração.
CO.OP.E.RA.TIVE, *s.*, cooperativa; *adj.*, coopérativo.
CO.OP.E.RA.TOR, *s.*, cooperador, colaborador.
CO.OPT *US*, **CO-OPT** *UK*, *v.*, cooptar.
CO.OR.DI.NATE, *s.*, coordenada (mapa, gráfico); *v.*, coordenar.
CO.OR.DI.NA.TION, *s.*, coordenação, direção.
CO.OR.DI.NA.TOR, *s.*, coordenador.
COO.TIE, *s.*, piolho.
CO-OWN.ER, *s.*, coproprietário.
CO-OWN.ER.SHIP, *s.*, copropriedade.
COP, *s.*, polícia, guarda policial; *v.*, prender.
CO-PART.NER, *s.*, sócio.
COPE, *v.*, lutar, contender; enfrentar.
COPI.ER, *s.*, copista.
CO.PI.LOT, *s.*, copiloto (avião).
CO.PI.OUS, *adj.*, copioso, abundante, farto.
CO.PI.OUS.NESS, *s.*, abundância, fartura, copiosidade.
COP-OUT, *s.*, desculpa, pretexto; aquele que se esquiva.
COP.PER, *s.*, cobre; utensílio de cobre; *col.*, policial.
COP.PICE, *s.*, o mesmo que *copse*.
COPSE, *s.*, capão, matagal, capoeira.
COP.U.LA, *s.*, ligação; *Gram.*, cópula.
COP.U.LATE, *v.*, copular.
COP.U.LA.TION, *s.*, copulação; ligação, união; coito.
COP.Y, *s.*, cópia, reprodução; *v.*, reproduzir, copiar.
COP.Y.BOOK, *s.*, caderno; *Com.*, copiador.
COPY-DESK, *s.*, revisão e redação final de jornal ou revista.
COPY.ING, *s.*, ato de copiar; reprodução, cópia.
COPY.RIGHT, *s.*, direitos do autor.
COP.Y TYP.IST, *s.*, *UK* digitador.
CO.QUE.TRY, *s.*, galanteio, coqueteria.

CORAL · 424 · COSMONAUT

COR.AL, s., coral, recife de coral.
CORD, s., corda, cabo, fio, linha.
COR.DIAL, adj., cordial.
COR.DIAL.LY, adv., cordialmente.
COR.DIAL.I.TY, s., cordialidade, sinceridade, afeição.
CORD.LESS, adj., Elet., sem fio.
COR.DON, s., cordão de isolamento.
COR.DU.ROY, s., veludo cotelê; adj., de cotelê.
CORE, s., caroço, centro, âmago.
CORE.LESS, adj., sem caroço.
CO.RE.LI.GION.IST, s., correligionário, partidário.
COR.ER, s., descaroçador de frutas.
CORGI, s., ração de cão; raça de cão do País de Gales.
CO.RI.AN.DER, s., Bot., coentro.
CORK, s., cortiça, rolha; v., colocar rolha.
CORK.AGE, s., taxa de desarrolhamento de vinho em restaurantes e hotéis.
CORK.ED, adj., arrolhado, rolhado; com gosto de rolha.
CORK.SCREW, s., saca-rolhas.
CORN, s., cereal, trigo, milho, aveia.
CORN BREAD, s., broa ou bolo de fubá.
COR.NEA, s., Anat., córnea.
COR.NER, s., esquina, ângulo, canto, escanteio; v., encurralar, encurvar.
COR.NER FLAG, s., Esp., bandeirinha de escanteio (futebol).
COR.NER KICK, s., Esp., cobrança de escanteio (futebol).
COR.NER SHOP, s., UK loja da esquina, loja do bairro.
COR.NER.STONE, s., pedra fundamental; fundamento, alicerce.
COR.NET, s., Mús., cornetim, corneta; UK casquinha de sorvete.
CORN.FIELD, s., UK campo de trigo; **CORN-FIELD**, US milharal.
CORN.FLAKES, s., flocos de milho.
CORN.FLOOR, s., celeiro.
CORN.FLOUR, s., amido de milho, maisena.
CORN-FLOWER, s., Bot., espiga de milho.
COR.NICE, s., Arq., cornija.
CORN.STARCH, s., o mesmo que cornflour.
CORN-TRADE, s., comércio de cereais.
COR.NU.CO.PI.A, s., Lit., cornucópia; fig., riqueza.
CORN.Y, adj., batido, antiquado, banal; granuloso.
CO.ROL.LA, s., Bot., corola.
COR.OL.LARY, s., corolário.
CO.RO.NA, s., coroa.
COR.O.NAL, s., coroa, grinalda; ornato de cabeça; adj., coronal.
COR.O.NA.RY, adj., coronário, coronal.
COR.O.NA.TION, s., coroação (de um monarca).
COR.O.NER, s., médico legista.
COR.PO.RAL, adj., corporal, corpóreo; s., Mil., cabo.
COR.PO.RATE, adj., corporativo; incorporado; coletivo.
COR.PO.RA.TION, s., município, junta; sociedade, corporação.
COR.PO.RA.TIVE, adj., corporativo.
COR.PO.RA.TIV.ISM, s., corporativismo.
COR.PO.RA.TOR, s., membro de uma corporação.
COR.PO.RE.AL, adj., corpóreo.
COR.PO.RE.I.TY, s., corporeidade.
COR.POR.I.FI.CA.TION, s., corporificação.
CORPS, s., unidade, corpo.

CORPSE, s., cadáver, defunto.
COR.PU.LENT, adj., corpulento.
COR.PUS, s., coleção de obras literárias; corpo.
COR.PUS.CLE, s., corpúsculo; glóbulo.
COR.PUS.CU.LAR, adj., corpuscular.
COR.RAL, s., curral.
COR.RA.SION, s., erosão.
COR.RECT, adj., correto, exato.
COR.REC.TION, s., correção.
COR.REC.TIVE, adj., s., corretivo.
COR.RECT.LY, adv., corretamente.
COR.RECT.NESS, s., correção; justeza.
COR.REC.TOR, s., corretor, revisor; corretivo.
COR.RE.LATE, v., correlacionar.
COR.RE.LA.TION, s., correlação.
COR.RE.LA.TIVE, s. e adj., correlativo.
COR.RE.LA.TIV.I.TY, s., correlatividade; correlação.
COR.RE.SPOND, v., corresponder.
COR.RE.SPON.DENCE, s., correspondência.
COR.RE.SPON.DENT, s., correspondente (de jornal, tevê etc.); correlativo; adj., correspondente, conforme.
COR.RE.SPON.DING, adj., correspondente.
COR.RI.DOR, s., local de passagem: corredor.
COR.RI.GI.BLE, adj., corrigível.
COR.ROB.O.RATE, v., corroborar.
COR.ROB.O.RA.TION, s., corroboração.
COR.RODE, v., corroer.
COR.RO.SION, s., corrosão.
COR.RO.SIVE, adj., corrosivo.
COR.RU.GATE, s., enrugar, franzir.
COR.RU.GAT.ED, adj., enrugado, corrugado; ondulado.
COR.RUPT, adj., corrupto; v., corromper.
COR.RUPT.ER, s., corruptor, sedutor.
COR.RUPT.I.BLE, adj., corruptível; perecível.
COR.RUP.TION, s., corrupção.
COR.RUP.TIVE, adj., corruptivo.
COR.SAGE, s., US pequeno buquê usado no vestido.
COR.SAIR, s., corsário, pirata.
COR.SET, s., espartilho; cinta (para mulheres).
COR.TEX, s., córtex, córtice.
COR.TI.CAL, s., cortical.
COR.TI.COID, s., Med., corticoide.
COR.TI.SONE, s., Med., cortisona.
COS, conj., UK abrev. de because; Mat., abrev. de cosine: cosseno.
COSH, s., UK cassete (de policial); v., bater com cassete.
CO.SIG.NA.TO.RY, s., consignatário.
CO-SIGN.ER, s., consignatário; avalista.
CO.SINE, s., Mat., cosseno.
COS.I.NESS, s., comodidade.
COS LET.TUCE, s., alface crespa.
COS.MET.IC, s., cosmético.
COS.ME.TI.CIAN, s., esteticista.
COS.MIC, adj., cósmico.
COS.MOG.O.NAL, adj., cosmogônico.
COS.MOG.O.NY, s., Astron., cosmogonia.
COS.MOG.RA.PHY, s., cosmografia.
COS.MOL.OGIC, adj., cosmológico.
COS.MOL.O.GIST, s., cosmólogo.
COS.MOL.O.GY, s., cosmologia.
COS.MO.NAUT, s., cosmonauta.

COSMOPOLITAN ··425··· COVERING

COS.MOP.O.LITAN, *adj.*, cosmopolita, cosmopolitano.
COS.MOP.O.LITE, *s.*, cosmopolita.
COS.MOS, *s.*, cosmos, universo.
COS.SET, *v.*, acarinhar, afagar; *s.*, animal de estimação.
COST, *s.*, custo, preço, custas; *v.*, custar.
CO-STAR, *s., Cin.*, TV, coadjuvante (ator/atriz).
COST-EF.FECT.IVE, *adj.*, custo-beneficio; lucrativo, rentável.
COST-EF.FECT.IVE.NESS, *s.*, rentabilidade.
COST.ING, *s.*, custo.
COS.TIVE, *adj.*, constipado.
COS.TIVE.NESS, *s.*, prisão de ventre, constipação.
COS.TLY, *adj.*, oneroso; caro; dispendioso; de grande valor.
COST-PRICE, *s.*, preço de custo.
COS.TUME, *s.*, traje, vestimenta; short para banho.
CO.SY, *adj.*, aconchegante, confortável.
COT.TAGE, *s.*, casa de campo.
COT.TAGE CHEESE, *s., US* queijo *cottage*; *UK* requeijão.
COT.TON, *s.*, algodão.
COT.TON BUD, COT.TON SWAB, *s.*, cotonete.
COT.TON-WOOL, *s.*, algodão bruto; chumaço de algodão.
COUCH, *v.*, deitar, recostar, estirar-se.
COU.CHETTE, *s., UK* cama (trem ou navio, para uma pessoa).
COU.GAR, *s., Zool.*, puma; suçuarana.
COUGH, *v.*, tossir; *s.*, tosse.
COUGH.ING, *s.*, tossidela, tossido; *adj.*, que tosse.
COULD, *v.*, passado do *v.* can.
COULDN'T, *v., abrev.* de *could not*.
COULD'VE, *v., abrev.* de *could have*.
COUN.CIL, *s.*, conselho.
COUN.CIL.LOR, *s.*, vereador.
COUN.SEL, *s.*, consulta, conselho; opinião.
COUN.SEL.EE, *s.*, orientando.
COUN.SEL.ING *US*, **COUN.SEL.LING** *UK*, *s.*, aconselhamento, orientação; terapia.
COUN.SEL.LOR, *s.*, conselheiro, orientador; *US* advogado.
COUNT, *v.*, contar; *s.*, contagem; conde.
COUNT.A.BLE, *adj.*, contável.
COUNT.DOWN, *s.*, contagem regressiva.
COUN.TE.NANCE, *s.*, semblante, rosto; fisionomia; aprovação; *v.*, aprovar.
COUNT.ER, *s.*, balcão, guichê, ficha; *v.*, contrair.
COUN.TER.ACT, *v.*, neutralizar, anular.
COUN.TER.AT.TACK, *s.*, contra-ataque.
COUN.TER.BAL.ANCE, *s.*, contrapeso; *v.*, contrabalançar.
COUN.TER.CHARGE, *s.*, contestação, recriminação.
COUN.TER.CLAIM, *s.*, reivindicação.
COUN.TER.CLOCK.WISE, *adj.*, anti-horário; *adv.*, em sentido anti-horário.
COUN.TER.ES.PI.O.NAGE, *s.*, contra-espionagem.
COUN.TER.FEIT, *s.*, falsificação; *v.*, falsificar.
COUN.TER.FOIL, *s.*, talão.
COUN.TER.INTEL.LI.GENCE, *s., Mil.*, contra-inteligência; contra-informação; contra-espionagem.
COUN.TER.MAND, *s.*, contraordem; revogação; *v.*, revogar.
COUN.TER.MEA.SURE, *s.*, contramedida; medida defensiva.
COUN.TER.OF.FEN.SIVE, *s.*, contraofensiva.
COUN.TER.OF.FER, *s.*, contraoferta.
COUN.TER.PANE, *s.*, coberta para dormir, colcha.
COUN.TER.POINT, *s. Mús.*, contraponto.
COUN.TER.PRO.DUC.TIVE, *adj.*, contraprodutivo,

contraproducente.
COUN.TER.REV.O.LU.TION, *s.*, contrarrevolução.
COUN.TER.SIGN, *v.*, autenticar.
COUNT.ESS, *s.*, condessa.
COUNT.ING, *s.*, contagem, cálculo; *adj.*, relativo a cálculo.
COUNT.LESS, *adj.*, inumerável.
COUN.TRY, *s.*, país, terra, nação, região, localidade.
COUN.TRY-CLUB, *s.*, clube de campo.
COUN.TRY.FOLK, *s.*, gente do campo.
COUN.TRY.MAN, *s.*, camponês, caipira.
COUN.TRY.SIDE, *s.*, campo, sítio, interior, sertão.
COUN.TRY.WIDE, *adj.*, relativo ao país inteiro.
COUN.TRY.WOM.AN, *s.*, compatriota (mulher); camponesa.
COUN.TY, *s.*, condado.
COUN.TY COURT, *s., UK* tribunal regional.
COUN.TY TOWN, *s., UK* sede do condado.
COUP, *s.*, golpe de mestre.
COU.PLE, *s.*, casal, par, parelha; *v.*, emparelhar, juntar dois.
COU.PLING, *s.*, ligação, união.
COU.PON, *s.*, cupão, vale.
COUR.AGE, *s.*, coragem, valentia.
COU.RA.GEOUS, *adj.*, corajoso.
COU.RA.GEOUS.LY, *adv.*, corajosamente, intrepidamente.
COU.RA.GEOUS.NESS, *s.*, coragem, valentia, intrepidez.
COUR.GETTE, *s.*, abobrinha.
COU.RI.ER, *s.*, correio, mensageiro, guia turístico.
COURSE, *s.*, curso, progresso, direção, processo; *v.*, rumar, acossar.
COURSE.BOOK, *s.*, apostila, polígrafo, livro de curso.
COURSE.WORK, *s.*, trabalho de curso.
COURS.ING, *s.*, currida; caça com cães.
COURT, *s.*, corte, tribunal; *v.*, cortejar, namorar.
COUR.TE.OUS, *adj.*, cortês, polido, educado.
COUR.TE.OUS.LY, *adv.*, cortesmente.
COUR.TE.OUS.NESS, *s.*, cortesia, polidez.
COUR.TE.SAN, *s.*, cortesã; prostituta de luxo.
COUR.TE.SY, *s.*, cortesia.
COUR.TI.ER, *s.*, cortesão, bajulador.
COURT.HOUSE, *s.*, palácio da justiça.
COURT-MAR.TIAL, *s.*, corte marcial; *v.*, submeter a uma corte marcial.
COURT OF AP.PEALS *US*, **COURT OF AP.PEAL** *UK*, *s.*, tribunal de apelação.
COURT OF IN.QUIR.Y, *s.*, comissão de inquérito; tribunal de investigação.
COURT-ROOM, *s.*, sala de tribunal.
COURT.SHIP, *s.*, galanteio.
COURT.YARD, *s.*, pátio.
COUS.IN, *s.*, primo, prima.
COVE, *s.*, enseada, angra, refúgio; *v.*, arquear, fazer uma abóbada.
COV.E.NANT, *s.*, convênio, pacto; *Rel.*, aliança; *Jur.*, contrato.
COV.E.NANT.ED, *adj.*, respaldado por contrato.
COV.E.NANT.ER, *s.*, contratante.
COV.ER, *v.*, cobrir ou fazer reportagem, percorrer, revestir; *s.*, tampa.
COV.ER.AGE, *s.*, cobertura, informe.
COV.ER.ALLS, *s. pl., US* macacão.
COV.ER CHARGE, *s.*, taxa de *couvert* em restaurantes.
COV.ER GIRL, *s.*, garota da capa de revista.
COV.ER.ING, *s.*, cobertura, coberta; capa (vestuário); *fig.*,

COVERLESS ··426·· CREEK

pretexto.
COV.ER.LESS, *adj.*, descoberto.
COV.ER OVER, *v.*, cobrir.
COV.ERT, *adj.*, abrigado; secreto, oculto; dissimulado; *s.*, abrigo.
COV.ER-UP, *s.*, encobrimento (da verdade), disfarce.
COV.ET, *v.*, cobiçar.
COV.E.TOUS, *adj.*, ambicioso, ganancioso.
COW, *s.*, vaca; fêmea de animal.
COW.ARD, *adj.*, covarde, cobarde.
COW.ARD.ICE, *s.*, covardia.
COW.ARD.LY, *adv.*, covardemente.
COW.BOY, *s.*, vaqueiro, peão, boiadeiro.
COW.ER, *v.*, encolher-se de medo; esconder-se.
COW.HERD, *s.*, vaqueiro.
COW.HIDE, *s.*, couro bovino, relho.
COWL.NECK, *s.*, gola drapeada; capuz.
CO-WORK.ER, *s.*, colega de trabalho; colaborador.
COW.PAT, *s.*, *col.*, estrume de vaca.
COW.SHED, *s.*, estábulo.
COX, *s.*, *col.*, o mesmo que *coxswain.*
COX.SWAIN, *s.*, *Náut.*, timoneiro; mestre de embarcação.
COY, *adj.*, tímido, envergonhado; *v.*, envergonhar-se.
COY.LY, *adv.*, recatadamente, timidamente.
COY.NESS, *s.*, timidez, modéstia.
COY.OTE, *s.*, coiote.
CPU, *s.*, *Inform.*, *abrev.* de *Central Processing Unit* (Unidade Central de Processamento).
CRAB, *s.*, caranguejo, siri; *v.*, criticar, rebaixar, arranhar, ferir.
CRAB.BED, *adj.*, de mau humor.
CRACK, *s.*, rachadura, brecha; *v.*, quebrar, rachar, partir.
CRACK.DOWN, *s.*, endurecimento (na lei, em relação a algo).
CRACK.ED, *adj.*, rachado, quebrado; *col.*, doido.
CRACK.ER, *s.*, biscoito.
CRACK.ERS, *adj.*, *UK* doido.
CRACK.ING, *s.*, estalo, ruído de rachadura.
CRACK.LE, *v.*, estalar, crepitar.
CRACK.LING, *s.*, crepitação.
CRACK.POT, *s.*, excêntrivo; *adj.*, maluco.
CRA.DLE, *s.*, berço; *v.*, pôr no berço.
CRAFT, *s.*, arte, ofício.
CRAFT.I.LY, *adv.*, astuciosamente.
CRAFT.I.NESS, *s.*, astifício, astúcia.
CRAFTS.MAN, *s.*, artesão, artífice.
CRAFTS.MAN.SHIP, *s.*, habilidade, destreza, perícia.
CRAFTS.WOM.AN, *s.*, artesã.
CRAFT.Y, *adj.*, astuto, esperto, sagaz, vivo.
CRAG, *s.*, penhasco, rochedo.
CRAG.GY, *adj.*, penhasco, escarpado; traços fortes (no rosto).
CRAGS.MAN, *s.*, montanhista, alpinista.
CRAM, *s.*, empanturramento; abarrotamento; *v.*, abarrotar; fartar-se; forçar; *col.*, estudar muito.
CRAMP, *s.*, cãibra.
CRAMPED, *adj.*, apertado, restrito; relatico a espasmo de câimbras.
CRAM.PON, *s.*, gancho de ferro; ponta, ponteira.
CRAN.BER.RY, *s.*, *Bot.*, mirtilo; uva-do-monte; oxicoco.
CRANE, *s.*, guindaste; *v.*, alçar com guindaste.
CRA.NI.UM, *s.*, crânio.
CRANK, *s.*, manivela.
CRANK.SHAFT, *s.*, virabrequim.

CRANK.Y, *adj.*, excêntrico, débil.
CRAN.NY, *s.*, fenda, fissura; rachadura.
CRAPE, *s.*, crepe.
CRAP.PY, *adj.*, *col.*, de péssima qualidade.
CRAPS, *s.*, *US* jogo de dados.
CRA.PUL.ENCE, *s.*, crapulice, embriaguez.
CRASH, *s.*, choque, batida de carros; estrondo, desastre, falência.
CRASH-LAND, *v.*, aterrissar forçosamente.
CRASH LAND.ING, *s.*, aterrissagem forçada.
CRA.SIS, *s.*, crase.
CRASS, *adj.*, grosseiro.
CRASS.NESS, *s.*, grosseria, estupidez.
CRATE, *s.*, engraçado; caixote; *v.*, encaixotar.
CRA.TER, *s.*, cratera.
CRA.VAT, *s.*, gravata.
CRAVE, *v.*, ansiar; almejar.
CRAV.EN, *s.* e *adj.*, covarde.
CRAV.EN.NESS, *s.*, covardia.
CRAV.ER, *s.*, suplicante, requerente.
CRAV.ING, *s.*, desejo ardente, súplica.
CRAW, *s.*, papo de aves.
CRAWL, *v.*, arrastar-se, engatinhar como nenê, andar muito devagar.
CRAY.FISH, *s.*, *Zool.*, lagostim; camarão-d'água-doce.
CRAY.ON, *s.*, lápis de cera; *v.*, desenhar com lápis de cera.
CRAZE, *s.*, moda; loucura.
CRAZED, *adj.*, enlouquecido, demente.
CRA.ZI.NESS, *s.*, loucura, demência, desvario.
CRA.ZY, *adj.*, louco, doido, maluco, desvairado.
CREAK, *s.*, rangido; *v.*, ranger.
CREAK.Y, *adj.*, que range.
CREAM, *s.*, creme, nata; *v.*, desnatar, transformar alimentos em purê.
CREAM CRACKER, *s.*, *UK* bolacha ou biscoito (de água e sal).
CREAMY, *adj.*, cremoso, cor de creme.
CREASE, *s.*, ruga, dobra; *v.*, dobrar, enrugar.
CREASED, *adj.*, amarrotado, amassado, franzido.
CRE.ATE, *v.*, criar, produzir.
CRE.A.TION, *s.*, criação.
CRE.A.TIVE, *adj.*, criativo.
CRE.A.TIV.I.TY, *s.*, criatividade.
CRE.A.TOR, *s.*, criador, inventor.
CREA.TURE, *s.*, criatura, ser, vivente, ente, animal.
CRE.DENCE, *s.*, crédito, fé.
CRE.DEN.TIALS, *s. pl.*, credenciais.
CRED.I.BIL.I.TY, *s.*, credibilidade.
CRED.I.BLE, *adj.*, crível.
CRED.IT, *s.*, crédito, mérito; acreditar, crer.
CRED.IT.A.BLE, *adj.*, louvável, honroso.
CRED.IT AC.COUNT, *s.*, *UK* conta de crédito.
CRED.IT CARD, *s.*, cartão de crédito.
CRED.IT LIM.IT *UK*, **CRED.IT LINE** *US*, *s.*, limite de crédito.
CRED.I.TOR, *s.*, credor.
CRED.IT TRANS.FER, *s.*, transferência bancária.
CRED.IT.WOR.THY, *adj.*, digno de crédito.
CRE.DU.LI.TY, *s.*, credulidade.
CRED.U.LOUS, *adj.*, crédulo.
CREED, *s.*, credo.
CREEK, *s.*, *US* riाccho; *UK* enseada.

CREEP — 427 — CROW

CREEP, v., deslizar.
CREEP.ER, s., trepadeira.
CREEP.Y, adj., medroso; horripilante.
CRE.MATE, v., cremar.
CRE.MA.TION, s., cremação.
CRE.MA.TO.RY, adj., s., crematório.
CREN.EL, s., ameia; seteira.
CREPE, s., crepe.
CREP.I.TANT, adj., crepitante.
CREP.I.TATE, v., crepitar.
CREP.I.TA.TION, s., crepitação.
CRE.PUS.CU.LAR, adj., crepuscular.
CRE.PUS.CULE, s., crepúsculo.
CRES.CENT, s., crescente, meia-lua.
CRESS, s., agrião.
CREST, s., crista; penacho; topete; cume; Her., brasão.
CREST.FAL.LEN, adj., desanimado.
CREST.ING, s., Arq., balaustrada.
CRE.TIN, adj., s., cretino, idiota.
CRE.TIN.ISM, s., cretinismo, idiotismo.
CRE.VASSE, s., fenda (de geleira), fissura.
CREV.ICE, s., rachadura, fenda, fissura.
CREW, s., tripulação (navio, avião); col., bando.
CREW.MAN, s., tripulante; membro da equipe.
CRIB, s., berço, manjedoura; v., copiar, plagiar, furtar.
CRIB.BER, s., plagiador.
CRICK, s., cãibra.
CRICK.ET, s., grilo, críquete, banquinho de madeira.
CRICK.ETER, s., jogador de críquete.
CRI.ER, s., leiloeiro; gritador, pregoeiro.
CRIME, s., crime, delito.
CRIM.I.NAL, s., criminoso; adj., criminal.
CRIM.I.NAL.I.TY, s., criminalidade.
CRIM.I.NAL.I.ZE, v., criminalizar.
CRIM.I.NAL LAW, s., Jur., direito penal.
CRIM.I.NAL LAW.YER, s., Jur., criminalista.
CRIM.I.NATE, v., incriminar, acusar.
CRIM.I.NOL.O.GIST, s., criminologista.
CRIM.I.NOL.O.GY, s., criminologia.
CRIMP, s., ondulação; ruga; dobra, prega; v., ondular; enrugar; dobrar; amassar.
CRIM.PLE, s., aleijado, paralítico; coxo; v., mutilar, aleijar.
CRIM.PLED, adj., enrugado, ondulado, amassado.
CRIM.SON, adj., carmesim; s., a cor carmesim, vermelho.
CRINGE, s., bajulação, servilismo; v., encolher-se, rebaixar-se, bajular.
CRING.ER, s., bajulador, servil.
CRIN.KLE, s., ruga; ondulação; v., enrugar(-se); encrespar(-se).
CRIP.PLE, s., aleijado; v., aleijar.
CRIP.PLING, adj., Med., incapacitante; paralisante; devastador.
CRI.SIS, s., crise.
CRISP, adj., crespo, enrugado; crocante; quebradiço; viçoso.
CRISP.BREAD, s., biscoito de centeio (para dieta).
CRISP.Y, adj., crocante, quebradiço; encrespado.
CRISS-CROSS, adj., cruzado, xadrez; v., entrecruzar-se.
CRI.TE.RI.ON, s., critério.
CRIT.IC, adj., crítico.
CRIT.I.CAL, adj., crítico; grave (situação).
CRIT.I.CAL.LY, adv., criticamente, gravemente; criteriosamente.

CRIT.I.CISM, s., crítica.
CRIT.I.CIZE, v., criticar.
CRI.TIQUE, s., crítica (comentário ou artigo).
CROAK, v., coaxar.
CRO.CHET, s., crochê; v., fazer crochê.
CROCK.ER.Y, s., louça de barro.
CROC.O.DILE, s., crocodilo.
CROC.O.DIL.I.AN, s., Zool., crocodiliano (espécime dos crocodilianos); adj., referente aos crocodilianos.
CRO.CUS, s., açafrão.
CROFT, s., UK sítio; chácara.
CROIS.SANT, s., Fr., pãozinho enrolado em forma de meia-lua.
CROOK, s., gancho, curva, curvatura; vigarista; v., curvar, perverter.
CROOK.ED, adj., arqueado; tortuoso; col., desonesto; adv., desonestamente.
CROON, s., UK canto monótono; v., cantarolar.
CROP, s., colheita, safra; v., plantar, semear, colher.
CROP.PER, s., tombo, queda; fracasso; cultivador; meeiro.
CRO.QUET, s., croqué (jogo de campo).
CRO.QUETTE, s., croquete.
CROSS, s., cruz, cruzamento; v., cruzar, atravessar.
CROSS.BAR, s., trave (do gol); barra transversal (bicicleta).
CROSS.BONES, s pl., dois ossos cruzados sob uma caveira.
CROSS.BOW, s., Mil., besta (arma medieval).
CROSS.BREED, s., híbrido, cruza (animais).
CROSS-CHECK, v., conferir com cruzamento de dados.
CROSS CUL.TU.RAL, adj., intercultural.
CROSS-DRESS, v., vestir-se de mulher (o homem) ou de homem (a mulher).
CROSSED LINE, s., linha cruzada.
CROSS-EYED, s., estrabismo.
CROSS-FER.TIL.IZE, v., fecundar por cruzamento.
CROSS FIRE, s., fogo cruzado.
CROSS.ING, s., cruzamento; encruzilhada; faixa de segurança; travessia.
CROSS-LEGGED, adj., de pernas criuzadas.
CROSS.LY, adv., com irritação.
CROSS.NESS, s., mau humor.
CROSS-PUR.POSES, s. pl., mal-entendido.
CROSS-QUES.TION, s., interrogatório cruzado; v., inquirir novamente.
CROSS-REF.ER, v., remeter; fazer referência (cruzada).
CROSS-REF.ER.ENCE, s., referência cruzada.
CROSS.ROADS, s., cruzamento, trevo.
CROSS-SEC.TION, s., corte transversal; grupo ou amostra representativa.
CROSS.WALK, s., US faixa de segurança para pedestres.
CROSS.WAYS, adv., o mesmo que crosswise.
CROSS WIND, s., vento lateral.
CROSS.WISE, adv., transversalmente, em diagonal.
CROSS.WORD, s., palavras cruzadas.
CROTCH.ET, s., mania; capricho; Mús., semínima.
CROTCH.ETY, adj., rabugento.
CROTCH.ET.I.NESS, s., excentricidade.
CROUCH, s., agachamento; humilhação; v., curvar-se; armar o bote (animal).
CROUP, s., crupe; garupa.
CROU.PI.ER, s., Fr., crupiê.
CROW, s., corvo.

CROWBAR ··428·· CUMULATIVE

CROW.BAR, *s.*, pé de cabra.
CROWD, *s.*, multidão; grupo, turma; *v.*, aglomerar(-se); lotar; empurrar.
CROWD.ED, *adj.*, lotado, repleto.
CROWN, *s.*, coroa, topo, cimo.
CROWN COURT, *s.*, tribunal com júri.
CROWNED, *adj.*, coroado, real; que tem crista.
CROWN.ING, *adj.*, supremo, glorioso; *s.*, coroamento.
CROWN PRINCE, *s.*, príncipe herdeiro.
CROW'S FEET, *s. pl.*, pés de galinha.
CRU.CIAL, *adj.*, crucial, vital.
CRU.CIAL.LY, *adv.*, crucialmente.
CRU.CI.BLE, *s.*, *Quím.*, cadinho, crisol.
CRU.CI.FIED, *adj.*, crucificado; *fig.*, atormentado.
CRU.CI.FIX, *s.*, crucifixo.
CRU.CI.FIX.ION, *s.*, crucificação; grande sofrimento, provação.
CRU.CI.FY, *v.*, crucificar, afligir, atormentar.
CRUDE, *adj.*, bruto, duro; grosseiro.
CRUDE.LY, *adv.*, cruamente, grosseiramente.
CRU.DI.TY, *s.*, crueza.
CRU.EL, *adj.*, cruel.
CRU.EL.LY, *adv.*, cruelmente, brutalmente.
CRU.EL.TY, *s.*, crueldade.
CRUET, *s.*, galheta.
CRUISE, *s.*, cruzeiro; *v.*, fazer um cruzeiro.
CRUIS.ER, *s.*, *Náut.*, cruzador.
CRUIS.ER.WEIGHT, *s.*, *Esp.*, peso meio-pesado (boxe).
CRUMB, *s.*, migalha (comida, pão); pedacinho, fragmento.
CRUM.BLE, *s.*, tipo de doce de frutas cozido ao forno; *v.*, esmigalhar(-se); desmoronar.
CRUM.BLY, *adj.*, farelento, friável.
CRUM.MY, *adj.*, *col.*, sem valor, fajuto.
CRUM.PET, *s.*, bolo fino assado; *UK col.*, mulher atraente, gostosa.
CRUIS.ING, *s.*, cruzeiro.
CRUM.PLE, *v.*, amassar, amarrotar.
CRUNCH, *v.*, mastigar, morder, esmagar.
CRUNCHY, *adj.*, crocante.
CRU.SADE, *s.*, cruzada; campanha obstinada (contra ou a favor de algo); *v.*, fazer campanha ou cruzada.
CRU.SA.DER, *s.*, *Hist.*, cruzado; cavaleiro das cruzadas.
CRUSH, *s.*, esmagamento, compressão; *v.*, esmagar, espremer.
CRUSH.ER, *s.*, esmagador, compressor.
CRUSH.ING, *adj.*, esmagador.
CRUST, *s.*, crosta, côdea.
CRUS.TA.CEA, *s.*, crustáceos.
CRUST.Y, *adj.*, coberto de crosta.
CRUTCH, *s.*, muleta.
CRUX, *s.*, ponto crucial.
CRY, *s.*, grito, *v.*, gritar.
CRY-BA.BY, *s.*, *col.*, chorão.
CRY.ING, *s.*, grito, berro, choro.
CRY.O.GEN.IC, *adj.*, criogênico.
CRY.O.GENY, *s.*, *Fís.*, criogenia.
CRY OUT, *v.*, gritar.
CRYPT, *s.*, cripta.
CRYPTIC, *adj.*, enigmático, secreto, oculto.
CRYP.TO.GRAM, *s.*, criptograma.
CRYP.TOG.RA.PHY, *s.*, criptografia.

CRYS.TAL, *s.*, cristal.
CRYS.TAL-CLEAR, *adj.*, claro como cristal, transparente.
CRYS.TAL.LINE, *adj.*, cristalino.
CRYS.TAL.LI.ZA.TION, *v.*, cristalização.
CRYS.TAL.LIZE, *v.*, cristalizar.
CRYS.TAL.LOG.RA.PHY, *s.*, cristalografia.
CUB, *s.*, filhote, cria; *v.*, dar à luz, parir.
CUB.AGE, *s.*, cubagem; volume.
CU.BAN, *s.* e *adj.*, que é ou natural ou habitante de Cuba; cubano.
CUB.BISH, *adj.*, desajeitado.
CUB.BY, *s.*, cubículo.
CUB.BY.HOLE, *s.*, o mesmo que *cubby*.
CUBE, *s.*, cubo.
CUBE ROOT, *s.*, *Mat.*, raíz cúbica.
CU.BIC, *adj.*, cúbico.
CU.BI.CLE, *s.*, cubículo.
CUB.ISM, *s.*, *Art.*, cubismo.
CUB.IST, *s.*, *Art.*, cubista.
CUB SCOUT, *s.*, lobinho (escoteiro mirim).
CUCK.OO, *s.*, cuco.
CUCK.OO CLOCK, *s.*, relógio cuco.
CU.CUM.BER, *s.*, pepino.
CUD, *s.*, bolo alimentar dos ruminantes; *v.*, ruminar; *fig.*, meditar.
CUD.DLE, *s.*, abraço; *v.*, abraçar(-se); afagar.
CUD.DLY, *adj.*, mimoso.
CUD.DLY TOY, *s.*, brinquedo de pelúcia.
CUD.GEL, *s.*, cacete, bastão; *v.*, bater com cacete, bastonar.
CUE, *s.*, sugestão, palpite; taco de bilhar, trança; *fig.*, sinal; *v.*, dar sugestão ou palpite; entrançar.
CUFF, *s.*, punho.
CUFF LINK, *s.*, abotoadura.
CUI.SINE, *s.*, culinária, arte de cozer.
CUL-DE-SAC, *s.*, *Fr.*, beco sem saída.
CU.LI.NARY, *adj.*, culinário.
CUL.LEN.DER, *s.*, coador, peneira.
CULL, *s.*, refugo; selecionar, separar; extermínio (de animais); *v.*, abater, exterminar (animais).
CUL.MI.NATE, *v.*, culminar.
CUL.MI.NA.TION, *s.*, culminação, auge, conclusão, término.
CU.LOTTES, *s. pl.*, culote, saia-calça.
CUL.PA.BIL.I.TY, *s.*, culpabilidade.
CUL.PA.BLE, *adj.*, culpável.
CUL.PRIT, *s.*, culpado; acusado.
CULT, *s.*, culto.
CUL.TIC, *adj.*, de culto.
CUL.TI.VA.BLE, *adj.*, cultivável.
CUL.TI.VATE, *v.*, cultivar.
CUL.TI.VAT.ED, *adj.*, culto; refinado; cultivado (o solo).
CUL.TI.VA.TION, *s.*, cultivo.
CUL.TUR.AL, *adj.*, cultural.
CUL.TURE, *s.*, cultura.
CUL.TURED, *adj.*, culto; refinado; civilizado; cultivado.
CUL.VERT, *s.*, bueiro.
CUM.BER, *v.*, obstruir, impedir; *s.*, impedimento; obstáculo.
CUM.IN, *s.*, *Bot.*, cominho.
CU.MU.LATE, *v.*, acumular, amontoar; *adj.*, acumulado, amontoado.
CU.MU.LA.TION, *s.*, acumulação.
CU.MU.LA.TIVE, *adj.*, cumulativo.

CUNNING ···429··· CYST

CUN.NING, s., esperteza, astúcia; adj., esperto, malandro.
CUP, s., chávena, taça.
CUP.BOARD, s., armário, guarda-louças.
CUP.CAKE, s., bolinho assado coberto com glacê.
CUP HOLD.ER, s., Esp., atual campeão de campeonato.
CU.PID, s., fig., cupido; Mit., Cupido (Cupid).
CU.PID.I.TY, s., cupidez, cobiça, ganância.
CU.PO.LA, s., Arq., cúpula.
CUP TIE, s., UK jogo eliminatório.
CUR.ABIL.I.TY, s., curabilidade.
CUR.A.BLE, adj., curável.
CU.RATE, s., cura; coadjutor, pároco auxiliar.
CU.RA.TIVE, adj., s., curativo.
CU.RA.TOR, s., Jur., curador, tutor; conservador (de museu).
CURB, s., controle; restrição; meio-fio; v., controlar; pôr freio.
CURD, s., coalhada, ricota, requeijão; v., coalhar.
CURD CHEESE, s., UK requeijão.
CUR.DLE, v., coalhar (leite); coagular (sangue).
CURE, s., cura, tratamento; v., curar.
CURE-ALL, s., panaceia.
CUR.FEW, s., toque de recolher; toque de sino à noite.
CUR.RING, s., processo de salgar, de curar, de defumar.
CU.RI.OS.I.TY, s., curiosidade, raridade; adj., raro.
CU.RI.OUS, adj., curioso, intrometido.
CU.RI.OUSLY, adv., curiosamente.
CURL, s., cacho, onda (de fumaça); v., encrespar, encara-colar; enrolar.
CURL.ER, s., rolo; enrolador de cabelo; jogador de curling.
CURL.ING, s., encrespamento; adj., encaracolado; Esp., jogo escocês no gelo.
CURL.Y, adj., encaracolado, ondulado.
CUR.RANT, s., groselha; Bot., groselheira; UK uva-passa.
CUR.REN.CY, s., moeda corrente; uso geral; circulação.
CUR.RENT, s., corrente, torrente; adj., atual, corrente, conhecido.
CUR.RENT AC.COUNT, s., Com., conta corrente.
CUR.RENT.LY, adj., atualmente, correntemente.
CUR.RIC.U.LAR, adj., curricular.
CUR.RIC.U.LUM, s., curriculum vitae; programa, roteiro.
CUR.RIC.U.LUM VITAE, s., Lat., curriculum vitae; currículo.
CUR.RI.ER.Y, s., curtume; curtidor.
CUR.RISH, adj., rude, ordinário; desprezível.
CUR.RISH.NESS, s., grosseria, brutalidade, rudeza.
CUR.RY, s., caril (condimento); v., esfregar um cavalo; fig., surrar (alguém).
CURSE, s., maldição, praga; desgraça; v., maldizer, xingar.
CURS.ED, adj., maldito, abominável; detestável.
CURS.ED.LY, adj., abominavelmente, detestavelmente.
CURS.ING, s., blasfêmia; xingamento.
CUR.SIVE, adj., cursivo.
CUR.SOR, s., cursor.
CUR.SO.RI.LY, adv., apressadamente, superficialmente.
CUR.SO.RY, adj., apressado, sem atenção.
CURT, adj., seco, brusco, ríspido; breve.
CUR.TAIN, s., cortina; v., cobrir com cortina.
CUR.TAIL, v., encurtar; resuzir.
CUR.TAIL.MENT, s., redução, restrição.
CURT.SY, s., reverência; v., reverenciar; respeitar.
CUR.VA.CEOUS, adj., cheia de curvas (mulher).
CUR.VA.TURE, s., curvatura.
CURVE, v., curvar, encurvar; s., curva.

CURVED, adj., curvo, curvado.
CUSH.ION, s., almopfada; amortecedor; v., almofadar; amortecer.
CUSH.Y, adj., col., mole, fácil; confortável.
CUSS, s., maldição.
CUSS.ED, adj., amaldiçoado, desgraçado.
CUS.TARD, s., nata, creme.
CUS.TO.DI.AL, adj., custódio.
CUS.TODI.AN, s., guarda; zelador.
CUS.TO.DY, s., custódia; proteção.
CUS.TOM, s., costume, tradição, hábito.
CUS.TOM.ARY, adj., costumeiro.
CUS.TOM-BUILT, adj., personalizado; feito sob encomenda.
CUS.TOM.ER, s., cliente.
CUS.TOM-MADE, adj., feito sob encomenda.
CUS.TOMS, s., alfândega.
CUS.TOMS OF.FICER, s., fiscal de alfândega.
CUT, s., corte, redução, v., cortar, reduzir.
CUT AND PASTE, v., Inform., recortar e colar.
CU.TA.NE.OUS, adj., cutâneo.
CUTE, adj., fofo, bonitinho, gracioso.
CUT GLASS, s., vidro lapidado.
CU.TI.CLE, s., cutícula.
CU.TIS, s., cútis, epiderme.
CUT.LASS, s., alfanje.
CUT.LER, s., cuteleiro.
CUT.LER.Y, s., talheres; cutelaria.
CUT.LET, s., costeleta (iguaria).
CUT-OFF, s., UK prazo, limite.
CUT.OFF, s., US atalho, picada.
CUT.OUT, s., desenho para recortar; disjuntor.
CUT-PRICE, s., preço reduzido.
CUT.TER, s., cortador; Cin., editor.
CUT.TING, adj., mordaz; s., corte; talho; roçada; redução de gastos.
CUT.UP, s., col., US indivíduo espalhafatoso.
CUT UP, adj., UK col., chateado.
CY.A.NIDE, s., Quím., cianeto, cianureto.
CY.BER.NE.TICS, s., cibernética.
CY.BER.SPACE, s., Inform., ciberespaço (internet).
CY.CLE, s., ciclo, bicicleta; v., andar de bicicleta.
CY.CLIC, adj., cíclico.
CY.CLING, s., ciclismo.
CY.CLING HEL.MET, s., capacete de ciclismo.
CY.CLIST, s., ciclista.
CYL.IN.DER, s., cilindro.
CY.CLONE, s., ciclone.
CYG.NET, s., filhote de cisne.
CY.LIN.DRIC, adj., o mesmo que cylindrical.
CY.LIN.DRI.CAL, adj., cilíndrico.
CY.MA, s., cimalha.
CYM.BALS, s. pl., Mús., címbalos, pratos.
CYN.IC, adj., cínico; céptico.
CYN.I.CAL, adj., cínico; céptico.
CYN.I.CAL.LY, adv., cinicamente; cepticamente.
CYN.I.CISM, s., cinismo.
CY.PHER, s., o mesmo que cipher.
CY.PRESS, s., Bot., cipreste.
CYP.RIAN, s. e adj., natural ou habitante de Chipre, cipriota.
CYP.RI.OT, s., o mesmo que Cyprian.
CYST, s., cisto.

CYSTIC

CYST.IC, *adj.*, cístico.
CYST.IC FI.BRO.SIS, *s., Med.*, fibrose cística.
CYS.TI.TIS, *s., Med.*, cistite.
CY.TOL.O.GY, *s.*, citologia.

CZECHOSLOVAK

CZAR, *s.*, czar.
CZECH, *s. e adj.*, natural ou habitante da República Tcheca, tcheco.
CZECH.O.SLO.VAK, *s.*, checoslovaco.

D

D, *s.*, quarta letra do alfabeto inglês; algarismo romano 500 (D).
DAB, *s.*, toque leve, palmadinha; *v.*, tocar de leve.
DAB.BLE, *v.*, agitar a água, chapinhar; salpicar; borrifar.
DAB.STER, *s.*, esperto, finório, esperto.
DACHS.HUND, *s.*, dachshund (raça de cão).
DAD, *s.*, papai, papá.
DAD.DY, *s.*, papai.
DAD.DY LONG.LEGS, *s.*, pernilongo.
DAF.FO.DIL, *s., Bot.*, narciso.
DAFT, *adj., Bot.*, imbecil, tolo, idiota, cretino.
DAFT.NESS, *s.*, tolice, imbecilidade, cretinice.
DAG.GER, *s.*, punhal, adaga, arma branca.
DAHL.IA, *s., Bot.*, dália.
DAI.LY, *adj.*, diário, cotidiano; *s.*, jornal, diário; *adv.*, diariamente.
DAI.LY RATE, *s.*, diária de hotel.
DAIN.TI.LY, *adv.*, delicadamente.
DAIN.TI.NESS, *s.*, delicadeza, finura, polidez; iguaria.
DAIN.TY, *s.*, iguaria fina, gulodice; *adj.*, delicado, delicioso, gracioso.
DAIRY, *s.*, fábrica de laticínios, leiteria.
DAI.RY CAT.TLE, *s.*, gado leiteiro.
DAI.RY FARM, *s.*, fazenda de gado leiteiro.
DAI.RY PROD.UCTS, *s. pl.*, laticínios.
DA.IS, *s.*, estrado.
DAI.SY, *s.*, margarida, bonina.
DALE, *s., Lit.*, vale.
DAL.LI.ER, *s.*, brincalhão, galhofeiro.
DAL.MA.TIAN, *s.*, dálmata (raça de cão).
DAM, *s.*, dique, represa, barragem; *v.*, represar, impedir, segurar.
DA.MA.GE, *s.*, dano, prejuízo, perda; *v.*, prejudicar, danificar, estragar.
DAM.AGES, *s. pl., Jur.*, danos, indenização.
DAM.AGED, *s.*, prejudicado, danificado, avariado.
DAM.AG.ING, *adj.*, prejudicial, danoso.
DAME, *s.*, senhora, dama, dona de casa.
DAMN, *v.*, condenar, censurar; blasfemar; *s.*, maldição; *adj., col.*, maldito.
DAM.NA.BLE, *adj.*, danável, condenável.
DAM.NA.TION, *s., Rel.*, maldição, condenação, danação.
DAMNED, *adj.*, maldito, danado; *s.*, os que foram condenados ao inferno.
DAM.NI.FY, *v.*, prejudicar, danificar, avariar.
DAMN.ING, *adj.*, condenatório.
DAMP, *s.*, umidade, abatimento; *v.*, umedecer, desanimar.
DAMP.EN, *v.*, umedecer, molhar.
DAMP.ER, *s.*, abafador, amortecedor.
DAMP.NESS, *s.*, umidade.
DAM.SEL, *s.*, moça, garota, donzela.
DANCE, *s.*, dança, baile; *v.*, dançar.
DANCE FLOOR, *s.*, pista de dança.
DANCE HALL, *s.*, salão de baile.
DANC.ER, *s.*, bailarino, dançarino.
DAN.CING, *s.*, dança; *adj.*, dançante.
DAN.DE.LI.ON, *s., Bot.*, dente-de-leão, dandélio.
DAN.DLE, *v.*, embalar, acariciar, acarinhar.
DAN.DRUFF, *s.*, caspa.
DAN.DY, *s.*, dândi, janota.
DAN.DY FE.VER, *s., Med.*, dengue.
DANE, *adj., s.*, dinamarquês.
DAN.GER, *s.*, perigo.
DAN.GER.OUS, *adj.*, perigoso.
DAN.GER.OUS DRIV.ING, *s., Jur.*, direção perigosa.
DAN.GER.OUS.LY, *adv.*, perigosamente.
DAN.GER.OUS.NESS, *s.*, perigo, ameaça.
DAN.GLE, *v.*, balançar(-se), bambolear(-se); oscilar.
DAN.GLER, *s.*, galanteador, mulherengo; insistente.
DAN.ISH, *adj., s.*, dinamarquês.
DANK, *s.*, lugar úmido, umidade; *adj.*, úmido, molhado.
DAP.PER, *adj.*, garboso; esperto; ativo.
DAP.PLED, *adj.*, malhado, pintado.
DARE, *v.*, provocar, desafiar, ousar.
DARE.DEV.IL, *s.*, indivíduo intrépido; *adj.*, intrépido, valentão.
DAR.ING, *adj.*, audacioso, corajoso; *s.*, audácia, coragem, valentia.
DARK, *s.*, escuridão, noite, trevas; *adj.*, escuro, moreno; *v.*, escurecer.
DARK.EN, *v.*, escurecer, tornar escuro.
DARK.EN.ER, *s.*, escurecedor.
DARK GLASS.ES, *s. pl.*, óculos escuros.
DARK HORSE, *s., fig.*, alasão.
DARK.NESS, *s.*, escuridão; trevas, obscuridade.
DARK.ROOM, *s.*, câmara escura.
DARKY, *s.*, negro, preto, mulato.
DAR.LING, *adj., s.*, querido, querida.
DARN, *s.*, remendo; praga; *v.*, remendar; amaldiçoar; *adj.*, maldito; *excl.*, que droga!.
DAR.NEL, *s.*, joio.
DARN.ING, *s.*, cerzidura, remendo.
DART, *s.*, dardo, flecha; pence (costura).
DASH, *s.*, hífen, travessão, arremesso, choque; *v.*, arremessar, bater.
DASH.BOARD, *s.*, painel, quadro de instrumentos.
DASH.ING, *adj.*, atraente, elegante; espirituoso, vivo.
DAS.TARD.LY, *adj.*, cruel; covarde, pusilânime.
DA.TA, *s.*, dados, informes, detalhes.
DA.TA BANK, *s.*, banco de dados.
DA.TA.BASE, *s.*, base (ou banco) de dados.
DA.TA PROC.ES.SING, *s.*, processamento de dados.
DA.TA PROC.ES.SOR, *s.*, processador de dados.
DATE, *s.*, data, época, prazo; tâmara; *v.*, datar, marcar data, namorar.
DATE BACK, *v.*, ser datado em.

DATEBOOK   ···432···   DECAHEDRON

DATE.BOOK, *s., US* agenda.
DAT.ED, *adj.*, antiquado.
DA.TIVE, *adj., s.*, dativo.
DAUB, *s.*, mancha, sujeira, borrão; *v.*, pintar grosseiramente; *fig.*, encobrir (faltas).
DAUGH.TER, *s.*, filha.
DAUGH.TER-IN-LAW, *s.*, nora.
DAUNT, *v.*, assustar, atemorizar.
DAV.EN.PORT, *s.*, escrivaninha.
DAW, *s.*, gralha; tipo imbecil.
DAW.DLE, *s.*, vadio, malandro; *v.*, vadiar, não fazer nada.
DAWN, *s.*, madrugada, alvorada, aurora; *v.*, amanhecer, raiar o dia.
DAWN.ING, *s.*, alvorada, amanhecer.
DAY, *s.*, dia, jornada.
DAY.BOOK, *s.*, diário.
DAY.BREAK, *s.*, amanhecer.
DAY.DREAM, *s.*, devaneio, sonho; *v.*, devanear, sonhar acordado.
DAY-DREAM.ER, *s.*, devaneador.
DAY.LIGHT, *s.*, luz do dia.
DAY NUR.SE.RY, *s.*, creche.
DAY OFF, *s.*, dia de folga.
DAY ROOM, *s.*, sala de estar.
DAY SCHOOL, *s.*, escolar diurna, externato.
DAY SHIFT, *s.*, turno de dia.
DAY-TIME, *s.*, dia (do nascer ao pôr do sol).
DAY-TO-DAY, *adj.*, cotidiano.
DAZE, *s.*, atordoamento; ofuscação; *v.*, atordoar.
DAZ.ZLE, *s.*, deslumbramento; *v.*, ofuscar, deslumbrar.
DAZ.ZLE.MENT, *s.*, deslumbramento.
DAZ.ZLING, *adj.*, ofuscante, fascinante.
D-DAY, *s., Mil.*, dia D.
DEA.CON, *s.*, diácono.
DEA.CON.ESS, *s.*, diaconisa.
DE.AC.TI.VATE, *v.*, desativar.
DEAD, *adj., s.*, morto, defunto, falecido.
DEAD-BEAT, *s., US* malandro, vadio.
DEAD.EN, *v.*, amortecer, abrandar; abafar; endurecer; matar.
DEAD.HEAD, *v.*, podar.
DEAD-HOUSE, *s.*, necrotério.
DEAD LET.TER, *s., fig.*, letra morta.
DEAD-LINE, *s.*, prazo final.
DEAD.LOCK, *s.*, impasse, paralisação, beco; *v.*, chegar a nada.
DEAD.LOCKED, *adj.*, paralisado (situação indefinida).
DEAD LOSS, *s.*, prejuízo total.
DEAD.LY, *adj.*, mortal, fatal, mortífero.
DEAD.PAN, *adj.*, inexpressivo (rosto); sem emoção.
DEAD TIME, *s.*, tempo ocioso.
DEAD WATER, *s.*, água parada.
DEAD.WOOD *US*, **DEAD WOOD** *UK*, *s.*, água parada.
DEAF, *adj.*, surdo.
DEAF-AID, *s., UK* aparelho de surdez.
DEAF.EN, *v.*, ensurdecer.
DEAF.EN.ING, *adj.*, ensurdecedor.
DEAF.EN.ING.LY, *adv.*, ensurdecedoramente.
DEAF-MUTE, *s.*, surdo-mudo.
DEAF.NESS, *s.*, surdez.
DEAL, *s.*, acordo, quantidade, porção; *v.*, negociar, fazer um acordo, jogar.

DEAL.ER, *s.*, negociante, comerciante; jogador que distribui as cartas.
DEAL.ER.SHIP, *s.*, revendedor.
DEAL.INGS, *s. pl.*, conduta; relações comerciais, negócios (com alguém).
DEAN, *s.*, reitor de universidade, deão, decano.
DEAR, *adj.*, querido, querida, caro; custoso, caro, dispendioso.
DEAR.LY, *adv.*, caro (de custo elevado); de muito apreço, ternamente, afetuosamente.
DEARTH, *s.*, carência, penúria, carestia, fome, escassez.
DE.AR.TIC.U.LATE, *v.*, desarticular.
DEAR.Y, *s.*, queridinho(a).
DEATH, *s.*, morte, óbito, falecimento.
DEATH-BED, *s.*, leito de morte; agonia derradeira.
DEATH CER.TIF.I.CATE, *s.*, certidão de óbito.
DEATH.LESS, *adj.*, imortal.
DEATH.LESS.NESS, *s.*, imortalidade, eternidade.
DEATH.LIKE, *adj.*, cadavérico.
DEATH.LY, *adj.*, mortal; *adv.*, mortalmente.
DEATH PEN.AL.TY, *s.*, pena de morte.
DEATH RATE, *s.*, índice de mortalidade.
DEATH ROW, *s.*, corredor da morte.
DEATH SEM.TENCE, *s., Jur.*, sentença de morte.
DEATHS.MAN, *s.*, carrasco.
DEB, *s., abrev.* de *debutant*.
DE.BALL, *v., vulg.*, castrar, capar.
DE.BAR, *v.*, privar de, excluir; impedir, proibir.
DE.BARK, *v.*, desembarcar.
DE.BAR.KA.TION, *s.*, desembarque.
DE.BASE, *v.*, degradar(-se) rebaixar, humilhar.
DE.BASE.MENT, *s.*, degradação.
DE.BATE, *s.*, debate, contenda; *v.*, debater.
DE.BAUCH, *s.*, deboche, escárnio; *v.*, debochar, escarnecer.
DE.BAUCH.ED, *adj.*, devasso, depravado.
DE.BAUCH.ERY, *s.*, deboche, depravação.
DE.BEN.TURE, *s.*, debênture, título de dívida.
DE.BIL.I.TATE, *v.*, debilitar, enfraquecer.
DE.BIL.I.TAT.ED, *adj.*, debilitado, enfraquecido.
DE.BIL.I.TAT.ING, *adj.*, enfraquecedor.
DE.BIL.I.TA.TION, *s.*, debilitação.
DE.BIL.I.TY, *s.*, debilidade, fraqueza.
DEB.IT, *s.*, débito, dívida; *v.*, debitar, lançar em dívida.
DEB.IT CARD, *s.*, cartão de crédito.
DEB.O.NAIR, *adj.*, garboso; afável, cortês.
DEB.O.NAIR.LY, *adv.*, afavelmente, garbosamente.
DEB.O.NAIR.NESS, *s.*, afabilidade, cortesia, garbo.
DE.BOUCH, *v.*, desembocar; sair, emergir.
DE.BOUCH.MENT, *s.*, desembocadura, saída.
DE.BRIEF, *v.*, interrogar (ao término de uma missão).
DE.BRIEF.ING, *s.*, relato após término de missão.
DE.BRIS, *s.*, ruínas, restos, escombros.
DEBT, *s.*, dívida, endividamento.
DEBT.OR, *s.*, devedor.
DÉ.BUT, *s.*, estreia.
DEB.U.TANT, **DEB.U.TANTE**, *s.*, debutante, estreante.
DE.CADE, *s.*, década.
DEC.A.DENCE, *s.*, decadência.
DEC.A.DENT, *adj., s.*, decadente.
DE.CAF.FE.IN.AT.ED COF.FEE, *s.*, café descafeinado.
DECA.GRAM, *s.*, decagrama.
DECA.HE.DRON, *s., Geom.*, decaedro.

DECALCIFICATION · 433 · DEEPEN

DE.CAL.CI.FI.CA.TION, *s.*, *Quím.*, descalcificação.
DE.CAL.CI.FY, *v.*, descalcificar.
DECA.LI.TRE, *s.*, decalitro.
DECA.LOGUE, *s.*, decálogo.
DE.CAMP, *v.*, decampar; escapar, safar(-se).
DE.CANT, *v.*, decantar, despejar.
DE.CANT.ER, *s.*, licoreira; vaso para decantar licores.
DECAPITALIZATION, *s.*, descapitalização.
DE.CAP.I.TAL.ISE(-IZE), *v.*, descapitalizar.
DE.CAP.I.TATE, *v.*, decapitar, degolar.
DE.CAP.I.TA.TION, *s.*, decapitação.
DEC.A.POD, *s.*, *Zool.*, decápode.
DECA.SYL.LAB.IC, *adj.*, decassílabo.
DE.CATH.LETE, *s.*, decatleta.
DE.CATH.LON, *s.*, *Esp.*, decatlo.
DE.CAY, *s.*, ruína, decadência, declínio; *v.*, decair, apodrecer, arruinar.
DE.CEASE, *s.*, desenlace, morte, óbito, falecimento; *v.*, morrer, falecer.
DE.CEASED, *s.*, morto, finado; *adj.*, falecido.
DE.CE.DENT, *s.*, *Jur.*, pessoa falecida.
DE.CEIT, *s.*, engano, fraude; falsidade, engodo.
DE.CEIT.FUL, *adj.*, enganoso.
DE.CEIT.FUL.NESS, *s.*, falsidade, aparência enganosa.
DE.CEIV.A.BIL.I.TY, *s.*, tapeação, logro; falha.
DE.CEIV.A.BLE, *adj.*, enganoso, falível.
DE.CEIVE, *v.*, enganar, lograr, ludibriar.
DE.CEIV.ER, *s.*, enganador, impostor.
DE.CEIV.ING.LY, *s.*, enganosamente, fraudulentamente.
DE.CEL.ER.ATE, *v.*, desacelerar.
DE.CEM.BER, *s.*, dezembro.
DE.CEN.CY, *s.*, decência, honradez, decoro.
DE.CEN.NA.RY, *s.*, decênio.
DE.CEN.NI.AL, *adj.*, decenal.
DE.CENT, *adj.*, decente, digno, honrado.
DE.CENT.LY, *adv.*, decentemente; razoavelmente.
DE.CENT.NESS, *s.*, decência, decoro.
DE.CEN.TRAL.IZA.TION, *s.*, descentralização.
DE.CEN.TRAL.IZE, *v.*, descentralizar.
DE.CEP.TI.BLE, *adj.*, iludível.
DE.CEP.TION, *s.*, decepção, fraude, engano.
DE.CEP.TIVE, *adj.*, ilusório, enganoso.
DE.CEP.TIVE.LY, *adv.*, enganosamente.
DEC.I.BEL, *s.*, decibel.
DE.CIDE, *v.*, decidir, resolver, solucionar; sentenciar, julgar.
DE.CID.ED, *adj.*, decidido, resolvido; evidente.
DE.CID.ED.LY, *adv.*, decididamente.
DE.CID.ING VOTE, *adj.*, voto de Minerva.
DE.CID.U.OUS, *adj.*, decíduo, efêmero, caduco.
DE.CID.U.OUS TOOTH, *s.*, dente de leite.
DECI.GRAM, *s.*, decigrama.
DEC.I.MAL, *adj.*, *s.*, decimal.
DEC.I.MAL SYS.TEM, *s.*, sistema decimal.
DEC.I.MATE, *v.*, dizimar, liquidar.
DE.CI.PHER, *v.*, decifrar, entender, explicar.
DE.CI.SION, *s.*, decisão, resolução, sentença.
DE.CI.SION-MAK.ING, *s.*, tomada de decisão.
DE.CI.SIVE, *adj.*, decisivo, resolutivo.
DE.CI.SIVE.LY, *adv.*, decisivamente, decididamente.
DE.CI.SIVE.NESS, *s.*, determinação.
DECK, *s.*, *Náut.*, convés, coberta de navio, tombadilho; *Arq.*, plataforma; *v.*, ornar, enfeitar; cobrir.
DECK-CHAIR, *s.*, espreguiçadeira.
DECKED, *adj.*, adornado, enfeitado.
DECK-HAND, *s.*, taifeiro, marujo.
DE.CLAIM, *v.*, recitar, declamar.
DE.CLAIM.ER, *s.*, declamador.
DEC.LA.MA.TION, *s.*, declamação.
DE.CLAM.A.TO.RY, *adj.*, declamatório, bombástico.
DE.CLAR.ANT, *s.*, *Jur.*, declarante.
DEC.LA.RA.TION, *s.*, declaração, dito, afirmação.
DEC.LA.RA.TIVE, *adj.*, declarativo.
DE.CLAR.A.TO.RY, *adj.*, declaratório, afirmativo.
DE.CLARE, *v.*, declarar, revelar, proclamar, afirmar, depor.
DE.CLARED, *adj.*, declarado, confessado.
DE.CLAS.SI.FY, *v.*, tornar público, revelar.
DEC.LI.NA.TION, *s.*, declinação, inclinação, descida, decadência.
DE.CLINE, *s.*, declínio; *v.*, declinar, recusar.
DE.CLINE, *s.*, declínio, diminuição; *v.*, diminuir, recusar.
DE.CLIV.I.TOUS, *adj.*, inclinado, ladeirento.
DE.CLIV.I.TY, *s.*, declive, declividade, inclinação, ladeira, descida.
DE.CODE, *v.*, decodificar.
DE.COD.ER, *s.*, decodificador.
DE.COL.LATE, *v.*, degolar, decapitar.
DE.COL.LA.TION, *s.*, degolação, decapitação.
DE.COL.O.NI.SA.TION, *s.*, descolonização.
DE.COL.OR.ANT, *s. e adj.*, descorante.
DE.COL.OR.ATE, *v.*, descolorir; *adj.*, descolorido.
DE.COM.POSE, *v.*, decompor.
DE.COM.POSITION, *s.*, decomposição.
DE.COM.POUND, *v.*, recompor.
DE.COM.PRES.SION, *s.*, descompressão.
DE.CON.GEST.ANT, *s.*, descongestionante.
DE.CON.TAM.I.NATE, *v.*, descontaminar.
DEC.O.RATE, *v.*, decorar, ornar, enfeitar.
DEC.O.ROUS, *adj.*, decoroso, honesto, sério.
DE.CO.RUM, *s.*, decoro.
DE.COY, *s.*, chamariz, isca; *v.*, atrair; apanhar pássaros.
DE.CREASE, *s.*, diminuição, decrescimento; *v.*, diminuir.
DE.CREAS.ING, *adj.*, decrescente.
DE.CREE, *s.*, decreto; sentença; edital; *v.*, decretar.
DE.CREP.IT, *adj.*, decrépito; caduco.
DE.CRES.CENT, *adj.*, decrescente.
DE.CRI.MI.NAL.I.SA.TION *UK*, **DE.CRI.MI.NAL.I.ZA.TION** *US*, *s.*, discriminalização.
DE.CRY, *v.*, censurar, advertir, admoestar.
DEC.U.PLE, *adj.*, *s.*, décuplo.
DED.I.CATE, *v.*, dedicar, oferecer.
DED.I.CAT.ED, *adj.*, dedicado.
DED.I.CA.TION, *s.*, dedicação, oferenda, dedicatória.
DE.DUCE, *v.*, deduzir, conjeturar, inferir.
DE.DU.CI.BLE, *adj.*, que se pode deduzir.
DE.DUCT, *v.*, deduzir, subtrair, diminuir.
DE.DUC.TION, *s.*, dedução, subtração, diminuição.
DEED, *s.*, ação, feito, proeza; *Jur.*, escritura; *v.*, transferir por escritura.
DEEM, *v.*, julgar, avaliar, estimar.
DEEM.STER, *s.*, juiz.
DEEP, *adj.*, fundo, profundo, baixo; *s.*, profundidade; abismo.
DEEP.EN, *v.*, afundar, aprofundar.

DEEPENING   •• 434 ••   DELAYED

DEEP.EN.ING, *adj.*, que se aprofunda (crise, recessão econômica).
DEEP FREEZE, *s.*, congelador, freezer.
DEEP-FRY, *v.*, fritar (algo) com muito óleo.
DEEPLY, *adv.*, profundamente.
DEEP-ROOT.ED, *adj.*, arraigado, enraizado.
DEEP-SEA, *s.*, mar profundo; *adj.*, submarino.
DEEP-SEAT.ED, *adj.*, profundamente arraigado, entranhado.
DEEP SLEEP, *s.*, sono profundo.
DEER, *s.*, *Zool.*, nome genérico para cervídeos (veado, cervo, gamo etc.).
DEER-STALKER, *s.*, chapéu de copa baixa, boné com abas.
DE-ESCALATE, *v.*, suavizar.
DE.FACE, *v.*, desfigurar, deformar.
DE.FACE.MENT, *s.*, desfiguração, mutilação.
DE.FAL.CA.TION, *s.*, desfalque.
DEF.A.MA.TION, *s.*, difamação, calúnia.
DEFAM.A.TO.RY, *adj.*, difamatório.
DE.FAME, *v.*, difamar, caluniar, desonrar.
DE.FAM.ER, *s.*, difamador, caluniador.
DE.FAULT, *s.*, falta, descuido, negligência; *v.*, negligenciar, estar ausente.
DE.FAULT.ER, *s.*, inadimplente.
DE.FAULT VAL.UE, *s.*, *Inform.*, valor padrão.
DE.FEAT, *s.*, derrota, revés, frustração; *v.*, derrotar, desbaratar.
DE.FEAT.ISM, *s.*, derrotismo.
DE.FEAT.IST, *s.* e *adj.*, derrotista.
DEF.E.CATE, *v.*, defecar.
DE.FECT, *s.*, defeito, deficiência, falha, vício.
DE.FEC.TION, *s.*, defecção, deserção.
DE.FEC.TIVE, *adj.*, defeituoso.
DE.FEC.TOR, *adj.*, desertor.
DE.FENCE *UK*, **DEFENSE** *US*, *s.*, defesa.
DE.FENCE.LESS *UK*, **DE.FENSE.LESS** *US*, *adj.*, indefeso, desamparado.
DE.FENCE.LESS.LY, *adv.*, indefensavelmente.
DE.FEND, *v.*, defender, preservar, amparar.
DE.FEND.ANT, *s.*, RÉU (também *fem.*: ré).
DE.FEN.DER, *s.*, defensor.
DE.FENSE *US*, *s.*, o mesmo que *defence UK.*
DE.FENSE.LESS *US*, *adj.*, o mesmo que *defenceless.*
DE.FEN.SI.BLE, *adj.*, defensível.
DE.FEN.SI.BLY, *adv.*, defensivamente, defensivelmente.
DE.FEN.SIVE, *adj.*, defensivo, receoso (alguém); *s.*, (na) defensiva (atitude).
DE.FEN.SIVE.LY, *adv.*, defensivamente.
DE.FER, *v.*, adiar, diferir, protelar.
DE.FER.A.BLE, *adj.*, adiável.
DEF.ER.ENCE, *s.*, deferência.
DEF.E.REN.TIAL, *adj.*, deferente.
DE.FI.ANCE, *s.*, desafio, provocação, rebeldia.
DE.FI.ANT, *adj.*, desafiador.
DE.FI.ANT.LY, *adv.*, desafiadoramente.
DE.FI.CIEN.CY, *s.*, deficiência, insuficiência, falta.
DE.FI.CIENT, *adj.*, deficiente, defeituoso, falho.
DEF.I.CIT, *s.*, déficit, deficiência, o que falta.
DE.FI.ER, *s.*, desafiador, desafiante.
DE.FILE, *s.*, desfiladeiro, garganta; *v.*, desonrar, corromper, manchar.
DE.FIN.A.BLE, *adj.*, definível.
DE.FINE, *v.*, definir.

DEF.I.NITE, *adj.*, definitivo, evidente, claro, determinado.
DEF.I.NITE.LY, *adv.*, definitivamente.
DEF.I.NITE.NESS, *s.*, limitação, precisão, certeza.
DEF.I.NI.TION, *s.*, definição.
DE.FIN.I.TIVE, *adj.*, definitivo, conclusivo, terminativo.
DEF.LA.GRATE, *v.*, deflagrar.
DEF.LA.GRA.TION, *s.*, deflagração.
DEF.LA.GRAT.OR, *s.*, deflagrador.
DE.FLATE, *v.*, esvaziar; *fig.*, diminuir, desanimar.
DE.FLA.TION, *s.*, esvaziamento; *Econ.*, deflação.
DE.FLA.TION.AR.Y, *adj.*, *Econ.*, deflacionário.
DE.FLECT, *v.*, desviar.
DE.FLEC.TION, *s.*, desvio, deflexão.
DE.FLEC.TIVE, *adj.*, flexível; refrativo.
DE.FLO.RA.TION, *s.*, defloração, violação, estupro.
DE.FLOW.ER, *v.*, deflorar, desflorar; violar.
DE.FO.LI.ANT, *s.*, desfolhante.
DE.FOR.EST, *v.*, desflorestar, desmatar.
DE.FOR.ES.TA.TION, *v.*, desflorestamento, desmatamento.
DE.FORM, *v.*, deformar, distorcer.
DE.FORM.A.BLE, *adj.*, deformável.
DE.FORMED, *adj.*, deformado, disforme.
DE.FOR.MA.TION, *s.*, deformação, distorção.
DE.FOR.MI.TY, *s.*, deformidade.
DE.FRAUD, *v.*, fraudar, trapacear, adulterar.
DE.FRAU.DA.TION, *s.*, defraudação, fraude, logro, trapaça.
DE.FRAY, *v.*, custear.
DE.FROST, *v.*, degelar, descongelar.
DEFT, *adj.*, destro, hábil, habilidoso, perito.
DEFT.LY, *adv.*, agilmente, primorosamente.
DEFT.NESS, *s.*, destreza, habilidade, primor.
DE.FUNCT, *adj.*, defunto, morto, extinto, falecido.
DE.FUSE, *v.*, desativar, neutralizar; *fig.*, acalmar
DE.FY, *v.*, desafiar, provocar.
DE.GEN.ER.ATE, *v.*, degenerar; *adj.*, degenerado.
DE.GEN.E.RA.TION, *s.*, degeneração.
DEG.RA.DATION, *s.*, degradação.
DE.GRADE, *v.*, degradar, aviltar, rebaixar, humilhar.
DE.GRAD.ED, *adj.*, degredado, infame.
DE.GRAD.ING, *adj.*, degradante.
DE.GREASE, *v.*, desengraxar.
DE.GREE, *s.*, título, diploma, degrau, grau.
DE.GUST, *v.*, degustar, provar.
DE.GUS.TA.TION, *s.*, degustação.
DE.HU.MAN.IZE(-ISE), *v.*, desumanizar, bestializar.
DE.HU.MID.I.FY, *v.*, desumedecer, desumidificar.
DE.HY.DRATE, *v.*, desidratar.
DE.HY.DRA.TION, *s.*, desidratação.
DE-ICE, *v.*, descongelar.
DEIC.TIC, *adj.*, demonstrativo, direto.
DE.IF.IC, *adj.*, deífico, divino.
DEIGN, *v.*, condescender; conceder.
DE.I.TY, *s.*, divindade.
DE.JECT, *v.*, desanimar, deprimir, abater.
DE.JECT.ED, *adj.*, abatido, desanimado.
DE.JEC.TION, *s.*, depressão, abatimento, desânimo.
DE.LATE, *v.*, delatar.
DE.LA.TION, *s.*, delatação.
DE.LA.TOR, *s.*, delator.
DE.LAY, *v.*, retardar, demorar, atrasar; *s.*, demora, atraso.
DE.LAY.ED, *adj.*, atrasado.

DELAYED-ACTION ··435·· DEMOTE

DE.LAYED-AC.TION, *adj.*, de ação retardada.
DE.LEC.TA.BLE, *adj.*, gostoso, deleitoso.
DE.LEC.TA.BLE.NESS, *s.*, deleite, prazer, gosto.
DE.LEC.TA.BLY, *adv.*, com deleite, deliciosamente.
DEL.E.GA.CY, *s.*, delegacia, delegação, representação.
DEL.E.GATE, *s.*, delegado; *v.*, delegar, autorizar.
DEL.E.GA.TION, *s.*, delegação, autorização, permissão.
DE.LETE, *v.*, deletar, apagar, extinguir, eliminar.
DEL.E.TE.RI.OUS, *adj.*, deletério, danoso.
DEL.E.TE.RI.OUS.LY, *adv.*, nocivamente, perniciosamente.
DE.LE.TION, *s.*, exclusão, anulação.
DE.LIB.ER.ATE, *v.*, deliberar, considerar; *adj.*, intencional, ponderado.
DE.LIB.ER.ATE.LY, *adv.*, deliberadamente.
DE.LIB.ER.ATE.NESS, *s.*, propósito, intenção, cautela.
DE.LIB.ER.A.TION, *s.*, deliberação, consideração, decisão.
DE.LIB.ER.A.TIVE, *adj.*, deliberativo, deliberante.
DEL.I.CA.CY, *s.*, delicadeza, gentileza, sensibilidade; guloseima.
DEL.I.CATE, *adj.*, delicado, cortês, gentil, sensível.
DEL.I.CATE.LY, *adv.*, delicadamente, suavemente.
DEL.I.CATE.NESS, *s.*, delicadeza, fragilidade.
DEL.I.CATES.SEN, *s.*, delicatessem (mercearia fina).
DE.LI.CIOUS, *adj.*, delicioso, gostoso, saboroso.
DE.LI.CIOUS.LY, *adv.*, deliciosamente.
DE.LI.CIOUS.NESS, *s.*, delícia, prazer, deleite, gostosura.
DEL.ICT, *s.*, delito, crime, culpa.
DE.LIGHT, *s.*, prazer, deleite, maravilha, delícia; *v.*, deleitar, aprazer.
DE.LIGHT.ED, *adj.*, muito contente, encantado.
DE.LIGHT.ED.NESS, *s.*, encanto, deleite, delícia.
DE.LIGHT.FUL, *adj.*, encantador.
DE.LIGHT.FUL.LY, *adv.*, encantadoramente.
DE.LIM.IT, *v.*, delimitar, limitar, confinar.
DE.LIM.I.TA.TION, *s.*, delimitação.
DE.LIN.E.ATE, *v.*, delinear, traçar.
DE.LIN.E.A.TION, *s.*, delineação, delineamento.
DE.LIN.E.A.TOR, *s.*, delineador.
DE.LIN.QUEN.CY, *s.*, delinquência, criminalidade.
DE.LIN.QUENT, *adj.*, *s.*, delinquente.
DEL.I.RA.TION, *s.*, delírio.
DE.LIR.I.OUS, *adj.*, delirante.
DE.LIR.I.OUS.LY, *adj.*, delirantemente.
DE.LIR.I.UM, *s.*, *Med.*, delírio.
DEL.ISH, *s.*, *adj.*, *col.*, delicioso.
DE.LIV.ER, *v.*, libertar, resgatar, soltar; entregar; distribuir.
DE.LIV.ER.ANCE, *s.*, libertação, libertação, resgate; parto.
DE.LIV.ER.ER, *s.*, entregador; libertador.
DE.LIV.ER.Y, *s.*, libertação, livramento; entrega; expedição; redenção, sentença; parto.
DELIVERY ROOM, *s.*, sala de parto.
DEL.TA, *s.*, delta (de um rio); quarta letra do alfabeto grego.
DE.LUDE, *v.*, iludir, enganar, fraudar.
DE.LUD.ER, *s.*, enganador.
DEL.UGE, *s.*, dilúvio; enxurrada; *v.*, inundar, alagar.
DE.LU.SION, *s.*, desilusão, ilusão.
DE.LU.SO.RY, *adj.*, ilusório, enganador.
DE LUXE, *adj.*, de luxo, luxuoso.
DELVE, *v.*, pesquisar, sondar; procurar (em bolsa, armário etc.).

DE.MAG.NET.I.SA.TION, *s.*, desmagnetização.
DE.MAG.NET.ISE(-IZE), *v.*, desmagnetizar.
DEM.A.GOG.IC, *adj.*, demagógico.
DEM.A.GOG.IC.AL, *adj.*, demagógico.
DEM.A.GOGUE, *s.*, demagogo.
DEM.A.GOGY, *s.*, demagogia.
DE.MAND, *v.*, postular, exigir, demandar, reivindicar; *s.*, exigência.
DE.MAND.ING, *adj.*, exigente.
DE.MAR.CATE, *v.*, demarcar, limitar.
DE.MAR.CA.TION, *s.*, demarcação.
DE.MA.TE.RI.AL.ISE(-IZE), *v.*, desmaterializar.
DE.MEAN, *v.*, rebaixar, humilhar.
DE.MEAN.ING, *adj.*, humilhante.
DE.MEAN.OUR *UK*, **DEMEANOR** *US*, *s.*, comportamento, conduta.
DE.MENT, *v.*, enlouquecer, tornar-se demente.
DE.MENT.ED, *adj.*, demente.
DE.MEN.TIA, *s.*, demência, loucura, desvario.
DEM.E.RAR.A SUG.AR, *s.*, açúcar mascavo.
DE.MER.IT, *s.*, demérito.
DEM.I.GOD, *s.*, *Mit.*, semideus.
DEM.I.GOD.DESS, *s.*, *Mit.*, semideusa.
DEM.I.JOHN, *s.*, garrafão empalhado (ger. de vinho).
DE.MIL.I.TA.RISE *US*, **DE.MIL.I.TA.RIZE** *UK*, *v.*, desmilitarizar.
DE.MISE, *s.*, falecimento, óbito.
DE.MIS.SION, *s.*, demissão.
DE.MIST, *v.*, *UK* desembaçar (para-brisa).
DEM.I.TONE, *s.*, *Mus.*, meio-tom, semitom.
DE.MO.BI.LISATION *US*, **DE.MO.BI.LIZATION** *UK*, *s.*, desmobilização.
DE.MO.BI.LIZE, *v.*, desmobilizar.
DE.MOC.RA.CY, *s.*, democracia.
DEM.O.CRAT, *s.*, democrata.
DEM.O.CRA.TIC, *adj.*, democrático.
DE.MOC.RA.TI.SA.TION *US*, **DE.MOC.RA.TI.ZA.TION** *UK*, *s.*, democratização.
DE.MOC.RA.TISE(-TIZE), *v.*, democratizar.
DE.MO.GRAPH.IC, *adj.*, demográfico.
DE.MOG.RA.PHY, *s.*, demografia.
DE.MOL.ISH, *v.*, demolir.
DE.MOL.ISH.ER, *s.*, demolidor.
DEM.O.LI.TION, *s.*, demolição, destruição.
DE.MON, *s.*, demônio, satã, satanás, diabo.
DE.MO.NI.AC, *adj.*, demoníaco.
DE.MON.ISE(-IZE), *v.*, demonizar, endemoninhar.
DE.MON.ISM, *s.*, demonismo.
DE.MON.OL.O.GY, *s.*, demonologia.
DEM.ON.STRA.BLE, *adj.*, demonstrável.
DEM.ON.STRABLY, *adv.*, demonstravelmente.
DEM.ON.STRATE, *v.*, demonstrar, manifestar, expor.
DEM.ON.STRA.TION, *s.*, demonstração.
DEM.ON.STRA.TIVE, *adj.*, efusivo, convincente concludente; *s.*, *Gram.*, demonstrativo (*pron.* ou *adj.*).
DEM.ON.STRA.TOR, *s.*, demonstrador; aquele que faz protesto em passeata.
DE.MOR.AL.I.SA.TION, **DE.MOR.AL.I.ZA.TION**, *s.*, desmoralização.
DE.MOR.AL.IZE, *v.*, desmoralizar.
DE.MOTE, *v.*, degradar; rebaixar.

DEMOTION ··· 436 ··· DERIVATIVE

DE.MO.TION, s., rebaixamento.
DE.MOUNT, v., desmontar (aparelhos, móveis etc.).
DE.MOUNT.A.BLE, adj., desmontável.
DE.MURE, adj., sério; recatado.
DE.MYS.TI.FI.CA.TION, s., desmistificação.
DE.MYS.TI.FY, v., desmistificar.
DEN, s., covil; antro; espelunca; aposento; v., viver em caverna.
DE.NA.TION.AL.ISE, **DE.NA.TION.AL.IZE**, v., desnacionalizar.
DENE, s., duna; monte de areia.
DEN.GUE, s., Med., dengue.
DE.NI.A.BLE, adj., negável.
DE.NI.AL, s., negação; refutação; negativa.
DEN.I.GRATE, v., difamar; denegrir.
DEN.IM, s., tecido de brim; dinims, s. pl.: jeans.
DEN.IM JACK.ET, s., jaqueta jeans.
DEN.I.ZEN, s., estrangeiro naturalizado.
DE.NOM.I.NATE, v., denominar; nomear; indicar.
DE.NOM.I.NA.TION, s., denominação; indicação.
DE.NOM.I.NA.TOR, s., denominador.
DE.NO.TA.TION, s., denotação; designação; indicação.
DE.NOTE, v., denotar; indicar; mostrar.
DE.NOTE.MENT, s., sinal; indicação.
DE.NOUE.MENT, s., desfecho.
DE.NOUNCE, v., denunciar.
DENSE, adj., denso; espesso; fechado; compacto.
DENSE.LY, adv., densamente.
DEN.SI.TY, s., densidade.
DENT, v., amassar; s., entalhe; dente (de engrenagem).
DEN.TAL, adj., dental; dentário.
DEN.TAL FLOSS, s., fio dental.
DEN.TAL OF.FICE, s., consultório dentário.
DEN.TAL PLATE, s., dentadura postiça.
DEN.TATE, adj., dentado.
DEN.TIST, s., dentista; odontólogo.
DEN.TIST.RY, s., odontologia.
DEN.TURES, s. pl., dentadura.
DE.NUDE, v., desnudar; despir.
DE.NUN.CI.ATE, v., denunciar; delatar.
DE.NUN.CI.A.TION, s., denúncia.
DE.NY, v., negar; recusar.
DE.O.DOR.ANT, s., desodorante.
DE.O.DOR.I.SA.TION, **DE.O.DOR.I.ZA.TION**, s., desodorização; desinfecção.
DE.ODOR.ISE(-IZE), v., desodorizar; desinfetar.
DE.PART, v., ir; partir; andar; sair.
DE.PART.MENT, s., departamento; seção; repartição.
DE.PART.MEN.TAL.ISE, v., departamentalizar.
DE.PAR.TURE, s., partida; saída; ida.
DE.PAR.TURE LOUNGE, s., sala de embarque.
DE.PEND, v., depender; sujeitar-se.
DE.PEND.A.BLE, adj., confiável; fidedigno.
DE.PEND.ANT, s., dependente.
DE.PEN.DENCE, s., dependência.
DE.PEN.DEN.CY, s., dependência (território etc.).
DE.PEND.ENT, s., dependente; adj., dependente; subordinado; que tem auxílio de (alguém).
DE.PICT, v., retratar; pintar.
DEP.I.LATE, v., depilar.
DEP.I.LA.TION, s., depilação.

DE.PLETE, v., reduzir, esvaziar, esgotar.
DE.PLE.TION, s., redução; depleção; sangria.
DE.PLOR.A.BLE, adj., deplorável.
DE.PLOR.A.TION, s., deploração, lamentação.
DE.PLORE, v., deplorar.
DE.PLOY, v., dispor.
DE.PLOY.MENT, s., disposição; Mil., preparação de tropas.
DE.PLUME, v., depenar.
DE.PO.NENT, s., deponente, depoente, declarante.
DE.POP.U.LATE, v., despovoar.
DE.POP.U.LAT.ED, adj., despovoado.
DE.POP.U.LA.TION, s., despovoamento, despovoação.
DE.PORT, v., deportar.
DE.POR.TA.TION, s., deportação.
DE.POSE, v., depor.
DE.POS.IT, s., depósito (de valores em banco), penhor; sedimento; Geol., jazida; aluvião.
DE.POS.IT AC.COUNT, s., US depósito a prazo; UK conta remunerada.
DE.POS.I.TA.RY, s., depositário (quem recebe em depósito).
DEP.O.SI.TION, s., Jur., depoimento; deposição; depósito; Geol., aluvião.
DE.POS.I.TOR, s., depositante.
DE.POT, s., depósito, armazém.
DE.PRAVE, v., depravar, viciar, corromper, estragar.
DE.PRAVED, adj., depravado, corrompido.
DE.PRAV.I.TY, s., depravação.
DEP.RE.CATE, v., censurar, desaprovar; protestar.
DEP.RE.CA.TION, s., desaprovação.
DE.PRE.CI.ATE, v., depreciar, desvalorizar.
DE.PRE.CI.A.TION, s., depreciação.
DEP.RE.DATE, v., depredar, destruir, saquear.
DEP.RE.DATION, s., depredação.
DE.PRESS, v., deprimir, reduzir.
DE.PRES.SANT, s., Med., sedativo, calmante.
DE.PRESSED, adj., deprimido, desanimado.
DE.PRESS.ING, adj., deprimente.
DE.PRES.SION, s., depressão.
DE.PRES.SIVE, s., depressivo.
DEP.RI.VA.TION, s., privação.
DE.PRIVE, v., privar de.
DE.PRIVED, adj., necessitado.
DEPTH, s., profundidade, profundeza; abismo; gravidade.
DEP.U.TA.TION, s., delegação, deputação.
DE.PUTE, v., delegar.
DEP.U.TISE(-IZE), v., atuar como delegado; substituir oficialmente alguém.
DEP.U.TY, s., ajudante do delegado; adj., adjunto; suplente.
DE.RAIL, v., descarrilar (trem).
DE.RAIL.MENT, s., descarrilamento.
DE.RANGED, adj., perturbado, transtornado.
DER.E.LICT, adj., abandonado.
DER.E.LIC.TION, s., abandono, desamparo.
DE.RIDE, v., ridicularizar, zombar, escarnecer.
DE.RID.ING, s., zombaria, desprezo, escárnio.
DE.RI.SION, s., escárnio, zombaria.
DE.RI.SIVE, adj., zombeteiro, ridículo.
DE.RI.SO.RY, adj., irrisório; ridículo.
DER.I.VA.TION, s., derivação.
DE.RIV.A.TIVE, s., Gram., derivado; adj., derivativo; pej., não original.

DERIVE ··437·· DETONATOR

DE.RIVE, *v.*, derivar, provir, proceder de.
DERM, *s.*, *Anat.*, derme, pele.
DER.MA.TI.TIS, *s.*, *Med.*, dermatite.
DER.MA.TOL.O.GIST, *s.*, dermatologista.
DER.MA.TOL.O.GY, *s.*, dermatologia.
DER.RIK, *s.*, grua, guindaste.
DERV, *s.*, óleo diesel.
DE.SAL.I.NATE, *v.*, dessalinizar.
DES.CANT, *s.*, *Mus.*, contraponto.
DE.SCEND, *v.*, descer, baixar, descender.
DE.SCEND.ANT, *s.*, descendente, filho; *adj.*, descendente.
DE.SCEND.ING, *adj.*, descendente.
DE.SCENT, *s.*, descida, descendência.
DE.SCRIBE, *v.*, descrever.
DE.SCRIP.TION, *s.*, descrição.
DE.SCRIP.TIVE, *adj.*, descritivo.
DES.E.CRAT, *v.*, profanar.
DES.E.CRATE, *v.*, profanar.
DES.E.CRA.TION, *s.*, profanação.
DE.SEG.RE.GATE, *v.*, desagregar.
DE.SEG.RE.GA.TION, *s.*, desagregação.
DE.SE.LECT, *v.*, excluir de uma seleção.
DES.ERT, *s.*, deserto; *v.*, desertar, tornar deserto, abandonar.
DE.SERT.ER, *s.*, desertor.
DE.SER.TION, *s.*, *Mil.*, deserção; abandono (pessoa).
DE.SERVE, *v.*, merecer, ser digno de.
DE.SERVED, *adj.*, merecido.
DE.SERV.ED.LY, *adv.*, merecidamente.
DE.SERV.ING, *adj.*, meritório.
DES.IC.CATE, *v.*, dessecar, desidratar; *adj.*, enxuto, seco.
DE.SID.ER.ATE, *v.*, desejar, querer, pretender.
DE.SIGN, *s.*, desenho, esboço, projeto, propósito; *v.*, projetar.
DES.IG.NATE, *v.*, designar, indicar, nomear; *adj.*, designado, indicado.
DES.IG.NA.TION, *s.*, designação; nome.
DE.SIGNED, *adj.*, intencional, proposital.
DE.SIGN.ER, *s.*, desenhista; projetista.
DE.SIR.A.BIL.I.TY, *s.*, qualidade de ser desejável.
DE.SIR.A.BLE, *adj.*, desejável, proveitoso, agradável.
DE.SIRE, *s.*, desejo, anseio; *v.*, querer, desejar, ansiar por.
DE.SIR.OUS, *adj.*, desejoso; cobiçoso.
DE.SIST, *v.*, desistir, renunciar.
DE.SIS.TANCE, *s.*, renúncia, desistência.
DESK, *s.*, carteira escolar, escrivaninha; secretária; balcão de aeroporto.
DESK CLERK, *s.*, *US* recepcionista.
DESK.TOP, *adj.*, *Comp.*, computador de mesa.
DES.O.LATE, *v.*, desolar, despovoar; *adj.*, despovoado, deserto.
DES.O.LATE.LY, *adv.*, desoladamente.
DES.O.LATE.NESS, *s.*, desolação.
DES.O.LA.TION *s.*, aflição, desolação, sofrimento.
DE.SPAIR, *v.*, desesperar, perder a esperança; *s.*, desespero.
DE.SPAIR.ING, *adj.*, desesperador.
DE.SPAIR.ING.LY, *adv.*, desesperadamente.
DES.PATCH, *v.*, o mesmo que *dispatch*.
DES.PER.ATE, *adj.*, desesperado; desesperador.
DES.PER.ATE.NESS, *s.*, desespero, desesperança; fúria.
DES.PER.ATE.LY, *adv.*, desesperadamente.
DES.PER.A.TION, *s.*, desespero, desesperança.
DES.PI.CA.BLE, *adj.*, desprezível.

DES.PI.CA.BLE.NESS, *s.*, desprezo, vileza, baixeza.
DE.SPISE, *v.*, desprezar.
DE.SPITE, *prep.*, apesar de, não obstante.
DE.SPOIL, *v.*, despojar, espoliar, furtar.
DE.SPOIL.MENT, *s.*, despojamento, espoliação.
DE.SPOND, *v.*, desanimar, desesperar.
DE.SPOND.ENT, *adj.*, desanimado.
DES.POT, *s.*, déspota, tirano.
DES.POT.IC, *adj.*, despótico.
DES.PO.TISM, *s.*, despotismo.
DES.SERT, *s.*, sobremesa.
DES.SERT SPOON, *s.*, colher de sobremesa.
DE.STA.BIL.ISE(-IZE), *v.*, desestabilizar.
DES.TI.NA.TION, *s.*, destino, direção, lugar.
DES.TINE, *v.*, destinar, remeter, designar.
DES.TI.NY, *s.*, destino, sorte, futuro.
DES.TI.TUTE, *adj.*, necessitado, miserável, destituído.
DES.TI.TU.TION, *s.*, privação, pobreza, carência.
DE.STROY, *v.*, destruir.
DE.STROY.A.BLE, *adj.*, destrutível.
DE.STROY.ER, *s.*, destruidor, exterminador; *Náut.*, contratorpedeiro.
DE.STRUC.TION, *s.*, destruição.
DE.STRUC.TIVE, *adj.*, destrutivo.
DE.STRUC.TIVE.LY, *adv.*, destrutivamente.
DE.STRUC.TOR, *s.*, destruidor, exterminador.
DES.UL.TO.RY, *adj.*, inconstante, sem propósito, desinteressado.
DE.TACH, *v.*, destacar, separar, desprender.
DE.TACH.A.BLE, *adj.*, removível, destacável.
DE.TACHED, *adj.*, imparcial; destacado.
DE.TACH.MENT, *s.*, desinteresse, desapego; *Mil.*, destacamento.
DE.TAIL, *s.*, detalhe, ninharia; *v.*, detalhar, pormenorizar.
DE.TAILED, *adj.*, detalhado.
DE.TAIN, *v.*, deter, prender.
DE.TAIN.EE, *s.*, detento, detido, preso.
DE.TAIN.ER, *s.*, detenção.
DE.TECT, *v.*, detectar, perceber, notar.
DE.TEC.TION, *s.*, detecção, revelação.
DE.TEC.TIVE, *s.*, detetive.
DE.TEC.TIVE NOVEL, *s.*, *Lit.*, romance policial.
DE.TEN.TION, *s.*, detenção.
DE.TECT.OR, *s.*, detector (aparelho); denunciador.
DE.TEN.TION, *s.*, detenção (de suspeito); prisão; castigo.
DE.TER, *v.*, desanimar, desalentar-se.
DE.TER.GENT, *s.*, detergente.
DE.TE.RI.O.RATE, *v.*, piorar, deteriorar, degenerar.
DE.TE.RI.O.RA.TION, *s.*, deterioração; ruína.
DE.TER.MI.NATE, *adj.*, determinado.
DE.TER.MI.NATE.NESS, *s.*, determinação; firmeza.
DE.TER.MI.NA.TION, *s.*, determinação, resolução.
DE.TER.MINE, *v.*, demarcar, determinar, decidir.
DE.TER.MINED, *adj.*, determinado; resoluto.
DE.TER.RENT, *adj.*, dissuasão, dissuasivo; *s.*, estorvo.
DE.TEST, *v.*, detestar.
DE.TEST.A.BLE, *adj.*, detestável.
DE.THRONE, *v.*, destronar.
DET.O.NATE, *v.*, detonar; explodir.
DET.O.NA.TION, *s.*, detonação.
DET.O.NA.TOR, *s.*, detonador.

DETOUR · 438 · DIFFERENT

DE.TOUR, s., desvio; v., voltear.
DE.TOX, s., col., desintoxicar.
DE.TOX.I.CATION, s., desintoxification.
DE.TRACT, v., destratar, difamar, caluniar.
DE.TRACT.ING, s., calúnia; adj., detrativo, calunioso.
DE.TRAC.TION, s., detração, calúnia.
DE.TRACT.OR, s., detrator, caluniador.
DET.RI.MENT, s., detrimento, dano, prejuízo.
DET.RI.MEN.TAL, adj., prejudicial.
DE.TRI.TION, s., Geol., detrição.
DE.TRI.TUS, s. Geol., detrito.
DEUCE, s., Esp., empate (tênis); número dois (cartas, dados).
DE.VAL.U.ATE, v., desvalorizar.
DE.VAL.U.A.TION, s., desvalorização (moeda).
DE.VAL.UE, v., desvalorizar.
DEV.AS.TATE, v, devastar, arrasar.
DEV.AS.TAT.ED, adj., devastado (lugar); fig., arruinado, arrasado.
DEV.AS.TAT.ING, adj., devastador, avassalador, desolador.
DEV.AS.TA.TION, s., devastação, desolação.
DE.VEL.OP, v., desenvolver, revelar, progredir, avançar, evoluir.
DE.VEL.OP.ER, s., empreendedor, desenvolvedor.
DE.VEL.OP.ING COUN.TRY, s., país em desenvolvimento.
DE.VEL.OP.MENT, s., desenvolvimento, progresso, evolução.
DE.VI.ANT, s., pessoa anormal; adj., anormal, pervertido.
DE.VI.ATE, v., desviar(-se) (do normal), afastar(-se).
DE.VI.A.TION, s., desvio.
DE.VICE, s., aparelho, dispositivo; plano; artifício, estratagema.
DEV.IL, s., diabo, demônio.
DEV.IL.ISH, adj., diabólico; adv., diabolicamente.
DEV.IL.ISH.LY, adv., diabolicamente.
DEV.IL.ISH.NESS, s., diabrura; qualidade diabólica.
DEV.IL-MAY-CARE, adj., inconsequente, imprudente.
DEV.IL'S AD.VO.CATE, s., advogado do diabo.
DE.VI.OUS, adj., desviado, divergente; fig., desonesto.
DE.VI.OUS.NESS, s., desonestidade.
DE.VISE, v., inventar, imaginar; deixar por testamento.
DE.VIS.ER, s., inventor; autor.
DE.VI.TAL.IZE, v., desvitalizar.
DE.VOID, adj., destituído, desprovido (de algo).
DE.VO.LU.TION, s., devolução, entrega.
DE.VOLVE, v., devolver, entregar, transferir, transmitir.
DE.VOTE, v., devotar, dedicar(-se).
DE.VOT.ED, adj., dedicado; devoto; zeloso.
DE.VOT.ED.LY, adv., devotadamente, dedicadamente.
DEV.O.TEE, s., devoto, dedicado.
DE.VO.TION, s., devoção, dedicação.
DE.VO.TION.AL, adj., devoto, beato.
DE.VOUR, v., devorar.
DE.VOUT, adj., s., devoto.
DEW, s., orvalho.
DEX.TER.I.TY, s., destreza, habilidade, capacidade.
DEX.TER.OUS, adj., ágil, hábil.
DEX.TER.OUS.LY, adv., destramente.
DEX.TER.OUS.NESS, s., agilidade, destreza.
DEX.TRAL, adj., destro, da mão direita.
DI.A.BE.TES, s., diabetes.
DI.A.BET.IC, s., diabético(a); adj., diabético.
DI.A.BOL.IC, adj., diabólico.

DI.A.BOL.ICAL, adj., o mesmo que diabolic.
DI.A.BOL.ICAL.LY, adj., diabolicamente, perversamente.
DI.AC.O.NATE, s., diaconato.
DI.A.DEM, s., diadema.
DI.AER.E.SIS, s., Gram., trema, diérese.
DI.AG.NOSE, v., diagnosticar.
DI.AG.NOS.TIC, adj., Med., diagnóstico.
DI.AG.NO.SIS, s., diagnóstico.
DI.AG.O.NAL, adj., diagonal.
DI.AG.ONAL.LY, adv., diagonalmente.
DI.A.GRAM, s., diagrama.
DI.A.GRAM.MA.TIC, adj., diagramático.
DI.AL, s., mostrador (relógio); indicador; v., discar, medir.
DI.AL.ING CODE, **DI.AL.LING CODE**, s., código de discagem.
DI.A.LECT, s., dialeto.
DI.A.LEC.TIC, s., dialética; adj., dialético.
DI.A.LEC.TICS, s., dialética.
DI.A.LOGUE, **DI.A.LOG**, s., diálogo, colóquio.
DI.AL.Y.SIS, s., Quím., diálise; Gram., diérese.
DI.AM.E.TER, s., diâmetro.
DI.A.MET.RI.CAL.LY, adv., diametralmente.
DI.A.MOND, s., diamante, losango.
DI.A.MOND WED.DING, s., bodas de diamante.
DI.A.PER, s., fralda, pano de linho, guardanapo.
DI.APH.A.NOUS, adj., diáfano, transparente, lúcido.
DI.A.PHRAGM, s., diafragma.
DI.AR.RHOEA, s., diarreia.
DI.A.RY, s., diário.
DIB, v., mergulhar.
DICE, s. pl., dados; jogo de dados; v., jogar dados; cortar em cubinhos.
DIC.EY, adj., incerto.
DI.CHOT.O.MY, s., dicotomia.
DICK, s., col., sujeito, detetive; vulg., pênis.
DIC.TATE, v., ditar; s., ditado.
DIC.TA.TION, s., ditado, ordem.
DIC.TA.TOR, s., ditador.
DIC.TA.TOR.SHIP, s., ditadura.
DIC.TION, s., dicção.
DIC.TIO.NARY, s., dicionário.
DID, v., passado do verbo do.
DI.DAC.TIC, adj., didático.
DI.DAC.TI.CISM, s., didática, didatismo.
DID.DLE, v., col., perder tempo; UK col., passar a perna; vulg., transar.
DIDN'T, abrev. de did not.
DIE, v., morrer, falecer.
DIE-HARD, s., teimoso.
DI.ER.E.SIS, s., o mesmo que diaeresis.
DIE.SEL, s., diesel.
DIE.SEL EN.GINE, s., motor a diesel.
DIE.SEL FUEL, **DIE.SEL OIL**, s., óleo diesel.
DIET, s., dieta, regime; v., fazer dieta.
DI.E.TER, s., aquele que faz dieta.
DI.E.TET.IC, adj., dietético.
DI.E.TET.ICS, s. pl., dietética.
DI.E.TI.CIAN, s., nutricionista.
DIF.FER, v., diferir, ser diferente, discordar, divergir.
DIF.FER.ENCE, s., diferença, diversidade, divergência.
DIF.FER.ENT, adj., diferente.

DIFFERENTIAL ··· 439 ··· DIRT

DIF.FER.EN.TIAL, *s.*, diferencial.
DIF.FER.EN.TI.ATE, *v.*, diferenciar, discriminar.
DIF.FER.ENT.LY, *adv.*, diferentemente.
DIF.FI.CULT, *adj.*, difícil, complicado.
DIF.FI.CUL.TY, *s.*, dificuldade, complicação.
DIF.FI.DENCE, *s.*, difidência, desconfiança, timidez.
DIF.FUSE, *v.*, difundir, espalhar; *adj.*, difuso, espalhado, esparramado.
DIF.FU.SION, *s.*, difusão.
DIG, *s.*, escavação; *v.*, cavar, escavar, revolver terra.
DI.GEST, *v.*, digerir, assimilar, aprender; *s.*, resumo, compêndio.
DI.GES.TION, *s.*, digestão.
DI.GEST.IVE, *s.*, digestivo, medicamento para digestão.
DI.GEST.IVE SYS.TEM, *s.*, sistema digestivo.
DIG.GER, *s.*, escavador, escavadeira (máquina).
DIG.IT, *s.*, dígito, dedo; medida.
DIG.I.TAL, *adj.*, digital.
DIG.I.TAL.LY, *adv.*, digitalmente.
DIG.I.TA.TION, *s.*, digitação.
DIG.I.TISE(-IZE), *v.*, digitalizar.
DI.GLAD.I.ATE, *v.*, digladiar, lutar.
DI.GLAD.I.A.TION, *s.*, digladiação, combate.
DIG.NI.FIED, *adj.*, digno, dignificado.
DIG.NI.FY, *v.*, dignificar, honrar, prestigiar.
DIG.NI.TA.RY, *s.*, dignitário.
DIG.NI.TY, *s.*, dignidade, honra.
DI.GRESS, *v.*, desviar(-se) do assunto, digressionar.
DI.GRES.SION, *s.*, digressão.
DI.GRES.SIVE, *adj.*, digressivo.
DIGS, *s. pl.*, pensão.
DIKE, *s.*, dique, represa, açude.
DI.LAC.ER.ATE, *v.*, dilacerar.
DI.LAC.ER.A.TION, *s.*, dilaceração.
DI.LAP.I.DATE, *v.*, dilapidar; demolir, dissipar.
DI.LAP.I.DAT.ED, *adj.*, em ruínas.
DI.LAP.I.DA.TION, *s.*, dilapidação, deterioração.
DI.LAT.A.BLE, *adj.*, dilatável.
DI.LA.TA.TION, *s.*, dilatação, aumento.
DI.LATE, *v.*, dilatar.
DI.LEM.MA, *s.*, dilema.
DIL.ET.TANTE, *s.*, diletante.
DIL.ET.TANTISM, *s.*, diletantismo.
DIL.I.GENCE, *s.*, diligência, demanda; aplicação, cuidado.
DIL.I.GENT, *adj.*, diligente, aplicado, zeloso.
DILL, *s.*, *Bot.*, aneto, endro.
DIL.LER, *s.*, *col.*, filme, show, peça de terror.
DIL.LY-DAL.LY, *v.*, embromar, vadiar.
DIL.U.ENT, *s.*, *Quím.*, diluente.
DI.LUTE, *v.*, diluir.
DI.LUT.ER, *s.*, diluidor.
DI.LU.TION, *s.*, diluição.
DI.LU.VI.AL, *adj.*, diluviano, diluvial.
DI.LU.VI.UM, *s.*, dilúvio.
DIM, *v.*, ofuscar, escurecer; *adj.*, escuro, ofuscado, sombrio, baço.
DIME, *s.*, moeda americana de prata de dez cents.
DI.MEN.SION, *s.*, dimensão, tamanho, grandeza.
DI.MEN.SIONAL, *adj.*, dimensório, dimensível.
DI.MIN.ISH, *v.*, diminuir, apequenar.
DI.MIN.ISHED, *adj.*, diminuído, reduzido.

DI.MIN.ISH.ING, *s.*, diminuição; *adj.*, diminuidor.
DIM.I.NU.TION, *s.*, diminuição.
DI.MIN.U.TIVE, *adj.*, diminuto; *Gram.*, diminutivo.
DIM.LY, *adv.*, fracamente, vagamente.
DIM.MER SWITCH, *s.*, *Elet.*, regulador de iluminação.
DIM.MISH, *adj.*, obscuro, de pouca clareza.
DIM.NESS, *s.*, obscuridade; sem clareza.
DIM.PLE, *s.*, covinha (no rosto).
DIM-WITTED, *s.*, *col.*, estúpido.
DIN, *s.*, rumor, zoeira.
DINE, *v.*, jantar, comer à noite.
DINE OUT, *v.*, jantar fora de casa.
DIN.ER, *s.*, quem janta; pequeno restaurante.
DING, *s.*, som de sino; *v.*, tinir.
DING-DONG, *s.*, badalada (de sino, de campainha).
DIN.GHY, *s.*, *Náut.*, pequeno barco, escaler.
DIN.GO, *s.*, *Zool.*, dingo (cão da Austrália).
DIN.GY, *adj.*, sujo, desbotado.
DIN.ING, *s.*, vagão restaurante nos trens.
DIN.ING-CAR, *s.*, vagão-restaurante.
DIN.ING-HOUR, *s.*, hora de jantar.
DIN.ING-ROOM, *s.*, sala de jantar.
DIN.ING-TA.BLE, *s.*, mesa de sala de jantar.
DIN.NER, *s.*, jantar, ceia.
DIN.NER JACK.ET, *s.*, paletó de cor preta; smoking.
DIN.NER SERVICE, *s.*, aparelho de jantar.
DIN.NER TABLE, *s.*, o mesmo que *dining-table*.
DIN.NER-TIME, *s.*, o mesmo que *dinner-hour*.
DI.NO.SAUR, *s.*, dinossauro.
DI.NO.SAU.RI.AN, *s.*, dinossauro; *adj.*, relativo a dinossauro.
DINT, *s.*, golpe; meio; *v.*, golpear; *by ~ of:* por meio de.
DI.OC.ESE, *s.*, diocese.
DI.ODE, *s.*, *Eletron.*, diodo.
DIP, *s.*, mergulho, banho de mar, inclinação; *v.*, mergulhar, molhar-se.
DIPH.THE.RIA, *s.*, difteria.
DIPH.THONG, *s.*, ditongo.
DI.PLO.MA, *s.*, diploma.
DI.PLO.MA.CY, *s.*, diplomacia.
DIP.LO.MAT, *s.*, diplomata.
DI.PLO.MAT.IC, *adj.*, diplomático; hábil, sagaz.
DI.PLO.MAT.IC CORPS, *s.*, dorpo diplomático.
DI.PLO.MED, *adj.*, diplomado.
DIRE, *adj.*, terrível.
DI.RECT, *v.*, dirigir, conduzir, administrar; *adj.*, direito, reto.
DI.RECT CUR.RENT, *s.*, corrente contínua.
DI.REC.TION, *s.*, direção, indicação, condução.
DI.REC.TIVE, *s.*, diretriz; ordem oficial; *adj.*, diretivo.
DI.RECT.LY, *adv.*, diretamente.
DI.RECT MAIL, *s.*, mala-direta.
DI.RECT.RESS, *s.*, diretora.
DI.RECT.OR, *s.*, diretor.
DI.RECT.O.RATE, *s.*, diretório, diretoria.
DI.RECT.OR-GEN.ER.AL, *s.*, diretor-geral.
DI.REC.TOR.SHIP, *s.*, cargo de diretor.
DI.REC.TO.RY, *s.*, comissão diretora; lista telefônica, lista de endereços.
DIRE.NESS, *s.*, pavor, medo, terror.
DIRGE, *s.*, música fúnebre, canção triste.
DIR.I.GI.BIL.I.TY, *s.*, dirigibilidade.
DIRT, *s.*, sujeira, lodo, imundície, sujidade.

DIRT-CHEAP ··440·· DISDAIN

DIRT-CHEAP, *adj.*, baratíssimo; *adv.*, bem barato.
DIRT-TRACK, *s.*, estrada de terra.
DIRTY, *adj.*, sujo, imundo, sórdido.
DIS.ABIL.I.TY, *s.*, inabilidade, incapacidade.
DIS.A.BLE, *v.*, incapacitar.
DIS.A.BLED, *adj.*, incapacitado.
DIS.A.BLE.MENT, *s.*, incapacidade, inabilidade.
DIS.A.BUSE, *v.*, desiludir, desabusar.
DIS.AC.CUS.TOM, *v.*, desacostumar, perder o hábito.
DIS.AD.VAN.TAGE, *s.*, desvantagem, desfavor.
DIS.AD.VAN.TAGED, *adj.*, desamparado, desfavorecido.
DIS.AD.VAN.TA.GEOUS, *adj.*, desvantajoso.
DIS.AF.FECT, *adj.*, desafeto, desleal, infiel.
DIS.AF.FECT.ED, *adj.*, insatisfeito, desafeiçoado.
DIS.AF.FEC.TION, *s.*, insatisfação.
DIS.A.GREE, *v.*, discordar.
DIS.A.GREE.A.BLE, *adj.*, desagradável.
DIS.AGREED, *adj.*, discordante, contrário, oposto.
DIS.A.GREE.MENT, *s.*, divergência, discordância; discussão.
DIS.AL.LOW, *v.*, rejeitar, desaprovar, anular.
DIS.AP.PEAR, *v.*, desaparecer.
DIS.AP.PEAR.ANCE, *s.*, desaparecimento; falecimento; extinção.
DIS.AP.POINT, *v.*, desapontar, decepcionar.
DIS.AP.POINT.ED, *adj.*, desapontado; decepcionado.
DIS.AP.POINT.ING, *adj.*, decepcionante, desapontador.
DIS.AP.POINT.MENT, *s.*, desapontamento, frustração.
DIS.AP.PRO.BA.TION, *s.*, desaprovação, negativa.
DIS.AP.PROV.AL, *s.*, desaprovação.
DIS.AP.PROVE, *v.*, desaprovar, não aceitar.
DIS.AP.PROV.ING, *adj.*, desaprovador, desaprovativo.
DIS.ARM, *v.*, desarmar.
DIS.AR.MA.MENT, *s.*, desarmamento.
DIS.AR.MING, *adj.*, que desarma; *fig.*, irresistível.
DIS.AR.MING.LY, *adv.*, apaziguadoramente; *fig.*, irresistivelmente.
DIS.AR.RAY, *v.*, desorganizar, desordenar; *s.*, desordem, confusão.
DIS.AR.TIC.U.LATE, *v.*, desarticular; desunir.
DIS.AR.TIC.U.LA.TION, *s.*, desarticulação.
DIS.AS.SEM.BLE, *v.*, separar, desmontar, desarmar.
DIS.AS.SEM.BLY, *s.*, separação, desmontagem.
DIS.AS.SO.CI.ATE, *v.*, desassociar; desligar.
DI.SAS.TER, *s.*, desastre, calamidade.
DI.SAS.TER A.REA, *s.*, área de calamidade pública.
DI.SAS.TROUS, *adj.*, desastroso, calamitoso.
DI.SAS.TROUS.LY, *adv.*, desastrosamente; desastradamente.
DIS.BAND, *v.*, dispersar, debandar.
DIS.BE.LIEF, *s.*, incredulidade, descrença.
DIS.BE.LIEVE, *v.*, descrer, desconfiar.
DIS.BURSE, *v.*, desembolsar, gastar.
DISC, *s.*, disco.
DIS.CARD, *s.*, descarte; *v.*, descartar, jogar fora.
DIS.CARD.ED, *adj.*, descartado, rejeitado.
DIS.CERN, *v.*, discernir, perceber.
DIS.CERN.I.BLE, *adj.*, discernível, perceptível.
DIS.CERN.I.BLE.NESS, *s.*, discernimento, perceptibilidade.
DIS.CERN.ING, *adj.*, perspicaz, sagaz.
DIS.CHARGE, *s.*, descarga, demissão, soltura; *v.*, descarregar, desempenhar.
DIS.CHARG.ER, *s.*, descarregador.

DIS.CI.PLE, *s.*, discípulo, aprendiz.
DIS.CI.PLI.NAR.IAN, *s.*, disciplinador.
DIS.CI.PLI.NA.RY, *adj.*, disciplinar.
DIS.CI.PLINE, *s.*, disciplina; *v.*, disciplinar, educar.
DIS.CI.PLINED, *adj.*, disciplinado.
DISC.JOCKEY, *s.*, disc-jóquei; programador musical.
DIS.CLAIM, *v.*, negar.
DIS.CLAIM.ER, *s.*, negação, retratação.
DIS.CLA.MA.TION, *s.*, repúdio.
DIS.CLOSE, *v.*, revelar, abrir.
DIS.CLO.SURE, *s.*, revelação, divulgação.
DIS.CO, *s.*, discoteca.
DIS.COG.RA.PHY, *s.*, discografia.
DIS.COL.OR.A.TION, *s.*, descoloração.
DIS.COL.OR.MENT, *s.*, descoloramento.
DIS.COL.OR *US*, **DIS.COL.OUR** *UK*, *v.*, descolorar, descolorir.
DIS.COM.FORT, *s.*, desconforto, inquietação.
DIS.CON.CERT, *v.*, desconcertar, desordenar.
DIS.CON.CERT.ING, *adj.*, desconcertante.
DIS.CON.NECT, *v.*, desconectar, desligar; *adj.*, desconectado, desconexo, separado.
DIS.CON.NECT.ED, *adj.*, desconectado, desconexo, separado.
DIS.CON.NEC.TION, *s.*, desconexão, separação.
DIS.CON.TENT, *s.*, descontentamento; *v.*, descontentar.
DIS.CON.TENT.MENT, *s.*, descontentamento.
DIS.CON.TIN.UE, *v.*, descontinuar, interromper.
DIS.CON.TI.NU.I.TY, *s.*, descontinuidade.
DIS.CON.TINUOUS, *adj.*, descontínuo, interrompido.
DIS.CORD, *s.*, discórdia; *v.*, discordar.
DIS.CORDANT, *adj.*, discordante.
DIS.CO.THEQUE, *s.*, discoteca.
DIS.COUNT, *s.*, desconto; *v.*, descontar.
DIS.COUNT-RATE, *s.*, taxa de desconto.
DIS.COU.RAGE, *v.*, desanimar, desencorajar, intimidar.
DIS.COUR.AGE.MENT, *s.*, desânimo, desencorajamento.
DIS.COUR.A.GING, *adj.*, desanimador, desencorajador.
DIS.COURSE, *s.*, discurso, oração; *v.*, discursar, falar.
DIS.COURS.ER, *s.*, orador.
DIS.COUR.TE.OUS, *adj.*, descortês.
DIS.COUR.TE.SY, *s.*, descortesia.
DIS.COV.ER, *v.*, descobrir, achar, encontrar, inventar.
DIS.COV.ER.ER, *s.*, descobridor, explorador.
DIS.COV.ERY, *s.*, descoberta, descobrimento.
DIS.CRED.IT, *v.*, descrer, desacreditar, desconfiar.
DIS.CREET, *adj.*, discreto.
DIS.CREET.LY, *adv.*, discretamente.
DIS.CREP.AN.CY, *s.*, discrepância.
DIS.CRETE, *adj.*, distinto, discreto.
DIS.CRETE.LY, *adv.*, distintamente.
DIS.CRE.TION, *s.*, discrição.
DIS.CRE.TION.A.RY, *adj.*, discricionário.
DIS.CRIM.I.NATE, *v.*, discriminar.
DIS.CRIM.I.NAT.ING, *adj.*, discriminador, distintivo; perspicaz.
DIS.CRIM.I.NA.TION, *s.*, discriminação, distinção; perspicácia.
DIS.CRIM.I.NA.TIVE, *adj.*, distintivo, discriminador.
DIS.CUS, *s.*, disco.
DIS.CUSS, *v.*, discutir, analisar.
DIS.CUS.SION, *s.*, discussão.
DIS.DAIN, *s.*, desdém, desprezo; *v.*, desdenhar.

DISDAINFUL ·· 441 ·· DISPENSATION

DIS.DAIN.FUL, *adj.*, desdenhoso.
DIS.EASE, *s.*, doença.
DIS.EASED, *adj.*, doente.
DIS.EM.BARK, *v.*, desembarcar.
DIS.EM.BAR.KA.TION, *s.*, desembarque.
DIS.EM.BOD.Y, *v.*, desincorporar; *Mil.*, dar baixa.
DIS.EM.BOD.IED, *adj.*, desincorporado; desencarnado.
DIS.EM.BOW.EL, *v.*, estripar.
DIS.EN.CHANT, *v.*, desencantar.
DIS.EN.CHANT.ED, *adj.*, desencantado.
DIS.EN.CHANT.MENT, *s.*, desencantamento.
DIS.EN.GAGE, *v.*, desembaraçar, desatar, soltar; desengatar.
DIS.EN.GAGE.MENT, *s.*, desembaraçamento; exoneração; ócio.
DIS.EN.TAIL, *v.*, desvincular.
DIS.EN.TAN.GLE, *v.*, desenredar, desembaraçar.
DIS.E.QUIL.I.BRATE, *v.*, desequilibrar.
DIS.FA.VOUR *UK*, **DIS.FA.VOR** *US*, *s.*, desfavor.
DIS.FIG.URE, *v.*, desfigurar.
DIS.GORGE, *v.*, vomitar.
DIS.GRACE, *s.*, desgraça, desonra; *v.*, desgraçar; desonrar.
DIS.GRACE.FUL, *adj.*, desgraçado, vergonhoso.
DIS.GRUN.TLE, *v.*, decepcionar, desapontar.
DIS.GRUN.TLED, *adj.*, decepcionado.
DIS.GUISE, *s.*, disfarce, fingimento; *v.*, disfarçar, dissimular.
DIS.GUST, *s.*, desgosto, repugnância; *v.*, repugnar, desgostar, enojar.
DIS.GUST.ING, *adj.*, nojento, repulsivo, odioso.
DISH, *s.*, prato, travessa.
DISH AER.I.AL, *s.*, antena parabólica.
DISH AN.TEN.NA, *s.*, o mesmo que *dish aerial*.
DIS.HAR.MO.NY, *s.*, desarmonia.
DIS.HEART.EN, *v.*, desalentar, desanimar.
DIS.HEART.EN.ING, *adj.*, desanimador, desencorajador.
DI.SHEV.ELLED *UK*, **DI.SHEV.ELED** *US*, *adj.*, desalinhado, desgrenhado.
DISH.CLOTH, *s.*, pano de louça.
DISH.FUL, *s.*, prato cheio de comida.
DIS.HON.EST, *adj.*, desonesto.
DIS.HON.ES.TY, *s.*, desonestidade.
DIS.HON.OR *US*, **DIS.HON.OUR** *UK*, *s.*, desonra; *v.*, desonrar.
DIS.HON.OR.A.BLE *US*, **DIS.HON.OUR.A.BLE** *UK*, *adj.*, desonroso, vergonhoso.
DIS.HON.OR.A.BLY *US*, **DIS.HON.OUR.A.BLY** *UK*, *adv.*, desonrosamente.
DISH OUT, *v.*, repartir.
DISH TOWEL, *s.*, pano de prato.
DISH.WASH.ER, *s.*, máquina de lavar louça.
DISH.Y, *col.*, *UK* gato(a) (diz-se a pessoas atraentes).
DIS.IL.LU.SION, *s.*, desilusão; *v.*, desiludir.
DIS.IL.LU.SION.ED, *adj.*, desiludido.
DIS.IL.LU.SION.MENT, *s.*, desilusão.
DIS.IN.CEN.TIVE, *s.*, desestímulo.
DIS.IN.CLINE, *v.*, indispor, malquerer.
DIS.IN.CLINED, *adj.*, indisposto (a fazer algo), desinclinado.
DIS.IN.FECT, *v.*, desinfetar.
DIS.IN.FEC.TANT, *s.*, desinfetante.
DIS.IN.FOR.MA.TION, *s.*, desinformação.
DIS.IN.GEN.U.OUS, *adj.*, dissimulado, insincero.
DIS.IN.HER.IT, *v.*, deserdar.
DIS.IN.TE.GRATE, *v.*, desintegrar, fragmentar, desfazer-se.

DIS.IN.TE.GRA.TION, *s.*, desintegração, fragmentação, desmoronamento.
DIS.IN.TEREST, *s.*, desinteresse, imparcialidade; altruísmo.
DIS.IN.TEREST.ED, *adj.*, desinteressado.
DIS.IN.VEST.MENT, *s.*, *Econ.*, desinvestimento.
DIS.JOIN, *v.*, separar, desconectar.
DIS.JOINT, *v.*, desconjuntar, separar.
DIS.JOINT.ED, *adj.*, desconjuntado, deslocado.
DIS.JUNCT, *adj.*, separado, desunido.
DIS.JUNC.TION, *s.*, disjunção, separação.
DISK, *s.*, disco; disquete.
DIS.KETTE, *s.*, disquete.
DIS.LIKE, *s.*, aversão, desgosto, desagrado.
DIS.LO.CATE, *v.*, deslocar, distanciar; desordenar, desarticular.
DIS.LO.CA.TION, *s.*, deslocação, desarticulação.
DIS.LODGE, *v.*, desalojar(-se), despejar, expulsar.
DIS.LOY.AL, *adj.*, desleal.
DIS.LOY.AL.TY, *s.*, deslealdade, perversidade.
DIS.MAL, *adj.*, sombrio, deprimente, lúgubre.
DIS.MAL.NESS, *s.*, lugubridade, melancolia.
DIS.MAN.TLE, *v.*, desmantelar; desmontar.
DIS.MAY, *s.*, consternação, tristeza; *v.*, entristecer, consternar.
DIS.MEM.BER, *v.*, desmembrar.
DIS.MISS, *v.*, despedir, demitir; rejeitar, descartar.
DIS.MISS.AL, *s.*, demissão, dispensa; repúdio.
DIS.MOUNT, *v.*, desmontar (cavalo, moto); desarmar, desmantelar.
DIS.MOUNT.ING, *s.*, desmontagem (moto, cavalo); *fig.*, desmonte (de aparelho).
DIS.OBE.DI.ENCE, *s.*, desobediência.
DIS.OBE.DI.ENT, *adj.*, desobediente, rebelde.
DIS.OBEY, *v.*, desobedecer.
DIS.OR.DER, *s.*, desordem, balbúrdia, confusão; *v.*, desordenar.
DIS.OR.DER.ED, *adj.*, desordenado; *Med.*, perturbado.
DIS.OR.DER.LY, *adj.*, desordenado, indisciplinado; *adv.*, desordenadamente.
DIS.OR.DER.LY CON.DUCT, *s.*, *Jur.*, perturbação da ordem.
DIS.OR.GA.NISE(-IZE), *v.*, desorganizar, desordenar, badernar.
DIS.OR.GAN.ISED(-IZED), *adj.*, desorganizado.
DIS.O.RI.ENT, *v.*, desorientar, confundir.
DIS.O.RI.EN.TA.TION, *s.*, desorientação.
DIS.OWN, *v.*, rejeitar, refutar, renegar, repudiar.
DIS.PAR.AGE, *v.*, depreciar, desacreditar.
DIS.PAR.AGE.MENT, *s.*, depreciação, menosprezo.
DIS.PAR.AG.ING, *adj.*, depreciativo.
DIS.PA.RATE, *s.*, disparate; *adj.*, diverso, díspar.
DIS.PAR.I.TY, *s.*, disparidade, desigualdade.
DIS.PAS.SION, *s.*, imparcialidade; indiferença.
DIS.PAS.SION.ATE, *adj.*, imparcial.
DIS.PATCH, *s.*, remessa, despacho, urgência; *v.*, despachar, mandar.
DIS.PATCH.ER, *s.*, despachante, expedidor.
DIS.PEL, *v.*, dissipar, dissipar.
DIS.PEND, *v.*, despender, gastar; dissipar.
DIS.PEN.SA.BLE, *adj.*, dispensável.
DIS.PEN.SA.RY, *s.*, dispensa.
DIS.PEN.SA.TION, *s.*, ato de dispensar; distribuição, repartição.

DISPENSE ·· 442 ·· DIVERGE

DIS.PENSE, v., dispensar, repartir; administrar, oferecer, preparar.
DIS.PENS.ER, s., dispensador; distribuidor de medicamentos.
DIS.PENS.ING CHEM.IST *UK*, **DIS.PENS.ING PHAR.MA. CIST** *US*, s., farmacêutico(a).
DIS.PER.SAL, s., dispersão.
DIS.PERSE, v., dispersar, espalhar.
DIS.PIR.IT.ED, *adj.*, desalentado, desanimado.
DIS.PIR.IT.ING, *adj.*, desanimador.
DIS.PLACE, v., deslocar.
DIS.PLACED PER.SON, s., exilado; refugiado.
DIS.PLACE.MENT, s., deslocamento, desalojamento.
DIS.PLAY, s., demonstração, exposição; v., exibir; mostrar.
DIS.PLEASE, v., ofender, incomodar, aborrecer.
DIS.PLEA.SURE, s., desprazer, desgosto.
DIS.POS.A.BLE, s., descartável; *adj.*, disponível, à disposição, descartável.
DIS.POS.AL, s., descarte; disponibilidade; alienação.
DIS.POSE, v., dispor, ajustar, colocar.
DIS.PO.SI.TION, s., disposição, ordenamento.
DIS.POS.SESS, v., despojar (alguém de algo); desapossar.
DIS.PRO.POR.TION, s., desproporção, disparidade.
DIS.PRO.POR.TION.ATE, *adj.*, desproporcional.
DIS.PROVE, v., refutar.
DIS.PU.TA.TION, s., disputa, discussão, debate.
DIS.PUTE, v., disputar, contender; s., disputa, contenda, luta.
DIS.QUAL.I.FI.CA.TION, s., desqualificação.
DIS.QUAL.I.FY, v., desqualificar.
DIS.QUI.ET, s., inquietação, desassossego.
DIS.RE.GARD, v., ignorar, não ver.
DIS.RE.PAIR, s., maus estado (de conservação).
DIS.REP.U.TA.BLE, *adj.*, desacreditado; de má reputação.
DIS.RE.PUTE, s., descrédito; infâmia, ignomínia.
DIS.RE.SPECT, v., desrespeitar; s., desrespeito.
DIS.RE.SPECT.FUL, *adj.*, desrespeitoso.
DIS.ROBE, v., despir, desnudar.
DIS.RUPT, v., destacar, perturbar.
DIS.RUP.TION, s., transtorno, interrupção; ruptura; rompimento.
DIS.RUP.TIVE, *adj.*, perturbador; rompedor; destruidor.
DIS.SAT.IS.FAC.TION, s., insatisfação, descontentamento.
DIS.SAT.IS.FIED, *adj.*, insatisfeito, descontente.
DIS.SECT, v., dissecar.
DIS.SEC.TION, s., dissecação.
DIS.SEM.I.NATE, v., disseminar.
DIS.SEM.I.NA.TION, s., disseminação.
DIS.SEM.I.NA.TOR, s., disseminador.
DIS.SEN.SION, s., dissensão, divergência.
DIS.SENT, s., divergência, discordância.
DIS.SENT.ER, s., dissidente.
DIS.SENT.ING, *adj.*, dissidente., discordante.
DIS.SERT, v., dissertar, discorrer.
DIS.SER.TA.TION, s., dissertação, redação.
DIS.SERV.ICE, s., desserviço.
DIS.SI.DENCE, s., dissidência.
DIS.SI.DENT, s., dissidente.
DIS.SIM.I.LAR, *adj.*, diferente, dissimilar.
DIS.SIM.U.LATE, v., dissimular, disfarçar.
DIS.SI.PATE, v., dissipar, gastar.
DIS.SI.PAT.ED, *adj.*, dissipado, esbanjado, desregrado.
DIS.SO.CI.ATE, v., dissociar, desunir; desagregar.

DIS.SO.LUTE, *adj.*, dissoluto, devasso.
DIS.SO.LU.TION, s., dissolução.
DIS.SOLVE, v., dissolver, desmanchar.
DIS.SUADE, v., dissuadir.
DIS.TANCE, s., distância, lonjura; v., distanciar, estar distante.
DIS.TANT, *adj.*, distante, afastado, longe.
DIS.TANT.LY, *adj.*, à distância, de longe; *fig.*, friamente.
DIS.TASTE, s., desagrado, repugnância.
DIS.TASTEFUL, *adj.*, desagradável, repugnante.
DIS.TEM.PER, s., destempero, mau humor; *Art.*, pintura à têmpera; v., destemperar, irritar.
DIS.TEND.ED, *adj.*, dilatado.
DIS.TIL, v., distilar.
DIS.TIL.LER, s., destilador.
DISTIL.LE.RY, s., destilaria.
DIS.TINCT, *adj.*, distinto, claro, evidente.
DIS.TINC.TION, s., distinção.
DIS.TINC.TIVE, *adj.*, característico, distintivo, particular.
DIS.TINC.TLY, *adv.*, distintamente, claramente.
DIS.TIN.GUISH, v., distinguir, diferenciar.
DIS.TIN.GUISH.ED, *adj.*, distinto, ilustre.
DIS.TIN.GUISH.ING, *adj.*, peculiar, característico.
DIS.TORT, v., distorcer.
DIS.TORT.ED, *adj.*, distorcido.
DIS.TOR.TION, s., distorção.
DIS.TRACT.ED, *adj.*, distraído, desatento; louco, demente.
DIS.TRAC.TION, s., distração, diversão; transtorno, demência.
DIS.TRAUGHT, *adj.*, distraído; transtornado, perturbado.
DIS.TRESS, s., angústia; v., angustiar, afligir.
DIS.TRESS.ED, *adj.*, angustiado; desamparado.
DIS.TRESS.ING, *adj.*, angustiante.
DIS.TRESS.FUL, *adj.*, angustiado, aflito, consternado.
DIS.TRIB.UTE, v., distribuir, dividir.
DIS.TRIB.UT.ING, *adj.*, distribuidor.
DIS.TRI.BU.TION, s., distribuição.
DIS.TRIB.U.TOR, s., distribuidor (comercial).
DIS.TRICT, s., distrito, região, zona.
DIS.TRUST, v., desconfiar, descrer; s., desconfiança.
DIS.TRUST.FUL, *adj.*, desconfiado.
DIS.TURB, v., perturbar, atrapalhar, transtornar.
DIS.TURB.ANCE, s., distúrbio, perturbação; transtorno.
DIS.TURB.ED, *adj.*, perturbado, preocupado.
DIS.TURB.ING, *adj.*, perturbador.
DIS.U.NI.TY, s., desunião, discórdia.
DISUSE, s., desuso; v., desusar.
DISUSED, *adj.*, abandonado, desusado, arcaico.
DI.SYL.LA.BLE, s., dissílabo.
DITCH, s., fosso, vala; trincheira; v., cavar fosso; *col.*, livrar-se.
DITCHER, s., cavador de fosso.
DITHER, s., estremecimento; *col.*, confusão; v., tremer; hesitar, vacilar.
DIT.TO, s., dito; v., copiar; *adv.*, idem, como anteriormente.
DIURETIC, s., diurético.
DI.UR.NAL, *adj.*, diurno, diário, quotidiano.
DIVA, s., diva.
DI.VA.GATE, v., divagar.
DI.VAN, s., divã.
DIVE, v., mergulhar; s., mergulho.
DIV.ER, s., mergulhador.
DI.VERGE, v., divergir.

DIVERGENCE ··443·· DORMANT

DI.VER.GENCE, *s.*, divergência.
DI.VER.GENT, *adj.*, divergente.
DI.VERSE, *adj.*, diverso.
DI.VER.SI.FI.CA.TION, *s.*, diversificação.
DI.VER.SI.FY, *v.*, diversificar.
DI.VER.SION, *s.*, diversão; desvio.
DI.VER.SI.TY, *s.*, diversidade.
DI.VERT, *v.*, divertir, distrair.
DI.VEST, *v.*, despir; privar (alguém de algo), livrar-se de.
DI.VIDE, *v.*, dividir, repartir, bifurcar.
DI.VID.ED, *adj.*, dividido; desunido.
DIV.I.DEND, *s.*, dividendo.
DI.VID.ERS, *s. pl.*, compasso.
DI.VID.ING, *adj.*, divisor, distribuidor.
DI.VID.ING LINE, *s.*, linha divisória.
DI.VINE, *adj.*, divino, sagrado; *v.*, adivinhar.
DI.VINE.LY, *adv.*, divinamente, encantadoramente.
DI.VIN.ER, *s.*, adivinho.
DIV.ING, *s.*, mergulho; salto (de trampolim).
DIV.ING BOARD, *s.*, trampolim.
DIV.ING SUIT, *s.*, escafandro.
DI.VIN.I.TY, *s.*, divindade.
DI.VIS.I.BLE, *adj.*, *Mat.*, divisível.
DI.VI.SION, *s.*, divisão, repartição.
DI.VI.SIVE, *adj.*, que causa divisão, divisor.
DI.VI.SOR, *s.*, divisor.
DI.VORCE, *s.*, *Jur.*, divórcio; *v.*, divorciar.
DI.VOR.CEE, *s.*, divorciado(a).
DI.VULGE, *v.*, divulgar, publicar.
DIZ.ZI.NESS, *s.*, tontura.
DIZ.ZY, *adj.*, tonto.
DNA, *s.*, *abrev.* de *deoxyribonucleic*: ácido desoxirribonucleico.
DO, *v. aux.*, fazer.
DO.A.BLE, *adj.*, exequível, factível.
DO.BER.MAN TER.RI.ER, *s.*, doberman (raça de cão).
DOC.ILE, *adj.*, dócil, afável, manso.
DO.CIL.I.TY, *s.*, docilidade.
DOCK, *s.*, doca; banco dos réus; *v.*, atracar.
DOCK.ER, *s.*, estivador.
DOCK.LANDS, *s. pl.*, *UK* região das docas.
DOCK.YARD, *s.*, estaleiro.
DOC.TOR, *s.*, doutor, médico.
DOC.TOR.ATE, *s.*, doutorado.
DOC.TRINE, *s.*, doutrina.
DOC.U.MENT, *s.*, documento; *v.*, documentar.
DOCUMENTARY, *adj.*, documentário (que tem valor documentativo).
DOC.U.MEN.TA.TION, *s.*, documentação.
DOD.DER.ING, **DOD.DER.Y**, *adj.*, *col.*, senil.
DOD.DLE, *s.*, *UK* barbada.
DODGE, *v.*, esquivar-se, fugir de; *s.*, *col.*, mutreta.
DODG.Y, *adj.*, *UK* desonesto; arriscado; fraco.
DOE, *s.*, corça (também fêmea do coelho, antílope etc.).
DOER, *s.*, agente, autor, fazedor.
DOES, *v.*, terceira pess. do sing., presente do indicativo, do verbo *to do*.
DOESN'T, *abrev.* de *does not*.
DOG, *s.*, cachorro, cão; *v.*, seguir, perseguir.
DOG COL.LAR, *s.*, coleira de cachorro.
DOG-EARED, *adj.*, com orelhas (caderno, livro).
DOG.FISH, *s.*, *Zool.*, cação.

DOG FOOD, *s.*, ração para cachorro.
DOG.GED, *adj.*, persistente.
DOG.GISH, *adj.*, relativo aos cães, canino.
DOG.GONE, **DOG.GONED**, *adj.*, *col.*, *US* maldito.
DOG.GY BAG, *s.*, cachorrinho.
DOG.MA, *s.*, dogma.
DOG.MAT.IC, *adj.*, dogmático.
DOG.MA.TIZE, *v.*, dogmatizar.
DOG PAD.DLE, *s.*, nado estilo cachorrinho.
DOGS.BOD.Y, *s.*, *UK* faz-tudo, burro de carga.
DO.INGS, *s. pl.*, afazeres, atividades.
DOLE.FUL, *adj.*, lúgubre.
DOLL, *s.*, boneca.
DOL.LAR, *s.*, dólar.
DOL.LOP, *s.*, *col.*, monte.
DOLL'S HOUSE *UK*, **DOLL.HOUSE** *US*, *s.*, casa de bonecas.
DOL.LY, *s.*, bonequinha.
DO.LOR.OUS, *adj.*, doloroso, aflitivo.
DO.LOUR, *s.*, angústia, aflição.
DOL.PHIN, *s.*, golfinho.
DOLT, *s.*, imbecil, idiota, bobo.
DO.MAIN, *s.*, domínio.
DO.MAIN NAME, *s.*, *Comp.*, nome de domínio.
DOME, *s.*, *Arq.*, domo.
DO.MES.TIC, *adj.*, doméstico, da casa.
DO.MES.TIC AP.PLI.ANCE, *s.*, eletrodoméstico.
DO.MES.TI.CATE, *v.*, domesticar, domar, amansar, civilizar.
DO.MES.TI.CAT.ED, *adj.*, domesticado.
DO.MES.TI.CI.TY, *s.*, domesticidade; vida caseira.
DO.MI.CILE, *s.*, domicílio, casa, residência.
DO.MI.CIL.I.A.RY, *adj.*, domiciliar.
DOM.I.NANCE, *s.*, dominância; predominância.
DOM.I.NANT, *adj.*, predominante, influente.
DOM.I.NATE, *v.*, dominar.
DOM.I.NA.TING, *adj.*, dominador.
DOM.I.NA.TION, *s.*, domínio.
DOM.I.NEER.ING, *adj.*, dominador.
DO.MIN.ION, *s.*, dominação; domínio.
DOM.I.NO, *s.*, peça de dominó.
DOM.I.NOES, *s. pl.*, jogo de dominó.
DON, *s.*, *UK* professor universitário, professor universitária.
DO.NATE, *v.*, doar.
DO.NA.TION, *s.*, doação.
DONE, *adj.*, pronto, assado; aceito socialmente.
DON.KEY, *s.*, burro, asno, jumento.
DO.NOR, *s.*, doador.
DO.NOR CARD, *s.*, carteira de doador.
DON'T, *abrev.* de *do not*.
DOO.DLE, *s.*, rabisco; *v.*, rabiscar.
DOOM, *s.*, destino.
DOOMED, *adj.*, condenado; fadado a.
DOOR, *s.*, porta.
DOOR.BELL, *s.*, campainha.
DOOR-HAN.DLE, *s.*, maçaneta.
DOOR-KNOB, *s.*, maçaneta.
DOOR.MAN, *s.*, porteiro.
DOOR-MAT, *s.*, porteiro.
DOOR.STEP, *s.*, degrau.
DOOR-TO-DOOR, *adj.*, de porta em porta (vendedor).
DOPE.Y, *adj.*, *col.*, tonto, grogue.
DOR.MANT, *adj.*, inativo.

DORMITORY 444 DRAWL

DOR.MI.TO.RY, s., dormitório.
DOR.MOUSE, s., rato-silvestre.
DOR.SAL, adj., dorsal.
DOS, s., abrev. de *Disk Operating System*: Sistema Operacional em Disco, DOS.
DOS.AGE, s., dosagem, posologia.
DOSE, s., dose; v., dosar.
DOS.SI.ER, s., dossiê.
DOT, s., mancha, ponto; v., salpicar.
DO.TAGE, s., decrepitude, senilidade.
DOTE, v., caducar; estar caído de amores; disparar.
DOT.ING, adj., apaixonado; zonzo.
DOT.TED LINE, s., linha pontilhada ou tracejada.
DOT.TY, adj., estúpido, louco.
DOU.BLE, adj., s., duplo; v., dobrar, duplicar.
DOU.BLE ACT, s., Teat., dupla de intérpretes.
DOU.BLE A.GENT, s., agente duplo (espionagem).
DOU.BLE BASS, s., Mús., contrabaixo.
DOU.BLE BED, s., cama de casal.
DOU.BLE CHIN, s., papada.
DOU.BLE-CLICK, s., Comp., duplo clique; v., clicar duas vezes.
DOU.BLE.NESS, s., duplicidade.
DOU.BLE-PARK, v., estacionar em fila dupla.
DOU.BLE ROOM, s., quarto de casal.
DOU.BLY, adv., duplamente.
DOUBT, s., dúvida, incerteza; v., duvidar.
DOUBT.FUL, adj., duvidoso.
DOUBT.LESS, adv., sem dúvida.
DOUGH, s., massa (de farinha); col., grana.
DOUGH.NUT, s., tipo de rosquinha.
DOUR, adj., austero.
DOUSE, v., jogar água em; encharcar.
DOVE, s., pomba.
DOVE.TAIL, v., combinar.
DOW.DY, adj., deselegante.
DOWN, adv., para baixo; prep., embaixo de, sob; s., penugem.
DOWN.BEAT, adj., col., sombrio.
DOWN.CAST, adj., abatido, cabisbaixo.
DOWN.ER, s., col., calmante.
DOWN.FALL, s., queda, ruína.
DOWN.GRADE, v., rebaixar.
DOWN.HEART.ED, adj., desacorçoado.
DOWN.HILL, adj., íngreme; fig., canja; de mau a pior.
DOWN.LOAD, s., Comp., baixar (dados para o computador).
DOWN.MAR.KET, adj., de baixa qualidade; adv., com qualidade ruim.
DOWN PAY.MENT, s., entrada.
DOWN.PLAY, v., minimizar.
DOWN.POUR, s., aguaceiro.
DOWN.RIGHT, adj., inequívoco, franco; vertical; adv., a prumo; completamente.
DOWN.SIDE, s., desvantagem.
DOWN.SIZE, v., reduzir em tamanho.
DOWN.STAIRS, adj., andar de barco.
DOWN.STREAM, s.f., a jusante.
DOWN TIME, s., tempo ocioso.
DOWN-TO-EARTH, adj., realista.
DOWN.TOWN, adj., US do centro (da cidade); adv., em direção do centro (da cidade).
DOWN.TROD.DEN, adj., oprimido; calcado sob os pés.
DOWN.TURN, s., decréscimo.

DOWN.WARD, adj., declinante, descendente; adv., downwards, downwardly: abaixo; declinantemente.
DOW.RY, s., dote.
DOZ, s., dúzia.
DOZE, v., dormitar.
DOZEN, s., dúzia.
DOZY, adj., sonolento; UK col., retardado.
DR, s., abrev. de doctor: doutor(a), Dr., Dra.
DRAB, adj., apagado, de cor parda; monótono.
DRA.CO.NI.AN, adj., draconiano, inflexível, cruel.
DRAFT, s., rascunho, esboço; ordem de pagamento, saque; Mil., destacamento; v., esboçar; Mil., destacar.
DRAFT.EE, s., Mil., US recruta, incorporado.
DRAFT.Y, adj., inútil, imprestável.
DRAG, v., dragar, arrastar.
DRAG.BOAT, s., draga.
DRAG-LINE, s., cabo de reboque.
DRAG.MAN, s., pescador que usa rede de arrasto.
DRAG-NET, s., rede de arrasto; batida policial.
DRAG.ON, s., dragão.
DRAG.ON.FLY, s., Zool., libélula.
DRA.GOON, s., soldado 'dragão' de cavalaria; v., oprimir com soldados dragões.
DRAG-QUEEN, s., transformista, travesti.
DRAG RACE, s., Esp., corrida de carros envenenados.
DRAGS.MAN, s., condutor de carruagem.
DRAIN, s., dreno, bueiro; v., drenar, esvaziar.
DRAIN.ER, s., escoadouro, escoador.
DRAIN.AGE, s., drenagem, esgoto.
DRAIN.ING, s., escoamento, drenagem.
DRAIN-BOARD, s., escorredor de louça.
DRAKE, s., pato macho, marreco macho.
DRAM, s., trago (de aguardente); gole de líquido.
DRA.MA, s., drama, teatro.
DRA.MAT.IC, adj., dramático.
DRA.MAT.IC.AL.LY, adv., dramaticamente; drasticamente.
DRAM.A.TIST, s., dramaturgo.
DRA.MA.TI.ZA.TION, s., dramatização.
DRA.MA.TIZE, v., dramatizar.
DRAPE, s., US cortina, tapeçaria; v., drapejar; colocar suavemente; vestir, decorar.
DRA.PER, s., negociante de tecidos; decorador; loja de tecidos.
DRAS.TIC, adj., drástico.
DRAS.TI.CAL.LY, adv., drasticamente.
DRAUGHT UK, **DRAFT** US, s., esboço, rascunho; carga; corrente de ar; v., traçar, esboçar.
DRAUGHT BEER, s., chope.
DRAUGHT-BOARD, s., UK tabuleiro de damas.
DRAUGHTS, s. pl., UK jogo de damas.
DRAW, s., ato de puxar, atrativo, sorte; v., desenhar, puxar, fechar.
DRAW.BACK, s., inconveniente; Com., desconto.
DRAW.BRIDGE, s., ponte levadiça.
DRAW.ER, s., gaveta.
DRAW.ERS, s. pl., ceroulas.
DRAW.ING, s., desenho.
DRAW.ING BOARD, s., prancheta de desenho.
DRAW.ING-PIN, s., UK tachinha, percevejo.
DRAW.ING-ROOM, s., sala de estar.
DRAWL, s., fala arrastada; v., falar de forma arrastada.

DRAWN   •• 445 ••   DUB

DRAWN, *v.*, *pp* de *draw*; *adj.*, traçado, esboçado; tirado; indeciso; cansado; fechado (cortina).

DRAWN-OUT, *adj.*, esticado.

DRAW.STRING, *s.*, cordão.

DREAD, *s.*, medo, pavor, terror; *v.*, temer.

DREAD.FUL, *adj.*, terrível, pavoroso.

DREAD LOCKS, *s. pl.*, penteado estilo rastafari.

DREAM, *s.*, sonho; *v.*, sonhar.

DREAM.ER, *s.*, sonhador.

DREAM.I.LY, *adj.*, sonhadoramente.

DREAM.I.NESS, *s.*, fantasia, utopia.

DREAM.LIKE, *adj.*, como em sonho, de sonho.

DREAM.Y, *adj.*, sonhador, fantasioso, distraído.

DREA.RY, *adj.*, monótono, aborrecido.

DREDGE, *s.*, draga; rede de arrasto; *v.*, dragar; pescar com rede de arrasto.

DREDGER, *s.*, máquina de dragar, draga; pescador que usa rede de arrasto.

DREGS, *s. pl.*, sedimento, borra; *fig.*, ralé.

DRENCH, *v.*, encharcar.

DRESS, *s.*, vestido, traje, roupa; *v.*, vestir.

DRES.SAGE, *s.*, adestramento.

DRESS CIRCLE, *s.*, *Teat.*, balcão.

DRESS.ER, *s.*, o que veste; o que faz curativos; *Teat.*, camareiro; *US* cômoda, toucador; aparador.

DRESS.ING, *s.*, ação de vestir(-se); tempero, molho; curativo.

DRESS.ING GOWN, *s.*, roupão, robe.

DRESS.ING ROOM, *s.*, *Esp.*, vestiário; *Teat.*, camarim.

DRESS.ING TA.BLE, *s.*, penteadeira, toucador.

DRESS.MAK.ER, *s.*, costureiro, costureira.

DRESS.MAK.ING, *s.*, costura.

DRESS SHIRT, *s.*, camisa social.

DRESSY, *adj.*, elegante.

DRIB.BLE, *s.*, baba, saliva; filete de água; garoa; *v.*, babar; pingar; *Esp.*, driblar

DRIED, *v. imp.* e *p.p.* de **TO DRY**, seco.

DRIED FRUIT, *s.*, fruta seca.

DRIED MILK, *s.*, leite em pó.

DRIED-UP, *adj.*, ressecado, seco.

DRIFT, *s.*, flutuação (à mercê de marés e ventos); impulso, tendência; *v.*, flutuar; ir à deriva; amontoar(-se).

DRIFT.ER, *s.*, nômade, andarilho; vagabundo; *Náut.*, barco que usa rede de arrasto.

DRILL, *s.*, furadeira, broca; sulco para semear; exercício, manobra; *v.*, furar, perfurar; instruir, treinar.

DRINK, *s.*, bebida, trago, gole; *v.*, beber, servir-se de bebida.

DRINK.A.BLE, *adj.*, potável.

DRINK.ER, *s.*, bebedor; beberrão.

DRINK.ING, *s.*, ato de beber; *adj.*, para beber.

DRINK.ING FOUN.TAIN, *s.*, bebedouro.

DRINK.ING WA.TER, *s.*, água potável.

DRIP, *s.*, gota, goteira.

DRIP.PING, *adj.*, encharcado, ensopado; que pinga.

DRIVE, *s.*, passeio de carro, trajeto; energia, vigor; *v.*, guiar, dirigir.

DRIVE-IN, *s.*, *US* restaurante ou lanchonete que serve no carro; *autocine*.

DRIV.EL, *s.*, baba, saliva; *col.*, tolice, bobagem.

DRIVE OFF, *v.*, expulsar, mandar embora.

DRIV.ER, *s.*, motorista, dirigente de carro ou trem.

DRIV.ER'S LI.CENSE *US*, **DRIV.ING LI.CENCE** *UK*, *s.*, carteira de motorista.

DRIVE.WAY, *s.*, entrada para carros (em garagem).

DRIV.ING, *adj.*, forte; relativo à ação de dirigir veículos.

DRIV.ING FORCE, *s.*, força motriz.

DRIV.ING SCHOOL, *s.*, autoescola.

DRIZ.ZLE, *s.*, chuvisco, garoa; *v.*, garoar, chuviscar.

DRIZ.ZLY, *adj.*, chuvoso, garoento.

DROLL, *adj.*, engraçado, cômico, alegre.

DROM.E.DARY, *s.*, dromedário.

DRONE, *s.*, *Zool.*, zangão; zunido; *fig.*, ocioso, vadio; tipo de avião teleguiado.

DROOL, *v.*, babar; salivar; *fig.*, babar por alguém.

DROOP, *v.*, encurvar-se, pender; fechar-se; murchar; desanimar, definhar.

DROP, *s.*, gota, pingo, pingente; *v.*, deixar cair, baixar, descer.

DROPS, *s. pl.*, *Med.*, gotas (de medicamento líquido).

DROP.LET, *s.*, gotícula.

DROP.OUT, *s.*, pessoa que abandona os estudos, marginalizado.

DROP.PER, *s.*, conta-gotas.

DROP.PING, *s.*, escoamento; *adj.*, gotejante.

DROP.PINGS, *s. pl.*, excremento de animais.

DROP.SY, *s.*, hidropisia.

DROSS, *s.*, escória, restos, sobras.

DROUGHT, *s.*, seca.

DROVE, *v.*, *ps.* de *drive*; *s.*, multidão; rebanho, manada.

DROWN, *v.*, afogar, diminuir o som.

DROWSE, *v.*, dormitar, dormir de leve.

DROW.SY, *adj.*, sonolento.

DRUB, *v.*, espancar, bater, surrar, dar uma tunda.

DRUDGE, *s.*, escravo do trabalho; *v.*, labutar arduamente.

DRUDG.ER.Y, *s.*, trabalho pesado.

DRUG, *s.*, remédio, medicamento, droga.

DRUG.GIST, *s.*, farmacêutico.

DRUG.STORE, *s.*, drogaria.

DRUID, *s.*, druida.

DRUM, *s.*, *Mús.*, tambor; tambor de óleo, barril; *v.*, rufar, tocar tambor; retumbar.

DRUM.BEAT, *s.*, toque de tambor, rufo.

DRUM MA.JOR.ETTE, *s.*, baliza (pessoa que vai à frente em desfiles cívicos ou esportivos manejando um bastão).

DRUM.MER, *s.*, *Mús.*, baterista; *US* caixeiro-viajante.

DRUMS, *s. pl.*, *Mús.*, bateria.

DRUNK, *v.*, *pp* de *drink*; *v.*, bêbedo, beberrão.

DRUNK.ARD, *s.*, beberrão, bêbado.

DRUNK.EN.NESS, *s.*, bebedeira, embriaguez.

DRY, *adj.*, seco, sem chuva; *v.*, secar, enxugar.

DRY-CLEAN, *v.*, lavar a seco.

DRY CLEAN.ER, *s.*, tinturaria.

DRY CLEAN.ING, *s.*, lavagem a seco.

DRY.ER, *s.*, secador.

DRY ICE, *s.*, gelo seco.

DRY LAND, *s.*, terra firme.

DRY LAW, *s.*, Lei Seca.

DRY.LY, DRI.LY, *adv.*, secamente.

DRY.NESS, *s.*, seca, aridez; aspereza, secura; monotonia.

DU.AL, *adj.*, dual, duplo.

DU.A.LISM, *s.*, dualismo.

DUAL NA.TION.AL.I.TY, *s.*, dupla nacionalidade.

DU.AL.I.TY, *s.*, dualidade.

DUB, *s.*, charco; pessoa inepta; *v.*, *Cin.* e *TV*, dublar filme;

DUBBED   •• 446 ••   DYSTROPHY

conferir titular a alguém.
DUB.BED, *adj., Cin. e TV*, dublado.
DU.BI.ETY, *s.*, dubiedade, dúvida.
DU.BI.OUS, *adj.*, duvidoso, incerto.
DU.BI.TA.TION, *s.*, dúvida.
DUCH.ESS, *s.*, duquesa.
DUCHY, *s.*, ducado.
DUCK, *s.*, pato.
DUCK.LING, *s.*, patinho.
DUCT, *s.*, tubo, canal; *Anat.*, ducto.
DUD, *s., col.*, coisa sem valor; *US* fracasso; *adj.*, falso, sem valor, inútil; que falhou (bomba).
DUDE, *s.*, almofadinha, grã-fino.
DUE, *adj.*, devido, aguardado.
DU.EL, *s.*, duelo, luta, contenda.
DUKE, *s.*, duque.
DUL.CET, *adj.*, doce, suave, afável, meigo.
DUL.CI.FY, *v.*, dulcificar, adoçar, suavizar.
DULL, *adj.*, nublado; sem brilho; triste; mouco; monótono; *v.*, atenuar (dor); tornar(-se) estúpido.
DULL.ISH, *adj.*, aborrecido, chato; um pouco estúpido.
DUL.LY, *adv.*, pesadamente, estupidamente.
DULY, *adv.*, devidamente, propriamente.
DUMB, *adj.*, mudo, calado; *US col.*, parvo; *v.*, emudecer.
DUMB.BELL, *s.*, haltere; *US col.*, estúpido.
DUMB.FOUND, *v.*, emudecer; confundir; assombrar; pasmar.
DUMB.NESS, *s.*, mudez, taciturnidade; *US* estupidez.
DUMB.STRUCK, *adj.*, emudecido, pasmado.
DUM.MY, *s.*, pessoa taciturna; postiço; manequim; estúpido; *adj.*, falso; emudecido.
DUM.MY RUM, *s.*, teste simulado, ensaio.
DUMP, *s.*, depósito de lixo, lixeira; *v.*, depositar, jogar fora; deixar cair; *Com.*, liquidar.
DUMP TRUCK, *s.*, caminhão basculante (de lixo).
DUMP.ING, *s.*, descarregamento; *no ~*: "proibido jogar lixo"; *Com.*, abaixo do preço de custo.
DUMP.ING GROUND, *s.*, depósito.
DUMP.LING, *s., Cul.*, bolinho de massa de pão.
DUMPS, *s. pl.*, depressão, tristeza.
DUMP.STER, *s.*, caçamba de lixo.
DUMP.Y, *adj.*, atarracado; maltrapilho.
DUNCE, *s.*, burro, estúpido.
DUNE, *s.*, duna.
DUNG, *s.*, estrume, esterco.
DUN.GA.REES, *s.*, *UK* macacão de trabalhador (de brim).
DUN.GEON, *s.*, masmorra; torre de vigia.
DUNK, *s.*, ato de molhar; *v.*, molhar.
DUO, *s.*, duo, dupla.
DU.O.DE.NUM, *s.*, duodeno.

DUPE, *s.*, tolo, otário; *v.*, enganar, lograr.
DU.PLEX, *s.*, *US* apartamento dúplex; *adj.*, dúplex, dúplice.
DU.PLI.CATE, *s.*, duplicação, cópia; *v.*, duplicar, copiar, fotocopiar.
DU.PLI.CA.TION, *s.*, duplicação.
DU.PLIC.I.TY, *s.*, duplicidade, ambiguidade, falsidade.
DU.RA.BIL.I.TY, *s.*, durabilidade, duração.
DU.RA.BLE, *adj.*, durável.
DU.RA.TION, *s.*, duração.
DU.RESS, *s.* coerção, coação; ameaça.
DUR.ING, *prep.*, durante.
DUSK, *s.*, crepúsculo, lusco-fusco, anoitecer; *v.*, anoitecer.
DUSKY, *adj.*, escuro, escurecido.
DUST, *s.*, pó, poeira.
DUST.BIN, *s.*, *US* lata de lixo.
DUST.CART, *s.*, *UK* caminhão de lixo.
DUST.ER, *s.*, pano para pó.
DUST.MAN, *s.*, lixeiro.
DUST MITE, *s.*, ácaro do pó.
DUST.PAN, *s.*, pá de lixo.
DUST.Y, *adj.*, empoeirado.
DUTCH, *adj.*, *s.*, holandês, batavo.
DU.TI.A.BLE, *adj.*, tributável.
DU.TI.FUL, *adj.*, cumpridor, que executa.
DU.TI.FUL.NESS, *s.*, cumprimento do dever.
DU.TY, *s.*, dever; taxa, imposto.
DUTY.FREE, *adj.*, livre de impostos; *s.*, loja de aeroporto.
DU.VET, *s.*, edredão.
DWARF, *s.*, anão, anã; *adj.*, pequenino, anão; *v.*, tornar menor; sobrepujar.
DWELL, *v.*, morar, habitar.
DWELL.ER, *s.*, morador, habitante.
DWELL.ING, *s.*, habitação, moradia.
DWIN.DLE, *v.*, diminuir, minguar, encolher-se.
DYE, *s.*, tinta, tintura; *v.*, tingir.
DYE.ING, *s.*, tintura; *adj.*, que tinge, tingidor.
DY.ER, *s.*, tintureiro.
DY.ING, *s.*, ato de morrer; *adj.*, agonizante, que está para se extinguir.
DYKE, *s.*, dique, represa.
DY.NAM.IC, *adj.*, dinâmico.
DY.NAM.ICS, *s.*, dinâmica.
DY.NA.MITE, *s.*, dinamite; *v.*, dinamitar.
DY.NA.MO, *s.*, dínamo.
DY.NAS.TY, *s.*, dinastia.
DYS.EN.TERY, *s.*, disenteria.
DYS.LEX.I.A, *s., Med.*, dyslexia.
DYS.LEX.IC, *adj.*, disléxico.
DYS.TRO.PHY, *s., Med.*, distrofia.

E, *s.*, quinta letra do alfabeto inglês.
EACH, *adj.*, cada; *pron.*, cada, cada um, cada qual.
EA.GER, *adj.*, ansioso, zeloso, ávido.
EA.GER.LY, *adv.*, ansiosamente; zelosamente.
EA.GER.NESS, *s.*, ânsia, avidez, zelo, impaciência.
EA.GLE, *s.*, águia.
EA.GLET, *s.*, filhote de águia.
EAR, *s.*, ouvido, orelha, audição; *v.*, espigar.
EAR.ACHE, *s.*, dor de ouvido.
EAR.DROPS, *s. pl.*, brincos.
EAR.DRUM, *s.*, *Anat.*, tímpano.
EARL, *s.*, conde.
EAR.LI.ER, *adj.*, anterior; *adv.*, antes.
EAR.LI.EST, *adj.*, primeiro; *adv.*, no mínimo.
EAR.LOBE, *s.*, lóbulo da orelha.
EAR.LY, *adj.*, cedo, matinal, precoce; *adv.*, de madrugada, em breve.
EAR.MARK, *v.*, destinar; marcar, assinalar; *s.*, marca na orelha de animais (rural).
EARN, *v.*, ganhar, lucrar.
EARN.ER, *s.*, ganhador; assalariado.
EAR.NEST, *s.*, seriedade, determinação; *adj.*, sério, honesto, determinado.
EAR.NEST.LY, *adv.*, seriamente.
EAR.NEST.NESS, *s.*, seriedade, severidade; zelo, dedicação.
EARN.INGS, *s. pl.*, salário, vencimento, ordenado.
EAR.PHONES, *s. pl.*, fones de ouvido.
EAR.PIECE, *s.*, audiofone (receptor de telefone).
EAR.PLUGS, *s. pl.*, protetores de ouvido.
EAR.RING, *s.*, brinco.
EAR.SHOT, *s.*, alcance da voz.
EAR-SPLIT.TING, *adj.*, ensurdecedor.
EARTH, *s.*, terra, globo terrestre, mundo, chão; *v.*, enterrar, ligar à terra.
EARTH.EN, *adj.*, terroso, térreo (feito de barro).
EARTH.EN.WARE, *adj.*, de barro, de louça (cerâmica).
EARTH.LING, *s.*, habitante da terra, terráqueo.
EARTH.LY, *adj.*, terrestre, térreo, mundano, profano.
EARTH.QUAKE, *s.*, terremoto, sismo.
EARTH.SHAK.ING, *adj.*, que tem importância fundamental.
EARTH.SHAT.TER.ING, *adj.*, *UK* surpreendente.
EARTH TREM.OR, *s.*, tremor de terra.
EARTH.WARD, *adj.*, em direção à terra.
EARTH.WORM, *s.*, minhoca.
EARTH.Y, *adj.*, terreno, terrestre; ordinário, vulgar; objetivo.
EAR.WAX, *s.*, cera de ouvido.
EAR.WIG, *s.*, *Zool.*, lacraia; *v.*, tagarelar.
EASE, *s.*, tranquilidade, sossego, conforto, bem-estar; *v.*, aliviar, atenuar.
EASE.FUL, *adj.*, tranquilo, sossegado, confortável.
EA.SEL, *s.*, cavalete.
EASE.MENT, *s.*, facilidade, conforto, vantagem.

EAS.I.LY, *adv.*, facilmente.
EAS.I.NESS, *s.*, facilidade, conforto, docilidade.
EAST, *s.*, leste, este, oriente.
EAST.BOUND, *adj.*, em direção a leste.
EAST.ER, *s.*, Páscoa.
EAST.ER EGG, *s.*, ovo de Páscoa.
EAST.ER.LY, *adj.*, leste, do leste.
EAST.ERN, *adj.*, oriental, do leste, levantino.
EAST.WARD, *adj.*, ao leste; *adj. e adv.*, oriental, para leste.
EAST.WARDS, *s.*, leste; *adv.*, para o leste.
EASY, *adj.*, fácil, leve, cômodo, confortável; *adv.*, facilmente.
EAS.Y CHAIR, *s.*, poltrona.
EAS.Y.GO.ING, *adj.*, descontraído.
EAT, *v.*, comer.
EAT.ABLE, *s. pl.*, víveres, alimentos.
EATER, *s.*, comedor.
EAT.ER.Y, *s.*, lugar que vende refeições.
EAT IN, *v.*, comer em casa.
EAT.ING-HOUSE, *s.*, restaurante, lanchonete.
EAVES, *s.*, beirada, beiral.
EA.VES.DROP, *v.*, bisbilhotar.
EBB, *s.*, maré baixa, vazante, refluxo; *v.*, diminuir, baixar, refluir.
EBB TIDE, *s.*, maré baixa, baixa mar, vazante.
EB.O.NY, *s.*, ébano, cor escura; *adj.*, escuro, negro, feito de ébano.
EBUL.LI.ENCE, *s.*, ebulição, fervura; excitação.
EBUL.LIENT, *adj.*, ebuliente, fervente; exaltado.
EB.UL.LI.ION, *s.*, ebulição, fervura; entusiasmo.
E-BUSI.NESS, *s.*, negócio eletrônico (empresa de internet).
EC.CEN.TRIC, *adj.*, excêntrico, exótico, estranho.
EC.CEN.TRIC.I.TY, *s.*, excentricidade.
EC.CLE.SI.AS.TIC, *adj., s.*, eclesiástico.
ECH.E.LON, *s.*, *Mil.*, escalão; hierarquia militar; *v.*, escalonar.
E.CHI.NO.DERM, *s.*, *Zool.*, equinoderma.
ECHO, *s.*, eco; repetição; *v.*, ecoar, ressoar.
ECH.O.CAR.DI.O.GRAM, *s.*, *Med.*, ecocardiograma.
EC.LAMP.SI.A, *s.*, *Med.*, eclâmpsia.
EC.LEC.TIC, *adj.*, eclético.
E.CLIPSE, *s.*, eclipse, escurecimento; *v.*, eclipsar-se, sumir.
EC.O.LOG.IC, *adj.*, ecológico.
EC.O.LOG.IC.AL, *adj.*, ecológico.
EC.O.LOG.IC.AL.LY, *adv.*, ecologicamente.
E.COL.O.GIST, *s.*, ecologista.
E.COL.O.GY, *s.*, ecologia.
E-COM.MERCE, *s.*, comércio eletrônico (vendas pela internet).
EC.O.NOM.IC, *adj.*, econômico, produtivo, lucrativo.
EC.O.NOM.I.CAL, *adj.*, econômico.
EC.O.NOM.ICS, *s.*, economia.
ECON.O.MIST, *s.*, economista.
E.CON.O.MIZE(-ISE), *v.*, economizar.

ECONOMY · 448 · EKE

E.CON.O.MY, *s.*, economia.
E.CON.O.MY CLASS, *s.*, classe econômica.
E.CO.SYS.TEM, *s.*, ecossistema.
ECO-TOUR.ISM, *s.*, ecoturismo.
ECO-TOUR.IST, *s.*, ecoturista.
EC.STA.SY, *s.*, êxtase.
EC.STAT.IC, *s.*, extático (estado de êxtase); *adj.*, extasiado.
EC.STAT.IC.AL.LY, *adv.*, em êxtase, extaticamente.
EC.UA.DOR.IAN, *adj., s.*, equatoriano.
E.CU.MEN.IC, *adj.*, ecumênico, universal.
EC.U.MEN.I.CAL, *adj.*, ecumênico.
EC.ZE.MA, *s.*, eczema.
ED.DY, *s.*, redemoinho; *v.*, redemoinhar.
EDEN, *s.*, éden, paraíso.
EDEN.TATE, *adj.*, desdentado.
EDGE, *s.*, canto, beira, bainha; margem; fio; corte; *v.*, afiar, amolar; embainhar, margear.
EDGED, *adj.*, afiado, pontiagudo; orlado.
EDGE.WAYS, *adv.*, lateralmente, pelo lado.
EDG.ER, *s.*, afiador, amolador.
EDGE.WAYS, *adv.*, lateralmente.
EDG.ING, *s.*, borda, guarnição; fita, franja.
EDG.Y, *adj.*, nervoso, inquieto; preocupado.
ED.I.BIL.I.TY, *s.*, comestibilidade.
ED.I.BLE, *adj.*, comestível, digerível.
E.DICT, *s.*, edital, lei, ordem.
ED.I.FI.CA.TION, *s.*, edificação.
ED.I.FI.CA.TO.RY, *adj.*, edificante, santificante.
ED.I.FICE, *s.*, edifício, prédio.
ED.I.FY, *v.*, edificar, instruir, ensinar.
ED.I.FY.ING, *adj.*, edificante.
ED.IT, *v.*, editar, publicar, editorar.
EDI.TION, *s.*, edição; publicação, impressão.
ED.I.TOR, *s.*, editor, redator, jornalista.
ED.I.TO.RI.AL, *adj., s.*, editorial.
ED.I.TO.RI.AL.IST, *s.*, editorialista.
ED.I.TRESS, *s.*, editora.
ED.U.CATE, *v.*, educar, instruir, preparar.
ED.U.CATED, *adj.*, educado, culto.
ED.U.CA.TION, *s.*, educação, ensino.
ED.U.CA.TION.AL, *adj.*, educacional; educativo.
ED.U.CA.TION.IST, *s.*, educador.
ED.U.CA.TIVE, *adj.*, educativo, instrutivo.
ED.U.CA.TOR, *s.*, educador, pedagogo.
E.DUCE, *v.*, deduzir, eduzir.
E.DU.CI.BLE, *adj.*, deduzível.
EDUC.TION, *s.*, dedução.
EEL, *s., Zool.*, enguia.
EER.IE, *adj.*, sinistro, lúgubre, misterioso.
EF.FACE, *v.*, obscurecer, apagar, extinguir.
EF.FACE.MENT, *s.*, anulamento, extinção, obliteração.
EF.FECT, *s.*, efeito; resultado; eficiência; *v.*, efetuar, fazer, realizar.
EF.FEC.TIVE, *adj.*, efetivo, eficaz.
EF.FEC.TIVE.LY, *adv.*, efetivamente, eficazmente.
EF.FEC.TIVE.NESS, *s.*, eficácia, eficiência, efetividade.
EF.FEC.TIVES, *s. pl.*, contingente (efetivo de um exército).
EF.FECT.LESS, *adj.*, ineficiente, inútil; ineficaz.
EF.FEC.TU.ATE, *v.*, efetuar, executar, concretizar.
EF.FEC.TU.A.TION, *s.*, efetuação, realização.
EF.FE.MI.NATE, *adj.*, efeminado, afeminado; mulherengo; fraco.
EF.FE.MI.NA.TION, *s.*, efeminação.
EF.FER.VESCE, *v.*, efervescer, ferver.
EF.FER.VES.CENT, *adj.*, efervescente; *fig.*, animado.
EF.FETE, *adj.*, cansado, fraco, gasto.
EF.FI.CA.CIOUS, *adj.*, eficaz, eficiente.
EF.FI.CA.CY, *s.*, eficácia.
EF.FI.CIENCY, *s.*, eficiência.
EF.FI.CIENT, *adj.*, eficiente, competente.
EF.FI.CIENT.LY, *adv.*, eficientemente.
EF.FI.GY, *s.*, efígie, imagem, figura.
EF.FLU.ENT, *s.*, efluente.
EF.FLU.VI.UM, *s., Lat.*, eflúvio, exalação.
EF.FLO.RESCE, *v.*, eflorescer.
EF.FLO.RES.CENCE, *s.*, eflorescência.
EF.FORT, *s.*, esforço, empenho, tentativa.
EF.FORT.FUL, *adj.*, trabalhoso, penoso.
EF.FORT.LESS, *adj.*, com desenvoltura, fácil.
EF.FORT.LESS.LY, *adv.*, facilmente.
EF.FRON.TER.Y, *s.*, descaramento.
EF.FRON.TER.Y, *s.*, descaramento.
EF.FUL.GENCE, *s.*, fulgor, brilho, resplendor.
EF.FUL.GENT, *adj.*, fulgurante, resplandecente.
EF.FUL.GENT.LY, *adv.*, fulgurantemente.
EF.FUSE, *v.*, efundir, derramar, espalhar.
EF.FU.SION, *s.*, efusão, chá, eflúvio.
EF.FU.SIVE, *adj.*, efusivo.
EF.FU.SIVE.LY, *adv.*, efusivamente.
E.GAL.I.TAR.I.AN, *s., adj.*, igualitário.
EGG, *s.*, ovo; óvulo, germe.
EGG-AP.PLE, *s., Bot.*, berinjela (fruto).
EGG.BEAT.ER, *s.*, batedeira de ovos.
EGG.CUP, *s.*, oveiro.
EGG.ING, *s.*, postura de ovos.
EGG.PLANT, *s., Bot., US* berinjela.
EGG.SHELL, *s.*, casca de ovos.
EGG WHISK, *s.*, batedor de ovos.
EGG WHITE, *s.*, clara de ovo.
EGG YOLK, *s.*, gema de ovo.
E.GO, *s.*, ego, eu.
E.GO.CEN.TRIC, *adj.*, egocêntrico.
E.GO.ISM, *s.*, egoísmo.
E.GO.IST, *s.*, egoísta.
E.GO.IST.IC, *adj.*, egoísta.
E.GRESS, *s.*, saída, egresso.
EGYP.TIAN, *adj., s.*, egípcio.
EI.DER.DOWN, *s.*, edredão.
EIGHT, *num.*, oito.
EIGH.TEEN, *num.*, dezoito.
EIGH.TEENTH, *s., num.*, décimo oitavo.
EIGHTH, *num.*, oitavo.
EIGHT.I.ETH, *num.*, octagésimo.
EIGHT.Y, *num.*, oitenta.
EIRE, *s., Ir,* República da Irlanda.
EI.THER, *pron.*, cada um, um ou outro; ambos.
E.JAC.U.LATE, *v.*, ejacular.
E.JAC.U.LA.TION, *s.*, ejaculação.
E.JECT, *v.*, lançar, jogar, ejetar, expelir.
E.JEC.TION, *s.*, ejeção, lançamento.
E.JEC.TOR, *s., Tec.*, ejetor.
EKE, *v.*, esticar, racionar.

ELABORATE · 449 · ELONGATED

E.LAB.O.RATE, v., aperfeiçoar, elaborar; adj., elaborado, aperfeiçoado.
E.LAB.O.RATE.LY, adv., detalhadamente.
E.LAB.O.RA.TION, s., elaboração.
E.LAPSE, v., transcorrer.
E.LAS.TIC, adj., elástico, flexível.
E.LAS.TIC.AT.ED, adj., elástico.
E.LAS.TIC BAND, s., UK elástico.
E.LAS.TIC.I.TY, s., elasticidade.
E.LAT.ED, adj., exultante.
E.LA.TION, s., exultação.
EL.BOW, s., cotovelo; v., acotovelar.
EL.BOW-CHAIR, s., poltrona, cadeira de braços.
EL.DER, adj., mais velho, o mais velho; s., pessoa idosa, ancião.
EL.DER.BER.RY, s., Bot., fruto do sabugueiro; sabugueiro.
EL.DER.LY, s., idoso(s); adj., de idade mais avançada.
EL.DER.SHIP, s., primogenitura.
EL.DEST, adj., mais velho, o mais velho.
E.LECT, s., os eleitos, os escolhidos; v., eleger, escolher, selecionar.
E.LEC.TION, s., eleição, escolha.
E.LEC.TION CAM.PAIGN, s., campanha eleitoral.
E.LEC.TION.EER.ING, s., propaganda eleitoral.
E.LEC.TIVE, s., disciplina opcional (estudo); adj., eletivo; elegível.
E.LEC.TIVE.LY, adv., por eleição.
E.LEC.TIVE.NESS, s., elegibilidade.
E.LEC.TOR, s., eleitor, votante.
E.LEC.TOR.AL, adj., eleitoral.
E.LEC.TOR.AL COL.LEGE, s., US colégio eleitoral.
E.LEC.TOR.ATE, s., eleitorado.
E.LEC.TRIC, adj., elétrico.
E.LEC.TRIC.AL, adj., elétrico.
E.LEC.TRIC.AL EN.GI.NEER, s., engenheiro eletricista.
E.LEC.TRIC.AL EN.GI.NEER.ING, s., engenharia elétrica.
E.LEC.TRIC.AL.LY, adv., eletricamente.
E.LEC.TRIC.AL SHOCK US, **E.LEC.TRIC SHOCK** UK, s., choque elétrico.
E.LEC.TRIC ARC, s., Eletr., arco elétrico ou voltaico.
E.LEC.TRIC CHAIR, s., cadeira elétrica.
E.LEC.TRIC COOKER, s., fogão elétrico.
E.LEC.TRIC CUR.RENT, s., corrente elétrica.
E.LEC.TRIC FENCE, s., cerca elétrica.
E.LEC.TRIC FIELD, s., Eletr., campo elétrico.
E.LEC.TRIC FIX.TURES, s. pl., instalações elétricas.
E.LEC.TRIC GUI.TAR, s., guitarra elétrica.
E.LEC.TRI.CIAN, s., eletricista.
E.LEC.TRIC.I.TY, s., eletricidade.
E.LEC.TRI.FI.CA.TION, s., eletrificação.
E.LEC.TRI.FY, v., eletrificar; eletrizar.
E.LEC.TRI.FY.ING, adj., fig., eletrizante.
E.LEC.TRO.CAR.DI.O.GRAM, s., Med., eletrocardiograma.
E.LEC.TRO.CAR.DI.OG.RA.PHY, s., Med., eletrocardiografia.
E.LEC.TRO.CUTE, v., eletrocutar.
E.LEC.TRO.CU.TION, s., eletrocussão.
E.LEC.TRODE, s., eletrodo.
E.LEC.TRO.EN.CEPH.A.LO.GRAM, s., eletroencefalograma.
E.LEC.TRO.EN.CEPH.A.LOG.RA.PHY, s., eletroencefalografia.
E.LEC.TROL.Y.SIS, s., eletrólise.

E.LEC.TRO.MAG.NET, s., eletroímã.
E.LEC.TRO.MAG.NET.IC, adj., eletromagnético.
E.LEC.TRO.MAG.NE.TISM, s., eletromagnetismo.
E.LEC.TRO.MO.TIVE, adj., eletromotor.
E.LEC.TRON, s., elétron.
E.LEC.TRON.IC, adj., eletrônico.
E.LEC.TRON.IC MAIL, s., correio eletrônico.
E.LEC.TRON.IC OR.GAN.IZ.ER, s., agenda eletrônica.
E.LEC.TRON.ICS, s., eletrônica.
E.LEC.TRON VOLT, s., Fís., elétron-volt.
E.LEC.TRO.PLATE, v., galvanizar, pratear.
E.LEC.TRO.PLAT.ED, adj., galvanizado.
E.LEC.TRO.PLAT.ING, s., galvanoplastia.
E.LEC.TRO.STAT.ICS, s., eletrostática.
EL.E.GANCE, s., elegância.
EL.E.GANT, adj., elegante, garboso.
EL.E.GANT.LY, adv., elegantemente, brilhantemente.
EL.E.GI.AC, s., elegíaco; adj., elegíaco, melancólico.
EL.E.GY, s., elegia.
EL.E.MENT, s., elemento, componente, fundamento.
EL.E.MEN.TAL, adj., elementar, básico.
EL.E.MEN.TAL.LY, adv., elementarmente.
EL.E.MEN.TA.RI.LY, adv., elementarmente, basicamente.
EL.E.MEN.TA.RI.NESS, s., elementaridade.
EL.E.MEN.TA.RY, adj., elementar.
EL.E.MEN.TA.RY SCHOOL, s., US escolar primária.
EL.E.PHANT, s., Zool., elefante.
EL.E.PHAN.TI.A.SIS, s., Med., elefantíase.
EL.E.VATE, v., elevar, levantar, alçar.
EL.E.VAT.ED, adj., elevado; digno, nobre; s., elevado.
EL.E.VA.TION, s., elevação, altura, altitude.
EL.E.VA.TOR, s., elevador, ascensor.
ELEV.EN, num., onze.
ELEV.ENTH, num., undécimo, décimo primeiro.
ELF, s., elfo, duende.
E.LIC.IT, v., eliciar; extrair; concluir.
E.LIDE, v., elidir, suprimir; eliminar (palavras de um texto); resumir.
EL.I.GI.BIL.I.TY, s., elegibilidade.
EL.I.GI.BLE, adj., elegível.
ELIM.I.NATE, v., eliminar, erradicar, tirar tudo.
ELIM.I.NA.TION, s., eliminação.
ELIM.I.NA.TOR, s., Esp., eliminatória (competição).
ELI.SION, s., Gram., elisão.
É.LITE, s., Fr., elite; nata, flor.
E.LIT.ISM, s., elitismo.
E.LIT.IST, s., elitista.
ELIX.IR, s., elixir.
E.LIZ.A.BE.THAN, adj., elisabetano.
EL.LIPSE, s., elipse.
EL.LIP.TIC, adj., elíptico.
ELK, s., Zool., alce.
EL.LIPSE, s., Geom., elipse.
EL.LIP.TIC.AL, adj., elíptico.
EL.LIP.TIC.AL.LY, adv., elipticamente.
ELM, s., Bot., olmo.
EL.O.CU.TION, s., elocução; dicção; eloquência.
EL.O.CU.TION.A.RY, adj., retórico.
EL.O.CU.TION.IST, s., orador, declamador.
E.LON.GATE, v., alongar, prolongar; esticar.
E.LON.GATED, adj., alongado.

ELOPE · · 450 · · EMPIRICISM

E.LOPE, *v.*, fugir (com o namorado ou para casar).
EL.O.QUENCE, *s.*, eloquência.
EL.O.QUENT, *adj.*, eloquente.
EL.O.QUENT.LY, *adv.*, eloquentemente.
ELSE, *adj.*, outro, diverso; *adv.*, em vez de; *conj.*, senão.
ELSE.WHERE, *adv.*, alhures, em outro lugar.
E.LU.CI.DATE, *v.*, elucidar, explicar, explanar.
E.LU.CI.DA.TION, *v.*, elucidação, explicação.
E.LU.CI.DA.TIVE, *adj.*, elucidativo.
E.LUDE, *v.*, iludir, fugir, esquivar-se.
E.LU.SION, *s.*, ardil, estratagema, artifício.
E.LU.SIVE, *adj.*, enganoso, ilusório.
E.LU.SIVE.LY, *adv.*, ardilosamente.
E.LU.TRI.ATE, *v.*, *Quím.*, decantar, purificar.
E.MA.CI.ATE, *v.*, emaciar, definhar, emagrecer.
E.MA.CI.ATED, *adj.*, emagrecido.
E-MAIL, *s.*, *Comp.*, correio eletrônico.
E-MAIL ADDRESS, *s.*, *Comp.*, endereço eletrônico.
EM.A.NATE, *v.*, emanar, proceder, vir de.
EM.A.NA.TION, *s.*, emanação, revelação; *fig.*, origem.
E.MAN.CI.PATE, *v.*, emancipar, livrar.
E.MAN.CI.PA.TION, *s.*, emancipação.
E.MAS.CU.LATE, *v.*, emascular, castrar; *fig.*, enfraquecer.
E.MAS.CU.LA.TION, *s.*, emasculação, castração; fraqueza.
EM.BALM, *v.*, embalsamar.
EM.BAL.MER, *s.*, embalsamador.
EM.BANK, *v.*, colocar dique; represar; terraplanar.
EM.BANK.MENT, *s.*, dique, barragem, aterro.
EM.BAR.GO, *s.*, proibição, embargo, veto.
EM.BARK, *v.*, embarcar.
EM.BAR.KA.TION, *s.*, embarque.
EM.BAR.RASS, *v.*, envergonhar; atrapalhar, dificultar.
EM.BAR.RASSED, *adj.*, perplexo, envergonhado.
EM.BAR.RASS.ING, *adj.*, embaraçoso, inoportuno.
EM.BAR.RASS.MENT, *s.*, vergonha, estorvo, empecilho.
EM.BAS.SY, *s.*, embaixada.
EM.BAT.TLED, *adj.*, em combate; preparado para o combate.
EM.BED, *v.*, enterrar; encaixar; fixar.
EM.BED.DED, *adj.*, enterrado; *fig.*, enraizado.
EM.BEL.LISH, *v.*, embelezar, ornamentar.
EM.BEL.LISH.MENT, *s.*, embelezamento.
EMB.ER, *s.*, tição, brasa, borralho.
EMB.ERS, *s. pl.*, brasa.
EM.BEZ.ZLE, *v.*, desviar, fraudar, desfalcar.
EM.BEZ.ZLE.MENT, *s.*, desfalque, desvio, fraude.
EM.BEZ.ZLER, *s.*, fraudador.
EM.BIT.TER, *v.*, azedar, amargar, angustiar.
EM.BIT.TERED, *adj.*, amargurado, cínico.
EM.BIT.TER.MENT, *s.*, amargura, aflição.
EM.BLAZE, *v.*, acender, incendiar; iluminar (com fogo).
EM.BLA.ZON, *v.*, *Her.*, brasonar; decorar; exaltar.
EM.BLA.ZON.ER, *s.*, artista de armas e brasões; aquele que exalta.
EM.BLEM, *s.*, emblema.
EM.BLEM.AT.IC, *adj.*, emblemático.
EM.BOD.I.MENT, *s.*, encarnação, personificação.
EM.BODY, *v.*, incorporar, personificar.
EM.BO.LISM, *s.*, *Med.*, embolia; embolismo.
EM.BOSS, *v.*, modelar ou gravar em relevo.
EM.BOSS.ED, *adj.*, em relevo.
EM.BOSS.ING, *s.*, relevo.

EM.BOSS.MENT, *s.*, relevo, gravura em relevo.
EM.BOW.ER, *v.*, cobrir com folhar ou ramos; envolver.
EM.BRACE, *v.*, abraçar, dar um abraço.
EM.BRACE.MENT, *s.*, abraço.
EM.BROI.DER, *v.*, bordar; enfeitar.
EM.BROI.DER.ER, *adj.*, bordador, bordadeira.
EM.BROI.DER.ED, *adj.*, bordado.
EM.BROI.DER.Y, *s.*, bordado; ornamento, enfeite.
EM.BROIL, *v.*, embrulhar, complicar.
EM.BRY.O, *s.*, embrião, feto.
EM.BRY.OL.O.GY, *s.*, embriologia.
EM.BRY.ONIC, *s.*, embrionário.
E.MEND, *v.*, corrigir, emendar.
E.MEND.A.BLE, *adj.*, emendável, corrigível.
E.MEND.ATE, *v.*, emendar, corrigir.
E.MEN.DA.TION, *s.*, correção, emenda.
E.MER.ALD, *s.*, esmeralda.
E.MERGE, *v.*, emergir, sair, vir para fora.
EMER.GENCE, *s.*, emergência.
E.MER.GEN.CY, *s.*, emergência.
E.MER.GEN.CY EXIT, *s.*, saída de emergência.
E.MER.GEN.CY LAND.ING, *s.*, pouso de emergência.
E.MER.GENT, *adj.*, emergente.
E.MER.I.TUS, *adj.*, *s.*, jubilado; aposentado.
E.MERSED, *adj.*, emerso.
E.MER.SION, *s.*, emersão.
E.MER.Y, *s.*, esmeril.
E.MER.Y BOARD, *s.*, lixa de unhas.
E.MET.IC, *adj.*, *Med.*, emético (que provoca vômitos).
EM.I.GRANT, *s.*, emigrante.
EM.I.GRATE, *v.*, emigrar.
EM.I.GRA.TION, *s.*, emigração.
EM.I.GRA.TOR, *s.*, emigrante.
EM.I.NENCE, *s.*, eminência.
EM.I.NENT, *adj.*, eminente.
EM.I.NENT.LY, *adv.*, eminentemente.
E.MIR, *s.*, emir.
E.MIR.ATE, *s.*, emirado.
EM.IS.SARY, *s.*, emissário, mensageiro.
E.MIS.SION, *s.*, emissão; emanação.
E.MIT, *v.*, emitir.
E.MOL.LIENT, *s.*, emoliente.
E.MOL.U.MENT, *s.*, emolumento, pagamento.
E.MO.TI.CON, *s.*, (*emotion+icon*) *Comp.*, figuras que expressam emoções em mensagens eletrônicas.
E.MO.TION, *s.*, emoção.
E.MO.TION.AL, *adj.*, emotivo, emocionado, comovente.
E.MO.TION.AL.LY, *adv.*, emocionalmente.
E.MO.TION.LESS, *adj.*, sem emoção.
E.MO.TIVE, *adj.*, emotivo, sensível.
EM.PA.THY, *s.*, *Psic.*, empatia.
EM.PER.OR, *s.*, imperador.
EM.PHA.SIS, *s.*, ênfase.
EM.PHA.SIZE, *v.*, enfatizar, destacar, salientar.
EM.PHAT.IC, *adj.*, enfático, saliente.
EM.PHAT.ICAL.LY, *adv.*, enfaticamente.
EM.PHY.SE.MA, *s.*, *Med.*, enfizema.
EM.PIRE, *s.*, império.
EM.PIR.IC, *s.*, empírico, charlatão; *adj.*, empírico.
EM.PIR.IC.AL, *adj.*, empírico.
EM.PIR.I.CISM, *s.*, empirismo; charlatanice.

EMPIRISM · 451 · ENERGETICS

EM.PIR.ISM, *s.*, empirismo.
EM.PLOY, *v.*, empregar, usar, utilizar.
EM.PLOY.A.BLE, *adj.*, empregável.
EM.PLOY.EE, *s.*, empregado.
EM.PLOY.ER, *s.*, empregador, patrão.
EM.PLOY.MENT, *s.*, emprego, trabalho, ocupação.
EM.PLOY.MENT A.GEN.CY, *s.*, agência de empregos.
EM.PLOY.MENT OF.FICE, *s.*, agência de empregos (atendimento).
EM.PO.RI.UM, *s.*, empório; estabelecimento comercial.
EM.POW.ER, *v.*, autorizar; *fig.*, permitir, capacitar.
EM.POW.ER.MENT, *s.*, autorização.
EM.PRESS, *s.*, imperatriz.
EMP.TI.NESS, *s.*, vazio, vácuo; *fig.*, nulidade, ostentação.
EMP.TY, *v.*, esvaziar, evacuar, desocupar; *adj.*, vazio, desocupado.
EMP.TY.HAND.ED, *adv.*, de mãos vazias.
EMU, *s.*, *Zool.*, ema.
EM.UL.ATE, *v.*, emular, rivalizar, competir.
EM.U.LA.TION, *s.*, emulação, rivalidade.
EM.U.LA.TOR, *s.*, êmulo; rival, competidor; *Comp.*, emulador.
EM.U.LOUS, *adj.*, emulador; ambicioso; *Ant.*, invejoso.
EM.U.LOUS.LY, *adv.*, com emulação, ambiciosamente.
EMUL.SION, *s.*, emulsão.
EN.A.BLE, *v.*, habilitar, capacitar, permitir.
EN.ACT, *v.*, ordenar, decretar, promulgar, legalizar.
EN.ACT.MENT, *s.*, lei, decreto, promulgação.
EN.AC.TOR, *s.*, legislador, executivo da lei.
EN.AM.EL, *s.*, esmalte; *v.*, esmaltar.
E.NAM.ELLED, **E.NAM.ELED**, *adj.*, esmaltado.
EN.AM.OR, **EN.AM.OUR**, *v.*, enamorar(-se); apaixonar(-se).
EN.AM.ORED, *adj.*, enamorado, cativo, apaixonado.
EN.CAGE, *v.*, engaiolar, prender, encarcerar.
EN.CAMP, *v.*, acampar; formar acampamento.
EN.CAMP.MENT, *s.*, acampamento.
EN.CAP.SU.LATE, *v.*, encapsular; condensar; *fig.*, resumir.
EN.CAP.SU.LAT.ED, *adj.*, encapsulado.
EN.CASE, *v.*, encaixotar, colocar dentro, encerrar.
EN.CASE.MENT, *s.*, encaixotamento.
EN.CASH, *v.*, *UK* descontar (cheque).
EN.CEPH.A.LOG.RA.PHY, *s.*, *Med.*, encefalografia.
EN.CHAIN, *v.*, prender com corrente, acorrentar; prender.
EN.CHAIN.MENT, *s.*, encadeamento; ligação.
EN.CHANT, *v.*, encantar, enfeitiçar.
EN.CHANT.ED, *adj.*, encantado.
EN.CHANT.ER, *s.*, encantador, mágico, feiticeiro.
EN.CHANT.ING, *adj.*, encantador, fascinante.
EN.CHANT.MENT, *s.*, encantamento, sedução.
EN.CHASE, *v.*, gravar (em pedra, metal etc.); cravejar, engastar; *fig.*, adornar (com relevo, engaste).
EN.CIR.CLE, *v.*, cercar, circundar, circular.
EN.CLAVE, *s.*, enclave.
EN.CLIT.IC, *s.*, enclítica; *adj.*, enclítico.
EN.CLOSE, *v.*, fechar, encerrar, cercar; incluir, anexar.
EN.CLO.SURE, *s.*, cerca, cercado.
EN.COM.PASS, *v.*, abranger, cercar.
EN.CORE, *s.*, bis; *excl.*, bis!.
EN.COUN.TER, *s.*, encontro; *v.*, encontrar, achar, topar com.
EN.COUR.AGE, *v.*, encorajar, animar, entusiasmar, estimular.
EN.COUR.AGE.MENT, *s.*, estímulo, encorajamento.
EN.COUR.AG.ING, *adj.*, incentivador.

EN.COUR.AG.ING.LY, *adv.*, animadoramente.
EN.CROACH, *v.*, apossar(-se) de algo, abusar, invadir.
EN.CROACH.ER, *s.*, transgressor; usurpador, invasor.
EN.CRUST, *v.*, incrustar, embutir.
EN.CRUST.A.TION, *s.*, incrustração.
EN.CRUST.ED, *adj.*, encrustado.
EN.CRYPT, *v.*, *Comp.*, criptografar.
EN.CRYP.TION, *s.*, criptografia.
EN.CUM.BER, *v.*, onerar; sobrecarregar; dificultar, impedir.
EN.CUM.BRANCE, *s.*, ônus; dependente (pessoa); dificuldade, estorvo.
EN.CYC.LI.CAL, *s.*, encíclica, *adj.*, encíclico.
EN.CY.CLO.PE.DIA, *s.*, enciclopédia.
EN.CY.CLO.PE.DIST, *s.*, enciclopedista.
END, *s.*, fim, ponta, final, término; *v.*, acabar, pôr fim, terminar.
EN.DAN.GER, *v.*, pôr em perigo, arriscar, expor.
EN.DAN.GER.ED SPE.CIES, *s.*, espécies em perigo (de extinção).
EN.DEAR, *v.*, encarecer, levantar o preço; ser amável, agradar.
EN.DEARED, *adj.*, amado.
EN.DEAR.ING, *adj.*, simpático.
EN.DEAR.MENT, *s.*, carinho, apreço, amor, ternura.
EN.DEAV.OUR, *s.*, empenho, esforço; *v.*, esforçar-se, empenhar-se.
EN.DEM.IC, *adj.*, endêmico; *s.*, doença endêmica; endemia.
END.ING, *s.*, fim, término, final, conclusão.
EN.DIVE, *s.*, endívia, chicória.
END.LESS, *adj.*, interminável, inesgotável.
END.LESS.LY, *adv.*, interminavelmente.
END.LESS.NESS, *s.*, eternidade, perpetuidade.
END.MOST, *adj.*, o mais distante, o mais longe.
EN.DOG.A.MY, *s.*, endogamia.
EN.DOG.E.NOUS, *adj.*, endógeno.
EN.DO.ME.TRI.UM, *s.*, *Med.*, endométrio.
EN.DORSE, *v.*, endossar cheque; endossar documento.
EN.DOR.SEE, *s.*, endossado.
EN.DORSE.MENT, *s.*, endosso; *UK* pontos (na carteira de motorista).
EN.DO.SCOPE, *s.*, *Med.*, endoscópio.
EN.DOS.CO.PY, *s.*, *Med.*, endoscopia.
EN.DO.SKEL.E.TON, *s.*, *Anat.*, endoesqueleto.
EN.DO.SPERM, *s.*, *Bot.*, endosperma.
EN.DOW, *v.*, doar, dar, proporcionar, dotar.
EN.DOW.ER, *s.*, doador, dotador.
EN.DOW.MENT, *s.*, dote.
EN.DUE, *v.*, dotar, vestir ; doar.
EN.DUR.A.BLE, *adj.*, suportável.
EN.DUR.A.BLY, *adj.*, suportavelmente.
EN.DUR.ANCE, *s.*, resistência, paciência, duração, persistência.
EN.DURE, *v.*, aguentar, suportar, tolerar.
EN.DUR.ER, *s.*, tolerante, quem suporta; sofredor.
EN.DUR.ING, *adj.*, sofredor, paciente, tolerante; duradouro.
END.US.ER, *s.*, usuário final, consumidor final.
END.WAYS *UK*, **END.WISE** *US*, *adv.*, de frente; ponta a ponta; de pé, em pé; longitudinalmente.
EN.E.MA, *s.*, *Med.*, enema; clister, lavagem intestinal.
EN.E.MY, *s.*, inimigo, adversário.
EN.ER.GET.IC, *adj.*, energético.
EN.ER.GET.ICS, *s.*, *Fil.*, energética.

ENERGISE(-IZE) ·· 452 ·· ENTHUSIAST

EN.ER.GISE(-IZE), *v.*, energizar; agir com energia.
EN.ER.GY, *s.*, energia.
EN.ER.VA.TION, *s.*, enfraquecimento, enervamento.
EN.FEE.BLE, *v.*, enfraquecer, debilitar.
EN.FEE.BLE.MENT, *s.*, enfraquecimento, debilitação.
EN.FET.TER, *v.*, acorrentar; *fig.*, escravizar; constranger.
EN.FOLD, *v.*, *Lit.*, envolver(-se).
EN.FORCE, *v.*, obrigar, forçar, fazer cumprir, coagir, constranger.
EN.FORCE.A.BLE, *adj.*, obrigatório; aplicável.
EN.FOR.CED.LY, *adv.*, obrigatoriamente, forçosamente.
EN.FORCE.MENT, *s.*, coação, obrigação, constrangimento.
EN.FRAN.CHISE, *v.*, emancipar, liberar, conceder direitos civis.
EN.GAGE, *v.*, empenhar (com palavra), comprometer(-se), combinar noivado, engajar-se; cativar; *Tec.*, engrenar.
EN.GAGED, *adj.*, ocupado; comprometido (noivo); *Tec.*, engrenado.
EN.GAGED TONE, *s.*, *UK* sinal de ocupado (telefone).
EN.GAGE.MENT, *s.*, compromisso, engajamento, noivado.
EN.GAGE.MENT RING, *s.*, anel de noivado, aliança de noivado.
EN.GA.GING, *adj.*, atraente, atrativo, insinuante.
EN.GA.GING.LY, *adv.*, atraentemente; insinuantemente.
EN.GEN.DER, *v.*, engendrar, plasmar, gerar, criar.
EN.GINE, *s.*, motor, engenho; locomotiva.
EN.GINE DRIV.ER, *s.*, maquinista.
EN.GI.NEER, *s.*, engenheiro, técnico, maquinista de locomotiva.
EN.GI.NEER.ING, *s.*, engenharia.
EN.GINE HOUSE, *s.*, casa de máquinas.
EN.GINE FIT.TER, *s.*, mecânico, montador.
EN.GINE.RY, *s.*, maquinaria; engenhos (bélicos).
ENG.LAND, *s.*, Inglaterra.
ENG.LISH, *adj.*, *s.*, inglês.
EN.GLISH.MAN, *s.*, inglês.
EN.GLISH.WOM.AN, *s.*, inglesa.
EN.GRAFT, *v.*, enxertar, implantar, colocar dentro.
EN.GRAVE, *v.*, gravar.
EN.GRAV.ER, *s.*, gravador.
EN.GRAV.ING, *s.*, gravura.
EN.GROSS, *v.*, passar a limpo, absorver, apoderar-se.
EN.GROSS.ED, *adj.*, absorto.
EN.GROSS.ER, *s.*, copista.
EN.GROSS.ING, *adj.*, absorvente.
EN.GULF, *v.*, engolir, tragar.
EN.HANCE, *v.*, enfatizar, salientar, aumentar.
EN.HANCE.MENT, *v.*, aumento, melhoria; *Comp.*, realçamento.
ENIG.MA, *s.*, enigma.
ENIG.MAT.IC, *adj.*, enigmático.
EN.JOIN, *v.*, mandar, impor, ordenar, prescrever.
EN.JOY, *v.*, usufruir, desfrutar, gostar de.
EN.JOY.A.BLE, *adj.*, agradável.
EN.JOY.MENT, *s.*, prazer.
EN.LACE, *v.*, enlaçar, envolver.
EN.LARGE, *v.*, alargar, aumentar, dilatar.
EN.LARGE.MENT, *s.*, ampliação, aumento, dilatação.
EN.LAR.GER, *v.*, ampliador (aquilo que aumenta).
EN.LIGHT.EN, *v.*, esclarecer.
EN.LIGHT.ENED, *adj.*, esclarecido.
EN.LIGHT.EN.ING, *adj.*, esclarecedor.

EN.LIGHT.EN.MENT, *s.*, esclarecimento.
EN.LIST, *v.*, angariar; *Mil.*, recrutar, alistar(-se).
EN.LIST.ED, *adj.*, recrutado.
EN.LIST MAN, *s.*, *Mil.*, US recruta.
EN.LIST.MENT, *s.*, alistamento, recrutamento.
EN.LIV.EN, *v.*, avivar, animar, divertir.
EN.MESH, *v.*, enredar, embaralhar, emaranhar.
EN.MI.TY, *s.*, inimizade.
EN.NO.BLE, *v.*, enobrecer, engrandecer, honorificar.
EN.NO.BLE.MENT, *s.*, enobrecimento.
E.NOL.O.GY, *s.*, enologia.
E.NOR.MI.TY, *s.*, enormidade, amplidão.
E.NOR.MOUS, *adj.*, enorme.
E.NOR.MOUS.LY, *adv.*, enormemente.
E.NOUGH, *adj.*, suficiente, bastante.
E.NOUNCE, *v.*, enunciar.
EN.QUIRE, *v.*, o mesmo que *inquire*.
EN.QUIR.Y, *s.*, o mesmo que *inquiry*.
EN.RAGE, *v.*, enfurecer, encolerizar.
EN.RAGED, *adj.*, enfurecido.
EN.RAGE.MENT, *s.*, enfurecimento.
EN.RAPT, *adj.*, arrebatado, enlevado.
EN.RAP.TURE, *v.*, arrebatar, enlevar, maravilhar.
EN.RICH, *v.*, enriquecer.
EN.RICH.MENT, *v.*, enriquecimento; melhoramento.
EN.ROL, EN.ROLL, *v.*, matricular(-se); inscrever(-se).
EN.ROL.MENT, EN.ROLL.MENT, *s.*, inscrição, matrícula, alistamento.
EN ROUTE, *adv.*, vindo de, a caminho; *interj.*, marche!.
EN.SAN.GUINE, *v.*, ensanguentar.
EN.SCONCE, *v.*, abrigar; ocultar.
EN.SCONCED, *adj.*, acomodado, instalado.
EN.SEM.BLE, *s.*, conjunto, união.
EN.SHRINE, *v.*, estar amparado (em algo).
EN.SIGN, *s.*, bandeira.
EN.SLAVE, *v.*, escravizar, dominar, subjugar.
EN.SLAVE.MENT, *s.*, escravidão.
EN.SLAV.ER, *s.*, escravizador, escravizante.
EN.SUE, *v.*, seguir, suceder, vir depois.
EN.SU.ING, *adj.*, seguinte.
EN.SURE, *v.*, assegurar.
EN.TAIL, *v.*, implicar.
EN.TAN.GLED, *adj.*, envolvido, emaranhado, intricado.
EN.TANGLE.MENT, *s.*, envolvimento.
EN.TER, *v.*, entrar em, associar-se, inscrever-se.
EN.TER.ING, *adj.*, entrante.
EN.TE.RI.TIS, *s.*, *Med.*, enterite.
EN.TER KEY, *s.*, *Comp.*, tecla "enter".
EN.TER.PRISE, *s.*, empresa, empreendimento.
EN.TER.PRIS.ER, *s.*, empreendedor.
EN.TER.PRIS.ING, *adj.*, empreendedor.
EN.TER.TAIN, *v.*, entreter, divertir, receber.
EN.TER.TAIN.ER, *s.*, artista.
EN.TER.TAIN.ING, *adj.*, divertido.
EN.TER.TAIN.MENT, *s.*, divertimento, diversão.
EN.THRAL, *v.*, cativar, subjugar; *fig.*, encantar, enfeitiçar.
EN.THRAL.LING, *adj.*, fascinante.
EN.THRONE, *v.*, entronizar.
EN.THUSE, *v.*, entusiasmar, animar, estimular.
EN.THU.SI.ASM, *s.*, entusiasmo.
EN.THU.SI.AST, *s.*, entusiasta.

ENTHUSIASTIC ··453·· EQUINOX

EN.THU.SI.AS.TIC, *adj.*, entusiástico, animador.
EN.THU.SI.AS.TI.CAL.LY, *adv.*, entusiasticamente.
EN.TICE, *v.*, atrair, seduzir; instigar.
EN.TICE.MENT, *s.*, sedução; atração; incitação.
EN.TI.CER, *s.*, sedutor, instigador.
EN.TI.CING, *adj.*, sedutor, tentador.
EN.TIRE, *adj.*, inteiro.
EN.TIRE.LY, *adv.*, inteiramente, totalmente.
EN.TIRE.NESS, *s.*, totalidade.
EN.TIRE.TY, *s.*, em sua totalidade.
EN.TI.TLE, *v.*, intitular, designar; autorizar.
EN.TI.TLE.MENT, *s.*, direito (de posse).
EN.TI.TY, *s.*, ente; entidade.
EN.TOMB, *v.*, enterrar, sepultar.
EN.TOMB.MENT, *s.*, sepultamento, enterro.
EN.TO.MOL.O.GY, *s.*, entomologia.
EN.TOU.RAGE, *s.*, companhia, séquito; meio (de pessoas).
EN.TRAILS, *s. pl.*, entranhas.
EN.TRAN.CE, *s.*, chegada, entrada, ingresso, porta, acesso.
EN.TRAN.CE FORM, *s.*, formulário para registro, ficha.
EN.TRANT, *s.*, aquele que entra; principiante; participante.
EN.TRAP, *v.*, prender, pegar em armadilha.
EN.TRAP.MENT, *s.*, armadilha; logro.
EN.TREAT, *v.*, suplicar, pedir, solicitar.
EN.TREAT.Y, *s.*, súplica.
EN.TRENCH, *v.*, entricheirar(-se); *fig.*, defender-se.
EN.TRENCH.MENT, *s.*, entrincheiramento, *fig.*, defesa.
EN.TRE.PRE.NEUR, *s., Fr.*, empresário.
EN.TRE.PRE.NEUR.I.AL, *adj.*, empresarial.
EN.TRO.PY, *s., Fís.*, entropia.
EN.TRUST, *v.*, confiar.
EN.TRUST.ED, *adj.*, incumbido.
EN.TRY, *s.*, entrada, ingresso, saguão, anotação, apontamento.
EN.TRY VISA, *s.*, visto de entrada (em um país).
EN.TWINE, *v.*, enlaçar, entrelaçar.
E.NU.MER.ATE, *v.*, enumerar.
E.NU.MER.A.TION, *s.*, enumeração.
E.NUN.CI.ATE, *v.*, enunciar, pronunciar, prolatar.
E.NUN.CI.A.TION, *s.*, enunciação.
E.NUN.CI.A.TOR, *s.*, enunciador.
EN.VEL.OP, *v.*, envolver.
EN.VE.LOPE, *s.*, envelope.
EN.VEL.OP.MENT, *s.*, envolvimento; envoltório, embrulho; *Mil.*, cerco.
EN.VEN.OM, *v.*, envenenar, irritar.
EN.VI.A.BLE, *adj.*, invejável; desejável.
EN.VI.OUS, *adj.*, invejoso.
EN.VI.OUS.LY, *adv.*, com inveja.
EN.VI.OUS.NESS, *s.*, inveja.
EN.VI.RON, *v.*, rodear, cercar, estar em torno.
EN.VI.RON.MENT, *s.*, meio ambiente, arredores, cercanias.
EN.VI.RON.MEN.TAL, *adj.*, ambiental, circundante.
EN.VI.RON.MEN.TAL.ISM, *s.*, ambientalismo.
EN.VI.RON.MEN.TAL.IST, *s.*, ambientalista.
EN.VI.RON.MENT.AL.LY, *adv.*, ecologicamente.
ENVIRONS, *s. pl.*, arredores, cercanias, imediações.
EN.VIS.AGE, *v.*, prever; enfrentar; considerar; examinar.
EN.VI.SION, *v.*, prever.
ENVOY, *s.*, enviado.
EN.VY, *s.*, inveja; *v.*, invejar.

EN.VY.ING.LY, *adv.*, invejosamente.
EN.WIND, *v.*, enrolar (em bobina).
EN.WRAP, *v.*, envolver; revestir.
EN.ZYME, *s., Quím.*, enzima.
E.O.CENE, *s., Geol.*, época eocena; *adj.*, eoceno.
E.PHEM.ERA, *s.*, efemeridade; coisa efêmera.
E.PHEM.ER.IS, *s.*, efemérides.
EPHEM.EROUS, *adj.*, efêmero.
EP.IC, *s.*, epopeia; *adj.*, épico.
EPI.CEN.TER, EPI.CEN.TRE, *s., Geol.*, epicentro (de abalo sísmico).
EPI.CURE, *s.*, epicurista; gastrônomo; sensualista.
EPI.CUR.ISM, *s.*, epicurismo.
EPI.DEM.IC, *adj.*, epidêmico; *s.*, epidemia.
EPI.DEM.I.OL.O.GY, *s.*, epidemiologia.
EPI.DER.MIS, *s.*, epiderme.
EPI.GLOT.TIS, *s., Anat.*, epiglote.
EPI.GRAM, *s.*, epigrama.
EPI.GRAPH, *s.*, epígrafe.
E.PIG.RA.PHY, *s.*, epigrafia.
EPI.LEP.SY, *s.*, epilepsia.
EPI.LEP.TIC, *adj.*, epiléptico.
EPI.LOGUE, EPI.LOG, *s.*, epílogo.
E.PIPH.A.NY, *s.*, epifania; *Epiphany*: dia de Reis.
E.PIS.CO.PA.CY, *s.*, diocese, episcopado, bispado.
E.PIS.CO.PAL, *adj.*, episcopal.
EPI.SODE, *s.*, episódio, fato, momento.
EPI.SOD.IC, *adj.*, episódico.
E.PIS.TE.MOL.O.GY, *s.*, epistemologia.
E.PIS.TLE, *s.*, epístola, carta.
EPI.TAPH, *s.*, epitáfio.
EPI.THET, *s.*, epíteto.
E.PIT.O.ME, *s.*, epítome.
E.PIT.O.MIZE(-ISE), *v.*, personificar, ser um exemplo perfeito; resumir.
EP.OCH, *s.*, época.
EP.O.NYM, *s.*, epônimo.
E.PON.Y.MOUS, *adj.*, epônimo.
EP.O.PEE, *s.*, epopeia.
E.QUA.BIL.I.TY, *s.*, uniformidade, igualdade.
E.QUA.BLE, *adj.*, plácido, sereno, uniforme.
E.QUAL, *s.*, igual, equitativo.
E.QUAL.I.TY, *s.*, igualdade.
E.QUAL.IZE, *v.*, igualar.
E.QUAL.I.ZER, *s.*, igualador; *Tec.*, equalizador; *Esp.*, gol de empate.
E.QUAL.LY, *adv.*, igualmente, uniformemente.
E.QUA.NIM.I.TY, *s.*, equanimidade.
E.QUA.NIM.OUS, *adj.*, equânime, justo, imparcial.
E.QUA.TE, *v.*, igualar; equiparar; *Mat.*, equivaler.
E.QUA.TION, *s.*, equação.
E.QUA.TOR, *s.*, equador, paralelo.
E.QUA.TO.RI.AL, *adj.*, equatorial.
E.QUES.TRI.AN, *adj.*, equestre.
E.QUI.DIS.TANT, *adj.*, equidistante.
E.QUIL.I.BRATE, *v.*, equilibrar.
E.QUIL.I.BRA.TION, *s.*, equilíbrio, equilibramento.
E.QUIL.I.BRIST, *s.*, equilibrista.
E.QUI.LIB.RI.UM, *s.*, equilíbrio.
E.QUINE, *adj.*, equino.
E.QUI.NOX, *s.*, equinócio.

EQUIP ··454·· ETHER

E.QUIP, *v.*, equipar, munir, fornecer.
EQ.UI.PAGE, *s.*, equipamento, equipagem.
E.QUIP.MENT, *s.*, equipamento; *Mil.*, armamento.
EQ.UI.TA.BLE, *adj.*, equitativo.
EQ.UI.TA.TION, *s.*, equitação.
EQ.UI.TY, *s.*, equidade, justiça, paridade.
E.QUIV.A.LENCE, *s.*, equivalência, igualdade.
E.QUIV.A.LENT, *s.*, equivalência; *adj.*, equivalente.
E.QUIV.O.CAL, *adj.*, ambíguo, duvidoso; confuso.
E.QUIV.O.CAL.NESS, *s.*, equívoco.
E.QUIV.O.CATE, *v.*, equivocar, equivocar-se, usar de ambiguidades.
E.QUIV.O.CA.TION, *s.*, equívoco, erro, engano.
E.RA, *s.*, era, época.
E.RAD.I.CATE, *v.*, erradicar, eliminar, arrancar.
E.RAD.I.CA.TION, *s.*, erradicação, eliminação.
E.RAS.ABLE, *adj.*, apagável, desmanchável.
E.RASE, *v.*, apagar, desmanchar, desgraçar.
E.RAS.ER, *s.*, apagador, objeto para apagar.
E.RA.SION, *s. Med.*, raspagem.
E.RA.SURE, *s.*, rasura, raspadura.
ERE, *conj.*, antes de, antes que.
E.RECT, *v.*, erigir, levantar, alçar; *adj.*, levantado, ereto, alçado.
E.REC.TILE, *adj.*, erétil.
E.REC.TING, *s.*, construção, edificação.
E.REC.TION, *s.*, ereção; construção, montagem.
E.RECT.LY, *adv.*, em pé; a prumo.
ER.GO.NOM.IC, *adj.*, ergonômico.
ER.GO.NOM.ICS, *s.*, ergonomia.
ERITREAN, *adj.*, *s.*, eritreu; habitante da Eritreia.
ER.MINE, *s.*, *Zool.*, arminho; pele de arminho.
ERODE, *v.*, corroer, provocar erosão.
EROGENOUS ZONE,
ERO.SION, *s.*, erosão.
EROT.IC, *adj.*, erótico.
E.R.O.TISM, *s.*, erotismo.
ERR, *v.*, errar, falhar, enganar, enganar-se.
ER.RAND, *s.*, mensagem, missão, recado.
ER.RAND BOY, *s.*, mensageiro.
ER.RANT, *s.*, errante, vagabundo.
ER.RAT.IC, *adj.*, irregular; errático.
ER.RA.TUM, *s.*, errata.
ER.RO.NE.OUS, *adj.*, errôneo.
ER.ROR, *s.*, erro.
ERST.WHILE, *adj.*, antigo.
E.RUCT.ATE, *v.*, arrotar.
E.RUC.TA.TION, *s.*, arroto.
ER.U.DITE, *adj.*, erudito.
ER.U.DITE.NESS, *s.*, erudição.
E.RUPT, *v.*, entrar em erupção.
E.RUP.TION, *s.*, erupção.
ESA, *s.*, *abrev.* de *European Space Agency*: Agência Espacial Europeia.
ES.CA.LADE, *v.*, escalar, subir, ascender; *s.*, escalada.
ES.CA.LATE, *v.*, escalar; subir por escada rolante, intensificar, aumentar.
ES.CA.LA.TION, *s.*, intensificação, aumento.
ES.CA.LA.TOR, *s.*, escada rolante.
ES.CAP.A.BLE, *adj.*, escapável; evitável.
ES.CA.PADE, *s.*, escapada, fuga; traquinice.
ES.CAPE, *s.*, fuga, escapada; *v.*, escapar, fugir, evadir-se.

ES.CAP.ISM, *s.*, *Psic.*, escapismo.
ES.CAP.IST, *s.*, *Psic.*, escapista; *adj.*, relativo ao escapismo.
ES.CARP, *s.*, escarpa, talude; *v.*, escarpar.
ES.CARP.MENT, *s.*, escarpa, alcantil.
ES.CHEW, *v.*, evitar; abster.
ES.CHEW.AL, *s.*, abstenção; ação de evitar.
ES.CORT, *s.*, escolta, acompanhante; *v.*, acompanhar.
ES.KI.MO, *s.*, esquimó; *adj.*, esquimó.
E.SOPH.A.GUS, *s.*, *Anat.*, esôfago.
ES.O.TER.IC, *adj.*, esotérico.
ES.PA.DRILLE, *s.*, alpargata.
ES.PE.CIAL, *adj.*, especial, particular, único.
ES.PE.CIAL.LY, *adv.*, especialmente, sobretudo, preferentemente.
ES.PE.RAN.TO, *s.*, esperanto.
ES.PI.O.NAGE, *s.*, espionagem.
ES.PLA.NADE, *s.*, esplanada.
ES.POUSE, *v.*, esposar, abraçar, abarcar.
ES.PRES.SO, *s.*, *It.*, café de máquina.
ES.PY, *v.*, avistar, divisar, ver.
ESS, *s.*, décima letra do alfabeto inglês.
ES.SAY, *s.*, ensaio; *v.*, tentar, pretender, ensaiar.
ES.SAY.IST, *s.*, ensaísta.
ES.SENCE, *s.*, essência, âmago.
ES.SEN.TIAL, *adj.*, essencial.
ES.SEN.TI.AL.I.TY, *s.*, essencialidade.
ES.SEN.TI.AL.LY, *adv.*, essencialmente.
ES.TAB.LISH, *v.*, estabelecer, instituir, firmar, assentar.
ES.TAB.LISH.ED, *adj.*, estabelecido, aceito, fundado.
ES.TAB.LISH.ER, *s.*, fundador, instituidor.
ES.TAB.LISH.MENT, *s.*, estabelecimento, instituição, fundação; *the Establishment*: a classe governante.
ES.TATE, *s.*, fazenda, bens, patrimônio, estado.
ES.TATE A.GEN.CY, *s.*, agência imobiliária.
ES.TATE A.GENT, *s.*, corretor de imóveis.
ES.TEEM, *s.*, estima, consideração; *v.*, estimar, prezar, amar.
ES.TEEMED, *adj.*, respeitado, estimado.
ES.THET.IC, *adj.*, o mesmo que *aesthetic*.
ES.TI.MA.BLE, *adj.*, estimável.
ES.TI.MA.BLE.NESS, *s.*, apreço, estima, respeito.
ES.TI.MATE, *v.*, calcular, estimar, avaliar; *s.*, cálculo, orçamento.
ES.TI.MAT.ED, *adj.*, estimado, calculado.
ES.TI.MA.TION, *s.*, estimativa, cálculo, avaliação.
ES.TI.MA.TIVE, *adj.*, estimado, estimativo.
ES.TO.NIAN, *s.* e *adj.*, estoniano; habitante da Estônia.
ES.TOP, *v.*, impedir, obstruir.
ES.TRADE, *s.*, palco, estrado, plataforma.
ES.TRANGE, *v.*, alienar, alhear; apartar(-se), afastar(-se).
ES.TRANGED, *adj.*, separado, apartado.
ES.TRO.GEN, *s.*, *Quím.*, estrógeno, estrogênio.
ES.TU.ARY, *s.*, estuário.
ESU.RI.ENCE, *s.*, miséria, fome, indigência.
ESU.RI.ENT, *adj.*, faminto, miserável, indigente.
ETCH, *v.*, gravar com água-forte.
ETCH.ING, *s.*, arte ou gravura feita com água-forte.
E.TER.NAL, *adj.*, eterno, perene, perpétuo.
E.TER.NAL.LY, *adv.*, eternamente.
E.TERNE, *adj.*, *Arc.*, eterno.
E.TER.NITY, *s.*, eternidade, perenidade.
E.THER, *s.*, éter.

ETHEREAL ··455·· EVOLVE

E.THEREAL, *adj.*, etéreo; *fig.*, puro, elevado.
ETH.IC, *adj.*, ético.
ETH.ICAL, *adj.*, ético.
ETHI.CS, *s.*, ética.
ETHI.O.PI.AN, *s.*, *adj.*, etíope; habitante da Etiópia.
ETH.NIC, *adj.*, étnico, racial.
ETH.NOG.RA.PHY, *s.*, etnografia.
ETH.NOL.O.GY, *s.*, etnologia.
ETHOL.O.GY, *s.*, etologia.
ETHOS, *s.*, sistema de valores.
ET.I.QUETTE, *s.*, etiqueta, boas maneiras sociais.
ET.Y.MO.LOG.IC, *adj.*, etimológico.
ET.Y.MOL.O.GIST, *s.*, etimologista.
ET.Y.MOL.O.GY, *s.*, etimologia.
EU.CA.LYP.TUS, *s.*, eucalipto.
EU.CHA.RIST, *s.*, eucaristia.
EU.CHA.RIS.TIC, *adj.*, eucarístico.
EU.GEN.IC, *adj.*, eugênico.
EU.GEN.ICS, *s.*, eugenia.
EU.LO.GIS.TIC, *adj.*, elogioso, louvador.
EU.LO.GI.UM, *s.*, elogio, louvor, tributo.
EU.LO.GIZE, *v.*, elogiar, louvar, enaltecer.
EU.LO.GIZ.ER, *s.*, elogiador, louvador.
EU.LO.GY, *s.*, elogio, louvor.
EU.NUCH, *adj.*, *s.*, eunuco.
EU.PHE.MISM, *s.*, eufemismo.
EU.PHE.MIS.TIC, *adj.*, eufemístico.
EU.PHE.MIZE, *v.*, eufemizar.
EU.PHON.IC, *adj.*, eufônico, suave, brando.
EU.PHO.NY, *s.*, eufonia, harmonia.
EU.PHO.RIA, *s.*, euforia.
EU.PHO.RIC, *adj.*, eufórico.
EUR.A.SIA, *s.*, Eurásia.
EU.RA.SIAN, *adj.*, eurasiano (relativo à Eurásia); *s.*, indivíduo eurasiano.
EU.RE.KA, *interj.*, heureca!
EU.RO, *s.*, *col.*, euro (moeda).
EU.RO.CEN.TRIC, *s.*, eurocêntrico (centrado na Europa).
EU.RO.CUR.REN.CY, *s.*, moeda europeia.
EU.RO.PE, *s.*, Europa.
EU.RO.PEAN, *s.*, *adj.*, europeu.
EU.RO.PEAN COM.MU.NI.TY, *s.*, Comunidade Europeia.
EU.RO.PE.AN.ISE(-IZE), *v.*, europeizar.
EU.RO.PEAN PAR.LIA.MENT, *s.*, Parlamento Europeu.
EU.RO.PEAN U.NION, *s.*, União Europeia.
EU.THA.NA.SIA, *s.*, eutanásia.
E.VAC.U.ATE, *v.*, evacuar, esvaziar.
E.VAC.U.A.TION, *s.*, evacuação.
E.VAC.U.EE, *s.*, evacuado.
E.VADE, *v.*, fugir, escapar, evadir(-se).
E.VAL.U.ATE, *v.*, avaliar, estimar, calcular.
E.VAL.U.A.TION, *s.*, avaliação, cálculo, estimativa.
EV.A.NESCE, *v.*, esvanecer, dissipar.
EV.A.NES.CENCE, *s.*, esvanecimento.
E.VAN.GEL, *s.*, evangelho.
E.VAN.GEL.IC.AL, *adj.*, evangélico; protestante.
E.VAN.GEL.ISE(-IZE), *v.*, evangelizar.
E.VAN.GEL.IST, *s.*, evangelista.
E.VAN.GE.LI.ZA.TION, *s.*, evangelização.
E.VAP.OR.A.BLE, *adj.*, evaporável.
E.VAP.O.RATE, *v.*, evaporar, evaporar-se.

E.VAP.O.RA.TION, *s.*, evaporação.
E.VA.SION, *s.*, evasão.
E.VA.SIVE, *adj.*, evasivo; ambíguo.
E.VA.SIVE.NESS, *s.*, atitude evasiva.
EVE, *s.*, véspera, vigília, anoitecer.
E.VEN, *v.*, entardecer, equilibrar, emparelhar; *adj.*, plano, liso, calmo.
E.VEN.FALL, *s.*, noitinha; o cair da noite.
E.VEN-HAND.ED, *adj.*, justo, imparcial.
E.VEN.ING, *s.*, tarde, noite.
E.VEN.ING CLASS, *s.*, aula noturna.
E.VEN.ING DRESS, *s.*, vestido de noite; traje a rigor.
E.VEN.ING STAR, *s.*, estrela vespertina.
E.VEN.LY, *adv.*, regularmente, igualmente, exatamente, imparcialmente.
E.VEN.NESS, *s.*, regularidade, igualdade; lisura.
E.VEN.SONG, *s.*, *Rel.*, oração da tarde.
E.VENT, *s.*, evento, fato, acontecimento.
E.VEN-TEM.PERED, *adj.*, equilibrado, calmo, tranquilo.
E.VENT.FUL, *adj.*, emocionante, agitado, movimentado, corrido.
EVEN.TU.AL, *adj.*, eventual, possível, final.
EVEN.TU.AL.I.TY, *s.*, eventualidade.
EVEN.TU.AL.LY, *adv.*, finalmente; no fim.
EVEN.TU.ATE, *v.*, acontecer, suceder.
EV.ER, *adv.*, sempre, toda hora, *conj.*, depois que.
EV.ER.GLADE, *s.*, *US* charco, pantanal.
EV.ER.GREEN, *s.*, *Bot.*, sempre-viva.
EV.ER.LAST.ING, *adj.*, eterno, perene.
EV.ER.MORE, *adj.*, eternamente, para sempre.
E.VER.SION, *adj.*, eversão, reviramento.
EV.ERY, *adj.*, cada, todo.
EV.ERY.BODY, *pron.*, todos, todo mundo.
EV.ERY.DAY, *adj.*, diário, comum, cotidiano.
EV.ERY.ONE, *pron.*, todos, todo mundo.
EV.ERY.PLACE, *adj.*, em todo lugar.
EV.ERY.THING, *pron.*, tudo.
EV.ERY.WAY, *adv.*, de todas as maneiras, de todos os modos.
EV.ERY.WHERE, *adv.*, em toda parte, em todo lugar.
E.VICT, *v.*, despejar.
E.VIC.TION, *s.*, despejo.
EV.I.DENCE, *s.*, evidência, prova, testemunho; *v.*, evidenciar, provar.
EV.I.DENT, *adj.*, evidente, claro, provado.
EV.I.DENT.LY, *adj.*, evidentemente, obviamente.
EV.I.DEN.TIAL, *adj.*, indicativo, evidencial.
E.VIL, *s.*, mal, maldade, ruindade; *adj.*, mau, maldoso.
E.VIL.DO.ER, *s.*, malfeitor.
E.VIL-MIND.ED, *adj.*, malicioso, malvado.
EVIL.NESS, *s.*, maldade, ruindade.
E.VINCE, *v.*, evidenciar; provar.
E.VIS.CER.ATE, *v.*, eviscerar, estripar.
EV.O.CA.TION, *s.*, evocação.
EV.O.CA.TIVE, *adv.*, evocativo.
E.VOKE, *v.*, evocar, lembrar.
EV.O.LU.TION, *s.*, evolução, desenvolvimento.
EV.O.LU.TION.A.RY, *adj.*, evolucionário, evolutivo.
EV.O.LU.TION.IST, *s.*, evolucionista.
EV.O.LU.TIVE, *adj.*, evolutivo.
E.VOLV.A.BLE, *adj.*, progressista, desenvolvível.
E.VOLVE, *v.*, desenvolver.

EWE ••456••• EXHILARATE

EWE, *s.*, ovelha.
EX.AC.ER.BATE, *v.*, exacerbar, agravar.
EX.AC.ER.BA.TION, *s.*, exacerbação.
EX.ACT, *adj.*, exato, justo, meticuloso.
EX.ACT.ING, *adj.*, exigente, exato, preciso.
EX.AC.TI.TUDE, *s.*, exatidão, precisão.
EX.ACT.LY, *adv.*, exatamente.
EX.ACT.NESS, *s.*, exatidão.
EX.AG.GER.ATE, *v.*, exagerar.
EX.AG.GER.AT.ED, *adj.*, exagerado.
EX.AG.GER.A.TION, *s.*, exagero.
EX.ALT, *v.*, exaltar, enaltecer, engrandecer.
EX.ALT.ED, *adj.*, sublime, elevado, nobre; exaltado.
EX.AL.TA.TION, *s.*, exaltação.
EX.AM, *s.*, exame.
EX.AM.I.NA.BLE, *adj.*, examinável.
EX.AM.I.NA.TION, *s.*, exame, verificação, investigação.
EX.AM.INE, *v.*, examinar, verificar, investigar.
EX.AM.IN.ER, *s.*, examinador, investigador.
EX.AM.PLE, *s.*, exemplo, modelo; *v.*, exemplificar.
EX.AS.PER.ATE, *v.*, exasperar, incomodar, irritar.
EX.AS.PER.AT.ING, *adj.*, exasperador, irritante.
EX.AS.PER.A.TION, *s.*, exasperação, incômodo.
EX.CA.VATE, *v.*, escavar; cavar.
EX.CA.VA.TION, *s.*, escavação; fosso.
EX.CA.VA.TOR, *s.*, escavadeira (máquina); escavador.
EX.CEED, *v.*, exceder, ser a mais, suplantar, ultrapassar.
EX.CEED.ING, *adj.*, excessivo.
EX.CEED.ING.LY, *adv.*, excessivamente.
EX.CEL, *v.*, exceder; sobressair, superar.
EX.CEL.LENCE, *s.*, excelência.
EX.CEL.LEN.CY, *s.*, Excelência (título honorífico); *Your/His* ~: Sua Excelência.
EX.CEL.LENT, *adj.*, excelente.
EX.CEPT, *prep.*, exceto; *v.*, excluir.
EX.CEPT.ING, *prep.*, com exceção de.
EX.CEP.TION, *s.*, exceção.
EX.CEP.TION.AL, *adj.*, excepcional.
EX.CEP.TION.AL.LY, *adv.*, excepcionalmente.
EX.CERPT, *s.*, excerto, extrato; *v.*, extratar, extrair.
EX.CESS, *s.*, excesso; abuso; desregramento; *adj.*, excessivo.
EX.CESS FARE, *s.*, sobretaxa.
EX.CES.SIVE, *adj.*, excessivo; exagerado; anormal.
EX.CES.SIVE.LY, *adv.*, excessivamente.
EX.CES.SIVE.NESS, *s.*, exagero, excessividade.
EX.CHANGE, *s.*, troca, câmbio, permuta.
EX.CHANGE RATE, *s.*, taxa de câmbio.
EX.CHANG.ER, *s.*, cambista, permutador.
EX.CI.SE, *s.*, imposto, taxa; *v.*, cortar; *Med.*, extrair.
EX.CI.SION, *s.*, amputação, corte.
EX.CIT.ABIL.I.TY, *s.*, excitabilidade.
EX.CIT.A.BLE, *adj.*, excitável; irritável.
EX.CI.TANT, *adj.*, excitante.
EX.CI.TA.TION, *s.*, excitação.
EX.CITE, *v.*, excitar, provocar.
EX.CITED, *adj.*, excitado; agitado, nervoso.
EX.CITE.MENT, *s.*, excitação, excitamento, emoção.
EX.CIT.ING, *adj.*, excitante; emocionante.
EX.CLAIM, *v.*, exclamar.
EX.CLA.MA.TION, *s.*, exclamação.
EX.CLA.MA.TIONS, *s. pl.*, gritaria.

EX.CLUDE, *v.*, excluir; excetuar.
EX.CLU.SION, *s.*, exclusão.
EX.CLU.SIVE, *adj.*, exclusivo; único.
EX.CLU.SIVE.LY, *adv.*, exclusivamente; restritamente.
EX.COM.MU.NI.CATE, *v.*, excomungar.
EX.COM.MU.NI.CATION, *s.*, excomunhão.
EX.CRE.MENT, *s.*, excremento.
EX.CRES.CENCE, *s.*, excrescência.
EX.CRE.TE, *v.*, excretar, evacuar.
EX.CRE.TION, *s.*, excreção.
EX.CRU.CI.ATE, *v.*, excruciar, atormentar.
EX.CRU.CI.A.TING, *adj.*, excruciante, penoso.
EX.CRU.CI.A.TION, *s.*, tormento, suplício.
EX.CUL.PATE, *v.*, desculpar.
EX.CUL.PA.TION, *s.*, desculpa.
EX.CUR.SION, *s.*, excursão.
EX.CUR.SION.IST, *s.*, excursionista.
EX.CUS.A.BLE, *adj.*, desculpável.
EX.CUSE, *v.*, desculpar, escusar.
EX-DI.REC.TO.RY, *adj.*, *UK* que não consta da lista telefônica.
EX.E.CRA.BLE, *adj.*, execrável.
EX.E.CRA.BLY, *adv.*, execravelmente.
EX.E.CRATE, *v.*, execrar; abominar; amaldiçoar.
EX.E.CRA.TION, *s.*, execração.
EX.E.CU.TA.BLE, *adj.*, executável.
EX.E.CUTE, *v.*, executar, cumprir, desempenhar, realizar.
EX.E.CUT.ER, *s.*, executor.
EX.E.CU.TION, *s.*, execução.
EX.E.CU.TION.ER, *s.*, carrasco.
EX.E.CU.TIVE, *s.*, *Com.*, executivo, diretor; *adj.*, executivo.
EX.E.CU.TOR, *s.*, inventariante, testamenteiro.
EX.E.GE.SIS, *s.*, exegese.
EX.E.GET.IC, *adj.*, exegético.
EX.EM.PLAR, *s.*, exemplar, modelo.
EX.EM.PLA.RY, *adj.*, exemplar, modelar.
EX.EM.PLI.FY, *v.*, exemplificar, dar como modelo.
EX.EMPT, *s.*, isento (de algum dever); *v.*, isentar, eximir; *adj.*, isento, livre.
EX.EMP.TION, *s.*, isenção, dispensa.
EX.ER.CI.SA.BLE, *adj.*, aplicável, praticável.
EX.ER.CISE, *s.*, exercício; *v.*, exercer, agir, trabalhar.
EX.ER.CI.TA.TION, *s.*, exercício, prática, treino.
EX.ERT, *v.*, exercer; aplicar; esforçar(-se); mostrar; manifestar.
EX.ER.TION, *s.*, esforço, empenho.
EX GRA.TI.A, *adv.*, *adj.*, *Lat.*, como um favor, de favor.
EX.HA.LA.TION, *s.*, exalação.
EX.HALE, *v.*, exalar, expirar.
EX.HAUST, *s.*, descarga, escapamento; exaustor; *v.*, esgotar, usar, consumir; esvaziar.
EX.HAUST.ED, *adj.*, exausto.
EX.HAUST.ING, *adj.*, exaustivo, fatigante.
EX.HAUS.TION, *s.*, exaustão.
EX.HAUS.TIVE, *adj.*, exaustivo.
EX.HAUS.TIVE.LY, *adv.*, exaustivamente.
EX.HIB.IT, *v.*, mostrar, exibir; *s.*, obra exposta.
EX.HI.BI.TION, *s.*, exibição, mostra.
EX.HI.BI.TION.ISM, *s.*, exibicionismo.
EX.HI.BI.TION.IST, *s.*, exibicionista.
EX.HI.BI.TOR, *s.*, expositor.
EX.HIL.A.RATE, *v.*, divertir, alegrar.

EXHILARATING ·· 457 ·· EXPRESSIONIST

EX.HIL.A.RA.TING, *adj.*, estimulante, divertido.
EX.HORT, *v.*, exortar.
EX.HOR.TA.TION, *s.*, exortação, moção, recomendação.
EX.HU.MA.TION, *s.*, exumação.
EX.HUME, *v.*, exumar, desenterrar.
EX.I.GENCE, *s.*, exigência, urgência.
EX.I.GEN.CY, *s.*, exigência.
EX.I.GENT, *adj.*, exigente.
EX.I.GU.ITY, *s.*, exiguidade.
EX.IG.U.OUS, *adj.*, exíguo, parco, reduzido.
EX.ILE, *s.*, exílio, exilado, *v.*, exilar.
EX.IL.ED, *adj.*, exilado.
EX.IL.I.TY, *s.*, sutileza, delicadeza.
EX.IM.I.OUS, *adj.*, exímio.
EX.IST, *v.*, existir, ser, viver.
EX.IS.TENCE, *s.*, existência, vida.
EX.IST.ENT, *adj.*, existente, atual.
EX.IS.TEN.TIAL, *adj.*, existencial.
EX.IS.TEN.TIAL.ISM, *s., Filos.*, existencialismo.
EX.IS.TEN.TIAL.IST, *s.*, existencialista.
EX.IST.ING, *adj.*, o mesmo que *existent*.
EX.IT, *s.*, saída; *v.*, sair.
EX.IT VISA, *s.*, visto de saída.
EX.O.DUS, *s.*, êxodo.
EX OF.FI.CI.O, *adv., Lat.*, em virtude do cargo.
EX.ON.ER.ATE, *v.*, exonerar, desobrigar.
EX.ON.ER.A.TION, *s.*, exoneração, desculpa, desobrigação.
EX.OR.BI.TANCE, *s.*, exorbitância, exagero, excesso.
EX.OR.BI.TANT, *adj.*, exorbitante.
EX.OR.CISM, *s.*, exorcismo.
EX.OR.CIST, *s.*, exorcista.
EX.OR.CIZE, *v.*, exorcizar, expulsar os demônios.
EX.O.TER.IC, *adj.*, exotérico.
EX.OT.IC, *adj.*, exótico.
EX.PAND, *v.*, expandir, aumentar, dilatar.
EX.PANSE, *s.*, extensão.
EX.PAN.SION, *s.*, expansão, desenvolvimento, propagação.
EX.PAN.SION.ISM, *s.*, expansionismo.
EX.PAN.SIVE, *adj.*, expansivo.
EX.PA.TRI.ATE, *v.*, expatriar, desterrar.
EX.PECT, *v.*, esperar, aguardar, supor.
EX.PEC.TAN.CY, *s.*, expectativa.
EX.PECT.ANT, *s.*, expectante; *adj.*, ansioso, esperançoso.
EX.PECT.ANT.LY, *adv.*, ansiosamente.
EX.PECT.ANT MOTH.ER, *s.*, gestante.
EX.PEC.TA.TION, *s.*, expectativa.
EX.PEC.TO.RANT, *s.*, expectorante.
EX.PEC.TO.RATE, *v.*, expectorar.
EX.PE.DIENT, *s.*, expediente; *adj.*, pertinente, apropriado.
EX.PE.DITE, *v.*, expedir, apressar.
EX.PE.DI.TION, *s.*, expedição.
EX.PE.DI.TION.A.RY FORCE, *s.*, força expedicionária.
EX.PEL, *v.*, expelir, expulsar, retirar de.
EX.PEND, *v.*, gastar.
EX.PEND.A.BLE, *adj.*, dispensável, descartável.
EX.PEND.I.TURE, *s.*, despesa, gasto.
EX.PENSE, *s.*, gasto, despesa.
EX.PEN.SIVE, *adj.*, caro, de preço alto.
EX.PE.RI.ENCE, *s.*, experiência; *v.*, experimentar, conhecer.
EX.PE.RI.ENCED, *adj.*, experiente, experimentado, perito.
EX.PER.I.MENT, *s.*, experiência, experimentação; *v.*,

experimentar.
EX.PER.I.MEN.TAL, *adj.*, experimental.
EX.PER.I.MEN.TAL.IZE, *v.*, experimentar.
EX.PER.I.MEN.TA.TION, *s.*, experimentação.
EX.PERT, *adj.*, hábil, esperto, perito; *s.*, experto, especialista.
EX.PER.TISE, *s.*, perícia.
EX.PI.ATE, *v.*, expiar, pagar as penas.
EX.PI.A.TION, *s.*, expiação, pagamento de penas.
EX.PIRE, *v.*, expirar, expelir, morrer.
EX.PI.RY, *s.*, vencimento, término.
EX.PI.RY DATE, *s.*, data de vencimento.
EX.PLAIN, *v.*, explanar, explicar, esclarecer.
EX.PLA.NA.TION, *s.*, explanação, explicação.
EX.PLA.NA.TORY, *adj.*, explicativo, explanatório.
EX.PLE.TIVE, *s.*, imprecação; *Gram.*, a partícula expletiva;
  adj., expletivo, completivo.
EX.PLI.CA.BLE, *adj.*, explicável.
EX.PLI.CATE, *v.*, explicar, esclarecer, explanar.
EX.PLI.CA.TION, *s.*, explicação.
EX.PLI.CA.TIVE, *adj.*, explicativo.
EX.PLIC.IT, *adj.*, explícito.
EX.PLIC.IT.LY, *adv.*, explicitamente, claramente.
EX.PLODE, *v.*, explodir.
EX.PLOD.ENT, *s.*, explosivo.
EX.PLOD.ER, *s.*, detonador.
EX.PLOIT, *v.*, explorar, utilizar-se, aproveitar-se; *s.*, façanha,
  bravura.
EX.PLOI.TA.TION, *s.*, exploração; aproveitamento.
EX.PLOI.TA.TIVE, *adj.*, explorador.
EX.PLOIT.ER, *s.*, explorador.
EX.PLO.RA.TION, *s.*, exploração.
EX.PLO.RA.TION.IST, *s.*, explorador (de minérios).
EX.PLO.RA.TIVE, *adj.*, exploratório.
EX.PLO.RA.TORY, *adj.*, o mesmo que *explorative*.
EX.PLORE, *v.*, explorar, pesquisar, examinar.
EX.PLOR.ER, *s.*, explorador, investigador.
EX.PLO.SION, *s.*, explosão, estouro.
EX.PLO.SIVE, *s.*, explosivo; *adj.*, explosivo.
EX.PLO.SIVE.LY, *adv.*, de modo explosivo.
EX.PO.NENT, *s.*, expoente; defensor, representante.
EX.PO.NEN.TIAL, *adj., Mat.*, exponencial.
EX.PORT, *v.*, exportar; *s.*, exportação.
EX.PORT.ABLE, *adj.*, exportável.
EX.POR.TA.TION, *s.*, exportação.
EX.PORT.ER, *s.*, exportador.
EX.POSE, *v.*, expor, apresentar, exibir, desmascarar.
EX.POSED, *adj.*, desprotegido, exposto.
EX.POS.ER, *s.*, expositor.
EX.PO.SI.TION, *s.*, exposição.
EX.PO.SI.TIVE, *adj.*, expositivo, elucidativo.
EX.PO.SI.TOR, *s.*, expositor, explicador.
EX.PO.SURE, *s.*, exposição (a algo), exibição, revelação,
  publicidade.
EX.POUND, *v.*, expor, explicar, apresentar.
EX.PRESS, *v.*, expressar, despachar; *adj.*, expresso, claro;
  s., rápido.
EX.PRESS.I.BLE, *adj.*, exprimível.
EX.PRES.SION, *s.*, expressão.
EX.PRESS.NESS, *s.*, clareza.
EX.PRES.SION.ISM, *s.*, expressionismo.
EX.PRES.SION.IST, *s., adj.*, expressionista.

EXPRESSIONLESS ·· 458 ·· EXTORTION

EX.PRES.SION.LESS, *adj.*, inexpressivo.
EX.PRES.SIVE, *adj.*, expressivo, enérgico.
EX.PRES.SIVE.LY, *adv.*, expressivamente, energicamente.
EX.PRES.SIV.I.TY, *s.*, expressividade.
EX.PRESS.LY, *adv.*, expressamente, claramente.
EX.PRESS-WAY, *s.*, autoestrada, rodovia.
EX.PRO.PRI.ATE, *v.*, expropriar, desapropriar.
EX.PRO.PRI.A.TION, *s.*, expropriação.
EX.PUL.SION, *s.*, expulsão.
EX.PUR.GATE, *v.*, expurgar, purificar.
EX.QUI.SITE, *adj.*, seleto, raro; fino, delicado; *s., col.*, janota.
EX.QUI.SITE.LY, *adv.*, finamente; perfeitamente.
EX.QUI.SITE.NESS, *s.*, maravilha, requinte.
EX.SAN.GUINE, *adj.*, exangue, anêmico.
EX.SCIND, *v.*, cortar.
EX.SERT, *v.*, amputar, cortar, retirar.
EX.SERV.ICE.MAN, *s.*, ex-combatente.
EX.TANT, *adj.*, existente, sobrevivente.
EX.TEM.PO.RA.NE.OUS, *adj.*, extemporâneo.
EX.TEM.PO.RARY, *adj.*, extemporâneo.
EX.TEM.PO.RI.ZA.TION, *s.*, extemporização, improvisamento.
EX.TEM.PO.RISE(-IZE), *v.*, improvisar, extemporizar.
EX.TEND, *v.*, dilatar, estender, aumentar.
EX.TEND.A.BLE, *adj.*, prorrogável; expansível.
EX.TEND.ED, *adj.*, estendido; extensivo.
EX.TEND.ED.LY, *adv.*, prolongadamente, extensivamente.
EX.TEN.SION, *s.*, extensão, acréscimo, expansão, aumento.
EX.TEN.SION COURSE, *s.*, curso de extensão.
EX.TEN.SIVE, *adj.*, extensivo, amplo, vasto, considerado.
EX.TEN.SIVE.LY, *adv.*, amplamente, extensivamente.
EX.TEN.SIVE.NESS, *s.*, extensão, grandeza, amplitude.
EX.TENT, *s.*, extensão, alcance, tamanho.
EX.TEN.U.ATE, *v.*, diminuir, atenuar, suavizar.
EX.TEN.U.AT.ING, *adj.*, atenuante.
EX.TEN.U.AT.ING.LY, *adv.*, atenuantemente.
EX.TEN.U.A.TION, *s.*, atenuação, suavização.
EX.TE.RI.OR, *adj.*, externo, exterior; *s.*, exterior.
EX.TE.RI.OR.I.TY, *s.*, exterioridade.
EX.TE.RI.OR.LY, *adv.*, exteriormente, externamente.
EX.TER.MI.NATE, *v.*, exterminar, liquidar, acabar.
EX.TER.MI.NA.TION, *s.*, extermínio.
EX.TER.MI.NA.TOR, *s.*, exterminador, destruidor.
EX.TER.NAL, *s.*, exterioridade, aparência; formalidade; *adj.*, externo, exterior; estranho.
EX.TER.NAL AER.I.AL, *s.*, antena externa.
EX.TER.NAL.ISE(-IZE), *v.*, exteriorizar; externar.
EX.TER.RES.TRI.AL, *adj.*, extraterrestre.
EX.TER.RI.TO.RI.AL, *adj.*, extraterritorial.
EX.TINCT, *adj.*, extinto, terminado, acabado.
EX.TINC.TION, *s.*, extinção.
EX.TIN.GUISH, *v.*, extinguir, liquidar, acabar.
EX.TIN.GUISH.ER, *s.*, extintor, apagador (de incêndio).
EX.TIN.GUISH.MENT, *s.*, extinção.
EX.TIR.PATE, *v.*, extirpar, erradicar.
EX.TIR.PA.TION, *s.*, extirpação, erradicação.
EX.TOL, *v.*, exaltar, enaltecer, louvar.
EX.TORT, *v.*, extorquir.

EX.TOR.TION, *s.*, extorsão.
EX.TOR.TION.ATE, *adj.*, extorsivo.
EX.TRA, *adj.*, extra, extraordinário, adicional; *s.*, extra, extraordinário.
EX.TRACT, *s.*, extrato; *v.*, extrair, arrancar, tirar de, extorquir.
EX.TRACT.A.BLE, *adj.*, extraível.
EX.TRAC.TION, *s.*, extração.
EX.TRAC.TIVE, *adj.*, extrativo.
EX.TRACT.OR, *s.*, extrator, centrífuga; *UK* exaustor.
EX.TRA.CUR.RIC.U.LAR, *adj.*, extracurricular.
EX.TRA.DITE, *v.*, extraditar, expulsar.
EX.TRA.DI.TION, *s.*, extradição.
EX.TRA.JU.DI.CIAL, *adj.*, extrajudicial.
EX.TRA.MAR.I.TAL, *adj.*, extraconjugal.
EX.TRA.NE.OUS, *adj.*, irrelevante; externo; estranho, alheio.
EX.TRA-OF.FI.CIAL, *adj.*, extraoficial.
EX.TRAOR.DI.NA.RI.LY, *adv.*, extraordinariamente.
EX.TRAOR.DI.NARY, *adj.*, extraordinário.
EX.TRAP.O.LATE, *v.*, extrapolar, exceder.
EX.TRA.SEN.SO.RY, *adj.*, extrassensorial.
EX.TRA.TER.RES.TRI.AL, *adj.*, o mesmo que *exterrestrial*.
EX.TRAV.A.GANCE, *s.*, extravagância.
EX.TRAV.A.GANT, *adj.*, extravagante, perdulário.
EX.TRAV.A.SATE, *v.*, extravasar.
EX.TREME, *adj.*, *s.*, extremo.
EX.TREME.LY, *adv.*, extremamente.
EX.TREME SPORTS, *s. pl.*, esportes radicais.
EX.TREM.ISM, *s.*, extremismo, radicalismo.
EX.TREM.IST, *s.*, extremista.
EX.TREM.I.TIES, *s. pl.*, extremidades.
EX.TREM.I.TY, *s.*, extremidade; suma gravidade.
EX.TRI.CATE, *v.*, soltar, livrar, desembaraçar.
EX.TRI.CA.TION, *s.*, desembaraço.
EX.TRIN.SIC, *adj.*, extrínseco, externo, exterior.
EX.TRO.VERT, *adj.*, *Psic.*, extrovertido.
EX.TRUDE, *v.*, expulsar, retirar; *Tec.*, prensar.
EX.TRUD.ED, *adj.*, *Tec.*, prensado.
EX.U.BER.ANCE, *s.*, exuberância.
EX.U.BER.ANT, *adj.*, exuberante.
EX.U.BER.ATE, *v.*, exuberar, tornar-se exuberante.
EX.UDE, *v.*, suar, exsudar.
EX.ULT, *v.*, exultar, regozijar.
EX.UL.TANCE, *s.*, exultação, alegria, regozijo.
EX.UL.TANT, *adj.*, exultante, triunfante.
EYE, *s.*, olho, buraco de agulha; *v.*, olhar, observar, fixar.
EYE.BALL, *s.*, globo ocular.
EYE.BROW, *s.*, sobrancelha.
EYED, *adj.*, que tem olhos.
EYE DROPS, *s. pl.*, colírio.
EYE.GLASS, *s.*, lente; monóculo; óculos.
EYE.LASH, *s.*, pestana, cílio.
EYE.LET, *s.*, ilhó.
EYE-LEVEL, *adj.*, à altura dos olhos.
EYE.LID, *s.*, pálpebra.
EYE.LI.NER, *s.*, delineador.
EYE.SIGHT, *s.*, vista, visão, olhar.
EYE.WIT.NESS, *s.*, testemunha ocular.

F, s., sexta letra do alfabeto inglês; *Mús.*, fá.
F, *abrev.* de Fahrenheit.
FA, s., fá.
FA.BLE, s., fábula, história, narração, alegoria.
FA.BLED, *adj.*, lendário, fictício, fabuloso.
FA.BLER, s., fabulista.
FAB.RIC, s., tecido, pano, fazenda, ficção; v., fingir, inventar.
FAB.RI.CANT, s., fabricante, aquele que manufatura.
FAB.RI.CATE, v., fabricar, confeccionar, manufaturar.
FAB.RI.CA.TION, s., fabricação, construção.
FAB.U.LIST, s., fabulista; *fig.*, mentiroso.
FAB.U.LOUS, *adj.*, fabuloso, extraordinário, lendário.
FAB.U.LOUS.LY, *adv.*, fabulosamente.
FA.ÇADE, s., *Ant.*, fachada, frontispício.
FACE, s., face, rosto, cara, fisionomia; superfície; v., enfrentar.
FACE.A.BLE, *adj.*, encarável, enfrentável.
FACE-CLOTH, s., pano de rosto.
FACE-CREAM, s., creme para o rosto.
FACE-GUARD, s., capacete ou viseira de proteção.
FACE.LESS, *adj.*, sem rosto, anônimo; sem personalidade.
FACE-LIFT.ING, s., *Med.*, cirurgia plástica para retirar as rugas.
FACE POW.DER, s., pó de arroz (cosmético).
FACE-SAV.ING, *adj.*, para salvar as aparências.
FAC.ET, s., faceta.
FA.CE.TIOUS, *adj.*, brincalhão.
FA.CE.TIOUS.LY, *adv.*, de forma brincalhona ou irônica.
FA.CE.TIOUS.NESS, s., zombaria; modos de zombeteiro.
FA.CIAL, *adj.*, facial.
FAC.ILE, *adj.*, fácil, simples, afável, dócil, superficial.
FA.CIL.I.TATE, v., facilitar.
FA.CIL.I.TA.TION, s., facilitação.
FA.CIL.I.TY, s., facilidade, habilidade.
FA.CING, s., revestimento, cobertura; *adj.*, oposto.
FAC.SIM.I.LE, s., fac-símile, cópia.
FACT, s., fato, acontecimento, caso, ocorrência.
FAC.TION, s., facção, partido, seita.
FAC.TION.AL, *adj.*, faccional, faccionário.
FAC.TIOUS, *adj.*, faccioso, partidário, sectário.
FAC.TIOUS.NESS, s., faccionismo; partidarismo.
FAC.TOR, s., fator.
FAC.TO.RI.AL, s., *Mat.*, fatorial; *adj.*, fatorial.
FAC.TO.RY, s., fábrica, usina, estabelecimento.
FACT SHEET, s., *UK* informativo.
FAC.TU.AL, *adj.*, fatual, real.
FAC.TU.AL.LY, *adv.*, realmente, efetivamente.
FAC.UL.TA.TIVE, *adj.*, facultativo, não obrigatório.
FAC.UL.TY, s., faculdade; direito, capacidade, habilidade.
FAD, s., moda passageira, modismo, mania.
FAD.DISH, *adj.*, maníaco, caprichoso.
FAD.DY, *adj.*, caprichoso; chato.
FADE, v., murchar, desbotar, enfraquecer, apagar-se.
FAD.ED, *adj.*, desbotado.

FAD.ING, *adj.*, murcho, pálido, que definha, desbotamento.
FAE.CAL, *adj.*, fecal.
FAE.CES, FE.CES, s. *pl.*, fezes.
FA.ER.Y, s., o mesmo que *fairy*.
FAG, s., trabalho penoso ou chato; *col.*, cigarro.
FAG END, s., sobra, resto; *UK* bagana.
FAGGED, *adj.*, *col.*, *UK* muito cansado.
FAG.GING, *adj.*, cansativo, fatigante.
FAG.GOT, s., feixe, molho de lenha, trouxa; *col.*, homossexual; v., enfeixar.
FAH.REN.HEIT, s., Fahrenheit (escala termométrica, representação: F).
FAIL, v., faltar, falhar; reprovar, rodar; extinguir(-se); enfraquecer.
FAILED, *adj.*, fracassado.
FAIL.ING, s., fraqueza; *prep.*, na falta de; *adj.*, que falta ou falha; debilitado.
FAIL-SAFE, *adj.*, protegido contra falhas.
FAIL.URE, s., falta, falha, fracasso, deficiência, omissão.
FAINT, s., desmaio, desfalecimento; *adj.*, débil, fraco; v., desmaiar.
FAINT.ING, s., desfalecimento; *adj.*, desmaiado.
FAINT.ISH, *adj.*, fraco, desmaiado.
FAINT.LY, *adv.*, fracamente; tenuemente.
FAINT.ISH, *adj.*, fraco, débil.
FAINT.NESS, s., debilidade, fraqueza.
FAIR, *adj.*, belo, claro, louro, íntegro; s., beleza, namorada.
FAIR.GROUND, s., parque de exposições.
FAIR-HAIRED, *adj.*, loiro.
FAI.RI.LY, *adv.*, fantasticamente.
FAIR.LY, *adv.*, absolutamente, regularmente, justamente.
FAIR-MIND.ED, *adj.*, justo, honesto.
FAIR.NESS, s., alvura, beleza, formosura.
FAIR PLAY, s., jogo limpo, honestidade.
FAIR-WEATH.ER, *adj.*, de bons ventos, de tempos prósperos.
FAIRY, s., fada, duende.
FAIR.Y.LAND, s., mundo das fadas.
FAIR.Y-LIGHTS, s. *pl.*, luzes de decoração de Natal.
FAIR.Y-TALE, s., conto de fadas.
FAITH, s., fé, crença, credulidade, convicção, religião; verdade.
FAITH.FUL, *adj.*, fiel, correto.
FAITH.FUL.LY, *adv.*, fielmente; cordialmente.
FAITH.FUL.NESS, s., fidelidade, lealdade, retidão.
FAITH HEAL.ER, s., curandeiro.
FAITH.LESS, *adj.*, incrédulo, sem fé.
FAITH.LESS.NESS, s., incredulidade, falta de fé.
FAKE, s., truque, fraude; *adj.*, falso; v., falsear, enganar, fraudar, fingir.
FAK.ER, s., falsificador.
FA.KIR, s., faquir.
FAL.CON, s., *Zool.*, falcão.

FALCONRY · 460 · FASHIONER

FAL.CON.RY, s., falcoaria.
FAL.DE.RAL, s., ninharia, bagatela, frivolidade.
FALL, s., queda, tombo, baixa, diminuição; **FALLS**, s. pl.: cataratas; v., cair, baixar, levar tombo.
FAL.LA.CIOUS, adj., falacioso.
FAL.LA.CY, s., falácia (argumento falso), engano.
FAL.LEN, adj., caído, prostrado.
FALL-BACK, v., retroceder; s., retirada.
FALL GUY, s., US bode expiatório.
FAL.LI.BIL.I.TY, s., falibilidade.
FAL.LI.BLE, adj., falível.
FAL.LI.BLY, adv., falivelmente.
FALL.ING, s., queda, rebaixamento.
FAL.LO.PIAN TUBE, s., Anat., trompa de Falópio.
FALL.OUT, s., Fís., chuva radiativa.
FAL.LOW, adj., alqueivado (terra sem cultivo); fulvo.
FALSE, adj., falso, inverídico, desonesto, infiel, adulterado.
FALSE DEAL.ER, s., embusteiro.
FALSE.FACE, s., máscara.
FALSE.HOOD, s., falsidade, engano, desonestidade.
FALSE.LY, adv., falsamente, erroneamente.
FALSE.NESS, s., falsidade.
FALSE.STEP, s., escorregadela.
FAL.SET.TO, s., Mús., falsete; adv., em falsete.
FAL.SI.FI.CA.TION, s., falsificação.
FAL.SI.FI.ER, s., falsificador, falsário.
FAL.SI.FY, v., falsificar, adulterar, corromper.
FAL.SI.TY, s., falsidade; mentira.
FAL.TER, v., vacilação, hesitação; v., gaguejar, hesitar, vacilar.
FAL.TER.ING, s., hesitação, vacilação.
FAME, s., fama, notoriedade, celebridade; v., celebrar, notabilizar.
FAMED, adj., afamado, célebre.
FA.MIL.IAR, adj., familiar, conhecido.
FA.MIL.IAR.I.TY, s., familiaridade, conhecimento.
FA.MIL.I.AR.I.ZA.TION, s., familiarização.
FA.MIL.IAR.IZE, v., familiarizar.
FAM.I.LY, s., família, descendência, linhagem.
FAM.I.LY CIR.CLE, s., círculo familiar.
FAM.I.LY PLAN.NING, s., planejamento familiar.
FAM.I.LY TREE, s., árvore genealógica.
FAM.INE, s., carência, carestia, penúria, fome.
FAM.ISHED, adj., col., faminto.
FAM.ISH.ING, adj., faminto, esfomeado.
FAM.OUS, adj., famoso, conhecido, célebre.
FA.MOUS.NESS, s., fama, celebridade, notoriedade.
FAN, s., leque, abanador; ventilador; col., fã, aficionado; v., abanar; arejar; ventilar.
FA.NAT.IC, s., fanático, fã.
FA.NAT.I.CAL.LY, adv., fanaticamente.
FA.NAT.I.CISM, s., fanatismo.
FA.NAT.I.CIZE, v., fanatizar.
FAN CLUB, s., fã-clube.
FAN.CIED, adj., imaginário.
FAN.CIES, s. pl., docinhos decorados.
FAN.CI.FUL, adj., fantástico, imaginoso, esquisito.
FAN.CI.FUL.LY, adv., fantasticamente, caprichosamente.
FAN.CY, s., fantasia, imaginação, capricho; v., imaginar, fantasiar, julgar.
FAN.CY BALL, s., baile à fantasia.
FAN.CY DRESS, s., fantasia (traje).

FAN.CY-DRESS PARTY, s., festa à fantasia.
FAN.CY GOODS, s. pl., artigos de luxo.
FAN.CY PRIC.ES, s., preços muito altos.
FAN.DAN.GO, s., fandango (dança espanhola).
FAN.FARE, s., fanfarra.
FANG, s., colmilho (dente canino); presa (de cobra).
FAN.LIGHT, s., claraboia.
FAN.NER, s., abanador; joeira.
FA.TAS.ISE(-IZE), v., fantasiar, sonhar acordado.
FAN.TAS.TIC, adj., fantástico, extraordinário, fantasioso; s., fantasista.
FAN.TAS.TI.CAL.LY, adv., fantasticamente.
FAN.TA.SY, s., fantasia, imaginação, utopia, ideal.
FAN.ZINE, s., fanzine (fanatic magazine: revista de fãs sobre TV, cinema, rádio etc.).
FAQ, s., abrev. de frequently asked questions (perguntas frequentes feitas por usuários).
FAR, s., o distante; adj., distante, longínquo.
FAR.A.WAY, adj., longínquo, remoto; distraído, ausente.
FARCE, s., farsa.
FAR.CI.CAL, adj., ridículo, cômico.
FARE, s., custo de uma passagem; bandeirada/táxi; v., passar bem ou mal.
FAR EAST, s., Extremo Oriente.
FARE.WELL, s., adeus, despedida.
FAR-FETCHED, adj., forçado; afetado, não natural.
FAR.I.NA.CEOUS, adj., farináceo, farinhoso.
FARM, s., fazenda, chácara, sítio; v., cultivar, plantar, criar gado.
FARM.ER, s., fazendeiro, granjeiro, agricultor.
FARM-HAND, s., peão, colono (da área rural).
FARM.HOUSE, s., casa de fazenda, quinta, granja.
FARM.ING, s., agricultura, cultura, lavoura.
FARM.STEAD, s., US granja, quinta.
FARM.YARD, s., pátio de fazenda.
FAR-OFF, adj., distante, afastado, longínquo.
FAR POINT, s., o ponto distinguível mais distante.
FAR-REACHING, adj., de longo alcance; abrangente.
FAR.RI.ER, s., ferrador (de cavalos), ferreiro.
FAR-SIGHT.ED, adj., prudente, perspicaz; Med., hipermetrope.
FART, s., vulg., peido (gás intestinal); v., peidar.
FAR.THER, adv., mais longe; adj., mais afastado, mais distante.
FAR.THEST adj., longíssimo, o mais distante.
FAS.CIA, s., fachada; painel (de carro); capa frontal (de dispositivo móvel).
FAS.CI.CLE, s., fascículo.
FAS.CI.NATE, v., fascinar, encantar.
FAS.CI.NAT.ED, adj., fascinado, encantado.
FAS.CI.NAT.ING, adj., fascinante.
FAS.CI.NA.TION, s., fascinação, encanto.
FAS.CISM, s., fascismo.
FAS.CIST, s., adj., fascita.
FASH.ION, s., maneira, moda, talhe, costume; v., moldar, dar forma.
FASH.ION.A.BLE, adj., próprio da moda, elegante.
FASH.ION.A.BLE, s., elegância (dentro da moda).
FASH.ION.A.BLY, adv., elegantemente; à moda.
FASH.ION DE.SIGN.ER, s., estilista, costureiro.
FASH.ION DIS.PLAY, s., desfile de modas.
FASH.IONED, adj., elaborado ou adaptado conforme a moda.
FASH.ION.ER, s., costureiro, modista, estilista.

FASHION SHOW · 461 · FEDERALIZATION

FASH.ION SHOW, *s.*, o mesmo que *fashion display*.
FAST, *adj.*, rápido, permanente, firme; *s.*, jejum, abstinência; *v.*, jejuar.
FAST-FOOD, *s.*, comida pronta, comida pronta na hora.
FAS.TEN, *v.*, fixar, firmar, prender.
FAS.TEN.ER, *s.*, presilha, fecho, prendedor.
FAS.TEN.ING, *s.*, fechadura, trinco, fecho; fixação, presilha.
FAST FOOD, *s.*, fast-food (serviço que prepara e serve comida rápida).
FAS.TID.I.OUS, *adj.*, fastidioso, enjoativo.
FAST.ING, *s.*, jejum; *adj.*, de jejum.
FAST LANE, *s.*, pista de alta velocidade.
FAT, *adj.*, gordo, grande, grosso; *s.*, gordura, banha; *v.*, engordar.
FA.TAL, *adj.*, fatal, mortal, letal.
FA.TAL.ISM, *s.*, fatalismo.
FA.TAL.IST, *s.*, fatalista.
FA.TAL.IS.TIC, *adj.*, fatalista.
FA.TAL.I.TY, *s.*, fatalidade, sorte, destino, desgraça, acidente fatal.
FA.TAL.LY, *adv.*, fatalmente, mortalmente.
FAT BODY, *s.*, *Med.*, tecido adiposo.
FATE, *s.*, sorte, destino, fado.
FAT.ED, *adj.*, fadado, predestinado.
FATE.FUL, *adj.*, fatídico, decisivo.
FAT.HEAD, *adj.*, tolo, bobo, imbecil.
FA.THER, *s.*, pai; padre (membro da Igreja católica); *Father*: Pai, Deus; *v.*, ser o pai de; procriar.
FA.THER.HOOD, *s.*, paternidade.
FA.THER-IN-LAW, *s.*, sogro.
FA.THER.LAND, *s.*, pátria, terra de nascimento.
FA.THER.LESS, *adj.*, órfão, órfão de pai.
FA.THER.LY, *adj.*, paternal, paterno.
FA.THER'S DAY, *s.*, Dia dos Pais.
FATH.OM, *s.*, *Náut.*, braça; *fig.*, profundidade, penetração; *v.*, penetrar, sondar.
FA.TID.IC, *adj.*, fatídico; profético.
FA.TIGUE, *s.*, fadiga, cansaço, afã, trabalho.
FA.TI.GUING, *adj.*, fatigante, cansativo, tedioso.
FAT.LESS, *s.*, sem gordura.
FAT.NESS, *s.*, gordura, corpulência.
FAT.TED, *adj.*, engordado, cevado.
FAT.TEN, *v.*, engordar; aumentar de peso.
FAT.TEN.ING, *adj.*, que engorda.
FAT.TY, *s.*, *pej.*, gorducho; *adj.*, gorduroso, adiposo.
FA.TU.I.TY, *s.*, fatuidade, tolice.
FAT.U.OUS, *adj.*, fátuo, presunçoso, tolo; ilusório.
FAT.U.OUS.LY, *adv.*, fatuamente, tolamente.
FAT.U.OUS.NESS, *s.*, fatuidade, tolice.
FAU.CET, *s.*, torneira.
FAULT, *s.*, culpa, defeito; *adj.*, culpado, defeituoso, errado, errôneo.
FAULT.I.NESS, *s.*, imperfeição, defeito.
FAULT.LESS, *adj.*, sem defeito, impecável.
FAULT.LESS.LY, *adv.*, impecavelmente, perfeitamente.
FAUN, *s.*, *Mit.*, fauno.
FAULT.Y, *adj.*, defeituoso.
FAU.NA, *s.*, fauna.
FA.VOR, *s.*, favor; *v.*, favorecer, auxiliar.
FA.VOR.A.BLE, *adj.*, favorável.
FA.VOR.A.BLE.NESS, *s.*, benevolência.

FA.VOR.A.BLY, *adv.*, favoravelmente.
FA.VORED, *adj.*, favorecido, preferido.
FA.VOR.ITE, *s.*, favorito, predileto; *adj.*, predileto.
FA.VOR.IT.ISM, *s.*, favoritismo; preferência.
FA.VOR.LESS, *adj.*, desprestigiado, desfavorecido.
FA.VOUR *UK*, *s.*, o mesmo que *favor*.
FA.VOUR.ABLE *UK*, *adj.*, o mesmo que *favorable*.
FA.VOUR.A.BLE.NESS *UK*, *s.*, o mesmo que *favorableness*.
FA.VOUR.A.BLY *UK*, *adv.*, o mesmo que *favorably*.
FA.VOUR.ED *UK*, *adj.*, o mesmo que *favored*.
FA.VOUR.ITE *UK*, *s.*, o mesmo que *favorite*.
FA.VOUR.LESS *UK*, *adj.*, o mesmo que *favorless*.
FA.VOUR.IT.ISM *UK*, *s.*, o mesmo que *favoritism*.
FAWN, *v.*, adular, bajular; *s.*, cervo jovem; *adj.*, castanho-amarelado.
FAWN.ER, *s.*, adulador, bajulador; puxa-saco.
FAWN.ING, *s.*, lisonja, adulação; *adj.*, adulador, servil.
FAWN.ING.LY, *s.*, servilmente.
FAX, *s.*, fax, fac-símile; *v.*, remeter um fax.
FAY, *s.*, fada.
FAZE, *v.*, perturbar, aborrecer, intimidar; *gír.*, grilar.
FBI, *s.*, *US abrev.* de *Federal Bureau of Investigation*: Agência Federal de Investigação, FBI.
FEAL, *adj.*, fiel, leal; *v.*, esconder.
FE.AL.TY, *adj.*, fidelidade, lealdade; *Ant.*, vassalagem.
FEAR, *s.*, medo; *v.*, temer, ter medo.
FEAR.FUL, *adj.*, medroso, temeroso; pavoroso, medonho.
FEAR.FUL.LY, *adv.*, timidamente; terrivelmente.
FEAR.FUL.NESS, *s.*, timidez, medo, temor; pavor, terror.
FEAR.ING, *adj.*, receoso, temeroso; *s.*, receio, temor.
FEAR.LESS, *adj.*, sem medo, destemido.
FEAR.LESS.LY, *adv.*, destemidamente.
FEAR.SOME, *adj.*, terrível, espantoso.
FEA.SI.BIL.I.TY, *s.*, viabilidade.
FEA.SI.BLE, *adj.*, viável.
FEAST, *s.*, festa, banquete, ágape; *v.*, festejar, banquetear-se.
FEAT, *s.*, façanha, feito; destreza.
FEATH.ER, *s.*, pena, pluma.
FEATH.ER-BED, *s.*, colchão de penas.
FEATH.ERED, *adj.*, emplumado; alado; ligeiro.
FEATH.ER.ING, *s.*, plumagem.
FEATH.ER.LESS, *s.*, implume.
FEATH.ER-WEIGHT, *s.*, *Esp.*, peso-pena (boxe).
FEA.TURE, *s.*, feição, fisionomia, rosto, reportagem; *v.*, caracterizar.
FEA.TURED, *adj.*, de destaque, destacado (pessoa).
FEA.TURE-FILM, *s.*, longa metragem (filme).
FEA.TURE.LESS, *adj.*, sem traços característicos.
FEB.RI.FUGE, *s.*, *Med.*, febrífugo, remédio para baixar a febre.
FE.BRILE, *adj.*, febril.
FEB.RU.ARY, *s.*, fevereiro.
FE.CAL *US*, **FAE.CAL** *UK*, *adj.*, fecal.
FE.CES *US*, **FAE.CES** *UK*, *s. pl.*, fezes.
FECK.LESS, *adj.*, fraco; imprestável; displicente.
FE.CUND, *adj.*, fecundo, fértil, produtivo.
FE.CUN.DATE, *v.*, fecundar, fertilizar.
FE.CUN.DA.TION, *s.*, fecundação, fertilização.
FE.CUN.DI.TY, *s.*, fecundidade, fertilidade.
FED.ER.AL, *adj.*, federal.
FED.ER.AL.ISM, *s.*, federalismo.
FED.ER.AL.I.ZA.TION, *s.*, federalização (usa-se também

FEDERALIZE •• 462 •• FETTER

federalisation).

FED.ER.AL.IZE, *v.*, federalizar (usa-se também *federalize*).

FED.ER.A.TION, *s.*, federação, confederação.

FED.ER.A.TIVE, *adj.*, federativo.

FED.ER.A.TIVE.LY, *adv.*, de modo federativo.

FED UP, *adj.*, farto, cheio (de alguém).

FEE, *s.*, propriedade, honorários, propina, taxa; *v.*, pagar, gratificar.

FEE.BLE, *adj.*, fraco, débil, ineficaz.

FEE.BLE-MIND.ED, *adj.*, parvo, imbecil.

FEE.BLE.NESS, *s.*, fraqueza, debilidade.

FEE.BLY, *adv.*, fracamente, debilmente; sem convicção.

FEED, *s.*, alimento, alimentação, comida, refeição, sustento; ração, forragem; *v.*, alimentar; abastecer.

FEED.ER, *s.*, alimentador (de animais), comedouro; o animal que come; *Eletr.*, cabo alimentador.

FEED.BACK, *s.*, resposta; processo de avaliação; *Eletr.*, realimentação, regeneração; *adj.*, de regeneração.

FEED.ING, *s.*, alimentação, comida, pastagem; *adj.*, que alimenta.

FEED.ING-BOT.TLE, *s.*, mamadeira.

FEEL, *s.*, tato, sensação, percepção; *v.*, sentir, perceber, notar.

FEEL.ER, *s.*, quem sente; antena de bicho.

FEEL.ING, *s.*, sensação, sentimento, percepção.

FEET, *s. pl.*, pés.

FEIGN, *v.*, fingir.

FEIGNED, *adj.*, fingido, dissimulado; inventado.

FEIGNED.LY, *adv.*, fingidamente, falsamente.

FEIGN.ED.NESS, *s.*, fingimento.

FEINT, *s.*, finta, simulação.

FEIST.Y, *adj.*, mal-humorado, irascível; espirituoso, arrojado.

FE.LIC.I.TATE, *v.*, felicitar, dar parabéns.

FE.LIC.I.TA.TION, *s.*, felicitação, parabéns, congratulação.

FE.LIC.I.TOUS, *adj.*, oportuno, apropriado; feliz, venturoso.

FE.LIC.I.TOUS.LY, *adv.*, felizmente.

FE.LIC.I.TY, *s.*, felicidade, ventura, contentamento.

FE.LINE, *adj.*, *s.*, felino.

FELL, *s.*, derrubada (árvores); *v.*, cortar, derrubar (árvores); *fells UK*: charneca; *adj.*, cruel, desumano.

FELL.ER, *s.*, lenhador.

FEL.LOW, *s.*, companheiro, camarada, colega.

FEL.LOW-CIT.I.ZEN, *s.*, concidadão.

FEL.LOW-FEEL.ING, *s.*, sentimento de solidariedade.

FEL.LOW-MAN, *s.*, parceiro; pessoa muito humana.

FEL.LOW.SHIP, *s.*, amizade, coleguismo, companheirismo.

FEL.ON, *s.*, réu, criminoso, delinquente; *adj.*, cruel, malvado.

FEL.O.NY, *s.*, felonia, crime, delito.

FELT, *s.*, feltro; artigo feito de feltro.

FELT-TIP PEN, FELT PEN, *s.*, caneta hidrográfica.

FE.MALE, *s.*, fêmea, mulher; *adj.*, feminino, feminil.

FEME, *s.*, *Jur.*, mulher, esposa.

FEM.I.NAL.I.TY, *s.*, feminilidade.

FEM.I.NINE, *adj.*, feminino.

FEM.I.NISM, *s.*, feminismo.

FEM.I.NIST, *s.*, feminista.

FE.MIN.I.TY, *s.*, feminilidade.

FEM.I.NIZE(-ISE), *v.*, feminizer(-se); efeminar(-se).

FE.MUR, *s.*, *Anat.*, fêmur.

FEN, *s.*, pântano, paul, charco, brejo.

FENCE, *s.*, cerca, cercado, grade; *v.*, cercar.

FENCED, *adj.*, cercado, fortificado.

FEN.CI.BLE, *adj.*, que pode se defender; bem fortificado.

FENC.ING, *s.*, *Esp.*, esgrima; cercas, estacaria, material para fazer cerca.

FEND, *v.*, defender(-se), desviar (de golpe), rechaçar.

FENDER, *s.*, proteção, defesa; para-lama; guarda-fogo.

FEN.NEL, *s.*, *Bot.*, funcho, erva-doce.

FEN.NY, *adj.*, pantanoso.

FENS, *s. pl.*, *UK* pântano.

FE.RA.CIOUS, *adj.*, feraz, fecundo.

FE.RAC.I.TY, *s.*, feracidade, fertilidade.

FE.RAL, *adj.*, feroz, selvagem.

FE.RINE, *adj.*, ferino, feroz, selvagem.

FER.MENT, *s.*, fermento; *v.*, fermentar.

FER.MENT.ED, *adj.*, fermentado.

FER.MEN.TA.TION, *s.*, fermentação.

FER.MI.UM, *s.*, *Quím.*, férmio.

FERN, *s.*, feto, samambaia.

FE.RO.CIOUS, *adj.*, feroz; cruel, violento.

FE.RO.CIOUS.LY, *adv.*, ferozmente.

FE.RO.CIOUS.NESS, *s.*, ferocidade, crueldade, violência.

FE.ROC.I.TY, *s.*, ferocidade.

FER.RE.OUS, *adj.*, férreo.

FER.RET, *s.*, *Zool.*, furão; *v.*, vasculhar; *fig.*, esmiuçar.

FER.RI.FE.ROUS, *adj.*, ferrífero (que produz ferro).

FER.RIS WHEEL, *s.*, roda-gigante.

FER.ROUS, *adj.*, *Quím.*, ferroso.

FER.RU.GI.NOUS, *adj.*, ferruginoso.

FER.RY, *s.*, balsa, barco para travessias; *v.*, transportar por barco.

FER.RY-BOAT, *s.*, balsa, barco para travessias.

FER.RY.MAN, *s.*, barqueiro, balseiro.

FER.TILE, *adj.*, fértil, fecundo, produtivo.

FER.TIL.I.TY, *s.*, fertilidade.

FER.TI.LI.ZA.TION, *s.*, fertilização; *Biol.*, fecundação (usa-se também *fertilisation*).

FER.TIL.IZE(-ISE), *v.*, fertilizar.

FER.TIL.IZ.ER(-ISER), *s.*, adubo, fertilizante.

FER.VENT, *adj.*, fervente, ardente; *fig.*, fervoroso, apaixonado.

FER.VENT.LY, *adv.*, fervorosamente.

FER.VOR *US*, **FER.VOUR** *UK*, *s.*, fervor, abrasamento; ardor, veemência.

FES.TAL, *adj.*, festivo.

FES.TER, *s.*, pústula; *v.*, inflamar-se, supurar; *fig.*, corromper-se.

FES.TER.ING, *v.*, supuração;

FES.TI.VAL, *s.*, festival, festa.

FES.TIVE, *adj.*, festivo.

FES.TIVE.LY, *adv.*, festivamente.

FES.TIV.I.TIES, *s. pl.*, festividades.

FES.TIV.I.TY, *s.*, festa, festividade.

FES.TOON, *s.*, festão, grinalda; *v.*, enfeitar, engrinaldar.

FE.TAL, *adj.*, o mesmo que *foetal*.

FETCH, *v.*, ir buscar; mandar vir; alcançar.

FETCH.ER, *s.*, aquele que vai buscar, ou trazer, algo.

FETCH.ING, *adj.*, *col.*, atraente.

FETE, FÊTE, *s.*, festa, festejo, festa beneficente; *v.*, festejar.

FET.ID, FOET.ID, *adj.*, fétido, fedido.

FE.TISH(-ICH), *s.*, fetiche; amuleto, talismã.

FE.TISH.ISM, *s.*, fetichismo (usa-se também *fetichism*).

FE.TOR, *s.*, FÉTIDO.

FET.TER, *s.*, ferros, grilhões, algemas; trava; *v.*, prender,

FETTERED   ·· 463 ··   FILTHY

algemar.

FET.TERED, *adj.*, acorrentado, algemado; impedido.

FET.TLE, *s.*, condição; forma; *in good ~*: em boa forma.

FE.TUS, *s.*, o mesmo que *foetus.*

FEUD, *s.*, disputa, contenda, rixa; *Ant.*, feudo.

FEU.DAL, *adj.*, feudal.

FEU.DAL.ISM, *s.*, feudalismo.

FEU.DA.TO.RY, *s., adj.*, feudatário, vassalo.

FE.VER, *s., Med.*, febre; *fig.*, febre; agitação; *v.*, ter febre, causar febre.

FE.VER.ED, *adj.*, febril; exaltado.

FE.VER.ISH, *adj., Med.*, febril; *fig.*, frenético, inconstante.

FE.VER.OUS, *adj.*, febricitante; febril.

FEW, *adj., pron.*, poucos, poucas.

FEW.ER, *adj.*, menos.

FEW.EST, *adj.*, mínimo, a menor quantidade.

FI.AN.CÉ, *s.*, noivo.

FI.AN.CÉE, *s.*, noiva.

FI.AS.CO, *s.*, fiasco.

FIB, *s.*, mentira, lorota, peta; *v.*, mentir.

FIB.BER, *s.*, mentiroso.

FI.BER *US*, **FI.BRE** *UK*, *s.*, fibra.

FI.BER.GLASS *US*, **FI.BRE.GLASS** *UK*, *s.*, fibra de vidro.

FI.BER OP.TICS, *s., Fis.*, transmissão (de dados) por fibra óptica.

FI.BRIL.LA.TION, *s., Med.*, fibrilação.

FI.BRO.SIS, *s., Med.*, fibrose.

FI.BROUS, *adj.*, fibroso.

FIB.U.LA, *s., Anat.*, fíbula, (perônio: termo fora de uso).

FICK.LE, *adj.*, inconstante, volúvel.

FIC.TION, *s.*, ficção; *adj.*, ficcional.

FIC.TION.AL, *adj.*, fictício, imaginário.

FIC.TION.AL.ISE(-IZE), *v.*, romancear (escrita), adaptar.

FIC.TION.IST, *s.*, ficcionista.

FIC.TI.TIOUS, *adj.*, fictício.

FID.DLE, *s.*, rabeca, violino; *v.*, tocar rabeca, tocar violino; remexer; burlar.

FID.DLER, *s.*, rabequista, violinista; embusteiro.

FID.DLY, *adj., col.*, trabalhoso.

FI.DEL.I.TY, *s.*, fidelidade.

FIDG.ET, *s.*, pessoa irrequieta; *v.*, ficar inquieto; incomodar; remexer-se.

FIDG.ET.Y, *adj., col.*, irrequieto; impaciente.

FI.DU.CIAL, *adj.*, fiducial, confiado.

FI.DU.CI.A.RY, *adj.*, fiduciário; *s.*, fiduciário, confidente.

FIEF, *s.*, feudo.

FIELD, *s.*, campo; área, especialidade.

FIELD-GLAS.SES, *s. pl.*, binóculo.

FIELD-MOUSE, *s.*, ratazana; *Zool.*, arganaz.

FIELD STUD.Y, *s.*, estudo de campo.

FIELD.WORK, *s.*, trabalho (científico) de campo.

FIEND, *s.*, demônio.

FIEND.ISH, *s.*, diabólico, demoníaco.

FIERCE, *adj.*, feroz, violento.·

FIERCE.LY, *adv.*, ferozmente, furiosamente.

FIERCE.NESS, *s.*, ferocidade, crueldade, maldade, violência.

FIERI.LY, *adv.*, fogosamente, furiosamente.

FIER.Y, *adj.*, chamejante; abrasador; cor de fogo; *fig.*, ardente, apaixonado; explosivo.

FIFA, *s.*, FIFA (abrev. de *Fédération Internationale de Football Association*).

FIF.TEEN, *num.*, quinze.

FIF.TEENTH, *s.*, décimo quinto.

FIFTH, *num.*, quinto.

FIF.TI.ETH, *num.*, quinquagésimo(a).

FIF.TY, *num.*, cinquenta.

FIF.TY-FIF.TY, *adv.*, meio a meio.

FIG, *s., Bot.*, figo; figueira.

FIGHT, *s.*, batalha, luta, briga.

FIGHT.ER, *s.*, lutador, batalhador, combatente.

FIGHT.ING, *s.*, luta, combate.

FIG.MENT, *s.*, imaginação, invenção, ficção.

FIG.TREE, *s.*, figueira, planta que produz figo.

FIG.UR.ABLE, *adj.*, figurável.

FIG.U.RANT, *s.*, figurante.

FIG.U.RA.TION, *s.*, figuração.

FIG.U.RA.TIVE, *adj.*, figurativo.

FIG.U.RA.TIVE.LY, *adv.*, metaforicamente, figurativamente.

FIG.URE, *s.*, figura, desenho, silhueta, forma.

FIG.URED, *adj.*, figurado; figurativo.

FI.GU.RINE, *s.*, estatueta (de cerâmica ou metal).

FIJIAN, *s., adj.*, fijiano (natural da ou pertencente à República de Fiji).

FIL.A.MENT, *s.*, filamento.

FIL.A.MEN.TA.RY, *adj.*, filamentar, filamentoso.

FIL.A.MEN.TOUS, *adj.*, filamentoso, fibroso.

FILCH, *v.*, surrupiar, furtar.

FILCH.ING, *s.*, furto, roubo.

FILE, *s.*, pasta, arquivo, fichário; lista; lixa, fio, arame, espeto; *v.*, lixar, arquivar, fichar.

FILE CARD, *s.*, ficha de arquivo.

FILE CLERK, *s.*, o mesmo que *filing clerk.*

FIL.ER, *s.*, limador.

FILE.NAME, *s., Comp.*, nome de arquivo.

FI.LET *US*, **FIL.LET** *UK*, *s.*, filé (de boi ou porco).

FIL.IAL, *adj.*, filial.

FIL.I.A.TION, *s.*, filiação; adoção.

FIL.I.BUS.TER, *s.*, filibusteiro, corsário, pirata; *v.*, piratear.

FIL.I.GREE, *s.*, filigrana.

FIL.ING CLERK, *s.*, arquivista, arquivador.

FIL.I.PI.NO(A), *s., adj.*, filipino(a) (natural ou habitante das Filipinas).

FILL, *s.*, suficiência, abastecimento; *v.*, encher, acumular, fartar.

FILL.ED, *adj.*, recheado.

FILL.ER, *s.*, enchedor; enchimento (para rachaduras).

FILL-IN, *s., col.*, tapa-buraco.

FILL.ING, *s.*, recheio; *Oftal.*, obturação; *adj.*, que enche, que sacia ou satisfaz.

FIL.LIP, *s.*, estímulo, incentivo; piparote; *v.*, incentivar.

FIL.LY, *s.*, égua de pouca idade, potranca.

FILM, *s.*, filme, película, fita de cinema, véu; *v.*, filmar, velar.

FILM-CAR.TRIDGE, *s.*, filme de rolo.

FILM.ING, *s.*, filmagem.

FILM-MAK.ER, *s.*, cineasta ou produtor de filmes.

FILM.Y, *adj.*, fino, delgado; turvo, translúcido; opaco.

FIL.TER, *s.*, filtro; *v.*, filtrar.

FIL.TER.A.BLE, *adj.*, filtrável.

FIL.TER.ING, *s.*, filtragem.

FILTH, *s.*, sujidade, sujeira, imundície.

FILTH.I.NESS, *s.*, sujeira, imundície.

FILTH.Y, *adj.*, sujo, imundo.

FILTRATE   ··464··   FISSION

FIL.TRATE, *v.*, filtrar; *s.*, líquido filtrado.
FIL.TRA.TION, *s.*, filtração, filtragem.
FIN, *s.*, nadadeira, barbatana, asa; *v.*, nadar com barbatana, mover as asas.
FIN.A.BLE, *adj.*, que está sujeito a multa.
FI.NAL, *adj.*, final, último, definitivo.
FI.NAL DE.MAND, *s.*, ultimato, último aviso.
FI.NA.LE, *s.*, *It.*, *Mús.*, final (sinfônica, ópera, teatro).
FI.NAL.IST, *s.*, finalista.
FI.NAL.I.TY, *s.*, finalidade.
FI.NAL.IZE(-ISE), *v.*, finalizar, completar, concluir.
FI.NAL.LY, *adv.*, finalmente.
FI.NANCE, *s.*, finanças, fundos; *v.*, financiar.
FI.NAN.CIAL, *adj.*, financeiro.
FI.NAN.CIAL.LY, *adv.*, financeiramente.
FI.NAN.CIER, *s.*, financeiro, financista.
FI.NAN.CING, *s.*, financiamento.
FINCH, *s.*, *Zool.*, tentilhão.
FIND, *v.*, encontrar, achar, descobrir.
FIND.ER, *s.*, achador, descobridor; *Com.*, promotor de negócios, intermediário.
FIND.ING, *s.*, descoberta, achado.
FIND.INGS, *s. pl.*, constatações (com provas ou fatos).
FINE, *adj.*, fino, excelente, ótimo; delicado; *adv.*, bem; *s.*, multa; *v.*, multar.
FINE ARTS, *s. pl.*, belas-artes.
FINE-LOOK.ING, *adj.*, atraente, fascinante, elegante.
FINE.LY, *adv.*, finamente.
FINE.NESS, *s.*, fineza, delicadeza, sutileza.
FIN.ER.Y, *s.*, elegância; refinamento.
FI.NESSE, *s.*, finura, delicadeza; destreza.
FIN.GER, *s.*, dedo; *v.*, manusear, apalpar, tocar com os dedos.
FIN.GERED, *adj.*, digitado, de dedos; que tem dedos.
FIN.GER.ING, *s.*, manejo; *Mus.*, dedilhado.
FIN.GER-MARK, *s.*, marca ou mancha feita por dedo.
FIN.GER-NAIL, *s.*, unha (dos dedos das mãos).
FIN.GER-PRINT, *s.*, impressão digital.
FIN.GER-STALL, *s.* dedeira.
FIN.GER-TIP, *s.*, ponta do dedo.
FIN.ING, *s.*, afinação; clarificação.
FI.NIS, *s.*, fim, termo.
FIN.ISH, *s.*, fim; *v.*, terminar, acabar, finalizar.
FIN.ISHED, *adj.*, terminado, completo; liquidado.
FIN.ISH.ING, *s.*, acabamento, conclusão.
FIN.ISH(ING) LINE, *s.*, *Esp.*, linha de chegada.
FI.NITE, *adj.*, finito.
FI.NI.TE.LY, *adv.*, limitadamente.
FI.NITE.NESS, *s.*, limitação, limite, marco.
FIN.LAND.ER, *s.*, *adj.*, finlandês (que vive na, ou habita a Finlândia).
FINN, *s.*, finlandês.
FINN.ISH, *s.*, finlandês (língua da Finlândia).
FIORD, *s.*, fiorde.
FIR, *s.*, *Bot.*, abeto.
FIR-AP.PLE, *s.*, pinhão.
FIRE, *s.*, fogo, incêndio; *v.*, disparar, atirar, estimular.
FIRE A.LARM, *s.*, alarme contra fogo.
FIRE.ARM, *s.*, arma de fogo.
FIRE-BOMB, *s.*, bomba incendiária.
FIRE-BRI.GADE, *s.*, corpo de bombeiros.
FIRE-CUR.TAIN, *s.*, cortina de fogo.

FIRE-DOOR, *s.*, porta corta-fogo.
FIRE-EAT.ER, *s.*, engolidor de fogo (circo); *fig.*, briguento.
FIRE ES.CAPE, *s.*, saída de emergência; escada de incêndio.
FIRE EX.TIN.GUISH.ER, *s.*, extintor de incêndio.
FIRE FIGHT.ER, *s.*, bombeiro (florestal).
FIRE-HY.DRANT, *s.*, hidrante.
FIRE.MAN, *s.*, bombeiro.
FIRE.PLACE, *s.*, lareira.
FIRE.PLUG, *s.*, o mesmo que *fire-hydrant*.
FIRE.PROOF, *adj.*, à prova de fogo.
FIRE-RISK, *s.*, perigo de incêndio.
FIRE.SIDE, *s.*, lareira; o calor produzido pela lareira.
FIRE-WALL, *s.*, muro guarda-fogo; *Inform.*, *firewall*: programa de segurança.
FIRE.WOOD, *s.*, lenha.
FIRE.WORKS, *s.*, fogos de artifício.
FIR.ING, *s.*, ato de acender; *Mil.*, tiroteio.
FIR.ING SQUAD, *s.*, *Mil.*, pelotão de fuzilamento.
FIRM, *s.*, firma, empresa; *adj.*, firme; *v.*, firmar.
FIR.MA.MENT, *s.*, firmamento, céu.
FIRM.LY, *adv.*, firmemente.
FIRM.NESS, *s.*, firmeza.
FIRST, *adj.*, primeiro; *adv.*, primeiramente; *s.*, primeira marcha de carro.
FIRST AID, *s.*, primeiros socorros.
FIRST AID.ER, *s.*, socorrista.
FIRST-CLASS, *adj.*, de primeira classe.
FIRST COUS.IN, *s.*, primo-irmão.
FIRST DE.GREE, *adj.*, de primeiro grau.
FIRST FLOOR, *s.*, *US* andar térreo; *UK* primeiro andar.
FIRST-HAND, *adv.*, em primeira mão.
FIRST LADY, *s.*, primeira-dama.
FIRST LIEU.TEN.ANT, *s.*, *Mil.*, primeiro-tenente.
FIRST.LY, *adv.*, primeiramente; o mesmo que *first*.
FISRST MATE, *s.*, *Náut.*, imediato.
FIRST NAME, *s.*, nome de batismo, prenome.
FIRST SER.GEANT, *s.*, *Mil.*, primeiro-sargento.
FIRST WORLD WAR, *s.*, *Hist.*, Primeira Guerra Mundial (usa-se também *World War I* ou *Great War*).
FIS.CAL, *adj.*, fiscal.
FISH, *s.*, peixe; *v.*, pescar.
FISH-BOWL, *s.*, aquário.
FISH-CAKE, *s.*, bolinho de peixe.
FISH.ER, *s.*, pescador.
FISH.ER.MAN, *s.*, pescador.
FISH.ERY, *s.*, indústria de pesca; pescaria.
FISH FARM, *s.*, viveiro de peixes.
FISH.HOOK, *s.*, anzol.
FISH.ING, *s.*, pesca, pescaria.
FISH.ING-BOAT, *s.*, barco de pesca.
FISH.ING-LINE, *s.*, linha de pescar.
FISH.ING-ROD, *s.*, vara de pescar.
FISH.MON.GER, *s.*, peixeiro.
FISH NET, *s.*, rede de pesca.
FISH SHOP, *s.*, peixaria.
FISH SLICE, *s.*, escumadeira.
FISH TANK, *s.*, tanque de peixes (viveiro de peixes).
FISH-TAIL, *s.*, rabo de peixe; *adj.*, semelhante a rabo de peixe; *v.*, nadar como um rabo de peixe.
FISH.Y, *adj.*, de peixe; *fig.*, duvidoso.
FIS.SION, *s.*, fendimento; *Fís.*, *Quím.*, fissão (atômica).

FISSIPARISM   ••465••   FLAW

FIS.SIP.A.RISM, *s.*, *Biol.*, fissiparidade.
FIS.SURE, *s.*, fissura, fenda.
FIS.SURED, *s.*, fendido, rachado, fissurado.
FIST, *s.*, punho.
FIS.TU.LA, *s.*, fístula.
FIT, *s.*, ajuste, ajustamento; *adj.*, bom, próprio, apto; *v.*, assentar, ajustar.
FIT.FUL, *adj.*, espasmódico, intermitente.
FIT.MENT, *s.*, móvel.
FIT.NESS, *s.*, boa saúde, boa forma.
FIT.TED, *adj.*, adequado, na medida; provido.
FIT.TER, *s.*, adaptador; *Tec.*, montador (de motores).
FIT.TING, *s.*, ajustamento, encaixe, montagem; prova (de roupa); *fittings*, *s.pl.*: acessórios; *adj.*, apropriado.
FIT.TING ROOM, *s.*, lugar de provar de roupas, provador.
FIVE, *num.*, cinco.
FIVE.FOLD, *adj.*, quíntuplo, quintuplicado.
FIX, *v.*, fixar, pregar, grudar, preparar.
FIX.ABLE, *adj.*, fixável.
FIX.A.TED, *adj.*, fixado; obcecado.
FIX.A.TION, *s.*, fixação.
FIXED, *adj.*, fixado, fixo; seguro.
FIXED I.DE.A, *adj.*, ideia fixa.
FIXED.LY, *adv.*, fixamente.
FIX.ED.NESS, *s.*, fixidez, firmeza.
FIX.ER, *s.*, fixador.
FIX.ING, *s.*, fixação; adaptação; conserto; *fixings*, *s.pl.*: adornos.
FIX.I.TY, *s.*, fixidez, estabilidade.
FIX.TURE, *s.*, fixação, fixidez; instalação, acessório; *fig.*, figura constante.
FIX-UP, *s.*, melhoria, reparo.
FIZZ, *v.*, assobiar, zunir.
FIZZ.ER, *s.*, assobiador.
FIZ.ZLE, *s.*, efervescência, assobio, crepitação; *v.*, sibilar, assobiar.
FIZZY, *adj.*, gasoso, com gás.
FLAB, *s.*, facidez.
FLAB.BER.GAST, *v.*, pasmar, espantar.
FLAB.BER.GAST.ED, *adj.*, perplexo.
FLAB.BI.LY, *adv.*, flacidamente, debilmente.
FLAB.BY, *adj.*, flácido.
FLAC.CID, *adj.*, flácido; mole; fraco.
FLAC.CID.I.TY, *s.*, flacidez, moleza.
FLAG, *s.*, bandeira, estandarte; lousa; *v.*, sinalizar com bandeira; desanimar.
FLAG.EL.LATE, *v.*, flagelar, açoitar, surrar.
FLAG.EL.LA.TION, *s.*, flagelação, flagelo, açoitamento.
FLA.GEL.LUM, *s.*, *Lat.*, flagelo, açoite.
FLAGGED, *adj.*, pavimentado (de pedras).
FLAG.GING, *s.*, lajeamento; *adj.*, pendente; flácido; cansado.
FLA.GI.TIOUS, *adj.*, mau, perverso, ruim, malvado.
FLA.GI.TIOUS.NESS, *s.*, perversidade, maldade.
FLAG.ON, *s.*, frasco, jarro, garrafão.
FLAG.POLE, *s.*, mastro de bandeira.
FLA.GRAN.CY, *s.*, flagrante, imprevisto.
FLA.GRANT, *adj.*, flagrante, evidente, claro.
FLA.GRANT.LY, *adv.*, flagrantemente.
FLAG.SHIP, *s.*, nau capitânia; *col.*, carro-chefe.
FLAG.STONE, *s.*, laje (pedra de pavimentação).
FLAIL, *v.*, debulhar (cereais) ; agitar(-se); açoitar.

FLAIR, *s.*, talento, capacidade, tirocínio, habilidade.
FLAK, *s.*, *Mil.*, fogo antiaéreo; *fig.*, críticas.
FLAKE, *s.*, floco, lasca; fagulha; *v.*, lascar(-se); escamar.
FLAKE OUT, *v.*, cair de cansaço.
FLAK.Y, *adj.*, escamoso; lascado, folhado; *col.*, extravagante.
FLAK.Y PAS.TRY, *s.*, massa folhada, mil-folhas.
FLAM, *s.*, mentira, engano, logro.
FLAM.BÉ, *adj.*, *Cul.*, flambado; *v.*, flambar.
FLAM.BOY.ANT, *adj.*, extravagante, chamativo; chamejante.
FLAME, *s.*, chama; *v.*, inflamar, arder.
FLAME.PROOF, *adj.*, à prova de fogo.
FLAME-THROW.ER, *s.*, *Mil.*, lança-chamas.
FLAM.ING, *adj.*, inflamado, cheio de chamas.
FLA.MIN.GO, *s.*, *Zool.*, flamingo.
FLAM.MA.BLE, *adj.*, inflamável.
FLAM.Y, *adj.*, flamejante, ardente.
FLAN, *s.*, torta, bolo.
FLANGE, *s.*, flange, bordo; aro; *v.*, bordear.
FLANK, *s.*, flanco; *v.*, flanquear, ladear.
FLAN.NEL, *s.*, toalha de rosto, flanela.
FLAN.NEL.ETTE, *s.*, flanela de algodão; baetilha.
FLAP, *s.*, aba, dobra; *v.*, oscilar, bater, ondular.
FLAP-JACK, *s.*, *US* espécie de panqueca; *UK* biscoito de aveia.
FLAR.ING, *adj.*, brilhante.
FLASH, *s.*, brilho, clarão, furo de reportagem; *v.*, brilhar, cintilar.
FLASH-BACK, *s.*, recuo no tempo, volta, retorno.
FLASH BULB, *s.*, *Fot.*, lâmpada de flash.
FLASH.ER, *s.*, *UK* pisca-pisca; *fig.*, exibicionista.
FLASH FLOOD, *s.*, enchente repentina.
FLASH GUN, *s.*, *Fot.*, disparador de flash.
FLASH.LIGHT, *s.*, lanterna de bolso.
FLASK, *s.*, garrafa térmica; frasco; cantil.
FLAT, *s.*, superfície plana, planície, pântano; *adj.*, plano, vazio, liso.
FLAT-FOOT.ED, *adj.*, que tem pés chatos; *UK* de calças curtas; desajeitado.
FLAT.LET, *s.*, pequeno apartamento.
FLAT.LY, *adv.*, de modo chato ou plano; monotonamente.
FLAT.MATE, *s.*, colega de apartamento.
FLAT.NESS, *s.*, lisura, planura, nivelamento; vulgaridade.
FLAT SCREEN, *s.*, tela plana (TV).
FLAT.TEN, *v.*, aplainar, nivelar, alisar; tornar monótono.
FLAT.TER, *v.*, lisonjear, bajular, cortejar; *s.*, assentador (de terreno).
FLAT.TER.ER, *s.*, lisonjeiro, bajulador.
FLAT.TER.ING, *adj.*, lisonjeiro, favorável, favorecedor.
FLAT.TERY, *s.*, bajulação, adulação.
FLAT.TING, *s.*, alisamento; ato de passar o ferro elétrico.
FLAT.U.LENCE, *s.*, flatulência.
FLAT.U.LENT, *adj.*, flatulento; cheio de si, inflado, vaidoso.
FLAT.WARE, *s.*, talheres; louças.
FLAUNT, *s.*, ostentação; pompa; *v.*, ostentar; tremular (ao vento).
FLAU.TIST, *s.*, flautista.
FLA.VOUR, *s.*, sabor; *v.*, condimentar, temperar.
FLA.VOUR.ING, *s.*, tempero, condimento.
FLA.VOUR.LESS, *adj.*, insípido, sem sabor.
FLA.VOUR.OUS, *adj.*, saboroso; aromático.
FLAW, *s.*, defeito, falha, fenda; *v.*, quebrar, inutilizar, fender.

FLAWED   •• 466 ••   FLOUNCE

FLAWED, *adj.*, defeituoso, imperfeito.
FLAW.LESS, *adj.*, impecável.
FLAW.Y, *adj.*, imperfeito, defeituoso; manchado; ventoso.
FLAX, *s.*, linho.
FLAX.EN, *adj.*, de linho.
FLAX.SEED, *s.*, linhaça (semente).
FLAX.Y, *adj.*, de linho, como linho.
FLAY, *v.*, esfolar, tirar a pele, despir.
FLAY.ER, *s.*, esfolador.
FLEA, *s.*, pulga.
FLEA.BITE, *s.*, picada de pulga; bagatela.
FLEA MAR.KET, *s.*, mercado das pulgas (de quinquilharias).
FLECK, *s.*, pinta, mancha; *v.*, salpicar, mosquear.
FLECKED, *adj.*, manchado, salpicado.
FLECK.LESS, *adj.*, imaculado.
FLEDGE, *v.*, criar penas (para voo), emplumar(-se).
FLEDGED, *adj.*, emplumado, quase pronto para voar.
FLEDGE.LESS, *adj.*, implume.
FLEDGE.LING, FLEDG.LING, *adj.*, ave novata e prestes a voar; *fig.*, frangote.
FLEE, *v.*, fugir, escapar.
FLEECE, *s.*, velo, tosão, lã; *v.*, tosquiar, tosar, espoliar.
FLEECED, *adj.*, lanoso; *fig.*, espoliado, usurpado.
FLEER.ING, *s.*, zombaria, escárnio; *v.*, escarnecer, zombar.
FLEET, *s.*, frota, esquadra.
FLEET.ING, *adj.*, passageiro, transitório.
FLEET.LY, *adv.*, velozmente, ligeiramente.
FLEET.NESS, *s.*, velocidade, rapidez.
FLEM.ING, *s.*, flamingo.
FLEM.ING, *s.*, flamengo (o habitante de Flandres).
FLEM.ISH, *s.*, flamengo e língua dos flamengos; *adj.*, flamengo (de Flandres).
FLESH, *s.*, carne polpuda; gordura, robustez; *v.*, descarnar (couro), alimentar com carne.
FLESH-FLY, *s.*, mosca varejeira.
FLESH.I.NESS, *s.*, gordura, corpulência.
FLESH.Y, *adj.*, carnudo, gordo; carnal, corpóreo, mundano.
FLETCH, *v.*, cobrir com penas as flechas.
FLETCH.ER, *s.*, aquele que faz flechas.
FLEX, *s.*, *Elet.*, fio, cabo; *v.*, flexionar.
FLEX.I.BIL.I.TY, *s.*, flexibilidade.
FLEX.I.BLE, *adj.*, flexível.
FLEX.I.BLY, *adv.*, flexivelmente.
FLEX.ION, *s.*, flexão.
FLEX.I.TIME, *s.*, horário flexível.
FLICK, *s.*, pancada leve, chicotada, piparote.
FLICK.ER, *v.*, tremular, vacilar, bruxulear; *s.*, vacilação, centelha.
FLI.ER, *s.*, aviador.
FLIGHT, *s.*, voo, fuga, lance de escada.
FLIGHT AT.TEND.ANT, *s.*, comissário de bordo.
FLIGHT CREW, *s.*, tripulação de voo.
FLIGHT.I.LY, *adv.*, caprichosamente.
FLIGHT RECORDER, *s.*, gravação de voo.
FLIGHT.Y, *adj.*, descuidado, frívolo.
FLIM.SY, *s.*, papel fino para cópia; *adj.*, frágil, franzino.
FLINCH, *s.*, recuo; vacilação; *v.*, recuar, encolher-se, vacilar.
FLINCH.ING, *s.*, vacilante, hesitante, trêmulo.
FLIN.DERS, *s.*, fragmentos.
FLING, *s.*, arremesso, pulo; *v.*, atirar(-se), arrojar(-se); arruinar.
FLINT, *s.*, pedra, sílex.

FLINT.I.NESS, *s.*, dureza, insensibilidade.
FLINT.STONE, *s.*, pederneira.
FLIP, *s.*, sacudida, estalido; *v.*, sacudir, mover bruscamente.
FLIP-FLOPS, *s. pl.*, chinelo de dedo.
FLIP.PANT, *adj.*, petulante, leviano; loquaz.
FLIP.PANT.LY, *adv.*, petulantemente.
FLIP.PER, *s.*, barbatana.
FLIP.PING, *adv.*, absolutamente; *adj.*, *col.*, *UK* maldito.
FLIP SIDE, *s.*, *col.*, lado B; *fig.*, o outro lado.
FLIRT, *v.*, namorar, namoricar, flertar; *s.*, namoradinho.
FLIR.TA.TION, *s.*, namoro, namorisco.
FLIR.TA.TIOUS, *adj.*, galanteador.
FLIT, *s.*, adejo, voo; *v.*, esvoaçar.
FLIT.ER, *v.*, esvoaçar, voejar, voar.
FLIT.ING, *s.*, voo rápido.
FLOAT, *s.*, boia, caixa; *v.*, flutuar, boiar.
FLOAT.A.BLE, *adj.*, flutuável, navegável.
FLOAT.AGE, *s.*, flutuação.
FLOAT.ER, *s.*, o que flutua; *US* vira-casaca.
FLOAT.ING, *adj.*, flutuante, móvel.
FLOAT.ING.LY, *adv.*, de modo flutuante.
FLOAT.Y, *adj.*, que é capaz de flutuar.
FLOC, *s.*, floco.
FLOCK, *s.*, bando; estofamento (com lã); *v.*, andar em bando; estofar (com lã).
FLOE, *s.*, banquisa (geleira flutuante).
FLOG, *v.*, açoitar.
FLOG.GER, *s.*, açoitador.
FLOOD, *s.*, enchente, inundação, enxurrada; *v.*, inundar, alagar.
FLOOD.ING, *s.*, inundação, alagamento.
FLOOD.LIGHT, *s.*, holofote; *v.*, iluminar com holofote.
FLOOD.LIT, *adj.*, iluminado por holofotes.
FLOOD-TIDE, *s.*, preamar, maré alta (maré-enchente).
FLOOR, *s.*, chão, piso, andar, assoalho; *v.*, assoalhar, pavimentar.
FLOOR.BOARD, *s.*, tábua de assoalho.
FLOOR CLOTH, *s.*, pano de chão.
FLOOR.ER, *s.*, muro.
FLOOR.ING, *s.*, chão, assoalho.
FLOOR LAMP, *s.*, *US* abajur de pé.
FLOOR.WAX, *s.*, cera para assoalho.
FLOP, *s.*, fracasso; *v.*, fracassar.
FLOP.PY, *adj.*, desengonçado.
FLOP.PI.LY, *adv.*, desajeitadamente.
FLOP.PY DISCK, *s.*, *Comp.*, *Ant.*, disquete (disco flexível).
FLO.RA, *s.*, flora.
FLO.RAL, *adj.*, floral; florido.
FLO.RES.CENCE, *s.*, florescência.
FLO.RES.CENT, *adj.*, florescente.
FLO.RET, *s.*, florzinha.
FLO.RI.AT.ED, *adj.*, floreado (ornamentos florais).
FLO.RI.CUL.TURE, *s.*, floricultura.
FLO.RI.CUL.TUR.IST, *s.*, floricultor.
FLOR.ID, *adj.*, florido.
FLOR.IST, *s.*, florista.
FLOSS, *s.*, fio de seda; seda crua; penugem; *dental floss*: fio dental.
FLOT.SAM, *s.*, restos de naufrágio; *fig.*, gente desocupada.
FLOUNCE, *s.*, gesto de indignação; safanão; babado; *v.*, fazer ar de indignação.

FLOUNCING · 467 · FOOLHARDY

FLOUNC.ING, s., apetrechos para babados.
FLOUN.DER, s., ato de se debater; *Zool.*, solha (peixe linguado); v., debater-se; tropeçar, atrapalhar-se.
FLOUR, s., farinha; v., enfarinhar, moer.
FLOUR.ISH, v., florescer; menear.
FLOUR.ISH.ING, *adj.*, viçoso, próspero, florescente.
FLOURY, *adj.*, farinhento, farinhoso.
FLOUT, s., escárnio, zombaria; v., desrespeitar, desprezar.
FLOW, s., fluxo, circulação; v., circular, correr, ondular.
FLOW.ER, s., flor, escol, elite, v., florescer, florir.
FLOW.ER BED, s., canteiro de flores.
FLOW.ERED, *adj.*, florido, floreado.
FLOW.ER.ING, *adj.*, florescente; s., florescência, desabrocho.
FLOW.ER.LESS, *adj.*, sem flores.
FLOW.ER.POT, s., vaso.
FLOW.ER.Y, *adj.*, florido; floreado, poético.
FLOW.ING, *adj.*, corrente, que flui; *fig.*, esvoaçante, ondeante.
FLU, s., *col.*, gripe, influenza.
FLUC.TU.ATE, v., flutuar.
FLUC.TU.A.TION, s., flutuação, vacilação.
FLUE, s., fumeiro (chaminé); tubo para ar ou fumaça; penugem; *Mús.*, tubo da flauta.
FLU.EN.CY, s., fluência.
FLU.ENT, *adj.*, fluente, eloquente.
FLU.ENT.LY, *adv.*, fluentemente.
FLUFF, s., penugem, buço; v., afofar (com felpa).
FLUFF.Y, *adj.*, macio, fofo.
FLU.ID, *adj.*, s., fluido.
FLU.ID.I.TY, s., fluidez.
FLUMP, v., cair ou jogar-se ao chão; s., baque surdo.
FLUNK, s., *col., US* fracasso; v., fracassar; reprovar em exame.
FLUN.KEY, s., lacaio, serviçal.
FLU.OR, s., o mesmo que *fluorine*.
FLU.O.RES.CENT, *adj.*, fluorescente.
FLU.O.RES.CENT LIGHT, s., luz fluorescente.
FLUOR.I.DATE, v., adicionar flúor em.
FLUOR.INE, s., *Quím.*, flúor.
FLUR.RY, s., lufada; atividade, animação.
FLUSH, s., rubor, brilho; v., ruborizar-se.
FLUSHED, *adj.*, empolgado, cheio de orgulho; ruborizado.
FLUSH.ING, s., rubor.
FLUS.TER, s., agitação; atrapalhação; v., agitar, atrapalhar.
FLUS.TERED, *adj.*, atrapalhado.
FLUTE, s., *Mús.*, flauta.
FLUT.IST *UK*, s., o mesmo que *flautist*.
FLUT.TER, s., adejo; o bater de asas; *Med.*, taquicardia; v., esvoaçar, voejar; alvoroçar-se.
FLU.VI.AL, *adj.*, fluvial.
FLUX, s., fluxo.
FLY, s., *Zool.*, mosca; voo; v., voar, viajar de avião; flutuar; saltar; *fig.*, fugir.
FLY.A.WAY, s., fujão, fugitivo; *adj.*, folgado (roupa); *fig.*, leviano.
FLY IN, v., chegar ou vir de avião.
FLY.ING, s., aviação.
FLY.ING-OF.FICER, s., tenente-aviador.
FLY.ING SAL.CER, s., disco voador.
FLY.O.VER, s., viaduto.
FLY.PAST, s., *UK* apresentação aérea.
FLY.WEIGHT, s., *Esp.*, peso-mosca (boxe).
FOAL, s., potro; v., dar cria (a égua).
FOAM, s., espuma, espuma de borra; v., espumar.

FOAM.Y, *adj.*, espumoso, espumante.
FO.CAL, *adj.*, focal.
FO.CAL.I.SA.TION, v., focalização, focagem (usa-se também *focalization*).
FO.CAL.ISE(-IZE), v., focar, enfocar, focalizar.
FOCAL POINT, s., ponto central, foco.
FOCUS, s., foco (visão); v., focar, enfocar; focalizar.
FOD.DER, s., forragem; v., alimentar o gado com forragem.
FOE, s., inimigo; adversário.
FOE.TAL, *adj.*, *Anat.*, fetal.
FOE.TID, *adj.*, o mesmo que *fetid*.
FOE.TUS, s., *Anat.*, feto.
FOG, s., nevoeiro, cerração; v., enevoar-se.
FOG.BOUND, *adj.*, *Náut.*, impedido devido a nevoeiro.
FO.GEY, s., o mesmo que *foggy*.
FOG.HORN, s., buzina de nevoeiro.
FOG.GI.NESS, s., nebulosidade.
FOG.GY, *adj.*, enevoado, nevoento, brumoso.
FOG LAMP, s., farol de neblina (veículos).
FOI.BLE, *adj.*, fraco, frágil.
FOIL, s., rasto (de caça); derrota, frustração; v., frustrar; derrotar.
FOIL.ING, s., rasto (de cervídeo).
FOIST, v., impingir.
FOLD, s., dobra, prega, ruga; curral; v., dobrar, enrugar, vincar.
FOLD.A.WAY, *adj.*, o mesmo que *fold-up*.
FOLD.ER, s., dobrador; pasta para papéis; folheto dobrado.
FOLD.ING, *adj.*, dobrável.
FOLD-UP, *adj.*, dobrável, dobradiça.
FO.LI.AGE, s., folhagem.
FO.LI.ATE, *adj.*, próprio de folhagem; v., enfeitar com folhagens.
FOLK, s., gente, povo; *adj.*, popular; familiares, parentes, pais.
FOLK.LORE, s., folclore.
FOLK MU.SIC, s., música folclórica.
FOLK.SY, *adj.*, *col., US* amigável.
FOL.LI.CLE, s., *Bot.*, folículo.
FOL.LIC.U.LAR, *adj.*, folicular.
FOL.LOW, s., ato de seguir, seguimento; v., seguir, acompanhar.
FOL.LOW.ER, s., seguidor, sequaz.
FOL.LOW.ING, *adj.*, s., seguinte, adepto, seguidor.
FOL.LOW-UP, s., continuação (de contrato); *Com.*, circular; *adj.*, complementar; frequente.
FOL.LY, s., loucura, desvario.
FO.MENT, v., fomentar.
FO.MENT.ER, s., fomentador.
FOND, *adj.*, amigo, carinhoso; muito amoroso; crédulo.
FON.DLE, v., acariciar, afagar.
FOND.LING, s., carinho, afago.
FOND.LY, *adv.*, carinhosamente, ingenuamente.
FOND.NESS, s., carinho, afago, ternura, carícia.
FONT, s., *Rel.*, pia batismal; *Comp.*, tipo, fonte.
FOOD, s., comida, alimento.
FOOD CHAIN, s., cadeia alimentar.
FOOD MIX.ER, s., batedeira.
FOOD PROC.ES.SOR, s., multiprocessador de alimentos.
FOOD.STUFF, s., gêneros alimentícios, comida.
FOOL, *adj.*, tolo, imbecil; v., enganar, lograr.
FOOL.ERY, s., loucura, imbecilidade, tolice, desvario.
FOOL.HAR.DY, *adj.*, temerário, imprudente.

FOOLISH · 468 · FORGETFULNESS

FOOL.ISH, *adj.*, tolo, bobo, imbecil.
FOOL.ISH.LY, *adv.*, tolamente.
FOOL.ISH.NESS, *s.*, tolice, loucura.
FOOL.PROOF, *adj.*, à prova de acidentes, seguro.
FOOT, *s.*, pé, pata, medida de 304mm.
FOOT.AGE, *s.*, comprimento na escala de pés.
FOOT-AND-MOUTH DIS.EASE, *s.*, febre aftosa.
FOOT.BALL, *s.*, futebol.
FOOT.BAL.LER, *s.*, *UK* jogador de futebol, futebolista.
FOOT.BALL POOLS, *s. pl.*, *UK* loteria esportiva.
FOOT.BRIDGE, *s.*, passarela.
FOOT.GEAR, *s.*, calçado.
FOOT.HOLD, *s.*, apoio para os pés.
FOOT.ING, *s.*, posição; giro, andada.
FOOT.LIGHTS, *s. pl.*, ribalta.
FOOT.MAN, *s.*, lacaio, serviçal.
FOOT.MARK, *s.*, pisada, marca de pegada.
FOOT.NOTE, *s.*, nota de rodapé.
FOOT.PATH, *s.*, caminho, atalho, desvio.
FOOT.PRINT, *s.*, pegada, indício.
FOOT.STEP, *s.*, passo (som); pegada; degrau; *fig.*, exemplo.
FOOT.WEAR, *s.*, calçado.
FOP.PISH, *adj.*, afetado, ridículo.
FOR, *prep.*, para, por, por causa de, apesar de.
FOR.AGE, *s.*, forragem; pilhagem; *v.*, dar forragem (ao gado); saquear.
FOR.AY, *s.*, incursão, pilhagem; *v.*, saquear, pilhar.
FOR.BEAR, *v.*, não querer, reprimir, abster-se.
FOR.BEAR.ING, *adj.*, controlado, paciente.
FOR.BID, *v.*, proibir; negar, vedar.
FOR.BID.DANCE, *s.*, proibição.
FOR.BID.DEN, *adj.*, proibido.
FOR.BID.DING, *adj.*, repulsive, ameaçador.
FOR.BY, *adv.*, *prep.*, além disso, perto de, ao lado de.
FORCE, *s.*, força; *v.*, forçar.
FORCE.A.BLE, *adj.*, forçoso, obrigatório.
FORCED, *adj.*, forçado, obrigado.
FORCED LAND.ING, *s.*, aterrissagem forçada.
FORCED.NESS, *s.*, constrangimento, coação.
FORCE.FUL, *adj.*, rigoroso, enérgico, forte.
FORCE.FUL.LY, *adv.*, vigorosamente, energicamente.
FORCE.FUL.NESS, *s.*, força, violência; vigor, poder.
FOR.CEPS, *s.*, fórceps.
FORCES, *s. pl.*, forças armadas; tropas.
FOR.CI.BLE, *adj.*, eficaz, enérgico, à força.
FORC.IBLE.NESS, *s.*, força.
FOR.CI.BLY, *adv.*, energicamente; à força.
FORD, *s.*, vau; *v.*, passar a vau, atravessar um rio a pé.
FORE, *s.*, *Náut.*, proa, parte dianteira; *adj.*, dianteiro, prévio; *adv.*, anteriormente.
FORE.ARM, *s.*, *Anat.*, antebraço; *v.*, armar antecipadamente.
FORE.BEAR, *s.*, antepassado.
FORE.BODE, *v.*, pressagiar, prognosticar, vaticinar; agourar.
FORE.BOD.ING, *s.*, mau presságio, pressentimento.
FORE.CAST, *s.*, previsão, prognóstico; *v.*, prever, prognosticar, prevenir.
FORE.CAST.ER, *s.*, meteorologista, analista (de mercado).
FORE.COURT, *s.*, adro, átrio.
FORE.DATE, *v.*, antedatar.
FORE.FA.THERS, *s. pl.*, antepassados, ascendentes.
FORE.FIN.GER, *s.*, dedo indicador.

FORE.FOOT, *s.*, pata dianteira de um quadrúpede.
FORE.FRONT, *s.*, vanguarda, frente; *in the ~*: em primeiro plano.
FORE.GO.ING, *adj.*, antecedente, precedente.
FORE.GROUND, *s.*, primeiro plano.
FORE.HEAD, *s.*, testa.
FOR.EIGN, *adj.*, estrangeiro, exterior, estranho.
FOR.EIGN AFFAIRS, *s. pl.*, relações exteriores.
FOR.EIGN AID, *s.*, ajuda internacional.
FOR.EIGN BOD.Y, *s.*, corpo estranho.
FOR.EIGN CURRENCY, *s.*, moeda estrangeira.
FOR.EIGN.ER, *s.*, estrangeiro, forasteiro.
FOR.EIGN EXCHANGE, *s.*, taxa de câmbio.
FOR.EIGN.ISM, *s.*, estrangeirismo.
FOR.EIGN OFFICE, *s.*, *Brit.*, Ministério das Relações Exteriores.
FORE.JUDGE, *v.*, prejulgar, julgar antecipadamente.
FORE.KNOW.A.BLE, *adj.*, previsível.
FORE.KNOWL.EDGE, *s.*, previsão.
FORE.LAND, *s.*, cabo, promontório.
FORE.LEG, *s.*, perna dianteira.
FORE.MAN, *s.*, capataz, mestre, chefe.
FORE.MOST, *adj.*, principal, antes de mais nada.
FORE.NAME, *s.*, prenome.
FORE.NOON, *s.*, manhã.
FORE.PART, *s.*, parte dianteira.
FORE.RUN, *v.*, preceder; antecipar, prevenir
FORE.RUN.NER, *s.*, precursor; presságio; antepassado.
FORE.SEE, *v.*, prever, antever.
FORE.SAID, *adj.*, supra referido.
FORE.SEE.A.BLE, *adj.*, previsível.
FORE.SHAD.OW, *v.*, prenunciar.
FORE.SIGHT, *s.*, previdência.
FORE.SKIN, *s.*, prepúcio.
FOR.EST, *s.*, floresta; *v.*, arborizar.
FOR.EST.ED, *adj.*, arborizado.
FORE.STALL, *v.*, prevenir, evitar.
FOR.EST.ER, *s.*, guarda-florestal.
FOR.EST.RY, *s.*, silvicultura.
FORE.TELL, *v.*, predizer, prenunciar.
FORE.TELL.ER, *s.*, profeta.
FORE.THOUGHT, *s.*, premeditação, antecipação, prudência.
FORE.TO.KEN, *s.*, prenúncio; *v.*, prenunciar.
FOR.EV.ER, *adj.*, para sempre.
FORE.WARN, *v.*, prevenir, acautelar.
FORE.WARD, *s.*, prefácio.
FORE.WOMAN, *s.*, contramestra; chefe (de seção).
FORE.WORD, *s.*, prefácio, apresentação.
FOR.FEIT, *s.*, falta, omissão, crime; *v.*, perder, ser confiscado de.
FOR.FEIT.ABLE, *adj.*, confiscável.
FOR.FEI.TURE, *s.*, multa, confisco.
FOR.GATH.ER, *v.*, reunir-se, juntar-se, associar-se.
FORGE, *s.*, forja; fornalha; *v.*, forjar, trabalhar na forja; falsificar, adulterar.
FORGED, *adj.*, forjado.
FORG.ER, *s.*, forjador, ferreiro; falsificador, enganador.
FOR.GER.Y, *s.*, falsificação; *fig.*, mentira, invenção.
FOR.GET, *v.*, esquecer, olvidar.
FOR.GET.FUL, *adj.*, esquecido.
FOR.GET.FUL.NESS, *s.*, esquecimento.

FORGETTER   ·· 469 ··   FRACTIONARY

FOR.GET.TER, *s.*, esquecido, descuidado.
FORG.ING, *s.*, forjamento; *fig.*, falsificação.
FOR.GIV.A.BLE, *adj.*, perdoável.
FOR.GIVE, *v.*, perdoar, escusar, desculpar.
FOR.GIVE.NESS, *s.*, desculpa, perdão.
FOR.GIV.ING, *adj.*, indulgente, bondoso, generoso.
FOR.GO, *v.*, renunciar a, abrir mão de; desistir de.
FORK, *s.*, garfo, bifurcação; *v.*, bifurcar-se.
FORK.ED.NESS, *s.*, bifurcação, encruzilhada.
FORK.LIFT, *s.*, empilhadeira.
FORK.Y, *adj.*, bifurcado.
FOR.LORN, *adj.*, desesperado, abandonado.
FORKY, *adj.*, bifurcado.
FORM, *s.*, forma, tipo, formulário; *v.*, formar, criar, formular.
FOR.MAL, *adj.*, formal, oficial, cerimonioso.
FOR.MAL.ISM, *s.*, formalismo.
FOR.MAL.I.TIES, *s.*, formalidades.
FOR.MAL.I.TY, *s.*, formalidade, formalismo.
FOR.MAL.IZE, *v.*, formalizar.
FOR.MAL.LY, *adv.*, formalmente, oficialmente.
FOR.MAT, *s.*, formato; *v.*, formatar.
FOR.MA.TION, *s.*, formação.
FORM.A.TIVE, *adj.*, formativo.
FOR.MENT, *v.*, fomentar, promover, estimular.
FOR.MENT.A.TION, *s.*, fomento, estímulo, incentivo.
FOR.MENT.ER, *s.*, fomentador, incentivador.
FOR.MER, *adj.*, antigo, velho, anterior; *s.*, formador, autor, criador.
FOR.MER.LY, *adv.*, antigamente.
FORM.FIT.TING, *adj.*, colante (traje).
FORM.FUL, *adj.*, em boa forma.
FOR.MIC.ANT, *adj.*, formigante.
FOR.MI.CA.RY, *s.*, formigueiro.
FOR.MI.DA.BLE, *adj.*, formidável, descomunal, terrível, atemorizante.
FORM.LESS, *adj.*, disforme, amorfo.
FOR.MU.LA, *s.*, fórmula.
FOR.MU.LARY, *s.*, formulário; *adj.*, próprio de fórmula.
FOR.MU.LATE, *v.*, formular.
FOR.MU.LA.TION, *s.*, formulação.
FOR.NI.CATE, *v.*, fornicar.
FOR.NI.CA.TION, *s.*, fornicação.
FOR.SAKE, *v.*, abandonar.
FOR.SAK.EN, *s.*, abandonado, desamparado.
FOR.SAK.ING, *s.*, abandono, desamparo.
FOR.SWEAR, *v.*, abjurar, repudiar, negar, renegar.
FORT, *s.*, forte.
FOR.TE, *s.*, forte, ponto ou lado forte.
FORTH, *adv.*, *Lit.*, adiante, em diante.
FORTH.COM.ING, *adj.*, próximo, vizinho, disponível.
FORTH.RIGHT, *adj.*, franco, sincero.
FORTH.WITH, *adv.*, em seguida, a seguir.
FOR.TI.ETH, *num.*, quadragésimo.
FOR.TI.FI.CA.TION, *s.*, fortificação.
FOR.TI.FIED, *adj.*, fortificado.
FOR.TI.FIED WINE, *s.*, vinho licoroso.
FOR.TI.FY, *v.*, fortificar, fortalecer.
FOR.TI.TUDE, *s.*, fortaleza, força.
FORT.NIGHT, *s.*, quinzena, 15 dias.
FORT.NIGHT.LY, *s.*, período quinzenal; *adj.*, quinzenal.
FOR.TRESS, *s.*, fortaleza.

FOR.TU.ITOUS, *adj.*, fortuito, casual, imprevisto.
FOR.TU.ITY, *s.*, casualidade.
FOR.TU.NATE, *adj.*, afortunado, feliz, com sorte.
FOR.TU.NATE.LY, *adv.*, felizmente, afortunadamente.
FOR.TU.NATE.NESS, *s.*, felicidade, bom êxito.
FOR.TUNE, *s.*, fortuna, sorte, ventura.
FOR.TUNE-TELL.ER, *s.*, adivinho; cartomante.
FOR.TY, *num.*, quarenta.
FO.RUM, *s.*, foro, fórum; *Hist.*, praça pública (Roma antiga).
FOR.WARD, *adj.*, para a frente, adiantado, futuro; atacante no jogo; *v.*, expedir, remeter.
FOR.WARD.ER, *s.*, expedidor, despachante; promotor, estimulador.
FOR.WARD.ING, *s.*, expedição, remessa, despacho.
FOR.WARD.LY, *adv.*, ousadamente.
FOR.WARD.NESS, *s.*, zelo, ardor; progresso; presunção, audácia.
FOR.WORN, *adj.*, cansado, exausto.
FOSS, *s.*, fosso.
FOS.SIL, *s.*, fóssil.
FOS.SIL.I.SA.TION, *s.*, fossilização.
FOS.SIL.ISE(-IZE), *v.*, fossilizar.
FOS.TER, *adj.*, adotivo, de criação; *v.*, nutrir, alimentar; patrocinar; educar, cultivar.
FOS.TER CHILD, *s.*, filho de criação.
FOS.TER.ING, *adj.*, benéfico; *s.*, amparo, benefício.
FOS.TER.LING, *s.*, filho adotivo; protegido.
FOS.TER PAR.ENTS, *s. pl.*, pais de criação.
FOUL, *adj.*, horrível, obsceno; *s.*, falta; *v.*, sujar, emporcalhar.
FOUL MOUTHED, *adj.*, desbocado.
FOUND, *v.*, fundar, fundir.
FOUN.DA.TION, *s.*, fundação, base.
FOUN.DER, *s.*, fundador, iniciador; *v.*, naufragar, afundar-se (navio); mancar (cavalo).
FOUN.DERED, *adj.*, trôpego, cansado.
FOUND.ER MEMBER, *s.*, membro-fundador, sócio-fundador.
FOUND.ING, *s.*, fundição.
FOUND.RY, *s.*, fundição.
FOUN.TAIN, *s.*, chafariz, fonte.
FOUN.TAIN-PEN, *s.*, caneta tinteiro.
FOUR, *num.*, quatro.
FOUR.FOLD, *adj.*, quádruplo.
FOUR-FOOT.ED, *adj.*, quadrúpede.
FOUR-LEAVED CLO.VER, *s.*, trevo de quatro folhas.
FOUR.TEEN, *num.*, quatorze, catorze.
FOUR.TEENTH, *num.*, décimo quarto.
FOURTH, *num.*, *adj.*, quarto.
FOWL, *s.*, ave de criação; *v.*, caçar aves selvagens.
FOWL.ER, *s.*, criador de aves.
FOX, *s.*, *Zool.*, raposa; *fig.*, sagaz, astuto; *v.*, lograr.
FOX-CUB, *s.*, filhote de raposa.
FOX.GLOVE, *s.*, dedal, dedaleira.
FOX.HOLE, *s.*, *Mil.*, trincheira; toca de raposa.
FOX.HUNT.ING, *s.*, caça à raposa.
FOX.I.NESS, *s.*, astúcia, esperteza.
FOX TER.RI.ER, *s.*, fox terrier (raça de cão).
FOXY, *adj.*, astuto, esperto.
FOY.ER, *s.*, saguão (de hotel, teatro); vestíbulo.
FRAC.TION, *s.*, fração, fragmento, parte.
FRAC.TION.AL, *adj.*, fracionário.
FRAC.TION.AR.Y, *adj.*, fracionário.

FRACTIONATION   •• 470 ••   FRIEZE

FRAC.TION.A.TION, *s.*, fracionamento.
FRAC.TIOUS, *adj.*, zangado, irritadiço.
FRAC.TIOUS.NESS, *s.*, irascibilidade, mau humor.
FRAC.TURE, *s.*, fratura; fenda, ruptura; fratura de osso; *v.*, fraturar (osso); quebrar.
FRAG.ILE, *adj.*, frágil.
FRAG.ILE.NESS, *s.*, fragilidade.
FRA.GIL.I.TY, *s.*, fragilidade.
FRAG.MENT, *s.*, fragmento.
FRAG.MEN.TA.RY, *adj.*, fragmentário, incompleto.
FRAG.MENT.ED, *adj.*, fragmentado.
FRA.GRANCE, *s.*, fragrância, aroma, perfume.
FRA.GRANT, *adj.*, fragrante, perfumado, aromatizado.
FRA.GRANT.LY, *adv.*, com fragrância, perfumadamente.
FRAIL, *adj.*, fraco, frágil, quebradiço.
FRAIL.NESS, *s.*, fragilidade, fraqueza.
FRAIL.TY, *s.*, fragilidade, fraqueza, delicadeza.
FRAME, *s.*, moldura, armação; quadro; *v.*, emoldurar, cercar; expressar.
FRAME OF MIND, *s.*, estado de espírito.
FRAME.WORK, *s.*, estrutura, base, armação, madeiramento.
FRANC, *s.*, franco (moeda).
FRANCE, *s.*, França.
FRAN.CHISE, *s.*, franquia, concessão; direito de voto.
FRAN.CHISE.MENT, *s.*, isenção, concessão, privilégio.
FRAN.CIS.CAN, *adj.*, *s.*, franciscano.
FRANK, *adj.*, franco; *v.*, franquear.
FRANK.ER, *s.*, franqueador.
FRANK.LY, *adv.*, francamente, abertamente.
FRANK.NESS, *s.*, franqueza, sinceridade.
FRAN.TIC, *adj.*, frenético, fora de si; *US gir.*, maravilhoso.
FRAN.TICAL.LY, *adv.*, freneticamente.
FRA.TER.NAL, *adj.*, fraternal, fraterno.
FRA.TER.NI.SA.TION, *s.*, fraternização (usa-se também *fraternization*).
FRAT.ER.NISE(-IZE), *v.*, fraternizar, confraternizar.
FRA.TER.NI.TY, *s.*, fraternidade, irmandade.
FRAT.RI.CIDE, *s.*, fatricídio, fratricída.
FRAUD, *s.*, fraude, engano; impostor.
FRAUD.U.LENCE, *s.*, fraudulência; engano, embuste.
FRAUD.U.LENT, *adj.*, fraudulento.
FRAUGHT, *adj.*, carregado, repleto; *UK col.*, preocupado.
FRAY, *s.*, rixa, briga, guerra; rasgão (tecido); *v.*, esfiapar, desgastar(-se), puir (tecido); cansar-se.
FRAY.ED, *adj.*, esfiapado; *fig.*, desgastado.
FRAZ.ZLE, *s.*, *US col.*, farrapo, trapo; exaustão; *v.*, esfarrapar; exaurir(-se).
FRAZ.ZLED, *adj.*, *col.*, exausto; confuso.
FREAK, *adj.*, *col.*, *pej.*, excêntrico, esquisito; *s.*, aberração, anomalia.
FREAK.ISH, *adj.*, excêntrico, exótico.
FRECK.LE, *s.*, sarda.
FRECK.LED, *adj.*, sardento.
FRECK.LY, *adj.*, o mesmo que *freckled*.
FREE, *adj.*, livre, solto, desocupado, grátis, gratuito; *v.*, libertar, livrar, soltar.
FREE.BIE, *s.*, *col.*, *US* brinde.
FREE.BOO.TER, *s.*, pirata.
FREE.BOOT.ING, *s.*, saque, pilhagem.
FREE.DOM, *s.*, liberdade.
FREE EN.TER.PRISE, *s.*, livre iniciativa (privada).

FREE FALL, *s.*, queda livre.
FREE.GIFT, *s.*, brinde.
FREE HAND, *s.*, carta branca; *adj.*, à mão livre.
FREE.LANCE, *adj.*, autônomo.
FREE.LY, *adv.*, livremente, generosamente, voluntariamente.
FREE.MAN, *s.*, liberto, cidadão.
FREE.MA.SON, *s.*, maçon.
FREE.MA.SON.RY, *s.*, maçonaria.
FREE SAM.PLE, *s.*, amostra grátis.
FREE SPEECH, *s.*, liberdade de expressão.
FREE.THINK.ER, *s.*, livre-pensador.
FREE-TRADE, *s.*, livre comércio.
FREE.WAY, *s.*, autoestrada.
FREEZE, *v.*, gelar, congelar; *s.*, geada, congelamento.
FREEZ.ER, *s.*, congelador, frizer.
FREEZ.ING, *adj.*, glacial, gelado.
FREIGHT, *s.*, carga, frete.
FREIGHT.ER, *s.*, cargueiro (navio); carregador.
FREIGHT.AGE, *s.*, frete, fretagem.
FREIGHT TRAIN, *s.*, *US* trem de carga.
FRENCH, *adj.*, *s.*, francês, franco, gaulês.
FRENCH FRIES, *s. pl.*, *Cul.*, batatas fritas.
FRENCH.IFY, *v.*, afrancesar.
FRENCH.MAN, *s.*, francês.
FRENCH TOAST, *s.*, *Cul.*, rabanada.
FRENCH.WOM.AN, *s.*, francesa.
FRE.NET.IC, *adj.*, frenético.
FREN.ZIED, *adj.*, agitado, incontrolável, desvairado.
FREN.ZIED.LY, *adv.*, freneticamente.
FREN.ZY, *s.*, frenesi, furor.
FRE.QUENCE, *s.*, frequência.
FRE.QUENT, *adj.*, frequente.
FRE.QUENT.ER, *s.*, frequentador.
FRE.QUENT.LY, *adv.*, frequentemente.
FRESH, *adj.*, fresco, novo, recente; *adv.*, recentemente.
FRESH.EN, *v.*, refrescar; tornar-se mais frio.
FRESH.ER, *s.*, *col.*, *UK* calouro.
FRESH.ET, *s.*, inundação, alagamento, cheia.
FRESH.LY, *adv.*, recentemente.
FRESH.MAN, *s.*, calouro, novato.
FRESH.NESS, *s.*, freesco, frescor; originalidade, novidade.
FRESH.WA.TER, *adj.*, de água doce; *US fig.*, provinciano.
FRET, *v.*, afligir, afligir-se, irritar; *s.*, irritação, raiva.
FRET.FUL, *adj.*, irritado, aborrecido, incomodado.
FRET.SAW, *s.*, serra tico-tico, serrote.
FREU.DI.AN, *adj.*, freudiano.
FRIAR, *s.*, frade, frei.
FRI.ARY, *s.*, convento de frades.
FRIC.AS.SEE, *s.*, fricassê; *v.*, preparar um fricassê.
FRIC.TION, *s.*, fricção, atrito.
FRIC.TION.AL.LY, *adv.*, com fricção, por atrito.
FRI.DAY, *s.*, sexta-feira.
FRIDGE, *s.*, *abrev.* de *refrigerator*, refrigerador.
FRIEND, *s.*, amigo.
FRIEND.ED, *adj.*, que tem amigos.
FRIEND.LESS, *adj.*, sem amigos.
FRIEND.LI.NESS, *s.*, amizade.
FRIEND.LY, *adj.*, simpático, amistoso, amigável.
FRIEND.SHIP, *s.*, amizade.
FRIES, *s. pl.*, *abrev.* de *French fries*, batatas fritas.
FRIEZE, *s.*, friso.

FRIGATE
·· 471 ··
FUNDED

FRIG.ATE, s., *Náut.*, fragata.
FRIGHT, s., temor, pavor, terror; v., assustar, apavorar.
FRIGHT.EN, v., assustar.
FRIGHT.ENED, *adj.*, amedrontado.
FRIGHT.EN.ING, *adj.*, assustador.
FRIGHT.FUL, *adj.*, terrível, pavoroso, horrível.
FRIG.ID, *adj.*, frígido, frio.
FRI.GID.I.TY, s., frigidez.
FRILL, s., rufo, babado (traje ou decoração); *col.*, frescura.
FRILL.Y, *adj.*, que tem babados.
FRINGE, s., franja, orla, borda, margem; v., franjar, orlar.
FRISK, s., salto, pulo, brincadeira, cambalhota; v., brincar, saltar, dançar.
FRISK.I.NESS, s., alegria, vivacidade, contentamento.
FRISK.Y, *adj.*, alegre, animado.
FRIT.TER, s., pedaço, fragmento, bolinho de carne; v., fragmentar, gastar.
FRI.VOL.I.TY, s., frivolidade, bagatela.
FRIV.O.LOUS, *adj.*, frívolo, fútil.
FRIZZ, s., frisado ou crespo (cabelos); v., frisar, encrespar(-se).
FRIZZ.Y, *adj.*, crespo, frisado, encrespado.
FRO, *adv.*, de, atrás, para trás.
FROCK, s., vestido, saia, roupa.
FROG, s., *Zool.*, rã.
FROG.MAN, s., homem-rã.
FROG-MARCH, v., arrastar (levando alguém) à força.
FROL.IC, v., brincar, folgar, gracejar; s., brincadeira, alegria, travessura.
FROM, *prep.*, de, da parte, a partir de, desde, da parte de.
FROND, s., fronde, copa de árvore.
FRONT, s., fronte, dianteira, fachada, frente; v., olhar de frente.
FRONT.AGE, s., frente, fachada principal.
FRONT.AL, *adj.*, frontal, fronteiro.
FRON.TIER, s., fronteira.
FRONT LINE, s., linha de frente.
FRONT MAN, s., apresentador (TV); representante.
FRONT-PAGE, *adj.*, primeira página (jornal).
FRONT ROOM, s., sala de estar.
FRONT-RUN.NER, s., *Esp.*, favorito (para vencer ou liderar).
FRON.TIS.PIECE, s., frontispício, fachada, frente.
FROST, s., gelo, geada; v., gelar, congelar.
FROST.ED, *adj.*, coberto por geada; congelado; fosco; *US Cul.*, coberto com glacê.
FROST.I.NESS, s., frio excessivo.
FROST.ING, s., glacê; superfície fosca de vidro ou metal.
FROST.Y, *adj.*, coberto de gelo, gelado, glacial.
FROTH, s., espuma; v., espumar.
FROTH.Y, *adj.*, espumoso; *UK* espumante; fútil.
FRO.WARD, *adj.*, insubmisso, teimoso.
FROWN, s., cenho franzido, carranca; v., franzir o cenho.
FROWN.ING, *adj.*, carrancudo.
FROWST, s., cheiro de mofo.
FROWS.TY, *adj.*, mofento.
FRO.ZEN, *adj.*, gelado, congelado; *fig.*, paralisado de medo.
FRO.ZEN.LY, *adv.*, friamente, enregeladamente.
FRUC.TIF.ER.OUS, *adj.*, frutífero.
FRUC.TI.FI.CA.TION, s., frutificação.
FRUC.TI.FY, v., frutificar.
FRU.GAL, *adj.*, frugal.
FRU.GAL.I.TY, s., frugalidade.
FRUIT, s., fruta, fruto; v., frutificar.

FRUIT-CAKE, s., *Cul.*, bolo com passas; *fig.*, maluco, pirado.
FRUIT.ER, s., árvore frutífera, fruteira; fruticultor.
FRUIT.ER.ER, s., vendedor de frutas, fruteiro.
FRUIT.FUL, *adj.*, frutuoso, fértil, proveitoso.
FRU.I.TION, s., fruição, usufruto, gozo.
FRUIT JUICE, s., suco de frutas.
FRUIT.LESS, *adj.*, infrutífero, em vão.
FRUIT MA.CHINE, s., *UK* caça-níqueis.
FRUMP.ISH, *adj.*, desleixado.
FRUS.TRATE, v., frustrar.
FRUS.TRAT.ED, *adj.*, frustrado.
FRUS.TRAT.ING, *adj.*, frustrante.
FRUS.TRA.TION, s., frustração.
FRY, v., fritar; s., fritada.
FRY.ING-PAN, s., frigideira.
FUCH.SI.A, s., *Bot.*, fúcsia.
FUD.DLE, s., bebedeira; confusão; v., embebedar-se; aturdir.
FUD.DLED, *adj.*, confuso.
FUDGE, s., *Cul.*, fondant (doce de açúcar); *fig.*, lorota; v., inventar, falsificar.
FU.EL, s., combustível; v., fornecer combustível.
FUG, s., mofo, cheiro de mofo.
FU.GA.CIOUS, *adj.*, fugaz, transitório, efêmero.
FU.GAC.I.TY, s., fugacidade.
FU.GI.TIVE, s., fugitivo.
FU.GI.TIVE.NESS, s., fugacidade, volatilidade.
FUL.CRUM, s., apoio, fulcro, base, sustentáculo.
FUL.FIL, v., cumprir, realizar, satisfazer, completar.
FUL.FILL.ING, *adj.*, gratificante.
FUL.FILL.MENT, s., realização, satisfação.
FUL.GU.RATE, v., fulgurar, brilhar, resplandecer.
FULL, *adj.*, cheio, completo, folgado; v., complementar, totalizar.
FULL MOON, s., lua cheia.
FULL.NESS, s., plenitude, abundância.
FULL-PAGE, *adj.*, página inteira (anúncio impresso).
FULL-SIZED, *adj.*, tamanho natural; adulto.
FULL.STOP, s., ponto final (pontuação).
FULL TIME, *adj.*, de tempo integral.
FUL.LY, *adv.*, completamente, totalmente.
FUL.MI.NANT, *adj.*, fulminante.
FUL.MI.NATE, v., fulminar.
FUL.MI.NA.TING, *adj.*, fulminante.
FUL.NESS, s., plenitude, força.
FUL.SOME, *adj.*, exagerado.
FUL.VOUS, *adj.*, s., fulvo, louro.
FUME, v., fumegar.
FU.MI.GATE, v., defumar.
FUM.Y, *adj.*, cheio de fumaça, fumegante.
FUN, s., brincadeira, graça, gracejo; v., brincar, divertir-se, gracejar.
FUNC.TION, s., função, exercício, uso; v., funcionar, trabalhar.
FUNC.TION.AL, *adj.*, funcional, prático.
FUNC.TION.ARY, s., funcionário.
FUND, s., fundo, fonte; capital; *funds s.pl.*: fundos; v., financiar.
FUN.DA.MENT, s., fundamento, base; *col.*, assento, traseiro.
FUN.DA.MEN.TAL, *adj.*, básico, fundamental.
FUN.DA.MEN.TAL.ISM, s., fundamentalismo.
FUN.DA.MEN.TAL.LY, *adv.*, fundamentalmente, basicamente.
FUND.ED, *adj.*, consolidado, fundado, baseado.

FUNDING ··472·· FUZZY

FUND.ING, *s.*, financiamento.
FU.NER.AL, *s.*, funeral, sepultamento.
FU.NE.RAL, *s.*, funeral, enterro.
FUN.FAIR, *s.*, parque de diversões.
FUN.GOUS, *adj.*, fungoso.
FUN.GUS, *s.*, fungo; bolor, mofo.
FUNK, *s.*, medo, embaraço, temor; tipo de música; *v.*, fugir, intimidar.
FUNK.I.NESS, *s.*, medo, pavor, timidez.
FUNK.Y, *adj.*, *Mús.*, ritmo rústico e vibrante; *gír.*, batuta; malcheiroso; apavorado.
FUN.NEL, *s.*, funil; chaminé; *v.*, passar por funil; encaminhar(-se).
FUN.NI.LY, *adv.*, comicamente, curiosamente, estranhamente.
FUN.NY, *adj.*, engraçado, divertido, estranho, diferente.
FUN.NY BONE, *s.*, parte nervosa do cotovelo; senso de humor.
FUN.NY FARM, *s.*, *US col.*, manicômio.
FUR, *s.*, pele de animal, crosta; *v.*, forrar com peles, formar crosta.
FUR.BISH, *v.*, polir, limpar.
FUR.CATE, *v.*, bifurcar; *adj.*, bifurcado.
FUR COAT, *s.*, casaco de peles.
FU.RI.OUS, *adj.*, furioso.
FU.RI.OUS.LY, *adv.*, furiosamente, violentamente.
FU.RI.OUS.NESS, *s.*, fúria, raiva, ira, furor.
FURLED, *adj.*, dobrado.
FUR.LOUGH, *s.*, licença.
FUR.NACE, *s.*, forno, fornalha.
FUR.NISH, *v.*, fornecer, prover, sortir, equipar, aparelhar.
FUR.NISH.ED, *adj.*, mobiliado.
FUR.NISH.INGS, *s. pl.*, mobiliário, mobília.
FUR.NI.TURE, *s.*, mobília, móveis, acessórios.
FU.ROR, *s.*, furor.
FUR.RI.ER, *s.*, peleiro (vendedor de peles).

FUR.ROW, *s.*, ruga, sulco.
FUR.ROW.ED, *adj.*, enrugado, lavrado.
FUR.RY, *adj.*, peludo.
FUR.THER, *adj.*, novo, adicional; *adv.*, mais longe, mais; *v.*, promover.
FUR.THER.ANCE, *s.*, adiantamento.
FUR.THER.MORE, *adv.*, além do mais, além disso, ademais.
FUR.THER.MOST, *adj.*, o mais longe.
FUR.THEST, *adj.*, *adv.*, o mais distante.
FUR.TIVE, *adj.*, furtivo.
FUR.TIVE.LY, *adv.*, furtivamente.
FU.RUN.CLE, *s.*, furúnculo.
FU.RY, *s.*, fúria, ira.
FUSE, *s.*, fusível, espoleta; *v.*, fundir, fundir-se.
FUSE-BOX, *s.*, caixa de fusíveis.
FUSED, *adj.*, *Elet.*, com fusível.
FU.SE.LAGE, *s.*, fuselagem.
FUS.IBLE, *adj.*, fusível.
FU.SIL, *s.*, tipo de espingarda; *adj.*, derretido; *Elet.*, fusível.
FU.SIL.IER, *s.*, *Mil.*, fuzileiro.
FU.SIL.LADE, *s.*, fuzilaria; *v.*, fuzilar; atacar com fogo cerrado.
FU.SION, *s.*, fusão.
FUSS, *s.*, barulho, escândalo.
FUSSY, *adj.*, exigente, complicado.
FUS.TI.GATE, *v.*, fustigar, açoitar.
FUS.TI.GA.TION, *s.*, fustigação.
FUS.TY, *adj.*, bolorento, mofado.
FU.TILE, *adj.*, fútil, inútil.
FU.TILE.NESS, *s.*, futilidade.
FU.TIL.I.TY, *s.*, futilidade.
FU.TURE, *adj.*, *s.*, futuro.
FU.TUR.IS.TIC, *adj.*, futurístico, futurista.
FU.TU.RI.TY, *s.*, futuro, futuridade.
FUZZ, *s.*, flocos, partículas finas; penugem.
FUZZ.Y, *adj.*, penugento; encrespado; vago, difuso.

G

G, *s.*, sétima letra do alfabeto inglês; sol *(mús.)*; grama.
GAB, *s.*, conversa, colóquio; *v.*, palrar, conversar, tagarelar.
GAB.AR.DINE, *s.*, gabardina.
GAB.BLE, *s.*, conversa, tagarelice, palavrório; *v.*, tagarelar, falar.
GAB.BLER, *s.*, falador, tagarela.
GAB.O.NESE, *s., adj.*, gabonense (do ou natural do Gabão).
GA.BY, *s.*, simplório, tolo, ingênuo.
GAD, *s.*, talhadeira, estilete; *v.*, vaguear.
GAD.ABOUT, *s.*, vagabundo, errante.
GAD.GET, *s.*, coisa, aparelho, engenhoca, insignificância.
GAEL.IC, *adj.*, gaélico (da ou relativo à Gália).
GAFFE, *s.*, gafe.
GAG, *s.*, mordaça, impedimento, brincadeira; amordaçar, silenciar.
GAGE, *s.*, penhor, fiança, desafio; *v.*, caucionar, dar em penhor.
GAG.ING, *s.*, aferição.
GAI.E.TY, *s.*, alegria, divertimento; esplendor.
GAI.LY, **GAY.LY**, *adv.*, alegremente, despreocupadamente.
GAIN, *s.*, ganho, lucro, benefício, salário, vantagem; *v.*, ganhar, lucrar.
GAIN.ABLE, *adj.*, ganhável, lucrável.
GAIN.ER, *s.*, beneficiário, ganhador.
GAIN.FUL, *adj.*, lucrativo, vantajoso.
GAIN.FUL.LY, *adv.*, vantajosamente, lucrativamente.
GAIN.FUL.NESS, *s.*, lucro, ganho, proveito.
GAIN.ING, *s.*, lucro.
GAIN.SAY, *s.*, contradição; negação; *v.*, contradizer, negar.
GAIT, *s.*, passo, modo de andar; *v.*, adestrar (cavalo) no andamento.
GAI.TERS, *s. pl.*, polainas, perneiras.
GA.LA, *s.*, festa, gala.
GA.LAC.TIC, *adj., Astron.*, galáctico.
GAL.AX.Y, *s., Astron.*, galáxia.
GALE, *s.*, ventania, vento.
GAL.I.LE.AN, *adj., s.*, galileu (da ou relativo à Galileia).
GALL, *s.*, fel, bílis, amargor; ódio; *v.*, mortificar.
GAL.LANT, *adj.*, galante, cortês, namorador; *v.*, namorar, galantear.
GAL.LANT.LY, *adv.*, galantemente, corajosamente.
GAL.LANT.RY, *s.*, galantaria; valentia, galanteio.
GALL BLAD.DER, *s., Anat.*, vesícula biliar.
GAL.LE.ON, *s., Náut.*, galeão.
GAL.LER.Y, *s.*, galeria; galeria de artes.
GAL.LEY, *s.*, galé, galera (navio movido a remo).
GAL.LIC, *adj., s.*, gaulês.
GAL.LI.CISM, *s.*, galicismo.
GAL.LI.NA.CEOUS, *adj.*, galináceo.
GALL.ING, *s.*, escoriação, esfolamento; *adj.*, irritante; que esfola.
GAL.LI.VANT, *v., col.*, perambular, vagabundear.
GAL.LON, *s.*, galão.
GAL.LOP, *s.*, galope; *v.*, galopar.
GAL.LOP.ING, *adj.*, galopante.
GAL.LOWS, *s. pl.*, forca; estrutura para ou semelhante à forca; enforcamento.
GALL.STONE, *s., Med.*, cálculo biliar.
GA.LORE, *adj.*, em abundância.
GA.LOSH, *s.*, galocha; *galoshes*, *s.pl.*, galochas.
GAL.VAN.IC, *adj.*, galvânico.
GAL.VA.NI.ZA.TION, *s.*, galvanização.
GAL.VA.NIZE, *v.*, galvanizar.
GAM.BI.AN, *adj.*, gambiano (de, ou nativo de Gâmbia).
GAM.BLE, *s., col.*, aposta, jogo; *v.*, apostar, arriscar.
GAM.BLER, *s.*, apostador, jogador.
GAM.BLING, *s.*, jogo de azar; *adj.*, que se refere ao jogo.
GAM.BOL, *s.*, cabriola; *v.*, cabriolar, saltar.
GAME, *s.*, jogo, partida; truque, brincadeira; caça; *v.*, jogar, apostar; *adj.*, valente, decidido; *col.*, coxo.
GAMES.MAN.SHIP, *s.*, artimanha para vencer um jogo.
GAM.ING, *s.*, jogo (por dinheiro).
GAM.MA RAY, *s., Fís.*, raio gama.
GAM.MON, *s.*, presunto; truque, mentira; gamão (jogo); *v.*, enganar.
GAMP, *s., col.*, guarda-chuva (grande).
GAM.UT, *s.*, gama, série.
GAN.DER, *s., Zool.*, ganso (macho); espiada, olhadela, tolo, bobo.
GANG, *s.*, equipe, turma, quadrilha, gangue.
GANG.LAND, *s.*, submundo do crime.
GAN.GLING, **GAN.GLY**, *adj.*, desajeitado, magro.
GANG.PLANK, *s., Náut.*, prancha (pequena ponte entre o barco e o cais).
GAN.GRENE, *v.*, gangrenar; *s.*, gangrena.
GAN.GRE.NOUS, *adj.*, gangrenoso.
GANG.STER, *s.*, gângster, bandido, criminoso.
GANG.WAY, *s.*, corredor em cinema e ônibus.
GAN.TRY, *s.*, canteiro, cavalete; ponte de guindaste rolante.
GAP, *s.*, fenda, racha, buraco, hiato; *v.*, fender, abrir.
GAPE, *s.*, bocejo, boquiaberto; *v.*, ficar boquiaberto, bocejar.
GAP.ER, *s.*, aquele que boceja; pasmo.
GAP.ING, *adj.*, boquiaberto; aberto (camisa), escancarado, que boceja.
GA.RAGE, *s.*, garagem, oficina de carros.
GARB, *s.*, garbo, elegância, vestuário; *v.*, vestir.
GAR.BAGE, *s.*, lixo, refugo.
GAR.BAGE CAN, *s.*, lata de lixo.
GAR.BAGE COL.LEC.TOR, *s.*, lixeiro.
GAR.BAGE TRUCK, *s.*, caminhão de lixo.
GAR.BLE, *s.*, adulteração, falsificação; *v.*, adulterar, falsificar; escolher.
GAR.BLED, *adj.*, adulterado.
GAR.BOIL, *s.*, desordem, tumulto.

GARDEN ·· 474 ·· GENERAL OFFICER

GAR.DEN, s., jardim, jardim público, parque urbano.
GAR.DEN.ER, s., jardineiro.
GAR.DE.NIA, s., Bot., gardênia.
GAR.DEN.ING, s., jardinagem.
GAR.GLE, v., gargarejar; s., gargarejo.
GAR.GLING, s., gargarejo.
GAR.GOYLE, s., gárgula.
GAR.ISH, adj., pomposo, de cor forte, vivo, berrante, luminoso.
GAR.LAND, s., coroa, grinalda; v., engrinaldar.
GAR.LIC, s., Bot., alho.
GAR.LICK.Y, adj., com alho, com cheiro de alho.
GAR.MENT, s., peça de roupa.
GAR.NER, s., celeiro, paiol; v., enceleirar, colocar em celeiro.
GAR.NET, s., granada.
GAR.NI.TURE, s., guarnição, enfeite.
GAR.RET, s., sótão.
GAR.RI.SON, s., Mil., guarnição, tropas; v., guarnecer.
GAR.RU.LOUS, s., palrador, tagarela.
GAR.TER, s., liga; v., prender com liga.
GARTH, s., pátio interno, jardim.
GAS, s., gás, gasolina; v., sufocar com gás.
GAS BAG, s., balão de gás.
GAS CHAM.BER, s., câmara de gás.
GAS COOK.ER, s., UK fogão a gás.
GAS CYL.IN.DER, s., botijão de gás.
GAS.E.LIER, s., lampião a gás, fogareiro a gás.
GAS.E.OUS, adj., gasoso.
GAS FIRE, s., UK aquecedor a gás.
GASH, s., talho, corte, facada; v., cortar, ferir.
GAS HOL.DER, s., botijão de gás.
GASKET, s., gaxeta.
GAS.I.FI.CA.TION, s., gaseificação.
GAS.I.FY, s., gaseificar.
GAS.MAN, s., vendedor de gás.
GAS MASK, s., máscara contra gases.
GAS.O.GENE, s., gasogênio.
GAS.O.LINE, s., gasolina.
GAS.OM.E.TER, s., gasômetro.
GASP, s., ofegação, arfada, suspiro; v., ofegar, arfar.
GAS.SI.NESS, s., vaidade, presunção, loquacidade.
GAS STA.TION, s., posto de gasolina.
GAS.SY, adj., gasoso, cheio de gás.
GAS.TRIC, adj., gástrico.
GAS.TRI.TIS, s., gastrite.
GAS.TRO.EN.TE.RI.TIS, s., Med., gastroenterite.
GAS.TRO.NOM.IC, adj., gastronômico.
GAS.TRON.O.MY, s., gastronomia.
GAS.WORKS, s., refinaria de gás.
GATE, s., portão; v., fechar o portão.
GÂ.TEAU, s., Fr., UK bolo recheado e coberto com creme.
GATE.CRASH, v., entrar como penetra (em festa).
GATE-CRASH.ER, s., penetra (de festa).
GATE.HOUSE, s., portaria, guarita.
GATE.KEEPER, s., porteiro.
GATE.POST, s., mourão.
GATE.WAY, s., passagem, passadiço, portão.
GATH.ER, v., colher flores, apanhar flores.
GATH.ER.ER, s., coletor, cobrador.
GATH.ER.ING, s., reunião, encontro, assembleia.
GAUCHE, adj., inábil, desajeitado, canhestro.

GAU.DY, adj., apelativo, chamativo.
GAUGE, GAGE, s., pluviômetro, medidor de combustível; calibre; v., estimar, calcular; calibrar, aferir.
GAUG.ER, s., medidor, aferidor.
GAUG.ING, s., medida.
GAUL.ISH, adj., s., gaulês, francês.
GAUNT, adj., magro, esquelético; desolado.
GAUNT.LET, s., manopla; luva de punho largo; corredor polonês; críticas duras.
GAUZE, s., gaze.
GAUZY, adj., próprio de gaze, referente a gaze.
GAV.EL, v., martelo; v., dividir.
GAWK.Y, adj., tolo, bobo, inábil.
GAY, adj., homossexual, aparatoso.
GAY.LY, adv., alegremente, despreocupadamente.
GAY.NESS, s., jovialidade; homossexualidade.
GAZE, v., olhar fixamente, fixar, mirar, observar.
GA.ZE.BO, s., varanda, terraço, belvedere.
GA.ZELLE, s., Zool., gazela, antílope.
GA.ZETTE, s., gazeta (jornal); v., publicar em diário oficial.
GAZ.ET.TEER, s., dicionário geográfico.
GEAR, s., equipamento, engrenagem, marcha de carro.
GEAR.BOX, s., caixa de marcha.
GEAR.ING, s., engrenagem, encaixe.
GECK.O, s., Zool., lagartixa.
GEE, interj., credo!, ora bolas!
GEE.ZER, s., esquisito.
GEI.GER COUNT.ER, s., contador Geiger.
GEI.SHA, s., gueixa.
GEL, s., Quím., gel, v., tomar forma de gel, engrossar.
GEL.A.TINE, GEL.A.TIN, s., gelatina.
GE.LAT.I.NI.ZA.TION, s., gelatinização.
GE.LAT.I.NOUS, adj., gelatinoso.
GE.LA.TION, s., gelificação; congelação.
GELD, v., castrar, capar; adj., castrado, eunuco, mutilado.
GELD.ING, s., animal capado; castração.
GEL.ID, adj., gélido, gelado.
GE.LID.I.TY, s., gelidez.
GE.LID.NESS, s., friagem, frialdade, frio.
GEM, s., gema, joia; v., cobrir com joias, enfeitar com joias.
GEM.ATE, v., Biol., reproduzir-se por gemação (brotamento).
GEM.I.NATE, adj., geminado, duplo, unido; v., geminar.
GEM.I.NA.TION, s., geminação.
GEM.MA, s., Biol., gema (vegetal, broto); rebento.
GEM.MA.TION, s., Biol., gemação, brotamento.
GEM.STONE, s., pedra preciosa.
GEN, s., UK informações.
GEN.DER, s., Gram., gênero; v., gerar, engendrar.
GENE, s., gene.
GEN.E.AL.O.GIST, s., genealogista.
GEN.E.AL.O.GY, s., genealogia.
GEN.ER.AL, s., general; adj., geral.
GEN.ER.AL.IST, adj., generalista.
GEN.ER.AL.I.TY, s., generalidade.
GEN.ER.AL.IZ.ABLE, adj., generalizável.
GEN.ER.AL.I.ZA.TION, s., generalização.
GEN.ER.AL.IZE, v., generalizar.
GEN.ER.AL KNOWL.EDGE, s., cultura geral.
GEN.ER.AL.LY, adv., geralmente, comumente, em geral.
GEN.ER.AL.MEET.ING, s., assembleia geral.
GEN.ER.AL OF.FI.CER, s., Mil., oficial-general.

GENERAL-PURPOSE ··475·· GHASTLY

GEN.ER.AL-PUR.POSE, *adj.*, de uso geral.
GEN.ER.AL.SHIP, *s.*, generalato.
GEN.ER.AL STRIKE, *s.*, greve geral.
GEN.ER.ATE, *v.*, gerar, produzir, procriar, engendrar.
GEN.ER.A.TION, *s.*, geração.
GEN.ER.A.TIVE, *adj.*, generativo, produtivo.
GEN.ER.A.TOR, *s.*, gerador.
GE.NER.IC, *adj.*, genérico.
GEN.ER.OS.I.TY, *s.*, generosidade.
GEN.ER.OUS, *adj.*, generoso, magnânimo.
GEN.ER.OUS.LY, *adv.*, generosamente.
GEN.ER.OUS.NESS, *s.*, generosidade.
GEN.E.SIS, *s.*, gênese, origem, gênesis, começo, alfa.
GE.NET.IC, *adj.*, genético.
GE.NET.I.CAL.LY MOD.I.FIED, *adj.*, geneticamente modificado.
GE.NET.IC CODE, *s.*, código genético.
GE.NET.IC EN.GI.NEER.ING, *s.*, engenharia genética.
GE.NET.I.CIST, *s.*, geneticista.
GE.NET.ICS, *s.*, genética.
GE.NIAL, *adj.*, simpático, cordial, alegre, comunicativo.
GE.NIAL.I.TY, *s.*, cordialidade, alegria, simpatia, comunicabilidade.
GE.NI.AL.LY, *adv.*, cordialmente, alegremente.
GE.NIE, *s.*, gênio, espírito, fantasma.
GEN.I.TAL, *adj.*, genital, sexual.
GE.NIUS, *s.*, gênio.
GEN.O.CIDE, *s.*, genocídio.
GE.NOME, *s.*, genoma.
GEN.RE, *s.*, gênero, estilo.
GENT, *s.*, *abrev.* de *gentleman*: cavalheiro; *col.*, nobre; *adj.*, gentil, elegante.
GEN.TEEL, *adj.*, fino, refinado, cavalheiresco.
GEN.TEEL.LY, *adv.*, distintamente.
GEN.TILE, *adj.*, *s.*, gentio, pagão.
GEN.TLE, *s.*, pessoa de boa família; *adj.*, educado, gentil, suave.
GEN.TLE.MAN, *s.*, senhor, cavalheiro, nobre, pessoa educada.
GEN.TLE.MAN.LY, *adj.*, cavalheiresco, bem-educado.
GEN.TLE.MAN.SHIP, *s.*, cavalheirismo.
GEN.TLE.NESS, *s.*, doçura, suavidade, gentileza.
GEN.TLE.WOM.AN, *s.*, senhora, dama.
GEN.TLY, *adv.*, suavemente; gentilmente; lentamente.
GEN.TRI.FI.CA.TION, *s.*, enobrecimento.
GEN.TRY, *s.*, alta burguesia; pequena nobreza.
GEN.U.FLECT, *v.*, ajoelhar, genuflectir.
GEN.U.FLEC.TION, *s.*, genuflexão.
GEN.U.INE, *adj.*, genuíno, legítimo, autêntico.
GEN.U.INE.LY, *adv.*, genuinamente, sinceramente.
GEN.U.INE.NESS, *s.*, genuinidade, legitimidade.
GE.NUS, *s.*, gênero.
GE.OD.E.SY, *s.*, geodésia.
GE.O.DY.NAM.ICS, *s.*, geodinâmica, tectônica.
GE.OG.RA.PHER, *s.*, geógrafo.
GEO.GRAPH.IC, *adj.*, geográfico.
GE.OG.RA.PHY, *s.*, geografia.
GEO.LOG.IC, *adj.*, geológico.
GE.OL.O.GIST, *s.*, geólogo.
GE.OL.O.GY, *s.*, geologia.
GE.OM.E.TER, *s.*, geômetra.

GE.O.MET.RIC, *adj.*, geométrico.
GE.OM.E.TRY, *s.*, geometria.
GE.O.MOR.PHOL.O.GY, *s.*, geomorfologia.
GE.O.POL.I.TICS, *s.*, geopolítica.
GEORGIAN, *s.*, *adj.*, georgiano (da, ou natural da Geórgia - país).
GE.O.SCI.ENCE, *s.*, geociência.
GE.O.THER.MAL, *adj.*, geotérmico.
GE.RA.NI.UM, *s.*, *Bot.*, gerânio.
GER.BIL, *s.*, *Zool.*, gerbo (pequeno roedor).
GE.RENT, *s.*, gerente, administrador.
GE.RI.AT.RIC, *adj.*, geriátrico.
GE.RI.AT.RICS, *s.*, *Med.*, geriatria.
GERM, *s.*, germe, micróbio, vírus.
GER.MAN, *adj.*, *s.*, alemão.
GER.MAN.IZE, *v.*, germanizar.
GER.MAN MEA.SLES, *s.*, *Med.*, rubéola.
GER.MAN.IC, *adj.*, germânico.
GER.MAN.IZE, *v.*, germanizar, tornar alemão.
GER.MA.NY, *s.*, Alemanha.
GERM CELL, *s.*, *Biol.*, gameta: célula germinativa.
GER.MEN, *s.*, germe.
GER.MI.CIDE, *s.*, germicida.
GER.MI.NAL, *adj.*, germinal.
GER.MI.NATE, *v.*, germinar, surgir, brotar, nascer.
GER.MI.NA.TION, *s.*, germinação, nascença.
GER.MI.NA.TIVE, *adj.*, germinativo, germinante.
GERM.Y, *adj.*, contaminado, infestado de germes.
GER.ON.TOL.O.GY, *s.*, *Med.*, gerontologia.
GER.UND, *s.*, *Gram.*, gerúndio.
GE.STALT, *s.*, *Psic.*, gestaltismo.
GES.TA.TION, *s.*, gestação, gravidez.
GES.TIC.U.LATE, *v.*, gesticular, fazer gestos.
GES.TIC.U.LA.TION, *s.*, gesticulação.
GES.TIC.U.LA.TO.RY, *adj.*, gesticulador.
GES.TURE, *s.*, gesto.
GET, *v.*, ficar, obter, receber, ganhar, aprender, suceder, causar, pegar.
GET-AT-ABLE, *adj.*, acessível.
GET ABOUT, *v.*, espalhar-se.
GET AFTER, *v.*, perseguir.
GET AT, *v.*, alcançar, atacar, agredir.
GET AWAY, *v.*, ir, partir, sair.
GET-A.WAY, *s.*, fuga, escapada.
GET BACK, *v.*, regressar, retornar, voltar.
GET BEHIND, *v.*, atrasar-se, demorar-se.
GET BEYOND, *v.*, ultrapassar, passar além.
GET IN, *v.*, entrar, adentrar.
GET OFF, *v.*, descer do ônibus, sair de um carro, trem.
GET OUT, *v.*, retirar-se, sair.
GET.TER, *s.*, adquirente.
GET.TING, *s.*, compra, aquisição, lucro.
GET-TO.GETH.ER, *v.*, reunir-se, agrupar-se, ajuntar-se.
GET UP, *v.*, levantar(-se), vestir-se; organizar, preparar, começar, tramar.
GETUP, *s.*, traje; *gír.*, vestimenta.
GEY.SER, *s.*, gêiser, fonte de água quente.
GHA.NA.IAN, **GHA.NIAN**, *adj.*, *s.*, ganense (de, ou natural de Gana).
GHAST.LI.NESS, *s.*, horror, palidez.
GHAST.LY, *adj.*, horrível, macabro, assustador; pálido,

GHERKIN · 476 · GLASS

abatido; *adv.*, horrivelmente, lividamente.
GHER.KIN, *s.*, pepino em conserva.
GHET.TO, *s.*, gueto.
GHOST, *s.*, espírito, fantasma.
GHOST.LI.NESS, *s.*, espiritualidade.
GHOST.LY, *adj.*, fantasmagórico; espiritual.
GHOST TOWN, *s.*, cidade fantasma.
GHOST.WHRITE, *v.*, executar papel de escritor em nome de outro.
GHOST.WHRIT.ER, *s.*, escritor contratado que escreve em nome de outro.
GHOUL, *s., Mit.*, espírito maléfico que se alimenta de túmulos; *pej.*, demônio.
GHOUL.ISH, *adj.*, macabro.
GI.ANT, *s.*, gigante; *adj.*, gigantesco.
GI.ANT.LIKE, *adj.*, gigantesco.
GIB.BER, *s.*, vozerio; *v.*, tagarelar, algaraviar.
GIB.BER.ISH, *s.*, bobagem, asneira; algaravia.
GIB.BET, *s.*, forca, patíbulo; *v.*, enforcar; *fig.*, expor ao desprezo público.
GIB.BON, *s., Zool.*, gibão.
GIB.BOS.I.TY, *s.*, corcunda, protuberância.
GIB.BOUS, *adj.*, curvo, curvado, corcunda.
GIBE, *s.*, deboche, escárnio; *v.*, escarnecer, debochar.
GIB.ER, *s.*, debochador, escarnecedor.
GIB.ING, *s.*, zombaria; *adj.*, escarnecedor.
GIB.LETS, *s. pl.*, miúdos de aves, cabidela.
GID.DY, *adj.*, que sente tonteira, tonto; leviano; *v.*, tontear; fazer papel de bobo.
GIFT, *s.*, presente, dádiva, talento.
GIFT.ED, *adj.*, dotado, talentoso.
GIFT.WARE, *s.*, artigos de presente.
GIFT.WRAP, *s.*, papel de presente; *v.*, embrulhar para presente.
GIGABYTE, *s., Comp.*, gigabyte (*símb.*: GB).
GI.GAN.TE.AN, *adj.*, gigânteo, gigantesco
GI.GAN.TIC, *adj.*, gigantesco.
GI.GAN.TISM, *s.*, gigantismo.
GIG.GLE, *s.*, risadinha; *v.*, dar risadinhas, zombar.
GIG.GLER, *s.*, escarnecedor, zombeteiro.
GIGGLY, *adj.*, com riso bobo.
GIGOLO, *s., pej.*, gigolô.
GILD, *v.*, dourar, enfeitar, embelezar.
GILD.ED, *adj.*, dourado; *fig.*, afortunado.
GILD.ER, *s.*, dourador.
GILD.ING, *s.*, douração, decoração, enfeite.
GIL.LIE, *s.*, jovem, moço, criado.
GILL, *s.*, guelra, brânquia (*ger.* no *pl.*: *gills*); córrego; vale estreito e profundo; *col.*, moça.
GILT, *s.*, camada de ouro, dourado, brilho; *gír.*, dinheiro; leitoa; *adj.*, dourado.
GILT EDGED, *adj.*, de máxima garantia.
GIM.CRACK, *s.*, bugiganga; *adj.*, sem valor.
GIM.CRACK.ER.Y, *s.*, bugigangas, quinquilharias.
GIM.LET, *s.*, verruma, furador; *v.*, furar com verruma; *adj.*, perfurante.
GIN, *s.*, gim (bebida alcoólica).
GIN.GER, *s., Bot.*, gengibre; *col.*, vivacidade; *gír.*, pessoa ruiva.
GIN.GER.LI.NESS, *s.*, cuidado, cautela.
GIN.GER.LY, *adj.*, cuidadoso; *adv.*, cuidadosamente.
GIN.GER.Y, *adj.*, condimentado (com gengibre); ruivo.

GIN.GI.VA, *s., Anat.*, gengiva.
GIN.GI.VAL, *adj.*, próprio das gengivas.
GIN.GI.VI.TIS, *s., Med.*, gengivite.
GIN.SENG, *s., Bot.*, ginseng.
GIP.SY, *s.*, cigano.
GI.RAFFE, *s., Zool.*, girafa.
GIR.A.SOL, *s., Min.*, girassol (tipo de opala).
GIRD, *v.*, envolver, cingir; zombar; *s.*, zombaria.
GIRD.ER, *s.*, viga mestra.
GIR.DLE, *s.*, cinta, cinto; espartilho; cerca; cercado; *v.*, cercar.
GIR.DLER, *s.*, cinteiro.
GIRL, *s.*, moça, jovem, garota.
GIRL.FRIEND, *s.*, amiga, namorada, garota.
GIRL.HOOD, *s.*, mocidade, juventude, adolescência.
GIRL.ISH, *adj.*, juvenil, próprio de moça.
GIRL SCOUT, *s.*, escoteira, bandeirante.
GI.RO, *s.*, transferência de crédito bancário.
GIRT, *adj.*, amarrado (com cinto); *v.*, cintar.
GIRTH, *s.*, circunferência; cinturão; *v.*, medir a cintura, cingir.
GIST, *s.*, essencial.
GIVE, *s.*, cessão, cedência; *v.*, dar, entregar, prover; conceder; dedicar; presentear; aplicar; transmitir.
GIVE-AND-TAKE, *s.*, troca, intercâmbio; *pej.*, toma-lá-dá-cá.
GIVE BACK, *v.*, devolver.
GIV.EN, *v., p.p.*, de *to give*; *adj.*, determinado; disposto; *Mat.*, dado, conhecido.
GIV.ER, *s.*, doador.
GIV.IN, *s.*, dádiva, presente, oferta.
GIZ.ZARD, *s.*, moela (de aves).
GLA.BROUS, *adj.*, glabro, liso.
GLA.CIAL, *adj.*, glacial.
GLA.CIAL.LY, *adv.*, de modo glacial.
GLA.CI.ATE, *v.*, cobrir com geleira.
GLA.CI.A.TION, *s., Geol.*, glaciação.
GLA.CIER, *s.*, geleira.
GLAD, *adj.*, satisfeito, contente; contentar, satisfazer.
GLAD.DEN, *v.*, contentar, alegrar, satisfazer.
GLADE, *s.*, clareira, picada em floresta.
GLAD.I.A.TOR, *s.*, gladiador.
GLAD.LY, *adv.*, com satisfação, alegremente,
GLAD.NESS, *s.*, alegria, felicidade, satisfação.
GLAD.SOME, *adj.*, alegre, agradável.
GLAIR, *s.*, clara de ovo (ou com a sua aparência).
GLAIR.Y, *adj.*, viscoso (como clara de ovo).
GLAM.OR.OUS, *adj.*, glamouroso, encantador.
GLAM.OR.OUS, *adj.*, glamoroso(a), atraente.
GLAM.OR.OUS.LY, *adv.*, de modo glamoroso ou fascinante.
GLAM.OUR *UK*, **GLAM.OR** *US*, *s.*, glamour, fascinação, encanto, brilho; *v.*, encantar, fascinar.
GLAM.OUR.IZE, *v.*, exaltar, tornar belo; romancear, fantasiar.
GLANCE, *s.*, olhadela, golpe de vista; indireta; *v.*, olhar alguém de relance; reluzir; insinuar.
GLANC.ING, *adj.*, oblíquo (reflexão, olhar).
GLAND, *s.*, glândula.
GLAN.DU.LAR, *adj.*, glandular.
GLAN.DULE, *s.*, glândula.
GLAN.DUL.OUS, *adj.*, glandular.
GLARE, *s.*, olhar penetrante, encarada; clarão, brilho; *v.*, fulminar (alguém) com o olhar, encarar; luzir, cegar.
GLAR.ING, *adj.*, evidente; ofuscante; de olhar fixo.
GLASS, *s.*, vidro, cristal, copo; *v.*, envidraçar, refletir.

GLASSBLOWING ··477·· GNARLED

GLASS.BLOW.ING, s., fabricação ou modelagem de vidro a quente, assopro de vidro.
GLASS-CUT.TER, s., corta-vidros, cortador de vidro.
GLASSES, s. pl., óculos.
GLASS FI.BER, s., fibra de vidro.
GLASS FOUN.DRY, s., fábrica de vidro.
GLASS.FUL, adj., copo cheio.
GLASS.HOUSE, s., estufa; *UK* prisão militar.
GLASS SNAKE, s., Zool., cobra-de-vidro.
GLASS WARE, s., objetos de cristal, vidraria.
GLASS.WORK.ER, s., vidreiro.
GLASS.WORKS, s., vidraria.
GLASSY, adj., vítreo, cristalino.
GLAU.CO.MA, s., Med., glaucoma.
GLAU.COUS, adj., glauco, verde-mar, verde-azulado.
GLAZE, v., envidraçar, vitrificar; colocar vidros; esmaltar; s., esmalte, cobertura vitrificada.
GLAZED, adj., vítreo, lustroso, vitrificado, esmaltado.
GLAZ.ER, s., esmaltador, vitrificador.
GLA.ZIER, s., vidraceiro.
GLAZ.ING, s., esmaltagem, vitrificação.
GLEAM, s., lampejo; centelha; vislumbre, brilhar; v., cintilar, vislumbrar.
GLEAM.Y, adj., luminoso, brilhante, esplendente.
GLEAN, v., colher informações, pesquisar.
GLEBE, s., terra, torrão, gleba.
GLEBE-HOUSE, s., casa paroquial.
GLEE, s., alegria, felicidade, satisfação, contentamento.
GLEE CLUB, s., sociedade de canto; grupo de cantores.
GLEED, s., brasa, cinza quente.
GLEE.FUL, adj., jovial, alegre, satisfeito, contente.
GLEET, s., Med., gonorreia.
GLEET.Y, adj., com corrimento.
GLEN, s., vale.
GLIB, adj., lisonjeiro, adulador, conversador.
GLIB.LY, adv., loquazmente; pej., com muita lábia.
GLIDE, s., deslize, deslizamento; v., deslizar, escorregar.
GLID.ER, s., Aeron., planador (avião ou piloto).
GLID.ING, s., voo de planador.
GLIM.MER, s., luz fraca, ideia vaga; v., vislumbrar, luzir pouco.
GLIMPSE, s., olhada rápida, vislumbre; v., ver de relance.
GLINT, s., resplendor, raio de luz; v., reluzir, brilhar.
GLIS.TEN, s., brilho, cintilação; v., brilhar, resplandecer.
GLITCH, s., falha técnica, pane.
GLIT.TER, s., brilho, resplendor; v., brilhar, resplandecer.
GLIT.TER.ING, adj., reluzente, brilhante, deslumbrante.
GLITZY, adj., deslumbrante.
GLOAT, s., satisfação maligna; v., tripudiar (de algo); sentir-se bem com a desgraça alheia.
GLO.BOS.I.TY, s., esfericidade, globosidade.
GLOB.U.LAR, adj., globular, esférico.
GLOB.ULE, s., glóbulo.

GLOOM, s., escuridão, tristeza, melancolia; v., escurecer, ficar triste.
GLOOM.I.NESS, s., obscuridade, escuridão, tristeza, melancolia.
GLOOM.STER, s., col., pessoa agourenta.
GLOOM.Y, adj., escuro, triste, melancólico.
GLOP, s., col., gororoba.
GLO.RI.A, s., auréola, brilho.
GLO.RI.FI.CA.TION, s., glorificação, celebração, clímax.
GLO.RI.FY, v., glorificar, celebrar, enaltecer.
GLO.RI.OUS, adj., glorioso, magnífico, extraordinário.
GLO.RI.OUS.LY, adv., gloriosamente.
GLO.RI.OUS.NESS, s., glória, triunfo, apoteose, brilho.
GLO.RY, s., glória; v., gloriar, exaltar, enaltecer.
GLOSS, s., polimento, lustro, brilho; glosa; v., polir, lustrar; glosar.
GLOS.SA.RI.AL, adj., relativo à glossário.
GLOS.SA.RIST, s., dicionarista, compilador de um glossário.
GLOS.SA.RY, s., glossário, dicionário.
GLOS.SO.LO.GY, s., glossologia.
GLOSS.ER, s., polidor, polidor; glosador.
GLOSS.I.LY, adv., com lustro.
GLOSS.I.NESS, s., lustro.
GLOS.SOL.O.GY, s., glossologia, glotologia.
GLOSS OVER, v., encobrir, esconder.
GLOSS.Y, adj., lustroso.
GLOT.TIS, s., Anat., glote.
GLOT.TOL.O.GY, s., glotologia.
GLOVE, s., luva; v., enluvar, calçar luvas.
GLOVE COM.PART.MENT, s., porta-luvas (automóvel).
GLOVE PUP.PET, s., fantoche, marionete em forma de luva.
GLOVEE, s., luveiro.
GLOW, v., brilhar, arder; s., brilho, esplendor.
GLOWER, v., olhar ameaçadoramente (para alguém).
GLOW.ING, adj., resplandecente, brilhante.
GLOW-WORM, s., Zool., vaga-lume, pirilampo.
GLOZE, v., iludir, enganar, lisonjear, glosar.
GLU.COSE, s., glicose.
GLUE, s., cola; v., colar.
GLU.EY, adj., viscoso, pegajoso, colante.
GLU.EY.NESS, s., viscosidade.
GLUM, adj., melancólico.
GLUM.NESS, s., mau humor.
GLUT, s., abundância, fartura, copiosidade; v., fartar, saturar, encher.
GLU.TEN, s., Quím., glúten.
GLU.TE.US, s., músculo glúteo; glutei, s.pl., glúteos, músculos das nádegas.
GLU.TI.NIZE, v., tornar pegajoso ou viscoso.
GLU.TI.NOUS, adj., glutinoso, pegajoso, empapado.
GLUT.TON, s., glutão, comilão; Zool., glutão.
GLUT.TON.IZE, v., comer muito, exceder-se no comer.
GLUT.TON.OUS, adj., voraz, comilão.
GLUT.TONY, s., glutonaria; gula.
GLY.CE.MI.A, s., Med., glicemia.
GLYC.ER.IN, s., Quím., glicerina.
GLY.CO.GEN, s., Quím., glicogênio.
GNAR, v., grunhir, rosnar.
GNARL, s., nó (na madeira); v., torcer, deformar.
GNARRED, adj., grunhido, rosnado.
GNARLED, adj., nodoso, sulcado, áspero.

GNARLY · 478 · GORGE

GNARL.Y, *adj.*, cheio de nós, nodoso.
GNASH, *v.*, ranger os dentes.
GNAT, *s.*, mosquito, maruim.
GNAW, *v.*, roer, corroer, morder.
GNAW.ER, *s.*, roedor.
GNAW.ING, *adj.*, que rói, roedor.
GNEISS, *s.*, *Geol.*, gnaisse.
GNOME, *s.*, gnomo.
GNU, *s.*, gnu.
GO, *v.*, ir, partir, sair, viajar, andar, funcionar, ser, passar, caminhar.
GO AFTER, *v.*, ir atrás de, perseguir.
GOAD, *s.*, aguilhão, espora; *v.*, aguilhoar; aferroar; instigar, provocar.
GO-A.HEAD, *s.*, ato de avançar; ambição, vigor; *adj.*, ativo, dinâmico.
GOAL, *s.*, meta, objetivo; *Esp.*, gol (ponto do futebol).
GOAL.IE, *s.*, *col.*, goleiro.
GOAL.KEEP.ER, *s.*, *Esp.*, goleiro (futebol).
GOAL LINE, *s.*, *Esp.*, linha de fundo (futebol).
GOAL POST, *s.*, *Esp.*, travessão da trave (futebol).
GO AT, *v.*, atirar-se a, jogar-se a.
GOAT, *s.*, cabra, bode.
GOAT.EE, *s.*, cavanhaque (também se usa *goatee beard*).
GOAT.HERD, *s.*, pastor de cabras.
GOAT'S CHEESE, *s.*, queijo de cabra.
GOAT.ISH, *adj.*, caprino; sensual, erótico, lascivo.
GOAT.LING, *s.*, cabrito.
GO A.WAY, *v.*, ir-se, ir embora, partir, sumir.
GO BACK, *v.*, voltar, retornar.
GOB, *s.*, boca, escarro, esputo; mina abandonada; *UK* matraca; *v.*, escarrar.
GOB.BET, *s.*, pedaço (de carne), parte, bocado.
GOB.BLE, *s.*, grugulejo (a voz do peru); *v.*, grugulejar; devorar, engolir rapidamente.
GOB.BLEE, *s.*, comilão; *US col.*, peru macho.
GO-BE.TWEEN, *s.*, intermediário.
GOB.LET, *s.*, copo, taça.
GOB.LIN, *s.*, duende travesso, trasgo.
GOD, *s.*, deus, deidade; *God*: Deus; *v.*, deificar, endeusar.
GOD.CHILD, *s.*, afilhado.
GOD.DAM, *adj.*, maldito.
GOD.DAUGHT.ER, *s.*, afilhada.
GOD.DESS, *s.*, deusa.
GOD.FA.THER, *s.*, padrinho.
GOD.FOR.SAK.EN, *adj.*, abandonado ou esquecido (por Deus).
GOD.HOOD, *s.*, divindade, natureza divina.
GOD.LESS, *adj.*, *s.*, ateu, incrédulo, ímpio.
GOD.LIKE, *adj.*, divino, sacro, santo.
GOD.LI.NESS, *s.*, devoção, religiosidade.
GOD.LY, *adj.*, devoto, pio; divino.
GOD.MOTH.ER, *s.*, madrinha.
GOD.PAR.ENTS, *s. pl.*, padrinhos.
GOD.SEND, *s.*, dádiva de Deus.
GOD.SON, *s.*, afilhado.
GO.ER, *s.*, frequentador; batalhador, empreendedor.
GO.FER, *s.*, serviçal.
GOG.GLE, *s.*, ato de arregalar os olhos; óculos de natação; *v.*, arregalar os olhos.
GO IN, *v.*, entrar.

GO.ING, *s.*, andamento, andada, partida, ida.
GOLD, *s.*, ouro; *fig.*, dinheiro, riqueza; *adj.*, áureo, dourado, de ouro.
GOLD DIG.GER, *s.*, garimpeiro.
GOLD-DIG.GING, *s.*, garimpagem; garimpo.
GOLD-DUST, *s.*, ouro em pó.
GOLD.EN, *adj.*, dourado, de ouro.
GOLD.EN AGE, *s.*, idade de ouro.
GOLD.EN EA.GLE, *s.*, *Zool.*, águia-real.
GOLD.EN MEAN, *s.*, meio-termo, moderação.
GOLD.EN WED.DING, *s.*, bodas de ouro.
GOLD-FILLED, *adj.*, folhado a ouro.
GOLD.FISH, *s.*, *Zool.*, peixe-dourado.
GOLD MEDAL, *s.*, medalha de ouro.
GOLD MINE, *s.*, mina de ouro.
GOLD.SMITH, *s.*, ourives.
GOLD.SMITH.RY, *s.*, ourivesaria.
GO.LEM, *s.*, *Heb.*, golem; autômato.
GOLF, *s.*, golfe.
GOLF.ER, *s.*, jogador de golfe.
GOL.GO.THA, *s.*, Gólgota, calvário.
GON.DO.LA, *s.*, gôndola.
GON.DO.LIER, *s.*, gondoleiro.
GONE, *v.*, *pp.* de *to go*; *adj.*, ido; pronto; consumido, gasto; esgotado; desfeito; fraco.
GON.OR.RHOE.A, *s.*, *Med.*, gonorreia, blenorragia.
GONG, *s.*, gongo.
GOOD, *adj.*, bom, bondoso, educado, polido; *s.*, bem.
GOOD AF.TER.NOON, *s.*, boa-tarde (saudação).
GOOD-BE.HAV.IOUR, *s.*, boa conduta.
GOOD-BYE, *interj.*, adeus.
GOOD DEED, *s.*, boa ação.
GOOD EVE.NING, *s.*, boa-noite (saudação).
GOOD FEL.LOW, *s.*, companheiro.
GOOD FRI.DAY, *s.*, Sexta-Feira Santa.
GOOD-HU.MOURED, *adj.*, bem-humorado.
GOOD-LOOK.ING, *adj.*, bonito.
GOOD LOOKS, *s. pl.*, boa aparência.
GOOD LUKS, *s.*, boa sorte.
GOOD MAN.NERS, *s. pl.*, boas maneiras.
GOOD MORN.ING, *s.*, bom-dia (saudação).
GOOD.NESS, *s.*, bondade, benevolência.
GOOD NIGHT, *s.*, boa-noite (saudação).
GOODS, *s.*, bens, posses, mercadoria.
GOODS STA.TION, *s.*, estação de carga.
GOODS TRAIN, *s.*, trem de carga.
GOOD.WILL, *s.*, benevolência, boa vontade.
GOODY, *adj.*, bonachão, ingênuo; *s.*, *col.*, galã; gulodices; *interj.*, ótimo!.
GOO.EY, *adj.*, *col.*, grudento.
GOOF, *s.*, *col.*, pateta, palerma, mancada; *v.*, dar mancada, ficar à toa.
GOOF.Y, *adj.*, *col.*, pateta, tonto, simplório.
GOOSE, *s.*, ganso; *geese*, *s. pl.*, gansos.
GOOSE.BER.RY, *s.*, *Bot.*, groselha.
GOOSE-STEP, *s.*, passo de ganso (marcha); *v.*, marchar em passo de ganso.
GO.PHER, *s.*, esquilo.
GORE, *s.*, *Lit.*, sangue (derramado, coagulado); pedaço de pano triangular; *v.*, ferir com chifres (touro).
GORGE, *s.*, desfiladeiro, garganta.

GORGEOUS ··479·· GRASS

GOR.GEOUS, *adj.*, magnífico, maravilhoso, deslumbrante.
GOR.GEOUS.LY, *adv.*, esplendidamente.
GOR.GEOUS.NESS, *s.*, esplendor, deslumbramento.
GOR.GON.ZO.LA, *s.*, gorgonzola (queijo).
GO.RIL.LA, *s.*, *Zool.*, gorila.
GORM.LESS, *adj.*, *UK pej.*, burro.
GO ROUND, *v.*, circular, rodear.
GOR.Y, *adj.*, sangrento, ensanguentado.
GOS.PEL, *s.*, evangelho; *fig.*, verdade absoluta; *Mús.*, gospel (música cristã popular).
GOS.PEL.LER, *s.*, evangelista.
GOS.SA.MER, *s.*, teia de aranha; *adj.*, fino, tênue.
GOS.SIP, *s.*, mexericos, fofoca; *v.*, mexericar.
GOS.SIPY, *adj.*, metido, bisbilhoteiro.
GOTH, *s.*, *Hist.*, godo; *fig.*, bárbaro.
GOTH.IC, *s.*, gótico (estilo artístico e literário); *adj.*, gótico, medieval.
GOUGE, *s.*, goiva, cinzel, formão; *v.*, goivar, cinzelar; arrancar o olho.
GOU.LASH, *s.*, gulash (prato húngaro de carne).
GOURD, *s.*, *Bot.*, abóbora; cuia, cabaça.
GOUR.MET, *s.*, *Fr.*, gourmet, gastrônomo.
GOUT, *s.*, *Med.*, gota (doença).
GOUTI.NESS, *s.*, *Med.*, gota, artritismo.
GOV.ERN, *v.*, governar, dirigir.
GOV.ERN.A.BIL.I.TY, *s.*, governabilidade.
GOV.ERN.A.BLE, *adj.*, governável, obediente.
GOV.ER.NANCE, *s.*, governo, autoridade.
GOV.ER.NESS, *s.*, governanta; professora particular.
GOV.ERN.ING, *adj.*, governante.
GOV.ERN.MENT, *s.*, governo.
GOV.ERN.MEN.TAL, *adj.*, governamental.
GOV.ER.NOR, *s.*, governador, diretor.
GOWN, *s.*, beca, toga; vestido.
GRAB, *s.*, agarramento; *v.*, agarrar; apanhar; *gír.*, prender.
GRACE, *s.*, graça, favor, elegância; *v.*, honrar, enfeitar.
GRACE.FUL, *adj.*, elegante, gracioso.
GRACE.LESS, *adj.*, sem graça, canhestro.
GRA.CIOUS, *adj.*, gracioso; elegante, afável.
GRA.CIOUS.LY, *adv.*, graciosamente, afavelmente.
GRA.CIOUS.NESS, *s.*, afabilidade, graça, benignidade.
GRA.DA.TION, *s.*, gradação.
GRADE, *s.*, grau, classe; *v.*, classificar.
GRAD.ER, *s.*, graduador.
GRADE SCHOOL, *s.*, *US* escolar primária.
GRA.DI.ENT, *s.*, declive, encosta; gradiente.
GRAD.ING, *s.*, nivelamento, classificação, graduação.
GRAD.U.AL, *adj.*, gradual, gradativo.
GRAD.U.AL.LY, *s.*, declive; *Mat.*, gradiente.
GRAD.U.ATE, *s.*, graduado, licenciado; *v.*, licenciar-se.
GRAD.U.A.TED, *adj.*, graduado.
GRAD.U.ATE SCHOOL, *s.*, *US* escolar de pós-graduação.
GRAD.U.A.TION, *s.*, graduação, formatura.
GRAF.FI.TI, *s.*, grafite, pichação.
GRAFT, *s.*, enxerto (planta); labuta; suborno; *v.*, enxertar (planta).
GRAIN, *s.*, grão, cereal; fibra; *v.*, granular.
GRAIN.Y, *adj.*, granuloso, granulado.
GRAM, *s.*, grama (unidade de peso).
GRAMA, *s.*, grama, erva, capim.
GRA.MIN.E.AE, *s. pl.*, *Bot.*, gramíneas.

GRA.MIN.E.OUS, *adj.*, gramíneo.
GRAM.MAR, *s.*, gramática.
GRAM.MAR.I.AN, *s.*, gramático.
GRAM.MAT.IC, *adj.*, gramatical.
GRAM.MAT.IC.AL, *adj.*, gramatical.
GRAMME, *s.*, grama (ver *gram*).
GRAMOPHONE, *s.*, gramofone, fonógrafo.
GRAM.PUS, *s.*, *Zool.*, orca (cetáceo).
GRAN, *s.*, *UK fam.*, vó (de vovó).
GRA.NA.RY, *s.*, celeiro.
GRAND, *adj.*, magnífico; ambicioso; ilustre; *col.*, excelente.
GRAND.CHILD, *s.*, neto, neta.
GRAND.CHILD.REN, *s.*, netos.
GRAND.DAD, *s.*, *fam.*, vovô.
GRAND.DAUGHT.ER, *s.*, neta.
GRAN.DEUR, *s.*, grandeza, maravilha.
GRAND DUCH.ESS, *s.*, grã-duquensa.
GRAND DUKE, *s.*, grão-duque.
GRAN.DEUR, *s.*, grandeza, majestade, magnificência.
GRAND.FA.THER, *s.*, avô.
GRAN.DI.OSE, *adj.*, grandioso, maravilhoso, imponente.
GRAND.CHILD.REN, *s.*, netos.
GRAN.DI.OS.I.TY, *s.*, grandiosidade.
GRAND.MA, *s.*, *fam.*, vovó.
GRAND-MAS.TER, *s.*, grão-mestre.
GRAND.MOTH.ER, *s.*, avó.
GRAND.PA, *s.*, *fam.*, vovô.
GRAND.PAR.ENTS, *s. pl.*, avós.
GRAND.SON, *s.*, neto.
GRANGE, *s.*, granja, chácara.
GRANG.ER, *s.*, granjeiro, chacareiro.
GRAN.ITE, *s.*, granito.
GRA.NIT.IC, *adj.*, granítico.
GRAN.NY, *s.*, *fam.*, vovó.
GRA.NO.LA, *s.*, *US* granola.
GRANT, *v.*, conceder, deferir, anuir; *s.*, bolsa de estudo, subsídio.
GRANT.OR, *s.*, outorgante.
GRAN.U.LAR, *adj.*, granular.
GRAN.U.LATE, *v.*, granular, tornar granulado.
GRAN.U.LATED SUGAR, *s.*, açúcar cristal.
GRAN.U.LA.TION, *s.*, granulação.
GRAN.ULE, *s.*, grânulo.
GRAN.U.LOUS, *adj.*, granuloso, granulado.
GRAPE, *s.*, *Bot.*, uva, videira.
GRAPE.FRUIT, *s.*, pomelo, toranja.
GRAPE.VINE, *s.*, videira, parreira.
GRAPH, *s.*, gráfico.
GRAPH.IC, *s.*, gráfico.
GRAPH.IC ART.IST, *s.*, artista gráfico.
GRAPH.ICS, *s.*, artes gráficas.
GRAPH.ITE, *s.*, grafite.
GRA.PHOL.O.GY, *s.*, grafologia.
GRAPH PA.PER, *s.*, papel milimetrado ou quadriculado.
GRAP.NEL, *s.*, arpéu (pequena âncora).
GRAP.PLE, *v.*, atracar-se; lutar, brigar; *fig.*, estar às voltas com (uma ideia, um caso etc.).
GRAP.PLING I.RON, *s.*, arpéu, gancho.
GRAPY, *adj.*, feito com uva.
GRASP, *v.*, pegar, agarrar, segurar, compreender.
GRASP.ING, *adj.*, avaro, avarento.
GRASS, *s.*, relva, gramado, grama, relvado.

GRASS CUTTER •• 480 ••• GRIP

GRASS CUT.TER, *s.*, máquina de cortar grama.
GRASS.HOP.PER, *s.*, *Zool.*, gafanhoto.
GRASS.LAND, *s.*, pastagem, gramado.
GRASS SNAKE, *s.*, cobra d'água.
GRASSY, *adj.*, coberto de grama, ervoso.
GRATE, *s.*, grade, grelha; lareira; *v.*, ranger, ralar.
GRATE.FUL, *adj.*, grato, agradecido.
GRATE.FUL.LY, *adv.*, agradecidamente.
GRATE.FUL.NESS, *s.*, agradecimento, gratidão.
GRAT.ER, *s.*, ralador.
GRAT.I.FI.CA.TION, *s.*, gratificação, satisfação.
GRAT.I.FY, *v.*, satisfazer, contentar, agradar.
GRAT.I.FY.ING, *adj.*, gratificante.
GRAT.ING, *adj.*, áspero; *s.*, grade.
GRATIS, *adv.*, grátis.
GRAT.I.TUDE, *s.*, gratidão.
GRA.TU.I.TOUS, *adj.*, gratuito, grátis.
GRA.TU.I.TY, *s.*, gratuidade, gratificação, gorjeta.
GRAVE, *s.*, sepultura, cova; *Gram.*, acento grave; *adj.*, grave, sério; solene; *v.*, gravar, esculpir.
GRAVE AC.CENT, *s.*, *Gram.*, acento grave.
GRAVE DIG.GER, *s.*, coveiro.
GRAV.EL, *s.*, cascalho, pedregulho.
GRAVE.NESS, *s.*, gravidade, seriedade, respeito.
GRAV.ER, *s.*, gravador; buril.
GRAVE.STONE, *s.*, lápide (de túmulo).
GRAVE.YARD, *s.*, cemitério.
GRAV.ID, *adj.*, grávida.
GRAV.I.TATE, *s.*, gravitar.
GRAV.I.TA.TION, *s.*, gravitação.
GRAV.I.TY, *s.*, gravidade, seriedade.
GRA.VURE, *s.*, gravura.
GRA.VY, *s.*, molho de carne, caldo de carne.
GRAZE, *s.*, pasto; *v.*, pastar, pastorear.
GRA.ZIER, *s.*, negociante de gado.
GRAZ.ING, *s.*, pasto.
GRAY, *s.*, o mesmo que *grey*.
GREASE, *s.*, graxa, sebo, gordura; *v.*, untar, engraxar; *fig.*, subornar.
GREASY, *adj.*, gorduroso, engordurado, escorregadio.
GREAT, *adj.*, grande, genial, forte.
GREAT-AUNT, *s.*, tia-avó.
GREAT BEAR, *s.*, *Astron.*, Ursa Maior.
GREAT.COAT, *s.*, sobretudo (traje).
GREAT-GRAND.CHIL.DREN, *s.*, bisnetos.
GREAT-GRAND.DAUGHT.ER, *s.*, bisneta.
GREAT-GRAND.FA.THER, *s.*, bisavô.
GREAT-GRAND.MOTH.ER, *s.*, bisavó.
GREAT-GRAND.SON, *s.*, bisneto.
GREAT.HEART.ED, *adj.*, benigno, benevolente.
GREAT.LY, *adv.*, muito; imensamente, grandemente.
GREAT.NESS, *s.*, grandeza, magnitude.
GREAT WALL OF CHI.NA, *s.*, a Grande Muralha da China.
GREAT WAR, *s.*, a Grande Guerra.
GRE.CIAN, *adj.*, *s.*, grego.
GREECE, *s.*, Grécia.
GREED, *s.*, cobiça, ganância, avidez.
GREED.I.LY, *adv.*, gulosamente.
GREED.Y, *adj.*, guloso, ganancioso.
GREEK, *adj.*, *s.*, grego.
GREEN, *adj.*, verde, inexperiente, simplório; *s.*, verde, verdor.

GREEN.BACK, *s.*, *US col.*, nota de dólar.
GREEN BEAN, *s.*, *Bot.*, vagem.
GREEN.ER, *s.*, novato, principiante.
GREEN.ERY, *s.*, verdura.
GREEN.HOUSE, *s.*, estufa.
GREEN.FLY, *s.*, *Zool.*, pulgão.
GREEN.GRO.CER, *s.*, verdureiro.
GREEN.HORN, *s.*, *US* recém-chegado; novato.
GREEN.HOUSE, *s.*, estufa para plantas.
GREEN.HOUSE EF.FECT, *s.*, efeito estufa.
GREEN.HOUSE GAS, *s.*, gás de efeito estufa.
GREEN.ISH, *adj.*, esverdeado.
GREEN.LAND.ER, *s.*, groenlandês.
GREEN.NESS, *s.*, verdura.
GREEN.SWARD, *s.*, relva, relvado, gramado.
GREEN.WOOD, *s.*, floresta verde.
GREEN.Y, *adj.*, verdoso, esverdeado.
GREET, *v.*, cumprimentar, saudar, acolher, receber, dirigir-se.
GREET.ING, *s.*, cumprimento, saudação.
GRE.GAR.I.OUS, *adj.*, gregário.
GRE.GO.RI.AN, *adj.*, *s.*, gregoriano.
GRE.NADE, *s.*, granada.
GRE.NA.DI.AN, **GRE.NA.DAN**, *adj.*, *s.*, granadino (de ou nativo de Granada).
GREN.A.DIER, *s.*, granadeiro.
GREY, *s.*, cor cinza; *v.*, ter cor cinza, acinzentar; *adj.*, cinzento, gris.
GREY-HAIRED, *adj.*, grisalho.
GREY-HEAD, *s.*, cabeça grisalha, cãs.
GREY.HOUND, *s.*, galgo (cachorro grande e esguio).
GREY.ING, **GRAY.ING**, *adj.*, cinzento, acinzentado.
GREY MAT.TER, *s.*, *Med.*, massa cinzenta; *col.*, inteligência.
GRID, *s.*, grade, grelha.
GRID.DLE, *s.*, chapa de ferro; forma para bolo.
GRID.I.RON, *s.*, grelha; *US* campo de futebol americano.
GRID.LOCK, *s.*, engarrafamento; caos organizacional.
GRID REF.ER.ENCE, *s.*, coordenada.
GRIEF, *s.*, aflição, tristeza.
GRIEV.ANCE, *s.*, queixa, mágoa, injustiça.
GRIEVE, *v.*, afligir, molestar, ofender.
GRIEV.ING, *s.*, luto; *adj.*, de luto.
GRIEV.OUS, *adj.*, doloroso, penoso, atroz, repugnante.
GRIEV.OUS.LY, *adv.*, gravemente, dolorosamente.
GRILL, *s.*, grelha, comida grelhada; *v.*, grelhar, assar em grelha.
GRIM, *adj.*, severo, rígido, repugnante.
GRI.MACE, *s.*, trejeito, careta.
GRI.MACER, *s.*, careteiro, aquele que faz caretas.
GRIM, *s.*, severo, rígido; horrível.
GRIME, *s.*, sujeira, fuligem; *v.*, encardir, sujar.
GRIM.I.LY, *adv.*, encardidamente.
GRIM.LY, *adv.*, severamente, rigidamente.
GRIM.Y, *adj.*, sujo, encardido.
GRIN, *s.*, sorriso aberto; *v.*, abrir um sorriso.
GRIND, *s.*, moedura, trituramento; *v.*, moer, triturar, picar.
GRIND.ER, *s.*, moleiro, moedor, afiador; o dente molar.
GRIND.ING, *adj.*, molestador, opressivo.
GRIND.STONE, *s.*, pedra de amolar, rebolo.
GRIN.NING, *adj.*, sorridente.
GRIP, *s.*, ação de apertar, força da mão (no aperto de mão); *v.*, agarrar, segurar, apertar.

GRIPE   ••481••   GUILELESS

GRIPE, *s.*, ato de agarrar, pressão; controle, domínio; *v.*, agarrar, apertar; oprimir.

GRIPES, *s. pl.*, dores de barriga.

GRIP.ING, *adj.*, opressivo; dor cortante.

GRIPPE, *s., Med.*, gripe.

GRIS.KIN, *s.*, lombo de porco.

GRIS.LY, *adj.*, horrendo, medonho.

GRIST, *s.*, grão inteiro (que não foi moído); forragem.

GRIS.TLE, *s.*, cartilagem.

GRIST.LY, *adj.*, cartilaginoso.

GRIT, *s.*, grão, pedregulho, grão de areia; *v.*, friccionar, roer.

GRIT.TY, *adj.*, arenoso, em grânulos; *US* corajoso.

GRIZ.ZLE, *adj.*, cinzento, cor cinza.

GRIZ.ZLY, *s., Zool.*, urso-pardo; *adj.*, cor cinza, cinzento.

GROAN, *s.*, gemido, suspiro; *v.*, gemer, suspirar, sofrer.

GROAN.ING, *s.*, gemido, suspiro.

GRO.CER, *s.*, merceeiro, vendedor.

GRO.CER.IES, *s.*, mantimentos, víveres.

GRO.CERY, *s.*, armazém, empório, mercearia.

GROG, *s.*, grogue, embriagado.

GROG.GI.NESS, *s.*, embriaguez, bebedeira.

GROG.GY, *adj.*, grogue, embriagado, bêbado.

GROIN, *s., Anat.*, virilha.

GROOM, *s.*, noivo; cavalariço; *v.*, tratar (de cavalo); preparar(-se); arrumar(-se); cortar (pelo de animal).

GROOMS.MAN, *s.*, padrinho do noivo.

GROOVE, *s.*, ranhura, encaixe, entalhe; *v.*, entalhar, escavar, sulcar.

GROPE, *v.*, acariciar; tatear; tentar (algo) às cegas.

GROSS, *adj.*, grosseiro, ordinário, bruto; *s.*, massa, parte principal.

GROSS.LY, *adv.*, inteiramente, extremamente.

GROSS.NESS, *s.*, grosseria, rudeza.

GRO.TESQUE, *adj.*, grotesco.

GROT.TO, *s.*, gruta, caverna.

GROUCH, *s.*, resmungão; *v.*, resmungar, reclamar.

GROUCH.Y, *adj.*, mal-humorado, nervoso.

GROUND, *s.*, terra, solo, chão, soalho; *v.*, pôr no chão, depor.

GROUND FLOOR, *s.*, andar térreo.

GROUND.ING, *s.*, conhecimentos básicos; castigo.

GROUND.LESS, *adj.*, infundado, sem razão.

GROUND-NUT, *s., UK* amendoim.

GROUND-PLAN, *s., Arquit.*, planta baixa.

GROUNDS, *s. pl.*, solo, chão; jardim (terreno em torno de uma casa).

GROUND.WORK, *s.*, base, preparação.

GROUP, *s.*, grupo, conjunto, classe; *v.*, agrupar, reunir.

GROUP.ER, *s., Zool.*, garoupa (peixe).

GROUP.IE, *s.*, tiete, fã.

GROUP.ING, *s.*, agrupamento, série, classe.

GROUP THER.A.PY, *s.*, terapia de grupo.

GROUSE, *s., Zool.*, tetraz (galo silvestre); queixa; *v.*, queixar-se.

GROUT, *s.*, argamassa, reboco; *v.*, rebocar, passar argamassa.

GROUT.ING, *s.*, acabamento com reboco.

GROVE, *s.*, bosque, arvoredo.

GROV.EL, *v.*, rastejar, arrastar-se; *fig.*, humilhar-se.

GROW, *v.*, crescer, germinar, brotar, arraigar-se, criar raízes.

GROW.ER, *s.*, plantador, produtor, agricultor.

GROW.ING, *s.*, crescimento, cultivo; *adj.*, crescente.

GROWL, *s.*, rosnado, rangido, resmungo; *v.*, rosnar, rugir.

GROWN, *adj.*, crescido, avolumado, desenvolvido.

GROWN-UP, *adj.*, adulto, crescido; *s.*, adulto.

GROWTH, *s.*, crescimento, aumento, desenvolvimento.

GROWTH RATE, *s., Econ.*, taxa de crescimento.

GRUB, *s.*, larva, lagarta; *gir.*, boia (comida fria).

GRUB.BY, *adj.*, encardido, sujo; bichado.

GRUDGE, *s.*, rancor, ódio, aversão; *v.*, invejar, fazer de má vontade.

GRUDG.ING, *adj.*, relutante; de má vontade, rancoroso.

GRUDG.ING.LY, *adv.*, com relutância, com aversão.

GRU.EL.LING, *adj.*, duro, difícil, árduo, penoso.

GRUE.SOME, *adj.*, repulsivo, horrível.

GRUE.SOME.LY, *adv.*, horrivelmente.

GRUFF, *s.*, brusco, repentino, rouco.

GRUM.BLE, *v.*, resmungar, bufar, reclamar.

GRUM.BLER, *s.*, resmungão, reclamador, neurótico.

GRUM.BLING, *s.*, resmungo; *adj.*, resmungão; rabugento; ranzinza.

GRUMP.I.NESS, *s.*, rabugice.

GRUMP.Y, *adj.*, rabugento, aborrecido, áspero, amuado.

GRUNGE, *s.*, aversão a padrões estabelecidos; sujeira; *Mús.*, grunge.

GRUNT, *s.*, grunhido, resmungo; *v.*, grunhir, resmungar.

GUAR.AN.TEE, *s.*, garantia, fiança, caução; *v.*, garantir, afiançar, abonar.

GUAR.AN.TOR, *s.*, fiador.

GUAR.AN.TY, *s.*, garantia, fiança, caução.

GUARD, *s.*, guarda, vigia, sentinela, vigilante; *v.*, viajar, defender.

GUARD DOG, *s.*, cão de guarda.

GUARD.ED, *adj.*, cauteloso.

GUARD.IAN, *s.*, protetor, guardião, tutor.

GUARD.I.AN AN.GEL, *s.*, anjo da guarda.

GUARD.IAN.SHIP, *s.*, tutela, tutoria, proteção.

GUARD.RAIL, *s.*, proteção lateral em uma via.

GUARDS.MAN, *s.*, sentinela; *UK* soldado da Guarda Real.

GUA.TE.MA.LAN, *s., adj.*, guatemalteco (da, ou natural da Guatemala).

GUA.VA, *s., Bot.*, goiaba.

GUER.RIL.LA, *s.*, guerrilha, guerrilheiro.

GUESS, *s.*, suposição, hipótese; *v.*, conjeturar, adivinhar, imaginar.

GUESS.A.BLE, *adj.*, adivinhável.

GUESS.TI.MATE, *s., col.*, estimativa aproximada.

GUESS.WORK, *s.*, adivinhação, conjectura.

GUEST, *s.*, hóspede, convidado.

GUEST.HOUSE, *s.*, pensão, hospedaria; casa de hóspedes.

GUEST.ROOM, *s.*, quarto de hóspedes.

GUEST STAR, *s.*, atriz ou ator convidado (TV, *Cin.*, Teat.).

GUF.FAW, *s.*, gargalhada; *v.*, gargalhar.

GUID.ANCE, *s.*, orientação, liderança.

GUIDE, *s.*, guia, sinal, vestígio, roteiro; *v.*, guiar, conduzir, levar.

GUIDE DOG, *s.*, cão-guia (cão de assistência ao cego).

GUIDE.BOOK, *s.*, guia de viagem.

GUIDE.LINE, *s.*, diretriz, princípio.

GUID.ING, *adj.*, norteador.

GUILD, GILD, *s.*, grêmio, associação, sociedade.

GUILE, *s.*, fraude, malícia, astúcia.

GUILE.FUL, *adj.*, malicioso, astucioso, astuto.

GUILE.LESS, *adj., Lit.*, cândido, sem malícia.

GUILLOTINE · 482 · GYVE

GUIL.LO.TINE, *s.*, guilhotina, máquina para cortar papel; *v.*, guilhotinar.

GUILT, *s.*, culpa, criminalidade.

GUILT.I.LY, *adv.*, de modo culpável.

GUILTY, *adj.*, culpado, criminoso, condenável.

GUIN.EA, *s., Hist.*, guinéu (antiga moeda inglesa de ouro).

GUIN.EA-FOWL, *s., Zool.*, galinha-d'angola.

GUIN.EA-PIG, *s., Zool.*, porquinho-da-índia.

GUISE, *s.*, aparência, aspecto.

GUI.TAR, *s., Mús.*, guitarra, violão, viola.

GUI.TAR.IST, *s.*, violonista, guitarrista.

GULCH, *s.*, ravina.

GULF, *s.*, golfo, baía, braço de mar; abismo, garganta; tragar, devorar.

GULF.STREAM, *s.*, Corrente do Golfo do México.

GULL, *s.*, gaivota; tolo, bobo; *v.*, enganar, lograr, seduzir.

GUL.LERY, *s.*, fraude, logro, engano.

GUL.LET, *s.*, goela, esôfago.

GUL.LI.BLE, *adj.*, ingênuo, crédulo.

GUL.LY, *s.*, bueiro, barranco, sarjeta, fossa.

GULP, *v.*, engolir, tragar, devorar; *s.*, gole, trago.

GUM, *s.*, goma, cola; gengiva (também *gums, pl.*); *v.*, colar.

GUM.BOIL, *s., Med.*, abscesso na gengiva.

GUM-BOOTS, *s. pl., UK* galochas, botas de borracha.

GUMMED, *adj.*, adesivo.

GUM.MING, *s.*, engomadura.

GUM.MY, *adj.*, grudento, pegajoso; pastoso.

GUMP.TION, *s.*, iniciativa, senso prático.

GUM-SHOE, *s., US* detetive.

GUN, *s.*, canhão, espingarda, arma de fogo, revólver; *v.*, atirar com arma.

GUN-DOG, *s.*, cão de caça (também *hunting dog*).

GUN.FIRE, *s.*, tiroteio.

GUNK, *s., gir.*, meleca.

GUN.MAN, *s.*, pistoleiro.

GUN.NER, *s.*, artilheiro.

GUN.NING, *s.*, caça, tiro.

GUN.POW.DER, *s.*, pólvora.

GUN.SHOT, *s.*, tiro com arma de fogo; distância de tiro.

GUN.SMITH, *s.*, armeiro.

GUR.GLE, *s.*, gorgolejo; balbucio (bebê); *v.*, gorgolejar; balbuciar (bebê).

GUSH, *s.*, erupção, torrente, jato, arroubo; *v.*, jorrar, transbordar.

GUSH.ING, *adj.*, que jorra; efusivo, arrebatado, sentimental.

GUSH.ING.LY, *adv.*, efusivamente.

GUSH.Y, *adj.*, sentimental, efusivo.

GUS.SET, *s.*, nesga (de pano etc.); *v.*, reforçar com nesga.

GUST, *s.*, lufada de vento, toró, pé de vento, trovoada.

GUST.Y, *adj.*, tempestuoso.

GUS.TA.TION, *s.*, gustação, experimentação, ato de provar.

GUSTY, *adj.*, tempestuoso, borrascoso, violento.

GUT, *s.*, intestino, tripa, entranhas; *v.*, estripar.

GUT.TER, *s.*, sarjeta, calha; *v.*, escavar, colocar calhas.

GUT.TER.ING, *s.*, gotejamento, calhas.

GUT.TER.MAN, *s.*, camelô, comerciante informal.

GUT.TER.SNIPE, *s.*, menino de rua, moleque.

GUT.TUR.AL, *adj.*, gutural.

GUT.TY, *adj.*, corpulento.

GUV, *s., gir.*, chefe.

GUY, *s.*, corda, cabo; *US* rapaz; *v.*, firmar, aguentar, segurar; ridicularizar.

GUY.ANA, *s.* Guiana.

GUY.A.NESE, *s.*, guianense.

GUY.ROPE, *s.*, corda, amarra.

GUZ.ZLE, *v.*, engolir com gula, empanturrar-se, comer muito, esbanjar.

GUZ.ZLER, *s.*, glutão, comilão.

GYM, *s.*, ginásio, ginástica.

GYM.KHA.NA, *s.*, gincana; competição entre grupos.

GYM.NA.SI.UM, *s.*, ginásio.

GYM.NAST, *s.*, ginasta.

GYM.NAST.IC, *adj.*, ginástico.

GYM.NAST.ICS, *s.*, ginástica.

GY.NE.COL.O.GY, GY.NAE.COL.O.GY, *s.*, ginecologia.

GY.NE.CO.LOG.I.CAL, *adj.*, ginecológico.

GY.NE.COL.O.GIST, *s.*, ginecologista.

GY.RATE, *v.*, girar, rodar.

GY.RA.TION, *s.*, giro, rotação.

GY.RO.SCOPE, *s.*, giroscópio.

GYVE, *s.*, algemas, grilhões; *v.*, algemar.

H

H, s., oitava letra do alfabeto inglês; *abrev.* de hora.
HA.BE.AS COR.PUS, s., *Lat., Jur.*, habeas corpus.
HAB.ER.DASH.ER, s., *UK* loja de armarinhos; *US* vendedor ou balconista de loja de roupas masculinas.
HAB.ER.DASH.ER.Y, s., *UK* artigos de armarinho; armarinho; *US* loja de roupas masculinas.
HA.BIL.I.TATE, v., habilitar.
HA.BIL.I.TA.TION, s., *Arc.*, habilitação.
HAB.IT, s., hábito, costume, usança; traje, hábito; v., habitar, acostumar.
HAB.IT.A.BLE, *adj.*, habitável.
HAB.IT.A.BLE.NESS, s., habitabilidade.
HAB.IT.ANT, s., habitante, morador.
HAB.I.TAT, s., **HÁBITAT**.
HAB.I.TA.TION, s., habitação, moradia.
HA.BIT.U.AL, *adj.*, habitual, costumeiro, tradicional.
HA.BIT.U.AL.LY, *adv.*, habitualmente.
HA.BIT.U.ATE, v., habituar, acostumar, habitualizar.
HAB.I.TUDE, s., *Arc.*, hábito, costume, usança.
HA.CHURE, s., hachura, v., hachurar, sombrear.
HA.CI.EN.DA, s., fazenda, estância.
HACK, v., cortar, talhar, entalhar; s., corte, fenda, carro de aluguel, táxi.
HACK.A.MORE, s., cabresto.
HACK.ER, s., *Comp.*, entusiasta de computador; pirata de computador.
HACK.IE, s., *col., US* taxista.
HACK.ING, *adj.*, contador, entalhador; tosse seca; s., *Comp.*, pirataria em computador, acesso ilegal.
HACK.LE, s., gramadeira; pelos eriçados no dorso; v., gramar (o linho); cortar, talhar; despedaçar.
HACK.LES, s. *pl.*, pelos eriçados no dorso; enfurecer alguém.
HACK.LE FLY, s., isca de pesca artificial.
HACK.NEYED, *adj., pej.*, batido, comum, banal.
HACK.SAW, s., serra para metais.
HAD, *part., adj.*, tido, havido.
HAD.DOCK, s., *Zool.*, hadoque (peixe que se assemelha ao bacalhau).
HADN'T, *contr.* de had not.
HAE.MA.TOL.O.GY, s., o mesmo que *hematology*.
HAE.MO.GLO.BIN, s., o mesmo que *hemoglobin*.
HAE.MO.PHIL.IA, s., *Med.*, o mesmo que *hemophilia*.
HAEM.OR.RHAGE, s., *Med.*, o mesmo que *hemorrhage*.
HAEM.OR.RHOIDS, s., *Med.*, o mesmo que *hemorrhoids*.
HAG, s., bruxa, feiticeira, megera.
HAG.GARD, *adj.*, faminto, abatido.
HAG.GARD.NESS, s., exaustão.
HAG.GISH, *adj.*, feio, velho, horrendo, abominável, nojento.
HAG.GLE, s., regateio, pechincha; v., regatear, pechinchar.
HAG.GLING, s., pechincha, regateio, ato de pechinchar.
HAG.I.OG.RA.PHY, s., hagiografia (biografia dos santos).
HAG.RID.DEN, *adj.*, atormentado, perturbado.
HAG.RIDE, v., atormentar, perturbar.
HAIL, s., granizo, saraiva; saudação; v., chover pedras, cair granizo; saudar, cumprimentar.
HAIL.STONE, s., granizo.
HAIL.STORM, s., chuva de granizo.
HAIR, s., cabelo, pelo.
HAIR.BRUSH, s., escova de cabelos.
HAIR.CUT, s., corte de cabelo.
HAIR.DRESS.ER, s., cabeleireiro.
HAIR.DO, s., *col.*, penteado.
HAIR.DRESS.ER, s., cabeleireiro.
HAIR.DRESS.ING, s., atividade de cabeleireiro; penteado.
HAIR.DRY.ER, s., secador de cabelos.
HAIR GEL, s., gel fixador.
HAIR.LINE, s., contorno do cabelo.
HAIRED, *adj.*, cabeludo, peludo.
HAIR.LESS, *adj.*, calvo, sem cabelos.
HAIR.PIN, s., grampo de cabelos.
HAIR SPRAY, s., laquê.
HAIR STYLE, s., estilo de penteado.
HAIR STYL.IST, s., cabeleireiro(a).
HAIRY, *adj.*, cabeludo, peludo.
HAI.TIAN, s., *adj.*, haitiano.
HAKE, s., *Zool.*, merluza (peixe do mar conhecido na culinária também como pescada).
HA.LA.TION, s., halo, auréola.
HALE, *adj.*, forte, vigoroso, robusto; v., puxar, arrastar.
HALE.NESS, s., vigor, força.
HALF, s., metade, meio bilhete; semestre; *adj.*, meio; parcial; *adv.*, pela metade, pela metade.
HALF-BACK, s., meio campo, médio volante (futebol).
HALF-BACKED, *adj.*, meio assado (bolo, pão); *fig.*, mal elaborado; imaturo.
HALF-BROTH.ER, s., meio-irmão.
HALF-HEART.ED, *adj.*, indiferente, desanimado.
HALF HOUR, s., meia hora.
HALF-HOUR.LY, *adj.*, a cada meia hora.
HALF-MOON, s., meia-lua.
HALF-SIS.TER, s., meia-irmã.
HALF-TIME, s., meio tempo.
HALF-TRUTH, s., meia verdade.
HALF-YEAR.LY, *adj.*, semestral.
HAL.I.TO.SIS, s., *Med.*, halitose.
HALL, s., entrada, saguão, átrio.
HAL.LE.LU.JAH, *excl.*, aleluia!
HALL.MARK, s., marca.
HAL.LOW, v., santificar, consagrar.
HAL.LOW.ED, *adj.*, sagrado, santo.
HAL.LOW.EEN, s., dia 31 de outubro, Dia das Bruxas.
HAL.LOW.MAS, s., *Rel.*, Dia de Todos os Santos.
HAL.LU.CI.NATE, s., alucinar, desvairar.
HAL.LU.CI.NA.TION, s., alucinação.

HALLUCINATORY ·· 484 ·· HARD ROCK

HAL.LU.CI.NA.TO.RY, *adj.*, alucinante.
HAL.LU.CI.NO.GEN, *s.*, alucinógeno.
HAL.LU.CI.NO.GEN.IC, *adj.*, alucinógeno.
HALL.WAY, *s.*, sala de entrada, corredor.
HA.LO, *s.*, halo, auréola; *fig.*, prestígio; *v.*, aureolar.
HAL.O.GEN, *s.*, *Quím.*, halogênio.
HALT, *s.*, parada (para descanso); *v.*, parar (lentamente); deter(-se) ou fazer deter.
HAL.TER, *s.*, cabresto, corda, laço, forca; *v.*, encabrestar, amarrar.
HAL.TER.NECK, *adj.*, (vestido) de frente única.
HALT.ING, *adj.*, vacilante.
HALT.ING PLACE, *s.*, ponto de parada.
HALVE, *v.*, dividir ao meio, cortar pela metade.
HAM, *s.*, presunto, fiambre; *col.*, ator canastrão; *v.*, *col.*, atuar com exagero.
HA.MATE, *adj.*, curvo (como gancho).
HAM.BURG.ER, *s.*, hambúrguer.
HAM-FIST.ED, *adj.*, desajeitado.
HAM.LET, *s.*, aldeia, localidade, aldeola, vila.
HAM.MER, *s.*, martelo; *v.*, martelar, bater com força.
HAM.MOCK, *s.*, rede para descansar.
HAM.MY, *adj.*, afetado, muito artificial.
HAM.PER, *s.*, cesto de roupa; estorvo; *v.*, obstruir, dificultar.
HAM.STER, *s.*, *Zool.*, hamster (espécie de roedor).
HAM.STRING, *s.*, tendão do jarrete; *v.*, cortar o tendão; *fig.*, impedir, paralisar.
HAND, *s.*, mão, ponteiro; letra, cartada.
HAND BACK, *v.*, devolver.
HAND.BAG, *s.*, valise, maleta de mão, sacola.
HAND.BALL, *s.*, *Esp.*, handebol.
HAND.BILL, *s.*, panfleto.
HAND.BOOK, *s.*, manual, guia de mão.
HAND.CART, *s.*, carrinho de mão.
HAND.CLASP, *s.*, aperto de mão.
HAND.CUFF, *s.*, algema; *handcuffs*, *s.pl.*, algemas; *v.*, algemar.
HAND-GLASS, *s.*, lente para leitura.
HAND.I.CAP, *s.*, *Esp.*, desvantagem dada a adversário forte; obstáculo; *v.*, impor desvantagem ao mais forte.
HAND.I.CAPPED, *adj.*, deficiente.
HAND.I.CRAFT, *s.*, artesanato.
HAND.I.NESS, *s.*, destreza, perícia.
HAN.DLE, *s.*, manivela, cabo, alça, trinco; *v.*, guiar, manobrar; manejar; manipular; lidar com.
HAN.DLE-BAR, *s.*, guidão (de bicicleta).
HAN.DLER, *s.*, manipulador; treinador (de pugilistas); *UK* carregador de bagagens.
HAND.KER.CHIEF, *s.*, lenço.
HAND.MADE, *adj.*, feito à mão.
HAND-OUT, *s.*, donativos (alimentos, roupas); folheto informativo; nota à imprensa.
HAND.OVER, *s.*, devolução (de uma compra).
HAND.RAIL, *s.*, corrimão.
HAND.SAW, *s.*, serrote (serra manual).
HAND.SHAKE, *s.*, aperto de mão.
HAND.SOME, *adj.*, belo, bonito, elegante.
HAND.STAND, *s.*, ação de plantar bananeira.
HANDS UP!, *interj.*, mãos ao alto!
HAND.WORK, *s.*, trabalho manual.
HAND.WRIT.ING, *s.*, caligrafia, letra.
HAND.WRIT.TEN, *adj.*, escrito à mão.

HAND.Y, *adj.*, À MÃO; hábil; acessível; prático.
HAND.Y.MAN, *s.*, faz-tudo.
HANG, *v.*, pendurar, enforcar.
HAN.GAR, *s.*, hangar.
HANG-DOG, *adj.*, envergonhado.
HANG.ER, *s.*, cabide.
HANG.ER-ON, *s.*, parasita.
HANG GLIDER, *s.*, asa delta.
HANG GLID.ING, *s.*, *Esp.*, voo livre (com asa-delta).
HANG.ING, *s.*, forca, enforcamento; suspensão (no ar); *hangings*, *s.pl.*: tapeçarias; *adj.*, dependurado.
HANG.MAN, *s.*, carrasco.
HANG.O.VER, *s.*, restos; ressaca de bebedeira.
HANG-UP, *s.*, problema complexo e preocupante.
HANK, *s.*, novelo; alça; madeixa.
HAN.KER, *s.*, desejar, querer muito, ansiar por.
HAN.KER.ING, *s.*, desejo ardente, anelo fortíssimo.
HAN.KY, HAN.KIE, *s.*, *abrev.* de *handkerchief*: lenço, lencinho.
HAP, *s.*, ventura; casualidade; *v.*, acontecer por acaso; suceder.
HAP.HAZ.ARD, *s.*, acaso; *adj.*, casual; caótico, desordenado.
HAP.LESS, *adj.*, infeliz, desgraçado, infausto.
HAP.LESS.NESS, *s.*, infelicidade, desgraça.
HAP.PEN, *v.*, acontecer, suceder, ocorrer.
HAP.PEN.ING, *s.*, acontecimento.
HAP.PI.LY, *adj.*, felizmente.
HAP.PI.NESS, *s.*, felicidade.
HAP.PY, *adj.*, feliz, contente, satisfeito.
HAP.PY HOUR, *s.*, *happy hour* (hora de confraternizar no começo da noite).
HA.RANGUE, *s.*, arenga, ladainha; *v.*, arengar.
HA.RASS, *v.*, importunar, aborrecer, perturbar.
HA.RASSED, *adj.*, perturbado, molestado; esgotado, tenso.
HAR.ASS.MENT, *s.*, aborrecimento; perseguição, assédio.
HAR.BIN.GER, *s.*, *Lit.*, precursor, arauto; *v.*, anunciar.
HAR.BOUR, HAR.BOR, *s.*, porto; *v.*, abrigar, acolher, proteger.
HAR.BOUR.ER, *s.*, *UK* hospedeiro.
HAR.BOUR.LESS, *adj.*, *UK* desabrigado.
HARD, *adj.*, duro, difícil, complicado, árduo, severo, rígido.
HARD.BACK, *s.*, livro encadernado, *adj.*, de capa dura.
HARD-BIT.TEN, *adj.*, duro, inflexível, intratável.
HARD-BOIL, *v.*, cozinhar ovo (bem fervido).
HARD-BOILED, *adj.*, bem cozido (ovo); *fig.*, impassível.
HARD.COV.ER, *adj.*, de capa dura (caderno, livro).
HARD CUR.REN.CY, *s.*, *Econ.*, moeda forte.
HARD DISK, *s.*, *Comp.*, disco rígido.
HARD DRUGS, *s. pl.*, drogas pesada.
HARD.EN, *v.*, endurecer, insensibilizar.
HARD.ENED, *adj.*, endurecido; habitual.
HARD.EN.ING, *s.*, endurecimento, firmeza, dureza.
HARD FEEL.INGS, *s. pl.*, ressentimentos.
HARD-HEAD.ED, *adj.*, realista; teimoso.
HARD-HEART.ED, *adj.*, insensível, cruel.
HARD-HEART.ED.LY, *adv.*, cruelmente.
HAR.DI.HOOD, *s.*, coragem, valentia, intrepidez.
HAR.DI.NESS, *s.*, coragem, valentia, denodo.
HARD LA.BOUR, *s.*, trabalhos forçados.
HARD-LIN.ER, *s.*, linha-dura, radical.
HARD.LY, *adv.*, apenas, somente, mal, logo que.
HARD.NESS, *s.*, dureza, firmeza; dificuldade; insensibilidade.
HARD ROCK, *s.*, *Mús.*, rock pauleira.

HARDSHIP · 485 · HEADHUNTER

HARD.SHIP, s., privação, apuro, dificuldade.
HARD SHOUL.DER, s., acostamento de via.
HARD.WARE, s., ferragens, material componente de um computador.
HARD.WOOD, s., madeira dura (de lei).
HARD.WEAR.ING, adj., durável (vestimenta).
HARD WORK, s., trabalho pesado.
HARD.Y, adj., forte, robusto, resistente; audacioso.
HARE, s., Zool., lebre.
HARE.LIP, s., Med., lábio leporino.
HAR.EM, s., harém.
HAR.I.COT, s., Bot., feijão-branco; vagem do feijão.
HARK, v., ouvir com atenção.
HAR.LE.QUIN, s., arlequim.
HAR.LOT, s., meretriz, prostituta, vagabunda.
HARM, s., mal, dano; v., prejudicar, fazer mal a.
HARM.FUL, adj., prejudicial, nocivo, danoso.
HARM.FUL.NESS, s., maldade, prejuízo, dano.
HARM.LESS, adj., inofensivo, inocente.
HARM.LESS.LY, adv., sem causar dano; inofensivamente.
HAR.MON.IC, s., som harmônico; adj., harmônico.
HAR.MON.I.CA, s., harmônica, gaita.
HAR.MON.ICS, s., Mús., harmonia.
HAR.MO.NI.OUS, adj., harmonioso; concordante.
HAR.MO.NI.OUS.NESS, s., harmonia, musicalidade.
HAR.MO.NIZE, v., harmonizar.
HAR.MO.NI.ZER, s., harmonizador.
HAR.MO.NY, s., harmonia, concordância.
HAR.NESS, s., arreio (cavalo); andador (bebê); ant., arnês, armadura; v., arrear; aproveitar.
HAR.NESS.ER, s., aquele que arreia cavalos.
HARP, s., harpa; v., tocar harpa.
HARP.IST, s., Mús., harpista.
HAR.POON, s., arpão; v., arpoar, pegar com o arpão.
HAR.PY, s., Zool., harpia; Mit., harpia.
HAR.ROW, s., rastelo; v., rastelar; angustiar.
HAR.ROW.ING, adj., angustiante.
HAR.ROW.ING.LY, adv., aflitivamente.
HAR.RY, v., maltratar, assolar, destruir.
HARSH, adj., duro, forte; áspero; desolado.
HARSH.LY, adv., severamente, duramente, asperamente.
HARSH.NESS, s., severidade, dureza, aspereza.
HARTS.HORN, s., Quím., carbonato de amônia (sal de amônia).
HAR.VEST, s., colheita, safra; produto do esforço; v., colher, ceifar; armazenar.
HAS, ps do verbo to have (3ª pessoa: he/she/it has).
HASH, s., Cul., picadinho (carne moída com batata); hash up: UK confusão.
HASH.ISH, s., haxixe.
HASN'T, contr. de has not.
HAS.SLE, s., col., amolação, discussão; v., amolar, incomodar.
HASTE, s., pressa, rapidez; v., apressar (o passo).
HAS.TEN, v., apressar-se, acelerar, ter pressa.
HAST.I.LY, adv., apressadamente; às pressas.
HAST.Y, adj., ligeiro, apressado, precipitado.
HAT, s., chapéu; v., colocar chapéu, cobrir com chapéu.
HAT.BOX, s., chapeleira.
HATCH, s., choco; ninhada, cria; traço fino (desenho); Náut., escotilha; v., chocar, incubar; fazer traços finos.
HATCH.ER, s., chocadeira, incubadora.

HATCH.ER.Y, s., o mesmo que hatcher.
HATCH.ET, s., machadinha.
HATCH.ING, s., incubação, ato de chocar; ato de sombrear desenho.
HATCH.WAY, s., escotilha.
HATE, s., ódio, aversão; v., odiar, detestar.
HATE.A.BLE, adj., detestável.
HATE.FUL, adj., odioso, odiento.
HATE.FUL.LY, adv., odiosamente.
HAT.ER, s., aquele que tem ódio.
HAT.ING, s., ódio, rancor.
HAT.MAK.ER, s., chapeleiro.
HA.TRED, s., ódio, rancor, raiva.
HAUGH.NESS, s., arrogância.
HAUGH.TI.NESS, s., arrogância, orgulho exacerbado.
HAUGH.TY, adj., arrogante.
HAUL, v., puxar, arrastar; s., ato de arrastar; pilhagem.
HAUL.AGE, s., ato de arrastar; transporte, frete.
HAUL.ER, s., aquele que puxa ou arrasta; transportador (usa-se também haulier).
HAUL.ING, s., reboque, transporte.
HAUNCH, s., quadril, anca, quarto traseiro vacum.
HAUNT, s., lugar preferido, retiro, toca; v., assombrar (por fantasmas), perseguir.
HAUNT.ED HOUSE, s., casa mal-assombrada.
HAUNT.ING, adj., inesquecível, obcecante.
HAUT.BOY, s., Mús., oboé.
HAU.TEUR, s., arrogância, soberba, vaidade.
HAVE, v., aux., ter, haver, possuir, deter, conseguir.
HA.VEN, s., porto; refúgio, abrigo.
HAVEN'T, contr. de have not.
HAV.ER.SACK, s., mochila.
HAV.ING, s. pl., bens, haveres.
HAV.OC, s., destruição.
HÁ.WAI.IAN, s., adj., havaiano.
HAWK, s., Zool., falcão; pigarro; fig., embusteiro; v., caçar com falcão; pigarrear; vender mercadorias na rua.
HAWK.ER, s., falcoeiro; camelô, mascate.
HAWK.ING, s., falcoaria.
HAY, s., feno; v., arrumar ou preparar o feno.
HAY.STACK, s., palheiro, paiol.
HAY-WIRE, s., arame de fardos de feno; adj., biruta, enlouquecido.
HAZ.ARD, s., risco, perigo; v., aventurar-se, arriscar-se.
HAZ.ARD.OUS, s., perigoso, arriscado.
HAZ.ARD.OUS.NESS, s., perigo, periculosidade.
HAZE, s., névoa, cerração; v., enevoar, nublar.
HA.ZEL, s., Bot., aveleira; adj., castanho-claro.
HA.ZEL.NUT, s., avelã.
HAZ.I.NESS, s., cerração, névoa, nebulosidade.
HAZY, adj., nublado, escuro, enevoado.
HE, pron., ele, aquele; s., menino, homem.
HEAD, s., cabeça, ponta, frente, chefe, diretor.
HEAD.ACHE, s., dor de cabeça.
HEAD.BAND, s., faixa para a cabeça, bandana.
HEAD.BOARD, s., cabeceira.
HEAD COLD, s., resfriado.
HEAD.DRESS, s., touca.
HEAD.ER, s., Esp., cabeçada (futebol).
HEAD.HUNT, v., contratar.
HEAD.HUNT.ER, s., caça-talentos; recrutador de executivos.

HEADINESS · 486 · HEGEMONY

HEAD.I.NESS, *s.*, teimosia, obstinação, cabeça dura.
HEAD.ING, *s.*, cabeçalho.
HEAD.LAND, *s.*, promontório.
HEAD.LIGHT, *s.*, farol.
HEAD.LESS, *adj.*, decapitado, sem cabeça.
HEAD.LIGHT, *s.*, farol de carro.
HEAD.LINE, *s.*, manchete; notícia principal.
HEAD.MAN, *s.*, chefe, dirigente, diretor.
HEAD.MAS.TER, *s.*, diretor de escola.
HEAD OF.FICE, *s.*, sede, matriz.
HEAD-ON, *adj.*, frontal, de frente; *adv.*, frontalmente, de frente.
HEAD.PHONES, *s. pl.*, fones de ouvido.
HEAD.QUAR.TERS, *s.*, sede de empresa, quartel-general.
HEAD.REST, *s.*, apoio para a cabeça.
HEAD.ROOM, *s.*, pé-direito, medida do piso até o teto.
HEAD.SHIP, *s.*, direção, domínio, chefia.
HEADS.MAN, *s.*, carrasco, verdugo.
HEAD.STONE, *s.*, lápide.
HEAD.STRONG, *adj.*, cabeça-dura, obstinado.
HEAD TEACHER, *s.*, diretor (de escola).
HEAD.WORD, *s.*, entrada (em dicionário), verbete.
HEAD.WORK, *s.*, trabalho intelectual.
HEAD.Y, *adj.*, emocionante; inebriante; estimulante; impetuoso.
HEAL, *v.*, curar, sarar.
HEAL.ING, *s.*, cura; *adj.*, saudável, curativo.
HEAL OVER, *v.*, curar, sarar.
HEALTH, *s.*, saúde.
HEALTH CEN.TRE, *s.*, *UK* centro de saúde.
HEALTH FOOD, *s.*, alimento saudável ou natural.
HEALTH.FUL, *adj.*, saudável, sanado, são, curado.
HEALTH.FUL.NESS, *s.*, saúde.
HEALTH.SOME, *adj.*, saudável.
HEALTH.Y, *adj.*, saudável, saneado, são.
HEAP, *s.*, montÃO, pilha; *v.*, amontoar.
HEAR, *v.*, ouvir, escutar, sentir, perceber.
HEAR.ER, *s.*, ouvinte, auditor, quem ouve.
HEAR FROM, *v.*, receber notícias, ser informado.
HEAR.ING, *s.*, audição, ouvido; interrogatório.
HEAR.ING AID, *s.*, *Med.*, aparelho auditivo, audiofone.
HEARK.EN, *v.*, ouvir atentamente.
HEAR.SAY, *s.*, boato, história.
HEARSE, *s.*, carro funerário.
HEART, *s.*, *Anat.*, coração (sist. cardiovascular); centro, núcleo, âmago, local central, copas; *fig.*, amor, coragem.
HEART.ACHE, *s.*, sofrimento, angústia.
HEART AT.TACK, *s.*, *Med.*, ataque cardíaco.
HEART.BEAT, *s.*, batida do coração, pulsação do coração.
HEART.BREAK, *s.*, sofrimento, mágoa.
HEART.BREAK.ING, *adj.*, de partir o coração.
HEART.BRO.KEN, *adj.*, de coração partido.
HEART.BURN, *s.*, azia (queimação no estômago).
HEART.BURN.ING, *s.*, rancor, ressentimento, ciúme.
HEART-DIS.EASE, *s.*, *Med.*, cardiopatia.
HEART.ED, *adj.*, de coração (*big-hearted*: de grande generosidade, *cold-hearted*: desalmado).
HEART.EN.ING, *adj.*, animador, encorajamento.
HEART.FELT, *adj.*, de todo o coração, sincero, franco.
HEARTH, *s.*, lar, morada, lareira, forno.
HEART.I.NESS, *s.*, cordialidade, amizade, sinceridade.
HEART.LAND, *s.*, área central (na política e economia).

HEART.LESS, *adj.*, cruel, sem coração; sem ânimo.
HEART.LESS.NESS, *s.*, crueldade, covardia.
HEART.LESS.LY, *s.*, cruelmente, melancolicamente.
HEART RATE, *s.*, batimento cardíaco.
HEART.SICK, *adj.*, melancólico, deprimido.
HEART.WARM.ING, *adj.*, agradável, gratificante.
HEART.Y, *adj.*, amável; animado, enérgico, sincero, genuíno; substancioso (alimento).
HEAT, *s.*, calor, ardor, excitação, entusiasmo; *v.*, aquecer, esquentar; excitar(-se), inflamar.
HEAT.ED, *adj.*, aquecido (ambiente); esquentado, exaltado.
HEAT.ER, *s.*, aquecedor; *gír.*, ferro (revólver).
HEATH, *s.*, charneca; urzal.
HEA.THEN, *adj.*, *s.*, pagão, não batizado.
HEA.THEN.ISM, *s.*, paganismo; brutalidade.
HEATH.ER, *s.*, *Bot.*, urze.
HEAT.ING, *s.*, aquecimento, calefação.
HEAT-RE.SIS.TANT, *adj.*, resistente ao calor.
HEAT.STROKE, *s.*, insolação.
HEAT WAVE, *s.*, onda de calor.
HEAVE, *v.*, puxar, empurrar, levantar, alçar; *s.*, hasteamento.
HEAV.EN, *s.*, céu, paraíso, éden; Divina Providência.
HEAV.EN.LI.NESS, *s.*, divindade.
HEAV.EN.LY, *adj.*, celeste, celestial, divino.
HEAV.I.LY, *adv.*, excessivamente, severamente, pesadamente, profundamente.
HEAV.I.NESS, *s.*, peso; preguiça; aflição.
HEAV.Y, *adj.*, pesado, duro, resistente; violento; rústico.
HEAV.Y IN.DUS.TRY, *s.*, indústria pesada.
HEAV.Y NEWS, *s. pl.*, más notícias.
HEAV.Y WEIGHT, *adj.*, *Esp.*, peso-pesado (boxe).
HEB.DOM.A.DAL, *adj.*, hebdomadário, semanal.
HE.BRA.IC, *adj.*, hebraico.
HE.BREW, *adj.*, *s.*, hebraico, hebreu.
HEC.A.TOMB, *s.*, hecatombe, matança, destruição.
HECK, *s.*, vara para pescar.
HECK.LE, *v.*, importunar, incomodar, interromper.
HECK.LER, *s.*, aquele que interrompe conversas com perguntas chatas.
HECT.ARE, *s.*, hectare.
HEC.TIC, *adj.*, *col.*, muito agitado; febril.
HEC.TIC FE.VER, *s.*, tuberculose, tísica.
HEC.TO.ME.TER, *s.*, hectômetro (equivalente a 100 metros).
HEC.TOR, *s.*, valentão, metido; *v.*, maltratar, machucar.
HE.DERA, *s.*, era, erva trepadeira.
HEDGE, *s.*, cerca viva; *v.*, dar evasivas.
HEDGE.HOG, *s.*, *Zool.*, porco-espinho.
HEDGE.ROW, *s.*, sebe, cerca viva.
HE.DON.ISM, *s.*, *Fis.*, hedonismo.
HE.DON.IST, *s.*, hedonista.
HEED, *s.*, atenção, cuidado; *v.*, dar atenção, ter cuidado.
HEED.FUL, *adj.*, cuidadoso, cauteloso.
HEED.FUL.NESS, *s.*, cuidado, atenção, cautela.
HEED.LESS, *adj.*, desatento, descuidado, negligente.
HEED.LESS.NESS, *s.*, descuido, insensatez.
HEEL, *s.*, *Anat.*, calcanhar; salto do sapato; *v.*, pregar salto em.
HEEL.ER, *s.*, sapateiro que conserta saltos; *pej.*, sabujo de político.
HEFT.Y, *adj.*, *col.*, robusto, vultoso, alto.
HEG.E.MON.IC, *adj.*, hegemônico.
HE.GE.MO.NY, *s.*, hegemonia, supremacia, domínio.

HEIFER ··487·· HESITANCY

HEIF.ER, s., novilha, bezerra.
HEIGHT, s., tamanho, altura, estatura.
HEIGHT.EN, v., levantar, elevar, aumentar; fortificar.
HEI.NOUS, adj., odioso, nefando, asqueroso, perverso, cruel.
HEI.NOUS.NESS, s., atrocidade, perversidade.
HEIR, s., herdeiro.
HEIR.DOM, s., herança, direito a herdar.
HEIR.ESS, s., herdeira.
HEIR.LOOM, s., relíquia (peça antiga ou de herança de família).
HEIST, s., roubo, assalto.
HE.LI.COP.TER, s., helicóptero.
HE.LI.O.CEN.TRIC, adj., Astron., heliocêntrico.
HE.LI.OG.RA.PHY, s., heliografia.
HE.LI.O.GRA.VURE, s., heliogravura.
HE.LI.PORT, s., heliporto.
HE.LI.UM, s., Quím., hélio.
HE.LIX, s., hélice.
HELL, s., inferno.
HE'LL, contr. de he will.
HELL-BENT, adj., totalmente decidido; inescrupuloso.
HEL.LEN.IC, adj., helênico.
HEL.LE.NISM, s., helenismo.
HEL.LE.NIS.TIC, adj., helenístico.
HELL.ISH, adj., infernal.
HELL.MOUTH, s., boca do inferno.
HEL.LO!, interj., oi!, olá! Salve!
HELM, s., elmo; Náut., leme (de navio); direção.
HEL.MET, s., elmo, capacete.
HEL.MINTH, s., Zool., helminto (verme do intestino).
HELMS.MAN, s., Náut., timoneiro.
HELP, s., ajuda, auxílio; v., ajudar, socorrer, auxiliar.
HELP.ER, s., ajudante, auxiliar.
HELP.FUL, adj., prestativo, prestimoso, solícito.
HELP.FUL.NESS, s., obsequiosidade, utilidade, assistência.
HELP.FUL.LY, adv., proveitosamente, utilmente.
HELP.ING, s., ajuda; porção (de alimento).
HELP.LESS, adj., indefeso, abandonado.
HELP.LESS.LY, adv., sem ajuda; impotentemente.
HELP LINE, s., apoio emocional por telefone.
HELP.MATE, s., colega, companheiro, ajudante.
HEL.TER-SKEL.TER, s., pressa, precipitação; UK tobogã gigante; adv., desordenadamente, confusamente.
HEL.VE.TIAN, adj., s., helvético, suíço.
HEL.VET.IC, adj., helvético, suíço.
HEM, s., bainha, margem; pigarro; v., embainhar, colocar na bainha; pigarrear.
HE.MA.TITE, s., Min., hematita.
HE.MA.TOL.O.GY, s., hematologia.
HEM.I.SPHERE, s., hemisfério.
HEM.I.SPHER.IC, adj., hemisférico.
HEM.LINE, s., altura da bainha (vestido saia).
HE.MO.GLO.BIN, s., hemoglobina.
HE.MO.PHIL.I.A, s., Med., hemofilia.
HE.MO.PHIL.I.AC, s., Med., hemofílico.
HEM.OR.RHAGE, s., hemorragia; v., ter ou sofrer hemorragia.
HEM.OR.RHOIDS, s., Med., hemorroidas..
HEMP, s., Bot., cânhamo.
HEMP.EN, s., de cânhamo.
HEN, s., galinha, fêmea de qualquer ave.
HENCE, adv., daqui a, por isso, por esse motivo; v., afastar-se.

HENCE.FORTH, adv., daqui em diante, doravante.
HENCH.MAN, s., pej., capanga; jagunço.
HEN.NA, s., Bot., hena; v., aplicar hena.
HEN.NERY, s., galinheiro.
HEN.PECK, v., dominar o marido.
HEN.PECK.ET, adj., pej., submisso, dominado.
HE.PAT.IC, adj., hepático.
HEP.A.TI.TIS, s., Med., hepatite.
HER, pron., a, lhe, seu, sua.
HER.ALD, s., arauto, mensageiro; v., anunciar, conclamar.
HE.RAL.DIC, adj., heráldico.
HER.ALD.RY, s., heráldica (ciência dos brasões).
HERB, s., erva; ervas aromáticas; gír., maconha.
HER.BA.CEOUS, , adj., herbáceo.
HERB.AGE, s., pasto, pastagem.
HERB.AL.IST, s., herbanário; Arc., botânico.
HER.BI.CIDE, s., herbicida.
HER.BI.VORE, s., herbívoro.
HER.BIV.O.ROUS, adj., herbívoro.
HER.CU.LE.AN, adj., hercúleo, que tem força fenomenal.
HERD, s., rebanho; v., compor um rebanho, arrebanhar, associar, reunir.
HERDS.MAN, s., pastor, boiadeiro, vaqueiro.
HERE, adv., aqui, neste local.
HERE.ABOUT, adv., por aqui, nas vizinhanças.
HERE.AF.TER, adv., daqui por diante.
HERE.BY, adv., por meio deste ou disto, por isto.
HER.E.DIT.A.MENT, s., herança, propriedades.
HE.RED.I.TAR.I.LY, adv., por herança.
HE.RED.I.TA.RY, adj., hereditário.
HE.RED.I.TY, s., hereditariedade.
HERE.FROM, adv., disto, daqui.
HERE.IN, adv., aqui dentro, incluso, incluído.
HERE.IN.TO, adv., neste lugar.
HER.E.SY, s., heresia.
HER.E.TIC, s., herege.
HE.RET.I.CAL, adj., herético.
HERE.WITH, adv., com isto.
HER.I.TA.BLE, adj., herdável, que se pode herdar.
HER.IT.AGE, s., herança.
HER.IT.OR, s., herdeiro.
HER.MAPH.RO.DITE, s., hermafrodita.
HER.ME.NEU.TIC, s., hermenêutica.
HER.MET.IC, adj., hermético, fechado.
HER.MET.I.CAL.LY, adv., hermeticamente.
HER.MIT, s., ermitão, eremita.
HER.MIT.AGE, s., eremitério; lugar solitário.
HER.NIA, s., Med., hérnia.
HE.RO, s., herói, protagonista de uma cena.
HE.RO.IC, adj., heroico.
HER.O.IN, s., Quím., heroína (droga).
HER.O.INE, s., heroína (mulher de valor).
HER.O.ISM, s., heroísmo.
HER.ON, s., Zool., garça.
HER.PES, s., Med., herpes.
HER.PET.IC, adj., Med., herpético.
HER.RING, s., Zool., arenque.
HERS, pron., lhe (a ela), seu, sua, dela.
HER.SELF, pron., si, se, ela mesma, ele mesmo.
HE'S, contr. de he is, he has.
HES.I.TAN.CY, s., hesitação, vacilação.

HESITANT
•• 488 ••
HISTORIC PLACES

HES.I.TANT, *adj.*, hesitante, vacilante.
HES.I.TANT.LY *adv.*, indecisamente.
HES.I.TATE, *v.*, hesitar, vacilar.
HES.I.TA.TION, *s.*, hesitação, vacilação.
HET.ERO.DOX, *adj.*, heterodoxo.
HET.ERO.GE.NEOUS, *adj.*, heterogêneo.
HET.ERO.NY.MOUS, *s.*, heterônimo.
HET.ERO.SEX.U.AL, *adj.*, heterossexual.
HET-UP, *adj.*, nervoso, uma pilha de nervos.
HEW, *v.*, cortar, cortar com machado.
HEX, *s., col.*, praga; bruxa.
HEX.A.GON, *s.*, hexágono.
HEX.AG.O.NAL, *adj.*, hexagonal.
HEY, *interj.*, ei!
HEY.DAY, *s.*, auge, apogeu.
HI, *interj.*, oi!, olá!
HI.A.TUS, *s.*, hiato.
HI.BER.NAL, *adj.*, invernal, hibernal.
HI.BER.NATE, *v.*, hibernar.
HI.BER.NA.TION, *s.*, hibernação.
HI.BIS.CUS, *s., Bot.*, hibisco.
HIC.CUP, HIC.COUGH, *s.*, soluço; *v.*, soluçar.
HICK, *s., col.*, caipira.
HID.DEN, *v., pp* de *hide*; *adj.*, secreto, escondido, oculto; embutido.
HIDE, *s.*, couro, pele; *v.*, esconder(-se), ocultar; *col.*, espancar.
HIDE AND SEEK, *s.*, esconde-esconde.
HIDE.AWAY, *s.*, esconderijo; *adj.*, escondido.
HIDE.BOUND, *adj.*, de pele colada aos ossos (gado); *fig.*, mesquinho; *pej.*, antiquado, careta.
HID.E.OUS, *adj.*, horrível, medonho, horrendo.
HID.E.OUS.NESS, *s.*, horror, feiura, pavor.
HIDE.OUT, *s.*, esconderijo (de criminosos).
HID.ER, *s.*, aquele que esconde.
HID.ING, *s.*, sova, surra; ato de esconder-se.
HID.ING PLACE, *s.*, esconderijo.
HI.ER.AR.CHIC, *adj.*, hierárquico.
HI.ER.AR.CHI.CAL, *adj.*, hierárquico.
HI.ER.AR.CHY, *s.*, hierarquia.
HI.ER.O.GLYPH, *s.*, hieróglifo (melhor no *pl. hieroglyphics*: hieróglifos).
HI-FI, *s.*, sistema *hi-fi* (abrev. de *high fidelity*).
HIGH, *adj.*, alto, forte, elevado, grande, superior.
HIGH AL.TAR, *s.*, altar-mor.
HIGH.BROW, *adj.*, intelectual, erudito; *s., col.*, sabichão.
HIGH CHAIR, *s.*, cadeira alta de bebê.
HIGH-CLASS, *adj.*, de alta classe; de qualidade superior.
HIGH COM.MAND, *s., Mil.*, alto comando.
HIGH COURT, *s.*, Suprema Corte.
HIGH.ER, *adj.*, superior.
HIGH.ER ED.U.CA.TION, *s.*, ensino superior.
HIGH FI.DEL.I.TY, *s.*, alta fidelidade (*abrev.: hi-fi*).
HIGH FLY.ING, *adj.*, ambicioso.
HIGH-HAND.ED, *adj.*, arbitrário, despótico; embusteiro.
HIGH-HAT, *adj.*, arrogante, grã-fino, janota.
HIGH-HEELED, *adj.*, de salto alto.
HIGH.LAND, *s.*, montanhas.
HIGH.LAND.ER, *s.*, montanhês, escocês.
HIGH-LEV.EL, *adj.*, de alto nível, do alto escalão.
HIGH.LIGHT, *s., fig.*, ponto alto, destaque; *v.*, realçar, enfatizar.
HIGH.LY, *adv.*, altamente; favoravelmente.

HIGH.NESS, *s.*, alteza; *His/Her* ~: Sua Majestade.
HIGH POINT, *s.*, ponto culminante.
HIGH-RISK, *adj.*, de alto risco.
HIGH SCHOOL, *s., US* escolar secundária, ensino médio.
HIGH-SPEED, *adj.*, de alta velocidade.
HIGH-TECH, *adj.*, de alta tecnologia (abrev. de *high-technology*).
HIGH TECH.NOL.O.GY, *s.*, alta tecnologia.
HIGH TIDE, *s.*, maré alta; *fig.*, ponto culminante.
HIGH.WAY, *s.*, autoestrada, rodovia.
HI.JACK, *v.*, sequestrar (avião, ônibus).
HI.JACK.ER, *s.*, sequestrador.
HIKE, *s.*, marcha, caminhada; marchar, caminhar, andar, ir.
HIK.ER, *s.*, caminhante, pedestre.
HIK.ING, *s.*, excursão a pé, caminhada.
HI.LA.RI.OUS, *adj.*, hilário, hilariante, engraçado; contente.
HI.LAR.I.TY, *s.*, hilaridade; alegria.
HILL, *s.*, colina, cômoro, elevação; *v.*, amontoar.
HILL.OCK, *s.*, pequena colina, outeiro.
HILL.SIDE, *s.*, encosta, ladeira, declive.
HILL.TOP, *s.*, topo do morro; *adj.*, no topo do morro.
HILL.Y, *adj.*, montanhoso.
HILT, *s.*, cabo (de faca ou espada).
HILT.ED, *adj.*, que tem cabo.
HIM, *pron.*, o, lhe (a ele).
HIM.SELF, *pron.*, ele mesmo, ela mesma, si, se, o, lhe.
HIND, *s., Zool.*, corça; *adj.*, traseiro, posterior.
HIND.ER, *v.*, retardar, atrapalhar, obstruir; *adj.*, traseiro.
HIN.DER.ER, *s.*, aquele que atrapalha, estorvador.
HIND.LEG, *s.*, perna traseira.
HIND.MOST, *adv.*, mais atrasado.
HIN.DRANCE, *s.*, obstáculo, atrasos.
HIN.DU, *adj., s.*, hindu, indiano.
HIN.DU.ISM, *s.*, hinduísmo.
HINGE, *s.*, dobradiça; *v.*, colocar dobradiças.
HIN.NY, *s., Zool.*, mulo, mula.
HINT, *s.*, insinuação, ideia, palpite; *v.*, insinuar.
HIN.TER.LAND, *s.*, interior (de um Estado ou país).
HIP, *s.*, quadril, anca; *adj.*, moderno, em harmonia; *interj., abrev.* de *hip*, hip hurra!.
HIP-BONE, *s., Anat.*, osso ilíaco.
HIP-HOP, *s., Mús.*, hip-hop.
HIP.PIE, *s.*, hippie (contra-cultura da década de 60).
HIP.PO, *s., abrev.* de *hippopotamus.*, hipopótamo.
HIP.PO.DROME, *s., Zool.*, hipódromo.
HIP.PO.POT.A.MUS, *s.*, hipopótamo.
HIRE, *v.*, alugar carro; *s.*, aluguel.
HIR.ER, *s.*, alugador, locatário.
HIR.PLE, *v.*, coxear.
HIS, *pron.*, o, seu, seus, sua, suas, os.
HIS.PAN.IC, *s., adj.*, hispânico.
HISS, *v.*, assobiar, vaiar, assuar; *s.*, assobio, vaia.
HIST!, *interj.*, psiu!, silêncio!
HIS.TOL.O.GY, *s.*, histologia.
HIS.TO.RI.AN, *s.*, historiador.
HIS.TOR.IC, *adj.*, histórico.
HIS.TOR.I.CAL, *adj.*, histórico.
HIS.TOR.I.CAL.LY, *adv.*, historicamente.
HIS.TOR.I.CIZE, *v.*, tornar histórico, historicizar.
HIS.TO.RIC.I.TY, *s.*, historicidade.
HIS.TOR.IC PLACES, *s. pl.*, lugares históricos.

HISTORIC SITE ·· 489 ·· HONDURAN

HIS.TOR.IC SITE, *s.*, patrimônio histórico (também se usa *heritage centre*).
HIS.TO.RY, *s.*, história.
HIS.TRI.ON.IC, *adj.*, histriônico, teatral; que não é sincero.
HIS.TRI.ON.ICS, *s. pl.*, arte teatral; *pej.*, melodrama.
HIT, *s.*, golpe, pancada; sorte; crítica; *v.*, dar uma pancada; atingir.
HITCH, *s.*, puxão, obstáculo, nó; ação de amarrar; *v.*, atar, amarrar, prender.
HITCH.HIKE, *v.*, viajar de carona.
HITCH.HIK.ER, *s.*, caroneiro(a).
HITCH.ING, *s.*, amarração.
HI-TECH, *s.*, alta tecnologia, tecnologia de ponta.
HITH.ER, *adj.*, junto, deste lado, mais perto; *adv.*, para cá.
HITH.ER.TO, *adv.*, até agora, até aqui.
HIT PA.RADE, *s.*, parada de sucessos.
HIT.TER, *s.*, rebatedor (beisebol); acerto, sorte.
HIV, *s.*, *HIV* (abrev. de *Human Immunodeficiency Virus*: Vírus da Imunodeficiência Humana).
HIVE, *s.*, colmeia, cortiço, enxame.
HIVES, *s.*, *Med.*, urticária.
HOAR, *s.*, brancura, velhice; geada; *adj.*, grisalho, antigo.
HOARD, *s.*, mealheiro, acúmulo (às escondidas); *v.*, juntar, acumular.
HOARD.ING, *s.*, provisionamento às escondidas, economias; tapume, tabique.
HOAR-FROST, *s.*, geada.
HOAR.I.NESS, *s.*, brancura (de cabelos grisalhos), velhice.
HOARSE, *adj.*, rouco.
HOARSE.LY, *adv.*, roucamente.
HOARSE.NESS, *s.*, rouquidão.
HOAX, *s.*, trote, logro, embuste; *v.*, pregar peça, fraudar.
HOAX.ER, *s.*, aquele que passa trote, embusteiro.
HOB.BLE, *s.*, coxeadura; *fig.*, embaraço; *v.*, coxear, mancar; estorvar, impedir.
HOB.BLER, *s.*, manco, coxo.
HOB.BLING.LY, *s.*, de modo manco.
HOB.BY, *s.*, passatempo, diversão, lazer.
HOB.GO.BLIN, *s.*, duende, bicho-papão.
HOB.NOB, *v.*, conversar; beber (com amigos); *adv.*, a esmo.
HOCK, *s.*, jarrete; penhor, débito; prego; *v.*, jarretar; empenhar (valores); pôr no prego.
HOCK.EY, *s.*, *Esp.*, hóquei.
HO.CUS-PO.CUS, *s.*, truque, artifício; *v.*, enganar, iludir.
HOD, *s.*, cocho de pedreiro; padiola de carvão.
HOE, *s.*, enxada; *v.*, cavar com enxada, capinar.
HOE.CAKE, *s.*, bolo de milho.
HOE.DOWN, *s.*, quadrilha (dança, música); festa.
HOER, *s.*, carpidor, capinador.
HOG, *s.*, porco capado; *pej.*, comilona; *v.*, cortar pelo ou crina; *col.*, dono da estrada, comer e beber muito.
HOG.GERY, *s.*, porcaria, sujeira, imundície; grosseria.
HOG-TIE, *v.*, amarrar as quatro patas; algemar; *fig.*, frustrar.
HOIST, *v.*, alçar, içar.
HOKE, *v.*, exagerar (falar mais do que é); falsificar.
HOLD, *s.*, ato de segurar, impressão (de alguém); cadeia; *v.*, pegar, conter, segurar, ter, realizar; resistir.
HOLD-ALL, *s.*, mala de mão, *UK holdall*: mochila.
HOLD.ER, *s.*, proprietário, dono; recipiente; detentor de títulos.
HOLD.ING, *s.*, ato de segurar; propriedade rural; ações;

adj., controlador.
HOLD-UP, *s.*, assalto à mão armada; atraso, empecilho.
HOLD WITH, *v.*, concordar com.
HOLE, *s.*, buraco, furo; cova; *v.*, cavar, esburacar.
HOL.I.DAY, *s.*, férias, dia de folga, feriado; dia santo.
HOL.I.DAY-MAK.ER, *s.*, excursionista.
HO.LI.NESS, *s.*, santidade.
HO.LISM, *s.*, *Fil.*, holismo.
HOL.LAND, *s.*, Holanda (condado de *Netherlands*).
HOL.LAND.ER, *adj.*, *s.*, holandês.
HOL.LER, *s.*, grito; *v.*, gritar.
HOL.LOW, *s.*, cavidade; *adj.*, oco, vazio, côncavo, falso.
HOL.LOW.NESS, *s.*, concavidade; falsidade.
HOL.LY, *s.*, *Bot.*, azevinho.
HO.LO.CAUST, *s.*, holocausto.
HOL.O.CENE, *s.*, *adj. Geol.*, holoceno (época do período quaternário).
HO.LO.GRAM, *s.*, *Fís.*, holograma.
HOLS, *s. pl.*, *UK* férias, folgas.
HOL.STER, *s.*, coldre.
HO.LY, *s.*, santuário; *adj.*, sagrado, santo, puro, santificado.
HO.LY BI.BLE, *s.*, Bíblia Sagrada.
HO.LY COM.MU.NION, *s.*, Sagrada Comunhão.
HO.LY GRAIL, *s.*, Santo Graal.
HOM.AGE, *s.*, homenagem; *v.*, homenagear.
HOME, *s.*, lar, casa, morada; pátria, país.
HOME AD.DRESS, *s.*, endereço residencial.
HOME BANK.ING, *s.*, página bancária na internet.
HOME-COM.ING, *s.*, volta ao lar (depois de uma ausência).
HOME DE.LIV.ER.Y, *s.*, entrega em domicílio.
HOME-LAND, *s.*, terra pátria, terra natal.
HOME.LESS, *adj.*, sem casa, sem teto.
HOME.LY, *adj.*, simples, rústico; inculto.
HOME.MADE, *s.*, caseiro, feito em casa.
HO.MEO.PATH, *s.*, o mesmo que *homoeopath*.
HO.MEO.PATH.IC, *adj.*, o mesmo que *homoeopathic*.
HO.ME.OP.A.THY, *s.*, o mesmo que *homoeopathy*.
HOME-OWN.ER, *s.*, proprietário da casa.
HOME PAGE, *s.*, página inicial de um site de internet.
HOME-SPUN, *adj.*, feito em casa (pano); *fig.*, tosco.
HOME.WARD, *adj.*, de regresso; *homewards*, *adv.*, para casa.
HOME.WORK, *s.*, trabalho de casa, tarefa.
HO.MI.CIDE, *s.*, homicida; homicídio.
HOM.ING, *adj.*, que se refere ao instinto do lar.
HOM.ING PI.GEON, *s.*, pombo-correio.
HOM.I.LY, *s.*, homilia, sermão, prédica.
HO.MOE.O.PATH, *s.*, homeopata.
HO.MOE.O.PATH.IC, *adj.*, homeopático.
HO.MOE.OP.A.THY, *s.*, homeopatia.
HO.MO.GE.NE.I.TY, *s.*, homogeneidade.
HO.MOG.E.NEOUS, *adj.*, homogêneo.
HO.MO.GE.NIZE, *v.*, homogeneizar.
HO.MOL.O.GOUS, *adj.*, homólogo.
HO.MOL.O.GY, *s.*, homologia.
HOM.O.NYM, *s.*, homônimo.
HO.MO.PHO.BI.A, *s.*, homofobia.
HO.MO.PHO.BIC, *adj.*, homofóbico.
HO.MO.PHONE, *s.*, homófono.
HO.MO.SEX.U.AL, *s.*, *adj.*, homossexual.
HO.MO.SEX.U.AL.I.TY, *s.*, homossexualismo.
HON.DU.RAN, *s.*, *adj.*, hondurenho.

HONE   •• 490 ••   HOUSEHOLD

HONE, *s.*, pedra de amolar; *v.*, afiar, amolar; aprimorar.

HON.EST, *adj.*, honesto, correto, franco, sincero.

HON.EST.LY, *adv.*, honestamente; sinceramente.

HON.ES.TY, *s.*, honestidade, honradez, sinceridade.

HON.EY, *s.*, mel; doçura; *v.*, adoçar; *adj.*, estimado.

HONEY-BEE, *s.*, *Zool.*, abelha operária.

HON.EY.COMB, *s.*, favo de mel.

HON.EYED, *adj.*, melífero.

HON.EY-MOON, *s.*, lua de mel.

HONK, *s.*, buzina; *v.*, buzinar.

HON.OR.ARY, *adj.*, honorário, grátis, não remunerado.

HON.OR.I.FIC, *adj.*, honorífico.

HON.OUR, *v.*, honrar, prestigiar; *s.*, honra, prestígio.

HON.OUR.A.BLE *UK*, **HON.OR.A.BLE** *US*, *adj.*, honrado.

HON.OUR.A.BLY *UK*, **HON.OR.A.BLY** *US*, *adv.*, honrosamente.

HOOCH, *s.*, *col.*, bebida alcoólica (ilegal).

HOOD, *s.*, capuz, capota de carro, tampa de panela.

HOOD.ED, *adj.*, mascarado; coberto, vedado.

HOOD.LUM, *s.*, arruaceiro, criminoso.

HOOD.WINK, *v.*, enganar, lograr.

HOO.EY, *s.*, *col.*, bobagem.

HOOF, *s.*, unha (de animal), casco, pata.

HOOK, *s.*, gancho, anzol, armadilha, laço; *v.*, fisgar, pescar com anzol.

HOOKED, *adj.*, curvo, curvado; *col.*, atraído, obcecado.

HOOK.ER, *s.*, *Náut.*, barco de pesca pequeno; *col.*, prostituta.

HOO.LI.GAN, *s.*, desordeiro, baderneiro.

HOOP, *s.*, arco; *v.*, arcar, pôr arcos em.

HOOPED, *adj.*, arqueado.

HOOT, *v.*, buzinar tocar, piar, chiar.

HOOT.ER, *s.*, buzina, sirene.

HOO.VER, *s.*, aspirador; *v.*, aspirar.

HOP, *s.*, pulo; salto; pulinho (viagem curta de avião); *Bot.*, lúpulo; *gir.*, ópio; *v.*, pular, saltar; viajar.

HOPE, *s.*, esperança, fé, espera; *v.*, esperar, ter esperança.

HOPE CHEST, *s.*, baú do enxoval.

HOPE.FUL, *adj.*, esperançoso, crédulo, otimista.

HOPE.FUL.LY, *adv.*, esperançosamente, com sorte.

HOPE.LESS, *adj.*, desesperado, angustiado, sem fé.

HOP.PER, *s.*, saltador; inseto pulador; tremonha (de moinho).

HOP-SCOTCH, *s.*, amarelinha (jogo infantil).

HORDE, *s.*, horda, multidão, bando, leva.

HO.RI.ZON, *s.*, horizonte.

HO.RI.ZON.TAL, *s.*, plano horizontal; *adj.*, horizontal.

HOR.MO.NAL, *adj.*, hormonal.

HOR.MONE, *s.*, hormônio.

HORN, *s.*, chifre, corno, galho; buzina de carro.

HORNED, *adj.*, cornífero, cornudo, galhudo.

HOR.NET, *s.*, *Zool.*, vespão.

HORN.Y, *adj.*, feito de chifre, calejado; excitado (sexualmente).

HORO.GRAPHY, *s.*, horografia.

HOR.O.LOGE, *s.*, cronômetro, relógio.

HOR.O.LOG.ER, *s.*, fabricante de relógios, relojoeiro.

HORO.SCOPE, *s.*, horóscopo.

HOR.REN.DOUS, *adj.*, horrendo, horrível, nefando.

HOR.RI.BLE, *adj.*, horrível, terrível, pavoroso, medonho.

HOR.RI.BLY, *adv.*, horrivelmente, terrivelmente.

HOR.RID, *adj.*, horrível, hórrido.

HOR.RID.NESS, *s.*, horror, pavor.

HOR.RIF.IC, *adj.*, horrendo, horroroso.

HOR.RI.FY, *v.*, horrorizar.

HOR.ROR, *s.*, horror.

HOR.ROR-STRUCK, *adj.*, em pânico.

HORSE, *s.*, *Zool.*, cavalo; *fig.*, garanhão; *v.*, montar a cavalo.

HORSE.BACK, *s.*, dorso de cavalo; *adv.*, a cavalo.

HORSE.BOX *UK*, **HORSE-CAR** *US*, *s.*, reboque para transportar cavalos.

HORSE-DOC.TOR, *s.*, veterinário.

HORSE.FLY, *s.*, *Zool.*, mutuca.

HORSE.MAN, *s.*, cavaleiro.

HORSE.MAN.SHIP, *s.*, equitação, cavalaria.

HORSE.POW.ER, *s.*, cavalo-vapor.

HORSE.RAD.ISH, *s.* *Bot.*, raiz-forte, rábano-picante.

HORSE.SHOE, *s.*, ferradura.

HORSE.WOM.AN, *s.*, cavaleira, amazona.

HORSY, *adj.*, equino, referente a cavalos.

HOR.TI.CUL.TURE, *s.*, horticultura.

HOR.TI.CUL.TUR.IST, *s.*, horticultor.

HO.SAN.NA, *interj.*, hosana.

HOSE, *s.*, mangueira, meias, tubo de mangueira.

HOSE.PIPE, *s.*, mangueira (para líquidos).

HO.SIERY, *s.*, meias, roupas íntimas.

HOS.PICE, *s.*, albergue, abrigo, asilo.

HOS.PI.TA.BLE, *adj.*, hospitaleiro.

HOS.PI.TA.BLE.NESS, *s.*, hospitalidade.

HOS.PI.TAL, *s.*, hospital.

HOS.PI.TAL.I.TY, *s.*, hospitalidade.

HOS.PI.TAL.IZE, *v.*, hospitalizar.

HOST, *s.*, anfitrião; apresentador de TV ou rádio; hóstia.

HOS.TAGE, *s.*, refém.

HOS.TEL, *s.*, albergue, hospedaria, alojamento.

HOS.TEL.RY, *s.*, estalagem; o mesmo que *hostel*.

HOSTESS, *s.*, anfitriã, hospedeira, recepcionista, garçonete.

HOS.TILE, *adj.*, hostil, adverso, agressivo.

HOS.TIL.I.TIES, *s. pl.*, hostilidades, ressentimentos.

HOS.TIL.I.TY, *s.*, hostilidade.

HOT, *adj.*, quente, quentíssimo, picante.

HOTCH-POTCH, *s.*, mixórdia, mistura; carne com legumes.

HOT DOG, *s.*, cachorro-quente.

HO.TEL, *s.*, hotel.

HO.TE.LIER, *s.*, hoteleiro, gerente de hotel.

HOT.FOOT, *adv.*, *Lit.*, apressadamente.

HOT.HEAD, *s.*, pessoa colérica.

HOT.HEAD.ED, *adj.*, temerário, colérico.

HOT.HOUSE, *s.*, estufa.

HOT LINE, *s.*, linha direta, linha de emergência.

HOT.LY, *adv.*, calorosamente, veementemente.

HOT.NESS, *s.*, calor, ardor, furor, ardência.

HOT SPOT, *s.*, lugar da moda; *Pol.*, área de tensão.

HOT-TEM.PERED, *adj.*, esquentado, irritável.

HOT-WA.TER BOT.TLE, *s.*, garrafa térmica.

HOUND, *v.*, perseguir, ir atrás, acossar.

HOUR, *s.*, hora.

HOUR.GLASS, *s.*, ampulheta.

HOUR.LY, *adv.*, de hora em hora.

HOUSE, *s.*, casa, residência, moradia; câmara, assembleia; *v.*, alojar.

HOUSE.BREAK.ING, *s.*, arrombamento de casa.

HOUSE.COAT, *s.*, roupão.

HOUSE.HOLD, *s.*, casa, família, lar, residência.

HOUSEHOLDER ··491·· HYACINTH

HOUSE.HOLD.ER, s., chefe de família, patrão.
HOUSE.KEEP.ER, s., governante, aia.
HOUSE.KEEP.ING, s., tarefas domésticas; administração e organização interna de um negócio.
HOUSE.WIFE, s., dona de casa, proprietária.
HOUSE.WORK, s., afazeres domésticos, serviços caseiros.
HOUSE-OWN.ER, s., proprietário (da casa).
HOUSE.WORK, s., trabalho doméstico.
HOV.EL, s., casebre, cabana, choça.
HOV.ER, v., pairar, voejar, flutuar no ar.
HOV.ER.CRAFT, s., veículo que se desloca sobre colchões de ar.
HOW, adv., como, quanto.
HOW.EVER, adv. e conj., todavia, contudo, não obstante.
HOWL, s., uivo, bramido, berro; v., uivar, berrar, urrar.
HOWL.ER, s., uivador, berrador; col., burrada, asneira.
HOWL.ING, adj., uivante; fig., imenso, extremo.
HUB, s., cubo de roda, centro.
HUB.BUB, s., algazarra, balbúrdia, confusão, bagunça.
HUB.CAP, s., calota de roda de carro.
HUCK.LE, s., anca.
HUD.DLE, s., amontoado (pessoas ou coisas); desordem, confusão; v., amontoar(-se), apertar-se (pessoas).
HUE, s., cor, colorido, matiz.
HUFF, s., mau humor; v., estar ofegante, bufar, ofender.
HUFF.I.NESS, s., arrogância, soberba, vaidade.
HUFF.Y, adj., arrogante, soberbo, vaidoso, petulante, atrevido.
HUG, s., abraço, estreitamento; v., abraçar, apertar.
HUGE, adj., imenso, grande, enorme.
HUGE.LY, adv., imensamente, enormemente.
HUGE.NESS, s., vastidão, amplidão.
HU.GE.NOT, s., Hist., huguenote.
HULK, s., carcaça, brutamontes; v., mover-se de modo pesado e lento.
HULK.ING, adj., gigantesco, grosseiro, desajeitado, lento.
HULL, s., casco de navio, fuselagem.
HUM, v., zumbir, zunir, cantarolar.
HU.MAN, adj., humano.
HU.MANE, adj., humano.
HU.MANE.LY, adv., humanamente.
HU.MAN.ISM, s., humanismo.
HU.MAN.IST, s., humanista.
HU.MAN.I.TA.RI.AN, adj., humanitário.
HU.MAN.I.TIES, s., humanidades, cultura clássica.
HU.MAN.I.TY, s., humanidade.
HU.MAN.I.ZA.TION, s., humanização.
HU.MAN.IZE, v., humanizar.
HU.MAN.LY, adv., humanamente.
HU.MAN NA.TURE, s., natureza humana.
HU.MAN RACE, s., raça humana.
HU.MAN RE.SOURCES, s. pl., recursos humanos.
HU.MAN RIGHTS, s. pl., direitos humanos.
HUM.BLE, adj., humilde, respeitoso; v., humilhar.
HUM.BLY, adv., humildemente.
HUM.BUG, s., fraude, tapeação; hipocrisia; v., tapear.
HUM.DRUM, adj., monótono, aborrecido, enfadonho.
HU.MER.US, s., Anat., úmero.
HU.MID, adj., úmido.
HU.MID.I.TY, s., umidade.
HU.MIL.I.ATE, v., humilhar, rebaixar.
HU.MIL.I.AT.ING, adj., humilhante.

HU.MIL.I.A.TION, s., humilhação, degradação.
HU.MIL.I.TY, s., humildade.
HUM.MING.BIRD, s., beija-flor, colibri.
HU.MOR.IST, s., humorista.
HU.MOR.OUS, adj., humorístico, cômico, engraçado.
HU.MOUR, HU.MOR, s., humorismo, humor, comicidade.
HUMP, s., corcunda, pequeno monte; v., corcovar, dobrar.
HUMP.BACK, s., corcunda, corcova.
HU.MUS, s., húmus.
HUNCH, s., corcova; intuição, pressentimento; v., curvar-se.
HUNCH.BACK, s., corcunda, corcova.
HUN.DRED, num., cem, cento, centena.
HUN.DRED.FOLD, adj., cêntuplo.
HUN.DRETH, num., centésimo.
HUN.GAR.I.AN, adj., s., húngaro.
HUN.GA.RY, s., Hungria.
HUN.GER, s., fome; desejo; v., estar com fome, estar desejoso.
HUN.GER STRIKE, s., greve de fome; v., fazer greve de fome.
HUN.GER.STRUK, s., faminto, esfomeado.
HUNG.OVER, s., ressaca.
HUN.GRI.LY, adv., com fome.
HUN.GRY, adj., faminto, esfomeado.
HUNK, s., col., pedaço, naco; homem atraente.
HUNT, v., caçar, perseguir; s., caça, caçada.
HUNT DOWN, v., caçar algo, alguém.
HUNT.ER, s., caçador.
HUNT.ING, s., caça.
HUNT.RESS, s., caçadora.
HUNTS.MAN, s., organizador de caçada.
HUR.DLE, s., Esp., barreira (corrida); dificuldade; v., cercar; Esp., saltar sobre barreiras.
HURL, v., arremessar, atirar, lançar, jogar, gritar, berrar.
HUR.RAH!, interj., hurra!, viva!; v., saudar, dar vivas.
HUR.RAY, interj., excl., viva! hurra!
HUR.RI.CANE, s., furacão, tormenta.
HUR.RIED, s., apressado.
HUR.RIED.LY, adv., apressadamente, precipitadamente.
HUR.RY, s., pressa, afobamento; v., apressar-se, ter pressa.
HURT, v., magoar, ferir, machucar.
HURT.FUL, adj., danoso, ofensivo, prejudicial.
HURT.FUL.LY, adv., prejudicialmente.
HURT.ING, s., ofensa, mágoa, sofrimento.
HUR.TLE, s., colisão, choque; v., lançar, arremessar, precipitar, colidir.
HUS.BAND, s., marido, esposo; v., poupar.
HUS.BAND.RY, s., criação de gado; agricultura.
HUSH, s., silêncio, quietude, calma; v., silenciar, aquietar, acalmar.
HUSK, s., casca (de semente), folhelho; v., debulhar, descascar.
HUS.KI.NESS, s., rouquidão, voz áspera.
HUSK.Y, s., Zool., husky (cão dos esquimós); adj., rouco; cascudo (de casca).
HUS.SY, s., moça, jovem esperta.
HUS.TINGS, s. pl., UK campanha eleitoral.
HUS.TLE, s., situação excitante; atividade confusa; pressa; v., apressar; forçar; empurrar.
HUT, s., choupana, choça, cabana; v., viver em barraca.
HUTCH, s., coelheira.
HY.A.CINTH, s., jacinto.

HYAENA ··492·· HYSTERICS

HY.AE.NA, *s., Zool.,* hiena.
HY.BRID, *s.,* híbrido.
HY.BRID.ISM, *s.,* hibridismo.
HY.DRAN.GEA, *s., Bot.,* hortência.
HY.DRANT, *s.,* hidrante.
HY.DRATE, *s., Quím.,* hidrato; *v.,* hidratar.
HY.DRAU.LIC, *adj.,* hidráulico.
HY.DRAU.LICS, *s.,* hidráulica.
HY.DRO, *s., UK abrev.* de estância hidromineral, spa.
HY.DRO.CAR.BON, *s., Quím.,* hicrocarboneto.
HY.DRO.GEN, *s.,* hidrogênio.
HY.DRO.GEN.ATE, *v., Quím.,* hidrogenar.
HY.DRO.GEN BOMB, *s.,* bomba de hidrogênio.
HY.DROG.RA.PHY, *s.,* hidrografia.
HY.DROL.O.GY, *s.,* hidrologia.
HY.DROM.E.TER, *s.,* hidrômetro.
HY.DRO.PHO.BIA, *s.,* hidrofobia.
HY.DRO.PLANE, *s.,* hidroplano.
HY.DRO.PON.ICS, *s. pl.,* hidropônica.
HY.DRO.SPHERE, *s.,* hidrosfera.
HY.DRO.THER.A.PY, *s., Med.,* hidroterapia.
HY.DROUS, *adj.,* hidratado, aquoso.
HY.DROX.I.DE, *s., Quím.,* hidróxido.
HY.E.NA, *s.,* o mesmo que *hyaena*.
HY.GIENE, *s.,* higiene.
HY.GIEN.IC, *adj.,* higiênico.
HY.GROM.E.TER, *s.,* higrômetro.
HY.GROM.E.TRY, *s.,* higrometria.
HY.MEN, *s., Anat.,* hímen.
HYMN, *s.,* hino, canto; *v.,* celebrar, cantar um hino.
HYM.NAL, *s.,* hinário, conjunto de hinos.
HYPE, *s.,* propaganda exagerada; agulha hipodérmica; engodo; *v.,* fazer propaganda exagerada; ludibriar.
HY.PER, *adj., col.,* enérgico, ativo.

HY.PER.AC.TIVE, *adj.,* hiperativo.
HY.PER.AC.TIV.I.TY, *s.,* hiperatividade.
HY.PER.BO.LA, *s.,* hiperboloide.
HY.PER.BO.LE, *s.,* hipérbole, exagero retórico.
HY.PER.CRIT.I.CIZE, *v.,* criticar exageradamente.
HY.PER.IN.FLA.TION, *s., Econ.,* hiperinflação.
HY.PER.MAR.KET, *s.,* hipermercado.
HY.PER.SEN.SI.TIVE, *adj.,* hipersensível.
HY.PER.TEN.SION, *s.,* hipertensão.
HY.PER.TEXT, *s., Comp.,* hipertexto.
HY.PER.TRO.PHY, *s.,* hipertrofia.
HY.PER.VEN.TI.LATE, *v.,* hiperventilar.
HY.PHEN *s.,* hífen.
HYP.NO.SIS, *s.,* hipnose.
HYP.NOT.IC, *s., Med.,* hipnótico, narcótico; *adj.,* hipnótico.
HYP.NO.TISM, *s.,* hipnotismo.
HYP.NO.TIST, *s.,* hipnotizador.
HYP.NO.TIZE, *v.,* hipnotizar.
HY.PO.CHON.DRIA, *s.,* hipocondria.
HY.POC.RI.SY, *s.,* hipocrisia.
HYP.O.CRITE, *s.,* hipócrita.
HY.PO.DERM, *s.,* hipoderme.
HY.PO.DER.MIC NEE.DLE, *s.,* seringa hipodérmica.
HY.POT.E.NUSE, *s.,* hipotenusa.
HY.POTH.E.CATE, *v.,* hipotecar.
HY.PO.THER.MI.A, *s.,* hipotermia.
HY.POTH.E.SIS, *s.,* hipótese.
HY.POTH.E.SIZE, *v.,* fazer hipóteses, hipotetizar.
HY.PO.THET.IC, *adj.,* hipotético.
HYS.TER.EC.TO.MY, *s., Med.,* histerectomia.
HYS.TE.RIA, *s.,* histeria.
HYS.TER.IC, *adj.,* histérico.
HYS.TER.ICS, *s. pl.,* crise histérica, histeria.

I

I, *s.*, nona letra do alfabeto inglês.
I, *pron.*, eu; núm. romano 1.
I.AMB, *s.*, jambo.
I.BE.RI.AN, *s.*, ibero; *adj.*, ibérico.
I.BE.RI.AN PEN.IN.SU.LA, *s.*, *Geogr.*, Península Ibérica.
I.BIS, *s.*, *Zool.*, íbis (ave pernalta).
IC.AR.US, *s.*, *Mit.*, Ícaro.
ICE, *s.*, gelo, sorvete; *v.*, gelar, congelar, esfriar.
ICE AGE, *s.*, *Geol.*, era glacial.
ICE.BERG, *s.*, icebergue.
ICE BAG, *s.*, bolsa de gelo.
ICE.BERG LET.TUCE, *s.*, *Bot.*, alface-americana.
ICE BLUE, *s.*, cor azul-claro; *adj.*, azul-claro.
ICE.BOAT, *s.*, navio quebra-gelo.
ICE.BOX, *s.*, *US* geladeira.
ICE.BREAK.ER, *s.*, o mesmo que *iceboat*.
ICE BUCK.ET, *s.*, balde de gelo.
ICE CAP, *s.*, calota polar.
ICE-COLD, *adj.*, gelado, geladíssimo.
ICE.CREAM, *s.*, sorvete.
ICE CUBE, *s.*, cubo de gelo.
ICED, *adj.*, com gelo, coberto com glacê.
ICE FLOE, *s.*, banquisa.
ICE HOCK.EY, *s.*, *Esp.*, hóquei sobre o gelo.
ICE.LAND, *s.*, *Geogr.*, Islândia.
ICE.LAND.ER, *s.*, islandês.
ICE.LAND.IC, *adj.*, s., islandês(a).
ICE LOL.LY, *s.*, picolé.
ICE PICK, *s.*, picador de gelo.
ICE POINT, *s.*, *Fís.*, temperatura ou ponto de congelamento (de um líquido).
ICE-RINK, *s.*, pista para patinação.
ICE SKATE, *s.*, patim (para o gelo); *v.*, patinar no gelo.
ICE SKAT.ER, *s.*, patinador no gelo.
ICE SKAT.ING, *s.*, *Esp.*, patinação sobre gelo, praticar patinação (sobre gelo).
ICH.NOL.O.GY, *s.*, icnologia (estudo das impressões fósseis).
ICH.THY.OL.O.GY, *s.*, ictiologia (estudo dos peixes).
ICH.THY.OPH.A.GY, *s.*, ictiofagia (hábito de se alimentar de peixes).
ICH.THY.O.SAU.RUS, *s.*, ictiossauro (réptil pré-histórico dos mares).
IC.I.LY, *adv.*, friamente.
IC.I.NESS, *s.*, congelamento, frio intenso; frigidez.
IC.ING, *s.*, glacê.
IC.ING SU.GAR, *s.*, açúcar de confeiteiro.
ICK.Y, *s.*, pessoa chata; *adj.*, chato, desagradável.
I.CON, *s.*, ícone.
I.CON.IC, *adj.*, icônico.
I.CON.O.CLAST, *s.*, iconoclasta.
I.CON.O.GRAPH.IC, *adj.*, iconográfico.
I.CO.NOG.RA.PHY, *s.*, iconografia (estudo de imagens).
I.CO.NOL.A.TRY, *s.*, iconolatria (adoração das imagens).
IC.TUS, *s.*, *Med.*, batimento do pulso.
ICY, *adj.*, gelado, congelado.
ID, *s.*, *Psic.*, id (estrutura psíquica responsável pelo instinto).
I'D, *contr.*, de *I would, I had, I would*.
I.DE.A, *s.*, ideia, pensamento.
I.DE.AL, *adj., s.*, ideal.
I.DE.AL.ISM, *s.*, idealismo.
I.DE.AL.IST, *s.*, idealista.
I.DE.AL.I.ZA.TION, *s.*, idealização.
I.DE.AL.IZE, *v.*, idealizar.
I.DE.AL.LY, *adv.*, idealmente, perfeitamente.
I.DEM, *pron.*, *Lat.*, o mesmo.
I.DEN.TI.CAL, *adj.*, idêntico.
I.DEN.TI.CAL.LY, *adv.*, identicamente.
I.DEN.TI.CAL.NESS, *s.*, identidade.
I.DEN.TIC.AL TWINS, *s. pl.*, gêmeos idênticos.
I.DEN.TI.FI.A.BLE, *adj.*, identificável.
I.DEN.TI.FI.CA.TION, *s.*, identificação.
I.DEN.TI.FI.CA.TION CARD, *s.*, carteira de identidade.
I.DEN.TI.FI.ER, *s.*, identificador.
I.DEN.TI.FY, *v.*, identificar.
I.DEN.TI.TY, *s.*, identidade.
I.DEN.TI.TY CARD, *s.*, identidade; crachá.
I.DEN.TI.TY PA.PERS, *s. pl.*, documentos de identidade.
I.DEN.TI.TY PA.RADE, *s.*, identificação.
ID.E.O.GRAM, *s.*, ideograma.
ID.E.OG.RA.PHY, *s.*, ideografia.
I.DE.O.LOG.I.CAL, *adj.*, ideológico.
I.DE.OL.O.GIST, *s.*, ideólogo.
I.DE.OL.O.GY, *s.*, ideologia.
ID.I.O.CY, *s.*, idiotismo, imbecilidade, burrice.
ID.I.OM, *s.*, idioma, língua; linguagem; idiomatismo.
ID.I.OM.AT.IC, *adj.*, idiomático.
ID.I.O.SYN.CRA.SY, *s.*, idiossincrasia.
ID.I.O.SYN.CRAT.IC, *adj.*, idiossincrásico, peculiar.
ID.I.OT, *s.*, idiota, imbecil.
ID.I.OT.IC, *adj.*, idiota.
ID.IO.TISM, *s.*, idiotismo, idiotice.
ID.I.OT.IZE, *v.*, idiotizar, tornar idiota.
I.DLE, *v.*, ficar à toa, não fazer nada; *s.*, indolente; *adj.*, inativo, ocioso.
I.DLE CA.PAC.I.TY, *s.*, *Econ.*, capacidade ociosa (de uma empresa).
I.DLER, *s.*, preguiçoso, desocupado.
I.DLE TALK, *s.*, conversa fiada.
I.DLY, *adv.*, preguiçosamente, casualmente, à toa.
I.DOL, *s.*, ídolo.
I.DOL.A.TER, *s.*, idólatra.
I.DOL.A.TRY, *s.*, idolatria.
I.DOL.IST, *s.*, idólatra.
I.DOL.I.ZA.TION, *s.*, adoração de ídolos.

IDOLIZE(-ISE) •• 494 •• IMMERSION HEATER

I.DOL.IZE(-ISE), *v.*, idolatrar.
I.DYLL *UK*, **I.DYL** *US*, *s.*, idílio (amor poético).
I.DYL.LIC, *adj.*, idílico.
IF, *conj.*, se, caso, mesmo que, ainda que.
IF.FY *adj.*, inseguro.
IG.LOO, *s.*, iglu.
IG.NE.OUS, *adj.*, ígneo, incandescente.
IG.NIT.ABLE, *adj.*, inflamável.
IG.NITE, *v.*, incendiar, inflamar, acender, colocar fogo.
IG.NI.TION, *s.*, ignição.
IG.NI.TION KEY, *s.*, chave de ignição (de motores).
IG.NO.BLE, *adj.*, ignóbil, vil, desprezível.
IG.NO.MIN.I.OUS, *adj.*, ignominioso.
IG.NO.MIN.Y, *s.*, ignomínia, vileza, infâmia.
IG.NO.RA.MUS, *s.*, ignorante.
IG.NO.RANCE, *s.*, ignorância.
IG.NO.RANT, *adj.*, ignorante, desinformado.
IG.NORE, *v.*, ignorar, desconhecer, fazer pouco caso.
I.GUA.NA, *s.*, iguana.
I.KON, *s.*, o mesmo que *icon*.
IL.E.UM, *s., Anat.*, íleo.
IL.I.AC, *adj., Anat.*, ilíaco.
ILL, *adj.*, doente, danoso, nocivo; *s.*, mal.
I'LL, *contr.* de *I will, I shall*.
ILL-AD.VISED, *adj.*, imprudente, insensato.
ILL-AF.FECT.ED, *adj.*, mal-intencionado.
ILL-BRED, *adj.*, malcriado.
ILL-CON.SID.ERED, *adj.*, impoderado.
ILL-DIS.POSED, *adj.*, de má vontade, malévolo, maligno.
IL.LE.GAL, *adj.*, ilegal.
IL.LE.GAL.I.TY, *s.*, ilegalidade.
IL.LE.GAL.LY, *adv.*, ilegalmente.
IL.LEG.I.BIL.I.TY, *s.*, ilegibilidade.
IL.LEG.I.BLE, *adj.*, ilegível.
IL.LE.GIT.I.MA.CY, *s.*, ilegitimidade.
IL.LE.GIT.I.MATE, *adj.*, ilegítimo.
ILL-E.QUIP.PED, *adj.*, despreparado, incapaz, desequipado.
ILL-FAT.ED, *adj.*, malfadado.
ILL FEEL.ING, *s.*, ressentimento, rancor.
ILL-FOUND.ED, *adj.*, infundado.
ILL-GOT, *adj.*, adquirido com desonestidade.
ILL-GOT.TEN GAINS, *s. pl.*, ganhos ilícitos.
ILL HEALTH, *s.*, má saúde.
IL.LIC.IT, *adj.*, ilícito.
IL.LIC.IT.LY, *adv.*, ilicitamente.
IL.LIC.IT.NESS, *s.*, ilegalidade, ilicitude.
IL.LIM.IT.A.BLY, *adv.*, ilimitadamente.
ILL-IN.FORMED, *adj.*, mal informado.
IL.LIN.I.UM, *s., Quím.*, ilínio (elemento de nº atômico 61).
IL.LIT.ER.A.CY, *s.*, ignorância, analfabetismo.
IL.LIT.ER.ATE, *s., adj.*, iletrado, analfabeto.
ILL-JUDGED, *adj.*, sem juízo, precipitado.
ILL-MAN.NERED, *adj.*, mal-educado, rude, grosseiro.
ILL.NESS, *s.*, doença.
IL.LOG.I.CAL, *adj.*, ilógico.
ILL-SUITED, *adj.*, inadequado.
ILL-TEM.PERED, *adj.*, mal-humorado.
ILL-TIMED, *adj.*, inoportuno.
ILL-TREAT, *v.*, maltratar.
ILL-TREAT.MENT, *s.*, maus-tratos.
IL.LUDE, *v.*, enganar, iludir.

IL.LU.MI.NATE, *v.*, iluminar, esclarecer, aclarar.
IL.LU.MI.NAT.ED, *adj.*, iluminado; iluminura.
IL.LU.MI.NAT.ING, *adj.*, esclarecedor, que ilumina (com ideias).
IL.LU.MI.NA.TION, *s.*, iluminação.
IL.LU.MINE, *v.*, iluminar, aclarar.
ILL-USE, *v.*, maltratar.
IL.LU.SION, *s.*, ilusão.
IL.LU.SION.ISM, *s.*, ilusionismo.
IL.LU.SION.IST, *s.*, ilusionista.
IL.LU.SO.RY, *adj.*, ilusório.
IL.LUS.TRATE, *v.*, ilustrar, exemplificar.
IL.LUS.TRAT.ED, *adj.*, ilustrado.
IL.LUS.TRA.TION, *s.*, ilustração, exemplo.
IL.LUS.TRA.TIVE, *adj.*, ilustrativo; explicativo.
IL.LUS.TRA.TOR, *s.*, ilustrador; explicador.
IL.LUS.TRI.OUS, *adj.*, ilustre, renomado, nobre.
ILL WILL, *s.*, hostilidade, animosidade.
I'M, *contr.* de *I am*.
IM.AGE, *s.*, imagem.
IMA.GE.RY, *s.*, imagem; imagens, figuras; fantasias.
IMAG.IN.ABLE, *adj.*, imaginável.
IMAG.IN.ABLY, *adj.*, imaginariamente.
IMAG.I.NA.RY, *adj.*, imaginário.
IMAG.I.NA.TION, *s.*, imaginação.
IMAG.I.NA.TIVE, *adj.*, imaginativo.
IMAG.INE, *v.*, imaginar, achar, supor, crer.
IM.AG.IN.ING, *s. pl.*, imaginação; *imaginings s.pl.: Lit.*, fantasias.
I.MA.GO, *s.*, imago.
I.MAM, *s., Rel.*, imã, imame (líder muçulmano).
IM.BAL.ANCE, *s.*, desigualdade.
IM.BE.CILE, *s.*, imbecil, idiota, tolo.
IM.BE.CIL.I.TY, *s.*, imbecilidade.
IM.BIBE, *v.*, embeber (de um líquido); assimilar.
IM.BRUE, *v.*, pôr de molho, mergulhar; manchar.
IM.BUE, *v.*, imbuir, inocular.
IM.I.TATE, *v.*, imitar.
IM.I.TA.TION, *s.*, imitação.
IM.I.TA.TOR, *s.*, imitador.
IM.MAC.U.LATE, *adj.*, imaculado, sem mancha, puro.
IM.MAC.U.LATELY, *adv.*, imaculadamente, impecavelmente.
IM.MA.TE.RI.AL, *adj.*, imaterial, incorpóreo.
IM.MA.TE.RI.AL.I.TY, *s.*, imaterialidade.
IM.MA.TURE, *adj.*, imaturo, precoce, verde.
IM.MA.TURE.NESS, *s.*, imaturidade, prematuridade.
IM.MA.TU.RI.TY, *s.*, imaturidade.
IM.MEAS.UR.A.BLE, *adj.*, incomensurável.
IM.MEAS.UR.A.BLE.NESS, *s.*, imensurabilidade.
IM.ME.DI.A.CY, *s.*, imediatismo, urgência.
IM.ME.DI.ATE, *adj.*, imediato, súbito, urgente, próximo.
IM.ME.DI.ATE.LY, *adv.*, imediatamente; diretamente; *conj.*, assim que.
IM.MED.I.CA.BLE, *adj.*, incurável.
IM.ME.MO.RI.AL, *adj.*, imemorial.
IM.MENSE, *adj.*, imenso, enorme, vasto, amplo.
IM.MENSE.LY, *adv.*, imensamente.
IM.MENSE.NESS, *s.*, imensidão, enormidade, vastidão.
IM.MEN.SI.TY, *s.*, imensidão, imensidade.
IM.MERSE, *v.*, imergir, submergir.
IM.MER.SION, *s.*, imersão, submersão.
IM.MER.SION HEAT.ER, *s.*, ebulidor.

IMMIGRANT ·· 495 ·· IMPLEMENT

IM.MI.GRANT, *adj., s.*, imigrante.
IM.MI.GRA.TION, *s.*, imigração.
IM.MI.NENCE, *s.*, iminência, proximidade, urgência.
IM.MI.NENT, *adj.*, iminente, próximo.
IM.MO.BILE, *adj.*, imóvel.
IM.MO.BIL.I.TY, *s.*, imobilidade.
IM.MO.BI.LI.ZA.TION, *s.*, imobilização.
IM.MO.BI.LIZE, *v.*, imobilizar.
IM.MOD.ER.ATE, *adj.*, imoderado, excessivo, demasiado.
IM.MOD.ER.A.TION, *s.*, imoderação, desmando.
IM.MOD.EST, *adj.*, vaidoso, imodesto, indecente.
IM.MO.LA.TION, *s.*, imolação, sacrifício, dificuldade.
IM.MOR.AL, *adj.*, imoral.
IM.MO.RAL.I.TY, *s.*, imoralidade.
IM.MO.RAL.LY, *adv.*, imoralmente.
IM.MOR.TAL, *adj.*, imortal.
IM.MOR.TAL.I.TY, *s.*, imortalidade.
IM.MOR.TAL.I.ZA.TION, *v.*, imortalização.
IM.MOR.TAL.IZE, *v.*, imortalizar.
IM.MOV.A.BIL.I.TY, *s.*, imobilidade.
IM.MOV.A.BLE, *adj.*, imóvel, fixo, inflexível.
IM.MUNE, *adj.*, imune.
IM.MUNE SYS.TEM, *s., Anat.*, sistema imunológico.
IM.MU.NI.TY, *s.*, imunidade.
IM.MU.NI.ZA.TION, *s., Med.*, imunização.
IM.MU.NIZE, *v.*, imunizar.
IM.MU.NO.DE.FI.CIEN.CY, *s.*, imunodeficiência.
IM.MU.NOLOGY, *s.*, imunologia.
IM.MU.RE, *v.*, murar; prender.
IM.MU.TA.BIL.I.TY, *s.*, imutabilidade.
IM.MU.TA.BLE, *adj.*, imutável.
IM.MU.TA.BLY, *adv.*, imutavelmente.
IMP, *s.*, criança travessa, diabinho, moleque.
IM.PACT, *s.*, colisão, impacto; *v.*, colidir, imprensar.
IM.PAIR, *v.*, prejudicar, enfraquecer.
IM.PAIRED, *adj.*, prejudicado, debilitado.
IM.PAIR.MENT, *s.*, prejuízo, depreciação.
IM.PALE, *v.*, empalar, perfurar, espetar.
IM.PALE.MENT, *s.*, empalação.
IM.PART, *v.*, dar, conceder, comunicar.
IM.PAR.TIAL, *adj.*, imparcial, justo.
IM.PAR.TIAL.I.TY, *s.*, imparcialidade.
IM.PAR.TIAL.LY, *adv.*, imparcialmente.
IM.PAR.TI.BLE, *adj.*, impartível, indivisível.
IM.PASS.A.BLE, *adj.*, intransitável.
IM.PASSE, *s.*, impasse.
IM.PAS.SIONED, *adj.*, apaixonado.
IM.PAS.SIVE, *adj.*, impassível.
IM.PAS.SIVE.NESS, *s.*, indiferença, impassividade.
IM.PA.TIENCE, *s.*, impaciência.
IM.PA.TIENT, *adj.*, impaciente.
IM.PA.TIENT.LY, *adv.*, impacientemente.
IM.PAY.ABLE, *adj.*, impagável.
IM.PEACH, *v.*, acusar, contestar, pôr em dúvida, denunciar.
IM.PEACH.A.BLE, *adj.*, que pode ser acusado, que pode ser impedido.
IM.PEACH.ER, *s.*, acusador.
IM.PEACH.MENT, *s.*, acusação, contestação; *Pol.*, impedimento (de exercer cargo).
IM.PEC.CA.BLE, *adj.*, impecável.
IM.PEC.CA.BLY, *adv.*, impecavelmente.

IM.PEC.CANT, *adj.*, livre de pecado.
IM.PE.CU.NI.OUS, *adj.*, indigente.
IM.PEDE, *v.*, impedir, perturbar, incomodar.
IM.PED.I.MENT, *s.*, impedimento, empecilho, obstáculo.
IM.PED.I.TIVE, *adj.*, impeditivo.
IM.PEL, *v.*, impelir, empurrar.
IM.PEL.LENT, *adj.*, impulsor, impelente.
IM.PEL.LER, *s.*, impulsor; rotor.
IM.PEND, *v.*, pender, pairar; ser iminente, urgir, ameaçar.
IM.PEND.ING, *adj.*, iminente, próximo.
IM.PEN.E.TRA.BLE, *adj.*, impenetrável.
IM.PEN.E.TRA.BLY, *adv.*, impenetravelmente.
IM.PER.A.TIVE, *adj.*, imperioso, imperativo, obrigado, vital.
IM.PE.RA.TOR, *s., Lat.*, imperador, soberano.
IM.PER.CEP.TI.BLE, *adj.*, imperceptível.
IM.PER.CEP.TI.BLY, *adv.*, imperceptivelmente.
IM.PER.FECT, *adj.*, imperfeito, falho, defeituoso.
IM.PER.FEC.TI.BIL.I.TY, *s.*, imperfectibilidade.
IM.PER.FEC.TION, *s.*, imperfeição, prejuízo, defeito.
IM.PE.RI.AL, *adj.*, imperial.
IM.PE.RI.AL.ISM, *s.*, imperialismo.
IM.PE.RI.AL.IST, *s., adj.*, imperialista.
IM.PER.IL, *v.*, pôr em perigo; expor.
IM.PE.RI.OUS, *adj.*, imperioso.
IM.PE.RI.OUS.LY, *adv.*, imperiosamente.
IM.PER.ME.ABLE, *adj.*, impermeável.
IM.PER.ME.ABLE.NESS, *s.*, impermeabilidade.
IM.PER.SON.AL, *adj.*, impessoal.
IM.PER.SON.AL.I.TY, *s.*, impersonalidade, impessoalidade.
IM.PER.SON.AL.IZE, *v.*, impessoalizar, tornar impessoal.
IM.PER.SON.AL.LY, *adv.*, impessoalmente.
IM.PER.SON.ATE, *v.*, personificar; imitar, fingir.
IM.PER.SON.A.TION, *s.*, personificação, imitação.
IM.PER.SON.A.TOR, *s.*, imitador, impostor.
IM.PER.TI.NENCE, *s.*, impertinência, teimosia.
IM.PER.TI.NENT, *adj.*, impertinente.
IM.PER.TURB.ABLE, *adj.*, imperturbável.
IM.PER.TURB.A.BLY, *adv.*, imperturbavelmente.
IM.PER.VI.OUS, *adj.*, impermeável, inacessível.
IM.PER.VI.OUS.LY, *adv.*, inacessivelmente.
IM.PER.VI.OUS.NESS, *s.*, impenetrabilidade, inacessibilidade.
IM.PE.TRATE, *v.*, impetrar, suplicar.
IM.PET.U.OS.I.TY, *s.*, impetuosidade, afobamento, pressa.
IM.PET.U.OUS, *adj.*, impetuoso, arrojado, precipitado.
IM.PET.U.OUS.LY, *adv.*, impetuosamente.
IM.PE.TUS, *s.*, ímpeto, impulso, arrojo, salto.
IM.PINGE, *v.*, chocar, colidir, ir de encontro.
IM.PINGE.MENT, *s.*, colisão, choque, embate.
IM.PI.OUS, *adj.*, ímpio, incrédulo, descrente.
IMP.ISH, *adj.*, travesso, levado.
IMP.ISH.NESS, *s.*, travessura.
IM.PLA.CA.BIL.I.TY, *s.*, implacabilidade.
IM.PLA.CA.BLE, *adj.*, implacável, inexorável.
IM.PLANT, *v.*, implantar, fixar, firmar, estabelecer.
IM.PLAN.TA.TION, *s.*, implantação.
IM.PLANT.ER, *s.*, implantador, colocador.
IM.PLAU.SI.BIL.I.TY, *s.*, implausibilidade, improbabilidade.
IM.PLAU.SI.BLE, *adj.*, implausível.
IM.PLAU.SI.BLY, *adv.*, improvavelmente.
IM.PLE.MENT, *s.*, implemento, utensílio, instrumento; *v.*, efetivar.

IMPLEMENTATION ·· 496 ·· INADVERTENCE

IM.PLE.MEN.TA.TION, s., implementação.
IM.PLI.CATE, v., implicar, comprometer.
IM.PLI.CA.TION, s., implicação, complicação, envolvimento.
IM.PLIC.IT, adj., implícito, subentendido, irrestrito.
IM.PLIC.ITLY, adv., implicitamente, absolutamente.
IM.PLIC.IT.NESS, s., subentendido.
IM.PLIED, adj., subentendido.
IM.PLODE, v., implodir.
IM.PLORE, v., implorar, suplicar, pedir, solicitar.
IM.PLOR.ER, s., suplicante, implorador, pedinte.
IM.PLOR.ING.LY, adv., suplicantemente.
IM.PLY, v., conter, encerrar, significar, deduzir.
IM.PO.LITE, adj., descortês, indelicado.
IM.PO.LITE.NESS, s., impolidez, descortesia.
IM.PON.DER.A.BIL.I.TY, s., imponderabilidade.
IM.PON.DER.A.BLE, adj., imponderável.
IM.PORT, s., importação, importância, valor; v., importar, significar.
IM.POR.TANCE, s., importância, presunção, consideração.
IM.POR.TANT, adj., importante, influente, significativo.
IM.POR.TANT.LY, adv., de modo importante.
IM.POR.TA.TION, s., importação.
IM.PORT.ER, s., importador.
IM.PORTS, s., produtos importados.
IM.POR.TU.NATE, adj., inoportuno, desfavorável.
IM.POR.TUNE, v., importunar.
IM.POSE, v., impor, obrigar a.
IM.POS.ER, s., impostor.
IM.POS.ING, adj., imponente.
IM.PO.SI.TION, s., imposição.
IM.POS.SI.BIL.I.TY, s., impossibilidade.
IM.POS.SI.BLE, adj., impossível.
IM.POS.SI.BLY, adv., impossivelmente.
IM.POST, s., imposto, tributo, taxa.
IM.POS.TOR, s., impostor, charlatão, falso, enganador.
IM.POS.TURE, s., impostura, embuste.
IM.PO.TENCE, s., impotência.
IM.PO.TENT, adj., impotente.
IM.POUND, v., Jur., apreender.
IM.POV.ER.ISH, v., empobrecer, tornar-se pobre.
IM.POV.ER.ISHED, adj., empobrecido.
IM.POV.ER.ISH.MENT, s., empobrecimento.
IM.PRAC.TI.CA.BIL.I.TY, s., impraticabilidade.
IM.PRAC.TI.CA.BLE, adj., impraticável.
IM.PRAC.TI.CAL, adj., pouco prático.
IM.PRE.CATE, s., imprecar, amaldiçoar, maldizer.
IM.PRE.CA.TION, s., imprecação, maldição.
IM.PRE.CISE, adj., impreciso, inexato.
IM.PREG.NA.BLE, adj., invulnerável, imbatível, inexpugnável.
IM.PREG.NA.BLY, adv., invencivelmente.
IM.PREG.NA.TE, v., fecundar, emprenhar; impregnar; adj., fecundado, prenhe; impregnado.
IM.PREG.NAT.ED, adj., prenhe; impregnado.
IM.PREG.NA.TION, s., fecundação; impregnação.
IM.PRESS, s., impressão, carimbo, marca; v., impressionar, imprimir.
IM.PRES.SION, s., impressão, estampa, sinal, caricatura.
IM.PRES.SION.ABLE, adj., impressionável.
IM.PRES.SION.ISM, s., Art., impressionismo.
IM.PRES.SION.IST, adj., Art., impressionista.
IM.PRES.SIVE, adj., impressionante; impressivo.

IM.PREST, s., empréstimo.
IM.PRINT, v., imprimir; s., impressão, ficha catalográfica do livro.
IM.PRINT.ED, adj., marcado.
IM.PRIS.ON, v., encarcerar, aprisionar, pôr na cadeia.
IM.PRIS.ON.MENT, s., cadeia, prisão, encarceramento.
IM.PROB.A.BIL.I.TY, s., improbabilidade.
IM.PROB.A.BLE, adj., improvável, duvidoso.
IM.PROB.A.BLY, adv., improvavelmente.
IM.PROB.I.TY, s., improbidade, desonestidade, safadeza.
IM.PROMP.TU, s., improviso; adj., improvisado; adv., improvisadamente.
IM.PROP.ER, adj., impróprio; inexato, indecente.
IM.PRO.PRI.E.TY, s., impropriedade.
IM.PROVE, v., melhorar, aperfeiçoar, cultivar.
IM.PROVED, adj., melhorado.
IM.PROVE.MENT, s., melhoria, aperfeiçoamento; progresso.
IM.PROV.I.DENCE, s., imprevidência, imprudência.
IM.PROV.I.DENT, adj., imprevidente, descurado, descuidado.
IM.PROV.ING, adj., proveitoso; salutar; edificante.
IM.PROV.ING.LY, adv., proveitosamente.
IM.PRO.VI.SA.TION, s., improvisação.
IM.PRO.VISE, v., improvisar, inventar.
IM.PRO.VIS.ER, s., improvisador.
IM.PRU.DENCE, s., imprudência.
IM.PRU.DENT, adj., imprudente.
IM.PRU.DENT.LY, adj., imprudentemente.
IM.PU.DIC.I.TY, s., impudícia.
IM.PUGN, v., impugnar, opor-se, refutar, recusar.
IM.PUGN.A.BLE, adj., impugnável.
IM.PUGN.A.TION, s., impugnação.
IM.PUGN.ER, s., impugnador.
IM.PULSE, s., impulso, ímpeto; v., agir por impulso.
IM.PUL.SION, s., impulsão, impulso.
IM.PUL.SIVE, adj., impulsivo, desenfreado.
IM.PUL.SIVE.LY, adv., impulsivamente.
IM.PUL.SIVE.NESS, s., impulsividade.
IM.PU.NI.TY, s., impunidade.
IM.PURE, adj., impuro, manchado.
IM.PU.RI.TY, s., impureza, impudícia.
IM.PUT.A.BLE, adj., imputável.
IM.PU.TA.TION, s., imputação.
IM.PUTE, v., imputar, atribuir, ligar com.
IN, prep., em, dentro, de, por, a, com, durante; s. abrev. de polegada.
IN.ABIL.I.TY, s., inabilidade, incapacidade.
IN.AC.CES.SI.BIL.I.TY, s., inacessibilidade.
IN.AC.CES.SI.BLE, adj., inacessível.
IN.AC.CU.RA.CY, s., imprecisão, incorreção.
IN.AC.CU.RATE, adj., impreciso, incorreto.
IN.AC.CU.RATE.LY, adv., incorretamente.
IN.AC.TION, s., inação, inércia.
IN.AC.TI.VATE, v., tornar inativo.
IN.AC.TIVE, adj., inativo, parado.
IN.AC.TIV.I.TY, s., inatividade.
IN.AD.E.QUA.CY, s., incapacidade, insuficiência.
IN.AD.E.QUATE, adj., inadequado, insuficiente.
IN.AD.E.QUATE.LY, adv., inadequadamente.
IN.AD.MIS.SI.BIL.I.TY, s., inadmissibilidade.
IN.AD.MIS.SI.BLE, adj., inadmissível.
IN.AD.VERT.ENCE, s., inadvertência, descuido.

INADVERTENT · 497 · INCOMMODIOUS

IN.AD.VERT.ENT, *adj.*, acidental, inadvertido.
IN.AD.VERT.ENT.LY, *adv.*, inadvertidamente, acidentalmente.
IN.AD.VIS.A.BLE, *adj.*, desaconselhável.
IN.ALIEN.ABLE, *adj.*, inalienável.
IN.ALIEN.ABLE.NESS, *s.*, inalienabilidade.
IN.ANE, *adj.*, vazio, oco, inane, fútil, inútil.
IN.ANE.LY, *adv.*, de modo vazio, futilmente.
IN.AN.I.MATE, *adj.*, inanimado, inerte, parado.
IN.A.NI.TION, *s.*, inanição, debilidade, fraqueza.
INAN.I.TY, *s.*, inanidade, inércia, nulidade, imobilidade.
IN.AP.PEAS.ABLE, *adj.*, inexorável, implacável, definitivo.
IN.AP.PE.TENCE, *s.*, inapetência.
IN.AP.PE.TENT, *adj.*, inapetente.
IN.AP.PLI.CA.BLE, *adj.*, inaplicável, inadequado.
IN.AP.PROACH.ABLE, *adj.*, inacessível, inaproximável.
IN.AP.PROACH.A.BLY, *adv.*, inacessivelmente.
IN.AP.PRO.PRI.ATE, *adj.*, inadequado, impróprio, inservível.
IN.APT, *adj.*, inapto, inábil, incapaz.
IN.AP.TI.TUDE, *s.*, inaptidão, incapacidade, inabilidade.
IN.AR.TIC.U.LATE, *adj.*, inarticulado, indistinto; mudo.
IN.AR.TIC.U.LATE.NESS, *s.*, sem articulação.
IN.AS.MUCH, *adv.*, visto que, dado que; na medida em que; *conj.*, porquanto, porque.
IN.AT.TEN.TION, *s.*, desatenção, incúria, negligência.
IN.AT.TEN.TIVE, *adj.*, desatento, descuidado, desleixado.
IN.AU.DI.BIL.I.TY, *s.*, inaudibilidade.
IN.AU.DI.BLE, *adj.*, inaudível.
IN.AU.GU.RAL, *adj.*, inaugural, inicial.
IN.AU.GU.RATE, *v.*, inaugurar, iniciar.
IN.AU.GU.RA.TION, *s.*, inauguração, início, abertura.
IN.AUS.PI.CIOUS; *adj.*, de mau agouro, pouco propício, desfavorável.
IN.AUS.PI.CIOUS.LY, *adv.*, desfavoravelmente.
IN-BE.TWEEN, *s.*, intermediário; intervalo; *adj.*, intermediário.
IN.BOARD, *adj.*, *adv.*, a bordo.
IN.BORN, *adj.*, inato, congênito.
IN-BOUND, *adj.*, *US* retornando à casa; esperado (de viagem).
IN.BRED, *adj.*, inato, congênito, consangüíneo.
IN.BREED, *v.*, procriar, criar na família.
IN.BREED.ING, *s.*, endogamia, procriação consangüínea.
IN.BUILT, *adj.*, diz-se do que é inerente (a pessoas ou coisas).
IN.CAL.CU.LA.BLE, *adj.*, incalculável.
IN.CAL.CU.LA.BLY, *adj.*, incalculavelmente.
IN.CAN.DESCE, *v.*, incandescer.
IN.CAN.DES.CENCE, *s.*, incandescência.
IN.CAN.DES.CENT, *adj.*, incandescente.
IN.CAN.TA.TION, *s.*, feitiço, palavras mágicas.
IN.CA.PA.BIL.I.TY, *s.*, incapacidade, inabilidade.
IN.CA.PA.BLE, *adj.*, incapaz, inábil.
IN.CA.PAC.I.TATE, *v.*, incapacitar.
IN.CA.PAC.I.TAT.ED, *adj.*, incapacitado.
IN.CA.PAC.I.TY, *s.*, incapacidade, inabilidade.
IN.CAR.CER.ATE, *v.*, encarcerar, aprisionar, colocar na cadeia.
IN.CAR.CER.A.TION, *s.*, encarceramento, aprisionamento.
IN.CAR.NATE, *adj.*, encarnado, avermelhado; *v.*, encarnar.
IN.CAR.NA.TION, *s.*, encarnação.
IN.CASE, *v.*, encaixar, envolver, encaixotar.
IN.CAU.TION, *s.*, descuido, falta de cautela, negligência.
IN.CAU.TIOUS, *adj.*, incauto, imprudente, negligente.
IN.CEN.DI.ARY, *adj.*, incendiário.

IN.CENSE, *s.*, incenso; *v.*, irritar, incomodar.
IN.CEN.TIVE, *s.*, incentivo, estímulo.
IN.CEN.TÌVIZE(-ISE), *v.*, incentivar.
IN.CEPT, *v.*, ingerir, deglutir, comer.
IN.CEP.TION, *s.*, origem, começo.
IN.CEP.TIVE, *adj.*, iniciador, principiante.
IN.CER.TI.TUDE, *s.*, incerteza.
IN.CES.SANT, *adj.*, incessante, ininterrupto.
IN.CES.SANT.LY, *adv.*, incessantemente.
IN.CEST, *s.*, incesto.
IN.CES.TU.OUS, *adj.*, incestuoso.
INCH, *s.*, polegada; *abrev.*, in.
IN.CHO.ATE, *adj.*, começado, iniciado, incipiente; *v.*, começar, iniciar.
IN.CHO.A.TION, *s.*, princípio, início, começo.
IN.CI.DENCE, *s.*, incidência.
IN.CI.DENT, *s.*, incidente, evento, fato, acontecimento.
IN.CI.DEN.TAL, *adj.*, incidental; *s.*, incidente.
IN.CI.DEN.TAL.LY, *adv.*, por acaso, a propósito.
IN.CI.DEN.TAL MU.SIC, *s.*, música de fundo.
IN.CIN.ER.ATE, *v.*, incinerar, queimar, reduzir a cinzas.
IN.CIN.ER.A.TION, *s.*, incineração.
IN.CIN.ER.A.TOR, *s.*, incinerador.
IN.CIP.I.ENT, *adj.*, incipiente, iniciante.
IN.CISE, *v.*, fazer uma incisão, cortar, talhar.
IN.CISED, *adj.*, inciso, cortado; gravado.
IN.CI.SION, *s.*, incisão, corte, talho.
IN.CI.SIVE, *adj.*, incisivo, eficaz; penetrante.
IN.CI.SOR, *s.*, incisivo; *incisors*, *s.pl.: Anat.*, incisivos (dentes).
IN.CI.SO.RY, *adj.*, incisório.
IN.CITANT, *s.*, incitador.
IN.CI.TA.TION, *s.*, incitação, incitamento, estímulo.
IN.CITE, *v.*, incitar, estimular, provocar.
IN.CITE.MENT, *s.*, incitamento, estímulo.
IN.CIT.ING, *adj.*, incitante, estimulante, que provoca.
IN.CI.VIL.I.TY, *s.*, incivilidade; descortesia.
IN.CLEM.ENT, *adj.*, inclemente, duro, ríspido.
IN.CLIN.ABLE, *adj.*, inclinável, inclinado, pendente.
IN.CLI.NA.TION, *s.*, inclinação, tendência, pendor, vocação.
IN.CLINE, *s.*, inclinação, tendência; *v.*, inclinar, tender para, curvar.
IN.CLINED, *adj.*, inclinado, propenso.
IN.CLOSE, *v.*, incluir, conter, reter, cercar, rodear.
IN.CLOSURE, *s.*, cerca, cercado.
IN.CLUDE, *v.*, incluir, colocar dentro.
IN.CLUD.ED, *adj.*, incluído, incluso.
IN.CLUD.ING, *prep.*, inclusive.
IN.CLU.SION, *s.*, inclusão.
IN.CLU.SIVE, *adj.*, incluso, incluído.
IN.CLU.SIVE.LY, *adv.*, inclusivamente.
IN.CO.HER.ENCE, *s.*, incoerência, incongruência.
IN.CO.HER.ENT, *adj.*, incoerente.
IN.CO.HE.SION, *s.*, incoesão.
IN.COME, *s.*, renda, lucro.
IN.COMER, *s.*, recém-chegado, recém-vindo.
IN.COME TAX, *s.*, imposto de renda.
IN.COM.ING, *adj.*, de chegada, que chega, recebido (carta, telefone), que assume um cargo.
IN.COM.MEN.SU.RA.BLE, *adj.*, incomensurável.
IN.COM.MODE, *v.*, incomodar, perturbar.
IN.COM.MO.DI.OUS, *adj.*, incômodo.

INCOMMUNICABLE ·· 498 ·· INDEPENDENT

IN.COM.MU.NI.CA.BLE, *adj.*, incomunicável.
IN.COM.MU.NI.CA.BLE.NESS, *s.*, incomunicabilidade.
IN.COM.MU.NI.CA.DO, *adj.*, incomunicável.
IN.COM.PA.RA.BIL.I.TY, *s.*, incomparabilidade.
IN.COM.PA.RA.BLE, *adj.*, incomparável.
IN.COM.PA.RA.BLY, *adv.*, incomparavelmente.
IN.COM.PAT.I.BIL.I.TY, *s.*, incompatibilidade.
IN.COM.PA.TI.BLE, *adj.*, incompatível.
IN.COM.PA.TI.BLY, *adv.*, incompativelmente.
IN.COM.PE.TENCE, *s.*, incompetência.
IN.COM.PE.TENT, *adj.*, incompetente.
IN.COM.PLETE, *adj.*, incompleto, não terminado.
IN.COM.PRE.HEN.SI.BLE, *adj.*, incompreensível.
IN.COM.PRE.HEN.SI.BLY, *adv.*, incompreensivelmente.
IN.COM.PRE.HEN.SION, *s.*, incompreensão.
IN.CON.CEIV.ABLE, *adj.*, inconcebível.
IN.CON.CLU.SIVE, *adj.*, inconclusivo; inconsequente:
IN.CON.GRU.ENT, *adj.*, incongruente.
IN.CON.GRU.OUS, *adj.*, incôngruo, impróprio, inconveniente.
IN.CON.SE.QUENCE, *s.*, inconsequência.
IN.CON.SE.QUENT, *adj.*, inconsequente, desmiolado.
IN.CON.SE.QUEN.TIAL, *adj.*, insignificante, irrelevante.
IN.CON.SID.ER.A.BLE, *adj.*, desprezível, insignificante; *adv.*, de modo não considerável.
IN.CON.SIS.TEN.CY, *s.*, inconsistência, incompatibilidade.
IN.CON.SIS.TENT, *adj.*, inconsistente.
IN.CON.SOL.ABLE, *adj.*, inconsolável.
IN.CON.SPIC.U.OUS, *adj.*, discreto, inconspícuo.
IN.CON.STAN.CY, *s.*, inconstância, mutabilidade.
IN.CON.STANT, *adj.*, inconstante, volúvel.
IN.CON.TEST.A.BLE, *adj.*, incontestável.
IN.CON.TEST.A.BLY, *adv.*, incontestavelmente.
IN.CON.TI.NENCE, *s.*, incontinência.
IN.CON.TI.NENT, *adj.*, incontinente.
IN.CON.TROL.LA.BLE, *adj.*, incontrolável.
IN.CON.TRO.VER.TI.BLE, *adj.*, incontrovertível, incontestável.
IN.CON.VEN.I.ENCE, *s.*, inconveniência, despudor; *v.*, incomodar.
IN.CON.VEN.I.ENT, *adj.*, inconveniente.
IN.CON.VEN.I.ENT.LY, *adv.*, inconvenientemente.
IN.COR.PO.RA.BLE, *adj.*, passível de ser incorporado.
IN.COR.PO.RATE, *v.*, incorporar, conter; *adj.*, incorporado, unido.
IN.COR.PO.RA.TION, *s.*, incorporação, ligação, associação.
IN.COR.RECT, *adj.*, incorreto.
IN.COR.RI.GI.BIL.I.TY, *s.*, incorrigibilidade.
IN.COR.RI.GI.BLE, *adj.*, incorrigível.
IN.COR.RUPT, *adj.*, incorrupto, íntegro.
IN.COR.RUPT.I.BLE, *adj.*, incorruptível.
IN.CREASE, *s.*, aumento; *v.*, aumentar, crescer.
IN.CREASED, *adj.*, intensificado, em crescimento.
IN.CREAS.ING, *adj.*, crescente, que aumenta.
IN.CREAS.ING.LY, *adv.*, de modo crescente, cada vez mais.
IN.CRED.I.BIL.I.TY, *s.*, incredibilidade.
IN.CRED.I.BLE, *adj.*, incrível, inacreditável.
IN.CRED.I.BLY, *adv.*, inacreditavelmente.
IN.CRE.DU.LI.TY, *s.*, incredulidade, descrença.
IN.CRED.U.LOUS, *adj.*, incrédulo, descrente.
IN.CRE.MENT, *s.*, incremento.
IN.CRIM.I.NATE, *v.*, incriminar, acusar, culpar.
IN.CRIM.I.NAT.ING, *adj.*, incriminatório.

IN.CRUST, *v.*, incrustar, fixar.
IN.CRUS.TA.TION, *s.*, incrustação.
IN.CRUSTED, *adj.*, incrustado.
IN.CU.BATE, *v.*, incubar, chocar.
IN.CUL.CATE, *v.*, inculcar, impingir.
IN.CU.BA.TION, *s.*, incubação.
IN.CU.BA.TIVE, *adj.*, incubador.
IN.CU.BA.TOR, *s.*, incubadora, estufa.
IN.CU.BUS, *s.*, íncubo; pesadelo.
IN.CUL.CATE, *v.*, inculcar.
IN.CUL.PATE, *v.*, culpar, incriminar, acusar.
IN.CUM.BEN.CY, *s.*, incumbência.
IN.CUM.BENT, *s.*, pessoa incumbida (de algo); *adj.*, com incumbência; que jaz ou pesa sobre.
IN.CUR, *v.*, incorrer em.
IN.CUR.A.BIL.I.TY, *s.*, incurabilidade.
IN.CUR.ABLE, *adj.*, incurável.
IN.CUR.SION, *s.*, incursão; *Mil.*, invasão.
IN.CUR.VATE, *v.*, encurvar, dobrar; *adj.*, encurvado.
IN.CUR.VA.TION, *s.*, encurvamento, curvatura.
IN.CURVE, *v.*, curvar, dobrar.
IN.DA.GATE, *v.*, indagar.
IN.DEBT.ED, *adj.*, que deve, endividado.
IN.DE.CEN.CY, *s.*, indecência, indecoro, despudor.
IN.DE.CENT, *adj.*, indecente, inadequado.
IN.DE.CI.PHER.A.BLE, *adj.*, indecifrável, ilegível.
IN.DE.CI.SION, *s.*, indecisão, incerteza.
IN.DE.CI.SIVE, *adj.*, indecisivo, hesitante.
IN.DE.CI.SIVE.LY, *adv.*, indecisivamente.
IN.DE.CI.SIVE.NESS, *s.*, indecisão, hesitação.
IN.DE.CO.ROUS, *adj.*, indecoroso.
IN.DEED, *adv.*, realmente, certamente, na verdade, de fato; *interj.*, decerto!, deveras!, realmente!.
IN.DE.FAT.I.GA.BLE, *adj.*, infatigável, incansável.
IN.DE.FEA.SI.BLE, *adj.*, irrevogável, inalienável.
IN.DE.FECT.I.BLE, *adj.*, idefectível.
IN.DE.FEN.SI.BLE, *adj.*, indefensável.
IN.DE.FIN.A.BLE, *adj.*, indefinível.
IN.DEF.I.NITE, *adj.*, indefinido, indeciso.
IN.DEF.I.NITE ARTICLE, *s.*, *Gram.*, artigo indefinido.
IN.DEF.I.NITE.LY, *adv.*, indefinidamente.
IN.DEL.I.BLE, *adj.*, indelével, inapagável.
IN.DEL.I.BLY, *adv.*, indelevelmente.
IN.DEL.I.CA.CY, *s.*, indelicadeza, polidez, finura.
IN.DEL.I.CATE, *adj.*, indelicado, grosseiro, incivilizado, rude.
IN.DEM.NI.FI.CA.TION, *s.*, indenização, pagamento.
IN.DEM.NI.FY, *v.*, indenizar, ressarcir prejuízos.
IN.DEM.NI.TY, *s.*, garantia, indenização, compensação, reparação.
IN.DENT, *s.*, chanfro, abertura de parágrafo; *v.*, dentear, cortar, recortar; abrir parágrafo; encomendar; certificar.
IN.DENT.ED, *adj.*, denteado, serrilhado; encomendado.
IN.DEN.TION, *s.*, recuo, recuo de parágrafo.
IN.DEN.TA.TION, *s.*, denteação, reentrância (superfície); chanfro; recuo (de parágrafo).
IN.DEN.TURE, *s.*, contrato de aprendizagem; recorte; escritura; *v.*, colocar (alguém) para aprender (ofício).
IN.DE.PEN.DENCE, *s.*, independência, liberdade.
IN.DE.PEN.DENCE DAY, *s.*, Dia da Independência.
IN.DE.PEN.DENCY, *s.*, independência.
IN.DE.PEN.DENT, *adj.*, independente, livre, justo.

INDEPENDENTLY   •• 499 ••   INEBRIANT

IN.DE.PEN.DENT.LY, *adv.*, independentemente.
IN.DE.PEN.DENT SCHOOL, *s.*, *UK* escola privada.
IN-DEPTH, *adj.*, exaustivo, em profundidade, detalhado.
IN.DE.SCRIB.A.BLE, *adj.*, indescritível.
IN.DE.STRUC.TI.BLE, *adj.*, indestrutível, firme.
IN.DE.TER.MIN.ABLE, *adj.*, indeterminável.
IN.DE.TER.MI.NATE, *adj.*, indeterminado.
IN.DE.TER.MI.NATE.NESS, *s.*, indeterminação, indecisão.
IN.DE.TER.MI.NED, *adj.*, indeterminado, irresoluto; inconstante.
IN.DE.TER.MIN.ISM, *s.*, *Fil.*, indeterminismo.
IN.DEX, *s.*, index, índice remissivo; agulha (de instrumento).
IN.DEX-FIN.GER, *s.*, (dedo) indicador.
IN.DEX-LINKED, *adj.*, indexado (à inflação).
IN.DIA, *s.*, Índia.
IN.DI.AN, *adj.*, *s.*, indiano; índio.
IN.DI.AN BLUE, *s.*, índigo (corante azul).
IN.DI.AN INK *UK*, **IN.DI.A INK** *US*, *s.*, nanquim (tinta).
IN.DI.AN O.CEAN, *s.*, Oceano Índico.
IN.DI.AN SUM.MER, *s.*, veranico.
IN.DI.A RUB.BER, *s.*, borracha natural (látex da seringueira).
IN.DI.CATE, *v.*, indicar, sugerir, apresentar.
IN.DI.CA.TION, *s.*, indicação, indício.
IN.DIC.A.TIVE, *adj.*, indicativo; *s.*, *Gram.*, modo indicativo.
IN.DI.CA.TOR, *s.*, indicador, pessoa ou coisa que indica.
IN.DICT, *v.*, acusar, culpar, processar.
IN.DICT.A.BLE, *adj.*, indiciável, acusável.
IN.DICT.EE, *s.*, acusado, réu.
IN.DICT.ER, *s.*, acusador, processante.
IN.DICT.MENT, *s.*, *Jur.*, indiciamento.
IN.DIE, *adj.*, *col.*, independente.
IN.DIES, *s.*, Índias (durante as grandes navegações).
IN.DIF.FER.ENCE, *s.*, indiferença.
IN.DIF.FER.ENT, *s.*, pessoa neutra; *adj.*, indiferente, imparcial, apático; medíocre.
IN.DI.GENCE, *s.*, indigência, miséria.
IN.DIG.E.NOUS, *adj.*, nativo, indígena; inerente.
IN.DI.GENT, *adj.*, *s.*, indigente, carente, necessitado.
IN.DI.GEST.ED, *adj.*, indigesto, indigerível.
IN.DI.GES.TI.BLE, *adj.*, indigesto; *fig.*, incompreensível, complicado.
IN.DI.GES.TION, *s.*, indigestão, zangado.
IN.DIG.NANT, *adj.*, indignado.
IN.DIG.NANT.LY, *adv.*, indignadamente.
IN.DIG.NA.TION, *s.*, indignação.
IN.DIG.NI.TY, *s.*, indignidade.
IN.DI.GO, *s.*, anil, cor azul.
IN.DI.RECT, *adj.*, indireto.
IN.DI.RECT.LY, *adv.*, indiretamente.
IN.DI.RECT SPEECH, *s.*, *Gram.*, discurso indireto.
IN.DI.RECT TAX.A.TION, *s.*, *Econ.*, impostos indiretos.
IN.DIS.CERN.I.BLE, *adj.*, indiscernível, imperceptível.
IN.DIS.CI.PLINE, *s.*, indisciplina.
IN.DIS.CREET, *adj.*, indiscreto.
IN.DIS.CRE.TION, *s.*, indiscrição.
IN.DIS.CRIM.I.NATE, *adj.*, indiscriminado.
IN.DIS.CRIM.I.NATE.LY, *adv.*, indiscriminadamente.
IN.DIS.CRIM.I.NA.TION, *s.*, indiscriminação.
IN.DIS.PEN.SA.BLE, *adj.*, indispensável.
IN.DIS.POSE, *v.*, indispor, inimizar, provocar.
IN.DIS.POSED, *adj.*, indisposto (por saúde); com má vontade.

IN.DIS.PO.SI.TION, *s.*, indisposição, aversão, mal-estar.
IN.DIS.SOL.U.BLE, *adj.*, indissolúvel.
IN.DIS.TINCT, *adj.*, indistinto, confuso.
IN.DIS.TINCT.LY, *adv.*, indistintamente.
IN.DIS.TIN.GUISH.A.BLE, *adj.*, indistinguível.
IN.DITE, *v.*, *Arc.*, escrever, redigir, compor.
IN.DIT.ER, *s.*, *Arc.*, indivíduo; *adj.*, individual, pessoal.
IN.DI.VID.U.AL, *adj.*, individual, particular; *s.*, indivíduo.
IN.DI.VID.U.AL.ISM, *s.*, individualismo.
IN.DI.VID.U.AL.IST, *s.*, individualista.
IN.DI.VID.U.AL.IST.IC, *adj.*, individualista.
IN.DI.VID.U.AL.I.TY, *s.*, individualidade.
IN.DI.VID.U.AL.IZE(-ISE), *v.*, individualizar.
IN.DI.VID.U.AL.LY, *adv.*, individualmente.
IN.DI.VIS.I.BLE, *adj.*, indivisível.
IN.DOC.ILE, *adj.*, indócil, rebelde, revoltado.
IN.DO.CIL.I.TY, *s.*, indocilidade.
IN.DOC.TRI.NATE, *v.*, doutrinar, catequizar.
IN.DOC.TRI.NA.TION, *s.*, doutrinação.
IN.DO-EU.RO.PE.AN, *s.*, *adj.*, indo-europeu.
IN.DO.LENCE, *s.*, indolência, preguiça, ócio.
IN.DO.LENT, *adj.*, indolente.
IN.DOM.I.TA.BLE, *adj.*, indomável.
IN.DO.NE.SIAN, *s.*, indonésio.
IN.DOOR, *adj.*, interno, interior, de dentro de casa.
IN.DOORS, *adv.*, internamente; em casa.
IN.DORSE, *v.*, endossar, aprovar, deferir.
IN.DU.BI.TA.BIL.I.TY, *s.*, indubitabilidade.
IN.DU.BI.TA.BLE, *adj.*, indubitável.
IN.DU.BI.TA.BLY, *adv.*, indubitavelmente.
IN.DUCE, *v.*, induzir, provocar, causar.
IN.DUCE.MENT, *s.*, persuasão, estímulo, incentivo.
IN.DUC.ER, *s.*, induzidor.
IN.DU.CI.BLE, *adj.*, induzível.
IN.DUCT, *v.*, estabelecer, instalar, ajeitar.
IN.DUC.TILE, *adj.*, indúctil.
IN.DUC.TION, *s.*, indução; apresentação, introdução.
IN.DUC.TION OR.DER, *s.*, *Mil.*, convocação para o serviço militar.
IN.DUC.TIVE, *adj.*, indutivo.
IN.DUC.TOR, *s.*, indutor; introdutor.
IN.DULGE, *v.*, favorecer, ser indulgente, satisfazer, tolerar.
IN.DUL.GENCE, *s.*, satisfação, indulgência.
IN.DUL.GENT, *adj.*, indulgente.
IN.DULT, *s.*, indulto, perdão.
IN.DUS.TRI.AL, *adj.*, industrial.
IN.DUS.TRI.AL.IST, *s.*, industrial.
IN.DUS.TRI.AL.I.ZA.TION, **IN.DUS.TRI.AL.I.SA.TION**, *s.*, industrialização.
IN.DUS.TRI.AL.IZE(-ISE), *v.*, industrializar.
IN.DUS.TRI.AL IN.JU.RY, *s.*, acidente de trabalho.
IN.DUS.TRI.AL PARK, **IN.DUS.TRI.AL ES.TATE**, *s.*, parque industrial.
IN.DUS.TRI.OUS, *adj.*, industrioso, trabalhador diligente; *adv.*, industriosamente.
IN.DUS.TRI.OUS.NESS, *s.*, diligência.
IN.DUS.TRY, *s.*, indústria, diligência, aplicação, trabalho.
IN.DWEL, *v.*, morar, residir, habitar, viver.
IN.DWELL.ER, *s.*, morador, habitante.
IN.DWELL.ING, *s.*, moradia, residência.
IN.E.BRI.ANT, *adj.*, inebriante, embriagante, intoxicante.

INEBRIATE ·· 500 ·· INFORMATICS

IN.E.BRI.ATE, v., inebriar, embriagar, embebedar.
IN.E.BRI.AT.ED, adj., inebriado, embriagado.
IN.E.BRI.E.TY, s., embriaguez, bebedeira.
IN.ED.I.BLE, adj., não comestível.
IN.EF.FA.BLE, adj., inefável, doce.
IN.EF.FA.BLY, adv., inefavelmente.
IN.EF.FECT.IVE, adj., ineficaz, inútil.
IN.EF.FEC.TU.AL, adj., ineficaz, inútil.
IN.EF.FI.CA.CIOUS, adj., ineficaz, ineficiente.
IN.EF.FI.CA.CY, s., ineficácia.
IN.EF.FI.CIEN.CY, s., ineficiência.
IN.EF.FI.CIENT, adj., ineficiente.
IN.EL.E.GANT, adj., deselegante; grosseiro.
IN.EL.I.GI.BLE, adj., inelegível.
IN.EPT, adj., inepto.
IN.EPT.I.TUDE, s., inépcia, ineptidão, incompetência.
IN.EPTLY, adv., ineptamente.
IN.E.QUAL.I.TY, s., desigualdade.
IN.EQ.UI.TA.BLE, adj., injusto.
IN.EQ.UI.TY, s., injustiça.
IN.E.RAD.I.CA.BLE, adj., inerradicável, inextirpável.
IN.ER.RA.BLE, adj., infalível.
IN.ER.RA.BLY, adv., infalivelmente.
IN.ERT, adj., inerte, parado, imóvel.
IN.ER.TIA, s., inércia.
IN.ER.TIAL, adj., Fís., inercial.
IN.ES.CAP.A.BLE, adj., inescapável, inevitável.
IN.ES.SEN.TIAL, adj., que não é essencial, dispensável.
IN.ES.TI.MA.BLE, adj., inestimável.
IN.EV.I.TA.BLE, adj., inevitável.
IN.EV.I.TA.BLY, adv., inevitavelmente.
IN.EX.ACT, adj., inexato.
IN.EX.AC.TI.TUDE, s., inexatidão.
IN.EX.CUS.A.BLE, adj., indesculpável.
IN.EX.O.RA.BLE, adj., inexorável.
IN.EX.PENS.IVE, adj., econômico, barato.
IN.EX.PE.RI.ENCE, s., inexperiência, despreparo.
IN.EX.PE.RI.ENCED, adj., inexperiente.
IN.EX.PERT, adj., inábil, despreparado.
IN.EX.PLI.CA.BLE, adj., inexplicável.
IN.EX.PLI.CA.BLY, adv., inexplicavelmente.
IN.EX.PLOR.ABLE, adj., inexplorável.
IN.EX.PRESS.IVE, adj., inexpressivo.
IN.EX.PUG.NA.BLE, adj., inexpugnável.
IN.EX.TRI.CA.BLE, adj., inextricável.
IN.EX.TRI.CA.BLY, adv., inextricavelmente.
IN.FAL.LI.BIL.I.TY, s., infalibilidade.
IN.FAL.LI.BLE, adj., infalível.
IN.FA.MOUS, adj., infame, abominável, detestável.
IN.FA.MY, s., infâmia.
IN.FAN.CY, s., infância.
IN.FANT, s., bebê, nenê, criança, infante.
IN.FAN.TI.CIDE, s., infanticídio.
IN.FAN.TILE, adj., infantil.
IN.FAN.TRY, s., Mil., infantaria.
IN.FAT.U.ATE, v., apaixonar; adj., apaixonado.
IN.FAT.U.ATED, adj., obcecado, apaixonado, enrabichado.
IN.FAT.U.A.TION, s., paixão louca, paixão profunda.
IN.FECT, v., infectar, contagiar, contaminar.
IN.FECT.ED, adj., infectado.
IN.FEC.TION, s., infecção, contágio.

IN.FEC.TIOUS, adj., infeccioso, contagioso.
IN.FEC.TIVE, adj., infeccioso.
IN.FE.LIC.I.TY, s., infelicidade, infortúnio.
IN.FER, v., inferir, deduzir, perceber.
IN.FER.ABLE, adj., deduzível.
IN.FER.ENCE, s., inferência, conclusão.
IN.FE.RI.OR, adj., inferior; s., inferior, subordinado.
IN.FE.RI.OR.I.TY, s., inferioridade.
IN.FER.NAL, adj., infernal.
IN.FER.NO, s., inferno.
IN.FER.TILE, adj., estéril, infértil.
IN.FER.TIL.I.TY, s., infertilidade, infecundidade.
IN.FEST, v., infestar.
IN.FES.TA.TION, s., infestação, praga.
IN.FEST.ED, adj., infestado.
IN.FI.DEL, adj., s., infiel.
IN.FI.DEL.I.TY, s., infidelidade.
IN.FIGHT.ING, s., disputa interna; Esp., luta com o oponente muito próximo (boxe).
IN.FIL.TRATE, v., infiltrar, infiltrar-se, enfiar-se, penetrar.
IN.FIL.TRA.TION, s., infiltração.
IN.FI.NITE, adj., infinito.
IN.FI.NITE.LY, adv., infinitamente.
IN.FI.NITE.NESS, s., infinidade.
IN.FIN.I.TES.I.MAL, adj., infinitesimal.
IN.FIN.I.TIVE, s., Gram., infinitivo (modo verbal); adj., infinitivo.
IN.FIN.I.TUDE, s., infinidade, imensidade.
IN.FIN.I.TY, s., infinito, infinidade.
IN.FIRM, adj., fraco, débil, instável.
IN.FIR.MA.RY, s., enfermaria.
IN.FIR.MI.TY, s., enfermidade, fraqueza.
IN.FLAME, v., inflamar, arder.
IN.FLAMED, adj., Med., inflamado.
IN.FLAM.MA.BLE, adj., inflamável.
IN.FLAM.MA.TION, s., inflamação.
IN.FLAM.MA.TORY, adj., inflamatório, incitante, insuflador.
IN.FLA.TABLE, adj., inflável.
IN.FLATE, v., inflar; Econ., inflacionar.
IN.FLAT.ED, adj., inflado, exagerado; Econ., inflacionado.
IN.FLA.TION, s., inchação, arrogância; Econ., inflação.
IN.FLA.TIONARY, adj., Econ., inflacionário.
IN.FLA.TION RATE, s., Econ., taxa de inflação.
IN.FLEC.TION, s., inflexão; flexão; curvatura.
IN.FLEX.I.BLE, adj., inflexível.
IN.FLICT, v., infligir, impor, obrigar a.
IN.FLIC.TION, s., inflição, castigo; fardo.
IN.FLICTIVE, s., infligidor.
IN.FLO.RES.CENCE, s., Bot., inflorescência.
IN.FLOW, s., influxo.
IN.FLU.ENCE, s., influência; v., influir, influenciar.
IN.FLU.ENT, adj., influente.
IN.FLU.EN.TIAL, adj., influente.
IN.FLU.EN.ZA, s., Med., gripe.
IN.FLUX, s., influxo, afluxo, afluência.
IN.FO, s., abrev. de information: informação.
IN.FORM, v., informar.
IN.FOR.MAL, adj., informal.
IN.FOR.MAL.I.TY, s., informalidade.
IN.FOR.MAL.LY, adv., informalmente.
IN.FORM.ANT, s., informante.
IN.FOR.MAT.ICS, s., Comp., informática.

INFORMATION ·· 501 ·· INOPPORTUNE

IN.FOR.MA.TION, *s.*, informação, informe, conhecimento.
IN.FORM.A.TIVE, *adj.*, informativo; instrutivo.
IN.FORMED, *adj.*, informado; instruído.
IN.FORM.ER, *s.*, informante; delator.
IN.FRACT, *v.*, infringir, quebrar a lei, delinquir.
IN.FRAC.TION, *s.*, infração, transgressão.
IN.FRAC.TOR, *s.*, infrator, transgressor, delinquente.
IN.FRA.RED, *s.*, *adj.*, infravermelho.
IN.FRA.STRUC.TURE, *s.*, infraestrutura.
IN.FRE.QUENT, *adj.*, infrequente.
IN.FRINGE, *v.*, infringir, transgredir.
IN.FRINGE.MENT, *s.*, transgressão, infração.
IN.FRING.ER, *s.*, infrator, transgressor, delinquente.
IN.FU.RI.ATE, *v.*, enfurecer.
IN.FU.RI.AT.ING, *adj.*, enfurecedor.
IN.FUSE, *v.*, infundir.
IN.FU.SION, *s.*, infusão.
IN.GE.NIOUS, *adj.*, engenhoso, esperto, perito.
IN.GE.NIOUS.NESS, *s.*, engenho, talento, habilidade.
IN.GE.NUE, *s.*, ingênua, inocente (menina).
IN.GE.NU.I.TY, *s.*, engenho, habilidade, esperteza, capacidade.
IN.GEN.U.OUS, *adj.*, ingênuo, inocente; franco.
IN.GEN.U.OUS.LY, *adv.*, ingenuamente, sinceramente.
IN.GEST, *v.*, ingerir.
IN.GLO.RI.OUS, *adj.*, inglório, inglorioso; vergonhoso.
IN.GOT, *s.*, lingote.
IN.GRAIN, *v.*, arraigar, enraizar.
IN.GRAINED, *adj.*, enraizado, arraigado.
IN.GRATE, *s.*, indivíduo ingrato.
IN.GRA.TI.ATE, *v.*, congraçar-se.
IN.GRA.TI.AT.ING, *adj.*, insinuante, lisonjeiro.
IN.GRAT.I.TUDE, *s.*, ingratidão.
IN.GRE.DI.ENT, *s.*, ingrediente.
IN.GRESS, *s.*, ingresso, entrada, acesso.
IN.GRES.SION, *s.*, ação de entrar, ingressão, ingresso.
IN.GROWN, *adj.*, encravado.
IN.HAB.IT, *v.*, habitar.
IN.HAB.IT.ABLE, *adj.*, habitável.
IN.HAB.I.TANT, *s.*, habitante.
IN.HAB.I.TA.TION, *s.*, habitação.
IN.HA.LA.TION, *s.*, inalação.
IN.HALE, *v.*, inalar, inspirar, tragar.
IN.HAL.ER, *s.*, *Med.*, inalador.
IN.HERE, *v.*, estar inerente, ligar-se.
IN.HER.ENCE, *s.*, inerência, ligação, ligadura.
IN.HER.ENT, *adj.*, inerente.
IN.HER.ENT.LY, *adv.*, inerentemente, intrinsecamente.
IN.HER.IT, *v.*, herdar, receber por herança.
IN.HER.I.TANCE, *s.*, herança.
IN.HER.I.TOR, *s.*, herdeiro.
IN.HIB.IT, *v.*, inibir, impedir.
IN.HIB.IT.ED, *adj.*, inibido.
IN.HI.BI.TION, *s.*, inibição.
IN.HOS.PI.TA.BLE, *adj.*, inospitaleiro, inóspito.
IN.HU.MAN, *adj.*, inumano, desumano.
IN.HU.MAN.I.TY, *s.*, desumanidade.
IN.HU.MA.TION, *s.*, inumação; sepultamento.
IN.HUME, *v.*, inumar, sepultar, enterrar.
IN.IM.I.TA.BLE, *adj.*, inimitável.
IN.IQ.UI.TOUS, *adj.*, iníquo.

IN.IQ.UI.TY, *s.*, iniquidade.
INI.TIAL, *adj.*, *s.*, inicial; *v.*, colocar as iniciais em.
INI.TIAL.IZE(-ISE), *v.*, *Comp.*, inicializar.
INI.TIAL.LY, *adv.*, inicialmente.
INI.TI.ATE, *s.*, principiante; *adj.*, iniciado, instruído; *v.*, iniciar, originar; instruir.
INI.TI.AT.ED, *adj.*, instruído, inteirado.
INI.TI.A.TION, *s.*, iniciação, princípio, início.
INI.TIA.TIVE, *s.*, iniciativa.
INI.TI.A.TOR, *s.*, iniciador.
IN.JECT, *v.*, injetar, inocular, dar injeção.
IN.JEC.TION, *s.*, injeção.
IN.JU.DI.CIOUS, *adj.*, sem juízo, imprudente.
IN.JUNC.TION, *s.*, injunção, determinação, ordem; mandado judicial; interdito.
IN.JURE, *v.*, injuriar, ofender, prejudicar.
IN.JU.RI.OUS, *adj.*, injurioso, ofensivo, prejudicial.
IN.JU.RY, *s.*, injúria, insulto; injustiça; lesão, ferimento.
IN.JUS.TICE, *s.*, injustiça.
INK, *s.*, tinta; *v.*, cobrir com tinta, borrar com tinta.
INK-HOLD.ER, *s.*, tinteiro (reservatório de tinta para caneta-tinteiro).
INK.LING, *s.*, boato; suspeita; insinuação.
INK-PAD, *s.*, almofada para carimbos.
INK.STAND, *s.*, tinteiro (para canetas).
INK-WELL, *s.*, tinteiro (de mesa).
INK.Y, *adj.*, sujo de tinta; como tinta.
IN.LAID, *adj.*, incrustado, marcheteado, embutido.
IN.LAND, *s.*, interior (de um país); *adj.*, interior (afastado do mar); *adv.*, para o interior.
IN-LAWS, *s.*, sogros.
IN.LET, *s.*, baía, enseada, angra.
IN.MATE, *s.*, pessoa que co-habita (em casa); recluso (em prisão).
IN.MOST, *adj.*, interior, íntimo, profundo.
INN, *s.*, hospedaria, taberna, bar.
IN.NARDS, *s. pl.*, *col.*, entranhas, vísceras.
IN.NATE, *adj.*, inato, congênito.
IN.NER, *adj.*, interno, interior.
IN.NING, *s.*, *Esp.*, turno, a vez de jogar.
IN.NO.CENCE, *s.*, inocência.
IN.NO.CEN.CY, *s.*, inocência.
IN.NO.CENT, *adj.*, inocente.
IN.NOC.U.OUS, *adj.*, inócuo.
IN.NO.VATE, *v.*, inovar.
IN.NO.VA.TION, *s.*, inovação.
IN.NO.VA.TIVE, *adj.*, inovador.
IN.NO.VA.TOR, *s.*, inovador.
IN.NU.EN.DO, *s.*, insinuação, indireta, sugestão.
IN.NU.MER.ABLE, *adj.*, incontável, inumerável.
IN.NU.MER.OUS, *adj.*, inumerável.
IN.OB.SERV.ANCE, *s.*, inobservância.
IN.OC.U.LATE, *v.*, inocular, injetar; vacinar.
IN.OC.U.LA.TION, *s.*, inoculação.
IN.O.DOR.OUS, *adj.*, inodoro.
IN.OF.FEN.SIVE, *adj.*, inofensivo.
IN.OP.ER.A.BLE, *adj.*, *Med.*, que não se pode operar; impraticável.
IN.OP.ER.A.TIVE, *adj.*, ineficaz.
IN.OP.ER.A.TIVE.NESS, *s.*, ineficácia.
IN.OP.POR.TUNE, *adj.*, inoportuno.

INORDINATE   •• 502 •••   INSTRUCTION

IN.OR.DI.NATE, *adj.*, excessivo, desmesurado, irregular.
IN.OR.DI.NATE.LY, *adv.*, de forma desmesurada, desordenadamente.
IN.OR.GAN.IC, *adj.*, inorgânico.
IN.OX.I.DA.BLE, *adj.*, inoxidável.
IN.OX.I.DIZE. *v.*, tornar inoxidável.
IN-PA.TIENT, *s.*, paciente interno, internado.
IN.PUT, *s.*, entrada, investimento, informação para o computador.
IN.QUI.ET, *adj.*, inquieto.
IN.QUI.ETUDE, *s.*, inquietude.
IN.QUIRE, *v.*, inquirir, buscar informações.
IN.QUIR.ING, *s.*, interrogador.
IN.QUI.RY, *s.*, pergunta, inquirição.
IN.QUI.SI.TION, *s.*, inquisição, investigação.
IN.QUI.SI.TIVE, *adj.*, curioso.
IN.ROAD, *s.*, invasão, transgressão; *to make inroads into*: abrir caminho, fazer progresso.
IN.RUSH, *s.*, invasão.
IN.SA.LU.BRI.OUS, *adj.*, insalubre.
IN.SA.LU.BRI.TY, *s.*, insalubridade.
IN.SANE, *adj.*, insano, louco, doido, desvairado.
IN.SAN.I.TA.RY, *adj.*, insalubre, anti-higiênico.
IN.SAN.I.TY, *s.*, insanidade, loucura, desvario.
IN.SA.TIA.BLE, *adj.*, insaciável.
IN.SCRIBE, *v.*, inscrever.
IN.SCRIP.TION, *s.*, inscrição.
IN.SCRIP.TION.AL, *adj.*, inscrição, inscritível.
IN.SCRU.TA.BLE, *adj.*, inescrutável, impenetrável.
IN.SECT, *s.*, inseto.
IN.SECT BITE, *s.*, picada de inseto.
IN.SEC.TI.CIDE, *s.*, inseticida.
IN.SEC.TION, *s.*, incisão.
IN.SEC.TIV.O.ROUS, *adj.*, insetívoro.
IN.SECT RE.PEL.LENT, *s.*, repelente para insetos.
IN.SE.CURE, *adj.*, inseguro.
IN.SE.CU.RI.TY, *s.*, insegurança.
IN.SEM.I.NATE, *v.*, inseminar, fecundar.
IN.SEM.I.NA.TION, *s.*, inseminação.
IN.SEN.SATE, *adj.*, insensato.
IN.SEN.SI.BIL.I.TY, *s.*, insensibilidade.
IN.SEN.SI.BLE, *adj.*, inconsciente, insensível.
IN.SEN.SI.TIVE, *adj.*, insensível.
IN.SEN.TI.ENT, *adj.*, inanimado.
IN.SEP.A.RA.BLE, *adj.*, inseparável.
IN.SERT, *v.*, inserir, introduzir, colocar dentro; *s.*, suplemento.
IN.SER.TION, *s.*, inserção.
IN-SER.VICE TRAIN.ING, *s.*, *UK* treinamento no serviço.
IN.SET, *s.*, detalhe; inserção; influxo; *v.*, inserir.
IN.SHORE, *adj.*, costeiro, litorâneo: *adv.*, perto da costa.
IN.SIDE, *s.*, interior, parte interna, entranhas; *prep.*, dentro de.
IN.SIDE STO.RY, *s.*, história íntima.
IN.SID.ER, *s.*, indivíduo pertencente a um grupo ou organização; aquele que está bem informado.
IN.SID.I.OUS, *adj.*, insidioso.
IN.SIGHT, *s.*, discernimento, conhecimento, compreensão, critério.
IN.SIGHT.FUL, *adj.*, criterioso, compreensivo.
IN.SIG.NIA, *s.*, insígnia, emblema.
IN.SIG.NIF.I.CANCE, *s.*, insignificância.
IN.SIG.NIF.I.CANT, *adj.*, insignificante, sem valor.

IN.SIN.CERE, *adj.*, insincero.
IN.SIN.U.ATE, *v.*, insinuar, sugerir, dar a entender.
IN.SIN.U.A.TING, *adj.*, insinuante, insinuativo.
IN.SIN.U.A.TION, *s.*, insinuação, sugestão.
IN.SIN.CER.I.TY, *s.*, insinceridade.
IN.SIP.ID, *adj.*, insípido, sem gosto, sem sabor, enfadonho.
IN.SIST, *v.*, insistir, persistir, sustentar.
IN.SIS.TENCE, *s.*, insistência.
IN.SIST.ENT, *adj.*, insistente.
IN.SO.BRI.E.TY, *s.*, destemperança, imoderação, sem sobriedade.
IN.SO.FAR, *conj.*, na medida em que, à medida que.
IN.SO.LA.TION, *s.*, insolação.
IN.SOLE, *s.*, palmilha.
IN.SO.LENCE, *s.*, insolência.
IN.SO.LENT, *adj.*, insolente, atrevido, petulante.
IN.SOL.U.BIL.I.TY, *s.*, insolubilidade.
IN.SOL.U.BLE, *adj.*, insolúvel.
IN.SOL.VEN.CY, *s.*, insolvência, falência.
IN.SOL.VENT, *adj.*, insolvente.
IN.SOM.NIA, *s.*, insônia.
IN.SOM.NI.AC, *s.*, insone; *adj.*, que tem insônia.
IN.SO.MUCH, *adv.*, a tal ponto que, tanto que.
IN.SPECT, *v.*, inspecionar, examinar, verificar.
IN.SPEC.TION, *s.*, inspeção, vistoria, exame.
IN.SPEC.TOR, *s.*, inspetor, fiscal.
IN.SPI.RA.TION, *s.*, inspiração, influência, tendência.
IN.SPIRE, *v.*, inspirar, incutir, insuflar, sugerir.
IN.SPIRED, *adj.*, inspirado.
IN.SPIR.ING, *adj.*, inspirador, estimulante.
IN.SPIR.IT, *v.*, estimular, entusiasmar, excitar, animar.
IN.STA.BIL.I.TY, *s.*, instabilidade.
IN.STA.BLE, *adj.*, instável, inseguro.
IN.STALL, *v.*, instalar, colocar, nomear.
IN.STAL.LA.TION, *s.*, instalação.
IN.STALL.MENT, *s.*, prestação, parte (de história: livro, série de TV); instalação; montagem.
IN.STANCE, *s.*, exemplo, instância; *v.*, exemplificar, dar como exemplo.
IN.STANT, *s.*, instante, momento; *adj.*, instantâneo, imediato, súbito.
IN.STAN.TA.NE.OUS, *adj.*, instantâneo, rápido.
IN.STANT.LY, *adv.*, imediatamente, instantaneamente.
IN.STEAD, *adv.*, em vez disso, em lugar de.
IN.STEP, *s.*, peito do pé.
IN.STI.GATE, *v.*, instigar, fomentar, suscitar.
IN.STI.GA.TION, *s.*, instigamento, instigação.
IN.STI.GA.TOR, *s.*, instigador.
IN.STIL, *v.*, instilar, inocular, infundir, injetar.
IN.STINCT, *s.*, instinto; *adj.*, instintivo, excitado, entusiasmado.
IN.STINC.TIVE, *adj.*, instintivo, involuntário.
IN.STINC.TIVE.LY, *adv.*, instintivamente.
IN.STI.TUTE, *s.*, instituto, instituição, sociedade; *v.*, instituir, nomear.
IN.STI.TU.TION, *s.*, instituição, instituto, costume, praxe.
IN.STI.TU.TION.AL, *adj.*, institucional.
IN.STI.TU.TION.AL.IZE(-ISE), *v.*, institucionalizar.
IN.STI.TU.TION.AL.IZED(-ISED), *adj.*, institucionalizado.
IN.STI.TU.TOR, *s.*, instituidor, fundador.
IN.STRUCT, *v.*, instruir, doutrinar, catequizar.
IN.STRUC.TION, *s.*, instrução.

INSTRUCTIVE ··503·· INTEREST RATE

IN.STRUC.TIVE, *adj.*, instrutivo.
IN.STRUC.TOR, *s.*, instrutor.
IN.STRUC.TRESS, *s.*, instrutora, professora.
IN.STRU.MENT, *s.*, instrumento, ferramenta, utensílio; *v.*, instrumentar.
IN.STRU.MEN.TAL, *adj.*, instrumental; *s.*, *Mús.*, instrumental.
IN.STRU.MEN.TAL.ISM, *s.*, *Fil.*, instrumentalismo.
IN.STRU.MEN.TAL.IST, *s.*, *Mús.*, instrumentalista.
IN.STRU.MEN.TA.TION, *s.*, instrumentação.
IN.SUB.OR.DI.NATE, *adj.*, insubordinado, indisciplinado, rebelde.
IN.SUB.OR.DI.NA.TION, *s.*, insubordinação.
IN.SUB.STAN.TIAL, *adj.*, frágil, pouco substancioso.
IN.SUF.FER.A.BLE, *adj.*, insuportável.
IN.SUF.FI.CIEN.CY, *s.*, insuficiência.
IN.SUF.FI.CIENT, *adj.*, insuficiente.
IN.SUF.FLATE, *v.*, insuflar, encher de ar.
IN.SU.LAR, *adj.*, insular; isolado, limitado; *fig.*, tacanho.
IN.SU.LATE, *v.*, isolar, segregar, separar.
IN.SU.LA.TION, *s.*, isolamento, solidão.
IN.SU.LIN, *s.*, *Med.*, insulina.
IN.SULT, *s.*, insulto; *v.*, insultar, ofender.
IN.SULT.ING, *adj.*, insultante, ofensivo.
IN.SU.PER.A.BLE, *adj.*, insuperável.
IN.SUR.ABLE, *adj.*, segurável.
IN.SUR.ANCE, *s.*, seguro; segurança.
IN.SUR.ANCE BROK.ER, *s.*, corretor de seguros.
IN.SUR.ANCE POL.I.CY, *adj.*, apólice de seguro.
IN.SUR.ANCE PRE.MI.UM, *s.*, prêmio do seguro.
IN.SURE, *v.*, segurar.
IN.SURED, *adj.*, segurado (contra algo); assegurado; *s.*, o segurado(a).
IN.SUR.ER, *s.*, segurador.
IN.SUR.GENT, *adj.*, *s.*, rebelde, revoltado, insubordinado.
IN.SUR.MOUNT.A.BLE, *adj.*, intransponível, insuperável.
IN.SUR.REC.TION, *s.*, insurreição, revolta.
IN.SUS.CEP.TI.BLE, *adj.*, insuscetível, insensível.
IN.TACT, *adj.*, intacto, íntegro, ileso, indene.
IN.TACT.NESS, *s.*, integridade, inteireza, totalidade.
IN.TAKE, *s.*, ingestão; ingresso; orifício por onde entra, entrada.
IN.TAN.GI.BLE, *adj.*, intangível.
IN.TE.GRAL, *adj.*, integrante, essencial, integral.
IN.TE.GRAL.LY, *adv.*, integralmente.
IN.TE.GRANT, *adj.*, integrante.
IN.TE.GRATE, *v.*, integrar, completar, integrar-se.
IN.TE.GRAT.ED, *adj.*, integrado.
IN.TE.GRAT.ED CIR.CUIT, *s.*, *Eletr.*, circuito integrado.
IN.TE.GRA.TION, *s.*, integração.
IN.TEG.RI.TY, *s.*, integridade, retidão.
IN.TEL.LECT, *s.*, intelecto.
IN.TEL.LEC.TU.AL, *adj.*, *s.*, intelectual.
IN.TEL.LEC.TU.AL.ISM, *s.*, intelectualismo.
IN.TEL.LEC.TU.AL.I.TY, *s.*, intelectualidade.
IN.TEL.LEC.TU.AL.IZE, *v.*, intelectualizar.
IN.TEL.LI.GENCE, *s.*, inteligência; informações confidenciais.
IN.TEL.LI.GENCE QUO.TIENT, *s.*, *Psic.*, quociente de inteligência (QI).
IN.TEL.LI.GENCE TEST, *s.*, teste de inteligência.
IN.TEL.LI.GENT, *adj.*, *s.*, inteligente.
IN.TEL.LI.GENT.LY, *adv.*, inteligentemente.

IN.TEL.LI.GI.BLE, *adj.*, inteligível.
IN.TEM.PER.ATE, *adj.*, intemperado, excessivo, descomedido.
IN.TEND, *v.*, pretender, propor-se.
IN.TEN.DANCE, *s.*, intendência.
IN.TEN.DANT, *s.*, intendente.
IN.TEND.ED, *adj.*, planejado.
IN.TENSE, *adj.*, intenso, emocional, sensitivo.
IN.TENSE.LY, *adv.*, intensamente.
IN.TENSE.NESS, *s.*, intensidade, força, arrojo.
IN.TEN.SI.FI.CA.TION, *s.*, intensificação.
IN.TEN.SI.FI.ER, *s.*, intensificador, ampliador.
IN.TEN.SI.FY, *v.*, intensificar.
IN.TEN.SI.TY, *s.*, intensidade.
IN.TEN.SIVE, *adj.*, intensivo.
IN.TEN.SIVE CARE, *s.*, tratamento intensivo.
IN.TEN.SIVE CARE U.NIT, *s.*, unidade de tratamento intensivo (UTI).
IN.TENT, *s.*, intenção; *adj.*, atento, concentrado em.
IN.TEN.TION, *s.*, intenção, propósito, desejo.
IN.TEN.TION.AL, *adj.*, intencional.
IN.TEN.TION.AL.I.TY, *s.*, intencionalidade.
IN.TEN.TION.AL.LY, *adv.*, intencionalmente.
IN.TEN.TLY, *adv.*, atentamente.
IN.TER, *v.*, enterrar, sepultar.
IN.TER.ACT, *v.*, interagir.
IN.TER.AC.TION, *s.*, interação.
IN.TER.AC.TIVE, *adj.*, interativo, que possui interação; *Comp.*, que oferece interatividade (programa).
IN.TER.AC.TIV.I.TY, *s.*, *Comp.*, interatividade.
IN.TER.CA.LATE, *v.*, intercalar, interpor.
IN.TER.CEDE, *v.*, interceder, pedir, suplicar.
IN.TER.CED.ER, *s.*, intercessor.
IN.TER.CEPT, *v.*, interceptar, deter, segurar.
IN.TER.CEP.TION, *s.*, interceptação.
IN.TER.CES.SION, *s.*, intercessão, pedido.
IN.TER.CHANGE, *s.*, câmbio, intercâmbio, permuta; trocar, cambiar.
IN.TER.CHANGE.A.BLE, *adj.*, intercambiável, permutável.
IN.TER.CITY, *adj.*, intermunicipal, interurbano.
IN.TER.COM, *s.*, intercomunicador.
IN.TER.COM.MU.NI.CATE, *v.*, intercomunicar.
IN.TER.COM.MU.NI.CA.TION, *s.*, intercomunicação.
IN.TER.CON.NECT, *v.*, interligar, ligar-se.
IN.TER.CON.NECT.ED, *adj.*, interligado.
IN.TER.CON.TI.NEN.TAL, *adj.*, intercontinental.
IN.TER.COS.TAL, *s.*, *Anat.*, músculo intercostal; *adj.*, intercostal.
IN.TER.COURSE, *s.*, intercurso, intercâmbio, relação; relacionamento (social, sexual).
IN.TER.DE.NOM.I.NA.TION.AL, *adj.*, que envolve denominações diferentes.
IN.TER.DE.PART.MENT.AL, *adj.*, interdepartamental.
IN.TER.DE.PEND.ENCE, *s.*, interdependência, dependência.
IN.TER.DE.PEND.ENT, *adj.*, interdependente.
IN.TER.DICT, *s.*, interdito; *v.*, interdizer, vetar, proibir.
IN.TER.DIC.TION, *s.*, interdição, proibição, veto.
IN.TER.DIS.CI.PLIN.ARY, *s.*, interdisciplinar.
IN.TER.EST, *s.*, interesse, atração; *Com.*, juros, lucro; *v.*, interessar, cativar.
IN.TER.EST.ED, *adj.*, interessado.
IN.TER.EST FREE, *adj.*, sem juros.
IN.TER.EST RATE, *s.*, taxa de juro.

INTERESTING ·· 504 ·· INTRANSIGENT

IN.TER.EST.ING, *adj.*, interessante.
IN.TER.FACE, *s.*, interface; *Comp.*, interface.
IN.TER.FERE, *v.*, interferir, intervir.
IN.TER.FER.ENCE, *s.*, interferência, intromissão.
IN.TER.FER.ING, *adj.*, que interfere; *pej.*, intrometido.
IN.TER.GA.LAC.TIC, *adj.*, intergaláctico.
IN.TER.GLA.CI.AL, *adj.*, *Geol.*, interglaciário.
IN.TER.IM, *adj.*, interino, momentâneo; *s.*, ínterim, meio tempo.
IN.TE.RI.OR, *adj.*, interior, interno; *s.*, interior.
IN.TE.RI.OR DEC.O.RA.TOR, *s.*, decorador de interiores.
IN.TE.RI.OR.LY, *adv.*, intimamente.
IN.TER.JECT, *v.*, interpor, intercalar, injetar.
IN.TER.JEC.TION, *s.*, interjeição; parada, interrupção.
IN.TER.LACE, *v.*, entrelaçar.
IN.TER.LACE.MENT, *s.*, entrelaçamento.
IN.TER.LEAVE, *v.*, intercalar (alguma coisa com outra).
IN.TER.LINE, *v.*, pôr nas entrelinhas.
IN.TER.LINK, *v.*, ligar, encadear, concatenar.
IN.TER.LOCK, *v.*, engrenar, engatar; encaixar; entrelaçar.
IN.TER.LOC.U.TION, *s.*, interlocução.
IN.TER.LOC.U.TOR, *s.*, interlocutor.
IN.TER.LOP.ER, *s.*, intruso.
IN.TER.LUDE, *s.*, intervalo; interlúdio; *v.*, intervalar.
IN.TER.MAR.RY, *v.*, casar (dentro da família); miscigenar, mestiçar.
IN.TER.ME.DI.ARY, *s.*, intermediário.
IN.TER.ME.DI.ATE, *adj.*, intermediário, mediador; *v.*, intermediar.
IN.TER.ME.DI.A.TOR, *s.*, mediador.
IN.TER.MENT, *s.*, enterro, sepultamento, funeral.
IN.TER.MI.NA.BLE, *adj.*, interminável.
IN.TER.MIN.GLE, *v.*, misturar, misturar-se.
IN.TER.MIS.SION, *s.*, intervalo, interrupção.
IN.TER.MIT, *v.*, interromper.
IN.TER.MIT.TENCE, *s.*, intermitência.
IN.TER.MIT.TENT, *adj.*, intermitente. ·
IN.TER.MIX, *v.*, misturar(-se).
IN.TERN, *s.*, *US* médico interno; estagiário; interno; *v.*, internar.
IN.TER.NAL, *s.*, natureza interna; foro íntimo; *adj.*, interno, intrínseco.
IN.TER.NAL.IZE(-ISE), *v.*, internalizar; incorporar.
IN.TER.NAL.LY, *adv.*, internamente.
IN.TER.NA.TION.AL, *adj.*, internacional.
IN.TER.NA.TION.AL DATE LINE, *s.*, linha internacional (de mudança) de data.
IN.TER.NA.TION.AL.LY, *adv.*, internacionalmente.
IN.TER.NA.TION.AL.ISM, *s.*, internacionalismo.
IN.TER.NA.TION.AL RELATIONS, *s. pl.*, relações internacionais.
IN.TER.NA.TION.AL.I.ZA.TION, *s.*, internacionalização.
IN.TER.NA.TION.AL.IZE(-ISE), *v.*, internacionalizar.
IN.TER.NE.CINE, *adj.*, mortal, letal.
IN.TER.NEE, *s.*, recluso; internado.
INTERNET, *s.*, internet.
IN.TER.NET CA.FÉ, *s.*, cibercafé.
IN.TERN.MENT, *s.*, internamento, internação.
IN.TER.PEL.LANT, *s.*, *adj.*, interpelante.
IN.TER.PEL.LA.TION, *s.*, interpelação; *Jur.*, intimação.
IN.TER.PER.SON.AL, *adj.*, interpessoal.
IN.TER.PLAY, *s.*, interação; *v.*, interagir.
IN.TER.PO.LATE, *v.*, interpolar.

IN.TER.PO.LA.TION, *s.*, interpolação.
IN.TER.POSAL, *s.*, interposição.
IN.TER.POSE, *v.*, interpor.
IN.TER.PO.SI.TION, *s.*, interposição.
IN.TER.PRET, *v.*, interpretar, traduzir, verter.
IN.TER.PRE.TA.TION, *s.*, interpretação, tradução.
IN.TER.PRET.ER, *s.*, intérprete, tradutor.
IN.TER.PRET.ING, *s.*, interpretação.
IN.TER.RA.CIAL, *adj.*, inter-racial.
IN.TER.RELATE, *v.*, correlacionar(-se), relacionar(-se).
IN.TER.RO.GATE, *v.*, interrogar, questionar.
IN.TER.RO.GA.TION, *s.*, interrogação.
IN.TER.RO.GA.TIVE, *adj.*, *s.*, *Gram.*, interrogativo; pronome interrogativo.
IN.TER.ROG.A.TOR, *s.*, interrogador.
IN.TER.ROG.A.TO.RY, *s.*, interrogatório.
IN.TER.RUPT, *v.*, interromper, parar, seccionar.
IN.TER.RUPT.ER, *s.*, interruptor.
IN.TER.RUP.TION, *s.*, interrupção.
IN.TER.SECT, *v.*, cruzar, ocorrer um trevo, cruzar-se, entroncar-se.
IN.TER.SEC.TION, *s.*, interseção.
IN.TER.SPERSE, *v.*, entremear(-se).
IN.TER.STATE, *s.*, *US* rodovia interestadual; *adj.*, interestadual.
IN.TER.STEL.LAR, *adj.*, *Astron.*, interestelar.
IN.TER.UR.BAN, *s.*, trem interurbano; *adj.*, interurbano.
IN.TER.VAL, *s.*, intervalo.
IN.TER.VENE, *v.*, intervir, ocorrer, acontecer.
IN.TER.VEN.TION, *s.*, intervenção.
IN.TER.VEN.TION.IST, *s.*, *adj.*, intervencionista.
IN.TER.VEN.TOR, *s.*, *Rel.*, mediador (eclesiástico).
IN.TER.VIEW, *s.*, entrevista; *v.*, entrevistar.
IN.TER.VIEW.EE, *s.*, indivíduo entrevistado.
IN.TER.WEAVE, *v.*, entrelaçar(-se); ligar, misturar.
IN.TER.VIW.ER, *s.*, entrevistador.
IN.TES.TATE, *adj.*, intestado (que não fez ou não foi incluído em testamento).
IN.TES.TI.NAL, *adj.*, intestinal.
IN.TES.TINE, *adj.*, interno, intestino; *intestines s.pl.: Anat.*, intestino, vísceras, tripas.
IN.TI.MA.CY, *s.*, intimidade.
IN.TI.MATE, *adj.*, íntimo, particular; *v.*, intimar; insinuar, propor.
IN.TI.MATE.LY, *adv.*, intimamente.
IN.TI.MA.TION, *s.*, intimação; insinuação.
IN.TIM.I.DATE, *v.*, intimidar.
IN.TIM.I.DAT.ING, *adj.*, intimidador, ameaçador, assustador.
IN.TIM.I.DA.TION, *v.*, intimidação.
IN.TO, *prep.*, em, para, dentro de, para.
IN.TOL.ER.A.BLE, *adj.*, intolerável.
IN.TOL.ER.ANCE, *s.*, intolerância.
IN.TOL.ER.ANT, *s.*, indivíduo intolerante; *adj.*, intolerante.
IN.TO.NATE, *v.*, entoar.
IN.TO.NA.TION, *s.*, entonação, entoação; modulação.
IN.TOX.I.CANT, *adj.*, intoxicante, inebriante.
IN.TOX.I.CATE, *v.*, intoxicar, embriagar.
IN.TOX.I.CA.TING, *adj.*, inebriante, embriagante; *Med.*, intoxicante.
IN.TOX.I.CA.TION, *s.*, intoxicação.
IN.TRACT.A.BLE, *adj.*, intratável, insolúvel.
IN.TRA.MU.RAL, *adj.*, intramuros.
IN.TRAN.SI.GENT, *s.*, indivíduo intransigente; *adj.*,

INTRANSITIVE ··505·· IRISH

intransigente.
IN.TRAN.SI.TIVE, *s., Gram.,* verbo intransitivo; *adj.,* intransitivo.
IN.TRANS.MIS.SI.BLE, *adj.,* intransmissível.
IN.TRA.U.TER.INE, *adj., Med.,* intrauterino.
IN.TRA.VE.NOUS, *adj.,* intravenoso.
IN-TRAY, *s.,* caixa ou receptáculo para correspondência.
IN.TREP.ID, *adj.,* intrépido, valente, denodado.
IN.TRI.CA.CY, *s.,* complexidade, intrincamento.
IN.TRIGUE, *s.,* intriga; *v.,* intrigar.
IN.TRI.GUING, *adj.,* intrigante.
IN.TRIN.SIC, *adj.,* intrínseco.
IN.TRO, *s., col.,* introdução; *pref.,* para dentro.
IN.TRO.DUCE, *v.,* introduzir.
IN.TRO.DUC.TION, *s.,* introdução.
IN.TRO.DUC.TIVE, *adj.,* introdutivo.
IN.TRO.SPEC.TION, *s.,* introspecção.
IN.TRO.DUC.TO.RY, *adj.,* introdutório.
IN.TRO.SPEC.TION, *s., Psic.,* introspecção.
IN.TRO.SPEC.TIVE, *adj.,* introspectivo.
IN.TRO.VER.SION, *s., Psic.,* introversão.
IN.TRO.VERT, *adj., s.,* introvertido.
IN.TRO.VERT.ED, *adj.,* introvertido, absorto.
IN.TRUDE, *v.,* intrometer-se.
IN.TRUD.ER, *s.,* intruso.
IN.TRU.SION, *s.,* intromissão.
IN.TU.IT, *v.,* intuir.
IN.TU.I.TION, *s.,* intuição.
IN.TU.I.TIVE, *adj.,* intuitivo.
IN.TU.I.TIVE.LY, *adv.,* intuitivamente.
IN.U.IT, *adj., s.,* esquimó, inuíte (relativo ou pertencente aos grupos esquimós).
IN.UN.DATE, *v.,* inundar.
IN.UN.DA.TION, *s.,* inundação.
IN.URE, *v.,* acostumar, habituar.
IN.URE.MENT, *s.,* costume, hábito.
IN.UTIL.I.TY, *s.,* inutilidade.
IN.VADE, *v.,* invadir.
IN.VAD.ER, *s.,* invasor.
IN.VAD.ING, *adj.,* invasor.
IN.VAL.ID, *s.,* indivíduo inválido; *adj.,* inválido, fraco; nulo, sem valor, ilegal; *v.,* invalidar.
IN.VAL.ID CHAIR, *s., des.,* cadeira de rodas (melhor: *wheelchair*).
IN.VAL.I.DATE, *v.,* invalidar, anular, desfazer.
IN.VAL.I.DA.TION, *s.,* invalidação.
IN.VAL.ID.I.TY, *s.,* invalidez.
IN.VAL.U.A.BLE, *adj.,* valioso, inestimável.
IN.VA.RI.A.BLE, *adj.,* invariável.
IN.VA.RI.A.BLY, *adv.,* invariavelmente.
IN.VA.SION, *s.,* invasão.
IN.VA.SIVE, *adj.,* invasivo, agressivo.
IN.VEC.TIVE, *s.,* invectiva, injúria.
IN.VEI.GLE, *v.,* aliciar, enganar.
IN.VEIGH, *v.,* invectivar, ofender, injuriar, destratar, xingar.
IN.VENT, *v.,* inventar.
IN.VENT.ER, *s.,* inventor.
IN.VEN.TION, *s.,* invenção, invento; ficção.
IN.VEN.TIVE, *adj.,* inventivo.
IN.VENT.OR, *s.,* inventor.
IN.VEN.TO.RY, *s.,* inventário; estoque; *v.,* inventariar.
IN.VEN.TO.RY CON.TROL, *s.,* controle de estoque.

IN.VERSE, *adj., s.,* inverso.
IN.VER.SION, *s.,* inversão.
IN.VERT, *s.,* invertido; *v.,* inverter; converter.
IN.VER.TE.BRATE, *adj., s.,* invertebrado.
IN.VERT.ED, *adj.,* inverso, invertido; homossexual.
IN.VERT.ED COM.MAS, *s. pl.,* aspas.
IN.VEST, *v.,* investir.
IN.VES.TI.GABLE, *adj.,* investigável.
IN.VES.TI.GATE, *v.,* investigar.
IN.VES.TI.GA.TION, *s.,* investigação.
IN.VES.TI.GA.TIVE, *adj.,* investigador, de investigação.
IN.VES.TI.GA.TOR, *s.,* investigador.
IN.VES.TI.TURE, *s.,* investidura (que dá autoridade ou posse).
IN.VEST.MENT, *s.,* investimento.
IN.VEST.MENT TRUST, *s., Com.,* fundo de investimento.
IN.VES.TOR, *s.,* investidor.
IN.VID.I.OUS, *adj.,* invejoso, injusto.
IN.VIG.I.LATE, *v.,* vigiar, fiscalizar.
IN.VIG.I.LA.TOR, *s.,* vigilante, vigia; *UK* fiscal.
IN.VIG.O.RATE, *v.,* revigorar, fortificar, fortalecer.
IN.VIG.OR.AT.ING, *adj.,* revigorante, estimulante.
IN.VIN.CI.BLE, *adj.,* invencível.
IN.VI.O.LA.BLE, *adj.,* inviolável.
IN.VI.O.LATE, *adj.,* inviolado, íntegro.
IN.VIS.I.BIL.I.TY, *s.,* invisibilidade.
IN.VIS.I.BLE, *adj.,* invisível.
IN.VIS.I.BLE INK, *s.,* tinta invisível.
IN.VI.TA.TION, *s.,* convite.
IN.VITE, *v.,* convidar.
IN.VIT.ER, *s.,* o que convida, convidador.
IN.VIT.ING, *adj.,* convidativo, tentador.
IN VI.TRO FER.TI.LI.ZA.TION, *s.,* fertilização *in vitro.*
IN.VOICE, *s.,* fatura, documento de cobrança; *v.,* faturar.
IN.VOKE, *v.,* invocar, chamar.
IN.VO.LU.CRE, *s.,* invólucro.
IN.VOL.UN.TARY, *adj.,* involuntário.
IN.VO.LU.TION, *s.,* involução; complicação.
IN.VOLVE, *v.,* envolver, implicar.
IN.VOLVED, *adj.,* envolvido; complicado, confuso.
IN.VOLVE.MENT, *s.,* envolvimento.
IN.VUL.NER.A.BLE, *adj.,* invulnerável.
IN.WARD, *s.,* interior, interno; íntimo, imo, profundo.
IN.WARD.LY, *adv.,* intimamente, por dentro.
IN.WARDS, *s. pl.,* vísceras; *adv.,* para dentro, na intimidade.
IO.DATE, *s., Quím.,* iodato.
I.O.DINE, *s., Quím.,* iodo.
I.ON, *s., Fís.,* íon.
I.O.TA, *s.,* muito pouco, pouquinho; iota (letra grega).
I.RAN, *s.,* Irã.
IRA.NI.AN, *adj., s.,* iraniano.
I.RAQ, *s.,* Iraque.
I.RA.QI, *s.,* iraquiano.
I.RAS.CI.BLE, *adj.,* irascível, irritável.
I.RATE, *adj.,* irado, irritado, enfurecido, brabo.
IRE, *s.,* ira, raiva, cólera, brabeza.
IRE.FUL, *adj.,* raivoso, irado, irritado.
IRE.LAND, *s.,* Irlanda.
IR.I.DES.CENT, *adj.,* iridescente.
I.RID.I.UM, *s., Quím.,* irídio.
I.RIS, *s., Anat.,* íris.
I.RISH, *adj., s.,* irlandês.

IRISHMAN ··506·· IVY

I.RISH.MAN, *s.*, irlandês.
IRK, *v.*, aborrecer, enfadar, incomodar.
IRK.SOME, *adj.*, aborrecido, enfadonho.
IRON, *s.*, ferro; ferro de passar roupa; *v.*, passar a ferro.
IRON.IC, *adj.*, irônico.
I.RON.I.CAL, *adj.*, irônico.
I.RON.I.CAL.LY, *adv.*, ironicamente.
I.RON.ING, *v.*, passar roupa a ferro.
I.RON.ING BOARD, *s.*, tábua de passar roupa.
I.RON LUNG, *s.*, *Med.*, pulmão de aço.
I.RON.MONG.ER, *s.*, ferreiro.
I.RON.WORK, *s.*, armação de ferro.
I.RON.WORKS, *s. pl.*, siderúrgica, fundição.
IRO.NY, *s.*, ironia.
IR.RA.DI.ATE, *v.*, irradiar.
IR.RA.TIO.NAL, *adj.*, irracional.
IR.RA.TIO.NAL.I.TY, *s.*, irracionalidade.
IR.REC.OG.NIS.A.BLE, *adj.*, irreconhecível.
IR.REC.ON.CIL.ABLE, *adj.*, irreconciliável.
IR.RE.COV.ER.A.BLE, *adj.*, irrecuperável.
IR.RE.CU.SA.BLE, *adj.*, irrecusável.
IR.RE.DEEM.ABLE, *adj.*, irremediável.
IR.RE.DUC.IBLE, *adj.*, irredutível.
IR.REF.U.TA.BLE, *adj.*, irrefutável.
IR.REG.U.LAR, *adj.*, irregular.
IR.REG.U.LAR.I.TY, *s.*, irregularidade.
IR.REG.U.LAR.LY, *adv.*, irregularmente.
IR.REL.E.VANCE, *s.*, irrelevância.
IR.REL.E.VANT, *adj.*, irrelevante.
IR.RE.LIG.IOUS, *adj.*, descrente.
IR.RE.ME.DI.A.BLE, *adj.*, irremediável.
IR.REP.A.RA.BLE, *adj.*, irreparável.
IR.RE.PLACE.ABLE, *adj.*, insubstituível.
IR.RE.PRE.HEN.SI.BLE, *adj.*, irrepreensível, prefeito.
IR.RE.PRESS.I.BLE, *adj.*, irreprimível.
IR.RE.PROACH.A.BLE, *adj.*, irreprochável, irrepreensível.
IR.RE.SIST.I.BIL.I.TY, *s.*, irresistibilidade.
IR.RE.SIST.I.BLE, *adj.*, irresistível.
IR.RES.O.LU.TE, *adj.*, irresoluto.
IR.RES.O.LU.TE.NESS, *s.*, irresolução.
IR.RES.PEC.TIVE, *adj.*, sem consideração.
IR.RE.SPON.SI.BLE, *s.*, *adj.*, irresponsável.
IR.RE.TRIEV.A.BLE, *adj.*, irrecuperável, insubstituível.
IR.REV.ER.ENCE, *s.*, irreverência.
IR.REV.ER.ENT, *adj.*, irreverente.
IR.RE.VERS.I.BLE, *adj.*, irreversível.
IR.REV.O.CA.BLE, *adj.*, irrevogável.
IR.RIG.ABLE, *adj.*, irrigável.
IR.RI.GATE, *v.*, irrigar.
IR.RI.GA.TION, *s.*, irrigação.
IR.RI.TA.BLE, *adj.*, irritável.
IR.RI.TANT, *s.*, (indivíduo ou situação) irritante; *adj.*, irritante.
IR.RI.TATE, *v.*, irritar, enfurecer.
IR.RI.TAT.ED, *adj.*, irritado.

IR.RI.TAT.ING, *adj.*, irritante.
IR.RI.TA.TION, *s.*, irritação.
IR.RUP.TION, *s.*, irrupção.
IS, *v.*, 3ª pes. do sing. do pres. do indic. de *to be*.
ISH.MA.EL.ITE, *adj.*, *s.*, ismaelita, descendente de Ismael.
IS.LAM, *s.*, islamismo.
IS.LAM.IC, *adj.*, islâmico.
IS.LAM.ISM, *s.*, islamismo.
IS.LAM.IST, *s.*, islamista.
IS.LAM.ITE, *s.*, islamita.
IS.LAND, *s.*, ilha.
IS.LAND.ER, *s.*, ilhéu, ilhoa.
ISLE, *s.*, ilhota, ilha, ilhazinha.
ISN'T, *contr.* de *is not*.
I.SO.BAR, *s.*, *Meteor.*, linha isobárica.
I.SOG.A.MY, *s.*, *Biol.*, isogamia.
I.SO.LATE, *v.*, isolar.
I.SO.LA.TED, *adj.*, isolado, afastado.
I.SO.LA.TION, *s.*, isolamento.
I.SO.LA.TION.ISM, *s.*, isolacionismo.
I.SO.MER, *s.*, *Quím.*, isômero.
I.SOS.CE.LES TRI.AN.GLE, *s.*, triângulo isósceles.
I.SO.MET.RIC, *adj.*, isométrico.
I.SO.THER.MAL, *adj.*, isotérmico.
I.SO.TOPE, *s.*, *Quím.*, isótopo.
IS.RA.EL.I, *adj.*, *s.*, israelense.
IS.RA.EL.ITE, *adj.*, *s.*, israelita.
IS.SUE, *s.*, questão, tema, edição.
IS.SU.ER, *s.*, emissor.
ISTH.MUS, *s.*, istmo.
IT, *pron.*, ele, ela, o, a, lhe, isto, isso.
IT, *s.*, TI (Tecnologia da Informação).
I.TAL.IAN, *adj.*, *s.*, italiano.
I.TAL.IAN.ISM, *s.*, italianismo.
I.TAL.IAN.IZE, *v.*, italianizar.
IT.A.LY, *s.*, Itália.
ITCH, *s.*, comichão, coceira; *v.*, sentir coceira, sentir comichão.
ITCH.I.NESS, *s.*, comichão, coceira.
ITCH.Y, *adj.*, que provoca coceira.
I.TEM, *s.*, item, assunto, tema, notícia.
I.TEM.IZE, *v.*, pormenorizar, detalhar.
IT.ER.ATE, *v.*, reiterar, repetir, tornar a fazer.
IT.ER.A.TION, *s.*, reiteração.
I.TIN.ER.ANT, *adj.*, itinerante.
I.TIN.ER.A.RY, *s.*, itinerário.
I.TIN.ER.ATE, *v.*, andar, viajar de um lugar para o outro.
ITS, *pron.*, seu, sua.
IT'S, *contr.* de *it is*, *it has*.
IT.SELF, *pron.*, si mesmo.
I'VE, *contr.*, de *I have*.
IVO.RY, *s.*, marfim, cor de marfim.
I.VO.RY TOW.ER, *s.*, *fig.*, torre de marfim.
IVY, *s.*, hera, trepadeira.

J, s., décima letra do alfabeto inglês.
JAB, s., golpe, facada, estocada; v., picar, furar, esfaquear, apunhalar.
JAB.BER, s., tagarelice, falatório; v., tagarelar, palrar, falar muito.
JAC.A.RAN.DA, s., *Tupí*, *Bot.*, jacarandá (árvore nativa do Brasil).
JAC.ENT, *adj.*, jacente.
JA.CINTH, s., jacinto.
JACK, s., Joãozinho (apelido), homem do povo, camarada, colega; *Tec.*, macaco, guincho.
JACK.AL s., *Zool.*, chacal; *fig.*, vigarista, trapaceiro.
JACK.ASS, s., asno, burro, jumento; tolo, imbecil.
JACK.DAW, s., *Zool.*, gralha.
JACK.ET, s., jaqueta, paletó, casaco; sobrecapa de livro.
JACK.ET CROWN, s., *Odont.*, coroa de jaqueta.
JACK.ET PO.TA.TO, s., batata assada com pele.
JACK.HAM.MER, s., britadeira.
JACK IN, v., abandonar, largar, deixar.
JACK-IN-THE-BOX, s., caixa de surpresa.
JACK KNIFE, s., canivete (grande); v., canivetear.
JACK-OF-ALL-TRADES, s., *col.*, pau pra toda obra.
JACK OFF, s., pessoa estúpida.
JACK.POT, s., sorte grande, fortuna.
JACK RAB.BIT, s., *Zool.*, lebre.
JACK-STRAW, s., espantalho (boneco de palha).
JACK UP, v., levantar automóvel com macaco; subir, aumentar.
JAC.O.BE.AN, *adj.*, *Pol.*, jacobino.
JAC.O.BIN.ISM, s., *Pol.*, jacobinismo.
JAC.TA.TION, s., jactância; *Med.*, jactação.
JAC.U.LATE, v., jacular, arremessar.
JAC.U.LA.TION, s., jaculação.
JADE, s., jade, pedra; v., fatigar-se.
JAD.ED, *adj.*, estafado, exausto; usado.
JAG, s., entalhe, dente; v., dentear, entalhar.
JAG.GED, *adj.*, denteado, recostado.
JAG, s., corte, dente de serra; v., dentear, pontear.
JAG.UAR, s., *Tupí*, *Zool.*, jaguar, onça.
JAH.VEH, s., Javé, Jeová, Deus.
JAIL, s., cadeia, prisão, xilindró; v., prender, pôr na cadeia, encarcerar.
JAIL-BIRD, s., *col.*, preso, reincidente.
JAIL BREAK, s., fuga de prisão.
JAIL.ER, s., carcereiro.
JA.LOU.SIE, s., persiana, veneziana.
JAKE, *adj.*, *col.*, ótimo, excelente.
JAM, s., aperto, esmagamento, geleia; v., esmagar, apertar, obstruir.
JA.MAI.CAN, *adj.*, s., jamaicano.
JAMB, s., *Arq.*, batente, umbral.
JAM.BA.LA.IA, s., *Cul.*, *US* prato típico da Luisiana.

JAM.BO.REE, s., reunião mundial de escoteiros.
JAM.MING, s., interferência em ondas de rádio.
JAM.MY, *adj.*, viscoso, pastoso.
JAM-PACKED, *adj.*, *col.*, apinhado.
JAN.GLE, v., soar com estridência.
JAN.GLING, s., altercação; estridência (som metálico); *adj.*, estridente.
JAN.I.TOR, s., bedel, zelador, porteiro.
JAN.U.ARY, s., janeiro.
JA.PAN, s., Japão.
JAP.A.NESE, *adj.*, s., japonês, nipônico.
JAR, s., jarro, vaso, pote; estridor, ruído, rangido, dissonância; v., chiar, ranger, estridular; brigar.
JA.RA.RA.CA, s., *Tupí*, *Zool.*, jararaca.
JAR.FUL, s., quantidade que contém um pote ou jarro.
JAR.GON, s., jargão.
JAR.RING, s., dissonância; *adj.*, que discorda; dissonante.
JAS.MINE, s., *Bot.*, jasmim, jasmim-vermelho.
JAUN.DICE, s., *Med.*, icterícia; *fig.*, inveja, ciúme; v., causar icterícia; *fig.*, invejar; ter ciúme.
JAUN.DICED, *adj.*, *Med.*, ictérico; *fig.*, invejoso, pessimista.
JAUNT, s., excursão, passeio; v., excursionar, passear.
JAUN.TI.LY, *adv.*, alegremente; garbosamente.
JAUN.TY, *adj.*, alegre, jovial, animado, vivo.
JAV.A.NESE, s., *adj.*, javanês.
JAVE.LIN, s., dardo, azagaia.
JAW, s., mandíbula, maxila, *fig.*, tagarelice; jaws: maxilar que inclui os dentes; v., tagarelar; bater boca.
JAW-BONE, s., osso de maxilar (de um crânio); queixada.
JAW-BREAK.ER, s., britador de pedras; *fig.*, *col.*, bala quebra-queixo; palavra de difícil pronúncia.
JAZZ, s., *Mús.*, jazz; *col.*, vivacidade; v., animar, dançar.
JAZZ.ER, s., compositor ou músico de *jazz*, jazzista.
JAZZ.Y, *adj.*, *Mús.*, jazzístico; animado; chamativo.
JEAL.OUS, *adj.*, ciumento, cioso, desconfiado, invejoso.
JEAL.OUS.LY, *adv.*, invejosamente; zelosamente.
JEAL.OU.SY, s., ciúme, desconfiança, inveja, zelo.
JEAN, s., *US* tipo de tecido forte.
JEANS, s., roupa confeccionada com tecido especial; *fig.*, calças (de brim), macacão.
JEEP, s., jipe.
JEER, s., zombaria, escarnecimento; v., zombar, escarnecer.
JEER.ING, s., zombaria; *adj.*, zombeteiro.
JE.HO.VAH, s., *Rel.*, Jeová.
JE.JUNE, *adj.*, ingênuo, ávido, faminto, magro.
JE.JUNE.LY, *adv.*, avidamente.
JE.JUNE.NESS, s., avidez, magreza, secura, fome.
JELL, s., gelatina, geleia; v., gelatinizar(-se), ficar gelatinoso.
JEL.LI.FY, v., gelatinizar.
JEL.LY, s., gelatina, geleia; v., tornar gelatinoso.
JEL.LY BEAN, s., bala de jujuba
JEL.LY-FISH, s., *Zool.*, água-viva, medusa.

JELLYROLL ·· 508 ·· JOURNEY-WORK

JEL.LY.ROLL, *s.*, rocambole; *US vulg.*, vulva; cópula.
JEN.KINS, *s.*, *col.*, cronista; *pej.*, bajulador.
JEOP.ARD.IZE(-ISE), *v.*, arriscar, pôr em perigo.
JEOP.AR.DY, *s.*, perigo, risco; *v.*, correr perigo, arriscar-se.
JER.E.MI.AD, *s.*, lamúria, choradeira.
JERK, *s.*, empurrão, solavanco, puxão; *v.*, sacudir, empurrar, lançar; charquear.
JERK.I.LY, *adv.*, abruptamente; aos empurrões.
JER.KIN, *s.*, jaqueta, jaleco.
JERK.Y, *adj.*, abrupto; aos trancos.
JER.RY-CAN, *s.*, galão de gasolina.
JER.SEY, *s.*, malha, suéter, camisola, tipo de tecido.
JES.SA.MINE, *s.*, *Bot.*, jasmim.
JEST, *s.*, gracejo, troça, brincadeira, graça, zombaria; *v.*, gracejar, galhofar.
JEST.ER, *s.*, zombador, gracejador, bobo, palhaço.
JEST.FUL, *adj.*, gracejador.
JEST.ING, *s.*, gracejo, galhofa; *adj.*, zombeteiro.
JE.SU.IT, *s.*, jesuíta.
JES.U.IT.IC, *adj.*, jesuítico.
JE.SUS, *s.*, Jesus, Cristo.
JET, *s.*, jato, jorro, azeviche, esguicho; *v.*, jorrar, sair a jato.
JET-BLACK, *s.*, cor de azeviche, cor escura.
JET EN.GINE, *s.*, motor a jato.
JET PRO.PELLED, *adj.*, de propulsão a jato; *col.*, rápido.
JET.TON, *s.*, ficha de jogo.
JET-SKI, *s.*, veículo a motor que desliza na água.
JET.TY, *s.*, quebra-mar.
JEW, *s.*, judeu, israelita, hebreu, judia, hebreia.
JEW.ISH, *adj.*, judeu, judia.
JEW.EL, *s.*, joia, pedra preciosa; *v.*, enfeitar com joias.
JEW.EL.LER, *s.*, joalheiro.
JEW.EL.LERY, *s.*, joias, pedrarias.
JIB, *s.*, *Náut.*, bujarrona; *v.*, tombar a vela; *fig.*, mudar de rumo.
JIBE, *s.*, zombaria.
JIF.FY, *s.*, *col.*, instante.
JIG, *s.*, jiga, dança; *v.*, dançar, sacudir-se, dançar uma jiga.
JIG.GER, *s.*, *Zool.*, bicho-de-pé; pessoa que ginga; *col.*, coqueteleira.
JIG.GLE, *s.*, sacudida, sacolejo; *v.*, gingar, balançar-se, sacudir-se.
JIG.SAW, *s.*, serrote, serra.
JI.HAD, *s.*, jihad.
JILT, *s.*, namoradeira; *v.*, dar o fora em quem se ama, flertar.
JIN.GLE, *s.*, som, tinido, música de propaganda; *v.*, soar, tinir, retinir.
JIN.GO.IST, *s.*, chauvinista, xenófobo.
JINX, *s.*, objeto ou ser que traz azar, azar; *Bras.*, caipora.
JINXED, *adj.*, azarado.
JIT.TER, *s.*, *US* nervoso; *jitters*, *s.pl.*: nervos à flor da pele.
JIT.TER.Y, *adj.*, *col.*, nervoso.
JIVE, *s.*, burburinho; *US Mús.*, *jazz*; *v.*, dançar *jazz*.
JOB, *s.*, obra, empreitada, tarefa, dever; *v.*, trabalhar, fazer biscates.
JOB.BER, *s.*, operário, trabalhador, empreiteiro; especulador.
JOB.BERY, *s.*, especulação, agiotagem, desonestidade em negócios.
JOB.BING, *s.*, negociata, usura, especulação; *adj.*, *UK* que trabalha por empreitada.
JOB CENTRE, *s.*, *UK* agência de empregos.
JOB-COB.BLER, *s.*, sapateiro que faz remendos.

JOB DES.CRIP.TION, *s.*, descrição do cargo.
JOB.LESS, *adj.*, desempregado, desocupado.
JOB LOT, *s.*, lote (de mercadorias).
JOCK.EY, *s.*, jóquei, velhaco; *v.*, montar um cavalo, enganar.
JOCK.STRAP, *s.*, sunga.
JO.COSE, *adj.*, jocoso, satisfeito, brincalhão.
JO.COSE.NESS, *s.*, jocosidade, brincadeira.
JOC.U.LAR, *adj.*, divertido, engraçado.
JOC.U.LAR.I.TY, *s.*, jovialidade, alegria, satisfação.
JODH.PURS, *s. pl.*, culote.
JOG, *s.*, sacudida, empurrão, cutucada; *v.*, sacudir, empurrar, mover.
JOG.GER, *s.*, *Esp.*, corredor; praticante de *cooper*.
JOG.GING, *s.*, *Esp.*, corrida, *cooper*.
JOG.GLE, *s.*, estremeção, solavanco; *v.*, estremecer, sacudir, saltar.
JOHN.NY.CAKE, *s.*, *US* pão de milho.
JOIN, *s.*, junção, união, encaixe; *v.*, juntar, atar, reunir, associar-se.
JOIN.DER, *s.*, união, coadunação.
JOIN.ER, *s.*, marceneiro.
JOIN.ER.Y, *s.*, marcenaria.
JOIN.ING, *s.*, junção.
JOINT, *s.*, junta, junção, laço, união; *v.*, ligar, unir; *adj.*, unido, ligado.
JOINT AC.COUNT, *s.*, conta conjunta.
JOINT-OWN.ER, *s.*, sócio, proprietário.
JOINT.ED, *adj.*, articulado.
JOINT.LY, *adv.*, conjuntamente, juntamente.
JOINT VEN.TURE, *s.*, empreendimento conjunto (em que participam duas ou mais empresas).
JOIST, *s.*, viga, barrote, travessa; *v.*, sustentar com barrote.
JOKE, *s.*, piada, chiste, brincadeira; *v.*, brincar, gracejar, zombar.
JOK.EY, *adj.*, *UK* engraçado.
JOK.ER, *s.*, piadista, brincalhão, zombador, cláusula leonina.
JOK.ING, *s.*, gracejo, piada, brincadeira.
JOKES.TRESS, *s.*, *US* comediante feminina.
JOL.LI.TY, *s.*, jovialidade, regozijo, alegria, satisfação.
JOL.LY, *adj.*, alegre, festivo, divertido, feliz; *v.*, festejar, celebrar, alegrar.
JOLT, *s.*, sacudida, solavanco, choque; *v.*, sacudir.
JOLT.ING, *s.*, solavanco, sacudida.
JOS.TLE, *s.*, colisão, choque; *v.*, acotovelar, empurrar, colidir, abalroar.
JOT, *s.*, um jota, ninharia, insignificância; *v.*, tomar apontamentos.
JOT.TER, *s.*, bloco de notas.
JOT.TING, *s.*, nota, apontamento, anotação.
JOT.TINGS, *s. pl.*, recadinhos.
JOULE, *s.*, *Fís.*, joule (unidade de trabalho e medida).
JOUNCE, *s.*, empurrão, solavanco, sacudidela; *v.*, empurrar, agitar.
JOUR.NAL, *s.*, jornal, revista, periódico, diário, gazeta.
JOUR.NAL.ESE, *s.*, *pej.*, jornalês (jargão jornalístico).
JOUR.NAL.ISM, *s.*, jornalismo.
JOUR.NAL.IST, *s.*, jornalista, articulista.
JOUR.NEY, *s.*, jornada, viagem, excursão; *v.*, viajar, excursionar.
JOUR.NEY-WORK, *s.*, dia de trabalho, jornada de trabalho, tarefa.

JOUST ·· 509 ·· JUT

JOUST, *s., Esp.,* justa, torneio; *v.,* justar, competir.
JO.VIAL, *adj.,* jovial, alegre, risonho, sorridente.
JO.VI.AL.I.TY, *s.,* jovialidade, satisfação, alegria.
JO.VI.ALY, *adv.,* jovialmente, alegremente.
JOWL, *s.,* rosto, cara, bochecha, mandíbula, maxilar.
JOWLS, *s. pl.,* bochechas.
JOWL.Y, *adv.,* de mandíbula saliente.
JOY, *s.,* alegria, regozijo, júbilo; *v.,* alegrar-se, contentar-se, ficar feliz.
JOY.FUL, *adj.,* alegre, feliz, jovial.
JOY.FUL.LY, *adv.,* alegremente.
JOY.LESS, *adj.,* triste, tristonho, infeliz.
JOY-RIDE, *s.,* passeio em carro roubado; *v.,* andar em carro roubado.
JOY.RID.ER, *s.,* ladrão de carro.
JOY.STICK, *s.,* manche, alavanca de controle em jogos de micro, avião.
JU.BI.LANT, *adj.,* jubilante, triunfante.
JU.BI.LATE, *v.,* regozijar-se, alegrar-se, jubilar, exultar.
JU.BI.LA.TION, *s.,* júbilo.
JU.BI.LEE, *s.,* jubileu, aniversário, comemoração.
JU.DA.IC, *adj.,* judaico.
JU.DA.ISM, *s.,* judaísmo.
JU.DA.IZE, *v.,* judaizar.
JUD.DER, *v., UK* sacudir intensamente.
JUDG.MENT, *s.,* julgamento, juízo, discernimento; condenação; parecer.
JUDG.MENT HALL, *s.,* sala de audiências.
JUDG.MENT SEAT, *s.,* foro, tribunal.
JUDGE, *v.,* juiz, juíza, árbitro; *v.,* julgar, arbitrar, examinar, conhecer.
JUDG.ER, *s.,* juiz, árbitro; crítico.
JUDG.ES, *s. pl., Bib.,* juízes.
JUDGE.SHIP, *s.,* magistratura, juizado, cargo de juiz.
JUDG.E'S OR.DER, *s.,* mandato judicial.
JU.DI.CA.BLE, *adj.,* julgável, ajuizável.
JU.DI.CA.TIVE, *adj.,* judicial, judicativo.
JU.DI.CIAL, *adj.,* judicial.
JU.DI.CIA.LY, *adv.,* judicialmente.
JU.DI.CIA.RY, *adj.,* judiciário; *s.,* o poder judiciário.
JU.DI.CIOUS, *adj.,* judicioso.
JU.DI.CIOUS.NESS, *s.,* juízo, discernimento.
JU.DO, *s., Esp.,* judô.
JU.DO.IST, *s.,* judoísta, judoca.
JUG, *s.,* jarro; *v.,* estufar, rechear, cozer a fogo lento.
JUG.GER.NAUT, *s.,* jamanta.
JUG.GLE, *s.,* prestidigitação, malabarismo; *v.,* fazer malabarismo.
JUG.GLER, *s.,* prestidigitador, malabarista.
JUG.U.LAR, *s.,* jugular, veia jugular; *adv.,* jugular.
JUICE, *s.,* suco, sumo.
JUI.CI.LY, *adv.,* de modo suculento.
JUICY, *adj.,* suculento, sumarento, cheio de sumo.
JU.JIT.SU, *s.,* jiu-jitsu (tipo de luta livre, sem armas).
JU.LIAN, *adj., s.,* juliano.
JU.LY, *s.,* julho.
JUM.BLE, *s.,* desordem, confusão, mistura; *v.,* misturar, embaralhar.
JUM.BO, *s.,* colosso, algo grandioso; avião-jumbo; *adj.,* gigantesco.
JUM.BO JET, *s.,* jumbo (avião).

JUM.BO-SIZED, *adj.,* gigantesco.
JUMP, *s.,* salto, pulo, óbice; *v.,* saltar, pular, assustar, disparar.
JUMP.ED-UP, *adj., UK pej.,* pretencioso.
JUMP.ER, *s.,* blusa, pulôver, colete, avental.
JUMP.I.LY, *adv.,* nervosamente.
JUMP.I.NESS, *s.,* nervosismo.
JUMP.ING, *s.,* salto, pulo; *s.,* saltador, pulador.
JUMP JET, *s.,* aeronave de decolagem vertical.
JUMP START, *v.,* fazer ligação direta.
JUMP.SUIT, *s.,* macacão.
JUM.PY, *adj.,* nervoso, irrequieto.
JUN., *abrev.* de *June:* junho; *abrev.* de *Junior; s.,* júnior.
JUNC.TION, *s.,* junção, conexão, cruzamento, entroncamento, trevo.
JUNC.TION BOX, *s.,* caixa de ligação.
JUNC.TURE, *s.,* conjuntura, momento, contexto, encontro, crise.
JUNE, *s.,* junho.
JUN.GLE, *s.,* mata, floresta, selva.
JUN.GLE CAT, *s., Zool.,* gato selvagem (africano e asiático).
JUN.GLE GYM, *s., US* trepa-trepa (estrutura metálica em parques públicos para as crianças).
JU.NIOR, *s.,* júnior, jovem; *adj.,* júnior, mais novo, filho de.
JU.NI.OR DOC.TOR, *s.,* médico residente.
JU.NI.OR SCHOOL, *s.,* escola primária.
JU.NI.PER, *s.,* junípero.
JUNK, *s.,* junco; velharias, trastes; *v.,* jogar fora, descartar.
JUNK FOOD, *s.,* comida pronta de *fast-food.*
JUNK.IE, *s., col.,* viciado (em drogas).
JUNK MAIL, *s., pej.,* lixo eletrônico.
JUNK SHOP, *s.,* brechó.
JUN.TA, *s.,* junta (conselho administrativo); junta militar.
JU.PI.TER, *s., Mit.,* Júpiter (pai dos deuses romanos).
JU.RAS.SIC, *s., Geol.,* período jurássico.
JU.RID.I.CAL, *adj.,* jurídico.
JU.RIS.CON.SULT, *s.,* jurisconsulto, advogado.
JU.RIS.DIC.TION, *s.,* jurisdição.
JU.RIS.DIC.TION.AL, *adj.,* jurisdicional.
JU.RIS.PRU.DENCE, *s.,* jurisprudência.
JU.RIS.PRU.DENT, *s.,* jurista; *adj.,* jurisprudente.
JU.RIST, *s.,* jurista, advogado.
JURY BOX, *s.,* tribunal do júri.
JU.ROR, *s.,* jurado.
JU.RY, *s.,* júri.
JU.RY.MAN, *s.,* jurado.
JUS, *s.,* direito, jus.
JUST, *adj.,* justo, imparcial, legal; *adv.,* apenas, justamente, somente.
JUS.TICE, *s.,* justiça, equidade; juiz, magistrado.
JUST.ICE OF THE PEACE, *s.,* Juiz de Paz.
JUS.TI.CIA.RY, *s.,* juiz.
JUS.TI.FI.A.BIL.I.TY, *s.,* justificabilidade.
JUS.TI.FI.A.BLE, *adj.,* justificável.
JUS.TI.FI.A.BLY, *adv.,* justificavelmente.
JUS.TI.FI.CA.TION, *s.,* justificação.
JUS.TI.FI.CA.TO.RY, *adj.,* justificativo, justificatório.
JUS.TI.FIED, *adj.,* justificado.
JUS.TI.FI.ER, *s.,* justificador, defensor.
JUS.TI.FY, *v.,* justificar.
JUST.NESS, *s.,* justiça; justo.
JUT, *s.,* saliência, ressalto; *v.,* sobressair, ressaltar, destacar.

JUTE · 510 · JUXTAPOSITIONAL

JUTE, *s.*, juta.
JU.VE.NILE, *adj.*, juvenil, adolescente; *s.*, menor de idade.
JU.VE.NILE COURT, *s.*, juizado de menores.
JU.VE.NILE DE.LIN.QUENT, *s.*, delinquente juvenil.

JUX.TA.POSE, *v.*, justapor, colocar junto.
JUX.TA.PO.SI.TION, *s.*, justaposição.
JUX.TA.PO.SI.TION.AL, *adj.*, justaposto.

K, *s.*, décima primeira letra do alfabeto inglês.
KAA.BA, *s.*, caaba (principal templo de oração dos muçulmanos que fica em Meca).
KA.KI, *s., Bot.,* caqui (fruto do caquizeiro).
KAIL.YARD, *s.*, horta.
KALE, *s.*, couve-crespa.
KA.LEI.DO.SCOPE, *s.*, caleidoscópio.
KA.LEI.DO.SCOP.IC, *adj.*, caleidoscópico.
KA.LENDS, *s. pl.,* calendas.
KA.LI.AN, *s.*, narguilé.
KAM.PU.CHE.AN, *s., adj.,* cambojano.
KAN.GA.ROO, *s.*, canguru.
KANT.I.AN, *adj.*, kantiano.
KA.O.LIN, *s.*, caulim.
KA.PUT, *adj., col.,* acabado, arruinado.
KAR.A.O.KE, *s.*, karaokê.
KAR.AT, *s., US* quilate (símb.: k).
KA.RA.TE, *s.*, karatê, luta corporal.
KAY.AK, *s.*, caiaque.
KE.BAD, *s., Cul.,* churrasquinho árabe picante.
KEEL, *s.*, quilha de navio, chata, barcaça; *v.*, mostrar a quilha, soçobrar.
KEEN, *adj.*, vivo, agudo, grande, mordaz, acirrado, vivaz, fogoso.
KEEN.LY, *adv.*, atentamente, profundamente, vivamente.
KEEN.NESS, *s.*, entusiasmo, intensidade, perspicácia.
KEEP, *s.*, sustento, alimentação, prisão; *v.*, deter, ter, possuir, proteger.
KEEP.ER, *s.*, proprietário, dono, carcereiro, capataz, zelador, guardador.
KEEP.ING, *s.*, manutenção, alimentação, cuidado, guarda.
KEEP.SAKE, *s.*, recordação, lembrança, presente.
KEG, *s.*, barril, tonel.
KELP, *s. Bot.,* alga marinha; *fig.*, dinheiro de trabalho duro.
KEN, *s.*, alcance visual, horizonte; compreensão.
KELT, *s* celta.
KEN, *s.*, círculo visual, alcance do conhecimento; *v.*, perceber.
KEN.NEL, *s.*, canil, casinha para cães; *v.*, abrigar cães.
KEN.YAN, *s., adj.,* queniano.
KER.A.TIN, *s.*, ceratina, queratina.
KERB, *s.*, meio-fio, borda de calçada, passeio.
KERB.STONE, *s.*, marco de pedra; pedra de meio-fio.
KER.CHIEF, *s.*, lenço de cabeça.
KER.MESS, *s.*, o mesmo que *kermis*.
KER.MIS, *s.*, quermesse, festa pública.
KER.NEL, *s.*, grão de milho; parte comestível da noz; *fig.*, núcleo, centro; *v.*, envolver.
KER.O.SENE, *s.*, querosene.
KES.TREL, *s.*, falcão europeu.
KETCH, *s.*, caiaque, chalupa, canoa.
KETCH.UP, *s.*, "ketchup", molho picante de tomate.
KET.TLE, *s.*, chaleira, caldeirão.
KET.TLE.DRUM, *s., Mús.,* tímpano, timbale.
KEY, *s.*, chave, chaveta, código, solução, decifração; *v.*, chavear, encaixar.
KEY.BOARD, *s.*, teclado.
KEY.HOLE, *s.*, buraco de fechadura.
KEY.NOTE, *s., Mús.,* nota tônica; *fig.*, ideia básica; *v.*, dar a nota tônica.
KEY.PAD, *s., Comp.,* teclado numérico.
KEY PUNCH, *s., US* máquina de perfurar cartões.
KEY-RING, *s.*, argola para chaves.
KEY.STONE, *s.*, pedra fundamental, pedra angular; *fig.*, viga mestra, base.
KEY.STROKE, *s., Comp.,* toque de tecla, ato de teclar.
KEY WORD, *s.*, palavra-chave.
KG, *abrev.* de *kilogram*: quilograma.
KHA.KI, *adj.*, cáqui; *s.*, a cor cáqui.
KHA.LIF, *s.*, o mesmo que *caliph*: califa.
KHAN, *s., Hist.,* cã (título de rei em nações da Ásia).
KHAN.ATE, *s.*, canato (domínio de um cã).
KHZ, *Fís., abrev.* de *kilohertz*: quilohertz.
KIB.BE, *s., Cul. Árabe,* quibe (comida árabe).
KIB.BUTZ, *s., Heb.,* kibutz (fazenda coletiva agrícola em Israel).
KICK, *s.*, pontapé, chute, coice; *v.*, chutar, dar um pontapé, escoicear.
KICK.ER, *s.*, chutador, escoiceador.
KICK.ING, *s.*, chute, patada, coice.
KICK-OFF, *s.*, pontapé inicial; *fig., col., UK* começo.
KID, *s.*, criança, garoto; cabrito, pele de cabrito; *v.*, zombar, tratar como criança.
KID.DY, *s.*, criancinha, garoto.
KID.NAP, *v.*, sequestrar, raptar.
KID.NAP.PER, *s.*, sequestrador, raptor.
KID.NAP.PING *UK*, **KID.NA.PING** *US*, *s.*, sequestro, rapto.
KID.NEY, *s., Anat.,* rim; *fig.*, temperamento; espécie.
KID.NEY BEAN, *s., Bot.,* feijão comum; feijão-roxo.
KID.NEY MA.CHINE, *s., Med.,* hemodialisador.
KILL, *v.*, matar, assassinar, trucidar; *s.*, assassinato, matança.
KILL.ER, *s.*, assassino, matador, criminoso.
KILL.ING, *s.*, assassinato, matança, crime, homicídio.
KILL.JOY, *s.*, estraga-prazeres.
KILN, *s.*, forno, estufa; *v.*, secar, ressecar.
KI.LO, *s.*, quilo, quilograma.
KI.LO.CAL.O.RIE, *s., Fís.,* quilocaloria.
KI.LO.GRAM.ME, *s.*, quilograma, quilo.
KI.LO.ME.TER, *s.*, quilômetro.
KI.LO.ME.TRE, *s.*, quilômetro.
KILO.WATT, *s., Eletr.,* quilowatt.
KILT, *s.*, saiote usado pelos escoceses.
KI.MO.NO, *s.*, quimono.
KIN, *s.*, família, parentes, afins, parentesco, parentela.
KIND, *s.*, tipo, espécie, gênero, raça; *adj.*, gentil, generoso,

KINDERGARTEN · · 512 · · KNOW-NOTHING

amável.

KIN.DER.GAR.TEN, s., jardim de infância.

KIND-HEART.ED, adj., de bom coração, bondoso.

KIN.DLE, v., acender, inflamar, pôr fogo; incitar, entusiasmar; dar cria.

KIN.DLING, s., gravetos.

KIND.LY, adj., amável, bondoso, suave, gentil; adv., amavelmente.

KIND.NESS, s., bondade, amabilidade, suavidade, gentileza.

KIN.DRED, s., parentela, parentesco, afim; adj., aparentado, similar.

KIN.E.MAT.IC, adj., cinemático.

KIN.E.MAT.ICS, s., cinemática.

KI.NET.IC, adj., cinético; ativo.

KI.NET.ICS, s., Fís., cinética.

KIN-FOLKS, s. pl., parentes; o mesmo que kinsfolk.

KING, s., rei, soberano, monarca; líder.

KING.DOM, s., monarquia, reinado, reino.

KING.HOOD, s., soberania, realeza.

KING.LIKE, adj., régio, real.

KING.PIN, s., pino mestre; col., manda-chuva, chefe.

KING-SIZED, adj., de tamanho maior (que o comum).

KINK, s., enroscamento, dobra, nó; torcicolo; fig., imperfeição; v., enroscar, torcer.

KINK.Y, adj., retorcido, encarapinhado; excêntrico, pervertido.

KIN.LESS, adj., sem parentes.

KINS.FOLK, s., parentes, parentesco.

KIN.SHIP, s., parentesco, consanguinidade; similaridade.

KI.OSK, s., quiosque.

KIP, s., col., sesta, cochilo; v., UK tirar cochilo.

KIP.PER, s., salmão ou arenque defumado.

KIR.MESS, s., o mesmo que kermis: quermesse.

KIRSCH, s., quirche.

KISS, s., beijo, ósculo, toque leve; v., beijar, oscular.

KISS.A.BLE, adj., adorável, que se tem vontade de beijar.

KISS OF LIFE, s., fig., técnica de respiração boca a boca.

KISS.ER, s., beijador; gír., boca; ass-kisser: puxa-saco.

KISS.ING, s., beijo, ato de beijar.

KIT, s., estojo, equipamento, kit, caixa de ferramentas, conjunto de ferramentas; v., montar.

KIT BAG, s., mochila de viagem (ger. de soldado).

KITCH.EN, s., cozinha.

KITCH.EN.ETTE, s., fr., quitinete (pequeno apartamento com copa e cozinha).

KITCH.EN GARD.EN, s., horta.

KITCH.EN ROLL, s., toalha de papel (em rolo).

KITCH.EN.WARE, s., utensílios para cozinha.

KITE, s., pipa, papagaio; v., soltar pipa.

KITSCH, s., kitsch (estilo de mau gosto, brega).

KIT.TEN, s., gatinho (gato novo).

KIT.TEN.ISH, adj., felino; travesso, galanteador.

KIT.TLE, adj., caprichoso, rabugento, melindroso, intratável.

KITTY, s., gatinho; vaquinha (arrecadação de fundos).

KI.WI, s., quiuí (ave neozelandesa); col., neozelandês; o mesmo que kiwifruit.

KI.WI.FRUIT, s., Bot., quiuí, quivi.

KLEP.TO.MA.NIA, s., Med., cleptomania.

KLEP.TO.MA.NIAC, adj., cleptomaníaco; s., cleptômano.

KM, abrev. de kilometer, s., km, quilômetro.

KNACK, s., destreza, habilidade, competência.

KNACK.ER, s., abatedor (de animais); v., esgotar, exaurir; abater (animais).

KNACK.ERED, adj., col., UK exausto, acabado.

KNAP.SACK, s., mochila.

KNAR, s., nó de madeira.

KNAR.RY, adj., nodoso.

KNAVE, s., velhaco, cafajeste, tratante; valete no baralho.

KNAV.ERY, s., velhacaria, cafajestice, safadeza.

KNEAD, v., amassar.

KNEE, s., joelho; cotovelo, joelheira; v., ajoelhar-se, cair de joelhos.

KNEE.CAP, s., rótula.

KNEE-DEEP, adj., da altura dos joelhos.

KNEE-HIGH, adj., à altura dos joelhos.

KNEEL, v., ajoelhar-se, ficar de joelhos, genuflectir-se.

KNELL, s., dobre fúnebre, toque de sinos para falecimento; v., dobrar.

KNICK.ERS, s. pl., UK calcinha (roupa íntima).

KNICK-KNACK, s., bagatela; penduricalho.

KNIFE, s., faca, lâmina; v., esfaquear, apunhalar, ferir com faca.

KNIGHT, s., cavaleiro, fidalgo, cavalo no jogo de xadrez.

KNIGHT.HOOD, s. fidalguia, título dos cavaleiros.

KNIT, v., tricotar, fazer tricô, entretecer, tecer, entrelaçar.

KNIT.TED, adj., de malha.

KNIT.TING, s., tricô, trabalho de tricô.

KNIT.TING NEE.DLE, s., agulha de tricô.

KNIT.TER, s., tecelão, quem tece malha.

KNIT.WEAR, s., malha, roupa de malha.

KNIVES, s., facas.

KNOB, s., maçaneta de porta, punho, puxador, botão de rádio, TV.

KNOB.BLY, adj., nodoso, ossudo, encaroçado.

KNOCK, s., pancada, golpe, batida; v., bater, surrar, dar pancadas.

KNOCK.ED, adj., derrubado, batido.

KNOCK.ER, s., aldrava, batedor (de porta).

KNOCK.ING, s., ato de bater; pancada, pancadaria.

KNOCK-KNEED, adj., de pernas tortas (joelhos para dentro).

KNOCK-ON EF.FECT, s., UK efeito dominó.

KNOCK OUT, v., deixar inconsciente, derrotar, abater.

KNOCK-OUT, s., nocaute, derrubada do adversário.

KNOLL, s., colina, outeiro, cômoro; dobre de sinos; v., tanger os sinos.

KNOP, s., botão de flor, botão, saliência.

KNOT, s., laço, nó, laçada, módulo; v., laçar, amarrar.

KNOT.TY, adj., cheio de nós, nodoso; fig., complicado.

KNOUT, s., cnute, chicote, azorrague; v., chicotear, surrar.

KNOW, s., conhecimento; v., conhecer, saber, reconhecer, identificar.

KNOW-ALL, s., pej., sabichão.

KNOW.ER, s., conhecedor, sabedor.

KNOW-HOW, s., conhecimento, experiência, domínio de uma técnica.

KNOW.ING, s., sabedoria, compreensão; adj., inteligente, sagaz.

KNOW.ING.LY, adv., conscientemente; sabiamente.

KNOW.ING.NESS, s., esperteza, sagacidade, perspicácia.

KNOWL.EDGE, s., conhecimento, saber.

KNOWL.EDGE.A.BLE, adj., entendido, informado.

KNOWN, adj., conhecido, declarado, reconhecido.

KNOW-NOTH.ING, s., ignorante, muito ignorante.

KNUCKLE

KNUCK.LE, *s.*, nó dos dedos; articulação, junta; *v.*, render-se, submeter.
KNURL, *s.*, saliência, nó, borda.
KO.A.LA, *s.*, *Zool.*, coala.
KOOK, *s.*, *US col.*, biruta, maluco.
KOOK.Y, *adj.*, *US col.*, maluco; diferente.
KO.RAN, *s.*, Corão.
KO.REA, *s.*, Coreia.

KO.RE.AN, *s.*, *adj.*, coreano.
KOW.TOW, *s.*, ato de prostrar-se até tocar o chão, reverência.
KU-KLUX-KLAN, *s.*, sociedade secreta americana que tem o racismo como ideologia.
KUNG FU, *s.*, kung fu, tipo de luta chinesa.
KURD, *s.*, curdo.
KURD.ISH, *adj.*, *s.*, curdo.
KW, *abrev.* de *kilowatt*: quilowatt.

L, *s.*, décima segunda letra do alfabeto inglês; litro.
L, *s* algarismo romano, que vale 50.
LA, *s.*, lá.
LAB, *s., col., US* laboratório.
LAB.A.RUM, *s.*, lábaro.
LA.BEL, *s.*, rótulo, etiqueta, letreiro, legenda; *v.*, etiquetar, rotular.
LA.BI.AL, *adj.*, labial.
LA.BI.ATE, *adj.*, labiado.
LA.BI.O.DEN.TAL, *s., adj., Fonol.*, labiodental.
LA.BI.O.NA.SAL, *s., Fonol.*, labionasal.
LA.BI.O.VE.LAR, *s., adj., Fonol.*, labiovelar (fonema).
LAB.O.RA.TO.RY, *s.*, laboratório.
LA.BO.RI.OUS, *adj.*, laborioso, trabalhador, diligente.
LA.BO.RI.OUS.LY, *adj.*, laboriosamente.
LA.BO.RI.OUS.NESS, *s.*, laboriosidade, diligência.
LA.BOUR, *s.*, trabalho, labor, mão de obra, fadiga; *v.*, trabalhar, labutar.
LA.BOUR DAY, *s.*, Dia do Trabalho.
LA.BOURED *UK*, **LA.BORED** *US*, *adj.*, elaborado, apurado; forçado (não natural).
LA.BOUR.ER, *s.*, trabalhador, operário.
LA.BOUR FORCE, *s.*, mão de obra.
LA.BOUR.ING, *s.*, trabalho, esforço.
LA.BOUR LAW, *s.*, lei trabalhista.
LA.BOUR MAR.KET, *s., Econ.*, mercado de trabalho.
LA.BOUR PAINS, *s. pl.*, dores de parto.
LA.BOUR RE.LA.TIONS, *s. pl.*, relações trabalhistas.
LAB.RA.DOR, *s.*, labrador (raça de cão).
LAB.Y.RINTH, *s.*, labirinto.
LAB.Y.RIN.THINE, *s.*, labiríntico; *fig.*, intrincado.
LAB.Y.RIN.THI.TIS, *s., Med.*, labirintite.
LACE, *s.*, cordão, laço, cadarço; renda; *v.*, atar, apertar.
LACE.MAK.ING, *s.*, fabricação de renda.
LAC.ER.ATE, *v.*, machucar, lacerar, ferir.
LAC.ER.ANT, *adj.*, dilacerante, lacerante, aflitivo.
LAC.ER.A.TION, *s., Med.*, laceração; tormento.
LACE-UP, *adj.*, de cordões; *s., UK* sapato de amarrar.
LACH.RY.MAL, *adj.*, lacrimal.
LACH.RY.MOSE, *adj.*, lacrimoso.
LAC.ING, *s.*, ato de amarrar, atar; laço.
LA.CIN.I.ATE, *adj.*, franjado.
LACK, *s.*, falta, carência, necessidade; *v.*, faltar, carecer, necessitar.
LACK.A.DAI.SI.CAL, *adj.*, desinteressado, apático, lânguido.
LACK.EY, *s.*, lacaio, servente, criado.
LACK.ING, *adj.*, carente, necessitado.
LACK.LUS.TRE *UK*, **LACK.LUS.TER** *US*, *adj.*, sem brilho, desbotado.
LA.CON.IC, *adj.*, lacônico, breve.
LA.CON.I.CAL.LY, *adv.*, laconicamente.
LAC.O.NISM, *s.*, laconismo.

LAC.QUER, *s.*, laca, verniz.
LAC.QUER.ER, *s.*, laqueador.
LAC.QUER.ING, *s.*, envernizamento.
LAC.TA.TION, *s.*, lactação.
LAC.TE.OUS, *adj.*, lácteo, leitoso.
LAC.TIC ACID, *s., Quím.*, ácido lático.
LAC.TOSE, *s., Quím.*, lactose.
LA.CU.NA, *s.*, omissão, lacuna, cavidade.
LA.CUS.TRINE, *adj.*, lacustre.
LA.CY, *adj.*, rendado, que imita ou é semelhante à renda.
LAD, *s.*, rapaz, moço, garoto; *col.*, camarada.
LAD.DER, *s.*, escada de mão.
LAD.DIE, *s.*, rapazinho, rapazelho.
LAD.DISH, *adj.*, machão.
LADE, *s.*, foz de rio; *v.*, carregar, despachar, empilhar.
LAD.EN, *adj.*, carregado.
LA.DI.DA, *adj., pej.*, afetado, pedante.
LA.DIES, *s. pl.*, senhoras, damas; *ladies*': toalete feminino.
LA.DIES' ROOM, *s.*, toalete feminino.
LAD.ING, *s.*, carregamento, carga.
LA.DLE, *s.*, concha para sopa.
LA.DY, *s.*, senhora, dama; esposa, dona.
LA.DY.BIRD *UK*, **LA.DY.BUG** *US*, *s., Zool.*, joaninha (inseto da família dos Coccinelídeos).
LA.DY-IN-WAIT.ING, *s.*, dama de companhia (da rainha).
LA.DY.LIKE, *adj.*, elegante, fino, refinado, distinto.
LA.DY.SHIP, *s.*, *her/your* ~ : sua/vossa senhoria.
LAG, *s.*, retardamento, atraso; *v.*, atrasar-se, retardar-se, encarcerar.
LA.GER, *s.*, cerveja leve e clara.
LAG.GARD, *s.*, retardatário; *adj.*, vagaroso, atrasado, tardio.
LAG.GING, *adj.*, demorado, vagaroso, lento.
LA.GOON, *s.*, lagoa, lago.
LA.IC, *adj., s.*, laico, leigo.
LA.ICAL, *adj.*, laico, secular, mundano, profano.
LA.ICAL.LY, *adv.*, de modo leigo.
LA.IC.I.TY, *s.*, laicidade.
LA.I.CI.ZA.TION, *s.*, laicização.
LAID, *adj.*, que tem sulcos.
LAID-BACK, *adj., col.*, descontraído, sem pressa.
LAIR, *s.*, covil, toca.
LAIR.AGE, *s.*, curral.
LAITY, *s.*, laicidade.
LAKE, *s.*, lago.
LAKE.SHORE, *s.*, margem de lago.
LAKE.SIDE, *adj.*, às margens (do lago).
LA.MA, *s.*, lama (sacerdote budista).
LAMB, *s.*, cordeiro, carne de cordeiro; *v.*, parir ovelha.
LAM.BASTE, **LAM.BAST**, *v.*, surrar, repreender rudemente; *fig., col.*, criticar severamente.
LAM.BEN.CY, *s.*, leveza, agilidade.
LAMB.KIN, *s.*, cordeirinho.

LAMBLIKE   •• 515 ••   LARYNX

LAMB.LIKE, *adj.*, dócil, inocente, manso.
LAMB.SKIN, *s.*, pele de cordeiro.
LAMB'S-WOOL, *s.*, lã de cordeiro.
LAME, *adj.*, coxo, manco, fraco; *v.*, estropiar, aleijar.
LAME DUCK, *adj.*, *fig.*, *US* parlamentar em final de mandato; empresa inadimplente; *s.*, *fig.*, fracasso; inútil.
LAME.LY, *adv.*, imperfeitamente; de forma não convincente, de modo coxo.
LAME.NESS, *s.*, manqueira; defeito, falha.
LAM.I.NAT.ED, *adj.*, laminado.
LA.MENT, *s.*, lamento, reclamação, queixa; *v.*, lamentar-se, queixar-se.
LA.MEN.TA.BLE, *adj.*, lamentável.
LA.MEN.TA.BLY, *adv.*, lamentavelmente.
LAM.EN.TA.TION, *s.*, lamentação, lamento.
LA.MENT.ING, *s.*, lamentação; *adj.*, lamuriento, lamuriante.
LAM.I.NA, *s.*, lâmina.
LAM.I.NATE, *v.*, laminar, reduzir a lâminas.
LAMP, *s.*, lâmpada, lanterna, lamparina.
LAMP-BLACK, *s.*, fuligem, negro de fumo, sujeira.
LAMP.ION, *s.*, lampião, lamparina.
LAMP.LIGHT.ER, *s.*, acendedor de lampiões.
LAM.POON, *s.*, pasquim; *v.*, difamar, satirizar.
LAMP.POST, *s.*, poste de luz.
LAMP.SHADE, *s.*, abajur.
LANCE, *s.*, lança.
LAN.CER, *s.*, lanceiro.
LAN.CET, *s.*, lanceta.
LAN.CI.NATE, *v.*, lancinar, afligir.
LAND, *s.*, terra, país, terras, propriedades; *v.*, desembarcar, aterrar.
LAND.CAR.RIAGE, *s.*, transporte por terra.
LAND.ED, *adj.*, com terras; fundiário.
LAND.ED GEN.TRY, *s. pl.*, (aristocrata) proprietário de terras.
LAND.FORCE, *s.*, exército de terra.
LAND.HOLD.ER, *s.*, proprietário de terras, sitiante, fazendeiro.
LAND.ING, *s.*, pouso, aterrissagem; desembarque; plataforma.
LAND.ING CRAFT, *s.*, *Mar.*, barcaça de desembarque militar.
LAND.ING FIELD, *s.*, *Aeron.*, campo de pouso, aeródromo.
LAND.ING GEAR, *s.*, trem de aterrissagem.
LAND.ING STRIP, *s.*, pista de aterrissagem.
LAND.LA.DY, *s.*, dona, proprietária de bar ou pub.
LAND.LOCKED, *adj.*, cercado de terra, sem acesso ao mar.
LAND.LORD, *s.*, dono, proprietário de bar ou pub.
LAND.MARK, *s.*, marco, limite, local conhecido.
LAND.MINE, *s.*, mina terrestre (bomba).
LAND OF.FICE, *s.*, cartório de registro de terras.
LAND.OWN.ER, *s.*, proprietário de terras, latifundiário.
LAND.SCAPE, *s.*, paisagem, panorama; *v.*, ajardinar.
LAND.SCAPE-PAINT.ER, *s.*, pintor paisagista.
LAND.SCAP.IST, *s.*, paisagista (pintor).
LAND.SLIDE, *s.*, desabamento, desmoronamento, grande vitória.
LAND.SLIP, *s.*, deslizamento de terra.
LAND.WARD, *adj.*, que se dirige para terra; *adv.*, em direção a terra.
LAND.WARDS, *adv.*, em direção a terra.
LAND.WORK.ER, *s.*, agricultor, lavrador.
LANE, *s.*, travessa, beco, viela, rota.

LAN.GOUS.TINE, *s.*, lagostim.
LAN.GUAGE, *s.*, linguagem, língua, estilo.
LAN.GUAGE LA.BOR.A.TORY, *s.*, laboratório de línguas.
LAN.GUID, *adj.*, lânguido, frágil, debilitado.
LAN.GUID.LY, *adv.*, languidamente.
LAN.GUID.NESS, *s.*, languidez; prostração.
LAN.GUISH, *v.*, definhar, enfraquecer-se.
LAN.GUISH.MENT, *s.*, desfalecimento, abatimento.
LAN.GUISH.ING, *s.*, lânguido, abatido, desfalecido.
LAN.GUISH.MENT, *s.*, languidez, langor, fraqueza.
LAN.GUOR, *s.*, langor, fraqueza, abatimento.
LAN.GUOR.OUS, *adj.*, langoroso.
LA.NIF.ER.OUS, *adj.*, lanífero, lanígero.
LANK.I.NESS, *s.*, o mesmo que *lankness*.
LANK.Y, *adj.*, magro, esbelto, fino, delgado, magricela.
LANK.NESS, *s.*, magreza.
LAN.O.LIN, *s.*, lanolina.
LA.NU.GI.NOUS, *adj.*, lanuginoso; coberto com lanugem.
LAN.TERN, *s.*, lanterna; farol; claraboia.
LAO.TIAN, *s.*, *adj.*, laosiano (natural ou relativo ao Laos).
LAP, *s.*, regaço, colo, descanso, disco rotativo, volta completa em uma pista; *v.*, lamber, embrulhar.
LAP.A.RO.SCOPY, *s.*, *Med.*, laparoscopia.
LAP DOG, *s.*, **CÃO**zinho de estimação.
LA.PEL, *s.*, lapela.
LAP.I.DATE, *v.*, lapidar, apedrejar, matar a pedradas.
LAP.I.DA.TION, *s.*, lapidação, apedrejamento.
LAP.I.DOSE, *adj.*, pedregoso.
LAP.IN, *s.*, pelo ou pele de coelho; coelho.
LAP.PER, *s.*, dobrador; embrulhador; esmerilhador; lambedor.
LAP.PET, *s.*, aba, fralda.
LAPSE, *s.*, lapso, espaço, período; negligência; *v.*, escoar, passar.
LAPSED, *adj.*, descrente.
LAP.TOP, *s.*, (computador) portátil, *laptop*, *notebook*.
LAR.BOARD, *s.*, *Náut.*, bombordo.
LAR.CE.NER, *s.*, ladrão, gatuno.
LAR.CE.NOUS, *adj.*, ladrão.
LAR.CE.NY, *s.*, furto, roubo, apropriação indébita.
LARD, *s.*, banha de porco; *v.*, engordar; lardear (carne).
LAR.DER, *s.*, despensa.
LAR.DON, *s.*, toicinho que se usa para lardear carne.
LARD.Y, *adj.*, gorduroso.
LARGE, *s.*, largo, amplo, grande.
LARGE IN.TES.TINE, *s.*, *Anat.*, intestino grosso.
LARGE.LY, *adv.*, basicamente; grandemente, em grande parte.
LARGE.NESS, *s.*, grandeza, amplidão.
LARGE-SCALE, *adj.*, de grande escala.
LAR.GESS, *s.*, donativo, dádiva, presente.
LAR.GESSE, *s.*, generosidade.
LARK, *s.*, *Zool.*, cotovia; *col.*, brincadeira; *v.*, fazer brincadeiras.
LARK.SPUR, *s.*, espora.
LARK.Y, *adj.*, brincalhão, traquinas, travesso.
LAR.RI.KIN, *s.*, indivíduo arruaceiro; *adj.*, arruaceiro.
LAR.VA, *s.*, larva.
LAR.VATE, *adj.*, mascarado, dissimulado.
LAR.YN.GI.TIS, *s.*, *Med.*, laringite.
LAR.YN.GOL.O.GIST, *s.*, *Med.*, laringologista.
LAR.YN.GOL.O.GY, *s.*, laringologia.
LAR.YNX, *s.*, laringe.

LASAGNA ··516·· LAXLY

LA.SA.GNA, LA.SA.GNE, *s., It.*, lasanha.
LAS.CIV.I.OUS, *adj.*, lascivo, devasso.
LAS.CIV.I.OUS.NESS, *s.*, lascívia, devassidão.
LA.SER, *s.*, laser, raio laser.
LA.SER BEAM, *s.*, feixe de laser, raio laser.
LAS.ER PRINT.ER, *s.*, impressora a laser.
LASH, *s.*, chicotada, cílio; *v.*, chicotear, açoitar, surrar.
LASH.ER, *s.*, açoitador.
LASS, *s.*, moça, jovem, garota.
LASS.IE, *s.*, mocinha, garotinha.
LAS.SI.TUDE, *s.*, cansaço, fadiga, esgotamento.
LAS.SO, *s.*, laço; *v.*, laçar, pegar com o laço.
LAST, *s.*, último; fim; *adj.*, último, derradeiro; *adv.*, em último lugar; *v.*, durar; preservar.
LAST-DITCH, *adj.*, derradeiro.
LAST.ING, *adj.*, duradouro, permanente.
LAST.ING.LY, *adj.*, duradouramente.
LAST.ING.NESS, *s.*, duração; solidez.
LAST.LY, *adv.*, recentemente, por último; por fim, finalmente.
LAST NAME, *s.*, sobrenome.
LAST POST, *s.*, última coleta, toque de recolher.
LAST QUAR.TER, *s.*, quarto minguante (lua)
LAST RITES, *s. pl.*, últimos sacramentos, extrema-unção.
LAST STRAW, *s.*, a gota d'água; o último dissabor.
LAST WORD, *s.*, a palavra final.
LATCH, *s.*, trinco, fecho, tranca; *v.*, fechar.
LATCH.KEY, *s.*, chave de trinco.
LATE, *adj.*, atrasado, tardio, lento; *adv.*, tarde.
LATE.COM.ER, *s.*, retardatário.
LATE.LY, *adv.*, ultimamente, recentemente.
LA.TEN.CY, *s.*, latência.
LATE.NESS, *s.*, demora, atraso.
LATE-NIGHT, *adj.*, noturno, da noite.
LA.TENT, *adj.*, latente.
LA.TENT.LY, *adv.*, latentemente.
LAT.ER, *adj.*, posterior; *adv.*, mais tarde, depois.
LAT.ER.AL, *adj.*, lateral.
LAT.ER.AL.I.TY, *s.*, lateralidade.
LAT.EST, *adj.*, último.
LA.TEX, *s.*, látex.
LATH, *s.*, sarrafo, ripa; *v.*, cobrir com ripas.
LATHE, *s.*, torno mecânico.
LATH.ER, *s.*, espuma; *v.*, ensaboar, fazer espuma; *col.*, passar um sabão, surrar, espancar.
LATH.ER.ING, *s.*, sova, surra, ensaboadela.
LAT.IN, *s.*, latim; *adj.*, latino.
LAT.IN-AMER.I.CAN, *s.*, latino-americano.
LAT.IN.ISM, *s.*, latinismo.
LA.TIN.I.TY, *s.*, latinidade.
LAT.IN.I.ZA.TION, *v.*, latinização.
LAT.IN.IZE, *v.*, latinizar.
LAT.ISH, *adv.*, um pouco tarde.
LAT.I.TUDE, *s.*, latitude, largura, clima.
LA.TRINE, *s.*, latrina, privada.
LAT.TER, *adj.*, último, posterior; recente, moderno.
LAT.TER-DAY, *adj.*, contemporâneo, moderno.
LAT.TER.LY, *adv.*, recentemente, ultimamente.
LAT.TICE, *s.*, treliça, rótila; *v.*, entrelaçar.
LAT.TICED, *adj.*, treliçado; engradado
LAT.VI.AN, *s., adj.*, letão (natural ou relativo à Letônia).
LAUD, *s.*, louvor, elogio; *v.*, louvar, exaltar, enaltecer.

LAUD.A.BLE, *adj.*, louvável.
LAUD.A.BLY, *adv.*, louvavelmente.
LAUGH, *s.*, gargalhada, riso, risada; *v.*, rir, gargalhar, dar risada.
LAUGH.ABLE, *adj.*, ridículo, risível, absurdo.
LAUGH.ING, *s.*, riso, risada; *adj.*, risonho.
LAUGH.ING GAS, *s.*, gás hilariante.
LAUGH.ING.STOCK, *s.*, motivo de riso.
LAUGH.TER, *s.*, riso, risada.
LAUNCH, *s.*, lancha; lançamento.
LAUNCH PAD, *s.*, Aeron., plataforma de lançamento.
LAUNCH.ER, *s.*, lançador.
LAUNCH.ING, *s.*, lançamento.
LAUNCH.ING PAD, *s.*, o mesmo que *launch pad*.
LAUN.DER, *v.*, lavar e passar; *col.*, lavar.
LAUN.DER.ER, *s.*, pessoa que lava, lavador, lavadeira.
LAUN.DER.ETTE, *s.*, lavanderia automatizada.
LAUN.DRESS, *s.*, lavadeira.
LAUN.DRY, *s.*, lavanderia.
LAUN.DRY BAS.KET, *s.*, cesto de roupa suja.
LAU.RE.ATE, *v.*, laurear.
LAU.RE.A.TION, *s.*, ato de laurear, laureação.
LAU.REL, *s.*, louro; *laurels s.pl.*, lauréis.
LAU.RELED, *adj.*, US laureado.
LA.VA, *s.*, lava.
LA.VA.BO, *s.*, lavabo.
LA.VA.TION, *s.*, lavação, lavagem, limpeza.
LAV.A.TO.RY, *s.*, banheiro, privada, toalete.
LAV.A.TO.RY PA.PER, *s.*, papel higiênico.
LAVE, *v.*, lavar, banhar.
LAV.EN.DER, *s.*, lavanda, alfazema; *v.*, perfumar, aromatizar.
LAV.ISH, *adj.*, generoso, pródigo, excessivo; *v.*, dissipar, esbanjar.
LAV.ISH.ER, *s.*, esbanjador.
LAV.ISH.LY, *adv.*, generosamente, prodigamente.
LAV.ISH.NESS, *s.*, prodigalidade.
LAW, *s.*, lei, norma, mandamento, foro, jurisprudência.
LAW-A.BID.ING, *adj.*, obediente à lei.
LAW-BREAK.ER, *s.*, transgressor da lei; infrator.
LAW-BREAK.ING, *s.*, infração, transgressão da lei; *adj.*, transgressor.
LAW COURT, *s.*, tribunal de justiça.
LAW.FUL, *adj.*, legal, legítimo.
LAW.FUL.LY, *adv.*, licitamente, legitimamente.
LAW.FUL.NESS, *s.*, legalidade.
LAW.LESS, *adj.*, ilegal, ilegítimo.
LAW.LESS.LY, *adv.*, ilegalmente.
LAW.MAK.ER, *s.*, legislador.
LAW.MAK.ING, *s.*, ato de legislar; *adj.*, legislativo.
LAWN, *s.*, relvado.
LAWN MOW.ER, *s.*, cortador de grama.
LAWN PAR.TY, *s.*, US recepção ao ar livre.
LAWN TEM.NIS, *s.*, Esp., jogo de tênis em gramado.
LAW SCHOOL, *s.*, escola de direito.
LAW.YER, *s.*, advogado, causídico, notário.
LAW.YER.ING, *s.*, advocacia.
LAX, *adj.*, flácido, solto; negligente; ambíguo, vago.
LAX.A.TIVE, *s.*, laxante; *adj.*, laxativo.
LAX.A.TION, *s.*, laxação, relaxamento.
LAX.I.TY, *s.*, lassidão, frouxidão.
LAX.LY, *adv.*, frouxamente.

LAY   •517••   LEFT WING

LAY, *s.*, situação, postura; *adj.*, leigo; *v.* colocar, pôr, derrubar, preparar.
LAY-ABOUT, *s.*, *UK col.*, vadio, preguiçoso.
LAY DAYS, *s. pl.*, *Náut.*, prazo contado em dias para atracação.
LAY.ER, *s.*, camada, leito; *v.*, mergulhar.
LAY.ETTE, *s.*, enxoval de bebê.
LAY IN, *v.*, armazenar.
LAY.MAN, *s.*, leigo.
LAY-OFF, *s.*, demissão.
LAY.OUT, *s.*, desenho, disposição de móveis, ordem em um ambiente.
LAY.O.VER, *s.*, *US* parada (em viagem), escala (de viagem).
LA.ZAR, *s.*, lázaro, leproso.
LA.ZAR-LIKE, *adj.*, lazarento.
LAZE, *v.*, vadiar, vagabundear.
LA.ZI.LY, *adv.*, preguiçosamente.
LA.ZI.NESS, *s.*, preguiça.
LAZ.ING, *adj.*, preguiçoso, vadio.
LA.ZY, *adj.*, preguiçoso.
LA.ZY-BONES, *s.*, *col.*, preguiçoso.
LEA, *s.*, prado, pradaria, várzea, campina.
LEACH, *s.*, lixívia; *v.*, lixiviar.
LEAD, *s.*, chumbo, sonda, conduta, guia, cabo, protagonista; *v.*, conduzir, dirigir, comandar, persuadir,jogar de mão.
LEAD.ED, *adj.*, com chumbo, chumbado.
LEAD.EN, *adj.*, plúmbeo.
LEAD.ER, *s.*, líder, comandante, chefe.
LEAD.ER.SHIP, *s.*, liderança, comando, condução.
LEAD.ING, *s.*, direção, liderança, comando; *adj.*, principal, primeiro.
LEAD.ING LIGHT, *s.*, luz de guia; *fig.*, figura central.
LEAD.ING MAN, *s.*, protagonista, ator principal.
LEAD.LINE, *s.*, sonda.
LEAD TIME, *s.*, *Com.*, prazo de entrega.
LEAF, *s.*, folha, folhagem, pétala, chapa; *v.*, cobrir de folhas, folhear.
LEAF.LESS, *adj.*, sem folhas, desfolhado.
LEAF.LET, *s.*, folhinha, folheto.
LEAFY, *adj.*, frondoso, copado, cheio de folhas.
LEAGUE, *s.*, liga, aliança, confederação; *v.*, associar-se, unir-se, ligar-se.
LEAK, *s.*, fuga, vazamento, rombo; *v.*, escoar, vazar, derramar, gotejar.
LEAK.AGE, *s.*, escoamento, vazamento, derrame.
LEAK.I.NESS, *s.*, vazamento, escoamento.
LEAK.ING, *s.*, derrame, vazamento, escoamento.
LEAK.Y, *adj.*, com juros.
LEAN, *s.*, carne magra, inclinação; *adj.*, magro, pobre; *v.*, tender, inclinar-se.
LEAN.ING, *s.*, inclinação, propensão, *adj.*, inclinado, desviado.
LEAN.LY, *adv.*, pobremente.
LEAN-TO, *s.*, alpendre, hangar; *adj.*, com uma inclinação (telhado).
LEAP, *s.*, salto, pulo; saltar, pular, arremessar-se.
LEAP DAY, *s.*, o dia 29 de fevereiro.
LEAP-FROG, *s.*, jogo de pular carniça; *v.*, *fig.*, aproveitar-se de.
LEAP YEAR, *s.*, ano bissexto.
LEAP.ING, *s.*, salto, pulo.
LEARN, *v.*, aprender, compreender, decorar, assimilar.
LEARN.ED, *adj.*, aprendido; culto, erudito, versado.
LEARN.ED.NESS, *s.*, erudição, aprendizagem.

LEARN.ER, *s.*, principiante, aprendiz.
LEARN.ING, *s.*, saber, aprendizagem.
LEAS.A.BLE, *adj.*, arrendável.
LEASE, *s.*, *Jur.*, arrendamento, contrato de locação; *v.*, arrendar, alugar.
LEASE.BACK, *s.*, contrato em que se estabelece a venda e arrendamento de uma propriedade vendida.
LEASE.HOLD, *s.*, arrendamento; *adj.*, arrendado; *adv.*, em arrendamento.
LEASE.HOLD.ER, *s.*, arrendatário.
LEASH, *s.*, correia, trela; *v.*, controlar, atrelar.
LEAST, *s.*, o mínimo; *adj.*, menor, mínimo; *adv.*, menos; *at ~ :* ao menos.
LEAST.WAYS, *adv.*, ao menos, pelo menos.
LEATH.ER, *s.*, couro; *v.*, cobrir com couro, revestir com couro.
LEATH.ERN, *adj.*, feito de couro.
LEATH.ERY, *adj.*, semelhante a couro.
LEAVE, *s.*, licença, partida; *v.*, partir, ir, viajar, abandonar, sobrar, falecer; cobrir-se de folhas.
LEAVED, *adj.*, frondoso, copado, umbroso.
LEAV.EN, *s.*, fermento, levedura; *v.*, fermentar, levedar.
LEAV.EN.ING, *s.*, fermentação, levedura.
LEAVE OF OB.SENCE, *s.*, licença.
LEAV.ING, *s.*, partida, saída, ida.
LEB.A.NESE, *s.*, *adj.*, libanês (natural do ou referente ao Líbano).
LEB.A.NON, *s.*, Líbano.
LECH, *adj.*, *col.*, desejo sexual; devasso; *v.*, sentir desejo sexual.
LECH.ER, *adj.*, lascivo, devasso.
LECH.ER.OUS, *adj.*, lascivo, luxurioso.
LECH.ER.Y, *s.*, lascívia.
LECTERN, *s.*, atril (apoio para livros, esp. a Bíblia).
LEC.TION, *s.*, trecho da Bíblia lido em serviços religiosos.
LEC.TURE, *s.*, preleção, conferência, palestra; *v.*, palestrar, lecionar; repreender.
LEC.TURE HALL, *s.*, salão de conferências, sala de aula (em sistema de palestra).
LEC.TURE THEA.TRE, *s.*, anfiteatro, salão de conferências.
LEDGE, *s.*, borda, orla; saliência, parapeito.
LEDGED, *adj.*, que tem borda.
LED.GER, *s.*, livro-razão na contabilidade.
LEE, *s.*, *Náut.*, sotavento; abrigo para o vento; *adj.*, a sotavento; em abrigo do vento.
LEECH, *s.*, sanguessuga; *fig.*, parasita, sugador; *v.*, sangrar (com sanguessugas); *fig.*, sugar.
LEEK, *s.*, alho-poró.
LEER, *s.*, modo de olhar de soslaio, de modo malicioso; *v.*, olhar de soslaio, olhar de malícia.
LEE.WAY, *s.*, liberdade de ação; tolerância; declinação da rota.
LEFT, *s.*, esquerda, lado esquerdo; *adv.*, à esquerda.
LEFT-HAND, *adj.*, canhoto; esquerda (mão); à esquerda.
LEFT-HAND.ED, *s.*, canhoto; desajeitado, ambíguo; estúpido.
LEFT-HAND.ER, *s.*, canhoto.
LEFT.ISM, *s.*, *Pol.*, esquerdismo.
LEFT.IST, *s.*, *Pol.*, esquerdista.
LEFT.LY, *adv.*, com a mão esquerda; ambiguamente, desajeitadamente.
LEFT.OVERS, *s.*, sobras, restos.
LEFT WING, *s.*, *Pol.*, ala da esquerda.

LEFT WINGER · 518 · LEVELLER

LEFT WING.ER, s., *Pol.*, ala esquerdista.
LEFT.Y, s., *col.*, canhoto; *Pol.*, esquerdista; *adv.*, de mão esquerda.
LEG, s., perna, pata, pé, suporte, trecho de um trajeto.
LEG.A.CY, s., legado, herança, doação.
LE.GAL, *adj.*, legal, legítimo, justo, lícito.
LE.GAL.ISM, s., legalismo.
LE.GAL.IST, s., legalista.
LE.GAL.I.TY, s., legalidade.
LE.GAL.I.ZA.TION, s., legalização.
LE.GAL.IZE(ISE), v., legalizar.
LE.GAL.LY, *adv.*, legalmente.
LE.GAL TEM.DER, s., moeda corrente.
LE.GATE, s., legado, delegado; v., legar.
LE.GA.TION, s., legação, missão diplomática.
LEG.END, s., lenda, legenda, mito, fábula.
LEG.END.AR.Y, *adj.*, lendário.
LEG.GINGS, s. *pl.*, calças compridas de malha femininas.
LEG.GY, *adj.*, pernas compridas e bonitas; de longo caule (planta).
LEG.I.BILITY, s., legibilidade.
LEG.I.BLE, *adj.*, legível, evidente, óbvio.
LEG.I.BLY, *adv.*, de forma legível.
LEG.IS.LATE, v., legislar.
LEG.IS.LA.TION, s., legislação.
LEG.IS.LA.TIVE, *adj.*, legislativo.
LEG.IS.LA.TOR, s., legislador.
LEG.IS.LA.TURE, s., legislatura.
LE.GIST, s., legista.
LE.GIT.I.MA.CY, s., legitimidade.
LE.GIT.I.MATE, v., legitimar, tornar legítimo; *adj.*, legítimo, lídimo.
LE.GIT.I.MATE.LY, *adv.*, legitimamente.
LE.GIT.I.MAT.IZE(-ISE), v., legitimar, legalizar, validar.
LE.GI.TI.MIST, s., *adj.*, legitimista.
LE.GIT.I.MI.ZA.TION, s., legitimação.
LE.GIT.I.MIZE(-ISE), v., legitimar.
LEG-ROOM, s., espaço para pôr as pernas.
LE.GUME, s., legume.
LE.GU.MI.NOUS, *adj.*, leguminoso.
LEG-WARM.ERS, s. *pl.*, polainas.
LEG.WORK, s., trabalho de campo; *col.* trabalho externo.
LEISH.MAN.I.A.SIS, s., *Med.*, leishmaniose.
LEI.SURE, s., lazer, ócio, folga; *adj.*, desocupado, ocioso.
LEI.SURE CEN.TRE, s., centro de lazer.
LEI.SURED, *adj.*, desocupado, ocioso, livre.
LEM.MING, s., *Zool.*, lemingue; *fig.*, marionete.
LEM.ON, s., limão, limoeiro; *adj.*, cor de limão.
LEM.ON.ADE, s., limonada.
LEM.ON-JUICE, s., suco de limão.
LEM.ON SQUEEZ.ER, s., espremedor de limão.
LEM.ON TREE, s., *Bot.*, limoeiro.
LE.MUR, s., *Zool.*, lêmure.
LEND, v., emprestar.
LEND.ER, s., mutuante.
LEND.ING, s., empréstimo.
LEND.ING LI.BRA.RY, s., biblioteca pública.
LENGHT, s., comprimento, extensão, duração.
LENGHT.EN, v., alongar, encompridar.
LENGHT.WAYS, *adv.*, ao comprido.
LENGHT.Y, *adj.*, comprido, longo, alongado, esticado.

LE.NI.ENCE, s., suavidade, brandura, clemência, indulgência.
LENIENCY, s., leniência, indulgência; calma, brandura.
LE.NIENT, *adj.*, brando, indulgente.
LE.NI.ENT.LY, *adv.*, calmamente, suavemente.
LEN.I.TIVE, *adj.*, s., lenitivo.
LEN.I.TY, s., indulgência.
LENS, s., lente, objetiva.
LENT, s., *Rel.*, quaresma.
LENT.EN, *adj.*, *Rel.*, quaresmal; parcimonioso, escasso.
LEN.TIL, s., lentilha.
LE.O.NINE, *adj.*, leonino.
LEOP.ARD, s., *Zool.*, leopardo.
LEOP.ARD.ESS, s., *Zool.*, fêmea do leopardo.
LEP.ER, s., leproso, hanseniano.
LEP.I.DOP.TER.OUS, *adj.*, *Zool.*, lepidóptero.
LEP.O.RINE, *adj.*, leporino (relativo à lebre).
LEP.RO.SAR.I.UM, s., leprosário (hospital para leprosos).
LEP.RO.SY, s., lepra, mal de Hansen.
LEP.ROUS, *adj.*, leproso, hanseniano.
LEP.TON, s., *Fís.*, lépton.
LEP.TO.SPI.ROU.SIS, s., *Med.*, leptospirose.
LES.BI.AN, s., lésbica; *adj.*, lésbico.
LES.BI.AN.ISM, s., lesbianismo.
LE.SION, s., lesão, machucadura, contusão.
LE.SIONED, *adj.*, lesionado.
LESS, s., menos; *adj.*, menor, inferior; *adv.*, menos.
LES.SEE, s., arrendatário, locatário.
LESS.EN, v., diminuir, reduzir.
LESS.ER, *adj.*, menor, inferior.
LES.SON, s., lição, aula; v., repreender, recriminar.
LES.SOR, s., locador, arrendador.
LEST, *conj.*, a fim de que não.
LET, v., deixar, permitir, concordar, aceitar, fazer com que.
LET.DOWN, s., decepção, desapontamento.
LE.THAL, *adj.*, letal, mortal.
LE.THAL.I.TY, *adj.*, letalidade.
LE.THAR.GIC, *adj.*, letárgico.
LETH.AR.GY, s., letargia.
LET INTO, v., deixar entrar, entrar.
LET ON, v., revelar.
LET'S, *contr.* de *let us.*
LET.TER, s., letra, carta, tipo; v., rotular, marcar com letras.
LET.TER.BOX, s., caixa postal.
LET.TER-CASE, s., carteira (para dinheiro e documentos).
LET.TERED, *adj.*, letrado, erudito.
LET.TER.HEAD, s., cabeçalho.
LET.TER.ING, s., letras, caracteres; rótulo; inscrição.
LET.TER OPEN.ER, s., abridor de cartas.
LET.TIC, s., *adj.*, letão (natural ou relativo à Letônia).
LET.TISH, s., letão (idioma); *adj.*, letão (relativo aos letões).
LET.TUCE, s., *Bot.*, alface.
LET-UP, s., pausa, interval; afrouxamento.
LEU.CO.CYTE, s., *Biol.*, leucócito.
LEU.KE.MI.A, s., *Med.*, leucemia.
LE.VEE, s., dique, represa.
LEV.EL, s., nível, plano horizontal, altura, estrato; v., nivelar, aplainar.
LEV.EL CROS.SING, s., passagem de nível.
LEV.EL-HEAD.ED, *adj.*, US equilibrado, criterioso, sensato.
LEV.EL PEG.GING, *adj.*, igualado.
LEV.EL.LER, s., nivelador.

LEVELLING ··519·· LIGAMENTOUS

LEV.EL.LING, *s.*, nivelamento.
LEV.EL UP, *v.*, nivelar.
LE.VEL.LY, *adv.*, ao nível.
LE.VER, *s.*, alavanca; *v.*, usar (como) alavanca.
LEV.ER.AGE, *s.*, ação de emprego de alavanca; *Econ.*, alavancagem; *fig.*, influência.
LEV.I.A.BLE, *adj.*, tributável, que se pode taxar.
LEV.I.A.THAN, *s.*, leviatã, gigante.
LEV.I.GATE, *v.*, pulverizar, moer, triturar.
LEV.I.TATE, *v.*, levitar.
LEV.I.TA.TION, *s.*, levitação.
LEV.I.TY, *s.*, leviandade, futilidade.
LEVY, *s.*, tributo, imposto, arrecadação; *v.*, arrecadar, cobrar impostos.
LEWD, *adj.*, devasso, obsceno, lascivo, carnal.
LEWD.LY, *adv.*, lubricamente, lascivamente.
LEX.I.CAL, *adj.*, lexical.
LEX.I.CON, *s.*, léxico, dicionário, glossário.
LI.ABIL.I.TY, *s.*, responsabilidade, dívida, dependência.
LIABLE, *adj.*, sujeito a.
LIAISE, *v.*, fazer contato, criar vínculos.
LI.AI.SON, *s.*, ligação, liame.
LI.A.NA, **LI.A.NE**, *s.*, liana, cipó.
LI.AR, *s.*, mentiroso.
LI.BA.TION, *s.*, libação.
LIB.BER, *s., col.*, feminista (palavra informal para *liberationist*).
LI.BEL, *s.*, libelo, ataque, difamação; *v.*, caluniar, difamar.
LI.BEL.LING, *s.*, difamação.
LI.BEL.LOUS *UK*, **LI.BEL.OUS** *US*, *adj.*, difamatório.
LIB.ER.AL, *adj.*, liberal, dadivoso, generoso.
LIB.ER.AL ARTS, *s. pl.*, ciências humanas, humanidades.
LIB.ER.AL.ISM, *s.*, liberalismo.
LIB.ER.AL.I.TY, *s.*, liberalidade.
LIB.ER.AL.I.ZA.TION, *s.*, liberalização.
LIB.ER.AL.IZE(-ISE), *v.*, liberalizar.
LIB.ER.AL MIND.ED, *adj.*, liberal.
LIB.ER.ATE, *v.*, liberar, libertar.
LIB.ER.A.TION, *s.*, liberação, libertação.
LIB.ER.A.TION.IST, *s.*, aquele que defende libertação; defensor da revolução sexual ou feminismo.
LIB.ER.A.TOR, *s.*, libertador.
LI.BER.I.AN, *s., adj.*, liberiano (natural da ou relativo à Libéria).
LIB.ER.TAR.I.AN, *s.*, libertário.
LIB.ER.TIN.AGE, *s.*, libertinagem, devassidão.
LIB.ER.TINE, *s.*, libertino.
LIB.ER.TY, *s.*, liberdade.
LI.BID.I.NOUS, *adj.*, libidinoso, devasso, lascivo.
LI.BI.DO, *s., Psic.*, libido.
LI.BRAR.I.AN, *s.*, bibliotecário.
LI.BRAR.I.AN.SHIP, *s.*, biblioteconomia.
LI.BRAR.Y, *s.*, biblioteca.
LI.BRAR.Y SCI.ENCE, *s.*, biblioteconomia.
LI.BRATE, *v.*, equilibrar, librar.
LI.BRA.TION, *s.*, libração, oscilação.
LI.BRET.TO, *s., It., Mús.*, libreto (texto de ópera).
LIB.YA, *s.*, Líbia.
LIB.YAN, *adj., s.*, líbio (natural da ou relativo à Síria).
LICE, *s.*, piolhos.
LI.CENCE, *s.*, licença; carteira de motorista.
LI.CENSE, *s.*, licença, autorização; *v.*, licenciar, autorizar.
LI.CENSED, *adj.*, autorizado (a fazer algo).

LI.CEN.SEE, *s.*, licenciado.
LI.CEN.SURE, *s.*, licenciatura; licenciamento.
LI.CEN.TI.ATE, *adj.*, licenciado.
LI.CEN.TIOUS, *adj., pej.*, licencioso.
LI.CEN.TIOUS.LY, *adv.*, licenciosamente.
LI.CHEN, *s.*, líquen.
LIC.IT, *adj.*, lícito, permitido.
LIC.IT.LY, *adv.*, licitamente.
LICK, *s.*, lambida, golpe, pancada; *v.*, lamber, bater, dar pancada.
LICK.ER.ISH, *adj.*, saboroso, delicado.
LICK.ING, *s.*, ação de lamber; *fig.*, surra.
LIC.O.RICE, *s.*, alcaçuz; *adj.*, de alcaçuz.
LID, *s.*, tampa; pálpebra.
LI.DO, *s.*, piscina pública; praia lacustre.
LIE, *s.*, mentira; antro; *v.*, deitar-se, estar deitado, encontrar-se; mentir.
LIE DE.TEC.TOR, *s.*, detector de mentiras.
LIE-DOWN, *v.*, descansar.
LIEF, *adv.*, de bom grado, agradavelmente.
LIEGE, *s.*, feudatário; suserano; *adj.*, feudal, suserano.
LIE-IN, *s.*, ato de ficar na cama até tarde.
LIEN, *s.*, hipoteca, penhor, garantia.
LIEU.TEN.ANC.Y, *s.*, posto de tenente.
LIEU.TEN.ANT, *s., Mil.*, tenente.
LIEU.TEN.ANT COLO.NEL, *s., Mil.*, tenente-coronel.
LIEU.TEN.ANT GOV.ER.NOR, *s.*, representante governador.
LIEVE, *adv.*, agradavelmente; o mesmo que *lief*.
LIFE, *s.*, vida, existência, duração, conduta, animação, biografia.
LIFE-AND-DEATH, *adj.*, de vida ou morte; de importância fundamental.
LIFE AN.NU.I.TY, *s.*, renda vitalícia.
LIFE BELT, *s.*, cinto salva-vidas.
LIFE.BLOOD, *s., fig.*, força vital, sangue vital.
LIFE.BOAT, *s.*, barco salva-vidas; lancha de salvamento.
LIFE BUOY, *s.*, boia salva-vidas.
LIFE EX.PEC.TAN.CY, *s.*, expectativa de vida.
LIFE.GUARD, *s.*, salva-vidas.
LIFE IM.PRIS.ON.MENT, *s.*, prisão perpétua.
LIFE IN.SUR.ANCE, *s.*, seguro de vida.
LIFE JACK.ET, *s.*, colete salva-vidas.
LIFE.LESS, *adj.*, inerte, sem vida, morto.
LIFE.LIKE, *adj.*, natural, próprio, realista.
LIFE.LINE, *s.*, corda de segurança; *fig.*, cordão umbilical.
LIFE.LONG, *adj.*, vitalício, eterno, perene.
LIFE PRE.SERV.ER, *s., US* cinto salva-vidas.
LIFE RAFT, *s.*, balsa salva-vidas.
LIFE.SAV.ER, *s.*, salva-vidas (equipamento); ajuda na hora certa.
LIFE SEM.TENCE, *s.*, pena de prisão perpétua.
LIFE-SIZE, *adj.*, em tamanho natural.
LIFE SPAN, *s.*, vida, vida útil.
LIFE.STYLE, *s.*, estilo de vida.
LIFE.TIME, *s.*, vida (tempo de), existência; *adj.*, vitalício.
LIFT, *s.*, levantamento, ascensor, carga; *v.*, levantar, erguer, alçar.
LIFT.ER, *s.*, aquele que levanta ou ergue; aparelho que ergue.
LIFT-OFF, *s.*, decolagem de avião; *v.*, decolar, alçar voo.
LIG.A.MENT, *s.*, ligamento, ligação.
LIG.A.MEN.TOUS, *adj.*, ligamentoso.

LIGATE · 520 · LIONIZE(-ISE)

LI.GATE, *v.*, ligar.
LI.GA.TION, *s.*, ligação, liame.
LIG.A.TURE, *s.*, ligadura, atadura.
LIGHT, *s.*, luz, claridade, brilho; luz diurna; leve, ágil; *v.*, acender, iluminar, brilhar; aliviar, pousar; golpear.
LIGHT BULB, *s.*, lâmpada incandescente.
LIGHT CREAM, *s.*, creme leve.
LIGHT.ED, *adj.*, iluminado, aceso.
LIGHT.EN, *v.*, clarear, iluminar(-se), brilhar; aliviar, tornar-se leve; alegrar(-se).
LIGHT.ER, *s.*, isqueiro, acendedor; barca, barcaça.
LIGHT-FIN.GERED, *adj.*, gatuno, mão-leve, dedos ligeiros.
LIGHT-HEAD.ED, *adj.*, insensato, tonto.
LIGHT-HEAD.ED.LY, *adj.*, insensatamente, levianamente.
LIGHT-HEART.ED, *adj.*, despreocupado, alegre.
LIGHT.HOUSE, *s.*, farol.
LIGHT IN.DUS.TRY, *s.*, indústria leve.
LIGHT.ING, *s.*, iluminação.
LIGHT.LESS, *adj.*, sem luz, escuro, apagado.
LIGHT.LY, *adv.*, ligeiramente, levemente; levianamente.
LIGHT ME.TER, *s.*, *Opt.*, fotômetro.
LIGHT.NESS, *s.*, leveza, destreza, rapidez.
LIGHT.NING, *s.*, relâmpago, brilho, raio.
LIGHT OP.E.RA, *s.*, *Mús.*, opereta.
LIGHT PEN, *s.*, caneta óptica.
LIGHTS, *s. pl.*, semáforo; luzes (de palco); *fig.*, ideias, opiniões.
LIGHT.SOME, *adj.*, claro, brilhante.
LIGHT.SOME.LY, *adv.*, claramente, alegremente, despreocupadamente.
LIGHT.SOME.NESS, *s.*, alegria, regozijo, luminosidade.
LIGHTS-OUT, *s.*, hora de apagar as luzes; *Mil.*, toque de recolher.
LIGHT.WEIGHT, *s.*, *Esp.*, peso-leve (boxe); joão-ninguém; *adj.*, leve; *pej.*, de pouca expressão.
LIGHT-YEAR, *s.*, *Astron.*, ano-luz.
LIKE, *s.*, gosto, preferência, amor, semelhante; *v.*, gostar, amar, semelhar, parecer, querer, desejar, agradar.
LIKE.ABLE, *adj.*, simpático, agradável, afável, popular.
LIKE.LI.HOOD, *s.*, probabilidade, plausibilidade; sinal, indício.
LIKE.LI.NESS, *s.*, semelhança, igualdade, verossimilhança.
LIKE.LY, *adj.*, provável, possível, promissor, adequado; *adv.*, provavelmente.
LIKE-MIND.ED, *adj.*, da mesma opinião.
LIK.EN, *v.*, assemelhar, parecer, comparar.
LIKE.NESS, *s.*, semelhança; imagem; aparência.
LIKE.WISE, *adv.*, da mesma maneira; *conj.*, outrossim, também.
LIK.ING, *s.*, simpatia, afeição, amizade.
LI.LAC, *s.*, a cor lilás; *adj.*, lilás.
LILT, *s.*, canção alegre, cadência; *v.*,
LILT.ING, *adj.*, melodioso, cadenciado.
LILY, *s.*, *Bot.*, lírio, açucena, flor-de-lis; *adj.*, branco, alvo, puro, cândido.
LIMB, *s.*, membro (braço, perna), galho, ramificação; limbo, borda, orla; *Rel.*, limbo.
LIMBED, *adj.*, com membros.
LIM.BER, *v.*, tornar-se flexível; *adj.*, flexível, ágil.
LIMB.LESS, *adj.*, sem membros.
LIM.BO, *s.*, limbo, prisão; exílio, ostracismo.
LIME, *s.*, *Bot.*, lima (lima-da-pérsia, limão-galego).
LIME.LIGHT, *s.*, notoriedade; refletor; o centro das atenções; *v.*, evidenciar.
LIME.STONE, *s.*, pedra calcária.
LIM.IT, *s.*, limite, marco; *v.*, limitar, demarcar, restringir.
LIM.IT.A.BLE, *adj.*, restringível, limitável.
LIM.I.TARY, *adj.*, limítrofe.
LIM.I.TA.TION, *s.*, limitação.
LIM.IT.ED, *adj.*, limitado.
LIM.IT.ED COM.PA.NY, *s.*, companhia limitada.
LIM.IT.ED E.DI.TION, *s.*, edição limitada.
LIM.IT.ER, *s.*, aquele que limita.
LIM.IT.LESS, *adj.*, limitado.
LI.MO, *s.*, *abrev.* de *limousine*: limosine.
LIM.OU.SINE, *s.*, limusina.
LIMP, *s.*, ato de coxear; *v.*, coxear, mancar; *adj.*, flexível, mole.
LIMP.ER, *s.*, coxo, manco.
LIM.PID, *adj.*, límpido, claro, puro, calmo.
LIM.PID.I.TY, *s.*, limpidez, clareza, claridade.
LIMP.ING.LY, *adv.*, mancando, coxeando.
LIMP.NESS, *s.*, fraqueza, debilidade.
LIMY, *adj.*, calcário, lodoso, viscoso.
LINE, *s.*, linha, corda, fio, fila, ruga; *v.*, enfileirar, alinhar, riscar.
LIN.E.AGE, *s.*, linhagem, estirpe, descendência.
LIN.E.MENT, *s.*, lineamento; contorno.
LIN.E.AR, *adj.*, linear.
LIN.E.AR.I.TY, *s.*, linearidade.
LIN.E.AR.LY, *adv.*, linearmente.
LIN.E.A.TION, *s.*, esboço, lineamento.
LINE DRAW.ING, *s.*, desenho feito a traço.
LIN.EN, *s.*, linho, roupas de cama, roupa branca; *adj.*, feito de linho.
LINEN BAS.KET, *s.*, cesto de roupa suja.
LIN.ER, *s.*, transatlântico.
LINE.UP, *s.*, formação em linha; escalação; fila de identificação (de suspeitos).
LIN.GER, *v.*, demorar(-se), persistir; prolongar; protelar.
LIN.GER, *v.*, demorar.
LIN.GE.RIE, *s.*, *Fr.*, lingerie.
LIN.GER.ING, *adj.*, prolongado, lento, demorado.
LIN.GUAL.LY, *adv.*, mediante o uso da língua.
LIN.GUIST, *s.*, linguista.
LIN.GUIS.TIC, *adj.*, linguístico.
LIN.GUIS.TICS, *s.*, linguística.
LIN.I.MENT, *s.*, linimento, loção, unguento.
LIN.ING, *s.*, forro, revestimento de parede, etc.
LINK, *s.*, elo, aro, ligação, conexão, vínculo; *v.*, vincular, conectar, ligar.
LINK.AGE, *s.*, ligação, conexão, vínculo, sistema articulado.
LINK.ED, *adj.*, relacionado, unido; acoplado.
LINK.ING, *s.*, ligação, conexão, união.
LINKS, *s.*, *Esp.*, campo de golfe.
LINK-UP, *s.*, conexão, acoplamento.
LINN, *s.*, cachoeira, catarata, queda-d'água.
LI.NO, **LI.NO.LE.UM**, *s.*, linóleo.
LIN.O.TYPE, *s.*, linotipo.
LIN.SEED OIL, *s.*, óleo de linhaça.
LINT, *s.*, gase, fiapos ou retalhos de fibras de algodão; *US* bolinhas que se forma em tecido puído.
LI.ON, *s.*, leão.
LION CUB, *s.*, filhote de leão.
LI.ON.ESS, *s.*, leoa.
LI.ON.IZE(-ISE), *v.*, tratar como celebridade, endeusar.

LIP ·· 521 ·· LOB

LIP, s., lábio, beiço; v., tocar com os lábios, murmurar, beijar.
LIP.O.SUC.TION, s., *Med.*, lipoaspiração.
LIPPED, *adj.*, que tem lábios.
LIP-READ, v., ler nos lábios.
LIP-READ.ING, s., leitura labial.
LIP.STICK, s., batom.
LI.QUATE, v., liquefazer, derreter.
LIQ.UE.FAC.TION, s., liquefação.
LIQ.UE.FIED, *adj.*, liquefeito.
LIQ.UE.FY, v., liquefazer, derreter, desmanchar.
LI.QUEUR, s., licor.
LIQ.UID, *adj.*, s., líquido.
LIQ.UI.DATE, v., liquidar.
LIQ.UI.DA.TION, s., liquidação.
LIQ.UI.DA.TOR, s., liquidante (em finanças).
LI.QUID.I.TY, s., liquidez (em finanças); condição de ser líquido.
LIQ.UID.IZE(-ISE), v., liquidificar, liquefazer.
LIQ.UID.IZER, s., liquidificador (ver também: *blender*).
LIQ.UID.LY, *adv.*, liquidamente, fluidamente.
LIQ.UID.NESS, s., liquidez.
LIQ.UOR, s., bebida alcoólica, aguardente, licor; caldo (de cozidos).
LI.QUO.RICE, s., o mesmo que *licorice*: alcaçuz.
LI.RA, s., *It.*, lira (moeda italiana).
LIS.BON, s., Lisboa.
LISP, s., ceceio, cicio; v., cecear, ciciar.
LISP.ER, s., aquele que cicia.
LIS.SOM, *adj.*, flexível, ágil.
LIS.SOME, *adj.*, *Lit.*, grácil, esbelto.
LIST, s., lista, rol, relação; ourela; prazer, desejo; v., registrar; listar, fazer uma lista; orlar; agradar, desejar.
LIST.ED, *adj.*, registrado, listado, relacionado.
LIS.TEN, v., escutar, ouvir, perceber.
LIS.TEN.ER, s., ouvinte.
LIST.EN IN, v., ouvir conversa alheia.
LIS.TEN.ING, s., ato de ouvir, audição.
LIST.ING, s., listagem.
LIST.LESS *adj.*, apático, indiferente, murcho.
LIST.LESS.LY *adv.*, indiferentemente, apaticamente.
LIST.LESS.NESS, s., indiferença, apatia.
LIST PRICE, s., preço de catálogo, preço de tabela.
LIT.A.NY, s., ladainha; litania.
LIT.ER.A.CY, s., alfabetização.
LIT.ER.AL, *adj.*, literal, ao pé da letra.
LIT.ER.AL.I.TY, s., literalidade, sentido literal.
LIT.ER.AL.IZE(-ISE), s., interpretar literalmente (ao pé da letra).
LIT.ER.AL.LY, *adv.*, literalmente.
LIT.ER.AR.I.LY, *adv.*, literariamente.
LIT.ER.ARY *adj.*, literário.
LIT.ER.ATE, *adj.*, alfabetizado, letrado, instruído.
LIT.ER.A.TOR, s., literato.
LIT.ER.A.TURE, s., literatura.
LITHE, *adj.*, ágil, rápido, destro.
LITHE.LY, *adv.*, flexivelmente.
LITHE.NESS, s., agilidade, rapidez, destreza.
LITH.I.UM, s., *Quím.*, lítio.
LITH.O.GRAPH, s., litografia; v., litografar.
LI.THOG.RA.PHY, s., litografia.
LITH.U.A.NI.AN, s., *adj.*, lituano (natural da ou relativo à Lituânia).

LIT.I.GA.BLE, *adj.*, litigável.
LIT.I.GANT, *adj.*, s., litigante.
LIT.I.GATE, v., litigar, contender.
LIT.I.GA.TION, s., litígio, contenda, disputa.
LI.TI.GIOUS, *adj.*, litigioso, contencioso.
LI.TRE, LI.TER, s., litro.
LIT.TER, s., liteira, maca, padiola, desordem; v., espalhar feno, dar à luz uma ninhada.
LIT.TER.BAG, s., *US* cesto de lixo.
LIT.TLE, *adj.*, pequeno, pouco, breve, fraco; *adv.*, pouco; s., pouca coisa.
LIT.TLE FIN.GER, s., dedo mínimo, mindinho.
LIT.TLE.NESS, s., ninharia, bagatela, pequena quantidade, pequenez.
LIT.TO.RAL, *adj.*, s., litoral.
LIT-UP, *adj.*, bêbado.
LI.TUR.GIC, *adj.*, litúrgico.
LIT.UR.GY, s., liturgia.
LIV.ABLE, *adj.*, habitável, suportável.
LIV.A.BLE.NESS, s., habitabilidade.
LIVE, v., viver, existir, subsistir, estar, ser, morar.
LIVED, *adj.*, de vida, com vida, existente, vivente.
LIVE-IN, *adj.*, residente.
LIVE.LI.HOOD, s., subsistência, meio de vida.
LIVE.LI.NESS, s., vida, vigor, vivência, vivacidade.
LIVE.LONG, *adj.*, inteiro.
LIVE.LY, *adj.*, vivo.
LI.VEN, v., animar(-se).
LIV.ER, s., fígado; habitante.
LIV.ER.ISH, *adj.*, que sofre do fígado; irritado, irascível.
LIV.ER.Y, s., libré, farda; marca distintiva.
LIVE WIRE, s., cabo com corrente; pessoa dinâmica, empreendedor.
LIVE.STOCK, s., gado, rebanho.
LIV.ID, *adj.*, lívido, pálido; furioso.
LI.VID.I.TY, s., lividez, palidez.
LIV.ING, s., vivo; sustento; *adj.*, vivo, estimulante; habitável.
LIV.ING.LY, *adv.*, realisticamente.
LIV.ING-ROOM, s., sala de estar.
LIV.ING STAN.DARD, s., padrão de vida.
LIX.IV.I.UM, s., lixívia.
LIZ.ARD, s., qualquer animal dos Lacertídeos: lagarto, lagartixa, camaleão, etc.
LLA.MA, s., *Zool.*, llama.
LOAD, s., carga, peso, carregamento; v., carregar, pesar, oprimir.
LOAD.ED, *adj.*, *col.*, bêbado; forrado, cheio da grana; tendencioso, ardiloso.
LOAD.ER, s., carregador (de carga); escavadeira.
LOAD.ING, s., carga; sobretaxa.
LOAD.ING BAY, s., zona de carga e descarga.
LOAD.STONE, s., pedra-ímã.
LOAF, s., pão de forma.
LOAFER, s., mocassim.
LOAN, s., empréstimo; v., emprestar.
LOATH, *adj.*, relutante.
LOATHE, v., detestar, odiar, ter aversão.
LOATH.ING, s., asco, repugnância, nojo, ódio.
LOATH.SOME, *adj.*, repugnante.
LOB, v., arremessar, lançar; *Esp.*, rebater (tênis).

LOBBY · 522 · LOOKING-GLASS

LOB.BY, *s.*, saguão, entrada; grupo de pressão política; *v.*, pressionar, fazer *lobby*.
LOB.BY.IST, *s.*, *Pol.*, lobista.
LOBE, *s.*, *Anat.*, lóbulo (lobo do cérebro ou pulmões).
LO.BOT.O.MIZE(-ISE), *v.*, *Med.*, realizar lobotomia.
LO.BOT.O.MY, *s.*, *Med.*, lobotomia.
LOB.STER, *s.*, *Zool.*, lagosta, lagostim.
LOB.ULE, *s.*, lóbulo.
LO.CAL, *adj.*, local; *s.*, trem local.
LO.CAL AN.ES.THET.IC, *s.*, anestesia local.
LOCAL AU.THO.RI.TY, *s.*, autoridade local.
LOCAL CALL, *s.*, chamada local.
LOCALE, *s.*, localidade, lugar, sítio.
LO.CAL.I.TY, *s.*, localidade.
LO.CAL.I.ZA.BLE, *adj.*, localizável.
LO.CAL.I.ZA.TION, *s.*, localização.
LO.CAL.IZE(-IZE), *v.*, localizar.
LO.CAL.LY, *adv.*, localmente.
LO.CAL TIME, *s.*, hora local.
LO.CATE, *v.*, localizar, situar.
LO.CAT.ED, *adj.*, localizado, sito, situado.
LO.CA.TION, *s.*, local, situação, posição.
LOCH, *s.*, *UK* lago.
LOCK, *s.*, fechadura; eclusa, comporta; *v.*, chavear, fechar, travar.
LOCK.A.BLE, *adj.*, com fechadura; que pode ser trancado.
LOCK.ER, *s.*, armário, baú; compartimento com chave.
LOCK.ER ROOM, *s.*, vestiário (esportivo).
LOCK.ET, *s.*, medalhão.
LOCK.JAW, *s.*, *Med.*, espasmo causado pelo tétano.
LOCK.OUT, *s.*, locaute, greve de patrões.
LOCK.RAM, *s.*, estopa.
LOCK.SMITH, *s.*, serralheiro, chaveiro.
LOCK.UP, *s.*, prisão, cadeia.
LOCO, *s.*, *col.*, *US* louco, doido; *s.*, *col.*, *UK* locomotiva.
LO.CO.MO.TE, *v.*, locomover(-se).
LO.CO.MO.TION, *s.*, locomoção.
LO.CO.MO.TIVE, *s.*, locomotiva; *adj.*, locomotivo.
LO.CO.MO.TIV.I.TY, *s.*, locomotividade.
LO.CO.MO.TOR, *adj.*, locomotor.
LO.CUM, *s.*, interino, substituto temporário.
LO.CUST, *s.*, *Zool.*, gafanhoto.
LO.CU.TION, *s.*, locução, frase, expressão verbal.
LO.CU.TO.RY, *s.*, locutório, parlatório.
LODGE, *s.*, portaria, guarita; alojamento; choupana, loja maçônica; *v.*, hospedar-se; alojar-se, apresentar.
LODGE.MENT, *s.*, alojamento.
LODG.ER, *s.*, inquilino, hóspede.
LODG.ING, *s.*, alojamento, casa, moradia, habitação.
LOFT, *s.*, sótão.
LOFTY, *adj.*, soberbo, arrogante, orgulhoso.
LOG, *s.*, tora, tronco, cepo, lenho; *v.*, cortar, derrubar árvores.
LOG.A.RITHM, *s.*, *Mat.*, logaritmo (*abrev.*: log).
LOG-BOOK, *s.*, *Náut.*, diário de bordo; livro de registro.
LOG CA.BIN, *s.*, cabana (feita de troncos).
LOG.GER, *s.*, madeireiro.
LOG.GER.HEAD, *s.*, tolo, cabeça-oca; tartaruga marinha.
LOG-HOUSE, *s.*, cabana feita de troncos.
LOG.IC, *s.*, *Fil.*, lógica.
LOG.I.CAL, *adj.*, lógico, racional, metódico.
LOG.I.CAL.LY, *adv.*, logicamente.

LOG.I.CIZE(-ISE), *v.*, argumentar.
LO.GIS.TIC, *adj.*, logístico.
LO.GIS.TICS, *s.*, logística.
LOG.MAN, *s.*, lenhador.
LOGO, *s.*, *col.*, logotipo.
LOG-ROL.LING, *s.*, *US Pol.*, troca de favores.
LO.GY, *adj.*, *US col.*, vagaroso, pesado.
LOIN, *s.*, quadril, lombo, carne de lombo assada.
LOIN.CLOTH, *s.*, tanga.
LOI.TER, *v.*, demorar, vadiar, atrasar-se, perder tempo.
LOLL, *v.*, recostar-se, refestelar-se.
LOLL.ING.LY, *adv.*, preguiçosamente.
LOL.LI.POP, *s.*, pirulito.
LOL.LY, *s.*, *col.*, pirulito; *UK* picolé; *gír.*, *UK* grana.
LON.DON, *s.*, Londres.
LON.DON.ER, *s.*, londrino(a).
LONE, *adj.*, solitário, só, retirado; solteira, viúva.
LONE.LI.NESS, *s.*, solidão, isolamento.
LONE.LY, *adj.*, solitário, só.
LON.ER, *s.*, solitário (por opção).
LONE.SOME, *adj.*, *US col.*, solitário, só, isolado.
LONG, *adj.*, longo, comprido, extenso; *adv.*, durante, longamente.
LONG.BOAT, *s.*, escaler, chalupa; lancha.
LONG-DIS.TANCE, *adj.*, de longa distância, remoto.
LONG-DIS.TANCE CALL, *s.*, *Telef.*, chamada de longa distância.
LONG-DRAWN, *adj.*, prolongado; extenso.
LONG-DRAWN-OUT, *adj.*, interminável.
LON.GEV.I.TY, *s.*, longevidade.
LONG-HAIRED, *adj.*, de pelo comprido (animal).
LONG.HAND, *s.*, escrita à mão.
LONG.ING, *s.*, desejo, anseio; desejo ardente; *adj.*, ansioso, ardente.
LONG.ING.LY, *adv.*, ansiosamente, ardentemente.
LON.GI.TUDE, *s.*, longitude.
LONG JOHNS, *s. pl.*, ceroulas.
LONG JUMP, *s.*, *Esp.*, salto em distância.
LONG-LIVED, *adj.*, duradouro, longevo.
LONG-LOST, *adj.*, perdido há muito tempo.
LONG-PLAY.ING RE.CORD, *s.*, disco de vinil: *long-play* (LP).
LONG-RANGE, *adj.*, de longo alcance; de longo prazo.
LONG-RUN.NING, *adj.*, de muita duração; que já dura muito tempo.
LONG.SHORE.MAN, *s.*, estivador.
LONG-STAND.ING, *adj.*, de longa data.
LONG-SUF.FER.ING, *s.*, paciência, resignação; *adj.*, sofrido; paciente, resignado.
LONG-TERM, *adj.*, a longo prazo.
LONG WAVES, *s. pl.*, ondas longas (de rádio).
LONG.WAYS, *adv.*, ao comprido, longitudinalmente.
LONG-WIND.ED, *adj.*, de grande fôlego; cansativo.
LOO, *s.*, casa de banho.
LOO.BY, *adj.*, tolo, bobo.
LOOK, *v.*, olhar, parecer, fixar-se em; *s.*, olhar, olhadela, vista.
LOOK AFTER, *v.*, cuidar de, tratar com.
LOOK-A.LIKE, *s.*, sósia.
LOOK BACK, *v.*, lembrar, recordar, relembrar.
LOOK.ER, *s.*, pessoa que olha; *gír.* pessoa atraente.
LOOK.ING, *s.*, olhar, olhada.
LOOK.ING-GLASS, *s.*, espelho.

LOOKOUT ··523·· LUBRICOUS

LOOK.OUT, *s.*, posto de observação, vigia, vigilância.
LOOK OVER, *v.*, examinar, verificar.
LOOM, *s.*, tear, cabo de remo; *v.*, aparecer, agigantar-se, surgir um vulto.
LOOM.ING, *s.*, miragem, ilusão, visão; *adj.*, indefinido.
LOON, *s.*, pateta, bobo.
LOON.I.NESS, *s.*, maluquice.
LOO.NY, *adj.*, adoidado, meio doido; *s.*, tolo, pateta, bobo, imbecil.
LOOP, *s.*, laço; *v.*, enlaçar, fazer uma curva acentuada.
LOOP.HOLE, *s.*, saída, buraco, abertura.
LOOSE, *adj.*, solto, livre, frouxo.
LOOSE CHANGE, *s.*, trocado (dinheiro ou moedas).
LOOS.EN, *v.*, soltar, desatar, afrouxar, desprender.
LOOSE FIT.TING, *adj.*, frouxo, folgado (roupa).
LOOSE-LEAF BIND.ER, *s.*, pasta de folhas removíveis.
LOOSE.LY, *adv.*, imprecisamente; sem apertar, livremente.
LOOSE.NESS, *s.*, frouxidão; diarreia.
LOOT, *s.*, pilhagem, saque, despojos; *v.*, saquear, pilhar.
LOOT.ER, *s.*, saqueador.
LOOT.ING, *s.*, saque, pilhagem; *adj.*, de pilhagem.
LOP, *v.*, podar, desbastar; *s.*, ramos cortados, ramos podados.
LOPE, *s.*, trote (cavalo), caminhar ligeiro; *v.*, trotar (cavalo), andar a passos largos e ligeiros.
LOP.PER, *s.*, podador.
LOP.PING, *s.*, poda, desbaste.
LOP-SID.ED, *adj.*, assimétrico, distorcido, inclinado para um lado.
LO.QUA.CIOUS, *adj.*, loquaz, falador; tagarela.
LO.QUA.CIOUS.LY, *adv.*, loquazmente.
LO.QUA.CIOUS.NESS, *s.*, loquacidade.
LORD, *s.*, senhor, amo, patrão; *v.*, dominar, elevar, governar.
LORD.LI.NESS, *s.*, dignidade; arrogância.
LORD.LY, *adj.*, nobre arrogante.
LORD.SHIP, *s.*, *UK your/his ~* : Vossa/Sua Senhoria.
LORE, *s.*, tradição, crença popular; erudição.
LORN, *adj.*, sem parentes, sem amigos.
LOR.RY, *s.*, caminhão, carro; **LORRY DRIVER**, *s.*, caminhoneiro.
LOSE, *v.*, perder.
LOS.ER, *s.*, perdedor, derrotado.
LOS.ING, *adj.*, vencido, derrotado.
LOSS, *s.*, perda, derrota.
LOSS LEAD.ER, *s.*, artigo em liquidação, chamariz.
LOST, *adj.*, perdido.
LOST CAUSE, *s.*, causa perdida.
LOST PROP.ER.TY OF.FICE, *s.*, *UK* setor de achados e perdidos.
LOT, *s.*, lote, porção, quantidade; *v.*, lotear, dividir em lotes.
LO.TION, *s.*, loção.
LOT.TERY, *s.*, loteria.
LOT.TO, *s.*, loto (jogo).
LO.TUS, *s.*, loto, lótus.
LOUD, *adj.*, forte, alto, rumoroso, estrepitoso; *adv.*, espalhafatosamente.
LOUD-HAIL.ER, *s.*, megafone.
LOUD.ISH, *adj.*, um pouco alto.
LOUD.LY, *adv.*, alto (voz alta); espalhafatosamente.
LOUD.MOUTH, *adj.*, tagarela, gasguita, fofoqueiro.
LOUD.NESS, *s.*, ruído, sonoridade, rumor, barulho.
LOUD.SPEAK.ER, *s.*, alto-falante.

LOUGH, *s.*, lago (na Irlanda).
LOUNGE, *s.*, sala de estar; sala de espera; ociosidade; *v.*, recostar-se; espreguiçar-se; vadiar.
LOUNGE-LIZ.ARD, *s.*, parasita social; *gír.*, pilantra.
LOUNGE SUIT, *s.*, traje social, terno; traje de passeio.
LOUR, *s.*, rosto carrancudo, face carregada; *v.*, mostrar-se severo.
LOUSE, *s.*, piolho.
LOUSY, *adj.*, piolhento; ruim, péssimo.
LOUT, *s.*, rústico.
LOV.ABLE, *adj.*, louvável, adorável, simpático.
LOV.A.BLE.NESS, *s.*, amabilidade, simpatia.
LOV.A.BLY, *s.*, amavelmente.
LOVE, *s.*, amor; grande afeição; *v.*, amar, gostar de, adorar, preferir.
LOVE-AF.FAIR, *s.*, caso (de amor).
LOVE-FEAST, *s.*, ágape; banquete de confraternização.
LOVE-GOD, *s.*, cupido.
LOVE.LESS, *adj.*, sem amor.
LOVE LET.TER, *s.*, carta de amor.
LOVE-LIFE, *s.*, vida amorosa.
LOVE.LI.NESS, *s.*, amabilidade, beleza, graciosidade.
LOVE.LY, *adj.*, encantador, fascinante, apaixonante, belo.
LOVE-MAK.ING, *s.*, relação sexual.
LOV.ER, *s.*, amante.
LOV.ER.LIKE, *adj.*, amoroso.
LOVE-SICK, *adj.*, doente de amor, apaixonado.
LOVE-SONG, *s.*, canção de amor.
LOVE-STO.RY, *s.*, história de amor.
LOV.ING, *adj.*, carinhoso, encantador.
LOV.ING.LY, *adv.*, carinhosamente, afetuosamente.
LOW, *s.*, aquilo que é ou está baixo; *adj.*, baixo, doente, pessimista; degradado; *v.*, balir, mugir.
LOW-BROW, *s.*, homem de pouca cultura; *adj.*, de baixo nível intelectual, inculto.
LOW-CAL.O.RIE, *adj.*, de baixa caloria.
LOW-COM.E.DY, *s.*, *Teat.*, comédia burlesca.
LOW-CUT, *adj.*, decotado.
LOW-DOWN, *adj.*, truque baixo; *col.*, fatos concretos.
LOW.ER, *adj.*, mais baixo, inferior; *v.*, rebaixar, abaixar, reduzir.
LOW.ER CLASS, *s.*, as classes baixas, proletariado.
LOW.ER.ING, *adj.*, ameaçador, sombrio.
LOW.ER.MOST, *adj.*, o mais baixo, ínfimo.
LOW-KEY, *adj.*, discreto, retraído.
LOW.LANDS, *s. pl.*, planície.
LOW.LI.NESS, *s.*, humildade, vileza, torpeza.
LOW.LY, *adj.*, humilde, modesto; *adv.*, humildemente.
LOW-PAID, *adj.*, mal pago.
LOW-RISE, *adj.*, baixo (para prédios, torres, etc.).
LOW SEA.SON, *s.*, baixa estação (turismo).
LOW TIDE, *s.*, maré baixa.
LOY.AL, *adj.*, leal.
LOY.AL.ISM, *s.*, legalismo.
LOY.AL.IST, *s.*, leal (ao governo).
LOY.AL.TY, *s.*, lealdade.
LOZ.ENGE, *s.*, losango (formato); pastilha (para a garganta).
LU.BRI.CANT, *adj.*, *s.*, lubrificante.
LU.BRI.CATE, *v.*, lubrificar.
LU.BRI.CA.TION, *s.*, lubrificação.
LU.BRIC.I.TY, *s.*, lubricidade; lascívia.
LU.BRI.COUS, *adj.*, lúbrico; lascivo.

LUCENCE ·· 524 ·· LYRICISM

LU.CEN.CE, s., brilho, luminosidade.
LU.CEN.CY, s., brilho, fulgor, resplendor.
LU.CENT, adj., luzente, brilhante, luminoso.
LU.CENT, adv., luminosamente, brilhantemente.
LU.CERNE, s., Bot., alfafa.
LU.CID, adj., lúcido; claro, nítido; compreensível.
LU.CID.LY, adv., lucidamente, claramente.
LU.CID.I.TY, s., lucidez, brilho, luminosidade, clareza.
LUCK, s., acaso, sorte, felicidade.
LUCK.I.LY, adv., afortunadamente.
LUCK.I.NESS, s., felicidade, ventura.
LUCK.LESS, adj., desafortunado.
LUCK.Y, adj., afortunado, ditoso, sortudo.
LUCK.Y CHARM, s., amuleto.
LU.CRA.TIVE, adj., lucrativo.
LU.CRA.TIVE.NESS, s., lucratividade.
LU.CRE, s., lucro, proveito.
LU.DI.CROUS, adj., ridículo.
LU.DO, s., ludo (jogo).
LUG, s., puxão, arrasto; v., arrastar, puxar.
LUG.GAGE, s., bagagem.
LUG.GAGE RACK, s., porta-bagagem (automóvel, trem etc.); bagageiro.
LUG.GAGE VAN, s., UK vagão de bagagem (trem).
LU.GU.BRI.OUS, adj., lúgubre.
LU.GU.BRI.OUS.LY, adv., lugubremente.
LUKE.WARM, adj., tépido, morno; indiferente.
LUKE.WARM.NESS, s., tibieza, tepidez, mornidão.
LULL, s., calmaria, pausa; v., acalmar, aquietar; embalar alguém.
LULL.A.BY, s., cantiga de ninar.
LUM.BA.GO, s., Med., lumbago (dor na região lombar).
LUM.BAR, adj., lombar.
LUM.BER, s., trastes, restos, madeira serrada, tábua.
LUM.BER.ER, s., madeireiro (cortador de madeira na mata).
LUM.BER.ING, adj., desengonçado; pesado.
LUM.BER.JACK, s., madeireiro, lenhador.
LUM.BER-MILL, s., serraria.
LUM.BER-ROOM, s., recinto para guardar madeira cortada.
LUM.BER.YARD, s., depósito de madeira.
LU.MI.NOS.I.TY, s., luminosidade.
LU.MI.NOUS, adj., luminoso.
LU.MI.NOUS.LY, adv., luminosamente, claramente.
LUMP, s., pedaço (de carvão); torrão (de açúcar); caroço; Med., tumor; v., agrupar; amontoar; empelotar.
LUMP.ER, s., estivador.
LUMP.ISH, adj., pesado, grosseiro.
LUMPY, adj., encaroçado.
LU.NA.CY, s., loucura, demência.
LU.NAR, adj., lunar.
LU.NA.TIC, adj., lunático.
LUNCH, s., lanche, almoço, merenda; v., lanchar, comer, alimentar-se.
LUN.CHEON.ETTE, s., lanchonete.
LUNCH.EON VOU.CHER, s., tíquete-refeição.
LUNCH.TIME, s., hora de almoço.
LU.NETTE, s., luneta.
LUNG, s., Anat., pulmão.
LUNG CAN.CER, s., Med., câncer de pulmão.

LUNGE, s., bote, estocada; v., arremessar-se, investir (para frente), dar o bote; estocar.
LU.PINE, s., Bot., tremoço; adj., relativo a lobo.
LURCH, s., desamparo, abandono, solavanco; v., balançar.
LURCH.ING, s., solavanco.
LURE, s., isca, engodo, engano; v., engodar, enganar, seduzir.
LU.RID, adj., lúrido, pálido, lívido, branco, esbranquiçado.
LURK, v., espreitar, emboscar.
LURK.ING, adj., que segue rondando.
LURK.ING.LY, adv., à espreita.
LUS.CIOUS, adj., suculento (fruta), saboroso; vistoso (cor); atraente.
LUS.CIOUS.LY, adv., deliciosamente; sensualmente.
LUS.CIOUS.NESS, s., delícia; doçura; sedução.
LUSH, adj., exuberante, luxuriante, viçoso, suculento; s., gír., beberrão.
LUSH.NESS, s., viço, exuberância, sumo.
LUST, s., luxo, luxúria, concupiscência.
LUST.FUL, adj., sensual, luxurioso.
LUST.FUL.NESS, s., luxúria, lascívia.
LUS.TRA.TION, s., lustração, polimento.
LUSTRE, s., lustre, brilho.
LUS.TROUS, adj., lustroso, brilhante, reluzente.
LUS.TI.LY, adv., vigorosamente.
LUS.TRATE, v., purificar.
LUS.TRA.TION, v., purificação.
LUS.TRE, s., lustre, brilho, esplendor.
LUSTY, adj., robusto, forte.
LUTE, s., alaúde.
LU.TE.CI.UM, s., Quím., lutécio (elemento de nº atômico 71).
LU.THER.AN, adj., s., Rel., luterano.
LU.THER.AN.ISM, s., Rel., luteranismo.
LUX, s., Ópt., lux.
LUX.ATE, v., luxar, provocar uma luxação.
LUX.A.TION, s., luxação.
LUXE, s., luxo.
LUX.U.RI.ANT, adj., luxuriante, viçoso.
LUX.U.RI.ATE, v., deleitar-se.
LUX.U.RI.OUS, adj., luxuoso, esplêndido.
LUX.U.RY, s., luxo, fausto, delícia.
LUX.U.RY GOODS, s., pl., artigos de luxo.
LY.CE.UM, s., liceu.
LY.CHEE, s., Bot., lichia.
LYE, s., soda cáustica; lixívia.
LY.ING, s., mentira.
LY.ING-IN, s., resguardo (após o parto)
LYMPH, s., linfa.
LYM.PHO.MA, s., Med., linfoma.
LYNCH, v., linchar (executar sumariamente).
LYNCH.ER, s., linchador.
LYNCH.ING, s., linchamento.
LYNX, s., Zool., lince.
LYRE, s., Mús., lira.
LYR.IC, adj., lírico; s., lírica.
LYR.I.CAL, adj., lírico.
LYR.I.CAL.NESS, adj., lirismo.
LYRICISM, s., Lit., o mesmo que lyricalness.

M, s., décima terceira letra do alfabeto inglês.
M, num., número mil em algarismo romano.
MA, s., abrev. de mamãe.
MA.CA.BRE, adj., macabro.
MAC.AD.AM, s., macadame.
MAC.AD.AM.I.ZA.TION, s., macadamização, macadame.
MAC.AD.AM.IZE(-ISE), v., macadamizar.
MAC.A.RON.IC, adj., macarrônico (relativo às línguas latinas).
MAC.A.RO.NI, s., It., macarrão.
MACE, s., maça, clava, bastão; Bot., flor de noz-moscada.
MAC.E.DO.NI.AN, s., adj., macedônico, macedônio.
MAC.ER.ATE, v., macerar.
MAC.ER.AT.ED, adj., macerado.
MAC.ER.A.TION, s., maceração.
MACH, s., Aeron. unidade de velocidade de voo equivalente à do som (1.469 km/h).
MA.CHE.TE, s., machete (faca para cortar cana).
MACH.I.A.VEL.LI.AN, adj., maquiavélico.
MACH.I.A.VEL.LI.AN.ISM, s., maquiavelismo.
MACH.I.NATE, v., maquinar, tramar, engendrar, conspirar.
MACH.I.NA.TION, s., maquinação, conspiração, trama.
MA.CHINE, s., máquina, mecanismo, carro, autômato.
MA.CHIN.ERY, s., maquinaria, mecanismo.
MA.CHINE-GUN, s., metralhadora; v., metralhar.
MA.CHIN.IST, s., maquinista, engenheiro, mecânico.
MA.CHO, s., macho; adj., viril, corajoso; pej., machista.
MACK.EREL, s., Zool., cavala (peixe de água salgada).
MACK.IN.TOSH, s., capa de chuva.
MAC.RO, adj., Econ., grande, generalizado.
MAC.RO.BI.OT.IC, adj., macrobiótico.
MAC.RO.COSM, s., macrocosmo.
MAC.RO.E.CO.NOM.ICS, s., Econ., macroeconomia.
MAC.U.LA, s., mácula, mancha.
MAC.U.LATE, v., macular, manchar, sujar; adj., maculado, manchado.
MAC.U.LAT.ED, adj., maculado, manchado.
MAD, adj., louco, desvairado, tolo, furioso, brabo, enfurecido.
MAD.A.GAS.CAN, s., adj., malgaxe.
MAD.AM, s., senhora.
MAD.CAP, s., louco, maluco; adj., descontrolado, excêntrico.
MAD.DEN, v., enlouquecer, enfurecer, enraivecer.
MAD.DEN.ING, adj., enlouquecedor.
MAD.DING, adj., louco, raivoso.
MADE, adj., part., feito, fabricado, terminado.
MADE-CIR.CUIT, s., circuito fechado.
MADE-TO-MEA.SURE, adj., sob medida.
MADE-UP, adj., maquiado, preparado, falso, esfarrapado.
MAD.HOUSE, s., hospício, manicômio.
MAD.LY, adv., alucinadamente, loucamente.
MAD.MAN, s., louco, doido, alienado, desvairado.
MAD.NESS, s., loucura, demência, raiva.
MA.DON.NA, s., Nossa Senhora, estátua de Nossa Senhora.
MAD.RI.GAL, s., madrigal.
MAD.WOM.AN, s., louca.
MA.ES.TRO, s., maestro, regente.
MAG, s., col., revista.
MAG.A.ZINE, s., revista, periódico; armazém, paiol.
MAG.A.ZIN.IST, s., articulista de revista.
MA.GEN.TA, s., a cor magenta; adj., magenta.
MAG.GOT, s., larva de mosca.
MA.GI.AN, s., mago; adj., relativo aos reis magos.
MAG.IC, adj., mágico; s., magia.
MAG.I.CAL, adj., mágico.
MAG.IC CAR.PET, s., tapete mágico.
MAG.IC EYE, s., UK olho mágico.
MAG.IC WAND, s., varinha mágica.
MA.GI.CIAN, s., mágico, prestidigitador, bruxo.
MAG.IS.TE.RI.AL, adj., dominador; Jur., magistral.
MAG.IS.TRA.CY, s., magistratura.
MAG.IS.TRATE, s., magistrado, juiz.
MAG.IS.TRA.TURE, s., Jur., o mesmo que magistracy: magistratura.
MAG.NA.NIM.I.TY, s., magnanimidade.
MAG.NAN.I.MOUS, adj., magnânimo.
MAG.NATE, s., magnata, pessoa muito rica.
MAG.NE.SIA, s., magnésia.
MAG.NE.SI.UM, s., Quím., magnésio.
MAG.NET, s., Fís., ímã; fig., atrativo.
MAG.NET.IC, adj., magnético, imantizado.
MAG.NET.IC DISK, s., disco magnético.
MAG.NET.IC FIELD, s., campo magnético.
MAG.NET.IC TAPE, s., fita magnética.
MAG.NE.TISM, s., magnetismo, imã.
MAG.NET.I.ZA.BLE, adj., magnetizável.
MAG.NET.I.ZA.TION, s., magnetização.
MAG.NET.IZE(-ISE), v., magnetizar, imantar.
MAG.NET.IZER(-ISER), s., magnetizador.
MAG.NE.TO.ME.TER, s., Fís., magnetômetro.
MAG.NE.TO.MET.RY, s., Fís., magnetometria.
MAG.NI.FI.CA.TION, s., ampliação, aumento.
MAG.NIF.I.CENCE, s., magnificência.
MAG.NIF.I.CENT, adj., magnífico, grandioso, brilhante.
MAG.NIF.I.CENT.LY, adv., magnificamente.
MAG.NI.FI.ER, s., ampliador, lente de aumento.
MAG.NI.FY, v., magnificar, engrandecer, aumentar.
MAG.NI.FY.ING GLASS, s., lente de aumento, lupa.
MAG.NI.TUDE, s., magnitude.
MAG.NO.LI.A, s., magnólia; creme.
MAG.NUM, s., garrafa para conter 1,5 litro de um líquido.
MAG.PIE, s., Zool., pega (ave da família dos corvídeos); tagarela.
MAG.YAR adj., s., magiar, húngaro.
MA.HA.RA.JAH, s., marajá (príncipe da Índia).
MA.HOG.A.NY, s., Bot., mogno; adj., feito de mogno.

MAHOMET ·· 526 ·· MAMMOTH

MA.HOM.ET, *s.*, Maomé.

MAID, *s.*, donzela, solteira, senhorita; criada, empregada.

MAID.EN, *s.*, donzela, senhorita, solteirona; *adj.*, solteira.

MAID.EN.HEAD, *s.*, virgindade, hímen.

MAID.EN NAME, *s.*, nome de solteira.

MAIDEN.HOOD, *s.*, virgindade; estado ou tempo de solteira.

MAID.EN.LI.NES, *s.*, candura; modéstia; pureza.

MAID.EN.LY, *adv.*, modestamente; *adj.*, virginal, puro; gentil.

MAID.EN NAME, *s.*, nome de solteira.

MAID.SERV.ANT, *s.*, criada.

MAIL, *s.*, correio, correspondência; armadura; *v.*, remeter cartas pelo correio; encouraçar.

MAIL.ABLE, *adj.*, que se pode remeter por correio.

MAIL.BAG, *s.*, sacola do carteiro.

MAIL.BOX, *s.*, caixa de correio, caixa de correspondência.

MAILED, *adj.*, expedido (pelo correio); armado, blindado.

MAIL.ER, *s.*, aquele que leva o correio ou cartas ao correio; máquina de endereçar.

MAIL.ING LIST, *s.*, lista de endereços.

MAIL.MAN, *s.*, *US* carteiro.

MAIL OR.DER, *s.*, pedido por reembolso postal.

MAIL.SHOT, *s.*, mala-direta.

MAIM, *s.*, mutilação, aleijamento, defeito físico; *v.*, mutilar, aleijar.

MAIN, *s.*, força física; cano, esgoto, oceano, mar alto; *adj.*, fundamental, principal.

MAIN COURSE, *s.*, *Cul.*, prato principal; *Náut.*, vela mestra.

MAIN FRAME, *s.*, *Comp.*, *mainframe* (principal unidade de processamento e armazenamento de dados).

MAIN.LAND, *s.*, continente; terra firme.

MAIN LINE, *s.*, linha-tronco (ferrovia); *Eletr.*, linha principal.

MAIN.LY, *adv.*, principalmente.

MAIN.SAIL, *s.*, *Náut.*, vela-mestra.

MAIN.STREAM, *adj.*, tendência predominante e atual.

MAIN.TAIN, *v.*, manter, conservar, afirmar.

MAIN.TAIN.ABLE, *adj.*, suportável.

MAIN.TAIN.ER, *s.*, mantenedor.

MAIN.TE.NANCE, *s.*, manutenção, sustento, alimentação.

MAIN.TE.NANCE OR.DER, *s.*, *Jur.*, obrigação de pensão (divórcio).

MAIZE, *s.*, *Bot.*, milho.

MA.JES.TIC, *adj.*, majestoso, grandioso.

MA.JES.TI.CAL.LY, *adv.*, majestosamente.

MAJ.ES.TY, *s.*, majestade.

MA.JOR, *s.*, major; *adj.*, maior, principal.

MA.JOR.ETTE, *s.*, baliza; o mesmo que *drum majorette.*

MA.JOR GEN.ER.AL, *s.*, *Mil.*, general de divisão.

MA.JOR.I.TA.RIAN, *adj.*, majoritário.

MA.JOR.I.TY, *s.*, maioria.

MA.JUS.CULE, *s.*, maiúscula (letra); *adj.*, maiúsculo.

MAK.A.BLE, *adj.*, realizável.

MAKE, *v.*, fazer, fabricar, produzir; *s.*, marca, feitura, feitio, forma.

MAKE-BE.LIEVE, *s.*, faz de conta; *v.*, fingir, fazer de conta.

MAKE FOR, *v.*, dirigir-se, rumar.

MAKE.OVER, *s.*, aperfeiçoamento, transformação; *v.*, *make over.* refazer.

MAK.ER, *s.*, fabricante, criador, inventor.

MAKE.SHIFT, *s.*, paliativo; *adj.*, provisório, improvisado.

MAKE-UP, *s.*, maquiagem, pintura; caráter; composição; *v.*, *make up for.* *US* compensar.

MAKE.WEIGHT, *s.*, contrapeso, para alcançar o peso.

MAK.ING, *s.*, fabricação, produção; criação; potencialidade.

MAL.AD.JUST.ED, *adj.*, desajustado, mal-ajustado.

MAL.AD.JUST.MENT, *s.*, desajuste; ajustamento defeituoso.

MAL.A.DY, *s.*, doença, enfermidade.

MAL.AISE, *s.*, mal-estar, indisposição.

MAL.AP.RO.POS, *adj.*, inconveniente, que fala palavrões.

MA.LAR.IA, *s.*, malária.

MA.LA.WI.AN, *s.*, *adj.*, malauiano.

MA.LAY, *s.*, malaio (habitante ou natural da Malásia).

MA.LAY.AN, *adj.*, malaio (relativo aos malaios ou à Malásia).

MA.LAY.SIA, *s.*, Malásia.

MA.LAY.SIAN, *s.*, *adj.*, malaio.

MAL.CON.TENT, *adj.*, *s.*, descontente, infeliz.

MALE, *s.*, macho, varão, sexo masculino: *adj.*, masculino, viril.

MAL.E.DICT, *v.*, amaldiçoar.

MAL.E.DIC.TION, *s.*, maldição.

MAL.E.FAC.TOR, *s.*, malfeitor.

MA.LEF.I.CENT, *adj.*, maléfico, maldoso.

MALE NURSE, *s.*, enfermeiro.

MA.LEV.O.LENT, *adj.*, malévolo.

MAL.FEA.SANCE, *s.*, prevaricação.

MAL.FORMED, *adj.*, malformado, deficiente físico.

MAL.FUNC.TION, *s.*, mau funcionamento; *v.*, funcionar mal.

MA.LIC, *adj.*, próprio da maçã.

MAL.ICE, *s.*, malícia, despudor.

MA.LI.CIOUS, *adj.*, malicioso, maldoso, malevolente.

MA.LIGN, *adj.*, maligno, pernicioso, maldoso; *v.*, difamar, caluniar.

MA.LIG.NANCE, *s.*, malignidade, virulência.

MA.LIG.NANT, *adj.*, maligno, diabólico.

MA.LIG.NI.TY, *s.*, malignidade, maldade.

MA.LIGN.LY, *adv.*, malignamente, maldosamente.

MA.LIGN.ER, *s.*, caluniador, injuriador.

MA.LIN.GER, *v.*, fazer-se de doente.

MA.LIN.GER.ER, *s.*, *Mil.*, doente fingido para evitar serviço.

MALL, *s.*, centro comercial; *shopping mall*: shopping center.

MAL.LARD, *s.*, *Zool.*, pato-real (tipo de marreco).

MAL.LEA.BIL.I.TY, *s.*, maleabilidade.

MAL.LEA.BLE, *adj.*, maleável.

MAL.LET, *s.*, marreta, malho, maço.

MAL.LOW, *s.*, *Bot.*, malva.

MAL.NOUR.ISHED, *adj.*, subnutrido.

MAL.NU.TRI.TION, *s.*, má nutrição, má alimentação.

MAL.ODOR.OUS, *adj.*, malcheiroso, fétido.

MAL.ODOR.OUS.NESS, *s.*, fedor, fedentina.

MAL.PO.SI.TION, *s.*, má posição.

MAL.PRAC.TICE, *s.*, malversação, falta profissional.

MALT, *s.*, malte; *v.*, preparar o malte para cerveja.

MAL.TREAT, *v.*, maltratar, atormentar.

MAL.TREAT.MENT, *s.*, mau trato, tormento.

MAM.MA, *s.*, mama, mamãe.

MAM.MAL, *s.*, mamífero.

MAM.MA.LIA, *s.*, *Lat.*, mamíferos.

MAM.MA.LI.AN, *adj.*, mamífero.

MAM.MAL.O.GY, *s.*, mamalogia (ramo da zoologia que estuda os mamíferos).

MAM.MA.RY, *adj.*, *Anat.*, mamário.

MAM.MOG.RA.PHY, *s.*, *Med.*, mamografia.

MAM.MON, *s.*, avareza; riqueza de influência maléfica.

MAM.MOTH, *s.*, mamute.

MAMMY •• 527 •• MAPLE SYRUP

MAM.MY, *s.*, mamãe; ama de leite preta.
MAN, *s.*, homem, varão, ser humano, pessoa, indivíduo; *v.*, colocar soldados, tripular, equipar.
MAN.A.CLE, *s.*, algemas, grilhetas; *v.*, algemar, prender, manietar.
MAN.AGE, *v.*, arranjar-se, dirigir, administrar, manejar.
MAN.AGE.A.BIL.I.TY, *s.*, maneabilidade.
MAN.AGE.A.BLE, *adj.*, controlável, manejável, dominável, viável; dócil.
MAN.AGE.MENT, *s.*, administração, direção, governo.
MAN.AG.ER, *s.*, gerente, administrador.
MAN.AG.ER.ESS, *s.*, gerente.
MAN.A.GE.RI.AL, *adj.*, gerencial, administrativo.
MAN.AG.ING DI.RECT.OR, *s.*, diretor administrativo.
MAN.A.TEE, *s.*, *Zool.*, peixe-boi.
MAN-CHILD, *s.*, filho varão.
MAN.CHU, *s.*, *adj.*, manchu (originário da ou relativo à Manchúria).
MAN.CHU.RI.AN, *adj.*, manchu (da Manchúria).
MAN.DA.MUS, *s.*, *Jur.*, mandado, despacho.
MAN.DA.RIN, *s.*, mandarim; tangerina; cor amarelo-alaranjada.
MAN.DATE, *s.*, mandato, delegação.
MAN.DA.TO.RY, *s.*, mandatário.
MAN.DI.BLE, *s.*, mandíbula, maxilar inferior.
MAN.DI.O.CA, *s.*, *Bot.*, mandioca, aipim.
MAN.DO.LIN, *s.*, *Mús.*, bandolim.
MAN.DRAG.O.RA, *s.*, *Bot.*, mandrágora; raiz ou fruto dessa planta.
MAN.DRAKE, *s.*, o mesmo que *mandragora*.
MAN.DRILL, *s.*, *Zool.*, mandril (babuíno gigante).
MANE, *s.*, juba, crina.
MAN-EAT.ER, *adj.*, canibal, antropófago.
MANED, *adj.*, que tem crina ou juba.
MA.NEU.VER, *s.*, manobra, evolução; *v.*, manobrar, dirigir.
MAN.FUL, *adj.*, másculo, varonil, viril, corajoso.
MAN.FUL.NESS, *s.*, coragem, valentia.
MAN.GA.NESE, *s.*, manganês.
MANGE, *s.*, ronha (tipo de sarna).
MAN.GER, *s.*, manjedoura.
MANGE.TOUT, *s.*, *Bot.*, ervilha-torta.
MAN.GLE, *v.*, destroçar, mutilar; *fig.*, assassinar.
MAN.GO, *s.*, manga, mangueira.
MAN.GROVE, *s.*, *Bot.*, mangue.
MAN.GY, *adj.*, sarnento, chaguento.
MAN-HAN.DLE, *v.*, matratar.
MAN.HOLE, *s.*, bueiro, boca de lobo.
MAN.HOOD, *s.*, idade adulta, varonilidade, masculinidade.
MAN.HOUR, *s.*, *Econ.*, hora-homem de trabalho.
MAN.HUNT, *s.*, perseguição (a um indivíduo por crime).
MA.NI.A, *s.*, mania.
MA.NI.AC, *adj.*, maníaco.
MAN.IC, *adj.*, *Psic.*, maníaco.
MAN.IC-DE.PRES.SIVE, *adj.*, *s.*, maníaco-depressivo.
MAN.I.CURE, *s.*, manicure; *v.*, tratar das unhas das mãos e pés.
MAN.I.FEST, *s.*, manifesto; *v.*, manifestar, declarar; *adj.*, manifesto.
MAN.I.FES.TANT, *s.*, manifestante.
MAN.I.FES.TA.TION, *s.*, manifestação, declaração.
MAN.I.FEST.LY, *adv.*, manifestamente, claramente.

MAN.I.FES.TO, *s.*, manifesto, declaração, proclamação.
MAN.I.FOLD, *s.*, cópia; *v.*, mimeografar, reproduzir; *adj.*, muitos.
MAN.I.FOLD, *s.*, mimeógrafo, fotocopiadora, xérox.
MAN.I.FOLD.NESS, *s.*, multiplicidade.
MAN.I.KIN, *s.*, manequim, boneco.
MA.NIL.A, *adj.*, de papel-manilha.
MAN.I.OC, *s.*, mandioca, aipim, macaxeira.
MA.NIP.U.LATE, *v.*, manipular.
MA.NIP.U.LA.TION, *s.*, manipulação.
MA.NIP.U.LA.TIVE, *adj.*, manipulatório, manipulador.
MA.NIP.U.LA.TOR, *s.*, manipulador.
MAN.KIND, *s.*, humanidade, gênero humano, espécie humana.
MAN.LIKE, *adj.*, característico do homem, viril, varonil.
MAN.LI.NESS, *s.*, masculinidade, virilidade; coragem.
MAN.LY, *adj.*, másculo, varonil, viril.
MAN-MADE, *adj.*, produzido pelo homem, artificial, sintético.
MAN.NA, *s.*, maná.
MANNED, *adj.*, tripulado.
MAN.NE.QUIN, *s.*, manequim.
MAN.NER, *s.*, modo, maneira, comportamento, procedimento.
MAN.NERED, *adj.*, educado, cortês, polido, gentil.
MAN.NER.ISM, *s.*, maneirismo; trejeito, afetação.
MAN.NISH, *adj.*, másculo, varonil, viril.
MA.NOEU.VRA.BLE *UK*, **MA.NOE.VRA.BLE** *US*, *adj.*, manobrável.
MA.NOEU.VRE *UK*, **MA.NEU.VER** *US*, *s.*, manobra; *v.*, manobrar, manejar.
MA.NOEU.VRER, *s.*, manobreiro.
MA.NOM.E.TER, *s.*, manômetro.
MAN.OR, *s.*, solar (mansão de verão).
MAN.POW.ER, *s.*, potencial humano, mão de obra, capacidade.
MAN.SERV.ANT, *s.*, criado, servo, empregado.
MAN.SION, *s.*, mansão, palácio, palacete.
MAN-SIZE, *adj.*, de tamanho grande (para homem adulto).
MAN.SLAUGH.TER, *s.*, matança, assassinato involuntário.
MAN-SLAY.ER, *s.*, homicida.
MAN.TEL, *s.*, cornija ou consolo de lareira.
MAN.TEL.PIECE, *s.*, o mesmo que *mantel*.
MAN.TLE, *s.*, manto, capa; *v.*, cobrir, tampar.
MAN-TO-MAN, *adj.*, de homem para homem.
MAN.U.AL, *s.*, manual, compêndio: *adj.*, manual, feito à mão.
MAN.U.AL.LY, *adv.*, manualmente.
MAN.U.AL WORK, *s.*, trabalho braçal ou manual.
MAN.U.AL WORK.ER, *s.*, trabalhador braçal, operário.
MAN.U.FAC.TO.RY, *s.*, fábrica, oficina.
MAN.U.FAC.TURE, *s.*, manufatura, fabricação; *v.*, manufaturar.
MAN.U.FAC.TUR.ER, *s.*, fabricante, manufaturador.
MAN.U.FAC.TUR.ING, *s.*, manufatura, fabricação.
MAN.U.FAC.TUR.ING IN.DUS.TRIES, *s. pl.*, indústrias manufatureiras.
MA.NURE, *s.*, estrume, adubo; *v.*, adubar, estrumar, fertilizar.
MA.NUR.ER, *s.*, adubador.
MA.NUR.ING, *s.*, fertilização, adubação.
MAN.U.SCRIPT, *s.*, manuscrito.
MANY, *adj.*, *pron.*, muitos, muitas.
MAP, *s.*, mapa; *v.*, mapear, desenhar mapas.
MA.PLE, *s.*, *Bot.*, bordo (tipo de árvore).
MA.PLE SYR.UP, *s.*, xarope de bordo.

MAR · 528 · MASSEUR

MAR, v., estragar, frustrar, arruinar.
MAR.A.THON, s., maratona.
MAR.A.THON RUNNER, s., maratonista.
MA.RAUD, v., saquear, pilhar.
MA.RAUD.ER, s., gatuno, saqueador.
MA.RAUD.ING, adj., saqueador.
MAR.BLE, s., mármore; adj., marmóreo.
MARCH, s., março.
MARCH, s., marcha, passeata; v., marchar, fazer passeata.
MARCH.ER, s., marchador, indivíduo que marcha.
MARCH.ING, s., marcha.
MAR.CHIO.NESS, s., marquesa.
MARE, s., égua (fêmea do cavalo).
MAR.GA.RINE, s., margarina.
MARGE, s., Lit., borda, margem; col., margarina.
MAR.GIN, s., margem, orla, borda; v., margear, orlar, marginar.
MAR.GIN.AL, adj., secundário, marginal, à margem.
MAR.GIN.AL.IZE(-ISE), v., marginalizar; deixar à margem.
MAR.GIN.AL.LY, adv., marginalmente; ligeiramente.
MAR.I.AN, adj., mariano, referente a Nossa Senhora.
MARI.GOLD, s., malmequer.
MAR.I.JUA.NA, s., maconha, marijuana.
MA.RI.NA, s., Náut., marina.
MAR.I.NADE, s., marinada; alimento em escabeche.
MAR.I.NATE, v., marinar, pôr em vinha d'alhos.
MA.RINE, s., fuzileiro naval americano; adj., marinho.
MA.RINE BI.OL.O.GY, s., biologia marinha.
MAR.I.NER, s., marinheiro.
MAR.I.O.NETTE, s., Fr., marionete.
MAR.I.TAL, adj., marital, matrimonial, conjugal.
MAR.I.TAL STA.TUS, s., estado civil.
MAR.I.TIME, adj., marítimo.
MAR.JO.RAM, s., manjerona.
MARK, s., marca, sinal, impressão, símbolo, alvo; v., marcar, assinalar, distinguir, indicar, escolher, designar.
MARK AS, v., marcar, rotular, etiquetar.
MARKED, adj., marcado, marcante; notável.
MARKED.LY, adv., maradamente; notavelmente.
MARK.ER, s., marcador, rotulador.
MAR.KET, s., mercado, supermercado; v., comerciar, comercializar.
MAR.KET.A.BIL.I.TY, s., negociabilidade.
MAR.KET.A.BLE, adj., vendável, negociável, comercializável.
MAR.KET ANAL.Y.SIS, s., análise de mercado.
MAR.KET-DAY, s., dia de feira.
MAR.KET.EER, s., pessoa especializada em mercadologia; Bras., marqueteiro.
MAR.KET.ER, s., feirante.
MAR.KET GAR.DEN, s., horta (para comercializar).
MAR.KET.ING, s., marketing, propaganda para vendas; mercadologia.
MAR.KET.PLACE, s., mercado, praça de vendas.
MAR.KET-PRICE, s., Econ., preço de mercado.
MAR.KET RE.SEARCH, s., pesquisa de mercado.
MAR.KET VAL.UE, s., Econ., valor de mercado.
MARK.ING, s., marcação, marca, marca de revisão.
MARKS.MAN, s., atirador (profissional).
MARKS.MAN.SHIP, s., pontaria, perícia no tiro ao alvo.
MARK.UP, s., margem de lucro; remarcação, aumento de preço.
MARK UP, v., remarcar preço, aumentar preço.

MAR.MA.LADE, s., marmelada, doce, geleia.
MAR.MOT, s., Zool., marmota.
MA.ROON, s., a cor castanha; adj., castanho; v., abandonar em local deserto.
MA.ROONED, adj., abandonado.
MAR.QUEE, s., toldo.
MAR.QUET.RY, s., marchetaria.
MAR.QUIS, s., marquês.
MAR.RIAGE, s., casamento,matrimônio, núpcias.
MAR.RIAGE CER.TIF.I.CATE, s., certidão de casamento.
MAR.RIAGE RING, s., aliança.
MAR.RIED, adj., casado, esposado, matrimonial.
MAR.RON, adj., cor castanha, castanho.
MAR.ROW, s., medula, tutano; essência.
MAR.RY, v., casar, desposar, unir em matrimônio.
MARS, s., Astron., Marte (planeta); Mit., Marte (deus da guerra).
MARSH, s., **PÂNTANO.**
MARSHAL, s., marechal, chefe de polícia; v., ordenar, dispor, dirigir.
MARSH.LAND, s., pantanal, área pantanosa.
MARSH.MAL.LOW, s., marshmallow.
MARSHY, adj., pantanoso.
MAR.SU.PI.AL, adj., s., marsupial.
MART, s., mercado, feira.
MAR.TIAL, adj., marcial, guerreiro, lutador.
MAR.TIAL ARTS, s. pl., artes marciais.
MAR.TIAL LAW, s., Mil., lei marcial.
MAR.TIAN, s., adj., marciano.
MAR.TIN, s., Zool., martinete (andorinha de asas longas).
MAR.TYR, s., mártir; v., martirizar, torturar, atormentar.
MAR.TYR.ED, adj., martirizado.
MAR.TYR.DOM, s., martírio, tortura.
MAR.VEL, s., maravilha, prodígio, magia; v., maravilhar-se, admirar.
MAR.VEL.OUS, adj., maravilhoso, mágico, extraordinário.
MARX.ISM, s., marxismo.
MARX.IST, s., adj., marxista.
MAR.ZI.PAN, s., maçapão.
MAS.CA.RA, s., rímel.
MAS.COT, s., mascote.
MAS.CU.LINE, s., masculino; adj., masculino, viril, forte.
MAS.CU.LINE.NESS, s., masculinidade, virilidade.
MASH, s., mistura, pasta, mingau, purê; v., misturar, triturar.
MASHED PO.TA.TOES, s., Cul., purê de batata.
MASK, s., máscara; v., mascarar, esconder o rosto com máscara.
MASKED, adj., mascarado, disfarçado.
MASK.ER, s., mascarado.
MAS.OCH.ISM, s., Psic., masoquismo.
MAS.OCH.IST, s., Psic., masoquista.
MAS.OCH.IST.IC, adj., Psic., masoquista.
MA.SON, s., mação, pedreiro; maçom.
MA.SON.IC, adj., maçônico.
MA.SON.RY, s., alvenaria, maçonaria.
MAS.QUER.ADE, s., baile de máscaras, disfarce; v., mascarar-se, disfarçar-se.
MASS, s., missa, liturgia da missa.
MASS, s., massa, multidão; v., reunir-se, concentrar-se.
MAS.SA.CRE, s., massacre, carnificina; v., massacrar.
MAS.SAGE, s., massagem; v., massagear, fazer massagens.
MAS.SEUR, s., massagista.

MASSEUSE   •• 529 •••   MAYPOLE

MAS.SEUSE, *s.*, massagista (mulher).
MAS.SIVE, *adj.*, maciço, compacto, enorme.
MAS.SIVE.LY, *adv.*, enormemente; pesadamente.
MAS.SIVE.NESS, *s.*, solidez.
MASS ME.DI.A, *s. pl.*, meios de comunicação de massa.
MASS-PRO.DUCE, *v.*, produzir em massa ou em série.
MASS PRO.DUC.TION, *s.*, produção em massa.
MAST, *s.*, mastro, poste.
MAS.TEC.TO.MY, *s., Med.*, mastectomia.
MAS.TER, *s.*, mestre, senhor, patrão, professor; *v.*, dominar, controlar.
MAS.TER BED.ROOM, *s.*, quarto principal.
MAS.TER.FUL, *adj.*, autoritário, dominador, magistral, destro.
MAS.TER.FUL.LY, *adv.*, autoritariamente, imperiosamente; habilmente.
MAS.TER-KEY, *s.*, chave-mestra.
MAS.TER.LESS, *adj.*, sem dono, sem mestre.
MAS.TER.LI.NESS, *s.*, mestria, habilidade.
MAS.TER.LY, *adj.*, magistral; *adv.*, magistralmente.
MAS.TER.MIND, *s.*, o cabeça de um grupo; *v.*, planejar.
MAS.TER OF CER.E.MO.NIES, *s.*, mestre de cerimônias.
MAS.TER.PIECE, *s.*, obra-prima.
MAS.TER PLAN, *s.*, plano-mestre.
MAS.TER'S DE.GREE, *s.*, mestrado.
MAS.TER.STROKE, *s.*, golpe de mestre.
MAS.TER.WORK, *s.*, obra-prima.
MAS.TER.Y, *s.*, domínio, autoridade, poder.
MAS.TI.CATE, *v.*, mastigar, morder.
MAS.TI.CA.TION, *s.*, mastigação.
MAS.TIFF, *s.*, mastim, cão.
MAS.TI.TIS, *s., Med.*, mastite (inflamação nas mamas).
MAS.TO.DON, *s., Arq.*, mastodonte.
MAS.TUR.BATE, *s.*, masturbar(-se).
MAS.TUR.BA.TION, *s.*, masturbação.
MAT, *s.*, esteira, capacho, tapete; *v.*, esteirar, entrançar.
MATCH, *s.*, fósforo, jogo, luta, partida; *v.*, emparelhar, casar, competir.
MATCH.A.BLE, *adj.*, comparável.
MATCH.BOX, *s.*, caixa de fósforos.
MATCH.ING, *adj.*, que combina (cores, vestuário, arranjo).
MATCH.LESS, *adj., Lit.*, incomparável, ímpar.
MATCH.MAK.ER, *s.*, casamenteiro; fabricante de fósforos.
MATCH POINT, *s., Esp.*, último ponto do *set* no tênis.
MATCH.STICK, *s.*, palito de fósforo.
MATE, *s.*, colega, camarada, cônjuge, macho/fêmea (animais); xeque-mate (xadrez); *v.*, casar, unir.
MA.TE.RI.AL, *s.*, material, matéria, ingrediente, tecido, anotações.
MA.TE.RI.AL.ISTIC, *s.*, materialista.
MA.TE.RI.AL.ISM, *s.*, materialismo.
MA.TE.RI.AL.IST, *s.*, materialista.
MA.TE.RI.AL.I.ZA.TION, *v.*, materialização.
MA.TE.RI.AL.IZE(-ISE), *v.*, materializar.
MA.TE.RI.AL.LY, *adv.*, materialmente, essencialmente.
MA.TE.RIAL.NESS, *s.*, materialidade.
MA.TER.NAL, *adj.*, maternal.
MA.TER.NAL.LY, *adv.*, maternalmente.
MA.TER.NI.TY, *s.*, maternidade (condição de mãe); *adj.*, de ou relativo à maternidade.
MA.TER.NI.TY DRESS, *s.*, vestido de gestante.
MA.TER.NI.TY HOS.PI.TAL, *s.*, maternidade.

MA.TER.NI.TY WARD, *s.*, sala de maternidade.
MATH, *s., col.*, matemática.
MATH.E.MAT.IC, *adj.*, matemático; exato.
MATH.E.MA.TI.CAL, *adj.*, matemático.
MATH.E.MA.TI.CIAN, *s.*, matemático.
MATH.E.MAT.ICS, *s.*, matemática (ciência).
MAT.I.NÉE, *s.*, matinê.
MAT.ING, *s.*, acasalamento, cruzamento.
MA.TRI.ARCH, *s.*, matriarca.
MA.TRI.ARCH.ATE, *s.*, matriarcado.
MA.TRI.CIDE, *s.*, matricídio; matricida.
MA.TRIC.U.LATE, *v.*, matricular, matricular-se.
MA.TRIC.U.LA.TION, *s.*, matrícula.
MAT.RI.MO.NIAL, *adj.*, matrimonial.
MAT.RI.MO.NY, *s.*, matrimônio, casamento.
MA.TRIX, *s.*, matriz, madre.
MA.TRON, *s.*, enfermeira-chefe; matrona.
MA.TRON.IZE(ISE), *v., fig.*, cuidar de, tutelar.
MA.TRON.LY, *adj.*, matronal; *adv.*, matronalmente.
MATT, *adj.*, fusco, opaco, sem brilho.
MATTE, *s.*, resíduo metálico; fosco (acabamento).
MAT.TED, *adj.*, embaraçado, emaranhado.
MAT.TER, *s.*, assunto, tema, questão, matéria, substância.
MAT.TER.Y, *adj.*, purulento.
MAT.TING, *s.*, esteira, capacho, tapete.
MAT.TOCK, *s.*, enxadão.
MAT.TRESS, *s.*, colchão.
MAT.U.RATE, *v.*, maturar, amadurecer, fazer amadurecer.
MAT.U.RA.TION, *s.*, maturação.
MA.TURE, *adj.*, maduro, amadurecido; *v.*, amadurecer.
MA.TURE.NESS, *s.*, maturidade; vencimentos de títulos.
MA.TU.RI.TY, *s.*, maturidade.
MA.TU.TI.NAL, *adj.*, matutinal, matutino.
MA.TU.TI.NE, *adj.*, matutino, matinal.
MAUD.LIN, *s.*, sentimentalismo; *adj.*, sentimental, embriagado.
MAUL, *s.*, marreta, malho; *v.*, malhar, espancar.
MAUL.ER, *s.*, boxeador, pugilista; malhador.
MAUN.DER, *v.*, murmurar, divagar, rosnar, dizer bobagens.
MAU.RI.TA.NI.AN, *s., adj.*, mauritano (também *Mauretanian*).
MAU.RI.TI.AN, *s., adj.*, mauriciano (pertencente ou relativo às Ilhas Maurício).
MAU.SO.LE.UM, *s.*, mausoléu.
MAUVE, *s.*, cor de malva; *adj.*, da cor de malva, lilás.
MAV.ER.ICK, *s., adj.*, inconformista.
MAWK.ISH, *adj.*, enjoativo, repugnante, lamuriento.
MAX.IL.LA, *s.*, osso maxilar.
MAX.IL.LARY, *adj.*, maxilar.
MAX.IM, *s.*, máxima.
MAX.I.MIZE(-ISE), *v.*, maximizar.
MAX.I.MUM, *s.*, máximo.
MAY, *s.*, maio.
MAY.DAY, *s.*, sinal de socorro: SOS.
MAY DAY, *s.*, 1º de Maio (Dia do Trabalho).
MAY.BE, *adv.*, talvez, quiçá.
MAY.FLY, *s., Zool.*, efemérida (inseto).
MAY.HEM, *s.*, caos.
MAYN'T, *contr.* de *may not*.
MAY.ON.NAISE, *s.*, maionese.
MAY.OR, *s.*, prefeito.
MAYOR.ESS, *s.*, prefeita; esposa de prefeito.
MAY.POLE, *s.*, mastro da festa do dia Primeiro de Maio.

MAY'VE · 530 · MELANOMA

MAY'VE, *contr. may have.*
MAZE, *s.*, labirinto, confusão; *v.*, confundir, embaraçar.
MA.ZI.LY, *adv.*, confusamente.
MBA, *s.*, MBA - *Master of Business Administration*: mestre em Administração de Empresas.
MC.CAR.THY.ISM, *s., Pol.*, macartismo.
ME, *pron.*, me, mim, eu.
MEAD.OW, *s.*, prado, campina.
MEAD.OW MOUSE, *s., Zool.*, rato silvestre.
MEA.GER, *adj.*, magro, escasso.
MEA.GRE, *adj.*, escasso, magro, estéril.
MEAL, *s.*, refeição, farinha; *v.*, comer, alimentar-se.
MEAL.TIME, *s.*, hora da refeição.
MEAL.Y, *adj.*, farináceo, farinhento; *fig.*, pálido.
MEAL.Y-MOUTHED, *adj., pej.*, hipócrita, fingido.
MEAN, *s.*, meio, meio-termo, média; *adj.*, sovina, mesquinho, médio.
MEAN-BORN, *adj.*, de origem humilde.
ME.AN.DER, *s.*, meandro, sinuosidade; *v.*, serpentear, vagar; divagar.
ME.AN.DER.INGS, *s. pl.*, zigue-zague.
MEAN.ING, *s.*, sentido, significado.
MEAN.ING.FUL, *adj.*, significativo; sério.
MEAN.ING.LESS, *adj.*, sem sentido, fútil.
MEAN.ING.LY, *adv.*, significativamente.
MEAN.LY, *adv.*, vilmente.
MEAN.NESS, *s.*, baixeza, vileza, pobreza, maldade.
MEANS, *s.*, meio; *v.*, querer dizer.
MEAN.TIME, *adv.*, entrementes; *conj.*, entretanto.
MEA.SLES, *s., Med.*, sarampo.
MEA.SLY, *adj.*, miserável.
MEAS.UR.A.BLE, *adj.*, mensurável.
MEAS.UR.A.BLY, *adv.*, mensuravelmente.
MEAS.URE, *s.*, medida, extensão, proporção, fita métrica. métrica.
MEAS.URED, *adj.*, medido, ponderado, uniforme.
MEAS.URED.LY, *adj.*, uniformemente, ritimadamente.
MEA.SURE.LESS, *adj.*, imenso, infinito.
MEA.SURE.MENT, *s.*, medida, medição.
MEA.SUR.ER, *s.*, medidor.
MEA.SUR.ING, *s.*, medição.
MEAT, *s.*, carne, alimento, comida, refeição.
MEAT PIE, *s., UK* torta de carne.
MEAT.BALL, *s.*, almôndega.
ME.A.TUS, *s.*, meato.
MEATY, *adj.*, carnudo.
ME.CHAN.IC, *s.*, mecânico.
ME.CHAN.I.CAL, *adj.*, mecânico.
ME.CHAN.ICS, *s.*, mecânica.
MECH.A.NISM, *s.*, mecanismo.
MECH.A.NI.ZA.TION, *s.*, mecanização.
MECH.A.NIZE, *v.*, mecanizar.
MED.AL, *s.*, medalha.
ME.DAL.LION, *s.*, medalhão.
MED.AL.LIST *UK*, **MED.AL.IST** *US*, *s.*, medalhista.
MED.DLE, *v.*, interferir, intrometer-se, meter-se.
MED.DLER, *s.*, intruso, intrometido.
MED.DLE.SOME, *adj.*, metido, intrometido.
MED.DLE.SOME.NESS, *s.*, intromissão.
MED.DLING, *s.*, intromissão, ingerência.
ME.DIA, *s.*, mídia, meio de comunicação; *news media, s.pl.*:

veículos de comunicação.
ME.DI.AE.VAL, *adj.*, o mesmo que *medieval*.
ME.DI.AN, *s., Mat.*, número que é a média de uma série; *adj.*, mediano, intermediário.
ME.DI.ATE, *v.*, mediar.
ME.DI.ATE.NESS, *s.*, mediação, intervenção.
ME.DI.A.TION, *s.*, mediação.
ME.DI.A.TOR, *s.*, mediador.
MED.IC, *s., col.*, estudante de medicina; médico.
MED.I.CA.BLE, *adj.*, medicável.
MED.I.CAL, *adj.*, médico; *s.*, exame médico; check-up.
MED.I.CAL CER.TIF.I.CATE, *s.*, atestado médico.
MED.I.CA.MENT, *s.*, medicamento, remédio.
ME.DI.CA.MEN.TOUS, *adj.*, medicamentoso.
MED.I.CATE, *v.*, medicar, tratar.
MED.I.CAT.ED, *adj.*, medicinal.
MED.I.CA.TION, *s.*, medicação.
ME.DIC.I.NAL, *adj.*, medicinal.
MED.I.CINE, *s.*, medicina, remédio.
MED.I.CO, *s.*, médico, acadêmico de medicina.
ME.DI.E.VAL, *adj.*, medieval.
ME.DI.O.CRE, *adj., s.*, medíocre.
ME.DI.OC.RI.TY, *s.*, mediocridade.
MED.I.TATE, *v.*, meditar, refletir, pensar.
MED.I.TA.TION, *s.*, meditação.
MED.I.TA.TIVE, *adj.*, meditativo, pensativo.
MED.I.TER.RA.NEAN, *s.*, Mediterrâneo.
ME.DI.UM, *s.*, médio, meio-termo, médium; *adj.*, médio, mediano.
ME.DI.UM-DRY, *adj.*, semisseco.
ME.DI.UM-SIZED, *adj.*, de tamanho médio.
ME.DI.UM WAV.ES, *s. pl.*, ondas médias (rádio).
MED.LEY, *s.*, mistura, coletânea; *adj.*, misturado, confuso.
ME.DUL.LA, *s.*, medula.
ME.DU.SA, *s., Zool.*, água-viva; medusa.
ME.DU.SA, *s., Mit.*, Medusa (górgona que tinha serpentes no lugar de cabelos).
MEED, *s.*, prêmio, presente.
MEEK, *adj.*, manso.
MEEK.LY, *adv.*, docilmente.
MEET, *s.*, reunião, encontro; *v.*, encontrar, reunir, conhecer, ajuntar-se.
MEET.ING, *s.*, reunião, encontro, assembleia.
MEET.ING PLACE, *s.*, ponto de encontro.
MEET.NESS, *s.*, propriedade, conveniência.
MEGA, *adj.*, mega (abrangente e muito grande).
MEG.A.BIT, *s., Comp.*, megabit (um milhão de *bits*).
MEG.A.HERTZ, *s.*, megahertz.
MEG.A.LO.MA.NIA, *s.*, megalomania.
MEG.A.LO.MA.NI.AC, *s.*, megalômano; *adj.*, megalomaníaco.
MEG.A.PHONE, *s.*, megafone.
MEG.A.TON, *s., Fís.*, megaton.
MEG.A.WATT, *s.*, megawatt.
MEL.A.MINE, *s., Quím.*, melanina.
MEL.AN.CHO.LIA, *s.*, melancolia, alienação, doença mental.
MEL.AN.CHOL.Y, *s.*, melancolia, depressão; *adj.*, melancólico, triste.
MEL.AN.CHOL.IC, *adj.*, melancólico.
MEL.A.NE.SI.AN, *s., adj.*, melanésio.
ME.LANGE, *s.*, mistura; miscelânea.
MEL.A.NO.MA, *s., Med.*, melanoma.

MELIORATE   •• 531 ••   MESSENGER

ME.LIO.RATE, *v.*, melhorar.
MEL.LOW, *adj.*, melodioso, suave.
ME.LOD.IC, *adj., Mús.*, melódico.
ME.LO.DI.OUS, *adj.*, melodioso, harmonioso, musical.
ME.LO.DI.OUS.NESS, *s.*, melodia.
MEL.O.DIST, *s.*, melodista.
MEL.O.DRA.MA, *s., Teat.*, melodrama.
MEL.O.DRA.MAT.IC, *adj.*, melodramático.
MEL.O.DY, *s.*, melodia.
ME.LON, *s.*, melão.
MELT, *s.*, fundição, metal fundido; *v.*, fundir, derreter, dissolver.
MELT.A.BLE, *adj.*, fundível.
MELT.DOWN, *s.*, fusão.
MELT.ER, *s.*, fundidor, cadinho.
MELT.ING POINT, *s.*, ponto de fusão.
MELT.ING-POT, *s.*, crisol; mistura racial e cultural.
MEM.BER, *s.*, membro; sócio, associado.
MEM.BER.SHIP, *s.*, qualidade de membro (de uma socie-dade); associação.
MEM.BER.SHIP CARD, *s.*, carteira de sócio.
MEM.BRANE, *s.*, membrana.
ME.MEN.TO, *s.*, memento, memorial.
MEMO, *s.*, memorando, nota, bilhete.
MEM.OIR, *s.*, memória, autobiografia.
MEM.O PAD, *s.*, rascunho de memorando.
MEM.O.RA.BIL.IA, *s. pl.*, memorabilia.
MEM.O.RA.BLE, *adj.*, memorável.
MEM.O.RA.BLY, *adv.*, memoravelmente.
MEM.O.RAN.DUM, *s.*, memorando.
ME.MO.RI.AL, *s.*, memorial, monumento de memórias.
ME.MO.RI.AL.IST, *s.*, memorialista; aquele que faz uma petição.
MEM.O.RI.ZA.TION, *s.*, memorização.
MEM.O.RIZE, *v.*, decorar, memorizar.
MEM.O.RY, *s.*, memória, recordação, lembrança.
MEM.O.RY CARD, *s., Comp.*, placa de memória.
MEN, *s. pl.*, homens.
MEN.ACE, *v.*, ameaçar; *s.*, ameaça.
MEN.A.CING, *adj.*, ameaçador.
MAN.A.CING.LY, *adv.*, ameaçadoramente.
ME.NAG.ER.IE, *s.*, reserva particular de animais.
MEND, *v.*, consertar, remendar.
MEN.DA.CIOUS, *adj.*, mentiroso, falso.
MEN.DAC.I.TY, *s.*, mentira, mendacidade, falsidade.
MEND.ER, *s.*, consertador, reparador.
MEN.DI.CAN.CY, *s.*, mendicância.
MEN.DI.CANT, *adj.*, mendicante, mendigo, pedinte.
MEN.DIC.I.TY, *s.*, mendicidade; mendicância.
MEND.ING, *s.*, remendo, roupas a concertar.
MEN.FOLK, *s. pl.*, homens (em geral).
ME.NI.AL, *s.*, lacaio, criado; *adj.*, servil, simplório.
MEN.IN.GI.TIS, *s., Med.*, meningite.
MEN.O.PAUSE, *s.*, menopausa.
MEN'S ROOM, *s.*, banheiro dos homens.
MEN.STRU.AL, *adj.*, menstrual.
MEN.STRU.ATE, *v.*, menstruar.
MEN.STRU.A.TION, *s.*, menstruação.
MEN.SU.RA.BIL.I.TY, *s.*, mensurabilidade.
MEN.SU.RA.BLE, *adj.*, mensurável.
MEN.SU.RA.TION, *s.*, medição, medida.
MENS.WEAR, *s.*, roupa masculina.

MEN.TAL, *adj.*, mental.
MEN.TAL HOS.PI.TAL, *s.*, hospital psiquiátrico.
MENT.AL.IST, *s.*, pessoa que lê mentes.
MEN.TAL.I.TY, *s.*, mentalidade.
MEN.TAL.LY, *adv.*, mentalmente.
MEN.THOL, *s.*, mentol.
MEN.THO.LAT.ED, *adj.*, mentolado.
MEN.TION, *s.*, menção, lembrança; *v.*, mencionar, referir.
MEN.TION.ABLE, *s.*, referível, citável.
MEN.TOR, *s.*, mentor.
MENU, *s.*, menu, cardápio.
MER.CAN.TILE, *adj.*, mercantil.
MER.CAN.TIL.ISM, *s., Econ.*, mercantilismo.
MER.CAN.TIL.IST, *s., adj., Com.*, mercantilista.
MER.CE.NARY, *adj., s.*, mercenário.
MER.CER.Y, *s.*, loja de tecidos.
MER.CHAN.DISE, *s.*, mercadoria; *v.*, negociar, mercantilizar.
MER.CHAN.DIS.ING, *s.*, propaganda.
MER.CHANT, *s.*, comerciante, negociante, mercador.
MER.CHANT SHIP, *s.*, navio mercante.
MER.CI.FUL, *adj.*, misericordioso, piedoso, bondoso.
MER.CI.FUL.LY, *adv.*, misericordiosamente.
MER.CI.FUL.NESS, *s.*, misericórdia, bondade.
MER.CI.LESS, *adj.*, desumano, cruel, perverso.
MER.CI.LESS.LY, *adv.*, impiedosamente.
MER.CU.RI.AL, *s.*, mercurial; *adj.*, mercurial (que contém mercúrio); *Lit.*, volúvel; ativo, vivo.
MER.CU.RY, *s.*, mercúrio; *v.*, limpar com solução de mercúrio.
MER.CU.RY, *s., Astron.*, Mercúrio (planeta); *Mit.*, Mercúrio (deus romano do comércio).
MER.CY, *s.*, piedade, compaixão, misericórdia.
MER.CY KILL.ING, *s.*, eutanásia.
ME.RE, *adj.*, mero, simples.
MERE.LY, *adv.*, meramente, simplesmente, apenas.
MER.E.TRI.CIOUS, *adj.*, falacioso.
MER.E.TRI.CIOUS.NESS, *s.*, vida ou conduta de meretriz.
MERGE, *v.*, fundir(-se); juntar.
MER.GER, *s.*, fusão (de companhias).
ME.RID.IAN, *adj., s.*, meridiano; *s.*, zênite.
ME.RID.I.O.NAL, *adj.*, meridional.
ME.RINGUE, *s., Cul.*, merengue, suspiro.
MER.IT, *s.*, mérito, merecimento, vantagem; *v.*, merecer.
MER.I.TOC.RA.CY, *s.*, meritocracia.
MER.I.TO.RI.OUS, *adj.*, meritório, merecedor.
MER.MAID, *s., Mit.*, sereia.
MER.MAN, *s., Mit.*, Tritão (deus do mar).
MER.RI.LY, *adv.*, divertidamente, alegremente.
MER.RI.MENT, *s.*, alegria, contentamento, felicidade.
MER.RI.NESS, *adj.*, alegre, jovial, feliz, satisfeito.
MER.RY, *adj.*, feliz; Merry Christmas!, Feliz Natal.
MAR.RY.MAK.ER, *s., Arc.*, folião.
MAR.RY-MAK.ING, *s., Lit.*, pândega, folia; festividade.
MER.RY-GO-ROUND, *s.*, carrossel.
MES.CA.LINE, *s., Farm.*, mescalina.
MESH, *s.*, malha; *v.*, prender com rede; enredar, enredar-se.
MES.MER.IZE, *s.*, hipnotizar, mesmerizar, magnetizar.
MES.ON, *s., Fís.*, méson (tipo de partícula subatômica).
MESS, *s.*, confusão, baderna; rancho.
MES.SAGE, *s.*, mensagem, recado; *v.*, passar uma mensagem.
MES.SEN.GER, *s.*, mensageiro.

M

MESSIAH · ·532· · MIFFED

MES.SI.AH, s., Rel., Messias, Cristo.
MES.SI.AN.IC, adj., messiânico.
MES.SI.NESS, s., desordem.
MES.SING, s., rancho, ato de arranchar, agrupamento.
MESS.MATE, s., comensal, conviva, companheiro de mesa.
MESSY, adj., desorganizado, confuso, sujo.
MET, v., ps, pp de *meet* (encontrar-se, conhecer).
ME.TAB.O.LISM, s., metabolismo.
ME.TAB.O.LIZE, v., metabolizar.
MET.AL, s., metal; v., cobrir com metal.
ME.TAL.LIC, adj., metálico.
MET.AL.LIZE(-ISE), v., metalizar.
MET.AL.LUR.GIC, adj., metalúrgico.
MET.AL.LUR.GIST, s., metalurgista, metalúrgico.
MET.AL.LUR.GY, s., metalurgia.
MET.AL.WORK, s., trabalho em metal.
MET.AL.WORK.ER, s., ferreiro.
MET.A.MOR.PHOSE, s., metamorfose; v., metamorfosear.
MET.A.MOR.PHO.SIS, s., metamorfose.
MET.A.PHOR, s., metáfora.
MET.A.PHYS.I.CAL, adj., metafísico.
MET.A.PHYS.ICS, s., metafísica.
ME.TAS.TA.SIS, s., Med., metástase.
METE, v., medir, repartir.
ME.TE.OR, s., meteoro.
ME.TE.OR.IC, adj., meteórico; atmosférico; efêmero, fugaz.
ME.TE.OR.ITE, s., meteorito.
ME.TE.O.RO.LOG.IC, adj., meteorológico.
ME.TE.O.RO.LOG.ICAL, adj., meteorológico.
ME.TE.O.ROL.O.GIST, s., meteorologista.
ME.TE.O.ROL.O.GY, s., meteorologia.
ME.TER, s., medidor, parquímetro.
METH.ANE, s., Quím., metano.
METH.A.NOL, s., Quím., metanol.
METH.OD, s., método.
ME.THOD.I.CAL, adj., metódico.
ME.THOD.I.CAL.LY, adv., metodicamente.
METH.OD.IST, s., Rel., metodista; adj., relativo a metodista.
METH.OD.IZE, v., metodizar, organizar.
METH.OD.OL.O.GY, s., metodologia.
ME.TIC.U.LOUS, adj., meticuloso.
ME.TIC.U.LOUS.LY, adv., meticulosamente.
ME.TON.Y.MY, s., metonímia.
METRE, s., metro.
MET.RIC, adj., métrico.
MET.RIC SYS.TEM, s., sistema métrico.
MET.RO, s., Fr., metrô.
ME.TROP.O.LIS, s., metrópole, cidade, capital.
MET.RO.POL.I.TAN, adj., metropolitano.
MET.TLE, s., brio, coragem, valor, denodo, ânimo.
MEW, s., miado; gaivota; v., miar;.
MEW.ING, s., miado.
MEWL, v., choramingar, chorar, lamentar.
MEX.I.CAN, adj., s., mexicano.
MEX.I.CO, s., México.
MEZ.ZA.NINE, s., mezanino, sobreloja.
MG, abrev. de *milligram*: miligrama.
MHZ, abrev. de *megahertz*: megahertz.
MI, s., mi.
MIAOW, s., miar.
MI.CA, s., mica.

MICE, s., pl. de *mouse*: camundongos.
MI.AS.MA, s., miasma.
MI.CRO, s., micro; pref., micro.
MI.CROBE, s., micróbio.
MI.CROB.IAL, adj., microbial, microbiano.
MI.CRO.BI.OL.O.GIST, s., microbiologista.
MI.CRO.BI.OL.O.GY, s., microbiologia.
MI.CRO.CIR.CUIT, s., microcircuito.
MI.CRO.CLI.MATE, s., microclima.
MI.CRO.CHIP, s., *microchip*, circuito gravado.
MI.CRO.COM.PUT.ER, s., microcomputador, computador.
MI.CRO.COSM, s., microcosmo.
MI.CRO.EC.O.NOM.ICS, s., microeconomia.
MI.CRO.FILM, s., microfilme.
MI.CROG.RA.PHY, s., micrografia.
MI.CRO.LIGHT, s., ultraleve.
MI.CROM.E.TER, s., micrômetro.
MI.CRON, s., mícron.
MI.CRO.OR.GAN.ISM, s., Biol., microorganismo.
MI.CRO.PHONE, s., microfone.
MI.CRO.PHYS.ICS, s., microfísica.
MI.CRO.PRO.CES.SOR, s., microprocessador.
MI.CRO SCOOT.ER, s., patinete.
MI.CRO.SCOPE, s., microscópio.
MI.CRO.SCOP.IC, adj., microscópico, minucioso.
MI.CROS.CO.PY, s., microscopia.
MI.CRO.SEC.OND, s., microssegundo.
MI.CRO.SUR.GE.RY, s., microcirurgia.
MI.CRO.WAVE, s., micro-ondas.
MIC.TU.RATE, v., mictar, urinar.
MID, adj., meio, médio, semi, hemi.
MID.AIR, s., adj., no ar, acima do solo.
MID.DAY, s., meio-dia.
MID.DLE, s., meio, cintura; adj., meio, médio.
MID.DLE AGED, s., meia-idade.
MID.DLE CLASS, s., classe média.
MID.DLE COURSE, s., meio-termo.
MID.DLE EAST, s., Oriente Médio.
MID.DLE FIN.GER, s., dedo médio.
MED.DLE.MAN, s., intermediário.
MID.DLE NAME, s., nome do meio.
MID.DLING, adj., médio, mediano.
MID.FIELD, s., Esp., meio-campo (futebol).
MIDGE, s., mosquito.
MIDG.ET, s., anão.
MID.LANG, s., parte central de um país, região interiorana.
MID.NIGHT, s., meia-noite.
MID.POINT, s., Geom., ponto central.
MID.RIFF, s., barriga; diafragma.
MIDST, s., meio, centro; adv., entre, no meio.
MID.STREAM, s., no meio da corrente (de um rio, de uma atividade).
MID.SUM.MER, s., pleno verão.
MID.WAY, adv., a meio caminho.
MID.WEEK, adv., no meio da semana.
MID.WINTER, adv., no meio do inverno, em pleno inverno.
MID.WIFE, s., parteira.
MID.WIFE.RY, s., trabalho de parteira.
MIEN, s., ar, aparência, semblante, feição.
MIFF, s., col., zanga; v., ofender.
MIFFED, adj., col., amuado.

MIGHT

MINISTRANT

MIGHT, *s.*, poder, força; *v., ps* de *may*: poder.
MIGHT.I.LY, *adv.*, poderosamente; imensamente.
MIGHT.N'T, *contr.* might not.
MIGHT'VE, *contr.* might have.
MIGHT.Y, *adj.*, poderoso, forte.
MI.GRAINE, *s.*, enxaqueca.
MI.GRANT, *adj.*, migrante.
MI.GRATE, *v.*, migrar.
MI.GRA.TION, *s.*, migração.
MI.GRA.TOR, *s.*, migrante.
MI.GRA.TO.RY, *adj.*, migratório.
MI.KA.DO, *s.*, micado (imperador do japão).
MILCH, *adj.*, lácteo, referente a leite.
MILD, *adj.*, suave, brando, afável, tenro, lenitivo, compassivo.
MILD.EN, *v.*, suavizar, abrandar.
MIL.DEW, *s., Bot.*, míldio (praga de videira); mofo.
MILD.LY, *adv.*, moderadamente.
MILD MAN.NERED, *adj.*, gentil, educado.
MILD.NESS, *s.*, suavidade, ternura, pena, compaixão.
MILE, *s.*, milha.
MILE.AGE, *s.*, milhagem.
MILE.OM.E.TER, *s.*, odômetro, marcador de milhagem.
MILE.STONE, *s.*, marco miliário; *fig.*, marco.
MI.LIEU, *s.*, meio, ambiente (social).
MIL.I.TAN.CY, *s.*, militância, luta, confiança.
MIL.I.TANT, *s.*, militante, adepto.
MIL.I.TA.RI.ZA.TION, *s.*, militarização.
MIL.I.TA.RISM, *s.*, militarismo.
MIL.I.TA.RIST, *s.*, militarista.
MIL.I.TA.RIZE(-ISE), *v.*, militarizar.
MIL.I.TA.RIZED ZONE, *s.*, zona militarizada.
MIL.I.TAR.Y, *s.*, exército; *adj.*, militar; bélico.
MIL.I.TAR.Y PO.LICE, *s.*, polícia militar.
MIL.I.TAR.Y SER.VICE, *s.*, serviço militar.
MIL.I.TATE, *v.*, influenciar; impedir.
MI.LI.TIA, *s.*, milícia.
MILK, *s.*, leite; *v.*, ordenhar, mungir, chupar.
MILK CHOCO.LATE, *s.*, chocolate ao leite.
MILK.ER, *s.*, ordenhador; quem tira leite.
MILK.ING, *s.*, ordenha.
MILK.MAID, *s.*, leiteira.
MILK.MAN, *s.*, leiteiro.
MILK-SHAKE, *s.*, milk-shake (leite batido com sorvete).
MILK.TOOTH, *s.*, dente de leite.
MILK.Y, *adj.*, leitoso.
MILK.Y WAY, *s., Astron.*, Via Látea.
MILL, *s.*, moinho, moedor de café, engenho; *v.*, redemoinhar.
MILLED, *adj.*, moído, triturado.
MIL.LE.NA.RY, *adj., s.*, milenário, milênio.
MIL.LEN.NI.UM *s.*, milênio, mil anos, milenário.
MIL.LE.PEDE, *s.*, centopeia.
MILL.ER, *v.*, moleiro.
MIL.LES.I.MAL, *s.*, milésima; *adj.*, milésimo.
MIL.LET, *s.*, painço (milho miúdo).
MIL.LI.BAR, *s.*, milibar (em meteorologia).
MIL.LI.GRAM, *s.*, miligrama.
MIL.LI.GRAM.ME, *s.*, miligrama.
MIL.LI.LI.TRE, *s.*, mililitro.
MIL.LI.ME.TRE(-TER), *s.*, milímetro.
MIL.LI.NER.Y, *s.*, chapelaria (para senhoras).
MIL.LION, *s.*, milhão.

MIL.LION.AIRE, *s.*, milionário.
MIL.LIONTH, *s., adj.*, milionésimo.
MIL.LI.SEC.OND, *s.*, milisegundo.
MILL.STONE, *s.*, pedra de moinho, mó.
MILL.WHEEL, *s.*, roda de azenha.
MI.LORD, *s.*, milorde.
MILT, *s.*, ova de peixes.
MIME, *s.*, mímica; *v.*, fazer mímica, imitar.
MIM.E.O.GRAPH, *s.*, mimeógrafo.
MI.ME.SIS, *s.*, mimetismo; imitação.
MI.ME.TIC, *adj.*, mimético.
MIM.IC, *adj.*, mímico; *v.*, imitar.
MIM.IC.RY, *s.*, mímica, imitação.
MI.MO.SA, *s., Bot.*, mimosa (tipo de planta leguminosa).
MIN.A.RET, *s.*, minarete.
MI.NA.TO.RY, *adj.*, ameaçador.
MINCE, *s.*, carne moída, recheio; *v.*, moer, triturar.
MINC.ER, *s.*, moedor de carne.
MINC.ING, *adj.*, afetado, efeminado.
MIND, *s.*, mente, intelecto; *v.*, cuidar, tomar conta de, preocupar-se.
MIND-BEND.ING, *adj., col.*, confuso.
MIND.ER, *s.*, quem cuida de crianças; guarda-costas.
MIND.FUL, *adj.*, atento; ciente (de algo).
MIND.FUL.NESS, *s.*, cuidado, atenção, preocupação.
MIND.LESS, *adj.*, sem sentido; tedioso.
MIND READ.ING, *s.*, ato de ler pensamentos.
MINE, *pron.*, meu, minha; *s.*, mina.
MINE DE.TEC.TOR, *s., Mil.*, detetor de minas.
MINE.FIELD, *s.*, campo minado.
MINE.LAY.ER, *s.*, navio lança-minas.
MIN.ER, *s.*, mineiro.
MIN.ER.AL, *v.*, mineralizar.
MIN.ER.AL.I.ZA.TION, *s.*, mineralização.
MIN.ER.AL.IZE(-ISE), *v.*, mineralizar.
MIN.ER.AL.O.GY, *s.*, mineralogia.
MIN.ER.AL OIL, *s.*, querosene.
MIN.ER.AL WA.TER, *s.*, água mineral.
MIN.E.STRO.NE, *s.*, sopa *minestrone*.
MINE.SWEEP.ER, *s.*, caça-minas (navio).
MIN.GLE, *v.*, misturar(-se); matizar; combinar(-se).
MIN.GLING, *s.*, mistura.
MIN.I, *s.*, minissaia.
MIN.IA.TURE, *s.*, miniatura; *adj.*, em miniatura.
MIN.I.BUS, *s.*, micro-ônibus.
MIN.I.CAB, *s., UK* mini-táxi.
MIN.I-COM.PUT.ER, *s.*, minicomputador.
MIN.I.KIN, *adj.*, pequeno, diminuto, reduzido, ínfimo.
MIN.IM, *s., Mús.*, mínima (nota musical).
MIN.I.MAL, *adj.*, mínimo.
MIN.I.MAL.IST, *s.*, minimalista (estilo artístico).
MIN.I.MIZE, *v.*, reduzir, minimizar.
MIN.I.MUM, *s.*, **MÍNIMO;** *adj.*, mínimo.
MIN.I.MUM WAGE, *s.*, salário mínimo.
MIN.ING, *s.*, mineração; *adj.*, mineiro.
MIN.ION, *s., pej.*, subordinado, lacaio.
MIN.ISH, *v.*, diminuir, reduzir, apequenar.
MIN.I-SKIRT, *s.*, minissaia.
MIN.IS.TER, *s.*, ministro, pastor.
MIN.IS.TE.RI.AL, *adj.*, ministerial.
MIN.IS.TRANT, *s., adj.*, ministrante.

MINISTRATION · · 534 · · MISREPRESENTATION

MIN.IS.TRA.TION, *s.*, administração, governo, agência, sacerdócio.
MIN.IS.TRY, *s.*, ministério.
MINK, *s.*, visom, pele de visom.
MINK COAT, *s.*, casaco de visom.
MIN.NOW, *s.*, peixinho (de água doce).
MI.NOR, *adj.*, menor, sem importância, menor de idade.
MI.NOR ROAD, *s.*, caminho secundário.
MI.NOR.I.TY, *s.*, minoria; menoridade.
MIN.STER, *s.*, mosteiro, catedral.
MIN.STER, *s.*, catedral.
MIN.STREL, *s.*, menestrel.
MINT, *s.*, hortelã; *v.*, cunhar moeda; *s.*, casa da moeda.
MINT.AGE, *s.*, moeda cunhada.
MINT.ER, *s.*, moedeiro.
MIN.U.ET, *s.*, minueto.
MI.NUS, *s.*, *Mat.*, sinal de menos; *adj.*, *Mat.*, negativo, desprovido de.
MI.NUS.CULE, *s.*, letra minúscula, *adj.*, minúsculo.
MI.NUS SIGN, *s.*, sinal de menos (-).
MI.NUTE, *s.*, minuto, instante, momento.
MIN.UTE, *adj.*, miúdo, minúsculo; exato, preciso.
MI.NUTE.NESS, *s.*, minuciosidade.
MI.NU.TI.AE, *s. pl.*, minúcias.
MIR.A.CLE, *s.*, milagre.
MI.RAC.U.LOUS, *adj.*, miraculoso, milagroso.
MI.RAC.U.LOUS.LY, *adv.*, milagrosamente.
MI.RAGE, *s.*, ilusão, miragem.
MIRE, *s.*, lodo, lama, lodaçal; *v.*, enlamear, atolar.
MIR.ROR, *s.*, espelho, retrovisor; modelo; *v.*, espelhar, refletir.
MIRTH, *s.*, risada, jovialidade, alegria.
MIRTH.FUL, *adj.*, alegre, jovial, satisfeito, risonho.
MIRTH.LESS, *adj.*, tristonho, triste.
MIRY, *adj.*, lamacento.
MIS.AD.VEN.TURE, *s.*, desgraça, infelicidade, infortúnio.
MIS.AD.VISE, *v.*, aconselhar mal.
MIS.AN.THROPE, *s.*, misantropo.
MIS.AN.THRO.PIST, *s.*, misantropo.
MIS.AN.THRO.PY, *s.*, misantropia.
MIS.AP.PLI.CA.TION, *s.*, má aplicação, abuso, sonegação.
MIS.AP.PLY, *v.*, dar má aplicação, fazer mau uso.
MIS.AP.PRE.HEND, *v.*, entender mal.
MIS.AP.PRE.HENSION, *s.*, mal-entendido.
MIS.AP.PRO.PRI.ATE, *v.*, desviar, sonegar; apropriar-se ilegalmente.
MIS.AP.PRO.PRI.A.TION, *s.*, desvio, apropriação indevida.
MIS.BE.HAVE, *v.*, comportar-se mal, agir de modo errado.
MIS.BE.HAVI.OUR, *s.*, mau comportamento; má conduta.
MIS.BE.LIEVE, *v.*, descrer, acreditar em algo errado, estar errado.
MIS.CAL.CU.LATE, *v.*, calcular mal, calcular errado.
MIS.CAL.CU.LA.TION, *s.*, erro de cálculo.
MIS.CALL, *v.*, dar nome errado.
MIS.CAR.RIAGE, *s.*, aborto natural; *fig.*, fracasso.
MIS.CAR.RY, *v.*, abortar; *fig.*, fracassar, malograr.
MIS.CEL.LA.NEOUS, *adj.*, diverso, vário, variado, misturado.
MIS.CEL.LA.NY, *s.*, miscelânea.
MIS.CHANCE, *s.*, infelicidade, desgraça.
MIS.CHIEF, *s.*, dano, prejuízo; travessura, diabrura.
MIS.CHIE.VOUS, *adj.*, travesso, brincalhão, peralta, moleque.
MIS.CON.CEIVE, *adj.*, com interpretação errônea; *v.*, entender mal.
MIS.CON.CEIVED, *adj.*, mal concebido.
MIS.CON.DUCT, *s.*, má conduta; má administração; *v.*, agir mal.
MIS.CON.STRUE, *v.*, interpretar erroneamente.
MIS.COUNT, *v.*, contar mal, errar a conta, enganar-se nas contas.
MIS.CRE.ANT, *adj.*, vil, desprezível, miserável.
MIS.DEED, *s.*, delito, crime, culpa.
MIS.DE.MEAN, *v.*, comportar-se mal.
MIS.DE.MEAN.OR, *s.*, *Jur.*, má conduta; contravenção.
MIS.DI.RECT, *v.*, dirigir mal, guiar mal, administrar mal.
MIS.DI.RECT.ED, *adj.*, mal dirigido, mal endereçado.
MIS.DOING, *s.*, delito, culpa, falta, erro.
MI.SER, *s.*, sovina, avarento, avaro, unha de fome.
MIS.ER.ABLE, *adj.*, miserável, triste, deprimido.
MIS.ER.A.BLY, *adv.*, miseravelmente, tristemente, de forma lamentável.
MI.SER.LY, *adj.*, mesquinho, miserável; avaro.
MIS.ERY, *s.*, tristeza, miséria, depressão.
MIS.FAITH, *s.*, descrença.
MIS.FIRE, *s.*, falha em detonação; falha na ignição; *v.*, não disparar, não dar partida; fracassar.
MIS.FIT, *s.*, desajuste; pessoa desajustada.
MIS.FOR.TUNE, *s.*, desgraça, infelicidade.
MIS.GIV.ING, *s.*, receio, desconfiança.
MIS.GOV.ERN, *v.*, governar mal, desgovernar.
MIS.GUIDE, *v.*, extraviar, perder o rumo, desviar, desencaminhar.
MIS.GUID.ED, *adj.*, mal orientado; desencaminhado, equivocado.
MIS.HAN.DLE, *v.*, lidar mal, administrar mal.
MIS.HAP, *s.*, infortúnio, desgraça, desastre.
MIS.HEAR, *v.*, ouvir mal.
MISH.MASH, *s.*, *col.*, mixórdia, confusão.
MIS.IN.FORM, *v.*, informar mal, dar informações erradas.
MIS.IN.FOR.MA.TION, *s.*, informação errada.
MIS.IN.TER.PRET, *v.*, interpretar mal, traduzir de modo errado.
MIS.JUDGE, *v.*, julgar mal, fazer juízo errado.
MIS.JUDGE.MENT, *s.*, julgamento errôneo.
MIS.LAY, *v.*, extraviar, perder, desviar.
MIS.LEAD, *v.*, enganar, corromper.
MIS.LEAD.ING, *adj.*, enganoso.
MIS.MAN.AGE, *v.*, administrar mal.
MIS.MAN.AGE.MENT, *s.*, má administração.
MIS.MATCH, *v.*, combinar mal.
MIS.NO.MER, *s.*, termo impróprio, designação incorreta.
MI.SOG.Y.NIST, *s.*, misógino.
MI.SOG.Y.NY, *s.*, misoginia.
MIS.PLACE, *v.*, deixar fora de lugar; extraviar, perder o rumo, desviar.
MIS.PLACED, *adj.*, inapropriado; deixado fora de lugar.
MIS.PRINT, *s.*, erro de impressão.
MIS.PRI.SION, *s.*, menosprezo, desprezo, relaxamento.
MIS.PRO.NOUNCE, *v.*, pronunciar mal.
MIS.QUOTE, *v.*, citar erradamente, dizer de modo errado.
MIS.READ, *v.*, ler ou interpretar erroneamente.
MIS.RE.PORT, *s.*, informação errônea, informe errado.
MIS.REP.RE.SENT, *v.*, deturpar; fazer falsa imagem de.
MIS.REP.RE.SEN.TA.TION, *s.*, deturpação, má interpretação;

MISRULE · 535 · MOISTURIZE(-ISE)

informação falsa.

MIS.RULE, *s.*, desgoverno, confusão.

MISS, *s.*, senhorita, jovem, moça.

MISS.HAP.EN, *adj.*, disforme, desengonçado.

MIS.SILE, *s.*, míssil, projétil, foguete, bomba.

MISS.ING, *adj.*, perdido, desaparecido; extraviado.

MISS.ING PER.SON, *s.*, pessoa desaparecida.

MIS.SION, *s.*, missão, expedição.

MIS.SION.ARY, *s.*, missionário.

MIS.SIVE, *s.*, missiva, carta.

MIS.SPELL, *v.*, soletrar ou escrever mal.

MIS.SPEL.LING, *s.*, erro de ortografia.

MIS.SPEND, *v.*, dissipar, desperdiçar, estragar.

MISSY, *s.*, senhorita, jovem.

MIST, *s.*, neblina, névoa, bruma, cerração; *v.*, enevoar, cobrir de bruma.

MIS.TAKE, *s.*, engano, erro, falha; *v.*, falhar, entender mal.

MIS.TAK.EN.LY, *adv.*, equivocadamente.

MIS.TER, *s.*, senhor; *abrev.:* Mr.

MIS.TIME, *v.*, calcular mal o tempo.

MIST.I.NESS, *s.*, tempo enevoado, tempo coberto de nuvens.

MIS.TRANS.LATE, *v.*, traduzir erradamente, verter de modo errado.

MIS.TRANS.LA.TION, *s.*, tradução incorreta.

MIS.TREAT, *v.*, maltratar.

MIS.TREAT.MENT, *s.*, mau trato.

MIS.TRESS, *s.*, professora, mestra; amante, amásia.

MIS.TRI.AL, *s.*, julgamento incorreto, processo nulo.

MIS.TRUST, *v.*, desconfiar de, desacreditar, temer.

MIS.TRUST.FUL, *adj.*, desconfiado.

MIST.Y, *adj.*, nebuloso, obscuro.

MIS.UN.DER.STAND, *v.*, entender mal, interpretar de modo errado.

MIS.UN.DER.STAND.ING, *s.*, equívoco, mal-entendido, desentendimento.

MIS.USE, *s.*, abuso, desvio, uso errado; *v.*, abusar, desviar.

MITE, *s.*, *Zool.*, tipo de acarino ou bicho do queijo.

MIT.I.GANT, *adj.*, mitigante, suavizante.

MIT.I.GATE, *v.*, mitigar, suavizar, atenuar, abrandar.

MIT.I.GAT.ING, *adj.*, atenuante.

MIT.I.GA.TION, *s.*, mitigação.

MI.TRE, *s.*, mitra (insígnia ou dignidade episcopal).

MITT, *s.*, luva.

MIT.TEN, *s.*, manguito; *Esp.*, luva do baseball.

MIT.TI.MUS, *s.*, mandado de prisão.

MIX, *v.*, misturar; *s.*, mistura, combinação.

MIXED, *adj.*, misto, misturado; confuso.

MIXED-A.BIL.I.TY, *adj.*, *UK* de vários níveis de habilidades (em sala de aula).

MIXED BLESS.ING, *s.*, lado bom e outro ruim.

MIXED E.CON.O.MY, *s.*, economia mista (empresas particulares e mistas).

MIXED UP, *adj.*, confuso; envolvido.

MIX.ER, *s.*, batedeira, misturador.

MIX.TURE, *s.*, mistura, mescla.

MIX-UP, *s.*, *col.*, engano, confusão.

MIZ.ZLE, *s.*, garoa, chuvinha, chuva miúda; *v.*, garoar, chuviscar.

MKT, *abrev.* de *market*: mercado.

ML, *abrev.* de *millilitre*: mililitro.

MM, *abrev.* de *millimeter(-tre)*: milímetro.

MNE.MON.IC, *adv.*, mnemônico.

MNE.MON.ICS, *s.*, mnemônica.

MOAN, *s.*, gemido, queixume; *v.*, lamentar-se, queixar-se, resmungar.

MOAN.FUL, *adj.*, queixoso, lastimoso.

MOAN.ING, *s.*, gemidos, reclamação, queichas.

MOAT, *s.*, fosso; *v.*, proteger ou circundar com fossos.

MOB, *s.*, plebe, ralé, raia miúda, gentalha; *v.*, tumultuar, badernar.

MO.BILE, *adj.*, móvel, inconstante, fútil, volátil, volúvel.

MO.BILE HOME, *s.*, trailer (casa sobre rodas).

MO.BILE LI.BRA.RY, *s.*, biblioteca ambulante (em ônibus).

MO.BILE PHONE, *s.*, telefone celular.

MO.BIL.I.TY, *s.*, mobilidade.

MO.BI.LI.ZA.TION, *s.*, mobilização.

MO.BI.LIZE, *v.*, mobilizar.

MOC.CA.SIN, *s.*, sapato mocassim.

MOCK, *s.*, zombaria, escárnio; *v.*, escarnecer, ridicularizar; *adj.*, falso.

MOCK.ERY, *s.*, escárnio, zombaria, ridicularização.

MOCK.ING, *adj.*, zombeteiro.

MOCK.ING.BIRD, *s.*, *Zool.*, tordo imitador (pássaro que imita outras aves).

MOCK-UP, *s.*, modelo em tamanho natural.

MODE, *s.*, modo, meio.

MOD.EL, *s.*, molde, modelo, maquete, exemplo; *v.*, modelar, moldar.

MO.DEM, *s.*, modem.

MOD.ER.ATE, *v.*, moderar, aquietar, restringir; *adj.*, moderado.

MOD.ER.ATE.LY, *adv.*, moderadamente.

MOD.ER.A.TION, *s.*, moderação.

MOD.ER.A.TOR, *s.*, moderador; *Rel.*, presidente de assembleia protestante; *Fís.*, material reator.

MOD.ERN, *adj.*, moderno.

MOD.ERN.ISM, *s.*, modernismo.

MOD.ERN.IST, *s.*, modernista.

MOD.ER.NI.TY, *s.*, modernidade.

MOD.ERN.I.ZA.TION, *s.*, modernização.

MOD.ERN.IZE, *v.*, modernizar.

MOD.EST, *adj.*, modesto.

MOD.EST.LY, *adv.*, modestamente, ligeiramente.

MOD.ES.TY, *s.*, modéstia.

MOD.I.FI.CA.TION, *s.*, modificação.

MOD.I.FY, *v.*, modificar.

MOD.ISH, *adj.*, da moda, que está na moda.

MOD.U.LAR, *v.*, modular o tom, modular um conjunto.

MOD.U.LATE, *v.*, modular; regular, ajustar.

MOD.U.LATED, *adj.*, modulado.

MOD.U.LA.TION, *s.*, modulação.

MOD.U.LA.TOR, *s.*, modulador.

MOD.ULE, *s.*, módulo.

MOG.GY, *s.*, *col.*, *UK* gato.

MO.GUL, *s.*, mogol, mongol; magnata.

MO.HAM.MED.AN, *adj.*, *s.*, maometano.

MO.HI.CAN, *s.*, *adj.*, moicano (também *Mohegan*).

MOI.E.TY, *s.*, metade, quinhão.

MOIL, *s.*, trabalho difícil, labuta; *v.*, cansar, estafar, labutar.

MOIST, *adj.*, úmido, molhado, chuvoso.

MOIST.EN, *v.*, umedecer, molhar.

MOIS.TURE, *s.*, umidade.

MOIS.TUR.IZE(-ISE), *v.*, umectar, hidratar.

MOISTURIZER · 536 · · MORALITY

MOIS.TUR.IZ.ER, *s.*, hidratante (creme para a pele).
MOKE, *s.*, jumento, burro, asno, jegue.
MO.LAR, *s.*, molar, dente molar; *adj.*, próprio para moer.
MO.LAS.SES, *s.*, melado.
MOLE, *s.*, toupeira; dique, cais, porto; *v.*, cavar, escavar.
MO.LEC.U.LAR, *adj.*, molecular.
MOL.E.CULE, *s.*, molécula.
MO.LEST, *v.*, molestar, perturbar, assediar.
MO.LES.TA.TION, *s.*, molestação.
MO.LEST.ER, *s.*, molestador.
MOL.LI.FY, *v.*, abrandar, suavizar, atenuar.
MOL.LUSC, *s.*, molusco.
MOL.LY, *s.*, indivíduo do sexo masculino, mas efeminado.
MOL.LY.COD.DLE, *v., col.*, mimar, estragar.
MOL.TEN, *adj.*, fundido, derretido, liquefeito.
MOM, *s., col., US* MÃE.
MO.MENT, *s.*, momento.
MO.MEN.TA.RI.LY, *adv.*, momentaneamente, *US* imediatamente.
MO.MEN.TARY, *adj.*, momentâneo, instantâneo.
MO.MEN.TOUS, *adj.*, momentoso, significativo.
MO.MEN.TUM, *s.*, momento.
MOM.MA, MOM.MY, *s., col., US* mamãe, mãezinha.
MON.A.CAL, *adj.*, o mesmo que *monastic*.
MON.ARCH, *s.*, monarca, soberano.
MO.NAR.CHIC, *adj.*, monárquico.
MON.AR.CHIST, *s.*, monarquista.
MON.AR.CHY, *s.*, monarquia.
MON.AS.TERY, *s.*, monastério, mosteiro.
MO.NAS.TIC, *adj.*, monástico.
MON.DAY, *s.*, segunda-feira.
MON.E.TAR.ISM, *s., Econ.*, monetarismo.
MON.E.TAR.IST, *s., adj., Econ.*, monetarista.
MON.E.TAR.Y, *adj.*, monetário.
MON.EY, *s.*, dinheiro, moeda.
MON.EY.BOX, *s.*, cofrinho.
MON.EYED, *adj.*, abastado, endinheirado.
MON.EY.LEND.ER, *s.*, agiota, prestamista.
MON.EY.LESS, *adj.*, sem dinheiro, pobre.
MON.EY.MAK.ER, *s.*, negócio rendoso, *fig.*, mina de ouro.
MON.EY.MAK.ING, *adj.*, rentável, lucrativo.
MON.EY.MAN, *s., Econ.*, finacista, finaciador.
MON.EY MAR.KET, *s.*, mercado monetário ou financeiro.
MON.GO.LIAN, *adj., s.*, mongol.
MON.GO.LISM, *s., Med.*, mongolismo, síndrome de Down.
MON.GREL, *s.*, cão, vira-lata.
MO.NI.TION, *s.*, advertência, admoestação, aviso.
MON.I.TOR, *s.*, monitor, instrutor, monitor de TV; *v.*, monitorar.
MON.I.TO.RY, *adj.*, admonitório.
MONK, *s.*, monge.
MON.KEY, *s., Zool.*, macaco.
MON.KEY-NUT, *s., col.*, amendoim (também *peanut*).
MON.KEY-WRENCH, *s.*, chave inglesa.
MONK.HOOD, *s.*, monaquismo.
MONK.ISH, *s.*, monacal, fradal.
MONO, *adj.*, mono.
MONO.CHROME, *adj.*, monocromo, de uma única cor.
MON.O.CLE, *s.*, monóculo.
MO.NOC.U.LAR, *adj.*, que tem um olho.
MON.O.CUL.TURE, *s., Agric.*, monocultura.
MO.NOG.A.MIST, *s.*, monógamo.

MO.NOG.A.MOUS, *adj.*, monógamo.
MO.NOG.A.MY, *s.*, monogamia.
MONO.GRAM, *s.*, monograma.
MON.O.LIN.GUAL, *adj.*, monolíngue.
MON.O.LITH, *adj.*, monólito.
MON.O.LITH.IC, *adj.*, monolítico.
MONO.LOGUE, *s.*, monólogo.
MON.O.PLANE, *s.*, monoplano.
MO.NOP.O.LIST, *s.*, monopolista.
MO.NOP.O.LIZE, *v.*, monopolizar.
MO.NOP.O.LY, *s.*, monopólio.
MON.O.RAIL, *s.*, monotrilho, monocarril (para trem).
MON.O.SYL.LAB.IC, *adj.*, monossilábico.
MON.O.SYL.LA.BLE, *s.*, monossílabo.
MON.O.THE.ISM, *s.*, monoteísmo.
MON.O.THE.IST, *s.*, monoteísta.
MON.O.TONE, *s.*, produção de sons em um só tom, mono-tonia; *adj.*, monótono, enfadonho.
MO.NOT.O.NOUS, *adj.*, monótono.
MO.NOT.O.NOUS.LY, *adv.*, monotonamente.
MO.NOT.O.NY, *s.*, monotonia.
MON.OX.IDE, *s.*, monóxido.
MON.SI.GNOR, *s.*, monsenhor.
MON.SOON, *s.*, monção (vento); estação chuvosa da Índia.
MON.STER, *s.*, monstro.
MON.STROS.I.TY, *s.*, monstruosidade.
MON.STROUS, *adj.*, monstruoso.
MON.TAGE, *s., Fr.*, montagem (cenário etc.).
MONTH, *s.*, mês.
MONTH.LY, *adj.*, mensal; *adv.*, mensalmente.
MON.U.MENT, *s.*, monumento.
MON.U.MEN.TAL, *adj.*, monumental, descomunal.
MOO, *v.*, mugir, berrar; *s.*, mugido.
MOOD, *s.*, humor, atmosfera.
MOOD.I.NESS, *s.*, capricho, rabugem, teimosia.
MOODY, *adj.*, caprichoso, teimoso, rabugento.
MOON, *s.*, lua; *v.*, andar à toa.
MOON.BEAN, *s., Lit.*, raio de luar.
MOON.LIGHT, *s.*, luar; *v.*, fazer um biscate.
MOON.LIGHT.ING, *s.*, trabalho extra, bico.
MOON.LIT, *adj.*, enluarado.
MOON.SCAPE, *s.*, paisagem lunar.
MOON.STRUCK, *adj.*, lunático, doido, desvairado.
MOONY, *adj.*, sonhador, sentimental, do mundo da lua.
MOOR, *s., UK* brejo; *v.*, atracar, ancorar.
MOOR, *s.*, mouro, sarraceno.
MOOR.ISH, *adj.*, pantanoso, lodoso.
MOOR.LAND, *s.*, terra pantanosa, banhado.
MOOSE, *s., Zool., US* alce.
MOOT, *v.*, debater, discutir; *s.*, discussão, debate.
MOP, *s.*, esfregão; *v.*, esfregar.
MOP-BOARD, *s.*, rodapé.
MOPE, *s.*, palerma; *v., pej.*, lastimar-se.
MOP.ED, *s., UK* bicicleta motorizada.
MOP.ISH, *adj.*, triste, aborrecido.
MOR.AL, *adj.*, moral; moralidade, costumes.
MO.RALE, *adj.*, moral, ânimo, disposição.
MOR.AL.ISM, *s.*, moralismo.
MOR.AL.IST, *s.*, moralista.
MOR.AL.IS.TIC, *adj., pej.*, moralista.
MOR.RAL.I.TY, *s.*, moralidade.

MORALIZATION ··537·· MOUSETRAP

MOR.AL.I.ZA.TION, *s.*, moralização.
MOR.AL.IZE, *v.*, moralizar.
MOR.AL.LY, *adv.*, moralmente.
MO.RASS, *s.*, brejo, pântano; emaranhado, confusão.
MOR.A.TO.RI.UM, *s.*, moratória.
MOR.BID, *adj.*, mórbido, doentio, doente.
MOR.BID.I.TY, *s.*, morbidez, doença.
MORE, *adv.*, mais.
MO.REL, *s.*, cogumelo.
MORE.OVER, *adv.*, além disso, além do mais.
MORGUE, *s.*, morgue, necrotério.
MOR.I.BUND, *adj.*, moribundo, agonizante, morrente.
MOR.MON, *s.*, mórmon.
MORN.ING, *s.*, manhã, madrugada.
MO.ROC.CAN, *adj.*, *s.*, marroquino.
MO.ROC.CO, *s.*, Marrocos.
MO.RON, *s.*, *col.*, idiota, imbecil.
MO.RON.IC, *adj.*, estúpido, imbecil.
MO.ROSE, *adj.*, melancólico, taciturno; rabugento.
MOR.PHIA, *s.*, o mesmo que *morfine*.
MOR.PHINE, *s.*, morfina.
MOR.PHO.LOG.IC, *adj.*, morfológico.
MOR.PHOL.O.GY, *s.*, morfologia.
MORSE CODE, *s.*, código morse.
MORSE, *s.*, morsa.
MOR.SEL, *s.*, pedacinho, bocado.
MOR.TAL, *adj.*, mortal.
MOR.TAL.I.TY, *s.*, mortalidade.
MOR.TAL.LY, *adv.*, mortalmente; fatalmente.
MOR.TAL.LY RATE, *s.*, taxa de mortalidade.
MOR.TAR, *s.*, argamassa; morteiro; almofariz.
MOR.TAR.BOARD, *s.*, desempenadeira de pedreiro; barrete de formatura.
MORT.GAGE, *s.*, hipoteca; *v.*, hipotecar.
MORT.GA.GEE, *s.*, credor hipotecário.
MORT.GAG.OR, *s.*, devedor hipotecário.
MOR.TI.CIAN, *s.*, *US* agente funerário.
MORT.I.FER.OUS, *adj.*, mortífero, mortal, letal.
MOR.TI.FI.CA.TION, *s.*, mortificação; tormento.
MOR.TI.FIED, *adj.*, mortificado.
MOR.TI.FY, *v.*, mortificar, sacrificar.
MOR.TISE, *s.*, malhete, entalhe; *v.*, malhetar, entalhar.
MOR.TU.ARY, *s.*, necrotério.
MO.SA.IC, *s.*, mosaico.
MOS.COW, *s.*, Moscou.
MOSQUE, *s.*, mesquita.
MOS.QUI.TO, *s.*, mosquito.
MOSS, *s.*, musgo; *v.*, cobrir com musgo.
MOSSY, *adj.*, musgoso, cheio de musgo.
MOST, *s.*, a maior parte, o maior número; *adj.*, o mais; *adv.*, o mais.
MOST.LY, *adv.*, principalmente; a maioria das vezes.
MOTE, *s.*, partícula.
MO.TEL, *s.*, motel.
MOTH, *s.*, mariposa, traça.
MOTH.BALL, *s.*, naftalina, bola de naftalina.
MOTH-EAT.EN, *adj.*, que está roído pelas traças.
MOTH.ER, *s.*, mãe; *v.*, cuidar de criança como mãe.
MOTH.ER.BOARD, *s.*, *Comp.*, placa-mãe.
MOTH.ER.HOOD, *s.*, maternidade.
MOTH.ER-IN-LAW, *s.*, sogra.

MOTH.ER.LAND, *s.*, pátria.
MOTH.ER LAN.GUAGE, *s.*, língua materna; idioma pátrio.
MOTH.ER.LESS, *s.* órfão de mãe.
MOTH.ER.LY, *adj.*, maternal.
MOTH.ER-OF-PEARL, *s.*, madrepérola.
MOTH.ER'S DAY, *s.*, Dia das Mães.
MOTH.ER SU.PE.RI.OR, *s.*, *Rel.*, madre superiora.
MOTH.ER-TO-BE, *s.*, futura mãe.
MOTH.ER TONGUE, *s.*, língua materna.
MO.TIF, *s.*, motivo, razão.
MO.TION, *s.*, movimento, gesto.
MO.TION.LESS, *adj.*, imóvel.
MO.TION PIC.TURE, *s.*, *US* filme (cinema).
MO.TI.VATE, *v.*, motivar, incentivar.
MO.TI.VAT.ED, *adj.*, motivado.
MO.TI.VA.TION, *s.*, motivação.
MO.TI.VA.TOR, *s.*, motivador.
MO.TIVE, *s.*, motivo.
MO.TIV.I.TY, *s.*, potência do motor.
MOT.LEY, *adj.*, heterogêneo, multicolor.
MO.TO.CROSS, *s.*, *Esp.*, *motocross* (corrida de motocicletas em pista de barro com obstáculos).
MO.TOR, *s.*, motor, carro.
MO.TOR.BIKE, *s.*, moto, motocicleta.
MO.TOR.BOAT, *s.*, barco a motor.
MO.TOR.BUS, *s.*, ônibus.
MO.TOR.CADE, *s.*, *Bras.*, carreata.
MO.TOR.CAR, *s.*, *UK* automóvel.
MO.TOR.CY.CLE, *s.*, motocicleta.
MO.TOR.CY.CLIST, *s.*, motociclista.
MO.TOR.ING, *adj.*, *UK* automobilístico.
MO.TOR.IST, *s.*, motorista.
MO.TOR.IZE(-ISE), *v.*, motorizar.
MO.TOR RAC.ING, *s.*, corrida automobilística.
MO.TOR SCOOT.ER, *s.*, lambreta.
MO.TOR VE.HI.CLE, *s.*, veículo motorizado.
MO.TOR.WAY, *s.*, rodovia, autoestrada.
MOT.TLE, *v.*, matizar, colorir com várias cores.
MOT.TLED, *adj.*, com manchas, sarapintado.
MOT.TO, *s.*, mote, lema; *Mús.*, motivo.
MOULD, *s.*, molde, mofo, bolor.
MOULD.ER, *s.*, moldador, carpinteiro; *v.*, pulverizar, reduzir a pó.
MOULD.I.NESS, *s.*, mofo, bolor.
MOULD.ING, *s.*, moldura, modelação.
MOULD.Y *UK*, **MOLDY** *US*, *adj.*, mofado.
MOUND, *s.*, pilha, monte; *v.*, amontoar.
MOUNT, *s.*, monte; *v.*, montar, trepar, subir, ascender.
MOUN.TAIN, *s.*, montanha.
MOUN.TAIN CHAIN, *s.*, cadeia de montanhas.
MOUN.TAIN.EER, *s.*, montanhista, alpinista.
MOUN.TAIN.EER.ING, *s.*, mantanhismo, alpinismo.
MOUN.TAIN.OUS, *adj.*, montanhoso.
MOUN.TAIN RANGE, *s.*, cadeia de montanhas, cordilheira.
MOUNT.ED, *adj.*, montado (em cavalo).
MOURN, *v.*, chorar, lamentar.
MOURN.ER, *s.*, enlutado.
MOURN.FUL, *adj.*, desolado, triste.
MOUSE, *s.*, camundongo, rato; *Comp.*, periférico que move o cursor na tela; *v.*, caçar ratos; espreitar.
MOUSE.TRAP, *s.*, ratoeira.

MOUSSE · 538 · MUSHROOM

MOUSSE, s., musse, doce, sobremesa.
MOUS.TACHE, s., bigode.
MOUTH, s., boca, entrada, foz; v., comer, mastigar, abocanhar, morder.
MOUTH.FUL, s., bocado.
MOUTH.LESS, adj., sem boca.
MOUTH.OR.GAN, s., Mús., harmônica, gaita de boca.
MOUTH.PIECE, s., bocal; fig., porta-voz.
MOUTH.WASH, s., antisséptico bucal.
MOUTH-WA.TER.ING, adj., de dar água na boca.
MOV.ABLE, adj., móvel.
MOV.ABLE.NESS, s., mobilidade.
MOVE, s., movimento, lance, jogada; mudança; v., mover-se, mexer-se.
MOVE BACK, v., voltar.
MOVE.MENT, s., movimento, gesto, mudança.
MOV.ER, s., motor.
MOV.IE, s., filme, cinema.
MOV.IE.GO.ER, s., US cinéfilo.
MOV.IE STAR, s., US estrela de cinema.
MOV.IE THEA.TER(TRE), s., cinema.
MOV.ING, adj., comovente.
MOV.ING STAIR.CASE, s., escada rolante.
MOW, v., colher, cortar.
MOW DOWN, v., chacinar, liquidar, matar.
MOW.ER, s., colhedor, cortador.
MO.ZAM.BI.CAN, s., adj., moçambicano.
MO.ZAM.BIQUE, s., Moçambique.
MR., abrev. de Mister: Sr., Senhor.
MRS., abrev. de Misstress: Sra., Senhora.
MUCH, pron., muito, adj., muito.
MUCH.NESS, s., quantidade, totalidade.
MUCK, s., sujeira, sujidade; v., sujar.
MUCK.I.NESS, s., imundície, sujeira.
MUCKY, adj., sujo, imundo, emporcalhado.
MU.CUS, s., muco.
MUD, s., lama, lodo; v., enlamear.
MUD.DLE, s., confusão, trapalhada; v., confundir, atrapalhar.
MUD.DLED, adj., confuso.
MUD.DY, adj., lamacento, lodoso; confuso; v., turvar, enlamear; confundir.
MUDG.ER, s., prevaricador
MUD.GUARD, s., para-lamas.
MUD.SLING.ING, s., Pol., difamação (em campanha eleitoral).
MUES.LI, s., granola, musli.
MUFF, s., regalo; protetor de orelhas ou mãos; v., col., inábil, errar, perder.
MUF.FIN, s., tipo de pão leve e doce.
MUF.FLE, v., abafar o som; agasalhar, abrigar.
MUF.FLED, adj., agasalhado.
MUG, s., caneca, caneco; v., assaltar.
MUG.GER, s., crocodilo.
MUG.GING, s., assalto.
MUG.GY, adj., úmido, molhado, abafado.
MUG SHOT, s., foto de identificação policial.
MU.LAT.TO, s., mulato.
MUL.BER.RY, s., amora.
MULCT, v., enganar, defraudar.
MULE, s., mula, burra.
MUL.ISH, adj., teimoso.
MUL.ISH.NESS, s., teimosia, obstinação.

MULL, v., refletir sobre.
MUL.LAH, s., Islam, mulá (professor ou erudito).
MULLED WINE, s., quentão.
MUL.LET, s., Zool., tainha, mugem.
MUL.LI.ON, s., caixilho.
MUL.TI.COL.ORED US, **MUL.TI.COL.OURED** UK, adj., multicolor.
MUL.TI-CUL.TU.RAL, adj., multicultural.
MUL.TI.FORM, adj., multiforme.
MUL.TI.LAT.ER.AL, adj., multilateral.
MUL.TI.ME.DI.A, adj., multimídia.
MUL.TI.MIL.LION.AIRE, s., multimilionário.
MUL.TI.NA.TION.AL, adj., multinacional.
MUL.TI.PLE, adj., s., múltiplo.
MUL.TI.PLE-CHOICE, adj., de múltipla escolha (em teste).
MUL.TI.PLE SCLE.RO.SIS, s., Med., esclerose múltipla.
MUL.TI.PLI.CA.TION, s., multiplicação.
MUL.TI.PLI.CA.TION SIGN, s., sinal de multiplicação.
MUL.TI.PLI.CA.TION TA.BLE, s., tabuada.
MUL.TI.PLIC.I.TY, s., multiplicidade.
MUL.TI.PLI.ER, s., multiplicador.
MUL.TI.PLY, v., multiplicar.
MUL.TI.PUR.POSE, adj., multiuso.
MUL.TI.STO.RY US, **MUL.TI.STO.REY** UK, s., edifício-garagem; adj., com muitos andares.
MUL.TI.TUDE, s., multidão.
MUL.TI.TU.DI.NOUS, adj., múltiplo, numeroso, diverso.
MUM, s., col., mãe, mamãe.
MUM.BLE, v., resmungar, murmurar, reclamar.
MUM.BLER, s., resmungão, murmurador.
MUM.BLING, s., murmuração.
MUM.MI.FI.CA.TION, s., mumificação.
MUM.MI.FY, v., mumificar.
MUM.MY, s., múmia; col., UK mamãe; v., mumificar.
MUMP.ER, s., mendigo.
MUMPS, s., papeira.
MUNCH, v., mascar, mastigar.
MUN.DANE, adj., mundano, trivial, profano.
MUNG, s., gír., coisa desagradável.
MU.NIC.I.PAL, adj., municipal.
MU.NIC.I.PAL.I.TY, s., municipalidade.
UM.NIF.I.CENT, adj., munificente, generoso.
MU.NI.TIONS, s., munições.
MU.RAL, s., mural, quadro pintado na parede.
MUR.DER, s., assassinato, homicídio; v., assassinar, matar.
MUR.DER.ER, s., assassino.
MUR.DER.ESS, s., assassina.
MUR.DER.ING, s., assassinato, homicídio.
MUR.DER.OUS, adj., assassino, homicida; aniquilador.
MURE, v., murar, emparedar, encarcerar.
MURK.I.NESS, s., escuridão, trevas, noite.
MURKY, adj., escuro, negro, turvo, enegrecido.
MUR.MUR, s., murmúrio, sussurro; v., murmurar.
MUR.PHY, s., batata.
MUS.CLE, s., músculo; força, energia.
MUS.CO.VITE, adj., s., moscovita.
MUS.CU.LAR, adj., muscular.
MUS.CU.LA.TURE, s., musculatura.
MUSE, s., musa; v., pensar, meditar.
MU.SE.UM, s., museu.
MUSH.ROOM, s., cogumelo, fungo.

MUSHY   ·· 539 ··   MYTHOLOGY

MUSH.Y, *adj.*, mole, piegas; sentimentaloide.
MU.SIC, *s.*, música.
MU.SI.CAL, *adj.*, musical, melodioso, harmonioso.
MU.SI.CAL IN.STRU.MENT, *s.*, instrumento musical.
MU.SI.CAL.LY, *adv.*, musicalmente, harmoniosamente.
MU.SI.CAL.NESS, *s.*, musicalidade, harmonia, melodia.
MU.SIC-HALL, *s.*, sala de espetáculo; teatro de variedades.
MU.SI.CIAN, *s.*, músico.
MU.SIC STAND, *s.*, atril para partituras.
MUSK, *s.*, almíscar; perfume de almíscar.
MUSK.ET, *s.*, mosquete, arma de fogo antiga.
MUSK.ET.EER, *s.*, mosqueteiro.
MUSK.RAT, *s.*, *Zool.*, rato-almiscarado.
MUSKY, *adj.*, almiscarado.
MUS.LEM, *s.*, *adj.*, muçulmano.
MUS.LIN, *s.*, musselina.
MUSS, *s.*, desordem, balbúrdia, confusão; *v.*, desordenar, badernar.
MUS.SEL, *s.*, mexilhão.
MUS.SUL.MAN, *s.*, muçulmano, maometano.
MUST, *v.*, ter de, dever, ser forçado a.
MUS.TACHE, *s.*, o mesmo que *moustache*: bigode.
MUS.TARD, *s.*, mostarda.
MUS.TER, *s.*, revista de tropas; *v.*, passar tropas em revista; reunir, juntar.
MUST.N'T, *contr.* de *must not*: não dever.
MUST'VE, *contr.* de *must have*: deve ter.
MUS.TY, *adj.*, mofado, com cheiro de mofo.
MU.TA.BIL.I.TY, *s.*, mutabilidade.
MU.TA.BLE, *adj.*, mutável, volúvel, transitório, efêmero.
MU.TANT, *s.*, *adj.*, mutante.
MU.TATE, *v.*, mudar, alterar, transformar.
MU.TA.TION, *s.*, mutação, transformação.
MUTE, *adj.*, mudo.
MUT.ED, *adj.*, suave, discreto, contido; mudo, silencioso.
MUTE.LY, *adv.*, silenciosamente.
MUTE.NESS, *s.*, mudez; silêncio.
MU.TI.LATE, *v.*, mutilar, deformar.
MU.TI.LA.TION, *s.*, mutilação.
MU.TI.NEER, *s.*, amotinado, rebelde.
MU.TI.NOUS, *adj.*, amotinado, revoltado, rebelde.
MU.TI.NOUS.NESS, *s.*, revolta, rebeldia, tumulto, revolução.
MU.TI.NY, *s.*, motim; *v.*, amotinar-se.

MUT.ISM, *s.*, mutismo, silêncio, mudez.
MUTT, *s.*, *col.*, tolo, bobo; *UK* vira-lata.
MUT.TER, *s.*, murmúrio, resmungo; *v.*, murmurar, resmungar.
MUT.TER.ER, *s.*, resmungão.
MUT.TER.ING, *s.*, resmungo, murmúrio.
MUT.TON, *s.*, carne de carneiro.
MU.TU.AL, *adj.*, mútuo, recíproco.
MU.TU.AL.ISM, *s.*, *Biol.*, mutualismo, simbiose.
MU.TU.AL.I.TY, *s.*, mutualidade, reciprocidade.
UM.TU.AL.LY, *adv.*, mutuamente.
MUZ.ZLE, *s.*, focinho, mordaça, boca de arma de fogo; *v.*, amordaçar.
MUZ.ZY, *adj.*, absorto, distraído.
MY, *pron.*, meu, minha, meus, minhas.
MY.CO.SIS, *s.*, *Med.*, micose.
MY.O.CAR.DI.UM, *s.*, *Anat.*, miocárdio.
MY.OPE, *s.*, míope.
MY.O.PIA, *s.*, miopia.
MY.O.PIC, *adj.*, míope.
MYO.SO.TIS, *s.*, miosótis.
MYR.I.AD, *s.*, miríade.
MYRRH, *s.*, mirra.
MYR.TLE, *s.*, *Bot.*, murta, mirto.
MY.SELF, *pron.*, eu mesmo, a mim mesmo.
MYS.TE.RI.OUS, *adj.*, misterioso.
MYS.TE.RI.OUS.LY, *adv.*, misteriosamente.
MYS.TERY, *s.*, mistério.
MYS.TER.Y TOUR, *s.*, passeio-surpresa de ônibus em locais turísticos.
MYS.TIC, *adj.*, *s.*, místico.
MYS.TI.CAL, *adj.*, místico, misterioso.
MYS.TI.CISM, *s.*, misticismo.
MYS.TI.FI.CA.TION, *s.*, mistificação.
MYS.TI.FIED, *adj.*, perplexo, desconcertado.
MYS.TI.FY, *v.*, mistificar.
MYS.TI.FY.ING, *adj.*, desconcertante.
MYS.TIQUE, *s.*, mística.
MYTH, *s.*, mito.
MYTH.IC, *adj.*, mítico, fabuloso.
MYTH.I.CAL, *adj.*, mítico; falso.
MYTH.O.LOG.IC, *adj.*, mitológico.
MYTH.O.LOG.I.CAL, *adj.*, mitológico.
MY.THOL.O.GY, *s.*, mitologia.

N, s., décima quarta letra do alfabeto inglês.
NAB, v., arrebatar subitamente, pegar, pegar em flagrante.
NA.BOB, s., nababo, ricaço, milionário.
NA.CELLE, s., Aeron., nacele, nacela.
NA.CRE, s., madrepérola; nácar.
NA.CRE.OUS, adj., nacarado.
NA.DIR, s., nadir; Astron., ponto oposto ao zênite; fig., ponto mais baixo.
NAFF, adj., gír., brega, vulgar, sem valor.
NAG, s., cavalo ruim, pangaré, matungo; v., resmungar, incomodar.
NAG.GER, s., resmungão.
NAG.GING, adj., agitado, briguento, implicante.
NA.ÏF, adj., Fr., o mesmo que naïve.
NAIL, s., neil, s., prego, unha, garra; v., pregar, fixar, agarrar.
NAIL-BRUSH, s., escova para unhas.
NAIL-CLIP.PERS, s. pl., cortador de unhas.
NAIL FILE, s., lixa de unha.
NAIL POL.ISH, s., o mesmo que nail varnish.
NAIL SCIS.SORS, s. pl., tesoura para unhas.
NAIL VAR.NISH, s., esmalte para unhas.
NA.ÏVE, NA.ÏF, adj., Fr., ingênuo, tolo, inocente, simplório.
NA.IVE.LY, adv., ingenuamente.
NA.KED, adj., despido, nu, exposto, desprotegido.
NA.KED.LY, adv., de forma nua.
NA.KED.NESS, s., nudez, exposição, falta de proteção.
NA.KED EYE, s., olho nu, olho desarmado.
NAME, s., nome, sobrenome, título, autoridade, renome; v., nomear, chamar, citar, dar nome.
NAME-DROP.PER, s., blasonador.
NAME.LESS, adj., sem nome, anônimo, inominado.
NAME.LY, adv., isto é, a saber.
NAME.SAKE, s., homônimo, xará, quem tem o mesmo nome.
NA.MIB.IAN, s., adj., namibiano.
NAN, s., col., UK vó.
NA.NISM, s., Med., nanismo.
NAN.NY, s., ama, aia.
NAN.NY-GOAT, s., cabra.
NA.NO.SE.COND, s., Fís., nanossegundo.
NA.NO.TECH.NOL.O.GY, s., nanotecnologia.
NAP, s., soneca, sesta, cochilo; s., cochilar, dormitar, ficar desprevenido.
NAPE, s., nuca.
NAPH.THA, s., nafta.
NAPH.THA.LENE, s., Quím., naftalina.
NAP.KIN, s., guardanapo.
NAP.PER, adj., dorminhoco.
NAP.PING, s., sesta, dormida, dormidela.
NAP.PY, s., UK fralda.
NAR.CIS.SISM, s., narcisismo.
NAR.CIS.SIS.TIC, adj., narcisista.
NAR.CIS.SUS, s., Bot., narciso.

NAR.CO.SIS, s., narcose.
NAR.COT.IC, adj., s., narcótico.
NAR.CO.TIZE, v., narcotizar.
NARK, s., col., dedo-duro, informante; v., irritar.
NAR.RATE, v., narrar, contar, referir, relatar.
NAR.RA.TION, s., narração, conto, narrativa, história.
NAR.RA.TIVE, s., narrativa.
NAR.RA.TOR, s., narrador, cronista, historiador.
NAR.ROW, s., desfiladeiro, estreito, braço de mar; v., estreitar, apertar; adj., estreito, apertado, restrito.
NAR.ROW.ING, s., aperto, restrição.
NAR.ROW.LY, adv., estreitamente; minuciosamente; por pouco, por um triz.
NAR.ROW-MIND.ED, adj., tacanho.
NAR.ROW.NESS, s., estreiteza, pequenez, restrição.
NASA, abrev. de National Aeronautics and Space Administration: Administração Nacional da Aeronáutica e Espaço.
NA.SAL, adj., nasal.
NA.SAL.A.TION, s., nasalização.
NA.SAL.I.ZA.TION, v., nasalização.
NA.SAL.IZE, v., nasalar, nasalizar.
NAS.CENT, adj., nascente.
NAS.TI.LY, adv., sordidamente, vilmente.
NAS.TI.NESS, s., torpeza, maldade.
NA.STUR.TIUM, s., Bot., nastúrcio, capuchinha.
NAS.TY, adj., sórdido, mau, maldoso, repugnante, vexatório.
NA.TAL, adj., natal.
NA.TAL.I.TY, s., natalidade.
NA.TA.TION, s., natação.
NA.TA.TO.RI.AL, adj., natatório.
NA.TION, s., nação, país, povo.
NA.TION.AL, adj., nacional.
NA.TION.AL AN.THEM, s., hino nacional.
NA.TION.AL FLAG, s., bandeira nacional.
NA.TION.AL DRESS, s., roupas típicas.
NA.TION.AL.ISM, s., nacionalismo.
NA.TION.AL.IST, s., nacionalista.
NA.TION.AL.IS.TIC, adj., nacionalista.
NA.TION.AL.I.TY, s., nacionalidade.
NA.TION.AL.I.ZA.TION, s., nacionalização.
NA.TION.AL.IZE, v., nacionalizar.
NA.TION.AL.IZED, adj., nacionalizado.
NA.TION.AL.LY, adv., nacionalmente.
NA.TION.AL PARK, s., parque nacional.
NA.TION.AL SERV.ICE, s., Mil., serviço militar.
NA.TION STATE, s., estado-nação.
NA.TION.WIDE, s., âmbito nacional, contexto nacional.
NA.TIVE, adj., nativo, natural, genuíno, inato, puro.
NA.TIV.I.TY, s., natividade; Natividade de Jesus Cristo.
NA.TRON, s., sódio.
NAT.TER, s., bate-papo; v., bater um papo, papear.
NAT.TY, adj., elegante, boa pinta.

NATURAL ··541·· NEGLIGENT

NAT.U.RAL, *adj.*, natural, ingênuo, oriundo, nativo, inato.
NAT.U.RAL CHILD.BIRTH, *s.*, *Med.*, parto natural.
NAT.U.RAL GAS, *s.*, gás natural.
NAT.U.RAL HIS.TO.RY, *s.*, ciências naturais, história natural.
NAT.U.RAL.ISM, *s.*, naturalismo.
NAT.U.RAL.IST, *s.*, naturalista.
NAT.U.RAL.I.ZA.TION, *s.*, naturalização.
NAT.U.RAL.IZE, *v.*, naturalizar.
NAT.U.RAL.IZE(-ISE), *v.*, naturalizar(-se).
NAT.U.RAL.LY, *adv.*, naturalmente; pór natureza; logicamente.
NAT.U.RAL.NESS, *s.*, naturalidade.
NAT.U.RAL PAR.ENT, *s.*, pai biológico.
NAT.U.RAL PER.SON, *s.*, *Econ.*, pessoa física.
NAT.U.RAL RE.SOURC.ES, *s. pl.*, recursos naturais.
NAT.U.RAL SCI.ENCE, *s.*, ciências natuais.
NAT.U.RAL SE.LEC.TION, *s.*, seleção natural.
NA.TURE, *s.*, natureza, índole.
NA.TURE RE.SERVE, *s.*, reserva natural.
NA.TUR.ISM, *s.*, naturismo, nudismo.
NA.TUR.IST, *s.*, naturista, nudista.
NAUGHT, *s.*, nada; zero (0); *adj.*, sem valor.
NAUGH.TY, *adj.*, desobediente, travesso, malcriado, mau.
NAU.SEA, *s.*, náusea, repugnância, enjoo.
NAU.SE.ANT, *adj.*, nauseante, enjoativo, repugnante.
NAU.SE.ATE, *v.*, nausear, enjoar, provocar nojo.
NAU.SE.A.TING, *s.*, nauseante, enjoativo, repugnante.
NAU.SEOUS, *adj.*, nauseabundo, repugnante, enjoativo, nojento.
NAU.TI.CAL, *adj.*, náutico.
NAU.TI.CAL MILE, *s.*, *Náut.*, milha náutica.
NAU.TI.LUS, *s.*, náutilo, argonauta.
NA.VAL, *adj.*, naval, marítimo, próprio do mar.
NA.VAL OF.FICE, *s.*, oficial da marinha.
NAVE, *s.*, nave (igreja).
NA.VEL, *s.*, umbigo, centro, meio.
NA.VEL-STRING, *s.*, *Anat.*, cordão umbilical.
NAV.I.GA.BIL.I.TY, *s.*, navegabilidade.
NAV.I.GA.BLE, *adj.*, navegável.
NAV.I.GATE, *v.*, navegar, pilotar uma nave.
NAV.I.GA.TION, *s.*, navegação.
NAV.I.GA.TION.AL, *adj.*, navegacional; marítimo, náutico.
NAV.I.GA.TOR, *s.*, navegador.
NA.VY, *s.*, esquadra, conjunto das forças marítimas, armada.
NA.VY BLUE, *s.*, a cor azul-marinho; *adj.*, azul-marinho.
NAZ.A.RENE, *adj.*, *s.*, nazareno.
NAZE, *s.*, cabo, promontório.
NA.ZI, *adj.*, *s.*, nazista, nazi.
NA.ZISM, *s.*, nazismo.
NE.AN.DER.THAL, *s.*, *Antr.*, homem de neandertal; *adj.*, neandertal.
NEAR, *adj.*, vizinho, próximo; *adv.*, perto; *prep.*, perto de; *v.*, aproximar.
NEAR.BY, *adj.*, próximo; *adv.*, perto, nas vizinhanças; à mão.
NEAR EAST, *s.*, Oriente Próximo.
NEAR.LY, *adv.*, quase.
NEAR MISS, *s.*, quase colisão; acidente evitado por um triz.
NEAR.NESS, *s.*, proximidade, cercanias, vizinhança; intimidade.
NEARSIDE, *s.*, lado oposto ao do condutor (do veículo).
NEAR.SIGHT.ED, *s.*, míope.
NEAT, *adj.*, ajeitado, arrumado, organizado, limpo, asseado.

NEAT.LY, *adv.*, habilmente, organizadamente, com capricho.
NEAT.NESS, *s.*, capricho, asseio, ordem.
NEB, *s.*, bico, ponta, pena de escrever.
NEB.U.LA, *s.*, nebulosa, galáxia.
NEB.U.LOS.I.TY, *s.*, nebulosidade, cerração, enevoamento.
NEB.U.LOUS, *adj.*, nebuloso, enevoado.
NEC.ES.SAR.I.LY, *adv.*, necessariamente, obrigatoriamente.
NEC.ES.SARY, *adj.*, necessário, preciso, obrigatório.
NE.CES.SI.TATE, *v.*, necessitar, obrigar, exigir, tornar necessário.
NE.CES.SI.TY, *s.*, necessidade, exigência, requisito; carência, pobreza.
NECK, *s.*, pescoço, gola, gargalo, estreito, istmo.
NECK-BAND, *s.*, colarinho, gola de camisa.
NECK.ER.CHIEF, *s.*, lenço para pescoço.
NECK.LACE, *s.*, colar.
NECK.LINE, *s.*, decote.
NECK.TIE, *s.*, gravata.
NE.CROL.O.GIC, *adj.*, necrológico.
NE.CROL.O.GY, *s.*, necrologia.
NEC.RO.MAN.CY, *s.*, necromancia.
NEC.RO.PHO.BI.A, *s.*, *Psic.*, necrofobia.
NE.CROP.O.LIS, *s.*, necrópole, cemitério.
NEC.ROP.SY, *s.*, necropsia, autópsia.
NE.CRO.SIS, *s.*, necrose.
NEC.TAR, *s.*, néctar.
NEC.TAR.INE, *s.*, nectarina.
NÉE, **NEE**, *adj.*, *Fr.*, em solteira, nascida (relativo ao nome).
NEED, *s.*, necessidade, carência, falta, dificuldade; *v.*, necessitar, precisar.
NEED.FUL, *adj.*, necessário, preciso, indispensável.
NEED.NESS, *s.*, pobreza, indigência, carência.
NEE.DLE, *s.*, agulha, bússola; *v.*, alfinetar, costurar, usar a agulha.
NEE.DLE.POINT, *s.*, bordado; qualquer ponto fino.
NEE.DLER, *s.*, fabricante de agulhas.
NEED.LESS, *adj.*, inútil, desnecessário.
NEED.LESS.LY, *adv.*, desnecessariamente.
NEED.LESS.NESS, *s.*, inutilidade.
NEE.DLE-WOM.AN, *s.*, costureira, costureira.
NEE.DLE.WORK, *s.*, bordado, costura.
NEEDN'T, *contr.* de *need not*.
NEED.Y, *adj.*, necessitado, carente.
NE.FAR.I.OUS, *adj.*, nefando, abominável, nojento.
NE.GATE, *v.*, negar, desmentir.
NE.GA.TION, *s.*, negação, negativa.
NEG.A.TIVE, *s.*, negativo, negativo de foto, negação, veto; *v.*, negar.
NEG.A.TIVE.NESS, *s.*, o mesmo que *negativity*.
NEG.A.TIV.ISM, *s.*, negativismo, pessimismo, nulidade.
NEG.A.TIV.I.TY, *s.*, negatividade.
NE.GLECT, *s.*, negligência, relaxamento; *v.*, negligenciar, descuidar.
NE.GLECT.ED, *adj.*, abandonado (criança); negligenciado (jardim).
NE.GLECT.ER, *s.*, negligente, descuidado.
NE.GLECT.FUL, *adj.*, negligente, desleixado, descuidado.
NE.GLECT.FUL.NESS, *s.*, negligência, relaxamento.
NEG.LI.GEE, *s.*, roupão, chambre (de mulher).
NEG.LI.GENCE, *s.*, negligência, relaxamento, descuido.
NEG.LI.GENT, *adj.*, *s.*, negligente.

NEGLIGENTLY · 542 · NEW ZEALANDER

NEG.LI.GENT.LY, *adv.*, negligentemente.
NEG.LI.GI.BLE, *adj.*, desprezível, insignificante.
NE.GO.TIA.BIL.I.TY, *s.*, negociabilidade, a arte de negociar.
NE.GO.TIA.BLE, *adj.*, negociável.
NE.GO.TI.ATE, *v.*, negociar, intermediar, resolver conflitos.
NE.GO.TI.A.TION, *s.*, negociação, negócio.
NE.GO.TI.A.TOR, *s.*, negociador.
NE.GRO, *adj.*, *s.*, negro, preto.
NEIGH, *s.*, relincho; *v.*, relinchar, rinchar.
NEIGH.BOUR *UK*, **NEIGH.BOR** *US*, *s.*, vizinho.
NEIGH.BOUR.HOOD *UK*, **NEIGH.BOR.HOOD** *US*, *s.*, vizinhança, cercanias.
NEIGH.BOUR.ING *UK*, **NEIGH.BOR.ING** *US*, *adj.*, vizinho, próximo, contíguo, perto.
NEI.THER, *pron.*, nenhum, nem um nem outro.
NEM.E.SIS, *s.*, nêmesis; castigo (merecido); ruína; oponente.
NE.O.CLAS.SI.CAL, *adj.*, neoclássico.
NE.O.CLAS.SI.CISM, *s.*, *Arq.*, neoclassicismo.
NE.O.CO.LO.NI.AL.ISM, *s.*, *Pol.*, *Econ.*, neocolonialismo.
NEO.LITH.IC, *adj.*, *Antr.*, neolítico.
NE.OL.O.GISM, *s.*, neologismo.
NE.OL.O.GY, *s.*, neologia.
NEON, *s.*, *Quím.*, néon; neônio (elem. químico de nº 10).
NE.ON LIGHT, *s.*, luz de néon.
NE.ON SIGN, *s.*, letreiro de néon.
NEO.PHYTE, *s.*, neófito, principiante, noviço.
NEP.A.LESE, *s.*, *adj.*, nepalês (habitante do ou relativo ao Nepal).
NE.PALI, *s.*, nepali, nepalês (nativo do ou a língua do Nepal).
NEPH.EW, *s.*, sobrinho.
NE.PHRI.TIS *s.*, nefrite.
NEP.O.TISM, *s.*, nepotismo.
NEP.TUNE, *s.*, *Astron.*, Netuno; *Mit.*, Netuno (deus do mar).
NERD, *s.*, *gír.*, nerd (pouco sociável).
NERVE, *s.*, nervo; coragem, afoiteza, vigor,descaramento; *v.*, animar.
NERVED, *adj.*, vigoroso, forte, robusto.
NERVE GAS, *s.*, *Quím.*, gás asfixiante.
NERVE-RACK.ING, *adj.*, *Quím.*, gás angustiante ou irritante.
NER.VOUS, *adj.*, nervoso, agitado, apreensivo.
NERV.OUS BREAK.DOWN, *s.*, esgotamento nervoso.
NERV.OUS.NESS, *s.*, nervosismo.
NERV.OUS SYS.TEM, *s.*, sistema nervoso.
NERV.OUS WRECK, *s.*, pessoa nervosa; pilha de nervos.
NER.VURE, *s.*, nervura de folha de planta.
NERV.Y, *adj.*, nervoso; *US* petulante, irritável.
NEST, *s.*, ninho, toca, covil; *v.*, aninhar-se, colocar-se em ninho.
NES.TLE, *v.*, abrigar, aninhar, proteger, abraçar.
NEST.LING, *s.*, passarinho, filhote de pássaro.
NET, *s.*, rede, malha, armadilha; *v.*, lançar a rede, pegar com a rede.
NETH.ER, *adj.*, inferior, mais baixo.
NETH.ER.LAND.ER, *adj.*, *s.*, holandês, batavo, flamengo.
NETH.ER.LANDS, *s. pl.*, Holanda, Países-Baixos.
NETH.ER.MOST, *adj.*, o mais baixo, o ínfimo.
NET.TLE, *s.*, urtiga; *v.*, irritar, incomodar, perturbar, exacerbar.
NET.TLED, *adj.*, ofendido, ressentido.
NET.TLING, *s.*, irritação,exasperação, incômodo.
NET.WORK, *s.*, rede; rede de comunicações (rádio, TV, computadores etc.).

NET.WORK.ING, *s.*, estabelecimento de uma rede (rádio, TV, computadores etc.).
NEU.RAL, *adj.*, neural.
NEU.RAL.GIA, *s.*, neuralgia, nevralgia.
NEU.RAL.GIC, *adj.*, nevrálgico.
NEUR.AS.THE.NIA, *s.*, neurastenia.
NEU.RO.LOG.I.CAL, *adj.*, neurológico.
NEU.ROL.O.GIST, *s.*, neurologista.
NEU.ROL.O.GY, *s.*, neurologia.
NEU.RON, *s.*, neurônio.
NEU.ROP.A.THY, *s.*, *Med.*, neuropatia.
NEU.RO.SIS, *s.*, neurose.
NEU.ROT.IC, *adj.*, *s.*, neurótico.
NEU.TER, *s.*, neutro, gênero neutro, ponto morto; *adj.*, assexuado, neutro.
NEU.TRAL, *adj.*, neutro, imparcial; *s.*, ponto morto/carro, nação neutra.
NEU.TRAL.ISM, *s.*, neutralismo, neutralidade.
NEU.TRAL.I.TY, *s.*, neutralidade.
NEU.TRAL.I.ZA.TION, *s.*, neutralização.
NEU.TRAL.IZE, *v.*, neutralizar, anular.
NEU.TRON, *s.*, *Fís.*, nêutron.
NEV.ER, *adv.*, nunca; nunca mais, jamais.
NEV.ER-END.ING, *adj.*, interminável.
NEV.ER.MORE, *adv.*, nunca, jamais, nunca mais.
NEV.ER.THE.LESS, *conj.*, todavia, não obstante, contudo.
NEW, *adj.*, novo, recente, moderno, fresco, complementar, atual.
NEW BLOOD, *s.*, *fig.*, sangue novo; renovação.
NEW.BORN, *s.*, recém-nascido.
NEW.COMER, *s.*, recém-vindo, recém-chegado.
NEW-FOUND, *adj.*, recém-descoberto (algo ou alguém).
NEW.ISH, *adj.*, quase novo.
NEW.LY, *adv.*, novamente; recentemente.
NEW.LY-WEDS, *s. pl.*, recém-casados.
NEW MOON, *s.*, lua nova (fase lunar).
NEW.NESS, *s.*, novidade.
NEWS, *s.*, notícias, novidades, noticiário.
NEWS A.GEN.CY, *s.*, agência de notícias.
NEWS-BOY, *s.*, rapaz que vende jornais, jornaleiro.
NEWS.CAST, *s.*, noticiário, jornal (rádio, TV).
NEWS.CAST.ER, *s.*, locutor, noticiarista, repórter.
NEWS CON.FER.ENCE, *s.*, entrevista coletiva.
NEWS.DEAL.ER, *s.*, vendedor de jornais e revistas.
NEWS.FLASH, *s.*, plantão de notícias, boletim extraordinário.
NEWS.GROUP, *s.*, *Comp.*, grupo de notícias.
NEWS.LET.TER, *s.*, boletim de notícias (por escrito).
NEWS.MAN, *s.*, jornalista, repórter.
NEWS.PA.PER, *s.*, jornal, diário, gazeta.
NEWS.PA.PER.MAN, *s.*, repórter, jornalista (jornal).
NEWS.PRINT, *s.*, jornal impresso; papel-jornal (onde se imprime jornal).
NEWS.ROOM, *s.*, sala de redação.
NEWS-SHEET, *s.*, folheto informativo.
NEWS-STAND, *s.*, banca de jornais.
NEWS.WOR.THY, *adj.*, que é de interesse jornalístico.
NEWSY, *adj.*, noticioso.
NEWT, *s.*, *Zool.*, espécie de salamandra.
NEW TES.TA.MENT, *s.*, *Rel.*, Novo Testamento.
NEW YEAR, *s.*, Ano-Novo.
NEW ZEA.LAND.ER, *s.*, neozelandês.

NEXT ·· 543 ·· NOMINEE

NEXT, *adj., s.*, próximo, vizinho, seguinte; *adv.*, depois, logo.
NEX.US, *s.*, nexo, vínculo, ligação.
NIB, *s.*, ponta, bico de pena; *v.*, apontar, fazer a ponta.
NIB.BLE, *v.*, mordiscar, beliscar, morder.
NIC.A.RA.GUA, *s.*, Nicarágua.
NIC.A.RA.GUAN, *adj., s.*, nicaraguense.
NICE, *adj.*, simpático, amável, atencioso, agradável, belo.
NICE-LOOK.ING, *adj.*, pessoa atraente.
NICE.LY, *adv.*, bem; agradavelmente; educadamente.
NICE.NESS, *s.*, simpatia, agradabilidade, gentileza, delicadeza.
NICE.TY, *s.*, delicadeza, sutileza; refinamento.
NICHE, *s.*, nicho.
NICK, *s.*, corte, entalhe, incisão, momento; *v.*, entalhar, cortar, inserir.
NICK.EL, *s.*, níquel; *v.*, niquelar, cobrir com níquel.
NICK.NAME, *s.*, apelido, alcunha; *v.*, apelidar, alcunhar.
NIC.O.TINE, *s.*, nicotina.
NIECE, *s.*, sobrinha.
NIF.TY, *adj.*, elegante, estiloso, chique.
NI.GE.RIA, *s.*, Nigéria.
NI.GE.RI.AN, *adj., s.*, nigeriano.
NIG.GARD, *s., adj.*, avaro, mesquinho.
NIG.GARD.LY, *adj.*, avarento, miserável; *adv.*, mesquinhamente.
NIG.GLE, *s.*, preocupação, aborrecimento; *v.*, aborrecer; criticar.
NIGH, *adv., prep.*, perto de, próximo.
NIGHT, *s.*, noite.
NIGHT.CAP, *s.*, touca de dormir; bebida que se toma antes de deitar.
NIGHT CLOTHES, *s. pl.*, pijama, roupa de dormir.
NIGHT.CLUB, *s.*, clube noturno.
NIGHT.DRESS, *s.*, camisola.
NIGHT.FALL, *s.*, anoitecer, crepúsculo.
NIGHT.IN.GALE, *s.*, rouxinol.
NIGHT.LIFE, *s.*, vida noturna.
NIGHT.LIGHT, *s.*, luz fraca que se deixa acesa à noite.
NIGHT.LY, *adj.*, noturno; *adv.*, à noite, de noite.
NIGHT.MARE, *s.*, pesadelo.
NIGHT.MAR.ISH, *adj.*, horripilante, aterrador.
NIGHT OWL, *s.*, notívago; coruja.
NIGHT POR.TER, *s.*, porteiro noturno.
NIGHT SCHOOL, *s.*, escola noturna.
NIGHT SHIRT, *s.*, camisolão (para homens).
NIGHT.SPOT, *s.*, clube noturno.
NIGHT.STICK, *s.*, *US* cassetete (de policial).
NIGHT-TIME, *s.*, noite.
NIGHT-WATCH.MAN, *s.*, guarda-noturno.
NIGHT.WEAR, *s.*, roupa de dormir.
NIGHTY, *adj.*, noturno; *adv.*, a cada noite.
NIGHT-SHIRT, *s.*, camisola.
NIGHT-TIME, *s.*, noite.
NI.HIL.IST, *s.*, niilista.
NI.HIL.ISM, *s.*, niilismo.
NI.HIL.IS.TIC, *adj.*, niilista.
NIL, *s.*, nada, zero.
NIM.BLE, *adj.*, ágil, rápido, ligeiro, vivo.
NIM.BLE.NESS, *s.*, agilidade, rapidez.
NIM.BLY, *adv.*, agilmente.
NIM.BUS, *s.*, *Met.*, nimbo, nuvem baixa de chuva; *Rel.*, nimbo,

auréola, halo.
NINE, *num.*, nove.
NINE.TEEN, *num.*, dezenove.
NINE.TEENTH, *num.*, décimo nono.
NINE.TI.ETH, *num.*, nonagésimo.
NINE.TY, *num.*, noventa.
NIN.NY, *s.*, tolo, simplório, parvo, bobo.
NINTH, *num.*, nono.
NIP, *v.*, beliscar, mordiscar; *s.*, beliscão, picada, mordida.
NIP.PER, *s.*, garra; rapaz, menino; *UK* criancinha.
NIP.PLE, *s.*, mamilo, bico de seio.
NIP.PON, *s.*, Japão.
NIP.PON.ESE, *adj., s.*, japonês, nipônico.
NIP.PY, *adj.*, *UK* fresquinho; *US* frio, penetrante; pungente, mordaz.
NIT, *s.*, **LÊNDEA**; *UK* bobão, idiota.
NIT.PICK.ING, *s.*, detalhismo; *adj.*, minucioso, detalhista.
NI.TRATE, *s.*, nitrato.
NI.TRIC AC.ID, *s.*, ácido nítrico.
NI.TRO.GEN, *s.*, *Quím.*, nitrogênio, azoto.
NI.TRO.GLYC.ER.IN, *s.*, nitroglicerina.
NI.TROUS, *adj.*, nitroso.
NIT.WIT, *s.*, *UK* bobão, idiota.
NIX, *s.*, nada, ninguém.
NO, *adv.*, não; *s.*, negativa; recusa; *Teat.*, no (teatro clássico japonês).
NO.AH'S ARK, *s.*, arca de Noé.
NO.BIL.I.AR.Y, *adj.*, nobiliário.
NO.BIL.I.TY, *s.*, nobreza, aristocracia.
NO.BLE, *adj.*, nobre, relativo à nobreza; *adj.*, nobre, fidalgo.
NO.BLE.MAN, *s.*, nobre (homem), fidalgo.
NO.BLE.NESS, *s.*, nobreza, grandeza, magnificência.
NO.BLE.WOM.AN, *s.*, mulher nobre.
NO.BLY, *adv.*, nobremente, generosamente.
NO.BODY, *pron.*, ninguém, nenhuma pessoa.
NOC.TUR.NAL, *adj.*, noturno.
NOC.TUR.NE, *s.*, *Mús.*, noturno (composição musical).
NOD, *s.*, aceno de cabeça, aquiescência, ordem; *v.*, acenar com a cabeça.
NODE, *s.*, nó, nódulo.
NOD.U.LAR, *adj.*, nodoso.
NOD.ULE, *s.*, nódulo.
NOD.UL.OUS, *adj.*, nodoso.
NO.EL, *s.*, *Lit.*, noel, Natal, canção de natal.
NO.HOW, *adv.*, de modo algum.
NOISE, *s.*, barulho, ruído, estrépito, clamor; *v.*, estrepitar, fazer barulho, falar demais.
NOISE.LESS, *adj.*, silencioso, silente, sem barulho.
NOISE.LESS.LY, *adv.*, silenciosamente.
NOISE.LESS.NESS, *s.*, silêncio.
NOIS.I.LY, *adv.*, ruidosamente.
NOISY, *adj.*, barulhento, ruidoso, estrepitoso, rumoroso.
NO.MAD, *adj., s.*, nômade.
NO.MAD.IC, *adj.*, nômade.
NO-MAN'S LAND, *s.*, *Mil.*, terra de ninguém.
NO.MEN.CLA.TURE, *s.*, nomenclatura.
NOM.I.NAL, *adj.*, nominal.
NOM.I.NAL.LY, *adv.*, nominalmente, teoricamente.
NOM.I.NATE, *v.*, nomear, referir, mencionar.
NOM.I.NA.TION, *s.*, nomeação.
NOM.I.NEE, *s.*, nomeado.

NONAGE ··544·· NOTIFY

NON.AGE, *s.*, menoridade.
NO.NA.GE.NAR.I.AN, *adj., s.*, nonagenário.
NON-AG.GRES.SION, *s.*, não agressão.
NON-AL.CO.HOL.IC, *adj.*, não alcoólico, sem álcool.
NON-BE.LIEV.ER, *s.*, descrente.
NON-BREAK.A.BLE, *adj.*, inquebrável.
NON.CHA.LANT, *adj.*, indiferente; calmo, sereno.
NON.CHA.LANT.LY, *adv.*, indiferentemente.
NON-COM.MIT.TAL, *adj.*, evasivo; esquivo, hesitante.
NON.CON.FORM.IST, *s.*, inconformista; rebelde; *adj.*, inconformista.
NON.CON.FORM.I.TY, *s.*, inconformismo, rebeldia.
NON-CO.OP.ER.A.TION, *s.*, não cooperação.
NON.DE.SCRIPT, *adj.*, desinteressante; indefinível.
NON-DRINK.ER, *s.*, abstêmio.
NONE, *pron.*, ninguém, nenhum, nada.
NON.ENT.I.TY, *s.*, nulidade; não existência, joão-ninguém.
NON-ES.SEN.TIAL, *adj.*, supérfluo, dispensável.
NONE.THE.LESS, *adv.*, contudo, não obstante.
NON-E.VENT, *s.*, desapontamento, decepção.
NON-EX.IS.TENT, *adj.*, não existente, inexistente.
NON-FIC.TION, *s.*, não ficção.
NON-HE.RO, *s.*, anti-herói.
NON-NE.GO.TI.A.BLE, *adj.*, não negociável.
NON-OB.SERV.ANCE, *s.*, inobservância.
NON-OP.ER.A.TION.AL, *adj.*, inoperante.
NON.PLUS, *s.*, confusão, balbúrdia, perplexidade; *v.*, confundir, embaraçar.
NON-PRO.LIF.ER.A.TION, *s.*, não proliferação (de armas).
NON-RE.TURN.A.BLE, *adj.*, não retornável.
NON.SENSE, *s.*, absurdo, disparate, contrassenso.
NON.SEN.SI.CAL, *adj.*, absurdo, sem sentido.
NON-SKID, *adj.*, antiderrapante.
NON-SMOK.ER, *s.*, não fumante.
NON-SMOK.ING, *adj.*, relativo à área onde é proibido fumar.
NON-STICK, *adj.*, antiaderente.
NON-STOP, *adj.*, contínuo, ininterrupto.
NON-SUIT, *s.*, processo anulado por falta de provas; *v.*, anular processo.
NOO.DLE, *s.*, talharim; tolo, bobo, imbecil.
NOOK, *s.*, canto, recanto, local ermo, retiro.
NOON, *s.*, meio-dia, apogeu.
NO ONE, *pron.*, o mesmo que *nobody*; ninguém.
NOON.DAY, *s.*, meio-dia; *adj.*, meridional.
NOOSE, *s.*, laço, nó corrediço; *v.*, fazer um nó; preparar uma armadilha.
NO PARK.ING, *s.*, estacionamento proibido.
NOR, *conj.*, nem, também não.
NOR.DIC, *adj., s.*, nórdico.
NORM, *s.*, norma, regra, mandamento, padrão.
NOR.MAL, *adj.*, normal, regular.
NOR.MAL.I.TY, *s.*, normalidade.
NOR.MAL.I.ZA.TION, *s.*, normalização.
NOR.MAL.IZE(-ISE), *v.*, normalizar.
NOR.MAL.LY, *adv.*, normalmente.
NOR.MAN, *adj., s.*, normando.
NORSE, *adj., s.*, escandinavo.
NORTH, *s.*, norte, setentrião; *adj.*, nórdico, setentrional; *v.*, ir para o norte.
NORTH AMER.I.CAN, *adj., s.*, norte-americano.
NORTH.BOUND, *adj.*, com direção norte.

NORTH-EAST, *s.*, nordeste.
NORTH.EAST.ER.LY, *adj.*, nordeste, nordestino; *adv.*, em direção nordeste.
NORTH.ER.LY, *adj.*, ao norte, do norte; boreal; *adv.*, em direção norte.
NORTH.ERN, *adj.*, do norte, nórdico, setentrional.
NORTH.ERN.ER, *s.*, habitante do norte.
NORTH.ERN LIGHTS, *s.*, aurora boreal.
NORTH.ERN.MOST, *adj.*, o mais setentrional, o mais ao norte.
NORTH KO.RE.AN, *s., adj.*, norte-coreano.
NORTH POLE, *s.*, Polo Norte.
NORTH-STAR, *s.*, estrela polar.
NORTH.WARD, *adj.*, para o norte; *adv.*, o mesmo que *northwards*.
NORTH.WARDS, *adv.*, em direção ao norte.
NORTH-WEST, *s.*, noroeste.
NORTH.WEST.ER.LY, *adj.*, a noroeste; do noroeste; *adv.*, em direção ao noroeste.
NOR.WAY, *s.*, Noruega.
NOR.WE.GIAN, *adj., s.*, norueguês.
NOSE, *s.*, nariz, focinho, olfato, faro, bico; *v.*, cheirar, focinhar, procurar.
NOSE.BAND, *s.*, focinheira.
NOSE.BLEED, *s.*, hemorragia pelo nariz.
NOSE.CONE, *s.*, ogiva.
NOSE.DIVE, *s., Aeron.*, mergulho de nariz (avião); *v.*, mergular (avião).
NOSE.GAY, *s.*, buquê, ramalhete, maço de flores.
NOSH, *s., col.*, rango, boia.
NOSH-UP, *s., col.*, comilança.
NOS.TAL.GI.A, *s.*, nostalgia, saudade.
NOS.TAL.GIC, *adj.*, nostálgico.
NOS.TRIL, *s.*, narina.
NOSY, *adj.*, metido, abelhudo, bisbilhoteiro.
NOT, *adv.*, não.
NO.TA.BIL.I.TY, *s.*, notabilidade.
NO.TA.BLE, *s.*, pessoa notável; *adj.*, notável, famoso, célebre.
NO.TA.BLE.NESS, *s.*, celebridade, fama.
NO.TA.BLY, *adv.*, notavelmente, especialmente, claramente.
NO.TA.RY, *s.*, notário, tabelião.
NO.TA.TION, *s.*, anotação, nota, notação.
NOTCH, *s.*, entalhe; *fig., col.*, ponto, grau.
NOTE, *s.*, nota, bilhete, aviso, anotação, nota musical; *v.*, anotar, tomar nota, observar.
NOTE.BOOK, *s.*, caderno; microcomputador portátil, agenda, agenda eletrônica.
NOT.ED, *adj.*, conhecido, renomado, famoso.
NOTE.LESS, *adj.*, desconhecido, obscuro.
NOTE.PAD, *s.*, bloco de notas.
NOTE.PA.PER, *s.*, papel de carta.
NOTE.WOR.THI.LY, *adv.*, notavelmente.
NOTE.WOR.THY, *adj.*, digno de nota.
NOTH.ING, *s.*, nada, zero, coisa nenhuma, nulidade.
NOTH.ING.NESS, *s.*, nada, inexistência.
NO.TICE, *s.*, aviso, notícia, anúncio, aviso prévio, prazo, notificação, informação.
NO.TICE.A.BLE, *adj.*, notável, digno de nota.
NO.TICE.A.BLY, *adv.*, notavelmente, visivelmente.
NO.TICE BOARD, *s.*, quadro de avisos.
NO.TI.FI.CA.TION, *s.*, notificação, aviso, informação.
NO.TI.FY, *v.*, notificar, avisar, intimar.

NOTION •• 545 •• NYMPHOMANIA

NO.TION, s., noção, conhecimento elementar, ideia, opinião.
NO.TION.AL, adj., nocional; imaginário, hipotético.
NO.TO.RI.E.TY, s., notoriedade, fama.
NO.TO.RI.OUS, adj., notório, público; pej., famigerado, de má fama.
NO.TO.RI.OUS.LY, adv., notoriamente.
NOT.WITH.STAND.ING, conj., no entanto, não obstante.
NOUGHT, s., zero.
NOUN, s. substantivo, nome.
NOUR.ISH, v., alimentar, nutrir, sustentar.
NOUR.ISH.ABLE, adj., nutrível, alimentável.
NOUR.ISH.ING adj., nutritivo, alimentício.
NOUR.ISH.MENT, s., alimento, nutrimento, comida.
NOV.EL, s., novela, romance; adj., novo, novel, recente.
NOV.EL.IST, s., novelista.
NOV.EL.TY, s., novidade.
NO.VEM.BER, s., novembro.
NOV.ICE, s., noviço, neófito, iniciante, principiante, novato.
NO.VI.TI.ATE, s., noviciado; aprendizado.
NOW, adv., agora, hoje, atualmente, neste momento.
NOW.A.DAYS, adv., atualmente, hoje em dia.
NO.WAY, adv., de modo algum, de forma alguma.
NO.WHERE, adj., a lugar nenhum, em nenhum lugar.
NO.WISE, adv., de modo algum.
NOX.IOUS, adj., nòcivo, prejudicial, danoso.
NOZ.ZLE, s., boca, bico.
NU.ANCE, s., nuança, matiz, meio tom.
NUB, s., US essência.
NUB.BLE, s., nó, protuberância.
NU.BI.AN, s., adj., núbio.
NU.BILE, adj., núbil.
NU.CLE.AR, adj., nuclear.
NU.CLE.AR FAM.I.LY, s., família nuclear (pai, mãe, filhos).
NU.CLE.AR PHYS.ICS, s., física nuclear.
NU.CLE.AR WAR, s., guerra nuclear.
NU.CLE.AR WEAP.ON, s., arma nuclear.
NU.CLE.US, s., núcleo.
NUDE, adj., nu, despido, sem roupas, descoberto, liso.
NUDGE, v., acotovelar, cutucar.
NUD.ISM, s., nudismo.
NUD.IST, s., nudista.
NU.DI.TY, s., nudez.
NUG.GET, s., pepita; pérola; col., novidade, boato.
NUI.SANCE, s., incômodo, aborrecimento, tipo desagradável; praga.
NULL, adj., nulo, sem validade; v., anular, invalidar.
NUL.LI.FI.CA.TION, s., anulação, invalidade.
NUL.LI.FI.ER, s., anulador.
NUL.LI.FY, v., anular, invalidar, nulificar.
NUL.LI.TY, s., nulidade.
NUMB, adj., entorpecido, paralisado, dormente; v., paralisar, entorpecer.
NUMB.ER, s., número, algarismo, soma; v., numerar, quantificar.

NUM.BER.ER, s., numerador.
NUM.BER.LESS, adj., inumerável, incontável; não numerado.
NUM.BER ONE, s., número um; o mais importante.
NUM.BER.PLATE, s., placa de veículo com número de licenciamento.
NU.MER.A.BLE, adj., numerável.
NU.ME.RA.CY, s., facilidade com números.
NU.MER.AL, s., numeral.
NU.MER.ATE, v., numerar, enumerar.
NU.MER.IC, adj., numérico.
NU.MER.I.CAL, adj., o mesmo que numeric.
NU.MER.OL.O.GY, s., numerologia.
NU.MER.OUS, adj., numeroso, abundante.
NU.MIS.MAT.ICS, s., numismática.
NUM.MA.RY, adj., numerário.
NUM.SKULL, adj., tolo, néscio, bobo, imbecil.
NUN, s., freira, monja.
NUN.CIO, s., núncio.
NUN.LIKE, adj., tal como freiras.
NUN.NERY, s., convento de freiras.
NUP.TIAL, adj., nupcial, matrimonial.
NURSE, s., enfermeira, ama-seca, governanta, aia; v., trabalhar como enfermeira, criar.
NURSE.MAID, s., ama-seca, babá.
NURS.ER.Y, s., creche, berçário, quarto de crianças, viveiro.
NURS.ER.Y NURSE, s., enfermeira de berçário; ama-seca.
NURS.ER.Y RHYME, s., poema ou cantiga infantil.
NURS.ER.Y SCHOOL, s., pré-escola, jardim de infância; creche.
NURS.ING, s., enfermagem, cuidados.
NUR.TURE, v., nutrir, alimentar; s., criação, educação, alimentação.
NUT, s., noz; porca de parafuso.
NUT-BROWN, adj., cor de castanha, acastanhado.
NUT.CASE, s., col., pirado, desequilibrado.
NUT.CRACK.ER, s., quebra-nozes.
NUT.HATCH, s., pica-pau.
NUT.MEG, s., noz-moscada.
NU.TRI.ENT, adj., s., nutriente.
NU.TRI.MENT, s., nutrimento, alimentação, sustento.
NU.TRI.TION, s., nutrição, alimentação.
NU.TRI.TION.AL, adj., nutritivo.
NU.TRI.TION.IST, s., nutricionista.
NU.TRI.TIOUS, adj., nutritivo.
NU.TRI.TIVE, adj., nutritivo.
NUT.SHELL, s., casca de noz.
NUT.TER, s., colhedor de nozes; col., louco, maníaco.
NUT.TING, s., colheira de nozes.
NUT.TY, adj., com sabor de noz.
NUZ.ZLE, v., fossar (com o focinho); col., fuçar, bisbilhotar.
N.Y.C., abrev. de New York City: cidade de Nova York.
NY.LON, s., náilon, fibra sintética.
NYMPH, s., ninfa.
NYM.PHO.MA.NIA, s., Med., ninfomania.

O, décima quinta letra do alfabeto inglês; s., zero (na leitura de números).
OAF, s., imbecil, tolo, idiota, simplório, parvo.
OAK, s., carvalho; adj., próprio do carvalho.
OAK.LING, s., carvalho novo.
OA.KUM, s., estopa, estopa para calafetar.
OAR, s., remo, remador; v., remar.
OARLOCK, s., US Náut., tolete.
OARS.MAN, s., remador.
OA.SIS, s., oásis.
OAT, s., aveia, flauta de pastor.
OAT.CAKE, s., bolo feito de aveia.
OATEN, adj., de aveia.
OAT.FIELD, s., campo de aveia, aveal.
OATH, s., juramento; praga, palavrão.
OATH.BREAK.ER, s., perjuro, juramento falso.
OAT.MEAL, s., farinha de aveia.
OB.DU.RATE, adj., teimoso, obstinado, duro.
OB.DU.RA.TION, s., teimosia, insistência.
OBE.DI.ENCE, s., obediência, atendimento.
OBE.DI.ENT, adj., obediente, atencioso, submisso.
OBE.DI.ENT.LY, adv., obedientemente.
OBEI.SANCE, s., reverência, mesura, deferência, respeito.
OBEI.SANT.LY, adv., mesuradamente.
OBE.LISK, s., obelisco.
OBESE, adj., obeso, gordo, barrigudo.
OBESE.NESS, s., obesidade, gordura excessiva.
OBE.SI.TY, s., obesidade.
OBEY, v., obedecer, acatar, respeitar.
OB.FUS.CATE, v., ofuscar, atordoar (com brilho).
OB.FUS.CA.TION, s., ofuscação, deslumbramento, brilho intenso.
OBIT, s., óbito, falecimento, obituário, morte.
OBIT.U.ARY, s., obituário, necrologia.
OB.JECT, s., objeto, coisa, objetivo, propósito; v., objetar, alegar, contrapor-se.
OB.JECT GLASS, s., Opt., lente objetiva.
OB.JEC.TI.FY, v., objetivar, pretender, colimar.
OB.JEC.TION, s., objeção, oposição, contraposição.
OB.JEC.TION.A.BLE, adj., censurável; repreensível.
OB.JEC.TION.A.BLY, adv., censuravelmente.
OB.JEC.TIVE, adj., s., objetivo.
OB.JEC.TIVE.LY, adv., objetivamente.
OB.JEC.TIVE.NESS, s., objetividade.
OB.JEC.TIV.ISM, s., objetivismo.
OB.JEC.TIV.I.TY, s., objetividade, imparcialidade.
OB.JEC.TOR, s., opositor.
OB.JUR.GATE, v., censurar, admoestar, advertir.
OB.JUR.GA.TION, s., censura, advertência, admoestação.
OB.JUR.GA.TO.RY, adj., objurgatório.
OB.LA.TION, s., oblação, oferenda.
OB.LI.GATE, v., obrigar, constranger, forçar a.
OB.LI.GA.TION, s., obrigação, constrangimento, compromisso, dever.
OB.LIG.A.TOR, s., devedor.
OB.LIG.A.TO.RI.LY, adv., obrigatoriamente.
OB.LIG.A.TO.RY, adj., obrigatório, forçado.
O.BLIGE, v., favorecer, obrigar, forçar.
OB.LI.GEE, s., credor.
O.BLIG.ING, adj., amável, obsequiador, gentil, cortês.
OB.LI.GOR, s., devedor.
OB.LIQUE, adj., oblíquo, indeciso, indeterminado.
OB.LIQUE CASE, s., Gram., caso oblíquo.
OB.LIQUE.LY, adv., obliquamente, indiretamente.
OB.LIQUE.NESS, s., obliquidade, indecisão.
OB.LIT.ER.ATE, v., obliterar, apagar, retirar, esquecer.
OB.LIT.ER.A.TION, s., obliteração, esquecimento.
OB.LIV.I.ON, s., esquecimento.
OB.LIV.I.OUS, adj., esquecido; distraído; inconsciente.
OB.LONG, adj., oblongo, retangular; s., retângulo, figura oblonga.
OB.NOX.IOUS, adj., odioso, detestável, nojento, intragável.
OB.NOX.IOUS.LY, adv., odiosamente.
OB.NU.BI.LA.TION, s., Lit., obnubilação, obscuridade.
O.BOE, s., Mús., oboé.
O.BO.IST, s., oboísta.
OB.RO.GA.TION, s., ob-rogação.
OB.SCENE, adj., obsceno, devasso.
OB.SCENE.LY, adv., obscenamente.
OB.SCEN.I.TY, s., obscenidade, devassidão.
OB.SCU.RANT, s., adj., obscurantista.
OB.SCU.RANT.ISM, s., obscurantismo, ignorância.
OB.SCU.RA.TION, s., obscurecimento; obscuridade.
OB.SCURE, adj., obscuro, ignorado, ambíguo; v., ocultar, escurecer; s., obscuridade.
OB.SCURE.LY, adv., obscuramente; confusamente.
OB.SCU.RI.TY, s., obscuridade, escuridão, ambiguidade, incerteza.
OB.SE.CRATE, v., implorar, rogar.
OB.SE.QUIES, s. pl., exéquias.
OB.SE.QUI.OUS, adj., obsequioso, atencioso, cortês.
OB.SERV.A.BLE, adj., observável, que se percebe, notável.
OB.SERV.A.BLY, adv., visivelmente; notavelmente.
OB.SER.VANCE, s., observação, acompanhamento, hábito.
OB.SER.VANT, adj., observador, observante.
OB.SER.VA.TION, s., observação, exame, verificação.
OB.SER.VA.TION.AL, adj., col., empírico, observacional (observação pessoal).
OB.SER.VA.TO.RY, s., observatório.
OB.SERVE, v., observar, cumprir, respeitar.
OB.SERV.ER, s., observador; espectador; vigia; Pol., analista.
OB.SERV.ING, adj., observador.
OB.SESS, v., obcecar(-se), obsedar.
OB.SES.SION, s., obsessão, ideia fixa, mania.

OBSESSIONAL ·· 547 ·· OESTROGEN

OB.SES.SION.AL, *adj.*, obsessivo.
OB.SES.SIVE, *adj.*, obsessivo.
OB.SID.I.AN, *s.*, obsidiana.
OB.SO.LES.CENSE, *s.*, obsolescência, velhice, desuso.
OB.SO.LES.CENT, *adj.*, antiquado, obsolescente.
OB.SO.LETE, *adj.*, obsoleto.
OB.STA.CLE, *s.*, obstáculo, empecilho, óbice, impedimento.
OB.STA.CLE RACE, *s., Esp.*, corrida de obstáculos (cavalos).
OB.STET.RIC, *adj.*, obstétrico.
OB.STE.TRI.CIAN, *s.*, obstetra, médico parteiro, parteiro, parteira.
OB.STET.RICS, *s.*, obstetrícia, obstétrica.
OB.STI.NA.CY, *s.*, obstinação, teimosia.
OB.STI.NATE, *adj.*, obstinado, teimoso.
OB.STI.NATE.LY, *adv.*, obstinadamente.
OB.STREP.ER.OUS, *adj.*, ruidoso, estrepitoso, barulhento.
OB.STREP.ER.OUS.NESS, *s.*, ruído, barulho, rumor, estrépito.
OB.STRUCT, *v.*, estorvar, incomodar, perturbar, obstruir.
OB.STRUCT.ED, *adj.*, obstruído, impedido, incomodado.
OB.STRUCT.ER, *s.*, obstrutor.
OB.STRUC.TION, *s.*, obstrução, obstáculo, óbice.
OB.STRUC.TIVE, *adj.*, obstrutivo.
OB.TAIN, *v.*, obter, conseguir, lograr.
OB.TAIN.A.BLE, *adj.*, obtenível, disponível.
OB.TAIN.ER, *s.*, obtentor.
OB.TAIN.MENT, *s.*, obtenção.
OB.TRUDE, *v.*, impor com violência, impor.
OB.TRU.SIVE, *adj.*, inconveniente; intruso; penetrante.
OB.TRU.SIVE.LY, *adv.*, intrusamente, importunamente.
OB.TU.RATE, *v.*, obturar, fechar, tapar.
OB.TU.RA.TION, *s.*, obturação.
OB.TUSE, *adj.*, obtuso.
OB.VERSE, *s.*, reverso, anverso; *adj.*, de frente.
OB.VERT, *v.*, voltar, dirigir para, reverter, pôr do avesso.
OB.VERT.ING, *adj.*, revertido, do avesso.
OB.VI.ATE, *v.*, obviar, prevenir.
OB.VI.OUS, *adj.*, óbvio, evidente, claro.
OB.VI.OUS.LY, *adv.*, obviamente.
OB.VI.OUS.NESS, *s.*, obviedade, evidência.
OC.CA.SION, *s.*, ocasião, fato, acontecimento, momento.
OC.CA.SION.AL, *adj.*, ocasional, momentâneo, acidental.
OC.CA.SION.AL.LY, *adv.*, ocasionalmente, vez por outra.
OC.CA.SION.ER, *s.*, ocasionador, causador.
OC.CIDENT, *s.*, ocidente, poente.
OC.CI.DEN.TAL, *adj.*, ocidental.
OC.CIP.I.TAL, *s., Anat.*, osso occipital; *adj.*, relativo ao osso occipital.
OC.CLUDE, *v.*, fechar, tapar.
OC.CLU.SION, *s.*, oclusão, fechamento.
OC.CLU.SIVE, *adj.*, oclusivo.
OC.CULT, *v.*, ocultar, esconder, dissimular; *adj.*, oculto, secreto, dissimulado.
OC.CUL.TA.TION, *s.*, ocultação, ocultamento.
OC.CULT.ISM, *s.*, ocultismo.
OC.CULT.NESS, *s.*, ocultação, confidência, segredo.
OC.CU.PAN.CY, *s.*, ocupação, posse.
OC.CU.PANT, *s.*, ocupante; *fig.*, inquilino.
OC.CU.PA.TION, *s.*, ocupação, profissão, trabalho.
OC.CU.PA.TION.AL, *adj.*, ocupacional.
OC.CU.PA.TION.AL DES.EASE, *s., Med.*, doença ocupacional.

OC.CU.PA.TION.AL THER.A.PY, *s.*, terapia ocupacional.
OC.CU.PI.ED, *adj.*, ocupado, aplicado, atarefado, diligente.
OC.CU.PI.ER, *s.*, ocupante.
OC.CU.PY, *v.*, ocupar, acomodar-se, morar.
OC.CUR, *v.*, ocorrer, acontecer, suceder.
OC.CUR.RENCE, *s.*, ocorrência, fato, acontecimento, evento, sucesso.
O.CEAN, *s.*, oceano; *fig.*, imensidão.
O.CEAN.I.AN, *s., adj.*, oceânico; oceaniense.
O.CEAN.IC, *adj.*, oceânico.
O.CEAN LIN.ER, *s.*, transatlântico.
O.CEAN.OG.RA.PHER, *s.*, oceanógrafo.
O.CEAN.OG.RA.PHY, *s.*, oceanografia.
O.CHRE, *s., ocre; adj.*, cor de ocre.
O'CLOCK, *abrev.* de *of the clock*: pelo relógio; *five ~*: cinco horas (pelo relógio).
OC.TA.GON, *s.*, octógono.
OC.TA.GON.AL, *adj.*, octogonal, octangular.
OC.TA.HE.DRON, *s., Geom.*, octaedro.
OC.TAVE, *s., Mús.*, oitava.
OC.TA.VO, *adj.*, oitavo.
OC.TO.BER, *s.*, outubro.
OC.TO.GE.NAR.I.AN, *adj., s.*, octogenário.
OC.TET, *s., Mús.*, octeto.
OC.TO.PUS, *s., Zool.*, polvo, octópode.
OC.TUPLE, *adj., num.*, óctuplo.
OC.U.LAR, *adj.*, ocular, visual.
OC.U.LIST, *s.*, oculista, oftalmologista.
ODA.LISQUE, *s.*, odalisca.
ODD, *adj.*, excelente, ótimo, ocasional, casual, esquisito, excêntrico, estranho.
ODD.BALL, *s., US col.*, esquisitão, excêntrico; *adj.*, esquisito, excêntrico.
ODD.ISH, *adj.*, meio esquisito.
ODD.I.TY, *s.*, esquisitice, excentricidade, extravagância, coisa estranha.
ODD JOBS, *s. pl.*, biscates, bicos.
ODD.LY, *adv.*, estranhamente.
ODD.MENTS, *s. pl.*, retalhos, restos, sobras; ninharias.
ODD.NESS, *s.*, desigualdade, excentricidade, esquisitice.
ODDS, *s. pl.*, vantagem (em favor de); lanbujem; disputa.
ODE, *s.*, ode.
ODI.OUS, *adj.*, odioso, nojento.
O.DI.OUS.LY, *adv.*, odiosamente.
O.DI.OUS.NESS, *s.*, ódio, odiosidade, aversão, repugnância.
O.DOM.E.TER, *s.*, odômetro.
O.DON.TAL.GI.A, *s.*, odontalgia (dor nos dentes).
O.DON.TAL.GY, *s.*, o mesmo que *odontalgia*.
O.DON.TOL.O.GIST, *s.*, odontologista, dentista, odontólogo.
O.DON.TOL.O.GY, *s.*, odontologia.
O.DOR.IF.ER.OUS, *adj.*, odorífero, aromatizado, perfumado.
O.DOUR.LESS, O.DOR.LESS, *adj.*, inodoro.
O.DOR.OUS, *adj.*, perfumado, aromático.
O.DOUR *UK,* **O.DOR** *US, s.*, odor, perfume; cheiro, fedor.
OD.YS.SEY, *s.*, odisséia.
OE.CU.MEN.I.CAL, EC.U.MEN.I.CAL, *adj.*, ecumênico; universal, geral.
OE.DE.MA *UK,* **E.DE.MA** *US, s., Med.*, edema, tumor.
OE.NOL.O.GY, *s.*, enologia.
OE.SOPH.A.GUS *UK,* **E.SOPH.A.GUS** *US, s., Anat.*, esôfago.
OES.TRO.GEN *UK,* **ES.TRO.GEN** *US*, estrogênio (hormônio

OF ·· 548 ·· OMELET

feminino).

OF, *prep.*, de, por, devido, entre.

OFF, *adj.*, cancelado, desligado, ausente; *prep.*, fora de, fora.

OFF-BAL.ANCE, *adj.*, desequilibrado; desprevenido; *adv.*, sem equilíbrio; desprevenidamente.

OFF-CEN.TRE *UK*, **OFF-CEN.TER** *US*, *adj.*, *adv.*, fora do centro.

OFF-COL.OUR *UK*, **OFF-COL.OR** *US*, *adj.*, indisposto, meio doente.

OFF-DAY, *s.*, *col.*, dia livre, dia de folga.

OF.FAL, *s.*, restos de comida, sobras.

OF.FENCE *UK*, **OF.FENSE** *US*, *s.*, delito, crime, ofensa, injúria, ataque, desgosto.

OF.FENCE.LESS, *adj.*, inofensivo, inocente.

OF.FEND, *v.*, ofender, injuriar, magoar, desgostar, escandalizar.

OF.FEND.ED, *adj.*, ofendido.

OF.FEND.ER, *s.*, ofensor, transgressor, delinquente.

OF.FEND.ING, *adj.*, ofensor.

OF.FENSE, *s.*, o mesmo que *offence*.

OF.FEN.SIVE, *adj.*, ofensivo.

OF.FEN.SIVE.NESS, *s.*, agressividade, caráter ofensivo.

OF.FER, *s.*, oferta, oferenda, dádiva, oferecimento; *v.*, oferecer, ofertar, doar.

OF.FER.ER, *s.*, oferente, ofertador.

OF.FER.ING, *s.*, oferta, dádiva, oferenda.

OF.FER.TO.RY, *s.*, ofertório, oferecimento.

OFF-GUARD, *adj.*, desprevenido.

OFF-HAND, *adj.*, brusco, repentino; informal; *adv.*, repentinamente.

OF.FICE, *s.*, escritório, gabinete, cargo, função, posto, seção, préstimos.

OF.FICE BOY, *s.*, estafeta, mensageiro, office-boy.

OF.FICE.HOLD.ER, *s.*, funcionário público.

OF.FICE HOURS, *s. pl.*, horas de expediente.

OF.FIC.ER, *s.*, oficial, diretor, agente, administrador, ministro, dirigente.

OF.FI.CIAL, *adj.*, *s.*, oficial; servidor público.

OF.FI.CIAL.DOM, *s.*, burocracia, administração pública.

OF.FI.CIAL.LY, *adv.*, oficialmente.

OF.FI.CI.ATE, *v.*, oficiar, empreender algo oficial.

OF.FI.CIOUS, *adj.*, oficioso, metido, intrometido.

OF.FI.CIOUS.LY, *adj.*, oficiosamente.

OFF.ING, *s.*, largo, mar alto; *in the ~*: iminente, num futuro próximo.

OFF-KEY, *adj.*, *Mús.*, desafinado, destoante, dissonante; *adv.*, desafinadamente.

OFF-LI.CENCE, *s.*, *UK* loja de bebidas alcoólicas.

OFF LIM.ITS, *adj.*, *Mil.*, relativo à área proibida.

OFF.LINE, *adj.*, fora de linha.

OFF.PUT.ING, *adj.*, desagradável, desconcertante.

OFF-SEA.SON, *adj.*, fora de temporada.

OFF.SET, *s.*, *offset*, processo de impressão; *v.*, compensar, equiparar.

OFF.SHORE, *adj.*, costeiro, litorâneo.

OFF.SIDE, *s.*, *Esp.*, impedimento (futebol); *adj.*, na lateral, do lado errado; *Esp.*, impedido (futebol).

OFF.SPRING, *s.*, descendência, filhos, prole.

OFF.STAGE, *adj.*, *Teat.*, de bastidores; *adv.*, nos bastidores.

OF.TEN, *adv.*, muitas vezes, frequentemente, amiúde.

O.GI.VAL, *adj.*, ogival.

O.GIVE, *s.*, ogiva.

O.GLE, *s.*, tipo de olhar ansioso; *v.*, olhar com ansiedade.

O.GRE, *s.*, ogro, bicho papão.

OHM, *s.*, *Eletr.*, ohm (unidade de resistência elétrica).

OIL, *s.*, óleo, petróleo; azeite; *v.*, lubrificar, azeitar, passar óleo, untar.

OIL.CAN, *s.*, almotolia.

OIL CHANGE, *s.*, troca de óleo (motor).

OIL-COL.OR, *s.*, tinta a óleo.

OIL FIELD, *s.*, campo petrolífero, bacia petrolífera.

OIL FILTER, *s.*, filtro de óleo.

OIL-FIRED, *adj.*, a óleo (que usa óleo como combustível).

OIL IN.DUS.TRY, *s.*, indústria petrolífera.

OIL.MAN, *s.*, negociante ou proprietário de ramo petrolífero.

OIL PAINT, *s.*, o mesmo que *oil-color*: tinta a óleo.

OIL-PAINT.ING, *s.*, pintura a óleo.

OIL RIG, *s.*, plataforma petrolífera.

OIL.SKIN, *s.*, oleado, capa.

OIL SLIK, *s.*, mancha de óleo.

OIL TANK.ER, *s.*, navio petroleiro; caminhão tanque.

OIL WELL, *s.*, poço petrolífero.

OILY, *adj.*, oleoso, gorduroso, banhoso.

OINT.MENT, *s.*, unguento, pomada.

O.K., *abrev.* de *okay*; *adj.*, *adv.*, tudo bem, ótimo, certo, aprovado.

OKRA, *s.*, quiabo.

OLD, *adj.*, velho, antigo, anterior.

OLD AGE, *s.*, velhice.

OLD.EN, *adj.*, velho, antigo.

OLD-FASH.IONED, *adj.*, fora de moda, obsoleto, velho.

OLD-FO.GY, *s.*, indivíduo antiquado; *adj.*, antiquado.

OLD-FO.GY.ISH, *adj.*, antiquado, obsoleto.

OLD MAID, *s.*, solteirona; pessoa pudica.

OLD MAS.TER, *s.*, grande mestre (de pintura); artista dos séc. XV a XVIII.

OLD.NESS, *s.*, velhice, antiguidade.

OLD TES.TA.MENT, *s.*, *Rel.*, Antigo Testamento.

OLD-TIME, *adj.*, dos velhos tempos.

OLD WORLD, *s.*, Velho Mundo (Eurásia e África).

OLE.AG.I.NOUS, *adj.*, oleaginoso; oleoso.

OLE.AG.I.NOUS.NESS, *s.*, oleosidade.

O.LE.IC, *adj.*, oleico.

O.LE.IN, *s.*, *Quím.*, oleína.

OLEO.MAR.GA.RINE, *s.*, margarina.

OL.I.GARCH, *s.*, oligarca.

OL.I.GAR.CHIC, *adj.*, oligárquico.

OL.I.GAR.CHY, *s.*, oligarquia.

OL.I.GO.CENE, *s.*, *Geol.*, oligoceno.

OL.I.GOP.O.LY, *s.*, oligopólio.

OLIO, *s.*, mistura, miscelânea.

OL.IVE, *s.*, azeitona, oliveira.

OL.IVE GREEN, *adj.*, verde-oliva.

OL.IVE-OIL, *s.*, azeite de oliva.

OL.IVE TREE, *s.*, *Bot.*, oliveira.

O.LYM.PI.AD, *s.*, olimpíada.

O.LYM.PI.AN, *adj.*, olímpico; *fig.*, fenomenal.

O.LYM.PIC, *adj.*, olímpico.

O.LYM.PIC GAMES, *s. pl.*, olimpíadas, jogos olímpicos.

O.LYM.PUS, *s.*, Olimpo.

OM.BUDS.MAN, *s.*, *ombudsman*.

OM.E.LET, *s.*, omelete.

OMEN ·· 549 ·· OPPONENT

O.MEN, *s.*, agouro, presságio; *v.*, augurar, pressagiar.
OMENED, *adj.*, fatal, fatídico.
OM.I.NOUS, *adj.*, ominoso, agourento.
OM.I.NOUS.LY, *adv.*, ominosamente.
O.MIS.SION, *s.*, omissão, lacuna, falta.
O.MIT, *v.*, omitir, deixar fora, excluir.
OM.NI.BUS, *s.*, ônibus.
OM.NIP.O.TENCE, *s.*, onipotência.
OM.NIP.O.TENT, *adj.*, onipontente.
OM.NI.PRES.ENCE, *s.*, onipresença, ubiquidade.
OM.NI.PRES.ENT, *adj.*, onipresente.
OM.NI.SCIENCE, *s.*, onisciência.
OM.NIS.CIENT, *adj.*, onisciente.
OM.NIV.O.ROUS, *adj.*, *s.*, onívoro.
ON, *prep.*, sobre, em, em cima de.
ONCE, *adv.*, uma vez, outrora, antigamente; *prep.*, depois que.
ONCE-O.VER, *s.*, *gír.*, corrida de olhos, uma olhada rápida.
ON-COM.ING, *s.*, chegada, aproximação; *adj.*, próximo.
ONE, *num.*, um; *adj.*, único, típico.
ONE-EYED, *adj.*, caolho, cego somente de um olho.
ONE-LEG.GED, *adj.*, coxo, manco; *s.*, perneta.
ONE-LIN.ER, *adj.*, piada curta.
ONE-MAN, *adj.*, individual, solo.
ONE.NESS, *s.*, unidade, identidade.
ONE-NIGHT STAND, *s.*, *US* apresentação única; *col.*, relacionamento passageiro.
ONE-OFF, *adj.*, único; *adj.*, exclusivo.
ONER.OUS, *adj.*, oneroso, pesado.
ONE-PAR.ENT FAM.I.LY, *s.*, família que possui apenas um dos pais.
ONE.ER.OUS, *adj.*, oneroso.
ONE.ER.OUS.NESS, *s.*, onerosidade.
ONE.SELF, *pron.*, se, si; si mesmo, si próprio.
ONE-SID.ED, *adj.*, parcial, injusto, desigual.
ONE-SID.ED.NESS, *s.*, imparcialidade.
ONE.TIME, *adj.*, antigo, anterios, do passado.
ONE-WAY, *adj.*, de sentido único, de mão única.
ON.GO.ING, *s.*, avanço, progresso; *adj.*, em andamento; atual; adiantado.
ON.ION, *s.*, cebola.
ON.IONY, *adj.*, acebolado, igual a cebola.
ON.LINE, *s.*, *Comp.*, em linha, em conexão direta.
ON-LOOK.ER, *s.*, espectador.
ON-LOOK.ING, *s.*, assistência, plateia; *adj.*, que presencia.
ONLY, *adv.*, somente, apenas; *adj.*, único, só; *conj.*, exceto, porém.
ON.O.MAT.O.POE.IA, *s.*, onomatopeia.
ON.RUSH, *s.*, carga, arremetida.
ON-SCREEN, *adj.*, *adv.*, *Comp.*, na tela.
ON.SET, *s.*, início, começo; assalto, ataque.
ON.SHORE, *adj.*, terrestre, em terra; *adv.*, em terra, para a terra.
ON.SIDE, *adj.*, *adv.*, em posição legal.
ON.SLAUGHT, *s.*, investida, assalto furioso.
ON.TO, *prep.*, para, a, em, sobre; ciente de, por dentro.
ON.TOL.O.GY, *s.*, ontologia.
O.NUS, *s.*, ônus, carga, peso, obrigação, responsabilidade.
ON.WARD, *adv.*, para frente, adiante; *adj.*, avançado, adiantado.
ON.YX, *s.*, *Min.*, ônix.
OO.DLES, *s. pl.*, *gír.*, grande quantidade de algo, montão.

OOF, *s.*, *gír.*, grana; *interj.*, uff!; que vergonha!
OOH, *interj.*, aah!
OOPS, *interj.*, opa!
OOZE, *s.*, limo, lodo; infusão; *v.*, correr líquidos; escoar líquidos, pingar, gotejar.
O.PAC.I.TY, *s.*, opacidade; obscuridade.
O.PAL, *s.*, *Min.*, opala.
O.PAL.ES.CENT, *s.*, opalescente.
O.PAQUE, *adj.*, opaco, fusco, embaçado.
O.PAQUE.NESS, *s.*, opacidade.
O.PEN, *s.*, clareira, abertura; *adj.*, aberto, livre, franco, irrestrito; *v.*, abrir, descerrar, franquear, liberar.
O.PEN.A.BLE, *adj.*, que pode ser aberto.
O.PEN-AIR, *s.*, ar livre; *adj.*, ao ar livre; no sereno.
O.PEN-AND-SHUT, *adj.*, evidente.
O.PNE DAY, *s.*, dia de visitação pública.
O.PEN-END.ED, *adj.*, de ponta aberta; ilimitado.
O.PEN-HEART.ED, *adj.*, de coração aberto; franco; generoso.
O.PEN-MAR.KET, *s.*, mercado livre.
O.PEN.ER, *s.*, abridor.
O.PEN.ING, *s.*, abertura, orifício; inauguração, estreia; início; oportunidade; *adj.*, primeiro, inicial.
O.PEN.ING TIME, *s.*, *UK* horário de abrir.
O.PEN-LET.TER, *s.*, carta aberta.
O.PEN.LY, *adv.*, abertamente.
O.PEN MAR.KET, *s.*, *Econ.*, mercado aberto ou livre.
O.PEN-MIND.ED, *adj.*, compreensivo; liberal, sem preconceitos.
O.PEN-MOUTHED, *adj.*, boquiaberto; guloso, ávido.
O.PEN.NESS, *s.*, franqueza; abertura; vastidão.
O.PEN-PLAN, *s.*, sem divisórias.
O.PEN-PRISON, *s.*, prisão em regime aberto.
O.PEN SEASON, *s.*, temporada aberta (caça ou pesca).
O.PEN U.NI.VER.SI.TY, *s.*, *UK* universidade aberta.
O.PER.A, *s.*, *lt.*, *Mús.*, ópera.
O.PER.A HOUSE, *s.*, teatro lírico.
O.PERA SING.ER, *s.*, cantor lírico.
OP.ER.ANT, *adj.*, operante.
OP.ER.ATE, *v.*, fazer funcionar, colocar em funcionamento, funcionar.
OP.ER.AT.IC, *adj.*, lírico, de ópera.
OP.ER.AT.ING, *s.*, funcionamento; *adj.*, operante, operador.
OP.ER.AT.ING SYS.TEM, *s.*, *Comp.*, sistema operacional.
OP.ER.A.TION, *s.*, operação, funcionamento; cirurgia.
OP.ER.A.TION.AL, *adj.*, operacional.
OP.ER.A.TIVE, *s.*, trabalhador, operário; *US* detetive; *adj.*, vigente, operante, em vigor (lei).
OP.ER.A.TOR, *s.*, operador, operante, manipulador.
OP.ER.ET.TA, *s.*, *lt.*, opereta.
O.PHID.I.A, *s. pl.*, ofídios.
O.PH.THAL.MI.A, *s.*, oftalmologia.
OPH.THAL.MOL.O.GIST, *s.*, oftalmologista.
OPH.THAL.MOL.O.GY, *s.*, oftalmologia.
O.PINE, *v.*, opinar, julgar, dar sugestão.
O.PIN.ION, *s.*, opinião, parecer, julgamento.
O.PIN.ION.AT.ED, *adj.*, teimoso, cabeça-dura.
O.PIN.ION.AT.ED.NESS, *s.*, teimosia, obstinação.
O.PIN.ION FOR.MER, *s.*, formador de opinião.
OPI.UM, *s.*, ópio.
OP.PO.NEN.CY, *s.*, oposição, antagonismo.
OP.PO.NENT, *s.*, oponente, adversário.

OPPORTUNE · · 550 · · ORION

OP.POR.TUNE, *adj.*, oportuno.
OP.POR.TUNE.NESS, *s.*, oportunidade.
OP.POR.TUN.ISM, *s.*, oportunismo.
OP.POR.TUN.IST, *s.*, oportunista.
OP.POR.TU.NI.TY, *s.*, oportunidade.
OP.POSE, *v.*, opor-se, estar contra.
OP.POSED, *adj.*, oposto, contrário.
OP.POS.ER, *s.*, opositor, adversário, antagonista.
OP.POS.ING, *adj.*, oposto, contrário.
OP.PO.SITE, *s.*, oposto, contrário, adversário; *adj.*, oposto, contrário, oponente.
OP.PO.SI.TION, *s.*, oposição.
OP.PRESS, *v.*, oprimir.
OP.PRESSED, *adj.*, oprimido.
OP.PRES.SION, *s.*, opressão.
OP.PRES.SIVE, *adj.*, opressivo, tirânico; sufocante.
OP.PRES.SIVE.NESS, *s.*, opressão, opressividade.
OP.PRES.SOR, *s.*, opressor, carrasco, ditador, tirano.
OP.PRO.BRI.OUS, *adj.*, infamante, humilhante.
OP.PRO.BRI.OUS.NESS, *s.*, opróbrio, vergonha, humilhação.
OP.PRO.BRI.UM, *s.*, opróbrio, vergonha.
OP.PUGN.ANCY, *s.*, oposição, confronto.
OPT, *v.*, optar, escolher.
OP.TA.TIVE, *s.*, *Gram.*, modo optativo; *adj.*, optativo.
OP.TIC, *adj.*, óptico.
OP.TI.CAL, *adj.*, óptico; visual.
OP.TI.CAL FI.BRE *UK*, **OP.TI.CAL FI.BER** *US*, *s.*, *Opt.*, fibra óptica.
OP.TI.CAL READ.ING, *s.*, *Comp.*, leitura óptica.
OP.TI.CIAN, *s.*, oculista.
OP.TICS, *s.*, óptica.
OP.TI.MAL, *adj.*, ideal, favorável, ótimo.
OP.TI.MISM, *s.*, otimismo.
OP.TI.MIST, *s.*, otimista.
OP.TI.MIST.IC, *adj.*, otimista.
OP.TI.MIZE, *v.*, otimizar; ser otimista.
OP.TI.MUM, *adj.*, ótimo.
OPTION, *s.*, opção, direito de optar em um negócio, escolha.
OP.TION.AL, *adj.*, opcional, facultativo.
OP.TOM.E.TRY, *s.*, optometria.
OP.U.LENCE, *s.*, opulência, riqueza, abundância.
OP.U.LENT, *adj.*, opulento, farto, abastado, rico.
OPUS.CULE, *s.*, opúsculo.
OR, *conj.*, ou, senão.
OR.A.CLE, *s.*, oráculo.
O.RAL, *adj.*, oral, falado.
O.RAL.LY, *adv.*, oralmente; por via oral.
ORANG, *s.*, *abrev.*, orangotango.
OR.ANGE, *s.*, laranja; *adj.*, cor de laranja, alaranjado.
OR.ANGE.ADE, *s.*, laranjada.
OR.ANGE-BLOS.SOM, *s.*, flor de laranjeira.
OR.ANGE JUICE, *s.*, suco de laranja.
OR.ANGE.RY, *s.*, laranjal.
OR.ANGE TREE, *s.*, *Bot.*, laranjeira.
O.RANG.U.TAN, *s.*, orangotango.
ORA.TION, *s.*, oração, discurso, alocução.
OR.A.TOR, *s.*, orador.
OR.A.TO.RI.O, *s.*, *Mús., Rel.*, oratório.
OR.A.TO.RY, *s.*, oratório.
ORB, *s.*, esfera, globo; *v.*, tornar esférico.
OR.BIC.U.LAR, *adj.*, orbicular.

OR.BIT, *s.*, órbita; *v.*, orbitar.
OR.BIT.AL, *adj.*, orbital.
ORC, *s.*, *Zool.*, orca.
OR.CHARD, *s.*, pomar, vergel.
OR.CHES.TRA, *s.*, orquestra.
OR.CHES.TRAL, *adj.*, orquestral.
OR.CHES.TRATE, *v.*, orquestrar.
OR.CHES.TRA.TION, *s.*, orquestração, conjunto de instrumentos.
OR.CHID, *s.*, *Bot.*, orquídea.
OR.CHIS, *s.*, orquídea.
OR.DAIN, *v.*, ordenar, comandar, decidir, decretar.
OR.DAIN.ER, *s.*, ordenador, quem decreta.
OR.DEAL, *s.*, provação, ordálio.
OR.DER, *s.*, ordem, encomenda, pedido; *v.*, ordenar, pôr em ordem, arrumar, pedir.
OR.DER.ING, *s.*, disposição.
OR.DER.LI.NESS, *s.*, regularidade, método.
OR.DER.LESS, *adj.*, desorganizado, confuso, embaralhado, desajustado.
OR.DER.LY, *s.*, ordenança, assistente hospitalar; *adj.*, organizado, ordenado.
OR.DI.NAL, *adj.*, ordinal; número ordinal.
OR.DI.NANCE, *s.*, lei, regulamento; ritual; costume.
OR.DI.NAR.I.LY, *adv.*, ordinariamente, comumente.
OR.DI.NARY, *adj.*, ordinário, comum, usual; ordinário, vulgar.
OR.DI.NA.TION, *s.*, ordenação.
ORD.NANCE, *s.*, *Mil.*, arsenal, artilharia.
ORE, *s.*, minério.
OR.GAN, *s.*, órgão.
OR.GAN.IC, *adj.*, orgânico.
OR.GAN.IC.AL.LY, *adv.*, organicamente.
OR.GAN.IC CHEM.IS.TRY, *s.*, química orgânica.
OR.GAN.ISM, *s.*, organismo.
OR.GAN.IST, *s.*, organista.
OR.GA.NI.ZA.TION, *s.*, organização.
OR.GA.NI.ZA.TION.AL, *adj.*, organizacional.
OR.GAN.IZE(-ISE), *v.*, organizar.
OR.GAN.IZED, *adj.*, organizado.
OR.GAN.IZED LA.BOUR, *s.*, mão de obra sindicalizada.
OR.GAN.IZ.ER, *s.*, organizador.
OR.GASM, *s.*, orgasmo.
OR.GY, *s.*, orgia, bacanal.
O.RI.ENT, *s.*, oriente, leste, nascente, levante; *v.*, orientar(-se); encaminhar, guiar; *adj.*, *Lit.*, oriental.
O.RI.ENT, *s.*, Extremo Oriente; *the Orient*: a Ásia ou países do leste da Ásia como China, Japão e Índia.
O.RI.EN.TAL, *v.*, orientar, orientar-se; colocar no rumo, rumar.
O.RI.EN.TATE, *v.*, orientar(-se).
O.RI.EN.TA.TION, *s.*, orientação.
O.RI.FICE, *s.*, buraco, orifício.
OR.I.GA.MI, *s.*, *Jap.*, origami.
OR.I.GIN, *s.*, origem.
O.RIG.I.NAL, *adj.*, original, genuíno.
O.RIG.I.NAL.I.TY, *s.*, originalidade.
O.RIG.I.NAL.LY, *adv.*, originalmente.
O.RIG.I.NAL SIN, *s.*, pecado original.
O.RIG.I.NATE, *v.*, originar-se, surgir, começar, iniciar.
O.RIG.I.NA.TION, *s.*, origem, causa, princípio.
O.RIG.I.NA.TOR, *s.*, originador, causador, autor, criador.
O.RION, *s.*, *Astron., Mit.*, órion.

ORISON ·· 551 ·· OUTLAST

OR.I.SON, s., oração, reza.
OR.NA.MENT, s., ornato, ornamento, enfeite.
OR.NA.MEN.TAL, adj., ornamental, que enfeita.
OR.NA.MEN.TA.TION, s., ornamentação, enfeite.
OR.NATE, adj., ornado, adornado.
OR.NATE.LY, adv., ornadamente, com adornos.
OR.NE.RY, adj., col., genioso, intratável.
OR.NI.THOL.O.GIST, s., ornitólogo, ornitologista.
OR.NI.THOL.O.GY, s., ornitologia.
OR.NI.THO.RHYN.CHUS, s., Zool., ornitorrinco.
OROG.RA.PHY, s., orografia.
O.ROL.O.GY, s., orologia, o mesmo que *orography*.
OR.PHAN, s., órfão.
OR.PHAN.AGE, s., orfanato.
OR.PHAN.HOOD, s., orfandade.
OR.PHE.AN, adj., orfeico; musical.
OR.PHIC., adj., órfico.
OR.RERY, s., planetário.
OR.THO.DON.TI.A, s., ortodontia.
OR.THO.DON.TIST, s., ortodontista.
OR.THO.DOX, adj., s., ortodoxo.
OR.THO.DOXY, s., ortodoxia.
OR.THO.EPY, s., ortoépia.
OR.THO.GRAPH.IC, adj., ortográfico.
OR.THOG.RA.PHY, s., ortografia.
OR.THO.PAE.DIC, adj., ortopédico.
OR.THO.PAE.DICS, s., ortopedia.
OR.THO.PAE.DIST UK, **OR.THO.PE.DIST** US, s., ortopedista.
OR.THO.PAE.DIC UK, **OR.THO.PE.DIC** US, adj., ortopédico.
OS.CIL.LATE, v., oscilar, vacilar, titubear.
OS.CIL.LAT.ING, adj., oscilante, vacilante.
OS.CIL.LA.TION, s., oscilação, vacilação, hesitação.
OS.CIL.LA.TOR, s., oscilador.
OS.CIL.LA.TOR.Y, adj., oscilatório, oscilante.
OS.CIL.LO.SCOPE, s., Eletr., osciloscópio.
OS.CU.LATE, v., oscular, beijar.
OS.CU.LA.TION, s., beijo, osculação.
OS.MO.SIS, s., osmose.
OS.MO.SIS, s., o mesmo que *osmose*.
OS.SE.OUS, adj., ósseo.
OS.SI.FIED, adj., ossificado.
OS.SI.FY, v., ossificar.
OS.SU.ARY, s., ossário.
OS.TEN.SI.BLE, adj., ostensivo.
OS.TEN.SIB.IL.I.TY, s., ostensibilidade.
OS.TEN.SI.BLY, adv., ostensivamente.
OS.TEN.SIVE, adj., o mesmo que *ostensible*.
OS.TEN.TA.TION, s., ostentação, exibição, barulho.
OS.TEN.TA.TIOUS, adj., ostentoso, pomposo.
OS.TEN.TA.TIOUS.NESS, s., pomposidade.
OS.TE.OL.O.GIST, s., osteologista.
OS.TE.OL.O.GY, s., osteologia.
OS.TE.O.PATH, s., osteopata.
OS.TE.OP.A.THY, s., Med., osteopatia (doença nos ossos).
OS.TE.O.PO.RO.SIS, s., Med., osteoporose.
OS.TI.ARY, s., hostiário, local para guardar as hóstias na igreja.
OS.TRA.CISM, s., ostracismo, exílio.
OS.TRA.CIZE, v., exilar, desterrar, condenar ao ostracismo.
OS.TRICH, s., Zool., avestruz.
OTH.ER, adj., pron., outro, outra; outros, outras.

OTH.ER HALF, s., outra metade.
OTH.ER.WISE, adj., diferente; adv., de resto; de outra maneira, por outro lado.
OTH.ER.NESS, s., diversidade.
OTH.ER.WORLD.LY, adj., de outro mundo, sobrenatural, espiritual, místico.
OTI.OSE, adj., ocioso, vadio, malandro.
OTI.OS.I.TY, s., ociosidade.
OT.TER, s., lontra.
OUCH, excl., ai!
OUNCE, s., Zool., onça (felino); onça (medida de peso); fig., an ~ of: um pouco de.
OUR, pron., nosso.
OURS, pron., nosso, nossa, nossos, nossas.
OUR.SELVES, pron. pl., nós, nós mesmos, nós mesmas.
OUST, v., expulsar.
OUST.ER, s., desapropriação.
OUT, s., espaço aberto, local fora; v., expulsar, desligar; adv., fora, para fora.
OUT.AGE, s., Comp., Eletr., interrupção, parada.
OUT-AND-OUT, adj., completo, absoluto.
OUT.BACK, s., interior, cafundó.
OUT.BAL.ANCE, v., predominar, preponderar; exceder (no peso).
OUT.BID, s., Com., lance maior; v., cobrir um lance; sobrepujar.
OUT.BORN, adj., s., nascido no estrangeiro, estrangeiro.
OUT.BOUND, adj., de ida, de saída; Náut., de longo curso.
OUT BOX, s., caixa destinada para enviar; Comp., oubox: caixa de saída (correio eletrônico).
OUT.BREAK, s., deflagração, surto, erupção, eclosão; v., eclodir, irromper.
OUT.BUILD.ING, s., pavilhão, anexo, dependência do prédio principal.
OUT.BURST, s., explosão; acesso (de raiva).
OUT.CAST, s., pária, proscrito, exilado; adj., exilado, desterrado, abandonado.
OUT.CLASS, v., rejeitado, proscrito; adj., exilado, desterrado.
OUT.COME, s., resultado, consequência, efeito.
OUT.CROP, s., Geol., afloramento.
OUT.CRY, s., grito, berro, clamor, tumulto; v., berrar, gritar, exclamar.
OUT.DIS.TANCE, v., deixar para trás; fig., ultrapassar.
OUT.DO, v., ultrapassar, exceder, ir além.
OUT.DOOR, s., cartaz publicitário, outdor; adj., exposto, colocado ao ar livre.
OUT.ER, adj., exterior, externo, fora, ao ar livre.
OUT.ER.MOST, adj., o mais afastado, o mais longe.
OUTER SPACE, s., espaço exterior (interplanetário).
OUTER WEAR, s., roupa de cima; capa de chuva; sobretudo.
OUT.FIT, s., roupa, vestimenta; col., agrupamento, turma.
OUT.FIT.TER, s., confecção de roupas; abastecedor, fornecedor.
OUT.FLANK, v., Mil., flanquear; fig., passar a perna.
OUT.GO.ING, s., partida, saída, eflúvio, despesas.
OUT.GROW, v., crescer em excesso, crescer demais.
OUT.GUARD, s., sentinela, vigilância, guarda avançada.
OUT.HOUSE, s., varanda, anexo externo, alpendre.
OUT.ING, s., passeio, excursão, caminhada.
OUT.LAND, s., estrangeiro, terras estrangeiras, exterior.
OUT.LAND.ER, s., estrangeiro, forasteiro.
OUT.LAST, v., exceder no tempo, ir além do tempo previsto.

OUTLAW   •• 552 ••   OVERCAST

OUT.LAW, s., fora da lei, proscrito, criminoso; v., proscrever, declarar fora da lei.

OUT.LAY, s., despesa, desembolso.

OUT.LET, s., saída, escoamento, posto de vendas; tomada elétrica; v., escoar.

OUT.LINE, s., contorno, esboço, silhueta, sumário; v., esboçar, delinear.

OUT.LIVE, v., sobreviver, subsistir.

OUT.LI.VER, s., sobrevivente.

OUT.LOOK, s., perspectiva, panorama, ponto de vista, previsão.

OUT.LY.ING, adj., remoto, distante, afastado.

OUT.MA.NOEU.VRE UK, **OUT.MA.NEU.VRE** US, v., manobrar melhor que; passar a perna em.

OUT.MOD.ED, adj., afastado, antiquado, obsoleto, arcaico.

OUT.NUM.BER, v., exceder em número.

OUT-OF-DATE, adj., sem validade de data, obsoleto.

OUT-OF-DOORS, adj., ao ar livre, fora, fora de casa.

OUT.PACE, v., sobrepujar, passar de alguém, ultrapassar.

OUT.PASS, v., ultrapassar, exceder.

OUT.PA.TIENT, s., paciente ambulatorial.

OUT.PLACE.MENT, s., Com., recolocação (de emprego).

OUT.PLAY, v., superar; jogar melhor que.

OUT.POST, s., posto avançado, guarita.

OUT.PUT, s., produção, rendimento; saída.

OUTRAGE, s., ultraje, injúria, escândalo, abuso; v., injuriar, ultrapassar, abusar.

OUT.RAGED, adj., indignado, ultrajado; com raiva.

OUT.RA.GEOUS, adj., ultrajante, injurioso, escandaloso, abusivo.

OUT.RANK, v., exceder em hierarquia.

OUT.REACH, v., alcançar, conseguir, passar.

OUT.RID.ER, s., escolta, batedor.

OUT.RIGHT, adj., sincero, franco; adv., completamente, imediatamente.

OUT.ROOT, v., extirpar, erradicar, arrancar.

OUT.RUN, v., correr mais que, ultrapassar, exceder.

OUT.SELL, v., vender mais, vender mais caro.

OUT.SET, s., início, começo, princípio.

OUT.SHINE, v., exceder em brilho, brilhar muito.

OUT.SIDE, s., exterior, aparência; adj., externo, exterior; adv., para fora, sem.

OUT.SID.ER, s., estranho, forasteiro, intruso.

OUT.SIZE, s., tamanho extragrande; adj., enorme, extragrande.

OUT.SIZED, adj., enorme.

OUT.SKIRT, s., limite, margem, borda; outskirts: arredores.

OUT.SMART, v., passar a perna em.

OUT.SOURCE, v., Com., terceirizar.

OUT.SOURC.ING, s., Com., terceirização.

OUT.SPO.KEN, adj., franco, sincero.

OUT.SPREAD, s., expanção; v., expandir(-se), estender; adj., estendido.

OUT.STAND, v., demorar-se, parar.

OUT.STAND.ING, adj., saliente, notável, destado; pendente, a receber.

OUT.STA.TION, s., posto avançado, posto fronteiriço.

OUT.STAY, v., permanecer mais tempo que, abusar da hospitalidade de.

OUT.STRETCHED, adj., estendido, esticado.

OUT.STRIP, v., superar, ultrapassar, tomar a dianteira.

OUT-TAKE, s., sobras de filme ou vídeo recusados na edição final.

OUT.TOP, v., exceder, ir além de, ultrapassar.

OUT-TRAY, s., bandeja de entradas e saídas (em escritório).

OUT.VOTE, v., vencer obtendo mais votos que (outrém).

OUT.WARD, adj., externo, de aparência externa, aparente; adv., do lado de fora, para fora.

OUT.WARD.LY, adv., aparentemente, externamente.

OUT.WARD.NESS, s., exterioridade.

OUT.WARDS, adv., US para fora.

OUT.WEIGH, v., pesar mais que; ter mais valor ou importância que.

OUT.WIT, v., exceder, ser mais esperto, exceder em esperteza.

OUT.WORK, s., fortificação, fortaleza exterior, trabalho externo.

OVAL, adj., oval.

O.VAR.I.AN, adj., do ovário, ovariano.

O.VAR.I.UM, s., ovário, oveiro.

O.VA.RY, s., o mesmo que ovarium.

O.VATE, adj., ovalado, com formato de ovo, oval.

O.VA.TION, s., ovação.

OV.EN, s., forno; v., assar no forno.

OV.EN.BIRD, s., joão-de-barro.

OV.EN.PROOF, adj., refratário, resistente a temperaturas variadas.

OV.EN.WARE, s., louça refratária.

OVER, s., excesso, demasia; adj., excedente; adv., por cima, em cima, demais.

O.VER.A.BUN.DANCE, s., superabundância.

O.VER.A.BUN.DANT, adj., superabundante.

O.VER.ACT, v., fazer com excessivo zelo; Teat., exagerar na atuação.

O.VER.AC.TIVE, adj., muito ativo.

O.VER.ALL, s., adj., total, global; adv., completamente, em toda parte, especialmente.

O.VER.ARM, adj., por cima do ombro, com o braço levantado; adv., por cima do ombro.

O.VER.AWE, v., intimidar, atemorizar, assustar.

O.VER.AWE, v., intimidar.

O.VER.BAL.ANCE, s., preponderância; v., perder o equilíbrio; prevalecer.

O.VER.BEAR, v., sobrepujar, oprimir, vencer.

O.VER.BEAR.ING, adj., autoritário, mandão, dominador, categórico.

O.VER.BOARD, adv., ao mar; to fall ~ : cair ao mar.

O.VER.BOIL, v., ferver demais, cozinhar muito, exceder no cozimento.

O.VER.BOOK, s., excesso de reservas; v., ter mais reservas que lugares.

O.VER.BUILD, v., construir além do necessário, superlotar de construções; construir sobre.

O.VER.BRIM, v., transbordar, vazar.

O.VER.BUR.DEN, s., sobrecarga; v., sobrecarregar.

OVER.BUSY, adj., demasiadamente ocupado, muito ocupado.

O.VER.CAME, v., pp de overcome: superou, conquistou.

O.VER.CAP.I.TAL.IZE(-ISE), v., sobrecapitalizar.

O.VER.CARE, s., solicitude, cuidado.

O.VER.CARE.FUL, adj., cuidadoso, solícito, cuidadoso em excesso.

O.VER.CAST, v., obscurecer, toldar, entristecer; adj., nublado, toldado.

OVERCHARGE ··553·· OVERSTOCK

O.VER.CHARGE, *s.*, sobrecarga, preço alto; *v.*, sobrecarregar, cobrar demais.

O.VER.COAT, *s.*, sobretudo.

O.VER.COME, *v.*, superar, sobrepujar, dominar.

O.VER.CON.FI.DENT, *adj.*, confiante em excesso.

O.VER.COOK.ED, *adj.*, cozido em demasia.

O.VER.CROWD, *v.*, abarrotar, superlotar.

O.VER.CROWD.ING, *s.*, superlotação, superpovoação.

O.VER.DO, *v.*, abusar, exagerar; cozinhar demasiadamente.

O.VER.DONE, *adj.*, passado do ponto; cozido demais; exagerado; *v.*, *pp* de *overdo*.

O.VER.DOSE, *s.*, overdose, dose excessiva.

O.VER.DRAFT, *s.*, saldo bancário negativo.

O.VER.DRAW, *v.*, *Com.*, ficar no negativo; exagerar (no gasto).

O.VER.DUE, *adj.*, atrasado, tardio, demorado.

O.VER.EA.GER, *adj.*, ansioso demais.

O.VER EA.SY, *adj.*, *Cul.*, *US* diz-se de ovos fritos dos dois lados.

O.VER.EAT, *v.*, comer em excesso, comer demais.

O.VER.EM.PHA.SIZE(-ISE), *v.*, enfatizar demais.

O.VER.ES.TI.MATE, *v.*, estimar em demasia, preferir a tudo.

O.VER.EX.CITE, *v.*, superexcitar; superexaltar.

O.VER.EX.POSE, *v.*, *Fot.*, superexpor.

O.VER.FALL, *s.*, queda-d'água, cachoeira.

O.VER.FEED, *v.*, saciar, saturar, encher.

O.VER.FILL, *v.*, encher demais.

O.VER.FLOW, *s.*, inundação, transbordamento; *v.*, transbordar, inundar.

O.VER.FLY, *v.*, voar sobre, voar por cima.

O.VER.GROW, *v.*, cobrir com vegetação, crescer muito.

O.VER.GROWN, *adj.*, coberto de vegetação.

O.VER.GROWTH, *s.*, vegetação viçosa.

O.VER.HAND, *s.*, superioridade, supremacia.

O.VER.HANG, *s.*, projeção, saliência; *v.*, pender, projetar-se, estender-se sobre.

O.VER.HAUL, *s.*, revisão, vistoria; *v.*, inspecionar, vistoriar, revisar.

O.VER.HEAD, *s.*, despesas; *adj.*, na parte de cima, aéreo; *adv.*, por cima, em cima.

O.VER.HEAR, *v.*, ouvir por acaso, escutar, entreouvir.

O.VER.HEAT, *v.*, aquecer demais, esquentar em excesso.

O.VER.HOUR, *s.*, hora extra no trabalho.

O.VER.JOY, *s.*, arrebatamento, grande alegria; *v.*, dar uma grande alegria.

O.VER.JOYED, *adj.*, supercontente; cheio de alegria.

O.VER.KILL, *s.*, *Mil.*, poder arrasador (em massa); *v.*, destruir com força desproporcional.

O.VER.LADE, *v.*, sobrecarregar.

O.VER.LAND, *adj.*, *adv.*, por terra,por via terrestre.

O.VER.LAP, *s.*, superposição; coincidência; *v.*, sobrepor, justapor; coincidir; envolver.

O.VER.LAY, *s.*, revestimento, capa, cobertura, colcha; *v.*, cobrir, revestir.

O.VER.LAY.ING, *s.*, cobertura, revestimento, camada.

O.VER.LEAF, *adv.*, no verso, atrás.

O.VER.LEAP, *v.*, saltar por cima, omitir, deixar de lado.

O.VER.LOAD, *s.*, sobrecarga; *v.*, sobrecarregar.

O.VER.LONG, *adj.*, *adv.*, longo demais; demorado demais.

O.VER.LOOK, *s.*, ato de olhar; omissão; *v.*, contemplar, admirar, olhar.

O.VER.LORD, *s.*, *Lit.*, senhor supremo; *v.*, reger, dominar.

O.VER.LY, *adv.*, excessivamente, demais.

O.VER.MAN, *s.*, inspetor.

O.VER.MAN.NING, *s.*, excesso de mão de obra.

O.VER.MAS.TER, *v.*, dominar, subjugar, conter.

O.VER.MUCH, *adj.*, demasiado; *adv.*, demasiadamente.

O.VER.NIGHT, *s.*, a tarde do dia anterior; *adj.*, noturno; que dura um pernoite; *adv.*, da noite para o dia.

O.VER.PAID, *v.*, *pp* de *overpay*; *adj.*, pago em excesso.

O.VER.PASS, *s.*, viaduto, passagem elevada; *v.*, transpor, passar por cima, vencer.

O.VER.PAST, *adj.*, passado, superado, transposto.

O.VER.PAY, *v.*, pagar em excesso, pagar a mais.

O.VER.PLAY, *v.*, exagerar; suprepujar, vencer; representar melhor que; fazer melhor do que é realmente.

O.VER.PLUS, *s.*, excedente, sobra, demasia, excesso.

O.VER.POP.U.LATE, *v.*, superpovoar.

O.VER.POP.U.LATION, *s.*, superpopulação.

O.VER.POW.ER, *s.*, excesso de força, domínio; *v.*, dominar, subjugar, vencer.

O.VER.POW.ER.ING, *adj.*, dominante, sufocante, opressor; irresistível, esmagador.

O.VER.PRESS, *v.*, oprimir, perseguir, castigar.

O.VER.PRICED, *adj.*, muito caro.

O.VER.PRO.TEC.TIVE, *adj.*, superprotetor.

O.VER.PRO.DUC.TION, *s.*, superprodução, produção excessiva.

O.VER.RATE, *v.*, superestimar, estimar em demasia.

O.VER.RATED, *adj.*, superestimado.

O.VER.REACH, *s.*, embuste, fraude; *v.*, ir longe demais, dar o passo maior que a perna.

O.VER.RE.ACT, *v.*, reagir exageradamente.

O.VER.RIDE, *v.*, dominar, sobrepujar; passar por cima.

O.VER.RID.ING, *adj.*, predominante.

O.VER.RIPE, *adj.*, maduro demais.

O.VER.RULE, *v.*, negar, indeferir, desconsiderar, desautorizar.

O.VER.RUN.NING, *s.*, invasão.

O.VER.SEA, *adj.*, ultramarino, além-mar, transatlântico.

O.VER.SEE, *v.*, inspecionar, vistoriar, vigiar, rever.

O.VER.SEER, *s.*, inspetor, vistoriador.

O.VER.SHADE, *v.*, escurecer, nublar, sombrear.

O.VER.SHAD.OW, *v.*, escurecer, sombrear, ofuscar.

O.VER.SHOOT, *v.*, *ps* e *pp* de *overshot*; passar por cima; exceder o alvo; *fig.*, passar do limite.

O.VER.SHOT, *adj.*, ultrapassado, excedido; *col.*, bêbado.

O.VER.SIGHT, *s.*, deslize, descuido; chefia, superintendência.

O.VER.SIM.PLI.FI.CA.TION, *s.*, simplificação excessiva.

O.VER.SIM.PLI.FY, *v.*, simplificar demais.

O.VER.SKIRT, *s.*, sobressaia.

O.VER.SLEEP, *v.*, dormir em excesso, dormir demais, dormir além da hora.

O.VER.SNOW, *v.*, cobrir com neve, nevar muito.

O.VER.SPEND, *v.*, gastar além da conta; torrar, exaurir (recursos).

O.VER.SPILL, *s.*, *UK* excesso de população.

O.VER.SPREAD, *v.*, espalhar, espargir, estender.

O.VER.STAFFED, *adj.*, com excesso de funcionários.

O.VER.STATE, *v.*, exagerar, sair dos limites.

O.VER.STAY, *v.*, ficar tempo demais; abusar da hospitalidade.

O.VER.STEP, *v.*, ultrapassar, exceder, passar por cima de.

O.VER.STOCK, *s.*, estoque excessivo; *v.*, abarrotar, acumular, encher demais.

OVERSUPPLY ··554·· OZONE LAYER

O.VER.SUP.PLY, *s.*, abundância, copiosidade.

O.VERT, *adj.*, aberto, público, manifesto.

O.VER.TAKE, *v.*, ultrapassar, passar além de.

O.VER.TAX, *v.*, exagerar nos impostos, sobrecarregar nos impostos.

O.VER.THROW, *s.*, deposição, destituição; *v.*, depor, destituir, derrubar; subverter, destruir.

O.VER.TIME, *s.*, horas extras, serão; *v.*, passar do tempo.

O.VER.TLY, *adv.*, abertamente, publicamente.

O.VER.TONES, *s. pl.*, insinuações.

O.VER.TOP, *v.*, exceder, dominar, subjugar.

O.VER.TURE, *s.*, abertura de uma música.

O.VER.TURN, *s.*, transtorno, reviravolta; *v.*, virar, derrubar, anular, aniquilar.

O.VER.USE, *s.*, uso demasiado; *v.*, usar demais.

O.VER.VAL.UE, *v.*, encarecer, exagerar o preço, cobrar valor exagerado.

O.VER.WEIGHT, *s.*, sobrepeso, peso excessivo; *v.*, pesar em excesso, pesar muito.

O.VER.VIEW, *s.*, visão geral, resumo.

O.VER.WEEN.ING, *adj.*, desmedido, presunçoso, arrogante.

O.VER.WHELM, *v.*, esmagar, oprimir, subjugar; inundar.

O.VER.WHELM.ING, *adj.*, opressivo, impressionante, esmagador.

O.VER.WHELM.ING.LY, *adv.*, opressivamente, esmagadoramente.

O.VER.WORK, *s.*, trabalho extra; *v.*, trabalhar em excesso, exagerar no trabalho.

O.VER.WORN, *adj.*, gasto pelo trabalho.

O.VER.WROUGHT, *adj.*, extenuado; muito nervoso; esmerado, elaborado.

O.VI.FORM, *adj.*, oviforme, oval.

O.VINE, *adj.*, ovino.

O.VIP.A.ROUS, *adj.*, ovíparo.

OV.U.LATE, *v.*, *Biol.*, ovular; *adj.*, ovulado.

O.VU.LA.TION, *s.*, *Biol.*, ovulação.

O.VULE, *s.*, óvulo.

OWE, *v.*, dever a alguém, ter dívidas.

OW.ING, *adj.*, devido; *owing to*, *prep.*: devido a.

OWL, *s.*, coruja, mocho.

OWN, *v.*, ter, possuir, reconhecer, confessar.

OWN.ER, *s.*, dono, possuidor, proprietário.

OWN.ER-OC.CU.PI.ER, *s.*, *UK* proprietário de casa ou apartamento onde mora.

OWN.ER.SHIP, *s.*, posse, propriedade.

OWN GOAL, *s.*, *Esp.*, gol contra (futebol).

OX, *s.*, boi.

OX.CART, *s.*, carro de boi.

OX.EN, *s.*, bois.

OX.EYE, *s.*, olho de boi.

OX.ID, *s.*, *Quím.*, óxido.

OX.ID.A.BLE, *adj.*, oxidável.

OX.I.DANT, *s.*, oxidante.

OX.I.DATE, *v.*, oxidar.

OX.I.DA.TION, *s.*, oxidação.

OX.IDE, *s.*, o mesmo que *oxid*.

OX.I.DIZE, *v.*, oxidar.

OX.MAN, *s.*, boiadeiro, vaqueiro.

OX.TAIL, *s.*, rabo de boi; *Cul.*, rabada.

OX.TAIL SOUP, *s.*, *Cul.*, rabada.

OX.Y.GEN, *s.*, *Quím.*, oxigênio (elem. de nº atômico 8).

OX.Y.GEN.ATE, *v.*, oxigenar.

OX.Y.GEN.A.TION, *s.*, oxigenação.

OX.Y.GEN.AT.ED-WA.TER, *s.*, água oxigenada.

OX.Y.GEN.IZ.A.BLE, *adj.*, oxigenável.

OX.Y.GEN MASK, *s.*, máscara de oxigênio.

OXY.TONE, *s.*, *Gram.*, oxítono.

OY.ER, *s.*, audiência.

OYS.TER, *s.*, ostra.

O.ZONE, *s.*, *Quím.*, ozônio.

O.ZONE LAY.ER, *s.*, camada de ozônio.

P, décima sexta letra do alfabeto inglês; *abrev.* de penny, pence.
PA, *s.*, papá, papai.
PAB.U.LUM, *s.*, sustento, pasto, alimento.
PA.CA, *s.*, *Zool.*, paca.
PACE, *s.*, passo, passada, medida, movimento; *v.*, andar a passo; compassar.
PACED, *adj.*, de passo.
PACE-MAK.ER, *s.*, *Med.*, marca-passo; *Esp.*, atleta que estabelece o ritmo da corrida.
PACE-SET.TER, *s.*, *US* atleta que regula o ritmo da corrida.
PACH.Y.DERM, *s.*, *Zool.*, paquiderme.
PACH.Y.DER.MI.A, *s.*, *Med.*, paquidermia.
PA.CIF.IC, *adj.*, pacífico, calmo, tranquilo, sossegado; *The ~ Ocean*: Oceano Pacífico.
PAC.I.FI.CA.TION, *s.*, pacificação.
PAC.I.FI.ER, *s.*, pacificador.
PAC.I.FISM, *s.*, pacifismo.
PAC.I.FIST, *s.*, pacifista.
PAC.I.FY, *v.*, pacificar, acalmar.
PACK, *s.*, bando, matilha; pacote, carga, fardo, mochila; encher, arrumar a mala.
PACK.AGE, *s.*, pacote, embrulho, fardo; *v.*, acondicionar, empacotar, enfardar.
PACK.AGE TOUR, *s.*, pacote de viagem turística.
PACK.AG.ING, *s.*, embalagem.
PACKED, *adj.*, lotado, cheio, repleto.
PACKED LUNCH, *s.*, almoço levado em marmita, merenda.
PACKED OUT, *adj.*, *col.*, *UK* apinhado.
PACK.ER, *s.*, enfardador, empacotador.
PACK.ET, *s.*, pacote, maço de cigarros.
PACK-HORSE, *s.*, cavalo de carga.
PACK ICE, *s.*, banquisa, massa de gelo flutuante.
PACK.ING, *s.*, embalagem, empacotamento.
PACK.ING CASE, *s.*, engradado ou caixote de embalagem.
PACT, *s.*, pacto, tratado, ajuste, aliança, convenção.
PAD, *s.*, almofada, enchimento, bloco para notas; *v.*, acolchoar, encher.
PAD.DED, *adj.*, revestido, forrado, acolchoado.
PAD.DED CELL, *s.*, cela acolchoada (para perturbados).
PAD.DING, *s.*, revestimento, acolchoamento, enchimento.
PAD.DLE, *s.*, remo; ato de patinhar (na água); *v.*, remar; patinhar, chapinhar.
PAD.DLER, *s.*, remador.
PAD.DLING POOL, *s.*, piscina infantil (para a criança chapinhar).
PAD.DOCK, *s.*, recinto fechado nos hipódromos, cercado.
PAD.DY, *s.*, arros com casca, arrozal.
PAD.DY FIELD, *s.*, arrozal.
PAD.DY WAG.ON, *s.*, *col.*, camburão; *col.*, *UK* tintureiro.
PAD.LOCK, *s.*, cadeado.
PAE.DI.AT.RICS *UK*, **PE.DI.AT.RICS** *US*, *s.*, pediatria.
PAE.DO.PHILE *UK*, **PE.DO.PHILE** *US*, *s.*, pedófilo.
PA.EL.LA, *s.*, *Es.*, paella.
PA.GAN, *adj.*, *s.*, pagão.
PA.GAN.ISM, *s.*, paganismo.
PA.GAN.IZE, *v.*, paganizar.
PAGE, *s.*, página, trecho, passagem; *v.*, paginar, mandar chamar.
PAG.EANT, *s.*, desfile com pompa, cortejo cívico.
PAG.EAN.TRY, *s.*, fausto, esplendor, pompa.
PAGE.BOY, *s.*, pagem; penteado feminino em estilo francês (tipo chanel).
PAG.ER, *s.*, paginador; pager (aparelho eletrônico de mensagens).
PAG.I.NATE, *v.*, paginar, folhear.
PAG.I.NA.TION, *s.*, paginação.
PAG.ING, *s.*, paginação.
PA.GO.DA, *s.*, pagode (templo pagão).
PAID, *adj.*, remunerado, pago.
PAIL, *s.*, balde.
PAIN, *s.*, dor, sofrimento, tormento; *v.*, atormentar, afligir, magoar, causar dor.
PAINED, *adj.*, aflito, atormentado, consternado.
PAIN.FUL, *adj.*, doloroso, aflitivo, magoado.
PAIN.FUL.LY, *adv.*, dolorosamente.
PAIN.KIL.LER, *s.*, analgésico, calmante.
PAIN.LESS, *adj.*, indolor, sem dor.
PAIN.LESS.LY, *adv.*, de forma indolor.
PAINS.TAK.ING, *s.*, esmero, apuro, diligência; *adj.*, esmerado, minucioso; assíduo.
PAINS.TAK.ING.LY, *adv.*, meticulosamente, esmeradamente.
PAINT, *s.*, pintura, tinta; *v.*, pintar.
PAINT.BOX, *s.*, estojo de tintas; estojo para maquiagem.
PAINT.BRUSH, *s.*, pincel, broxa.
PAINT.ED, *adj.*, pintado.
PAINT.ER, *s.*, pintor, pintor de paredes.
PAINT.ING, *s.*, pintura, tela, quadro.
PAINT STRIP.PER, *s.*, removedor de tinta.
PAINT-WORK, *s.*, pintura.
PAINT.Y, *adj.*, sujo de tinta, manchado de tinta.
PAIR, *s.*, par, dupla, parelha, casal; *v.*, emparelhar, juntar, unir.
PA.JA.MAS, *s.*, pijama.
PA.KI.STAN, *s.*, Paquistão.
PA.KI.STANI, *adj.*, *s.*, paquistanês.
PAL, *s.*, colega, camarada, companheiro.
PAL.ACE, *s.*, palácio.
PA.LAE.OG.RA.PHY *UK*, **PA.LE.OG.RA.PHY** *US*, *s.*, paleografia.
PA.LAE.ON.TOL.O.GY *UK*, **PA.LE.ON.TOL.O.GY** *US*, *s.*, paleontologia.
PAL.AT.ABLE, *adj.*, palatável, saboroso, gostoso.
PAL.A.TAL, *adj.*, *s.*, palatal.
PAL.ATE, *s.*, *Anat.*, palato.

PALATIAL •• 556 •• PARABLE

PA.LA.TIAL, *adj.*, palaciano; *fig.*, suntuoso.
PA.LAV.ER, *s.*, debate; palavreado, balbúrdia; *v.*, palavrear.
PALE, *adj.*, pálido, fraco, claro; *v.*, empalidecer.
PALE ALE, *s.*, cerveja clara.
PALE.NESS, *s.*, palidez.
PA.LE.O.CENE, *adj.*, *Geol.*, paleoceno.
PA.LE.OG.RA.PHY, *s.*, *US* paleografia.
PA.LE.O.LITH.IC, *adj.*, *Geol.*, paleolítico.
PA.LE.OL.O.GY, *s.*, paleologia.
PA.LE.ON.TOL.O.GY *US*, *s.*, paleontologia.
PA.LE.O.ZO.IC, *s.*, *Geol.*, Era Paleozoica; *adj.*, paleozoico.
PAL.ES.TINE, *s.*, Palestina.
PAL.ES.TIN.IAN, *adj.*, *s.*, palestino.
PAL.ETTE, *s.*, paleta; conjunto de cores usado por artista.
PAL.ETTE KNIFE, *s.*, espátula de pintor.
PAL.IN.DROME, *s.*, palíndromo.
PAL.ING, *s.*, paliçada.
PALL, *s.*, mortalha, pálio; *US* caixão (defunto); *fig.*, cortina (fumaça); *v.*, cobrir com mortalha; enfraquecer.
PALL.BEAR.ER, *s.*, carregador do caixão funerário.
PAL.LI.A.TIVE, *adj.*, *s.*, paliativo.
PAL.LID, *adj.*, pálido, descorado, empalidecido.
PAL.LOR, *s.*, palidez, palor.
PALM, *s.*, palma, palma da mão, palmeira; *v.*, empalmar; trapacear, fraudar.
PAL.MATE, *adj.*, espalmado.
PALM.IST.RY, *s.*, quiromancia.
PALM OIL, *s.*, azeite de dendê.
PALM SUN.DAY, *s.*, Domingo de Ramos.
PALM TREE, *s.*, *Bot.*, palmeira.
PALMY, *adj.*, palmífero, florescente, próspero.
PALP, *v.*, apalpar.
PAL.PA.BLE, *adj.*, palpável.
PAL.PA.BLY, *adv.*, palpavelmente, obviamente.
PAL.PATE, *v.*, apalpar.
PAL.PI.TATE, *v.*, palpitar.
PAL.PI.TA.TION, *s.*, palpitação; *palpitations*, *s.pl.*, palpitações.
PAL.SY, *s.*, *Med.*, paralisia; entorpecimento, marasmo.
PAL.TER, *v.*, simular, enganar, barganhar, lograr.
PAL.TRY, *adj.*, irrisório, ridículo; vil, torpe.
PAM.PAS, *s. pl.*, pampas; *adj.*, relativo aos pampas.
PAM.PAS-GRASS, *s.*, *Bot.*, capim-dos-pampas.
PAM.PER, *v.*, mimar, acarinhar.
PAM.PHLET, *s.*, panfleto.
PAM.PHLET.EER, *s.*, panfletário.
PAN, *s.*, frigideira, caçarola, prato, tacho, tina; *v.*, garimpar, fritar, criticar.
PAN.A.CEA, *s.*, panaceia.
PA.NACHE, *s.*, penacho; *fig.*, bravata, elã.
PAN.A.MA, *s.*, panamá (tipo de chapéu).
PAN-A.MER.I.CAN, *adj.*, pan-americano.
PAN.CAKE, *s.*, panqueca.
PAN.CAKE DAY, *s.*, dia da panqueca; Terça-feira de Carnaval.
PAN.CAKE ROLL, *s.*, *Cul.*, rolinho primavera.
PAN.CRE.AS, *s.*, *Anat.*, pâncreas.
PAN.DA, *s.*, *Zool.*, panda, urso panda.
PAN.DA CAR, *s.*, *UK* patrulha policial.
PAN.DECT, *s.*, tratado, acordo, ajuste, acerto.
PAN.DE.MI.A, *s.*, *Med.*, pandemia.

PAN.DE.MO.NI.UM, *s.*, pandemônio.
PAN.DE.MY, *s.*, *Med.*, pandemia
PAN.DER, *s.*, alcoviteiro.
PANE, *s.*, vidraça, vidro, chapa, almofada; *v.*, envidraçar, forrar com madeira.
PANED, *adj.*, envidraçado; almofadado.
PAN.EL, *s.*, painel, almofada, barra.
PAN.FUL, *s.*, panelada, panela cheia.
PANG, *s.*, dor repentina; aflição, ânsia, acesso (de culpa, de fome).
PAN.IC, *s.*, pânico, temor; *v.*, temer, entrar em pânico.
PAN.ICK.Y, *adj.*, amedrontado; aterrorizante.
PAN.IC-STRICK.EN, *adj.*, em pânico, apavorado.
PAN.NIER, *s.*, alforge, cesto, paneiro.
PAN.NI.KIN, *s.*, panelinha, copo de metal.
PAN.O.PLY, *s.*, *Hist.*, panóplia.
PAN.O.RAMA, *s.*, panorama.
PAN.O.RA.MIC, *adj.*, panorâmico.
PA.NSY, *s.*, amor-perfeito.
PANT, *s.*, arquejo, palpitação; *v.*, arquejar, palpitar, latejar, almejar.
PAN.THE.ISM, *s.*, panteísmo.
PAN.THE.IST, *s.*, panteísta.
PAN.THER, *s.*, *Zool.*, pantera.
PANT.IES, *s. pl.*, cuecas, calcinhas.
PAN.TO, *s.*, *col.*, o mesmo que *pantomime*.
PAN.TO.FLE, *s.*, pantufa, chinelo.
PAN.TO.MIME, *s.*, pantomima; *v.*, fazer pantomima.
PAN.TO.GRAPH, *s.*, pantógrafo.
PAN.TRY, *s.*, despensa, copa.
PANTS, *s.*, cuecas, ceroulas.
PANTY, *s.*, cueca, calcinha.
PANT.Y.HOSE, *s.*, meia-calça.
PAP, *s.*, papa, mingau.
PA.PA, *s.*, papai.
PA.PA.CY, *s.*, papado; governo papal.
PA.PAL, *adj.*, papal.
PAP.A.RAZ.ZO, *s.*, *It.*, fotógrafo *free lancer*.
PA.PA.YA, *s.*, *Es.*, *Bot.*, mamoeiro; mamão.
PA.PER, *s.*, papel, jornal, pedaço de papel; artigo; *v.*, revestir com papel.
PA.PER.BACK, *s.*, brochura, livro não encadernado.
PA.PER BAG, *s.*, saquinho de papel.
PA.PER.BOARD, *s.*, papelão, papel grosso.
PA.PER.BOY, *s.*, jornaleiro.
PA.PER CLIP, *s.*, clipe para papel.
PA.PER CUT.TER, *s.*, guilhotina, máquina para cortar papel.
PA.PER HAND.KER.CHIEF, *s.*, lenço de papel.
PA.PER KNIFE, *s.*, espátula, abridor de cartas.
PA.PER-MON.EY, *s.*, papel-moeda.
PA.PER SHOP, *s.*, banca de revistas e jornais.
PA.PER.WEIGHT, *s.*, peso para papéis.
PA.PER.WORK, *s.*, papelada; registro de dados.
PA.PIST, *s.*, *pej.*, papista; *adj.*, papista.
PA.PRI.KA, *s.*, páprica, pimentão doce.
PA.PUA, *s.*, Papua.
PAP.U.AN, *s.*, *adj.*, papua.
PA.PUA NEW GUIN.EA, *s.*, Papua Nova Guiné.
PAR, *s.*, paridade, igualdade; *v.*, colocar a par.
PAR.A, *s.*, *col.*, o mesmo que *paratrooper*.
PAR.A.BLE, *s.*, parábola, alegoria.

PARABOLA · 557 · PAROLE

PA.RAB.O.LA, s., parábola, figura matemática.
PAR.A.BOL.IC, adj., parabólico.
PARA.CHUTE, s., paraquedas.
PARA.CHUT.IST, s., paraquedista.
PA.RADE, s., parada, desfile, ostentação, passeata; v., ostentar, desfilar, mostrar.
PAR.A.DIGM, s., paradigma, modelo, padrão, exemplar.
PAR.A.DIG.MAT.IC, adj., paradigmático.
PAR.A.DISE, s., paraíso, éden, local agradável; felicidade.
PAR.A.DIS.IC, adj., paradisíaco.
PAR.A.DOX, s., paradoxo; v., exprimir-se por paradoxos.
PAR.A.DOX.I.CAL, adj., paradoxal.
PAR.A.DOX.I.CAL.LY, adv., paradoxalmente.
PAR.AF.FIN, s., parafina.
PAR.AF.FIN OIL, s., querosene.
PAR.AF.FIN WAX, s., parafina.
PAR.A.GLID.ING, s., voo de parapente.
PAR.A.GON, s., modelo, padrão, protótipo; v., comparar.
PAR.A.GRAPH, s., parágrafo.
PAR.A.GUAY, s., Paraguai.
PAR.A.GUAY.AN, s., adj., paraguaio.
PAR.A.KEET, s., periquito.
PAR.AL.LAX, s., Astron., paralaxe.
PAR.AL.LEL, s., paralelo, linha paralela, analogia, correspondência; v., comparar.
PAR.AL.LEL BARS, s. pl., Esp., barras paralelas (ginástica olímpica).
PAR.AL.LEL.E.PI.PED, s., paralelepípedo.
PAR.A.LYZE(-YSE), v., paralisar, entorpecer, parar.
PAR.A.LYZED(-YSED), adj., Med., paralizado; col., muito ébrio.
PA.RAL.Y.SIS, s., paralisia.
PAR.A.LYT.IC, adj., s., paralítico.
PAR.A.MED.IC, s., paramédico, socorrista (usa-se também *paramedics*).
PAR.A.MED.I.CAL, adj., paramédico.
PA.RAM.E.TER, s., parâmetro.
PAR.A.MIL.I.TAR.Y, adj., paramilitar.
PAR.A.MOUNT, s., chefe máximo; adj., vital, fundamental; soberano, superior, supremo.
PARA.NOIA, s., paranoia.
PAR.A.NOI.AC, s., adj., paranoico.
PAR.A.NOID, adj., paranoico, desconfiado.
PAR.A.NOR.MAL, adj., Psic., paranormal.
PARA.NYMPH, s., paraninfo, padrinho.
PAR.A.PET, s., parapeito.
PAR.A.PHER.NA.LIA, s., parafernália.
PARA.PHRASE, s., paráfrase; v., parafrasear.
PARA.PLE.GIA, s., paraplegia.
PARA.PLE.GIC, adj., paraplégico.
PARA.PSY.CHOL.O.GY, s., parapsicologia.
PAR.AS.CEND.ING, s., voo de parapente.
PAR.A.SITE, s., parasita.
PAR.A.SIT.IC, adj., parasita, parasítico, parasitário.
PAR.A.SOL, s., guarda-sol, guarda-chuva, sombrinha.
PARA.TROOP.ER, s., paraquedista (do exército).
PAR.BOIL, v., cozer de leve, cozinhar um pouco.
PAR.CEL, s., parcela, quantia, pacote, embrulho; pedaço; v., embrulhar, lotear.
PAR.CEL.ING *US*, **PAR.CEL.LING** *UK*, s., parcelamento; *UK* loteamento.
PAR.CEL POST, s., serviço de encomenda postal.

PAR.CE.NARY, s., herança.
PARCH, v., tostar, secar, ressecar.
PARCHED, adj., seco, ressecado, crestado.
PARCH.MENT, s., pergaminho.
PARCH.ING, adj., abrasador.
PARD, s., leopardo.
PAR.DON, s., perdão, indulto, indulgência; v., perdoar, desculpar, absolver.
PAR.DON.ABLE, adj., perdoável.
PAR.DON.ING, adj., indulgente, generoso.
PARE, v., aparar, desbastar, cortar, podar.
PAR.ENT, s., parente, pai ou mãe; *parents*: pais.
PAR.ENT.AGE, s., parentesco, parentela, família.
PA.REN.TAL, adj., dos pais, paterno, parental.
PA.REN.TAL.LY, adv., paternalmente.
PA.RENT COM.PA.NY, s., o mesmo que *parenthouse*: matriz.
PA.REN.THET.IC(-ICAL), adj., parentético; episódico; entre parênteses.
PA.REN.THE.SIS, s., parêntese.
PAR.ENT.HOOD, s., paternidade, maternidade.
PAR.ENT.HOUSE, s., Com., matriz, sede.
PAR.ENT.ING, s., cuidado dos pais.
PAR.ENT.LESS, adj., órfão, que perdeu os pais.
PA.RI.AH, s., pária.
PA.RI.E.TAL, s., parietal.
PAR.ING, s., poda, desbaste.
PAR.INGS, s., aparas; pele, casca.
PAR.ISH, s., paróquia; adj., paroquial.
PAR.ISH COUN.CIL, s., junta paroquial; *UK* conselho distrital.
PA.RISH.ION.ER, s., paroquiano.
PAR.ISH PRIEST, s., pároco.
PA.RI.SIAN, adj., s., parisiense.
PAR.I.TY, s., paridade, igualdade.
PARK, s., parque; estacionamento; v., estacionar, transformar em parque.
PARK.ING, s., estacionamento, local para estacionamento.
PARK.ING ME.TER, s., parquímetro.
PARK.ING-PLACE, s., vaga de estacionamento.
PARK.ING TICK.ET, s., multa por estacionamento proibido.
PAR.KIN.SON'S DIS.EASE, s., Med., mal de Parkinson.
PARK.LAND, s., parque, área do parque (com árvores e gramado).
PARK.WAY, s., avenida ampla e arborizada, alameda.
PARK.Y, adj., col., *UK* frio, fresco.
PAR.LANCE, s., conversação, linguajar, modo de falar.
PAR.LEY, s., parlamentação, discussão; v., parlamentar, conferenciar, discutir.
PAR.LIA.MENT, s., parlamento.
PAR.LIA.MEN.TAR.I.AN, s., parlamentar.
PAR.LIA.MEN.TAR.ISM, s., parlamentarismo.
PAR.LIA.MEN.TA.RY, s., parlamentar.
PARL.ING, s., conferência, debate, discussão.
PAR.LOR, PAR.LOUR, s., sala de visitas; gabinete, saleta.
PAR.LOUS, adj., precário, arriscado, perigoso.
PAR.ME.SAN (CHEESE), s., queijo tipo parmesão.
PAR.NAS.SI.AN, adj., s., parnasiano.
PA.RO.CHI.AL, adj., interiorano, provincial; paroquial.
PA.RO.CHI.AL SCHOOL, s., *US* escola paroquial.
PAR.O.DY, s., paródia; v., parodiar.
PA.ROLE, s., palavra, promessa oral, senha; juramento; liberar mediante palavra.

PARONYM ·· 558 ·· PATENTED

PAR.O.NYM, s., Gram., cognato, parônimo.
PAR.OX.YSM, s., paroxismo.
PAR.OX.Y.TONE, s., paroxítono.
PAR.QUET, s., parquê, assoalho de tacos, taco; v., revestir com tacos.
PAR.RI.CIDE, s., parricida; parricídio.
PAR.ROT, s., Zool., papagaio.
PAR.ROT FASH.ION, adj., como papagaio; adv., de modo mecânico, como papagaio.
PAR.RY, v., desviar ou aparar (golpes); esquivar-se, evitar.
PARSE, v., analisar gramaticalmente, analisar.
PAR.SI.MO.NI.OUS, adj., parcimonioso, simples, frugal, avarento, avaro.
PAR.SI.MO.NY, s., parcimônia, poupança, economia.
PARS.ING, s., análise gramatical.
PARS.LEY, s., salsa.
PAR.SON, s., pároco, padre, clérigo, pastor, vigário.
PART, s., parte, parcela, porção, cena, capítulo, divisão; v., dividir, partir, separar.
PART.AGE, s., partilha, divisão.
PAR.TAKE, v., partilhar, participar, compartilhar.
PAR.TAK.ER, s., participante, apaniguado, cúmplice.
PAR.TAK.ING, s., participação.
PAR.TIAL, adj., parcial, faccioso, fracionário.
PAR.TIAL.I.TY, s., parcialidade.
PAR.TIAL.LY, adv., parcialmente.
PAR.TIAL.LY SIGHT.ED, adj., com visão parcial.
PART.I.BLE, adj., partível, divisível.
PAR.TIC.I.PANT, s., participante.
PAR.TIC.I.PATE, v., participar de.
PAR.TIC.I.PA.TION, s., participação.
PAR.TIC.I.PA.TO.RY, adj., participativo.
PAR.TI.CI.PLE, s., particípio.
PAR.TI.CLE, s., partícula, parcela, parte.
PAR.TI-COL.OURED, adj., multicor, matizado.
PAR.TIC.U.LAR, s., particular, qualquer indivíduo; adj., particular, específico, único.
PAR.TIC.U.LAR.I.TY, s., particularidade, especialidade, minuciosidade, pormenor.
PAR.TIC.U.LAR.IZE, v., particularizar.
PAR.TIC.U.LAR.LY, adv., particularmente, especialmente; muito.
PART.ING, s., despedida; divisão; partida, saída; UK repartição; fig., morte; adj., de partido; fig., moribundo.
PAR.TI.SAN, s., partidário; guerrilheiro; adj., partidário.
PAR.TI.TION, s., partição, divisão, divisória, seção; v., dividir, repartir.
PART.LY, adv., em parte, parcialmente.
PART.NER, s., sócio, parceiro; par, cônjuge, consorte.
PART.NER.SHIP, s., parceria; sociedade, participação.
PAR.TRIDGE, s., Zool., perdiz.
PART-TIME, adj., meio período; adv., em meio período.
PAR.TU.RI.ENT, s., parturiente; adj., parturiente.
PAR.TU.RI.TION, s., parturição, parto.
PAR.TY, s., partido, festa; parte interessada, litigante, processante.
PAR.TY WALL, s., parede-meia; parede divisória.
PAR.VE.NU, s., novo-rico; adj., novo-rico.
PAS.QUIM, s., pasquim, jornal satírico.
PASS, s., passagem, passo, desfiladeiro, estreito, vão; v., passar, transpor, atravessar.

PASS.A.BLE, adj., passável, aceitável, livre; tolerável.
PASS.A.BLY, adv., aceitavelmente, toleravelmente.
PAS.SAGE, s., passagem, corredor, trânsito, caminho, travessia, trecho de livro.
PAS.SAGE.WAY, s., corredor, passagem; galeria.
PASS AWAY, v., falecer.
PASS.BOOK, s., caderneta.
PAS.SEN.GER, s., passageiro.
PAS.SER, s., passante, caminhante.
PAS.SER-BY, s., transeunte, passante.
PAS.SIB.I.LI.TY, s., passibilidade.
PAS.SING, adj., passageiro, transitório, efêmero.
PAS.SION, s., paixão.
PAS.SION.AL, s., passional, passioneiro; adj., passional.
PAS.SION.ATE, adj., apaixonado.
PAS.SION.ATE.LY, adv., apaixonadamente.
PAS.SION FRUIT, s., Bot., maracujá.
PAS.SION.LESS, adj., impassível, desapaixonado.
PAS.SIVE, adj., passivo.
PAS.SIVE.LY, adv., passivamente.
PAS.SIV.I.TY, s., paciência, passividade, inércia.
PASS.KEY, s., chave mestra; chave pessoal ou privativa.
PASS.LESS, adj., intransitável; desprovido de passaporte.
PASS.PORT, s., passaporte.
PASS TO, v., passar para.
PASS.WORD, s., senha, contrassenha.
PAST, s., passado, tempo passado; adj., passado, findo; prep., por, adiante de.
PAS.TA, s., massa, massas de culinária.
PASTE, s., pasta, massa; cola, grude; Cul., patê; v., colar, grudar.
PAS.TEL, s., pastel.
PASTE-UP, s., Tipog., pestape, colagem.
PAS.TEUR.I.ZA.TION, s., pasteurização.
PAS.TEUR.IZE(-ISE), v., pasteurizar.
PAS.TICHE, s., Art., pastiche; imitação.
PAS.TIL, s., pastilha.
PAS.TIME, s., passatempo.
PAST.I.NESS, s., qualidade de pastoso.
PAS.TOR, s., pastor, pároco.
PAS.TO.RAL, s., bucólico, pastoril; Rel., pastoral.
PAST PAR.TI.CI.PLE, s., Gram., particípio passado.
PAST PER.FECT, s., Gram., pretérito mais-que-perfeito.
PAS.TRY, s., massa, bolo.
PAS.TRY.COOK, s., pasteleiro.
PAST TENSE, s., Gram., passado ou pretérito.
PAS.TUR.AGE, s., pastagem, pasto, comida.
PAS.TURE, s., pasto, comida, refeição.
PAS.TURE.LAND, s., pastagem, terra pastoril.
PAST.Y, s., Cul., pastelão de carne; adj., pastoso; pálido.
PAT, s., pancadinha, tapinha; v., bater de leve, dar tapinhas.
PATCH, s., retalho, pedaço de fazenda, sinal, remendo; v., remendar, consertar.
PATCH.ABLE, adj., remendável.
PATCH.ING, s., remendo, remendagem.
PATCH.WORK, s., colcha de retalhos.
PATCH.Y, adj., irregular, feito de remendos; incompleto.
PATE, s., cabeça.
PA.TEL.LA, s., patela, rótula, rótula do joelho.
PAT.ENT, s., patente; v., patentear, registrar.
PAT.ENT.ED, adj., patenteado, que tem registro de patente.

PATENTEE ·· 559 ·· PEANUT BUTTER

PAT.ENT.EE, *s.*, detentor de uma patente.
PAT.ENT LEATH.ER, *s.*, couro envernizado.
PAT.ENT.LY, *adv.*, evidentemente.
PA.TER, *s.*, pai.
PA.TER.NAL, *adj.*, paternal, paterno.
PA.TER.NAL.LY, *adv.*, paternalmente.
PA.TER.NAL.IST(IC), *adj.*, paternalista.
PA.TER.NI.TY, *s.*, paternidade.
PATH, *s.*, caminho,vereda, senda, trajeto, trajetória.
PA.THET.IC, *adj.*, patético, lastimável.
PA.THET.I.CAL.LY, *adv.*, pateticamente.
PATH.FIND.ER, *s.*, explorador, batedor, guia.
PATH.LESS, *adj.*, intransitável.
PATH.O.LOG.IC, *adj.*, patológico.
PATH.O.LOG.I.CAL, *adj.*, patológico.
PA.THOL.O.GIST, *s.*, patologista.
PA.THOL.O.GY, *s.*, patologia.
PA.THOS, *s.*, *Gr.*, patos (qualidade que desperta piedade; capacidade de comover-se); compaixão.
PATH.WAY, *s.*, caminho, estrada, trilha, senda.
PA.TIENCE, *s.*, paciência.
PA.TIENT, *adj.*, *s.*, paciente.
PA.TIENT.LY, *adv.*, pacientemente.
PAT.I.NA, *s.*, pátina.
PA.TIO, *s.*, pátio.
PA.TIS.SE.RIE, *s.*, *Fr.*, loja de bolos e tortas.
PA.TOIS, *s.*, *Fr.*, patoá, dialeto, regionalismo; jargão.
PA.TRI.ARCH, *s.*, patriarca.
PA.TRI.AR.CHY, *s.*, patriarcado.
PAT.RI.MO.NI.AL, *adj.*, patrimonial.
PAT.RI.MO.NY, *s.*, patrimônio.
PA.TRI.OT, *s.*, patriota.
PA.TRI.OT.IC, *adj.*, patriótico.
PA.TRI.OT.ISM, *s.*, patriotismo.
PA.TROL, *s.*, patrulha; *v.*, patrulhar.
PA.TROL CAR, *s.*, carro de patrulha; radiopatrulha.
PA.TROL.MAN, *s.*, patrulheiro, policial, soldado.
PA.TROL WAG.ON, *s.*, *US* camburão.
PA.TROL.WOM.AN, *s.*, patrulheira.
PA.TRON, *s.*, cliente, freguês.
PA.TRON.AGE, *s.*, patrocínio.
PA.TRON.ESS, *s.*, defensora.
PA.TRON.IZE(-ISE), *v.*, patrocinar; favorecer apadrinhar; ser cliente de.
PA.TRON.IZER, *s.*, protetor.
PA.TRON.IZ.ING, *adj.*, defensor; *pej.*, codecendente.
PA.TRON SAINT, *s.*, santo padroeiro(a).
PAT.RO.NYM.IC, *adj.*, patronímico.
PAT.TEN, *s.*, tamanco, soco.
PAT.TER, *s.*, jargão; tagarelice; ruído monótono; *v.*, tagarelar; tamborilar (chuva monótona).
PAT.TERN, *s.*, exemplo, amostra, padrão, molde; *v.*, copiar, imitar.
PAT.TERN MAK.ER, *s.*, modelador; aquele que faz moldes.
PAT.TY, *s.*, pequeno pastel, torta, empada.
PAU.CI.TY, *s.*, escassez, insuficiência, falta.
PAUNCH, *s.*, pança, barriga.
PAUNCH.Y, *adj.*, pançudo, barrigudo.
PAU.PER.DOM, *s.*, pobreza.
PAU.PER, *s.*, pobre.
PAU.PER.ISM, *s.*, pobreza, miséria, indigência.

PAU.PER.IZE(-ISE), *s.*, empobrecer.
PAUSE, *s.*, pausa, intervalo; *v.*, fazer uma pausa.
PAUS.ING, *s.*, pausa.
PAVE, *v.*, pavimentar, calçar, calcetar.
PAVED, *adj.*, calçado, pavimentado.
PAVE.MENT, *s.*, pavimento, pavimentação, calçamento; calçada, passeio.
PAVE.MENT ART.IST, *s.*, *UK* artista de rua.
PA.VIL.ION, *s.*, pavilhão, barraca, anexo.
PAV.ING, *s.*, calçamento, pavimento.
PAV.ING STONE, *s.*, paralelepípedo.
PAW, *s.*, pata, garra; *v.*, escavar.
PAW.KY, *adj.*, astuto, velhaco.
PAWN, *s.*, peão (peça de xadrez); *fig.*, títere, marionete; penhora; *v.*, penhorar.
PAWN.BRO.KER, *s.*, penhorista.
PAWN.ER, *s.*, empenhador.
PAWN.SHOP, *s.*, loja de penhores.
PAX, *s.*, paz.
PAY, *s.*, paga, pagamento, salário; *v.*, pagar, saldar, liquidar.
PAY.A.BLE, *adj.*, a pagar; lucrativo.
PAY.BACK, *s.*, *Com.*, recuperação de investimento.
PAY.CHEK, *s.*, contracheque, salário.
PAY.DAY, *s.*, dia de pagamento.
PAY.EE, *s.*, beneficiário.
PAY.ER, *s.*, pagador.
PAY.ING GUEST, *s.*, pensionista.
PAY.LOAD, *s.*, carga útil.
PAY.MAS.TER, *s.*, pagador (funcionário).
PAY.MENT, *s.*, pagamento, remuneração.
PAY.NIM, *s.*, pagão.
PAY OFF, *v.*, pagar, saldar.
PAY.O.LA, *s.*, gorjeta; *col.*, *US* suborno.
PAY PACK.ET, *s.*, *UK* envelope de pagamento; *col.*, salário.
PAY-PER-VIEW, *s.*, pay-per-view (taxa de TV por programa escolhido).
PAY.ROLL, *s.*, folha de pagamento, importância.
PAY.SLIP *UK*, **PAY.STUB** *US*, *s.*, contracheque.
PC, *s.*, *abrev.* de *personal computer*: computador pessoal.
PEA, *s.*, *Bot.*, ervilha.
PEACE, *s.*, paz, tranquilidade, ordem, harmonia, sossego, trabalho.
PEACE.A.BLE, *adj.*, pacífico, tranquilo.
PEACE.A.BLY, *adv.*, pacificamente.
PEACE.FUL, *adj.*, quieto, calmo, sereno, pacífico.
PEACE.FUL.NESS, *s.*, tranquilidade, sossego, quietude.
PEACE.MAK.ER, *s.*, pacificador, apaziguador.
PEACE OF.FER.ING, *s.*, bandeira branca, oferta de paz.
PEACE.TIME, *s.*, tempo ou período de paz.
PEACH, *s.*, *Bot.*, pêssego; *adj.*, cor de pêssego.
PEA.COCK, *s.*, *Zool.*, pavão.
PEA.COCK.ISH, *adj.*, vaidoso, fútil, volúvel.
PEAK, *s.*, cume, pico, cimo, ponta, auge, apogeu; viseira (de boné); *v.*, atingir o máximo; definhar, emagrecer.
PEAKED, *adj.*, pontiagudo; com viseira (boné); *col.*, doentio, macilento.
PEAK RATE, *s.*, tarifa máxima.
PEAK.Y, *adj.*, pontiagudo; *col.*, doentio, acabado.
PEAL, *s.*, repique de sinos, bimbalhar; *v.*, repicar, badalar.
PEA.NUT, *s.*, *Bot.*, amendoim.
PEA.NUT BUT.TER, *s.*, manteiga de amendoim.

PEAR ··560·· PENETRATING

PEAR, s., pera; *Bot.*, pereira.
PEARL, s., pérola.
PEARL.Y, *adj.*, perolado, nacarado.
PEAS.ANT, s., camponês.
PEAS.ANT.RY, s., classe camponesa.
PEA.SHOOT.ER, s., sarabatana.
PEAT, s., turfa.
PEAT.Y, *adj.*, turfoso.
PEB.BLE, s., calhau, seixo; v., apedrejar, pavimentar com pedras.
PE.CAN, s., *Bot.*, nogueira-pecã, noz-pecã.
PE.CAN PIE, s., torta de nozes.
PEC.CAN.CY, s., pecado, vício, defeito.
PECK, s., bicada; v., bicar, dar bicadas; picar.
PECK.ER, s., bico (de aves; chupeta de bebê); *Zool.*, pica-pau; *vulg.*, pênis; *gír.*, bom humor, vitalidade.
PECK.ING, s., bicada; picada.
PECK.ING OR.DER, s., hierarquia social; *gír.*, lei do mais forte.
PECK.ISH, *adj.*, esfomeado, faminto; irritadiço.
PEC.TO.RAL, s., peitoral; *Anat.*, músculo peitoral.
PEC.U.LATE, v., fraudar, furtar, defraudar.
PEC.U.LA.TION, s., concussão, fraude, peculato.
PE.CU.LIAR, *adj.*, peculiar, estranho.
PE.CU.LIAR.I.TY, s., peculiaridade, genuinidade, particularidade.
PE.CU.LIAR.LY, *adv.*, peculiarmente, estranhamente.
PE.CU.LI.UM, s., pecúlio.
PE.CU.NI.ARY, *adj.*, pecuniário.
PED.A.GOG.IC, *adj.*, pedagógico.
PED.A.GOG.IC.AL, *adj.*, pedagógico.
PED.A.GOG.ICS, s., pedagogia.
PED.A.GOGUE, s., pedagogo.
PED.A.GO.GY, s., pedagogia.
PED.AL, s., pedal; v., pedalar.
PED.A.LO, s., *UK* pedalinho.
PED.ANT, s., pedante.
PED.ANT.ISM, s., pedantismo.
PED.ANT.RY, s., pedantismo.
PED.DLE, v., espalhar (boatos); traficar (drogas); mascatear.
PED.DLER, s., traficante; mascate.
PED.ER.AST *US*, **PAED.ER.AST** *UK*, s., pederasta.
PED.ER.AS.TY *US*, **PAED.ER.AS.TY** *UK*, s., pederastia.
PED.ES.TAL, s., pedestal.
PE.DES.TRI.AN, s., pedestre, transeunte.
PE.DES.TRI.AN CROSS.ING, s., *UK* faixa de pesdestre.
PE.DES.TRI.AN.IZE(-ISE), v., transformar em área para pedestres; caminhar no passeio.
PE.DI.AT.RIC *US*, **PAE.DI.AT.RIC** *UK*, *adj.*, pediátrico.
PE.DI.A.TRI.CIAN *US*, **PAE.DI.A.TRI.CIAN** *UK*, s., pediatra.
PE.DI.AT.RICS *US*, **PAE.DI.AT.RICS** *UK*, s., pediatria.
PED.I.CURE, s., pedicuro.
PED.I.GREE, s., pedigree, raça, genealogia canina.
PED.LAR *UK*, **PED.DLER** *US*, s., mascate, traficante.
PE.DOM.E.TER, s., pedômetro.
PE.DO.PHILE *US*, **PAE.DO.PHILE** *UK*, s., pedófilo.
PE.DO.PHIL.I.A *US*, **PAE.DO.PHIL.I.A** *UK*, s., pedofilia.
PEE, s., *fam.*, *gír.*, xixi, urina; v., *gír.*, urinar, fazer xixi.
PEEK, s., espiadela, espreitadela; v., espiar, espreitar.
PEEL, s., casca; v., descascar.
PEEL.ER, s., descascador.
PEEL.INGS, s. *pl.*, cascas.

PEEP, s., espiada, olhadela, aurora; v., espreitar, espiar, raiar, romper.
PEEP.HOLE, s., vigia, olho mágico, orifício para espreitar.
PEER, v., observar, mirar, olhar com atenção.
PEER.AGE, s., pariato, nobreza.
PEER.ESS, s., esposa de nobre.
PEER GROUP, s., grupo de mesma faixa etária ou classe social.
PEER.LESS, *adj.*, insuperável, inigualável.
PEEVE, v., irritar, provocar, exacerbar, aborrecer.
PEEVED, *adj.*, aborrecido.
PEE.VISH, *adj.*, rabugento, obstinado, teimoso.
PEG, s., cabide, grampo, cavilha, pé; pregar, confinar, restringir.
PE.JO.RA.TIVE, *adj.*, pejorativo, depreciativo, humilhante.
PE.KIN, s., Pequim.
PE.KIN.ESE, s., pequinês (raça de cão); s., *adj.*, habitante de, ou relativo a Pequim.
PEL.AGE, s., pelagem.
PELF, s., produto de saque, pilhagem; bens, riquezas adquiridas ilicitamente.
PEL.I.CAN, s., *Zool.*, pelicano.
PEL.LET, s., bolinha, pelota; grânulo, pílula; bala, chumbinho (de armas); v., peletizar; formar bolinhas.
PEL.LI.CLE, s., película.
PELL-MELL, *adv.*, atropeladamente.
PEL.MET, s., sanefa, cortinado; *UK* bandô.
PEL.LU.CID, *adj.*, claro, diáfano, transparente.
PEL.LU.CID.I.TY, s., transparência.
PELT, s., pele; couro não curtido; pedrada, pancada; v., atirar pedras; golpear, bater; atacar (com palavras).
PEL.VIC, *adj.*, pélvico.
PEL.VIS, s., pélvis, bacia.
PEN, s., pena, caneta, estilo literário, expressão própria; redil, cercado, curral.
PE.NAL, *adj.*, penal, punível, castigável.
PE.NAL.IZE(-ISE), v., penalizar, infligir penas, punir.
PE.NAL.LY, *adv.*, de modo penal.
PE.NAL SET.TLE.MENT, s., colônia penal.
PEN.AL.TY, s., penalidade, castigo, pena, punição.
PEN.AL.TY CLAUSE, s., cláusula penal.
PEN.ANCE, s., penitência, arrependimento, sofrimento.
PEN-AND-INK, *adj.*, a tinta.
PEN-AND-INK DRAW.ING, s., desenho a bico de pena.
PENCE, s. *pl.*, *UK* o mesmo que *penny*.
PEN.CHANT, s., inclinação, propensão, predileção.
PEN.CIL, s., lápis, pincel fino; v., escrever com lápis, desenhar.
PEN.CIL CASE, s., estojo de canetas; lapiseira, porta-lápis.
PEN.CILED *US*, **PEN.CILLED** *UK*, *adj.*, pintado, desenhado; radiado.
PEN.CIL SHARP.EN.ER, s., apontador de lápis.
PEN.DANT, s., pingente.
PEN.DEN.CY, s., pendência.
PEND.ING, *adj.*, pendente; iminente; *prep.*, durante, até.
PEN.DU.LOUS, *adj.*, pendente, suspenso, pendular.
PEN.DU.LOUS.NESS, s., suspensão; vascilação; oscilação.
PEN.DU.LUM, s., pêndulo.
PEN.E.TRA.BIL.I.TY, s., penetrabilidade.
PEN.E.TRA.BLE, *adj.*, penetrável; *fig.*, suscetível.
PEN.E.TRATE, s., penetrar, entrar, adentrar.
PEN.E.TRAT.ING, *adj.*, penetrante.

PENETRATION •• 561 •• PERIPHERAL

PEN.E.TRA.TION, s., penetração.
PEN.FRIEND *UK*, **PEN PAL** *US*, s., amigo por correspondência; correspondente.
PEN.GUIN, s., *Zool.*, pinguim.
PEN.I.CIL.LIN, s., *Med., Quím.*, penicilina.
PEN.IN.SU.LA, s., península.
PE.NIS, s., *Anat.*, pênis.
PEN.I.TENCE, s., penitência.
PEN.I.TENT, s., penitente, arrependido; s., penitente.
PEN.I.TEN.TIA.RY, s., penitenciária.
PEN.KNIFE, s., canivete.
PEN.MAN.SHIP, s., caligrafia.
PEN NAME, s., pseudônimo.
PEN.NANT, s., bandeirola.
PEN.NATE, *adj.*, alado, emplumado, peniforme.
PEN.NI.LESS, *adj.*, sem dinheiro.
PEN.NY, s., *UK* pêni (centavo de libra).
PEN.NY-PINCH.ING, s., avarento, avareza; frugalidade; *adj.*, avaro.
PEN PAL, s., *US* amigo feito por correspondência.
PEN.SION, s., pensão, aposentadoria; v., aposentar, dar uma pensão.
PEN.SION.A.BLE, *adj.*, com direito à aposentadoria.
PEN.SION.ER, s., aposentado, pensionista.
PEN.SION FUND, s., fundo de pensão.
PEN.SIVE, *adj.*, pensativo.
PEN.STOCK, s., comporta, açude, dique, represa.
PEN.TA.GON, s., *Geom.*, pentágono.
PEN.TA.GRAM, s., pentagrama.
PEN.TA.TEUCH, s., *Rel.*, Pentateuco.
PEN.TATH.LETE, s., pentatleta.
PEN.TATH.LON, s., *Esp.*, pentatlo.
PEN.TE.COST, s., *Rel.*, Pentecostes.
PENT.HOUSE, s., alpendre, varanda, telheiro, cobertura.
PENT-UP, *adj.*, contido, reprimido.
PEN.UL.TI.MATE, *adj.*, penúltimo.
PEN.UM.BRA, s., penumbra.
PE.NU.RI.OUS, *adj.*, miserável, avaro, sovina.
PE.NU.RI.OUS.NESS, s., avareza; penúria.
PEN.U.RY, s., penúria, miséria.
PE.ON, s., soldado; servição; peão, trabalhador rural.
PEO.PLE, s. *pl.*, gente, pessoas, povo, pessoas de modo geral.
PEP, s., energia, dinamismo, vigor, disposição.
PEP.PER, s., pimenta; v., apimentar.
PEP.PER.BOX, s., *US* pimenteira.
PEP.PER.CORN, s., grão de pimenta; *fig.*, ninharia.
PEP.PER.ED, *adj.*, salpicado (de algo); crivado (de algo).
PEP.PER.ING, *adj.*, picante, ardente.
PEP.PER MILL, s., moedor de pimenta.
PEP.PER.MINT, s., *Bot.*, hortelã-pimenta.
PEP.PER POT, s., *UK* pimenteira.
PEP.PER TREE, s., *Bot.*, aroeira.
PEP.PERY, *adj.*, apimentado, picante.
PEP.TIC, *adj.*, digestivo.
PEP.TIC ULCER, s., *Med.*, úlcera péptica.
PER, *prep.*, por, mediante.
PER.AD.VEN.TURE, s., acaso, causalidade; possibilidade; incerteza; *adv.*, talvez, por acaso; possivelmente.
PER.AM.BU.LATE, v., perambular, andar, percorrer, inspecionar.

PER CAP.I.TA, *adj., adv., Lat.*, per capita.
PER CENT, *adv., Lat.*, por cento.
PER.CEIV.ABLE, *adj.*, perceptível.
PER.CEIVE, v., perceber, notar, compreender, entender, captar, ouvir.
PER.CENT.AGE, s., percentagem.
PER.CEP.TI.BLE, *adj.*, perceptível.
PER.CEP.TION, s., percepção.
PER.CEP.TIVE, *adj.*, perceptivo.
PER.CEP.TIVE.LY, *adv.*, de modo perspicaz, perceptivelmente.
PER.CIP.I.ENCE, s., percepção.
PERCH, s., poleiro; v., empoleirar-se, pousar.
PER.CO.LATE, v., coar, filtrar.
PER.CO.LA.TION, s., filtração; *Farm.*, percolação.
PER.CO.LA.TOR, s., cafeteira.
PER.CUSS, v., percutir, ferir.
PER.CUS.SION, s., percussão, choque.
PER.CUS.SION.IST, s., percussionista.
PER.DI.TION, s., perdição, ruína, desgraça.
PER.DU.RA.BLE, *adj.*, perdurável.
PER.DUR.ING, *adj.*, duradouro, durável.
PER.E.GRI.NATE, v., peregrinar, andar, viajar.
PER.E.GRI.NA.TION, s., peregrinação, romaria, viagem.
PER.EMP.TO.RY, *adj.*, peremptório, categórico.
PE.REN.NI.AL, *adj.*, perene, eterno.
PER.FECT, *adj.*, perfeito, completo; s., perfeito; v., aperfeiçoar, aprimorar.
PER.FEC.TION, s., perfeição.
PER.FEC.TION.ISM, s., perfeccionismo.
PER.FEC.TION.IST, s., perfeccionista.
PER.FECT.LY, *adv.*, perfeitamente.
PER.FID.I.OUS, *adj.*, pérfido, falso, traiçoeiro.
PER.FI.DY, s., perfídia, traição, falsidade.
PER.FO.RATE, v., perfurar.
PER.FO.RA.TION, s., perfuração.
PER.FORCE, *adv.*, forçosamente, necessariamente.
PER.FORM, v., realizar, fazer, concretizar.
PER.FOR.MANCE, s., performance, desempenho.
PER.FORM.ER, s., ator, atriz, executor; executor, realizador.
PER.FORM.ING ARTS, s. *pl.*, artes performáticas.
PER.FUME, s., perfume; v., perfumar, aromatizar.
PER.FUMED, *adj.*, perfumado.
PER.FUM.ER.Y, s., perfumaria.
PER.FUNC.TO.RY, *adj.*, superficial, feito às pressas, perfunctório; descuidado.
PER.FUSE, v., borrifar, aspergir; difundir.
PER.FU.SION, s., aspersão.
PER.HAPS, *adv.*, talvez.
PER.I.CAR.DI.UM, s., *Anat.*, pericárdio.
PER.IL, s., perigo, risco, problema.
PER.IL.OUS, *adj.*, perigoso.
PE.RIM.E.TER, s., perímetro.
PE.RI.OD, s., período, lapso de tempo, divisão, espaço; menstruação.
PE.RI.OD.IC, *adj.*, periódico.
PE.RI.OD.I.CAL, s., periódico; *adj.*, relativo a periódico.
PE.RI.OD.IC.I.TY, s., periodicidade.
PER.I.O.DON.TICS, s., periodontia.
PE.RI.OD PAINS, s. *pl.*, cólicas menstruais.
PER.I.PA.TET.IC, s., peripatético.
PE.RIPH.ER.AL, s., *adj.*, periférico.

PERIPHERY · 562 · PERVERTED

PE.RIPH.ERY, s., periferia.
PE.RIPH.RA.SIS, s., perífrase.
PER.I.SCOPE, s., periscópio.
PER.ISH, v., perecer, sucumbir, deteriorar-se.
PER.ISH.ABLE, adj., perecível, deteriorável.
PER.ISH.ING, adj., col., congelante; adv., col., de modo congelante.
PER.I.TO.NE.UM, s., Anat., peritônio.
PER.I.TO.NI.TIS, s., Med., peritonite.
PER.I.WIG, s., peruca, cabeleira postiça.
PER.JURE, v., perjurar, jurar falsamente.
PER.JUR.ER, s., perjuro.
PER.JU.RY, s., perjúrio, juramento falso.
PERK, s., col., mordomia, regalia.
PERK.Y, adj., animado, alegre, feliz, satisfeito.
PERM, s., abrev. para *permanent wave*: permanente de cabelo.
PER.MA.NENCE, s., permanência, perseverança, continuidade.
PER.MA.NENT, adj., permanente.
PER.MA.NENT.LY, adv., permanentemente.
PER.ME.ABIL.I.TY, s., permeabilidade.
PER.ME.A.BLE, adj., permeável.
PER.ME.ATE, v., permear, penetrar, difundir.
PER.MIS.SI.BLE, adj., permissível.
PER.MIS.SION, s., permissão, concessão, licença.
PER.MIS.SIVE, adj., permissivo.
PER.MIS.SIVE.NESS, s., tolerância, permissividade.
PER.MIT, s., licença; v., permitir, deixar, deferir.
PER.MU.TA.TION, s., permuta, câmbio, troca, permutação.
PER.MU.TA.BIL.I.TY, s., permutabilidade.
PER.MU.TA.BLE, adj., permutável.
PER.MUTE, v., permutar, trocar, cambiar.
PER.NI.CIOUS, adj., pernicioso, nocivo, danoso.
PER.NICK.ET.Y, adj., col., meticuloso, pedante; delicado, difícil.
PER.OX.IDE, s., Quím., peróxido, água oxigenada; v., oxigenar.
PER.PEND, v., ponderar, arrazoar, pensar, avaliar.
PER.PEN.DIC.U.LAR, adj., perpendicular.
PER.PE.TRATE, v., perpetrar, executar, realizar, cometer.
PER.PE.TRA.TION, s., perpetração.
PER.PE.TRA.TOR, s., perpetrador.
PER.PET.U.AL, adj., perpétuo, perene, eterno.
PER.PET.U.AL.LY, adv., perpetuamente, continuamente, constantemente.
PER.PET.U.AL MO.TION, s., modo-continuo.
PER.PET.U.ATE, v., perpetuar, perenizar, eternizar.
PER.PET.U.ATION, s., perpetuação.
PER.PE.TU.I.TY, s., perpetuidade, perenidade, eternidade.
PER.PLEX, v., deixar perplexo, desconcertar (alguém).
PER.PLEXED, adj., perplexo.
PER.PLEX.ING, adj., perplexo, complicado.
PER.PLEX.I.TY, s., perplexidade.
PER.QUI.SITE, s., Jur., direito, prerrogativa, privilégios adicionais.
PERSE, adj., azul-cinza.
PER.SE.CUTE, v., perseguir, incomodar, perturbar.
PER.SE.CU.TION, s., perseguição.
PER.SE.CU.TOR, s., perseguidor, opressor.
PER.SE.VER.ANCE, s., perseverança.
PER.SE.VER.A.TION, s., repetição excessiva, excesso.
PER.SE.VERE, v., perseverar, continuar, persistir.

PER.SIAN, adj., s., persa.
PER.SIST, v., persistir, perseverar.
PER.SIST.ENCE, s., persistência.
PER.SIST.ENT, adj., persistente.
PER.SIST.ENT.LY, adv., persistentemente, obstinadamente.
PER.SNICK.E.TY, adj., o mesmo que *pernicketi*.
PER.SON, s., pessoa; indivíduo.
PER.SO.NA, s., imagem, personagem, personalidade.
PER.SON.A.BLE, adj., atraente, bem-apessoado.
PER.SON.AGE, s., personagem, personalidade.
PER.SON.AL, adj., pessoal, individual, próprio.
PER.SON.AL AS.SIST.ANT, s., assistente particular.
PER.SON.AL HY.GIENE, s., higiene pessoal.
PER.SON.AL.I.TY, s., personalidade.
PER.SON.AL.IZE(-ISE), v., personalizar, tipificar; levar para o lado pessoal.
PER.SON.AL.IZED(-ISED), adj., personalizado.
PER.SON.AL.LY, adv., pessoalmente, em pessoa.
PER.SON.AL PRO.NOUM, s., Gram., pronome pessoal.
PER.SON.AL PROP.ER.TY, s., bens móveis.
PER.SON.AL RIGHTS, s. pl., direitos individuais.
PER.SON.ATE, v., personificar, representar; caracterizar; simular, fingir.
PER.SON.NEL, s., pessoal (de uma companhia), equipe (de trabalho).
PER.SON.I.FI.CA.TION, s., personificação.
PER.SON.I.FY, s., personificar.
PER.SPEC.TIVE, s., perspectiva.
PER.SPI.CA.CIOUS, adj., perspicaz, sagaz, inteligente.
PER.SPI.CAC.I.TY, s., perspicácia.
PER.SPI.RA.TION, s., transpiração, suor.
PER.SPIRE, v., suar, exsudar, transpirar.
PER.SUADE, v., persuadir, convencer, levar a.
PER.SUAD.ER, v., persuasor.
PER.SUA.SI.BLE, adj., persuasível, persuasivo.
PER.SUA.SION, s., persuasão, convencimento, convicção.
PER.SUA.SIVE, adj., persuasivo.
PER.SUA.SIVE.LY, adv., persuasivamente.
PERT, adj., atrevido, ousado, descarado, insolente.
PER.TAIN, v., pertencer, ser propriedade, concernir, referir-se.
PER.TI.NA.CIOUS, adj., pertinaz, teimoso, obstinado.
PER.TI.NAC.I.TY, s., pertinácia, teimosia.
PER.TI.NENCE, s., pertinência, relevância.
PER.TI.NENT, adj., pertinente, referente, concernente.
PERT.NESS, s., audácia, ousadia, atrevimento.
PER.TURB, v., perturbar, incomodar, aborrecer.
PER.TUR.BA.TION, s., perturbação, incômodo.
PER.TURBED, adj., perturbado.
PE.RUKE, s., peruca, cabeleira.
PE.RUS.AL, s., leitura atenta; leitura rápida.
PE.RUSE, v., ler com atenção; ler por cima.
PE.RU.VI.AN, adj., s., peruano, habitante do Peru.
PER.VADE, s., impregnar, penetrar, permear.
PER.VA.SION, s., penetração, infiltração.
PER.VA.SIVE, adj., penetrante; difundido, difuso.
PER.VERSE, adj., perverso, maldoso.
PER.VERSE.LY, adv., perversamente.
PER.VER.SION, s., perversão, corrupção, maldade.
PER.VER.SI.TY, s., perversidade.
PER.VERT, v., perverter, corromper; adj., pervertido.
PER.VERT.ED, adj., pervertido, distorcido.

PESTER ··563·· PHOTOGRAPHY

PES.TER, *v.*, incomodar, amolar, perturbar.
PES.SI.MISM, *s.*, pessimismo.
PES.SI.MIST, *s.*, pessimista.
PES.SI.MIS.TIC, *adj.*, pessimista.
PEST, *s.*, peste, pestilência, epidemia.
PEST.ER, *v.*, incomodar, perturbar.
PES.TER.ING, *adj.*, inoportuno, perturbador, abusivo.
PES.TI.CIDE, *s.*, pesticida.
PES.TI.LENCE, *s.*, pestilência, peste.
PES.TI.LENT, *adj.*, pestilento.
PES.TLE, *s.*, pilão; *v.*, pilar, triturar.
PET, *s.*, animal de estimação; *v.*, acariciar, acarinhar.
PET.AL, *s.*, pétala.
PE.TARD, *s.*, petardo, bomba.
PE.TER, *v.*, diminuir gradualmente, esgotar-se, ficar exausto.
PE.TER.MAN, *s.*, *UK* arrombador de cofres.
PE.TI.TION, *s.*, petição, pedido, requerimento; *v.*, peticionar, pedir, requerer.
PE.TI.TION.ER, *s.*, suplicante, peticionante, requerente.
PET NAME, *s.*, apelido carinhoso, alcunha.
PET.RI.FIED, *adj.*, petrificado.
PET.RI.FY, *v.*, petrificar.
PE.TRO.CHEM.I.CAL, *adj.*, petroquímico.
PE.TRO.DOL.LAR, *s.*, petrodólar.
PET.ROL, *s.*, gasolina; *v.*, abastecer com gasolina.
PET.RO.LA.TUM, *s.*, *Quím.*, petrolato, vaselina líquida.
PE.TRO.LE.OUS, *adj.*, petrolífero.
PE.TRO.LE.UM, *s.*, petróleo.
PE.TRO.LE.UM JEL.LY, *s.*, *UK* vaselina (*petrolatum*).
PE.TROL PUMP, *s.*, bomba de gasolina.
PE.TROL STA.TION, *s.*, *UK* posto de gasolina.
PE.TROL TANK, *s.*, *UK* tanque de gasolina.
PE.TROUS, *adj.*, pétreo, rochoso.
PET.TI.COAT, *s.*, anágua, combinação; saia.
PET.TI.NESS, *s.*, insignificância, ninharia, bagatela.
PET.TISH, *adj.*, rabugento, desagradável, aborrecido, ranzinza.
PET.TISH.NESS, *s.*, rabugice.
PET.TY, *adj.*, mesquinho, ridículo, insignificante.
PET.TY OF.FI.CER, *s.*, suboficial.
PET.U.LANCE, *s.*, petulância, atrevimento.
PET.U.LANT, *adj.*, petulante.
PE.TU.NIA, *s.*, petúnia.
PEW, *s.*, banco de igreja.
PEW.TER, *s.*, peltre (liga de estanho); objeto feito com essa liga.
PHA.LANGE, *s.*, *Anat.*, falange.
PHAL.LIC, *adj.*, fálico.
PHAL.LUS, *s.*, falo; *Anat.*, pênis.
PHAN.TASM, *s.*, fantasma.
PHAN.TAS.MA.GO.RIA, *s.*, fantasmagoria.
PHAN.TOM, *s.*, fantasma.
PHA.RAOH, *s.*, faraó.
PHAR.I.SA.IC, *s.*, farisaico.
PHAR.I.SEE, *s.*, fariseu; hipócrita.
PHAR.MA.CEU.TIC, *adj.*, farmacêutico.
PHAR.MA.CEU.TICS, *s.*, farmácia, ciência farmacêutica.
PHAR.MA.CIST, *s.*, farmacêutico, oficial de farmácia.
PHAR.MA.COL.O.GY, *s.*, farmacologia.
PHAR.MA.CY, *s.*, farmácia.
PHA.ROS, *s.*, farol, faro.

PHAR.YN.GI.TIS, *s.*, faringite.
PHAR.YNX, *s.*, *Anat.*, faringe.
PHA.SIC, *adj.*, relativo à fase, fásico.
PHASE, *s.*, fase.
PHD, *abrev.* de *Doctor of Philosophy*: título de doutor em ciências humanas.
PHEAS.ANT, *s.*, faisão.
PHE.NOM.E.NA, *s. pl.*, fenômenos.
PHE.NOM.E.NAL, *adj.*, fenomenal.
PHE.NOM.E.NOL.O.GY, *s.*, fenomenologia.
PHE.NOM.E.NON, *s.*, fenômeno, prodígio.
PHE.NO.TYPE, *s.*, *Biol.*, fenótipo.
PHI.AL, *s.*, frasco, vidro.
PHI.LAN.DER.ER, *s.*, namorador, sedutor.
PHI.LAN.THROPE, *s.*, filantropo.
PHI.LAN.THROP.IC, *adj.*, filantrópico, humanitário.
PHI.LAN.THRO.PIST, *s.*, filantropo.
PHI.LAN.THRO.PY, *s.*, filantropia.
PHI.LAT.E.LY, *s.*, filatelia.
PHIL.HAR.MON.IC, *s.*, *adj.*, filarmônica.
PHIL.IP.PINE, *s.*, *adj.*, filipino.
PHIL.IS.TINE, *s.*, *adj.*, filisteu.
PHI.LOL.O.GY, *s.*, filologia.
PHI.LOS.O.PHER, *s.*, filósofo.
PHIL.O.SOPH.IC, *adj.*, filosófico.
PHIL.O.SOPHI.CAL, *adj.*, filosófico.
PHIL.O.SOPH.IZE(-ISE), *v.*, filosofar.
PHIL.OS.O.PHY, *s.*, filosofia.
PHIL.TER, *s.*, filtro, poção mágica.
PHLEGM, *s.* fleuma.
PHLEG.MAT.IC, *adj.*, fleumático.
PHO.BIA, *s.*, fobia.
PHOE.NI.CIAN, *adj.*, *s.*, fenício.
PHOE.NIX, *s.*, fênix.
PHONE, *s.*, fonema; *abrev.* de *telephone*: telefone; *v.*, telefonar.
PHONE-BOOK *UK*, *s.*, lista telefônica.
PHONE-BOOTH *US*, *s.*, cabina de telefone.
PHONE-BOX *UK*, *s.*, cabine telefônica.
PHO.NET.IC, *adj.*, fonético.
PHO.NET.ICS, *s.*, fonética.
PHO.NIC, *adj.*, fônico; acústico.
PHO.NOL.O.GY, *s.*, fonologia.
PHO.NOM.E.TER, *s.*, fonômetro.
PHO.NY *US*, **PHO.NEY** *UK*, *s.*, impostor, embuste; *adj.*, falso, farsante; *v.*, falsificar.
PHOS.PHATE, *s.*, fosfato.
PHOS.PHO.RES.CENCE, *s.*, fosforescência.
PHOS.PHO.RIC, *adj.*, fosfórico, fosforescente.
PHOS.PHO.RUS, *s.*, fósforo.
PHO.TO, *s.*, foto.
PHO.TO.COM.PO.SI.TION, *s.*, fotocomposição.
PHO.TO.COPI.ER, *s.*, fotocopiadora.
PHO.TO.COPY, *s.*, fotocópia; *v.*, fotocopiar.
PHO.TO.ELEC.TRIC, *adj.*, *Fís.*, fotoelétrico.
PHO.TO-EN.GRAV.ING, *s.*, fotogravura.
PHO.TO.GE.NIC, *adj.*, fotogênico.
PHO.TO.GRAM, *s.*, *Cin.*, fotograma.
PHO.TO.GRAPH, *s.*, fotografia, foto; *v.*, fotografar.
PHO.TOG.RA.PHER, *s.*, fotógrafo.
PHO.TO.GRAPH.IC, *adj.*, fotográfico.
PHO.TOG.RA.PHY, *s.*, fotografia.

PHOTOMETER ··564·· PILGRIM

PHO.TOM.E.TER, s., fotômetro.
PHO.TOM.E.TRY, s., fotometria.
PHO.TON, s., *Fís.*, fóton.
PHO.TO.PHO.BI.A, s., *Med.*, fotofobia.
PHO.TO.SEN.SI.TIVE, adj., fotossensível.
PHO.TO.SYN.THE.SIS, s., *Quím., Bot.*, fotossíntese.
PHO.TO.TY.PY, s., *Tipog.*, fototipia.
PHRAS.AL, adj., frasal, frásico.
PHRASE, s., frase, expressão; elocução; v., expressar, redigir; exprimir.
PHRA.SE.OL.O.GIC, adj., fraseológico.
PHRASE.OL.O.GY, s., fraseologia.
PHRAS.ING, s., fraseologia.
PHRE.NET.IC, adj., frenético.
PHRE.NI.TIS, s., frenesi, delírio.
PHTHI.SIS, s., tísica, tuberculose.
PHY.LOG.E.NY, s., *Biol.*, filogenia.
PHYS.IC, s., remédio, purgante; v., purgar, dar remédio.
PHYS.I.CAL, adj., físico.
PHYS.I.CAL ED.U.CA.TION, s., educação física.
PHYS.I.CAL EX.AM.I.NA.TION, s., exame médico.
PHYS.I.CAL.LY, adv., fisicamente.
PHYS.I.CAL TRAIN.ING, s., treinamento físico.
PHY.SI.CIAN, s., médico, clínico.
PHYS.I.CIST, s., físico.
PHYS.ICS, s. pl., física.
PHYS.I.O, s., col., fisioterapeuta, fisioterapia.
PHYS.I.OG.NOM.IC, adj., fisionômico.
PHYS.I.OG.NO.MY, s., fisionomia.
PHYS.I.OL.O.GIST, s., fisiologista.
PHYS.I.OL.O.GY, s., fisiologia.
PHYS.I.O.THER.A.PIST, s., fisioterapeuta.
PHYS.I.O.THER.A.PY, s., fisioterapia.
PHY.SIQUE, s., físico, estrutura física.
PI, s., símbolo matemático.
PI.A.NIST, s., pianista.
PI.ANO, s., *Mús.*, piano.
PI.ANO AC.COR.DI.ON, s., *Mús.*, acordeão.
PIC.A.ROON, s., pirata, corsário, assaltante, safado.
PIC.CO.LO, s., *Mús.*, flautim.
PICK, s., picareta, enxadão; picada; v., picar, cavar, colher, apanhar, provocar.
PICK.AXE *UK*, **PICKAX** *US*, s., picareta, alvião, picão; v., trabalhar com picareta.
PICKED, adj., colhido, escolhido, selecionado.
PICK.ER, s., colhedor, apanhador, cavador, batedor.
PICK.ET, s., piquete, estaca, marco; v., cercar, limitar, piquetar, marcar.
PICK.ING, s., escolha, colheita.
PICK.LE, s., picles, conservas; v., conservar no tempero.
PICK.LED, adj., em conserva; col., bêbado.
PICK-ME-UP, s., col., estimulante, tônico.
PICK.POCK.ET, s., batedor de carteiras.
PICK-UP *US*, **PICK-UP** *UK*, s., picape, camioneta.
PICK.Y, adj., difícil de contentar, enjoado, exigente.
PIC.NIC, s., piquenique, passeio; v., passear, fazer um piquenique.
PIC.NICK.ER, s., participante de piquenique, excursionista.
PIC.TO.RI.AL, s., revista ilustrada; adj., ilustrado.
PIC.TURE, s., pintura, desenho, quadro, tela, filme; *pictures*: filmes; v., pintar, retratar, descrever.

PIC.TURE BOOK, s., livro ilustrado.
PIC.TURE.LY, adv., pictoricamente.
PIC.TURE RAIL, s., moldura para pinturas ou quadros.
PIC.TUR.ESQUE, adj., pitoresco.
PIC.TURE WIN.DOW, s., janela panorâmica.
PID.DLE, v., ficar à toa; col., urinar.
PID.DLING, adj., col., insignificante, irrisório.
PIDG.IN, s., pídgin (fala híbrida de duas ou mais línguas. Ex.: portunhol).
PIE, s., torta, pastelão; *fig.*, confusão.
PIECE, s., peça, pedaço, fatia, parte, coleção, amostra, obra.
PIECE.MEAL, adj., pouco a pouco, aos poucos, a pouco e pouco.
PIECE.WORK, s., trabalho por empreitada.
PIED, adj., vário, variado.
PIER, s., cais, molhe.
PIERCE, v., furar, penetrar, trespassar, perfurar.
PIERCED, s., furado.
PIERC.ING, adj., penetrante, cortante; s., piercing (adereço preso ao corpo com alfinete).
PIERC.ING.LY, adv., de modo penetrante, agudamente.
PI.E.TISM, s., carolice, pieguice, beatice.
PI.E.TY, s., piedade, fervor, respeito.
PIF.FLE, s., tolice, disparate, bagatela; v., dizer bobagens.
PIF.FLING, adj., col., ridículo.
PIG, s., *Zool.*, porco, suíno; *fig.*, glutão, porcalhão.
PI.GEON, s., *Zool.*, pombo, pomba.
PI.GEON.HOLE, s., escaninho; casinha do pombal; v., classificar, pôr no escaninho; engavetar.
PI.GEON-TOED, adj., com pés virados para dentro.
PIG.GERY, s., chiqueiro, sujeira, porcaria, pocilga.
PIG.GISH, adj., porcalhão, imundo; glutão; sórdido.
PIG.GY, s., porquinho, leitão, bácaro.
PIG.GY.BACK, s., ato de levar algo ou alguém nos ombros; v., levar algo ou alguém nos ombros.
PIG.GY.BANK, s., porquinho de colocar moedas, cofrinho.
PIG.HEAD.ED, adj., cabeçudo.
PIG IRON, s., ferro fundido, lingote.
PIG.LET, s., leitão; o mesmo que *piggy*.
PIG.MENT, s., pigmento.
PIG.MEN.TA.TION, s., pigmentação.
PIG.MY, s., pigmeu.
PIG.SKIN, s., couro de porco.
PIG.STY, s., pocilga, chiqueiro.
PIG.SWILL, s., lavagem (para porcos).
PIG.TAIL, s., rabo de porco; trança (de cabelo), rabicho.
PIG.WASH, s., lavagem (alimentação de porco).
PIKE, s., pico, cume, montanha, barreira; pedágio rodoviário.
PIKE.STAFF, s., haste de pique (lança de combate); *Zool.*, lúcio (peixe).
PI.LAS.TER, s., pilastra.
PIL.CHARD, s., sardinha.
PILE, s., pelo, pilha, monte, pira funerária.
PILE DRIV.ER, s., bate-estaca (de construção civil).
PILE UP, s., engavetamento (colisão de vários veículos); amontoado.
PIL.FER, v., furtar, desviar, roubar, enganar.
PIL.FER.AGE, s., roubo, furto.
PIL.FER.ER, s., ladrão, gatuno.
PIL.FER.ING, s., roubo, furto.
PIL.GRIM, s., peregrino, romeiro.

PILGRIMAGE   ••565••   PITUITARY

PIL.GRIM.AGE, s., peregrinação, romaria.
PILL, s., pílula, comprimido.
PIL.LAGE, s., pilhagem, saque, botim; v., pilhar, saquear.
PIL.LAR, s., pilar; v., suportar com pilares, firmar com pilares.
PIL.LAR-BOX, s., UK caixa coletora do correio.
PILL.BOX, s., caixa de comprimidos (remédio); Mil., casamata.
PIL.LION, s., assento traseiro de motocicleta; garupa.
PIL.LO.RY, s., pelourinho; v., fig., expor ao ridículo.
PIL.LOW, s., almofada, tavesseiro.
PIL.LOW.CASE, s., fronha.
PIL.LOWY, adj., macio, delicado, mole, suave.
PI.LOT, s., piloto; pilotar.
PI.LOT.AGE, s., pilotagem.
PI.MEN.TO, s., Bot., pimentão-doce.
PIMP, s., chulo, calão.
PIM.PLE, s., Med., espinha (erupção cutânea), pústula.
PIM.PLY, adj., espinhento (que está cheio de espinhas no rosto).
PIN, s., alfinete, pino; v., alfinetar, espetar.
PIN.A.FORE, s., avental.
PIN.BALL, s., fliperama.
PIN.CERS, s., torquês, pinça.
PINCH, s., beliscão, aperto, adversidade; v., beliscar, arrancar, extorquir.
PINCHED, adj., abatido, fraco; atormentado; apertado, comprimido.
PINCH.ING, s., beliscada, beliscão.
PIN.CUSH.ION, s., alfineteira.
PINE, s., pinheiro, pinho, madeira de pinheiro.
PINE.AP.PLE, s., ananás, abacaxi.
PINE CONE, s., pinha (de pinheiro).
PINE NEE.DLE, s., Bot., agulha (folha do pinheiro em forma de agulha).
PINE NUT, s., pinhão (semente comestível da pinha).
PINE TREE, s., Bot., pinheiro.
PINE.WOOD, s., pinheiral; madeira de pinho.
PIN.ERY, s., abacaxizal.
PING, s., assobio, silvo, sibilo; v., assobiar, silvar, sibilar.
PING-PONG, s., pingue-pongue, tênis de mesa.
PIN.GUID, adj., pingue, gordo, obeso.
PIN.HEAD, s., cabeça de alfinete; fig., ninharia; fig., tolo.
PIN.HOLE, s., furo de alfinete, buraquinho.
PINK, adj., cor-de-rosa, rosado; s., cravo, cravina.
PINK.EYE, s., Med., conjuntivite aguda; influenza.
PINK.IE, s., mindinho, minguinho (dedo mínimo).
PINK.ISH, adj., rosa-pálido.
PINK.Y, s., o mesmo que pinkie.
PIN.NA.CLE, s., pináculo, cume, auge, clímax.
PIN.NY, s., col., o mesmo que pinafore.
PIN.POINT, s., ponta muito aguçada; v., determinar com com precisão; identificar; adj., minúsculo, aguçado.
PIN.PRICK, s., alfinetada; aborrecimento, irritação.
PIN-STRIPE, s., risco (desenho em tecido), listra; adj., listrado.
PIN-STRIPED, adj., riscado, listrado.
PIN-UP, s., foto ou desenho de mulher bonita, sensual, ger. bem-humorado; adj., muito atraente.
PI.O.NEER, s., pioneiro.
PI.OUS, adj., pio, devoto, religioso.
PI.OUS.LY, adv., piamente, devotamente.
PI.OUS.NESS, s., piedade, devoção.
PIP, s., semente, caroço.

PIPE, s., cachimbo; gaita de foles; cano, tubo; v., tocar flauta, assobiar; cachimbar.
PIPE CLEAN.ER, s., limpador de cachimbo.
PIPE.LINE, s., gasoduto, oleoduto.
PIP.ER, s., tocador de gaita de foles; encanador.
PIP.ING, s., tubulação; adv., ardentemente.
PIP.ING HOT, adj., bem quente, fervente.
PIP.KIN, s., panela de barro, escudela, bacia.
PIP-SQUEAK, s., pej., coisa insignificante.
PI.QUAN.CY, s., picância, sabor picante, amargura, aspereza.
PI.QUANT, adj., picante, mordaz, intrigante.
PIQUE, s., ressentimento, amuo; v., melindrar, amuar, ressentir.
PI.QUET, s., piquete, estaca, marco.
PI.RA.CY, s., pirataria.
PI.RA.NHA, s., Zool., piranha (peixe).
PI.RA.RU.CU, s., Bras., Zool., pirarucu (peixe de rio).
PI.RATE, s., pirata, corsário; v., piratear.
PIR.OU.ETTE, s., pirueta.
PIS.CA.TO.RY, adj.,piscoso, piscatório.
PI.SCES, s., Astrol., Peixes.
PI.SCI.CUL.TURE, s., piscicultura.
PIS.MIRE, s., formiga.
PISS, s., vulg., urina; v., vulg., urinar.
PISSED, adj., vulg., de saco cheio; puto da vida.
PIS.TA.CHIO, s., Bot., pistache; pistaceira.
PIS.TOL, s., pistola; v., atirar com pistola.
PIS.TON, s., pistão (de motor).
PIT, s., fosso, cova, fossa; v., enterrar, colocar em cova, opor, escavar.
PIT BULL TER.RI.ER, s., pit bull terrier (raça de cão).
PITCH, s., piche, pez, lançamento, lote de coisas; tom musical; montar, lançar.
PITCH-BLACK, adj., preto como carvão.
PITCHED, adj., inclinado.
PITCHED BAT.TLE, s., batalha campal.
PITCH.ER, s., jarro.
PITCH.FORK, s., forcado, garfo de lavoura.
PITCH.I.NESS, s., escuridão, negrume, trevas.
PITCH.ING, s., Náut., arfagem; apresentação; pavimentação; adj., inclinado.
PIT.E.OUS, adj., comovente, lamentável, doloroso.
PIT.E.OUS.LY, adv., lamentavelmente, de modo comovente.
PIT.FALL, s., queda, alçapão, armadilha, perigo.
PITH, s., medula; tutano; fig., vigor, força; essência.
PIT.HEAD, s., entrada ou boca de mina.
PITH HELMET, s., chapéu de palha.
PITH.I.NESS, s., vigor, energia, força, robustez.
PITH.Y, adj., denso, contundente, incisivo, sucinto.
PIT.I.A.BLE, adj., lastimável, lamentável.
PIT.I.FUL, adj., comovente, tocante.
PIT.I.FUL.LY, adv., lamentavelmente, desprezivelmente.
PIT.I.FUL.NESS, s., misericórdia, piedade, compaixão.
PIT.I.LESS, adj., impiedoso, cruel.
PIT.TA BREAD, s., pão sírio.
PIT.TANCE, s., miséria.
PIT.TED, adj., corroído, picado, roído.
PIT.TER-PAT.TER, s., ruído contínuo e monótono (de passos, de chuva).
PIT.TING, s., corrosão.
PI.TU.I.TAR.Y, s., Anat., glândula pituitária, hipófise.

PITY ·· 566 ·· PLAYHOUSE

PITY, *s.*, piedade, pena, compaixão; *v.*, compadecer-se.
PIT.Y.ING, *adj.*, compassivo.
PIV.OT, *s.*, pivô, eixo; *v.*, girar.
PIX.EL, *s.*, *Comp.*, píxel.
PIX.IE, PIX.Y, *s.*, fada, fadinha.
PIX.Y, *s.*, fada, duende.
PIZ.ZA, *s.*, *It.*, pizza.
PIZ.ZAZZ, *s.*, *col.*, vitalidade, energia, entusiasmo.
PLA.CA.BLE, *adj.*, placável, brando.
PLAC.ARD, *s.*, placar, quadro de avisos.
PLA.CATE, *v.*, aplacar, apaziguar, acalmar.
PLA.CA.TO.RY, *adj.*, apaziguante.
PLACE, *s.*, lugar, posto, situação; *v.*, pôr, colocar, situar, alocar.
PLA.CE.BO, *s.*, *Med.*, placebo.
PLACE.MENT, *s.*, disposição; colocação, estágio.
PLA.CEN.TA, *s.*, *Anat., Bot.*, placenta.
PLAC.ER, *s.*, jazida, aluvião.
PLACE SET.TING, *s.*, talher; objeto(s) que compõe(m) a mesa.
PLAC.ET, *s.*, permissão.
PLAC.ID, *adj.*, plácido, sereno, calmo, tranquilo.
PLA.CID.I.TY, *s.*, placidez, serenidade, tranquilidade, calma.
PLAC.ID.LY, *adv.*, placidamente, calmamente.
PLA.GIA.RISM, *s.*, plágio.
PLA.GIA.RIST, *s.*, plagiador.
PLA.GIA.RIZE, *v.*, plagiar.
PLAGUE, *s.*, peste, praga, endemia; *v.*, atormentar, incomodar, perturbar.
PLAGUY, *adj.*, inoportuno, maldoso, ruim.
PLAICE, *s.*, *Zool.*, linguado.
PLAIN, *s.*, planície, planura, várzea; *adj.*, plano, liso, manifesto, evidente, natural.
PLAIN CHOCO.LATE, *s.*, chocolate meio amargo.
PLAIN-CLOTHES, *adj.*, à paisana.
PLAIN.LY, *s.*, claramente, francamente, completamente, abertamente.
PLAIN.NESS, *s.*, franqueza, clareza, lisura.
PLAIN SAILING, *s.*, navegação livre, caminho livre; *adj., fig.*, sem dificuldades.
PLAIN-SPOK.EN, *adj.*, franco, sincero.
PLAINT, *s.*, queixa, reclamação.
PLAIN.TIFF, *adj.*, queixoso, reclamante.
PLAIN.TIVE, *adj.*, queixoso.
PLAIT, *s.*, trança, dobra, prega; *v.*, trançar; preguear.
PLAN, *s.*, plano, proposta, projeto, programa; *v.*, planejar, fazer planos.
PLAN.CHETTE, *s.*, prancheta, mesa para desenho.
PLANE, *s.*, plano, nível, avião, plaina; *v.*, voar de avião, planar.
PLAN.ET, *s.*, *Astron.*, planeta.
PLAN.E.TAR.I.UM, *s.*, planetário.
PLAN.E.TAR.Y, *adj.*, planetário; errante; terrestre.
PLAN.GEN.CY, *s.*, plangência; sonoridade (ger. de lamento).
PLAN.GENT, *adj.*, plangente; sonoro (ger. triste).
PLAN.I.SPHERE, *s.*, planisfério.
PLANK, *s.*, prancha, tábua, suporte; *v.*, assoalhar, colocar tábuas.
PLANK.TON, *s.*, plancton.
PLAN.LESS, *adj.*, desorganizado, sem plano.
PLANNED, *adj.*, planejado.
PLAN.NER, *s.*, planejador, projetista, idealizador.
PLAN.NING, *s.*, planejamento.

PLANT, *s.*, planta, vegetal, máquina, fábrica, plantação; *v.*, plantar, semear, fundar.
PLAN.TAIN, *s.*, *Bot.*, banana-da-terra.
PLANT POT, *s.*, vaso de plantas.
PLAN.TA.TION, *s.*, plantação, vegetação, cobertura vegetal.
PLANT.ER, *s.*, plantador.
PLANT.ING, *s.*, plantação.
PLAQUE, *s.*, placa, broche, insígnia.
PLASH, *s.*, charco, poço; *v.*, enlamear, borrifar.
PLASHY, *adj.*, pantanoso, lamacento.
PLASM, *s.*, plasma, protoplasma.
PLAS.MA, *s.*, plasma.
PLAS.TER, *s.*, reboco, gesso, emplastro; *v.*, rebocar, remendar, emplastar.
PLAS.TER.BOARD, *s.*, chapa de gesso.
PLAS.TERED, *adj.*, emplastrado de gesso; *col.*, bêbado.
PLAS.TER.ER, *s.*, rebocador (construção civil); modelador (gesso).
PLAS.TER.ING, *s.*, ato de rebocar (contrução civil).
PLAS.TER.STONE, *s.*, gesso.
PLAS.TIC, *s.*, plástico, plástica, material de plástico; *adj.*, plástico, moldável.
PLAS.TIC BAG, *s.*, saco de plástico.
PLAS.TIC BUL.LET, *s.*, bala de borracha.
PLAS.TIC MON.EY, *s.*, cartão de crédito.
PLAS.TIC SUR.GE.RY, *s.*, *Med.*, cirurgia plástica.
PLAS.TIC WRAP, *s.*, *US* filme de PVC transparente de cozinha.
PLATE, *s.*, prato, chapa, gravura, lâmina, folha, baixela; *v.*, chapear, blindar.
PLA.TEAU, *s.*, platô, planalto, altiplano.
PLATE.FUL, *s.*, pratada, prato cheio.
PLATE-GLASS, *s.*, vidro laminado para espelhos.
PLAT.EN, *s.*, platina.
PLATE RACK, *s.*, escorredor de pratos.
PLAT.FORM, *s.*, plataforma, cais, palanque, programa partidário.
PLAT.ING, *s.*, galvanização, chapeamento.
PLAT.I.NUM, *s.*, platina.
PLAT.I.TUDE, *s.*, lugar comum, chavão, trivialidade, nariz de cera.
PLAT.I.TU.DI.NOUS, *adj.*, comum, trivial, ordinário, vulgar.
PLA.TON.IC, *adj.*, platônico.
PLA.TO.NISM, *s.*, platonismo.
PLA.TOON, *s.*, pelotão, grupo de soldados.
PLAT.TER, *s.*, travessa (de louça); *gir.*, disco de vinil.
PLAT.Y.PUS, *s.*, *Zool.*, ornitorrinco.
PLAU.DIT, *s.*, aplauso; *plaudits s.pl.*, aplausos.
PLAU.SI.BLE, *adj.*, plausível, razoável, aceitável.
PLAU.SI.BLY, *adv.*, plausivelmente, convincentemente.
PLAY, *s.*, jogo, peça, diversão, filme, brincadeira; *v.*, jogar, brincar, tocar instrumento.
PLAY.BILL, *s.*, cartaz de lançamento (teatro).
PLAY.BOY, *s.*, playboy, pessoa de festas, farrista.
PLAY.ER, *s.*, jogador, músico, tocador de instrumento musical.
PLAY.FEL.LOW, *s.*, amigo de infância.
PLAY.FUL, *adj.*, brincalhão.
PLAY.FUL.LY, *adv.*, divertidamente.
PLAY.GROUND, *s.*, pátio para recreio; local para jogos.
PLAY.GROUP, *s.*, jardim de infância.
PLAY.HOUSE, *s.*, cinema, teatro, casa de espetáculos.

PLAYING CARD · 567 · POACH

PLAY.ING CARD, s., carta de baralho.
PLAY.ING FIELD, s., quadra de esportes.
PLAY LIST, s., lista de músicas tocadas nas rádios, playlist.
PLAY.MATE, s., colega, companheiro, camarada.
PLAY OFF, s., jogo decisivo, jogo final, jogo de decisão; v., desempatar.
PLAY.PEN, s., chiqueirinho (cercadinho de criança).
PLAY.ROOM, s., sala de recração.
PLAY.SCHOOL, s., jardim de infância.
PLAY.THING, s., brinquedo; fig., joguete.
PLAY.TIME, s., recreio, folguedo.
PLAY.WRIGHT, s., dramaturgo, teatrólogo.
PLA.ZA, s., praça; centro ou complexo comercial.
PLEA, s., apelo, apelação, pretexto, disputa, litígio.
PLEACH, v., entretecer, encurvar ramos.
PLEAD, v., pleitear; Jur., defender, advogar.
PLEAD.ER, s., defensor, advogado.
PLEAD.ING, s., alegação, defesa.
PLEAS.ANT, adj., agradável, brincalhão, simpático.
PLEAS.ANT.NESS, s., deleite, amenidade.
PLEAS.ANT.LY, adv., agradavelmente.
PLEAS.ANT.RY, s., gracejo, graça, jovialidade.
PLEASE, interj., por favor!; v., agradar, dar prazer, satisfazer, deleitar.
PLEASED, adj., satisfeito, contente, agradado.
PLEAS.ING, adj., agradável, aprazível.
PLEAS.ING.LY, adv., agradavelmente.
PLEA.SUR.A.BLE, adj., aprazível, prazenteiro; agradável.
PLEA.SURE, s., prazer, agrado, satisfação.
PLEAT, s., dobra, prega, ruga; v., dobrar.
PLEAT.ED, adj., pregueado.
PLE.BE.IAN, adj., s., plebeu.
PLEB.IS.CITE, s., plebiscito.
PLEBS, s., plebe, ralé, raia miúda, gentalha, populaça.
PLEC.TRUM, s., Mús., palheta (para dedilhar).
PLEDGE, s., penhor, fiança, garantia, brinde, promessa; v., empenhar, caucionar.
PLEIS.TO.CENE, s., Geol., pleistoceno; adj., pleistoceno.
PLE.NA.RY, adj., plenário, pleno, completo.
PLE.NA.RY SES.SION, s., sessão plenária.
PLEN.I.TUDE, s., plenitude, totalidade.
PLEN.TI.FUL, adj., abundante, copioso, variado.
PLEN.TY, s., abundância, copiosidade.
PLE.O.NASM, s., Gram., pleonasmo.
PLETH.O.RA, s., Med., pletora; fig., excesso.
PLEU.RA, s., Anat., pleura.
PLEX.US, s., Anat., plexo; fig., emaranhado.
PLI.ABIL.I.TY, s., flexibilidade, docilidade, afabilidade.
PLI.A.BLE, PLI.ANT, adj., flexível; dócil, complacente.
PLI.AN.CY, s., flexibilidade, brandura.
PLI.ERS, s. pl., alicates.
PLIGHT, s., condição, situação, compromisso; v., comprometer, empenhar.
PLIM.SOLLS, s. pl., UK tênis, sapatos de ginástica.
PLOD, v., caminhar com dificuldade, caminhar pesadamente, labutar.
PLOD.DING, s., trabalho pesado, faina, labuta.
PLOT, s., conspiração, enredo, pedaço de terra, lote, conluio; v., delinear, marcar.
PLOT.TER, s., agrimensor, cartógrafo, maquinador.
PLOUGH, s., arado, máquina para arar, terra arada; v., arar,

lavrar, sulcar.
PLOUGH.ABLE, adj., arável, lavrável, cultivável.
PLOUGH.ER, s., arador, lavrador, agricultor.
PLOUGH.ING, s., lavra,. aradura; sulco de arado.
PLOUGH.SHARE UK, **PLOWSHARE** US, s., relha de arado.
PLOY, s., estratagema (para derrotar o adversário).
PLUCK, s., arrancada, puxão, determinação; v., arrancar, puxar, apanhar, reprovar.
PLUCK.I.NESS, s., valentia, bravura, coragem.
PLUCK.Y, adj., valente, corajoso.
PLUG, s., plugue, tomada elétrica, tampa para lavabo; v., tapar, fechar, arrolhar.
PLUM, s., ameixa, ameixeira, uva passa.
PLUM.AGE, s., plumagem.
PLUMB, s., prumo, nível; adj., aprumado, perpendicular; v., aprumar.
PLUMB.ER, s., encanador, bombeiro.
PLUMB.ING, s., encanamento.
PLUMB LINE, s., fio de prumo.
PLUME, s., pluma, pena, plumagem, prêmio; v., emplumar, alisar as penas.
PLUM.MET, s., prumo; v., mergulhar, despencar.
PLUM.MY, adj., gír., da cor da ameixa; UK afetado.
PLUMP, s., toró, aguaceiro, baque; v., cair, baquear, arremessar.
PLUMP.LY, adv., de modo súbito; verticalmente.
PLUMP.NESS, s., gordura, atrevimento.
PLUMP.Y, adj., gordo, cheio.
PLUM TREE, s., Bot., ameixeira.
PLUMY, adj., emplumado, plumoso, cheio de penas.
PLUN.DER, s., saque, pilhagem; saquear, pilhar, rapinar.
PLUN.DER.ER, s., saqueador, assaltante, ladrão.
PLUNGE, s., mergulho, imersão, queda, salto; mergulhar, submergir, cravar.
PLUNG.ER, s., mergulhador; desentupidor.
PLUNG.ING, adj., profundo.
PLUNK, s., som estridente; v., produzir som estridente.
PLU.PER.FECT, s., mais-que-perfeito.
PLU.RAL, adj., s., plural.
PLU.RAL.IST, s., adj., plurarista.
PLU.RAL.I.TY, s., pluralidade.
PLUS, s., sinal de adição, adv., mais; adj., aditivo, positivo.
PLUSH, s., pelúcia, felpudo; adj., de pelúcia; fig., suntuoso.
PLUSHY, adj., felpudo.
PLUS SIGN, s., sinal de mais (em matemática).
PLU.TO, s., Astron., Plutão (planeta); Mit., Plutão (deus romano).
PLU.TOC.RA.CY, s., plutocracia.
PLU.TO.CRAT, s., plutocrata.
PLU.TO.NI.UM, s., Quím., plutônio.
PLU.VI.AL, adj., pluvial, chuvoso, próprio da chuva.
PLU.VI.O.ME.TER, s., pluviômetro.
PLU.VI.OUS, adj., chuvoso.
PLY, s., dobra, prega; v., manipular, importunar, aplicar-se, diligenciar.
PLY.WOOD, s., compensado (madeira).
P.M., PM, abrev. de post meridiem (de tarde, à tarde).
PNEU.MAT.IC, adj., pneumático.
PNEU.MAT.ICS, s., pneumática.
PNEU.MO.NIA, s., pneumonia.
PNEU.MON.IC, adj., pulmonar.
POACH, v., pisar, pisotear, umedecer, reduzir, caçar às

POACHER · 568 · POLYETHYLENE

escondidas; atolar-se; escaldar ovos sem casca.

POACH.ER, s., caçador furtivo; *Cul.*, panela para cozinhar ovos.

POACH.ING, s., caça ilegal.

POACH.Y, *adj.*, lamacento.

P.O. BOX, s., caixa postal

POCK.ET, s., bolso, algibeira, bolsa; colocar no bolso, embolsar, reprimir-se.

POCK.ET.BOOK, s., livro de bolso; *UK* bolsa de senhora; *US* carteira.

POCK.ET.FUL, s., quantidade que cabe no bolso; *col.*, bolso cheio, monte.

POCK.ET.KNIFE, s., canivete.

POCK.ET MON.EY, s., dinheirinho; *col.*, mesada de criança.

POD, s., vagem; bolsa, saco; v., produzir vagens.

PODG.I.NESS, s., gordura.

PODGY, *adj.*, gordo, rechonchudo, obeso.

PO.DI.UM, s., pódio.

PO.EM, s., poema.

PO.E.SY, s., poesia, arte poética.

PO.ET, s., poeta, poetisa, vate.

PO.ET.AS.TER, s., poetastro.

PO.ET.ESS, s., poetisa.

PO.ET.IC, *adj.*, poético.

PO.ET.ICS, s., poética, arte poética.

PO.ET.RY, s., poesia.

PO.GO STICK, s., pula-pula (brinquedo de criança).

PO.GROM, s., massacre étnico.

POIGN.AN.CY, s., comoção, pungência.

POIGN.ANT, *adj.*, comovente.

POINT, s., ponto, fim, ponto essencial, sinal, mancha; v., apontar, indicar, referir.

POINT-BLANK, *adj., fig.*, categórico, direto, franco; *adv.*, diretamente.

POINT.ED, *adj.*, pontudo, irônico.

POINT.ED.LY, *adv.*, sugestivamente, intensionalmente.

POINT.ER, s., ponteiro, indicador.

POINT.ING, s., preenchimento, rejuntamento; ação de apontar.

POINT.LESS, *adj.*, sem ponta, inútil, desnecessário.

POINT.Y, *adj.*, significativo.

POISE, s., equilíbrio, elegância, garbo, pausa; v., equilibrar, balançar.

POISED, *adj.*, equilibrado; preparado; suspenso.

POI.SON, s., veneno, tóxico; v., envenenar, intoxicar.

POI.SON.ING, s., envenenamento.

POI.SON.OUS, *adj.*, venenoso, tóxico, danoso, nocivo.

POKE, s., empurrão, cutucada, canga para boi; v., empurrar, ressaltar, sobressair.

POK.ER, s., atiçador, intrometido; pôquer.

POK.ER FACE, s., rosto sem expressão; *UK* cara de pau.

POK.Y, POK.EY, *adj.*, apertado; maçante; maltrapilho.

PO.LAND, s., Polônia.

PO.LAR, *adj.*, polar.

PO.LAR BEAR, s., *Zool.*, urso polar.

PO.LAR.I.TY, s., polaridade.

PO.LAR.I.ZA.TION, s., polarização.

PO.LAR.IZE, v., polarizar.

POLE, *adj.*, s., polaco.

POLE, s., polo, vara, poste, mastro; v., suportar, impelir, empurrar com vara.

POLE.AXE *UK*, **POLE-AX** *US*, s., machadinha (arma); v., *fig.*, nocautear.

POLE.AXED, v., atordoado.

PO.LEM.IC, *adj.*, polêmico, contundente.

PO.LEM.ICS, s., polêmica.

POL.E.MIZE, v., polemizar.

POLE STAR, s., estrela polar; *fig.*, guia.

POLE-VAULT, s., *Esp.*, salto com vara.

PO.LICE, s., polícia; v., policiar, legalizar, regulamentar.

PO.LICE CAR, s., radiopatrulha.

PO.LICE DE.PART.MENT, s., *US* departamento de polícia.

PO.LICE DOG, s., cão policial.

PO.LICE.MAN, s., policial, agente de polícia.

PO.LICE STA.TION, s., *UK* delegacia.

PO.LICE.WOM.AN, s., policial, agente feminina de polícia.

POL.I.CY, s., diplomacia, habilidade política; apólice de seguro.

POL.I.CY.HOLD.ER, s., segurado.

PO.LI.O, s., *col.*, poliomielite.

PO.LIO.MY.ELI.TIS, s., *Med.*, poliomielite.

POL.ISH, *adj.*, s., polaco, polonês.

POL.ISH, s., graxa, lustro, polimento, cultura; v., lustrar, polir, engraxar.

POL.ISHED, *adj.*, polido, elegante.

POL.ISH.ING, s., polimento, lustro.

PO.LITE, *adj.*, polido, cortês, educado, fino.

PO.LITE.LY, *adv.*, educadamente.

PO.LITE.NESS, s., delicadeza, polidez, cortesia, educação, fineza.

POL.I.TIC, *adj.*, político, esperto, sagaz.

PO.LIT.I.CAL, *adj.*, político.

PO.LIT.I.CAL.LY, *adv.*, politicamente.

PO.LIT.I.CAL SCI.ENCE, s., ciência política.

POL.I.TI.CIAN, s., político.

PO.LIT.I.CIZE, v., politicar.

POL.I.TICS, s., política.

POL.KA, s., polca.

POL.KA DOT, s., padrão de bolinhas (em estampas).

POLL, s., votação, pesquisa, apuração; v., colher votos, votar, apurar votos.

POL.LEN, s., pólen; v., polinizar.

POLL.INATE *UK*, **POLLENATE** *US*, v., *Bot.*, polinizar.

POLL.INA.TION *UK*, **POLLENATION** *US*, s., *Bot.*, polinização.

POLL.ING, s., votação.

POLL.ING BOOTH, s., cabine de votação.

POLL.ING-DAY, s., dia de eleição.

POLL.ING STA.TION, s., zona eleitoral.

POL.LI.NIZE, s., *Bot.*, polinizar.

POL.LI.NIZ.ER, s., *Bot.*, polinizador.

POL.LU.TANT, s., poluente.

POL.LUTE, v., poluir, sujar, turvar.

POL.LUT.ED, v., poluído.

POL.LU.TION, s., poluição, sujeira, corrupção, depravação.

PO.LO, s., *Esp.*, polo.

PO.LO.NI.UM, s., *Quím.*, polônio (elem. radioativo).

PO.LO SHIRT, s., camisa polo.

POL.TER.GEIST, s., fantasma, espírito perturbador.

POL.Y.AN.THUS, s., *Bot.*, primavera-dos-jardins.

POL.Y BAG, s., *col.*, *UK* saco plástico.

POL.Y.ES.TER, s., poliéster.

POL.Y.ETH.YL.ENE, s., *Quím.*, polietileno.

POLYGAMIST ·· 569 ·· POSER

PO.LYG.A.MIST, s., polígamo.
PO.LYG.A.MOUS, adj., polígamo, poligâmico.
PO.LYG.A.MY, s., poligamia.
POL.Y.GLOT, adj., s., poliglota.
POL.Y.GON, s., Geom., polígono.
POL.Y.GRAPH, s., polígrafo.
POL.Y.HE.DRON, s., Geom., poliedro.
POL.Y.MER, s., Quím., polímero.
POL.Y.MOR.PHISM, s., Biol., polimorfismo.
POLY.NE.SIAN, s., adj., polinésio.
POLY.NO.MI.AL, s., Mat., polinômio (álgebra).
POL.YP, s., Med., pólipo.
PO.LYPH.O.NY, s., Mús., polifonia.
POL.Y.STY.RENE, s., Quím., isopor, poliestireno.
POL.Y.SYL.LA.BLE, s., polissílabo.
POL.Y.TECH.NIC, s., politécnica, escola politécnica.
POL.Y.THE.ISM, s., politeísmo.
POL.Y.THENE, s., Quím., o mesmo que polyethylene,
POL.Y.UN.SAT.U.RAT.ED, adj., poli-insaturado.
POL.Y.VA.LENT, adj., s., polivalente, versátil.
POL.Y.U.RE.THANE, s., Quím., poliuretano.
PO.MADE, s., pomada.
PO.MAN.DER, s., sachê aromático, caixinha de perfumes.
POME.GRAN.ATE, s., Bot., romã.
POM.MEL, s., maçaneta; botão do punho de espada; v., esmurrar.
POMP, s., pompa.
POM-POM, s., pompom.
POM.POS.I.TY, s., pomposidade, ostentação, exibição.
POMP.OUS, adj., pomposo, luxuoso.
PONCE, s., gír. cafetão; pej., marica.
PON.CHO, s., poncho.
POND, s., lago pequeno, lagoa, tanque; v., represar águas.
PON.DER, v., ponderar, meditar, raciocinar, refletir.
PON.DER.A.BIL.I.TY, s., ponderabilidade.
PON.DER.ING, adj., ponderado.
PONE, s., broa, pão de milho.
PON.IARD, s., punhal, adaga; v., apunhalar, esfaquear.
PON.TIFF, s., pontífice, papa.
PON.TIF.I.CATE, v., pontificado, papado.
PON.TOON, s., plataforma flutuante; barcaça; UK vinte-e-um (jogo de cartas).
PO.NY, s., pônei, cavalo pequeno; Lit., sinopse literária.
PO.NY E.DI.TION, s., edição abreviada.
POO.DLE, s., poodle (raça de cão).
POOH, interj., oras!, bobagem!
POOL, s., poça, quantia apostada, bolo; associação de empresas.
POOP, s., Náut., tombadilho; popa.
POOPED, adj., col., esgotado.
POOR, adj., pobre, inferior, ruim, deselegante, mirrado; s. pl., os pobres.
POOR.LY, adj., col., adoentado; UK mal; adv., pobremente; abjetamente; mal.
POOR.HOUSE, s., asilo, hospedaria para pobres.
POOR.NESS, s., pobreza, insuficiência; má qualidade.
POP, s., estouro, estrépito, detonação de arma de fogo; v., estourar, estalar.
POP.CORN, s., milho para pipocas.
POPE, s., papa.
POP.LAR, s., álamo.

POP.PLE, s., borbulho; v., borbulhar, deslizar, rolar.
POP.LIN, s., popeline (tecido de algodão).
POP.PER, s., UK presilha.
POP.PY, s., Bot., papoula.
POP.PY.COCK, s., col., conversa fiada; papo furado.
POP.U.LACE, s., povo, população.
POP.U.LAR, adj., popular, conhecido.
POP.U.LAR.I.TY, s., popularidade.
POP.U.LAR.IZE, v., popularizar.
POP.U.LAR.LY, adv., popularmente.
POP.U.LATE, v., povoar, habitar, divulgar.
POP.U.LATED, adj., povoado.
POP.U.LA.TION, s., população, povo.
POP.U.LIST, s., populista.
POP.U.LOUS, adj., populoso.
POP-UP, adj., com sistema de ejeção; com ilustrações tridimensionais (livro).
POR.CE.LAIN, s., porcelana.
PORCH, s., átrio, entrada; US varanda, alpendre.
POR.CU.PINE, s., porco-espinho.
PORE, s., poro; pore over: examinar atentamente.
PORK, s., carne de porco.
PORK.ER, s., porco cevado.
PORK.ING, s., porco, leitão, suíno.
PORK CHOP, s., costeleta de porco.
PORK PIE, s., pastelão de porco.
POR.KY, adj., gordo, obeso.
PORN, s., col., pornô.
POR.NOG.RA.PHY, s., pornografia.
PO.ROS.I.TY, s., porosidade.
PO.ROUS, adj., poroso.
POR.POISE, s., Zool., boto, toninha.
POR.RIDGE, s., mingau de cereal.
PORT, s., porto, ancoradouro, canal; portão, entrada, bombordo.
PORT.A.BIL.I.TY, s., portabilidade, ação de portar.
PORT.A.BLE, adj., portável, portátil.
POR.TAGE, s., transporte,carreto, frete, despesas.
POR.TAL, s., portal.
PORT.CUL.LIS, s., porta levadiça (de um castelo).
POR.TEND, v., pressagiar, prever, agourar, vaticinar.
POR.TENT, s., prognóstico, presságio, agouro, vaticínio.
POR.TEN.TOUS, adj., prodigioso, extraordinário, fantástico.
POR.TER, s., porteiro, portador, carregador.
PORT.FO.LIO, s., pasta, carteira, valise.
PORT.HOLE, s., Náut., vigia, portinhola.
POR.TION, s., porção, quantia, parte, fração; v., repartir, dividir.
PORT.LY, adj., corpulento.
POR.TRAIT, s., retrato, imagem, foto, fotografia.
POR.TRAIT.IST, s., retratista.
POR.TRAY, v., fotografar, retratar, reproduzir a imagem, pintar.
POR.TRAY.AL, s., retrato; representação pictórica; interpretação (filme).
POR.TU.GAL, s., Portugal.
POR.TU.GUESE, adj., s., português, língua portuguesa, habitante de Portugal.
POSE, s., pose, postura, conduta, atitude; v., posar, colocar-se, propor.
POS.ER, s., pergunta difícil; pessoa que posa; pej., fingido; col., quebra-cabeça.

POSEUR ·· 570 ·· POX

PO.SEUR, *s., col.*, fingido.
POS.IT, *v.*, postular; firmar, fixar.
PO.SI.TION, *s.*, posição, situação, cargo, função, ocupação, ponto de vista.
POS.I.TIVE, *adj.*, positivo, certo, real, concreto, definido.
POS.I.TIVE.LY, *adv.*, positivamente.
POS.I.TIV.ISM, *s.*, positivismo.
POS.SE, *s., US* destacamento policial.
POS.SESS, *v.*, possuir, ter, deter, reter; copular.
POS.SESSED, *adj.*, possuído, possesso.
POS.SES.SION, *s.*, posse, possessão; objetos pessoais.
POS.SES.SIVE, *adj.*, possessivo, dominador.
POS.SES.SIVE.LY, *adv.*, possessivamente.
POS.SES.SOR, *s.*, proprietário, possessor; *Jur.*, usufrutuário.
POS.SES.SO.RY, *s.*, possuidor.
POS.SI.BIL.I.TY, *s.*, possibilidade, circunstância, oportunidade.
POS.SI.BLE, *adj.*, possível.
POS.SI.BLY, *adv.*, possivelmente, talvez, quiçá.
POST, *s.*, correio, cargo, posto, poste, estação; *v.*, fixar em poste, pendurar.
POST.AGE, *s.*, postagem, porte, franquia.
POS.TAGE-STAMP, *s.*, selo postal.
POST.AL, *adj.*, postal.
POST.AL OR.DER, *s.*, vale postal.
POST.BOX, *s.*, caixa postal.
POST.CARD, *s.*, cartão postal, cartão, postal.
POST.CODE, *s.*, código postal, código de endereçamento postal, CEP.
POST.DATE, *s.*, pós-data; *v.*, pós-datar.
POST.ER, *s.*, cartaz, *v.*, afixar cartazes.
POS.TE.RI.OR, *adj.*, posterior.
POS.TE.RI.OR.I.TY, *s.*, posterioridade.
POS.TE.RI.OR.LY, *adv.*, posteriormente.
POS.TER.I.TY, *s.*, posteridade.
POST.ER PAINT, *s.*, têmpera.
POST.FACE, *s.*, posfácio.
POST.GRAD.U.ATE, *adj.*, *s.*, pós-graduado.
POST.HU.MOUS, *adj.*, póstumo, depois de falecido.
POST.HU.MOUS.LY, *adv.*, postumamente.
POS.TIL, *s.*, apostila, nota.
POST-IN.DUS.TRI.AL, *adj.*, pós-industrial.
POST.ING, *s.*, despacho pelo correio; nomeação (serviço).
POST.MAN, *s.*, carteiro.
POST.MARK, *s.*, carimbo postal; *v.*, carimbar.
POST.MAST.ER, *s.*, chefe do correio, gerente do correio.
POST.MIS.TRESS, *s.*, agente feminina do correio.
POST-MOR.TEM, *adj.*, *Lat.*, *post*-mortem: posterior à morte; *s.*, autópsia, necrópsia.
POST.NA.TAL, *adj.*, pós-natal, após o nascimento.
POST OFFICE, *s.*, agência postal, correio.
POST-OP.E.RA.TIVE, *adj.*, pós-operatório.
POST.PAID, *adj.*, comporte pago.
POST.PONE, *v.*, adiar, pospor, transferir.
POST.PONE.MENT, *s.*, adiamento.
POST.SCRIPT, *s.*, pós-escrito, P.S.
POS.TU.LATE, *s.*, postulado; *v.*, postular, peticionar.
POS.TU.LA.TION, *s.*, postulação, petição, exigência.
POS.TURE, *s.*, postura, atitude, conduta.
POS.TUR.ING, *s.*, pose, presunção, atitude.
POST.WAR, *adj.*, do pós-guerra.

PO.SY, *s.*, ramalhete, buquê.
POT, *s.*, pote, panela, vaso, vasilhame, caneca, urinol; *v.*, pôr em conserva.
PO.TA.BLE, *adj.*, potável.
POT.ASH, *s.*, potassa.
PO.TAS.SI.UM, *s.*, *Quím.*, potássio.
PO.TA.TION, *s.*, bebida, libação, trago, gole.
PO.TA.TO, *s.*, *Bot.*, batata, batata-doce, batata frita.
POT-BEL.LIED, *adj.*, pançudo, barrigudo.
PO.TEN.CY, *s.*, potência, força, vigor, energia, poder.
PO.TENT, *adj.*, poderoso, potente, forte, vigoroso, enérgico.
PO.TEN.TATE, *s.*, potentado.
PO.TEN.TIAL, *s.*, potencial, potencialidade; potencial.
PO.TEN.TI.AL.I.TY, *s.*, potencialidade.
PO.TEN.TIAL.LY, *adv.*, potencialmente.
POT.HERB, *s.*, hortaliça.
POT.HOLE, *s.*, buraco (de rua).
POTION, *s.*, poção, dose.
POT.LUCK, *s.*, *Cul.*, o que tiver para comer, o trivial.
POT PLANT, *s.*, planta de vaso.
POT.POUR.RI, *s.*, *Fr.*, *Mús.*, coletânea; pot-pourri.
POT ROAST, *s.*, carne assada.
POT.TAGE, *s.*, sopa, caldo.
POT.TED, *adj.*, de vaso; em conserva; *UK* condensado.
POT.TER, *s.*, oleiro.
POT.TERY, *s.*, olaria, cerâmica, louça de barro.
POT.WARE, *s.*, cerâmica.
POUCH, *s.*, bolso, algibeira, tabaqueira.
POUFFE, *s.*, *UK* pufe.
POULT, *s.*, frango, pinto.
POUL.TICE, *s.*, cataplasma; *v.*, aplicar cataplasma.
POUL.TER.ER, *s.*, galinheiro, vendedor de aves.
POUL.TRY, *s.*, carne de aves; aves domésticas.
POUNCE, *v.*, agarrar (algo); lançar-se (sobre alguém).
POUND, *s.*, curral para gado; libra, medida com 453,59g; *v.*, socar, bater, esmurrar.
POUND.AGE, *s.*, comissão, porcentagem, pagamento.
POUND.ING, *s.*, surra, golpe, pacada, batida; latejamento.
POUND STER.LING, *s.*, libra esterlina.
POUR, *s.*, aguaceiro, toró; *v.*, despejar, vazar, soltar, brotar, chover, fluir.
POUR.ER, *s.*, funil.
POUR.ING, *adj.*, torrencial, copioso, abundante.
POUT, *s.*, beiço; *v.*, fazer beiço.
POV.ER.TY, *s.*, pobreza, indigência, miséria.
POV.ER.TY LINE, *s.*, linha de pobreza.
POW.DER, *s.*, pó, pó de arroz, polvilho, pólvora; *v.*, polvilhar, empoar, salgar.
POW.DERED, *adj.*, em pó.
POW.DER ROOM, *s.*, toalete.
POW.DER.Y, *adj.*, poeirento; empoeirado.
POW.ER, *s.*, poder, força, autoridade, comando, energia, aparelho-motor, potência.
POW.ER.BOAT, *s.*, barco a motor.
POW.ER.FUL, *adj.*, forte, poderoso, dominador, enérgico.
POW.ER.FUL.LY, *adv.*, poderosamente.
POW.ER.HOUSE, *s.*, casa de máquinas.
POW.ER.LESS, *adj.*, fraco, impotente; ineficiente.
POW.ER POINT, *s.*, *UK* ponto de força, tomada elétrica.
POW.ER STRUC.TURE, *s.*, grupo dominador.
POX, *s.*, pústula, varíola.

PRACTICABLE ··571·· PREEMPTIVE

PRAC.TI.CA.BLE, *adj.*, praticável.
PRAC.TI.CA.BLY, *adv.*, de modo factível.
PRAC.TI.CAL, *adj.*, prático, praticável.
PRAC.TI.CAL.I.TY, *s.*, praticabilidade.
PRAC.TI.CAL.LY, *adv.*, praticamente.
PRAC.TICE, *s.*, prática, uso, costume, experiência, exercício; *v.*, praticar, exercitar.
PRAC.TICED *US*, **PRACTISED** *UK*, *adj.*, experiente, experimentado.
PRAC.TIC.ER *US*, **PRAC.TIS.ER** *UK*, *s.*, prático, profissional; praticante.
PRAC.TIS.ING *UK*, **PRAC.TIC.ING** *US*, que exerce (profissão); praticante (cristão, católico).
PRAC.TI.TION.ER, *s.*, pessoa que pratica a profissão (médico, etc.).
PRAG.MAT.IC, *s.*, pragmática; *adj.*, pragmático.
PRAG.MA.TISM, *s.*, pragmatismo.
PRAI.RIE, *s.*, pradaria, prado, campo, campina.
PRAISE, *s.*, louvor, aplauso, exaltação; *v.*, louvar, aplaudir, elogiar.
PRAISE.WOR.THY, *adj.*, louvável.
PRAM, *s.*, carrinho de bebê.
PRANCE, *v.*, empino; *v.*, empinar-se; emproar-se.
PRANG, *s.*, *col.*, *UK* desastre; *v.*, espatifar-se (avião).
PRANK, *s.*, logro, travessura, brincadeira; *v.*, brincar, fazer travessuras; adornar.
PRANK.ING, *s.*, enfeite, adorno.
PRANK.ISH, *adj.*, travesso, traquinas, brincalhão, peralta.
PRAT, *s.*, *UK* palerma.
PRATE, *s.*, tagarelice; *v.*, tagarelar, palrar.
PRAT.ER, *s.*, tagarela, palrador.
PRAT.TLE, *v.*, *pej.*, tagarelar.
PRATE, *s.*, tagarelice; *v.*, tagarelar, falar pelos cotovelos.
PRA.TIQUE, *s.*, prático de porto, piloto de navio em porto.
PRAWN, *s.*, camarão, lagostim.
PRAX.IS, *s.*, práxis, praxe, prática.
PRAY, *v.*, rezar, orar.
PRAY.ER, *s.*, oração, súplica, pedido, prece.
PRAYER.FUL, *adj.*, piedoso, devoto.
PREACH, *s.*, prédica, sermão; *v.*, pregar, predicar, aconselhar, catequizar.
PREACH.ER, *s.*, pregador (de sermões ou doutrinas).
PRE.AM.BLE, *s.*, preâmbulo, prefácio, abertura, exórdio.
PRE.AR.RANGE, *v.*, arranjar antes, predispor.
PRE.AR.RANGED, *adj.*, já combinado.
PRE.CAR.I.OUS, *adj.*, precário.
PRE.CAR.I.OUS.LY, *adv.*, precariamente.
PRE.CAST, *adj.*, pré-moldado.
PRE.CAU.TION, *s.*, precaução.
PRE.CAU.TIONARY, *adj.*, de precaução.
PRE.CAU.TIOUS, *adj.*, precavido, cauteloso.
PRE.CAU.TIOUS.LY, *adv.*, cautelosamente.
PRE.CEDE, *v.*, preceder, antecder.
PRE.CE.DENCE, *s.*, precedência, prioridade, antecedência.
PRE.CE.DENT, *s.*, precedente.
PRE.CED.ING, *adj.*, precedente, anterior, antecedente.
PRE.CEPT, *s.*, preceito, norma, determinação.
PRE.CEP.TOR, *s.*, preceptor, mestre, guia.
PRE.CES.SION, *s.*, precessão.
PRE.CINCT, *s.*, distrito policial; vizinhanças, arredores, cercanias.

PRE.CI.OS.I.TY, *s.*, preciosidade.
PRE.CIOUS, *adj.*, precioso.
PRE.CIOUS ME.TAL, *s.*, metal precioso.
PRE.CIOUS STONE, *s.*, pedra preciosa.
PREC.I.PICE, *s.*, precipício.
PRE.CIP.I.TAN.CY, *s.*, precipitação, afobamento.
PRE.CIP.I.TATE, *v.*, precipitar, afobar, acelerar.
PRE.CIP.I.TA.TION, *s.*, precipitação, afobamento.
PRE.CIP.I.TOUS, *adj.*, íngreme, escarpado; precipitado.
PRE.CISE, *adj.*, preciso, exato, detalhado.
PRE.CISE.LY, *adv.*, exatamente, precisamente.
PRE.CISE.NESS, *s.*, precisão, exatidão.
PRE.CI.SION, *s.*, precisão, exatidão.
PRE.CLUDE, *v.*, precludir, excluir.
PRE.CO.CIOUS, *adj.*, precoce.
PRE.CO.CIOUS.NESS, *s.*, precocidade.
PRE.COC.I.TY, *s.*, precocidade.
PRE.CON.CEIVED, *adj.*, preconcebido.
PRE.CON.CEP.TION, *s.*, preconcepção, ideia preconcebida, preconceito.
PRE.CON.DI.TION, *s.*, pré-condição, condição prévia.
PRE-COOK, *v.*, pré-cozinhar.
PRE.COOKED, *adj.*, pré-cozido.
PRE.CUR.SOR, *s.*, precursor.
PRE.DA.CEOUS, *adj.*, rapinante, de rapina.
PRE.DATE, *v.*, predatar, antedatar.
PRE.DA.TION, *s.*, predação, destruição.
PRED.A.TOR, *s.*, predador.
PRED.A.TO.RY, *adj.*, predador, voraz, destruidor.
PRE.DE.CEASE, *v.*, morrer antes de (alguém), morrer primeiro.
PRE.DE.CES.SOR, *s.*, predecessor, antecessor, antepassado.
PRE.DES.TI.NATE, *v.*, predestinar.
PRE.DES.TI.NA.TION, *s.*, predestinação, sina, destino.
PRE.DE.TER.MINE, *v.*, predeterminar, prefixar, preestabelecer.
PRE.DE.TER.MINED, *adj.*, predeterminado.
PRE.DIC.A.MENT, *s.*, aperto, apuro, situação difícil.
PRED.I.CATE, *s.*, predicado, qualidade, atributo; *v.*, afirmar, confirmar.
PRED.I.CA.TION, *s.*, predicação.
PRED.I.CA.TIVE, *adj.*, *s.*, predicativo.
PRE.DICT, *v.*, predizer, vaticinar, prever.
PRE.DICT.A.BLE, *adj.*, previsível.
PRE.DIC.TION, *s.*, previsão, predição.
PRE.DIC.TOR, *s.*, profeta.
PRE.DI.LEC.TION, *s.*, predileção, preferência.
PRE.DIS.POSE, *v.*, predispor.
PRE.DIS.PO.SI.TION, *s.*, predisposição, inclinação, rumo, tendência.
PRE.DOM.I.NANCE, *s.*, predominância, predomínio.
PRE.DOM.I.NANT, *adj.*, predominant.
PRE.DOM.I.NANT.LY, *adv.*, predominantemente.
PRE.DOM.I.NATE, *v.*, predominar, dominar.
PRE.DOM.I.NA.TION, *s.*, predominação, dominação.
PRE.EM.I.NENT, *adj.*, preeminente.
PRE.EM.I.NENCE, *s.*, preeminência, primazia.
PRE.EMPT, *v.*, obter por preempção; apropriar; *col.*, atecipar-se a.
PRE.EMPT.ION, *v.*, preempção; *col.*, apropriação antecipada.
PRE.EMP.TIVE, *adj.*, que envolve preempção, preventivo.

PREEN · 572 · PRESSURIZED(-ISED)

PREEN, v., alisar com o bico (ave); *fig.*, arrumar-se, enfeitar-se.
PRE-EX.IST, v., preexistir.
PRE-EX.IS.TENCE, s., preexistência.
PRE.FAB, s., casa pré-fabricada.
PRE.FAB.RI.CATE, v., pré-fabricar.
PREF.ACE, s., prefácio, preâmbulo; v., prefaciar.
PRE.FECT, s., prefeito, dirigente, monitor.
PRE.FEC.TURE, s., prefeitura, governo.
PRE.FER, v., preferir, escolher, dar preferência.
PREF.ER.ABLE, adj., preferível.
PREF.ER.A.BLY, adv., preferivelmente.
PREF.ER.ENCE, s., preferência, antecedência.
PREF.ER.EN.TIAL, adj., preferencial.
PRE.FER.MENT, s., promoção.
PRE.FIX, s., prefixo.
PREG.NAN.CY, s., gravidez, fertilidade.
PREG.NAN.CY TEST, s., teste de gravidez.
PREG.NANT, adj., grávida; fecundo; *fig.*, abundante.
PRE.HEAT, v., preaquecer.
PRE.HEN.SION, s., preensão.
PRE.HIS.TOR.IC, adj., pré-histórico.
PRE.HIS.TO.RY, s., pré-história.
PRE.IN.DUS.TRI.AL, adj., pré-industrial.
PRE.JUDGE, v., prejulgar, julgar antes.
PRE.JUDG.MENT, s., prejulgamento.
PREJ.U.DICE, s., preconceito.
PREJ.U.DICED, adj., preconceituoso, parcial.
PREJ.U.DI.CIAL, adj., prejudicial.
PREL.A.CY, s., prelazia, episcopado.
PRE.LIM.I.NARY, s., preliminar, abertura; *preliminaries s.pl.*, preliminares; eliminatórias; *US* prévias (eleições).
PRE.LIMS, s. pl., *UK* examens preliminares.
PRE.LUDE, s., prelúdio, abertura, prólogo; v., preludiar.
PRE.MA.TURE, adj., prematuro.
PRE.MA.TURE.NESS, adj., precocidade, prematuridade; precipitação.
PRE.MA.TURE.LY, adv., prematuramente.
PRE.MED.I.TATE, v., premeditar, pensar antes.
PRE.MED.I.TAT.ED, adj., premeditado.
PRE.MED.I.TA.TION, s., premeditação.
PRE.MEN.STRU.AL, adj., pré-menstrual.
PRE.MIER, s., primeiro ministro.
PREM.I.ERE, s., *Fr.*, estreia; adj., estreante.
PREM.I.ER.SHIP, s., cargo ou posição de primeiro-ministro.
PREM.ISE, s., premissa.
PRE.MI.UM, s., prêmio.
PRE.MO.NI.TION, s., premonição, pressentimento.
PRE.MON.I.TIVE, adj., premonitório.
PRE-NA.TAL, adj., pré-natal.
PRE.OC.CU.PA.TION, s., preocupação.
PRE.OC.CU.PIED, adj., preocupado, absorto.
PRE.OC.CU.PY, v., preocupar.
PRE.OR.DAIN, v., predeterminar, préordenar.
PRE-PACKED, adj., pré-embalado.
PRE.PAID, adj., com porte pago.
PREP.A.RA.TION, s., preparação, arrumação; s., preparativos.
PRE.PAR.A.TO.RY, s., preparativo; adj., preparatório.
PRE.PARE, v., preparar, aprontar, elaborar.
PRE.PARED, adj., preparado, pronto.
PRE.PAY, v., pagar antecipadamente.
PRE.PON.DER.ANCE, s., preponderância, hegemonia,

comando.
PRE.PON.DER.ANT.LY, adv., predominantemente, majoritariamente.
PRE.PON.DER.ATE, v., preponderar.
PREP.O.SI.TION, s., preposição.
PRE.POS.SESS.ING, adj., atraente, agradável, cativante.
PRE.POS.TER.OUS, adj., absurdo; irracional, ilógico.
PRE-RE.CORD, v., gravar (programa de TV, rádio), pré-gravar.
PRE.REQ.UI.SITE, s., pré-requisito.
PRE.ROG.A.TIVE, s., prerrogativa.
PRES.AGE, s., presságio, auspício, vaticínio; v., pressagiar.
PRES.BY.O.PIA, s., presbiopia.
PRES.BY.TER, s., presbítero.
PRES.BY.TER.Y, s., presbitério.
PRES.BY.TE.RI.AN, adj., s., presbiteriano.
PRE.SCI.ENCE, s., presciência, premonição.
PRE.SCI.ENT, adj., presciente.
PRE.SCHOOL, adj., pré-escolar.
PRE.SCRIBE, v., prescrever, receitar, indicar.
PRE.SCRIPT, s., preceito, norma, regra; adj., prescrito.
PRE.SCRIP.TION, s., prescrição, receita.
PRE.SCRIP.TIVE, adj. Gram., prescritivo; consagrado pelo uso.
PRES.ENCE, s., presença.
PRE.SENT, s., presente; adj., presente, atual, momentâneo; v., apresentar, ofertar.
PRES.ENT.A.BLE, adj., apresentável.
PRE.SEN.TA.TION, s., apresentação, demonstração, exposição.
PRE.SENT DAY, s., o momento atual; adj., que é atual; contemporâneo.
PRE.SENT.ER, s., apresentador.
PRE.SEN.TI.MENT, s., pressentimento, impressão.
PRES.ENT.LY, adv., presentemente, atualmente, em breve.
PRES.ER.VA.TION, s., preservação, conservação.
PRE.SER.VA.TIVE, s., conservante.
PRE.SERVE, v., conservar, preservar, manter; manter em conserva.
PRE.SERVED, adj., em conserva; conservado, preservado.
PRE.SERV.ER, s., preservador, preservativo (que preserva).
PRE.SET, v., prefixar, pré-ajustar, programar; adj., prefixado.
PRE-SHRUNK, adj., pré-encolhido (tecido).
PRE.SIDE, v., presidir, dirigir, comandar como presidente.
PRES.I.DEN.CY, s., presidência, comando, direção.
PRES.I.DENT, s., presidente.
PRES.I.DEN.TIAL, adj., presidencial.
PRESS, s., pressão, multidão; imprensa; prelo, prensa, impressora; v., apertar, oprimir, forçar.
PRESS A.GEN.CY, s., assessoria de imprensa.
PRESS CON.FE.RENCE, s., entrevista coletiva à imprensa.
PRESS.ED, adj., apertado, aflito, necessitado.
PRESS.ING, adj., urgente, apressado.
PRESS.MAN, s., jornalista; impressor, tipógrafo.
PRESS OF.FICE, s., departamento de imprensa.
PRESS RE.LEASE, s., matéria para publicação (jornal).
PRES.SURE, s., pressão, aperto, compressão, força, coação, pressão atmosférica.
PRES.SURE COOK.ER, s., panela de pressão.
PRES.SUR.I.ZA.TION, s., pressurização.
PRES.SUR.IZE(-ISE), v., pressurizar.
PRES.SUR.IZED(-ISED), adj., pressurizado.

PRESTIGE   ·· 573 ··   PRISSY

PRES.TIGE, *s.*, prestígio.
PRES.TI.GIOUS, *adj.*, prestigioso.
PRE.SUM.A.BLE, *adj.*, presumível.
PRE.SUM.A.BLY, *adv.*, presumivelmente.
PRE.SUME, *v.*, presumir, supor, achar, pensar.
PRE.SUMP.TION, *s.*, presunção, suposição, hipótese.
PRE.SUMP.TU.OUS, *adj.*, presunçoso.
PRE.SUP.POSE, *v.*, pressupor, imaginar, achar.
PRE.SUP.PO.SI.TION, *s.*, pressuposição, hipótese, suposição.
PRE.TENCE *UK*, **PRETENSE** *US*, *s.*, pretensão, ambição; fingimento, pretexto, simulação.
PRE.TEND, *v.*, fingir, simular.
PRE.TEN.SION, *s.*, pretensão.
PRE.TEN.TIOUS, *adj.*, pretensioso.
PRE.TEN.TIOUS.LY, *adv.*, pretenciosamente.
PRE.TEN.TIOUS.NESS, *s.*, pretensão, caráter pretensioso.
PRET.ER.IT, *s.*, pretérito.
PRET.ER.I.TION, *s.*, preterição, omissão.
PRE.TER.MIT, *v.*, preterir, deixar fora, omitir.
PRE.TEXT, *s.*, pretexto.
PRET.TI.FY, *v.*, embelezar.
PRET.TI.LY, *adv.*, encantadoramente, lindamente.
PRET.TI.NESS, *s.*, beleza, formosura, elegância.
PRET.TY, *adj.*, belo, formoso, elegante, bonito.
PRET.TY.ISH, *adj.*, abonitado, mais ou menos belo.
PRET.ZEL, *s.*, *Cul.*, rosca salgada em forma de laço.
PRE.VAIL, *v.*, vencer, triunfar.
PRE.VAIL.ING, *adj.*, predominante, prevalecente, decisivo.
PREV.A.LENCE, *s.*, prevalência, domínio, predomínio.
PREV.A.LENT, *adj.*, predominante, prevalecente.
PRE.VAR.I.CATE, *v.*, prevaricar, tergiversar.
PRE.VENT, *v.*, prevenir, impedir, obstar.
PRE.VENT.A.BLE, *adj.*, evitável.
PRE.VEN.TA.TIVE, *s.*, o mesmo que *preventive*.
PRE.VEN.TION, *s.*, prevenção, cuidado.
PRE.VEN.TIVE, *adj.*, preventivo.
PRE.VIEW, *s.*, pré-estreia; trailer (de filme); *v.*, assistir em pré-estreia; prever.
PRE.VI.OUS, *adj.*, prévio, anterior.
PRE.VI.OUS.LY, *adv.*, anteriormente, previamente, antes.
PRE.VI.OUS.NESS, *s.*, anterioridade, precedência.
PRE.VISE, *v.*, prever, vaticinar.
PRE.VI.SION, *v.*, previsão.
PRE.WAR, *adj.*, antes da guerra.
PRE-WASH, *s.*, pré-lavagem.
PREY, *s.*, rapina, saque, pilhagem; *v.*, saquear, pilhar, rapinar.
PRICE, *s.*, preço, valor, custo, recompensa; *v.*, colocar preço, avaliar.
PRICE CUR.RENT, *s.*, lista de preços.
PRICE.LESS, *adj.*, sem preço, impossível de ser pago.
PRICE LIST, *s.*, o mesmo que *price current*.
PRICE TAG, *s.*, etiqueta de preço (da mercadoria).
PRIC.EY, *adj.*, *col.*, caro (preço alto).
PRICK, *s.*, punctura, picada, ferroada, remorso; *v.*, picar, pungir, afligir, ferroar.
PRICK.ER, *s.*, picador, furador.
PRICK.LE, *s.*, espinho, ferrão; comichão, formigamento; *v.*, picar, ferroar; comichar, formigar.
PRICK.LY, *adj.*, espinhoso, espinhento, pontudo.
PRICK.LY HEAT, *s.*, *Med.*, brotoeja.

PRIDE, *s.*, orgulho, soberba, vaidade, exibição; *v.*, orgulhar-se, envaidecer-se.
PRIEST, *s.*, sacerdote, padre.
PRIEST.ESS, *s.*, sacerdotisa.
PRIEST.HOOD, *s.*, sacerdócio.
PRIEST.LIKE, *adj.*, sacerdotal, referente a sacerdote.
PRIG, *s.*, ladrão, pedante, presunçoso; *v.*, roubar, furtar.
PRIM, *adj.*, afetado, empertigado; *v.*, ter ar afetado.
PRI.MA.CY, *s.*, primazia, antecedência, superioridade.
PRI.MAL, *adj.*, primitivo, primeiro.
PRI.MA.RI.LY, *adv.*, primeiramente, principalmente.
PRI.MA.RY, *s.*, tema principal; eleição primária; *adj.*, primário, primitivo, essencial.
PRI.MA.RY E.LEC.TION, *s.*, *US* prévias (eleições).
PRI.MA.RY SCHOOL, *s.*, *UK* escola primária.
PRI.MA.RY TEACH.ER, *s.*, *UK* professor(a) de escola primária.
PRI.MATE, *s.*, *Zool.*, primata; *Rel.*, primaz; *adj.*, relativo aos primatas.
PRIME, *s.*, início, aurora, juventude, número primo; *adj.*, primitivo, primeiro.
PRIME MIN.IS.TER, *s.*, primeiro ministro.
PRIME.NESS, *s.*, excelência, primor.
PRIME NUM.BER, *s.*, *Mat.*, número primo.
PRIM.ER, *s.*, cartilha, livro de ensino elementar.
PRIME SCHOOL, *s.*, *US* escola primária.
PRIME TIME, *s.*, horário nobre (rádio, TV).
PRI.ME.VAL, *adj.*, pimitivo, primevo.
PRIM.I.TIVE, *adj.*, primitivo, elementar, rudimentar.
PRIM.I.TIV.ISM, *s.*, *Filos.*, *Art.*, primitivismo.
PRIM.NESS, *s.*, afetação, pedantismo, petulância.
PRI.MO.GEN.I.TURE, *s.*, primogenitura.
PRI.MOR.DI.AL, *adj.*, primitivo, primário, primordial.
PRINCE, *s.*, príncipe.
PRINCE.DOM, *s.*, principado.
PRINCE.LIKE, *adj.*, principesco.
PRINCE.LY, *adj.*, principesco; magnífico, suntuoso, generoso.
PRIN.CESS, *s.*, princesa.
PRIN.CI.PAL, *adj.*, principal, fundamental; *s.*, diretor.
PRIN.CI.PAL.I.TY, *s.*, principado.
PRIN.CI.PAL.LY, *adv.*, principalmente, principalmente.
PRIN.CI.PLED, *adj.*, de princípio.
PRIN.CI.PLE, *s.*, princípio, início, começo.
PRINT, *s.*, impressão, letra de forma, marca, vestígio, ato de imprimir; *v.*, gravar, imprimir, marcar, colocar sinais, copiar, fazer cópias.
PRINT.ER, *s.*, impressor.
PRINT.ERY, *s.*, oficina gráfica, gráfica, impressora.
PRINT.ING, *s.*, impressão, estampagem, tiragem, cópias.
PRINT-OUT, *s.*, *Comp.*, saída de impressora, impressão.
PRI.OR, *s.*, prior; *adj.*, prévio, anterior; mais importante.
PRI.OR.ATE, *s.*, priorado, priorato.
PRI.O.RI.TIZE(-ISE), *v.*, priorizar.
PRI.OR.I.TY, *s.*, prioridade, precedência.
PRI.OR.Y, *s.*, convento (dirigido por um prior).
PRISE, *v.*, erguer ou forçar com alavanca.
PRISM, *s.*, prisma.
PRIS.ON, *s.*, prisão, cárcere, cadeia.
PRIS.ON.ER, *s.*, preso, prisioneiro, encarcerado.
PRIS.SY, *adj.*, meticuloso em excesso; fresco; afetado.

PRISTINE ··574·· PROFIT-MAKING

PRIS.TINE, *adj.*, puro, imaculado.
PRI.VA.CY, *s.*, privacidade, solidão, segredo, confidência.
PRI.VATE, *s.*, soldado raso; *adj.*, privado, particular, reservado, individual, secreto.
PRI.VATE DE.TEC.TIVE, *s.*, detetive particular.
PRI.VATE EN.TER.PRISE, *s.*, empresa privada.
PRI.VATE EYE, *s.*, detetive particular.
PRI.VATE IN.VES.TI.GA.TOR, *s.*, investigador particular.
PRI.VATE.LY, *adv.*, privadamente.
PRI.VATE PROP.ER.TY, *s.*, propriedade privada.
PRI.VATE SCHOOL, *s.*, escola particular.
PRI.VA.TION, *s.*, privação, falta, carência, ausência.
PRIV.A.TIVE, *adj.*, privativo, reservado.
PRI.VAT.I.ZA.TION, *s.*, privatização.
PRI.VAT.IZE(-ISE), *v.*, privatizar, particularizar.
PRIV.ET, *s.*, *Bot.*, alfena, alfeneiro.
PRIV.I.LEGE, *s.*, privilégio, regalia, prerrogativa; *v.*, privilegiar, favorecer.
PRIV.I.LEGED, *adj.*, privilegiado.
PRIVY, *s.*, latrina, privada; *adj.*, particular, pessoal, individual.
PRIZE, *s.*, prêmio, presente, recompensa, privilégio; *v.*, avaliar, estimar, elogiar.
PRIZE GIV.ING, *s.*, entrega de prêmios.
PRIZE WIN.NER, *s.*, premiado.
PRO, *s.*, pró, vantagem; *adv.*, em favor.
PROB.A.BIL.I.TY, *s.*, probabilidade, possibilidade.
PROB.A.BLE, *adj.*, provável.
PROB.A.BLY, *adv.*, provavelmente.
PRO.BATE, *s.*, aprovação de um testamento, cópia legítima.
PRO.BA.TION, *s.*, provação, experimento, experiência, noviciado.
PRO.BA.TION.AL, *adj.*, probatório, experimental; em período de experiência.
PRO.BA.TION.AR.Y, *adj.*, o mesmo que *probational*.
PRO.BA.TION.ER, *s.*, aprendiz, noviço, principiante.
PROBE, *s.*, sonda, sindicância, investigação; *v.*, investigar, fazer sindicância.
PROB.ING, *adj.*, inquiridor, sondador; *s.*, sondagem.
PRO.BI.TY, *s.*, probidade.
PROB.LEM, *s.*, problema, questão, dificuldade, charada, enigma.
PROB.LEM.AT.IC, *adj.*, problemático.
PRO.CE.DUR.AL, *adj.*, *Jur.*, processual.
PRO.CE.DURE, *s.*, conduta, procedimento, comportamento, método.
PRO.CEED, *v.*, proceder, prosseguir, derivar, provir, continuar.
PRO.CEED.ING, *s.*, procedimento, prosseguimento, continuação.
PRO.CESS, *s.*, processo, progresso, curso, decurso; citação, intimação; *v.*, processar.
PRO.CES.SING, *s.*, *Comp.*, processamento.
PRO.CES.SION, *s.*, procissão, séquito, cortejo, marcha; *v.*, desfilar, andar.
PRO.CES.SOR, *s.*, *Comp.*, processador; *Cul.*, processador de alimentos.
PRO.CLAIM, *v.*, proclamar, apregoar, pregar, decretar, publicar.
PROC.LA.MA.TION, *s.*, proclamação, apregoamento.
PRO.CLIV.I.TY, *s.*, tendência, propensão, inclinação.
PRO.CRAS.TI.NATE, *v.*, procrastinar, protelar.
PRO.CRAS.TI.NA.TION, *s.*, procrastinação, protelação.

PRO.CRE.ATE, *v.*, procriar, gerar.
PRO.CRE.ATION, *s.*, procriação, geração, reprodução.
PRO.CRE.ATOR, *s.*, procriador.
PROC.TOL.O.GY, *v.*, *Med.*, proctologia.
PROC.TOR.IZE, *v.*, disciplinar, ordenar, organizar.
PROC.U.RA.CY, *s.*, procuradoria.
PROC.U.RA.TION, *s.*, procuração.
PROC.U.RA.TOR, *s.*, procurador.
PROC.U.RA.TO.RY, *s.*, *Jur.*, procuração.
PRO.CURE, *v.*, obter, conseguir, alcançar, somar; agir como procurador.
PRO.CUR.ER, *s.*, provedor; *pej.*, alcoviteiro.
PRO.CURE.MENT, *s.*, aquisição, obtenção; *Jur.*, mediação, intervenção.
PROD, *s.*, alfinetada, picada, cutucada, estímulo; *v.*, picar, cutucar, incitar.
PROD.I.GAL, *adj.*, pródigo.
PROD.I.GAL.I.TY, *s.*, prodigalidade.
PRO.DI.GIOUS, *adj.*, prodigioso, maravilhoso, estupendo, incomum.
PROD.I.GY, *s.*, maravilha, milagre, prodígio.
PRO.DUCE, *s.*, produto, artigo manufaturado, lucro; *v.*, produzir, exibir, gerar.
PRO.DUC.ER, *s.*, produtor.
PROD.UCT, *s.*, produto, fruto, artigo, resultado, consequência.
PRO.DUC.TION, *s.*, produção, manufatura, exibição, obra, criação.
PRO.DUC.TION CON.TROL, *s.*, controle de produção.
PRO.DUC.TION LINE, *s.*, linha de produção.
PRO.DUC.TION MAN.AG.ER, *s.*, gerente de produção.
PRO.DUC.TIVE, *adj.*, produtivo.
PRO.DUC.TIVE.LY, *adv.*, de modo produtivo.
PRO.DUC.TIV.I.TY, *s.*, produtividade.
PRO.EM, *s.*, prefácio.
PROF.A.NA.TION, *s.*, profanação.
PRO.FAN.I.TY, *s.*, obscenidade, indecência; blasfêmia.
PRO.FANE, *adj.*, profano, laico, secular, impuro; *v.*, profanar, manchar, desrespeitar.
PRO.FESS, *v.*, professar, fazer votos, prometer, confessar, reconhecer.
PRO.FESSED, *adj.*, declarado, pretenso.
PRO.FES.SION, *s.*, profissão, declaração, confissão; fé, crença.
PRO.FES.SION.AL, *adj.*, *s.*, profissional.
PRO.FES.SION.AL.ISM, *s.*, profissionalismo.
PRO.FES.SION.AL.LY, *adv.*, profissionalmente.
PRO.FES.SOR, *s.*, professor, mestre.
PRO.FES.SOR.SHIP, *s.*, *UK* cátedra; cadeira de professor em universidade.
PROF.FER, *s.*, oferenda, oferta; *v.*, ofertar, oferecer.
PRO.FI.CIEN.CY, *s.*, proficiência.
PRO.FI.CIENT, *adj.*, proficiente, versado, hábil.
PRO.FILE, *s.*, perfil, contorno, corte, talhe; *v.*, perfilar, moldar, modelar.
PROF.IT, *s.*, proveito, lucro, rendimento, benefício; *v.*, aproveitar, obter proveito.
PROF.IT.A.BIL.I.TY, *s.*, lucro, rentabilidade.
PROF.IT.A.BLE, *adj.*, lucrativo, rentável, proveitoso, vantajoso.
PROF.IT.A.BLY, *adv.*, com lucro, proveitosamente.
PROF.IT.EER.ING, *s.*, especulação, exploração.
PROF.IT-MA.KING, *s.*, obtenção de lucros; *adj.*, com fins

PROFIT MARGIN ··575·· PROPORTIONATE

lucrativos, rentável.
PROF.IT MAR.GIN, *s.*, margem de lucro.
PROF.IT SHAR.ING, *s.*, participação nos lucros.
PROF.LI.GATE, *adj.*, devasso, libertino.
PRO.FOUND, *adj.*, profundo.
PRO.FOUND.LY, *adv.*, profundamente, com profundidade.
PRO.FOUND.NESS, *s.*, profundidade.
PRO.FUN.DI.TY, *s.*, profundidade.
PRO.FUSE, *adj.*, profuso, abundante.
PRO.FUSE.LY, *adv.*, profusamente, abundantemente.
PRO.FU.SION, *s.*, profusão, copiosidade, abundância.
PRO.GEN.I.TOR, *s.*, progenitor.
PROG.E.NY, *s.*, progênie, prole.
PRO.GES.TER.ONE, *s.*, *Biol.*, progesterona.
PROG.NO.SIS, *s.*, prognóstico.
PROG.NOS.TI.CATE, *v.*, prognosticar, vaticinar, prever.
PROG.NOS.TI.CA.TION, *s.*, presságio, prognóstico.
PRO.GRAM, *s.*, *US* programa (espetáculo; projeto); *Comp.*, programa (*software*); *v.*, *Comp.*, programar.
PRO.GRAM.ME *UK*, **PRO.GRAM** *US*, *s.*, programa, roteiro; *v.*, programar.
PRO.GRAM.MER *UK*, **PRO.GRAM.ER** *US*, *s.*, programador.
PRO.GRAM.MING, *s.*, programação.
PROG.RESS, *s.*, progresso; *v.*, progredir, desenvolver.
PRO.GRES.SION, *s.*, progressão, avanço.
PRO.GRES.SIVE, *adj.*, progressivo.
PRO.GRES.SIVE.LY, *adv.*, progressivamente.
PRO.HIB.IT, *v.*, proibir, vetar.
PRO.HI.BI.TION, *s.*, proibição, veto, negativa.
PRO.HIB.I.TIVE, *adj.*, proibitivo.
PROJ.ECT, *s.*, projeto, plano, pesquisa, intento; *v.*, projetar, estimar, tentar.
PRO.JEC.TILE, *s.*, projétil.
PRO.JEC.TION, *s.*, projeção (filme, previsão), destaque, ênfase.
PRO.JEC.TION.IST, *s.*, *US* projecionista (operador de projetor de cinema).
PRO.JEC.TION ROOM, *s.*, *UK* sala de projeção.
PRO.JEC.TOR, *s.*, projetor.
PRO.LE.TAR.I.AN, *adj.*, proletário.
PRO.LE.TAR.I.AT, *s.*, proletariado.
PRO-LIFE, *adj.*, pró-vida.
PRO.LIF.ER.ATE, *v.*, proliferar, espalhar, difundir.
PRO.LIF.ER.A.TION, *s.*, proliferação.
PRO.LIF.IC, *adj.*, prolífico.
PRO.LIX, *adj.*, prolixo, longo, difuso, complexo.
PRO.LIX.I.TY, *s.*, prolixidade.
PRO.LOGUE, *s.*, prólogo, prefácio, início.
PRO.LONG, *v.*, prolongar.
PRO.LON.GA.TION, *s.*, prolongamento, prolongação.
PROM.E.NADE, *s.*, passeio, giro, convescote, piquenique.
PRO.ME.THI.UM, *s.*, *Quím.*, promécio.
PROM.I.NENCE, *s.*, proeminência, eminência, valor, importância.
PROM.I.NENT, *adj.*, proeminente, em evidência, protuberante.
PROM.I.NENT.LY, *adv.*, proeminentemente.
PRO.MIS.CU.I.TY, *s.*, promiscuidade.
PRO.MIS.CU.OUS, *adj.*, promíscuo.
PROM.ISE, *s.*, promessa, espera, esperança, compromisso, palavra.
PROM.IS.ER, *s.*, prometedor.

PROM.IS.ING, *adj.*, promissor.
PROM.IS.SO.RY NOTE, *s.*, *Jur.*, nota promissória.
PROM.ON.TO.RY, *s.*, promontório.
PRO.MOTE, *v.*, promover, divulgar.
PRO.MOT.ER, *s.*, patrocinador, divulgador.
PRO.MO.TION, *s.*, promoção.
PROMPT, *v.*, iniciar, impelir, recordar, sugerir; *Teat.*, deixa, ponto; *adj.*, pronto, alerta, rápido.
PROMPT.ER, *s.*, instigador; *Teat.*, o que dá o ponto.
PROMP.TI.TUDE, *s.*, prontidão, presteza.
PROMPT.LY, *adv.*, prontamente, imediatamente; pontualmente.
PROMPT.NESS, *s.*, prontidão, rapidez, presteza, pontualidade.
PRO.MUL.GATE, *s.*, promulgar, divulgar.
PRO.MUL.GA.TION, *s.*, promulgação, divulgação.
PRO.MUL.GA.TOR, *s.*, promulgador.
PRONE, *adj.*, inclinado, propenso, de borco, de bruços.
PRONG, *adj.*, forcado, dente de garfo; *v.*, forcar.
PRO.NOM.I.NAL, *adj.*, pronominal.
PRO.NOUN, *s.*, *Gram.*, pronome.
PRO.NOUNCE, *v.*, pronunciar, articular, declarar, afirmar.
PRO.NOUNCED, *adj.*, pronunciado, marcado; decidido.
PRO.NOUNCE.MENT, *s.*, pronunciamento, declaração.
PRO.NOUNC.ING, *s.*, pronúncia.
PRON.TO, *adv.*, *col.*, imediatamente.
PRO.NUN.CI.A.TION, *s.*, pronúncia, pronunciação.
PROOF, *s.*, prova, demonstração, exame, experiência, comprovante.
PROOF.READ, *v.*, *Tipog.*, revisar (provas).
PROOF.READ.ER, *s.*, *Tipog.*, revisor (de provas).
PROP, *s.*, estaca, escora, estepe.
PRO.PA.GAN.DA, *s.*, propaganda.
PRO.PA.GAN.DIST, *s.*, propagandista.
PROP.A.GATE, *v.*, propagar, difundir, divulgar.
PROP.A.GA.TION, *s.*, propagação, divulgação.
PROP.A.GA.TOR, *s.*, propagador.
PRO.PANE, *s.*, *Quím.*, propano.
PROP.AR.OX.Y.TONE, *s.*, proparoxítono.
PRO.PEL, *v.*, propelir, impelir.
PRO.PEL.LER, *s.*, propulsor, hélice.
PRO.PEN.SI.TY, *s.*, propensão, inclinação; gosto.
PROP.ER, *adj.*, próprio, particular, genuíno, característico, privativo, inerente.
PREP.ER.LY, *adv.*, adequadamente, corretamente, direito, bem, devidamente, convenientemente.
PROP.ER NOUM, *s.*, nome próprio.
PROP.ER.TY, *s.*, propriedade, característica, caráter; propriedade de bens de raiz.
PROPH.E.CY, *s.*, profecia, vaticínio.
PROPH.E.SY, *v.*, profetizar, vaticinar.
PROPH.ET, *s.*, profeta.
PRO.PHET.IC, *adj.*, profético.
PRO.PI.TI.ATE, *v.*, propiciar, favorecer, ajudar.
PRO.PI.TI.A.TION, *s.*, conciliação; *Teol.*, sacrifício.
PRO.PI.TIOUS, *adj.*, propício, favorável.
PRO.PO.NENT, *s.*, proponente, defensor.
PRO.POR.TION, *s.*, proporção.
PRO.POR.TION.AL, *adj.*, proporcional.
PRO.POR.TION.AL.I.TY, *s.*, proporcionalidade.
PRO.POR.TION.ATE, *v.*, proporcionar, conceder; *adj.*,

PROPOSAL ·· 576 ·· PROW

proporcional.
PRO.POS.AL, s., proposta, solicitação, pedido.
PRO.POSE, v., propor, expor, oferecer, indicar.
PRO.POSED, adj., proposto.
PROP.O.SI.TION, s., proposição, proposta.
PRO.POUND, v., propor, oferecer, indicar.
PRO.PRI.E.TARY, s., dono, proprietário, propriedade; adj., proprietário.
PRO.PRI.E.TOR, s., proprietário, dono.
PRO.PRI.E.TOR.I.AL, adj., proprietário, possessivo.
PRO.PRI.E.TY, s., retidão, decoro, decência; boas maneiras.
PRO.PUL.SION, s., propulsão, impulsão, impulso.
PRO.PUL.SIVE, adj., propulsivo, propulsor.
PRO.RATE, v., US ratear (fazer rateio).
PRO.RO.GA.TION, s., prorrogação, adiamento.
PRO.ROGUE, v., prorrogar, adiar.
PRO.SA.IC, adj., prosaico.
PRO.SCRIBE, s., proscrever, desterrar, condenar ao exílio, condenar.
PRO.SCRIP.TION, s., proscrição.
PROSE, s., prosa; v., escrever em prosa, usar de prosa.
PROS.E.CUTE, v., processar.
PROS.E.CU.TION, s., prosseguimento, execução; Jur., acusação; the ~ : a acusação.
PROS.E.CU.TOR, s., promotor.
PROS.E.LYTE, s., prosélito, sequaz, seguidor, sectário.
PROS.E.LY.TISM, s., proselitismo.
PROS.ER, s., prosador, escritor, narrador, cronista.
PROS.O.DY, s., prosódia.
PROS.PECT, s., prospecto, vista, perspectiva; v., pesquisar, investigar, explorar.
PROS.PECT.ING, s., prospecção.
PRO.SPEC.TIVE, adj., provável, esperado, aguardado, possível.
PRO.SPECT.IVE.NESS, s., prospeção, perspectiva, possibilidade.
PRO.SPEC.TOR, s., prospector (de minas), explorador.
PRO.SPEC.TUS, s., prospecto, folheto, informativo.
PROSP.ER, v., prosperar, melhorar.
PROS.PER.I.TY, s., prosperidade, melhoria.
PROS.PER.OUS, adj., próspero, progressivo.
PROS.TATE, s., Anat., próstata; adj., prostático.
PRO.STAT.IC, adj., prostático.
PROS.THE.SIS, s., Med., prótese; Gram., prótese, próstese.
PROS.TI.TUTE, s., prostituta, meretriz; v., dedicar-se à prostituição, prostituir-se.
PROS.TI.TU.TION, s., prostituição, meretrício.
PROS.TRATE, v., prostrar; abater, enfraquecer; adj., prostrado, debilitado.
PRO.TAG.O.NIST, s., protagonista, personagem principal, líder, guia.
PROT.A.SIS, s., prótese.
PRO.TECT, v., proteger, resguardar.
PRO.TECT.ING, adj., protetor.
PRO.TEC.TION, s., proteção.
PRO.TEC.TION.ISM, s., protecionismo.
PRO.TEC.TION.IST, s., protecionista.
PRO.TEC.TIVE, adj., protetor.
PRO.TEC.TIVE.NESS, s., sentimento de proteção.
PRO.TEC.TOR, s., protetor, tutor.
PRO.TEC.TOR.ATE, s., protetorado.

PRO.TEIN, s., Biol., Quím., proteína.
PRO.TEST, s., protesto, reclamação, queixa; v., protestar, reclamar, queixar-se.
PRO.TEST.ER, s., protestador, reclamante, manifestante.
PROT.ES.TANT, adj., s., protestante.
PROT.ES.TANT.ISM, s., protestantismo.
PRO.TES.TA.TION, s., protesto, reclamação.
PROTH.E.SIS, s., prótese.
PRO.TO.COL, s., protocolo, cerimonial, etiqueta.
PRO.TON, s., Fís., Quím., próton.
PRO.TO.TYPE, s., protótipo.
PRO.TO.ZO.AN, s., adj., protozoário.
PRO.TO.ZO.ON, s., protozoário.
PRO.TRACT, v., protrair, adiar, prolongar.
PRO.TRACT.ED, adj., prolongado.
PRO.TRAC.TOR, s., transferidor.
PRO.TRUDE, v., salientar-se, sobressair-se; fazer ressaltar.
PRO.TRU.SION, s., saliência, protuberância.
PRO.TU.BER.ANCE, s., protuberância, saliência, bossa.
PRO.TU.BER.ANT, adj., protuberante, saliente, destacado.
PROUD, adj., orgulhoso, vaidoso, arrogante; imponente, admirável; impetuoso.
PROUD.LY, adv., orgulhosamente; pej., arrogantemente.
PROV.ABLE, adj., provável, possível.
PROVE, v., provar, experimentar, tentar, comprovar, patentear, evidenciar.
PROV.EN, v., provado, comprovado, demonstrado.
PROV.E.NANCE, s., proveniência, origem, procedência.
PRO.VEN.ÇAL, s., adj., provençal.
PROV.EN.DER, s., forragem seca, ração animal, alimento para animais.
PROV.ER, s., provador, experimentador, degustador.
PROV.ERB, s., provérbio, máxima, dito, adágio.
PRO.VER.BI.AL, adj., proverbial.
PRO.VIDE, v., prover, fornecer, abastecer, suprir, providenciar.
PRO.VID.ED, adj., provido, fornecido, abastecido, suprido; conj., desde que, contanto que.
PROV.I.DENCE, s., providência.
PROV.I.DENT, adj., previdente, prudente, avisado.
PROV.I.DEN.TIAL, adj., providencial.
PRO.VID.ER, s., provedor, mantenedor.
PRO.VID.ING, conj., providing (that): desde que.
PROV.INCE, s., província, região, estado.
PRO.VIN.CIAL, adj., provinciano, provincial, caipira, interiorano.
PROV.ING, s., prova.
PRO.VI.SION, s., provisão, abastecimento, suprimento.
PRO.VI.SION.AL, adj., provisional, provisório.
PRO.VI.SION.AL.LY, adv., provisionalmente, provisoriamente, temporariamente.
PRO.VI.SO, s., Jur., condição, cláusula; prescrição.
PRO.VI.SO.RY, adj., provisório, condicional.
PROV.O.CA.TION, s., provocação.
PRO.VOC.A.TIVE, adj., provocativo; provocante, excitante.
PRO.VOC.A.TIVE.LY, adv., provocativamente, provocantemente.
PRO.VOKE, v., provocar, instigar, causar.
PRO.VOK.ER, s., provocador, instigador.
PRO.VOK.ING, adj., provocador; provocante.
PROVOST, s., diretor, chefe; UK reitor; prefeito (Escócia).
PROW, s., Náut., proa.

PROWESS · 577 · · PUMP

PROW.ESS, s., habilidade, destreza, rapidez.
PROWL, s., ronda, vigilância, sentinela; v., rondar, vigiar, andar a esmo.
PROWL CAR, s., US radiopatrulha.
PROW.LER, s., rondante; gatuno, vagabundo.
PROX.I.MATE, adj., próximo, vizinho, achegado, imediato.
PROX.IM.I.TY, s., proximidade, vizinhança, adjacência.
PROXY, s., procuração, procurador, representante; v., agir como procurador.
PRUDE, adj., pudico, melindroso.
PRU.DENCE, s., prudência, cuidado, cautela.
PRU.DENT, adj., prudente, cauteloso, cuidadoso.
PRU.DENT.LY, adv., prudentemente.
PRUD.ERY, s., afetação, melindre.
PRUD.ISH, s., afetado, melindroso, prudente.
PRUNE, s., ameixa seca.
PRUN.ING, s., poda, podadura.
PRU.RI.ENCE, s., prurido; lascívia.
PRU.RI.ENT, adj., pruriente; lascivo.
PRU.RI.TUS, s., Med., prurido.
PRUS.SIAN, adj., s., prussiano.
PRY, v., meter-se, intrometer-se, investigar.
PRY.ING, adj., intrometido, abelhudo; curioso, espreitador.
PSALM, s., salmo.
PSALM.IST, s., salmista.
PSEUDO, adj., pseudo, falso.
PSEU.DO.NYM, s., pseudônimo.
PSEU.DON.Y.MOUS, adj., pseudônimo.
PSO.RI.A.SIS, s., Med., psoríase.
PSYCH UP, v., col., preparar psicologicamente (expressão).
PSYCHE, s., psique.
PSYCH.E.DEL.IC, s., droga psicodélica; adj., psicodélico.
PSY.CHI.AT.RIC, adj., psiquiátrico.
PSY.CHI.A.TRIST, s., psiquiatra.
PSY.CHI.A.TRY, s., psiquiatria.
PSY.CHIC, adj., psíquico.
PSY.CHO.AN.A.LYSE, s., psicanalizar.
PSY.CHO.ANAL.Y.SIS, s., psicanálise.
PSY.CHO.AN.A.LYST, s., psicanalista.
PSY.CHO.LOG.IC, adj., psicológico.
PSY.CHO.LOG.IC.AL, adj., o mesmo que psichologic.
PSY.CHOL.O.GIST, v., psicólogo.
PSY.CHOG.RA.PHY, s., psicografia.
PSY.CHOL.O.GY, s., psicologia.
PSY.CHO.MO.TOR, adj., psicomotor.
PSY.CHO.PATH, s., psicopata.
PSY.CHO.SIS, s., Med., psicose.
PSY.CHO.SO.MAT.IC, adj., psicossomático.
PSY.CHO.THER.A.PY, s., psicoterapia.
PSY.CHOT.IC, adj., psicótico.
PUB, s., UK bar, pub.
PU.BER.TY, s., puberdade.
PU.BES, s., púbis.
PU.BES.CENCE, s., puberdade, pubescência.
PU.BES.CENT, adj., púbere.
PU.BIC, adj., Anat., pubiano.
PUB.LIC, s., público, povo, assistência; UK taberna, bar; adj., público, comum.
PUB.LI.CAN, s., UK dono de pub, taberneiro; publicano.
PUB.LI.CA.TION, s., publicação, proclamação, editoração.
PUB.LIC DO.MAIN, s., domínio público.

PUB.LIC HOL.I.DAY, s., feriado nacional.
PUB.LIC HOUSE, s., UK pub, bar.
PUB.LI.CIST, s., publicista, publicitário.
PUB.LIC.I.TY, s., publicidade, propaganda.
PUB.LI.CIZE, v., publicar, divulgar, propagar.
PUB.LIC.LY, adv., publicamente.
PUB.LIC OF.FICE, s., cargo público.
PUB.LIC O.PIN.ION, s., opinião pública.
PUB.LIC PROS.E.CU.TOR, s., Jur., promotor público.
PUB.LIC RE.LA.TIONS, s. pl., relações públicas.
PUB.LIC SCHOOL, s., UK escola particular; US escola pública.
PUB.LISH, v., publicar, divulgar.
PUB.LISH.ER, s., editor, publicador, divulgador.,
PUB.LISH.ING, s., setor editorial.
PUB.LISH.ING HOUSE, PUB.LISH.ING COM.PA.NY, s., editora.
PUCE, adj., marrom-avermelhado.
PUCK, s., duende, fantasma.
PUCK.ER, s., ruga, prega, dobra; v., amarrotar, enrugar, franzir.
PUD.DING, s., pudim, sobremesa.
PUD.DLE, s., poça, atoleiro, lamaçal; v., embaciar, ofuscar, turvar.
PU.ER.ILE, adj., pueril, infantil.
PU.ER.IL.I.TY, s., puerilidade, infantilidade.
PUER.TO RI.CAN, adj., porto-riquenho.
PUFF, s., sopro, baforada, lufada, bomba, protuberância; v., soprar, bufar, ofegar.
PUFFED OUT, adj., inchado (de machucado); UK ofegante, esbaforido.
PUF.FI.NESS, s., inchamento, intumescência; empolamento.
PUF.FY, adj., inchado.
PUG, s., dogue (tipo de cão de pelo curto); col., raposa; gír., pugilista.
PU.GI.LISM, s., pugilismo, luta.
PU.GI.LIST, s., pugilista.
PUG.NA.CIOUS, adj., belicoso; brigão, combativo.
PUG.NAC.I.TY, s., belicosidade, pugnacidade.
PUIS.SANCE, s., força, vigor, domínio.
PUKE, s., vômito; v., vomitar, lançar.
PULE, s., choro, gemido.
PULL, s., puxão, arranco, arrancada, força, gole; v., puxar, arrastar, colher, remover.
PUL.LEY, s., roldana; polia.
PULL OUT, s., Mil., retirada (de tropas); encarte (de revista).
PULL.OVER, s., pulôver, agasalho.
PUL.MO.NARY, adj., pulmonar.
PULP, s., polpa de frutas.
PUL.PIT, s., púlpito.
PULP.Y, adj., polposo, carnudo.
PUL.SAR, s., Astron., pulsar.
PUL.SATE, v., pulsar, latejar, arquejar.
PUL.SA.TION, s., pulsação, latejamento.
PULSE, s., pulso, cadência, compasso; legume.
PUL.VER.I.ZA.TION, s., pulverização.
PUL.VER.IZE, v., pulverizar.
PU.MA, s., puma.
PUM.ICE, s., pedra-pomes; v., limpar (com pedra-pomes).
PUM.MEL, v., esmurrar, surrar.
PUMP, s., bomba, sondagem; v., bombear, arrojar, esgotar.

PUMPERNICKEL · 578 · PUTT

PUM.PER.NICK.EL, s., pão de centeio integral.
PUMP.KIN s., abóbora.
PUN, s., trocadilho, jogo de palavras.
PUNCH, s., soco, murro, pancada, ímpeto, ponche; v., picar, socar, furar.
PUNCH BALL, PUNCH.ING BALL, s., saco de pancadas.
PUNCH.ER, s., furador.
PUNCH LINE, s., frase final (de uma história), arremate, *slogan* ou piada.
PUNCH-UP, s., *UK* briga (entre várias pessoas).
PUNCH.Y, *adj.*, *col.*, incisivo, forte, vigoroso; *col.*, bêbado.
PUNC.TIL.I.OUS, *adj.*, escrupuloso, preocupado.
PUNC.TIL.I.OUS.NESS, s., meticulosidade, detalhe.
PUNC.TU.AL, *adj.*, pontual.
PUNC.TU.AL.I.TY, s., pontualidade, exatidão, assiduidade.
PUNC.TU.AL.LY, *adv.*, pontualmente.
PUNC.TU.ATE, s., pontuar, enfatizar, destacar, realçar.
PUNC.TU.A.TION, s., pontuação, ênfase.
PUNC.TU.A.TION MARK, s., sinal de pontuação.
PUNC.TURE, s., punctura, buraco (feito por algo pontudo), furo (de pneu); v., perfurar, furar, puncionar.
PUN.DIT, s., especialista (em algum assunto).
PUN.GEN.CY, s., pungência, acidez, agrura.
PUN.GENT, *adj.*, pungente, forte, penetratante; mordaz.
PUN.ISH, v., punir, castigar.
PUN.ISH.ABLE, *adj.*, punível, castigável.
PUN.ISH.ING, *adj.*, penoso.
PUN.ISH.MENT, s., castigo, punição, pena.
PU.NI.TIVE, *adj.*, punitivo.
PUNK, s., rufião, punk.
PUN.NET, s., *UK* cesto (de frutas delicadas).
PUNT, s., barco a remo; ponto (em jogo de azar); v., navegar em barco a remo; pontuar (jogo).
PUNT.ER, s., *gír.*, *UK* jogador, apostador, cliente; *col.*, barqueiro (de barco a remo).
PU.NY, *adj.*, fraco, débil.
PUP, s., cachorrinho, filhote; *fig.*, meninote.
PU.PIL, s., pupila, pupilo, aluno, discípulo.
PUP.PET, s., marionete, fantoche, títere.
PUP.PET SHOW, s., teatro de marionetes.
PUP.PY, s., cachorrinho, filhote de cachorro.
PUP.PY FAT, s., dobrinhas de gordura (de bebê).
PUR.BLIND.NESS, s., cegueira relativa.
PUR.CHASE, s., compra, aquisição.
PUR.CHAS.ER, s., comprador.
PURE, *adj.*, puro.
PURE.BRED, s., puro-sangue; *adj.*, puro-sangue.
PU.RÉE, s., purê.
PURE.LY, *adv.*, puramente.
PURE.NESS, s., pureza.
PUR.GA.TION, s., purgação, limpeza.
PUR.GA.TIVE, s., purgante; *adj.*, purificador, purgador.
PUR.GA.TO.RY, s., purgatório.
PURGE, s., purgação, purgante; v., purgar, purificar, limpar, sanar.
PU.RI.FI.CA.TION, s., purificação, purgação.
PU.RI.FI.ER, s., purificador.
PU.RI.FY, v., purificar, purgar, limpar.
PU.RI.FY.ING, s., purificação.
PUR.IST, s., purista.
PU.RI.TAN, s., puritano.

PU.RI.TAN.I.CAL, *adj.*, *pej.*, puritano.
PU.RI.TAN.ISM, s., puritanismo.
PU.RI.TY, s., pureza.
PURL, s., laçada (de tricô); remoinho, ondulação; v., dar uma laçada (tricô); ondular.
PUR.LOIN, v., furtar, plagiar, roubar.
PUR.LOIN.ER, s., ladrão, gatuno.
PUR.PLE, *adj.*, purpúreo, roxo.
PUR.PORT, s., sentido, significado; v., significar; pretender; passar por.
PUR.POSE, s., propósito, objetivo, intenção.
PUR.POSE.FUL, *adj.*, decidido, resoluto, incisivo.
PUR.POSE.LY, *adv.*, propositadamente, deliberadamente.
PURR, s., ronrom; v., ronronar.
PURSE, s., bolsa, carteira, erário, dinheiro, caixa; v., enrugar, franzir.
PURS.ER, s., comissário de bordo, intendente naval.
PUR.SU.ANCE, s., prosseguimento, seguimento, continuação.
PUR.SU.ANT.LY, *adv.*, de acordo, de conformidade.
PUR.SUE, v., perseguir, procurar, seguir, adotar.
PUR.SU.ER, s., perseguidor.
PUR.SUIT, s., perseguição; caça; busca; atividade.
PU.RU.LENCE, s., purulência.
PU.RU.LENT, *adj.*, purulento.
PUR.VEY, v., prover, abastecer, suprir.
PUR.VEY.ANCE, s., abastecimento.
PUR.VEY.OR, s., fornecedor.
PUS, s., *Med.*, pus.
PUSH, s., empurrão, tentativa, emergência, impulso; v., empurrar, impulsionar.
PUSH BIKE, s., *UK* bicicleta.
PUSH-CART, s., carrinho de vendedor (empurrado a mão); carrinho de mão.
PUSHED, *adj.*, *col.*, carente de; com falta de; com dificuldade de.
PUSH.ER, s., aquele que empurra; propulsor; *gír.*, traficante de drogas.
PUSH.O.VER, s., coisa fácil de fazer, moleza; *col.*, otário.
PUSH-UP, s., *US* flexão (atividade física).
PUSHY, *adj.*, intrometido, metido.
PU.SIL.LA.NIM.I.TY, s., pusilanimidade.
PU.SIL.LAN.I.MOUS, *adj.*, pusilânime.
PUSS, s., *col.*, gatinho, bichano; *col.*, rapariga; *puss in boots*: gato de botas.
PUS.SY, s., gatinha; *pussy cat*: gatinho, pessoa fofa e delicada; *adj.*, *Med.*, purulento.
PUS.TU.LATE, v., criar pústulas; *adj.*, pustulento.
PUS.TU.LA.TION, s., pustulação.
PUT, s., lance, arremesso; v., pôr, colocar, meter, atribuir, guardar, expor, calcular.
PUT ABOVE, v., colocar acima de, pôr em cima de.
PU.TA.TIVE, *adj.*, putativo.
PUT DOWN, v., largar, pôr no chão; *col.*, humilhar, rebaixar; *UK* sacrificar.
PU.TRE.FAC.TION, s., putrefação.
PU.TRE.FY, v., apodrecer, putrefazer.
PU.TRID, *adj.*, pútrido, fedido, fedorento.
PU.TRID.I.TY, s., podridão.
PUTSH, s., golpe de Estado.
PUTT, s., *Esp.*, tacada leve (golfe); v., dar tacada leve.

PUT UPON

PUT UPON, *adj.*, explorado; *v.*, pôr por cima; *to feel* ~ : sentir-se usado.
PUZ.ZLE, *s.*, charada, quebra-cabeças, palavras cruzadas; *v.*, confundir, embaraçar.
PUZ.ZLED, *adj.*, embaraçado, complicado, confuso.
PUZ.ZLER, *s.*, embaraçador.
PUZ.ZLING, *adj.*, desconcertante, embaraçoso; enigmático.
PYG.MAE.AN, *adj.*, pigmeu.
PYG.MY, *s.*, pigmeu.
PY.JA.MAS, *s. pl.*, pijama (peças do pijama).
PY.LON, *s.*, pilão, poste, torre.

PYR.A.MID, *s.*, pirâmide.
PYRE, *s.*, pira, fogueira, pira funerária.
PY.REX, *s.*, pírex.
PY.ROG.RA.PHY, *s.*, pirografia.
PY.RO.MA.NI.AC, *s.*, piromaníaco.
PY.ROM.E.TER, *s.*, pirômetro.
PY.ROM.E.TRY, *s.*, pirometria.
PY.RO.TECH.NIC, *adj.*, pirotécnico.
PY.THAG.O.RE.AN, *adj.*, pitagórico.
PY.THON, *s.*, pitão, serpente.
PYX, *s.*, cibório, cálice, píxide.

Q, s., décima sétima letra do alfabeto inglês.
QUACK, s., grasnido de pato; v., grasnar; adj., charlatão.
QUACK.ERY, s., charlatanismo, curandeirismo.
QUAD, s. abrev. de *quadrangle*: quadrângulo; abrev. de *quadrupled*: quádruplo.
QUAD BIKE, s., col., quadriciclo.
QUAD.RAN.GLE, s., quadrângulo; adj., quadrangular.
QUA.DRAN.GU.LAR, adj., quadrangular.
QUAD.RANT, s., quadrante.
QUAD.RA.PHON.IC, adj., quadrafônico.
QUAD.RATE, s., quadrado, quadrilátero; v., quadrar; adj., quadrado.
QUAD.RA.TURE, s., quadratura.
QUAD.RI.LAT.ER.AL, adj., s., quadrilátero.
QUA.DRILLE, s., quadrilha.
QUA.DROON, s., quarteirão.
QUAD.RU.PED, adj., s., Zool., quadrúpede.
QUA.DRU.PLE, v., quadruplicar.
QUA.DRU.PLETS, s. pl., quadrigêmeos.
QUA.DRU.PLEX, adj., s., quádruplo.
QUA.DRU.PLI.CATE, v., quadruplicar; quadruplicado.
QUA.DRU.PLI.CA.TION, v., quadruplicação.
QUADS, s. pl., col., quadrigêmeos.
QUAFF, s., trago (de bebida); v., beber grandes goles (de bebida).
QUAG, s., pântano, charco, brejo, paul.
QUAG.MIRE, s., pântano, brejo.
QUAIL, s., codorniz; v., ceder, amedrontar-se.
QUAINT, adj., curioso, estranho, esquisito.
QUAINT.NESS, s., singularidade; esquisitice.
QUAKE, s., tremor, abalo sísmico; v., tremer, estremecer.
QUAK.ING, s., tremor; adj., trêmulo, tremente, medroso.
QUAL.I.FI.CA.TION, s., qualificação, requisito, modificação, título.
QUAL.I.FIED, adj., qualificado, capacitado, habilitado.
QUAL.I.FY, v., qualificar, capacitar, habilitar, educar, modificar.
QUAL.I.FY.ING, adj., qualificativo, qualificador; Esp., *qualifying round*: rodada preliminar (competição).
QUAL.I.TA.TIVE, adj., qualitativo.
QUAL.I.TY, s., qualidade, predicado.
QUALM, s., desânimo, desmaio, desfalecimento, náusea, dúvida.
QUALMS, s. pl., receio, escrúpulos.
QUAN.DA.RY, s., dilema, dúvida.
QUAN.TIC, s., quântico; Mat., quântica.
QUAN.TI.FI.A.BLE, adj., quantificável.
QUAN.TI.FY, s., UK quantidade; v., quantificar, avaliar.
QUAN.TI.TA.TIVE, adj., quantitativo.
QUAN.TI.TY, s., quantidade, valor, soma.
QUAN.TI.ZA.TION, s., quantização.
QUAN.TUM THEORY, s., Fís., teoria quântica.
QUAN.TUM ME.CHAN.ICS, s. pl., Fís., mecânica quântica.
QUAR.AN.TINE, s., quarentena.
QUARK, s., Cul., quark (queijo); Fís., quark (física atômica).
QUAR.REL, s., disputa, contenda, rixa, discussão; v., discutir, disputar, querelar.
QUAR.REL.LER, s., altercador, polemista, querelante.
QUAR.REL.SOM, adj., briguento, brigão, quereloso.
QUAR.REL.SOME, adj., briguento, irritado, irascível.
QUAR.RI.ER, s., cavouqueiro.
QUAR.RY, s., pedreira, caça, presa; v., tirar macadame, extrair pedras.
QUART, s., quarto, medida para líquidos com 1.136 litros.
QUART.ER, s., quarto, quarta parte, trimestre, quarteirão; v., esquartejar.
QUART.ER-BOUND, s., encadernado com lombada de couro.
QUAR.TER.DECK, s., Náut., tombadilho superior.
QUAR.TER.FI.NAL, s., Esp., quartas de final.
QUART.ER HOUR, s., um quarto de hora, quinze minutos.
QUAR.TER.ING, s., esquartejamento; aquartelamento.
QUAR.TET, s., quarteto.
QUARTZ, s., Min.; quartzo.
QUA.SAR, s., Astron., quasar.
QUASH, v., anular, destruir, suprimir.
QUA.TER.NA.RY, adj., quaternário.
QUA.TRAIN, s., quarteto, estrofe com quatro versos, quadra.
QUA.VER, s., Mús., colcheia; garganteio; tremor; v., tremer; falar com voz trêmula; trinar.
QUA.VER.ING, adj., trêmulo.
QUAY, s., cais, ancoradouro.
QUAY.SIDE, s., cais.
QUEA.SI.NESS, s., enjoo, náusea.
QUEA.SY, adj., enjoado.
QUEEN, s., rainha, dama, carta de baralho e peça no xadrez; v., coroar alguém rainha.
QUEEN BEE, s., Zool., abelha-mestra, abelha rainha.
QUEEN MOTH.ER, s., rainha-mãe (mãe de rei ou rainha).
QUEEN.LY, adj., régio, próprio de rainha.
QUEER, adj., esquisito, estranho, adoentado; v., arruinar, embaraçar.
QUELL, v., sufocar, reprimir, subjugar; abrandar, acalmar.
QUENCH, v., extinguir, debelar; suprimir, sufocar; saciar.
QUENCH.A.BLE, adj., extinguível, saciável.
QUER.IST, s., interrogador, curioso.
QUER.U.LOUS, adj., queixoso, choroso, quereloso.
QUE.RY, s., pergunta, questão, ponto de interrogação; v., perguntar, indagar.
QUEST, s., indagação, busca, pergunta; v., indagar, buscar, procurar.
QUES.TION, s., questão, pergunta, exame, disputa; v., examinar, perguntar, duvidar.
QUES.TION.ABLE, adj., questionável, duvidoso.
QUES.TION.ARY, s., questionário.

QUESTIONER ··581·· QUOTIENT

QUES.TION.ER, *s.*, interrogador, examinador.
QUES.TION.ING, *s.*, interrogatório; *adj.*, interrogativo.
QUES.TION MARK, *s.*, ponto de interrogação.
QUES.TION MAST.ER *UK*, **QUIZ.MAS.TER** *US*, *s.*, apresentador de show de perguntas.
QUES.TION.NAIRE, *s.*, questionário.
QUEUE, *s.*, fila; *v.*, fazer fila, enfileirar.
QUEUE-JUMP, *v.*, *UK* furar a fila.
QUIB.BLE, *s.*, ninharia, chorumela, *v.*, lamuriar-se por pouco.
QUIB.BLER, *s.*, pessoa que chora por ninharia; *Bras.*, cri-cri.
QUICK, *s.*, ser vivo, carne viva; *adj.*, rápido, vivo, ativo, intenso, èsperto.
QUICK.EN, *v.*, apressar, acelerar, estimular.
QUICK.LY, *adv.*, rapidamente, subitamente, de súbito.
QUICK.NESS, *s.*, rapidez, celeridade, pressa.
QUICK.SAND, *s.*, areia movediça.
QUICK.SIL.VER, *s.*, mercúrio.
QUICK.STEP, *s.*, dança de salão de passos rápidos; *Mil.*, passo acelerado.
QUICK-TEM.PERED, *adj.*, irritadiço.
QUICK-WIT.TED, *adj.*, arguto.
QUID, *s.*, *col.*, *UK* libra (esterlina).
QUI.ESCE, *v.*, emudecer, calar-se, ficar em silêncio.
QUI.ES.CENCE, *s.*, quietude, tranquilidade, paz, sossego.
QUI.ET, *s.*, sossego, paz, quietude; *adj.*, calmo, tranquilo; *v.*, aquietar, acalmar.
QUI.ET.EN, *v.*, acalmar, aquietar, tranquilizar, sossegar.
QUI.ET.IZE, *v.*, aquietar, acalmar.
QUI.ET.LY, *adv.*, quietamente, calmamente.
QUI.ET.NESS, *s.*, tranquilidade, quietude, sossego, calma, paz.
QUIFF, *s.*, *UK* topete, mecha de cabelos.
QUILL, *s.*, pluma, pena para escrever; *v.*, enrolar, dobrar.
QUILT, *s.*, colcha, acolchoado; *v.*, acolchoar, forrar.
QUILT.ED, *adj.*, acolchoado.
QUINCE, *s.*, marmelo.
QUIN.I.A, *s.*, quina, quinina.

QUI.NINE, *s.*, *Quím.*, quinina, quinino.
QUIN.QUAG.E.NA.RI.AN, *adj.*, *s.*, quinquagenário.
QUIN.QUEN.NIAL, *adj.*, quinquenal.
QUIN.QUEN.NIUM, *s.*, *Lat.*, quinquênio, lustro.
QUINS, **QUINTS**, *s. pl.*, *col.*, quíntuplos.
QUIN.TES.SEN.TIAL, *adj.*, fundamental; de característica central.
QUIN.TET, *s.*, quinteto.
QUIN.TU.PLE, *adj.*, *s.*, quíntuplo; *v.*, quintuplicar.
QUIN.TU.PLETS, *s. pl.*, quíntuplos.
QUIP, *s.*, escárnio, zombaria, sátira; *v.*, zombar, mofar, rir de.
QUIRK, *s.*, truque, subterfúgio, artimanha.
QUIRK.Y, *adj.*, peculiar.
QUIT, *v.*, renunciar, abandonar, partir, quitar; *adj.*, quite, livre.
QUITE, *adv.*, completamente, totalmente.
QUITS, *adj.*, quite, livre.
QUIT.TANCE, *s.*, quitação, recibo.
QUIT.TER, *s.*, molenga.
QUIV.ER, *s.*, aljava; *v.*, tremer, estremecer.
QUIV.ER.ING, *s.*, tremor; *adj.*, trêmulo.
QUIX.OT.IC, *adj.*, quixotesco.
QUIZ, *s.*, problema, enigma; *v.*, embaraçar, dificultar.
QUIS.MAS.TER, *s.*, animador de programa de perguntas.
QUIZ.ZI.CAL, *adj.*, zombeteiro, excêntrico, estranho.
QUOD, *s.*, prisão, cadeia, xadrez; *v.*, prender, encarcerar.
QUOIN, *s.*, ângulo, pedra angular, esquina; *v.*, firmar com pedra.
QUOITS, *s.*, jogo das argolas.
QUO.RUM, *s.*, *Lat.*, quórum.
QUOTA, *s.*, *Lat.*, quota, cota.
QUOT.ABLE, *adj.*, cotável, citável.
QUO.TA.TION, *s.*, cotação, citação.
QUO.TA.TION MARKS, *s. pl.*, aspas.
QUOTE, *s.*, citação, cotação; *v.*, citar, orçar, cotar.
QUO.TID.IAN, *adj.*, quotidiano, cotidiano, diário.
QUO.TIENT, *s.*, quociente, cociente.

R

R, décima oitava letra do alfabeto inglês.
RAB.BET, s., entalhe, encaixe; v., encaixar, entalhar.
RAB.BI, s., rabino, mestre.
RAB.BIT, s., coelho.
RAB.BI.TER, s., caçador de coelhos.
RAB.BLE, s., poviléu, plebe, ralé, povinho, populaça, gentalha; v., arruaçar, badernar.
RA.BID, adj., furioso, violento, raivento, hidrófobo.
RA.BI.ES, s., Vet., hodrofobia, raiva.
RAC.COON, s., Zool., racum (carnívoro noturno da Am. do Norte semelhante ao guaxinim).
RACE, s., corrida, competição, raça, raça humana, povo, canal; v., competir, correr; adj., US de corrida.
RACE.COURSE, s., pista de corridas, hipódromo.
RACE.HORSE, s., cavalo de corrida; *horses-racing*: corrida de cavalos.
RACE RIOT, s., conflito racial.
RACE-TRACK, s., pista de corridas, autódromo.
RACE-WALK.ING, s., Esp., marcha atlética.
RA.CHIT.IC, adj., raquítico.
RA.CHI.TIS, s., Med., raquitismo.
RA.CIAL, adj., racial.
RA.CIAL DIS.CRIM.I.NA.TION, s., discriminação racial.
RA.CIAL.ISM, s., o mesmo que *racism*.
RAC.I.LY, adv., vigorosamente, vivamente.
RA.CI.NESS, s., força, vigor, robustez, fortaleza.
RAC.ING, s., Esp., corrida; adj., de corrida.
RAC.ING CAR UK, **RACE CAR** US, s., carro de corrida.
RAC.ING DRIV.ER UK, **RACE DRIV.ER** US, s., piloto de corrida.
RAC.ISM, s., racismo.
RAC.IST, s., racista.
RACK, s., prateleira, cavalete, cabide, porta-bagagem; ruína, destroços.
RACK.ET s., barulho; extorsão, negociata, safadeza; raquete (jogo de tênis, andar na neve etc.).
RACK.ET.EER, s., extorsionário, escroque; v., obter dinheiro por extorsão.
RACK.ET.EER.ING, s., ato de obter dinheiro por extorsão.
RA.CON.TEUR, s., Fr., pessoa que conta histórias e anedotas.
RAC.QUET, s., raquete.
RACY, adj., corajoso, ousado, picante, mordaz.
RA.DAR, s., radar.
RA.DAR TRAP, s., radar eletrônico da polícia rodoviária.
RA.DI.AN, s., Mat., radiano.
RA.DI.ANCE, s., radiação, brilho, esplendor.
RA.DI.ANT, adj., radiante, brilhante, luminoso.
RA.DI.ATE, s., v., radiar, irradiar; propagar; transmitir pelo rádio; adj., raiado, radiado.
RA.DI.A.TION, s., radiação.
RA.DI.A.TIVE, adv., radiativo.
RA.DI.A.TOR, s., radiador; aquecedor.

RAD.I.CAL, adj., radical; adj., radical, extremo.
RAD.I.CAL.I.ZA.TION UK, **RAD.I.CAL.I.SA.TION** US, s., radicalização.
RAD.I.CAL.IZE(-ISE), v., radicalizar.
RAD.I.CAL.LY, adv., radicalmente.
RAD.I.CAL.ISM, s., radicalismo.
RAD.I.CAL.NESS, s., caráter radical, natureza, origem, princípio fundamental.
RA.DI.O, s., Quím., rádio (elem. radioativo); aparelho de rádio, radiotransmissão; v., transmitir por rádio.
RA.DI.O.AC.TIVE, adj., radioativo.
RA.DI.O.AC.TIVE WASTE, s., lixo radioativo.
RA.DI.O.AC.TIV.I.TY, s., radioatividade.
RA.DI.O A.LARM, s., rádio-relógio.
RA.DI.O-BROAD.CAST.ING, s., radiotransmissão.
RA.DI.O-CON.TROLLED, s., UK controle remoto
RADI.I FRE.QUEN.CY, s., radiofrequência.
RA.DI.O.GRAPH, s., radiografia, negativo de raios X (ou cópia); v., radiografar.
RA.DI.OG.RA.PHER, s., radiologista; radiógrafo.
RA.DI.OG.RA.PHY, s., radiografia.
RA.DI.OPH.O.NY, s., radiofonia.
RA.DI.OS.CO.PY, s., radioscopia.
RA.DI.O STA.TION, s., emissora de rádio, estação de radiodifusão.
RA.DI.O.THER.A.PIST, s., Med., radioterapeuta.
RA.DI.O.THER.A.PY, s., Med., radioterapia.
RAD.ISH, s., rabanete.
RA.DI.UM s., Quím., rádio (elem. radioativo).
RA.DI.US, s., Geom., raio; Anat., rádio (osso do antebraço).
RA.DON, s., Quím., radônio (elem. radioativo).
RAF.FI.A, s., Bot., ráfia (tipo de palmeira baixa da África).
RAF.FLE, s., rifa, sorteio; v., rifar, sortear.
RAFT, s., balsa, jangada.
RAFT.ER, s., viga, esteio, coluna.
RAG, s., trapo, farrapo, repreensão; jornaleco; *rags* s.pl.: trapos.
RAG.A.MUF.FIN, adj., s., vagabundo, esfarrapado.
RAG.BAG, s., sacola de trapos; fig., mixórdia, salada, mistura.
RAG DOLL, s., boneca de pano.
RAGE, s., raiva, ira, ódio, furor, violência; v., enfurecer-se, irritar-se.
RAGE.FUL, adj., raivoso, furioso, irado, irritado.
RAGE.FUL.LY, adv., raivosamente, furiosamente.
RAG.GED, adj., maltrapilho, esfarrapado, roto, pobre.
RAG.GING, adj., furioso, raivoso; feroz, intenso; espumoso.
RAG.MAN, s., negociante de coisas velhas.
RA.GOUT, s., Fr., Cul., ragu.
RAID, s., incursão, assalto, ataque, reide; v., atacar repentinamente, invadir.
RAID.ER, s., invasor, ladrão, assaltante.
RAIL, s., corrimão, parapeito, grade; trilho de ferrovia; v.,

RAILING ··583·· RASTA

xingar, insultar, cercar.
RAIL.ING, s., grade, parapeito; trilhos, materiais para trilhos.
RAIL.ROAD, s., ferrovia, estrada de ferro.
RAIL.WAY, s., estrada de ferro.
RAIL.WAY CAR, s., vagão.
RAIL.WAY EN.GINE, s., locomotiva.
RAIL.WAY LINE, s., linha de trem.
RAIL.WAY MAN, s., ferroviário.
RAIL.WAY STA.TION, s., estação ferroviária.
RAIN, s., chuva; v., chover, gotejar, garoar.
RAIN.BOW, s., arco-íris.
RAIN.COAT, s., impermeável, capa de chuva.
RAIN.DROP, s., gota de chuva, pingo de chuva.
RAIN.FALL s., chuva, aguaceiro.
RAIN FOR.EST, s., floresta tropical.
RAIN-GAUGE, s., pluviômetro.
RAIN.PROOF, adj., impermeável.
RAIN.STORM, s., pancada de chuva, temporal.
RAIN-WA.TER, s., água da chuva.
RAIN.Y, adj., chuvoso.
RAISE, s., aumento, elevação; v., elevar, levantar, engrande-
cer, ajuntar, criar, educar.
RAISED, adj., levantado, elevado; cultivado, crescido; em
relevo.
RAI.SIN, s., uva seca, passa.
RAJ, s., Hist., Império Britânico na Índia.
RA.JAH, s., rajá.
RAKE, s., ancinho, rodo, tipo dissoluto; v., limpar, ajuntar,
farrear, revolver, remexer.
RAKE-OFF, s., col., propina, lucro ilícito.
RAK.ER, s., ancinho, raspador.
RAK.ISH, adj., dissoluto, devasso, lascivo.
RAL.LY, s., reunião, reagrupamento; v., reunir, agrupar, ajun-
tar, organizar, reanimar.
RAL.LY.ING, s., rali (corrida de automóveis em vias públicas).
RAM, s., Zool., carneiro; aríete; Astrol., Áries; v., bater, golpear,
forçar, cravar.
RAM, abrev. de random access memory: memória de acesso
rápido; s., RAM.
RAM.A.DAN, s., Rel., ramadã.
RAM.BLE, s. ato de vaguear; v., vaguear, vagabundear.
RAM.BLER, s., vagabundo, errante, vadio.
RAM.BLING, s., divagação; passeio; adj., divagador, vaga-
bundo; incoerente, tortuoso.
RAM.E.KIN, s., ramequim, tigela de cerâmica que vai ao
forno.
RAM.I.FI.CA.TION, s., ramificação.
RAM.I.FY, v., ramificar(-se).
RAMP, s., rampa, declive, inclinação, fraude, embuste; v.,
pular, saltar.
RAM.PAGE, s., alvoroço, violência, barulho; v., fazer, pro-
mover, esbravejar.
RAM.PA.GEOUS, adj., violento, furioso.
RAM.PANT, adj., exuberante, desenfreado, desmedido.
RAM.PANT.LY, adv., exuberantemente.
RAM.PARTS, s. pl., muralha.
RAM.SHACK.LE, adj., periclitante; v., desmoronar, cair aos
pedaços.
RANCH, s., rancho, fazenda, estância, sítio.
RANCH.ER, s., fazendeiro, rancheiro.
RANCH HOUSE, s., casa de campo, casa na fazenda.

RAN.CID, adj., rançoso.
RAN.CID.I.TY, s., ranço, rançosidade.
RAN.COUR UK, **RAN.COR** US, s., rancor, ódio, aversão.
RAND, s., orla, borda, margem.
RAN.DOM, s., acaso; adj., fortuito, aleatório; adv., por acaso,
fortuitamente.
RAM.DOM.IZE(-ISE), v., escolher aleatoriamente.
RAN.DOM.LY, adv., ao acaso.
RANGE, s., cadeia, cordilheira, extensão, calibre; v., colocar,
arrumar, percorrer.
RANG.ER, s., guarda-florestal.
RANK, s., fila, fileira, posto, categoria, nível, graduação; v.,
enfileirar, organizar.
RANK.ING, s., classificação, categorização.
RAN.KLE, v., inflamar-se, irritar-se; causar (ou sentir) dor;
causar sentimento.
RAN.SACK, v., revistar, explorar, saquear, pilhar.
RAN.SOM, s., resgate, redenção, refém; v., resgatar, remir.
RAN.SOM.ER, s., resgatador, libertador.
RANT, s., fanfarrice; discurso violento ou bombástico; v., falar
asneira, arengar, usar de discurso bombástico.
RANT.ER, s., fanfarrão; bazofiador.
RANT.ING, s., falatório.
RAP, s., batidinha, batida na porta, pancada; Mús., rap; v.,
bater, dar uma pancada, berrar; arrebatar.
RA.PA.CIOUS, adj., rapace, de rapina; voraz, ávido.
RA.PA.CIOUS.NESS, s., rapacidade, ganância.
RA.PAC.I.TY, s., rapacidade, voracidade, ganância.
RAPE, s., roubo, estupro, violação; v., arrebentar, violentar,
raptar.
RAP.ID, adj., rápido; s., torrente.
RAP.ID-FIRE, s., Mil., fogo contínuo e intenso.
RA.PID.I.TY, s., rapidez, celeridade, presteza.
RA.PID.LY, adv., rapidamente.
RAP.ID.NESS, s., o mesmo que rapidity.
RAP.IST, s., estuprador.
RAP.PER, s., aquele que bate a porta; aldrava; gír., conver-
sador, falador; Mús., cantor de rap.
RAP.PORT, s., concordância, harmonia, conformidade.
RAP.PROCHE.MENT, s., reaproximação.
RAPT, adj., absorto (concentrado); enlevado, arrebatado.
RAPT.NESS, s., êxtase, arrebatamento.
RAP.TURE, s., êxtase, enlevo, arrebatamento.
RAP.TUR.OUS, adj., arrebatador, extasiante.
RARE, adj., raro, rarefeito, bom, extraordinário.
RA.RE.FIED, adj., rarefeito; exclusivo, ilustre.
RAR.E.FY, v., rarefazer, rarear.
RARE.LY, adv., raramente; magificamente.
RARE.NESS, s., raridade.
RAR.ING, adj., col., impaciente, ansioso.
RAR.I.TY, s., raridade.
RAS.CAL, s., patife, mau caráter; adj., desonesto.
RASE, v., arrasar, destruir, demolir.
RASH, adj., apressado, impetuoso; v., arrebatar, tirar, arrancar.
RASH.ER, s., fatia fina de bacon.
RASH.LY, adv., precipitadamente.
RASH.NESS, s., precipitação.
RASP, s., grosa, lima.
RASP.BER.RY, s., framboesa.
RASP.ING, adj., áspero, estridente, irritante.
RAS.TA, abrev. de Rastafarian; s., rastafári.

RASTAFARIAN ·· 584 ·· REALIZE(-ISE)

RAS.TA.FA.RI.AN, s., rastafári.

RAT, s., rato, ratazana; v., caçar ratos, furar greves, comportar-se de maneira vil.

RATCH.ET, s., catraca.

RATE, s., razão, taxa, preço, medida, padrão, imposto predial; v., taxar, cobrar imposto.

RATE.PAY.ER, s., contribuinte de imposto predial.

RAT.ER, s., avaliador.

RATH.ER, adv., um pouco, antes, quiçá, muito, preferivelmente.

RAT.I.FI.CA.TION, s., ratificação.

RAT.I.FY, v., ratificar, confirmar.

RAT.ING, s., avaliação; censura.

RA.TIO, s., razão, proporção.

RA.TI.O.CI.NA.TION, s., raciocínio, tirocínio.

RA.TION, s., ração; pl., mantimentos, víveres; v., raciocinar.

RA.TION.AL, adj., racional, razoável, justo.

RA.TION.ALE, s., fundamento lógico, análise racional.

RA.TION.AL.ISM, s., racionalismo.

RA.TION.AL.I.ZA.TION, s., racionalização.

RA.TION.AL.I.TY, s., racionalidade.

RA.TION.AL.IZE(-ISE), v., racionalizar, raciocinar, medir, ponderar, avaliar.

RATIONING, s., racionamento.

RAT RACE, s., competição acirrada.

RAT.TLE, s., matraca, chocalho, tagarelice; v., provocar ruído de matraca, chocalhar.

RAT.TLER, s., falador, tagarela.

RAT.TLE.SNAKE, s., cascavel.

RAT.TY, adj., col., andrajoso, esfarrapado, roto; gír., rabugento.

RAU.CITY, s., rouquidão.

RAU.COUS, adj., rouco, rouquenho; espalhafatoso.

RAUN.CHY, adj., obsceno, erótico, insinuante; gír., descuidado, de qualidade inferior.

RAV.AGE, s., devastação, destruição; v., devastar, destruir, arruinar, roubar.

RAV.AG.ING, s., saque; adj., devastador, assolador.

RAVE, s., delírio, fúria, raiva; v., delirar, tornar-se furioso, desvairar.

RA.VEN, s., Zool., corvo; pilhagem; rapina; adj., de cor preta; v., pilhar, saquear; viver de rapina.

RAV.E.NOUS, adj., famélico, esfomeado.

RAV.ER, s., pessoa delirante; UK festeiro.

RAV.IN, s., saque, pilhagem.

RA.VINE, s., ravina, desfiladeiro, garganta.

RAV.ING, s., desvario, delírio, delirante, alucinado; ~ lunatic: doido varrido.

RAV.ING.LY, adv., delirantemente, freneticamente.

RAV.I.O.LI, s., It., ravióli.

RAV.ISH, v., arrebatar, encantar, cativar; v., raptar, violar.

RAV.ISH.ING, adj., arrebatador, belíssimo; extasiante.

RAV.ISH.MENT, s., encanto, arrebatamento, sedução.

RAW, s., ferida, inflamação; adj., cru, insípido, bruto, novato, rude.

RAW DEAL, s., tratamento injusto, cruel.

RAW MA.TERI.AL, s., matéria-prima.

RAW.NESS, s., crueza, dureza, aspereza.

RAW WEA.THER, s., tempo úmido e frio.

RAY, s., raio de luz, linha, corrente elétrica, traço; raia.

RAY.ON, s., raion (tipo de fibra sedosa artificial).

RAZE, v., arrasar, destruir, aniquilar, extirpar, demolir.

RA.ZOR, s., navalha, gilete, aparelho para fazer a barba.

RA.ZOR BLADE, s., lâmina de barbear.

RA.ZOR-SHARP, adj., afiado; perspicaz.

RAZ.ZLE, s., festa animada e barulhenta.

RAZZ.MA.TAZZ, s., gír., alvoroço, balbúrdia, Bras., auê..

RE, s., ré.

REACH, s., alcance, extensão, limite, objetivo; v., alcançar, atingir, obter, esticar.

REACH.A.BLE, adj., acessível, alcançável.

REACT, v., reagir, retornar ao nível inicial.

RE.AC.TION, s., reação, reflexo; reflexos.

RE.AC.TION.ARY, adj., s., reacionário, revolucionário.

RE.AC.TI.VATE, v., reativar.

RE.AC.TI.VA.TION, s., reativação.

RE.ACT.IVE, adj., reativo.

RE.AC.TIV.I.TY, s., reatividade.

RE.AC.TOR, s., reator, reator nuclear.

READ, v., ler, entender, compreender.

READ.A.BIL.I.TY, s., legibilidade; leitura fácil e agradável.

READ.A.BLE, adj., legível, compreensível, inteligível.

READ BACK, v., reler, tornar a ler.

RE.AD.DRESS, v., reendereçar, mudar de endereço.

READ.ER, s., leitor, declamador, quem faz leituras nas reuniões.

READ.ER.SHIP, s., público leitor.

READ.I.NESS, s., prontidão, presteza, boa vontade, disposição.

READ.ING, s., leitura, revisão, correção, registro, interpretação.

READ.ING LAMP, s., lâmpada de leitura.

READ.ING ROOM, s., sala de leitura.

RE.AD.JUST, v., reajustar, consertar, refazer.

RE.AD.JUST.ABLE, adj., reajustável, reformável.

RE.AD.MIS.SION, s., readmissão.

RE.AD.MIT, v., readmitir, tornar a aceitar.

READ.OUT, s., Comp., exibição de dados; leitura de dados.

READ-THROUGH, s., olhada geral (para ambiente ou paisagem).

READ.Y, adj., pronto, preparado, disponível, fácil, acabado; adv., logo, imediatamente.

READ.Y-MADE, adj., pronto.

RE.AF.FIRM, v., reafirmar, confirmar.

RE.AF.FOR.EST UK, **RE.FOR.EST** US, v., reflorestar.

RE.AF.FOR.EST.A.TION UK, **RE.FOR.ES.TA.TION** US, s., reflorestamento.

RE.AGENT, s., reagente.

RE.AL, s., realidade, Real; adj., real, verdadeiro, verídico, legítimo, autêntico.

RE.AL ALE, UK cerveja artesanal.

RE.AL ES.TATE, s., bens imobiliários.

RE.A.LIGN, v., realinhar; Pol., reorganizar.

RE.A.LIGN.MENT, s., realinhamento; Pol., reestruturação.

RE.AL.ISM, s., realismo.

RE.AL.IST, s., realista.

RE.AL.IS.TIC, adj., realístico.

RE.AL.IS.TI.CAL.LY, adv., de forma realista, realisticamente.

RE.AL.I.TY, s., realidade, verdade.

RE.AL.I.ZA.BLE, adj., realizável; imaginável, concebível.

RE.AL.I.ZA.TION, s., realização.

RE.AL.IZE(-ISE), v., realizar, efetuar, concretizar, cumprir, conceber.

REALIZER(-ISER) ·· 585 ·· RECOMMENDATION

RE.AL.I.ZER(-ISER), s., realizador.
RE.AL.LO.CATE, v., realocar.
RE.AL.LY, adv., realmente, de fato; sem dúvida; muito; *really?*: é mesmo?; *really!*: francamente!
REALM, s., reino, domínio, estado.
RE.AL TIME, s., Comp., tempo ral.
RE.AL.TOR, s., US corretor de imóveis.
RE.AL.TY, s., bens de raiz.
REAM, s., resma.
RE.AN.I.MATE, v., reanimar, fazer reviver; adj., reanimado.
RE.AP.PEAR, v., reaparecer, ressurgir.
RE.AP.PEAR.ANCE, s., reaparição, reaparecimento.
RE.AP.PRAIS.AL, s., reavaliação, reexame.
RE.AP.PRAISE, v., reavaliar, reexaminar.
REAR, s., parte traseira, traseiro, traseira, retaguarda; v., criar, educar, erguer, empinar.
REAR.GUARD, s., retaguarda.
RE.ARM, v., rearmar.
RE.AR.MA.MENT, s., rearmamento.
REAR.MOST, adj., último (de uma fila).
RE.AR.RANGE, v., reorganizar; reajustar, reagrupar.
RE.AR.RANGE.MENT, s., reorganização, reajuste; rearranjo.
REAR.VIEW MIR.ROR, s., espelho retrovisor.
REA.SON, s., razão, raciocínio, bom-senso; v., raciocinar, pensar, meditar.
REA.SON.ABLE, adj., razoável.
REA.SON.A.BLY, adv., razoavelmente, sensatamente.
REA.SONED, adj., raciocinado, fundamentado.
REA.SON.ING, s., raciocínio.
RE.AS.SEM.BLE, v., reunir, reagrupar.
RE.AS.SERT, v., reafirmar, afirmar de novo.
RE.AS.SESS, v., reavaliar.
RE.AS.SESS.MENT, s., reavaliação.
RE.AS.SUR.ANCE, s., garantia, penhor.
RE.AS.SURE, v., tranquilizar, restaurar a confiança.
RE.AS.SUR.ING, adj., tranquilizador.
RE.BATE, s., abatimento, restituição; desconto; v., abater, descontar, restituir.
REB.EL, s., rebelde, revolucionário; v., rebelar-se, revoltar-se.
RE.BEL.LION, s., rebelião, revolta.
RE.BEL.LIOUS, s., rebelde, revolucionário, revoltado.
RE.BIRTH, s., renascimento.
RE.BORN, adj., renascido.
RE.BOUND, s., ressalto, repercussão, ricochete; v., ressaltar.
RE.BUFF, s., repulsa, negativa, recusa.
RE.BUILD, v., reconstruir, refazer, remontar.
RE.BUKE, s., reprimenda.
RE.BUT, v., refutar, retorquir, contradizer.
RE.BUT.TAL, s., refutação.
RE.CAL.CI.TRANT, adj., recalcitrante, obstinado, teimoso.
RE.CALL, s., revogação, chamada de volta; v., chamar de volta, revocar.
RE.CANT, v., retratar-se.
RE.CAP, s., pneu recapado; v., recauchutar um pneu, revestir, recapar.
RE.CAP.TURE, s., recaptura; v., recapturar, resgatar.
RE.CA.PIT.U.LATE, v., recapitular, rever.
RE.CEDE, v., recuar, retornar, regredir; baixar a maré, escassear.
RE.CED.ING, adj., vazante (maré).
RE.CEIPT, s., recibo, recepção, recebimento; v., quitar, dar recibo.

RE.CEIV.A.BLE, adj., a receber.
RE.CEIVE, v., receber, aceitar, receptar, hospedar; sofrer, tolerar.
RE.CEIV.ER, s., recebedor, destinatário; receptor (rádio,TV); receptador (drogas); curador; UK fone.
RE.CEIV.ER.SHIP, s., curadoria.
RE.CENT, adj., recente, novo, novel.
RE.CENT.LY, adv., recentemente.
RE.CEP.TA.CLE, s., receptáculo, recipiente.
RE.CEP.TION, s., recepção, acolhida, recebimento, audiência.
RE.CEP.TION.IST, s., recepcionista.
RE.CEP.TION ROOM, s., recepção.
RE.CEP.TIVE, adj., receptivo.
RE.CEP.TIVE.NESS, s., receptividade.
RE.CESS, s., recesso, intervalo, pausa, segredo; v., fazer uma pausa, descansar.
RE.CES.SION, s., ato de recuar; retrocesso; renúncia; Econ., recessão.
RE.CES.SION.A.RY, adj., recessivo.
RE.CES.SIVE, adj., recessivo.
RE.CHARGE, v., recarregar.
RE.CHARGE.A.BLE, adj., recarregável.
RE.CI.SION, s., rescisão, Jur., anulação.
REC.I.PE, s., receita.
RE.CIP.I.ENT, s., recipiente, recebedor.
RE.CIP.RO.CAL, adj., recíproco, mútuo.
RE.CIP.RO.CATE, v., retribuir; tornar recíproco.
RE.CIP.RO.CAL.NESS, s., reciprocidade.
REC.I.PROC.I.TY, s., reciprocidade.
RE.CIT.AL, s., Mús., recital, récita; exposição narrativa.
REC.I.TA.TION, s., recitação, declamação.
RE.CITE, v., recitar.
RE.CIT.ER, s., recitador, declamador.
RECK.LESS, adj., descuidado, imprudente, temerário.
RECK.LESS.NESS, s., imprudência, negligência.
RECK.ON, v., contar, calcular, avaliar, pensar, supor.
RECK.ON.ING, s., conta, cálculo.
RECK.ON.ER, s., contador, calculista.
RECK.ON.ING, s., cálculo, avaliação.
RE.CLAIM, s., reclamação, reivindicação; v., reclamar, reivindicar, aplainar.
RE.CLAIM.ING, s., reivindicação.
REC.LA.MA.TION, s., reclamação; recuperação; aproveitamento.
REC.LI.NATE, adj., reclinado, inclinado.
RE.CLINE, v., inclinar, inclinar-se, pender.
RE.CLUSE, s., recluso, eremita.
RE.CLU.SION, s., reclusão, detenção.
RE.CLU.SIVE, adj., recluso, retirado, solitário.
REC.OG.NI.TION, s., reconhecimento, identificação.
REC.OG.NI.ZA.BLE UK, **REC.OG.NI.SA.BLE** US, adj., reconhecível, identificável.
REC.OG.NIZE, v., reconhecer, identificar, confessar, saudar.
RE.COIL, s., recuo; rechaço; v., recuar, retroceder, rechaçar.
REC.OL.LECT, v., lembrar, recordar.
REC.OL.LEC.TION, s., recordação, lembrança.
REC.OM.MENCE, v., recomeçar.
REC.OM.MEND, v., recomendar, insinuar.
REC.OM.MEND.A.BLE, adj., recomendável.
REC.OM.MEN.DA.TION, s., recomendação, aconselhamento.

RECOMMIT ··586·· REDOUBTABLE

REC.OM.MIT, *v.*, reiterar o compromisso; encarregar; prender de novo.

REC.OM.PENSE, *s.*, recompensa, pagamento, indenização; *v.*, recompensar.

RE.COM.POSE, *v.*, recompor, refazer, reconstruir.

REC.ON.CILE, *v.*, reconciliar, harmonizar, ajustar, conciliar.

REC.ON.CIL.I.A.TION, *s.*, reconciliação, harmonização.

REC.ON.CIL.I.A.TO.RY, *adj.*, reconciliatório.

REC.ON.DITE, *adj.*, recôndito.

RE.CON.DI.TION, *v.*, recondicionar.

RE.CON.DUCT, *v.*, reconduzir.

RE.CON.NAIS.SANCE, *s.*, reconhecimento.

RE.CON.NECT, *v.*, reconectar, restabelecer contato.

RE.CON.NOI.TRE *UK*, **RECONNOITER** *US*, *v.*, fazer um reconhecimento, explorar, inspecionar.

RE.CON.QUER, *v.*, reconquistar.

RE.CON.QUEST, *s.*, reconquista.

RE.CON.SID.ER, *v.*, reconsiderar.

RE.CON.SID.E.RA.TION, *s.*, reconsideração.

RE.CON.STI.TUTE, *v.*, reconstituir, refazer, recompor.

RE.CON.STI.TU.TION, *s.*, reconstituição.

RE.CON.STRUCT, *v.*, reconstruir, refazer.

RE.CON.STRUC.TION, *s.*, reconstrução, restauração.

RE.CON.VENE, *v.*, reunir(-se) novamente.

RE.CORD, *s.*, registro, inscrição, protocolo, documento, arquivo; *v.*, registrar, anotar.

RE.CORD-BREAK.ER, *s.*, *Esp.*, recordista.

RE.CORD-BREAK.ING, *adj.*, que quebra recordes.

RE.CORD.ER, *s.*, gravador; anotador, registrador; *Mús.*, flauta doce.

RE.CORD.ING, *s.*, gravação musical.

RE.CORD LI.BRA.RY, *s.*, discoteca (coleção de discos).

RE.CORD PLAY.ER, *s.*, toca-discos.

RE.COUNT, *v.*, relatar.

RE.COUP, *v.*, recuperar, reaver.

RE.COUP.MENT, *s.*, indenização, pagamento de danos; desquite.

RE.COURSE, *s.*, recurso, ajuda, auxílio.

RE.COV.ER, *v.*, recuperar, refazer.

RE.COV.ER.A.BLE, *adj.*, recuperável; curável, reparável.

RE.COV.ERY, *s.*, recuperação, melhora.

REC.RE.ATE, *v.*, recrear.

REC.RE.A.TION, *s.*, recreio, recreação.

REC.RE.A.TION.AL, *adj.*, recreativo.

RE.CRE.A.TION ROOM, *s.*, *US* sala de jogos; sala de recreação.

RE.CRE.A.TIVE, *adj.*, recreativo, divertido, alegre.

RE.CRIM.I.NATE, *v.*, censurar, recriminar, advertir.

RE.CRIM.I.NA.TION, *s.*, recriminação.

RE.CRIM.I.NA.TIVE, *s.*, recriminatório.

RE.CRIM.I.NA.TOR, *s.*, recriminador.

RE.CROSS, *v.*, atravessar de novo, tornar a atravessar.

RE.CRU.DES.CENCE, *s.*, recrudescimento.

RE.CRUIT, *s.*, recruta, iniciante, novato; *v.*, recrutar.

RE.CRUIT.MENT, *s.*, recrutamento, alistamento.

REC.TAL, *adj.*, *Anat.*, retal.

RECT.AN.GLE, *s.*, retângulo.

REC.TAN.GU.LAR, *adj.*, retangular.

REC.TI.FI.A.BLE, *adj.*, retificável.

REC.TI.FI.CA.TION, *s.*, retificação, acerto.

REC.TI.FY, *v.*, retificar.

REC.TI.LIN.E.AR, *adj.*, retilíneo.

REC.TI.TUDE, *s.*, retidão, retitude, equidade.

REC.TOR, *s.*, reitor, dirigente; prior.

REC.TOR.ATE, *s.*, reitoria, reitorado.

REC.TO.RY, *s.*, reitoria; residência paroquial.

REC.TUM, *s.*, reto, intestino reto.

RE.CUM.BENT, *adj.*, deitado, recostado.

RE.CU.PER.ATE, *v.*, recuperar, recuperar-se, recompor.

RE.CU.PER.A.TION, *s.*, recuperação.

RE.CUR, *v.*, repetir-se.

RE.CUR.RENCE, *s.*, recorrência.

RE.CUR.RENT, *adj.*, que se repete, periódico.

RE.CUR.RING, *adj.*, recorrente, periódico.

RE.CY.CLA.BLE, *adj.*, reciclável.

RE.CY.CLE, *v.*, reciclar.

RE.CY.CLING, *s.*, reciclagem.

RED, *s.*, cor vermelha, rubor, vermelho; *adj.*, vermelho, ruivo, tinto; *v.*, avermelhar.

RE.DACT, *v.*, redigir, editar, escrever.

RE.DAC.TION, *s.*, redação, composição, escrito.

RE.DAC.TOR, *s.*, redator.

RED BLOOD CELL, *s.*, *Biol.*, glóbulo vermelho.

RED CARD, *s.*, *Esp.*, cartão vermelho (futebol).

RED CAR.PET, *s.*, tapete vermelho.

RED CRES.CENT, *s.*, Crescente Vermelho.

RED CROSS, *s.*, Cruz Vermelha.

RED DEER, *s.*, *Zool.*, veado.

RED.DEN, *v.*, avermelhar, tornar vermelho, ruborizar.

RED.DISH, *adj.*, avermelhado, ruborizado.

RED.DISH.NESS, *s.*, vermelhidão, ruborização.

RE.DEEM, *v.*, redimir; resgatar.

RE.DEEM.A.BLE, *adj.*, redimível, resgatável, reparável.

RE.DEEM.ER, *s.*, resgatador; redentor; *Rel.*, *the* ~ : o Redentor.

RE.DE.LIV.ER, *v.*, restituir, devolver.

RE.DE.LIV.ERY, *s.*, restituição, devolução.

RE.DEMP.TION, *s.*, redenção, libertação, liberação.

RE.DE.PLOY, *v.*, remanejar.

RE.DE.PLOY.MENT, *s.*, redisposição, renovação.

RE.DE.SIGN, *v.*, remodelar.

RE.DE.VEL.OP, *v.*, renovar.

RE.DE.VEL.OP.MENT, *s.*, renovação.

RED-FACED, *adj.*, corado.

RED-HAIRED, *adj.*, com cabelo ruivo, ruivo.

RED-HAND.ED, *adj.*, em flagrante, com sangue nas mãos.

RED.HEAD, *s.*, *col.*, ruiva; indivíduo ruivo.

RED-HOT, *adj.*, em brasa; *fig.*, furioso, excitado, apaixonado.

RED IN.DI.AN, *s.*, *US* pele vermelha (índio da Am. do Norte); também *redskin*.

RED.IN.TE.GRATE, *v.*, reintegrar, renovar, restaurar; *adj.*, renovado, refeito.

RED.IN.TE.GRA.TION, *s.*, reintegração, restauração.

RE.DI.RECT, *v.*, redirecionar, direcionar, desviar.

RE.DI.REC.TION, *s.*, redirecionamento.

RE.DIS.TRIB.UTE, *v.*, redistribuir.

RED.LY, *adv.*, de vermelho, avermelhadamente.

RED.NESS, *s.*, vermelhidão.

RE.DO, *v.*, refazer, recompor.

RED.O.LENCE, *s.*, perfume, aroma, odor.

RED.O.LENT, *adj.*, *Lit.*, perfumado, cheiroso, aromático.

RE.DOU.BLE, *v.*, redobrar, repetir.

RE.DOUBT.A.BLE, *adj.*, formidável, temível.

REDOUND ···587··· REGION

RE.DOUND, *v.*, redundar, contribuir.
RE.DRAFT, *s.*, novo projeto, esboço, novo saque (de conta bancária); *v.*, reescrever, reprojetar, ressacar.
RE.DRAW, *v.*, redesenhar.
RE.DRESS, *s.*, emenda, retificação, socorro; *v.*, emendar, retificar.
RED SEA, *s.*, *Geogr.*, Mar Vermelho.
RED.SKIN, *s.*, pele-vermelha, índio.
RED-TAPE, *s.*, formalidades; *fig.*, burocracia.
RE.DUCE, *v.*, reduzir, rebaixar, diminuir, dar outra forma.
RE.DUC.ER, *s.*, redutor.
RE.DUC.TION, *s.*, redução, abatimento.
RE.DUN.DAN.CY, *s.*, demissão, exoneração, desemprego.
RE.DUN.DANT, *adj.*, redundante, excessivo; supérfluo.
RE.DU.PLI.CATE, *v.*, reduplicar, duplicar, dobrar.
RE.DU.PLI.CA.TION, *s.*, duplicação, reduplicação.
RED.WOOD, *Bot.*, sequoia; pau-brasil.
RE-ECH.O, *s.*, repetição em eco; *v.*, repercutir, ecoar, ressoar.
REED, *s.*, *Bot.*, junco; *Mús.*, palheta (embocadura).
RE.ED.U.CATE, *v.*, reeducar, reabilitar.
REEF, *s.*, recife, escolho.
REEK, *s.*, fumo, vapor, fumaça; *v.*, esfumaçar, vaporizar, fumar.
REEL, *s.*, carretel, bobina, rolo, filme, molinete; *v.*, oscilar, bobinar, enrolar.
RE-ELECT, *v.*, reeleger.
RE-ELEC.TION, *, s.*, reeleição.
RE-EN.FORCE, *v.*, reforçar, fortificar; *s.*, reforço, fortalecimento.
RE-EN.ACT, *v.*, restabelecer, reviver.
RE-EN.TER, *v.*, reentrar; *Com.*, fazer novo lançamento.
RE-EN.TRY, *s.*, reentrada; ação de retornar à atmosfera (espaçonave); *Jur.*, retomada.
RE-ES.TAB.LISH, *v.*, restabelecer, recompor.
RE-ES.TAB.LISH.MENT, *s.*, restabelecimento, restauração, reconstrução.
RE-EX.AM.INE, *v.*, reexaminar, rever.
RE.FEC.TION, *s.*, refeição, refeição frugal.
RE.FEC.TORY, *s.*, refeitório.
RE.FER, *v.*, referir, contar, dirigir, recorrer.
REF.ER.EE, *s.*, árbitro; julgador; *v.*, arbitrar.
REF.ER.ENCE, *s.*, referência, menção, atenção.
REF.ER.EN.DUM, *s.*, referendum, referendo, plebiscito.
RE.FILL, *s.*, refil, carga nova; *v.*, reabastecer, recarregar.
RE.FILL.A.BLE, *adj.*, recarregável; que se pode reabastecer.
RE.FINE, *v.*, refinar.
RE.FINED, *adj.*, refinado, apurado.
RE.FINE.MENT, *s.*, refinamento, requinte.
RE.FIN.ERY, *s.*, refinaria, usina de refino.
RE.FIT, *v.*, compor, consertar, refazer, fazer.
RE.FLECT, *v.*, refletir, meditar, pensar, raciocinar.
RE.FLEC.TION, *s.*, reflexão.
RE.FLEC.TIVE, *adj.*, refletivo, brilhante; reflexivo.
RE.FLEC.TOR, *s.*, refletor.
RE.FLEX, *adj.*, *s.*, reflexo.
RE.FLEX.IVE, *adj.*, reflexivo.
RE.FLOW, *s.*, refluxo.
RE.FOR.EST, *v.*, o mesmo que *refforest*.
RE.FOR.ES.TA.TION, *s.*, o mesmo que *refforestation*.
RE.FORM, *s.*, reforma; *v.*, reformar.
REF.OR.MA.TION, *s.*, *Rel.*, *the* ~ : a Reforma (séc. XVI), que resultou no protestantismo.

REF.OR.MA.TION, *s.*, reforma, reestruturação, restabelecimento.
RE.FOR.MA.TO.RY, *s.*, reformatório.
RE.FORMED, *adj.*, reformado, corrigido, regenerado.
RE.FORM.ER, *s.*, reformador.
RE.FORM.IST, *s.*, *adj.*, reformista.
RE.FRACT, *v.*, refratar; refratar-se.
RE.FRAC.TION, *s.*, refração.
RE.FRAC.TO.RY, *adj.*, refratário.
RE.FRAIN, *v.*, abster-se de, deixar de.
RE.FRESH, *v.*, refrescar, reanimar, reabastecer, refrigerar.
RE.FRESHED, *adj.*, revigorado.
RE.FRESH.ER, *s.*, aquele ou aquilo que refresca; refrigerante, refresco; atualização.
RE.FRESH.ING, *adj.*, refrescante, calmante, repousante.
RE.FRESH.MENT, *s.*, refresco, refrigerante; lanche; descanso.
RE.FRESH.MENTS, *s. pl.*, comida ou bebida leve, lanche leve.
RE.FRIG.ER.ATE, *v.*, refrigerar, refrescar.
RE.FRIG.ER.A.TION, *s.*, refrigeração, refrescamento.
RE.FRIG.ER.A.TOR, *s.*, refrigerador, geladeira.
RE.FU.EL, *v.*, reabastecer.
REF.UGE, *s.*, refúgio, esconderijo; *v.*, refugiar-se, retirar-se.
REF.U.GEE, *s.*, refugiado.
REF.U.GEE CAMP, *s.*, campo de refugiados.
RE.FUND, *s.*, reembolso; *v.*, devolver, reembolsar.
RE.FUR.BISH, *v.*, renovar.
RE.FUR.BISH.MENT, *s.*, restauração, reforma.
RE.FUS.AL, *s.*, recusa, negação, negativa.
RE.FUSE, *s.*, refugo, lixo, sucata; *v.*, recusar, recusar-se, negar.
RE.FUSE COL.LEC.TION, *s.*, coleta de lixo.
RE.FUSE COL.LEC.TOR, *s.*, lixeiro.
RE.FUSE DUMP, *s.*, depósito de lixo.
RE.FUT.ABLE, *adj.*, refutável.
REF.U.TA.TION, *s.*, refutação, desmentido.
RE.FUTE, *v.*, refutar, contradizer, desmentir.
RE.GAIN, *v.*, recuperar, reaver.
RE.GAL, *adj.*, real, régio, próprio de um rei.
RE.GALE, *s.*, regalo, banquete; *v.*, regalar, banquetear; deleitar.
RE.GA.LI.A, *s. pl.*, *Lat.*, insígnias e regalias reais.
RE.GARD, *s.*, olhar, atenção, estima; *v.*, olhar fixamente, considerar, mirar.
RE.GARD.ING, *prep.*, com referência a, com respeito a.
RE.GARD.LESS, *adj.*, negligente, descuidado; não obstante; *adv.*, apesar de tudo.
RE.GAT.TA, *s.*, regata.
RE.GEN.CY, *s.*, regência.
RE.GEN.ER.ATE, *v.*, regenerar(-se), recuperar(-se), restaurar; ser reformado.
RE.GEN.E.RA.TION, *s.*, regeneração.
RE.GENT, *s.*, regente.
REG.I.CIDE, *v.*, regicídio; regicida.
RE.GIME, *s.*, regime, sistema de governo.
REG.I.MENT, *s.*, regimento, grupo de soldados; *v.*, arregimentar, recrutar.
REG.I.MEN.TA.TION, *s.*, arregimentação, sujeição a controle governamental.
RE.GI.MENT.ED, *adj.*, controlado, ordenado.
RE.GION, *s.*, região, zona, localidade.

REGIONAL ·· 588 ·· RELIGIOUSNESS

RE.GION.AL, *adj.*, regional.
REG.IS.TER, *s.*, registro, inscrição, arquivo, torneira; *v.*, registrar, inscrever.
REG.IS.TERED, *adj.*, registrado (oficialmente), inscrito, matriculado.
REG.IS.TERED TRADE.MARK, *s.*, marca registrada.
REG.IS.TRAR, *s.*, escrivão, registrador, oficial.
REG.IS.TRA.TION, *s.*, registro, matrícula, inscrição.
REG.IS.TRA.TION NUM.BER, *s.*, número de licença (veículo).
REG.IS.TRY, *s.*, registro, cartório.
REG.IS.TRY OF.FICE, *s.*, registro civil.
RE.GORGE, *v.*, vomitar; engolir, sorver.
RE.GRESS, *s.*, regresso, volta, retorno; *v.*, regressar, tornar, voltar, retornar.
RE.GRES.SION, *s.*, regressão, regresso.
RE.GRES.SOR, *s.*, aquele que regressa.
RE.GRES.SIVE, *adj.*, regressivo.
RE.GRET, *s.*, pesar, tristeza, arrependimento, desprazer; *v.*, lamentar, lastimar.
RE.GRET.FUL, *adj.*, pesaroso, lamentável, tristonho.
RE.GRET.FUL.LY, *adv.*, pesarosamente.
RE.GRET.TABLE, *adj.*, lastimável, lamentável.
RE.GRET.TA.BLY, *adv.*, lamentavelmente.
RE.GROUP, *v.*, reagrupar(-se).
REG.U.LA.BLE, *adj.*, regulável, ajustável.
REG.U.LAR, *s.*, soldado regular, clérigo, partidário; *adj.*, regular, normal, ordeiro.
REG.U.LAR.I.TY, *s.*, regularidade, habitualidade, ordem.
REG.U.LAR.I.ZA.TION *UK*, **REG.U.LAR.I.SA.TION** *US*, *s.*, regularização.
REG.U.LAR.IZE, *v.*, regularizar, normalizar.
REG.U.LAR.LY, *adv.*, regularmente, uniformemente.
REG.U.LATE, *v.*, regular, regularizar, ajustar.
REG.U.LA.TION, *s.*, regulamento, norma, regra.
RE.GUR.GI.TATE, *v.*, regurgitar, refluir; *pej.*, repetir como papagaio.
RE.HA.BIL.I.TATE, *v.*, reabilitar, recuperar, restaurar.
RE.HA.BIL.I.TA.TION, *s.*, reabilitação.
RE.HEARSE, *v.*, ensaiar, treinar; repetir; recitar.
RE.HEAT, *v.*, reaquecer.
REIGN, *s.*, reino, reinado, domínio, poder; *v.*, dominar, reinar, governar.
REIGN.ING, *adj.*, reinante, atual, prevalecente.
RE.IM.BURSE, *v.*, reembolsar, pagar, quitar, saldar.
RE.IM.BURSE.MENT, *s.*, reembolso.
RE.IM.PRESS, *v.*, reimprimir, reeditar.
RE.IM.PRINT, *v.*, reimprimir.
REIN, *s.*, rédea, refreamento, freio; *v.*, conduzir pelas rédeas, governar.
RE.IN.CAR.NA.TION, *s.*, reencarnação.
RE.IN.DEER, *s.*, *Zool.*, rena
RE.IN.FORCE, *s.*, reforço; *v.*, reforçar.
RE.IN.FORCE CON.CRETE, *s.*, concreto armado.
RE.IN.FORCE.MENT, *s.*, reforço, apoio.
REIN.LESS, *adj.*, descontrolado, desgovernado.
RE.IN.STATE, *v.*, readmitir, reinstalar, reintegrar.
RE.IN.STATE.MENT, *v.*, readmissão, reinstalação, reintegração.
RE.IN.SUR.ANCE, *s.*, resseguro.
RE.IN.TE.GRATE, *v.*, reintegrar, repor, recolocar.
RE.IN.TE.GRA.TION, *s.*, reintegração.

RE.IN.TRO.DUCE, *v.*, reintroduzir; reapresentar.
RE.IS.SUE, *s.*, reedição, reimpressão.
RE.IT.ER.ATE, *v.*, reiterar, refazer, repetir.
RE.JECT, *v.*, rejeitar, recusar, desprezar, negar.
RE.JEC.TION, *s.*, rejeição, desprezo, negativa.
RE.JOICE, *v.*, regozijar-se, alegrar-se, ficar satisfeito, alegrar-se.
RE.JOIC.ING, *s.*, regozijo, alegria.
RE.JOIN, *v.*, reunir, ajuntar, agrupar; responder, retrucar, retorquir.
RE.JOIND.ER, *s.*, réplica.
RE.JU.VE.NATE, *v.*, rejuvenescer, remoçar, tornar-se jovem.
RE.JU.VE.NA.TION, *s.*, rejuvenescimento.
RE.JU.VE.NES.CENCE, *s.*, rejuvenescimento, remoçamento.
RE.KIN.DLE, *v.*, reacender, reavivar, reanimar.
RE.LAPSE, *s.*, recaída, reincidência; *v.*, recair, reincidir.
RE.LATE, *v.*, relatar, contar, narrar, referir.
RE.LAT.ED, *adj.*, relacionado; aparentado (de alguém); afim.
RE.LA.TION, *s.*, relação, narração, conto, alusão; parente.
RE.LA.TION.AL, *adj.*, aparentado; *Comp.*, relacional.
RE.LA.TION.SHIP, *s.*, relação, relacionamento; ligação, afinidade; parentesco.
RE.LA.TIVE, *s.*, parente; o que é relativo; pronome, adjetivo ou advérbio relativos; *adj.*, relativo, referente.
RE.LA.TIVE.LY, *adv.*, relativamente.
RE.LA.TIV.ISM, *s.*, relativismo.
RE.LA.TIV.I.TY, *s.*, relatividade.
RE.LA.TIV.IZE(-ISE), *v.*, tornar relativo, relativizar.
RE.LAX, *v.*, relaxar, descontrair-se, pôr-se à vontade, descansar, repousar
RE.LAX.A.TION, *s.*, relaxamento, repouso, lazer, ócio.
RE.LAX.ING, *adj.*, relaxante, repousante.
RE.LAY, *s.*, revezamento, estação de muda no correio antigo; *v.*, revezar, substituir.
RE.LEASE, *s.*, liberação, desobrigação, escape; *v.*, soltar, liberar, livrar.
REL.E.GATE, *v.*, relegar, exilar, banir, deportar, afastar.
REL.E.GA.TION, *s.*, desterro, exílio, expatriamento.
RE.LENT, *v.*, condescender, ceder; abrandar, acalmar(-se); ter compaixão.
RE.LENT.LESS, *adj.*, inflexível, implacável.
RE.LENT.LESS.LY, *adv.*, inflexivelmente, implacavelmente.
REL.E.VANCE, *s.*, relevância, importância; relação.
REL.E.VANT, *adj.*, relevante, destacado, relativo, pertinente.
RE.LI.ABIL.I.TY, *s.*, confiança, seriedade, fidelidade.
RE.LI.ABLE, *adj.*, confiável, seguro.
RE.LI.A.BLY, *adv.*, confiantemente, com segurança.
RE.LI.ANCE, *s.*, confiança, fé; dependência.
RE.LI.ANT, *adj.*, confiante, seguro; dependente.
REL.IC, *s.*, relíquia, restos mortais.
REL.ICT, *s.*, viúva.
RE.LIEF, *s.*, alívio, socorro, assistência, apoio, remédio; relevo, saliência.
RE.LIEF MAP, *s.*, *Geogr.*, mapa de relevo.
RE.LIEF ROAD, *s.*, estrada marginal; *UK* desvio (na estrada).
RE.LIEVE, *v.*, aliviar, assistir, ajudar, substituir, desobrigar.
RE.LIEVED, *adj.*, aliviado.
RE.LI.GION, *s.*, religião, fé, crença, credo.
RE.LI.GION.LESS, *adj.*, sem religião, descrente.
RE.LI.GIOUS, *s.*, religioso, clérigo; *adj.*, religioso, devoto.
RE.LI.GIOUS.NESS, *s.*, religiosidade, fé; piedade.

RELINQUISH ·· 589 ·· REPATRIATE

RE.LIN.QUISH, *v.*, renunciar a, abandonar, desistir de, capitular.

REL.ISH, *s.*, gosto, sabor, tempero, condimento, entusiasmo; *v.*, saborear, degustar.

REL.ISH.A.BLE, *adj.*, gostoso, saboroso.

RE.LIVE, *v.*, reviver.

RE.LO.CATE, *v.*, realocar, transferir(-se).

RE.LO.CA.TION, *s.*, realocação.

RE.LUCT, *v.*, relutar, repugnar, resistir, opor-se.

RE.LUC.TANCE, *s.*, relutância, repugnância, oposição.

RE.LUC.TANT, *adj.*, relutante, hesitante.

RE.LUC.TANT.LY, *adv.*, relutantemente.

RE.LY, *v.*, confiar em, acreditar.

REM, *abrev. de Rapid Eye Movement*: movimento rápido dos olhos (um dos estágios do sono).

RE.MAIN, *s.*, sobra, resto, sobejo; *v.*, sobrar, restar, ficar, continuar.

RE.MAIN.DER, *s.*, resto, sobra, restante.

RE.MAIN.ING, *adj.*, restante.

RE.MAKE, *v.*, refazer, recompor, reconstruir.

RE.MAND, *s.*, devolução; *Jur., on ~*: sob prisão preventiva; *v.*, devolver; *Jur.*, reencarcerar.

RE.MARK, *s.*, comentário, observação; remarcação; *v.*, comentar, observar, reparar; remarcar.

RE.MARK.A.BLE, *adj.*, excepcional, extraordinário, notável.

RE.MARK.A.BLY, *adv.*, excepcionalmente.

RE.MAR.RY, *v.*, recasar-se, casar de novo.

RE.ME.DI.AL, *adj.*, medicinal.

REM.E.DY, *s.*, remédio, curativo; *v.*, curar, remediar, corrigir.

RE.MEM.BER, *v.*, recordar, lembrar, relembrar, transmitir lembranças.

RE.MEM.BRANCE, *s.*, lembrança, recordação, memorial.

RE.MIND, *v.*, lembrar, recordar.

RE.MIND.ER, *s.*, lembrança, lembrete.

REM.I.NISCE, *v.*, rememorar.

REM.I.NIS.CENCE, *s.*, reminiscência, lembrança, memória.

REM.I.NIS.CENT, *adj.*, rememorativo, recordativo.

RE.MISS, *adj.*, negligente, desleixado, lento.

RE.MIS.SION, *s.*, remissão, perdão, absolvição.

RE.MIS.SIVE, *adj.*, remissivo.

RE.MIT, *v.*, remeter, enviar, mandar, adiar, absolver, desistir, reconduzir à cadeia.

RE.MIT.TANCE, *s.*, remessa (de algo); remessa de valores.

RE.MIT.TEE, *s.*, destinatário.

RE.MIT.TER, *s.*, remetente.

REM.NANT, *s.*, resto, sobra; refugo; indício.

RE.MOD.EL, *v.*, remodelar, refazer.

RE.MON.STRATE, *v.*, protestar.

RE.MORSE, *s.*, remorso, escrúpulo, arrependimento.

RE.MORSE.FUL, *adj.*, arrependido, contrito.

RE.MORSE.LESS, *adj.*, sem remorso, desumano.

RE.MOTE, *adj.*, remoto, antigo, distante, indireto, mediato, afastado:

RE.MOTE CON.TROL, *s.*, controle remoto.

RE.MOTE.LY, *adv.*, remotamente.

RE.MOTE.NESS, *s.*, distanciamento, isolamento, distância; indiferença.

RE.MOULD *UK*, **REMOLD** *US*, *v.*, reformar, transformar, recriar.

RE.MOV.A.BLE, *adj.*, desmontável, removível.

RE.MOV.AL, *s.*, mudança, remoção; destituição.

RE.MOV.AL VAN, *s.*, *UK* caminhão de mudança.

RE.MOVE, *s.*, grau, degrau, distância, transferência, promoção; *v.*, remover, mudar.

RE.MOVED, *adj.*, afastado, distante, longínquo.

RE.MOV.ER, *s.*, removedor; solvente; aquele que faz mudanças.

RE.MU.NER.ATE, *v.*, remunerar, pagar, recompensar.

RE.MU.NER.A.TION, *s.*, remuneração.

RE.NAIS.SANCE, *s.*, Renascença, Renascimento.

RE.NAL, *adj.*, renal, próprio dos rins.

RE.NAME, *v.*, renomear.

RE.NA.SCENCE, *s.*, renascença, renascimento.

REND, *v.*, rasgar, fender, despedaçar, rachar, lacerar.

REN.DER, *v.*, retribuir, devolver, dar, pagar, submeter, fazer, tomar.

REN.DER.ING, *s.*, interpretação.

REN.DEZ.VOUS, *s.*, *Fr.*, encontro, ponto de encontro; *v.*, encontrar-se em ponto marcado.

REN.DI.TION, *s.*, rendição, capitulação; declamação, interpretação.

REN.E.GADE, *s.*, renegado, traidor, desertor; *v.*, desertar, trair.

RE.NEGE, *v.*, recusar, negar; deixar de cumprir (promessa).

RE.NE.GO.TI.ATE, *v.*, renegociar.

RE.NEW, *v.*, renovar, refazer, reanimar, reparar, recomeçar.

RE.NEW.A.BLE, *adj.*, renovável.

RE.NEW.AL, *s.*, renovação, renovamento, reforma.

REN.NET, *s.*, coalheira, coalho.

RE.NOUNCE, *v.*, renunciar, desistir, abandonar, repudiar.

RE.NOUNCE.MENT, *s.*, renúncia, desistência.

REN.O.VATE, *v.*, renovar, reformar, refazer, recompor; *adj.*, renovado, refeito.

REN.O.VA.TION, *s.*, renovação.

REN.O.VA.TOR, *s.*, renovador.

RE.NOWN, *s.*, renome, fama.

RE.NOWNED, *adj.*, renomado, famoso.

RENT, *s.*, aluguel, renda, arrendamento; racha, fenda; *v.*, alugar, arrendar.

RENT.AL, *s.*, aluguel.

RENT.ED, *adj.*, alugado.

RENT-FREE, *adj.*, sem aluguel, livre de aluguel.

RE.NUM.BER, *v.*, renumerar.

RE.NUN.CI.A.TION, *s.*, renúncia, desistência.

RE.OC.CU.PY, *v.*, reocupar.

REOCCURRENCE, *s.*

RE.OPEN, *v.*, reabrir, tornar a abrir.

RE.OR.GAN.I.ZA.TION, *s.*, reorganização.

RE.OR.GA.NIZE(-ISE), *v.*, reorganizar, recompor.

RE.O.RI.EN.TA.TION, *s.*, reorientação.

REP, *s.*, *col.*, *UK* representante; *abrev. de representative.*

RE.PAINT, *v.*, repintar, pintar de novo.

RE.PAIR, *s.*, reparo, conserto, reparação; *v.*, reparar, consertar, emendar.

RE.PAIR.MAN, *s.*, aquele que faz diversos tipos de consertos, reparador, remendeiro.

REP.A.RA.TION, *s.*, reparação, restauração, indenização, satisfação.

REP.A.RA.TIONS, *s. pl.*, indenizações, reparações (por danos causados).

RE.PAR.TEE, *s.*, réplica arguta.

RE.PAST, *s.*, refeição, ato de comer, comida.

RE.PA.TRI.ATE, *v.*, repatriar.

REPAY ·· 590 ·· RESCUER

RE.PAY, *v.*, reembolsar, retribuir.
RE.PAY.ING, *adj.*, lucrativo.
RE.PAY.MENT, *s.*, reembolso, devolução, retribuição.
RE.PEAL, *s.*, revogação, anulação; *v.*, revogar, anular, cassar.
RE.PEAT, *s.*, repetição, refrão; *v.*, repetir, reiterar, reproduzir.
RE.PEAT.ED, *adj.*, repetido.
RE.PEAT.ED.LY, *adv.*, repetidamente.
RE.PEL, *v.*, repelir, rechaçar, repudiar, rejeitar.
RE.PEL.LENT, *s.*, repelente; *adj.*, repelente, que repele, repugnante.
RE.PENT, *v.*, arrepender-se.
RE.PEN.TANCE, *s.*, arrependimento, contrição.
RE.PEN.TANT, *adj.*, arrependido, arrependimento; penitente.
RE.PER.CUS.SION, *s.*, repercussão.
REP.ER.TOIRE, *s.*, *Fr.*, repertório.
REP.ER.TO.RY, *s.*, repertório; depósito; inventário.
REP.E.TI.TION, *s.*, repetição, recitação.
RE.PET.I.TIOUS, *adj.*, repetitivo.
RE.PET.I.TIVE, *adj.*, o mesmo que *repetitious*.
RE.PINE, *v.*, murmurar, lamentar-se.
RE.PHRASE, *v.*, reformular a frase, dizer em outras palavras.
RE.PLACE, *v.*, recolocar, tornar a pôr no mesmo lugar, repor, restituir.
RE.PLACE.MENT, *s.*, substituição, recolocação, reposição.
RE.PLANT, *v.*, replantar.
RE.PLAY, *s.*, partida decisiva; reprodução.
RE.PLEN.ISH, *v.*, reabastecer, prover novamente.
RE.PLETE, *adj.*, repleto farto,, cheio, saciado.
REP.LI.CA, *s.*, réplica, reprodução, resposta.
REP.LI.CATE, *v.*, duplicar, replicar, fazer cópia.
REP.LI.CA.TION, *s.*, réplica, resposta; cópia; repercussão.
RE.PLY, *s.*, resposta, réplica; *v.*, responder, replicar, retorquir.
RE.PLY-PAID, *s.*, resposta comercial com porte pago.
RE.PORT, *s.*, reportagem, relatório, informação, notícia; *v.*, relatar, referir, noticiar.
RE.PORT.AGE, *s.*, reportagem.
RE.PORT CARD, *s.*, boletim escolar.
RE.PORT.ED.LY, *adv.*, segundo os comentários, pelo que se diz.
RE.PORT.ED SPEECH, *s.*, *Gram.*, discurso indireto.
RE.PORT.ER, *s.*, repórter, jornalista.
RE.PORT.ING, *s.*, reportagem, relatório de reportagem.
RE.POSE, *s.*, repouso, descanso, tranquilidade; *v.*, repousar, descansar.
RE.POSE.FUL, *adj.*, descansado, repousado, calmo, sossegado.
RE.POS.SESS, *v.*, retomar a posse de; recuperar, readquirir.
RE.POS.SES.SION, *s.*, reintegração de posse.
REP.RE.HEND, *v.*, repreender, censurar, advertir.
REP.RE.HEN.SI.BLE, *adj.*, repreensível.
REP.RE.HEN.SION, *s.*, repreensão, advertência, censura.
REP.RE.SENT, *v.*, representar, constituir, revelar, simbolizar, encenar.
REP.RE.SEN.TA.TION, *s.*, representação, imagem, figura, espetáculo.
REP.RE.SENT.A.TIVE, *s.*, substituto, representante; delegado, agente; *adj.*, representativo, representante; típico.
RE.PRESS, *v.*, reprimir, conter, subjugar, oprimir.
RE.PRESSED, *adj.*, reprimido, frustrado.
RE.PRES.SION, *s.*, repressão, opressão, subjugação.
RE.PRES.SIVE, *adj.*, repressivo.

RE.PRIEVE, *s.*, indulto, perdão, trégua; *v.*, indultar, adiar, aliviar.
REP.RI.MAND, *s.*, reprimenda, repreensão; *v.*, repreender.
RE.PRINT, *s.*, reedição, reimpressão; *v.*, reimprimir, reeditar.
RE.PRI.SAL, *s.*, represália, vingança, retaliação.
RE.PROACH, *s.*, repreensão, censura, vergonha; *v.*, repreender, advertir, difamar.
RE.PROACH.FUL, *adj.*, de reprovação.
REP.RO.BATE, *s.*, réprobo; *v.*, reprovar, condenar; *adj.*, réprobo, condenado.
RE.PRO.DUCE, *v.*, reproduzir, reproduzir-se; multiplicar, propagar.
RE.PRO.DUC.TION, *s.*, reprodução, propagação, imitação.
RE.PRO.DUC.TIVE, *adj.*, *Biol.*, reprodutor, reprodutivo.
RE.PRO.GRAM, *v.*, reprogramar.
RE.PROOF, *s.*, reprovação, repreensão, censura.
RE.PROV.ABLE, *adj.*, reprovável, censurável.
RE.PROV.AL, *s.*, censura, advertência, reprovação.
RE.PROVE, *v.*, reprovar, censurar, repreender.
RE.PROV.ING, *adj.*, de reprovação; repreensivo.
REP.TILE, *s.*, réptil.
RE.PUB.LIC, *s.*, república.
RE.PUB.LI.CAN, *adj.*, *s.*, republicano.
RE.PUB.LI.CA.TION, *s.*, republicação, reedição, reimpressão.
RE.PUB.LISH, *v.*, republicar, reproduzir, reeditar, reimprimir.
RE.PU.DI.ATE, *v.*, repudiar, rejeitar, renegar, negar.
RE.PU.DI.A.TION, *s.*, repúdio.
RE.PUG.NANCE, *s.*, repugnância, asco, aversão, nojo.
RE.PUG.NANT, *adj.*, repugnante, asqueroso, nojento.
RE.PULSE, *v.*, rejeitar, repudiar, repelir.
RE.PUL.SION, *s.*, aversão, repulsão, nojo.
RE.PUL.SIVE, *adj.*, repulsive.
REP.U.TA.BIL.I.TY, *s.*, respeitabilidade, respeito.
REP.UTA.BLE, *adj.*, de boa reputação.
REP.U.TA.TION, *s.*, reputação, fama, honra.
RE.PUTE, *v.*, reputar, estimar.
RE.PU.TED, *adj.*, de renome.
RE.PU.TED.LY, *adv.*, supostamente, segundo dizem.
RE.QUEST, *s.*, petição, requerimento, solicitação; *v.*, requerer, peticionar, solicitar.
RE.QUEST STOP, *s.*, *UK* parada solicitada (pelo passageiro ao motorista de ônibus).
RE.QUI.EM, *s.*, *Lat.*, réquiem.
RE.QUIRE, *v.*, requerer, pedir, solicitar, peticionar.
RE.QUIRED, *adj.*, necessário, exigido.
RE.QUIRE.MENT, *s.*, requerimento, exigência, necessidade, requisição.
REQ.UI.SITE, *s.*, requisito, pré-requisito.
REQ.UI.SI.TION, *s.*, requisição, requerimento, petição; *v.*, requisitar, confiscar.
RE.QUITE, *v.*, retribuir, recompensar, saldar, pagar.
RE.READ, *v.*, reler.
RE.REC.ORD, *v.*, regravar.
RE.ROUTE, *v.*, redirecionar, reencaminhar.
RE.RUN, *s.*, reprise, repetição; *v.*, reexibir, reimprimir.
RE.SALE, *s.*, revenda.
RE.SCHED.ULE, *v.*, reagendar, reprogramar; *Com.*, renegociar.
RES.CIND, *v.*, rescindir, revogar, quebrar, anular.
RE.SCIS.SION, *s.*, rescisão, anulação.
RES.CUE, *s.*, salvamento, liberação; *v.*, livrar, socorrer, ajudar.
RES.CU.ER, *s.*, libertador, salvador.

RESEAL ·· 591 ·· RESTRICTED

RE.SEAL, *v.*, fechar novamente.
RE.SEARCH, *s.*, pesquisa, investigação; *v.*, pesquisar, buscar, investigar.
RE.SEARCH.ER, *s.*, pesquisador.
RE.SEARCH WORK, *s.*, trabalho de pesquisa.
RE.SEAT, *v.*, reassentar, colocar de novo.
RE.SECT, *v.*, ressecar, secar.
RE.SELL, *v.*, revender, tornar a vender.
RE.SELL.ER, *s.*, revendedor.
RE.SEM.BLANCE, *s.*, semelhança.
RE.SEM.BLE, *v.*, assemelhar-se, parecer-se com, ser semelhante.
RE.SEM.BLING, *adj.*, semelhante, parecido.
RE.SENT, *v.*, ressentir-se com, magoar-se, ofender-se.
RE.SENT.FUL, *adj.*, ressentido.
RE.SENT.MENT, *s.*, ressentimento, rancor, ofensa.
RES.ER.VA.TION, *s.*, reserva, restrição, limitação.
RE.SERVE, *s.*, reserva, restrição, discrição; reservar, guardar, excluir.
RE.SERVED, *adj.*, reservado, discreto, restrito.
RE.SERVE PRICE, *s.*, *UK* preço mínimo (de venda).
RE.SERV.IST, *s.*, reservista.
RES.ER.VOIR, *s.*, *Fr.*, reservatório, tanque; reservatório natural, represa, açude.
RE.SET, *s.*, nova montagem, engaste; *v.*, engastar, remontar.
RE.SET.TLE, *v.*, reocupar (terras), tranquilizar, recolonizar, reassentar.
RE.SET.TLE.MENT, *s.*, ocupação (terras), recolonização, reassentamento.
RE.SHAPE, *v.*, reformar, remodelar.
RE.SHUF.FLE, *s.*, reorganização, rearranjo; *v.*, reorganizar, rearranjar; embaralhar de novo (cartas); reformar (casa).
RE.SIDE, *v.*, morar, habitar, viver, residir.
RES.I.DENCE, *s.*, residência, moradia, habitação.
RES.I.DENT, *s.*, residente, habitante, morador; *adj.*, residente.
RES.I.DEN.TIAL, *adj.*, residência; *UK* em regime de internato.
RES.I.DEN.TIAL AR.E.A, *s.*, área residencial.
RE.SID.U.AL, *adj.*, residual, restante; *s.*, saldo, resto.
RES.I.DUE, *s.*, resíduo, resto, sucata.
RE.SIGN, *v.*, renunciar, resignar-se, conformar-se, demitir-se.
RES.IG.NA.TION, *s.*, resignação, demissão, exoneração, submissão.
RES.IGNED, *adj.*, resignado.
RE.SIL.I.ENCE, *s.*, capacidade de recuperação.
RE.SIL.I.ENT, *adj.*, resiliente, elástico, resistente, que se recupera com rapidez.
RES.IN, *s.*, resina.
RE.SIST, *v.*, resistir, opor-se, repelir, impedir.
RE.SIS.TANCE, *s.*, resistência, oposição.
RE.SIS.TANT, *adj.*, *s.*, resistente.
RE.SIST.I.BIL.I.TY, *s.*, resistência, resistibilidade.
RE.SIST.LESS, *adj.*, irresistível.
RE.SIS.TOR, *s.*, *Eletr.*, resistor.
RES.O.LUTE, *adj.*, resoluto, firme, determinado, consciente.
RES.O.LUTE.LY, *adv.*, resolutamente.
RES.O.LUTE.NESS, *s.*, firmeza, determinação, resolução.
RE.SO.LU.TION, *s.*, resolução, determinação, firmeza.
RE.SOLV.ABLE, *adj.*, resolúvel.
RE.SOLVE, *s.*, resolução, decisão; *v.*, resolver, analisar, solucionar.
RES.O.NANCE, *s.*, ressonância, repetição, eco.

RES.O.NANT, *adj.*, ressonante, vibrante.
RES.O.NATE, *v.*, ressoar, ressonar, ecoar.
RE.SORT, *s.*, estância turística, complexo para veraneio.
RE.SOUND, *s.*, eco, ressonância; ressoar, ecoar.
RE.SOUND.ING, *adj.*, retumbante, estrondoso, ressonante.
RE.SOURCE, *s.*, recurso, meio, fonte, riqueza.
RE.SOURCE.FUL, *adj.*, habilidoso, hábil, desembaraçado.
RE.SOURCE.FUL.NESS, *s.*, versatilidade, desenvoltura.
RE.SPECT, *s.*, respeito, preferência, deferência; respeitar, cumprimentar, acatar.
RE.SPECT.A.BIL.I.TY, *s.*, respeitabilidade.
RE.SPECT.A.BLE, *adj.*, respeitável.
RE.SPECT.A.BLY, *adv.*, respeitavelmente.
RE.SPECT.ED, *adj.*, respeitado.
RE.SPECT.FUL, *adj.*, respeitoso, atencioso.
RE.SPECT.FUL.LY, *adv.*, respeitosamente.
RE.SPEC.TIVE, *adj.*, respectivo, relativo, pertinente.
RE.SPEC.TIVE.LY, *adv.*, respectivamente.
RES.PI.RA.TION, *s.*, respiração.
RES.PI.RA.TOR, *s.*, respirador, filtro, máscara de proteção.
RES.PIR.A.TO.RY, *adj.*, respiratório.
RE.SPIRE, *v.*, respirar.
RE.SPITE, *s.*, repouso, pausa, intervalo, prorrogação.
RE.SPLEN.DENCE, *s.*, resplendor, brilho.
RE.SPLEN.DENT, *adj.*, resplandecente, brilhante.
RE.SPOND, *v.*, responder, retrucar, reagir.
RE.SPON.DENT, *adj.*, correspondente.
RE.SPONSE, *s.*, resposta, réplica, responsório.
RE.SPON.SI.BIL.I.TY, *s.*, responsabilidade.
RE.SPON.SI.BLE, *adj.*, responsável; equilibrado.
RE.SPON.SI.BLY, *adv.*, responsavelmente.
RE.SPON.SIVE, *adj.*, responsivo, que responde bem, que corresponde, compreensível.
REST, *s.*, descanso, repouso, pausa, intervalo; resto, sobra; *v.*, descansar, repousar.
RES.TART, *s.*, reinício; *v.*, recomeçar; *Comp.*, reiniciar, ligar outra vez.
RE.STATE, *v.*, reformular; reafirmar, expor de novo.
RES.TAU.RANT, *s.*, restaurante.
RES.TAU.RANT CAR, *s.*, *UK* vagão restaurante.
REST.DAY, *s.*, dia de descanso, dia de repouso.
REST.ED, *adj.*, descansado.
REST.FUL, *adj.*, calmo, sossegado, tranquilo.
REST HOME, *s.*, casa de repouso, asilo, abrigo.
REST.ING, *s.*, descanso, sossego, repouso.
RES.TI.TU.TION, *s.*, restituição, indenização.
REST.IVE, *adj.*, inquieto, impaciente.
REST.LESS, *adj.*, inquieto, irrequieto, impaciente, agitado.
REST.LESS.LY, *adv.*, impacientemente; sem conseguir dormir.
RE.STOCK, *v.*, reabastecer.
RES.TO.RA.TION, *s.*, restauração, restituição, restabelecimento, reparo.
RE.STOR.A.TIVE, *s.*, tônico; *adj.*, revigorante, tônico.
RE.STORE, *v.*, restaurar, restituir, restabelecer.
RE.STOR.ER, *s.*, restaurador.
RE.STRAIN, *v.*, reprimir, frear, refrear, dominar.
RE.STRAINED, *adj.*, comedido, contido.
RE.STRAINT, *s.*, restrição, limitação; embaraço; prudência, controle; reclusão.
RE.STRICT, *v.*, restringir, reprimir, limitar.
RE.STRICT.ED, *adj.*, restrito, limitado; controlado.

RESTRICTION ·· 592 ·· REVIEW

RE.STRIC.TION, s., restrição, limitação, repressão.
RE.STRIC.TIVE, adj., restritivo.
REST ROOM, s., US banheiro.
RE.STRUC.TURE, v., reestruturar.
RE.SULT, s., resultado, consequência; v., resultar, originar, provir.
RE.SULT.ANT, adj., resultante.
RE.SUME, v., recomeçar, retomar, reassumir, recuperar.
RÉ.SU.MÉ, s., resumo, sumário, compêndio.
RE.SUMP.TION, s., retomada.
RE.SUR.FACE, v., repavimentar; vir à tona.
RE.SURGE, v., ressurgir, ressuscitar, rugir.
RE.SUR.GENCE, s., ressurgimento.
RES.UR.RECT, v., ressuscitar.
RES.UR.REC.TION, s., ressurreição.
RE.SUS.CI.TATE, v., ressuscitar, ressurgir, reanimar.
RE.SUS.CI.TA.TION, s., ressuscitação, ressuscitamento.
RE.TAIL, s., retalho, varejo, venda a varejo; v., retalhar, vender a varejo.
RE.TAIL.ER, s., varejista.
RE.TAIN, v., reter, manter, conservar, guardar.
RE.TAIN.ER, s., adiantamento; comissão, taxa; servente, atendente.
RE.TAIN.ING WALL, s., muro de arrimo.
RE.TAKE, v., retomar.
RE.TAL.I.ATE, v., retaliar, vingar-se.
RE.TAL.I.A.TION, s., retaliação, vingança, desforra.
RE.TARD, s., retardamento, demora, atraso; v., retardar, demorar.
RE.TARD.ED, adj., retardado; que sofre de atraso mental.
RETCH, v., ter ânsia de vômito, provocar vômito.
RE.TELL, v., repetir, tornar a dizer.
RE.TEN.TION, s., retenção, lembrança, memória.
RE.TEN.TIVE, adj., retentivo, que retém.
RET.I.CENCE, s., reticência, reserva, discrição.
RET.I.CENT, adj., reticente, reservado, discreto.
RET.I.NA, s., retina.
RET.I.NUE, s., séquito, comitiva, acompanhamento, cortejo.
RE.TIRE, v., retirar-se, afastar-se, aposentar-se, recolher-se, deitar-se, ir dormir.
RE.TIRED, adj., retirado, isolado; aposentado, reformado.
RE.TIRED.NESS, s., solidão, retiro.
RE.TIRE.MENT, s., retiro, afastamento, abandono, aposentadoria, intimidade.
RE.TIR.ING, adj., tímido, retraído; que vai se aposentar.
RE.TIR.ING ROOM, s., privada, banheiro, lavabo, lavatório.
RE.TORT, s., réplica, resposta; v., responder, retrucar, replicar, retorquir, rebater.
RE.TOUCH, s., retoque; v., retocar, modificar, recompor.
RE.TRACE, v., volver pelo mesmo caminho, voltar, tornar, rememorar.
RE.TRACT, v., retrair, recolher.
RE.TRACT.A.BLE, adj., retrátil.
RE.TRAC.TION, s., retratação.
RE.TRAIN, v., reciclar, retreinar.
RE.TRAIN.ING, s., reciclagem.
RE.TRANS.FER, v., retransferir, transferir de novo.
RE.TREAT, s., Mil., retirada; toque de recolher; refúgio, asilo; recuo.
RE.TRENCH.MENT, s., corte de gastos; economia; entrincheiramento.

RE.TRI.AL, s., novo julgamento.
RET.RI.BU.TION, s., retribuição, recompensa, castigo, pena, vingança.
RE.TRIEV.AL, s., recuperação.
RE.TRIEVE, v., reaver, recuperar, restaurar, corrigir, consertar.
RE.TRIEV.ER, s., perdigueiro (cão).
RE.TRIM, v., arranjar de novo, rearranjar.
RET.RO.ACT, v., retroagir, reagir.
RET.RO.ACT.IVE, adj., retroativo.
RET.RO.CEDE, v., retroceder, recuar, devolver.
RET.RO.CES.SION, s., retrocesso, recuo.
RET.RO.GRADE, adj., retrógrado, ultrapassado; v., regredir, retrogradar.
RET.RO.GRES.SIVE, adj., regressivo.
RET.RO.SPECT, s., retrospecto, rememorização; v., relembrar, rememorar.
RET.RO.SPEC.TIVE, adj., retrospectivo, retroativo.
RET.RO.SPEC.TIVE.LY, adv., retrospectivamente.
RE.TRY, v., julgar novamente.
RE.TURN, s., regresso, retorno, volta, devolução, retribuição; v., voltar, regressar.
RE.TURN.ABLE, adj., retornável, restituível.
RE.U.NI.FI.CA.TION, s., reunificação.
RE.UNION, s., reunião, encontro, assembleia.
RE.UNITE, v., reunir, unir, conciliar.
RE.U.SA.BLE, adj., reutilisável, reciclável.
RE.USE, s., reuso, reutilização; v., reutilizar.
REVALUE, v., valorizar; reavaliar.
RE.VAMP, v., reformar, consertar, redecorar.
RE.VEAL, v., revelar, manifestar, mostrar, divulgar.
RE.VEAL.ER, s., revelador.
RE.VEAL.ING, s., revelação; adj., esclarecedor, revelador.
REV.EIL.LE, s., Fr., toque da alvorada.
REV.EL, s., festança, folia; v., festejar, divertir-se muito, cair na gandaia.
REV.E.LA.TION, s., revelação, anúncio.
REV.E.LA.TOR, s., revelador.
REV.EL.LER, s., pândego, festeiro, farrista, dissoluto.
REV.EL.RY, s., festança, orgia, folia.
RE.VENGE, s., vingança, desforra, represália, vendeta; v., vingar-se.
REV.E.NUE, s., renda, rendimento, proventos, taxas, impostos.
RE.VER.BER.ATE, v., reverberar, advertir, ecoar, repercutir.
RE.VER.BER.A.TION, s., reverberação, reflexão.
REV.ER.ENCE, s., reverência, respeito, acatamento, deferência; v., reverenciar.
REV.ER.END, s., reverendo, clérigo, padre, pastor.
REV.ER.ENT, adj., reverente, respeitoso.
REV.ER.EN.TIAL, adj., reverencial; o mesmo que reverent.
REV.ER.IE, s., devaneio.
RE.VER.SAL, s., reviravolta, contratempo.
RE.VERSE, s., reverso, avesso, contrário, revés; v., inverter, transpor, abolir, anular.
RE.VERSE.LESS, adj., irreversível, imutável.
RE.VERS.I.BLE, adj., reversível.
RE.VERS.ING, s., inversão.
RE.VER.SION, s., reversão, volta.
RE.VERT, v., reverter, voltar, retroceder, retornar.
RE.VEST, v., revestir.
RE.VIEW, s., revista, inspeção de tropas, crítica literária,

REVIEWAL ··593·· RIGHTLY

revisão; v., rever, recapitular.
RE.VIEW.AL, s., crítica, resenha.
RE.VIEW.ER, s., crítico, revisor.
RE.VILE, s., ultraje, injúria, ofensa; v., ofender, injuriar, ultrajar, insultar.
RE.VISE, s., revisão, conserto, emenda; v., revisar, corrigir, consertar, emendar.
RE.VISED, adj., revisado.
RE.VI.SION, s., revisão, correção.
RE.VI.SION.IST, s., adj., revisionista.
RE.VIS.IT, v., revisitar.
RE.VI.TAL.IZE, v., revitalizar, reforçar.
RE.VIV.AL, s., renovação; ressurgimento; reapresentação.
RE.VIVE, v., reviver, ressuscitar, surgir, renascer, animar.
RE.VIV.I.FY, v., revivificar, reviver, reanimar.
REV.O.CA.TION, s., revogação, derrogação, negação.
RE.VOKE, v., revogar; renunciar.
RE.VOLT, s., revolta, insurreição, sedição; v., revoltar-se, rebelar-se, rebelar.
RE.VOLT.ER, s., revoltoso, rebelde, revolucionário.
RE.VOLT.ING, adj., revoltante, repugnante; rebelde.
REV.O.LU.TION, s., revolução, levante, ciclo, revolução dos planetas.
REV.O.LU.TION.ARY, s., revolucionário, sedicioso.
REV.O.LU.TION.IZE, v., revolucionar.
RE.VOLVE, v., revolver, girar, ponderar.
RE.VOLV.ER, s., revólver, pistola.
RE.VOLV.ING, adj., giratório, rotatório; revolvedor.
RE.VOLV.ING DOOR, s., porta giratória.
RE.VUE, s., revista, teatro de revista.
RE.VUL.SION, s., asco, repugnância.
RE.WARD, s., recompensa, gratificação; v., recompensar, gratificar.
RE.WARD.ING, adj., gratificante.
RE.WIND, v., rebobinar, voltar.
RE.WIRE, v., refazer a fiação elétrica.
RE.WORD, v., expressar de novo com outras palavras.
RE.WORK, v., reelaborar.
RE.WRITE, v., reescrever, escrever de novo, tornar a escrever.
REY.NARD, s., Zool., raposa.
RHAP.SO.DY, s., rapsódia, elocução.
RHEA, s., Zool., ema, nandu, tipo de avestruz.
RHET.O.RIC, s., retórica, eloquência.
RHE.TOR.I.CAL, adj., o mesmo que rhetoric.
RHEU.MAT.IC, adj., Med., reumático.
RHEU.MA.TISM, s., Med., reumatismo.
RHEU.MA.TOID AR.THRI.TIS, s., Med., artrite reumatoide.
RHINE.STONE, s., diamante falso; seixo do Reno.
RHI.NI.TIS, s., Med., rinite.
RHI.NO, s., col., Zool., rinoceronte.
RHI.NOC.ER.OS, s., Zool., rinoceronte.
RHI.NOL.O.GIST, s., rinologista.
RHO.DE.SIAN, s., adj., rodesiano.
RHOMB, s., rombo.
RHOM.BOID, s., romboide.
RHU.BARB, s., Bot., ruibarbo; col., vozerio.
RHUM.BA, s., Mús., rumba.
RHYME, s., rima; v., rimar, versificar com rima.
RHYTHM, s., ritmo, cadência, compasso.
RHYTHM AND BLUES, s., US música negra que deu origem

ao rock-and-roll.
RHYTH.MIC, adj., rítmico, compassado.
RIB, s., costela, viga de uma ponta, filé, nervura; v., colocar vigas, zombar.
RIB.ALD, adj., velhaco, safado, cafajeste, grosseiro, depravado.
RIB.ALD.RY, s., velhacaria, safadeza, libertinagem.
RIBBED, adj., canelado; que tem costelas; que tem reforço.
RIB.BON, s., fita, tira, banda, fita de máquina de escrever; v., colocar fita.
RIB CAGE, s., Anat., caixa torácica.
RICE, s., arroz.
RICE.FIELD, s., arrozal; arrozeira.
RICE.POWD.ER, s., pó de arroz.
RICH, s., rico, ricos; adj., riço, valioso, forte, fértil, suculento, cheio, suave.
RICH.ES, s., riqueza, riquezas.
RICH.LY, adv., ricamente, fartamente, esplendidamente.
RICH.NESS, s., riqueza, opulência, abundância, fertilidade, excelência.
RICH.TER SCALE, s., escala Richter.
RICK.ETS, s., Med., raquitismo.
RICK.ETY, adj., raquítico, fraco, débil, desnutrido.
RIC.O.CHET, v., ricochetear.
RID, v., libertar, livrar, liberar, desembaraçar.
RID.DANCE, s., libertação, liberação, desembaraço.
RID.DLE, s., enigma, charada, ambiguidade; v., decifrar, ler charada.
RID.DLED, adj., crivado, perfurado; cheio, saturado; infestado.
RIDE, s., passeio, passeio a cavalo, giro, percurso; v., cavalgar, passear, viajar, andar.
RID.ER, s., cavaleiro, amazona, viajante; ciclista, motociclista.
RIDGE, s., cume, cimo, pico; cumeeira, garupa; v., sulcar, arar.
RIDGY, adj., sulcado, arado, trilhado pelo arado.
RID.I.CULE, s., ridículo, mofa, zombaria; adj., ridículo; v., ridicularizar, mofar, rir de.
RI.DIC.U.LOUS, adj., ridículo.
RI.DIC.U.LOUS.LY, adv., ridiculamente.
RID.ING, s., equitação, cavalgada.
RID.ING SCHOOL, s., escola de equitação.
RIFE, adj., muito comum; predominante.
RIFF.RAFF, s., ralé, gentalha.
RI.FLE, s., rifle, carabina, fuzil; v., saquear, roubar, pilhar.
RI.FLER, s., saqueador, salteador, bandido.
RIFT, s., fenda, greta, rombo; v., rachar, fender, abrir.
RIG, s., equipamento, torre para perfurar; fraude, brincadeira; v., equipar, fraudar.
RIG.GER, s., especulador.
RIG.GING, s., Náut., cordame.
RIGHT, s., direito, justiça, reivindicação, prerrogativa, a Direita; adj., direito, reto, justo, honesto, bom, sadio, normal; adv., corretamente, com justiça.
RIGHT ANGLE, s., ângulo reto.
RIGHT.EOUS, adj., justo, reto, correto.
RIGHT.EOUS.NESS, s., honradez, retidão.
RIGHT.FUL, adj., legítimo, justo.
RIGHT.FUL.LY, adv., legitimamente.
RIGHT-HAND, adj., direito, o lado direito.
RIGHT-HAND.ED, adj., destro.
RIGHT.LESS, adj., destituído de direitos.
RIGHT.LY, adv., com razão, com justiça.

RIGHT-MINDED ·· 594 ·· ROCKER

RIGHT-MIND.ED, *adj.,* honrado, honesto; correto.
RIGHT.NESS, *s.,* retidão, justiça.
RIGHT.O, *excl., UK* certo!
RIGHT OF WAY, *s.,* preferencial (no trânsito), que tem a preferência; direito de passagem.
RIGHT WING, *s., Pol.,* ala da direita.
RIGHT WING.ER, *s.,* direitista.
RIG.ID, *adj.,* rígido, duro, inflexível.
RI.GID.I.TY, *s.,* rigidez, inflexibilidade.
RI.GID.LY, *adv.,* rigidamente.
RIG.MA.ROLE, *s., col.,* ladainha, palavrório; ritual; *adj.,* confuso, incoerente.
RIG.OR.OUS, *adj.,* rigoroso, severo, inflexível.
RIG.OR.OUS.LY, *adv.,* rigorosamente.
RIG.OUR, *s.,* rigor.
RIG-OUT, *s., UK* beca; traje.
RILE, *v.,* irritar, aborrecer, incomodar.
RILL, *s.,* regato, riacho, arroio, ribeiro; *v.,* fluir, deslizar como água.
RIM, *s.,* borda, orla, aro, margem.
RIND, *s.,* casca, película, crosta; *v.,* descascar.
RING, *s.,* anel, aro, argola; ringue, picadeiro, arena; toque de campainha; *v.,* telefonar, soar campainha, bimbalhar de sino, badalar.
RING.ER, *s.,* sineiro.
RING FIN.GER, *s.,* dedo anular.
RING.ING, *s.,* toque de sino, repicar, dobrar, bimbalhar.
RING.LEAD.ER, *s.,* cabeça, líder.
RING.LET, *s.,* argolinha; anel de cabelo.
RING.WAY, *s., UK* anel rodoviário.
RINK, *s.,* pista de patinação, rinque.
RINSE, *s.,* enxaguadura, lavagem; *v.,* lavar, bochechar.
RIOT, *s.,* distúrbio, motim, desordem, revolta; *v.,* amotinar, provocar distúrbios.
RI.OT.ER, *s.,* amotinador, sedicioso, revoltoso.
RI.OT.OUS, *adj.,* barulhento, turbulento; desenfreado, exuberante.
RIP, *s.,* rasgão, rasgo; *v.,* rasgar, dilacerar, romper; *adj.,* velhaco, patife, safado.
RIPE, *v.,* amadurecer, maturar; *adj.,* maduro, amadurecido, pronto, preparado.
RIPE.EN, *v.,* amadurecer, maturar, desenvolver.
RIPE.NESS, *s.,* madureza, desenvolvimento, maturidade, desenvolvimento.
RIP-OFF, *s., gír.,* roubo, surrupio, assalto; imitação barata.
RIP.PING, *s.,* ato de rasgar, rasgamento.
RIP.PLE, *s.,* ondulação, onda; *v.,* ondular, encrespar.
RIP.SAW *s.,* serrote.
RISE, *s.,* ascensão, promoção, subida, lance de escada, cheia; *v.,* subir, levantar, aumentar, ressuscitar, crescer, vir à superfície.
RIS.ER, *s.,* degrau, levantador.
RI.SI.BLE, *adj.,* risível.
RIS.ING, *s.,* levante, ascensão, revolta, ressurreição, tumor.
RISK, *s.,* risco, perigo; *v.,* arriscar, pôr em risco, expor ao perigo.
RISK.FUL, *adj.,* perigoso, arriscado.
RISK.LESS, *adj.,* sem perigo, seguro.
RISKY, *adj.,* arriscado, perigoso, temerário.
RI.SOT.TO, *s., It.,* risoto.
RIS.SOLE, *s.,* rissole, pastelão, empada recheada com carne.

RITE, *s.,* rito, cerimonial, ritual, cerimônia.
RIT.U.AL, *s.,* ritual, cerimonial; *adj.,* ritual, cerimonial.
RIT.U.AL.ISM, *s.,* ritualismo.
RIT.U.AL.IS.TIC, *adj.,* ritualista.
RI.VAL, *s.,* rival, êmulo, adversário; *v.,* rivalizar, emular, competir; *adj.,* rival.
RI.VAL.RY, *s.,* rivalidade, emulação, competição.
RIV.ER, *s.,* rio.
RIV.ER.BANK, *s.,* margem de rio.
RIV.ER.BED, *s.,* leito de rio, álveo.
RIV.ER.SIDE, *s.,* margem de rio.
RIV.ET, *s.,* rebite; *v.,* arrebitar, rebitar.
RIV.ET.ING, *s.,* rebitagem; *adj.,* fascinante.
RIV.U.LET, *s.,* ribeiro, riozinho, regato, arroio, córrego.
ROACH, *s., Zool.,* peixe semelhante à carpa; *US* barata; *gír.,* bagana.
ROAD, *s.,* caminho, estrada, via, rodovia.
ROAD.BLOCK, *s.,* barreira em rodovia.
ROAD.HOUSE, *s.,* hospedaria à beira da estrada, estalagem.
ROAD MAP, *s.,* mapa rodoviário.
ROAD ROL.LER, *s.,* rolo compressor.
ROAD.SIDE, *s.,* beira de estrada; *adj.,* à margem da estrada.
ROAD SIGN, *s.,* sinal ou placa de trânsito.
ROAD TAX, *s.,* imposto sobre veículos (semelhante ao IPVA).
ROAD TEST, *s.,* teste de estrada.
ROAD TRANS.PORT, *s.,* tranporte rodoviário.
ROAD.WAY, *s.,* estrada, rodovia, pista da estrada.
ROAM, *s.,* andança, passeio, caminhada ao léu; *v.,* vaguear, andar, girar, passear.
ROAM.ER, *s.,* errante, andarilho, caminhante.
ROAR, *s.,* rugido, urro, berro, bramido, barulho; *v.,* rugir, mugir, bramir, urrar, berrar.
ROAR.ING, *s.,* rugido, mugido, berro, bramido; *adj.,* estrondoso, estrepitoso.
ROAST, *s.,* assado, carne assada, assadura; *v.,* assar, tostar, assar muito.
ROAST.BEEF, *s.,* rosbife.
ROAST.ER, *s.,* assador, grelha.
ROAST.ING, *s.,* assadura; *adj.,* muito calor.
ROB, *v.,* roubar, furtar, assaltar, pilhar.
ROB.BER, *s.,* ladrão, assaltante.
ROB.BERY, *s.,* ladroagem, roubalheira, furto, roubo, rapina.
ROBE, *s.,* toga, beca, vestimenta.
ROB.IN, *s. Zool.,* certos pássaros norte-americanos e europeus: pintarroxos, tordos, etc.
RO.BOT, *s.,* robô.
RO.BOT.ICS, *s.,* robótica.
RO.BUST, *adj.,* robusto, forte, vigoroso, sadio, resoluto.
RO.BUS.TIOUS, *adj.,* robusto, vigoroso.
RO.BUS.TIOUS.LY, *adj.,* vigorosamente, robustamente.
RO.BUST.LY, *adv.,* vigorosamente.
ROCK, *s.,* rocha, pedra, penedo, balanço; *v.,* balançar, oscilar, embalar.
ROCK AND ROLL, ROCK'N'ROLL, *s., Mús.,* estilo musical norte-americano surgido nos anos de 1940.
ROCK-BOT.TOM, *s.,* nível baixíssimo, atingir o fundo do poço.
ROCK BREAK.ER, *s.,* britador.
ROCK CLIMB.ER, *s.,* alpinista.
ROCK CLIMB.ING, *s.,* alpinismo.
ROCK.ER, *s.,* berço, cadeira de balanço; apreciador de música rock.

ROCKET · 595 · ROUGHNESS

ROCK.ET, *s.*, foguete.
ROCK.ET LAUNCH.ER, *s.*, lança-foguetes; lançador de foguetes.
ROCK.ING CHAIR, *s.*, cadeira de balanço.
ROCK.ING HORSE, *s.*, cavalo de balanço (brinquedo).
ROCK.LESS, *adj.*, sem rochas, sem pedras.
ROCK SALT, *s.*, sal-gema.
ROCK.Y, *adj.*, rochoso, instável, oscilante.
RO.CO.CO, *s., Fr.*, estilo rococó; *adj.*, rococó.
ROD, *s.*, vara, haste, bastão; *fishing rod*: vara de pescar.
RO.DENT, *adj., s.*, roedor.
RO.DE.O, *s.*, rodeio.
ROE, *s.*, ova (de peixe).
ROE DEER, *s.*, cervo pequeno da Europa e Ásia, corço.
RO.GA.TION, *s.*, rogação, rogações, preces, pedidos.
ROGUE, *s.*, velhaco, safado, patife, cafajeste.
ROGU.ERY, *s.*, velhacaria, patifaria, safadeza.
ROGU.ISH, *adj.*, velhaco, safado, patife, maldoso.
ROIL, *v.*, turvar, perturbar, irritar.
ROIS.TER, *v.*, contar fanfarronices, alardear, vangloriar-se.
ROLE, *s.*, papel de artista, desempenho, função.
ROLL, *s.*, rolo, maço, cilindro, manobra, rol, lista; *v.*, rolar, enrolar, arregaçar, rufar.
ROLL.ER, *s.*, rolo, cilindro, roda, roldana, rolo compressor, laminador.
ROLL.ER.BLADE, *s.*, patim com rodas alinhadas uma atrás da doutra.
ROLL.ER COAST.ER, *s.*, montanha-russa.
ROLL.ER SKATE, *s.*, patim de rodas (com quatro rodas); *v.*, patinar.
ROL.LICK.ING, *adj.*, travesso, alegre, brincalhão.
ROLL.ING, *adj.*, ondulado.
ROLL.ING PIN, *s., Cul.*, rolo de macarrão.
RO.LY-PO.LY, *s.*, rocambole.
ROM, *s., Comp.*, *read-only memory*: memória de somente leitura; memória ROM.
RO.MAINE LET.TUCE, *s., US* alface romana.
RO.MAN, *adj., s.*, romano.
RO.MANCE, *s.*, romance, aventura amorosa, romantismo.
RO.MAN.ESQUE, *adj.*, românico.
RO.MA.NIA, *s.*, Romênia.
RO.MA.NIAN, *adj., s.*, romeno.
RO.MAN.ISM, *s.*, religião católica.
RO.MAN.I.ZA.TION, *s.*, romanização.
RO.MAN.IZE, *v.*, romanizar.
ROMAN NUMERALS,
RO.MAN.TIC, *adj.*, romântico.
RO.MAN.TI.CISM, *s.*, romantismo.
RO.MAN.TI.CIST, *s.*, artista adepto do romantismo, romântico.
ROM.A.NY, *s.*, cigano; romani (língua cigana); *adj.*, cigano ou relativo à língua romani.
ROME, *s.*, Roma.
ROM.ISH, *s.*, católico romano.
ROMP, *s.*, brincadeira, travessura, traquinagem; *v.*, brincar ruidosamente.
ROMP.ERS, *s. pl.*, macacão de criança.
ROMP.ISH, *adj.*, traquinas, moleque, travesso.
ROOF, *s.*, teto, telhado, cume, casa, abrigo; *v.*, cobrir com telhas, alojar, abrigar.
ROOF.ING, *s.*, material para a cobertura (telhado).
ROOF RACK, *s., UK* bagageiro (na capota do carro), porta-bagens.
ROOF TOP, *s.*, telhado (de casa).
ROOK, *s.*, torre no jogo de xadrez; trapaceiro; *v.*, trapacear, fraudar, furtar.
ROOK.IE, *s., col., US* novato.
ROOK.Y, *s.*, recruta, novato.
ROOM, *s.*, quarto, apartamento, cômodo, lugar, sala; morar em aposento.
ROOM.ER, *s.*, pensionista, sublocatário.
ROOM.ING HOUSE, *s., US* pensão.
ROOMY, *adj.*, espaçoso, amplo, folgado.
ROOST, *s.*, poleiro, galinheiro, abrigo para aves; *v.*, alojar, empoleirar, pernoitar.
ROOST.ER, *s.*, galo.
ROOT, *s.*, raiz, causa, origem, começo, raiz matemática; *v.*, enraizar, arraigar, radicar.
ROOT CROP, *s.*, tubérculos.
ROOT.ED, *adj.*, enraizado, arraigado.
ROOT.LESS, *adj.*, sem raízes, desarraigado.
ROOT.Y, *adj.*, que tem muitas raízes, radicoso.
ROPE, *s.*, corda, cabo, baraço, fileira; *v.*, amarrar, atar com corda, laçar.
ROPE LAD.DER, *s.*, escada de cordas.
RO.SA.RY, *s.*, rosário.
ROSE, *s.*, rosa, roseira; *adj.*, cor-de-rosa.
RO.SE.ATE, *adj.*, rosado, cor-de-rosa.
ROSE.BED, *s.*, canteiro de rosas.
ROSE.BUD, *s.*, botão de rosa.
ROSE.BUSH, *s.*, roseira.
ROSE-COL.OURED, *adj.*, cor-de-rosa.
ROSE.MARY, *s.*, alecrim.
ROSE-TREE, *s., Bot.*, roseira comum.
RO.SETTE, *s.*, roseta.
ROSE.WOOD, *s., Bot.*, pau-rosa (árvore da Amazônia).
ROS.IN, *s.*, resina, breu, pez.
ROS.TER, *s.*, lista; escala de plantão ou serviços; *v.*, listar.
ROS.TRUM, *s.*, tribuna, rostro; bico.
ROSY, *adj.*, rosado, rosáceo, cor-de-rosa, corado.
ROT, *s.*, podridão, putrefação; *v.*, apodrecer, putrefazer-se.
ROTA, *s.*, lista de turnos; relação, rol.
RO.TA.RY, *s.*, rotativa, máquina impressora; *adj.*, rotativo, giratório.
RO.TATE, *v.*, girar, rodar, revezar; *adj.*, em forma de roda.
RO.TA.TION, *s.*, rotação, revolução, movimento giratório, turno de revezamento.
ROTE, *s.*, rotina.
RO.TIS.SER.IE, *s.*, assadeira, churrasqueira, churrascaria.
ROT.TEN, *adj.*, podre, estragado, fedorento, corrupto.
ROT.TER, *s., gír.*, canalha, patife.
RO.TUND, *adj.*, rechonchudo, redondo, roliço.
ROU.BLE, *s.*, rublo, moeda russa.
ROUGE, *s.*, ruge, carmim, batom; *v.*, passar batom.
ROUGH, *adj.*, tosco, áspero, rouco, violento, ríspido, mau; *v.*, domesticar, tornar áspero.
ROUGH.AGE, *s.*, fibras.
ROUGH.CAST, *s.*, reboco.
ROUGH COP.Y, *s.*, esboço, rascunho.
ROUGH DI.A.MOND, *s., UK* diamante bruto.
ROUGH.EN, *v.*, tornar(-se) rústico, áspero; arrepiar, irritar.
ROUGH.LY, *adv.*, bruscamente; rusticamente.
ROUGH.NESS, *s.*, aspereza, dureza, grosseria, rudeza.

ROULETTE ·· 596 ·· RUMMAGE

ROU.LETTE, s., roleta.
ROUND, s., esfera, círculo, circunferência, anel, aro; v., arredondar, arcar, circundar.
ROUND.A.BOUT, s., desvio, caminho indireto; UK rotatória; carrossel; gira-gira; adj., indireto, vago.
ROUND.ED, adj., curvo, encurvado.
ROUND.ER, s., gír., que ronda bares e cabarés bebendo; beberrão, gastador.
ROUND.ING, s., arredondamento.
ROUND.LY, adv., redondamente, francamente, severamente.
ROUND.NESS, s., redondeza, esfericidade, clareza.
ROUND TA.BLE, s., mesa redonda, conferência.
ROUND TRIP, s., viagem de ida e volta.
ROUND.UP, s., resumo, apanhado geral; US rodeio.
ROUSE, s., alvorada, despertar; v., acordar, despertar.
ROUS.ING, adj., estimulante, incitador; extraordinário, excessivo; entusiástico, estrondoso (aplauso).
ROUT, s., derrota.
ROUTE, s., caminho, trajeto, via, rota, direção; determinar a rota.
ROUTE MARCH, s., Mil., marcha.
ROU.TINE, s., rotina, hábito; adj., rotineiro, habitual, usual.
ROU.TINE.LY, adv., frequentemente.
ROVE, s., ato de vaguear, passeio sem destino; v., vagar por, vaguear, errar, viajar sem rumo.
RO.VER, s., errante, andarilho, caminhante; vagabundo, pirata.
ROV.ING, adj., itinerante, nômade, errante.
ROW, s., fila, fileira, travessa, motim; v., enfileirar, remar, provocar desordem.
ROW.BOAT, s., barco a remo.
ROW.DI.NESS, s., tumulto, alvoroço; brutalidade.
ROW.DY, s., desordeiro, baderneiro, arruaceiro; adj., desordeiro.
ROW.ER, s., Esp., remador.
ROW HOUSE, s., US casa geminada.
ROW.ING, s., Esp., remo; remadura.
ROW.ING BOAT, s., UK barco a remo.
ROY.AL, adj., real, régio, majestoso.
ROY.AL BLUE, adj., azul-escuro, azul-imperial.
ROY.AL.ISM, s., realismo.
ROY.AL.IST, s., realista.
ROY.AL JELLY, s., geleia real.
ROY.AL.TY, s., realeza, posição real.
RPM, abrev. de revolutions per minute: revoluções por minuto, rotações por minuto.
RUB, s., esfrega, fricção, atrito, obstáculo, crítica; v., esfregar, atritar, roçar.
RUB.BER, s., borracha, galocha, pneu, grosa, lima; v., revestir com borracha.
RUB.BER BAND, s., elástico, borrachinha para papel.
RUB.BER BUL.LET, s., Mil., bala de borracha.
RUB.BER.IZE(-ISE), v., revestir(-se) de borracha.
RUB.BER PLANT, s., árvore da goma elástica; planta do látex; goma elástica.
RUB.BER STAMP, s., carimbo de borracha.
RUB.BER TREE, s., Bot., seringueira.
RUB.BER.Y, adj., borrachento, semelhante à borracha.
RUB.BING, s., fricção, atrito.
RUB.BISH, s., sucata, lixo, detritos, refugo.
RUB.BISH BAG, s., UK saco de lixo.

RUB.BISH.ING, adj., inútil, insignificante, sem valor.
RUB.BISH.Y, adj., col., porcaria, sem valor.
RUB.BLE, s., cascalho, pedregulho; entulho.
RUBE., s., US caipira, ingênuo, jeca.
RU.BE.FY, v., enrubescer, corar.
RU.BEL.LA, s., Med., rubéola.
RU.BE.O.LA, s., Med., sarampo (também measles).
RU.BI.OUS, adj., vermelho, rubro.
RU.BRIC, s., rubrica.
RU.BRI.CATE, v., rubricar.
RU.BY, s., rubi.
RUCK, s., prega, dobra, ruga; v., vincar, dobrar, enrugar.
RUCK.SACK, s., mochila.
RUC.TIONS, s. pl., tumulto, alvoroço.
RUD.DER, s., leme, timão.
RUD.DI.NESS, s., rudeza, grosseria, aspereza.
RUD.DY, adj., corado, avermelhado.
RUDE, adj., rude, áspero, grosseiro, mal-educado, malcriado.
RUDE.LY, adv., rudemente, bruscamente, violentamente.
RUDE.NESS, má criação, má educação, incivilidade.
RU.DI.MENT, s., rudimento, coisa elementar.
RU.DI.MEN.TAL, adj., rudimentar, elementar.
RU.DI.MEN.TA.RY, adj., rudimentar, fundamental, elementar; pouco desenvolvido.
RU.DI.MENTS, s., rudimentos, noções básicas.
RUE, s., pesar, compaixão, dó; v., sentir pena, penalizar-se, condoer-se.
RUE.FUL, adj., sentido, condoído, penalizado.
RUF.FI.AN, s., rufião, desordeiro, malvado; adj., brutal, perverso, malvado.
RUF.FLE, s., folho, tufo, ondulação, irritação; v., franzir, enrugar, irritar, amolar.
RUG, s., tapete, capacho; v., puxar, arrastar.
RUG.BY, s., rúgbi, futebol americano.
RUG.GED, adj., áspero, desigual, rugoso, austero, rigoroso, acidentado.
RUG.GED.NESS, s., aspereza.
RUG.GER, s., col., UK rúgbi.
RU.GOSE, adj., rugoso, enrugado, pregueado.
RU.IN, s., ruína, destruição, queda, bancarrota; v., arruinar, decair, falir, seduzir.
RU.IN.ATE, v., arruinar, destruir, aniquilar.
RU.IN.A.TION, s., ruína; desgraça, queda, derrocada.
RU.IN.OUS, adj., ruinoso, desastroso.
RULE, s., regra, norma, regulamento, domínio; régua; v., determinar, regrar, decidir.
RULED, adj., governado, dirigido, regrado.
RUL.ER, s., governador, dirigente, regente.
RUM, s., rum, aguardente.
RU.MA.NIAN, ROU.MA.NIAN, s., romeno (habitante de Romênia); adj., romeno.
RUM.BA, s., Mús., rumba (estilo de música e dança afro-cubana); v., dançar a rumba.
RUM.BLE, s., ruído surdo, assento traseiro, porta-bagagem; v., fazer ruído.
RUM.BUS.TIOUS, adj., impetuoso, enérgico; turbulento.
RU.MI.NANT, adj., s., ruminante.
RU.MI.NATE, v., ruminar, remoer; ponderar, considerar.
RU.MI.NA.TION, s., ruminação.
RUM.MAGE, s., busca minuciosa, desordem, confusão; v., investigar, vistoriar.

RUMMAGE SALE · 597 · RYE BREAD

RUM.MAGE SALE, *s.*, *US* bazar beneficente.
RUM.MY, *s.*, jogo de cartas; *adj.*, excêntrico, esquisito.
RU.MOUR, RUMOR, *s.*, rumor, boato; *v.*, espalhar boatos.
RU.MOUR.ER, *s.*, boateiro.
RUMP, *s.*, anca, garupa, nádega, parte traseira.
RUM.PLE, *s.*, ruga, prega, dobra, vinco; *v.*, enrugar, amarrotar, preguear.
RUM.PUS, *s.*, *col.*, balbúrdia, distúrbio, barulho.
RUN, *s.*, corrida, passeio de carro, trajeto, percurso, pista, temporada; *v.*, correr, apressar, fugir, atingir, perseguir, pesquisar.
RUN-A.ROUND, *s.*, *gír.*, subterfúgio, enrolar alguém.
RUN.AWAY, *s.*, trânsfuga, desertor, vagabundo, fugitivo.
RUN.DOWN, *s.*, relatório detalhado, resumo; explicação; decaída, enfraquecimento.
RUNG, *s.*, degrau, raio de roda.
RUN.NER, *s.*, corredor, mensageiro, espião, maquinista, corretor, anel.
RUN.NER-UP, *s.*, segundo colocado em um torneio ou competição.
RUN.NING, *s.*, corrida, direção, curso, contrabando; *adj.*, cursivo, corrente.
RUN.NING AC.COUNT, *s.*, conta-corrente.
RUN.NING COM.MEN.TA.RY, *s.*, comentário ao vivo.
RUN.NING RE.PAIRS, *s. pl.*, pequenos reparos.
RUN.NING WA.TER, *s.*, água corrente.
RUN.NY, *adj.*, que é mole; que goteja, que escorre.
RUNT, *s.*, filhote mais fraco; raquítico; *pej.*, baixinho, tampinha.
RUN-THROUGH, *s.*, ensaio; passada rápida.
RUN.WAY, *s.*, pista de aterrissagem; canal, trilha.
RUP.TURE, *s.*, ruptura, hérnia; *v.*, romper, quebrar.
RU.RAL, *adj.*, rural, campestre, do sítio.
RU.RAL.IST, *s.*, camponês, colono.
RUSE, *s.*, ardil, artimanha, manha, armadilha.

RUSH, *s.*, pressa, ímpeto, movimento, fúria; *v.*, impelir, empurrar, apressar-se, atacar.
RUSHED, *adj.*, apressado, feito às pressas.
RUSH HOUR, *s.*, hora do *rush*.
RUSH.ING, *s.*, carreira precipitada, ímpeto, arremetida; *adj.*, impetuoso.
RUSK, *s.*, rosca; biscoito.
RUS.SET, *s.*, cor avermelhada; *adj.*, avermelhado, ruivo.
RUS.SETY, *adj.*, moreno, trigueiro.
RUS.SIA, *s.*, Rússia.
RUS.SIAN, *adj.*, *s.*, russo.
RUS.SIAN ROU.LETTE, *s.*, roleta-russa.
RUST, *s.*, ferrugem, mofo, bolor; *v.*, enferrujar, mofar, criar bolor.
RUS.TIC, *s.*, pessoa rústica, camponês; *adj.*, rústico, agreste, rude, bruto.
RUS.TIC.I.TY, *s.*, rusticidade, vida rural, ignorância.
RUST.I.NESS, *s.*, estado de ferrugem.
RUS.TLE, *s.*, sussurro, murmúrio, ruído; *v.*, sussurrar, roçar, rugir.
RUST.LESS, *adj.*, sem ferrugem, desenferrujado.
RUST.PROOF, *adj.*, inoxidável.
RUS.TY, *adj.*, enferrujado, rançoso, bolorento.
RUT, *s.*, cio, excitação sexual de animais; sulco; *v.*, estar no cio.
RUTH, *s.*, pena, dó, compaixão.
RUTH.FUL, *adj.*, compassivo, penalizado, misericordioso.
RUTH.LESS, *adj.*, implacável, sem piedade, cruel.
RUTH.LESS.NESS, *adj.*, impiedoso.
RUT.TISH, *adj.*, lascivo, libidinoso.
RWAN.DAN, *s.*, *adj.*, ruandês.
RYE, *s.*, centeio.
RYE BREAD, *s.*, pão de centeio.

S, s., décima nona letra do alfabeto inglês.
SAB.BATH, s., sábado para os judeus, domingo para os cristãos, dia de descanso.
SAB.BAT.IC, adj., sabático.
SAB.BAT.I.CAL, s., período sabático; adj., em período sabático.
SA.BLE, s., Zool., zibelina; pele de marta; adj., da cor da marta; fig., escuro, sombrio.
SAB.O.TAGE, s., Fr., sabotagem; v., sabotar.
SAB.O.TEUR, s., Fr., sabotador.
SA.BRE, SA.BER, s., sabre.
SAC.CHA.RINE, s., sacarina.
SA.CHET, s., perfumador.
SACK, s., saco, saca, despedida; v., ensacar, exonerar, demitir.
SACK.ER, s., saqueador.
SACK.FUL, s., saca, sacada (o quanto cabe num saco).
SACK.ING, s., tecido grosseiro, linhagem.
SAC.RA.MENT, s., sacramento.
SAC.RA.MEN.TAL, adj., sacramental.
SA.CRED, adj., sagrado, sacro.
SAC.RI.FICE, s., sacrifício; v., sacrificar.
SAC.RI.LEGE, s., sacrilégio.
SAC.RI.LE.GIOUS, adj., sacrílego, injurioso.
SACRING, adj., sagrado, consagrado.
SAC.RIS.TAN, s., sacristão.
SAC.RIS.TY, s., sacristia.
SAC.RO.SANCT, adj., sacrossanto, sagrado.
SAD, adj., triste, tristonho, deplorável, lamentável, escuro, sombrio.
SAD.DEN, v., entristecer, tornar-se triste, deprimir.
SAD.DLE, s., sela, selim, assento de bicicleta; v., selar, pôr sela.
SAD.DLE.BAG, s., alforje.
SAD.DLER, s., seleiro.
SAD.IRON, s., ferro de passar roupa, ferro de engomar.
SA.DISM, s., sadismo, perversão.
SA.DIST, s., sádico, sadista.
SA.DIST.IC, adj., sádico.
SAD.LY, adv., tristemente, lamentavelmente.
SAD.NESS, s., tristeza, melancolia.
SAD.O.MAS.O.CHIS.TIC, adj., sadomasoquista.
SA.FA.RI, s., safári.
SAFE, s., cofre, caixa forte, guarda-comida; adj., seguro, ileso, imune, cauteloso.
SAFE-BREAK.ER, s., arrombador de cofre.
SAFE-CON.DUCT, s., salvaguarda, salvo-conduto.
SAFE.GUARD, s., salvaguarda, proteção, defesa.
SAFE HOUSE, s., esconderijo.
SAFE.KEEP.ING, s., proteção, custódia.
SAFE.LY, adv., seguramente, com segurança.
SAFE.NESS, s., segurança, certeza.
SAFE SEX, s., sexo seguro.
SAFE.TY, s., segurança, custódia.
SAFE.TY.BELT, s., salva-vidas; cinto de segurança.
SAFE.TY CATCH, s., trava de segurança.
SAFE.TY IS.LAND, s., ilha (calçada feita no meio de uma rua para separar as duas mÃOS).
SAFE.TY-PIN, s., pino de segurança.
SAFE.TY RAIL, s., corrimão.
SAFE.TY VALVE, s., válvula de segurança.
SAF.FRON, s., açafrão.
SAG, s., queda, caída; v., cair, afundar, desmanchar.
SA.GA, s., saga.
SA.GA.CIOUS, adj., sagaz, astuto, esperto, finório.
SA.GAC.I.TY, s., sagacidade.
SAGE, s., salva; sábio; adj., sábio, instruído, letrado.
SAGE.NESS, s., sabedoria, erudição, prudência.
SAG.GY, adj., que pode curvar-se ou cair.
SAG.IT.TA.RI.US, s., Astron., sagitário (constelação); signo do zodíaco.
SA.GO, s., sagu.
SA.HA.RA, s., Geogr., Saara (deserto).
SA.HA.RAN, adj., saariano.
SAID, adj., part., dito, referido, mencionado.
SAIL, s., vela de navio, velame, veleiro; v., velejar, viajar, navegar, singrar.
SAIL.BOAT, s., veleiro.
SAIL.CLOTH, s., lona (pano forte para fazer as velas para barcos).
SAIL.ING, s., navegação a vela, partida.
SAIL.ING SHIP, s., veleiro (também *sailboat*).
SAIL.OR, s., marinheiro, marujo, nauta.
SAINT, s., santa, santo; adj., santo; v., santificar, canonizar.
SAINT.HOOD, s., santidade.
SAINT.LIKE, adj., santo, piedoso, devoto, pio.
SAINT.LY, adj., como santo; santificado, santo, puro, pio.
SAKE, s., causa, motivo, razão, fim, finalidade.
SAL.ABLE, adj., vendável.
SAL.AD, s., alface, prato de verduras, frios.
SAL.AD BOWL, s., saladeira.
SAL.AD SPOOM, s., colher de salada.
SAL.A.MAN.DER, s., Zool., salamandra.
SAL.A.MI, s., salame.
SAL.A.RIED, adj., assalariado.
SAL.A.RY, s., salário.
SALE, s., venda, movimento de vendas, mercado.
SALE.ABLE, adj., vendável.
SALE.ROOM, s., sala de vendas; *US salesroom*.
SALES.MAN, s., vendedor, caixeiro, balconista.
SALES REP.RE.SEN.TA.TIVE, s., representante de vendas.
SALES TEAM, s., equipe de vendas.
SALES.WOM.AN, s., vendedora.
SA.LIENCE, s., saliência, destaque.

SALIENT ·· 599 ·· SATISFACTION

SA.LIENT, *adj.*, saliente, destacado, evidente, óbvio, claro.
SA.LINE, *s.*, salina, solução de cloreto de sódio e água; *adj.*, salino.
SA.LI.VA, *s.*, saliva, cuspe.
SAL.I.VATE, *v.*, salivar, produzir saliva.
SAL.I.VA.TION, *s.*, salivação.
SAL.LOW, *adj.*, amarelado, pálido, esmaecido.
SAL.LOW.NESS, *s.*, palidez.
SAL.LY, *s.*, gracejo, chiste.
SALM.ON, *s.*, *Zool.*, salmão.
SAL.MO.NEL.LA, *s.*, *Zool.*, salmonela.
SA.LON, *s.*, salão, sala, reunião; *beauty salon*: salão de beleza.
SA.LOON, *s.*, bar, salão, sala.
SALT, *s.*, sal de cozinha; *Quím.*, cloreto de sódio.
SALT CEL.LAR, **SALT SHAK.ER**, *s.*, saleiro (de mesa).
SALT.ED, *adj.*, salgado, com sal.
SALT.ERN, *s.*, salina, mina de sal.
SALT.ISH, *adj.*, um tanto salgado, salgado.
SALT.LESS, *adj.*, insosso, sem sal, insípido.
SALT.MINE, *s.*, salina, mina de sal.
SALT.PETRE, *s.*, salitre.
SALT.WA.TER, *s.*, água do mar; *adj.*, salgado, de água do mar.
SALTY, *adj.*, salgado.
SA.LU.BRI.OUS, *adj.*, salubre, saudável.
SA.LU.BRI.TY, *s.*, salubridade.
SAL.U.TARY, *adj.*, salutar.
SAL.U.TA.TION, *s.*, saudação.
SA.LUTE, *s.*, saudação, salva de tiros; continência; *v.*, saudar.
SAL.VAGE, *s.*, salvamento, recuperação; *v.*, salvar.
SAL.VA.TION, *s.*, salvação.
SALVE, *s.*, unguento, pomada, bálsamo, remédio; *v.*, untar, passar pomada.
SAL.VER, *s.*, bandeja, salva.
SAL.VIA, *s.*, salva, sálvia.
SAL.VO, *s.*, salva (de palmas, de artilharia).
SA.MAR.I.TAN, *adj.*, *s.*, samaritano.
SAM.BA, *s.*, *Mús.*, samba (música e dança brasileiras); *v.*, sambar.
SAME, *pron.*, *adj.*, mesmo, mesma, o mesmo, a mesma.
SAME.NESS, *s.*, monotonia, mesmice; uniformidade, identidade.
SA.MO.AN, *s.*, *adj.*, samoano.
SAM.PLE, *s.*, amostra, prova; *v.*, examinar, provar, degustar.
SAN.ABLE, *adj.*, sanável, curável.
SAN.A.TO.RI.UM, *s.*, sanatório, hospital, casa de saúde; *US sanitorium.*
SANC.TI.FI.CA.TION, *s.*, santificação.
SANC.TI.FY, *v.*, santificar.
SANC.TION, *s.*, sanção, autorização, confirmação; *v.*, sancionar, autorizar.
SANC.TI.TY, *s.*, santidade.
SANC.TU.ARY, *s.*, santuário, refúgio.
SANC.TUM, *s.*, lugar sagrado, santuário.
SAND, *s.*, areia, local de areia; *v.*, arear.
SAN.DAL, *s.*, sandália.
SAN.DAL.WOOD, *s.*, *Bot.*, sândalo.
SAND-BAG, *s.*, saco de areia.
SAND-BANK, *s.*, banco de areia.
SAND.CASTLE, *s.*, castelo de areia.
SAND DUNE, *s.*, duna (de areia).

SAND.ER, *s.*, lixadeira.
SAND.GLASS, *s.*, ampulheta.
SAND.PA.PER, *s.*, lixa; *v.*, lixar.
SAND.PIT *UK*, **SAND.BOX** *US*, *s.*, caixa de areia.
SAND.STONE, *s.*, arenito.
SAND-STORM, *s.*, tempestade de areia.
SAND.WICH, *s.*, sanduíche; *v.*, imprensar, colocar no meio de duas partes.
SANDY, *adj.*, arenoso, amarelado.
SANE, *adj.*, são, sadio, saudável, sensato, racional, ajuizado.
SAN.GUI.NARY, *adj.*, sanguinário.
SAN.GUINE, *adj.*, sanguíneo, vivo.
SAN.I.FY, *v.*, sanear, higienizar.
SAN.I.TAR.Y, *adj.*, sanitário, higiênico, limpo.
SAN.I.TAR.Y NAP.KIN, *s.*, *US* absorvente higiênico
SAN.I.TAR.Y TOW.EL, *s.*, *UK* absorvente higiênico.
SAN.I.TATE, *v.*, sanear.
SAN.I.TA.TION, *s.*, instalações sanitárias; serviço público de saúde.
SAN.I.TIZE(-ISE), *v.*, sanear, desinfetar; limpar, polir.
SAN.I.TY, *s.*, sanidade mental, juízo, bom senso.
SAN.SCRIT, *s.*, sânscrito.
SAN.TA CLAUS, *s.*, Papai Noel.
SAP, *s.*, seiva, humor; *v.*, esgotar, minar, sangrar.
SAP.FUL, *adj.*, cheio de seiva, viçoso, vigoroso.
SA.PID.I.TY, *s.*, gosto, sabor.
SA.PI.ENCE, *s.*, sapiência, sabedoria.
SAP.LING, *s.*, árvore nova, muda.
SAP.O.NA.CEOUS, *adj.*, saponáceo.
SAP.PHIRE, *s.*, safira.
SAR.A.CEN, *adj.*, *s.*, sarraceno.
SAR.CASM, *s.*, sarcasmo.
SAR.CAS.TIC, *adj.*, sarcástico.
SAR.COPH.A.GUS, *s.*, sarcófago.
SAR.DINE, *s.*, sardinha.
SAR.DON.IC, *adj.*, sardônico, mordaz.
SA.RI, *s.*, sari.
SA.RONG, *s.*, sarongue.
SAR.SA.PA.RIL.LA, *s.*, salsaparrilha.
SAR.TO.RI.AL, *adj.*, relativo a alfaiate; bem vestido; *Anat.*, relativo ao músculo sartório.
SASH, *s.*, faixa, cinturão, cinta.
SAS.SY, *adj.*, *col.*, *US* descarado, insolente.
SA.TAN, *s.*, satã, satanás, diabo.
SA.TAN.IC, *adj.*, satânico.
SATCH.EL, *s.*, mochila escolar.
SATE, *v.*, saciar, fartar, satisfazer.
SAT.ED, *adj.*, farto, satisfeito.
SAT.EL.LITE, *s.*, satélite.
SAT.EL.LITE DISH, *s.*, antena parabólica.
SA.TIA.BLE, *adj.*, saciável.
SA.TI.ATE, *v.*, saciar, fartar, satisfazer.
SA.TI.ETY, *s.*, saciedade, fartura.
SAT.IN, *s.*, cetim; *adj.*, acetinado; *v.*, acetinar, dar brilho de cetim.
SAT.IRE, *s.*, sátira, crítica, ironia.
SA.TIR.IC, *adj.*, satírico, irônico, crítico.
SA.TIR.I.CAL, *adj.*, satírico.
SAT.I.RIST, *s.*, satirista.
SAT.I.RIZE, *v.*, satirizar.
SAT.IS.FAC.TION, *s.*, satisfação, contentamento; indenização,

SATISFACTORY ··600·· SCENIC

pagamento.

SAT.IS.FAC.TO.RY, *adj.*, satisfatório.

SAT.IS.FIED, *adj.*, satisfeito, contente, farto, saciado.

SAT.IS.FY, *v.*, satisfazer, fartar, contentar, indenizar, agradar.

SAT.IS.FY.ING, *adj.*, satisfatório , agradável.

SAT.U.RATE, *v.*, saturar, fartar, satisfazer; *adj.*, saturado, farto, satisfeito.

SAT.U.RA.TED, *adj.*, saturado, impregnado.

SAT.U.RA.TION, *s.*, saturação, saciedade.

SAT.UR.DAY, *s.*, sábado.

SAT.URN, *s.*, *Astron.*, Saturno (sexto planeta do sistema solar); *Mit.*, deus da agricultura romano.

SA.TYR, *s.*, sátiro.

SA.TY.RIC, *adj.*, satírico.

SAUCE, *s.*, molho, tempero, condimento; *v.*, temperar, condimentar.

SAUCE-BOAT, *s.*, molheira.

SAUCE.PAN, *s.*, panela, caçarola.

SAUC.ER, *s.*, pires.

SAU.CY, *adj.*, atrevido, descarado, petulante.

SAL.DI A.RA.BI.AN, *s.*, *adj.*, árabe-saudita.

SAU.ER.KRAUT, *s.*, chucrute.

SAU.NA, *s.*, sauna.

SAUN.TER, *s.*, passeio, volta, giro; *v.*, andar ao léu, saracotear.

SAU.SAGE, *s.*, salsicha, linguiça.

SAV.AGE, *s.*, selvagem, bárbaro, pessoa bruta; *adj.*, bruto, rude, grosseiro, cruel.

SAVAGENESS,

SAV.AGE.RY, *s.*, selvajaria, barbaridade, grosseria.

SAV.AN.NAH, *s.*, *Geogr.*, savana.

SA.VANT, *s.*, sábio, cientista.

SAVE, *v.*, salvar, economizar, ganhar, defender, proteger, abrigar; *prep.*, exceto.

SAV.ER, *s.*, salvador, libertador.

SAV.ING, *s.*, economia; *pl.*, economias.

SAV.INGS, *s. pl.*, economias.

SAV.INGS AC.COUNT, *s.*, conta remunerada (como caderneta de poupança).

SA.VIOUR *UK*, **SA.VIOR** *US*, *s.*, salvador.

SA.VOUR *UK*, **SA.VOR** *US*, *s.*, sabor, gosto; *v.*, saborear, degustar, apreciar, provar.

SA.VOUR.Y, **SA.VOR.Y**, *adj.*, saboroso, gostoso; salgado.

SAW, *s.*, serra, serrote; *v.*, serrar.

SAW.DUST, *s.*, serradura, serragem.

SAW.ER, *s.*, serrador.

SAW-MILL, *s.*, serraria.

SAW.YER, *s.*, serrador.

SAX, *s.*, *col.*, saxofone.

SAX.ON, *adj.*, *s.*, saxão; *adj.*, saxônico.

SAX.O.PHONE, *s.*, saxofone.

SAXOPHONIST, *s.*, saxofonista.

SAY, *s.*, palavra, fala, discurso; *v.*, dizer, falar, exprimir.

SAY.ING, *s.*, ditado, provérbio.

SAY-SO, *s.*, *col.*, *US* ordem, palavra, permissão.

SCAB, *s.*, casca ou crosta de ferida; *Med.*, sarna; *gír.*, *US* fura-greve.

SCAB.BY, *adj.*, coberto de feridas; sarnento.

SCA.BIES, *s.*, sarna.

SCA.BI.OUS, *adj.*, sarnento.

SCA.BROUS, *adj.*, escabroso, áspero, rude.

SCAF.FOLD, *s.*, cadafalso, patíbulo, armação para enforcamento.

SCAF.FOLD.ING, *s.*, andaime.

SCALD, *s.*, escaldamento, queimadura; *v.*, escaldar, queimar, esterilizar.

SCALD.ING, *s.*, escaldadura; queimadura; *adj.*, escaldante.

SCALE, *s.*, escala; escama, caspa, crosta, cascão, graduação, balança; *v.*, escalar, subir, medir, ascender, pesar.

SCAL.ING, *s.*, escalada.

SCAL.LION, *s.*, *Bot.*, *US* cebolinha-verde.

SCAL.LOP, *s.*, *Zool.*, vieira (molusco comestível); *v.*, cozinhar em concha de vieiras.

SCALP, *s.*, couro cabeludo do crânio; *v.*, escalpelar, tirar o couro da cabeça.

SCAL.PEL, *s.*, escalpelo, bisturi.

SCAMP, *s.*, velhaco, patife, cafajeste, safado.

SCAM.PER, *s.*, corrida; *v.*, fugir rapidamente; correr.

SCAM.PI, *s.*, camarões fritos ao alho.

SCAN, *v.*, examinar, esquadrinhar, explorar, investigar, ajustar a *TV*.

SCAN.DAL, *s.*, escândalo, desonra, desgraça, difamação, calúnia.

SCAN.DAL.IZE, *v.*, escandalizar, desonrar, ofender, chocar.

SCAN.DAL.OUS, *adj.*, escandaloso, ofensivo, difamador, vergonhoso.

SCAN.DI.NA.VIAN, *s.*, *adj.*, escandinavo.

SCAN.NER, *s.*, explorador, examinador; *Comp.*, copiadora digital, escâner; *Med.*, tomógrafo.

SCANT, *v.*, restringir, limitar, confinar; *adj.*, escasso, limitado, restrito.

SCANT.NESS, *s.*, insuficiência, escassez, limitação, carência.

SCAN.TLE, *v.*, cortar em pedaços, picar, fracionar.

SCANTY, *adj.*, escasso, insuficiente, limitado.

SCAPE.GOAT, *s.*, bode expiatório.

SCAR, *s.*, cicatriz, sinal; *v.*, cicatrizar, marcar.

SCARCE, *adj.*, escasso, raro, incomum.

SCARCE.LY, *adv.*, raramente, apenas, mal.

SCARCE.NESS, *s.*, falta, carência, escassez, raridade.

SCAR.CITY, *s.*, escassez.

SCARE, *s.*, susto, espanto, assombro, pânico; *v.*, espantar, assustar.

SCARE.CROW, *s.*, espantalho.

SCARE.MON.GER, *s.*, alarmista.

SCARF, *s.*, cachecol, xale, lenço para a cabeça.

SCAR.LET, *adj.*, *s.*, vermelho.

SCAR.LET FE.VER, *s.*, *Med.*, escarlatina.

SCARP, *s.*, escarpa; *v.*, escarpar.

SCARY, *adj.*, assustador, assustado, medroso.

SCATH.ING, *adj.*, mordaz; rigoroso.

SCAT.TER, *v.*, espalhar, dispersar.

SCAT.TER.BRAINED, *adj.*, *col.*, desmiolado.

SCAT.TERED, *adj.*, espalhado, disperso.

SCAT.TY, *adj.*, *col.*, *UK* maluco, louco.

SCAV.ENGE, *v.*, varrer, limpar.

SCAV.EN.GER, *s.*, varredor de rua; animal que se alimenta de carniça.

SCE.NA, *s.*, cena.

SCE.NAR.IO, *s.*, cenário, panorama.

SCENE, *s.*, cenário, panorama, paisagem, escândalo, decoração teatral.

SCEN.ER.Y, *s.*, paisagem; *Teat.*, cenário.

SCE.NIC, *adj.*, pitoresco, cênico.

SCENIC ROUTE •• 601 •• SCRATCH PAD

SCEN.IC ROUTE, *s.*, rota turística.
SCEN.O.GRAPH.IC, *adj.*, cenográfico.
SCE.NOG.RA.PHY., *s.*, cenografia.
SCENT, *s.*, cheiro, aroma, perfume, faro; pista, pegada.
SCENT.ED, *adj.*, cheiroso, perfumado.
SCEP.TER, *s.*, cetro.
SCEP.TIC, SKEP.TIC, *adj., s.*, céptico.
SCEP.TI.CISM, SKEP.TI.CISM, *s.*, ceticismo.
SCEP.TRE, SCEP.TER, *s.*, cetro.
SCHED.ULE, *s.*, lista, programa, roteiro, tabela, horário; *v.*, tabelar, planejar, datar.
SCHE.MAT.IC, *adj.*, esquemático.
SCHEME, *s.*, esquema, maquinação, plano, sistema, método; *v.*, conspirar, maquinar.
SCHEM.ING, *adj.*, que faz intriga; intrigante.
SCHISM, *s.*, cisma, segregação, separação.
SCHIST, *s.*, xisto.
SCHIZ.O.PHRE.NI.A, *s., Med.*, esquizofrenia.
SCHIZ.O.PHREN.IC, *adj., Med.*, esquizofrênico.
SCHMALTZ, *s.*, gordura; *fig.*, sentimentalismo.
SCHO.LAR, *s.*, aluno, escolar, estudante; sábio, erudito, sabido.
SCHOL.AR.SHIP, *s.*, sabedoria, erudição; bolsa de estudos.
SCHO.LAS.TIC, *s.*, escolástico; *adj.*, escolástico, educacional.
SCHOOL, *s.*, escola, colégio, universidade; aulas, corpo docente; *v.*, educar, ensinar.
SCHOOL AGE, *s.*, idade escolar.
SCHOOL.BOOK, *s.*, livro escolar.
SCHOOL.BOY, *s.*, aluno.
SCHOOL.CHILD, *s.*, aluno (ainda criança).
SCHOOL DIN.NER, *s.*, *UK* merenda escolar.
SCHOOL FRIEND, *s.*, colega de aula.
SCHOOL.GIRL, *s.*, aluna.
SCHOOL.ING, *s.*, educação, instrução, ensino, capacitação escolar.
SCHOOL.MAS.TER, *s.*, professor, mestre-escola.
SCHOOL.ROOM, *s.*, sala de aula.
SCHOOL.TEACH.ER, *s.*, professor.
SCHOOL.WORK, *s.*, trabalho escolar, lição de casa.
SCHOOL YEAR, *s.*, ano escolar.
SCHOO.NER, *s.*, escuna.
SCI.AT.IC, *adj.*, ciático.
SCI.AT.I.CA, *s., Med.*, dor no nervo ciático.
SCI.ENCE, *s.*, ciência, sabedoria, erudição.
SCI.ENCE FIC.TION, *s., Lit.*, ficção científica.
SCI.ENCE PARK, *s.*, parque industrial de alta tecnologia.
SCI.EN.TIF.IC, *adj.*, científico.
SCI.EN.TIST, *s.*, cientista, sábio, pesquisador.
SCI-FI, *abrev.* de *science fiction*: ficção científica.
SCIN.TIL.LATE, *v.*, cintilar, brilhar.
SCIN.TIL.LA.TION, *s.*, cintilação, brilho, luminosidade.
SCIS.SION, *s.*, cisão, divisão, partição.
SCIS.SORS, *s. pl.*, tesouras.
SCLE.RO.SIS, *s., Med.*, esclerose.
SCLE.ROT.IC, *adj.*, esclerosado.
SCOFF, *s.*, zombaria, desprezo, escárnio; *v.*, zombar, escarnecer, mofar, ridicularizar.
SCOFF.ER, *s.*, zombador, escarnecedor, mofador.
SCOLD, *v.*, repreender, xingar.
SCONCE, *s.*, candeeiro, fortaleza; *v.*, fortificar.
SCOOP, *s.*, pá, concha, cavidade; espátula; furo jornalístico;

v., cavar, tirar com concha.
SCOOT, *s.*, corrida; *v.*, correr, fugir, andar apressadamente.
SCOOT.ER, *s.*, patinete; motoneta, lambreta.
SCOPE, *s.*, escopo, objetivo, âmbito, abrangência, oportunidade, contexto.
SCORCH, *s.*, queimadura leve; *v.*, chamuscar, queimar.
SCORCH.ER, *s.*, dia muito quente, escaldante; pessoa que abusa da velocidade na estrada.
SCORCH.ING, *adj., col.*, escaldante (tempo).
SCORE, *s.*, escore, contagem, dívida, razão, motivo; *v.*, sulcar, arar, fazer pontos.
SCORE.BOARD, *s., Esp.*, placar.
SCOR.ER, *s.*, marcador de pontos.
SCORN, *s.*, desprezo, escárnio, desdém; desprezar, desdenhar, escarnecer.
SCORN.FUL, *adj.*, desdenhoso, zombador, escarnecedor.
SCOR.PI.O, *s., Astron.*, Escorpião (constelação); *Astrol.*, Escorpião (signo do zodíaco).
SCOR.PI.ON, *s.*, escorpião.
SCOT, *s.*, escocês, escocesa.
SCOTCH, *adj., s.*, escocês, habitante da Escócia, dialeto escocês; uísque escocês.
SCOT.FREE, *adj.*, isento de impostos, livre de taxas.
SCOT.LAND, *s.*, Escócia.
SCOTS, *adj.*, escocês, escocesa.
SCOT.TISH, *adj.*, escocês.
SCOUN.DREL, *s.*, salafrário, patife, cafajeste; *adj.*, patife, safado, tratante.
SCOUR, *s.*, corrente, correnteza, lavação, *v.*, procurar, limpar, lavar, polir, perseguir.
SCOUR.ER, *s.*, esponja de aço.
SCOURGE, *s.*, flagelo, tormento, aflição, dor.
SCOUT, *s.*, batedor, explorador, escoteiro; *v.*, espiar, observar, examinar; *boy scout*, *s.*: escoteiro; *girl scout*, *s.*: escoteira.
SCOUT.MAST.ER, *s.*, chefe dos escoteiros.
SCOWL, *s.*, olhar de zanga, carranca; *v.*, fazer olhar de zanga, franzir a testa.
SCRAB.BLE, *s.*, ação de arrastar-se; rabisco, garatuja; *v.*, raspar; arranhar; rabiscar.
SCRAG.GY, *adj.*, magro, fino, esquelético.
SCRAM, *v., gír.*, chispar, picar a mula.
SCRAM.BLE, *s.*, escalada íngreme, luta; *v.*, subir, ascender, lutar.
SCRAM.BLED EGGS, *s. pl., Cul.*, ovos mexidos.
SCRAM.BLER, *s.*, o que se arrasta; *Comp.*, misturador; *Esp.*, moto de estrada de terra, *off-road*.
SCRAP, *s.*, pedaço, fragmento, resto, recorte; *v.*, despedaçar, fragmentar, esmagar.
SCRAP.BOOK, *s.*, álbum de recortes.
SCRAPE, *s.*, ruído de arranhão ou raspagem; *fig.*, dificuldade; *v.*, raspar, arranhar, roçar; economizar.
SCRAP.ER, *s.*, raspador; avarento.
SCRAP HEAP, *s.*, monte de sucata; *fig.*, menosprezo.
SCRAP.ING, *s.*, raspagem.
SCRAP.INGS, *s. pl.*, raspas; economias.
SCRAP METAL, *s.*, sucata, ferro-velho.
SCRAP.PY, *adj., pej.*, desconexo, incoerente; *gír.*, briguento.
SCRATCH, *s.*, arranhão, esfoladura, raspagem; *v.*, arranhar, riscar, marcar, labutar.
SCRATCH.ER, *s.*, raspador, raspadeira.
SCRATCH PAD, *s.*, bloco de rascunho.

SCRATCH PAPER · 602 · SEARCH-LIGHT

SCRATCH PA.PER, s., papel de rascunho.
SCRATCH.Y, adj., rangido, estridente (som); áspero, que pinica (tecido); esfarrapado.
SCRAWL, s., rabisco, garatuja, letra ilegível; v., rabiscar, garatujar, escrever mal.
SCRAW.NY, adj., magro, magricela, esquelético.
SCREAM, s., grito, berro; v., gritar, berrar, guinchar, rir alto.
SCREAM.ING, s., gritaria; adj., penetrante, agudo.
SCREE, s., acúmulo de pedras soltas em penhasco; seixo.
SCREECH, s., guincho, grito forte, bramido, berro; v., guinchar, berrar, bramir.
SCREEN, s., biombo, divisória, tapume, para-brisa; v., abrigar, esconder, examinar.
SCREEN.ING, s., exame médico.
SCREEN.PLAY, s., roteiro (de cinema).
SCREEN.WRIT.ER, s., roteirista (de cinema).
SCREW, s., parafuso, porca, hélice; v., parafusar, atarraxar, montar, forçar, obrigar.
SCREW.BALL, s., gír., cabeça oca, pessoa excêntrica.
SCREW.DRIV.ER, s., chave de fenda.
SCREW.NUT, s., porca de parafuso.
SCRIB.BLE, s., rabisco; v., rabiscar.
SCRIBE, s., escriba, copista, escrevente; v., escrever, copiar.
SCRIM.MAGE, s., escaramuça, contenda, disputa, luta.
SCRIMP, v., US economizar com exagero; estreitar, limitar; mesquinhar.
SCRIPT, s., argumento, roteiro, texto, escrita, caligrafia, enredo de um filme.
SCRIPT.ED, adj., com roteiro, roteirizado; programado; redigido (para servir de modelo).
SCRIP.TURES, s. pl., Bíblia, Sagradas Escrituras.
SCRIPT.WRIT.ER, s., roteirista (para cinema, TV, rádio etc.).
SCRIV.EN.ER, s., escriturário, secretário.
SCROLL, s., rolo de papel ou pergaminho; Comp., mover, rolar.
SCROLL BAR, s., Comp., barra de rolagem.
SCROOGE, s., pej., avaro, avarento, miserável.
SCRO.TUM, s., escroto.
SCROUNGE, v., furtar, roubar, tirar de alguém.
SCROUNG.ER, s., aquele que vive às custas dos outros, parasita.
SCRUB, s., capoeira, mato, mata, moita; v., esfregar, varrer, lavar, trabalhar.
SCRUBY, adj., infeliz, inferior, miserável.
SCRUFF, s., pescoço, nuca.
SCRUF.FY, adj., imundo, sujo; bagunçado.
SCRUMP.TIOUS, adj., col., delicioso.
SCRUNCH, v., amassar; mover com rangidos; estalar.
SCRUNCH.IE, s., elástico de cabelo.
SCRU.PLE, s., escrúpulo, hesitação, remorso; v., hesitar, titubear, vacilar.
SCRU.PU.LOUS, adj., escrupuloso, hesitante.
SCRU.PU.LOUS.LY, adv., escrupulosamente, totalmente.
SCRU.TI.NEER, s., escrutinador, conferente de votos em eleição.
SCRU.TI.NIZE, v., escrutinar, examinar, conferir votos.
SCRU.TI.NI.ZER(-ISER), v., escrutinador.
SCRU.TI.NY, s., escrutínio, exame; apuração de votos.
SCUBA DIV.ING, s., Esp., mergulho executado com tubo de oxigênio para longo período.
SCUD, s., fuga precipitada, vento forte, chuvisco; v., chover, correr, fugir.

SCUFF, s., arranhão, raspagaem; v., arrastar, raspar; gastar, riscar.
SCUF.FLE, s., luta corporal, tumulto, pugilato, enxada; v., lutar, brigar, arrastar os pés.
SCULL, s., ginga (tipo de remo), gingação; v., remar; gingar.
SCUL.LERY, s., UK área de serviço; copa (área para lavar e guardar a louça).
SCULP, v., esculpir.
SCULPT, v., esculpir.
SCULP.TOR, s., escultor.
SCUM, s., espuma, escuma, ralé, escória; v., escumar, formar espuma.
SCUM.MER, v., escumadeira.
SCUP.PER, v., Náut., afundar; fig., UK arruinar, destruir, aniquilar.
SCURF, s., caspa.
SCUR.RIL.OUS, adj., difamatório.
SCUR.RY, s., pressa, correria; v., fugir, começar a correr.
SCUR.VI.NESS, s., baixeza, vileza, baixaria.
SCUR.VY, s., Med., escorbuto.
SCUT.TLE, s., cesto, balde; corrida, passeio; escotilha; v., correr, afundar um navio.
SCYTHE, s., segadeira, foice, alfanje; v., ceifar, cortar, colher.
SEA, s., mar, oceano, onda, movimento das ondas, dilúvio.
SEA AIR, s., ar do mar; maresia.
SEA-BIRD, s., ave marinha.
SEA.BOARD, s., costa, litoral.
SEA-BREEZE, s., brisa do mar.
SEA.FAR.ER, s., navegante, marinheiro.
SEA.FAR.ING, adj., navegante; do mar.
SEA.FOOD, s., marisco.
SEA FRONT, s., beira-mar, orla marinha.
SEA.GO.ING, adj., de alto-mar.
SEA.GULL, s., Zool., gaivota.
SEA-HORSE, s., Zool., cavalo-marinho.
SEAL, s., Zool., foca; selo, brasão; v., selar, fechar.
SEA LANE, s., rota marítima.
SEA.LANT, s., selador.
SEA LEVEL, s., nível do mar.
SEAL.ING WAX, s., lacre (cera para lacrar documentos ou cartas).
SEA LION, s., Zool., leão-marinho.
SEAM, s., costura, sutura, ligação, cicatriz, sulco; v., costurar, coser, fender.
SEA-MAID, s., sereia.
SEA-MAN, s., marinheiro, marujo.
SEA.MAN.SHIP, s., náutica, marinhagem, marinheiraria.
SEA MILE, s., milha marítima.
SEAM.LESS, adj., sem costura.
SEAM.STRESS, s., costureira.
SEAM.Y, adj., que tem costuras; fig., péssimo, sórdido.
SEA-PLANE, s., hidroavião (avião que pousa na água).
SEAR, s., marca, sinal de queimadura; v., queimar, cauterizar, secar, murchar.
SEARCH, s., busca, procura, pesquisa; v., procurar, buscar, investigar.
SEARCH EN.GINE, s., Comp., mecanismo de busca.
SEARCH.ER, s., pesquisador, investigador.
SEARCH.ING, s., pesquisa, inspeção, exame; adj., perspicaz, minucioso, penetrante.
SEARCH-LIGHT, s., farol, holofote.

SEARCH-WARRANT ·· 603 ·· SELECTED

SEARCH-WAR.RANT, *s.*, mandado de busca policial em uma residência.
SEAR.ING, *adj.*, contundente, intenso; abrasador, causticante.
SEA SALT, *s.*, sal marinho.
SEA.SHORE, *s.*, costa, litoral, beira-mar, praia.
SEA.SICK, *adj.*, enjoado, enojado.
SEA.SICK.NESS, *s.*, enjoo do mar, nojo.
SEA.SIDE, *s.*, praia, orla marinha; litoral; *adj.*, costeiro.
SEA.SON, *s.*, estação do ano, temporada; *v.*, temperar, condimentar, sazonar, madurar.
SEA.SON.AL, *adj.*, sazonal, próprio da estação.
SEA.SONED, *adj.*, maduro, experiente; temperado (alimento).
SEA.SON.ING, *s.*, tempero, condimento.
SEAT, *s.*, assento, cadeira, poltrona, traseiro, nádegas, fundilho; *v.*, sentar-se, assentar-se, empossar, colocar, instituir.
SEAT BELT, *s.*, cinto de segurança.
SEAT.ED, *adj.*, sentado.
SEAT.ING, *s.*, assento; acomodação.
SEA UR.CHIN, *s.*, *Zool.*, ouriço do mar.
SEA-WALL, *s.*, quebra-mar, dique, molhe.
SEA.WA.TER, *s.*, água do mar.
SEA.WEED, *s.*, alga marinha.
SEA.WOR.THY, *adj.*, em condições de navegar (embarcação).
SE.BA.CEOUS, *adj.*, sebáceo, gorduroso.
SEC.A.TEURS, *s. pl.*, *Fr.*, *UK* tesoura para podar.
SE.CEDE, *v.*, separar-se, retirar-se, abandonar.
SE.CES.SION, *s.*, secessão, separação, cisão.
SE.CLUDE, *v.*, excluir, segregar.
SE.CLUD.ED, *adj.*, afastado, retirado, isolado.
SE.CLU.SION, *s.*, segregação, exclusão.
SEC.OND, *s.*, *num.*, segundo; segundo (do relógio); *adj.*, segundo; subordinado; *adv.*, em segundo lugar.
SEC.OND.AR.Y, *adj.*, secundário.
SEC.OND.AR.Y SCHOOL, *s.*, escola secundária.
SEC.OND BEST, *adj.*, segundo melhor (em algo).
SEC.OND-CLASS, *adj.*, de segunda classe.
SEC.OND COUS.IN, *s.*, primo em segundo grau.
SEC.OND.HAND, *adj.*, de segunda mão, usado.
SEC.OND-IN-COM.MAND, *s.*, o segundo em comando, vice-comandante, suplente.
SEC.OND.LY, *adv.*, em segundo lugar.
SEC.OND.MENT, *s.*, *Mil.*, transferência temporária.
SE.CRE.CY, *s.*, segredo, sigilo.
SE.CRET, *adj.*, secreto; *s.*, segredo.
SEC.RE.TAR.I.AT, *s.*, secretariado, secretaria.
SEC.RE.TAR.Y, *s.*, secretária, secretário.
SEC.RE.TAR.Y-GEN.E.RAL, *s.*, secretário-geral.
SEC.RE.TARY.SHIP, *s.*, secretariado.
SE.CRETE, *v.*, secretar, expelir; segregar; ocultar.
SE.CRE.TION, *s.*, secreção.
SE.CRE.TIVE, *adj.*, reservado, discreto, segredista; que secreta.
SE.CRET.LY, *adv.*, secretamente.
SE.CRET.NESS, *s.*, segredo, sigilo.
SE.CRET SERV.ICE, *s.*, serviço secreto.
SECT, *s.*, seita.
SEC.TAR.I.AN, *adj.*, sectário, sequaz.
SEC.TA.RY, *s.*, sectário, fanático.
SEC.TION, *s.*, seção, divisão, departamento.
SEC.TOR, *s.*, setor.
SEC.U.LAR, *adj.*, secular, leigo.

SEC.U.LAR.ISM, *s.*, secularismo.
SEC.U.LAR.IST, *s.*, secularista.
SEC.U.LAR.I.ZA.TION, *v.*, secularização.
SEC.U.LAR.IZE(-ISE), *v.*, secularizar.
SE.CURE, *adj.*, seguro, firme, rígido; *v.*, segurar, guardar, proteger, atar, ligar.
SE.CURE.LY, *adv.*, seguramente, firmemente.
SE.CU.RI.TY, *s.*, segurança, fiança, garantia, apólice.
SE.CU.RI.TY COUN.CIL, *s.*, Conselho de Segurança da ONU.
SE.DAN, *s.*, *US* sedã.
SE.DAN CHAIR, *s.*, liteira.
SE.DATE, *adj.*, calmo, sossegado, descansado; *v.*, sedar.
SE.DA.TION, *s.*, sedação.
SED.A.TIVE, *adj.*, sedativo, calmante.
SED.EN.TARY, *adj.*, sedentário.
SED.I.MENT, *s.*, sedimento, depósito, camada básica.
SE.DI.TION, *s.*, sedição, motim, revolta.
SE.DI.TIOUS, *adj.*, sedicioso, revoltoso, amotinado.
SE.DUCE, *v.*, seduzir, persuadir, convencer, corromper.
SE.DUC.ER, *s.*, sedutor.
SE.DUC.TION, *s.*, sedução.
SE.DUC.TIVE, *adj.*, sedutor, atraente.
SED.U.LOUS, *adj.*, diligente, assíduo, trabalhador, dinâmico.
SEE, *v.*, ver, perceber, olhar, observar, espiar, perceber, notar, descobrir, assistir.
SEED, *s.*, semente, grão, bulbo, broto, prole, esperma, muda; *v.*, semear, plantar.
SEED.ER, *s.*, semeador.
SEED.LESS, *adj.*, sem semente.
SEED.LING, *s.*, muda (planta).
SEED.Y, *adj.*, espigado; *col.*, abatido; surrado, maltrapilho.
SEEK, *v.*, procurar, solicitar, tentar.
SEEK.ER, *s.*, investigador.
SEEK.ING, *s.*, procura, busca.
SEEM, *v.*, parecer, dar a impressão de.
SEEM.ING, *s.*, aparência, parecer, opinião.
SEEM.ING.LY, *adv.*, aparentemente.
SEEM.LI.NESS, *s.*, decoro.
SEEM.LY, *adj.*, decoroso, decente, pudico.
SEEP, *v.*, penetrar, infiltrar-se.
SEER, *s.*, vidente, profeta.
SEETHE, *s.*, ebulição; *v.*, ferver; ficar com muita raiva.
SEE.SAW, *s.*, gangorra, balanço, vaivém; *v.*, balançar, oscilar, brincar na gangorra.
SEG.MENT, *s.*, segmento, parte, divisão, seção; *v.*, segmentar.
SEG.MEN.TA.TION, *s.*, segmentação.
SEG.RE.GATE, *v.*, segregar, afastar; *adj.*, segregado, afastado, separado.
SEG.RE.GAT.ED, *adj.*, segregado.
SEG.RE.GA.TION, *s.*, segregação, afastamento.
SEIS.MIC, *adj.*, sísmico.
SEIS.MO.GRAPH, *s.*, sismógrafo.
SEIS.MOL.O.GY, *s.*, sismologia.
SEIZE, *v.*, pegar, agarrar, pescar, entender, apreender, confiscar, capturar, ligar.
SEI.ZURE, *s.*, apreensão, confiscação, sequestro, embargo, ataque, derrame cerebral.
SEL.DOM, *adv.*, raramente.
SE.LECT, *v.*, selecionar, escolher; *adj.*, seleto, escolhido, fino, especial, exclusivo.
SE.LECT.ED, *adj.*, escolhido, selecionado.

SELECTION ··604·· SEPTIC

SE.LEC.TION, s., seleção, escolha.
SE.LEC.TIVE, adj., seletivo.
SE.LEC.TOR, s., seletor; Esp., selecionador.
SE.LE.NI.UM, s., Quím., selênio (elem. de nº atômico 34).
SELF, pron., mesmo, mesma; próprio, própria.
SELF-AD.HE.SIVE, adj., auto-adesivo.
SELF-AS.SUR.ANCE, s., autoconfiança.
SELF-AS.SURED, adj., seguro de si, autoconfiante.
SELF-CEN.TRED, adj., egocêntrico, egoísta.
SELF-CLEAN.ING, adj., autolimpante.
SELF-CON.FESSED, adj., assumido.
SELF-CON.FI.DENCE, s., autoconfiança.
SELF-CON.SCIOUS, adj., inibido, tímido, constrangido.
SELF-CON.TAINED, adj., reservado, retraído; independente.
SELF-CON.TROL, s., autodomínio.
SELF-DE.FENCE, s., legítima defesa.
SELF-DE.NI.AL, s., abnegação.
SELF-DE.TER.MI.NA.TION, s., autodeterminação.
SELF-DIS.CI.PLINE, s., autodisciplina.
SELF-ED.U.CAT.ED, adj., autodidata.
SELF-EM.PLOYED, adj., autônomo.
SELF-ES.TEEM, s., autoestima, amor-próprio.
SELF-GOV.ERN.ING, s., autônomo.
SELF-HELP, s., autoajuda.
SELF-IM.POR.TANT, adj., presunçoso.
SELF-IN.TER.EST, s., egoísmo, interesse próprio.
SELF.ISH, adj., egoísta.
SELF.ISH.NESS, s., egoísmo.
SELF.LESS, adj., abnegado.
SELF-POR.TRAIT, s., autorretrato.
SELF-PRES.ER.VA.TION, s., autodefesa.
SELF-RE.GARD, s., amor-próprio; pej., narcisismo.
SELF-RE.LI.ANT, adj., independente; autoconfiante.
SELF-RE.SPECT, s., amor próprio.
SELF.SAME, adj., mesmo, idêntico, igual.
SELF-SER.VICE, s., self-service, serviço para si mesmo.
SELF-SUF.FI.CIENT, adj., autossuficiente.
SELF-TAUGHT, s., autodidata.
SELF-WILLED, adj., teimoso, cabeçudo.
SELL, v., vender; vender-se.
SELL-BY DATE, s., UK prazo de validade.
SELL.ER, s., vendedor.
SELL.ING, s., venda, ato de vender.
SELL.ING PRICE, s., preço de venda.
SELL-OUT, s., col., sucesso de bilheteria; liquidação; adj., esgotado (ingresso).
SEL.LO.TAPE, s., fita adesiva.
SELTZ.ER, s., água mineral de soda.
SEL.VAGE, s., borda, margem, borda; v., orlar, margear.
SE.MAN.TIC, adj., semântico.
SEM.A.PHORE, s., semáforo.
SEM.BLANCE, s., aparência, semelhança, imagem.
SE.MEN, s., sêmen.
SE.MES.TER, s., semestre.
SEM.I.CIR.CLE, s., semicírculo.
SEM.I.CIR.CU.LAR, s., semicircular.
SEM.I.CO.LON, s., ponto e vírgula.
SEM.I.CON.DUC.TOR, s., semicondutor.
SEM.I.FI.NAL, s., semifinal.
SEM.I.FI.NAL.IST, s., semifinalista.
SEM.I.NAL, adj., seminal; original, muito influente.

SEM.I.NAR, s., seminário, curso.
SEM.I.NARY, s., seminário.
SEM.I.OT.ICS, s., semiótica.
SEM.I-PRE.CIOUS, adj., semiprecioso.
SEM.I-SKIMMED MILK, adj., UK leite semidesnatado.
SEM.ITE, s., semita.
SEMI.TROP.I.CAL, adj., subtropical.
SEM.O.LI.NA, s., semolina, sêmola.
SEN.ATE, s., senado.
SEN.A.TOR, s., senador.
SEND, v., enviar, mandar, remeter, expedir.
SEND.ER, s., remetente.
SEN.E.GAL.ESE, s., adj., senegalês.
SE.NILE, adj., senil.
SE.NIL.I.TY, s., senilidade, velhice.
SEN.I.OR, adj., sênior, mais velho, mais antigo.
SEN.I.OR CIT.I.ZEN, s., idoso.
SEN.IOR.I.TY, s., antiguidade, senioridade.
SEN.SA.TION, s., sensação, percepção, sentimento.
SEN.SA.TION.AL, adj., sensacional.
SEN.SA.TION.AL.ISM, adj., sensacionalismo.
SEN.SA.TION.AL.IST, s., sensacionalista; adj., pej., sensacionalista.
SENSE, s., senso, sentido, sensação; v., sentir, perceber.
SENSE.LESS, adj., insensato, tolo, desajuizado.
SEN.SI.BIL.I.TIES, s. pl., sentimentos, emoções.
SEN.SI.BIL.I.TY, s., sensibilidade.
SEN.SI.BLE, adj., sensível, sensato.
SEN.SI.TIVE, adj., sensível, delicado; s., sensitivo (extrassensorial).
SEN.SI.TIVE.NESS, s., sensibilidade, suscetibilidade.
SEN.SI.TIV.I.TY, s., o mesmo que sensitiveness.
SEN.SI.TI.ZA.TION, s., sensibilização.
SEN.SOR, s., Fis., sensor.
SEN.SO.RI.AL, adj., sensorial.
SEN.SU.AL, adj., sensual.
SEN.SU.AL.ISM, s., sensualismo.
SEN.SU.AL.I.TY, s., sensualidade, libidinismo, lascívia.
SEN.SU.AL.LY, adv., sensualmente, voluptuosamente.
SEN.SU.OUS, adj., sensual.
SEN.TENCE, s., frase, período, sentença; v., sentenciar, condenar, absolver.
SEN.TEN.TIOUS, adj., sentencioso.
SEN.TI.MENT, s., sentimento, opinião, parecer.
SEN.TI.MEN.TAL, adj., sentimental, emotivo, sensível.
SEN.TI.MEN.TAL.ISM, s., sentimentalismo.
SEN.TI.MEN.TAL.I.TY, s., sentimentalidade.
SEN.TI.NEL, s., sentinela, guarda.
SEN.TRY, s., sentinela.
SEP.A.RA.BLE, adj., separável.
SEP.A.RATE, v., separar, apartar, desligar; adj., separado, apartado.
SEP.A.RAT.ED, adj., separado, afastado.
SEP.A.RATE.LY, adv., separadamente.
SEP.A.RATE.NESS, s., separação.
SEP.A.RA.TION, s., separação.
SEP.A.RA.TISM, s., separatismo.
SEP.A.RA.TIST, s., separatista.
SEPIA, adj., sépia.
SEP.TEM.BER, s., setembro.
SEP.TIC, adj., séptico.

SEPTICAEMIA ··605·· SHADE

SEP.TI.CAE.MI.A *UK,* **SEP.TI.CE.MI.A** *US, s., Med.,* septicemia.
SEP.UL.CHRE *UK,* **SEP.UL.CHER** *US, s., Lit.,* sepulcro.
SEP.TU.A.GE.NAR.I.AN, *adj., s.,* septuagenário.
SE.PUL.CHRAL, *adj.,* sepulcral.
SEP.UL.TURE, *s.,* sepultura, cova.
SE.QUEL, *s.,* resultado, consequência, continuação, sequência.
SE.QUENCE, *s.,* sequência, série, continuidade.
SE.QUES.TER, *v.,* o mesmo que *sequestrate.*
SE.QUES.TRATE, *v.,* sequestrar, raptar.
SE.QUIN, *s.,* lantejoula.
SE.QUOI.A, *s., Bot.,* sequoia.
SER.APH, *s.,* serafim.
SERB, *s., adj.,* sérvio.
SER.BI.AN, *s., adj.,* sérvio.
SER.BO-CRO.A.TIAN, *, s., adj.,* servo-croata.
SER.E.NADE, *s.,* serenata; *v.,* fazer serenata, cantar serenatas.
SE.RENE, *adj.,* sereno, calmo, tranquilo.
SE.RENE.LY, *adv.,* serenamente.
SE.REN.I.TY, *s.,* serenidade, calmaria, calma.
SERF, *s.,* servo, serviçal, escravo.
SERF.DOM, *s.,* servidão, escravidão.
SERGE, *s.,* sarja.
SER.GEANT, *s.,* sargento.
SE.RI.AL, *s.,* série, seriado, sequência de um filme durante dias.
SE.RI.AL.IZE(-ISE), *v.,* publicar em folhetim.
SE.RI.AL KILL.ER, *s.,* assassino em série.
SE.RI.AL NUM.BER, *s.,* número de série.
SE.RIES, *s.,* série.
SER.IF, *s., Tipog.,* serifa.
SE.RIG.RA.PHY, *s., Tipog.,* serigrafia.
SE.RI.OUS, *adj.,* sério, severo, importante, grave.
SE.RI.OUS.LY, *adv.,* seriamente.
SE.RI.OUS.NESS, *s.,* seriedade.
SER.MON, *s.,* sermão.
SER.O.TO.NIN, *s., Med.,* serotonina.
SER.PENT, *s.,* serpente, cobra.
SER.RAT.ED, *adj.,* serrilhado, dentado.
SE.RUM, *s.,* soro.
SER.VANT, *s.,* servo, empregado.
SERVE, *v.,* servir, atender, passar por, cumprir pena, trabalhar como criado.
SERV.ER, *s.,* servidor.
SER.VICE, *s.,* serviço, culto religioso, revisão de carro.
SERV.ICE.A.BLE, *adj.,* prático, útil; durável, resistente.
SERV.ICE.MAN, *s., Mil.,* homem em serviço militar.
SERV.ICE STA.TION, *s.,* bomba de gasolina; serviços de posto de gasolina (restaurante, oficina etc.).
SERV.ICE.WOM.AN, *s., Mil.,* mulher em serviço militar.
SER.VI.ETTE, *s.,* guardanapo.
SER.VILE, *adj.,* servil.
SER.VIL.I.TY, *s.,* servilidade, servilismo, baixeza.
SERV.ING, *s.,* porção (de comida); *adj.,* servil, que serve.
SERV.I.TOR, *s.,* servidor, criado, serviçal.
SERV.I.TUDE, *s.,* servidão, escravidão.
SES.A.ME, *s., Bot.,* gergelim, sésamo.
SES.SION, *s.,* sessão.
SET, *s.,* jogo, conjunto, aparelho elétrico, série, facção,

forma, ajuste, desvio, cenário; *v.,* pôr, colocar, fixar, endurecer, solidificar.
SET.BACK, *s.,* revés, contratempo.
SET POINT, *s., Esp.,* ponto que fecha um set: *set point* (no tênis ou outro esporte análogo).
SET-SQUARE, *s.,* *UK* esquadro (para desenho).
SET.TEE, *s.,* sofá.
SET.TER, *s.,* cão de caça.
SET.TING, *s.,* cenário, pôr do sol.
SET.TLE, *s.,* sofá, poltrona; *v.,* assentar, estabelecer, decidir, fixar, fixar residência.
SET.TLED, *adj.,* estabelecido, estável.
SET.TLE.MENT, *s.,* liquidação, acordo, fixação, arranjo, pagamento, fundação.
SET.TLER, *s.,* colono, fazendeiro.
SET-UP, *s., col.,* estrutura, armação.
SEV.EN, *num.,* sete, número sete.
SEV.EN.FOLD, *adj.,* sétuplo; *adv.,* sete vezes.
SEV.EN.TEEN, *num.,* dezessete.
SEV.EN.TEENTH, *num.,* décimo sétimo.
SEV.ENTH, *num.,* sétimo.
SEV.EN.TI.ETH, *num.,* septuagésimo.
SEV.EN.TY, *num.,* setenta.
SEV.ER, *v.,* cortar, partir, dividir, rachar.
SEV.ER.AL, *pron.,* vário, vários, vária, várias; algum, alguns.
SEV.ER.ANCE, *s.,* rompimento, separação, corte.
SEV.ER.ANCE PAY, *s.,* indenização por demissão.
SE.VERE, *adj.,* severo, austero, sério, violento, rígido.
SE.VERE.LY, *adv.,* gravemente, severamente.
SE.VER.I.TY, *s.,* severidade, rigor, austeridade.
SEW, *v.,* costurar.
SEW.AGE, *s.,* detritos, esgotos.
SEW.ER, *s.,* cano de esgoto, encanamento.
SEW.ER.AGE, *s.,* sistema ou rede de esgoto.
SEW.ING, *s.,* costura.
SEW.ING MA.CHINE, *s.,* máquina de costura.
SEW UP, *v.,* coser, costurar.
SEX, *s.,* sexo; *adj.,* sexual, próprio do sexo.
SEX.A.GE.NAR.I.AN, *s.,* sexagenário.
SEX AP.PEAL, *s.,* atração sexual.
SEX ED.U.CA.TION, *s.,* educação sexual.
SEX.ISM, *s.,* sexismo.
SEX.IST, *s., adj.,* sexista.
SEX.LESS, *adj.,* assexuado, sem sexo.
SEX.TET, *s.,* sexteto.
SEX.TU.PLE, *s.,* sêxtuplo; *v.,* multiplicar por seis; *adj.,* sêxtuplo.
SEX.TU.PLET, *s.,* sêxtuplo, grupo de seis; criança nascida de um parto com seis bebês.
SEX.U.AL, *adj.,* sexual.
SEX.U.AL HA.RASS.MENT, *s.,* assédio sexual.
SEX.U.AL IN.TER.COURSE, *s.,* intercurso sexual, coito.
SEX.U.AL.I.TY, *s.,* sexualidade.
SEX.U.AL.LY TRANS.MIT.TED DES.EASE, *s., Med.,* doença sexualmente transmissível (DST).
SEX.Y, *adj.,* séxi, sensual, lascivo.
SF, SF, *abrev.* de *science fiction:* ficção científica.
SGT, *abrev.* para *Sergeant:* sargento.
SHAB.BY, *adj.,* esfarrapado, maltrapilho, usado.
SHACK, *s.,* choupana, cabana, barraca.
SHACK.LE, *s.,* algema; corrente, elo; *v.,* algemar, impedir.
SHADE, *s.,* sombra, abajur, tom, matiz; *v.,* sombrear, matizar.

SHADINESS ··606·· SHIELD

SHAD.I.NESS, *s.*, escuridão, sombra, trevas.
SHAD.ING, *s.*, sombreado.
SHAD.OW, *s.*, sombra; *v.*, acompanhar, seguir de perto sem ser visto, perseguir.
SHAD.OW.Y, *adj.*, escuro, obscuro; vago.
SHAD.Y, *adj.*, sombreado, sombrio.
SHAFT, *s.*, poço; haste, lança; *v.*, ludibriar, trapacear. ‹
SHAG.GY, *adj.*, desgrenhado.
SHAH, *s.*, xá.
SHAKE, *s.*, abalo, agitação, vibração, terremoto, bebida batida; *v.*, agitar, derrubar.
SHAKE-DOWN, *s.*, *US* extorsão, chantagem; revista, busca.
SHAKE.SPEAR.E.AN, *adj.*, shakespeariano.
SHAKE-UP, *s.*, reestruturação; *v.*, reestruturar (um negócio); falar duro; sacudir, agitar.
SHAK.ING, *s.*, abalo, tremor, agitação; *adj.*, agitado, tremido.
SHAK.Y, *adj.*, trêmulo, débil, instável; *col.*, duvidoso.
SHALE, *s.*, xisto.
SHALL, *v. aux.*, (para exprimir: intenção, obrigação, permição; formar futuro; formar perguntas) dever, estar.
SHAL.LOW, *s.*, baixio, local raso; *v.*, tornar raso; *adj.*, raso, superficial.
SHAM, *s.*, fraude, fingimento, pretexto, logro; *v.*, pretender, fingir, fraudar.
SHAM.BLES, *s.*, matadouro, matança, confusão.
SHAME, *s.*, vergonha, humilhação, degradação, desgraça; *v.*, envergonhar, degradar.
SHAME.FACED, *adj.*, envergonhado, tímido.
SHAME.FUL, *adj.*, vergonhoso, degradado.
SHAME.FUL.NESS, *s.*, vergonha, humilhação.
SHAME.LESS, *adj.*, desavergonhado.
SHAM.MY, *s.*, *Zool.*, camurça (cabra montês); couro desse animal.
SHAM.POO, *s.*, xampu, massagem; *v.*, lavar, massagear, lavar o cabelo.
SHAM.ROCK, *s.*, trevo, trifólio.
SHAN.DY, *s.*, *UK* bebida em que se mistura cerveja com limonada.
SHAN'T, *contr.* de shall not.
SHAN.TY, *s.*, cabana, choça, choupana.
SHAN.TY.TOWN, *s.*, bairro com barracos; favela.
SHAPE, *s.*, forma, molde, formação, modelo; *v.*, moldar, formar, dar forma, adaptar.
SHAPED, *adj.*, com forma de, em forma de.
SHAPE.LESS, *adj.*, sem forma, disforme, informe.
SHAPE.LY, *adj.*, formoso, bem formado, simétrico.
SHARD, *s.*, caco (fragmento de vidro ou cerâmica).
SHARE, *s.*, parte, cota, ação, fração; *v.*, ter em comum, partilhar, dividir, ter interesse.
SHARE.HOLD.ER, *s.*, acionista.
SHARE-OUT, *s.*, compartilhamento, divisão.
SHARE.WARE, *s.*, *Comp.*, shareware (programa gratuito disponibilizado por tempo limitado).
SHARK, *s.*, tubarão; tipo velhaco.
SHARP, *s.*, sustenido; *adj.*, afiado, pontiagudo, agudo, acre, desonesto, marcado.
SHARP.EN, *v.*, afiar, amolar, aguçar.
SHARP.EN.ER, *s.*, afiador, amolador; apontador de lápis.
SHARP.ER, *s.*, vigarista, trapaceiro, velhaco.
SHARP-EYED, *adj.*, perspicaz.
SHARP.LY, *adj.*, claramente, exatamente; bruscamente,

repentinamente, fortemente.
SHARP.NESS, *s.*, severidade, agudeza; dureza; perspicácia, esperteza.
SHARP.SHOOT.ER, *s.*, atirador de elite.
SHARP-WIT.TED, *adj.*, perspicaz, sagaz.
SHAT.TER, *v.*, despedaçar, fragmentar, rachar, perturbar, destruir, arrasar, assolar.
SHAT.TERED, *adj.*, arrasado; despedaçado; *UK* extenuado.
SHAT.TER.ING, *adj.*, arrasador, devastador; *UK* extenuante.
SHAVE, *s.*, barbeamento; navalha, gilete; *v.*, barbear, fazer a barba, raspar a barba.
SHAV.EN, *adj.*, barbeado, com a barba feita.
SHAV.ER, *s.*, barbeiro, aparelho para fazer a barba.
SHAV.ING, *s.*, ato de barbear(-se); *adj.*, barbeado.
SHAV.ING BRUSH, *s.*, pincel de barba.
SHAV.ING CREAM, *s.*, creme de barbear.
SHAV.ING FOAM, *s.*, espuma de barbear.
SHAV.INGS, *s. pl.*, lascas, cavacos; aparas de metal.
SHAWL, *s.*, xale, cachecol; *v.*, colocar xale.
SHE, *pron.*, ela.
SHEAF, *s.*, feixe, maço (também usado no *pl.*: shaves).
SHEAR, *v.*, tosquiar.
SHEAR.ING, *s.*, tosquia.
SHEATH, *s.*, bainha; camisa de Vênus, preservativo, camisinha.
SHEATHE, *v.*, embainhar.
SHEATH KNIFE, *s.*, faca com bainha.
SHED, *s.*, barracão, galpão; *v.*, perder; desfazer(-se); derramar, verter.
SHE'D, *contr.* de she had, she would.
SHEEN, *s.*, brilho, resplendor, luminosidade.
SHEEP, *s.*, carneiro, ovelha.
SHEEP.DOG, *s.*, cão pastor.
SHEEP.ISH, *adj.*, encabulado, embaraçado.
SHEEP.ISH.LY, *adv.*, timidamente, encabuladamente.
SHEEP.SKIN, *s.*, pele de carneiro.
SHEER, *adj.*, puro, diáfano, transparente, translúcido.
SHEET, *s.*, lençol, folha de papel, chapa, lâmina, camada.
SHEET ICE, *s.*, camada de gelo (sobre telhado, estrada).
SHEET.ING, *s.*, pano de lençol; forro.
SHEIK, *s.*, xeique, xeque.
SHELF, *s.*, estante, prateleira, banco de areia; (também no *pl.*: shelves: prateleiras).
SHELL, *s.*, casca, concha, aparência; bomba, granada; *v.*, descascar, bombardear.
SHE'LL, *contr.* de she will, she shall.
SHELL.FISH, *s.*, crustáceo, molusco, marisco; frutos do mar.
SHEL.LING, *s.*, bombardeio.
SHELL SHOCK, *s.*, trauma de guerra.
SHELT.ER, *s.*, defesa, coberta, refúgio, abrigo; *v.*, proteger, abrigar, esconder.
SHEL.TERED, *adj.*, protegido, coberto.
SHELVE, *v.*, descartar, pôr na prateleira; adiar.
SHELV.ING, *s.*, prateleiras (para estante).
SHEP.HERD, *s.*, pastor, zagal; *v.*, proteger, guiar, zelar.
SHEP.HERD.ESS, *s.*, pastora.
SHER.BET, *s.*, suco em pó; *US* sorvete de frutas.
SHER.IFF, *s.*, xerife.
SHER.RY, *s.*, xerez (tipo de vinho espanhol).
SHE'S, *contr.* de she is, she has.
SHIELD, *s.*, escudo, proteção, defesa; *v.*, proteger, defender,

SHIFT · 607 · SHOUT

cobrir, servir de escudo.
SHIFT, s., mudança, turno, troca, esquema, truque; v., mudar, variar, mudar de rumo.
SHIFT KEY, s., Comp., tecla "shift".
SHIFT.LESS, adj., folgado, indolente.
SHIFT.ING, s., esperteza, astúcia, mudança.
SHIFT.Y, adj., esperto, sagaz, astuto, finório.
SHI.ITE, s., adj., xiita.
SHIL.LING, s., xelim.
SHIL.LY-SHAL.LY, v., vacilar, titubear.
SHIM.MER, s., bruxuleio, cintilação; v., bruxulear, tremeluzir.
SHIN, s., canela da perna.
SHIN-BONE, s., Anat., tíbia (osso).
SHINE, s., brilho, lustre, resplendor, luminosidade; v., brilhar, luzir, reluzir, ressaltar.
SHIN.GLE, s., seixos, cascalho, pedrinha, pedregulho.
SHIN.ING, adj., brilhante.
SHIN PADS, s. pl., caneleira.
SHINY, adj., lustroso, brilhante, luminoso.
SHIP, s., navio, embarcação, vapor; v., embarcar, colocar a bordo, enviar, mandar.
SHIP.BUILD.ER, s., empresa de construção de navios, estaleiro.
SHIP.BUILD.ING, s., construção naval.
SHIP.MAS.TER, s., capitão de navio mercante.
SHIP.MENT, s., embarque, carregamento.
SHIP.PER, s., expedidor, exportador.
SHIP.PING, s., remessa, transporte marítimo, navegação.
SHIP.PING COM.PA.NY, s., companhia de navegação.
SHIP.SHAPE, adj., em ordem.
SHIP.WRECK, s., naufrágio, desastre, malogro.
SHIP.WRECKED, s., naufrágio; v., naufragar.
SHIP.YARD, s., estaleiro.
SHIRE, s., condado.
SHIRK, v., escapar, esquivar(-se), safar(-se).
SHIRK.ER, s., ocioso, vadio.
SHIRT, s., camisa, blusa.
SHIRT.Y, adj., UK estúpido; zangado.
SHIT, s., fezes, porcaria; vulg., merda, bosta; v., evacuar; vulg., cagar.
SHIV.ER, s., tremor, arrepio, pedaço; v., tremer, estremecer.
SHIV.ER.ING, s., arrepio, calafrio, tremor de frio.
SHOAL, s., cardume, bando, multidão, baixio.
SHOCK, s., choque, choque elétrico, susto, trauma; v., pregar um susto, escandalizar.
SHOCK-AB.SORB.ER, s., amortecedor (de veículos).
SHOCKED, adj., chocado.
SHOCK.ING, adj., revoltante, chocante.
SHOCK.PROOF, adj., à prova de choque.
SHOCK TROOPS, s. pl., tropa de choque.
SHOD, adj., calçado, ferrado (cavalo); v., ps, pp de shoe.
SHOD.DY, adj., de má qualidade, inferior, ordinário.
SHOE, s., sapato, ferradura; v., ferrar, colocar ferradura.
SHOE.BRUSH, s., escova de sapatos.
SHOE.HORN, s., calçadeira (para sapato).
SHOE.LACE, s., cadarço, cordão de sapato.
SHOE.LESS, adj., descalço.
SHOE.MAK.ER, s., sapateiro.
SHOE POL.ISH, s., graxa de sapato.
SHOE RE.PAIRER, s., sapateiro.
SHOE.SHOP, s., loja que vende calçados; sapataria.

SHOE.STRING, s., cadarço; ninharia, bagatela.
SHOO, interj., xô! (para espantar).
SHOOT, s., tiro, chute, caça, rebento, broto, filmagem; v., atirar, matar, dar tiro.
SHOOT.ER, s., atirador.
SHOOT.ING, s., caça, ação de atirar, tiroteio, fuzilamento.
SHOOT.ING STAR, s., estrela cadente.
SHOOT-OUT, s., tiroteio.
SHOP, s., loja, oficina; v., fazer compras.
SHOP FLOOR, s., chão de fábrica; trabalhadores braçais de uma fábrica.
SHOP.KEEP.ER, s., lojista, comerciante.
SHOP.LIFT.ER, s., ladrão de lojas.
SHOP.LIFT.ING, s., furto em loja.
SHOP.PER, s., comprador.
SHOP.PING, s., compras.
SHOP.PING CART, s., US carrinho de compras.
SHOP.PING LIST, s., lista de compras.
SHOP.PING MALL, s., US shopping center.
SHORE, s., costa, praia, litoral; v., escorar, estaquear, reforçar.
SHORE.LINE, s., litoral, linha costeira.
SHORN, adj., cortado, raspado, tosquiado.
SHORT, s., short, calças curtas, som curto, curto-circuito; adj., curto, breve, baixo, pequeno, insuficiente, pouco, ab-rupto, rude.
SHORT.AGE, s., escassez, carência, falta.
SHORT.BREAD, s., biscoito.
SHORT CIR.CUIT, s., Eletr., curto circuito.
SHORT COM.ING, s., defeito, falha, falta.
SHORT.CUT, s., atalho.
SHORT.EN, v., encurtar, abreviar, resumir.
SHORT.EN.ING, s., encurtamento; Cul., gordura vegetal.
SHORT.FALL, s., déficit.
SHORT.HAND, s., taquigrafia, estenografia.
SHORT.HAND.ED, adj., com falta de pessoal.
SHORT.HAND TYP.IST, s., UK taquígrafo.
SHORT-HAUL, adj., de curta distância.
SHORT LIST, s., lista curta de selecionados; v., UK escolher nomes para uma pequena lista.
SHORT-LIVED, adj., efêmero, fugaz.
SHORT.LY, adv., imediatamente, em breve.
SHORT.NESS, s., brevidade, concisão.
SHORTS, s. pl., calças curtas; shorts.
SHORT-SIGHT.ED, adj., míope.
SHORT STO.RY, s., Lit., conto.
SHORT-TEM.PERED, adj., pavio curto, irritadiço.
SHORT WAVE, s., onda curta (rádio).
SHORT.Y, s., baixinho, homem de pouca altura.
SHOT, s., tiro, chumbo, injeção, projétil, descarga, fotografia.
SHOT.GUN, s., espingarda.
SHOT PUT, s., Esp., lançamento de peso.
SHOULD, v. aux., dever.
SHOUL.DER, s., ombro, costas, quarto dianteiro; v., pôr nos ombros, carregar.
SHOUL.DER BAG, s., bolsa a tiracolo.
SHOUL.DER-BLADE, s., Anat., omoplata.
SHOUL.DER PAD, s., ombreira, enchimento.
SHOUL.DER-STRAP, s., alça.
SHOULD.N'T, contr. de should not.
SHOULD'VE, contr. de should have.
SHOUT, s., grito, berro, gargalhada; v., berrar, gritar, rir alto,

SHOVE ·· 608 ·· SIGNALLING

gargalhar.
SHOVE, *s.*, empurrão; *v.*, empurrar, impulsionar, atropelar.
SHOV.EL, *s.*, escavadeira.
SHOW, *s.*, show, espetáculo, apresentação, exposição; *v.*, mostrar, exibir, expor.
SHOW BIZ, SHOW BUSI.NESS, *s.*, mundo dos espetáculos, *show business.*
SHOW.CASE, *s.*, vitrine, mostruário.
SHOW.DOWN, *s.*, acerto de contas; confronto.
SHOW.ER, *s.*, aguaceiro, enxurrada; expositor, mostrador.
SHOW.ER CAP, *s.*, touca de banho.
SHOW.ER.PROOF, *adj.*, impermeável.
SHOW.ER.Y, *adj.*, chuvoso.
SHOW.ING, *s.*, projeção, exibição.
SHOW.MAN, *s.*, empresário, homem de espetáculos.
SHOWN, *v.*, *ps* de *show.*
SHOW-OFF, *s.*, *col.*, exibido.
SHOW.PIECE, *s.*, atração principal.
SHOW.ROOM, *s.*, sala de exposições, mostruário.
SHOW.Y, *adj.*, chamativo.
SHRAP.NEL, *s.*, estilhaços.
SHRED, *s.*, tira, pedaço, fragmento; *v.*, cortar em tiras, despedaçar.
SHRED.DER, *s.*, picador de papel; triturador (de alimentos).
SHREW, *s.*, bruxa, mulher encrenqueira, megera; víbora.
SHREWD, *adj.*, inteligente, astuto, sagaz, perspicaz.
SHREWD.NESS, *s.*, astúcia, esperteza, sagacidade.
SHRIEK, *s.*, grito, guincho; *v.*, gritar.
SHRILL, *adj.*, agudo, estridente.
SHRIMP, *s.*, camarão.
SHRINE, *s.*, santuário.
SHRINK, *v.*, encolher, reduzir-se.
SHRINK.AGE, *s.*, encolhimento, redução, apequenamento.
SHRINK.ING, *s.*, contração, encolhimento.
SHRIV.EL, *v.*, murchar, encolher, enrugar(-se).
SHROUD, *s.*, mortalha, coberta; *v.*, amortalhar, cobrir, envolver.
SHRUB, *s.*, arbusto.
SHRUB.BER.Y, *s.*, arbustos.
SHRUG, *s.*, encolhimento dos ombros; *v.*, encolher os ombros; dar de ombros.
SHRUNK.EN, *adj.*, contraído, murcho.
SHUCK, *s.*, casca, vagem.
SHUD.DER, *s.*, estremecimento, tremor, tremedeira; *v.*, estremecer, tremer.
SHUF.FLE, *s.*, mistura, confusão, arrasto; *v.*, embaralhar, transferir, arrastar (os pés).
SHUF.FLER, *s.*, trapaceiro, enganador.
SHUF.FLING, *s.*, confusão, evasiva.
SHUN, *v.*, evitar, esquivar.
SHUNT, *s.*, desvio; *v.*, desviar; trocar de via férrea (trem).
SHUNT.ER, *s.*, locomotiva de manobras.
SHUSH, *excl.*, psit; cale-se!
SHUT, *v.*, fechar, tapar, tampar, cerrar.
SHUT.TER, *s.*, veneziana, folha de janela.
SHUT.TLE, *s.*, naveta, lançadeira, vaivém, máquina de costura.
SHUT.TLE.COCK, *s.*, peteca.
SHY, *s.*, sobressalto; *adj.*, tímido, reservado, medroso; *v.*, espantar-se, recuar.
SHY.LY, *adv.*, timidamente.
SHY.NESS, *s.*, timidez, acanhamento.

SI, *s.*, nota musical si.
SI.A.MESE, *s.*, *adj.*, siamês.
SI.A.MESE TWINS, *s. pl.*, irmãos siameses.
SI.BE.RI.AN, *adj.*, *s.*, siberiano.
SIB.I.LANT, *s.*, consoante sibilante, sibilo; *adj.*, sibilante.
SIB.LING, *s.*, irmão, irmã.
SI.CIL.I.AN, *s.*, *adj.*, siciliano.
SICK, *pl.*, doentes; *adj.*, doente, enfermo, enjoado, aflito; *v.*, açular, instigar, atacar.
SICK BAY, *s.*, enfermaria.
SICK.EN, *v.*, ficar doente, adoentar-se.
SICK.EN.ING, *adj.*, repugnante, enjoativo.
SICK.LE, *s.*, foice.
SICK.LI.NESS, *s.*, indisposição, náusea, mal-estar.
SICK.LY, *adj.*, doente, enfermiço, adoentado, enfermo.
SICK.NESS, *s.*, doença, enfermidade, náusea, enjoo, enfado.
SICK.NESS BEM.E.FIT, *s.*, seguro-saúde.
SIDE, *s.*, lado, flanco, margem, face, superfície, aspecto, declive, grupo; *v.*, tomar partido, ser favorável a; *adj.*, lateral, de lado.
SIDE-BOARD, *s.*, guarda-louça, aparador, armário.
SIDE-BOARDS, *s. pl.*, costeletas, suíças.
SIDE-BURNS, *s. pl.*, o mesmo que *sideboards.*
SIDE-CAR, *s.*, assento acoplado à lateral de uma motocicleta, sidecar.
SIDE-DISH, *s.*, acompanhamento, guarnição.
SIDE-EF.FECT, *s.*, efeito colateral.
SIDE-KICK, *s.*, *gir.*, pareceiro, cupincha, comparsa.
SIDE.LIGHT, *s.*, luz lateral do carro.
SIDE-LINE, *s.*, atividade paralela, bico (trabalho).
SIDE.LINES, *s. pl.*, *Esp.*, linha lateral (do campo).
SIDE.LONG, *adj.*, de lado, de soslaio; *adv.*, lateralmente.
SIDE-ON, *adj.*, lateral; *adv.*, de lado.
SIDE-SHOW, *s.*, espetáculo colocado no intervalo de um grande espetáculo.
SIDE-STEP, *v.*, passo para o lado; evadir, evitar
SIDE STREET, *s.*, estrada secundária.
SIDE.TRACK, *s.*, desvio, beco, rua sem saída.
SIDE.WALK, *s.*, calçada, passeio.
SIDE.WAY, *s.*, estrada secundária, rua lateral.
SIDE.WAYS, *s.*, estrada vicinal; *adj.*, lateral; *adv.*, lateralmente; de um lado.
SID.ING, *s.*, *US* tapume.
SI.DLE, *v.*, andar de lado.
SIEGE, *s.*, *Mil.*, sítio, cerco; *v.*, sitiar, cercar.
SI.ER.RA LE.ONE.AN, *s.*, *adj.*, serra-leonês.
SI.ES.TA, *s.*, *Es.*, sesta, cochilo (após o almoço).
SIEVE, *s.*, peneira; *v.*, peneirar.
SIFT, *v.*, peneirar, examinar, vistoriar.
SIGH, *s.*, suspiro; *v.*, suspirar, falar aos suspiros.
SIGHT, *s.*, vista, visão, espetáculo, visibilidade, mira; *v.*, ver, avistar, olhar, observar.
SIGHT.ING, *s.*, pontaria.
SIGHT-SEE.ING, *s.*, turismo.
SIGHT-SE.ER, *s.*, turista.
SIGN, *s.*, sinal, marca, gesto, letreiro, tabuleta; *v.*, assinar, subscrever, contratar.
SIG.NAL, *s.*, aviso, notícia, senha; *v.*, sinalizar, dar sinais, fazer sinais.
SIG.NAL.IZE, *v.*, assinalar, marcar, distinguir.
SIG.NAL.LING, *s.*, sinalização.

SIGNALMAN ·· 609 ·· SITCOM

SIG.NAL.MAN, *s.*, sinaleiro.
SIG.NA.TO.RY, *s.*, signatário.
SIG.NA.TURE, *s.*, assinatura, sinal musical, abertura de programa radiofônico.
SIG.NIF.I.CANCE, *s.*, importância, significação, significado.
SIG.NIF.I.CANT, *adj.*, significante.
SIG.NI.FI.CA.TION, *s.*, significação, significado.
SIG.NIF.I.CANT.LY, *adv.*, significantemente.
SIG.NI.FY, *s.*, significar, representar, expressar, demonstrar, exibir.
SIGN.POST, *s.*, placa com sinalização; indicação; *v.*, indicar, guiar.
SI.LENCE, *s.*, silêncio, calma, sossego; *v.*, silenciar, calar-se.
SI.LENC.ER, *s.*, silenciador.
SI.LENT, *adj.*, silencioso, calmo, quieto, calado, mudo.
SI.LENT.LY, *adv.*, em silêncio; silenciosamente.
SI.LENT PART.NER, *s.*, sócio comanditário.
SI.LI.CI.UM, *s.*, *Quím.*, silício (elem. de nº atômico 14).
SIL.I.CON, *s.*, *Quím.*, o mesmo que *silicium*.
SIL.I.CONE, *Quím.*, silicone.
SIL.I.CON VAL.LEY, *s.*, Vale do Silício.
SIL.HOU.ETTE, *s.*, silhueta.
SILK, *s.*, seda, tecido feito com seda; *adj.*, sedoso, feito de seda.
SILK.WORM, *s.*, bicho-da-seda.
SILKY, *adj.*, sedoso, de seda, macio.
SILL, *s.*, soleira de porta.
SIL.LY, *s.*, pessoa boba; *adj.*, bobo, ridículo, tolo.
SI.LO, *s.*, silo.
SILT, *s.*, sedimento, limo, lodo; *v.*, entupir, obstruir.
SILT.Y, *adj.*, lodoso.
SIL.VER, *s.*, prata, moedas de prata; prataria; *adj.*, feito de prata, argênteo; *v.*, pratear.
SIL.VER.IZE, *v.*, pratear, cobrir com prata.
SIL.VER SCREEN, *s.*, *col.*, tela de cinema, cinema.
SIL.VER.SMITH, *s.*, prateiro: pessoa que trabalha com prata.
SIL.VER.WARE, *s.*, prataria.
SIL.VER WED.DING, *s.*, bodas de prata.
SIL.VERY, *adj.*, prateado, argênteo, argentino.
SIM.I.LAR, *adj.*, similar, semelhante, parecido.
SIM.I.LAR.I.TY, *s.*, similaridade, semelhança.
SIM.I.LAR.LY, *adv.*, similarmente, da mesma forma.
SIM.I.LE, *adj.*, símile, semelhante.
SIM.MER, *s.*, cozimento em fogo lento; *v.*, cozer em fogo lento, cozinhar devagar.
SIM.PER, *s.*, sorriso bobo; *v.*, sorrir bobamente.
SIM.PER.ING, *adj.*, idiota, imbecil.
SIM.PLE, *adj.*, simples, ingênuo, simplório.
SIM.PLE-MINDED, *adj.*, simplório; ignorante; sincero.
SIM.PLE.TON, *s.*, idiota, imbecil, tolo.
SIM.PLIC.I.TY, *s.*, simplicidade.
SIM.PLI.FI.CA.TION, *s.*, simplificação.
SIM.PLI.FY, *v.*, simplificar.
SIM.PLIS.TIC, *adj.*, simplista.
SIM.PLY, *adv.*, simplesmente.
SIM.U.LATE, *v.*, simular, disfarçar.
SIM.U.LA.TION, *s.*, simulação.
SIM.U.LA.TOR, *s.*, simulador.
SI.MUL.TA.NE.ITY, *s.*, simultaneidade.
SI.MUL.TA.NEOUS, *adj.*, simultâneo.
SI.MUL.TA.NE.OUS.LY, *adv.*, simultaneamente.

SIN, *s.*, pecado, ofensa, delito; *v.*, pecar.
SINCE, *adv.*, desde então, depois; *prep.*, desde; *conj.*, desde que.
SIN.CERE, *adj.*, sincero, franco.
SIN.CERE.LY, *adv.*, sinceramente.
SIN.CER.I.TY, *s.*, sinceridade.
SINE, *s.*, *Mat.*, seno.
SIN.EW, *s.*, tendão, nervo.
SIN.EW.Y, *adj.*, musculoso.
SIN.FUL, *adj.*, pecaminoso, pecador, cheio de pecados.
SING, *v.*, cantar.
SIN.GA.PORE, *s.*, Cingapura (país).
SIN.GA.PORE.AN, *s.*, *adj.*, cingapuriano.
SINGE, *v.*, chamuscar.
SING.ER, *s.*, cantor.
SIN.GHA.LESE, *s.*, *adj.*, cingalês (nativo de ou relativo ao Sri Lanka).
SING.ING, *s.*, canto, canção.
SIN.GLE, *s.*, bilhete de ida, algo individual; *v.*, escolher; *adj.*, só, único, solteiro.
SIN.GLE BED, *s.*, cama de solteiro.
SIN.GLE EU.RO.PE.AN MAR.KET, *s.*, Mercado Comum Europeu.
SIN.GLE FILE, *s.*, fila indiana.
SIN.GLE-HAND.ED, *adj.*, sozinho, só.
SIN.GLE-MIND.ED, *adj.*, determinado, resoluto, franco.
SIN.GLE.NESS, *s.*, singeleza, simplicidade.
SIN.GLE PA.RENT, *s.*, pai solteiro ou mãe solteira.
SIN.GLES BAR, *s.*, *US* bar (para solteiros).
SING.SONG, *adj.*, canção monótona; *adj.*, monótono (em ritmo).
SIN.GU.LAR, *adj.*, singular, excepcional, único.
SIN.GU.LAR.I.TY, *s.*, singularidade.
SIN.GUL.AR.LY, *adv.*, especialmente, singularmente, individualmente.
SIN.HA.LESE, *s.*, *adj.*, o mesmo que *Singhalese*.
SIN.IS.TER, *adj.*, sinistro.
SI.NIS.TRAL, *adj.*, esquerdo, sinistro.
SINK, *s.*, pia, lava-louça, esgoto, fossa; *v.*, afundar, descer, cair, deprimir-se, cavar.
SINK.AGE, *s.*, imersão, mergulho.
SIN.LESS, *adj.*, sem pecados.
SIN.NER, *s.*, pecador, pecadora.
SIN.U.OS.I.TY, *s.*, sinuosidade.
SIN.U.OUS, *adj.*, sinuoso.
SI.NUS, *s.*, *Anat.*, seios paranasais.
SI.NUS.I.TIS, *s.*, *Med.*, sinusite.
SIP, *s.*, gole, trago, gole pequeno; *v.*, beber aos goles pequenos, bebericar.
SI.PHON, *s.*, sifão, tubo.
SIR, *s.*, senhor, título de reverência.
SI.REN, *s.*, sirene; sereia, ninfa, mulher belíssima.
SIR.LOIN, *s.*, pedaço ou bife de lombo da vaca.
SI.SAL, *s.*, sisal.
SIS.SY, *s.*, maricas, pessoa afeminada.
SIST.ER, *s.*, irmã; enfermeira-chefe; freira, religiosa.
SIST.ER.HOOD, *s.*, congregação, irmandade.
SISTER-IN-LAW, *s.*, cunhada.
SIT, *v.*, sentar, sentar-se, assentar-se, acomodar, ter assento, ocupar cargo.
SIT.COM, *s.*, *abrev.* de *situation comedy*: comédia de costumes,

SIT DOWN · · 610 · · SLAUGHTER

seriado de TV ger. com risadas ao fundo.
SIT DOWN, *v.*, sentar-se, assentar-se.
SITE, *s.*, saite, lugar, posição, página na Internet; terreno, sítio.
SIT.TER, *s.*, quem senta ou fica sentado.
SIT.TING, *s.*, ato de sentar; sessão, reunião; horário de funcionamento, turnos.
SIT.TING DUCK, *s.*, pessoa indefesa.
SIT.TING ROOM, *s.*, sala de estar.
SIT.U.ATE, *adj.*, situado, colocado, posto.
SIT.U.AT.ED, *adj.*, estabelecido, situado; colocado.
SIT.U.ATION, *s.*, situação, posição.
SIT UP, *s.*, *Esp.*, exercícios abdominais.
SIX, *num.*, seis.
SIX.FOLD, *adj.*, *num.*, sêxtuplo.
SIX.TEEN, *num.*, dezesseis.
SIX.TEENTH, *num.*, décimo sexto.
SIXTH, *num.*, sexto.
SIXTH SENSE, *s.*, sexto sentido.
SIX.TI.ETH, *num.*, sexagésimo.
SIX.TY, *num.*, sessenta.
SIZE, *s.*, tamanho, extensão, medida, volume, quantidade, número de sapato.
SIZE.A.BLE, *adj.*, considerável.
SIZ.ZLE, *s.*, chiado, berro; *v.*, chiar.
SKATE, *s.*, patim, patinete; *v.*, patinar.
SKATE.BOARD, *s.*, skate.
SKATE.BOARD.ER, *s.*, skatista.
SKAT.ER, *s.*, patinador.
SKAT.ING, *s.*, patinagem, patinação.
SKAT.ING RINK, *s.*, rinque de patinação; pista de patinação no gelo.
SKEIN, *s.*, madeixa; *v.*, enroscar.
SKEL.E.TAL, *adj.*, esquelético.
SKEL.E.TON, *s.*, esqueleto, carcaça, armação, projeto.
SKEP, *s.*, cesto, colmeia.
SKETCH, *s.*, croqui, esboço, desenho, cena; *v.*, esboçar, desenhar.
SKETCH.BOOK, *s.*, rascunho, caderno para borrão.
SKETCH.PAD, *s.*, bloco para desenhos.
SKETCH.Y, *adj.*, esboço, incompleto, pouco detalhado.
SKEW, *adj.*, oblíquo, inclinado.
SKEW.ER, *s.*, espeto; *v.*, espetar.
SKI, *s.*, esqui; *v.*, esquiar.
SKID, *s.*, escorregão, derrapada, deslizador; *v.*, deslizar, derrapar.
SKI.ER, *s.*, esquiador.
SKI JUMP, *s.*, *Esp.*, salto de esqui; rampa para saltos de esqui.
SKI.ING, *s.*, esqui, ato de esquiar.
SKIL.FUL, **SKILL.FUL**, *adj.*, habilidoso, hábil.
SKIL.FUL.LY, **SKILL.FUL.LY**, *adv.*, habilmente.
SKILL, *s.*, habilidade, perícia, capacidade, destreza.
SKILLED, *adj.*, habilidoso, especializado, hábil.
SKIL.LET, *s.*, caçarola; *US* frigideira.
SKIM, *s.*, escuma, espuma; *v.*, escumar, espumar, desnatar, roçar. ■
SKIM.MER, *s.*, escumadeira.
SKIM.MILK, **SKIMED MILK**, *adj.*, desnatado.
SKIMP, *v.*, mesquinhar(-se), economizar; restringir.
SKIMP.Y, *adj.*, pequeno sumário; avarento, mesquinho.
SKIN, *s.*, pele, casca, couro, crosta; *v.*, tirar a pele, pelar,

esfolar, descascar.
SKIN-DEEP, *adj.*, superficial.
SKIN.FLINT, *s.*, pão-duro, sovina.
SKIN.HEAD, *s.*, *UK* jovem rebelde de cabeça rapada de tendência neonazista, *skinhead*.
SKIN.NER, *s.*, esfolador.
SKIN.NY, *adj.*, magro, magricela.
SKINT, *adj.*, pelado, quebrado, sem um tostão.
SKIN-TIGHT, *adj.*, colante (roupa); roupa muito justa.
SKIP, *s.*, salto, pulo, balde; *v.*, saltar, pular; omitir.
SKIP.PER, *s.*, capitão de pequeno navio de pesca.
SKIP.PING, *s.*, pulo, salto; *Esp.*, pular corda; *adj.*, pulante.
SKIP.PING ROPE, *s.*, corda de pular.
SKIR.MISH, *s.*, escaramuça; *v.*, escaramuçar.
SKIRT, *s.*, saia, borda, bainha; *v.*, marginar, orlar, limitar, ladear.
SKIRT.ING, *s.*, rodapé.
SKIRTING BOARD,
SKIT, *s.*, sátira, paródia, esquete.
SKIT.TISH, *adj.*, inquieto, esquivo, arisco.
SKIT.TLE *s.*, pau, pino.
SKIVE, *v.*, matar aula; enrolar, fazer hora; desbastar, aparar.
SKIV.VY, *s.*, serviçal, empregada doméstica.
SKUL.DUG.GER.Y, *s.*, *US* trapaça, desonestidade.
SKULK, *s.*, medroso, covarde; *v.*, esconder-se.
SKULL, *s.*, caveira, crânio, cabeça.
SKULL.CAP, *s.*, solidéu, quipá, boné.
SKUNK, *Zool.*, jaritataca (nome popular: gambá); *col.*, pessoa vil.
SKY, *s.*, céu, firmamento, tempo, paraíso.
SKY.CAP, *s.*, *US* carregador (em aeroporto).
SKY.DIVE, *v.*, saltar de paraquedas.
SKY.DIVER, *s.*, paraquedista.
SKY.DIV.ING, *s.*, paraquedismo.
SKY.LARK, *s.*, *Zool.*, cotovia (laverca).
SKY.LIGHT, *s.*, clarabóia.
SKY-LINE, *s.*, linha do horizonte, horizonte.
SKY.SCRAP.ER, *s.*, arranha-céu.
SLAB, *s.*, laje, bloco de pedra; *v.*, desbastar, cortar.
SLACK, *s.*, parte solta de algo; *adj.*, desmazelado, descuidado, frouxo.
SLACK.EN, *v.*, reduzir, afrouxar, diminuir (velocidade); relaxar.
SLAG, *s.*, escória, escombros.
SLAG-HEAP, *s.*, bota-fora, entulho.
SLAM, *s.*, batida forte de porta, estrondo, crítica dura; *v.*, fechar com estrondo, bater.
SLAND.ER, *s.*, difamação, calúnia; *v.*, difamar, caluniar.
SLAN.DER.OUS, *adj.*, caluniador, difamador.
SLANG, *s.*, gíria, calão, jargão; *v.*, usar de jargão.
SLANT, *s.*, declive, ladeira, inclinação; ponto de vista; *v.*, inclinar, inclinar-se.
SLANT.ING, *adj.*, oblíquo, inclinado.
SLAP, *s.*, tapa, bofetada, bofetão; *v.*, dar um tapa, esbofetear.
SLAP-DASH, *adj.*, desleixado, relachado.
SLAP.STICK, *s.*, pastelão (comédia), palhaçada; burlesco.
SLAP-UP, *adj.*, formidável, de primeira (festa, jantar).
SLASH, *v.*, cortar, talhar, lascar, golpear.
SLAT, *s.*, sarrafo, ripa, tira.
SLATE, *s.*, ardósia, lousa; *v.*, cobrir com telhas de ardósia, criticar violentamente.
SLAUGHT.ER, *s.*, matança, carnificina, massacre; *v.*, abater,

SLAUGHTER-HOUSE ··611·· SMACK

matar, massacrar.
SLAUGHT.ER-HOUSE, s., matadouro.
SLAV, adj., s., eslavo.
SLAVE, s., escravo, servo; v., trabalhar como escravo, trabalhar muito.
SLA.VER, s., escravocrata, dono de escravos.
SLAV.ERY, s., escravidão.
SLAV.IC, s., adj., eslavo.
SLAV.ISH, adj., serviçal, servil, escravo.
SLA.VO.NI.AN, s., esloveno, eslavo; adj., esloveno.
SLA.VON.IC, s., adj., o mesmo que Slavic.
SLAY, v., matar, assassinar.
SLAY.ER, s., matador, assassino.
SLEA.ZY, adj., pobre, esquálido, sujo; sórdido.
SLEDGE, s., trenó; marreta, malho.
SLEDGE-HAM.MER, s., marreta, malho.
SLEEK, adj., brilhoso, macio, sedoso; polido, insinuante.
SLEEP, s., sono, soneca; v., dormir, tirar uma soneca, descansar.
SLEEP.ER, s., quem dorme, dorminhoco, dormente; vagão-dormitório.
SLEEP.I.LY, adv., sonolentamente, preguiçosamente.
SLEEP.I.NESS, s., sonolência, torpor.
SLEEP.ING, s., sono, dormida, descanso.
SLEEP.ING BAG, s., saco de dormir.
SLEEP.ING CAR, s., vagão-leito (de trem).
SLEEP.LESS, adj., sem sono, insone; irriquieto.
SLEEP.LESS.NESS, s., insônia.
SLEEP.WALK.ER, s., sonâmbulo.
SLEEPY, adj., sonolento.
SLEET, s., chuva com neve ou com granizo.
SLEEVE, s., manga, luva, conexão, capa de disco; v., colocar mangas.
SLEEVE.LESS, s., sem mangas.
SLEIGH, s., trenó.
SLEND.ER, adj., esbelto, delgado, fino, elegante, insuficiente.
SLEUTH, s., col., detetive, investigador.
SLICE, s., fatia, rodela, espátula, faca, pedaço; v., fatiar, cortar, talhar, dividir.
SLICK, s., lugar liso; v., alisar, lustrar; adj., liso, escorregadio, jeitoso, hábil, esperto.
SLICK.ER, s., US capa de chuva comprida.
SLIDE, s., eslaide, diapositivo, deslizamento, escorregão; v., deslizar, escorregar.
SLID.ER, s., cursor, corrediça.
SLIDE-RULE, s., régua de cálculo.
SLIGHT, s., desprezo, menoscabo; v., desprezar, desconsiderar; adj., franzino, fraco.
SLIGHT.ING, adj., desprezivo, desdenhoso.
SLIGHT.LY, adv., levemente.
SLIM, v., emagrecer, afinar; adj., fino, delgado, esbelto.
SLIME, s., lodo, lama, limo, muco.
SLIM.LINE, adj., muito delgado, magro, leve.
SLIM.MING, s., emagrecimento; adj., emagrecedor.
SLIM.Y, adj., coberto de lodo; lodoso, viscoso; fig., fingido.
SLING, s., estilingue, funda, bodoque; lançamento; v., atirar, arremessar, lançar.
SLING.BACK, s., sandália.
SLING.SHOT, s., estilingue, bodoque; atiradeira, catapulta.
SLIP, s., escorregão, lapso, erro, coberta, fronha; v., andar, mover-se, escapar, passar.

SLIP DOWN, v., escorregar.
SLIP-ON, s., pulôver.
SLIP.PAGE, s., deslizamento, deslize.
SLIP.PED DISK, s., Med., hérnia de disco.
SLIP.PER, s., chinelo.
SLIP.PERY, adj., escorregadio, liso, enganoso, obsceno.
SLIP.SHOD, adj., desleixado, descuidado.
SLIP.STREAM, s., rastro; turbilhão da hélice; Lit., ficção slipstream (que mistura gêneros).
SLIP-UP, s., col., US mancada; engano sem prejuízos.
SLIT, s., fenda, greta, corte, racha; v., fender, rachar.
SLITH.ER, s., escorregadela; v., escorregar, deslizar, derrapar.
SLI.VER, s., lasca, pedaço, fatia; v., lascar, fatiar.
SLOB.BER, s., baba; v., babar.
SLOG, s., labuta, trabalhar sem descanso; chatice.
SLO.GAN, s., slogan, frase de efeito, dito, máxima, lema, grito de guerra.
SLOOP, s., Náut., chalupa (tipo de barco a vela).
SLOP, s., líquido derramado; v., derramar, transbordar; pieguice.
SLOPE, s., declive, ladeira, rampa, encosta; v., inclinar-se, estar inclinado.
SLOP.ING, adj., inclinado, declivado.
SLOP.PI.NESS, s., umidade, lama, sujeira.
SLOP.PY, adj., molhado, úmido, lamacento, descuidado.
SLOSH, s., lama, limo, sujeira, neve.
SLOUGH, s., lamaçal; fig., desespero; pele de cobra, casca de ferida; v., mudar, pender, largar, deixar.
SLOT, s., ranhura, fenda; fazer uma fenda.
SLOT MA.CHINE, s., máquina automática (de salgadinhos ou refrigerantes).
SLOTH, s., preguiça, indolência, vadiagem.
SLO.VAK, s., adj., eslaco.
SLO.VA.KI.AN, s., adj., eslovaco.
SLOV.EN, s., pessoa relaxada; adj., sujo, relaxado, descuidado.
SLO.VE.NIA, s., Eslovênia.
SLO.VE.NI.AN, s., adj., esloveno.
SLOV.EN.LY, adj., desalinhado, relaxado, desleixado.
SLOW, adj., lento, bronco, vagaroso, tardio; adv., tardio, lentamente; v., ir lento.
SLOW.DOWN, s., desaceleração; redução de atividade.
SLOW.LY, adv., lentamente, devagar.
SLOW MO.TION, s., velocidade baixa, câmera lenta.
SLOW.NESS, s., lentidão, vagareza, vagar.
SLUDGE, s., lama, barro, lodo.
SLUG, s., Zool., lesma.
SLUG.GISH, adj., molenga, lerdo; moroso.
SLUICE, s., eclusa, comporta, dique, canal; v., soltar a água; abrir comporta.
SLUM.BER, s., sono leve, soneca.
SLUMP, s., queda brusca na economia, baixa, colapso, depressão.
SLUR, s., calúnia, difamação, afronta; v., balbucear.
SLURP, s., beber líquido fazendo barulho, golada.
SLUSH, s., neve meio deretida; lodo, lama.
SLUT, s., pej., mulher relaxada; vulg., piranha.
SLY, adj., esperto, sagaz, astuto, malicioso, safado, velhaco.
SLY.NESS, s., astúcia, esperteza.
SMACK, s., sabor; palmada, estalo dos lábios, beijoca; v., bater, cheirar, beijocar.

SMALL ··612·· SNOWY

SMALL, *s.*, tipo pequeno, coisa pequena; *adj.*, pequeno, diminuto, trivial, baixo.
SMALL CHANGE, *s.*, toco miúdo.
SMALL.HOLD.ING, *s.*, chácara, minifúndio.
SMALL.POX, *s.*, varíola.
SMALL-SCALE, *adj.*, em tamanho reduzido.
SMARM.Y, *adj., col.*, adulador, puxa-saco.
SMART, *s.*, dor aguda; *v.*, sofrer, sentir dor aguda; *adj.*, elegante, vivo, esperto, forte.
SMART.EN, *v.*, tornar bonito, embelezar.
SMASH, *s.*, colisão, choque, rompimento, estrondo, falência, desastre; *v.*, quebrar, esmagar, romper, arruinar, falir.
SMASHED, *adj.*, bêbado, mamado; quebrado, esmagado.
SMASH.ING, *adj., col.*, esmagador, fenomenal.
SMAT.TER, *s.*, conhecimento superficial; *v.*, falar sem conhecimento.
SMAT.TER.ING, *s.*, noções, conhecimento superficial.
SMEAR, *s.*, mancha, nódoa; *v.*, manchar, sujar, enodoar, macular.
SMELL, *s.*, cheiro, olfato, aroma, odor, fedor; *v.*, cheirar, sentir cheiro, emitir cheiro.
SMELL.Y, *adj., col.*, malcheiroso, fedorento.
SMELT, *v.*, fundir (metal), derreter, refinar.
SMILE, *s.*, sorriso; *v.*, sorrir, olhar com alegria.
SMIL.EY, *adj.*, sorridente.
SMIL.ING, *s.*, sorriso; *adj.*, sorridente, risonho.
SMIRK, *s.*, sorriso afetado.
SMITE, *s.*, soco, pancada; *v.*, bater, golpear, ferir, matar.
SMITH, *s.*, ferreiro; forjador.
SMITH.ERY, *s.*, ferraria, forja.
SMITH.Y, *s.*, forja; ferraria, oficina de ferreiro.
SMIT.TEN, *adj.*, afetado, encantado.
SMOCK, *s.*, guarda-pó, avental.
SMOG, *s.*, nevoeiro misturado com fumaça.
SMOKE, *s.*, fumo, fumaça, charuto, cigarro, cachimbo; *v.*, fumar, pitar, defumar.
SMOKED, *adj.*, defumado.
SMOK.ER, *s.*, fumador; recinto próprio para fumantes.
SMOK.ING, *s.*, ato ou hábito de fumar, fumegante.
SMOK.Y, *adj.*, fumegante, defumado; cheio de fumaça, enfumaçado.
SMOL.DER *US*, **SMOUL.DER** *UK*, *s.*, combustão sem fogo (fumaça), brasa; *v.*, fumegar, arder.
SMOOCH, *v., col.*, dar amassos (carinhos).
SMOOTH, *s.*, polimento, alisamento; *v.*, polir, alisar; *adj.*, liso, plano, macio, calmo.
SMOOTH.LY, *adv.*, suavemente, calmamente.
SMOOTH.NESS, *s.*, maciez, lisura; tranquilidade, doçura.
SMOTH.ER, *s.*, fumaceira; *v.*, abafar, sufocar, asfixiar; apagar, reprimir, reter.
SMUDGE, *s.*, mancha, nódoa, marca; *v.*, sujar, manchar, enodoar, macular.
SMUG, *adj.*, presunçoso.
SMUG.GLE, *v.*, contrabandear; trazer ou levar algo escondido.
SMUG.GLER, *s.*, contrabandista.
SMUG.GLING, *s.*, contrabando.
SMUG.NESS, *s.*, comodidade; *pej.*, presunção.
SMUT, *s.*, fuligem, sujeira, mancha; obscenidade; *v.*, sujar, manchar, macular.
SMUT.TY, *adj.*, sujo, manchado, indecente, obsceno.
SNACK, *s.*, lanche, merenda.

SNACK BAR, *s.*, lanchonete.
SNAG, *s.*, ponta de galho; rasgão; empecilho; *v.*, rasgar (por prender em algo); pegar; atrapalhar, impedir.
SNAIL, *s.*, caracol.
SNAKE, *s.*, serpente, cobra, víbora.
SNAP, *s.*, estalo, estalido, ruptura, foto, cadeado; *v.*, estalar, quebrar, ceder, morder.
SNAP.SHOT, *s.*, foto instantânea.
SNARE, *s.*, armadilha, cilada, emboscada; *v.*, enredar, pegar com armadilha.
SNARL, *s.*, rosnado; *v.*, rosnar.
SNARL.ING, *adj.*, rabugento.
SNARL-UP, *s.*, confusão, rolo.
SNATCH, *s.*, trecho, pedacinho, fragmento; *v.*, pegar, agarrar, roubar; *gír.*, sequestrar.
SNATCH.ER, *s.*, assaltante, sequestrador.
SNAZZY, *adj.*, chamativo, atraente, atual, moderno.
SNEAK, *v.*, andar furtivamente, mover-se às escondidas.
SNEAK.ERS, *s.*, tênis.
SNEAK.ING, *adj.*, furtivo, encoberto, oculto.
SNEAK.Y, *adj.*, furtivo, sorrateiro.
SNEER, *s.*, riso de escárnio, sarcasmo; *v.*, sorrir ou rir com escárnio, zombar.
SNEEZE, *s.*, espirro; *v.*, espirrar.
SNICK.ER, **SNIG.GER**, *s.*, riso dissimulado e zombeteiro; *v.*, rir por dentro, rir entredentes.
SNIFF, *s.*, fungada, inalação, fungadela; *v.*, fungar, aspirar com ruído; assoar o nariz.
SNIFF.ER DOG, *s.*, cão farejador.
SNIF.FLE, *s.*, fundada; *v.*, fungar.
SNIG.GER, *s., v.*, o mesmo que *snicker*.
SNIP, *s.*, corte, incisão, tesourada, palpite; *v.*, cortar com tesoura, cortar em pedaços.
SNIPE, *v.*, atirar de tocaia, emboscar; criticar (alguém).
SNIP.ER, *s.*, franco-atirador.
SNIP.PET, *s.*, pedacinho, fragmento, recorte (de notícia).
SNIV.EL, *s.*, choramingo; muco nasal; *v.*, chorar, choramingar.
SNOB, *s.*, esnobe, pretensioso, petulante, pernóstico.
SNOB.BERY, *s.*, esnobismo, pedantismo.
SNOB.BISH, *adj.*, esnobe, pretencioso.
SNOG, *s.*, *UK* beijo apaixonado; *v.*, beijar apaixonado.
SNOOKER, *s.*, jogo de bilhar; *v.*, *UK* ludibriar.
SNOOP, *v., col.*, bisbilhotar, futricar.
SNOOP.ER, *s.*, bisbilhoteiro, mexeriqueiro.
SNOOT.Y, *adj.*, metido, esnobe, afetado.
SNOOZE, *s.*, soneca, dormidela; *v.*, tirar uma soneca.
SNORE, *s.*, ronco; *v.*, roncar.
SNOR.ING, *s.*, ronco; *adj.*, que ronca, roncador.
SNORT, *s.*, bufo, resfôlego; *v.*, bufar, resfolegar; roncar.
SNOT.TY, *adj., col.*, ranhoso, melequento; presunçoso, arrogante.
SNOUT, *s.*, focinho, tromba.
SNOW, *s.*, neve, nevada, névasca; *v.*, nevar.
SNOW-DRIFT, *s.*, amontoado ou monte de neve.
SNOW.FALL, *s.*, nevada, nevasca, caída de neve.
SNOW.FLAKE, *s.*, floco de neve.
SNOW.MAN, *s.*, boneco de neve.
SNOW.SHOE, *s.*, raquete de neve.
SNOW.STORM, *s.*, nevasca, tempestade de neve.
SNOWY, *adj.*, nevado, nevoso, coberto de neve.

SNUB ··613·· SOME

SNUB, s., repulsa, repúdio; v., desdenhar, desprezar, menosprezar.

SNUFF, s., rapé, tabaco; pavio queimado; v., cheirar, aspirar rapé, apagar vela.

SNUFF.BOX, s., caixinha de rapé.

SNUF.FLE, s., ato de bufar, bufo; fala fanhosa; v., fungar, cheirar, cheirar.

SNUG, v., confortar, acomodar; adj., confortável, acomodado, agasalhado.

SNUG.GLE, v., aconchegar(-se), aninhar(-se).

SO, adv., assim, deste modo, tão, de tal modo, muito, então, por isso.

SOAK, s., pequena molhada; v., embeber, molhar, ensopar.

SOAKED, adj., ensopado, empapado, molhado; col., bêbado.

SOAK.ING, adj., que molha.

SOAKY, adj., molhado, ensopado, impregnado.

SOAP, s., sabão; v., ensaboar.

SOAP BUB.BLE, s., bolha de sabão.

SOAP DISH, s., saboneteira.

SOAP-OP.ER.A, s., novela (de TV ou rádio).

SOAP POW.DER, s., sabão em pó.

SOAPY, adj., ensaboado, coberto de sabão.

SOAR, v., pairar, planar; v., elevar(-se).

SOAR.ING, adj., elevado, exorbitante, sublime.

SOB, s., soluço; v., soluçar.

SOB.BING, s., soluço; adj., soluçante.

SO.BER, adj., sóbrio; v., tornar(-se) sóbrio.

SOBER.ING, adj., sóbrio, sisudo, circunspecto.

SO.BRI.E.TY, s., sobriedade.

SO-CALLED, adj., assim chamado.

SOC.CER, s., futebol.

SO.CIA.BIL.I.TY, s., sociabilidade.

SO.CIA.BLE, s., US reunião; adj., sociável.

SO.CIAL, s., encontro social; adj., social.

SO.CIAL DE.MOC.RA.CY, s., Pol., social-democracia.

SO.CIAL.ISM, s., socialismo.

SO.CIAL.IST, s., socialista.

SO.CIAL.IZE, v., socializar.

SO.CIAL LIFE, s., vida social.

SO.CIAL.LY, adv., socialmente.

SO.CIAL OR.DER, s., ordem social, regime.

SO.CIAL SCI.ENCE, s., ciência social.

SO.CIAL SE.CU.RI.TY, s., seguro social.

SO.CIAL SERV.ICE, s., serviço de assistência social.

SO.CI.E.TY, s., sociedade, associação.

SO.CIO.ECO.NOM.IC, adj., socioeconômico.

SO.CI.O.LOG.IC.AL, adj., sociológico.

SO.CI.OL.O.GIST, s., sociólogo.

SO.CI.OL.O.GY, s., sociologia.

SOCK, s., meia, meia curta, soquete.

SOCK.ET, s., cavidade; encaixe; Eletr., tomada.

SOD, s., relvado, gramado, grama, terreno com grama; v., cobrir com grama, gramar.

SO.DA, s., soda, barrilha, soda cáustica.

SO.DA WA.TER, s., água gasosa, soda.

SO.DAL.I.TY, s., congregação, confraria.

SOD.DEN, adj., encharcado, úmido; estúpido; v., encharcar, embriagar.

SO.DI.UM, s., sódio.

SO.FA, s., sofá.

SO.FA-BED, s., sofá-cama.

SOFT, adj., suave, leve, meigo, bom, fino, liso, macio, delicado.

SOFT.BALL, s., Esp., softball (jogo parecido com o baseball).

SOFT DRINK, s., US refresco.

SOFT.EN, v., amolecer, amaciar, mitigar, acalmar, esmaecer.

SOF.TEN.ER, s., amaciante (de roupas), amortecedor; mitigador.

SOFT.LY, adv., suavemente, gentilmente, tenuemente.

SOFT.NESS, s., maciez, moleza, delicadeza, generosidade.

SOFT.WARE, s., programa de informática, software, conteúdo do programa.

SOFT.Y, s., col., fracote, moleirão; manteiga derretida.

SOG.GY, adj., empapado, encharcado.

SOIL, s., solo, terra, terra para plantar, país; sujeira, esterco, brejo; v., sujar, desonrar.

SOILED, adj., sujo.

SO.JOURN, s., estada, permanência rápida em; v., permanecer por curto tempo.

SO.LACE, s., consolo, conforto, alívio; v., consolar, confortar, aliviar.

SO.LAR, adj., solar, próprio do sol.

SO.LAR EN.ER.GY, s., energia solar.

SO.LAR SYS.TEM, s., sistema solar.

SOL.DER, s., solda; soldar.

SOL.DIER, s., soldado,militar; v., servir o exército.

SOL.DIERY, s., tropa, soldadesca, grupo de soldados.

SOLD, v., ps e pp de to sell.

SOLD OUT, adj., esgotado (que vendeu tudo).

SOLE, s., sola dos pés, sola, sola de sapato; adj., só, sozinho, solteiro; v., pôr sola.

SOL.EMN, adj., solene.

SO.LEM.NI.TY, s., solenidade, festividade, cerimônia.

SOL.EM.NI.ZA.TION, s., solenização.

SOL.EM.NIZE, v., solenizar, ritualizar.

SO.LIC.IT, v., solicitar, pedir, requerer, procurar, buscar.

SO.LIC.I.TA.TION, s., solicitação.

SO.LIC.I.TOR, s., requerente, solicitante; advogado.

SO.LIC.I.TOUS, adj., solícito, ansioso.

SO.LIC.I.TUDE, s., solicitude.

SOL.ID, adj., sólido, robusto, forte, maciço; s., corpo sólido, sólido.

SOL.I.DAR.I.TY, s., solidariedade.

SOL.ID FUEL, s., combustível sólido (carvão, lenha).

SO.LID.I.FY, v., solidificar, tornar sólido.

SOL.ID.LY, adv., solidamente, firmemente.

SO.LIL.O.QUY, s., monólogo, solilóquio.

SOL.I.TARY, adj., solitário, só, isolado, retirado, único.

SOL.I.TUDE, s., solidão, isolamento.

SO.LO, s., Mús., solo; adv., só.

SO.LO.IST, s., Mús., solista.

SOL.STICE, s., solstício.

SOL.U.BLE, adj., solúvel.

SO.LU.TION, s., solução.

SOLVE, v., resolver, solver, solucionar.

SOL.VEN.CY, s., solvência, resolução.

SOL.VENT, adj., s., solvente.

SO.MA.LI, s., adj., somali.

SO.MA.LIA, s., Somália.

SOM.BRE, SOM.BER, adj., sombrio, escuro, triste, lúgubre.

SOME, adj., um, uma, um pouco, algum, alguma, alguém, cerca de, mais ou menos.

SOMEBODY ··614·· SPACE

SOME.BODY, *pron.*, alguém.
SOME DAY, *adv.*, algum dia (no futuro).
SOME.HOW *adv.*, de qualquer maneira, por uma razão ou outra.
SOME.ONE, *pron.*, alguém.
SOME.PLACE, *adv.*, *US* o mesmo que *somewhere*.
SOM.ER.SAULT,
SOME.THING, *pron.*, alguma coisa, algo.
SOME.TIME, *adv.*, algum dia, outra vez, em alguma ocasião.
SOME.TIMES, *adv.*, por vezes, às vezes, de vez em quando.
SOME.WAY, *adv.*, de algum modo.
SOME.WHAT, *adv.*, um tanto.
SOME.WHERE, *adv.*, em algum lugar, em alguma parte.
SOM.NAM.BU.LISM, *s.*, sonambulismo.
SON, *s.*, filho.
SO.NAR, *s.*, sonar.
SO.NA.TA, *s.*, *It.*, *Mús.*, sonata.
SONG, *s.*, canção, canto, som melodioso, melodia, poesia.
SON.IC, *adj.*, sônico.
SON-IN-LAW, *s.*, genro.
SON.NET, *s.*, soneto.
SON.NY, *s.*, meu filho, filhinho.
SON.SHIP, *s.*, filiação.
SOON, *adv.*, logo, brevemente, cedo, imediatamente.
SOON.ER, *adv.*, antes, mais cedo.
SOOT, *s.*, fuligem; *v.*, sujar de fuligem.
SOOTHE, *v.*, acalmar, sossegar, aquietar, aliviar.
SOOTH.ING, *adj.*, calmante, tranquilizante.
SOOTH.SAY.ER, *s.*, vate, profeta, vaticinador, adivinho.
SOOT.Y, *adj.*, fuliginoso, escuro, preto.
SO.PHIS.TI.CAT.ED, *adj.*, sofisticado.
SO.PHIS.TI.CA.TION, *s.*, sofisticação.
SOP.O.RIF.IC *adj.*, soporífico.
SOP.PING, *adj.*, molhado, empapado.
SOP.PY, *adj.*, molhado, embebido; *UK* pieguice.
SO.PRA.NO, *s.*, *It.*, *Mús.*, soprano; *adj.*, de soprano.
SOR.BET, *s.*, sorvete.
SOR.CER.ER, *s.*, feiticeiro, mágico, bruxo.
SOR.CER.ESS, *s.*, feiticeira, bruxa.
SOR.CER.Y, *s.* bruxaria, feitiçaria, magia.
SOR.DID, *adj.*, sórdido, imundo, sujo.
SOR.DID.NESS, *s.*, sordidez, imundície, sujeira.
SORE, *s.*, ferida, chaga; *adj.*, ferido, dolorido; inflamável.
SORE.LY, *adv.*, extremamente, grandemente, muito.
SO.ROR.I.TY, *s.*, irmandade, associação de irmãs; clube de moças (de universidade).
SOR.REL, *s.*, *Bot.*, azeda (planta azedinha), alazão (cavalo).
SOR.ROW, *s.*, tristeza, mágoa, dor, pesar, aborrecimento.
SOR.ROW.FUL, *adj.*, triste, magoado, pesaroso, aborrecido.
SOR.RY, *adj.*, triste, magoado, pesaroso, arrependido, melancólico.
SORT, *s.*, tipo, espécie, caráter; *v.*, classificar, tipificar, selecionar, organizar.
SORT.ING, *s.*, escolha, distribuição, classificação.
SOS, *s.*, *Náut.*, chamada telegráfica por socorro.
SO-SO, *adv.*, mais ou menos, assim, assim; *adv.*, regularmente.
SOT, *s.*, beberrão, cachaceiro, ébrio; *v.*, embriagar-se.
SOUF.FLÉ, *s.*, *Fr.*, *Cul.*, suflê.
SOUGHT, *v.*, *ps* e *pp* de *to seek*.
SOUL, *s.*, alma, criatura, ser, espírito.
SOUL-DES.TROY.ING, *adj.*, arrasador, deprimente.

SOUL.FUL, *adj.*, emocionante, sentimental.
SOUL.LESS, *adj.*, sem alma, desalmado.
SOUL MATE, *s.*, alma gêmea.
SOUL MU.SIC, *s.*, *Mús.*, ritmo popular dos negros norte-americanos.
SOUND, *s.*, som, ruído, tom; estreito, *Med.*, sonda; *adj.*, são, saudável, forte, sólido; *v.*, soar, tocar; sondar.
SOUND BAR.RI.ER, *s.*, barreira do som.
SOUND EFFECTS, *s.pl.*, efeitos sonoros (usados em cinema, teatro, rádio etc.).
SOUND.ING, *s.*, ato de soar; sondagem, investigação (de opinião); *adj.*, ressoante, retumbante.
SOUND.LY, *adv.*, salutarmente; profundamente, firmemente, razoavelmente, inteiramente.
SOUND.NESS, *s.*, estabilidade, integridade; sanidade; segurança.
SOUND.PROOF, *adj.*, à prova de som; *v.*, fazer isolamento acústico.
SOUND.TRACK, *s.*, *Cin.*, trilha sonora.
SOUND-WAVE, *s.*, *Fís.*, onda sonora.
SOUP, *s.*, sopa.
SOUP PLATE, *s.*, prato de sopa, prato fundo.
SOUP.SPOON, *s.*, prato de sopa.
SOUR, *s.*, algo azedo; *adj.*, azedo, acre, ácido, amargo; *v.*, azedar, aborrecer.
SOURCE, *s.*, fonte, nascente.
SOUR.NESS, *s.*, azedume; *fig.*, mau humor.
SOUTH, *s.*, sul, direção sul, meridião; *adj.*, sul, meridional.
SOUTH-AMER.I.CAN, *adj.*, *s.*, sul-americano.
SOUTH.BOUND, *adj.*, na direção sul.
SOUTH-EAST, *s.*, sudeste.
SOUTH.EASTERLY, *adj.*, de sudeste; *adv.*, em direção ao sudeste.
SOUTH-EASTERN, *adj.*, ao sudeste; do sudeste.
SOUTH.ER.LY, *adj.*, ao sul, meridional.
SOUTH.ERN, *adj.*, direcionado para o sul, sulista, meridional.
SOUTH.ERN.ER, *s.*, *adj.*, sulista.
SOUTH KO.RE.AN, *s.*, *adj.*, sul-coreano.
SOUTH VIET.NAM.ESE, *s.*, *adj.*, sul-vietnamita.
SOUTH.WARD, *adv.*, para o sul, em direção ao sul.
SOUTH-WEST, *s.*, sudoeste.
SOUTH.WEST.ER.LY, *adj.*, ao sudoeste; *adv.*, para o sudeste.
SOUTH-WEST.ERN, *adj.*, para o sudoeste, do sudoeste.
SOUTH YE.MEN, *s.*, Iêmen do Sul.
SOU.VE.NIR, *s.*, suvenir, lembrança, recordação.
SOV.ER.EIGN, *s.*, soberano, governante.
SOV.ER.EIGN.TY, *s.*, soberania, soberania, poder, mando.
SO.VI.ET, *adj.*, *s.*, soviético.
SO.VI.ET U.NION, *s.*, *Hist.*, antiga União Soviética.
SOW, *s.*, porca, fêmea do porco; *v.*, semear.
SOW.ER, *s.*, semeador.
SOX, *s. pl.*, *US* meias curtas (variação de *socks*).
SOY, *s.*, soja.
SOYA, *s.*, soja.
SOY.A BEAN, *s.*, grão de soja.
SOY SAUCE, *s.*, molho de soja.
SOZ.ZLED, *adj.*, *UK* pinguço.
SPA, *s.*, estância termal, balneário com água quente.
SPACE, *s.*, espaço, local, área, superfície, lapso de tempo; *v.*, espaçar, criar espaços.

SPACE AGE ··615·· SPIN

SPACE AGE, s., era espacial.
SPACE.CRAFT, s., nave espacial.
SPACE.MAN, s., cosmonauta, astronauta.
SPACE SHUT.TLE, s., ônibus espacial.
SPAC.ING, s., Tipog., espacejamento.
SPA.CIOUS, adj., espaçoso.
SPADE, s., pá; espada.
SPA.GHET.TI, s., espaguete.
SPAIN, s., Espanha.
SPAM, s., Comp., spam (publicidade ou mensagem de conteúdo indesejado em massa); v., enviar spam.
SPAN, s., período (de tempo); palmo (medida); vão; gama; v., medir palmos; abarcar.
SPAN.IARD, adj., s., espanhol.
SPAN.IEL, s., spaniel (raça de cão).
SPAN.ISH, adj., s., espanhol.
SPAN.ISH A.MER.I.CA, s., Hist., América espanhola.
SPAN.ISH A.MER.I.CAN, s., adj., hispano-americano.
SPANK, s., golpe, palmada; v., bater, golpear, chicotear.
SPAN.NER, s., chave inglesa.
SPAR, s., mastro, verga.
SPARE, s., peça sobressalente, reserva; v., economizar, dispor de; adj., excedente.
SPARE TIME, s., tempo livre.
SPAR.ING, adj., parco, modesto, frugal; infulgente.
SPAR.ING.LY, adv., frugalmente, com moderção.
SPARK, s., chispa, faísca, brilho, luz; v., reluzir, faiscar, brilhar.
SPAR.KLE, s., clarão, brilho; v., faiscar, brilhar, cintilar.
SPAR.KLER, s., o que brilha ou cintila; col., diamante.
SPARK.LING, adj., cintilante, faiscante, brilhante; fig., vivaz.
SPARK.LING WINE, s., vinho espumante.
SPAR.ROW, s., pardal.
SPARSE, adj., esparso, ralo, disperso.
SPAR.TAN, s., espartano; fig., indivíduo austero; adj., espartano; fig., austero.
SPAS.TIC, adj., espasmódico.
SPASM, s., espasmo.
SPAS.MOD.IC, adj., espasmódico.
SPAT, s., discussão; rusga; v., ps e pp de spit: cuspir.
SPATE, s., torrente, enchente, avalanche.
SPA.TIAL, adj., espacial (espaço comum ou espaço estelar).
SPAT.TER, v., respingar, borrifar.
SPAT.U.LA, s., espátula.
SPAY; v., Vet., castrar, esterilizar (animal).
SPAWN, s., ovas, ova, cria, ovo; v., criar, gerar.
SPEAK, v., falar, dizer, discursar, conversar.
SPEAK.ER, s., orador, falante, repórter, alto-falante.
SPEAK.ING, adj., discurso, fala.
SPEAR, s., lança; v., lancear.
SPEAR.HEAD, s., ponta de lança; v., liderar, encabeçar.
SPEC, s., especificação; v., espicificar.
SPE.CIAL, adj., especial, extra.
SPE.CIAL.IST, s., especialista; adj., especializado.
SPE.CI.AL.I.TY, s., especialidade.
SPE.CIAL.IZE, v., especializar.
SPE.CIAL.LY, adv., especialmente, realmente.
SPE.CIAL.TY, s., especialização; especialidade; peculiaridade.
SPE.CIES, s., espécies, ervas.
SPE.CIF.IC, adj., específico, único, próprio.
SPE.CIF.I.CAL.LY, adv., especificamente.

SPEC.I.FI.CA.TION, s., especificação.
SPEC.I.FY, v., especificar.
SPEC.I.MEN, s., espécime, amostra, exemplar.
SPEC.I.MEN SIG.NA.TURE, s., assinatura reconhecida em cartório.
SPECK, s., mancha, pinta, salpico; v., manchar, salpicar, colocar pinta.
SPECK.LED, adj., manchado.
SPECS, s., óculos.
SPEC.TA.CLE, s., espetáculo.
SPEC.TAC.U.LAR, adj., espetacular.
SPEC.TA.TOR, s., espectador, assistente.
SPEC.TRE, s., espectro.
SPEC.TRUM, s., Fís., espectro; fig., gama.
SPEC.U.LATE, v., especular, verificar.
SPEC.U.LA.TION, s., especulação, ideia, verificação.
SPEC.U.LA.TIVE, adj., especulativo.
SPEC.U.LA.TOR, s., especulador.
SPEECH, s., fala, discurso.
SPEECH.LESS, adj., mudo, sem fala, silencioso.
SPEED, s., velocidade, rapidez, pressa; v., acelerar, apressar, correr.
SPEED.BOAT, s., lancha.
SPEED.ING, s., excesso de velocidade.
SPEED-LIM.IT, s., limite de velocidade.
SPEE.DO, s., UK velocímetro; o mesmo que speedometer.
SPEED.OM.E.TER, s., velocímetro.
SPEED.Y, adj., veloz, rápido, imediato, célere.
SPE.LE.OL.O.GY, s., Geol., espeleologia.
SPELL, s., palavra mágica, encanto, magia, fascinação; v., pressagiar, soletrar.
SPELL.BOUND, adj., encantado, fascinado.
SPELL.CHECK, s., Comp., correção ortográfica; v., verificar ortografia.
SPELL.CHECK.ER, s., Comp., corretor ortográfico.
SPELL.ING, s., ortografia.
SPENSE, s., despensa.
SPEND, v., gastar, despender, consumir, passar.
SPEND.ER, s., gastador, esbanjador.
SPEND.ING, s., gastança, despesa; gastos.
SPEND.THRIFT, s., esbanjador, perdulário; adj., gastador.
SPENT, adj., gasto, consumido; cansado, exausto.
SPERM, s., esperma.
SPERM-WHALE, s., Zool., cachalote (espécie de baleia).
SPEW, s., vômito; v., vomitar.
SPHERE, s., esfera.
SPHER.I.CAL, adj., esférico, redondo, globular.
SPHINC.TER, s., Anat., esfíncter.
SPHINX, s., esfinge.
SPICE, s., condimento, tempero, sabor, especiaria; v., condimentar, temperar.
SPIC.ERY, s., especiaria.
SPICY, adj., condimentado, temperado.
SPI.DER, s., Zool., aranha.
SPIEL, s., papo, lábia.
SPIKE, s., ponta, espigão, cume; espiga.
SPIK.Y, adj., espinhoso, pontiagudo; adj., irritável.
SPILL, s., derramamento, aguaceiro, toró; v., derramar, entornar, despejar.
SPILL.AGE, s., derramamento, derrame.
SPIN, s., parafuso, rotação, movimento rápido; v., fiar, torcer,

SPINACH · 616 · SPRINKLER

puxar, esticar.
SPIN.ACH, s., espinafre.
SPI.NAL COL.UMN, s.,Anat., coluna vertebral.
SPI.NAL CORD, s., Anat., medula espinal.
SPIN.DLE, s., fuso; eixo (de vitrola); barra, poste.
SPIN.DLY, adj., alto, magro, espigado, espichado.
SPINE, s., espinha dorsal, espinha, suporte, espinho, ponta, saliência.
SPINE-CHIL.LING, adj., horripilante, aterrorizante.
SPINE.LESS, adj., sem espinhos; invertebrado; fig., fraco.
SPIN.NING, s., fiação.
SPIN-OFF, s., Com., subsidiária; benefício, subproduto.
SPIN.STER, s., solteira, solteirona.
SPI.RAL, s., espiral, mola; adj., espiralado; v., formar espiral, elevar os preços.
SPIRE, s., pináculo; cone; espiral; v., afilar-se.
SPIR.IT, s., espírito, alma, fantasma, ânimo, coragem; s. pl., bebidas alcoólicas.
SPIR.IT.ED, adj., espirituoso, animado, entusiasmado.
SPIR.IT.U.AL, adj., espiritual.
SPIR.IT.U.AL.ISM, s., espiritualismo.
SPIR.IT.U.AL.IST, s., espiritualista.
SPIR.I.TU.AL.I.TY, s., espiritualidade.
SPIR.I.TU.OUS, adj., espirituoso, alcoólico.
SPIT, s., saliva, cuspida, cuspe, espeto para carne; v., pôr no espeto, espetar; cuspir.
SPITE, s., rancor, ressentimento, ódio; v., ofender, injuriar, odiar.
SPITE.FUL, adj., despeitado, rancoroso.
SPIT.TING IM.AGE, s., semelhança perfeita.
SPIT.TLE, s., saliva, cuspe.
SPLASH, s., borrifo, esguicho, espirro; v., chapinhâr, espirrar, molhar.
SPLAY, v., alargar, aumentar.
SPLEEN, s., baço, mau humor, melancolia.
SPLEEN.FUL, adj., rabugento, irritadiço, impertinente, insuportável.
SPLEN.DID, adj., esplêndido, maravilhoso.
SPLEN.DID.LY, adv., esplendidamente.
SPLEN.DOUR, SPLEN.DOR, s., esplendor, brilho.
SPLICE, s., encaixe, junção; v., encaixar, entrelaçar.
SPLINT, s., tala; v., entalar, encanar.
SPLIN.TER, s., lasca, estilhaço; v., lascar, estilhaçar.
SPLIN.TER GROUP, s., grupo dissidente.
SPLIT, s., fenda, brecha, greta, cisão, divisão; v., cindir, rachar, fender, separar.
SPLIT-LEV.EL, adj., dúplex; duplo.
SPLIT PERS.ON.AL.I.TY, s., Psic., dupla personalidade.
SPLIT.TING, adj., que racha; agudo; estridente.
SPLUT.TER, s., estralo, azáfama; v., balbuciar; algaraviar.
SPOIL, s., despojos, saque, pilhagem; v., arruinar, danificar, estragar, saquear.
SPOILED, adj., estragado, deteriorado; mimado (criança ou pessoa).
SPOIL.ER, s., desmancha-prazeres; sabotador, saqueador.
SPOIL SPORT, s., col., desmancha-prazeres.
SPOKE, s., raio (da roda); v., ps de to speak: falar.
SPOKES.MAN, s., porta-voz.
SPOKES.PER.SON, s., porta-voz, orador.
SPOKES.WOM.AN, s., oradora.
SPONGE, s., esponja; bolo, pão de ló; parasita; v., lavar com

esponja, esfregar.
SPONGE-CAKE, s., Cul., pão de ló.
SPONGY, adj., esponjoso.
SPON.SOR, s., patrocinador, quem patrocina esporte com fins de propaganda; v., patrocinar, apadrinhar.
SPON.SOR.SHIP, s., patrocínio, garantia.
SPON.TA.NE.I.TY, s., espontaneidade.
SPON.TA.NE.OUS, adj., espontâneo.
SPON.TA.NE.OUS.LY, adv., espontaneamente.
SPOOF, s., remedo, sátira; paródia; v., remedar, parodiar.
SPOOK, s., assombração, espectro; v., US assustar, espantar.
SPOOK.Y, adj., assombrado, fantasmagórico.
SPOOL, s., carretel, bobina, rolo de filme; v., enrolar, bobinar.
SPOON, s., colher.
SPOON.FUL, s., colherada.
SPO.RAD.IC, adj., esporádico.
SPORT, s., esporte, desporto, atletismo, divertimento; v., brincar, jogar, divertir-se.
SPORT.FUL, adj., alegre, brincalhão; zombador, irônico.
SPORT.ING, adj., esportivo.
SPORTS.MAN, s., esportista, desportista (homem).
SPORTS.WEAR, s., roupa esportiva (casual); roupa para prática de esportes.
SPORTS.WOM.AN, s., atleta.
SPORTY, adj., desportivo, esportivo.
SPOT, s., marca, local, ponto, pinta, espaço publicitário; v., notar, marcar, manchar.
SPOT.LESS, adj., imaculado, impecável.
SPOT.LIGHT, s., luz, farol, holofote, refletor.
SPOT-ON, adj., col., UK certeiro.
SPOT.TY, adj., manchado, marcado, salpicado.
SPOUSE, s., cônjuge, consorte.
SPOUT, s., jato, jorro, esguicho; bica, cano, goteira; v., jorrar, esguichar; discursar; arengar.
SPRAIN, s., torção, distensão; v., torcer, distender.
SPRAWL, s., expansão, alastramento, esparramar(-se); v., estirar-se, expandir-se; espreguiçar-se.
SPRAWL.ING, adj., expansível; espaçoso, vasto.
SPRAY, s., borrifo, vaporizador, spray; v., borrifar, vaporizar, pulverizar.
SPRAY CAN, s., lata de aerossol.
SPRAY PAINT, s., tinta spray.
SPREAD, s., expansão, difusão, diferença entre preço de oferta e procura; v., espalhar.
SPREAD.ING, adj., extensivo, expansivo.
SPREAD.SHEET, s., Comp., planilha eletrônica.
SPREE, s., farra, folia; v., fazer farra, farrear.
SPRIG, s., broto, ramo, rebento, vergôntea.
SPRIGHT.LY, adj., vivo, esperto; adv., alegremente.
SPRING, s., primavera, salto, pulo; v., saltar, pular, nascer, brotar.
SPRING.BOARD, s., trampolim.
SPRING-CLEAN, v., fazer uma faxina geral.
SPRING.ER, s., saltador, pulador.
SPRING ON.ION, s., Bot., UK cebolinha verde.
SPRING ROLL, s., UK rolinho primavera.
SPRING.TIME, s., primavera.
SPRING.Y, adj., flexível, elástico.
SPRIN.KLE, s., chuvisco; v., espalhar, pulverizar, polvilhar.
SPRIN.KLER, s., regador, sistema de proteção contra incêndios por chuveirinho.

SPRINKLING   •• 617 ••   STANCE

SPRIN.KLING, s., salpicado, pitada, aspersão.
SPRINT, s., corrida (de velocidade); v., correr, percorrer.
SPRINT.ER, s., corredor.
SPRITE, s., espírito, fantasma.
SPROCK.ET, s., roda dentada.
SPROUT, s., broto; col., jovem; v., brotar, desabrochar; surgir, nascer; desenvolver.
SPRUCE, s., Bot., abeto vermelho; adj., arrumado; v., enfeitar(-se), arrumar(-se).
SPRY, adj., esperto, vivaz; alerta, rápido.
SPUD, s., pá estreita; col., batata; v., escavar, carpir.
SPUNK, s., isca.
SPUR, s., espora, estímulo; v., incitar, estimular.
SPU.RI.OUS, adj., espúrio, falso, bastardo.
SPURN, s., rejeição; v., desprezar, recusar, rejeitar.
SPURT, s., jorro, esguicho, jato; v., jorrar, esguichar com força.
SPUT.TER, s., saliva.
SPY, s., espião, espia; v., espiar, olhar, espionar, verificar.
SPY.ING, s., espionagem.
SQUAB.BLE, s., discussão, briga; v., brigar, altercar, discutir.
SQUAD, s., esquadra, pelotão, seleção, time.
SQUAD CAR, s., rádio patrulha.
SQUAD.RON, s., esquadrão, pelotão.
SQUAL.ID, adj., esquálido; sujo, miserável.
SQUALL, s., tempestade, lufada de vento, pé de vento.
SQUA.LOR, s., sordidez.
SQUA.MOUS, adj., escamoso, coberto de escamas.
SQUAN.DER, v., desperdiçar, dissipar.
SQUARE, v., quadrado, praça, quadra, simetria; v., esquadrar, dividir em quadras.
SQUARED, adj., quadrado.
SQUARE DANCE, s., Mús., quadrilha; v., dançar a quadrilha.
SQUARE.LY, adv., de modo quadrado; honestamente.
SQUARE ROOT, s., Mat., raiz quadrada.
SQUASH, s., squash, esporte; abóbora, polpa, baque; v., espremer, amassar, apertar.
SQUASHY, adj., amassado, espremido.
SQUAT, s., agachamento adj., agachado; v., agachar-se.
SQUAT.TER, s., US intruso (ilegalmente).
SQUAWK, s., guincho, chio; v., guinchar, chiar.
SQUEAK, s., guincho; v., guinchar, chiar, ranger.
SQUEAK.Y, adj., guinchante, rangente.
SQUEAL, s., grunhido, guincho, grito agudo; v., chiar, grunhir.
SQUEA.MISH, adj., sensível, delicado.
SQUEEZE, s., aperto, compressão; galho (problema); abraçar; v., apertar, espremer, comprimir; extrair à força.
SQUEEZ.ER, s., espremedor (eletrodoméstico); prensa.
SQUELCH, s., respingo; v., chapinhar.
SQUIB, s., busca-pé, rojão; Lit., conto humorístico, sátira; v., soltar fogos; escrever sátiras.
SQUID, s., Zool., lula.
SQUIFFED, adj., o mesmo que squiffy.
SQUIFF.Y, adj., gír., meio embriagado.
SQUIG.GLE, s., rabisco; v., rabiscar.
SQUINT, s., olhada, estrabismo; v., piscar, olhar, olhar de soslaio, ser vesgo.
SQUIRE, s., UK proprietário rural, fazendeiro.
SQUIRM, s., contorção; entrelaçamento; v., contorcer-se; entrelaçar.
SQUIR.REL, s., Zool., esquilo.
SQUIRT, s., esguicho, jato, jorro; v., esguichar, jorrar.

SRI LAN.KA, s., Sri Lanka.
SRI LAN.KAN, s., adj., habitante de ou relativo a Sri Lanka.
ST, abrev. de saint: santo.
STAB, s., facada, punhalada, pontada; v., esfaquear, apunhalar, ferir com faca.
STAB.BING, s., ato de atacar (com faca); adj., agudo, penetrante (dor).
STA.BIL.I.TY, s., estabilidade.
STA.BI.LIZE, v., estabilizar.
STA.BIL.I.ZER, s., estabilizador; o que se usa para estabilizar.
STA.BLE, adj., estável; firme, seguro; estábulo, estrebaria.
STACK, s., pilha, monte; col., chaminé; v., empilhar, amontoar.
STA.DI.UM, s., estádio.
STAFF, s., pessoal, quadro de assessores, grupo; v., assessorar com pessoas, ajudar.
STAF.FING, s., preenchimento de vagas.
STAG, s., cervo, veado.
STAGE, s., palco, teatro, ator, elenco, andaime; v., encenar, representar no palco.
STAGE-COACH, s., diligência, carruagem.
STAGE NAME, s., pseudônimo, nome artístico.
STAG.GER, s., vertigem, tontura; v., cambalear, estontear, vacilar, hesitar, confundir.
STAG.GER.ING, adj., cambaelante, titubeante; assombroso, inacreditável.
STAG.ING, s., andaime, plataforma; ensaio, encenação (teatro).
STAG.NAN.CY, s., estagnação, parada.
STAG.NANT, adj., estagnado, quieto; lento, parado; podre.
STAG.NATE, v., estagnar, parar.
STAG.NA.TION, s., estagnação.
STAID, adj., sério, adequado, sossegado.
STAIN, s., mancha, tinta, nódoa; v., manchar, macular, sujar.
STAINED, adj., manchado.
STAIN.ER, s., tintureiro.
STAIR, s., escadaria, escada, degrau.
STAIR.WAY, s., escadaria.
STAIR.CASE, s., escadaria, escada.
STAKE, s., estaca, poste, moirão, aposta; v., fixar, estaquear, pôr piquetes, apostar.
STAKE.OUT, s., vigilância, vigia.
STA.LAC.TITE, s., estalactite.
STA.LAG.MITE, s., estalagmite.
STALE, adj., velho, rançoso; dormido (pão); estragado.
STALE.MATE, s., empate (no xadrez); impasse; v., chegar a um impasse.
STALK, s., talo, caule, haste, tronco; caçar por emboscada, andar sem ruído.
STALL, s., estábulo, baia; banca de frutas e verduras; v., ter animal na baia.
STAL.LION, s., garanhão.
STA.MEN, s., Bot., estame.
STAM.I.NA, s., energia, vigor, estamina.
STAM.MER, s., gagueira; v., gaguejar.
STAMP, s., selo, timbre, carimbo; v., selar, carimbar carta, timbrar.
STAM.PEDE, s., debandada, estouro (boiada); v., estourar, debandar; correr (em pânico).
STAMP.ER, s., estampador, impressor.
STAMP.ING, s., estampagem.
STANCE, s., postura (corporal, de opinião).

STAND

·· 618 ··

STENOGRAPHER

STAND, s., estante, postura, ponto de táxi, tribuna; v., estar em pé, encontrar-se.

STAN.DARD, s., standard, padrão, gabarito, critério; adj., padronizado, regular.

STAN.DARD.IZE, v., estandardizar, padronizar.

STAND.ARD TIME, s., hora oficial.

STAND-BY, s., auxílio, apoio; adj., preparado, a postos, pronto.

STAND-IN, s., suplente.

STAND.ING, s., ato de ficar de pé; reputação, posição; adj., de pé, ereto; estável, estabelecido.

STAND.POINT, s., ponto de vista.

STAND.STILL, s., parada, imobilização, paralisação.

STAND-UP, adj., de pé, ereto, rígido.

STAN.ZA, s., estância, estrofe.

STA.PLE, s., grampo; adj., básico (de primeira necessidade); importante; v., segurar com grampo.

STA.PLER, s., grampeador.

STAR, s., estrela; estrela de cinema, pessoa famosa; v., ser a estrela de um evento.

STAR.BOARD, s., estibordo; adj., a estibordo.

STARCH, s., amido, fécula.

STARCH.Y, adj., engomado; que contém amido.

STAR.DOM, s., estrelato.

STAR.DUST, s., Astron., poeria estelar; col., devaneio.

STARE, s., olhar fixo; v., olhar fixamente, mirar, fixar, fitar.

STAR.FISH, s., estrela-do-mar.

STARK, adj., total, completo, rígido, acabado; adv., totalmente, completamente.

STARK-NAKED, adj., nu, pelado, em pelo.

STAR.LET, s., estrelinha; atriz nova que se destaca.

STAR.LIGHT, s., luz das estrelas.

STAR.LIT, adj., iluminado pelas estrelas.

STAR.RY, adj., estrelado.

STAR.RY-EYED, adj., sonhador; iludido.

START, s., partida, começo, princípio, impulso, vantagem; v., partir, começar, assustar.

START.ER, s., autor, motor de arranque, arranque de carro; juiz; entradas.

START.ING, s., começo, início, sobressalto.

START.ING POINT, s., ponto de partida.

STAR.TLE, v., assustar, alarmar.

START.LING, adj., assustador, alamante.

STAR.VA.TION, s., fome.

STARVE, v., passar fome, morrer de fome.

STARV.ING, adj., faminto, esfomeado.

STATE, s., estado, situação, contexto, cargo, nação, país, governo; v., declarar, exprimir, expor, referir, determinar; adj., formal, cerimonial, próprio do governo.

STATE.LESS, adj., sem pátria.

STATE.LY, adj., majestoso, imponente; adv., majestosamente.

STATE.MENT, s., afirmação, declaração; Com., extrato de banco, balanço.

STATE.SIDE, adj., dos Estados Unidos; adv., nos Estados Unidos.

STATES.MAN, s., estadista, político renomado.

STATIC, s., estática (eletricidade, rádio, TV); adj., estático.

STAT.ICS, s. pl., Fís., estática.

STA.TION, s., estação, estação emissora, ponto de parada; v., parar, estacionar.

STA.TION.ARY, adj., estacionário, fixo.

STA.TION.ER, s., dono de papelaria.

STA.TION.ER.Y, s., artigos de papelaria ou escritório.

STA.TION HOUSE, s., delegacia, quartel de bombeiros.

STA.TION WAG.ON, s., US camioneta, col., perua.

STAT.IST, s., estadista.

STA.TIS.TIC, s., estatística.

STAT.IS.TI.CIAN, s., estatístico.

STA.TIS.TICS, s., estatística.

STAT.UE, s., estátua.

STAT.U.ESQUE, adj., como estátua; escultural, belo.

STAT.U.ETTE, s., estatueta.

STAT.URE, s., estatura, altura, dimensão, desenvolvimento.

STA.TUS, s., status, posição, condição, estatuto.

STA.TUS BAR, s., Comp., barra de status.

STA.TUS QUO, s., Lat., status quo.

STAT.UTE, s., estatuto.

STAT.UTE BOOK, s., UK código civil.

STAT.U.TO.RY, adj., estatutário.

STAUNCH, adj., constante, leal, fiel; v., estancar.

STAVE, s., bastão, vara; Mús., pauta; v., quebrar; romper-se.

STAY, s., estadia, estada, permanência, paralisação; v., permanecer, ficar, hospedar-se.

STAY.ING-POW.ER, s., resistência.

STEAD, s., sítio, lugar, lugarejo.

STEAD.FAST, adj., firme, estável.

STEAD.I.LY, adv., gradualmente; firmemente, calmamente.

STEAD.Y, adj., regular, constante; inalterável, inabalável; firme, sensato; v., fixar, firmar, estabilizar(-se).

STEAK, s., bife, pequeno filé, churrasquinho.

STEAK.HOUSE, s., churrascaria.

STEAL, s., roubo, furto; v., roubar, furtar.

STEAL.ER, s., ladrão, gatuno, gato.

STEAL.ING, s., furto, roubo.

STEALTH, s., ação clandestina, dissimulação; furto.

STEALTH.Y, adj., furtivo, dissimulado.

STEAM, s., vapor; v., cozer a vapor, evaporar, fumegar.

STEAM.BOAT, s., barco a vapor.

STEAM-EN.GINE, s., máquina a vapor.

STEAM.ER, s., navio a vapor, vapor.

STEAM I.RON, s., ferro de passar roupas a vapor.

STEAM.Y, adj., cheio de vapor; col., quente, excitante.

STEEL, s., aço, adj., de aço.

STEEL-WOOL, s., palha de aço.

STEEL.WORK.ER, s., operário de usina siderúrgica.

STEEL.WORKS, s., siderúrgica (também steel mill).

STEEL.Y, adj., como aço, duro; acerado.

STEEP, s., precipício, declive forte; adj., íngreme, áspero, abrupto; infusão; v., macerar, extrair, colocar para macerar.

STEE.PLE, s., campanário, torre.

STEE.PLE.CHASE, Esp., corrida de obstáculos.

STEEP.LY, adv., abruptamente, consideravelmente.

STEER, s., boi, novilho; v., dirigir, guiar carro, governar.

STEER.ING, s., direção de veículo.

STEERS.MAN, s., timoneiro, dirigente.

STEL.LAR, adj., estelar.

STEM, s., talo, haste, caule; Gram., raiz; v., proceder, derivar; parar, estancar.

STEM CELL, s., Biol., célula-tronco.

STENCH, s., fedor, mau cheiro.

STEN.CIL, s., estêncil, matriz para reproduzir figuras ou escritos.

STE.NOG.RA.PHER, s., estenógrafo, taquígrafo.

STENOGRAPHY ·· 619 ·· STOPOVER

STE.NOG.RA.PHY, s., estenografia.
STEP, s., passo, degrau, sinal, pulo, andar.
STEP BOARD, s., estribo.
STEP.BROTH.ER, s., meio-irmão.
STEP.CHILD, s., enteado, enteada.
STEP.DAUGH.TER, s., enteada.
STEP.FA.THER, s., padrasto.
STEP-LAD.DER, s., escada de mão.
STEP.MOTH.ER, s., madrasta.
STEP.PING-STONE, s., degrau; *fig.*, trampolim.
STEP.SIS.TER, s., meia-irmã.
STEP.SON, s., enteado.
STE.REO, s., estereofônico; *adj.*, estéreo, estereofônico.
STE.REO.PHON.IC, *adj.*, estereofônico.
STE.REO.TYPE, s., estereótipo; *v.*, estereotipar.
STER.ILE, *adj.*, estéril, esterilizado.
STER.IL.I.TY, s., esterilidade.
STER.IL.I.ZA.TION, s., esterilização.
STER.IL.IZE, *v.*, esterilizar.
STER.LING, s., libra esterlina.
STERN, s., *Náut.*, popa; *adj.*, duro, inflexível.
STERN.LY, *adv.*, severamente, duramente.
STER.OID, s., *Quím.*, esteroide.
STETH.O.SCOPE, s., estetoscópio.
STE.VE.DORE, s., estivador.
STEW, s., guisado, carne cozida, ensopado; *v.*, cozinhar, ensopar.
STEW.ARD, s., comissário de bordo.
STEW.ARD.ESS, s., comissária de bordo, aeromoça.
STICK, s., pau, cacete, bastão, galho, acha; *v.*, furar, matar, apunhalar, destruir.
STICK.ER, s., autocolante.
STICK.ING, *adj.*, aderente.
STICK-ON, *adj.*, autocolante.
STICK.PIN, s., alfinete de gravata.
STICK-UP, s., *gír.*, *US* assalto à mão armada.
STICK.Y, *adj.*, grudento, adesivo; gomado; úmido e abafado (clima); *fig.*, desastrado.
STIFF, s., caipira, matuto; *adj.*, rijo, duro, forte, teso, emperrado.
STIFF.EN, *v.*, endurecer, enrijecer(-se); firma-se; aumentar (preços).
STIF.FEN.ER, s., fixador, endurecedor.
STIFF.NESS, s., rigidez, dureza, tesão.
STI.FLE, *v.*, abafar, conter, reprimir, suprimir.
STI.FLING, *adj.*, sufocante, asfixiante.
STIG.MA, s., estigma.
STIG.MA.TIZE, *v.*, estigmatizar.
STILE, s., lance, degrau, escada; torquinete.
STILL, *adj.*, parado, fixo; *adv.*, ainda, contudo, entretanto, todavia.
STILL.BORN, *adj.*, natimorto.
STILL LIFE, s., natureza-morta (arte); *still-life*, *adj.*, relativo à natureza-morta.
STILL.NESS, s., calma, silêncio, tranquilidade.
STILTED, *adj.*, artificial, afetado, forçado.
STILT, s., perna-de-pau; estaca.
STIM.U.LANT, s., estimulante.
STIM.U.LATE, *v.*, estimular.
STIM.U.LAT.ING, *adj.*, estimulante.
STIM.U.LA.TION, s., estimulação, estímulo; incentivo.

STIM.U.LUS, s., estímulo.
STING, s., ferroada, picada, ferrão; picar, aguilhoar, ferroar.
STING.ING NET.TLE, s., *Bot.*, urtiga.
STING.Y, *adj.*, avaro, sovina, pão-duro.
STINK, s., fedor, mau cheiro; *v.*, feder, cheirar mal; ter reputação duvidosa.
STINK.ING, *adj.*, fedorento, fétido, podre; *adv.*, extremamente.
STINT, s., limite, tarefa, economia; *v.*, restringir, limitar, poupar.
STI.PEND, s., estipêndio, salário.
STIP.U.LATE, *v.*, estipular, determinar.
STIP.U.LA.TION, s., estipulação, condição, acordo.
STIR.RING, *adj.*, excitante.
STIR.RUP, s., estribo.
STITCH, s., pontada (dor); porção; ponto (cosura); *v.*, dar pontos; suturar; costurar, alinhavar.
STITCH.ING, s., ponto, costura.
STOAT, s., *Zool.*, arminho.
STOCK, s., estoque, provisão, fornecimento, suprimento, reserva, gado, linhagem, estirpe, títulos; *v.*, fornecer, prover, abastecer, armazenar.
STOCK.ADE, s., paliçada; cerca; *US* prisão militar; *v.*, proteger, fortificar.
STOCK.BRO.KER, s., corretor.
STOCK CAR, s., carro comum com motor preparado para corridas.
STOCK.HOLD.ER, s., acionista.
STOCK.ING, s., meia; meia fina comprida (de mulher).
STOCK.IST, s., estoquista, varegista.
STOCK.PILE, s., estoque, suprimento; *v.*, estocar, armazenar.
SOTCK ROOM, s., depósito.
STOCK.Y, *adj.*, reforçado, corpulento, forte.
STODG.Y, *adj.*, enfadonho; indigesto, pesado.
STO.IC, *adj.*, estoico.
STOICAL, *adj.*, estoico.
STO.I.CISM, s., estoicismo.
STOKE, *v.*, alimentar (o fogo), remexer (o fogo).
STOK.ER, s., foguista.
STOL.ID, *adj.*, estólido, impassível, apático.
STOM.ACH, s., estômago, barriga, ventre, pança.
STOM.ACH-ACHE, s., dor de estômago.
STOM.ACH UL.CER, s., *Med.*, úlcera de estômago.
STONE, s., pedra, cálculo; rocha, caroço; *v.*, colocar pedras, apedrejar, descaroçar.
STONE-MA.SON, s., pedreiro.
STOMP, s., sapateado; *v.*, pisotear, pisar.
STONE AGE, s., idade da pedra.
STONED, *adj.*, *UK* bêbado, doidão.
STONE.MA.SON, s., canteiro.
STONE.WALL, *v.*, obstruir, embromar.
STONE.WARE, s., faiança, louças, objetos de barro.
STON.Y, *adj.*, pedregoso.
STOOGE, s., palhaço (comédia); boneco, joguete.
STOOL, s., banquinho, genuflexório; dedo-duro; copa de árvore, toco; fezes; *v.*, delatar; brotar; evacuar fezes.
STOOP, s., inclinação para frente; sacada; poste, pilar; *v.*, dobrar-se, inclinar(-se).
STOP, s., parada, pausa, interrupção, obstáculo; *v.*, parar, interromper, deter-se.
STOP.GAP, s., substituto, paliativo; quebra-galho, *UK* tapa-buraco.
STOP.O.VER, s., *US* parada (em viagem), estância; pulo,

STOPPAGE ··620·· STRIPTEASE

passada.

STOP.PAGE, *s.*, greve, obstrução, impedimento.

STOP.PER, *s.*, tampa, tampo, rolha.

STOP.PING, *s.*, *UK* trem pinga-pinga (com paradas em todas as estações); parada, pausa.

STOP.WATCH, *s.*, cronômetro.

STOR.AGE, *s.*, armazenagem, armazenamento.

STORE, *s.*, provisão, armazenagem, fornecimento, mercado; *pl.*, víveres.

STORE.HOUSE, *s.*, *US* depósito, armazém; *fig.*, mina (do tesouro).

STORE.KEEP.ER, *s.*, gerente (de loja), lojista.

STORE.ROOM, *s.*, almoxarifado.

STOR.EY, *s.*, andar de um prédio.

STORK, *s.*, cegonha.

STORM, *s.*, tempestade, tormenta; *v.*, enfurecer, atormentar, assaltar.

STORM.ING, *s.*, assalto, ataque; tempestuosidade; *adj.*, tempestuoso.

STORM.Y, *adj.*, tempestuoso, tormentoso; colérico.

STO.RY, *s.*, estória, lenda, fato folclórico, mentira.

STORY.BOOK, *s.*, livro de contos; *adj.*, relativo a contos de fada.

STORY.TEL.LER, *s.*, contador de histórias.

STOUT, *s.*, cerveja preta e forte; *adj.*, corpulento, robusto; potente.

STOUT.NESS, *s.*, corpulência, firmeza, solidez.

STOVE, *s.*, fogão, estufa.

STOW, *s.*, *gír.*, cessar; acabar com; guardar, arrumar; alojar; empacotar.

STOW.AWAY, *s.*, passageiro clandestino.

STOW.ER, *s.*, estivador.

STRAD.DLE, *v.*, escarranchar (sentar de pernas abertas); atravessar (ponte), cruzar.

STRAFE, *v.*, *Mil.*, metralhar.

STRAG.GLE, *v.*, ficar par trás, desgarrar-se; errar, vagar.

STRAG.GLER, *s.*, retardatário; pessoa errante.

STRAIGHT, *adj.*, franco, direto; reto, liso; simples, convencional; *adv.*, corretamente, diretamente.

STRAIGHT.A.WAY, *adv.*, imediatamente; em seguida.

STRAIGHT.EN, *v.*, endireitar, tornar reto, sério.

STRAIN, *s.*, tensão, esforço; luxação, estirpe; forçar, distorcer, estirar.

STRAINED, *adj.*, cansado, forçado; coado.

STRAIN.ER, *s.*, coador.

STRAIN.ING, *s.*, esforço.

STRAIT, *s.*, estreito, garganta.

STRAIT JACK.ET, *s.*, camisa de força.

STRAND, *s.*, filamento, fibra, cordão; praia, costa; *v.*, desatar fios; encalhar; fracassar.

STRAND.ED, *adj.*, encalhado; *fig.*, fracassado.

STRANGE, *s.*, estranho, estrangeiro, desconhecido.

STRANGE.LY, *adv.*, estranhamente.

STRANG.ER, *s.*, estrangeiro, forasteiro, estranho, desconhecido.

STRANGLE.HOLD, *s.*, gravata (luta); *fig.*, influência repressora sobre alguém.

STRAN.GU.LATE, *v.*, estrangular, sufocar.

STRAN.GU.LA.TION, *s.*, estrangulamento, sufocação.

STRAP, *s.*, tira, correia, alça, cordão; *v.*, segurar, atar com tira.

STRAP.LESS, *adj.*, sem alça.

STRAP.PING, *adj.*, forte, robusto.

STRAT.A.GEM, *s.*, estratagema.

STRA.TE.GIC, *adj.*, estratégico.

STRAT.E.GIST, *s.*, estrategista.

STRAT.E.GY, *s.*, estratégia.

STRAT.I.FIED, *adj.*, estratificado.

STRA.TO.SPHERE, *s.*, estratosfera.

STRA.TUM, *s.*, *Geol.*, camada; *Sociol.*, camada social.

STRAW, *s.*, palha, palhinha; ninharia, bagatela.

STRAW.BER.RY, *s.*, morango.

STRAY, *v.*, extraviar-se, perder-se, desviar-se; *adj.*, extraviado, perdido, desviado.

STREAK, *s.*, camada, faixa, listra; raio (de tempestade); traço, temperamento; *v.*, correr como um raio.

STREAKED, *adj.*, riscado, listrado, raiado.

STREAKY, *adj.*, riscado, listrado, raiado; instável, irregular; nervoso.

STREAM, *s.*, riacho, ribeiro, fluxo, torrente; *v.*, correr, fluir, deslizar.

STREAM.ER, *s.*, fita, serpentina; bandeirola, flâmula.

STREAM.LINE, *v.*, dar forma aerodinâmica; racionalizar.

STREAM.LINED, *adj.*, aerodinâmico; racionalizado, simplificado.

STREET, *s.*, rua, via.

STREET.CAR, *s.*, *UK* bonde; *US* carro elétrico.

STRENGTH, *s.*, força, firmeza, resistência, robustez.

STRENGTH.EN, *v.*, fortificar, robustecer, tonificar.

STRESS, *s.*, estresse, pressão, tensão, cansaço; *v.*, destacar, realçar, enfatizar.

STRESSED, *adj.*, estressado.

STRESS.FUL, *adj.*, estressante, exaustivo.

STRETCH, *s.*, extensão, trecho, alongamento; *v.*, esticar, alargar, estender.

STRETCH.ER, *s.*, o que estica, esticador; maca, padiola.

STRETCH.Y, *adj.*, elástico, felxível.

STREW, *s.*, espalhar, espargir, difundir.

STRICK.EN, *adj.*, ferido, machucado, atacado.

STRICT, *adj.*, rigoroso, austero, severo.

STRICT.LY, *adv.*, rigidamente, estritamente, exatamente.

STRICT.NESS, *s.*, severidade, rigor, austeridade.

STRIDE, *s.*, passos largos, passadas longas; *v.*, caminhar a passos largos, transpor.

STRI.DENT, *adj.*, estridente.

STRIFE, *s.*, conflito, contenda, discussão.

STRIKE, *s.*, greve, ataque; *v.*, bater em, descobrir, estar em greve, atacar, destruir.

STRIKE.BOUND, *adj.*, paralisado(a) por greve.

STRIKE.BREAK.ER, *s.*, fura-greve.

STRIK.ER, *s.*, grevista.

STRIK.ING, *s.*, ato de bater, toque; *adj.*, impressionante, notável.

STRING, *s.*, cordão, fio, réstia, corda, instrumento de cordas, barbante, embira.

STRIN.GENT, *adj.*, estrito, limitado, rigoroso.

STRING.Y, *adj.*, fibroso.

STRIP, *s.*, tira, faixa, risca; *v.*, despir, desnudar, despir-se, despojar-se.

STRIPE, *s.*, listra, faixa; galão.

STRIPED, *adj.*, listrado.

STRIP.PER, *s.*, quem pratica o estriptise.

STRIP.TEASE, *s.*, estriptise, desnudamento artístico.

STRIPY
·· 621 ··
SUBSIST

STRIP.Y, *adj.*, listrado, riscado.

STRIVE, *v.*, esforçar-se, lutar por, empenhar-se.

STRIV.ING, *s.*, esforço, empenho.

STROKE, *s.*, golpe, soco, pancada, derrame cerebral; afago; *v.*, afagar, acariciar.

STROLL, *s.*, volta, passeio, giro; *v.*, passear, andar, girar, dar uma volta.

STRONG-BOX, *s.*, caixa-forte.

STRONG.HOLD, *s.*, fortaleza; *fig.*, baluarte.

STRONG.LY, *adv.*, fortemente, solidamente.

STRUC.TUR.AL, *adj.*, estrutural, próprio de estrutura.

STRUC.TUR.AL.LY, *adv.*, estruturalmente.

STRUC.TURE, *s.*, estrutura, construção, edifício.

STRUG.GLE, *s.*, luta, combate, contenda; *v.*, lutar, batalhar, contender, porfiar.

STRUG.GLER, *s.*, lutador, combatente.

STRUG.GLING, *adj.*, esforçado.

STRUM, *s.*, dedilhado; *v.*, dedilhar.

STRYCH.NINE, *s.*, *Quím.*, estricnina.

STRUT, *s.*, escora, suporte, apoio; *v.*, escorar, suportar.

STUB, *s.*, toco (de lápis); canhoto (de cheque); cepa; curto; *v.*, roçar; dar topada (com o pé).

STUB.BLE, *s.*, barba curta e espetada; restolho.

STUB.BORN, *adj.*, teimoso, obstinado, cabeça-dura.

STUB.BORN.LY, *adv.*, teimosamente, obstinadamente.

STUB.BORN.NESS, *s.*, teimosia, obstinação.

STUB.BY, *adj.*, atarracado; toco.

STUC.CO, *s.*, estuque, reboco; *v.*, rebocar, estucar.

STUCK, *adj.*, preso, emperrado, empacado; *v.*, *ps* e *pp* de *sitck*: prender.

STUD.DED, *adj.*, cravejado, adornado.

STU.DENT, *s.*, estudante, aluno.

STUD.IED, *adj.*, estudado, pensado.

STU.DI.O, *s.*, estúdio, ateliê.

STU.DI.OUS, *adj.*, estudioso, aplicado, diligente, assíduo.

STU.DI.OUS.LY, *adv.*, cuidadosamente, estudiosamente.

STUDY, *s.*, estudo, sala de aula, aplicação; estudar.

STUFF, *s.*, matéria, material, matéria-prima, coisa; *v.*, rechear, encher, parar, estofar.

STUFFED, *adj.*, *col.*, empanturrado; *Cul.*, recheado; empalhado.

STUFF.ING, *s.*, *Cul.*, recheio; estofamento, enchimento.

STUFF.Y, *adj.*, abafado, sufocante; conservador, retrógado.

STUM.BLE, *s.*, falha, erro, lapso, deslize; *v.*, tropeçar, derrapar, cambalear.

STUMP, *s.*, cepo, toco; coto; *v.*, deixar perplexo; *US* percorrer em camapanha eleitoral.

STUN, *s.*, aturdimento, pasmaria; *v.*, aturdir, pasmar, espantar.

STUNNED, *adj.*, chocado, assombrado.

STUN.NING, *adj.*, chocante; deslumbrante, imponente.

STUNT, *s.*, proeza, peripécia, façanha.

STUNT.ED, *adj.*, definhado, mirrado.

STUNT MAN, *s.*, *Cin.*, dublê (homem).

STUNT WOM.AN, *s.*, *Cin.*, dublê (mulher).

STU.PE.FY, *v.*, estupefazer, espantar, deixar estupefato.

STU.PEN.DOUS, *adj.*, estupendo, assombroso.

STU.PID, *adj.*, idiota, imbecil, estúpido.

STU.PID.I.TY, *s.*, estupidez, imbecilidade, idiotice.

STU.PID.LY, *adv.*, estupidamente.

STU.POR, *s.*, estupor, espanto.

STUR.DY, *adj.*, robusto, forte; firme, inflexível.

STUR.GEON, *s.*, *Zool.*, esturjão.

STY, *s.*, chiqueiro, curral, pocilga, antro; terçol; *v.*, viver em chiqueiro, viver em sujidade.

STYE, *s.*, terçol (também *sty*).

STYLE, *s.*, estilo, conduta, modo de vida, elegância.

STYL.ISH, *adj.*, de estilo, elegante.

STYL.IST, *s.*, estilista.

STY.LUS, *s.*, agulha (de toca-discos); buril; *Comp.*, caneta gráfica.

SUA.SION, *s.*, persuasão, convencimento.

SUAVE, *adj.*, suave, doce, melífluo.

SUB, *s.*, *Esp.*, *col.*, substituto, reserva; *abrev.* de *submarine*: submarino; *v.*, substituir.

SUB.COM.MIT.TEE, *s.*, subcomitê.

SUB.CONS.CIOUS, *adj.*, subconsciente.

SUB.CONS.CIOUS.LY, *adv.*, de forma subconsciente.

SUB.CON.TI.NENT, *s.*, subcontinente.

SUB.CON.TRACT, *v.*, subcontratar, terceirizar.

SUB.CUL.TURE, *s.*, subcultura.

SUB.DI.VIDE, *v.*, subdividir.

SUB.DI.VI.SION, *s.*, subdivisão.

SUB.DUE, *v.*, subjugar, dominar, vencer.

SUB.DUED, *adj.*, brando, calmo; quieto; vencido; tênue (luz), escuro.

SUB.ED.I.TOR, *s.*, subeditor.

SUB.HEAD.ING, *s.*, subtítulo.

SUB.HU.MAN, *adj.*, subumano.

SUB.JECT, *s.*, assunto, tema, objeto, tópico, súdito; sujeito, motivo; *v.*, subjugar, dominar, sujeitar, submeter.

SUB.JEC.TION, *s.*, sujeição, dominação, submissão.

SUB.JEC.TIVE, *adj.*, subjetivo, pessoal.

SUB.JEC.TIVE.LY, *adv.*, subjetivamente.

SUB.JUNC.TIVE, *s.*, subjuntivo; *adj.*, *Gram.*, subjuntivo.

SUB.LIME, *adj.*, sublime, divino.

SUB.LIME.LY, *adv.*, sublimemente.

SUB.LIM.I.NAL, *adj.*, *Psic.*, subliminar.

SUB.MA.RINE, *s.*, submarino.

SUB.MERGE, *v.*, submergir, imergir, afundar-se, mergulhar.

SUB.MIS.SION, *s.*, submissão, sujeição.

SUB.MIS.SIVE, *adj.*, submisso, dócil.

SUB.MIT, *v.*, submeter, subjugar, sujeitar, submeter-se.

SUB.OR.DI.NATE, *adj.*, subordinado, submisso.

SUB.OR.DI.NATE CLAUSE, *s.*, *Gram.*, oração subordinada.

SUB.OR.DI.NA.TION, *s.*, subordinação; submissão.

SUB.ORN, *v.*, subornar, enganar, falsear.

SUB.OR.NA.TION, *s.*, suborno.

SUB.ROU.TINE, *s.*, *Comp.*, sub-rotina.

SUB.SCRIBE, *v.*, subscrever.

SUB.SCRIB.ER, *s.*, assinante de jornal, revista.

SUB.SCRIP.TION, *s.*, subscrição, assinatura.

SUB.SEC.TION, *s.*, subseção.

SUB.SE.QUENT, *adj.*, subsequente.

SUB.SERV.I.ENT, *adj.*, subserviente.

SUB.SET, *s.*, *Mat.*, subconjunto.

SUB.SIDE, *v.*, acalmar (emoção); baixar (nível), diminuir (inchaço); decantar; ceder, afundar.

SUB.SI.DENCE, *s.*, subsidência; abaixamento; ato de acalmar-se.

SUB.SID.I.ARY, *adj.*, secundário.

SUB.SI.DIZE, *v.*, subsidiar, auxiliar, ajudar.

SUB.SI.DY, *s.*, subsídio, auxílio, ajuda, apoio.

SUB.SIST, *v.*, subsistir.

SUBSISTENCE · 622 · SUN

SUB.SIS.TENCE, s., subsistência.
SUB.SOIL, s., subsolo.
SUB.STANCE, s., substância, matéria.
SUB.STAND.ARD, adj., que está abaixo do padrão.
SUB.STAN.TIAL, adj., substancial, material, sólido.
SUB.STAN.TIAL.LY, adv., substancialmente.
SUB.STAN.TI.ATE, adj., substancioso, pertinente.
SUB.STAN.TIVE, s., substantivo; adj., real, certo.
SUB.STI.TUTE, s., substituto.
SUB.STI.TU.TION, s., substituição.
SUB.TI.TLE, s., subtítulo; Cin., legenda; v., Cin., legendar.
SUB.TER.FUGE, s., subterfúgio, desculpa, pretexto.
SUB.TER.RA.NEAN, adj. s., subterrâneo.
SUB.TLE, adj., sutil, tênue.
SUB.TLE.TY, s., sutileza, delicadeza.
SUB.TLY, adv., sutilmente.
SUB.TO.TAL, s., subtotal.
SUB.TRACT, v., subtrair, deduzir, descontar.
SUB.TRAC.TION, s., subtração; Mat., diminuição, subtração.
SUB.TROP.I.CAL, adj., subtropical.
SUB.URB, s., subúrbio.
SUB.UR.BAN, adj., suburbano.
SUB.UR.BI.A, s., subúrbio.
SUB.VEN.TION, s., subvenção, ajuda.
SUB.VER.SION, s., subversão, desordem, revolta.
SUB.VER.SIVE, s., adj., subversivo.
SUB.VERT, v., subverter, minar.
SUB.WAY, s., metrô, trem subterrâneo em cidades.
SUC.CEED, v., suceder, ter êxito, obter sucesso, dar-se bem.
SUC.CEED.ING, adj., seguinte, subsequente.
SUC.CESS, s., sucesso, êxito.
SUC.CESS.FUL, adj., bem-sucedido, de sucesso.
SUC.CESS.FUL.LY, adv., com sucesso.
SUC.CES.SION, s., sucessão, série, descendência, sequência.
SUC.CES.SIVE, adj., sucessivo.
SUC.CES.SOR, s., sucessor.
SUC.CINCT, adj., resumido, breve, conciso, sucinto.
SUC.CINT.LY, adj., sucintamente.
SUC.CU.LENT, adj., suculento, saboroso.
SUC.CUMB, v., sucumbir, falecer, perecer, morrer.
SUC.CUR.SAL, s., sucursal.
SUCH, adj., semelhante, igual; adv., tanto, tão.
SUCK, s., chupada, sucção; v., chupar, sorver, mamar.
SUCK.ER, s., ventosa; pirulito; chupador (só para animal); fig., fã, gír., babaca; col., trouxa.
SUCK.LE, v., amamentar.
SU.CROSE, s., sacarose.
SUC.TION, s., sucção.
SU.DAN, s., Sudão (país).
SU.DA.NESE, s., adj., sudanês.
SUD.DEN, adj., subitâneo, repentino, inesperado.
SUD.DEN.LY, adv., repentinamente.
SUD.DEN.NESS, s., rapidez; brusquidão.
SUDS, s. pl., espuma ou bolhas de sabão.
SUE, v., processar, peticionar contra outrem, mover um processo.
SUEDE, s., camurça.
SUET, s., sebo.
SUF.FER, v., sofrer, aguentar, suportar, tolerar.
SUF.FER.ANCE, s., condescendência, tolerância, paciência.

SUF.FER.ER, s., paciente; sofredor.
SUF.FER.ING, s., sofrimento, dor, aflição.
SUF.FICE, v., ser suficiente, bastar; satisfazer.
SUF.FI.CIEN.CY, s., suficiência.
SUF.FI.CIENT, adj., suficiente, bastante.
SUF.FI.CIENT.LY, adv., suficientemente.
SUF.FIX, s., sufixo.
SUF.FO.CATE, v., sufocar, asfixiar, matar por sufocação.
SUF.FO.CA.TION, s., sufocação, asfixia.
SUF.FRAGE, s., sufrágio, voto, direito de voto.
SUF.FUSE, v., espalhar, encher, derramar, cobrir, banhar.
SUG.AR, s., açúcar; v., açucarar, adoçar.
SUG.AR-BEET, s., beterraba.
SUG.AR BOWL, s., açucareiro.
SUG.AR.CANE, s., Bot., cana-de-açúcar.
SUG.ARED, adj., adoçado.
SUG.AR.Y, adj., muito doce, açucarado; pej., meloso.
SUG.GEST, v., sugerir, propor, lembrar, insinuar.
SUG.GES.TION, s., sugestão, insinuação, proposição.
SUG.GEST.IVE, adj., sugestivo, indicativo.
SU.I.CID.AL, adj., suicida.
SUI.CIDE, s., suicida; suicídio.
SUIT, s., terno de roupa, processo, caso judicial, naipe, petição; v., vestir, ajustar.
SUIT.ABIL.I.TY, s., conveniência, necessidade.
SUIT.A.BLE, adj., adequado, apropriado, certo.
SUIT.A.BLY, adv., apropriadamente.
SUIT.CASE, s., maleta.
SUITE, s., conjunto de quartos, conjunto de salas em um hotel.
SUIT.ED, adj., apropriado, adequado.
SUIT.OR, s., pretendente.
SULK, v., ficar emburrado, amuar.
SULK.Y, adj., emburrado; rabugento.
SUL.LEN, adj., rabujento, amuado, teimoso, melindroso.
SUL.PHATE UK, **SUL.FATE** US, s., Quim., sulfato.
SUL.PHUR UK, **SUL.FUR** US, s., enxofre.
SUL.PHU.RIC AC.ID UK, **SUL.FU.RIC AC.ID** US, s., Quim., ácido sulfúrico.
SUL.TAN, s., sultão.
SUL.TA.NA, s., sultana.
SUL.TRY, adj., abafado, quente; opressivo.
SUM, s., soma, total, cálculo.
SU.MA.TRA, s., Sumatra (país).
SU.MA.TRAN, s., adj., habitante de, ou relativo à Sumatra.
SUM.MA.RI.LY, adv., sumariamente.
SUM.MA.RIZE, v., resumir, sumarizar, compendiar, sintetizar.
SUM.MA.RY, s., sumário, resumo, compêndio, síntese.
SUM.MA.TION, s., soma, adição; somatório; recapitulação.
SUM.MER, s., verão.
SUM.MER.TIME, s., verão; temporada de verão.
SUMMER TIME, s., UK horário de verão.
SUM.MER.Y, adj., de verão.
SUM.MING UP, s., resumo, súmula; summing-up: recapitulação.
SUM.MIT, s., cúpula; cume, pico; auge.
SUM.MON, v., convocar, intimar; citar; concentrar, reunir.
SUM.MONS, s., Jur., intimação; v., Jur., intimar.
SU.MO, s., Jap., Esp., sumô (luta japonesa).
SUMP.TU.OUS, adj., suntuoso.
SUN, s., sol.

SUNBATHE

SUN.BATHE, v., tomar banho de sol.
SUN.BATHER, s., banhista.
SUN.BEAM, s., raio de sol.
SUN.BURN, s., queimadura de sol.
SUN.DAE, s., *sundae* (tipo de sorvete com coberturas).
SUN.DAY, s., domingo.
SUN.DI.AL, s., relógio de sol.
SUN.DOWN, s., pôr do sol.
SUN-DRIED, adj., seco ao sol, desidratado.
SUN.FLOW.ER, s., girassol.
SUN.GLAS.SES, s., óculos de sol.
SUNK.EN, adj., submerso, afundado; embutido.
SUN.LITHT, s., luz do sol.
SUN.LIT, adj., ensolarado.
SUN.NI, s., adj., sunita.
SUN.NY, adj., ensolarado, cheio de sol.
SUN.RISE, s., nascer do sol, nascente.
SUN.ROOF, s., teto solar.
SUN.SET, s., pôr do sol.
SUN.SHADE, s., guarda-sol; sombrinha; dossel, toldo.
SUN.SHINE, s., luz do sol; luz solar.
SUN SPOT, s., *Astron.*, mancha solar.
SUN.STROKE, s., insolação.
SUN.TAN, s., bronzeado do sol.
SUN.TANNED, adj., bronzeado.
SU.PER.ABUN.DANCE, s., superabundância.
SU.PERB, adj., soberbo.
SU.PER.CIL.I.OUS, adj., convencido, arrogante.
SU.PER.FI.CIAL, adj., superficial.
SU.PER.FLU.OUS, adj., supérfluo.
SU.PE.RI.OR, s., adj., superior.
SU.PE.RI.OR.I.TY, s., superioridade; *pej.*, arrogância.
SU.PER.LA.TIVE, s., *Gram.*, superlativo; adj., excelente.
SU.PER.MAN, s., super-homem.
SU.PER.MAR.KET, s., supermercado.
SU.PER.NAT.U.RAL, adj., sobrenatural.
SU.PER.STAR, s., superstar, estrela (pessoa famosa).
SU.PER.STI.TION, s., superstição.
SU.PER.STI.TIOUS, adj., supersticioso.
SU.PER.STORE, s., hipermercado.
SUP.PER, s., jantar.
SUP.PLANT, v., suplantar, vencer.
SUP.PLE, adj., flexível, dócil; elástico, maleável.
SUP.PLE.MENT, s., suplemento, complemento; v., completar.
SUP.PLE.MEN.TA.RY, adj., suplementar.
SUP.PLI.CANT, s., suplicante, pedinte, requerente.
SUP.PLI.CA.TION, s., súplica, pedido, petição.
SUP.PLI.ER, s., fornecedor, abastecedor.
SUP.PLY, s., suprimento, fornecimento, provisão; v., fornecer, abastecer, suprir.
SUP.PORT, s., suporte, apoio, auxílio; v., apoiar, ajudar, manter.
SUP.PORT.ER, s., partidário; *Esp.*, torcedor.
SUP.POSE, v., supor, imaginar, achar, fazer uma hipótese.
SUP.POSED, adj., suposto, pretenso.
SUP.POS.ED.LY, adv., supostamente.
SUP.POS.ING, conj., se, caso, supondo que.
SUP.POS.I.TO.RY, s., supositório.
SUP.PRESS, v., suprimir, tirar, contar, oprimir.
SUP.PRES.SION, s., supressão.
SUP.PRES.SOR, s., supressor.

SUSTENANCE

SU.PRA.NA.TION.AL, adj., supranacional.
SU.PREM.A.CY, s., supremacia, domínio.
SU.PREME, adj., supremo, máximo, o maior.
SU.PRE.MO, s., *col.*, *UK* manda-chuva.
SUR.CHARGE, s., sobrecarga, sobretaxa, sobrepeso.
SURE, adj., certo, seguro, convencido, fiel.
SURE.FIRE, adj., *col.*, certeiro.
SURE.LY, adv., com certeza, seguramente.
SURE.TY, s., garantia, segurança, fiança.
SURF, s., surfe, rebentação das ondas, ressaca.
SUR.FACE, s., superfície, face, lado; v., revestir, vir à tona.
SURF.BOARD, s., prancha de surfe.
SUR.FEIT, s., excesso.
SURF.ER, s., surfista; *Comp.*, internauta.
SURF.ING, s., surfe.
SURGE, s., onda, vaga, turbilhão; *Eletr.*, sobretensão; v., aumentar, avançar; subir, crescer.
SUR.GEON, s., cirurgião, médico.
SUR.GERY, s., cirurgia, sala de operação, consultório.
SU.RI.NA.ME, s., Suriname (país).
SUR.LY, adj., ríspido, de mau humor, rude.
SUR.MISE, s., conjetura; imaginação; v., imaginar; supor.
SUR.MOUNT, v., galgar; superar, vencer.
SUR.NAME, s., apelido, sobrenome.
SUR.PASS, s., ultrapassar, superar.
SUR.PLUS, s., excedente, superávit; adj., excedente.
SUR.PRISE, s., surpresa, espanto; v., surpreender.
SUR.PRISED, adj., surpreso.
SUR.PRIS.ING, adj., surpreedente.
SUR.PRIS.ING.LY, adv., surpreendentemente.
SUR.RE.AL, adj., surreal.
SUR.RE.AL.ISM, s., surrealismo.
SUR.RE.AL.IST, s., adj., surrealista.
SUR.REN.DER, s., rendição; v., render-se; entregar(-se), renunciar a.
SUR.REP.TI.TIOUS, adj., subreptício, furtivo, oculto, tácito.
SUR.RO.GATE, s., substituto, suplente, sub-rogado; v., substituir, sub-rogar.
SUR.ROUND, v., circundar, rodear, cercar.
SUR.ROUND.ING, adj., circundante, vizinho; relacionado.
SUR.TAX, s., sobretaxa.
SUR.VEIL.LANCE, s., vigilância, cuidado, atenção.
SUR.VEY, s., visão, vistoria, inspeção, mapa, levantamento; v., inspecionar, vistoriar.
SUR.VEY.OR, s., agrimensor, inspetor, vistoriador.
SUR.VIV.AL, s., sobrevivência.
SUR.VIVE, v., sobreviver, perdurar, durar, continuar.
SUR.VI.VOR, s., sobrevivente.
SUS.CEP.TI.BLE, adj., suscetível.
SUS.PECT, adj., s., suspeito; v., suspeitar, desconfiar.
SUS.PEND, v., suspender, interromper, cessar, remover.
SUS.PEND.ER, s., liga; *Med.*, cinta ortopédica; *suspenders*: US suspensórios, UK cintas-ligas.
SUS.PENSE, s., incerteza, dúvida, ansiedade.
SUS.PEN.SION, s., suspensão.
SUS.PI.CION, s., suspeita, dúvida.
SUS.PI.CIOUS, adj., suspeitoso, suspeito, desconfiado.
SUS.PI.CIOUS.LY, adv., suspeitosamente.
SUS.TAIN, v., sustentar, manter, alimentar; sofrer, afligir-se.
SUS.TAIN.A.BLE, adj., sustentável.
SUS.TE.NANCE, s., alimento, sustento, mantimento,

SUTURE

624

SYPHILIS

subsistência.

SU.TURE, *s., Med.,* sutura; costura.

SVELTE, *adj.,* esbelto.

SWA.HI.LI, *s., adj.,* suaíli (povo ou relativo a esse povo da costa leste africana de Zanzibar.)

SWAL.LOW, *s.,* andorinha.

SWAMP, *s.,* brejo, pântano, charco; *v.,* atolar.

SWAN, *s.,* cisne.

SWAP, *s.,* troca, permuta, acordo para troca de pagamentos; *v.,* trocar, permutar.

SWARM, *s.,* enxame de abelhas, multidão, grande quantidade; *v.,* enxamear.

SWARTH.Y, *adj.,* escuro, moreno.

SWAS.TI.KA, *s.,* suástica, cruz gamada.

SWAT, *s.,* golpe, pancada; *v.,* esmagar, amassar, matar.

SWATCH, *s.,* amostra.

SWATHE, *s.,* bandagem, faixa; *v.,* enfaixar, envolver, embrulhar.

SWAT.TER, *s.,* mata-moscas.

SWAY, *s.,* influência; *v.,* balançar; influenciar, convencer.

SWA.ZI.LAND, *s.,* Swazilândia (país).

SWEAR, *v.,* jurar, prestar juramento; praguejar, blasfemar.

SWEAR.ING, *s.,* juramento; praga, blasfêmia, imprecação.

SWEAR.WORD, *s.,* palavrão.

SWEAT, *s.,* suor, transpiração; suar, transpirar.

SWEAT.BAND, *s.,* faixa antitranspirante.

SWEAT.ER, *s.,* camisola; suéter, pulôver.

SWEAT.SHIRT, *s.,* pulôver, blusão de moleton.

SWEAT.SHOP, *s., pej.,* emprego onde se trabalha muito e se paga pouco.

SWEATY, *adj.,* suado.

SWEDE, *adj., s.,* sueco.

SWE.DEN, *s.,* Suécia.

SWED.ISH, *s.,* língua sueca.

SWEEP, *s.,* varredura, varrição; curva, volta; área, região; *v.,* varrer, escovar; roçar; dragar, escavar; vasculhar.

SWEEP.ER, *s.,* varredor.

SWEEP.ING, *s.,* varredura; limpeza; *adj.,* radical, completo, amplo; curvo.

SWEEP.STAKE, *s.,* loteria de corrida de cavalos; bolão (jogo).

SWEET, *s.,* coisa doce, doce, sobremesa; *adj.,* doce, açucarado, suave.

SWEET-AND-SOUR, *adj.,* agridoce.

SWEET CORN, *s., US* milho verde.

SWEET.EN, *s.,* adoçar, colocar açúcar em.

SWEET.EN.ER, *s.,* adoçante; *fig.,* suborno.

SWEET.EN.ING, *s.,* adoçante.

SWEET.HEART, *s.,* querido(a), amado(a); namorado(a).

SWEET.NESS, *s.,* doçura; delicadeza; perfume.

SWEET POTATO, *s., Bot.,* batata-doce.

SWEET SHOP, *s., UK* confeitaria.

SWELL, *s.,* aumento, inchação, onda, vaga, vagalhão; *v.,* crescer, inchar, dilatar.

SWELL.ING, *s.,* inchação, intumescência, inchaço.

SWEL.TER.ING, *adj.,* abafado, sufocante.

SWIFT, *s.,* andorinha; *adj.,* rápido, célere, rápido.

SWIFT.LY, *adj.,* rapidamente, velozmente.

SWIFT.NESS, *s.,* velociade, rapidez.

SWIG, *s.,* trago, gole.

SWILL, *s.,* lavagem; *v.,* enxaguar.

SWIM, *s.,* ato de nadar, nado, natação; *v.,* nadar, flutuar, estar inundado.

SWIM.MER, *s.,* nadador.

SWIMMING, *s.,* natação.

SWIM.MING POOL, *s.,* piscina.

SWIM.MING SUIT, *s.,* trajes para banho, roupa de banho.

SWIN.DLE, *s.,* fraude, logro; *v.,* fraudar, defraudar, enganar.

SWIM.SUIT, *s.,* traje de banho.

SWINE, *s.,* porco; velhaco, calhorda, cafajeste.

SWING, *s.,* balanço, oscilação, ritmo; *v.,* balançar, oscilar.

SWING.ING, *s.,* suingue; *adj.,* animado, alegre; descontraído.

SWIPE, *s.,* pancada, ato de bater; *v.,* golpear; passar, roubar.

SWIRL, *s.,* redemoinho; espiral; *v.,* rodopiar, girar.

SWISH, *adj., s.,* suíço.

SWISS, *s., adj.,* suíço.

SWISS CHARD, *s., Bot.,* acelga.

SWITCH, *s.,* interruptor, interrupção; *v.,* mudar, interromper.

SWITCH.BLADE, *s., US* canivete.

SWITCHED-ON, *adj., gír.,* ligado, antenado, por dentro.

SWIV.EL, *s.,* girador, tornel; *v.,* girar (sobre um tornel).

SWIT.ZER.LAND, *s.,* Suíça.

SWOON, *s.,* desmaio; *v.,* desmaiar, desfalecer, esmorecer.

SWOOP, *s.,* arremetida (avião), investida; *v.,* precipitar-se; investir; arremeter (avião).

SWORD, *s.,* espada.

SWORD.ISH, *s.,* peixe-espada.

SWORDS.MAN, *s.,* esgrimista, espadachim.

SWOT, *s., gír., UK* estudante esfoçado, cê-dê-efe.

SYL.LA.BLE, *s.,* sílaba.

SYL.LA.BUS, *s.,* programa (de uma disciplina).

SYM.BOL, *s.,* símbolo.

SYM.BOL.IC, *adj.,* simbólico.

SYM.BOL.IZE(-ISE), *v.,* simbolizar.

SYM.BOL.ISM, *s.,* simbolismo.

SYM.MET.RIC, *adj.,* simétrico.

SYM.MET.RI.CAL, *adj.,* simétrico.

SYM.ME.TRY, *s.,* simetria.

SYM.PA.THET.IC, *adj.,* simpático, agradável.

SYM.PA.THIZE, *v.,* simpatizar com, entender.

SYM.PA.THI.ZER(-ISER), *s.,* simpatizante.

SYM.PA.THY, *s.,* simpatia, compreensão, compaixão.

SYM.PHON.IC, *adj.,* sinfônico.

SYM.PHO.NY, *s.,* sinfonia.

SYM.PO.SIUM, *s.,* simpósio.

SYMP.TOM, *s.,* sintoma, indício, suspeita.

SYMP.TO.MAT.IC, *adj.,* sintomático.

SYN.A.GOGUE, *s.,* sinagoga.

SYNC, *s., col.,* sincronização ; *v.,* sincronizar.

SYN.CHRO.NIZE, *v.,* sincronizar.

SYN.CO.PA.TED, *adj.,* sincopado, abreviado.

SYN.DROME, *s.,* síndrome.

SYN.OD, *s.,* sínodo.

SYN.O.NYM, *s.,* sinônimo.

SYN.ON.Y.MOUS, *adj.,* sinônimo.

SYN.OP.SIS, *s.,* sinopse, resumo, síntese.

SYN.TAX, *s.,* sintaxe.

SYN.THE.SIS, *s.,* síntese.

SYN.THE.SIZE(-ISE), *v.,* sintetizar.

SYN.THE.SIZER, *s., Mús.,* sintetizador.

SYN.THET.IC, *adj.,* sintético.

SYPH.I.LIS, *s.,* sífilis.

SYRIA

SYR.IA, *s.*, Síria.
SYR.IAN, *s., adj.*, sírio.
SY.RINGE, *s.*, seringa.
SYR.UP, *s.*, xarope.

SYSTEMATIZE

SYS.TEM, *s.*, sistema, método, modo.
SYS.TEM.AT.IC, *adj.*, sistemático, metódico.
SYS.TEM.A.TIZE, *v.*, sistematizar.

T

T, vigésima letra do alfabeto inglês.
TAB, s., tira, aba, lingueta, alça; etiqueta de roupa.
TAB.ER.NA.CLE, s., tabernáculo.
TAB.BY, s., tafetá, gato malhado; adj., listrado, malhado, tigrado.
TA.BLE, s., mesa; refeição, comida; platô, tabela, lista; v., colocar na mesa, listar.
TA.BLE.CLOTH, s., toalha de mesa.
TA.BLE FOOT.BALL, s., pebolim.
TA.BLE.LAND, s., planalto.
TA.BLE LAMP, s., luminária, candeeiro.
TA.BLE.SPOON, s., colher de sopa.
TAB.LET, s., tabuleta, bloco de papel; comprimido.
TA.BLE TEN.NIS, s., Esp., tênis de mesa.
TA.BLE WINE, s., vinho de mesa.
TAB.LOID, s., tabloide.
TA.BOO, s., tabu.
TAB.U.LAR, adj., tabular.
TAB.U.LATE, v., tabular, dar forma de tabela.
TA.CHOM.E.TER, s., tacômetro.
TACHY.GRAPHY, s., taquigrafia.
TAC.IT, adj., tácito, implícito, oculto.
TAC.I.TURN, adj., taciturno, tristonho.
TA.CO, s., taco (comida mexicana).
TACK, s., tacha, prego; v., prender, fixar com tacha.
TACK.LE, s., aparelho, equipamento, guincho; v., manejar, tentar resolver, agarrar.
TACKY, adj., pegajoso.
TACT, s., tato, diplomacia, postura.
TACT.FUL, adj., tático.
TACT.FUL.LY, adv., taticamente, diplomaticamente.
TAC.TIC, adj., tático.
TAC.TIC.AL, adj., tático.
TAC.TICS, s., tática.
TAC.TIL.I.TY, s., tactilidade, perceptibilidade.
TAC.TILE, adj., tátil, palpável.
TACT.LESS, adj., insensível; sem diplomacia.
TACT.LESS.LY, adv., indelicadamente.
TAD.POLE, s., girino.
TAF.FE.TA, s., tafetá.
TAE.NIA, s., Zool., tênia.
TAF.FY, s., caramelo (bala), puxa-puxa.
TAG, s., etiqueta.
TAG.RAG, s., canalha, calhorda, safado, cafajeste.
TA.HI.TI, s., Taiti (país).
TA.HI.TIAN, s., adj., taitiano.
TAIL, s., rabo, cauda, cauda de avião, parte traseira; v., pôr um rabo.
TAIL.BACK, s., UK engarrafamento (trânsito).
TAIL.COAT, s., fraque.
TAIL.GATE, s., porta traseira.
TAIL.LESS, adj., pitoco, sem cauda.
TAI.LOR, s., alfaiate.
TAI.LORED, adj., feito sob medida.
TAINT, s., nódoa, mancha, mácula; v., manchar, enodoar, macular.
TAINT.ED, adj., manchado, estragado, contaminado.
TAI.WAN, s., Taiwan (país).
TAI.WANESE, s., adj., taiwanês.
TA.JIK.I.STAN, TADZ.HIK.I.STAN, s., Tajiquistão ou Tadjiquistão (país).
TAKE, v., tomar, requerer, fotografar, exigir, agendar, pegar, tolerar.
TAKE A.WAY UK, s., o mesmo que take-out.
TA.KEN, v., pp de take.
TAKE.OFF, s., decolagem.
TAKE-OUT, s., comida para viagem; Bras., quentinha.
TAKE.O.VER, s., aquisição, posse; tomada de posse; conquista.
TAK.ER, s., tomador, comprador.
TAK.ING, s., tomada, apreensão, arresto.
TAK.ING.NESS, s., sedução, fascinação, atração.
TAKINGS,
TALC, s., Min., talco (industrial).
TALE, s., conto, enredo, narrativa.
TAL.ENT, s., talento.
TAL.ENT.ED, adj., talentoso.
TAL.IS.MAN, s., talismã.
TALK, s., conversa, fala, conversação, discurso, conselho; v., falar, conversar, dizer.
TALK.A.TIVE, adj., loquaz, tagarela.
TALK.ER, s., falador, falante, tagarela, palrador.
TALK.ING, s., conversa, conversação, tagarelice.
TALK.SHOW s., programa de rádio ou TV, entrevistando pessoas.
TALL, adj., alto, grande, elevado, exagerado.
TALL.BOY, s., cômoda, armário com gaveta.
TALL.NESS, s., altura, estatura, dimensão.
TAL.LY, s., conta, registro, cálculo, rótulo, marca; v., marcar, designar, controlar.
TAL.MUD, s., Rel., Talmude.
TAM.A.BIL.I.TY, s., docilidade, afabilidade.
TAM.A.RIND, s., Bot., tamarindo.
TAM.BOUR, s., Mús., tambor.
TAM.BOU.RINE, s., Mús., pandeiro, tamborim.
TAME, v., amansar, domesticar, domar, submeter, dominar, sujeitar.
TAME.LY, adv., mansamente, docilmente.
TAM.ER, s., domador(a).
TAM.PON, s., tampão (de algodão).
TAN, s., cor bronzeada; Bot., tanino; adj., castanho, bronzeado; v., bronzear(-se).
TAN.DEM, s., tandem (tipo de bicicleta).
TANG, s., sabor forte.

TANGA   •• 627 •••   TECHNOLOGICAL

TAN.GA, *s.*, tanga (traje de banho de tamanho reduzido).
TAN.GENT, *s.*, tangente.
TAN.GER.INE, *s.*, tangerina.
TAN.GI.BLE, *adj.*, tangível.
TAN.GLE, *s.*, emaranhamento; confusão; *v.*, emaranhar, entrelaçar; complicar, enredar.
TAN.GLED, *adj.*, emaranhado, enrolado, confuso.
TAN.GO, *s.*, tango (música e dança argentinas); *v.*, dançar o tango.
TANG.Y, *adj.*, picante, ácido; forte (cheiro).
TANK, *s.*, tanque, depósito.
TANK.ER, *s.*, navio-tanque, caminhão-tanque.
TAN.NERY, *s.*, curtume, fábrica para curtir couros.
TANNED, *adj.*, bronzeado, moreno; curtido (couro).
TAN.NIN, *s.*, tanino.
TAN.NING, *s.*, curtimento.
TAN.TA.LIZE(-ISE), *v.*, atormentar, provocar, tentar.
TAN.TRUM, *s.*, acesso de fúria; birra, pirraça.
TANZANIA, *s.*, Tanzânia.
TAN.ZA.NIAN, *s.*, *adj.*, tanzaniano.
TAP, *s.*, torneira, pancadinha, batida leve; *v.*, bater de leve, remendar, destampar.
TAP DANCE, *s.*, sapateado (dança).
TA.PER, *s.*, vela, círio, diminuição; *v.*, diminuir, afilar.
TAPE.WORM, *s.*, tênia.
TA.PIR, *s.*, anta, tapir.
TAP.I.O.CA, *s.*, tapioca (fécula de mandioca).
TAP.PET, *s.*, bravo, alavanca.
TAP.STER, *s.*, taberneiro, empregado de bar, dono de bar.
TAR, *s.*, piche, alcatrão; marujo, marinheiro; *v.*, pichar.
TA.RAN.TU.LA, *s.*, tarântula, aranha.
TAR.DI.NESS, *s.*, lentidão, demora.
TAR.DY, *adj.*, lento, moroso, vagaroso.
TAR.GET, *s.*, objetivo, alvo; *v.*, dirigir, orientar (na direção de); selecionar (canal de TV).
TAR.GET.A.BLE, *adj.*, que pode ser alvejado.
TAR.IFF, *s.*, tarifa.
TAR.NISH, *v.*, embaciar, embaçar, manchar, sujar.
TAR.OT, *s.*, tarô.
TAR.PAU.LIN, *s.*, lona encerada; material encerado.
TAR.RA.GON, *s.*, *Bot.*, estragão.
TAR.SUS, *s.*, tarso.
TART, *s.*, torta.
TAR.TAN, *s.*, estilo escocês de desenho em xadrez; *tartan.*
TAR.TAR, *s.*, tártaro.
TART.NESS, *s.*, acidez, azedume, amargor.
TASK, *s.*, tarefa, dever.
TASK.ING, *s.*, empreitada, tarefa.
TASK.MAS.TER, *s.*, capataz.
TAS.MA.NIA, *s.*, *Geogr.*, Tasmânia (ilha e estado australiano).
TAS.MA.NI.AN, *s.*, *adj.*, tasmaniano.
TAST.ABLE, *adj.*, degustável, saboroso.
TASTE, *s.*, gosto, sabor, paladar; *v.*, provar, experimentar, degustar, saborear.
TASTE BUD, *s.*, *Anat.*, papila gustativa.
TASTE.FUL, *adj.*, gostoso, saboroso; fino.
TASTE.FUL.LY, *adv.*, com bom gosto, esteticamente fino.
TASTE.FUL.NESS, *s.*, gosto, paladar; discernimento.
TASTE.LESS, *adj.*, insosso; insípido, sem gosto.
TAST.ER, *s.*, degustador, provador.
TASTY, *adj.*, saboroso, gostoso, delicioso.

TAT, *s.*, *pej.*, *UK* bugigangas; *v.*, bilrar, fazer bilro.
TAT.TER, *s.*, farrapo, andrajo, traste; *v.*, esfarrapar.
TAT.TERED, *adj.*, esfarrapado, maltrapilho.
TAT.TERS, *s.*, farrapo, trapo, frangalhos.
TAT.TOO, *s.*, tatuagem; *v.*, tatuar.
TAT.TOOIST, *s.*, tatuador.
TAT.TY, *adj.*, esfarrapado, escangalhado, *pej.*, reles, enxovalhado.
TAUNT, *s.*, zombaria, mofa, escárnio; *v.*, zombar, escarnecer.
TAUT, *adj.*, retesado, firme; teso, esticado.
TAU.TEN, *v.*, esticar(-se), retesar.
TAU.TOL.O.GY, *s.*, *Gram.*, tautologia.
TAV.ERN, *s.*, taverna, estalagem, bar.
TAW.DRY, *adj.*, *pej.*, mau gosto, espalhafatoso.
TAW.NY, *adj.*, ruivo, fulvo, trigueiro.
TAX, *s.*, taxa, imposto; *v.*, tributar, taxar, sobrecarregar.
TAX.A.BLE, *adj.*, tributável.
TAX.A.TION, *s.*, taxação, tributação.
TAX-FREE, *adj.*, livre de impostos.
TAX.I, *s.*, táxi.
TAX.I.DER.MIST, *s.*, taxidermista.
TAX.I.ME.TER, *s.*, taxímetro.
TAX.ING, *s.*, taxação; *adj.*, árduo, exigente, oneroso.
TAX.MAN, *s.*, *col.*, coletor de impostos.
TAX.PAY.ER, *s.*, contribuinte (de impostos).
TAX YEAR, *s.*, ano fiscal; exercício (também *fiscal year*).
TEA, *s.*, chá, refeição de final de tarde.
TEA BAG, *s.*, saquinho de chá.
TEACH, *v.*, ensinar, instruir, educar, dar aula, lecionar.
TEACH.ER, *s.*, professor.
TEACH.ING, *s.*, ensino, magistério.
TEACH.ING AID, *s.*, *Educ.*, ensino; material pedagógico.
TEA-CLOTH, *s.*, toalhinha de mesa para chá; pano de prato.
TEA.CUP, *s.*, chávena ou xícara de chá.
TEAM, *s.*, time, esquadra.
TEAM.STER, *s.*, *US* caminhoneiro.
TEAM.WORK, *s.*, equipe de trabalho, grupo de trabalho.
TEA PAR.TY, *s.*, chá da tarde.
TEA.POT, *s.*, bule de chá.
TEAR, *s.*, lágrima; *v.*, rasgar.
TEAR.DROP, *s.*, gota de lágrima, lágrima; pingente de brilhante.
TEAR.FUL, *adj.*, choroso, lacrimoso.
TEAR GAS, *s.*, gás lacrimogêneo.
TEAR.ING, *adj.*, apressado; furioso.
TEASE, *s.*, caçoador; *v.*, caçoar; pedir com insistência.
TEAS.ER, *s.*, importunador, implicante; *teaser.*
TEA.SPOON, *s.*, colher de chá.
TEA-STRAIN.ER, *s.*, coador de chá.
TEAT, *s.*, teta.
TEA.TIME, *s.*, hora do chá.
TEA TOW.EL, *s.*, pano de prato.
TECH.NIC, *s.*, técnica; arte, prática.
TECH.NI.CAL, *adj.*, técnico.
TECH.NI.CAL.LY, *adv.*, tecnicamente.
TECH.NI.CI.AN, *s.*, técnico.
TECH.NIQUE, *s.*, o mesmo que *technic.*
TECH.NICS, *s.*, técnica, tecnologia.
TECH.NO, *s.*, *Mús.*, *techno* (música eletrônica).
TECH.NO.CRAT, *s.*, tecnocrata.
TECH.NO.LOG.IC.AL, *adj.*, tecnológico.

TECHNOLOGY ·· 628 ·· TERMINOLOGY

TECH.NOL.O.GY, s., tecnologia.
TED.DY, s., ursinho de pelúcia.
TE.DIOUS, adj., tedioso, fastidioso, aborrecido.
TE.DI.UM, s., tédio, aborrecimento.
TEEM, v., abundar, enxamear, pulular; UK chover torrencialmente.
TEEN.AGE, adj., adolescente.
TEEN.AG.ER, s., adolescente, jovem.
TEENS, s., abrev. de teenager: adolescente (dos 13 aos 19 anos).
TEE.NY, s., col., miudinho, pequenininho.
TEE SHIRT, s., camiseta.
TEE.TER, s., vaivém; v., vacilar, hesitar; balançar.
TEETH, s. pl., dentes.
TEETHE, v., nascer dos dentes, endentecer.
TEETH.ING, s., dentição.
TEE.TO.TAL, s., abstêmio; adj., abstinente.
TEE.TO.TAL.ISM, s., abstenção de bebidas alcoólicas.
TEL.E.COM.MU.NI.CA.TIONS, s., telecomunicações.
TEL.E.FILM, s., filme de televisão.
TEL.E.GRAM, s., telegrama.
TEL.E.GRAPH, s., telégrafo.
TE.LEG.RA.PHER, s., telegrafista.
TEL.E.GRAPH.IC, adj., telegráfico.
TE.LEG.RA.PHIST, s., telegrafista.
TE.LEG.RA.PHY, s., telegrafia.
TE.LEM.E.TRY, s., telemetria.
TE.LEP.A.THY, s., telepatia.
TELE.PHONE, s., telefone; v., telefonar.
TEL.E.PHONE BOOK, s., UK lista telefônica.
TEL.E.PHONE CALL, s., chamada telefônica; telefonema.
TEL.E.PHONE NUM.BER, s., número de telefone.
TELE.PHON.ER, s., telefonista.
TE.LE.PHON.IST, s., telefonista.
TELE.PHO.NY, s., telefonia.
TEL.E.PLAY, s., roteiro para filme de televisão.
TEL.E.VIEW, v., assistir à televisão.
TEL.E.SCOPE, s., telescópio.
TEL.E.VI.SION, s., televisão.
TEL.E.VI.SION STA.TION, s., emissora de televisão.
TEL.EX, s., telex; v., remeter comunicação por telex.
TELL, v., dizer, contar, narrar, falar, distinguir.
TELL.ER, s., caixa (de banco); escrutinador (contador de votos).
TELL.ING, adj., revelador, contundente, vigoroso.
TELL.LY, s., abrev. de televisão.
TE.MER.I.TY, s., temeridade.
TEMP, s., temporário, interino.
TEM.PER, s., temperamento, humor, modo de ser; v., moderar, controlar.
TEM.PERA, s., têmpera.
TEM.PER.A.MENT, s., temperamento.
TEM.PER.A.MEN.TAL, adj., temperamental.
TEM.PER.ANCE, s., temperança, moderação.
TEM.PER.ATE, adj., temperado, clima temperado.
TEM.PER.A.TURE, s., temperatura.
TEM.PERED, adj., contido, comedido, suave; disposto; temperado (aço).
TEM.PEST, s., tempestade, furacão.
TEM.PES.TU.OUS, adj., tempestuoso (tempo); tumultuoso.
TEM.PLATE, s., molde, modelo, padrão.

TEM.PLE, s., templo.
TEM.PLET, s., o mesmo que template.
TEM.PO.RAL, adj., temporal, mundano; s., temporal, têmpora.
TEM.PO.RAR.I.LY, adv., temporariamente.
TEM.PO.RAR.Y, adj., passageiro, transitório, temporário, fugaz.
TEM.PO.RIZE, s., temporizar, contemporizar.
TEMPT, v., tentar; instigar, seduzir.
TEMP.TA.TION, s., tentação, sedução.
TEMPT.ER, s., tentador, sedutor.
TEMPT.ING, adj., tentador, convidativo.
TEN, num., dez.
TEN.A.BLE, adj., sustentável; defensável; estável.
TEN.A.BLY, adv., sustentavelmente.
TE.NA.CIOUS, adj., tenaz, persistente, teimoso.
TE.NAC.I.TY, s., tenacidade.
TENANCY, s., aluguel, arrendamento.
TEN.ANT, s., inquilino.
TEND, v., cuidar, zelar, tomar conta, prestar atenção.
TEN.DEN.CY, s., tendência, inclinação, pendor.
TEN.DER, s., proposta, prova, carne macia; adj., tenro, macio; v., oferecer, provar.
TEN.DER.IZE(-ISE), v., amaciar, tornar tenra (carne).
TEN.DER.LY, adv., ternamente, carinhosamente.
TEN.DER.NESS, s., ternura, suavidade; maciez.
TEN.DON, s., tendão.
TEN.DRIL, s., Bot., gavinha; cacho (de cabelo).
TEN.E.BROUS, adj., tenebroso, terrível.
TEN.E.MENT, s., prédio de apartamentos, cortiço.
TEN.ET, s., princípio, dogma.
TEN.NER, s., col., UK nota de dez libras.
TEN.FOLD, adj., décuplo.
TEN.NIS, s., tênis.
TEN.NIS BALL, s., bola de tênis.
TENSE, adj., tenso, rígido, estressado.
TENSED UP, adj., tenso.
TEN.SION, s., tensão.
TEN.SI.TY, s., tensidade, tensão, rigidez.
TENT, s., tenda, barraca.
TEN.TA.CLE, s., tentáculo.
TENTH, num., décimo.
TE.NU.ITY, s., tenuidade.
TEN.U.OUS, adj., tênue, rarefeito; delgado, fino.
TEN.U.OUS.LY, adv., tenuemente, sutilmente.
TEN.URE, s., posse de uma propriedade; estabilidade no emprego.
TEPEE, s., US tenda indígena.
TEP.ID, adj., tépido, morno.
TE.PID.I.TY, s., tepidez, mornidade.
TE.QUI.LA, s., Bot., tequila (agave azul), aguardente feita dessa planta.
TER.CEN.TE.NA.RY, s., tricentenário.
TERM, s., termo, palavra; expressão, período, trimestre escolar, cláusulas contratuais.
TER.MI.NA.BLE, adj., limitável; revogável; terminável.
TER.MI.NAL, s., final; terminal (estação de trem, ônibus, aeroporto); adj., terminal, final.
TER.MI.NAL.LY, adv., no fim.
TER.MI.NATE, v., terminar, concluir, finalizar.
TER.MI.NA.TION, s., término, limitação.
TER.MI.NOL.O.GY, s., terminologia.

TERMINUS · 629 · THEY

TER.MI.NUS, s., terminal, ponto final; fim, final, término.
TER.MITE, s., Zool., cupim, térmite.
TERM.LESS, adj., ilimitado, sem limite.
TER.RA, s., terra.
TER.RACE, s., terraço, fila de casas, casas ladeadas.
TER.RACED, adj., escalonado, em fileira.
TER.RA-COT.TA, s., terracota (do It.: terra cotta).
TER.RAIN, s., terreno.
TER.RES.TRI.AL, adj., terrestre.
TER.RI.BLE, adj., terrível, pavoroso, horroroso.
TER.RI.BLY, adv., terrivelmente.
TER.RI.ER, s., terrier (raça de cão).
TER.RIF.IC, adj., formidável, fabuloso; enorme; interj., legal.
TER.RI.FIED, adj., aterrorizado.
TER.RI.FY, v., apavorar, aterrorizar, amedrontar.
TER.RI.FY.ING, adj., horripilante, aterrorizante.
TER.RINE, s., terrina (recipiente de barro para cozinhar).
TER.RI.TO.RI.AL, adj., territorial.
TER.RI.TO.RY, s., território.
TER.ROR, s., terror.
TERRORISM, s., terrorismo.
TER.ROR.IST, s., terrorista.
TER.ROR.IZE, v., aterrorizar, apavorar, terrificar.
TER.RY, s., tecido felpudo, atoalhado.
TERSE, adj., seco; curto, grosso; consiso, sucinto.
TERSE.LY, adv., sucintamente, concisamente.
TER.TIAR.Y, adj., terciário.
TEST, s., teste, prova, exame; v., testar, examinar, verificar.
TES.TA.MENT, s., testamento; the Old/New Testament: o Velho/Novo Testamento.
TEST BAN, s., suspensão de testes nucleares.
TEST-DRIVE, v., test-drive (testar um veículo antes de comprá-lo).
TES.TER, s., provador, degustador, experimentador.
TES.TI.CLE, s., testículo.
TES.TI.FY, s., testemunhar, depor, ser testemunha judicial.
TES.TI.MO.NI.AL, s., atestado, certidão; homenagem, testemunho; adj., de honra, de testemunho.
TES.TI.MO.NY, s., testemunho, depoimento.
TES.TI.NESS, s., mau humor, rabugice, irascibilidade.
TEST.ING, s., prova, experimentação, ensaio.
TES.TOS.TER.ONE, s., Med., testosterona.
TES.TY, adj., teimoso, obstinado, cabeça-dura, irascível.
TET.A.NUS, s., tétano.
TETCH.Y, adj., rabugento, irritável.
TETH.ER, s., corda, corrente; v., apear, amarrar, acorrentar.
TEXT, s., texto, livro, livro didático, leitura didática.
TEXT.BOOK, s., livro escolar.
TEX.TILE, adj., têxtil.
TEX.TU.AL, adj., textual.
TEX.TURE, s., textura.
THAI.LAND, s., Tailândia.
THAMES, s., Tâmisa.
THAN, conj., que, do que.
THANK, v., agradecer; s., agradecimento; interj., obrigado/obrigada.
THANK.FUL, adj., agradecido, grato.
THANK.FUL.LY, adv., agradecidamente.
THANK.LESS, adj., ingrato.
THANKS.GIV.ING, s., ação de graças.
THANK YOU, excl., obrigado!; s., agradecimento.

THAT, pron., adj., esse, essa; aquele, aquela; pron., isso, aquilo, quem, qual; adv., tão.
THATCHED, adj., com telhado de palha.
THAW, s., degelo, descongelamento; v., degelar, derreter; descongelar.
THE, art., o, a, os, as.
THE.ATRE, THE.ATER, s., teatro.
THE.AT.RI.CAL, adj., teatral.
THE.AT.RI.CAL.ISM, s., teatralidade, teatralismo.
THEFT, s., roubo.
THEIR, pron., seu, sua, seus, suas, dele, dela, deles, delas.
THEIRS, pron., o seu, a sua, os seus, as suas.
THE.ISM, s., teísmo.
THEM, pron., os, as, lhes, a eles, a elas.
THE.MAT.IC, adj., temático.
THEME, s., tema.
THEM.SELVES, pron., elas mesmas, eles mesmos; a si próprios, a si próprias; a si mesmos, a si mesmas.
THEN, adv., naquele tempo, logo, depois; conj., então, portanto, nesse caso.
THENCE, adv., dali, daquele lugar.
THENCE.FORTH, adv., desde então.
THE.OC.RA.CY, s., teocracia.
THEO.LO.GIAN, s., teólogo.
THE.OL.O.GY, s., teologia.
THE.O.REM, s., teorema.
THE.O.REM.AT.IC, adj., relativo a teorema.
THE.O.RET.IC, adj., teórico, teorético.
THE.O.RET.I.CAL.LY, adv., teoricamente, em teoria.
THE.O.RE.TI.CIAN, s., teórico.
THEORIST, s., teórico, teorista.
THE.O.RI.ZA.TION, s., teorização.
THE.O.RIZE(-ISE), v., teorizar, trabalhar com teorias.
THE.O.RY, s., teoria, ideia.
THER.A.PEU.TICS, s., terapêutica.
THER.A.PIST, s., terapeuta.
THER.A.PY, s., terapia.
THERE, adv., ali, lá, acolá, além.
THERE.AF.TER, adv., depois disso.
THERE.BY, adv., assim, deste modo.
THERE.FORE, conj., portanto.
THERE.FROM, adv., disto, daquilo, daí.
THERE.IN, adv., nisto, nisso, naquele lugar, lá.
THERE.OF, adv., disto, disso, daquilo.
THERE'S, contr. de there is: há, existe.
THERE.TO, adv., àquilo, a isso; além disso, para isso.
THERE.UP.ON, adv., nisto, nisso, naquilo, por causa disso.
THERE.WITH, adv., com isso, com aquilo.
THE.RI.AC, s., antídoto.
THER.MAL, adj., térmico.
THER.MIC, adj., térmico.
THER.MOM.E.TER, s., termômetro.
THER.MOM.E.TRY, s., termometria.
THER.MO.DY.NAM.ICS, s., termodinâmica.
THER.MO.NU.CLE.AR, adj., termonuclear.
THER.MO.PLAS.TIC, s., adj., termoplástico.
THER.MO.STAT, s., termostato.
THE.SAU.RUS, s., tesouro, dicionário de sinônimos.
THESE, pron., pl., estes, estas.
THE.SIS, s., tese.
THEY, pron., eles, elas.

THEY'RE · 630 · THUNDERSTRUCK

THEY'RE, *contr.* de *they are*: eles/elas são.
THICK, *adj.*, espesso, denso, grosso.
THICK.EN, *v.*, adensar-se, espessar-se; engrossar.
THICK.ET, *s.*, moita, matagal.
THICK.LY, *adv.*, espessamente; em camadas grossas.
THICK.NESS, *s.*, espessura, grossura, densidade.
THICK.SET, *adj.*, robusto, atarracado.
THIEF, *s.*, ladrão, gatuno.
THIEVE, *v.*, roubar, furtar, surrupiar.
THIGH, *s.*, coxa.
THIGH.BONE, *s.*, *Anat.*, fêmur.
THIM.BLE, *s.*, dedal.
THIN, *v.*, afinar, adelgar, diminuir; *adj.*, fino, estreito, magro, delgado, franzino.
THINE, *pron.*, o teu, a tua, os teus, as tuas.
THING, *s.*, coisa, objeto, assunto, tema; *pl.* pertences, objetos.
THINK, *v.*, pensar, achar, imaginar.
THINK.ER, *s.*, pensador, raciocinador.
THINK.ING, *s.*, pensamento, meditação, raciocínio, reflexão.
THIN.LY, *adv.*, em fatias finas, em camadas finas.
THIN.NER, *s.*, *Quím.*, tíner.
THIN.NESS, *s.*, magreza, tenuidade.
THIRD, *num.*, terceiro, terço.
THIRD-CLASS,
THIRD.ING, *s.*, a terça parte.
THIRD.LY, *adv.*, em terceiro lugar.
THIRST, *s.*, sede.
THIRSTY, *adj.*, sedento.
THIR.TEEN, *num.*, treze.
THIR.TEENTH, *num.*, décimo terceiro.
THIR.TI.ETH, *num.*, trigésimo.
THIR.TY, *num.*, trinta.
THIS, *pron.*, este, esta, isto.
THIS.TLE, *s.*, cardo (planta com espinhos); *adv.*, para cá.
THITH.ER, *adj.*, de lá; *adv.*, para ali, para lá.
THONG, *s.*, taga (de banho); *US* sandália.
THO.RAC.IC, *adj.*, torácico.
THO.RAX, *s.*, tórax.
THORN, *s.*, espinho.
THORN.Y, *adj.*, espinhento.
THOR.OUGH, *adj.*, minucioso, detalhado, metódico.
THOR.OUGH.BRED, *s.*, puro-sangue; *adj.*, bem-educado.
THOR.OUGH.FARE, *s.*, via, passagem, caminho.
THOR.OUGH.LY, *adv.*, completamente; a fundo.
THOR.OUGH.NESS, *s.*, profundade, eficácia, perfeição.
THOSE, *pron.*, *pl.*, esses, essas.
THOUGH, *conj.*, embora, se bem que, no entanto.
THOUGHT, *s.*, pensamento, ideia, reflexão, meditação.
THOUGHT.FUL, *adj.*, pensativo, meditativo.
THOUGHT.FUL.NESS, *s.*, ar pensativo; meditação, consideração.
THOUGHT.LESS, *adj.*, indelicado; irrefletido, imprudente.
THOUGHT.LESS.NESS, descuido, negligência; indelicadeza.
THOU.SAND, *num.*, mil.
THOU.SANDTH, *num.*, milésimo.
THRASH, *s.*, sova, tunda, espancamento; *v.*, surrar, bater, espancar.
THRASH.ING, *s.*, surra, sova, espancamento.
THREAD, *s.*, fio, barbante; linha (que passa na agulha); *v.*, enfiar (na agulha); passar; abrir caminho.
THREAD.BARE, *adj.*, puído, gasto; manjado (argumento).

THREAT, *s.*, ameaça, perigo.
THREAT.EN, *v.*, ameaçar, meter medo.
THREAT.EN.ING, *adj.*, ameaçador.
THREE, *s.*, três.
THREE.FOLD, *num.*, triplo.
THRESH, *v.*, debulhar.
THREE.SOME, *s.*, trio; tríade, trindade.
THRESH.OLD, *s.*, limiar; soleira (da porta).
THRICE, *adv.*, três vezes.
THRIFT, *s.*, economia, poupança.
THRIFT.NESS, *s.*, economia, parcimônia.
THRILL, *s.*, vibração, estremecimento, emoção, sensação; *v.*, emocionar, entusiasmar; vibrar, tremer.
THRILLED, *adj.*, emocionado; entusiasmado, excitado.
THRILL.ER, *s.*, filme ou romance de suspense.
THRILL.ING, *adj.*, emocionante, animado.
THRIVE, *v.*, crescer, desenvolver(-se), prosperar.
THRIVING, *adj.*, próspero; florescente.
THROAT, *s.*, garganta.
THROAT.Y, *adj.*, gutural, rouco.
THROB, *s.*, batimento, pulso, pulsação, emoção; *v.*, pulsar, bater, palpitar.
THROE, *s.*, espasmo, pontada; dor forte; agonia; *throes* *s.pl.*: dores do parto.
THROM.BO.SIS, *s.*, *Med.*, trombose.
THRONE, *s.*, trono.
THRONG, *s.*, aglomeração, multidão; *v.*, aglomerar(-se), amontoar(-se).
THROT.TLE, *s.*, acelerador (automóvel), afogador; válvula (do controle do combustível).
THROUGH, *prep.*, por, através de, durante, por meio de, devido a; *adj.*, direto.
THROUGH.OUT, *prep.*, durante todo, por todo; por; *adv.*, completamente; o tempo todo.
THROUGH.PUT, *s.*, rendimento (trabalho); taxa de transferência.
THROW, *s.*, arremesso, tiro, lançamento; *v.*, jogar, atirar, lançar, arremessar.
THROW.AWAY, *adj.*, descartável.
THROW.BACK, *s.*, retrocesso; regresso; revés.
THROW-IN, *s.*, *Esp.*, arremesso de mão, lateral (futebol).
THROWN, *v.*, *pp* de *throw*: arremessar; *adj.*, torcido (seda).
THRU, *prep.*, através.
THRUSH, *s.*, *Zool.*, tordo, melro; *Med.*, afta.
THRUST, *s.*, empuxo, impulso, golpe; *v.*, empurrar, impulsionar.
THRUST.ING, *s.*, empurrão; agressivo.
THRU.WAY, *s.* US autoestrada, rodovia.
THUD, *s.*, baque; *v.*, dar um baque seco; baquear.
THUG, *s.*, criminoso, facínora, bandido.
THUMB, *s.*, polegar.
THUMB.NAIL, *s.*, unha do polegar; *adj.*, breve, conciso.
THUMP, *s.*, murro, soco, golpe, baque; *v.*, esmurrar, golpear.
THUND.ER, *s.*, trovão; *v.*, trovejar.
THUN.DER.BOLT, *s.*, raio, corisco.
THUN.DER.CLAP, *s.*, trovão, trovoada.
THUN.DER.CLOUD, *s.*, nuvem carregada (que relampeja).
THUN.DER.ING, *adj.*, enorme, descomunal; fulminante.
THUN.DER.OUS, *adj.*, fulminante, pavoroso, terrível.
THUN.DER.STORM, *s.*, temporal.
THUN.DER.STRUCK, *adj.*, *fig.*, atônito; *Lit.*, fulminado.

THUNDERY ·· 631 ·· TOASTER

THUN.DER.Y, *adj.*, carregado, tempestuoso.
THURS.DAY, *s.*, quinta-feira.
THUS, *adv.*, assim, dessa maneira.
THWART, *v.*, frustrar, impedir.
THYME, *s.*, tomilho.
THY.ROID, *s.*, tiroide.
TI.AR.A, *s.*, tiara; dignidade pontifícia.
TIB.IA, *s.*, *Anat.*, tíbia.
TIC, *s.*, tique, cacoete.
TICK, *s.*, tique-taque, sinal, marca; carrapato; *v.*, marcar, produzir o som de tique-taque.
TICK.ET, *s.*, tíquete, bilhete, passagem, entrada para espetáculo, etiqueta.
TICK.LE, *s.*, titilação, coceira; *v.*, coçar, fazer cócegas.
TICK.LING, *s.*, cócegas.
TICK.LISH, *adj.*, coceguento; sensível; crítico.
TICK-TACK, *s.*, tique-taque.
TICK-TACK-TOE, *s.*, *US* jogo da velha.
TID.DLY, *adj.*, *gír.*, minúsculo; *gír.*, *UK* bebaço.
TIDE, *s.*, maré, fluxo, tendência do tempo; *v.*, navegar com a maré.
TIDE.MARK, *s.*, linha ou marca de maré alta.
TI.DI.LY, *adv.*, ordenadamente, asseadamente.
TI.DI.NESS, *s.*, asseio, higiene.
TID.INGS, *s. pl.*, *Lit.*, novas; informações.
TI.DY, *adj.*, asseado, arrumado; *v.*, arrumar, limpar.
TIE, *s.*, fita, corda, cordel; vínculo; *v.*, amarrar, ligar, atar.
TIE BREAK, *s.*, *Esp.*, último *set* para desempatar (tênis).
TIE.PIN, *s.*, alfinete de gravata.
TIER, *s.*, camada, fileira, fila; renque; *v.*, empilhar, enfileirar.
TIFF, *s.*, trago, gole; *v.*, beber, tragar, engolir.
TI.GER, *s.*, tigre.
TI.GER.ISH, *adj.*, feroz, próprio do tigre.
TIGHT, *adj.*, apertado, justo; teso, esticado, firme; *adv.*, firmemente.
TIGHT.EN, *v.*, esticar, apertar, estender.
TIGHT.FIST.ED, *s.*, *col.*, pão-duro.
TIGHT.NESS, *s.*, aperto.
TIGHT-LIPPED, *adj.*, calado; de poucas palavras.
TIGHT.LY, *adv.*, justamente, firmemente; bem esticado.
TIGHT.ROPE, *s.*, corda bamba.
TI.GRESS, *s.*, tigre fêmea.
TIL.DE, *s.*, til.
TILE, *s.*, telha, azulejo, ladrilho.
TILED, *adj.*, telha (cobertura); ladrilhado, azulejado.
TIL.ING, *s.*, colocação de ladrilhos; pisos, azulejos, telhas.
TILL, *s.*, caixa registradora; *conj.*, até que; *v.*, amanhar, cultivar a terra.
TILL.AGE, *s.*, lavoura, agricultura.
TIL.LER, *s.*, lavrador, agricultor, colono, sitiante.
TILT, *s.*, declive, inclinação; lona, toldo; *v.*, inclinar, pender, balançar; cobrir com lona.
TIM.BER, *s.*, madeira (de construção); viga; *adj.*, de madeira.
TIM.BERED, *adj.*, de madeira, revestido com madeira.
TIME, *s.*, tempo, época, era, hora, momento; *v.*, medir o tempo, marcar o tempo.
TIME BOMB, *s.*, bomba-relógio.
TIMED, *adj.*, cronometrado, com tempo determinado.
TIME.KEEP.ER, *s.*, indivíduo pontual.
TIME.LESS, *adj.*, perene, eterno, perpétuo.
TIME.LY, *adj.*, oportuno, em tempo; *adv.*, cedo, em boa hora.

TIME OFF, *s.*, folga (tempo de folga).
TIME.PIECE, *s.*, relógio, cronômetro.
TIMER, *s.*, temporizador, cronômetro; *Esp.*, cronometrista.
TIME-SAV.ING, *adj.*, que economiza tempo.
TIME.TA.BLE, *s.*, horário; quadro de horários.
TIME ZONE, *s.*, fuso horário.
TIM.ID, *adj.*, tímido, timorato, acanhado.
TI.MID.I.TY, *s.*, timidez, acanhamento, vergonha.
TIM.ID.LY, *adv.*, timidamente.
TIM.ING, *s.*, regulação de tempo (para algo); cronometragem; *timing*.
TIM.O.ROUS, *adj.*, tímido, acanhado, envergonhado.
TIM.PA.NO, *s.*, *Mús.*, tímpano.
TIN, *s.*, estanho, lata de estanho.
TIN CAN, *s.*, lata.
TINC.TURE, *s.*, tintura, tingimento; *v.*, tingir, colorir.
TIN.DER.BOX, *s.*, isqueiro.
TIN.FOIL, *s.*, papel alumínio; folha de estanho.
TINGE, *s.*, tom, matiz, coloração; toque (de sabor), sensação.
TIN.GLE, *s.*, formigamento; *v.*, formigar.
TI.NI.NESS, *s.*, pequenez, finura.
TINK.ER, *s.*, funileiro; fig.; remendagem; *adj.*, biltre; atabalhoado; *v.*, remendar, soldar.
TIN.KLE, *v.*, tinir, fazer tinir.
TIN.KLING, *s.*, tinido.
TIN.MAN, *s.*, funileiro.
TINNED, *adj.*, US enlatado (comida).
TIN-O.PEN.ER, *s.*, abridor de lata.
TIN.SEL, *s.*, lantejoula; enfeite que cintila.
TINT, *s.*, tinta para cabelo, matiz, cor.
TINTED, *adj.*, pintado, colorido, tingido.
TINY, *adj.*, diminuto, minúsculo.
TIP, *s.*, ponta, fim, gorjeta; *v.*, dar uma gorjeta.
TIP.PLE, *s.*, bebida alcoólica; *v.*, beber sempre bebida alcoólica.
TIP.PLER, *s.*, bebedor.
TIP.PLING, *s.*, bebedeira, embriaguez.
TIP.TOE, *s.*, ponta do pé; *v.*, andar nas pontas dos pés.
TI.RADE, *s.*, tirada, discurso, diatribe, crítica violenta.
TIRE, *s.*, enfeite, adorno; pneu; *v.*, cansar-se, aborrecer, aborrecer-se; enfeitar.
TIRED, *adj.*, cansado, esgotado.
TIRED.NESS, *s.*, cansaço, fadiga.
TIRE.LESS, *s.*, cançasso.
TIRE.SOME, *adj.*, cansativo, enfadonho.
TIR.ING, *adj.*, enfadonho, fatigante.
TI.SANE, *s.*, tisana, infusão.
TIS.SUE, *s.*, tecido, lenço de papel.
TITHE, *s.*, dízimo, décima parte.
TIT.IL.LATE, *v.*, excitar(-se), estimular.
TIT.I.VATE, *v.*, arrumar(-se), enfeitar(-se), ataviar(-se).
TI.TLE, *s.*, título.
TI.TLED, *adj.*, nobre, com título de nobreza.
TIT.TER, *s.*, riso nervoso; *v.*, rir baixinho.
TIT.U.LAR, *adj.*, *s.*, titular.
TO, *prep.*, para, a, até, de; *adv.*, em direção a, para diante.
TOAD, *s.*, *Zool.*, sapo.
TOAD.STOOL, *s.*, cogumelo venenoso.
TOAD.Y, *adj.*, bajulador, servil, adulador.
TOAST, *s.*, torrada, pão torrado; *v.*, torrar.
TOAST.ER, *s.*, torradeira.

TOBACCO · · 632 · · TOTEM

TO.BAC.CO, s., tabaco, fumo.
TO.BA.CO.NIST, s., vendedor de tabaco.
TO.BOG.GAN, s., tobogã.
TOD, s., raposa.
TO.DAY, adv., hoje.
TOD.DLE, s., passo incerto; v., dar os primeiros passos, (como criança); vagar.
TOD.DLER, s., criança que começa a andar.
TOD.DY, s., grogue; ponche; suco de certas palmeiras.
TO-DO, s., gír., confusão, tumulto.
TOE, s., dedo do pé, bico do sapato.
TOE.HOLD, s., ponto de apoio (para o pé); fig., trampolim.
TOE.NAIL, s., unha do pé.
TOF.FEE, s., caramelo, bala.
TO.FU, s., tofu (tipo de queijo de soja japonês).
TO.GA, s., toga.
TO.GETH.ER, adv., juntos.
TO.GE.THER.NESS, s., união (familiar); camaradagem.
TO.GO, s., Togo (país).
TO.GO.LESE, s., adj., togolês.
TOGS, s. pl., traje, roupa.
TOIL, s., afã, labuta, trabalho, faina; v., trabalhar, labutar.
TOI.LET, s., banheiro, privada; local para higiene pessoal.
TOI.LET BAG, s., nécessaire.
TOI.LET PA.PER, s., papel higiênico.
TO.KEN, s., prova, símbolo, sinal, ficha.
TOL.ER.A.BIL.I.TY, s., tolerabilidade.
TOL.ER.A.BLE, adj., tolerável; sofrível.
TOL.ER.A.BLY, adv., toleravelmente, regularmente.
TOL.ER.ANCE, s., tolerância.
TOL.ER.ANT, adj., tolerante.
TOL.ER.ATE, v., tolerar, suportar, permitir.
TOL.ER.A.TION, s., tolerância.
TOLL, s., taxa, tributo, pedágio; badalada (de sino); v., cobrar taxas, tributar; dobrar os sinos.
TOLL.BOOTH, s., cabine de pedágio.
TOLL-FREE, adj., livre de taxa, gratuito.
TO.MA.TO, s., tomate.
TOMB, s., túmulo, sepultura, cova, tumba.
TOMB.STONE, s., lápide, pedra do túmulo.
TOM.CAT, s., gato.
TOME, s., tomo, volume, exemplar.
TOM.MY, s., soldado do exército inglês.
TO.MOR.ROW, adv., amanhã.
TON, s., tonelada.
TO.NAL, adj., tonal (em relação à tonalidade).
TO.NAL.I.TY, s., tonalidade, tom.
TONE, s., tom, tonalidade; v., entoar, dar o tom.
TON.ER, s., tônico; tintura; toner (para fotocopiadora).
TONGS, s. pl., pinça, tenaz.
TONGUE, s., língua.
TON.IC, adj., tônico.
TO.NIGHT, adv., esta noite, hoje, hoje à noite.
TON.NAGE, s., tonelagem.
TONNE, s., tonelada métrica.
TON.SIL, s., amígdala.
TON.SIL.LI.TIS, s., amigdalite.
TOO, adv., demais, muito, demasiadamente.
TOOL, s., ferramenta, ferramental.
TOOL BOX, s., caixa de ferramentas.
TOOT, s., buzinada; v., buzinar.

TOOTH, s., dente.
TOOTH.ACHE, s., dor de dentes.
TOOTH.BRUSH, s., escova de dentes.
TOOTH.LESS, adj., desdentado.
TOOTH.PASTE, s., pasta de dentes.
TOOTH.PICK, s., palito para dentes.
TOO.TLE, v., flautear baixo; col., passear.
TOP, s., cume, cimo, pico; adj., máximo, altíssimo; v., exceder, estar alto.
TO.PAZ, s., topázio.
TOP.COAT, s., sobretudo (leve).
TOP HAT, s., cartola.
TOP.IC, s., tópico, tema, assunto.
TOP.IC.AL, adj., atual, da atualidade; tópico.
TOP.KNOT, s., topete (cabelo).
TOP.LESS, s., topless, falta da parte superior do biquíni ou maiô.
TOP-LEVEL, adj., referente ao mais alto nível.
TOP.MOST, adj., o mais alto, supremo.
TO.POG.RA.PHER, s., topógrafo.
TO.POG.RA.PHY, s., topografia.
TOPPED, adj., coberto de (ou por algo).
TOP.PING, s., cobertura; Cul., glacê.
TOP.PLE, v., tombar, derrubar; vir abaixo, fazer cair.
TOP.RANK.ING, adj., proeminente; do mais alto nível.
TOP-SECRET, adj., ultra secreto, secretíssimo.
TOP.SOIL, s., parte superficial do solo, solo arável.
TORCH, s., tocha, archote.
TO.RE.A.DOR, s., toureiro.
TOR.MENT, s., tormento, aflição, suplício, dor; v., atormentar, afligir.
TOR.MENT.OR, s., atormentador.
TOR.NA.DO, s., tornado, furacão.
TOR.PE.DO, s., torpedo.
TOR.PID.I.TY, s., torpor, entorpecimento, inanição.
TOR.POR, s., torpor, inércia.
TOR.RE.FAC.TION, s., torrefação.
TOR.RE.FY, v., torrar.
TOR.RENT, s., torrente, caudal.
TOR.REN.TIAL, adj., torrencial.
TOR.RID, adj., tórrido, causticante.
TOR.SION, s., torção.
TOR.SO, s., torso, busto.
TORT, s., dano, prejuízo.
TORT.OISE, s., Zool., tartaruga.
TORT.OISE SHELL, s., couraça de tartaruga; adj., de tartaruga.
TOR.TU.OUS, adj., tortuoso, sinuoso; traiçoeiro.
TOR.TU.OS.I.TY, s., tortuosidade.
TOR.TURE, s., tortura, suplício; v., torturar, supliciar.
TOR.TUR.ER, s., torturador.
TOSS, v., atirar, arremessar, lançar.
TO.TAL, s., total, soma total; adj., total; v., somar, calcular, totalizar.
TO.TAL.I.TAR.I.AN, s., adepto do totalitarismo; adj., totalitário.
TO.TAL.I.TAR.I.AN.ISM, s., totalitarismo.
TO.TAL.I.TY, s., totalidade, soma total.
TO.TAL.IZE(ISE), v., totalizar.
TO.TAL.I.ZER(ISER), s., totalizador.
TO.TAL.LY, adv., totalmente.
TO.TEM, s., totem.

TOTTER · 633 · TRANSFORMATION

TOT.TER, s., cambaleio; v., cambalear.

TOUCH, s., toque, tato, contato, apalpadela; v., tocar, apalpar, contatar.

TOUCH.A.BLE, adj., palpável, contatável.

TOUCH.DOWN, s., aterrissagem, aterragem (avião).

TOUCHED, adj., comovido.

TOUCH.ING, adj., tocante, comovente.

TOUCH.STONE, s., pedra de toque, padrão, critério, medida.

TOUCH.Y, adj., sensível, irritável.

TOUGH, s., valentão; adj., resistente, forte, robusto; duro, difícil.

TOUGH.EN, v., endurecer, fortalecer, enrijecer.

TOUGH.NESS, s., firmeza, força; resistência.

TOU.PEE, s., peruca.

TOUR, s., viagem, excursão; v., viajar, excursionar.

TOUR.ER, s., turista; carro de turismo.

TOUR.ING, adj., itinerante, de turismo; em turnê.

TOUR.ISM, s., turismo.

TOUR.IST, s., turista, viajante.

TOUR.IST.Y, adj., pej., turístico (para gringo).

TOUR.NA.MENT, s., torneio.

TOUR.NI.QUET, s., torniquete.

TOU.SLE, v., despentear, desgrenhar.

TOUT, s., cambista; v., agenciar, revender.

TOW, s., reboque; v., rebocar.

TO.WARD, TO.WARDS, prep., para, em direção a; defronte de; com relação a.

TOW.AGE, s., reboque, reboque de carro.

TO.WARD, prep., em direção a.

TOW.EL, s., toalha.

TOW.ER, s., torre, torreão, espigão.

TOW.ER.ING, adj., altíssimo, muito alto; muito grande.

TOWN, s., cidade.

TOWN COUN.CIL, s., câmara municipal.

TOWN.ISH, adj., urbano, citadino.

TOWN PLAN.NING, s., urbanismo.

TOWN.SHIP, s., distrito municipal; municipalidade.

TOW TRUCK, s., US guincho, reboque.

TOX.IC, adj., tóxico.

TOX.I.CANT, s., veneno, tóxico.

TOX.IN, s., toxina.

TOY, s., brinquedo.

TOY.SHOP, s., loja de brinquedos.

TRACE, s., traço, vestígio, sinal; v., traçar, verificar, seguir os vestígios.

TRA.CING, s., decalque, cópia (desenho no traço).

TRACK, s., sinal, marca, vestígio, caminho, trajetória; v., seguir a pista.

TRACK.AGE, s., reboque.

TRACK.ING, s., reboque.

TRACK.SUIT, s., abrigo esportivo.

TRACT, s., região, localidade, zona; panfleto.

TRAC.TA.BIL.I.TY, s., afabilidade, delicadeza.

TRAC.TATE, s., tratado, discurso.

TRAC.TION, s., tração.

TRAC.TOR, s., trator.

TRADE, s., comércio, negócio; v., comerciar, negociar.

TRADE BAR.RI.ER, s., barreira comercial, embargo comercial.

TRADE FAIR, s., feira industrial.

TRADE.MARK, s., marca registrada.

TRADE NAME, s., nome comercial, Com., razão social.

TRAD.ER, s., comerciante, negociante.

TRADES.MAN, s., comerciante, negociante.

TRADE UN.ION, s., sindicato trabalhista.

TRAD.ING, s., comércio; adj., mercantil.

TRA.DI.TION, s., tradição.

TRA.DI.TION.AL, adj., tradicional.

TRA.DI.TION.AL.LY, adv., tradicionalmente.

TRAF.FIC, s., tráfico, trânsito, tráfego.

TRAF.FIC CIR.CLE, s., US anel viário.

TRAF.FIC IS.LAND, s., canteiro central de uma estrada (separando as pistas).

TRAF.FICK.ER, s., traficante.

TRAF.FIC LIGHT, s., semáforo.

TRAG.E.DY, s., tragédia.

TRAG.IC, adj., trágico.

TRAG.IC.AL.LY, adv., tragicamente.

TRAIL, s., trilha, rastro; faro; picada; v., arrastar; rastejar; andar atrás de; andar lentamente; Esp., perder (jogo).

TRAIL.ER, s., reboque, treiler, amostra de trechos de um filme.

TRAIL.ING, s., reboque, treiler.

TRAIN, s., trem, sucessão de fatos; v., treinar, capacitar, preparar.

TRAINED, adj., treinado, especializado.

TRAIN.EE, s., aprendiz, estagiário.

TRAIN.ER, s., treinador, instrutor.

TRAIN.ING, s., treino, treinamento; instrução; adj., de treino.

TRAIPSE, v., col., vaguear, vadiar.

TRAIT, s., traço, sinal, caráter, característica, predicado.

TRAI.TOR, s., traidor.

TRAI.TRESS, s., traidora.

TRA.JECT, s., trajeto, roteiro.

TRA.JEC.TO.RY, s., trajetória.

TRAM, s., bonde; tram car: bonde elétrico.

TRAMP, s., vagabundo.

TRAM.PLE, s., barulho de pisar, tropel; v., pisar; calcar; esmagar.

TRAM.PO.LINE, s., trampolim.

TRANCE, s., transe, torpor, êxtase.

TRAN.QUIL, adj., Lit., tranquilo.

TRAN.QUIL.LI.TY, TRAN.QUIL.I.TY US, s., tranquilidade.

TRAN.QUIL.LIZE UK, **TRAN.QUIL.IZE** US, v., tranquilizar.

TRAN.QUIL.LIZER UK, **TRAN.QUIL.IZER** US, s., tranquilizador.

TRANS.ACT, v., negociar, comerciar.

TRANS.AC.TION, s., transação, negócio.

TRANS.AT.LAN.TIC, adj., transatlântico.

TRANS.CEIV.ER, s., aparelho de rádio transmissor-receptor.

TRAN.SCEND, v., transcender, exceder, ir além.

TRAN.SCEN.DENCE, s., transcendência.

TRAN.SCRIBE, v., transcrever, reproduzir.

TRAN.SCRIPT, s., transcrição, cópia, reprodução.

TRANS.FER, v., transferir, mudar, deslocar.

TRANS.FER.A.BLE, adj., transferível.

TRANS.FER.ENCE, s., transferência.

TRANS.FIG.U.RA.TION, s., transfiguração.

TRANS.FIG.URE, v., transfigurar.

TRANS.FIX, v., trespassar.

TRANS.FORM, v., transformar, mudar.

TRANS.FOR.MA.TION, s., transformação, mudança.

TRANSFORMER · 634 · TRICKERY

TRANS.FORM.ER, *s.*, transformador.
TRANS.FU.SION, *s.*, transfusão.
TRANS.GEN.IC, *adj.*, transgênico, transgenético.
TRANS.GRESS, *v.*, transgredir, violar, desrespeitar.
TRANS.GRES.SION, *s.*, transgressão, violação; desrespeito.
TRAN.SIENT, *adj.*, transitório, pessoa em trânsito; *adj.*, transitório, breve.
TRAN.SIT, *s.*, trânsito, tráfego, passagem.
TRAN.SI.TION, *s.*, transição, passagem, mudança.
TRAN.SI.TION.AL, *adj.*, transicional.
TRAN.SI.TIVE, *adj.*, transitivo.
TRAN.SI.TO.RY, *adj.*, transitório, passageiro.
TRANS.LATE, *s.*, verter, traduzir.
TRANS.LA.TION, *s.*, tradução, versão, interpretação; *Fis.*, translação.
TRANS.LA.TOR, *s.*, tradutor, intérprete.
TRANS.LU.CENT, *adj.*, translúcido.
TRANS.MI.GRA.TION, *s.*, transmigração.
TRANS.MIS.SION, *s.*, transmissão.
TRANS.MIT, *v.*, transmitir, enviar, remeter, mandar.
TRANS.MIT.TER, *s.*, transmissor.
TRANS.MU.TA.TION, *s.*, transmutação.
TRAN.SOM, *s.*, trave, travessa.
TRANS.PAR.EN.CY, *s.*, transparência, diafaneidade.
TRANS.PAR.ENT, *adj.*, transparente; evidente, óbvio.
TRAN.SPIRE, *v.*, transpirar, suar; tornar público.
TRANS.PLANT, *v.*, transplantar; *s.*, transplante.
TRANS.PORT, *s.*, transporte; *v.*, transportar.
TRANS.PORT.A.BIL.I.TY, *s.*, possibilidade de transporte.
TRANS.PORT.A.BLE, *adj.*, transportável.
TRANS.POR.TA.TION, *s.*, transporte.
TRANS.PORT.ER, *s.*, cegonheira (caminhão de transporte de automóveis).
TRANS.POSE, *v.*, transpor.
TRANS.SEX.U.AL, *adj.*, transexual.
TRANS.VER.SAL, *adj.*, transversal.
TRANS.VER.SAL.I.TY, *s.*, transversalidade.
TRANS.VES.TITE, *s.*, travesti.
TRAP, *s.*, armadilha, arapuca; cilada, ardil; *v.*, armar (alçapão); ficar preso, pegar, deter.
TRA.PEZE, *s.*, trapézio.
TRAP.PER, *s.*, caçador.
TRAP.PINGS, *s. pl.*, arreio decorado; *fig.*, decoração, pompa.
TRASH, *s.*, lixo, rejeitos.
TRASH.CAN, *s.*, *US* lata do lixo.
TRASHY, *adj.*, desprezível, descartável.
TRAU.MA, *s.*, trauma.
TRAU.MAT.IC, *adj.*, traumático.
TRAU.MA.TIZE(-ISE), *v.*, traumatizar, angustiar, afligir.
TRAV.EL, *s.*, viagem; *v.*, viajar, percorrer lugares.
TRAV.EL A.GEN.CY, *s.*, agência de viagens.
TRAV.EL A.GENT, *s.*, agente de viagens.
TRAV.ELLED *UK*, **TRAV.ELED** *US*, *adj.*, viajado, com experiência.
TRAV.EL.LER *UK*, **TRAV.EL.ER** *US*, *s.*, caixeiro viajante.
TRAV.EL.LING *UK*, **TRAV.EL.ING** *US*, *s.*, viagem; *adj.*, de viagem, viajante; itinerante.
TRAV.EL.LING SALES.MAN, *s.*, caixeiro-viajante.
TRAVERSE, *s.*, travessia; passagem; *v.*, atravessar.
TRAV.ES.TY, *s.*, paródia.
TRAWL, *s.*, rede de arrasto; arrastão; espinhel; *v.*, pescar

com rede de arrasto; investigar; vasculhar.
TRAWL.ER, *s.*, *Náut.*, traineira.
TRAY, *s.*, bandeja, cesta, cesto.
TREACH.ER.OUS, *adj.*, traidor, traiçoeiro; *adv.*, traiçoeiramente.
TREACH.ER.Y, *s.*, traição.
TREA.CLE, *s.*, *UK* melado.
TREAD, *s.*, banda de rodagem (pneu); sola; passos; *v.*, pisar, esmagar com os pés.
TREAD.LE, *s.*, pedal, *v.*, pedalar.
TREAD.MILL, *s.*, esteira (para exercícios); roda de moinho.
TREA.SON, *s.*, traição.
TREA.SURE, *s.*, tesouro, joia; *v.*, apreciar, admirar.
TREA.SUR.ER, *s.*, tesoureiro.
TREA.SUR.Y, *s.*, tesouraria; departamento de finanças; *Treasury Departmen: US* Ministério da Fazenda.
TREAT, *s.*, festim, prazer, satisfação.
TREAT.MENT, *s.*, tratamento.
TREB.LE CLEF, *s.*, *Mús.*, clave de sol.
TREA.TY, *s.*, tratado, acordo, combinação.
TRE.BLE, *adj.*, tríplice; *v.*, triplicar.
TREE, *s.*, árvore, planta.
TREE-LINED, *adj.*, arborizado.
TREE-TRUNK, *s.*, tronco (de árvore).
TRE.FOIL, *s.*, trevo, folha com três pontas.
TREK, *s.*, jornada, viagem, caminhada.
TREL.LIS, *s.*, latada, pérgola.
TREM.BLE, *v.*, tremer.
TER.MEN.DOUS, *adj.*, tremendo, enorme, espantoso.
TER.MEN.DOUS.LY, *adv.*, tremendamente.
TREM.OR, *s.*, tremor, tremida.
TREM.U.LANT, *adj.*, trêmulo, tremente.
TREM.U.LOUS, *adj.*, trêmulo, vacilante.
TRENCH, *s.*, trincheira.
TRENCH.ANT, *adj.*, mordaz, agudo; sincero.
TREND, *s.*, tendência, pendor, inclinação.
TREP.I.DA.TION, *s.*, trepidação, exaltação, alarme.
TRES.PASS, *s.*, intrusão, delito, abuso; pecado; *v.*, invadir, abusar, violar, transgredir.
TRES.PASS.ER, *s.*, invasor, transgressor, violador.
TRESS, *s.*, trança, madeixa.
TRES.TLE, *s.*, cavalete.
TREY, *s.*, três, terno.
TRI.AL, *s.*, *Jur.*, julgamento, interrogatório; teste; experimento; *adj.*, judicial; experimental.
TRI.AN.GLE, *s.*, triângulo.
TRI.AN.GU.LAR, *adj.*, triangular.
TRIATH.LON, *s.*, *Esp.*, triatlo.
TRIB.AL, *adj.*, tribal; *adv.*, de modo tribal.
TRIBE, *s.*, tribo.
TRIB.U.LA.TION, *s.*, tribulação, sofrimento, tormento.
TRI.BU.NAL, *s.*, tribunal.
TRI.BUNE, *s.*, tribuna; tribuno, orador.
TRIB.U.TAR.Y, *s.*, *Geogr.*, afluente; *adj.*, afluente; tributável, tributário.
TRIB.UTE, *s.*, tributo, homenagem.
TRICE, *v.*, levantar; *Náut.*, içar; amarrar; *in a ~*: num instante.
TRI.CEPS, *s.*, *Anat.*, tríceps.
TRICK, *s.*, truque, habilidade, peça, fraude, logro.
TRICK.ER, *s.*, enganador, trapaceiro.
TRICK.ER.Y, *s.*, trapaça, malandragem.

TRICKLE   •• 635 ••   TRUSTER

TRICK.LE, *s.*, fio (de água); gotejamento, pingo; *v.*, gotejar, escoar.

TRICK.STER, *s.*, trapaceiro, velhaco, impostor.

TRICKSY, *s.*, brincalhão.

TRICK.Y, *adj.*, enrolado, complicado; enganador.

TRI.COT, *s.*, tricô; roupa de malha.

TRI.CY.CLE, *s.*, triciclo.

TRI.DENT, *s.*, tridente.

TRIED, *v.*, *ps* e *pp* de *try*; *adj.*, provado, experimentado.

TRI.EN.NI.AL, *adj.*, trienal; *s.*, triênio.

TRI.ER, *s.*, batalhador; provador

TRI.FLE, *s.*, ninharia; *Cul.*, pavê.

TRI.FLING, *adj.*, *pej.*, insignificante, frívolo.

TRIG.GER, *s.*, gatilho.

TRIG.O.NOM.E.TRY, *s.*, trigonometria.

TRIL.BY, *s.*, chapéu de feltro.

TRILL, *s.*, gorjeio; *v.*, trilar, gorjear.

TRIL.LION, *s.*, *US* bilhão; *UK* quintilhão; *trillions*, *s.pl.*: *col.*, um monte de, zilhões.

TRIL.O.GY, *s.*, trilogia.

TRIM, *s.*, decoração, ornamento; *v.*, arranjar, ordenar, organizar, ajustar, equipar.

TRIM.MING, *s.*, enfeite, ornato.

TRIM.NESS, *s.*, asseio, higiene, elegância.

TRIN.I.DAD.IAN, *s.*, *adj.*, trinitário (relativo a, ou habitante de Trinidad e Tobago).

TRIN.KET, *s.*, adorno, enfeite; bijuteria.

TRIN.I.TY, *s.*, trindade.

TRI.NO.MI.AL, *adj.*, *s.*, trinômio.

TRIO, *s.*, trio.

TRIP, *s.*, viagem, excursão; *v.*, andar, caminhar, viajar; tropeçar.

TRI.PAR.TITE, *adj.*, tripartite, tripartido.

TRIPE, *s.*, entranhas, tripas, vísceras, bucho.

TRIPH.THONG, *s.*, tritongo.

TRIP.LE, *s.m.*, *adj.*, triplo, tríplice.

TRIP.LE JUMP, *s.*, *Esp.*, salto triplo.

TRIP.LET, *s.*, trigêmeo.

TRIP.LETS, *s. pl.*, trigêmeos.

TRIP.LI.CATE, *adj.*, triplicado.

TRI.POD, *s.*, tripé.

TRIP.PER, *s.*, escursionista, viajante, turista.

TRIP.WIRE, *s.*, fio que se estica para fazer uma armadilha.

TRI.SYL.LAB.IC, *adj.*, trissilábico.

TRI.SYL.LA.BLE, *s.*, trissílabo.

TRITE, *adj.*, *pej.*, banal, trivial, batido, usado.

TRIT.NESS, *s.*, banalidade, vulgaridade.

TRI.UMPH, *s.*, triunfo, vitória; *v.*, triunfar.

TRI.UM.PHAL, *adj.*, triunfal.

TRI.UM.PHANT, *adj.*, triunfante.

TRI.UM.PHANT.LY, *adv.*, triunfantemente.

TRI.UM.VI.RATE, *s.*, *Hist.*, triunvirato.

TRIV.ET, *s.*, suporte de três pernas para pratos, trempe, tripé.

TRIV.I.A, *s.*, trivialidades.

TRIV.I.AL, *adj.*, trivial, comum, vulgar, ordinário.

TRIV.I.AL.I.TY, *s.*, trivialidade, banalidade.

TRIV.I.AL.IZE(-ISE), *v.*, trivializar.

TRO.JAN, *adj.*, *Hist.*, troiano.

TROLL, *s.*, trasgo, ogro (do mito escandinavo); *v.*, iscar (peixe).

TROL.LEY, *s.*, *US* trole, bonde; *UK* vagonete; carrinho.

TROL.LEY BUS, *s.*, ônibus elétrico.

TROM.BONE, *s.*, *Mús.*, trombone.

TROOP, *s.*, tropa, grupo, bando.

TROOP.ER, *s.*, soldado de cavalaria; *US* polícia militar.

TROOP.SHIP, *s.*, *Náut.*, navio-transporte.

TRO.PHY, *s.*, troféu.

TROP.IC, *s.*, trópico.

TROP.I.CAL, *adj.*, tropical.

TROP.IC OF CAN.CER, *s.*, *Geogr.*, Trópico de Câncer.

TROP.IC OF CAP.RI.CORN, *s.*, *Geogr.*, Trópico de Capricórnio.

TROP.ICS, *s.*, região trópica; *the* ~ : os trópicos.

TROT, *s.*, trote, passo rápido; *v.*, trotar, andar apressadamente.

TROT.TER, *s.*, trotador (cavalo); *gír.*, pé de porco (para alimento).

TROT.TING, *s.*, trote.

TROU.BLE, *s.*, problema, dificuldade, preocupação; *v.*, incomodar, perturbar.

TROU.BLED, *adj.*, preocupado, agitado, perturbado.

TROU.BLE.MAKER, *s.*, desordeiro, encrequeiro, agitador.

TROU.BLER, *s.*, incomodador, perturbador.

TROU.BLE.SHOOT.ER, *s.*, conciliador, árbitro.

TROU.BLE.SOME, *adj.*, incômodo, desagradável.

TROUGH, *s.*, cocho, gamela, tina; calha de moinho; depressão ou parte baixa entre ondas.

TROUNCE, *v.*, castigar, surrar; vencer.

TROUPE, *s.*, trupe, companhia teatral.

TROU.SERS, *s. pl.*, calças compridas.

TROUS.SEAU, *s.*, *Fr.*, enxoval de noiva.

TROUT, *s.*, truta.

TROW, *v.*, pensar, cogitar, refletir, crer.

TROW.EL, *s.*, colher de pedreiro, trolha; pá de jardim; *v.*, alisar reboco com trolha.

TRU.AN.CY, *s.*, ociosidade, falta (na escola).

TRU.ANT, *s.*, ocioso; gazeteiro, aluno que mata aulas.

TRUCE, *s.*, armistício, trégua.

TRUCK, *s.*, caminhão, vagão.

TRUCK.ER, *s.*, caminhoneiro.

TRUCK.ING, *s.*, transporte por caminhão.

TRU.CU.LENCE, *s.*, truculência, barbaridade.

TRU.CU.LENT, *adj.*, truculento.

TRUDGE, *s.*, caminhada difícil; *v.*, caminhar com dificuldade, arrastar-se.

TRUE, *adj.*, verdadeiro, correto, genuíno.

TRUF.FLE, *s.*, trufa.

TRU.ISM, *s.*, truísmo, clichê.

TRU.LY, *adv.*, verdadeiramente, sinceramente.

TRUE.NESS, *s.*, verdade, sinceridade, genuinidade.

TRUMP, *s.*, trunfo (carta); *v.*, trunfar (jogar cartas).

TRUM.PET, *s.*, trombeta.

TRUM.PET.ER, *s.*, *Mús.*, trompetista.

TRUN.CATE, *v.*, truncar, cortar, amputar.

TRUN.CHEON, *s.*, cacete, pau.

TRUN.DLE, *v.*, empurrar; rodar lentamente.

TRUNK, *s.*, trónco, tronco de pessoa, tromba de elefante.

TRUSS, *s.*, *Med.*, cinta para hérnia, funda; *v.*, atar, amarrar, fixar.

TRUST, *s.*, confiança, fé; *v.*, confiar, acreditar, crer.

TRUSTED, *adj.*, confiado, de confiança.

TRUS.TEE, *s.*, curador; membro de conselho diretor.

TRUS.TEE.SHIP, *s.*, curadoria, administração.

TRUST.ER, *s.*, quem confia, fiador.

TRUSTINESS ··· 636 ··· TWILL

TRUST.I.NESS, *s.*, fidelidade, confiança.
TRUST.WOR.THY, *adj.*, fidedigno, honrado, fiel.
TRUST.Y, *adj.*, fiel, confiável.
TRUTH, *s.*, verdade.
TRUTH.FUL, *adj.*, sincero, verdadeiro, verídico.
TRY, *s.*, tentativa; *v.*, julgar, examinar, provar, cansar, fatigar.
TRY.ING, *adj.*, difícil, árduo.
TSAR, *s.*, czar.
T-SHIRT, *s.*, camiseta.
TUB, *s.*, tina, banheira.
TU.BA, *s.*, *Mús.*, tuba.
TUB.BY, *adj.*, gorducho.
TUBE, *s.*, cano, tubo, câmara do pneu; metrô.
TU.BER.CLE, *s.*, tubérculo.
TU.BER.CU.LO.SIS, *s.*, tuberculose.
TU.BER.CU.LOUS, *adj.*, tuberculoso.
TUB.ING, *s.*, tubulação, encanamento.
TUCK, *s.*, dobra, prega; *v.*, comprimir, enfiar, meter.
TUES.DAY, *s.*, terça-feira.
TUFT, *s.*, penacho, tufo.
TUG.BOAT, *s.*, rebocador (barco).
TU.LIP, *s.*, tulipa.
TUM.BLE, *s.*, queda, caída; *v.*, cair, tombar.
TUM.BLE-DOWN, *adj.*, em ruínas; prestes a cair.
TUM.BLER, *s.*, copo; acrobata; pombo volteador; joão-teimoso (boneco).
TU.ME.FAC.TION, *s.*, tumefação, inchamento.
TU.ME.FY, *v.*, inchar, intumescer.
TU.MID, *adj.*, túmido, inchado.
TUM.MY, *s.*, barriga, estômago.
TU.MOUR, **TU.MOR**, *s.*, tumor.
TU.MULT, *s.*, tumulto, confusão, baderna.
TU.MUL.TU.OUS, *adj.*, tumultuoso.
TUN, *s.*, tonel, barril, pipa.
TU.NA, *s.*, *Zool.*, atum.
TUN.DRA, *s.*, *Geogr.*, tundra.
TUNE, *s.*, melodia, tonalidade, canção; *v.*, afinar, sintonizar, cantar afinado.
TUNE.FUL, *adj.*, melodioso, musical.
TUNE.FUL.LY, *adv.*, melodiosamente.
TUNE.LESS, *adj.*, dissonante, sem melodia.
TUNG.STEN, *s.*, *Quím.*, tungstênio.
TU.NIC, *s.*, túnica.
TU.NI.SIA, *s.*, Tunísia.
TU.NI.SIAN, *s.*, *adj.*, tunisiano.
TUN.NEL, *s.*, túnel, galeria.
TUN.NY, *s.*, *Zool.*, atum.
TUR.BAN, *s.*, turbante.
TUR.BID, *adj.*, túrbido, turvo, lodoso; confuso.
TUR.BINE, *s.*, turbina.
TUR.BO, *s.*, turbo.
TUR.BOT, *s.*, *Zool.*, linguado, rodovalho.
TUR.BU.LENCE, *s.*, turbulência.
TUR.BU.LENT, *adj.*, turbulento.
TU.REEN, *s.*, terrina, sopeira.
TURF, *s.*, gramado; turfa; *v.*, cobrir com grama, gramar.
TUR.FY, *adj.*, coberto de grama, gramado, turfoso.
TUR.GID, *adj.*, túrgido, , inchado; *fig.*, empolado.
TURK, *adj.*, *s.*, turco.
TUR.KEY, *s.*, *Zool.*, peru.
TUR.KEY, *s.*, Turquia.

TUR.KI.STAN, **TUR.KE.STAN**, *s.*, Turquistão (país).
TURK.ISH, *s.*, língua turca; *adj.*, turco.
TURK.MEN.I.AN, *adj.*, turcomeno.
TURK.MEN.I.STAN, *s.*, Turcomenistão (país).
TUR.KO.MAN, *s.*, turcomano.
TUR.MOIL, *s.*, desordem, perturbação.
TURN, *s.*, turno, volta, tendência, curva de estrada; *v.*, dar volta, virar, girar.
TURN.A.BOUT, *s.*, reviravolta, mudança radical.
TURN BACK, *v.*, voltar, retornar.
TURN.COAT, *s.*, *pej.*, vira-casaca, desertor.
TURNED OFF, *adj.*, *gír.*, livre do vício da droga, limpo.
TURN.ER, *s.*, torneiro.
TURN.ING, *s.*, torneamento; desvio, travessa; *adj.*, decisivo.
TUR.NIP, *s.*, nabo.
TURN.KEY, *s.*, chaveiro, carcereiro.
TURN.OUT, *s.*, comparecimento (espectador participante).
TURN.OVER, *s.*, rotatividade de empregados; total de negócios.
TURN.PIKE, *s.*, posto de pedágio, estrada com pedágio.
TURN.ROUND, **TURN.A.ROUND**, *s.*, reviravolta; tempo médio de permanência.
TURN.STILE, *s.*, catraca, roleta.
TURN-UP, *s.*, punho; *UK* bainha; *turnup s.*: barra italiana (em calça).
TUR.PEN.TINE, *s.*, terebentina, aguarrás.
TURPS, *s.*, *UK* aguarrás.
TUR.QUOISE, *s.*, turquesa.
TUR.RET, *s.*, torre pequena; *Mil.*, torre de tiro.
TUR.TLE, *s.*, *Zool.*, tartaruga.
TUSK, *s.*, presa.
TUSK.ER, *s.*, animal com grandes dentes (ex.: elefante).
TUS.SLE, *s.*, briga, luta; *v.*, brigar, lutar, disputar.
TU.TE.LAGE, *s.*, tutoria, tutela, guarda.
TU.TE.LAR, *adj.*, tutelar.
TU.TOR, *s.*, tutor, preceptor, professor universitário.
TU.TOR.AGE, *s.*, supervisão, tutela, ensino.
TU.TO.RI.AL, *s.*, tutorial.
TU.TU, *s.*, tutu (roupa de bailarina).
TUX.E.DO, *s.*, *US* traje a rigor, smoking.
TV, *s.*, *abrev.* de *television*: televisão.
TWAD.DLE, *s.*, tagarelice, sem importância; *v.*, tagarelar.
TWANG, *s.*, som metálico, som vibrante, som nasalado.
TWEAK, *s.*, beliscão; *v.*, beliscar.
TWEE, *adj.*, engraçadinho; *pej.*, piegas.
TWEED, *s.*, tecido de lã.
TWEET, *s.*, pio; *v.*, piar.
TWEEZE, *v.*, puxar ou tirar com pinça.
TWEEZ.ERS, *s.*, pinça pequena.
TWELFTH, *num.*, décimo segundo, duodécimo.
TWELVE, *num.*, doze.
TWEN.TIES, *s. pl.*, casa dos vinte (anos ou números de 20 a 29).
TWEN.TI.ETH, *num.*, vigésimo.
TWEN.TY, *num.*, vinte.
TWERP, *s.*, *gír.*, *UK* bobo, imbecil.
TWICE, *adv.*, duas vezes.
TWID.DLE, *v.*, girar, virar; brincar com os dedos polegares.
TWIG, *s.*, graveto, ramo, galho.
TWI.LIGHT, *s.*, crepúsculo.
TWILL, *s.*, sarja (tipo de tecido).

TWIN   •• 637 ••   TYROLEAN

TWIN, *s.*, gêmeo idêntico, gêmeo.
TWIN BEDS, *s. pl.*, duas camas de solteiro.
TWINE, *s.*, cordão, barbante; *v.*, enlaçar, enrolar (em algo).
TWINGE, *s.*, pontada, ferroada; remorso; *v.*, doer, atormentar.
TWIN.KLE, *s.*, cintilação, brilho; *v.*, cintilar, brilhar.
TWIRL, *s.*, giro, rodopio; *v.*, girar, rodopiar; torcer.
TWIRL.ING, *s.*, volta, giro.
TWIST, *s.*, torção, giro, mudança imprevista, tipo de dança; *v.*, torcer, enrolar.
TWIST.ED, *adj.*, torcido; distorcido, deturpado.
TWIST.ER, *s.*, ciclone; US tornado.
TWIST.Y, *adj.*, sinuoso; torcido, tortuoso.
TWIT, *s.*, imbecil, idiota, pateta.
TWITCH, *s.*, puxão, contração, empurrão; *v.*, contrair-se.
TWIT.TER, *s.*, gorjeio, chilro; *v.*, gorjear.
TWO, *num.*, dois.
TWO-FACED, *adj.*, de duas caras, falso.
TWO.FOLD, *num.*, duplo, duplicado.
TWO.SOME, *s.*, casal, par, parelha; grupo de duas pessoas; *adj.*, de dois, de duas (pessoas).
TWO.STEP, *s.*, dança de passo duplo (dois pra lá, dois pra cá).
TWO-WAY, *s.*, dois sentidos, caminho com dois sentidos; *adj.*, de duas vias.
TY.COON, *s.*, magnata.
TYM.PA.NUM, *s.*, tímpano.

TYPE, *s.*, tipo, espécie, padrão; *v.*, datilografar, digitar.
TYPE.FACE, *s.*, tipo de letra.
TYPE.SCRIPT, *s.*, datilografia, cópia datilográfica.
TYPE.SET.TER, *s.*, tipografia; composição (de tipos em tipografia).
TYPE.SET.TING, *s.*, composição (para impressão).
TYPE.WRITE, *v.*, datilografar.
TYPE.WRIT.ER, *s.*, máquina de escrever.
TYPE.WRIT.ING, *s.*, datilografia.
TY.PHOID, *s.*, febre tifoide.
TY.PHOON, *s.*, tufão, furacão.
TY.PHUS, *s.*, tifo.
TYP.I.CAL, *adj.*, típico.
TYPICALLY, *adv.*, tipicamente, habitualmente.
TYP.I.FY, *v.*, tipificar, simbolizar.
TYP.ING, *s.*, datilografia.
TYP.IST, *s.*, datilógrafo, datilógrafa.
TY.PO, *s., col.*, erro tipográfico.
TY.POG.RA.PHER, *s.*, tipógrafo.
TY.POG.RA.PHY, *s.*, tipografia.
TY.RAN.NI.CAL, *adj.*, tirânico.
TYR.AN.NIZE, *v.*, tiranizar, massacrar.
TYR.AN.NY, *s.*, tirania.
TYR.ANT, *s.*, tirano, déspota.
TYRE, *s.*, pneu.
TY.RO.LE.AN, **TY.RO.LESE**, *adj., s.*, tirolês.

U

U, s., vigésima primeira letra do alfabeto inglês.
U.BIQ.UI.TOUS, adj., ubíquo, onipresente.
UBIQ.UI.TY, s., ubiquidade.
UD.DER, s., úbere.
UFO, abrev. de *unidentified flying object*: objeto voador não identificado, OVNI.
UGAN.DA, s., Uganda (país).
UGAN.DAN, s., adj., ugandense.
UG.LI.FY, v., enfear, tornar feio.
UG.LI.NESS, s., feiura, fealdade.
UG.LY, adj., feio, repulsivo, mau, desagradável.
UL.CER, s., úlcera.
UK, abrev. de *United Kingdom*: Reino Unido, RU.
U.KRAINE, s., Ucrânia (país).
U.KRAIN.I.AN, s., adj., ucraniano.
UL.CER.ATE, v., ulcerar, provocar úlcera.
UL.CER.A.TED, adj., ulcerado.
UL.CER.OUS, adj., ulceroso.
UL.STER, s., Irlanda do Norte.
UL.TE.RI.OR, adj., ulterior, posterior.
UL.TI.MATE, adj., último, final.
UL.TI.MATE.LY, adv., finalmente, por fim, enfim.
UL.TI.MA.TUM, s., ultimato.
UL.TRA.MA.RINE, adj., ultramarino.
UL.TRA.SON.IC, adj., ultrassônico.
UL.TRA.SOUND, s., ultrassom.
UL.TRA.VI.O.LET, adj., ultravioleta.
UM.BER, s., sombreado; v., sombrear, provocar sombra.
UM.BIL.I.CAL, adj., umbilical.
UM.BIL.I.CUS, s., Anat., umbigo.
UM.BRA, s., sombra, assombração.
UM.BRAGE, s., sombra, suspeita, desconfiança.
UM.BRA.GEOUS, adj., umbroso, sombrio.
UM.BREL.LA, s., guarda-chuva.
UM.PIRE, s., árbitro de jogo; v., arbitrar, conduzir, apitar.
UMP.TEEN, adj., inúmero, inúmeros.
UMP.TEENTH, adj., num., col., enésimo.
UN.A.BASH.ED, adj., imperturbável; desavergonhado.
UN.A.BAT.ED, adj., incessante, constante; que não diminui.
UN.ABLE, adj., incapaz, inábil, impotente, despreparado.
UN.A.BRIDGED, adj., não abreviado, completo, integral.
UN.AC.CEPT.ABLE, adj., inaceitável.
UN.AC.COUNT.ABLE, adj., inexplicável.
UN.AC.COUNT.A.BLY, adv., inexplicavelmente.
UN.AC.COUNTED FOR, adj., desaparecido, inexplicado; de que não se presta contas.
UN.AC.CUS.TOMED, adj., desacostumado, estranho, inusual.
UN.AD.VISED, adj., indiscreto.
UN.AF.FECT.ED, adj., leal, sincero, discreto, franco, fiel.
UN.AL.LOW.ABLE, adj., inadmissível.
UN.ALTER.ED, adj., inalterado.
UNA.NIM.I.TY, s., unanimidade.

UN.AP.PROVED, adj., desaprovado, não aprovado.
UN.AC.QUAINT.ED, adj., que desconhece, alheio, estranho.
UN.A.FRAID, adj., destemido.
UN.AM.BIG.U.OUS, adj., inequívoco.
U.NA.NIM.I.TY, s., unanimidade.
U.NAN.I.MOUS, adj., unânime.
U.NAN.I.MOUS.LY, adv., unanimemente.
UN.AN.NOUNCED, adj., não anunciado; adv., sem anunciar.
UN.AP.PEAL.ING, adj., desagradável.
UN.AP.PROACH.A.BLE, adj., inacessível, reservado, intratável; incomparável.
UN.ARM, v., desarmar, tornar desarmado.
UN.ARMED, adj., desarmado.
UN.ASHAMED, adj., descarado, desavergonhado.
UN.AT.TACHED, adj., solto, liberado, livre.
UN.AT.TAIN.A.BLE, adj., inatingível.
UN.AT.TEND.ED, adj., desacompanhado, só; sem vigilância; abandonado; sem ataduras (ferida).
UN.AU.THO.RIZED, adj., não autorizado, desautorizado.
UN.AVAIL.ING, adj., inútil.
UN.A.VOID.A.BLE, adj., inevitável; *Jur.*, irrevogável.
UN.A.VOID.A.BLY, adv., inevitavelmente, irrevogavelmente.
UN.A.WARE, adj., desconhecedor, que não percebe, inconsciente.
UN.BAL.ANCE, v., desequilibrar.
UN.BAL.ANCED, adj., desequilibrado; desajustado.
UN.BEAR.A.BLE, adj., insuportável, insustentável.
UN.BEAR.A.BLY, adv., insuportavelmente.
UN.BEAT.A.BLE, adj., imbatível.
UN.BE.COM.ING, adj., indecente, indecoroso, despudorado.
UN.BE.LIEF, s., descrença, descrédito, incredulidade.
UN.BE.LIEV.A.BLE, adj., inacreditável; *interj.*, incrível!.
UN.BE.LIEV.A.BLY, adv., incrivelmente, inacreditavelmente.
UN.BE.LIEV.ER, s., incrédulo, descrente, céptico, agnóstico.
UN.BEND, v., relaxar; afrouxar, soltar; desencurvar; endireitar.
UN.BEND.ING, adj., intransigente, exigente, obstinado.
UN.BI.ASED, adj., imparcial, justo.
UN.BID.DEN, adj., espontâneo, natural.
UN.BLEM.ISHED, adj., imaculado, irrepreensível, *fig.*, irretocável.
UN.BLOCK, v., desbloquear, desentupir.
UN.BOLT, v., destrancar, desaferrolhar.
UN.BOIL.ED, adj., cru, não cozido.
UN.BORN, adj., por nascer, nascituro, futuro.
UN.BOUND.ED, adj., ilimitado, imenso, sem limites.
UN.BREAK.A.BLE, adj., inquebrável.
UN.BRI.DLED, adj., desenfreado; desembestado (cavalo).
UN.BUT.TON, v., desabotoar.
UN.BUR.DEN, v., descarregar.
UN.CAN.NY, adj., estranho, esquisito.
UN.CAR.ING, adj., desatencioso, insensível.
UN.CEAS.ING, adj., contínuo, continuado.

UNCEREMONIOUS   •• 639 ••   UNDERTOW

UN.CER.E.MO.NI.OUS, *adj.*, abrupto, descortês.
UN.CER.E.MO.NI.OUS.LY, *adv.*, abruptamente.
UN.CER.TAIN, *adj.*, incerto, improvável, indeciso.
UN.CHAIN, *v.*, libertar, liberar.
UN.CHAL.LENGED, *adj.*, inquestionável, inconteste.
UN.CHANGED, *adj.*, inalterado, imutável.
UN.CHANG.ING, *adj.*, imutável.
UN.CHAR.AC.TER.IS.TIC, *adj.*, incomum, fora do comum.
UN.CHAR.I.TA.BLE, *adj.*, mesquinho, insensível.
UN.CHAR.TED, *adj.*, não cartografado, inexplorado.
UN.CHAS.TI.TY, *s.*, despudor, impureza.
UN.CHECKED, *adj.*, incontrolado, desenfreado; *adv.*, sem restrições.
UN.CIV.IL, *adj.*, incivil, grosseiro, bruto.
UN.CIV.IL.IZED(ISED), *adj.*, incivilizado, selvagem.
UN.CLAIMED, *adj.*, não reclamado, não buscado.
UN.CLAS.SI.FIED, *adj.*, não classificado; não confidencial.
UNCLE, *s.*, tio.
UN.CLEAN, *adj.*, sujo, imundo, porco, sórdido.
UN.CLEAN.NESS, *s.*, impureza, sujeira, sujidade, imundície.
UN.CLEAR, *adj.*, confuso, indistinto, obscuro.
UN.CLOSE, *v.*, abrir, desabotoar, desabrochar.
UN.CLOTHED, *adj.*, despido, nu, pelado.
UN.CO, *adj.*, raro, singular, único.
UN.COM.FORT.A.BLE, *adj.*, desconfortável; *fig.*, desagradável.
UN.COM.FORT.A.BLY, *adv.*, desconfortavelmente.
UN.COM.MON, *adj.*, incomum, raro, singular.
UN.COM.PRE.HEND.ING, *adj.*, descomplicado.
UN.COM.PRO.MIS.ING, *adj.*, inflexível, resoluto.
UN.CON.CERN, *s.*, indiferença.
UN.CON.CERNED, *adj.*, indiferente, insensível, despreocupado.
UN.CON.DI.TION.AL, *adj.*, incondicional.
UN.CON.NECT.ED, *adj.*, desconectado, desligado, desatado.
UN.CON.SCIOUS, *adj.*, inconsciente.
UN.CON.SCIOUS.LY, *adv.*, inconscientemente.
UN.CON.STI.TU.TION.AL, *adj.*, inconstitucional.
UN.CON.TROL.LA.BLE, *adj.*, incontrolável.
UN.COOKED, *adj.*, cru, não cozido.
UN.CORK, *v.*, desarrolhar; abrir (garrafa).
UN.COR.RECT.ED, *adj.*, incorreto, não correto.
UN.COR.RUPT, *adj.*, incorrupto, sério, puro.
UN.COUTH, *adj.*, rude, grosseiro, bruto, bárbaro.
UN.COV.ER, *v.*, destampar, destapar, descobrir.
UNC.TION, *s.*, unção, ungimento.
UN.CUL.TURED, *adj.*, inculto, não cultivado.
UN.CURL, *v.*, alisar (cabelo), desenrolar(-se), soltar(-se).
UN.CUT, *adj.*, inteiro, inteiriço, não cortado.
UN.DAM.AGED, *adj.*, intacto, incólume.
UN.DAT.ED, *adj.*, não datado.
UN.DAUNT.ED, *adj.*, destemido, inabalável.
UN.DE.CID.ED, *adj.*, indeciso, hesitante, vacilante.
UN.DE.CID.ED.NESS, *s.*, indecisão, hesitação.
UN.DE.FEND.ED, *adj.*, indefeso, sem defesa.
UN.DE.FINED, *adj.*, indefinido.
UN.DE.MAND.ING, *adj.*, pouco exigente; complacente.
UN.DE.NI.A.BLE, *adj.*, inegável.
UN.DE.NI.A.BLY, *adj.*, inegavelmente.
UN.DER, *prep.*, debaixo de, sob, segundo, de acordo com; *adv.*, debaixo.
UN.DER-AGE, *adj.*, menor, menor de idade, adolescente.

UN.DER.BUY, *v.*, comprar por preço menor, pagar menos do que vale.
UN.DER.COAT, *s.*, primeira demão (de tinta).
UN.DER.COV.ER, *adj.*, secreto, sigiloso, clandestino, tácito.
UN.DER.ES.TI.MATE, *v.*, subestimar, não avaliar certo.
UN.DER.DE.VEL.OPED, *adj.*, subdesenvolvido.
UN.DER.EM.PLOY.MENT, *s.*, subemprego.
UN.DER.ES.TI.MATE, *v.*, subestimar.
UN.DER.FEED, *adj.*, desnutrido.
UN.DER.FOOT, *adv.*, sob os pés; embaixo, debaixo.
UN.DER.GO, *v.*, passar por, aguentar, suportar; submeter-se a.
UN.DER.HAND, *adj.*, clandestino, oculto; desleal, fingido, ardiloso.
UN.DER.GRAD.U.ATE, *s.*, universitário.
UN.DER.GROUND, *s.*, metrô, grupo clandestino; *adj.*, subterrâneo, clandestino.
UN.DER.LAY, *s.*, forração, camada, base; *v.*, forrar, calçar.
UN.DER.LEASE, *s.*, sublocação; *v.*, sublocar.
UN.DER.LINE, *v.*, sublinhar, destacar.
UN.DER.LIN.EN, *s.*, roupa íntima.
UN.DER.LING, *s.*, subalterno.
UN.DER.LY.ING, *adj.*, subjacente; *fig.*, secreto, oculto.
UN.DER.MINE, *v.*, solapar, minar, colocar minas.
UN.DER.MEN.TIONED, *adj.*, abaixo mencionado.
UN.DER.MOST, *adj.*, ínfimo, o mais baixo.
UN.DER.NEATH, *s.*, parte inferior; *adv.*, embaixo, debaixo, abaixo, por baixo; *prep.*, debaixo de; sob o aspecto de.
UN.DER.PAID, *adj.*, mal pago. •
UN.DER.PANTS, *s. pl.*, *col.*, cueca.
UN.DER.PASS, *s.*, passagem subterrânea.
UN.DER.PLAY, *s.*, truque; *v.*, minimizar; menosprezar.
UN.DER.PRAISE, *v.*, desprezar, menosprezar, desdenhar.
UN.DER.PRICE, *s.*, preço abaixo do real; *v.*, cotar preço abaixo do valor real.
UN.DER.RATED, *adj.*, subestimado.
UN.DER.SCORE, *v.*, sublinhar, salientar, ressaltar.
UN.DER.SEA, *adj.*, submarino.
UN.DER.SELL, *v.*, vender por preço inferior.
UN.DER.SET, *s.*, ressaca.
UN.DER.SHIRT, *s.*, *US* camiseta.
UN.DER.SIDE, *s.*, local inferior.
UN.DER.SIGNED, *s.*, abaixo-assinado.
UN.DER.SKIRT, *s.*, anágua.
UN.DER.STAND, *v.*, entender, compreender.
UN.DER.STAND.A.BLE, *adj.*, compreensível.
UN.DER.STAND.A.BLY, *adv.*, compreensivelmente.
UN.DER.STAND.ING, *s.*, entendimento, compreensão; acordo; *adj.*, compreensivo.
UN.DER.STATE, *v.*, atenuar, abrandar.
UN.DER.STAT.ED, *adj.*, sóbrio; atenuado.
UN.DER.STATE.MENT, *s.*, atenuação (de uma afirmação).
UN.DER.STOOD, *adj.*, compreendido, entendido.
UN.DER.STUD.Y, *s.*, *Teat.*, substituto (ator); *v.*, estudar fala de ator para poder substituí-lo.
UN.DER.TAK.ER, *s.*, agente funerário; empresário.
UN.DER.TAK.ING, *s.*, incumbência, tarefa; promessa, garantia.
UN.DER.TONE, *s.*, voz baixa, meio-tom; insinuação (significado subjacente).
UN.DER.TOW, *s.*, ressaca, contracorrente.

UNDERVALUE ·· 640 ·· UNINTELLIGENT

UN.DER.VAL.UE, *v.*, subavaliar, subestimar.
UN.DER.WA.TER, *adj.*, subaquático, submerso.
UN.DER.WAY, *adv.*, encaminhado, em andamento.
UN.DER.WEAR, *s.*, cueca, roupa íntima.
UN.DER.WORLD, *s.*, submundo, baixo-mundo.
UN.DER.WRITE, *v.*, subscrever, assinar; comprometer-se com.
UN.DER.WRIT.ER, *s.*, seguradora, segurador, corretor de seguros.
UN.DER.WRIT.ING, *s.*, seguro.
UN.DER.WRIT.TEN, *adj.*, abaixo-assinado, subscrito.
UN.DE.SIR.ABLE, *adj.*, indesejável, impróprio.
UN.DE.TER.MI.NATE, *adj.*, indeterminado.
UN.DE.TERRED, *adj.*, valente, ousado, decidido.
UN.DE.VEL.OPED, *adj.*, subdesenvolvido, não explorado; embrionário, em desenvolvimento.
UN.DIES, *s. pl.*, roupas íntimas; *lingerie.*
UN.DIG.NI.FIED, *adj.*, indecoroso, impróprio, indigno.
UN.DIS.CI.PLINED, *adj.*, indisciplinado.
IN.DIS.COV.ERED, *adj.*, oculto, clandestino.
UN.DIS.PUT.ED, *adj.*, incontestável, irrefutável.
UN.DIS.TIN.GUISHED, *adj.*, sem graça, sem qualidade; indistinto.
UN.DIS.TRACT.ED, *adj.*, atento, atencioso.
UN.DIS.TURBED, *adj.*, impassível, tranquilo.
UN.DI.VID.ED, *adj.*, inteiro, indiviso.
UN.DO, *v.*, desatar, desmanchar.
UN.DO.ING, *s.*, ruína, desgraça.
UN.DONE, *adj.*, incompleto, inacabado.
UN.DOUBT.ED, *adj.*, indubitável, incontestável.
UN.DOUBT.ED.LY, *adv.*, indubitavelmente, certamente.
UN.DRESS, *s.*, nudez; *v.*, despir(-se).
UN.DRESSED, *adj.*, despido; em roupa caseira.
UN.DUE, *adj.*, impróprio, incorreto, inadequado.
UN.DU.LANT, *adj.*, ondulante.
UN.DU.LATE, *v.*, ondular.
UN.DU.LY, *adv.*, demasiadamente; indevidamente.
UN.DY.ING, *adj.*, imortal, perene, eterno.
UN.EARTH, *v.*, desenterrar, descobrir.
UN.EARTH.LY, *adj.*, sobrenatural.
UN.EARNED, *adj.*, imerecido.
UN.EASY, *adj.*, preocupado, incômodo, desconfortável.
UN.EAT.A.BLE, *adj.*, indigesto, intragável.
UN.ECO.NOM.IC, *adj.*, antieconômico.
UN.ED.U.CAT.ED, *adj.*, iletrado, analfabeto, não escolarizado.
UN.EM.PLOYED, *adj.*, desempregado.
UN.EM.PLOY.MENT, *s.*, desemprego.
UN.EN.VI.A.BLE, *adj.*, não invejável.
UN.EQUAL, *adj.*, desigual, irregular.
UN.EQUIV.O.CAL, *adj.*, inequívoco, evidente, claro.
UN.ERR.ING, *adj.*, infalível.
UN.ETH.I.CAL, *adj.*, antiético.
UN.E.VEN, *adj.*, desigual, irregular, desnivelado.
UN.E.VENT.FUL, *adj.*, calmo, tranquilo, sossegado.
UN.EX.CEP.TION.AL, *adj.*, usual, diário, corrente.
UN.EX.PE.RI.ENCED, *adj.*, inexperiente.
UN.EX.PECT.ED, *adj.*, inesperado.
UN.EX.PECT.ED.LY, *adv.*, inesperadamente.
UN.EX.PRES.SIVE, *adj.*, inexpressivo.
UN.FAIR.NESS, *s.*, injustiça, deslealdade, infidelidade.
UN.FAIL.ING, *adj.*, infalível.

UN.FAIR, *adj.*, injusto.
UN.FAIR.LY, *adv.*, injustamente.
UN.FAIR.NESS, *s.*, injustiça.
IN.FAITH.FUL, *adj.*, infiel.
UN.FAL.TER.ING, *adj.*, firme, decidido, resoluto.
UN.FASH.ION.A.BLE, *adj.*, fora de moda.
UN.FAS.TEN, *v.*, desatar.
UN.FA.VOUR.A.BLE, *adj.*, desfavorável.
UN.FEEL.ING, *adj.*, insensível.
UN.FET.TER, *v.*, soltar, colocar em liberdade.
UN.FIN.ISHED, *adj.*, incompleto, inacabado, não lapidado.
UN.FIT, *adj.*, for a de forma; inadequado (para algo).
UN.FLAG.GING, *adj.*, inesgotável, incansável.
UN.FLAP.PA.BLE, *adj., col.*, inabalável.
UN.FOLD, *v.*, desdobrar.
UN.FORE.SEE.A.BLE, *adj.*, imprevisível.
UN.FORE.SEEN, *adj.*, imprevisto.
UN.FOR.GET.TA.BLE, *adj.*, inesquecível.
UN.FOR.GIV.A.BLE, *adj.*, imperdoável.
UN.FORMED, *adj.*, não formado, informe.
UN.FOR.TU.NATE, *adj.*, infortunado, infeliz.
UN.FOR.TU.NATE.LY, *adv.*, infelizmente.
UN.FOUND.ED, *adj.*, infundado.
UN.FRIEND.LY, *adj.*, inamistoso, hostil, adverso; insensível.
UN.FRUIT.FUL, *adj.*, infrutífero, estéril.
UN.FURL, *v.*, estender, desdobrar, esticar.
UN.GEN.ER.OUS, *adj.*, mesquinho.
UN.GLOR.I.OUS, *adj.*, inglório, modesto.
UN.GOD.LY, *adj.*, ímpio, ateu, malvado.
UN.GOV.ERN.ABLE, *adj.*, ingovernável.
UN.GRACE.FUL, *adj.*, sem graça, desgracioso, insosso.
UN.GRATE.FUL, *adj.*, ingrato, desagradável, mal-agradecido.
UN.GRATE.FUL.NESS, *s.*, ingratidão.
UN.GUENT, *s.*, unguento.
UN.GUAL, *s.*, unha, garra.
UN.HAP.PY, *adj.*, infeliz, triste, tristonho, infortunado, desgraçado.
UN.HAP.PY.NESS, *s.*, infelicidade.
UN.HARMED, *adj.*, ileso, indene.
UN.HEALTHY, *adj.*, insalubre, doentio, doente.
UN.HEED.ED, *adj.*, despercebido, ignorado.
UN.HEED.ING, *adj.*, negligente, descuidado, despreocupado, relapso.
UN.HOOK, *v.*, desenganchar, desprender.
UN.HOPED, *adj.*, inesperado.
UN.HOUSE, *v.*, desalojar, despejar.
UN.HURT, *adj.*, ileso.
UNICEF, *abrev.* de *United Nations Children's Fund*: Fundo das Nações Unidas para a Infância, UNICEF.
U.NI.CORN, *s.*, unicórnio (animal mitológico).
U.NI.CY.CLE, *s.*, monociclo.
U.NI.FI.CA.TION, *s.*, unificação.
U.NI.FORM, *adj.*, *s.*, uniforme.
U.NI.FORM.LY, *adv.*, uniformemente.
U.NI.FOR.MI.TY, *s.*, uniformidade.
U.NI.FY, *v.*, unificar, unir, reunir.
U.NI.FY.ING, *adj.*, unificador.
UNI.LAT.ER.AL, *adj.*, unilateral.
UN.IN.FORMED, *adj.*, incauto, imprudente.
UN.IN.HA.BI.TED, *adj.*, desabitado.
UN.IN.TEL.LI.GENT, *adj.*, imbecil, não inteligente.

UNINTENTIONAL ··641·· UNREPEATABLE

UN.IN.TEN.TION.AL, *adj.*, involuntário, sem intenção.
UN.IN.TER.EST.ED, *adj.*, desinteressado, indiferente.
UN.IN.TER.RUPT.ED, *adj.*, contínuo, ininterrupto.
UN.IN.VIT.ED, *adj.*, não convidado; intruso.
UNION, *s.*, união; sindicato.
U.NION.IZE(-ISE), *v.*, sindicalizar(-se).
U.NION.IZED(-ISED), *adj.*, sindicalizado.
U.NIQUE, *adj.*, único, ímpar.
U.NIQUE.LY, *adv.*, singularmente, exclusivamente.
UNI.SEX, *adj.*, unissexo.
U.NI.SON, *s.*, harmonia, concordância; *Mús.*, uníssono.
U.NIT, *s.*, unidade, equipe, grupo.
U.NITE, *v.*, unir, aderir; juntar(-se).
U.NIT.ED, *adj.*, unido, combinado.
U.NIT.ED AR.AB EMIR.ATES, *s.*, Emirados Árabes Unidos (reino).
U.NIT.ED KING.DOM, *s.*, Reino Unido (reino).
U.NIT.ED NA.TIONS, *s.*, Nações Unidas (organização).
U.NIT.ED STATES, *s.*, Estados Unidos (país).
UNI.TARY, *adj.*, unitário, total.
UNITE, *v.*, unir, ligar, reunir.
UNI.TY, *s.*, unidade.
UNI.VER.SAL, *adj.*, universal.
UNI.VER.SAL.ISM, *s.*, universalismo.
UNI.VER.SAL.I.TY, *s.*, universalidade.
UNI.VER.SAL.IZE, *v.*, universalizar.
UNI.VERSE, *s.*, universo.
UNI.VER.SI.TY, *s.*, universidade.
UN.JUST, *adj.*, injusto.
UN.JUS.TI.FI.ABLE, *adj.*, injustificável.
UN.JUS.TI.FIED, *adj.*, injustificado.
UN.JUST.NESS, *s.*, injustiça.
UN.KEMPT, *adj.*, despenteado, desgrenhado.
UN.KIND, *adj.*, maldoso, cruel, perverso.
UN.KIND.LY, *adv.*, indelicadamente.
UN.KNOW.ING, *adj.*, ignorante, iletrado, estúpido.
UN.KNOWN, *adj.*, desconhecido, ignoto.
UN.LACE, *v.*, desatar, desamarrar.
UN.LAW.FUL, *adj.*, ilegal.
UN.LEARN, *v.*, desaprender.
UN.LESS, *conj.*, a menos que.
UN.LIKE, *adj.*, diferente, diverso; *prep.*, ao contrário de, ao invés de.
UN.LIKE.LY, *adj.*, improvável, inverossímil; estranho.
UN.LIM.IT.ED, *adj.*, ilimitado, infinito.
UN.LIS.TED, *adj.*, não listado, fora da lista.
UN.LOCK, *v.*, abrir, destrancar, destravar.
UN.LUCK.I.LY, *adv.*, infelizmente; desgraçadamente.
UN.LUCKY, *adj.*, infeliz, mal-humorado, taciturno.
UN.MAKE, *v.*, destruir, arruinar, depor.
UN.MANNED, *adj.*, não tripulado.
UN.MARKED, *adj.*, sem marca.
UN.MAR.RIED, *adj.*, solteiro.
UN.MASK, *v.*, desmascarar; revelar.
UN.MAT.CHED, *adj.*, inigualável, ímpar.
UN.MEA.SUR.ABLE, *adj.*, imensurável.
UN.MER.CI.FUL, *adj.*, cruel, impiedoso, perverso.
UN.MIND.FUL, *adj.*, descuidado, insensível, indiferente.
UN.MIS.TAK.A.BLE, *adj.*, inconfundível; inequívoco.
UN.MIXED, *adj.*, puro, não misturado.
UN.MOV.ABLE, *adj.*, imóvel, inarredável.

UN.NAMED, *adj.*, anônimo.
UN.NAT.U.RAL, *adj.*, pouco natural; desnaturado; artificial.
UN.NEC.ES.SARY, *adj.*, desnecessário.
UN.NERVE, *v.*, enervar, enfraquecer.
UN.NERV.ING, *adj.*, enervante; inquietante.
UN.NO.TICED, *adj.*, desapercebido, despercebido.
UN.NUM.BERED, *adj.*, inumerável.
UNO, *abrev.* de *United Nations Organization*: Organização das Nações Unidas, ONU.
UN.OB.SERV.ANCE, *s.*, inobservância, descuido.
UN.OB.SERVED, *adj.*, desapercebido, despercebido.
UN.OC.CU.PIED, *adj.*, vago, desocupado, livre.
UN.OF.FEN.SIVE, *adj.*, inofensivo.
UN.OB.TRU.SIVE, *adj.*, discreto, modesto, moderado.
UN.OPENED, *adj.*, fechado.
UN.OWNED, *adj.*, sem dono.
UN.PACK, *v.*, desempacotar, desembrulhar, desfazer (as malas); *Comp.*, descompactar.
UN.PAID, *adj.*, não pago, não ressarcido.
UN.PAR.DON.ABLE, *adj.*, imperdoável.
UN.PEO.PLE, *v.*, despovoar.
UN.PER.TURBED, *adj.*, calmo, sossegado, impassível.
UN.PICK, *v.*, descosturar, desfazer, desmanchar, desatar.
UN.PIT.Y.ING, *adj.*, cruel, malvado, maldoso, perverso.
UN.PLUG, *v.*, desligar, desconectar, desarrolhar, destampar.
UN.PO.LITE, *adj.*, descortês, malcriado, grosseiro.
UN.POP.U.LAR, *adj.*, impopular.
UN.PRE.DICT.A.BLE, *adj.*, imprevisível.
UN.PRE.TEN.TIOUS, *adj.*, despretensioso.
UN.PRICED, *adj.*, sem preço.
UN.PRINTED, *adj.*, não impresso.
UN.PRO.DUC.TIVE, *adj.*, improdutivo.
UN.PROF.IT.ABLE, *adj.*, inútil.
UN.PRO.PI.TIOUS, *adj.*, desfavorável, não propício.
UN.PROVED, *adj.*, não provado.
UN.PUB.LISHED, *adj.*, inédito (obra), não publicado.
UN.PUNC.TU.AL.I.TY, *s.*, impontualidade.
UN.PUN.ISHED, *adj.*, impune.
UN.QUAL.I.FIED, *adj.*, desqualificado; inadequado, impróprio; ilimitado, absoluto, completo.
UN.QUES.TION.A.BLE, *adj.*, inquestionável.
UN.QUES.TION.ING, *adj.*, incondicional, sem perguntar.
UN.QUI.ET, *adj.*, inquieto, agitado, perturbado.
UN.READ, *adj.*, iletrado, não lido, ignorante.
UN.REAL, *adj.*, irreal, ilusório.
UN.RE.AL.I.TY, *s.*, irrealidade.
UN.REA.SON, *s.*, absurdo.
UN.RE.CLAIMED, *adj.*, não reclamado.
UN.REC.OG.NIZ.A.BLE *UK*, **UN.REC.OGNISABLE** *US*, *adj.*, irreconhecível.
UN.REC.OG.NIZED(-ISED), *adj.*, não reconhecido, inconfesso.
UN.REC.ON.CIL.A.BLE, *adj.*, irreconciliável.
UN.RE.HEARSED, *adj.*, *Teat.*, improvisado, não ensaiado.
UN.RE.LAXED, *adj.*, não relaxado.
UN.RE.LIEVED, *adj.*, não socorrido.
UN.RE.MEM.BERED, *adj.*, esquecido.
UN.RE.MIT.TING, *adj.*, incessante, contínuo.
UN.RE.PAID, *adj.*, não reembolsado.
UN.RE.PAIR.A.BLE, *adj.*, irreparável.
UN.RE.PEAT.A.BLE, *adj.*, irrepetível.

UNREST · · 642 · · UPLANDER

UN.REST, *s.*, inquietação, distúrbio, confusão.
UN.RE.STORED, *adj.*, não recuperado.
UN.RE.STRAINED, *adj.*, desenfreado, incontido.
UN.RE.STRICT.ED, *adj.*, irrestrito, ilimitado.
UN.RIGHT.FUL, *adj.*, injusto, perverso, malvado.
UN.RIPE, *adj.*, verde, imaturo, não maduro.
UN.ROBE, *v.*, desnudar, tirar a roupa, pelar.
UN.ROLL, *v.*, desenrolar.
UN.RUL.I.NESS, *s.*, indisciplina, desordem.
UN.RU.LY, *adj.*, indisciplinado, desobediente, teimoso; sem lei.
UN.SAFE, *adj.*, inseguro, perigoso.
UN.SALE.ABLE, *adj.*, não vendável.
UN.SAT.IS.FAC.TO.RY, *adj.*, insatisfatório.
UN.SAT.IS.FIED, *adj.*, insatisfeito.
UN.SA.VOUR.I.NESS, *s.*, insipidez.
UN.SAY, *v.*, desdizer, desmentir.
UN.SCATHED; *adj.*, incólume, ileso, são e salvo.
UN.SCHED.ULED, *adj.*, imprevisto, não programado.
UN.SCREW, *v.*, desparafusar.
UN.SCRIP.TED, *adj.*, improvisado, de improviso.
UN.SCRU.PU.LOUS, *adj.*, inescrupuloso.
UN.SEAT, *v.*, derrubar, depor.
UN.SEA.WOR.THY, *adj.*, inegável.
UN.SEE.ING, *adj.*, invisível, oculto, escondido.
UN.SEEM.LY, *adj.*, inconveniente, impróprio, inadequado.
UN.SEEN, *adj.*, despercebido, invisível.
UN.SELF.ISH, *adj.*, desinteressado.
UN.SET.TLE, *v.*, inquietar; alterar, deslocar; instabilizar.
UN.SETTLED, *adj.*, inquieto, instável; incerto, inseguro.
UN.SETTL.ING, *adj.*, inquietante, perturbador.
UN.SHAVED, UN.SHAV.EN, *adj.*, com a barba por fazer.
UN.SHAK.EN, *adj.*, firme, imóvel.
UN.SHEATHE, *v.*, desembainhar.
UN.SHOD, *adj.*, descalço.
UN.SO.CIA.BIL.I.TY, *s.*, insociabilidade.
UN.SOLD, *adj.*, não vendido.
UN.SO.LIC.IT.ED, *adj.*, não solicitado, não pedido.
UN.SOLVED, *adj.*, não solucionado, não resolvido.
UN.SPAR.ING, *adj.*, generoso, bondoso.
UN.SPEAK.A.BLE, *adj.*, indizível, indescritível, terrível.
UN.SPE.CI.FIED, *adj.*, indefinido, não específico.
UN.SPENT, *adj.*, não gasto.
UN.SPOILED, *adj.*, incólume, intocado.
UN.SPO.KEN, *adj.*, não falado.
UN.STA.BIL.I.TY, *s.*, instabilidade.
UN.STA.BLE, *adj.*, instável, inseguro, sem firmeza.
UN.STEAD.Y, *adj.*, inseguro, oscilante; inconsistente.
UN.STOP.PA.BLE, *adj.*, inevitável
UN.STRUC.TURED, *adj.*, desorganizado, desestruturado.
UN.SUC.CESS.FUL, *adj.*, frustrado, mal sucedido.
UN.SUP.PORT.ABLE, *adj.*, insuportável.
UN.SURE, *adj.*, inseguro, incerto.
UN.SUIT.A.BLE, *adj.*, inconveniente, inapropriado.
UN.SUS.PECT.ED, *adj.*, insuspeito.
UN.SWEET.ENED, *adj.*, sem açúcar.
UN.SYM.PA.THET.IC, *adj.*, antipático, insensível.
UN.TAPPED, *adj.*, inexplorado.
UN.TAUGHT, *adj.*, ignorante, analfabeto, iletrado.
UN.TAXED, *adj.*, isento de impostos, não tributado.
UN.TEN.A.BLE, *adj.*, insustentável.

UN.THANK.FUL, *adj.*, ingrato, mal-agradecido.
UN.THINK.A.BLE, *adj.*, inconcebível, inimaginável.
UN.THRIFT.Y, *adj.*, pródigo.
UN.TI.DY, *adj.*, desordenado, desarrumado, desleixado.
UN.TIE, *v.*, soltar, desatar, desmanchar.
UN.TIL, *prep.*, até; *conj.*, até que.
UN.TIME.LY, *adj.*, prematuro, inoportuno; intempestivo; *adv.*, precocemente, inoportunamente.
UN.TIR.ING, *adj.*, incansável.
UN.TOLD, *adj.*, inédito, inestimável.
UN.TOUCHED, *adj.*, intato, inteiro, ileso, intocado.
UN.TO.WARD, *adj.*, inconveniente; adverso; indócil.
UN.TRAINED, *adj.*, indisciplinado, desordeiro.
UN.TRANS.FER.ABLE, *adj.*, intransferível.
UN.TROU.BLED, *adj.*, calmo, inquieto, tranquilo.
UN.TRUE, *adj.*, falso, errado.
UN.TRUE.NESS, *s.*, mentira, falsidade.
UN.TRUTH, *s.*, mentira, falsidade.
UN.TRUTH.FUL, *adj.*, mentiroso, insincero.
UN.US.A.BLE, *adj.*, imprestável, inutilizável.
UN.USED, *adj.*, sem uso, novo, completo.
UN.U.SU.AL, *adj.*, raro, incomum, invulgar, singular.
UN.U.SU.AL.LY, *adv.*, excepcionalmente, invulgarmente, raramente.
UN.VAR.I.ABLE, *adj.*, invariável.
UN.VARY.ING, *adj.*, invariável.
UN.VEIL, *v.*, desvelar, desvendar, expor; descerrar.
UN.VERSED, *adj.*, inexperiente, ignorante, desconhecedor.
UN.WANT.ED, *adj.*, indesejado, indesejável, malquisto.
UN.WAR.RANT.ED, *adj.*, não garantido.
UN.WASHED, *adj.*, sujo, imundo, não lavado.
UN.WEL.COME, *adj.*, inoportuno, aborrecido.
UN.WELL, *adj.*, indisposto, adoentado.
UN.WHOLE.SOME, *adj.*, insalubre, doentio.
UN.WISE, *adj.*, imprudente, desavisado.
UN.WIT.TING, *adj.*, inconsciente, involuntário.
UN.WIT.TING.LY, *adv.*, inadvertidamente, involuntariamente.
UN.WOR.THY, *adj.*, indigno, desprezível.
UN.WRIT.TEN, *adj.*, não escrito, tácito, presumido, oral.
UN.YIELD.ING, *adj.*, inflexível; teimoso; firme, duro.
UN.YOKE, *v.*, libertar-se, soltar-se, sair do jugo.
UN.ZIP, *v.*, abrir o zíper (de); *Comp.*, descompactar.
UP, *prep.*, para cima, em cima, em, sobre, através de; *adv.*, para cima, para o alto.
UP.BEAT, *s.*, bom êxito; *adj.*, otimista.
UP.BRAID, *v.*, advertir, censurar, criticar, admoestar.
UP.BRING.ING, *s.*, educação, formação (educacional).
UP.CAST, *adj.*, erguido, levantado, alçado.
UP.DATE, *v.*, atualizar, pôr em dia.
UP.END, *v.*, por(-se) de pé; virar de ponta-cabeça.
UP.FRONT, *adj.*, franco, direto, expansivo; *adv.*, diretamente.
UP.GRADE, *s.*, upgrade, subida, elevação; *v.*, melhorar, remodelar, atualizar.
UP.HEAV.AL, *s.*, transtorno, confusão.
UP.HILL, *adj.*, íngreme, elevado; árduo, *adv.*, para cima, arduamente.
UP.HOLD.ER, *s.*, apoio, sustentáculo, reforço.
UP.HOL.STER, *v.*, acolchoar, estofar.
UP.KEEP, *s.*, manutenção, cuidado.
UP.LAND, *s.*, *Geogr.*, planalto, terreno elefado; *adj.*, no planalto.
UP.LAND.ER, *s.*, terreno montanhoso, elevado; *adj.*,

UPLIFT · 643 · UZBEKISTAN

montanhoso.

UP.LIFT, s., exaltação (espiritual); *fig.*, enaltecer; extasiar.

UP.ON, *prep.*, em cima, sobre, por cima de.

UP.PER, s., superior, parte superior; *adj.*, superior, mais alto.

UP.PER-CLASS, *adj.*, referente à classe alta.

UP.PER-CRUST, *adj.*, da alta roda.

UP.PER HOUSE, s., *UK* Câmara dos Lordes.

UP.PER.MOST, *adj.*, o mais alto.

UP.RAISE, v., levantar, erguer, exaltar, louvar.

UP.RIGHT, *adj.*, ereto, reto, vertical.

UP.RIS.ING, s., revolta, rebeldia, revolução.

UP.ROAR, s., algazarra, tumulto, protesto.

UP.ROAR.I.OUS, *adj.*, barulhento.

UP.ROOT, v., arrancar (raiz); desarraigar; erradicar; extirpar.

UP.SET, s., reviravolta, revés, contrariedade; v., virar, perturbar, incomodar.

UP.SET.TING, *adj.*, inquietante, perturbador.

UP.SHOT, s., conclusão, resultado, arremate, finalização.

UP.SIDE DOWN, *adv.*, de cabeça para baixo; de modo confuso; *upside-down adj.*: de ponta-cabeça, confuso.

UP.STAIRS, s., andar superior; *adv.*, em cima, na parte superior; *adj.*, superior.

UP.STAGE, v., ofuscar outro ator, roubar a cena de; *adj.*, soberbo.

UP.STAND.ING, *adj.*, honrado, honesto; em pé, ereto.

UP.START, s., novo-rico, tipo indigesto.

UP.STATE, s., interior (de um Estado); *adj.*, no interior; *adv.*, para o interior.

UP.SURGE, s., aumento de (algo); inchação; irrupção, excitação.

UP.TAKE, s., entendimento, compreensão (de texto/fato).

UP.TIGHT, *adj.*, nervoso.

UP.TOWN, *adj.*, *US* na parte alta da cidade; *US* suburbano; *adv.*, para a parte alta da cidade.

UP.TURN, s., ato de virar para cima; *fig.*, melhoria; v., virar para cima, levantar, erguer(-se).

UP.TURNED, *adj.*, virado para cima; tombado.

UP.WARD, *adj.*, dirigido para cima, superior; *adv.*, para cima, por cima, cima (também *upwards*).

URAE.MIA, s., uremia.

URA.NI.UM, s., urânio.

U.RA.NUS, s., *Astron.*, planeta Urano; *Mit.*, Urano (deus grego).

UR.BAN, *adj.*, urbano, citadino.

UR.BANE, *adj.*, urbano, cortês, gentil.

UR.BAN.I.TY, s., urbanidade, gentileza, polidez.

UR.BAN.IZE(-ISE), v., urbanizar.

UREA, s., ureia.

URE.THRA, s., uretra.

URET.IC, *adj.*, urético.

UR.GEN.CY, s., urgência, pressa, insistência.

UR.GENT, *adj.*, urgente.

UR.GENT.LY, *adv.*, urgentemente.

URI.NAL, s., urinol.

URI.NATE, v., urinar.

URINE, s., urina.

URL, *abrev.* de *Uniform Resource Locator*: Localizador Padrão de Recursos, URL.

URN, s., urna.

URU.GUAY, s., Uruguai.

URU.GUAY.AN, *adj.*, s., uruguaio.

US, *pron.*, nos; nós.

US, *abrev.* de *United States*: Estados Unidos (país), EU.

USA, s., *abrev.* de *United States of America*: Estados Unidos da América, EUA.

US.A.BLE, *adj.*, usável, utilizável.

US.AGE, s., uso, usança.

USB, *Comp.*, *abrev.* de *Universal Serial Bus*: Porta Serial Universal, USB.

USE, s., uso, emprego, utilidade; v., usar, empregar, utilizar.

USED, *adj.*, usado; usual; segunda mão.

USE.FUL, *adj.*, útil, proveitoso, utilizado.

USE.FUL.NESS, s., utilidade.

USE.LESS, *adj.*, inútil

USE.LESS.NESS, s., inutilidade.

US.ER, s., usuário, consumidor.

USE UP, v., esgotar, terminar, acabar.

USSR, *Hist.*, *abrev.* de *Union of Soviet Socialist Republic*: União das Repúblicas Socialistas Soviéticas, URSS.

U.SU.AL, *adj.*, usual, corriqueiro, habitual.

U.SU.AL.NESS, s., uso, emprego, costume.

U.SU.FRUCT, s., usufruto.

U.SU.RER, s., usurário.

U.SURP, v., usurpar, tirar, pegar.

U.SUR.PA.TION, s., usurpação.

U.SU.RY, s., usura, sovinice.

U.TEN.SIL, s., utensílio.

U.TER.US, s., útero.

U.TIL.I.TAR.I.AN, *adj.*, utilitário, funcional.

U.TIL.I.TY, s., utilidade.

U.TIL.I.ZA.BLE, s., utilizável, aproveitável.

U.TIL.I.ZA.TION, s., utilização.

U.TI.LIZE(-ISE), v., utilizar, usar.

U.TI.LIZER(-ISER), s., o que utiliza.

U.T.MOST, *adj.*, maior, superior.

U.TO.PIA, s., utopia.

U.TO.PI.AN, *adj.*, utópico.

UT.TER, *adj.*, total, completo, incondicional; v., emitir proferir.

UT.TER.ANCE, s., declaração, dito, fala.

UT.TER.LY, *adv.*, totalmente, completamente.

U.VU.LA, s., úvula.

UX.O.RI.AL, *adj.*, uxório.

UX.OR.I.CIDE, s., uxoricida.

UX.O.RI.OUS, *adj.*, submisso à mulher; maricas, afeminado.

UZ.BEK, s., *adj.*, usbeque.

UZ.BEK.I.STAN, s., Usbequistão (país).

V, s., vigésima segunda letra do alfabeto inglês; V: número 5, romano.
VA.CAN.CY, s., vacância, vaga, lacuna, quarto de hotel desocupado.
VA.CANT, adj., vago, vazio, livre, desocupado, abandonado.
VA.CANT.LY, adv., distraidamente, ociosamente.
VA.CATE, v., desocupar, esvaziar, liberar.
VA.CA.TION, s., férias, feriado, período de descanso.
VA.CA.TION.ER, s., US veranista; pessoa em férias.
VAC.CI.NATE, v., vacinar.
VAC.CI.NA.TION, s., Med., vacinação.
VAC.CINE, s., Med., vacina.
VAC.IL.LATE, v., vacilar, hesitar, titubear.
VAC.IL.LA.TION, s., vacilação, hesitação, titubeio.
VAC.U.UM, s., vácuo.
VAG.A.BOND, s., vagabundo.
VA.GI.NA, s., Anat., vagina.
VAG.I.NAL, adj., vaginal.
VAGRANCY, s., vagabundagem.
VA.GRANT, s., vagabundo.
VAGUE, adj., vago.
VAGUE.LY, adv., vagamente, distraidamente, levemente.
VAGUE.NESS, s., incerteza, vagueza, indefinição.
VAIN, adj., vão, vaidoso.
VAIN.GLO.RY, s., vanglória, vaidade, soberba.
VAIN.LY, adv., em vão; futilmente, vaidosamente.
VAIN.NESS, s., vaidade, soberba.
VA.LET, s., camareiro, criado, aio, pagem.
VAL.ID, adj., válido.
VAL.I.DATE, v., validar, valorizar.
VA.LID.I.TY, s., validade.
VAL.EN.TINE'S DAY, s., Dia dos Namorados (Dia de São Valentim, em 14 de fevereiro).
VAL.ET, s., Fr., camareiro; valete, pagem; v., trabalhar como camareiro.
VAL.LEY, s., vale.
VAL.I.ANT, adj., valente, destemido.
VAL.ID, adj., válido.
VAL.I.DATE, v., validar, legitimar, corroborar, ratificar.
VA.LID.I.TY, s., validade; validez.
VAL.OUR, s., valor, valentia, denodo.
VAL.U.A.BLE, adj., valioso, precioso.
VAL.U.A.TION, s., avaliação; orçamento.
VAL.UE, s., valor, importância, preço, valia; v., valorizar, avaliar.
VAL.UED, adj., estimado; valioso.
VAL.U.ER, s., avaliador.
VALVE, s., válvula.
VAMP, s., mulher fascinante.
VAM.PIRE, s., vampiro.
VAM.PIR.ISM, s., vampirismo.
VAN, s., camioneta, furgão, van.
VAN.DAL, s., vândalo.
VAN.DAL.ISE, v., vandalizar.
VAN.DAL.ISM, s., vandalismo.
VAN.GUARD, s., vanguarda.
VA.NIL.LA, s., baunilha.
VAN.ISH, v., desaparecer, sumir.
VAN.I.TY, s., vaidade, soberba.
VAN.TAGE, s., vantagem.
VA.POR.I.ZA.TION, s., vaporização.
VA.POR.IZE, v., vaporizar.
VA.POUR, s., vapor.
VA.POURY, adj., vaporoso.
VAR.I.ABIL.I.TY, s., variabilidade.
VARI.A.BLE, s., variável; adj., variável, irregular, inconstante; Mat., variável.
VAR.I.ANCE, s., diferença, variância, discrepância.
VAR.I.ANT, adj., s., variante.
VAR.I.A.TION, s., variação.
VAR.I.CEL.LA, s., varicela.
VAR.I.COSE VEINS, s. pl., varizes.
VAR.I.CES, s., varizes.
VAR.IED, adj., vário, variado.
VA.RI.E.TY, s., variedade, diversidade.
VA.RI.O.LA, s., varíola.
VAR.NISH, s., verniz; v., envernizar.
VAR.NISHED, adj., envernizado.
VAR.NISH.ER, s., polidor, lustrador
VAR.Y, v., variar, mudar, trocar.
VAR.Y.ING, adj., variado, diverso.
VAS.CU.LAR, adj., vascular.
VASE, s., vaso.
VASC.U.LAR, adj., Biol., vascular.
VAS.CU.LAR.I.ZA.TION, s., Med., vascularização.
VAS.EC.TO.MY, s., Med., vasectomia.
VAS.E.LINE, s., vaselina.
VAST, adj., vasto, amplo, enorme.
VAS.TI.TUDE, s., vastidão, imensidão, imensidade.
VAST.LY, adv., vastamente, enormemente, muito.
VAST.NESS, s., o mesmo que vastitude: vastidão.
VAT, s., tina, cuba, vaza.
VAT.I.CAN, s., Vaticano.
VAULT, s., caixa-forte; arco, abóbada; cripta; v., saltar, pular; arquear.
VAULT.ING HORSE, s., Esp., cavalo (aparelho de ginástica olímpica).
VAUNT.ED, adj., alardeado, pomposo.
VAUNT.ER, s., alardeador, fanfarrão, gabador.
VEAL, s., vitela (carne).
VEER, v., virar, tornar.
VEGAN, s., adj., vegetariano (rígido).
VEG.E.TA.BLE, s., vegetal, legume, hortaliça; adj., vegetal.
VEG.E.TAR.I.AN, s., adj., vegetariano.

VEGETARIANISM ·· 645 ·· VICIOUS

VEG.E.TAR.I.AN.ISM, *s.*, vegetarianismo.
VEG.E.TATE, *v.*, vegetar; *Bot.*, crescer; *fig.*, viver como vegetal.
VEG.E.TA.TION, *s.*, vegetação.
VEG.GIE, *adj., col., UK* vegetariano.
VE.HE.MENCE, *s.*, veemência.
VE.HE.MENT, *adj.*, veemente, ardente, violento.
VE.HE.MENT.LY, *adv.*, veementemente; violentamente.
VE.HI.CLE, *s.*, veículo.
VE.HIC.U.LAR, *adj.*, veicular, relativo a veículos automotores.
VEIL, *s.*, véu; *fig.*, manto; *v.*, cobrir com véu; velar, vendar.
VEILED, *adj.*, velado.
VEIN, *s.*, veia; nervura.
VEINY, *adj.*, venenoso, detentor de veias.
VE.LOC.I.PEDE *s.*, velocípede.
VE.LOC.I.TY, *s.*, velocidade.
VE.LOUR, *s.*, tecido aveludado.
VE.LUM, *s.*, véu.
VEL.VET, *s.*, veludo; *adj.*, aveludado.
VE.NAL, *adj.*, venal.
VE.NAL.I.TY, *s.*, venalidade, corrupção.
VEND, *v.*, vender.
VEND.OR, *s.*, vendedor, fornecedor.
VE.NEER, *s.*, compensado (madeira), embutido; *fig.*, aparência; *v.*, embutir, chapear (com madeira).
VEN.ER.A.BLE, *adj.*, venerável.
VEN.ER.ATE, *v.*, venerar.
VEN.ER.A.TION, *s.*, veneração.
VEN.ERY, *s.*, caça, caçada.
VE.NE.TIAN BLIND, *s.*, veneziana, persiana.
VEN.GEANCE, *s.*, vingança, vendeta.
VE.NIAL, *adj.*, venial.
VEN.OM, *s.*, veneno.
VEN.OM.OUS, *adj.*, venenoso, peçonhento; maldoso.
VENT, *s.*, saída, passagem ou abertura de ar; vento; *v.*, expelir (ar); descarregar (frustrações).
VEN.TI.LATE, *v.*, ventilar, arejar.
VEN.TI.LA.TION, *s.*, ventilação, arejamento.
VEN.TI.LA.TOR, *s.*, ventilador.
VEN.TRI.CLE, *s.*, ventrículo.
VEN.TRIL.O.QUIST, *s.*, ventríloquo.
VEN.TURE, *s.*, empreendimento, atuação comercial; *v.*, arriscar, tentar.
VEN.TURE.SOME, *adj.*, aventureiro, empreendedor ousado.
VE.NUS, *s., Astron.*, planeta Vênus; *Mit.*, Vênus (deusa romana do amor e da beleza); *fig.*, mulher bela.
VE.RA.CIOUS, *adj.*, verídico, verdadeiro, veráz.
VE.RAC.I.TY, *s.*, veracidade.
VE.RAN.DA, *s.*, varanda.
VERB, *s.*, verbo.
VER.BAL, *adj.*, verbal, oral.
VER.BAL.LY, *adv.*, verbalmente, oralmente.
VER.BA.TIM, *adj., Lat.*, literal, textual; *adv.*, literalmente.
VER.BOSE, *adj.*, prolixo; verboso, loquaz.
VER.DAN.CY, *s.*, verdura.
VER.DICT, *s.*, veredicto, sentença, decisão judicial.
VER.DURE, *s.*, verdura.
VERGE, *s.*, borda, margem, beira, limite; *v.*, beirar; limitar; pender, tender (inclinando-se).
VER.GER, *s.*, sacristão.
VER.I.FI.CA.TION, *s.*, verificação, exame.
VER.I.FY, *v.*, verificar, inspecionar, vistoriar.

VER.I.TA.BLE, *adj.*, legítimo, verdadeiro, genuíno.
VER.I.TY, *s.*, verdade.
VER.MI.CEL.LI, *s.*, aletria.
VER.MI.CIDE, *s.*, vermicida.
VER.MI.FUGE, *s.*, vermífugo, *adj.*, vermífugo.
VER.MIL.ION, *s.*, a cor vermelho-alaranjado; *adj.*, vermelhão, vermelho-alaranjado.
VER.MIN.OUS, *adj.*, verminoso.
VER.MOUTH, *s.*, vermute.
VER.NAC.U.LAR, *s.*, vernáculo, língua-mãe.
VER.RU.CA, *s.*, verruga.
VER.SA.TILE, *adj.*, versátil, plástico.
VER.SA.TIL.I.TY, *s.*, versatilidade, flexibilidade.
VERSE, *s.*, verso, estrofe.
VERSED, *adj.*, versado, hábil.
VER.SI.CLE, *s.*, versículo.
VER.SI.FY, *v.*, versificar, fazer versos.
VER.SION, *s.*, versão.
VER.SUS, *prep.*, versus, contra, em oposição.
VER.TE.BRA, *s.*, vértebra.
VER.TE.BRATE, *s.*, vertebrado.
VER.TI.CAL, *adj.*, vertical.
VER.TI.CAL.I.TY, *s.*, verticalidade.
VER.TI.CAL.LY, *adv.*, verticalmente.
VER.TIG.I.NOUS, *adj.*, vertiginoso.
VER.TI.GO, *s.*, vertigem.
VERVE, *s.*, verve, vivacidade.
VER.Y, *adv.*, muito, bastante.
VES.I.CA, *s.*, bexiga.
VES.I.CLE, *s.*, vesícula.
VES.PER.TINE, *adj.*, vespertino.
VES.PERS, *s.*, vésperas.
VEST, *s., UK* camiseta; *US* colete; *v.*, investir, dar posse a, dotar.
VES.PI.ARY, *s.*, vespeiro.
VES.TAL, *s.*, vestal, virgem; *adj.*, vestal.
VES.TI.BULE, *s.*, vestíbulo, saguão, átrio.
VES.TIGE, *s.*, vestígio.
VEST.MENT, *s.*, veste, vestimenta, roupas.
VET.E.RAN, *s.*, veterano de guerra.
VET.ER.I.NAR.I.AN, *s., adj.*, veterinário.
VET.ER.I.NARY, *s.*, veterinário.
VE.TO, *s.*, veto; *v.*, vetar, proibir.
VET.TING, *s.*, exame minucioso, investigação; escrutínio.
VEX, *v.*, vexar; atormentar, afligir.
VEX.A.TION, *s.*, vexação, irritação.
VI.A, *prep.*, via, por meio de, por via de.
VI.A.BIL.I.TY, *s.*, viabilidade.
VI.A.BLE, *adj.*, viável.
VIA.DUCT, *s.*, viaduto.
VI.AND, *s.*, vianda, carne.
VI.BRANT, *adj.*, vibrante, entusiasmado, animado.
VI.BRATE, *v.*, vibrar, festejar.
VI.BRA.TOR, *s.*, vibrador.
VIC.AR, *s.*, vigário.
VICE, *s.*, vício, defeito, vezo; torno mecânico.
VICE-CHAN.CEL.LOR, *s.*, vice-chanceler.
VICE-PRES.I.DENT, *s.*, vice-presidente.
VICE-VER.SA, *adv.*, vice-versa; reciprocamente.
VI.CIN.I.TY, *s.*, proximidade, adjacência, vizinhança.
VI.CIOUS, *adj.*, vicioso, violento, cruel.

VICIOUSNESS   •• 646 ••   VIZ

VI.CIOUS.NESS, *s.*, violência, crueldade; vício.
VI.CIS.SI.TUDE, *s.*, vicissitude, mudança.
VIC.TIM, *s.*, vítima.
VIC.TIM.IZE(ISE), *v.*, vitimar.
VIC.TO.RI.AN, *s.*, *Hist.*, vitoriano; *adj.*, vitoriano (relativo à Rainha Vitória, 1819-1901).
VIC.TO.RI.OUS, *adj.*, vitorioso, vencedor.
VIC.TO.RY, *s.*, vitória. .
VI.DE.LI.CET, *adv.*, isto é, a saber (*prep.*, *abrev.*: *viz*).
VID.E.O, *s.*, vídeo (programa gravado para televisão); *adj.*, vídeo (relativo à televisão ou à imagem em tela).
VI.DE.O.CAS.SETTE, *s.*, fita de videocassete.
VI.DE.O.CON.FER.ENCE, *s.*, videoconferência.
VI.DE.O GAME, *s.*, videogame, videogueime, videojogo.
VI.DE.O.TAPE, *s.*, videoteipe; *v.*, gravar em videoteipe.
VIE, *v.*, competir, concorrer.
VI.ET.NAM, *s.*, Vietnã (país).
VI.ET.NAM.ESE, *s.*, *adj.*, vietnamita.
VIEW, *s.*, vista, ponto de vista, perspectiva, parecer.
VIEW.ER, *s.*, telespectador, visor.
VIEW.FIND.ER, *s.*, *Fot.*, visor.
VIEW.POINT, *s.*, ponto de vista.
VIG.IL, *s.*, vigília.
VIG.I.LANCE, *s.*, vigilância.
VIG.I.LANT, *adj.*, vigilante.
VIG.I.LAN.TE, *s.*, membro de grupo de vigilantes; justiceiro; *adj.*, justiceiro.
VIG.OR.OUS, *adj.*, vigoroso, vivaz.
VIG.OUR, VIGOR, *s.*, vigor, força, robustez.
VILE, *adj.*, vil, infame, repulsivo.
VIL.I.FY, *v.*, envilecer, aviltar, difamar.
VIL.LAGE, *s.*, aldeia, povoado, localidade.
VIL.LAG.ER, *s.*, aldeão. .
VIL.LAIN, *s.*, vilão, biltre, patife, safado.
VIN.DI.CATE, *v.*, vingar, justiçar, justificar.
VIN.DI.CA.TION, *s.*, vingança.
VIN.E.GAR, *s.*, vinagre.
VINE.YARD, *s.*, vinhedo, vinha.
VIN.AI.GRETTE, *s.*, molho vinagrete.
VIN.DI.CATE, *v.*, vindicar, justificar.
VIN.DI.CA.TOR, *s.*, vindicador, protetor, defensor.
VIN.DIC.TIVE, *adj.*, vingativo.
VINE, *s.*, *Bot.*, videira, vinha; *Bot.*, trepadeira.
VIN.E.GAR, *s.*, vinagre; *fig.*, mau humor.
VIN.E.GAR.ISH, *adj.*, avinagrado.
VINE.YARD, *s.*, vinhedo.
VIN.I.CUL.TURE, *s.*, vinicultura, viticultura.
VI.NO, *s.*, *col.*, vinho.
VIN.TAGE, *s.*, vindima, colheita de uva.
VINT.NER, *s.*, produtor ou comerciante de vinhos, taberneiro.
VI.NYL, *s.*, vinil.
VI.O.LA, *s.*, *Mús.*, viola; *Bot.*, violeta.
VI.O.LATE, *v.*, violar.
VI.O.LA.TION, *s.*, violação.
VI.O.LENCE, *s.*, violência.
VI.O.LENT, *adj.*, violento; furioso; duro, extremo, ardente.
VI.O.LENT.LY, *adv.*, violentamente.
VI.O.LET, *s.*, violeta; *adj.*, violeta, da cor de violeta.
VI.O.LIN, *s.*, *Mús.*, violino.
VI.O.LIN.IST, *s.*, violinista.
VI.O.LON.CEL.LIST, *s.*, violoncelista.

VI.O.LON.CEL.LO, *s.*, *Mús.*, violoncelo.
VI.O.LONE, *s.*, *Mús.*, contrabaixo.
VI.PER, *s.*, víbora, serpente, cobra.
VIR.GIN, *adj.*, *s.*, virgem.
VIR.GIN.AL, *s.*, *adj.*, virginal.
VIR.GIN.I.TY, *s.*, virgindade, celibato.
VIR.GO, *s.*, *Astron.*, Virgem (constelação); *Astrol.*, Virgem (signo do zodíaco).
VI.RID.I.TY, *s.*, verdor, verdura, viço.
VIR.ILE, *adj.*, viril.
VI.RIL.I.TY, *s.*, virilidade.
VI.ROL.O.GY, *s.*, virologia.
VIR.TU.AL, *adj.*, virtual.
VIR.TUE, *s.*, virtude, vantagem.
VIR.TU.OUS, *adj.*, virtuoso; honrado, íntegro.
VIR.TU.OUS.I.TY, *s.*, virtuosismo, virtuosidade.
VIR.U.LENCE, *s.*, virulência.
VIR.U.LENT, *adj.*, virulento.
VI.RUS, *s.*, vírus.
VI.SA, *s.*, visto, sinal.
VIS.CERA, *s.*, vísceras, intestinos.
VIS.CER.AL, *adj.*, visceral; *fig.*, instintivo, intuitivo.
VIS.COSE, *s.*, *Quím.*, viscose (solução); viscose (fio ou tecido).
VIS.COS.I.TY, *s.*, viscosidade.
VIS.COUNT, *s.*, visconde.
VIS.COUS, *adj.*, viscoso, pegajoso.
VISE, *s.*, *US* torno de mesa; *v.*, tornear.
VIS.I.BIL.I.TY, *s.*, visibilidade.
VIS.I.BLE, *adj.*, visível.
VIS.I.BLY, *adv.*, visivelmente.
VI.SION, *s.*, vista, visão, panorama.
VI.SION.AR.Y, *s.*, *adj.*, visionário.
VIS.IT, *s.*, visita; *v.*, visitar, fazer visitas.
VIS.I.TOR, *s.*, visitante, turista.
VIS.OR, *s.*, viseira.
VIS.TA, *s.*, vista, imagem, panorama, perspectiva.
VI.SU.AL, *adj.*, visual.
VI.SU.AL.I.ZA.TION, *s.*, visualização.
VI.SU.AL.IZE(-ISE), *v.*, visualizar.
VIS.U.AL.LY, *adv.*, visualmente.
VI.TAL, *adj.*, vital, essencial, fundamental.
VI.TAL.I.TY, *s.*, vitalidade, vigor, energia.
VI.TAL.IZE(-ISE), *v.*, vitalizar, revigorar.
VI.TAL.I.ZER(-ISER), *s.*, vitalizador.
VIT.AL.LY, *adv.*, extremamente.
VI.TA.MIN, *s.*, vitamina.
VI.TI.ATE, *v.*, viciar, corromper.
VI.TI.CUL.TURE, *s.*, viticultura.
VIT.RE.OUS, *adj.*, vítreo, vitroso.
VIT.RI.FI.CA.TION, *s.*, vitrificação.
VIT.RI.FY, *v.*, vitrificar.
VI.TU.PER.A.TION, *s.*, vituperação, advertência.
VI.VA.CIOUS, *adj.*, vivaz, animado, comunicativo.
VI.VAC.I.TY, *s.*, vivacidade, ânimo.
VIV.ID, *adj.*, vívido, claro, evidente.
VIV.ID.LY, *adv.*, vividamente; com cores vivas.
VIV.I.FI.CA.TION, *s.*, vivificação.
VIV.I.FY, *v.*, vivificar.
VIV.I.SEC.TION, *s.*, vivissecção.
VIX.EN, *s.*, *Zool.*, fêmea da raposa; *fig.*, megera.
VIZ, *prep.*, *abrev.* de *videlicet*: a saber, isto é.

VIZIER ··•647··· VULVA

VI.ZIER, VI.ZIR, *s.* vizir.
VO.CA.BLE, *s.,* vocábulo, termo, palavra.
VO.CAB.U.LARY, *s.,* vocabulário.
VO.CAL, *adj.,* vocal; franco, sincero.
VO.CAL.ISM, *s.,* vocalismo.
VO.CAL.IST, *s.,* vocalista.
VO.CAL.IZE, *v.,* vocalizar, pronunciar.
VO.CA.TION, *s.,* vocação.
VO.CA.TION.AL, *adj.,* vocacional, profissional.
VOC.A.TIVE, *adj., s.,* vocativo.
VO.CIF.ER.ATE, *v.,* vociferar.
VO.CIF.ER.OUS, *adj.,* vociferante.
VOD.KA, *s.,* vodca (bebida russa).
VOGUE, *s.,* moda, voga, evidência.
VOID, *s.,* vazio, vácuo; *adj.,* nulo, vazio.
VOL.A.TILE, *adj.,* volátil.
VOL.A.TIL.I.ZA.TION, *s.,* volatilização.
VOL.A.TIL.IZE(-ISE), *v.,* volatilizar.
VOL.CA.NIC, *adj.,* vulcânico.
VOL.CA.NO, *s.,* vulcão.
VOL.I.TION, *s.,* volição, vontade (de escolha).
VOLLEY, *s.,* rajada (tiroteio); *fig.,* torrente; *Esp.,* voleio; *v.,* dar voleio.
VOL.LEY.BALL, *s.,* vôlei, voleibol.
VOLT, *s.,* volt.
VOLT.AGE, *s.,* voltagem.
VOL.U.BIL.I.TY, *s.,* volubilidade, loquacidade.
VOL.UME, *s.,* volume, peso; capacidade.
VOL.U.MI.NOUS, *adj.,* volumoso; que ocupa muito espaço.

VOL.UN.TAR.I.LY, *adv.,* voluntariamente.
VOL.UN.TARY, *adj.,* voluntário, que trabalha de graça.
VOL.UN.TEER, *s.,* voluntário; *v.,* oferecer gratuitamente.
VO.LUP.TU.OUS, *adj.,* voluptuoso, sensual, libidinoso.
VO.LUP.TU.OUS.NESS, *s.,* volúpia, sensualidade, luxúria.
VOM.IT, *s.,* vômito; *v.,* vomitar.
VOO.DOO, *s.,* vodu.
VO.RA.CIOUS, *adj.,* voraz.
VO.RAC.I.TY, *s.,* voracidade, rapacidade.
VOR.TEX, *s.,* turbilhão.
VOTE, *s.,* voto, votação, sufrágio; *v.,* votar, sufragar.
VOT.ER, *s.,* eleitor, votante.
VOT.ING, *s.,* votação, sufrágio.
VOUCH, *v.,* garantir, dar garantia, assegurar.
VOUCH.ER, *s.,* garantia, tíquete, senha, cartão, vale.
VOW, *s.,* voto.
VOW.EL, *s.,* vogal.
VOY.AGE, *s.,* viagem, itinerário.
VOY.AG.ER, *s.,* viajante.
VOY.EUR, *s., Fr.,* voyeur.
VOY.EUR.ISM, *s., Fr.,* voyeurismo.
VUL.GAR, *adj.,* vulgar, ordinário, popular.
VUL.GAR.I.TY, *s.,* vulgaridade, grosseria.
VUL.GAR.IZE, *v.,* vulgarizar, popularizar.
VUL.NER.A.BIL.I.TY, *s.,* vulnerabilidade.
VUL.NER.A.BLE, *adj.,* vulnerável; sensível, influenciável.
VUL.NER.A.BLY, *adv.,* vulneravelmente.
VUL.TURE, *s.,* abutre.
VUL.VA, *s.,* vulva.

W, s., vigésima terceira letra do alfabeto inglês.
WACK.I.NESS, s., gír., US excentricidade, maluquice.
WACK.Y, adj., excêntrico, extravagante.
WAD, s., chumaço, maço (dinheiro), pilha (documentos); v., estofar.
WAD.DING, s., forro, entretela.
WADE, v., andar com dificuldade, caminhar; patinhar.
WAD.ING-POOL, s., piscina para crianças.
WA.FER, s., bolacha doce.
WAF.FLE, s., Cul., waffle (tipo de biscoito); lenga-lenga; v., ser evasivo, enrolar.
WAFT, v., flutuar.
WAFT.AGE, s., transporte (pela água).
WAG, v., sacudir, menear, mexer.
WAGE, s., salário, vencimento.
WA.GER, s., aposta.
WAG.GISH, adj., brincalhão, jocoso.
WAG.GLE, s., balanço, meneio; v., balançar, menear.
WAG.GON-LIT, s., vagão-dormitório.
WAG.GON, s., vagão.
WAIL, s., lamento, queixa, gemido; v., lamentar-se, gemer.
WAIL.ING, s., choramingo, queixume; lamentação.
WAIN, s., carro, carroça, veículo.
WAIST, s., cintura (do corpo).
WAIST.BAND, s., cós, cintura da calça.
WAIST.COAT, s., colete.
WAIST.LINE, s., medida da cintura.
WAIT, s., espera; v., esperar, aguardar.
WAIT.ER, s., garçom.
WAIT.ING, s., espera, serviço.
WAIT.RESS, s., garçonete.
WAIVE, v., renunciar, abrir mão de; protelar.
WAIV.ER, s., desistência; Jur., renúncia.
WAKE, s., esteira; velório; v., acordar, despertar.
WAKEN, v., despertar, acordar; avivar.
WAK.ING, s., vigilância, vigília.
WALES, s., País de Gales.
WALK, s., passeio, excursão, caminhada, andada, passo; v., andar, caminhar.
WALK.ER, s., caminhante, pedestre, andante.
WALK.ING, s., andar, caminhada, andada.
WALK.ING DIC.TION.AR.Y, s., dicionário ambulante (pessoa que fala difícil).
WALK-ON, s., figurante (teatro); adj., de figurante.
WALK.OUT, s., greve branca (greve que favorece patrões).
WALK.O.VER, s., UK vitória fácil, barbada.
WALKWAY, s., passarela (de pedestres).
WALL, s., muro, parede.
WAL.LA.BY, s., Zool., canguru pequeno.
WALLED, adj., murado, cercado por muros.
WAL.LET, s., carteira (de homem).
WAL.LOP, s., surra; v., surrar.

WAL.LOW, s., chafurda; v., chafurdar.
WALL.PA.PER, s., papel de parede.
WAL.LY, s., UK pateta, bobo.
WAL.NUT, s., noz; nogueira.
WAL.RUS, s., morsa.
WALTZ, s., valsa; v., valsar, dançar valsa.
WAND, s., varinha mágica.
WAN.DER, v., perambular, vagar, divagar.
WAN.DER.ER, s., vagabundo.
WAN.DER.ING, adj., divagante, ambulante.
WANE, v., diminuir, decrescer.
WAN.GLE, v., col., arranjar, conseguir, dar um jeito.
WAN.NA.BE, s., aspirante a músico; col., US aquele que deseja ser igual a outro.
WAN.NESS, s., palidez.
WANT, v., desejar, querer, necessitar, exigir.
WANT.AGE, s., falta, carência.
WANT.ED, adj., procurado (pela polícia); desejado.
WANTING, adj., carente.
WAN.TON, adj., gratuito, irresponsável.
WAN.TON.NESS, s., lascívia.
WAR, s., guerra.
WARD, s., ala (hospital); enfermaria; distrito eleitoral; Jur., tutelado.
WAR.DEN, s., administrador de hotel, diretor.
WAR.DER, s., carcereiro.
WARD.ROBE, s., guarda-roupas.
WARE, s., mercadoria, gêneros alimentícios.
WARE.HOUSE, s., armazém, depósito.
WARES, s., mercadorias.
WAR.FARE, s., guerra, combate, disputa (de gangues).
WARHEAD, s., Mil., ogiva (míssil).
WAR.I.LY, adv., cautelosamente; com desconfiança.
WAR.I.NESS, s., cautela, cuidado, precaução.
WAR.LOCK, s., bruxo, feiticeiro, mago.
WARM, adj., quente.
WARM-HEART.ED, adj., afetuoso, amável, simpático.
WARM.LY, adv., calorosamente; efusivamente.
WARM.NESS, s., cordialidade; entusiasmo; tepidez.
WAR.MON.GER, s., belicista, provocador.
WARMTH, s., calor, quentura, calor humano.
WARN, v., avisar, prevenir, acautelar.
WARN.ING, s., advertência, aviso, chamada de atenção.
WARP, s., urdidura; empenamento; v., distorcer, deformar; empenar.
WARPED, adj., curvo, empenado.
WAR.RANT, s., autorização, mandado judicial, patente.
WAR.RANT.ER, s., fiador.
WAR.RAN.TY, s., garantia.
WAR.REN, s., toca de coelho, coelheira; labirinto, confusão.
WAR.RING, adj., rival, contrário, oposto.
WAR.RIOR, s., guerreiro.

WARSHIP ·· 649 ·· WEDGE

WAR.SHIP, *s.*, navio de guerra.
WART, *s.*, verruga.
WART.Y, *adj.*, verruguento.
WAR.TIME, *s.*, tempo de guerra; *adj.*, tempo de guerra.
WARY, *adj.*, receoso, cauteloso; prudente.
WAS, *v., ps* de *to be*.
WASH, *v.*, lavar, limpar; *s.*, lavagem, limpeza.
WASH.A.BLE, *adj.*, lavável.
WASH.BA.SIN, *s.*, lavatório.
WASH.CLOTH, *s.*, toalha de rosto.
WASHED-OUT, *adj.*, desbotado; *fig.*; esgotado, abatido.
WASHED-UP, *adj., col.*, liquidado, acabado; abatido.
WASH.ING, *s.*, lavagem, banho; roupa lavada; roupa para lavar.
WASH.OUT, *s., col.*, fracasso, desastre; solapamento.
WASH.ROOM, *s.*, banheiro; *US* lavabo.
WASN'T, *contr.* de *was not*.
WASHY, *adj.*, úmido, molhado, lavado.
WASP, *s., Zool.*, vespa.
WASP.ISH, *adj., fig.*, mordaz, rabugento; semelhante à vespa.
WAST.AGE, *s.*, desgaste, desperdício, perda.
WASTE, *s.*, sobra, refugo; *adj.*, de sobra, refugado; residual; de esgoto; *v.*, desperdiçar, devastar, assolar.
WAST.ED, *adj.*, desperdiçado, perdido, arruinado, debilitado; *col.*, drogado.
WASTE.FUL, *adj.*, esbanjador, pródigo; devastador.
WASTE.LAND, *s.*, terreno deserto, solo improdutivo.
WAST.ER, *s.*, gastador, pródigo, esbanjador.
WATCH, *s.*, relógio; vigília, vigia, guarda; *v.*, vigiar, contemplar, olhar; cuidar.
WATCH.DOG, *s.*, cão de guarda; *fig.*, guardião.
WATCH.ER, *s.*, vigia, vigilante, guarda.
WATCH.FUL, *adj.*, atento, vigilante, cauteloso.
WATCH.MA.KER, *s.*, relojoeiro.
WATCH.MAN, *s.*, guarda, vigia, segurança.
WATCH.STRAP, *s.*, pulseira de relógio.
WATCH.WORD, *s.*, palavra de ordem, lema; *Mil.*, senha.
WA.TER, *s.*, água; *v.*, regar, molhar, lacrimejar.
WA.TER.COL.OUR, *s.*, aquarela.
WA.TER.COURSE, *s.*, córrego, riacho, canal.
WA.TER.CRESS, *s.*, agrião.
WA.TER.FALL, *s.*, queda d'água, cachoeira, cascata.
WA.TER.FRONT, *s.*, margem, orla marítima, beira-mar; *adj.*, na margem.
WA.TER GATE, *s.*, comporta.
WA.TER HOLE, *s.*, olho d'água, cisterna, cacimba.
WA.TER.ING CAN, *s.*, o mesmo que *watering pot*.
WA.TER.ING POT, *s.*, regador.
WA.TER LI.LY, *s., Bot.*, nenúfar, ninfeia, vitória-régia.
WA.TER.LINE, *s., Náut.*, linha-d'água.
WA.TER MAIN, *s.*, adutora; grande tubo de água.
WA.TER.MAN, *s.*, barqueiro.
WA.TER.MARK, *s.*, marca d'água (em papel); marca do nível de água.
WA.TER.MEL.ON, *s.*, melancia.
WA.TER POLO, *s., Esp.*, polo aquático.
WA.TER.PROOF, *adj., s.*, impermeável; *adj.*, à prova d'água.
WA.TERS.HED, *s., Geogr.*, linha divisória de águas.
WA.TER.SIDE, *s.*, margem de rio; beira-mar; costa; *adj.*, ribeirinho, lacustre.
WA.TER.SPOUT, *s.*, tromba d'água.

WA.TER.TIGHT, *adj.*, à prova d'água, hermético; *fig.*, seguro; explícito, claro.
WA.TERY, *adj.*, úmido, molhado, aquoso.
WATT, *s., Eletr.*, watt.
WATT.AGE, *s., Eletr.*, voltagem, potência em *watts*.
WAVE, *s.*, onda, sinal, ondulação; *v.*, acenar com a mão.
WAVED, *adj.*, ondulado, cheio de ondas.
WA.VER, *s.*, oscilação; hesitação; *v.*, vacilar, hesitar; sacudir, oscilar, tremer; esvoaçar.
WA.VER.ING, *adj.*, indeciso, hesitante.
WAV.Y, *adj.*, ondulado, ondulante; flutuante.
WAX, *s.*, cera; *v.*, passar cera.
WAX.EN, *adj.*, de cera; lustroso; semelante à cera, pálido.
WAX.WORKS, *s.*, museu de cera.
WAXY, *adj.*, de cera.
WAY, *s.*, caminho, via, estrada, percurso, direção, hábito.
WAY.FAR.ER, *s.*, viajante.
WAY.LAY, *v.*, abordar; tocaiar.
WAY OUT, *s.*, saída; *adj., col.*, *way-out*: arrojado.
WAY.WARD, *adj., col.*, incorrigível; caprichoso, indócil.
W.C., *s.*, banheiro, privada, toalete.
WE, *pron.*, nós.
WEAK, *adj.*, fraco, frágil, débil.
WEAK.EN, *v.*, enfraquecer(-se), debilitar.
WEAK.LING, *s., pej.*, fracote.
WEAK.LY, *adv.*, fracamente.
WEAK.NESS, *s.*, fraqueza, debilidade.
WEAL, *s.*, vergão, vinco (de chicotada).
WEALTH, *s.*, riqueza, abundância, copiosidade.
WEALTH.Y, *adj.*, rico, endinheirado; abundante.
WEAN, *v.*, desmamar (bebê), desaleitar, despegar.
WEAP.ON, *s.*, arma.
WEAR, *s.*, uso, desgaste, perda; *v.*, vestir, desgastar, calçar.
WEAR.A.BLE, *adj.*, usável, que se pode usar.
WEA.RI.LY, *adv.*, com cansaço; cansativamente.
WEA.RI.NESS, *s.*, cansaço, aborrecimento.
WEAR.ING, *adj.*, fatigante, exaustivo.
WEA.RY, *adj.*, cansado, deprimido.
WEA.SEL, *s., Zool.*, doninha.
WEATH.ER, *s.*, tempo.
WEATH.ER.COCK, *s.*, cata-vento.
WEATH.ERED, *adj.*, marcado, deteriorado, gasto (com o tempo).
WEATH.ER.MAN, *s.*, meteorologista.
WEAVE, *s.*, tecedura, trama (de tecido); *v.*, tecer, costurar; trançar.
WEAV.ER, *s.*, tecelão.
WEAV.ING, *s.*, tecelagem.
WEB, *s.*, teia, tecido; *fig.*, rede; *Comp.*, *Web* (rede mundial de computadores).
WEB.BING, *s.*, borda de tapete; tira de tecido resistente.
WEB.CAM, *s., Comp.*, câmera para conexão de internet, *webcam*.
WEB.CAST, *s., Comp.*, transmissão ao vivo pela internet.
WEB DE.SIGN.ER, *s.*, *web designer* (desenvolvedor de páginas da *web*).
WEB.PHONE, *s.*, telefone via internet, *webphone*.
WEB.STER, *s.*, tecelão.
WED.DING, *s.*, casamento.
WED.DING CAKE, *s.*, bolo de casamento.
WEDGE, *s.*, cunha; *fig.*, calço; *v.*, usar cunha.

WEDLOCK · 650 · WHITE GOODS

WED.LOCK, *s.*, casamento, matrimônio.

WEDNES.DAY, *s.*, quarta-feira.

WEE, *adj.*, pequeninho, minúsculo; de madrugada; *US col.*, xixi.

WEED.Y, *adj.*, cheio de ervas daninhas; franzinho, magro, fracote.

WEEK.DAY, *s.*, dia de semana.

WEEK.END, *s.*, fim de semana.

WEEK.LY, *s.*, semanário; *adj.*, semanal; *adv.*, semanalmente.

WEEP, *v.*, *pp* e *ps* de *wept*: chorar.

WEEP.Y, *adj.*, choroso, lacrimoso.

WEFT, *s.*, trama, tecido.

WEIGHT, *s.*, peso.

WEIGHT.A.BLE, *adj.*, pesável.

WEIGHT.ED, *adj.*, com peso.

WEIGHT.LESS.NESS, *s.*, anti-gravidade; ausência de peso; imponderabilidade.

WEIGHT.Y, *adj.*, pesado.

WEIR, *s.*, represa, açude, dique.

WEIRD, *adj.*, estranho, esquisito.

WEL.COME, *s.*, acolhida, recepção; *adj.*, bem-vindo.

WEL.COM.ING, *s.*, acolhida, acolhimento.

WELD, *s.*, solda; *v.*, soldar.

WELD.ER, *s.*, soldador.

WEL.FARE, *s.*, bem-estar; saúde social; *adj.*, de assistência social.

WELL, *s.*, poço.

WELL-BAL.ANCED, *adj.*, bem equilibrado; equilibrado.

WELL-BE.ING, *s.*, bem-estar.

WELL-BRED, *adj.*, bem-educado, polido, fino.

WELL-DONE, *adj.*, bem-feito; *Cul.*, bem passado.

WELL HEAD, *s.*, nascente, fonte.

WEL.LIES, *s. pl.*, *UK* botas impermeáveis (também *wellington*).

WEL.LING.TON, *s.*, bota impermeável de cano alto.

WELL-KNOWN, *adj.*, conhecido, familiar.

WELL-TIMED, *adj.*, oportuno; em tempo apropriado.

WEL.LY, *s.*, *UK* o mesmo que *wellies*.

WELSH, *adj.*, *s.*, galês.

WEL.TER, *s.*, confusão, rebuliço; *v.*, rolar, rebolar-se.

WEND.Y HOUSE, *s.*, casinha de brinquedo.

WERE.WOLF, *s.*, lobisomem.

WEST, *s.*, oeste; *adv.*, para oeste.

WEST.BOUND, *adj.*, em direção a oeste.

WEST.ERN, *s.*, filme americano de ação dos tempos da colonização; *adj.*, ocidental.

WEST.ERN.IZE(-ISE), *v.*, ocidentalizar.

WEST.ERN.MOST, *adj.*, o mais ocidental.

WEST IN.DI.AN, *s.*, *adj.*, antilhano.

WEST.WARD *adv.*, para o oeste, em direção ao oeste. *westwards*

WET, *s.*, chuva, umidade; *adj.*, úmido, molhado, ensopado ; *v.*, molhar, umedecer.

WET.NESS, *s.*, umidade, umedecimento.

WE'VE, *contr.* de *we have*.

WACK, *s.*, *gír.*, *UK* cara, sujeito; *adj.*, *US* droga, porcaria.

WHALE, *s.*, *Zool.*, baleia.

WHAL.ING, *s.*, pesca de baleias; baleação.

WHAM, *excl.*, bum! (barulho de impacto).

WHARF, *s.*, cais, molhe.

WHAT, *pron.*, que, o que, aquilo; quê? o quê?

WHAT.EV.ER, *pron.*, tudo aquilo que, qualquer coisa que.

WHAT.NOT, *s.*, estante; *pron.*, coisas assim, outras coisas mais.

WHEAT, *s.*, trigo.

WHEE.DLE, *v.*, obter por astúcia, conseguir por logro, conseguir por adulação.

WHEEL, *s.*, roda, roda do leme; *v.*, dar voltas, girar, empurrar algo com rodas.

WHEEL.BAR.ROW, *s.*, carrinho de mão.

WHEEL.BASE, *s.*, distância entre eixos.

WHEEL.CHAIR, *s.*, cadeira de rodas.

WHEEZE, *s.*, respiração ofegante; *v.*, ofegar, resfolegar.

WHEEZ.Y, *adj.*, ofegante, resfolegante.

WHELK, *s.*, *Zool.*, búzio, caramujo.

WHEN, *adv.*, quando; *conj.*, ao passo que.

WHENCE, *adv.*, donde, de que lugar.

WHENCE.SO.EV.ER, *adv.*, de qualquer lugar.

WHEN.EV.ER, *adv.*, quando, toda vez que; quando quer que; sempre (que); *conj.*, sempre que, toda vez que.

WHERE, *s.*, cenário, lugar; *adv.* e *conj.*, onde?, onde, aonde.

WHERE.A.BOUTS, *s.*, paradeiro; *adv.*, onde, por onde.

WHERE.AS, *conj.*, enquanto, ao passo que, considerando que.

WHERE.BY, *pron.*, pelo qual.

WHERE.OF, *adv.*, do que.

WHER.EV.ER, *adv.* e *conj.*, para onde quer que; seja onde for; onde? para onde?

WHERE.UP.ON, *conj.*, formal; ao que, do que.

WER.RY, *s.*, barco.

WHETH.ER, *conj.*, se.

WHET, *v.*, aguçar, despertar, estimular; amolar, afiar.

WHICH, *pron.*, que, qual, quais, o qual, a qual.

WHICH.EV.ER, *pron.*, qualquer, quaisquer.

WHIFF, *s.*, cheirinho, cheiro, odor; *fig.*, sopro.

WHILE, *s.*, tempo, período; *conj.*, enquanto, ao mesmo tempo que, contanto.

WHIM, *s.*, capricho, extravagância.

WHIM.PER, *s.*, queixa, lamento, lamúria; *v.*, chorar, lamuriar-se, soluçar.

WHIM.SY, *s.*, capricho, teimosia, mania.

WHINE, *s.*, gemido; grito; *v.*, gemer, queixar-se; gritar.

WHINGE, *v.*, lamuriar, choramingar.

WHIP, *s.*, chicote; *v.*, chicotear, bater, espancar, sovar.

WHIP.PER, *s.*, açoitador (com chicote).

WHIP.PET, *s.*, whippet, galgo (cão grande e esguio, próprio para corrida).

WHIP.PING, *s.*, açoite, espancamento.

WHIRL, *s.*, redemoinho, giro, rodopio; tumulto, confusão; *v.*, rodopiar.

WHIRL.POOL, *s.*, remoinho.

WHIRL.WIND, *s.*, redemoinho de vento, vendaval; furacão.

WHISK, *s.*, batedeira; *v.*, mover com rapidez.

WHIS.KER, *s.*, bigode,(de gato, rato); bigode; *whiskers s.pl.*: suíças, costeletas.

WHIS.KY, *s.*, uísque.

WHIS.PER, *s.*, murmúrio, sussurro; *v.*, murmurar.

WHIS.PER.ING, *s.*, cochicho(s), sussurro(s); boato(s).

WHIST, *s.*, uíste (certo jogo de cartas).

WHIS.TLE, *s.*, apito; assobio; *v.*, apitar, assobiar.

WHIT, *s.*, bocado, pitada; *not a ~* : nem um pouco.

WHITE, *adj.*, branco, pálido, alvo, cândido.

WHITE GOODS, *s. pl.*, eletrodomésticos (linha branca); roupas brancas (lençóis, toalhas).

WHITE-HAIRED ··651·· WISDOM

WHITE-HAIRED, *adj.*, grisalho (cabelos).
WHIT.EN, *v.*, branquear, alvejar, caiar.
WHITE.NESS, *s.*, brancura, alvura, palidez.
WHIT.EN.ER, *s.*, branqueador, alvejante.
WHITE SAUCE, *s.*, molho branco.
WHITE TRASH, *s., pej., US* branquelo, branco pobre.
WHITE.WASH, *s.*, cal.
WHIT.SUN, *s.*, Pentecostes.
WHIT.TLE, *v.*, cortar, cortar com faca.
WHIZ, *s.*, zumbido, zunido, ruído estridente.
WHO, *pron.*, quem?, que; oqual, osquais.
WHO.EV.ER, *pron.*, quem quer que.
WHOLE, *s.*, totalidade; *adj.*, todo, integral, completo; *pron.*, todo.
WHOLE-HEART.ED, *adj.*, sincero, cordial, sério.
WHOLE.MEAL, *adj.*, integral, completo, total.
WHOLE NOTE, *s., Mús.*, semibreve.
WHOLE.SALE, *s.*, venda por atacado, venda em grande quantidade.
WHOLE.SOME, *adj.*, saudável, sadio, são.
WHOL.LY, *adv.*, inteiramente, totalmente.
WHOM, *pron.*, quem?; quem.
WHOM.SO.EV.ER, *pron.*, quem quer que seja.
WHOOP, *s.*, grito, berro; grito de guerra; pio (coruja); tosse (de engasgo); *v.*, gritar, bradar; piar.
WHOOP.EE, *interj.*, oba! hip hurra!; *s.*, festividade ruidosa.
WHOOPS, *interj.*, opa! ops!
WHOOSH, *s.*, som sibilante, rajada (de vento); esguicho; *v.*, soprar forte; esguichar.
WHOP, *v., col.*, derrubar, derrotar, espancar; som de soco.
WHOP.PER, *s., col.*, mentira deslavada, exagero; colosso.
WHOP.PING, *adj., col.*, imenso, colossal.
WHORE, *s.*, prostituta, meretriz, rameira.
WHO'RE, *contr.* de *who are*.
WHOSE, *pron.*, de quem, do qual, da qual.
WHO.SO.EV.ER, *pron.*, seja quem for, quem quer que.
WHO'VE, *contr.* de *who have*.
WHY, *pron.*, por que, por quê?; *conj.*, porque.
WICK, *s.*, pavio, mecha.
WICK.ER, *s.*, vime.
WICK.ET, *s.*, portinhola, cancela; *UK Esp.*, meta (críquete).
WIDE, *adj.*, largo, vasto, grande, amplo.
WIDE-A.WAKE, *adj.*, desperto, atento; de olhos abertos.
WIDE.LY, *adv.*, largamente, amplamente.
WID.EN, *v.*, alargar, ampliar, aumentar.
WIDE.NESS, *s.*, largura, amplitude.
WIDE-OPEN, *adj.*, escancarado, arregalado, todo aberto.
WID.OW, *s.*, viúva.
WID.OW.ER, *s.*, viúvo.
WID.OW.HOOD, *s.*, viuvez.
WIDE.SPREAD, *adj.*, disseminado, muito espalhado, comum.
WID.OW, *s.*, viúva.
WID.OWED, *adj.*, viúvo(a); enviuvado(a); *fig.*, abandonado.
WID.OW.ER, *s.*, viúvo (homem).
WIDTH, *s.*, largura.
WIELD, *v., UK* manejar, controlar; exercer (autoridade).
WIFE, *s.*, esposa, consorte.
WIG, *s.*, peruca.
WIG.GLE, *v.*, balanço, meneio; *v.*, balançar, oscilar, menear(-se).
WIG.GLY, *adj.*, ondulado, sinuoso, serpeante.
WIG.WAM, *s., US* tenda (dos índios norte-americanos).

WILD, *adj.*, selvagem, silvestre, furioso, bárbaro, insensato.
WILD.CAT, *s., Zool.*, gato selvagem; *Zool.*, lince.
WIL.DE.BEEST, *s., Zool.*, gnu.
WIL.DER.NESS, *s.*, sertão, terra inculta e bravia, local ermo.
WILD FLOW.ER, *s., Bot.*, planta silvestre; flor silvestre.
WILD FOWL, *s., Zool.*, qualquer ave silvestre.
WILD.LIFE, *s.*, animais e plantas selvagens.
WILD.LY, *adv.*, de modo selvagem, agrestemente; selvagemente; ameaçadoramente; extremamente.
WILE, *s.*, truque, esperteza; *wiles s.pl.:* artimanhas.
WIL.FUL *UK*, **WILLFUL** *US*, teimoso, voluntarioso; proposital.
WILL, *s.*, desejo, vontade, testamento; *v.*, querer, desejar.
WILLED, *adj.*, com boa vontade, pronto, propenso.
WILL.ING, *adj.*, disposto; inclinado a; prestativo; concordante.
WILL.ING.LY, *adv.*, de bom grado.
WILL.ING.NESS, *s.*, boa vontade, disposição, prontidão.
WIL.LOW, *s.*, salgueiro.
WIL.LOW.Y, *adj.*, longilíneo, esbelto, flexível.
WILL POW.ER, *s.*, força de vontade.
WIL.LY, *s., UK gír.* vulgar para pênis.
WILT, *s.*, murchar, definhar, esmorecer.
WILY, *adj.*, esperto, sagaz, astuto, inteligente.
WIMP, *s.*, pessoa fraca; *pej.*, maricão.
WIN, *s.*, vitória; *v.*, vencer, superar, ganhar.
WINCE, *s.*, recuo, contração (de dor); *v.*, recuar (reação); contrair-se (de dor ou de vergonha).
WINCH, *s.*, guindaste, guincho; manivela; *v.*, levantar (algo) com guindaste.
WIND, *s.*, vento, fôlego, aragem.
WIND.ED, *adj.*, sem fôlego.
WIND.FALL, *s.*, golpe de sorte.
WIND.ING, *s.*, curva, dobra, enrolamento; *adj.*, sinuoso; tortuoso, enrolado; torcido.
WIND.MILL, *s.*, moinho de vento.
WIN.DOW, *s.*, janela.
WIN.DOW LEDGE, *s.*, parapeito de janela.
WIN.DOW.PANE, *s.*, vidraça.
WIN.DOW SHADE, *s., US* persiana.
WIND.PIPE, *s., Anat.*, traqueia.
WIND.SCREEN, *s.*, para-brisa.
WIND SOCK, *s., Aeron.*, biruta.
WIND.SURF.ER, *s.*, prancha de windsurf; windsurfista.
WIND.SURF.ING, *s., Esp.*, surfe à vela.
WIND.Y, *adj.*, com vento, cheio de vento.
WINE, *s.*, vinho.
WINE CEL.LAR, *s.*, adega.
WING, *s.*, asa, para-lama.
WING.SPAN, *s.*, envergadura (da asa).
WINK, *s.*, piscada; *v.*, piscar.
WIN.KLE, *s., Zool.*, caramujo.
WIN.NER, *s.*, vencedor, conquistador.
WIN.NING, *s.*, ato de vencer; *adj.*, vencedor, vitorioso; atraente, sedutor.
WIN.NINGS, *s. pl.*, lucros, ganhos, proveito.
WIN.SOME, *adj.*, atraente, encantador.
WIN.TER, *s.*, inverno.
WIN.TRY, *adj.*, invernal, hibernal, invernoso.
WIPE, *s.*, limpeza, higiene; *v.*, limpar, higienizar.
WIRE, *s.*, arame, fio, telegrama; *v.*, colocar fios elétricos.
WIR.ING, *s.*, instalação elétrica.
WIS.DOM, *s.*, sabedoria, prudência, ciência.

WISE   ·· 652 ··   WORTH

WISE, *adj.*, prudente, sábio, sensato, erudito.

WISE.LY, *adv.*, sabiamente.

WISH, *s.*, desejo, vontade; *v.*, querer, desejar.

WISH.FUL, *adj.*, desejoso.

WISP, *s.*, mecha, tufo (cabelo); *fig.*, fragmento, bocado.

WISP.Y, *adj.*, ralo, delgado, fino; insignificante; em tufos.

WIST.FUL, *adj.*, melancólico, triste, saudoso.

WIT, *s.*, pessoa espirituosa; sagacidade; juízo.

WITCH, *s.*, bruxa.

WITCH.CRAFT, *s.*, bruxaria, feitiçaria.

WITCH DOC.TOR, *s.*, feiticeiro, curandeiro.

WITCH HUNT, *s.*, caça às bruxas.

WITH, *prep.*, com.

WITH.DRAW, *v.*, retirar, sacar (dinheiro); retrair, recolher(-se), remover; privar de; *Mil.*, recuar.

WITH.DRAW.AL, *s.*, retirada, saque; remoção, afastamento.

WITHE, *s.*, vime, junco.

WITH.ER, *v.*, secar, murchar, definhar; debilitar(-se).

WITH.ERED, *adj.*, murcho, seco, mirrado.

WITH.HOLD, *v.*, reter, conservar; negar.

WITH.IN, *prep.*, dentro de.

WITH.OUT, *prep.*, sem.

WITH.STAND, *v.*, resistir a, aguentar, opor-se.

WIT.NESS, *s.*, testemunha; testemunho; *v.*, testemunhar, presenciar.

WIT.TER, *v.*, *col.*, *UK* dizer abobrinhas.

WIT.TI.CISM, *s.*, dito sagaz, observação espirituosa, graça.

WIT.TY, *adj.*, espirituoso, arguto; gracioso, satírico, mordaz.

WIVE, *v.*, desposar(-se), casar(-se); tomar como esposa.

WIVES, *s. pl.*, esposas.

WIZ.ARD, *s.*, feiticeiro.

WIZ.EN, *v.*, murchar, secar; *adj.*, murcho, seco.

WIZ.ENED, *adj.*, seco, murcho; enrugado, rugoso.

WOB.BLE, *s.*, balanço, bamboleio; *v.*, cambalear; balançar, tremer, oscilar.

WOB.BLY, *adj.*, vacilante; *col.*, molenga, bambo.

WOE, *s.*, mágoa, dor, sofrimento.

WOK, *s.*, tipo de panela chinesa, *wok*.

WOLD, *s.*, bosque.

WOLF, *s.*, lobo.

WOM.AN, *s.*, mulher.

WOM.AN.HOOD, *s.*, sexo feminino, feminilidade.

WOM.AN.IZER(ISER), *s.*, *pej.*, conquistador, mulherengo, galinha.

WOM.AN.LY, *adj.*, feminino.

WOMB, *s.*, útero.

WOM.EN'S LIB.E.RA.TION, *s.*, movimento de libertação feminina.

WON, *v.*, *ps* e *pp* de *to win*.

WON.DER, *s.*, maravilha, espetáculo; *v.*, maravilhar, admirar, desejar.

WON.DER.FUL, *adj.*, maravilhoso, espetacular, prodigioso.

WON.DER.FUL.LY, *adv.*, maravilhosamente, notavelmente.

WON.DER.LAND, *s.*, país das maravilhas; paraíso.

WON.DROUS, *adj.*, maravilhoso, prodigioso.

WON.KY, *adj.*, vacilante, inseguro; torto.

WONT, *s.*, hábito, costume, prática; *adj.*, acostumado, habitual, de praxe.

WON'T, *contr.* de *will not*.

WOO, *v.*, namorar, flertar, fazer a corte.

WOOD, *s.*, madeira, floresta, mata.

WOOD.ED, *adj.*, arborizado.

WOOD.EN, *adj.*, de madeira; *fig.*, desajeitado, sem jeito.

WOOD.LAND, *s.*, mata, floresta, bosque.

WOOD.MAN, *s.*, guarda-florestal.

WOOD.PECK.ER, *s.*, pica-pau.

WOOD.WORK, *s.*, carpintaria.

WOOD.WORM, *s.*, *Zool.*, caruncho, carcoma.

WOOF, *s.*, uivo; cãozinho (infantil); trama, tecido; *v.*, latir, ladrar; tramar, blefar.

WOOL, *s.*, lã.

WOOL.LY, *adj.*, de lã, lanoso; *US* incerto, confuso.

WOOL.LY HEAD.ED, *adj.*, desatinado; cheio de fantasias, cheio de idealismos.

WOOZ.Y, *adj.*, atordoado; *gír.*, alcoolizado.

WORCES.TER SAUCE, *s.*, molho inglês.

WORD, *s.*, palavra, termo, notícia, comentário; *v.*, redigir, escrever.

WORD.ING, *s.*, palavreado, fraseado.

WORD PRO.CES.SOR, *s.*, *Comp.*, processador de textos.

WORD.Y, *adj.*, *pej.*, prolixo, floreado.

WORK, *s.*, trabalho, labuta, emprego, serviço; *v.*, trabalhar, funcionar, moldar.

WORK.A.BLE, *adj.*, viável, utilizável, executável.

WORK.A.HOL.IC, *s.*, pessoa fanática por trabalho.

WORK.BENCH, *s.*, bancada (de mecânico); banca (de trabalho).

WORK.BOOK, *s.*, livro-texto; livro de exercícios.

WORKED-UP, *adj.*, exaltado.

WORK.ER, *s.*, trabalhador, operário.

WORK.HOUSE, *s.*, *UK* albergue, asilo; *US* casa de correção.

WORK.ING, *s.*, operação, procedimento de trabalho; *adj.*, em operação; que trabalha, trabalhador; ativo.

WORK LOAD, *s.*, carga de trabalho.

WORK.MAN, *s.*, trabalhador, operário.

WORK.MAN.SHIP, *s.*, qualidade (de trabalho), obra, manufatura, acabamento.

WORK.MATE, *s.*, colega de trabalho.

WORK OF ART, *s.*, obra de arte.

WORK.OUT, *s.*, treinamento, prática, prova, experiência.

WORK.ROOM, *s.*, sala de trabalho.

WORK.SHOP, *s.*, oficina, lição prática.

WORLD, *s.*, mundo, globo; *adj.*, mundial, global.

WORLD.LY, *adj.*, mundano, terreno; secular, profano.

WORLD-WEAR.Y, *adj.*, entediado; cansado do mundo ou da vida.

WORLD-WIDE, *adj.*, mundial; *adv.*, no mundo inteiro.

WORM, *s.*, verme, minhoca; lagarta; *v.*, mover-se como verme; rastejar; caçar vermes (pássaros).

WORN, *v.*, *pp* de *to wear*; *adj.*, surrado, gasto; exausto.

WORN-OUT, *adj.*, usado, gasto; exausto.

WOR.RIED, *adj.*, preocupado, ansioso, angustiado.

WOR.RY, *s.*, preocupação; *v.*, preocupar.

WOR.RY.ING, *adj.*, preocupante, inquietador.

WORSE, *adj.*, *adv.*, pior; o pior, péssimo.

WORS.EN, *v.*, piorar, agravar.

WORS.EN.ING, *s.*, piora; *adj.*, que piora.

WOR.SHIP, *s.*, adoração, veneração.

WOR.SHIP.PER, *s.*, devoto (de uma religião).

WORST, *adv.*, pior; *s.*, o pior (de todos).

WOR.STED, *s.*, lã penteada.

WORTH, *s.*, valor, merecimento.

WORTHLESS ··653·· WRY

WORTH.LESS, *adj.*, imprestável, inútil, sem valor.
WORTH.WHILE, *adj.*, que a pena, lucrativo.
WOR.THY, *adj.*, merecedor, justo, digno.
WOULD, *v. aux.*, usado em frases interrogativas, para formar o futuro do pretérito e expressar condição.
WOULD-BE, *adj.*, aspirante, suposto, imaginário.
WOULDN'T, *contr.* de *would not*.
WOULD'VE, *contr.* de *would have*.
WOUND, *v.*, ferir, machucar, lesar.
WOUND.ED, *adj.*, ferido, machucado.
WOUND.ING, *adj.*, prejudicial, danoso.
WOW, *s., col.*, sucesso, estouro; *v.*, empolgar; *interj.*, uau!, oba! magnífico!
WRAITH, *s.*, fantasma, espírito, espectro.
WRAN.GLE, *s.*, briga, luta, pugilato.
WRAP, *s.*, xale, capa.
WRAP.PER, *s.*, embalagem, papel de bala; manta, envoltório; empacotador.
WRAP.PING, *s.*, embrulho, invólucro; empacotamento.
WRATH, *s.*, raiva, ira, cólera.
WRATH.FUL, *adj.*, raivoso, irritado, furioso.
WREATH, *s.*, coroa (de flores), grinalda; festão.
WRECK, *s.*, destroços, restos, ruína; *v.*, destruir, destroçar.
WRECK.AGE, *s.*, escombros, destroços; soçobro; restos; naufrágio.
WRECK.ER, *s.*, demolidor, destroçador, saqueador; *US* guincho, reboque; barco salva-vidas.
WRENCH, *s.*, chave inglesa, puxada; *v.*, separar, separar com dor.
WREST, *v.*, arrancar, extrair.

WRES.TLE, *v.*, derrubar, lutar (luta livre); combater, brigar.
WRES.TLER, *s., Esp.*, lutador de luta livre.
WRES.TLING, *s., Esp.*, luta livre.
WRETCH, *adj.*, desgraçado; infeliz, desditoso, safado.
WRETCH.ED, *adj.*, infeliz, desprezível, vil.
WRIG.GLE, *s.*, movimento de zigue-zague; *v.*, serpear; ziguezaguear; mexer(-se), retorcer(-se).
WRING, *v.*, torcer, apertar, sufocar.
WRING.ING, *s.*, torcedura, aperto.
WRIN.KLE, *s.*, ruga, prega; *v.*, enrugar,.dobrar-se.
WRIN.KLED, *adj.*, enrugado, franzido, com prega.
WRIST, *s.*, pulso.
WRIST.BAND, *s.*, pulseira (de relógio), punho de camisa.
WRIST.WATCH, *s.*, relógio de pulso.
WRIT, *s.*, mandado judicial.
WRITE, *v.*, escrever, redigir.
WRITE OFF, *v.*, cancelar.
WRIT.ER, *s.*, escritor.
WRITE UP, *v.*, redigir.
WRITHE, *v.*, contorcer(-se), retorcer(-se).
WRIT.ING, *s.*, escrita, letra, caligrafia.
WRIT.ING DESK, *s.*, escrivaninha.
WRIT.ING PA.PER, *s.*, papel de carta.
WRONG, *s.*, injustiça; *adj.*, errado, mau, injusto, equivocado; *adv.*, mal, erradamente.
WRONG.FUL, *adj.*, injusto, ilegal; nocivo, ofensivo.
WRONG.LY, *adv.*, injustamente, erroneamente.
WRONG.NESS, *s.*, injustiça, safadeza.
WRY, *adj.*, irônico, mordaz.

X, *s.*, vigésima quarta letra do alfabeto inglês; número 10 romano (X).
XAN.A.DU, *s.*, Xanadu.
XANT.HOUS, *adj.*, mongólico, amarelo.
X-CHRO.MO.SOME, *s., Biol.*, cromossomo X (designa o sexo feminino).
XE.NO.PHO.BIA, *s.*, xenofobia.
XE.ROG.RA.PHY, *s.*, xerografia.
XEROX, *s.*, Xerox (marca registrada); cópia xerográfica; *v.*, xerografar.
XMAS, *abrev.* de Christmas (Natal).
X-RAT.ED, *adj.*, obsceno, pornográfico, brutal (diz-se de filmes).
X-RAY, *s.*, radiografia; *v.*, radiografar.
XY.LO.GRAPH, *s.*, xilogravura.
XY.LOG.RA.PHER, *s.*, xilógrafo (artista).
XY.LOG.RA.PHY, *s.*, xilografia.
XY.LOL, *s., Quím.*, xilol, xilênio.
XY.LO.NITE, *s.*, celuloide.
XY.LO.PHONE, *s., Mús.*, xilofone.
XY.LO.PHON.IST, *s., Mús.*, xilofonista.

Y, s., vigésima quinta letra do alfabeto inglês.
YACHT, s., iate.
YACHT.ING, s., iatismo.
YACHTS.MAN, s., iatista.
YACHTS.WOM.AN, s., iatista (mulher).
YAHOO, s., brutamontes, selvagem.
YAK, s., Zool., iaque (boi do tibete).
YAM, s., Bot., inhame; cará.
YANK, s., adj., abrev. de Yankee: ianque.
YANK, s., col., arranco, puxão; v., col., arrancar, tirar.
YAN.KEE, s., adj., ianque.
YAP, v., ganir, gemer.
YARD, s., jarda, medida de 91,4cm.
YARD.STICK, s., padrão de medida.
YASH.MAK, s., burca.
YAWN, s., bocejo; v., bocejar.
YAWN.ER, s., bocejador.
YEAH, adv., col., sim.
YEAN.LING, s., cordeirinho, cabritinho ou ovelhinha.
YEAR, s., ano.
YEAR.BOOK, s., anuário.
YEAR.LING, s., potro, filhote (animal).
YEAR.LY, adj., anual.
YEARN, v., ansiar por, aspirar a, pretender, desejar.
YEARN.ING, s., ânsia, aspiração; adj., ansioso.
YEAST, s., fermento, levedura.
YELL, s., grito, berro, urro; v., gritar, berrar.
YEL.LOW, adj., amarelo.
YEL.LOW CARD, s., Esp., cartão amarelo (futebol).
YEL.LOW FEVER, s., Med., febre amarela.
YEL.LOW.ISH, adj., amarelado.
YEL.LOW.NESS, s., amarelidão.
YELP, s., latido, uivo; v., latir, uivar.
YE.MEN, s., Iêmen (país).
YE.ME.NI, s., adj., iemenita.
YEN, s., iene (moeda japonesa).
YEO.MAN, s., sitiante, dono de pequena propriedade agrícola.
YEP, adv., gír., sim.
YES, adv., sim.
YES MAN, s., pej., aquele que concorda com seu superior, capacho.
YES.TER, adj., passado, ido, transcorrido, último; adv., ontem.
YES.TER.DAY, s., ontem; adv., ontem.
YET, adv., ainda; conj., contudo, porém, mas.
YID.DISH, s., iídiche (língua de parte dos judeus); adj., iídiche (relativo a esse idioma).
YIELD, s., colheita; v., produzir, render, ceder.
YIP.PEE, interj., oba!
YO, interj., ei!
YODEL, s., canto típico dos tiroleses; v., cantar à moda dos tiroleses.
YO.GURT, YOGHURT, YOGHOURT, s., iogurte.
YOKE, s., junta de bois, junta, jugo.
YOKEL, s., pej., caipira, camponês, rústico.
YOLK, s., gema de ovo.
YOU, pron., tu, você, senhor, vós, vocês; o, os, a, as, lhe, contigo, convosco.
YOU'D, contr. de you had, you would.
YOU'LL, contr. de you will.
YOUNG, s., juventude; adj., jovem, moço; s., filhote, cria de bicho.
YOUNG.ER, adj., mais novo.
YOUNG.ISH, adj., novato, bem novo.
YOUNG MAN, s., rapaz, moço.
YOUNG.NESS, s., juventude, mocidade; inexperiência.
YOUNG WO.MAN, s., rapariga, moça.
YOUNG.STER, s., moço, jovem, rapaz.
YOUR, pron., seu, sua, teu, tua, vosso, vossa.
YOU'RE, contr. de you are.
YOURS, pron. poss., teu(s), tua(s), seu(s), sua(s), de você(s), do(s) senhor(es), da(s) senhora(s).
YOUR.SELF, pron., tu mesmo, você mesmo, si mesmo.
YOUR.SELVES, pron., vós mesmos, vocês mesmos.
YOUTH, s., juventude, mocidade.
YOUTH.FUL, adj., jovem, moço.
YOUTH.FUL.LY, adv., vigorosamente, de modo juvenil.
YOUTH.FUL.NESS, s., juventude, mocidade; viço.
YOU'VE, contr. de you have.
YO.YO, s., ioiô; gír., pessoa indecisa.
YU.GO.SLAV, YU.GO.SLAV.IAN, adj., s., iugoslavo.
YUM.MY, adj., col., delicioso.
YUP.PIE, YUP.PY, s., iupi.

Z, s., vigésima sexta letra do alfabeto inglês.
ZAIRE, ZAÏRE, s., Zaire (país).
ZAIREAN, ZAÏREAN, s., adj., zairense.
ZAM.BE.ZI, ZAMBESI, s., Zambezi (país)
ZAM.BI.A, s., Zâmbia (país).
ZAM.BI.AN, s., adj., zambiano.
ZA.NY, s., palhaço, tolo, pateta; adj., bobo, tolo, imbecil.
ZAP, v., zapear (passar os canais de TV); despachar (matar), atacar, fulminar; cozinhar (no microondas).
ZEAL, s., fervor, entusiasmo, ânimo.
ZEAL.OT, s., zelote, fanático, entusiasta.
ZEAL.OUS, adj., zeloso.
ZE.BRA, s., zebra.
ZE.NITH, s., zênite, cume, cimo, pico.
ZEPH.YR, s., zéfiro, aura, aragem, vento brando.
ZEP.PE.LIN, s., zepelim.
ZE.RO, s., zero.
ZEST, s., sabor, entusiasmo, prazer, deleite.
ZEST.FUL, adj., saboroso, gotoso, prazeroso.
ZE.TA, s., zeta, dzeta (sexta letra do alfabeto grego).
ZEUG.MA, s., zeugma, silepse.
ZIB.EL.INE, s., pele de zibelina (marta).
ZIK.KU.RAT, s., Hist., o mesmo que ziggurat.
ZIG.GU.RAT, s., Hist., zigurate.
ZIG.ZAG, s., zigue-zague; v., zigue-zaguear.
ZILCH, s., nulidade, nada, zero.
ZIM.BA.BWE, s., Zimbábue (país).
ZIM.BA.BWE.AN, s., adj., zimbabuano.
ZINC, s., Quím., zinco; v., zincar.
ZINC.IF.ER.OUS, adj., zincífero.
ZINC.I.FI.CA.TION, s., zincagem, galvanização.
ZINC.I.FIED, adj., zincado, galvanizado.
ZINC.I.FY, v., zincar, galvanizar.
ZINC.OUS, adj., zincífero.
ZI.ON, s., Sião.
ZI.ON.ISM, s., sionismo.
ZI.ON.IST, s., adj., sionista.
ZIP, s., zunido, silvo, fecho, zíper; fechar o zíper.
ZIP CODE, s., US código de endereçamento postal (CEP).
ZIP.PER, s., zíper.
ZIP.PY, adj., col., possante, cheio de energia; alegre, vivo.
ZIR.CON, s., Min., zircão.
ZIR.CO.NI.UM, s., Quím., zircônio.
ZIT, s., acne, espinha; US mancha na pele.
ZITH.ER, s., Mús., cítara.
ZO.DI.AC, s., zodíaco.
ZO.DI.A.CAL, adj., zodiacal.
ZOM.BIE, s., zumbi; (também zombi).
ZO.NA.TION, s., zoneamento.
ZONE, s., zona, região, localidade.
ZOO, s., zoo, zoológico.
ZO.OG.E.NY, s., zoogenia.
ZO.O.GE.OG.RA.PHY, s., zoogeografia.
ZO.O.LOG.IC, adj., zoológico
ZO.O.LOG.I.CAL, adj., UK zoológico.
ZO.OL.O.GIST, s., zoólogo.
ZO.OL.O.GY, s., zoologia.
ZOOM, v., zunir, zumbir, subir um aclive com rapidez.
ZO.OM.E.TRY, s., zoometria.
ZOOM LENS, s., Ópt., lente para dar efeito zum; zum.
ZO.O.MOR.PHIC, adj., zoomorfo.
ZO.O.MOR.PHISM, s., zoomorfismo.
ZO.ON.O.SIS, s., Biol., zoonose.
ZO.O.SPERM, s., Biol., zoosperma.
ZO.O.SPHERE, s., Ecol., zoosfera.
ZO.RIL, s., Zool., zorrilho.
ZUC.CHI.NI, s., Bot., abobrinha italiana.
ZU.LU, adj., s., zulu, povo africano.
ZY.GO.MA, s., zigoma.
ZY.GO.TE, s., Biol., zigoto.